CASES AND MATERIALS

DOMESTIC RELATIONS

SIXTH EDITION

by

WALTER WADLINGTON
James Madison Professor of Law Emeritus
University of Virginia School of Law

RAYMOND C. O'BRIEN
Professor of Law
The Catholic University of America

FOUNDATION PRESS

2007

© 1970, 1974, 1978, 1984, 1990, 1995, 1998, 2002 FOUNDATION PRESS

© 2007 By FOUNDATION PRESS

      395 Hudson Street

      New York, NY 10014

      Phone Toll Free 1–877–888–1330

      Fax (212) 367–6799

      foundation-press.com

Printed in the United States of America

ISBN 978–1–59941–064–7

 TEXT IS PRINTED ON 10% POST CONSUMER RECYCLED PAPER

WW

For Derek and Kim
"Open your eyes and see! The fields are shining for harvest."

ROB

John L. Garvey
"The one who walks in the way of integrity shall be in my service."

*

PREFACE TO THE SIXTH EDITION

The fact that this is the sixth edition of this casebook reflects the enormity of change in family law since the casebook's inception. We continue to employ the words "Domestic Relations" rather than "family law" because we believe that the former offers a comprehensive title in which the developments in interpersonal relationships will continue to find reconstruction. Phenomena contributing to the change in domestic relations would include the ever-expanding list of options offered to adults in their desire to self-order their relationships, the expanding definition of marriage and marriage-like partnerships, the continued erosion of interspousal immunity and testimonial privilege, and a quickened pace to the distribution of marital property and spousal support. And throughout all editions of the casebook there has been increasing federal encroachment on what had heretofore been matters left solely to the discretion of the states. Interestingly, federal incursion into domestic relations has occurred during a time of judicial and legislative federalism. All of these issues contribute to the dynamism of domestic relations.

Each edition of the casebook has sought to balance the changes that have occurred with the need to provide continuity with what has gone before. A knowledge of what has gone before is important to understand what the new does. Addition of a case, the deletion of another, or the substitution of a NOTE or statute is always done with attention to the fact that professors may have used one or the other to great advantage in a class and any change will precipitate at least modest concern (or perhaps stronger reaction). But often there has been a reversal–as with Lawrence v. Texas–or a decided change in the majority of cases–as with Kantaras v. Kantaras–or the focus has shifted completely, as with Gonzales v. Carhart. We assure those using this new edition that we have sought to limit the changes to those we thought clearly necessary, maintaining continuity with previous editions. This reflects our continued concern that professors can use the materials with an eclectic approach in structuring their courses. This is important when one realizes that they can be used in two, three or four hour courses, and in several different offerings, and they do not mandate a specific ordering.

Several themes in this new edition will be recognized by users of previous editions. We have continued our efforts to provide particularly good discussion cases. The casebook method of teaching law, even with its variations today, calls for cases offering the professor the opportunity to "springboard" from the facts and issue specifically raised in it to other possibly relevant rules and principles and to speculate on the need for and course of future changes. Often the cases are teaching tools themselves, condensing decades of decisions and refinements into a few pages of instructive history.

Another theme is the inclusion of state and federal statutes that provide a fixed point of reference in some discussion. All too often students may be lulled into a common law mentality, without the discipline of analyzing and deciphering statutes. We offer selected statutes in an effort to provide the professor a vehicle through which legislation may be integrated into the course. For example, at the federal level, the ADOPTION AND SAFE FAMILIES ACT OF 1997, and the DEFENSE OF MARRIAGE ACT. Examples of state statutory enactments include Florida's SAFE HAVEN STATUTE and Maryland's STANDBY GUARDIANSHIP law. Also included are some of the uniform laws proposed by the National Conference of Commissioners on Uniform State Laws.

Continuing state expansion of individual liberties guaranteed by the state, not the federal, constitution, provided another major theme. During the last decades of the twentieth century state courts in Hawaii reasoned that state constitutional grounds of privacy and equal protection justified same sex marriage. Later, in Massachusetts, the state supreme court would compel the state legislature to provide marriage licenses to same sex couples. State courts or legislatures in Vermont, New Hampshire, Connecticut and New Jersey would precipitate civil unions, a status spreading to other states. Countless law review articles now testify to additional interpretations of other state constitutions, providing an expansive list of liberties and enforceable claims. These deal with issues such as reproductive rights, de facto parenthood, gender inequality, custody and relocation, domestic violence, and interspousal tort immunity. State courts had become laboratories of domestic relations change.

The casebook consists of nine chapters. In Chapter I, students are introduced to the changing concepts of marriage and family. Increasing private ordering among adults has fashioned a "function" family, providing legitimacy for relationships heretofore excluded under a "form" family construct. Distinctions between the function and form families is analyzed in the material concerning the uniqueness of marriage, and then the federal and state challenges to marriage and other intimate relationships. Of interest in the constitutional evolution is the overruling of Bowers v. Hardwick by Lawrence v. Texas. And in Gonzales v. Carhart the Supreme Court ruled on an abortion statute and formed a new majority.

Getting married is the subject of Chapter II. The controversy over same sex marriage contributes to the discussion of the unique role that marriage has played in history. Entering into the status of marriage was both an entry into an economic relationship and a moral realm where the married couple enjoyed protection in part because the state was always a third-party to the relationship. While the incidents of annulment have waned with the increasing frequency of no-fault divorce, states continue to monitor entry into common law and statutory marriage. There is more widespread recognition of the rights of putative spouses, and a definite trend has developed regarding the ability of a transsexual to enter into a valid marriage.

Chapter III details the significant changes that have occurred in the legal relationship of husband and wife. The last three decades of the twentieth century witnessed a steady erosion of the antiquated concept of "oneness" of husband and wife, gradually replaced by a "marital partnership" of two equals. With this new partnership there have arisen opportunities for spousal tort suits, civil and criminal claims for assault, sodomy and rape, and reduction in the opportunities for invoking the spousal privilege. In reference to domestic violence the courts and the legislatures continue to parse the distinction between privacy and imminent fear of bodily harm. But the status of marriage still can be a significant bulwark in reference to the necessity of support, presumptions of parentage associated with reproductive technologies, and medical care. This chapter will also establish a framework for division of marital property (community property) and divorce, all to be discussed more fully later.

Chapter IV presents the procedural and substantive mechanisms by which an otherwise valid marriage may be dissolved. Every state now has a no-fault ground for divorce, some states eliminating all marital fault grounds. While "covenant marriage" is an option for couples, few states make it available. Many experts in the field and The AMERICAN LAW INSTITUTE'S PRINCIPLES OF THE LAW OF FAMILY DISSOLUTION: ANALYSIS AND RECOMMENDATIONS (2000) criticize the use of marital fault as a factor in the division of marital property. And in the tug-of-war among the states for divorce jurisdiction there are suggestions regarding making the entire process simpler.

Chapter V offers two approaches to the division of marital property. First, the professor may choose to introduce students to the community property approach evidenced by the New Mexico decision of Ruggles v. Ruggles, and the California statutes illustrating the equal division modus operandi inherent in community property states. Second, the New York statute offers to those professors utilizing the common law method of distribution an excellent list of equitable factors to consider in the division of property. In either jurisdiction, Chapter V offers a discussion of support, reimbursement and rehabilitation, and then discusses the division of assets. The handling of marital and separate property continues to change; options, goodwill, disability benefits, imputing income, and limits upon support are all discussed. Likewise, child support, although governed by state statutory guidelines, may be increased under certain circumstances. Rebutting the guideline amount is a consistent theme in litigation and the parameters are discussed. Finally, this lengthy chapter provides the basic rules for income tax and bankruptcy applicability (though these are covered in much greater detail in those specialized courses), and the ability of parties to limit or structure support through private ordering is featured, along with enforcement orders.

Pertinent to the modern age, the legal and biological relationship of parent and child are offered in Chapter VI. Cases explore the limits of assisted reproduction and parenthood, and the new UNIFORM PARENTAGE ACT, promulgated by the National Conference of Commissioners on Uniform State Laws, has been adopted by an increasing number of states. Nonetheless, the cases, articles and statutes provided seek to provide a framework through which future discussion, cases, and legislation might evolve.

Chapter VII concerns the state's interest in the protection of children, most often against the competing claims of parents who seek to make decision on their behalf, and almost always involving discipline, medical care, education, neglect and simple control. The Supreme Court, interpreting the Due Process Clause, has strengthened the presumptive rights of parents, but increasingly, parents are being held accountable for failure to perform parental duties and concomitantly, parental availability for tort suit by a child against a parent.

Chapter VIII involves the modern arena of litigation, custody and visitation of children. To assist in sorting through the various rules and presumptions, we have gathered the cases, statutes and law review articles into three constructs. The constructs, each prompting a different series of questions, involve disputes between parents, between parents and third parties, and between parents and the states. Admittedly, the range of litigation may exceed these in this modern age, but the vast majority of cases involve these three and certainly from them it is possible to extrapolate and reason to additional conclusions. There are recent additions to the discussion too. Increasingly, the UNIFORM CHILD CUSTODY JURISDICTION AND ENFORCEMENT ACT has gained dominance, augmented by the federal PARENTAL KIDNAPING PREVENTION ACT, and the INTERNATIONAL CHILD ABDUCTION REMEDIES ACT. Internationally, there is the HAGUE CONVENTION ON THE CIVIL ASPECTS OF INTERNATIONAL CHILD ABDUCTION.

Chapter IX identifies issues associated with termination of parental rights, and also initiation of new relationships through adoption. State procedures continue to provide the mechanism for temporary and permanent involuntary removal of children from parental care. But federal constitutional protections apply to safeguard the parental guarantee of Due Process of law. Enactment of the federal ADOPTION AND SAFE FAMILIES ACT OF 1997 has shifted the burden to parents to cooperate with state efforts at reunification, thereby making it more feasible to permanently place dependent children. In addition, federal funds have been appropriated and additional statutes passed to subsidize adoptions of "special needs" children. Any delay or denial of adoption based on race, color, or national origin is prohibited under the federal INTERETHNIC ADOPTION ACT. New Mexico's OPEN ADOPTION ACT is an example of a state effort to promote adoption by allowing an adopted child to continue contact with biological parents. All of these efforts address the concern of all to provide a child with permanence, balanced against the often competing interests of the biological parents, state and federal agencies, and competition for funds.

Because of the proliferation of statutes and related developments in domestic relations, it may be useful to consider as supplements two other books by the same authors of the casebook: FAMILY LAW STATUTES, INTERNATIONAL CONVENTIONS AND UNIFORM LAWS (3d ed. 2007), and FAMILY LAW IN PERSPECTIVE (2d ed. 2007). Both books are published by Foundation Press.

Finally, the authors wish to extend our sincere appreciation to Adam Bitter for his excellent research assistance.

WALTER WADLINGTON
wwadlington@earthlink.
net

RAYMOND C. O'BRIEN
obrien@law.edu

*

NOTE ON EDITING

Some citations, footnotes, and text have been omitted in order to keep the materials at manageable size for a several hour credit course, or to eliminate portions of a decision focusing on an unrelated issue. When some footnotes have been omitted, those that have been retained bear the original numbering from the reporter or other source from which the passage was excerpted. Some citations to cases and secondary material (including some "string" citations with brief explanatory notes about cases in the string) have been omitted without notes or symbols indicating their omission. Ellipses, or brackets summarizing omitted text, indicate whether other text has been deleted in the editing process.

SPECIAL ACKNOWLEDGMENT

We thank the National Conference of Commissioners on Uniform State Laws for their permission to reprint excerpts from copyrighted text of their various UNIFORM LAWS.

*

TABLE OF WEB SITES

Subject

Child Support Guidelines/Child Support Information
http://www.acf.hhs.gov/programs/cse/ [This is the website for the U.S. Office of Child Support Enforcement, within HHS.]
http://www.child support collections.com/ [Gives an overview of the child support laws in the states, and contains general information on child support enforcement.]
http://www.acf.hhs.gov/programs/cse/pubs/2003/reports/prelim-datareport/table 9. [U.S. Department of Health and Human Services, Office of Child Support Enforcement.]
http://www.uifsa.com. [UIFSA Home Page.]

Counseling Resources
http://www.divorcenet.com
http://www.divorcesource.com/archives/counseling.shtml

Domestic Partnerships
http://www.thetaskforce.org/ [This is the website of the National Gay and Lesbian Task Force.]

Domestic Violence
http://www.usdoj.gov/ovw/ [U.S. Department of Justice's Office on Violence Against Women.]
http://wwwhrc.org. [Human Rights Campaign.]

Drugs and Child Protection
http://www.childwelfare.gov/systemwide/laws_policies/statutes/drug-exposed.cfm [Contains information on state statutes regarding parental drug use as child abuse.]
http://www.cwla.org/advocacy/nationalfactsheet06.htm [Website from the Child Welfare League of America. In addition to a broad range of other information, it contains some statistics on children and substance abuse.]

Health Care Directives
http://www.helpguide.org/elder/advance_directive_end_of_life_care.htm [Information on the use of health care directives and living wills.]
http://www.agingwithdignity.org. [General information of planning for incapacity.]
http://www.nhpco.org. [National Hospice and Palliative Care Organization, providing information on end of life decisionmaking.]
http://www.mayoclinic.com. [Mayo Clinic's Advance Directive Resources.]

Subject

IN VITRO FERTILIZATION

http://www.americanpregnancy.org/infertility/ivf.html [This site is run by the American Pregnancy Association, and contains general information on in vitro fertilization, the variations on IVF; and information on pregnancy in general.]

PARENTAL ALIENATION

http://www.parentalalienation.com/ [General site on parental alienation.]

SCHOOL VOUCHERS

http://www.topix.net/education/school vouchers [This is a news site on the issue of school vouchers.]

http://www.ncsl.org/programs/educ/VoucherMain.htm [This is link for the National Conference of State Legislatures; provides an overview of the issue.]

http://childrenfirstamerica.org/legislation.htm.

SPOUSAL SUPPORT

http://www.divorceinfo.com/alimony.htm

http://www.divorcehq.com/alimony.html

UNMARRIED COHABITANTS

http://www.census.gov/population/www/socdemo/hh fam.html [Provides statistics.]

WOMAN'S SUPPORT RESOURCES

http://www.divorcesupport.com/search/women.shtml [Resources specific to women.]

*

SUMMARY OF CONTENTS

TABLE OF CONTENTS

*

TABLE OF CASES

Principal cases are in bold type. Non-principal cases are in roman type. References are to Pages.

DOMESTIC RELATIONS

*

CHAPTER I

CHANGING CONCEPTS OF MARRIAGE AND FAMILY

A. FUNCTION VERSUS FORM IN "FAMILY" RELATIONSHIPS

City of Ladue v. Horn

Missouri Court of Appeals, Eastern District, Division Three, 1986.
720 S.W.2d 745.

■ CRANDALL, JUDGE.

Defendants, Joan Horn and E. Terrence Jones, appeal from the judgment of the trial court in favor of plaintiff, City of Ladue (Ladue), which enjoined defendants from occupying their home in violation of Ladue's zoning ordinance and which dismissed defendants' counterclaim. We affirm.

The case was submitted to the trial court on stipulated facts. Ladue's Zoning Ordinance No. 1175 was in effect at all times pertinent to the present action. Certain zones were designated as one-family residential. The zoning ordinance defined family as: "One or more persons related by blood, marriage or adoption, occupying a dwelling unit as an individual housekeeping organization." The only authorized accessory use in residential districts was for "[a]ccommodations for domestic persons employed and living on the premises and home occupations." The purpose of Ladue's zoning ordinance was broadly stated as to promote "the health, safety, morals and general welfare" of Ladue.

In July, 1981, defendants purchased a seven-bedroom, four-bathroom house which was located in a single-family residential zone in Ladue. Residing in defendants' home were Horn's two children (aged 16 and 19) and Jones's one child (age 18). The two older children attended out-of-state universities and lived in the house only on a part-time basis. Although defendants were not married, they shared a common bedroom, maintained a joint checking account for the household expenses, ate their meals together, entertained together, and disciplined each other's children. Ladue made demands upon defendants to vacate their home because their household did not comprise a family, as defined by Ladue's zoning ordinance, and therefore they could not live in an area zoned for single-family dwellings. When defendants refused to vacate, Ladue sought to enjoin defendants' continued violation of the zoning ordinance. Defendants counterclaimed, seeking a declaration that the zoning ordinance was constitutionally void.

1

They also sought attorneys' fees and costs. The trial court entered a permanent injunction in favor of Ladue and dismissed defendants' counterclaim. Enforcement of the injunction was stayed pending this appeal.

Preliminarily, we note that the ordinance in question clearly restricts the use of the property rather than the character of the structure. It is therefore a legal impossibility to uphold the validity of the ordinance and, at the same time, permit defendants to occupy their residence.

In Missouri, the scope of appellate review in zoning matters is limited; and the reviewing court may not substitute its judgment for that of the zoning authority. A zoning ordinance is presumed valid. The legislative body is vested with broad discretion and the appellate court cannot interfere unless it is shown that the legislative body has acted arbitrarily.

. . .

Capsulated, defendants' attack on Ladue's ordinance is three-pronged. First, the zoning limitations foreclose them from exercising their right to associate freely with whomever they wish. Roberts v. United States Jaycees, 468 U.S. 609, 104 S.Ct. 3244, 82 L.Ed.2d 462 (1984). Second, their right to privacy is violated by the zoning restrictions. Stanley v. Georgia, 394 U.S. 557, 89 S.Ct. 1243, 22 L.Ed.2d 542 (1969). Third, the zoning classification distinguishes between related persons and unrelated persons. United States Dept. of Agriculture v. Moreno, 413 U.S. 528, 93 S.Ct. 2821, 37 L.Ed.2d 782 (1973). Defendants allege that the United States and Missouri Constitutions grant each of them the right to share his or her residence with whomever he or she chooses. They assert that Ladue has not demonstrated a compelling, much less rational, justification for the overly proscriptive blood or legal relationship requirement in its zoning ordinance.

Defendants posit that the term "family" is susceptible to several meanings. They contend that, since their household is the "functional and factual equivalent of a natural family," the ordinance may not preclude them from living in a single-family residential Ladue neighborhood. See, e.g., McMinn v. Town of Oyster Bay, 66 N.Y.2d 544, 498 N.Y.S.2d 128, 488 N.E.2d 1240 (Ct.App.1985). Defendants argue in their brief as follows:

> The record amply demonstrates that the private, intimate interests of Horn and Jones are substantial. Horn, Jones, and their respective children have historically lived together as a single family unit. They use and occupy their home for the identical purposes and in the identical manners as families which are biologically or maritally related.

To bolster this contention, defendants elaborate on their shared duties, as set forth earlier in this opinion. Defendants acknowledge the importance of viewing themselves as a family unit, albeit a "conceptual family" as opposed to a "true non-family," in order to prevent the application of the ordinance.[3]

---

3. The distinction between "conceptual" or "non-traditional" families and true non-families may well be a distinction without a difference, the distinction resting in

The fallacy in defendants' syllogism is that the stipulated facts do not compel the conclusion that defendants are living as a family. A man and woman living together, sharing pleasures and certain responsibilities, does not *per se* constitute a family in even the conceptual sense. To approximate a family relationship, there must exist a commitment to a permanent relationship and a perceived reciprocal obligation to support and to care for each other. See, e.g., State ex rel. Ellis v. Liddle, 520 S.W.2d 644, 650 (Mo.App.1975). Only when these characteristics are present can the conceptual family, perhaps, equate with the traditional family. In a traditional family, certain of its inherent attributes arise from the legal relationship of the family members. In a non-traditional family, those same qualities arise in fact, either by explicit agreement or by tacit understanding among the parties.

While the stipulated facts could arguably support an inference by the trial court that defendants and their children comprised a non-traditional family, they do not compel that inference. Absent findings of fact and conclusions of law, we cannot assume that the trial court's perception of defendants' familial status comported with defendants' characterization of themselves as a conceptual family. In fact, if a finding by the trial court that defendants' living arrangement constituted a conceptual family is critical to a determination in defendants' favor, we can assume that the court's finding was adverse to defendants' position. Ordinarily, given our deference to the decision of the trial court, that would dispose of this appeal. We decline, however, to restrict our ruling to such a narrow basis. We therefore consider the broader issues presented by the parties. We assume, *arguendo,* that the sole basis for the judgment entered by the trial court was that defendants were not related by blood, marriage or adoption, as required by Ladue's ordinance.

We first consider whether the ordinance violates any federally protected rights of the defendants. Generally, federal court decisions hold that a zoning classification based upon a biological or a legal relationship among household members is justifiable under constitutional police powers to protect the public health, safety, morals or welfare of the community.

More specifically, the United States Supreme Court has developed a two-tiered approach by which to examine legislation challenged as violative of the equal protection clause. If the personal interest affected by the ordinance is fundamental, "strict scrutiny" is applied and the ordinance is sustained only upon a showing that the burden imposed is necessary to protect a compelling governmental interest. If the ordinance does not contain a suspect class or impinge upon a fundamental interest, the more relaxed "rational basis" test is applied and the classification imposed by the ordinance is upheld if any facts can reasonably justify it. McGowan v.

speculation and stereotypical presumptions. Further, recognition of the conceptual family suffers from the defect of commanding inquiry into who are the users rather than focusing on the use itself. See generally Note, City of Santa Barbara v. Adamson: An Associational Right of Privacy and the End of Family Zones, 69 Calif.L.Rev. 1052, 1068–70 (1981).

Maryland, 366 U.S. 420, 426, 81 S.Ct. 1101, 1105, 6 L.Ed.2d 393 (1961). Defendants urge this court to recognize that their interest in choosing their own living arrangement inexorably involves their fundamental rights of freedom of association and of privacy.

In Village of Euclid v. Ambler Realty Co., 272 U.S. 365, 47 S.Ct. 114, 71 L.Ed. 303 (1926) and in Nectow v. City of Cambridge, 277 U.S. 183, 48 S.Ct. 447, 72 L.Ed. 842 (1928), the United States Supreme Court also established the due process parameters of permissible legislation. The ordinance in question must have a "foundation in reason" and bear a "substantial relation to the public health, the public morals, the public safety or the public welfare in its proper sense."

In the Village of Belle Terre v. Boraas, 416 U.S. 1, 94 S.Ct. 1536, 39 L.Ed.2d 797 (1974), the court addressed a zoning regulation of the type at issue in this case. The court held that the Village of Belle Terre ordinance involved no fundamental right, but was typical of economic and social legislation which is upheld if it is reasonably related to a permissible governmental objective. The challenged zoning ordinance of the Village of Belle Terre defined family as:

> One or more persons related by blood, adoption or marriage, living and cooking together as a single housekeeping unit [or] a number of persons but not exceeding two (2) living and cooking together as a single housekeeping unit though not related by blood, adoption, or marriage....

The court upheld the ordinance, reasoning that the ordinance constituted valid land use legislation reasonably designed to maintain traditional family values and patterns.

The importance of the family was reaffirmed in Moore v. City of East Cleveland, 431 U.S. 494, 97 S.Ct. 1932, 52 L.Ed.2d 531 (1977), wherein the United States Supreme Court was confronted with a housing ordinance which defined a "family" as only certain closely related individuals. Consequently, a grandmother who lived with her son and two grandsons was convicted of violating the ordinance because her two grandsons were first cousins rather than brothers. The United States Supreme Court struck down the East Cleveland ordinance for violating the freedom of personal choice in matters of marriage and family life. The court distinguished *Belle Terre* by stating that the ordinance in that case allowed all individuals related by blood, marriage or adoption to live together; whereas East Cleveland, by restricting the number of related persons who could live together, sought "to regulate the occupancy of its housing by slicing deeply into the family itself." The court pointed out that the institution of the family is protected by the Constitution precisely because it is so deeply rooted in the American tradition and that "[o]urs is by no means a tradition limited to respect for the bonds uniting the members of the nuclear family."

Here, because we are dealing with economic and social legislation and not with a fundamental interest or a suspect classification, the test of constitutionality is whether the ordinance is reasonable and not arbitrary and bears a rational relationship to a permissible state objective. . . .

Ladue has a legitimate concern with laying out guidelines for land use addressed to family needs. . . . The question of whether Ladue could have chosen more precise means to effectuate its legislative goals is immaterial. Ladue's zoning ordinance is rationally related to its expressed purposes and violates no provisions of the Constitution of the United States. Further, defendants' assertion that they have a constitutional right to share their residence with whomever they please amounts to the same argument that was made and found unpersuasive by the court in *Belle Terre.*

We next consider whether the Ladue ordinance violates any rights of defendants protected by the Missouri Constitution. Defendants rely on several Missouri cases which they allege have "expanded the definition of 'family.'" We disagree with defendants' conclusion.

In State ex rel. Ellis v. Liddle, 520 S.W.2d 644 (Mo.App.1975), the zoning ordinance divided the term "family" into two distinct categories, as follows:

> First, "one or more persons related by blood, marriage, or adoption living together in one dwelling unit" in a "common household" including servants, guests, boarders, roomers or lodgers. The ordinance places no limitation on the number of such persons occupying the dwelling unit. Second, persons "not related by blood, marriage, or adoption". Such occupancy may not exceed 10 persons in any one dwelling unit.

Id. at 650. Given this definition, the court permitted the operation of a group home for six to eight juvenile boys and two "teaching parents" in a single-family residential neighborhood in Maryville, Missouri. The court stated that it was clear that, *"both under the specific terms of the ordinance* and under common law" (emphasis added), the operation of the group home did no violence to the single-family residence requirement.

In City of Vinita Park v. Girls Sheltercare, Inc., 664 S.W.2d 256 (Mo.App.1984), this court allowed the use of a single-family residence as a girls' group home operated by the Juvenile Court of St. Louis County in the City of Vinita Park. The Vinita Park Zoning Ordinance defined family as "[o]ne or more persons related by blood or marriage occupying a premises and living as a single housekeeping unit." Id. at 258. The housing ordinance contained a more expansive definition of family:

> [A]n individual or married couple and the children thereof and no more than two other persons related directly to the individual or married couple by blood or marriage and not more than three persons not related by blood or marriage living together as a single housekeeping unit in a dwelling unit.

Id. at 259 n. 1.

The court stated that, although the group did not "conform to the letter of either of the *ordinances* which defines family," it did conform to

"the spirit of the *ordinances.*" Id. at 259. (emphasis added). After addressing the "family" issue, the court addressed what it referred to as the
"pivotal issue" of the case concerning what limitations there are on the
power of a municipality to zone public uses. The court held that "the
leasing of the premises pursuant to the statutory authority for the county
and juvenile court to establish a group home is a governmental function
(use) and thereby immune from the City of Vinita Park's zoning ordinance."

In both of these cases, the reviewing court looked to the definition of
family as set forth in the ordinance. Defendants' argument that these cases
"expand" the definition of family is unpersuasive. The clear implication of
these cases is that the appellate court will give deference to a zoning
ordinance, particularly when there is no overriding governmental interest
or statutory authority to negate the legislative prerogative to define family
based upon biological or legal relationships.

For purposes of its zoning code, Ladue has in precise language defined
the term family. It chose the definition which comports with the historical
and traditional notions of family; namely, those people related by blood,
marriage or adoption. That definition of family has been upheld in numerous Missouri decisions. See, e.g., London v. Handicapped Facilities Board of
St. Charles County, 637 S.W.2d 212 (Mo.App.1982) (group home not a
"family" as used in restrictive covenant); Feely v. Birenbaum, 554 S.W.2d
432 (Mo.App.1977) (two unrelated males not a "family" as used in restrictive covenant); Cash v. Catholic Diocese, 414 S.W.2d 346 (Mo.App.1967)
(nuns not a "family" as used in a restrictive covenant).

Decisions from other state jurisdictions have addressed identical constitutional challenges to zoning ordinances similar to the ordinance in the
instant case. The reviewing courts have upheld their respective ordinances
on the ground that maintenance of a traditional family environment
constitutes a reasonable basis for excluding uses that may impair the
stability of that environment and erode the values associated with traditional family life.

The essence of zoning is selection; and, if it is not invidious or
discriminatory against those not selected, it is proper. There is no doubt
that there is a governmental interest in marriage and in preserving the
integrity of the biological or legal family. There is no concomitant governmental interest in keeping together a group of unrelated persons, no matter
how closely they simulate a family. Further, there is no state policy which
commands that groups of people may live under the same roof in any
section of a municipality they choose.

. . .

NOTES

Same Sex Families. The *Ladue* decision supported the traditional or "form" definition of family when challenged by what works or what "functions" for the parties themselves. A later case heard by the New York Court of Appeals provided a seminal decision supporting a functional definition of family over a city's regulation of rent control (which happens to involve two persons of the same sex). *See* Braschi v. Stahl Assocs. Co., 74 N.Y.2d 201, 544 N.Y.S.2d 784, 543 N.E.2d 49 (1989). Appellant and decedent, two adult males not related by blood, marriage, or adoption, had resided in a rent controlled apartment with the lease solely in the name of the decedent. The New York City Rent and Eviction Regulation allowed the landlord to evict the appellant since his name was not on the lease and he was not "the surviving spouse of the deceased tenant or some other member of the deceased tenant's family who has been living with the tenant." Eviction allowed the landlord to raise the rent. In supporting the claim to a function family and thus allowing the appellant to remain, the court found the two men had:

> lived together as life partners for more than ten years. They regarded one another, and were regarded by family and friends, as spouses. The two men's families were aware of the nature of their relationship, and they regularly visited each other's families and attended family functions together, as a couple . . .

> In addition, to their interwoven social lives, appellant clearly considered the apartment his home. He lists the apartment as his address on his driver's license and passport, and receives all his mail at the apartment address. Moreover, appellant's tenancy was known to the Building's superintendent and doormen, who viewed the two men as a couple.

> Financially, the two men shared all obligations including a household budget. The two were authorized signatories for three safe deposit boxes, they maintained joint savings and checking accounts, and joint credit cards. In fact, rent was often paid with a check from their joint checking account. Additionally, Blanchard [the decedent] executed a power of attorney in appellant's favor so that appellant could make the necessary decisions—financial, medical and personal—for him during his illness. Finally, appellant was the named beneficiary of Blanchard's life insurance policy, as well as the primary legatee and co-executor of Blanchard's estate.

The New York Court of Appeals held that appellant was not excluded, as a matter of law, from seeking protection from eviction under the law. [The case was certified to them only as to this question.] Arriving at this result, the court concluded that the term "family" as used in the rent control law:

> should not be rigidly restricted to those people who have formalized their relationship by obtaining, for instance, a marriage certificate or an adoption order. The intended protection against sudden eviction should not rest on fictitious legal distinctions or genetic history, but instead should find its foundation in the reality of family life. In the context of eviction, a more realistic, and certainly equally valid, view of a family includes two adult life-time partners whose relationship is

long-term and characterized by an emotional and financial commitment and interdependence. This view comports with our society's traditional concept of "family" and with the expectations of individuals who live in such nuclear units ... In fact, Webster's Dictionary defines "family" first as a "group of people united by certain convictions or common affiliation" [Webster's Ninth New Collegiate Dictionary 448 (1984); *see*, Ballantine's Law Dictionary 456 (3rd ed. 1969) ("family" defined as "[p]rimarily, the collective body of persons who live in one house and under one head or management"); ...] Hence, it is reasonable to conclude that, in using the term "family," the Legislature intended to extend protection to those who reside in households having all of the normal familial characteristics. Appellant Braschi should therefore be afforded the opportunity to prove that he and Blanchard had such a household.

This definition of "family" is consistent with both of the competing purposes of the rent control laws: the protection of the individuals from sudden dislocation and gradual transition to a free market system. Family members, whether or not related by blood or law, who have always treated the apartment as their family home will be protected against the hardship of eviction following the death of the named tenant, thereby furthering the Legislature's goal of preventing dislocation and preserving family units which might otherwise be broken apart upon eviction. This approach will foster the transition from rent control to rent stabilization by drawing a distinction between those individuals who are, in fact, genuine family members, and those who are mere roommates [*see* N.Y. Real Prop. Law § 235f. (McKinney 1987); Yorkshire Towers Co. v. Harpster, 510 N.Y.S.2d 976 (1986)], or newly discovered relatives hoping to inherit the rent controlled apartment after the existing tenant's death.

In a footnote the court sought to distinguish the decision from zoning matters:

... the definition of family we adopt here for purposes of the non-eviction protection of the rent control laws is completely unrelated to the concept of "functional family," as that term has developed under this court's decisions in the context of zoning ordinances. Those decisions focus on a locality's power to use its zoning powers in such a way as to impinge upon an individual's ability to live under the same roof with another individual. They have absolutely no bearing on the scope of non-eviction protection provided by § 2204.6(d).

There was serious concern after Braschi as to what objective limits might be imposed on the practical aspects of rent control in New York. For a good discussion of this aspect of the changing definition of family, *see* David D. Haddock and Daniel D. Polsby, *Family as a Rational Classification*, 74 WASH. U. L. Q. 15 (1996). In a decision related to expansion of family definition, the New York Supreme Court has upheld the New York City Domestic Partnership Law, empowering the city to enter into insurance contracts or health plans for non-married city workers and their designated non-marital families. The court held that the decision results from previous decisions in New York courts expanding the definition of family. *See* Slattery v. City of New York, 266 A.D.2d 24, 697 N.Y.S.2d 603 (1999). But the New York Supreme Court has held that the survivor of a homosexual relationship in which the parties were in a "spousal relationship" was not entitled to a right of election against the decedent's Last Will and Testament. The state statutory term of "surviving spouse" does not include homosexual life partners. The court rejected an argument based on the holding in *Braschi*. *See* In re Estate of Cooper, 187 A.D.2d 128, 592 N.Y.S.2d 797 (1993).

Also after the *Braschi* decision in 1989, businesses initiated employee incentives whereby non-marital partners, most often of the same sex, could register and share in economic benefits offered by the business. Most often the benefits consisted of insurance coverage, bereavement leave, and any other perks of that particular business. The focus was on providing similar benefits to married and unmarried couples. *See* Raymond C. O'Brien, *Domestic Partnership: Recognition and Responsibility,* 32 SAN DIEGO L. REV. 163, 177–181 (1995). Businesses called these arrangements "domestic partnerships." Eventually local and state governments provided similar benefits to employees and today, California has one of the most extensive domestic partnership arrangements ever envisioned. From domestic partnership a further evolution occurred with the arrival of "reciprocal beneficiaries" in Hawaii and then "civil unions" presently available in Vermont, Connecticut, and New Jersey. This will be discussed in more detail *infra*. While a very few opposite sex couples may enter into these arrangements, they were devised to provide economic benefits to same sex adults living in committed relationships, as in *Braschi*, but unable to marry.

Opposite Sex Unmarried Families. Opposite sex couples are precluded, except in very narrow circumstances, from entering into civil unions, reciprocal beneficiary, or domestic partnerships. The rationale for their exclusion is their ability to enter into marriage. Nonetheless, courts have increasingly recognized the rights of unmarried opposite sex couples to privately order their economic, parental, and social obligations. The issue has always been whether unmarried couples should be able to utilize economic benefits that heretofore had been reserved to married couples. For example, when non-marital cohabitants marry after a period of non-marital cohabitation, some courts have been willing to consider as marital property subject to division *all* of the property acquired when the parties were cohabiting, not just property acquired during the actual marriage. *See, e.g., In re* Marriage of Timm, 200 Or.App. 621, 117 P.3d 301 (2005). *But see* Bunyard v. Bunyard, 828 So.2d 775 (Miss. 2002) (court unwilling to treat separate property acquired during premarital cohabitation as marital property when couple divorced). Also, courts have been willing to enforce orders of support between the two unmarried parties. *See, e.g.,* Gormley v. Robertson, 120 Wash.App. 31, 83 P.3d 1042 (2004). And based on the equities involved, particularly the need to avoid unjust enrichment, courts have enforced oral agreements between unmarried cohabitants even after the death of one of the parties. *See, e.g.,* Byrne v. Laura, 52 Cal.App.4th

1054, 60 Cal.Rptr.2d 908 (Cal. Ct. App. 1997); Olver v. Fowler, 131 Wash.App. 135, 126 P.3d 69 (2006), *review granted*, 158 Wash.2d 1006, 143 P.3d 829 (Oct. 11, 2006) (No. 78321–7). Not all states have been as accommodating. Minnesota, for example, requires there to be an express written agreement between the parties to be enforceable. *See* MINN. STAT. ANN. § 513.075 (West 2002). And some courts require cohabitation warranting enforcement. *See, e.g.,* Levine v. Konvitz, 383 N.J.Super. 1, 890 A.2d 354 (App.Div. 2006) (court refused to enforce a promise of support after the couple had a 70–year non-marital relationship because there had never been cohabitation), *certification denied*, 186 N.J. 607, 897 A.2d 1061 (2006).

Non-marital Couples, Landlords and the First Amendment. Some states have extended protection against bias to non-marital couples. For example, states have statutes that specifically prohibit discrimination based on marital status. Thus, when non-married partners seek to rent a residence, obtain loans or register as domestic partners, employers, landlords and lenders are prohibited from refusing benefits. Often objections against extending benefits to non-marital partners are based on the Free Exercise Clause of the First Amendment. An example of such a refusal is Smith v. Fair Employment and Housing Commission, 12 Cal.4th 1143, 51 Cal.Rptr.2d 700, 913 P.2d 909 (1996), *cert. denied*, 521 U.S. 1129, 117 S.Ct. 2531, 138 L.Ed.2d 1031 (1997). At issue was the California Fair Employment and Housing Act 12955 that provides in part that: "It shall be unlawful: (a) For the owner of any housing accommodation to discriminate against any person because of the race, color, religion, sex, *marital status*, national origin, ancestry, familial status, or disability of that person" [emphasis added]. Evelyn Smith, a member of Bidwell Presbyterian Church in Chico, California, refused to rent one of her four rental units to anunmarried couple because she

> believes that sex outside of marriage is sinful, and that it is a sin for her to rent her units to people who will engage in non-marital sex on her property. [She] believes God will judge her if she permits people to engage in sex outside of marriage in her rental units and that if she does so, she will be prevented from meeting her deceased husband in the hereafter.

Id. at 912. The California Supreme Court held that the state's ban against marital status discrimination did not substantially burden the landlord's free exercise and the landlord must comply with the Fair Employment and Housing Act and rent to the non-married couple. Other states have reached similar results. *See, e.g.,* Swanner v. Anchorage Equal Rights Commission, 874 P.2d 274 (Alaska 1994), *cert. denied*, 513 U.S. 979, 115 S.Ct. 460, 130 L.Ed.2d 368 (1994), and McCready v. Hoffius, 459 Mich. 131, 586 N.W.2d 723 (1998), where the Michigan Supreme Court held that the state's interest in providing equal access to such a fundamental need as housing outweighs the landlord's sincerely held religious beliefs; if landlords wish to participate in the rental housing market they must comply with the state statute. *See* Jane Rutherford, *Religion, Rationality, and Special Treatment*,

9 WM. & MARY BILL RTS. J. 303 (2001); Michael W. McConnell, *The Problem of Singling Out Religion*, 50 DEPAUL L. REV. 1 (2000).

First Amendment religious exemption continues to arise in cases other than housing discrimination. Other examples would include vaccination of children, medical care and treatment of children, education, parental supervision, and even the use of controlled substances in religious ceremonies. The following decision is illustrative.

Catholic Charities of Sacramento Inc. v. Superior Court

Supreme Court of California, 2004.
32 Cal.4th 527, 10 Cal.Rptr.3d 283, 85 P.3d 67, cert. denied 125 S.Ct. 53.

■ WERDEGAR, J.

In this case, we address a church-affiliated employer's constitutional challenges to the Women's Contraception Equity Act (WCEA), under which certain health and disability insurance contracts must cover prescription contraceptives. The plaintiff employer, which opposes contraceptives on religious grounds, claims the statute violates the establishment and free exercise clauses of the United States and California Constitutions. (U.S. Const., 1st Amend.; Cal. Const., art. I, § 4.) The lower courts rejected the employer's claims. We affirm.

The Legislature enacted the WCEA in 1999 to eliminate gender discrimination in health care benefits and to improve access to prescription contraceptives. Evidence before the Legislature showed that women during their reproductive years spent as much as 68 percent more than men in out-of-pocket health care costs, due in large part to the cost of prescription contraceptives and the various costs of unintended pregnancies, including health risks, premature deliveries and increased neonatal care. Evidence also showed that, while most health maintenance organizations (HMO's) covered prescription contraceptives, not all preferred provider organization (PPO) and indemnity plans did. As a result, approximately 10 percent of commercially insured Californians did not have coverage for prescription contraceptives.

The Legislature chose to address these problems by regulating the terms of insurance contracts. The WCEA does not require any employer to offer coverage for prescription drugs. Under the WCEA, however, certain health and disability insurance plans that cover prescription drugs must cover prescription contraceptives. As an exception, the law permits a "religious employer" to request a policy that includes drug coverage but excludes coverage for "contraceptive methods that are contrary to the religious employer's religious tenets." Health and Safety Code section 1367.25 governs group health care service plan contracts; Insurance Code section 10123.196 governs individual and group disability insurance policies.

Plaintiff Catholic Charities of Sacramento, Inc. (hereafter Catholic Charities) is a California nonprofit public benefit corporation. (See Corp.

Code, § 5110 et seq.) Although independently incorporated, Catholic Charities describes itself as "operated in connection with the Roman Catholic Bishop of Sacramento" and as "an organ of the Roman Catholic Church." The nonprofit corporation "offer[s] a multitude of social services and private welfare programs to the general public, as part of the social justice ministry of the Roman Catholic Church." These services and programs include "providing immigrant resettlement programs, elder care, counseling, food, clothing and affordable housing for the poor and needy, housing and vocational training of the developmentally disabled and the like."

Catholic Charities offers health insurance, including prescription drug coverage, to its 183 full-time employees through group health care plans underwritten by Blue Shield of California and Kaiser Permanente. Catholic Charities does not, however, offer insurance for prescription contraceptives because it considers itself obliged to follow the Roman Catholic Church's religious teachings, because the Church considers contraception a sin, and because Catholic Charities believes it cannot offer insurance for prescription contraceptives without improperly facilitating that sin.

As mentioned, the WCEA permits a "religious employer" to offer prescription drug insurance without coverage for contraceptives that violate the employer's religious tenets. (Health & Saf. Code, § 1367.25, subd. (b).) The act defines a "religious employer" as "an entity for which each of the following is true: [¶] (A) The inculcation of religious values is the purpose of the entity. [¶] (B) The entity primarily employs persons who share the religious tenets of the entity. [¶] (C) The entity serves primarily persons who share the religious tenets of the entity. [¶] (D) The entity is a nonprofit organization as described in Section 6033(a)(2)(A)I or iii, of the Internal Revenue Code of 1986, as amended." (*Ibid.*) The cited provisions of the Internal Revenue Code exempt, from the obligation to file an annual return, "churches, their integrated auxiliaries, and conventions or associations of churches" (26 U.S.C. § 6033(a)(2)(A)(I)) and "the exclusively religious activities of any religious order" (*id.*, § 6033(a)(2)(A)(I) and (iii)).

Catholic Charities does not qualify as a "religious employer" under the WCEA because it does not meet any of the definition's four criteria. (See Health & Saf. Code, § 1367.25, subd. (b)(1)(A)–(D).) The organization candidly acknowledges this in its complaint, offering the following explanation: "The corporate purpose of Catholic Charities is not the direct inculcation of religious values. Rather, [its] purpose . . . is to offer social services to the general public that promote a just, compassionate society that supports the dignity of individuals and families, to reduce the causes and results of poverty, and to build healthy communities through social service programs such as counseling, mental health and immigration services, low-income housing, and supportive social services to the poor and vulnerable. Further, Catholic Charities does not primarily employ persons who share its Roman Catholic religious beliefs, but, rather, employs a diverse group of persons of many religious backgrounds, all of whom share [its] Gospel-based commitment to promote a just, compassionate society that supports the dignity of individuals and families. Moreover, Catholic Charities serves people of all faith backgrounds, a significant majority of [whom] do not share [its] Roman Catholic faith. Finally, ... Catholic Charities, although an exempt organization under 26 U.S.C. § 501(c)(3), is not a nonprofit organization pursuant to [s]ection 6033(a)(2)(A)(I) or (iii) of the Internal Revenue Code of 1986. Consequently, ... Catholic Charities is not entitled ... to an exemption from the mandate imposed by [the WCEA]."

As mentioned, the WCEA implicitly permits any employer to avoid covering contraceptives by not offering coverage for prescription drugs. But this option, according to Catholic Charities, does not eliminate all conflict between the law and its religious beliefs. Catholic Charities feels obliged to offer prescription drug insurance to its employees under what it describes as the "Roman Catholic religious teaching" that "an employer has a moral obligation at all times to consider the well-being of its employees and to offer just wages and benefits in order to provide a dignified livelihood for the employee and his or her family."

Perceiving no option consistent with both its beliefs and the law, Catholic Charities filed this action seeking a declaratory judgment that the WCEA is unconstitutional and an injunction barring the law's enforcement. Defendants are the State of California, the Department of Managed Health Care and the Department of Insurance ... Catholic Charities' challenges to the WCEA arise under the establishment and free exercise clauses of the United States and California Constitutions. (U.S. Const., 1st Amend.; Cal. Const., art. I, § 4.) The superior court, finding no reasonable likelihood that Catholic Charities would prevail on the merits, denied its motion for a preliminary injunction. Catholic Charities sought review of this ruling by petition for writ of mandate, which the Court of Appeal denied. We granted review of the Court of Appeal's decision.

Catholic Charities, in its brief to this court, asserts eight constitutional challenges to the WCEA. All refer to the religion clauses of the federal and state Constitutions. (U.S. Const., 1st Amend.; Cal. Const., art. I, § 4.) Catholic Charities begins with a set of three arguments to the effect that the WCEA impermissibly interferes with the autonomy of religious organizations. (See 10 Cal.Rptr.3d p. 294, 85 P.3d p. 76 et seq., *post.*) Next, Catholic Charities claims the WCEA impermissibly burdens its right of free exercise. As part of this claim, Catholic Charities offers four arguments for subjecting the WCEA to strict scrutiny, despite the United States Supreme Court's holding that the right of free exercise does not excuse compliance with neutral, generally applicable laws. (*Employment Div., Ore. Dept. of Human Res. v. Smith* (1990) 494 U.S. 872, 876–890, 110 S.Ct. 1595, 108 L.Ed.2d 876; see 10 Cal.Rptr.3d p. 299, 85 P.3d p. 81 et seq., *post.*) Finally, Catholic Charities contends the WCEA fails even the rational basis test. (See p. 315, 85 P.3d p. 94 et seq., *post.*)

A. Religious Autonomy

1. Interference with matters of religious doctrine and internal church governance

... Catholic Charities asserts that the Legislature, in enacting the WCEA, violated the rule of church property cases by interfering with matters of internal church governance and by rejecting the Catholic Church's decision that prescription contraceptives are sinful. These assertions are incorrect. This case does not implicate internal church governance; it implicates the relationship between a nonprofit public benefit corporation and its employees, most of whom do not belong to the Catholic Church. Only those who join a church impliedly consent to its religious governance on matters of faith and discipline. (*Watson, supra,* 13 Wall. 679, 80 U.S. 679, 729.) Certainly the WCEA conflicts with Catholic Charities' religious beliefs, but this does not mean the Legislature has decided a religious question. Congress has created, and the high court has resolved, similar conflicts between employment law and religious beliefs without deciding religious questions and without reference to the church property cases. (E.g., *Tony and Susan Alamo Foundation v. Sec'y of Labor* (1985) 471 U.S. 290, 303–306, 105 S.Ct. 1953, 85 L.Ed.2d 278 [religious organization must comply with federal minimum wage laws]; *United States v. Lee* (1982) 455 U.S. 252, 256–261, 102 S.Ct. 1051, 71 L.Ed.2d 127 [Amish employer must pay Social Security and unemployment taxes].) Neither does this case require us to decide any religious questions. Instead, we need only apply the usual rules for assessing whether state-imposed burdens on religious exercise are constitutional. (See *Church of Lukumi Babalu Aye, Inc. v. Hialeah* (1993) 508 U.S. 520, 531–533, 113 S.Ct. 2217, 124 L.Ed.2d 472; *Employment Div., Ore. Dept. of Human Res. v. Smith, supra,* 494 U.S. 872, 876–882, 110 S.Ct. 1595.) This we do below, in the context of Catholic Charities' separate claims under the free exercise clause. (See 10 Cal. Rptr.3d p. 299, 85 P.3d p. 81 et seq., *post.*)

. . .

2. DISTINCTION BETWEEN RELIGIOUS AND SECULAR ACTIVITIES

Catholic Charities next argues that the First Amendment forbids the government to "premis[e] a religious institution's eligibility for an exemption from government regulation upon whether the activities of the institution are deemed by the government to be 'religious' or 'secular'. . . ." The argument is directed against the four statutory criteria an employer must satisfy to claim exemption from the WCEA as a "religious employer." (Health & Saf. Code, § 1367.25, subd. (b)(1)(A)–(D); see 10 Cal.Rptr.3d p. 292, 85 P.3d p. 75, *ante.*) The argument lacks merit.

The exception to the WCEA accommodates religious exercise by relieving statutorily defined "religious employers" (Health & Saf. Code, § 1367.25, subd. (b)) of the burden of paying for contraceptive methods that violate their religious beliefs. The United States Supreme Court has long recognized that the alleviation of significant governmentally created burdens on religious exercise is a permissible legislative purpose that does not offend the establishment clause. (*Corporation of Presiding Bishop v. Amos* (1978) 483 U.S. 327, 334–335, 107 S.Ct. 2862, 97 L.Ed.2d 273; *Hobbie v. Unemployment Appeals Comm'n of Fla.* (1987) 480 U.S. 136, 144–145, 107 S.Ct. 1046, 94 L.Ed.2d 190; cf. *Employment Div., Ore. Dept. of Human*

Res. v. Smith, supra, 494 U.S. 872, 890, 110 S.Ct. 1595.) Such legislative accommodations would be impossible as a practical matter if the government were, as Catholic Charities argues, forbidden to distinguish between the religious entities and activities that are entitled to accommodation and the secular entities and activities that are not. In fact, Congress and the state legislatures have drawn such distinctions for this purpose, and laws embodying such distinctions have passed constitutional muster. (E.g., *Corporation of Presiding Bishop v. Amos, supra,* 483 U.S. 327, 334–340, 107 S.Ct. 2862 [upholding statutory exemption of "religious" employers from liability for religious discrimination; 42 U.S.C. § 2000e–1(a)]; *East Bay Asian Local Development Corp. v. State of California* (2000) 24 Cal.4th 693, 704–718, 102 Cal.Rptr.2d 280, 13 P.3d 1122 [upholding state laws exempting "religiously affiliated" organizations from landmark preservation laws, Gov.Code, §§ 25373, subds. (c) & (d), 37361, subd. (c)].)

. . .

Our conclusion that the government may properly distinguish between secular and religious entities and activities for the purpose of accommodating religious exercise does not mean that any given statute purporting to draw such distinctions necessarily passes muster under the free exercise clause. "[A] law targeting religious beliefs as such is never permissible," and a court " 'must survey meticulously the circumstances of governmental categories to eliminate, as it were, religious gerrymanders.' " (*Church of Lukumi Babalu Aye, Inc. v. Hialeah, supra,* 508 U.S. 520, 533–534, 113 S.Ct. 2217, quoting *Walz v. Tax Commission* (1970) 397 U.S. 664, 696, 90 S.Ct. 1409, 25 L.Ed.2d 697 (conc. opn. of Harlan, J.).) We address below Catholic Charities' separate argument that the WCEA's definition of "religious employer" in fact embodies a legislative effort to target Catholic organizations for unfavorable treatment. (See 10 Cal.Rptr.3d p. 303, 85 P.3d p. 84 et seq., *post.*)

3. EXCESSIVE ENTANGLEMENT

Catholic Charities contends that the WCEA's exemption for "religious employer[s]" (Health & Saf. Code, § 1367.25, subd. (b)) violates the establishment clause by mandating an entangling inquiry into the employer's religious purpose and into its employees' and clients' religious beliefs. The argument refers to the first three of the four statutory criteria for identifying a "religious employer," namely, whether "[t]he inculcation of religious values is the purpose of the entity" (*id.,* subd. (b)(1)(A)), whether "[t]he entity primarily employs persons who share the religious tenets of the entity" (*id.,* subd. (b)(1)(B)), and whether "[t]he entity serves primarily persons who share the religious tenets of the entity" (*id.,* subd. (b)(1)(C)). A law that fosters an excessive governmental entanglement with religion can for that reason violate the establishment clause. (*Lemon v. Kurtzman* (1971) 403 U.S. 602, 612–613, 91 S.Ct. 2105, 29 L.Ed.2d 745.)[6] Moreover,

---

6. The court in *Lemon v. Kurtzman, supra,* 403 U.S. 602, 91 S.Ct. 2105, 29 L.Ed.2d 745, "gleaned from [its prior] cases" three tests for determining whether a statute violates the establishment clause: "First, the statute must have a secular legislative pur-

recent judicial opinions have criticized rules and laws that invite official "trolling through a person's or institution's religious beliefs." (*Mitchell v. Helms* (2000) 530 U.S. 793, 828, 120 S.Ct. 2530, 147 L.Ed.2d 660 (plur. opn. of Thomas, J.); *University of Great Falls v. N.L.R.B.* (D.C.Cir.2002) 278 F.3d 1335, 1342–1348.)

The argument might have merit as applied to a hypothetical employer that sought to qualify under the WCEA's exemption for religious employers (Health & Saf. Code, § 1367.25, subd. (b)) but objected on establishment clause grounds to an entangling official effort to verify that its purpose was the inculcation of religious values, and that it primarily employed and served persons who shared its religious tenets. But Catholic Charities candidly alleges in its complaint that it does not qualify under the exemption because it does not satisfy any of the four criteria. More specifically, Catholic Charities concedes that its purpose is not the inculcation of religious values, that it does not primarily hire and serve Catholics, and that it does not fall within either of the relevant provisions of the Internal Revenue Code (26 U.S.C. § 6033(a)(2)(A)(I) and (iii), cited in Health & Saf. Code, § 1367.25, subd. (b)(1)(D)). Consequently, no entangling inquiry into Catholic Charities' purpose or beliefs, or the beliefs of its employees and clients, has occurred or is likely to occur. Therefore, even if in some other case the statute might require an entangling inquiry, in this case, as applied to Catholic Charities, the establishment clause offers no basis for holding the statute unconstitutional.

B. FREE EXERCISE OF RELIGION

Catholic Charities argues the WCEA violates the free exercise clauses of the federal and state Constitutions (U.S. Const., 1st Amend.; Cal. Const., art. I, § 4) by coercing the organization to violate its religious beliefs, in that the WCEA, by regulating the content of insurance policies, in effect requires employers who offer their workers insurance for prescription drugs to offer coverage for prescription contraceptives. Catholic Charities wishes to offer insurance, but may not facilitate the use of contraceptives without violating its religious beliefs.

. . .

The general rule affirmed in *Smith, supra,* 494 U.S. 872, 110 S.Ct. 1595, would at first glance appear to dispose of Catholic Charities' free exercise claim. The WCEA's requirements apply neutrally and generally to all employers, regardless of religious affiliation, except to those few who satisfy the statute's strict requirements for exemption on religious grounds. (Health & Saf. Code, § 1367.25, subd. (b).) The act also addresses a matter the state is free to regulate; it regulates the content of insurance policies for the purpose of eliminating a form of gender discrimination in health

pose; second its principal or primary effect must be one that neither advances nor inhibits religion . . .; finally, the statute must not foster 'an excessive governmental entangle-ment with religion.' " (*Id.,* at pp. 612–613, 91 S.Ct. 2105, quoting *Walz v. Tax Commission, supra,* 397 U.S. 664, 674, 90 S.Ct. 1409.)

benefits. The act conflicts with Catholic Charities' religious beliefs only incidentally, because those beliefs happen to make prescription contraceptives sinful. Accordingly, it appears Catholic Charities may successfully challenge the WCEA only by demonstrating an exception to the general rule.

. . .

2. RELIGIOUS GERRYMANDER

Our analysis does not end with the conclusion that the WCEA is facially neutral towards religion. The First Amendment requires more than facial neutrality. It protects against " 'subtle departures from neutrality' " and "governmental hostility which is masked as well as overt." (*Lukumi, supra,* 508 U.S. 520, 534, 113 S.Ct. 2217, quoting *Gillette v. United States, supra,* 401 U.S. 437, 452, 91 S.Ct. 828.) Thus, a court " 'must survey meticulously the circumstances of governmental categories to eliminate, as it were, religious gerrymanders.' " (*Ibid.,* quoting *Walz v. Tax Commission, supra,* 397 U.S. 664, 696, 90 S.Ct. 1409 (conc. opn. of Harlan, J.).) Catholic Charities argues the Legislature gerrymandered the WCEA to deny the benefit of the exemption to Catholic organizations. The law discriminates, Catholic Charities contends, both against the Catholic Church and against religious organizations of any denomination that engage in charitable work, as opposed to work that is purely spiritual or evangelical.

We find no merit in the argument that the WCEA discriminates against the Catholic Church. It was at the request of Catholic organizations that the Legislature added an exception permitting religious employers to deny coverage for "contraceptive methods that are contrary to the religious employer's religious tenets." (Health & Saf. Code, § 1367.25, subd. (b).) Because most religions do not object to prescription contraceptives, most religious employers are subject to the WCEA. The Legislature's decision to grant preferential treatment to religious employers who do object is justifiable as an accommodation of religious exercise under the principles discussed above. (*Amos, supra,* 483 U.S. 327, 334–335, 107 S.Ct. 2862.) That the exemption is not sufficiently broad to cover all organizations affiliated with the Catholic Church does not mean the exemption discriminates against the Catholic Church.[9]

. . .

9. Indeed, rather than discriminating against the Catholic Church, the WCEA can more plausibly be viewed as benefiting the Catholic Church in practical effect, since no other religious group opposed to prescription contraceptives has been identified. But the WCEA does not for this reason violate the establishment clause. A law intended not to discriminate among religions but to alleviate a governmentally created burden on religious exercise does not necessarily violate the establishment clause, even though only a single religion in need of accommodation has been identified, if the law is phrased neutrally, to allow for the possibility that other as-yet-unidentified religions in need of the same accommodation will be able to claim it. (See, e.g., *Kong v. Scully* (9th Cir.2003) 341 F.3d 1132; *Children's Health. Is A Legal Duty v. Min De Parle* (8th Cir.2000) 212 F.3d 1084; *Droz v. Commissioner of I.R.S.* (9th Cir.1995) 48 F.3d 1120.)

Catholic Charities' intent may be to argue that the WCEA discriminates against charitable social work *as a religious practice*. Such an argument would implicate "[t]he principle that government, in pursuit of legitimate interests, cannot in a selective manner impose burdens only on conduct motivated by religious belief...." (*Lukumi, supra,* 508 U.S. 520, 543, 113 S.Ct. 2217.) Applying this principle, the high court in *Lukumi* held unconstitutional an ordinance that permitted the killing of animals for food or sport, but not in religious rituals. The ordinance had " 'every appearance of a prohibition that society is prepared to impose upon [Santeria worshippers] but not upon itself.' " (*Id.,* at p. 545, 113 S.Ct. 2217, quoting *The Florida Star v. B.J.F.* (1989) 491 U.S. 524, 542, 109 S.Ct. 2603, 105 L.Ed.2d 443.) The WCEA is not similar. If a religiously affiliated organization fails to qualify for exemption because its purpose is something other than the "inculcation of religious values" (Health & Saf. Code, § 1367. 25, subd. (b)(1)(A)), then the result is simply that the organization becomes subject to the same obligations that apply to all other employers. Because the WCEA applies to all nonreligious employers engaged in charitable social work, no argument can logically be made that the WCEA imposes a burden on charitable social work only when performed for religious reasons.

As additional support for its claim that the WCEA's purpose is to discriminate against the Catholic Church, Catholic Charities contends the Legislature drafted the "religious employer" exception (Health & Saf. Code, § 1367.25, subd. (b)) with the specific intention of excluding Catholic hospitals and social service agencies like Catholic Charities. Catholic Charities draws an analogy to *Lukumi, supra,* 508 U.S. 520, 540–542, 113 S.Ct. 2217, in which the high court considered specific statements by members of the Hialeah City Council as evidence that the ordinance prohibiting animal sacrifice was intended to suppress the Santeria religion. Catholic Charities' assertions about the legislative history of the WCEA do not justify a similar conclusion in this case.

According to Catholic Charities, the history of the WCEA suggests the Legislature intended the law to close a "Catholic gap" in insurance coverage for prescription contraceptives. The evidence does not support the contention. The phrase "Catholic gap" appears only in Catholic Charities' brief, not in the legislative history. Catholic Charities refers to the Senate testimony of a representative of Planned Parenthood, which opposed any exception for religious employers. Explaining that organization's position, the witness stated: "Primarily our intent was to close the gap in insurance coverage for contraception and prescription benefit plans. Our concern with granting an exemption is that that defeats the original purpose of the bill." The "gap" to which the witness apparently referred was the gap identified by a national consulting firm's 1999 study of health insurance for prescription contraceptives. This study, which received much attention in the Legislature, concluded that approximately 10 percent of commercially insured Californians did not already have insurance coverage for prescription contraceptives. The study identified this minority not as the employees of Catholic organizations, but as persons covered by PPO and indemnity plans. While most HMO's covered prescription contraceptives, not all PPO and indemnity plans did. Catholic Charities' assertion that the purpose of the WCEA was to close a "Catholic gap" rather than a statewide statistical gap in coverage has no apparent evidentiary support.[11]

Next, Catholic Charities argues the Legislature deliberately narrowed the statutory exception for "religious employer[s]" (Health & Saf. Code, § 1367.25, subd. (b)) to include as few Catholic organizations as possible and specifically to exclude Catholic hospitals and social service organizations. The legislative history does show that the bill's sponsors argued against a broader exception. The bill's Senate sponsor, for example, stated in a committee hearing that "the intention of the authors as it relates to creating a religious exemption may not be the same intentions of the religions themselves in wanting to be exempted. [¶] The intention of the religious exemption in both these bills is an intention to provide for exemption for what is religious activity. The more secular the activity gets, the less religiously based it is, and the more we believe that they should be required to cover prescription drug benefits for contraception." Catholic Charities describes this and similar statements as evidence that the Legislature targeted specific Catholic organizations for disadvantageous treatment. But we have already examined and rejected that argument. The law treats some Catholic organizations more favorably than all other employers by exempting them; nonexempt Catholic organizations are treated the same as all other employers.

. . .

C. RATIONAL BASIS

Catholic Charities' final challenge to the WCEA is that it violates the rational basis test. More specifically, Catholic Charities argues the State has defined the exempt category of "religious employer" (Health & Saf. Code, § 1367.25, subd. (b)) with arbitrary criteria. "In effect," according to Catholic Charities, "the Legislature decided that any religious institution that employs individuals of other faiths or that ministers to persons of all faiths (or no faith)—in effect any 'missionary' church or church with social outreach—is not sufficiently 'religious' to qualify for exemption," and that these classifications are "wholly unrelated to any legitimate state interest."

The argument lacks merit. The WCEA's exemption for religious organizations, even if not applicable to Catholic Charities, rationally serves the legitimate interest of complying with the rule barring interference with the relationship between a church and its ministers. (See *ante*, 10 Cal.Rptr.3d at p. 296, 85 P.3d at p. 78 et seq.) Although the high court has not spoken

---

11. Catholic Charities also argues that the Legislature acted out of antipathy and spite towards the Catholic Church. Through this argument, Catholic Charities seeks to compare the Legislature's consideration of the WCEA with the Hialeah City Council's decision (see *Lukumi, supra,* 508 U.S. 520, 113 S.Ct. 2217) to ban animal sacrifice as a way of suppressing the Santeria religion. In discussing the council's decision, the high court noted that Hialeah city officials had castigated Santeria as an "abomination to the Lord" and "the worship of demons," and that a public crowd attending the city council's meeting had interrupted with jeers and taunts the President of the Santeria Church. (*Id.,* at p. 541, 113 S.Ct. 2217.) The legislative history of the WCEA discloses no comparable antipathy to the Catholic Church.

on the subject, the lower federal courts have held that the constitutionally based ministerial exemption survives the decision in *Smith, supra,* 494 U.S. 872, 110 S.Ct. 1595.... Most organizations entitled to invoke the ministerial exemption will be involved in the "inculcation of religious values," which the first criterion requires. (Health & Saf. Code, § 1367.25, subd. (b)(1)(A).) many will also satisfy the WCEA's fourth exemption criterion, which requires that a religious employer qualify for federal tax exemption as a church, an integrated auxiliary of a church, a convention or association of churches, or a religious order. (See 26 U.S.C. § 6033(a)(2)(A)(I) and (iii), cited in Health & Saf. Code, § 1367.25, subd. (b)(1)(D).) If in any case the constitutionally required ministerial exception were broader than the statutory exemption, the former would of course take precedence.

The second criterion, to which Catholic Charities specifically objects as lacking a rational basis, requires that an employer "primarily employ [ ] persons who share the religious tenets of the entity." (Health & Saf. Code, § 1367.25, subd. (b)(1)(B).) This provision, in effect, accommodates religious employers more broadly than the ministerial exemption requires by extending the WCEA's exemption to employees who could not fall within the ministerial exemption. The provision has the legitimate, rational purpose of accommodating a state-imposed burden on religious exercise. (*Amos, supra,* 483 U.S. 327, 334–335, 107 S.Ct. 2862.)

The third criterion, to which Catholic Charities also objects, is problematic. To qualify under it, an employer must "serve[ ] primarily persons who share the religious tenets of the entity." (Health & Saf. Code, § 1367.25, subd. (b)(1)(C).) To imagine a legitimate purpose for such a requirement is difficult. Reading the provision literally, a hypothetical soup kitchen run entirely by the ministers of a church, which inculcates religious values to those who come to eat (thus satisfying the first, second, and fourth criteria), would lose its claim to an exemption from the WCEA if it chose to serve the hungry without discrimination instead of serving coreligionists only. The Legislature may wish to address this problem. Catholic Charities, however, cannot successfully challenge the WCEA on this ground because the organization concedes it does not qualify under any of the criteria for exemption, including the relatively objective terms of the federal tax statute cited in the fourth criterion. (Health & Saf. Code, § 1367.25, subd. (b)(1)(D).) Catholic Charities thus cannot qualify for exemption in any event.

The decision of the Court of Appeal is affirmed.

■ WE CONCUR: GEORGE, C.J., BAXTER, CHIN, and MORENO, JJ.

[The separate concurring opinion by KENNARD, J. and the dissenting opinion by BROWN, J. have been omitted.]

B.   MAKING YOUR OWN DEAL: CONTRACTUAL ARRANGEMENTS AS AN ALTERNATIVE TO MARRIAGE

Increasingly, both opposite and same sex couples are cohabiting in nonmarital relationships with no intention of entering into marriage, either statutory or common law. More than roommates and often seeking to express their functional family in terms of contracts, these couples seek to have their economic interests recognized within the context of a sexual relationship. The ability of adults to form non-marital contractual relationships which often mimic a marital relationship is the subject of non-marital contracting, both when the contract is explicit or implicit. The following cases and materials thus question the availability of contractual relationships for non-marital couples, the role of the judiciary in enforcing them, the appropriate venue for litigation, evolution to domestic partnership, and the pitfalls attendant when the couple's relationship resembles too intimately the institution of marriage.

1. THE MARVIN TRILOGY

Marvin v. Marvin (I)

Supreme Court of California, In Bank, 1976.
18 Cal.3d 660, 134 Cal.Rptr. 815, 557 P.2d 106.

■ TOBRINER, JUSTICE.

During the past 15 years, there has been a substantial increase in the number of couples living together without marrying. Such non-marital relationships lead to legal controversy when one partner dies or the couple separates. Courts of Appeal, faced with the task of determining property rights in such cases, have arrived at conflicting positions: two cases (In re Marriage of Cary (1973) 34 Cal.App.3d 345, 109 Cal.Rptr. 862; Estate of Atherley (1975) 44 Cal.App.3d 758, 119 Cal.Rptr. 41) have held that the Family Law Act (Civ.Code, § 4000 et seq.) requires division of the property according to community property principles, and one decision (Beckman v. Mayhew (1975) 49 Cal.App.3d 529, 122 Cal.Rptr. 604) has rejected that holding. . . .

We conclude: (1) The provisions of the Family Law Act do not govern the distribution of property acquired during a non-marital relationship; such a relationship remains subject solely to judicial decision. (2) The courts should enforce express contracts between non-marital partners except to the extent that the contract is explicitly founded on the consideration of meretricious sexual services. (3) In the absence of an express contract, the court should inquire into the conduct of the parties to determine whether that conduct demonstrates an implied contract, agreement of partnership or joint venture, or some other tacit understanding between the parties. The courts may also employ the doctrine of quantum meruit, or equitable remedies such as constructive or resulting trusts, when warranted by the facts of the case.

In the instant case plaintiff and defendant lived together for seven years without marrying; all property acquired during this period was taken in defendant's name. When plaintiff sued to enforce a contract under which she was entitled to half the property and to support payments, the trial court granted judgment on the pleadings for defendant, thus leaving him with all property accumulated by the couple during their relationship. Since the trial court denied plaintiff a trial on the merits of her claim, its decision conflicts with the principle stated above, and must be reversed.

1. *The factual setting of this appeal.*

. . .

Plaintiff avers that in October of 1964 she and defendant "entered into an oral agreement" that while "the parties lived together they would combine their efforts and earnings and would share equally any and all property accumulated as a result of their efforts whether individual or combined." Furthermore, they agreed to "hold themselves out to the general public as husband and wife" and that "plaintiff would further render her services as a companion, homemaker, housekeeper and cook to . . . defendant."

Shortly thereafter plaintiff agreed to "give up her lucrative career as an entertainer [and] singer" in order to "devote her full time to defendant . . . as a companion, homemaker, housekeeper and cook;" in return defendant agreed to "provide for all of plaintiff's financial support and needs for the rest of her life."

Plaintiff alleges that she lived with defendant from October of 1964 through May of 1970 and fulfilled her obligations under the agreement. During this period the parties as a result of their efforts and earnings acquired in defendant's name substantial real and personal property, including motion picture rights worth over $1 million. In May of 1970, however, defendant compelled plaintiff to leave his household. He continued to support plaintiff until November of 1971, but thereafter refused to provide further support.

On the basis of these allegations plaintiff asserts two causes of action. The first, for declaratory relief, asks the court to determine her contract and property rights; the second seeks to impose a constructive trust upon one half of the property acquired during the course of the relationship.

Defendant demurred unsuccessfully, and then answered the complaint. Following extensive discovery and pretrial proceedings, the case came to trial. Defendant renewed his attack on the complaint by a motion to dismiss. Since the parties had stipulated that defendant's marriage to Betty Marvin did not terminate until the filing of a final decree of divorce in January 1967, the trial court treated defendant's motion as one for judgment on the pleadings augmented by the stipulation.

After hearing argument the court granted defendant's motion and entered judgment for defendant. Plaintiff moved to set aside the judgment and asked leave to amend her complaint to allege that she and defendant reaffirmed their agreement after defendant's divorce was final. The trial court denied plaintiff's motion, and she appealed from the judgment.

2. *Plaintiff's complaint states a cause of action for breach of an express contract.*

. . .

Defendant first and principally relies on the contention that the alleged contract is so closely related to the supposed "immoral" character of the relationship between plaintiff and himself that the enforcement of the contract would violate public policy. He points to cases asserting that a contract between non-marital partners is unenforceable if it is "involved in" an illicit relationship or made in "contemplation" of such a relationship. A review of the numerous California decisions concerning contracts between non-marital partners, however, reveals that the courts have not employed such broad and uncertain standards to strike down contracts. The decisions instead disclose a narrower and more precise standard: a contract between non-marital partners is unenforceable only *to the extent* that it *explicitly* rests upon the immoral and illicit consideration of meretricious sexual services.

. . .

. . . [W]e base our opinion on the principle that adults who voluntarily live together and engage in sexual relations are nonetheless as competent as any other persons to contract respecting their earnings and property rights. Of course, they cannot lawfully contract to pay for the performance of sexual services, for such a contract is, in essence, an agreement for prostitution and unlawful for that reason. But they may agree to pool their earnings and to hold all property acquired during the relationship in accord with the law governing community property; conversely they may agree that each partner's earnings and the property acquired from those earnings remains the separate property of the earning partner. So long as the agreement does not rest upon illicit meretricious consideration, the parties may order their economic affairs as they choose, and no policy precludes the courts from enforcing such agreements.

In the present instance, plaintiff alleges that the parties agreed to pool their earnings, that they contracted to share equally in all property acquired, and that defendant agreed to support plaintiff. The terms of the contract as alleged do not rest upon any unlawful consideration. We therefore conclude that the complaint furnishes a suitable basis upon which the trial court can render declaratory relief. The trial court consequently erred in granting defendant's motion for judgment on the pleadings.

3. *Plaintiff's complaint can be amended to state a cause of action founded upon theories of implied contract or equitable relief.*

As we have noted, both causes of action in plaintiff's complaint allege an express contract; neither assert any basis for relief independent from the contract. In In re Marriage of Cary, 34 Cal.App.3d 345, 109 Cal.Rptr. 862, however, the Court of Appeal held that, in view of the policy of the Family Law Act, property accumulated by non-marital partners in an actual family relationship should be divided equally. Upon examining the *Cary* opinion, the parties to the present case realized that plaintiff's alleged relationship with defendant might arguably support a cause of action independent of any express contract between the parties. The parties have therefore briefed and discussed the issue of the property rights of a non-marital partner in the absence of an express contract. Although our conclusion that plaintiff's complaint states a cause of action based on an express contract alone compels us to reverse the judgment for defendant, resolution of the *Cary* issue will serve both to guide the parties upon retrial and to resolve a conflict presently manifest in published Court of Appeal decisions.

Both plaintiff and defendant stand in broad agreement that the law should be fashioned to carry out the reasonable expectations of the parties. Plaintiff, however, presents the following contentions: that the decisions prior to *Cary* rest upon implicit and erroneous notions of punishing a party for his or her guilt in entering into a non-marital relationship, that such decisions result in an inequitable distribution of property accumulated during the relationship, and that *Cary* correctly held that the enactment of the Family Law Act in 1970 overturned those prior decisions. Defendant in response maintains that the prior decisions merely applied common law principles of contract and property to persons who have deliberately elected to remain outside the bounds of the community property system.[11] *Cary*, defendant contends, erred in holding that the Family Law Act vitiated the force of the prior precedents.

. . .

In summary, we believe that the prevalence of non-marital relationships in modern society and the social acceptance of them, marks this as a time when our courts should by no means apply the doctrine of the unlawfulness of the so-called meretricious relationship to the instant case. As we have explained, the nonenforceability of agreements expressly providing for meretricious conduct rested upon the fact that such conduct, as the word suggests, pertained to and encompassed prostitution. To equate the non-marital relationship of today to such a subject matter is to do violence to an accepted and wholly different practice.

We are aware that many young couples live together without the solemnization of marriage, in order to make sure that they can successfully later undertake marriage. This trial period, preliminary to marriage, serves as some assurance that the marriage will not subsequently end in dissolu-

---

11. We note that a deliberate decision to avoid the strictures of the community property system is not the only reason that couples live together without marriage. Some couples may wish to avoid the permanent commitment that marriage implies, yet be willing to share equally any property acquired during the relationship; others may fear the loss of pension, welfare, or tax benefits resulting from marriage (see Beckman v. Mayhew, 49 Cal.App.3d 529, 122 Cal.Rptr. 604). Others may engage in the relationship as a possible prelude to marriage. In lower socio-economic groups the difficulty and ex- pense of dissolving a former marriage often leads couples to choose a non-marital relationship; many unmarried couples may also incorrectly believe that the doctrine of common law marriage prevails in California, and thus that they are in fact married. Consequently we conclude that the mere fact that a couple have not participated in a valid marriage ceremony cannot serve as a basis for a court's inference that the couple intend to keep their earnings and property separate and independent; the parties' intention can only be as ascertained by a more searching inquiry into the nature of their relationship.

tion to the harm of both parties. We are aware, as we have stated, of the pervasiveness of non-marital relationships in other situations.

The mores of the society have indeed changed so radically in regard to cohabitation that we cannot impose a standard based on alleged moral considerations that have apparently been so widely abandoned by so many. Lest we be misunderstood, however, we take this occasion to point out that the structure of society itself largely depends upon the institution of marriage, and nothing we have said in this opinion should be taken to derogate from that institution. The joining of the man and woman in marriage is at once the most socially productive and individually fulfilling relationship that one can enjoy in the course of a lifetime.

We conclude that the judicial barriers that may stand in the way of a policy based upon the fulfillment of the reasonable expectations of the parties to a non-marital relationship should be removed. As we have explained, the courts now hold that express agreements will be enforced unless they rest on an unlawful meretricious consideration. We add that in the absence of an express agreement, the courts may look to a variety of other remedies in order to protect the parties' lawful expectations.[24]

The courts may inquire into the conduct of the parties to determine whether that conduct demonstrates an implied contract or implied agreement of partnership or joint venture, or some other tacit understanding between the parties. The courts may, when appropriate, employ principles of constructive trust or resulting trust. Finally, a non-marital partner may recover in quantum meruit for the reasonable value of household services rendered less the reasonable value of support received if he can show that he rendered services with the expectation of monetary reward.[25]

Since we have determined that plaintiff's complaint states a cause of action for breach of an express contract, and, as we have explained, can be amended to state a cause of action independent of allegations of express contract,[26] we must conclude that the trial court erred in granting defendant a judgment on the pleadings.

The judgment is reversed and the cause remanded for further proceedings consistent with the views expressed herein.

24. We do not seek to resurrect the doctrine of common law marriage, which was abolished in California by statute in 1895. Thus we do not hold that plaintiff and defendant were "married," nor do we extend to plaintiff the rights which the Family Law Act grants valid or putative spouses; we hold only that she has the same rights to enforce contracts and to assert her equitable interest in property acquired through her effort as does any other unmarried person.

25. Our opinion does not preclude the evolution of additional equitable remedies to protect the expectations of the parties to a non-marital relationship in cases in which existing remedies prove inadequate; the suitability of such remedies may be determined in later cases in light of the factual setting in which they arise.

26. We do not pass upon the question whether, in the absence of an express or implied contractual obligation, a party to a non-marital relationship is entitled to support payments from the other party after the relationship terminates.

■ CLARK, JUSTICE (concurring and dissenting).

The majority opinion properly permits recovery on the basis of either express or implied in fact agreement between the parties. These being the issues presented, their resolution requires reversal of the judgment. Here, the opinion should stop.

This court should not attempt to determine all anticipated rights, duties and remedies within every meretricious relationship—particularly in vague terms. Rather, these complex issues should be determined as each arises in a concrete case.

The majority broadly indicates that a party to a meretricious relationship may recover on the basis of equitable principles and in quantum meruit. However, the majority fails to advise us of the circumstances permitting recovery, limitations on recovery, or whether their numerous remedies are cumulative or exclusive. Conceivably, under the majority opinion a party may recover half of the property acquired during the relationship on the basis of general equitable principles, recover a bonus based on specific equitable considerations, and recover a second bonus in quantum meruit.

The general sweep of the majority opinion raises but fails to answer several questions. First, because the Legislature specifically excluded some parties to a meretricious relationship from the equal division rule of Civil Code section 4452, is this court now free to create an equal division rule? Second, upon termination of the relationship, is it equitable to impose the economic obligations of lawful spouses on meretricious parties when the latter may have rejected matrimony to avoid such obligations? Third, does not application of equitable principles—necessitating examination of the conduct of the parties—violate the spirit of the Family Law Act of 1969, designed to eliminate the bitterness and acrimony resulting from the former fault system in divorce? Fourth, will not application of equitable principles reimpose upon trial courts the unmanageable burden of arbitrating domestic disputes? Fifth, will not a quantum meruit system of compensation for services—discounted by benefits received—place meretricious spouses in a better position than lawful spouses? Sixth, if a quantum meruit system is to be allowed, does fairness not require inclusion of all services and all benefits regardless of how difficult the evaluation?

When the parties to a meretricious relationship show by express or implied in fact agreement they intend to create mutual obligations, the court should enforce the agreement. However, in the absence of agreement, we should stop and consider the ramifications before creating economic obligations which may violate legislative intent, contravene the intention of the parties, and surely generate undue burdens on our trial courts.

By judicial overreach, the majority perform a nunc pro tunc marriage, dissolve it, and distribute its property on terms never contemplated by the parties, case law or the Legislature.

NOTE

After the California Supreme Court's decision, the dispute eventuated in a trial between the two celebrities that was a popular media event. Lee

Marvin was ordered to pay Michelle $104,000 to assist with her economic rehabilitation. The opinion of the Los Angeles Superior Court may be found at 5 Fam.L.Rptr. 3077 (Apr. 24, 1979). It can properly be called **Marvin II.**

Marvin v. Marvin (III)

Court of Appeal, Second District, Division 3, 1981.
122 Cal.App.3d 871, 176 Cal.Rptr. 555.

■ COBEY, ASSOCIATE JUSTICE.

Defendant, Lee Marvin, appeals from that portion of a judgment ordering him to pay to plaintiff, Michelle Marvin, the sum of $104,000, to be used by her primarily for her economic rehabilitation.

. . .

This statement of facts is taken wholly from the findings of the trial court, which tried the case without a jury. The parties met in June 1964 and started living together occasionally in October of that year. They lived together almost continuously (except for business absences of his) from the spring of 1965 to May or June of 1970, when their cohabitation was ended at his insistence. This cohabitation was the result of an initial agreement between them to live together as unmarried persons so long as they both enjoyed their mutual companionship and affection.

More specifically, the parties to this lawsuit never agreed during their cohabitation that they would combine their efforts and earnings or would share equally in any property accumulated as a result of their efforts, whether individual or combined. They also never agreed during this period that plaintiff would relinquish her professional career as an entertainer and singer in order to devote her efforts full time to defendant as his companion and homemaker generally. Defendant did not agree during this period of cohabitation that he would provide all of plaintiff's financial needs and support for the rest of her life.

Furthermore, the trial court specifically found that: (1) defendant has never had any obligation to pay plaintiff a reasonable sum as and for her maintenance; (2) plaintiff suffered no damage resulting from her relationship with defendant, including its termination and thus defendant did not become monetarily liable to plaintiff at all; (3) plaintiff actually benefited economically and socially from the cohabitation of the parties, including payment by defendant for goods and services for plaintiff's sole benefit in the approximate amount of $72,900.00, payment by defendant of the living expenses of the two of them of approximately $221,400.00, and other substantial specified gifts;[3] (4) a confidential and fiduciary relationship never existed between the parties with respect to property; (5) defendant was never unjustly enriched as a result of the relationship of the parties or

---

3. The trial court also found that "Defendant made a substantial financial effort to launch Plaintiff's career as a recording singer and to continue her career as a nightclub singer."

of the services performed by plaintiff for him or for them; (6) defendant never acquired any property or money from plaintiff by any wrongful act.

The trial court specifically found in support of its challenged rehabilitation award that the market value of defendant's property at the time the parties separated exceeded $1 million, that plaintiff at the time of the trial of this case had been recently receiving unemployment insurance benefits, that it was doubtful that plaintiff could return to the career that she had enjoyed before the relationship of the parties commenced, namely, that of singer, that plaintiff was in need of rehabilitation—i.e., to learn new employable skills, that she should be able to accomplish such rehabilitation in two years and that the sum of $104,000 was not only necessary primarily for such rehabilitation, but also for her living expenses (including her debts) during this period of rehabilitation, and that defendant had the ability to pay this sum forthwith.

Moreover, the trial court concluded as a matter of law that inasmuch as defendant had terminated the relationship of the parties and plaintiff had no visible means of support, "in equity", she had a right to assistance by defendant until she could become self-supporting. The trial court explained that it fixed the award at the highest salary that the plaintiff had ever earned, namely, $1,000 a week for two years, although plaintiff's salary had been at that level for only two weeks and she ordinarily had earned less than one-half that amount weekly.

. . .

The trial court apparently based its rehabilitative award upon two footnotes in the opinion of our Supreme Court in this case. (Marvin v. Marvin (1976) 18 Cal.3d 660, 134 Cal.Rptr. 815, 557 P.2d 106.) These are footnotes 25 and 26, which respectively read as follows:

"Our opinion does not preclude the evolution of additional equitable remedies to protect the expectations of the parties to a non-marital relationship in cases in which existing remedies prove inadequate; the suitability of such remedies may be determined in later cases in light of the factual setting in which they arise." (Id., at p. 684, 134 Cal.Rptr. 815, 557 P.2d 106.)

"We do not pass upon the question whether, in the absence of an express or implied contractual obligation, a party to a non-marital relationship is entitled to support payments from the other party after the relationship terminates." (Id. at p. 685, 134 Cal.Rptr. 815, 557 P.2d 106.)

There is no doubt that footnote 26 opens the door to a support award in appropriate circumstances. Likewise, under footnote 25, equitable remedies should be devised "to protect the expectations of the parties to a non-marital relationship." The difficulty in applying either of these footnotes in the manner in which the trial court has done in this case is that, as already pointed out, the challenged limited rehabilitative award of the trial court is not within the issues of the case as framed by the pleadings and there is nothing in the trial court's findings to suggest that such an award is warranted to protect the expectations of *both* parties.

Quite to the contrary, as already noted, the trial court expressly found that plaintiff benefited economically and socially from her relationship with defendant and suffered no damage therefrom, even with respect to its termination. Furthermore, the trial court also expressly found that defendant never had any obligation to pay plaintiff a reasonable sum as and for her maintenance and that defendant had not been unjustly enriched by reason of the relationship or its termination and that defendant had never acquired anything of value from plaintiff by any wrongful act.

Furthermore, the special findings in support of the challenged rehabilitative award merely established plaintiff's need therefor and defendant's ability to respond to that need. This is not enough. The award, being nonconsensual in nature, must be supported by some recognized underlying obligation in law or in equity. A court of equity admittedly has broad powers, but it may not create totally new substantive rights under the guise of doing equity.

The trial court in its special conclusions of law addressed to this point attempted to state an underlying obligation by saying that plaintiff had a right to assistance from defendant until she became self-supporting. But this special conclusion obviously conflicts with the earlier, more general, finding of the court that defendant has never had and did not then have any obligation to provide plaintiff with a reasonable sum for her support and maintenance and, in view of the already-mentioned findings of no damage (but benefit instead), no unjust enrichment and no wrongful act on the part of defendant with respect to either the relationship or its termination, it is clear that no basis whatsoever, either in equity or in law, exists for the challenged rehabilitative award. . . .

The judgment under appeal is modified by deleting therefrom the portion thereof under appeal, namely, the rehabilitative award of $104,000 to plaintiff, Michelle Marvin. As modified it is affirmed.

. . .

NOTES

The California Supreme Court in *Marvin* was willing to enforce non-marital contracts between parties who were also involved in a sexual relationship because of the court's recognition of a shift in public attitude towards non-marital cohabitation. A decade earlier, the Supreme Court allowed for interracial marriage because of an evolving social order. *See* Loving v. Virginia, 388 U.S. 1, 87 S.Ct. 1817, 18 L.Ed.2d 1010 (1967). Twenty years after *Marvin*, the Supreme Court of Hawaii would base its decision to require the state of Hawaii to demonstrate a compelling state interest to prevent persons of the same sex from marrying on an evolving social order. *See* Baehr v. Lewin, 74 Haw. 530, 852 P.2d 44 (1993). For recent statistics on nonmarital cohabitation, *see* United States Census

Bureau, Families and Living Arrangements, www.census.gov/population/ www/socdemo/hh-fam.html (last visited Jan.9, 2007).

The willingness of a court to enforce a contract between unmarried cohabitants after *Marvin* has depended on a variety of factors. For example, is the contract express or implied? Does the contract resemble too many prerequisites historically reserved to marriage? Does the bargaining positions between the parties invoke equitable considerations? Consider the following situations:

Express Contracts. Express written contracts between adult cohabiting partners that resemble business rather than marital arrangements, are most likely to be enforced by the courts. *See, e.g.*, Roach v. Puera, 534 N.W.2d 560 (Minn.Ct.App.1995), refusing to enforce an agreement between cohabitants that was not in writing. Courts are willing to enforce agreements that divide property and finances, but limit inclusion of equitable remedies that give the appearance of establishing common law marriage or provide equitable remedies reserved to married couples upon divorce. *See, e.g.*, Wilcox v. Trautz, 427 Mass. 326, 693 N.E.2d 141 (1998). Examples of such equitable remedies would be temporary support for unmarried cohabitants, *see* Friedman v. Friedman, 20 Cal.App.4th 876, 24 Cal.Rptr.2d 892 (1993); or award of attorney fees as in a marital dissolution proceeding. *See* Western Community Bank v. Helmer, 48 Wash.App. 694, 740 P.2d 359 (1987), *but see*, In re Cooke, 93 Wash.App. 526, 969 P.2d 127 (1999), allowing attorney fees within the context of cohabitation if incurred in defending against a baseless and improper suit. If such remedies are made express within the cohabitation contract as economic elements, they would be enforceable.

Implied Contracts. The vast majority of contracts between cohabiting persons are less than express, they are oral and thus seek enforcement through implied or equitable remedies. Michelle Marvin sought enforcement of such an arrangement in *Marvin*. Courts are more reluctant to infer obligations when the agreement between the parties may seem "gratuitous," *see* Morone v. Morone, 50 N.Y.2d 481, 429 N.Y.S.2d 592, 413 N.E.2d 1154 (1980):

> Absent an express agreement, there is no frame of reference against which to compare the testimony presented and the character of the evidence that can be presented becomes more evanescent. There is, therefore, substantially greater risk of emotion-laden afterthought, not to mention fraud, in attempting to ascertain by implication what services, if any, were rendered gratuitously and what compensation, if any, the parties intended to be paid. *Id.* at 1157.

Some courts are more willing to apply equitable principles. For example, the Washington Court of Appeals applied a community property presumption to property acquired during a seven year non-marital cohabitation between a man and a woman. *See* Koher v. Morgan, 93 Wash.App. 398, 968 P.2d 920 (1998). The Supreme Court of Washington has previously held that property acquired during cohabitation may be distributed upon just and equitable principles based on: "continuous cohabitation, duration of the relationship, purpose of the relationship, pooling of resources and services for joint projects, and the intent of the parties." Connell v. Francisco, 127 Wn.2d 339, 898 P.2d 831, 833 (1995). Other courts are willing to divide property acquired by the parties during cohabitation based mainly upon demonstrated intent. *See, e.g.,* Pinto and Smalz, 153 Or.App. 1, 955 P.2d 770 (1998). Some courts impose a constructive trust to avoid fraud when cohabitation engenders trust and excessive financial contribution by the plaintiff. *See* Williams v. Lynch, 245 A.D.2d 715, 666 N.Y.S.2d 749 (1997). But recovery is difficult as courts regard services rendered during cohabitation as "presumably gratuitous." *See* Featherston v. Steinhoff, 226 Mich.App. 584, 575 N.W.2d 6 (1997), and if cohabitation is prohibited by statute between unmarried persons, difficulty of recovery is aggravated. *See, e.g.,* Davis v. Davis, 643 So.2d 931 (Miss.1994).

Agreements between parties may be enforced even after the death of one of the cohabitants. *See, e.g.,* Byrne v. Laura, 52 Cal.App.4th 1054, 60 Cal.Rptr.2d 908 (1997). And the fact that cohabiting parties are members of the same sex will not bar recovery. The New York Supreme Court allowed recovery under an agreement between two lesbians upon the termination of their 14–year relationship. The court relied upon an express contract executed between the parties after their separation and the case could be addressed outside the context of cohabitation and under contract law. Silver v. Starrett, 176 Misc.2d 511, 674 N.Y.S.2d 915 (1998).

Hewitt v. Hewitt

Supreme Court of Illinois, 1979.
77 Ill.2d 49, 31 Ill.Dec. 827, 394 N.E.2d 1204.

■ Underwood, Justice:

The issue in this case is whether plaintiff Victoria Hewitt, whose complaint alleges she lived with defendant Robert Hewitt from 1960 to 1975 in an unmarried, family-like relationship to which three children have been born, may recover from him "an equal share of the profits and properties accumulated by the parties" during that period.

Plaintiff initially filed a complaint for divorce, but at a hearing on defendant's motion to dismiss, admitted that no marriage ceremony had taken place and that the parties have never obtained a marriage license. In dismissing that complaint the trial court found that neither a ceremonial nor a common law marriage existed; that since defendant admitted the paternity of the minor children, plaintiff need not bring a separate action under the Paternity Act to have the question of child support determined; and directed plaintiff to make her complaint more definite as to the nature of the property of which she was seeking division.

Plaintiff thereafter filed an amended complaint alleging the following bases for her claim: (1) that because defendant promised he would "share his life, his future, his earnings and his property" with her and all of defendant's property resulted from the parties' joint endeavors, plaintiff is entitled in equity to a one-half share; (2) that the conduct of the parties evinced an implied contract entitling plaintiff to one-half the property accumulated during their "family relationship"; (3) that because defendant fraudulently assured plaintiff she was his wife in order to secure her services, although he knew they were not legally married, defendant's property should be impressed with a trust for plaintiff's benefit; (4) that because plaintiff has relied to her detriment on defendant's promises and devoted her entire life to him, defendant has been unjustly enriched.

The factual background alleged or testified to is that in June 1960, when she and defendant were students at Grinnell College in Iowa, plaintiff became pregnant; that defendant thereafter told her that they were husband and wife and would live as such, no formal ceremony being necessary, and that he would "share his life, his future, his earnings and his property" with her; that the parties immediately announced to their respective parents that they were married and thereafter held themselves out as husband and wife; that in reliance on defendant's promises she devoted her efforts to his professional education and his establishment in the practice of pedodontia, obtaining financial assistance from her parents for this purpose; that she assisted defendant in his career with her own special skills and although she was given payroll checks for these services she placed them in a common fund; that defendant, who was without funds at the time of the marriage, as a result of her efforts now earns over $80,000 a year and has accumulated large amounts of property, owned either jointly with her or separately; that she has given him every assistance a wife and mother could give, including social activities designed to enhance his social and professional reputation.

The amended complaint was also dismissed, the trial court finding that Illinois law and public policy require such claims to be based on a valid marriage. The appellate court reversed, stating that because the parties had outwardly lived a conventional married life, plaintiff's conduct had not "so affronted public policy that she should be denied any and all relief" (62 Ill.App.3d 861, 869, 20 Ill.Dec. 476, 482, 380 N.E.2d 454, 460), and that plaintiff's complaint stated a cause of action on an express oral contract. We granted leave to appeal. Defendant apparently does not contest his obligation to support the children, and that question is not before us.

The appellate court, in reversing, gave considerable weight to the fact that the parties had held themselves out as husband and wife for over 15 years. The court noted that they lived "a most conventional, respectable and ordinary family life" that did not openly flout accepted standards, the "single flaw" being the lack of a valid marriage. Indeed the appellate court went so far as to say that the parties had "lived within the legitimate boundaries of a marriage and family relationship of a most conventional sort", an assertion which that court cannot have intended to be taken literally. Noting that the Illinois Marriage and Dissolution of Marriage Act does not prohibit non-marital cohabitation and that the Criminal Code of 1961 makes fornication an offense only if the behavior is open and notorious, the appellate court concluded that plaintiff should not be denied relief on public policy grounds.

In finding that plaintiff's complaint stated a cause of action on an express oral contract, the appellate court adopted the reasoning of the California Supreme Court in the widely publicized case of Marvin v. Marvin (1976), 18 Cal.3d 660, 134 Cal.Rptr. 815, 557 P.2d 106, quoting extensively therefrom. . . .

. . .

It is apparent that the *Marvin* court adopted a pure contract theory, under which, if the intent of the parties and the terms of their agreement are proved, the pseudo-conventional family relationship which impressed the appellate court here is irrelevant; recovery may be had unless the implicit sexual relationship is made the explicit consideration for the agreement. In contrast, the appellate court here, as we understand its opinion, would apply contract principles only in a setting where the relationship of the parties outwardly resembled that of a traditional family. It seems apparent that the plaintiff in *Marvin* would not have been entitled to recover in our appellate court because of the absence of that outwardly appearing conventional family relationship.

The issue of whether property rights accrue to unmarried cohabitants can not, however, be regarded realistically as merely a problem in the law of express contracts. Plaintiff argues that because her action is founded on an express contract, her recovery would in no way imply that unmarried cohabitants acquire property rights merely by cohabitation and subsequent separation. However, the *Marvin* court expressly recognized and the appellate court here seems to agree that if common law principles of express contract govern express agreements between unmarried cohabitants, common law principles of implied contract, equitable relief and constructive trust must govern the parties' relations in the absence of such an agreement. In all probability the latter case will be much the more common, since it is unlikely that most couples who live together will enter into express agreements regulating their property rights. (Bruch, Property Rights of De Facto Spouses, Including Thoughts on the Value of Homemakers' Services, 10 Fam.L.Q. 101, 102 (1976).) The increasing incidence of non-marital cohabitation referred to in *Marvin* and the variety of legal remedies therein sanctioned seem certain to result in substantial amounts of litigation, in which, whatever the allegations regarding an oral contract, the proof will necessarily involve details of the parties' living arrangements.

Apart, however, from the appellate court's reliance upon *Marvin* to reach what appears to us to be a significantly different result, we believe there is a more fundamental problem. We are aware, of course, of the increasing judicial attention given the individual claims of unmarried cohabitants to jointly accumulated property, and the fact that the majority of courts considering the question have recognized an equitable or contractual basis for implementing the reasonable expectations of the parties unless sexual services were the explicit consideration. The issue of unmarried cohabitants' mutual property rights, however, as we earlier noted, cannot appropriately be characterized solely in terms of contract law, nor is it limited to considerations of equity or fairness as between the parties to such relationships. There are major public policy questions involved in determining whether, under what circumstances, and to what extent it is desirable to accord some type of legal status to claims arising from such relationships. Of substantially greater importance than the rights of the immediate parties is the impact of such recognition upon our society and the institution of marriage. Will the fact that legal rights closely resembling those arising from conventional marriages can be acquired by those who deliberately choose to enter into what have heretofore been commonly referred to as "illicit" or "meretricious" relationships encourage formation of such relationships and weaken marriage as the foundation of our family-based society? In the event of death shall the survivor have the status of a surviving spouse for purposes of inheritance, wrongful death actions, workmen's compensation, etc.? And still more importantly: what of the children born of such relationships? What are their support and inheritance rights and by what standards are custody questions resolved? What of the sociological and psychological effects upon them of that type of environment? Does not the recognition of legally enforceable property and custody rights emanating from non-marital cohabitation in practical effect equate with the legalization of common law marriage—at least in the circumstances of this case? And, in summary, have the increasing numbers of unmarried cohabitants and changing mores of our society reached the point at which the general welfare of the citizens of this State is best served by a return to something resembling the judicially created common law marriage our legislature outlawed in 1905?

Illinois' public policy regarding agreements such as the one alleged here was implemented long ago in Wallace v. Rappleye (1882), 103 Ill. 229, 249, where this court said: "An agreement in consideration of future illicit cohabitation between the plaintiffs is void." This is the traditional rule, in force until recent years in all jurisdictions....

It is true, of course, that cohabitation by the parties may not prevent them from forming valid contracts about independent matters, for which it is said the sexual relations do not form part of the consideration. Those courts which allow recovery generally have relied on this principle to reduce the scope of the rule of illegality. Thus, California courts long prior to *Marvin* held that an express agreement to pool earnings is supported by independent consideration and is not invalidated by cohabitation of the parties, the agreements being regarded as simultaneous but separate. More recently, several courts have reasoned that the rendition of housekeeping and homemaking services such as plaintiff alleges here could be regarded as the consideration for a separate contract between the parties, severable from the illegal contract founded on sexual relations....

The real thrust of plaintiff's argument here is that we should abandon the rule of illegality because of certain changes in societal norms and attitudes. It is urged that social mores have changed radically in recent years, rendering this principle of law archaic. It is said that because there are so many unmarried cohabitants today the courts must confer a legal status on such relationships. This, of course, is the rationale underlying some of the decisions and commentaries. If this is to be the result, however, it would seem more candid to acknowledge the return of varying forms of common law marriage than to continue displaying the naivete we believe involved in the assertion that there are involved in these relationships contracts separate and independent from the sexual activity, and the assumption that those contracts would have been entered into or would continue without that activity.

Even if we were to assume some modification of the rule of illegality is appropriate, we return to the fundamental question earlier alluded to: If resolution of this issue rests ultimately on grounds of public policy, by what body should that policy be determined? *Marvin*, viewing the issue as governed solely by contract law, found judicial policy-making appropriate. Its decision was facilitated by California precedent and that State's no-fault divorce law. In our view, however, the situation alleged here was not the kind of arm's length bargain envisioned by traditional contract principles, but an intimate arrangement of a fundamentally different kind. The issue, realistically, is whether it is appropriate for this court to grant a legal status to a private arrangement substituting for the institution of marriage sanctioned by the State. The question whether change is needed in the law governing the rights of parties in this delicate area of marriage-like relationships involves evaluations of sociological data and alternatives we believe best suited to the superior investigative and fact-finding facilities of the legislative branch in the exercise of its traditional authority to declare public policy in the domestic relations field. That belief is reinforced by the fact that judicial recognition of mutual property rights between unmarried cohabitants would, in our opinion, clearly violate the policy of our recently enacted Illinois Marriage and Dissolution of Marriage Act. Although the Act does not specifically address the subject of non-marital cohabitation, we think the legislative policy quite evident from the statutory scheme.

The Act provides:

"This Act shall be liberally construed and applied to promote its underlying purposes, which are to:

(1) provide adequate procedures for the solemnization and registration of marriage;

(2) strengthen and preserve the integrity of marriage and safeguard family relationships." (Ill.Rev.Stat.1977, ch. 40, par. 102.)

We cannot confidently say that judicial recognition of property rights between unmarried cohabitants will not make that alternative to marriage more attractive by allowing the parties to engage in such relationships with greater security. As one commentator has noted, it may make this alternative especially attractive to persons who seek a property arrangement that the law does not permit to marital partners. (Comment, 90 Harv.L.Rev. 1708, 1713 (1977).) This court, for example, has held void agreements releasing husbands from their obligation to support their wives. In thus potentially enhancing the attractiveness of a private arrangement over marriage, we believe that the appellate court decision in this case contravenes the Act's policy of strengthening and preserving the integrity of marriage.

The Act also provides: "Common law marriages contracted in this State after June 30, 1905 are invalid." (Ill.Rev.Stat.1977, ch. 40, par. 214.) The doctrine of common law marriage was a judicially sanctioned alternative to formal marriage designed to apply to cases like the one before us. . . .

While the appellate court denied that its decision here served to rehabilitate the doctrine of common law marriage, we are not persuaded. Plaintiff's allegations disclose a relationship that clearly would have constituted a valid common law marriage in this State prior to 1905. . . . It is of course true, as plaintiff argues, that unlike a common law spouse she would not have full marital rights in that she could not, for example, claim her statutory one-third share of defendant's property on his death. The distinction appears unimpressive, however, if she can claim one-half of his property on a theory of express or implied contract.

Further, in enacting the Illinois Marriage and Dissolution of Marriage Act, our legislature considered and rejected the "no-fault" divorce concept that has been adopted in many other jurisdictions, including California. Illinois appears to be one of three States retaining fault grounds for dissolution of marriage. Certainly a significantly stronger promarriage policy is manifest in that action, which appears to us to reaffirm the traditional doctrine that marriage is a civil contract between three parties—the husband, the wife and the State. The policy of the Act gives the State a strong continuing interest in the institution of marriage and prevents the marriage relation from becoming in effect a private contract terminable at will. This seems to us another indication that public policy disfavors private contractual alternatives to marriage.

Lastly, in enacting the Illinois Marriage and Dissolution of Marriage Act, the legislature adopted for the first time the civil law concept of the putative spouse. The Act provides that an unmarried person may acquire the rights of a legal spouse only if he goes through a marriage ceremony and cohabits with another in the good-faith belief that he is validly married. When he learns that the marriage is not valid his status as a putative spouse terminates; common law marriages are expressly excluded. The legislature thus extended legal recognition to a class of non-marital relationships, but only to the extent of a party's good-faith belief in the existence of a valid marriage. Moreover, during the legislature's deliberations on the Act *Marvin* was decided and received wide publicity. These circumstances in our opinion constitute a recent and unmistakable legislative judgment disfavoring the grant of mutual property rights to knowingly unmarried cohabitants. . . .

. . .

We do not intend to suggest that plaintiff's claims are totally devoid of merit. Rather, we believe that our statement in Mogged v. Mogged (1973) 55 Ill.2d 221, 225, 302 N.E.2d 293, 295, made in deciding whether to abolish a judicially created defense to divorce, is appropriate here:

> "Whether or not the defense of recrimination should be abolished or modified in Illinois is a question involving complex public-policy considerations as to which compelling arguments may be made on both sides. For the reasons stated hereafter, we believe that these questions are appropriately within the province of the legislature, and that, if there is to be a change in the law of this State on this matter, it is for the legislature and not the courts to bring about that change."

We accordingly hold that plaintiff's claims are unenforceable for the reason that they contravene the public policy, implicit in the statutory scheme of the Illinois Marriage and Dissolution of Marriage Act, disfavoring the grant of mutually enforceable property rights to knowingly unmarried cohabitants. The judgment of the appellate court is reversed. . . .

Watts v. Watts

Supreme Court of Wisconsin, 1987.
137 Wis.2d 506, 405 N.W.2d 303.

■ Shirley S. Abrahamson, Justice.

This is an appeal from a judgment of the circuit court for Dane County, William D. Byrne, Judge, dismissing Sue Ann Watts' amended complaint . . . for failure to state a claim upon which relief may be granted. . . . [W]e reverse the judgment of the circuit court and remand the cause to the circuit court for further proceedings consistent with this opinion.

The case involves a dispute between Sue Ann Evans Watts, the plaintiff, and James Watts, the defendant, over their respective interests in property accumulated during their non-marital cohabitation relationship which spanned 12 years and produced two children. . . .

The plaintiff commenced this action in 1982. The plaintiff's amended complaint alleges the following facts, which for purposes of this appeal must be accepted as true. The plaintiff and the defendant met in 1967, when she was 19 years old, was living with her parents and was working full time as a nurse's aide in preparation for a nursing career. Shortly after the parties met, the defendant persuaded the plaintiff to move into an apartment paid for by him and to quit her job. According to the amended complaint, the defendant "indicated" to the plaintiff that he would provide for her.

Early in 1969, the parties began living together in a "marriage-like" relationship, holding themselves out to the public as husband and wife. The plaintiff assumed the defendant's surname as her own. Subsequently, she gave birth to two children who were also given the defendant's surname. The parties filed joint income tax returns and maintained joint bank accounts asserting that they were husband and wife. The defendant insured the plaintiff as his wife on his medical insurance policy. He also took out a life insurance policy on her as his wife, naming himself as the beneficiary. The parties purchased real and personal property as husband and wife. The plaintiff executed documents and obligated herself on promissory notes to lending institutions as the defendant's wife.

During their relationship, the plaintiff contributed childcare and home-making services, including cleaning, cooking, laundering, shopping, running errands, and maintaining the grounds surrounding the parties' home. Additionally, the plaintiff contributed personal property to the relationship which she owned at the beginning of the relationship or acquired through gifts or purchases during the relationship. She served as hostess for the defendant for social and business-related events. The amended complaint further asserts that periodically, between 1969 and 1975, the plaintiff cooked and cleaned for the defendant and his employees while his business, a landscaping service, was building and landscaping a golf course.

From 1973 to 1976, the plaintiff worked 20–25 hours per week at the defendant's office, performing duties as a receptionist, typist, and assistant bookkeeper. From 1976 to 1981, the plaintiff worked 40–60 hours per week at a business she started with the defendant's sister-in-law, then continued and managed the business herself after the dissolution of that partnership. The plaintiff further alleges that in 1981 defendant made their relationship so intolerable that she was forced to move from their home and their relationship was irretrievably broken. Subsequently, the defendant barred the plaintiff from returning to her business.

The plaintiff alleges that during the parties' relationship, and because of her domestic and business contributions, the business and personal wealth of the couple increased. Furthermore, the plaintiff alleges that she never received any compensation for these contributions to the relationship and that the defendant indicated to the plaintiff both orally and through his conduct that he considered her to be his wife and that she would share equally in the increased wealth.

The plaintiff asserts that since the breakdown of the relationship the defendant has refused to share equally with her the wealth accumulated through their joint efforts or to compensate her in any way for her contributions to the relationship.

The plaintiff's first legal theory to support her claim against the property accumulated during the cohabitation is that the plaintiff, defendant, and their children constitute a "family," thus entitling the plaintiff to bring an action for property division under sec. 767.02(1)(h), Stats. 1985–86,[2] and to have the court "divide the property of the parties and divest and transfer the title of any such property" pursuant to sec. 767.255, 1985–86.[3]

---

2. Sec. 767.02(1)(h), Stats. 1985–86, provides that "Actions affecting the family are: ... (h) For property division."

3. Sec. 767.255, Stats. 1985–86, provides in relevant part:

"Upon every judgment of annulment, divorce or legal separation, *or in rendering a*

The plaintiff asserts that the legislature intended secs. 767.02(1)(h) and 767.255, which usually govern division of property between married persons in divorce or legal separation proceedings, to govern a property division action between unmarried cohabitants who constitute a family. The plaintiff points out that secs. 767.02(1)(h) and 767.255 are part of chapter 767, which is entitled "Actions Affecting the Family," and that in 1979 the legislature deliberately changed the title of the chapter from "Actions Affecting Marriage" to "Actions Affecting the Family."[4] The legislature has failed to provide any definition for "family" under ch. 767, or for that matter under any chapter of the Family Code.

The plaintiff relies on Warden v. Warden, 36 Wash.App. 693, 676 P.2d 1037 (1984), to support her claim for relief under secs. 767.02(1)(h) and 767.255. In *Warden,* the Washington court of appeals held that the statute providing guidelines for property division upon dissolution of marriage, legal separation, etc., could also be applied to divide property acquired by unmarried cohabitants in what was "tantamount to a marital family except for a legal marriage." Warden, 36 Wash.App. at 698, 676 P.2d at 1039. *Warden* is remarkably similar on its facts to the instant case. The parties in *Warden* had lived together for 11 years, had two children, held themselves out as husband and wife, acquired property together, and filed joint tax returns. On those facts, the Washington court of appeals held that the trial court correctly treated the parties as a "family" within the meaning of the Washington marriage dissolution statute. In addition, the trial court had considered such statutory factors as the length and purpose of the parties' relationship, their two children, and the contributions and future prospects of each in determining their respective shares of the property.

Although the *Warden* case provides support for the plaintiff's argument, most courts which have addressed the issue of whether marriage dissolution statutes provide relief to unmarried cohabitants have either rejected or avoided application of a marriage dissolution statute to unmarried cohabitants.[6]

---

judgment in an action under s. 767.02(1)(h), the court shall divide the property of the parties and divest and transfer the title of any such property accordingly." (emphasis supplied)

4. Laws of 1979, ch. 352, sec. 19.

In a supplemental submission, and at oral argument, the plaintiff analogized its interpretation of sec. 767.255 to this court's adoption of a broad definition of "family" in the context of zoning and land use. See, e.g. Crowley v. Knapp, 94 Wis.2d 421, 437, 288 N.W.2d 815 (1980), in which this court stated that a "family" in that context "may mean a group of people who live, sleep, cook, and eat upon the premises as a single housekeeping

unit." In *Crowley,* the court adopted a definition of "family" serving that public policy favoring the free and unrestricted use of property.

By contrast, the plaintiff here has failed to convince us that extending the definition of "family" in this case to include unmarried cohabitants will further in any way the expressed public policy of ch. 767 to promote marriage and the family.

6. For a discussion of whether cohabitation should be viewed as analogous to marriage, see Fineman, Law and Changing Patterns of Behavior: Sanctions on Non–Marital Cohabitation, 1981 Wis.L.Rev. 275, 316–32.

The purpose of statutory construction is to ascertain the intent of the legislature and give effect to that intent. If the language of the statute is unclear, the court will endeavor to discover the legislature's intent as disclosed by the scope, history, context, subject matter and purpose of the statute.

While we agree with the plaintiff that some provisions in ch. 767 govern a mother, father, and their children, regardless of marriage,[7] upon our analysis of sec. 767.255 and the Family Code, we conclude that the legislature did not intend sec. 767.255 to extend to unmarried cohabitants.

When the legislature added what is now sec. 767.255 in 1977 as part of the no fault divorce bill, it stated that its "sole purpose" was "to promote an equitable and reasonable adjudication of the economic and custodial issues involved in *marriage* relationships."[8] (emphasis supplied) Moreover, the unambiguous language of sec. 767.255 and the criteria for property division listed in sec. 767.255 plainly contemplate that the parties who are governed by that section are or have been married.[9] Finally, secs. 767.02(1)(h) and 767.255 were both in existence before the 1979 legislature changed the title of ch. 767 from "Marriage" to "Family." A change in the title of the chapter would not change the import of these statutory provisions.

Furthermore, the Family Code emphasizes marriage. The entire Family Code, of which ch. 767 is an integral part, is governed generally by the provisions of sec. 765.001(2), which states in part that "[i]t is the intent of chs. 765 to 768 to promote the stability and best interests of *marriage and the family*. . . . *Marriage* is the institution that *is the foundation of family and of society.* Its stability is basic to morality and civilization, and of vital interest to society and the state." (emphasis supplied) Section 765.001(3) further states that "[c]hapters 765 to 768 shall be liberally construed to effect the objectives of sub. (2)." The conclusion is almost inescapable from this language in sec. 765.001(2)(3) that the legislature not only intended chs. 765–768 to protect and promote the "family," but also intended "family" to be within the "marriage" context.[10]

---

7. The plaintiff correctly points out that ch. 767 includes actions for determining paternity, which are not dependent upon the marital status of the parents. See, secs. 767.45–767.53, Stats. 1985–86.

8. 1977 Wis.Laws ch. 105, § 1(4).

9. Some of the criteria listed under sec. 767.255, Stats. (1985–86), are as follows:

"(1) The length of the marriage.

"(2) The property brought to the marriage by each party.

. . .

"(3) The contribution of each party to the marriage, giving appropriate eco-

nomic value to each party's contribution in homemaking and child care services.

. . .

"(11) Any written agreement made by the parties before or during the *marriage* concerning any arrangement for property distribution; . . ." (emphasis supplied).

10. When the legislature abolished criminal sanctions for cohabitation in 1983, it nevertheless added a section to the criminal code stating that while the state does not regulate private sexual activity of consenting adults, the state does not condone or encourage sexual conduct outside the institution of

The statutory prohibition of marriages which do not conform to statutory requirements, sec. 765.21, Stats. 1985–86,[11] further suggests that the legislature intended that the Family Code applies, for the most part, to those couples who have been joined in marriage according to law.

.   .   .

The plaintiff urges that the defendant, as a result of his own words and conduct, be estopped from asserting the lack of a legal marriage as a defense against the plaintiff's claim for property division under sec. 767.255. As support for her position, the plaintiff cites a 1905 Tennessee case and two law review articles that do no more than cite to the Tennessee case law.[12]

Although the defendant has not discussed this legal theory, we conclude that the doctrine of "marriage by estoppel" should not be applied in this case. We reach this result primarily because we have already concluded that the legislature did not intend sec. 767.255 to govern property division between unmarried cohabitants.[13] We do not think the parties' conduct should place them within the ambit of a statute which the legislature did not intend to govern them.

The plaintiff's third legal theory on which her claim rests is that she and the defendant had a contract to share equally the property accumulated during their relationship. The essence of the complaint is that the parties had a contract, either an express or implied in fact contract, which the defendant breached.

Wisconsin courts have long recognized the importance of freedom of contract and have endeavored to protect the right to contract. A contract will not be enforced, however, if it violates public policy. A declaration that the contract is against public policy should be made only after a careful balancing, in the light of all the circumstances, of the interest in enforcing a particular promise against the policy against enforcement. Courts should be reluctant to frustrate a party's reasonable expectations without a

marriage. The legislature adopted the language of sec. 765.001 that "[m]arriage is the foundation of family and society. Its stability is basic to morality and civilization, and of vital interest to society and this state." Sec. 944.01, Stats. 1985–86.

11.   Common law marriages were abolished in 1917. Sec. 765.21, Stats. 1985–86, provides that marriages contracted in violation of specified provisions of ch. 765 are void.

12.   Plaintiff cites to Smith v. North Memphis Savings Bank, 115 Tenn. 12, 89 S.W. 392 (Tenn.1905), which is one of the more "recent" in a series of Tennessee cases to apply "marriage by estoppel." The plaintiff also cites Comment, Property Rights Upon Termination of Unmarried Cohabitation: Marvin v. Marvin, 90 Harv.L.Rev. 1708, 1711–12 (1977); and Weyrauch, Informal and Formal Marriage—An Appraisal of Trends in Family Organization, 28 U.Chi.L.Rev. 88, 105 (1960). Weyrauch cites to Tennessee law, and the comment cites to Weyrauch.

13.   This court has previously rejected application of the "marriage by estoppel" doctrine in certain cases. In Eliot v. Eliot, 81 Wis. 295, 299, 51 N.W. 81, 82 (1892), a man was held not estopped from pleading that he was under age to be married in an annulment action he brought, even though he fraudulently induced the defendant into marriage. Accord Swenson v. Swenson, 179 Wis. 536, 540–41, 192 N.W. 70, 72 (1923).

corresponding benefit to be gained in deterring "misconduct" or avoiding inappropriate use of the judicial system.

The defendant appears to attack the plaintiff's contract theory on three grounds. First, the defendant apparently asserts that the court's recognition of plaintiff's contract claim for a share of the parties' property contravenes the Wisconsin Family Code. Second, the defendant asserts that the legislature, not the courts, should determine the property and contract rights of unmarried cohabiting parties. Third, the defendant intimates that the parties' relationship was immoral and illegal and that any recognition of a contract between the parties or plaintiff's claim for a share of the property accumulated during the cohabitation contravenes public policy.

The defendant rests his argument that judicial recognition of a contract between unmarried cohabitants for property division violates the Wisconsin Family Code on Hewitt v. Hewitt, 77 Ill.2d 49, 31 Ill.Dec. 827, 394 N.E.2d 1204 (1979). In *Hewitt* the Illinois Supreme Court concluded that judicial recognition of mutual property rights between unmarried cohabitants would violate the policy of the Illinois Marriage and Dissolution Act because enhancing the attractiveness of a private arrangement contravenes the Act's policy of strengthening and preserving the integrity of marriage. The Illinois court concluded that allowing such a contract claim would weaken the sanctity of marriage, put in doubt the rights of inheritance, and open the door to false pretenses of marriage.

We agree with Professor Prince and other commentators that the *Hewitt* court made an unsupportable inferential leap when it found that cohabitation agreements run contrary to statutory policy and that the *Hewitt* court's approach is patently inconsistent with the principle that public policy limits are to be narrowly and exactly applied.[14]

Furthermore, the Illinois statutes upon which the Illinois Supreme Court rested its decision are distinguishable from the Wisconsin statutes. The Illinois Supreme Court relied on the fact that Illinois still retained "fault" divorce and that cohabitation was unlawful. By contrast, Wisconsin abolished "fault" in divorce in 1977 and abolished criminal sanctions for non-marital cohabitation in 1983.[15]

The defendant has failed to persuade this court that enforcing an express or implied in fact contract between these parties would in fact violate the Wisconsin Family Code. The Family Code, chs. 765–768 Stats.

---

14. Prince, Public Policy Limitations in Cohabitation Agreements: Unruly Horse or Circus Pony, 70 Minn.L.Rev. 163, 189–205 (1985).

15. Both Illinois and Wisconsin have abolished common law marriages. In our view this abolition does not invalidate a private cohabitation contract. Cohabitation agreements differ in effect from common law marriage. There is a significant difference between the consequences of achieving common law marriage status and of having an enforceable cohabitation agreement.

In Latham v. Latham, 274 Or. 421, 426–27, 547 P.2d 144, 147 (1976), the Oregon supreme court found that the Legislature's decriminalization of cohabitation represented strong evidence that enforcing agreements made by parties during cohabitation relationships would not be contrary to Oregon public policy.

1985–86, is intended to promote the institution of marriage and the family. We find no indication, however, that the Wisconsin legislature intended the Family Code to restrict in any way a court's resolution of property or contract disputes between unmarried cohabitants.

The defendant also urges that if the court is not willing to say that the Family Code proscribes contracts between unmarried cohabiting parties, then the court should refuse to resolve the contract and property rights of unmarried cohabitants without legislative guidance. The defendant asserts that this court should conclude, as the *Hewitt* court did, that the task of determining the rights of cohabiting parties is too complex and difficult for the court and should be left to the legislature. We are not persuaded by the defendant's argument. Courts have traditionally developed principles of contract and property law through the case-by-case method of the common law. While ultimately the legislature may resolve the problems raised by unmarried cohabiting parties, we are not persuaded that the court should refrain from resolving such disputes until the legislature gives us direction. Our survey of the cases in other jurisdictions reveals that *Hewitt* is not widely followed.

We turn to the defendant's third point, namely, that any contract between the parties regarding property division contravenes public policy because the contract is based on immoral or illegal sexual activity. The defendant does not appear to make this argument directly. It is not well developed in the brief, and at oral argument defendant's attorney indicated that he did not find this argument persuasive in light of the current community mores, the substantial number of unmarried people who cohabit, and the legislature's abolition of criminal sanctions for cohabitation. Although the parties in the instant case cohabited at a time when cohabitation was illegal, the defendant's counsel at oral argument thought that the present law should govern this aspect of the case. Because illegal sexual activity has posed a problem for courts in contract actions, we discuss this issue even though the defendant did not emphasize it.

Courts have generally refused to enforce contracts for which the sole consideration is sexual relations, sometimes referred to as "meretricious" relationships. See In Matter of Estate of Steffes, 95 Wis.2d 490, 514, 290 N.W.2d 697 (1980), citing Restatement of Contracts Section 589 (1932). Courts distinguish, however, between contracts that are explicitly and inseparably founded on sexual services and those that are not. This court, and numerous other courts, have concluded that "a bargain between two people is not illegal merely because there is an illicit relationship between the two so long as the bargain is independent of the illicit relationship and the illicit relationship does not constitute any part of the consideration bargained for and is not a condition of the bargain." Steffes, supra, 95 Wis.2d at 514, 290 N.W.2d 697.

While not condoning the illicit sexual relationship of the parties, many courts have recognized that the result of a court's refusal to enforce contract and property rights between unmarried cohabitants is that one party keeps all or most of the assets accumulated during the relationship, while the other party, no more or less "guilty," is deprived of property which he or she has helped to accumulate.

The *Hewitt* decision, which leaves one party to the relationship enriched at the expense of the other party who had contributed to the acquisition of the property, has often been criticized by courts and commentators as being unduly harsh.[18] Moreover, courts recognize that their refusal to enforce what are in other contexts clearly lawful promises will not undo the parties' relationship and may not discourage others from entering into such relationships. Tyranski v. Piggins, 44 Mich.App. 570, 577, 205 N.W.2d 595 (1973). A harsh, per se rule that the contract and property rights of unmarried cohabiting parties will not be recognized might actually encourage a partner with greater income potential to avoid marriage in order to retain all accumulated assets, leaving the other party with nothing.

One Wisconsin case which requires discussion in this context is Smith v. Smith, 255 Wis. 96, 38 N.W.2d 12. In *Smith,* one of the parties to a common law marriage discovered that such marriages were not legal, demanded that the defendant marry her, was refused, and sought equitable property division. The court denied her claim. Although we find the harsh result in *Smith* troubling, we need not overrule it because *Smith* is distinguishable from the instant case.

The plaintiff in *Smith* was seeking equitable property division under the marriage dissolution statutes. Like the court in *Smith,* we have decided that those statutes are unavailable to an unmarried person. The plaintiff in this case, however, rests her claim on theories of recovery other than those of the plaintiff in *Smith.* The *Smith* court ruled that the plaintiff had based her claim for property division solely on the fact of the couple's illegal common law marriage. In other words, the plaintiff in that case had not alleged facts necessary to find that the couple had agreed to share their property, independent from their sexual relationship.

In *Smith,* the problem was inadequate pleading by the plaintiff. In this case, the plaintiff has alleged many facts independent from the parties' physical relationship which, if proven, would establish an express contract or an implied in fact contract that the parties agreed to share the property accumulated during the relationship.

The plaintiff has alleged that she quit her job and abandoned her career training upon the defendant's promise to take care of her. A change in one party's circumstances in performance of the agreement may imply an agreement between the parties.

In addition, the plaintiff alleges that she performed housekeeping, childbearing, childrearing, and other services related to the maintenance of

---

18. See Prince, Public Policy Limitations on Cohabitation Agreements: Unruly Horse or Circus Pony, 70 Minn.L.Rev. 163, 189–205 (1985); Oldham & Caudill, A Reconnaissance of Public Policy Restrictions upon Enforcement of Contracts between Cohabitants, 18 Fam.L.Q. 93, 132 (Spring 1984); Comment, Marvin v. Marvin: Five Years Later, 65 Marq.L.Rev. 389, 414 (1982).

the parties' home, in addition to various services for the defendant's business and her own business, for which she received no compensation. Courts have recognized that money, property, or services (including housekeeping or childrearing) may constitute adequate consideration independent of the parties' sexual relationship to support an agreement to share or transfer property. See Tyranski, supra, 44 Mich.App. at 574, 205 N.W.2d at 597; Carlson v. Olson, 256 N.W.2d 249, 253–254 (1977); Carroll v. Lee, 148 Ariz. 10, 14, 712 P.2d 923, 927 (1986); . . .[19]

According to the plaintiff's complaint, the parties cohabited for more than twelve years, held joint bank accounts, made joint purchases, filed joint income tax returns, and were listed as husband and wife on other legal documents. Courts have held that such a relationship and "joint acts of a financial nature can give rise to an inference that the parties intended to share equally." Beal v. Beal, 282 Or. 115, 122, 577 P.2d 507, 510 (1978). The joint ownership of property and the filing of joint income tax returns strongly implies that the parties intended their relationship to be in the nature of a joint enterprise, financially as well as personally.

Having reviewed the complaint and surveyed the law in this and other jurisdictions, we hold that the Family Code does not preclude an unmarried cohabitant from asserting contract and property claims against the other party to the cohabitation. We further conclude that public policy does not necessarily preclude an unmarried cohabitant from asserting a contract claim against the other party to the cohabitation so long as the claim exists independently of the sexual relationship and is supported by separate consideration. Accordingly, we conclude that the plaintiff in this case has pleaded the facts necessary to state a claim for damages resulting from the defendant's breach of an express or an implied in fact contract to share with the plaintiff the property accumulated through the efforts of both parties during their relationship. . . .

The plaintiff's fourth theory of recovery involves unjust enrichment. Essentially, she alleges that the defendant accepted and retained the benefit of services she provided knowing that she expected to share equally in the wealth accumulated during their relationship. She argues that it is unfair for the defendant to retain all the assets they accumulated under these circumstances and that a constructive trust should be imposed on the property as a result of the defendant's unjust enrichment. In his brief, the defendant does not attack specifically either the legal theory or the factual allegations made by the plaintiff.

19. Until recently, the prevailing view was that services performed in the context of a "family or marriage relationship" were presumed gratuitous. However, that presumption was rebuttable. See Steffes, 95 Wis.2d at 501, 290 N.W.2d at 703–704. In *Steffes,* we held the presumption to be irrelevant where the plaintiff can show either an express or implied agreement to pay for those services, even where the plaintiff has rendered them "with a sense of affection, devotion and duty." Id. 95 Wis.2d at 503, 290 N.W.2d at 703–704. For a discussion of the evolution of thought regarding the economic value of homemaking services by cohabitants, see Bruch, Property Rights of De Facto Spouses Including Thoughts on the Value of Homemakers' Services, 10 Fam.L.Q. 101, 110–14 (Summer 1976).

Unlike claims for breach of an express or implied in fact contract, a claim of unjust enrichment does not arise out of an agreement entered into by the parties. Rather, an action for recovery based upon unjust enrichment is grounded on the moral principle that one who has received a benefit has a duty to make restitution where retaining such a benefit would be unjust.

. . .

In Wisconsin, an action for unjust enrichment, or quasi contract, is based upon proof of three elements: (1) a benefit conferred on the defendant by the plaintiff, (2) appreciation or knowledge by the defendant of the benefit, and (3) acceptance or retention of the benefit by the defendant under circumstances making it inequitable for the defendant to retain the benefit.

The plaintiff has cited no cases directly supporting actions in unjust enrichment by unmarried cohabitants, and the defendant provides no authority against it. This court has previously extended such relief to a party to a cohabitation in Estate of Fox, 178 Wis. 369, 190 N.W. 90 (1922). In *Fox*, the plaintiff was a woman who had believed in good faith that she was married to the decedent, when in fact she was not. The court found that the decedent "husband" had "by fraudulent representations induced the plaintiff to enter into the illicit relationship." Under those circumstances, the court reasoned that it was "just and logical" to infer "from the nature of the transaction" that "the supposed husband [can be] held to have assumed to pay [for services rendered by his 'spouse'] because in point of law and equity it is just that he should pay."

In *Fox,* the court expressly refused to consider whether the same result would necessarily follow in other circumstances. Thus, *Fox* does not supply explicit support for the plaintiff's position here where she does not claim that she thought the parties were actually married.

The *Steffes* case, however, does provide additional support for the plaintiff's position. Although *Steffes* involved a claim for recovery in contract by an unmarried cohabitant for the value of services she performed for the decedent, the same equitable principles that governed that case would appear to apply in a case where the plaintiff is seeking recovery based upon unjust enrichment. In *Steffes,* the court cited with approval a statement by the trial judge that "[t]he question I have in mind is why should the estate be enriched when that man was just as much a part of the illicit relationship as she was and not let her have her fair dues. I don't understand that law that would interpret unjust enrichment that way and deprive one and let the other benefit and do it on the basis that there was an illicit relationship but not equally held against the both...." Steffes, supra, 95 Wis.2d at 508, 290 N.W.2d 697.

As part of his general argument, the defendant claims that the court should leave the parties to an illicit relationship such as the one in this case essentially as they are found, providing no relief at all to either party....

As we have discussed previously, allowing no relief at all to one party in a so-called "illicit" relationship effectively provides total relief to the other, by leaving that party owner of all the assets acquired through the efforts of both. Yet it cannot seriously be argued that the party retaining all the assets is less "guilty" than the other. Such a result is contrary to the principles of equity. Many courts have held, and we now so hold, that unmarried cohabitants may raise claims based upon unjust enrichment following the termination of their relationships where one of the parties attempts to retain an unreasonable amount of the property acquired through the efforts of both.

In this case, the plaintiff alleges that she contributed both property and services to the parties' relationship. She claims that because of these contributions the parties' assets increased, but that she was never compensated for her contributions. She further alleges that the defendant, knowing that the plaintiff expected to share in the property accumulated, "accepted the services rendered to him by the plaintiff" and that it would be unfair under the circumstances to allow him to retain everything while she receives nothing. We conclude that the facts alleged are sufficient to state a claim for recovery based upon unjust enrichment.

As part of the plaintiff's unjust enrichment claim, she has asked that a constructive trust be imposed on the assets that the defendant acquired during their relationship. . . . To state a claim on the theory of constructive trust the complaint must state facts sufficient to show (1) unjust enrichment and (2) abuse of a confidential relationship or some other form of unconscionable conduct. The latter element can be inferred from allegations in the complaint which show, for example, a family relationship, a close personal relationship, or the parties' mutual trust. These facts are alleged in this complaint or may be inferred. Therefore, we hold that if the plaintiff can prove the elements of unjust enrichment to the satisfaction of the circuit court, she will be entitled to demonstrate further that a constructive trust should be imposed as a remedy.

The plaintiff's last alternative legal theory on which her claim rests is the doctrine of partition. . . .

In Wisconsin partition is a remedy under both the statutes and common law. Partition applies generally to all disputes over property held by more than one party. This court has already held, in Jezo v. Jezo, 19 Wis.2d 78, 81, 119 N.W.2d 471 (1963), that the principles of partition could be applied to determine the respective property interests of a husband and wife in jointly owned property where the divorce law governing property division did not apply. . . . Jezo appears to say that persons, regardless of their marital status, may sue for partition of property.

Apart from citing the partition statutes, the plaintiff relies heavily on Carlson v. Olson, supra, 256 N.W.2d at 255, in which the Minnesota supreme court approved the application of common law partition principles to augment partition statutes on facts very similar to those in this case.[22]

22. In *Carlson,* as in the instant case, the parties held themselves out to be married. The parties filed joint income tax returns and maintained joint bank accounts.

Carlson is one of a number of cases similar to the fact situation in the case at bar in which the court used the partition remedy to protect the interests of both parties to a non-marital cohabitation relationship in the property acquired during their relationship. See, e.g., Carroll v. Lee, 148 Ariz. 10, 14, 712 P.2d 923 (1986) (partition allowed where parties acquired property in joint title through joint common effort and for a common purpose and parties had implied partnership or joint enterprise agreement).

. . .

In this case, the plaintiff has alleged that she and the defendant were engaged in a joint venture or partnership, that they purchased real and personal property as husband and wife, and that they intended to share all the property acquired during their relationship. In our opinion, these allegations, together with other facts alleged in the plaintiff's complaint (e.g., the plaintiff's contributions to the acquisition of their property) and reasonable inferences therefrom, are sufficient under Wisconsin's liberal notice pleading rule to state a claim for an accounting of the property acquired during the parties' relationship and partition. . . .

NOTE

While the *Hewitt* case probably received more attention, *Watts* (or its approach) is followed in a much larger number of jurisdictions. For instance, in Bright v. Kuehl, 650 N.E.2d 311 (Ind.App.1995), an Indiana court rejected the analysis of *Hewitt* and allowed a claim for both contract and unjust enrichment.

Anastasi v. Anastasi

United States District Court, District of New Jersey, 1982.
544 F.Supp. 866.

■ DEBEVOISE, DISTRICT JUDGE.

Plaintiff instituted this action in the Chancery Division of the Superior Court of New Jersey, charging that defendant had breached his agreement "to provide plaintiff with all of her financial support and needs for the rest of her life". Defendant removed the case to the federal court . . . on the basis of diversity of citizenship. I raised the question whether the case should be remanded to the state court on the ground that it is within the domestic relations exception to federal jurisdiction notwithstanding that there is diversity of citizenship. After briefing and oral argument I concluded that under applicable New Jersey law the action was akin to a contract

---

The major difference between *Carlson* and the instant case is that in *Carlson,* the plaintiff's contribution was limited to homemaking and childcare. That contribution was found sufficient to imply an agreement to share all the property accumulated during the parties' relationship. In this case, the plaintiff allegedly contributed business services and personal property as well as homemaking and childcare services.

action rather than a domestic relations action and therefore the domestic relations exception to jurisdiction did not require remand. Anastasi v. Anastasi, 532 F.Supp. 720 (D.N.J.1982).

In reaching my conclusion I relied heavily upon two New Jersey cases which dealt with agreements for life support entered into by two cohabiting but unmarried persons. Kozlowski v. Kozlowski, 80 N.J. 378, 403 A.2d 902 (1979); Crowe v. DeGioia, 179 N.J.Super. 36, 430 A.2d 251 (App.Div.1981). Each held that such agreements were to be treated under the rules established by the law of contracts. In Crowe v. DeGioia the Court (with one judge dissenting) reversed an order of the trial court awarding plaintiff weekly support payments *pendente lite,* requiring defendant to pay plaintiff's outstanding medical, dental, drug and other bills, permitting plaintiff the exclusive use of defendant's dwelling, and requiring defendant to continue to pay all costs, enjoining defendant from disposing of his assets and awarding plaintiff a counsel fee *pendente lite.*

In ruling as I did I stated:

> I conclude that the exception will apply only if two conditions are met: first, the state exhibits a significant interest in this kind of relationship akin to the state's interest in the marriage and the parent-child relationships; and, second, in order to protect this interest a court must make the same kinds of inquiries that have traditionally brought into play the domestic relations exception.
>
> . . .
>
> Had the views of the trial court and of the dissenting opinion on appeal prevailed in *DeGioia,* I would have concluded that the domestic relations exception to jurisdiction should be applied were such an action instituted in the federal court. The state would have evidenced a sufficient interest in the relationship of unmarried couples to have devised legal mechanisms to protect the parties upon dissolution of the relationship. It would be necessary for a court to inquire into the details of the relationship and into the financial circumstances of the parties. It would be necessary to do this on a continuing basis at least during the course of the litigation. This is precisely what the domestic relations exception is designed to avoid.

Anastasi v. Anastasi, supra, at 724, 725.

On July 8, 1982 the New Jersey Supreme Court reversed the judgment of the Appellate Division of the Superior Court in Crowe v. DeGioia, 90 N.J. 126, 447 A.2d 173 (1982). The Supreme Court ruled that Crowe should be permitted to remain in the home, that support payments to meet "her minimal needs" should be continued *pendente lite,* and that "necessary" medical, dental and pharmaceutical bills should continue to be paid by DeGioia. The Supreme Court held that DeGioia should not be restrained from transferring his assets and that costs and counsel fees should not be awarded in the application for temporary relief. Observing that the Chancery Division rather than the Law Division was the more appropriate forum for the case, the Court stated:

Moreover, a similarity exists between many of the issues and proofs in this type of case and those in a matrimonial action, the exclusive province of the Chancery Division under R. 4:75. Consequently, in this case, as we anticipate will be true in the majority of such cases, the Chancery Division is the appropriate forum. Selection of the Law or Chancery Division in future cases should reflect the responsible exercise of judgment by counsel, subject to the control of the court, to best achieve a just result in this evolving cause of action.

At 138, 447 A.2d 173.

After the New Jersey Supreme Court's opinion was issued I directed the parties to show cause why the instant action should or should not be remanded to the state courts. A hearing was held and I conclude that in the present posture of New Jersey law this kind of case is within the domestic relations exception to jurisdiction and must be remanded.

New Jersey's Supreme Court emphasized that it was not awarding alimony because "alimony may be awarded only in a matrimonial action for divorce or nullity". It was, it stated, "applying traditional equitable principles" in an attempt to "achieve substantial justice" by adjusting "the rights and duties of parties in light of the realities of their relationship". At 135, 447 A.2d 173.

For federal jurisdictional purposes, it is immaterial what label is ascribed to the actions New Jersey courts are now required to take in "palimony" cases. What matters is not the label but rather the function the courts are called upon to perform. As delineated by the New Jersey Supreme Court, a palimony case applying New Jersey law is a domestic relations case within the exception to federal jurisdiction.

In Crowe v. DeGioia the Supreme Court defined a significant state interest in living relationships established by agreement rather than by formal marriage. It noted the frequency of such relationships and the need to protect the interests of the parties to them, stating:

> Increasing numbers of unmarried couples live together. The number of households comprised of unmarried partners rose from approximately 12,000 in 1960 to more than 1.5 million in 1980. U.S. Bureau of Census, Dept. of Commerce, 1960 Census of Population, "Persons by Family Characteristics," Table 15 (1960) and Current Population Report, Series P–20, No. 365, "Marital Status in Living Arrangements," Table 7 (1980). Although plaintiff need not be rewarded for cohabiting with defendant, she should not be penalized simply because she lived with him in consideration of a promise for support. Our endeavor is to shape a remedy that will protect the legally cognizable interests of the parties and serve the needs of justice.

At 135, 447 A.2d 173.

The Court evidently contemplates that palimony actions will be commenced with increasing frequency and in its opinion provided guidance as to the Division of the Superior Court in which such actions should be filed—normally the Chancery Division. At 137, 447 A.2d 173.

Not only does Crowe v. DeGioia announce a significant state interest in the consensual live-in relationship, it requires that in order to protect this interest a trial court must make the same kinds of inquiries that have traditionally brought into play the domestic relations exception to federal jurisdiction. In Crowe v. DeGioia the Court's rationale requires a finding of a reasonable basis for one of the parties to remain in the non-marital home. It requires a finding of the minimal needs of the moving party in order to form a basis for an award of interim support payments. It requires a finding as to the necessity of medical, dental and pharmaceutical bills. Final resolution of the controversy will inevitably require extensive probing into many other issues similar to those in a matrimonial action in order "to best achieve a just result in this evolving cause of action".

. . . [T]hese are the kinds of inquiries and judgments which the state courts are best equipped to handle. They are the kinds of inquiries and judgments which, under the domestic relations exception to jurisdiction, may not be made by federal courts.

For these reasons the case will be remanded to the Superior Court of New Jersey, Chancery Division. . . .

NOTE

Non–Marital Partnerships and the Domestic Relations Exception to Federal Jurisdiction. In Barber v. Barber, 62 U.S. 582, (21 How.) 582, 584, 16 L.Ed. 226 (1858), the Supreme Court of the United States said in dictum:

> We disclaim altogether any jurisdiction in the courts of the United States upon the subject of divorce, or for the allowance of alimony, either as an original proceeding in chancery or as an incident to divorce *a vinculo,* or to one from bed and board.

That statement led to what became known as a "domestic relations exception" to subject matter jurisdiction in federal courts. Under this doctrine, even though with diversity of citizenship and the requisite jurisdictional amount in controversy, federal courts will not hear divorce cases. In the past, the exception was far wider; some believe that longstanding inaccessibility to federal courts even to challenge arbitrary state regulation of marriage and divorce contributed significantly to the slow pace of reform until only two or three decades ago. Considerable question has been voiced about the appropriate scope and even the desirability of an exception, and there are signs that it is now beginning to erode. Even so, there continue to be strong views that federal courts should abstain from hearing family law matters. Such a position was articulated by Justice Rehnquist as recently as 1982 in his dissenting opinion in Santosky v. Kramer:

> If ever there were an area in which federal courts should heed the admonition of Justice Holmes that "a page of history is worth a volume of logic," it is in the area of domestic relations. This area has been left to the states from time immemorial, and not without good reason.

455 U.S. 745, 769, 102 S.Ct. 1388, 71 L.Ed.2d 599 (1982).

In Ankenbrandt v. Richards, 504 U.S. 689, 112 S.Ct. 2206, 119 L.Ed.2d 468 (1992), the Supreme Court of the United States was asked to decide whether the exception should apply to tort suits brought in federal court solely pursuant to diversity jurisdiction. Justice White, seeking a firmer foundation for the federal domestic relations exception than the century and one-half old *Barber*, wrote that the exception cannot be found explicitly within the Constitution but rather in the power of Congress to grant jurisdiction under Article III. He explained that

> Article I, § 8, cl. 9, for example, authorizes Congress "[t]o constitute Tribunals inferior to the supreme Court" and Article III, § 1, states that "[t]he judicial Power of the United States shall be vested in one supreme Court, and in such inferior courts as the Congress may from time to time ordain and establish." The court cases state the rule that "if inferior courts were created, [Congress was not] required to invest them with all the jurisdiction it was authorized to bestow under Article III. Palmore v. United States, 411 U.S. 389, 401."

Id. at 697.

. . .

> We thus are content to rest our conclusion that a domestic relations exception exists as a matter of statutory construction not on the accuracy of the historical justifications on which it was based, but rather on Congress' apparent acceptance of this construction of the diversity jurisdiction . . . .

Id. at 700.

. . .

> We conclude, therefore, that the domestic relations exception, as articulated by this Court since *Barber*, divests the federal courts of power to issue divorce, alimony, and child custody decrees. Given the long passage of time without any expression of congressional dissatisfaction, we have no trouble today reaffirming the validity of the exception as it pertains to divorce and alimony decrees and child custody orders.

Id. at 706–7.

The Court concluded that there was no domestic relations exception in tort cases such as *Ankenbrandt*, where one former spouse sued another on behalf of children alleged to have been abused. Nonetheless, Justice White did state that there may be future instances when subject matter jurisdiction may be proper but in which there could exist sufficient grounds to warrant abstention from exercising jurisdiction:

> It is not inconceivable, however, that in certain circumstances, the abstention principles might be relevant even when the parties do not seek a divorce, alimony or child custody. This would be so when a case presents "difficult questions of state law bearing on policy problems of substantial public import whose importance transcends the result in

the case then at bar." ... Such might well be the case if a federal suit were filed prior to effectuation of a divorce, alimony or child custody decree, and the suit depended on a determination of the status of the parties.

Id. at 700.

Justice Blackmun concurred in the judgment of the court, but refused to accept the majority's holding that the exception is found within the statutory basis. He preferred to find its basis in "discretionary abstention" rather than any "mandatory limit" but denied that the diversity statute contains an exception for domestic relations matters.

What significance should the court's decision in *Ankenbrandt* have with regard to the legal nature of "living together" contracts?

CALIFORNIA FAMILY CODE (West 2004 and 2005 Cum. Supp.)

§ 297. Domestic partners and partnership; establishment

(a) Domestic partners are two adults who have chosen to share one another's lives in an intimate and committed relationship of mutual caring.

(b) A domestic partnership shall be established in California when both persons file a Declaration of Domestic Partnership with the Secretary of State pursuant to this division, and, at the time of filing, all of the following requirements are met:

(1) Both persons have a common residence.

(2) Neither person is married to someone else or is a member of another domestic partnership with someone else that has not been terminated, dissolved, or adjudged a nullity.

(3) The two persons are not related by blood in a way that would prevent them from being married to each other in this state.

(4) Both persons are at least 18 years of age.

(5) Either of the following:

(A) Both persons are members of the same sex.

(B) One or both of the persons meet the eligibility criteria under Title II of the Social Security Act as defined in 42 U.S.C. Section 402(a) for old-age insurance benefits or Title XVI of the Social Security Act as defined in 42 U.S.C. Section 1381 for aged individuals. Notwithstanding any other provision of this section, persons of opposite sexes may not constitute a domestic partnership unless one or both of the persons are over the age of 62.

(6) Both persons are capable of consenting to the domestic partnership.

(c) "Have a common residence" means that both domestic partners share the same residence. It is not necessary that the legal right to possess the common residence be in both of their names. Two people have a common residence even if one or both have additional residences. Domestic partners do not cease to have a common residence if one leaves the common residence but intends to return.

§ 297.5. Rights, protections and benefits; responsibilities; obligations and duties under law; date of registration as equivalent of date of marriage

(a) Registered domestic partners shall have the same rights, protections, and benefits, and shall be subject to the same responsibilities, obligations, and duties under law, whether they derive from statutes, administrative regulations, court rules, government policies, common law, or any other provisions or sources of law, as are granted to and imposed upon spouses.

(b) Former registered domestic partners shall have the same rights, protections, and benefits, and shall be subject to the same responsibilities, obligations, and duties under law, whether they derive from statutes, administrative regulations, court rules, government policies, common law, or any other provisions or sources of law, as are granted to and imposed upon former spouses.

(c) A surviving registered domestic partner, following the death of the other partner, shall have the same rights, protections, and benefits, and shall be subject to the same responsibilities, obligations, and duties under law, whether they derive from statutes, administrative regulations, court rules, government policies, common law, or any other provisions or sources of law, as are granted to and imposed upon a widow or a widower.

(d) The rights and obligations of registered domestic partners with respect to a child of either of them shall be the same as those of spouses. The rights and obligations of former or surviving registered domestic partners with respect to a child of either of them shall be the same as those of former or surviving spouses.

(e) To the extent that provisions of California law adopt, refer to, or rely upon, provisions of federal law in a way that otherwise would cause registered domestic partners to be treated differently than spouses, registered domestic partners shall be treated by California law as if federal law recognized a domestic partnership in the same manner as California law.

(f) Registered domestic partners shall have the same rights regarding nondiscrimination as those provided to spouses.

(g) Notwithstanding this section, in filing their state income tax returns, domestic partners shall use the same filing status as is used on their federal income tax returns, or that would have been used had they filed federal income tax returns. Earned income may not be treated as community property for state income tax purposes.

(h) No public agency in this state may discriminate against any person or couple on the ground that the person is a registered domestic partner rather than a spouse or that the couple are registered domestic partners rather than spouses, except that nothing in this section applies to modify eligibility for long-term care plans pursuant to Chapter 15 (commencing with Section 21660) of Part 3 of Division 5 of Title 2 of the Government Code.

(i) This act does not preclude any state or local agency from exercising its regulatory authority to implement statutes providing rights to, or imposing responsibilities upon, domestic partners.

(j) This section does not amend or modify any provision of the California Constitution or any provision of any statute that was adopted by initiative.

(k) This section does not amend or modify federal laws or the benefits, protections, and responsibilities provided by those laws.

(*l*) Where necessary to implement the rights of registered domestic partners under this act, gender-specific terms referring to spouses shall be construed to include domestic partners.

(m)(1) For purposes of the statutes, administrative regulations, court rules, government policies, common law, and any other provision or source of law governing the rights, protections, and benefits, and the responsibilities, obligations, and duties of registered domestic partners in this state, as effectuated by this section, with respect to community property, mutual responsibility for debts to third parties, the right in particular circumstances of either partner to seek financial support from the other following the dissolution of the partnership, and other rights and duties as between the partners concerning ownership of property, any reference to the date of a marriage shall be deemed to refer to the date of registration of a domestic partnership with the state.

(2) Notwithstanding paragraph (1), for domestic partnerships registered with the state before January 1, 2005, an agreement between the domestic partners that the partners intend to be governed by the requirements set forth in Sections 1600 to 1620, inclusive, and which complies with those sections, except for the agreement's effective date, shall be enforceable as provided by Sections 1600 to 1620, inclusive, if that agreement was fully executed and in force as of June 30, 2005.

§ 299. Termination of registered domestic partnership; filing of Notice of Termination of Domestic Partnership; conditions; effective date; setting aside termination; jurisdiction

(a) A registered domestic partnership may be terminated without filing a proceeding for dissolution of domestic partnership by the filing of a Notice of Termination of Domestic Partnership with the Secretary of State pursuant to this section, provided that all of the following conditions exist at the time of the filing:

(1) The Notice of Termination of Domestic Partnership is signed by both registered domestic partners.

(2) There are no children of the relationship of the parties born before or after registration of the domestic partnership or adopted by the parties after registration of the domestic partnership, and neither of the registered domestic partners, to their knowledge, is pregnant.

(3) The registered domestic partnership is not more than five years in duration.

(4) Neither party has any interest in real property wherever situated, with the exception of the lease of a residence occupied by either party which satisfies the following requirements:

(A) The lease does not include an option to purchase.

(B) The lease terminates within one year from the date of filing of the Notice of Termination of Domestic Partnership.

(5) There are no unpaid obligations in excess of the amount described in paragraph (6) of subdivision (a) of Section 2400, as adjusted by subdivision (b) of Section 2400, incurred by either or both of the parties after registration of the domestic partnership, excluding the amount of any unpaid obligation with respect to an automobile.

(6) The total fair market value of community property assets, excluding all encumbrances and automobiles, including any deferred compensation or retirement plan, is less than the amount described in paragraph (7) of subdivision (a) of Section 2400, as adjusted by subdivision (b) of Section 2400, and neither party has separate property assets, excluding all encumbrances and automobiles, in excess of that amount.

(7) The parties have executed an agreement setting forth the division of assets and the assumption of liabilities of the community property, and have executed any documents, title certificates, bills of sale, or other evidence of transfer necessary to effectuate the agreement.

(8) The parties waive any rights to support by the other domestic partner.

(9) The parties have read and understand a brochure prepared by the Secretary of State describing the requirements, nature, and effect of terminating a domestic partnership.

(10) Both parties desire that the domestic partnership be terminated.

(b) The registered domestic partnership shall be terminated effective six months after the date of filing of the Notice of Termination of Domestic Partnership with the Secretary of State pursuant to this section, provided that neither party has, before that date, filed with the Secretary of State a notice of revocation of the termination of domestic partnership, in the form and content as shall be prescribed by the Secretary of State, and sent to the other party a copy of the notice of revocation by first-class mail, postage prepaid, at the other party's last known address. The effect of termination of a domestic partnership pursuant to this section shall be the same as, and shall be treated for all purposes as, the entry of a judgment of dissolution of a domestic partnership.

(c) The termination of a domestic partnership pursuant to subdivision (b) does not prejudice nor bar the rights of either of the parties to institute an action in the superior court to set aside the termination for fraud, duress, mistake, or any other ground recognized at law or in equity. A court may set aside the termination of domestic partnership and declare the termination of the domestic partnership null and void upon proof that the parties did not meet the requirements of subdivision (a) at the time of the filing of the Notice of Termination of Domestic Partnership with the Secretary of State.

(d) The superior courts shall have jurisdiction over all proceedings relating to the dissolution of domestic partnerships, nullity of domestic partnerships, and legal separation of partners in a domestic partnership. The dissolution of a domestic partnership, nullity of a domestic partnership, and legal separation of partners in a domestic partnership shall follow the same procedures, and the partners shall possess the same rights, protections, and benefits, and be subject to the same responsibilities, obligations, and duties, as apply to the dissolution of marriage, nullity of marriage, and legal separation of spouses in a marriage, respectively, except as provided in subdivision (a), and except that, in accordance with the consent acknowledged by domestic partners in the Declaration of Domestic Partnership form, proceedings for dissolution, nullity, or legal separation of a domestic partnership registered in this state may be filed in the superior courts of this state even if neither domestic partner is a resident of, or maintains a domicile in, the state at the time the proceedings are filed.

§ 299.2. Recognizing same sex unions from another jurisdiction as a valid domestic partnership

A legal union of two persons of the same sex, other than a marriage, that was validly formed in another jurisdiction, and that is substantially equivalent to a domestic partnership as defined in this part, shall be recognized as a valid domestic partnership in this state regardless of whether it bears the name domestic partnership.

NOTE

Domestic partnership has increased in scope and practice, as the California legislation indicates. The statutes above went into effect on January 1, 2005. California now applies retroactive standing to a decedent's domestic partner in wrongful death cases, Bouley v. Long Beach Memorial Med. Ctr., 127 Cal.App.4th 601, 25 Cal.Rptr.3d 813 (2005), and concomitantly, there is no denial of equal protection in denying that same right to unmarried couples of the opposite sex. Opposite sex couples may not enter into domestic partnerships unless one of them is at least 62 years of age or eligible for age-based benefits under the Social Security Act. Ability of opposite sex couples to marry and their refusal to do so indicates a lack of commitment that the court found a rational reason for different treatment. Holguin v. Flores, 122 Cal.App.4th 428, 18 Cal.Rptr.3d 749 (2004). But in Montana the state constitution's equal protection clause demands that same sex domestic partners be provided with health benefits at Montana University if the state provides such benefits to the declared common law spouses of heterosexual employees. Snetsinger v. Montana Univ. Sys., 325 Mont. 148, 104 P.3d 445 (2004).

Suggested Reading: Grace Ganz Blumberg, *Legal Recognition of Same-Sex Conjugal Relationships: The 2003 California Domestic Partner Rights and Responsibilities Act in Comparative Civil Rights and Family Law Perspectives*, 51 UCLA L. REV. 1555–1617 (2004); Margaret F. Brinig *and* Steven L. Nock, *Marry Me, Bill: Should Cohabitation be the (Legal) Default Option?*, 64 LA. L. REV. 403–442 (2004); Ann Laquer Estin, *Embracing Tradition: Pluralism in American Family Law*, 63 MD. L. REV. 540–604 (2004).

C.   MARRIAGE: THE RELIGIOUS HERITAGE

The jurisprudence of the ecclesiastical courts, defined as courts having jurisdiction over matters pertaining to religion, had a direct influence over what we now regard as "family law" or domestic relations. When matrimonial causes were transferred from the English ecclesiastical courts to the statutory Divorce Court in 1857, the continued relevance of much of the old canon law was assured not only by the necessity of recourse to precedent, but by explicit statutory authorization of reference to antecedent ecclesiastical practice. This ecclesiastical practice had a long history. According to Professor Joseph Martos in DOORS TO THE SACRED (1991) at 360: "With the coming of the dark ages in Europe after the fall of the Roman empire, churchmen were called upon more and more to decide marriage cases. Centuries before, Constantine had given them authority to act as judges in certain civil matters, and now that authority grew as the regular judicial system collapsed." By the fifteenth century, the ecclesiastical courts of the Roman Catholic Church supervised the granting of annulments to those who could prove that their present marriage was invalid by canonical standards.

During the sixteenth century, the Protestant Reformers, including Henry VIII, no stranger to divorce and remarriage, denied that marriage was a sacrament. Martin Luther was an outspoken reformer. According to Professor Martos at pages 373–74:

> Marriage was instituted by God, said Luther, but not as a sacrament in the Roman sense. Rather it was a natural and social institution which accordingly fell under the natural and civil law, not church law. "No one can deny that marriage is an external and secular matter, like food and clothing, houses and land, subject to civil supervision" (On Matrimonial Matters). Thus the church should leave "each city and state to its own customs and practices in this regard" (Short

Catechism, Preface). The role of the clergy should be to advise and counsel Christians about marriage, not to pass laws about it and judge marriage cases. Civil governments, on the other hand, had a right to make marriage laws because all authority ultimately comes from God, and so in the secular world they acted in God's name. They could not be expected to pass laws that were in strict conformity with the ideals of the gospel, but at the same time they were morally obliged to keep within the bounds set by the laws of nature in enacting legislation for the good of society.

By the time the ecclesiastical courts had transferred responsibility for domestic relations to the civil divorce courts, England had experienced more than three hundred years of the Protestant Reformation. Explicitly rejected was the doctrine of the Roman Catholic Church that marriage was a sacrament; instead marriage was purely a contractual matter between the parties with varying degrees of church involvement and state supervision. This is the heritage of the American colonies and much of the practice in the United States today. Nonetheless, all Christian denominations conceptualize marriage in Hebrew scriptural terms: "But from the beginning of creation God made them male and female. This is why a man must leave father and mother, and the two shall become one body. They are no longer two, therefore, but one body. So what God has united, man must not divide." This central tenet is the norm; it has been adopted into current ecclesiastical documents.

At the close of the Second Vatican Council of the Roman Catholic Church, in 1965, 2900 bishops from throughout the world, adopted this definition of marriage (AUSTIN FLANNERY, O.P., (ED.) VATICAN COUNCIL II 950 (1975) (*quoting from Pastoral Constitution on the Church in the Modern World* § 48)):

> The intimate partnership of life and the love which constitutes the married state has been established by the creator and endowed by him with its own proper laws: it is rooted in the contract of its partners, that is, in their irrevocable personal consent. It is an institution confirmed by the divine law and receiving its stability, even in the eyes of society, from the human act by which the partners mutually surrender themselves to each other; for the good of the partners, of the children, and of society this sacred bond no longer depends on human decision alone. For God himself is the author of marriage and has endowed it with various benefits and with various ends in view: all of these have a very important bearing on the continuation of the human race, on the personal development and eternal destiny of every member of the family, on the dignity, stability, peace, and prosperity of the family and of the whole human race.

The ecclesiastical law heritage forms the basis of much of family law in the United States. Its practices, definitions, prohibitions, structures and history affect marriage qualifications, divorce grounds and custody determinations. Often, as the cases demonstrate, this ecclesiastical law heritage is the basis upon which secular society both seeks to limit individual freedom and, contrastingly, safeguard individual possibility.

D.   MARRIAGE: THE STATE'S INTEREST

The definition of marriage is more static than the evolving contractual relationships described in non-marital contracts and domestic partnerships. Intimately connected to the religious underpinnings of most Americans, the status of the relationship has undergone little challenge, and to date, each challenge has resulted in an affirmation of what has come to be an agreed-upon definition of marriage. In the middle of the nineteenth century, the following summary was offered by JOEL P. BISHOP, COMMENTARIES ON THE LAW OF MARRIAGE AND DIVORCE, Vol. 1, pages 1–4 (6th Ed. 1881):

> **§ 3.   Marriage Defined.** Marriage, as distinguished from the agreement to marry and form the act of becoming married, is the civil status of one man and one woman united for life, for the discharge, to each other and the community, of the duties legally incumbent upon those whose association is founded on the distinction of sex.
>
> **Source of Marriage—Further of the Definition.** The source of marriage is the law of nature, whence it has flowed into the municipal laws of every civilized country, and into the general law of nations. And since it can exist only in pairs, and since none are compelled, but all who are capable are permitted, to assume it,—marriage may be said to proceed ... from a civil contract between one man and one woman of the needful physical and civil capacity. While the contract remains a mere agreement to marry, it is not essentially different from the other executory civil contracts; it does not superinduce the status; and on its violation, action may be maintained by the injured party to recover his damages of the other. But when it is executed in what the law accepts as a valid marriage, its nature as a contract is merged in the higher nature of the status. And though the new relation—that is, the status—retains some similitude reminding of its origin, the contract does in truth no longer exist, but the parties are governed by the law of husband and wife.

UNIFORM MARRIAGE AND DIVORCE ACT (1970)*

§ 201.   [Formalities]

Marriage is a personal relationship between a man and a woman arising out of a civil contract to which the consent of the parties is essential. A marriage licensed, solemnized, and registered as provided in this Act is valid in this State. A marriage may be contracted, maintained, invalidated, or dissolved only as provided by law.

[This and subsequent excerpts from the Uniform Marriage and Divorce Act and other Uniform Acts are reprinted with permission from the National Council of Commissioners on Uniform State Laws.]

FLORIDA MARRIAGE PREPARATION AND PRESERVATION ACT OF 1998

§ 741.04(1). [Marriage License Issued]

No county court judge or clerk of the circuit court in this state shall issue a license for the marriage of any person unless there shall be first presented and filed with him or her an affidavit in writing, signed by both parties to the marriage, providing the social security numbers ... of each party, made and subscribed before some person authorized by law to administer an oath, reciting the true and correct ages of such parties; unless both such parties shall be over the age of 18 years, ... and unless one party is a male and the other party is a female. Pursuant to the federal Personal Responsibility and Work Opportunity Reconciliation Act of 1996, each party is required to provide his or her social security number in accordance with this section.... Disclosure of social security numbers ... obtained through this requirement shall be limited to the purpose of administration of the Title IV–D program for child support enforcement.

§ 741.0305(1). [Marriage Fee Reduction for Completion of Premarital Preparation Course]

A man and a woman who intend to apply for a marriage license ... may, together or separately, complete a premarital preparation course of not less than 4 hours. Each individual shall verify completion of the course by filing with the application a valid certificate of completion from the course provider, which certificate shall specify whether the course was completed by personal instruction, videotape instruction, instruction via other electronic medium, or a combination of those methods. All individuals who complete a premarital preparation course pursuant to this section must be issued a certificate of completion at the conclusion of the course by their course provider. Upon furnishing such certificate when applying for a marriage license, the individuals shall have their marriage license fee reduced by $32.50.

NOTE

The notion of marriage as a civil contract results from the rejection of the ecclesiastical or sacramental character of marriage existent prior to the Reformation in the mid-sixteenth century. The Protestant Reformers, their ideas carried to America from Europe, regarded marriage as a matter for the civil authorities to administer. Marriage as an "institution" may be attributed to Blackstone's adherence to a contract formula. 1 Commentaries 432. Story, Conflict of Law § 108 (2d ed. 1841). Joel Bishop, at least by his own admission, was responsible for the wide acceptance of the concept "status". Bishop's Commentaries on the Law of Marriage and Divorce, which underwent half a dozen editions between 1852 and 1891, was a major factor in the development of family law during the nineteenth century. He described this in an Introduction to his text of Criminal Procedure (3d ed. 1880), in which he set forth his strong (and by no mean modest) views about the influences of his writings:

Let [the reader] carefully examine the books on marriage and divorce, as they were before our present author wrote. He will learn that there has never been a legal subject upon which our tribunals have been in so much confusion and conflict. He will see that my book consisted, in large part, of a cleaning up of questions of difficulty; not by leaving plain what was before obscure, and making smooth the ways which were before rough. Let him then follow down the decisions of our courts to the present time. He will find that, as often as the views of the book were seen and *understood*, they were adopted by the courts; and that, not only is this the rule, but to it there is no exception. Id. at xv.

Maynard v. Hill

Supreme Court of the United States, 1888.
125 U.S. 190, 8 S.Ct. 723, 31 L.Ed. 654.

■ MR. JUSTICE FIELD.

. . .

Marriage, as creating the most important relation in life, as having more to do with the morals and civilization of a people than any other institution, has always been subject to the control of the legislature. That body prescribes the age at which parties may contract to marry, the procedure or form essential to constitute marriage, the duties and obligations it creates, its effects upon the property rights of both, present and prospective, and the acts which may constitute grounds for its dissolution.

. . .

. . . [W]hilst marriage is often termed by text writers and in decisions of courts a civil contract—generally to indicate that it must be founded upon the agreement of the parties, and does not require any religious ceremony for its solemnization—it is something more than a mere contract. The consent of the parties is of course essential to its existence, but when the contract to marry is executed by the marriage, a relation between the parties is created which they cannot change. Other contracts may be modified, restricted, or enlarged, or entirely released upon the consent of the parties. Not so with marriage. The relation once formed, the law steps in and holds the parties to various obligations and liabilities. It is an institution, the maintenance of which in its purity the public is deeply interested, for it is the foundation of the family and of society, without which there would be neither civilization nor progress. This view is well expressed by the Supreme Court of Maine in Adams v. Palmer, 51 Me. 481, 483[:]

"When the contracting parties have entered into the married state, they have not so much entered into a contract as into a new relation, the rights, duties, and obligations of which rest not upon their agreement, but upon the general law of the State, statutory or common, which defines and prescribes those rights, duties, and obligations. They are of law, not of contract. It was of contract that the relation should be established, but being established, the power of the parties as to its extent or duration is at an end. Their rights under it are determined by the will of the sovereign, as evidenced by law. They can neither be modified nor changed by any agreement of parties. It is a relation for life, and the parties cannot terminate it at any shorter period by virtue of any contract they may make. The reciprocal rights arising from this relation, so long as it continues, are such as the law determines from time to time, and none other." And again: "It is not, then, a contract within the meaning of the clause of the Constitution which prohibits the impairing the obligation of contracts. It is, rather, a social relation, like that of parent and child, the obligations of which arise not from the consent of concurring minds, but are the creation of the law itself; a relation the most important, as affecting the happiness of individuals, the first step from barbarism to incipient civilization, the purest tie of social life and the true basis of human progress."

NOTE

The small number of early constitutional law decisions dealing with domestic relations are known largely from pithy or otherwise quotable passages that are not always remembered or cited in appropriate context. Maynard v. Hill provides an example of this. The facts of the case are widely forgotten. It was an equity suit seeking to compel the transfer of lands in the Washington Territory that were registered in a public land settlement. Plaintiffs were children of the settler's first wife, from whom the settler had obtained a divorce by a legislative act of the Territorial Assembly. The validity of such a divorce was at issue because the wife of a resident settling initially as a married man would take no interest in the title subsequently acquired by him if the pair divorced before completion of the settlement period.

SUGGESTED CHANGES: CONCEPTS OF MARRIAGE

"Covenant marriage" has been widely publicized, but only three States have adopted legislation to recognize it. *See* La. Rev. Stat. Ann. § 9:272 (West 2000); added to by La. Legis. 249 (2006); Ariz. Rev. Stat. § 25–901 (2000) and Ark. Code Ann. § 9–11–801 (2001). It can hardly be defined as a new species of marriage because its basic effect is that the parties may elect to have their union terminable only on specific (usually fault) grounds rather than breakdown. Ironically it is in principle a form of contractual alteration of some of the key provisions regarding marriage dissolution. A soon to be published study is S.L. Nock, J.W. Wright, and C. Sanchez, Covenant Marriage and the Marriage Movement, Rutgers U. Press (2008).

Fisher v. Fisher

Court of Appeals of New York, 1929.
250 N.Y. 313, 165 N.E. 460.

■ Kellogg, J. In this action for a separation the complaint alleges "that the parties hereto were duly married on the 24th day of October, 1925." The answer denies the allegation. Concededly, on the day named the parties to the action were on board the steamship Leviathan, then on the high seas, bound from the port of New York to Southampton, England. When the ship was 40 miles out from the port of New York, its captain performed a marriage ceremony, wherein these parties were the principals. In the course of the ceremony the captain asked the plaintiff if she took the defendant for her husband, asked the defendant if he took the plaintiff for his wife, received an affirmative answer from each, and thereupon pronounced them man and wife. Cohabitation of the principals followed the ceremony. The only question which survives for discussion here is this: Were the parties upon the occasion in question lawfully united in marriage?

It is elementary that marriage is a civil contract; that the law deals with it as it does with all other contracts; that it pronounces a marriage to be valid wherever a man and woman, able and willing to contract, do, per verba de praesenti, promise to become husband and wife. A formal ceremony of marriage, whether in due form or not, must be assumed to be by consent, and, therefore, prima facie a contract of marriage per verba de praesenti. According to the common law of all Christendom, consensual marriages—i.e., marriages resting simply on consent per verba de praesenti—between competent parties, are valid marriages.... The sanction which the law of civilized nations bestows upon marriages by mere consent is of course not inclusive of marriages which civilization commonly condemns.... Otherwise, regulations restrictive of the common right of marriage by mere consent, or imposing conditions upon it, are exceptional; they depend upon local statutes, and, as in other cases of exceptions, if one claims that a case falls within them, the burden is upon him to show the fact.... [A]lthough no law of any state, territory or district of the United States, *sanctioning* the marriage of the parties to this action, may have followed the ship Leviathan upon the high seas, in the absence of any such law which *condemned* the marriage, we think that they were lawfully married. It becomes necessary now to inquire whether a controlling law of any state did condemn the marriage.

The defendant, prior to the performance of the marriage ceremony in question, was already a married man. His former wife had procured, in this jurisdiction, a decree of divorce against him, dissolving the marriage on the ground of adultery. According to the terms of the decree and the laws of this state the defendant was forbidden to remarry during the life of his then wife. The wife, who procured the decree, is still living. It is well settled that the provisions of our statute forbidding the remarriage of a party who has been divorced for adultery have no extraterritorial effect; that a subsequent marriage of the guilty party, during the life of the innocent party, in a sister state, if valid in that state, will be recognized here as a lawful marriage. The question then arises, Did the laws of the State of New York follow the steamship Leviathan in its journey upon the high seas?

"The Steamship Leviathan of New York, N.Y." was registered in the port of New York. The certificate of registry specifies that the "United States of America represented by the United States Shipping Board is the only owner of the vessel called the Leviathan of New York, N.Y." On the high seas it flew the flag of the United States. A ship in the open sea is regarded by the law of nations as a part of the territory whose flag such ship carries. Wharton, Conflict of Laws, § 356. Wharton says: "As between the several states in the American Union, a ship at sea is presumed to belong to the state in which it is registered." For this statement the sole authority is Crapo v. Kelly, 16 Wall. 610, 21 L.Ed. 430. We think that the learned author misconceived the decision in that case. The ship there considered was a vessel owned by residents of the state of Massachusetts. It was, likewise, registered at a port within the state of Massachusetts. As we read the case, the court decided that the vessel was a Massachusetts ship, not because it had a Massachusetts registry, but because its owners were citizens of Massachusetts. The court said: "Again, the owners of this vessel and the assignees in insolvency were citizens of Massachusetts, and subject to her laws. It is not doubted that a sale of property between them of property on board of this vessel, or of the vessel itself, would be regulated by the laws of Massachusetts." In The Havana (C.C.A.) 64 F. 496, it was held that a vessel owned by a New Jersey corporation, although registered in New York, was a New Jersey vessel. In International Nav. Co. v. Lindstrom (C.C.A.) 123 F. 475, it was said: "It is plain that the New York statute did not reach the case, because, inasmuch as the steamship belonged to a citizen of New Jersey, it was a vessel of that state, notwithstanding its registry in New York." ... We think it clear, under the authorities, that the laws which follow a ship upon the high seas are the laws of the state where the owner resides, not the laws of the state within which the ship is registered. Therefore, if we assume that the United States was the owner of the steamship Leviathan, the laws of the state of New York did not follow the ship as a part of its territory, since the United States certainly is not domiciled in that state. The presumption of the validity of the marriage, therefore, was not destroyed by proof that one of the parties thereto, within the state of New York, was incompetent to marry.

We have hitherto assumed that the marriage in question had not the positive sanction of any Federal statute, or of the common law of any state, territory or district of the United States, carried upon the high seas by the steamship Leviathan. We think the fact is otherwise.

Congress had provided that: "Every vessel making voyages from a port in the United States to any foreign port" should have an official log book; that every master of such a vessel should make entry therein of "Every marriage taking place on board, with the names and ages of the parties." Mason's U.S. Code, vol. 3, title 46, § 201 (46 U.S.C.A. § 201), "Every marriage taking place on board" is certainly inclusive of marriages other than those sanctioned by the municipal laws of the state of the ship's ownership. We take it that Congress had thus recognized that on board a ship at sea, notwithstanding the absence of municipal laws so carried, there is nevertheless a law of marriage. That law can be none other than the law, common to all nations, which pronounces valid all consensual marriages between a man and woman who are, in the view of all civilized people, competent to marry. In this view, the marriage between the parties to this action, by force of a federal statute, which Congress was fully empowered to enact, was a valid marriage.

If the federal statute cannot thus be interpreted, then we think that the common law of the District of Columbia prevailed to give sanction to the marriage. We have thus far assumed that the title to the steamship Leviathan was in the United States. The certificate of registry so states, and the referee has so found. Moreover, the respondent does not appear to have disputed the point. However, we think that such was not the fact. An act of Congress of June 5, 1920, provided in part as follows: "All vessels . . . acquired by the President . . . in pursuance of the joint resolution entitled 'Joint Resolution authorizing the President to take over for the United States the possession and title of any vessel within its jurisdiction, which at the time of coming therein was owned in whole or in part by any corporation, citizen, or subject of any nation with which the United States may be at war, or was under register of any such nation, and for other purposes,' approved May 12, 1917, . . . are hereby transferred to the board. . . ." (46 U.S.C.A. § 863). The "board" is the United States Shipping Board. The steamship Leviathan was a vessel of the class referred to by the joint resolution. . . . It seems to be clear, therefore, that the title to the steamship Leviathan was in the United States Shipping Board. That board had its domicile in the District of Columbia. Therefore, if the law of Congress referred to did not occupy the field, the law of the District of Columbia in relation to marriage followed the steamship on its journey upon the high seas, and was controlling. . . .

In the absence of proof of the statutes of the District, we must assume that the common law, which would give sanction to the marriage in question, prevails in the District of Columbia; that this law obtained on board the steamship Leviathan when upon the high seas; that the marriage between the parties was, therefore, legal. . . .

NOTES

Is marriage "universal" or "state specific"? In seeking an answer to this question, one can ask whether marriage on an unclaimed island in mid-ocean or a vessel on the high seas will be recognized without resort to consideration of either the domicile of the parties or some jurisdiction with contacts to the locus that might be used for validation. Note how the court went through such a process of identification in *Fisher*. In Moore v. Neff, 629 S.W.2d 827 (Tex.App.1982), the appellant pursued her claim that she had become the lawful wife of the late Howard Hughes through a marriage ceremony aboard an unidentified yacht off the coast of California. No marriage license had been issued, and subsequently the appellant married three other individuals. The Texas court held that she was estopped from asserting a marriage at sea. According to newspaper reports, appellant subsequently settled her claim against the estate of Howard Hughes for a sum that she described as being in "not more than eight figures". An attorney for two Hughes heirs said it was "substantially less than eight figures." *See* N.Y. TIMES, May 26, 1983, at A14, col. 4.

Recognition of foreign country marriages. Occasionally courts have confronted the argument that another country's "marriage" is so contrary to the forum's definition of the institution that an action asserting rights based on such a union should be precluded. This problem has been raised with regard to marriages from jurisdictions that permit polygamy (*e.g.* People v. Ezeonu, 155 Misc.2d 344, 588 N.Y.S.2d 116) (Sup.Ct., Bronx Co.1992) (bigamous marriage was repugnant to public policy); single gender marriages; or virtually free dissolubility. In Nachimson v. Nachimson [1930] P. 217 (C.A.), a British court faced the last fact situation in an action for separation filed by one of the parties. In 1924 the couple had gone through a "marriage" ceremony in Moscow, their domicile then being Russia. They had cohabited in England during 1925, but the respondent alleged that he had dissolved the union in 1929 under Russian law by an ex parte registration of such fact with the Consulate General of the U.S.S.R. in Paris. It was against the background of this very liberal Russian rule as to dissolubility which existed at the time of the marriage, as opposed to the British concept of marriage as a union between one man and one woman for life, that the question whether the parties had ever been married became an issue. Although the lower court had determined that no marriage had come into being, this was reversed by the Court of Appeal, Lord Hanworth stating:

> It may be that our minds, trained to regard marriage as in most cases sanctified by religious rites—in others by a civil procedure not less binding—recoil at the recognition of a union capable of being dissolved so easily as the marriage of these spouses when contracted in Russia appears to have been. Nevertheless that marriage has the essential legal ingredients. It is the union of one man and one woman to the exclusion of all others; it is to last for life unless it is dissolved in a manner that is made definite and final by registration. It was duly entered into in accordance with the forms required by the lex loci of the domicile of the parties to it. I find myself unable consistently with the authorities, to criticize or to weigh the strength that ought to be attached to the tie which form the nexus and union of the spouses or to qualify the essence of the marriage by consideration of the means whereby it may be dissolved if and when that question fails to be determined by the law of the domicile of the parties. . . .

Foreign marriages that differ from those solemnized in the United States may be the subject of renewed interest as a result of increased international recognition of single gender marriage. Belgium, Canada, Denmark, Iceland, the Netherlands, Norway, South Africa, Spain and Sweden either have or are moving toward some legal recognition of single gender marriages. Rex Wocker, *Same–Sex Marriage, Nordic Style*, 726 ADVOCATE 26 (1997), reports that:

> In Denmark, where "gay marriage" has been legal the longest, 2,083 gay or lesbian couples had tied the knot as of January 1, 1996,

according to the nation's sole gay newspaper, PAN–Bladet. Seventeen percent of the couples (357) later divorced, and 219 marriages ended when a partner died. More male couples have gotten hitched than female couples—1.449 versus 643. Danish lesbians also have a higher divorce rate—23%, compared with 14% for gay men.

The United States Congress, anticipating issues of recognition, passed the Defense of Marriage Act, 1 U.S.C.A. § 7 with the following definition of "marriage" and "spouse":

> In determining the meaning of any Act of Congress, or of any ruling, regulation, or interpretation of the various administrative bureaus and agencies of the United States, the word "marriage" means only a legal union between one man and one woman as husband and wife, and the word "spouse" refers only to a person of the opposite sex who is a husband or a wife.

E. REGULATING MARRIAGE AND OTHER INTIMATE RELATIONSHIPS: SOME CONSTITUTIONAL DIMENSIONS

Sharma v. Sharma

Court of Appeals of Kansas, 1983.
8 Kan.App.2d 726, 667 P.2d 395.

■ FOTH, CHIEF JUDGE:

The defendant, Mridula Niranjan Sharma, appeals from an order granting a divorce to her husband, Niranjan Sharma. The parties are citizens of India and Hindus of high caste. The wife contends that the order dissolving her marriage violates her constitutionally guaranteed right of free exercise of religion. She informs us that the Hindu religion does not recognize divorce, and that if she returns to India as a divorced woman, her family and friends will treat her as though she were dead. The husband disputes this, but even assuming that the wife's interpretation of Hindu personal law is accurate, we must affirm.

It has long been recognized that under the First Amendment of the United States Constitution, freedom of belief is absolute. The law may, however, regulate conduct prompted by religious beliefs when the individual's interest in the free exercise of religion is outweighed by a compelling state interest. Sherbert v. Verner, 374 U.S. 398, 403, 83 S.Ct. 1790, 1793–94, 10 L.Ed.2d 965 (1963); Reynolds v. United States, 98 U.S. 145, 25 L.Ed. 244 (1878).

The wife contends that Wisconsin v. Yoder, 406 U.S. 205, 92 S.Ct. 1526, 32 L.Ed.2d 15 (1972), requires that her religious beliefs prevail. We disagree. In *Yoder*, the United States Supreme Court found that the State's requirement of compulsory school attendance until age 16 was in irreconcilable conflict with the religious beliefs of the Amish defendants. Formal high school education beyond the eighth grade not only exposes Amish children to values that they reject as influences that alienate man from God, but it also takes them away from the traditional training that imparts the attitudes and skills necessary for life in the Amish community. 406 U.S. 211–212, 92 S.Ct. at 1531. This is not such a case, for the granting of a divorce to the husband does not deny the wife her religious freedom.

We find only one case in which the present issue has been considered, Williams v. Williams, 543 P.2d 1401 (Okl.1975), cert. denied 426 U.S. 901, 96 S.Ct. 2220, 48 L.Ed.2d 826 (1976). In response to a wife's contention that the divorce granted to her husband contravened the religious vows taken by the parties and the authority of God, the Bible, and Jesus Christ, the Oklahoma Supreme Court stated:

> "The action of the trial court only dissolved the civil contract of marriage between the parties. No attempt was made to dissolve it ecclesiastically. Therefore, there is no infringement upon her constitutional right of freedom of religion. She still has her constitutional prerogative to believe that in the eyes of God, she and her estranged husband are ecclesiastically wedded as one, and may continue to exercise that freedom of religion according to her belief and conscience. Any transgression by her husband of their ecclesiastical vows, is, in this instance, outside the jurisdiction of the court." 543 P.2d at 1403.

We agree with the Oklahoma court's analysis and find it applicable here. The wife here may take such view of their relationship after the decree as her religion requires, but as a matter of law the civil contract has been dissolved.

In addition, the husband apparently does not share his wife's religious beliefs about divorce, since he sought the decree. Under these circumstances, to compel him to remain married because of the wife's religious beliefs would be to prefer her beliefs over his. Any such preference is prohibited by the Establishment Clause of the First Amendment. The government may not "aid one religion, aid all religions, or prefer one religion over another." Everson v. Board of Education, 330 U.S. 1, 15, 67 S.Ct. 504, 511, 91 L.Ed. 711 (1947).

We discern no constitutional infirmity in the decree dissolving the marriage. . . .

Reynolds v. United States

Supreme Court of the United States, 1878.
98 U.S. 145, 25 L.Ed. 244.

Error to the Supreme Court of the Territory of Utah. This is an indictment found in the District Court for the third judicial district of the Territory of Utah, charging George Reynolds with bigamy, in violation of section 5352 of the Revised Statutes, which omitting its exceptions, is as follows:—

"Every person having a husband or wife living, who marries another, whether married or single, in a Territory, or other place over which the United States have exclusive jurisdiction, is guilty of bigamy, and shall be punished by a fine of not more than $500, and by imprisonment for a term of not more than five years."

. . .

Evidence was admitted that showed that the prisoner had married Mary Ann Tuddenham, and subsequently had married Amelia Jane Schofield, during the lifetime of said Mary....

... The jury found him guilty ... and the judgment that he be imprisoned at hard labor for a term of two years, and pay a fine of $500, rendered by the District Court, having been affirmed by the Supreme Court of the Territory, he sued out this writ of error.

■ WAITE, C.J.

... On the trial, the plaintiff in error, the accused proved that at the time of his alleged second marriage he was, and for many years before had been a member of the Church of Jesus Christ of Latter–Day Saints, commonly called the Mormon Church, and a believer in its doctrines; that it was an accepted doctrine of that church "that it was the duty of the male members of said church, circumstances permitting, to practice polygamy; ... that this duty was enjoined by different books which the members of said church believed to be of divine origin, and among others the Holy Bible, and also, that the members of the church believed that the practice of polygamy was directly enjoined upon the male members thereof by the Almighty God, in a revelation to Joseph Smith, the founder and prophet of said church; and that failing or refusing to practice polygamy by such male members of said church, when circumstances would admit, would be punished, and that the penalty for such failure and refusal would be damnation of the life to come." He also proved "that he had received permission from the recognized authorities in said church to enter into polygamous marriage; ... and that such marriage ceremony was performed under and pursuant to the doctrines of said church."

Upon this proof he asked the court to instruct the jury that if they found from the evidence that he "was married as charged—if he was married—in pursuance of and in conformity with what he believed at the time to be a religious duty, that the verdict must be 'not guilty.' " This request was refused, and the court did charge "that there must have been a criminal intent, but that if the defendant under the influence of a religious belief that it was right,—under an inspiration, if you please, that it was right,—deliberately married a second time, having a first wife living, the want of consciousness of evil intent—the want of understanding on his part that he was committing a crime—did not excuse him; but the law inexorably in such case implied the criminal intent."

Upon this charge and refusal to charge the question is raised whether religious belief can be accepted as a justification of an overt act made criminal by the law of the land....

Congress cannot pass a law for the government of the Territories which shall prohibit the free exercise of religion. The first amendment to the Constitution expressly forbids such legislation. Religious freedom is guaranteed everywhere throughout the United States, so far as congressional interference is concerned. The question to be determined is, whether the law now under consideration comes within this prohibition.

The word "religion" is not defined in the Constitution. We must go elsewhere, therefore, to ascertain its meaning, and nowhere more appropriately, we think, than to the history of the times in the midst of which the provision was adopted. The precise point of the inquiry, is what is the religious freedom which has been guaranteed. . . .

Polygamy has always been odious among the northern and western nations of Europe, and, until the establishment of the Mormon Church, was almost exclusively a feature of the life of Asiatic and of African people. At common law, the second marriage was always void (2 Kent Com. 79), and from the earliest history of England polygamy has been treated as an offence against society. After the establishment of the ecclesiastical courts, and until the time of James I., it was punished through the instrumentality of those tribunals, not merely because ecclesiastical rights had been violated, but because upon the separation of the ecclesiastical courts from the civil the ecclesiastical were supposed to be the most appropriate for the trial of matrimonial causes and offences against the rights of marriage, just as they were for testamentary causes and the settlement of the estates of deceased persons.

By the statute of 1 James I. (c. 11), the offence, if committed in England or Wales, was made punishable in the civil courts, and the penalty was death. As this statute was limited in its operation to England and Wales, it was at a very early period re-enacted, generally with some modifications, in all the colonies. In connection with the case we are now considering, it is a significant fact that on the 8th day of December, 1788, after the passage of the act establishing religious freedom, and after the convention of Virginia had recommended as an amendment to the Constitution of the United States the declaration in a bill of rights that "all men have an equal, natural, and unalienable right to the free exercise of religion, according to the dictates of conscience," the legislature of that State substantially enacted the statute of James I., death penalty included, because, as recited in the preamble, "it hath been doubted whether bigamy or polygamy be punishable by the laws of this Commonwealth." 12 Hening's Stat. 691. From that day to this we think it may safely be said there never has been a time in any State of the Union when polygamy has not been an offence against society, cognizable by the civil courts and punishable with more or less severity. In the face of all this evidence, it is impossible to believe that the constitutional guaranty of religious freedom was intended to prohibit legislation in respect to this most important feature of social life. Marriage, while from its very nature, a sacred obligation, is nevertheless, in most civilized nations, a civil contract, and usually regulated by law. Upon it society may be said to be built, and out of its fruits spring social relations and social obligations and duties, with which government is necessarily required to deal. In fact, according as monogamous or polygamous marriages are allowed, do we find the principles on which the government of the people, to a greater or less extent rests....

In our opinion, the statute immediately under consideration is within the legislative power of Congress.... This being so, the only question which remains is, whether those who make polygamy a part of their religion are excepted from the operation of the statute. If they are, then those who do not make polygamy a part of their religious belief may be found guilty and punished, while those who do, must be acquitted and go free. This would be introducing a new element into criminal law. Laws are made for government of actions, and while they cannot interfere with mere religious belief and opinions, they may with practices. Suppose one believed that human sacrifices were a necessary part of religious worship, would it be seriously contended that the civil government under which he lived could not interfere to prevent a sacrifice? Or if a wife religiously believed it was her duty to burn herself upon the funeral pile of her dead husband would it be beyond the power of the civil government to prevent her carrying her belief into practice?

So here, as a law of the organization of society under the exclusive dominion of the United States, it provided that plural marriage shall not be allowed. Can a man excuse his practices to the contrary because of his religious belief? To permit this would be to make the professed doctrines of religious belief superior to the law of the land, and in effect to permit every citizen to become a law unto himself. Government could exist only in name under such circumstances.

... Every act necessary to constitute the crime was knowingly done. ... The only defence of the accused in this case is his belief that the law ought not to have been enacted. It matters not that his belief was a part of his professed religion: it was still belief, and belief only....

Judgment affirmed.

NOTE

Polygamy was present among the kings of Israel in the Hebrew scripture. "She [Abigail] became his wife, and David also married Ahinoam of Jezreel. Thus both of them were his wives ..." (1 Samuel 25:42–3). In America, it was practiced by Mormons in Illinois and also in Utah, but at no time did a large percentage of the Mormon population engage in polygamous marriages. As early as 1862 there was federal legislation against the practice, but the law had little effect. Some twenty years later the Edmunds law was passed, later supplemented by the Edmunds–Tucker law. This legislation introduced a stricter campaign against polygamy in Utah and other territories where the practice prevailed. Men and women were fined and imprisoned, and some Mormon leaders were driven into exile. Pursuant to the Enabling Act through which Utah became a state in 1896, the Utah Constitution, Art. III, § 1, provides:

> Perfect toleration of religious sentiment is guaranteed. No inhabitant of this state shall ever be molested in person or property on account of his or her mode of religious worship; but polygamous or plural marriages are forever prohibited.

For an excellent historical account of the introduction of the Mormon religion into Utah, *see* Society of Separationists, Inc. v. Whitehead, 870 P.2d 916 (Utah 1993) (where the Supreme Court of Utah held that a city's council's practice of permitting prayer during a portion of the council's meeting did not violate provision of Utah Constitution prohibiting expenditure of public money to support religious exercise). Also, Sanderson v. Tryon, 739 P.2d 623 (Utah 1987), where the Supreme Court of Utah held that a parent's practice of polygamy is, taken alone, not a sufficient reason to make a custody award or to permit a meaningful review of a custody award on appeal.

Reynolds is usually cited as recognizing state authority to define marriage as monogamous and to impose sanctions based on polygamy. What would its effect be on a state's decision to permit polygamy or polyandry (or both) because of a demographic imbalance between the sexes? Would it have any further impact on determining the scope of state authority to redefine marriage in other contexts?

Buchholz v. Buchholz

Supreme Court of Nebraska, 1976.
197 Neb. 180, 248 N.W.2d 21.

■ Per Curiam.

[The trial court's rejection of a wife's argument that Nebraska's divorce statutes are unconstitutional was upheld.]

Respondent's first contention is that she has a property right in the marriage. Although not entirely clear from her brief, she apparently believes that the decree of divorce deprives her of a substantial property interest in violation of the Fourteenth Amendment's due process clause. Respondent cites no case in point but seeks to compare the situation with that of a tenured job holder who loses his position "without fault." See Perry v. Sindermann, 408 U.S. 593, 92 S.Ct. 2694, 33 L.Ed.2d 570.

.   .   .

The proposition here presented was directly in issue in In re Marriage of Walton, 28 Cal.App.3d 108, 104 Cal.Rptr. 472. The California law is similar to our own. The court stated: "Similarly, Wife's contention that the dissolution of her marriage on the ground of irreconcilable differences under The Family Law Act unconstitutionally deprives her of a vested interest in her married status cannot be sustained. Certainly a wife has a legitimate interest in her status as a married woman, but, separate and apart from marital property and support rights as to which Wife makes no contention, we entertain some doubt whether her interest in her status as a married woman constitutes property within the purview of the due process clauses of article I, section 13 of the California Constitution and the Fourteenth Amendment to the United States Constitution. In any event, in view of the state's vital interest in the institution of marriage and the state's plenary power to fix the conditions under which the marital status may be created or terminated, it is clear that Wife could have no vested interest in the state's maintaining in force the grounds for divorce that existed at the time of her marriage. Her interest, however it be classified, was subject to the reserve power of the state to amend the law or enact additional laws for the public good and in pursuance of public policy...."

We agree that the marriage contract does not create a property right in the marital status. A marriage is not a property interest but is, in essence, a personal relationship subject to dissolution on terms fixed by state law.

NOTE

In 1964, the Anglican Archbishop of Canterbury appointed a committee to review the existing English divorce law. In 1966 that committee produced the Mortimer Report that recommended that divorces be granted in England on the ground of the breakdown of marriage. The state of California, in 1969, acting upon a recommendation of a committee of its own, was the first state to replace traditional fault grounds with non-fault marital breakdown. Today, each state has a non-fault ground that allows for dissolution of marriage without regard to the fault of a party.

Griswold v. Connecticut

Supreme Court of the United States, 1965.
381 U.S. 479, 85 S.Ct. 1678, 14 L.Ed.2d 510.

■ MR. JUSTICE DOUGLAS delivered the opinion of the Court.

Appellant Griswold is Executive Director of the Planned Parenthood League of Connecticut. Appellant Buxton is a licensed physician and a professor at the Yale Medical School who served as Medical Director for the League at its Center in New Haven—a center open and operating from November 1 to November 10, 1961, when appellants were arrested.

They gave information, instruction, and medical advice to *married persons* as to the means of preventing conception. They examined the wife and prescribed the best contraceptive device or material for her use. Fees were usually charged, although some couples were serviced free.

The statutes whose constitutionality is involved in this appeal are §§ 53–32 and 54–196 of the General Statutes of Connecticut (1958 rev.). The former provides:

"Any person who uses any drug, medicinal article or instrument for the purpose of preventing conception shall be fined not less than fifty dollars or imprisoned not less than sixty days nor more than one year or be both fined and imprisoned."

Section 54–196 provides:

"Any person who assists, abets, counsels, causes, hires or commands another to commit any offense may be prosecuted and punished as if he were the principal offender."

The appellants were found guilty as accessories and fined $100 each, against the claim that the accessory statute as so applied violated the Fourteenth Amendment. . . .

Coming to the merits, we are met with a wide range of questions that implicate the Due Process Clause of the Fourteenth Amendment. . . . We do not sit as a super-legislature to determine the wisdom, need, and propriety of laws that touch economic problems, business affairs, or social conditions. This law, however, operates directly on an intimate relation of husband and wife and their physician's role in one aspect of that relation.

The association of people is not mentioned in the Constitution nor in the Bill of Rights. The right to educate a child in a school of the parents' choice—whether public or private or parochial—is also not mentioned. Nor is the right to study any particular subject or any foreign language. Yet the First Amendment has been construed to include certain of those rights.

By Pierce v. Society of Sisters [268 U.S. 510, 45 S.Ct. 571], the right to educate one's children as one chooses is made applicable to the States by the force of the First and Fourteenth Amendments. By Meyer v. State of Nebraska [262 U.S. 390, 43 S.Ct. 625], the same dignity is given the right to study the German language in a private school. In other words, the State may not, consistently with the spirit of the First Amendment, contract the spectrum of available knowledge. The right of freedom of speech and press includes not only the right to utter or to print, but the right to distribute, the right to receive, the right to read and freedom of inquiry, freedom of thought, and freedom to teach—indeed the freedom of the entire university community. . . . Without those peripheral rights the specific rights would be less secure. And so we reaffirm the principle of the Pierce and the Meyer cases.

In NAACP v. State of Alabama, 357 U.S. 449, 462, 78 S.Ct. 1163, 1172, we protected the "freedom to associate and privacy in one's associations," noting that freedom of association was a peripheral First Amendment right. Disclosure of membership lists of a constitutionally valid association, we held, was invalid "as entailing the likelihood of a substantial restraint upon the exercise by petitioner's members of their right to freedom of association." Ibid. In other words, the First Amendment has a penumbra where privacy is protected from governmental intrusion. In like context, we have protected forms of "association" that are not political in the customary sense but pertain to the social, legal, and economic benefit of the members. NAACP v. Button, 371 U.S. 415, 430–431, 83 S.Ct. 328, 336–337, 9 L.Ed.2d 405. . . .

Those cases involved more than the "right of assembly"—a right that extends to all irrespective of their race or ideology. De Jonge v. State of Oregon, 299 U.S. 353, 57 S.Ct. 255, 81 L.Ed. 278. The right of "association," like the right of belief (West Virginia State Board of Education v. Barnette, 319 U.S. 624, 63 S.Ct. 1178), is more than the right to attend a meeting; it includes the right to express one's attitudes or philosophies by membership in a group or by affiliation with it or by other lawful means. Association in that context is a form of expression of opinion; and while it is not expressly included in the First Amendment its existence is necessary in making the express guarantees fully meaningful.

The foregoing cases suggest that specific guarantees in the Bill of Rights have penumbras, formed by emanations from those guarantees that help give them life and substance. . . . Various guarantees create zones of privacy. The right of association contained in the penumbra of the First Amendment is one, as we have seen. The Third Amendment in its prohibition against the quartering of soldiers "in any house" in time of peace without the consent of the owner is another facet of that privacy. The Fourth Amendment explicitly affirms the "right of the people to be secure in their persons, houses, papers, and effects, against unreasonable searches and seizures." The Fifth Amendment in its Self–Incrimination Clause enables the citizen to create a zone of privacy which government may not force him to surrender to his detriment. The Ninth Amendment provides: "The enumeration in the Constitution, of certain rights, shall not be construed to deny or disparage others retained by the people." . . .

The present case, then, concerns a relationship lying within the zone of privacy created by several fundamental constitutional guarantees. And it concerns a law which, in forbidding the *use* of contraceptives rather than regulating their manufacture or sale, seeks to achieve its goals by means having a maximum destructive impact upon that relationship. Such a law cannot stand in light of the familiar principle, so often applied by this Court, that a "governmental purpose to control or prevent activities constitutionally subject to state regulation may not be achieved by means which sweep unnecessarily broadly and thereby invade the area of protected freedoms." NAACP v. Alabama, 377 U.S. 288, 307, 84 S.Ct. 1302, 1314, 12 L.Ed.2d 325. Would we allow the police to search the sacred precincts of marital bedrooms for telltale signs of the use of contraceptives? The very idea is repulsive to the notions of privacy surrounding the marriage relationship.

We deal with a right of privacy older than the Bill of Rights—older than our political parties, older than our school system. Marriage is a coming together for better or for worse, hopefully enduring, and intimate to the degree of being sacred. It is an association that promotes a way of life, not causes; a harmony in living, not political faiths; a bilateral loyalty, not commercial or social projects. Yet it is an association for as noble a purpose as any involved in our prior decisions.

Reversed.

■ Mr. Justice Goldberg who The Chief Justice and Mr. Justice Brennan join, concurring.

. . .

The language and history of the Ninth Amendment reveal that the Framers of the Constitution believed that there are additional fundamental rights, protected from governmental infringement, which exist alongside those fundamental rights specifically mentioned in the first eight constitutional amendments.

The Ninth Amendment reads, "The enumeration in the Constitution, of certain rights, shall not be construed to deny or disparage others retained by the people." The Amendment is almost entirely the work of James Madison. It was introduced in Congress by him and passed the House and Senate with little or no debate and virtually no change in language. It was proffered to quiet expressed fears that a bill of specifically enumerated rights could not be sufficiently broad to cover all essential rights and that the specific mention of certain rights would be interpreted as a denial that others were protected. . . .

The Connecticut statutes here involved deal with a particularly important and sensitive area of privacy—that of the marital relation and the marital home. This Court recognized in Meyer v. Nebraska, supra, that the right "to marry, establish a home and bring up children" was an essential part of the liberty guaranteed by the Fourteenth Amendment. In Pierce v. Society of Sisters, the Court held unconstitutional an Oregon Act which forbade parents from sending their children to private schools because such an act "unreasonably interferes with the liberty of parents and guardians to direct the upbringing and education of children under their control." As this Court said in Prince v. Massachusetts, 321 U.S. 158, at 166, 64 S.Ct. 438, at 442, 88 L.Ed. 645, the Meyer and Pierce decisions "have respected the private realm of family life which the state cannot enter."

I agree with Mr. Justice Harlan's statement in his dissenting opinion in Poe v. Ullman, 367 U.S. 497, 551–552, 81 S.Ct. 1752, 1781:

"Certainly the safeguarding of the home does not follow merely from the sanctity of property rights. The home derives its pre-eminence as the seat of family life. And the integrity of that life is something so fundamental that it has been found to draw to its protection the principles of more than one explicitly granted Constitutional right. . . . Of this whole 'private realm of family life' it is difficult to imagine what is more private or more intimate than a husband and wife's marital relations."

The entire fabric of the Constitution and the purposes that clearly underlie its specific guarantees demonstrate that the rights to marital privacy and to marry and raise a family are of similar order and magnitude as the fundamental rights specifically protected.

Although the Constitution does not speak in so many words of the right of privacy in marriage, I cannot believe that it offers these fundamental rights no protection. . . .

Finally, it should be said of the Court's holding today that it in no way interferes with a State's proper regulation of sexual promiscuity or misconduct. As my Brother Harlan so well stated in his dissenting opinion in Poe v. Ullman, supra, 367 U.S. at 553, 81 S.Ct. at 1782.

> "Adultery, homosexuality and the like are sexual intimacies which the State forbids . . . but the intimacy of husband and wife is necessarily an essential and accepted feature of the institution of marriage, an institution which the State not only must allow, but which always and in every age it has fostered and protected. It is one thing when the State exerts its power either to forbid extra-marital sexuality . . . or to say who may marry, but it is quite another when, having acknowledged a marriage and the intimacies inherent in it, it undertakes to regulate by means of the criminal law the details of that intimacy."

In sum, I believe that the right of privacy in the marital relation is fundamental and basic—a personal right "retained by the people" within the meaning of the Ninth Amendment. Connecticut cannot constitutionally abridge this fundamental right, which is protected by the Fourteenth Amendment from infringement by the States. I agree with the Court that petitioners' convictions must therefore be reversed.

[The concurring opinions of Justices Harlan and White, and the dissenting opinions of Justices Black and Stewart are omitted.]

NOTE

Language from the several opinions in *Griswold*, which was decided by a plurality, continues to be cited widely for all sorts of propositions. The preceding excerpts were selected because of their discussion of a right of marital privacy. Nonetheless, the right of privacy—actually personal autonomy—will appear frequently in many of the cases throughout other areas of family law.

Eisenstadt v. Baird

Supreme Court of the United States, 1972.
405 U.S. 438, 92 S.Ct. 1029, 31 L.Ed.2d 349.

■ MR. JUSTICE BRENNAN delivered the opinion of the Court.

Appellee William Baird was convicted at a bench trial in the Massachusetts Superior Court under Massachusetts General Laws c. 272, § 21, first, for exhibiting contraceptive articles in the course of delivering a lecture on contraception to a group of students at Boston University and, second, for giving a young woman a package of Emko vaginal foam at the close of his address.[1] The Massachusetts Supreme Judicial Court unanimously set aside the conviction for exhibiting contraceptives on the ground that it violated Baird's First Amendment rights, but by a four-to-three vote sustained the conviction for giving away the foam. Commonwealth v. Baird, 355 Mass. 746, 247 N.E.2d 574 (1969). Baird subsequently filed a petition for a Federal writ of habeas corpus, which the District Court dismissed. 310 F.Supp. 951 (1970). On appeal, however, the Court of Appeals for the First Circuit vacated the dismissal and remanded the action with directions to grant the writ discharging Baird. 429 F.2d 1398 (1970). This appeal by the Sheriff of Suffolk County, Massachusetts, followed. . . .

Massachusetts General Laws c. 272, § 21, under which Baird was convicted, provides a maximum five-year term of imprisonment for "whoever . . . gives away . . . any drug, medicine, instrument or article whatever for the prevention of conception," except as authorized in § 21A. Under § 21A, "[a] registered physician may administer to or prescribe for any married person drugs or articles intended for the prevention of pregnancy or conception. [And a] registered pharmacist actually engaged in the business of pharmacy may furnish such drugs or articles to any married person presenting a prescription from a registered physician." As interpreted by the State Supreme Judicial Court, these provisions make it a felony for anyone, other than a registered physician or pharmacist acting in accordance with the terms of § 21A, to dispense any article with the intention that it be used for the prevention of conception. The statutory scheme distinguishes among three distinct classes of distributees—*first,* married persons may obtain contraceptives to prevent pregnancy, but only from doctors or druggists on prescription; *second,* single persons may not obtain contraceptives from anyone to prevent pregnancy; and, *third,* married or single persons may obtain contraceptives from anyone to prevent not pregnancy, but the spread of disease. . . .

The legislative purposes that the statute is meant to serve are not altogether clear. In Commonwealth v. Baird, supra, the Supreme Judicial Court noted only the State's interest in protecting the health of its citizens: "[T]he prohibition in § 21," the court declared, "is directly related to" the State's goal of "preventing the distribution of articles designed to prevent conception which may have undesirable, if not dangerous, physical consequences." 355 Mass., at 753, 247 N.E.2d, at 578. In a subsequent decision, Sturgis v. Attorney General, Mass., 260 N.E.2d 687, 690 (1970), the court, however, found "a second and more compelling ground for upholding the statute"—namely, to protect morals through "regulating the private sexual lives of single persons."[3] The Court of Appeals, for reasons that will appear,

---

1. The Court of Appeals below described the recipient of the foam as "an unmarried adult woman." 429 F.2d 1398, 1399 (1970). However, there is no evidence in the record about her marital status.

3. Appellant suggests that the purpose of the Massachusetts statute is to promote marital fidelity as well as to discourage premarital sex. Under § 21A, however, contraceptives may be made available to married persons without regard to whether they are living with their spouses or the uses to which the contraceptives are to be put. Plainly the

did not consider the promotion of health or the protection of morals through the deterrence of fornication to be the legislative aim. Instead, the court concluded that the statutory goal was to limit contraception in and of itself—a purpose that the court held conflicted "with fundamental human rights" under Griswold v. Connecticut, 381 U.S. 479, 85 S.Ct. 1678 (1965), where this Court struck down Connecticut's prohibition against the use of contraceptives as an unconstitutional infringement of the right of marital privacy. 429 F.2d, at 1401–1402.

We agree that the goals of deterring premarital sex and regulating the distribution of potentially harmful articles cannot reasonably be regarded as legislative aims of §§ 21 and 21A. And we hold that the statute, viewed as a prohibition on contraception *per se,* violates the rights of single persons under the Equal Protection Clause of the Fourteenth Amendment.

... The question for our determination in this case is whether there is some ground of difference that rationally explains the different treatment accorded married and unmarried persons under Massachusetts General Laws c. 272, §§ 21 and 21A.[7] For the reasons that follow, we conclude that no such ground exists.

First. Section 21 stems from Stat.1879, c. 159, § 1, which prohibited, without exception, distribution of articles intended to be used as contraceptives. In Commonwealth v. Allison, 227 Mass. 57, 62, 116 N.E. 265, 266 (1917), the Massachusetts Supreme Judicial Court explained that the law's "plain purpose is to protect purity, to preserve chastity, to encourage continence and self restraint, to defend the sanctity of the home, and thus to engender in the State and nation a virile and virtuous race of men and women." Although the State clearly abandoned that purpose with the enactment of § 21A at least insofar as the illicit sexual activities of married persons are concerned, see n. 3 supra, the court reiterated in Sturgis v. Attorney General, supra, that the object of the legislation is to discourage premarital sexual intercourse. Conceding that the State could, consistently with the Equal Protection Clause, regard the problems of extramarital and premarital sexual relations as "[e]vils ... of different dimensions and proportions, requiring different remedies," Williamson v. Lee Optical Co., 348 U.S. 483, 489, 75 S.Ct. 461, 465, 99 L.Ed. 563 (1955), we cannot agree that the deterrence of premarital sex may reasonably be regarded as the purpose of the Massachusetts law.

It would be plainly unreasonable to assume that Massachusetts has prescribed pregnancy and the birth of an unwanted child as punishment for fornication, which is a misdemeanor under Massachusetts General Laws c.

---

legislation has no deterrent effect on extramarital sexual relations.

7. Of course, if we were to conclude that the Massachusetts statute impinges upon fundamental freedoms under *Griswold,* the statutory classification would have to be not merely *rationally related* to a valid public purpose but *necessary* to the achievement of a *compelling* state interest. E.g., Shapiro v. Thompson, 394 U.S. 618, 89 S.Ct. 1322, 22 L.Ed.2d 600 (1969); Loving v. Virginia, 388 U.S. 1, 87 S.Ct. 1817, 18 L.Ed.2d 1010 (1967). But just as in Reed v. Reed, supra, we do not have to address the statute's validity under that test because the law fails to satisfy even the more lenient equal protection standard.

272, § 18. Aside from the scheme of values that assumption would attribute to the State, it is abundantly clear that the effect of the ban on distribution of contraceptives to unmarried persons has at best a marginal relation to the proffered objective. What Mr. Justice Goldberg said in Griswold v. Connecticut, supra, 381 U.S. at 498, 85 S.Ct. at 1689, 14 L.Ed.2d 510 (concurring opinion), concerning the effect of Connecticut's prohibition on the use of contraceptives in discouraging extra-marital sexual relations, is equally applicable here. "The rationality of this justification is dubious, particularly in light of the admitted widespread availability to all persons in the State of Connecticut, unmarried as well as married, of birth-control devices for the prevention of disease, as distinguished from the prevention of conception." Like Connecticut's laws, §§ 21 and 21A do not at all regulate the distribution of contraceptives when they are to be used to prevent not pregnancy, but the spread of disease. Commonwealth v. Corbett, 307 Mass. 7, 29 N.E.2d 151 (1940), cited with approval in Commonwealth v. Baird, 355 Mass., at 754, 247 N.E.2d, at 579. Nor, in making contraceptives available to married persons without regard to their intended use, does Massachusetts attempt to deter married persons from engaging in illicit sexual relations with unmarried persons. Even on the assumption that the fear of pregnancy operates as a deterrent to fornication, the Massachusetts statute is thus so riddled with exceptions that deterrence of premarital sex cannot reasonably be regarded as its aim.

Moreover, §§ 21 and 21A on their face have a dubious relation to the State's criminal prohibition on fornication. As the Court of Appeals explained, "Fornication is a misdemeanor [in Massachusetts], entailing a thirty dollar fine, or three months in jail. Violation of the present statute is a felony, punishable by five years in prison. We find it hard to believe that the legislature adopted a statute carrying a five-year penalty for its possible, obviously by no means fully effective, deterrence of the commission of a ninety-day misdemeanor." 429 F.2d, at 1401. Even conceding the legislature a full measure of discretion in fashioning remedies for fornication, and recognizing that the State may seek to deter prohibited conduct by punishing more severely those who facilitate than those who actually engage in its commission, we, like the Court of Appeals, cannot believe that in this instance Massachusetts has chosen to expose the aider and abetter who simply *gives away* a contraceptive to *20* times the *90–day* sentence of the offender himself. The very terms of the State's criminal statutes, coupled with the *de minimis* effect of §§ 21 and 21A in deterring fornication, thus compel the conclusion that such deterrence cannot reasonably be taken as the purpose of the ban on distribution of contraceptives to unmarried persons.

Second. Section 21A was added to the Massachusetts General Laws by Stat.1966, c. 265, § 1. The Supreme Judicial Court in Commonwealth v. Baird, supra, held that the purpose of the amendment was to serve the health needs of the community by regulating the distribution of potentially harmful articles. It is plain that Massachusetts had no such purpose in mind before the enactment of § 21A. As the Court of Appeals remarked, "Consistent with the fact that the statute was contained in a chapter dealing with 'Crimes Against Chastity, Morality, Decency and Good Order,' it was cast only in terms of morals. A physician was forbidden to prescribe contraceptives even when needed for the protection of health.'' Commonwealth v. Gardner, 1938, 300 Mass. 372, 15 N.E.2d 222., 429 F.2d, at 1401. Nor did the Court of Appeals "believe that the legislature [in enacting § 21A] suddenly reversed its field and developed an interest in health. Rather, it merely made what it thought to be the precise accommodation necessary to escape the *Griswold* ruling." Ibid.

Again, we must agree with the Court of Appeals. If health were the rationale of § 21A, the statute would be both discriminatory and overbroad. Dissenting in Commonwealth v. Baird, 355 Mass., at 758, 247 N.E.2d, at 581, Justices Whittemore and Cutter stated that they saw "in § 21 and § 21A, read together, no public health purpose. If there is need to have a physician prescribe (and a pharmacist dispense) contraceptives, that need is as great for unmarried persons as for married persons." The Court of Appeals added: "If the prohibition [on distribution to unmarried persons] is to be taken to mean that the same physician who can prescribe for married patients does not have sufficient skill to protect the health of patients who lack a marriage certificate, or who may be currently divorced, it is illogical to the point of irrationality." 429 F.2d, at 1401.[8] Furthermore, we must join the Court of Appeals in noting that not all contraceptives are potentially dangerous.[9] As a result, if the Massachusetts statute were a health measure, it would not only invidiously discriminate against the unmarried, but also be overbroad with respect to the married, a fact that the Supreme Judicial Court itself seems to have conceded in Sturgis v. Attorney General, Mass., 260 N.E.2d, at 690, where it noted that "it may well be that certain contraceptive medication and devices constitute no hazard to health, in which event it could be argued that the statute swept too broadly in its prohibition." "In this posture," as the Court of Appeals concluded, "it is impossible to think of the statute as intended as a health measure for the unmarried, and it is almost as difficult to think of it as so intended even as to the married." 429 F.2d, at 1401.

---

8. Appellant insists that the unmarried have no right to engage in sexual intercourse and hence no health interest in contraception that needs to be served. The short answer to this contention is that the same devices the distribution of which the State purports to regulate when their asserted purpose is to forestall pregnancy are available without any controls whatsoever so long as their asserted purpose is to prevent the spread of disease. It is inconceivable that the need for health controls varies with the purpose for which the contraceptive is to be used when the physical act in all cases is one and the same.

9. The Court of Appeals stated, 429 F.2d at 1401:

"[W]e must take notice that not all contraceptive devices risk 'undesirable . . . [or] dangerous physical consequences.' It is 200 years since Casanova recorded the ubiquitous article which, perhaps because of the birthplace of its inventor, he termed a 'redingote anglais.' The reputed nationality of the condom has now changed, but we have never heard criticism of it on the side of health. We cannot think that the legislature was unaware of it, or could have thought that it needed a medical prescription. We believe the same could be said of certain other products."

But if further proof that the Massachusetts statute is not a health measure is necessary, the argument of Justice Spiegel, who also dissented in Commonwealth v. Baird, 355 Mass., at 759, 247 N.E.2d, at 582, is conclusive: "It is at best a strained conception to say that the Legislature intended to prevent the distribution of articles 'which may have undesirable, if not dangerous, physical consequences.' If that was the Legislature's goal, § 21 is not required" in view of the federal and State laws *already* regulating the distribution of harmful drugs. We conclude, accordingly, that, despite the statute's superficial earmarks as a health measure, health, on the face of the statute, may no more reasonably be regarded as its purpose than the deterrence of premarital sexual relations.

Third. If the Massachusetts statute cannot be upheld as a deterrent to fornication or as a health measure, may it, nevertheless, be sustained simply as a prohibition on contraception? The Court of Appeals analysis "led inevitably to the conclusion that, so far as morals are concerned, it is contraceptives per se that are considered immoral—to the extent that *Griswold* will permit such a declaration." 429 F.2d, at 1401–1402. The Court of Appeals went on to hold, id., at 1402:

> "To say that contraceptives are immoral as such, and are to be forbidden to unmarried persons who will nevertheless persist in having intercourse, means that such persons must risk for themselves an unwanted pregnancy, for the child, illegitimacy, and for society, a possible obligation of support. Such a view of morality is not only the very mirror image of sensible legislation; we consider that it conflicts with fundamental human rights. In the absence of demonstrated harm, we hold it is beyond the competency of the state."

We need not and do not, however, decide that important question in this case because, whatever the rights of the individual to access to contraceptives may be, the rights must be the same for the unmarried and the married alike.

If under *Griswold* the distribution of contraceptives to married persons cannot be prohibited, a ban on distribution to unmarried persons would be equally impermissible. It is true that in *Griswold* the right of privacy in question inhered in the marital relationship. Yet the marital couple is not an independent entity with a mind and heart of its own, but an association of two individuals each with a separate intellectual and emotional make-up. If the right of privacy means anything, it is the right of the *individual*, married or single, to be free from unwarranted governmental intrusion into matters so fundamentally affecting a person as the decision whether to bear or beget a child. See Stanley v. Georgia, 394 U.S. 557, 89 S.Ct. 1243.[10]

---

10. In Stanley, 394 U.S., at 564, 89 S.Ct., at 1247, the Court stated:

"[A]lso fundamental is the right to be free, except in very limited circumstances, from unwanted governmental intrusions into one's privacy.

" 'The makers of our Constitution undertook to secure conditions favorable to the pursuit of happiness. They recognized the significance of man's spiritual nature, of his feelings and of his intellect. They knew that only a part of the pain,

See also Skinner v. Oklahoma ex rel. Williamson, 316 U.S. 535, 62 S.Ct. 1110 (1942); Jacobson v. Massachusetts, 197 U.S. 11, 29, 25 S.Ct. 358, 362 (1905).

On the other hand, if *Griswold* is no bar to a prohibition on the distribution of contraceptives, the State could not, consistently with the Equal Protection Clause, outlaw distribution to unmarried but not to married persons. In each case the evil, as perceived by the State, would be identical, and the underinclusion would be invidious.

... We hold that by providing dissimilar treatment for married and unmarried persons who are similarly situated, Massachusetts General Laws c. 272, §§ 21 and 21A, violate the Equal Protection Clause. The judgment of the Court of Appeals is affirmed.

NOTE

Justice Douglas joined the opinion of the Court but filed a separate concurring opinion expressing his view that it was "a simple First Amendment case" which could have been affirmed on that narrower ground. He added that "The teachings of Baird and those of Galileo might be of a different order; but the suppression of either is equally repugnant." 405 U.S. 438, 457, 92 S.Ct. 1029, 31 L.Ed.2d 349.

Justice White concurred in the result reached by the Court, filing a separate opinion in which Mr. Justice Blackmun joined. He stated that "Had Baird distributed a supply of the so-called 'pill', I would sustain his conviction" under the Massachusetts law, and added:

> That Baird could not be convicted for distributing Emko to a married person disposes of this case. Assuming *arguendo* that the result would be otherwise had the recipient been unmarried, nothing has been placed in the record to indicate her marital status. The State has maintained that marital status is irrelevant because an unlicensed person cannot legally dispense vaginal foam either to married or unmarried persons. This approach is plainly erroneous and requires the reversal of Baird's conviction; for on the facts of this case, it deprives us of knowing whether Baird was in fact convicted for making a constitutionally protected distribution of Emko to a married person. Id. at 462–64.

Chief Justice Burger dissented and also disagreed with the concurring opinion of Justice White, stating that: "The need for dissemination of information on birth control is not impinged in the slightest by limiting the

pleasure and satisfactions of life are to be found in material things. They sought to protect Americans in their beliefs, their thoughts, their emotions, and their sensations. They conferred, as against the Government, the right to be let alone— the most comprehensive of rights and the right most valued by civilized man.' Olmstead v. United States, 277 U.S. 438, 478, 48 S.Ct. 564, 572 (1928) (Brandeis, J., dissenting)...."

distribution of medicinal substances to medical and pharmaceutical channels as Massachusetts has done by statute." Id. at 470.

Does *Baird* guarantee a right to procreate, within or without marriage? Does it suggest any clear limitation on distinctions that can be made between permissible conduct of parties in other contexts based upon being married rather than single?

Roe v. Wade

Supreme Court of the United States, 1973.
410 U.S. 113, 93 S.Ct. 705, 35 L.Ed.2d 147.

■ MR. JUSTICE BLACKMUN delivered the opinion of the Court.

. . .

The Texas statutes that concern us here are Arts. 1191–1194 and 1196 of the State's Penal Code, Vernon's Ann.P.C. These make it a crime to "procure an abortion," as therein defined, or to attempt one, except with respect to "an abortion procured or attempted by medical advice for the purpose of saving the life of the mother." Similar statutes are in existence in a majority of the States.

. . .

Jane Roe,[4] a single woman who was residing in Dallas County, Texas, instituted this federal action in March 1970. . . . She sought a declaratory judgment that the Texas criminal abortion statutes were unconstitutional on their face, and an injunction restraining the defendant from enforcing the statutes.

Roe alleged that she was unmarried and pregnant; that she wished to terminate her pregnancy by an abortion "performed by a competent, licensed physician, under safe, clinical conditions"; that she was unable to get a "legal" abortion in Texas because her life did not appear to be threatened by the continuation of her pregnancy; and that she could not afford to travel to another jurisdiction in order to secure a legal abortion under safe conditions. She claimed that the Texas statutes were unconstitutionally vague and that they abridged her right of personal privacy, protected by the First, Fourth, Fifth, Ninth, and Fourteenth Amendments. By an amendment to her complaint Roe purported to sue "on behalf of herself and all other women" similarly situated.

. . .

It perhaps is not generally appreciated that the restrictive criminal abortion laws in effect in a majority of States today are of relatively recent vintage. Those laws, generally proscribing abortion or its attempt at any time during pregnancy except when necessary to preserve the pregnant woman's life, are not of ancient or even of common-law origin. Instead,

---

4.   The name is a pseudonym.

they derive from statutory changes effected, for the most part, in the latter half of the 19th century.

. . .

In this country, the law in effect in all but a few States until mid–19th century was the pre-existing English common law. Connecticut, the first State to enact abortion legislation, adopted in 1821 that part of Lord Ellenborough's Act that related to a woman "quick with child." The death penalty was not imposed. Abortion before quickening was made a crime in that State only in 1860. In 1828, New York enacted legislation that, in two respects, was to serve as a model for early anti-abortion statutes. First, while barring destruction of an unquickend fetus as well as a quick fetus, it made the former only a misdemeanor, but the latter second-degree man-slaughter. Second, it incorporated a concept of therapeutic abortion by providing that an abortion was excused if it "shall have been necessary to preserve the life of such mother, or shall have been advised by two physicians to be necessary for such purpose." By 1840, when Texas had received the common law, only eight American States had statutes dealing with abortion. It was not until after the War Between the States that legislation began generally to replace the common law. Most of these initial statutes dealt severely with abortion after quickening but were lenient with it before quickening. Most punished attempts equally with completed abortions. While many statutes included the exception for an abortion thought by one or more physicians to be necessary to save the mother's life, that provision soon disappeared and the typical law required that the procedure actually be necessary for that purpose.

Gradually, in the middle and late 19th century the quickening distinc-tion disappeared from the statutory law of most States and the degree of the offense and the penalties were increased. By the end of the 1950's a large majority of the jurisdictions banned abortion, however and whenever performed, unless done to save or preserve the life of the mother. The exceptions, Alabama and the District of Columbia, permitted abortion to preserve the mother's health. Three States permitted abortions that were not "unlawfully" performed or that were not "without lawful justifica-tion," leaving interpretation of those standards to the courts. In the past several years, however, a trend toward liberalization of abortion statutes has resulted in adoption, by about one-third of the States, of less stringent laws, most of them patterned after the ALI Model Penal Code, § 230.3....

It is thus apparent that at common law, at the time of the adoption of our Constitution, and throughout the major portion of the 19th century, abortion was viewed with less disfavor than under most American statutes currently in effect. Phrasing it another way, a woman enjoyed a substan-tially broader right to terminate a pregnancy than she does in most States today. At least with respect to the early stage of pregnancy, and very possibly without such a limitation, the opportunity to make this choice was present in this country well into the 19th century. Even later, the law continued for some time to treat less punitively an abortion procured in early pregnancy.

6. *The position of the American Medical Association.*

. . .

In 1970, after the introduction of a variety of proposed resolutions, and of a report from its Board of Trustees, a reference committee noted "polarization of the medical profession on this controversial issue"; division among those who had testified; a difference of opinion among AMA councils and committees; "the remarkable shift in testimony" in six months, felt to be influenced "by the rapid changes in state laws and by the judicial decisions which tend to make abortion more freely available;" and a feeling "that this trend will continue." On June 25, 1970, the House of Delegates adopted preambles and most of the resolutions proposed by the reference committee. The preambles emphasized "the best interests of the patient," "sound clinical judgment," and "informed patient consent," in contrast to "mere acquiescence to the patient's demand." The resolutions asserted that abortion is a medical procedure that should be performed by a licensed physician in an accredited hospital only after consultation with two other physicians and in conformity with state law, and that no party to the procedure should be required to violate personally held moral principles. Proceedings of the AMA House of Delegates 220 (June 1970). The AMA Judicial Council rendered a complementary opinion.

. . .

8. *The position of the American Bar Association.*

At its meeting in February 1972 the ABA House of Delegates approved, with 17 opposing votes, the Uniform Abortion Act that had been drafted and approved the preceding August by the Conference of Commissioners on Uniform State Laws.[40] 58 A.B.A.J. 380 (1972).

40. "Section 1. (*Abortion Defined; When Authorized.*)

"(a) 'Abortion' means the termination of human pregnancy with an intention other than to produce a live birth or to remove a dead fetus.

"(b) An abortion may be performed in this state only if it is performed:

"(1) by a physician licensed to practice medicine (or osteopathy) in this state or by a physician practicing medicine (or osteopathy) in the employ of the government of the United States or of this state, (and the abortion is performed (in the physician's office or in a medical clinic, or) in a hospital approved by the (Department of Health) or operated by the United States, this state, or any department, agency, or political subdivision of either;) or by a female upon herself upon the advice of the physician; and

"(2) within (20) weeks after the commencement of the pregnancy (or after (20) weeks only if the physician has reasonable cause to believe (i) there is a substantial risk that continuance of the pregnancy would endanger the life of the mother or would gravely impair the physical or mental health of the mother, (ii) that the child would be born with grave physical or mental defect, or (iii) that the pregnancy resulted from rape or incest, or illicit intercourse with a girl under the age of 16 years).

"Section 2. (Penalty.) Any person who performs or procures an abortion other than authorized by this Act is guilty of a (felony) and, upon conviction thereof, may be sentenced to pay a fine not exceeding ($1,000) or to imprisonment (in the state penitentiary) not exceeding (5 years), or both."

VII

Three reasons have been advanced to explain historically the enactment of criminal abortion laws in the 19th century and to justify their continued existence.

It has been argued occasionally that these laws were the product of a Victorian social concern to discourage illicit sexual conduct. Texas, however, does not advance this justification in the present case, and it appears that no court or commentator has taken the argument seriously. . . .

A second reason is concerned with abortion as a medical procedure. . . . [I]t has been argued that a State's real concern in enacting a criminal abortion law was to protect the pregnant woman, that is, to restrain her from submitting to a procedure that placed her life in serious jeopardy.

Modern medical techniques have altered this situation. Appellants and various amici refer to medical data indicating that abortion in early pregnancy, that is, prior to the end of the first trimester, although not without its risk, is now relatively safe. Mortality rates for women undergoing early abortions, where the procedure is legal, appear to be as low as or lower than the rates for normal childbirth. Consequently, any interest of the State in protecting the woman from an inherently hazardous procedure, except when it would be equally dangerous for her to forgo it, has largely disappeared. . . .

The third reason is the State's interest—some phrase it in terms of duty—in protecting prenatal life. Some of the argument for this justification rests on the theory that a new human life is present from the moment of conception. The State's interest and general obligation to protect life then extends, it is argued, to prenatal life. Only when the life of the pregnant mother herself is at stake, balanced against the life she carries within her, should the interest of the embryo or fetus not prevail. Logically, of course, a legitimate state interest in this area need not stand or fall on acceptance of the belief that life begins at conception or at some other point prior to life birth. In assessing the State's interest, recognition may be given to the less rigid claim that as long as at least potential life is involved, the State may assert interests beyond the protection of the pregnant woman alone.

Parties challenging state abortion laws have sharply disputed in some courts the contention that a purpose of these laws, when enacted, was to protect prenatal life. Pointing to the absence of legislative history to support the contention, they claim that most state laws were designed solely to protect the woman. Because medical advances have lessened this concern, at least with respect to abortion in early pregnancy, they argue that with respect to such abortions the laws can no longer be justified by any state interest. . . .

VIII

The Constitution does not explicitly mention any right of privacy. In a line of decisions, however, going back perhaps as far as Union Pacific R. Co.

v. Botsford, 141 U.S. 250, 251, 11 S.Ct. 1000, 1001, 35 L.Ed. 734 (1891), the Court has recognized that a right of personal privacy, or a guarantee of certain areas or zones of privacy, does exist under the Constitution. In varying contexts, the Court or individual Justices have, indeed, found at least the roots of that right in the First Amendment. . . .

This right of privacy, whether it be founded in the Fourteenth Amendment's concept of personal liberty and restrictions upon state action, as we feel it is, or, as the District Court determined, in the Ninth Amendment's reservation of rights to the people, is broad enough to encompass a woman's decision whether or not to terminate her pregnancy. The detriment that the State would impose upon the pregnant woman by denying this choice altogether is apparent. Specific and direct harm medically diagnosable even in early pregnancy may be involved. Maternity, or additional offspring, may force upon the woman a distressful life and future. Psychological harm may be imminent. Mental and physical health may be taxed by child care. There is also the distress, for all concerned, associated with the unwanted child, and there is the problem of bringing a child into a family already unable, psychologically and otherwise, to care for it. In other cases, as in this one, the additional difficulties and continuing stigma of unwed motherhood may be involved. All these are factors the woman and her responsible physician necessarily will consider in consultation.

On the basis of elements such as these, appellant and some amici argue that the woman's right is absolute and that she is entitled to terminate her pregnancy at whatever time, in whatever way, and for whatever reason she alone chooses. With this we do not agree. Appellant's arguments that Texas either has no valid interest at all in regulating the abortion decision, or no interest strong enough to support any limitation upon the woman's sole determination, are unpersuasive. The Court's decisions recognizing a right of privacy also acknowledge that some state regulation in areas protected by that right is appropriate. As noted above, a State may properly assert important interests in safeguarding health, in maintaining medical standards, and in protecting potential life. At some point in pregnancy, these respective interests become sufficiently compelling to sustain regulation of the factors that govern the abortion decision. The privacy right involved, therefore, cannot be said to be absolute. In fact, it is not clear to us that the claim asserted by some amici that one has an unlimited right to do with one's body as one pleases bears a close relationship to the right of privacy previously articulated in the Court's decisions. The Court has refused to recognize an unlimited right of this kind in the past. Jacobson v. Massachusetts, 197 U.S. 11, 25 S.Ct. 358, 49 L.Ed. 643 (1905) (vaccination); Buck v. Bell, 274 U.S. 200, 47 S.Ct. 584, 71 L.Ed. 1000 (1927) (sterilization).

We, therefore, conclude that the right of personal privacy includes the abortion decision, but that this right is not unqualified and must be considered against important state interests in regulation.

. . .

IX

. . .

A. The appellee and certain amici argue that the fetus is a "person" within the language and meaning of the Fourteenth Amendment. In support of this, they outline at length and in detail the well-known facts of fetal development. If this suggestion of personhood is established, the appellant's case, of course, collapses, for the fetus' right to life would then be guaranteed specifically by the Amendment. The appellant conceded as much on reargument. On the other hand, the appellee conceded on reargument that no case could be cited that holds that a fetus is a person within the meaning of the Fourteenth Amendment.

The Constitution does not define "person" in so many words. [The opinion reviews the use of the term in various parts of the Constitution, concluding that in nearly all the instances cited, "the use of the word is such that it has application only postnatally"].

All this, together with our observation, supra, that throughout the major portion of the 19th century prevailing legal abortion practices were far freer than they are today, persuades us that the word "person," as used in the Fourteenth Amendment, does not include the unborn "moment of conception."

This conclusion, however, does not of itself fully answer the contentions raised by Texas, and we pass on to other considerations.

B. The pregnant woman cannot be isolated in her privacy. She carries an embryo and, later, a fetus, if one accepts the medical definitions of the developing young in the human uterus. See Dorland's Illustrated Medical Dictionary 478–479, 547 (24th ed. 1965). The situation therefore is inherently different from marital intimacy, or bedroom possession of obscene material, or marriage, or procreation, or education, with which Eisenstadt and Griswold, Stanley, Loving, Skinner and Pierce and Meyer were respectively concerned. As we have intimated above, it is reasonable and appropriate for a State to decide that at some point in time another interest, that of health of the mother or that of potential human life, becomes significantly involved. The woman's privacy is no longer sole and any right of privacy she possesses must be measured accordingly.

Texas urges that, apart from the Fourteenth Amendment, life begins at conception and is present throughout pregnancy, and that, therefore, the State has a compelling interest in protecting that life from and after conception. We need not resolve the difficult question of when life begins. When those trained in the respective disciplines of medicine, philosophy, and theology are unable to arrive at any consensus, the judiciary, at this point in the development of man's knowledge, is not in a position to speculate as to the answer.

It should be sufficient to note briefly the wide divergence of thinking on this most sensitive and difficult question. There has always been strong support for the view that life does not begin until live birth. . . . As we have noted, the common law found greater significance in quickening. Physicians and their scientific colleagues have regarded that event with less interest and have tended to focus either upon conception, upon live birth, or upon the interim point at which the fetus becomes "viable," that is, potentially able to live outside the mother's womb, albeit with artificial aid. Viability is usually placed at about seven months (28 weeks) but may occur earlier, even at 24 weeks. The Aristotelian theory of "mediate animation," that held sway throughout the Middle Ages and the Renaissance in Europe, continued to be official Roman Catholic dogma until the 19th century, despite opposition to this "ensoulment" theory from those in the Church who would recognize the existence of life from the moment of conception. The latter is now, of course, the official belief of the Catholic Church. As one brief amicus discloses, this is a view strongly held by many non-Catholics as well, and by many physicians. Substantial problems for precise definition of this view are posed, however, by new embryological data that purport to indicate that conception is a "process" over time, rather than an event, and by new medical techniques such as menstrual extraction, the "morning-after" pill, implantation of embryos, artificial insemination, and even artificial wombs.

In areas other than criminal abortion, the law has been reluctant to endorse any theory that life, as we recognize it, begins before live birth or to accord legal rights to the unborn except in narrowly defined situations and except when the rights are contingent upon life birth. For example, the traditional rule of tort law denied recovery for prenatal injuries even though the child was born alive. That rule has been changed in almost every jurisdiction. In most States, recovery is said to be permitted only if the fetus was viable, or at least quick, when the injuries were sustained, though few courts have squarely so held. In a recent development, generally opposed by the commentators, some States permit the parents of a stillborn child to maintain an action for wrongful death because of prenatal injuries. Such an action, however, would appear to be one to vindicate the parents' interest and is thus consistent with the view that the fetus, at most, represents only the potentiality of life. Similarly, unborn children have been recognized as acquiring rights or interests by way of inheritance or other devolution of property, and have been represented by guardians ad litem. Perfection of the interests involved, again, has generally been contingent upon live birth. In short, the unborn have never been recognized in the law as persons in the whole sense.

X

In view of all this, we do not agree that, by adopting one theory of life, Texas may override the rights of the pregnant woman that are at stake. We repeat, however, that the State does have an important and legitimate interest in preserving and protecting the health of the pregnant woman, whether she be a resident of the State or a non-resident who seeks medical consultation and treatment there, and that it has still another important and legitimate interest in protecting the potentiality of human life. These interests are separate and distinct. Each grows in substantiality as the woman approaches term and, at a point during pregnancy, each becomes "compelling."

With respect to the State's important and legitimate interest in the health of the mother, the "compelling" point, in the light of present medical knowledge, is at approximately the end of the first trimester. This is so because of the now-established medical fact, referred to above at 725, that until the end of the first trimester mortality in abortion may be less than mortality in normal childbirth. It follows that, from and after this point, a State may regulate the abortion procedure to the extent that the regulation reasonably relates to the preservation and protection of maternal health. Examples of permissible state regulation in this area are requirements as to the qualifications of the person who is to perform the abortion; as to the licensure of that person; as to the facility in which the procedure is to be performed, that is, whether it must be a hospital or may be a clinic or some other place of less-than-hospital status; as to the licensing of the facility; and the like.

This means, on the other hand, that, for the period of pregnancy prior to this "compelling" point, the attending physician, in consultation with his patient, is free to determine, without regulation by the State, that, in his medical judgment, the patient's pregnancy should be terminated. If that decision is reached, the judgment may be effectuated by an abortion free of interference by the State.

With respect to the State's important and legitimate interest in potential life, the "compelling" point is at viability. This is so because the fetus then presumably has the capability of meaningful life outside the mother's womb. State regulation protective of fetal life after viability thus has both logical and biological justifications. If the State is interested in protecting fetal life after viability, it may go so far as to proscribe abortion during that period, except when it is necessary to preserve the life or health of the mother.

Measured against these standards, Art. 1196 of the Texas Penal Code, in restricting legal abortions to those "procured or attempted by medical advice for the purpose of saving the life of the mother," sweeps too broadly. The statute makes no distinction between abortions performed early in pregnancy and those performed later, and it limits to a single reason, "saving" the mother's life, the legal justification for the procedure. The statute, therefore, cannot survive the constitutional attack made upon it here.

. . .

To summarize and to repeat:

1. A state criminal abortion statute of the current Texas type, that excepts from criminality only a *life-saving* procedure on behalf of the mother, without regard to pregnancy stage and without recognition of the other interests involved, is violative of the Due Process Clause of the Fourteenth Amendment.

(a) For the stage prior to approximately the end of the first trimester, the abortion decision and its effectuation must be left to the medical judgment of the pregnant woman's attending physician.

(b) For the stage subsequent to approximately the end of the first trimester, the State, in promoting its interest in the health of the mother, may, if it chooses, regulate the abortion procedure in ways that are reasonably related to maternal health.

(c) For the stage subsequent to viability, the State in promoting its interest in the potentiality of human life may, if it chooses, regulate, and even proscribe, abortion except where it is necessary, in appropriate medical judgment, for the preservation of the life or health of the mother.

2. The State may define the term "physician," as it has been employed in the preceding paragraphs of this Part XI of this opinion, to mean only a physician currently licensed by the State, and may proscribe any abortion by a person who is not a physician as so defined.

. . .

This holding, we feel, is consistent with the relative weights of the respective interests involved, with the lessons and examples of medical and legal history, with the lenity of the common law, and with the demands of the profound problems of the present day. The decision leaves the State free to place increasing restrictions on abortion as the period of pregnancy lengthens, so long as those restrictions are tailored to the recognized state interests. The decision vindicates the right of the physician to administer medical treatment according to his professional judgment up to the points where important state interests provide compelling justifications for intervention. Up to those points, the abortion decision in all its aspects is inherently, and primarily, a medical decision, and basic responsibility for it must rest with the physician. If an individual practitioner abuses the privilege of exercising proper medical judgment, the usual remedies, judicial and intra-professional, are available.

. . .

[The concurring opinion of Justice Stewart and the dissent of Justice Rehnquist have been omitted.]

Gonzales v. Carhart

Supreme Court of the United States, 2007.
___ U.S. ___, 127 S.Ct. 1610, ___ L.Ed.2d ___.

■ Justice Kennedy delivered the opinion of the Court.

These cases require us to consider the validity of the Partial–Birth Abortion Ban Act of 2003 (Act), 18 U.S.C. § 1531 (2000 ed., Supp. IV), a federal statute regulating abortion procedures. In recitations preceding its operative provisions the Act refers to the Court's opinion in *Stenberg v. Carhart*, 530 U.S. 914 (2000), which also addressed the subject of abortion procedures used in the later stages of pregnancy. Compared to the state statute at issue in *Stenberg*, the Act is more specific concerning the instances to which it applies and in this respect more precise in its coverage. We conclude the Act should be sustained against the objections lodged by the broad, facial attack brought against it.

. . .

The Act proscribes a particular manner of ending fetal life, so it is necessary here, as it was in *Stenberg*, to discuss abortion procedures in some detail. Three United States District Courts heard extensive evidence describing the procedures. In addition to the two courts involved in the instant cases the District Court for the Southern District of New York also considered the constitutionality of the Act. *Nat. Abortion Federation v. Ashcroft*, 330 F. Supp. 2d 436 (2004). It found the Act unconstitutional, *id.*, at 493, and the Court of Appeals for the Second Circuit affirmed, *Nat. Abortion Federation v. Gonzales*, 437 F. 3d 278 (2006). The three District Courts relied on similar medical evidence; indeed, much of the evidence submitted to the *Carhart* court previously had been submitted to the other two courts. 331 F. Supp. 2d, at 809–810. We refer to the District Courts' exhaustive opinions in our own discussion of abortion procedures.

Abortion methods vary depending to some extent on the preferences of the physician and, of course, on the term of the pregnancy and the resulting stage of the unborn child's development. Between 85 and 90 percent of the approximately 1.3 million abortions performed each year in the United States take place in the first three months of pregnancy, which is to say in the first trimester. *Planned Parenthood*, 320 F. Supp. 2d, at 960, and n. 4; App. in No. 05–1382, pp. 45–48. The most common first-trimester abortion method is vacuum aspiration (otherwise known as suction curettage) in which the physician vacuums out the embryonic tissue. Early in this trimester an alternative is to use medication, such as mifepristone (commonly known as RU–486), to terminate the pregnancy. *Nat. Abortion Federation, supra,* at 464, n. 20. The Act does not regulate these procedures.

Of the remaining abortions that take place each year, most occur in the second trimester. The surgical procedure referred to as "dilation and evacuation" or "D&E" is the usual abortion method in this trimester. *Planned Parenthood*, 320 F. Supp. 2d, at 960–961. Although individual techniques for performing D&E differ, the general steps are the same.

A doctor must first dilate the cervix at least to the extent needed to insert surgical instruments into the uterus and to maneuver them to evacuate the fetus. *Nat. Abortion Federation, supra*, at 465; App. in No. 05–1382, at 61. The steps taken to cause dilation differ by physician and gestational age of the fetus. See, *e.g., Carhart*, 331 F. Supp. 2d, at 852, 856, 859, 862–865, 868, 870, 873–874, 876–877, 880, 883, 886. A doctor often begins the dilation process by inserting osmotic dilators, such as laminaria (sticks of seaweed), into the cervix. The dilators can be used in combination with drugs, such as misoprostol, that increase dilation. The resulting amount of dilation is not uniform, and a doctor does not know in advance how an individual patient will respond. In general the longer dilators remain in the cervix, the more it will dilate. Yet the length of time doctors employ osmotic dilators varies. Some may keep dilators in the cervix for two days, while others use dilators for a day or less. *Nat. Abortion Federation, supra*, at 464–465; *Planned Parenthood, supra*, at 961.

After sufficient dilation the surgical operation can commence. The woman is placed under general anesthesia or conscious sedation. The doctor, often guided by ultrasound, inserts grasping forceps through the woman's cervix and into the uterus to grab the fetus. The doctor grips a fetal part with the forceps and pulls it back through the cervix and vagina, continuing to pull even after meeting resistance from the cervix. The friction causes the fetus to tear apart. For example, a leg might be ripped off the fetus as it is pulled through the cervix and out of the woman. The process of evacuating the fetus piece by piece continues until it has been completely removed. A doctor may make 10 to 15 passes with the forceps to evacuate the fetus in its entirety, though sometimes removal is completed with fewer passes. Once the fetus has been evacuated, the placenta and any remaining fetal material are suctioned or scraped out of the uterus. The doctor examines the different parts to ensure the entire fetal body has been removed. See, *e.g., Nat. Abortion Federation, supra*, at 465; *Planned Parenthood, supra*, at 962.

Some doctors, especially later in the second trimester, may kill the fetus a day or two before performing the surgical evacuation. They inject digoxin or potassium chloride into the fetus, the umbilical cord, or the amniotic fluid. Fetal demise may cause contractions and make greater dilation possible. Once dead, moreover, the fetus' body will soften, and its removal will be easier. Other doctors refrain from injecting chemical agents, believing it adds risk with little or no medical benefit. *Carhart, supra*, at 907–912; *Nat. Abortion Federation, supra*, at 474–475.

The abortion procedure that was the impetus for the numerous bans on "partial-birth abortion," including the Act, is a variation of this standard D&E. See M. Haskell, Dilation and Extraction for Late Second Trimester Abortion (1992), 1 Appellant's App. in No. 04–3379 (CA8), p. 109 (hereinafter Dilation and Extraction). The medical community has not reached unanimity on the appropriate name for this D&E variation. It has been referred to as "intact D&E," "dilation and extraction" (D&X), and "intact D&X." *Nat. Abortion Federation, supra*, at 440, n. 2; see also F. Cunningham et al., Williams Obstetrics 243 (22d ed. 2005) (identifying the procedure as D&X); Danforth's Obstetrics and Gynecology 567 (J. Scott, R. Gibbs, B. Karlan, & A. Haney eds. 9th ed. 2003) (identifying the procedure as intact D&X); M. Paul, E. Lichtenberg, L. Borgatta, D. Grimes, & P. Stubblefield, A Clinician's Guide to Medical and Surgical Abortion 136 (1999) (identifying the procedure as intact D&E). For discussion purposes this D&E variation will be referred to as intact D&E. The main difference between the two procedures is that in intact D&E a doctor extracts the fetus intact or largely intact with only a few passes. There are no comprehensive statistics indicating what percentage of all D&Es are performed in this manner.

Intact D&E, like regular D&E, begins with dilation of the cervix. Sufficient dilation is essential for the procedure. To achieve intact extraction some doctors thus may attempt to dilate the cervix to a greater degree. This approach has been called "serial" dilation. *Carhart, supra*, at 856, 870, 873; *Planned Parenthood, supra*, at 965. Doctors who attempt at the outset to perform intact D&E may dilate for two full days or use up to 25 osmotic dilators. See, *e.g.*, Dilation and Extraction 110; *Carhart, supra*, at 865, 868, 876, 886.

In an intact D&E procedure the doctor extracts the fetus in a way conducive to pulling out its entire body, instead of ripping it apart. One doctor, for example, testified:

> "If I know I have good dilation and I reach in and the fetus starts to come out and I think I can accomplish it, the abortion with an intact delivery, then I use my forceps a little bit differently. I don't close them quite so much, and I just gently draw the tissue out attempting to have an intact delivery, if possible." App. in No. 05–1382, at 74.

Rotating the fetus as it is being pulled decreases the odds of dismemberment. *Carhart, supra*, at 868–869; App. in No. 05–380, pp. 40–41; 5 Appellant's App. in No. 04–3379 (CA8), p. 1469. A doctor also "may use forceps to grasp a fetal part, pull it down, and re-grasp the fetus at a higher level—sometimes using both his hand and a forceps—to exert traction to retrieve the fetus intact until the head is lodged in the [cervix]." *Carhart*, 331 F. Supp. 2d, at 886–887.

Intact D&E gained public notoriety when, in 1992, Dr. Martin Haskell gave a presentation describing his method of performing the operation. Dilation and Extraction 110–111. In the usual intact D&E the fetus' head lodges in the cervix, and dilation is insufficient to allow it to pass. See, *e.g., ibid.*; App. in No. 05–380, at 577; App. in No. 05–1382, at 74, 282. Haskell explained the next step as follows:

> "At this point, the right-handed surgeon slides the fingers of the left [hand] along the back of the fetus and 'hooks' the shoulders of the fetus with the index and ring fingers (palm down).

> "While maintaining this tension, lifting the cervix and applying traction to the shoulders with the fingers of the left hand, the surgeon takes a pair of blunt curved Metzenbaum scissors in the right hand. He carefully advances the tip, curved down, along the spine and under his middle finger until he feels it contact the base of the skull under the tip of his middle finger.

> "[T]he surgeon then forces the scissors into the base of the skull or into the foramen magnum. Having safely entered the skull, he spreads the scissors to enlarge the opening.

> "The surgeon removes the scissors and introduces a suction catheter into this hole and evacuates the skull contents. With the catheter still

in place, he applies traction to the fetus, removing it completely from the patient." H. R. Rep. No. 108–58, p. 3 (2003).

This is an abortion doctor's clinical description.

. . .

Dr. Haskell's approach is not the only method of killing the fetus once its head lodges in the cervix, and "the process has evolved" since his presentation. *Planned Parenthood*, 320 F. Supp. 2d, at 965. Another doctor, for example, squeezes the skull after it has been pierced "so that enough brain tissue exudes to allow the head to pass through." App. in No. 05–380, at 41; see also *Carhart, supra,* at 866–867, 874. Still other physicians reach into the cervix with their forceps and crush the fetus' skull. *Carhart, supra,* at 858, 881. Others continue to pull the fetus out of the woman until it disarticulates at the neck, in effect decapitating it. These doctors then grasp the head with forceps, crush it, and remove it. *Id.,* at 864, 878; see also *Planned Parenthood, supra,* at 965.

Some doctors performing an intact D&E attempt to remove the fetus without collapsing the skull. See *Carhart, supra,* at 866, 869. Yet one doctor would not allow delivery of a live fetus younger than 24 weeks because "the objective of [his] procedure is to perform an abortion," not a birth. App. in No. 05–1382, at 408–409. The doctor thus answered in the affirmative when asked whether he would "hold the fetus' head on the internal side of the [cervix] in order to collapse the skull" and kill the fetus before it is born. *Id.,* at 409; see also *Carhart, supra,* at 862, 878. Another doctor testified he crushes a fetus' skull not only to reduce its size but also to ensure the fetus is dead before it is removed. For the staff to have to deal with a fetus that has "some viability to it, some movement of limbs," according to this doctor, "[is] always a difficult situation." App. in No. 05–380, at 94; see *Carhart, supra,* at 858.

D&E and intact D&E are not the only second-trimester abortion methods. Doctors also may abort a fetus through medical induction. The doctor medicates the woman to induce labor, and contractions occur to deliver the fetus. Induction, which unlike D&E should occur in a hospital, can last as little as 6 hours but can take longer than 48. It accounts for about five percent of second-trimester abortions before 20 weeks of gestation and 15 percent of those after 20 weeks. Doctors turn to two other methods of second-trimester abortion, hysterotomy and hysterectomy, only in emergency situations because they carry increased risk of complications. In a hysterotomy, as in a cesarean section, the doctor removes the fetus by making an incision through the abdomen and uterine wall to gain access to the uterine cavity. A hysterectomy requires the removal of the entire uterus. These two procedures represent about .07% of second-trimester abortions. *Nat. Abortion Federation*, 330 F. Supp. 2d, at 467; *Planned Parenthood, supra,* at 962–963.

. . .

The Act responded to *Stenberg* in two ways. First, Congress made factual findings. Congress determined that this Court in *Stenberg* "was required to accept the very questionable findings issued by the district court judge," § 2(7), 117 Stat. 1202, notes following 18 U.S.C. § 1531 (2000 ed., Supp. IV), p. 768, ¶ (7) (Congressional Findings), but that Congress was "not bound to accept the same factual findings," *ibid.*, ¶ (8). Congress found, among other things, that "[a] moral, medical, and ethical consensus exists that the practice of performing a partial-birth abortion ... is a gruesome and inhumane procedure that is never medically necessary and should be prohibited." *Id.*, at 767, ¶ (1).

Second, and more relevant here, the Act's language differs from that of the Nebraska statute struck down in *Stenberg*. See 530 U.S., at 921–922 (quoting Neb. Rev. Stat. Ann. §§ 28–328(1), 28–326(9) (Supp. 1999)). The operative provisions of the Act provide in relevant part:

"(a) Any physician who, in or affecting interstate or foreign commerce, knowingly performs a partial-birth abortion and thereby kills a human fetus shall be fined under this title or imprisoned not more than 2 years, or both. This subsection does not apply to a partial-birth abortion that is necessary to save the life of a mother whose life is endangered by a physical disorder, physical illness, or physical injury, including a life-endangering physical condition caused by or arising from the pregnancy itself. This subsection takes effect 1 day after the enactment.

"(b) As used in this section—

"(1) the term 'partial-birth abortion' means an abortion in which the person performing the abortion—

"(A) deliberately and intentionally vaginally delivers a living fetus until, in the case of a head-first presentation, the entire fetal head is outside the body of the mother, or, in the case of breech presentation, any part of the fetal trunk past the navel is outside the body of the mother, for the purpose of performing an overt act that the person knows will kill the partially delivered living fetus; and

"(B) performs the overt act, other than completion of delivery, that kills the partially delivered living fetus; and

"(2) the term 'physician' means a doctor of medicine or osteopathy legally authorized to practice medicine and surgery by the State in which the doctor performs such activity, or any other individual legally authorized by the State to perform abortions: *Provided, however,* That any individual who is not a physician or not otherwise legally authorized by the State to perform abortions, but who nevertheless directly performs a partial-birth abortion, shall be subject to the provisions of this section.

. . .

"(d)(1) A defendant accused of an offense under this section may seek a hearing before the State Medical Board on whether the physician's conduct was necessary to save the life of the mother whose life was endangered by a physical disorder, physical illness, or physical injury, including a life-endangering physical condition caused by or arising from the pregnancy itself.

"(2) The findings on that issue are admissible on that issue at the trial of the defendant. Upon a motion of the defendant, the court shall delay the beginning of the trial for not more than 30 days to permit such a hearing to take place.

"(e) A woman upon whom a partial-birth abortion is performed may not be prosecuted under this section, for a conspiracy to violate this section, or for an offense under section 2, 3, or 4 of this title based on a violation of this section." 18 U.S.C. § 1531 (2000 ed., Supp. IV).

The Act also includes a provision authorizing civil actions that is not of relevance here. § 1531(c).

C

The District Court in *Carhart* concluded the Act was unconstitutional for two reasons. First, it determined the Act was unconstitutional because it lacked an exception allowing the procedure where necessary for the health of the mother. 331 F. Supp. 2d, at 1004–1030. Second, the District Court found the Act deficient because it covered not merely intact D&E but also certain other D&Es. *Id.,* at 1030–1037.

The Court of Appeals for the Eighth Circuit addressed only the lack of a health exception. 413 F. 3d, at 803–804. The court began its analysis with what it saw as the appropriate question—"whether 'substantial medical authority' supports the medical necessity of the banned procedure." *Id.,* at 796 (quoting *Stenberg*, 530 U.S., at 938). This was the proper framework, according to the Court of Appeals, because "when a lack of consensus exists in the medical community, the Constitution requires legislatures to err on the side of protecting women's health by including a health exception." 413 F. 3d, at 796. The court rejected the Attorney General's attempt to demonstrate changed evidentiary circumstances since *Stenberg* and considered itself bound by *Stenberg*'s conclusion that a health exception was required. 413 F. 3d, at 803 (explaining "[t]he record in [the] case and the record in *Stenberg* [were] similar in all significant respects"). It invalidated the Act. *Ibid.*

The District Court in *Planned Parenthood* concluded the Act was unconstitutional "because it (1) pose[d] an undue burden on a woman's ability to choose a second trimester abortion; (2) [was] unconstitutionally vague; and (3) require[d] a health exception as set forth by ... *Stenberg*." 320 F. Supp. 2d, at 1034–1035.

The Court of Appeals for the Ninth Circuit agreed. Like the Court of Appeals for the Eighth Circuit, it concluded the absence of a health exception rendered the Act unconstitutional. The court interpreted *Stenberg* to require a health exception unless "there is *consensus in the medical community* that the banned procedure is never medically necessary to preserve the health of women.'' 435 F. 3d, at 1173. Even after applying a deferential standard of review to Congress' factual findings, the Court of Appeals determined ''substantial disagreement exists in the medical community regarding whether'' the procedures prohibited by the Act are ever necessary to preserve a woman's health. *Id.*, at 1175–1176.

The Court of Appeals concluded further that the Act placed an undue burden on a woman's ability to obtain a second-trimester abortion. The court found the textual differences between the Act and the Nebraska statute struck down in *Stenberg* insufficient to distinguish D&E and intact D&E. 435 F. 3d, at 1178–1180. As a result, according to the Court of Appeals, the Act imposed an undue burden because it prohibited D&E. *Id.*, at 1180–1181.

Finally, the Court of Appeals found the Act void for vagueness. *Id.*, at 1181. Abortion doctors testified they were uncertain which procedures the Act made criminal. The court thus concluded the Act did not offer physicians clear warning of its regulatory reach. *Id.*, at 1181–1184. Resting on its understanding of the remedial framework established by this Court in *Ayotte v. Planned Parenthood of Northern New Eng.*, 546 U.S. 320, 328–330 (2006), the Court of Appeals held the Act was unconstitutional on its face and should be permanently enjoined. 435 F. 3d, at 1184–1191.

. . .

... Whatever one's views concerning the *Casey* joint opinion, it is evident a premise central to its conclusion—that the government has a legitimate and substantial interest in preserving and promoting fetal life— would be repudiated were the Court now to affirm the judgments of the Courts of Appeals.

Casey involved a challenge to *Roe v. Wade*, 410 U.S. 113 (1973). The opinion contains this summary:

> "It must be stated at the outset and with clarity that *Roe*'s essential holding, the holding we reaffirm, has three parts. First is a recognition of the right of the woman to choose to have an abortion before viability and to obtain it without undue interference from the State. Before viability, the State's interests are not strong enough to support a prohibition of abortion or the imposition of a substantial obstacle to the woman's effective right to elect the procedure. Second is a confirmation of the State's power to restrict abortions after fetal viability, if the law contains exceptions for pregnancies which endanger the woman's life or health. And third is the principle that the State has legitimate interests from the outset of the pregnancy in protecting the health of the woman and the life of the fetus that may become a child. These principles do not contradict one another; and we adhere to each." 505 U.S., at 846 (opinion of the Court).

Though all three holdings are implicated in the instant cases, it is the third that requires the most extended discussion; for we must determine whether the Act furthers the legitimate interest of the Government in protecting the life of the fetus that may become a child.

To implement its holding, *Casey* rejected both *Roe*'s rigid trimester framework and the interpretation of *Roe* that considered all previability regulations of abortion unwarranted. 505 U.S., at 875–876, 878 (plurality opinion). On this point *Casey* overruled the holdings in two cases because they undervalued the State's interest in potential life. See *id.,* at 881–883 (joint opinion) (overruling *Thornburgh v. American College of Obstetricians and Gynecologists,* 476 U.S. 747 (1986) and *Akron v. Akron Center for Reproductive Health, Inc.,* 462 U.S. 416 (1983)).

We assume the following principles for the purposes of this opinion. Before viability, a State "may not prohibit any woman from making the ultimate decision to terminate her pregnancy." 505 U.S., at 879 (plurality opinion). It also may not impose upon this right an undue burden, which exists if a regulation's "purpose or effect is to place a substantial obstacle in the path of a woman seeking an abortion before the fetus attains viability." *Id.,* at 878. On the other hand, "[r]egulations which do no more than create a structural mechanism by which the State, or the parent or guardian of a minor, may express profound respect for the life of the unborn are permitted, if they are not a substantial obstacle to the woman's exercise of the right to choose." *Id.,* at 877. *Casey,* in short, struck a balance. The balance was central to its holding. We now apply its standard to the cases at bar.

. . .

Respondents agree the Act encompasses intact D&E, but they contend its additional reach is both unclear and excessive. Respondents assert that, at the least, the Act is void for vagueness because its scope is indefinite. In the alternative, respondents argue the Act's text proscribes all D&Es. Because D&E is the most common second-trimester abortion method, respondents suggest the Act imposes an undue burden. In this litigation the Attorney General does not dispute that the Act would impose an undue burden if it covered standard D&E.

We conclude that the Act is not void for vagueness, does not impose an undue burden from any overbreadth, and is not invalid on its face.

The Act punishes "knowingly perform[ing]" a "partial-birth abortion." § 1531(a) (2000 ed., Supp. IV). It defines the unlawful abortion in explicit terms. § 1531(b)(1).

First, the person performing the abortion must "vaginally delive[r] a living fetus." § 1531(b)(1)(A). The Act does not restrict an abortion procedure involving the delivery of an expired fetus. The Act, furthermore, is inapplicable to abortions that do not involve vaginal delivery (for instance, hysterotomy or hysterectomy). The Act does apply both previability and postviability because, by common understanding and scientific terminology, a fetus is a living organism while within the womb, whether or not it is viable outside the womb. See, *e.g., Planned Parenthood,* 320 F. Supp. 2d, at 971–972. We do not understand this point to be contested by the parties.

Second, the Act's definition of partial-birth abortion requires the fetus to be delivered "until, in the case of a head-first presentation, the entire fetal head is outside the body of the mother, or, in the case of breech presentation, any part of the fetal trunk past the navel is outside the body of the mother." § 1531(b)(1)(A) (2000 ed., Supp. IV). The Attorney General concedes, and we agree, that if an abortion procedure does not involve the delivery of a living fetus to one of these "anatomical 'landmarks' "—where, depending on the presentation, either the fetal head or the fetal trunk past the navel is outside the body of the mother—the prohibitions of the Act do not apply. Brief for Petitioner in No. 05–380, p. 46.

Third, to fall within the Act, a doctor must perform an "overt act, other than completion of delivery, that kills the partially delivered living fetus." § 1531(b)(1)(B) (2000 ed., Supp. IV). For purposes of criminal liability, the overt act causing the fetus' death must be separate from delivery. And the overt act must occur after the delivery to an anatomical landmark. This is because the Act proscribes killing "the partially delivered" fetus, which, when read in context, refers to a fetus that has been delivered to an anatomical landmark. *Ibid.*

Fourth, the Act contains scienter requirements concerning all the actions involved in the prohibited abortion. To begin with, the physician must have "deliberately and intentionally" delivered the fetus to one of the Act's anatomical landmarks. § 1531(b)(1)(A). If a living fetus is delivered past the critical point by accident or inadvertence, the Act is inapplicable. In addition, the fetus must have been delivered "for the purpose of performing an overt act that the [doctor] knows will kill [it]." *Ibid.* If either intent is absent, no crime has occurred. This follows from the general principle that where scienter is required no crime is committed absent the requisite state of mind.

Respondents contend the language described above is indeterminate, and they thus argue the Act is unconstitutionally vague on its face. "As generally stated, the void-for-vagueness doctrine requires that a penal statute define the criminal offense with sufficient definiteness that ordinary people can understand what conduct is prohibited and in a manner that does not encourage arbitrary and discriminatory enforcement." *Kolender v. Lawson*, 461 U.S. 352, 357 (1983); *Posters 'N' Things, Ltd. v. United States*, 511 U.S. 513, 525 (1994). The Act satisfies both requirements.

The Act provides doctors "of ordinary intelligence a reasonable opportunity to know what is prohibited." *Grayned v. City of Rockford*, 408 U.S. 104, 108 (1972). Indeed, it sets forth "relatively clear guidelines as to prohibited conduct" and provides "objective criteria" to evaluate whether a doctor has performed a prohibited procedure. *Posters 'N' Things, supra*, at 525–526. Unlike the statutory language in *Stenberg* that prohibited the delivery of a "substantial portion" of the fetus—where a doctor might question how much of the fetus is a substantial portion—the Act defines the line between potentially criminal conduct on the one hand and lawful abortion on the other ... Doctors performing D&E will know that if they do not deliver a living fetus to an anatomical landmark they will not face criminal liability.

This conclusion is buttressed by the intent that must be proved to impose liability. The Court has made clear that scienter requirements alleviate vagueness concerns. *Posters 'N' Things, supra*, at 526; see also *Colautti v. Franklin*, 439 U.S. 379, 395 (1979) ("This Court has long recognized that the constitutionality of a vague statutory standard is closely related to whether that standard incorporates a requirement of *mens rea*"). The Act requires the doctor deliberately to have delivered the fetus to an anatomical landmark. § 1531(b)(1)(A) (2000 ed., Supp. IV). Because a doctor performing a D&E will not face criminal liability if he or she delivers a fetus beyond the prohibited point by mistake, the Act cannot be described as "a trap for those who act in good faith." *Colautti, supra*, at 395 (internal quotation marks omitted).

Respondents likewise have failed to show that the Act should be invalidated on its face because it encourages arbitrary or discriminatory enforcement. *Kolender, supra*, at 357. Just as the Act's anatomical landmarks provide doctors with objective standards, they also "establish minimal guidelines to govern law enforcement." *Smith v. Goguen*, 415 U.S. 566, 574 (1974). The scienter requirements narrow the scope of the Act's prohibition and limit prosecutorial discretion. It cannot be said that the Act "vests virtually complete discretion in the hands of [law enforcement] to determine whether the [doctor] has satisfied [its provisions]." *Kolender, supra*, at 358 (invalidating a statute regulating loitering). Respondents' arguments concerning arbitrary enforcement, furthermore, are somewhat speculative. This is a preenforcement challenge, where "no evidence has been, or could be, introduced to indicate whether the [Act] has been enforced in a discriminatory manner or with the aim of inhibiting [constitutionally protected conduct]." *Hoffman Estates v. Flipside, Hoffman Estates, Inc.*, 455 U.S. 489, 503 (1982). The Act is not vague.

We next determine whether the Act imposes an undue burden, as a facial matter, because its restrictions on second-trimester abortions are too broad. A review of the statutory text discloses the limits of its reach. The Act prohibits intact D&E; and, notwithstanding respondents' arguments, it does not prohibit the D&E procedure in which the fetus is removed in parts.

The Act prohibits a doctor from intentionally performing an intact D&E. The dual prohibitions of the Act, both of which are necessary for criminal liability, correspond with the steps generally undertaken during this type of procedure. First, a doctor delivers the fetus until its head lodges in the cervix, which is usually past the anatomical landmark for a breech presentation. See 18 U.S.C. § 1531(b)(1)(A) (2000 ed., Supp. IV). Second, the doctor proceeds to pierce the fetal skull with scissors or crush it with forceps. This step satisfies the overt-act requirement because it kills the fetus and is distinct from delivery. See § 1531(b)(1)(B). The Act's intent requirements, however, limit its reach to those physicians who carry out the intact D&E after intending to undertake both steps at the outset.

The Act excludes most D&Es in which the fetus is removed in pieces, not intact. If the doctor intends to remove the fetus in parts from the outset, the doctor will not have the requisite intent to incur criminal liability. A doctor performing a standard D&E procedure can often "tak[e] about 10–15 'passes' through the uterus to remove the entire fetus." *Planned Parenthood*, 320 F. Supp. 2d, at 962. Removing the fetus in this manner does not violate the Act because the doctor will not have delivered the living fetus to one of the anatomical landmarks or committed an additional overt act that kills the fetus after partial delivery. § 1531(b)(1) (2000 ed., Supp. IV).

A comparison of the Act with the Nebraska statute struck down in *Stenberg* confirms this point. The statute in *Stenberg* prohibited "deliberately and intentionally delivering into the vagina a living unborn child, or a substantial portion thereof, for the purpose of performing a procedure that the person performing such procedure knows will kill the unborn child and does kill the unborn child." 530 U.S., at 922 (quoting Neb. Rev. Stat. Ann. § 28–326(9) (Supp. 1999)). The Court concluded that this statute encompassed D&E because "D&E will often involve a physician pulling a 'substantial portion' of a still living fetus, say, an arm or leg, into the vagina prior to the death of the fetus." 530 U.S., at 939. The Court also rejected the limiting interpretation urged by Nebraska's Attorney General that the statute's reference to a "procedure" that "kill[s] the unborn child" was to a distinct procedure, not to the abortion procedure as a whole. *Id.,* at 943.

Congress, it is apparent, responded to these concerns because the Act departs in material ways from the statute in *Stenberg*. It adopts the phrase "delivers a living fetus," § 1531(b)(1)(A) (2000 ed., Supp. IV), instead of "delivering ... a living unborn child, or a substantial portion thereof," 530 U.S., at 938 (quoting Neb. Rev. Stat. Ann. § 28–326(9) (Supp. 1999)). The Act's language, unlike the statute in *Stenberg*, expresses the usual meaning of "deliver" when used in connection with "fetus," namely, extraction of an entire fetus rather than removal of fetal pieces. See Stedman's Medical Dictionary 470 (27th ed. 2000) (defining deliver as "[t]o assist a woman in childbirth" and "[t]o extract from an enclosed place, as the fetus from the womb, an object or foreign body"); see also I. Dox, B. Melloni, G. Eisner, & J. Melloni, The HarperCollins Illustrated Medical Dictionary 160 (4th ed. 2001); Merriam Webster's Collegiate Dictionary 306 (10th ed. 1997). The Act thus displaces the interpretation of "delivering" dictated by the Nebraska statute's reference to a "substantial portion" of the fetus. *Stenberg, supra,* at 944 (indicating that the Nebraska "statute itself specifies that it applies *both* to delivering 'an intact unborn child' *or* 'a substantial portion thereof' "). In interpreting statutory texts courts use the ordinary meaning of terms unless context requires a different result. See, *e.g.,* 2A N. Singer, Sutherland on Statutes and Statutory Construction § 47:28 (rev. 6th ed. 2000). Here, unlike in *Stenberg*, the language does not require a departure from the ordinary meaning. D&E does not involve the delivery of a fetus because it requires the removal of fetal parts that are ripped from the fetus as they are pulled through the cervix.

The identification of specific anatomical landmarks to which the fetus must be partially delivered also differentiates the Act from the statute at issue in *Stenberg*. § 1531(b)(1)(A) (2000 ed., Supp. IV). The Court in *Stenberg* interpreted "substantial portion" of the fetus to include an arm or a leg. 530 U.S., at 939. The Act's anatomical landmarks, by contrast, clarify that the removal of a small portion of the fetus is not prohibited. The landmarks also require the fetus to be delivered so that it is partially "outside the body of the mother." § 1531(b)(1)(A). To come within the ambit of the Nebraska statute, on the other hand, a substantial portion of the fetus only had to be delivered into the vagina; no part of the fetus had to be outside the body of the mother before a doctor could face criminal sanctions. *Id.*, at 938–939.

By adding an overt-act requirement Congress sought further to meet the Court's objections to the state statute considered in *Stenberg*. Compare 18 U.S. C. § 1531(b)(1) (2000 ed., Supp. IV) with Neb. Rev. Stat. Ann. § 28–326(9) (Supp. 1999). The Act makes the distinction the Nebraska statute failed to draw (but the Nebraska Attorney General advanced) by differentiating between the overall partial-birth abortion and the distinct overt act that kills the fetus. See *Stenberg*, 530 U.S., at 943–944. The fatal overt act must occur after delivery to an anatomical landmark, and it must be something "other than [the] completion of delivery." § 1531(b)(1)(B). This distinction matters because, unlike intact D&E, standard D&E does not involve a delivery followed by a fatal act.

The canon of constitutional avoidance, finally, extinguishes any lingering doubt as to whether the Act covers the prototypical D&E procedure. "[T]he elementary rule is that every reasonable construction must be resorted to, in order to save a statute from unconstitutionality." *Edward J. DeBartolo Corp. v. Florida Gulf Coast Building & Constr. Trades Council*, 485 U.S. 568, 575 (1988) (quoting *Hooper v. California*, 155 U.S. 648, 657 (1895)). It is true this longstanding maxim of statutory interpretation has, in the past, fallen by the wayside when the Court confronted a statute regulating abortion. The Court at times employed an antagonistic "canon of construction under which in cases involving abortion, a permissible reading of a statute [was] to be avoided at all costs." *Stenberg, supra*, at 977 (Kennedy, J., dissenting) (quoting *Thornburgh*, 476 U.S., at 829 (O'Connor, J., dissenting)). *Casey* put this novel statutory approach to rest. *Stenberg, supra*, at 977 (Kennedy, J., dissenting). *Stenberg* need not be interpreted to have revived it. We read that decision instead to stand for the uncontroversial proposition that the canon of constitutional avoidance does not apply if a statute is not "genuinely susceptible to two constructions." *Almendarez–Torres v. United States*, 523 U.S. 224, 238 (1998); see also *Clark v. Martinez*, 543 U.S. 371, 385 (2005). In *Stenberg* the Court found the statute covered D&E. 530 U.S., at 938–945. Here, by contrast, interpreting the Act so that it does not prohibit standard D&E is the most reasonable reading and understanding of its terms.

Contrary arguments by the respondents are unavailing. Respondents look to situations that might arise during D&E, situations not examined in *Stenberg*. They contend—relying on the testimony of numerous abortion doctors—that D&E may result in the delivery of a living fetus beyond the

Act's anatomical landmarks in a significant fraction of cases. This is so, respondents say, because doctors cannot predict the amount the cervix will dilate before the abortion procedure. It might dilate to a degree that the fetus will be removed largely intact. To complete the abortion, doctors will commit an overt act that kills the partially delivered fetus. Respondents thus posit that any D&E has the potential to violate the Act, and that a physician will not know beforehand whether the abortion will proceed in a prohibited manner. Brief for Respondent Planned Parenthood et al. in No. 05–1382, p. 38.

This reasoning, however, does not take account of the Act's intent requirements, which preclude liability from attaching to an accidental intact D&E. If a doctor's intent at the outset is to perform a D&E in which the fetus would not be delivered to either of the Act's anatomical landmarks, but the fetus nonetheless is delivered past one of those points, the requisite and prohibited scienter is not present. 18 U.S.C. § 1531(b)(1)(A) (2000 ed., Supp. IV). When a doctor in that situation completes an abortion by performing an intact D&E, the doctor does not violate the Act. It is true that intent to cause a result may sometimes be inferred if a person "knows that that result is practically certain to follow from his conduct." 1 LaFave § 5.2(a), at 341. Yet abortion doctors intending at the outset to perform a standard D&E procedure will not know that a prohibited abortion "is practically certain to follow from" their conduct. *Ibid.* A fetus is only delivered largely intact in a small fraction of the overall number of D&E abortions. *Planned Parenthood*, 320 F. Supp. 2d, at 965.

The evidence also supports a legislative determination that an intact delivery is almost always a conscious choice rather than a happenstance. Doctors, for example, may remove the fetus in a manner that will increase the chances of an intact delivery. See, *e.g.*, App. in No. 05–1382, at 74, 452. And intact D&E is usually described as involving some manner of serial dilation. See, *e.g.*, Dilation and Extraction 110. Doctors who do not seek to obtain this serial dilation perform an intact D&E on far fewer occasions. See, *e.g.*, *Carhart*, 331 F. Supp. 2d, at 857–858 ("In order for intact removal to occur on a regular basis, Dr. Fitzhugh would have to dilate his patients with a second round of laminaria"). This evidence belies any claim that a standard D&E cannot be performed without intending or foreseeing an intact D&E.

Many doctors who testified on behalf of respondents, and who objected to the Act, do not perform an intact D&E by accident. On the contrary, they begin every D&E abortion with the objective of removing the fetus as intact as possible. See, *e.g.*, *id.*, at 869 ("Since Dr. Chasen believes that the intact D&E is safer than the dismemberment D&E, Dr. Chasen's goal is to perform an intact D&E every time"); see also *id.*, at 873, 886. This does not prove, as respondents suggest, that every D&E might violate the Act and that the Act therefore imposes an undue burden. It demonstrates only that those doctors who intend to perform a D&E that would involve delivery of a living fetus to one of the Act's anatomical landmarks must adjust their conduct to the law by not attempting to deliver the fetus to either of those points. Respondents have not shown that requiring doctors to intend dismemberment before delivery to an anatomical landmark will prohibit the vast majority of D&E abortions. The Act, then, cannot be held invalid on its face on these grounds.

Under the principles accepted as controlling here, the Act, as we have interpreted it, would be unconstitutional "if its purpose or effect is to place a substantial obstacle in the path of a woman seeking an abortion before the fetus attains viability." *Casey*, 505 U.S., at 878 (plurality opinion). The abortions affected by the Act's regulations take place both previability and postviability; so the quoted language and the undue burden analysis it relies upon are applicable. The question is whether the Act, measured by its text in this facial attack, imposes a substantial obstacle to late-term, but previability, abortions. The Act does not on its face impose a substantial obstacle, and we reject this further facial challenge to its validity.

The Act's purposes are set forth in recitals preceding its operative provisions. A description of the prohibited abortion procedure demonstrates the rationale for the congressional enactment. The Act proscribes a method of abortion in which a fetus is killed just inches before completion of the birth process. Congress stated as follows: "Implicitly approving such a brutal and inhumane procedure by choosing not to prohibit it will further coarsen society to the humanity of not only newborns, but all vulnerable and innocent human life, making it increasingly difficult to protect such life." Congressional Findings (14)(N), in notes following 18 U.S.C. § 1531 (2000 ed., Supp. IV), p. 769. The Act expresses respect for the dignity of human life.

Congress was concerned, furthermore, with the effects on the medical community and on its reputation caused by the practice of partial-birth abortion. The findings in the Act explain:

> "Partial-birth abortion ... confuses the medical, legal, and ethical duties of physicians to preserve and promote life, as the physician acts directly against the physical life of a child, whom he or she had just delivered, all but the head, out of the womb, in order to end that life." Congressional Findings (14)(J), *ibid.*

There can be no doubt the government "has an interest in protecting the integrity and ethics of the medical profession." *Washington v. Glucksberg*, 521 U.S. 702, 731 (1997); see also *Barsky v. Board of Regents of Univ. of N. Y.*, 347 U.S. 442, 451 (1954) (indicating the State has "legitimate concern for maintaining high standards of professional conduct" in the practice of medicine). Under our precedents it is clear the State has a significant role to play in regulating the medical profession.

Casey reaffirmed these governmental objectives. The government may use its voice and its regulatory authority to show its profound respect for the life within the woman. A central premise of the opinion was that the Court's precedents after *Roe* had "undervalue[d] the State's interest in potential life." 505 U.S., at 873 (plurality opinion); see also *id.*, at 871. The plurality opinion indicated "[t]he fact that a law which serves a valid purpose, one not designed to strike at the right itself, has the incidental effect of making it more difficult or more expensive to procure an abortion cannot be enough to invalidate it." *Id.,* at 874. This was not an idle assertion. The three premises of *Casey* must coexist. See *id.,* at 846 (opinion of the Court). The third premise, that the State, from the inception of the pregnancy, maintains its own regulatory interest in protecting the life of the fetus that may become a child, cannot be set at naught by interpreting *Casey*'s requirement of a health exception so it becomes tantamount to allowing a doctor to choose the abortion method he or she might prefer. Where it has a rational basis to act, and it does not impose an undue burden, the State may use its regulatory power to bar certain procedures and substitute others, all in furtherance of its legitimate interests in regulating the medical profession in order to promote respect for life, including life of the unborn.

The Act's ban on abortions that involve partial delivery of a living fetus furthers the Government's objectives. No one would dispute that, for many, D&E is a procedure itself laden with the power to devalue human life. Congress could nonetheless conclude that the type of abortion proscribed by the Act requires specific regulation because it implicates additional ethical and moral concerns that justify a special prohibition. Congress determined that the abortion methods it proscribed had a "disturbing similarity to the killing of a newborn infant," Congressional Findings (14)(L), in notes following 18 U. S. C. § 1531 (2000 ed., Supp. IV), p. 769, and thus it was concerned with "draw[ing] a bright line that clearly distinguishes abortion and infanticide." Congressional Findings (14)(G), *ibid.* The Court has in the past confirmed the validity of drawing boundaries to prevent certain practices that extinguish life and are close to actions that are condemned. *Glucksberg* found reasonable the State's "fear that permitting assisted suicide will start it down the path to voluntary and perhaps even involuntary euthanasia." 521 U. S., at 732–735, and n. 23.

Respect for human life finds an ultimate expression in the bond of love the mother has for her child. The Act recognizes this reality as well. Whether to have an abortion requires a difficult and painful moral decision. *Casey, supra,* at 852–853 (opinion of the Court). While we find no reliable data to measure the phenomenon, it seems unexceptionable to conclude some women come to regret their choice to abort the infant life they once created and sustained. See Brief for Sandra Cano et al. as *Amici Curiae* in No. 05–380, pp. 22–24. Severe depression and loss of esteem can follow. See *ibid.*

In a decision so fraught with emotional consequence some doctors may prefer not to disclose precise details of the means that will be used, confining themselves to the required statement of risks the procedure entails. From one standpoint this ought not to be surprising. Any number of patients facing imminent surgical procedures would prefer not to hear all details, lest the usual anxiety preceding invasive medical procedures become the more intense. This is likely the case with the abortion procedures here in issue. See, *e.g., Nat. Abortion Federation,* 330 F. Supp. 2d, at 466, n.

22 ("Most of [the plaintiffs'] experts acknowledged that they do not describe to their patients what [the D&E and intact D&E] procedures entail in clear and precise terms"); see also *id.*, at 479.

It is, however, precisely this lack of information concerning the way in which the fetus will be killed that is of legitimate concern to the State. *Casey, supra*, at 873 (plurality opinion) ("States are free to enact laws to provide a reasonable framework for a woman to make a decision that has such profound and lasting meaning"). The State has an interest in ensuring so grave a choice is well informed. It is self-evident that a mother who comes to regret her choice to abort must struggle with grief more anguished and sorrow more profound when she learns, only after the event, what she once did not know: that she allowed a doctor to pierce the skull and vacuum the fast-developing brain of her unborn child, a child assuming the human form.

It is a reasonable inference that a necessary effect of the regulation and the knowledge it conveys will be to encourage some women to carry the infant to full term, thus reducing the absolute number of late-term abortions. The medical profession, furthermore, may find different and less shocking methods to abort the fetus in the second trimester, thereby accommodating legislative demand. The State's interest in respect for life is advanced by the dialogue that better informs the political and legal systems, the medical profession, expectant mothers, and society as a whole of the consequences that follow from a decision to elect a late-term abortion.

It is objected that the standard D&E is in some respects as brutal, if not more, than the intact D&E, so that the legislation accomplishes little. What we have already said, however, shows ample justification for the regulation. Partial-birth abortion, as defined by the Act, differs from a standard D&E because the former occurs when the fetus is partially outside the mother to the point of one of the Act's anatomical landmarks. It was reasonable for Congress to think that partial-birth abortion, more than standard D&E, "undermines the public's perception of the appropriate role of a physician during the delivery process, and perverts a process during which life is brought into the world." Congressional Findings (14)(K), in notes following 18 U.S.C. § 1531 (2000 ed., Supp. IV), p. 769. There would be a flaw in this Court's logic, and an irony in its jurisprudence, were we first to conclude a ban on both D&E and intact D&E was overbroad and then to say it is irrational to ban only intact D&E because that does not proscribe both procedures. In sum, we reject the contention that the congressional purpose of the Act was "to place a substantial obstacle in the path of a woman seeking an abortion." 505 U.S., at 878 (plurality opinion).

The Act's furtherance of legitimate government interests bears upon, but does not resolve, the next question: whether the Act has the effect of imposing an unconstitutional burden on the abortion right because it does not allow use of the barred procedure where "necessary, in appropriate medical judgment, for [the] preservation of the . . . health of the mother." *Ayotte*, 546 U. S., at 327–328 (quoting *Casey, supra*, at 879 (plurality opinion)). The prohibition in the Act would be unconstitutional, under precedents we here assume to be controlling, if it "subject[ed] [women] to significant health risks." *Ayotte, supra,* at 328; see also *Casey, supra,* at 880 (opinion of the Court). In *Ayotte* the parties agreed a health exception to the challenged parental-involvement statute was necessary "to avert serious and often irreversible damage to [a pregnant minor's] health." 546 U.S., at 328. Here, by contrast, whether the Act creates significant health risks for women has been a contested factual question. The evidence presented in the trial courts and before Congress demonstrates both sides have medical support for their position.

Respondents presented evidence that intact D&E may be the safest method of abortion, for reasons similar to those adduced in *Stenberg.* See 530 U.S., at 932. Abortion doctors testified, for example, that intact D&E decreases the risk of cervical laceration or uterine perforation because it requires fewer passes into the uterus with surgical instruments and does not require the removal of bony fragments of the dismembered fetus, fragments that may be sharp. Respondents also presented evidence that intact D&E was safer both because it reduces the risks that fetal parts will remain in the uterus and because it takes less time to complete. Respondents, in addition, proffered evidence that intact D&E was safer for women with certain medical conditions or women with fetuses that had certain anomalies. See, e.g., *Carhart,* 331 F. Supp. 2d, at 923–929; *Nat. Abortion Federation, supra,* at 470–474; *Planned Parenthood,* 320 F. Supp. 2d, at 982–983.

These contentions were contradicted by other doctors who testified in the District Courts and before Congress. They concluded that the alleged health advantages were based on speculation without scientific studies to support them. They considered D&E always to be a safe alternative. See, e.g., *Carhart, supra,* at 930–940; *Nat. Abortion Federation,* 330 F. Supp. 2d, at 470–474; *Planned Parenthood,* 320 F. Supp. 2d, at 983.

There is documented medical disagreement whether the Act's prohibition would ever impose significant health risks on women. See, *e.g., id.,* at 1033 ("[T]here continues to be a division of opinion among highly qualified experts regarding the necessity or safety of intact D&E"); see also *Nat. Abortion Federation, supra,* at 482. . . .

The question becomes whether the Act can stand when this medical uncertainty persists. The Court's precedents instruct that the Act can survive this facial attack. The Court has given state and federal legislatures wide discretion to pass legislation in areas where there is medical and scientific uncertainty. . . .

This traditional rule is consistent with *Casey,* which confirms the State's interest in promoting respect for human life at all stages in the pregnancy. Physicians are not entitled to ignore regulations that direct them to use reasonable alternative procedures. The law need not give abortion doctors unfettered choice in the course of their medical practice, nor should it elevate their status above other physicians in the medical community. In *Casey* the controlling opinion held an informed-consent requirement in the abortion context was "no different from a requirement that a doctor give certain specific information about any medical procedure." 505 U.S., at 884 (joint opinion). . . .

The conclusion that the Act does not impose an undue burden is supported by other considerations. Alternatives are available to the prohibited procedure. As we have noted, the Act does not proscribe D&E. One District Court found D&E to have extremely low rates of medical complications. *Planned Parenthood, supra*, at 1000. Another indicated D&E was "generally the safest method of abortion during the second trimester." *Carhart*, 331 F. Supp. 2d, at 1031; see also *Nat. Abortion Federation, supra*, at 467–468 (explaining that "[e]xperts testifying for both sides" agreed D&E was safe). In addition the Act's prohibition only applies to the delivery of "a living fetus." 18 U.S.C. § 1531(b)(1)(A) (2000 ed., Supp. IV). If the intact D&E procedure is truly necessary in some circumstances, it appears likely an injection that kills the fetus is an alternative under the Act that allows the doctor to perform the procedure.

The instant cases, then, are different from *Planned Parenthood of Central Mo. v. Danforth*, 428 U.S. 52, 77–79 (1976), in which the Court invalidated a ban on saline amniocentesis, the then-dominant second-trimester abortion method. The Court found the ban in *Danforth* to be "an unreasonable or arbitrary regulation designed to inhibit, and having the effect of inhibiting, the vast majority of abortions after the first 12 weeks." *Id.,* at 79. Here the Act allows, among other means, a commonly used and generally accepted method, so it does not construct a substantial obstacle to the abortion right.

In reaching the conclusion the Act does not require a health exception we reject certain arguments made by the parties on both sides of these cases. On the one hand, the Attorney General urges us to uphold the Act on the basis of the congressional findings alone. Brief for Petitioner in No. 05–380, at 23. Although we review congressional factfinding under a deferential standard, we do not in the circumstances here place dispositive weight on Congress' findings. The Court retains an independent constitutional duty to review factual findings where constitutional rights are at stake. See *Crowell v. Benson*, 285 U.S. 22, 60 (1932) ("In cases brought to enforce constitutional rights, the judicial power of the United States necessarily extends to the independent determination of all questions, both of fact and law, necessary to the performance of that supreme function").

As respondents have noted, and the District Courts recognized, some recitations in the Act are factually incorrect. See *Nat. Abortion Federation*, 330 F. Supp. 2d, at 482, 488–491. Whether or not accurate at the time, some of the important findings have been superseded. Two examples suffice. Congress determined no medical schools provide instruction on the prohibited procedure. Congressional Findings (14)(B), in notes following 18 U. S. C. § 1531 (2000 ed., Supp. IV), p. 769. The testimony in the District Courts, however, demonstrated intact D&E is taught at medical schools. *Nat. Abortion Federation, supra*, at 490; *Planned Parenthood*, 320 F. Supp. 2d, at 1029. Congress also found there existed a medical consensus that the prohibited procedure is never medically necessary. Congressional Findings

(1), in notes following 18 U.S.C. § 1531 (2000 ed., Supp. IV), p. 767. The evidence presented in the District Courts contradicts that conclusion. See, e.g., *Carhart, supra*, at 1012–1015; *Nat. Abortion Federation, supra*, at 488–489; *Planned Parenthood, supra*, at 1025–1026. Uncritical deference to Congress' factual findings in these cases is inappropriate.

On the other hand, relying on the Court's opinion in *Stenberg*, respondents contend that an abortion regulation must contain a health exception "if 'substantial medical authority supports the proposition that banning a particular procedure could endanger women's health.'" Brief for Respondents in No. 05–380, p. 19 (quoting 530 U.S., at 938); see also Brief for Respondent Planned Parenthood et al. in No. 05–1382, at 12 (same). As illustrated by respondents' arguments and the decisions of the Courts of Appeals, *Stenberg* has been interpreted to leave no margin of error for legislatures to act in the face of medical uncertainty. *Carhart*, 413 F. 3d, at 796; *Planned Parenthood*, 435 F. 3d, at 1173; see also *Nat. Abortion Federation*, 437 F. 3d, at 296 (Walker, C. J., concurring) (explaining the standard under *Stenberg* "is a virtually insurmountable evidentiary hurdle").

A zero tolerance policy would strike down legitimate abortion regulations, like the present one, if some part of the medical community were disinclined to follow the proscription. This is too exacting a standard to impose on the legislative power, exercised in this instance under the Commerce Clause, to regulate the medical profession. Considerations of marginal safety, including the balance of risks, are within the legislative competence when the regulation is rational and in pursuit of legitimate ends. When standard medical options are available, mere convenience does not suffice to displace them; and if some procedures have different risks than others, it does not follow that the State is altogether barred from imposing reasonable regulations. The Act is not invalid on its face where there is uncertainty over whether the barred procedure is ever necessary to preserve a woman's health, given the availability of other abortion procedures that are considered to be safe alternatives.

The considerations we have discussed support our further determination that these facial attacks should not have been entertained in the first instance. In these circumstances the proper means to consider exceptions is by as-applied challenge. The Government has acknowledged that preenforcement, as-applied challenges to the Act can be maintained. Tr. of Oral Arg. in No. 05–380, pp. 21–23. This is the proper manner to protect the health of the woman if it can be shown that in discrete and well-defined instances a particular condition has or is likely to occur in which the procedure prohibited by the Act must be used. In an as-applied challenge the nature of the medical risk can be better quantified and balanced than in a facial attack.

The latitude given facial challenges in the First Amendment context is inapplicable here. Broad challenges of this type impose "a heavy burden" upon the parties maintaining the suit. *Rust v. Sullivan*, 500 U.S. 173, 183 (1991). What that burden consists of in the specific context of abortion statutes has been a subject of some question. Compare *Ohio v. Akron Center for Reproductive Health*, 497 U.S. 502, 514 (1990) ("[B]ecause appellees are making a facial challenge to a statute, they must show that no set of circumstances exists under which the Act would be valid" (internal quotation marks omitted)), with *Casey*, 505 U.S., at 895 (opinion of the Court) (indicating a spousal-notification statute would impose an undue burden "in a large fraction of the cases in which [it] is relevant" and holding the statutory provision facially invalid). See also *Janklow v. Planned Parenthood, Sioux Falls Clinic*, 517 U.S. 1174 (1996). We need not resolve that debate.

As the previous sections of this opinion explain, respondents have not demonstrated that the Act would be unconstitutional in a large fraction of relevant cases. *Casey, supra*, at 895 (opinion of the Court). We note that the statute here applies to all instances in which the doctor proposes to use the prohibited procedure, not merely those in which the woman suffers from medical complications. It is neither our obligation nor within our traditional institutional role to resolve questions of constitutionality with respect to each potential situation that might develop. "[I]t would indeed be undesirable for this Court to consider every conceivable situation which might possibly arise in the application of complex and comprehensive legislation." *United States v. Raines*, 362 U.S. 17, 21 (1960) (internal quotation marks omitted). For this reason, "[a]s-applied challenges are the basic building blocks of constitutional adjudication." Fallon, As–Applied and Facial Challenges and Third–Party Standing, 113 Harv. L. Rev. 1321, 1328 (2000).

The Act is open to a proper as-applied challenge in a discrete case.... No as-applied challenge need be brought if the prohibition in the Act threatens a woman's life because the Act already contains a life exception. 18 U.S.C. § 1531(a) (2000 ed., Supp. IV).

* * *

Respondents have not demonstrated that the Act, as a facial matter, is void for vagueness, or that it imposes an undue burden on a woman's right to abortion based on its overbreadth or lack of a health exception. For these reasons the judgments of the Courts of Appeals for the Eighth and Ninth Circuits are reversed.

It is so ordered.

■ Justice Thomas, with whom Justice Scalia joins, concurring.

I join the Court's opinion because it accurately applies current jurisprudence, including *Planned Parenthood of Southeastern Pa. v. Casey*, 505 U.S. 833 (1992). I write separately to reiterate my view that the Court's abortion jurisprudence, including *Casey* and *Roe v. Wade*, 410 U.S. 113 (1973), has no basis in the Constitution. See *Casey, supra*, at 979 (SCALIA, J., concurring in judgment in part and dissenting in part); *Stenberg v. Carhart*, 530 U.S. 914, 980–983 (2000) (THOMAS, J., dissenting)....

■ JUSTICE GINSBURG, with whom JUSTICE STEVENS, JUSTICE SOUTER, and JUSTICE BREYER join, dissenting.

In *Planned Parenthood of Southeastern Pa. v. Casey*, 505 U.S. 833, 844 (1992), the Court declared that "[l]iberty finds no refuge in a jurisprudence of doubt." There was, the Court said, an "imperative" need to dispel doubt as to "the meaning and reach" of the Court's 7–to–2 judgment, rendered nearly two decades earlier in *Roe v. Wade*, 410 U.S. 113 (1973). 505 U.S., at 845. Responsive to that need, the Court endeavored to provide secure guidance to "[s]tate and federal courts as well as legislatures throughout the Union," by defining "the rights of the woman and the legitimate authority of the State respecting the termination of pregnancies by abortion procedures." *Ibid.*

Taking care to speak plainly, the *Casey* Court restated and reaffirmed *Roe*'s essential holding. 505 U.S., at 845–846. First, the Court addressed the type of abortion regulation permissible prior to fetal viability. It recognized "the right of the woman to choose to have an abortion before viability and to obtain it without undue interference from the State." *Id.*, at 846. Second, the Court acknowledged "the State's power to restrict abortions *after fetal viability*, if the law contains exceptions for pregnancies which endanger the woman's life *or health*." *Ibid.* (emphasis added). Third, the Court confirmed that "the State has legitimate interests from the outset of the pregnancy in protecting *the health of the woman* and the life of the fetus that may become a child." *Ibid.* (emphasis added).

In reaffirming *Roe*, the *Casey* Court described the centrality of "the decision whether to bear . . . a child," *Eisenstadt v. Baird*, 405 U.S. 438, 453 (1972), to a woman's "dignity and autonomy," her "personhood" and "destiny," her "conception of . . . her place in society." 505 U.S., at 851–852. Of signal importance here, the *Casey* Court stated with unmistakable clarity that state regulation of access to abortion procedures, even after viability, must protect "the health of the woman." *Id.*, at 846.

Seven years ago, in *Stenberg v. Carhart*, 530 U.S. 914 (2000), the Court invalidated a Nebraska statute criminalizing the performance of a medical procedure that, in the political arena, has been dubbed "partial-birth abortion."[1] With fidelity to the *Roe–Casey* line of precedent, the Court held the Nebraska statute unconstitutional in part because it lacked the requisite protection for the preservation of a woman's health. *Stenberg*, 530 U.S., at 930; cf. *Ayotte v. Planned Parenthood of Northern New Eng.*, 546 U.S. 320, 327 (2006).

Today's decision is alarming. It refuses to take *Casey* and *Stenberg* seriously. It tolerates, indeed applauds, federal intervention to ban nationwide a procedure found necessary and proper in certain cases by the American College of Obstetricians and Gynecologists (ACOG). It blurs the line, firmly drawn in *Casey*, between previability and postviability abor-

---

1. The term "partial-birth abortion" is neither recognized in the medical literature nor used by physicians who perform second-trimester abortions. See *Planned Parenthood Federation of Am. v. Ashcroft*, 320 F. Supp. 2d 957, 964 (ND Cal. 2004), aff'd, 435 F. 3d 1163 (CA9 2006). The medical community refers to the procedure as either dilation & extraction (D&X) or intact dilation and evacuation (intact D&E). See, *e.g.*, *ante*, at 5; *Stenberg v. Carhart*, 530 U.S. 914, 927 (2000).

tions. And, for the first time since *Roe*, the Court blesses a prohibition with no exception safeguarding a woman's health.

I dissent from the Court's disposition. Retreating from prior rulings that abortion restrictions cannot be imposed absent an exception safeguarding a woman's health, the Court upholds an Act that surely would not survive under the close scrutiny that previously attended state-decreed limitations on a woman's reproductive choices.

As *Casey* comprehended, at stake in cases challenging abortion restrictions is a woman's "control over her [own] destiny." 505 U.S., at 869 (plurality opinion). See also *id.*, at 852 (majority opinion).[2] "There was a time, not so long ago," when women were "regarded as the center of home and family life, with attendant special responsibilities that precluded full and independent legal status under the Constitution." *Id.*, at 896–897 (quoting *Hoyt v. Florida*, 368 U.S. 57, 62 (1961)). Those views, this Court made clear in *Casey*, "are no longer consistent with our understanding of the family, the individual, or the Constitution." 505 U.S., at 897. Women, it is now acknowledged, have the talent, capacity, and right "to participate equally in the economic and social life of the Nation." *Id.*, at 856. Their ability to realize their full potential, the Court recognized, is intimately connected to "their ability to control their reproductive lives." *Ibid.* Thus, legal challenges to undue restrictions on abortion procedures do not seek to vindicate some generalized notion of privacy; rather, they center on a woman's autonomy to determine her life's course, and thus to enjoy equal citizenship stature. See, *e.g.*, Siegel, Reasoning from the Body: A Historical Perspective on Abortion Regulation and Questions of Equal Protection, 44 Stan. L. Rev. 261 (1992); Law, Rethinking Sex and the Constitution, 132 U. Pa. L. Rev. 955, 1002–1028 (1984).

> In keeping with this comprehension of the right to reproductive choice, the Court has consistently required that laws regulating abortion, at any stage of pregnancy and in all cases, safeguard a woman's health. See, *e.g.*, *Ayotte*, 546 U.S., at 327–328 ("'[O]ur precedents hold ... that a State may not restrict access to abortions that are necessary, in appropriate medical judgment, for preservation of the life or health of the [woman].'" (quoting *Casey*, 505 U.S., at 879 (plurality opinion))); *Stenberg*, 530 U.S., at 930 ("Since the law requires a health exception in order to validate even a postviability abortion regulation, it at a minimum requires the same in respect to previability regulation."). See also *Thornburgh v. American College of Obstetricians and Gynecologists*, 476 U.S. 747, 768–769 (1986) (invalidating a *post*-viability abortion regulation for "fail[ure] to require that [a pregnant woman's] health be the physician's paramount consideration").

2. *Planned Parenthood of Southeastern Pa. v. Casey*, 505 U.S. 833, 851–852 (1992), described more precisely than did *Roe v. Wade*, 410 U.S. 113 (1973), the impact of abortion restrictions on women's liberty. *Roe*'s focus was in considerable measure on "vindicat[ing] the right of the physician to administer medical treatment according to his professional judgment." *Id.*, at 165.

We have thus ruled that a State must avoid subjecting women to health risks not only where the pregnancy itself creates danger, but also where state regulation forces women to resort to less safe methods of abortion. See *Planned Parenthood of Central Mo. v. Danforth*, 428 U.S. 52, 79 (1976) (holding unconstitutional a ban on a method of abortion that "force[d] a woman ... to terminate her pregnancy by methods more dangerous to her health"). See also *Stenberg*, 530 U.S., at 931 ("'[Our cases] make clear that a risk to ... women's health is the same whether it happens to arise from regulating a particular method of abortion, or from barring abortion entirely.'"). Indeed, we have applied the rule that abortion regulation must safeguard a woman's health to the particular procedure at issue here—intact dilation and evacuation (D&E).[3]

In *Stenberg*, we expressly held that a statute banning intact D&E was unconstitutional in part because it lacked a health exception. 530 U.S., at 930, 937. We noted that there existed a "division of medical opinion" about the relative safety of intact D&E, *id.*, at 937, but we made clear that as long as "substantial medical authority supports the proposition that banning a particular abortion procedure could endanger women's health," a health exception is required, *id.*, at 938. We explained:

> "The word 'necessary' in *Casey*'s phrase 'necessary, in appropriate medical judgment, for the preservation of the life or health of the [pregnant woman],' cannot refer to an absolute necessity or to absolute proof. Medical treatments and procedures are often considered appropriate (or inappropriate) in light of estimated comparative health risks (and health benefits) in particular cases. Neither can that phrase require unanimity of medical opinion. Doctors often differ in their estimation of comparative health risks and appropriate treatment. And

---

3. (D&E) is the most frequently used abortion procedure during the second trimester of pregnancy; intact D&E is a variant of the D&E procedure. See *ante*, at 4, 6; *Stenberg*, 530 U.S., at 924, 927; *Planned Parenthood*, 320 F. Supp. 2d, at 966. Second-trimester abortions (*i.e.*, midpregnancy, previability abortions) are, however, relatively uncommon. Between 85 and 90 percent of all abortions performed in the United States take place during the first three months of pregnancy. See *ante*, at 3 . . . .

Adolescents and indigent women, research suggests, are more likely than other women to have difficulty obtaining an abortion during the first trimester of pregnancy. Minors may be unaware they are pregnant until relatively late in pregnancy, while poor women's financial constraints are an obstacle to timely receipt of services. See Finer, Frohwirth, Dauphinee, Singh, & Moore, Timing of Steps and Reasons for Delays in Obtaining Abortions in the United States, 74 Contra-

ception 334, 341–343 (2006). See also Drey et al., Risk Factors Associated with Presenting for Abortion in the Second Trimester, 107 Obstetrics & Gynecology 128, 133 (Jan. 2006) (concluding that women who have second-trimester abortions typically discover relatively late that they are pregnant). Severe fetal anomalies and health problems confronting the pregnant woman are also causes of second-trimester abortions; many such conditions cannot be diagnosed or do not develop until the second trimester. See, *e.g.*, Finer, *supra*, at 344; F. Cunningham et al., Williams Obstetrics 242, 290, 328–329, (22d ed. 2005); cf. Schechtman, Gray, Baty, & Rothman, Decision–Making for Termination of Pregnancies with Fetal Anomalies: Analysis of 53,000 Pregnancies, 99 Obstetrics & Gynecology 216, 220–221 (Feb. 2002) (nearly all women carrying fetuses with the most serious central nervous system anomalies chose to abort their pregnancies).

Casey's words 'appropriate medical judgment' must embody the judicial need to tolerate responsible differences of medical opinion...." *Id.*, at 937 (citation omitted).

Thus, we reasoned, division in medical opinion "at most means uncertainty, a factor that signals the presence of risk, not its absence." *Ibid.* "[A] statute that altogether forbids [intact D&E].... consequently must contain a health exception." *Id.*, at 938. See also *id.*, at 948 (O'Connor, J., concurring) ("Th[e] lack of a health exception necessarily renders the statute unconstitutional.").

In 2003, a few years after our ruling in *Stenberg*, Congress passed the Partial–Birth Abortion Ban Act—without an exception for women's health. See 18 U.S.C. § 1531(a) (2000 ed., Supp. IV)[4]. The congressional findings on which the Partial–Birth Abortion Ban Act rests do not withstand inspection, as the lower courts have determined and this Court is obliged to concede. *Ante*, at 35–36. See *National Abortion Federation v. Ashcroft*, 330 F. Supp. 2d 436, 482 (SDNY 2004) ("Congress did not ... carefully consider the evidence before arriving at its findings."), aff'd *sub nom. National Abortion Federation v. Gonzales*, 437 F. 3d 278 (CA2 2006). See also *Planned Parenthood Federation of Am. v. Ashcroft*, 320 F. Supp. 2d 957, 1019 (ND Cal. 2004) ("[N]one of the six physicians who testified before Congress had ever performed an intact D&E. Several did not provide abortion services at all; and one was not even an obgyn.... [T]he oral testimony before Congress was not only unbalanced, but intentionally polemic."), aff'd, 435 F. 3d 1163 (CA9 2006); *Carhart v. Ashcroft*, 331 F. Supp. 2d 805, 1011 (Neb. 2004) ("Congress arbitrarily relied upon the opinions of doctors who claimed to have no (or very little) recent and relevant experience with surgical abortions, and disregarded the views of doctors who had significant and relevant experience with those procedures."), aff'd, 413 F. 3d 791 (CA8 2005).

Many of the Act's recitations are incorrect. See *ante*, at 35–36. For example, Congress determined that no medical schools provide instruction on intact D&E. § 2(14)(B), 117 Stat. 1204, notes following 18 U.S.C. § 1531 (2000 ed., Supp. IV), p. 769, ¶ (14)(B) (Congressional Findings). But in fact, numerous leading medical schools teach the procedure. See *Planned Parenthood*, 320 F. Supp. 2d, at 1029; *National Abortion Federation*, 330 F. Supp. 2d, at 479. See also Brief for ACOG as *Amicus Curiae* 18 ("Among the schools that now teach the intact variant are Columbia, Cornell, Yale, New York University, Northwestern, University of Pittsburgh, University of Pennsylvania, University of Rochester, and University of Chicago.").

---

4. The Act's sponsors left no doubt that their intention was to nullify our ruling in *Stenberg*, 530 U.S. 914. See, *e.g.*, 149 Cong. Rec. 5731 (2003) (statement of Sen. Santorum) ("Why are we here? We are here because the Supreme Court defended the indefensible.... We have responded to the Supreme Court."). See also 148 Cong. Rec. 14273 (2002) (statement of Rep. Linder) (rejecting proposition that Congress has "no right to legislate a ban on this horrible practice because the Supreme Court says [it] cannot").

More important, Congress claimed there was a medical consensus that the banned procedure is never necessary. Congressional Findings (1), in notes following 18 U.S.C. § 1531 (2000 ed., Supp. IV), p. 767. But the evidence "very clearly demonstrate[d] the opposite." *Planned Parenthood*, 320 F. Supp. 2d, at 1025. See also *Carhart*, 331 F. Supp. 2d, at 1008–1009 ("[T]here was no evident consensus in the record that Congress compiled. There was, however, a substantial body of medical opinion presented to Congress in opposition. If anything . . . the congressional record establishes that there was a 'consensus' in favor of the banned procedure."); *National Abortion Federation*, 330 F. Supp. 2d, at 488 ("The congressional record itself undermines [Congress'] finding" that there is a medical consensus that intact D&E "is never medically necessary and should be prohibited." (internal quotation marks omitted)).

Similarly, Congress found that "[t]here is no credible medical evidence that partial-birth abortions are safe or are safer than other abortion procedures." Congressional Findings (14)(B), in notes following 18 U.S.C. § 1531 (2000 ed., Supp. IV), p. 769. But the congressional record includes letters from numerous individual physicians stating that pregnant women's health would be jeopardized under the Act, as well as statements from nine professional associations, including ACOG, the American Public Health Association, and the California Medical Association, attesting that intact D&E carries meaningful safety advantages over other methods. See *National Abortion Federation*, 330 F. Supp. 2d, at 490. See also *Planned Parenthood*, 320 F. Supp. 2d, at 1021 ("Congress in its findings . . . chose to disregard the statements by ACOG and other medical organizations."). No comparable medical groups supported the ban. In fact, "all of the government's own witnesses disagreed with many of the specific congressional findings." *Id.*, at 1024.

In contrast to Congress, the District Courts made findings after full trials at which all parties had the opportunity to present their best evidence. The courts had the benefit of "much more extensive medical and scientific evidence . . . concerning the safety and necessity of intact D&Es." *Planned Parenthood*, 320 F. Supp. 2d, at 1014; cf. *National Abortion Federation*, 330 F. Supp. 2d, at 482 (District Court "heard more evidence during its trial than Congress heard over the span of eight years.").

During the District Court trials, "numerous" "extraordinarily accomplished" and "very experienced" medical experts explained that, in certain circumstances and for certain women, intact D&E is safer than alternative procedures and necessary to protect women's health. *Carhart*, 331 F. Supp. 2d, at 1024–1027; see *Planned Parenthood*, 320 F. Supp. 2d, at 1001 ("[A]ll of the doctors who actually perform intact D&Es concluded that in their opinion and clinical judgment, intact D&Es remain the safest option for certain individual women under certain individual health circumstances, and are significantly safer for these women than other abortion techniques, and are thus medically necessary."); cf. *ante*, at 31 ("Respondents presented evidence that intact D&E may be the safest method of abortion, for reasons similar to those adduced in *Stenberg*.").

According to the expert testimony plaintiffs introduced, the safety advantages of intact D&E are marked for women with certain medical conditions, for example, uterine scarring, bleeding disorders, heart disease, or compromised immune systems. See *Carhart*, 331 F. Supp. 2d, at 924–929, 1026–1027; *National Abortion Federation*, 330 F. Supp. 2d, at 472–473; *Planned Parenthood*, 320 F. Supp. 2d, at 992–994, 1001. Further, plaintiffs' experts testified that intact D&E is significantly safer for women with certain pregnancy-related conditions, such as placenta previa and accreta, and for women carrying fetuses with certain abnormalities, such as severe hydrocephalus. See *Carhart*, 331 F. Supp. 2d, at 924, 1026–1027; *National Abortion Federation*, 330 F. Supp. 2d, at 473–474; *Planned Parenthood*, 320 F. Supp. 2d, at 992–994, 1001. See also *Stenberg*, 530 U.S., at 929; Brief for ACOG as *Amicus Curiae* 2, 13–16.

Intact D&E, plaintiffs' experts explained, provides safety benefits over D&E by dismemberment for several reasons: *First*, intact D&E minimizes the number of times a physician must insert instruments through the cervix and into the uterus, and thereby reduces the risk of trauma to, and perforation of, the cervix and uterus—the most serious complication associated with nonintact D&E. See *Carhart*, 331 F. Supp. 2d, at 923–928, 1025; *National Abortion Federation*, 330 F. Supp. 2d, at 471; *Planned Parenthood*, 320 F. Supp. 2d, at 982, 1001. *Second*, removing the fetus intact, instead of dismembering it *in utero*, decreases the likelihood that fetal tissue will be retained in the uterus, a condition that can cause infection, hemorrhage, and infertility. See *Carhart*, 331 F. Supp. 2d, at 923–928, 1025–1026; *National Abortion Federation*, 330 F. Supp. 2d, at 472; *Planned Parenthood*, 320 F. Supp. 2d, at 1001. *Third*, intact D&E diminishes the chances of exposing the patient's tissues to sharp bony fragments sometimes resulting from dismemberment of the fetus. See *Carhart*, 331 F. Supp. 2d, at 923–928, 1026; *National Abortion Federation*, 330 F. Supp. 2d, at 471; *Planned Parenthood*, 320 F. Supp. 2d, at 1001. *Fourth*, intact D&E takes less operating time than D&E by dismemberment, and thus may reduce bleeding, the risk of infection, and complications relating to anesthesia. See *Carhart*, 331 F. Supp. 2d, at 923–928, 1026; *National Abortion Federation*, 330 F. Supp. 2d, at 472; *Planned Parenthood*, 320 F. Supp. 2d, at 1001. See also *Stenberg*, 530 U.S., at 928–929, 932; Brief for ACOG as *Amicus Curiae* 2, 11–13.

Based on thoroughgoing review of the trial evidence and the congressional record, each of the District Courts to consider the issue rejected Congress' findings as unreasonable and not supported by the evidence. See *Carhart*, 331 F. Supp. 2d, at 1008–1027; *National Abortion Federation*, 330 F. Supp. 2d, at 482, 488–491; *Planned Parenthood*, 320 F. Supp. 2d, at 1032. The trial courts concluded, in contrast to Congress' findings, that "significant medical authority supports the proposition that in some circumstances, [intact D&E] is the safest procedure." *Id.*, at 1033 (quoting *Stenberg*, 530 U.S., at 932); accord *Carhart*, 331 F. Supp. 2d, at 1008–1009, 1017–1018; *National Abortion Federation*, 330 F. Supp. 2d, at 480–482;[5] cf.

---

5. Even the District Court for the Southern District of New York, which was more skeptical of the health benefits of intact D&E, see *ante*, at 32, recognized: "[T]he Gov-

Stenberg, 530 U.S., at 932 ("[T]he record shows that significant medical authority supports the proposition that in some circumstances, [intact D&E] would be the safest procedure.").

The District Courts' findings merit this Court's respect. See, *e.g.*, Fed. Rule Civ. Proc. 52(a); *Salve Regina College v. Russell*, 499 U.S. 225, 233 (1991). Today's opinion supplies no reason to reject those findings. Nevertheless, despite the District Courts' appraisal of the weight of the evidence, and in undisguised conflict with *Stenberg*, the Court asserts that the Partial–Birth Abortion Ban Act can survive "when . . . medical uncertainty persists." *Ante*, at 33. This assertion is bewildering. Not only does it defy the Court's longstanding precedent affirming the necessity of a health exception, with no carve-out for circumstances of medical uncertainty, see *supra*, at 4–5; it gives short shrift to the records before us, carefully canvassed by the District Courts. Those records indicate that "the majority of highly-qualified experts on the subject believe intact D&E to be the safest, most appropriate procedure under certain circumstances." *Planned Parenthood*, 320 F. Supp. 2d, at 1034. See *supra*, at 9–10.

The Court acknowledges some of this evidence, but insists that, because some witnesses disagreed with the ACOG and other experts' assessment of risk, the Act can stand. *Ante*, at 32–33, 37. In this insistence, the Court brushes under the rug the District Courts' well-supported findings that the physicians who testified that intact D&E is never necessary to preserve the health of a woman had slim authority for their opinions. They had no training for, or personal experience with, the intact D&E procedure, and many performed abortions only on rare occasions. See *Planned Parenthood*, 320 F. Supp. 2d, at 980; *Carhart*, 331 F. Supp. 2d, at 1025; cf. *National Abortion Federation*, 330 F. Supp. 2d, at 462–464. Even indulging the assumption that the Government witnesses were equally qualified to evaluate the relative risks of abortion procedures, their testimony could not erase the "significant medical authority support[ing] the proposition that in some circumstances, [intact D&E] would be the safest procedure." *Stenberg*, 530 U.S., at 932.[6]

ernment's own experts disagreed with almost all of Congress's factual findings"; a "significant body of medical opinion" holds that intact D&E has safety advantages over non-intact D&E; "[p]rofessional medical associations have also expressed their view that [intact D&E] may be the safest procedure for some women"; and "[t]he evidence indicates that the same disagreement among experts found by the Supreme Court in *Stenberg* existed throughout the time that Congress was considering the legislation, despite Congress's findings to the contrary." *National Abortion Federation*, 330 F. Supp. 2d, at 480–482.

6. The majority contends that "[i]f the intact D&E procedure is truly necessary in some circumstances, it appears likely an injection that kills the fetus is an alternative under the Act that allows the doctor to perform the procedure." *Ante*, at 34–35. But a "significant body of medical opinion believes that inducing fetal death by injection is almost always inappropriate to the preservation of the health of women undergoing abortion because it poses tangible risk and provides no benefit to the woman." *Carhart v. Ashcroft*, 331 F. Supp. 2d 805, 1028 (Neb. 2004) (internal quotation marks omitted), aff'd, 413 F. 3d 791 (CA8 2005). In some circumstances, injections are "absolutely [medically] contraindicated." 331 F. Supp.

The Court offers flimsy and transparent justifications for upholding a nationwide ban on intact D&E *sans* any exception to safeguard a women's health. Today's ruling, the Court declares, advances "a premise central to [*Casey*'s] conclusion"—*i.e.*, the Government's "legitimate and substantial interest in preserving and promoting fetal life." *Ante*, at 14. See also *ante*, at 15 ("[W]e must determine whether the Act furthers the legitimate interest of the Government in protecting the life of the fetus that may become a child."). But the Act scarcely furthers that interest: The law saves not a single fetus from destruction, for it targets only a *method* of performing abortion . . . . .

Delivery of an intact, albeit nonviable, fetus warrants special condemnation, the Court maintains, because a fetus that is not dismembered resembles an infant. *Ante,* at 28. But so, too, does a fetus delivered intact after it is terminated by injection a day or two before the surgical evacuation, *ante,* at 5, 34–35, or a fetus delivered through medical induction or cesarean, *ante,* at 9. Yet, the availability of those procedures—along with D&E by dismemberment—the Court says, saves the ban on intact D&E from a declaration of unconstitutionality. *Ante,* at 34–35. Never mind that the procedures deemed acceptable might put a woman's health at greater risk. . . .

Ultimately, the Court admits that "moral concerns" are at work, concerns that could yield prohibitions on any abortion. See *ante*, at 28 ("Congress could . . . conclude that the type of abortion proscribed by the Act requires specific regulation because it implicates additional ethical and moral concerns that justify a special prohibition."). Notably, the concerns expressed are untethered to any ground genuinely serving the Government's interest in preserving life. By allowing such concerns to carry the day and case, overriding fundamental rights, the Court dishonors our precedent. See, *e.g.*, *Casey*, 505 U.S., at 850 ("Some of us as individuals find abortion offensive to our most basic principles of morality, but that cannot control our decision. Our obligation is to define the liberty of all, not to mandate our own moral code."); *Lawrence v. Texas*, 539 U.S. 558, 571 (2003) (Though "[f]or many persons [objections to homosexual conduct] are not trivial concerns but profound and deep convictions accepted as ethical and moral principles," the power of the State may not be used "to enforce these views on the whole society through operation of the criminal law." (citing *Casey*, 505 U.S., at 850)).

Revealing in this regard, the Court invokes an antiabortion shibboleth for which it concededly has no reliable evidence: Women who have abortions come to regret their choices, and consequently suffer from "[s]evere

2d, at 1027. See also *id.*, at 907–912; *National Abortion Federation*, 330 F. Supp. 2d, at 474–475; *Planned Parenthood*, 320 F. Supp. 2d, at 995–997. The Court also identifies medical induction of labor as an alternative. See *ante*, at 9. That procedure, however, requires a hospital stay, *ibid.*, rendering it inaccessible to patients who lack financial re-

sources, and it too is considered less safe for many women, and impermissible for others. See *Carhart*, 331 F. Supp. 2d, at 940–949, 1017; *National Abortion Federation*, 330 F. Supp. 2d, at 468–470; *Planned Parenthood*, 320 F. Supp. 2d, at 961, n. 5, 992–994, 1000–1002.

depression and loss of esteem." *Ante*, at 29.[7] Because of women's fragile emotional state and because of the "bond of love the mother has for her child," the Court worries, doctors may withhold information about the nature of the intact D&E procedure. *Ante*, at 28–29. The solution the Court approves, then, is *not* to require doctors to inform women, accurately and adequately, of the different procedures and their attendant risks. Cf. *Casey*, 505 U.S., at 873 (plurality opinion) ("States are free to enact laws to provide a reasonable framework for a woman to make a decision that has such profound and lasting meaning."). Instead, the Court deprives women of the right to make an autonomous choice, even at the expense of their safety.[8]

7. The Court is surely correct that, for most women, abortion is a painfully difficult decision. See *ante*, at 28. But "neither the weight of the scientific evidence to date nor the observable reality of 33 years of legal abortion in the United States comports with the idea that having an abortion is any more dangerous to a woman's long-term mental health than delivering and parenting a child that she did not intend to have. . . ." Cohen, Abortion and Mental Health: Myths and Realities, 9 Guttmacher Policy Rev. 8 (2006); see generally Bazelon, Is There a Post–Abortion Syndrome? N.Y. Times Magazine, Jan. 21, 2007, p. 40. See also, *e.g.*, American Psychological Association, APA Briefing Paper on the Impact of Abortion (2005) (rejecting theory of a postabortion syndrome and stating that "[a]ccess to legal abortion to terminate an unwanted pregnancy is vital to safeguard both the physical and mental health of women"); Schmiege & Russo, Depression and Unwanted First Pregnancy: Longitudinal Cohort Study, 331 British Medical J. 1303 (2005) (finding no credible evidence that choosing to terminate an unwanted first pregnancy contributes to risk of subsequent depression); Gilchrist, Hannaford, Frank, & Kay, Termination of Pregnancy and Psychiatric Morbidity, 167 British J. of Psychiatry 243, 247–248 (1995) (finding, in a cohort of more than 13,000 women, that the rate of psychiatric disorder was no higher among women who terminated pregnancy than among those who carried pregnancy to term); Stodland, The Myth of the Abortion Trauma Syndrome, 268 JAMA 2078, 2079 (1992) ("Scientific studies indicate that legal abortion results in fewer deleterious sequelae for women compared with other possible outcomes of unwanted pregnancy. There is no evidence of an abortion trauma syndrome."); American Psychological Association, Council

Policy Manual: (N)(I)(3), Public Interest (1989) (declaring assertions about widespread severe negative psychological effects of abortion to be "without fact"). But see Cougle, Reardon, & Coleman, Generalized Anxiety Following Unintended Pregnancies Resolved Through Childbirth and Abortion: A Cohort Study of the 1995 National Survey of Family Growth, 19 J. Anxiety Disorders 137, 142 (2005) (advancing theory of a postabortion syndrome but acknowledging that "no causal relationship between pregnancy outcome and anxiety could be determined" from study); Reardon et al., Psychiatric Admissions of Low–Income Women following Abortion and Childbirth, 168 Canadian Medical Assn. J. 1253, 1255–1256 (May 13, 2003) (concluding that psychiatric admission rates were higher for women who had an abortion compared with women who delivered); cf. Major, Psychological Implications of Abortion—Highly Charged and Rife with Misleading Research, 168 Canadian Medical Assn. J. 1257, 1258 (May 13, 2003) (critiquing Reardon study for failing to control for a host of differences between women in the delivery and abortion samples).

8. Eliminating or reducing women's reproductive choices is manifestly *not* a means of protecting them. When safe abortion procedures cease to be an option, many women seek other means to end unwanted or coerced pregnancies. See, *e.g.*, World Health Organization, Unsafe Abortion: Global and Regional Estimates of the Incidence of Unsafe Abortion and Associated Mortality in 2000, pp. 3, 16 (4th ed. 2004) ("Restrictive legislation is associated with a high incidence of unsafe abortion" worldwide; unsafe abortion represents 13% of all "maternal" deaths); Henshaw, Unintended Pregnancy and Abortion: A Public Health Perspective, in A Clinician's

This way of thinking reflects ancient notions about women's place in the family and under the Constitution—ideas that have long since been discredited. Compare, *e.g.*, *Muller v. Oregon*, 208 U.S. 412, 422–423 (1908) ("protective" legislation imposing hours-of-work limitations on women only held permissible in view of women's "physical structure and a proper discharge of her maternal funct[ion]"); *Bradwell v. State*, 16 Wall. 130, 141 (1873) (Bradley, J., concurring) ("Man is, or should be, woman's protector and defender. The natural and proper timidity and delicacy which belongs to the female sex evidently unfits it for many of the occupations of civil life. . . . The paramount destiny and mission of woman are to fulfil[l] the noble and benign offices of wife and mother."), with *United States v. Virginia*, 518 U.S. 515, 533, 542, n. 12 (1996) (State may not rely on "overbroad generalizations" about the "talents, capacities, or preferences" of women; "[s]uch judgments have . . . impeded . . . women's progress toward full citizenship stature throughout our Nation's history"); *Califano v. Goldfarb*, 430 U.S. 199, 207 (1977) (gender-based Social Security classification rejected because it rested on "archaic and overbroad generalizations" "such as assumptions as to [women's] dependency" (internal quotation marks omitted)).

> Though today's majority may regard women's feelings on the matter as "self-evident," *ante*, at 29, this Court has repeatedly confirmed that "[t]he destiny of the woman must be shaped . . . on her own conception of her spiritual imperatives and her place in society." *Casey*, 505 U.S., at 852. See also *id.*, at 877 (plurality opinion) ("[M]eans chosen by the State to further the interest in potential life must be calculated to inform the woman's free choice, not hinder it."); *supra*, at 3–4.

In cases on a "woman's liberty to determine whether to [continue] her pregnancy," this Court has identified viability as a critical consideration. See *Casey*, 505 U.S., at 869–870 (plurality opinion). "[T]here is no line [more workable] than viability," the Court explained in *Casey*, for viability is "the time at which there is a realistic possibility of maintaining and nourishing a life outside the womb, so that the independent existence of the second life can in reason and all fairness be the object of state protection that now overrides the rights of the woman. . . . In some broad sense it might be said that a woman who fails to act before viability has consented to the State's intervention on behalf of the developing child." *Id.*, at 870.

Today, the Court blurs that line, maintaining that "[t]he Act [legitimately] appl[ies] both previability and postviability because . . . a fetus is a living organism while within the womb, whether or not it is viable outside the womb." *Ante*, at 17. Instead of drawing the line at viability, the Court refers to Congress' purpose to differentiate "abortion and infanticide"

Guide to Medical and Surgical Abortion 11, 19 (M. Paul, E. Lichtenberg, L. Borgatta, D. Grimes, & P. Stubblefield eds. 1999) ("Before legalization, large numbers of women in the United States died from unsafe abortions."); H. Boonstra, R. Gold, C. Richards, & L. Finer, Abortion in Women's Lives 13, and fig. 2.2 (2006) ("as late as 1965, illegal abortion still accounted for an estimated . . . 17% of all officially reported pregnancy-related deaths"; "[d]eaths from abortion declined dramatically after legalization").

based not on whether a fetus can survive outside the womb, but on where a fetus is anatomically located when a particular medical procedure is performed. See *ante*, at 28 (quoting Congressional Findings (14)(G), in notes following 18 U.S.C. § 1531 (2000 ed., Supp. IV), p. 769).

One wonders how long a line that saves no fetus from destruction will hold in face of the Court's "moral concerns." See *supra*, at 15; cf. *ante*, at 16 (noting that "[i]n this litigation" the Attorney General "does not dispute that the Act would impose an undue burden if it covered standard D&E"). The Court's hostility to the right *Roe* and *Casey* secured is not concealed. Throughout, the opinion refers to obstetrician-gynecologists and surgeons who perform abortions not by the titles of their medical specialties, but by the pejorative label "abortion doctor." *Ante*, at 14, 24, 25, 31, 33. A fetus is described as an "unborn child," and as a "baby," *ante*, at 3, 8; second-trimester, previability abortions are referred to as "late-term," *ante*, at 26; and the reasoned medical judgments of highly trained doctors are dismissed as "preferences" motivated by "mere convenience," *ante*, at 3, 37. Instead of the heightened scrutiny we have previously applied, the Court determines that a "rational" ground is enough to uphold the Act, *ante*, at 28, 37. And, most troubling, *Casey*'s principles, confirming the continuing vitality of "the essential holding of *Roe*," are merely "assume[d]" for the moment, *ante*, at 15, 31, rather than "retained" or "reaffirmed," *Casey*, 505 U.S., at 846.

The Court further confuses our jurisprudence when it declares that "facial attacks" are not permissible in "these circumstances," *i.e.*, where medical uncertainty exists. *Ante*, at 37; see *ibid*. ("In an as-applied challenge the nature of the medical risk can be better quantified and balanced than in a facial attack."). This holding is perplexing given that, in materially identical circumstances we held that a statute lacking a health exception was unconstitutional on its face. *Stenberg*, 530 U.S., at 930; see *id*., at 937 (in facial challenge, law held unconstitutional because "significant body of medical opinion believes [the] procedure may bring with it greater safety for *some patients*" (emphasis added)). . . .

Without attempting to distinguish *Stenberg* and earlier decisions, the majority asserts that the Act survives review because respondents have not shown that the ban on intact D&E would be unconstitutional "in a large fraction of relevant cases." *Ante*, at 38 (citing *Casey*, 505 U.S., at 895). But *Casey* makes clear that, in determining whether any restriction poses an undue burden on a "large fraction" of women, the relevant class is *not* "all women," nor "all pregnant women," nor even all women "seeking abortions." 505 U.S., at 895. Rather, a provision restricting access to abortion, "must be judged by reference to those [women] for whom it is an actual rather than an irrelevant restriction," *ibid*. Thus the absence of a health exception burdens *all* women for whom it is relevant—women who, in the judgment of their doctors, require an intact D&E because other procedures would place their health at risk.[9] Cf. *Stenberg*, 530 U.S., at 934 (accepting

---

9. Eliminating or reducing women's reproductive choices is manifestly *not* a means of protecting them. When safe abortion procedures cease to be an option, many women

the "relative rarity" of medically indicated intact D&Es as true but not "highly relevant"—for "the health exception question is whether protecting women's health requires an exception for those infrequent occasions"); *Ayotte*, 546 U.S., at 328 (facial challenge entertained where "[i]n some very small percentage of cases . . . women . . . need immediate abortions to avert serious, and often irreversible damage to their health"). It makes no sense to conclude that this facial challenge fails because respondents have not shown that a health exception is necessary for a large fraction of second-trimester abortions, including those for which a health exception is unnecessary: The very purpose of a health *exception* is to protect women in *exceptional* cases.

If there is anything at all redemptive to be said of today's opinion, it is that the Court is not willing to foreclose entirely a constitutional challenge to the Act. "The Act is open," the Court states, "to a proper as-applied challenge in a discrete case." *Ante,* at 38; see *ante,* at 37 ("The Government has acknowledged that preenforcement, as-applied challenges to the Act can be maintained."). But the Court offers no clue on what a "proper" lawsuit might look like. See *ante,* at 37–38. Nor does the Court explain why the injunctions ordered by the District Courts should not remain in place, trimmed only to exclude instances in which another procedure would safeguard a woman's health at least equally well. Surely the Court cannot mean that no suit may be brought until a woman's health is immediately jeopardized by the ban on intact D&E. A woman "suffer[ing] from medical complications," *ante,* at 38, needs access to the medical procedure at once and cannot wait for the judicial process to unfold. See *Ayotte*, 546 U.S., at 328.

The Court appears, then, to contemplate another lawsuit by the initiators of the instant actions. In such a second round, the Court suggests, the challengers could succeed upon demonstrating that "in discrete and well-defined instances a particular condition has or is likely to occur in which the procedure prohibited by the Act must be used." *Ante,* at 37. One may anticipate that such a preenforcement challenge will be mounted swiftly, to ward off serious, sometimes irremediable harm, to women whose health would be endangered by the intact D&E prohibition.

---

seek other means to end unwanted or coerced pregnancies. See, *e.g.*, World Health Organization, Unsafe Abortion: Global and Regional Estimates of the Incidence of Unsafe Abortion and Associated Mortality in 2000, pp. 3, 16 (4th ed. 2004) ("Restrictive legislation is associated with a high incidence of unsafe abortion" worldwide; unsafe abortion represents 13% of all "maternal" deaths); Henshaw, Unintended Pregnancy and Abortion: A Public Health Perspective, in A Clinician's Guide to Medical and Surgical Abortion 11, 19 (M. Paul, E. Lichtenberg, L. Borgatta, D. Grimes, & P. Stubblefield eds. 1999) ("Before legalization, large numbers of women in the United States died from unsafe abortions."); H. Boonstra, R. Gold, C. Richards, & L. Finer, Abortion in Women's Lives 13, and fig. 2.2 (2006) ("as late as 1965, illegal abortion still accounted for an estimated . . . 17% of all officially reported pregnancy-related deaths"; "[d]eaths from abortion declined dramatically after legalization").

The Court envisions that in an as-applied challenge, "the nature of the medical risk can be better quantified and balanced." *Ibid*. But it should not escape notice that the record already includes hundreds and hundreds of pages of testimony identifying "discrete and well-defined instances" in which recourse to an intact D&E would better protect the health of women with particular conditions. See *supra*, at 10–11. Record evidence also documents that medical exigencies, unpredictable in advance, may indicate to a well-trained doctor that intact D&E is the safest procedure. See *ibid*. In light of this evidence, our unanimous decision just one year ago in *Ayotte* counsels against reversal. See 546 U.S., at 331 (remanding for reconsideration of the remedy for the absence of a health exception, suggesting that an injunction prohibiting unconstitutional applications might suffice).

The Court's allowance only of an "as-applied challenge in a discrete case," *ante*, at 38—jeopardizes women's health and places doctors in an untenable position. Even if courts were able to carve-out exceptions through piecemeal litigation for "discrete and well-defined instances," *ante*, at 37, women whose circumstances have not been anticipated by prior litigation could well be left unprotected. In treating those women, physicians would risk criminal prosecution, conviction, and imprisonment if they exercise their best judgment as to the safest medical procedure for their patients. The Court is thus gravely mistaken to conclude that narrow as-applied challenges are "the proper manner to protect the health of the woman." Cf. *ibid*.

IV

As the Court wrote in *Casey*, "overruling *Roe*'s central holding would not only reach an unjustifiable result under principles of *stare decisis*, but would seriously weaken the Court's capacity to exercise the judicial power and to function as the Supreme Court of a Nation dedicated to the rule of law." 505 U.S., at 865. "[T]he very concept of the rule of law underlying our own Constitution requires such continuity over time that a respect for precedent is, by definition, indispensable." *Id*., at 854. See also *id*., at 867 ("[T]o overrule under fire in the absence of the most compelling reason to reexamine a watershed decision would subvert the Court's legitimacy beyond any serious question.").

Though today's opinion does not go so far as to discard *Roe* or *Casey*, the Court, differently composed than it was when we last considered a restrictive abortion regulation, is hardly faithful to our earlier invocations of "the rule of law" and the "principles of *stare decisis*." Congress imposed a ban despite our clear prior holdings that the State cannot proscribe an abortion procedure when its use is necessary to protect a woman's health. See *supra*, at 7, n. 4. Although Congress' findings could not withstand the crucible of trial, the Court defers to the legislative override of our Constitution-based rulings. See *supra*, at 7–9. A decision so at odds with our jurisprudence should not have staying power.

In sum, the notion that the Partial–Birth Abortion Ban Act furthers any legitimate governmental interest is, quite simply, irrational. The

Court's defense of the statute provides no saving explanation. In candor, the Act, and the Court's defense of it, cannot be understood as anything other than an effort to chip away at a right declared again and again by this Court—and with increasing comprehension of its centrality to women's lives. See *supra*, at 3, n. 2; *supra*, at 7, n. 4. When "a statute burdens constitutional rights and all that can be said on its behalf is that it is the vehicle that legislators have chosen for expressing their hostility to those rights, the burden is undue." *Stenberg*, 530 U.S., at 952 (Ginsburg, J., concurring) (quoting *Hope Clinic v. Ryan*, 195 F. 3d 857, 881 (CA7 1999) (Posner, C. J., dissenting)).

* * *

For the reasons stated, I dissent from the Court's disposition and would affirm the judgments before us for review.

Lawrence v. Texas

Supreme Court of the United States, 2003.
539 U.S. 558, 123 S.Ct. 2472, 156 L.Ed.2d 508.

■ Justice Kennedy delivered the opinion of the Court.

Liberty protects the person from unwarranted government intrusions into a dwelling or other private places. In our tradition the State is not omnipresent in the home. And there are other spheres of our lives and existence, outside the home, where the State should not be a dominant presence. Freedom extends beyond spatial bounds. Liberty presumes an autonomy of self that includes freedom of thought, belief, expression, and certain intimate conduct. The instant case involves liberty of the person both in its spatial and more transcendent dimensions.

I

The question before the Court is the validity of a Texas statute making it a crime for two persons of the same sex to engage in certain intimate sexual conduct.

In Houston, Texas, officers of the Harris County Police Department were dispatched to a private residence in response to a reported weapons disturbance. They entered an apartment where one of the petitioners, John Geddes Lawrence, resided. The right of the police to enter does not seem to have been questioned. The officers observed Lawrence and another man, Tyron Garner, engaging in a sexual act. The two petitioners were arrested, held in custody over night, and charged and convicted before a Justice of the Peace.

The complaints described their crime as "deviate sexual intercourse, namely anal sex, with a member of the same sex (man)." App. to Pet. for Cert. 127a, 139a. The applicable state law is Tex. Penal Code Ann. § 21.06(a) (2003). It provides: "A person commits an offense if he engages in deviate sexual intercourse with another individual of the same sex." The statute defines "[d]eviate sexual intercourse" as follows:

"(A) any contact between any part of the genitals of one person and the mouth or anus of another person; or

"(B) the penetration of the genitals or the anus of another person with an object." § 21.01(1).

The petitioners exercised their right to a trial *de novo* in Harris County Criminal Court. They challenged the statute as a violation of the Equal Protection Clause of the Fourteenth Amendment and of a like provision of the Texas Constitution. Tex. Const., Art. 1, § 3a. Those contentions were rejected. The petitioners, having entered a plea of *nolo contendere,* were each fined $200 and assessed court costs of $141.25. App. to Pet. for Cert. 107a–110a.

The Court of Appeals for the Texas Fourteenth District considered the petitioners' federal constitutional arguments under both the Equal Protection and Due Process Clauses of the Fourteenth Amendment. After hearing the case en banc the court, in a divided opinion, rejected the constitutional arguments and affirmed the convictions. 41 S.W.3d 349 (Tex.App.2001). The majority opinion indicates that the Court of Appeals considered our decision in *Bowers v. Hardwick,* 478 U.S. 186, 106 S.Ct. 2841, 92 L.Ed.2d 140 (1986), to be controlling on the federal due process aspect of the case. *Bowers* then being authoritative, this was proper.

We granted certiorari, 537 U.S. 1044, 123 S.Ct. 661, 154 L.Ed.2d 514 (2002), to consider three questions:

"1. Whether Petitioners' criminal convictions under the Texas 'Homosexual Conduct' law—which criminalizes sexual intimacy by same sex couples, but not identical behavior by different-sex couples—violate the Fourteenth Amendment guarantee of equal protection of laws?

"2. Whether Petitioners' criminal convictions for adult consensual sexual intimacy in the home violate their vital interests in liberty and privacy protected by the Due Process Clause of the Fourteenth Amendment?

"3. Whether *Bowers v. Hardwick,* 478 U.S. 186, 106 S.Ct. 2841, 92 L.Ed.2d 140 (1986), should be overruled?" Pet. for Cert. i.

The petitioners were adults at the time of the alleged offense. Their conduct was in private and consensual.

II

We conclude the case should be resolved by determining whether the petitioners were free as adults to engage in the private conduct in the exercise of their liberty under the Due Process Clause of the Fourteenth Amendment to the Constitution. For this inquiry we deem it necessary to reconsider the Court's holding in *Bowers.*

There are broad statements of the substantive reach of liberty under the Due Process Clause in earlier cases, including *Pierce v. Society of Sisters,* 268 U.S. 510, 45 S.Ct. 571, 69 L.Ed. 1070 (1925), and *Meyer v. Nebraska,* 262 U.S. 390, 43 S.Ct. 625, 67 L.Ed. 1042 (1923); but the most pertinent beginning point is our decision in *Griswold v. Connecticut,* 381 U.S. 479, 85 S.Ct. 1678, 14 L.Ed.2d 510 (1965).

In *Griswold* the Court invalidated a state law prohibiting the use of drugs or devices of contraception and counseling or aiding and abetting the use of contraceptives. The Court described the protected interest as a right to privacy and placed emphasis on the marriage relation and the protected space of the marital bedroom. *Id.,* at 485, 85 S.Ct. 1678.

After *Griswold* it was established that the right to make certain decisions regarding sexual conduct extends beyond the marital relationship. In *Eisenstadt v. Baird,* 405 U.S. 438, 92 S.Ct. 1029, 31 L.Ed.2d 349 (1972), the Court invalidated a law prohibiting the distribution of contraceptives to unmarried persons. The case was decided under the Equal Protection Clause, *id.,* at 454, 92 S.Ct. 1029; but with respect to unmarried persons, the Court went on to state the fundamental proposition that the law impaired the exercise of their personal rights, *ibid.* It quoted from the statement of the Court of Appeals finding the law to be in conflict with fundamental human rights, and it followed with this statement of its own:

> "It is true that in *Griswold* the right of privacy in question inhered in the marital relationship.... If the right of privacy means anything, it is the right of the *individual,* married or single, to be free from unwarranted governmental intrusion into matters so fundamentally affecting a person as the decision whether to bear or beget a child." *Id.,* at 453, 92 S.Ct. 1029.

The opinions in *Griswold* and *Eisenstadt* were part of the background for the decision in *Roe v. Wade,* 410 U.S. 113, 93 S.Ct. 705, 35 L.Ed.2d 147 (1973). As is well known, the case involved a challenge to the Texas law prohibiting abortions, but the laws of other States were affected as well. Although the Court held the woman's rights were not absolute, her right to elect an abortion did have real and substantial protection as an exercise of her liberty under the Due Process Clause. The Court cited cases that protect spatial freedom and cases that go well beyond it. *Roe* recognized the right of a woman to make certain fundamental decisions affecting her destiny and confirmed once more that the protection of liberty under the Due Process Clause has a substantive dimension of fundamental significance in defining the rights of the person.

In *Carey v. Population Services Int'l,* 431 U.S. 678, 97 S.Ct. 2010, 52 L.Ed.2d 675 (1977), the Court confronted a New York law forbidding sale or distribution of contraceptive devices to persons under 16 years of age. Although there was no single opinion for the Court, the law was invalidated. Both *Eisenstadt* and *Carey,* as well as the holding and rationale in *Roe,* confirmed that the reasoning of *Griswold* could not be confined to the protection of rights of married adults. This was the state of the law with respect to some of the most relevant cases when the Court considered *Bowers v. Hardwick.*

The facts in *Bowers* had some similarities to the instant case. A police officer, whose right to enter seems not to have been in question, observed

Hardwick, in his own bedroom, engaging in intimate sexual conduct with another adult male. The conduct was in violation of a Georgia statute making it a criminal offense to engage in sodomy. One difference between the two cases is that the Georgia statute prohibited the conduct whether or not the participants were of the same sex, while the Texas statute, as we have seen, applies only to participants of the same sex. Hardwick was not prosecuted, but he brought an action in federal court to declare the state statute invalid. He alleged he was a practicing homosexual and that the criminal prohibition violated rights guaranteed to him by the Constitution. The Court, in an opinion by Justice White, sustained the Georgia law. Chief Justice Burger and Justice Powell joined the opinion of the Court and filed separate, concurring opinions. Four Justices dissented. 478 U.S., at 199, 106 S.Ct. 2841 (opinion of Blackmun, J., joined by Brennan, Marshall, and STEVENS, JJ.); *id.*, at 214, 106 S.Ct. 2841 (opinion of STEVENS, J., joined by Brennan and Marshall, JJ.).

The Court began its substantive discussion in *Bowers* as follows: "The issue presented is whether the Federal Constitution confers a fundamental right upon homosexuals to engage in sodomy and hence invalidates the laws of the many States that still make such conduct illegal and have done so for a very long time." *Id.*, at 190, 106 S.Ct. 2841. That statement, we now conclude, discloses the Court's own failure to appreciate the extent of the liberty at stake. To say that the issue in *Bowers* was simply the right to engage in certain sexual conduct demeans the claim the individual put forward, just as it would demean a married couple were it to be said marriage is simply about the right to have sexual intercourse. The laws involved in *Bowers* and here are, to be sure, statutes that purport to do no more than prohibit a particular sexual act. Their penalties and purposes, though, have more far-reaching consequences, touching upon the most private human conduct, sexual behavior, and in the most private of places, the home. The statutes do seek to control a personal relationship that, whether or not entitled to formal recognition in the law, is within the liberty of persons to choose without being punished as criminals.

This, as a general rule, should counsel against attempts by the State, or a court, to define the meaning of the relationship or to set its boundaries absent injury to a person or abuse of an institution the law protects. It suffices for us to acknowledge that adults may choose to enter upon this relationship in the confines of their homes and their own private lives and still retain their dignity as free persons. When sexuality finds overt expression in intimate conduct with another person, the conduct can be but one element in a personal bond that is more enduring. The liberty protected by the Constitution allows homosexual persons the right to make this choice.

Having misapprehended the claim of liberty there presented to it, and thus stating the claim to be whether there is a fundamental right to engage in consensual sodomy, the *Bowers* Court said: "Proscriptions against that conduct have ancient roots." *Id.*, at 192, 106 S.Ct. 2841. In academic writings, and in many of the scholarly *amicus* briefs filed to assist the Court in this case, there are fundamental criticisms of the historical premises relied upon by the majority and concurring opinions in *Bowers*. Brief for Cato Institute as *Amicus Curiae* 16–17; Brief for American Civil Liberties Union et al. as *Amici Curiae* 15–21; Brief for Professors of History et al. as *Amici Curiae* 3–10. We need not enter this debate in the attempt to reach a definitive historical judgment, but the following considerations counsel against adopting the definitive conclusions upon which *Bowers* placed such reliance.

At the outset it should be noted that there is no longstanding history in this country of laws directed at homosexual conduct as a distinct matter. Beginning in colonial times there were prohibitions of sodomy derived from the English criminal laws passed in the first instance by the Reformation Parliament of 1533. The English prohibition was understood to include relations between men and women as well as relations between men and men. See, *e.g., King v. Wiseman,* 92 Eng. Rep. 774, 775 (K.B.1718) (interpreting "mankind" in Act of 1533 as including women and girls). Nineteenth-century commentators similarly read American sodomy, buggery, and crime-against-nature statutes as criminalizing certain relations between men and women and between men and men. See, *e.g.,* 2 J. Bishop, Criminal Law § 1028 (1858); . . . J. May, The Law of Crimes § 203 (2d ed. 1893). The absence of legal prohibitions focusing on homosexual conduct may be explained in part by noting that according to some scholars the concept of the homosexual as a distinct category of person did not emerge until the late 19th century. See, e.g., J. Katz, The Invention of Heterosexuality 10 (1995); J. D'Emilio & E. Freedman, Intimate Matters: A History of Sexuality in America 121 (2d ed. 1997) ("The modern terms *homosexuality* and *heterosexuality* do not apply to an era that had not yet articulated these distinctions"). Thus early American sodomy laws were not directed at homosexuals as such but instead sought to prohibit nonprocreative sexual activity more generally. This does not suggest approval of homosexual conduct. It does tend to show that this particular form of conduct was not thought of as a separate category from like conduct between heterosexual persons.

Laws prohibiting sodomy do not seem to have been enforced against consenting adults acting in private. A substantial number of sodomy prosecutions and convictions for which there are surviving records were for predatory acts against those who could not or did not consent, as in the case of a minor or the victim of an assault. As to these, one purpose for the prohibitions was to ensure there would be no lack of coverage if a predator committed a sexual assault that did not constitute rape as defined by the criminal law. Thus the model sodomy indictments presented in a 19th-century treatise, see 2 Chitty, *supra,* at 49, addressed the predatory acts of an adult man against a minor girl or minor boy. Instead of targeting relations between consenting adults in private, 19th-century sodomy prosecutions typically involved relations between men and minor girls or minor boys, relations between adults involving force, relations between adults implicating disparity in status, or relations between men and animals.

To the extent that there were any prosecutions for the acts in question, 19th-century evidence rules imposed a burden that would make a conviction more difficult to obtain even taking into account the problems always inherent in prosecuting consensual acts committed in private. Under then-prevailing standards, a man could not be convicted of sodomy based upon testimony of a consenting partner, because the partner was considered an accomplice. A partner's testimony, however, was admissible if he or she had not consented to the act or was a minor, and therefore incapable of consent. See, *e.g.,* F. Wharton, Criminal Law 443 (2d ed. 1852); 1 F. Wharton, Criminal Law 512 (8th ed. 1880). The rule may explain in part the infrequency of these prosecutions. In all events that infrequency makes it difficult to say that society approved of a rigorous and systematic punishment of the consensual acts committed in private and by adults. The longstanding criminal prohibition of homosexual sodomy upon which the *Bowers* decision placed such reliance is as consistent with a general condemnation of nonprocreative sex as it is with an established tradition of prosecuting acts because of their homosexual character.

The policy of punishing consenting adults for private acts was not much discussed in the early legal literature. We can infer that one reason for this was the very private nature of the conduct. Despite the absence of prosecutions, there may have been periods in which there was public criticism of homosexuals as such and an insistence that the criminal laws be enforced to discourage their practices. But far from possessing "ancient roots," *Bowers,* 478 U.S., at 192, 106 S.Ct. 2841, American laws targeting same sex couples did not develop until the last third of the 20th century. The reported decisions concerning the prosecution of consensual, homosexual sodomy between adults for the years 1880–1995 are not always clear in the details, but a significant number involved conduct in a public place. See Brief for American Civil Liberties Union et al. as *Amici Curiae* 14–15, and n. 18.

It was not until the 1970's that any State singled out same sex relations for criminal prosecution, and only nine States have done so. [Cases and statutes omitted.]

In summary, the historical grounds relied upon in *Bowers* are more complex than the majority opinion and the concurring opinion by Chief Justice Burger indicate. Their historical premises are not without doubt and, at the very least, are overstated.

It must be acknowledged, of course, that the Court in *Bowers* was making the broader point that for centuries there have been powerful voices to condemn homosexual conduct as immoral. The condemnation has been shaped by religious beliefs, conceptions of right and acceptable behavior, and respect for the traditional family. For many persons these are not trivial concerns but profound and deep convictions accepted as ethical and moral principles to which they aspire and which thus determine the course of their lives. These considerations do not answer the question before us, however. The issue is whether the majority may use the power of the State to enforce these views on the whole society through operation of the criminal law. "Our obligation is to define the liberty of all, not to mandate our own moral code." *Planned Parenthood of Southeastern Pa. v. Casey,* 505 U.S. 833, 850, 112 S.Ct. 2791, 120 L.Ed.2d 674 (1992).

Chief Justice Burger joined the opinion for the Court in *Bowers* and further explained his views as follows: "Decisions of individuals relating to homosexual conduct have been subject to state intervention throughout the history of Western civilization. Condemnation of those practices is firmly rooted in Judeao–Christian moral and ethical standards." 478 U.S., at 196, 106 S.Ct. 2841. As with Justice White's assumptions about history, scholarship casts some doubt on the sweeping nature of the statement by Chief Justice Burger as it pertains to private homosexual conduct between consenting adults. See, *e.g.,* Eskridge, Hardwick and Historiography, 1999 U. Ill. L.Rev. 631, 656. In all events we think that our laws and traditions in the past half century are of most relevance here. These references show an emerging awareness that liberty gives substantial protection to adult persons in deciding how to conduct their private lives in matters pertaining to sex. "[H]istory and tradition are the starting point but not in all cases the ending point of the substantive due process inquiry." *County of Sacramento v. Lewis,* 523 U.S. 833, 857, 118 S.Ct. 1708, 140 L.Ed.2d 1043 (1998) (KENNEDY, J., concurring).

This emerging recognition should have been apparent when *Bowers* was decided. In 1955 the American Law Institute promulgated the Model Penal Code and made clear that it did not recommend or provide for "criminal penalties for consensual sexual relations conducted in private." ALI, Model Penal Code § 213.2, Comment 2, p. 372 (1980). It justified its decision on three grounds: (1) The prohibitions undermined respect for the law by penalizing conduct many people engaged in; (2) the statutes regulated private conduct not harmful to others; and (3) the laws were arbitrarily enforced and thus invited the danger of blackmail. ALI, Model Penal Code, Commentary 277–280 (Tent. Draft No. 4, 1955). In 1961 Illinois changed its laws to conform to the Model Penal Code. Other States soon followed. Brief for Cato Institute as *Amicus Curiae* 15–16.

In *Bowers* the Court referred to the fact that before 1961 all 50 States had outlawed sodomy, and that at the time of the Court's decision 24 States and the District of Columbia had sodomy laws. 478 U.S., at 192–193, 106 S.Ct. 2841. Justice Powell pointed out that these prohibitions often were being ignored, however. Georgia, for instance, had not sought to enforce its law for decades. *Id.,* at 197–198, n. 2, 106 S.Ct. 2841 ("The history of nonenforcement suggests the moribund character today of laws criminalizing this type of private, consensual conduct").

The sweeping references by Chief Justice Burger to the history of Western civilization and to Judeo–Christian moral and ethical standards did not take account of other authorities pointing in an opposite direction. A committee advising the British Parliament recommended in 1957 repeal of laws punishing homosexual conduct. The Wolfenden Report: Report of the Committee on Homosexual Offenses and Prostitution (1963). Parliament enacted the substance of those recommendations 10 years later. Sexual Offences Act 1967, § 1.

Of even more importance, almost five years before *Bowers* was decided the European Court of Human Rights considered a case with parallels to *Bowers* and to today's case. An adult male resident in Northern Ireland alleged he was a practicing homosexual who desired to engage in consensual homosexual conduct. The laws of Northern Ireland forbade him that right. He alleged that he had been questioned, his home had been searched, and he feared criminal prosecution. The court held that the laws proscribing the conduct were invalid under the European Convention on Human Rights. *Dudgeon v. United Kingdom,* 45 Eur. Ct. H.R. (1981). Authoritative in all countries that are members of the Council of Europe (21 nations then, 45 nations now), the decision is at odds with the premise in *Bowers* that the claim put forward was insubstantial in our Western civilization.

In our own constitutional system the deficiencies in *Bowers* became even more apparent in the years following its announcement. The 25 States with laws prohibiting the relevant conduct referenced in the *Bowers* decision are reduced now to 13, of which 4 enforce their laws only against homosexual conduct. In those States where sodomy is still proscribed, whether for same sex or heterosexual conduct, there is a pattern of nonenforcement with respect to consenting adults acting in private. The State of Texas admitted in 1994 that as of that date it had not prosecuted anyone under those circumstances. *State v. Morales,* 869 S.W.2d 941, 943.

Two principal cases decided after *Bowers* cast its holding into even more doubt. In *Planned Parenthood of Southeastern Pa. v. Casey,* 505 U.S. 833, 112 S.Ct. 2791, 120 L.Ed.2d 674 (1992), the Court reaffirmed the substantive force of the liberty protected by the Due Process Clause. The *Casey* decision again confirmed that our laws and tradition afford constitutional protection to personal decisions relating to marriage, procreation, contraception, family relationships, child rearing, and education. *Id.,* at 851, 112 S.Ct. 2791. In explaining the respect the Constitution demands for the autonomy of the person in making these choices, we stated as follows:

"These matters, involving the most intimate and personal choices a person may make in a lifetime, choices central to personal dignity and autonomy, are central to the liberty protected by the Fourteenth Amendment. At the heart of liberty is the right to define one's own concept of existence, of meaning, of the universe, and of the mystery of human life. Beliefs about these matters could not define the attributes of personhood were they formed under compulsion of the State." *Ibid.*

Persons in a homosexual relationship may seek autonomy for these purposes, just as heterosexual persons do. The decision in *Bowers* would deny them this right.

The second post-*Bowers* case of principal relevance is *Romer v. Evans,* 517 U.S. 620, 116 S.Ct. 1620, 134 L.Ed.2d 855 (1996). There the Court struck down class-based legislation directed at homosexuals as a violation of the Equal Protection Clause. *Romer* invalidated an amendment to

Colorado's constitution which named as a solitary class persons who were homosexuals, lesbians, or bisexual either by "orientation, conduct, practices or relationships," *id.,* at 624, 116 S.Ct. 1620 (internal quotation marks omitted), and deprived them of protection under state antidiscrimination laws. We concluded that the provision was "born of animosity toward the class of persons affected" and further that it had no rational relation to a legitimate governmental purpose. *Id.,* at 634, 116 S.Ct. 1620.

As an alternative argument in this case, counsel for the petitioners and some *amici* contend that *Romer* provides the basis for declaring the Texas statute invalid under the Equal Protection Clause. That is a tenable argument, but we conclude the instant case requires us to address whether *Bowers* itself has continuing validity. Were we to hold the statute invalid under the Equal Protection Clause some might question whether a prohibition would be valid if drawn differently, say, to prohibit the conduct both between same sex and different-sex participants.

Equality of treatment and the due process right to demand respect for conduct protected by the substantive guarantee of liberty are linked in important respects, and a decision on the latter point advances both interests. If protected conduct is made criminal and the law which does so remains unexamined for its substantive validity, its stigma might remain even if it were not enforceable as drawn for equal protection reasons. When homosexual conduct is made criminal by the law of the State, that declaration in and of itself is an invitation to subject homosexual persons to discrimination both in the public and in the private spheres. The central holding of *Bowers* has been brought in question by this case, and it should be addressed. Its continuance as precedent demeans the lives of homosexual persons.

The stigma this criminal statute imposes, moreover, is not trivial. The offense, to be sure, is but a class C misdemeanor, a minor offense in the Texas legal system. Still, it remains a criminal offense with all that imports for the dignity of the persons charged. The petitioners will bear on their record the history of their criminal convictions. Just this Term we rejected various challenges to state laws requiring the registration of sex offenders. *Smith v. Doe,* 538 U.S. 84, 123 S.Ct. 1140, 155 L.Ed.2d 164 (2003); *Connecticut Dept. of Public Safety v. Doe,* 538 U.S. 1, 123 S.Ct. 1160, 155 L.Ed.2d 98 (2003). We are advised that if Texas convicted an adult for private, consensual homosexual conduct under the statute here in question the convicted person would come within the registration laws of at least four States were he or she to be subject to their jurisdiction. Pet. for Cert. 13, and n. 12 (citing Idaho Code §§ 18–8301 to 18–8326 (Cum.Supp.2002); La.Code Crim. Proc. Ann., §§ 15:540–15:549 (West 2003); Miss.Code Ann. §§ 45–33–21 to 45–33–57 (Lexis 2003); S.C.Code Ann. §§ 23–3–400 to 23–3–490 (West 2002)). This underscores the consequential nature of the punishment and the state-sponsored condemnation attendant to the criminal prohibition. Furthermore, the Texas criminal conviction carries with it the other collateral consequences always following a conviction, such as notations on job application forms, to mention but one example.

The foundations of *Bowers* have sustained serious erosion from our recent decisions in *Casey* and *Romer*. When our precedent has been thus weakened, criticism from other sources is of greater significance. In the United States criticism of *Bowers* has been substantial and continuing, disapproving of its reasoning in all respects, not just as to its historical assumptions. See, *e.g.,* C. Fried, Order and Law: Arguing the Reagan Revolution—A Firsthand Account 81–84 (1991); R. Posner, Sex and Reason 341–350 (1992). The courts of five different States have declined to follow it in interpreting provisions in their own state constitutions parallel to the Due Process Clause of the Fourteenth Amendment, see *Jegley v. Picado,* 349 Ark. 600, 80 S.W.3d 332 (2002); *Powell v. State,* 270 Ga. 327, 510 S.E.2d 18, 24 (1998); *Gryczan v. State,* 283 Mont. 433, 942 P.2d 112 (1997); *Campbell v. Sundquist,* 926 S.W.2d 250 (Tenn.App.1996); *Commonwealth v. Wasson,* 842 S.W.2d 487 (Ky.1992).

To the extent *Bowers* relied on values we share with a wider civilization, it should be noted that the reasoning and holding in *Bowers* have been rejected elsewhere. The European Court of Human Rights has followed not *Bowers* but its own decision in *Dudgeon v. United Kingdom.* See *P.G. & J.H. v. United Kingdom,* App. No. 00044787/98, & ¶ 56 (Eur.Ct.H. R., Sept. 25, 2001); *Modinos v. Cyprus,* 259 Eur. Ct. H.R. (1993); *Norris v. Ireland,* 142 Eur. Ct. H.R. (1988). Other nations, too, have taken action consistent with an affirmation of the protected right of homosexual adults to engage in intimate, consensual conduct. See Brief for Mary Robinson et al. as *Amici Curiae* 11–12. The right the petitioners seek in this case has been accepted as an integral part of human freedom in many other countries. There has been no showing that in this country the governmental interest in circumscribing personal choice is somehow more legitimate or urgent.

The doctrine of *stare decisis* is essential to the respect accorded to the judgments of the Court and to the stability of the law. It is not, however, an inexorable command. *Payne v. Tennessee,* 501 U.S. 808, 828, 111 S.Ct. 2597, 115 L.Ed.2d 720 (1991) ("*Stare decisis* is not an inexorable command; rather, it 'is a principle of policy and not a mechanical formula of adherence to the latest decision' ") (quoting *Helvering v. Hallock,* 309 U.S. 106, 119, 60 S.Ct. 444, 84 L.Ed. 604 (1940)). In *Casey* we noted that when a Court is asked to overrule a precedent recognizing a constitutional liberty interest, individual or societal reliance on the existence of that liberty cautions with particular strength against reversing course. 505 U.S., at 855–856, 112 S.Ct. 2791; see also *id.,* at 844, 112 S.Ct. 2791 ("Liberty finds no refuge in a jurisprudence of doubt"). The holding in *Bowers,* however, has not induced detrimental reliance comparable to some instances where recognized individual rights are involved. Indeed, there has been no individual or societal reliance on *Bowers* of the sort that could counsel against overturning its holding once there are compelling reasons to do so. *Bowers* itself causes uncertainty, for the precedents before and after its issuance contradict its central holding.

The rationale of *Bowers* does not withstand careful analysis. In his dissenting opinion in Bowers Justice STEVENS came to these conclusions:

"Our prior cases make two propositions abundantly clear. First, the fact that the governing majority in a State has traditionally viewed a particular practice as immoral is not a sufficient reason for upholding a law prohibiting the practice; neither history nor tradition could save a law prohibiting miscegenation from constitutional attack. Second, individual decisions by married persons, concerning the intimacies of their physical relationship, even when not intended to produce offspring, are a form of 'liberty' protected by the Due Process Clause of the Fourteenth Amendment. Moreover, this protection extends to intimate choices by unmarried as well as married persons." 478 U.S., at 216, 106 S.Ct. 2841 (footnotes and citations omitted).

Justice STEVENS' analysis, in our view, should have been controlling in *Bowers* and should control here.

Bowers was not correct when it was decided, and it is not correct today. It ought not to remain binding precedent. *Bowers v. Hardwick* should be and now is overruled.

The present case does not involve minors. It does not involve persons who might be injured or coerced or who are situated in relationships where consent might not easily be refused. It does not involve public conduct or prostitution. It does not involve whether the government must give formal recognition to any relationship that homosexual persons seek to enter. The case does involve two adults who, with full and mutual consent from each other, engaged in sexual practices common to a homosexual lifestyle. The petitioners are entitled to respect for their private lives. The State cannot demean their existence or control their destiny by making their private sexual conduct a crime. Their right to liberty under the Due Process Clause gives them the full right to engage in their conduct without intervention of the government. "It is a promise of the Constitution that there is a realm of personal liberty which the government may not enter." *Casey, supra,* at 847, 112 S.Ct. 2791. The Texas statute furthers no legitimate state interest which can justify its intrusion into the personal and private life of the individual.

Had those who drew and ratified the Due Process Clauses of the Fifth Amendment or the Fourteenth Amendment known the components of liberty in its manifold possibilities, they might have been more specific. They did not presume to have this insight. They knew times can blind us to certain truths and later generations can see that laws once thought necessary and proper in fact serve only to oppress. As the Constitution endures, persons in every generation can invoke its principles in their own search for greater freedom.

The judgment of the Court of Appeals for the Texas Fourteenth District is reversed, and the case is remanded for further proceedings not inconsistent with this opinion.

■ Justice O'Connor, concurring in the judgment.

The Court today overrules *Bowers v. Hardwick,* 478 U.S. 186, 106 S.Ct. 2841, 92 L.Ed.2d 140 (1986). I joined *Bowers,* and do not join the Court in overruling it. Nevertheless, I agree with the Court that Texas' statute banning same sex sodomy is unconstitutional. See Tex. Penal Code Ann. § 21.06 (2003). Rather than relying on the substantive component of the Fourteenth Amendment's Due Process Clause, as the Court does, I base my conclusion on the Fourteenth Amendment's Equal Protection Clause.

The Equal Protection Clause of the Fourteenth Amendment "is essentially a direction that all persons similarly situated should be treated alike." *Cleburne v. Cleburne Living Center, Inc.*, 473 U.S. 432, 439, 105 S.Ct. 3249, 87 L.Ed.2d 313 (1985); see also *Plyler v. Doe*, 457 U.S. 202, 216, 102 S.Ct. 2382, 72 L.Ed.2d 786 (1982). Under our rational basis standard of review, "legislation is presumed to be valid and will be sustained if the classification drawn by the statute is rationally related to a legitimate state interest." *Cleburne v. Cleburne Living Center, supra,* at 440, 105 S.Ct. 3249; see also *Department of Agriculture v. Moreno*, 413 U.S. 528, 534, 93 S.Ct. 2821, 37 L.Ed.2d 782 (1973); *Romer v. Evans*, 517 U.S. 620, 632–633, 116 S.Ct. 1620, 134 L.Ed.2d 855 (1996); *Nordlinger v. Hahn*, 505 U.S. 1, 11–12, 112 S.Ct. 2326, 120 L.Ed.2d 1 (1992).

Laws such as economic or tax legislation that are scrutinized under rational basis review normally pass constitutional muster, since "the Constitution presumes that even improvident decisions will eventually be rectified by the democratic processes." *Cleburne v. Cleburne Living Center, supra,* at 440, 105 S.Ct. 3249; see also *Fitzgerald v. Racing Assn. of Central Iowa*, 539 U.S. 103, 123 S.Ct. 2156, 156 L.Ed.2d 97 (2003); *Williamson v. Lee Optical of Okla., Inc.*, 348 U.S. 483, 75 S.Ct. 461, 99 L.Ed. 563 (1955). We have consistently held, however, that some objectives, such as "a bare ... desire to harm a politically unpopular group," are not legitimate state interests. *Department of Agriculture v. Moreno, supra,* at 534, 93 S.Ct. 2821. See also *Cleburne v. Cleburne Living Center, supra,* at 446–447, 105 S.Ct. 3249; *Romer v. Evans, supra,* at 632, 116 S.Ct. 1620. When a law exhibits such a desire to harm a politically unpopular group, we have applied a more searching form of rational basis review to strike down such laws under the Equal Protection Clause.

We have been most likely to apply rational basis review to hold a law unconstitutional under the Equal Protection Clause where, as here, the challenged legislation inhibits personal relationships. In *Department of Agriculture v. Moreno,* for example, we held that a law preventing those households containing an individual unrelated to any other member of the household from receiving food stamps violated equal protection because the purpose of the law was to " 'discriminate against hippies.' " 413 U.S., at 534, 93 S.Ct. 2821. The asserted governmental interest in preventing food stamp fraud was not deemed sufficient to satisfy rational basis review. *Id.,* at 535–538, 93 S.Ct. 2821. In *Eisenstadt v. Baird,* 405 U.S. 438, 447–455, 92 S.Ct. 1029, 31 L.Ed.2d 349 (1972), we refused to sanction a law that discriminated between married and unmarried persons by prohibiting the distribution of contraceptives to single persons. Likewise, in *Cleburne v. Cleburne Living Center, supra,* we held that it was irrational for a State to require a home for the mentally disabled to obtain a special use permit when other residences—like fraternity houses and apartment buildings—did not have to obtain such a permit. And in *Romer v. Evans,* we disallowed a state statute that "impos[ed] a broad and undifferentiated disability on a single named group"—specifically, homosexuals. 517 U.S., at 632, 116 S.Ct. 1620.

The statute at issue here makes sodomy a crime only if a person "engages in deviate sexual intercourse with another individual of the same sex." Tex. Penal Code Ann. § 21.06(a) (2003). Sodomy between opposite-sex partners, however, is not a crime in Texas. That is, Texas treats the same conduct differently based solely on the participants. Those harmed by this law are people who have a same sex sexual orientation and thus are more likely to engage in behavior prohibited by § 21.06.

The Texas statute makes homosexuals unequal in the eyes of the law by making particular conduct—and only that conduct—subject to criminal sanction. It appears that prosecutions under Texas' sodomy law are rare. See *State v. Morales,* 869 S.W.2d 941, 943 (Tex.1994) (noting in 1994 that § 21.06 "has not been, and in all probability will not be, enforced against private consensual conduct between adults"). This case shows, however, that prosecutions under § 21.06 *do* occur. And while the penalty imposed on petitioners in this case was relatively minor, the consequences of conviction are not. It appears that petitioner's convictions, if upheld, would disqualify them from or restrict their ability to engage in a variety of professions, including medicine, athletic training, and interior design. See, *e.g.,* Tex. Occ.Code Ann. § 164.051(a)(2)(B) (2003 Pamphlet) (physician); § 451.251(a)(1) (athletic trainer); § 1053.252(2) (interior designer). Indeed, were petitioners to move to one of four States, their convictions would require them to register as sex offenders to local law enforcement. See, *e.g.,* Idaho Code § 18–8304 (Cum.Supp.2002); La. Stat. Ann. § 15:542 (West Cum.Supp.2003); Miss.Code Ann. § 45–33–25 (West 2003); S.C.Code Ann. § 23–3–430 (West Cum.Supp.2002); cf. *ante,* at 2482.

And the effect of Texas' sodomy law is not just limited to the threat of prosecution or consequence of conviction. Texas' sodomy law brands all homosexuals as criminals, thereby making it more difficult for homosexuals to be treated in the same manner as everyone else. Indeed, Texas itself has previously acknowledged the collateral effects of the law, stipulating in a prior challenge to this action that the law "legally sanctions discrimination against [homosexuals] in a variety of ways unrelated to the criminal law," including in the areas of "employment, family issues, and housing." *State v. Morales,* 826 S.W.2d 201, 203 (Tex.App.1992).

Texas attempts to justify its law, and the effects of the law, by arguing that the statute satisfies rational basis review because it furthers the legitimate governmental interest of the promotion of morality. In *Bowers,* we held that a state law criminalizing sodomy as applied to homosexual couples did not violate substantive due process. We rejected the argument that no rational basis existed to justify the law, pointing to the government's interest in promoting morality. 478 U.S., at 196, 106 S.Ct. 2841. The only question in front of the Court in *Bowers* was whether the substantive component of the Due Process Clause protected a right to engage in homosexual sodomy. *Id.,* at 188, n. 2. *Bowers* did not hold that moral disapproval of a group is a rational basis under the Equal Protection Clause to criminalize homosexual sodomy when heterosexual sodomy is not punished.

This case raises a different issue than *Bowers:* whether, under the Equal Protection Clause, moral disapproval is a legitimate state interest to justify by itself a statute that bans homosexual sodomy, but not heterosexual sodomy. It is not. Moral disapproval of this group, like a bare desire to harm the group, is an interest that is insufficient to satisfy rational basis review under the Equal Protection Clause. See, *e.g., Department of Agriculture v. Moreno, supra,* at 534, 93 S.Ct. 2821; *Romer v. Evans,* 517 U.S., at 634–635, 116 S.Ct. 1620. Indeed, we have never held that moral disapproval, without any other asserted state interest, is a sufficient rationale under the Equal Protection Clause to justify a law that discriminates among groups of persons.

Moral disapproval of a group cannot be a legitimate governmental interest under the Equal Protection Clause because legal classifications must not be "drawn for the purpose of disadvantaging the group burdened by the law." *Id.,* at 633, 116 S.Ct. 1620. Texas' invocation of moral disapproval as a legitimate state interest proves nothing more than Texas' desire to criminalize homosexual sodomy. But the Equal Protection Clause prevents a State from creating "a classification of persons undertaken for its own sake." *Id.,* at 635, 116 S.Ct. 1620. And because Texas so rarely enforces its sodomy law as applied to private, consensual acts, the law serves more as a statement of dislike and disapproval against homosexuals than as a tool to stop criminal behavior. The Texas sodomy law "raise[s] the inevitable inference that the disadvantage imposed is born of animosity toward the class of persons affected." *Id.,* at 634, 116 S.Ct. 1620.

Texas argues, however, that the sodomy law does not discriminate against homosexual persons. Instead, the State maintains that the law discriminates only against homosexual conduct. While it is true that the law applies only to conduct, the conduct targeted by this law is conduct that is closely correlated with being homosexual. Under such circumstances, Texas' sodomy law is targeted at more than conduct. It is instead directed toward gay persons as a class. "After all, there can hardly be more palpable discrimination against a class than making the conduct that defines the class criminal." *Id.,* at 641, 116 S.Ct. 1620 (SCALIA, J., dissenting) (internal quotation marks omitted). When a State makes homosexual conduct criminal, and not "deviate sexual intercourse" committed by persons of different sexes, "that declaration in and of itself is an invitation to subject homosexual persons to discrimination both in the public and in the private spheres." *Ante,* at 2482.

Indeed, Texas law confirms that the sodomy statute is directed toward homosexuals as a class. In Texas, calling a person a homosexual is slander *per se* because the word "homosexual" "impute[s] the commission of a crime." *Plumley v. Landmark Chevrolet, Inc.,* 122 F.3d 308, 310 (C.A.5

1997) (applying Texas law); see also *Head v. Newton,* 596 S.W.2d 209, 210 (Tex.App.1980). The State has admitted that because of the sodomy law, *being* homosexual carries the presumption of being a criminal. See *State v. Morales,* 826 S.W.2d, at 202–203 ("[T]he statute brands lesbians and gay men as criminals and thereby legally sanctions discrimination against them in a variety of ways unrelated to the criminal law"). Texas' sodomy law therefore results in discrimination against homosexuals as a class in an array of areas outside the criminal law. See *ibid.* In *Romer v. Evans,* we refused to sanction a law that singled out homosexuals "for disfavored legal status." 517 U.S., at 633, 116 S.Ct. 1620. The same is true here. The Equal Protection Clause " 'neither knows nor tolerates classes among citizens.' " *Id.,* at 623, 116 S.Ct. 1620 (quoting *Plessy v. Ferguson,* 163 U.S. 537, 559, 16 S.Ct. 1138, 41 L.Ed. 256 (1896) (Harlan, J. dissenting)).

A State can of course assign certain consequences to a violation of its criminal law. But the State cannot single out one identifiable class of citizens for punishment that does not apply to everyone else, with moral disapproval as the only asserted state interest for the law. The Texas sodomy statute subjects homosexuals to "a lifelong penalty and stigma. A legislative classification that threatens the creation of an underclass . . . cannot be reconciled with" the Equal Protection Clause. *Plyler v. Doe,* 457 U.S., at 239, 102 S.Ct. 2382 (Powell, J., concurring).

Whether a sodomy law that is neutral both in effect and application, see *Yick Wo v. Hopkins,* 118 U.S. 356, 6 S.Ct. 1064, 30 L.Ed. 220 (1886), would violate the substantive component of the Due Process Clause is an issue that need not be decided today. I am confident, however, that so long as the Equal Protection Clause requires a sodomy law to apply equally to the private consensual conduct of homosexuals and heterosexuals alike, such a law would not long stand in our democratic society. In the words of Justice Jackson:

> "The framers of the Constitution knew, and we should not forget today, that there is no more effective practical guaranty against arbitrary and unreasonable government than to require that the principles of law which officials would impose upon a minority be imposed generally. Conversely, nothing opens the door to arbitrary action so effectively as to allow those officials to pick and choose only a few to whom they will apply legislation and thus to escape the political retribution that might be visited upon them if larger numbers were affected." *Railway Express Agency, Inc. v. New York,* 336 U.S. 106, 112–113, 69 S.Ct. 463, 93 L.Ed. 533 (1949) (concurring opinion).

That this law as applied to private, consensual conduct is unconstitutional under the Equal Protection Clause does not mean that other laws distinguishing between heterosexuals and homosexuals would similarly fail under rational basis review. Texas cannot assert any legitimate state interest here, such as national security or preserving the traditional institution of marriage. Unlike the moral disapproval of same sex relations—the asserted state interest in this case—other reasons exist to promote the institution of marriage beyond mere moral disapproval of an excluded group.

A law branding one class of persons as criminal based solely on the State's moral disapproval of that class and the conduct associated with that class runs contrary to the values of the Constitution and the Equal Protection Clause, under any standard of review. I therefore concur in the Court's judgment that Texas' sodomy law banning "deviate sexual intercourse" between consenting adults of the same sex, but not between consenting adults of different sexes, is unconstitutional.

■ JUSTICE SCALIA, with whom THE CHIEF JUSTICE and JUSTICE THOMAS join, dissenting.

"Liberty finds no refuge in a jurisprudence of doubt." *Planned Parenthood of Southeastern Pa. v. Casey,* 505 U.S. 833, 844, 112 S.Ct. 2791, 120 L.Ed.2d 674 (1992). That was the Court's sententious response, barely more than a decade ago, to those seeking to overrule *Roe v. Wade,* 410 U.S. 113, 93 S.Ct. 705, 35 L.Ed.2d 147 (1973). The Court's response today, to those who have engaged in a 17–year crusade to overrule *Bowers v. Hardwick,* 478 U.S. 186, 106 S.Ct. 2841, 92 L.Ed.2d 140 (1986), is very different. The need for stability and certainty presents no barrier.

Most of the rest of today's opinion has no relevance to its actual holding—that the Texas statute "furthers no legitimate state interest which can justify" its application to petitioners under rational-basis review. *Ante,* at 2484 (overruling *Bowers* to the extent it sustained Georgia's anti-sodomy statute under the rational-basis test). Though there is discussion of "fundamental proposition[s]," *ante,* at 2477, and "fundamental decisions," *ibid.* nowhere does the Court's opinion declare that homosexual sodomy is a "fundamental right" under the Due Process Clause; nor does it subject the Texas law to the standard of review that would be appropriate (strict scrutiny) if homosexual sodomy *were* a "fundamental right." Thus, while overruling the *outcome* of *Bowers,* the Court leaves strangely untouched its central legal conclusion: "[R]espondent would have us announce ... a fundamental right to engage in homosexual sodomy. This we are quite unwilling to do." 478 U.S., at 191, 106 S.Ct. 2841. Instead the Court simply describes petitioners' conduct as "an exercise of their liberty"—which it undoubtedly is—and proceeds to apply an unheard-of form of rational-basis review that will have far-reaching implications beyond this case. *Ante,* at 2476.

I

I begin with the Court's surprising readiness to reconsider a decision rendered a mere 17 years ago in *Bowers v. Hardwick.* I do not myself believe in rigid adherence to *stare decisis* in constitutional cases; but I do believe that we should be consistent rather than manipulative in invoking the doctrine. Today's opinions in support of reversal do not bother to distinguish—or indeed, even bother to mention—the paean to *stare decisis* coauthored by three Members of today's majority in *Planned Parenthood v. Casey.* There, when *stare decisis* meant preservation of judicially invented abortion rights, the widespread criticism of *Roe* was strong reason to *reaffirm* it:

"Where, in the performance of its judicial duties, the Court decides a case in such a way as to resolve the sort of intensely divisive controversy reflected in *Roe*[,] . . . its decision has a dimension that the resolution of the normal case does not carry. . . . [T]o overrule under fire in the absence of the most compelling reason . . . would subvert the Court's legitimacy beyond any serious question." 505 U.S., at 866–867, 112 S.Ct. 2791.

Today, however, the widespread opposition to *Bowers,* a decision resolving an issue as "intensely divisive" as the issue in *Roe,* is offered as a reason in favor of *overruling* it. See *ante,* at 2482–2483. Gone, too, is any "enquiry" (of the sort conducted in *Casey*) into whether the decision sought to be overruled has "proven 'unworkable,' " *Casey, supra,* at 855, 112 S.Ct. 2791.

Today's approach to *stare decisis* invites us to overrule an erroneously decided precedent (including an "intensely divisive" decision) *if:* (1) its foundations have been "eroded" by subsequent decisions, *ante,* at 2482; (2) it has been subject to "substantial and continuing" criticism, *ibid.*; and (3) it has not induced "individual or societal reliance" that counsels against overturning, *ante,* at 2483. The problem is that *Roe* itself—which today's majority surely has no disposition to overrule—satisfies these conditions to at least the same degree as *Bowers.*

A preliminary digressive observation with regard to the first factor: The Court's claim that *Planned Parenthood v. Casey, supra,* "casts some doubt" upon the holding in *Bowers* (or any other case, for that matter) does not withstand analysis. *Ante,* at 2480. As far as its holding is concerned, *Casey* provided a *less* expansive right to abortion than did *Roe, which was already on the books when* Bowers *was decided.* And if the Court is referring not to the holding of *Casey,* but to the dictum of its famed sweet-mystery-of-life passage, *ante,* at 2481 (" 'At the heart of liberty is the right to define one's own concept of existence, of meaning, of the universe, and of the mystery of human life' "): That "casts some doubt" upon either the totality of our jurisprudence or else (presumably the right answer) nothing at all. I have never heard of a law that attempted to restrict one's "right to define" certain concepts; and if the passage calls into question the government's power to regulate *actions based on* one's self-defined "concept of existence, etc.," it is the passage that ate the rule of law.

I do not quarrel with the Court's claim that *Romer v. Evans,* 517 U.S. 620, 116 S.Ct. 1620, 134 L.Ed.2d 855 (1996), "eroded" the "foundations" of *Bowers*' rational-basis holding. See *Romer, supra,* at 640–643, 116 S.Ct. 1620 (SCALIA, J., dissenting). But *Roe* and *Casey* have been equally "eroded" by *Washington v. Glucksberg,* 521 U.S. 702, 721, 117 S.Ct. 2258, 138 L.Ed.2d 772 (1997), which held that *only* fundamental rights which are " 'deeply rooted in this Nation's history and tradition' " qualify for anything other than rational basis scrutiny under the doctrine of "substantive due process." *Roe* and *Casey,* of course, subjected the restriction of abortion to heightened scrutiny without even attempting to establish that the freedom to abort *was* rooted in this Nation's tradition.

Bowers, the Court says, has been subject to "substantial and continuing [criticism], disapproving of its reasoning in all respects, not just as to its historical assumptions." *Ante*, at 2483. Exactly what those nonhistorical criticisms are, and whether the Court even agrees with them, are left unsaid, although the Court does cite two books. See *ibid*. (citing C. Fried, Order and Law: Arguing the Reagan Revolution—A Firsthand Account 81–84 (1991); R. Posner, Sex and Reason 341–350 (1992)).[1] Of course, *Roe* too (and by extension *Casey*) had been (and still is) subject to unrelenting criticism, including criticism from the two commentators cited by the Court today. See Fried, *supra*, at 75 ("Roe was a prime example of twisted judging"); Posner, *supra*, at 337 ("[The Court's] opinion in *Roe* (3)27 fails to measure up to professional expectations regarding judicial opinions"); Posner, Judicial Opinion Writing, 62 U. Chi. L.Rev. 1421, 1434 (1995) (describing the opinion in *Roe* as an "embarrassing performanc[e]").

That leaves, to distinguish the rock-solid, unamendable disposition of *Roe* from the readily overrulable *Bowers*, only the third factor. "[T]here has been," the Court says, "no individual or societal reliance on *Bowers* of the sort that could counsel against overturning its holding...." *Ante*, at 2483. It seems to me that the "societal reliance" on the principles confirmed in *Bowers* and discarded today has been overwhelming. Countless judicial decisions and legislative enactments have relied on the ancient proposition that a governing majority's belief that certain sexual behavior is "immoral and unacceptable" constitutes a rational basis for regulation. See, *e.g., Williams v. Pryor*, 240 F.3d 944, 949 (C.A.11 2001) (citing *Bowers* in upholding Alabama's prohibition on the sale of sex toys on the ground that "[t]he crafting and safeguarding of public morality ... indisputably is a legitimate government interest under rational basis scrutiny"); *Milner v. Apfel*, 148 F.3d 812, 814 (C.A.7 1998) (citing *Bowers* for the proposition that "[l]egislatures are permitted to legislate with regard to morality ... rather than confined to preventing demonstrable harms"); *Holmes v. California Army National Guard* 124 F.3d 1126, 1136 (C.A.9 1997) (relying on *Bowers* in upholding the federal statute and regulations banning from military service those who engage in homosexual conduct); *Owens v. State*, 352 Md. 663, 683, 724 A.2d 43, 53 (1999) (relying on *Bowers* in holding that "a person has no constitutional right to engage in sexual intercourse, at least outside of marriage"); *Sherman v. Henry*, 928 S.W.2d 464, 469–473 (Tex.1996) (relying on *Bowers* in rejecting a claimed constitutional right to commit adultery). We ourselves relied extensively on *Bowers* when we concluded, in *Barnes v. Glen Theatre, Inc.*, 501 U.S. 560, 569, 111 S.Ct. 2456, 115 L.Ed.2d 504 (1991), that Indiana's public indecency statute furthered "a substantial government interest in protecting order and morality," *ibid.*, (plurality opinion); see also *id.*, at 575, 111 S.Ct. 2456

---

1. This last-cited critic of *Bowers* actually writes: "*[Bowers]* is correct nevertheless that the right to engage in homosexual acts is not deeply rooted in America's history and tradition." Posner, Sex and Reason, at 343.

(SCALIA, J., concurring in judgment). State laws against bigamy, same sex marriage, adult incest, prostitution, masturbation, adultery, fornication, bestiality, and obscenity are likewise sustainable only in light of *Bowers'* validation of laws based on moral choices. Every single one of these laws is called into question by today's decision; the Court makes no effort to cabin the scope of its decision to exclude them from its holding. See *ante,* at 2480 (noting "an emerging awareness that liberty gives substantial protection to adult persons in deciding how to conduct their private lives *in matters pertaining to sex*" (emphasis added)). The impossibility of distinguishing homosexuality from other traditional "morals" offenses is precisely why *Bowers* rejected the rational-basis challenge. "The law," it said, "is constantly based on notions of morality, and if all laws representing essentially moral choices are to be invalidated under the Due Process Clause, the courts will be very busy indeed." 478 U.S., at 196, 106 S.Ct. 2841.[2]

What a massive disruption of the current social order, therefore, the overruling of *Bowers* entails. Not so the overruling of *Roe,* which would simply have restored the regime that existed for centuries before 1973, in which the permissibility of and restrictions upon abortion were determined legislatively State-by-State. *Casey,* however, chose to base its *stare decisis* determination on a different "sort" of reliance. "[P]eople," it said, "have organized intimate relationships and made choices that define their views of themselves and their places in society, in reliance on the availability of abortion in the event that contraception should fail." 505 U.S., at 856, 112 S.Ct. 2791. This falsely assumes that the consequence of overruling *Roe* would have been to make abortion unlawful. It would not; it would merely have *permitted* the States to do so. Many States would unquestionably have declined to prohibit abortion, and others would not have prohibited it

2. While the Court does not overrule *Bowers* holding that homosexual sodomy is not a "fundamental right," it is worth noting that the "societal reliance" upon that aspect of the decision has been substantial as well. See 10 U.S.C. § 654(b)(1) ("A member of the armed forces shall be separated from the armed forces ... if ... the member has engaged in ... a homosexual act or acts"); *Marcum v. McWhorter,* 308 F.3d 635, 640–642 (C.A.6 2002) (relying on *Bowers* in rejecting a claimed fundamental right to commit adultery); *Mullins v. Oregon,* 57 F.3d 789, 793–794 (C.A.9 1995) (relying on *Bowers* in rejecting a grandparent's claimed "fundamental liberty interes[t]" in the adoption of her grandchildren); *Doe v. Wigginton,* 21 F.3d 733, 739–740 (C.A.6 1994) (relying on *Bowers* in rejecting a prisoner's claimed "fundamental right" to on-demand HIV testing); *Schowengerdt v. United States,* 944 F.2d 483, 490 (C.A.9 1991) (relying on *Bowers* in upholding a bisexual's discharge from the armed services); *Charles v. Baesler,* 910 F.2d 1349, 1353 (C.A.6 1990) (relying on *Bowers* in rejecting fire department captain's claimed "fundamental" interest in a promotion); *Henne v. Wright,* 904 F.2d 1208, 1214–1215 (C.A.8 1990) (relying on *Bowers* in rejecting a claim that state law restricting surnames that could be given to children at birth implicates a "fundamental right"); *Walls v. Petersburg,* 895 F.2d 188, 193 (implicates a "fundamental right"); *Walls v. Petersburg,* 895 F.2d 188, 193 (C.A.4 1990) (relying on *Bowers* in rejecting substantive-due-process challenge to a police department questionnaire that asked prospective employees about homosexual activity); *High Tech Gays v. Defense Industrial Security Clearance Office,* 895 F.2d 563, 570–571 (C.A.9 1990) (relying on *Bowers* holding that homosexual activity is not a fundamental right in rejecting—on the basis of the rational-basis standard—an equal-protection challenge to the Defense Department's policy of conducting expanded investigations into backgrounds of gay and lesbian applicants for secret and top-secret security clearance).

within six months (after which the most significant reliance interests would have expired). Even for persons in States other than these, the choice would not have been between abortion and childbirth, but between abortion nearby and abortion in a neighboring State.

To tell the truth, it does not surprise me, and should surprise no one, that the Court has chosen today to revise the standards of *stare decisis* set forth in *Casey.* It has thereby exposed *Casey*'s extraordinary deference to precedent for the result-oriented expedient that it is.

II

Having decided that it need not adhere to *stare decisis,* the Court still must establish that *Bowers* was wrongly decided and that the Texas statute, as applied to petitioners, is unconstitutional.

Texas Penal Code Ann. § 21.06(a) (2003) undoubtedly imposes constraints on liberty. So do laws prohibiting prostitution, recreational use of heroin, and, for that matter, working more than 60 hours per week in a bakery. But there is no right to "liberty" under the Due Process Clause, though today's opinion repeatedly makes that claim. *Ante,* at 2478 ("The liberty protected by the Constitution allows homosexual persons the right to make this choice"); *ante,* at 2481 (" 'These matters . . . are central to the liberty protected by the Fourteenth Amendment' "); *ante,* at 2483 ("Their right to liberty under the Due Process Clause gives them the full right to engage in their conduct without intervention of the government"). The Fourteenth Amendment *expressly allows* States to deprive their citizens of "liberty," *so long as "due process of law" is provided:*

> "No state shall . . . deprive any person of life, liberty, or property, *without due process of law.*" Amdt. 14 (emphasis added).

Our opinions applying the doctrine known as "substantive due process" hold that the Due Process Clause prohibits States from infringing *fundamental* liberty interests, unless the infringement is narrowly tailored to serve a compelling state interest. *Washington v. Glucksberg,* 521 U.S., at 721, 117 S.Ct. 2258. We have held repeatedly, in cases the Court today does not overrule, that *only* fundamental rights qualify for this so-called "heightened scrutiny" protection—that is, rights which are " 'deeply rooted in this Nation's history and tradition,' " *ibid.* See *Reno v. Flores,* 507 U.S. 292, 303, 113 S.Ct. 1439, 123 L.Ed.2d 1 (1993) (fundamental liberty interests must be "so rooted in the traditions and conscience of our people as to be ranked as fundamental" (internal quotation marks and citations omitted)); *United States v. Salerno,* 481 U.S. 739, 751, 107 S.Ct. 2095, 95 L.Ed.2d 697 (1987) (same). See also *Michael H. v. Gerald D.,* 491 U.S. 110, 122, 109 S.Ct. 2333, 105 L.Ed.2d 91 (1989) ("[W]e have insisted not merely that the interest denominated as a 'liberty' be 'fundamental' . . . but also that it be an interest traditionally protected by our society"); *Moore v. East Cleveland,* 431 U.S. 494, 503, 97 S.Ct. 1932, 52 L.Ed.2d 531 (1977) (plurality opinion); *Meyer v. Nebraska,* 262 U.S. 390, 399, 43 S.Ct. 625, 67 L.Ed. 1042 (1923) (Fourteenth Amendment protects "those privileges *long recognized at common law* as essential to the orderly pursuit of happiness by free men" (emphasis added)).[3] All other liberty interests may be abridged or abrogated pursuant to a validly enacted state law if that law is rationally related to a legitimate state interest.

Bowers held, first, that criminal prohibitions of homosexual sodomy are not subject to heightened scrutiny because they do not implicate a "fundamental right" under the Due Process Clause, 478 U.S., at 191–194, 106 S.Ct. 2841. Noting that "[p]roscriptions against that conduct have ancient roots," *id.*, at 192, 106 S.Ct. 2841, that "[s]odomy was a criminal offense at common law and was forbidden by the laws of the original 13 States when they ratified the Bill of Rights," *ibid.*, and that many States had retained their bans on sodomy, *id.*, at 193, Bowers concluded that a right to engage in homosexual sodomy was not " 'deeply rooted in this Nation's history and tradition,' " *id.*, at 192, 106 S.Ct. 2841.

The Court today does not overrule this holding. Not once does it describe homosexual sodomy as a "fundamental right" or a "fundamental liberty interest," nor does it subject the Texas statute to strict scrutiny. Instead, having failed to establish that the right to homosexual sodomy is " 'deeply rooted in this Nation's history and tradition,' " the Court concludes that the application of Texas's statute to petitioners' conduct fails the rational-basis test, and overrules *Bowers'* holding to the contrary, see *id.*, at 196, 106 S.Ct. 2841. "The Texas statute furthers no legitimate state interest which can justify its intrusion into the personal and private life of the individual." *Ante,* at 2484.

I shall address that rational-basis holding presently. First, however, I address some aspersions that the Court casts upon *Bowers'* conclusion that homosexual sodomy is not a "fundamental right"—even though, as I have said, the Court does not have the boldness to reverse that conclusion.

III

The Court's description of "the state of the law" at the time of *Bowers* only confirms that *Bowers* was right. *Ante,* at 2477. The Court points to *Griswold v. Connecticut,* 381 U.S. 479, 481–482, 85 S.Ct. 1678, 14 L.Ed.2d 510 (1965). But that case *expressly disclaimed* any reliance on the doctrine of "substantive due process," and grounded the so-called "right to privacy" in penumbras of constitutional provisions *other than* the Due Process Clause. *Eisenstadt v. Baird,* 405 U.S. 438, 92 S.Ct. 1029, 31 L.Ed.2d 349 (1972), likewise had nothing to do with "substantive due process"; it invalidated a Massachusetts law prohibiting the distribution of contracep-

---

3. The Court is quite right that "history and tradition are the starting point but not in all cases the ending point of the substantive due process inquiry," *ante,* at 2480. An asserted "fundamental liberty interest" must not only be "deeply rooted in this Nation's history and tradition," *Washington v. Glucksberg,* 521 U.S. 702, 721, 117 S.Ct. 2258 (1997), but it must *also* be "implicit in the concept of ordered liberty," so that "neither liberty nor justice would exist if [it] were sacrificed," *ibid.* Moreover, liberty interests unsupported by history and tradition, though not deserving of "heightened scrutiny," are *still* protected from state laws that are not rationally related to any legitimate state interest. *Id.,* at 722, 117 S.Ct. 2258. As I proceed to discuss, it is this latter principle that the Court applies in the present case.

tives to unmarried persons solely on the basis of the Equal Protection Clause. Of course *Eisenstadt* contains well known dictum relating to the "right to privacy," but this referred to the right recognized in *Griswold*—a right penumbral to the *specific* guarantees in the Bill of Rights, and not a "substantive due process" right.

Roe v. Wade recognized that the right to abort an unborn child was a "fundamental right" protected by the Due Process Clause. 410 U.S., at 155, 93 S.Ct. 705. The *Roe* Court, however, made no attempt to establish that this right was " 'deeply rooted in this Nation's history and tradition' "; instead, it based its conclusion that "the Fourteenth Amendment's concept of personal liberty . . . is broad enough to encompass a woman's decision whether or not to terminate her pregnancy" on its own normative judgment that anti-abortion laws were undesirable. See *id.,* at 153, 93 S.Ct. 705. We have since rejected *Roe*'s holding that regulations of abortion must be narrowly tailored to serve a compelling state interest, see *Planned Parenthood v. Casey,* 505 U.S., at 876, 112 S.Ct. 2791 (joint opinion of O'CONNOR, KENNEDY, and SOUTER, JJ.); *id.,* at 951–953, 112 S.Ct. 2791 (REHNQUIST, C. J., concurring in judgment in part and dissenting in part)—and thus, by logical implication, *Roe*'s holding that the right to abort an unborn child is a "fundamental right." See 505 U.S., at 843–912, 112 S.Ct. 2791 (joint opinion of O'CONNOR, KENNEDY, and SOUTER, JJ.) (not once describing abortion as a "fundamental right" or a "fundamental liberty interest").

After discussing the history of antisodomy laws, *ante,* at 2478–2480, the Court proclaims that, "it should be noted that there is no longstanding history in this country of laws directed at homosexual conduct as a distinct matter," *ante,* at 2478. This observation in no way casts into doubt the "definitive [historical] conclusion," *id.,* on which *Bowers* relied: that our Nation has a longstanding history of laws prohibiting *sodomy in general*—regardless of whether it was performed by same sex or opposite-sex couples:

> "It is obvious to us that neither of these formulations would extend a fundamental right to homosexuals to engage in acts of consensual sodomy. Proscriptions against that conduct have ancient roots. *Sodomy* was a criminal offense at common law and was forbidden by the laws of the original 13 States when they ratified the Bill of Rights. In 1868, when the Fourteenth Amendment was ratified, all but 5 of the 37 States in the Union had *criminal sodomy laws.* In fact, until 1961, all 50 States outlawed *sodomy,* and today, 24 States and the District of Columbia continue to provide criminal penalties for *sodomy* performed in private and between consenting adults. Against this background, to claim that a right to engage in such conduct is 'deeply rooted in this Nation's history and tradition' or 'implicit in the concept of ordered liberty' is, at best, facetious." 478 U.S., at 192–194, 106 S.Ct. 2841 (citations and footnotes omitted; emphasis added).

It is (as *Bowers* recognized) entirely irrelevant whether the laws in our long national tradition criminalizing homosexual sodomy were "directed at homosexual conduct as a distinct matter." *Ante,* at 2478. Whether homosexual sodomy was prohibited by a law targeted at same sex sexual relations or by a more general law prohibiting both homosexual and heterosexual sodomy, the only relevant point is that it *was* criminalized—which suffices to establish that homosexual sodomy is not a right "deeply rooted in our Nation's history and tradition." The Court today agrees that homosexual sodomy was criminalized and thus does not dispute the facts on which *Bowers actually* relied.

Next the Court makes the claim, again unsupported by any citations, that "[l]aws prohibiting sodomy do not seem to have been enforced against consenting adults acting in private." *Ante,* at 2479. The key qualifier here is "acting in private"—since the Court admits that sodomy laws *were* enforced against consenting adults (although the Court contends that prosecutions were "infrequent," *ibid.*). I do not know what "acting in private" means; surely consensual sodomy, like heterosexual intercourse, is rarely performed on stage. If all the Court means by "acting in private" is "on private premises, with the doors closed and windows covered," it is entirely unsurprising that evidence of enforcement would be hard to come by. (Imagine the circumstances that would enable a search warrant to be obtained for a residence on the ground that there was probable cause to believe that consensual sodomy was then and there occurring.) Surely that lack of evidence would not sustain the proposition that consensual sodomy on private premises with the doors closed and windows covered was regarded as a "fundamental right," even though all other consensual sodomy was criminalized. There are 203 prosecutions for consensual, adult homosexual sodomy reported in the West Reporting system and official state reporters from the years 1880–1995. See W. Eskridge, Gaylaw: Challenging the Apartheid of the Closet 375 (1999) (hereinafter Gaylaw). There are also records of 20 sodomy prosecutions and 4 executions during the colonial period. J. Katz, Gay/Lesbian Almanac 29, 58, 663 (1983). *Bowers'* conclusion that homosexual sodomy is not a fundamental right "deeply rooted in this Nation's history and tradition" is utterly unassailable.

Realizing that fact, the Court instead says: "[W]e think that our laws and traditions in the past half century are of most relevance here. These references show *an emerging awareness* that liberty gives substantial protection to adult persons in deciding how to conduct their private lives *in matters pertaining to sex.*" *Ante,* at 2480 (emphasis added). Apart from the fact that such an "emerging awareness" does not establish a "fundamental right," the statement is factually false. States continue to prosecute all sorts of crimes by adults "in matters pertaining to sex": prostitution, adult incest, adultery, obscenity, and child pornography. Sodomy laws, too, have been enforced "in the past half century," in which there have been 134 reported cases involving prosecutions for consensual, adult, homosexual sodomy. Gaylaw 375. In relying, for evidence of an "emerging recognition," upon the American Law Institute's 1955 recommendation not to criminalize " 'consensual sexual relations conducted in private,' " *ante,* at 2480, the Court ignores the fact that this recommendation was "a point of resistance in most of the states that considered adopting the Model Penal Code." Gaylaw 159.

In any event, an "emerging awareness" is by definition not "deeply rooted in this Nation's history and tradition[s]," as we have said "fundamental right" status requires. Constitutional entitlements do not spring into existence because some States choose to lessen or eliminate criminal sanctions on certain behavior. Much less do they spring into existence, as the Court seems to believe, because *foreign nations* decriminalize conduct. The *Bowers* majority opinion *never* relied on "values we share with a wider civilization," *ante,* at 2483, but rather rejected the claimed right to sodomy on the ground that such a right was not " 'deeply rooted in *this Nation's* history and tradition,' " 478 U.S., at 193–194, 106 S.Ct. 2841 (emphasis added). *Bowers'* rational-basis holding is likewise devoid of any reliance on the views of a "wider civilization," see *id.,* at 196, 106 S.Ct. 2841. The Court's discussion of these foreign views (ignoring, of course, the many countries that have retained criminal prohibitions on sodomy) is therefore meaningless dicta. Dangerous dicta, however, since "this Court . . . should not impose foreign moods, fads, or fashions on Americans." *Foster v. Florida,* 537 U.S. 990, n., 123 S.Ct. 470, 154 L.Ed.2d 359 (2002) (THOMAS, J., concurring in denial of certiorari).

IV

I turn now to the ground on which the Court squarely rests its holding: the contention that there is no rational basis for the law here under attack. This proposition is so out of accord with our jurisprudence—indeed, with the jurisprudence of *any* society we know—that it requires little discussion.

The Texas statute undeniably seeks to further the belief of its citizens that certain forms of sexual behavior are "immoral and unacceptable," *Bowers, supra,* at 196, 106 S.Ct. 2841—the same interest furthered by criminal laws against fornication, bigamy, adultery, adult incest, bestiality, and obscenity. *Bowers* held that this *was* a legitimate state interest. The Court today reaches the opposite conclusion. The Texas statute, it says, "furthers *no legitimate state interest* which can justify its intrusion into the personal and private life of the individual," *ante,* at 2484 (emphasis added). The Court embraces instead Justice STEVENS' declaration in his *Bowers* dissent, that "the fact that the governing majority in a State has traditionally viewed a particular practice as immoral is not a sufficient reason for upholding a law prohibiting the practice," *ante,* at 2483. This effectively decrees the end of all morals legislation. If, as the Court asserts, the promotion of majoritarian sexual morality is not even a *legitimate* state interest, none of the above-mentioned laws can survive rational-basis review.

* * *

Today's opinion is the product of a Court, which is the product of a law-profession culture, that has largely signed on to the so-called homosexual agenda, by which I mean the agenda promoted by some homosexual activists directed at eliminating the moral opprobrium that has traditionally attached to homosexual conduct. I noted in an earlier opinion the fact that the American Association of Law Schools (to which any reputable law school *must* seek to belong) excludes from membership any school that refuses to ban from its job-interview facilities a law firm (no matter how small) that does not wish to hire as a prospective partner a person who openly engages in homosexual conduct. See *Romer, supra,* at 653, 116 S.Ct. 1620.

One of the most revealing statements in today's opinion is the Court's grim warning that the criminalization of homosexual conduct is "an invitation to subject homosexual persons to discrimination both in the public and in the private spheres." *Ante,* at 2482. It is clear from this that the Court has taken sides in the culture war, departing from its role of assuring, as neutral observer, that the democratic rules of engagement are observed. Many Americans do not want persons who openly engage in homosexual conduct as partners in their business, as scoutmasters for their children, as teachers in their children's schools, or as boarders in their home. They view this as protecting themselves and their families from a lifestyle that they believe to be immoral and destructive. The Court views it as "discrimination" which it is the function of our judgments to deter. So imbued is the Court with the law profession's anti-anti-homosexual culture, that it is seemingly unaware that the attitudes of that culture are not obviously "mainstream"; that in most States what the Court calls "discrimination" against those who engage in homosexual acts is perfectly legal; that proposals to ban such "discrimination" under Title VII have repeatedly been rejected by Congress, see Employment Non–Discrimination Act of 1994, S. 2238, 103d Cong., 2d Sess. (1994); Civil Rights Amendments, H.R. 5452, 94th Cong., 1st Sess. (1975); that in some cases such "discrimination" is *mandated* by federal statute, see 10 U.S.C. § 654(b)(1) (mandating discharge from the armed forces of any service member who engages in or intends to engage in homosexual acts); and that in some cases such "discrimination" is a constitutional right, see *Boy Scouts of America v. Dale,* 530 U.S. 640, 120 S.Ct. 2446, 147 L.Ed.2d 554 (2000).

Let me be clear that I have nothing against homosexuals, or any other group, promoting their agenda through normal democratic means. Social perceptions of sexual and other morality change over time, and every group has the right to persuade its fellow citizens that its view of such matters is the best. That homosexuals have achieved some success in that enterprise is attested to by the fact that Texas is one of the few remaining States that criminalize private, consensual homosexual acts. But persuading one's fellow citizens is one thing, and imposing one's views in absence of democratic majority will is something else. I would no more *require* a State to criminalize homosexual acts—or, for that matter, display *any* moral disapprobation of them—than I would *forbid* it to do so. What Texas has chosen to do is well within the range of traditional democratic action, and its hand should not be stayed through the invention of a brand-new "constitutional right" by a Court that is impatient of democratic change. It is indeed true that "later generations can see that laws once thought necessary and proper in fact serve only to oppress," *ante,* at 2484; and when that happens, later generations can repeal those laws. But it is the premise of our system that those judgments are to be made by the people, and not imposed by a governing caste that knows best.

One of the benefits of leaving regulation of this matter to the people rather than to the courts is that the people, unlike judges, need not carry things to their logical conclusion. The people may feel that their disapprobation of homosexual conduct is strong enough to disallow homosexual marriage, but not strong enough to criminalize private homosexual acts—and may legislate accordingly. The Court today pretends that it possesses a similar freedom of action, so that that we need not fear judicial imposition of homosexual marriage, as has recently occurred in Canada (in a decision that the Canadian Government has chosen not to appeal). See *Halpern v. Toronto,* 2003 WL 34950 (Ontario Ct.App.); Cohen, Dozens in Canada Follow Gay Couple's Lead, Washington Post, June 12, 2003, p. A25. At the end of its opinion—after having laid waste the foundations of our rational-basis jurisprudence—the Court says that the present case "does not involve whether the government must give formal recognition to any relationship that homosexual persons seek to enter." *Ante,* at 2484. Do not believe it. More illuminating than this bald, unreasoned disclaimer is the progression of thought displayed by an earlier passage in the Court's opinion, which notes the constitutional protections afforded to "personal decisions relating to *marriage,* procreation, contraception, family relationships, child rearing, and education," and then declares that "[p]ersons in a homosexual relationship may seek autonomy for these purposes, just as heterosexual persons do." *Ante,* at 2482 (emphasis added). Today's opinion dismantles the structure of constitutional law that has permitted a distinction to be made between heterosexual and homosexual unions, insofar as formal recognition in marriage is concerned. If moral disapprobation of homosexual conduct is "no legitimate state interest" for purposes of proscribing that conduct, *ante,* at 2484; and if, as the Court coos (casting aside all pretense of neutrality), "[w]hen sexuality finds overt expression in intimate conduct with another person, the conduct can be but one element in a personal bond that is more enduring," *ante,* at 2478; what justification could there possibly be for denying the benefits of marriage to homosexual couples exercising "[t]he liberty protected by the Constitution," *ibid.*? Surely not the encouragement of procreation, since the sterile and the elderly are allowed to marry. This case "does not involve" the issue of homosexual marriage only if one entertains the belief that principle and logic have nothing to do with the decisions of this Court. Many will hope that, as the Court comfortingly assures us, this is so.

The matters appropriate for this Court's resolution are only three: Texas's prohibition of sodomy neither infringes a "fundamental right" (which the Court does not dispute), nor is unsupported by a rational relation to what the Constitution considers a legitimate state interest, nor denies the equal protection of the laws. I dissent.

■ Justice Thomas, dissenting.

I join Justice SCALIA's dissenting opinion. I write separately to note that the law before the Court today "is . . . uncommonly silly." *Griswold v.*

Connecticut, 381 U.S. 479, 527, 85 S.Ct. 1678, 14 L.Ed.2d 510 (1965) (Stewart, J., dissenting). If I were a member of the Texas Legislature, I would vote to repeal it. Punishing someone for expressing his sexual preference through noncommercial consensual conduct with another adult does not appear to be a worthy way to expend valuable law enforcement resources.

Notwithstanding this, I recognize that as a member of this Court I am not empowered to help petitioners and others similarly situated. My duty, rather, is to "decide cases 'agreeably to the Constitution and laws of the United States.' " *Id.,* at 530, 85 S.Ct. 1678. And, just like Justice Stewart, I "can find [neither in the Bill of Rights nor any other part of the Constitution a] general right of privacy," *ibid.,* or as the Court terms it today, the "liberty of the person both in its spatial and more transcendent dimensions," *ante,* at 2475.

NOTE

The aftermath of the Supreme Court's majority decision, especially the dissent by Justice Antonin Scalia, has been less than anticipated. For example, the U.S. District Court for the District of Utah has affirmed federal and state prohibition of polygamy. The challenge to the polygamy ban was based on *Lawrence,* and as a violation of free exercise of religion, freedom of association, and the right to privacy. Bronson v. Swensen, No. 2:04–CV21–TS, 394 F.Supp.2d 1329 (D. Utah 2005). Also, in New York, legislation that allows only opposite sex couples to marry is rationally related to procreation and child-rearing and thus constitutional in spite of the *Lawrence* decision. Seymour v. Holcomb, 7 Misc.3d 530, 790 N.Y.S.2d 858 (Sup. Ct. 2005). Likewise, *Lawrence* does not provide that same sex couples have a fundamental right to adopt. Lofton v. Secretary of the Department of Children & Family Servs., 358 F.3d 804 (11th Cir. 2004); Wilson v. Ake, 354 F. Supp. 2d 1298 (M.D. Fla. 2005). As to sexual mores, Virginia's anti-fornication statute is void as it cannot be distinguished from the sodomy statute in *Lawrence* and therefore infringes on a person's liberty interest. Martin v. Ziherl, 269 Va. 35, 607 S.E.2d 367 (2005). But after *Lawrence,* Alabama can continue to criminalize the sale of sexual devices marketed primarily for sexual stimulation. Williams v. Attorney Gen. of Ala., 378 F.3d 1232 (11th Cir. 2004).

Loving v. Virginia

Supreme Court of the United States, 1967.
388 U.S. 1, 87 S.Ct. 1817, 18 L.Ed.2d 1010.

■ Mr. Chief Justice Warren delivered the opinion of the Court.

This case presents a constitutional question never addressed by this Court: whether a statutory scheme adopted by the State of Virginia to prevent marriages between persons solely on the basis of racial classifications violates the Equal Protection and Due Process Clauses of the Fourteenth Amendment. For reasons which seem to us to reflect the central meaning of those constitutional commands, we conclude that these statutes cannot stand consistently with the Fourteenth Amendment.

In June 1958, two residents of Virginia, Mildred Jeter, a Negro woman, and Richard Loving, a white man, were married in the District of Columbia pursuant to its laws. Shortly after their marriage, the Lovings returned to Virginia and established their marital abode in Caroline County. At the October Term, 1958, of the Circuit Court of Caroline County, a grand jury issued an indictment charging the Lovings with violating Virginia's ban on interracial marriages. On January 6, 1959, the Lovings pleaded guilty to the charge and were sentenced to one year in jail; however, the trial judge suspended the sentence for a period of 25 years on the condition that the Lovings leave the State and not return to Virginia together for 25 years. . . .

After their convictions, the Lovings took up residence in the District of Columbia. On November 6, 1963, they filed a motion in the state trial court to vacate the judgment and set aside the sentence on the ground that the statutes which they had violated were repugnant to the Fourteenth Amendment. The motion not having been decided by October 28, 1964, the Lovings instituted a class action in the United States District Court for the Eastern District of Virginia requesting that a three-judge court be convened to declare the Virginia antimiscegenation statutes unconstitutional and to enjoin state officials from enforcing their convictions. On January 22, 1965, the state trial judge denied the motion to vacate the sentences, and the Lovings perfected an appeal to the Supreme Court of Appeals of Virginia. On February 11, 1965, the three-judge District Court continued the case to allow the Lovings to present their constitutional claims to the highest state court.

The Supreme Court of Appeals upheld the constitutionality of the antimiscegenation statutes and, after modifying the sentence, affirmed the convictions.[2] The Lovings appealed this decision. . . .

The two statutes under which appellants were convicted and sentenced are part of a comprehensive statutory scheme aimed at prohibiting and punishing interracial marriages. The Lovings were convicted of violating § 20–58 of the Virginia Code:

> "*Leaving State to evade law.*—If any white person and colored person shall go out of this State, for the purpose of being married, and with the intention of returning, and be married out of it, and afterwards return to and reside in it, cohabiting as man and wife, they shall be punished as provided in § 20–59, and the marriage shall be governed by the same law as if it had been solemnized in this State. The fact of their cohabitation here as man and wife shall be evidence of their marriage."

2.   206 Va. 924, 147 S.E.2d 78 (1966).

Section 20–59, which defines the penalty for miscegenation, provides:

"Punishment for marriage.—If any white person intermarry with a colored person, or any colored person intermarry with a white person, he shall be guilty of a felony and shall be punished by confinement in the penitentiary for not less than one nor more than five years."

Other central provisions in the Virginia statutory scheme are § 20–57, which automatically voids all marriages between "a white person and a colored person" without any judicial proceeding, and §§ 20–54 and 1–14 which, respectively, define "white persons" and "colored persons and Indians" for purposes of the statutory prohibitions.[4] The Lovings have never disputed in the course of this litigation that Mrs. Loving is a "colored person" or that Mr. Loving is a "white person" within the meanings given those terms by the Virginia statutes.

Virginia is now one of 16 States which prohibit and punish marriages on the basis of racial classifications. Penalties for miscegenation arose as an incident to slavery and have been common in Virginia since the colonial period. The present statutory scheme dates from the adoption of the Racial Integrity Act of 1924, passed during the period of extreme nativism which followed the end of the First World War. The central features of this Act, and current Virginia law, are the absolute prohibition of a "white person" marrying other than another "white person," a prohibition against issuing marriage licenses until the issuing official is satisfied that the applicants' statements as to their race are correct, certificates of "racial composition" to be kept by both local and state registrars, and the carrying forward of earlier prohibitions against racial intermarriage.

---

4. Section 20–54 of the Virginia Code provides:

"Intermarriage prohibited; meaning of term 'white persons.'—It shall hereafter be unlawful for any white person in this State to marry any save a white person, or a person with no other admixture of blood than white and American Indian. For the purpose of this chapter, the term 'white person' shall apply only to such person as has no trace whatever of any blood other than Caucasian; but persons who have one-sixteenth or less of the blood of the American Indian and have no other non-Caucasic blood shall be deemed to be white persons. All laws heretofore passed and now in effect regarding the intermarriage of white and colored persons shall apply to marriages prohibited by this chapter." Va. Code Ann. § 20–54 (1960 Repl.Vol.).

The exception for persons with less than one-sixteenth "of the blood of the American Indian" is apparently accounted for, in the words of a tract issued by the Registrar of the State Bureau of Vital Statistics, by "the de-sire of all to recognize as an integral and honored part of the white race the descendants of John Rolfe and Pocahontas...." Plecker, The New Family and Race Improvement, 17 Va.Health Bull., Extra No. 12, at 25–26 (New Family Series No. 5, 1925), cited in Wadlington, The Loving Case; Virginia's Anti–Miscegenation Statute in Historical Perspective, 52 Va.L.Rev. 1189, 1202, n. 93 (1966).

Section 1–14 of the Virginia Code provides:

"Colored persons and Indians defined.— Every person in whom there is ascertainable any Negro blood shall be deemed and taken to be a colored person, and every person not a colored person having one fourth or more of American Indian blood shall be deemed an American Indian; except that members of Indian tribes existing in this Commonwealth having one fourth or more of Indian blood and less than one sixteenth of Negro blood shall be deemed tribal Indians." Va.Code Ann. § 1–14 (1960 Repl.Vol.).

In upholding the constitutionality of these provisions in the decision below, the Supreme Court of Appeals of Virginia referred to its 1955 decision in Naim v. Naim, 197 Va. 80, 87 S.E.2d 749, as stating the reasons supporting the validity of these laws. In *Naim*, the state court concluded that the State's legitimate purposes were "to preserve the racial integrity of its citizens," and to prevent "the corruption of blood," "a mongrel breed of citizens," and "the obliteration of racial pride," obviously an endorsement of the doctrine of White Supremacy. Id., at 90, 87 S.E.2d at 756. The court also reasoned that marriage has traditionally been subject to state regulation without federal intervention, and, consequently, the regulation of marriage should be left to exclusive state control by the Tenth Amendment.

While the state court is no doubt correct in asserting that marriage is a social relation subject to the State's police power, Maynard v. Hill, 125 U.S. 190, 8 S.Ct. 723, 31 L.Ed. 654 (1888), the State does not contend in its argument before this Court that its powers to regulate marriage are unlimited notwithstanding the commands of the Fourteenth Amendment. Nor could it do so in light of Meyer v. State of Nebraska, 262 U.S. 390, 43 S.Ct. 625, 67 L.Ed. 1042 (1923), and Skinner v. State of Oklahoma, 316 U.S. 535, 62 S.Ct. 1110, 86 L.Ed. 1655 (1942). Instead, the State argues that the meaning of the Equal Protection Clause, as illuminated by the statements of the Framers, is only that state penal laws containing an interracial element as part of the definition of the offense must apply equally to whites and Negroes in the sense that members of each race are punished to the same degree. Thus, the State contends that, because its miscegenation statutes punish equally both the white and the Negro participants in an interracial marriage, these statutes, despite their reliance on racial classifications do not constitute an invidious discrimination based upon race. The second argument advanced by the State assumes the validity of its equal application theory. The argument is that, if the Equal Protection Clause does not outlaw miscegenation statutes because of their reliance on racial classifications, the question of constitutionality would thus become whether there was any rational basis for a State to treat interracial marriages differently from other marriages. On this question, the State argues, the scientific evidence is substantially in doubt and, consequently, this Court should defer to the wisdom of the state legislature in adopting its policy of discouraging interracial marriages.

Because we reject the notion that the mere "equal application" of a statute containing racial classifications is enough to remove the classifications from the Fourteenth Amendment's proscription of all invidious racial discriminations, we do not accept the State's contention that these statutes should be upheld if there is any possible basis for concluding that they serve a rational purpose....

There can be no question but that Virginia's miscegenation statutes rest solely upon distinctions drawn according to race. The statutes proscribe generally accepted conduct if engaged in by members of different races. Over the years, this Court has consistently repudiated "[d]istinctions between citizens solely because of their ancestry" as being "odious to a free people whose institutions are founded upon the doctrine of equality." Hirabayashi v. United States, 320 U.S. 81, 100, 63 S.Ct. 1375, 1385, 87 L.Ed. 1774 (1943). At the very least, the Equal Protection Clause demands that racial classifications, especially suspect in criminal statutes, be subjected to the "most rigid scrutiny," Korematsu v. United States, 323 U.S. 214, 216, 65 S.Ct. 193, 194, 89 L.Ed. 194 (1944), and, if they are ever to be upheld, they must be shown to be necessary to the accomplishment of some permissible state objective, independent of the racial discrimination which it was the object of the Fourteenth Amendment to eliminate. . . .

There is patently no legitimate overriding purpose independent of invidious racial discrimination which justifies this classification. The fact that Virginia prohibits only interracial marriages involving white persons demonstrates that the racial classifications must stand on their own justification, as measures designed to maintain White Supremacy.[11] We have consistently denied the constitutionality of measures which restrict the rights of citizens on account of race. There can be no doubt that restricting the freedom to marry solely because of racial classifications violates the central meaning of the Equal Protection Clause.

These statutes also deprive the Lovings of liberty without due process of law in violation of the Due Process Clause of the Fourteenth Amendment. The freedom to marry has long been recognized as one of the vital personal rights essential to the orderly pursuit of happiness by free men.

Marriage is one of the "basic civil rights of man," fundamental to our very existence and survival. Skinner v. State of Oklahoma, 316 U.S. 535, 541, 62 S.Ct. 1110, 1113, 86 L.Ed. 1655 (1942). To deny this fundamental freedom on so unsupportable a basis as the racial classifications embodied in these statutes, classifications so directly subversive of the principle of equality at the heart of the Fourteenth Amendment, is surely to deprive all the State's citizens of liberty without due process of law. The Fourteenth Amendment requires that the freedom of choice to marry not be restricted by invidious racial discriminations. Under our Constitution, the freedom to marry or not marry, a person of another race resides with the individual and cannot be infringed by the State.

. . .

NOTE

Almost two decades before *Loving* reached the United States Supreme Court, California's highest court declared that State's anti-miscegenation

---

11. Appellants point out that the State's concern in these statutes, as expressed in the words of the 1924 Act's title, "An Act to Preserve Racial Integrity," extends only to the integrity of the white race. While Virginia prohibits whites from marrying any nonwhite (subject to the exception for the descendants of Pocahontas), Negroes, Orientals, and any other racial class may intermarry without statutory interference.

Appellants contend that this distinction renders Virginia's miscegenation statutes arbitrary and unreasonable even assuming the constitutional validity of an official purpose to preserve "racial integrity." We need not reach this contention because we find the racial classifications in these statutes repugnant to the Fourteenth Amendment, even assuming an even-handed state purpose to protect the "integrity" of all races.

statute unconstitutional as a violation of equal protection guarantees and also as "too vague and uncertain to be enforceable regulations of a fundamental right...." Perez v. Sharp, 32 Cal.2d 711, 198 P.2d 17 (1948). The concurring opinion of Carter, J., drew special attention in legal circles because it relied in part on the Charter of the United Nations.

For further discussion of the development of miscegenation bans, *see* Walter Wadlington, *The Loving Case: Virginia's Anti–Miscegenation Statute in Historical Perspective*, 52 VA.L.REV. 1189 (1966). For an argument that the framers of the Fourteenth Amendment did not mean it to affect anti-miscegenation laws, *see* Alfred Avins, *Anti–Miscegenation Laws and the Fourteenth Amendment: The Original Intent*, 52 VA. L. REV. 1224 (1966).

Zablocki v. Redhail

Supreme Court of the United States, 1978.
434 U.S. 374, 98 S.Ct. 673, 54 L.Ed.2d 618.

■ MR. JUSTICE MARSHALL delivered the opinion of the Court.

At issue in this case is the constitutionality of a Wisconsin statute, Wis.Stat. §§ 245.10(1), (4), (5) (1973), which provides that members of a certain class of Wisconsin residents may not marry, within the State or elsewhere, without first obtaining a court order granting permission to marry. The class is defined by the statute to include any "Wisconsin resident having minor issue not in his custody and which he is under an obligation to support by any court order or judgment." The statute specifies that court permission cannot be granted unless the marriage applicant submits proof of compliance with the support obligation and, in addition, demonstrates that the children covered by the support order "are not then and are not likely thereafter to become public charges." No marriage license may lawfully be issued in Wisconsin to a person covered by the statute, except upon court order; any marriage entered into without compliance with § 245.10 is declared void; and persons acquiring marriage licenses in violation of the section are subject to criminal penalties.

. . .

Appellee Redhail is a Wisconsin resident who, under the terms of § 245.10, is unable to enter into a lawful marriage in Wisconsin or elsewhere so long as he maintains his Wisconsin residency. The facts, according to the stipulation filed by the parties in the District Court, are as follows. In January 1972, when appellee was a minor and a high school student, a paternity action was instituted against him in Milwaukee County Court, alleging that he was the father of a baby girl born out of wedlock on July 5, 1971. After he appeared and admitted that he was the child's father, the court entered an order on May 12, 1972, adjudging appellee the father and ordering him to pay $109 per month as support for the child until she reached 18 years of age. From May 1972 until August 1974, appellee was unemployed and indigent, and consequently was unable to make any support payments.

On September 27, 1974, appellee filed an application for a marriage license with appellant Zablocki, the County Clerk of Milwaukee County, and a few days later the application was denied on the sole ground that appellee had not obtained a court order granting him permission to marry, as required by § 245.10. Although appellee did not petition a state court thereafter, it is stipulated that he would not have been able to satisfy either of the statutory prerequisites for an order granting permission to marry. First, he had not satisfied his support obligations to his illegitimate child, and as of December 1974 there was an arrearage in excess of $3,700. Second, the child had been a public charge since her birth, receiving benefits under the Aid to Families with Dependent Children program. It is stipulated that the child's benefit payments were such that she would have been a public charge even if appellee had been current in his support payments.

.   .   .

The leading decision of this Court on the right to marry is Loving v. Virginia, 388 U.S. 1 (1967). In that case, an interracial couple who had been convicted of violating Virginia's miscegenation laws challenged the statutory scheme on both equal protection and due process grounds. The Court's opinion could have rested solely on the ground that the statutes discriminated on the basis of race in violation of the Equal Protection Clause. But the Court went on to hold that the laws arbitrarily deprived the couple of a fundamental liberty protected by the Due Process Clause, the freedom to marry. . . .

. . . [R]ecent decisions have established that the right to marry is part of the fundamental "right of privacy" implicit in the Fourteenth Amendment's Due Process Clause. . . .*

It is not surprising that the decision to marry has been placed on the same level of importance as decisions relating to procreation, childbirth, child-rearing, and family relationships. As the facts of this case illustrate, it would make little sense to recognize a right of privacy with respect to other matters of family life and not with respect to the decision to enter the relationship that is the foundation of the family in our society. The woman whom appellee desired to marry had a fundamental right to seek an abortion of their expected child, see Roe v. Wade, supra, or to bring the child into life to suffer the myriad social, if not economic, disabilities that the status of illegitimacy brings, see Trimble v. Gordon, 430 U.S. 762, 768–770, and n. 13 (1977); Weber v. Aetna Casualty & Surety Co., 406 U.S. 164, 175–176 (1972). Surely, a decision to marry and raise the child in a traditional family setting must receive equivalent protection. And, if appellee's right to procreate means anything at all, it must imply some right to enter the only relationship in which the State of Wisconsin allows sexual relations legally to take place.[11]

* The opinion quotes from Griswold v. Connecticut, 381 U.S. 479, 486 (1965).

11. Wisconsin punishes fornication as a criminal offense:

By reaffirming the fundamental character of the right to marry, we do not mean to suggest that every state regulation which relates in any way to the incidents of or prerequisites for marriage must be subjected to rigorous scrutiny. To the contrary, reasonable regulations that do not significantly interfere with decisions to enter into the marital relationship may legitimately be imposed. The statutory classification at issue here, however, clearly does interfere directly and substantially with the right to marry.

Under the challenged statute, no Wisconsin resident in the affected class may marry in Wisconsin or elsewhere without a court order, and marriages contracted in violation of the statute are both void and punishable as criminal offenses. Some of those in the affected class, like appellee, will never be able to obtain the necessary court order, because they either lack the financial means to meet their support obligations or cannot prove that their children will not become public charges. These persons are absolutely prevented from getting married. Many others, able in theory to satisfy the statute's requirements, will be sufficiently burdened by having to do so that they will in effect be coerced into foregoing their right to marry. And even those who can be persuaded to meet the statute's requirements suffer a serious intrusion into their freedom of choice in an area in which we have held such freedom to be fundamental.

When a statutory classification significantly interferes with the exercise of a fundamental right, it cannot be upheld unless it is supported by sufficiently important state interests and is closely tailored to effectuate only those interests.... Appellant asserts that two interests are served by the challenged statute: the permission-to-marry proceeding furnishes an opportunity to counsel the applicant as to the necessity of fulfilling his prior support obligations; and the welfare of the out-of-custody children is protected. We may accept for present purposes that these are legitimate and substantial interests, but, since the means selected by the State for achieving these interests unnecessarily impinge on the right to marry, the statute cannot be sustained.

There is evidence that the challenged statute, as originally introduced in the Wisconsin Legislature, was intended merely to establish a mechanism whereby persons with support obligations to children from prior marriages could be counselled before they entered into new marital relationships and incurred further support obligations. Court permission to marry was to be required, but apparently permission was automatically to be granted after counselling was completed. The statute actually enacted, however, does not expressly require or provide for any counselling whatsoever, nor for any automatic granting of permission to marry by the court, and thus it can hardly be justified as a means for ensuring counselling of the persons within its coverage. Even assuming that counselling does take place—a fact as to which there is no evidence in the record—this interest obviously cannot support the withholding of court permission to marry once counselling is completed.

"Whoever has sexual intercourse with a person not his spouse may be fined not more than $200 or imprisoned not more than 6 months or both." Wis.Stat. § 944.15 (1973).

With regard to safeguarding the welfare of the out-of-custody children, appellant's brief does not make clear the connection between the State's interest and the statute's requirements. At argument, appellant's counsel suggested that, since permission to marry cannot be granted unless the applicant shows that he has satisfied his court-determined support obligations to the prior children and that those children will not become public charges, the statute provides incentive for the applicant to make support payments to his children. This "collection device" rationale cannot justify the statute's broad infringement on the right to marry.

First, with respect to individuals who are unable to meet the statutory requirements, the statute merely prevents the applicant from getting married, without delivering any money at all into the hands of the applicant's prior children. More importantly, regardless of the applicant's ability or willingness to meet the statutory requirements, the State already has numerous other means for exacting compliance with support obligations, means that are at least as effective as the instant statute's and yet do not impinge upon the right to marry. Under Wisconsin law, whether the children are from a prior marriage or were born out of wedlock, court-determined support obligations may be enforced directly via wage assignments, civil contempt proceedings, and criminal penalties. And, if the State believes that parents of children out of their custody should be responsible for ensuring that those children do not become public charges, this interest can be achieved by adjusting the criteria used for determining the amounts to be paid under their support orders.

There is also some suggestion that § 245.10 protects the ability of marriage applicants to meet support obligations to prior children by preventing the applicants from incurring new support obligations. But the challenged provisions of § 245.10 are grossly underinclusive with respect to this purpose, since they do not limit in any way new financial commitments by the applicant other than those arising out of the contemplated marriage. The statutory classification is substantially overinclusive as well: given the possibility that the new spouse will actually better the applicant's financial situation, by contributing income from a job or otherwise, the statute in many cases may prevent affected individuals from improving their ability to satisfy their prior support obligations. And, although it is true that the applicant will incur support obligations to any children born during the contemplated marriage, preventing the marriage may only result in the children being born out of wedlock, as in fact occurred in appellee's case. Since the support obligation is the same whether the child is born in or out of wedlock, the net result of preventing the marriage is simply more illegitimate children.

The statutory classification created by §§ 245.101(1), (4), (5) thus cannot be justified by the interests advanced in support of it. The judgment of the District Court is, accordingly,

Affirmed.

■ MR. JUSTICE POWELL, concurring in the judgment.

I concur in the judgment of the Court that Wisconsin's restrictions . . . cannot meet applicable constitutional standards. I write separately because the majority's rationale sweeps too broadly in an area which traditionally has been subject to pervasive state regulation. The Court apparently would subject all state regulation which "directly and substantially" interferes with the decision to marry in a traditional family setting to "critical examination" or "compelling state interest" analysis. Presumably, "reasonable regulations that do not significantly interfere with the decision to enter into the marital relationship may legitimately be imposed." The Court does not present, however, any principled means for distinguishing between the two types of regulations. Since state regulation in this area typically takes the form of a prerequisite or barrier to marriage or divorce, the degree of "direct" interference with the decision to marry or to divorce is unlikely to provide either guidance for state legislatures or a basis for judicial oversight.

. . . [I]t is fair to say that there is a right of marital and familial privacy which places some substantive limits on the regulatory power of government. But the Court has yet to hold that all regulation touching upon marriage implicates a "fundamental right" triggering the most exacting judicial scrutiny.

. . . [Noting that Loving v. Virginia is the principal authority cited by the majority, the opinion explains that because of the issue of racial discrimination] *Loving* involved a denial of a "fundamental freedom" on a wholly unsupportable basis—the use of classifications "directly subversive of the principle of equality at the heart of the Fourteenth Amendment. . . ." It does not speak to the level of judicial scrutiny of, or governmental justification for, "supportable" restrictions on the "fundamental freedom" of individuals to marry or divorce.

In my view, analysis must start from the recognition of domestic relations as "an area that has long been regarded as a virtually exclusive province of the States." Sosna v. Iowa, 419 U.S. 393, 404 (1975). The marriage relation traditionally has been subject to regulation, initially by the ecclesiastical authorities, and later by the secular state. As early as Pennoyer v. Neff, 95 U.S. 714, 734–735 (1877), this Court noted that a State "has absolute right to prescribe the conditions upon which the marriage relation between its own citizens shall be created, and the causes for which it may be dissolved." The State, representing the collective expression of moral aspirations, has an undeniable interest in ensuring that its rules of domestic relations reflect the widely held values of its people.

. . . State regulation has included bans on incest, bigamy, and homosexuality, as well as various preconditions to marriage, such as blood tests. Likewise, a showing of fault on the part of one of the partners traditionally has been a prerequisite to the dissolution of an unsuccessful union. A "compelling state purpose" inquiry would cast doubt on the network of restrictions that the States have fashioned to govern marriage and divorce.

State power over domestic relations is not without constitutional limits. The Due Process Clause requires a showing of justification "when the government intrudes on choices concerning family living arrangements" in a manner which is contrary to deeply rooted traditions. Moore v. City of East Cleveland, Ohio, 431 U.S. 494, 499, 503–504 (1977) (plurality opinion). Due process constraints also limit the extent to which the State may monopolize the process of ordering certain human relationships while excluding the truly indigent from that process. Boddie v. Connecticut, 401 U.S. 371 (1971). Furthermore, under the Equal Protection Clause the means chosen by the State in this case must bear "a fair and substantial relation" to the object of the legislation.

The Wisconsin measure in this case does not pass muster under either due process or equal protection standards. Appellant identifies three objectives which are supposedly furthered by the statute in question: (I) a counseling function; (ii) an incentive to satisfy outstanding support obligations; and (iii) a deterrent against incurring further obligations. The opinion of the Court amply demonstrates that the asserted counseling objective bears no relation to this statute. . . .

The so-called "collection device" rationale presents a somewhat more difficult question. I do not agree with the suggestion in the Court's opinion that a State may never condition the right to marry on satisfaction of existing support obligations simply because the State has alternative methods of compelling such payments. To the extent this restriction applies to persons who are able to make the required support payments but simply wish to shirk their moral and legal obligation, the Constitution interposes no bar to this additional collection mechanism. The vice inheres not in the collection concept, but in the failure to make provision for those without the means to comply with child support obligations. I draw support from Justice Harlan's opinion in Boddie v. Connecticut. In that case, the Court struck down filing fees for divorce actions as applied to those wholly unable to pay, holding "that a State may not, consistent with the obligations imposed on it by the Due Process Clause of the Fourteenth Amendment, preempt the right to dissolve this legal relationship without affording all citizens access to the means it has prescribed for doing so." 401 U.S. at 383. The monopolization present in this case is total, for Wisconsin will not recognize foreign marriages that fail to conform to the requirements of § 245.10.

The third justification, only obliquely advanced by appellant, is that the statute preserves the ability of marriage applicants to support their prior issue by preventing them from incurring new obligations. The challenged provisions of § 245.10 are so grossly underinclusive with respect to this objective, given the many ways that additional financial obligations may be incurred by the applicant quite apart from a contemplated marriage, that the classification "does not bear a fair and substantial relation to the object of the legislation." Craig v. Boren, 429 U.S., at 211 (Powell, J., concurring). . . .

■ [The concurring opinions of CHIEF JUSTICE BURGER, JUSTICES STEWART, and STEVENS, and the dissent of JUSTICE REHNQUIST, have been omitted.]

NOTE

Is there really a fundamental right to marry? Is it "implicit in the concept of ordered liberty"? *See* Palko v. State of Connecticut, 302 U.S. 319, 325, 58 S.Ct. 149, 82 L.Ed. 288 (1937). Note the language in the concurring opinion of Justice Powell in *Zablocki* that "A 'compelling state purpose' inquiry would cast doubt on the network of restrictions that the States have fashioned to govern marriage and divorce." But the Court has said that "marriage involves interests of basic importance in our society", Boddie v. Connecticut, 401 U.S. 371, 376, 91 S.Ct. 780, 28 L.Ed.2d 113 (1971); has pointed to "the favored treatment of marriages", Califano v. Jobst, 434 U.S. 47, 58, 98 S.Ct. 95, 54 L.Ed.2d 228 (1977); and has given "categorical preference" to marriage (Michael H. v. Gerald D., 491 U.S. 110, 129, 109 S.Ct. 2333, 105 L.Ed.2d 91 (1989)). Of course the Court in Loving v. Virginia, 388 U.S. 1, 12, 87 S.Ct. 1817, 18 L.Ed.2d 1010 (1967), stated that "marriage is one of the 'basic civil rights of man', fundamental to our very existence and survival...." If marriage is a fundamental right, is it so because marriage has as its traditional purpose the procreation and raising of children?

In *The Right to Marry and Divorce: A New Look At Some Unanswered Questions*, 63 WASH.U.L.Q. 577 (1985), Professor Cathy Jones examined prevalent restrictions on marriage and concluded that most or all would fail a true "fundamental rights/strict scrutiny" approach. However, she suggests several ways in which courts might interpret or apply *Zablocki* to avoid upsetting "economic or moral reality."

Singer v. Hara

Court of Appeals of Washington, 1974.
11 Wn.App. 247, 522 P.2d 1187.

■ SWANSON, CHIEF JUDGE.

Appellants Singer and Barwick, both males, appeal from the trial court's order denying their motion to show cause by which they sought to compel King County Auditor Lloyd Hara to issue a marriage license to them....

Appellants argue three basic assignments of error, namely, (1) the trial court erred in concluding that the Washington marriage statutes, RCW 26.04.010 et seq., prohibit same sex marriages; (2) the trial court's order violates the Equal Rights Amendment (ERA) to the Washington State Constitution, Const. art. 31, § 1; and (3) the trial court's order violates the eighth, ninth and fourteenth amendments to the United States Constitution.[1]

---

1. Appellants also list as an "assignment of error" the assertion that the trial court's order "was based on the erroneous and fallacious conclusion that same sex marriages are destructive to society." In support of this assertion, appellants devote nearly 40 pages of their brief to what they characterize as a discussion of "the concept of homosexuality and same sex marriages through the eyes of other important disciplines—that of

[After reviewing the Washington legislation, the court found that] [t]he trial court correctly concluded that the applicable marriage statutes do not permit same sex marriage.

Appellants next argue that if, as we have held, our state marriage laws must be construed to prohibit same sex marriages, such laws are unconstitutional when so applied. In this context, we consider appellants' second assignment of error which is directed to the proposition that the state prohibition of same sex marriages violates the ERA which recently became part of our state constitution[4].... [T]o our knowledge, no court in the nation has ruled upon the legality of same sex marriage in light of an equal rights amendment. The ERA provides, in relevant part:

> Equality of rights and responsibility under the law shall not be denied or abridged on account of sex.

In seeking the protection of the ERA, appellants argue that the language of the amendment itself leaves no question of interpretation and that the essential thrust of the ERA is to make sex an impermissible legal classification. Therefore, they argue, to construe state law to permit a man to marry a woman but at the same time to deny him the right to marry another man is to construct an unconstitutional classification "on account of sex." In response to appellants' contention, the state points out that all same sex marriages are deemed illegal by the state, and therefore argues that there is no violation of the ERA so long as marriage licenses are denied equally to both male and female pairs. In other words, the state suggests that appellants are not entitled to relief under the ERA because they have failed to make a showing that they are somehow being treated differently by the state than they would be if they were females. Appellants suggest, however, that the holdings in Loving v. Virginia, 388 U.S. 1, 9, 87 S.Ct. 1817, 18 L.Ed.2d 1010 (1967); Perez v. Lippold, 32 Cal.2d 711, 198 P.2d 17 (1948), and J.S.K. Enterprises, Inc. v. City of Lacey, 6 Wash.App. 43, 492 P.2d 600 (1971), are contrary to the position taken by the state. We disagree.

In *Loving,* the state of Virginia argued that its anti-miscegenation statutes did not violate constitutional prohibitions against racial classifica-

---

the sociologists, theologians, scientists, and doctors." Appellants state that "a basic understanding of homosexuals and society is a precondition to an enlightened discussion of the legal grounds raised...." Although we do not quarrel with that proposition, we deem it appropriate to observe that appellants' discussion in that regard does not present a legal argument, nor is there any evidence in the record to suggest that the trial court in fact based its order on the "erroneous and fallacious conclusion" to which appellants take exception. Therefore, while we recognize that appellants have presented a valuable context for the discussion of their legal points, we have endeavored to confine this opinion to discussion of the legal issues presented without attempting to present our views on matters of sociology, theology, science and medicine.

4. HJR 61, commonly known as the "equal rights amendment," was approved by the voters November 7, 1972, and became effective December 7, 1972. Const. amend. 61, adding article 31. The language of the ERA is substantially similar to the federal ERA now before the states for ratification as the twenty-seventh amendment to the United States Constitution.

tions because the statutes affected both racial groups equally. The Supreme Court, noting that "the fact of equal application does not immunize the statute from the very heavy burden of justification which the Fourteenth Amendment has traditionally required of state statutes drawn according to race," held that the Virginia laws were founded on an impermissible racial classification and therefore could not be used to deny inter-racial couples the "fundamental" right to marry. The California court made a similar ruling as to that state's anti-miscegenation law in *Perez.*

Although appellants suggest an analogy between the racial classification involved in *Loving* and *Perez* and the alleged sexual classification involved in the case at bar, we do not find such an analogy. The operative distinction lies in the relationship which is described by the term "marriage" itself, and that relationship is the legal union of one man and one woman. Washington statutes, specifically those relating to marriage (RCW 26.04) and marital (community) property (RCW 26.16), are clearly founded upon the presumption that marriage, as a legal relationship, may exist only between one man and one woman who are otherwise qualified to enter that relationship.[6] Similarly although it appears that the appellate courts of this state until now have not been required to define specifically what constitutes a marriage, it is apparent from a review of cases dealing with legal questions arising out of the marital relationship that the definition of marriage as the legal union of one man and one woman who are otherwise qualified to enter into the relationship not only is clearly implied from such cases, but also was deemed by the court in each case to be so obvious as not to require recitation.... Finally, the courts known by us to have considered the question have all concluded that same sex relationships are outside of the proper definition of marriage. Jones v. Hallahan, 501 S.W.2d 588 (Ky.1973); Baker v. Nelson, 291 Minn. 310, 191 N.W.2d 185 (1971); Anonymous v. Anonymous, 67 Misc.2d 982, 325 N.Y.S.2d 499 (1971). Appellants have cited no authority to the contrary.

Given the definition of marriage which we have enunciated, the distinction between the case presented by appellants and those presented in *Loving* and *Perez* is apparent. In *Loving* and *Perez,* the parties were barred from entering into the marriage relationship because of an impermissible racial classification. There is no analogous sexual classification involved in the instant case because appellants are not being denied entry into the marriage relationship because of their sex; rather, they are being denied entry into the marriage relationship because of the recognized definition of that relationship as one which may be entered into only by two persons who are members of the opposite sex.[8] As the court observed in Jones v.

6. In this regard, we are aided by the rule of statutory construction that words of a statute must be understood in their usual and ordinary sense in the absence of a statutory definition to the contrary....

8. Appellants argue that *Loving* and *Perez* are analogous to the case at bar notwithstanding what might be the "definition" of marriage. They argue that at the time *Loving* and *Perez* were decided, marriage *by definition* barred interracial marriages and that the *Loving* and *Perez* courts changed that definition through their interpretation of the Fourteenth Amendment. Appellants

Hallahan, supra, 501 S.W.2d at 590: "In substance, the relationship proposed by the appellants does not authorize the issuance of a marriage license because what they propose is not a marriage." *Loving* and *Perez* are inapposite.

J.S.K. Enterprises, Inc. v. City of Lacey, supra, is also factually and legally dissimilar to the case at bar. In that case, this court held that a city ordinance which permitted massagists to administer massages only to customers of their own sex constituted discrimination on the basis of sex, prohibited by the equal protection clause of the fourteenth amendment to the United States Constitution, and also violated RCW 49.12.200, relating to the right of women to pursue any employment. We see no analogy between the right of women to administer massages to men and the question of whether the prohibition against same sex marriages is unconstitutional. The right recognized in *J.S.K. Enterprises, Inc.* on the basis of principles applicable to employment discrimination has nothing to do with the question presented by appellants.

Appellants apparently argue, however, that notwithstanding the fact that the equal protection analysis applied in *Loving, Perez* and *J.S.K. Enterprises, Inc.* may render those cases distinguishable from the case at bar, the absolute language of the ERA requires the conclusion that the prohibition against same sex marriages is unconstitutional. In this context, appellants suggest that definition of marriage, as the legal union of one man and one woman, in and of itself, when applied to appellants, constitutes a violation of the ERA. Therefore, appellants contend, persons of the same sex must be presumed to have the constitutional right to marry one another in the absence of a countervailing interest or clear exception to the ERA.

Appellants cite no case law in support of their position, but direct our attention to the analysis set forth in Note, The Legality of Homosexual Marriage, 82 Yale L.J. 573 (1973), and in Brown, Emerson, Falk & Freedman, The Equal Rights Amendment: A Constitutional Basis for Equal Rights for Women, 80 Yale L.J. 871 (1971). The latter article, however, is clearly written in the context of the impact of the ERA upon the rights of women and men as individuals and the authors make no suggestion that the ERA requires a change in the definition of marriage to include same sex relationships.[9] The authors suggest that the ERA prohibition of sex dis-

---

suggest that the ERA operates in a manner analogous to the Fourteenth Amendment to require us to change the definition of marriage to include same sex marriages. We disagree. The *Loving* and *Perez* courts did not change the basic definition of marriage as the legal union of one man and one woman; rather, they merely held that the race of the man or woman desiring to enter that relationship could not be considered by the state in granting a marriage license. In other words, contrary to appellants' contention, the

Fourteenth Amendment did not require any change in the definition of marriage and, as we hold today, neither does the ERA....

9. The authors describe the basic principle of the ERA in part as follows, at 889: "The basic principle of the Equal Rights Amendment is that sex is not a permissible factor in determining the legal rights of women, or of men. This means that the treatment of any person by the law may not be based upon the circumstance that such person is of one sex or the other. The law does, of course,

crimination is "absolute," meaning that one person may not be favored over another where sex is the only distinguishing factor between the two. In that context, the authors state at 892:

> From this analysis it follows that the constitutional mandate must be absolute. The issue under the Equal Rights Amendment cannot be different but equal, reasonable or unreasonable classification, suspect classification, fundamental interest, or the demands of administrative expediency. Equality of rights means that sex is not a factor. This at least is the premise of the Equal Rights Amendment.

The author of the note, The Legality of Homosexual Marriage, supra, applies the aforementioned analysis of the ERA in the totally different context of same sex relationships and thus concludes that the ERA requires that such relationships be accommodated by state marriage laws. We are not persuaded by such reasoning. We do not believe that approval of the ERA by the people of this state reflects any intention upon their part to offer couples involved in same sex relationships the protection of our marriage laws. A consideration of the basic purpose of the ERA makes it apparent why that amendment does not support appellants' claim of discrimination. The primary purpose of the ERA is to overcome discriminatory legal treatment as between men and women "on account of sex." The popular slogan, "Equal pay for equal work," particularly expresses the rejection of the notion that merely because a person is a woman, rather than a man, she is to be treated differently than a man with qualifications equal to her own.

Prior to adoption of the ERA, the proposition that women were to be accorded a position in the law inferior to that of men had a long history.[10]

impose different benefits or different burdens upon different members of the society. That differentiation in treatment may rest upon particular characteristics or traits of the persons affected, such as strength, intelligence, and the like. But under the Equal Rights Amendment the existence of such a characteristic or trait to a greater degree in one sex does not justify classification by sex rather than by the particular characteristic or trait. Likewise the law may make different rules for some people than for others on the basis of the activity they are engaged in or the function they perform. But the fact that in our present society members of one sex are more likely to be found in a particular activity or to perform a particular function does not allow the law to fix legal rights by virtue of membership in that sex. In short, sex is a prohibited classification."

10. For example, Mr. Justice Bradley, in his concurring opinion upholding the refusal of a state court to license a woman to practice law in Bradwell v. Illinois, 83 U.S. (16 Wall.) 130, 21 L.Ed. 442 (1872), stated in part at 141:

[T]he civil law, as well as nature herself, has always recognized a wide difference in the respective spheres and destinies of man and woman. Man is, or should be, woman's protector and defender. The natural and proper timidity and delicacy which belongs to the female sex evidently unfits it for many of the occupations of civil life. The constitution of the family organization, which is founded in the divine ordinance, as well as in the nature of things, indicates the domestic sphere as that which properly belongs to the domain and functions of womanhood. The harmony, not to say identity, of interests and views which belong, or should belong, to the family institution is repugnant to the idea of a woman adopting a distinct and independent career from that of her husband. . . .

. . . The paramount destiny and mission of woman are to fulfil the noble and benign offices of wife and mother. This is the law of the Creator.

Thus, in that context, the purpose of the ERA is to provide the legal protection, as between men and women, that apparently is missing from the state and federal Bills of Rights, and it is in light of that purpose that the language of the ERA must be construed. To accept the appellants' contention that the ERA must be interpreted to prohibit statutes which refuse to permit same sex marriages would be to subvert the purpose for which the ERA was enacted by expanding its scope beyond that which was undoubtedly intended by the majority of the citizens of this state who voted for the amendment.

We are of the opinion that a common-sense reading of the language of the ERA indicates that an individual is afforded no protection under the ERA unless he or she first demonstrates that a right or responsibility has been denied solely because of that individual's sex. Appellants are unable to make such a showing because the right or responsibility they seek does not exist. The ERA does not create any new rights or responsibilities, such as the conceivable right of persons of the same sex to marry one another; rather, it merely insures that existing rights and responsibilities, or such rights and responsibilities as may be created in the future, which previously might have been wholly or partially denied to one sex or to the other, will be equally available to members of either sex. The form of discrimination or difference in legal treatment which comes within the prohibition of the ERA necessarily is of an invidious character because it is discrimination based upon the fortuitous circumstance of one's membership in a particular sex per se. This is not to say, however, that the ERA prohibits all legal differentiations which might be made among males and females. A generally recognized "corollary" or exception to even an "absolute" interpretation of the ERA is the proposition that laws which differentiate between the sexes are permissible so long as they are based upon the unique physical characteristics of a particular sex, rather than upon a person's membership in a particular sex per se. See Brown, Emerson, Falk & Freedman, The Equal Rights Amendment: A Constitutional Basis for Equal Rights for Women, supra at 893–96.

In the instant case, it is apparent that the state's refusal to grant a license allowing the appellants to marry one another is not based upon appellants' status as males, but rather it is based upon the state's recognition that our society as a whole views marriage as the appropriate and desirable forum for procreation and the rearing of children. This is true even though married couples are not required to become parents and even though some couples are incapable of becoming parents and even though not all couples who produce children are married. These, however, are exceptional situations. The fact remains that marriage exists as a protected legal institution primarily because of societal values associated with the propagation of the human race. Further, it is apparent that no same sex couple offers the possibility of the birth of children by their union. Thus the refusal of the state to authorize same sex marriage results from such impossibility of reproduction rather than from an invidious discrimination "on account of sex." Therefore, the definition of marriage as the legal union of one man and one woman is permissible as applied to appellants, notwithstanding the prohibition contained in the ERA, because it is founded upon the unique physical characteristics of the sexes, and appellants are not being discriminated against because of their status as males per se. In short, we hold the ERA does not require the state to authorize same sex marriage.

Appellants' final assignment of error is based primarily upon the proposition that the state's failure to grant them a marriage license violates the Equal Protection Clause of the Fourteenth Amendment to the United States Constitution. The threshold question presented involves the standard by which to measure appellants' constitutional argument. We have held that the effect of our state marriage statutes is to prohibit same sex marriages, and as a general proposition such statutes must be presumed constitutional. See Aetna Life Ins. Co. v. Washington Life & Disability Ins. Guar. Ass'n, 83 Wash.2d 523, 520 P.2d 162 (1974). The operative effect of such a presumption is that the statutory classification in question—the exclusion of same sex relationships from the definition of marriage—does not offend the Equal Protection Clause if it rests upon some reasonable basis.

Appellants contend, however, that a standard stricter than such a "reasonable basis" test must be applied to the operation of our state marriage laws. Appellants point out that a fundamental right—the right to marry—is at stake in the instant litigation, ... Moreover, appellants, reasoning primarily by analogy from *Loving* and related cases, argue that the statutory prohibition against same sex marriages constitutes a classification based upon sex. Therefore, appellants urge that the applicable standard under the Equal Protection Clause requires that the classification be deemed "inherently suspect" and one which may not be sustained unless the state demonstrates that a "compelling state interest" so requires.

We do not take exception to the proposition that the Equal Protection Clause of the Fourteenth Amendment requires strict judicial scrutiny of legislative attempts at sexual discrimination. Our state Supreme Court has held that a legislative classification based upon sex is inherently suspect, Hanson v. Hutt, 83 Wash.2d 195, 517 P.2d 599 (1973), as has a plurality of the United States Supreme Court, Frontiero v. Richardson, 411 U.S. 677, 93 S.Ct. 1764, 36 L.Ed.2d 583 (1973). As we have already held in connection with our discussion of the ERA, however, appellants do not present a case of sexual discrimination. Appellants were not denied a marriage license because of their sex; rather, they were denied a marriage license because of the nature of marriage itself.

Appellants appear to recognize the distinction we make because they also argue that the definition of marriage as it is reflected in our marriage statutes constitutes an inherently suspect classification because it discriminates against homosexuals as a group. In other words, appellants appear to present the alternative argument that although they are not being discriminated against because they are males, they are being discriminated against because they happen to be homosexual.

Although appellants present argument to the contrary, we agree with the state's contention that to define marriage to exclude homosexual or any other same sex relationships is not to create an inherently suspect legislative classification requiring strict judicial scrutiny to determine a compelling state interest. The state contends that the exclusion of same sex relationships from our marriage statutes may be upheld under the traditional "reasonable basis" or "rational relationship" test to which we have previously made reference. We agree.

There can be no doubt that there exists a rational basis for the state to limit the definition of marriage to exclude same sex relationships. Although, as appellants contend, other cultures may have fostered differing definitions of marriage, marriage in this state, as elsewhere in the nation, has been deemed a private relationship of a man and a woman (husband and wife) which involves "interests of basic importance in our society." See Boddie v. Connecticut, 401 U.S. 371, 376, 91 S.Ct. 780, 785, 28 L.Ed.2d 113 (1971). Accordingly, subject to constitutional limitations, the state has exclusive dominion over the legal institution of marriage and the state alone has the "prerogative of creating and overseeing this important institution." Coleman v. Coleman, 32 Ohio St.2d 155, 160, 291 N.E.2d 530, 534 (1972).

We do not seek to define in detail the "interests of basic importance" which are served by retaining the present definition of marriage as the legal union of one man and one woman. The societal values which are involved in this area must be left to the examination of the legislature. For constitutional purposes, it is enough to recognize that marriage as now defined is deeply rooted in our society. Although, as appellants hasten to point out, married persons are not required to have children or even to engage in sexual relations, marriage is so clearly related to the public interest in affording a favorable environment for the growth of children that we are unable to say that there is not a rational basis upon which the state may limit the protection of its marriage laws to the legal union of one man and one woman. Under such circumstances, although the legislature may change the definition of marriage within constitutional limits, the constitution does not require the change sought by appellants. As the court observed in Baker v. Nelson, supra, 291 Minn. at 312, 313, 191 N.W.2d at 186:

> The institution of marriage as a union of man and woman, uniquely involving the procreation and rearing of children within a family, is as old as the book of Genesis. . . . This historic institution manifestly is more deeply founded than the asserted contemporary concept of marriage and societal interests for which petitioners contend. The due process clause of the Fourteenth Amendment is not a charter for restructuring it by judicial legislation.

.   .   .

. . . [W]e hold that the trial court correctly concluded that the state's denial of a marriage license to appellants is required by our state statutes and permitted by both the state and federal constitutions.

NOTES

Hawaii. Baehr v. Lewin, 74 Haw. 530, 852 P.2d 44 (1993).The case that went further than any other to date in seeking to establish the right of persons of the same sex to marry was *Baehr*. Two female couples, Genora Dancel and Nina Baehr, and Tammy Rodrigues and Antoinette Pregil, plus one male couple, Pat Lagon and Joseph Melillo met all of the state requirements for marriage but were denied a license because each couple was of the same sex and thus not capable of forming a valid marriage under Hawaii law. The plaintiffs then challenged the state's denial based on guarantees of privacy, equal protection and due process under the state constitution. The Hawaii Supreme Court disregarded the issue of homosexuality, but did hold that the state constitution's prohibition of discrimination based on sex classifications required the state to justify its denial of a marriage license to the plaintiffs by compelling state interests.

The court's holding demanded strict scrutiny of the state's denial even though the state, as had been done before, argued the definition of marriage itself precluded the possibility of discrimination: "the right of persons of the same sex to marry one another does not exist because marriage, by definition and usage, means a special relationship between a man and a woman." *Id.*, 852 P.2d at 61 [quoting the state's brief]. The Hawaii court found this argument to be "circular and unpersuasive." *Id.* Instead, borrowing from the example of the Supreme Court in *Loving v. Virginia*, the court allowed that the definition of marriage could change: "customs change with an evolving social order." *Id.* at 63. In remanding the case to the circuit court for hearings, the court ruled that:

> [the statute] is presumed to be unconstitutional . . . unless Lewin, as an agent of the State of Hawaii, can show that (a) the statute's sex-based classification is justified by compelling state interests and (b) the statute is narrowly drawn to avoid unnecessary abridgements of the applicant couples' constitutional rights. *Id.* at 67.

On December 3,1996, the Circuit Court of Hawaii held that the State of Hawaii had not established a compelling state interest to prohibit persons of the same sex from being entitled to a license to marry and notified the state supreme court of its holding. *See* Baehr v. Miike, Civ. No. 91–1394, 1996 WL 694235 (Haw.Cir.Ct.Dec.3, 1996). The country waited to see if the state supreme court would then require the state to issue licenses to the plaintiffs and arguably others similarly situated, thus providing the possibility of state-recognized same sex marriage. But while the country waited, the Hawaii legislature passed two bills. The first went into effect on July 8, 1997 permitting reciprocal beneficiary relationships to be established between persons at least 18 years old, neither party may be married or be a party to another reciprocal beneficiary relationship, and they must be barred from marrying one another under state law. If a couple qualifies, the benefits conferred exceed any provided under domestic partnership; the benefits are meant to mirror those given to married couples. Included would be: surviving spouse elective share rights, inheritance, workers compensation survivorship, and legal standing relating to wrongful death and victims' rights. *See* Haw. Rev. Stat. § 560:2–202 (1998). The reciprocal beneficiary legislation is a domestic partnership arrangement, having none of the marriage-like requirements of license to enter and grounds for dissolution as will be found in the Vermont Civil Union legislation.

The second bill enacted by the legislature provided for a constitutional amendment allowing the Hawaii legislature the right to restrict marriage to persons of the opposite sex: "The legislature shall have the power to reserve marriage to opposite sex couples." The constitutional amendment passed in November 1998. *See* Hawaii Const., art. I, § 23. Then, in December 1999, the Supreme Court of Hawaii ruled that: "The marriage amendment has rendered the plaintiffs' complaint moot" and ordered the judgement of the circuit court be reversed. *See* Baehr v. Miike, 92 Hawai'i 634, 994 P.2d 566 (1999). This judgement ended the possibility for same sex marriage in Hawaii, but left in place the nation's most comprehensive version of domestic partnership.

Alaska. Brause v. Bureau of Vital Statistics, No. 3AN–95–6562 CI, 1998 WL 88743 (Alaska Super.1998). The court held that under the privacy provision of the Alaska Constitution, persons have a fundamental right to choose a life partner. Thus, the state must demonstrate a compelling state interest to deny a marriage license to same sex couples. Before the litigation could take on the character of that in Hawaii, citizens in Alaska voted on November 3, 1998, to amend the state constitution to define marriage as being between one man and one woman. *See* Alaska Const., art. I, § 25. This ended the constitutional challenge.

Statutory Definitions of Marriage. Following the litigation in Hawaii and Alaska, many states enacted legislation defining marriage as being between a man and a woman. The statutes were passed so as to deny the legitimacy of marriage between same sex couples and to deny recognition of any same sex marriage celebrated outside of the state. For example, in a controversial ballot initiative, Proposition 22, voters in California voted to amend the California Family Code so as to prohibit recognition of gay marriage in the state. *See* Ben White, *Californians Vote to Ban Recognition of Gay Marriage*, Wash. Post, Mar. 8, 2000, at A21. Also, the Federal government enacted the Defense of Marriage Act, 110 Stat. 2419 (1996), amending 28 U.S.C.A. § 1738C & 1 U.S.C.A. § 7. The word marriage as used in the statute means only a legal union between one man and one woman, and the word spouse refers only to a person of the opposite sex who is a husband or wife. Furthermore, the Act provides that no state, territory, or possession of the United States, or Indian Tribe, shall be required to give effect to any public act, record, or judicial proceeding of any other state, territory, possession, or tribe respecting a relationship between persons of the same sex that is treated as a marriage. *See generally* Jenne R. Shui-

Kunze, Note, *The Defenseless Marriage Act: The Constitutionality of the Defense of Marriage Act as an Extension of Congressional Power Under the Full Faith and Credit Clause*, 48 CASE W. RES. L. REV. 351 (1998); Larry Kramer, *Same–Sex Marriage, Conflict of Laws, and the Unconstitutional Public Policy Exception*, 106 YALE L. J. 1965 (1997); Jon–Peter Kelley, Note, *An Act of Infidelity: Why the Defense of Marriage Act is Unfaithful to the Constitution*, 7 CORNELL J. L. & PUB. POL'Y 203 (1997).

Massachusetts. Based on the Massachusetts Constitution's guarantees of due process and equal protection, the Supreme Judicial Court of Massachusetts ruled that the state may no longer deny the protections, benefits and obligations conferred by civil marriage to two individuals of the same sex. Goodridge v. Department of Pub. Health, 440 Mass. 309, 798 N.E.2d 941 (2003). Borrowing from the liberty protections announced in *Lawrence*, and the developing understanding of the invidious quality of discrimination identified in *Loving*, the court ruled that there was no longer even a rational basis for the state to forbid marriage license to persons of the same sex. Subsequently, the state began issuing marriage licenses to same sex couples who could demonstrate that they were residents of Massachusetts. Massachusetts statutes stipulate that before the state may issue a marriage license to a nonresident of Massachusetts, a state official must be satisfied "that such person is not prohibited from intermarrying by the laws of the jurisdiction where he or she resides." MASS. GEN. LAWS ANN. ch. 207, § 12 (West 1998). Dissenting justices argued that the state's legislature's denial of marriage licenses to same sex couples is rationale and deserves deference by the courts. In effect the dissenting justices argued that same sex marriage must be left to the legislative process, otherwise courts could use the liberty and due process clauses as vehicles to enforce judicial social policies. Such action is prohibited under separation of powers. As this casebook goes to press the Massachusetts legislature is grappling with whether or not to include on the 2008 ballot a voter referendum to provide a state constitutional amendment defining marriage as between a man and a woman. Such an amendment would not affect the validity of already solemnized same sex marriage, but it would prohibit future marriages between persons of the same sex after the effective date of the amendment.

Vermont, New Hampshire, Connecticut and New Jersey. Baker v. Vermont, 170 Vt. 194, 744 A.2d 864. On December 20, 1999, the Vermont Supreme Court ruled that the Common Benefits Clause of the Vermont Constitution requires that same sex couples receive the same benefits and protections as married couples under state law. The court held that, "viewed in the light of history, logic, and experience, we conclude that none of the interests asserted by the State provides a reasonable and just basis for the continued exclusion of same sex couples from benefits incident to a civil marriage license under Vermont law." *Id.* at 886. And thus, "the current statutory scheme [marriage restricted to opposite-sex persons] shall remain in effect for a reasonable period of time to enable the Legislature to consider and enact implementing legislation in an orderly and expeditious fashion." *Id.* at 887. During April 2000, Vermont enacted An Act Relating to Civil Unions. *See* Vermont H. 847 (2000). *See* William N. Eskridge, Jr., *Equality Practice: Liberal Reflections on the Jurisprudence of Civil Unions*, 64 Alb. L. Rev. 853 (2001); Mark Strasser, *Equal Protection at the Crossroads; on Baker, Common Benefits, and Facial Neutrality*, 42 Ariz. L. Rev. 935 (2000); Greg Johnson, *Vermont Civil Unions: The New Language of Marriage*, 25 Vt. L. Rev. 15 (2000); Michael Mello, *For Today I'm Gay: the Unfinished Battle for Same–Sex Marriage in Vermont*, 25 Vt. L. Rev. 149 (2000).

Connecticut introduced civil unions in 2005 (2005 Conn. Pub. Acts 13), and in October 2006, the New Jersey Supreme Court, in a decision similar to Vermont's seven years earlier, ruled that the state constitution's equal protection guarantee requires that same sex couples be afforded on equal terms the same benefits enjoyed by opposite sex couples within the existing marriage statutes. *See* Lewis v. Harris, 188 N.J. 415, 908 A.2d 196 (2006). By so ruling, the highest state court allowed the legislature to create a separate civil union status, thus permitting the exclusion of the status of marriage as a benefit to be obtained. The state court refused to hold that there is a fundamental right to same sex marriage, but held that an existing comprehensive domestic partnership law was not sufficiently extensive in providing benefits to same sex couples. The New Jersey legislature passed the civil union legislation on December 14, 2006. *See* 2006 N.J. Sess. Law Serv. ch. 103 (West). In addition to permitting same sex couples all protections and responsibilities under the law as are granted to spouses in marriage, the statute also recognizes civil unions validly entered into in other jurisdictions.

VERMONT STATUTES ANN., TIT. 4, 8, 15, 18 (2006)

§ 1202. Requisites of a valid civil union

For a civil union to be established in Vermont, it shall be necessary that the parties to a civil union satisfy all of the following criteria:

(1) Not be a party to another civil union or a marriage.

(2) Be of the same sex and therefore excluded from the marriage laws of this state.

(3) Meet the criteria and obligations set forth in 18 V.S.A. chapter 106.

§ 1204. Benefits, protections and responsibilities of parties to a civil union

(a) Parties to a civil union shall have all the same benefits, protections and responsibilities under law, whether they derive from statute, administrative or court rule, policy, common law or any other source of civil law, as are granted to spouses in a marriage.

(b) A party to a civil union shall be included in any definition or use of the terms "spouse," "family," "immediate family," "dependent," "next of kin," and other terms that denote the spousal relationship, as those terms are used throughout the law.

(c) Parties to a civil union shall be responsible for the support of one another to the same degree and in the same manner as prescribed under law for married persons.

(d) The law of domestic relations, including annulment, separation and divorce, child custody and support, and property division and maintenance shall apply to parties to a civil union.

(e) The following is a nonexclusive list of legal benefits, protections and responsibilities of spouses, which shall apply in like manner to parties to a civil union:

(1) laws relating to title, tenure, descent and distribution, intestate succession, waiver of will, survivorship, or other incidents of the acquisition, ownership, or transfer, inter vivos or at death, of real or personal property, including eligibility to hold real and personal property as tenants by the entirety (parties to a civil union meet the common law unity of person qualification for purposes of a tenancy by the entirety);

(2) causes of action related to or dependent upon spousal status, including an action for wrongful death, emotional distress, loss of consortium, dramshop, or other torts or actions under contracts reciting, related to, or dependent upon spousal status;

(3) probate law and procedure, including nonprobate transfer;

(4) adoption law and procedure;

(5) group insurance for state employees under 3 V.S.A. § 631, and continuing care contracts under 8 V.S.A. § 8005;

(6) spouse abuse programs under 3 V.S.A. § 18;

(7) prohibitions against discrimination based upon marital status;

(8) victim's compensation rights under 13 V.S.A. § 5351;

(9) workers' compensation benefits;

(10) laws relating to emergency and non-emergency medical care ad treatment, hospital visitation and notification, including the Patient's Bill of Rights under 18 V.S.A. chapter 42 and the Nursing Home Residents' Bill of Rights under 33 V.S.A. chapter 73;

(11) terminal care documents under 18 V.S.A. chapter 111, and durable power of attorney for health care execution and revocation under 14 V.S.A. chapter 121;

(12) family leave benefits under 21 V.S.A. chapter 5, subchapter 4A;

(13) public assistance benefits under state law;

(14) laws relating to taxes imposed by the state or a municipality other than estate taxes;

(15) laws relating to immunity from compelled testimony and the marital communication privilege;

(16) the homestead rights of a surviving spouse under 27 V.S.A. § 105 and homestead property tax allowance under 32 V.S.A. § 6062;

(17) laws relating to loans to veterans under 8 V.S.A. § 1849;

(18) the definition of family farmer under 10 V.S.A. § 272;

(19) laws relating to the making, revoking and objecting to anatomical gifts by others under 18 V.S.A. § 5240;

(20) state pay for military service under 20 V.S.A. § 1544;

(21) application for absentee ballot under 17 V.S.A. § 2532;

(22) family landowner rights to fish and hunt under 10 V.S.A. § 4253;

(23) legal requirements for assignment of wages under 8 V.S.A. § 2235; and

(24) affirmance of relationship under 15 V.S.A. § 7.

(f) The rights of parties to a civil union, with respect to a child of whom either becomes the natural parent during the term of the civil union, shall be the same as those of a married couple, with respect to a child of whom either spouse becomes the natural parent during the marriage.

§ 1206. Dissolution of civil unions

The family court shall have jurisdiction over all proceedings relating to the dissolution of civil unions. The dissolution of civil unions shall follow the same procedures and be subject to the same substantive rights and obligations that are involved in the dissolution of marriage in accordance with chapter 11 of this title, including any residency requirements.

§ 5164. Persons Authorized to Certify Civil Unions

Civil unions may be certified by a supreme court justice, a superior court judge, a district judge, a judge of probate, an assistant judge, a justice of the peace or by a member of the clergy residing in this state and ordained or licensed, or otherwise regularly authorized by the published laws or discipline of the general conference, convention or other authority of his or her faith or denomination or by such a clergy person residing in an adjoining state or country, whose parish, church, temple, mosque or other religious organization lies wholly or in part in this state, or by a member of the clergy residing in some other state of the United States or in the Dominion of Canada, provided he or she has first secured from the probate court of the district within which the civil union is to be certified, a special authorization, authorizing him or her to certify the civil union if such probate judge determines that the circumstances make the special authorization desirable. Civil unions among the Friends or Quakers, the Christadelphian Ecclesia and the Baha'i Faith may be certified in the manner used in such societies.

NOTE

Discussion on Same Sex Marriage Alternatives. Vermont, New Hampshire, New Jersey and Connecticut provide civil union benefits for persons of the same sex. Such a status is the most similar to marriage because it requires a license, a ceremony, and in the event of dissolution, filing for dissolution just as though there had been a marriage. Reciprocal beneficiaries, now available in Hawaii, more resembles domestic partnership, allowing a same sex couple to register a partner or delete a registered partner at will. Finally, the domestic partnership statute adopted in California is the most extensive in the United States, providing a list of benefits similar to those enjoyed by married couples. The three legal arrangements are particularly pertinent to gay and lesbian persons. For commentary, see Carlos A. Ball, *This is Not Your Father's Autonomy: Lesbian and Gay Rights From a Feminist and Relational Perspective,* 28 HARV. J. L. & GENDER 345–379 (2005); Ariela R. Dubler, *From McLaughlin v. Florida to Lawrence v. Texas: Sexual Freedom and the Road to Marriage,* 106 COLUM. L. REV. 1165–1187 (2006); Kris Franklin, *The "Authoritative Moment": Exploring the Boundaries of Interpretation in the Recognition of Queer Families,* 32 WM. MITCHELL L. REV. 655–718 (2006); Julie A. Greenberg and Marybeth Herald, *You Can't Take It With You: Constitutional Consequences of Interstate Gender–Identity Rulings,* 80 WASH. L. REV. 887–942 (2005); Johanna L. Grossman, *Resurrecting Comity: Revisiting the Problem of Non–Uniform Marriage Laws,* 84 OR. L. REV. 433–488 (2005); Jill Elaine Hasday, *Intimacy and Economic Exchange,* 119 HARV. L. REV. 491–530 (2005); Dominick Vetri, *The Gay Codes: Federal & State Laws Excluding Gay & Lesbian Families,* 41 WILLAMETTE L. REV. 881–940 (2005).

CHAPTER II

GETTING MARRIED

A. INTRODUCTION

Each state maintains its own rules about who can marry and what must be done to achieve marital status within its territory. In recent years there has been some movement toward uniformity, but significant differences remain among some jurisdictions regarding such matters as premarital testing, minimum age, prohibited degrees of kinship between parties and ceremonial requirements. The origins and purposes of many of the rules (some of which are deeply rooted in antiquated custom or religious tradition) often have been forgotten or are ignored. It was long questioned whether any constitutional challenges could be made to even the most arbitrary or discriminatory state regulation. Only with decisions of the Supreme Court of the United States in cases such as Loving v. Virginia, 388 U.S. 1, 87 S.Ct. 1817, 18 L.Ed.2d 1010 (1967), and Zablocki v. Redhail, 434 U.S. 374, 98 S.Ct. 673, 54 L.Ed.2d 618 (1978), did it become clear that state limitations on marriage could be gauged in the courts by a constitutional yardstick. Subsequent awareness of the newly defined constitutional vulnerability led many state legislatures to substantially revise many of their marriage laws, eliminating or revising many antiquarian provisions. Even so, the task of cleaning up and modernizing is by no means finished.

A UNIFORM MARRIAGE AND DIVORCE ACT, 9 U.L.A. 156, first promulgated in 1970 and later amended in 1971 and 1973, deals with many of the problems raised in this chapter. Although it has been adopted in substantial part by only a small number of states, it was highly influential in the early reform of divorce grounds and matrimonial property law by providing model language and approaches at times when legislatures were ready to act quickly.

Today marriage is in a time of reshaping, with a strange combination of old rules and new challenges to them accompanied by a strong trend toward expanded private ordering. *See* Walter Wadlington, *Marriage: An Institution in Transition and Redefinition*, Chapter 11 in CROSS CURRENTS: FAMILY LAW AND POLICY IN THE U.S. AND ENGLAND (2001).

B. COURTSHIP AND THE MARRIAGE PROMISE

Compared with the extensive body of legislation and jurisprudence regarding who can marry and how to achieve marital status, legal regulation of the parties' conduct during "courtship" long has been a matter of *laissez faire.* Provisions that encroach on the activities of the parties often are vestiges from an earlier period in which attitudes toward nonmarital sexual relations and the rights and roles of women differed considerably from those of today. The legal encroachments (many of them now abolished) consisted principally of (1) bans on sexual intercourse between unmarried adults; (2) attempts at specific enforcement of promises to marry through a mélange of tort, contract or penal sanctions; (3) definition of the permissible scope of third party intervention to arrange, encourage, or discourage "pairing" between specific individuals; and (4) rules and principles for deciding ownership of property transferred in contemplation of marriages that did not take place.

Debate continues about whether marriage should be easy to achieve and divorce hard to obtain, or vice versa. As a practical matter, obstacles to marriage have been increasingly minimal. And divorce, now more often a matter of negotiation than litigation, is far easier to obtain than it was only several decades ago.

1. ENFORCING A PROMISE TO MARRY

Wightman v. Coates

Supreme Judicial Court of Massachusetts, 1818.
15 Mass. 1, 8 Am.Dec. 77.

ASSUMPSIT on a promise to marry the plaintiff, and a breach thereof by refusal, and having married another woman.

■ PARKER, C. J. We can conceive of no more suitable ground of application to the tribunals of justice for compensation, than that of a violated promise to enter into a contract, on the faithful performance of which the interest of all civilized countries so essentially depends. When two parties, of suitable age to contract, agree to pledge their faith to each other, and thus withdraw themselves from that intercourse with society which might probably lead to a similar connection with another; the affections being so far interested as to render a subsequent engagement not probable or desirable; and one of the parties wantonly and capriciously refuses to execute the contract, which is thus commenced, the injury may be serious, and circumstances may often justify a claim of pecuniary indemnification.

When the female is the injured party, there is generally more reason for a resort to the laws, than when the man is the sufferer.... A deserted female, whose prospects in life may be materially affected by the treachery of the man, to whom she has plighted her vows, will always receive from a jury the attention which her situation requires.... It is also for the publick interest, that conduct tending to consign a virtuous woman to celibacy, should meet with that punishment, which may prevent it from becoming common. That delicacy of the sex, which happily in this country gives the man so much advantage over the woman, in the intercourse which leads to matrimonial engagements, requires for its protection and continuance the aid of the laws.

Stanard v. Bolin

Supreme Court of Washington, En Banc, 1977.
88 Wn.2d 614, 565 P.2d 94.

■ HAMILTON, ASSOCIATE JUSTICE.

This appeal presents the question of whether the common-law action for breach of promise to marry should be abolished. The trial court concluded that the action was contrary to public policy and dismissed the plaintiff's (appellant's) complaint ... for failure to state a claim upon which relief can be granted. We accepted review and conclude that the action is not contrary to public policy.

In October, 1974, plaintiff and defendant (respondent) were introduced to each other by mutual friends, and their courtship developed soon thereafter. During the course of their courtship, defendant assured plaintiff that he was worth in excess of $2 million, was planning to retire in 2 years, and that the two of them would then travel. Defendant also promised plaintiff that she would never have to work again and that he would see to the support of her two teen-age boys. He also promised to see that the plaintiff's mother would never be in need.

On September 22, 1975, plaintiff accepted defendant's proposal of marriage. Thereafter, defendant took her to a jewelry store and purchased an engagement ring and matching wedding rings. The parties found a suitable home for their residence and signed the purchase agreement as husband and wife. At the insistence of defendant, plaintiff placed her home on the market for sale and sold most of her furniture at a public auction. The parties set December 13, 1975, as their wedding date, reserved a church, and engaged a minister to perform the service. Dresses for plaintiff, her mother, and the matron of honor were ordered, and a reception was arranged at a local establishment. The parties began informally announcing their plans to a wide circle of friends. After the wedding date was set, plaintiff's employer hired another person and requested plaintiff to assist in teaching the new employee the duties of her job.

On November 13, 1975, defendant informed plaintiff that he would not marry her. This came as a great shock to plaintiff and caused her to become ill and lose sleep and weight. Plaintiff sought medical advice and was treated by her physician. Plaintiff also had to take her home off the market and repurchase furniture at a cost in excess of that which she received for her older furniture. In addition, plaintiff was forced to cancel all wedding plans and reservations, and to explain to her matron of honor, her mother, and her children, that she was not marrying. Plaintiff was also obliged to return wedding gifts and to face her friends and neighbors, each of whom felt entitled to an explanation.

In her first claim for relief, plaintiff sought damages to compensate her for her pain, impairment to health, humiliation, and embarrassment. Plaintiff's second claim sought damages to compensate her for her loss of expected financial security.

The breach-of-marriage-promise action has its origins in the common law. Professor Clark, a well-known authority on family law, has posited that 17th Century English conceptions of marriage as largely a property transaction caused the English common-law courts to intervene in a subject matter which, up until the 17th Century, had been almost exclusively under the jurisdiction of the ecclesiastical courts. See H. Clark, The Law of Domestic Relations in the United States 2 (1968) (hereafter cited as Clark). In any event, the action was carried forward into the common law of Washington and was recognized by this court as early as 1905. Because the action has its origins in the common law and has not been acted upon by the legislature, it is proper for us to reexamine it and determine its continued viability in light of present-day society.

The breach-of-promise-to-marry action is one not easy to classify. Although the action is treated as arising from the breach of a contract (the contract being the mutual promises to marry), the damages allowable more closely resemble a tort action. Thus, the plaintiff may recover for loss to reputation, mental anguish, and injury to health, in addition to recovering for expenditures made in preparation for the marriage and loss of the pecuniary and social advantages which the promised marriage offered. In addition, some states allow aggravated damages for seduction under promise to marry and for attacks by the defendant on the plaintiff's character. Furthermore, some states allow punitive damages when the defendant's acts were malicious or fraudulent. . . .

The action in its present form is subject to almost uniform criticism by the commentators, although our research has not disclosed any cases in which a court has abolished the action.[1] In essence, these criticisms are: (1) the action is used as an instrument of oppression and blackmail; (2) engaged persons should be allowed to correct their mistakes without fear of publicity and legal compulsion; (3) the action is subject to great abuse at the hands of gullible and sympathetic juries; (4) it is wrong to allow under the guise of contract an action that is essentially tortious and penal in nature; and (5) the measure of damages is unjust because damages are allowed for loss of social and economic position, whereas most persons marry for reasons of mutual love and affection. See, e.g., Brown, Breach of Promise Suits, 77 U.Pa.L.Rev. 474 (1929); Wright, The Action for Breach of the Marriage Promise, 10 Va.L.Rev. 361 (1924); . . . Although some of these criticisms are not without merit, we do not believe they justify an outright abolishment of the action.

When two persons agree to marry, they should realize that certain actions will be taken during the engagement period in reliance on the mutual promises to marry. Rings will be purchased, wedding dresses and other formal attire will be ordered or reserved, and honeymoon plans with

---

1. The action has been abolished or modified by statute in some states. [The footnote cites statutes in Alabama, California, Colorado, Connecticut, Florida, Indiana, Maine, Maryland, Massachusetts, Michigan, Nevada, New Hampshire, New Jersey, New York, Pennsylvania, West Virginia, Wisconsin, and Wyoming. Many other states, including Virginia, also have abolished the action.]

their attendant expenses will be made. Wedding plans, such as the rental of a church, the engagement of a minister, the printing of wedding invitations, and so on, will commence. It is also likely that the parties will make plans for their future residence, such as purchasing a house, buying furniture, and the like. Further, at the time the parties decide to marry, they should realize that their plans and visions of future happiness will be communicated to friends and relatives and that wedding gifts soon will be arriving. When the plans to marry are abruptly ended, it is certainly foreseeable that the party who was unaware that the future marriage would not take place will have expended some sums of money and will suffer some forms of mental anguish, loss to reputation, and injury to health. We do not feel these injuries should go unanswered merely because the breach-of-promise-to-marry action may be subject to abuses; rather, an attempt should be made to eradicate the abuses from the action.

One major abuse of the action is allowing the plaintiff to bring in evidence of the defendant's wealth and social position. This evidence is admissible under the theory that the plaintiff should be compensated for what she or he has lost by not marrying the defendant.

Although damages for loss of expected financial and social position more closely resemble the contract theory of recovery than the other elements of damages for breach of promise to marry, we do not believe these damages are justified in light of modern society's concept of marriage. Although it may have been that marriages were contracted for material reasons in 17th Century England, marriages today generally are not considered property transactions, but are, in the words of Professor Clark, "the result of that complex experience called being in love." A person generally does not choose a marriage partner on the basis of financial and social gain; hence, the plaintiff should not be compensated for losing an expectation which he or she did not have in the first place. Further, the breach-of-promise-to-marry action is based on injuries to the plaintiff, and evidence of the defendant's wealth tends to misdirect the jury's attention when assessing the plaintiff's damages towards an examination of the defendant's wealth rather than the plaintiff's injuries.

Professor McCormick has concluded that evidence of the defendant's wealth has a more potent effect upon the size of the verdict than any instruction on damages. See C. McCormick, Handbook on the Law of Damages 399, n. 36 (1935). If this is so, then it presents a very strong reason for disallowing any evidence of the defendant's wealth and social position. We conclude that damages for loss of expected financial and social position should no longer be recoverable under the breach-of-promise-to-marry action. This means that evidence of the defendant's wealth and social position becomes immaterial in assessing the plaintiff's damages.

Other damages subject to criticism are those damages given for mental anguish, loss to reputation, and injury to health. It is argued that these injuries are "so vague and so little capable of measurement in dollars that they give free rein to the jury's passions, prejudices and sympathies." See Clark, supra at 12. This argument has little merit, for it places no faith in the jury's ability to evaluate objectively the evidence regarding plaintiff's injuries and render a just verdict. If a jury's verdict is tainted by passion or prejudice, or is otherwise excessive, the trial court and the appellate court have the power to reduce the award or order a new trial. Lack of ability to quantify damages in exact dollar amounts does not justify abolishing the breach-of-promise-to-marry action. In her complaint plaintiff alleged that she had suffered pain, impairment to health, humiliation, and embarrassment as a result of the defendant's breach of his promise to marry. If this is true, and we must assume it is for purposes of review, then she is entitled to compensation for these injuries.

. . .

We also do not believe the action should be abolished so that engaged persons are free from compulsion to choose whether to end an engagement. Although the policy of the state should not be to encourage a person to marry when he or she has begun to have second thoughts about a prospective mate, it is also the policy of the state to afford an avenue of redress for injuries suffered due to the actions of another. Allowing recovery for injuries, which are foreseeable at the time of entering into the relationship, should not be denied on the presumption the defendant would rather enter into the marriage than pay damages for the injuries caused. Furthermore, it is hard to conceive of a plaintiff suing a defendant in order to coerce the defendant into a marriage which would be unstable at best. It is possible that there may be such a plaintiff, but that is no reason for abolishing the action for all plaintiffs, for that would cause most plaintiffs to go uncompensated for their injuries at the expense of a few unworthy plaintiffs.

In conclusion, we have decided that the breach-of-promise-to-marry action should be retained as a quasi-contract, quasi-tort action for the recovery of the foreseeable special and general damages which are caused by a defendant's breach of promise to marry. However, the action is modified to the extent that a plaintiff cannot recover for loss of expected financial and social position, because marriage is no longer considered to be a property transaction.

. . .

■ UTTER, ASSOCIATE JUSTICE (dissenting).

I believe the change advocated does not go far enough. Motive of the defendant may still, apparently, be considered in assessing damages. Where the breach of promise to marry is wanton or deliberate, the effect is to allow exemplary damages, contrary to the public policy of our state. Wyman v. Wallace, 15 Wash.App. 395, 549 P.2d 71 (1976). In *Wyman*, the Court of Appeals abolished the action for alienation of affections of a spouse by an unrelated third person on the ground, among others, that "the element of punishment is so inextricably interwoven into any award of damages for alienation of the affections of a spouse that the true nature of the award is punitive." This is no less true in this case than it was in *Wyman*. In addition, in 1973 our state adopted a new dissolution of marriage act. The establishment of the fact that a marriage is "irretrievably broken" is now a sufficient ground for dissolution, with no finding of fault necessary. The trial judge observed in his memorandum decision on motion to dismiss:

> The current public policy expressed in the 1973 Dissolution Act is to disregard fault in the judicial determination of property rights at the dissolution of a marriage. Fault is not to be considered in determining which party shall have the decree. There are no damages as such in a dissolution. Is it not obvious, however, that one of the parties to a dissolution suffers at least as much humiliation, embarrassment, mental suffering and loss of financial expectation and security as does a party to the breakup of an engagement?
>
> It is significant that there was no divorce by judicial decree at common law when the breach of promise action came into being. Tupper v. Tupper, 63 Wash.2d 585 [388 P.2d 225]. Should not the public policy declared in the divorce statutes be applicable to engagements? I believe it is.

. . .

I believe these criticisms are sufficient grounds, given the recently enunciated policy of the state in the dissolution of marriage act, to justify our abolition of this now obsolete, judicially created, cause of action.

NOTES

In Wildey v. Springs, 47 F.3d 1475 (1995) the United States Court of Appeals for the Fourth Circuit offered a historical perspective of the breach of promise action:

> The action for the breach of a promise to marry is of antique vintage. First conceived as a creature of the English ecclesiastical courts, the action was originally used to pressure a reluctant lover into fulfilling a marital promise. W.J. Brockelbank, *The Nature of the Promise to Marry—A Study in Comparative Law*, 41 ILL.L.REV. 1, 3 (1946); Michael Grossberg, GOVERNING THE HEARTH: LAW AND THE FAMILY IN NINETEENTH-CENTURY AMERICA 34 (1985). The common law eventually adopted the action, however, and permitted the recovery of monetary damages. Although developed by English courts, the action found its way into the American colonies and was later used by post-revolutionary American lawyers.
>
> The action served dual ideals in colonial America. On the one hand, a breach of promise action continued to appeal to vestiges of the older notion that marriage was a property transaction completed after complex family negotiations. Grossberg, supra, at 35. But on the other hand, the action began to pay tribute to the emerging ideal that marriage was a sacred contract premised upon affection and emotional commitment. Id. The suits soon became utilized almost universally by women, and were justified by lawmakers largely on these grounds. Id. at 37. Marriage was considered necessary to secure both a woman's

social and financial security. Margaret F. Brinig, *Rings and Promises*, 6 J.LAW, ECONOMICS, AND ORGANIZATION 203, 204–05 (1990). But more importantly, the actions, and the judges who were willing to enforce them, recognized that promises to marry sometimes occasioned a loss of virginity. Id. at 205. Because of the importance the society of that day placed on premarital chastity, the economic and social harm suffered by a jilted woman were often reflected in large damage awards. Id.

The actions were characterized by a lack of legal formality peculiar for the law of that time. Foreign observers noted that, unlike wills or commercial contracts, little was needed to support an allegation that the parties had become engaged. Grossberg, supra, at 51. Consequently, appellate courts deferred widely to jury determinations in credibility contests. Id. at 49. Traditional rules relating to damages, too, were relaxed. Despite the originally contractual nature of the action, judges refused to confine the damage measure to immediate loss. Instead, they permitted recovery for elements such as mental anguish and a loss of social position. Id. at 43.

Largely because of the perceived vagaries of the suits, the actions had fallen into disrepute by the early twentieth century. Three principal reasons are given for their decline in popularity. The first is the unfounded use of the suit, given the lax standards of proof, to extort out-of-court settlements. Brockelbank, supra, at 13; Note, *Heartbalm Statutes and Deceit Actions*, 83 Mich.L.Rev. 1770, 1776 (1985). Second, the excessive damages awarded prompted disdain for the actions. Id. at 1774. Finally, the ideals that the action served came to be viewed as anachronistic. The greater social and economic freedom incident to women's entry into the workforce meant that the loss of an initial suitor posed a lower threat to future prospects than it might have in the nineteenth century. Grossberg, supra, at 55.

The court pointed out that "As concerns grew, legislatures began to act." By today, about half of the states have abolished the action either by statute or jurisprudence, typically eliminating other "heart balm" actions as well. New York Civil Rights Law (McKinney 1992) is an example of a broad abolition statute:

§ **80–a.** The rights of action to recover sums of money as damages for alienation of affections, criminal conversation, seduction, or breach of contract to marry are abolished. No act done within this state shall operate to give rise, either within or without this state, to any such right of action. No contract to marry made or entered into in this state shall operate to give rise, either within or without this state to any cause or right of action for its breach.

§ **81.** It shall be unlawful for any person, either as a party or attorney, or in behalf of either, to file, serve or cause to be filed or served, or threaten to file, serve or cause to be filed or served, any process or pleading, in any court of the state, setting forth or seeking to recover a sum of money upon any cause of action abolished by this article, whether such cause of action arose within or without the state.

. . .

§ 83. Any person who violates any of the provisions of this article shall be guilty of a felony which shall be punishable by a fine of not less than one thousand dollars nor more than five thousand dollars, or by imprisonment for a term of not less than one year nor more than five years, or by both such fine and imprisonment, in the discretion of the court.

§ 84. This article shall be liberally construed to effectuate its objects and purposes and the public policy of the state as hereby declared. . . . Nothing contained in this article shall be construed as a repeal of any provision of the penal law or the criminal procedure law or any other law relating to criminal or quasi-criminal actions or proceedings.

In 1935 Illinois also abolished the common law cause of action but in *Heck v. Schupp*, 394 Ill. 296, 68 N.E.2d 464, 466 (1946), the state's Supreme Court set that statute aside as unconstitutional under the Illinois Constitution's requirement that a legal remedy be provided for all injuries. The Illinois legislature then enacted a statute sharply limiting the time in which an action should be brought, allowing recovery only for actual damages, and requiring notice to be given within three months from the date that the breach of promise occurred. 740 Ill. Comp. St. § 15/1 et seq (West 1993). It was under that statute that the breach of promise action reached the courts in *Wildey*, supra. Although the lower court initially returned a verdict in favor of the plaintiff, this was reversed on appeal because her notice had not provided the defendant with the date on which the parties became engaged, as required in the Breach of Promise Act. Id. at § 15/4.

Possible defenses to an action for breach of promise to marry include fraudulent misrepresentation or concealment, insanity at time of the engagement, development of certain serious illnesses or physical conditions, or that the plaintiff was married at the time of the engagement.

Seduction. The common law tort of seduction still exists in some jurisdictions. According to the earlier rationale, a defendant's conduct must have consisted of "such solicitations, importunities, misrepresentations, knowingly false promises or artifices, including a false promise to marry for the purpose of seduction, which lead the plaintiff, a chaste unmarried woman, to deviate from the path of rectitude. . . ." Breece v. Jett, 556 S.W.2d 696, 707 (Mo.App.1977). The action thus centered on the element of fraud. Not all jurisdictions recognized the seduction action, which once was available only to a father who could collect damages for loss of the services of his daughter. The requirement of parental "loss of services" eventually was retained only as a fiction and by now has largely disappeared, sometimes through specific statutory provision. With its elimination, some courts and legislatures allowed women to bring seduction actions in their own right for damages based on reputation loss, embarrassment, or other such harm In Franklin v. Hill, 264 Ga. 302, 444 S.E.2d 778 (1994), the

Supreme Court of Georgia held their state's statute giving parents a cause of action for seduction of their unmarried daughter unconstitutional. The decision was based on gender discrimination in violation of the equal protection clause of the Georgia Constitution because only men could be civilly liable under the statute.

Judicial Interpretation to Avoid Circumvention of the Bans. Some lawyers faced with anti-heart balm laws urged courts to interpret their provisions respecting breach of promise as abolishing only actions based explicitly on failure to carry out a promise to marry. They filed similar controversies to court, ostensibly based on other legal theories. In Thibault v. Lalumiere, 318 Mass. 72, 60 N.E.2d 349 (1945), a plaintiff proceeded on a theory of assault and battery, alleging that "as a result of defendant's behavior the plaintiff was caused to acquiesce in and submit to defendant's embraces and caresses." Plaintiff's attorney also sought to recover for defendant's deceit and fraud in making a promise that he knew plaintiff would rely on but which he did not intend to carry out. Rejecting plaintiff's contentions, the Supreme Judicial Court of Massachusetts pointed out that the State's statute:

> not only abolished the right of action for breach of promise but it went farther and abolished any form of action, whatever its form, that was based upon such a breach. The breach is no longer a legal wrong. . . .
> Actions in tort for fraud have been held to be within the prohibition of such statutes and any other cause of action that originates in the breach of promise of marriage. The plaintiff's cause of action arises out of a breach of promise of marriage and she cannot circumvent the statute by bringing an action in tort for damages so long as the direct or underlying cause of her injury is the breach of promise of marriage.

However, in Tuck v. Tuck, 14 N.Y.2d 341, 251 N.Y.S.2d 653, 200 N.E.2d 554 (1964), New York's Court of Appeals held that despite Civil Rights Law § 80 "an action for deceit will lie where the defendant has induced the plaintiff to 'marry' and cohabit with him on the fraudulent representation that he was unmarried. . . ." The court accounted for this distinction by pointing out that:

> The woman who permits herself to be seduced by a *promise* of marriage knows full well that she is entering into an immoral and meretricious relationship. Completely lacking in such a case—grounded solely upon a breach of promise—is the change of status or, more precisely, the good faith supposed change of status on the part of the woman deceived. In the present case, at least according to the allegations of the complaint which we must at this stage accept as true, the plaintiff believed, in good faith, that the ceremony, performed by one apparently an official and in the presence of witnesses, was what it seemed to be, that she was legally married to this defendant and that their subsequent cohabitation was truly as husband and wife.

In another variation on this plot, the Supreme Judicial Court of Maine dealt with an action by parents of a minor to recover compensatory and punitive damages for defendant's breach of a promise to marry their minor daughter and for malicious and intentional infliction of mental suffering by plaintiffs as a resulting from failure to seasonably inform them that he intended not to show for the wedding. The court concluded that the policy considerations barring actions for damages for breach of promise to marry in a suit based on fraud or deceit apply equally to an action for intentional infliction of mental distress so far as it arises in the context of a breach of promise to marry. Waddell v. Briggs, 381 A.2d 1132 (Me.1978).

2.   GIFTS IN CONTEMPLATION OF MARRIAGE

Vigil v. Haber

Supreme Court of New Mexico, 1994.
119 N.M. 9, 888 P.2d 455.

■ FRANCHINI, JUSTICE.

Glenn Haber appeals from an order adjudging that Haber's former fiancee, Jannel M. Vigil, should be given permanent possession of an engagement ring she received from Haber. We hold that the ring was a conditional gift dependent upon the parties' marriage, that the question of whose fault it was that the engagement was broken is irrelevant, and that therefore the ring should be returned to Haber.

. . . Haber and Vigil exchanged engagement rings in February 1992. Unfortunately, their relationship deteriorated and each accused the other of threats and assaults. In May 1992 the couple separated and Vigil filed for a temporary order of protection. A special hearing commissioner resolved all protection issues and determined that the parties should return the rings they had given to each other. Haber immediately returned the ring he had, along with some of Vigil's other possessions. At a later hearing, however, Vigil objected to returning the engagement ring Haber had given to her. The commissioner instructed the Santa Fe Police to hold the ring until the dispute was resolved and referred the matter to the district court.

Haber filed a motion in district court for an order to release the ring to him. After a hearing, the court determined that Vigil canceled the wedding plans but that she justifiably did so because of Haber's misconduct. The court then ordered that Vigil should keep the ring because Haber caused the failure of the condition (marriage) upon which the gift was based.

.   .   .

Determination of the ownership of an engagement gift does not require a finding of who caused breakup of the engagement. The issue raised in this case is one of first impression in New Mexico. In determining who should be granted possession of an engagement ring in cases in which the marriage has not occurred, courts in other states have used a rationale "based upon a contract theory, i.e., the ring is a symbol of an agreement to marry. If that agreement is not performed, then the parties should be restored to the status quo." Spinnell v. Quigley, 56 Wash.App. 799, 785 P.2d 1149, 1150 (1990). Using a kind of equitable estoppel, some courts at common law have created a policy exception to the rule that engagement gifts should be returned. Under this exception, if the marriage is not finalized because the donor breached the marriage agreement, the donor may not benefit from his breach by regaining the ring given as an engagement gift. The rationale for the exception is that " '[n]o man should take advantage of his own wrong.' " Id. (quoting Mate v. Abrahams, 62 A.2d 754, 755 (N.J.1948)). The practice of determining possession based upon fault is the majority rule. Aronow v. Silver, 223 N.J.Super. 344, 538 A.2d 851, 852 (Ct.Ch.Div.1987). However, application of this rationale makes changing one's mind about the choice of a marriage partner legally wrong unless the court determines that the donor was justified in changing his or her mind.

Following a modern trend, legislatures and courts have moved toward a policy that removes fault-finding from the personal-relationship dynamics of marriage and divorce. New Mexico was the first state to legislatively recognize "no-fault" divorce. State ex rel. DuBois v. Ryan, 85 N.M. 575, 577, 514 P.2d 851, 853 (1973); see NMSA 1978, § 40–4–1(A) (Repl. Pamp.1994) (stating grounds for divorce includes incompatibility). When determining whether a divorce should be granted on grounds of incompatibility, fault is not relevant to the determination. "[U]sually the conduct of both spouses contributes to the failure of a marriage[;] ... establishing guilt and innocence is not really useful." Dixon v. Dixon, 107 Wis.2d 492, 319 N.W.2d 846, 851 (1982). We agree with the court in Brown v. Thomas, 127 Wis.2d 318, 379 N.W.2d 868, 873 (Ct.App.1985), cert. denied, 127 Wis.2d 572, 383 N.W.2d 64 (1986), that the policy statements that govern "our approach to broken marriages [are] equally relevant to broken engagements." See also Gaden v. Gaden, 29 N.Y.2d 80, 323 N.Y.S.2d 955, 962, 272 N.E.2d 471, 476 (1971) (holding that the question of fault or guilt is irrelevant to the breaking of an engagement and subsequent duty to return gifts given in anticipation of marriage).

In Gaden, the court stated that the result of basing entitlement to keep engagement gifts on the fault of another would "encourage every disappointed donee to resist the return of engagement gifts by blaming the donor for the breakup of the contemplated marriage, thereby promoting dramatic courtroom accusations and counter-accusations of fault." Id. That is exactly what happened in this case. In attempting to prove that her cancellation of the marriage was justified, Vigil introduced testimony that Haber had physically abused her. Haber testified that Vigil made her own contributions to the domestic conflict. The trial court stated that it would not find that one side was lying and one side was telling the truth, but ultimately determined that it was Haber's fault that the engagement was broken. The court applied the exception to the common-law principle that the parties should be returned to the status quo, but the court also ordered Vigil to pay to Haber the value of the ring Haber had returned to her, which was approximately $500.00.

We agree that "fault, in an engagement setting, cannot be ascertained," Aronow, 538 A.2d at 853, and follow the lead of Iowa, New Jersey, New York, and Wisconsin in holding that when the condition precedent of marriage fails, an engagement gift must be returned. See Fierro v. Hoel, 465 N.W.2d 669, 672 (Iowa Ct.App.1990) (holding engagement ring is inherently conditional and rejecting any fault approach to determining whether the ring should be returned to the donor); Aronow, 538 A.2d at 854; . . . see also John D. Perovich, Annotation, Rights in Respect of Engagement & Courtship Presents When Marriage Does Not Ensue, 46 A.L.R.3d 578, § 2[b], at 583–84,§ 12.5, at 92 (1972 & Supp. 1994) ("[A]pplication of fault concepts . . . is inconsistent with the modern trend toward the abandonment of fault in domestic relations cases and other actions. . . . [T]he only relevant inquiry in such cases is whether the condition under which the gift was made has failed."). "If the wedding is called off, for whatever reason, the gift is not capable of becoming a completed gift and must be returned to the donor." Fierro, 465 N.W.2d at 672. Of course, this holding has no application to those situations in which the parties have agreed in advance to the final disposition of engagement gifts; those gifts, by agreement, are not conditioned upon marriage. Likewise, this holding has no bearing on post-breakup settlement agreements.

. . . It is uncontroverted that the engagement ring was given to Vigil on condition and in contemplation of marriage. The condition having failed, Haber is entitled to return of the ring and Vigil is not required to pay to Haber the value of the ring that he returned to her. The order of the trial court is vacated and we remand for entry of an order releasing the ring to Haber.

NOTE

In Heiman v. Parrish, 262 Kan. 926, 942 P.2d 631 (1997), the Supreme Court of Kansas concluded that the no-fault line of cases was persuasive with regard to return of an engagement ring after the engagement had been called off. In its opinion the court asked reflectively

What is fault or the unjustifiable calling off of an engagement?

By way of illustration, should courts be asked to determine which of the following grounds for breaking an engagement is fault or justified? (1) The parties have nothing in common; (2) one party cannot stand prospective in-laws; (3) a minor child of one of the parties is hostile to and will not accept the other party; (4) an adult child of one of the parties will not accept the other party; (5) the parties' pets do not get along; (6) a party was too hasty in proposing or accepting the proposal; (7) the engagement was a rebound situation which is now regretted; (8) one party has untidy habits that irritate the other; or (9) the parties' have religious differences. The list could be endless.

CALIFORNIA CIVIL CODE (West 1988)

§ 1590.   Gifts in contemplation of marriage; recovery

Where either party to a contemplated marriage in this State makes a gift of money or property to the other on the basis or assumption that the marriage will take place, in the event that the donee refuses to enter into the marriage as contemplated or that it is given up by mutual consent, the donor may recover such gift or such part of its value as may, under all of the circumstances of the case, be found by a court or jury to be just.

NOTE

Some of the original anti-heart balm statutes were so strict in their language that suits to recover property given on condition of marriage might not be permitted. New York's Civil Rights Law (McKinney 1992) eventually was amended to provide that

§ **80–b.** Nothing in this article contained shall be construed to bar a right of action for the recovery of a chattel, the return of money or securities, or the value thereof at the time of such transfer, or the rescission of a deed to real property when the sole consideration for the transfer of the chattel, money or securities or real property was a contemplated marriage which has not occurred, and the court may, if in its discretion justice so requires, (1) award the defendant a lien upon the chattel, securities or real property for monies expended in connection therewith or improvements made thereto, (2) deny judgment for the recovery of the chattel or securities or for rescission of the deed and award money damages in lieu thereof.

3.   THIRD PARTY INTERVENTION

Inducing breach of a contract can be tortious under some circumstances, but such an action has long been considered unavailable with regard to agreements or promises to marry. *See* Brown v. Glickstein, 347 Ill.App. 486, 107 N.E.2d 267 (1952). One policy explanation is that parents, other relatives and friends of the contracting parties should be free to counsel them concerning an agreement that is so important to society.

There remains an antiquarian body of law dealing with commercial intervention in the courtship process. The generally accepted rule long was that contracts to procure a spouse in return for monetary consideration were unenforceable. Despite this, marriage brokers continued to thrive during the period in which the rule was being developed. Although advertisements in the Yellow Pages of some metropolitan telephone books suggest that providers of such services are still actively in business, technological advance has spawned the modern but less romantic practice of matching potential mates through computer profiles. Many newspapers also regularly offer personal advertising sections for persons seeking mates.

C.   MARRIAGE PROCEDURES, FORMAL AND INFORMAL

1.   INFORMAL OR "COMMON LAW" MARRIAGE

Meister v. Moore

United States Supreme Court, 1877.
96 U.S. 76, 24 L.Ed. 826.

■ MR. JUSTICE STRONG delivered the opinion of the court.

The learned judge of the Circuit Court instructed the jury, that, if neither a minister nor a magistrate was present at the alleged marriage of

William A. Mowry and the daughter of Indian Pero, the marriage was invalid under the Michigan Statute; and this instruction is now alleged to have been erroneous. It certainly withdrew from the consideration of the jury all evidence, if any there was, of informal marriage by contract per verba de praesenti. That such a contract constitutes a marriage at common law there can be no doubt. . . . Marriage is everywhere regarded as a civil contract. Statutes in many of the States, it is true, regulate the mode of entering into the contract, but they do not confer the right. Hence they are not within the principle, that where a statute creates a right and provides a remedy for its enforcement, the remedy is exclusive. No doubt, a statute may take away a common law right; but there is always a presumption that the Legislature has no such intention, unless it be plainly expressed. A statute may declare that no marriages shall be valid unless they are solemnized in a prescribed manner; but such an enactment is a very different thing from a law requiring all marriages to be entered into in the presence of a magistrate or a clergyman, or that it be preceded by a license, or publication of banns, or be attested by witnesses. Such formal provisions may be construed as merely directory, instead of being treated as destructive of a common law right to form the marriage relation by words of present assent. And such, we think, has been the rule generally adopted in construing statutes regulating marriage. Whatever directions they may give respecting its formation or solemnization, courts have usually held a marriage good at common law to be good notwithstanding the statutes, unless they contain express words of nullity.

. . .

As before remarked, the statutes are held merely directory; because marriage is a thing of common right, because it is the policy of the State to encourage it, and because, as has sometimes been said, any other construction would compel holding illegitimate the offspring of many parents conscious of no violation of law.

NOTE

An even earlier case that greatly influenced the spread of the doctrine of informal consensual marriages in this country was Fenton v. Reed, 4 Johns. 52 (N.Y.1809). The decision presumably was written by James Kent, then Chief Justice of the Supreme Court of New York. The term "common law marriage" applied to contracts *per verba de praesenti* or *per verba de futuro cum copula,* probably derives from 2 Kent, Commentaries on American Law 87, a work first published in 1826. Already in Grisham v. State, 10 Tenn. 589 (1831), we find a court speaking of "a marriage by the common law." The early cases on common law marriage in the United States are collected in Koegel, Common Law Marriage and Its Development in the United States (1922). For more discussion of the subject *see* Walter O. Weyrauch, *Informal and Formal Marriage—An Appraisal of Trends in*

Family Organization, 28 U.Chi.L.Rev. 88 (1960), and Stuart J. Stein, *Common Law Marriage: Its History and Certain Contemporary Problems*, 9 J.Fam.Law 271 (1970).

Black, Common Law Marriage

2 U.Cin.L.Rev. 113, 131–32 (1928).

The rule accepted in the courts of the United States is Roman in concept if not in origin. It is not medieval but classical; it does not depend upon the notion of a promise being binding on the conscience and enforceable by a court of conscience. It is not metaphysical or sacramental but practical, depending wholly on proof of a status deliberately assumed and publicly maintained. Its sole difficulties are those of proof and lack of record.

The difficulties of proof are not otherwise than those necessarily incurred in litigation involving any other relation of life and courts have had always to come to decisions affecting not only properties in large amounts but life itself and human liberty, depending upon the veracity of statement and reliability of memory of witnesses whose personal interest may be as much involved in one issue as in another. So long as only human agencies can be employed to resolve human disputes, there is no particular reason for excluding a single class of controversies from hearing because of the hazard of mistake common to all. It is public policy that a public record be kept of marriages and that policy is defeated in the instance of common law marriage, but it is also public policy to prevent illegitimacy, to reduce promiscuity in sexual relations and to promote and encourage marriage. In government, a choice is always to be made between ends but a record of marriage is not an end in itself but a means towards social order. It is not wise to defeat social order for the sake of orderliness in method. The recognition of common law marriage does not involve the abandonment of ceremonial marriage. That form is sustained by social pressure and it is only by simulating it that irregular unions escape censure and ostracism.

Crosson v. Crosson

Court of Civil Appeals of Alabama, 1995.
668 So.2d 868.

■ CRAWLEY, JUDGE.

Bruce Crosson and Barbara Crosson were married in February 1982 in a ceremonial marriage. The Crossons were divorced in June 1993. It is undisputed that after the divorce Mr. Crosson asked his former wife to come back and be his wife. Mrs. Crosson (the "wife") accepted the invitation to move back in with Mr. Crosson (the "husband").[2] They began living together in August 1993.

---

2. Although the determination of whether the parties are, in fact, husband and wife is before this court, for convenience, they will be referred to as such.

Unknown to the wife, the husband married another woman in October 1994. Upon discovering that fact, the wife immediately sued for a divorce from the husband, contending that she was his common-law wife, and that he had committed adultery and bigamy, and that there was an irretrievable breakdown of the marriage.

The trial court found that the wife had failed to prove a common-law marriage and dismissed her complaint for divorce. At the conclusion of the testimony, the trial court stated:

> "When these [elements of common-law marriage] are met there is a presumption that a man and woman are married, however, that presumption does not exist where the parties are separated and one of the parties marries under a legal marriage. That is subject to rebuttal but it takes a very strong rebuttal to reach to the level of common law marriage to basically void a legal marriage or a ceremonial marriage.... [B]ased upon the testimony that has been presented the court has no recourse but to find that there did not exist a common law marriage at this time in this case and dismiss the petition for divorce."

The trial court's final judgment simply stated, "The Plaintiff's Complaint for Divorce is hereby DISMISSED, the Plaintiff having failed to prove the existence of a common law marriage." The trial court, in reaching its decision, applied this principle of law stated in White v. White, 225 Ala. 155, 158, 142 So. 524, 526 (1932): "[T]he presumption of an actual marriage from the fact of cohabitation, etc., is rebutted by the fact of a subsequent permanent separation, without apparent cause, and the actual marriage soon after of one of the parties." (Citations omitted.)

We must determine if the trial court erred in finding that a common-law marriage did not exist between the parties, on the basis that the husband's marriage to another vitiated the presumption of the common-law marriage between the parties.

The first issue is whether the parties entered into a common-law marriage.

> "This Court has recently reaffirmed the requirements for a common-law marriage in Alabama in Etheridge v. Yeager, 465 So.2d 378 (Ala.1985). In that opinion, citing various cases as precedent, we held that while no ceremony or particular words are necessary, there are common elements which must be present, either explicitly expressed or implicitly inferred from the circumstances, in order for a common-law marriage to exist. Those elements are: 1) capacity; 2) present, mutual agreement to permanently enter the marriage relationship to the exclusion of all other relationships; and 3) public recognition of the relationship as a marriage and public assumption of marital duties and cohabitation."

Boswell v. Boswell, 497 So.2d 479, 480 (Ala.1986) (citations omitted). "No specific words of assent are required; present intention is inferred from cohabitation and public recognition." Waller v. Waller, 567 So.2d 869, 869 (Ala.Civ.App.1990) (citation omitted). In Copeland v. Richardson, 551 So.2d 353, 355 (Ala.1989), our Supreme Court stated, "This Court has recognized valid common law marriages between parties who were once formally married to each other, when the proof has been sufficient to establish common law relationships." (Citations omitted.)

I. The Boswell Criteria

1. Capacity

Both parties testified that immediately after their divorce, neither party married anyone else and that there was no other impediment to their remarriage. Therefore, both parties had the capacity to enter into the marital relationship.

2. Present Mutual Agreement

The wife testified that she and the husband intended to enter into a marital relationship when "Bruce told me that he loved me and that he knew that he had made some mistakes, that I had taught him a very valuable lesson and that he loved me and *he wanted me to come back and be his wife and I did*." (Emphasis added.) The husband did not deny making this statement. The wife returned to the husband's home that day. Both stated that while living together they had sexual relations. The wife testified that this second relationship "was a lot better" than the previous marital relationship because during their prior marriage, the husband never "accepted" her children by a previous marriage. She further testified that before living together again, they talked about this problem, and that the husband said he loved her children and that he was sorry that he had treated them as he had. During their alleged common-law relationship, the parties signed an agreement allowing the wife's daughter and her family to place a mortgaged mobile home on these parties' real property. Under the terms of the divorce, the wife still had an interest in the land. The wife testified that, except for the husband's relationship with her children, there was no difference between the relationship she and he had had before the divorce and the relationship they had after they began living together in August 1993. The wife never dropped him as a beneficiary of her health insurance. The husband maintained insurance on the wife's automobile. The husband obtained a pistol license for the wife in December 1993 by signing her name to the license, which showed her address at the home where they were living together.

This case is similar to Copeland, wherein our Supreme Court affirmed a judgment based on a finding of a common-law marriage and held that the finding of the parties' present intent to become married upon their reunification was based upon the husband's asking the wife to " 'come and be my wife.' " 551 So.2d at 355. In Copeland, the wife promised at that time that she would try harder to get along with the husband's daughters.

The husband's only contradictory testimony as to their mutual assent to be married is his testimony that he dated others and that he and the others were seen together at restaurants. He did not tell the wife, and he contends that he did not intend to enter into an agreement to get married when the wife replied "maybe" to his proposal of marriage; however, the wife moved in and began living with him on the same day. The husband's subjective intent, i.e., any unexpressed intent he may have had not to be married, must yield to the reasonable conclusion to be drawn from his objective acts such as his failure to dispute what appeared to be a marital relationship. These acts speak for themselves. McGiffert v. State ex rel. Stowe, 366 So.2d 680 (Ala.1978).

Because the husband's subjective intent is insufficient to rebut the objective acts of the parties, we must take it as undisputed that when these parties began to live together they had a mutual agreement to permanently enter the marriage relationship, to the exclusion of all other relationships.

3. Public Recognition

The husband admitted that after she moved back to his home she kept her clothes, personal belongings, furnishings, etc., at the house, and that they shared household duties. The wife did not remove her wedding band when she was divorced. In April 1994, the parties filed a federal tax return for the year 1993, stating that their status was "married filing joint return." This return included a Schedule C, "Profit or Loss From Business," for the husband's installation business, which stated a net income of approximately one half of the parties' adjusted gross income. This return was signed following this statement: "Under penalties of perjury, I declare that I have examined this return and accompanying schedules and statements, and to the best of my knowledge and belief, they are true, correct, and complete."

The parties lived together until the wife's job required her to move to Mississippi in March 1994. The wife took an apartment in Mississippi, listing the husband as her "husband" on an application for utilities. Upon the husband's first visit to the wife's apartment, he went to the office where she worked to obtain a key to the apartment, and the office manager asked him if he was "Barbara's husband," to which he replied, "Yes." On that occasion, the husband was driving the wife's vehicle, and her grandson was with him. The husband picked up a U–Haul truck and assisted her in moving to Tupelo. The husband and the wife saw each other on weekends, with each party driving every other weekend to the home of the other.

On several social occasions the wife introduced him as her husband, and he made no comment regarding that introduction, but now contends that he made no comment because he did not want to embarrass his wife by correcting her. The same office manager testified that at a company picnic and at the office manager's home several months after that, the husband was introduced as the wife's husband, and that he did not on either occasion deny being her husband. Another office manager testified that she attended a company Christmas party in 1993 where the husband was introduced as the wife's husband, by a company manager and by the wife, and the husband made no denial. This office manager also testified that after the divorce the husband talked with her about the separation and stated that he wanted to be back together with his wife again. This court has held that a man's knowingly allowing himself to be referred to as someone's husband, on several occasions, presented an objective manifestation of a mutual assent to be husband and wife. O'Dell v. O'Dell, 57 Ala.App. 185, 326 So.2d 747 (1976).

These facts meet the required elements, stated in Boswell, supra, of capacity, present mutual agreement, and public recognition of the relationship as a marriage and public assumption of marital duties and cohabitation, thereby, inferring consent to enter a matrimonial relationship to the exclusion of all other relationships. Waller, supra.

II.   Issues in Rebuttal

1.   Discussion of Ceremonial Marriage

The husband contends that the relationship did not amount to a common-law marriage because they discussed having a ceremonial marriage, which never occurred. We disagree.

The husband admitted that on several occasions after the divorce he asked her to marry him, and she said "maybe." The wife stated that she agreed to remarry, but that they just never got around to having a ceremonial marriage. In Huffmaster v. Huffmaster, 279 Ala. 594, 188 So.2d 552 (1966), the court held that the evidence supported a finding of a common-law marriage between parties who had lived together continuously from 1933 until 1961, except for a few months in 1945 after a divorce, where the parties filed joint income tax returns as husband and wife subsequent to their divorce. As in this case, the wife in Huffmaster testified that the parties "just never did have time to get around to getting married." Id., 279 Ala. at 594–95, 188 So.2d at 553.

"[T]he intent to participate in a marriage ceremony in the future does not prove a couple's nonmarriage." Mattison v. Kirk, 497 So.2d 120, 123 (Ala.1986) (citation omitted) (overruled on other grounds, Carbon Hill Mfg., Inc. v. Moore, 602 So.2d 354 (Ala.1992)). The rule was enunciated in King v. King, 269 Ala. 468, 471, 114 So.2d 145, 147 (1959), where the court said: "The mere fact that the parties could not get together on the time when and the place where they were to have another ceremonial marriage is not sufficient to overcome the presumption of the common-law marriage." In Mattison, 497 So.2d at 123, the court noted, "It is not uncommon even for ceremonially married couples to have a second marriage ceremony—a sort of celebration and renewal of marriage vows." The fact that two people are planning a wedding ceremony does not mean that they are not presently married.

2.   Dating Others

The husband contends that he could not be found to have intended to be in a marital relationship, permanent and exclusive of all others, because he had dated other women and had been seen with them in public places, although the wife had no knowledge of these actions. We disagree.

Although the husband testified that he was dating "others," he identi-fied only one woman, Cheryl Gaddy Rollings, and he stated that he begin dating her in August 1994, one year after the wife had accepted his invitation to move in with him and become his wife. When asked why he did not tell the wife he was dating others, the husband stated, "Why should I? I don't have no ties with her. She is not—I'm not married to her."

"Once there is a marriage, common law or ceremonial, it is *not* 'transitory, ephemeral, or conditional.' Once married, by common law or by ceremony, the spouses are married. There is no such thing as being a 'little bit' married; and once married, one spouse's *liaison amoureuse* does not end the marital status, whether that status was created by common law or by ceremony, though it may afford the other spouse a ground for judicially terminating the legal relationship."

Adams v. Boan, 559 So.2d 1084, 1087 (Ala.1990) (citations omitted) (em-phasis in original).

3. Marriage to Another

The husband contends that his ceremonial marriage on October 1, 1994, to Cheryl Gaddy Rollings was evidence that could be considered by the trial court to rebut the presumption of an actual marriage between the husband and wife, based upon their cohabitation, etc. We disagree.

This principle, stated in White v. White, 225 Ala. 155, 142 So. 524 (1932), does not apply in this case, because, as discussed above, we must take it as undisputed that when the parties resumed living together in August 1993 they fully intended a marital relationship. This occurred when the wife accepted the husband's invitation to come back and be his wife; she agreed and moved in with him that same day.

"A subsequent asserting 'we knew we were not married' by a party to such an agreement [to enter into a marital relationship] will hardly vitiate a valid marriage where the *original* understanding was to presently enter into the marriage relationship, followed by a public recognition of the relationship." Huffmaster, 279 Ala. at 595, 188 So.2d at 554 (emphasis added).

"[T]he *operative time* is when the agreement is initially entered into, and once other conditions of public recognition and cohabitation are met the only ways to terminate a common-law marriage are by death or divorce. A party cannot legally terminate the marriage by simply changing his or her mind ... or by telling selected individuals, 'We're not really married.' "

Skipworth v. Skipworth, 360 So.2d 975, 977 (Ala.1978) (emphasis added). The operative time, in the instant case, was when the *husband* asked the wife to come back and be his wife *and she did* return for that purpose.

Because we must take it as undisputed that the parties intended to become husband and wife in August 1993, and because they immediately began public assumption of marital duties and cohabitation, we must conclude that a common-law marriage was formed and that the husband's marriage to another, a year later, could not "untie the knot." Therefore, the principle stated in White, and relied upon by the trial judge, is not applicable. The trial court misapplied the law to the facts, and no presumption of correctness exists as to the court's judgment. Griggs v. Driftwood Landing, Inc., 620 So.2d 582 (Ala.1993).

III.   Conclusion

The arguments raised to rebut the contention that these parties had a common-law marriage—(1) their discussion of a ceremonial marriage, (2) the husband's dating others, and (3) the husband's subsequent marriage to another—are, as discussed before, insufficient to rebut the facts suggesting a common-law marriage. The trial court's judgment that no marriage existed between the parties is against the great weight of the evidence. Also, as stated before, the trial court misapplied the law.

The trial court's judgment is reversed, and this case is remanded for further proceedings consistent with this opinion.

NOTE

Less than a quarter of the states still permit informal or "common law" marriages to be effected within their boundaries. Some jurisdictions abolished the practice through specific legislation. In others, courts construed formal requirements regarding solemnization as mandatory rather than directory. The drafters of the Uniform Marriage and Divorce Act purported not to take a stand regarding abolishing or maintaining common law marriage. Instead, it lists alternative Sections 211A and B, which either validate or invalidate such unions. The official Commentary explains:

> These alternatives are presented because the line of cleavage in the states, between those who consider the common law marriage to be a highly useful social institution and those which insist that all marriages *de jure* should be contracted in accordance with prescribed statutory formalities, proved impossible to erase.... The alternatives are a signal to the state legislatures that this issue should be re-examined even if the state is one of those which has already abolished common law marriage.

Despite the ostensible position of the commentators by virtue of taking no position on common law marriage, § 207(b), which provides that bigamous and certain other marriages are prohibited, includes a key curative part of common law marriage by providing that

> Parties to a marriage prohibited under this section who cohabit after removal of the impediment are lawfully married as of the date of removal of the impediment.

Some common law marriage jurisdictions are reluctant to hold that a marriage takes place almost automatically between parties who continue cohabitation after removal of an impediment that made the union void at the outset. In Byers v. Mount Vernon Mills, Inc., 268 S.C. 68, 231 S.E.2d

699 (1977), the parties had married while H still had a living wife. Their marriage thus was initially void, but six years later H divorced his first wife. Eleven years later he left his second "wife" and eventually married still another, with whom he was living at the time of his death. Even though the proceeding involved the question of eligibility for workers' compensation benefits, the court found that there had been no valid common law union between H and the second person with whom he had gone through a marriage ceremony. The court explained its test:

> The law is well settled in this state that the removal of an impediment to a marriage contract (the divorce in this case) does not convert an illegal bigamous marriage into a common law legal marriage. After the barrier to marriage has been removed, there must be a new mutual agreement, either by way of civil ceremony or by way of a recognition of the illicit relation and a new agreement to enter into a common law marriage arrangement.

Another problem on which there is disagreement concerns the effect of temporary cohabitation in a jurisdiction other than the domicile or residence of the parties. In Grant v. Superior Court In and For County of Pima, 27 Ariz.App. 427, 555 P.2d 895 (1976), it was alleged that the parties had gone a motel in Texas for a few hour, consummated their marriage after agreeing to be husband and wife, and then told another couple accompanying them that they were married. The rest of the day was spent in Mexico. The parties then returned to Arizona where they lived together and held themselves out as husband and wife. In refusing to recognize that a common law marriage was created under these circumstances, the Arizona court first pointed out that:

> The elements of such a relationship in Texas are (1) an agreement presently to be husband and wife; (2) living together and cohabiting as husband and wife; (3) holding each other out to the public as such.

In refusing to find that a marriage had been effected, they stated:

> It is not the requirement of domicile . . . that makes the difference, but rather the connection by the couple with the state that recognizes common law marriages. The only connection these parties had with the State of Texas was as mere transients.

Similarly, in Vaughn v. Hufnagel, 473 S.W.2d 124 (Ky.1971), appellant claimed to be decedent's wife and sought appointment as administratrix of his estate. In 1966 she and decedent, both Kentucky residents, had journeyed together to Ohio and registered in a motel there as Mr. and Mrs. Clarence Vaughn. According to appellant, while there "they exchanged mutual vows in marriage without witnesses or solemnization." Within 24 hours they returned to Kentucky with appellant "regaled in the customary diamond ring and wedding band" and they lived and held themselves out as man and wife in Kentucky until his death. In refusing to recognize appellant as the legal wife, the Court said:

> "[T]his state does not recognize common-law marriage within the boundary lines of this state, but may recognize one legalized in another

state. But it takes more than riding across the Ohio River to make one legal." Id. at 125.

Because a marriage valid at the place of celebration generally is valid elsewhere, the extraterritorial impact of common law marriage can be significant. Long after a state has formally abolished informal marriage by statute, its courts may be called on to determine whether a union was effected under prior law. In New York, where common law marriage after April 29, 1933 was abolished by statute, the Court of Appeals in 1974 was asked to determine the claims of rival widows seeking the estate of their husband who died in 1971. In re Estate of Benjamin, 34 N.Y.2d 27, 355 N.Y.S.2d 356, 311 N.E.2d 495 (1974). The Court found that a valid common law marriage had been effected with W–1 sometime between 1927 and 1933 and stated that: "Once a valid common-law marriage is entered into, a subsequent denial of the marriage or a change of mind by one of the parties does not invalidate the marriage." While the Surrogate had found at trial that because of the strong presumption as to the validity of the later ceremonial marriage there should be direct proof of the agreement *per verba de praesenti* in order to overcome this, the Court of Appeals said:

> ". . . [T]he agreement essential to a common-law marriage need not be proved in any direct way. Direct or circumstantial evidence may suffice. . . . Documentary evidence, cohabitation as husband and wife, acknowledgment, declarations, conduct and the like are all probative. . . . Cohabitation or reputation, or holding out to the world as man and wife, we have held, constitute evidence of a marital agreement and raise a presumption of common-law marriage."

In a strong dissent, Judge Gabrielli pointed out that the issue dividing the Court was whether there must be greater proof of an agreement to overcome the strong presumption of validity favoring the second ceremonial marriage. He noted that any evidence of events or occurrences after April 29, 1933 should not be used to establish the claimed marriage relationship.

The "curative powers" of common law marriage can serve as a double edged sword. Important to the outcome in any case can be the proclivity of the particular court to try to find a socially desirable solution under the circumstances by manipulating facts in terms of rules of evidence, or by the presumption of validity of the most recent marriage, the probative value of the initial ceremony, the presumption favoring legitimacy, or shifting the burden of proof. Significant in many cases is the context or proceeding in which the question is raised; the potential here is vast, including questions of the availability of the husband-wife privilege in criminal cases, whether a prior will was revoked, whether the appropriate action for dissolution should be divorce or annulment and what this will mean in terms of support, determination of an insurance beneficiary, or the ordering of heirs under intestacy laws.

For a sensitive discussion of the impact on women of abolishing common law marriage and whether it should be revived, *see* Cynthia Grant Bowman, *A Feminist Proposal to Bring Back Common Law Marriage*, 75 OREGON L. REV. 709 (1997).

UTAH CODE ANN. § 30–1–4.5 (Supp.2006)

§ 30–1–4.5. Validity of marriage not solemnized

(1) A marriage which is not solemnized according to this chapter shall be legal and valid if a court or administrative order establishes that it arises out of a contract between a man and a woman who:

(a) are of legal age and capable of giving consent;

(b) are legally capable of entering a solemnized marriage under the provisions of this chapter;

(c) have cohabited;

(d) mutually assume marital rights, duties, and obligations; and

(e) who hold themselves out as and have acquired a uniform and general reputation as husband and wife.

(2) The determination or establishment of a marriage under this section must occur during the relationship described in Subsection (1), or within one year following the termination of that relationship. Evidence of a marriage recognizable under this section may be manifested in any form, and may be proved under the same general rules of evidence as facts in other cases.

TEXAS FAMILY CODE, ANN. (Vernon 2006)

§ 2.401. Proof of Informal Marriage

(a) In a judicial, administrative, or other proceeding, the marriage of a man and woman may be proved by evidence that:

(1) a declaration of their marriage has been signed as provided by this subchapter; or

(2) the man and woman agreed to be married and after the agreement they lived together in this state as husband and wife and there represented to others that they were married.

(b) If a proceeding in which a marriage is to be proved as provided by Subsection (a)(2) is not commenced before the second anniversary of the date on which the parties separated and ceased living together, it is rebuttably presumed that the parties did not enter into an agreement to be married.

(c) A person under 18 years of age may not:

(1) be a party to an informal marriage; or

(2) execute a declaration of informal marriage under Section 2.402.

§ 2.402. Declaration and Registration of Informal Marriage

(a) A declaration of informal marriage must be signed on a form prescribed by the bureau of vital statistics and provided by the county clerk. Each party to the declaration shall provide the information required in the form.

(b) The declaration form must contain:

(1) a heading entitled "Declaration and Registration of Informal Marriage, _____ County, Texas";

(2) spaces for each party's full name, including the woman's maiden surname, address, date of birth, place of birth, including city, county, and state, and social security number, if any;

(3) a space for indicating the type of document tendered by each party as proof of age and identity;

(4) printed boxes for each party to check "true" or "false" in response to the following statement: "The other party is not related to me as:

(A) an ancestor or descendant, by blood or adoption;

(B) a brother or sister, of the whole or half blood or by adoption;

(C) a parent's brother or sister, of the whole or half blood or by adoption; or

(D) a son or daughter of a brother or sister, of the whole or half blood or by adoption";

(5) a printed declaration and oath reading: "I SOLEMNLY SWEAR (OR AFFIRM) THAT WE, THE UNDERSIGNED, ARE MARRIED TO EACH OTHER BY VIRTUE OF THE FOLLOWING FACTS: ON OR ABOUT (DATE) WE AGREED TO BE MARRIED, AND AFTER THAT DATE WE LIVED TOGETHER AS HUSBAND AND WIFE AND IN THIS STATE WE REPRESENTED TO OTHERS THAT WE WERE MARRIED. SINCE THE DATE OF MARRIAGE TO THE OTHER PARTY I HAVE NOT BEEN MARRIED TO ANY OTHER PERSON. THIS DECLARATION IS TRUE AND THE INFORMATION IN IT WHICH I HAVE GIVEN IS CORRECT.";

(6) spaces immediately below the printed declaration and oath for the parties' signatures; and

(7) a certificate of the county clerk that the parties made the declaration and oath and the place and date it was made.

NOTE

As its name suggests, common law marriage ordinarily is not a creature of statute. Laws such as those enacted in Utah and Texas were adopted to promote legal certainty about status when it is desired to formally establish that the parties were married some time in the past. What possible problems do they create or leave unresolved?

For discussion of whether federal law should also include other provisions that would give at least limited effect to de facto relationships that would not qualify as marriages or putative marriages under the laws of the parties' domiciles, *see* Robert M. Jarvis, *Rethinking the Meaning of the Phrase "Surviving Widow" in the Jones Act: Has the Time Come for Admiralty Courts to Fashion a New Law of Domestic Relations?*, 21 CAL.W.L.REV. 463 (1985). The use of state law to establish a common law marriage for federal criminal law purposes also has raised questions in some circumstances. In United States v. Seay, 718 F.2d 1279 (4th Cir. 1983), a U.S. Court of Appeals affirmed the conviction of a widow for making false statements to the Department of Labor and accepting benefits under the Federal Employee Compensation Act when she was not entitled to them. After the death of her husband on active military duty, defendant was eligible for FECA benefits until she remarried. Her subsequent prosecution turned on whether she had remarried in South Carolina through the "common law" method. In a dissenting opinion, Butzner, J. stated:

> In 32 states which do not recognize common law marriages, a soldier's widow can live with a man without forfeiting her pension or suffering prosecution for fraud because she signed the identical form the defendant signed. When the government through criminal prosecution draws a distinction between the marital status of soldiers' widows living in 18 states and those living in the other 32, the government should be prepared to give fair notice that signing a form, which it provides, is a criminal act in some states though innocent in others.

Id. at 1286–7.

2. CONFIDENTIAL MARRIAGE

CALIFORNIA FAMILY CODE (West 2004)

§ 500. Requirements for confidential marriages

When an unmarried man and an unmarried woman, not minors, have been living together as husband and wife, they may be married pursuant to this chapter by a person authorized to solemnize a marriage . . ., without the necessity of first obtaining health certificates.

§ 502. Inability to personally appear; issuance of license

If, for any reason, either or both of the parties to be married is physically unable to appear in person before the county clerk, a confidential marriage license shall be issued by the county clerk to the person solemnizing the marriage upon that person's presenting an affidavit to the county clerk, signed by the person and the parties to be married, explaining the reason for the inability to appear.

. . .

§ 506. Authentication of license; filing

(a) The confidential marriage license shall be presented to the person solemnizing the marriage.

(b) Upon performance of the ceremony, the confidential marriage certificate shall be filled out by the parties to the marriage and authenticated by the person solemnizing the marriage.

(c) The certificate shall be returned by the person solemnizing the marriage to the office of the county clerk in the county in which the license was issued within 10 days after the ceremony.

. . .

§ 511. Maintenance of marriage certificates; inspections; preservation of record; reproductions; disclosure of information.

(a) Except as provided in subdivision (b), the county clerk shall maintain confidential marriage certificates filed pursuant to Section 506 as permanent records which shall not be open to public 26 inspection except upon order of the court issued upon a showing of good cause.

(b) The county clerk shall keep all original certificates of confidential marriages for one year from the date of filing. After one year, the clerk may microfilm the certificates and dispose of the original certificates or microfilm the certificates and send the original certificates to the Office of the State Registrar. The county clerk shall promptly seal and store at least one original negative of each microphotographic film made in a manner and place as reasonable to ensure its preservation indefinitely against loss, theft, defacement, or destruction. The microphotograph shall be made in a manner that complies with the minimum standards or guidelines, or both, recommended by the American National Standards Institute or the Association for Information and Image Management. Every reproduction shall be deemed and considered an original. A certified copy of any reproduction shall be deemed and considered a certified copy of the original.

(c) The county clerk may conduct a search for a confidential marriage certificate for the purpose of confirming the existence of a marriage, but the date of the marriage and any other information contained in the certificate shall not be disclosed except upon order of the court.

(d) The county clerk shall, not less than quarterly, transmit copies of all original confidential marriage certificates retained, or originals of microfilmed confidential marriage certificates filed after January 1, 1982, to the State Registrar of Vital Statistics. The registrar may destroy the copies so transmitted after they have been indexed. The registrar may respond to an inquiry as to the existence of a marriage performed pursuant to this chapter, but shall not disclose the date of the marriage.

NOTE

"Confidential marriage" does not superimpose the status of marriage on an informal relationship, but rather allows parties who have had longstanding relationships (and may be considered by their friends as married) in a jurisdiction without common law marriage to go through a marriage ceremony without publicity.

3. STATUTORILY REQUIRED FORMALITIES

Carabetta v. Carabetta

Supreme Court of Connecticut, 1980.
182 Conn. 344, 438 A.2d 109.

■ PETERS, ASSOCIATE JUSTICE.

This is an appeal from the dismissal of an action for the dissolution of the marriage.... The trial court ... determined that the parties had never been legally married and thereupon granted the defendant's motion to dismiss....

... The plaintiff and the defendant exchanged marital vows before a priest in the rectory of Our Lady of Mt. Carmel Church of Meriden, on August 25, 1955, according to the rite of the Roman Catholic Church, although they had failed to obtain a marriage license. Thereafter they lived together as husband and wife, raising a family of four children, all of whose birth certificates listed the defendant as their father. Until the present action, the defendant had no memory or recollection of ever having denied that the plaintiff and the defendant were married.

The issue before us is whether, under Connecticut law, despite solemnization according to an appropriate religious ceremony, a marriage is void where there has been noncompliance with the statutory requirement of a marriage license. This is a question of first impression in this state. The trial court held that failure to obtain a marriage license was a flaw fatal to the creation of a legally valid marriage and that the court therefore lacked subject matter jurisdiction over an action for dissolution.

. . . .

The governing statutes at the time of the purported marriage between these parties contained two kinds of regulations concerning the requirements for a legally valid marriage. One kind of regulation concerned substantive requirements determining those eligible to be married.... The other kind of regulation concerns the formalities prescribed by the state for the effectuation of a legally valid marriage. These required formalities, in turn, are of two sorts: a marriage license and a solemnization. In Hames v. Hames, [163 Conn.] 599, 316 A.2d 379 [(1972)], we interpreted our statutes not to make void a marriage consummated after the issuance of a license but deficient for want of due solemnization. Today we examine the statutes in the reverse case, a marriage duly solemnized but deficient for want of a marriage license.

As to licensing, the governing statute in 1955 was a section entitled "Marriage licenses." It provided, in subsection (a): "No persons shall be joined in marriage until both have joined in an application ... for a license for such marriage." Its only provision for the consequence of noncompliance with the license requirement was contained in subsection (e): ". . . any person who shall join any persons in marriage without having received such [license] shall be fined not more than one hundred dollars." General Statutes (Rev.1949) § 7302, as amended by § 1280b (1951 Sup.) and by § 2250c (1953 Sup.).[3] Neither this section, nor any other, described as void a marriage celebrated without license.

As to solemnization, the governing section, entitled "Who may join persons in marriage," provided in 1955: "All judges and justices of the peace may join persons in marriage . . . and all ordained or licensed clergymen belonging to this state or any other state so long as they continue in the work of the ministry may join persons in marriage and all marriages attempted to be celebrated by any other persons shall be void; but all marriages which shall be solemnized according to the forms and usages of any religious denomination in this state shall be valid." General Statutes (Rev.1949) § 7306, as amended by § 1281b (1951 Sup.) and by § 2251c (1953 Sup.).[4] Although solemnization is not at issue in the case before us, this language is illuminating since it demonstrates that the legislature has on occasion exercised its power to declare expressly that failure to observe some kinds of formalities, e.g., the celebration of a marriage by a person not authorized by this section to do so, renders a marriage void. . . .

In the absence of express language in the governing statute declaring a marriage void for failure to observe a statutory requirement, this court has held in an unbroken line of cases since Gould v. Gould, 78 Conn. 242, 247, 61 A. 604 (1905), that such a marriage, though imperfect, is dissoluble rather than void. We see no reason to import into the language "[n]o persons shall be joined in marriage until [they have applied for] a license," a meaning more drastic than that assigned in Gould v. Gould, supra, to the statute that then provided that "[n]o man and woman, either of whom is epileptic . . . shall intermarry." Although the state may well have a legitimate interest in the health of those who are about to marry, Gould v. Gould held that the legislature would not be deemed to have entirely invalidated a marriage contract in violation of such health requirements unless the statute itself expressly declared the marriage to be void. Then as now, the legislature had chosen to use the language of voidness selectively, applying it to some but not to all of the statutory requirements for the creation of a legal marriage. Now as then, the legislature has the competence to choose to sanction those who solemnize a marriage without a marriage license rather than those who marry without a marriage license. In sum, we conclude that the legislature's failure expressly to characterize as void a marriage properly celebrated without a license means that such a marriage is not invalid.

Since the marriage that the trial court was asked to dissolve was not void, the trial court erred in granting the motion to dismiss for lack of jurisdiction over the subject matter. . . .

---

3. Now General Statutes § 46b–24.   **4.** Now General Statutes § 46b–22.

NOTES

Licensure. Marriage licensing goes back to colonial times, but such regulations developed slowly among the states. A Marriage Licensing Act making licensure essential to a valid marriage was recommended by the Commissioners on Uniform State Laws in 1911, but only two states adopted its substance while five others accepted some of its provisions.

All of the states have licensing laws today, but in some of them a valid marriage nevertheless may be effected without obtaining a license. This usually results from interpretation of the statutes as directory rather than mandatory. It also is consonant with the strong public policy of favoring the validity of marriages. Attempts to enforce requirements for licensure by imposing penalties against applicants for false statements, or against clerks for issuing licenses to unqualified persons, have largely been ineffective. Many of those who issue licenses do not seem to realize or accept the broad powers provided or implied in the statutes that confer their authority, and few states have evidenced interest in prosecuting persons who procure marriage licenses through false statements.

Some states require a specific waiting period before a marriage can be solemnized within its borders. Because neither domicil nor residence is required before a license can be obtained or a marriage performed in a particular jurisdiction, persons who wish to avoid such restrictions and marry immediately may simply go to another state without such a provision.

Ceremony. The history of English marriage rules may shed some light on the peculiarities of our own, but those developments probably are of little legal importance to us today except in discussions of informal marriage. Today each state generally specifies the persons who may perform marriages and the conditions that are placed on them. Ordinarily no specific form of ceremony is ordinarily required though some statutes do require specifically that the parties take each other as husband and wife. West Virginia has a "Ritual for ceremony of marriage by judges". W.Va. Stat. § 48–1–12b (Lexis 1999).

Despite specific designations of authority in the statutes, problems still arise regarding who has authority to solemnize marriages. For example, in Cramer v. Commonwealth, 214 Va. 561, 202 S.E.2d 911 (1974) the Supreme Court of Virginia held that "ordained" ministers of the Universal Life Church, Inc. did not qualify as "ministers" within the meaning of the Virginia statute describing who could celebrate the rites of marriage. The court noted that the organization's only dogma was "that each person believe that which is right and that each person shall judge for himself what is right", and that "Universal ministers are ordained, without question of their faith, for life for a free-will offering". It explained that:

> The interest of the state is not only in marriage as an institution, but in the contract between the parties who marry, and in the proper

memorializing of the entry into, and execution of, such a contract. In the proper exercise of its legislative authority it can require that the person who performs a marriage ceremony be certified or licensed.

In State v. Lynch, 301 N.C. 479, 272 S.E.2d 349 (1980), a bigamy conviction was reversed because the first marriage of the defendant, performed by a person holding only a mail order certificate purchased for $10.00 giving him "credentials of a minister" in the Universal Life Church, Inc., was invalid and thus the second marriage could not be bigamous.

Statutes in some jurisdictions provide that if the parties believed in good faith that the person who solemnized their marriage was legally authorized to do so, then lack of authority shall not be ground for annulment. In such cases, however, there may be criminal sanctions that can be imposed against the unauthorized person. *See, e.g.,* VA.STAT. §§ 20–28, 20–31.

4.   PROXY MARRIAGE

Proxy or "picture" marriages usually involve the situation in which a ceremony takes place between parties who are in different jurisdictions. One method for this is to designate a "stand-in" who appears for the absent party at the ceremony, with the idea that the law there should govern. Such marriages could not be effected in some states because of requirements that both parties be present at the ceremony. And federal law limits their recognition for immigration purposes regardless of local validity. According to 8 U.S.C. § 1101(a)(35) (2000):

> The term [sic] "spouse", "wife", or "husband" do not include a spouse, wife or husband by reason of any marriage ceremony where the contracting parties thereto are not physically present in the presence of each other, unless the marriage shall have been consummated.

Section 206 of the Uniform Marriage and Divorce Act contains the following provision specifically authorizing proxy marriages:

> (b) If a party to a marriage is unable to be present at the solemnization, he may authorize in writing a third person to act as his proxy. If the person solemnizing the marriage is satisfied that the absent party is unable to be present and has consented to the marriage, he may solemnize the marriage by proxy. If he is not satisfied, the parties may petition the [_____] court for an order permitting the marriage to be solemnized by proxy.

For general issues concerning the impact of immigration laws on marriage, see Kerry Abrams, *Immigration Law and the Regulation of Marriage*, 91 MINN. L. REV. 101 (2007).

D.   ANNULMENT AND ITS EFFECTS

1.   THE VOID–VOIDABLE DISTINCTION

An annulment action is brought to declare the legal invalidity of a particular union from its inception. A divorce action seeks to terminate a valid marriage as of a specific date after it came into legally recognized existence. Despite the simplicity of this conceptual framework, our legal treatment of annulment has been the subject of much confusion.

Some of the confused and confusing development characteristic of the action for annulment can be attributed to suspicion and lack of understanding of the ecclesiastical law from which it derives. The problems were further exacerbated from an early time by inconsistent use of terms. Coke and Blackstone, the two most venerated commentators on the common law, applied the term "divorce" to all forms of disestablishment of the marriage relationship. The reason lay not in their lack of analytical capacity, but in the fact that English courts often used "divorce" to describe the situation in which the ecclesiastical courts were prepared to say that a marriage never had occurred (annulment), the case in which a separation of the parties would be decreed for grave reasons such as adultery or cruelty (the separation from bed and board, or divorce *a mensa et thoro*), and the case in which the marriage was terminated and the parties were free to remarry afterward (the divorce *a vinculo matrimonii*). This confusion of terminology can be found occasionally even today. *See, e.g.*, Va.Code § 20–39.

The distinction between void and voidable unions is of considerable importance in most jurisdictions. Under the purist approach a void marriage, which usually offends some strong public policy of the state, needs no formal judicial action or declaration to establish its invalidity. It can be attacked by third persons, and the challenge may be instituted even after death of the parties. Cohabitation between them following removal of the impediment that caused their union to be void will not serve to "ratify" and thereby validate the original marriage (though in some jurisdictions a new common law marriage may take place). In states that recognize the void marriage concept in this "pure" form, courts nevertheless will entertain annulment actions in such cases in order to accord certainty to wealth transactions or legal relationships. However some states now require an action for annulment or declaration of invalidity to establish the nullity of what most jurisdictions would regard as void marriages. Others provide for at least limited ratification of what traditionally would be a void (and thus not ratifiable) marriage on removal of the disqualifying impediment.

A voidable marriage typically reflects encroachment on some lesser public policy. Such a union can be ratified by conduct of the parties after removal of the legal impediment that made it vulnerable and unless it is judicially annulled in timely fashion (before ratification, death of a party, or tolling of the action under an applicable statute of limitation), it is valid from its inception. Under the doctrine of "relation back", however, a voidable marriage that has been annulled by a court is deemed to be void *ab initio*. The harshness of such a rule that could affect legitimacy of children and property rights of the parties led to widespread adoption of various types of ameliorative statutes. Some jurisdictions even provide that a party can sue for divorce on a ground that conceptually should be the basis for annulment (for example, conduct or conditions dating from before the marriage).

Annulment provides an illustration of how law in practice does not necessarily mirror law as described in the books. Annulments sometimes have been granted on the joint request of parties who had no children and whose union was of short duration, even though the legal basis for such a ruling was highly tenuous. Historically this reflected both the difficulty of obtaining a divorce under the fault system and the widely held view that annulment was more acceptable socially than divorce. Also, annulment can be desirable for a person whose religious tenets are opposed to divorce. Attitudes about divorce have changed considerably with the advent of "breakdown" grounds, but the historic view of annulment as the less controversial alternative may be the major reason for its retention today when a persuasive case can be made that the action—at least when it involves only a voidable union—has become an anachronism.

In 1966 the Project of the Governor's Commission on the Family in California made the following observations:

Annulment is presently granted upon six grounds: incapability (i.e., non-age); prior valid marriage still existing ("innocent" bigamy); unsound mind; fraud; force; and physical incapacity. These grounds relate to impediments or defects theoretically existing before the marriage which prevent the marriage's valid formation, as opposed to divorce grounds which relate to post-marriage occurrences. They apply to voidable marriages; in other words, the marriages subject to these defects are nevertheless good until annulled.

Additionally, two classes of marriages are denominated void ab initio: Those which are knowingly bigamous, and those which are "incestuous" (i.e., within the prohibited degrees of consanguinity and affinity). Void marriages are not technically annulled, but are subject to a declaration of nullity sought by either party. Thus, failure to take legal action confers no validity upon a void marriage, while it has this effect upon a voidable marriage.

Annulments comprise less than 5% of all severance actions; 35% of them are grounded on bigamy, nearly 47% on fraud. It appears that the Courts in reality try to subsume a breakdown-of-marriage standard under the annulment grounds much as they attempt to subsume it under the divorce grounds; the ground of fraud in annulments is used in much the same way as the ground of extreme cruelty in divorce cases.

We are convinced that the essential question presented in the annulment of a voidable marriage does not differ from that presented in any dissolution of marriage case. To over-simply state the case, if the parties can live and function successfully with the alleged impediment, then the marriage is viable and should not be dissolved. If they cannot, then the marriage has broken down in fact and should be ended at law. We believe, therefore, that the successful operation of the Family Court demands that the same standard govern annulments of voidable marriages as governs other dissolution proceedings, and we recommend the elimination of the specific fault annulment grounds;

the removal of the annulment of voidable marriages as a separate form of action; and the coalescence of all dissolution proceedings (save for declarations of nullity in the case of void marriages) into a single form of action governed by a single standard.

. . .

In cases of void marriage, we recommend that the present declaration of nullity be preserved, and that either party should be able to apply to the Court for this form of declaratory relief. The statute proposed by the Commission affords protection of the property and support interests of an innocent spouse following a declaration of nullity, by analogy to the laws governing the division of community property and alimony.

Despite declarations such as this, the general legislative approach has been more along the lines of codifying traditional annulment rules carved out by the courts rather than melding it into the "break down" approach to marriage dissolution.

UNIFORM MARRIAGE AND DIVORCE ACT (1973)

§ 207. [Prohibited Marriages.]

(a) The following marriages are prohibited:

(1) a marriage entered into prior to the dissolution of an earlier marriage of one of the parties;

(2) a marriage between an ancestor and a descendant, or between a brother and a sister, whether the relationship is by the half or the whole blood, or by adoption;

(3) a marriage between an uncle and a niece or between an aunt and a nephew, whether the relationship is by the half or the whole blood, except as to marriages permitted by the established customs of aboriginal cultures.

(b) Parties to a marriage prohibited under this section who cohabit after removal of the impediment are lawfully married as of the date of removal of the impediment.

(c) Children born of a prohibited marriage are legitimate.

§ 208. [Declaration of Invalidity.]

(a) The [_____] court shall enter its decree declaring the invalidity of a marriage entered into under the following circumstances:

(1) a party lacked capacity to consent to the marriage at the time the marriage was solemnized, either because of mental incapacity or infirmity or because of the influence of alcohol, drugs, or other incapacitating substances, or a party was induced to enter into a marriage by force or duress, or by fraud involving the essentials of marriage;

(2) a party lacks the physical capacity to consummate the marriage by sexual intercourse, and at the time the marriage was solemnized the other party did not know of the incapacity;

(3) a party [was under the age of 16 years and did not have the consent of his parents or guardian and judicial approval or] was aged 16 or 17 years and did not have the consent of his parents or guardian or judicial approval; or

(4) the marriage is prohibited.

(b) A declaration of invalidity under subsection (a)(1) through (3) may be sought by any of the following persons and must be commenced within the times specified, but in no event may a declaration of invalidity be sought after the death of either party to the marriage:

(1) for a reason set forth in subsection (a)(1), by either party or by the legal representative of the party who lacked capacity to consent, no later than 90 days after the petitioner obtained knowledge of the described condition;

(2) for the reason set forth in subsection (a)(2), by either party, no later than one year after the petitioner obtained knowledge of the described condition;

(3) for the reason set forth in subsection (a)(3), by the underaged party, his parent or guardian, prior to the time the underaged party reaches the age at which he could have married without satisfying the omitted requirement.

Alternative A

[(c) A declaration of invalidity for the reason set forth in subsection (a)(4) may be sought by either party, the legal spouse in case of a bigamous marriage, the [appropriate state official], or a child of either party, at any time prior to the death of one of the parties.]

Alternative B

[(c) A declaration of invalidity for the reason set forth in subsection (a)(4) may be sought by either party, the legal spouse in case of a bigamous marriage, the [appropriate state official] or a child of either party, at any time, not to exceed 5 years following the death of either party.]

(d) Children born of a marriage declared invalid are legitimate.

(e) Unless the court finds, after a consideration of all relevant circumstances, including the effect of a retroactive decree on third parties, that the interests of justice would be served by making the decree not retroactive, it shall declare the marriage invalid as of the date of the marriage. The provisions of this Act relating to property rights of the spouses, maintenance, support, and custody of children on dissolution of marriage are applicable to non-retroactive decrees of invalidity.

McConkey v. McConkey

Supreme Court of Virginia, 1975.
216 Va. 106, 215 S.E.2d 640.

■ COCHRAN, JUSTICE.

. . .

[Clara and Edward McConkey were divorced in 1968. Edward was ordered to pay $200 monthly in alimony. In October 1971 Clara married

Calvin Sykes. In November 1971 Clara instituted an action against Sykes for divorce based on desertion or annulment based on fraud. A final decree of annulment was rendered in January 1973, after which she petitioned for reinstatement of alimony from Edward.]

Clara contends that, as her second marriage was declared void retrospectively, she should be restored to the same position and standing she enjoyed before she went through the second marriage ceremony. We do not agree.

Section 20–110 of the Code of 1950, as amended, provides:

> "If any person to whom alimony has been awarded shall thereafter marry, such alimony shall cease as of the date of such marriage."

We need not decide whether this statute would apply to a person to whom alimony has been awarded who thereafter is involved in a void marriage. Clara's marriage to Sykes was not void *ab initio*. There is no evidence that the marriage ceremony was invalid. The annulment was based upon fraud on the part of Sykes, so that the marriage was voidable if Clara desired to have it annulled. . . .

We have drawn a distinction between void and voidable marriages. A voidable marriage is "usually treated as a valid marriage until it is decreed void." Toler v. Oakwood Smokeless Coal Corp., 173 Va. 425, 432, 4 S.E.2d 364, 367 (1939). And the parties to a voidable marriage "are husband and wife unless and until the marriage is annulled." Payne v. Commonwealth, 201 Va. 209, 211, 110 S.E.2d 252, 254 (1959).

Clara's reliance on Robbins v. Robbins, 343 Mass. 247, 178 N.E.2d 281 (1961) is misplaced. There, the court held that an annulled voidable second marriage did not relieve the first husband of his obligation to make alimony payments under a divorce decree that was silent as to the effect of remarriage. The Massachusetts statute, however, required proof of a change of circumstances before the previous award of alimony could be altered, and the court found no such change of circumstances in the case under consideration. Moreover, in Surabian v. Surabian, 362 Mass. 342, 285 N.E.2d 909 (1972), the court held, in distinguishing Robbins v. Robbins, supra, that where a separation agreement incorporated in a divorce decree provided that alimony should terminate upon the wife's remarriage the annulment of her voidable second marriage did not reinstate the alimony.

It has been generally held that annulment of a voidable second marriage does not entitle the wife to reinstatement of alimony payments from her first husband, where there is a statute providing that alimony shall terminate upon the recipient's remarriage. Sefton v. Sefton, 45 Cal.2d 872, 291 P.2d 439 (1955); Flaxman v. Flaxman, 57 N.J. 458, 273 A.2d 567 (1971). Other jurisdictions have followed this rule even in the absence of such a statute. Evans v. Evans, 212 So.2d 107 (Fla.App.1968); Bridges v. Bridges, 217 So.2d 281 (Miss.1968); Chavez v. Chavez, 82 N.M. 624, 485

P.2d 735 (1971). And in New York, where there is now a statute authorizing the court, in annulment proceedings, to order the payment of alimony, it is held that the wife is no longer entitled to reinstate alimony upon annulment of a voidable marriage. Gaines v. Jacobsen, 308 N.Y. 218, 124 N.E.2d 290 312 (1954). Prior to the enactment of this statute the rule in New York had been to the contrary. . . .

We hold that where the divorced wife enters into a subsequent voidable marriage she thereby forfeits her right to alimony from her former husband. The husband has a right to assume the validity of the second marriage and to arrange his affairs accordingly. When his former wife voluntarily accepts the risk of a subsequent marriage, he should not be held accountable for her gullibility, mistake or misfortune. A voidable marriage may not be annulled for years. Indeed, in the present case the decree of annulment was entered more than a year after the marriage ceremony. To require the former husband to proceed during this period at his peril in making financial commitments that could be suddenly disrupted, through no fault of his, would be to penalize him for events beyond his control. We decline to do so.

NOTE

The facts of the *McConkey* case provide an illustration of how problems can arise because of the conceptual distinction between annulment and divorce. A factor that has influenced some courts in the past is whether the applicable state law provides for a possible support award to a spouse in an annulment action. Some states now permit such awards by statute, often on the same basis as alimony awards on divorce. After the Supreme Court of Utah, in Ferguson v. Ferguson, 564 P.2d 1380 (Utah 1977), held that an annulment should not automatically restore alimony awarded under a prior divorce decree and that trial courts could exercise sound discretion in ordering such reinstatement if necessary "to rectify serious inequity or injustice", the legislature enacted what is now UTAH CODE § 30–3–5(8) (LEXIS Supp. 2001) that provides:

> Unless a decree of divorce specifically provides otherwise, any order of the court that a party pay alimony to a former spouse automatically terminates upon the remarriage of that former spouse. However, if that marriage is annulled and found to be void ab initio, payment of alimony shall resume if the party paying alimony is made a party to the action of annulment and his rights are determined.

The problem can arise both with regard to judicial decrees for alimony and contractual provisions of separation and property settlement agreements. How would you word a decree or contractual provision to deal effectively with it?

The Virginia court did not rule in *McConkey* on what result it would reach if the "remarriage" under similar facts were void. Are there any good reasons, conceptual or practical, for treating void and voidable "remarriages" differently with respect to termination or resumption of alimony from a prior divorce?

In Shank v. Shank, 100 Nev. 695, 691 P.2d 872 (1984), the plaintiff had obtained an annulment of her second marriage because her new husband had not divorced his first wife. Plaintiff sought reinstatement of her first husband's alimony payments that had been terminated because of her remarriage. After reviewing the policy reasons generally asserted for not reviving such payments, the Supreme Court of Nevada held that:

> the term "remarriage" as used in the divorce decree and [the Nevada alimony statute] means the solemnization or ceremony of remarriage, without regard to whether the remarriage is later determined to be void or voidable.

In In Re Marriage of Cargill and Rollins, the Supreme Court of Colorado took a different tack, holding that "while an annulment of a marriage does not automatically reinstate a maintenance obligation from a previous marriage as a matter of law, such an obligation may be reinstated, depending on the facts and the equities of the situation." 843 P.2d 1335 (1993). Construing the term "remarriage" in their state's statute on termination of alimony to refer to achieving marital status rather than going through a marriage ceremony, the court stated that

> Manageable standards for a trial court to consider can be formulated. First, the mere fact that a party remarried, and later had that second marriage declared void, does not resurrect the ex-spouse's maintenance obligation. Instead, the trial court must look to the facts of the particular case. Among the factors to be considered are the length of the second marriage, whether the annulment of the second marriage was proper and should bind the first spouse, whether maintenance is being paid (or is more than theoretically payable) from the invalidated marriage, the circumstances of the parties, and whether the payor spouse would suffer substantial prejudice by reinstating maintenance payments. In sum, the district court should be guided by its role as a court of equity in such matters.

In Joye v. Yon, 345 S.C. 264, 547 S.E.2d 888 (App.2001), the South Carolina Court of Appeals held that alimony would be restored after an absolutely void marriage (the alimony recipient's putative husband had never been divorced from his prior wife), specifically rejecting the argument that "remarriage" could include such a union for determining alimony restoration. The court also noted that there was no indication in the record that the first husband (the alimony payor) had changed his financial position in reliance upon his wife's void union, and the time lapse was not great.

2. Putative Marriage

UNIFORM MARRIAGE AND DIVORCE ACT (1973)

[**§ 209. [Putative Spouse.]** Any person who has cohabited with another to whom he is not legally married in the good faith belief that he was married to that person is a putative spouse until knowledge of the fact that he is not legally married terminates his status and prevents acquisition of further rights. A putative spouse acquires the rights conferred upon a legal spouse, including the right to maintenance following termination of his status, whether or not the marriage is prohibited (Section 207) or declared invalid (Section 208). If there is a legal spouse or other putative spouses, rights acquired by a putative spouse do not supersede the rights of the legal spouse or those acquired by other putative spouses, but the court shall apportion property, maintenance, and support rights among the claimants as appropriate in the circumstances and in the interests of justice.]

LOUISIANA CIVIL CODE ANN. (West 1999)

Art. 96. Civil effects of absolutely null marriage; putative marriage

An absolutely null marriage nevertheless produces civil effects in favor of a party who contracted it in good faith for as long as that party remains in good faith.

When the cause of the nullity is one party's prior undissolved marriage, the civil effects continue in favor of the other party, regardless of whether the latter remains in good faith, until the marriage is pronounced null or the latter party contracts a valid marriage.

A marriage contracted by a party in good faith produces civil effects in favor of a child of the parties.

A purported marriage between parties of the same sex does not produce any civil effects.

Williams v. Williams

Nevada Supreme Court, 2004.
120 Nev. 559, 97 P.3d 1124.

■ Per Curiam.

This is a case of first impression involving the application of the putative spouse doctrine in an annulment proceeding. Under the doctrine, an individual whose marriage is void due to a prior legal impediment is treated as a spouse so long as the party seeking equitable relief participated in the marriage ceremony with the good-faith belief that the ceremony was legally valid. A majority of states recognize the doctrine when dividing property acquired during the marriage, applying equitable principles, based on community property law, to the division. However, absent fraud, the doctrine does not apply to awards of spousal support. While some states have extended the doctrine to permit spousal support awards, they have done so under the authority of state statutes.

We agree with the majority view. Consequently, we adopt the putative spouse doctrine in annulment proceedings for purposes of property division and affirm the district court's division of the property. However, we reject the doctrine as a basis of awarding equitable spousal support. Because Nevada's annulment statutes do not provide for an award of support upon annulment, we reverse the district court's award of spousal support.

On August 26, 1973, appellant Richard E. Williams underwent a marriage ceremony with respondent Marcie C. Williams. At that time, Marcie believed that she was divorced from John Allmaras. However, neither Marcie nor Allmaras had obtained a divorce. Richard and Marcie believed they were legally married and lived together, as husband and wife, for 27 years. In March 2000, Richard discovered that Marcie was not divorced from Allmaras at the time of their marriage ceremony.

In August 2000, Richard and Marcie permanently separated. In February 2001, Richard filed a complaint for an annulment. Marcie answered and counterclaimed for one-half of the property and spousal support as a putative spouse. In April 2002, the parties engaged in a one-day bench trial to resolve the matter.

At trial, Richard testified that had he known Marcie was still married, he would not have married her. He claimed that Marcie knew she was not divorced when she married him or had knowledge that would put a reasonable person on notice to check if the prior marriage had been dissolved. Specifically, Richard stated that Marcie should not have relied on statements from Allmaras that he had obtained a divorce because Marcie never received any legal notice of divorce proceedings. In addition, Richard claimed that in March 2000, when Marcie received a social security check in the name of Marcie Allmaras, Marcie told him that she had never been divorced from Allmaras. Marcie denied making the statement.

Marcie testified that she believed she was not married to her former husband, John Allmaras, and was able to marry again because Allmaras told her they were divorced. Marcie further testified that in 1971, she ran into Allmaras at a Reno bus station, where he specifically told her that they were divorced and he was living with another woman. According to Marcie, she discovered she was still married to Allmaras during the course of the annulment proceedings with Richard. Marcie testified that if she had known at any time that she was still married to Allmaras, she would have obtained a divorce from him.

During the 27 years that the parties believed themselves to be married, Marcie was a homemaker and a mother. From 1981 to 1999, Marcie was a licensed child-care provider for six children. During that time, she earned $460 a week. At trial, Marcie had a certificate of General Educational Development (G.E.D.) and earned $8.50 an hour at a retirement home. She was 63 years old and lived with her daughter because she could not afford to live on her own.

Both parties stipulated to the value of most of their jointly-owned property. At the time of the annulment proceeding, the parties held various items in their joint names, including bank accounts, vehicles, life insurance policies, a Sparks home, a radiator business, and a motorcycle.

The district court found that Marcie had limited ability to support herself. The district court also concluded that both parties believed they were legally married, acted as husband and wife, and conceived and raised two children. Marcie stayed home to care for and raise their children. Based upon these facts, the district court granted the annulment and awarded Marcie one-half of all the jointly-held property and spousal support. The district court did not indicate whether its award was based on the putative spouse doctrine or an implied contract and quantum meruit theory. The final judgment divided the parties' property so that each received assets of approximately the same value. It also ordered Richard to pay Marcie the sum of $500 per month for a period of four years as "reimbursement and compensation for the benefit received by [Richard] by way of [Marcie's] forgoing a career outside the home in order to care for [Richard] and their children." Richard timely appealed the district court's judgment.

A marriage is void if either of the parties to the marriage has a former husband or wife then living.[2] Richard and Marcie's marriage was void because Marcie was still married to another man when she married Richard. Although their marriage was void, an annulment proceeding was necessary to legally sever their relationship. An annulment proceeding is the proper manner to dissolve a void marriage and resolve other issues arising from the dissolution of the relationship.

First, Richard contends that Marcie is not entitled to one-half of their joint property because their marriage was void. Richard asserts that application of the putative spouse doctrine and quasi-community property principles was improper. Alternatively, Richard argues that if the district court relied on implied contract and quantum meruit theories, the district court should have divided the parties' residence according to this court's decision in *Sack v. Tomlin*,[4] which would provide Richard with 67 percent of the assets instead of 50 percent.

Second, Richard argues that the district court erred in awarding spousal support. Richard contends support is not permitted, absent statutory authority, under the putative spouse doctrine and that there is no basis in Nevada law for awarding compensation for services rendered during the marriage under a theory of quantum meruit.

Because the record does not reflect the basis for the district court's decision, resolution of Richard's contentions requires us to address the putative spouse doctrine.

Under the putative spouse doctrine, when a marriage is legally void, the civil effects of a legal marriage flow to the parties who contracted to marry in good faith.[5] That is, a putative spouse is entitled to many of the rights of an actual spouse. A majority of states have recognized some form of the doctrine through case law or statute.[7] States differ, however, on what

---

2. NRS 125.290(2).

4. 110 Nev. 204, 871 P.2d 298 (1994).

5. *Hicklin,* 509 N.W.2d at 631.

7. Christopher L. Blakesley, *The Putative Marriage Doctrine*, 60 Tul. L.Rev. 1 (1985); *see* Cal. Fam.Code § 2251 (West 1994); Colo.Rev.Stat. Ann. § 14–2–111 (West

exactly constitutes a "civil effect." The doctrine was developed to avoid depriving innocent parties who believe in good faith that they are married from being denied the economic and status-related benefits of marriage, such as property division, pension, and health benefits.[8]

The doctrine has two elements: (1) a proper marriage ceremony was performed, and (2) one or both of the parties had a good-faith belief that there was no impediment to the marriage and the marriage was valid and proper.[9] "Good faith" has been defined as an "honest and reasonable belief that the marriage was valid at the time of the ceremony."[10] Good faith is presumed. The party asserting lack of good faith has the burden of proving bad faith. Whether the party acted in good faith is a question of fact.[12] Unconfirmed rumors or mere suspicions of a legal impediment do not vitiate good faith " 'so long as no certain or authoritative knowledge of some legal impediment comes to him or her.' "[13] However, when a person receives reliable information that an impediment exists, the individual cannot ignore the information, but instead has a duty to investigate further. Persons cannot act " 'blindly or without reasonable precaution.' "[15] Finally, once a spouse learns of the impediment, the putative marriage ends.

We have not previously considered the putative spouse doctrine, but we are persuaded by the rationale of our sister states that public policy supports adopting the doctrine in Nevada. Fairness and equity favor recognizing putative spouses when parties enter into a marriage ceremony in good faith and without knowledge that there is a factual or legal impediment to their marriage. Nor does the doctrine conflict with Nevada's policy in refusing to recognize common-law marriages or palimony suits. In the putative spouse doctrine, the parties have actually attempted to enter into a formal relationship with the solemnization of a marriage ceremony, a missing element in common-law marriages and palimony suits. As a majority of our sister states have recognized, the sanctity of marriage is not undermined, but rather enhanced, by the recognition of the putative spouse doctrine. We therefore adopt the doctrine in Nevada.

We now apply the doctrine to the instant case. The district court found that the parties obtained a license and participated in a marriage ceremony on August 26, 1973, in Verdi, Nevada. The district court also found that Marcie erroneously believed that her prior husband, Allmaras, had terminated their marriage by divorce and that she was legally able to marry

---

2003); 750 Ill. Comp. Stat. Ann. 5/305 (West 1999); La. Civ.Code Ann. art. 96 (West 1999); Minn.Stat. Ann. § 518.055 (West 1990); Mont.Code Ann. § 40–1–404 (2003).

8. *See Cortes v. Fleming,* 307 So.2d 611, 613 (La.1973) (noting that the doctrine has been applied to issues involving legitimacy of children, workers' compensation benefits, community property, and inheritance).

9. Blakesley, *supra* note 7, at 6.

10. *Hicklin,* 509 N.W.2d at 631

12. *Galbraith v. Galbraith,* 396 So.2d 1364, 1369 (La.Ct.App.1981).

13. *Garduno v. Garduno,* 760 S.W.2d 735, 740 (Tex.App.1988) (quoting *Succession of Chavis,* 211 La. 313, 29 So.2d 860, 862 (1947)).

15. *Id.* (quoting *Chavis,* 29 So.2d at 863).

Richard. In so finding, the district court also necessarily rejected Richard's argument that Marcie acted unreasonably in relying on Allmaras' statements because she had never been served with divorce papers and that she had a duty to inquire about the validity of her former marriage before marrying Richard.

Although Richard's and Marcie's testimony conflicted on this issue, judging the credibility of the witnesses and the weight to be given to their testimony are matters within the discretion of the district court.[17] "This court reviews district court decisions concerning divorce proceedings for an abuse of discretion. Rulings supported by substantial evidence will not be disturbed on appeal."[18] Substantial evidence is that which a sensible person may accept as adequate to sustain a judgment.[19] We apply the same standard in annulment proceedings. The district court was free to disregard Richard's testimony, and substantial evidence supports the district court's finding that Marcie did not act unreasonably in relying upon Allmaras' representations. The record reflects no reason for Marcie to have disbelieved him and, thus, no reason to have investigated the truth of his representations. Although older case law suggests that a party cannot rely on a former spouse's representation of divorce, more recent cases indicate this is just a factor for the judge to consider in determining good faith. We conclude that the district court did not err in finding that Marcie entered into the marriage in good faith. She therefore qualifies as a putative spouse. We now turn to the effect of the doctrine on the issues of property division and alimony.

Community property states that recognize the putative spouse doctrine apply community property principles to the division of property, including determinations of what constitutes community and separate property. Since putative spouses believe themselves to be married, they are already under the assumption that community property laws would apply to a termination of their relationship. There is no point, therefore, in devising a completely separate set of rules for dividing property differently in a putative spouse scenario. We agree with this reasoning.

In some states, courts apply community property principles to divide property acquired during the purported marriage.[22] In other states, the property is considered to be held under joint tenancy principles and is divided equally between the parties. Regardless of the approach, all states that recognize the putative spouse doctrine divide assets acquired during the marriage in an equitable fashion. We conclude that the application of community property principles to a putative marriage, as indicated in *Sanguinetti v. Sanguinetti*,[24] is the better approach to the division of

---

17. *Castle v. Simmons*, 120 Nev. 98, ___, 86 P.3d 1042, 1046 (2004).

18. *Shydler v. Shydler*, 114 Nev. 192, 196, 954 P.2d 37, 39 (1998).

19. *See Schmanski v. Schmanski*, 115 Nev. 247, 251, 984 P.2d 752, 755 (1999).

22. *Sanguinetti v. Sanguinetti*, 69 P.2d 845, 847 (1937).

24. 69 P.2d at 847

property in such cases.[25] In this case, the district court treated the parties' property as quasi-community property and equally divided the joint property between the parties. Substantial evidence supports the district court's division, and we affirm the district court's distribution of the property.

States are divided on whether spousal support is a benefit or civil effect that may be awarded under the putative spouse doctrine. Although some states permit the award of alimony, they do so because their annulment statutes permit an award of rehabilitative or permanent alimony. At least one state, however, has found alimony to be a civil effect under the putative spouse doctrine even in the absence of a specific statute permitting an award of alimony.[28]

Nevada statutes do not provide for an award of alimony after an annulment. Thus, the cases in which alimony was awarded pursuant to statute are of little help in resolving this issue. In those cases, state legislatures had codified the putative spouse doctrine and specifically indicated that issues such as property division and alimony were to be resolved in the same manner as if the void marriage had been valid. Absent such a determination by the Nevada Legislature, we must look to the cases in which courts have either refused to award alimony in the absence of statutory authority, despite recognizing the doctrine for other purposes, or awarded spousal support based on the putative spouse doctrine.

In *McKinney v. McKinney,* the Georgia Supreme Court summarily stated that alimony is not available in an equitable action for annulment because the right to alimony depends upon a valid marriage.[31] This reflects the general rule expressed in *Poupart.* However, unlike *Poupart,* the Georgia Supreme Court does appear to have relied on the putative spouse doctrine in dividing the parties' property since it discussed concepts of good faith. Thus, it appears that the Georgia court declined to award alimony under the doctrine.

The California Supreme Court followed the same rationale in *Sanguinetti,* noting that a putative spouse has no right to an allowance of alimony. However, the California Supreme Court found that a putative spouse could maintain a claim under quantum meruit for the reasonable value of the services that the putative spouse rendered to the marriage if there was fraud or fault (such as cruelty) committed by the party opposing alimony.

25. Different rules may apply when one of the parties qualifies as a putative spouse and the other does not. When a person enters into the relationship with knowledge of an impediment and knowledge the marriage is not valid, some states have found the person who acted in bad faith is not entitled to benefit from the marriage. We do not reach this issue because the facts of this case involve two innocent putative spouses.

28. *Cortes v. Fleming,* 307 So.2d 611 (La.1973). While the Louisiana Supreme

Court did not rely on a statute specifically granting a putative spouse the right to alimony in its decision, the court did use an annulment statute as a basis of the award. The court indicated the term "civil effect" in the annulment statute was broad enough to include alimony. Nevada does not have similar language in its annulment statutes.

31. 242 Ga. 607, 250 S.E.2d 470, 472 (1978).

In a similar case, Kindle v. Kindle,[35] the Florida Court of Appeals upheld an award of alimony when the husband failed to disclose his previous marriage and was not divorced when he entered into a second marriage ceremony. Preston and Kikeu Kindle were married for 20 years when the court granted an annulment. At the time the couple married, Preston was already married, but he never disclosed this to Kikeu. The trial court found that Kikeu was an innocent victim of Preston's wrongdoing and awarded Kikeu permanent alimony. The Florida Court of Appeals upheld the permanent alimony award based on equitable principles. The court further stated that "[i]t would be grossly inequitable to deny alimony to a putative wife of a twenty-year marriage because the husband fraudulently entered into a marriage ceremony."[37]

Sanguinetti and *Kindle,* however, are distinguishable from the instant case. In those cases, the courts found fraud, bad faith or bad conduct, such as cruelty, to support the award of equitable alimony. In the instant case, Richard and Marcie each acted in good faith. Neither Richard nor Marcie knowingly defrauded the other, and there is no evidence of misconduct or bad faith.

We can find no case, and Marcie has cited to none, in which spousal support was awarded to a putative spouse absent statutory authority, fraud, bad faith or bad conduct. Although one commentator favors such awards on the theory that the purpose of the putative spouse doctrine is to fulfill the reasonable expectations of the parties,[38] we are unaware of any court adopting such a standard.

The putative spouse doctrine did not traditionally provide for an award of spousal support. Extensions of the doctrine have come through statute or findings of fraud and bad faith. As neither is present in this case, we decline to extend the doctrine to permit an award of spousal support when both parties act in good faith. Richard and Marcie's marriage was void, and there was no showing of bad faith or fraud by either party. Absent an equitable basis of bad faith or fraud or a statutory basis, the district court had no authority to grant the spousal support award, and we reverse that part of the judgment awarding spousal support.

We conclude that an annulment proceeding is the proper method for documenting the existence of a void marriage and resolving the rights of the parties arising out of the void relationship. We adopt the putative spouse doctrine and conclude that common-law community property principles apply by analogy to the division of property acquired during a putative marriage. However, the putative spouse doctrine does not permit an award of spousal support in the absence of bad faith, fraud or statutory authority. Therefore, we affirm that portion of the district court's order equally dividing the parties' property and reverse that portion of the order awarding spousal support.

35. 629 So.2d 176 (Fla.Dist.Ct.App. 1993).

37. *Id.* at 177.

38. Blakesley, *supra* note 7, at 43.

NOTE

The putative marriage doctrine provides a method for safeguarding the economic interests of a party to a void or voidable marriage that has been annulled if that party cohabited in good faith belief that the marriage was valid. Because the test for applying the doctrine is one of good faith, it is possible that a person may have more than one putative spouse at the same time.

Other approaches to dealing with this problem include common law marriage, the presumption of validity of the most recent union, and ameliorative statutes that confer certain incidents such as legitimacy of offspring. Until recently the putative marriage doctrine existed largely in community property states. Inclusion of optional § 209 in the Uniform Marriage and Divorce Act has led to more widespread adoption. A form of "putative spouse" test dealing with cases of ceremonialized marriages that are invalidated because of an unknown impediment also is contained in the federal Social Security law. 42 U.S.C.A. § 416(h)(1)(B)(i) (West Supp. 2001).

One question that might be raised with regard to U.M.D.A. § 209 is whether it affords adequate guidelines for apportionment in "multiple spouse" cases, as mandated in the final sentence of the section. The Comment to the Act states that "A fair and efficient apportionment standard is likely to be the length of time each spouse cohabited with the common partner." The Comment also makes it clear that the Act was not intended to abolish other equitable doctrines.

For a detailed examination of the putative marriage doctrine and its effects, *see* Christopher Blakesley, *The Putative Marriage Doctrine*, 60 Tul.L.Rev. 1 (1985).

E. Determining Legal Eligibility

1. Minimum Age Requirements

Moe v. Dinkins

United States District Court, Southern District of New York, 1981.
533 F.Supp. 623.

■ Motley, District Judge.

Plaintiffs Maria Moe, Raoul Roe and Ricardo Roe seek a judgment declaring unconstitutional, and enjoining the enforcement of, the parental consent requirement of New York Domestic Relations Law §§ 15.2 and 15.3. Section 15.2 provides that all male applicants for a marriage license between ages 16 and 18 and all female applicants between ages 14 and 18 must obtain "written consent to the marriage from both parents of the minor or minors or such as shall then be living...." Section 15.3 requires that a woman between ages 14 and 16 obtain judicial approval of the marriage, as well as the parental consent required by Section 15.2.

This action is now before the court on plaintiffs' motion for summary judgment declaring Section 15 unconstitutional and enjoining its enforcement. . . .

Plaintiff Raoul Roe was eighteen years old when this action was commenced. Plaintiff Maria Moe was fifteen years old. Plaintiff Ricardo Roe is their one year old son who was born out of wedlock. Plaintiffs live together as an independent family unit. In late November, 1978, Maria became pregnant by Raoul and in April, 1979, they moved into an apartment together. Maria requested consent from her mother, a widow, to marry Raoul, but Mrs. Moe refused, allegedly because she wishes to continue receiving welfare benefits for Maria. Maria and Raoul continue to be prevented from marrying because of Mrs. Moe's failure to give consent to the marriage as required by Section 15. Maria and Raoul allege that they wish to marry in order to cement their family unit and to remove the stigma of illegitimacy from their son, Ricardo.

In addition, Cristina Coe and Pedro Doe have moved to intervene as plaintiffs and additional class representatives in this action, pursuant to Fed.R.Civ.P. 24(b)(2), and for an order allowing them to proceed with this action under pseudonyms and without appointment of a guardian ad litem.

For the reasons discussed below, the motion for intervention is granted. Plaintiffs' motion for summary judgment declaring Section 15 unconstitutional is denied. This court holds that the parental consent requirement of Section 15 does not violate plaintiffs' constitutional rights.

Intervention

Proposed plaintiff-intervenor Cristina Coe is fifteen years old. Proposed plaintiff-intervenor Pedro Doe is seventeen years old. Cristina is eight months pregnant with Pedro's child. Cristina and Pedro reside in the home of Pedro's father and step-mother. In January 1981, when Cristina discovered she was pregnant, she and Pedro informed Cristina's mother of their desire to have their child and to marry. Mrs. Coe refused to give Cristina her consent to marry and arranged for Cristina to have an abortion. Cristina refused to keep the appointments her mother made for her at the abortion clinic. Consequently, Mrs. Coe told Cristina she wanted to have nothing more to do with her and that she was leaving the country to live in the Dominican Republic.

Cristina and Pedro wish to marry to express their commitment to and caring for each other, to legitimate their relationship, and to raise their child in accord with their beliefs in a traditional family setting sanctioned by law. They wish to marry before their child is born so that he or she will never have the stigma of illegitimacy attached to his or her life. However, Cristina and Pedro are precluded from petitioning for judicial approval to obtain a marriage license by operation of Section 15 because Mrs. Coe, Cristina's custodial parent, refuses to consent to the marriage.

Rule 24(b)(2) of the Federal Rules of Civil Procedure allows permissive intervention "when an applicant's claim or defense and the main action have a question of law or fact in common. . . ." The rule further provides that "[i]n exercising its discretion the court shall consider whether the intervention will unduly delay or prejudice the adjudication of the rights of the original parties."

The claims of Cristina and Pedro present the same legal issue presented by the present plaintiffs—whether the parental consent requirement of Section 15 is constitutional. Like plaintiffs Maria Moe and Raoul Roe, Cristina and Pedro wish to marry in order to cement their family unit and raise their child without the stigma of illegitimacy. Like Maria and Raoul, Cristina and Pedro are prevented from marrying by the parental veto imposed by Section 15. Intervention will not result in any delay or prejudice to the rights of the original parties or to the orderly process of this court.

In addition, plaintiffs argue that the intervention of Pedro and Cristina will present the court with a more complete picture of the impact of Section 15's parental consent requirement and will add to the representativeness of the named class members. Section 15 requires that Maria, who is now sixteen, must have parental consent to obtain a marriage license. Section 15 requires that Cristina must obtain judicial approval to marry, but precludes her from petitioning for judicial approval unless her parent has consented. While Maria has already borne a child, Cristina is now expecting a baby and is thus in a position to totally avoid the stigma of illegitimacy for her child.

Defendants object to the intervention of Cristina and Pedro on two grounds. First, defendants contend that Cristina and Pedro do not belong in the plaintiff class because New York law provides them with a means to obtain a marriage license without Cristina's mother's consent. Second, defendants argue that plaintiffs' motion for intervention should be denied because Cristina and Pedro have failed to reveal their true identities to defendants. The court finds both objections to be without merit.

Defendants state that under the New York Social Services Law a child less than eighteen years old may be declared abandoned by his or her parent. In that case, defendants contend, the Surrogate may grant letters of guardianship for the purpose of consenting to the teenager's marriage if marriage would be in the teenager's best interests. Defendants' contention is contrary to the ruling of the Court of Appeals in Moe v. Dinkins, supra, 635 F.2d at 1049, that in New York "the consent of a court-appointed guardian cannot bypass the statutory requirement of parental consent, regardless of the unfairness created by a refusal to grant permission." In that decision, the Court of Appeals rejected each of the alternative constructions of Section 15 posed by defendants which might allow an exception to the parental consent requirement.

Cristina's and Pedro's failure to reveal to defendants their true identities does not bar their intervention in this action. It is common for plaintiffs, both minors and those over the age of majority, to be permitted to proceed under a pseudonym where the case concerns matters of a highly sensitive and personal nature such as marriage and illegitimacy.

Defendants claim that the secrecy surrounding Cristina and Pedro precludes them from verifying the standing of Cristina and Pedro to challenge the constitutionality of Section 15. However, standing depends on what the complaint alleges. The proposed intervenor complaint filed by Cristina and Pedro alleges sufficient facts to demonstrate that they have the personal stake in the outcome of the controversy needed to confer standing.

. . .

Plaintiffs contend that Section 15 of the New York Domestic Relations Law,[1] requiring parental consent for the marriage of minors between the ages of fourteen and eighteen, deprives them of the liberty which is guaranteed to them by the Due Process Clause of the Fourteenth Amendment to the Federal Constitution.

A review of Supreme Court decisions defining liberties guaranteed by the Fourteenth Amendment reveals that activities relating to child-rearing and education of children, Pierce v. Society of Sisters, 268 U.S. 510, 45 S.Ct. 571, 69 L.Ed. 1070 (1925), procreation, Skinner v. Oklahoma, 316 U.S. 535, 62 S.Ct. 1110, 86 L.Ed. 1655 (1942), abortion, Roe v. Wade, 410 U.S. 113, 93 S.Ct. 705, 35 L.Ed.2d 147 (1973), family relations, Moore v. City of East Cleveland, 431 U.S. 494, 97 S.Ct. 1932, 52 L.Ed.2d 531 (1977), contraception, Carey v. Population Services International, 431 U.S. 678, 97 S.Ct. 2010, 52 L.Ed.2d 675 (1977), and, most recently, marriage, Zablocki v. Redhail, 434 U.S. 374, 98 S.Ct. 673, 54 L.Ed.2d 618 (1978), are constitutionally protected rights of individual privacy embodied within the concept

---

1. The pertinent parts of Section 15 are as follows:

(2) If it shall appear upon an application of the applicant as provided in this section or upon information required by the clerk that the man is under eighteen years of age and is not under sixteen years of age, or that the woman is under the age of eighteen and not under fourteen years of age, then the town or city clerk before he shall issue a license shall require the written consent to the marriage from both parents of the minor or minors or such as shall then be living, or if the parents of both are dead, then the written consent of the guardians of such minor or minors. If one of the parents has been missing and has not been seen or heard from for a period of one year preceding the time of the application for the license, although diligent inquiry has been made to learn the whereabouts of such parent, the town or city clerk may issue a license to such minor upon the sworn statement and consent of the other parent. If the marriage of the parents of such a minor has been dissolved by decree of divorce or annulment, the consent of the parent to whom the court which granted the decree has awarded custody of such minor shall be sufficient. If there is no parent or guardian of the minor or minors living to their knowledge then the town or city clerk shall require the written consent for the marriage of the person under whose care and government the minor or minors may be before a license shall be issued. If a parent of such minor has been adjudicated an incompetent, the town or city clerk may issue a license to such minor upon the production of a certified copy of such judgment so determining and upon the written consent of the other parent.

N.Y.Dom.Rel.Law § 15 (14 McKinney).

of liberty which the Due Process Clause of the Fourteenth Amendment was designed to protect.

However, neither *Zablocki* nor its predecessors arose in the context of state regulation of marriages of minors. In that respect, this is a case of first impression.

While it is true that a child, because of his minority, is not beyond the protection of the Constitution, the Court has recognized the State's power to make adjustments in the constitutional rights of minors. . . . This power to adjust minors' constitutional rights flows from the State's concern with the unique position of minors. In Bellotti v. Baird, 443 U.S. 622, 99 S.Ct. 3035, 61 L.Ed.2d 797 (1979), the Court noted "three reasons justifying the conclusion that the constitutional rights of children cannot be equated with those of adults: the peculiar vulnerability of children; their inability to make critical decisions in an informed and mature manner; and the importance of the parental role in child-rearing."

Likewise, marriage occupies a unique position under the law. It has been the subject of extensive regulation and control, within constitutional limits, in its inception and termination and has "long been regarded as a virtually exclusive province of the State." Sosna v. Iowa, 419 U.S. 393, 404, 95 S.Ct. 553, 559, 42 L.Ed.2d 532 (1975).

While it is evident that the New York law before this court directly abridges the right of minors to marry, *in the absence of parental consent*, the question is whether the State interests that support the abridgement can overcome the substantive protection of the Constitution. The unique position of minors and marriage under the law leads this court to conclude that Section 15 should not be subjected to strict scrutiny, the test which the Supreme Court has ruled must be applied whenever a state statute burdens the exercise of a fundamental liberty protected by the Constitution. Applying strict scrutiny would require determination of whether there was a compelling state interest and whether the statute had been closely tailored to achieve that state interest. The compelling state purpose necessitated by application of the strict scrutiny test "would cast doubt on a network of restrictions that the States have fashioned to govern marriage and divorce." Zablocki v. Redhail, 434 U.S. at 399, 98 S.Ct. at 688 (Powell, J., concurring). It is this court's view that Section 15 should be looked at solely to determine whether there exists a rational relation between the means chosen by the New York legislature and the legitimate state interests advanced by the State.

The State interests advanced to justify the parental consent requirement of Section 15 include the protection of minors from immature decision-making and preventing unstable marriages. The State possesses paternalistic power to protect and promote the welfare of children who lack the capacity to act in their own best interest. The State interests in mature decision-making and in preventing unstable marriages are legitimate under its *parens patriae* power.

An age attainment requirement for marriage is established in every American jurisdiction. The requirement of parental consent ensures that at least one mature person will participate in the decision of a minor to marry. That the State has provided for such consent in Section 15 is rationally related to the State's legitimate interest in light of the fact that minors often lack the "experience, perspective and judgment" necessary to make "important, affirmative choices with potentially serious consequences." Bellotti v. Baird, supra, 443 U.S. at 635–36, 99 S.Ct. at 3043–44.

Yet, plaintiffs fault the parental consent requirement of Section 15 as possibly arbitrary, suggesting that courts, as non-interested third parties, are in a better position to judge whether a minor is prepared for the responsibilities that attach to marriage. Although the possibility for parents to act in other than the best interest of their child exists, the law presumes that the parents "possess what the child lacks in maturity" and that "the natural bonds of affection lead parents to act in the best interest of their children." Parham v. J.R., 442 U.S. 584, 610, 99 S.Ct. 2493, 2508, 61 L.Ed.2d 101 (1979) (procedure for voluntary commitment of children under eighteen to state hospitals by their parents held constitutional). "That the governmental power should supercede parental authority in all cases because some parents" may act in other than the best interest of their children is "repugnant to the American tradition." Id. at 602–03, 99 S.Ct. at 2504. . . .

Plaintiffs also contend that Section 15 denied them the opportunity to make an individualized showing of maturity and denies them the only means by which they can legitimize their children and live in the traditional family unit sanctioned by law. On the other hand, New York's Section 15 merely delays plaintiffs' access to the institution of marriage. Moreover, the prohibition does not bar minors whose parents consent to their child's marriage. Assuming *arguendo* that the illegitimacy of plaintiff Moe's child and plaintiff Coe's yet unborn child is a harm, it is not a harm inflicted by Section 15. It is merely an incidental consequence of the lawful exercise of State power. The illegitimacy of plaintiffs' children, like the denial of marriage without parental consent, is a temporary situation at worst. A subsequent marriage of the parents legitimatizes the child, thereby erasing the mark of illegitimacy. The rights or benefits flowing from the marriage of minors are only temporarily suspended by Section 15. Any alleged harm to these rights and benefits is not inflicted by Section 15, but is simply an incidental consequence of the valid exercise of State power.

The fact that the State has elected to use a simple criterion, age, to determine probable maturity in the absence of parental consent, instead of requiring proof of maturity on a case by case basis, is reasonable, even if the rule produces seemingly arbitrary results in individual cases. "Simply because the decision of a parent is not agreeable to a child or because there is a [possible stigmatization of the child] does not automatically transfer power to make the decision from parents to some other agency or officer of the state." Parham v. J.R., 442 U.S. at 603, 99 S.Ct. at 2504.

Plaintiffs' reliance on the abortion and contraception cases is misplaced. . . . These cases can be distinguished from the instant case in that

> a pregnant minor's options are much different than those facing a minor in other situations, *such as deciding whether to marry*. A minor not permitted to marry before the age of maturity is required simply to postpone her decision. She and her intended spouse may preserve the opportunity for a later marriage should they continue to desire it.

Bellotti v. Baird, 443 U.S. at 642, 99 S.Ct. at 3047 (emphasis added). Giving birth to an unwanted child involves an irretrievable change in position for a minor as well as for an adult, whereas the temporary denial of the right to marry does not. Plaintiffs are not irretrievably foreclosed from marrying. The gravamen of the complaint, in the instant case, is not total deprivation but only delay.

This court concludes that Section 15's requirement of parental consent is rationally related to the State's legitimate interests in mature decision-making with respect to marriage by minors and preventing unstable marriages. It is also rationally related to the State's legitimate interest in supporting the fundamental privacy right of a parent to act in what the parent perceives to be the best interest of the child free from state court scrutiny. Section 15, therefore, does not offend the constitutional rights of minors but represents a constitutionally valid exercise of state power.

Accordingly, plaintiffs' motion for summary judgment in their favor is denied and summary judgment is entered in favor of defendants.

NOTE

Judge Motley's decision was upheld in Moe v. Dinkins, 669 F.2d 67 (2d Cir.1982), *cert. denied* 459 U.S. 827, 103 S.Ct. 61, 74 L.Ed.2d 64 (1982). In a short Per Curiam opinion the Court of Appeals concluded that:

> . . . Judge Motley was correct in testing the constitutionality of New York Domestic Relations Law § 15 by determining whether there exists a rational relation between the means chosen by the New York legislature and legitimate state interests in adopting and enforcing the restriction. In light of New York's important interest in promoting the welfare of children by preventing unstable marriages among those lacking the capacity to act in their best interests, we agree . . . that the New York statutory scheme passed constitutional muster.

Note that the parties were allowed to proceed under pseudonyms. Why shouldn't all domestic relations cases be treated anonymously by the reporters, particularly if judges insist on including intimate details that may be unnecessary to the *ratio decidendi* of the case? For one critic's largely unheeded plea for such an approach, *see* Walter Wadlington, *Portrait of the Judge as Popular Author: An Appeal for Anonymity and Restraint in Domestic Relations Cases*, 1 FAM.L.Q. 77 (1967).

UNIFORM MARRIAGE AND DIVORCE ACT (1973)

§§ 208(a)(3), 208(b)(3) (1973)

(*See* text at page 213, *supra.*)

NOTE

Problems regarding the minimum age for marriage today reflect influences as varying as medieval feudalism and contemporary wisdom about the capacity of adolescents. It is usually stated that the common law set the age of consent to marry at 14 for males and 12 for females. These ages were determined to establish a presumption of capacity to consummate. This was done in the heyday of feudalism when espousal of infants was common. A child who had completed the seventh year was presumed to possess capacity to consent to a future marriage. Such espousals were arranged by tenants holding by military tenure as a means of defeating their overlord's exercise of the feudal incident of marriage in the event of the tenant's decease during the child's minority. The contracts were voidable until the ages of 14 and 12 were reached, unless some act were done that established consummation in fact. This was the precise concatenation of events that the rule of marriage *per verba de futuro cum copula* was designed to cover. The church took the position that if the parties had reached the age of rational consent for a marriage and in fact married, the consent of the parents was immaterial and the marriage was valid. This was accepted by the temporal law where the consent of parent or guardian was relevant not to the validity of marriage but solely to questions of property. *See* Pollock & Maitland, History of English Law 389–90; Swinburne, Treatise of Spousals §§ 8–9.

In this country state legislatures typically have established one age at which a person is deemed fully competent to marry and another at which marriage can take place with parental consent. The ages for majority once were different for women and men in many jurisdictions though this had largely been changed even before similar discrimination in the context of child support provisions was declared unconstitutional in Stanton v. Stanton, 429 U.S. 501, 97 S.Ct. 717, 50 L.Ed.2d 723 (1977). Age can be an important factor for many legal concerns, ranging from juvenile court jurisdiction to eligibility for motor vehicle operators' licenses, but after ratification in 1971 of the 26th Amendment that accorded the vote at 18 in federal elections, many states acted to remove the bulk of disabilities of infancy at least by that age. (There has been a subsequent movement toward fixing a higher minimum age for purchase of alcoholic beverages.)

Problems about marriage capacity that reached the courts under this system often centered on the question whether a marriage below the age at which marriage is permitted with parental consent, or a marriage without parental consent but within the period in which parental consent would be effective to validate the union, is void, voidable or valid. Some courts drew from the old common law age rules to determine that above age 12 or 14 (or perhaps even 7) the marriage is at most voidable. And some held that marriage without parental consent at an age when the applicable statute would permit marriage with such consent, creates a perfectly valid union. The latter approach relegates the parental consent requirement to an *in terrorem* role.

In light of the previous rules, a key concern exists in some jurisdictions with regard to underage marriages that are never annulled and are ignored by the parties when they subsequently remarry. If such marriages are not void, then the remarriage may produce a bigamous union.

2. Kinship

Some restriction of sexual intercourse between closely related persons exists in nearly every society. Criminal prohibitions are found in all states of this country, with possible penalties ranging from a year to life imprisonment. This reflects variations both in the inclusiveness of specific prohibitions and differences in public policy concerning such bans. Parties who marry in the face of specific incest prohibitions typically find that their unions will be treated as either voidable or void depending on the closeness of their kinship.

The usually accepted reasons for barring sexual intercourse or marriage between close relatives are:

(1) negative eugenics, through which it is sought to limit the number of offspring with genetically undesirable traits;

(2) religious doctrine;

(3) minimizing internal family pressures and sexual competition and thus promoting family harmony;

(4) widely accepted social taboos;

(5) protecting young and dependent females against sexual imposition.

Variations in specific kin partnership restrictions can stem from differing views as to what interests are of greatest moment. Genetic concerns, for example, could be satisfied through limiting sexual intercourse only between consanguineous relatives. And since the utilitarian goal of the eugenicist is to guard against procreation of defective children, it is logical for kinship bans to be related to the degree of increased probability of homozygosis with respect to a particular trait—in other words, the chance that the offspring will receive an identical genetic contribution from each parent. Difficulties arise because geneticists disagree in their assessments of the relative dangers of inbreeding. Some fear that although prevention of mating between blood relatives may decrease the number of first generation defectives, it will increase the incidence of genetic disorders in later generations through dispersion of undesirable genes among the general population. Generally there has been a significant time lag between development of greater scientific understanding in genetics and the incorporation of these findings into the legal prohibitions dealing with incest.

Some persons view current incest laws as little more than a secular enforcement of religious tenets. Although one must acknowledge that in this area, like many others in the field of domestic relations, religious views clearly have had impact on the development of our laws,[1] churches today maintain varying restrictions concerning which kin marriages should be prohibited and it is questionable whether any single religious body could now strongly influence either the penal laws or those concerning marriage in this area. In some instances it is possible to obtain a church annulment of a marriage which the state might not consider legally void or voidable.

In theory, the interest in preserving family harmony should take into consideration the increased importance of the nuclear family and the lessened likelihood that extended kin groups will be living in the same household. A relatively new challenge is the accommodation of adoptive relatives within this framework. Adoptive relationship can exist independently of affinity or consanguinity. Some legislatures have banned marriages between siblings by adoption, but such a provision was invalidated in Israel v. Allen, 195 Colo. 263, 577 P.2d 762 (1978).

CALIFORNIA FAMILY CODE (West 2004)

§ 2200.   Incestuous marriages

Marriages between parents and children, ancestors and descendants of every degree, and between brothers and sisters of the half as well as the whole blood, and between uncles and nieces or aunts and nephews, are incestuous, and void from the beginning, whether the relationship is legitimate or illegitimate.

GEORGIA CODE ANN. (2004)

19-3-3. Degrees of relationship within which intermarriage prohibited; penalty; effect of prohibited marriage.

(a) Any person who marries a person to whom he knows he is related, either by blood or by marriage, as follows:

(1) Father and daughter or stepdaughter;

(2) Mother and son or stepson;

(3) Brother and sister of the whole blood or the half blood;

(4) Grandparent and grandchild;

(5) Aunt and nephew; or

(6) Uncle and niece

shall be punished by imprisonment for not less than one nor more than three years.

---

1. For a review of the Biblical background on the subject, see Leviticus 18:6–18; 20:11, 12, 14, 17, 19, 20, 21; 21:1–3.

(b) Marriages declared to be unlawful under subsection (a) of this Code section shall be void from their inception.

NOTE

Another statutory approach defines the prohibition in terms of degrees of kinship between the parties, almost universally using the civil law definition. This requires counting back to the nearest common ancestor in the ascending line of the parties, then descending to the person whose kin relationship degree is in question. Each link in the chain, both ascending and descending, counts as a degree; thus uncle and niece are related within three degrees. In some jurisdictions the degrees of relationship within which marriage is prohibited extend further than those to which criminal sanctions against incestuous sexual intercourse attach. What are the possible legal implications of this?

For further exploration of kinship based marriage restrictions in this country and a sensitive appraisal of whether the state interest justifies such widespread limitations, *see* Carolyn S. Bratt, *Incest Statutes and the Fundamental Right of Marriage: Is Oedipus Free to Marry?*, 18 FAM.L.Q. 257 (1984).

Singh v. Singh

Supreme Court of Connecticut, 1990.
213 Conn. 637, 569 A.2d 1112.

■ ARTHUR H. HEALEY, ASSOCIATE JUSTICE.

This is an appeal from the trial court's denial of the plaintiff's and the defendant's motion to open the 1984 judgment of annulment of their 1983 marriage in Connecticut. We transferred this case from the Appellate Court to this court pursuant to Practice Book § 4023. We find no error.

... The parties, David Singh (husband) and Seoranie Singh (wife), were married on January 13, 1983, in Hartford. In their complaint, seeking an annulment, they alleged that their 1983 marriage was entered into "upon the mistaken belief by both parties that they were not related," but "they [had only] recently discovered that they are uncle and niece." There were no issue of this marriage. In 1984, the court, Hon. Simon Cohen, state trial referee, rendered judgment of annulment declaring the marriage null and void after finding, inter alia, that "[t]he marriage was entered into upon the mistaken belief by both parties that they were legally qualified to marry," but that "[both parties] have recently discovered that they are uncle and niece."

Thereafter, in November, 1988, both parties filed a motion to open the judgment. That motion alleged that, although the judgment found that they were uncle and niece and, therefore, not legally qualified to marry, in fact, since the wife's mother is the husband's half sister, the wife is the husband's half niece and not his niece. The parties also maintained that they sought the annulment only because of the advice of counsel that their marriage was, "without question," incestuous and void under our statutory scheme. See General Statutes §§ 46b–21,[2] 53a–191.[3] In view of the fact that our statute concerning kindred who may not marry does not mention "half nieces" or "half uncles" and no Connecticut decision extends the scope of the law's prohibition to relatives of the half blood, the parties claimed that the marriage "might well be deemed lawful and valid." They further alleged that they were remarried in August, 1988, in California where, citing People v. Baker, 69 Cal.2d 44, 442 P.2d 675, 69 Cal.Rptr. 595 (1968), they assert that the California Supreme Court has determined that marriages between uncles and nieces of the half blood are not proscribed by that state's incest statute.[4]

The trial court, Kline, J., denied the motion to open the judgment of annulment. In doing so, it found that the wife was the daughter of her husband's half sister and that this half sister and the husband were descended from a common mother but different fathers. It noted that while there were some Connecticut cases[5] implicating the statute, there were no Connecticut cases specifically addressing the question whether persons of the half blood fall within the statutorily prohibited degrees of whole blood relationships. Further, the trial court not only said that a number of cases in other jurisdictions indicated that marriage or sexual intercourse between an uncle and niece of the half blood could be incestuous, but also opined that the texts seemed to be uniform that both at common law and by

2. General Statutes § 46b–21 provides: "(Formerly Sec. 46–1.) KINDRED WHO MAY NOT MARRY. No man may marry his mother, grandmother, daughter, granddaughter, sister, aunt, niece, stepmother or stepdaughter, and no woman may marry her father, grandfather, son, grandson, brother, uncle, nephew, stepfather or stepson. Any marriage within these degrees is void."

3. General Statutes § 53a–191 provides: "INCEST: CLASS D FELONY." (a) A person is guilty of incest when such person marries a person whom such person knows to be related to such person within any of the degrees of kindred specified in section 46b–21. "(b) Incest is a class D felony."

4. Despite this second marriage, the parties went on to contend in their motion to open that they would still face a "painful two year separation" unless the annulment judgment was opened. The reasons they advanced to support this latter claim of the two year delay was, they claim, due to certain amendments in November, 1986, to the Immigration and Nationality Act. The wife was a citizen of Guyana when she remarried her husband. She had been cited by the im-

migration authorities for exclusion as an "overstay" and was therefore precluded from applying for an "adjustment status" to permanent residency based on that marriage. Consequently, she will have to return to Guyana and cannot initiate an "adjustment status" application until she has completed two years of residence outside the United States. They emphasize in their motion that "their relationship has nothing in common with so-called 'green card marriages.'" A "green card" is a document which evidences an alien's permanent residence status in the United States. See United States v. Carpentier, 689 F.2d 21, 23 n. 5 (2d Cir.1982).

5. In this context, the trial court specifically referred to State v. Skinner, 132 Conn. 163, 43 A.2d 76 (1945), Catalano v. Catalano, 148 Conn. 288, 170 A.2d 726 (1961), and State v. Moore, 158 Conn. 461, 262 A.2d 166 (1969). It also referred to an opinion of the attorney general concerning the validity of a marriage between an uncle and his half niece under General Statutes (1930 Rev.) § 51–48, the precursor of the present statute, General Statutes § 46b–21. See 19 Opin. Atty. Gen. 281 (1935).

statute prohibited degrees of relationship by blood included persons of the half blood as well as of the whole blood. The court also stated that these authorities uniformly held that there is no distinction between the whole blood and half blood in computing the degrees within which marriages are prohibited as incestuous. The trial court also concluded that not only consanguinity but also the degree of the relationship between the parties was a basis for prohibiting certain marriages. Because § 46b–21 prohibits marriages between stepparents and stepchildren, the court inferred that it was not the actual blood relationship that appeared to concern the legislature but rather the degree or distance of the relationship between the parties indicating a legislative intent to prevent not only marriages of the whole blood but also those of the half blood. The trial court accordingly denied the motion to open and set aside the judgment of annulment. This appeal followed,

The issue to be decided is whether a marriage between persons related to one another as half uncle and half niece is incestuous under our statutory scheme and, therefore, void. See General Statutes §§ 46b–21, 53a–191. The parties maintain that such a marriage is not incestuous under our statutory law. The attorney general, who appeared as an amicus curiae, argued to the contrary. The determination of this question involves the interrelation and judicial interpretation of two statutes, §§ 46b–21 and 53a–191. This case, unlike State v. Skinner, 132 Conn. 163, 43 A.2d 76 (1945), or State v. Moore, 158 Conn. 461, 262 A.2d 166 (1969), to which counsel have referred, does not come before us on appeal from a conviction of the crime of incest. These cases, however, are instructive on the issue to be resolved in this case.[6]

Historically, marriage between certain relatives "has been disfavored by all nations during all ages." F. Keezer, Marriage and Divorce (3d Ed.1923) § 170; 1 C. Vernier, American Family Laws (1931) § 37; 1 H. Clark, Law of Domestic Relations in the United States (2d Ed.1987) § 2.9; see Gould v. Gould, 78 Conn. 242, 244, 61 A. 604 (1905). Although incest was punished by the ecclesiastical courts in England, it was not an indictable offense at common law and punishment was left entirely to the ecclesiastical courts. See People v. Baker, supra; Cecil v. Commonwealth, 140 Ky. 717, 719, 131 S.W. 781 (1910); ... "The ecclesiastical courts followed the interdiction of Levitical law which prohibited marriages between persons more closely related than fourth cousins unless a dispensation was procured from the Church of Rome; no distinction was made between persons related by affinity or consanguinity." People v. Baker, supra, 442 P.2d 675, 69 Cal.Rptr. 595; ... In 1540, during the reign of Henry VIII, a statute was passed regulating the degrees of relationship within which marriage was illegal. See 32 Henry 8, c. 38. That statute

---

6. Counsel have also stressed our decision in Catalano v. Catalano, 148 Conn. 288, 170 A.2d 726 (1961), which was an appeal from a probate decree, that required our interpretation of three statutes, i.e., the precursors of General Statutes §§ 46b–21 and 53a–191, as well as General Statutes § 46–6 ("when marriages in foreign countries are valid," now General Statutes § 46b–28).

limited the prohibitions against marriage to relatives closer than first cousins, and although the ecclesiastical courts approved of the statute, the courts continued to make no distinction between relatives by consanguinity or affinity. "Consanguinity" is a blood relationship. It is the connection or relation of persons descended from the same stock or common ancestor. Black's Law Dictionary (5th Ed.). It is distinguished from "affinity" which, in turn, is the connection existing in consequence of a marriage between each of the married persons and the kindred of the other spouse.

The initial departure of the American jurisdictions from the English law was to declare incest a crime. The crime of incest is purely statutory, and most states have a statute making it a crime. The statutes delineating incestuous relationships departed from the ecclesiastical law in two respects. The majority of states extended the criminal prohibitions to first cousins and beyond while other states imposed criminal penalties only where the relationship was that of consanguinity. As will be seen, Connecticut's incest statute followed the former course. While these statutes may vary in detail, they generally define incest as marriage or sexual intercourse between persons too closely related in consanguinity or affinity to be entitled to marry legally.

In Connecticut, incest has been a crime since the incest statute was enacted in 1702.... The 1702 act[8] prohibited marriages between persons within certain degrees of kinship including that of uncle and niece. Catalano v. Catalano, supra; Gould v. Gould, supra. In the 1875 revision, the language describing the degree of relationship, now appearing in § 46b–21, was adopted. General Statutes (1875 Rev.) § 1; Catalano v. Catalano, supra. There has been no substantive change in the language since that time.[9] Thus, since 1702, our incest statute has interdicted marriage between persons related by either consanguinity or affinity.

8. "The Acts and Laws of His Majesty's Colony of Connecticut in New England, Revision of 1702" contains: "An Act to prevent Incestuous Marriages" and provides in part: "That no man shall marry any woman within the degrees hereafter named in this Act, That is to say, No man shall marry his Grandfathers Wife, Wives Grandmother, Fathers Sister, Mothers Sister, Fathers Brothers Wife, Mothers Brothers Wife, Wives Fathers Sister, Wives Mothers Sister, Fathers Wife, Wives Mother; Daughter, Wives Daughter, Sons Wife, Sister, Brothers Wife, Wives Sister, Sons Daughter, Daughters Daughter, Sons Sons Wife, Daughters Sons Wife, Wives Sons Daughter, Wives Daughters Daughter, Brothers Daughter, Sisters Daughter, Brothers Sons Wife, Sisters Sons Wife, Wives Brothers Daughter, Wives Sisters Daughter; and if any man shall hereafter marry, or have carnal copulation with any woman, who is within the degrees before recited in this Act, every such Marriage shall be, and is hereby declared to be null and void; and all Children that shall hereafter be born of such Incestuous Marriage or Copulation, shall be for ever disabled to Inherit by Descent, or by being generally named in any Deed or Will, by Father or Mother." (Spelling as in original.)

9. The legislature, however, has had the statute before it in recent years. In 1978, it changed the third word of General Statutes § 46b–21 from "shall" to "may" after the words "No man" as well as after the words "no woman." Public Acts 1978, No. 78–230, § 3. At the same time, it amended the second sentence to provide: "Any marriage within these degrees is void" instead of "and, if any man or woman marries within the degrees aforesaid, said marriage shall be void."

Initially, the parties claim that the trial court erred by adhering to a line of cases dating from the interpretations of the incest statute during the reign of Henry VIII.[10] citing to the English statute of 32 Henry 8, c. 38. They concede that "[d]espite notable changes in sexual mores and in the very conditions which underlie the incest taboo itself, which have intervened since the time of Henry VIII, most Courts considering [the] question have been satisfied to mechanically reproduce the precedents of several hundred years ago." They, nevertheless, urge "a more modern approach to the construction of our incest statute" and maintain that they "rely upon a line of cases placing more emphasis on the rights of criminal defendants, and the importance of preserving bona fide marriages against the undue extension of statutory categories."[11] They claim that there are several compelling reasons for the statutory construction that they urge: (1) the plain language of § 46b–21 favors the construction allowing uncle-niece marriages between relatives of the half blood; (2) undue judicial extension of the prohibitions contained in § 46b–21 may lead to unfair prosecutions for the crime of incest under § 53a–191; (3) an unwarranted extension of the incest prohibition to include uncles and nieces of the half blood is inconsistent with proper respect for the preservation of bona fide marriages; and (4) since the prohibition of "uncle-niece marriages, especially those between relatives of half blood, are not the object of universal condemnation, the Court will not be at odds with 'natural law' if it adopts the construction [advocated] by [the parties]." We are not persuaded by any of these claims.

It is clear that § 46b–21 does not contain any language that expressly distinguishes between relatives of the whole blood and the half blood. It is also clear that although § 46b–21 is a civil statute, its interrelationship with § 53a–191, the criminal statute prohibiting incest, is such that both statutes may fairly be said to be in pari materia and so § 46b–21 is to be construed in this case in harmony with the law of which it forms a part. The infusion into § 53a–191 of the degrees of relationship set out in § 46b–21 as the predicate for the commission of the crime of incest invokes the rule of strict construction that is applied to criminal statutes. The United States Supreme Court has said: "That criminal statutes are to be construed strictly is a proposition which calls for the citation of no authority. But this does not mean that every criminal statute must be given the narrowest possible meaning in complete disregard of the purpose of the legislature." United States v. Bramblett, 348 U.S. 503, 509–10, 75 S.Ct. 504, 508, 99 L.Ed. 594 (1955). The same court also said: "No rule of construction, however, requires that a penal statute be strained and distorted in order to exclude conduct clearly intended to be within its scope—nor does any rule require that the act be given the 'narrowest meaning.' It is sufficient if the words are given their fair meaning in accord with the evident intent of [the

---

10. Henry VIII (1491–1547) reigned as King of England from 1509 to 1547.

11. Here, the parties refer us to three cases: People v. Baker, 69 Cal.2d 44, 442 P.2d 675, 69 Cal.Rptr. 595 (1968); People v. Wom-

ack, 167 Cal.App.2d 130, 334 P.2d 309 (1959); and State v. Bartley, 304 Mo. 58, 263 S.W. 95 (1924). Each of these cases is inapposite as we point out later in this opinion.

legislature]." United States v. Raynor, 302 U.S. 540, 552, 58 S.Ct. 353, 359, 82 L.Ed. 413 (1938). We have said: "Strict construction does not mean that a statute must be read in isolation. 'In construing a statute, common sense must be used, and courts will assume that the legislature intended to accomplish a reasonable and rational result.' ... 'The rule of strict construction does not require that the narrowest technical meaning be given to the words employed in a criminal statute in disregard of their context and in frustration of the obvious legislative intent.' " (Citations omitted.) In re Luis R., 204 Conn. 630, 635, 528 A.2d 1146 (1987). Such authority demonstrates that the rule of strict construction of penal statutes is not without limitation; the doctrine of strict construction is only one of the aids which is to be used in the construction of penal statutes. Other aids include such things as the statutory language itself, legislative history where available, the furthering of the policy and purposes fairly apparent from the statute which include the mischief sought to be proscribed and related statutes.

In our analysis, it is proper to explore further the state of the law as it was at the time that our incest statute was enacted in 1702. The fundamental case explicating the ecclesiastical law as it was deemed at the time was Butler v. Gastrill, supra. That case, which was decided in 1722, said: "And when we consider who are prohibited to marry by the Levitical Law,[12] we must not only consider the mere Words of the Law itself, but what, from a just and fair Interpretation, may be deduced from it." Id., 158. On the basis of early English cases discussing the prohibition of marriage within certain degrees, Halsbury said: "In reference to the prohibited degrees, relationship by the half blood is a bar to marriage equally with relationship by the whole blood." 16 Halsbury's Laws of England p. 284. Another noted text writer wrote: "The relationship by half blood is the same in [the consanguinity cases] as by whole blood; so that, for example, it is incestuous for a man to marry the daughter of his brother of the half blood, or the daughter of his half-sister." 1 J. Bishop, Marriage, Divorce and Separation § 748. It is fair to assume that, when the incest statute was enacted in 1702, the framers were aware of and adopted the interpretation of the ecclesiastical law as it then existed in England, thus treating the relation of the half blood like that of the whole blood.

There has been no substantive change since that time in our incest statute insofar as the degree of consanguinity within which marriage is proscribed. That is not without significance. Indeed, implicating the issue before us, in 1961, we said: "It has been the declared public policy of this state continuously since 1702 to prohibit marriages of uncle and niece and declare them void." Catalano v. Catalano, supra, 148 Conn. at 290, 170 A.2d 726. Our decisional law under the incest statute has been sparse. In Catalano, we held invalid a marriage between an uncle and a niece under

---

12. "A fair interpretation" of the statute of 32 Hen. 8, c. 38 has been said to forbid marriage outside the Levitical degrees. 1 J. Bishop, Marriage, Divorce and Separation (1891) § 737; see 1 J. Schouler, Husband and Wife (1882) § 15. The Levitical degrees are those degrees of kindred between a man and a woman which bar their marriage to each other as those degrees are set forth in the eighteenth chapter of Leviticus. Black's Law Dictionary (5th Ed.); Ballentine's Law Dictionary (1969).

our statutory scheme although the marriage was valid in Italy where it was performed. In that case, we noted that the "generally accepted rule" was that a marriage valid where the ceremony was performed was valid everywhere. Id., at 291, 170 A.2d 726. We pointed out, however, that there were certain exceptions to the rule, including one which regarded as invalid incestuous marriages between persons so closely related that their marriage was contrary to the strong public policy of the domicil. Id. In that context, we said: "That exception may be expressed in the terms of a statute or by necessary implication." Id.

Besides Catalano, two other cases merit discussion. In State v. Skinner, 132 Conn. 163, 43 A.2d 76 (1945), we held that the relationship of brother and half-sister was comprehended within the degrees of relationship forbidding marriage under the incest statute. In that case, we rejected the defendant brother's claim that the relationship of half-sister did not come within the statutory prohibition. Id., at 165, 43 A.2d 76. In doing so, we pointed out that the defendant "admitted in his brief that all the cases which [his counsel] have found are to the contrary and that public policy would indicate that relationship of the half blood should be included in the prohibition of the incest statute." Id. After referring to several cases from other jurisdictions that directly held that "brother" includes a brother of the half blood and that "sister" includes a sister of the half blood, we said: "In view of the purpose of the statute . . . its language, and the soundness of the decisions we have cited, we hold that the word sister, as used in the statute, applies to and includes a half sister."[13] Id.

In State v. Moore, 158 Conn. 461, 464, 262 A.2d 166 (1969), the defendant had been found guilty of incest[14] where the parties involved were the defendant and the nineteen year old daughter of the defendant's brother-in-law, that is, the daughter of the defendant's wife's brother. In reversing the incest conviction in Moore, we observed that the trial court "extended the meaning of § 46–1 (now § 46b–21) beyond its fair import." Id., at 465, 262 A.2d 166. In doing so, we referred to Skinner, pointing out that the relationship in that case contained the element of consanguinity and we also noted that that element appeared in all the relationships enumerated in § 46–1 (now § 46b–21) except the relationship of stepmother or stepdaughter and stepfather or stepson. Id., at 466, 262 A.2d 166. Moore then goes on to say: "The question at once arises as to why, in its enumeration of relationships which do not include the element of consan-

---

13. Long ago, albeit in a different context (the construction of a statute as to who would take in the event of a "lapsed" devise or legacy under a will) the only issue was whether the word "brother" or "sister" as used in that statute included half brothers. Seery v. Fitzpatrick, 79 Conn. 562, 65 A. 964 (1907). In Seery, we said: "In England it has long been settled that whenever the word 'brother' or 'sister' is used in a statute without limitation [as in the statute in Seery], it

includes half-brothers or half-sisters respectively." Id., at 563, 65 A. 964.

14. General Statutes § 53–223, at the time of State v. Moore, 158 Conn. 461, 262 A.2d 166 (1969), provided: "Every man and woman who marry or carnally know each other, being within any of the degrees of kindred specified in section 46–1, shall be imprisoned in the State Prison not more than 10 years."

guinity, the General Assembly saw fit to include only those of stepparent or a stepchild. In the application of the criminal law, it would be an unwarranted extension and presumption to assume that by specifying those relationships the legislature has intended to include others which lack the element of consanguinity. Had the legislative intent been to include what, in this case, would commonly be called a relationship of niece-in-law and uncle-in-law, it would have been a simple matter to say." Id. Therefore, the Moore court opined that, absent such a declaration, the trial court's construction "amounted to an unwarranted extension of its expressed meaning and intent." Id.

The parties stress that Moore is very supportive of their position. We do not agree for several reasons. First, the fact pattern in Moore was different from that in both Skinner and Catalano, as in the latter two cases, unlike Moore, a blood relationship was involved. Second, in Moore, we referred to Skinner, noting that, in Skinner, we not only pointed out that the relationship in that case "is embraced within the meaning of the statute" but also that in that relationship there was the element of consanguinity. State v. Moore, supra. In Moore, the element of consanguinity was absent but that of affinity was present. Moreover, in Moore, we did not qualify our holding in Skinner but acknowledged its viability. Finally, in Moore, we were not called upon to decide whether the statute proscribed marriage between two persons where each was a relative of the half blood although Skinner, fairly read, was a step in that direction.

Nor do we overlook, in reaching our conclusion, those cases that the parties urge us to rely upon in reaching "a more modern approach" to the construction of our incest statute. This approach, they claim, is one which places more emphasis on the rights of criminal defendants as well as "preserving bona fide marriages against the undue extension of statutory categories." They cite the following cases: People v. Baker, supra; People v. Womack, 167 Cal.App.2d 130, 334 P.2d 309 (1959); and State v. Bartley, 304 Mo. 58, 263 S.W. 95 (1924).

The parties place the greatest stress on People v. Baker, supra. A close reading of that case demonstrates that it is clearly inapposite. That case was an incest prosecution against Baker who had had sexual relations with his niece who was related to him by the half blood; that is, her mother was the defendant's half sister. The trial court found him guilty of incest. His principal claim on appeal was that the prohibition in California Penal Code § 285[15] against fornication by an uncle and his niece did not apply where they were related by the half blood. That statute provided in part: "Persons being within the degrees of consanguinity within which marriages are declared by law to be incestuous and void ... who commit fornication ...

---

15. California Penal Code § 285, which was enacted in 1872 and amended only in 1921, provided at the time of People v. Baker, 69 Cal.2d 44, 442 P.2d 675, 69 Cal.Rptr. 595 (1968), as follows: "Persons being within the degrees of consanguinity within which mar- riages are declared by law to be incestuous and void, who intermarry with each other, or who commit fornication or adultery with each other, are punishable by imprisonment in the state prison not less than one year nor more than fifty years."

with each other ... are punishable by imprisonment...." California Civil Code § 59 provided: "Marriages between parents and children, ancestors and descendants of every degree, and between brothers and sisters of the half as well as the whole blood, and between uncles and nieces or aunts and nephews, are incestuous, and void from the beginning, whether the relationship is legitimate or illegitimate." (Emphasis added.) The Baker court reversed the conviction. In doing so, it reasoned that the phrase "of the half as well as the whole blood" obviously referred to brothers and sisters and could not be interpreted also to modify "uncles and nieces" under established tenets of statutory construction. Moreover, by including relationships between brothers and sisters of the half blood and not so specifying as to more distant relatives, the Baker court reasoned that the legislature evinced the intention to exclude such persons from the statutory prohibition. People v. Baker, supra. In recognizing that various state statutes differ, it acknowledged that the more common type of statute extended the prohibition to uncles and nieces of the half blood even where half blood relationships were not mentioned.[16] The manifest dissimilarity of the California statute in Baker from our statutes affords little support for the claims of the parties in this case. Indeed, Baker itself expressly points this up when, after stating that incest is governed by specific statutes in the various states, it says that "the relevant decisions must be considered in the context of the statutory scheme peculiar to the particular state." Id., 69 Cal.2d 47, 442 P.2d 675, 69 Cal.Rptr. 595. We agree.

The Baker court addressed the earlier case of People v. Womack, supra. Womack posed the question whether an admitted act of sexual intercourse between the defendant Womack and the fourteen year old daughter of his half sister was incestuous under the same statutory scheme that existed in Baker. The California Court of Appeals had affirmed Womack's conviction of incest. In doing so, it construed the statutory scheme to include the defendant and the victim within those degrees of relationship between whom sexual intercourse was prohibited. In its decision, it observed that "[b]y definition, an uncle is a brother of one's father or mother, and no distinction is made between the whole and the half blood according to common and ordinary usage." People v. Womack, supra, 167 Cal.App.2d at 131, 334 P.2d 309. Baker not only referred to Womack but expressly "disapproved" of it as "being inconsistent with fundamental canons of construction of criminal statutes." Therefore, Womack hardly supports the parties in the case before us. Rather significantly, however, the Baker court explicitly did say: "Undeniably, the great weight of authority is in accord

---

16. As to that, the court in People v. Baker, 69 Cal.2d 44, 47, 442 P.2d 675, 69 Cal.Rptr. 595 (1968), said: "More commonly, the statute condemns various relationships without specifying the 'wholeness' of the blood as to any of them. In all reported decisions construing such a statute, the courts have extended its bans to uncles and nieces of the half blood by reasoning that 'uncle' in ordinary usage of the word includes a person of the half blood, and/or that under other statutes, relatives of the half blood are given the same legal status as those of the whole blood.... Either rationale is inapposite where the statute, as is true of Civil Code section 59, specifically deals with some half blood relations and not with others." (Citations omitted.)

with the result reached in Womack. (Note, 72 A.L.R.2d 706)'' and conceded that those decisions which represented the weight of authority were consonant with the English ecclesiastical law declaring a marriage between an uncle and niece of the half blood incestuous. People v. Baker, supra, 69 Cal.2d at 47, 442 P.2d 675, 69 Cal.Rptr. 595.

Finally, the parties refer us to State v. Bartley, supra, but that Missouri incest decision hardly buttresses their claim. The defendant Bartley, who had been convicted in the trial court, was a half brother of the mother of the young woman with whom he had had sexual intercourse, the relationship being that of uncle and niece of the half blood. The Missouri statute defining incest provided in part: ''Persons within the following degrees of consanguinity, to wit: Parents and children, including grandparents and grandchildren of every degree, brothers and sisters of the half as well as of the whole blood, uncles and nieces, aunts and nephews, who shall intermarry, or who shall commit adultery or fornication . . . shall be adjudged guilty of incest. . . .'' (Emphasis added.) Id., 304 Mo. at 61, 263 S.W. 95. In reversing the conviction, the Missouri Supreme Court adopted a strict construction of the statute against the state saying, inter alia, that ''[n]o one is to be made subject to such statutes by implication'' and ''[w]here one class of persons is designated as subject to its penalties, all others not mentioned are exonerated.'' Id., at 63, 263 S.W. 95. That case effectively held: ''When the Legislature mentioned brothers and sisters of the half blood it necessarily excluded all other relationships of the half blood.'' Id. Again, as in Baker and Womack, Bartley involved a statutory scheme quite dissimilar from ours. Each involves statutes that expressly provide for certain relationships of the half blood; ours does not.

In addition, the parties suggest that holding marriages between uncles and nieces of the half blood valid will place more emphasis on the rights of criminal defendants and the importance of preserving bona fide marriages against the undue extension of statutory categories. At the outset, we should point out that in this appeal there are no claims that the statutory scheme involved is unconstitutional. Moreover, this appeal does not come to us as a criminal matter. We are, therefore, disinclined to give any opinion, without any factual predicate, what effect upholding the parties' ''more emphasis on the rights of criminal defendants'' claim, because to do so would amount to an advisory opinion. Also, on that branch of their claim, we point out here, as we did in Lomas & Nettleton Co. v. Waterbury, 122 Conn. 228, 234, 188 A. 433 (1936), that ''[l]aw suits are not determined by a consideration of philosophy in the abstract, but by the application of legal principles to the facts of a particular case.''

Connecticut has its statutory scheme in place to implement its policy of delineating the relationships between persons under our jurisdiction who may properly enter into marriage. It has been for many years and still remains the declared public policy of the state. See Catalano v. Catalano, supra. The degrees of relationship within which marriages are prohibited are not, from what we have already said, words of art. Fairly read, the prohibition against intermarriage of those related by consanguinity can be understood to extend to those of the half blood as well as of the whole blood. In Skinner, which predated the case before us by a generation, we held that the words "brother" and "sister" included those of the half blood. "According to the common meaning of the word ['uncle'], it includes the half-brother of the [mother] and there is no distinction between the whole and half blood." 90 C.J.S. 1025. We believe that the same can be said of the term "niece," that is, that it comprehends the half blood as well as the whole blood. In doing so, we accord to each word its common meaning without frustrating legislative intent but rather enhancing it. Other courts have had no difficulty concluding that their statutes, although silent on the half blood matter, comprehend that relationship in "uncle-niece" incest cases. See, e.g., State v. Lamb, 209 Iowa 132, 227 N.W. 830 (1929); Commonwealth v. Ashey, supra, 248 Mass. at 260, 142 N.E. 788. In giving a statute its full meaning where that construction is in harmony with the context and policy of the statute, "there is no canon against using common sense in construing laws as saying what they obviously mean." Roschen v. Ward, 279 U.S. 337, (1929); Donnelley v. United States, 276 U.S. 505 (1928). We will attempt no encompassing definition of a "bona fide marriage" in the incest context. The parties have advanced none. We submit, however, that, given the common meaning of uncle and niece, as we have discussed it, what would constitute a "bona fide marriage" in the incest context should be decided on a case-by-case basis against the background of authority we have set out above. Therefore, contrary to the parties' claim, our interpretation of the statutory scheme does not constitute an "unwarranted extension" of the incest prohibition that "is inconsistent with proper respect for the preservation of bona fide marriages."

In conclusion, a marriage between persons related to one another as half-uncle and half-niece is void under General Statutes §§ 46b–21 and 53a–191 as incestuous.[17]

NOTE

Relationship through adoption. Many prohibitions on intermarriage based on kinship (or criminal incest penalties) address only relationships by consanguinity or affinity. In State v. Geile, 747 S.W.2d 757 (Mo.App.1988), the Missouri Court of Appeals, Eastern District held that Missouri's statutory's prohibition of marriage between uncle and niece did not extend to such a relationship created only through adoption. The applicable statute made no specific reference to adoption.

Some states have begun to include intermarriage bans between persons related only through adoption only, particularly siblings by adoption. Such

---

17. The fact that the General Assembly has expressly provided in 1987 that "[r]elatives of the half blood shall take the same share under [General Statutes § 45–276, entitled 'Distribution when there are no children or representatives of them']" is not in conflict with this conclusion. The 1987 statute, Public Acts 1987, No. 87–239, entitled "An Act Concerning Discrimination Between Relatives of the Whole and Half Blood," was enacted for a limited purpose. It did purport to affect the affairs of relatives in only a limited manner—to prevent discrimination between relatives of whole and half blood under our inheritance law where there are no children or representatives of them. That purpose does not implicate the issue we decide on this appeal.

a prohibition was held unconstitutional by the Supreme Court of Colorado in Israel v. Allen, 195 Colo. 263, 577 P.2d 762 (1978). The parents of the siblings by adoption had married when her daughter was 13 and his son was 18. The families had been living in different states beforehand. After the marriage, the husband adopted his new wife's daughter.

The specific language of the Colorado statute was based on UNIFORM MARRIAGE AND DIVORCE ACT § 207(2), which provides

> *Prohibited marriages.* (1) The following marriages are prohibited: . . . (b) A marriage between an ancestor and a descendant or between a brother and sister, whether the relationship is by the half or the whole blood or by adoption; . . .

The court stated that:

> At the outset, there is an issue as to whether or not marriage is a fundamental right in Colorado. If it is, defendant must show a compelling state interest in order to justify the unequal treatment of adopted brothers and sisters under the statute. Since we find, however, that the provision prohibiting marriage between adopted children fails even to satisfy minimum rationality requirements, we need not determine whether a fundamental right is infringed by this statute.

It was determined that the prohibition against intermarriage by brother and sister related by whole or half blood were severable from the stricken provision.

Should it make a difference if the adoption that creates the sibling relationship takes place after they are adults?

3.   PHYSICAL OR MENTAL INCAPACITY

Until the eugenics movement in the United States gained the ear of the legislature, the law of marriage had no preventive medicine program of its own. To be sure, the motive of healthy offspring underlay, among other reasons, the canon law rules against consanguineous marriages, but essentially these rules were enforced because they were regarded as God's law. Only two afflictions were recognized as grounds for annulment of a marriage: impotence, because it defeated the achievement of two of the ends of marriage; and lunacy and idiocy, because they went to the matter of consent. The church would grant a divorce *mensa et thoro* for reasons of disease only if positive danger of life threatened the healthy spouse. A bodily illness was regarded as a situation which demanded the exertion of conjugal fidelity.

The English ecclesiastical law that continued the traditions established earlier made virtually no innovations beyond expansion of the meaning of cruelty to embrace the endangering of health, which eventually was extended to infection with a venereal disease. The Matrimonial Causes Act of 1937 added epilepsy and communicable venereal disease to the grounds on which a marriage would be voidable.

In the United States there appeared little disposition at first to deal more liberally than the English courts had done. Until fairly recently, generations of litigants battered at the oft-repeated generalization that fraudulent misrepresentations as to good health could not vitiate a marriage contract. The immense authority of Bishop, and later Schouler, tended to preserve this generalization from assault. However, contemporaneously with the growth of the eugenics movement, and with increasing public awareness of the communicability of certain diseases, the granting of annulments for fraud in the concealment of venereal disease, tuberculosis, drug addiction, and mental disorders in a family, came to be regarded as a proper exercise of judicial authority.

Regulatory statutes dealing with physical and mental qualifications for marriage have extended from prohibitions against issuance of licenses or performance of marriage ceremonies when persons with certain conditions or illnesses are involved to declarations that particular unions will be void or voidable. Serological testing for venereal disease is widespread today and some states mandate that parties seeking marriage licenses be advised of the potentials and availability of genetic counseling. However, restrictions on marriage by persons with conditions such as epilepsy have been eliminated. A special contemporary concern deals with testing for AIDS or HIV. An Illinois requirement for such testing was introduced in 1987 but eliminated in 1989, though many states strongly encourage HIV testing prior to marriage.

Controversies about the health of parties entering marriage have arisen in a number of contexts, most frequent among them:

(1) annulment actions for want of consent by a party lacking capacity to understand the nature of marriage or awareness of the marital ceremony;

(2) annulment actions based on fraud in concealing or misrepresenting certain physical disabilities;

(3) actions to determine the validity or effect of statutory proscriptions against marriage;

(4) challenges to statutes limiting or barring issuance of marriage licenses to certain categories of persons;

(5) divorce actions in states that permit this on the basis of certain disabilities existing at the time of marriage that ordinarily would provide grounds only for annulment. Recent reforms have made such provisions increasingly rare.

UNIFORM MARRIAGE AND DIVORCE ACT

§ 208(a)(1), (2) (1973)

(For the text *see* p. 213, *supra*.)

Edmunds v. Edwards

Supreme Court of Nebraska, 1980.
205 Neb. 255, 287 N.W.2d 420.

■ Brodkey, Justice.

This case involves an action brought in the District Court for Douglas County on May 23, 1977, by Renne Edmunds, guardian of the estate of Harold Edwards (hereinafter referred to as Harold), against Inez Edwards (nee Ryan, hereinafter referred to as Inez), to annul the marriage of his ward Harold to Inez, which occurred on May 10, 1975. In his petition, the guardian alleged that the marriage was void for the reason that Harold did not have the mental capacity to enter into a marriage contract on that date, which allegation was specifically denied by Inez. In its order entered on November 27, 1978, following trial of the matter, the District Court found that Harold was mentally retarded, as that phrase is commonly used in medical science, but not to a degree which, under the law of the State of Nebraska, is of such a nature as to render him mentally incompetent to enter into the marriage relation, and that at the time of the marriage between Harold and Inez, Harold had sufficient capacity to understand the nature of the marriage contract and the duties and responsibilities incident to it, so as to be able to enter into a valid and binding marriage contract. The court therefore found that the marriage of Harold and Inez, which occurred on May 10, 1975, was, in fact and in law, a valid marriage and continues to exist as a valid marriage under the laws of the State of Nebraska, ... The guardian has appealed....

Harold was born on August 7, 1918, and was institutionalized at the Beatrice State Home as mentally retarded on September 25, 1939. He was a resident at the Beatrice State Home for a period of approximately 30 years. It was during this period that he first met Inez, who was also a patient of the home, and Bill Lancaster, who lived with Harold in Omaha after their release from the Beatrice State Home, and who has continued to reside with Harold and Inez since their marriage. Harold was placed in Omaha on November 14, 1969, and started a new life under the auspices of the Eastern Nebraska Community Office of Retardation (ENCOR), which was established in 1968 to provide alternatives for institutionalization of retarded persons at the Beatrice State Home and to assist in the normalization of the retarded in local communities. After coming to Omaha, Harold obtained employment as a food service worker in the Douglas County Hospital on February 16, 1970, and lived in a staffed ENCOR apartment from that time until shortly before his marriage in 1975. As will later be made apparent, he has functioned satisfactorily in that employment, and has received promotions and salary increases since commencing on that job. While under the auspices of ENCOR, Harold and Inez developed a romantic interest in each other and eventually decided to get married. The date of the marriage was postponed in order to afford the couple the opportunity to have premarital sex counseling and marriage counseling from the pastor of their church in Omaha. They were married by Reverend Verle Holsteen, pastor of the First Baptist Church in Omaha, Nebraska, and their friends, staff members of ENCOR, and out-of-state relatives attended the wedding in that church. The guardian did not bring this action to annul the marriage for a period of approximately 2 years after the date of the marriage ceremony.

. . .

According to testimony in the record, mental retardation refers basically to delayed intellectual function and developmental delays usually associated from the time early in life and persisting throughout life. There are various degrees of mental retardation according to the official diagnostic system or nomenclature of the American Medical Association. Those degrees are mild, moderate, severe, and profound. Formerly, there was older nomenclature that defined the degrees of mental retardation as idiot, imbecile, and moron. The older classification of idiot is now encompassed under the two new groupings of "profound" and "severe;" the older classification of "imbecile" is now encompassed within the range of moderate mental retardation; and the older term "moron" is today classified as mild mental retardation. The expert medical witnesses for both parties agree that Harold falls within the classification of mild mental retardation.

The guardian first called his medical expert, Dr. Robert Mitchell, a psychologist connected with Creighton University in Omaha. Dr. Mitchell expressed the opinion that he did not believe Harold was competent to enter into a valid marriage, but admitted on cross-examination that being mildly mentally retarded did not automatically preclude a person from marriage. He also testified that he had asked Harold during his examinations and consultations what marriage meant, to which Harold responded "For life," and also "You stay married forever." Harold told Dr. Mitchell during the interview that he wanted to get married. Dr. Mitchell also stated: "[I] found no evidence from him or the way he behaved in my interview that he was attempting to get out of the marriage, he seemed very happy with the marriage. . . ." Dr. Mitchell also testified: "It is much better, I think, to refer to Mr. Edwards as a person who is fifty-nine years of age who is not as bright as most people. But he has had fifty-nine years of experience, and he is an adult, and physiologically he is matured, as well."

The medical expert witness called by the defendant was Dr. Frank J. Menolascino, a psychiatrist specializing in the field of mental retardation, and author of numerous books and articles upon the subject. He was well acquainted with Harold, having first met him in 1959 when he was doing work at the Beatrice State Home, and had seen Harold many times since that time. He had examined Harold in December 1977, and again in July 1978, during the week Dr. Menolascino testified. He testified that Harold was not functioning below the mildly retarded range and that the tests reflected that a great deal of Harold's difficulty appeared to be primarily a lack of training. Harold told him he was marrying a lady he had known at the Beatrice State Home and that he had had premarital counseling from the minister of his church and also sexual counseling. Dr. Menolascino also testified that he had asked Harold why he wanted to get married, and

Harold replied, "I don't want to be lonely." Harold had been married approximately 2 ½ years before Dr. Menolascino saw him in December of 1977, and his mental status was "remarkably similar to the one I had seen in the past in the '60s." Dr. Menolascino was asked: "Doctor, do you believe that you have an opinion as to whether Mr. Edwards was capable of understanding the nature of a marriage within the paradigm you have discussed in May of 1975?" and he answered: "Yes, he was able to." He further testified that in his examination of Harold in December 1977, he questioned whether Harold was even mildly retarded, but at the subsequent examination, he concluded that Harold was mildly retarded, upper level. On cross-examination Dr. Menolascino was asked: "In your opinion, do you think that Harold Edwards understands the fact that he is liable for Mrs. Edwards' bills if she goes to a store and runs up some bills?" to which he replied: "Yes." He was then asked: "Do you think he understands the fact that if he gets a divorce he might have to pay alimony?" His reply to that question was: "I am not sure. I am not sure...."

In addition to the medical witnesses who testified, there was also evidence adduced from various lay witnesses. Renne Edmunds, the guardian, testified that he first met Harold about April 8, 1975, although the date of the inception of the guardianship was October 18, 1972. At that time Harold was already under the care and guidance of ENCOR. Edmunds testified: "It was my conclusion that he [Harold] could not not only manage a fund of thirty thousand, he couldn't manage the small purchases, as well." He testified that he refused to pay certain expenses of the wedding because they were not compensable from guardianship funds. He admits that he was told about the marriage taking place, and that he had filed no action to prevent the marriage, which took place May 10, 1975. His annulment action was filed approximately 2 years later. Harry John Naasz, an adviser for ENCOR, who was Harold's supervisor, testified that he had assisted Harold in making preparations for the marriage including obtaining of blood tests and the marriage certificate. He had discussed the forthcoming wedding with Harold: "Can you tell us what you discussed concerning the marriage? A. We discussed what it would mean, what it would mean living together, sharing their lives. Q. And what did Harold express to you? A. He wanted to get married. Q. What did he say that led you to believe that he might understand marriage? A. He mentioned to me that he understood, too that it was a commitment to each other, that Inez would be living there." Mr. Naasz did admit in his testimony that at the beginning he did have some question in his mind about whether Harold understood marriage. He later referred the couple for marriage counseling.

David Bones, an employee of Planned Parenthood in Omaha and Council Bluffs, and also an ordained minister in the United Methodist Church, testified with reference to premarital sex counseling he had given to Harold and Inez on April 16, 1975. He testified: "As I recall, we talked some about the responsibility of economics, we talked about what kind of things they liked to do together, which is the common things we talk to most folks about. Q. Was there a response from Harold as to what kind of things they liked to do together? A. Well, the thing that I recall—and I cannot swear that it is a specific—specifically a statement made—that, you know, Harold and Inez together talked about their enjoying just being together and being together in the sense of arms around each other, holding each other, holding hands, kidding one another, those things were a nice part of their experience as they were, and it appeared to us—.'' Bones testified that he basically completed his premarital sex course with Harold and Inez and that Harold appeared to understand it and nodded his head.

Reverend Verle Holsteen, who was the pastor of the First Baptist Church on Park Avenue in Omaha, and who was the officiating officer at the marriage between Harold and Inez, testified that he had known Inez since 1971 and Harold since 1974, and they attended his church regularly. He gave them premarital counseling and recalls having had three sessions with them. He asked Harold if he understood what they were talking about and Harold said yes. Reverend Holsteen performed the wedding ceremony and attended the reception which was held at the First Baptist Church parlor. He recalls church members being present, as well as friends of Harold and Inez from ENCOR and relatives from California. He stated: "My perception of their relationship to each other is that they get along well, that they enjoy being together. I have never had either one of them come to me and say, you know, I have a problem with the other. Q. Do you have an opinion on whether or not Harold understood the nature of marriage at the time you counseled him? . . . A. My feeling at the moment was that Harold understood as best he could, as anyone does." Reverend Holsteen testified on cross-examination: "I felt that Harold understood that if things followed through that he would be married to Inez." He was asked whether he had some doubt in his mind as to whether Harold understood what a marriage contract was all about and he replied: "By observing him I would say that he would not understand as much as other people what a marriage contract would be about. But I recognized, and I stand by this, that they would get along well together." On redirect-examination he was asked: "Reverend, your testimony is, you did have some concern initially about his capacity? A. Yes, I did. Q. And is it also, then, your testimony that after talking to Harold and Inez your reservations were resolved? . . . A. I would say yes, they were resolved."

Also testifying at the trial was Elizabeth Cartwright, an employee of ENCOR, who monitors Harold and Inez' finances. She testified that when Harold gets paid at the Douglas County Hospital he signs his check, takes it to the bank, deposits all the money except $40, and gives Inez $20 and he keeps $20. She does not have to go to the bank with him. Elizabeth Cartwright also testified that Inez is quite a bit sharper than Harold and she helps him around. She also testified about an incident involving the loss of Harold's wedding ring. She stated: "Just recently Harold lost his wedding band and he called me up at work and was very much upset and stated that he lost his wedding band, and he said to me that it was exchanged to him on his wedding day, Inez gave it to him, he wanted another wedding band. So in talking with Inez and Harold they came to the conclusion that they would purchase another one at Crossroads, and they withdrew money from their savings account for the first time and purchased a wedding band. Harold selected it." She also testified, however, that Harold cannot figure his finances and needs assistance.

The final witness offering testimony at the trial was John Taylor, personnel director for the Civil Service Commission for Douglas County. He testified that Harold was first employed by the Douglas County Hospital on February 16, 1970, in the food service department, and that Harold has been promoted since and has received pay increases since February 1970, reflecting good job performance. Neither party to the marriage testified at the trial.

We now examine some established rules of law which we believe are applicable to this case. We first consider the nature of the marriage contract. Section 42–101, R.R.S.1943, provides: "In law, marriage is considered a civil contract, to which the consent of the parties capable of contracting is essential." Although by statute, marriage is referred to as a "civil contract," we have held: "That it is not a contract resembling in any but the slightest degree, except as to the element of consent, any other contract with which the courts have to deal, is apparent upon a moment's reflection.... What persons establish by entering into matrimony, is not a contractual relation, but a social *status*; and the only essential features of the transactions are that the participants are of legal capacity to assume that status, and freely consent so to do." University of Michigan v. McGuckin, 64 Neb. 300, 89 N.W. 778 (1902). Also, in Willits v. Willits, 76 Neb. 228, 107 N.W. 379 (1906), we stated that while our law defines marriage as a civil contract, it differs from all other contracts in its consequences to the body politic, and for that reason in dealing with it or with the status resulting therefrom the state never stands indifferent, but is always a party whose interest must be taken into account.

Another statutory provision of which we must take cognizance in this appeal is section 42–103, R.R.S.1943, which provides: "Marriages are void ... (2) when either party, at the time of marriage, is insane or mentally incompetent to enter into the marriage relation;...." This statute was reiterated, and other applicable rules with reference to competency to enter into a marriage relationship were reviewed in Homan v. Homan, 181 Neb. 259, 147 N.W.2d 630 (1967), wherein we stated: "The petition alleged that the ward was mentally incompetent at the time of the marriage. By statute a marriage is void 'when either party is insane or an idiot at the time of marriage, and the term idiot shall include all persons who from whatever cause are mentally incompetent to enter into the marriage relation.' § 42–103, R.S.Supp., 1965.

"A marriage contract will not be declared void for mental incapacity to enter into it unless there existed at the time of the marriage such a want of understanding as to render the party incapable of assenting thereto. Fischer v. Adams, 151 Neb. 512, 38 N.W. 337. Mere weakness or imbecility of mind is not sufficient to void a contract of marriage unless there be such a mental defect as to prevent the party from comprehending the nature of the contract and from giving his fee [sic] and intelligent consent to it.

"Absolute inability to contract, insanity, or idiocy will void a marriage, but mere weakness of mind will not unless it produces a derangement sufficient to avoid all contracts by destroying the power to consent. Aldrich v. Steen, 71 Neb. 33, 98 N.W. 445; Adams v. Scott, 93 Neb. 537, 141 N.W. 148. A marriage is valid if the party has sufficient capacity to understand the nature of the contract and the obligations and responsibilities it creates. Fischer v. Adams, supra; Kutch v. Kutch, 88 Neb. 114, 129 N.W. 169.

. . .

"A marriage is presumed valid, and the burden of proof is upon the party seeking annulment. Adams v. Scott, supra."

It is the general rule that the existence of a valid marriage is a question of fact. In this case the trier of fact was the court and the court had all the foregoing evidence, summarized above, before it. Concededly, much of the evidence with reference to the capacity of Harold to enter into the marriage contract was conflicting and disputed. An action to annul a marriage, being an action in equity, is governed by the provisions of section 25–1925, R.R.S.1943, which provides: "In all appeals from the district court to the Supreme Court in suits in equity, wherein review of some or all of the findings of fact of the district court is asked by the appellant, it shall be the duty of the Supreme Court to retry the issue or issues of fact involved in the finding or findings of fact complained of upon the evidence preserved in the bill of exceptions, and upon trial de novo of such question or questions of fact, reach an independent conclusion as to what finding or findings are required under the pleadings and all the evidence, without reference to the conclusion reached in the district court or the fact that there may be some evidence in support thereof." However, it is also the well-established rule that where the evidence on material questions of fact is in irreconcilable conflict, this court will, in determining the weight of the evidence, consider the fact that the trial court observed the witnesses and their manner of testifying, and therefore must have accepted one version of the facts rather than the opposite. This rule has been applied both in annulment actions and in divorce actions.

Applying this rule to the present case, we conclude, therefore, that the trial court was correct in dismissing the guardian's petition to annul the marriage of his ward, and that its action in this regard should be and hereby is affirmed.

NOTE

Would it be better policy to use a test of whether a party with mental deficiency or disability understands the nature of marriage or a test as to that person's ability to function effectively as a spouse or a parent? Should the law differentiate its test for marital capacity between a physically robust party who suffers from feeblemindedness at a young age and an older person who suffers from senility that cannot be reversed?

Temporary mental incapacity can affect the validity of a marriage if the condition exists at the time of the ceremony and ratification does not take place after the disability has terminated. In Mahan v. Mahan, 88 So.2d 545 (Fla.1956), a wife sought annulment of her marriage on the ground that at the time of the ceremony she was so intoxicated by "alcoholic stimulants" that she was not in possession of her mental faculties and was incapable of forming conscious consent to the marriage. The husband answered that he could neither admit nor deny the allegations because at the time of the alleged marriage he was so intoxicated that he could not state whether he was ever married. There was corroboration of the intoxication of both parties by witnesses who traveled with them when the marriage occurred, and there was evidence that the marriage was not followed by cohabitation. Annulment was granted, the court finding the evidence sufficient to establish that at the time of the marriage the wife was incapable of entering a binding agreement.

Rickards v. Rickards

Supreme Court of Delaware, 1960.
53 Del. 134, 166 A.2d 425.

■ WOLCOTT, JUSTICE. This is an appeal by the husband from a judgment of the Superior Court of New Castle County granting an annulment of marriage at the suit of the wife. . . .

The action was based upon 13 Del.C. § 1551, which provides as one ground for annulment of marriages:

> "Incurable physical impotency, or incapacity for copulation, at the suit of either party; if the party making the application was ignorant of such impotency or incapacity at the time of the marriage."

. . .

It serves no purpose to review the details of the evidence. We . . . are satisfied that the ruling below to the effect that the wife had sustained the burden of proving that the husband was sexually impotent at least as to her, was probably incurable as a "pure form" sexual deviate, and by reason thereof had an incapacity for copulation with the wife, was correct.

We think it also established beyond doubt that the husband's incapacity was entirely due to psychic causes. The evidence is clear that he suffered from no physical defect of a sexually incapacitating nature. We think it apparent that psychogenic causes had made the husband physically unable to copulate, at least with the woman he had married.

The question before us, therefore, is whether 13 Del.C. § 1551 permits the annulment of a marriage when the cause of impotency is psychic rather than physical in origin.

The wife argues that the statute, being in the alternative, permits proof of either "incurable physical impotency" or "incapacity for copulation" for any recognized medical reason. This argument was rejected by the Superior Court in S. v. S., 3 Terry 192, 29 A.2d 325, when it held that the second phrase was merely explanatory of the word "impotency", and that the ground of annulment authorized by the statute was incurable physical impotency. If the questions were of first instance in this State we would have some doubt as to the propriety of the construction, but we do not re-examine it for, in the view we take of the case, it is unnecessary to do so. Consequently, we neither approve nor disapprove the rule of S. v. S.

We think this statutory ground for annulment of marriage is an incurable physical inability on the part of one spouse to copulate with the other. This being so, it follows that whether the inability stems from physical or mental defects, provided in either case that the resulting condition is incurable, the requirement of the statute is met. . . .

The husband does not argue strenuously against the conclusion that impotency under that statute may be the result of psychic causes. The main thrust of his argument is that the wife has failed to establish *incurable* impotency. . . .

The husband is, of course, correct in maintaining that the asserted impotency must be incurable, but in the case before us we think this fact has been established to a reasonable certainty by the testimony of the psychiatrist who not only had examined him but who for a period of time had had him under treatment. In the opinion of this doctor, the husband "probably" could be classed as incurably physically impotent. It is true that the doctor testified that it was possible to treat the husband's psychic troubles, but the fair import of his testimony is that the possibility of a cure was remote. The trial judge concluded that the doctor's opinion was that the husband was incurably physically impotent. We think this conclusion correct from the evidence. . . .

For the foregoing reasons, we affirm that portion of the judgment appealed from granting an annulment. . . .

NOTE

In Tompkins v. Tompkins, 92 N.J.Eq. 113, 111 A. 599 (Ch.Div.1920), a young couple had lived together for five years but the wife was still a virgin. In the wife's annulment action, the husband "vigorously protested his virility but admitted the non-consummation of the marriage. . . ." The court applied the "doctrine of triennial cohabitation," ostensibly a rule from the Roman law which had been applied in English courts: "The essence of the doctrine is, that if the wife be a virgin and apt after three years' cohabitation, the husband will be presumed to be impotent, and the burden will be upon him to overcome the presumption of proof that he is not at fault." The court added:

The burden, then, being shifted to the husband to excuse or justify the plight of his wife, the question comes to one of belief in his story of forbearance for five years, under most trying circumstances, simply because sexual intercourse was painful and distressing to her I have misgivings. Such solicitude of a groom is noble, of a husband, heroic. Few have the fortitude to resist the temptations of the honeymoon. But human endurance has its limitations. When nature demands its due, youth is prodigal in the payment. Men are still cavemen in the pleasures of the bed. The sex may be more temperate, but none the less passionate, and heedless of the penalty. They do not shirk the initiation nor shrink from the consequences. The husband's plea does not inspire confidence. Common experience discredits it. And if, in fact, he had the physical power, and refrained from sexual intercourse during the five years he occupied the same bed with his wife, purely out of sympathy for her feelings, he deserves to be doubted for not having asserted his rights, even though she balked.

The presumption of impotency has not been overcome and a decree of nullity will be advised. 111 A. 599, at 601.

Another set of problems can arise when annulment of a marriage is requested on the ground of impotence although children have been born of the union. This possibility exists in several situations, as illustrated by judicial opinions.

In T. v. M., 100 N.J.Super. 530, 242 A.2d 670 (Ch.Div.1968), the court described the annulment action before it, based on physical and incurable impotence, as being "of novel impression in New Jersey and, perhaps in this country, in that the wife, while still a virgin, with an intact hymen, suffered a miscarriage during the marriage." Medical testimony described this anomaly as resulting from a "splash pregnancy" caused by the husband's ejaculation against the wife's vulva during an unsuccessful attempt at normal intercourse. The court granted the annulment based on the wife's impotence after outlining the rather extensive medical testimony in the case. One wonders whether the same decision would have been reached had a child been born. Is a "penetration" rule necessary, or can it be argued that a marriage is "consummated" when the wife gives birth to a child sired by her husband?

Considering that a man may be impotent for annulment purposes even though capable of reproduction and of intercourse with women other than his wife, it is easily possible that through homologous artificial insemination (AIH), which utilizes the husband's semen, such an "impotent" husband might nevertheless father a child by his wife. In L. v. L., [1949] 1 All E.R. 141, a husband and wife gave birth to a child through AIH though they had never copulated together. The court granted the wife an annulment even though the child would be illegitimate under English law at that time. In Gursky v. Gursky, 39 Misc.2d 1083, 242 N.Y.S.2d 406 (1963), an annulment was granted to a wife who established that there had been no consummation of the marriage. The court then faced the problem of determining the status of a child born through heterologous artificial insemination (AID) to which the husband had consented after medical advice concerning his own incapacity. Although the child was considered illegitimate, the husband was required to make support payments after the annulment on a theory of implied contract or equitable estoppel.

Kantaras v. Kantaras

District Court of Appeal of Florida, Second District, 2004.
884 So.2d 155.

■ FULMER, JUDGE.

Linda Kantaras appeals from a final judgment dissolving her marriage to Michael Kantaras. This appeal presents an issue of first impression in Florida: whether a postoperative female-to-male transsexual person can validly marry a female under the current law of this state. We hold that the law of this state does not provide for or allow such a marriage; therefore, we reverse the final judgment and remand for the trial court to declare the marriage of the parties void ab initio.

In 1959 Margo Kantaras was born a female in Ohio. In 1986 Margo changed her name to Michael John Kantaras, and in 1987 Michael underwent sex reassignment, which included hormonal treatments, a total hysterectomy, and a double mastectomy. In 1988 Michael met Linda, and Linda learned of Michael's surgeries. Linda, who was pregnant by a former boyfriend, gave birth to a son in June 1989. Linda and Michael applied for a marriage license with Michael representing that he[1] was male. The two married in July 1989 in Florida. In September 1989, Michael applied to adopt Linda's son, with Michael representing to the court that he was Linda's husband. Linda gave birth to a daughter in 1992 after Linda underwent artificial insemination with the sperm of Michael's brother.

In 1998 Michael filed a petition for dissolution of marriage seeking to dissolve his marriage to Linda and to obtain custody of both children. Linda answered and counterpetitioned for dissolution and/or annulment claiming that the marriage was void ab initio because it violated Florida law that bans same sex marriage. Linda claimed that the adoption of her son was void because it violated Florida's ban on homosexual adoption, and she claimed that Michael was not the biological or legal father of her daughter.

After a lengthy trial, the trial court entered an order finding that Michael was legally a male at the time of the marriage, and thus, the trial court concluded that the marriage was valid. The trial court also concluded that Michael was entitled to primary residential custody of the two children.

In outlining its reasons for determining that Michael was male at the time of the marriage, the trial court stated, in part:

1. Our references to Michael Kantaras as "he" throughout this opinion are not in- tended to carry a legal significance.

24. Michael at the date of marriage was a male based on the persuasive weight of all the medical evidence and the testimony of lay witnesses in this case, including the following:

(a) As a child, while born female, Michael's parents and siblings observed his male characteristics and agreed he should have been born a "boy."

(b) Michael always has perceived himself as a male and assumed the male role doing house chores growing up, played male sports, refused to wear female clothing at home or in school and had his high school picture taken in male clothing.

(c) Prior to marriage he successfully completed the full process of transsexual reassignment, involving hormone treatment, irreversible medical surgery that removed all of his female organs inside of his body, including having a male reconstructed chest, a male voice, a male configured body and hair with beard and moustache, and a naturally developed penis.

(d) At the time of the marriage his bride, Linda was fully informed about his sex reassignment status, she accepted along with his friends, family and wor[k] colleagues that Michael in his appearance, characteristics and behavior was perceived as a man. At the time of the marriage he could not assume the role of a woman.

(e) Before and after the marriage he has been accepted as a man in a variety of social and legal ways, such as having a male driving license; male passport; male name change; male modification of his birth certificate by legal ruling; male participation in legal adoption proceedings in court; and as a male in an artificial insemination program, and participating for years in school activities with the children of this marriage as their father. All of this, was no different than what Michael presented himself as at the date of marriage.

25. Michael was born a heterosexual transsexual female. That condition [which] is now called "Gender Identity Dysphoria," was diagnosed for Michael in adulthood some twenty (20) years after birth. Today and at the date of marriage, Michael had no secondary female identifying characteristics and all reproductive female organs were absent, such as ovaries, fallopian tubes, cervix, womb, and breasts. The only feature left is a vagina which Dr. Cole testified was not typically female because it now had a penis or enlarged, elongate[d] clitoris.

26. Michael after sex reassignment or triatic treatments would still have a chromosomal patter [sic] (XX) of a woman but that is a presumption. No chromosomal tests were performed on Michael during the course of his treatment at the Rosenberg Clinic.

27. Chromosomes are only one factor in the determination of sex and they do not overrule gender or self identity, which is the true test or identifying mark of sex. Michael has always, for a lifetime, had a self-identity of a male. Dr. Walter Bockting, Dr. Ted Huang and Dr.

Collier Cole, all testified that Michael Kantaras is now and at the date of marriage was medically and legally "male."

28. Under the marriage statute of Florida, Michael is deemed to be male, and the marriage ceremony performed in the Sandford [sic] County Court house on July 18, 1989, was legal.

The issue in this case involves the interplay between the Florida statutes governing marriage and the question of whether Michael Kantaras was legally male or female when he married Linda. We first address the relevant statutes and then discuss our reasons for concluding that the trial court erred in finding that Michael was male at the time of the marriage.

The Florida Legislature has expressly banned same sex marriage. As amended in 1977 by chapter 77–139, Laws of Florida, the statute governing the issuance of a marriage license, at the time one was issued in this case, provided that no license shall be issued unless one party is a male and the other a female:No county court judge or clerk of the circuit court in this state shall issue a license for the marriage of any person unless there shall be first presented and filed with him an affidavit in writing, signed by both parties to the marriage, made and subscribed before some person authorized by law to administer an oath, . . . and unless one party is a male and the other party is a female. § 741.04(1), Fla. Stat. (1987). In 1997, the legislature enacted the Florida Defense of Marriage Act, prohibiting marriage between persons of the same sex:

(1) Marriages between persons of the same sex entered into in any jurisdiction, whether within or outside the State of Florida, the United States, or any other jurisdiction, either domestic or foreign, or any other place or location, or relationships between persons of the same sex which are treated as marriages in any jurisdiction, whether within or outside the State of Florida, the United States, or any other jurisdiction, either domestic or foreign, or any other place or location, are not recognized for any purpose in this state.

(2) The state, its agencies, and its political subdivisions may not give effect to any public act, record, or judicial proceeding of any state, territory, possession, or tribe of the United States or of any other jurisdiction, either domestic or foreign, or any other place or location respecting either a marriage or relationship not recognized under subsection (1) or a claim arising from such a marriage or relationship.

(3) For purposes of interpreting any state statute or rule, the term "marriage" means only a legal union between one man and one woman as husband and wife, and the term "spouse" applies only to a member of such a union.

§ 741.212, Fla. Stat. (Supp.1998).

Courts in Ohio, Kansas, Texas, and New York have addressed issues involving the marriage of a postoperative transsexual person, and in all cases the courts have invalidated or refused to allow the marriage on the grounds that it violated state statutes or public policy. In the case of *In re Ladrach,* 32 Ohio Misc.2d 6, 513 N.E.2d 828 (Probate 1987), the court found that a postoperative male-to-female transsexual was not permitted to marry a male.

> "[T]here is no authority in Ohio for the issuance of a marriage license to consummate a marriage between a post-operative male to female transsexual person and a male person." *Id.* at 832.

> This court is charged with the responsibility of interpreting the statutes of this state.... Since the case at bar is apparently one of first impression in Ohio, it is this court's opinion that the legislature should change the statutes, if it is to be the public policy of the state of Ohio to issue marriage licenses to post-operative transsexuals.

> *Id.*

More recently an Ohio appellate court agreed with the decision in *Ladrach* and affirmed a trial court's denial of a marriage license to a postoperative female-to-male transsexual and a female. *See In re A Marriage License for Nash,* Nos.2002–T–0149, 2002–T–0179, 2003 WL 23097095 (Ohio Ct.App. Dec. 31, 2003). Noting that "Ohio, like most states, has a clear public policy that authorizes and recognizes marriages only between members of the opposite sex," the court concluded that the term "male" as used in the marriage statute does not include a female-to-male postoperative transsexual. *Id.* at 5–6. Agreeing with the court in *Ladrach* that it was the responsibility of the legislature to change the public policy, the court stated that it was "loath to expand the statutory designation of individuals who may marry through judicial legislation." *Id.* at 7.

The Kansas Supreme Court declared a marriage void after it found that a postoperative male-to-female transsexual was not a woman. *See In re Estate of Gardiner,* 273 Kan. 191, 42 P.3d 120 (2002), *cert. denied,* 537 U.S. 825, 123 S.Ct. 113, 154 L.Ed.2d 36 (2002). *Gardiner,* a probate case, involved the question of who was the rightful heir to the intestate estate of Marshall Gardiner: Gardiner's son, Joe, or J'Noel Gardiner, a male-to-female transsexual who married Marshall Gardiner the year before his death. *Id.* at 122. Joe sought summary judgment on the ground that J'Noel's marriage to Marshall was void. *Id.* at 123. The district court granted summary judgment concluding that the marriage was void under Kansas law on the ground that J'Noel was a male. *Id.* The court of appeals reversed and directed the district court to determine whether J'Noel was male or female at the time the marriage license was issued, taking into account a number of factors in addition to chromosomes. *Id.* at 132–34. The Supreme Court of Kansas granted Joe's petition for review and reversed the decision of the court of appeals, concluding that the district court had properly entered summary judgment on the ground that J'Noel's marriage to Marshall was void. *Id.* at 136–37.

The supreme court concluded that the issue on appeal was one of law, not fact, and it involved the interpretation of the Kansas statutes. *Id.* at 135. The court recognized that "[t]he fundamental rule of statutory construction is that the intent of the legislature governs." *Id.* After discussing the common meaning of the terms sex, male, and female, the court stated:

The words "sex," "male," and "female" in everyday understanding do not encompass transsexuals. The plain, ordinary meaning of "persons of the opposite sex" contemplates a biological man and a biological woman and not persons who are experiencing gender dysphoria. A male-to-female post-operative transsexual does not fit the definition of a female. The male organs have been removed, but the ability to "produce ova and bear offspring" does not and never did exist. There is no womb, cervix, or ovaries, nor is there any change in his chromosomes. As the *Littleton* court noted, the transsexual still "inhabits . . . a male body in all aspects other than what the physicians have supplied." 9 S.W.3d at 231. J'Noel does not fit the common meaning of female.

Id. at 135.

In response to the court of appeals' conclusion that a question remained as to whether J'Noel was a female at the time the license was issued for the purpose of the statute, the supreme court stated:

We do not agree that the question remains. We view the legislative silence to indicate that transsexuals are not included. If the legislature intended to include transsexuals, it could have been a simple matter to have done so. We apply the rules of statutory construction to ascertain the legislative intent as expressed in the statute. We do not read into a statute something that does not come within the wording of the statute.

Id. at 136 (citation omitted). The supreme court stated further:

[T]he legislature clearly viewed "opposite sex" in the narrow traditional sense. . . . We cannot ignore what the legislature has declared to be the public policy of this state. Our responsibility is to interpret [the statute] and not to rewrite it. . . . If the legislature wishes to change public policy, it is free to do so; we are not. To conclude that J'Noel is of the opposite sex of Marshall would require that we rewrite [the statute].

Id. at 136–37. The supreme court concluded that "the validity of J'Noel's marriage to Marshall is a question of public policy to be addressed by the legislature and not by this court." *Id.* at 137.

In *Littleton v. Prange,* 9 S.W.3d 223 (Tex.App.1999), the Texas court found a marriage between a man and a postoperative male-to-female transsexual void. Christie Littleton, the transsexual, married Jonathon Mark Littleton in Kentucky in 1989. *Id.* at 225. After Jonathon's death in 1996, Christie sued Dr. Prange for medical malpractice in her capacity as Jonathon's surviving spouse. *Id.* The doctor moved for summary judgment asserting that Christie was a man and could not be the surviving spouse of another man. *Id.* The trial court agreed and granted summary judgment. *Id.*

The appeals court concluded that the case presented a pure question of law.

Id. at 230.

> In our system of government it is for the legislature, should it choose to do so, to determine what guidelines should govern the recognition of marriages involving transsexuals. . . .

> It would be intellectually possible for this court to write a protocol for when transsexuals would be recognized as having successfully changed their sex. . . . But this court has no authority to fashion a new law on transsexuals, or anything else. We cannot make law when no law exists: we can only interpret the written word of our sister branch of government, the legislature.

Id. at 230. The court concluded "as a matter of law, that Christie Littleton is a male. As a male, Christie cannot be married to another male. Her marriage to Jonathon was invalid, and she cannot bring a cause of action as his surviving spouse." *Id.* at 231.

New York courts have also refused to recognize transsexual marriage. *See Anonymous v. Anonymous,* 67 Misc.2d 982, 325 N.Y.S.2d 499 (1971); *Frances B. v. Mark B.,* 78 Misc.2d 112, 355 N.Y.S.2d 712 (1974). In *Frances B.,* the plaintiff, a woman, filed an annulment action claiming that, prior to the marriage, the defendant (a postoperative female-to-male transsexual) fraudulently represented himself as a male, although the defendant did not have male sex organs and was still a woman. 355 N.Y.S.2d at 713. The defendant moved to amend his answer to include a counterclaim for divorce on the ground of abandonment. *Id.* at 714. The court, noting the public policy that the marriage relationship exists for the purpose of begetting offspring, concluded that the defendant's sex reassignment surgery did not enable the defendant to perform male sexual functions in a marriage:

> Assuming, as urged, that defendant was a male entrapped in the body of a female, the record does not show that the entrapped male successfully escaped to enable defendant to perform male functions in a marriage. Attempted sex reassignment by mastectomy, hysterectomy, and androgenous hormonal therapy, has not achieved that result.

Id. at 717.

Thus, the court concluded that, as a matter of law, the defendant had no basis to counterclaim for divorce. *Id.* at 716–17.

There is one case in the United States that has permitted transsexual marriage. In *M.T. v. J.T.,* 140 N.J.Super. 77, 355 A.2d 204 (1976), the husband sought an annulment on the ground that his wife was a male-to-female transsexual. The New Jersey court rejected the husband's argument, upheld the validity of the marriage, and affirmed a judgment of the lower court obligating the husband to support the transsexual as his wife. 355 A.2d at 211. After considering the medical evidence, the court held that when a transsexual person has successfully undergone sex-reassignment and can fully function sexually in the reassigned sex, then the person could marry legally as a member of the sex finally indicated. *Id.* at 210–11.

In sum, it has been established that an individual suffering from the condition of transsexualism is one with a disparity between his or her genitalia or anatomical sex and his or her gender, that is, the individual's strong and consistent emotional and psychological sense of sexual being. A transsexual in a proper case can be treated medically by certain supportive measures and through surgery to remove and replace existing genitalia with sex organs which will coincide with the person's gender. If such sex reassignment surgery is successful and the postoperative transsexual is, by virtue of medical treatment, thereby possessed of the full capacity to function sexually as a male or female, as the case may be, we perceive no legal barrier, cognizable social taboo, or reason grounded in public policy to prevent that person's identification at least for purposes of marriage to the sex finally indicated.

Id. at 210–11.

In the case before us, the trial court relied heavily on the approach taken by an Australian family court in *In re Kevin,* (2001) 28 Fam. L.R. 158, *aff'd,* 30 Fam. L.R. 1 (Austl.Fam.Ct.2003) (pagination of Lexis printout), which the trial court believed "correctly states the law in modern society's approach to transsexualism." In that case, the Australian court took the view that courts must recognize advances in medical knowledge and practice and found that a female-to-male transsexual should be considered a man for purposes of marriage. Australia prohibits same sex marriage; nevertheless, the court ruled that a marriage between a woman and a postoperative female-to-male transsexual was valid. In affirming the trial court, the Family Court of Australia stated in its conclusion:

> Should the words "man" and "marriage" as used in the Marriage Act 1961 bear their contemporary ordinary everyday meaning?
>
> . . .
>
> Unless the context requires a different interpretation, the words "man" and "woman" when used in legislation have their ordinary contemporary meaning according to Australian usage. That meaning includes postoperative transsexuals as men or women in accordance with their sexual reassignment. . . .

30 Fam. L.R. 1 at 48.

On appeal, Michael argues that the trial court properly adopted the approach taken by the Australian court.

He further argues that the approach taken by the majority of courts in the United States that have addressed the issue of transsexual marriage ignore modern medical science. We disagree.

The controlling issue in this case is whether, as a matter of law, the Florida statutes governing marriage authorize a postoperative transsexual to marry in the reassigned sex. We conclude they do not. We agree with the Kansas, Ohio, and Texas courts in their understanding of the common meaning of male and female, as those terms are used statutorily, to refer to immutable traits determined at birth. Therefore, we also conclude that the trial court erred by declaring that Michael is male for the purpose of the marriage statutes. Whether advances in medical science support a change in the meaning commonly attributed to the terms male and female as they are used in the Florida marriage statutes is a question that raises issues of public policy that should be addressed by the legislature. Thus, the question of whether a postoperative transsexual is authorized to marry a member of their birth sex is a matter for the Florida legislature and not the Florida courts to decide. Until the Florida legislature recognizes sex-reassignment procedures and amends the marriage statutes to clarify the marital rights of a postoperative transsexual person, we must adhere to the common meaning of the statutory terms and invalidate any marriage that is not between persons of the opposite sex determined by their biological sex at birth. Therefore, we hold that the marriage in this case is void ab initio.

Our holding that the marriage is void ab initio does not take into consideration the best interests of the children involved in this case. While we recognize that the trial judge went to great lengths to determine the best interests of the children, the issue of deciding primary residential custody was dependent on the trial court's conclusion that the marriage was valid. We do not attempt to undertake a determination of the legal status of the children resulting from our conclusion that the marriage is void. The legal status of the children and the parties' property rights will be issues for the trial court to examine in the first instance on remand.

Reversed and remanded with directions to grant the counterpetition for annulment declaring the marriage between the parties void ab initio.

■ COVINGTON AND WALLACE, JJ., concur.

NOTE

Advances in medical technology have made sex transfer surgery more widely available, thus precipitating legal issues such those reviewed in the *Kantaras* decision.

The Florida court describes the various approaches taken among the states that have considered the issue, as well as a few foreign judgments. At present, recognition of the validity of the marriage of a transsexual if there is a proper congruence of anatomy and genitalia remains the distinct minority view. See M.T. v. J.T., 140 N.J.Super. 77, 355 A.2d 204 (App. Div.), *cert. denied*, 71 N.J. 345, 364 A.2d 1076. 71 N.J. 345, 364 A.2d 1076 (1976).

While Kantaras addresses the issue of whether a valid marriage occurred, there are concomitant issues than can arise. Depending on the validity of the marriage, persons may qualify for many benefits associated with testate and intestate administration. *See, e.g., In re* Estate of Gardiner, 29 Kan.App.2d 92, 22 P.3d 1086 (2001) (son sought to replace transsexual spouse of father upon father's death, *aff'd in part, rev'd in part*, 273 Kan. 191, 42 P.3d 120 (2002). In Littleton v. Prange, 9 S.W.3d

223 (Tex. App. 1999), a transsexual sought to bring a medical malpractice action as the surviving spouse but the court denied the claim because of the invalidity of the marriage. During the pendency of the action, the plaintiff had obtained a new birth certificate in Texas listing her as a female. The state statutes provide a procedure for amendment of a birth record that is "incomplete or proved by satisfactory evidence to be inaccurate." The court noted that the birth certificate was not binding on it as to the gender of the plaintiff at the time of the marriage.

Some states now have specific provisions for changing birth or other records after an individual has undergone surgery for sex reassignment. *See, e.g.,* CAL HEALTH & SAFETY CODE §§ 103425–103445 (West 2006); LA. REV. STAT. ANN.§ 40:62 (2001); VA. CODE ANN. § 32.1–269(E) (2004). Generally, these statutes do not specifically address whether a person may remarry as a member of the reassigned sex after the surgical procedure. If a court decides the marriage is invalid, the issues of putative spouse or nonmarital contract may arise.

4. EXISTING MARRIAGE

Reynolds v. United States

Supreme Court of the United States, 1878.
98 U.S. 145, 8 Otto 145, 25 L.Ed. 244.

(For the text of the opinion *see* p. 69, *supra*.)

F. WHAT LAW GOVERNS?

In re Marriage of Sumners

Court of Appeals of Missouri, Southern District, Division 2, 1983.
645 S.W.2d 205.

■ HOGAN, JUDGE.

This is an action to dissolve a marriage. By amended answer filed with leave of court, defendant Jerry Lee Sumners challenged the jurisdiction of the court over the subject matter of the action. The trial court heard and determined the matter as provided by Rule 55.27(c). It concluded the parties' marriage was void and dismissed the action. Plaintiff appeals.

The defendant has been married four times. He married Alma, his first wife, by whom he has two children, in Kansas in September 1955. Defendant and Alma were divorced on December 30, 1957, but were remarried in Oklahoma the following month. Defendant and Alma were again divorced in Kansas on September 29, 1961. At some time in 1961, defendant moved from Wichita to Omaha. He married Patricia O'Neil in Nebraska on December 12, 1961. Patricia sued the defendant for divorce in the District

Court of Douglas County, at Omaha, in 1963. On October 18, 1963, that court entered a default decree awarding Patricia an "absolute divorce." The decree concludes: "IT IS FURTHER ORDERED THAT NEITHER PARTY TO THIS DIVORCE MAY REMARRY WITHIN SIX MONTHS OF THE DATE OF THIS DECREE." Defendant testified he received a copy of this decree shortly after it was entered. The record is entirely silent concerning Patricia after the divorce; it may be inferred from the Nebraska decree that she was present when that decree was entered on October 18, 1963.

The defendant began courting the plaintiff in July or early August 1963. The ardor of their courtship increased, and plaintiff became defendant's paramour approximately 1 month after the decree was issued. Plaintiff's knowledge of the terms of the decree was made an issue on trial. We do not regard her appreciation of its effect controlling. It is fairly inferable that she became aware of its content during the early years of the parties' marriage, but we regard the defendant's knowledge of the prohibition against remarriage as superior to hers. Nebraska law would charge defendant with knowledge of the terms of the decree.

Defendant proposed marriage to the plaintiff "[f]ormally with a diamond ring on December 14th of 1963." The parties immediately made plans to be married in Iowa, even though they were residents of Omaha and intended to remain in Nebraska. They finally decided to be married at a church 250 miles east of Omaha. The church is designated the "Little Brown Church in the Vale." Both parties testified the name of the church had romantic appeal. With deference, we think candor was better served by defendant's answer when he was closely cross-examined about the parties' choice of matrimonial forum. Defendant testified that he and the plaintiff had discussed a plan to be married and chose the church in Iowa because "there was a waiting period in the State of Nebraska, and when [plaintiff] come [sic] up pregnant, naturally, she was going to show, and we didn't want her friends and everyone else to know that we had to get married. So, in my own way of thinking, going into the State of Iowa, I thought we [would] legally, to a point, be married, because I knew there was a waiting period in Nebraska." A marriage ceremony was performed at the "Little Brown Church in the Vale," in Chickasaw County, Iowa, on January 31, 1964, a little more than 3 months after defendant's divorce from Patricia.

The parties lived together in Nebraska as husband and wife from the date of their marriage in 1964 until November 15, 1968. In 1968 they moved to Lawrence County, Missouri, and thereafter lived together as husband and wife, except for one period of separation, until they were finally separated on February 23, 1980. Proof of the parties' cohabitation is abundant; they are the natural parents of a son born August 18, 1964, another son born October 4, 1965, a third son born December 22, 1967, and a daughter born December 23, 1974. All these children have attended school in Missouri and have been held out as the parties' children. Since 1965, the parties have filed joint income tax returns as husband and wife; they have acquired several parcels of realty as tenants by the entirety.

[The opinion traces the elaborate course of the litigation, noting that defendant's answer in May 1980 admitted "the existence of a lawful marriage" with plaintiff.]

... On September 16, 1981, the defendant moved to file an amended answer, alleging that when the original answer was filed in May 1980, counsel was unaware of the provisions of Nebraska law but that subsequent research had disclosed that the defendant's Nebraska divorce did not terminate his marital status for 6 months. The amended answer sets up in paragraph 7 that "[t]he parties were never married" because at the time the Iowa ceremony was celebrated, the Nebraska decree had not become final and therefore the Iowa marriage was void. The defendant was permitted to file this amended answer, and a hearing was held to determine the parties' marriage status on November 10, 1981. On November 23, 1981, the cause was dismissed.

... We have recited the procedural facts only to give cast or color to the basic nature of the controversy before the trial court and the appeal before this court. We would carefully note and have it most clearly understood that we suggest no impropriety whatever upon the part of the defendant nor his counsel; the fact of lawful marriage is jurisdictional. We do believe, though we cannot be sure, that the real matter in issue is the same matter presented in most dissolution appeals: The award and distribution of marital assets.

When the validity of a marriage has been assailed in a divorce or other proceeding, our courts have applied a rule of law called a "presumption." At least since 1860, Missouri has consistently adhered to the presumption that a second or subsequent marriage is valid. Sometimes it has been said that the presumption is a "presumption of law." The nature and incidents of the presumption were stated at length by our Supreme Court in Carr v. Carr, 232 S.W.2d 488, 489 (Mo.1950):

> "Defendant, who asserted the invalidity of his marriage to plaintiff, had the burden of proof upon the issue, even though the issue required proof of a negative fact difficult to prove.... And where a valid first marriage has been shown, as in the instant case, it may be presumed that, at the time of the second marriage, the first marriage had been dissolved, either by a decree of divorce, or by the death of the former spouse.... The presumption of the validity of the last marriage may be repelled only by the most cogent and satisfactory evidence...."

.   .   .

The defendant relies, primarily, upon the statutory law of Nebraska. At the time defendant was divorced from Patricia O'Neil, Nebraska law provided that a divorce did not become final or operative until 6 months after trial and decision, R.S. 42–340 (1943), and the Supreme Court of Nebraska quite uniformly held that a decree of divorce rendered in Nebraska did not operate to terminate the marital status for 6 months. His principal argument both here and in the trial court is that because the Nebraska decree did not operate to dissolve the marital status for 6 months and he remarried within the interlocutory period, his marriage to the plaintiff is polygamous and void.

The hiatus in the defendant's argument and in his proof is that neither the trial court nor this court has been presented with any evidence tending to show what became of Patricia O'Neil after the decree was rendered. The Nebraska decree recites that Patricia appeared in court on October 18, 1963, and we suppose this recital may be taken as proof she was alive at that time. Nonetheless, plaintiff and defendant were not married until January 31, 1964. The defendant argues that when a person is shown to be alive at a given time the law presumes that he remains alive until the contrary is shown, or, in the absence of proof, a different presumption arises. Such is indeed the law of this state. However, it has been held by our courts and others that when the presumption of the validity of a marriage conflicts with the presumption of the continuance of life, and there are no circumstances in evidence to aid the presumption of continued life, the presumption of validity of the marriage is stronger and will prevail. In this case, there is no evidence to aid the presumption of continued life; there is no basis for any inference that when she and defendant finally separated, Patricia was in robust health; there is, indeed, no basis for any factual conclusion other than that Patricia was alive on October 18, 1963. The defendant has failed to sustain his burden to show that he had a wife living when he married the plaintiff.

Neither would it be decisive if, upon remand, defendant were able to adduce proof that Patricia O'Neil was seen alive and healthy after he married the plaintiff. What the defendant actually relies on, in this case, is not the invalidity of his marriage, but the ineffectiveness of his divorce. Such position is taken after defendant has cohabited with plaintiff as his wife for 16 years, with one period of separation, has sired four children by the plaintiff and has judicially admitted, though not conclusively, that the plaintiff is his lawful wife. It is generally recognized that a person may be precluded from attacking the validity of a foreign divorce decree if, under the circumstances it would be inequitable for him to do so.[1] The position of the American Law Institute is that:

> "... In general, it may be said that a person who obtains a divorce and then remarries will not be permitted to attack the validity of the divorce in order to free himself from his obligations to his second spouse or in order to claim an inheritance from the estate of the first spouse...." Restatement (Second) of Conflicts of Laws § 74, Comment b.

In Missouri, this rule of preclusion or estoppel has been applied to prevent one spouse from claiming an inheritance or interest in the estate of a deceased spouse. See, e.g., Crane v. Deacon, 253 S.W. 1068, 1072–1073[10] (Mo.1923) (husband sought to prove his divorce collusive in order

---

1. See, generally, Restatement (Second) of Conflict of Laws § 74 (1971); R. Leflar, American Conflicts Law § 226 (1977) [hereinafter Leflar]; H. Clark, Estoppel Against Jurisdictional Attack on Decrees of Divorce, 70 Yale L.J. 45 (1960).

to claim share of deceased wife's estate); Buffington v. Carty, 195 Mo. 490, 499, 93 S.W. 779, 780 (1906) (lapse of time prevented equitable claim to an interest in the property of former wife from whom plaintiff was invalidly divorced).... Perhaps the most straightforward application of the principle of law we have in mind was made in Littlefield v. Littlefield, 199 Mo.App. 456, 203 S.W. 636 (1918). There the court held that remarriage, perhaps with knowledge that her divorce was invalid, precluded the plaintiff from asserting a claim in her former husband's property.

We are not particularly concerned, however, with establishing that our courts have, in the past, called the preclusion an "estoppel." What we have in mind is the principle that "the person who produced the misleading situation cannot, as against persons who may (or may not) have thought the divorce to be valid, set up its invalidity when later that invalidity seems advantageous to him." Leflar, supra, § 226, p. 461. This statement comports with the Restatement view that the rule of preclusion applies when, under the circumstances, it would be inequitable to permit a particular person to challenge the validity of a divorce decree. Restatement (Second) of Conflict of Laws § 74, Comment b.

This notion of preclusion, or estoppel, or quasi-estoppel to which the quoted authorities speak was elucidated in Spellens v. Spellens, 49 Cal.2d 210, 317 P.2d 613 (1957). The facts are somewhat different from those presented here, but there is some similarity in that the parties had entered into a marriage of questionable validity after the wife obtained an interlocutory decree which did not dissolve the wife's former marital status. The court stated, in the course of its opinion, 317 P.2d at 618–619:

> "... The theory is that the marriage is not made valid by reason of the estoppel but that the estopped person may not take a position that the divorce or latter marriage was invalid.... 'To hold otherwise protects neither the welfare nor morals of society but, on the contrary, such holding [would be] a flagrant invitation to others to attempt to circumvent the law, cohabit in unlawful state, and when tired of such situation, apply to the courts for a release from the indicia of the marriage status' ... [and] [f]rom a pragmatic viewpoint, judicial invalidation of irregular foreign divorces and attendant remarriages ... is a [wholly ineffective] sanction against an institution whose charm lies in its immediate respectability...."

This "estoppel" doctrine has been applied in many jurisdictions in widely variant factual situations. While such an approach to the merits of this appeal would be less satisfactory than resolution upon the principle that the presumption of validity has not been dispelled, it has the virtue of consonance with established constitutional and conflict of laws principles. It has been held, and we believe, that U.S. Const. Art. IV, § 1 and its implementing legislation, 28 U.S.C.A. § 1738, compel us to recognize foreign divorce decrees as they relate to the marital status, Urbanek v. Urbanek, 503 S.W.2d 434, 439[2] (Mo.App.1973), and as we tried in wholly inappropriate language and with minimal success to explain in Marriage of Bradford, 557 S.W.2d 720, 726–727[9] (Mo.App.1977), 28 U.S.C.A. § 1738 requires us to give a foreign divorce decree that effect upon the marital status which it would have in the state where the decree was rendered. The preclusion rule of the Restatement does no violence to this requirement. A judgment by estoppel does not validate a void marriage contracted before an interlocutory decree has dissolved the marital status; it only estops a party or the parties from attacking the validity of the foreign decree if it would be inequitable for him—or them—to do so.

Moreover, in this case, the application of orthodox principles of conflict of laws leads us to the same conclusion we have reached by applying the presumption that the marriage was valid. The validity of the marriage in the first instance must be determined by looking to the law of the state where it was contracted. If we assume that Iowa would not recognize the marriage because the Nebraska decree had not terminated defendant's marital status, ordinary principles of choice of law would require us to look to Iowa's rules of conflict of laws. Robert Leflar, supra, § 220, p. 445, n. 3. When we do so, we find that Iowa clearly holds it is the law of the forum which determines whether a party is estopped to attack the validity of a foreign divorce decree. In re Marriage of Winegard, 278 N.W.2d 505, 509–510[4][5] (Iowa 1979), cert. denied sub nom. Winegard v. Gilvin, 444 U.S. 951, 100 S.Ct. 425, 62 L.Ed.2d 321 (1979); ... The parties are domiciled here, and this court would hold the defendant estopped to deny the efficiency of the Nebraska decree even if it were shown that Patricia was alive and well when the parties were married in Iowa.

As the record lies before us, we hold the defendant failed to rebut the presumption that the parties' marriage was valid. The trial court erroneously applied the law to the facts, the judgment of dismissal is reversed and the trial court is directed to reinstate the cause on its docket.

THE LEGACY OF ENOCH ARDEN

The social and legal problems created by the return of a lost or missing spouse have long been of concern. Our laws that attempt to deal with them in the context of remarriage have been broadly dubbed "Enoch Arden Laws" after the seaman in Tennyson's poem. But unlike that character, who chose not to disturb the new relationships created during his absence, one who returns in today's litigious world more often is prepared to go to court to get the legal problems sorted out. Some of the legislative responses did no more than provide a safeguard against bigamy prosecution against one spouse who had remarried in good faith belief of the other's death. This, of course, would not clear up the possibility that the second marriage was void, and the presumption of its validity might be overcome by proving that neither party had obtained a dissolution. Other statutes provided a means for dissolving the first marriage through judicial action. Some states did not label such a procedure "divorce". (New York, for example, called it "Dissolution of marriage on ground of absence" and thus long maintained its assertion that adultery was its only divorce ground.) Failure to comply with the statutory requirements could lead to litigation in which allegations of estoppel and "unclean hands" would be traded. The Pennsylvania statute that follows is an example of a provision that grants a degree of judicial discretion and can permit remarriage without having to wait for passage of an arbitrary time period.

23 PENNSYLVANIA CONS. STAT. ANN. (West 2001)

§ 1701. Decree that spouse of applicant is presumed decedent

(a) Finding of death.—When the spouse of an applicant for a marriage license has disappeared or is absent from the place of residence of the spouse without being heard of after diligent inquiry, the court, aided by the report of a master if necessary, upon petition of the applicant for a marriage license, may make a finding and decree that the absentee is dead and the date of death if notice to the absentee has been given as provided in subsection (d) and either of the applicants is and for one year or more prior to the application has been a resident of this Commonwealth.

(b) Presumption from absence.—When the death of the spouse of an applicant for a marriage license is in issue, the unexplained absence from the last known place of residence and the fact that the absentee has been unheard of for seven years may be sufficient ground for finding that the absentee died seven years after the absentee was last heard from.

(c) Exposure to specific peril.—The fact that an absentee spouse was exposed to a specific peril of death may be a sufficient ground for finding that the absentee died less than seven years after the absentee was last heard from.

(d) Notice to absentee—The court may require advertisement in an newspapers as the court, according to the circumstances of the case, deems advisable. . . .

(e) Remarriage after decree of presumed death.—Even though the absentee spouse declared to be presumed dead is in fact alive, the remarriage of the spouse who has obtained a license to marry and a decree of presumed death of the former spouse shall be valid for all purposes as though the former marriage had been terminated by divorce, and all property of the presumed decedent shall be administered and disposed of as provided by Title 20 (relating to decedents, estates and fiduciaries).

§ 1702. Marriage during existence of former marriage

(a) General rule.—If a married person, during the lifetime of the other person with whom the marriage is in force, enters into a subsequent marriage pursuant to the requirements of this part and the parties to the marriage live together thereafter as husband and wife, and the subsequent marriage was entered into by one or both of the parties in good faith in the full belief that the former spouse was dead or that the former marriage has been annulled or terminated by a divorce, or without knowledge of the former marriage, they shall, after the impediment to their marriage has been removed by the death of the other party to the former marriage or by annulment or divorce, if they continue to live together as husband and wife in good faith on the part of one of them, be held to have been legally married from and immediately after the date of death or the date of the decree of annulment or divorce.

. . .

(b) False rumor of death of spouse.—Where a remarriage has occurred upon false rumor of the death of a former spouse in appearance well-founded but there has been no decree of presumed death, the remarriage shall be void and subject to annulment by either party to the remarriage as provided by section 3304 (relating to grounds for annulment of void marriages), and the returning spouse shall have cause for divorce as provided in section 3301 (relating to grounds for divorce).

(c) Criminal penalties.—Where the remarriage was entered into in good faith, neither party to the remarriage shall be subject to criminal prosecution for bigamy.

NOTE

§ 1703 of the Pennsylvania statute provides that after the death of either party, no inquiry will be made into the validity of a marriage because of consangunity.

RESTATEMENT (2d) OF CONFLICT OF LAWS

§ 6. Choice of Law Principles

(1) A court, subject to constitutional restrictions, will follow a statutory directive of its own state on choice of law.

(2) When there is no such directive, the factors relevant to the choice of the applicable rule of law include

(a) the needs of the interstate and international systems,

(b) the relevant policies of the forum,

(c) the relevant policies of other interested states and the relative interests of those states in the determination of the particular issue,

(d) the protection of justified expectations,

(e) the basic policies underlying the particular field of law,

(f) certainty, predictability and uniformity of result, and

(g) ease in the determination and application of the law to be applied.

§ 283. Validity of Marriage

(1) The validity of a marriage will be determined by the local law of the state which, with respect to the particular issue, has the most significant relationship to the spouses and the marriage under the principles stated in § 6.

(2) A marriage which satisfies the requirements of the state where the marriage was contracted will everywhere be recognized as valid unless it violates the strong public policy of another state which has the most significant relationship to the spouses and the marriage.

Comment on Subsection (1):

. . .

c. *Purpose of rule.* The interest of a state in having one of its marriage rules applied will depend upon the purpose sought to be achieved by that rule and upon the relation of the state to the marriage and to the parties. So the state where the spouses were domiciled before the marriage and where they made their home immediately thereafter has an obvious interest in the application of a rule forbidding the marriage of persons within certain degrees of relationship. On the other hand, such a state may have little interest in the application to an out-of-state marriage of a rule regulating the form in which a marriage should be celebrated. By way of contrast, the state where the marriage was celebrated may have a real interest in the application to non-residents of a rule regulating the form that a marriage ceremony should take and little interest in the application of a rule directed to incestuous marriages.

Comment on Subsection (2):

. . .

f. *Formalities.* The state where the marriage was celebrated, or, in the case of a common law marriage, the state where the parties cohabited while holding themselves out to be man and wife, is the state which will usually be primarily concerned with the question of formalities. These include such matters as:

1. the necessity of a license;
2. the necessity of a formal ceremony;
3. the person to perform the ceremony;
4. the manner of the performance of the ceremony.

If the requirements of this state have been complied with, the marriage will not be held invalid in other states for lack of necessary formalities except in the unusual situation where such a result is required by the strong policy of another state which has the most significant relationship to the spouses and the marriage.

g. *"Common law" marriage.* Whether a marriage can be created without formal ceremony is a question relating to formalities. If the acts relied upon to create the marriage meet the requirements of the state where the acts took place, the marriage will not be held invalid for lack of the necessary formalities except in the unusual circumstances stated in Comment *f.* A marriage without ceremony is commonly called a common law marriage.

h.   Validity in respects other than formalities. The interest of the state where the marriage was contracted relates primarily to the question whether there has been compliance with the formalities prescribed by its local law. Other considerations lead to the upholding of the validity of a marriage which meets the requirements of this state in other respects. The validity of a marriage is of utmost concern to the parties and their children; so the choice of the applicable law should be simple and easy in application and should point to the law most likely to have been consulted by the parties. Furthermore, there is a strong inclination to uphold a marriage because of the hardship that might otherwise be visited upon the parties and their children. Finally, differences among the marriage laws of various states usually involve only minor matters of debatable policy rather than fundamentals. All of these factors together support the general rule that a marriage which meets the requirements of the state where the marriage was contracted will be held valid everywhere. So, for example, a marriage will usually be valid everywhere if it complies with the requirements of the state where it was contracted as to such matters as:

1.   the capacity of either party to marry;

2.   whether the consent of a parent or guardian is necessary;

3.   whether the parties are within one of the forbidden degrees of relationship;

4.   physical examination before marriage.

i.   Marriage which does not meet the requirements of the state where it was contracted. Upholding the validity of a marriage is . . . a basic policy in all states. The fact that a marriage does not comply with the requirements of the state where it was contracted should not therefore inevitably lead to the conclusion that the marriage is invalid. To begin with, the requirement that was not satisfied may not be mandatory, at least in the case of a marriage between nonresidents, in the state where the marriage was contracted with the result that the marriage would be valid even under the local conceptions of that state. But even if the requirement is a mandatory one, the marriage should not necessarily be held invalid in other states provided that it would be valid under the local law of some other state having a substantial relation to the parties and the marriage. The marriage should not be held invalid in such a case unless the intensity of the interest of the state where the marriage was contracted in having its invalidating rule applied outweighs the policy of protecting the expectations of the parties by upholding the marriage and the interest of the other state with the validating rule in having this rule applied.

The state where the marriage was contracted has a substantial interest in having persons who marry within its territory comply with its local requirements as to formalities at least to the extent that these requirements are mandatory. As to such mandatory requirements, the state where the marriage was contracted may well be the state of dominant interest and, if so, there is good reason for its invalidating rule to be applied.

The state where the marriage was contracted will probably have no similar interest in the application to a marriage between nonresidents of such of its marriage rules as do not relate to formalities. So, for example, there would seem to be little reason to invalidate a marriage between first cousins by application of a rule of the state where the marriage was contracted if such a marriage would be valid under the local law of the state where the parties were domiciled both before and immediately following their marriage. Upholding the validity of the marriage in such a case by application of the validating rule of the state of domicil would seem required by the fact that the latter state has the dominant interest in the issue to be decided and by the choice-of-law policy which favors protection of the justified expectations of the parties by upholding the marriage.

. . .

§ 284. Incidents of Foreign Marriage

A state usually gives the same incidents to a foreign marriage which is valid under the principles stated in § 283, that it gives to a marriage contracted within its territory.

Comment: . . .

c. When giving of incident would be contrary to strong policy of state. A state will not give a particular incident to a foreign marriage when to do so would be contrary to its strong local policy. The state will not do so even though the marriage was valid in the state where it was contracted and even though the incident in question would be granted in that state. A denial of a particular incident on the grounds stated in this Comment does not deny the validity of the marriage.

The mere fact that the marriage itself would have been invalid if contracted in the state is not a sufficient ground for the denial of a particular incident. An incident should not be denied except when such denial is required by a strong policy of the state.

A state may deny one incident to a foreign marriage and at the same time allow the marriage other incidents. So a state may prohibit the parties to a polygamous marriage from cohabiting within its territory. Yet it may recognize the legitimacy of the children of such a marriage and the economic interests of the spouses, such as a right to support on the part of one spouse against the other and the marital property interests or forced share, or intestate share, of one spouse in the local assets of the other. Again, a state may not permit a wife to acquire her husband's nationality, and yet may permit the spouses to cohabit within its territory and enjoy normal economic interests in each other's property.

NOTE

The RESTATEMENT OF CONFLICTS (2D) and its approach to choice of law in marriage are sensitively appraised in Hans Baade, *Marriage and Divorce in American Conflicts Law: Governmental–Interests Analysis and the Restatement (Second)*, 72 COLUM.L.REV. 329 (1972). For further discussion of marriage conflicts law, past and present (with some suggestions for the future), see David Engdahl, *Proposal for a Benign Revolution in Marriage Law and Marriage Conflicts Law,* 55 Iowa L.Rev. 56 (1969).

CALIFORNIA FAMILY CODE (West 2004)

§ 308.   Foreign marriages; validity

A marriage contracted outside this state that would be valid by the laws of the jurisdiction in which the marriage was contracted is valid in this state.

NOTE

Determining what law should govern in determining validity of a marriage between first cousins was a key concern in In re Estate of Levie, 50 Cal.App.3d 572, 123 Cal.Rptr. 445 (1975), involving the precursor of the Code article above, Cal.Civ.Code § 4104. The parties were residents of California who went through a marriage ceremony in Nevada that satisfied procedural requirements there. One of the parties died intestate in California approximately a year later after they had held themselves out as husband and wife in the good faith belief that they were married. In determining the validity of the marriage, and thus respondent's eligibility as a surviving spouse entitled to priority, the Court of Appeal held:

> Decedent and respondent, as first cousins, could lawfully have been married in California.... But it is conceded by respondent that the marriage ceremony performed in Nevada was invalid in that state because of the parties' consanguinity....

> Appellant contends, citing Civil Code section 4104, that because the attempted marriage was void in Nevada, the state where contracted, it is void in California. It is true that the statute (and a predecessor enactment, former Civil Code section 63) do not speak expressly of the invalidity in California of a marriage which was void where performed. But the statute by implication adopts the common law rule that "the law of the place of marriage controls the question of its validity." (Colbert v. Colbert (1946) 28 Cal.2d 276, 280, 169 P.2d 633, 635; ...)

> Citing Hurtado v. Superior Court (1974) 11 Cal.3d 574, 114 Cal.Rptr. 106, 522 P.2d 666, respondent presents a choice-of-law analysis in support of an argument that because the parties were eligible to marry in California their attempted marriage should be treated as valid in California judicial proceedings. But Civil Code section 4104 is a legislative direction governing the choice of law. Under the stipulated facts it must be concluded that the invalid Nevada marriage is not to be treated as valid in California.

Singh v. Singh

Supreme Court of Connecticut, 1990.
213 Conn. 637, 569 A.2d 1112.

(The text of the opinion appears at p. 275, *supra.*)

NOTE

Uniform Marriage Evasion Act. In 1912 the UNIFORM MARRIAGE EVASION ACT was approved by the National Conference of Commissioners on Uniform State Laws. It provided that:

1. If any person residing and intending to continue to reside in this state who is disabled or prohibited from contracting marriage under the laws of this state shall go into another state or country and there contract a marriage prohibited and declared void by the laws of this state, such marriage shall be null and void for all purposes in this state with the same effect as though such prohibited marriage had been entered into in this state.

2. No marriage shall be contracted in this state by a party residing and intending to continue to reside in another state or jurisdiction if such marriage would be void if contracted in such other state or jurisdiction, and every marriage celebrated in this state in violation of this provision shall be null and void.

. . .

The act was adopted (sometimes in modified form) by only five states. In 1943 it was withdrawn. HANDBOOK OF THE NATIONAL CONFERENCE OF COMMISSIONERS ON UNIFORM STATE LAWS 64 (1943). Some states still have specific "evasion" statutes. Such a provision was involved in Loving v. Virginia, *supra* at p. 153.

CHAPTER III

HUSBAND AND WIFE: CHANGING ROLES, RIGHTS AND DUTIES

A. TWO PERSONS, NOT ONE

Our law long imposed substantial disabilities on women. Some of these may be traced to the necessities of military organization, to which so much of the social structure in the early feudal period was subservient. Others can be accounted for only by reference to scriptural texts that allotted women a subordinate position in the scheme of human affairs. From the very beginning English law drew a distinction between the single woman (feme sole) and the married woman (feme covert) with respect to their capacities and what was called their "abilities". The feme sole was conceded a legal capacity a little less than that of a male (she was excluded from public functions) but in the exercise of private rights she was almost completely competent. The feme covert not only had greatly reduced legal capacity, but her abilities—her competence to transact in the sphere of private law, were almost totally suspended during coverture. In one of the earliest sources of English law it is explained that the married woman is *sub virga*—under the rod of her husband—attributing to him an authority and power of command that lingered in the criminal law of this century and retained a qualified recognition in statutes that proclaimed the husband to be the head of the family. But the most important result of this ancient conception was the control that the husband was permitted to assume over the wife's realty. If the wife at time of marriage was seised of an estate of inheritance in land, the husband, upon the marriage, became seised of the freehold *jure uxoris*, and took the rents and profits during their joint lives. If the wife at the time of marriage had an estate for life or for the life of another, the husband became seised of such estate in the right of his wife and was entitled to profits. To these rights the courts eventually applied theories of guardianship and devised means to prevent alienation without the wife's consent. Personal property that the wife had possessed in her own right vested immediately and absolutely in the husband.

The correlative duties upon the husband were: (1) he was liable for his wife's prenuptial debts and torts, although he was discharged if there was no recovery for these during coverture; and (2) he was liable to maintain his wife, but this was limited to necessaries suitable to the couple's station in life. If the wife incurred debts for such necessaries the husband was obliged to pay the debts, at first only if agency or ratification could be established, but eventually on the theory that such purchases were made for his use.

The status of the married woman was affected even more profoundly through the law's absorption of the biblical concept that upon marriage man and woman became one flesh.[1] In the hands of the temporal courts this notion was translated into the proposition that man and wife are one person—a notion hardly consistent with the theory of guardianship and the wife's situation of being *sub potestate*, a patent recognition of the individual identities of the spouses. Nevertheless, a variety of rules came to be justified on the "one person" theory. Some of the oldest of these rules related to the matter of rank or condition; for example, a bondwoman marrying a freeman acquired freedom during coverture. In the case of feoffments to husband and wife they did not take by moieties, but both were seised by the entireties. Similarly, the incapacity of husband and wife to contract with each other was explained on the theory that they were but one person in the law.[2]

It was not feasible to introduce the "one person" theory into the field of procedure. The solutions found in respect of real actions reflect the substantive law; that is to say, although the wife's capacities were in suspense, she possessed nevertheless an ultimate proprietary right. Consequently, action for the recovery of land was given to husband and wife and neither could sue without the other. Conversely, it was against husband and wife that action must be brought to recover land that was held in the right of the wife. With the development of delictual actions another set of circumstances forced the recognition of the wife's identity. From time immemorial the married woman had been deemed capable of committing wrongs. In respect of crimes she was almost completely *sui juris*. Consequently, when tort actions developed the law was not prepared to acquit her of delictual liability. To provide an adequate remedy against one whom law and custom had made judgment proof, it was early established that the action must lie against husband and wife. The former might answer alone, but the converse was not true. In the course of time the notion of the wife's subjection to her husband caused some alteration in older conceptions of liability through acceptance of a presumption that tortious acts of a feme covert were done at the coercion or instigation of the husband. But the manner of bringing an action remained the same.

The rules about joinder also applied in cases of torts done to the wife's person, though where the action was founded on the special damage done to the husband he alone could bring the action. Classical examples of the latter are alienation of affections, enticement and criminal conversation, all of which were originally founded on an interference with a property right.

The rigors of the complex of rules respecting the feme covert that developed at common law were eventually mollified in certain particulars through the elaboration of various expedients that the Court of Chancery

---

1. Genesis 2:24; Matthew 19:5,6; Mark 10:8.

2. See Williams, *The Legal Unity of Husband and Wife*, 10 Mod.L.Rev. 16 (1947).

took under its protective wing. These related to matters of property and were possible only because of the trust device. The intervention of Chancery was based not so much upon a fixed design of extending the married woman's rights as upon a policy of enabling a person (usually a father) who gave or settled property on a woman even though she was married, to insure she would have it as her own and be able to deal with it independently of her husband. The prudent settlor would convey the property to a trustee, in whom legal title was vested, to hold for the benefit of the woman in accordance with the terms of the trust, upon which her actual powers of disposition also depended. Chancery by degrees worked out the idea that a trustee must deal with the property in accordance with her directions. Eventually it also became settled that it was not necessary that property be vested in trustees, but if it be given or devised to a feme covert for her separate use the husband would be held to be trustee for her. In the latter half of the eighteenth century, a further safeguard against overreaching by the husband was perfected by means of the clause introduced into wills and settlements known as the restraint on anticipation, whereby the married woman could neither alienate her property nor charge it with her debts.[3]

The equitable separate estate of married women was introduced into America during the colonial period and after the Revolution there was wholesale reception of the English rules. But this institution was predicated upon the possession in the settlor or testator of a respectable corpus of property and consequently was less adapted to the needs of a democratic society than it had been to the order of things in England. The social ferment that characterized the first half of the 19th century in America exemplified by extension of political democracy, anti-slavery agitation, the "rise of the common man", the beginnings of organized labor, the movement for agrarian reform and expansion of public education, inevitably swept in its wake the emancipation of married women. Abetted by sympathetic males and able and articulate female reformers, a relatively brief period of polemics and propaganda resulted in the initial married woman's property statute in the state of Mississippi (1839). This act was permissive, but in Maine, the first northern state to pass such legislation (1844), the statute was mandatory. The objective of the reformers was that all property a woman should bring to her marriage and any she might thereafter acquire should be her sole and separate property, not subject to the disposal or control of the husband. Early statutes in some states, such as Massachusetts, fell short of this, but as the movement gained momentum over a period of some forty years the substance of the program was achieved. The property acts were succeeded by statutes or judicial decisions lifting procedural disabilities, then by acts making explicit the wife's power to contract (in some states exclusive of her husband), permitting direct conveyances of land between spouses, and eventually the bestowal of a right of action for injury even as against her husband.

3. This was abolished by § 1, Married Women (Restraint upon Anticipation) Act, 1949, 12, 13 & 14 Geo. 6 c. 78.

Although a federal Equal Rights Amendment to the Constitution was not ratified, legislative and judicial action continues. Increased application of the equal protection clause of the Fourteenth Amendment to sex-based discrimination cases, statutes dealing with sex based discrimination in employment and credit transactions, and "Equal Rights" provisions in revised state constitutions, are having significant impact. These achievements reflect a combination of changing social attitudes as well as activism by women's groups. Although there are differing views among the latter about appropriate methods of approach to abolish discrimination, there are common basic goals such as ending wage, employment, and other discrimination based on sex; sharing of child raising and housekeeping roles and providing adequate participation in the financial fortunes of the family based on contributions other than wage earning; erasing stereotypes that depict woman as an ornament, an instrument for gratification of male sex desires, or a breeding machine; and securing greater personal autonomy for women within and without marriage. Two challenging studies that examine modern movements toward family "reform" in historical perspective and offer frameworks for future approaches to the structure of the family, are Frances E. Olsen, *The Family and the Market*, 96 HARV.L.REV. 1497 (1983), and Mary Ann Glendon, THE NEW FAMILY AND THE NEW PROPERTY (1981). For a sensitive appraisal of family law in the second half of the 20th century, *see* Michael Grossberg, *How to Give the Present a Past? Family Law in the United States 1950–2000*, Chapter 1 in CROSS CURRENTS: FAMILY LAW AND POLICY IN THE UNITED STATES AND ENGLAND (2001).

B.   NAMES IN THE FAMILY
1.   A MARRIED WOMAN'S NAME

Stuart v. Board of Supervisors of Elections

Court of Appeals of Maryland, 1972.
266 Md. 440, 295 A.2d 223.

■ MURPHY, CHIEF JUDGE. Mary Emily Stuart and Samuel H. Austell, Jr., were married in Virginia on November 13, 1971 and shortly thereafter, took up residence in Columbia, Howard County, Maryland. In accordance with the couple's oral antenuptial agreement, Stuart continued, after the marriage, to use and be exclusively known by her birth given ("maiden") name and not by the legal surname of her husband.

On March 2, 1972, Stuart undertook to register to vote in Howard County in her birth given name. After disclosing to the registrar that she was married to Austell but had consistently and nonfraudulently used her maiden name, she was registered to vote in the name of Mary Emily Stuart.

On March 16, 1972 the Board of Supervisors of Elections for Howard County notified Stuart by letter that since under Maryland law "a woman's legal surname becomes that of her husband upon marriage," she was required by Maryland Code, Article 33, § 3–18(c) to complete a "Request for Change of Name" form or her registration would be cancelled. Stuart did not complete the form and her registration was cancelled on April 4, 1972.

Stuart promptly challenged the Board's action.... [S]he maintained that she was properly registered to vote in her birth given name, that being her true and correct name; that under the English common law, in force in Maryland, a wife could assume the husband's name if she desired, or retain her own name, or be known by any other name she wished, so long as the name she used was not retained for a fraudulent purpose; and that since the only name she ever used was Mary Emily Stuart the Board had no right to cancel her voter registration listed in that name.

... Evidence was adduced showing that the oral antenuptial agreement between Stuart and Austell that she would retain her maiden name was a matter of great importance to both parties. Stuart testified that her marriage to Austell was "based on the idea that we're both equal individuals and our names symbolize that." ...

There was evidence showing that the practice of the Board requiring a married woman to use the surname of her husband dated back to 1936; that the practice was a uniform one throughout the State and was adopted to provide some trail of identification to prevent voter fraud; that if a married woman could register under different names the identification trail would be lost; and that the only exception permitted to the requirement that married women register under their husbands' surnames was if the name was changed by court order.

By opinion filed May 10, 1972, Judge Mayfield concluded "that a person may adopt and use any name chosen in the absence of fraudulent intent or purpose"; that the use by Stuart of her maiden name was without fraudulent intent or purpose; that it is the law of Maryland that "the use by the wife of the husband's surname following marriage, while the same have been initially based upon custom and usage, is now based on the common law of England, which law has been duly adopted as the law of this State"; that under the provisions of the Code, Article 33, § 3–18(a)(3) clerks of courts, as therein designated, are required to notify Boards of Supervisors of Elections of the "present names" of females over the age of eighteen years residing within the State "whose names have been changed by marriage"; that by subsection (c) of § 3–18, the Boards, upon being advised of a "change of name by marriage," are required to give notification "that such ... change of name by marriage ... has been reported to the board, and shall require the voter to show cause within two weeks ... why his registration should not be cancelled"; that § 3–18 appeared "to be in conformity with the common law," as espoused in such cases as People ex rel. Rago v. Lipsky, 327 Ill.App. 63, 63 N.E.2d 642 (1945) and Forbush v. Wallace, 341 F.Supp. 217 (M.D.Ala.1971), aff'd per curiam 405 U.S. 970, 92 S.Ct. 1197, 31 L.Ed.2d 246 (1972);* that the "statutory requirements [of

---

* The three-judge District Court in *For-bush* *upheld the constitutionality of Ala-* *bama's regulation requiring a married woman to use her husband's surname in*

§ 3–18] are in accordance with the law which says that upon marriage the wife takes the surname of her husband"; that the provisions of § 3–18 do not deprive Stuart of her right to use her maiden name, nor of her right to vote, but require only that she "register to vote under her 'legal' name, . . . based upon the broad general principle of the necessity for proper record keeping and the proper and most expedient way of identifying the person who desires to vote."[1]

From the court's order denying her petitions to correct the voter registry and to restore her name thereto, Stuart has appealed. She claims on appeal, as she did below, that a woman's surname upon marriage does not become that of her husband by operation of the common law in force in Maryland and that nothing in the provisions of § 3–18(a)(3) and (c) mandates a contrary result.

What constitutes the correct legal name of a married woman under common law principles is a question which has occasioned a sharp split of authorities, crystallized in the conflicting cases of State ex rel. Krupa v. Green, 114 Ohio App. 497, 177 N.E.2d 616 (1961), relied upon by Stuart, and People ex rel. Rago v. Lipsky, supra, adopted by the lower court as its principal authority for denying the petitions. *Green* approved the voter registration of a married woman in her birth given name which she had openly, notoriously and exclusively used subsequent to her marriage, and held that she could use that name as a candidate for public office. The court held:

> "It is only *by custom*, in English speaking countries, that a woman, upon marriage, adopts the surname of her husband in place of the surname of her father." Id. 177 N.E.2d at 619 (Emphasis in original.)

Lipsky refused to allow a married woman to remain registered to vote under her birth given name on the basis of

> ". . . the long-established custom, policy and rule of the common law among English-speaking peoples whereby a woman's name is changed

---

obtaining a driver's license. The Supreme Court's affirmance was without opinion and was based upon Alabama common law.— EDITORS' NOTE.

1. In pertinent part, § 3–18(a)(3) and (c) provides:

"(a) *Reports to be made by certain public agencies.* Reports to the board shall be made by the several officials in Baltimore City at least once each month, and in the several counties, by the last days of January and July in each year, as follows:

. . .

"(3) The clerk of the Court of Common Pleas in Baltimore City and the clerk of the circuit court for each county shall file with said respective boards the former and present names of all female residents of said city or county, as the case may be, over the age of twenty-one years, whose names have been changed by marriage since the date of the last such report.

. . .

"(c) *Notification to show cause before cancellation.* Whenever the . . . change of name by marriage . . . is reported as above provided, the board shall cause to be mailed to the address of such voter . . . a notification that such . . . change of name by marriage . . . has been reported to the board, and shall require the voter to show cause within two weeks . . . why his registration should not be cancelled. . . ."

by marriage and her husband's surname becomes *as a matter of law* her surname." Id. 63 N.E.2d at 645 (Emphasis supplied.) . . .

We think the lower court was wrong in concluding that the principles enunciated in *Lipsky* represent the law of Maryland. We have heretofore unequivocally recognized the common law right of any person, absent a statute to the contrary, to "adopt any name by which he may become known, and by which he may transact business and execute contracts and sue or be sued." Romans v. State, 178 Md. 588, 597, 16 A.2d 642, 646. In the context of the name used in an automobile liability insurance contract, we approved the consistent nonfraudulent use by a married woman of a surname other than that of her lawful husband in Erie Insurance Exchange v. Lane, 246 Md. 55, 227 A.2d 231. Citing with approval Everett v. Standard Acc. Ins. Co., 45 Cal.App. 332, 187 P. 996 (1919), we summarized its holding as follows:

> "The court . . . held that because the insured had been known as Everett for twenty-two years before the policy was issued, a representation that his name was Everett was not a misrepresentation, although his name before had been Cowie, since a man may lawfully change his name without resorting to legal proceedings and by general usage or habit acquire another." *Erie,* 246 Md. at 62–63, 227 A.2d at 236.

If a married woman may lawfully adopt an assumed name (which, in *Erie,* was neither her birth given name nor the name of her lawful husband) without legal proceedings, then we think Maryland law manifestly permits a married woman to retain her birth given name by the same procedure of consistent, nonfraudulent use following her marriage. In so concluding, we note that there is no statutory requirement in the Code, . . . that a married woman adopt her husband's surname. Consistent with the common law principle referred to in the Maryland cases, we hold that a married woman's surname does not become that of her husband where, as here, she evidences a clear intent to consistently and nonfraudulently use her birth given name subsequent to her marriage. Thus, while under *Romans*, a married woman may choose to adopt the surname of her husband—this being the long-standing custom and tradition which has resulted in the vast majority of married women adopting their husbands' surnames as their own—the mere fact of the marriage does not, as a matter of law, operate to establish the custom and tradition of the majority as a rule of law binding upon all.

. . . [W]e believe the rule we enunciate today is founded upon the English common law incorporated into the laws of Maryland by Article 5 of the Maryland Declaration of Rights. The question of English common law was considered by the Ohio Court of Appeals in State ex rel. Krupa v. Green, supra, 177 N.E.2d at 619:

> "In England, from which came our customs with respect to names, a woman is permitted to retain her maiden surname upon marriage if she so desires.

"M. Turner–Samuels, in his book on 'The Law of Married Women' at page 345, states:

> "In England, custom has long since ordained that a married woman takes her husband's name. This practice is not invariable; not compellable by law. . . . A wife may continue to use her maiden, married, or any other name she wishes to be known by. . . ."

. . .

Under the common law of Maryland, as derived from the common law of England, Mary Emily Stuart's surname thus has not been changed by operation of law to that of Austell solely by reason of her marriage to him. On the contrary, because of her exclusive, consistent, nonfraudulent use of her maiden name, she is entitled to use the name Mary Emily Stuart unless there is a statute to the contrary. . . .

Nothing in the language of § 3–18(a)(3) or (c) purports to compel *all* married women to register to vote in their husbands' surname. Since Mary Emily Stuart did not undergo a "change of name by marriage," this Section merely requires her to show cause to the Board that she consistently and nonfraudulently used her birth given name rather than her husband's surname following marriage.

In light of our disposition of the common law issue, we find it unnecessary to reach the constitutional issues raised by the appeal.

Order dismissing petitions vacated. . . .

RESUMING A BIRTH NAME

During marriage. When a married woman adopts her husband's surname, there are differing views about what she should do if she wishes to resume her former name even though the union has not been dissolved. Under the common law doctrine it would seem that she need not resort to judicial action. But in order to foster certainty and to avoid repeated explanations to various agencies or other entities many women prefer to utilize the name change provisions generally provided by state statutes. *See, e.g.,* VA.CODE § 8.01–217 (LEXIS 2000). So long as the change is not designed to accomplish a fraudulent purpose, such statutes should be applicable. *See* In re Miller, 243 S.E.2d 464 (Va.1978).

The California Attorney General published an opinion that states that a person has the freedom to change his or her name and to use whatever name he or she selects, subject only to qualifications as to fraud. Nonetheless, the Attorney General admitted that use of statutory procedures are often beneficial since this procedure would provide an official document. *See* Opinion N. 00–205, Cal. Atty. Gen., recited in 83 Op. Atty Gen. Cal. 136 (2000).

After Divorce. It is common today that statutes specifically authorize a woman who took her husband's name on marriage to resume her birth name after divorce. Although some trial courts in states with seemingly discretionary statutes have balked at restoring a divorced woman's surname, ostensibly out of concern about possible detriment to her children, appellate courts have taken a less restrictive view. Sneed v. Sneed, 585 P.2d 1363 (Okl.1978); Klein v. Klein, 373 A.2d 86 (Md.App.1977); Egner v. Egner, 133 N.J.Super. 403, 337 A.2d 46 (1975). In Peniston v. Peniston, 511 S.W.2d 675 (Ky.1974) a trial court's refusal to restore the wife's former surname upon divorce was upheld when the request was made by the husband.

2. Names for Children

Henne v. Wright

United States Court of Appeals, 8th Circuit, 1990.
904 F.2d 1208, cert. denied 498 U.S. 1032, 111 S.Ct. 692, 112 L.Ed.2d 682 (1991).

■ Bright, Senior Circuit Judge.

. . . Plaintiffs brought this action under 42 U.S.C. § 1983 individually and as next friends to their daughters alleging that Neb.Rev.Stat. § 71–640.01 (1986) unconstitutionally infringes their fundamental fourteenth amendment right to choose surnames for their daughters other than those prescribed. The defendants appeal, contending that the district court erred in the following respects: (1) plaintiffs lack standing; (2) plaintiffs failed to join certain parties necessary for a just adjudication under Fed.R.Civ.P. 19(a); and (3) Neb.Rev.Stat. § 71–640.01 does not unconstitutionally infringe a fundamental right. We reject defendants' first two contentions but are persuaded by the third and therefore reverse.

I. BACKGROUND

On April 4, 1985, Debra Henne gave birth to Alicia Renee Henne at a hospital in Lincoln, Nebraska. Following Alicia's birth, Debra completed a birth certificate form at the request of a hospital employee. Debra listed Gary Brinton as the father and entered the name Alicia Renee Brinton in the space provided for the child's name. Brinton, also present at the hospital, completed and signed a paternity form.

At the time of the birth, Debra was still married to Robert Henne. Although Debra and Robert Henne had filed for a divorce prior to Alicia's birth, the decree dissolving the marriage did not become final until after the birth. As a result of her marital status, hospital personnel, acting on instructions from the Department of Health, informed Debra that she could not surname her daughter "Brinton." Debra then filled out a second birth certificate form, entering the child's name as Alicia Renee Henne and leaving blank the space provided for the father's name. Robert Henne has never claimed to be Alicia's father and, pursuant to the divorce decree, pays no child support for her.

Almost three years later, on February 4, 1988, Debra Henne went in person to the Bureau of Vital Statistics of the Nebraska Department of Health and requested that Alicia's surname be changed to Brinton and that

Gary Brinton be listed on the birth certificate as the father. Debra produced a signed statement personally acknowledging Gary Brinton as Alicia's biological father. She also presented a signed acknowledgement of paternity from Gary Brinton and a letter from him requesting that the birth certificate be changed. Personnel at the Bureau of Vital Statistics, acting indirectly at the direction of defendants Cooper and Wright, denied Debra's request. Other than her visit to the Bureau of Vital Statistics and this action, Debra has made no attempt to change Alicia's surname.

On June 17, 1988, at St. Elizabeth's Hospital in Lincoln, Nebraska, Linda Spidell gave birth to a daughter, Quintessa Martha Spidell. Linda wished to give Quintessa the surname "McKenzie," the same surname as her other two children, who were born in California. Hospital personnel, acting upon instructions from the Department of Health, informed Linda that Quintessa could not be surnamed McKenzie and that if Linda did not complete the birth certificate form the hospital would enter Quintessa's last name as Spidell. Linda completed the form, entering "Spidell" as Quintessa's surname and leaving blank the space provided for the father's name.

Linda surnamed her other children McKenzie simply because she liked that name and not because of any familial connection. For that reason, and because she wishes all three children to share the same name, she wants Quintessa surnamed McKenzie. Linda was not married at the time of Quintessa's birth or at the time of this action and there has been no judicial determination of paternity. At trial, however, both Linda and Ray Duffer, who lives with Linda and her children, testified that Duffer is Quintessa's biological father. Other than this action, Linda has made no attempt to change Quintessa's surname.

Defendant Dr. Gregg F. Wright heads the Nebraska Department of Health. The Nebraska Department of Health assists the governor in executing and administering certain laws, including Neb.Rev.Stat. § 71–640.01, the law at issue in this action. Defendant Stanley S. Cooper directs the Bureau of Vital Statistics of the Nebraska Department of Health. In this capacity he ensures that all birth records are filed and maintained in accordance with the laws of Nebraska, including section 71–640.01.

These defendants and the Nebraska Department of Health are responsible for furnishing forms and instructions for use in completing birth certificates to hospitals throughout Nebraska. These birth certificate forms and instructions implement Neb.Rev.Stat. § 71–640.01, which restricts the choice of surnames that can be entered on a birth certificate. Hospital personnel and Nebraska authorities denied plaintiffs their choice of surnames pursuant to this statute.

Debra Henne brought this suit on behalf of herself and her minor child Alicia Renee Henne in federal district court against defendants Wright and Cooper in their official capacities, alleging that Neb.Rev.Stat. § 71–640.01, as implemented and enforced by defendants, violated the Federal Constitution. Linda Spidell later intervened as an additional plaintiff on her own behalf and on behalf of her minor child Quintessa Martha Spidell.

Following a bench trial, the court ruled that the constitutional right to privacy protects a parent's right to name his or her child. The court did not specifically identify the appropriate level of scrutiny by which to examine Neb.Rev.Stat. § 71–640.01. The court held that the justifications for the statute asserted by the defendants failed to satisfy even a minimal level of constitutional scrutiny. . . .

II. DISCUSSION

[In parts A and B the court rejects defendants' arguments that plaintiffs lack standing. As to the argument regarding failure to join presumed and putative fathers as necessary parties, the court notes that it was unnecessary to "enter this thicket" because of their disposition of the plaintiffs' constitutional claims.]

C. Fundamental Right

Defendants contend that the district court erred in holding Neb.Rev. Stat. § 71–640.01[5] unconstitutional. The district court held that an extension of the fourteenth amendment right of privacy protects a parent's right to name his or her child and that the statute failed to survive even minimal scrutiny. We determine that the fourteenth amendment right of privacy does not protect the specific right at issue here and that the statute rationally furthers legitimate state interests.

This case presents the issue whether a parent has a fundamental right to give a child a surname at birth with which the child has no legally established parental connection. We frame the issue this way because each plaintiff wishes to enter on her daughter's birth certificate a surname proscribed by section 71–640.01. Debra Henne wishes to enter the surname of the alleged father (Brinton) without first obtaining a judicial determination of paternity. Linda Spidell wishes to enter a surname (McKenzie) with which her daughter has no connection other than that Linda has already given that name to her two other children. We note, however, that while

---

5. Section 71–640.01 states: The information pertaining to the name of an infant born in this state and reported on a birth certificate, filled out and filed pursuant to sections 71–601 to 71–648, shall comply with the following: (1) If the mother was married at the time of either conception or birth of the child, or at any time between conception and birth, the name of such mother's husband shall be entered on the certificate as the father of the child and the surname of the child shall be entered on the certificate as being (a) the same as that of the husband, unless paternity has been determined otherwise by a court of competent jurisdiction, (b) the surname of the mother, (c) the maiden surname of the mother, or (d) the hyphenated surname of both parents; (2) If the mother was not married at the time of either conception or birth of the child, or at any time between conception and birth, the name of the father shall not be entered on the certificate without the written consent of the mother and the person named as the father, in which case and upon the written request of both such parents the surname of the child shall be that of the father or the hyphenated surname of both parents; (3) In any case in which paternity of a child is determined by a court of competent jurisdiction, the name of the father shall be entered on the certificate in accordance with the finding of the court and the surname of the child may be entered on the certificate the same as the surname of the father; (4) In all other cases, the surname of the child shall be the legal surname of the mother; and (5) If the father is not named on the certificate, no other information about the father shall be entered thereon.

section 71–640.01 requires that a child have some legally established parental connection to the surname entered on the birth certificate,[6] it does not prevent either plaintiff from ever giving her daughter the desired surname.[7] The district court overlooked this important distinction in characterizing the issue as whether parents generally possess a fundamental right to name a child. This case does not present that broad issue.

Whether there is a fundamental right to give a child a surname at birth with which the child has no legally established parental connection will dictate the appropriate level of constitutional scrutiny for evaluating Neb.Rev.Stat. § 71–640.01. Specifically, if the statute significantly infringes a right deemed fundamental under the fourteenth amendment right of privacy then we must rigorously scrutinize the asserted justifications for the statute. Otherwise, we analyze the statute under the highly deferential rational basis standard of review applicable to most economic and social legislation challenged under the fourteenth amendment.

We now turn to the question whether the right at issue is fundamental. A long line of Supreme Court cases have established that "liberty" under the fourteenth amendment encompasses a right of personal privacy to make certain decisions free from intrusive governmental regulation absent compelling justification. See, e.g., Zablocki v. Redhail, 434 U.S. at 374, 98 S.Ct. at 673 (fundamental right to marriage); Moore v. City of East Cleveland, 431 U.S. 494, 97 S.Ct. 1932, 52 L.Ed.2d 531 (1977) (fundamental right to live with relatives); Roe v. Wade, 410 U.S. 113, 93 S.Ct. 705, 35 L.Ed.2d 147 (1973) (fundamental right to an abortion); Loving v. Virginia, 388 U.S. 1, 87 S.Ct. 1817, 18 L.Ed.2d 1010 (1967) (fundamental right to interracial marriage). Two of the earliest right to privacy cases, Meyer v. Nebraska, 262 U.S. 390, 43 S.Ct. 625, 67 L.Ed. 1042 (1923) (fundamental right to instruct a child in a foreign language), and Pierce v. Society of Sisters, 268 U.S. 510, 45 S.Ct. 571, 69 L.Ed. 1070 (1925) (fundamental right to send child to a non-public school), established the existence of a fundamental right to make child rearing decisions free from unwarranted governmental intrusion. See Roe v. Wade, 410 U.S. at 153, 93 S.Ct. at 727. Meyer and Pierce do not, however, establish an absolute parental right to make decisions relating to children free from government regulation. See

6. Thus, Alicia Henne could have been given her mother's surname, her mother's maiden surname or the surname of the presumed father, but not the surname of the alleged father without a judicial determination of paternity. Neb.Rev.Stat. § 71–640.01(1). Quintessa Spidell could have been given her mother's surname, id. § 71–640.01(4), the surname of a person named as the father if that person requested so in writing, id. § 71–640.01(2), or the surname of a person found by a court of competent jurisdiction to be the father, id. § 71–640.01(3).

7. Debra Henne could enter the surname Brinton on her daughter's birth certificate by obtaining a judicial determination of paternity on the part of Gary Brinton. Neb.Rev.Stat. § 71–640.01(1)(a). Linda Spidell could enter the surname McKenzie on her daughter's birth certificate only by first changing her own surname to McKenzie. Nebraska law provides a procedure, however, whereby either child's name could later be changed. Neb.Rev.Stat. §§ 61–101 to 61–104 (1986). See also Spatz v. Spatz, 199 Neb. 332, 258 N.W.2d 814 (1977). Moreover, under Nebraska law any civil action can be brought in forma pauperis if necessary. Neb.Rev.Stat. §§ 25–2301 to 25–2310 (1986 & Supp.1988).

Prince v. Massachusetts, 321 U.S. 158, 166, 64 S.Ct. 438, 442, 88 L.Ed. 645 (1944) ("[N]either rights of religion nor rights of parenthood are beyond limitation"); Stanley v. Illinois, 405 U.S. 645, 652, 92 S.Ct. 1208, 1213, 31 L.Ed.2d 551 (1972) (state has legitimate interest in separating neglectful parents from child); Jehovah's Witnesses v. King County Hosp., 278 F.Supp. 488, 504 (W.D.Wash.1967) (three judge panel) (state may intervene in parents' religiously motivated decision refusing medically necessary blood transfusion for children), aff'd, 390 U.S. 598, 88 S.Ct. 1260, 20 L.Ed.2d 158 (1968) (per curiam).

In determining whether a right not enumerated in the Constitution qualifies as fundamental, we ask whether the right is "deeply rooted in this Nation's history and tradition," Moore v. City of East Cleveland, 431 U.S. at 503, 97 S.Ct. at 1938. We proceed cautiously in this area of the law, ever mindful that the judiciary "is the most vulnerable and comes nearest to illegitimacy when it deals with judge-made constitutional law having little or no cognizable roots in the language or even the design of the Constitution." Id. at 544, 97 S.Ct. at 1958 (White, J., dissenting).

While Meyer and Pierce extended constitutional protection to parental decisions relating to child rearing, the parental rights recognized in those cases centered primarily around the training and education of children.... By contrast, the parental decision in this case relates to the choice of a child's surname. This subject possesses little, if any, inherent resemblance to the parental rights of training and education recognized by Meyer and Pierce. Thus, as the district court rightly recognized, constitutional protection for the right to choose a non-parental surname at birth must flow, if at all, from an extension of Meyer and Pierce. Furthermore, any logical extension of Meyer and Pierce has to be grounded in the tradition and history of this nation. See Moore v. City of East Cleveland, 431 U.S. at 503, 97 S.Ct. at 1938; Bowers v. Hardwick, 478 U.S. 186, 192, 106 S.Ct. 2841, 2844, 92 L.Ed.2d 140 (1986). Given this standard, we necessarily conclude that plaintiffs have presented no fundamental right.

The custom in this country has always been that a child born in lawful wedlock receives the surname of the father at birth, see, e.g., Secretary of the Commonwealth v. City of Lowell, 373 Mass. 178, 366 N.E.2d 717, 725 (1977); ..., and that a child born out of wedlock receives the surname of the mother at birth, see, e.g., Buckley v. State, 19 Ala.App. 508, 98 So. 362, 363 (1923); ...

While some married parents now may wish to give their children the surname of the mother or a hyphenated surname consisting of both parents' surname, and some unmarried mothers may wish to give their children the surname of the father, we can find no American tradition to support the extension of the right of privacy to cover the right of a parent to give a child a surname with which that child has no legally recognized parental connection. Plaintiffs therefore have not asserted a right that is fundamental under the fourteenth amendment right of privacy and Neb. Rev.Stat. § 71–640.01 need only rationally further legitimate state interests to withstand constitutional scrutiny.

The district court in this case held that section 71–640.01 failed to survive even minimal scrutiny. Other federal courts reviewing statutes restricting the choice of surnames have taken similar positions. Nevertheless, for the reasons discussed below, we determine that the Nebraska statute passes minimal scrutiny, i.e., the rational basis test.

A law must be upheld under the rational basis test unless it bears no rational relation to a legitimate state interest. . . .

We determine that the law rationally furthers at least three legitimate state interests: the state's interest in promoting the welfare of children, the state's interest in insuring that the names of its citizens are not appropriated for improper purposes and the state's interest in inexpensive and efficient record keeping. Specifically, a reasonable legislature could believe that in most cases a child's welfare is served by bearing a surname possessing a connection with at least one legally verifiable parent. Furthermore, the legislature could reasonably perceive that in the absence of a law such as section 71–640.01, the name of a non-parent could be improperly appropriated to achieve a deliberately misleading purpose, such as the creation of a false implication of paternity. Finally, the legislature could reasonably conclude that it is easier and cheaper to verify and index the birth records of a person who has a surname in common with at least one legally verifiable parent. The district court's review of the evidence buttresses this conclusion. 711 F.Supp. at 515.[8] Although the Nebraska legislature could perhaps tailor the statute to more closely serve these purposes, we cannot say that section 71–640.01 bears no rational relationship to the state's legitimate interests. We therefore reject plaintiffs' contention that Neb.Rev.Stat. § 71–640.01 unconstitutionally restricts their parental rights.

. . . [T]he district court's judgment is reversed.

■ ARNOLD, CIRCUIT JUDGE, concurring in part and dissenting in part.

. . . The fundamental right of privacy, in my view, includes the right of parents to name their own children, and the State has shown no interest on the facts of these cases sufficiently compelling to override that right. . . .

A few salient facts are worth repeating. Debra Henne wants to give her daughter the surname of the little girl's father. The father is willing. He has acknowledged his fatherhood. The man to whom Ms. Henne was married when the baby was born has no objection. Linda Spidell wants to name her daughter "McKenzie," which is neither her name nor the name

---

8. The district court noted that the defendants offered evidence that section 71–640.01 promotes inexpensive and efficient indexing and access of birth records. Nevertheless, the court stated that

"[i]n keeping with the admonishment of [Stanley v. Illinois, 405 U.S. 645, 656, 92 S.Ct. 1208, 1215, 31 L.Ed.2d 551 (1972)], I find that the state's interest in efficiency and cost savings loses its legitimacy when compared to the constitutional right at issue here." 711 F.Supp. at 515. In Stanley, the Supreme Court in effect ruled that the state's interests in administrative efficiency did not withstand heightened scrutiny. Here, however, defendants need only demonstrate that the law rationally furthers legitimate state interests.

of the child's father. The choice is not so eccentric as it seems, however: Ms. Spidell's two other children are named "McKenzie," and it is quite natural to desire that all of one's three children have the same surname. Again, no one with a personal interest objects. Ray Duffer, the man who lives with Ms. Spidell, is the child's father, and "McKenzie" is fine with him.

The government, in the person of the State of Nebraska, says no to both mothers. The most plausible reason it offers is administrative convenience.[1] Records are easier to keep and use if every person has the surname of "at least one legally verifiable parent." Ante, at 1215. This interest is legitimate, and the statute under challenge is rationally related to it. If the appropriate level of constitutional scrutiny were the rational-basis test, I would agree that the law is valid. But if a fundamental right is at stake, the State must show a compelling interest, which it has wholly failed to do. So the case comes down to this: Do parents have a fundamental right to name their own children?

The question could well be analyzed as a First Amendment issue. What I call myself or my child is an aspect of speech. When the State says I cannot call my child what I want to call her, my freedom of expression, both oral and written, is lessened. And if the First Amendment is at stake, everyone would concede that the State could not win without showing a compelling interest. But the parties have not presented the case in First Amendment terms, either here or in the District Court. It would be unfair for an appellate court to decide the case on that basis, at least without a chance for additional briefing.

So we address the case in terms of the right of privacy. This is trickier ground than the First Amendment. There is a Speech Clause, but no "Privacy Clause" as such. The right of privacy is not the beneficiary of explicit textual protection in the federal Constitution. It is an unenumerated right. There are such things in constitutional law, however. We know that much (if we know little else) from the Ninth Amendment. The Founders of this Nation deeply believed that the individual took primacy over government. People existed, and had rights, before there was such a thing as government. Government might protect or recognize rights, but rights, some of them anyway, existed before government and independently of it, and would continue to exist after government had been destroyed. The source of rights was not the State, but, as the Declaration of Independence put it, the "Creator."

---

1. It is also true, as the Court says, ante, at 1215, that allowing an unfettered choice of surname could enable parents to imply falsely that someone was the father of the child. In the example I put at the oral argument, I would have an interest in keeping a stranger from naming her child "Richard S. Arnold, Jr.," and the State would have an interest in defending my reputation against such a false implication. Nothing of the kind is involved in the present cases. Moreover, the State might have an interest in the matter if the child's parents could not agree on a surname. Again, no such issue is presented by these cases.

It is perfectly true, and the Court is right to emphasize, that unelected judges should tread with great caution when dealing "with judge-made constitutional law having little or no cognizable roots in the language or even the design of the Constitution." Moore v. City of East Cleveland, 431 U.S. 494, 544, 97 S.Ct. 1932, 1958, 52 L.Ed.2d 531 (1977) (White, J., dissenting). But the proposition that unenumerated rights exist is both textually demonstrable (the Ninth Amendment) and sanctified by Supreme Court precedent. The right to travel, for example, was recognized long before the modern debate over the right of privacy, and even before the passage of the Due Process Clause of the Fourteenth Amendment, with its open-ended reference to liberty, created a textual basis for limitations on the power of States not contained in the words of the original Constitution. See Crandall v. Nevada, 73 U.S. (6 Wall.) 35, 18 L.Ed. 744 (1867).

The real question is, not whether there is a right of privacy (see also the Fourth Amendment for a modicum of textual support), but how do you tell what it includes? The limits of the right remain controversial, and no doubt they will continue to be tested by litigation. Precedent tells us at least this much, though: family matters, including decisions relating to child rearing and marriage, are on almost everyone's list of fundamental rights. See, e.g., Zablocki v. Redhail, 434 U.S. 374, 383, 98 S.Ct. 673, 679, 54 L.Ed.2d 618 (1978), and the other cases cited by the Court, ante, at 1214. The right to name one's child seems to me, if anything, more personal and intimate, less likely to affect people outside the family, than the right to send the child to a private school, Pierce v. Society of Sisters, 268 U.S. 510, 45 S.Ct. 571, 69 L.Ed. 1070 (1925), or to have the child learn German, Meyer v. Nebraska, 262 U.S. 390, 43 S.Ct. 625, 67 L.Ed. 1042 (1923). We know, moreover, from Roe v. Wade, 410 U.S. 113, 93 S.Ct. 705, 35 L.Ed.2d 147 (1973), that these women had a fundamental right to prevent their children from being born in the first place. It is a bizarre rule of law indeed that says they cannot name the children once they are born. If there was ever a case of the greater including the less, this ought to be it.

So I do not see the right being claimed here as an "extension" of prior cases. It is rather well within the principle of those cases. A person's name is, in a sense, her identity, her personality, her being. I take it the Court would not deny a citizen the right to choose her own name, absent some compelling governmental interest. No more should we deny her the right to choose her child's name. The child has, at birth, no will of her own, and her parents should be allowed to speak for her. There is something sacred about a name. It is our own business, not the government's.

Having labeled the present claim as an "extension" of existing law, the Court goes on to say that extensions may be permitted only if they are "deeply rooted in this Nation's history and tradition," Moore v. City of East Cleveland, supra, 431 U.S. at 503, 97 S.Ct. at 1938. It then asks whether there is an "American tradition to support the extension of the right of privacy to cover the right of a parent to give a child a surname with which that child has no legally recognized parental connection." Having satisfied itself that there is no such tradition, the Court rejects what it characterizes as an "extension" of the right of privacy.

As is often the case, how one phrases a question has a great deal to do with the answer one gets. To illustrate the point, I refer to some aspects of tradition about names that the Court does not mention. In the beginning, surnames were unknown. They "were not considered of controlling importance until the reign of Queen Elizabeth, 1558–1603." Note, What's in a Name?, 2 N.Y.L.Rev. 1, 1 (1924). "The surname, in its origin, was not, as a rule, inherited from the father, but was either voluntarily adopted by the son or conferred upon him by his neighbors...." Ibid.[2] Fundamentally, names were not inherited. They were something people chose for themselves. "There [was] no such thing as the 'legal name' of a person in the sense that he may not lawfully adopt or acquire another. By the common law a man [sic] may name himself, or change his name at will, and this without solemnity or formality of any kind; or he may acquire a name by reputation, general usage or habit." Id. at 2 (citations omitted). Even after statutes were passed to provide a fixed procedure for changing one's name, the statutes were treated as merely supplementary to the common law. One could use the statute if desired, but the old do-it-yourself right simply to assume a new name still existed. Smith v. United States Cas. Co., 197 N.Y. 420, 90 N.E. 947, 950 (1910).

The early tradition, then, did not restrict one's own choice of a surname. "You could freely select any name you chose, whether it was your parents' surname or not...." Names were people's own business, not the government's. One's name did not have to be that of a legally recognized parent.

. . .

The cases cited so far on the question of tradition are all rather old; and it may fairly be asked, whether any tradition that once existed still obtains. There is good evidence that the answer is yes. See, e.g., Hauser v. Callaway, 36 F.2d 667, 669 (8th Cir.1929) ("A man's name for all practical and legal purposes is the name by which he is known and called in the community where he lives and is best known."). The most recent case on the point I have found, Walker v. Jackson, 391 F.Supp. 1395, 1402 (E.D.Ark.1975) (three-judge court) (Webster, Henley, and Eisele, JJ.), squarely holds that under the common law of Arkansas—which has not been changed by statute—a person can change his name at will in the absence of fraud.

So far as the choice of one's own name is concerned, then, it seems well established that the tradition, still extant, is a complete absence of statutory prohibition. Certainly there is no pattern of positive law denying such a right of self-determination. I take it that the Court would concede that

---

2. The older authorities on names uniformly refer to "fathers," "sons," and what "a man" might choose for a name. I take it everyone would concede today that mothers, daughters, and women in general are legally entitled to the benefit of whatever tradition was formerly expressed in male terms.

there is a fundamental right to choose one's own name. There is no "societal tradition of enacting laws *denying* [this] interest," Michael H. v. Gerald D., 491 U.S. 110, 109 S.Ct. 2333, 2341 n. 2, 105 L.Ed.2d 91 (1989) (plurality opinion) (emphasis in original), and that seems to be the standard that has recently attracted more votes than any other on the Supreme Court.

This Court, however, phrases the question more narrowly: is there a tradition supporting "the right of a parent to give a child a surname with which that child has no legally recognized parental connection"? I grant that there is no such tradition: what the plaintiffs in this case want to do is unusual. Few parents, no doubt, have done or wanted to do it in the past, and few would want to do it now. But, by the same token, there is no solid tradition of legislation denying any such right, and under Michael H., supra, that is the relevant question. In the absence of any tradition either way on the precise point, we should look, I submit, to the tradition we do have. People may choose or change their own names without leave of government. It is only a small step to extend the same right to their children's names. Children are, during infancy anyway, simply legal extensions of their parents for many purposes.

So I would hold that the right asserted here is fundamental, and that the State has no interest compelling enough to override it in the circumstances of this case. In attempting to do so, the State intrudes intolerably into what should be a private decision, one of the basic liberties of the citizen. . . .

NOTES

Disputes between parents. In Marriage of Gulsvig, 498 N.W.2d 725 (Iowa 1993), the Supreme Court of Iowa held that it was in the best interests of the child of the divorcing parents to retain the mother's surname, which was also that of her second husband. (Acting alone, the mother had effected a change on the birth certificate.) The court noted that the mother had given assurance that she would retain her name if she remarried, and her suggestion that the father receive generous visitation was construed as indicating that she wanted him to have strong ties with the child. The parents were awarded joint custody, with the mother having primary physical care of the child. Harris, J. dissented, stating although hedid not object to the majority's disapproval of the outdated rule giving fathers virtually absolute power to append their surname to a child, he believed that in the absence of an agreement between the parents, they should select a surname used by one of them during their relationship. In a separate dissent, Snell, J. provided a history of names in various societies and concluded that:

> The legal standard that should be applied in this case of determining the child's name at birth should be more stringent than what is applied by the majority of courts in applications to change a name. In name change cases involving minors, the noncustodial father's name is

entitled to be given significant consideration and a change is not warranted unless there is clear and convincing evidence that it is in the child's best interests to change its name.

. . .

No name change case has been cited and I have found none in the United States that has sanctioned the stripping of a father's name from his child when he is without fault and the placing of another man's name on the child with whom the child has no biological or legal relationship. I do not believe a divorced father, who is without fault, should have to face the distinct possibility of losing not only the custody of his children but of having his name forever excised from their being. To approve [the mother's] unilateral and deceitful act on the principle of promoting family unity is not an affirmation of the equality of women, which I support, but an assault on the dignity of man. The noncustodial father's role is reduced to that of an anonymous sperm donor, finance provider and unwelcome visitor. At once, history is ignored, custom rejected and genealogy abjured.

In Hamby v. Jacobson, 769 P.2d 273 (Utah App.1989), the Utah Court of Appeals faced the question whether two children should bear the surname of their father or their custodial mother after their parents divorced. Rejecting arguments that there should be a presumption that the paternal surname should be used or a rebuttable presumption that the custodial parent's decision should govern, the court determined that "the best interests of the child is the paramount consideration in determining whether a child's name should be changed." *Id.* at 277. The court explained that:

In determining a child's best interests, courts have considered factors including: 1) the child's preference in light of the child's age and experience; 2) the effect of a name change on the development and preservation of the child's relationship with each parent; 3) the length of time a child has used a name; 4) the difficulties, harassment or embarrassment a child may experience from bearing the present or proposed name; 5) the possibility that a different name may cause insecurity and lack of identity, and 6) the motive or interests of the custodial parent. We believe that these factors and perhaps others may be relevant, but that courts should apply only those factors present in the particular circumstances of each case. Further, because the child's best interests is dependent upon the particular facts in a case, the court should enter findings of fact which state the reasons for granting or denying the application to change the child's name.

We also point out that lip-service to the best interests of the child should not be used as a subterfuge to nevertheless perpetuate the paternal preference.

The Montana Supreme Court cited a societal preference for preserving the male's lineage through use of the father's surname, but held that this was improper, the test must be gender neutral and based solely on what is in the best interest of the child. When a child has carried the mother's surname for the first 18 months of his life, was baptized with her name, she will be his primary caretaker, she and the child's half-sibling have the same last name, and she has said she will not change her name even if she remarries, then it is in the child's best interest to have her name. *See* Workman v. Olszewski, 297 Mont. 327, 993 P.2d 667 (1999). And the court may issue a restraining order barring the child from such things as travel when a parent does not comply with an order concerning the child's name. *See, e.g.*, Howard v. Cornell, 134 Idaho 403, 3 P.3d 528 (2000).

The New Jersey Supreme Court has ruled that the child's primary caretaker has a presumptive right to change the name of the child and that the primary caretaker does not need to show how the change would promote the best interests of the child prior to doing so. In departing from the "best interest of the child" test, the court has ruled that the non-primary caretaker parent has the burden to rebut the presumption. Ronan v. Adely, 182 N.J. 103, 861 A.2d 822 (2004). In spite of New Jersey's approach, other courts still rely upon the best interest of the child test when resolving disputes between parents over the name of the child. *See, e.g.*, Poindexter v. Poindexter, 360 Ark. 538, 203 S.W.3d 84 (2005); *In re* Name Change of Perez, 105 Ohio St. 3d 1440, 822 N.E.2d 811 (2005); In re Petition of Carter, 640 S.E.2d 96 (W.Va. Nov. 9, 2006). Likewise, courts have used the best interest of the child test when considering the child's right to use the father's name when the parents are not married. *See, e.g.*, Scoggins v. Trevino, 200 S.W.3d 832 (Tex. App. 2006)(listing twelve factors to consider).

C. TRANSACTIONS BETWEEN SPOUSES

FLORIDA CONSTITUTION, ART. 10, § 5

There shall be no distinction between married women and married men in the holding, control, disposition, or encumbering of their property, both real and personal; except that dower or curtesy may be established and regulated by law.

FLORIDA STATUTES ANNOTATED (West 2000)

§ 708.08. Married women's rights: separate property

(1) Every married woman is empowered to take charge of and manage and control her separate property, to contract and to be contracted with, to sue and be sued, to sell, convey, transfer, mortgage, use, and pledge her real and personal property and to make, execute, and deliver instruments of every character without the joinder or consent of her husband in all respects as fully as if she were unmarried. Every married woman has and may exercise all rights and powers with respect to her separate property, income, and earnings and may enter into, obligate herself to perform, and enforce contracts or undertakings to the same extent and in like manner as

if she were unmarried and without the joinder or consent of her husband. Any claim or judgment against a married woman shall not be a claim or lien against her inchoate right of dower in her husband's separate property. All conveyances, contracts, transfers, or mortgages of real property or any interest in it, executed by a married woman without the joinder of her husband before or after the effective date of the 1968 Constitution of Florida, are as valid and effective as though the husband had joined.

MASSACHUSETTS GENERAL LAWS ANNOTATED, CHAPTER 209 (West 1998)

§ 2.   Married woman; power to contract

A married woman may make contracts, oral and written, sealed and unsealed, in the same manner as if she were sole, and may make such contracts with her husband.

§ 3.   Transfers between husband and wife

Transfers between husband and wife. Transfers of real and personal property between husband and wife shall be valid to the same extent as if they were sole.

§ 4.   Married woman; work and labor; presumption

Work and labor performed by a married woman for a person other than her husband and children shall, unless there is an express agreement on her part to the contrary, be presumed to be performed on her separate account.

§ 5.   Married woman; acting as fiduciary

A married woman may be an executrix, administratrix, guardian, conservator, trustee or receiver, and may bind herself and the estate which she represents without any act or assent of her husband.

§ 6.   Married woman; power to sue and be sued

A married woman may sue and be sued in the same manner as if she were sole; but this section shall not authorize suits between husband and wife except in connection with contracts entered into pursuant to the authority contained in section two.

§ 7.   Married woman; liabilities

A married woman shall not be liable for her husband's debts, nor shall her property be liable to be taken on an execution against him. But a married woman shall be liable jointly with her husband for debts due, to the amount of one hundred dollars in each case, for necessaries furnished with her knowledge or consent to herself or her family, if she has property to the amount of two thousand dollars or more.

§ 8.   Husband; liability for wife's debts

A husband shall not be liable upon a cause of action which originated against his wife prior to their marriage, or to pay a judgment recovered against her.

§ 9.   Husband; liability on contracts concerning separate property of wife

Contracts made by a married woman relative to her separate property, trade, business, labor or services shall not bind her husband or render him or his property liable therefor; but she and her separate property shall be liable on such contracts in the same manner as if she were sole.

§ 13.   Marriage settlements

The preceding sections shall not invalidate a marriage settlement or contract.

NOTES

The "sewing machine exception". A special "spot zoning" type of authorization, no doubt reflecting mercantile concerns of the time, was Pa.Stat.Ann. tit. 48, § 33. Enacted in 1872, it provided that "all contracts made by married women, in the purchase of sewing machines for their own use, shall be binding, without the necessity of the husband joining in the same." The statute was not repealed until 1982.

The slow erosion of a restrictive common law rule. In Romeo v. Romeo, 84 N.J. 289, 418 A.2d 258 (1980), a wife sought dependency benefits under New Jersey's Workers' Compensation Act based on the husband's death while working for the Newark tavern and restaurant of which she was sole proprietor. The husband, a salaried employee, was shot to death and robbed while on a trip to the bank to deposit checks and withdraw cash for the business. The issue before the court was whether the common law rule that contracts between spouses are unenforceable prevented a valid employment relationship. Prior case law had interpreted state legislation to continue the common law rule. In at least partially reversing this and allowing the wife's compensation claim, the Supreme Court of New Jersey first pointed to the "complete erosion" of "the theory of spousal unity of person and interest", and concluded that:

> In spite of the genuine interests served by the common law rule against enforcement of interspousal contracts, it could become an instrument of injustice were we to accept uncritically the assumption that any enforcement would promote discord. Thus, in assessing the continued vitality of the common law rule we must apply the asserted justification of marital harmony to the particular type of contractual relationship for which recognition is sought.

. . . [T]here are several reasons why the State's interest in protecting marital harmony does not support a denial of workers' compensation coverage.

[T]he terms of workers' compensation coverage cannot be negotiated by the parties. The scheme is provided entirely by statute and is not subject to "bargain and sale" or modification. The financial security provided by the prompt and certain recovery inherent in workers' compensation would probably enhance marital harmony rather than detract from it. Further, since the employer is required to insure its employees, both the suit and any recovery would effectively be against an insurance company rather than the spouse.

. . .

These factors distinguish the present case from one in which remedies are sought for the breach of an interspousal employment contract. Since the latter action would involve elements of domestic relations as well as contract law, it might be better left to the flexible powers of a court of equity. We are not here required to resolve that issue, however. The question before us is whether the common law rule against interspousal contracts, despite its demonstrated weaknesses in the workers' compensation setting, will be allowed to stand as a bar to recovery under the Workers' Compensation Act. We believe that to do so would permit the rule to become an instrument of injustice.

418 A.2d 264.

Changes in the relationship between spouses parallel changes in approaches towards equality in general, sexism, racism, the definition of family and reproductive control. For a textbook addressing each of these issues, *see* CATHERINE A. MACKINNON, SEX EQUALITY: FAMILY LAW (2001). In general, *see* Katherine B. Silbaugh, *Accounting for Family Change.* (Reviewing June Carbone, FROM PARTNERS TO PARENTS: THE SECOND REVOLUTION IN FAMILY LAW.), 89 GEO. L. J. 923 (2001); John Witte, Jr., *The Goods and Goals of Marriage*, 76 NOTRE DAME L. REV. 1019 (2001); Joseph W. McKnight, *Family Law: Husband and Wife*, 53 SMU L. REV. 995 (2000); Raymond C. O'Brien, *The Reawakening of Marriage*, 102 W. VA. L. REV. 339 (1999).

D. SUPPORT DURING MARRIAGE

McGuire v. McGuire

Supreme Court of Nebraska, 1953.
157 Neb. 226, 59 N.W.2d 336.

■ MESSMORE, JUSTICE. The plaintiff, Lydia McGuire, brought this action in equity in the district court for Wayne County against Charles W. McGuire, her husband, as defendant, to recover suitable maintenance and support money, and for costs and attorney's fees. Trial was had to the court and a decree was rendered in favor of the plaintiff.

The district court decreed that the plaintiff was legally entitled to use the credit of the defendant and obligate him to pay for certain items in the nature of improvements and repairs, furniture, and appliances for the household in the amount of several thousand dollars; required the defendant to purchase a new automobile with an effective heater within 30 days; ordered him to pay travel expenses of the plaintiff for a visit to each of her daughters at least once a year; that the plaintiff be entitled in the future to pledge the credit of the defendant for what may constitute necessaries of life; awarded a personal allowance to the plaintiff in the sum of $50 a month; awarded $800 for services for the plaintiff's attorney; and as an alternative to part of the award so made, defendant was permitted, in agreement with plaintiff, to purchase a modern home elsewhere.

The defendant filed a motion for new trial which was overruled. From this order the defendant perfected appeal to this court.

. . .

The record shows that the plaintiff and defendant were married in Wayne, Nebraska, on August 11, 1919. At the time of the marriage the defendant was a bachelor 46 or 47 years of age and had a reputation for more than ordinary frugality, of which the plaintiff was aware. She had visited in his home and had known him for about 3 years prior to the marriage. After the marriage the couple went to live on a farm of 160 acres located in Leslie precinct, Wayne County, owned by the defendant and upon which he had lived and farmed since 1905. The parties have lived on this place ever since. The plaintiff had been previously married. Her first husband died in October 1914, leaving surviving him the plaintiff and two daughters. He died intestate, leaving 80 acres of land in Dixon County. The plaintiff and each of the daughters inherited a one-third interest therein. At the time of the marriage of the plaintiff and defendant the plaintiff's daughters were 9 and 11 years of age. By working and receiving financial assistance from the parties to this action, the daughters received a high school education in Pender. One daughter attended Wayne State Teachers College for 2 years and the other daughter attended a business college in Sioux City, Iowa, for 1 year. Both of these daughters are married and have families of their own.

On April 12, 1939, the plaintiff transferred her interest in the 80–acre farm to her two daughters. The defendant signed the deed.

At the time of trial plaintiff was 66 years of age and the defendant nearly 80 years of age. No children were born to these parties. The defendant had no dependents except the plaintiff.

The plaintiff testified that she was a dutiful and obedient wife, worked and saved, and cohabited with the defendant until the last 2 or 3 years. She worked in the fields, did outside chores, cooked, and attended to her household duties such as cleaning the house and doing the washing. For a number of years she raised as high as 300 chickens, sold poultry and eggs, and used the money to buy clothing, things she wanted, and for groceries. She further testified that the defendant was the boss of the house and his word was law; that he would not tolerate any charge accounts and would not inform her as to his finances or business; and that he was a poor companion. The defendant did not complain of her work, but left the impression to her that she had not done enough. On several occasions the plaintiff asked the defendant for money. He would give her very small amounts, and for the last 3 or 4 years he had not given her any money nor provided her with clothing, except a coat about 4 years previous. The defendant had purchased the groceries the last 3 or 4 years, and permitted her to buy groceries, but he paid for them by check. There is apparently no complaint about the groceries the defendant furnished. The defendant had not taken her to a motion picture show during the past 12 years. They did not belong to any organizations or charitable institutions, nor did he give her money to make contributions to any charitable institutions. . . . For the past 4 years or more, the defendant had not given the plaintiff money to purchase furniture or other household necessities. Three years ago he did purchase an electric, wood-and-cob combination stove which was installed in the kitchen, also linoleum floor covering for the kitchen. The plaintiff further testified that the house is not equipped with a bathroom, bathing facilities, or inside toilet. The kitchen is not modern. She does not have a kitchen sink. Hard and soft water is obtained from a well and cistern. She has a mechanical Servel refrigerator, and the house is equipped with electricity. There is a pipeless furnace which she testified had not been in good working order for 5 or 6 years, and she testified she was tired of scooping coal and ashes. She had requested a new furnace but the defendant believed the one they had to be satisfactory. She related that the furniture was old and she would like to replenish it, at least to be comparable with some of her neighbors; that her silverware and dishes were old and were primarily gifts, outside of what she purchased; that one of her daughters was good about furnishing her clothing, at least a dress a year, or sometimes two; that the defendant owns a 1929 Ford coupé equipped with a heater which is not efficient, and on the average of every 2 weeks he drives the plaintiff to Wayne to visit her mother; and that he also owns a 1927 Chevrolet pickup which is used for different purposes on the farm. The plaintiff was privileged to use all of the rent money she wanted to from the 80–acre farm, and when she goes to see her daughters, which is not frequent, she uses part of the rent money for that purpose, the defendant providing no funds for such use. The defendant ordinarily raised hogs on his farm, but the last 4 or 5 years has leased his farm land to tenants, and he generally keeps up the fences and the buildings. At the present time the plaintiff is not able to raise chickens and sell eggs. She has about 25 chickens. The plaintiff has had three abdominal operations for which the defendant has paid. She selected her own doctor, and there were no restrictions placed in that respect. When she has requested various things for the home or personal effects, defendant has informed her on many occasions that he did not have the money to pay for the same. She would like to have a new car. She visited one daughter in Spokane,

Washington, in March 1951 for 3 or 4 weeks, and visited the other daughter living in Fort Worth, Texas, on three occasions for 2 to 4 weeks at a time. She had visited one of her daughters when she was living in Sioux City some weekends. The plaintiff further testified that she had very little funds, possibly $1,500 in the bank which was chicken money and money which her father furnished her, he having departed this life a few years ago; and that use of the telephone was restricted, indicating that defendant did not desire that she make long distance calls, otherwise she had free access to the telephone.

It appears that the defendant owns 398 acres of land with 2 acres deeded to a church, the land being of the value of $83,960; that he has bank deposits in the sum of $12,786.81 and government bonds in the amount of $104,500; and that his income, including interest on the bonds and rental for his real estate, is $8,000 or $9,000 a year. There are apparently some Series E United States Savings Bonds listed and registered in the names of Charles W. McGuire or Lydia M. McGuire purchased in 1943, 1944, and 1945, in the amount of $2,500. Other bonds seem to be in the name of Charles W. McGuire, without a beneficiary or co-owner designated. The plaintiff has a bank account of $5,960.22. This account includes deposits of some $200 and $100 which the court required the defendant to pay his wife as temporary allowance during the pendency of these proceedings. One hundred dollars was withdrawn on the date of each deposit.

The defendant assigns as error that the decree is not supported by sufficient evidence; that the decree is contrary to law; that the decree is an unwarranted usurpation and invasion of defendant's fundamental and constitutional rights; and that the court erred in allowing fees for the plaintiff's attorney.

While there is an allegation in the plaintiff's petition to the effect that the defendant was guilty of extreme cruelty towards the plaintiff, and also an allegation requesting a restraining order be entered against the defendant for fear he might molest plaintiff or take other action detrimental to her rights, the plaintiff made no attempt to prove these allegations and the fact that she continued to live with the defendant is quite incompatible with the same.

. . . [T]here are no cases cited by the plaintiff and relied upon by her from this jurisdiction or other jurisdictions that will sustain the action such as she has instituted in the instant case.

. . . [In] Anshutz v. Anshutz, 16 N.J.Eq. 162, . . . it was said that while a wife had no right to the interference of the court for her maintenance until her abandonment or separation, there might be an abandonment or separation, within the sound construction of the statute, while the parties continued to live under the same roof, as where the husband utterly refused to have intercourse with his wife, or to make any provision for her maintenance, and thus he might seclude himself in a portion of his house, take his meals alone or board elsewhere than in his house, and so as effectively separate himself from his wife and refuse to provide for her as in case of actual abandonment, although in whatever form it might exist it must be an abandonment. . . .

There are also several cases, under statutes of various states, in which separate maintenance was refused the wife, where the husband and wife were living in the same house. These cases are to the effect that it is an indispensable requirement of a maintenance statute that the wife should be living separate and apart from her husband without her fault, and that therefore, a wife living in the same house with her husband, occupying a different room and eating at a different time, was not entitled to separate maintenance.

In the instant case the marital relation has continued for more than 33 years, and the wife has been supported in the same manner during this time without complaint on her part. The parties have not been separated or living apart from each other at any time. In the light of the cited cases it is clear, especially so in this jurisdiction, that to maintain an action such as the one at bar, the parties must be separated or living apart from each other.

The living standards of a family are a matter of concern to the household, and not for the courts to determine, even though the husband's attitude toward his wife, according to his wealth and circumstances, leaves little to be said in his behalf. As long as the home is maintained and the parties are living as husband and wife it may be said that the husband is legally supporting his wife and the purpose of the marriage relation is being carried out. Public policy requires such a holding. It appears that the plaintiff is not devoid of money in her own right. She has a fair-sized bank account and is entitled to use the rent from the 80 acres of land left by her first husband, if she so chooses.

. . .

Reversed and remanded with directions to dismiss.

■ YEAGER, JUSTICE (dissenting).

. . .

In the light of what the decisions declare to be the basis of the right to maintain an action for support, is there any less reason for extending the right to a wife who is denied the right to maintenance in a home occupied with her husband than to one who has chosen to occupy a separate abode?

If the right is to be extended only to one who is separated from the husband equity and effective justice would be denied where a wealthy husband refused proper support and maintenance to a wife physically or mentally incapable of putting herself in a position where the rule could become available to her.

It is true that in all cases examined which uphold the right of a wife to maintain an action in equity for maintenance the parties were living apart, but no case has been cited or found which says that separation is a condition precedent to the right to maintain action in equity for maintenance. Likewise none has been cited or found which says that it is not.

In primary essence the rule contemplates the enforcement of an obligation within and not without the full marriage relationship. The reasoning contained in the opinions sustaining this right declare that purpose.

.   .   .

I think however that the court was without proper power to make any of the awards contained in the decree for the support and maintenance of the plaintiff except the one of $50 a month.

From the cases cited herein it is clear that a husband has the obligation to furnish to his wife the necessaries of life. These decisions make clear that for failure to furnish them the wife may seek allowances for her support and maintenance. However neither these decisions nor any others cited or found support the view contended for by plaintiff that the court may go beyond this and impose obligations other than that of payment of money for the proper support and maintenance of the wife.

.   .   .

NOTE

Obviously it is difficult for most law students in the first decade of the 21st century to identify vicariously with life in rural Nebraska in the middle of the 20th century. Even so, it is important to understand that the *McGuire* case was long used a poignant example of the need for reform of marital property and divorce law. *See,* e.g., Martha Fineman, *Implementing Equality: Ideology, Contradiction and Social Change. A Study of Rhetoric and Results in the Regulation of the Consequences of Divorce,* 1983 Wis. L.Rev. 789, 855. It should be understood that although some judges might have thought the remedy for a wife in Mrs. McGuire's situation was divorce, in many states at that time (and some still) the departure of a spouse without a ground for divorce could result in forfeiture or significant curtailment of alimony or other economic rights. One should ask how many of the basic problems remain today (even considered in terms of different creature comfort standards). For example, we have easier divorce, though abandonment or desertion still may limit alimony in some states and it is questionable whether economic treatment such as that described above would amount to cruelty or constructive desertion as a divorce ground. The changing ways in which marriage may be regarded as an economic partnership in many jurisdictions will be addressed in Chapter 5, *infra.*

NEW YORK FAMILY COURT ACT (McKinney 1999)

§ 412.   Married person's duty to support spouse

A married person is chargeable with the support of his or her spouse and, if possessed of sufficient means or able to earn such means, may be required to pay for his or her support a fair and reasonable sum, as the court may determine, having due regard to the circumstances of the respective parties.

VIRGINIA CODE ANN. (2004)

§ 20–61. Any spouse who without cause deserts or willfully neglects or refuses or fails to provide for the support and maintenance of his or her spouse . . . shall be guilty of a misdemeanor. . . .

GENDER–BASED DISCRIMINATION AND THE "NECESSARIES DOCTRINE"

Under the common law "necessaries" doctrine which was accepted widely in this country, a husband was responsible for necessary goods and services furnished to his wife by third parties. In Schilling v. Bedford County Memorial Hospital, Inc., 225 Va. 539, 303 S.E.2d 905 (1983), defendant was sued by a hospital seeking to recover for health care services it had rendered to his wife. Overruling a trial court decision that the husband was responsible for the treatment as a necessary under Va.Code § 55–37 (a codification of the common law), the Supreme Court of Virginia held that because the law imposed financial responsibility on a husband but not a wife it was an unconstitutional, gender-based discrimination under Article I, § 11 of the Virginia Constitution (Virginia's equal rights provision) as well as the equal protection clause of the Fourteenth Amendment to the U.S. Constitution. The court specifically rejected the hospital's argument that unequal treatment is justified by financial inequities facing women. They explained that the doctrine was rooted in outdated assumptions "as to the proper role of males and females in our society."

Courts in some jurisdictions have simply construed the "necessaries doctrine" in modern fashion to impose a duty on wives as well as husbands. See, e.g., Richland Memorial Hospital v. Burton, 282 S.C. 159, 318 S.E.2d 12 (1984). However, Virginia's response was added by statute after the Schilling case because the court determined that such a change should be a matter for the General Assembly. Va. Code Ann. § 55–37 (2004) now provides that:

> Except as otherwise provided in this section, a spouse shall not be responsible for the other spouse's contract or tort liability to a third party, whether such liability arose before or after the marriage. The doctrine of necessaries as it existed at common law shall apply equally to both spouses, except where they are permanently living separate and apart, but shall in no event create any liability between such spouses as to each other. No lien arising out of a judgment under this section shall attach to the judgment debtors' principal residence held by them as tenants by the entireties.

Are there good reasons to maintain the "necessaries doctrine" today or should it be abolished entirely, even if it does not discriminate based on gender? As a practical matter, widespread use of the joint credit card may have diminished the number of cases that otherwise might arise.

CALIFORNIA FAMILY CODE (West 2004)

§ 914.   Personal liability for debts incurred by spouse; separate property applied to satisfaction of debt

(a) Notwithstanding Section 913, a married person is personally liable for the following debts incurred by the person's spouse during marriage:

(1) A debt incurred for necessaries of life of the person's spouse while the spouses are living together.

(2) Except as provided in Section 4302, a debt incurred for common necessaries of life of the person's spouse while the spouses are living separately.

(b) The separate property of a married person may be applied to the satisfaction of a debt for which the person is personally liable pursuant to this section. If separate property is so applied at a time when nonexempt property in the community estate or separate property of the person's spouse is available but is not applied to the satisfaction of the debt, the married person is entitled to reimbursement to the extent such property was available.

(c)(1) Except as provided in paragraph (2), the statute of limitations set forth in Section 366.2 of the Code of Civil Procedure shall apply if the spouse for whom the married person is personally liable dies.

(2) If the surviving spouse had actual knowledge of the debt prior to expiration of the period set forth in Section 366.2 and the personal representative of the deceased spouse's estate failed to provide the creditor asserting the claim under this section with timely written notice of the probate administration of the estate in the manner provided for pursuant to Section 9050 of the Probate Code, the statute of limitations set forth in Section 337 or 339, as applicable, shall apply.

State v. Clark

Supreme Court of Washington, En Banc, 1977.
88 Wn.2d 533, 563 P.2d 1253.

■ Hicks, Associate Justice.

In January 1976, following a jury trial, M'Lissa Clark Daling was convicted of one count of possession of a controlled substance (a felony) and one count of possession of marijuana (a misdemeanor). She wishes an appellate review of her trial at public expense. From a finding of nonindigency by the trial court, she petitions this court. The sole issue on appeal is the indigency of petitioner. If she is indigent, she is entitled to an appeal at public expense. . . .

The record upon which we are asked to act is sketchy in the extreme. However, it appears that M'Lissa Clark was arrested June 12, 1975, and a trial took place in September. A mistrial resulted and the matter was reset for trial in January 1976. In November 1975, after the mistrial but prior to her new trial, M'Lissa Clark married Jay Daling.

Following the marriage, the couple moved to the Waterville area where Jay Daling owned 250 acres of wheat land. This land had been inherited by him some years preceding the marriage.

In January 1976, M'Lissa Daling was tried and convicted. After the conviction, she requested appellate review at public expense for the reason that she was an indigent. . . .

Upon considering petitioner's request and in examining the resources available to her, the trial court found that, while petitioner's separate assets and the marital community assets were insufficient, her husband had ample assets to finance an appeal. There was no indication in the record whether Jay Daling was willing or unwilling to finance an appeal and, consequently, the trial court made no finding in that regard. The trial court concluded that petitioner, M'Lissa Clark Daling, was not an indigent person entitled to an appeal at public expense. . . .

At the time of petitioner's marriage in November, her husband was aware that the trial of his bride was scheduled for January. Marriage, under the circumstances, carried the risk that his spouse might be found guilty and be required to spend some time in confinement, absent an appeal. In point of fact, petitioner's sentence was deferred except for 25 days in the county jail.

Assuming, as we must, that petitioner's desired appeal has probable merit and that it is not frivolous, should petitioner's spouse in this instance be obliged to finance any appeal that may be taken? . . .

After analyzing a number of cases, amicus concludes that the husband should not be responsible for the wife's appeal in this case. We do not agree.

RCW 26.16.200 provides:

> Neither husband or wife is liable for the debts or liabilities of the other incurred before marriage, nor for the separate debts of each other, nor is the rent or income of the separate property of either liable for the separate debts of the other: *Provided,* That the earnings and accumulations of the husband shall be available to the legal process of creditors for the satisfaction of debts incurred by him prior to marriage, and the earnings and accumulations of the wife shall be available to the legal process of creditors for the satisfaction of debts incurred by her prior to marriage. For the purpose of this section neither the husband nor the wife shall be construed to have any interest in the earnings of the other: *Provided Further,* That no separate debt may be the basis of a claim against the earnings and accumulations of either a husband or wife unless the same is reduced to judgment within three years of the marriage of the parties.

RCW 26.16.205 provides:

> The expenses of the family and the education of the children, including stepchildren, are chargeable upon the property of both husband and wife, or either of them, and in relation thereto they may be sued jointly or separately: *Provided,* That with regard to stepchildren, the obligation shall cease upon the termination of the relationship of husband and wife.

While the act of M'Lissa Clark for which she was tried occurred before she became Mrs. Daling, the trial in which she was convicted occurred after her marriage. Following her trial, she decided she wanted an appeal. There was no obligation for appeal costs before that time. The expense of this appeal, while related to an antenuptial act, is not an antenuptial debt. Thus, RCW 26.16.200 and cases decided thereunder regarding antenuptial debts are not apposite in this instance. Would the expense of an appeal in this case be a separate debt of the wife, collectible solely from her assets, or is the family-support statute (RCW 26.16.205) applicable?

RCW 26.16.205 has been the law of this state since 1881. Family-expense statutes, such as this, are generally considered to be at least as broad as the common-law duty to provide "necessaries" for the family. Should liability extend to providing a criminal appeal for a wife from a husband's separate property? This is a question of first impression in this state.

The Supreme Court of Colorado had such a case before it in Read v. Read, 119 Colo. 278, 202 P.2d 953 (1949). There the wife had been convicted of murder in the second degree, a divorce action was in progress, she was destitute, and the question of the expenses of an appeal in the criminal matter was before the court. The trial court's order provided that the husband should finance the appeal. On review the Supreme Court of Colorado, after determining that the husband was liable for necessaries, said at page 285, 202 P.2d at page 957:

> The question then posed is whether court costs, attorney fees and incidental expenses incurred in the defense of the criminal case by the wife, and a review of the judgment therein, are necessaries for which the husband is liable. Such necessaries include food, wearing apparel, medicines and medical attention, a habitation and necessary furniture and other articles for the wife's protection in society, consistent with the husband's ability to pay, and such articles and things as are necessary for her sustenance as well as preservation of her health and comfort. The term "necessaries" is incapable of exact definition; its meaning is variable, depending upon the circumstances, financial and otherwise, of the parties. We have said that plaintiff is entitled to have the judgment of conviction reviewed by this court and the necessity for expenses incurred therewith is as apparent and as vital as would be medical expenses incurred in case of her illness. Suffering and anguish resulting from her conviction may be as serious and disastrous as bodily ailments. The trial court found that plaintiff is destitute and that her husband is financially able to bear the expenses incurred in reviewing her conviction. The court further found that such allowed expenses were "necessaries." If they are such, defendant is liable therefor.... Under the attendant circumstances the expenses in pre-

senting her case in this court for review are "necessaries" for which defendant is liable, and the allowances thereof by the trial court were, under the circumstances here presented, right and proper.

. . .

Minnesota finds legal services for a wife to be a "necessary" under proper circumstances. In an action against the husband for legal services and expenses incurred in procuring the legal restoration of the wife's competency, the plaintiff's attorney prevailed. The husband had not wanted the services and he had said he would not pay for them. The court found that under the circumstances attorney fees and expenses were "necessaries," and the obligation to provide them was enforced against the husband. Carr v. Anderson, 154 Minn. 162, 191 N.W. 407 (1923).

We are persuaded that legal expenses, including a review of trial court proceedings, falls within the purview of RCW 26.16.205 as a family expense when a criminal action is involved and a spouse's liberty is at stake. It would follow that the separate assets of Jay Daling, petitioner's husband, may be considered in determining whether M'Lissa Clark Daling is an indigent person. The trial court did consider Jay Daling's separate assets when it found that petitioner was not an indigent person. The trial court was correct.

We find the above dispositive of the matter before us, however, we find it necessary to consider one more case. Christiansen v. Dept. of Social Security, 15 Wash.2d 465, 131 P.2d 189 (1942), a departmental 3–judge opinion with two judges concurring in the result, holding that a wife's separate property is not a "resource" of the husband's such as to preclude him from eligibility for a senior-citizen grant, was not cited by petitioner or amicus curiae, nor did either discuss the family-expense statute. In *Christiansen,* the Department of Social Security, through its acting director, denied respondent's application for a senior-citizen grant solely on the ground that his wife had assets readily convertible into cash in the amount of $1454. The Department contended this was a resource of the husband even though it was conceded to be the separate property of the wife. The husband was 87 years old and the wife was 67. She had not made application for a grant.

In its contention that the wife's separate property was a "resource" of the husband when he applied for a senior-citizen grant, the Department relied on RCW 26.16.205 (Rem.Rev.Stat. § 6906) as construed and applied in In re DeNisson, 197 Wash. 265, 84 P.2d 1024 (Wash. 1938). In that case, the wife had been adjudged mentally incompetent and a guardian had been appointed for her estate. This court held that necessary living expenses of her destitute husband were part of the "expenses of the family," and in the guardianship proceedings, gave him an allowance for his support from the wife's separate estate. *DiNisson* was found to be inapplicable in *Christiansen* because "no court has assumed jurisdiction of her [Mrs. Christiansen's] person or of her property." Nor could any form of action be brought by the husband or in his behalf to compel his wife to make him an allowance in anticipation of the accrual of debts to be incurred for his support.

In addition to finding *DeNisson* not controlling, the court stated the following facts as reasons for finding no resource in the wife's separate property: the wife's failure to support the husband would not be grounds for divorce; she would not be liable to criminal prosecution for failure to support her husband even though financially able to do so, though the reverse would not be true; and if the wife sues for divorce, she could not be compelled to pay temporary support during the pendency of the action.

We find that, with the passage of time and changes in statutes, the above reasons are today questionable. A wife now may be criminally liable for failure to support her husband under such circumstances as her husband would be liable for failure to support her. RCW 26.20.030. In marriage dissolution proceedings, the obligations of the wife and husband are the same. RCW 26.09.050, .090. We do not find *Christiansen* persuasive in the case at bench and we confine it to its facts.

The order of the trial court denying petitioner's motion for order of indigency is affirmed. . . .

NOTE

Family expense statutes generally were enacted for the benefit of creditors. For a historical background of this type of legislation, *see* 3 Chester G. Vernier, American Family Laws 102–108 (1935). Many were enacted in the 1920s and 1930s. Minn.Stat.Ann. § 519.05 (West 2006), revised in 2001, now provides:

> (a) A spouse is not liable to a creditor for any debts of the other spouse. Where husband and wife are living together, they shall be jointly and severally liable for necessary medical services that have been furnished to either spouse, and necessary household articles and supplies furnished to and used by the family. Notwithstanding this paragraph, in a proceeding under chapter 518 the court may apportion such debt between the spouses.

> (b) Either spouse may close a credit card account or other unsecured consumer line of credit on which both spouses are contractually liable, by giving written notice to the creditor.

E.   Testimonial Privilege, Torts and Crimes Between Spouses

1.   Testimonial Privilege

Trammel v. United States

Supreme Court of the United States, 1980.
445 U.S. 40, 100 S.Ct. 906, 63 L.Ed.2d 186.

■ Mr. Chief Justice Burger delivered the opinion of the Court.

We granted certiorari to consider whether an accused may invoke the privilege against adverse spousal testimony so as to exclude the voluntary testimony of his wife.

. . . .

On March 10, 1976, petitioner Otis Trammel was indicted with two others, Edwin Lee Roberts and Joseph Freeman, for importing heroin into the United States from Thailand and the Philippine Islands and for conspiracy to import heroin in violation of 21 U.S.C.A. §§ 952(a), 962(a), and 963. The indictment also named six unindicted co-conspirators, including petitioner's wife Elizabeth Ann Trammel.

According to the indictment, petitioner and his wife flew from the Philippines to California in August 1975, carrying with them a quantity of heroin. Freeman and Roberts assisted them in its distribution. Elizabeth Trammel then travelled to Thailand where she purchased another supply of the drug. On November 3, 1975, with four ounces of heroin on her person, she boarded a plane for the United States. During a routine customs search in Hawaii, she was searched, the heroin was discovered, and she was arrested. After discussions with Drug Enforcement Administration agents, she agreed to cooperate with the Government.

Prior to trial on this indictment, petitioner moved to sever his case from that of Roberts and Freeman. He advised the court that the Government intended to call his wife as an adverse witness and asserted his claim to a privilege to prevent her from testifying against him. At a hearing on the motion, Mrs. Trammel was called as a Government witness under a grant of use immunity. She testified that she and petitioner were married in May 1975 and that they remained married.[1] She explained that her cooperation with the Government was based on assurances that she would be given lenient treatment. She then described in considerable detail, her role and that of her husband in the heroin distribution conspiracy.

After hearing this testimony, the District Court ruled that Mrs. Trammel could testify in support of the Government's case to any act she observed during the marriage and to any communication "made in the presence of a third person"; however, confidential communications between petitioner and his wife were held to be privileged and inadmissible. The motion to sever was denied.

At trial, Elizabeth Trammel testified within the limits of the court's pretrial ruling; her testimony, as the Government concedes, constituted virtually its entire case against petitioner. He was found guilty on both the substantive and conspiracy charges. . . .

In the Court of Appeals petitioner's only claim of error was that the admission of the adverse testimony of his wife, over his objection, contravened this Court's teaching in Hawkins v. United States, 358 U.S. 74, 79 S.Ct. 136, 3 L.Ed.2d 125 (1958), . . .

---

1. In response to the question whether divorce was contemplated, Mrs. Trammel testified that her husband had said that "I would go my way and he would go his."

The privilege claimed by petitioner has ancient roots. Writing in 1628, Lord Coke observed that "it hath been resolved by the Justices that a wife cannot be produced either against or for her husband." 1 Coke, A Commentarie upon Littleton 6b (1628). See, generally, 8 J. Wigmore, Evidence § 2227, (McNaughton rev. 1961). This spousal disqualification sprang from two canons of medieval jurisprudence: first, the rule that an accused was not permitted to testify in his own behalf because of his interest in the proceeding; second, the concept that husband and wife were one, and since the woman had no recognized separate legal existence, the husband was that one. From those two now long-abandoned doctrines, it followed that what was inadmissible from the lips of the defendant-husband was also inadmissible from his wife.

Despite its medieval origins, this rule of spousal disqualification remained intact in most common-law jurisdictions well into the 19th century.... [I]t was not until 1933, in Funk v. United States, 290 U.S. 371, 54 S.Ct. 212, 78 L.Ed. 369, that this Court abolished the testimonial disqualification in the federal courts, so as to permit the spouse of a defendant to testify in the defendant's behalf. *Funk*, however, left undisturbed the rule that either spouse could prevent the other from giving adverse testimony. The rule thus evolved into one of privilege rather than one of absolute disqualification.

The modern justification for this privilege against adverse spousal testimony is its perceived role in fostering the harmony and sanctity of the marriage relationship. Notwithstanding this benign purpose, the rule was sharply criticized. Professor Wigmore termed it "the merest anachronism in legal theory and an indefensible obstruction to truth in practice." The Committee on the Improvement of the Law of Evidence of the American Bar Association called for its abolition. 63 American Bar Association Reports, at 594–595 (1938). In its place, Wigmore and others suggested a privilege protecting only private marital communications, modeled on the privilege between priest and penitent, attorney and client, and physician and patient.[5]

These criticisms influenced the American Law Institute, which, in its 1942 Model Code of Evidence, advocated a privilege for marital confidences, but expressly rejected a rule vesting in the defendant the right to exclude all adverse testimony of his spouse. See American Law Institute, Model Code of Evidence, Rule 215 (1942). In 1953 the Uniform Rules of Evidence, drafted by the National Conference of Commissioners on Uniform State Laws, followed a similar course; it limited the privilege to confidential communications and "abolishe[d] the rule, still existing in some states, and

---

5. This Court recognized just such a confidential marital communications privilege in Wolfle v. United States, 291 U.S. 7, 54 S.Ct. 279, 78 L.Ed. 617 (1934), and in Blau v. United States, 340 U.S. 332, 71 S.Ct. 301, 95 L.Ed. 306 (1951). In neither case, however, did the Court adopt the Wigmore view that the communications privilege be substituted *in place of* the privilege against adverse spousal testimony. The privilege as to confidential marital communications is not at issue in the instant case; accordingly, our holding today does not disturb *Wolfle* and *Blau*.

largely a sentimental relic, of not requiring one spouse to testify against the other in a criminal action." See Rule 23(e) and comments. Several state legislatures enacted similarly patterned provisions into law.

In Hawkins v. United States, 358 U.S. 74, 79 S.Ct. 136, 3 L.Ed.2d 125 (1958), this Court considered the continued vitality of the privilege against adverse spousal testimony in the federal courts. There the District Court had permitted petitioner's wife, over his objection, to testify against him. With one questioning concurring opinion, the Court held the wife's testimony inadmissible.... Also rejected was the Government's suggestion that the Court modify the privilege by vesting it in the witness spouse, with freedom to testify or not independent of the defendant's control. The Court viewed this proposed modification as antithetical to the widespread belief, evidenced in the rules then in effect in a majority of the States and in England, "that the law should not force or encourage testimony which might alienate husband and wife, or further inflame existing domestic differences."

Hawkins, then, left the federal privilege for adverse spousal testimony where it found it, continuing "a rule which bars the testimony of one spouse against the other unless both consent." Id., at 78. Accord, Wyatt v. United States, 362 U.S. 525, 528 (1960).[7]

.   .   .

The Federal Rules of Evidence acknowledge the authority of the federal courts to continue the evolutionary development of testimonial privileges in federal criminal trials "governed by the principles of the common law as they may be interpreted ... in the light of reason and experience." Fed.Rule Evid. 501. Cf. Wolfle v. United States, supra, at 12 (1934). The general mandate of Rule 501 was substituted by the Congress for a set of privilege rules drafted by the Judicial Conference Advisory Committee on Rules of Evidence and approved by the Judicial Conference of the United States and by this Court. That proposal defined nine specific privileges, including a husband-wife privilege which would have codified the *Hawkins* rule and eliminated the privilege for confidential marital communications. See Fed.Rule of Evid., Proposed Rule 505. In rejecting the proposed rules and enacting Rule 501, Congress manifested an affirmative intention not to freeze the law of privilege. Its purpose rather was to "provide the courts with the flexibility to develop rules of privilege on a case-by-case basis," 120 Cong.Rec. 40891 (1974) (statement of Rep. Hungate), and to leave the door open to change.

---

7. The decision in *Wyatt* recognized an exception to *Hawkins* for cases in which one spouse commits a crime against the other. 362 U.S., at 526, 80 S.Ct., at 902. This exception placed on the ground of necessity, was a longstanding one at common law. See Lord Audley's Case, 123 Eng.Rep. 1140 (1931); 8 Wigmore § 2239. It has been expanded since then to include crimes against the spouse's property, and in recent years crimes against children of either spouse, United States v. Allery, 526 F.2d 1362 (C.A.8 1975). Similar exceptions have been found to the confidential marital communications privilege.

Although Rule 501 confirms the authority of the federal courts to reconsider the continued validity of the *Hawkins* rule, the long history of the privilege suggests that it ought not to be casually cast aside. That the privilege is one affecting marriage, home, and family relationships—already subject to much erosion in our day—also counsels caution.

.   .   .

Since 1958, when *Hawkins* was decided, support for the privilege against adverse spousal testimony has been eroded further. Thirty-one jurisdictions, including Alaska and Hawaii, then allowed an accused a privilege to prevent adverse spousal testimony. The number has now declined to 24. In 1974, the National Conference on Uniform State Laws revised its Uniform Rules of Evidence, but again rejected the *Hawkins* rule in favor of a limited privilege for confidential communications. See Uniform Rules of Evidence, Rule 504. That proposed rule has been enacted in Arkansas, North Dakota, and Oklahoma—each of which in 1958 permitted an accused to exclude adverse spousal testimony. The trend in state law toward divesting the accused of the privilege to bar adverse spousal testimony has special relevance because the law of marriage and domestic relations are concerns traditionally reserved to the states. See Sosna v. Iowa, 419 U.S. 393, 404 (1975). Scholarly criticism of the *Hawkins* rule has also continued unabated.

.   .   .

It is essential to remember that the *Hawkins* privilege is not needed to protect information privately disclosed between husband and wife in the confidence of the marital relationship—once described by this Court as "the best solace of human existence." Stein v. Bowman, 13 Pet., at 223. Those confidences are privileged under the independent rule protecting confidential marital communications. The *Hawkins* privilege is invoked, not to exclude private marital communications but rather to exclude evidence of criminal acts and of communications made in the presence of third persons.

No other testimonial privilege sweeps so broadly. The privileges between priest and penitent, attorney and client, and physician and patient limit protection to private communications. These privileges are rooted in the imperative need for confidence and trust. The priest-penitent privilege recognizes the human need to disclose to a spiritual counselor, in total and absolute confidence, what are believed to be flawed acts or thoughts and to receive priestly consolation and guidance in return. The lawyer-client privilege rests on the need for the advocate and counselor to know all that relates to the client's reasons for seeking representation if the professional mission is to be carried out. Similarly, the physician must know all that a patient can articulate in order to identify and to treat disease; barriers to full disclosure would impair diagnosis and treatment.

The *Hawkins* rule stands in marked contrast to these three privileges. Its protection is not limited to confidential communications; rather it permits an accused to exclude all adverse spousal testimony. As Jeremy

Bentham observed more than a century and a half ago, such a privilege goes far beyond making "every man's house his castle," and permits a person to convert his house into "a den of thieves." 5 Rationale of Judicial Evidence 340 (1827). It "secures, to every man, one safe and unquestionable and ever ready accomplice for every imaginable crime." Id., at 338.

The ancient foundations for so sweeping a privilege have long since disappeared. Nowhere in the common-law world—indeed in any modern society—is a woman regarded as chattel or demeaned by denial of a separate legal identity and the dignity associated with recognition as a whole human being. Chip by chip, over the years those archaic notions have been cast aside so that "[n]o longer is the female destined solely for the home and the rearing of the family, and only the male for the marketplace and the world of ideas." Stanton v. Stanton, 421 U.S. 7, 14, 15, 95 S.Ct. 1373, 1377, 1378, 43 L.Ed.2d 688 (1975).

The contemporary justification for affording an accused such a privilege is also unpersuasive. When one spouse is willing to testify against the other in a criminal proceeding—whatever the motivation—their relationship is almost certainly in disrepair; there is probably little in the way of marital harmony for the privilege to preserve. In these circumstances, a rule of evidence that permits an accused to prevent adverse spousal testimony seems far more likely to frustrate justice than to foster family peace.[12] Indeed, there is reason to believe that vesting the privilege in the accused could actually undermine the marital relationship. For example, in a case such as this, the Government is unlikely to offer a wife immunity and lenient treatment if it knows that her husband can prevent her from giving adverse testimony. If the Government is dissuaded from making such an offer, the privilege can have the untoward effect of permitting one spouse to escape justice at the expense of the other. It hardly seems conducive to the preservation of the marital relation to place a wife in jeopardy solely by virtue of her husband's control over her testimony.

Our consideration of the foundations for the privilege and its history satisfy us that "reason and experience" no longer justify so sweeping a rule as that found acceptable by the Court in *Hawkins.* Accordingly, we conclude that the existing rule should be modified so that the witness spouse alone has a privilege to refuse to testify adversely; the witness may be neither compelled to testify nor foreclosed from testifying. This modification—vesting the privilege in the witness spouse—furthers the important public interest in marital harmony without unduly burdening legitimate law enforcement needs.

Here, petitioner's spouse chose to testify against him. That she did so after a grant of immunity and assurances of lenient treatment does not render her testimony involuntary. Accordingly, the District Court and the

---

12. It is argued that abolishing the privilege will permit the Government to come between husband and wife, pitting one against the other. That, too, misses the mark. Neither *Hawkins,* nor any other privilege, prevents the Government from enlisting one spouse to give information concerning the other or to aid in the other's apprehension. It is only the spouse's testimony in the courtroom that is prohibited.

Court of Appeals were correct in rejecting petitioner's claim of privilege, and the judgment of the Court of Appeals is affirmed.

NOTE

Spousal privilege may be limited by statute. For example, in Commonwealth v. Kirkner, 569 Pa. 499, 805 A.2d 514 (2002), the Pennsylvania Supreme Court ruled on the admissibility of testimony given by a spouse against her husband who had been charged with simple assault and harassment of her The state statute eliminated the spousal privilege in criminal proceedings for bodily injury between husband and wife, and thus the privilege could not be used no matter what effect the wife's testimony would have upon her spouse. The court's opinion demonstrated that the common law privilege is unavailable whenever revoked by statute.

2. SEXUAL ASSAULT OR RAPE

Warren v. State

Supreme Court of Georgia, 1985.
255 Ga. 151, 336 S.E.2d 221.

■ SMITH, JUSTICE.

"When a woman says I do, does she give up her right to say I won't?"[1] This question does not pose the real question because rape and aggravated sodomy are not sexual acts of an ardent husband performed upon an initially apathetic wife,[3] they are acts of violence that are accompanied with physical and mental abuse and often leave the victim with physical and psychological damage that is almost always long lasting.[4] Thus we find the more appropriate question: When a woman says "I do" in Georgia does she give up her right to State protection from the violent acts of rape and

---

1. Griffin, In 44 States, It's Legal to Rape Your Wife, 21 Student Lawyer. Another question posed is: "But if you can't rape your wife, who[m] can you rape?" Freeman, "But If You Can't Rape Your Wife, Who[m] Can You Rape?": The Marital Rape Exemption Re-examined. 15 Family Law Quarterly (1981).

3. Georgia has recognized both spouses' right to say "I won't" under the domestic law, by providing that before refusal of sexual intercourse rose to the level of cruel treatment in divorce, the refusal had to be "a denial, that ... was wilful, persistent and without justification and done with an intent to cast him off as a husband completely and forever." Harkness v. Harkness, 228 Ga. 184, 186, 184 S.E.2d 566 (1971).

4. "When you have been intimately violated by a person who is supposed to love and protect you, it can destroy your capacity for intimacy with anyone else. Moreover, many wife victims are trapped in a reign of terror and experience repeated sexual assaults over a period of years. When you are raped by a stranger you have to live with a frightening memory. When you are raped by your husband, you have to live with your rapist." National Center on Women and Family Law, Clearing House Review, November, 1984, citing Dr. David Finkelhor's testimony and statement in support of H.B. 516 to remove spousal exemption to sexual assault offenses to the Judiciary Committee, New Hampshire State Legislature (Mar. 25, 1981), p. 745.

aggravated sodomy performed by her husband? The answer is no.[5] We affirm.

The appellant, Daniel Steven Warren, was indicted by a Fulton County Grand Jury for the rape and aggravated sodomy of his wife. They were living together as husband and wife at the time. The appellant filed a pre-trial general demurrer and motion to dismiss the indictment. After a hearing, the motions were denied. The appellant sought and was issued a certificate of immediate review and filed an application for an interlocutory appeal which was granted by this court.

1.   The appellant asserts that there exists within the rape statute an implicit marital exclusion that makes it legally impossible for a husband to be guilty of raping his wife.

Until the late 1970's there was no real examination of this apparently widely held belief. Within the last few years several jurisdictions have been faced with similar issues and they have decided that under certain circumstances a husband can be held criminally liable for raping his wife.

What is behind the theory and belief that a husband could not be guilty of raping his wife? There are various explanations for the rule and all of them flow from the common law attitude toward women, the status of women and marriage.

Perhaps the most often used basis for the marital rape exemption is the view set out by Lord Hale[6] in 1 Hale P.C. 629. It is known as Lord Hale's contractual theory. The statement attributed to Lord Hale used to support the theory is: "but a husband cannot be guilty of a rape committed by himself upon his lawful wife, for by their mutual matrimonial consent and contract the wife hath given up herself in this kind unto her husband which she cannot retreat."

There is some thought that the foundation of his theory might well have been the subsequent marriage doctrine of English law, wherein the perpetrator could, by marrying his victim, avoid rape charges. It was thus argued as a corollary, rape within the marital relationship would result in the same immunity.[7]

---

5. It would be incongruous to find both spouses have a right under the domestic law to refuse a normal and mutual satisfying function of married life, and at the same time find that wives have no protection under the criminal law in the event their husbands engage in the violent conduct defined as rape.

6. Hale was Chief Justice of the Court of King's Bench from 1671 until 1675 when he resigned at age 66, one year before his death. A book based on his manuscripts was published in 1736, and the first American edition of the book was published in America in 1847, 1 M. Hale, Pleas of the Crown. Although we could not find a Georgia case

that cited Hale's implied consent theory, we found a case that gives us a glimpse into Hale's world of more than three hundred years ago. "In 2 P.C. 290, this great judge and illustrious author says, 'But of all difficulties in evidence, there are two sorts of crimes that give the greatest difficulty, namely, rapes and witchcraft, ...'" Smith v. State, 77 Ga. 705, 712 (1886).

7. The laws in America changed that doctrine, "[t]he general rule apart from statute is that the subsequent marriage of the parties is no bar to a prosecution for rape. [Cit.] ..." 9 A.L.R. 339.

Another theory stemming from medieval times is that of a wife being the husband's chattel or property. Since a married woman was part of her husband's property, nothing more than a chattel, rape was nothing more than a man making use of his own property.

A third theory is the unity in marriage or unity of person theory that held the very being or legal existence of a woman was suspended during marriage, or at least was incorporated and consolidated into that of her husband. In view of the fact that there was only one legal being, the husband, he could not be convicted of raping himself.

These three theories have been used to support the marital rape exemption. Others have tried to fill the chasm between these three theories with justifications for continuing the exemption in the face of changes in the recognition of women, their status, and the status of marriage. Some of the justifications include: Prevention of fabricated charges; Preventing wives from using rape charges for revenge; Preventing state intervention into marriage so that possible reconciliation will not be thwarted. A closer examination of the theories and justifications indicates that they are no longer valid, if they ever had any validity.

Hale's implied consent theory was created[8] at a time when marriages were irrevocable and when all wives promised to "love, honor, and obey" and all husbands promised to "love, cherish, and protect until death do us part." Wives were subservient to their husbands, her identity was merged into his, her property became his property, and she took his name for her own.

There have been dramatic changes in women's rights and the status of women and marriage. Today our State Constitution provides that, "no person shall be deprived of life, *liberty,* or property except by due process," (Emphasis supplied.) Art. 1, § 1, Para. 1, and "protection to *person* and property is the paramount duty of government and shall be impartial and complete. No person shall be denied the equal protection of the laws." (Emphasis supplied.) Art. 1, § 2, Para. 2. Our State Constitution also provides that each spouse has a right to retain his or her own property. Art. 1, § 1, Para. 27. Our statutory laws provide that, "[t]he rights of citizens include, *without limitation,* the following: (1) The right of *personal security,* [and] (2) The right of *personal liberty* ..." (Emphasis supplied.) OCGA § 1–2–6. Women in Georgia "are entitled to the privilege of the elective franchise and have the right to hold any civil office or perform any civil function as fully and completely as do male citizens." OCGA § 1–2–7. Couples who contemplate marriage today may choose either spouse's surname or a combination of both names for their married surname, OCGA § 19–3–33.1. No longer is a wife's domicile presumed to be that of her

8. Hale cited no legal authority for his proposition, "[t]hus the marital exemption rule expressly adopted by many of our sister states has its ORIGIN in a bare, extra-judicial declaration made some 300 years ago. Such a declaration cannot itself be considered a definite and binding statement of the common law, although legal commentators have often restated the rule since the time of Hale without evaluating its merits, [cits.]" State v. Smith, 85 N.J. 193, 426 A.2d 38, 41 (1981).

husband, OCGA § 19–2–3 and no longer is the husband head of the family with the wife subject to him. OCGA § 19–3–8. Marriages are revocable without fault by either party, OCGA § 19–5–3(13); either party, not just the husband, can be required to pay alimony upon divorce, OCGA § 19–6–1; and both parties have a joint and several duty to provide for the maintenance, protection, and education of their children, OCGA § 19–7–2. Couples may write antenuptial agreements in which they are able to decide, prior to marriage, future settlements, OCGA § 19–3–62; and our legislature has recognized that there can be violence in modern family life and it has enacted special laws to protect family members who live in the same household from one another's violent acts, Ga.L.1981, 880; OCGA § 19–13–1 et seq.

Today, many couples write their own marriage vows in which they specifically decide the terms of their marriage contract. Certainly no normal woman who falls in love and wishes " 'to marry, establish a home and bring up children' . . . a central part of the *liberty* protected by the Due Process Clause, [Cits.]" (Emphasis supplied.) Zablocki v. Redhail, 434 U.S. 374, 384, 98 S.Ct. 673, 679, 54 L.Ed.2d 618 (1978), would knowingly include an irrevocable term to her revocable marriage contract that would allow her husband to rape her. Rape "is highly reprehensible, both in a moral sense and in its almost total contempt for the personal integrity and autonomy of the female victim. . . . Short of homicide, it is the 'ultimate violation of self.' " Coker v. Georgia, 433 U.S. 584, 599, 97 S.Ct. 2861, 2869, 53 L.Ed.2d 982 (1977). It is incredible to think that any state would sanction such behavior by adding an implied consent term *to all marriage contracts* that would leave *all* wives with no protection under the law from the "ultimate violation of self," *Coker,* supra, 97 S.Ct. at 2869, simply because they choose to enter into a relationship that is respected and protected by the law. The implied consent theory to spousal rape is without logical meaning, and *obviously conflicts* with our Constitutional and statutory laws and our regard for all citizens of this State.

One would be hard pressed to argue that a husband can rape his wife because she is his chattel. Even in the darkest days of slavery when slaves were also considered chattel, rape was defined as "the carnal knowledge of a female whether free or slave, forcibly and against her will." Georgia Code, § 4248, p. 824 (1863). Both the chattel and unity of identity rationales have been cast aside. "No where in the common law world—[or] in any modern society—is a woman regarded as chattel or demeaned by denial of a separate legal identity and the dignity associated with recognition as a whole human being." Trammel v. United States, 445 U.S. 40, 52, 100 S.Ct. 906, 913, 63 L.Ed.2d 186 (1980).

We find that none of the theories have any validity. The justifications likewise are without efficacy. There is no other crime we can think of in which *all of the victims are denied protection* simply because someone might fabricate a charge; there is no evidence that wives have flooded the district attorneys with revenge filled trumped-up charges, and once a marital relationship is at the point where a husband rapes his wife, state intervention is needed for the wife's protection.[10]

There never has been an expressly stated marital exemption included in the Georgia rape statute. Furthermore, our statute never included the word "unlawful" which has been widely recognized as signifying the incorporation of the common law spousal exclusion. Commonwealth v. Chretien, 338 Mass. 123, 417 N.E.2d 1203, 1208 (1981). A reading of the statute indicates that there is no marital exclusion. "A person commits the offense of rape when he has carnal knowledge of a female forcibly and against her will." OCGA § 16–6–1. We need not decide whether or not a common law marital exemption became part of our old statutory rape law, because the rape statute that was similar to the common law definition[12] was specifically repealed in 1968, and our new broader statute, OCGA § 16–6–1, was enacted in its place which plainly on its face includes a husband.[13]

2.   The appellant contends that there is an implicit marital exclusion within the aggravated sodomy statute that makes it legally impossible for a husband to be guilty of an offense of aggravated sodomy performed upon his wife.

Sodomy was originally defined as "the carnal knowledge and connection against the order of nature by man with man, or in the same unnatural manner with woman." Laws 1833, Cobb's 1851 Digest, p. 787. The punishment for sodomy was "imprisonment at labor in the penitentiary for and during the natural life of the person convicted of this detestable crime." Laws 1833, Id.

Under the original rape and sodomy statutes, a man accused of rape could defend by alleging that the victim consented. If the consent could be proven, he could not be guilty of rape, because the third element of the offense "against her will" would be missing. One accused of sodomy could not defend by alleging consent, as lack of consent was not an element of the offense, and "[w]here a man and a woman voluntarily have carnal knowledge and connection against the order of nature with each other, they are both guilty of sodomy, . . ." Comer v. State, 21 Ga.App. 306, 94 S.E. 314 (1917). Thus an allegation of consent would only go to show the other

---

10. The state intervenes in cases of assault, OCGA §§ 16–5–20; 16–5–21 and battery, OCGA §§ 16–5–23; 16–5–24 and in other forms of family violence, OCGA § 19–13–1 et seq., and we have recognized that assault and battery are involved in rape. Hardy v. State, 159 Ga.App. 854, 285 S.E.2d 547 (1981).

12. "Rape is the carnal knowledge of a female, forcibly and against her will."

13. When our Criminal Code was revised, the drafters relied upon the Illinois Criminal Code and the Model Penal Code. Both Codes included within their rape stat-

utes an explicit marital exemption. "A male person . . . who has sexual intercourse with a female, not his wife, by force and against her will commits rape." Ill.Rev.Stat. § 11.1; "A male who has sexual intercourse with a female not his wife is guilty of rape if; . . ." Section 213.1 Model Penal Code. Our Legislature could have, but did not, include the words "not his wife." They chose instead to add the words "A person," which broadens the statute and which is in keeping with the enunciated purposes of the code. OCGA § 16–1–2.

party's guilt. "One who voluntarily participates in an unnatural act of sexual intercourse with another is also guilty of sodomy. One who does not so participate is not guilty." Perryman v. State, 63 Ga.App. 819, 823, 12 S.E.2d 388 (1940).

In 1968 the sodomy statute was specifically repealed, and two new offenses were enacted, sodomy and aggravated sodomy. There can be no common law marital exemption under the aggravated sodomy statute based on "implied consent," when the statute was enacted in 1968 and when there clearly was no marital exemption for sodomy based on "consent" under the original sodomy statute.

3. The appellant contends that if we find no marital exemptions under the rape and aggravated sodomy statutes it would be a new interpretation of the criminal law, and to apply the statutes to him would deprive him of his due process rights.

"All the Due Process Clause requires is that the law give sufficient warning that men may conduct themselves so as to avoid that which is forbidden. [Cit.]" Rose v. Locke, 423 U.S. 48, 50, 96 S.Ct. 243, 46 L.Ed.2d 185 (1975). Both the rape and aggravated sodomy statutes are broadly written and they are plain on their face. This is a first application of these statutes to this particular set of facts, this is not an unforeseeable judicial enlargement of criminal statutes that are narrowly drawn.

. . .

Judgment affirmed.

NOTE

In People v. Liberta, 64 N.Y.2d 152, 485 N.Y.S.2d 207, 474 N.E.2d 567 (1984), the New York Court of Appeals struck down both the marital and gender exemptions in that State's criminal rape statute. The case involved a defendant husband who had been judicially ordered to move out and remain away from the marital home. Although the court found that under such a protective order he was statutorily "not married" at the time of the rape, it nevertheless concluded that the marital exemption for rape was unconstitutional. In doing so, they specifically rejected several possible rationales in support of the exemption. These included possible fabrication of complaints by vindictive wives, the right of marital privacy, the interest in promoting reconciliation between parties, and the argument that marital rape is less serious than other rapes and therefore is adequately dealt with under other statutes such as those on assault. The court concluded:

> The question . . . is whether the Legislature would prefer to have statutes which cover forcible rape and sodomy, with no exemption for married men who rape or sodomize their wives and no exception made for females who rape males, or instead to have no statutes proscribing forcible rape and sodomy. In any case where a court must decide whether to sever an exemption or instead declare an entire statute a nullity it must look at the importance of the statute, the significance of

the exemption within the over-all statutory scheme, and the effects of striking down the statute. . . . Forcible sexual assaults have historically been treated as serious crimes and certainly remain so today. . . . Statutes prohibiting such behavior are of the utmost importance, and to declare such statutes a nullity would have a disastrous effect on the public interest and safety. The inevitable conclusion is that the Legislature would prefer to eliminate the exemptions and thereby preserve the statutes. Accordingly we choose the remedy of striking the marital exemption . . . and the gender exemption . . . , so that it is now the law of this State that any person who engages in sexual intercourse or deviate sexual intercourse with any other person by forcible compulsion is guilty of either rape in the first degree or sodomy in the first degree. Because the statutes under which the defendant was convicted are not being struck down, his conviction is affirmed.

VIRGINIA CODE ANN. (Supp. 2006)

§ 18.2–61. Rape

A. If any person has sexual intercourse with a complaining witness, whether or not his or her spouse, or causes a complaining witness, whether or not his or her spouse, to engage in sexual intercourse with any other person and such act is accomplished (i) against the complaining witness's will, by force, threat or intimidation of or against the complaining witness or another person; or (ii) through the use of the complaining witness's mental incapacity or physical helplessness; or (iii) with a child under age 13 as the victim, he or she shall be guilty of rape.

B. A violation of this section shall be punishable, in the discretion of the court or jury, by confinement in a state correctional facility for life or for any term not less than five years; the penalty for a violation of subdivision A (iii), where the offender is more than three years older than the victim, if done in the commission of, or as part of the same course of conduct as, or as part of a common scheme or plan . . . shall include a mandatory minimum term of confinement of 25 years. If the term of confinement imposed for any violation of subdivision A (iii), where the offender is more than three years older than the victim, is for a term less than life imprisonment, the judge shall impose, in addition to any active sentence, a suspended sentence of no less than 40 years. This suspended sentence shall be suspended for the remainder of the defendant's life, subject to revocation by the court.

There shall be a rebuttable presumption that a juvenile over the age of 10 but less than 12, does not possess the physical capacity to commit a violation of this section. In any case deemed appropriate by the court, all or part of any sentence imposed for a violation under this section against a spouse may be suspended upon the defendant's completion of counseling or therapy, if not already provided, in the manner prescribed under [the statute] if, after consideration of the views of the complaining witness and such other evidence as may be relevant, the court finds such action will promote maintenance of the family unit and will be in the best interest of the complaining witness. C. Upon a finding of guilt under this section, when a spouse is the complaining witness in any case tried by the court without a jury, the court, without entering a judgment of guilt, upon motion of the defendant who has not previously had a proceeding against him for violation of this section dismissed pursuant to this subsection and with the consent of the complaining witness and the attorney for the Commonwealth, may defer further proceedings and place the defendant on probation pending completion of counseling or therapy, if not already provided, in the manner prescribed under [the statute]. If the defendant fails to so complete such counseling or therapy, the court may make final disposition of the case and proceed as otherwise provided. If such counseling is completed as prescribed under [the statute]. The court may discharge the defendant and dismiss the proceedings against him if, after consideration of the views of the complaining witness and such other evidence as may be relevant, the court finds such action will promote maintenance of the family unit and be in the best interest of the complaining witness.

NOTE

Vermont has joined those states holding that consent to sexual contact may not be presumed in a tort action for sexual battery between spouses. The Vermont Supreme Court ruled that implied consent was based on an "arcane common law" and that today there is no difference under Vermont's criminal provision for sexual assault between marital and nonmarital status. *In re* Estate of Peters, 171 Vt. 381, 765 A.2d 468 (2000). In State v. Willis, 223 Neb. 844, 394 N.W.2d 648 (1986), the Supreme Court of Nebraska held that whatever basis may have existed for assuming that the common law doctrine of spousal exclusion was applicable to its former state rape law, it was abrogated when the legislature enacted its new sexual assault law. *See generally* Timothy S. Mehok, Recent Development, *The Fifth Circuit Takes a Look at Federal Tort Claims in the Context of Sexual Battery.* (Leleux v. United States, 178 F.3d 750 (5th Cir.1999)), 75 TUL. L. REV. 549 (2000).

3.   CRIMES INVOLVING SPOUSAL PROPERTY

Cladd v. State

Supreme Court of Florida, 1981.
398 So.2d 442.

■ ALDERMAN, JUSTICE.

The sole issue presented for review is whether a husband, who is physically but not legally separated from his wife, can be guilty of burglary when he enters premises, possessed only by the wife and in which he has no ownership or possessory interest, without the wife's consent and with intent to commit an offense therein.... We hold that the Second District

[Court of Appeal] correctly decided that, under the particular facts of this case, the defendant could be guilty of burglary of his estranged wife's apartment. . . .

The factual situation is narrow. The defendant and his wife had been separated for approximately six months, although there was no formal separation agreement or restraining order. He had no ownership or possessory interest in his wife's apartment and had at no time lived there. One morning, he broke through the locked door of her apartment with a crowbar, struck her, and attempted to throw her over the second floor stair railing. The next morning, he again attempted to break into her apartment but left when the police arrived.

The defendant was charged with burglary and attempted burglary.[2] Although conceding that his wife did not in fact consent to his entry into her apartment, he moved to dismiss the charges on the basis that since the victim was his wife, he was licensed or invited to enter her apartment as a matter of law. He then contended that, if he had the right to enter the apartment, he could not be guilty of burglary or attempted burglary. Relying upon Vazquez v. State [350 So.2d 1094 (Fla.App.1977)], the trial court dismissed the charges. The State appealed, and the Second District, expressly disagreeing with the rationale of the Third District in *Vazquez,* reversed. The Second District held that although each spouse may have the legal right to the other's company, this does not include the right to break and enter the other's apartment *with intent to commit an offense therein.*

In *Vazquez,* the Third District held that since the husband in that case had the legal right to be with his wife, he could not be guilty of burglary when he broke into her apartment. Judge Haverfield, however, expressing the view later adopted by the Second District, dissented to the reversal of the burglary conviction. Pointing out that the victim's wife had the sole possessory rights to the apartment and that defendant had gained entrance only by actually breaking down the door and finding that the evidence was sufficient to sustain the burglary conviction, he concluded that the wife's apartment was not a marital abode and defendant no longer had a legal right to be there.

Later, in Wilson v. State, 359 So.2d 901 (Fla. 3d DCA), cert. denied, 365 So.2d 716 (Fla.1978), the Third District addressed the issue of whether entry into a father-in-law's home, where defendant's wife was temporarily residing, with intent to assault her constituted burglary. Distinguishing *Vazquez* on the basis that, in *Wilson,* the premises were possessed by the wife's father, the Third District affirmed defendant's burglary conviction and said that the husband's legal right to be with his wife did not establish consent where the wife was living in premises which were not solely possessed by her. The right of consortium alone was not sufficient to give

---

2. Burglary means entering or remaining in a structure or a conveyance with the intent to commit an offense therein, unless the premises are at the time open to the public or the defendant is licensed or invited to enter or remain. Section 810.02, Florida Statutes (1977). It is a crime that involves primarily the invasion of possessory property rights of another. Cannon v. State, 102 Fla. 928, 136 So. 695 (1931).

the husband a right of entry into these premises. Yet, the legal right of consortium was the basis upon which the Third District premised its determination of implied consent in *Vazquez*.

We reject the defendant's contention that the marriage relationship and the right of consortium deriving therefrom preclude the State from ever establishing the nonconsensual entry requisite to the crime of burglary, and we disapprove the Third District's contrary ruling in *Vazquez*. Since burglary is an invasion of the possessory property rights of another, where premises are in the sole possession of the wife, the husband can be guilty of burglary if he makes a nonconsensual entry into her premises with intent to commit an offense, the same as he can be guilty of larceny of his wife's separate property. In State v. Herndon, 158 Fla. 115, 27 So.2d 833 (1946), discussing a wife's separate property rights, we held that a husband could be charged with the larceny of his wife's separate property, and we explained:

> In a society like ours, where the wife owns and holds property in her own right, where she can direct the use of her personal property as she pleases, where she can engage in business and pursue a career, it would be contrary to every principle of reason to hold that a husband could ad lib appropriate her property. If the common-law rule was of force, the husband could collect his wife's pay check, he could direct its use, he could appropriate her separate property and direct the course of her career or business if she has one. We think it has not only been abrogated by law, it has been abrogated by custom, the very thing out of which the common law was derived.

27 So.2d at 835. The defendant's consortium rights did not immunize him from burglary where he had no right to be on the premises possessed solely by his wife independent of an asserted right to consortium.

The defendant's estranged wife was in sole possession of the premises into which he broke with intent to assault her. The district court correctly reversed the trial court's dismissal of the burglary and attempted burglary charges.

. . .

■ BOYD, JUSTICE, dissenting.

Under long-established principles of Anglo–American law, one of the essential incidents of the marital state is the right of spouses to the company and comfort of one another. This right is referred to as the right of consortium.

Consortium is so basic as an incident of marriage that it should not be undermined except by a clear legislative statement of the public policy of this state. The legislature should reconcile the matter of consortium rights with the elements of any crime, and should do so very carefully when dealing in the context of a crime carrying a possible sentence of life imprisonment. See § 810.02(2), Fla.Stat. (1977).

. . .

The legislature has met a number of times since the principles of the *Vazquez* and *Wilson* cases were announced. I believe the fact that the legislature failed to modify or clarify the burglary statute in response to the judicial development of these principles indicates that the legislative intent was properly derived in those cases.

. . .

■ England, Justice, dissenting.

Like an anxious Pandora endeavoring to stuff the ills of the world back into her box, the majority endeavors to confine interspousal crimes to the factual situation of this case. As Pandora and the world sadly learned, however, once the box is opened there is no way to contain the ephemeral evils which escape.

The majority today holds that one spouse may commit burglary against another. This new common law doctrine has emanations which go far beyond this case. This becomes evident when the case is viewed preliminarily from the perspective of what is *not* here involved.

First, this is not a prosecution for assault. Any discussion with regard to the husband's physical abuse or intended physical abuse of his wife is extraneous to the legal question presented. Mr. Cladd may or may not be prosecuted for his violent acts toward his wife's person. Whether that occurs is beside the point.

Second, this case does not involve spouses who are divorced, legally separated, or already in court in a pending dissolution proceeding. The husband and wife here are married, and there is no objective, legal manifestation that their marriage or interpersonal relations are being unwound. That they live apart, it will be seen, is quite irrelevant to the legal issue posed.

Third, this case does not entail a situation where separately-owned property, purchased or inherited by the wife, was established as a residence apart from her husband's. The record here only shows that Mrs. Cladd's living accommodations were separate from her husband's. We do not know who purchased the furnishings and fixtures, whether they came from a residence which had been occupied jointly, or even whether the separate abode was a second or alternative home.

When these matters are removed from the *legal* considerations, this case boils down to a husband's uninvited entry onto premises which the wife occupies away from the marital home. This situation is legally indistinguishable from other situations in which a separate residence is maintained by one or both spouses and in which one is temporarily residing, such as a summer home, a winter ski lodge, a vacation cottage at the seashore, a temporary, rented, haven from marital incompatibility, a remote wing or separate building on jointly occupied property (such as a studio-garage in which one spouse alone works), or even a separate bedroom in which one spouse may be seeking a retreat in the marital home. The record of this proceeding nowhere indicates that the wife had a separate possessory interest in the property she placed in her separate facility. We do not know whether the six-month separation of these spouses was the result of estrangement, a mutually agreed-upon cooling off period, a segregated vacation plan, or some other reason. Mr. Cladd here, I submit, was simply charged with illegal entry into a place where his wife claimed sanctuary from their common residence. The manner of entry and the purpose for entry may prompt judicial concerns for the wife's welfare, but the parties' motives or state of mind will prove an unreliable touchstone for criminal prosecutions of this sort, I predict.

The effect of today's decision is to bring prosecuting attorneys into marital disputes in a way which is unprecedented in Florida or elsewhere. I confess I am not comfortable with the Third District's analysis of the basis for rejecting burglary prosecutions in these situations—a right of cohabitation or consortium. Those concepts connote marital harmony, and here we have obvious discord. I am quite comfortable, however, with the thought that our criminal courts should not be involved, in fact or as a threat, in domestic disputes which involve an invasion of one spouse's claim of separateness or privacy. Personal assaults, I repeat, are different, and in those cases perhaps different considerations should pertain.

NOTE

A.L.I. MODEL PENAL CODE § 223.1(4) provides that: "It is not a defense that a theft was from the actor's spouse, except that misappropriation of household and personal effects, or other property normally accessible to both spouses, is theft only if it occurs after the parties have ceased living together."

4. INSTITUTIONAL RESPONSES TO VIOLENCE BETWEEN SPOUSES

State ex rel. Williams v. Marsh

Supreme Court of Missouri, 1982.
626 S.W.2d 223.

■ HIGGINS, JUDGE.

Denise Williams petitions this court for a writ of mandamus to compel the trial court to issue an order of protection, an order restraining her husband from entering her dwelling and a temporary order of custody as authorized by The Adult Abuse Act, §§ 455.010–.085, RSMo Supp.1980. In a separate action she appeals the trial court's dismissal of her petition filed under Chapter 455, RSMo Supp.1980. The appeal was consolidated with the mandamus action because both present the same issues concerning the trial court's determination that Chapter 455, RSMo Supp.1980 violates a number of provisions of the Missouri and United States Constitutions. The preliminary writ is made peremptory; the judgment of dismissal is reversed, and the cause is remanded for further proceedings consistent with the writ herein issued.

After a hearing on plaintiff's petition for an *ex parte* order of protection, the trial court found: plaintiff, Denise Williams, and respondent, Edward M. Williams were married; one child was born of the marriage; the couple had been living separately for approximately five months prior to the hearing, plaintiff having custody of the child; respondent's home address was unknown although his place of employment was known[1] and his estimated wages were $1,000 per month; during the separation respondent provided no support or maintenance to plaintiff or the child with the exception of a small amount of clothing for the child; plaintiff leased or rented her residence individually; on November 13, 1980, and on numerous previous occasions, respondent (a 230 lbs., former Golden Gloves boxer) "intentionally, knowingly and wilfully beat petitioner ... causing ... serious physical injury ... requiring petitioner to be hospitalized ..." for 12 days. The court concluded: respondent was a former adult household member whose actions constituted abuse; he had purposely placed petitioner in apprehension of immediate physical injury; and thus plaintiff had "shown an unqualified right to the temporary relief available under §§ 455.035 and 455.045."

The court dismissed the petition because it held the Adult Abuse Act, in general and specifically §§ 455.035, .045 and .085, RSMo Supp.1980 unconstitutional, and thus unenforceable.

The Adult Abuse Act was adopted by the Missouri Legislature on June 13, 1980, and became effective August 13, 1980. It was adopted by the Missouri Legislature as a result of an increased awareness nationally of the prevalence of domestic violence and of the need to protect the victims of that violence.[2] It is part of a nationwide trend to legislate in this area. Existing remedies such as peace bonds, regular criminal process, and tort law have proved to be less than adequate in aiding the victims of abuse and in preventing further abuse.

An adult who is abused by a present or former adult household member, may petition the circuit court for relief under the Act. Two types of relief are available: *ex parte* orders issued without notice to the respondent or a hearing, and orders issued after notice and an on record hearing.

---

1. All attempts to notify respondent husband of this appeal have failed; communication by mail sent to him at his alleged place of employment has been returned.

2. See, e.g., Domestic Violence and Legislation with Respect to Domestic Violence: Hearings Before the Subcommittee on Child and Human Development, 95th Cong., 2d Sess. (1978) (hereinafter cited as Domestic Violence Hearings); D. Martin, Battered Wives (1976); M. Straus, R. Gelles & S. Steinmetz, Behind Closed Doors (1980); Buzawa & Buzawa, Legislative Responses to the Problem of Domestic Violence in Michigan, 25 Wayne L.Rev. 859 (1979); Freeman, Le Vice Anglais? Wife–Battering in English and American Law, 11 Fam.L.Q. 199 (1977); Gayford, Wife–Battering: A Preliminary Survey of 100 Cases, 1 Brit.Med.J. 194 (1975); Gelles, Abused Wives: Why Do They Stay, 38 J. Marr. & Fam. 659 (1976); Taub, Ex Parte Proceedings in Domestic Violence Situations: Alternative Frameworks for Constitutional Scrutiny, 9 Hofstra L.Rev. 95 (1980); Comment, Spouse Abuse: A Novel Remedy for a Historic Problem, 84 Dick.L.Rev. 147 (1979); Comment, Wife Beating: Law and Society Confront the Castle Door, 15 Conz.L.Rev. 171 (1979); Note, The Battered Wife's Dilemma: To Kill or Be Killed, 32 Hastings L.J. 895 (1980).

Violation of an *ex parte* order of protection of which the respondent has notice or of a full order of protection is declared to be a class C misdemeanor for which the respondent may be arrested without a warrant.

. . .

The trial court held that plaintiff had "an unqualified right to the . . . relief available under the Act." This ruling confers upon the plaintiff standing to argue in support of the Act because from it she derives an actual and justiciable interest susceptible of protection.

. . .

The trial court ruled that the Act violates Mo.Const. art. III, § 23, which provides that "[n]o bill shall contain more than one subject which shall be clearly expressed in its title . . ." because it contains provisions relating to children, i.e., custody and support, rather than relating exclusively to adults, and thus contains more than one subject. The title of Senate Bill 524 is "an Act relating to the abuse of adults by an adult household member, with penalty provisions." The test to determine if a title violates § 23 is whether "all of the provisions of the statute fairly relate to the same subject, have a natural connection therewith or are the incidents or the means to accomplish its purpose." State ex rel. Jardon v. Industrial Development Authority, 570 S.W.2d 666, 677 (Mo.banc 1978). The subject of the Act is adult abuse; the purpose of the Act is to protect household members by preventing further violence. The question is whether the child custody provisions fairly relate to the subject of adult abuse and promote the purpose of the Act.

Studies have shown that the victim of adult abuse is usually a woman. In a large percentage of families, children have been present when the abuse occurred. In one study, fifty-four percent of the battered women interviewed reported that their husbands had committed acts of violence against their children as well as against them. Even if the child is not physically injured, he likely will suffer emotional trauma from witnessing violence between his parents. Abuse appears to be perpetuated through the generations; an individual who grows up in a home where violence occurs is more likely either to abuse others as an adult or to be a victim of abuse. Adult abuse, therefore, is a problem affecting not only the adult members of a household but also the children. The most compelling reason for an abused woman to remain in the home subject to more abuse is her financial dependency; this is particularly true for the women with children. The orders pertaining to child custody, support, and maintenance are all fairly related to and serve the purpose of aiding victims of domestic violence and preventing future incidents of adult abuse.

The court held that §§ 455.035–.045 of the Act facially violate the due process guarantees of U.S. Const., amend. XIV and Mo. Const. art. I, § 10 by permitting a respondent to be deprived of constitutionally protected interests prior to notice or an adversary hearing. The trial court found the *ex parte* orders of protection constitutionally infirm because the Act, on its face, may be applied to exclude a respondent from his home or from contact with his children for a fifteen day period prior to notice or hearing. The trial judge concedes that the goal of the statute is legitimate and important, but nevertheless ruled it unconstitutional because of its impact on important personal rights. He reached this conclusion by finding: that the facts upon which an *ex parte* order may be issued are not easily verifiable and thus not appropriate for presentation by affidavit to the court, as required by Mitchell v. W.T. Grant Co., 416 U.S. 600, 617–18, 94 S.Ct. 1895, 1905, 40 L.Ed.2d 406 (1974); and that there is no procedure by which the respondent can dissolve the *ex parte* orders. Fuentes v. Shevin, 407 U.S. 67, 86, 92 S.Ct. 1983, 1997, 32 L.Ed.2d 556 (1972).

Sections 455.020–.035, RSMo Supp.1980 set out the procedure for obtaining an *ex parte* order of protection. The person seeking an order of protection files a verified petition with the clerk of the circuit court or, if the court is unavailable, with "any available circuit or associate circuit judge in the city or county having jurisdiction...." The judge may grant the *ex parte* orders only "for good cause shown" which is defined as "[a]n immediate and present danger of abuse to the petitioner." "Abuse" is defined as "inflicting, other than by accidental means, or attempting to inflict physical injury, on an adult or purposely placing another adult in apprehension of immediate physical injury." Section 455.010(1), RSMo Supp.1980. Three orders may be issued *ex parte:* restraining the respondent from further acts of abuse; restraining the respondent from entering the family dwelling unit; and granting temporary custody of any minor children. The statute permits an order restraining the respondent from entering the family dwelling unit to issue in favor of a spouse who otherwise has no property interest in the home. An *ex parte* order of protection remains in effect until the hearing, which is to be held "[n]ot later than fifteen days after the filing of a petition...." Sections 455.035–.045, RSMo Supp.1980.

The due process guarantee is intended to protect an individual against arbitrary acts of the government. Furthermore, it protects the right to use and enjoy one's property without governmental interference. Before the guarantee of due process comes into play, however, there must be a deprivation by the government of a constitutionally protected interest. Mathews v. Eldridge, 424 U.S. 319, 332, 96 S.Ct. 893, 901, 47 L.Ed.2d 18 (1976). The interests which are subject to temporary deprivation through the issuance of an *ex parte* order constitute significant liberty and property interests falling "within the purview of the Due Process Clause."[8] See Fuentes v. Shevin, 407 U.S. at 90, 92 S.Ct. at 1999; ... Thus the procedures available under the Act must meet the constitutional standard.

Notice and an opportunity to be heard must be provided by the state in a meaningful manner prior to deprivation of a protected interest. This rule is not necessarily applied when there is only a temporary taking, as is the

---

8. Defendant contends that two interests are involved; in his home and in custody of the children. In some cases there may be a third protected interest—the liberty interest of a respondent in his reputation. See Taub, supra note 2, at 104–06. Any one of these interests may be sufficient to warrant procedural safeguards required by the Due Process Clause.

case here. Due process is a flexible concept; the same procedures need not be applied in all instances. The extent and nature of procedures depends upon weighing of the private interests affected and the governmental functions involved. The United States Supreme Court in Mathews v. Eldridge identified a third factor to be considered in the balancing formula; the risk of erroneous deprivation using the existing procedures....

The first factor is the private interest affected. The respondent has two private interests at stake; a property interest in one's home and a liberty interest in custody of one's children. These interests are significant, the importance of which has been emphasized by the United States Supreme Court. See cases, supra.

The second factor in the balancing formula is the governmental interest. The Adult Abuse Act is an exercise of the state's police power. Through the procedures established to aid victims of domestic violence, the legislature promotes the general health, welfare, and safety of its citizens. The magnitude of the problem of domestic violence is evidenced by statistics compiled by the FBI in 1973 which indicate that one-fourth of all homicides in the United States occur within the family. The petitioner's interests which are protected by the state in furthering its interests are the same as those of the respondent. The parties, irrespective of marital status, may own or rent the dwelling jointly, although under the Act this is not required. If it becomes unsafe for both parties to remain in the home, one may need to be excluded. The choice is reduced to the victim of the abuse leaving or the court ordering the abuser to leave. Parents may have an equal interest in maintaining custody of their children.[10] Both interests are important and have been accorded deference by the courts.

The Missouri Legislature has established a mechanism whereby the state can intervene when abuse of one adult by another household member occurs or is threatened and thus prevent further violence. State legislatures have broad power to enact laws to protect the general health, welfare, and safety. States also have been given deference in adopting reasonable summary procedures when acting under their police power.

The third factor in the test in Mathews v. Eldridge is "the fairness and reliability of the existing pretermination procedures, and the probable value, if any, of additional procedural safeguards." ...

An *ex parte* order of protection is analogous to a temporary restraining order because both are injunctions issued prior to notice or hearing. *Ex parte* orders restraining acts of abuse or entrance into the dwelling are issued upon a showing of "an immediate and present danger of abuse to the petitioner." Section 455.035, RSMo Supp.1980. As in a proceeding to obtain any other restraining order, the petitioner must satisfy the court

---

10. This differs from those cases where the state is attempting to remove children from the custody of the natural parent, see, e.g., Stanley v. Illinois, 405 U.S. 645, 92 S.Ct. 1208, 31 L.Ed.2d 551 (1972), and vest custody in the court. Here, one parent retains custody.

that grounds exist to justify granting this order.[11] This will, in most instances, require the petitioner to appear personally before the court at which time the credibility of the petitioner can be tested.[12] In addition, the judge may be able to see first hand "the evidence of violence manifested in burns, cuts, bruises, and fractures." Boyle v. Boyle, supra note 4, slip op. at 7. If the petitioner is unable to appear because of injuries, this may be alleged and proof thereof will allow the court to determine that there is "[a]n immediate and present danger of abuse."

A protection order, if granted, remains in effect until the hearing which is to be held "[n]ot later than fifteen days after the filing of a petition." Section 455.040.1, RSMo Supp.1980. This sets a maximum period that the order could be effective without some hearing. Nothing in the statute suggests that the respondent could not obtain an earlier hearing. Concerning other restraining orders, Rule 92.02(b) provides that a party against whom a temporary restraining order has been issued may, upon two days' (or shorter time if the court so prescribes) notice to the opposing party, receive a hearing on the order. This rule is equally applicable to orders issued under the Act. The statute requires that the petition, notice of the hearing date, and any *ex parte* order of protection be served upon the respondent. Section 455.040.2, RSMo Supp.1980. The court at the same time may include in the notice information regarding the respondent's right to request an earlier hearing and the procedure to be followed.

The Supreme Court in Fuentes v. Shevin, outlined categories of cases where outright seizures have been allowed. 407 U.S. at 91, 92 S.Ct. at 2000. The first is where seizure has been directly necessary to secure an important governmental or general public interest; the second is where there has been a special need for prompt action; the third is where the state has kept strict control over its monopoly of legitimate force: there is a government official responsible for determining that seizure was necessary under standards set out in "narrowly drawn statutes."

The Act meets the foregoing standards. The Act is directly necessary to secure important governmental interests, i.e., protection of victims of abuse and prevention of further abuse. The situation where the challenged Act is to be applied are those where prompt action is necessary, i.e., when there is "[a]n immediate and present danger of abuse"—the only time the *ex parte* order may be issued. The government has kept strict control over its powers. Only a judge in his discretion, may issue the *ex parte* orders. This differs from the procedure where "[p]rivate parties, serving their own private advantage, may unilaterally invoke state power to replevy goods from another" disapproved in Fuentes v. Shevin, supra at 93, 92 S.Ct. at

11. The determination made by the court in adult abuse cases is also analogous to a probable cause determination for issuance of a warrant "on oath or affirmation of the complainant." Rule 21.04. See Rule 21.05. The forms issued by this Court for seeking relief under the Act similarly require verification and as such are affidavits of facts upon which the Court may act. Sections 455.020, 455.025, RSMo. See also Order, Supreme Court of Missouri, en banc, August 8, 1980.

12. Judge Marsh, in this case, conducted an *ex parte* hearing on Mrs. Williams' petition.

2001. Under the Adult Abuse Act, the petitioner requests the court to act on his or her behalf. The court, not the clerk, must issue the order and the orders are not to be issued routinely but only after the petitioner has filed a verified petition showing good cause.

... The interests and procedures considered, these *ex parte* order provisions comply with due process requirements because they are a reasonable means to achieve the state's legitimate goal of preventing domestic violence, and afford adequate procedural safeguards prior to and after any deprivation occurs.

The court found that the Act is unconstitutional because it authorizes imprisonment for debt in violation of Mo. Const. art. I, § 11 by making criminal failure to pay support orders. The statute makes criminal violation of the *ex parte* order of protection, of which the respondent has notice, and violation of a full order of protection. The statute sets forth no punishment for violation of ancillary orders dealing with child support, maintenance, or attorney's fees. Therefore, there can be no imprisonment for debt and the Act does not violate Mo. Const. art. I, § 11.

The trial court held the Act void for vagueness because it fails to give adequate warning as to what conduct is proscribed and thus violates U.S. Const. amend. XIV and Mo. Const., art. I, § 10. . . .

Vagueness, as a due process violation, takes two forms. One is the lack of notice given a potential offender because the statute is so unclear that "men of common intelligence must necessarily guess at its meaning." The other is that the statute fails to set out "explicit standards" for those who must apply it, resulting in arbitrary and discriminatory application.

As to the former, "[i]f terms or words used in the statute are of common usage and are understandable by persons of ordinary intelligence, they satisfy the constitutional requirements as to definiteness and certainty." Prokopf v. Whaley, 592 S.W.2d 819, 824 (Mo.banc 1980); State v. Williams, 473 S.W.2d 382 (Mo.1971).

Section 455.085.3, RSMo Supp.1980 states:

> Violation of the terms and conditions of an *ex parte* order of protection, of which the respondent has notice, shall be a class C misdemeanor. Violation of the terms and conditions of a full order of protection shall be a class C misdemeanor.

Under this section violation of an *ex parte* order is a misdemeanor only if "respondent has notice." This section provides the individual subject to an *ex parte* order an absolute right to be personally served with notice expressly stating what conduct on his or her part is criminal. See also § 455.040.2, RSMo Supp.1980. A full protection order may be issued only after a hearing on record, and notice and an opportunity to be heard is given to the respondent. Sections 455.010(5) and 455.040, subd. 2, RSMo Supp.1980 require personal service of the full order of protection. There are only two (full protection) or three (*ex parte*) limited orders which may be issued against respondent. For example, an *ex parte* order may state that respondent (named) shall not abuse, threaten to abuse, molest, disturb the peace of the petitioner (named), enter the dwelling unit (house, apartment) of the petitioner, or interfere with petitioners custody of children (named). From the face of these sections it is clear that contravention of the specific orders which are limited in number and of which the respondent is personally informed is a violation of § 455.085.3, RSMo Supp.1980.

It is further determined that to insure that the respondent has knowledge, the notice served upon him should expressly include a statement informing him that a violation of the order is a class C misdemeanor and stating the maximum penalty associated therewith. This is required by the clear intent expressed by the legislature in §§ 455.010(4), (5), 455.040.1, 2 and 455.085, RSMo Supp.1980, that respondent be informed by complete notification. See again Order, Supreme Court, August 8, 1980.

The Act provides sufficient direction and guidance for the judges who must apply it. The protection orders are to issue only when an "immediate and present danger of abuse to the petitioner" is found. Section 455.035, RSMo Supp.1980. Abuse is further defined as "inflicting, other than by accidental means, or attempting to inflict physical injury, on an adult or purposely placing another adult in apprehension of immediate physical injury." Section 455.010(1), RSMo Supp.1980. "On a challenge to a statute or ordinance as being unconstitutionally vague ... the language is to be treated by applying it to the facts at hand." Prokopf v. Whaley, 592 S.W.2d at 824. The trial court expressly found that the evidence was "overwhelming and abundantly clear that petitioner has shown all of the elements required by Chapter 455 that would otherwise (if not for the constitutional issues) entitle her to the relief she seeks" and that petitioner had shown "an unqualified right to the temporary relief." This demonstrates that no arbitrary or discriminatory application is presently or potentially in issue. The trial court was fully aware of the standards for granting relief and how to apply the Act.

> [The Court also rejected the argument that the Act violated requirements of separation and non-delegation of power in the Missouri Constitution.]

The trial court held that § 455.085, RSMo Supp.1980 authorizes warrantless arrest under conditions which violate the Fourth Amendment of the United States Constitution, made applicable to the states through the Fourteenth Amendment, Mapp v. Ohio, 367 U.S. 643, 81 S.Ct. 1684, 6 L.Ed.2d 1081 (1961), and by art. I, § 15 of the Missouri Constitution. It is contended that this section permits an arrest in the arrestee's home without a warrant, consensual entry, or exigent circumstances, and is thus void "on its face", citing Payton v. New York, 445 U.S. 573, 100 S.Ct. 1371, 63 L.Ed.2d 639 (1980).

In Sibron v. New York, 392 U.S. 40, 88 S.Ct. 1889, 20 L.Ed.2d 917 (1968), the United States Supreme Court refused to engage in the abstract and unproductive exercise of laying the extraordinary elastic categories of [a statute permitting "stop and frisks"] next to the categories of the Fourth Amendment in an effort to determine whether the two are in some sense compatible, [because] [t]he constitutional validity of a warrantless search is pre-eminently the sort of question which can only be decided in the concrete factual context of the individual case. In this respect it is quite different from the question of the adequacy of the procedural safeguards written into a statute which purports to authorize the issuance of search warrants in certain circumstances. The statute in Sibron v. New York, supra, is similar to § 455.085, RSMo Supp.1980 in that both generally authorize activities which may or may not be offensive to the Fourth Amendment. With the purpose of settling questions regarding the facial validity of the Act, this contention is addressed with the admonition that official actions violate the Fourth Amendment and not general authorization statutes such as the one examined in Sibron v. New York, supra.

Section 455.085.1, RSMo Supp.1980 authorizes warrantless arrest where probable cause exists to believe that a violation of a protection order has occurred. Generally, warrantless arrests upon probable cause for felonies or misdemeanors may constitutionally be authorized by statute. However, a warrantless arrest in the arrestee's home is impermissible absent consent to enter or exigent circumstances. Payton v. New York, 445 U.S. at 590, 100 S.Ct. at 1382. It is the warrantless in-home seizure which defendant argues is impermissibly authorized by § 455.085.1, RSMo Supp. 1980. Section 455.085.2 states:

> The same procedures, including those designed to protect constitutional rights, shall be applied to the respondent as those applied to any individual detained in police custody.

Procedurally it is required that when an in-home arrest occurs either a warrant or consent to enter the house be obtained or that exigent circumstances exist. These procedures are "designed to protect constitutional rights" and are to "be applied to the respondent", § 455.085.2, RSMo Supp.1980.

This section does not authorize unconstitutional arrests; and if such an arrest were to occur under the guise of the Act then the respondent would be entitled to the same remedy as "any individual detained in police custody."

The presumptive constitutionality of the Adult Abuse Act is not overcome by any of the attacks presented.

. . .

■ BARDGETT, JUDGE, concurring in part.

I concur in the result reached and in the principal opinion except for that portion upholding the constitutionality of § 455.085.3 which makes the violation of an order of protection a crime—a class C misdemeanor.

This is not a criminal case and the question whether the misdemeanor conviction of one for violation of a protective order could be constitutionally upheld ought, in my opinion, await that kind of case. My reservations about this matter flow from the fact that the conduct of a spouse does not become a crime unless and until the judge so declares and then only with respect to that one person. This *law* does not prohibit certain conduct as criminal generally but rather leaves it to a judge to decide whether certain conduct, if engaged in in the future, will be criminal only as to a particular person. Certain acts of an abusive type are criminal by general law—assault and battery—and are a crime regardless of who commits them, but that is not the case under § 455.085.3. I have no particular difficulty with contempt proceedings which may involve incarceration for the violation of an injunctive order—an order of protection—but that is not a crime.

The statute does not make the act of entering one's home a crime. The only time that act becomes a criminal act is when, and if, a judge declares it to be criminal by prohibiting it in a protective order with respect to a particular person. Thus, § 455.085.3 delegates to a judge the power to say what conduct constitutes a crime and whether or not certain conduct, if engaged in by a particular person, will be a crime. The drug cases are not analogous. In those cases the *administrative agency* identified the drug which produced the statutorily proscribed effects and the possession of that drug was then prohibited *generally* as to all people. Neither the agency nor a judge decided that possession of the drug by a particular *person* would be a crime, but that possession of the drug by others would not be a crime.

I believe it highly questionable whether a crime can, under our Constitution, be so personalized; nevertheless, the issue of the constitutionality of § 455.085.3 is unnecessary to the adjudication of this case. I therefore reserve judgment on that matter until the case occurs in which that issue is decisive. I concur in all other aspects of the principal opinion.

■ WELLIVER, JUDGE, dissenting.

. . .

When we permit child custody, support and maintenance provisions, usually found in Chapter 452, to be hidden behind the newly created term which we now denominate as "Adult Abuse", when we permit the orders contemplated by the act to be entered without notice or hearing, and, when we permit circuit judges to define the elements of crime on a case by case basis without notice or hearing, then we by judicial interpretation have rendered a nullity: (1) the long established rule of statutory construction that penal statutes must be strictly construed against the state, (2) the constitutional prohibition, Mo. Const. art. III, § 23, that "[n]o bill shall contain more than one subject which shall be clearly expressed in its title . . .," and (3) due process of law, U.S. Const.Amend. XIV, Mo. Const. art. I, § 10.

The Adult Abuse Act exhibits the fullest potential for creating nine new evils for every evil it would seek by its terms to correct.

NOTE

Other Statutes and Challenges. A survey published in 1985 revealed that every state had passed some form of legislation in response to concern about domestic violence, and that 37 of those included provision for some form of *ex parte* preliminary relief. *See* Note, *Ex Parte Protection*

Orders: Is Due Process Locked Out?, 58 TEMPLE L.Q. 841 (1985). The number of appellate cases involving due process challenges remains relatively small, and the basic statutes have been upheld in them. In addition to *Marsh, see* Schramek v. Bohren, 145 Wis.2d 695, 429 N.W.2d 501 (App.1988); and Marquette v. Marquette, 686 P.2d 990 (Okl.App.1984).

The scope of the domestic violence statutes has increased in response to varying circumstances. In H.E.S. v. J.C.S., 175 N.J. 309, 815 A.2d 405 (2003), the New Jersey Supreme Court was asked to review the procedural and substantive due process issues raised by the state's Domestic Violence Act. Specifically, the court was asked to decide if video surveillance by one spouse of the other spouse's bedroom can constitute one of the predicate offenses of domestic violence; also, whether receiving notice of the complaint less than twenty-four hours prior to trial violated the defendant's due process rights. The court quickly held that the faulty notice was inherently lacking in due process. As to whether the video surveillance of the plaintiff by the defendant constituted harassment, the court held that the presence of the camera did constitute harassment. Even though the plaintiff did not know of the existence of the video camera, the "totality of the circumstances" indicated that using the surveillance, the defendant was able to know private conversations and was more familiar with plaintiff's conduct. This knowledge allowed the defendant to act accordingly in causing injury to the plaintiff. In addition, the defendant's action constituted stalking under the state's applicable statute because the defendant purposefully acted against a specific person over a period of time in proximity to the plaintiff. It is reasonable to think that such a course of action would cause a reasonable person to fear bodily injury to himself or herself. The defendant may be charged with the crime as long as due process is afforded him. There have been similar cases. *See, e.g.,* United States v. Al–Zubaidy, 283 F.3d 804 (6th Cir. 2002)(VAWA's provision against interstate stalking is constitutional); People v. Sullivan, 53 P.3d 1181 (Colo. Ct. App. 2002 (placement of a global positioning system in plaintiff's care can constitute stalking)); Smith v. Martens, 279 Kan. 242, 106 P.3d 28 (2005)(state stalking statute is constitutional).

Remedies for Failure of Officials to Act. In 1977 Oregon adopted a broad "Abuse Prevention Act" designed to strengthen the legal protection for persons threatened with assault by present or former spouses or cohabitants. OR.REV.STAT. §§ 107.700–107.720 (1999). Included in the provisions of the Act is authorization for courts to issue temporary restraining orders, injunctions, and temporary child custody orders. In Nearing v. Weaver, 295 Or. 702, 670 P.2d 137 (1983), the Supreme Court of Oregon held that police officers who violated the statute can be held liable in tort to individuals intended to be beneficiaries who suffer resulting psychic or physical harm.

A different approach was taken in an earlier legal battle initiated in New York by twelve "battered wives" who asserted that probation and Family Court nonjudicial personnel had engaged in "a pattern of conduct calculated (1) to deter battered wives from filing petitions for orders of protection against their offending husbands, (2) to block them from meaningful access to Family Court judges empowered to issue temporary orders of protection, and (3) by failing to advise the wives that the defendants proffer of counseling is voluntary, to dissuade complainants from pursuing their legal remedies." *See* Bruno v. Codd, 47 N.Y.2d 582, 419 N.Y.S.2d 901, 393 N.E.2d 976 (1979). In its opinion, the New York Court of Appeals noted that 40% of all police night calls in New York City are said to involve problems of battered or threatened wives. The text of a consent decree that was negotiated with the police is reproduced in 4 FAM.L.REP. 3095 (July 18, 1978). For a comprehensive article that is a valuable resource on domestic violence cases and statutes, *see* Catherine F. Klein and Leslye E. Orloff, *Providing Legal Protection for Battered Women: An Analysis of State Statutes and Case Law*, 21 HOFSTRA L.REV. 801 (1993).

For a recent decision which holds the police not liable for failure to protect woman who was eventually killed by her estranged boyfriend, *see* Semple v. Moundsville, W.Va., 195 F.3d 708 (4th Cir.1999), *rev. denied*, 528 U.S. 1189, 120 S.Ct. 1243, 146 L.Ed.2d 102 (2000). As to police protection and liability in general, *see* Jeremy Daniel Kernodle, Note. *Policing the Police: Clarifying the Test for Holding the Government Liable Under 42 U.S.C. § 1983 and the State Created Danger Theory*, 54 VAND. L. REV. 165 (2001); Richard Emery & Ilann Margalit Maazel, *Why Civil Rights Lawsuits Do Not Deter Police Misconduct: The Conundrum of Indemnification and a Proposed Solution*, 28 FORD. Urb. L. J. 587 (2000).

The Massachusetts Abuse Prevention Law gives the following detailed rules regarding police handling of domestic violence cases, at 209A MASS. GEN. LAWS ANN. CH. 209A, § 6 (West 1998):

> Whenever any law officer has reason to believe that a family or household member has been abused or is in danger of being abused, such officer shall use all reasonable means to prevent further abuse. The officer shall take, but not be limited to the following action:
>
> (1) remain on the scene of where said abuse occurred or was in danger of occurring as long as the officer has reason to believe that at least one of the parties involved would be in immediate physical danger without the presence of a law officer. This shall include, but not be limited to remaining in the dwelling for a reasonable period of time;
>
> (2) assist the abused person in obtaining medical treatment necessitated by an assault, which may include driving the victim to the emergency room of the nearest hospital, or arranging for appropriate transportation to a health care facility, notwithstanding any law to the contrary;
>
> (3) assist the abused person in locating and getting to a safe place; including but not limited to a designated meeting place for a shelter or a family member's or friend's residence. The officer shall consider the victim's preference in this regard and what is reasonable under all the circumstances;

(4) give such person immediate and adequate notice of his or her rights. Such notice shall consist of handing said person a copy of the statement which follows below and reading the same to said person. Where said person's native language is not English, the statement shall be then provided in said person's native language whenever possible.

"You have the right to appear at the Superior, Probate and Family, District or Boston Municipal Court, if you reside within the appropriate jurisdiction, and file a complaint requesting any of the following applicable orders: (a) an order restraining your attacker from abusing you; (b) an order directing your attacker to leave your household, building or workplace; (c) an order awarding you custody of a minor child; (d) an order directing your attacker to pay support for you or any minor child in your custody, if the attacker has a legal obligation of support; and (e) an order directing your attacker to pay you for losses suffered as a result of abuse, including medical and moving expenses, loss of earnings or support, costs for restoring utilities and replacing locks, reasonable attorney's fees and other out-of-pocket losses for injuries and property damage sustained. For an emergency on weekends, holidays, or weeknights the police will refer you to a justice of the superior, probate and family, district, or Boston municipal court departments. You have the right to go to the appropriate district court or the Boston municipal court and seek a criminal complaint for threats, assault and battery, assault with a deadly weapon, assault with intent to kill or other related offenses. If you are in need of medical treatment, you have the right to request that an officer present drive you to the nearest hospital or otherwise assist you in obtaining medical treatment. If you believe that police protection is needed for your physical safety, you have the right to request that the officer present remain at the scene until you and your children can leave or until your safety is otherwise ensured. You may also request that the officer assist you in locating and taking you to a safe place, including but not limited to a designated meeting place for a shelter or a family member's or a friend's residence, or a similar place of safety. You may request a copy of the police incident report at no cost from the police department."

The officer shall leave a copy of the foregoing statement with such person before leaving the scene or premises.

(5) assist such person by activating the emergency judicial system when the court is closed for business;

(6) inform the victim that the abuser will be eligible for bail and may be promptly released; and

(7) arrest any person a law officer witnesses or has probable cause to believe has violated a temporary or permanent vacate, restraining, or no-contact order or judgment issued pursuant to section eighteen, thirty-four B or thirty-four C of chapter two hundred and eight, section thirty-two of chapter two hundred and nine, section three, four or five of this chapter, or sections fifteen or twenty of chapter two hundred

and nine C. When there are no vacate, restraining, or no-contact orders or judgments in effect, arrest shall be the preferred response whenever an officer witnesses or has probable cause to believe that a person:

(a) has committed a felony;

(b) has committed a misdemeanor involving abuse as defined in section one of this chapter;

(c) has committed an assault and battery in violation of section thirteen A of chapter two hundred and sixty-five.

The safety of the victim and any involved children shall be paramount in any decision to arrest. Any officer arresting both parties must submit a detailed, written report in addition to an incident report, setting forth the grounds for dual arrest.

No law officer investigating an incident of domestic violence shall threaten, suggest, or otherwise indicate the arrest of all parties for the purpose of discouraging requests for law enforcement intervention by any party.

No law officer shall be held liable in any civil action regarding personal injury or injury to property brought by any party to a domestic violence incident for an arrest based on probable cause when such officer acted reasonably and in good faith and in compliance with this chapter and the statewide policy as established by the secretary of public safety.

Whenever any law officer investigates an incident of domestic violence, the officer shall immediately file a written incident report in accordance with the standards of the officer's law enforcement agency and, wherever possible, in the form of the National Incident–Based Reporting System, as defined by the Federal Bureau of Investigation. The latter information may be submitted voluntarily by the local police on a monthly basis to the crime reporting unit of the criminal history systems board.

The victim shall be provided a copy of the full incident report at no cost upon request to the appropriate law enforcement department.

When a judge or other person authorized to take bail bails any person arrested under the provisions of this chapter, he shall make reasonable efforts to inform the victim of such release prior to or at the time of said release.

When any person charged with or arrested for a crime involving abuse under this chapter is released from custody, the court or the emergency response judge shall issue, upon the request of the victim, a written no-contact order prohibiting the person charged or arrested from having any contact with the victim and shall use all reasonable means to notify the victim immediately of release from custody. The victim shall be given at no cost a certified copy of the no-contact order.

During Spring of 2004, the en banc Court of Appeals for the Tenth Circuit held that a state statute that promised a process by which a restraining order issued against an abusive spouse would be given vitality through prompt and careful consideration by law enforcement officials, provided a basis for a procedural due process claim against the local municipality. Gonzales v. City of Castle Rock, 366 F.3d 1093 (10th Cir. 2004). But on June 27, 2005, in a 7–2 decision, the Supreme Court ruled that the city could not be sued under a 14th Amendment procedural claim. Town of Castle Rock, Colo. v. Gonzales, 545 U.S. 748, 125 S.Ct. 2796, 162 L.Ed.2d 658 (2005). Writing for the majority, Justice Scalia pointed out that the procedural component of the Due Process Clause does not protect everything that might be described as a benefit.

The Battered Spouse Profile. In prosecutions involving "battered wives" who contend that they have killed or injured their spouses in self-defense, attempts have been made to utilize a "profile" based on studies of the personality and behavior of other battered spouses. For discussion of this, *see* Ibn–Tamas v. United States, 407 A.2d 626 (D.C.App.1979); Myrna S. Raeder, *The Better Way: The Role of Batterer's Profiles and Expert "Social Framework" Background in Cases Implicating Domestic Violence,* 68 UNIVERSITY OF COLORADO LAW REVIEW 147–187 (1997); Myrna S. Raider, *The Admissibility of Prior Acts of Domestic Violence: Simpson and Beyond. (People v. Simpson: Perspectives on the Implications for the Criminal Justice System),* 69 U.S.C. L. REV. 1463 (1996); Hope Toffee, *Crazy Women, Unharmed Men, and Evil Children: Confronting the Myths about Battered People Who Kill Their Abusers, and the Argument for Extending Battering Syndrome Self–Defenses to All Victims of Domestic Violence,* 70 U.S.C. L. REV. 337–380 (1996); and Note, *The Battered Wife Syndrome and Self–Defense: A Legal and Empirical Dissent,* 72 VA.L.REV. 619 (1986).

Federal Response to Domestic Violence. In 1994 Congress passed the VIOLENCE AGAINST WOMEN ACT (VAWA), Pub. L. No. 103–322, §§ 40001–40703, 108 Stat. 1796, 1902–55. The Act encourages the states to implement programs addressing domestic violence, but the Act also creates criminal sanctions for interstate domestic violence and creates a federal civil rights remedy for a person victimized by gender-motivated violence. Under the civil rights provision a person may be compensated and receive punitive damages from the person who committed the violence. On May 15, 2000, the Supreme Court held that the civil rights provision of VAWA was an invalid exercise of Congress' power under the Commerce Clause and Section 5 of the 14th Amendment. *See* United States v. Morrison, 529 U.S. 598, 120 S.Ct. 1740, 146 L.Ed.2d 658 (2000). Nonetheless, that aspect of VAWA which makes it a federal crime to commit interstate domestic violence has been held to be constitutional. *See, e.g.,* United States v. Lankford, 196 F.3d 563 (5th Cir.1999); United States v. Page, 167 F.3d 325 (6th Cir.1999), rev. denied, 528 U.S. 1003, 120 S.Ct. 496, 145 L.Ed.2d 382 (1999). For a review, *see* CLARE DALTON and ELIZABETH M. SCHNEIDER, BATTERED WOMEN AND THE LAW 953–991 (2001); Judith Resnick, *The Programmatic Judiciary: Lobbying, Judging, and Invalidating the Violence Against Women Act,* 74 S. CAL. L. REV. 269 (2000); Elizabeth Villiers Gemmette, *Filling in the Silence: Domestic Violence, Literature and Law,* 32 Loy. U. Chi. L. J. 91 (2000). For an argument as to why the federal legislation should provide a civil cause of action, *see* Kerrie E. Maloney, *Gender Motivated Violence and the Commerce Clause: The Civil Rights Provision of the Violence Against Women Act After Lopez,* 96 COLUM. L. REV. 1876 (1996).

Other Approaches. A number of approaches are being tried for dealing with this serious and often devastating problem. Special shelter homes have become popular. Usually dependent on community or private donations for financial support, they can offer the battered spouse an immediate, practical alternative of safety and the possibility of counseling before a reunion, if indeed the latter goal is selected. In England the movement toward establishing such refuges was given impetus through wide circulation of a 1974 book, Scream Quietly or the Neighbours Will Hear, by Erin Pizzey. Special training for police officers to deal with the problems of family crisis is a popular governmental response.

A proposal that has met with very mixed reactions is enactment of a "spouse abuse reporting statute" patterned after legislation dealing with battered children. One concern is that such a statute would be personally demeaning to adults; the state role as *parens patriae* is considered justification for such intrusive intervention on behalf of children. For discussion of a lawyer's role, *see* Linda G. Mills, *On the Other Side of Silence: Effective Lawyering for Intimate Abuse,* 81 CORNELL. L. REV. 1225 (1996).

5. TORT ACTIONS BETWEEN SPOUSES

Bozman v. Bozman

Maryland Court of Appeals, 2003.
376 Md. 461, 830 A.2d 450.

■ BELL, CHIEF JUDGE.

Whether the common-law doctrine of interspousal tort immunity shall remain viable in Maryland is the issue we decide in this appeal. The Circuit Court for Baltimore County dismissed the complaint alleging malicious prosecution filed by William E. Bozman, the petitioner, against Nancie L. Bozman, the respondent, a judgment which the Court of Special Appeals affirmed. We shall reverse the judgment of the intermediate appellate court and, as urged by the petitioner, abrogate the doctrine of interspousal immunity.

The petitioner and the respondent were married in this State on August 16, 1968. On February 24, 2000, the petitioner initiated divorce proceedings against the respondent. As grounds, he pled adultery. The parties were divorced on March 12, 2001.

Shortly before the divorce was finalized, on January 20, 2001, the petitioner filed in the Circuit Court for Baltimore County a complaint sounding in malicious prosecution against the respondent. In that complaint, which consisted of one count, the petitioner alleged that, as a result of criminal charges, which the respondent brought against him on February 17, 2000, May 3, 2000 and July 19, 2000, he was arrested and charged with stalking, harassment and multiple counts of violation of a Protective Order. The petitioner further alleged that the charges were brought without probable cause, were deliberately fabricated to ensure that the petitioner would be arrested, and were in retaliation for the petitioner's initiation of the divorce proceedings and his unwillingness to make concessions in those proceedings. The respondent moved to dismiss the complaint. She argued, in support of that motion, *inter alia,* that the action was barred based upon the common law doctrine of interspousal tort immunity.

The Circuit Court granted the respondent's Motion to Dismiss, but with leave to amend. Thereafter, the petitioner filed an Amended Complaint. As she had done earlier, the respondent filed a motion to dismiss, relying, also as she had done before, on the doctrine of interspousal immunity. Responding to the motion to dismiss and relying on this Court's decision in *Lusby v. Lusby,* 283 Md. 334, 390 A.2d 77 (1978), in which the Court held that interspousal immunity was not a defense to a tort action between spouses where the conduct constituting the tort was "outrageous [and] intentional," *id.* at 335, 390 A.2d at 77, the petitioner argued that the defense was inapplicable under the facts he alleged; his multiple incarcerations and his being subjected to house arrest were sufficiently outrageous and intentional as to fall within the *Lusby* rule. Altogether, the petitioner claims, as a result of the respondent's false accusations, that he was incarcerated on five separate occasions, for periods ranging between one (1) and ten (10) days, and placed on home detention, which required that he wear an ankle monitoring bracelet for approximately eight (8) months.

On the same day that a hearing on the motion to dismiss was held, the petitioner filed a Second Amended Complaint. That complaint reiterated the allegations of the earlier complaint as Count I and added a second malicious prosecution count. That second malicious prosecution count alleged that, on February 2, 2001, the respondent filed, against the petitioner, additional charges of violating an *ex parte* order, which although ultimately dismissed, again resulted in the petitioner's incarceration and incurring an expense to be released. As he did in the initial complaint, the petitioner claimed that the respondent fabricated the charges, although, on this occasion, the momentum was different; it was in response to the initial malicious prosecution action and the respondent's inability to "prevail in her position" in the divorce proceedings. The petitioner specifically alleged that the dismissal of the charges referred to in Count II, one of the elements of a successful malicious prosecution action, occurred after the parties were divorced. Thus, he argued that that count was not subject to the interspousal immunity defense.

The trial court granted the respondent's Motion to Dismiss, ruling that the action was barred by the doctrine of interspousal immunity. The petitioner noted a timely appeal to the Court of Special Appeals.

In the intermediate appellate court, the petitioner challenged the trial court's dismissal of Count I of the Second Amended Complaint, arguing that it was error in light of this Court's decision in *Lusby,* because malicious prosecution is an outrageous, intentional tort to which inter-spousal immunity is not a defense. As to the dismissal of Count II of the Second Amended Complaint, the petitioner submitted that, not only was the conduct outrageous and intentional, but the cause of action for the malicious prosecution alleged in that count arose after the parties were legally divorced. Consequently, he argues, the doctrine of interspousal immunity is rendered inapplicable to that count, as well.

To be sure, the Court of Special Appeals "questioned the continued viability of" the doctrine of interspousal immunity. *Bozman v. Bozman,* 146 Md.App. 183, 195, 806 A.2d 740, 747 (2002), citing *Boblitz v. Boblitz,* 296 Md. 242, 462 A.2d 506, (1983). Characterizing it as an "antiquated doctrine" and stating that it "runs counter to present-day norms," *id.,* the intermediate appellate court commented:

> "We recognize that the doctrine may serve some practical purpose of preventing spouses from instituting suits in tort as a means of gaining an advantage in pending divorce proceedings or for some other improper reason. We remain unconvinced, however, that retention of this doctrine best reflects the will of the people of this State as evidence by, among other reforms, enactment of the Equal Rights Amendment in 1972."

Id. Nevertheless, it recognized that:

> "Regardless, we are bound to follow the dictates of the law as it presently exists in Maryland. The law is that interspousal immunity may be raised as a defense to a viable cause of action alleging an intentional tort so long as the tort is not 'outrageous,' as that term is used in *Lusby* and *Doe [v. Doe,* 358 Md. 113, 747 A.2d 617]."

Id. at 196, 806 A.2d at 747.

Therefore, the Court of Special Appeals addressed the issue that lay at the heart of the case, as submitted to it, the quality of the respondent's conduct and, more generally, the nature of the tort of malicious prosecution. More specifically, the court considered whether the tort, or at least the conduct that constituted the tort, came within the term, "outrageous," as defined in, and contemplated by, *Lusby.* It concluded:

> "Without minimizing in any way the harsh consequences to appellant wrought by appellee's behavior in this case, we cannot say that it is of comparable character to that addressed by the Court in *Lusby.* Appellee's actions in the instant case no doubt caused appellant to suffer significant humiliation and hardship. But they did not involve extreme violence of the most personal and invasive sort, the threat of death and a display of the means by which to carry out that threat, or the physical and psychic trauma that the victim in *Lusby* endured. We conclude, therefore, that the conduct that underlies appellant's claim of malicious prosecution is not, in and of itself, indicative of the sort of outrageous conduct contemplated by the *Lusby* exception to interspousal immunity."

Id. at 197–98, 806 A.2d at 748.[3] Accordingly, the intermediate appellate court held that "malicious prosecution is not so outrageous as to bring it within the narrow exception to the doctrine of interspousal immunity." The court affirmed the trial court's dismissal of Count I of the Second Amended Complaint. *Id.* at 186, 806 A.2d at 741.

. . .

We granted both petitions. *Bozman v. Bozman,* 372 Md. 429, 813 A.2d 257 (2002). We agree with the Court of Special Appeals, that the interspousal immunity doctrine is an antiquated rule of law which, in our view, runs counter to prevailing societal norms and, therefore, has lived out its usefulness. Accordingly, we shall answer the petitioner's first question in the affirmative and, so, complete the abrogation of the doctrine from the common law of this State. As a result, we need not, and shall not, address the other questions raised by the petitioner's petition or the respondent's cross-petition.

. . .

The doctrine of interspousal immunity in tort cases is a rule of law existing in the common law of Maryland. *Doe, supra,* 358 Md. at 119, 747 A.2d at 619 ("Prior to *Lusby,* the doctrine of interspousal immunity in tort cases was clearly recognized as part of the common law of this state."). In *Boblitz,* we noted that it is a rule of "ancient origin" and created "exclusively from judicial decisions." 296 Md. at 244, 462 A.2d at 507. "The rule at common law [was] that a married woman cannot maintain an action against her husband for injuries caused by his negligent or tortious act." *David v. David,* 161 Md. 532, 534, 157 A. 755, 756 (1932).

The rationale underlying the interspousal immunity rule has been discussed in our cases. In *David,* the Court stated: "The reason usually

---

3. Because one of the elements of the tort of intentional infliction of emotional distress, recognized by this Court in *Harris v. Jones,* 281 Md. 560, 566, 380 A.2d 611 (1977), is that the conduct must be "extreme and outrageous," the Court of Special Appeals relied heavily on this Court's cases addressing that tort. *Bozman v. Bozman,* 146 Md. App. 183, 198–200, 806 A.2d 740, 748–750 (2002). Noting that liability has been found in those cases only " 'where the conduct has been so outrageous in character, and so extreme in degree, as to go beyond all possible bounds of decency, and to be regarded as atrocious, and utterly intolerable in a civilized community,' " *id.* (quoting *Harris,* 281 Md. at 567, 380 A.2d at 615, in turn quoting Restatement (Second) of Torts, ch. 2, Emotional Distress, § 46 (1965)), the court cited *B.N. v. K.K.,* 312 Md. 135, 146, 538 A.2d 1175 (1988) ("one who knowingly engages in con-

duct that is highly likely to infect another with an incurable disease . . . has committed extreme and outrageous conduct.") and *Figueiredo–Torres v. Nickel,* 321 Md. 642, 654, 584 A.2d 69 (1991) (a psychologist retained to improve a marital relationship acts outrageously when he facilitates a romantic, sexual relationship with the spouse of a patient). The court also relied on those parent-child immunity doctrine cases, in which a minor child has been the victim of "cruel, inhuman or outrageous conduct at the hands of a parent." *Bozman,* 146 Md.App. at 199, 806 A.2d at 749, quoting *Eagan v. Calhoun,* 347 Md. 72, 75, 698 A.2d 1097 (1997) (father committed voluntary manslaughter of his children's mother); *see Mahnke v. Moore,* 197 Md. 61, 68, 77 A.2d 923 (1951) (father shot child's mother in child's presence, kept the child with the body for six days, then shooting self in front of the child).

given for that rule is the presumed legal identity of the husband and wife." *Id.* at 534, 157 A. at 756, quoting *Philips v. Barnet* 1 QB 436 (1876). A more complete statement of the rationale was provided in *Lusby,* 283 Md. at 338, 390 A.2d at 78–79, with attribution to Blackstone, (1 W. Blackstone, Commentaries, Book 1, Ch. 15, p. 442, 443):

> "By marriage, the husband and wife are one person in the law: that is, the very being of legal existence of the woman is suspended during the marriage, or at least is incorporated and consolidated into that of the husband: under whose wing, protection, and cover, she performs everything; and is therefore called in our law french a *feme-covert, foemina viro co-operta;* is said to be a *covert-baron,* or under the protection and influence of her husband, her *baron,* or *lord;* and her condition during her marriage is called *coverture.* Upon this principle, of a union of person in husband and wife, depend almost all the legal rights, duties and disabilities, that either of them acquire by the marriage."

> "He adds, in discussing the consequences of this union of husband and wife, 'If the wife be injured in her person or her property, she can bring no action for redress without her husband's concurrence, and in his name, as well as her own: neither can she be sued without making the husband a defendant.' "

. . .

The first breach of the interspousal immunity doctrine in Maryland occurred with our decision in *Lusby.* There, the wife brought a tort action against her husband for damages. As reported by the Court (283 Md. at 335, 390 A.2d at 77),

> "She alleged that while she was operating her motor vehicle on a public highway the husband 'pulled alongside of [her] in his pick-up truck and pointed a highpowered rifle at her.' She attempted to flee by increasing the speed of her car. She claimed that then 'another truck occupied by two (2) men, whose identities are unknown to [her] and who, [t]hereinafter are referred to [in the declaration] as John Doe and Richard Roe, cut and forced her off the road, nearly causing a collision.' ... After she stopped her car, the husband 'approached her automobile with a rifle pointed at her, opened her left door, ordered her to move over, forced his way into the automobile and began to drive the automobile.' They were followed by Doe in the husband's truck and Roe in the second truck. Thereafter, the wife 'was forced to enter [the husband's] truck with [the husband] and Richard Roe.' John Doe drove the wife's vehicle and the second truck was left parked. She alleged that her husband then struck her, 'tore [her] clothes off and did forcefully and violently, despite [her] desperate attempts to protect herself, carnally know [her] against her will and without her consent.' She further claimed that, with the aid and assistance of her husband, both Doe and Roe attempted to rape her. She said that following those events her husband 'and his two companions released [her] and [her

husband] told [her] that he would kill her if she informed anyone of the aforesaid events; and that he has continued to harass and threaten [her].' "

Id. at 335–36, 390 A.2d at 77–78. On these facts, the Court held, "under the facts and circumstances of this case, amounting to an outrageous, intentional tort, a wife may sue her husband for damages." *Id.* at 335, 390 A.2d at 77.

In rendering our decision, we stated, having noted the Legislature's inaction with regard to amending the Married Women's Act to ameliorate the effect of the interspousal immunity defense and the purpose of statutory construction in the interpretation of statutes:

> "For purposes of our decision here today . . . we need not be involved with statutory construction nor need we be involved with our prior cases other than for dicta appearing in them to the effect that one spouse may not sue another for tort. None of our prior cases has involved an intentional tort."

Id. at 357–58, 390 A.2d at 89. Nevertheless, before doing so, and, presumably, to inform the decision, we reviewed all of our cases addressing the interspousal immunity doctrine, *id.* at 340–46, 390 A.2d at 80–82, surveyed the cases on the subject from our sister jurisdictions, *id.* at 346–49, 390 A.2d at 82–84, considered the opinions of the commentators as to the doctrine's viability and justification, *id.* at 350, 390 A.2d at 84–85, and "examined the foundation upon which our [prior] holdings rest." *Id.* at 354–57, 390 A.2d at 86–88.

The review of our cases revealed consistent and uniform application of the doctrine, some questioning of the doctrine's underpinnings and that in none of those cases "has there been an allegation of an intentional tort, much less the outrageous conduct" involved in that case. *Id.* at 352, 390 A.2d at 86. Cases from other jurisdictions, the survey found, reflected a division on the issue of the continued viability of the interspousal immunity doctrine. *Id.* at 350, 390 A.2d at 84. On the other hand, the Court noted, the commentators were near unanimous in their criticism of the common law rule of immunity. *Id.* With regard to the examination of the prior holdings on the subject, the Court said:

> . . .

> Merely five years after *Lusby,* we were asked "to reexamine the interspousal immunity rule . . . and to declare that rule to be no longer viable in tort cases involving personal injury to a spouse resulting from the negligence of the other spouse." *Boblitz, supra,* 296 Md. at 244, 462 A.2d at 506. In that case, a wife sued her husband for injuries she sustained almost a year before the marriage, as a result, she alleged, of his negligence in the operation of an automobile. Pleading the parties' marital status and relying on *Hudson,* the husband moved for summary judgment, arguing that the wife's alleged cause of action had been extinguished by the marriage. *Id.* at 243, 462 A.2d at 506. The motion was granted and we issued the writ of certiorari to review the question previously stated. *Id.* at 244, 462 A.2d at

506. We reversed the summary judgment, in the process abrogating the interspousal immunity rule in this State as to cases sounding in negligence. *Id.* at 275, 462 A.2d at 522. We explained:

> "We share the view now held by the vast majority of American States that the interspousal immunity rule is unsound in the circumstances of modern life in such cases as the subject. It is a vestige of the past. We are persuaded that the reasons asserted for its retention do not survive careful scrutiny. They furnish no reasonable basis for denial of recovery for tortious personal injury. We find no subsisting public policy that justifies retention of a judicially created immunity that would bar recovery for injured victims in such cases as the present."

Id. at 273, 462 A.2d at 521. (citation omitted).

We arrived at that holding only after conducting a thorough and exhaustive review of the doctrine of interspousal immunity, including its history and rationale, the impact and effect of the doctrine on women and women's rights, the Maryland cases applying the doctrine and the foundation on which they rested, the application and acceptance of the doctrine in our sister states, and, in particular, the change that has occurred over time in the acceptance of the doctrine by the courts of those States, the views of the legal scholars and the academic community as to the continued viability of the doctrine, and the impact of abrogating the doctrine in negligence cases.

. . .

On two occasions in the last twenty-five years, this court has done an analysis of the interspousal immunity doctrine and its rational underpinnings, the reasons or justification offered for its existence and continued viability, and, on each occasion, found the doctrine and the foundation on which it was built to be lacking. We found the trend and, indeed, the great weight of authority, to be to move away from the doctrine and in favor of changing the common law to abolish it, either fully or partially. The majority of the States, we discovered, were of the view that the doctrine was outdated and served no useful purpose, that "there presently exists no cogent or logical reason why the doctrine of interspousal tort immunity should be continued." *Merenoff,* 388 A.2d at 962. As we have seen, this Court, in *Boblitz* expressed its adherence to this majority view, characterizing the doctrine as "unsound in the circumstances of modern life" and "a vestige of the past," for which "the reasons asserted for its retention do not survive careful scrutiny." 296 Md. at 273, 462 A.2d at 521. We continue of that view and, the trend toward abrogation having continued and the weight of authority having grown larger, we are fortified in that view.

. . .

We are not convinced. It has been held that "insofar as interspousal liability for tort is concerned there is no logical or legal reason for drawing a distinction between the two." *Klein v. Klein,* 58 Cal.2d 692, 26 Cal.Rptr.

102, 376 P.2d 70, 71 (1962). *See Beattie v. Beattie,* 630 A.2d 1096, 1101 ("[I]t appears that the rationale underlying the abrogation of the Doctrine in the context of negligence actions would apply to intentional torts."). *See also Price v. Price,* 732 S.W.2d 316, 319–320 (Tex.1987), expressing concern that partial abrogation of the doctrine, which would leave in place a bar to other actionable torts that would not exist in the case of unmarried persons, would amount to a repudiation of the state constitutional guarantee of equal protection of the laws.

In any event, California abrogated the doctrine in intentional tort cases in 1962. The respondent has not provided any demonstrative evidence that any of the questions or problems she posits as possible and, indeed, "undoubtedly will arise" have arisen in California or any where else for that matter. Moreover, the other States that have fully abrogated the doctrine or in cases of intentional torts, some quite a long time ago, e.g. *Brown v. Brown, supra,* 88 Conn. 42, 89 A. 889 (1914); *Gilman v. Gilman,* 78 N.H. 4, 95 A. 657 (N.H.1915); *Crowell v. Crowell,* 180 N.C. 516, 105 S.E. 206 (1920); *Penton v. Penton,* 223 Ala. 282, 135 So. 481 (1931); *Pardue v. Pardue,* 167 S.C. 129, 166 S.E. 101 (1932), provide an accurate barometer of what can be expected after abrogation and what they reveal is far different from the picture the respondent paints.

The overwhelming weight of authority supports the petitioner's argument that the interspousal immunity doctrine should be abrogated. Joining the many of our sister States that have already done so, we abrogate the interspousal immunity rule, a vestige of the past, whose time has come and gone, as to all cases alleging an intentional tort. As we did in *Boblitz,* 296 Md. at 275, 462 A.2d at 522, we shall apply the abrogation to this case and to all causes of action accruing after the date of the filing of this opinion.

JUDGMENT OF THE COURT OF SPECIAL APPEALS REVERSED. CASE REMANDED TO THAT COURT, WITH INSTRUCTIONS TO REVERSE THE JUDGMENT OF THE CIRCUIT COURT FOR BALTIMORE COUNTY AND REMAND THE CASE TO THAT COURT FOR PROCEEDINGS CONSISTENT WITH THIS OPINION. COSTS IN THIS COURT AND IN THE COURT OF SPECIAL APPEALS TO BE PAID BY THE RESPONDENT.

F. THIRD PARTY INTERFERENCE WITH THE RELATIONSHIP

A number of actions have been available in the past to deal with disruption of the marriage relationship by a third party, or with one spouse's injury based on harm caused to the other. Often the major concern at the outset had to do with economic incidents, though there also was concern about pride and personal affront. One should question seriously whether such actions are consistent with today's social habits as well as our concepts about individual rights. Indeed some such actions have been abolished by a significant number of jurisdictions, as explained in the discussion below about the principal actions that developed.

Alienation of Affections and Criminal Conversation. The purpose of an alienation of affections action is to provide redress against a third party who causes one spouse to lose affection for the other. Criminal conversation is a civil action that originally was available against a man who had sexual intercourse with the wife of the plaintiff. Proof of loss of affection or marital breakup was unnecessary because the early rationale for the action was that the husband might be the presumed father of any children produced by such an extramarital connection, or that question might be raised as to the legitimacy of his own offspring. It is also said to be grounded on the common law notion of a husband having a property right in the person of his wife. *See* Albertini v. Veal, 292 S.C. 561, 357 S.E.2d 716, 718 (App.1987). The action remained long after those conceptual underpinnings were forgotten, and jurisdictions where it has been retained generally have extended it to wives as well as husbands. As explained in Oppenheim v. Kridel, 236 N.Y. 156, 140 N.E. 227 (1923):

> whatever reasons there were for giving the husband at common law the right to maintain an action for adultery committed with his wife exist today in behalf of the woman for a like illegal act committed by her husband. If he had feelings and honor which were hurt by such improper conduct, who will say today that she has not the same, perhaps even a keener sense of the wrong done to her and to the home? If he considered it a defilement of the marriage bed, why should she not view it in the same light? The statements that he had a property interest in her body and a right to the personal enjoyment of his wife are archaic, unless used in a refined sense worthy of the times, and which give to the wife the same interest in her husband.

Many of the "anti-heart balm statutes", discussed in Chapter 1, eliminated civil damage actions for alienation or criminal conversation, based on their susceptibility to the same abuses that were perceived with regard to breach of promise and seduction actions. In Louisiana alienation of affections was never actionable. Moulin v. Monteleone, 165 La. 169, 115 So. 447 (1927). Some courts have abolished the action without specific legislation. Attempts to "relabel" the action generally have not been successful in the courts. For example, in Speer v. Dealy, 242 Neb. 542, 495 N.W.2d 911 (1993) the Supreme Court of Nebraska rejected a husband's action for tortious interference with the marital contract and intentional infliction of emotional distress against his wife's co-worker, with whom the wife allegedly was romantically involved. The court held that the husband could not recover on either theory because both were in essence claims for either alienation of affections or criminal conversation that had been abolished by statute.

Because the action is by a spouse against a third party, the courts looks to the interference with the marriage. The Kentucky Supreme Court allowed a suit against a priest for the tort of outrage when conduct amounts to intentional infliction of emotional distress. A married couple had gone to the priest for counseling and without the husband's knowledge or consent, the priest engaged in a sexual relationship with the wife.

Osborne v. Payne, 31 S.W.3d 911 (Ky.2000). Likewise, the Utah Supreme Court allowed a suit by a husband against his now ex-wife's paramour when he learned the wife had begun an affair with a man before marriage and continued it throughout the 25–year marriage, and that two of the wife's children had been fathered by the paramour. The court allowed the former husband to bring suit against the paramour on the grounds of alienation of affection and intentional infliction of emotional distress. Heiner v. Simpson, 23 P.3d 1041 (Utah 2001).

Loss of Consortium. At common law a husband had an action for the loss of his wife's services when she was injured by the tort of a third party. As in the case of other interferences with family relations, the loss that he sustained was gradually considered to include many other incidents such as the companionship and attentions of the spouse (consortium). Although a right to services might have to be alleged as a technical requirement, an actual showing of loss of services became relatively unimportant. And though the action originally had been developed in connection with intentional torts such as assault and battery, it was extended in this country to injury from negligent harms early in the present century. This is the strong majority position today, although a few states still follow an early rationale, which denied the continued existence of the husband's actions when he was no longer entitled to his wife's services because of the Married Women's Acts. In Virginia the action is forbidden by statute. VA.CODE ANN. § 55–36 (LEXIS 1998 Repl. Vol.).

Despite the action's originally being based on a husband's property right, jurisdictions that recognize recovery for loss of consortium today generally have extended it to a wife based on injuries to her husband. In Prill v. Hampton, 154 Wis.2d 667, 453 N.W.2d 909 (App.1990), a former wife sought to recover damages for loss of consortium after divorce and for "wrongful divorce" on the theory that her divorce was the direct result of injuries sustained by the husband as a result of the defendant's negligence in a motor vehicle accident. The Court of Appeals of Wisconsin found that "public policy considerations, including uncertainty of claims and unmanageable societal costs, require that damages for consortium be terminated when the marital relationship terminates." As to the action for "wrongful divorce," they stated that:

> This type of claim has not been recognized in the past and we refuse to recognize it now. We conclude that sound public policy reasons preclude claims that a spouse's injuries caused a divorce. While we recognize that there is a strong public policy that permits injured parties to recover damages for their injuries, we also recognize countervailing public policy considerations that should bar claims for wrongful divorce.
>
> Failure of a marriage is rarely attributable to a single cause. In some instances, there may be evidence that the spouse's injuries were, in part, the cause of the marriage's failure. For the jury to properly assess the amount of damages, however, it is necessary to show both a causal relationship and the extent or degree this factor played in the

failure of the marriage. Such an inquiry would open to scrutiny very personal issues, not only of the spouse claiming damages, but also of the injured spouse. This factor, along with the difficulty of the jury in determining the extent to which any single cause may have contributed to the failure of the marriage, requires that such claims be rejected.

The court added that the claim also could be regarded as essentially an alienation of affections action, which has been legislatively abolished.

G. Medical Care

Decision Making About Treatment. It is a widely accepted practice in the hospital and medical communities to obtain consent from one spouse for life threatening procedures to the other who is incapable of fully understanding the nature of the proposed treatment and the alternatives to it. This is despite the fact that the amount of the sparse precedent about the degree of authority that a spouse can exercise in such instances without formal appointment as a guardian or authorization under a health care directive. Are there potential conflicts of interest in such an approach? Another variation of this problem can arise when it is deemed necessary for someone to make a "substituted judgment" as to what the currently incompetent patient (including one in a persistent vegetative state) would have chosen for life prolonging under the circumstances. One can argue that a spouse is best prepared to do this in light of understanding based on the couple's intimate relationship. But in many cases it is the spouse who most likely will be affected financially by a decision to prolong care. Should this affect decisions about appointment to guardianship?

Widely enacted "Natural death acts" allow a competent person to make an advance declaration as to whether "heroic treatment" will be administered if the declarant later becomes incompetent and such treatment will only prolong the death process. Some of those statutes have taken the further step of providing a list of persons authorized to make such decisions if the terminal patient has not executed a declaration while competent. High in the hierarchy of "designated decision makers" in such laws is the patient's spouse. *See, e.g.,* Va.Code § 54.1–2986 (LEXIS 1998 Repl. Vol.). Louisiana's statute has a similar provision that is qualified by allowing decision making only by a spouse who is "not judicially separated". *See* La. R.S. 40:1299.58.5A(2)(c) (West 2001). Would you include such a qualification or would you expand it in any way?

A Duty to Seek Medical Assistance? Whether one spouse has any special duty to seek medical assistance for the other has been raised in several criminal prosecutions that involved unusual fact situations. In State v. Morgan, 86 Wash.App. 74, 936 P.2d 20 (1997), a husband was convicted for manslaughter based on his failure to fulfil his statutory and natural duty to summon aid for someone he had helped place in danger. The court stated that the Washington statute on family nonsupport makes it a crime for one to wilfully omit "to provide necessary food, clothing, shelter, or medical attendance to his or her spouse.... The violation of this statutory duty could provide the recklessness necessary for a manslaughter charge.'' The court found also that the husband had a duty under the circumstances independent of that in the statute, concluding that

> ... [The husband] had a statutory duty to provide medical care, a natural duty to provide medical help to his wife, and a duty to summon aid for someone he helped place in danger. His violation of this duty amounted to recklessness and was sufficient basis for the manslaughter charge. The court's denial of the motion to dismiss was proper.

See also, People v. Oliver, 210 Cal.App.3d 138, 258 Cal.Rptr. 138 (1989), and State v. Mally, 139 Mont. 599, 366 P.2d 868 (1961). However, the cases do not extend to instances in which one spouse acts in good faith at the request of the other who is competent. For further examination of this doctrine, *see* Commonwealth v. Konz, 498 Pa. 639, 450 A.2d 638 (1982); and Robbins v. Stephanski, 83 A.D.2d 271, 443 N.Y.S.2d 1016 (1981).

Case on Point, Terry Schiavo. The contest between Michael Schiavo, Terri Schiavo's husband, and her parents over who should have the authority to remove Terri's nutrition and hydration tube, precipitated intense national debate. The contest concerned who should make the medical decisions when the incapacitated person has not made his or her wishes known. Following the Florida Supreme Court decision in Bush v. Schiavo, 885 So.2d 321, the United States Supreme Court refused to hear an appeal brought by the governor in January 2005. Then, one day prior to when Terri Schiavo's feeding tube was to be removed at the request of the husband, the Florida Circuit Judge ordered a temporary stay upon a motion made by the parents that Terri's husband was not acting in his wife's best interests because of his personal involvement with another woman. The court eventually rejected the parents' assertion, the stay was then lifted, and the tube was removed on March 18, 2005. Consistently, the husband's position was that his wife had told him she would not want to continue living as she was then.

Sensing the federal courts would not intervene to overrule the husband's decision, the United States Senate and House of Representatives deliberated overnight to pass emergency legislation ''for the relief of the parents of'' Terri Schiavo. The president signed the legislation–The Schiavo Bill–during the pre-dawn hours on March 21, 2005. In essence, the federal legislation sought to provide to the parents of Terri Schiavo a federal cause of action regardless of whether there still remained state causes of action, and to issue any injunctive relief to safeguard Terri Schiavo's rights to continued medical treatment. In spite of the federal statute, the federal district court refused to issue injunctive relief, most importantly to reinsert the feeding tube, and the parents appealed again to the Florida Supreme Court and the United States Supreme Court. Both courts declined to intervene and Terri Schiavo died on March 31, 2005, thirteen days after the feeding tube was removed. Her husband ordered an autopsy on his wife to discover the extent of her brain damage, and then her body was cremated over the objections of her parents. *See* Laura Stanton, *The Battle over Terri Schiavo*, WASH. POST, Apr. 1, 2005, at A13.

The legal struggle between the spouse and the parents sparked intense legal, medical and religious controversy. *See, e.g.*, Timothy E. Quill, *Terri Schiavo–A Tragedy Compounded*, 352 NEW ENG. J. MED. 1630 (2005); Editorial, *Extraordinary Means*, COMMONWEAL, Apr. 8, 2005, at 5. The cost in Medicaid dollars of caring for persons such as Terri Schiavo is also being debated. *See, e.g.*, Jonathan Weisman & Ceci Connolly, *Schiavo Case Puts Face on Rising Medical Costs*, WASH. POST, Mar. 28, 2005, at A13. But the most significant impact may be the intense interest in advance medical planning as citizens wish to avoid placing themselves or their families in similar circumstances. *See, e.g.*, Lois Shepherd, *Shattering the Neutral Surrogate Myth in End-of-Life Decisionmaking: Terri Schiavo and Her Family*, 35 CUMBERLAND L. REV.575 (2005). A number of web sites offer information and forms concerning health care directives. *See, e.g.*, AGING WITH DIGNITY, at *http://www.agingwithdignity.org* (last visited Jan. 7, 2007); NAT'L HOSPICE & PALLIATIVE CARE ORG., at *http://www.nhpco.org* (last visited Jan. 7, 2007); MAYO CLINIC'S ADVANCE DIRECTIVE RES., at *http://www. mayoclinic.com* (last visited Jan. 7, 2007).

CHAPTER IV

MATRIMONIAL BREAKDOWN: GROUNDS AND JURISDICTION FOR DISSOLUTION OF MARRIAGE

A. THE PERSPECTIVE OF HISTORY

Lord Bryce observed in 1901 that our state divorce laws then constituted "the largest and the strangest, and perhaps the saddest, body of legislative experiments in the sphere of family law which free, self-governing communities have ever tried."[1] In large measure this condition reflected the powerfully entrenched moral and religious views about indissolubility of marriage except in the context of significant fault. This was exemplified by the editorial expression of Horace Greeley, who wrote in 1860 while campaigning against easier divorce, that "to the libertine, the egotist, the selfish, sensual seeker of personal and present enjoyment at whatever cost to others, the Indissolubility of Marriage is an obstacle, a restraint, a terror; and God forbid that it should ever cease to be."[2]

The mores have changed dramatically since 1860, or even 1960, with regard to divorce and the indissolubility of marriage. The view of a large segment of our population today is better summarized in the words of the modern bard, Paul Simon:

> I like to sleep with the windows open
>
> And you like to sleep with the windows closed
>
> So goodbye
>
> Goodbye
>
> Goodbye.[3]

Whether the new approaches to divorce are any less strange or sad may be debated, but they certainly constitute dramatic change. Even so, vestiges of the longstanding fault tradition remain, and it is important that we understand the history of divorce grounds and divorce as an institution in this country.

---

1. 2 J. Bryce, Studies in History and Jurisprudence 830 (1901).

2. N.Y. Tribune, April 7, 1860, quoted in M. Blake, The Road to Reno at 92 (1962).

3. The words are from the song "You're Kind", which can be found on the 1975 Paul Simon LP: "Still crazy after all these years."

At the beginning of the twentieth century the ecclesiastical heritage was still quite apparent in our divorce laws. The oldest part of the law was that inherited from ancient ecclesiastical jurisprudence respecting judicial separation—the divorce *a mensa et thoro.* Traditionally this had been a mere physical separation of the parties for cause, a remedy that extinguished none of the economic incidents of marriage and did not permit either party to remarry. It was so limited because of the tenet that a valid marriage was a sacrament and was by divine injunction indissoluble. In keeping with the emphasis which the church placed upon maintenance of the family, it offered a limited form of relief to the parties while seeking at the same time to insure that their obligations to society were performed.

The absolute divorce, known as the divorce *a vinculo matrimonii,* stems from the Protestant reformers' rejection of the sacramental character of marriage and their insistence that it should be a temporal matter. But Luther, who was first to assert this, did not take the next logical step— free divorce. The family was focal in his social philosophy and consequently it was only in cases of adultery or malicious desertion (both of which were considered subversive of family solidarity) that he was prepared to concede an absolute divorce, and even then with only the innocent party being set free to remarry.

The reform of dogma in England was effected along lines more conservative than those indicated by Luther. But an attempted reformation of the canon law failed of adoption and the main features of the old law were retained. With respect to divorce this meant that there was available only the separation, or divorce *a mensa et thoro.* It was not until 1698 that a private act itself indisputably dissolving the marriage was used. The instances thereafter continued to be rare.

The development of divorce jurisdiction in America after the Revolution proceeded along highly diverse lines. The legislative divorce, an imitation of the English parliamentary divorce, was universal. Only a few states, notably Virginia in 1827 and Maryland in 1830, undertook any early attempt to require judicial or quasi-judicial preliminaries. States with a chancery tradition committed jurisdiction to equity courts while in New England common law or probate courts had cognizance of divorce matters once they became a judicial function. Confusion between annulment and divorce was widespread. Many states retained a form of divorce *a mensa et thoro,* and variations developed so that such a decree eventually might be converted into a divorce *a vinculo.* Most important was the proliferation of grounds for divorce as legislatures backed away from the process of granting divorces by private bill and gave courts authority to dissolve marriages on proof of certain conduct regarded as antisocial according to the views of the day. These statutory grounds might be drafted with specificity, such as attempting the life of the other spouse "by poison or any other means showing malice"; or they might take on omnibus proportions, as in a Rhode Island law which, after listing a number of specific fault grounds, added that divorce could be granted "for any other gross misbehavior and wickedness, in either of the parties, repugnant to and in violation of the marriage covenant.''

In addition to the widespread legislative variations, an elaborate body of judicially created defenses developed around the conceptual base of fault as the condition for dissolution by divorce. Condonation, connivance and recrimination are still important in some jurisdictions.

In the 1960's major pressure for reform of this Kafkaesque process began to influence some legislatures. There was growing belief that our divorce laws more reflected nineteenth rather than twentieth century mores. There also was concern that many divorce courts had become infested with perjured testimony and collusive actions that often were overlooked by judges who felt that divorce could be a desirable social goal. If two parties wanted a divorce and were willing to fib a bit, they could be divorced in many jurisdictions through an uncontested proceeding. But if one spouse wished to thwart or substantially delay the other's divorce desires, this often could be achieved through contesting the action.

The basic approach of the divorce reform movement that developed momentum in the 1960's was to deemphasize the role of fault, at least in determining whether to dissolve a marriage. The thought was that there should be some reasonably simple and nontraumatic method for pronouncing the last legal rites over marriages that were in fact dead. Emphasis shifted from fixing blame or inflicting punishment to determining whether a union had broken down to the point that there was little or no hope for repair. Approaches that were offered ranged from "living apart" grounds with short enough separation periods to be workable, to new causes for divorce such as irremediable breakdown or irreconcilable differences that rendered the marriage no longer tenable. Some jurisdictions substituted the term "dissolution" for "divorce" to symbolize the magnitude of the break with past practices and to skirt any vestiges of social obloquy sometimes accompanying divorce in the past. The judicial transition was sometimes frustrating, with judges occasionally unable to change their prior thinking about divorce as a reward or punishment. Opponents of the new approach argued that making divorce too easy posed a threat to marriage as an institution; proponents countered that cultural factors, not divorce legislation, provide the major influence on marital breakdown.

Although the reform is by no means finished, divorce now can be obtained far more freely. The 1972 Statement of Social Principles of The United Methodist Church gives some idea of the modern recognition that divorce is an accepted part of our culture today:

> "We assert the sanctity of the marriage covenant. Marriage between a man and a woman has long been blessed by God and recognized by society.... In marriages where the partners are, even after thoughtful consideration and counsel, estranged beyond reconciliation, we recognize divorce and the right of divorced persons to remarry, and express our concern for the needs of the children of such union."

In Ritual in a New Day: An Invitation (1976), a volume created as part of an Alternative Rituals Project, the need for a Ritual for Divorce is discussed and several illustrative rituals are reproduced. Included are one in which both spouses participate, another involving only one of the spouses, and a third which can be incorporated into a remarriage ceremony. On the other hand, a substantial movement toward returning to fault based divorce has been launched in some jurisdictions.

For further review and analysis of divorce in this country, *see* Bryna Bogoch & Ruth Halperin–Kaddari, *Divorce Israeli Style: Professional Perceptions of Gender and Power in Mediated and Lawyer–Negotiated Divorces,* 28 LAW & POL'Y 137–163 (2006); James Herbie DiFonzo, *Customized Marriage,* 75 IND. L. J. 875 (2000); Mae Kuykendall, *Emerson Family Values: Claims to Duration and Renewal in American Narratives of Divorce, Love and Marriage,* 18 Hastings Women's L. J. 69–113 (2007); Robert R. Rains, *Disability and Family Relationships: Marriage Penalties and Support Anomalies,* 22 GA. ST. U. L. REV. 561–596 (2006); Laura Rosenbury, *Two Ways to End a Marriage: Divorce or Death,* 2005 UTAH L. REV. 1227–1290; Katherine Shaw Spaht, *Covenant Marriage Seven Years Later: Its As Yet Unfulfilled Promise,* 65 LA. L. REV. 605–634 (2005); Barbara Stark, *Rhetoric, Divorce and International Human Rights: The Limits of Divorce Reform for the Protection of Children,* 65 LA. L. REV. 1433–1456 (2005).

B. GROUNDS AND DEFENSES

Approximately one third of the states have eliminated all fault grounds and replaced them with some form of irretrievable breakdown, sometimes accompanied by the ground of insanity. Fault grounds still subsist in the other jurisdictions, and marital misconduct still can have substantial impact on financial awards, but every state has some form of "no fault" ground, though agreement between the parties may be necessary in an least one jurisdiction. Given the migratory nature of our population, it is important for attorneys to have a practical understanding of the fault system regardless of their own state's grounds, though no attempt is made here to review the many peculiar rules that have been engrafted onto it in various jurisdictions.

1. THE FAULT SCHEME

UTAH CODE ANN. (1999)

30–3–1 Procedure—Residence—Grounds.

(1) Proceedings in divorce are commenced and conducted as provided by law for proceedings in civil causes, except as provided in this chapter.

(2) The court may decree a dissolution of the marriage contract between the petitioner and respondent on the grounds specified in Subsec-

tion (3) in all cases where the petitioner or respondent has been an actual and bona fide resident of this state and of the county where the action is brought, or if members of the armed forces of the United States who are not legal residents of this state, where the petitioner has been stationed in this state under military orders, for three months next prior to the commencement of the action.

(3) Grounds for divorce:

(a) impotency of the respondent at the time of marriage;

(b) adultery committed by the respondent subsequent to marriage;

(c) willful desertion of the petitioner by the respondent for more than one year;

(d) willful neglect of the respondent to provide for the petitioner the common necessaries of life;

(e) habitual drunkenness of the respondent;

(f) conviction of the respondent for a felony;

(g) cruel treatment of the petitioner by the respondent to the extent of causing bodily injury or great mental distress to the petitioner;

(h) irreconcilable differences of the marriage;

(i) incurable insanity; or

(j) when the husband and wife have lived separately under a decree of separate maintenance of any state for three consecutive years without cohabitation.

(4) A decree of divorce granted under Subsection (3)(j) does not affect the liability of either party under any provision for separate maintenance previously granted.

(5)(a) A divorce may not be granted on the grounds of insanity unless: (i) the respondent has been adjudged insane by the appropriate authorities of this or another state prior to the commencement of the action; and (ii) the court finds by the testimony of competent witnesses that the insanity of the respondent is incurable.

(b) The court shall appoint for the respondent a guardian ad litem, who shall protect the interests of the respondent. A copy of the summons and complaint shall be served on the respondent in person or by publication, as provided by the laws of this state in other actions for divorce, or upon his guardian ad litem, and upon the county attorney for the county where the action is prosecuted.

(c) The county attorney shall investigate the merits of the case and if the respondent resides out of this state, take depositions as necessary, attend the proceedings, and make a defense as is just to protect the rights of the respondent and the interests of the state.

(d) In all actions the court and judge have jurisdiction over the payment of alimony, the distribution of property, and the custody and maintenance of minor children, as the courts and judges possess in other actions for divorce.

(e) The petitioner or respondent may, if the respondent resides in this state, upon notice, have the respondent brought into the court at trial, or have an examination of the respondent by two or more competent physicians, to determine the mental condition of the respondent. For this purpose either party may have leave from the court to enter any asylum or institution where the respondent may be confined. The costs of court in this action shall be apportioned by the court.

NOTE

Often the divorce statute becomes a hodgepodge of grounds, some better incorporated into suits for annulment (e.g., 3(a)), and some which include all of the other grounds (e.g., 3(h)). The rationale is that the statute has a long history with varying permutations. *See generally* Erik V. Wicks, Comment. *Fault–Based Divorce "Reforms," Archaic Survivals, and Ancients Lessons*, 46 WAYNE L. REV. 1565 (2000).

NEW YORK DOMESTIC RELATIONS LAW (McKinney 1999 & Supp. 2006)

§ 170. Action for divorce

An action for divorce may be maintained by a husband or wife to procure a judgment divorcing the parties and dissolving the marriage on any of the following grounds:

(1) The cruel and inhuman treatment of the plaintiff by the defendant such that the conduct of the defendant so endangers the physical or mental well being of the plaintiff as renders it unsafe or improper for the plaintiff to cohabit with the defendant.

(2) The abandonment of the plaintiff by the defendant for a period of one or more years.

(3) The confinement of the defendant in prison for a period of three or more consecutive years after the marriage of plaintiff and defendant.

(4) The commission of an act of adultery, provided that adultery for the purposes of articles ten, eleven, and eleven-A of this chapter, is hereby defined as the commission of an act of sexual intercourse, oral sexual conduct or anal sexual conduct, voluntarily performed by the defendant, with a person other than the plaintiff after the marriage of plaintiff and defendant. Oral sexual conduct and anal sexual conduct include, but are not limited to, sexual conduct as defined in subdivision two of section 130.00 and subdivision three of section 130.20 of the penal law.

(5) The husband and wife have lived apart pursuant to a decree or judgment of separation for a period of one or more years after the granting of such decree or judgment, and satisfactory proof has been submitted by

the plaintiff that he or she has substantially performed all the terms and conditions of such decree or judgment.

(6) The husband and wife have lived separate and apart pursuant to a written agreement of separation, subscribed by the parties thereto and acknowledged or proved in the form required to entitle a deed to be recorded, for a period of one or more years after the execution of such agreement and satisfactory proof has been submitted by the plaintiff that he or she has substantially performed all the terms and conditions of such agreement. Such agreement shall be filed in the office of the clerk of the county wherein either party resides. In lieu of filing such agreement, either party to such agreement may file a memorandum of such agreement, which memorandum shall be similarly subscribed and acknowledged or proved as was the agreement of separation and shall contain the following information: (a) the names and addresses of each of the parties, (b) the date of marriage of the parties, (c) the date of the agreement of separation and (d) the date of this subscription and acknowledgment or proof of such agreement of separation.

§ 173.   In an action for divorce there is a right to trial by jury of the issues of the grounds for granting the divorce.

§ 200.   Action for separation

An action may be maintained by a husband or wife against the other party to the marriage to procure a judgment separating the parties from bed and board, forever, or for a limited time, for any of the following causes:

1.   The cruel and inhuman treatment of the plaintiff by the defendant such that the conduct of the defendant so endangers the physical or mental well being of the plaintiff as renders it unsafe or improper for the plaintiff to cohabit with the defendant.

2.   The abandonment of the plaintiff by the defendant.

3.   The neglect or refusal of the defendant-spouse to provide for the support of the plaintiff-spouse where the defendant-spouse is chargeable with such support under the provisions of section thirty-two of this chapter or of section four hundred twelve of the family court act.

4.   The commission of an act of adultery by the defendant; except where such offense is committed by the procurement or with the connivance of the plaintiff or where there is voluntary cohabitation of the parties with the knowledge of the offense or where action was not commenced within five years after the discovery by the plaintiff of the offense charged or where the plaintiff has also been guilty of adultery under such circumstances that the defendant would have been entitled, if innocent, to a divorce, provided that adultery for the purposes of this subdivision is hereby defined as the commission of an act of sexual intercourse, oral sexual conduct or anal sexual conduct, voluntarily performed by the defendant, with a person other than the plaintiff after the marriage of plaintiff and defendant. Oral sexual conduct and anal sexual conduct include, but

are not limited to, sexual conduct as defined in subdivision two of section 130.00 and subdivision three of section 130.20 of the penal law.

5. The confinement of the defendant in prison for a period of three or more consecutive years after the marriage of plaintiff and defendant.

NOTE

The extensive list of grounds that are considered "faults" and grounds that are considered "no fault" raises questions as to choice: Must the party seeking a divorce choose one or the other, or can the party choose both in petitioning for a divorce? Is it possible for one party to choose one ground and the other party another? In Ebbert v. Ebbert, 123 N.H. 252, 459 A.2d 282 (1983), the trial court had approved a master's recommendation on cross libels for divorce that two decrees be awarded, one based on adultery and the other on irreconcilable differences. In overruling this decision on appeal, the Supreme Court of New Hampshire explained that the addition of "irreconcilable differences" as a ground did not repeal the original thirteen grounds based on fault, and held that:

> A party who seeks a divorce on a fault ground cannot be denied the opportunity to litigate on that basis merely because the other party has advanced irreconcilable differences as grounds for divorce.

Under the circumstances this would seem to require that the trial court determine whether breakdown of the marriage was caused by adultery or irreconcilable differences. Is such an approach consistent with the idea that a key reason for adding breakdown grounds is to lessen the bitterness that may be abetted by the divorce process? Some state statutes that mix both fault and no-fault grounds permit a court to make a finding of "fault" for alimony purposes without having to rest the divorce on such a ground. *See, e.g.*, VA. CODE ANN. § 20–107.1 (2004). Fault is an important consideration in the distribution of marital assets. Approximately half of the states allow marital or economic fault to be considered in the division of marital property or an award of spousal support, thus making fault of one or both of the parties a significant factor. For analysis and a list of specific states, *see* ALI, PRINCIPLES OF THE LAW OF FAMILY DISSOLUTION: ANALYSIS AND RECOMMENDATIONS, Proposed Final Draft Part I, Ch. 1, Introduction, 14–74 (Feb. 14, 1997). For example, the potential recipient's adultery is a complete bar to alimony, without regard to any other facts of the case, in Georgia, North Carolina, South Carolina, and West Virginia. *Id.* at 23. Proof of the adultery may be based simply on circumstances, but at least one court has held that neither judge nor jury should hold as a matter of law that two people cannot live in the same residence without engaging in sexual intercourse. Hughes v. Hughes, 33 Va.App. 160, 531 S.E.2d 654 (2000).

VIRGINIA CODE ANN. (2004)

§ 20–91. Grounds for divorce from bond of matrimony.

A. A divorce from the bond of matrimony may be decreed:

(1) For adultery; or for sodomy or buggery committed outside the marriage; . . .

(3) Where either of the parties subsequent to the marriage has been convicted of a felony, sentenced to confinement for more than one year and confined for such felony subsequent to such conviction, and cohabitation has not been resumed after knowledge of such confinement (in which case no pardon granted to the party so sentenced shall restore such party to his or her conjugal rights); or

. . .

(6) Where either party has been guilty of cruelty, caused reasonable apprehension of bodily hurt, or willfully deserted or abandoned the other, such divorce may be decreed to the innocent party after a period of one year from the date of such act;

. . .

(9)(a) On the application of either party if and when the husband and wife have lived separate and apart without any cohabitation and without interruption for one year. In any case where the parties have entered into a separation agreement and there are no minor children either born of the parties, born of either party and adopted by the other or adopted by both parties, a divorce may be decreed on application if and when the husband and wife have lived separately and apart without cohabitation and without interruption for six months. A plea of res adjudicata or of recrimination with respect to any other provision of this section shall not be a bar to either party obtaining a divorce on this ground; nor shall it be a bar that either party has been adjudged insane, either before or after such separation has commenced, but at the expiration of one year or six months, whichever is applicable, from the commencement of such separation, the grounds for divorce shall be deemed to be complete, and the committee of the insane defendant, if there be one, shall be made a party to the cause, or if there be no committee, then the court shall appoint a guardian ad litem to represent the insane defendant.

(b) This subsection (9) shall apply whether the separation commenced prior to its enactment or shall commence thereafter. Where otherwise valid, any decree of divorce hereinbefore entered by any court having equity jurisdiction pursuant to this subsection (9), not appealed to the Supreme Court of Virginia, is hereby declared valid according to the terms of said decree notwithstanding the insanity of a party thereto.

(c) A decree of divorce granted pursuant to this subsection (9) shall in no way lessen any obligation any party may otherwise have to support the spouse unless such party shall prove that there exists in the favor of such party some other ground of divorce under this section or § 20–95.B. A decree of divorce shall include each party's social security number, or other control number issued by the Department of Motor Vehicles. . . .

§ **20–95.**   Grounds for divorces from bed and board. A divorce from bed and board may be decreed for cruelty, reasonable apprehension of bodily hurt, willful desertion or abandonment.

NOTE

Former grounds 2, 4, 5, 7 and 8 of Va. Code § 20–91 were repealed but the General Assembly did not renumber the remaining ones.

Note that Virginia and New York still maintain both the divorce *a mensa et thoro,* or divorce from bed and board, and the divorce *a vinculo matrimonii,* or absolute divorce. Some states once provided substantially different grounds for the two actions, one of which can hardly be called a true divorce because neither party is free to remarry afterward. The practical effect of this in some cases could be that the "innocent" party who did not wish to remarry (or have his or her spouse remarry) could elect between the procedures. The Virginia Code provides that either party may merge a decree for divorce from bed and board into a decree for absolute divorce once the requisite statutory period has elapsed. Va. Code § 20–121. Are there any good reasons for maintaining the two actions today, particularly under a statute like Virginia's which has overlapping grounds?

Brady v. Brady

Court of Appeals of New York, 1985.
64 N.Y.2d 339, 486 N.Y.S.2d 891, 476 N.E.2d 290.

■ Wachtler, Chief Judge.

Plaintiff Edward Brady has brought this matrimonial action against his wife, defendant Dorothy Brady, seeking a divorce and sale of the marital residence. The complaint alleged, as grounds for obtaining a divorce, that Mrs. Brady committed acts constituting cruel and inhuman treatment and constructively abandoned plaintiff by refusing to engage in sexual relations with him (see, Domestic Relations Law § 170). The question presented is what conduct constitutes cruel and inhuman treatment in a "long-term" marriage so as to give rise to a cause of action for divorce. More specifically, we must determine whether the principles set forth in Hessen v. Hessen, 33 N.Y.2d 406, 353 N.Y.S.2d 421, 308 N.E.2d 891, with respect to the necessary showing of cruel and inhuman treatment in a long-term marriage, are still to be followed.

The parties were married in 1956 and have four children, who were born between 1957 and 1966. From May 1977 to September 1979, Mr. Brady lived in the marital residence on an infrequent basis and since September or October 1979 he has not resided there at all. Mr. Brady commenced this action for a divorce in 1981. His verified complaint set forth two causes of action, one for constructive abandonment and the other for cruel and inhuman treatment. Among the allegations relating to the claim of cruel and inhuman treatment were that Mrs. Brady, during 1976, struck him with objects, including a lamp and a vase, threatened him with a knife, attempted to choke him and frequently berated him. Her answer denied all of these allegations and set forth counterclaims for maintenance and child support, but not for a judgment of divorce.

At trial, plaintiff, with minimal corroboration, testified to the allegations in the complaint. Mrs. Brady, supported in much of her testimony by one of the Brady children, again denied the charges of constructive abandonment and cruel and inhuman treatment, and stated that she did not seek a divorce. The trial court, although apparently rejecting most of plaintiff's specific claims of cruel and inhuman treatment, granted him a divorce on that cause of action. The court termed the marriage a "dead" one, and concluded that based on the marital breakdown and the separation of the parties further cohabitation was improper. The court also awarded custody of the remaining infant child to Mrs. Brady, granted her exclusive use and occupancy of the marital residence until the emancipation of this child, at which time the residence would be sold, provided for the distribution of other marital property, and ordered plaintiff to make payments to her for maintenance and child support.

The Appellate Division, 101 A.D.2d 797, 475 N.Y.S.2d 470, unanimously modified the trial court judgment. The court found that plaintiff had not made out a cause of action for divorce based on cruel and inhuman treatment, and thus deleted the portions of the judgment granting plaintiff a divorce and ordering the sale of the marital residence upon the emancipation of the remaining infant child. We now affirm.

Prior to the 1966 amendments to the Domestic Relations Law, the sole ground for divorce in this State was adultery. The 1966 reforms added five additional grounds, one of which was, and remains, "The cruel and inhuman treatment of the plaintiff by the defendant such that the conduct of the defendant so endangers the physical or mental well being of the plaintiff as renders it unsafe or improper for the plaintiff to cohabit with the defendant" (Domestic Relations Law § 170[1], added by L.1966, ch. 254).

In Hessen v. Hessen, 33 N.Y.2d 406, 353 N.Y.S.2d 421, 308 N.E.2d 891, supra, we held that a plaintiff seeking a divorce under the cruel and inhuman treatment subdivision must show serious misconduct, and not mere incompatibility. Subsequent cases have established that a plaintiff, relying on this subdivision, must generally show a course of conduct by the defendant spouse which is harmful to the physical or mental health of the plaintiff and makes cohabitation unsafe or improper. The subdivision requires a finding of fault and thus a showing of irreconcilable or irremediable differences is insufficient by itself.

In *Hessen,* we also noted that the determination of whether conduct constituted cruel and inhuman treatment would depend, in part, on the length of the parties' marriage, because what might be considered substantial misconduct in the context of a marriage of short duration, might only be "transient discord" in that of a long-term marriage. Thus, courts in this State have required a high degree of proof of cruel and inhuman treatment where there is a marriage of long duration and an isolated act of mistreatment will rarely suffice.

At the time the *Hessen* case was decided, only a wife was able to collect alimony following a divorce. If, however, her "misconduct" entitled the husband to obtain a divorce on a ground such as cruel and inhuman treatment, she was precluded under Domestic Relations Law § 236 from receiving alimony or exclusive possession of the marital home.[1] Thus, the effect of granting a husband a divorce on the ground of his wife's cruel and inhuman treatment was a potential financial catastrophe to the wife. In *Hessen,* we noted that this negative effect could be particularly harmful where the defendant, as was the case therein, was a "dependent older woman" and this fact served as one of the bases for requiring a higher degree of proof of cruel and inhuman treatment in a long-term marriage.

In 1980, the Equitable Distribution Law was enacted and Domestic Relations Law § 236 was amended to provide, in part, that either spouse could be required to pay alimony ("maintenance"), and to eliminate the rule that misconduct by a spouse precludes receiving an award of alimony or exclusive possession of the marital home. The change with respect to the person who could be required to pay alimony was constitutionally required in light of the Supreme Court's 1979 decision in Orr v. Orr, 440 U.S. 268, 99 S.Ct. 1102, 59 L.Ed.2d 306, which held that the Alabama statutory scheme which imposed alimony obligations on husbands only violated the equal protection clause of the 14th Amendment to the United States Constitution. Plaintiff argues that the *Hessen* rule, as to long-term marriages, was designed to protect only women and thus can no longer be followed in view of the *Orr* decision. He also argues that there is no longer any reason to require a higher showing of misconduct in a long-term marriage as the spouse against whom the divorce is granted can receive alimony payments and exclusive possession of the marital home, and thus there is no danger that granting a divorce will be financially ruinous to a "dependent older woman".

If the evidentiary requirement set forth in *Hessen* with respect to marriages of long duration were applied only where the plaintiff was the husband, then there would likely be an equal protection violation. *Hessen,* however, has been and should be followed whether the plaintiff is the husband or the wife. Thus, plaintiff's constitutional argument is without merit. Plaintiff's contention that the rationale for the *Hessen* rule has been eliminated by the 1980 amendments to Domestic Relations Law § 236 is also unconvincing. That financial problems could have faced a middle aged woman against whom a cruelty divorce was granted was merely one of the bases for requiring a higher degree of proof of cruel and inhuman treatment in a long-term marriage. The fundamental reason for such a rule was, and remains, the commonsense notion that the conduct which a plaintiff

---

1. The only exception to this rule was where the plaintiff had waived his rights under that provision of the Domestic Relations Law and authorized the trial court to make such awards (Hessen v. Hessen, 33 N.Y.2d 406, 411, 353 N.Y.S.2d 421, 308 N.E.2d 891; Barry v. Barry, 93 A.D.2d 797, 460 N.Y.S.2d 601).

alleges as the basis for a cause of action must be viewed in the context of the entire marriage, including its duration, in deciding whether particular actions can properly be labeled as cruel and inhuman.

Therefore, we reaffirm the holding in *Hessen* that whether a plaintiff has established a cause of action for a cruelty divorce will depend, in part, on the duration of the marriage in issue. The existence of a long-term marriage does not, of course, serve as an absolute bar to the granting of a divorce for cruel and inhuman treatment, and even in such a marriage "substantial misconduct" might consist of one violent episode such as a severe beating.

It is not clear which, if any, of plaintiff's allegations were credited by the trial court. The trial court did conclude that plaintiff had not made a sufficient showing of cruel and inhuman treatment under *Hessen* in view of the duration of the marriage (26 years), but concluded that "the *[Hessen]* rule must be considered as no longer retaining its authority". The court went on to find that the Bradys' marriage was a "dead" one, and, "in its discretion", granted Mr. Brady a divorce on his cause of action for cruel and inhuman treatment. While the trial court does have broad discretion as to whether to grant a cruelty divorce, such a divorce cannot be granted simply because the court concludes that there is a "dead marriage".

. . .

NOTE

What constitutes "Cruelty"? Before enactment of "breakdown" grounds, nothing contributed more to the relaxation of the old stern standards of how divorce laws should be administered than judicial manipulation of the term "cruelty". This first became a divorce ground in our country at a time when woman, as the old phrase had it, was "under the rod of her husband," and consequently was supposed to be subject to his discipline. These ideas of subjection long survived the passage of Married Women's Acts, and affected judicial thinking about what conduct properly could be denominated cruel. This conservatism sometimes was abetted by statutory language; many state legislatures, spendthrift with adjectives, had stipulated that the ground must be extreme cruelty, intolerable cruelty, or cruel, barbarous and inhuman treatment. The looser, modern interpretations came in spite of such statutory exhortations.

Not only may statutory language vary, but courts may express greatly differing opinions as to what will constitute "cruelty" under statutes of similar wording. Physical violence may be required by some, while mental cruelty is enough for others. In Farrar v. Farrar, 553 S.W.2d 741 (Tenn. 1977), the evidence presented by plaintiff to establish cruelty included an extra-marital affair of the defendant. Whether mental cruelty should be a ground for divorce without proof of physical injury was long difficult to resolve in some jurisdictions. Eventually most courts found ways to handle the problem, just as they had in the evolution of tort law to permit recovery of damages for emotional harm alone.

The London Times, July 16, 1963, carried a short account of the case of Lines v. Lines, heard by the High Court of Justice: Probate and Admiralty. The wife sought a divorce based on cruelty. She complained that during the six months the parties lived together the husband persistently required her to tickle the soles of his feet, the top of his head, or his back. According to the report:

A week after the marriage the husband made his first request to the wife to tickle his feet after he removed his shoes and socks. The wife thought the request peculiar and at first refused, but the husband threatened not to talk to her. After that he asked to be tickled nearly every night, and sometimes it went on for four hours or more, even when they were watching television. If the wife refused to tickle him the husband sulked.

In January, 1959, the wife left the husband for two days, but returned on his promise to give up the tickling. For a few days his conduct improved, but he then started importuning again to be tickled.

The wife finally left in February 1959. Her doctor had said that she was then suffering from acute anxiety and could not keep her fingers still.

The husband had not desired to hurt the wife but had persisted in his demands to be tickled after being warned of the effect on her health. On the House of Lords authority of Gollins v. Gollins (The Times, June 28, 1963) the husband's conduct amounted to cruelty.

In Williams v. Williams, [1964] A.C. 698, 1963, 2 All E.R. 994, H.L., which involved a question of whether insanity could be a defense to cruelty, Lord Reid said:

To my mind, "cruelty" is a word that can take its meaning from its context: often it connotes blameworthiness but quite often it does not. Let me give one or two examples. Even in comparatively recent times practically everyone, including men of the highest integrity and intelligence who were quite as civilised as any of us, firmly believed that persecution in one form or another was not only excusable but was a moral duty. Few would deny that their acts were cruel, but I do not see how we can reasonably blame them for not having anticipated modern ideas. And is it a misuse of language to call a cat cruel? Again, when we speak of the cruel sea no doubt we personify the sea but do we blame it? So the law cannot just take "cruelty" in its ordinary or popular meaning, because that is too vague: we must decide what, if any, mental state is a necessary ingredient.

Proving Adultery. Adultery was universally included as a ground in fault-based divorce laws. New York long maintained that it was the State's only ground, though its liberal approach to annulment sometimes was used to expand the available causes for dissolution. The major problem that adultery presents is the matter of proof; from a practical point of view it often is either too ample or too meager. The first situation involves the collusive divorce in which evidence has been "staged" for ultimate presentation to an ostensibly unsuspecting referee or judge. This sort of deviousness was even a concern in the days of Chancellor Kent, who acknowledged having "had occasion to believe, in the exercise of a judicial cognizance over numerous cases of divorce, that the sin of adultery was sometimes committed on the part of the husband for the very purpose of divorce." 2 KENT, COMMENTARIES ON AMERICAN LAW 106 (13th ed.1884). Years later, another New York judge described to a committee on matrimonial law reform the sameness of the circumstantial evidence of adultery that reached his court regularly, noting:

> She is always in a sheer pink robe. It's never blue—always pink. And he is always in his shorts when they catch them.

N.Y. Herald Tribune, Oct. 1, 1965, p. 19, col. 4. Circumstantial evidence still may be used to prove adultery, but it must do more than simply establish a strong suspicion of guilt.

For an illustration of successful use of the physician-patient privilege by a wife whose husband sought to introduce evidence in support of his allegation that she had undergone an abortion after he had been sterilized and thus must have committed adultery, see Arsenaux v. Arsenaux, 428 So.2d 427 (La.1983).

Finally, the New Hampshire Supreme Court has ruled that the state's statute providing for a divorce based on the ground of adultery contemplates that adultery excludes all non-coital sex acts. Therefore, sexual contact between persons of the same sex or any act between persons of the same sex or any act between persons of the same sex or any act between persons of the opposite sex or with animals that does not include coitus is, by definition, not adultery for purposes of obtaining a divorce in the state. *In re* Blanchflower, 150 N.H. 226, 834 A.2d 1010 (2003).

Corroboration. In divorce actions corroboration by evidence other than testimony of the parties often is required in order to lessen the potential for collusion. *See, e.g.,* VA.CODE § 20–99 (LEXIS 2000 Repl. Vol.). In Graham v. Graham, 210 Va. 608, 172 S.E.2d 724 (1970), H sued W for divorce, alleging that she wilfully deserted him. W cross-claimed for divorce on the grounds of cruelty and constructive desertion. It was established by third party testimony that W had physically left the marital home; she justified her departure because of H's alleged cruelty, which could only be established by the testimony of the spouses. The court denied a divorce to either party, pointing out that W was justified in leaving home because of H's conduct, but a divorce could not be granted to her because there was no corroboration as required by statute. As a consolation, the court noted that since Virginia has a "living apart" ground for divorce the parties eventually would be able to dissolve their union legally.

Husband D. v. Wife D.

Family Court of Delaware, New Castle County, 1977.
383 A.2d 302.

■ WAKEFIELD, JUDGE.

This is the Court's decision concerning the contested divorce sought by Husband. The petition alleges misconduct "in that Respondent has been habitually drunk for a period in excess of two years from [sic] the date of the filing of this petition." The Court treats this as an allegation that Respondent was guilty of "habitual intemperance" which was "so destructive of the marriage relation that petitioner cannot reasonably be expected to continue in that relation" within the meaning of 13 Del.C. § 1503(5).

Mr. D. is presently 62 years of age and Mrs. D., 46. They were married in 1969 and lived together until they separated in July of 1976. Prior to and for a short period after their marriage, Petitioner worked full time. He went on disability about six months after the marriage and has worked only sporadically at odd jobs ever since. They both drank before and all during the marriage. Respondent did not drink as much prior to marriage and, according to Petitioner, she began to drink more heavily as time went on. All Respondent ever drank was beer, while Petitioner himself drank both beer and hard liquor in considerable quantity. He apparently handled alcohol better than she did. Petitioner stated that Respondent would go to the liquor store at 9:00 a.m. every morning, purchase beer and commence to drink throughout the day until bedtime. He admitted that he often drank with her but not all day and not every day. He testified that their only outside entertainment together was attendance at taprooms. She did attend a convention with him one time, got drunk, and embarrassed him. Petitioner admitted, however, that Respondent took good care of him and the house, cooked the meals, and stated, "I never wanted for anything."

The break-up occurred in July of 1976 when Petitioner arrived home from a convention to find his wife at the door in her underwear in an intoxicated condition. She called him "every name in the book" and he took his things and left. He returned for a couple of days around Christmas, when Respondent's brother was expected to be in Delaware. He did this in order to save her embarrassment, since the family did not know of the separation. Respondent had to be taken to the hospital because of alcohol and undernourishment on December 27 after both of them had "partied" for a couple of days. This was the third such hospitalization. Respondent, apparently, has maintained complete sobriety since but, despite this, there is no possibility of reconciliation. Respondent herself agreed that their relationship deteriorated over the last couple of years preceding the separation. She believes that Petitioner was just as much affected by alcohol as she was, but that he constantly complained about *her* problem to divert attention from *his*.

The Court concludes from the evidence that both parties were alcoholics—i.e., that both had acquired "such fixed, irresistible custom of frequent indulgence in intoxicating liquor with consequent drunkenness as to evidence a confirmed habit and inability to control the appetite for intoxicants." Lecates v. Lecates, Del.Super., 190 A. 294, 296 (1937). The difference in their drinking habits was one of degree only.

Respondent asserts that the divorce should be denied because (a) the parties drank together frequently and heavily before marriage and, hence, the situation was known to Petitioner at the time they were married, and (b) the fault must be so serious as to make it impossible for the other to endure. In addition, although not pleaded or argued by Respondent, the question of possible recrimination, condonation, or connivance is also present.

In addressing the last-mentioned issue, the opinion of then Superior Court Judge Herrmann in Muir v. Muir, Del.Super., 86 A.2d 857 (1952) is pertinent since the facts are somewhat similar. In that case, the court found that the defendant had been guilty of habitual drunkenness for a period of two years and held that the defense of connivance was available in habitual drunkenness cases "if it is found that the plaintiff 'procured or connived at the offense charged.' " However, the court rejected the defendant's contention that plaintiff was guilty of connivance because plaintiff himself made liquor available to her and drank with her himself, since he did not do so with the corrupt intent that she should become an habitual drunkard as defined in *Lecates,* supra. The court held:

> "Undoubtedly, the plaintiff's actions resulted in the presentation of temptation to the defendant. Unquestionably, he would have been more faithful to his marriage vows had he taken precautions to protect the defendant against her own weakness. As a matter of law, however, I do not believe that the plaintiff was obliged to forego his own proper and ordinary recreation at the risk of being charged with the corrupt intent to make his wife an habitual drunkard. It is concluded, therefore, that the evidence does not establish connivance by the plaintiff."

On the issue of condonation, the court in *Muir* held that the defense is not available in cases of habitual drunkenness, since that is a "continuing" cause of divorce.

While the defenses of condonation or connivance may not be available to Respondent in this case under the doctrine of *Muir,* there are two areas of distinction between that case and this—one of fact and the other of law.

In *Muir,* there was no finding that the plaintiff was himself an habitual drunkard or even had a serious drinking habit. Thus the court there did not have to deal with the question which the Court deems present in this case—whether a plaintiff who himself is guilty of fault may obtain a divorce from a spouse guilty of the same (or nearly the same) fault.

The second distinction is one of law. At the time of *Muir,* the law provided simply that "The causes for divorce from the bonds of matrimony shall be . . . (6) Habitual drunkenness for two years," whereas the present law permits the granting of a divorce for conduct "so destructive of the marriage relation that petitioner cannot reasonably be expected to continue in that relation; and . . . includes, as examples, . . . habitual intemperance." 13 Del.C. § 1503(5) and § 1505(b).

There are several possible legal theories upon which such a defense may be premised—clean hands, recrimination or failure to be the injured and innocent party. Under the law as it existed prior to June 4, 1974, it would appear that recrimination could be used only as a defense to adultery. See 13 Del.C. § 1523 and § 1524 (1974 ed.). When the new divorce law was first enacted in 1974, the defenses of recrimination, etc. were abolished, but effective March 29, 1976, 13 Del.C. § 1505 was again amended to insert the following language:

> "(c) Previously existing defenses to divorce of condonation, connivance, recrimination, insanity and lapse of time are preserved but only with respect to marriages characterized under subsection (b)(2) of this section."

Subsection (b)(2) of § 1505 authorizes divorce based upon misconduct. It is apparent that the legislature, by using the words "previously existing defenses," intended to reinstate those defenses as they existed prior to 1974, and under this interpretation recrimination would not be a defense, since under the prior law it was a defense only in adultery cases. The Court holds, therefore, that recrimination is not a defense available in this proceeding under the present law.

"Clean hands" or the absence of material fault by the petitioner has been applied in divorce cases in many states. See 1 Nelson, Divorce and Annulment, 2d ed. § 10.02 pp. 361–363. The doctrine of "clean hands" is actually an equitable defense and usually not applicable in divorce proceedings except where, by statute, such proceedings are specifically designated as equitable in nature. See Nelson, supra, § 10.02. Hence "clean hands" is not technically available as an affirmative defense in this jurisdiction, since our divorce law was originally vested in the Superior Court rather than the Court of Chancery. The Court need not pass upon the availability of "clean hands" as a defense, however, since there is another similar, analogous principle which applies.

The concept of divorce based on fault of the respondent has its correlative assumption that only an injured and innocent party may obtain a divorce. As stated in Nelson, supra, § 2.05 p. 25:

> "As a general proposition, to obtain a divorce one must be the 'injured and innocent' party. This requirement is sometimes imposed by statute, but seems to be regarded as inherent in the nature of the proceedings and within the legislative intent even when not explicitly stated."

And at p. 26:

> "This rule is one apart from the doctrine of recrimination, which goes farther and requires, for an absolute defense by way of recrimination, a counter-showing of existence of ground for divorce against the party seeking it. The same principle underlies both, but recrimination, properly speaking, is an affirmative defense, while the 'injured and innocent' party requirement may be, and commonly is, invoked by the court in uncontested cases and whenever it sees fit to do so, irrespective of defense."

While the Delaware statute does not specifically require the petitioner to be an "injured and innocent party," some of the Delaware cases do use similar terminology. See, for example, Woodall v. Woodall, Del.Super., 125 A.2d 504

(1956) where the court denied a divorce on grounds of desertion when plaintiff herself refused to consummate the marriage and refused to set up housekeeping with respondent away from petitioner's mother's home. There the court held:

> "Plaintiff, nevertheless, maintains she is entitled to a decree. To the contrary, he whose conduct itself amounts to grounds for divorce and which causes the other spouse to leave the marriage home is hardly in the position to maintain an action for wilful desertion...."

The court in *Woodall* quoted with approval from Nelson, supra, § 4.16 p. 102, in part, as follows:

> "Therefore, if the applicant by his conduct, *whether or not it would independently be ground for divorce,* brought about a situation so unpleasant or intolerable that the opposite spouse could not be expected to continue further cohabitation, the latter's cessation of cohabitation may be regarded as 'justified' and the applicant be denied a divorce because the fault was his and he was not an injured and innocent party. [Furthermore, it is the rule in most states *that if the parties are equally at fault* in bringing about the separation, neither can successfully accuse the other of desertion.]" [Emphasis added.]

The Court holds that the foregoing principles apply with like force and effect to a divorce on grounds of habitual intemperance, and that Petitioner in this case is not an "injured and innocent" party. While he is not solely at fault for causing the marital break-up, his own drinking habits were equal to or nearly as great as hers.

Even if this were not the case, the Court would deny the petition on another ground—that Respondent's conduct was not "so destructive of the marriage relation that petitioner cannot reasonably be expected to continue in that relation" within the meaning of 13 Del.C. § 1503. As stated previously, this language is new to the present divorce law, and the Court considers it to be a substantive change consistent with the legislature's desire to encourage "no fault" divorces and to discourage divorces based upon fault, except in the most egregious cases where one party commits acts so serious as to render further cohabitation by the injured and innocent party unreasonable. Under this theory, for example, a single act of adultery may no longer be ground for divorce unless it can also be shown that such act is so destructive of the marriage relationship as to render further cohabitation unreasonable.

In any event, under the facts of this case, the Court does not believe that the alcoholic tendencies of the wife were so severe as to render further cohabitation by the husband unreasonable. Except for one or two instances, he did not recite any misbehavior by the wife while drinking and certainly did not show that his life was seriously and adversely affected. Indeed, he stated that she performed her wifely household duties very well—cooked, cleaned, did the laundry, etc. Although their life together may not have been exciting and they may have been incompatible of temperament, the

Court cannot find that Petitioner's drinking was the sole cause of the marital break-up.

Decree of divorce denied.

NOTE

The court's reference in the *Husband D.* case to the fact that the wife continued to perform household duties even though intoxicated, raises the issue of what would constitute "constructive desertion" for purposes of obtaining a fault divorce on such a ground. In Ricketts v. Ricketts, 393 Md. 479, 903 A.2d 857 (2006), the husband and wife continued to live in the same house, but the husband filed for divorce and custody of the couple's children. In his petition, the husband alleged that the wife denied him marital relations and forced him from the marital bedroom, thus constructively deserting him. The court agreed with the husband. And even though Maryland law provided that custody to one parent may only be granted if the parties live apart, the court ruled that logic demanded that a custody award be granted under these facts since the court was willing to allow the same-house couple a divorce based on the ground of constructive desertion.

NEW YORK DOMESTIC RELATIONS LAW (McKinney 1999 & Supp. 2006)

§ 171.   **When divorce denied, although adultery proved**

In either of the following cases, the plaintiff is not entitled to a divorce, although the adultery is established:

1.   Where the offense was committed by the procurement or with the connivance of the plaintiff.

2.   Where the offense charged has been forgiven by the plaintiff. The forgiveness may be proven, either affirmatively, or by the voluntary cohabitation of the parties with the knowledge of the fact.

3.   Where there has been no express forgiveness, and no voluntary cohabitation of the parties, but the action was not commenced within five years after the discovery by the plaintiff of the offense charged.

4.   Where the plaintiff has also been guilty of adultery under such circumstances that the defendant would have been entitled, if innocent, to a divorce.

VIRGINIA CODE ANN. (2004)

§ 20–93.   **Insanity of guilty party after commencement of desertion no defense.** When the suit is for divorce from the bond of matrimony for willful desertion or abandonment, it shall be no defense that the guilty party has, since the commencement of such desertion, and within one year thereafter, become and has been adjudged insane, but at the expiration of one year from the commencement of such desertion the ground for divorce shall be deemed to be complete, and the committee of

the insane defendant, if there be one, shall be made a party to the cause, or if there be no committee, then the court shall appoint a guardian ad litem to represent the insane defendant. This section shall apply whether the desertion or abandonment commenced heretofore or shall commence hereafter.

§ **20–94. Effect of cohabitation after knowledge of adultery, sodomy or buggery; lapse of five years.** When the suit is for divorce for adultery, sodomy, or buggery, the divorce shall not be granted, if it appear that the parties voluntarily cohabited after the knowledge of the fact of adultery, sodomy or buggery, or that it occurred more than five years before the institution of the suit, or that it was committed by the procurement or connivance of the party alleging such act.

NOTES

Defenses to Fault Grounds. The New York and Virginia statutes illustrate the key defenses against fault based grounds. Although they were developed largely through judicial action, today it is common for them to be at least partially incorporated into statutes. Many have been eliminated or severely restricted. For example, Va.Code § 20–93 (LEXIS 2000 Repl. Vol.) overruled a prior judicial decision that allowed use of insanity as a defense to a divorce action based on desertion if the "guilty" party became incompetent after departing but before the full statutory separation period had passed. Pollard v. Pollard, 204 Va. 316, 130 S.E.2d 425 (1963). A rationale used by some courts to justify insanity as a defense was that it negated blameworthiness. The question of what test to apply (*M'Naghten* or *Durham,* for example) was not always clear. For further discussion *see* Walter Wadlington, *Divorce Without Fault Without Perjury*, 52 Va.L.Rev. 32, 43 (1966).

The classic defenses are collusion, condonation, connivance, and recrimination. In addition, some states provide statutes of limitation for certain grounds such as adultery. Collusion really is less a defense for the parties than a means for courts to deny a divorce to persons who fabricate evidence because both want a divorce and they have no grounds. Connivance involves "corrupt consent" of one party to conduct of the other that amounts to a divorce ground. *See* Gutzwiller v. Gutzwiller, 8 N.J.Super. 254, 74 A.2d 325 (App.Div.1950).

Condonation is one spouse's forgiveness of the other's marital misconduct that amounts to a fault divorce ground. Condonation can take place through specific agreement or continued cohabitation after knowledge of the offense. It is widely said to be conditional on the condonee thenceforth treating the condoner with "conjugal kindness"; breaking this condition can "revive" the original divorce ground. Although some courts occasionally have indicated that "a new ground" revives the old one, this is conceptually inaccurate because no such revival would be necessary if a new ground exists and can be proved. The more typical (and insidious) use of the doctrine allows for revival through misconduct falling short of a divorce ground or in cases of insufficient proof to establish the new violation as a ground.

Probably the best known and also the most criticized of fault defenses has been recrimination. Under this doctrine, if each party were to establish that the other had committed a marital offense amounting to a divorce ground, both would be precluded from obtaining a divorce. In such instances of dual fault the parties would be committed to a choice between living separately while remaining married or remaining together and probably hating it. Elaborate rules of gamesmanship developed around the defense over time. Some grounds were considered of lesser magnitude than others and only those of equal severity would counterbalance each other. In some jurisdictions a ground for divorce *a mensa et thoro* would not offset a ground for divorce *a vinculo matrimonii*. A variety of theories were advanced in support of the doctrine of recrimination: (1) the "clean hands" doctrine; (2) the theory that the parties are "in pari delicto"; (3) that there has been a breach of mutually dependent covenants; (4) the theory of compensation; and (5) that divorce is a remedy only for an innocent spouse. Some states finally provided by statute that courts could grant divorce despite a showing of fault on the part of both spouses. In other jurisdictions this doctrine, known as "comparative rectitude", was introduced judicially—sometimes even in the face of apparently contrary statutes. The classic example of the latter approach is the decision in De Burgh v. De Burgh, 39 Cal.2d 858, 250 P.2d 598 (1952), in which Traynor, J. laid down four guidelines for judicial use in such cases: The prospect of reconciliation, the effect of the marital conflict on the parties, the effect of the conflict upon third parties, and comparative guilt. An elaborate tracing of the history of the development of recrimination, said to have its origin in the Roman *actio rei uxoria,* is found in C. v. C., 54 N.J. 223, 254 A.2d 778 (1969), in which the New Jersey Supreme Court finally held that "in an uncontested case, absent extraordinary circumstances, a trial court should not on its own motion raise a recriminatory defense." The New Jersey legislature subsequently abolished recrimination and condonation as defenses to divorce. *See* N.J.Rev.Stat. § 2A:34–7 (West 2000).

Reconsidering fault divorce. As the materials in the remainder of the chapter illustrate, no-fault divorce made divorce available to the spouse "at fault" and eliminated the lengthy and often "steamy" trials that were needed to prove fault and address the common law defenses. The divorce rate doubled between 1960 and 1990. *See* Peter T. Kilborn, *Shifts in Families Reach a Plateau, Study Says*, N.Y. Times, Nov. 27, 1996, at A16. Gradually, arguments were made that "easy divorce" produced single parents who were unable to afford necessities for children, that changes in welfare made poverty more of a certainty in a single parent households, that quick and easy divorce hindered any early reconciliation, and that no-fault divorce devalued marriage and family. *See* Raymond C. O'Brien, *The Reawakening of Marriage*, 102 W. Va. L. Rev. 339 (1999); Patrick F. Fagan, *How Broken Families Rob Children of Their Chances for Future Prosperity*, recited in 25 Fam. L. Rpt. 1455 (Aug. 8, 1999); Laura Gatland, *Putting the Blame on No–Fault*, 83 A.B.A.J. 50 (1997); David Blankenhorn, *The State of the Family and the Family Policy Debate*, 36 Santa Clara L. Rev. 432

(1996); James McLindon, *Separate But Unequal: The Economic Disaster of Divorce for Women and Children*, 21 FAM. L. Q. 351 (1987).

In 1997, Louisiana became the first state to offer couples an opportunity to contract between themselves and enter into what has been termed a "covenant marriage." If a couple elects to do so they may sign a declaration of intent stating that they have received premarital counseling, promise to take reasonable efforts to preserve the marriage if marital difficulties arise, and intend to remain married for the rest of their lives. They thus limit the divorce grounds to those associated with fault. *See* LA. REV. STAT. ANN. § 9:272 (West 2000). Since adoption by Louisiana, Arizona and Arkansas have adopted their own versions of Covenant Marriage. *See* Covenant Marriage, ARIZ. REV. STAT. § 25–901 (2000) and Covenant Marriage Act, ARK. CODE ANN. § 9–11–801 (2001). For general comment on the legislation, *see* Katherine Shaw Spaht, *Covenant Marriage Seven Years Later: Its as Yet Unfulfilled Promise*, 65 La. L. Rev. 605–634 (2005); Amy L. Stewart, Note, *Covenant Marriage: Legislating Family Values*, 32 IND. L. REV. S509 (1999); Melissa Lawton, Note, *The Constitutionality of Covenant Marriage Laws*, 66 FORDHAM L. REV. 2471 (1998); Melissa S. LaBauve, *Covenant Marriages: A Guise for Lasting Commitment?* 43 LOY. L. REV. 421 (1997); Bruce Nolan, *Bishops Back Off Covenant Marriage*, NEW ORLEANS TIMES-PICAYUNE, Oct. 30, 1997 at A1; Ellen Goodman, a columnist with The Washington Post, suggests that covenant marriage offers couples a choice between "regular" and "high test" marriage. *See* Ellen Goodman, *Covenant Marriage*, WASH. POST, Aug. 16, 1997, at A24.

2.   INSANITY AS A GROUND

UTAH CODE ANN. (1999)

30–3–1(5)

For the text of this section *see* p. 360, *supra*.

VIRGINIA CODE ANN. (2004)

§ 20–91(9)

For the text of this section *see* p. 364, *supra*.

CALIFORNIA FAMILY CODE (West 2004)

§ 2312.   Incurable insanity

A marriage may be dissolved on the grounds of incurable insanity only upon proof, including competent medical or psychiatric testimony, that the insane spouse was at the time the petition was filed, and remains, incurably insane.

§ 2313.   Support of incurably insane spouse; order for support or bond

No dissolution of marriage granted on the ground of incurable insanity relieves a spouse from any obligation imposed by law as a result of the marriage for the support of the spouse who is incurably insane, and the court may make such order for support, or require a bond therefor, as the circumstances require.

NOTE

Insanity has long been an enumerated ground for divorce in some jurisdictions. Many of those provisions, however, required that the condition must be so extreme, the prognosis so bleak, or the length of institutionalization so great, that the ground was of little practical use. Some jurisdictions that have shifted almost entirely to a "breakdown" ground nevertheless have retained insanity as a separate cause. The generally accepted reason for this is concern by some about whether breakdown grounds should be applicable in the case of an insane spouse. This problem was faced earlier by several jurisdictions in cases involving "living separate and apart" grounds. For a mythical court opinion illustrating the problems of integrating insanity into the scheme of a hybrid divorce statute, *see* Walter Wadlington, *A Case of Insanity and Divorce*, 56 Va.L.Rev. 12 (1970).

3.   Breakdown: The New Standard

Generally classified as falling within the ambit of "breakdown" divorce or "no fault" dissolution grounds are:

(1) incompatibility, sometimes known as incompatibility of temperament;

(2) separation for a specific time period pursuant to agreement between the spouses, generally termed "voluntary separation";

(3) separation for a specific time period under breakdown circumstances whether or not both the parties desired or agreed to live apart, and without regard to the circumstances under which the separation commenced;

(4) a general category of laws that require no specific period of separation but only proof of "irretrievable breakdown", "irreconcilable differences", or some similarly phrased condition that ostensibly denotes that the marriage is dead. There may be crossbreeding between this ground and (3) to require a short separation period or at least to regard such a separation as creating a presumption that irretrievable breakdown has occurred.

(5) Provisions allowing for dissolution based on longstanding absence of one spouse under conditions by which his or her death is presumed.

Although category (1) grounds have a long history, their use and availability were quite limited until recently and they still are not very popular. Effectiveness and usage of category (2) and (3) grounds has depended on the length of the separation required. Today's typical "separation" statute requires at least six months or a year of living apart. Category (4) grounds were introduced in California and Iowa in 1970; the approach was embraced at the same time in the initial version of the Uniform Marriage and Divorce Act. Category (5) includes the so-called "Enoch Arden laws".

When a divorce ground is premised on a period of separation, the issue arises as to whether the intent to terminate the marriage must coincide with the time specified for the separation. For example, in Sinha v. Sinha, 515 Pa. 14, 526 A.2d 765 (1987), the state's statute required a three year period of separation to dissolve the marriage and the issue before the court was whether the statute required an intent to dissolve the marriage prior to the three year period. The husband and wife had been married in India, and then the husband came to America seeking an advanced degree. Even though the husband and wife corresponded regularly, the husband filed for divorce in 1979 but voluntarily dismissed the petition. In 1980 he filed for a divorce a second time on the ground that the couple had lived separate and apart for three years and the marriage was irretrievably broken. The court refused to allow the divorce based on physical separation alone, holding that at least one of the parties must have the intent to dissolve the marriage prior to the commencement of the three year period. In Gleason v. Gleason, 256 N.E.2d 513 (N.Y.1970), the court ruled that it is socially and morally undesirable to compel a couple whose marriage is dead to remain subject to its bonds. Based on this, the court was willing to apply the intent retroactively. To do otherwise would foster collusion and fraud and encourage couples to seek out-of-state divorces. Both of these cases illustrate how limited some separation statutes once were, and the differences in judicial willingness to construe them broadly. Today the more usual period of required separation is six months to a year.

UNIFORM MARRIAGE AND DIVORCE ACT (1973)

§ 302.   (a) The [ ] court shall enter a decree of dissolution of marriage if:

. . .

(2) the court finds that the marriage is irretrievably broken, if the finding is supported by evidence that (I) the parties have lived separate and apart for a period of more than 180 days next preceding the commencement of the proceeding, or (ii) there is serious marital discord adversely affecting the attitude of one or both of the parties toward the marriage;

(3) the court finds that the conciliation provisions of Section 305 either do not apply or have been met;

(4) to the extent it has jurisdiction to do so, the court has considered, approved, or provided for child custody, the support of any child entitled to

support, the maintenance of either spouse, and the disposition of property; or has provided for a separate, later hearing to complete these matters.

(b) If a party requests a decree of legal separation rather than a decree of dissolution of marriage, the court shall grant the decree in that form unless the other party objects.

§ 305. (a) If both of the parties by petition or otherwise have stated under oath or affirmation that the marriage is irretrievably broken, or one of the parties has so stated and the other has not denied it, the court, after hearing, shall make a finding whether the marriage is irretrievably broken.

(b) If one of the parties has denied under oath or affirmation that the marriage is irretrievably broken, the court shall consider all relevant factors, including the circumstances that gave rise to filing the petition and the prospect of reconciliation, and shall:

(1) make a finding whether the marriage is irretrievably broken; or

(2) continue the matter for further hearing not fewer than 30 nor more than 60 days later, or as soon thereafter as the matter may be reached on the court's calendar, and may suggest to the parties that they seek counseling. The court, at the request of either party shall, or on its own motion may, order a conciliation conference. At the adjourned hearing the court shall make a finding whether the marriage is irretrievably broken.

(c) A finding of irretrievable breakdown is a determination that there is no reasonable prospect of reconciliation.

NOTE

This version of section 302 was contained in the Act as approved by the House of Delegates of the American Bar Association in February 1974. The first version promulgated in 1970 did not contain the language referring to a specific period of separation or "serious marital discord". Between the original promulgation of the Act and the changes just mentioned, the Family Law Section of the American Bar Association proposed a Revised version of the Act which would have provided for one year of separation or "serious marital misconduct" affecting the physical or mental health of the petitioner. For the full text of the proposed revised statute, *see* 7 FAM.L.Q. 135 (1973). Ironically, it is the less restrictive early version of the Uniform Act that has served widely as a model for state legislation on the subject.

CALIFORNIA FAMILY CODE (West 2004)

§ 2310.   Grounds for dissolution or legal separation

Dissolution of the marriage or legal separation of the parties may be based on either of the following grounds, which shall be pleaded generally:

(a) Irreconcilable differences, which have caused the irremediable breakdown of the marriage.

(b) Incurable insanity.

§ 2311. Irreconcilable differences defined

Irreconcilable differences are those grounds which are determined by the court to be substantial reasons for not continuing the marriage and which make it appear that the marriage should be dissolved.

Husband W. v. Wife W.

Supreme Court of Delaware, 1972.
297 A.2d 39.

■ PER CURIAM:

In this divorce action brought upon the ground of incompatibility, the Trial Court held that the plaintiff failed to sustain his burden of showing no reasonable possibility of reconciliation....

.   .   .

The undisputed evidence ... shows: the parties had been separated and living apart for almost one and a half years; recurrent violent quarrels involved the police and the Family Court on numerous occasions to the extent that on October 7, 1970, a Judge of that Court remarked about the frequency of the difficulties and, on December 30, 1970, the same judge stated "it is obvious that the marriage is finished and they are incompatible"; the defendant put lye in the plaintiff's food; she tried to stab him with an ice-pick or knife; she threw a brick through a window in a fit of temper: the plaintiff locked the defendant out of the house on a cold, winter day; he hit her over the head with a chair, hospitalizing her, and then presented the repaired chair to her as a souvenir; he hit her over the head with two other chairs on other occasions; he kicked her; he threatened her with a piece of iron; and he threatened to burn the house down.

In the light of that marital history, it is not surprising that ... when asked about the likelihood of reconciliation, the plaintiff testified: "No, sir, in no way, shape, or form"; and that, in response to the same question the defendant testified, in the probable understatement of the week: "I don't know if we could [reconcile] or not".

.   .   .

Reversed and remanded with direction to grant the decree of divorce.

NOTE

Courts often had a difficult time in defining the fault grounds of adultery, cruelty and desertion; no-fault grounds such as "incompatibility" offer similar perplexities. Incompatibility was one of the earliest no-fault grounds introduced in this country, but it failed to become the majority no-fault ground. The problem of definition, along with the failure to provide any guidelines for its application as a divorce ground, no doubt were responsible for its lack of acceptance. Definitional difficulties are compounded by the reluctance of parties to accede to a system which allows one of the parties to end the marriage, when the other thinks he or she is very compatible and willing to do even better to keep the marriage intact. *See, e.g.,* Shachter v. Shachter, 25 Fam. L. Rpt. 1207 (Ill. App. Ct. 1999), *rev. denied,* 526 U.S. 1005, 119 S.Ct. 1143, 143 L.Ed.2d 210 (1999), where former husband argued the no-fault ground deprived him of the liberty interest of sustaining his marriage and caring for his children, and that the state divided his property and income without a proper hearing to establish a reason for doing so. Or in Benson v. Benson, 25 Fam. L. Rpt. 1454 (Ala. Civ. App. 1999), *rev. denied,* 528 U.S. 816, 120 S.Ct. 55, 145 L.Ed.2d 48 (1999), when the issue was whether granting a divorce on incompatibility of temperament unconstitutionally violated one party's right to free exercise of religion when that religion teaches that adultery is the sole acceptable basis for divorce. In both instances the court granted the divorce based on the no-fault ground.

C. The Jurisdictional Jumble

1. Qualifying Domestic Divorce Decrees for Full Faith and Credit: The Significance of Domicile

In the United States cognizance of an action for divorce has traditionally depended upon the domicile of the petitioner. The original American statutes made the divorce remedy available to "inhabitants" of a state or required a period of residence therein before suit could be begun. Because of the prevalence of restrictive rules respecting the capacity of a married woman to sue in her own name, as if sole, and the rigid observance of the common law rule that under all circumstances her domicile was that of her spouse, obtaining a valid divorce in a state other than the one in which both parties lived was initially something which husbands could do more easily than wives.

In the 1840's the first statutes emancipating the married woman from common law limitations on her capacity were enacted. Insofar as these gave her the right to maintain or defend actions, the boon of the divorce remedy, where it had not been explicitly granted in divorce or separation statutes, was hers. There remained, however, the domicile problem where the husband had deserted, or where the wife to escape his cruelties had left his bed and board. In 1856 the Supreme Court of Rhode Island in the influential case of Ditson v. Ditson, 4 R.I. 87 held that where the husband committed an offense, or was guilty of such dereliction of duty in the marital relation as to entitle her to have the relation dissolved, the wife might (indeed must, to avoid condonation) establish a separate domicil of her own. Later developments in the law gave married women the power to become separately domiciled quite simply by applying the general rules governing the acquisition of domicil. Once a married woman had the power to obtain a domicil of her own, either spouse could move from the state of the marital home and seek divorce in another state.

From roughly the beginning of the 20th century the rules about divorce jurisdiction were a mixture of full faith and comity, even for decrees of sister states. The major question was whether in an *ex parte* divorce decree entitled to the full faith and credit required by Article IV, Section 1 of the Constitution[1] on the basis of one spouse's domicil or, as in the case of *in personam* judgments, must the defendant be personally before the court? In 1942 the Supreme Court of the United States in Williams v. North Carolina, 317 U.S. 287, 63 S.Ct. 207, 87 L.Ed. 279 (1942), decided that if due process requirements of notice were satisfied, an *ex parte* decree of the state of one spouse's domicile must be recognized throughout the nation by force of the Constitution. The reasons given are an interesting blend of theoretical and practical considerations:

> ... [D]ivorce decrees are more than *in personam* judgments. They involve the marital status of the parties. Domicil creates a relationship to the state which is adequate for numerous exercises of state power. Each state as a sovereign has a rightful and legitimate concern in the marital status of persons domiciled within its borders. The marriage relation creates problems of large social importance. Protection of offspring, property interests, and the enforcement of marital responsibilities are but a few of commanding problems in the field of domestic relations with which the state must deal. Thus it is plain that each state, by virtue of its command over its domiciliaries and its large interest in the institution of marriage can alter within its own borders the marriage status of the spouse domiciled there, even though the other spouse is absent.... 317 U.S. 287, 298, 299.

> ... Under the circumstances of this case, a man would have two wives, a wife two husbands. The reality of a sentence to prison proves that there is no mere play on words. Each would be a bigamist for living in one state with the only one with whom the other state would permit him lawfully to live. Children of the second marriage would be bastards in one state but legitimate in the other.... 317 U.S. 287, 299, 300.

> ... Certainly if decrees of a state altering the marital status of its domiciliaries are not valid throughout the Union even though the requirements of procedural due process are wholly met, a rule would be fostered which could not help but bring "considerable disaster to innocent persons" and "bastardize children hitherto supposed to be

---

1. Article IV, sec. 1 of the Constitution not only directs that "Full Faith and Credit shall be given in each State to the public Acts, Records, and Judicial Proceedings of every other State" but also provides that "Congress may by general laws prescribe the Manner in which such Acts, Records and Proceedings shall be proved, and the Effect thereof." Congress has exercised that power. By the Act of June 25, 1948, c. 646, 28 U.S.C.A. § 1738, Congress has provided that judgments "shall have the same full faith and credit in every court within the United States and its Territories and Possessions as they have by law or usage in the courts of such State, Territory or Possession from which they are taken."

the offspring of lawful marriage" (Mr. Justice Holmes dissenting in Haddock v. Haddock, supra, 201 U.S. at page 628, 26 S.Ct. at page 551), or else encourage collusive divorces. Beale, Constitutional Protection of Decrees for Divorce, 19 Harv.L.Rev. 586, 596. These intensely practical considerations emphasize for us the essential function of the full faith and credit clause in substituting a command for the former principles of comity.... 317 U.S. 287, 301.

The facts of the first *Williams* case can help place the holding in perspective. A man and a woman went from North Carolina to Nevada, where they resided for a sufficient time to meet the requirement of the latter's residence statute. After that they secured divorces from their separate spouses who remained in North Carolina, the state in which all of them previously had been domiciled. The divorced pair who had gone to Nevada then married each other there and returned to North Carolina where they cohabited as husband and wife. They were prosecuted and convicted in North Carolina under a law proscribing bigamous cohabitation. It was this holding that the Supreme Court overturned.

In a second *Williams* case, the State of North Carolina brought an action involving the same parties, asserting that because they never were validly domiciled in Nevada the decree need not be accorded recognition under the Full Faith and Credit Clause. They were again convicted, with the state court holding being upheld by the U.S. Supreme Court this time. Williams v. North Carolina, 325 U.S. 226, 65 S.Ct. 1092, 89 L.Ed. 1577 (1945). The Court held that, while the state of a spouse's domicil has the power to grant a divorce entitled to full faith and credit, the issue whether either spouse was, in fact, domiciled in the state of divorce is open for re-examination:

> It is one thing to reopen an issue that has been settled after appropriate opportunity to present their contentions has been afforded to all who had an interest in its adjudication. This applies also to jurisdictional questions. After a contest these cannot be relitigated as between the parties.... But those not parties to a litigation ought not to be foreclosed by the interested actions of others; especially not a State which is concerned with the vindication of its own social policy and has no means, certainly no effective means, to protect that interest against the selfish action of those outside its borders. The State of domiciliary origin should not be bound by an unfounded, even if not collusive, recital in the record of a court of another State. As to the truth or existence of a fact, like that of domicil, upon which depends the power to exert judicial authority, a State not a party to the exertion of such judicial authority in another State but seriously affected by it has a right, when asserting its own unquestioned authority, to ascertain the truth or existence of that crucial fact.... 325 U.S. 226, 230, 65 S.Ct. 1092, 1095, 89 L.Ed. 1577, 1582.

What is immediately before us is the judgment of the Supreme Court of North Carolina [224 N.C. 183, 29 S.E.2d 744]. We have authority to upset it only if there is want of foundation for the conclusion that Court reached. The conclusion it reached turns on its finding that the spouses who obtained the Nevada decrees were not domiciled there. The fact that the Nevada court found that they were domiciled there is entitled to respect, and more. The burden of undermining the verity which the Nevada decrees import rests heavily upon the assailant. But simply because the Nevada court found that it had power to award a divorce decree cannot, we have seen, foreclose reexamination by another State. Otherwise, as was pointed out long ago, a court's record would establish its power and the power would be proved by the record. Such circular reasoning would give one State a control over all the other States which the Full Faith and Credit Clause certainly did not confer. Thompson v. Whitman, supra [18 Wall. 457, 21 L.Ed. 897]. If this Court finds that proper weight was accorded to the claims of power by the court of one State in rendering a judgment the validity of which is pleaded in defense in another State, that the burden of overcoming such respect by disproof of the substratum of fact—here domicil—on which such power alone can rest was properly charged against the party challenging the legitimacy of the judgment that such issue of fact was left for fair determination by appropriate procedure, and that a finding adverse to the necessary foundation for any valid sister-State judgment was amply supported in evidence, we cannot upset the judgment before us. 325 U.S. 226, 233, 234, 65 S.Ct. 1092, 1097, 89 L.Ed. 1577, 1583–84.

In the second *Williams* case Mr. Justice Frankfurter asserted: "Under our system of law, judicial power to grant a divorce—jurisdiction, strictly speaking—is founded on domicil." 325 U.S. 226, 229, 65 S.Ct. 1092, 89 L.Ed. 1577. Does this mean that a divorce not granted on the basis of a spouse's domicil (say, on the basis of the presence of both parties) violates the Due Process Clause? Judge Goodrich of the United States Court of Appeals for the Third Circuit thought so. Writing in Alton v. Alton, 207 F.2d 667 (3d Cir.1953), a case involving a divorce granted to two Connecticut domiciliaries in the Virgin Islands whose statutes permitted the divorce of parties who had been personally served in the Islands or who had entered a general appearance, the judge stated:

> We think that adherence to the domiciliary requirement is necessary if our states are really to have control over the domestic relations of their citizens. The instant case would be typical. In the Virgin Islands incompatibility of temperament constitutes grounds for divorce. In Connecticut it does not. We take it that it is all very well for the Virgin Islands to provide for whatever matrimonial regime it pleases for people who live there. But the same privilege should be afforded to those who control affairs in Connecticut.

> Our conclusion is that the second part of this statute conflicts with the due process clause of the Fifth Amendment and the Organic Act. Domestic relations are a matter of concern to the state where a person is domiciled. An attempt by another jurisdiction to affect the relation of a foreign domiciliary is unconstitutional even though both parties are

in court and neither one raises the question. The question may well be asked as to what the lack of due process is. The defendant is not complaining. Nevertheless, if the jurisdiction for divorce continues to be based on domicile, as we think it does, we believe it to be lack of due process for one state to take to itself the readjustment of domestic relations between those domiciled elsewhere. The Supreme Court has in a number of cases used the due process clause to correct states which have passed beyond what that court has considered proper choice-of-law rules. . . . 207 F.2d 667, 676, 677.

Did Judge Goodrich mean the Courts of the Islands had no power to decree a divorce in the circumstances or that to use Virgin Islands' substantive divorce law would violate due process?

In either case the text of the Fourteenth Amendment creates a problem not happily resolved by Judge Goodrich. The text says: "no state shall deprive a *person* of life, liberty or property without due process of law." (Italics supplied) Neither of the Altons had complained of the action of the Islands' court. The trial court had refused on its own motion to decree the divorce.

Judge Hastie dissented but pointed out:

"But once the power to decide the case is based merely upon personal jurisdiction a court must decide as a separate question upon what basis, if any, the local substantive law of divorce can properly be applied to determine whether the plaintiff is entitled to the relief sought. In this case, if it should appear that Mr. and Mrs. Alton were both domiciled in Connecticut at the time of suit in the Virgin Islands and that their estrangement had resulted from conduct in the matrimonial home state, it may well be that under correct application of conflict of laws doctrine, and even under the due process clause, it is encumbent upon the Virgin Islands, lacking connection with the subject matter to apply the divorce law of some state that has such connection, here Connecticut. . . . " 207 F.2d 667, 685.

Judge Hastie's point reminds us that in many cases an out-of-state divorce would present few attractions if the conduct of the parties were to be judged by the same law that would judge it at home.

The Alton case became moot before the issue was decided by the Supreme Court. Alton v. Alton, 347 U.S. 965, 74 S.Ct. 774, 98 L.Ed. 1107 (1954). At a later time the issue was brought to the Supreme Court in Granville–Smith v. Granville–Smith, 349 U.S. 1, 75 S.Ct. 553, 99 L.Ed. 773 (1955). There the Court decided that the Virgin Islands' legislature had exceeded its powers under the Islands' Organic Act by passage of the Divorce Act. So the constitutional question remains unresolved. Note, however, the closing words of the dissent of Clark, J. (in which Black and Reed, JJ., joined):

Divorce is an intensely practical matter, and if a husband and wife domiciled in any State want a divorce enough, we all know that they can secure it in several of our States. This being so, I see no sense in striking down the Islands' law. There is no virtue in a state of the law the only practical effect of which would be to make New Yorkers fly 2,400 miles over land to Reno instead of 1,450 miles over water to the Virgin Islands.

The only vice of the Virgin Islands' statute, in an uncontested case like this, is that it makes unnecessary a choice between bigamy and perjury. I think the Court should not discourage this.... 349 U.S. 1, 28.

Over the years some other justices of the Supreme Court have expressed the view that domicil is not the fundamental basis of jurisdiction to divorce. For example, Rutledge, J., dissenting in Williams II, 325 U.S. 226, 244, 65 S.Ct. 1092, 89 L.Ed. 1577 et seq., and especially 260, n. 16, suggests that one year of residence could be adopted by the Supreme Court as the jurisdictional requirement for divorce. Justice Rutledge's suggestion was, of course, that divorce based on such residency would meet the standard of due process and also be entitled to full faith and credit.

Mr. Justice Murphy in his opinion in the second Williams case expressed the view that a state may grant divorces on bases other than domicil without offending Due Process even though such decrees may not be entitled to full faith and credit. Chief Justice Stone and Justice Jackson concurred in the Murphy opinion:

The State of Nevada has unquestioned authority, consistent with procedural due process, to grant divorces on whatever basis it sees fit to all who meet its statutory requirements. It is entitled, moreover, to give to its divorce decrees absolute and binding finality within the confines of its borders.

But if Nevada's divorce decrees are to be accorded full faith and credit in the courts of her sister states it is essential that Nevada have proper jurisdiction over the divorce proceedings. This means that at least one of the parties to each ex parte proceeding must have a bona fide domicil within Nevada for whatever length of time Nevada may prescribe. 325 U.S. 226, 239.

NOTES

The Restatement View. According to Restatement (Second) of Conflict of Laws § 72:

A state has power to exercise judicial jurisdiction to dissolve the marriage of spouses, neither of whom is domiciled in the state, if either spouse has such a relationship to the state as would make it reasonable for the state to dissolve the marriage.

In a case involving a service person's statute requiring only that the party be "a resident of this state ... or a member of the armed forces ... stationed in this state", the Washington Supreme Court held that the necessary nexus for divorce jurisdiction would be satisfied if the service party has maintained a continuous military presence during the 90 days required by the statute between the filing of the petition and the granting of divorce. The Court relied heavily on the Restatement provision quoted above, along with the Commissioner's Note to U.M.D.A. § 302(a)(1), after noting that the question whether a state court has jurisdiction to grant a divorce unless at least one party is a domiciliary "has created much controversy." In re Marriage of Ways, 85 Wn.2d 693, 538 P.2d 1225 (1975). Special problems may arise with regard to career members of the armed services because of difficulty in establishing domicile. A variation of this approach is to provide by statute for a presumption of domicile when the armed forces member has been stationed in the particular jurisdiction for a minimum period. *See, e.g.,* VA.CODE § 20–97.1 (LEXIS Repl. Vol. 2000).

Because the requirement of domicil is said to be imposed in order to assure that full faith and credit will be given to a decree in other states, it sometimes is postulated that a divorce decree may have internal validity without being entitled to mandatory recognition in other states. The Court in *Ways*, aware of this proposition, stated:

> "It has been suggested that it is possible for a state to grant a divorce or marriage dissolution valid only in the state that grants it, regardless of nexus, notwithstanding the Fourteenth Amendment as construed in Alton v. Alton, is to the contrary and notwithstanding the risk of nonrecognition by other states. Such a decree, however, would be alarmingly unreliable and misleading. Persons divorced in one state under a decree treated as valid there, might be considered married in another state to which the parties might travel on a visit or move temporarily or permanently. A construction of RCW 26.09.030 that could bring about so alarming a result would render the validity of subsequent marriages uncertain, create serious domestic problems in connection with children, particularly children of subsequent marriages entered into on the faith of the validity of the divorce, and would prejudicially affect property rights and their distribution insofar as they were dependent upon the validity or the invalidity of the marriage dissolution or its interstate recognition. It is unreasonable to believe that in enacting RCW 26.09.030 the state intended any such adverse consequences—consequences that would largely nullify the purposes of the statute so far as concerns members of the armed forces. Moreover, it is our duty to avoid rendering a statute unconstitutional by interpretation if by an alternative interpretation we may render it constitutional. . . .

> "To carry out the legislative intent in light of what has been stated, we hold the statute means the member of the armed forces must be stationed in this state continuously throughout the 90–day period described in the statute in order to confer jurisdiction upon the appropriate state court to enter a decree of dissolution." 538 P.2d at 1230–31.

Are RESTATEMENT (2D) § 72 and the *Ways* decision consistent with the first *Williams* case insofar as full faith and credit is concerned? For further analysis *see* Helen Garfield, *The Transitory Divorce Action: Jurisdiction in* the No–Fault Era, *58 TEX.L.REV. 501 (1980); Hans Baade,* Marriage and Divorce in American Conflicts Law: Governmental–Interests Analysis and the Restatement (Second), *72 COLUM.L.REV. 329, 334 et seq. (1972).*

Proposals for Legislation. A number of efforts were made by the late Senator McCarran of Nevada to obtain legislation defining the instances in which divorce decrees would be entitled to full faith and credit. One such proposal passed the Senate in 1952 but never was reported out of the House Judiciary Committee. For an account of that proposal and of the arguments favoring or opposing legislation of the sort generally, *see* J. D. Sumner, Jr., *Full Faith and Credit for Divorce Decrees—Present Doctrine and Possible Changes,* 9 VAND.L.REV. 1, 24–5 (1955).

State courts continue to wrestle with the Due Process Clause and with United States Supreme Court decisions when considering divorce jurisdiction. For example, in Von Schack v. Von Schack, 893 A.2d 1994 (Me. 2006), the Maine Supreme Judicial Court, in a case of first impression in the state, held that a divorcing resident's out-of-state spouse need not have minimum contacts with Maine in order for the state to enter a divorce judgment. Nonetheless, the out-of-state spouse must have notice of the proceeding and the divorce judgment must not involve property, parental rights, or support issues.

Annulment Jurisdiction. Jurisdiction to annul a marriage is not so widely regarded as requiring a prerequisite of domicil. The generally stated reason for this difference from divorce is that in annulment actions the law of the state where the marriage was celebrated or contracted usually controls, rather than the law of the domicil. *See* Whealton v. Whealton, 67 Cal.2d 656, 63 Cal.Rptr. 291, 432 P.2d 979 (1967). According to the RESTATEMENT (2D) OF CONFLICT OF LAWS (1971) § 76:

A state has power to exercise judicial jurisdiction to nullify a marriage from its beginning

(a) under the circumstances which would give the state jurisdiction to dissolve the marriage by divorce, or

(b) if the respondent spouse is personally subject to the judicial jurisdiction of the state, and it is either the state where the marriage was contracted or is the state whose local law governs the validity of the marriage under the rule of § 283.

A "Minimum contacts" Standard? For a suggestion that the jurisdictional standards of *Williams I* for ex parte divorces should be replaced with a "minimum contacts" standard, *see* E. Roy Hawkens, *The Effect of Shaffer v. Heitner on the Jurisdictional Standard in Ex Parte Divorces,* 18 FAM.L.Q. 311 (1984).

Sherrer v. Sherrer

Supreme Court of the United States, 1948.
334 U.S. 343, 68 S.Ct. 1087, 92 L.Ed. 1429.

■ MR. CHIEF JUSTICE VINSON delivered the opinion of the Court.

We granted certiorari in this case and in Coe v. Coe, 334 U.S. 378, 68 S.Ct. 1094, to consider the contention of petitioners that Massachusetts has failed to accord full faith and credit to decrees of divorce rendered by courts of sister States.

Petitioner Margaret E. Sherrer and the respondent, Edward C. Sherrer, were married in New Jersey in 1930, and from 1932 until April 3, 1944, lived together in Monterey, Massachusetts. Following a long period of marital discord, petitioner, accompanied by the two children of the marriage, left Massachusetts, on the latter date, ostensibly for the purpose of spending a vacation in the State of Florida.

On July 6, 1944, a bill of complaint for divorce was filed at petitioner's direction in the Circuit Court of the Sixth Judicial Circuit of the State of Florida. The bill alleged extreme cruelty as grounds for divorce and also alleged that petitioner was a "bona fide resident of the State of Florida." The respondent received notice by mail of the pendency of the divorce proceedings. He retained Florida counsel who entered a general appearance and filed an answer denying the allegations of petitioner's complaint, including the allegation as to petitioner's Florida residence.

On November 14, 1944, hearings were held in the divorce proceedings. Respondent appeared personally to testify with respect to a stipulation entered into by the parties relating to the custody of the children. Throughout the entire proceedings respondent was represented by counsel. Petitioner introduced evidence to establish her Florida residence and testified generally to the allegations of her complaint. Counsel for respondent failed to cross-examine or to introduce evidence in rebuttal.

The Florida court on November 29, 1944, entered a decree of divorce after specifically finding "that petitioner is a bona fide resident of the State of Florida, and that this court has jurisdiction of the parties and the subject matter in said cause; ... " Respondent failed to challenge the decree by appeal to the Florida Supreme Court.

On December 1, 1944, petitioner was married in Florida to one Henry A. Phelps, whom petitioner had known while both were residing in Massachusetts and who had come to Florida shortly after petitioner's arrival in that State. Phelps and petitioner lived together as husband and wife in Florida, where they were both employed, until February 5, 1945, when they returned to Massachusetts.

In June, 1945, respondent instituted an action in the Probate Court of Berkshire County, Massachusetts, which has given rise to the issues of this case. Respondent alleged that he is the lawful husband of petitioner, that the Florida decree of divorce is invalid, and that petitioner's subsequent marriage is void. Respondent prayed that he might be permitted to convey his real estate as if he were sole and that the court declare that he was living apart from his wife for justifiable cause. Petitioner joined issue on respondent's allegations.

In the proceedings which followed, petitioner gave testimony in defense of the validity of the Florida divorce decree. The Probate Court, however, resolved the issues of fact adversely to petitioner's contentions, found that she was never domiciled in Florida, and granted respondent the relief he had requested. The Supreme Judicial Court of Massachusetts affirmed the decree on the grounds that it was supported by the evidence and that the requirements of full faith and credit did not preclude the Massachusetts courts from reexamining the finding of domicile made by the Florida court.

At the outset, it should be observed that the proceedings in the Florida court prior to the entry of the decree of divorce were in no way inconsistent with the requirements of procedural due process.... It is clear that respondent was afforded his day in court with respect to every issue involved in the litigation, including the jurisdictional issue of petitioner's domicile. Under such circumstances, there is nothing in the concept of due process which demands that a defendant be afforded a secondary opportunity to litigate the existence of jurisdictional facts....

It should also be observed that there has been no suggestion that under the law of Florida, the decree of divorce in question is in any respect invalid or could successfully be subjected to the type of attack permitted by the Massachusetts court.

That the jurisdiction of the Florida court to enter a valid decree of divorce was dependent upon petitioner's domicile in that State is not disputed. This requirement was recognized by the Florida court which rendered the divorce decree, and the principle has been given frequent application in decisions of the State Supreme Court. But whether or not petitioner was domiciled in Florida at the time the divorce was granted was a matter to be resolved by judicial determination. Here, unlike the situation presented in Williams v. North Carolina, 1945, 325 U.S. 226, 65 S.Ct. 1092, 89 L.Ed. 1577, 157 A.L.R. 1366, the finding of the requisite jurisdictional facts was made in proceedings in which the defendant appeared and participated. The question with which we are confronted, therefore, is whether such a finding made under the circumstances presented by this case may, consistent with the requirements of full faith and credit, be subjected to collateral attack in the courts of a sister State in a suit brought by the defendant in the original proceedings.

. . .

... [We] hold that the Massachusetts courts erred in permitting the Florida divorce decree to be subjected to attack on the ground that petitioner was not domiciled in Florida at the time the decree was entered. Respondent participated in the Florida proceedings by entering a general appearance, filing pleadings placing in issue the very matters he sought subsequently to contest in the Massachusetts courts, personally appearing before the Florida court and giving testimony in the case, and by retaining attorneys who represented him throughout the entire proceedings. It has not been contended that respondent was given less than a full opportunity to contest the issue of petitioner's domicile or any other issue relevant to the litigation. There is nothing to indicate that the Florida court would not have evaluated fairly and in good faith all relevant evidence submitted to it.

Respondent does not even contend that on the basis of the evidence introduced in the Florida proceedings, that court reached an erroneous result on the issue of petitioner's domicile. If respondent failed to take advantage of the opportunities afforded him, the responsibility is his own. We do not believe that the dereliction of a defendant under such circumstances should be permitted to provide a basis for subsequent attack in the courts of a sister State on a decree valid in the State in which it was rendered.

. . .

It is urged further, however, that because we are dealing with litigation involving the dissolution of the marital relation, a different result is demanded from that which might properly be reached if this case were concerned with other types of litigation. . . .

But the recognition of the importance of a State's power to determine the incidents of basic social relationships into which its domiciliaries entered does not resolve the issues of this case. This is not a situation in which a State has merely sought to exert such power over a domiciliary. This is, rather, a case involving inconsistent assertions of power by courts of two States of the Federal Union and thus presents considerations which go beyond the interests of local policy, however vital. In resolving the issues here presented, we do not conceive it to be a part of our function to weigh the relative merits of the policies of Florida and Massachusetts with respect to divorce and related matters. Nor do we understand the decisions of this Court to support the proposition that the obligation imposed by Article IV, § 1, of the Constitution and the Act of Congress passed thereunder, amounts to something less than the duty to accord full faith and credit to decrees of divorce entered by courts of sister States. . . .

. . .

It is one thing to recognize as permissible the judicial reexamination of findings of jurisdictional fact where such findings have been made by a court of a sister State which has entered a divorce decree in ex parte proceedings. It is quite another thing to hold that the vital rights and interests involved in divorce litigation may be held in suspense pending the scrutiny by courts of sister States of findings of jurisdictional fact made by a competent court in proceedings conducted in a manner consistent with the highest requirements of due process and in which the defendant has participated. We do not conceive it to be in accord with the purposes of the full faith and credit requirement to hold that a judgment rendered under the circumstances of this case may be required to run the gantlet of such collateral attack in the courts of sister States before its validity outside of the State which rendered it is established or rejected. That vital interests are involved in divorce litigation indicates to us that it is a matter of greater rather than lesser importance that there should be a place to end such litigation. And where a decree of divorce is rendered by a competent court under the circumstances of this case, the obligation of full faith and credit requires that such litigation should end in the courts of the State in which the judgment was rendered.

Reversed.

[The dissent of Justice Frankfurter and Justice Murphy has been omitted.]

NOTES

Notice. An elementary and fundamental requirement of due process in any proceeding which is to be accorded finality is notice that is reasonably calculated, under all the circumstances, to apprise interested parties of the pendency of the action and afford them an opportunity to present their objections. The individual states have come up with various procedures for giving notice to an absent spouse in an ex parte divorce action, including constructive service through publication. As pointed out in Mullane v. Central Hanover Bank & Trust Co., 339 U.S. 306, 70 S.Ct. 652, 94 L.Ed. 865 (1950), however:

> "It would be idle to pretend that publication alone, as prescribed here, is a reliable means of acquainting interested parties of the fact that their rights are before the courts...."

The Superior Court of New Jersey, Appellate Division, holds that in the modern age, an e-mail address is a demonstration of due diligence in an effort to notify the other spouse of pending divorce action. The court vacated a default judgement of divorce when the husband had the wife's e-mail address but did not notify her of his divorce petition via the e-mail address which he had or any other means reasonably calculated to reach her. *See* Modan v. Modan, 327 N.J.Super. 44, 742 A.2d 611 (App.Div.2000).

A problem of res judicata? One may question whether the res judicata doctrine was correctly applied in the *Sherrer* and *Coe* cases. The doctrine is properly applicable to bind Mr. Sherrer in Massachusetts by the Florida finding as to the domicile issue only if the issue is the same in Massachusetts as it was in Florida. However, "domicile 1" may not be identical with "domicile 2." The definition of a legal concept depends upon the purpose which it is called to serve and the legal authority defining it.

It must be clear that in Massachusetts the question of domicile is a federal matter. The circumstances under which a divorce decree is entitled to full faith and credit (the jurisdiction to divorce under the full faith and credit clause) is certainly a federal question which ought to be reviewable by the Supreme Court of the United States. Did the Florida court have a *federal* question of domicil before it to decide? Mr. Sherrer could, indeed, have litigated a question labeled "domicile," but was it "domicile" within the meaning of the Florida divorce statutes or was it "domicile," a jurisdictional issue under the Constitution of the United States? Suppose Sherrer had successfully sought direct review of the Florida divorce from the Supreme Court of the United States. What would have been the federal issue to be decided respecting the power of Florida to divorce the Sherrers?

Did Mr. Sherrer, in the final analysis, find himself bound by failing to litigate a federal question in Florida (the jurisdictional basis of a divorce decree which is entitled to full faith and credit) which was not before the Florida court?

Courts have been consistent in seeking finality, terming it a principle founded in equity and common sense. *See, e.g.* Weston v. Jones, 603 N.W.2d 706 (S.D.1999) (when the husband was an active participant in an Indian tribal court's divorce court, he is estopped from later attacking the judgement on jurisdictional grounds).

Jurisdictional challenge by a third party. In 1951, the Supreme Court of the United States added a further gloss to the full faith and credit rules in Johnson v. Muelberger, 340 U.S. 581, 71 S.Ct. 474, 95 L.Ed. 552 (1951). Decedent's W_2 had obtained a Florida decree without complying with its 90 day residence requirement. He had appeared by attorney, had denied wrongful acts, but did not contest allegations re residence. He remarried and upon his death W_3 elected to take a statutory third under New York law. A child of the first marriage contested this election, claiming W_2's Florida decree was invalid. The New York Court of Appeals holding that the Florida decree bound only the parties themselves and under Florida law the child could attack the decree collaterally in Florida and so in New York was reversed. The Court said: "No Florida case has come to our attention holding that a child may contest in Florida its parent's divorce where the parent was barred from contesting, as here, by *res judicata*." New York cannot permit an attack by reason of the Full Faith and Credit Clause. "When a divorce cannot be attacked for lack of jurisdiction by parties actually before the court or strangers in the rendering state it cannot be attacked by them anywhere in the Union." Could the State of New York have attacked the Florida divorce in a bigamy prosecution against the decedent (while he lived) for his marriage to W_3? New York apparently permits children, who may inherit property, to attack the validity of a parent's divorce after the parent has died. By what reasoning was the plaintiff prevented from taking advantage of this New York rule? If it is argued that a child is prevented by the Florida decree, may she not properly respond: "That decree is invalid and I wish to demonstrate that fact?"

Injunctions. At one time injunctions occasionally were granted in some states against one spouse's obtaining a divorce elsewhere allegedly based on fraudulent assertions concerning jurisdiction, on the theory that irreparable injury otherwise might accrue to the spouse who remains at home. *See, e.g.,* Garvin v. Garvin, 302 N.Y. 96, 96 N.E.2d 721 (1951); Hammer v. Hammer, 278 App.Div. 396, 105 N.Y.S.2d 812 (1951), affirmed 303 N.Y. 481, 104 N.E.2d 864 (1952). However, in Rodgers v. Rodgers, 30 A.D.2d 548, 290 N.Y.S.2d 608 (1968), the court held that "Injunctive relief should not be granted permanently to prevent a defendant from establishing a bona fide residence in any sister State although one of its purposes is to institute an action for divorce. . . ."

Special appearance to contest jurisdiction. Procedural rules in some states allow a defendant to appear specially to contest jurisdiction without participating so as to invoke the rule of Sherrer v. Sherrer. *See, e.g.*, Spalding v. Spalding, 171 Conn. 220, 368 A.2d 14 (1976) (interpreting California procedure). The court in *Spalding* also held that unless there is a state statute to the contrary, the jurisdictional requirement of domicil is satisfied if domicil exists at the time of the commencement of the action but not on the day when judgment is rendered.

UNIFORM DIVORCE RECOGNITION ACT (1947), 9 U.L.A. 355 (1988)

§ 1. [Validity of Foreign Decree]

A divorce from the bonds of matrimony obtained in another jurisdiction shall be of no force or effect in this state, if both parties to the marriage were domiciled in this state at the time the proceeding for the divorce was commenced.

§ 2. [Evidence of Domicile]

Proof that a person obtaining a divorce from the bonds of matrimony in another jurisdiction was (a) domiciled in this state within twelve months prior to the commencement of the proceeding therefor, and resumed residence in this state within eighteen months after the date of his departure therefrom, or (b) at all times after his departure from this state, and until his return maintained a place of residence within this state, shall be prima facie evidence that the person was domiciled in this state when the divorce proceeding was commenced.

NOTE

The preceding Act has been withdrawn by the Commissioners on Uniform State Laws. It was adopted in only seven states: California, Nebraska, New Hampshire, North Dakota, Rhode Island, South Carolina and Wisconsin

MASSACHUSETTS GENERAL LAWS ANNOTATED, CHAPTER 208 (West 1998)

§ 39. Foreign divorces; validity

A divorce adjudged in another jurisdiction according to the laws thereof by a court having jurisdiction of the cause and of both the parties shall be valid and effectual in this commonwealth; but if an inhabitant of this commonwealth goes into another jurisdiction to obtain a divorce for a cause occurring here while the parties resided here, or for a cause which would not authorize a divorce by the laws of this commonwealth, a divorce so obtained shall be of no force or effect in this commonwealth.

Sosna v. Iowa

Supreme Court of the United States, 1975.
419 U.S. 393, 95 S.Ct. 553, 42 L.Ed.2d 532.

■ MR. JUSTICE REHNQUIST delivered the opinion of the Court.

Appellant Carol Sosna married Michael Sosna on September 5, 1964, in Michigan. They lived together in New York between October 1967 and August 1971, after which date they separated but continued to live in New York. In August 1972, appellant moved to Iowa with her three children, and the following month she petitioned the District Court of Jackson County, Iowa, for a dissolution of her marriage. Michael Sosna, who had been personally served with notice of the action when he came to Iowa to visit his children, made a special appearance to contest the jurisdiction of the Iowa court. The Iowa court dismissed the petition for lack of jurisdiction, finding that Michael Sosna was not a resident of Iowa and appellant had not been a resident of the State of Iowa for one year preceding the filing of her petition. In so doing the Iowa court applied the provisions of Iowa Code § 598.6 requiring that the petitioner in such an action be "for the last year a resident of the state."

. . .

The durational residency requirement under attack in this case is a part of Iowa's comprehensive statutory regulation of domestic relations, an area that has long been regarded as a virtually exclusive province of the States....

The statutory scheme in Iowa, like those in other States, sets forth in considerable detail the grounds upon which a marriage may be dissolved and the circumstances in which a divorce may be obtained. Jurisdiction over a petition for dissolution is established by statute in "the county where either party resides," Iowa Code § 598.2, and the Iowa courts have construed the term "resident" to have much the same meaning as is ordinarily associated with the concept of domicile. Korsrud v. Korsrud, 242 Iowa 178, 45 N.W.2d 848 (1951). Iowa has recently revised its divorce statutes, incorporating the no-fault concept, but it retained the one-year durational residency requirement.

The imposition of a durational residency requirement for divorce is scarcely unique to Iowa, since 48 States impose such a requirement as a condition for maintaining an action for divorce. As might be expected, the periods vary among the States and range from six weeks to two years. The one-year period selected by Iowa is the most common length of time prescribed.

Appellant contends that the Iowa requirement of one year's residence is unconstitutional for two separate reasons: *first*, because it establishes two classes of persons and discriminates against those who have recently exercised their right to travel to Iowa, . . . ; and, *second*, because it denies a litigant the opportunity to make an individualized showing of bona fide residence and therefore denies such residents access to the only method of legally dissolving their marriage. Boddie v. Connecticut, 401 U.S. 371, 91 S.Ct. 780 (1971).

State statutes imposing durational residency requirements were of course invalidated when imposed by States as a qualification for welfare payments, for voting, and for medical care. But none of those cases intimated that the States might never impose durational residency requirements, and such a proposition was in fact expressly disclaimed. What those cases had in common was that the durational residency requirements they struck down were justified on the basis of budgetary or record-keeping considerations which were held insufficient to outweigh the constitutional claims of the individuals. But Iowa's divorce residency requirement is of a different stripe. Appellant was not irretrievably foreclosed from obtaining some part of what she sought, as was the case with the welfare recipients in *Shapiro*, the voters in *Dunn*, or the indigent patient in *Maricopa County*. She would eventually qualify for the same sort of adjudication which she demanded virtually upon her arrival in the State. Iowa's requirement delayed her access to the courts, but, by fulfilling it, a plaintiff could ultimately obtain the same opportunity for adjudication which she asserts ought to be hers at an earlier point in time.

Iowa's residency requirement may reasonably be justified on grounds other than purely budgetary considerations or administrative convenience. Cf. Kahn v. Shevin, 416 U.S. 351, 94 S.Ct. 1734, 40 L.Ed.2d 189 (1974). A decree of divorce is not a matter in which the only interested parties are the State as a sort of "grantor," and a plaintiff such as appellant in the role of "grantee." Both spouses are obviously interested in the proceedings, since it will affect their marital status and very likely their property rights. Where a married couple has minor children, a decree of divorce would usually include provisions for their custody and support. With consequences of such moment riding on a divorce decree issued by its courts, Iowa may insist that one seeking to initiate such a proceeding have the modicum of attachment to the State required here.

Such a requirement additionally furthers the State's parallel interests in both avoiding officious intermeddling in matters in which another State has a paramount interest, and in minimizing the susceptibility of its own divorce decrees to collateral attack. A State such as Iowa may quite reasonably decide that it does not wish to become a divorce mill for unhappy spouses who have lived there as short a time as appellant had when she commenced her action in the state court after having long resided elsewhere. Until such time as Iowa is convinced that appellant intends to remain in the State, it lacks the "nexus between person and place of such permanence as to control the creation of legal relations and responsibilities of the utmost significance." Williams v. North Carolina, 325 U.S. 226, 65 S.Ct. 1092, 1095, 89 L.Ed. 1577 (1945). Perhaps even more importantly, Iowa's interests extend beyond its borders and include the recognition of its divorce decrees by other States under the Full Faith and Credit Clause of the Constitution, Art. IV, § 1. For that purpose, this Court has often stated that "judicial power to grant a divorce—jurisdiction, strictly speaking—is founded on domicil." *Williams*, supra; Andrews v. Andrews, 188 U.S. 14, 23 S.Ct. 237, 47 L.Ed. 366 (1903); Bell v. Bell, 181 U.S. 175, 21 S.Ct. 551, 45 L.Ed. 804 (1901). Where a divorce decree is entered after a finding of domicile in *ex parte* proceedings,[20] this Court has held that the finding of domicile is not binding upon another State and may be disregarded in the face of "cogent evidence" to the contrary. *Williams*, supra, 325 U.S. at 236, 65 S.Ct. at 1098. For that reason, the State asked to enter such a decree is entitled to insist that the putative divorce plaintiff satisfy something more than the bare minimum of constitutional requirements before a divorce may be granted. The State's decision to exact a one-year residency requirement as a matter of policy is therefore buttressed by a quite permissible inference that this requirement not only effectuates state substantive policy but likewise provides a greater safeguard against successful collateral attack than would a requirement of bona fide residence alone. This is precisely the sort of determination that a State in the exercise of its domestic relations jurisdiction is entitled to make.

We therefore hold that the state interest in requiring that those who seek a divorce from its courts be genuinely attached to the State, as well as a desire to insulate divorce decrees from the likelihood of collateral attack, requires a different resolution of the constitutional issue presented than was the case in *Shapiro*, supra, *Dunn*, supra, and *Maricopa County*, supra.

Nor are we of the view that the failure to provide an individualized determination of residency violates the Due Process Clause of the Fourteenth Amendment. Vlandis v. Kline, 412 U.S. 441, 93 S.Ct. 2230, 37 L.Ed.2d 63 (1973), relied upon by appellant, holds that Connecticut might not arbitrarily invoke a permanent and irrebuttable presumption of nonresidence against students who sought to obtain in-state tuition rates when that presumption was not necessarily or universally true in fact. But in *Vlandis* the Court warned that its decision should not "be construed to deny a State the right to impose on a student, as one element in demon-

---

20. When a divorce decree is not entered on the basis of *ex parte* proceedings, this Court held in Sherrer v. Sherrer, 334 U.S. 343, 351–352, 68 S.Ct. 1087, 1091, 92 L.Ed. 1429 (1948):

"[T]he requirements of full faith and credit bar a defendant from collaterally attacking a divorce decree on jurisdictional grounds in the courts of a sister State where there has been participation by the defendant in the divorce proceedings, where the defendant has been accorded full opportunity to contest the jurisdictional issues, and where the decree is not susceptible to such collateral attack in the courts of the State which rendered the decree."

Our Brother Marshall argues in dissent that the Iowa durational residency requirement "sweeps too broadly" since it is not limited to *ex parte* proceedings and could be narrowed by a waiver provision. But Iowa's durational residency requirement cannot be tailored in this manner without disrupting settled principles of Iowa practice and pleading. Iowa's rules governing special appearances made it impossible for the state court to know, either at the time a petition for divorce is filed or when a motion to dismiss for want of jurisdiction is filed, whether or not a defendant will appear and participate in the divorce proceedings. Iowa Rules of Civil Procedure 66, 104. The fact that the state legislature might conceivably adopt a system of waivers and revise court rules governing special appearances does not make such detailed rewriting appropriate business for the federal judiciary.

strating bona fide residence, a reasonable durational residency requirement." An individualized determination of physical presence plus the intent to remain, which appellant apparently seeks, would not entitle her to a divorce even if she could have made such a showing.[22] For Iowa requires not merely "domicile" in that sense, but residence in the State for a year in order for its courts to exercise their divorce jurisdiction.

In Boddie v. Connecticut, supra, this Court held that Connecticut might not deny access to divorce courts to those persons who could not afford to pay the required fee. Because of the exclusive role played by the State in the termination of marriages, it was held that indigents could not be denied an opportunity to be heard "absent a countervailing state interest of overriding significance." 401 U.S., at 377, 91 S.Ct., at 785. But the gravamen of appellant Sosna's claim is not total deprivation, as in *Boddie*, but only delay. The operation of the filing fee in *Boddie* served to exclude forever a certain segment of the population from obtaining a divorce in the courts of Connecticut. No similar total deprivation is present in appellant's case, and the delay which attends the enforcement of the one-year durational residency requirement is, for the reasons previously stated, consistent with the provisions of the United States Constitution.

Affirmed.

■ Mr. Justice Marshall, with whom Mr. Justice Brennan joins, dissenting.

. . . [T]he previous decisions of this Court make it plain that the right of marital association is one of the most basic rights conferred on the individual by the State. . . . I think it is clear beyond cavil that the right to seek dissolution of the marital relationship is of such fundamental importance that denial of this right to the class of recent interstate travelers penalizes interstate travel within the meaning of *Shapiro, Dunn,* and *Maricopa County.*

Having determined that the interest in obtaining a divorce is of substantial social importance, I would scrutinize Iowa's durational residency requirement to determine whether it constitutes a reasonable means of furthering important interests asserted by the State. The Court, however, has not only declined to apply the "compelling interest" test to this case, it has conjured up possible justifications for the State's restriction in a manner much more akin to the lenient standard we have in the past applied in analyzing equal protection challenges to business regulations. . . .

. . . . .

The Court's third justification seems to me the only one that warrants close consideration. Iowa has a legitimate interest in protecting itself

---

22. In addition to a showing of residence within the State for a year, Iowa Code § 598.6 requires any petition for dissolution to state "that the maintenance of the residence has been in good faith and not for the purpose of obtaining a marriage dissolution only." In dismissing appellant's petition in state court, Judge Keck observed that appellant had failed to allege good-faith residence.

against invasion by those seeking quick divorces in a forum with relatively lax divorce laws, and it may have some interest in avoiding collateral attacks on its decree in other States. These interests, however, would adequately be protected by a simple requirement of domicile—physical presence plus intent to remain—which would remove the rigid one-year barrier while permitting the State to restrict the availability of its divorce process to citizens who are genuinely its own.

The majority notes that in Williams v. North Carolina, 325 U.S. 226, 65 S.Ct. 1092, 89 L.Ed. 1577 (1945), the Court held that for *ex parte* divorces one State's finding of domicile could, under limited circumstances, be challenged in the courts of another. From this, the majority concludes that since Iowa's findings of domicile might be subject to collateral attack elsewhere, it should be permitted to cushion its findings with a one-year residency requirement.

For several reasons, the year's waiting period seems to me neither necessary nor much of a cushion. First, the *Williams* opinion was not aimed at States seeking to avoid becoming divorce mills. Quite the opposite, it was rather plainly directed at States that had cultivated a "quickie divorce" reputation by playing fast and loose with findings of domicile. If Iowa wishes to avoid becoming a haven for divorce seekers, it is inconceivable that its good-faith determinations of domicile would not meet the rather lenient full faith and credit standards set out in *Williams*.

A second problem with the majority's argument on this score is that *Williams* applies only to *ex parte* divorces. This Court has held that if both spouses were before the divorcing court, a foreign State cannot recognize a collateral challenge that would not be permissible in the divorcing State. Sherrer v. Sherrer, 334 U.S. 343, 68 S.Ct. 1087, 92 L.Ed.2d 1429 (1948). Therefore, the Iowa statute sweeps too broadly even as a defense to possible collateral attacks, since it imposes a one-year requirement whenever the respondent does not reside in the State, regardless of whether the proceeding is *ex parte*.

Third, even a one-year period does not provide complete protection against collateral attack. It merely makes it somewhat less likely that a second State will be able to find "cogent evidence" that Iowa's determination of domicile was incorrect. But if the Iowa court has erroneously determined the question of domicile, the year's residence will do nothing to preclude collateral attack under *Williams*.

Finally, in one sense the year's residency requirement may technically increase rather than reduce the exposure of Iowa's decrees to collateral attack. Iowa appears to be among the States that have interpreted their divorce residency requirements as being of jurisdictional import. Since a State's divorce decree is subject to collateral challenge in a foreign forum for any jurisdictional flaw that would void it in the State's own courts, New York ex rel. Halvey v. Halvey, 330 U.S. 610, 67 S.Ct. 903, 91 L.Ed. 1133 (1947), the residency requirement exposes Iowa divorce proceedings to attack both for failure to prove domicile and for failure to prove one year's residence. If nothing else, this casts doubt on the majority's speculation that Iowa's residency requirement may have been intended as a statutory shield for its divorce decrees. In sum, concerns about the need for a long residency requirement to defray collateral attacks on state judgments seem more fanciful than real. If, as the majority assumes, Iowa is interested in assuring itself that its divorce petitioners are legitimately Iowa citizens, requiring petitioners to provide convincing evidence of bona fide domicile should be more than adequate to the task.

I conclude that the course Iowa has chosen in restricting access to its divorce courts unduly interferes with the right to "migrate, resettle, find a new job, and start a new life." Shapiro v. Thompson, 394 U.S., at 629, 89 S.Ct., at 1328. . . .

[The dissenting opinion of JUSTICE WHITE has been omitted.]

2. COMITY FOR DECREES OF FOREIGN STATES

Perrin v. Perrin

United States Court of Appeals, Third Circuit, 1969.
408 F.2d 107.

■ MARIS, CIRCUIT JUDGE. This is an appeal by the defendant husband from a judgment of the District Court of the Virgin Islands granting to the plaintiff wife a divorce and the custody of their minor son, Daniel, now 9 years old. The parties, who were married in New York on September 10, 1954, are Swiss citizens. On February 8, 1967 the present plaintiff filed a petition in a court of the State of Chihuahua, Mexico, praying for a divorce from her husband, the present defendant. The plaintiff appeared personally in the Mexican proceeding. The defendant appeared by a duly empowered attorney at law and filed a consenting answer. On February 23, 1967 the Mexican court entered a decree of divorce, dissolving the marriage and awarding custody of the minor child to the defendant. . . .

In the latter part of November, 1967, the defendant arrived in St. Thomas from Martinique on the motor vessel Jolly Rover to engage in the charter business for the tourist season. The defendant had just returned from Switzerland where the minor child had been living with the defendant's parents and he brought the minor child to St. Thomas with him. . . . On January 29, 1968 the plaintiff filed . . . a complaint . . . against the defendant . . . praying for an absolute divorce and again seeking the custody of the minor child. A motion to dismiss this complaint for lack of jurisdiction of the subject matter and persons of the plaintiff and minor child was filed by the defendant and on March 7, 1968 was denied. . . .

The defendant's motion to dismiss the complaint was based, inter alia, upon the proposition that the court lacked jurisdiction of the subject matter because there was no existing marriage between the parties to dissolve, the marriage having been terminated a year previously by the Mexican divorce decree, an authenticated copy of which was annexed to the motion. In her brief opposing the motion the plaintiff attacked the validity of the Mexican divorce decree on the ground that neither party was domiciled in Mexico at the time it was rendered and that the Mexican court, therefore, lacked jurisdiction to render it. Thus was raised the question of the validity of the Mexican decree or, more precisely, the question whether the plaintiff can be heard to attack in this proceeding the validity of the Mexican decree which she herself had sought and obtained and in the entry of which the defendant had acquiesced.

. . .

It is true, as the plaintiff now argues, that domicile is regarded as the basis for jurisdiction to grant a divorce in the United States. Granville–Smith v. Granville–Smith, 1955, 349 U.S. 1, 75 S.Ct. 553, 99 L.Ed. 773. It is likewise true that a divorce decree may be collaterally attacked for lack of domiciliary jurisdiction, Williams v. North Carolina, 1945, 325 U.S. 226, 65 S.Ct. 1092, 89 L.Ed. 1577, 157 A.L.R. 1366, if the defendant was not personally served and did not appear. But it is equally well settled that if the defendant was personally served or did actually appear in the action he is estopped from impeaching the resulting divorce decree, whether the domiciliary jurisdiction was contested by the defendant, Sherrer v. Sherrer, 1948, 334 U.S. 343, 68 S.Ct. 1087, 92 L.Ed. 1429, 1 A.L.R.2d 1355, or was admitted by him, Coe v. Coe, 1948, 334 U.S. 378, 68 S.Ct. 1094, 92 L.Ed. 1451, 1 A.L.R.2d 1376.

The Sherrer and Coe cases involved . . . the full faith and credit clause of the federal Constitution. Here, however, we are dealing with a decree of a foreign state as to which the principles of comity, rather than full faith and credit, apply. Ordinarily, the recognition in the United States of such a foreign decree will depend upon whether at least one of the spouses was domiciled in the foreign state when the decree of divorce was rendered. Certainly "mail order" divorce decrees in which neither spouse has appeared personally in the foreign jurisdiction are not recognized here, and this appears to be equally true in the case of ex parte divorce decrees in which an absent defendant is served only extraterritorially or constructively and does not actually appear or file an answer in the action.

In the Mexican proceeding involved in the present case, however, as in the Coe case, a bilateral divorce is involved. For here, as there, the plaintiff was personally present in the foreign state and appeared in the foreign court and the defendant appeared in that court by counsel and filed a consenting answer. In Rosenstiel v. Rosenstiel, 1965, 16 N.Y.2d 64, 262 N.Y.S.2d 86, 209 N.E.2d 709, cert. den. 384 U.S. 971, 86 S.Ct. 1861, 16 L.Ed.2d 682, the Court of Appeals of New York was presented with the question whether such a bilateral divorce granted in the State of Chihuahua, Mexico, was entitled to recognition in New York State. In speaking for the Court of Appeals in that case Judge Bergan said, inter alia:

> "There is squarely presented to this court now for the first time the question whether recognition is to be given by New York to a matrimonial judgment of a foreign country based on grounds not accepted in New York, where personal jurisdiction of one party to the

marriage has been acquired by physical presence before the foreign court; and jurisdiction of the other has been acquired by appearance and pleading through an authorized attorney although no domicile of either party is shown within that jurisdiction; and 'residence' has been acquired by one party through a statutory formality based on brief contact.

"In cases where a divorce has been obtained without any personal contact with the jurisdiction by either party or by physical submission to the jurisdiction by one, with no personal service of process within the foreign jurisdiction upon, and no appearance or submission by, the other, decision has been against the validity of the foreign decree (Caldwell v. Caldwell, 298 N.Y. 146, 81 N.E.2d 60 (1948); Rosenbaum v. Rosenbaum, 309 N.Y. 371, 130 N.E.2d 902, 54 A.L.R.2d 1232 (1955)).

"Although the grounds for divorce found acceptable according to Mexican law are inadmissible in New York, and the physical contact with the Mexican jurisdiction was ephemeral, there are some incidents in the Mexican proceedings which are common characteristics of the exercise of judicial power.

"The former husband was physically in the jurisdiction, personally before the court, with the usual incidents and the implicit consequences of voluntary submission to foreign sovereignty. Although he had no intention of making his domicile there, he did what the domestic law of the place required he do to establish a 'residence' of a kind which was set up as a statutory prerequisite to institute an action for divorce. This is not our own view in New York of what a bona fide residence is or should be, but it is that which the local law of Mexico prescribes.

"Since he was one party to the two–party contract of marriage he carried with him legal incidents of the marriage itself, considered as an entity, which came before the court when he personally appeared and presented his petition. In a highly mobile era such as ours, it is needful on pragmatic grounds to regard the marriage itself as moving from place to place with either spouse, a concept which underlies the decision in Williams v. State of North Carolina I, 317 U.S. 287, p. 304, 63 S.Ct. 207, 87 L.Ed. 279, p. 289, 143 A.L.R. 1273.

"The voluntary appearance of the other spouse in the foreign court by attorney would tend to give further support to an acquired jurisdiction there over the marriage as a legal entity. In theory jurisdiction is an imposition of sovereign power over the person. It is usually exerted by symbolic and rarely by actual force, e.g., the summons as a symbol of force; the attachment and the civil arrest, as exerting actual force.

"But almost universally jurisdiction is acquired by physical and personal submission to judicial authority and in legal theory there seems to be ground to admit that the Mexican court at Juarez acquired jurisdiction over the former marriage of the defendant.

"It is true that in attempting to reconcile the conflict of laws and of State interests in matrimonial judgments entered in States of the United States, where the Constitution compels each to give full faith and credit to the judgments of the others, a considerable emphasis has been placed on domicile as a prerequisite to that compulsory recognition.... But domicile is not intrinsically an indispensable prerequisite to jurisdiction (cf. Stimson, Jurisdiction in Divorce Cases: The Unsoundness of the Domiciliary Theory, 42 Amer.Bar Assn.J. 222 (1956); Griswold, Divorce Jurisdiction and Recognition of Divorce Decrees—A Comparative Study, 65 Harv.L.Rev. 193, 228).

"The duration of domicile in sister States providing by statute for a minimal time to acquire domicile as necessary to matrimonial action jurisdiction is in actual practice complied with by a mere formal gesture having no more relation to the actual situs of the marriage or to true domicile than the formality of signing the Juarez city register. The difference in time is not truly significant of a difference in intent or purpose or in effect.

"The State or country of the true domicile has the closest real public interest in a marriage but, where a New York spouse goes elsewhere to establish a synthetic domicile to meet technical acceptance of a matrimonial suit, our public interest is not affected differently by a formality of one day than by a formality of six weeks.

"Nevada gets no closer to the real public concern with the marriage than Chihuahua...."

With these views we agree and we think that the case is ruled in principle by the Coe case. We find it impossible to believe that six weeks residence by Mr. Coe gave Nevada a greater or more real concern with his marriage than a day or two's residence in Chihuahua by Mrs. Perrin gave to that Mexican State. Although we recognize that there is a divergence of view on this question among American jurisdictions, we hold, as did the Court of Appeals of New York in that case, that "A balanced public policy now requires that recognition of the bilateral Mexican divorce be given rather than withheld and such recognition as a matter of comity offends no public policy" of this Territory. We are the more persuaded to this result in this case because the party who seeks to attack the Mexican decree is not the defendant in that case but rather the plaintiff who procured it upon her representation to the Mexican court that she resided in the City of Juarez. It follows that the plaintiff may not in this proceeding be heard to deny the validity of the Mexican divorce decree. Since by the terms of that decree her marriage with the defendant was dissolved on February 23, 1967, no marriage status remained to be terminated when the present complaint was filed....

. . .

The decree of the District Court will be reversed....

NOTE

In Dart v. Dart, 460 Mich. 573, 597 N.W.2d 82 (1999), *rev. denied*, 529 U.S. 1018, 120 S.Ct. 1418, 146 L.Ed.2d 311 (2000), the wife was present and represented by counsel at an English divorce proceeding when the court granted a decree of divorce and ordered a property division in accordance with English law which looks to the wife's financial needs in regard to large assets, rather than the division of marital assets. She later argued in a petition to deny comity to the English decree, that the property distribution was repugnant to Michigan due process of law and thus should be denied comity. The court rejected her appeal and awarded comity to the English decree. So too, in Hyde v. Hyde, 562 S.W.2d 194 (Tenn.1978), the wife had appeared in person to obtain a divorce in the Dominican Republic in 1974. The husband was represented in the proceeding by an attorney there who acted under the power of a attorney filed with the court. This satisfied the laws of the Dominican Republic regarding jurisdiction. Later, in 1976, the husband asked a court in Tennessee for either a declaratory judgement that the foreign divorce was valid or, in the alternative, a divorce by the Tennessee court. The petition alleged that the parties had settled their property rights and support obligations by contract and that they had submitted to the jurisdiction of the foreign court in good faith to obtain a no-fault divorce. The trial judge granted summary judgement holding that the foreign divorce was valid and enforceable, and the Divorce Referee appealed. The Supreme Court of Tennessee upheld the lower court's decision, noting that a state can look to its own public policy in determining whether to grant comity to another nation's decree. Tennessee, it pointed out, authorized the granting of divorces based on irreconcilable differences and the resolution of property and other rights through settlement agreements.

3. THE EFFECT OF LACHES AND ESTOPPEL

Kazin v. Kazin

Supreme Court of New Jersey, 1979.
81 N.J. 85, 405 A.2d 360.

■ HANDLER, J.

This case presents the question whether the plaintiff, who obtained a presumably void or voidable Mexican divorce from her first husband, should be allowed to maintain a matrimonial action against her present husband for divorce, alimony and equitable distribution or, alternatively, for separate maintenance. The circumstances reveal that defendant participated in plaintiff's decision to obtain a Mexican divorce from her former husband, and, following that divorce, defendant and plaintiff married and lived together for seven years, apparently believing themselves to be husband and wife. In Tonti v. Chadwick, 1 N.J. 531, 64 A.2d 436 (1949), the Court was presented with the same question under comparable circumstances and denied relief. We no longer find persuasive the reasoning of our earlier decision and decline to follow it. We rule in this case that the plaintiff is entitled to assert her matrimonial claims.

Plaintiff, Clara Kazin, was first married to Jesse Lawrence Liss on October 10, 1953. They had four children. Sometime prior to 1969, Liss left Clara and their children to live with another woman. Clara steadfastly refused to give him a divorce. In February of 1969, Clara met Michael Kazin, the defendant in this action, and shortly thereafter Michael proposed marriage. This led to Clara's obtaining a Mexican divorce from Liss on May 27, 1969. Less than one month later, on June 18, 1969, Clara and Michael married in this State and lived together until July 1976, when defendant moved out of their home.

In October 1976 plaintiff instituted an action for divorce on grounds of extreme cruelty and desertion and, by later amendment, adultery, seeking alimony and equitable distribution; in the alternative, she sought separate maintenance. Defendant filed an answer in which he denied that the parties were validly married to each other. He also counterclaimed for a judgment that the purported marriage between the parties was null and void on grounds that plaintiff's Mexican divorce was invalid and that her prior marriage was still in force. These allegations were reiterated as an affirmative defense after defendant was allowed by consent order to withdraw his counterclaim. Plaintiff was permitted by the same consent order, without the necessity of a formal reply, to continue to assert her previous defenses to the counterclaim, namely, estoppel, laches, fraud and unclean hands.

According to plaintiff, the plan to obtain a Mexican divorce originated with defendant, who arranged for a meeting of all interested parties, Clara, Liss, and himself, in the Newark law offices of his attorney. The attorney assured the parties that a Mexican divorce was perfectly legal. The parties also discussed Liss' support obligations. Based on Michael's promise to marry her and to provide for everything, plaintiff did not request support from Liss and agreed to accept minimal support for her four sons (with no provision for their college education). Liss agreed to sign all papers which he and his attorney believed were sufficient to confer jurisdiction on the Mexican court. Defendant then made all the arrangements for plaintiff to go to Mexico, paid all her expenses, and personally accompanied her there. Liss generally corroborated plaintiff's version of the circumstances surrounding the Mexican divorce. He stated that the Mexican divorce was defendant's idea and defendant wanted plaintiff to be divorced as soon as possible and had promised that he would take care of the children. Liss was assured by his own attorney that the Mexican divorce would be valid. Kazin's version of these events is somewhat different. He insisted that he was approached by Liss with respect to the Mexican divorce and that it was Liss' attorney rather than his who made the arrangements. He further maintained that he accompanied plaintiff only as far as El Paso, Texas, rather than to Mexico. It is clear that all of the parties relied upon the validity of the Mexican divorce. Following that divorce, Clara and Michael married and lived together as husband and wife for seven years. Liss also remarried and presently has two children from this union.

On cross-motions, the parties requested the trial court to decide on the pleadings and affidavits "whether or not defendant may raise the question of the invalidity of the Mexican divorce." The trial judge concluded, on the basis of Tonti v. Chadwick, that defendant was estopped from affirmatively asserting the invalidity of plaintiff's Mexican divorce, but that since the divorce was void, plaintiff could not prove a valid marriage and therefore was not entitled to either dissolution or support from defendant. On appeals by both parties, the Appellate Division upheld the judgment of the trial court, dismissing plaintiff's complaint....

. . .

It is clear that in Tonti v. Chadwick, the Court was responsive to a powerful legislative mandate against the facile termination of lawful marriages. It was felt that to apply, or withhold, estoppel to grant affirmative relief in such circumstances would be inconsistent with that policy and would enable the parties effectively to frustrate the objectives of the matrimonial laws, particularly those governing the dissolution of the marriage status. Those laws designedly made it quite difficult for a married person to obtain a divorce in this State. One seeking a divorce had to affix marital blame upon the other spouse. The statutory grounds for divorce were limited to relatively egregious forms of behavior, adultery, extreme cruelty, and willful desertion for at least two years. Moreover, the complainant was required to be blameless for the failure of the marriage. A legitimate claim for divorce could be defeated even by a guilty defendant if it could be established that the plaintiff engaged in marital conduct amounting to recrimination, condonation or unclean hands.

Our courts were generally faithful to these strict legislative commands, imposing heavy burdens upon the litigants in their quest for relief from an onerous or moribund marriage. Decisions mirrored the severity of this legislative policy in dealing with foreign divorces obtained by New Jersey domiciliaries. In particular, there was little tolerance shown for Mexican divorces obtained through the mails or by nominal appearances, exemplified by the New York decision of Caldwell v. Caldwell, 298 N.Y. 146, 81 N.E.2d 60 (Ct.App.1948), and echoed in our own cases.... The Court in Tonti v. Chadwick took pains to note the then-controlling statute nullified a divorce decree obtained by a New Jersey inhabitant in another state or country "for a cause which occurred while the parties resided in this state, or for a cause which is not ground for divorce under the laws of this state...." Tonti v. Chadwick, supra, 1 N.J., at 535–536, 64 A.2d at 438. This legislative policy, strongly paternalistic and protective toward the marriages of New Jersey domiciliaries, influenced judicial perceptions of the role of equity in such cases involving vulnerable foreign divorces. Absent constitutional full faith and credit or comity, some decisions tended to turn more on whether the foreign decrees were offensive to this State's public policy than on the real marital relationships, actual needs or comparative positions of the parties.

It would, nevertheless, be an overstatement to imply that courts even under prior laws were insensitive to equitable concerns or did not, within the constraints of the matrimonial statutes, conscientiously undertake to balance the equities as between parties. Many decisions demonstrated an appreciation of the need for a genuine weighing of the relative interests of the contestants. However, more important than these judicial antecedents in terms of the relevance of equitable principles in resolving matrimonial controversies has been the drastic change in the State's statutes in the matrimonial field.

The Divorce Reform Act of 1971 both repealed and substantially amended prior legislation controlling marital relationships. The differences in public policy wrought by this revision are fundamental. Significantly, the previous statute negating foreign divorces based on jurisdictional and substantive grounds inconsistent with our own, in some measure relied upon by the Court in Tonti v. Chadwick, was repealed, and no longer expresses the legislative attitude towards such matters. Grounds for divorce have been expanded and liberalized. Fault in the demise of a marriage is not presently a crucial concern. Matrimonial blame is merely one circumstance to be weighed in granting alimony and support. Adultery is not considered a per se bar to alimony, and support in the form of alimony is generally available in all matrimonial actions, including nullity.

Equitable principles have moved to the forefront. In the event of dissolution of the marriage, assets of the spousal partnership are to be divided equitably. The most important considerations in identifying and marshalling property for this purpose are the objective indicia of the true marital relationship of the parties, not simply the date of divorce or the formal filing of the divorce complaint. Interspousal agreements continue to be enforceable only to the extent they are fair. Further, the statutory abolition of the harsh traditional defenses of recrimination, condonation and unclean hands is added evidence of the ascendence of equitable principles as an integral aspect of the State's public policy toward domestic relations.

. . . Changed attitudes toward marriage and the burgeoning divorce rate, reflecting the temper of the times, have created new interpersonal problems, which have already impacted upon the courts. In this legal and social milieu, courts are well counseled to give full range to equitable doctrines in dealing with matrimonial controversies.

The equitable principle of estoppel has been applied broadly and in a wide variety of matrimonial cases. It has been recognized that "in cases involving foreign divorce decrees, as in other situations, . . . the application of the principles of equitable estoppel cannot be subjected to fixed and settled rules of universal application, but rests largely on the facts and circumstances of each particular case." Weber v. Weber, 200 Neb. 659, 666, 265 N.W.2d 436, 441 (Sup.Ct.1978); . . . The equitable rule precluding individuals from attacking foreign divorce decrees "[has] not [been] limited to situations of what might be termed 'true estoppel' where one party induces another to rely to his damage upon certain representations . . .",

Restatement (Second) of Conflict of Laws § 74, Comment b (1971), but has also encompassed situations sometimes termed "quasi-estoppel" where an individual is not permitted to "blow both hot and cold," taking a position inconsistent with prior conduct, if this would injure another, regardless of whether that person has actually relied thereon.

In the overwhelming majority of cases, estoppel has been applied to thwart a spouse from attacking his or her own divorce. Estoppel has also been applied, however, in situations analogous to that presented in this case, to prevent an individual from attacking his spouse's prior divorce.

In a number of cases, courts have forbidden a husband from attacking the prior divorce decree of his wife, where he took an active role in helping her to procure that decree. Estoppel has also been applied, however, where the second husband's involvement in his spouse's prior divorce was relatively passive but, in marrying her, he himself relied on that divorce. The doctrine estopping a party who marries in reliance upon a prior divorce from subsequently attacking that divorce has been widely endorsed. In cases in which several of these factors coalesce, as, for example, where the party seeking to attack the prior foreign divorce of a current spouse was not only aware of that decree but also assisted or helped in its procurement and, further, relied upon it by marrying that person, the claim for an estoppel is especially strong. Akin to the doctrine of estoppel as applied where there is a second marriage is the strong presumption in favor of the validity of the latest of two or more marriages, as well as the corollary presumption that a prior marriage has been lawfully terminated by death or divorce. These presumptions cast a heavy burden on the person objecting to the legality of the last marriage to prove its invalidity by clear and convincing evidence.

Not all courts have been persuaded that the estoppel doctrine is an appropriate judicial tool where there has been a remarriage. Some decisions have condemned application of the doctrine to uphold an invalid foreign divorce decree as tantamount to countenancing bigamy or conferring upon the parties the right to self-help in securing a divorce contrary to the laws of the jurisdiction. These approaches have in turn invited criticism. The State's concern over bigamous conduct need not be undermined by the estoppel doctrine invoked by private parties in civil matrimonial litigations. Clark, "Estoppel Against Jurisdictional Attack on Decrees of Divorce", [70 Yale L.J. 45, at 62 (1960)]. Many courts have expressed the view that it would be even more unseemly and inimical to a sound public policy to permit the spouse of a second marriage to act inconsistently with prior conduct in entering into that marriage. They have stressed that a spouse who has received the benefits of a second marriage should not be able to escape its obligations.

These views comport closely with our current matrimonial policies. Full weight should be given the legislative objectives governing divorce, which reflect a genuine concern for the realities of the marital relationship and allow the expeditious, orderly and fair dissolution of destroyed marriages and call for the protection, financial and otherwise, of the survivors of such marriages, including children. There remains little, if any, interest in encouraging the resurrection of deceased marriages, even if pronounced dead by other tribunals whose processes are not completely consistent with our own. In this context, the estoppel doctrine itself should be a reflection of that public policy and be applied, or not, in accordance with its demands in the circumstances of the given case.

Although the parties here offered different versions of the events which culminated in the Mexican divorce decree, certain matters are not disputed or contested and their differences do not militate against the application of the doctrine of estoppel. Defendant was hardly an ignorant or innocent bystander. He participated in some degree in the decision to obtain the divorce and admitted accompanying plaintiff on her trip to Mexico, at least as far as the border at El Paso. The parties married a month after the divorce and undertook the normal responsibilities of marriage, including the acquisition of a marital home and other assets and the mutual care of plaintiff's children by her first husband. Their married life together lasted for seven years. Additionally, defendant presumably knew that plaintiff's former husband, also in reliance upon the Mexican divorce, remarried and had two children from this second union. Thus, several factors, knowledge, participation, acceptance of benefits and subsequent marriage, establish defendant's nexus with plaintiff's foreign divorce. It would, in our view, be contrary to the public policy reflected in our current laws to permit defendant under these circumstances to attack the validity of his wife's prior Mexican divorce and to repudiate the obligations which he assumed in marrying plaintiff. To that end, he is estopped to assert these particular defenses to plaintiff's marital claims.

. . .

NOTE

In re Goode, 165 Or.App. 327, 997 P.2d 244 (2000), involved a Columbian woman who was married to a Columbian man when the two obtained a Dominican Republic divorce in 1984. The woman then moved to Oregon where she and a second man married. Nonetheless, six years after her marriage to the second husband she obtained an Oregon divorce from the first husband again. She then re-married the second husband in Oregon. A few years passed and she petitioned the Oregon court for a divorce from her second husband and he responded that their first marriage in 1984 was void because she was still married to the first husband then. He argued that the woman's first divorce should be denied comity and thus she was still married to the first husband at the time of her purported marriage to the second. His argument was that comity should not be granted by Oregon because neither of the parties was domiciled in the Dominican Republic at the time of the divorce and thus granting comity would reward forum shopping. Furthermore, the woman should be estopped from asserting the validity of the divorce in 1984 since her divorce from the same marriage six years later in Oregon was premised on her recognition that she was still married. The court rejected the man's arguments and awarded comity to the 1984 divorce. The court reasoned that estoppel is an equitable doctrine and since the man promoted and encouraged the Dominican Republic divorce he should not be able to claim the divorce was invalid in his suit claiming their marriage in 1984 was void.

In Staley v. Staley, 251 Md. 701, 248 A.2d 655 (1968), the wife left Maryland and obtained an ex parte Nevada divorce on January 20, 1965. The following day she married H_2 and one day after that returned with him to Maryland. H_1 was aware of the divorce during the month of the decree and some two months later learned of her remarriage. Wife and H_1 were in court together a number of times afterward concerning child custody, which was awarded to H_1 with visitation rights in wife. Some eighteen months after the Nevada decree, H_1 brought an action for divorce based on desertion. Wife asserted that H_1 was guilty of laches and, following a trial court's award of divorce, appealed on this ground and the question whether H_1 had sustained his burden of proof as to the Nevada court's lack of jurisdiction. Affirming the decision of the trial court, the Court of Appeals noted that the defense of laches requires both the plaintiff's negligence or lack of diligence in asserting his rights *and* prejudice or injury to the defendant; since wife had remarried one day after being divorced it was not considered possible to say that she had suffered prejudice as the result of action or inaction by H_1. As to wife's argument that her relations with her children were prejudiced by the delay because they would know that she had been living in adultery for eighteen months, the court said: "By her own acts she created the domestic situation which she now decries and must suffer the consequences."

In Bartsch v. Bartsch, 204 Va. 462, 132 S.E.2d 416 (1963), the Virginia Court of Appeals, reversing a lower court decision which had set aside a Nevada ex parte divorce decree, held that W_1 was barred by laches from asserting invalidity even for lack of jurisdiction. The divorce was granted in 1939 but the attack came after the husband's death in 1960. The court noted, without being explicit, that there was prejudice to W_2 who, along with W_1, sought to participate in the husband's estate. Some emphasis was placed on the fact that W_1 waited until the death of the husband, who was obviously a key witness, to bring the action.

A recurring problem involves a second spouse who wishes to annul a marriage because of the other spouse's jurisdictionally assailable prior divorce. The majority (though not universal) rule seems to be that such a collateral attack will not be permitted because the new spouse had no interest in the divorce proceeding when it was taking place. The result has been reached both in cases of complicity by the second spouse which would be tantamount to estoppel, and in cases in which there was no knowledge of the prior proceeding at the time. In the latter instance, the courts say that the new spouse simply has no standing to make the attack. *See, e.g.,* Leatherbury v. Leatherbury, 233 Md. 344, 196 A.2d 883 (1964); George v. King, 208 Va. 136, 156 S.E.2d 615 (1967). On the other hand, some courts may entertain an action for fraud in such cases. For a general discussion of estoppel against attacks on divorce decrees based on jurisdiction, *see* HOMER CLARK, THE LAW OF DOMESTIC RELATIONS 434 (2d ed. 1988).

4. THE DOCTRINE OF DIVISIBLE DIVORCE

Newport v. Newport

Supreme Court of Virginia, 1978.
219 Va. 48, 245 S.E.2d 134.

■ HARRISON, JUSTICE.

The issue here is whether in Virginia a wife's right to alimony survives an absolute divorce obtained by the husband in an *ex parte* proceeding in another state.

Elswick Newport and Flora Newport were married in 1947 and moved to Virginia in 1966. The husband, while stationed in Vietnam from April to November, 1972, wrote his wife that he intended to divorce her. Upon his return to the United States Elswick Newport established his residence in Nevada, and on April 2, 1973, he was awarded an *ex parte* divorce from appellee. The only relief granted the husband by the Nevada court was a decree "dissolving the bonds of matrimony heretofore and now existing between the parties".

In May, 1974, Flora Newport, who had been a resident of Fairfax County, Virginia, since 1966, filed her bill of complaint against appellant for separate maintenance and support, alleging that her husband had failed to provide her sufficient support and had left her in "necessitous circumstances". The husband filed an answer in which he alleged that his wife was not eligible for support since a final decree of divorce had been entered in his favor on April 2, 1973, by the Second Judicial District Court of the State of Nevada, in and for the County of Washoe. The husband also filed a cross-bill seeking a partition of their residence property then occupied by the wife. The lower court accorded full faith and credit to the Nevada divorce decree insofar as that decree terminated the marital status of the parties, but held that the Nevada court was without power to adjudicate the question of alimony between the parties, and that its decree dissolving the marriage did not terminate the wife's right to support.

Appellant claims that the court below was without authority, either by statute or under the provisions of the common law, to award the wife permanent alimony, as it did, after a final decree of divorce had been entered by a court of another state having jurisdiction to terminate the marriage. He relies upon Code § 20–107, which, in pertinent part, provides that:

> "Upon decreeing the dissolution of a marriage, and also upon decreeing a divorce, whether from the bond of matrimony or from bed and board, and upon decreeing that neither party is entitled to a divorce, the court may make such further decree as it shall deem expedient concerning

the estate and the maintenance and support of the parties, or either of them.... "[1]

Appellant argues that none of the situations detailed by the Code existed in the instant case when the lower court entered its final decree.

The cases which control generally our decision here are Vanderbilt v. Vanderbilt, 354 U.S. 416, 77 S.Ct. 1360, 1 L.Ed.2d 1456 (1957); Armstrong v. Armstrong, 350 U.S. 568, 76 S.Ct. 629, 100 L.Ed. 705 (1956); and Estin v. Estin, 334 U.S. 541, 68 S.Ct. 1213, 92 L.Ed. 1561 (1948). In *Estin* the wife obtained in New York a judgment of separation and an award of permanent monthly alimony. The husband moved to Nevada, became domiciled there, and obtained an absolute divorce from his wife in an action in which she was not personally served and did not appear. When the husband ceased making alimony payments, the wife sued for the arrearage and recovered a judgment in the New York court. The Supreme Court affirmed, holding that full faith and credit did not require that New York recognize the *ex parte* Nevada decree as one which terminated the wife's right under the decree of New York for alimony. The Court, applying the law of the State of New York, found that the right to alimony did survive the divorce decree, and that Nevada could not adjudicate the question of alimony because the wife was not personally served with process and did not appear. Mr. Justice Douglas, speaking for a majority of the Court, said:

"The result in this situation is to make the divorce divisible—to give effect to the Nevada decree insofar as it affects marital status and to make it ineffective on the issue of alimony. It accommodates the interests of both Nevada and New York in this broken marriage by restricting each State to the matters of her dominant concern.

"Since Nevada had no jurisdiction to alter respondent's rights in the New York judgment, we do not reach the further question whether in any event that judgment would be entitled to full faith and credit in Nevada. [Citations omitted.] And it will be time enough to consider the effect of any discrimination shown to out-of-state ex parte divorces when a State makes that its policy." 334 U.S. at 549, 68 S.Ct. at 1218–1219.

The decision in *Estin* left in doubt the status of a wife's right to alimony which had not been reduced to judgment prior to the entry for the husband of an *ex parte* divorce decree. See Annot., 28 A.L.R.2d 1378 (1953). In *Armstrong* the husband, a resident of Florida, obtained a constructive service divorce from his wife who was a resident of Ohio. In its decree the Florida court stated that the wife had "made no showing of any need on her part for alimony" and decreed that no award of alimony be made to her. Later the wife obtained a judgment in Ohio granting her alimony. The question before the Supreme Court was whether the action of the Ohio court in awarding alimony had the effect of denying full faith and credit to the Florida decree. The Supreme Court interpreted the Florida decree as

---

1. The 1977 amendment deleted "estate and the" following "concerning the" near the middle of the first sentence of the first paragraph of § 20–107.

being one which did not adjudicate the absent wife's right to alimony but merely asserted that it would not pass on the question of alimony, and that, therefore, the court in Ohio, where the wife resided, in awarding alimony to the wife, did not fail to give full faith and credit to the Florida decree.

Significantly, in a concurring opinion in *Armstrong,* written by Mr. Justice Black, and agreed to by Mr. Chief Justice Warren, Mr. Justice Douglas and Mr. Justice Clark, the view was expressed that Florida had in fact dealt with the question of alimony. The concurring Justices rested their opinion on the ground that a judgment denying alimony to a nonresident wife in an *ex parte* divorce proceeding was invalid as a matter of due process, and therefore the decree of the Florida court was not entitled to full faith and credit. Mr. Justice Black thought that *Estin* was controlling, and said:

> "The fact that Mrs. Estin's claim to support had been reduced to judgment prior to divorce while Mrs. Armstrong's had not is not a meaningful distinction. Mrs. Armstrong's right to support before judgment, like Mrs. Estin's right to support after judgment, is the kind of personal right which cannot be adjudicated without personal service. [Citation omitted.]" 350 U.S. at 577, 76 S.Ct. at 634.

The facts in *Vanderbilt* more nearly parallel the facts in the instant case. The parties there were married in 1948 and were living in California at the time of their separation in 1952. The wife moved to New York in February, 1953. In March, 1953, the husband filed suit for divorce in Nevada and obtained a decree of final divorce which provided that both husband and wife were "freed and released from the bonds of matrimony and all the duties and obligations thereof ...". The wife was not served with process in Nevada and did not appear.

In April, 1954, Mrs. Vanderbilt instituted an action in New York praying for separation from her husband and for alimony. The husband appeared specially and contended that the Full Faith and Credit Clause of the United States Constitution compelled the New York court to treat the Nevada divorce as having ended the marriage and as having destroyed any duty of support that he owed the wife. The New York court found the Nevada decree valid insofar as it effectively dissolved the marriage, but, nevertheless, directed the husband to make certain designated support payments to the wife. The Supreme Court, in an opinion by Mr. Justice Black, held:

> "The factor which distinguishes the present case from *Estin* is that here the wife's right to support had not been reduced to judgment prior to the husband's *ex parte* divorce. In our opinion this difference is not material on the question before us. Since the wife was not subject to its jurisdiction, the Nevada divorce court had no power to extinguish any right which she had under the law of New York to financial support from her husband. It has long been the constitutional rule that a court cannot adjudicate a personal claim or obligation unless it has jurisdiction over the person of the defendant. Here, the Nevada divorce court was as powerless to cut off the wife's support right as it would

have been to order the husband to pay alimony if the wife had brought the divorce action and he had not been subject to the divorce court's jurisdiction. Therefore, the Nevada decree, to the extent it purported to affect the wife's right to support, was void and the Full Faith and Credit Clause did not obligate New York to give it recognition." [Footnotes omitted.] 354 U.S. at 418–19, 77 S.Ct. at 1362–1363.

Counsel for appellant argues that *Estin, Armstrong* and *Vanderbilt* stand only for the proposition that whether the right of a wife to alimony survives an *ex parte* divorce decree which dissolves a marriage depends on the law of the state involved....

The entitlement of a wife to alimony was clearly established in West v. West, 126 Va. 696, 101 S.E. 876 (1920), where Judge Prentis, later Chief Justice, referring to a marriage between a man and a woman solemnized one day, that night consummated and terminated the following day, held:

"As the result of that marriage and condonation, he incurred responsibilities from which he cannot and should not escape. Among those responsibilities are his duty, under Code, 1919 sec. 5107, to pay the sums necessary for the maintenance of the woman and to enable her to carry on the suit, and, under section 5111, to pay such proper permanent alimony upon the dissolution of the marriage as the court may decree." 126 Va. at 699, 101 S.E. at 877.

The "divisible divorce concept" under which full faith and credit is given to a divorce decree as to dissolution of a marriage but not as to property and support rights, recognized in *Estin, Armstrong* and *Vanderbilt* was also recognized by us in Isaacs v. Isaacs, 115 Va. 562, 79 S.E. 1072 (1913). There the wife was awarded a divorce *a mensa et thoro* and alimony by a Virginia court. Subsequently, her husband obtained an absolute divorce from her in Kentucky and sought to interpose the Kentucky decree as a bar to enforcement of the wife's lien on his Virginia real estate for alimony payments. While both states had personal jurisdiction over the parties, the alimony awarded by the Virginia court was made before the Kentucky proceedings had been instituted. We recognized the Kentucky decree as a final dissolution of the marriage, but declined to give it effect as to termination of the lien for past and future installments of alimony payable under the Virginia decree.

Counsel for appellee understandably relies upon language found in Osborne v. Osborne, 215 Va. 205, 207 S.E.2d 875 (1974) to support her position. The Osbornes were married in 1962 and lived in Prince William County until 1970 when they moved to Texas. In July, 1971, the parties separated, and Mrs. Osborne returned to Prince William. In February, 1972, Osborne filed a petition in Texas for divorce. Although the wife was not served with process within the State of Texas, she made a general appearance and filed a general denial to Osborne's petition.

In August, 1972, Mrs. Osborne filed a suit in Prince William for an absolute divorce from her husband, alleging constructive desertion. Osborne was personally served with process and filed a plea in abatement asserting that all matters in controversy should be adjudicated in the Texas court. The lower court denied the plea and ordered Osborne to pay certain sums for child support and for alimony *pendente lite*. Thereafter, the Texas court granted Osborne an absolute divorce, gave Mrs. Osborne custody of the children, and directed him to pay $125 per month for the support of each child. Osborne then filed a second plea in abatement, seeking dismissal of the Prince William County, Virginia cause on the ground that all matters in controversy had been settled by the final judgment of the Texas court. The lower court overruled Osborne's plea in abatement, recognized the Texas decree of divorce as a dissolution of the Osborne marriage, but asserted continuing jurisdiction over the matters of child custody, child support and alimony. We held on appeal that the Texas decree must be given full faith and credit as to Mrs. Osborne's marital status, and as to her rights to property and support for herself.

Important to our decision in *Osborne* was the fact that Texas had personal jurisdiction over Mrs. Osborne and gave her the opportunity to litigate her rights. Further, the Texas statutes dealing with the division of property upon dissolution of a marriage provide that the court shall divide the estate of the parties in a manner that the court shall deem just and right. In making the division the court considers virtually the same factors that are considered by a Virginia court in awarding alimony. We said in *Osborne:* "Despite the significant distinctions in the assets that can be used, the flexibility available, and the duration of the award, we conclude that the Texas scheme of economic adjustment upon the dissolution of a marriage seeks to protect the same right as does the award of alimony in Virginia." 215 Va. at 210, 207 S.E.2d at 880. We concluded that if Mrs. Osborne should attempt to raise again in a Texas court the issue of the property division or support for herself, she would be barred by the principle of *res judicata;* and that we were bound by the Texas decision and could not permit Mrs. Osborne to relitigate in Virginia a right which had already been determined by the Texas court.

We have recognized that the general rule, supported by the great weight of authority, is that full faith and credit will be accorded a foreign divorce decree as to property and support rights, as well as to marital status, where the divorce court had personal jurisdiction over the parties; and further, that some jurisdictions have rejected the "divisible divorce" doctrine and have given full faith and credit for all purposes to all foreign *ex parte* divorce decrees. In *Osborne* we left open and undecided the question which is before us in the instant case. Here, the Nevada final decree of divorce was entered before, rather than after, permanent alimony was decreed by the trial court of Virginia. However, while Nevada had no personal jurisdiction over the wife, Virginia did have personal jurisdiction over the appellant-husband.

The considerations that permit the state of the matrimonial domicile to change the marital status of the parties by an *ex parte* divorce proceeding were well stated in *Estin,* where it was said:

"Marital status involves the regularity and integrity of the marriage relation. It affects the legitimacy of the offspring of marriage. It is the basis of criminal laws, as the bigamy prosecution in Williams v. North Carolina, 317 U.S. 287, 63 S.Ct. 207, 87 L.Ed. 279 (1942) dramatically illustrates. The State has a considerable interest in preventing bigamous marriages and in protecting the offspring of marriages from being bastardized. The interest of the State extends to its domiciliaries. The State should have the power to guard its interest in them by changing or altering their marital status and by protecting them in that changed status throughout the farthest reaches of the nation. For a person domiciled in one State should not be allowed to suffer the penalties of bigamy for living outside the State with the only one which the State of his domicile recognizes as his lawful wife. And children born of the only marriage which is lawful in the State of his domicile should not carry the stigma of bastardy when they move elsewhere. These are matters of legitimate concern to the State of the domicile. They entitle the State of the domicile to bring in the absent spouse through constructive service. In no other way could the State of the domicile have and maintain effective control of the marital status of its domiciliaries." 334 U.S. at 546–47, 68 S.Ct. at 1217.

The considerations which impel us to hold that the legal obligation of a husband to support his wife may not be extinguished by a court lacking personal jurisdiction of the wife are equally as strong. In Eaton v. Davis, 176 Va. 330, 338, 10 S.E.2d 893, 897 (1940), we observed:

"The word alimony comes from the Latin *alimonia,* 'sustenance,' and means, therefore, the sustenance or support of the wife by her divorced husband. It stems from the common-law right of the wife to support by her husband, which right, unless the wife by her own misconduct forfeits it, continues to exist even after they cease to live together. Alimony has as its sole object the support of the wife, and is not to be considered a property settlement upon a dissolution of the marriage. It may, however, take the form of either a lump-sum payment or the more usual periodic payments."

In summary, the duty of a husband to support his wife is a moral as well as a legal obligation; it is a marital duty, in the performance of which the public as well as the parties are interested; it is a duty which is an incident to the marriage state and arises from the relation of the marriage; and it is an inherent right which may be asserted in a divorce suit or in an independent suit therefor.

The right of a wife to support is of such importance to the community, as well as to the parties, that it survives an absolute divorce obtained by her husband in an *ex parte* proceeding in another state. Thus we affirm the decree of the lower court which accorded full faith and credit to the Nevada divorce decree insofar as that decree terminated the marital status of appellant and appellee; decreed that the Nevada court was without power to adjudicate the question of alimony; and held that the Nevada decree did not terminate appellee's right to support by appellant.

Affirmed.

NOTE

The concept of divisible divorce, in actuality, involves all of the following: marriage, divorce or annulment, spousal division of property or support, child support, and child custody or visitation. Each of these is divisible because each conceivably could be established or litigated in separate states under separate rules; enforcement or recognition is likewise distinctive for each. But usually the concept is addressed in the context of the separation of divorce from property or support rights, and whether a court has jurisdiction over a physically-absent spouse so as to allow for a property settlement that would comply with due process requirements. *See, e.g.,* Dawson–Austin v. Austin, 968 S.W.2d 319 (Tex.1998), *rev. denied*, 525 U.S. 1067, 119 S.Ct. 795, 142 L.Ed.2d 657 (1999), where the court held there was no minimum contact and hence no personal jurisdiction over the absent spouse when only assets moved to the state by the petitioning husband formed the basis for claimed jurisdiction.

Since jurisdiction for divorce requires jurisdiction over only one spouse, the burden is on the spouse who "sits tight" at home to second guess if the other will establish a true domicile for purposes of divorce. There also must be proper service of process upon the absent spouse. *See, e.g.,* Raymond v. Raymond, 343 Ark. 480, 36 S.W.3d 733 (2001). But even though one spouse may petition for divorce, this does not deprive the other of personal options. In Snider v. Snider, 209 W.Va. 771, 551 S.E.2d 693 (2001), the West Virginia Supreme Court reaffirmed the divisible divorce concept in a suit by the husband to dismiss West Virginia's jurisdiction over him concerning issues of alimony and equitable division of property. As in *Newport*, he argued that since Illinois already dissolved his marriage, West Virginia no longer had jurisdiction to adjudge the wife's personal rights. But the court held that since he had maintained a marital residence in West Virginia, owned real estate there, secured a loan from a state bank, and lived in that property when residing in the state, there were sufficient minimum contacts for jurisdiction over him to resolve the wife's claims even though his divorce in Illinois was entitled to recognition.

In re Marriage of Laine, 34 Kan.App.2d 519, 120 P.3d 802 (2005), involved another set of sit tight facts. The husband and wife had resided in Texas but then the husband moved to Kansas where he established residency and a new life. The wife filed for divorce in Texas and the husband responded there. At that time, the Texas court enjoined the husband from filing any other action concerning the marriage until the Texas court had the opportunity to rule. In spite of this, the husband filed for a divorce in Kansas and petitioned for an award of property he had acquired in Kansas. The Kansas court awarded him a divorce and various pension and investment funds. The wife did not appear in the Kansas proceedings, but did appeal, arguing that Texas had personal jurisdiction over both of the parties and that Texas alone had the right to award the divorce and divide any and all marital property. On appeal, the Kansas court agreed with the wife and set aside the husband's Kansas divorce and division of marital property, allowing the wife's sit tight policy to provide Texas with sole jurisdiction.

D. Special Problems of Service of Process

Kulko v. Superior Court of California

Supreme Court of the United States, 1978.
436 U.S. 84, 98 S.Ct. 1690, 56 L.Ed.2d 132.

■ Mr. Justice Marshall delivered the opinion of the Court.

The issue before us is whether, in this action for child support, the California state courts may exercise *in personam* jurisdiction over a nonresident, nondomiciliary parent of minor children domiciled within the State. For reasons set forth below, we hold that the exercise of such jurisdiction would violate the Due Process Clause of the Fourteenth Amendment.

Appellant Ezra Kulko married appellee Sharon Kulko Horn in 1959, during appellant's three-day stopover in California en route from a military base in Texas to a tour of duty in Korea. At the time of this marriage, both parties were domiciled in and residents of New York State. Immediately following the marriage, Sharon Kulko returned to New York, as did appellant after his tour of duty. Their first child, Darwin, was born to the Kulkos in New York in 1961, and a year later their second child, Ilsa, was born, also in New York. The Kulkos and their two children resided together as a family in New York City continuously until March 1972, when the Kulkos separated.

Following the separation, Sharon Kulko moved to San Francisco, California. A written separation agreement was drawn up in New York; in September 1972, Sharon Kulko flew to New York City in order to sign this agreement. The agreement provided, *inter alia,* that the children would remain with their father during the school year but would spend their Christmas, Easter and summer vacations with their mother. While Sharon Kulko waived any claim for her own support or maintenance, Ezra Kulko agreed to pay his wife $3,000 per year in child support for the periods when the children were in her care, custody and control. Immediately after execution of the separation agreement, Sharon Kulko flew to Haiti and procured a divorce there; the divorce decree incorporated the terms of the agreement. She then returned to California, where she remarried and took the name Horn.

The children resided with appellant during the school year and with their mother on vacations, as provided by the separation agreement, until December 1973. At this time, just before Ilsa was to leave New York to spend Christmas vacation with her mother, she told her father that she wanted to remain in California after her vacation. Appellant bought his daughter a one-way plane ticket, and Ilsa left, taking her clothing with her. Ilsa then commenced living in California with her mother during the school year and spending vacations with her father. In January 1976, appellant's other child, Darwin, called his mother from New York and advised her that he wanted to live with her in California. Unbeknownst to appellant, appellee Horn sent a plane ticket to her son, which he used to fly to California where he took up residence with his mother and sister.

Less than one month after Darwin's arrival in California, appellee Horn commenced this action against appellant in the California Superior Court. She sought to establish the Haitian divorce decree as a California judgment; to modify the judgment so as to award her full custody of the children; and to increase appellant's child support obligations. Appellant appeared specially and moved to quash service of the summons on the ground that he was not a resident of California and lacked sufficient "minimum contacts" with the State under International Shoe Co. v. Washington, 326 U.S. 310, 316, 66 S.Ct. 154, 158, 90 L.Ed. 95 (1945), to warrant the State's assertion of personal jurisdiction over him.

The trial court summarily denied the motion to quash, and appellant sought review in the California Court of Appeal by petition for a writ of mandate. Appellant did not contest the court's jurisdiction for purposes of the custody determination, but, with respect to the claim for increased support, he renewed his argument that the California courts lacked personal jurisdiction over him. The appellate court affirmed the denial of appellant's motion to quash, reasoning that, by consenting to his children's living in California, appellant had "caused an effect in th[e] state" warranting the exercise of jurisdiction over him. 133 Cal.Rptr. 627, 628 (1976).

The California Supreme Court granted appellant's petition for review, and in a 4–2 decision sustained the rulings of the lower state courts. 19 Cal.3d 514, 138 Cal.Rptr. 586, 564 P.2d 353 (1977). It noted first that the California Code of Civil Procedure demonstrated an intent that the courts of California utilize all bases of *in personam* jurisdiction "not inconsistent with the Constitution."[3] Agreeing with the court below, the Supreme Court stated that, where a nonresident defendant has caused an effect in the State by an act or omission outside the State, personal jurisdiction over the defendant in causes arising from that effect may be exercised whenever "reasonable." It went on to hold that such an exercise was "reasonable" in this case because appellant had "purposely availed himself of the benefits and protections of the laws of California" by sending Ilsa to live with her mother in California. While noting that appellant had not, "with respect to his other child, Darwin, caused an effect in [California]"—since it was appellee Horn who had arranged for Darwin to fly to California in January 1976—the court concluded that it was "fair and reasonable for defendant to be subject to personal jurisdiction for the support of both children, where

3. Section 410.10 of the California Code of Civil Procedure provides:

"A court of this state may exercise jurisdiction on any basis not inconsistent with the Constitution of this state or of the United States." The opinion below does not appear to distinguish between the requirements of the Federal and State Constitutions.

he has committed acts with respect to one child which confers [*sic*] personal jurisdiction and has consented to the permanent residence of the other child in California."

. . . We have concluded that jurisdiction by appeal does not lie, but, treating the papers as a petition for a writ of certiorari, we hereby grant the petition and reverse the judgment below.

The Due Process Clause of the Fourteenth Amendment operates as a limitation on the jurisdiction of state courts to enter judgments affecting rights or interests of nonresident defendants. See Shaffer v. Heitner, 433 U.S. 186, 198–200, 97 S.Ct. 2569, 2577, 53 L.Ed.2d 683 (1977). It has long been the rule that a valid judgment imposing a personal obligation or duty in favor of the plaintiff may be entered only by a court having jurisdiction over the person of the defendant. Pennoyer v. Neff, 95 U.S. 714, 732–733, 24 L.Ed. 565, 572 (1878); International Shoe Co. v. Washington, supra, 326 U.S., at 316, 66 S.Ct., at 158. The existence of personal jurisdiction, in turn, depends upon the presence of reasonable notice to the defendant that an action has been brought. Mullane v. Central Hanover Trust Co., 339 U.S. 306, 313–314, 70 S.Ct. 652, 656–657, 94 L.Ed. 865 (1950), and a sufficient connection between the defendant and the forum State as to make it fair to require defense of the action in the forum. In this case, appellant does not dispute the adequacy of the notice that he received, but contends that his connection with the State of California is too attenuated, under the standards implicit in the Due Process Clause of the Constitution, to justify imposing upon him the burden and inconvenience of defense in California.

The parties are in agreement that the constitutional standard for determining whether the State may enter a binding judgment against appellant here is that set forth in this Court's opinion in International Shoe Co. v. Washington, supra: that a defendant "have certain minimum contacts with [the forum state] such that the maintenance of the suit does not offend 'traditional notions of fair play and substantial justice.' "

. . .

Like any standard that requires a determination of "reasonableness," the "minimum contacts" test of *International Shoe* is not susceptible of mechanical application; rather, the facts of each case must be weighed to determine whether the requisite "affiliating circumstances" are present. Hanson v. Denckla, 357 U.S. 235, 246, 78 S.Ct. 1228, 1235, 2 L.Ed.2d 1283 (1958). We recognize that this determination is one in which few answers will be written "in black and white. The greys are dominant and even among them the shades are innumerable." Estin v. Estin, 334 U.S. 541, 545, 68 S.Ct. 1213, 1216, 92 L.Ed. 1561 (1948). But we believe that the California Supreme Court's application of the minimum contacts test in this case represents an unwarranted extension of *International Shoe* and would, if sustained, sanction a result that is neither fair, just, nor reasonable.

In reaching its result, the California Supreme Court did not rely on appellant's glancing presence in the State some 13 years before the events that led to this controversy, nor could it have. Appellant has been in California on only two occasions, once in 1959 for a three-day military stopover on his way to Korea, see p. 1694, supra, and again in 1960 for a 24–hour stopover on his return from Korean service. To hold such temporary visits to a State a basis for the assertion of *in personam* jurisdiction over unrelated actions arising in the future would make a mockery of the limitations on state jurisdiction imposed by the Fourteenth Amendment. Nor did the California court rely on the fact that appellant was actually married in California on one of his two brief visits. We agree that where two New York domiciliaries, for reasons of convenience, marry in the State of California and thereafter spend their entire married life in New York, the fact of their California marriage by itself cannot support a California court's exercise of jurisdiction over a spouse who remains a New York resident in an action relating to child support.

Finally, in holding that personal jurisdiction existed, the court below carefully disclaimed reliance on the fact that appellant had agreed at the time of separation to allow his children to live with their mother three months a year and that he had sent them to California each year pursuant to this agreement. As was noted below, to find personal jurisdiction in a State on this basis, merely because the mother was residing there, would discourage parents from entering into reasonable visitation agreements. Moreover, it could arbitrarily subject one parent to suit in any State of the Union where the other parent chose to spend time while having custody of their offspring pursuant to a separation agreement.[6] As we have emphasized,

> "The unilateral activity of those who claim some relationship with a nonresident defendant cannot satisfy the requirement of contact with the forum State.... [I]t is essential in each case that there be some act by which the defendant purposefully avails [him]self of the privilege of conducting activities within the forum State...." Hanson v. Denckla, supra, 357 U.S., at 253, 78 S.Ct., at 1240.

The "purposeful act" that the California Supreme Court believed did warrant the exercise of personal jurisdiction over appellant in California was his "actively and fully consent[ing] to Ilsa living in California for the school year ... and ... sen[ding] her to California for that purpose." We cannot accept the proposition that appellant's acquiescence in Ilsa's desire to live with her mother conferred jurisdiction over appellant in the California courts in this action. A father who agrees, in the interests of family harmony and his children's preferences, to allow them to spend more time in California than was required under a separation agreement can hardly be said to have "purposefully availed himself" of the "benefits and protec-

---

6. Although the separation agreement stated that appellee Horn resided in California and provided that child-support payments would be mailed to her California address, it also specifically contemplated that appellee might move to a different State. The agreement directed appellant to mail the support payments to appellee's San Francisco address or "any other address which the Wife may designate from time to time in writing."

tion" of California's laws. See Shaffer v. Heitner, supra, 433 U.S., at 216, 97 S.Ct., at 2586.[7]

Nor can we agree with the assertion of the court below that the exercise of *in personam* jurisdiction here was warranted by the financial benefit appellant derived from his daughter's presence in California for nine months of the year. This argument rests on the premise that, while appellant's liability for support payments remained unchanged, his yearly expenses for supporting the child in New York decreased. But this circumstance, even if true, does not support California's assertion of jurisdiction here. Any diminution in appellant's household costs resulted, not from the child's presence in California, but rather from her absence from appellant's home. Moreover, an action by appellee Horn to increase support payments could now be brought, and could have been brought when Ilsa first moved to California, in the State of New York;[8] a New York court would clearly have personal jurisdiction over appellant and, if a judgment were entered by a New York court increasing appellant's child support obligations, it could properly be enforced against him in both New York and California. Any ultimate financial advantage to appellant thus results not from the child's presence in California but from appellee's failure earlier to seek an increase in payments under the separation agreement.[10] The argument below to the contrary, in our view, confuses the question of appellant's liability with that of the proper forum in which to determine that liability.

In light of our conclusion that appellant did not purposefully derive benefit from any activities relating to the State of California, it is apparent that the California Supreme Court's reliance on appellant's having caused an "effect" in California was misplaced. This "effects" test is derived from the American Law Institute's Restatement (Second) of Conflicts § 37 (1971), which provides:

"A state has power to exercise judicial jurisdiction over an individual who causes effects in the state by an act done elsewhere with

---

7. The court below stated that the presence in California of appellant's daughter gave appellant the benefit of California's "police and fire protection, its school system, its hospital services, its recreational facilities, its libraries and museums...." 19 Cal.3d, at 522, 138 Cal.Rptr., at 589, 564 P.2d, at 356. But, in the circumstances presented here, these services provided by the State were essentially benefits to the child, not the father, and in any event were not benefits that appellant purposefully sought for himself.

8. Under the separation agreement, appellant is bound to "indemnify and hold [his] Wife harmless from any and all attorney fees, costs and expenses which she may incur by reason of the default of [appellant] in the performance of any of the obligations required to be performed by him pursuant to

the terms and conditions of this agreement." To the extent that appellee Horn seeks arrearages, her litigation expenses, presumably including any additional costs incurred by appellee as a result of having to prosecute the action in New York, would thus be borne by appellant.

10. It may well be that, as a matter of state law, appellee Horn could still obtain through New York proceedings additional payments from appellant for Ilsa's support from January 1974, when a *de facto* modification of the custody provisions of the separation agreement took place, until the present. See H. Clark, Domestic Relations § 15.2, at 500 (1968); cf. County of Santa Clara v. Hughes, 43 Misc.2d 559, 251 N.Y.S.2d 579 (1964).

respect to any cause of action arising from these effects unless the nature of the effects and of the individual's relationship to the state make the exercise of such jurisdiction unreasonable."[11]

While this provision is not binding on this Court, it does not in any event support the decision below. As is apparent from the examples accompanying § 37 in the Restatement, this section was intended to reach wrongful activity outside of the State causing injury within the State, see, e.g., Comment *a*, p. 157 (shooting bullet from one State into another), or commercial activity affecting state residents, ibid. Even in such situations, moreover, the Restatement recognizes that there might be circumstances that would render "unreasonable" the assertion of jurisdiction over the nonresident defendant.

The circumstances in this case clearly render "unreasonable" California's assertion of personal jurisdiction. There is no claim that appellant has visited physical injury on either property or persons within the State of California. Compare Hess v. Pawloski, 274 U.S. 352, 47 S.Ct. 632, 71 L.Ed. 1091 (1927). The cause of action herein asserted arises, not from the defendant's commercial transactions in interstate commerce, but rather from his personal, domestic relations.... Furthermore, the controversy between the parties arises from a separation that occurred in the State of New York; appellee Horn seeks modification of a contract that was negotiated in New York and that she flew to New York to sign....

Finally, basic considerations of fairness point decisively in favor of appellant's State of domicile as the proper forum for adjudication of this case, whatever the merits of appellee's underlying claim. It is appellant who has remained in the State of the marital domicile, whereas it is appellee who has moved across the continent.

. . .

In seeking to justify the burden that would be imposed on appellant were the exercise of *in personam* jurisdiction in California sustained, appellee argues that California has substantial interests in protecting the welfare of its minor residents and in promoting to the fullest extent possible a healthy and supportive family environment in which the children of the State are to be raised. These interests are unquestionably important. But while the presence of the children and one parent in California arguably might favor application of California law in a lawsuit in New York, the fact that California may be the " 'center of gravity' " for choice of law purposes does not mean that California has personal jurisdiction over the defendant. And California has not attempted to assert any particularized interest in trying such cases in its courts by, e.g., enacting a special jurisdictional statute.

California's legitimate interest in ensuring the support of children resident in California without unduly disrupting the children's lives, more-

---

11. Section 37 of the Restatement has effectively been incorporated into California law. See Judicial Council Comment (9) to California Code Civ.Proc. § 410.10.

over, is already being served by the State's participation in the Uniform Reciprocal Enforcement of Support Act of 1968. This statute provides a mechanism for communication between court systems in different States, in order to facilitate the procurement and enforcement of child-support decrees where the dependent children reside in a State that cannot obtain personal jurisdiction over the defendant. California's version of the Act essentially permits a California resident claiming support from a nonresident to file a petition in California and have its merits adjudicated in the State of the alleged obligor's residence, without either party having to leave his or her own State. Cal.Code Civ.Proc. § 1650 et seq. New York State is a signatory to a similar act. Thus, not only may plaintiff-appellee here vindicate her claimed right to additional child support from her former husband in a New York court, but the uniform acts will facilitate both her prosecution of a claim for additional support and collection of any support payments found to be owed by appellant.[15]

It cannot be disputed that California has substantial interests in protecting resident children and in facilitating child-support actions on behalf of those children. But these interests simply do not make California a "fair forum," Shaffer v. Heitner, supra, 433 U.S., at 215, 97 S.Ct., at 2586, in which to require appellant, who derives no personal or commercial benefit from his child's presence in California and who lacks any other relevant contact with the State, either to defend a child-support suit or to suffer liability by default.

.   .   .

Accordingly, we conclude that the appellant's motion to quash service, on the ground of lack of personal jurisdiction, was erroneously denied by the California courts. The judgment of the California Supreme Court is, therefore,

Reversed.

■ MR. JUSTICE BRENNAN, with whom MR. JUSTICE WHITE and MR. JUSTICE POWELL join, dissenting.

The Court properly treats this case as presenting a single narrow question. That question is whether the California Supreme Court correctly "weighed" "the facts," ante, at 1697, of this particular case in applying the settled "constitutional standard," id., at 1697, that before state courts may exercise *in personam* jurisdiction over a nonresident, nondomiciliary parent of minor children domiciled in the State, it must appear that the nonresident has "certain minimum contacts [with the forum state] such that the maintenance of the suit does not offend 'traditional notions of fair play and substantial justice.' " International Shoe Co. v. Washington, 326 U.S. 310, 316, 66 S.Ct. 154, 158, 90 L.Ed. 95 (1945). The Court recognizes that "this determination is one in which few answers will be written 'in black and

---

15. Thus, it cannot here be concluded, as it was in McGee v. International Life Insurance Co., 355 U.S., at 223–224, 78 S.Ct., at 201, with respect to actions on insurance contracts, that resident plaintiffs would be at a "severe disadvantage" if *in personam* jurisdiction over out-of-state defendants were sometimes unavailable.

white,' " ante, at 1697. I cannot say that the Court's determination against state court *in personam* jurisdiction is implausible, but, though the issue is close, my independent weighing of the facts leads me to conclude, in agreement with the analysis and determination of the California Supreme Court, that appellant's connection with the State of California was not too attenuated, under the standards of reasonableness and fairness implicit in the Due Process Clause, to require him to conduct his defense in the California courts. I therefore dissent.

NOTES

"Family law" long arm statutes. Many states have added specific family law provisions to their "long arm" statutes. Kan. Stat. Ann. § 6–308(b) (Supp. 2003) provides:

> Any person, whether or not a citizen or resident of this state, who in person or through an agent or instrumentality does any of the acts hereinafter enumerated, thereby submits the person and, if an individual, the individual's personal representative, to the jurisdiction of the courts of this state as to any cause of action arising from the doing of any of these acts:
>
> . . .
>
> (8) living in the marital relationship within the state notwithstanding subsequent departure from the state, as to all obligations arising for maintenance, child support or property settlement under article 16 of this chapter, if the other party to the marital relationship continues to reside in the state; . . .

Article 16, to which the statute refers, deals with divorce and maintenance.

As in the Kansas statute's reference to the marital relationship, other long arm statutes often refer to the "matrimonial domicile" at the commencement of the divorce action as the basis for jurisdiction. *See, e.g.,* Strickland v. Strickland, 272 Ga. 855, 534 S.E.2d 74 (2000). In the absence of specific statutory reference to long arm statute, the courts safeguard due process requirements through minimum contact requirements. *See, e.g.,* Sherlock v. Sherlock, 143 N.C.App. 300, 545 S.E.2d 757 (2001), where the court found sufficient minimum contact through the fact that husband administered his important legal, civic, personal, and financial affairs primarily from North Carolina. But in Bushelman v. Bushelman, 246 Wis.2d 317, 629 N.W.2d 795 (2001), the court held that a non-resident husband's consent to his wife and children living in Wisconsin, and his phone calls and letters to them, as well as his visits with them in the state, did not confer minimum contacts for personal jurisdiction. In Cooke v. Cooke, 277 Ga. 731, 594 S.E.2d 370 (2004), the court held that marital domicile of the absent party confers long arm in personam jurisdiction.

Burnham v. Superior Court. In Burnham v. Superior Court of California, 495 U.S. 604, 110 S.Ct. 2105, 109 L.Ed.2d 631 (1990) the petitioner, a New Jersey resident, had been served with a summons and divorce petition by his wife while he was visiting in California. His motion to quash the service was denied in the state courts, and the Supreme Court held that exercise of personal jurisdiction based on serving the defendant while he was in the state comported with traditional notions of fair play and substantial justice. In an opinion by Scalia, J., the court stated:

Petitioner's strongest argument, though we ultimately reject it, relies upon our decision in Shaffer v. Heitner, 433 U.S. 186, 97 S.Ct. 2569, 53 L.Ed.2d 683 (1977). In that case, a Delaware court hearing a shareholder's derivative suit against a corporation's directors secured jurisdiction quasi in rem by sequestering the out-of-State defendants' stock in the company, the situs of which was Delaware under Delaware law. Reasoning that Delaware's sequestration procedure was simply a mechanism to compel the absent defendants to appear in a suit to determine their personal rights and obligations, we concluded that the normal rules we had developed under International Shoe for jurisdiction over suits against absent defendants should apply—viz., Delaware could not hear the suit because the defendants' sole contact with the State (ownership of property there) was unrelated to the lawsuit. 433 U.S., at 213–215, 97 S.Ct., at 2584–2585.

It goes too far to say, as petitioner contends, that Shaffer compels the conclusion that a State lacks jurisdiction over an individual unless the litigation arises out of his activities in the State. Shaffer, like International Shoe, involved jurisdiction over an absent defendant, and it stands for nothing more than the proposition that when the "minimum contact" that is a substitute for physical presence consists of property ownership it must, like other minimum contacts, be related to the litigation. Petitioner wrenches out of its context our statement in Shaffer that "all assertions of state-court jurisdiction must be evaluated according to the standards set forth in International Shoe and its progeny," 433 U.S., at 212, 97 S.Ct., at 2584. When read together with the two sentences that preceded it, the meaning of this statement becomes clear: "The fiction that an assertion of jurisdiction over property is anything but an assertion of jurisdiction over the owner of the property supports an ancient form without substantial modern justification. Its continued acceptance would serve only to allow state-court jurisdiction that is fundamentally unfair to the defendant. 'We therefore conclude that all assertions of state-court jurisdiction must be evaluated according to the standards set forth in International Shoe and its progeny.' Ibid. (emphasis added). Shaffer was saying, in other words, not that all bases for the assertion of in personam jurisdiction (including, presumably, in-state service) must be treated alike and subjected to the 'minimum contacts' analysis of International Shoe; but rather that quasi in rem jurisdiction, that fictional 'ancient form,' and in personam jurisdiction, are really one and the same and must be treated alike—leading to the conclusion that quasi in rem jurisdiction, i.e., that form of in personam jurisdiction based upon a 'property ownership' contact and by definition unaccompanied by personal, in-state service, must satisfy the litigation-relatedness requirement of

International Shoe. The logic of Shaffer's holding—which places all suits against absent nonresidents on the same constitutional footing, regardless of whether a separate Latin label is attached to one particular basis of contact—does not compel the conclusion that physically present defendants must be treated identically to absent ones. As we have demonstrated at length, our tradition has treated the two classes of defendants quite differently, and it is unreasonable to read Shaffer as casually obliterating that distinction. International Shoe confined its 'minimum contacts' requirement to situations in which the defendant 'be not present within the territory of the forum,' " 326 U.S., at 316, 66 S.Ct., at 158, and nothing in Shaffer expands that requirement beyond that.

It is fair to say, however, that while our holding today does not contradict Shaffer, our basic approach to the due process question is different. We have conducted no independent inquiry into the desirability or fairness of the prevailing in-state service rule, leaving that judgment to the legislatures that are free to amend it; for our purposes, its validation is its pedigree, as the phrase "traditional notions of fair play and substantial justice" makes clear. Shaffer did conduct such an independent inquiry, asserting that " 'traditional notions of fair play and substantial justice' can be as readily offended by the perpetuation of ancient forms that are no longer justified as by the adoption of new procedures that are inconsistent with the basic values of our constitutional heritage." 433 U.S., at 212, 97 S.Ct., at 2584. Perhaps that assertion can be sustained when the "perpetuation of ancient forms" is engaged in by only a very small minority of the States. Where, however, as in the present case, a jurisdictional principle is both firmly approved by tradition and still favored, it is impossible to imagine what standard we could appeal to for the judgment that it is "no longer justified." While in no way receding from or casting doubt upon the holding of Shaffer or any other case, we reaffirm today our time-honored approach.... For new procedures, hitherto unknown, the Due Process Clause requires analysis to determine whether "traditional notions of fair play and substantial justice" have been offended. International Shoe, 326 U.S., at 316, 66 S.Ct., at 158. But a doctrine of personal jurisdiction that dates back to the adoption of the Fourteenth Amendment and is still generally observed unquestionably meets that standard.

E. CAN THE PROCESS BE SIMPLIFIED?

The complexity of the divorce process, often involving multiple states and due process concerns over forum shopping by spouses eager to avoid local state laws, prompts suggestions that the federal government take over the entire divorce mechanism and provide uniformity throughout the states. History and the resurgence of federalism mitigate against such proposals. *See generally*, Ronald M. Jacobs, *Defining the Line Between State and Federal Governance*, 69 GEO. WASH. L. REV. 135 (2001); Ernest A. Young, *Dual Federalism, Concurrent Jurisdiction, and the Foreign Affairs Exception*, 69 GEO. WASH. L. REV. 139 (2001); Linda H. Elrod, *Epilogue: Of Families, Federalization, and a Quest* for *Policy*. 33 FAM. L. Q. 843 (1999); STANLEY ELKINS & ERIC MCKITRICK, THE AGE OF FEDERALISM (1993); Ankenbrandt v. Richards, 504 U.S. 689, 112 S.Ct. 2206, 119 L.Ed.2d 468 (1992), affirming the domestic relations exception to federal subject matter jurisdiction. A more feasible approach is a trend towards mediation and the avoidance of attorneys in the process. Mediation may facilitate custody and visitation issues and even when there are few marital assets and the couple has no children, summary dissolution as is exemplified in the California statute that follows, would be helpful. There have been a few cases of alleged misconduct by mediators. *See, e.g.*, Vitakis–Valchine v. Valchine, 793 So.2d 1094, 2001 WL 953412 (Fla.App.2001). The mediator's misconduct may be a ground to overturn a marital agreement. As to mediation, *see generally* Marsha B. Freeman, *Divorce Mediation: Sweeping Conflicts Under the Rug, Time to Cleans House*, 78 U. DET. L. REV. 67 (2000); Judge Diane K. Vescovo, Allen S. Blair and Hayden D. Lait, *Ethical Dilemmas in Mediation,* 31 I. MIAMI L. REV. 59 (2000); Carol Bruch, *When to Use and When to Avoid Mediation*, 31 FAM. AND CONCILIATION COURTS REV. 101 (1993).

Divorce has become a matter of negotiation rather than litigation in many cases, as the material in the following chapters will reveal. Not surprisingly, disputes have reached the courts concerning roles which may be played by non-lawyers (e.g., selling forms, or helping complete them) without running afoul of proscriptions against unauthorized legal practice. But the majority of complaints have come from allegations or proof of lawyer misconduct. These include: (1) misuse of the legal process, Caudle v. Mendel, 994 P.2d 372 (Alaska 1999); (2) having sexual relationships with clients in a divorce action, *In re* Halverson, 140 Wn.2d 475, 998 P.2d 833 (2000); *see also In re* Tsoutsouris, 748 N.E.2d 856 (Ind.2001); Iowa Supreme Court Bd. of Professional Ethics and Conduct v. Furlong, 625 N.W.2d 711 (Iowa 2001); (3) equitable indemnity, Gursey Schneider & Co. v. Wasser, Rosenson & Carter, 90 Cal.App.4th 1367, 109 Cal.Rptr.2d 678 (2001), as modified on denial of rehearing, 2001 Cal. App. LEXIS 665 (Cal. Dist. Ct. App. Aug. 23, 2001); (4) malpractice, Fang v. Bock, 305 Mont. 322, 28 P.3d 456 (2001); (5) intentional infliction of emotional distress, Gaspard v. Beadle, 36 S.W.3d 229 (Tex.App.2001). For a general review of the attorney-client role in the process of divorce, *see* Carrie J. Menkel–Meadow, *When Winning Isn't Everything: The Lawyer as Problem Solver*, 28 HOFSTRA L. REV. 905 (2000); Marianne M. Jennings, *Moral Disengagement and Lawyers: Codes, Ethics, Conscience, and Some Great Movies*, 37 DUQ. L. REV. 637 (2000).

CHAPTER V

MARITAL BREAKDOWN: RESOLVING THE FINANCIAL CONCERNS

A. ALIMONY AND PROPERTY DISTRIBUTION: THE BASIC FRAMEWORKS

1. INTRODUCTION

Originally, support during marriage was the responsibility of the husband in return for the wife's services and sometimes the economic dowry the wife brought to the marriage. Likewise, after marriage alimony originated in English law as a continuing duty of support owed by husband to wife during a period of separation "from bed and board" described by the ecclesiastical courts as a divorce "*a mensa et thoro.*" During this period of support neither party could remarry because the bond of matrimony was indissoluble and still intact; thus support was part of the continuing duty owed by the husband to his wife. Today, support or maintenance awards during periods of physical and legal separation mirror this practice, but awards are made without reference to gender. Whenever a couple was able to obtain a Parliamentary divorce, one which allowed for the bond of matrimony to be severed absolutely (*a vinculo*), each spouse was able to marry another and technically the prior marriage and support duty of the prior spouse ceased. This complete cessation of marriage and support—a "clean break"—is attained infrequently in modern society and legislatures and courts grapple with two distinct elements of financial concern: (1) distribution of marital assets, and (2) providing for martial support, or what the American Law Institute terms compensatory spousal payments. A third financial concern is child support and this is addressed in a separate chapter, but nonetheless completes the legal spectrum of resolving financial concerns for purposes of entitlement and enforcement.

In making distributions of marital property and/or marital support, American jurisdictions may be grouped under two general classifications: (1) common law or equitable property states, and (2) community property states. More often than not there is overlap between these two in approach so that any precise delineation is impossible. Nonetheless, traditionally the common law states recognize title—ownership—in one of the marital partners and then use equitable principles to apportion between both parties. Community property states tend to disregard title in one partner with a presumption that everything acquired with spousal labor during the marriage is the property of the community in which each spouse has an undivided one-half interest without regard to equitable principles. Again, the two systems often overlap depending on state statutes and the discretion of the trial court, the latter being very extensive. Discretion in the distribution of the marital property and/or support payments will likely be based upon one or more of the following approaches:

(1) *Fault.* One of the oldest bases for awarding property or support is spousal misconduct: conduct which goes to the heart of the marriage (marital) or economic (dissipation or concealment). A number of common law and community property states allow courts to consider either or both types of fault, but some states adopt the position of the Uniform Marriage and Divorce Act and eliminate any consideration of fault as a basis for awarding property or support.

(2) *Station in Life/Need and Ability.* Using both property and support payments, courts seek to provide for "reimbursement" to a spouse who contributed to the enhanced earning capacity of the other, or "rehabilitation" after an extended period of service to the marital enterprise sacrificing personal earning capacity. To meet the spouse's need or to provide for a maintenance of the spouse's station in life, extended support payments are made, often resembling alimony. The American Law Institute uses the term compensatory payments to signify a shift from need and ability to loss and the necessity to compensate the loss a spouse experiences when the marriage ends and future economic gains yet-to-be-derived from the marriage are withdrawn. Spousal age, health and the length of the marriage will impact the duration of the support award when marital property is insufficient to divide at divorce and meet the goals of the court.

(3) *Economic Partnership.* Similar in approach to community property states which come closest to elimination of equitable distribution, the court defines assets derived from community labor and separates those retained as separate and divides the community/marital assets equally. Support may still be justified to either reimburse or rehabilitate (compensate) either spouse when community/marital assets are insufficient in achieving this goal. In rejecting equity this approach also denies recovery for non-economic expectations or disappointments.

(4) *Support.* As with station in life, equities, support or an unequal division of property may be justified to provide a standard of living for the child custodian spouse, or it may be necessary to prevent a non-income earning spouse from needing public welfare.

Each of these approaches has a basis in statute but its effect will be demonstrated in the discretion of the trial judge able to define property or utilize equitable distribution and order support when marital assets are insufficient. Judicial discretion is portentous. Any critique today of criteria must consider the rapidly changing public policy underpinnings of each, especially gender stereotyping, domestic violence, indissolubility of marriage, poverty and the single parent, expansion of tort remedies, practicality and collection techniques, and the contrast between individual and state control over the status of marriage. Additionally, because every state allows no-fault divorce and thus the ability of one spouse to unilaterally terminate the marriage in most jurisdictions, parties must plan for the unexpected.

The material presented offers two statutory models. New York is representative of the common law states acknowledgment of ownership through title. To indemnify either party the legislature adopted a list of equitable factors from which the court may choose to fairly apportion marital assets and, if necessary provide for support. Equitable distribution has actually decreased the importance of alimony as it was utilized to provide support for a former spouse with no title over property; alimony was premised upon the marriage itself. Divorce courts are given more authority to make division of property and support awards based on factors approved by the legislature, thus providing at least a basis for uniformity in the jurisdiction. Issues such as fault, duration of any award, and defining property such as income producing education and goodwill continue to challenge common law states.

The second statutory approach typifies community property states. California is most often used even though that state provides a "clean break" from equitable principles. Eight states and perhaps another, Wisconsin, have adopted the community property system of wealth transfer. This is a system originating with the Visigoth tribes in Europe and then the Spanish conquerors occupying parts of the United States. Title is unimportant, all property acquired during marriage being presumed to be community property and thus divided equally upon divorce. Spousal support is allowed but only in those instances to redress loss of earning capacity, expectations or the destruction or concealment of community assets.

Particular attention should be given to the ability of adult parties at the time of their marriage to structure the outcome of property distribution upon any separation or divorce through provisions accommodated in the Uniform Premarital Agreement Act. Fairness, full disclosure and the opportunity for attorneys to structure parties' expectations at the beginning of marriage, limit the courts and legislatures from artificially constructing what the parties could have expected or contributed. Increasingly, periods of non-marital cohabitation precede the marriage and this too deserves incorporation into marital agreements.

Finally, modern courts give the parties significant discretion to order economic affairs between themselves as long as such discretion does not impinge on the rights of children. Thus, parties may enter into post-nuptial agreements or separation agreements in contemplation of divorce. In such instances attorneys and mediators serve as negotiators with the various statutory models operating as default governors. Such negotiation involves expertise in taxation, bankruptcy, torts, contracts, federal and state enforcement techniques and of course professional responsibility. *See generally* www.divorcesupport.com/spousal/support/spousal.shtml.

2. APPROACH OF A COMMON LAW/EQUITABLE DISTRIBUTION STATE

All common law states have enacted statutory lists of equitable distribution factors to accommodate the fact that title to property may be held in the name of one spouse even though it was acquired during marriage as a result of marital labor. The factors are to be utilized by trial judges in a fair allocation of property, but preference among the factors is missing and hence the judges possess immense discretion. This promotes unpredictability in distribution. *See, e.g.,* Marsha Garrison, *How Do Judges Decide Divorce Cases? An Empirical Analysis of Discretionary Decision Making,* 74 N. CAR. L. REV. 401 (1996). For a state court analysis, *see* Charles P. Kindregan, Jr. and Monroe L. Inker, *A Quarter Century of Allocating Spousal Property Interests: The Massachusetts Experience,* 33 SUFF. L. REV. 11 (1999). Duration of marriage, contributions made to the acquisition of marital property and economic circumstances of the parties at the commencement of the marriage are among the most common factors in any statute. *See* ALI, PRINCIPLES OF THE LAW OF FAMILY DISSOLUTION: ANALYSIS AND RECOMMENDATIONS: PROPOSED FINAL DRAFT PART I, CH. 4, § 4:15, COMMENT A, 206–207 (FEB. 14, 1997). The New York state statute listing factors as equitable is a prime example of one state's common law approach. One author writes that the proportion of divorces in New York state where alimony was awarded declined from 21 percent to 12 percent after the state adopted its statute containing its equitable factors. *Id.* at 302, quoting Marsha Garrison, *Good Intentions Gone Awry: The Impact of New York's Equitable Distribution Law on Divorce Outcomes,* 57 BROOK. L. REV. 621, 697 (1991). But distinctions must be made between alimony (support) and division of marital property.

The statute is offered to provide a comprehensive exploration of a common law approach to the three financial concerns of this chapter: marital property, spousal support and child support. Specific definitions of what constitutes marital property, and issues concerning child support will be discussed specifically *infra.* For information concerning counseling, support and resources connected to divorce and support issues, *see* www. webcrawler.com/relationships/divorce or in www.divorcenet.com/fla.html.

NEW YORK DOMESTIC RELATIONS LAW (McKinney 2007)

§ 236, Part B.

NEW ACTIONS OR PROCEEDINGS

Maintenance and distributive award. 1. Definitions. Whenever used in this part, the following terms shall have the respective meanings hereinafter set forth or indicated:

a. The term "maintenance" shall mean payments provided for in a valid agreement between the parties or awarded by the court in accordance with the provisions of subdivision six of this part, to be paid at fixed intervals for a definite or indefinite period of time, but an award of maintenance shall terminate upon the death of either party or upon the recipient's valid or invalid marriage, or upon modification pursuant to paragraph (b) of subdivision nine of section two hundred thirty-six of this part or section two hundred forty-eight of this chapter.

b. The term "distributive award" shall mean payments provided for in a valid agreement between the parties or awarded by the court, in lieu of or to supplement, facilitate or effectuate the division or distribution of property where authorized in a matrimonial action, and payable either in a lump sum or over a period of time in fixed amounts. Distributive awards shall not include payments which are treated as ordinary income to the recipient under the provisions of the United States Internal Revenue Code.

c. The term "marital property" shall mean all property acquired by either or both spouses during the marriage and before the execution of a separation agreement or the commencement of a matrimonial action, regardless of the form in which title is held, except as otherwise provided in agreement pursuant to subdivision three of this part. Marital property shall not include separate property as hereinafter defined.

d. The term separate property shall mean:

(1) property acquired before marriage or property acquired by bequest, devise, or descent, or gift from a party other than the spouse;

(2) compensation for personal injuries;

(3) property acquired in exchange for or the increase in value of separate property, except to the extent that such appreciation is due in part to the contributions or efforts of the other spouse;

(4) property described as separate property by written agreement of the parties pursuant to subdivision three of this part.

e. The term "custodial parent" shall mean a parent to whom custody of a child or children is granted by a valid agreement between the parties or by an order or decree of a court.

f. The term "child support" shall mean a sum paid pursuant to court order or decree by either or both parents or pursuant to a valid agreement between the parties for care, maintenance and education of any unemancipated child under the age of twenty-one years.

2. Matrimonial actions. Except as provided in subdivision five of this part, the provisions of this part shall be applicable to actions for an annulment or dissolution of a marriage, for a divorce, for a separation, for a declaration of the nullity of a void marriage, for a declaration of the validity or nullity of a foreign judgment of divorce, for a declaration of the validity or nullity of a marriage, and to proceedings to obtain maintenance or a distribution of marital property following a foreign judgment of divorce, commenced on and after the effective date of this part. Any application which seeks a modification of a judgment, order or decree made in an action commenced prior to the effective date of this part shall be heard and determined in accordance with the provisions of part A of this section.

3. Agreement of the parties. An agreement by the parties, made before or during the marriage, shall be valid and enforceable in a matrimonial action if such agreement is in writing, subscribed by the parties, and acknowledged or proven in the manner required to entitle a deed to be recorded. Notwithstanding any other provision of law, an acknowledgment

of an agreement made before marriage may be executed before any person authorized to solemnize a marriage pursuant to subdivisions one, two and three of section eleven of this chapter. Such an agreement may include (1) a contract to make a testamentary provision of any kind, or a waiver of any right to elect against the provisions of a will; (2) provision for the ownership, division or distribution of separate and marital property; (3) provision for the amount and duration of maintenance or other terms and conditions of the marriage relationship, subject to the provisions of section 5–311 of the general obligations law, and provided that such terms were fair and reasonable at the time of the making of the agreement and are not unconscionable at the time of entry of final judgment; and (4) provision for the custody, care, education and maintenance of any child of the parties, subject to the provisions of section two hundred forty of this article. Nothing in this subdivision shall be deemed to affect the validity of any agreement made prior to the effective date of this subdivision.

4. Compulsory financial disclosure. a. In all matrimonial actions and proceedings in which alimony, maintenance or support is in issue, there shall be compulsory disclosure by both parties of their respective financial states. No showing of special circumstances shall be required before such disclosure is ordered. A sworn statement of net worth shall be provided upon receipt of a notice in writing demanding the same, within twenty days after the receipt thereof. In the event said statement is not demanded, it shall be filed with the clerk of the court by each party, within ten days after joinder of issue, in the court in which the proceeding is pending. As used in this part, the term "net worth" shall mean the amount by which total assets including income exceed total liabilities including fixed financial obligations. It shall include all income and assets of whatsoever kind and nature and wherever situated and shall include a list of all assets transferred in any manner during the preceding three years, or the length of the marriage, whichever is shorter; provided, however that transfers in the routine course of business which resulted in an exchange of assets of substantially equivalent value need not be specifically disclosed where such assets are otherwise identified in the statement of net worth. All such sworn statements of net worth shall be accompanied by a current and representative paycheck stub and the most recently filed state and federal income tax returns including a copy of the W–2(s) wage and tax statement(s) submitted with the returns. In addition, both parties shall provide information relating to any and all group health plans available to them for the provision of care or other medical benefits by insurance or otherwise for the benefit of the child or children for whom support is sought, including all such information as may be required to be included in a qualified medical child support order as defined in section six hundred nine of the employee retirement income security act of 1974 (29 USC 1169) including, but not limited to: (i) the name and last known mailing address of each party and of each dependent to be covered by the order; (ii) the identification and a description of each group health plan available for the benefit or coverage of the disclosing party and the child or children for whom support is sought; (iii) a detailed description of the type of coverage

available from each group health plan for the potential benefit of each such dependent; (iv) the identification of the plan administrator for each such group health plan and the address of such administrator; (v) the identification numbers for each such group health plan; and (vi) such other information as may be required by the court. Noncompliance shall be punishable by any or all of the penalties prescribed in section thirty-one hundred twenty-six of the civil practice law and rules, in examination before or during trial.

b. As soon as practicable after a matrimonial action has been commenced, the court shall set the date or dates the parties shall use for the valuation of each asset. The valuation date or dates may be anytime from the date of commencement of the action to the date of trial.

5. Disposition of property in certain matrimonial actions.

a. Except where the parties have provided in an agreement for the disposition of their property pursuant to subdivision three of this part, the court, in an action wherein all or part of the relief granted is divorce, or the dissolution, annulment or declaration of the nullity of a marriage, and in proceedings to obtain a distribution of marital property following a foreign judgment of divorce, shall determine the respective rights of the parties in their separate or marital property, and shall provide for the disposition thereof in the final judgment.

b. Separate property shall remain such.

c. Marital property shall be distributed equitably between the parties, considering the circumstances of the case and of the respective parties.

d. In determining an equitable disposition of property under paragraph c, the court shall consider:

(1) the income and property of each party at the time of marriage, and at the time of the commencement of the action;

(2) the duration of the marriage and the age and health of both parties;

(3) the need of a custodial parent to occupy or own the marital residence and to use or own its household effects;

(4) the loss of inheritance and pension rights upon dissolution of the marriage as of the date of dissolution;

(5) any award of maintenance under subdivision six of this part;

(6) any equitable claim to, interest in, or direct or indirect contribution made to the acquisition of such marital property by the party not having title, including joint efforts or expenditures and contributions and services as a spouse, parent, wage earner and homemaker, and to the career or career potential of the other party;

(7) the liquid or non-liquid character of all marital property;

(8) the probable future financial circumstances of each party;

(9) the impossibility or difficulty of evaluating any component asset or any interest in a business, corporation or profession, and the economic

desirability of retaining such asset or interest intact and free from any claim or interference by the other party;

(10) the tax consequences to each party;

(11) the wasteful dissipation of assets by either spouse;

(12) any transfer or encumbrance made in contemplation of a matrimonial action without fair consideration;

(13) any other factor which the court shall expressly find to be just and proper.

e. In any action in which the court shall determine that an equitable distribution is appropriate but would be impractical or burdensome or where the distribution of an interest in a business, corporation or profession would be contrary to law, the court in lieu of such equitable distribution shall make a distributive award in order to achieve equity between the parties. The court in its discretion, also may make a distributive award to supplement, facilitate or effectuate a distribution of marital property.

f. In addition to the disposition of property as set forth above, the court may make such order regarding the use and occupancy of the marital home and its household effects as provided in section two hundred thirty-four of this chapter, without regard to the form of ownership of such property.

g. In any decision made pursuant to this subdivision, the court shall set forth the factors it considered and the reasons for its decision and such may not be waived by either party or counsel.

h. In any decision made pursuant to this subdivision the court shall, where appropriate, consider the effect of a barrier to remarriage, as defined in subdivision six of section two hundred fifty-three of this article, on the factors enumerated in paragraph d of this subdivision.

6. Maintenance. a. Except where the parties have entered into an agreement pursuant to subdivision three of this part providing for maintenance, in any matrimonial action the court may order temporary maintenance or maintenance in such amount as justice requires, having regard for the standard of living of the parties established during the marriage, whether the party in whose favor maintenance is granted lacks sufficient property and income to provide for his or her reasonable needs and whether the other party has sufficient property or income to provide for the reasonable needs of the other and the circumstances of the case and of the respective parties. Such order shall be effective as of the date of the application therefor, and any retroactive amount of maintenance due shall be paid in one sum or periodic sums, as the court shall direct, taking into account any amount of temporary maintenance which has been paid. In determining the amount and duration of maintenance the court shall consider:

(1) the income and property of the respective parties including marital property distributed pursuant to subdivision five of this part;

(2) the duration of the marriage and the age and health of both parties;

(3) the present and future earning capacity of both parties;

(4) the ability of the party seeking maintenance to become self-supporting and, if applicable, the period of time and training necessary therefor;

(5) reduced or lost lifetime earning capacity of the party seeking maintenance as a result of having foregone or delayed education, training, employment, or career opportunities during the marriage;

(6) the presence of children of the marriage in the respective homes of the parties;

(7) the tax consequences to each party;

(8) contributions and services of the party seeking maintenance as a spouse, parent, wage earner and homemaker, and to the career or career potential of the other party;

(9) the wasteful dissipation of marital property by either spouse; (10) any transfer or encumbrance made in contemplation of a matrimonial action without fair consideration; and

(11) any other factor which the court shall expressly find to be just and proper.

b. In any decision made pursuant to this subdivision, the court shall set forth the factors it considered and the reasons for its decision and such may not be waived by either party or counsel.

c. The court may award permanent maintenance, but an award of maintenance shall terminate upon the death of either party or upon the recipient's valid or invalid marriage, or upon modification pursuant to paragraph (b) of subdivision nine of section two hundred thirty-six of this part or section two hundred forty-eight of this chapter.

d. In any decision made pursuant to this subdivision the court shall, where appropriate, consider the effect of a barrier to remarriage, as defined in subdivision six of section two hundred fifty-three of this article, on the factors enumerated in paragraph a of this subdivision.

7. Child Support. a. In any matrimonial action, or in an independent action for child support, the court as provided in section two hundred forty of this chapter shall order either or both parents to pay temporary child support or child support without requiring a showing of immediate or emergency need. The court shall make an order for temporary child support notwithstanding that information with respect to income and assets of either or both parents may be unavailable. Where such information is available, the court may make an order for temporary child support pursuant to section two hundred forty of this article. Such order shall, except as provided for herein, be effective as of the date of the application therefor, and any retroactive amount of child support due shall be support arrears/past due support and shall be paid in one sum or periodic sums, as

the court shall direct, taking into account any amount of temporary child support which has been paid. In addition, such retroactive child support shall be enforceable in any manner provided by law including, but not limited to, an execution for support enforcement pursuant to subdivision (b) of section fifty-two hundred forty-one of the civil practice law and rules. When a child receiving support is a public assistance recipient, or the order of support is being enforced or is to be enforced pursuant to section one hundred eleven-g of the social services law, the court shall establish the amount of retroactive child support and notify the parties that such amount shall be enforced by the support collection unit pursuant to an execution for support enforcement as provided for in subdivision (b) of section fifty-two hundred forty-one of the civil practice law and rules, or in such periodic payments as would have been authorized had such an execution been issued. In such case, the court shall not direct the schedule of repayment of retroactive support. The court shall not consider the misconduct of either party but shall make its award for child support pursuant to section two hundred forty of this article.

b.   Notwithstanding any other provision of law, any written application or motion to the court for the establishment of a child support obligation for persons not in receipt of family assistance must contain either a request for child support enforcement services which would authorize the collection of the support obligation by the immediate issuance of an income execution for support enforcement as provided for by this chapter, completed in the manner specified in section one hundred eleven-g of the social services law; or a statement that the applicant has applied for or is in receipt of such services; or a statement that the applicant knows of the availability of such services, has declined them at this time and where support enforcement services pursuant to section one hundred eleven-g of the social services law have been declined that the applicant understands that an income deduction order may be issued pursuant to subdivision (c) of section five thousand two hundred forty-two of the civil practice law and rules without other child support enforcement services and that payment of an administrative fee may be required. The court shall provide a copy of any such request for child support enforcement services to the support collection unit of the appropriate social services district any time it directs payments to be made to such support collection unit. Additionally, the copy of any such request shall be accompanied by the name, address and social security number of the parties; the date and place of the parties' marriage; the name and date of birth of the child or children; and the name and address of the employers and income payors of the party from whom child support is sought. Unless the party receiving child support has applied for or is receiving such services, the court shall not direct such payments to be made to the support collection unit, as established in section one hundred eleven-h of the social services law.

c.   The court shall direct that a copy of any child support or combined child and spousal support order issued by the court on or after the first day of October, nineteen hundred ninety-eight, in any proceeding under this section be provided promptly to the state case registry established pursuant to subdivision four-a of section one hundred eleven-b of the social services law.

8. Special relief in matrimonial actions. a. In any matrimonial action the court may order a party to purchase, maintain or assign a policy of insurance providing benefits for health and hospital care and related services for either spouse or children of the marriage not to exceed such period of time as such party shall be obligated to provide maintenance, child support or make payments of a distributive award. The court may also order a party to purchase, maintain or assign a policy of accident insurance or insurance on the life of either spouse, and to designate in the case of life insurance, either spouse or children of the marriage, or in the case of accident insurance, the insured spouse as irrevocable beneficiaries during a period of time fixed by the court. The obligation to provide such insurance shall cease upon the termination of the spouse's duty to provide maintenance, child support or a distributive award. A copy of such order shall be served, by registered mail, on the home office of the insurer specifying the name and mailing address of the spouse or children, provided that failure to so serve the insurer shall not effect the validity of the order.

b. In any action where the court has ordered temporary maintenance, maintenance, distributive award or child support, the court may direct that a payment be made directly to the other spouse or a third person for real and personal property and services furnished to the other spouse, or for the rental or mortgage amortization or interest payments, insurances, taxes, repairs or other carrying charges on premises occupied by the other spouse, or for both payments to the other spouse and to such third persons. Such direction may be made notwithstanding that the parties continue to reside in the same abode and notwithstanding that the court refuses to grant the relief requested by the other spouse.

c. Any order or judgment made as in this section provided may combine any amount payable to either spouse under this section with any amount payable to such spouse as child support or under section two hundred forty of this chapter.

9. Enforcement and modification of orders and judgments in matrimonial actions.

a. All orders or judgments entered in matrimonial actions shall be enforceable pursuant to section fifty-two hundred forty-one or fifty-two hundred forty-two of the civil practice law and rules, or in any other manner provided by law. Orders or judgments for child support, alimony and maintenance shall also be enforceable pursuant to article fifty-two of the civil practice law and rules upon a debtor's default as such term is defined in paragraph seven of subdivision (a) of section fifty-two hundred forty-one of the civil practice law and rules. The establishment of a default shall be subject to the procedures established for the determination of a mistake of fact for income executions pursuant to subdivision (e) of section fifty-two hundred forty-one of the civil practice law and rules. For the purposes of enforcement of child support orders or combined spousal and child support orders pursuant to section five thousand two hundred forty-one of the civil practice law and rules, a "default" shall be deemed to include amounts arising from retroactive support. The court may, and if a party shall fail or refuse to pay maintenance, distributive award or child support the court shall, upon notice and an opportunity to the defaulting party to be heard, require the party to furnish a surety, or the sequestering and sale of assets for the purpose of enforcing any award for maintenance, distributive award or child support and for the payment of reasonable and necessary attorney's fees and disbursements.

b.   Upon application by either party, the court may annul or modify any prior order or judgment as to maintenance or child support, upon a showing of the recipient's inability to be self-supporting or a substantial change in circumstance or termination of child support awarded pursuant to section two hundred forty of this article, including financial hardship. Where, after the effective date of this part, a separation agreement remains in force no modification of a prior order or judgment incorporating the terms of said agreement shall be made as to maintenance without a showing of extreme hardship on either party, in which event the judgment or order as modified shall supersede the terms of the prior agreement and judgment for such period of time and under such circumstances as the court determines. Provided, however, that no modification or annulment shall reduce or annul any arrears of child support which have accrued prior to the date of application to annul or modify any prior order or judgment as to child support. The court shall not reduce or annul any arrears of maintenance which have been reduced to final judgment pursuant to section two hundred forty-four of this chapter. No other arrears of mainte-nance which have accrued prior to the making of such application shall be subject to modification or annulment unless the defaulting party shows good cause for failure to make application for relief from the judgment or order directing such payment prior to the accrual of such arrears and the facts and circumstances constituting good cause are set forth in a written memorandum of decision. Such modification may increase maintenance or child support nunc pro tunc as of the date of application based on newly discovered evidence. Any retroactive amount of maintenance, or child support due shall, except as provided for herein, be paid in one sum or periodic sums, as the court directs, taking into account any temporary or partial payments which have been made. Any retroactive amount of child support due shall be support arrears/past due support. In addition, such retroactive child support shall be enforceable in any manner provided by law including, but not limited to, an execution for support enforcement pursuant to subdivision (b) of section fifty-two hundred forty-one of the civil practice law and rules. When a child receiving support is a public assistance recipient, or the order of support is being enforced or is to be enforced pursuant to section one hundred eleven-g of the social services law, the court shall establish the amount of retroactive child support and notify the parties that such amount shall be enforced by the support collection unit pursuant to an execution for support enforcement as provid-ed for in subdivision (b) of section fifty-two hundred forty-one of the civil practice law and rules, or in such periodic payments as would have been authorized had such an execution been issued. In such case, the court shall not direct the schedule of repayment of retroactive support. The provisions of this subdivision shall not apply to a separation agreement made prior to the effective date of this part.

c.   Notwithstanding any other provision of law, any written application or motion to the court for the modification or enforcement of a child support or combined maintenance and child support order for persons not in receipt of family assistance must contain either a request for child support enforcement services which would authorize the collection of the support obligation by the immediate issuance of an income execution for support enforcement as provided for by this chapter, completed in the manner specified in section one hundred eleven-g of the social services law; or a statement that the applicant has applied for or is in receipt of such services; or a statement that the applicant knows of the availability of such services, has declined them at this time and where support enforcement services pursuant to section one hundred eleven-g of the social services law have been declined that the applicant understands that an income deduction order may be issued pursuant to subdivision (c) of section five thousand two hundred forty-two of the civil practice law and rules without other child support enforcement services and that payment of an administrative fee may be required. The court shall provide a copy of any such request for child support enforcement services to the support collection unit of the appropriate social services district any time it directs payments to be made to such support collection unit. Additionally, the copy of such request shall be accompanied by the name, address and social security number of the parties; the date and place of the parties' marriage; the name and date of birth of the child or children; and the name and address of the employers and income payors of the party ordered to pay child support to the other party.

Unless the party receiving child support or combined maintenance and child support has applied for or is receiving such services, the court shall not direct such payments to be made to the support collection unit, as established in section one hundred eleven-h of the social services law.

d. The court shall direct that a copy of any child support or combined child and spousal support order issued by the court on or after the first day of October, nineteen hundred ninety-eight, in any proceeding under this section be provided promptly to the state case registry established pursuant to subdivision four-a of section one hundred eleven-b of the social services law.

3.   APPROACH OF A COMMUNITY PROPERTY STATE

Ruggles v. Ruggles

Supreme Court of New Mexico, 1993.
116 N.M. 52, 860 P.2d 182.

■ MONTGOMERY, JUSTICE.

We ... revisit a subject of recurring concern in our case law: the proper treatment, in a proceeding to dissolve a marriage, of the spouses' community property interest in an employer-sponsored retirement plan. We deem this subject to involve an issue of substantial public interest, . . . This Court discussed the subject most recently in *Schweitzer v. Burch,* 103 N.M. 612, 711 P.2d 889 (1985), in which we said (in what we shall see below was essentially dictum): "[U]pon dissolution of marriage, unless both parties agree otherwise, the trial court *must* divide community property retirement benefits on a 'pay as it comes in' basis." *Id.* at 615, 711 P.2d at 892 (emphasis added).

In the cases now under review, our Court of Appeals, in two 2–to–1 opinions by different panels, faithfully followed the *Schweitzer* "pay as it comes in" rule and held in effect that a nonemployee spouse is entitled, on dissolution of the marriage, to no monetary benefits representing his or her community interest in a retirement plan when the employee spouse has not yet retired. The nonemployee spouse's only entitlement on dissolution, the Court of Appeals held, is to an order that he or she will eventually, when the employee spouse actually retires and begins to receive payment of the pension provided for under the plan, receive payments of his or her share as they "come in." This is true even though the employee spouse's interest at the time of dissolution is, as it was in *Ruggles,* fully vested and matured. *Ruggles v. Ruggles,* 114 N.M. 63, 68–70, 834 P.2d 940, 945–47 (Ct.App. 1992); . . .

We now withdraw *Schweitzer*'s rigid "pay as it comes in" mandate and return to the more flexible pre-*Schweitzer* formulations that permitted a trial court to award to a nonemployee spouse in a marital dissolution all or a portion of his or her community interest in a retirement plan. We hold that the preferred method of dealing with these community assets is to treat them as all other community assets are treated on dissolution— namely, to value, divide, and distribute them (or other assets with equiva- lent value) to the divorcing spouses. We realize that in some cases, given the innumerable variations in pension plans and the infinite variety in the circumstances of individual divorcing couples, it will not be possible or practicable to achieve this preferred method of distribution and that other methods, including the "reserved jurisdiction" or "pay as it comes in" method, will have to be utilized. In cases such as the two before us, in which the employee spouse's interest is vested and matured, the desirabili- ty and feasibility of an immediate distribution to the nonemployee spouse are at their zenith. Consequently, we hold that in such cases the trial court should adopt as its first priority the making of a "lump sum" or other equivalent distribution to the nonemployee spouse. The Court of Appeals having ruled otherwise in these cases, its decisions are reversed and each case is remanded to the respective trial court for further proceedings consistent with this opinion.

. . .

Joseph and Nancy Ruggles were married on April 4, 1959. At the time of their marriage, Joseph was employed by Sandia Corporation ("Sandia") in Albuquerque, New Mexico. He began employment with Sandia on May 26, 1958, and remained continuously employed there through the time of trial. Sandia maintained a retirement plan for its employees, under which Joseph's interest was fully vested and matured at the time of trial;[2] he had become eligible to retire after thirty years' employment. The trial court found that as of the date of trial, June 28, 1988, Joseph would have been entitled to receive a pension of $1,570.71 per month had he elected to retire on that date. However, as of the date of trial he had not decided to retire and did not know when he would retire; he speculated that he might retire at age 63. At the time of trial he was 50.

The parties stipulated that as of June 28, 1988, Nancy owned a 48% interest in Joseph's Sandia pension benefits. Although they had entered into a comprehensive marital settlement agreement (discussed below), the agreement did not specifically provide when Nancy was to begin receiving her interest in the pension plan nor the specific dollar amount she was to receive, and these issues were disputed at trial. The court ruled that Nancy was entitled to receive 48% of $1,570.71, or $753.94, directly from Joseph, effective June 28, 1988, and continuing each month thereafter until Joseph's retirement from Sandia. At that time Nancy could receive her $753.94 directly from Sandia pursuant to a qualified domestic relations order ("QDRO").[3] The court also found that, if Joseph retired at the time of trial (at age 50), the then present value of the benefits he would receive from Sandia was $269,854.00; that if he retired at age 55, the present value of the benefits would be $182,000.00; and that if he retired at age 65, the present value would be $48,000.00. The court summed up these findings by declaring: "The present value of Joseph Ruggles's Sandia pension benefits drops every day that passes before retirement."

2. An employee's interest is "vested" when he or she has the right to receive retirement benefits at normal or early retirement, whether or not the employee continues to work for the employer until retirement. Steven R. Brown, *Berry v. Berry and the Division of Pension Benefits in Divorce and Post-Judgment Partition Actions,* 13 Community Prop.J., April 1986, at 30, 34. An employee generally becomes 100% vested after some minimum number of years of employment, but the vesting rate varies greatly among retirement plans. An employee's interest has "matured" when the employee is actually eligible to retire and receive benefits. *See id.* at 33. The maturity date is generally determined by the employee's age and years of employment. Phoebe Carter & John Myers, *Division and Distribution of the Community Interest in Defined Benefit Pensions: Schweitzer Reconsidered,* 18 N.M. L.Rev. 95, 100–01 (1988).

3. A QDRO is a mechanism by which a nonemployee spouse can receive his or her community share of an employee spouse's retirement benefits directly from the employer. QDRO's were created by the Retirement Equity Act of 1984, Pub.L. No. 98–397, 98 Stat. 1426 ("REA"). The REA created a limited exception to the broad antiassignment provisions of the Employee Retirement Income Security Act of 1974 ("ERISA") and the Internal Revenue Code of 1954 ("I.R.C.") to allow state courts, by order, to assign plan benefits if the state court order is a "qualified domestic relations order," or QDRO. Section 104, 98 Stat. at 1433 (amendment to ERISA) (codified as amended at 29 U.S.C. § 1056(d) (1988 & Supp. III 1991)); § 204, 98 Stat. at 1445 (amendment to I.R.C.) (codified as amended at I.R.C. §§ 401(a)(13), 414(p) (1988 & Supp. III 1991)).

As stated above, the Ruggles entered into a marital settlement agreement ("MSA") before trial. Article IV of the agreement purported to distribute the parties' community estate, including the community interest in each party's retirement benefits—Nancy's with her employer, the Albuquerque Public Schools (concerning which there is no issue on this appeal), and Joseph's with Sandia—in each case as earned from the date of marriage until February 1, 1988. The agreement did not specify when either spouse was to receive his or her community share of the other's benefits. Other provisions pertinent to the MSA will be noted later in this opinion.

At trial, each party contended that the MSA, insofar as it related to disposition of Nancy's entitlement to her community share of Joseph's retirement benefits, was unambiguous. Each party renews that contention on appeal, though Joseph also argued to the Court of Appeals that if the Court found the MSA ambiguous, it should be construed according to standard rules of construction governing ambiguous agreements. The trial court ruled that the agreement was not ambiguous and applied it in accordance with Nancy's contention: that she was entitled to receive $753.94 per month from Joseph commencing June 28, 1988, representing her interest in the Sandia pension benefits that Joseph would receive if he elected to retire at that time.

Joseph appealed to the Court of Appeals, arguing generally that the trial court's rulings contravened basic principles of community property law and misapplied the parties' MSA. The Court of Appeals agreed and reversed the trial court's judgment. In reaching its decision, the Court of Appeals first considered the parties' MSA. Although the Court agreed with the trial court that the agreement was unambiguous, it disagreed with the trial court as to the meaning of the agreement and concluded that the parties had agreed that Nancy would not receive her share of Joseph's benefits until he actually retired. *Ruggles,* 114 N.M. at 66–67, 834 P.2d at 943–44. The Court then stated that, while the MSA was binding on the parties, the trial court had discretion to modify it to ensure "fairness." It identified the fairness in question as "the equalized division of community property upon divorce." *Id.* at 67, 834 P.2d at 944.

The Court of Appeals then went on to discuss the trial court's order that Joseph pay Nancy her share of the retirement benefits before he actually retired. The Court gave three reasons for rejecting Nancy's argument that Joseph should not be able to time his retirement to deprive her of her share of their community property. First, the Court said that Nancy's position was contrary to *Schweitzer,* which requires distribution of retirement benefits on a "pay as it comes in basis." *Id.* at 69, 834 P.2d at 946. The Court's second reason was that delaying Nancy's receipt of benefits until Joseph actually retired did not deprive her of any rights because her rights derived from the community's rights; since the community's right to the benefits was always subject to Joseph's decision on when to retire, so too was her community interest upon dissolution of the marriage. *Id.* at 69–70, 834 P.2d at 946–47. Finally, as its third reason the

Court said that Joseph's postponement of retirement did not wholly delay Nancy's receipt of benefits since Nancy could immediately begin to receive a portion of her share of benefits directly from Sandia through a QDRO, which the trial court had found would amount to $182.98 per month. *Id.* at 70, 834 P.2d at 947. The Court remanded the case to the trial court with instructions to enter a QDRO for the amount Nancy could immediately begin receiving from Sandia.

Upon Nancy's petition, we granted certiorari.

. . .

We begin our analysis with a review of significant New Mexico cases dealing with the subjects of valuation, division, and distribution of a community's interest in retirement benefits upon dissolution of the spouses' marriage. In *LeClert v. LeClert,* 80 N.M. 235, 236, 453 P.2d 755, 756 (1969), this Court first held that retirement benefits are a form of employee compensation and are community property to the extent they are attributable to employment during coverture. In that case we affirmed an order directing payment to the nonemployee spouse of one-half of the community share of the employee spouse's (the husband's) military retirement benefits *as received.* The husband had been ordered to retire from the military, so there was no issue over whether his benefits were vested or matured. We commented: "[The husband's] retirement pay to which he was to become entitled [on retirement] cannot be considered a mere expectancy. . . ." *Id.*[6]

Several years after deciding *LeClert,* we issued our opinion in *Copeland v. Copeland,* 91 N.M. 409, 575 P.2d 99 (1978), which remained the leading case on the subject of this opinion until it was modified in *Schweitzer. Copeland* involved the division and distribution of vested but unmatured retirement benefits. We first concluded that unmatured benefits are community property subject to division *upon dissolution,* 91 N.M. at 412, 575 P.2d at 102, reasoning that it would be inequitable to consider such benefits to be a mere expectancy simply because they are subject to divestment by death, *see id.* at 411–12, 575 P.2d at 101–02. We noted that "[t]he cases are in agreement that at the time of the divorce the court must place a value on the pension rights and include it in the entire assets, then make a distribution of the assets equitably." *Id.* at 413, 575 P.2d at 103. Relying on cases from other community property jurisdictions, we pointed out that a determination of the discounted present value of the benefits at dissolution depends on a variety of factors, including, in addition to the

---

6. *LeClert* was overruled temporarily, insofar as it held that military retirement pay was part of the community property subject to division upon divorce, in *Espinda v. Espinda,* 96 N.M. 712, 713, 634 P.2d 1264, 1265 (1981), after the United States Supreme Court's decision in *McCarty v. McCarty,* 453 U.S. 210, 220–36, 101 S.Ct. 2728, 2735–43, 69 L.Ed.2d 589 (1981), which held that federal law precluded a state court from dividing military retirement pay pursuant to state community property laws. In 1982, however, Congress passed the Uniformed Services Former Spouses' Protection Act, Pub.L. No. 97–252, 96 Stat. 730 (1982) (codified as amended at 10 U.S.C. § 1408 (1988 & Supp. III 1991)), which had the effect of reversing the *McCarty* decision. This Court then reinstated *LeClert* in *Walentowski v. Walentowski,* 100 N.M. 484, 486, 672 P.2d657, 659 (1983).

possibility of the employee spouse's death, the possibility of termination of employment, the length of time remaining before the employee becomes eligible to retire and his or her interest matures, and the community's investment, if any, in the pension plan. *Id.* (citing *Brown v. Brown (In re Marriage of Brown),* 15 Cal.3d 838, 126 Cal.Rptr. 633, 544 P.2d 561, 567 (1976) (in bank); *Ramsey v. Ramsey,* 96 Idaho 672, 679, 535 P.2d 53, 60 (1975); and *Wilder v. Wilder,* 85 Wash.2d 364, 534 P.2d 1355, 1358 (1975) (en banc)). Quoting from *Wilder,* we recognized that "[t]here can be no set rule for determining every case and as in all other cases of property distribution, the trial court must exercise a wise and sound discretion." *Copeland,* 91 N.M. at 413, 575 P.2d at 103 (quoting *Wilder,* 534 P.2d at 1358).

> We continued in *Copeland:*
>
> It would appear that a flexible approach to this problem is needed. The trial court should make a determination of the present value of the unmatured pension benefits with a division of assets which includes this amount, or divide the pension on a "pay as it comes in" system. This way, if the community has sufficient assets to cover the value of the pension, an immediate division would make a final disposition; but, if the pension is the only valuable asset of the community and the employee spouse could not afford to deliver either goods or property worth the other spouse's interest, then the trial court may award the non-employee spouse his/her portion as the benefits are paid.*Id.* at 414, 575 P.2d at 104.

However, quoting from *In re Marriage of Brown,* 544 P.2d at 567, we cautioned that the trial court should observe "the fundamental principle that property attributable to community earnings must be divided equally *when the community is dissolved."* 91 N.M. at 411, 575 P.2d at 101 (emphasis added).

. . .

In 1985, this Court decided *Schweitzer* and in the process announced an abrupt departure from the principles of *Copeland* and its progeny. The issue was whether a beneficiary of the estate of a previously divorced nonemployee spouse, who upon her divorce had been awarded a share of her husband's monthly retirement benefit on a "pay as it comes in" basis, was entitled to continue to receive the benefits, which purportedly had been devised to the beneficiary by the decedent. In other words, was a deceased former spouse's right to receive her share of community property retirement benefits a devisable property right?

We answered that it was not. We held that community property retirement benefits that are awarded on a "pay as it comes in" basis are only inheritable or devisable up to the amount of the community contributions, if any, to the plan. An order dividing benefits on a "pay as it comes in" basis terminates, we held, on the death of either spouse unless the amount contributed by the community, if any, has not yet been paid out in benefits. *Schweitzer,* 103 N.M. at 615, 711 P.2d at 892.

There was thus no issue in *Schweitzer* about how a nonemployee spouse's community interest in a retirement plan should be distributed, or otherwise dealt with, upon divorce. Nevertheless, the Court stated: "We now modify *Copeland* prospectively to hold that upon dissolution of marriage, unless both parties agree otherwise, the trial court must divide community property retirement benefits on a 'pay as it comes in' basis." Id. After stating the actual holding of the case—that an order dividing benefits on a "pay as it comes in" basis terminates upon the death of either spouse (unless any amount contributed by the community has not yet been paid out in benefits)—the Court went on to explain the rationale for requiring distribution of all community retirement benefits on a "pay as it comes in" basis. We said that the reason for this requirement is to assure equity and fairness. Otherwise, the court could award a "lump sum" benefit in one case which would grant to the non-employee spouse an amount that might not ever be received if either spouse died before the projected benefits had been paid out; and on a "pay as it comes in" basis in another case, which would operate to the benefit of the employee spouse whose retirement income would not have to be divided after the non-employee spouse's death. The inequality would be compounded if the employee spouse died first, having received only a portion of his or her divided share but having paid the ex-spouse the present value of all of his or her estimated lifetime share under the lump sum decree.

. . .

Schweitzer firmly committed New Mexico to the "reserved jurisdiction" method of distributing the community interest in retirement benefits. The other principal method of distributing these benefits is the "lump sum" or "cash value" method. Under the lump sum method, retirement plan benefits are awarded to the employee spouse at the time of dissolution and assets of equivalent value are awarded to the nonemployee spouse. *See* L. Glenn Hardie, *Pay Now or Later: Alternatives in the Disposition of Retirement Benefits on Divorce,* 53 Cal.St.B.J. 106, 107 (1978). Under the reserved jurisdiction method, the court does not distribute the community interests at the time of dissolution, but reserves jurisdiction to distribute the benefits when the employee spouse actually receives them. *Id.; see also* Barbara A. DiFranza & Donald W. Parkyn, *Dividing Pensions on Marital Dissolution,* 55 Cal.St.B.J. 464, 466–68 (1980) (describing both methods and referring to lump sum method as "present cash value" method).

With respect to the specific issue involved in this case—whether a nonemployee spouse should receive her[9] community interest in a retire-

---

9. From this point on in this opinion, we shall use the feminine pronoun to refer to the nonemployee spouse and the masculine to refer to the employee spouse. We do this, despite our preference for gender neutrality in our opinions, for three reasons: (1) To avoid the incessant and sometimes awkward repetition of phrases such as "he or she," "her or his," "him/her," etc.; (2) because those are the roles of the spouses in *Ruggles,* which is the primary case triggering our review of this question on certiorari; and (3) because those will be the roles of the spouses in the majority of cases in today's society. Of course, the roles can be reversed, as *Mick* illustrates.

ment plan, or begin to receive it, upon dissolution when the employee spouse's interest is vested and matured, or should be required to wait until retirement benefits are actually paid before receiving, or beginning to receive, her share—only three of the eight community property states appear to have expressly considered the issue. All three of those states have ruled that, when the employee spouse's interest is vested and matured, the nonemployee spouse is entitled upon dissolution to immediate distribution of her share of retirement benefits: Arizona—*Koelsch v. Koelsch,* 148 Ariz. 176, 713 P.2d 1234 (1986) (en banc); California—*Gillmore v. Gillmore (In re Marriage of Gillmore),* 29 Cal.3d 418, 174 Cal.Rptr. 493, 629 P.2d 1 (1981); and Nevada—*Gemma v. Gemma,* 105 Nev. 458, 778 P.2d 429 (1989). Rulings in the other community property jurisdictions are somewhat ambivalent on whether courts should follow one method or the other, and in any event none appears to have addressed the precise issue considered in this case.[10]

In re Marriage of Gillmore is a leading case. There, the California Supreme Court held that the nonemployee spouse can immediately receive her community interest in the benefits from the employee spouse. The court stated, "A unilateral choice to postpone retirement cannot be manipulated so as to impair a spouse's interest in ... retirement benefits." *Gillmore,* 629 P.2d at 4. The court reasoned that the nonemployee spouse's interest would be impaired because she would be deprived of immediate enjoyment and management of her community property. *Id.* at 4 n. 4 (recognizing that "the timing of receipt and the control of an asset are important aspects of its value"). The court also said that the employee spouse cannot force the nonemployee spouse to share in the risk that the benefits could be forfeited if the employee spouse dies before retirement. *Id.* at 4.

The Arizona Supreme Court followed *Gillmore,* to a considerable extent, in *Koelsch.* In an extensive discussion covering various aspects of the subject considered in this opinion, the Arizona court held that a

---

10. The Texas Supreme Court has announced a clear preference for the "if, as, and when received" method of distributing retirement benefits, reasoning that it avoids the difficulties of computing present value. *Cearley v. Cearley,* 544 S.W.2d 661, 666 (Tex. 1976). However, the court apparently has never *required* use of that method, and at least one appellate court has affirmed a trial court's lump sum distribution of retirement benefits. *See May v. May,* 716 S.W.2d 705, 711–12 (Tex.Ct.App.1986). Both Idaho and Washington recognize discretion in their trial courts to make either a lump sum or a deferred distribution. As to Idaho, *see Shill v. Shill,* 100 Idaho 433, 439, 599 P.2d 1004, 1010 (1979); *see also Shill v. Shill,* 115 Idaho 115, 120, 765 P.2d 140, 145 (1988) (recognizing the issue presented in *Ruggles* and *Mick,* but declining to rule on it). As to Washington, *compare Bulicek v. Bulicek,* 59 Wash. App. 630, 800 P.2d 394, 398–99 (1990) (recognizing trial court's discretion and affirming award of benefits to a nonemployee spouse on an "as received" basis) *with Wilder v. Wilder,* 85 Wash.2d 364, 534 P.2d 1355, 1359 (1975) (en banc) (upholding trial court's order requiring employee spouse to pay nonemployee spouse her community property share of retirement benefits that were vested and matured upon dissolution). In Louisiana, trial courts similarly have flexibility to select an equitable method for distributing retirement benefits. *See Hare v. Hodgins,* 586 So.2d 118, 126–27 (La.1991) (stating that fixed percentage method, previously ordered in another case, was not the only permissible method of distributing retirement benefits).

nonemployee spouse's community interest in an employee spouse's matured retirement plan, when the employee wants to continue working, is to be valued and paid, or commenced to be paid, upon dissolution. The court recognized, however, that the trial court retains considerable discretion in selecting the appropriate method of payment. The court expressed a preference for the lump sum distribution method as providing a clean break between the parties and an unencumbered pension plan to the employee, as well as relieving the court of any further supervision over the parties' relationship. *Koelsch,* 148 Ariz. at 183, 713 P.2d at 1241.

The court continued that the nonemployee spouse's lump sum interest in the plan can be satisfied in several ways: by an award of cash or property equal to the value of the interest or by an installment obligation, which may or may not correspond with the amount the nonemployee spouse would receive if the employee spouse were to retire, and which may be secured by a lien on some or all of the employee spouse's separate property and may bear interest. *Id.* at 183, 713 P.2d at 1241. Further, "[i]f the lump sum method would be impossible or inequitable, the court can order that the non-employee spouse be paid a monthly amount equal to his or her share of the benefit which would be received if the employee spouse were to retire." *Id.* at 185, 713 P.2d at 1243.

For the reasons that appear below, we agree with *Koelsch* that the lump sum method is the preferable one for satisfying the nonemployee spouse's claim to her community interest in her spouse's retirement plan, and that the trial court should have discretion in implementing that method, alone or in combination with other methods, including in an appropriate case the reserved jurisdiction method, in distributing the nonemployee spouse's interest upon dissolution.

. . . .

Before applying the principles reviewed thus far in this opinion, we pause to remind ourselves of some equally important—indeed, fundamental—principles of community property law in New Mexico (and, so far as we are aware, in all other community property jurisdictions). First, it is axiomatic that each spouse in a marriage has a present, vested, one-half interest in the spouses' community property. This has been the law in this state at least since *Beals v. Ares,* 25 N.M. 459, 492–93, 185 P. 780, 790 (1919). The proposition has been reiterated countless times in our case law. . . .

Second, as we very recently recognized in *Swink v. Fingado,* 115 N.M. 275, 277, 850 P.2d 978, 990 (1993) (citing *Michelson v. Michelson,* 86 N.M. 107, 110, 520 P.2d 263, 266 (1974), and *Otto v. Otto,* 80 N.M. 331, 332, 455 P.2d 642, 643 (1969)), one of the chief incidents of community property lies in the district court's duty on dissolution to divide the property equally. Other cases, of course, can be cited to the same effect. . . .

Third, almost as a corollary to the rule requiring equal division of the community property on divorce, we have recognized the desirability of granting each spouse complete and immediate control over his or her share of the community property in order to ease the transition of the parties after dissolution. *Hertz v. Hertz,* 99 N.M. 320, 330, 657 P.2d 1169, 1179 (1983) (quoting *Cunningham v. Cunningham,* 96 N.M. 529, 531, 632 P.2d 1167, 1169 (1981)). In *Hertz* we reversed a trial court's order granting the divorcing spouses' residence to the husband and ordering him to pay the wife her community share of the residence through installments over a ten-year period. We held that the trial court erred in refusing to give the wife " 'complete and immediate control' of her interest in the community property." *Id.* at 330, 657 P.2d at 1169. Similarly, in *Chrane v. Chrane,* 98 N.M. 471, 649 P.2d 1384 (1982), we reversed a trial court's award to the wife of a life estate in the divorcing parties' residence. We reasoned that the effect of the court's award was to divest the husband of his equity in the property. *Id.* at 472, 649 P.2d at 1385. We accordingly directed the court on remand to order sale of the house and distribution of the proceeds to the parties within a reasonable time or to "make such other disposition of the home as will result in the husband receiving, within a reasonable time, his share of the value of the home." *Id.*

Immediately distributing community property on dissolution is of signal importance, not only because it eases the parties' transition following dissolution, but also because it furthers the important goal of minimizing future contact and conflict between divorcing spouses. Any court order that postpones distribution, thereby financially linking the parties to one another following a judgment of dissolution, invites future strife when one of the parties seeks to enforce the order. In the context of distribution of retirement benefits, several courts and commentators have identified severance of the parties' interest as an advantage of the lump sum distribution method over the reserved jurisdiction method. *Koelsch,* 148 Ariz. at 183, 713 P.2d at 1241 ("provides a clean break between the parties"); *Shill,* 100 Idaho at 437, 599 P.2d at 1008 ("effects a complete severance of the spouses' interests"); *Gemma,* 778 P.2d at 431 ("end[s] the parties' involvement with each other and finaliz[es] the divorce immediately in all respects"); Sherry A. Fabina, Note, *The Retirement Equity Act: An Accommodation of Competing Interests,* 63 Ind.L.J. 131, 143 (1987) ("avoid[s] future confrontations about financial matters").

With these principles in mind, we now apply them to the issues in these cases.

. . .

As noted above, the Court's concern in *Schweitzer* over the lump sum method was twofold: First, the court could award a "lump sum" benefit in one case which would grant to the non-employee spouse an amount that might not ever be received if either [FN[11]] spouse died before the projected benefits had been paid out; and on a "pay as it comes in" basis in another case, which would operate to the benefit of the employee spouse whose retirement income would not have to be divided after the non-employee spouse's death.

Thus, the Court focused its concern over the lump sum method on the potential inequality arising from the risk of forfeiture borne by the employee spouse: If he lived longer than his life expectancy, he would realize benefits in excess of those distributed to his ex-spouse on dissolution; if he died before retirement or before living out his life expectancy, with no ability to alienate or transmit at death the value of his pension rights, he would receive less than the value of the rights transferred to his former spouse at the time of divorce. As the Court of Appeals put it in *Ruggles* below, this Court in *Schweitzer* "was most concerned with the possibility of the employee spouse bearing all the risk of forfeiture and desired instead for both parties to bear the risk. . . . [The Supreme Court determined] that it is preferable for both spouses to bear the risk of forfeiture equally. . . ." 114 N.M. at 69, 834 P.2d at 946.

But we think it impossible to devise a system that, in all cases, will result in both spouses bearing the risk of forfeiture equally. Although this is the professed goal of the reserved jurisdiction or "pay as it comes in" method, its achievement of that goal is illusory. For, while the nonemployee spouse risks losing everything if her husband dies prematurely (*i.e.,* before retirement), the employee spouse walks away from the marriage dissolution secure in the knowledge that, if he lives past retirement, he will eventually have a pension to protect him in his retirement years. In the meantime, he has a *job.* He has a source of income (probably amounting to considerably more than the amount he would receive as a retirement pension) and the relative comfort of knowing that his income will probably increase, his eventual pension will probably increase, and upon retirement he will receive a guaranteed lifetime annuity. The nonemployee spouse, to be sure, has some of the same expectations as her former husband; depending on how long he lives and when he chooses to retire, she will eventually share in his pension (to the extent, probably, determined years before at the time of divorce). In the meantime, she may lack employment, and her future security depends entirely on when her ex-spouse decides to retire. The goals of effecting a clean break between the parties and of disentangling them from one another financially have been subverted, and the court has the prospect of relitigating the parties' precise shares of the pension payments when the employee decides to retire.

This is not an equal sharing of the risk.

. . .

In *Ruggles,* for the reasons and subject to the principles discussed below, we reverse the Court of Appeals and remand the case to the trial court to decide the parties' dispute over their marital settlement agreement. If the court finds that the parties agreed on when and how Nancy's share of Joseph's retirement benefits was to be paid to her, then that agreement should, of course, be enforced. We agree with *Schweitzer* that the rule for distribution of a nonemployee spouse's interest in a retirement plan, whatever the rule is, should be applied only in the absence of an agreement between the spouses on the subject. However, if the parties did not agree one way or the other on when and how Nancy was to receive her interest in Joseph's retirement plan, the court should reinstate its judgment awarding Nancy $753.94 per month as her community interest in Joseph's retirement plan. At the same time, we agree with the Court of Appeals that $182.98 of this amount should be paid directly by Joseph's employer, Sandia, through a QDRO. The court should enter such a QDRO, reduce Joseph's monthly obligation accordingly, and provide for Nancy's full entitlement to be paid to her on Joseph's actual retirement through an increased QDRO.

We acknowledge that this resolution of the parties' dispute does not comport with what we have described as the preferred method of satisfying a nonemployee spouse's community interest in an employee spouse's retirement plan—namely, a lump sum distribution, through other assets (including an installment obligation secured by a lien on other assets and bearing interest) and utilizing a QDRO to the maximum extent available, equal to the present cash value of her interest in the plan. However, Nancy has raised no issue about the court's failure to make a lump sum distribution, and Joseph has at no point contended that such a distribution was preferable to the manner in which the trial court divided the pension benefits. In any event, the parties' other assets have been divided pursuant to their MSA, and it would seem unwise to attempt to unscramble the eggs at this point. On remand, however, either party may request the court to revisit the questions of present-value determination and distribution, and the court may exercise its sound discretion in deciding how to deal with any such request.

. . .

We agree with the Court of Appeals that the MSA, fairly construed, reflects the parties' understanding that Joseph would continue working until well after the divorce. We further agree that the parties did not provide in their MSA, expressly or by implication, that Joseph would pay Nancy $753.94 per month from and after the dissolution of their marriage. However, we do not agree that the absence of such a provision from their written agreement necessarily means that the parties agreed that Nancy would not begin to receive any portion of her community share of Joseph's retirement plan until he actually retired. Unlike both the trial court and the Court of Appeals, we believe the MSA is ambiguous on this point and that further proceedings are necessary to resolve the ambiguity. If it cannot be resolved as an evidentiary or factual matter, then it follows that the parties made no agreement on the issue—their agreement simply failed to cover the point, and Nancy's entitlement to her share of Joseph's retirement benefits must be decided under the principles outlined previously in this opinion.

. . .

We therefore remand *Ruggles* to the trial court with directions to consider extrinsic evidence of the parties' intent as to distribution of Nancy's community share of the Sandia benefits. Any discussions between the parties on this issue are admissible to explain the terms of the agreement. Such evidence cannot be said to contradict the agreement when its meaning is not yet known. *C.R. Anthony,* 112 N.M. at 509, 817 P.2d at 243. The trial court might determine that the parties reached no agreement on this issue—that is, that they did not consider it and therefore did not agree on how to resolve it. A search for their intent would then be "fruitless." *See* Restatement (Second) of Contracts § 204 cmt. b. The court should then utilize the lump sum method to the extent feasible, as previously discussed, except that the court should not apply the lump sum method arbitrarily and without regard for the equities of the situation obtaining at that time. It is the burden of the party contesting the lump sum method to adduce a sufficient basis for denying a lump sum award. In the absence of findings to justify such a denial, the denial might well constitute an abuse of the trial court's discretion. With appropriate findings, the trial court may, as we have discussed, utilize other methods, in combination with or apart from the lump sum method.

Finally, we wish to comment on the Court of Appeals' statement in *Ruggles* that "the trial court had discretion to modify the terms of the agreement to assure fairness." 114 N.M. at 67, 834 P.2d at 944. The Court cited *Brister v. Brister,* 92 N.M. 711, 594 P.2d 1167 (1979), and *Wolcott v. Wolcott,* 101 N.M. 665, 687 P.2d 100 (Ct.App.1984), as support for this statement. Neither case supports the proposition that a court dividing community property in a dissolution proceeding has authority to modify the parties' agreed-upon division to assure "fairness." *Brister* involved modification of an award of alimony, as expressly permitted by statute. *Brister,* 92 N.M. at 713–14, 594 P.2d at 1169–70 (relying on NMSA 1978, § 40–4–7(B)(2)). *Wolcott* perhaps does provide inferential support for the proposition, but any such support is weak because the case involved unique facts (a prior court decree that the husband apparently sought to evade by entering into a subsequent separation agreement) and cited no authority itself except *Brister* and *Scanlon v. Scanlon,* 60 N.M. 43, 287 P.2d 238 (1955), which, like *Brister,* involved modification of an alimony or support agreement. *Id.* at 46, 54, 287 P.2d at 240, 246.

While this issue is not directly before us in this certiorari proceeding, we cannot let pass a remark that we believe is of questionable validity. Even Joseph Ruggles, the prevailing party in the Court of Appeals, asks us to disapprove the Court's dictum. We are inclined to agree with Joseph that a voluntary property settlement between divorcing spouses, dividing their community property as they see fit, is sacrosanct and cannot be upset by the court granting the divorce, absent fraud, duress, mistake, breach of fiduciary duty, or other similar equitable ground for invalidating an agreement. *See, e.g., Miller v. Miller,* 33 N.M. 132, 134, 262 P. 1007, 1007–08 (1928) (trial court that approved divorcing spouses' property settlement agreement could hardly have ruled otherwise "in the face of the voluntary property settlement made by the parties themselves ... which was not attacked for fraud, duress, or mistake."). *See also* NMSA 1978, § 40–2–2 (Repl.Pamp.1989) (Either spouse may enter into any transaction with the other which either might if unmarried, "subject, in transactions between themselves, to the general rules of common law which control the actions of persons occupying confidential relations with each other.'').

The decisions of the Court of Appeals in these cases are reversed, and each case is remanded to the district court where it arose for further proceedings consistent with this opinion.

NOTE

The New Mexico court emphasizes the standard that equal division of community assets is presumptive in community property states and furthermore, each of the parties should have complete and immediate control over his or her share at termination of the marriage. Distinct from community property is all separate property, defined as owned by one of the parties prior to marriage or acquired during marriage by gift, devise, bequest or descent. Separate property remains that of the individual holder and may only be utilized for distribution under particular circumstances, most notably child support or to rectify financial misconduct by the party with the separate property if there is insufficient community property. *See, e.g.,* ARIZ. REV. STAT. ANN. § 25–318(C) (1991). But any support order is distinct from property distribution; this principle applies in both community property and common law states. For a detailed examination of one state's community property laws, *see* GRACE GANZ BLUMBERG, COMMUNITY PROPERTY LAW IN CALIFORNIA (3d ed. 1999). California code provisions containing some of the points made by the court, but also emphasizing elements of community property distribution follow:

CALIFORNIA FAMILY CODE (West 2004)

§ 2550. Manner of division of community estate

Except upon the written agreement of the parties, or on oral stipulation of the parties in open court, or as otherwise provided in this division, in a proceeding for dissolution of marriage or for legal separation of the parties, the court shall, either in its judgment of dissolution of the marriage, in its judgment of legal separation of the parties, or at a later time if it expressly reserves jurisdiction to make such a property division, divide the community estate of the parties equally.

§ 2551. Characterization of liabilities; confirmation or assignment

For the purposes of division and in confirming or assigning the liabilities of the parties for which the community estate is liable, the court shall characterize liabilities as separate or community and confirm or assign them to the parties in accordance with Part 6 (commencing with Section 2620).

§ 2552. Valuation of assets and liabilities

(a) For the purpose of division of the community estate upon dissolution of marriage or legal separation of the parties, except as provided in subdivision (b), the court shall value the assets and liabilities as near as practicable to the time of trial.

(b) Upon 30 days' notice by the moving party to the other party, the court for good cause shown may value all or any portion of the assets and liabilities at a date after separation and before trial to accomplish an equal division of the community estate of the parties in an equitable manner.

§ 2553. Powers of court

The court may make any orders the court considers necessary to carry out the purposes of this division.

§ 2554. Failure to agree to voluntary division of property; submission to arbitration

(a) Notwithstanding any other provision of this division, in any case in which the parties do not agree in writing to a voluntary division of the community estate of the parties, the issue of the character, the value, and the division of the community estate may be submitted by the court to arbitration for resolution pursuant to Chapter 2.5 (commencing with Section 1141.10) of Title 3 of Part 3 of the Code of Civil Procedure, if the total value of the community and quasi-community property in controversy in the opinion of the court does not exceed fifty thousand dollars ($50,000). The decision of the court regarding the value of the community and quasi-community property for purposes of this section is not appealable.

(b) The court may submit the matter to arbitration at any time it believes the parties are unable to agree upon a division of the property.

. . .

§ 2602. Additional award or offset against existing property; award of amount determined to have been misappropriated

As an additional award or offset against existing property, the court may award, from a party's share, the amount the court determines to have been deliberately misappropriated by the party to the exclusion of the interest of the other party in the community estate.

B. TEMPORARY ALIMONY AND SEPARATE MAINTENANCE

UNIFORM MARRIAGE AND DIVORCE ACT (1973)

§ 304. [Temporary Order or Temporary Injunction]

(a) In a proceeding for dissolution of marriage or for legal separation, or in a proceeding for disposition of property or for maintenance or support following dissolution of the marriage by a court which lacked personal jurisdiction over the absent spouse, either party may move for temporary maintenance or temporary support of a child of the marriage entitled to support. The motion shall be accompanied by an affidavit setting forth the factual basis for the motion and the amounts requested.

(b) As a part of a motion for temporary maintenance or support or by independent motion accompanied by affidavit, either party may request the court to issue a temporary injunction for any of the following relief:

(1) restraining any person from transferring, encumbering, concealing, or otherwise disposing of any property except in the usual course of business or for the necessities of life, and, if so restrained, requiring him to notify the moving party of any proposed extraordinary expenditures made after the order is issued;

(2) enjoining a party from molesting or disturbing the peace of the other party or of any child;

(3) excluding a party from the family home or from the home of the other party upon a showing that physical or emotional harm would otherwise result;

(4) enjoining a party from removing a child from the jurisdiction of the court; and

(5) providing other injunctive relief proper in the circumstances.

(c) The court may issue a temporary restraining order without requiring notice to the other party only if it finds on the basis of the moving affidavit or other evidence that irreparable injury will result to the moving party if no order is issued until the time for responding has elapsed.

(d) A response may be filed within [20] days after service of notice of motion or at the time specified in the temporary restraining order.

(e) On the basis of the showing made and in conformity with Sections 308 and 309, the court may issue a temporary injunction and an order for temporary maintenance or support in amounts and on terms just and proper in the circumstance.

(f) A temporary order or temporary injunction:

(1) does not prejudice the rights of the parties or the child which are to be adjudicated at subsequent hearings in the proceeding;

(2) may be revoked or modified before final decree on a showing by affidavit of the facts necessary to revocation or modification of a final decree under Section 316;

(3) terminates when the final decree is entered or when the petition for dissolution or legal separation is voluntarily dismissed.

CALIFORNIA FAMILY CODE (West 2004)

§ 3600. Support orders

During the pendency of any proceeding for dissolution of marriage or for legal separation of the parties or under Division 8 (commencing with Section 3000) (custody of children) or in any proceeding where there is at issue the support of a minor child or a child for whom support is authorized under Section 3901 or 3910, the court may order (a) the husband or wife to pay any amount that is necessary for the support of the wife or husband, consistent with the requirements of subdivisions (i) and (m) of Section 4320 and Section 4325, or (b) either or both parents to pay any amount necessary for the support of the child, as the case may be.

NOTE

Temporary alimony, still widely known as alimony *pendente lite*, is designed to provide support for a spouse during the divorce action, along with contribution to attorneys' fees and other costs of maintaining or defending the action. At one time payments could go only to the wife, reflecting then prevalent stereotypes of roles within marriage. Such limitations generally were removed even before the U.S. Supreme Court's decision in Orr v. Orr, 440 U.S. 268, 99 S.Ct. 1102, 59 L.Ed.2d 306(1979), which set aside an Alabama statute providing that husbands, but not wives, could be required to pay alimony on divorce.

Despite the fact that temporary alimony is considered to be in some sense a continuation of the support duty while the parties are still married, from a strategic standpoint some attorneys express concern that the amount judicially fixed for it may also have an impact on setting the level of an eventual award of permanent alimony. The basis for this concern probably has been lessened with the approach to alimony widely incorporated in today's statutes that calls for initially determining the division of property and then deciding whether alimony or support is necessary.

Some jurisdictions provide an action for separate maintenance without divorce. In Capodanno v. Commissioner of Internal Revenue, 602 F.2d 64 (3d Cir.1979), a United States Court of Appeals held that persons who were living separately, with the husband making court ordered payments under New Jersey's separate maintenance statute, were still married and must file income tax returns as married persons. In some jurisdictions the action is based on equitable principles rather than statute. *See* Rodgers v. Rodgers, 349 So.2d 540 (Miss.1977). Both actions are distinct from the divorce *a mensa et thoro* and payments are not alimony *pendente lite*.

C. PERMANENT ALIMONY AND MAINTENANCE

UNIFORM MARRIAGE AND DIVORCE ACT (1973)

§ 308. [Maintenance]

(a) In a proceeding for dissolution of marriage, legal separation, or maintenance following a decree of dissolution of the marriage by a court which lacked personal jurisdiction over the absent spouse, the court may grant a maintenance order for either spouse only if it finds that the spouse seeking maintenance:

(1) lacks sufficient property to provide for his reasonable needs; and

(2) is unable to support himself through appropriate employment or is the custodian of a child whose condition or circumstances make it appropriate that the custodian not be required to seek employment outside the home.

(b) The maintenance order shall be in amounts and for periods of time the court deems just, without regard to marital misconduct, and after considering all relevant factors including:

(1) the financial resources of the party seeking maintenance, including marital property apportioned to him, his ability to meet his needs independently, and the extent to which a provision for support of a child living with the party includes a sum for that party as custodian;

(2) the time necessary to acquire sufficient education or training to enable the party seeking maintenance to find appropriate employment;

(3) the standard of living established during the marriage;

(4) the duration of the marriage;

(5) the age and the physical and emotional condition of the spouse seeking maintenance; and

(6) the ability of the spouse from whom maintenance is sought to meet his needs while meeting those of the spouse seeking maintenance.

NOTE

The removal of marital misconduct (fault) as a basis for maintenance in § 308(b) was a bold departure from the practice of permitting courts to consider both marital and economic conduct in awarding marital property or ordering spousal support. Half of the states follow this approach and eliminate considerations of marital misconduct unless it affects the other spouse's economic needs. Domestic violence, concealment of property or destruction of assets would be examples of misconduct affecting support. *See* CALIF. FAM. CODE § 4324, providing that an injured spouse is entitled to a prohibition of any temporary or permanent award for spousal support or medical, life, or other insurance benefits or payments from the injured spouse to the other. The American Law Institute allies itself with those states rejecting marital misconduct and suggests that tort law is a better remedy to address pain, suffering and emotional loss during marriage. *See* ALI, PRINCIPLES OF THE LAW OF FAMILY DISSOLUTION: ANALYSIS AND RECOMMENDATIONS: PROPOSED FINAL DRAFT PART I, CH. 1, INTRODUCTION, 29–43 (FEB. 14, 1997). For an argument suggesting fault may be appropriate, *see* Carl E. Schneider, *Marriage, Morals, and the Law: No–Fault Divorce and Moral Discourse*, 1994 UTAH L. REV. 503.

NEW YORK DOMESTIC RELATIONS LAW, § 236B, 5d(1)– (13) McKinney Supp. (2007)

(The text of this provision appears at pages 434, *supra*.)

CALIFORNIA FAMILY CODE (West 2004)

§ 4320.   Determination of amount due for support; considerations

In ordering spousal support under this part, the court shall consider all of the following circumstances:

(a) The extent to which the earning capacity of each party is sufficient to maintain the standard of living established during the marriage, taking into account all of the following:

(1) The marketable skills of the supported party; the job market for those skills; the time and expenses required for the supported party to acquire the appropriate education or training to develop those skills; and the possible need for retraining or education to acquire other, more marketable skills or employment.

(2) The extent to which the supported party's present or future earning capacity is impaired by periods of unemployment that were incurred during the marriage to permit the supported party to devote time to domestic duties.

(b)   The extent to which the supported party contributed to the attainment of an education, training, a career position, or a license by the supporting party.

(c) The ability of the supporting party to pay spousal support, taking into account the supporting party's earning capacity, earned and unearned income, assets, and standard of living.

(d) The needs of each party based on the standard of living established during the marriage.

(e) The obligations and assets, including the separate property, of each party.

(f) The duration of the marriage.

(g) The ability of the supported party to engage in gainful employment without unduly interfering with the interests of dependent children in the custody of the party.

(h) The age and health of the parties.

(i) Documented evidence of any history of domestic violence, as defined in Section 6211, between the parties, including, but not limited to, consideration of emotional distress resulting from domestic violence perpetrated against the supported party by the supporting party, and consideration of any history of violence against the supporting party by the supported party.

(j) The immediate and specific tax consequences to each party.

(k) The balance of the hardships to each party.

(*l*) The goal that the supported party shall be self-supporting within a reasonable period of time. Except in the case of a marriage of long duration as described in Section 4336, a "reasonable period of time" for purposes of this section generally shall be one-half the length of the marriage. However, nothing in this section is intended to limit the court's discretion to order support for a greater or lesser length of time, based on any of the other factors listed in this section, Section 4336, and the circumstances of the parties.

(m) The criminal conviction of an abusive spouse shall be considered in making a reduction or elimination of a spousal support award in accordance with Section 4325.

(n) Any other factors the court determines are just and equitable.

§ 4330.   Order of support; advice to support recipient

(a) In a judgment of dissolution of marriage or legal separation of the parties, the court may order a party to pay for the support of the other party an amount, for a period of time, that the court determines is just and reasonable, based on the standard of living established during the marriage, taking into consideration the circumstances as provided in Chapter 2 (commencing with Section 4320).

(b) When making an order for spousal support, the court may advise the recipient of support that he or she should make reasonable efforts to assist in providing for his or her support needs, taking into account the particular circumstances considered by the court pursuant to Section 4320, unless, in the case of a marriage of long duration as provided for in Section 4336, the court decides this warning is inadvisable.

Murphy v. Murphy
Supreme Court of Maine, 2003.
816 A.2d 814.

■ CLIFFORD, J.

Michael J. Murphy appeals and Stephanie Murphy cross-appeals from a divorce judgment entered in the District Court (Bangor, *Russell, J.*). Michael contends that the trial court erred in awarding transitional spousal support to cover Stephanie's dental and medical expenses. Michael also challenges the amount of the spousal support. Stephanie contends that the trial court erred in its determination and valuation of marital property, its division of marital property, and its failure to order Michael to pay her legal fees. We affirm the judgment.

The parties met and began living together over twenty-six years ago in New York. In 1980, they moved to Massachusetts and purchased a home as joint tenants. Michael worked for New England Electric for about ten years. During this time, the parties held themselves out as married. On July 5, 1985, their son Brendon was born, and the parties agreed that

Stephanie would stay at home and take care of him. Stephanie also home schooled Brendon. After approximately ten years in Massachusetts, Michael accepted a job with an engineering firm in Maine. Two years later, the parties bought the current marital home in Hampden using about $25,000 realized from the sale of their Massachusetts home. In 1993, Stephanie decided that they needed to be married because she was concerned that if anything happened to Michael she and Brendon would not be taken care of, so the couple married in October of 1993. In 1995, Michael started his own engineering consultant business. Stephanie helped Michael with the management of this business for about one year. In the fall of 1998, Stephanie began work as a psychiatric technician at Acadia Hospital. She was trained at the hospital and currently works full time.

The divorce proceeding was commenced in September of 2000. Prior to the trial, the couple sold real estate they owned in Brewer, and the net proceeds of approximately $4600 went to Stephanie.

After the parties separated, Michael and Brendon continued to live in the marital home in Hampden. The parties agreed that after the divorce, Brendon would continue to live with Michael, but would visit Stephanie whenever Brendon wanted and the parties would share parental rights and responsibilities. Stephanie lives in an apartment and shares expenses with a domestic partner, who earns approximately $28,000 a year. Stephanie previously took a sign language course and would like to go to college to earn a degree so that she could become an American sign language interpreter. She would be able to take some electives near where she lives, but would have to attend the University of Southern Maine for two years to take the core courses in sign language.

Stephanie testified that she is in need of a substantial amount of dental work. She estimated that the cost of the extractions and bridge work needed would be about $11,250. Stephanie also testified that she would like to continue in therapy to treat her depression, for which she takes prescription medication.

In Michael's financial statement, the marital home is valued at $119,300. Philip Cormier, a licensed real estate broker who conducted an appraisal on the property, testified that, if the property were placed on the market, he would suggest a listing price of $119,000 to $125,000 in order to sell the property within three or four months, and said that the property would probably yield a price of approximately $117,000. He acknowledged that the real estate market was doing well and that some houses were actually selling at list price or higher.

Michael has a retirement account from his ten years of employment in Massachusetts, prior to his marriage, which he rolled over into an account with A.G. Edwards when he left his job in Massachusetts. Michael testified that he has not added any money to this account since that time. The account has a value of approximately $115,000 and stands in Michael's name alone.

Michael's mother died in the late 1990s, and left an estate worth nearly half a million dollars. Prior to her death, Michael and his mother had a joint account with a value of about $43,000. After her death, Michael separated this account into two accounts in local banks. One account worth about $30,000 was placed in the parties' joint names, but was used only to pay costs of his mother's estate. Stephanie had a debit card for this joint account, but she never used it. After the parties had separated and the estate costs had been paid, Michael placed this money in his separate account. Michael was expected to receive $240,000 from his mother's estate and Brendon was expected to receive $120,000.

The court found the Hampden marital home to be worth $119,300 and awarded the property to Michael, with Michael assuming the balance on the mortgage of approximately $91,000. The court awarded the $4000 car to Michael and the $9000 car to Stephanie. The court set apart various other items of tangible personal property to each party, with items valued at $15,000 to Michael, and items worth $5000 to Stephanie.

The court determined that the $115,000 retirement account was Michael's nonmarital property. The court also determined that the money Michael is to receive from his mother's estate is nonmarital property. Thus, the court concluded that Michael had nonmarital assets of approximately $355,000, and Stephanie had none. Michael received approximately $78,300 and Stephanie $18,600 from the court's initial division of the marital estate,[1] but to ensure a more equitable division, the court ordered Michael to pay Stephanie $50,000.

The court found Stephanie's earning potential is approximately $18,000, and Michael's earning capacity to be about $90,000 a year. Although Stephanie has less income potential than Michael, given Stephanie and her partner's combined income, the court concluded that she could "maintain a reasonable standard of living without general support." Taking into account Stephanie's medical, dental, and educational needs, as well as her attorney fees obligation, the court awarded her transitional spousal support in the amount of $60,000.

II.   MICHAEL MURPHY'S APPEAL

A.   Spousal Support—Purposes

In contending that the trial court erred in awarding Stephanie transitional spousal support to cover her dental and medical expenses, Michael

---

1. Stephanie received a car worth $9000, tangible personal property worth $5000, and $4600 from the proceeds of the sale of the parties' Brewer property, which reaches a total of $18,600. Michael received the marital home worth $119,300, but also assumed the $91,000 mortgage. Michael also received a car worth $4000, tangible personal property worth $15,000, a business account totaling $13,000, and personal accounts totaling $1800. The actual total of these items is $62,100, but the court's order states it is $78,300. Neither party pointed out this mathematical inconsistency. It is possible that the $1800 figure was a typographical error that should have been $18,000, which would put Michael's total award of marital property at $78,300.

argues that those two categories do not fall within the definition of transitional support. We disagree.

Issues regarding spousal support are within the sound discretion of the trial court. *Noyes v. Noyes,* 662 A.2d 921, 922 (Me.1995). Title 19–A M.R.S.A. § 951–A(2) (Supp.2002), lists the five possible types of spousal support that a trial court may award, including general support and transitional support.[2] There is a rebuttable presumption that general support will not be awarded when the marriage is less than ten years in duration.[3] 19–A M.R.S.A. § 951–A(2)(A).

Id.

Transitional support, "may be awarded to provide for a spouse's transitional needs, including, *but not limited to:* (1) Short-term needs resulting from financial dislocations associated with the dissolution of the marriage; or (2) Reentry or advancement in the work force, including, but not limited to, physical or emotional rehabilitation services, vocational training and education." 19–A M.R.S.A. § 951–A(2)(B) (emphasis added). In determining an award of spousal support, the court must consider a number of factors, which include "health and disabilities of each party," and "any other factors the court considers appropriate."[4]

2. Title 19–A M.R.S.A. § 951–A (2) in pertinent part provides as follows:

2. Types of spousal support. The court may, after consideration of all factors set forth in subsection 5, award or modify spousal support for one or more of the following reasons.

A. General support may be awarded to provide financial assistance to a spouse with substantially less income potential than the other spouse so that both spouses can maintain a reasonable standard of living after the divorce.

(1) There is a rebuttable presumption that general support may not be awarded if the parties were married for less than 10 years as of the date of the filing of the action for divorce. There is also a rebuttable presumption that general support may not be awarded for a term exceeding 1/2 the length of the marriage if the parties were married for at least 10 years but not more than 20 years as of the date of the filing of the action for divorce.

(2) If the court finds that a spousal support award based upon a presumption established by this paragraph would be inequitable or unjust, that finding is sufficient to rebut the applicable presumption.

B. Transitional support may be awarded to provide for a spouse's transitional needs, including, but not limited to:

(1) Short-term needs resulting from financial dislocations associated with the dissolution of the marriage; or

(2) Reentry or advancement in the work force, including, but not limited to, physical or emotional rehabilitation services, vocational training and education.

. . .

Id.

3. Although Stephanie contends that she is entitled to an award of general support, the length of the marriage was eight years, and the trial court was not compelled to find that she overcame the presumption. *See* 19–A M.R.S.A. § 951–A(2).

4. Title 19–A M.R.S.A. § 951–A (5) provides as follows:

5. Factors. The court shall consider the following factors when determining an award of spousal support;

A. The length of the marriage;

B. The ability of each party to pay;

C. The age of each party;

D. The employment history and employment potential of each party;

The court's transitional support award in this case is based partly on Stephanie's health issues, her desire to receive counseling, her need for dental work, her obligation to pay attorney fees, and her need for more education and training. Michael challenges the court's consideration of Stephanie's counseling and dental work and contends that these items are not "transitional needs." The spousal support statute, however, does not specifically define the limits of "transitional needs," but rather provides that transitional needs "includ[e] but [are] not limited to" two broad categories. 19–A M.R.S.A. § 951–A (2)(B). Moreover, in determining an award of alimony, the court is required to consider the factors listed in § 951–A (5), including the health of the parties. 19–A M.R.S.A. § 951–A (5)(I). Accordingly, the transitional alimony award based in part on Stephanie's need for counseling and dental work is well within the trial court's discretion. *See Noyes,* 662 A.2d at 922.

B.   Spousal Support—Amount

Michael also argues that the trial court's award of $60,000 for transitional spousal support was excessive and beyond its discretion, contending that the evidence supports a transitional award of no more than $27,700. We disagree.

Stephanie has demonstrated a need for dental work, the need for legal representation in connection with this appeal, and that she will have to limit her work hours to accommodate her class schedule, and will be required to move to or commute to USM for two years. Furthermore, the statute provides that in determining an award of spousal support, the court must consider, among other factors, the income potential of the parties, their age, their standard of living, training and education, and their ability

E.   The income history and income potential of each party;

F.   The education and training of each party;

G.   The provisions for retirement and health insurance benefits of each party;

H.   The tax consequences of the division of marital property, including the tax consequences of the sale of the marital home, if applicable;

I.   The health and disabilities of each party;

J.   The tax consequences of a spousal support award;

K.   The contributions of either party as homemaker;

L.   The contributions of either party to the education or earning potential of the other party;

M.   Economic misconduct by either party resulting in the diminution of marital property or income;

N.   The standard of living of the parties during the marriage;

O.   The ability of the party seeking support to become self-supporting within a reasonable period of time;

P.   The effect of the following on a party's need for spousal support or a party's ability to pay spousal support:

(1) Actual or potential income from marital or nonmarital property awarded or set apart to each party as part of the court's distributive order pursuant to section 953; and

(2) Child support for the support of a minor child or children of the marriage pursuant to chapter 63; and

Q.   Any other factors the court considers appropriate.

Id.

to pay spousal support. 19–A M.R.S.A. § 951–A(5). Contrary to Michael's contention, the transitional award of $60,000 was reasonable, was in keeping with the purpose of transitional support and well within the trial court's discretion. *See Noyes,* 662 A.2d at 922.

II. STEPHANIE MURPHY'S CROSS–APPEAL

A. Determination, Valuation, and Distribution of Marital Property

Stephanie contends that the trial court erred in its determination, valuation, and division of the marital property. She argues that the court erred in its valuation of the marital home, that the IRA account in Michael's name was marital property, that the $30,000 previously in a joint account was marital property as well, and that the division of the marital property was not equitable.

1. The marital home in Hampden

The trial court's valuation of marital property is reviewed for clear error. *Robinson v. Robinson,* 2000 ME 101, ¶ 12, 751 A.2d 457, 460. The Hampden property was valued at $119,300 in Michael's financial statement, there was expert testimony that the property would be listed at $119,000 to $125,000, and that the market was doing well, and some homes were selling at list price or higher. The court's valuation of the marital home at $119,300 was not clear error. *See Robinson,* 2000 ME 101, ¶ 12, 751 A.2d at 460 (holding trial court's valuation of a business was not clearly erroneous because the court based its determination on an independent review of the evidence and the value was within the range provided by expert opinion).

2. Retirement account

A trial court's determination of whether property owned by the parties is part of the marital estate or is nonmarital, is reviewed for clear error. *Doucette v. Washburn,* 2001 ME 38, ¶ 7, 766 A.2d 578, 581. Such a determination made by the trial court will not be disturbed if it is supported by competent evidence in the record. *Id.*

Title 19–A M.R.S.A. § 953(2) (1998 & Supp.2002) defines "marital property" as "all property acquired by either spouse subsequent to the marriage" with five listed exceptions.[5] All property that is acquired during

---

5. Title 19–A M.R.S.A. § 953(2) provides as follows:

    2. Definition. For purposes of this section, "marital property" means all property acquired by either spouse subsequent to the marriage, except:

    A. Property acquired by gift, bequest, devise or descent;

    B. Property acquired in exchange for property acquired prior to the marriage or in exchange for property acquired by gift, bequest, devise or descent;

    C. Property acquired by a spouse after a decree of legal separation;

    D. Property excluded by valid agreement of the parties; and

    E. The increase in value of property acquired prior to the marriage and the increase in value of a spouse's nonmarital property as defined in paragraphs A to D.

    (1) "Increase in value" includes:

    (a) Appreciation resulting from market forces; and

the marriage is presumed to be marital property, pursuant to 19–A M.R.S.A. § 953(3), but the presumption can be overcome by the applicability of one or more of the exceptions.[6] One such exception, the increase in value of property that one spouse acquired prior to the marriage, contained in section 953(2)(E), was recently addressed in *Warner v. Warner,* 2002 ME 156, ¶¶ 27–35, 807 A.2d 607. In *Warner,* we explained the newly revised section 953(2)(E) as it related to one spouse's nonmarital stock as follows:

> Revised section 953(2)(E)(1)(a) establishes that to the extent a party demonstrates that the increase in value of a spouse's nonmarital stock resulted from "market forces," the increased value is nonmarital property regardless of whether the spouse or spouses played a substantial active role in managing the stock. In addition, sections 953(2)(E)(1)(b) and (2)(c) establish that to the extent a party demonstrates that the increase in value of a spouse's nonmarital stock resulted from reinvested income and capital gain, the increased value is nonmarital property unless it is also established that "either or both spouses had a substantial active role during the marriage in managing, preserving or improving the property." 19–A M.R.S.A. 953(2)(E)(1)(b) & (2)(c) (Supp.2002). *Warner,* 2002 ME 156, ¶ 31, 807 A.2d 607. Thus, the revised section 953(2)(E) makes clear that the increase of one spouse's nonmarital property that is attributable solely to market forces is also considered nonmarital property. *Id.* ¶ 27.

Michael's retirement account is a rollover account from his ten years of employment in Massachusetts prior to the parties' marriage, and Michael testified that the account has not been added to since that time. The account remains in Michael's name alone. Stephanie did not contest that the account was a rollover account from Michael's previous employer in Massachusetts. She provided no documents showing that her name had ever been on the account, nor did she show that any marital funds or effort had been applied to the account. The court's finding that the IRA account

---

(b) Appreciation resulting from reinvested income and capital gain unless either or both spouses had a substantial active role during the marriage in managing, preserving or improving the property.

(2) "Increase in value" does not include:

(a) Appreciation resulting from the investment of marital funds or property in the nonmarital property;

(b) Appreciation resulting from marital labor; and

(c) Appreciation resulting from reinvested income and capital gain if either or both spouses had a substantial active role during the marriage in managing, preserving or improving the property.

6. Title 19–A M.R.S.A. § 953(3) provides as follows:

3. Acquired subsequent to marriage. All property acquired by either spouse subsequent to the marriage and prior to a decree of legal separation is presumed to be marital property regardless of whether title is held individually or by the spouses in some form of coownership such as joint tenancy, tenancy in common, tenancy by the entirety or community property. The presumption of marital property is overcome by a showing that the property was acquired by a method listed in subsection 2.

Id.

was Michael's nonmarital property and was valued at $115,000 was not clear error. *See Doucette,* 2001 ME 38, ¶ 7, 766 A.2d at 581.

3. The $30,000 briefly held in a joint account

Stephanie challenges the trial court's determination that a $30,000 account standing in Michael's name was nonmarital property. She contends that because it had been in a joint account, it is marital property. Although property acquired by one spouse during the marriage is presumed to be marital property, that presumption may be rebutted by showing that the property falls under one of the exclusions listed in section 953(2), which includes property acquired by gift, bequest, or descent. 19–A M.R.S.A. § 953(2), (2)(A) & (3).

In *Chamberlin v. Chamberlin,* 2001 ME 167, 785 A.2d 1247, we upheld the trial court's determination that the plaintiff's property remained nonmarital even though it passed through the parties' joint checking account. The plaintiff's father had died and left the plaintiff an inheritance, which included $50,000 that was briefly placed in the parties' joint checking account before the plaintiff placed the funds in various investments in her own name. *Id.* ¶ 7, 785 A.2d at 1250. The plaintiff testified that she and the defendant had previously agreed that $50,000 of the inheritance was strictly her property. *Id.* In upholding the trial court's determination that the funds were nonmarital, we stated that "[i]n contrast to our holding in *Long* [*v. Long,* 1997 ME 171, ¶¶ 16–18, 697 A.2d 1317, 1323–24], we have never held that deposit accounts are subject to such automatic treatment as marital assets when funds are placed briefly in accounts, and we decline to do so now."[7] *Id.* ¶ 6, 785 A.2d at 1249.

After his mother's death, Michael placed $30,000 of a $43,000 joint account he held with his mother, into a joint account with Stephanie, for a brief period of time, but with the understanding that this money would be used for paying taxes of his mother's estate. Stephanie never accessed any of the funds from this account, which is now in Michael's name. Section 953(2)(A) excludes property acquired after a marriage by descent from being classified as marital property. 19–A M.R.S.A. § 953(2)(A). Contrary to Stephanie's contention, *Long* does not require that the $30,000 be considered marital property. The trial court's determination that inherited money briefly placed in a joint account remains nonmarital property is not clear error. *Chamberlin,* 2001 ME 167, ¶¶ 5–7, 785 A.2d at 1249–50.

4. The division of the marital property

Stephanie challenges the trial court's division of the martial property. Following the court's initial division of the marital property, it ordered

---

7. In *Long,* the defendant placed $35,000 that he realized from the sale of his nonmarital property in a joint savings account, and then invested that money in property in Maine that he owned in joint tenancy with his wife. 1997 ME 171, ¶ 2, 697 A.2d at 1319. We refused to apply the source of funds rule and held that real estate owned jointly by spouses was marital property regardless of who supplied the purchasing funds. *Id.* ¶¶ 16–18, 697 A.2d at 1323–24.

Michael to pay $50,000 to Stephanie to make the distribution more equitable.

Trial courts have broad discretion when dividing marital property, and we review the court's action for an abuse of discretion. *Robinson,* 2000 ME 101, ¶ 9, 751 A.2d at 459. Title 19–A M.R.S.A. § 953(1) provides that in a divorce action, "the court shall set apart to each spouse the spouse's property and shall divide the marital property in proportions the court considers just after considering all relevant factors."[8] The statute provides for a just distribution, which "is not synonymous with an equal distribution. . . . [w]e have made it clear that a court is not required to divide the marital property equally, but is required to make the division fair and just considering all of the circumstances of the parties." *Doucette,* 2001 ME 38, ¶ 24, 766 A.2d 578, 586.

Stephanie argues that she should be awarded more marital property because of her contributions to the home over the course of their relationship and because Michael has nonmarital property. The trial court, however, considered the factors set out in section 953 in dividing the property and required Michael to pay Stephanie $50,000. The division of marital property was within the trial court's discretion. *Robinson,* 2000 ME 101, ¶ 9, 751 A.2d at 459.

C. Attorney fees

Attorney fees awards in divorce actions are reviewed by this Court only for an abuse of discretion. *Warner,* 2002 ME 156, ¶ 54, 807 A.2d 607. Title 19–A M.R.S.A. § 952(3) (1998) provides that "[w]hen making a final decree, the court may order a party to pay reasonable attorney[ ] fees. Attorney[ ] fees awarded in the nature of support may be payable immediately or in installments." *Id.* This Court has previously recognized that the legislature has given trial courts broad discretion in determining whether or not to award attorney fees to a party in a divorce action. *Rosen v. Rosen,* 651 A.2d 335, 336 (Me.1994).

The trial court based its $60,000 transitional support award to Stephanie in part on her need to pay her divorce attorney. The court declined to directly award either party counsel fees, and determined that the parties should be responsible for their own attorney fees. Stephanie argues that Michael is in a better financial position and is more able to pay attorney fees. In *Rosen,* we said the parties' financial position is not the only factor to consider in determining an award of attorney fees. *Rosen,* 651 A.2d at 336–37. Rather, all relevant factors must be considered to reach a fair and

---

8. Title 19–A M.R.S.A. § 953(1) (1998) provides that the court must consider all relevant factors, which include the following:

A. The contribution of each spouse to the acquisition of the marital property, including the contribution of a spouse as homemaker;

B. The value of the property set apart to each spouse; and

C. The economic circumstances of each spouse at the time the division of property is to become effective, including the desirability of awarding the family home or the right to live in the home for reasonable periods to the spouse having custody of the children. *Id.*

just award. *Id.* at 336. As the trial court considered Stephanie's need to pay her attorney in awarding her transitional spousal support, the court did not abuse its discretion by failing to award her attorney fees directly.

The entry is:

Judgment affirmed.

NOTE

The *Murphy* decision illustrates the direction legislatures and courts have taken during the last forty years, that is, away from permanent alimony. At an earlier time, courts were willing to order alimony until death, remarriage, or a significant involuntary change of circumstances made payment unnecessary or impossible. *See, e.g.,* Olsen v. Olsen, 98 Idaho 10, 557 P.2d 604 (1976). Also, it was customary for husbands but not wives to pay alimony, but a decision by the Supreme Court of the United States held that an Alabama statute requiring this was unconstitutional discrimination. Orr v. Orr, 440 U.S. 268, 99 S.Ct. 1102, 59 L.Ed.2d 306 (1979). It took some time for the practice of gender neutrality to catch up with the law, as the *Pfohl* case illustrates. Today's cases, as depicted in *Murphy*, often involve couples cohabiting prior to marriage and a desire on the part of the court to divide the marital property and then to limit the general or transitional support to as short a period as possible. General support is for long term marriages and transitional support for shorter marriages, but in both instances courts seek to dissolve the economic ties as quickly, but as equitably, as possible.

Gender issues and questions continue to arise in the context of both division of marital property and orders of spousal support. *See, e.g.,* Alicia Brokars Kelly, *The Marital Partnership Pretense and Career Assets: the Ascendency of Self Over the Marital Community,* 81 B.U.L. REV. 59 (2001); Anne Lawton, *The Meritocracy Myth and the Illusion of Equal Employment Opportunity,* 85 MINN. L. REV. 587 (2000); Ann Estin, *Love and Obligation: Family Law and the Romance of Economics,* 36 WILLIAM AND MARY L. REV. 989 (1995); Jana Singer, *Alimony and Efficiency: The Gendered Costs and Benefits of the Economic Justification for Alimony,* 82 GEO. L. J. 2423 (1994); Milton C. Regan, Jr., *Spouses and Strangers: Divorce Obligations and Property Rhetoric,* 82 GEO. L. J. 2303 (1994). Some statutes direct the trial judge to consider the non-monetary contributions of homemakers. *See, e.g.,* W.VA. CODE § 48–2–32 (Supp. 1985); *see also* Katherine Silbaugh, *Turning Labor Into Love: Housework and the Law,* 92 NORTHWESTERN. U. L. REV. 1 (1996).

Pfohl v. Pfohl

District Court of Appeals of Florida, Third District, 1977.
345 So.2d 371.

■ HUBBART, JUDGE.

This is an action for dissolution of marriage in which the husband was awarded lump sum and rehabilitative alimony as well as attorneys' fees....

The major question presented for review is whether it is an abuse of discretion in a dissolution of marriage action for a trial court to award the husband $30,000 in lump sum alimony and $5,000 a month rehabilitative alimony for 18 months when: (1) the wife has a net worth of $4,250,000; (2) the parties shared an extremely high standard of living at first supported by the wife based on contributions to her from her father and thereafter based entirely on her own wealth during a nine year marriage; (3) the husband is 37 years old, unemployed with limited employment skills, in good physical, but impaired mental health, and in possession of approximately $200,000 assets most of which were received during the marriage from the wife.

Both parties contend that the trial judge abused his discretion. The wife argues that the husband is not entitled to any alimony; the husband argues that the amount of lump sum alimony is inadequate and that permanent, rather than rehabilitative alimony should have been awarded. We reject all these contentions and hold that the alimony awards herein were well within the discretion of the trial judge to make under the circumstances of this case.

Alimony has been traditionally considered an allowance which a husband is required to make in order to maintain his wife in the event of separation or divorce and is based on the common law obligation of a husband to support his wife. Floyd v. Floyd, 91 Fla. 910, 108 So. 896 (1926). In determining the amount of such alimony, the courts have established two criteria: (1) the husband's ability to pay, and (2) the needs of the wife, taking into consideration the standard of living shared by the parties to the marriage. Sisson v. Sisson, 336 So.2d 1129 (Fla.1976); Firestone v. Firestone, 263 So.2d 223 (Fla.1972).

Quite properly, these are criteria of the broadest nature, not susceptible to a precise formula automatically translatable into dollars and cents. We are dealing with a tragically human problem which touches peoples' lives during a period of immense personal crisis. One cannot dispense substantial justice in such explosive cases as if the answer lies in a computer or a rigid rule book. Mathematical exactness is neither possible nor desirable. The trial court of necessity has a wide discretion to apply the established criteria in fashioning a fair and equitable alimony award in the infinite variety of cases which come before it. . . .

The so-called "no fault" divorce law enacted by the Florida Legislature in 1971, represents a significant, but not totally radical departure from the historic conception of alimony. Section 61.08, Florida Statutes (1975) provides as follows:

"(1) In a proceeding for dissolution of marriage, the court may grant alimony to either party, which alimony may be rehabilitative or permanent in nature. In any award of alimony, the court may order periodic payments or payments in lump sum or both. The court may consider the adultery of a spouse and the circumstances thereof in determining whether alimony shall be awarded to such spouse and the amount of alimony, if any, to be awarded to such spouse.

(2) In determining a proper award of alimony, the court may consider any factor necessary to do equity and justice between the parties."

Under this statute, it is provided for the first time that a wife may be required to support her husband through alimony payments. This is in keeping with the current social trend toward establishing a more equitable relationship between the sexes.

.   .   .

Although this historic change in alimony law is far-reaching and we have not yet chartered its full effects, we can at least begin by stating that a husband's entitlement to alimony must stand on the same criteria as that of a wife. Lefler v. Lefler, 264 So.2d 112 (Fla. 4th DCA 1972). To be entitled to alimony, the husband must show a financial ability by the wife to pay for such an award coupled with a demonstrated need of the husband for support, taking into consideration the standard of living shared by the parties to the marriage.

Although in most marriages, the husband remains the sole provider of the family, with the wife making the home and raising the children, if any, an increasing number of marriages do not fit this mold. In some marriages, both parties work and jointly support the family, although the degree of support by either party may vary. In others, the wife is the sole support of the family unit with the husband fulfilling some non-economic role. It is in these non-traditional type marriages where the question of alimony for the husband may arise.

In the instant case, we are faced with such a non-traditional type of marriage. Although neither party did any serious work to financially support the family unit, the wife, rather than the husband, was the sole provider in this marriage. The husband resigned his employment at the request of the wife to live a life of luxury with his wife and family. Such fabulous wealth on the part of a woman who supports a marriage in which the husband is of modest means is not unknown in our society, but it certainly presents a case of unusual dimensions which we think the trial judge handled most reasonably upon the marriage's dissolution under the traditional criteria for awarding alimony.

As to the first criterion for awarding alimony, it is undisputed that the wife easily has the financial ability to pay for the alimony award in this case. She has a financial worth in excess of $4,000,000 and regularly maintains a checking account considerably greater than the total $120,000 alimony award for the husband. The award is therefore immune from attack as being beyond the financial means of the wife.

As to the second criterion for awarding alimony, the lump sum and rehabilitative alimony awards herein were commensurate with the need of the husband for temporary, although not permanent support, taking into consideration the standard of living shared by the parties to the marriage. The husband's limited employment opportunities, his impaired mental condition, and the very high standard of living to which the wife accustomed the husband to live during the marriage, are all critical factors in sustaining the trial court's exercise of discretion in fashioning the alimony award in this case.

The husband was a toy salesman for six years earning a modest salary which job he gave up at the request of the wife to devote full time to his life with the wife and family after a year and a half of marriage. Save for this limited service mainly as a figurehead in the businesses of his wife's family, he has been out of the employment market for the last seven and a half years of the marriage. At the time of the final hearing, he was unemployed, living with friends at a drastically reduced life style, having unsuccessfully attempted on a number of occasions to obtain employment, since the wife barred him from the marital homes. This impairment in a spouse's otherwise modest employment capacities caused in part by the supporting spouse's insistence that such work be terminated in favor of the family is a significant factor in sustaining an alimony award.

Added to this, is the husband's impaired mental condition. According to the uncontradicted testimony of an industrial psychologist, Dr. Marquit, the husband is suffering from a mental disorder which will require at least a year of intensive psychotherapy at considerable expense. He further testified that at present the husband is ill-suited for the employment market. We are in no position to second guess the trial judge's acceptance of this testimony based on his personal evaluation of Dr. Marquit as well as that of the husband. Certainly it is not beyond the realm of reasonable inference for the trial judge to have concluded that the husband's nine years of leisure class idleness followed by an abrupt end to his male cinderella existence when the wife literally threw him out of her home, at least partially brought on his current mental problems for which some period of rehabilitation is necessary. Such mental impairment, although temporary rather than permanent in nature, is a significant factor in sustaining an alimony award.

The husband's financial needs must also be measured in part by taking into consideration the extremely high standard of living to which the wife accustomed the husband through nine years of marriage. Firestone v. Firestone, 263 So.2d 223 (Fla.1972); Hausman v. Hausman, 330 So.2d 833 (Fla. 3d DCA 1976); Dash v. Dash, 284 So.2d 407 (Fla. 3d DCA 1973). The wife accustomed the husband to a life style which costs over $5,000 a month to maintain during a marriage which can hardly be described as a "marry in June and sue the following September" situation. Firestone v. Firestone, supra. In view of this fact, we cannot say that the limited eighteen month rehabilitative alimony plus lump sum alimony fashioned by the trial judge herein was an abuse of discretion. It was reasonably commensurate with the parties' high life style without at the same time creating an unreasonable charge on the wife for the rest of her life.

The wife argues that she accustomed the husband to such a high life style based on money she received from her father. It is true that the wife supported the marriage at first through contributions from the wife's father, but from 1972–1975 she supported the family unit entirely from her own separate estate. In our judgment, it is irrelevant how the wife lawfully acquired the money on which she supported the husband and family. The fact is she supported the family unit, not the husband. . . .

Rehabilitative alimony has been awarded to supplement means already available in an amount reasonably required during the post-marriage period to maintain a spouse until he or she in the exercise of reasonable efforts and endeavors is in a position of self support. It necessarily presupposes the potential for self support which is presently impaired. Lump sum alimony has been awarded as a payment of a definite sum or property in the nature of a final property settlement which serves a reasonable purpose such as rehabilitation or where the marriage's duration or the parties' financial position would make such an award advantageous to both parties. The alimony awards herein fit these traditional patterns and purposes for alimony.

The wife argues that the husband's $200,000 in assets acquired mainly by gift from the wife during the marriage, disqualifies the husband from receiving any alimony. We disagree. Although this is a significant factor in upholding the trial court's refusal to make the alimony permanent, we cannot say that this compels the result urged by the wife, particularly in view of the husband's demonstrated need for temporary, rehabilitative support. Except for the Sears stock, the husband's assets are non-income producing. And it has been held that a spouse is not required to deplete capital assets in order to maintain a prior standard of living. Gordon v. Gordon, 204 So.2d 734 (Fla. 3d DCA 1967). Moreover, alimony awards have been upheld where the spouse seeking alimony possessed assets comparable to that of the husband in this case. Harrison v. Harrison, 314 So.2d 812 (Fla. 3d DCA 1975).

The wife throughout these proceedings has attacked the husband's life style as parasitic and has warned that he should not be able to parlay such an existence into a $120,000 alimony award. The same criticism could be made of a good many wives who upon dissolution of a tragically flawed marriage have received alimony awards. We pass no judgment on the morality or social value of the marriage herein. Many Americans might very well regard the conduct of either party to this marriage with some cynicism. The work ethic is, after all, deeply ingrained in our mores. But we must take the marriage as we find it without passing judgment on the life style of either party. In a free society, there is room enough for many kinds of marriages, including this one. If and when such a marriage dissolves, it must be accorded equal treatment according to the standards for determining alimony set for all marriage dissolutions.

Moreover, the limited nature of the alimony awards herein should allay any fears that it will encourage any type of parasitic conduct. The husband has hardly been given a meal ticket for life; he has been given a temporary and limited assist to rehabilitate himself to a position of eventual self-support based on a demonstrated need. In this, we can find no abuse of discretion.

Turning now to the husband's cross appeal, we are not persuaded that the husband's demonstrated needs are so great that the trial court abused its discretion in refusing to make the alimony award permanent rather than rehabilitative and in refusing to award a greater lump sum alimony. As the wife accurately points out, the husband is a relatively young, well-educated man of 37, has excellent physical health although temporarily impaired mental health, has $200,000 in assets of his own, has some employment skills if only limited ones, and lives alone without custody of the parties' two children. We can see no reason why he could not properly rehabilitate himself within eighteen months with the alimony awarded herein. In the event that substantial rehabilitation does not occur by the end of eighteen months despite the husband's reasonable and diligent efforts, the husband can petition the court for modification of the alimony award.

The second question presented for review is whether it is an abuse of discretion in a dissolution of marriage action for a trial judge to set a $30,000 attorneys fee to be paid by the wife for the husband's attorneys where: (1) the wife has a net worth of $4,250,000; (2) the husband has a net worth of $200,000; (3) the husband's attorneys secure lump sum and rehabilitative alimony for the husband worth $120,000; (4) the husband's attorneys are eminent counsel who spent one hundred working hours plus twenty more hours of associate and law clerk time preparing for a unique, but not protracted or unduly complex litigation; and (5) the expert testimony puts a reasonable attorneys fee at $30,000.

The wife contends that she should not be required to pay the fee and that in any event, the fee was excessive. We reject these contentions and hold that the award of attorneys fees was well within the discretion of the trial judge to set under the circumstances of this case.

Much the same considerations which govern our decision on the alimony issue control the issue on attorneys fees. There is a demonstrated need for financial assistance for the husband to hire competent counsel which is not precluded by his possession of non-liquid, non-income producing assets. The wife unquestionably has the financial ability to pay for the fee.

The attorneys for the husband spent one hundred working hours preparing the case herein plus twenty more hours of associate and law clerk time. The case was a unique, but not protracted or unduly complex litigation. Expert testimony placed a reasonable attorneys fee at $30,000. The attorneys have been successful in securing an alimony award for the husband which is a singular accomplishment in the amount of $120,000. The husband's attorneys are also eminent counsel in the community.

The wife complains that the fee is excessive in view of the number of hours spent preparing the case. The law is well-settled, however, that attorneys fees should be awarded based in large measure on the quality of services rendered and not necessarily on the quantity of service. The elements usually considered in determining the amount of attorneys fees are: services rendered, responsibility incurred, the nature of the services, the skill required, the circumstances under which it was rendered, the ability of the litigant to respond, the value of the services to the client, and the beneficial results, if any, of the services. Measured by these standards, it is clear that the trial judge was well within his discretion in awarding attorneys fees for the husband in the amount of $30,000.

. . .

Affirmed.

NOTE

Payment of attorney fees in domestic cases is of considerable importance as was demonstrated in the court's decision. Other courts have also considered financial need in awarding fees. *See, e.g.,* Brady v. Brady, 39 S.W.3d 557 (Mo.App.2001), court ordered husband to pay wife's attorney fees in light of his marital misconduct and her financial constraints; Renfrow v. Draper, 232 F.3d 688 (9th Cir.2000), wife was entitled to recover attorney fees incurred in litigating the amount of the husband's debts in a bankruptcy proceeding; and Ex parte James, 764 S.2d 557 (Ala.1999), supporting a trial court's discretion in awarding $100,000 to the wife's attorney to be taken from the marital estate, of which two-thirds was granted to the husband. The award was justified because of the complexity and duration of the case.

CALIFORNIA FAMILY CODE (West 1994)

§ 20034. Attorney–Mediator; licensure and experience; duties; litigant hearing access

(a) An attorney, known as an Attorney–Mediator, shall be hired to assist the court in resolving child and spousal support disputes, to develop community outreach programs, and to undertake other duties as assigned by the court.

(b) The Attorney–Mediator shall be an attorney, licensed to practice in this state, with mediation or litigation experience, or both, in the field of family law.

(c) By local rule, the superior court may designate the duties of the Attorney–Mediator, which may include, but are not limited to, the following:

(1) Meeting with litigants to mediate issues of child support, spousal support, and maintenance of health insurance. Actions in which one or both of the parties are unrepresented by counsel shall have priority.

(2) Preparing support schedules based on statutory guidelines accessed through existing up-to-date computer technology.

(3) Drafting stipulations to include all issues agreed to by the parties, which may include issues other than those specified in Section 20031.

(4) If the parties are unable to resolve issues with the assistance of the Attorney–Mediator, prior to or at the hearing, and at the request of the court, the Attorney–Mediator shall review the paperwork, examine documents, prepare support schedules, and advise the judge whether or not the matter is ready to proceed.

(5) Assisting the clerk in maintaining records.

(6) Preparing formal orders consistent with the court's announced order in cases where both parties are unrepresented.

(7) Serving as a special master to hearing proceedings and making findings to the court unless he or she has served as a mediator in that case.

(8) Assisting the court with research and any other responsibilities which will enable the court to be responsive to the litigants' needs.

(9) Developing programs for bar and community outreach through day and evening programs, videotapes, and other innovative means that will assist unrepresented and financially disadvantaged litigants in gaining meaningful access to Family Court. These programs shall specifically include information concerning underutilized legislation, such as expedited temporary support orders (Chapter 5 (commencing with Section 3620) of Part 1 of Division 9), modification of support orders (Article 3 (commencing with Section 3680) of Chapter 6 of Part 1 of Division 9) and preexisting, court-sponsored programs, such as supervised visitation and appointment of attorneys for children.

(d) The court shall develop a protocol wherein all litigants, both unrepresented by counsel and represented by counsel, have ultimate access to a hearing before the court.

NOTE

Mediation cases continue to be decided. For example, in interpreting the state's Domestic Relations Arbitration Act, the Michigan Court of Appeals held that the statute required a hearing before an arbitrator may settle any matter by mediation. When the arbitrator met with the parties ex parte without holding a hearing, the couple is not bound by the arbitrator's award. Miller v. Miller, 264 Mich.App. 497, 691 N.W.2d 788 (2004). Likewise, the West Virginia Supreme Court of Appeals held that when one of the parties to a custody dispute withdrew consent to the mediated plan prior to the court's order adopting it, the court lacked the right to adopt a mediated agreement. Mason v. Mason, 216 W.Va. 328, 607 S.E.2d 434 (W. Va. 2004).

The possibility of making the process simpler continues to be the subject of exploration. *See, e.g.*, Marsha B. Freeeman, *Divorce Mediation: Sweeping Conflicts Under the Rug, Time to Clean House*, 78 U. DET. MERCY L. REV. 67 (2000); Judge Diane K. Vescovo, Allen S. Blair and Hayden D.

Lait, *Ethical Dilemmas in Mediation*, 31 U. MEM. L. REV. 59 (2000); Carrie J. Menkel–Meadow, *When Winning Isn't Everything: The Lawyer as Problem Solver*, 28 HOFSTRA L. REV. 925 (2000); Mariane M. Jennings, *Moral Disengagement and Lawyers: Codes, Ethics, Conscience, and Some Great Movies*, 37 DUQ. L. REV. 573 (1999).

Herndon v. Herndon

Supreme Court of South Dakota, 1981.
305 N.W.2d 917.

■ WUEST, CIRCUIT JUDGE.

This is an appeal from an order denying a reduction in child support payments and termination of alimony. We affirm.

The parties hereto were divorced in 1973 after seventeen years of marriage. There is no transcript of the original trial or any findings of fact and conclusions of law inasmuch as they were waived. It does appear that neither party had much property when they were married. After the marriage, appellant finished his training as a chiropractor and commenced a practice which he maintained with the help of appellee until the divorce. They accumulated property worth $200,000, which the trial court divided nearly equally. The decree further awarded appellee custody of the two sons with child support payments of $250 per child per month, and the additional sum of $600 per month for alimony. In addition, the court ordered a college trust fund of $20,000 per child, which was established. Appellee contributed $26,000 to the trust fund, and appellant contributed $14,000. In 1974 appellant applied for a termination of alimony and reduction in child support. The reduction in alimony was denied; however, the child support for the oldest boy was eliminated because he had married. In 1976 appellant again applied for a termination of alimony and a reduction in child support. Appellant asserted as changed circumstances for termination of alimony and reduction in child support payments appellee's employment income; appreciation of the assets awarded to appellee by the divorce decree; appellant's reduction in income; and appellant's health problems involving the use of his hands.

Appellant has severe osteoarthritic changes at the base of both thumbs at the metacarpal trapezoidal joint which is aggravated by his profession, in which he has to do a great deal of manipulation and massage. The thumbs remain swollen and his work causes increasing pain. X rays show that there has been loss of cartilage so that bone is rubbing on bone at the base of both thumbs. His physician has recommended fusion or locking the joint at the base of the thumb on each hand with two pins, and the building of a bone bridge with bone from another part of the body. This surgery would disable appellant from his profession for at least a year. This condition was urged as a changed circumstance at the 1974 hearing, the 1976 hearing, and at the last hearing now on appeal. As a result of the 1976 hearing, the court reduced the alimony payments to $250 per month but left the child support payment at $250. Neither party appealed.

As changed circumstances since the 1976 hearing, appellant has alleged appreciation of appellee's property awarded in the divorce decree; rental income of appellee's property and employment income of appellee; reduction of appellant's income; and sale of appellant's practice due to the condition of his hands. Appellant now lives in Arizona and no longer practices, although he has Arizona and California licenses. Evidence introduced at the most recent hearing established that there was no change in the condition of appellant's hands since 1974. Appellant maintained his practice until 1979, when it was sold.

The trial court held that there had not been a sufficient change of circumstances since 1976 to justify a reduction in support payments and termination of alimony. This Court has consistently held that there must be a change of circumstances to justify a change in alimony and child support payments. This Court does not sit as a trier of fact and will not disturb the decision of the trial court on questions of alimony and child support unless there is an abuse of discretion.

The term "abuse of discretion" refers to "a discretion exercised to an end or purpose not justified by, and clearly against, reason and evidence." Root v. Bingham, 26 S.D. 118, 120, 128 N.W. 132, 133 (1910), quoting from Murray v. Buell, 74 Wis. 14, 41 N.W. 1010 (1889).

Applying these principles to the case at bar, we are unable to say that the trial court abused its discretion. The condition of appellant's hands has remained unchanged since the hearings in 1974 and 1976. It is true that appellee's property has appreciated since 1976, but this has resulted largely through inflation, which has also affected the cost of rearing appellant's son. It is true that appellant has sold his practice and that he is not presently practicing his profession, resulting in reduced income; however, appellant has Arizona and California licenses, and there was some testimony that he may re-establish a practice in Sioux Falls. A person cannot voluntarily reduce his income in order to avoid alimony and support payments. Simmons v. Simmons, 67 S.D. 145, 290 N.W. 319 (1940). The evidence in this case does not show that appellant is unable to maintain a practice; to the contrary, it shows that appellant did continue practicing from 1974 until 1979.

. . .

■ HENDERSON, JUSTICE (concurring in part, dissenting in part).

I would reverse the trial court's order denying appellant a reduction in alimony. A review of the economic posture of the respective parties clearly indicates that appellee is not a needy recipient of alimony. On the contrary, her monetary status greatly exceeds that of her ex-husband.

First, as the trial court noted, appellant has experienced a "drastic reduction" in income since the 1976 proceedings. This reduction was caused by the necessity of appellant selling his chiropractic practice due to the chronically severe crippling of his hands. Appellant's present income consists of $828 per month from payments received on realty which appellant was forced to sell to support himself, his estranged wife and their child. Appellant also receives $551 as monthly accrued interest on savings accumulated during the years he was able to practice his profession. Between October of 1979 and October of 1980, appellant received one-third of the fees collected from his former patients through the chiropractor who purchased his practice. Currently, appellant is not a practicing chiropractor and, due to the arthritic condition of his hands, appears to have reached the end of his professional career.

In its correspondence to the parties' attorneys in December of 1979, the trial court stated that "it appears [appellant's] income level has dropped below $3,000 per month—and on the most conservative basis may have dropped below $2,000 per month. That is a substantial change in circumstances from 1976." I agree that a substantial change in circumstances has occurred since 1976, and point out that a mere change in circumstances is sufficient for a modification of alimony to occur. Blare v. Blare, 302 N.W.2d 787 (S.D.1981).

It is true, as the majority points out, that surgery might alleviate much of appellant's discomfort and possibly enable him to resume his chiropractic practice. I find it hard to fathom, however, the "voluntary" nature of appellant's income reduction. Agreed, appellant apparently does not wish to undergo the rather complex surgical procedure and resulting year of incapacitation. But does appellant's decision not to have surgery at the age of sixty necessarily mean he "voluntarily" reduced his income? Did appellant "voluntarily" cause the joints in his trained hands to swell-up, thereby inflicting upon himself such pain that work became a painful daily exercise in his profession? The answer to these questions is an obvious "no."

It is absurd to believe that appellant would avoid surgery merely to reduce his income, thereby possibly reducing his alimony obligation. This Court long ago concluded that the ability of the alimony obligor to pay is a paramount consideration in determining whether alimony obligations should be reduced. "The fact that the husband has suffered a serious impairment of health or physical condition ... since the entry of a decree for alimony or maintenance may authorize a reduction, suspension, or termination of alimony payments where his condition affects his ability to pay." Annot. 18 A.L.R.2d 45 (1951). It is unconscionable to require appellant to ply his profession with proficiency and pain (bone rubbing on bone) so as to enable appellee to enrich her already comfortable economic status.

Coupled with appellant's decreased ability to provide alimony is the fact that appellee cannot realistically be said to require alimony. Appellee is currently employed and grossing approximately $14,560 annually. Furthermore, she owns $209,306 worth of assets, including certificates of deposit which alone total over $100,000. At the hearing on the motion for modification, appellee testified that it cost her $8,336 per year to raise and adequately provide for the parties' son. When appellee's own income is added to appellant's child support obligation of $250 per month, appellee's yearly income comes to $17,560. It is significant that this total does not entail any interest and/or earnings accrued from appellee's stock, certificates of deposit, rental income, savings, or mutual funds. The record simply does not reflect that appellee needs alimony.

As the trial court stated, appellee's income and capital assets have increased since 1976. The trial court also pointed out, however, that inflation has offset this increase. If this be true, would not the same inflationary factors have even more severely eroded appellant's income, in light of the fact that appellant's income had decreased, not increased, over the same period of time? The answer is clearly a resounding "yes."

As I have recently expressed, the economic need of an alimony recipient must be considered when reviewing the equity of such an award. Lanphear v. Lanphear, 303 N.W.2d 576 (S.D.1981) (Henderson, Justice, concurring in part, dissenting in part); Herrboldt v. Herrboldt, 303 N.W.2d 571 (S.D.1981) (Henderson, Justice, dissenting). "The fact that the wife has acquired a substantial amount of property, or that her property has increased in value, after the entry of a decree for alimony or maintenance is an important consideration in determining whether and to what extent the decree should be modified." Annot. 18 A.L.R.2d 74 (1951).

In conclusion, I must agree with the Kentucky Court of Appeals when it stated that "[t]heoretically, alimony or maintenance is based in part on a consideration of the needs of the parties as well as their respective abilities to meet them." Gann v. Gann, 347 S.W.2d 540, 542 (Ky.App.1961). Applying this basic theory of equity to the particulars of this case, leads me to the inevitable conclusion that the trial court abused its discretion when it denied appellant's motion for a termination of alimony.

Bell v. Bell

Supreme Judicial Court of Massachusetts, 1984.
393 Mass. 20, 468 N.E.2d 859.

■ O'CONNOR, JUSTICE.

The plaintiff appealed to the Appeals Court from the dismissal of her contempt complaint against her former husband for his failure to continue support payments allegedly owed to her under a judgment of divorce. The Appeals Court, by a two-to-one decision, reversed the judgment of the Probate Court. Bell v. Bell, 16 Mass.App.Ct. 188, 197, 459 N.E.2d 109 (1983).... We affirm the judgment of the Probate Court.

The judgment of divorce was entered on April 28, 1976, effective as of November 28, 1975. It incorporated a separation agreement that provided in part that the defendant would make significant monthly alimony payments to the plaintiff for a period of fifteen years following the entry of a final judgment of divorce or until the "happening of the following contingencies: 1) the [w]ife's death, 2) the [w]ife's remarriage, and/or 3) [the w]ife's living together with a member of the opposite sex, so as to give the outward appearance of marriage at any time prior to May 1, 1981, whichever of the ... three contingencies happens first." The controversy concerns the interpretation and application of the third contingency provision (cohabitation clause). After a trial of the contempt matter, the judge made written findings and rulings. Based on his subsidiary findings with respect to the conduct of the plaintiff, we conclude that she "liv[ed] together with a member of the opposite sex, so as to give the outward appearance of marriage . . . prior to May 1, 1981."[1] It follows that the judge correctly ruled that the defendant's obligation to pay alimony had terminated and the contempt complaint was properly dismissed.

The judge found that following the judgment of divorce the plaintiff resided at the marital home in Cohasset on a regular basis until March, 1978. From March, 1978, until that summer she resided part of the time at the Cohasset home and part of the time in an apartment leased by a man identified as "J.R." From June, 1978, through October, 1979, she resided on a regular basis with J.R. in his apartment, and from October, 1979, to June, 1980, she resided with him at his apartment "for the most part." The judge also found that "[d]uring the period of time from June, 1978 through May, 1981, the plaintiff on a regular basis cohabited with J.R. . . . during which time they shared the same bedroom."

In addition, the judge made numerous detailed findings which we summarize briefly. The apartment lease stood solely in J.R.'s name. The plaintiff's name did not appear on the door or on the mailbox and she received her mail elsewhere. J.R. paid the rent and the plaintiff purchased the food and did most of the cooking and cleaning. Part of the furniture in the apartment was his and part of it was hers. They maintained separate bank accounts and never commingled assets. They took trips together and divided the costs. They socialized together. The plaintiff never represented to anyone that she was married to J.R. She never used his surname.

The cohabitation clause in question allowed the termination of alimony payments in the event that the plaintiff lived with a man "so as to give the outward appearance of marriage." It focused on the possibility of the plaintiff's sharing a home with a man, and it contemplated that that might occur in either of two ways: in a way that would create the appearance that the plaintiff and the man were married, or in a way that would not create such an appearance. Clearly, the parties thought that a man and a woman could live together in a way that would normally be associated with being married without their actually being married and without claiming or acknowledging a marriage relationship. It is difficult to conceive of what conduct the parties contemplated if that conduct did not at least include the plaintiff's sharing a bedroom with a man on a regular basis for approximately three years.

The Appeals Court held that it was the intention of the parties that alimony might be terminated only on the death or remarriage of the plaintiff, or "in circumstances so closely like marriage as to result in Mrs. Bell acquiring significant actual support or a new right to support from a

---

1. We consider the cohabitation clause to be unambiguous as applied to the facts of this case, and therefore we do not rely on parol evidence or on findings of the judge to determine the intent of the parties.

man prior to the specified date in 1981." Bell v. Bell, supra at 194, 459 N.E.2d 109. The Appeals Court correctly noted that, in the absence of a formally solemnized marriage, the plaintiff could not become entitled to support from a man except by a contract providing for it. Thus, in effect, the Appeals Court interpreted the separation agreement to provide for the termination of alimony in less than fifteen years only if the plaintiff died or remarried or, irrespective of appearances, if she actually received significant financial support from a man other than the defendant, or entered into a contract for support.

The plain language of the agreement cannot properly be ignored. The clause in question does not mention support or the plaintiff's continuing need for it in the absence of a new source. It would have been relatively easy for the parties to have expressly provided for the termination of alimony in the event of the plaintiff's being substantially supported by another man or becoming contractually entitled to such support. There was no need to subtly express that thought by a reference to the plaintiff's living with a man so as to give the outward appearance of marriage. The language is better suited, and we think was employed, to provide for termination of the plaintiff's right to alimony if she were to remarry or were to live as though she were remarried.

In arriving at its interpretation of the cohabitation clause as relieving the defendant of his alimony obligation only if the plaintiff were to receive substantial support or were to become contractually entitled to receive support from another man, the Appeals Court relied in part on a provision in the separation agreement that "neither the [h]usband nor the [w]ife will hereafter interfere with the personal liberty of the other, and each may lead his or her life free from any criticism or restraint by the other." Bell v. Bell, supra at 194, 459 N.E.2d 109. The court reasoned that, if the defendant were entitled to terminate alimony payments in response to the plaintiff's arrangement with J.R., the defendant could coerce the plaintiff's conduct in a way that was inconsistent with the intent of the parties as expressed in their agreement. Id. at 194–195, 459 N.E.2d 109. It is true that the disputed clause, as we interpret it, might give the plaintiff reason not to live with a man so as to give the outward appearance of marriage. It is also true that the provision permitting a termination of alimony in the event of the plaintiff's remarriage might give her reason to decide against remarriage. We think, however, that it is clear that the parties did not intend by the noninterference provision to preclude the defendant from possibly influencing the plaintiff's choices by terminating alimony payments in the event she were to remarry or were to live with a man in the manner of a married couple. Termination of alimony payments in such circumstances cannot be considered interference with the plaintiff's personal liberty or "criticism or restraint" within the meaning of the agreement.

Finally, the plaintiff argues that "[c]ohabitation clauses which operate to bar the receipt of support payments by the wife upon the commencement of a non-marital relationship with a man, unfairly discriminate against women, both pursuant to the equal protection clause of the United States

Constitution and the Massachusetts Equal Rights Amendment." The plaintiff's argument challenging the constitutionality of the provision appears for the first time on appeal to this court. Because this argument was not raised below, we decline to consider it.

Judgment of the Probate Court affirmed.

■ Wilkins, Justice (dissenting, with whom Liacos and Abrams, Justices, join).

The opinion of the Appeals Court presents a reasonable interpretation of the separation agreement, certainly a view preferable to that expressed in the opinion of this court. The court's opinion gives no effect to the provision in the separation agreement that neither party will "interfere with the personal liberty of the other, and each may lead his or her life free from any criticism or restraint of the other." We would reverse the judgment of the trial court by focusing on the crucial language of the separation agreement, and would thus ignore the details of the private arrangements between Mrs. Bell and J.R. that have influenced the opinion of this court and the majority and dissenting opinions of the Justices of the Appeals Court.

The question for decision is what the parties meant by the phrase "(3) [the w]ife's living together with a member of the opposite sex, so as to give the outward appearance of marriage at any time prior to May 1, 1981...." We know that the wife's living with a man would not alone terminate the husband's alimony obligation. The living together must have the appearance of marriage and that appearance must be outward. The court is wrong, therefore, in relying exclusively on the fact of "[Mrs. Bell's] sharing a bedroom with [J.R.] on a regular basis for approximately three years." That fact presents no outward appearance of anything. It was a private matter.

The significant point is that all the facts concerning the conduct and relationship of the wife and J.R. are equally consistent with a couple's not being married as they are with a couple's being married.[1] Couples, married and unmarried, share or do not share living and travel expenses when they live together. In today's society, for better or for worse, unmarried couples live together and, from that fact alone, no conclusion can fairly be drawn that such couples are married or that they give the outward appearance of marriage. The fact of sharing a bedroom over a period of time is thus inconclusive on the question of an outward appearance of marriage.

The disputed language would apply, however, if Mrs. Bell were to have held herself out as married to J.R. That fact would have given the outward

---

1. There is one fact which, if true, might indicate that Mrs. Bell and J.R. did not give the outward appearance of marriage. She testified that, during the entire time she had known J.R., she had dated other men and that she and J.R. had no arrangement by which she could not go out with other men. The opinion of the court ignores both this testimony concerning outward conduct and the trial judge's failure to consider it. The trial judge simply found that "on rare occasions [Mrs. Bell] brought someone other than J.R. to ... cocktail parties" at J.R.'s apartment.

appearance of marriage. The facts in this case incontestably show that Mrs. Bell made no such representation. It is not for us to apply our moral judgment to conclude that the sharing of a bedroom over a period of time should be treated as giving an outward appearance of marriage when in fact, in today's world, such a sharing of a bedroom gives no such appearance.

■ ABRAMS, JUSTICE (dissenting).

I cannot share the court's certitude that the plaintiff and her former husband agreed that his obligation to pay alimony would terminate if she shared a bedroom with another man "on a regular basis." A separation agreement incorporated in a judgment of divorce is not an ordinary contract, but a judicially sanctioned contract setting forth the allocation between former spouses of rights, responsibilities, and resources. Although wives today may be less economically dependent on their husbands than was the case in the past, it remains true that the typical alimony recipient is a woman who has sacrificed her earning capacity to her marriage and who, as an equitable and practical matter, must look to her former husband for financial support following a separation or divorce. Such women have little bargaining power and to a large extent must rely on judicial supervision to ensure that their entitlement to support is not made contingent on unjust and unreasonable conditions. See Knox v. Remick, 371 Mass. 433, 436–437, 358 N.E.2d 432 (1976). By giving its imprimatur to an interpretation of the Bells' separation agreement that hinges the plaintiff's entitlement to support on her conformity to life-style requirements imposed by the defendant, the court encourages economically-dominant husbands to meddle arbitrarily with the postdivorce lives of their wives, and thereby sends an unfortunate message to probate judges charged with scrutinizing such separate agreements to ensure that the agreements are "fair and reasonable." Knox v. Remick, supra at 436, 358 N.E.2d 432.

To be sure, there is nothing unreasonable about provisions allowing the defendant and others similarly situated to discontinue support payments in circumstances where the recipient's need is eliminated or met by another source. As construed by the court, the separation agreement and divorce judgment terminated the plaintiff's right to support solely because of her involvement in a relationship that does not have the defendant's approval, without any inquiry into its effect on her need for support and without reciprocal restraint on her husband.

Such a purely punitive elimination of support cannot be reconciled with the agreement's guarantee that "each [spouse] may lead his or her life free from any . . . restraint by the other." But even if, as the court decides, the unjustified limitation on the plaintiff's personal life imposed by a cutoff of support in the circumstances of this case is not plainly inconsistent with the terms of the Bells' agreement, public policy considerations should operate to preclude the result reached by the court. It is well established that a contractual restraint on fundamental private rights is subversive of public policy if it is "more onerous in its nature than is reasonably necessary for the proper fulfillment" of its purposes. Gleason v. Mann, 312

Mass. 420, 423–424, 425, 45 N.E.2d 280 (1942) (agreement that bound woman "to live a life of celibacy" unenforceable on public policy grounds where obligation "could be of no benefit" to employer). Compare Whitinsville Plaza, Inc. v. Kotseas, 378 Mass. 85, 102–103, 390 N.E.2d 243 (1979). By interpreting and enforcing the clause at issue here so as to give judicial sanction to a termination of support, the court allies itself with alimony payors who exercise their economic power in a manner that unreasonably interferes with the private, autonomous lives of the spouse from whom they have been divorced. I dissent.

NOTE

Husbands have also lost support payments because of cohabitation. *See, e.g.,* Baker v. Baker, 566 N.W.2d 806 (N.D.1997). Because payment of support—as compared to division of marital property—extends court supervision into the couple's future, material change in circumstances and specific events such as cohabitation may justify modification or termination of support. Remarriage or death are the traditional events triggering modification or elimination of support; retirement or changed financial circumstances are others. *See, e.g.,* Cal. Fam. Code §§ 4322, 4337. Some states authorize courts to order that a life insurance policy be maintained for the benefit of a supported spouse. *See, e.g.,* N.Y. Dom. Rel. Law § 236(B)(8)(a) (West 1999). Often couples will have an agreement delineating modification. Typically, however, courts are left to their own discretion. Some courts, either because of the equities involved or because of state statutes, provide support for a former spouse for an indefinite period. Most often this occurs when the supported spouse will have difficulty in becoming self-supporting. *See, e.g.,* Md. Code Ann., Fam. Law, § 11–106(c) (Supp. 1995); Minn. Stat. Ann. § 518.552(3).

Regarding cohabitation, the Principles takes the position that the establishment of a domestic partnership, or the maintenance of a common household for a continuous period of at least three months are bases upon which the court may suspend payments of support. *See* ALI, Principles of the Law of Family Dissolution: Analysis and Recommendations, Tentative Draft No. 4, § 5.10, 61–62 (April 10, 2000). Whether or not courts apply a standard of financial impact to the cohabitation is central. *See* Walter Wadlington, *Sexual Relations After Separation or Divorce: The New Morality and the Old and New Divorce Laws*, 63 Va. L. Rev. 249 (1977); Thomas Oldham, *Cohabitation by an Alimony Recipient Revisited*, 20 J. Fam. Law 615 (1981–82).

CALIFORNIA FAMILY CODE (West 1994)

§ 4323. Cohabitation with person of the opposite sex; rebuttable presumption of decreased need for support; modification or termination of support

(a)(1) Except as otherwise agreed to by the parties in writing, there is a rebuttable presumption, affecting the burden of proof, of decreased need for spousal support if the supported party is cohabiting with a person of the opposite sex. Upon a determination that circumstances have changed, the court may modify or terminate the spousal support as provided for in Chapter 6 (commencing with Section 3650) of Part 1.

(2) Holding oneself out to be the husband or wife of the person with whom one is cohabiting is not necessary to constitute cohabitation as the term is used in this subdivision.

(b) The income of a supporting spouse's subsequent spouse or nonmarital partner shall not be considered when determining or modifying spousal support.

(c) Nothing in this section precludes later modification or termination of spousal support on proof of change of circumstances.

GEORGIA CODE ANN. (Supp. 2006)

19–6–19

. . .

(b) Subsequent to a final judgment of divorce awarding periodic payment of alimony for the support of a spouse, the voluntary cohabitation of such former spouse with a third party in a meretricious relationship shall also be grounds to modify provisions made for periodic payments of permanent alimony for the support of the former spouse. As used in this subsection, the word "cohabitation" means dwelling together continuously and openly in a meretricious relationship with another person, regardless of the sex of the other person. In the event the petitioner does not prevail in the petition for modification on the ground set forth in this subsection, the petitioner shall be liable for reasonable attorney's fees incurred by the respondent for the defense of the action.

D. DIVIDING PROPERTY ON DIVORCE

UNIFORM MARRIAGE AND DIVORCE ACT (1973)

Alternative A

Section 307. [Disposition of Property.]

(a) In a proceeding for dissolution of a marriage, legal separation, or disposition of property following a decree of dissolution of marriage or legal separation by a court which lacked personal jurisdiction over the absent spouse or lacked jurisdiction to dispose of the property, the court, without regard to marital misconduct, shall, and in a proceeding for legal separation may, finally equitably apportion between the parties the property and assets belonging to either or both however and whenever acquired, and whether the title thereto is in the name of the husband or wife or both. In making apportionment the court shall consider the duration of the marriage, and prior marriage of either party, antenuptial agreement of the parties, the age, health, station, occupation, amount and sources of income, vocational skills, employability, estate, liabilities, and needs of each of the parties, custodial provisions, whether the apportionment is in lieu of or in addition to maintenance, and the opportunity of each for future acquisition of capital assets and income. The court shall also consider the contribution or dissipation of each party in the acquisition, preservation, depreciation, or appreciation in value of the respective estates, and the contribution of a spouse as a homemaker or to the family unit.

(b) In a proceeding, the court may protect and promote the best interests of the children by setting aside a portion of the jointly and separately held estates of the parties in a separate fund or trust for the support, maintenance, education, and general welfare of any minor, dependent, or incompetent children of the parties.

Alternative B

Section 307. [Disposition of Property.]

In a proceeding for dissolution of the marriage, legal separation, or disposition of property following a decree of dissolution of the marriage or legal separation by a court which lacked personal jurisdiction over the absent spouse or lacked jurisdiction to dispose of the property, the court shall assign each spouse's separate property to that spouse. It also shall divide community property, without regard to marital misconduct, in just proportions after considering all relevant factors including:

(1) contribution of each spouse to acquisition of the marital property, including contribution of a spouse as homemaker;

(2) value of the property set apart to each spouse;

(3) duration of the marriage; and

(4) economic circumstances of each spouse when the division of property is to become effective, including the desirability of awarding the family home or the right to live therein for a reasonable period to the spouse having custody of any children.

NEW YORK DOMESTIC RELATIONS LAW, § 236.B.5 (McKinney Supp. 2007)

(For the text of this statute, *see* p. 436, *supra*.)

NOTES

When does the accrual of marital property end? Because of the lack of clarity in some statutes questions have been raised about when a couple ceases to accrue marital property. In Portner v. Portner, 93 N.J. 215, 460 A.2d 115 (1983), the Supreme Court of New Jersey held that "for purposes of the equitable distribution of marital assets, a marriage is deemed to end on the day a valid complaint for divorce is filed that commences a proceeding culminating in a final judgment of divorce." In Anglin v. Anglin, 80 N.Y.2d 553, 592 N.Y.S.2d 630, 607 N.E.2d 777 (1992), the Court of Appeals of New York construed Domestic Relations Law § 236(B)(1)(c) to mean that a separation action does not, ipso facto, terminate the marital economic partnership and, therefore, does not preclude the subsequent accrual of marital property.

In Dobbyn v. Dobbyn, 57 Md.App. 662, 471 A.2d 1068 (1984), the parties agreed that the date of filing the petition would be used to determine what constituted marital property. However they disagreed on the date that should be used for establishing the value of assets such as securities, options, and commodities. The Court of Special Appeals of Maryland held that property should be valued as of the earlier time of their liquidation or the date that the parties were granted an absolute divorce.

Retroactivity. Questions about retroactivity have been raised in the early application of some of the new equitable jurisdiction statutes. Typically the statutes state some date after which all suits that are filed will be governed by the new provisions. In some states persons planning on filing for divorce gave careful thought to the timing of their actions to see whether the old or the new law would be more advantageous to them. The effective date of N.Y.DOM.REL. LAW § 236.B was July 19, 1980. In Motler v. Motler, 60 N.Y.2d 244, 469 N.Y.S.2d 586, 457 N.E.2d 691 (1983), a husband had commenced an action for divorce on July 17, 1980. The New York Court of Appeals was asked to decide whether it was error to grant the wife's motion to discontinue a counterclaim interposed in the suit after the effective date. The conceded purpose of discontinuing the claim was to permit her to commence a separate action under the new Equitable Distribution Law. The Court upheld the granting of the motion to allow discontinuance of the claim, distinguishing it from an earlier decision in which the defendant wife had filed her answer before the effective date of the statute.

Premarital cohabitation. Should property acquired by a couple during a period of premarital cohabitation be treated as separate or marital property if that couple later marries and then divorces? Increasingly, courts allow a judge to consider the cohabitation prior to marriage in apportioning the marital estate. *See, e.g.,* Northrop v. Northrop, 622 N.W.2d 219 (N.D. 2001); In re Rolf, 303 Mont. 349, 16 P.3d 345 (2000). And in Meyer v. Meyer, 239 Wis.2d 731, 620 N.W.2d 382 (2000), the Supreme Court of Wisconsin allowed the court to consider a spouse's premarital contribution to the other spouse's college and medical school education. Other courts specifically allow courts to divide assets acquired during cohabitation as marital property. *See, e.g.,* Matter of Marriage of Dubnicay, 113 Or.App. 61, 830 P.2d 608 (1992). Other courts take the position that the period of cohabitation and any assets acquired should not be considered in dividing assets at the end of the marriage. *See, e.g.,* In re Marriage of Crouch, 88 Ill.App.3d 426, 43 Ill.Dec. 580, 410 N.E.2d 580 (1980).

Hardy v. Hardy

Court of Appeals of South Carolina, 1993.
311 S.C. 433, 429 S.E.2d 811.

■ GARDNER, J.

The parties were married in 1957 and of the marriage two children were born, both now emancipated. At the time of the institution of the divorce, the wife was 57 years of age and the husband 58 years of age.

At the time of the divorce, Mr. Hardy owed in his name approximately $32,000 (exclusive of medical expenses); Mrs. Hardy owed in her name about $2,800.

The appealed order provided in pertinent part:

The Court is of the opinion that each party should be required to satisfy all indebtedness in their respective names, or for which they have been the primary payor in the past with the exception of real estate mortgages and car payments which will be paid by the party receiving the property.

We hold that the trial judge erred in reserving alimony for the wife. "[A]limony may be reserved when there is a 'determination that there exists an identifiable set of circumstances that is likely to generate a need for alimony in the reasonably near future.' " *Donahue v. Donahue,* 299 S.C. 353, 363, 384 S.E.2d 741, 747 (1989) (citations omitted). "If there is no need for alimony at the time of the trial, and no indication of physical or mental illness, foreseeable change in need in the future, or some other extenuating circumstance, a question of alimony should not be reserved." *Id.* at 363, 384 S.E.2d at 747.

We have carefully examined the record and we hold that, at the time of the final hearing, there was no present or foreseeable circumstance which would warrant the reservation of alimony. The wife is in good health, is drawing a pension from the State, and is selling real estate part-time. The circumstances where alimony may be reserved are not present in this case. We, accordingly, reverse that portion of the appealed order which reserves alimony to the wife.

We hold that the trial judge failed to recognize that the law relating to marital debts was materially impacted by S.C.Code Ann. section 20–7–472 (Supp.1991), which provides in pertinent part:

In making apportionment, the court must give weight in such proportion as it finds appropriate to all of the following factors:

* * *

(13) liens and any other encumbrances upon the marital property, which themselves must be equitably divided, or upon the separate property of either of the parties, *and any other existing debts incurred by the parties or either of them during the course of the marriage;* [Emphasis ours.]

* * *

(15) such other relevant factors as the trial court shall expressly enumerate in its order.

We hold that section 20–7–472 creates a presumption that a debt of either spouse incurred prior to marital litigation is a marital debt and must be factored in the totality of equitable apportionment. The presumption is rebuttable.

For purposes of equitable distribution, "marital debt" is debt incurred for the joint benefit of the parties regardless of whether the parties are legally jointly liable for the debt or whether one party is legally individually liable. *See Geer v. Geer,* 84 N.C.App. 471, 353 S.E.2d 427 (1987). *See also Allen v. Allen,* 287 S.C. 501, 339 S.E.2d 872 (Ct.App.1986).

In the equitable division of a marital estate, the estate which is to be equitably divided by the family court judge is the net estate, i.e., provision for the payment of marital debts must be apportioned as well as the apportionment of property itself. We hold this to be implicit in the above statute. We hold, therefore, that basically the same rules of fairness and equity which apply to the equitable division of marital property also apply to the division of marital debts.

We hold that the burden of proving a spouse's debt as non-marital rests upon that party who makes such assertion. If the trial judge finds that a spouse's debt was not made for marital purposes, we hold that it need not be factored in the court's equitable apportionment of the marital estate and the trial judge may require payment by the spouse who created the debt for non-marital purposes.

We hold that the words "in such proportion as it finds appropriate," as used in section 20–7–472 accord much discretion to the trial judge in providing for the payment of marital debts as a consideration in the equitable division of the marital estate.

In the instant case, the trial judge failed to recognize that section 20–7–472 creates a presumption that all debts regardless of who created them are marital debts; additionally, the trial judge failed to make a determination that the husband's debts were non-marital. We, accordingly, reverse that portion of the appealed order which requires each spouse to satisfy the debts which were in his or her name and remand this issue for determination in accordance with this decision. Upon remand, the trial court shall concurrently distribute the marital assets and the marital debts.

We find no merit to the remaining issues presented in this appeal, including the adultery issue. For the above reasons, we reverse that part of the appealed order which provides that alimony be reserved to the wife and we remand the issue of apportionment of marital debts and assets. Accordingly, the appealed order is affirmed in part, reversed in part and remanded for purposes of a new trial on the issue of the apportionment of marital debts and marital assets.

NOTE

Often, when a married couple files for divorce the only "property" consists of debt. How does the court define marital as compared to separate debt for division? The American Law Institute provides that marital property and marital debts are divided at dissolution so that the spouses receive net shares equal in value, although not necessarily identical in kind. *See* ALI, PRINCIPLES OF THE LAW OF FAMILY DISSOLUTION: ANALYSIS AND RECOMMENDATIONS: PROPOSED FINAL DRAFT PART I, CH. 4, § 4.15, 194 (Feb. 14, 1997). Nonetheless, when marital debts exceed marital assets, the ALI provides that courts may assign the excess unequally because a significant disparity exists between the spouses in their financial capacity, the participation in the decision to incur the debt, their consumption of the goods and services that the debt was incurred to acquire, or some combination of these factors. *Id.* at § 4.15(2)(c). California, a community property state, likewise provides that debts and assets be divided equally, but if community debts exceed community assets then the court may assign the excess debt as it deems "just and equitable, taking into account factors such as the parties' relative ability to pay." *See* CAL. FAM. CODE § 2622 (West 2001).

Mahoney v. Mahoney

Supreme Court of New Jersey, 1982.
91 N.J. 488, 453 A.2d 527.

■ PASHMAN, J.

Once again the Court must interpret this state's law regarding the distribution of marital property upon divorce. The question here is whether the defendant has the right to share the value of a professional business (M.B.A.) degree earned by her former husband during their marriage. The Court must decide whether the plaintiff's degree is "property" for purposes of N.J.S.A. 2A:34–23, which requires equitable distribution of "the property, both real and personal, which was legally and beneficially acquired . . . during the marriage." If the M.B.A. degree is not property, we must still decide whether the defendant can nonetheless recover the money she contributed to her husband's support while he pursued his professional education. For the reasons stated below, we hold that the plaintiff's professional degree is not property and therefore reject the defendant's claim that the degree is subject to equitable distribution. To this extent, we concur in the reasoning of the Appellate Division. Notwithstanding this concurrence, we reverse the judgment of the Appellate Division, which had the effect of denying the defendant any remedial relief for her contributions toward her husband's professional education and remand for further proceedings.

When the parties married in Indiana in 1971, plaintiff, Melvin Mahoney, had an engineering degree and defendant, June Lee Mahoney, had a bachelor of science degree. From that time until the parties separated in October 1978 they generally shared all household expenses. The sole exception was the period between September 1975 and January 1977, when the plaintiff attended the Wharton School of the University of Pennsylvania and received an M.B.A. degree.

During the 16–month period in which the plaintiff attended school, June Lee Mahoney contributed about $24,000 to the household. Her husband made no financial contribution while he was a student. Melvin's educational expenses of about $6,500 were paid for by a combination of veterans' benefits and a payment from the Air Force. After receiving his degree, the plaintiff went to work as a commercial lending officer for Chase Manhattan Bank.

Meanwhile, in 1976 the defendant began a part-time graduate program at Rutgers University, paid for by her employer, that led to a master's degree in microbiology one year after the parties had separated. June Lee worked full-time throughout the course of her graduate schooling.

In March 1979, Melvin Mahoney sued for divorce; his wife filed a counterclaim also seeking a divorce. In May 1980, the trial court granted dual judgments of divorce on the ground of 18 months continuous separation.

At the time of trial, plaintiff's annual income was $25,600 and defendant's income was $21,000. No claim for alimony was made. The parties owned no real property and divided the small amount of their personal property by agreement.

The only issue at trial was the defendant's claim for reimbursement of the amount of support she gave her husband while he obtained his M.B.A. degree. Defendant sought 50% of the $24,000 she had contributed to the household during that time, plus one-half of the $6,500 cost of her husband's tuition.

The trial court decided that defendant should be reimbursed, 175 N.J.Super. 443, 419 A.2d 1149 (Ch.Div.1980), holding that "the education and degree obtained by plaintiff, under the circumstances of this case, constitute a property right. . . ." However, the court did not attempt to determine the value of plaintiff's M.B.A. degree. Instead, finding that in this case "[t]o ignore the contributions of the sacrificing spouse would be . . . an unjust enrichment of the educated spouse," id. at 446, 419 A.2d 1149, the court ordered the award of a "reasonable sum as a credit [for] . . . the maintenance of the household and the support of plaintiff during the educational period." Plaintiff was ordered to reimburse his wife in the amount of $5,000, to be paid at the rate of $100 per month. The court did not explain why it chose this amount.

Plaintiff appealed to the Appellate Division, which reversed the award. 182 N.J.Super. 598, 442 A.2d 1062 (1982). It not only rejected defendant's claim for reimbursement but also held that neither a professional license nor an educational degree is "property" for the purposes of the equitable distribution statute. . . .

In rejecting defendant's claim for reimbursement, the Appellate Division disapproved of the attempt to measure the contributions of the parties to one another or to their marriage. The court cited with approval Wisner v. Wisner, 129 Ariz. 333, 631 P.2d 115, 123 (Ct.App.1981), where an Arizona appeals court stated:

> [I]t is improper for a court to treat a marriage as an arm's length transaction by allowing a spouse to come into court *after* the fact and make legal arguments regarding unjust enrichment. . . .

. . . [C]ourts should assume, in the absence of contrary proof, that the decision [to obtain a professional degree] was mutual and took into account what sacrifices the community [of husband and wife] needed to make in the furtherance of that decision. [emphasis in original]

The Appellate Division saw no need to distinguish contributions made toward a spouse's attainment of a license or degree from other contributions, calling such special treatment "a kind of elitism which inappropriately depreciates the value of all the other types of contributions made to each other by other spouses. . . ." 182 N.J.Super. at 613, 442 A.2d 1062. Finally, the court noted that in this case each spouse left the marriage "with comparable earning capacity and comparable educational achievements."

. . .

This case first involves a question of statutory interpretation. The Court must decide whether the Legislature intended an M.B.A. degree to be "property" so that, if acquired by either spouse during a marriage, its value must be equitably distributed upon divorce. In determining whether the Legislature intended to treat an M.B.A. degree as property under N.J.S.A. 2A:34–23, the Court gains little guidance from traditional rules of statutory construction. There is no legislative history on the meaning of the word "property" in the equitable distribution statute, N.J.S.A. 2A:34–23, and the statute itself offers no guidance. . . .

Regarding equitable distribution, this Court has frequently held that an "expansive interpretation [is] to be given to the word 'property,'" Gauger v. Gauger, 73 N.J. 538, 544, 376 A.2d 523 (1977). New Jersey courts have subjected a broad range of assets and interests to equitable distribution. . . .

This Court, however, has never subjected to equitable distribution an asset whose future monetary value is as uncertain and unquantifiable as a professional degree or license. The Appellate Division discussed at some length the characteristics that distinguish professional licenses and degrees from other assets and interests, including intangible ones, that courts equitably distribute as marital property. Quoting from In re Marriage of Graham, 194 Colo. 429, 574 P.2d 75, 77 (1978), in which the Colorado Supreme Court held that an M.B.A. degree is not subject to equitable distribution, the court stated:

> An educational degree, such as an M.B.A., is simply not encompassed even by the broad views of the concept of "property." It does not have an exchange value or any objective transferable value on an open market. It is personal to the holder. It terminates on death of the holder and is not inheritable. It cannot be assigned, sold, transferred, conveyed, or pledged. An advanced degree is a cumulative product of many years of previous education, combined with diligence and hard work. It may not be acquired by the mere expenditure of money. It is simply an intellectual achievement that may potentially assist in the future acquisition of property. In our view, it has none of the attributes

of property in the usual sense of that term. [182 N.J.Super. at 605, 442 A.2d 1062]

A professional license or degree is a personal achievement of the holder. It cannot be sold and its value cannot readily be determined. A professional license or degree represents the opportunity to obtain an amount of money only upon the occurrence of highly uncertain future events. By contrast, the vested but unmatured pension at issue in *Kikkert,* supra, entitled the owner to a definite amount of money at a certain future date.

The value of a professional degree for purposes of property distribution is nothing more than the possibility of enhanced earnings that the particular academic credential will provide. In Stern v. Stern, 66 N.J. 340, 345, 331 A.2d 257 (1975), we held that a lawyer's

> earning capacity, even where its development has been aided and enhanced by the other spouse . . . should not be recognized as a separate, particular item of property within the meaning of N.J.S.A. 2A:34–23. Potential earning capacity . . . should not be deemed property as such within the meaning of the statute. [footnote omitted][3]

Equitable distribution of a professional degree would similarly require distribution of "earning capacity"—income that the degree holder might never acquire. The amount of future earnings would be entirely speculative. Moreover, any assets resulting from income for professional services would be property acquired *after* the marriage; the statute restricts equitable distribution to property acquired *during* the marriage. N.J.S.A. 2A:34–23.

Valuing a professional degree in the hands of any particular individual at the start of his or her career would involve a gamut of calculations that reduces to little more than guesswork. As the Appellate Division noted, courts would be required to determine far more than what the degree holder could earn in the new career. The admittedly speculative dollar amount of

> earnings in the "enhanced" career [must] be reduced by the . . . income the spouse should be assumed to have been able to earn if otherwise employed. In our view [this] is ordinarily nothing but speculation, particularly when it is fair to assume that a person with the ability and motivation to complete professional training or higher education would probably utilize those attributes in concomitantly productive alternative endeavors. [182 N.J.Super. at 609, 442 A.2d 1062]

Even if such estimates could be made, however, there would remain a world of unforeseen events that could affect the earning potential—not to mention the actual earnings—of any particular degree holder.

---

3. A professional degree should not be equated with goodwill which, as we noted in *Stern,* may, in a given case, add economic worth to a property interest. Stern v. Stern, 66 N.J. at 346–47 n. 5, 331 A.2d 257 (1975).

A person qualified by education for a given profession may choose not to practice it, may fail at it, or may practice in a speciality, location or manner which generates less than the average income enjoyed by fellow professionals. The potential worth of the education may never be realized for these or many other reasons. An award based upon the prediction of the degree holder's success at the chosen field may bear no relationship to the reality he or she faces after the divorce. [DeWitt v. DeWitt, 98 Wis.2d 44, 296 N.W.2d 761, 768 (Ct.App.1980) (footnote omitted)]

Moreover, the likelihood that an equitable distribution will prove to be unfair is increased in those cases where the court miscalculates the value of the license or degree.

The potential for inequity to the failed professional or one who changes careers is at once apparent; his or her spouse will have been awarded a share of something which never existed in any real sense. [Id.]

The finality of property distribution precludes any remedy for such unfairness. "Unlike an award of alimony, which can be adjusted after divorce to reflect unanticipated changes in the parties' circumstances, a property division may not [be adjusted]." Id.

Because of these problems, most courts that have faced the issue have declined to treat professional degrees and licenses as marital property subject to distribution upon divorce. Several courts, while not treating educational degrees as property, have awarded the supporting spouse an amount based on the cost to the supporting spouse of obtaining the degree. In effect, the supporting spouse was reimbursed for her financial contributions used by the supported spouse in obtaining a degree.

Even if it were marital property, valuing educational assets in terms of their cost would be an erroneous application of equitable distribution law. As the Appellate Division explained, the cost of a professional degree "has little to do with any real value of the degree and fails to consider at all the nonfinancial efforts made by the degree holder in completing his course of study." 182 N.J.Super. at 610, 442 A.2d 1062. See also *DeWitt*, supra, 296 N.W.2d at 767. Once a degree candidate has earned his or her degree, the amount that a spouse—or anyone else—paid towards its attainment has no bearing whatever on its value. The cost of a spouse's financial contributions has no logical connection to the value of that degree.

As the Appellate Division correctly noted, "the cost approach [to equitable distribution] is plainly not conceptually predicated on a property theory at all but rather represents a general notion of how to do equity in this one special situation." 182 N.J.Super. at 610, 442 A.2d 1062. Equitable distribution in these cases derives from the proposition that the supporting spouse should be reimbursed for contributions to the marital unit that, because of the divorce, did not bear its expected fruit for the supporting spouse.

The trial court recognized that the theoretical basis for the amount of its award was not equitable distribution, but rather reimbursement. It held that "the education and degree obtained by plaintiff, under the circumstances of this case, constitute a property right *subject to equitable offset* upon the dissolution of the marriage." 175 N.J.Super. at 447, 419 A.2d 1149 (emphasis added). The court allowed a "reasonable sum as a credit . . . on behalf of the maintenance of the household and the support of the plaintiff during the educational period." Id. Although the court found that the degree was distributable property, it actually reimbursed the defendant without attempting to give her part of the *value* of the degree.

This Court does not support reimbursement between former spouses in alimony proceedings as a general principle. Marriage is not a business arrangement in which the parties keep track of debits and credits, their accounts to be settled upon divorce. Rather, as we have said, "marriage is a shared enterprise, a joint undertaking . . . in many ways it is akin to a partnership." Rothman v. Rothman, 65 N.J. 219, 229, 320 A.2d 496 (1974); see also Jersey Shore Medical Center–Fitkin Hospital v. Estate of Baum, 84 N.J. 137, 141, 417 A.2d 1003 (1980). But every joint undertaking has its bounds of fairness. Where a partner to marriage takes the benefits of his spouse's support in obtaining a professional degree or license with the understanding that future benefits will accrue and inure to both of them, and the marriage is then terminated without the supported spouse giving anything in return, an unfairness has occurred that calls for a remedy.

In this case, the supporting spouse made financial contributions towards her husband's professional education with the expectation that both parties would enjoy material benefits flowing from the professional license or degree. It is therefore patently unfair that the supporting spouse be denied the mutually anticipated benefit while the supported spouse keeps not only the degree, but also all of the financial and material rewards flowing from it.

Furthermore, it is realistic to recognize that in this case, a supporting spouse has contributed more than mere earnings to her husband with the mutual expectation that both of them—she as well as he—will realize and enjoy material improvements in their marriage as a result of his increased earning capacity. Also, the wife has presumably made personal financial sacrifices, resulting in a reduced or lowered standard of living. Additionally, her husband, by pursuing preparations for a future career, has foregone gainful employment and financial contributions to the marriage that would have been forthcoming had he been employed. He thereby has further reduced the level of support his wife might otherwise have received, as well as the standard of living both of them would have otherwise enjoyed. In effect, through her contributions, the supporting spouse has consented to live at a lower material level while her husband has prepared for another career. She has postponed, as it were, present consumption and a higher standard of living, for the future prospect of greater support and material benefits. The supporting spouse's sacrifices would have been rewarded had the marriage endured and the mutual expectations of both of them been fulfilled. The unredressed sacrifices—loss of support and reduction of the standard of living—coupled with the unfairness attendant upon the defeat of the supporting spouse's shared expectation of future advantages, further justify a remedial reward. In this sense, an award that is referable to the spouse's monetary contributions to her partner's education significantly implicates basic considerations of marital support and standard of living—factors that are clearly relevant in the determination and award of conventional alimony.

To provide a fair and effective means of compensating a supporting spouse who has suffered a loss or reduction of support, or has incurred a lower standard of living, or has been deprived of a better standard of living in the future, the Court now introduces the concept of reimbursement alimony into divorce proceedings. The concept properly accords with the Court's belief that regardless of the appropriateness of permanent alimony or the presence or absence of marital property to be equitably distributed, there will be circumstances where a supporting spouse should be reimbursed for the financial contributions he or she made to the spouse's successful professional training. Such reimbursement alimony should cover *all* financial contributions towards the former spouse's education, including household expenses, educational costs, school travel expenses and any other contributions used by the supported spouse in obtaining his or her degree or license.

This result is consistent with the remedial provisions of the matrimonial statute. N.J.S.A. 2A:34–23. A basic purpose of alimony relates to the quality of economic life to which one spouse is entitled and that becomes the obligation of the other. Alimony has to do with support and standard of living. We have recently recognized the relevance of these concepts in accepting the notion of rehabilitative alimony, which is consonant with the basic underlying rationale that a party is entitled to continue at a customary standard of living inclusive of costs necessary for needed educational training. Lepis v. Lepis, 83 N.J. 139, 155 n. 9, 416 A.2d 45.

The statute recognizes that alimony should be tailored to individual circumstances, particularly those relating to the financial status of the parties. Thus, in all actions for divorce (fault and no-fault) when alimony is awarded, the court should consider actual need, ability to pay and duration of the marriage. In a "fault" divorce, however, the court "may consider also the proofs made in establishing such ground in determining ... alimony ... that is fit, reasonable and just." N.J.S.A. 2A:34–23. There is nothing in the statute to suggest that the standards for awarding alimony are mutually exclusive. Consequently, the financial contributions of the parties during the marriage can be relevant. Financial dishonesty or financial unfairness between the spouses, or overreaching also can be material. The Legislature has not precluded these considerations. Nothing in the statute precludes the court from considering marital conduct—such as one spouse contributing to the career of the other with the expectation of material benefit—in fashioning alimony awards. See Lepis v. Lepis, supra. The flexible nature of relief in a matrimonial cause is also evidence by the equitable distribution remedy that is provided in the same section of the matrimonial statute.

The Court does not hold that every spouse who contributes toward his or her partner's education or professional training is entitled to reimbursement alimony. Only monetary contributions made with the mutual and shared expectation that both parties to the marriage will derive increased income and material benefits should be a basis for such an award. For example, it is unlikely that a financially successful executive's spouse who, after many years of homemaking, returns to school would upon divorce be required to reimburse her husband for his contributions toward her degree. Reimbursement alimony should not subvert the basic goals of traditional alimony and equitable distribution.

In proper circumstances, however, courts should not hesitate to award reimbursement alimony. Marriage should not be a free ticket to professional education and training without subsequent obligations. This Court should not ignore the scenario of the young professional who after being supported through graduate school leaves his mate for supposedly greener pastures. One spouse ought not to receive a divorce complaint when the other receives a diploma. Those spouses supported through professional school should recognize that they may be called upon to reimburse the supporting spouses for the financial contributions they received in pursuit of their professional training. And they cannot deny the basic fairness of this result.[5]

As we have stated, reimbursement alimony will not always be appropriate or necessary to compensate a spouse who has contributed financially to the partner's professional education or training. "Rehabilitative alimony" may be more appropriate in cases where a spouse who gave up or postponed her own education to support the household requires a lump sum or a short-term award to achieve economic self-sufficiency. The Court specifically approved of such limited alimony awards in Lepis v. Lepis, 83 N.J. 139, 155 n. 9, 416 A.2d 45 (1980), stating that we did "not share the view that only unusual cases will warrant the 'rehabilitative alimony' approach." However, rehabilitative alimony would not be appropriate where the supporting spouse is unable to return to the job market, or has already attained economic self-sufficiency.

Similarly, where the parties to a divorce have accumulated substantial assets during a lengthy marriage, courts should compensate for any unfair-

---

5. This decision recognizes the fairness of an award of reimbursement alimony for past contributions to a spouse's professional education that were made with the expectation of mutual economic benefit. We need not in the present posture of this case determine the degree of finality or permanency that should be accorded an award of reimbursement alimony as compared to conventional alimony. As noted, an award of reimbursement alimony combines elements relating to the support, standard of living and financial expectations of the parties with notions of marital fairness and avoidance of unjust enrichment. We must also recognize that, while these cases frequently illustrate common patterns of human behavior and experience among married couples, circumstances vary among cases. Consequently, it would be unwise to attempt to anticipate all of the ramifications that flow from our present recognition of a right to reimbursement alimony. We therefore leave for future cases questions as to whether and under what changed circumstances such awards may be modified or adjusted.

ness to one party who sacrificed for the other's education, not by reimbursement alimony but by an equitable distribution of the assets to reflect the parties' different circumstances and earning capacities. In *Rothman*, supra, the Court explicitly rejected the notion that courts should presume an equal division of marital property. 65 N.J. at 232 n. 6, 320 A.2d 496. "Rejecting any simple formula, we rather believe that each case should be examined as an individual and particular entity." Id. If the degree-holding spouse has already put his professional education to use, the degree's value in enhanced earning potential will have been realized in the form of property, such as a partnership interest or other asset, that is subject to equitable distribution. See *Stern*, supra, 65 N.J. at 346–47, 331 A.2d 257.

The degree holder's earning capacity can also be considered in an award of permanent alimony.[6] Alimony awards under N.J.S.A. 2A:34–23 must take into account the supporting spouse's ability to pay; earning capacity is certainly relevant to this determination. Our courts have recognized that a primary purpose of alimony, besides preventing either spouse from requiring public assistance, is "to permit the wife, who contributed during marriage to the accumulation of the marital assets, to share therein." Even though the enhanced earning potential provided by a degree or license is not "property" for purposes of N.J.S.A. 2A:34–23, it clearly should be a factor considered by the trial judge in determining a proper amount of alimony. If the degree holder's actual earnings turn out to diverge greatly from the court's estimate, making the amount of alimony unfair to either party, the alimony award can be adjusted accordingly.

We stated in *Stern,* supra, that while earning potential should not be treated as a separate item of property,

> [p]otential earning capacity is doubtless a factor to be considered by a trial judge in determining what distribution will be "equitable" and it is even more obviously relevant upon the issue of alimony. [66 N.J. at 345, 331 A.2d 257]

We believe that *Stern* presents the best approach for achieving fairness when one spouse has acquired a professional degree or license during the marriage. Courts may not make any permanent distribution of the value of professional degrees and licenses, whether based upon estimated worth or cost. However, where a spouse has received from his or her partner financial contributions used in obtaining a professional degree or license with the expectation of deriving material benefits for both marriage partners, that spouse may be called upon to reimburse the supporting spouse for the amount of contributions received.

---

6. It should be noted that alimony is not generally available for a self-supporting spouse under the laws of Minnesota, see *DeLa Rosa*, supra, 309 N.W.2d at 758, or Kentucky, see *Inman*, supra, 578 S.W.2d at 270, two states that have treated professional licenses as property. Those states are thus handicapped in their ability to do equity in situations where little or no marital property has been accumulated and the supporting spouse does not qualify for maintenance unless they treat professional licenses as property.

In the present case, the defendant's financial support helped her husband to obtain his M.B.A. degree, which assistance was undertaken with the expectation of deriving material benefits for both spouses. Although the trial court awarded the defendant a sum as "equitable offset" for her contributions, the trial court's approach was not consistent with the guidelines we have announced in this opinion. Therefore, we are remanding the case so the trial court can determine whether reimbursement alimony should be awarded in this case and, if so, what amount is appropriate.

The judgment of the Appellate Division is reversed and the cause remanded for further proceedings not inconsistent with this opinion.

CALIFORNIA FAMILY CODE (West 2004)

§ 2641.   Community contributions to education or training

(a) "Community contributions to education or training" as used in this section means payments made with community or quasi-community property for education or training or for the repayment of a loan incurred for education or training, whether the payments were made while the parties were resident in this state or resident outside this state.

(b) Subject to the limitations provided in this section, upon dissolution of marriage or legal separation of the parties:

(1) The community shall be reimbursed for community contributions to education or training of a party that substantially enhances the earning capacity of the party. The amount reimbursed shall be with interest at the legal rate, accruing from the end of the calendar year in which the contributions were made.

(2) A loan incurred during marriage for the education or training of a party shall not be included among the liabilities of the community for the purpose of division pursuant to this division but shall be assigned for payment by the party.

(c) The reimbursement and assignment required by this section shall be reduced or modified to the extent circumstances render such a disposition unjust, including, but not limited to, any of the following:

(1) The community has substantially benefited from the education, training, or loan incurred for the education or training of the party. There is a rebuttable presumption, affecting the burden of proof, that the community has not substantially benefited from community contributions to the education or training made less than 10 years before the commencement of the proceeding, and that the community has substantially benefited from community contributions to the education or training made more than 10 years before the commencement of the proceeding.

(2) The education or training received by the party is offset by the education or training received by the other party for which community contributions have been made.

(3) The education or training enables the party receiving the education or training to engage in gainful employment that substantially reduces the need of the party for support that would otherwise be required.

(d) Reimbursement for community contributions and assignment of loans pursuant to this section is the exclusive remedy of the community or a party for the education or training and any resulting enhancement of the earning capacity of a party. However, nothing in this subdivision limits consideration of the effect of the education, training, or enhancement, or the amount reimbursed pursuant to this section, on the circumstances of the parties for the purpose of an order for support pursuant to Section 4320.

(e) This section is subject to an express written agreement of the parties to the contrary.

NOTES

The American Law Institute takes the position that occupational licenses and educational degrees are not property divisible on divorce. *See* ALI, Principles of the Law of Family Dissolution: Analysis and Recommendations: Proposed Final Draft Part I, Ch. 4, § 4.07, 146 (Feb. 14, 1997). But "a spouse is entitled at divorce to reimbursement for the financial contributions made to the other spouse's education or training" under defined circumstances which allow for calculation. *Id.* at § 5.15, 383 (Feb. 14, 1997). Almost all courts and the ALI treat the degree as an intangible asset and inextricably attributable to the educated spouse's earning capacity and thus not property. The argument made by these jurisdictions is that relief should come from support or alimony. *See, e.g.,* Wilson v. Wilson, 388 N.W.2d 432 (Minn.App.1986).

Goodwill is another intangible asset. *See, e.g.,* Piscopo v. Piscopo, 232 N.J.Super. 559, 557 A.2d 1040 (App.Div.1989), where court held that celebrity's goodwill was marital property subject to division based on the celebrity's past earning capacity and the probability this will continue. The term has been defined as the excess value of the business's market value over its asset value. *See generally* Grace Blumberg, *Intangible Assets: Recognition and Valuation* § 23.05[1] in 2 Valuation and Distribution of Marital Property (1996). Other courts decline to treat goodwill as marital property in the absence of a sale of the asset and always simply earning potential when applied to professional persons. *See, e.g,* In re Marriage of Talty, 166 Ill.2d 232, 209 Ill.Dec. 790, 652 N.E.2d 330 (1995) and Sorensen v. Sorensen, 839 P.2d 774 (Utah 1992). Some courts make a distinction between property and earning potential. *See, e.g.,* In re Marriage of Schneider, 214 Ill.2d 152, 291 Ill.Dec. 601, 824 N.E.2d 177 (2005) (personal goodwill is an equitable factor and enterprise goodwill is marital property).

Personal injury is tangible but at issue is whether any settlement award is personal to the victim or part of the marital property. The Nebraska Supreme Court represents the majority approach deciding that any decision should be based on an analysis of the underlying purposes of the award rather than the mechanical approach which treats personal injury awards as entirely marital property. Compensation for pain, suffering, disfigurement, disability or loss of post-divorce earnings should not be considered marital property but the burden is upon the victim to demonstrate that the award was for these factors. If the award is to compensate for anything that would diminish the marital partnership the award is marital property. Parde v. Parde, 258 Neb. 101, 602 N.W.2d 657 (1999).

O'Brien v. O'Brien

Court of Appeals of New York, 1985.
66 N.Y.2d 576, 498 N.Y.S.2d 743, 489 N.E.2d 712.

■ SIMONS, JUDGE.

In this divorce action, the parties' only asset of any consequence is the husband's newly acquired license to practice medicine. The principal issue presented is whether that license, acquired during their marriage, is marital property subject to equitable distribution under Domestic Relations Law § 236(B)(5).

. . .

Plaintiff and defendant married on April 3, 1971. At the time both were employed as teachers at the same private school. Defendant had a bachelor's degree and a temporary teaching certificate but required 18 months of postgraduate classes at an approximate cost of $3,000, excluding living expenses, to obtain permanent certification in New York. She claimed, and the trial court found, that she had relinquished the opportunity to obtain permanent certification while plaintiff pursued his education. At the time of the marriage, plaintiff had completed only three and one-half years of college but shortly afterward he returned to school at night to earn his bachelor's degree and to complete sufficient premedical courses to enter medical school. In September 1973 the parties moved to Guadalajara, Mexico, where plaintiff became a full-time medical student. While he pursued his studies defendant held several teaching and tutorial positions and contributed her earnings to their joint expenses. The parties returned to New York in December 1976 so that plaintiff could complete the last two semesters of medical school and internship training here. After they returned, defendant resumed her former teaching position and she remained in it at the time this action was commenced. Plaintiff was licensed to practice medicine in October 1980. He commenced this action for divorce two months later. At the time of trial, he was a resident in general surgery.

During the marriage both parties contributed to paying the living and educational expenses and they received additional help from both of their families. They disagreed on the amounts of their respective contributions but it is undisputed that in addition to performing household work and managing the family finances defendant was gainfully employed throughout the marriage, that she contributed all of her earnings to their living and educational expenses and that her financial contributions exceeded those of plaintiff. The trial court found that she had contributed 76% of the parties' income exclusive of a $10,000 student loan obtained by defendant. Finding that plaintiff's medical degree and license are marital property, the court received evidence of its value and ordered a distributive award to defendant.

Defendant presented expert testimony that the present value of plaintiff's medical license was $472,000. Her expert testified that he had arrived at this figure by comparing the average income of a college graduate and that of a general surgeon between 1985, when plaintiff's residency would end, and 2012, when he would reach age 65. After considering Federal income taxes, an inflation rate of 10% and a real interest rate of 3% he capitalized the difference in average earnings and reduced the amount to present value. He also gave his opinion that the present value of defendant's contribution to plaintiff's medical education was $103,390. Plaintiff offered no expert testimony on the subject.

The court, after considering the life-style that plaintiff would enjoy from the enhanced earning potential his medical license would bring and defendant's contributions and efforts toward attainment of it, made a distributive award to her of $188,800, representing 40% of the value of the license, and ordered it paid in 11 annual installments of various amounts beginning November 1, 1982 and ending November 1, 1992. The court also directed plaintiff to maintain a life insurance policy on his life for defendant's benefit for the unpaid balance of the award and it ordered plaintiff to pay defendant's counsel fees of $7,000 and her expert witness fee of $1,000. It did not award defendant maintenance.

A divided Appellate Division . . . concluded that a professional license acquired during marriage is not marital property subject to distribution. It therefore modified the judgment by striking the trial court's determination that it is and by striking the provision ordering payment of the expert witness for evaluating the license and remitted the case for further proceedings.

On these cross appeals, defendant seeks reinstatement of the judgment of the trial court. Plaintiff contends that the Appellate Division correctly held that a professional license is not marital property but he also urges that the trial court failed to adequately explain what factors it relied on in making its decision, that it erroneously excluded evidence of defendant's marital fault and that the trial court's awards for attorneys and expert witness fees were improper.

The Equitable Distribution Law contemplates only two classes of property: marital property and separate property (Domestic Relations Law § 236[B][1][c], [d]). The former, which is subject to equitable distribution, is defined broadly as "*all* property acquired by either or both spouses during the marriage and before the execution of a separation agreement or the commencement of a matrimonial action, *regardless of the form in which title is held*" (Domestic Relations Law § 236[B][1][c] [emphasis added]; *see* § 236[B][5][b], [c]). Plaintiff does not contend that his license is excluded from distribution because it is separate property; rather, he claims that it is not property at all but represents a personal attainment in acquiring knowledge. He rests his argument on decisions in similar cases from other jurisdictions and on his view that a license does not satisfy common-law concepts of property. Neither contention is controlling because decisions in other States rely principally on their own statutes, and the legislative history underlying them, and because the New York Legislature deliberately went beyond traditional property concepts when it formulated the Equitable Distribution Law. Instead, our statute recognizes that spouses have an equitable claim to things of value arising out of the marital relationship and classifies them as subject to distribution by focusing on the marital status of the parties at the time of acquisition. Those things acquired during marriage and subject to distribution have been classified as "marital property" although, as one commentator has observed, they hardly fall within the traditional property concepts because there is no common-law property interest remotely resembling marital property. "It is a statutory creature, is of no meaning whatsoever during the normal course of a marriage and arises full-grown, like Athena, upon the signing of a separation agreement or the commencement of a matrimonial action." [Thus] [i]t is hardly surprising, and not at all relevant, that traditional common law property concepts do not fit in parsing the meaning of "marital property" (Florescue, "Market Value", *Professional Licenses and Marital Property: A Dilemma in Search of a Horn,* 1982 N.Y.St.Bar Assn. Fam.L.Rev. 13 [Dec.]). Having classified the "property" subject to distribution, the Legislature did not attempt to go further and define it but left it to the courts to determine what interests come within the terms of section 236(B)(1)(c).

We made such a determination in Majauskas v. Majauskas, 61 N.Y.2d 481, 474 N.Y.S.2d 699, 463 N.E.2d 15, holding there that vested but unmatured pension rights are marital property subject to equitable distribution. Because pension benefits are not specifically identified as marital property in the statute, we looked to the express reference to pension rights contained in section 236(B)(5)(d)(4), which deals with equitable distribution of marital property, to other provisions of the equitable distribution statute and to the legislative intent behind its enactment to determine whether pension rights are marital property or separate property. A similar analysis is appropriate here and leads to the conclusion that marital property encompasses a license to practice medicine to the extent that the license is acquired during marriage.

Section 236 provides that in making an equitable distribution of marital property, "the court shall consider: . . . (6) any equitable claim to, interest in, or direct or indirect contribution made to the acquisition of such marital property by the party not having title, including joint efforts or expenditures and contributions and services as a spouse, parent, wage earner and homemaker, and *to the career or career potential* of the other party [and] . . . (9) the impossibility or difficulty of evaluating any component asset or any interest in a business, corporation or *profession*" (Domestic Relations Law § 236[B][5][d][6], [9] [emphasis added]). Where equitable distribution of marital property is appropriate but "the distribution of an interest in a business, corporation or *profession* would be contrary to law" the court shall make a distributive award in lieu of an actual distribution of the property (Domestic Relations Law § 236[B][5][e] [emphasis added]). The words mean exactly what they say: that an interest in a profession or professional career potential is marital property which may be represented by direct or indirect contributions of the non-title-holding spouse, including financial contributions and nonfinancial contributions made by caring for the home and family.

The history which preceded enactment of the statute confirms this interpretation. Reform of section 236 was advocated because experience had proven that application of the traditional common-law title theory of property had caused inequities upon dissolution of a marriage. The Legislature replaced the existing system with equitable distribution of marital property, an entirely new theory which considered all the circumstances of the case and of the respective parties to the marriage. Equitable distribution was based on the premise that a marriage is, among other things, an economic partnership to which both parties contribute as spouse, parent, wage earner or homemaker. Consistent with this purpose, and implicit in the statutory scheme as a whole, is the view that upon dissolution of the marriage there should be a winding up of the parties' economic affairs and a severance of their economic ties by an equitable distribution of the marital assets. Thus, the concept of alimony, which often served as a means of lifetime support and dependence for one spouse upon the other long after the marriage was over, was replaced with the concept of maintenance which seeks to allow "the recipient spouse an opportunity to achieve [economic] independence" (Assembly Memorandum, 1980 N.Y.Legis.Ann., at 130).

The determination that a professional license is marital property is also consistent with the conceptual base upon which the statute rests. As this case demonstrates, few undertakings during a marriage better qualify as the type of joint effort that the statute's economic partnership theory is intended to address than contributions toward one spouse's acquisition of a professional license. Working spouses are often required to contribute substantial income as wage earners, sacrifice their own educational or career goals and opportunities for child rearing, perform the bulk of household duties and responsibilities and forego the acquisition of marital assets that could have been accumulated if the professional spouse had been employed rather than occupied with the study and training necessary to acquire a professional license. In this case, nearly all of the parties' nine-year marriage was devoted to the acquisition of plaintiff's medical license and defendant played a major role in that project. She worked continuously during the marriage and contributed all of her earnings to their joint effort, she sacrificed her own educational and career opportunities, and she traveled with plaintiff to Mexico for three and one-half years while he attended medical school there. The Legislature has decided, by its explicit reference in the statute to the contributions of one spouse to the other's profession or career, that these contributions represent investments in the economic partnership of the marriage and that the product of the parties' joint efforts, the professional license, should be considered marital property.

The majority at the Appellate Division held that the cited statutory provisions do not refer to the license held by a professional who has yet to establish a practice but only to a going professional practice. There is no reason in law or logic to restrict the plain language of the statute to existing practices, however, for it is of little consequence in making an award of marital property, except for the purpose of evaluation, whether the professional spouse has already established a practice or whether he or she has yet to do so. An established practice merely represents the exercise of the privileges conferred upon the professional spouse by the license and the income flowing from that practice represents the receipt of the enhanced earning capacity that licensure allows. That being so, it would be unfair not to consider the license a marital asset.

Plaintiff's principal argument, adopted by the majority below, is that a professional license is not marital property because it does not fit within the traditional view of property as something which has an exchange value on the open market and is capable of sale, assignment or transfer. The position does not withstand analysis for at least two reasons. First, as we have observed, it ignores the fact that whether a professional license constitutes marital property is to be judged by the language of the statute which created this new species of property previously unknown at common law or under prior statutes. Thus, whether the license fits within traditional property concepts is of no consequence. Second, it is an overstatement to assert that a professional license could not be considered property even outside the context of section 236(B). A professional license is a valuable property right, reflected in the money, effort and lost opportunity for employment expended in its acquisition, and also in the enhanced earning capacity it affords its holder, which may not be revoked without due process of law. That a professional license has no market value is irrelevant. Obviously, a license may not be alienated as may other property and for that reason the working spouse's interest in it is limited. The Legislature has recognized that limitation, however, and has provided for an award in lieu of its actual distribution (see, Domestic Relations Law § 236[B][5][e]).

Plaintiff also contends that alternative remedies should be employed, such as an award of rehabilitative maintenance or reimbursement for direct financial contributions. The statute does not expressly authorize retrospective maintenance or rehabilitative awards and we have no occasion to decide in this case whether the authority to do so may ever be implied from its provisions. It is sufficient to observe that normally a working spouse should not be restricted to that relief because to do so frustrates the purposes underlying the Equitable Distribution Law. Limiting a working spouse to a maintenance award, either general or rehabilitative, not only is contrary to the economic partnership concept underlying the statute but also retains the uncertain and inequitable economic ties of dependence that the Legislature sought to extinguish by equitable distribution. Maintenance is subject to termination upon the recipient's remarriage and a working spouse may never receive adequate consideration for his or her contribution and may even be penalized for the decision to remarry if that is the only method of compensating the contribution. As one court said so well, "[t]he function of equitable distribution is to recognize that when a marriage ends, each of the spouses, based on the totality of the contributions made to it, has a stake in and right to a share of the marital assets accumulated while it endured, not because that share is needed, but because those assets represent the capital product of what was essentially a partnership entity" (Wood v. Wood, 119 Misc.2d 1076, 1079, 465 N.Y.S.2d 475). The Legislature stated its intention to eliminate such inequities by providing that a supporting spouse's "direct or indirect contribution" be recognized, considered and rewarded (Domestic Relations Law § 236[B][5][d][6]).

Turning to the question of valuation, it has been suggested that even if a professional license is considered marital property, the working spouse is entitled only to reimbursement of his or her direct financial contributions (see, Note, Equitable Distribution of Degrees and Licenses: Two Theories Toward Compensating Spousal Contributions, 49 Brooklyn L.Rev. 301, 317–322). By parity of reasoning, a spouse's down payment on real estate or contribution to the purchase of securities would be limited to the money contributed, without any remuneration for any incremental value in the asset because of price appreciation. Such a result is completely at odds with the statute's requirement that the court give full consideration to both direct and indirect contributions "made to the acquisition of such marital property by the party not having title, including joint *efforts* or expenditures and *contributions and services as a spouse, parent,* wage earner *and homemaker*" (Domestic Relations Law 236[B][5][d][6] [emphasis added]). If the license is marital property, then the working spouse is entitled to an equitable portion of it, not a return of funds advanced. Its value is the enhanced earning capacity it affords the holder and although fixing the present value of that enhanced earning capacity may present problems, the problems are not insurmountable. Certainly they are no more difficult than computing tort damages for wrongful death or diminished earning capacity resulting from injury and they differ only in degree from the problems presented when valuing a professional practice for purposes of a distributive award, something the courts have not hesitated to do. The trial court retains the flexibility and discretion to structure the distributive award equitably, taking into consideration factors such as the working spouse's need for immediate payment, the licensed spouse's current ability to pay and the income tax consequences of prolonging the period of payment once it has received evidence of the present value of the license and the working spouse's contributions toward its acquisition and considered the remaining factors mandated by the statute, it may then make an appropriate distribution of the marital property including a distributive award for the professional license if such an award is warranted. When other marital assets are of sufficient value to provide for the supporting spouse's equitable portion of the marital property, including his or her contributions to the acquisition of the professional license, however, the court retains the discretion to distribute these other marital assets or to make a distributive award in lieu of an actual distribution of the value of the professional spouse's license.

. . .

Plaintiff also contends that the trial court erred in excluding evidence of defendant's marital fault on the question of equitable distribution. Arguably, the court may consider marital fault under factor 10, "any other factor which the court shall expressly find to be just and proper". Except in egregious cases which shock the conscience of the court, however, it is not a "just and proper" factor for consideration in the equitable distribution of marital property. That is so because marital fault is inconsistent with the underlying assumption that a marriage is in part an economic partnership and upon its dissolution the parties are entitled to a fair share of the marital estate, because fault will usually be difficult to assign and because introduction of the issue may involve the courts in time-consuming procedural maneuvers relating to collateral issues. We have no occasion to consider the wife's fault in this action because there is no suggestion that she was guilty of fault sufficient to shock the conscience.

. . .

Accordingly, in view of our holding that plaintiff's license to practice medicine is marital property, the order of the Appellate Division should be modified, with costs to defendant, by reinstating the judgment and the case remitted to the Appellate Division for determination of the facts, including the exercise of that court's discretion and, as so modified, affirmed. . . .

■ Meyer, Judge (concurring).

I concur in Judge Simons' opinion but write separately to point up for consideration by the Legislature the potential for unfairness involved in distributive awards based upon a license of a professional still in training.

An equity court normally has power to " 'change its decrees where there has been a change of circumstances' ". The implication of Domestic Relations Law § 236(B)(9)(b), which deals with modification of an order or decree as to maintenance or child support, is, however, that a distributive award pursuant to section 236(B)(5)(e), once made, is not subject to change. Yet a professional in training who is not finally committed to a career choice when the distributive award is made may be locked into a particular kind of practice simply because the monetary obligations imposed by the distributive award made on the basis of the trial judge's conclusion (prophecy may be a better word) as to what the career choice will be leaves him or her no alternative.

The present case points up the problem. A medical license is but a step toward the practice ultimately engaged in by its holder, which follows after internship, residency and, for particular specialties, board certification. Here it is undisputed that plaintiff was in a residency for general surgery at the time of the trial, but had the previous year done a residency in internal medicine. Defendant's expert based his opinion on the difference between the average income of a general surgeon and that of a college graduate of plaintiff's age and life expectancy, which the trial judge utilized, impliedly finding that plaintiff would engage in a surgical practice despite plaintiff's testimony that he was dissatisfied with the general surgery program he was in and was attempting to return to the internal medicine training he had been in the previous year. The trial judge had the right, of course, to discredit that testimony, but the point is that equitable distribution was not intended to permit a judge to make a career decision for a licensed spouse still in training. Yet the degree of speculation involved in the award made is emphasized by the testimony of the expert on which it was based. Asked whether his assumptions and calculations were in any way speculative, he replied: "Yes. They're speculative to the extent of, will Dr. O'Brien practice medicine? Will Dr. O'Brien earn more or less than the average surgeon earns? Will Dr. O'Brien live to age sixty-five? Will Dr. O'Brien have a heart attack or will he be injured in an automobile accident? Will he be disabled? I mean, there is a degree of speculation. That speculative aspect is no more to be taken into account, cannot be taken into account, and it's a question, again, Mr. Emanuelli, not for the expert but for the courts to decide. It's not my function nor could it be."

The equitable distribution provisions of the Domestic Relations Law were intended to provide flexibility so that equity could be done. But if the assumption as to career choice on which a distributive award payable over a number of years is based turns out not to be the fact (as, for example, should a general surgery trainee accidentally lose the use of his hand), it should be possible for the court to revise the distributive award to conform to the fact. And there will be no unfairness in so doing if either spouse can seek reconsideration, for the licensed spouse is more likely to seek reconsideration based on real, rather than imagined, cause if he or she knows that the nonlicensed spouse can seek not only reinstatement of the original award, but counsel fees in addition, should the purported circumstance on which a change is made turn out to have been feigned or to be illusory.

NOTES

Every other state and the American Law Institute excludes professional income-enhancing degrees from classification as marital property "because their value is inextricably intertwined with spousal skills or earning capacity, or post-marital spousal labor." ALI, PRINCIPLES OF THE LAW OF FAMILY DISSOLUTION: ANALYSIS AND RECOMMENDATIONS: PROPOSED FINAL DRAFT PART I, CH. 4, § 407, 151 (Feb. 14, 1997). New York's approach was reaffirmed in McSparron v. McSparron, 87 N.Y.2d 275, 639 N.Y.S.2d 265, 662 N.E.2d 745 (1995), where the court held that the value of a newly earned professional license may be measured by comparing average lifetime income of college graduates and the lifetime earnings of persons with such a license and then reducing the difference to it's present value. *Id.* at 751. The limitation on the degree being property subject to division upon divorce is that the non-degree earning spouse must contribute in a meaningful way to the attainment of the degree during marriage, not before the marriage or after separation. Gandhi v. Gandhi, 283 A.D.2d 782, 724 N.Y.S.2d 541 (2001).

Increase in value of the career of the plaintiff wife, (a prominent actress and model) was determined to be marital property in Golub v. Golub, 139 Misc.2d 440, 527 N.Y.S.2d 946 (Sup.Ct.1988). The court explained:

> There seems to be no rational basis upon which to distinguish between a degree, a license, or any other special skill that generates substantial income. In determining the value of marital property, all such income generating assets should be considered if they accumulated while the marriage endured. If one spouse has sacrificed and assisted the other in an effort to increase that other spouse's earning capacity, it should make no difference what shape or form that asset takes so long as it in fact results in an increased earning capacity . . .

> The noncelebrity spouse should be entitled to a share of the celebrity spouse's fame, limited, of course, by the degree to which that fame is attributable to the non-celebrity spouse. The source of the fame must still be traced to the marital efforts.

All of the community property states take the position that a degree is not property but that the supporting spouse is entitled to a share of the degree-holding spouse's earning capacity through reimbursement. *See, e.g.,* GRACE GANZ BLUMBERG, COMMUNITY PROPERTY IN CALIFORNIA 369–385 (3d. 1999). Professor Deborah Batts has examined and analyzed the various judicial approaches that have been taken on this subject and has included a set of appendices with a detailed summary of the burgeoning group of cases on the subject in *Remedy Refocus: In Search of Equity in "Enhanced Spouse/Other Spouse" Divorces*, 63 N.Y.U.L. REV. 751 (1988). For more general discussion, *see* Katherine Wells Meighan, *For Better of for Worse: A Corporate Finance Approach to Valuing Educational Degrees at Divorce*, 5 GEO. MASON L. REV. 193 (1997); Susan Etta Keller, *The Rhetoric of Marriage, Achievement, and Power: An Analysis of Judicial Opinions Considering the Treatment of Professional Degrees as Marital Property*, 21 VT. L. REV. 409 (1996). The issues are examined conceptually in the context of support payments in, Ira Mark Ellman, *The Theory of Alimony*, 77 CAL. L. REV. 1 (1989).

Christianson v. Christianson

Supreme Court of North Dakota, 2003.
671 N.W.2d 801.

■ SANDSTROM, JUSTICE.

Gerald Christianson is appealing a Northwest Judicial District Court judgment awarding Cecelia Christianson $900.00 per month in spousal support. Gerald Christianson argues that the district court erred in imputing income to him when determining his ability to pay, that Cecelia Christianson's needs as a disadvantaged spouse were not supported by the evidence, that temporary support should have been awarded, and that equalizing their income was inappropriate. Because we are unable to fully review the district court's finding that Cecelia Christianson is a disadvantaged spouse entitled to permanent support, we affirm that portion of its decision. Concluding the district court improperly calculated the amount of spousal support, we reverse and remand for proper calculation.

. . .

Gerald and Cecelia Christianson married in June 1968. Gerald Christianson sued Cecelia Christianson for divorce in January 2001. At the time of trial, Gerald Christianson was 56 and Cecelia Christianson was 58. Gerald Christianson has a Bachelor of Science Degree in Biology, a Master's Degree in School Administration, and a Specialist's Degree in Educational Leadership.

Gerald Christianson had been working as a Superintendent at Parshall High School in Parshall, North Dakota. Following the 1999–2000 school year, he retired and began drawing benefits from the North Dakota Teachers' Fund for Retirement. He gave up his position in anticipation of obtaining a "state job" as a grant administrator, but the job never materialized. Before retiring, Gerald Christianson had an annual salary of $56,000, and with benefits, his compensation was close to $65,000.

Gerald Christianson enrolled at North Dakota State University in Fargo, North Dakota, in August of 2000 to pursue a Specialist's Degree in Educational Leadership. The salary range for a person with this degree is between $50,000 and $90,000. While attending school at North Dakota State University, Gerald Christianson earned $692.00 per month as a graduate teaching assistant and $800.00 per month as a sales associate at Marshall Field's. Gerald Christianson's retirement income at the time gave him $2,273.86 per month. He forwarded $1,050.00 of that amount to Cecelia Christianson. Gerald Christianson is in good health, aside from occasional back pain.

Cecelia Christianson has a Bachelor of Science Degree in Elementary Education. She is employed as an elementary school teacher at Plaza School in Plaza, North Dakota, earning $24,500. She also works part-time at the Cenex Convenience Store in Parshall, earning from $300 to $350 per month.

On October 15, 2001, the district court awarded 60 percent of the marital property to Cecelia Christianson and 40 percent to Gerald Christianson. The district court found Cecelia Christianson to be a disadvantaged spouse and determined she could not be rehabilitated. The court awarded her permanent support in the amount of zero ($0.00) dollars. Given the fact that Gerald Christianson did not have full-time employment and was pursuing a degree, the court deferred setting the amount of spousal support until October 15, 2002.

The district court found Cecelia Christianson had low job security; the school where she teaches has declining enrollment, and at some point it may no longer be feasible to keep the school open. It found that she may find it difficult to obtain other employment as a teacher because there are many elementary school teachers and she is 58 years old and does not have a portfolio, which is required by many schools.

The district court also found the parties moved to different communities nine times during their marriage. It found these moves were made solely to advance Gerald Christianson's career, and little consideration was given to whether Cecelia Christianson could obtain a teaching job. It also found Cecelia Christianson's teaching career was interrupted by these moves; extended time away from the classroom does not look good on a resume. The district court found that being away from teaching also made it difficult for Cecelia Christianson to build retirement. Because the parties dipped into her retirement fund on four occasions, her retirement is a fraction of what it could have been. It also found that Cecelia Christianson has heel spurs in both feet and will eventually require surgery. Judgment was entered November 6, 2001.

On January 16, 2003, the district court again reviewed the issue of support. The court found Cecelia Christianson's needs as a disadvantaged spouse had become more pronounced since the divorce judgment had been entered; the A.G. Edwards stock portfolio awarded to her as part of the property division had sharply declined in value. The court also found that despite a concerted and good-faith attempt to obtain employment, Gerald Christianson has been unable to secure a position in the field of school administration. The court recognized that Gerald Christianson voluntarily gave up a $56,000 job, that the salary range for an individual possessing his type of degree is $50,000 to $90,000, and that his present earnings are significantly less than the prevailing amounts earned in the community by persons with a similar work history and occupational qualifications. The court found Gerald Christianson to be underemployed. The court used an equalization-of-income approach and imputed income to Gerald Christianson to set the support award at $900.00 per month. The amended judgment was entered on April 3, 2003.

Gerald Christianson argues that no authority exists for imputing income to him for the purpose of calculating spousal support, that equalization of income was inappropriate for this case, and that the district court improperly assessed his ability to pay.

He argues spousal support is not the same as child support, in which the imputation of income is authorized, and claims no such authority exists in the case of spousal support.

"Spousal support awards must be made in consideration of the disadvantaged spouse's needs and of the supporting spouse's needs and ability to pay." *Shields v. Shields*, 2003 ND 16, ¶ 10, 656 N.W.2d 712.

Cecelia Christianson can point to no North Dakota statutory or case law providing for the imputation of income in spousal support cases. Other states have permitted imputing income in some cases. *See, e.g., Moore v. Moore*, 242 Mich.App. 652, 619 N.W.2d 723, 724–25 (2000); *In re Marriage of Carrick*, 560 N.W.2d 407, 410 (Minn.Ct.App.1997); *Grady v. Grady*, 295

Ark. 94, 747 S.W.2d 77, 78–79 (1988). Even if it were allowed, it would not be appropriate for this case. *See id.* The district court found that despite a concerted and good-faith attempt on Gerald Christianson's part to obtain employment, he has come up empty-handed in his job search.[2]

Gerald Christianson claims that the use of an income-equalization approach to spousal support was not appropriate.

Equalization is not a goal of spousal support, and equalization of income between divorcing spouses is not a measure of spousal support although it is a factor that can be considered. *Sommers,* 2003 ND 77, ¶ 17, 660 N.W.2d 586. The amount of support ordered greatly exceeds Gerald Christianson's ability to pay and is not justified by "equalization of income."

We reverse, concluding the district court improperly imputed income to Gerald Christianson when it sought to equalize the parties' incomes. We remand to the district court for proper calculation of spousal support based upon the parties' needs and ability to pay.

Cecelia Christianson argues she should be awarded attorney fees on appeal because Gerald Christianson's actions have unreasonably increased the time and effort spent on the dispute.

"The principal factors to be considered for deciding the amount of attorney fees are need and ability to pay." *Mahoney v. Mahoney,* 1997 ND 149, ¶ 40, 567 N.W.2d 206. "An award of attorney's fees in litigation about marital obligations between former spouses does not depend entirely on the merits of each position, although whether one party's actions unreasonably increased the time and effort spent on the dispute can be a factor." *Id.*

Section 14–05–23, N.D.C.C., states that "during any time in which an action for separation or divorce is pending, the court, upon application of a party, may issue an order requiring ... payment of attorney fees." Under this section we have concurrent original jurisdiction with the district court to award attorney fees on appeal. *Severson v. Severson,* 482 N.W.2d 594, 596 (N.D.1992).

[A]s we are an appellate court and exercise original jurisdiction rarely, as attorney's fees and costs involve the necessity of determining facts, and as we ordinarily do not determine facts, we prefer that the district court initially make the determination of attorney's fees even in conjunction with an appeal to our Court. *McIntee v. McIntee,* 413 N.W.2d 366, 367 (N.D.1987). When a party to a divorce action makes a motion in this Court for an award of attorney's fees on appeal, we generally remand the issue to the district court for a determination. *Roen v. Roen,* 438 N.W.2d at 174.

Severson, at 596.

---

2. Contrary to the concurring and dissenting opinion's statement, at ¶ 36, the district court did *not* implicitly or explicitly find Gerald Christianson was "voluntarily underemployed."

We remand this case to the district court for a determination of whether attorney fees should be awarded to Cecelia Christianson and, if so, for what amount.

We reverse the district court's judgment as to the amount of spousal support and remand for further proceedings.

■ CAROL RONNING KAPSMER, J., concurs. GERALD W. VANDE WALLE, C.J., I concur in the result remanding this case for further proceedings.

[The separate opinion of NEUMANN, JUSTICE, concurring specially in the result, has been omitted.]

■ MARING, JUSTICE, concurring in part and dissenting in part.

I respectfully dissent from that part of the majority opinion holding that no authority exists allowing imputation of income for the purpose of calculating spousal support and that part holding equalization of income is inappropriate in this case. I concur in the remaining parts of the opinion, but would affirm the judgment of the trial court.

Gerald and Cecelia were married 33 years before divorcing and in dispute is the ultimate amount of the trial court's award of permanent spousal support to Cecelia. Gerald worked as superintendent at Parshall High School for the 1999–2000 school year and earned a total compensation package of $65,000. He voluntarily quit his position at the end of the school year in anticipation of a "state job" as a grant administrator. However, the "state job" never materialized and he enrolled at North Dakota State University ("NDSU") in August of 2000 to pursue a Specialist's Degree in Educational Leadership, which he obtained in May of 2002.

During his advanced degree education, Gerald, who was then 56 years of age, began drawing from his teacher's retirement fund. Gerald testified the salary range for an Education Leader in this area of the country is $50,000 to $90,000. He testified at trial that he had already applied for forty positions region-wide and had not been able to secure one.

The trial court found that while attending NDSU, Gerald was receiving $692 a month as a Graduate Teaching Assistant, $800 a month as a part-time salesperson at Marshall Fields, and $2,273.86 a month of retirement funds. Gerald testified he was sending Cecelia $1,050 a month. The trial court also found Gerald had voluntarily relinquished his superintendent position and that the decision was not a "truly joint decision" by Gerald and Cecelia. The trial court concluded Gerald's actions constituted economic fault. Additionally, the trial court determined Gerald spent $22,704.18 of the proceeds from annuities, in part, on costs associated with obtaining his advanced degree from NDSU. Accordingly, marital funds were used by Gerald to obtain his advanced education.

Cecelia is 58 years old and earns a salary of $24,500 a year as an elementary teacher plus $300 to $350 a month as a part-time worker at the Parshall Cenex Convenience Store. The trial court found that Cecelia supported Gerald's career advancement to the detriment of her own. They moved nine times to advance Gerald's career with little or no consideration for Cecelia's teaching career. Due to the frequent moves, Cecelia could not build her retirement, and what retirement she did have, was invaded on four separate occasions to help pay moving expenses or to pay for Gerald's advanced education. The trial court concluded that Cecelia is a disadvantaged spouse and is entitled to spousal support, but declined to set the amount until Gerald finished at NDSU and obtained full-time employment and, "in any event (i.e., whether Gerald obtains full-time employment or not) . . . no later than *October 15, 2002.*"

On October 15, 2002, Cecelia requested that the trial court review the spousal support award and alleged Gerald had a greater ability to pay than he did at the time of trial. On review, the trial court found that Cecelia's needs have become even more pronounced since the divorce judgment. It also found that "[d]espite a concerted and good faith attempt . . .," Gerald has come up empty in his job search, "*. . . at least in the field of school administration.*" (Emphasis added.) The trial court further found:

> Realistically, Cecelia cannot wait any longer to begin receiving support from Gerald. Recognizing that: 1. Gerald *voluntarily* gave up a $56,000.00 per year (plus benefits) superintendent's position at Parshall High School in order to obtain his advanced degree; 2. the salary range for an individual possessing this degree is $50,000.00 to $90,000.00; and, 3. Gerald's present earnings are significantly less than prevailing amounts earned in the community (of Bismarck, ND) by persons with similar work history and occupational qualifications, Gerald is "underemployed"—and equity dictates that the Court impute annual income of $50,000.00 to Gerald in calculating his spousal support obligation. When this is done, it can readily be seen that there is a substantial disparity between the incomes of Cecelia and Gerald—a disparity which the property division ordered by the Court did not ameliorate and which the Court believes *cannot* be readily adjusted by rehabilitative support given Cecelia's circumstances.

Our Court has held that the trial courts must consider the *Ruff–Fischer* guidelines in determining both the amount and duration of spousal support. *Sommer v. Sommer,* 2001 ND 191, ¶ 9, 636 N.W.2d 423. The factors include:

> the respective ages of the parties, their earning ability, the duration of the marriage and conduct of the parties during the marriage, their station in life, the circumstances and necessities of each, their health and physical condition, their financial circumstances as shown by the property owned at the time, its value at the time, its income-producing capacity, if any, whether accumulated before or after the marriage, and such other matters as may be material.

Id. (citation omitted).

The trial court in this case very carefully considered all the *Ruff–Fischer* factors including the needs of each party and the ability of the supporting spouse to pay. The trial court imputed income of $50,000 to Gerald based on Gerald's testimony that the salary range for an individual with his degree was $50,000 to $90,000 and that Gerald last earned a total compensation package of $65,000.

The majority opinion states that spousal support awards are to be made in consideration of need and ability to pay, without ever mentioning the *Ruff–Fischer* guidelines; that there is no authority to impute income; and that even if it were allowed the trial court found Gerald made a good faith attempt to obtain employment. The majority opinion overlooks that the trial court found Gerald had "voluntarily" quit his job and that this act constituted economic fault. The majority opinion also overlooks that the trial court noted Gerald may need to find full-time employment in another field and that he made no attempt to do this. With regard to Gerald's good faith attempt to find a job, the trial court clearly referenced only Gerald's attempt to find a school administration job as being made in "good faith." Implicitly the trial court found Gerald was "voluntarily" underemployed, and after having given him one year to resolve his employment status, the court imputed income.

A number of jurisdictions have found that where a party has voluntarily reduced his income, the court may impute income to arrive at an amount for spousal support. *See, e.g., Moore v. Moore,* 242 Mich.App. 652, 619 N.W.2d 723, 724–25 (2000) (citing *Healy v. Healy,* 175 Mich.App. 187, 437 N.W.2d 355 (1989)) (holding that a court can consider a voluntary reduction of income to determine the proper amount of alimony, and that if a court finds a party voluntarily reduced the party's income, the court may impute additional income to arrive at an appropriate alimony award); *Weller v. Weller,* 2002 Ohio 7125, ¶ 47, 2002 WL 31862681 (Ohio Ct.App. 2002) (quoting *Motycka v. Motycka,* 2001 Ohio 2162, 2001 WL 688886) (holding that a trial court has the discretion to impute income to parties for purposes of spousal support, "even if it is determined that a party has no income"); *Cox v. Cox,* 877 P.2d 1262, 1267 (Utah Ct.App.1994) (holding that after first determining a spouse is voluntarily unemployed or underemployed, it is appropriate to impute income) (citations omitted); *Grady v. Grady,* 295 Ark. 94, 747 S.W.2d 77, 78–79 (1988) (holding, in the proper circumstances, a trial court may impute income to a supporting spouse who voluntarily changes employment); *Grable v. Grable,* 307 Ark. 410, 821 S.W.2d 16, 20 (1991) (holding that a trial court may impute income); *In re Marriage of Stephenson,* 39 Cal.App.4th 71, 46 Cal.Rptr.2d 8, 14 (1995) (holding that if a "supporting spouse elects to retire early and to not seek reasonably remunerative available employment under the circumstances, then the court can properly impute income to that supporting spouse . . ."); *Kovar v. Kovar,* 648 So.2d 177, 178 (Fla.Dist.Ct.App.1994) (holding that when a supporting spouse voluntarily reduces his income, it is in the trial court's discretion to impute income); *Bronson v. Bronson,* 793 So.2d 1109, 1111 (Fla.Dist.Ct.App.2001) (same); *In re Marriage of Carrick,* 560 N.W.2d 407, 410 (Minn.Ct.App.1997) (holding that a trial court may impute a party's income to set maintenance, if it first finds that the party was underemployed in bad faith); *In re Marriage of Warwick,* 438 N.W.2d 673, 677 (Minn.Ct.App.1989) (extending earning capacity determination as an appropriate measure of income from child support to spousal support and concluding the rationale for child support is persuasive for maintenance).

In the present case, the trial court did not err in imputing income where it found Gerald was voluntarily underemployed; had only attempted a good faith search for employment as a school superintendent and not for other full-time employment; and the imputed amount of income was within the range of Gerald's testimony as to what he could earn as well as the history of his earnings.

To the extent that the majority opinion stands for the proposition that equalization of income is never appropriate when setting spousal support, I dissent. We have stated that "[a] valid consideration in awarding spousal support is balancing the burden created by divorce." *Marschner v. Marschner*, 2001 ND 4, 621 N.W.2d 339. We also have stated that "[r]elevant to a spousal support determination is the distribution of marital property, the liquid nature of the property, and the income-producing nature of property." *Id.* In this case, the parties net marital estate was minimal being only $38,885. Here, the evidence is that the award of $14,000 in the AG Edwards Account had been reduced to $7,000 and would provide little income to Cecilia.

Cecelia significantly contributed to Gerald's increased earning ability over a period of 33 years. Cecelia's earning ability will never approach Gerald's. Our Court has stated that a valid consideration in an award of spousal support is:

> whether there is a need to *equitably* balance the burdens created by the divorce where the parties cannot maintain the same standard of living apart as they enjoyed together. *See Wald v. Wald*, 556 N.W.2d 291, 297 (N.D.1996) ("We recognize a court must balance the burden created by a divorce when it is impossible to maintain two households at the pre-divorce standard of living."); *Wiege v. Wiege*, 518 N.W.2d 708, 712 (N.D.1994) ("The trial court's award of permanent support, combined with the rehabilitative support, *equitably* shares the overall reduction in the parties' separate standards of living and is not clearly erroneous.") (internal quotation marks omitted); *Wahlberg v. Wahlberg*, 479 N.W.2d 143, 145 (N.D.1992) ("Continuance of a standard of living is a valid consideration in spousal support determinations, *e.g., Bagan v. Bagan*, 382 N.W.2d 645 (N.D.1986), as is balancing the burdens created by the separation when it is impossible to maintain two households at the pre-divorce standard, *e.g., Weir v. Weir*, 374 N.W.2d 858 (N.D.1985).").

Sommer, 2001 ND 191, ¶ 10, 636 N.W.2d 423 (emphasis added).

Although, as in property division, equitable does not need to mean equal, equitable can mean equal. In *Glander v. Glander*, 1997 ND 192, 569 N.W.2d 262, our Court upheld an equalization of income between divorcing spouses. We noted that some jurisdictions reject equalization of income while others "have approved indefinite spousal support that resulted in equalizing post-divorce income." *Id.* Our Court concluded that "[w]hile arbitrary equalization of income between parting spouses would be questionable, we conclude the circumstances here justified it. In determining support, a court must 'balance the burden created by a divorce when it is impossible to maintain two households at the pre-divorce standard of living.' " *Id.* at ¶ 18 (citations omitted).

In *Riehl v. Riehl,* 1999 ND 107, 595 N.W.2d 10, our Court stated "[w]hile we have not endorsed the 'equalization of income between divorcing spouses,' (citation omitted) we conclude the period of spousal support in this case does not adequately address the burdens of the divorce." We reversed and remanded for the trial court to consider whether permanent spousal support would be equitable to offset the permanent economic disadvantage suffered by the wife in that case. *Id.*

I believe the trial court did not clearly err in equalizing the incomes through an award of spousal support under the facts and circumstances of this case. If Gerald wishes to decrease his spousal support payments upon his retirement, he may bring a motion for modification of the amount at that time. *See Sommer,* 2001 ND 191, 636 N.W.2d 423.

I respectfully dissent and would affirm the judgment of the trial court.

In re Marriage of Brown

Supreme Court of California, 1976.
15 Cal.3d 838, 126 Cal.Rptr. 633, 544 P.2d 561.

■ Tobriner, Justice.

Since French v. French (1941) 17 Cal.2d 775, 778, 112 P.2d 235, California courts have held that nonvested pension rights are not property, but a mere expectancy, and thus not a community asset subject to division upon dissolution of a marriage. . . .

Upon reconsideration of this issue, we have concluded that French v. French should be overruled and that the subsequent decisions which rely on that precedent should be disapproved. As we shall explain, the *French* rule cannot stand because nonvested pension rights are not an expectancy but a contingent interest in property; furthermore, the *French* rule compels an inequitable division of rights acquired through community effort. Pension rights, whether or not vested, represent a property interest; to the extent that such rights derive from employment during coverture, they comprise a community asset subject to division in a dissolution proceeding.

Before we turn to the facts of this appeal we must devote a few words to terminology. Some decisions that discuss pension rights, but do not involve division of marital property, describe a pension right as "vested" if the employer cannot unilaterally repudiate that right without terminating the employment relationship. As we explain later, we believe that these decisions correctly define the point at which a pension right becomes a property interest. In divorce and dissolution cases following French v. French, however, the term "vested" has acquired a special meaning; it refers to a pension right which is not subject to a condition of forfeiture if the employment relationship terminates before retirement.[1] We shall use the term "vested" in this latter sense as defining a pension right which survives the discharge or voluntary termination of the employee.

As so defined, a vested pension right must be distinguished from a "matured" or unconditional right to immediate payment. Depending upon the provisions of the retirement program, an employee's right may vest after a term of service even though it does not mature until he reaches retirement age and elects to retire. Such vested but immature rights are frequently subject to the condition, among others, that the employee survive until retirement.

The issue in the present case concerns the nonvested pension rights of respondent Robert Brown. General Telephone Company, Robert's employer, maintains a noncontributory pension plan in which the rights of the employees depend upon their accumulation of "points," based upon a combination of the years of service and the age of the employee. Under this plan, an employee who is discharged before he accumulates 78 points forfeits his rights; an employee with 78 points can opt for early retirement at a lower pension, or continue to work until age 63 and retire at an increased pension.

Gloria and Robert Brown married on July 29, 1950. When they separated in November of 1973, Robert had accumulated 72 points under the pension plan, a substantial portion of which is attributable to his work during the period when the parties were married and living together.[3] If he continues to work for General Telephone, Robert will accumulate 78 points on November 30, 1976. If he retires then, he will receive a monthly pension of $310.94; if he continues his employment until normal retirement age his pension will be $485 a month.

Relying on the *French* rule, the trial court held that since Robert had not yet acquired a "vested" right to the retirement pension, the value of his pension rights did not become community property subject to division by the court. It divided the remaining property, awarding Gloria the larger share but directing her to pay $1,742 to Robert to equalize the value received by each spouse. The court also awarded Gloria alimony of $75 per month. Gloria appeals from the portion of the interlocutory judgment that declares that Robert's pension rights are not community property and thus not subject to division by the court.

As we have stated, the fundamental theoretical error which led to the inequitable division of marital property in the present case stems from the seminal decision of French v. French, supra, 17 Cal.2d 775, 112 P.2d 235. Mrs. French claimed a community interest in the prospective retirement pay of her husband, an enlisted man in the Fleet Reserve. The court noted

1. See Article, The Identification and Division of Intangible Community Property: Slicing the Invisible Pie (1973) 6 U.C.Davis L.Rev. 26, 29–31.

3. Since it concluded that nonvested pension rights are not divisible as a community asset, the trial court did not determine what portion of Robert's pension rights is owned by the community.

that "under the applicable statutes the [husband] will not be entitled to such pay until he completes a service of 14 years in the Fleet Reserve and complies with all the requirements of that service." (P. 778, 112 P.2d p. 236.) It concluded that "At the present time, his right to retirement pay is an expectancy which is not subject to division as community property." (Ibid.)

In 1962 the Court of Appeal in Williamson v. Williamson, 203 Cal. App.2d 8, 21 Cal.Rptr. 164, explained the *French* rule, asserting that "To the extent that payment is, at the time of the divorce, subject to conditions which may or may not occur, the pension is an expectancy, not subject to division as community property."

Subsequent cases, however, have limited the sweep of *French*, holding that a vested pension is community property even though it has not matured or is subject to conditions within the employee's control. But although we have frequently reiterated the *French* rule in dictum, we have not previously had occasion to reexamine the merits of that rule.

Throughout our decisions we have always recognized that the community owns all pension rights attributable to employment during the marriage. The *French* rule, however, rests on the theory that nonvested pension rights may be community, but that they are not property; classified as mere expectancies, such rights are not assets subject to division on dissolution of the marriage.

We have concluded, however, that the *French* court's characterization of nonvested pension rights as expectancies errs. The term expectancy describes the interest of a person who merely foresees that he might receive a future beneficence, such as the interest of an heir apparent, or of a beneficiary designated by a living insured who has a right to change the beneficiary.[6] As these examples demonstrate, the defining characteristic of an expectancy is that its holder has no *enforceable right* to his beneficence.

Although some jurisdictions classify retirement pensions as gratuities, it has long been settled that under California law such benefits "do not derive from the beneficence of the employer, but are properly part of the consideration earned by the employee." Since pension benefits represent a form of deferred compensation for services rendered, the employee's right to such benefits is a contractual right, derived from the terms of the employment contract. Since a contractual right is not an expectancy but a chose in action, a form of property, we held in Dryden v. Board of Pension Commissioners, 6 Cal.2d 575, 579, 59 P.2d 104 (1936), that an employee

---

6. The cases discussing the interest of an insurance beneficiary clarify the distinction between an expectancy and a contractual right. "The interest of a beneficiary designated by an insured who has the right to change the beneficiary is, like that of a legatee under a will, a mere expectancy of a gift at the time of the insured's death." (Grimm v. Grimm (1945) 26 Cal.2d 173, 175–176, 157 P.2d 841, 842.) But if the holder acquires a contractual right to be named as beneficiary of the policy, his interest is no longer an expectancy, but a property right. (See Page v. Washington Mut. Life Ass'n (1942) 20 Cal.2d 234, 242, 125 P.2d 20.)

acquires a property right to pension benefits when he enters upon the performance of his employment contract.

Although *Dryden* involved an employee who possessed vested pension rights, the issue of nonvested rights came before us in Kern v. City of Long Beach, 29 Cal.2d 848, 179 P.2d 799 (1947). There a city employee contended that the city's repeal of a pension plan unconstitutionally impaired the obligation of contract. The city defended on the ground that the employee's pension rights had not vested at the time of the abrogation of the plan.

Ruling in favor of the employee, we stated in *Kern* that: "[T]here is little reason to make a distinction between the periods before and after the pension payments are due. It is true that an employee does not earn the right to a full pension until he has completed the prescribed period of service, but he has actually earned some pension rights as soon as he has performed substantial services for his employer. [Citations omitted.] He ... has then earned certain pension benefits, the payment of which is to be made at a future date.... [T]he mere fact that performance is in whole or in part dependent upon certain contingencies does not prevent a contract from arising, and the employing governmental body may not deny or impair the contingent liability any more than it can refuse to make the salary payments which are immediately due. Clearly, it cannot do so after all the contingencies have happened, and in our opinion it cannot do so at any time after a contractual duty to make salary payments has arisen, since a part of the compensation which the employee has at that time earned consists of his pension rights." (29 Cal.2d at p. 855, 179 P.2d at p. 803.)

Since we based our holding in *Kern* upon the constitutional prohibition against impairment of contracts, a prohibition applicable only to public entities, the private employer in Hunter v. Sparling (1948) 87 Cal.App.2d 711, 197 P.2d 807 contended that it could repudiate an employee's nonvested pension rights without liability. Rejecting that contention, the Court of Appeal cited the language from *Kern* quoted above and concluded that once the employee performed services in reliance upon the promised pension, he could enforce his right to a pension either under traditional contract principles of offer, acceptance and consideration or under the doctrine of promissory estoppel. In subsequent years the courts have repeatedly reaffirmed that a nonvested pension right is nonetheless a contractual right, and thus a property right.

... In other situations when community funds or effort are expended to acquire a conditional right to future income, the courts do not hesitate to treat that right as a community asset.[9] For example, in Waters v. Waters (1946) 75 Cal.App.2d 265, 170 P.2d 494, the attorney husband had a contingent interest in a suit pending on appeal at the time of the divorce; the court held that his fee, when and if collected, would be a community asset. Indeed in the several recent pension cases the courts have asserted

---

9. See Thiede, The Community Property Interest of the Non–Employee Spouse in Private Employee Retirement Benefits (1975) 9 U.S.F.L.Rev. 635, 656–661; Note, Retirement Pay: A Divorce in Time Saved Mine (1973) 24 Hastings L.J. 347, 354–356.

that vested but immature pensions are community assets although such pensions are commonly subject to the condition that the employee survive until retirement.

We conclude that French v. French, and subsequent cases erred in characterizing nonvested pension rights as expectancies and in denying the trial courts the authority to divide such rights as community property. This mischaracterization of pension rights has, and unless overturned, will continue to result in inequitable division of community assets. Over the past decades, pension benefits have become an increasingly significant part of the consideration earned by the employee for his services. As the date of vesting and retirement approaches, the value of the pension right grows until it often represents the most important asset of the marital community. A division of community property which awards one spouse the entire value of this asset, without any offsetting award to the other spouse, does not represent that equal division of community property contemplated by Civil Code section 4800.

The present case illustrates the point. Robert's pension rights, a valuable asset built up by 24 years of community effort, under the *French* rule would escape division by the court as a community asset solely because dissolution occurred two years before the vesting date. If, as is entirely likely, Robert continues to work for General Telephone Company for the additional two years needed to acquire a vested right, he will then enjoy as his separate property an annuity created predominantly through community effort. This "potentially whimsical result," as the Court of Appeal described a similar division of community property in In re Marriage of Peterson, 41 Cal.App.3d 642, 651, 115 Cal.Rptr. 184 (1974), cannot be reconciled with the fundamental principle that property attributable to community earnings must be divided equally when the community is dissolved.

Respondent does not deny that if nonvested pension rights are property, the *French* rule results in an inequitable division of that property. He maintains, however, that any inequity can be redressed by an award of alimony to the nonemployee spouse. Alimony, however, lies within the discretion of the trial court; the spouse "should not be dependent on the discretion of the court ... to provide her with the equivalent of what should be hers as a matter of absolute right." (In re Marriage of Peterson, supra, 41 Cal.App.3d 642, 651, 115 Cal.Rptr. 184, 191.)

Respondent and amicus further suggest that a decision repudiating the *French* rule would both impose severe practical burdens upon the courts and restrict the employee's freedom to change his place or terms of employment. We shall examine these contentions and point out why they do not justify a continued refusal by the courts to divide nonvested pension rights as a community asset.

In dividing nonvested pension rights as community property the court must take account of the possibility that death or termination of employment may destroy those rights before they mature. In some cases the trial court may be able to evaluate this risk in determining the present value of those rights. But if the court concludes that because of uncertainties affecting the vesting or maturation of the pension that it should not attempt to divide the present value of pension rights, it can instead award each spouse an appropriate portion of each pension payment as it is paid.[10] This method of dividing the community interest in the pension renders it unnecessary for the court to compute the present value of the pension rights, and divides equally the risk that the pension will fail to vest.

As respondent points out, an award of future pension payments as they fall due will require the court to continue jurisdiction to supervise the payments of pension benefits. Yet this obligation arises whenever the court cannot equitably award all pension rights to one spouse, whether or not such rights are vested; the claim of mere administrative burden surely cannot serve as support for an inequitable substantive rule which distinguishes between vested and nonvested rights. Despite the administrative burden such an award imposes, courts in the past have successfully divided *vested* pension rights by awarding each spouse a share in future payments. Courts can divide nonvested pension rights in like fashion.

Moreover, the practical consequence of the *French* rule has been historically that the court must often award alimony to the spouse who, deprived of any share in the nonvested pension rights, lacks resources to purchase the necessities of life. Judicial supervision of alimony awards, undertaken in the past, entails far more onerous a burden than supervision of future pension payment.

As to the claim that our present holding will infringe upon the employee's freedom of contract, we note that judicial recognition of the nonemployee spouse's interest in vested pension rights has not limited the employee's freedom to change or terminate his employment, to agree to a modification of the terms of his employment (including retirement benefits), or to elect between alternative retirement programs.[12] We do not conceive that judicial recognition of spousal rights in nonvested pensions will change the law in this respect. The employee retains the right to decide, and by his decision define, the nature of the retirement benefits owned by the community.

Robert finally contends that any decision overruling French v. French should be given purely prospective effect. Although as we explain our

---

10. Our suggestion in Phillipson v. Board of Administration, supra, 3 Cal.3d 32, 46, 89 Cal.Rptr. 61, 473 P.2d 765, that when feasible the trial court should award the employee all pension rights and compensate his spouse with other property of equal value, was not intended to tie the hands of the trial court. That court retains the discretion to divide the community assets in any fashion which complies with the provisions of Civil Code section 4800.

12. In Phillipson v. Board of Administration, supra, 3 Cal.3d 32, 89 Cal.Rptr. 61,

473 P.2d 765, the employee had absconded with most of the community assets; the trial court to equalize the division of community property awarded the spouse all of the employee's pension rights. Under those special circumstances we held that since the employee no longer enjoyed a beneficial interest in the rights, the divorce court could control the employee's election between alternative benefit programs. (3 Cal.3d at p. 48, 89 Cal.Rptr. 61, 473 P.2d 765.)

decision cannot be accorded complete retroactivity without upsetting final judgments of long standing, we believe the decision may properly govern any case in which no final judgment dividing the marital property has been rendered.

. . .

We conclude that our decision today should not apply retroactively to permit a nonemployee spouse to assert an interest in nonvested pension rights when the property rights of the marriage have already been adjudicated by a decree of dissolution or separation which has become final as to such adjudication, unless the decree expressly reserved jurisdiction to divide such pension rights at a later date. Our decision will apply retroactively, however, to any case in which the property rights arising from the marriage have not yet been adjudicated, to such rights if such adjudication is still subject to appellate review, or if in such adjudication the trial court has expressly reserved jurisdiction to divide pension rights.

. . .

In sum, we submit that whatever abstract terminology we impose, the joint effort that composes the community and the respective contributions of the spouses that make up its assets, are the meaningful criteria. The wife's contribution to the community is not one whit less if we declare the husband's pension rights not a contingent asset but a mere "expectancy." Fortunately we can appropriately reflect the realistic situation by recognizing that the husband's pension rights, a contingent interest, whether vested or not vested, comprise a property interest of the community and that the wife may properly share in it.

The judgment of the superior court is reversed and the cause remanded for further proceedings consistent with the views expressed herein.

NOTES

At one point in history the marital home was the most significant marital asset; today this preeminence often belongs to the pension funds. Other assets associated with marital labor have evolved as well. For a discussion, *see* Grace Ganz Blumberg, *Marital Property Treatment of Pensions, Disability Pay, Workers' Compensation, and Other Wage Substitutes: An Insurance, Or Replacement, Analysis*, 33 U.C.L.A. L. REV. 1250 (1986); Grace Ganz Blumberg, *Intangible Assets: Recognition and Valuation* § 23.08 in 2 VALUATION AND DISTRIBUTION OF MARITAL PROPERTY (1996). These assets/benefits are most often classified as wage substitutes and states have taken various approaches to their classification. For instance, state courts are willing to consider a pension's value in the division of marital assets, even though a state statute may bar dividing the pension itself as marital property. To accomplish its objective the court may accommodate the value of the pension by using other divisible property, similar to the approach taken when unable to divide Social Security or federal disability benefits. *See, e.g.*, Waln v. Waln, 280 Wis.2d 253, 694 N.W.2d 452 (2005).

(1) **Stock Options:** Nonvested stock options are considered marital property subject to division upon divorce if they are evidenced by a contract that will allow the employee the option to exercise the option during or after the marital period. Examples include Hiett v. Hiett, 158 S.W.3d 720 (Ark. Ct. App.2004) (stock options may be considered as divisible property and also for payment of support); *In re* Valence, 147 N.H. 663, 798 A.2d 35 (2002) (nonvested stock options are marital property if they are defined by contractual rights); and Otley v. Otley, 147 Md.App. 540, 810 A.2d 1 (2002)(stock options earned during marriage but payable after divorce are nonetheless marital property).

(2) **Deferred and accelerated compensation:** these benefits are marital property if earned—although not received—during the marital period. A separation incentive bonus that became available to an employee after entry of the divorce decree but before property division was non-marital property because the benefit did not accrue during the marriage. Sharber v. Sharber, 35 S.W.3d 841 (Ky.App.2001).

(3) **Accrued leave:** sick leave benefits are accumulated by the employee during employment in exchange for services rendered and are thus marital property for those periods employed, but the cash value is limited to any employee contractual terms. Purpura v. Kelly, 913 So.2d 110 (Fla. Dist. App. 2005).

(4) **Life insurance:** courts have held that a term life insurance policy is non-marital property, see Estate of Logan, 191 Cal.App.3d 319, 236 Cal.Rptr. 368 (1987), but the Maryland Court of Special Appeals has ruled that an irrevocable life insurance trust established by a man during his marriage for wife's benefit is marital property subject to equitable division upon divorce. Caccamise v. Caccamise, 130 Md.App. 505, 747 A.2d 221 (2000).

(5) **Severance pay:** Marriage of Wright, 140 Cal.App.3d 342, 189 Cal.Rptr. 336 (1983), severance pay received after separation is marital property if based on services performed during marriage or under a contractual agreement, but non-marital property if meant to compensate the employee for loss of employment after separation.

(6) **Cost of living adjustments to pension benefits:** Moore v. Moore, 114 N.J. 147, 553 A.2d 20 (1989), holds that the cost of living increases should be included in division of marital property if the benefits are not specifically attributable to post-separation employment.

(7) **Disability Payments:** The Principles published by the American Law Institute provide that "Disability pay and workers' compensation payments are marital property to the extent they replace income or benefits the recipient would have earned during the marriage but for the qualifying disability or injury." PRINCIPLES OF THE LAW OF FAMILY DISSOLUTION: ANALYSIS AND RECOMMENDATIONS § 4.08(2)(b) (2000). This view is represented in many state court decisions. *See, e.g.,* Beckley v. Beckley, 822 N.E.2d 158 (Ind. 2005) (disability payments paid as compensation for lost wages is subject to division as marital property); Lawson v. Hayden, 786 N.E.2d 756

(Ind. Ct. App. 2003) (payment is marital property if earned from employment taxes paid during the marriage); Metz v. Metz, 61 P.3d 383 (Wyo. 2003) (to be divisible disability payment must be a substitute for income earned during the marital period).

Mansell v. Mansell

Supreme Court of the United States, 1989.
490 U.S. 581, 109 S.Ct. 2023, 104 L.Ed.2d 675.

■ JUSTICE MARSHALL delivered the opinion of the Court.

In this appeal, we decide whether state courts, consistent with the federal Uniformed Services Former Spouses' Protection Act, 10 U.S.C. § 1408 (1982 ed. and Supp. V) (Former Spouses' Protection Act or Act), may treat, as property divisible upon divorce, military retirement pay waived by the retiree in order to receive veterans' disability benefits. We hold that they may not.

Members of the Armed Forces who serve for a specified period, generally at least 20 years, may retire with a pension. 10 U.S.C. § 3911 et seq. (Army) (1982 ed. and Supp. V); § 6321 et seq. (1982 ed. and Supp. V) (Navy and Marine Corps); § 8911 et seq. (1982 ed. and Supp. V) (Air Force). The amount of retirement pay a veteran is eligible to receive is calculated according to the number of years served and the rank achieved. §§ 3926 and 3991 (Army); §§ 6325–6327 (Navy and Marine Corps); § 8929 (Air Force). Veterans who became disabled as a result of military service are eligible for disability benefits. 38 U.S.C. § 310 (wartime disability); § 331 (peacetime disability). The amount of disability benefits a veteran is eligible to receive is calculated according to the seriousness of the disability and the degree to which the veteran's ability to earn a living has been impaired. §§ 314 and 355.

In order to prevent double dipping, a military retiree may receive disability benefits only to the extent that he waives a corresponding amount of his military retirement pay. § 3105.[1] Because disability benefits are exempt from federal, state, and local taxation, § 3101(a), military retirees who waive their retirement pay in favor of disability benefits increase their after-tax income. Not surprisingly, waivers of retirement pay are common.

California, like several other States, treats property acquired during marriage as community property. When a couple divorces, a state court divides community property equally between the spouses while each spouse retains full ownership of any separate property. See Cal.Civ.Code Ann. § 4800(a) (West 1983 and Supp.1989). California treats military retirement payments as community property to the extent they derive from military service performed during the marriage. See, e.g., Casas v. Thompson, 42

---

1. For example, if a military retiree is eligible for $1500 a month in retirement pay and $500 a month in disability benefits, he must waive $500 of retirement pay before he can receive any disability benefits.

Cal.3d 131, 139, 228 Cal.Rptr. 33, 37–38, 720 P.2d 921, 925, cert. denied, 479 U.S. 1012, 107 S.Ct. 659, 93 L.Ed.2d 713 (1986).

In McCarty v. McCarty, 453 U.S. 210, 101 S.Ct. 2728, 69 L.Ed.2d 589 (1981), we held that the federal statutes then governing military retirement pay prevented state courts from treating military retirement pay as community property. We concluded that treating such pay as community property would do clear damage to important military personnel objectives. We reasoned that Congress intended that military retirement pay reach the veteran and no one else. In reaching this conclusion, we relied particularly on Congress' refusal to pass legislation that would have allowed former spouses to garnish military retirement pay to satisfy property settlements. Finally, noting the distressed plight of many former spouses of military members, we observed that Congress was free to change the statutory framework.

In direct response to McCarty, Congress enacted the Former Spouses' Protection Act, which authorizes state courts to treat "disposable retired or retainer pay" as community property. 10 U.S.C. § 1408(c)(1).[2] " 'Disposable retired or retainer pay' " is defined as "the total monthly retired or retainer pay to which a military member is entitled," minus certain deductions. § 1408(a)(4) (1982 ed., Supp. V). Among the amounts required to be deducted from total pay are any amounts waived in order to receive disability benefits. § 1408(a)(4)(B).[3]

The Act also creates a payments mechanism under which the Federal Government will make direct payments to a former spouse who presents, to the Secretary of the relevant military service, a state-court order granting her a portion of the military retiree's disposable retired or retainer pay. This direct payments mechanism is limited in two ways. § 1408(d). First, only a former spouse who was married to a military member "for a period of 10 years or more during which the member performed at least 10 years of service creditable in determining the member's eligibility for retired or retainer pay," § 1408(d)(2), is eligible to receive direct community property payments. Second, the Federal Government will not make community property payments that exceed 50 percent of disposable retired or retainer pay. § 1408(e)(1).

Appellant Gerald E. Mansell and appellee Gaye M. Mansell were married for 23 years and are the parents of six children. Their marriage

2. The language of the Act covers both community property and equitable distribution States, as does our decision today. Because this case concerns a community property State, for the sake of simplicity we refer to § 1408(c)(1) as authorizing state courts to treat "disposable retired or retainer pay" as community property.

3. Also deducted from total military retirement pay are amounts: (a) owed by the military member to the United States; (b) required by law to be deducted from total pay, including employment taxes, and fines and forfeitures ordered by courts-martial; (c) properly deducted from federal, state, and local income taxes; (d) withheld pursuant to other provisions under the Internal Revenue Code; (e) deducted to pay government life insurance premiums; and (f) deducted to create an annuity for the former spouse. 10 U.S.C. § 1408(a)(4)(A)–(F) (1982 ed. and Supp. V).

ended in 1979 with a divorce decree from the Merced County, California, Superior Court. At that time, Major Mansell received both Air Force retirement pay and, pursuant to a waiver of a portion of that pay, disability benefits. Mrs. Mansell and Major Mansell entered into a property settlement which provided, in part, that Major Mansell would pay Mrs. Mansell 50 percent of his total military retirement pay, including that portion of retirement pay waived so that Major Mansell could receive disability benefits. In 1983, Major Mansell asked the Superior Court to modify the divorce decree by removing the provision that required him to share his total retirement pay with Mrs. Mansell. The Superior Court denied Major Mansell's request without opinion.

Major Mansell appealed to the California Court of Appeal, Fifth Appellate District, arguing that both the Former Spouses' Protection Act and the antiattachment clause that protects a veteran's receipt of disability benefits, 38 U.S.C. § 3101(a) (1982 ed. and Supp. IV),[4] precluded the Superior Court from treating military retirement pay that had been waived to receive disability benefits as community property. Relying on the decision of the Supreme Court of California in Casas v. Thompson, supra, the Court of Appeal rejected that portion of Major Mansell's argument based on the Former Spouses' Protection Act. *Casas* held that after the passage of the Former Spouses' Protection Act, federal law no longer pre-empted state community property law as it applies to military retirement pay. The *Casas* court reasoned that the Act did not limit a state court's ability to treat total military retirement pay as community property and to enforce a former spouse's rights to such pay through remedies other than direct payments from the Federal Government. 42 Cal.3d, at 143–151, 228 Cal.Rptr., at 40–46, 720 P.2d, at 928–933. The Court of Appeal did not discuss the antiattachment clause, 38 U.S.C. § 3101(a).[6] The Supreme Court of California denied Major Mansell's petition for review.

We noted probable jurisdiction, and now reverse.

Because domestic relations are preeminently matters of state law, we have consistently recognized that Congress, when it passes general legislation, rarely intends to displace state authority in this area. Thus we have held that we will not find preemption absent evidence that it is " 'positively required by direct enactment.' " *Hisquierdo,* supra, at 581, 99 S.Ct. at 808 (quoting Wetmore v. Markoe, 196 U.S. 68, 77, 25 S.Ct. 172, 176, 49 L.Ed. 390 (1904)). The instant case, however, presents one of those rare instances

---

4. That clause provides that veterans' benefits "shall not be assignable except to the extent specifically authorized by law, and . . . shall be exempt from the claim[s] of creditors, and shall not be liable to attachment, levy, or seizure by or under any legal or equitable process whatever, either before or after receipt by the [veteran]." 38 U.S.C. § 3101(a) (1982 ed. and Supp. IV).

6. Because we decide that the Former Spouses' Protection Act precludes States from treating as community property retirement pay waived to receive veterans disability benefits, we need not decide whether the anti-attachment clause, § 3101(a), independently protects such pay. See, e.g., Rose v. Rose, 481 U.S. 619, 107 S.Ct. 2029, 95 L.Ed.2d 599 (1987); Wissner v. Wissner, 338 U.S. 655, 70 S.Ct. 398, 94 L.Ed. 424 (1950).

where Congress has directly and specifically legislated in the area of domestic relations.

It is clear from both the language of the Former Spouses' Protection Act, and its legislative history, that Congress sought to change the legal landscape created by the *McCarty* decision.[7] Because pre-existing federal law, as construed by this Court, completely pre-empted the application of state community property law to military retirement pay, Congress could overcome the *McCarty* decision only by enacting an affirmative grant of authority giving the States the power to treat military retirement pay as community property.

The appellant and appellee differ sharply on the scope of Congress' modification of *McCarty*. Mrs. Mansell views the Former Spouses' Protection Act as a complete congressional rejection of *McCarty's* holding that state law is pre-empted; she reads the Act as restoring to state courts all pre-*McCarty* authority. Major Mansell, supported by the Solicitor General, argues that the Former Spouses' Protection Act is only a partial rejection of the *McCarty* rule that federal law preempts state law regarding military retirement pay.[8]

Where, as here, the question is one of statutory construction, we begin with the language of the statute. Mrs. Mansell's argument faces a formidable obstacle in the language of the Former Spouses' Protection Act. Section 1408(c)(1) of the Act affirmatively grants state courts the power to divide military retirement pay, yet its language is both precise and limited. It provides that "a court may treat disposable retired or retainer pay ... either as property solely of the member or as property of the member and his spouse in accordance with the law of the jurisdiction of such court." § 1408(c)(1). The Act's definitional section specifically defines the term "disposable retired or retainer pay" to exclude, *inter alia*, military retirement pay waived in order to receive veterans' disability payments. § 1408(a)(4)(B).[9] Thus, under the Act's plain and precise language, state courts have been granted the authority to treat disposable retired pay as community property; they have not been granted the authority to treat total retired pay as community property.

Mrs. Mansell attempts to overcome the limiting language contained in the definition, § 1408(a)(4)(B), by reading the Act as a garnishment statute

---

7. Congress also demonstrated its focus on *McCarty* when it chose June 25, 1981, the day before *McCarty* was decided, as the applicable date for some of the Act's provisions.

8. Although the Solicitor General has filed an *amicus* brief supporting Major Mansell, his initial *amicus* brief, filed before the Court noted jurisdiction, supported Mrs. Mansell.

9. The statute provides, in pertinent part:

" 'Disposable retired or retainer pay' means the total monthly retired or retainer pay to which a member is entitled

... less amounts which—

. . .

"(B) are required by law to be and are deducted from the retired or retainer pay of such member, including fines and forfeitures ordered by courts-martials, Federal employment taxes, and amounts waived in order to receive compensation under title 5 or title 38 [disability payments]." § 1408(a)(4)(B).

designed solely to set out the circumstances under which, pursuant to a court order, the Federal Government will make direct payments to a former spouse. According to this view, § 1408(a)(4)(B) defines "[d]isposable retired or retainer pay" only because payments under the federal direct payments mechanism are limited to amounts defined by that term.

The garnishment argument relies heavily on the Act's savings clause. That clause provides:

> "Nothing in this section shall be construed to relieve a member of liability for the payment of alimony, child support, *or other payments* required by a court order on the grounds that payments made out of disposable retired or retainer pay under this section have been made in the maximum amount permitted under [the direct payments mechanism]. Any such unsatisfied obligation of a member may be enforced by any means available under law other than the means provided under this section in any case in which the maximum amount permitted under ... [the direct payments mechanism] has been paid." § 1408(e)(6) (emphasis added).

Mrs. Mansell argues that, because the savings clause expressly contemplates "other payments" in excess of those made under the direct payments mechanism, the Act does not "attempt to tell the state courts what they may or may not do with the underlying property." For the reasons discussed below, we find a different interpretation more plausible. In our view, the savings clause serves the limited purpose of defeating any inference that the federal direct payments mechanism displaced the authority of state courts to divide and garnish property not covered by the mechanism. . . .

First, the most serious flaw in the garnishment argument is that it completely ignores § 1408(c)(1). Mrs. Mansell provides no explanation for the fact that the defined term—"disposable retired or retainer pay"—is used in § 1408(c)(1) to limit specifically and plainly the extent to which state courts may treat military retirement pay as community property.

Second, the view that the Act is solely a garnishment statute and therefore not intended to pre-empt the authority of state courts is contradicted not only by § 1408(c)(1), but also by the other subsections of § 1408(c). Sections 1408(c)(2), (c)(3), and (c)(4) impose new substantive limits on state courts' power to divide military retirement pay. Section 1408(c)(2) prevents a former spouse from transferring, selling, or otherwise disposing of her community interest in the military retirement pay.[10] Section 1408(c)(3) provides that a state court cannot order a military member to retire so that the former spouse can immediately begin receiving her portion of military retirement pay. And § 1408(c)(4) prevents spouses from forum shopping for a State with favorable divorce laws.[12]

---

10. The Senate Report expressly contemplates that § 1408(c)(2) will preempt state law. S.Rep. No. 97–502, p. 16 (1982).

12. A state court may not treat disposable retirement pay as community property unless it has jurisdiction over the military member by reason of (1) residence, other

Because each of these provisions pre-empts state law, the argument that the Act has no pre-emptive effect of its own must fail.[13] Significantly, Congress placed each of these substantive restrictions on state courts in the same section of the Act as § 1408(c)(1). We think it unlikely that every subsection of § 1408(c), except § 1408(c)(1), was intended to pre-empt state law.

In the face of such plain and precise statutory language, Mrs. Mansell faces a daunting standard. She cannot prevail without clear evidence that reading the language literally would thwart the obvious purposes of the Act. The legislative history does not indicate the reason for Congress' decision to shelter from community property law that portion of military retirement pay waived to receive veterans' disability payments. But the absence of legislative history on this decision is immaterial in light of the plain and precise language of the statute; Congress is not required to build a record in the legislative history to defend its policy choices.

Because of the absence of evidence of specific intent in the legislative history, Mrs. Mansell resorts to arguments about the broad purposes of the Act. But this reliance is misplaced because, at this general level, there are statements that both contradict and support her arguments. Her argument that the Act contemplates no federal pre-emption is supported by statements in the Senate Report and the House Conference Report that the purpose of the Act is to overcome the *McCarty* decision and to restore power to the States. But the Senate Report and the House Conference Report also contain statements indicating that Congress rejected the uncomplicated option of removing all federal pre-emption and returning unlimited authority to the States. Indeed, a bill that would have eliminated all federal preemption died in the Senate Committee.[17] Her argument that

than by military assignment in the territorial jurisdiction of the court, (2) domicile, or (3) consent. § 1408(c)(4). Although the Senate Committee had decided not to include any forum shopping restrictions, seeing "no need to limit the jurisdiction of the State courts by restricting the benefits afforded by this bill ..." S.Rep. No. 97–502, at 9, U.S.Code Cong. & Admin.News 1982, p. 1604, the House version of the bill contained the restrictions, and at conference, the Senate agreed to add them. H.R.Conf.Rep. No. 97–749, at 167.

13. That Congress intended the substantive limits in § 1408(c)(1) to be, to some extent, distinct from the limits on the direct payments mechanism contained in § 1408(d) is demonstrated by the legislative compromise that resulted in the direct payments mechanism being available only to former spouses who had been married to the military retiree for 10 years or more. § 1408(d)(2). Under the House version of the bill, military retirement pay could be treated as communi-

ty property only if the couple had been married for 10 years or more. H.R.Conf.Rep. No. 97–749, at 165. The Senate Committee had considered, but rejected, such a provision. S.Rep. No. 97–502, at 9–11. The conferees agreed to remove the House restriction. Instead, they limited the federal direct payments mechanism to marriages that had lasted 10 years or more. H.R.Conf.Rep. No. 97–749, at 166–167. Under this compromise, state courts have been granted the authority to award a portion of disposable military retired pay to former spouses who were married to the military member for less than 10 years but such former spouses may not take advantage of the direct payments mechanism.

17. Entitled "Nonpreemption of State law" the bill provided that "[f]or purposes of division of marital property of any member or former member of the armed forces upon dissolution of such member's marriage, the law of the State in which the dissolution of marriage proceeding was instituted shall be

Congress primarily intended to protect former spouses is supported by evidence that Members of Congress were moved by and responding to the distressed economic plight of military wives after a divorce.[18] But the Senate Report and the House debates contain statements which reveal that Congress was concerned as well with protecting the interests of military members.

Thus, the legislative history, read as a whole, indicates that Congress intended both to create new benefits for former spouses and to place limits on state courts designed to protect military retirees. Our task is to interpret the statute as best we can, not to second guess the wisdom of the congressional policy choice.... Given Congress' mixed purposes, the legislative history does not clearly support Mrs. Mansell's view that giving effect to the plain and precise language of the statute would thwart the obvious purposes of the Act.

We realize that reading the statute literally may inflict economic harm on many former spouses. But we decline to misread the statute in order to reach a sympathetic result when such a reading requires us to do violence to the plain language of the statute and to ignore much of the legislative history. Congress chose the language that requires us to decide as we do, and Congress is free to change it.

For the reasons stated above, we hold that the Former Spouses' Protection Act does not grant state courts the power to treat, as property divisible upon divorce, military retirement pay that has been waived to receive veterans disability benefits. The judgment of the California Court of Appeal is hereby reversed and the case is remanded for further proceedings not inconsistent with this opinion.

■ Justice O'Connor, with whom Justice Blackmun joins, dissenting.

. . .

Under the Court's reading of the Act as precluding the States from characterizing gross retirement pay as community property, a military retiree has the power unilaterally to convert community property into separate property and increase his after-tax income, at the expense of his ex-spouse's financial security and property entitlements. To read the statute as permitting a military retiree to pocket 30 percent, 50 percent, even

---

dispositive on all matters pertaining to the division of any retired, retirement, or retainer pay to which such member or former member is entitled or will become entitled." S. 1453, 97th Cong., 1st Sess. (1981).

18. The Senate Committee pointed out that "frequent change-of-station moves and the special pressures placed on the military spouse as a homemaker make it extremely difficult to pursue a career affording economic security, job skills and pension protection." S.Rep. No. 97–502, at 6, U.S.Code Cong. & Admin.News 1982, p. 1601. The language of

the Act, and much of its legislative history, is written in gender neutral terms and there is no doubt that the Act applies equally to both former husbands and former wives. But "it is quite evident from the legislative history that Congress acted largely in response to the plight of the military *wife*." Horkovich, Uniformed Services Former Spouses' Protection Act: Congress' Answer to *McCarty v. McCarty* Goes Beyond the Fundamental Question, 23 Air Force L.Rev. 287, 308 (1982–1983) (emphasis in original).

80 percent of gross retirement pay by converting it into disability benefits and thereby to avoid his obligations under state community property law, however, is to distort beyond recognition and to thwart the main purpose of the statute, which is to recognize the sacrifices made by military spouses and to protect their economic security in the face of a divorce. Women generally suffer a decline in their standard of living following a divorce. See Weitzman, The Economics of Divorce: Social and Economic Consequences of Property, Alimony and Child Support Awards, 28 UCLA L.Rev. 1181, 1251 (1981). Military wives face special difficulties because "frequent change-of-station moves and the special pressures placed on the military spouse as a homemaker make it extremely difficult to pursue a career affording economic security, job skills and pension protection." S.Rep. No. 97–502, at 6, U.S.Code Cong. & Admin.News 1982, p. 1601. The average military couple married for 20 years moves about 12 times, and military wives experience an unemployment rate more than double that of their civilian counterparts. Brief for Women's Equity Action League et al. as *Amicus Curiae* 10–11. Pensions, moreover, are often the single most valuable asset acquired by military couples. Id., at 18. Indeed, the one clear theme that emerges from the legislative history of the Act is that Congress recognized the dire plight of many military wives after divorce and sought to protect their access to their ex-husbands' military pensions. See S.Rep. No. 97–502, at 6; 128 Cong.Rec. 18318 (1982) ("[F]requent military moves often preclude spouses from pursuing their own careers and establishing economic independence. As a result, military spouses are frequently unable to vest in their own retirement plans or obtain health insurance coverage from a private employer. Military spouses who become divorced often lose all access to retirement and health benefits—despite a 'career' devoted to the military") (remarks of Rep. Schumer). See also id., at 18315, 18316, 18317, 18320, 18323, 18328. Reading the Act as not precluding States from characterizing retirement pay waived to receive disability benefits as property divisible upon divorce is faithful to the clear remedial purposes of the statute in a way that the Court's interpretation is not.

The conclusion that States may treat gross military retirement pay as property divisible upon divorce is not inconsistent with 38 U.S.C. § 3101(a) (1982 ed., Supp. V). This anti-attachment provision provides that veterans' disability benefits "shall not be liable to attachment, levy, or seizure by or under any legal or equitable process whatever, either before or after receipt by the beneficiary." Gaye Mansell acknowledges, as she must, that § 3101(a) precludes her from garnishing under state law Major Mansell's veterans' disability benefits in satisfaction of her claim to a share of his gross military retirement pay, just as § 1408(c)(1) precludes her from invoking the federal direct payments mechanism in satisfaction of that claim. To recognize that § 3101(a) protects the funds from a specific source, however, does not mean that § 3101(a) prevents Gaye Mansell from recovering her 50 percent interest in Major Mansell's gross retirement pay out of any income or assets he may have *other* than his veterans' disability benefits. So long as those benefits themselves are protected, calculation of Gaye Mansell's entitlement on the basis of Major Mansell's gross retirement pay does not constitute an "attachment" of his veterans' disability benefits. Section 3101(a) is designed to ensure that the needs of disabled veterans and their families are met, see Rose v. Rose, 481 U.S. 619, 634, 107 S.Ct. 2029, 2038, 95 L.Ed.2d 599 (1987), without interference from creditors. That purpose is fulfilled so long as the benefits themselves are protected by the anti-attachment provision.

In sum, under the Court's interpretation of the Former Spouses' Protection Act, the former spouses Congress sought to protect risk having their economic security severely undermined by a unilateral decision of their ex-spouse to waive retirement pay in lieu of disability benefits. It is inconceivable that Congress intended the broad remedial purposes of the statute to be thwarted in such a way. To be sure, as the Court notes, Congress sought to be "fair and equitable" to retired service members as well as to protect divorced spouses. Congress explicitly protected military members by limiting the percentage of disposable retirement pay subject to the federal garnishment remedy and by expressly providing that military members could not be forced to retire. Moreover, a retiree is still advantaged by waiving retirement pay in lieu of disability benefits: the pay which is waived is not subject to the federal direct payments mechanism, and the former spouse must resort instead to the more cumbersome and costly process of seeking a state garnishment order against the value of that waived pay. See H.R.Rep. No. 98–700, pp. 4–5 (1984) (discussing difficulties faced by ex-spouses in obtaining state garnishment orders). Even these state processes cannot directly attach the military retiree's disability benefits for purposes of satisfying a community property division given the strictures of the anti-attachment provision of 38 U.S.C. § 3101(a). There is no basis for concluding, however, that Congress sought to protect the interests of service members by allowing them unilaterally to deny their former spouses *any* opportunity to obtain a fair share of the couple's military pension.

It is now once again up to Congress to address the inequity created by the Court in situations such as this one. But because I believe that Congress has already expressed its intention that the States have the authority to characterize waived retirement pay as property divisible upon divorce, I dissent.

NOTE

When confronting the election dilemma presented by the federal Uniformed Services Former Spouses' Protection Act, some state courts have been willing to compensate the former non-military electing spouse with divisible assets not associated with the military disability payments. *See, e.g.*, Surratt v. Surratt, 85 Ark.App. 267, 148 S.W.3d 761 (2004); *In re* Marriage of Lodeski, 107 P.3d 1097 (Colo. Ct. App. 2004); Whitfield v. Whitfield, 373 N.J.Super. 573, 862 A.2d 1187 (2004). Thus, if there is alternative property courts may diminish or eliminate the hardship presented by the election. Such an approach is not prohibited by the statute.

Likewise, when an active duty soldier elected to take a "CSB/Redux Bonus" after fifteen years of military service, knowing that this would reduce the military pension, the former non-electing spouse had a right to share in the bonus to the extent that the former spouse's award of the pension would be reduced. Boedeker v. Larson, 44 Va.App. 508, 605 S.E.2d 764 (2004). In addition, courts have used a similar approach when contemplating the loss of future Social Security benefits. *See, e.g.*, Depot v. Depot, 893 A.2d 995 (Me. 2006).

Boggs v. Boggs

Supreme Court of the United States, 1997.
520 U.S. 833, 117 S.Ct. 1754, 138 L.Ed.2d 45.

■ JUSTICE KENNEDY delivered the opinion of the Court.

We consider whether the Employee Retirement Income Security Act of 1974 (ERISA), 88 Stat. 832, as amended, 29 U.S.C. § 1001 et seq., pre-empts a state law allowing a nonparticipant spouse to transfer by testamentary instrument an interest in undistributed pension plan benefits. Given the pervasive significance of pension plans in the national economy, the congressional mandate for their uniform and comprehensive regulation, and the fundamental importance of community property law in defining the marital partnership in a number of States, the question is of undoubted importance. We hold that ERISA pre-empts the state law.

Isaac Boggs worked for South Central Bell from 1949 until his retirement in 1985. Isaac and Dorothy, his first wife, were married when he began working for the company, and they remained husband and wife until Dorothy's death in 1979. They had three sons. Within a year of Dorothy's death, Isaac married Sandra, and they remained married until his death in 1989.

Upon retirement, Isaac received various benefits from his employer's retirement plans. One was a lump-sum distribution from the Bell System Savings Plan for Salaried Employees (Savings Plan) of $151,628.94, which he rolled over into an Individual Retirement Account (IRA). He made no withdrawals and the account was worth $180,778.05 when he died. He also received 96 shares of AT & T stock from the Bell South Employee Stock Ownership Plan (ESOP). In addition, Isaac enjoyed a monthly annuity payment during his retirement of $1,777.67 from the Bell South Service Retirement Program.

The instant dispute over ownership of the benefits is between Sandra (the surviving wife) and the sons of the first marriage. The sons' claim to a portion of the benefits is based on Dorothy's will. Dorothy bequeathed to Isaac one-third of her estate, and a lifetime usufruct in the remaining two-thirds. A lifetime usufruct is the rough equivalent of a common-law life estate. See La. Civ.Code Ann., Art. 535 (West 1980). She bequeathed to her sons the naked ownership in the remaining two-thirds, subject to Isaac's usufruct. All agree that, absent pre-emption, Louisiana law controls and that under it Dorothy's will would dispose of her community property interest in Isaac's undistributed pension plan benefits. A Louisiana state court, in a 1980 order entitled "Judgment of Possession," ascribed to Dorothy's estate a community property interest in Isaac's Savings Plan account valued at the time at $21,194.29.

Sandra contests the validity of Dorothy's 1980 testamentary transfer, basing her claim to those benefits on her interest under Isaac's will and 29 U.S.C. § 1055. Isaac bequeathed to Sandra outright certain real property including the family home. His will also gave Sandra a lifetime usufruct in the remainder of his estate, with the naked ownership interest being held by the sons. Sandra argues that the sons' competing claim, since it is based on Dorothy's 1980 purported testamentary transfer of her community property interest in undistributed pension plan benefits, is pre-empted by ERISA. The Bell South Service Retirement Program monthly annuity is now paid to Sandra as the surviving spouse.

After Isaac's death, two of the sons filed an action in state court requesting the appointment of an expert to compute the percentage of the retirement benefits they would be entitled to as a result of Dorothy's attempted testamentary transfer. They further sought a judgment awarding them a portion of: the IRA; the ESOP shares of AT & T stock; the monthly annuity payments received by Isaac during his retirement; and Sandra's survivor annuity payments, both received and payable.

In response, Sandra Boggs filed a complaint in the United States District Court for the Eastern District of Louisiana, seeking a declaratory judgment that ERISA pre-empts the application of Louisiana's community property and succession laws to the extent they recognize the sons' claim to an interest in the disputed retirement benefits. The District Court granted summary judgment against Sandra Boggs. 849 F.Supp. 462 (1994). It found that, under Louisiana community property law, Dorothy had an ownership interest in her husband's pension plan benefits built up during their marriage. The creation of this interest, the court explained, does not violate 29 U.S.C. § 1056(d)(1), which prohibits pension plan benefits from being "assigned" or "alienated," since Congress did not intend to alter traditional familial and support obligations. In the court's view, there was no assignment or alienation because Dorothy's rights in the benefits were acquired by operation of community property law and not by transfer from Isaac. Turning to Dorothy's testamentary transfer, the court found it effective because "[ERISA] does not display any particular interest in preserving maximum benefits to any particular beneficiary." 849 F.Supp., at 465.

A divided panel of the Fifth Circuit affirmed. 82 F.3d 90 (1996). The court stressed that Louisiana law affects only what a plan participant may do with his or her benefits after they are received and not the relationship between the pension plan administrator and the plan beneficiary. For the reasons given by the District Court, it found ERISA's pension plan anti-alienation provision, § 1056(d)(1), inapplicable to Louisiana's creation of Dorothy Boggs' community property interest in the pension plan benefits.

It concluded that the transfer of the interest from Dorothy to her sons was not a prohibited assignment or alienation, as this transfer was "two steps removed from the disbursement of benefits." Id., at 97.

Six members of the Court of Appeals dissented from the failure to grant rehearing en banc. 89 F.3d 1169 (1996). In their view, a testamentary transfer of an interest in undistributed retirement benefits frustrates ERISA's goals of securing national uniformity in pension plan administration and of ensuring that retirees, and their dependents, are the actual recipients of retirement income. They believed that Congress' creation of the qualified domestic relations order (QDRO) mechanism in § 1056(d)(3), whose requirements were not met by the 1980 judgment of possession, further supported their position. (A QDRO is a limited exception to the pension plan anti-alienation provision and allows courts to recognize a nonparticipant spouse's community property interest in pension plans under specific circumstances.)

[The court noted that there was a split between holdings of the Fifth and Ninth Circuits. The former includes the community property states of Louisiana and Texas, while the latter includes the community property states of Arizona, California, Idaho, Nevada, and Washington.]

. . . We now reverse.

. . .

This case lies at the intersection of ERISA pension law and state community property law. None can dispute the central role community property laws play in the nine community property States. It is more than a property regime. It is a commitment to the equality of husband and wife and reflects the real partnership inherent in the marital relationship. State community property laws, many of ancient lineage, "must have continued to exist through such lengths of time because of their manifold excellences and are not lightly to be abrogated or tossed aside." 1 W. de Funiak, Principles of Community Property 11 (1943). The community property regime in Louisiana dates from 1808 when the territorial legislature of Orleans drafted a civil code which adopted Spanish principles of community property. Id., at 85–89. Louisiana's community property laws, and the community property regimes enacted in other States, implement policies and values lying within the traditional domain of the States. These considerations inform our pre-emption analysis. See Hisquierdo v. Hisquierdo, 439 U.S. 572, 581, 99 S.Ct. 802, 808, 59 L.Ed.2d 1 (1979).

The nine community property States have some 80 million residents, with perhaps $1 trillion in retirement plans. See Brief for Estate Planning, Trust and Probate Law Section of the State Bar of California as Amicus Curiae 1. This case involves a community property claim, but our ruling will affect as well the right to make claims or assert interests based on the law of any State, whether or not it recognizes community property. Our ruling must be consistent with the congressional scheme to assure the security of plan participants and their families in every State. In enacting ERISA, Congress noted the importance of pension plans in its findings and declaration of policy, explaining: "[T]he growth in size, scope, and numbers of employee benefit plans in recent years has been rapid and substantial; . . . the continued well-being and security of millions of employees and their dependents are directly affected by these plans; . . . they are affected with a national public interest [and] they have become an important factor affecting the stability of employment and the successful development of industrial relations. . . ." 29 U.S.C. § 1001(a).

ERISA is an intricate, comprehensive statute. Its federal regulatory scheme governs employee benefit plans, which include both pension and welfare plans. All employee benefit plans must conform to various reporting, disclosure and fiduciary requirements, see §§ 1021–1031, 1101–1114, while pension plans must also comply with participation, vesting, and funding requirements, see §§ 1051–1086. The surviving spouse annuity and QDRO provisions, central to the dispute here, are part of the statute's mandatory participation and vesting requirements. These provisions provide detailed protections to spouses of plan participants which, in some cases, exceed what their rights would be were community property law the sole measure.

ERISA's express pre-emption clause states that the Act "shall supersede any and all State laws insofar as they may now or hereafter relate to any employee benefit plan. . . ." § 1144(a). We can begin, and in this case end, the analysis by simply asking if state law conflicts with the provisions of ERISA or operates to frustrate its objects. We hold that there is a conflict, which suffices to resolve the case. We need not inquire whether the statutory phrase "relate to" provides further and additional support for the pre-emption claim. Nor need we consider the applicability of field pre-emption. . . .

We first address the survivor's annuity and then turn to the other pension benefits.

Sandra Boggs, as we have observed, asserts that federal law pre-empts and supersedes state law and requires the surviving spouse annuity to be paid to her as the sole beneficiary. We agree.

The annuity at issue is a qualified joint and survivor annuity mandated by ERISA. Section 1055(a) provides: "Each pension plan to which this section applies shall provide that—'(1) in the case of a vested participant who does not die before the annuity starting date, the accrued benefit payable to such participant shall be provided in the form of a qualified joint and survivor annuity.'" ERISA requires that every qualified joint and survivor annuity include an annuity payable to a nonparticipant surviving spouse. The survivor's annuity may not be less than 50% of the amount of the annuity which is payable during the joint lives of the participant and spouse. § 1055(d)(1). Provision of the survivor's annuity may not be waived by the participant, absent certain limited circumstances, unless the spouse consents in writing to the designation of another beneficiary, which designation also cannot be changed without further spousal consent, witnessed by a plan representative or notary public. § 1055(c)(2). Sandra Boggs, as the surviving spouse, is entitled to a survivor's annuity under these provisions. She has not waived her right to the survivor's annuity, let alone consented to having the sons designated as the beneficiaries.

Respondents say their state-law claims are consistent with these provisions. Their claims, they argue, affect only the disposition of plan proceeds after they have been disbursed by the Bell South Service Retirement Program, and thus nothing is required of the plan. ERISA's concern for securing national uniformity in the administration of employee benefit plans, in their view, is not implicated. They argue Sandra's community property obligations, after she receives the survivor annuity payments, "fai[l] to implicate the regulatory concerns of ERISA." Fort Halifax Packing Co. v. Coyne, 482 U.S. 1, 15, 107 S.Ct. 2211, 2219, 96 L.Ed.2d 1 (1987).

We disagree. The statutory object of the qualified joint and survivor annuity provisions, along with the rest of § 1055, is to ensure a stream of income to surviving spouses. Section 1055 mandates a survivor's annuity not only where a participant dies after the annuity starting date but also guarantees one if the participant dies before then. See §§ 1055(a)(2), (e). These provisions, enacted as part of the Retirement Equity Act of 1984 (REA), Pub.L. 98–397, 98 Stat. 1426, enlarged ERISA's protection of surviving spouses in significant respects. Before REA, ERISA only required that pension plans, if they provided for the payment of benefits in the form of an annuity, offer a qualified joint and survivor annuity as an option entirely within a participant's discretion. 29 U.S.C. §§ 1055(a), (e) (1982 ed.). REA modified ERISA to permit participants to designate a beneficiary for the survivor's annuity, other than the nonparticipant spouse, only when the spouse agrees. § 1055(c)(2). Congress' concern for surviving spouses is also evident from the expansive coverage of § 1055, as amended by REA. Section 1055's requirements, as a general matter, apply to all "individual account plans" and "defined benefit plans." § 1055(b)(1). The terms are defined, for § 1055 purposes, so that all pension plans fall within those two categories. See § 1002(35). While some individual account plans escape § 1055's surviving spouse annuity requirements under certain conditions, Congress still protects the interests of the surviving spouse by requiring those plans to pay the spouse the nonforfeitable accrued benefits, reduced by certain security interests, in a lump-sum payment. § 1055(b)(1)(C).

ERISA's solicitude for the economic security of surviving spouses would be undermined by allowing a predeceasing spouse's heirs and legatees to have a community property interest in the survivor's annuity. Even a plan participant cannot defeat a nonparticipant surviving spouse's statutory entitlement to an annuity. It would be odd, to say the least, if Congress permitted a predeceasing nonparticipant spouse to do so. Nothing in the language of ERISA supports concluding that Congress made such an inexplicable decision. Testamentary transfers could reduce a surviving spouse's guaranteed annuity below the minimum set by ERISA (defined as 50% of the annuity payable during the joint lives of the participant and spouse). In this case, Sandra's annuity would be reduced by approximately 20%, according to the calculations contained in the sons' state-court filings. There is no reason why testamentary transfers could not reduce a survivor's annuity by an even greater amount. Perhaps even more troubling, the recipient of the testamentary transfer need not be a family member. For instance, a surviving spouse's § 1055 annuity might be substantially reduced so that funds could be diverted to support an unrelated stranger.

In the face of this direct clash between state law and the provisions and objectives of ERISA, the state law cannot stand. Conventional conflict pre-emption principles require pre-emption "where compliance with both federal and state regulations is a physical impossibility, ... or where state law stands as an obstacle to the accomplishment and execution of the full purposes and objectives of Congress." Gade v. National Solid Wastes Management Assn., 505 U.S. 88, 98, 112 S.Ct. 2374, 2383, 120 L.Ed.2d 73 (1992) (internal quotation marks and citation omitted). It would undermine the purpose of ERISA's mandated survivor's annuity to allow Dorothy, the predeceasing spouse, by her testamentary transfer to defeat in part Sandra's entitlement to the annuity § 1055 guarantees her as the surviving spouse. This cannot be. States are not free to change ERISA's structure and balance.

Louisiana law, to the extent it provides the sons with a right to a portion of Sandra Boggs'§ 1055 survivor's annuity, is pre-empted.

Beyond seeking a portion of the survivor's annuity, respondents claim a percentage of: the monthly annuity payments made to Isaac Boggs during his retirement; the IRA; and the ESOP shares of AT & T stock. As before, the claim is based on Dorothy Boggs' attempted testamentary transfer to the sons of her community interest in Isaac's undistributed pension plan benefits. Respondents argue further—and somewhat inconsistently—that their claim again concerns only what a plan participant or beneficiary may do once plan funds are distributed, without imposing any obligations on the plan itself. Both parties agree that the ERISA benefits at issue here were paid after Dorothy's death, and thus this case does not present the question whether ERISA would permit a nonparticipant spouse to obtain a devisable community property interest in benefits paid out during the existence of the community between the participant and that spouse.

A brief overview of ERISA's design is necessary to put respondents' contentions in the proper context. The principal object of the statute is to protect plan participants and beneficiaries.... Section 1001(c) explains that ERISA contains certain safeguards and protections which help guarantee the "equitable character and the soundness of [private pension] plans" in order to protect "the interests of participants in private pension plans and their beneficiaries." The general policy is implemented by ERISA's specific provisions. Apart from a few enumerated exceptions, a plan fiduciary must "discharge his duties with respect to a plan solely in the interest of the participants and beneficiaries." § 1104(a)(1). The assets of a plan, again with certain exceptions, are "held for the exclusive purposes of providing benefits to participants in the plan and their beneficiaries and defraying reasonable expenses of administering the plan." § 1103(c)(1). The Secretary of Labor has authority to create exemptions to ERISA's prohibition on certain plan holdings, acquisitions, and transactions, but only if doing so is in the interests of the plan's "participants and beneficiaries." § 1108(a)(2). Persons with an interest in a pension plan may bring a civil suit under ERISA's enforcement provisions only if they are either a participant or beneficiary. Section 1132(a)(1)(B), for instance, provides that a civil action may be brought "by a participant or beneficiary . . . to recover benefits due to him under the terms of his plan, to enforce his rights under the terms of the plan, or to clarify his rights to future benefits under the terms of the plan."

ERISA confers beneficiary status on a nonparticipant spouse or dependent in only narrow circumstances delineated by its provisions. For example, as we have discussed, § 1055(a) requires provision of a surviving spouse annuity in covered pension plans, and, as a consequence the spouse is a beneficiary to this extent. Section 1056's QDRO provisions likewise recognize certain pension plan community property interests of nonparticipant spouses and dependents. A QDRO is a type of domestic relations order which creates or recognizes an alternate payee's right to, or assigns to an alternate payee the right to, a portion of the benefits payable with respect to a participant under a plan. § 1056(d)(3)(B)(i). A domestic relations order, in turn, is any judgment, decree, or order that concerns "the provision of child support, alimony payments, or marital property rights to a spouse, former spouse, child, or other dependent of a participant" and is "made pursuant to a State domestic relations law (including a community property law)." §§ 1056(d)(3)(B)(ii). A domestic relations order must meet certain requirements to qualify as a QDRO. See §§ 1056(d)(3)(C)–(E). QDRO's, unlike domestic relations orders in general, are exempt from both the pension plan anti-alienation provision, § 1056(d)(3)(A), and ERISA's general pre-emption clause, § 1144(b)(7). In creating the QDRO mechanism Congress was careful to provide that the alternate payee, the "spouse, former spouse, child, or other dependent of a participant," is to be considered a plan beneficiary. §§ 1056(d)(3)(K), (J). These provisions are essential to one of REA's central purposes, which is to give enhanced protection to the spouse and dependent children in the event of divorce or separation, and in the event of death the surviving spouse. Apart from these detailed provisions, ERISA does not confer beneficiary status on nonparticipants by reason of their marital or dependent status.

Even outside the pension plan context and its anti-alienation restriction, Congress deemed it necessary to enact detailed provisions in order to protect a dependent's interest in a welfare benefit plan. Through a § 1169 "qualified medical child support order" a child's interest in his or her parent's group health care plan can be enforced. A "medical child support order" is defined as any judgment, decree, or order that concerns the provision of child support "made pursuant to a State domestic relations law (including a community property law) and relates to benefits under such plan." § 1169(a)(2)(B)(i). As with a QDRO, a "medical child support order" must satisfy certain criteria in order to qualify. See §§ 1169(a)(3)–(4). In accordance with ERISA's care in conforming entitlements to benefits with participant or beneficiary status, the statute treats a child subject to such a qualifying order as a participant for ERISA's reporting and disclosure requirements and as a beneficiary for other purposes. § 1169(a)(7).

The surviving spouse annuity and QDRO provisions, which acknowledge and protect specific pension plan community property interests, give rise to the strong implication that other community property claims are not consistent with the statutory scheme. ERISA's silence with respect to the right of a nonparticipant spouse to control pension plan benefits by testamentary transfer provides powerful support for the conclusion that the right does not exist. Cf. Massachusetts Mut. Life Ins. Co. v. Russell, 473 U.S. 134, 147–148, 105 S.Ct. 3085, 3092–3093, 87 L.Ed.2d 96 (1985). It should cause little surprise that Congress chose to protect the community property interests of separated and divorced spouses and their children, a traditional subject of domestic relations law, but not to accommodate testamentary transfers of pension plan benefits. As a general matter, "[t]he whole subject of the domestic relations of husband and wife, parent and child, belongs to the laws of the States and not to the laws of the United States." In re Burrus, 136 U.S. 586, 593–594, 10 S.Ct. 850, 853, 34 L.Ed. 500 (1890). Support obligations, in particular, are "deeply rooted moral responsibilities" that Congress is unlikely to have intended to intrude upon. See Rose v. Rose, 481 U.S. 619, 632, 107 S.Ct. 2029, 2037, 95 L.Ed.2d 599 (1987); see also id., at 636–640, 107 S.Ct., at 2039–2041 (O'CONNOR, J., concurring). In accord with these principles, Congress ensured that state domestic relations orders, as long as they meet certain statutory requirements, are not pre-empted.

We conclude the sons have no claim under ERISA to a share of the retirement benefits. To begin with, the sons are neither participants nor beneficiaries. A "participant" is defined as an "employee or former employee of an employer, or any member or former member of an employee organization, who is or may become eligible to receive a benefit." § 1002(7). A "beneficiary" is a "person designated by a participant, or by the terms of an employee benefit plan, who is or may become entitled to a benefit thereunder." § 1002(8). Respondents' claims are based on Dorothy Boggs' attempted testamentary transfer, not on a designation by Isaac Boggs or under the terms of the retirement plans. They do not even attempt to argue that they are beneficiaries by virtue of the judgment of possession qualifying as a QDRO.

An amicus, the Estate Planning, Trust and Probate Law Section of the State Bar of California, in support of respondents' position, points to pre-REA case law holding that ERISA does not pre-empt spousal community property interests in pension benefits, regardless of who is the plan participant or beneficiary. As did the District Court below, the amicus relies in particular upon In re Marriage of Campa, 89 Cal.App.3d 113, 152 Cal.Rptr. 362 (1979), in which the California Court of Appeals for the First District held that ERISA does not bar California courts from joining pension funds in marriage dissolution proceedings and ordering the pension plan to divide pension payments between the employee and his or her former nonparticipant spouse. We dismissed the pension plan's appeal for want of a substantial federal question, 444 U.S. 1028, 100 S.Ct. 696, 62 L.Ed.2d 664 (1980), and, although not entitled to full precedential weight, see Edelman v. Jordan, 415 U.S. 651, 670–671, 94 S.Ct. 1347, 1359–1360, 39 L.Ed.2d 662 (1974), that disposition constitutes a decision on the merits.... The state court in Marriage of Campa was not alone in refusing to find ERISA pre-emption in the divorce context. See, e.g., Stone v. Stone, 450 F.Supp. 919 (N.D.Cal.1978), aff'd, 632 F.2d 740 (C.A.9 1980), cert. denied, 453 U.S. 922, 101 S.Ct. 3158, 69 L.Ed.2d 1004 (1981); ... This judicial consensus, amicus argues, was codified by the QDRO provisions which were contained in the 1984 REA amendments. The amicus contends that since REA, or the pre-REA case law which it allegedly adopted, did not consider the community property rights of a nonparticipant spouse in the testamentary context, it should not be construed to pre-empt state law governing this different subject.

We disagree with this reasoning. It is true that the subject of testamentary transfers is somewhat removed from domestic relations law. The QDRO provisions address the rights of divorced and separated spouses, and their dependent children, which are the traditional concern of domestic relations law. The pre-REA federal common-law extension of § 1002(8)'s definition of "beneficiary" by courts in the context of marital dissolution was in part based on an appreciation of the fact that domestic relations law is primarily an area of state concern, see Marriage of Campa, supra, at 124, 152 Cal.Rptr., at 367–368, and the basic principle that a beneficiary's interest in a spendthrift trust, despite otherwise applicable protections, can be reached in the context of divorce and separation. See E. Griswold, Spendthrift Trusts 389–391 (2d ed.1947) (summarizing state case law); Restatement (Second) of Trusts § 157 (1959). The state court in Marriage of Campa took its implicit determination that the nonparticipant spouse was a beneficiary to its logical conclusion, forcing the pension plan to join the marital dissolution proceedings as a party and compelling it to pay the spouse her share of the pension benefits. Whether or not this extension of the definition of "beneficiary" was consistent with the statute then in force, these authorities are not applicable in light of the REA amendments. The QDRO and the surviving spouse annuity provisions define the scope of a nonparticipant spouse's community property interests in pension plans consistent with ERISA.

Respondents and their amicus in effect ask us to ignore § 1002(8)'s definition of "beneficiary" and, through case law, create a new class of persons for whom plan assets are to be held and administered. The statute is not amenable to this sweeping extratextual extension. It is unpersuasive to suggest that third parties could assert their claims without being counted as "beneficiaries." A plan fiduciary's responsibilities run only to participants and beneficiaries. § 1104(a)(1). Assets of a plan are held for the exclusive purposes of providing benefits to participants and beneficiaries and defraying reasonable expenses of administration. § 1103(c)(1). Reading ERISA to permit nonbeneficiary interests, even if not enforced against the plan, would result in troubling anomalies. Either pension plans would be run for the benefit of only a subset of those who have a stake in the plan or state law would have to move in to fill the apparent gaps between plan administration responsibilities and ownership rights, resulting in a complex set of requirements varying from State to State. Neither result accords with the statutory scheme.

The conclusion that Congress intended to pre-empt respondents' non-beneficiary, nonparticipant interests in the retirement plans is given specific and powerful reinforcement by the pension plan anti-alienation provision. Section 1056(d)(1) provides that "[e]ach pension plan shall provide that benefits provided under the plan may not be assigned or alienated." Statutory anti-alienation provisions are potent mechanisms to prevent the dissipation of funds. In Hisquierdo we interpreted an anti-alienation provision to bar a divorced spouse's interest in her husband's retirement benefits. See 439 U.S., at 583–590, 99 S.Ct., at 809–813. ERISA's pension plan anti-alienation provision is mandatory and contains only two explicit exceptions, see §§ 1056(d)(2), (d)(3)(A), which are not subject to judicial expansion. See Guidry v. Sheet Metal Workers Nat. Pension Fund, 493 U.S. 365, 376, 110 S.Ct. 680, 687, 107 L.Ed.2d 782 (1990). The anti-alienation provision can "be seen to bespeak a pension law protective policy of special intensity: Retirement funds shall remain inviolate until retirement." J. Langbein & B. Wolk, Pension and Employee Benefit Law 547 (2d ed.1995).

Dorothy's 1980 testamentary transfer, which is the source of respondents' claimed ownership interest, is a prohibited "assignment or alienation." An "assignment or alienation" has been defined by regulation, with certain exceptions not at issue here, as "[a]ny direct or indirect arrangement whereby a party acquires from a participant or beneficiary" an interest enforceable against a plan to "all or any part of a plan benefit payment which is, or may become, payable to the participant or beneficiary." 26 CFR § 1.401(a)–3(c)(1)(ii). Those requirements are met. Under Louisiana law community property interests are enforceable against a plan. See Eskine v. Eskine, 518 So.2d 505, 508 (La.1988). If respondents' claims were allowed to succeed they would have acquired, as of 1980, an interest in Isaac's pension plan at the expense of plan participants and beneficiaries.

As was true with survivors' annuities, it would be inimical to ERISA's purposes to permit testamentary recipients to acquire a competing interest in undistributed pension benefits, which are intended to provide a stream of income to participants and their beneficiaries. See Guidry, supra, at 376, 110 S.Ct., at 687 ("[The anti-alienation provision] reflects a considered congressional policy choice, a decision to safeguard a stream of income for pensioners . . . and their dependents . . ."). Pension benefits support participants and beneficiaries in their retirement years, and ERISA's pension plan safeguards are designed to further this end. See § 1001(c). Besides the anti-alienation provision, Congress has enacted other protective measures to guarantee that retirement funds are there when a plan's participants and beneficiaries expect them. There are, for instance, minimum funding standards for pension plans and a pension plan termination insurance program which guarantees benefits in the event a plan is terminated before being fully funded. See §§ 1082, 1301–1461. Under respondents' approach, retirees could find their retirement benefits reduced by substantial sums because they have been diverted to testamentary recipients. Retirement benefits and the income stream provided for by ERISA-regulated plans would be disrupted in the name of protecting a nonparticipant spouses' successors over plan participants and beneficiaries. Respondents' logic would even permit a spouse to transfer an interest in a pension plan to creditors, a result incompatible with a spendthrift provision such as § 1056(d)(1).

Community property laws have, in the past, been pre-empted in order to ensure the implementation of a federal statutory scheme. See, e.g., . . . Free v. Bland, 369 U.S. 663, 82 S.Ct. 1089, 8 L.Ed.2d 180 (1962); Hisquierdo v. Hisquierdo, 439 U.S. 572, 99 S.Ct. 802, 59 L.Ed.2d 1 (1979); McCarty v. McCarty, 453 U.S. 210, 101 S.Ct. 2728, 69 L.Ed.2d 589 (1981); Mansell v. Mansell, 490 U.S. 581, 109 S.Ct. 2023, 104 L.Ed.2d 675 (1989); . . . Free v. Bland, supra, is of particular relevance here. A husband had purchased United States savings bonds with community funds in the name of both spouses. Under Treasury regulations then in effect, when a co-owner of the bonds died, the surviving co-owner received the entire interest in the bonds. After the wife died, her son—the principal beneficiary of her will—demanded either one-half of the bonds or reimbursement for loss of the community property interest. The Court held that the regulations pre-empted the community property claim, explaining: "One of the inducements selected by the Treasury is the survivorship provision, a convenient method of avoiding complicated probate proceedings. Notwithstanding this provision, the State awarded full title to the co-owner but required him to account for half of the value of the bonds to the decedent's estate. Viewed realistically, the State has rendered the award of title meaningless." Id., at 669, 82 S.Ct., at 1093.

The same reasoning applies here. If state law is not pre-empted, the diversion of retirement benefits will occur regardless of whether the interest in the pension plan is enforced against the plan or the recipient of the pension benefit. The obligation to provide an accounting, moreover, as with the probate proceedings referred to in Free, is itself a burden of significant proportions. Under respondents' view, a pension plan participant could be forced to make an accounting of a deceased spouse's community property interest years after the date of death. If the couple had lived in several States, the accounting could entail complex, expensive, and time-consuming litigation. Congress could not have intended that pension benefits from pension plans would be given to accountants and attorneys for this purpose.

Respondents contend it is anomalous and unfair that a divorced spouse, as a result of a QDRO, will have more control over a portion of his or her spouse's pension benefits than a predeceasing spouse. Congress thought otherwise. The QDRO provisions, as well as the surviving spouse annuity provisions, reinforce the conclusion that ERISA is concerned with providing for the living. The QDRO provisions protect those persons who, often as a result of divorce, might not receive the benefits they otherwise would have had available during their retirement as a means of income. In the case of a predeceased spouse, this concern is not implicated. The fairness of the distinction might be debated, but Congress has decided to favor the living over the dead and we must respect its policy.

The axis around which ERISA's protections revolve is the concepts of participant and beneficiary. When Congress has chosen to depart from this framework, it has done so in a careful and limited manner. Respondents' claims, if allowed to succeed, would depart from this framework, upsetting the deliberate balance central to ERISA. It does not matter that respondents have sought to enforce their rights only after the retirement benefits have been distributed since their asserted rights are based on the theory that they had an interest in the undistributed pension plan benefits. Their state-law claims are pre-empted. The judgment of the Fifth Circuit is

Reversed.

■ [The dissenting opinion of JUSTICE BREYER, with whom JUSTICE O'CONNOR, THE CHIEF JUSTICE and JUSTICE GINSBURG join in part, is omitted.]

NOTE

Because the vast majority of pensions are encompassed by the federal statute ERISA (Employee Retirement Income Security Act), it is an important element of any state's marital property order. In order to provide payment from a covered plan to an alternate payee, the federal requirements allowing for a Qualified Domestic Relations Order (QDRO) must be satisfied. *See* Howard A. Massler, *Qualified Domestic Relations Orders* in 3 VALUATION AND DISTRIBUTION OF MARITAL PROPERTY (1996). Most jurisdictions have liberally construed the criteria by which a domestic relations order will qualify as a QDRO. *See, e.g.*, Stewart v. Thorpe Holding Co. Profit Sharing Plan, 207 F.3d 1143 (9th Cir.2000), *rev. denied* 531 U.S. 1074, 121 S.Ct. 768, 148 L.Ed.2d 668 (2001).

E. SUPPORT FOR CHILDREN

UNIFORM MARRIAGE AND DIVORCE ACT (1973)

§ 309. [Child Support]

In a proceeding for dissolution of marriage, legal separation, maintenance, or child support, the court may order either or both parents owing a duty of support to a child to pay an amount reasonable or necessary for his support, without regard to marital misconduct, after considering all relevant factors including:

> (1) the financial resources of the child;
>
> (2) the financial resources of the custodial parent;

(3) the standard of living the child would have enjoyed had the marriage not been dissolved;

(4) the physical and emotional condition of the child and his educational needs; and

(5) the financial resources and needs of the noncustodial parent.

NEW YORK DOMESTIC RELATIONS LAW, § 236(B)(7) (McKinney Supp. 2007)

(The text of this provision appears at pages 539, *supra*.)

Voishan v. Palma

Court of Appeals of Maryland, 1992.
327 Md. 318, 609 A.2d 319.

■ CHASANOW, JUDGE.

John and Margaret Voishan were divorced on June 26, 1981, by decree of the Circuit Court for Anne Arundel County. Margaret was awarded custody of their two daughters and John was ordered to pay $250 per week toward the girls' support. Over four years later, an order dated October 7, 1985 increased the amount of John's obligation for the support of both children to $1400 per month. The circuit court's order also awarded John certain detailed visitation rights.

On March 8, 1991, the circuit court's intercession was again sought to address John's request to find Margaret in contempt for violating the visitation order as well as Margaret's motion to modify child support. The Honorable Raymond G. Thieme, Jr. presided at that hearing and shortly thereafter entered an order finding that Margaret was not in contempt of court. That order also increased John's child support obligation for the one daughter who was still a minor from $700 per month to $1550 per month. John then appealed the modification of child support to the Court of Special Appeals. Because of the important issues raised on appeal, this Court granted certiorari before consideration by the intermediate appellate court. While Margaret failed to file an appellee's brief or respond to John's oral arguments, both the Maryland Chapter of the American Academy of Matrimonial Lawyers and the Attorney General of Maryland filed amici curiae briefs and presented oral argument.

This dispute requires the Court, for the first time, to address Maryland Code, (1984, 1991 Repl.Vol.) Family Law Article §§ 12–201 *et seq.* (the "guidelines").[1] The General Assembly enacted these guidelines in 1989 to comply with federal law and regulations. *See* 42 U.S.C. §§ 651–667 (1982 & 1984 Supp. II) and 45 C.F.R. § 302.56 (1989). The federal mandate required that the guidelines be established and "based on specific descriptive

---

1. Unless otherwise specified, all statutory references are to Maryland Code, (1984, 1991 Repl.Vol.) Family Law Article.

and numeric criteria and result in a computation of the support obligation." *Id.* When drafting the guidelines, the Maryland Senate Judicial Proceedings Committee had before it *Development of Guidelines For Child Support Orders: Advisory Panel Recommendations and Final Report,* U.S. Department of Health and Human Services' Office of Child Support Enforcement. This report explained that the need for the guidelines was threefold: (1) to "remedy a shortfall in the level of awards" that do not reflect the actual costs of raising children, (2) to "improve the consistency, and therefore the equity, of child support awards," and (3) to "improve the efficiency of court processes for adjudicating child support...."

After considering several different models recommended by the Advisory Panel on Child Support Guidelines, the General Assembly chose to base Maryland's guidelines on the Income Shares Model. *See* Senate Judicial Proceedings Committee, *Bill Analysis,* Senate Bill 49 (1989). The conceptual underpinning of this model is that a child should receive the same proportion of parental income, and thereby enjoy the standard of living, he or she would have experienced had the child's parents remained together. *Id. See also* Robert G. Williams, "Child Support Guidelines: Economic Basis and Analysis of Alternative Approaches," *Improving Child Support Practice* I–12 to I–13 (A.B.A.1986). Accordingly, the model establishes child support obligations based on estimates of the percentage of income that parents in an intact household typically spend on their children. *Id.* Consistent with this model, the legislature constructed the schedule in § 12–204(e), which sets forth the basic child support obligation for any given number of children based on combined parental income.

Following the Income Shares Model, Maryland's guidelines first require that the trial judge determine each parent's monthly "adjusted actual income." Section 12–201(d) states:

" 'Adjusted actual income' means actual income minus:

(1) preexisting reasonable child support obligations actually paid;

(2) except as provided in § 12–204(a)(2) of this subtitle, alimony or maintenance obligations actually paid; and

(3) the actual cost of providing health insurance coverage for a child for whom the parents are jointly and severally responsible."

After determining each parent's monthly "adjusted actual income," the judge then adds these two amounts together to arrive at the monthly "combined adjusted actual income" of the parents. *See* § 12–201(e). Having calculated the combined adjusted actual income of the parents, the judge can then determine whether that figure falls within the range of incomes found in the schedule of § 12–204(e). If the figure is within the schedule, the judge then locates the corresponding "basic child support obligation" for the given number of children. Where the monthly income falls between two amounts set forth in the schedule, § 12–204(c) dictates that the basic child support obligation is the same as the obligation specified for the next highest income level. The judge then divides this basic child support obligation between the parents in proportion to each of their adjusted actual incomes. § 12–204(a). The judge must then add together any work-related child care expenses, extraordinary medical expenses, and school and transportation expenses and allocate this total between the parents in proportion to their adjusted actual incomes. § 12–204(g)–(i). The amount of child support computed in this manner[2] is presumed to be correct, although this presumption may be rebutted by evidence that such amount would be unjust and inappropriate in a particular case. § 12–202(a)(2). In the instant case, evidence was presented at the March 8, 1991 hearing that John now earns $145,000 per year, while Margaret's annual income is $30,000. John does not contend that his actual income should be reduced by any expenses identified in § 12–201(d). Therefore, he computes a "combined adjusted actual income" of $175,000 a year or $14,583 per month in his argument to this Court. This combined income exceeds $10,000 per month, which is the highest income provided for in § 12–204(e). The legislature addressed this situation in § 12–204(d), which says: "If the combined adjusted actual income exceeds the highest level specified in the schedule in subsection (e) of this section, the court may use its discretion in setting the amount of child support."

While John's primary contention is that Judge Thieme abused his discretion in setting the monthly obligation at $1550, he first argues that the judge could not modify the amount of child support without making a threshold finding that there was a "material change of circumstance." *See* § 12–104(a). At the hearing before Judge Thieme, John's trial counsel never suggested that the parties' circumstances had not materially changed. In effect, John's trial counsel admitted that a material change in circumstances existed when she told Judge Thieme, "We're not arguing that [Margaret] shouldn't have an increase." Moreover, in more than doubling the amount of child support, Judge Thieme implicitly found that a change of circumstances had been shown. *See* § 12–202(b).

Having disposed of John's preliminary argument, we now reach his primary contention. John contends that the $1550 monthly child support award is inconsistent with the spirit and intent behind the Income Shares Model, and concludes that Judge Thieme abused his discretion in awarding that amount. John maintains that Judge Thieme accurately found that the parties' earnings created a ratio of 83 to 17 for John's and Margaret's respective percentages of their $175,000 combined annual income. John contends, however, that Judge Thieme erred in the manner in which he applied these percentages to arrive at the amount of $1550 per month for John's share of the obligation. Judge Thieme examined expense sheets for each of the parties and concluded that the "reasonable expenses of the

---

2. This is the proper procedure for cases other than shared physical custody cases. § 12–204(k). Where the parents share physical custody of the child, as defined by § 12–201(i), the judge shall multiply the basic child support obligation by one and one-half to determine the "adjusted basic child support obligation." *See* §§ 12–201(j) and 12–204(f). The judge then divides that amount "between the parents in proportion to their respective adjusted actual incomes." § 12–204(*l*) (1). After that, the judge calculates which parent owes payment to the other by applying the provisions of § 12–204(*l*)(2)–(5).

child" were $1873 each month. The judge then calculated 83% of that figure and rounded John's share of the obligation down to $1550.

John argues here, as he did below, that a "reasonable approach" would have been for the trial judge to assume that the maximum basic child support obligation listed in the schedule is not only applicable to combined monthly incomes of $10,000, but also applies to those in excess of $10,000 per month. Under the schedule in § 12–204(e), the maximum basic child support obligation of $1040 per month is presumptively correct for parties who have a combined monthly income of $10,000. John argues that $1040 per month should also provide the presumptively correct basic child support obligation for all combined monthly incomes over $10,000. While we believe that $1040 could provide the presumptive *minimum* basic award for those with combined monthly incomes above $10,000, we do not believe that the legislature intended to cap the basic child support obligation at the upper limit of the schedule. *See, e.g., Hinshelwood v. Hinshelwood,* 564 So.2d 141 (Fla. 5th DCA 1990); *In re Marriage of Van Inwegen,* 757 P.2d 1118, 1120 (Colo.App.1988). Had the legislature intended to make the highest award in the schedule the presumptive basic support obligation in all cases with combined monthly income over $10,000, it would have so stated and would not have granted the trial judge discretion in fixing those awards. Further, John's proposed approach creates an artificial ceiling and itself defeats the guidelines' policy that the child enjoy a standard of living consonant with that he or she would have experienced had the parents remained married. We are unpersuaded by John's argument that the legislature meant for all children whose parents earn more than $10,000 per month to have the same standard of living as those whose parents earn $10,000 per month.

Alternatively, John argues that Judge Thieme should have extrapolated from the guidelines to determine what the support obligation would have been had the schedule extended up to the parties' $14,583 monthly income. John notes that at the upper levels in the guidelines, the basic child support obligation for one child increases by $5 for every $100 rise in combined adjusted actual income. Extrapolating on that basis, John argues that the basic child support obligation would be $1270 per month ($4583/100 x $5 plus $1040). John also acknowledges that under the guidelines, in addition to the basic child support obligation—whatever that is computed to be, he has an obligation to pay 83% of the additional work-related child care expenses which, in the instant case, are $400 per month. *See* § 12–204(g). Taking 83% of the $1270 basic child support obligation plus 83% of the $400 work-related child care expenses, John argues, renders his portion of his daughter's support to be $1386 per month. Although slightly more generous than his earlier argument, which would leave the judge with no discretion, John's second contention is essentially that this Court should significantly restrict the judicial discretion granted by § 12–204(d) and allow judges very little latitude in deviating from the extrapolation method. John asks this Court to hold that Judge Thieme abused his discretion when he set the award $164 higher than the amount computed by John's strict extrapolation theory. While we believe that the trial judge should consider the underlying policies of the guidelines and strive toward congruous results, we think that Judge Thieme did not abuse his discretion in fixing the amount of this award.

The legislature has clearly enunciated that the policies of the guidelines are those embodied in the Income Shares Model. John also argues that this model relies on the assumption that the percentage of income expended on children decreases as parental income increases, and therefore the General Assembly could not have intended to permit an award in this case to exceed 10.4% of combined monthly income, the percentage represented by the schedule's maximum support obligation for one child. The legislative history, however, indicates that the General Assembly did not intend to impose a maximum percentage of income or any similar restraint on the judge's discretion in setting awards where the parents' combined adjusted actual income exceeds $10,000 per month. In the hearings on the guidelines, the General Assembly was asked repeatedly to circumscribe the discretion granted in § 12–204(d). The Fair Family Law Association of Maryland testified that "[t]he proposed statute leaves families with income above $10,000 a month ($120,000 a year) with absolutely no guidelines," and suggested that the schedule be amended to provide that "for family incomes greater than $10,000 per month the basic child support obligation shall be the same percentage of total family income as for income of $10,000 per month [10.4% for one child]." Senate Judicial Proceedings Committee, S.B. 49 Bill File (1989). Several members of Family Law Section of the Montgomery County Bar Association testified that "[l]eaving the amount of child support in upper income cases to the discretion of the court will not help us to predict results or settle cases. . . . We suggest that the table be extended, or that guidelines of some sort be provided." *Id.* Notwithstanding these pleas, the General Assembly did not change § 12–204(d) or address any specific comment to these concerns. Rather, it chose to rely on judicial discretion. We agree with the Attorney General's conclusion in its amicus curiae brief that

> "[i]mplicit in this judgment is the view that at very high income levels, the percentage of income expended on children may not necessarily continue to decline or even remain constant because of the multitude of different options for income expenditure available to the affluent. The legislative judgment was that at such high income levels judicial discretion is better suited than a fixed formula to implement the guidelines' underlying principle that a child's standard of living should be altered as little as possible by the dissolution of the family."

While the legislature specifically rejected the request for more explicit formulae for incomes above the schedule, the general principles from which the schedule was derived should not be ignored. *See* § 12–202(a), which provides that "in *any* proceeding to establish or modify child support . . . the court shall use the child support guidelines set forth in this subtitle." (emphasis added). To effectuate the legislative intent to improve the consistency of child support awards, trial judges should bear in mind the guidelines' underlying principles when deciding matters within their discretion. Extrapolation from the schedule may act as a "guide," but the judge may also exercise his or her own independent discretion in balancing

> "the best interests and needs of the child with the parents' financial ability to meet those needs. Factors which should be considered when setting child support include the financial circumstances of the parties, their station in life, their age and physical condition, and expenses in educating the children." (Citations omitted).

Unkle v. Unkle, 305 Md. 587, 597, 505 A.2d 849, 854 (1986). These principles expressed in the pre-guidelines *Unkle* decision are consistent with the underlying concept that the child's needs be met as they would have been absent the parents' divorce.

While we reject John's argument that Judge Thieme abused his discretion because he placed too *little* reliance on John's suggested mechanical extrapolation from the schedule, we also decline to adopt the position taken by the Maryland Chapter of the American Academy of Matrimonial Lawyers (the AAML) in their amicus curiae brief. The AAML basically argues that Judge Thieme abused his discretion because he placed too *much* reliance on a mechanical application of the guidelines. The AAML contends that the economic data from which the figures in the schedule were derived did not include empirical evidence of the actual household expenditures for children of high income parents. Because the research and data used in constructing the Income Shares Model did not contemplate these high-range combined parental incomes, the AAML argues, the model provides *no* assistance in calculating the proper amount of child support. Thus, the AAML concludes, "the trial court erred when it applied a rigid formula (relative percentage of parents' income)...."

In support of this conclusion, the AAML points out that the legislature did not include in § 12–204(d) the phrase which appears in § 12–204(a)(1), (g)(1), (h), and (i)—"shall be divided between the parents in proportion to their adjusted actual incomes." While the argument is not expressly articulated, the AAML seems to suggest that Judge Thieme should not have divided the child support obligation in an 83 to 17 ratio. We believe that Judge Thieme acted properly in apportioning the obligation based upon the parties' respective percentages of their combined adjusted actual income. Moreover this action was consonant with the principle, expressed in the Income Shares Model as well as pre-guidelines caselaw, that each parent "share the responsibility for parental support in accordance with their respective financial resources." *Rand v. Rand,* 280 Md. 508, 517, 374 A.2d 900, 905 (1977). Finally, Judge Thieme did not look only to the parties' incomes and calculate a particular percentage thereof. Rather, he determined the reasonable needs of the child and then calculated each parent's proportionate share.

The Court in *Rand* declined to "mandate any specific formula by which the chancellor is to calculate the amount of support to be charged against each parent" and left to the chancellor's discretion the manner of assessing financial resources. *Id.* The legislature has modified *Rand*'s holding, as § 12–201 now defines the manner in which the trial judge should determine each party's "adjusted actual income." This would seem to be the initial step in *any* proceeding to establish or modify child support, as the judge must first determine whether the parents' combined adjusted actual income falls within, above, or below the schedule range. Although § 12–204(d) itself does not contain specific language requiring that the judge divide the child support obligation "between the parents in proportion to their adjusted actual incomes," this principle certainly underlies the Income Shares Model. Consequently, we believe that Judge Thieme properly calculated the support obligation and divided it between the parties in proportion to their incomes.

. . .

While awards made under § 12–204(d) will be disturbed only if there is a clear abuse of discretion, a reviewing court must also be mindful that the federal call for child support guidelines was motivated in part by the need to improve the consistency of awards. Thus, the trial judge has somewhat more latitude than that argued by John, but not the unguided discretion of pre-guidelines cases as advocated by the AAML. Rather, we agree with the Attorney General's position that the guidelines do establish a rebuttable presumption that the maximum support award under the schedule is the minimum which should be awarded in cases above the schedule.[5] Beyond this the trial judge should examine the needs of the child in light of the parents' resources and determine the amount of support necessary to ensure that the child's standard of living does not suffer because of the parents' separation. Further, the judge should give some consideration to the Income Shares method of apportioning the child support obligation. Consequently, we conclude that Judge Thieme properly exercised his discretion in receiving evidence of the parents' financial circumstances, considering the needs of the child, and then apportioning the "reasonable expenses of the child."

. . .

JUDGMENT OF THE CIRCUIT COURT FOR ANNE ARUNDEL COUNTY AFFIRMED. COSTS TO BE PAID BY APPELLANT.

■ McAULIFFE, JUDGE, concurring.

I concur in the result. I do not believe that the legislature intended to authorize trial judges to ignore basic policy decisions made by the legislature with respect to the equitable establishment of child support, or to

---

5. The Maryland guidelines were "patterned after the Colorado child support guidelines." Senate Judicial Proceedings Committee, *Floor Report,* Senate Bill 49 (1989). While it appears the Colorado Supreme Court has not yet spoken on the issue, that state's intermediate appellate court has repeatedly held that in cases above the schedule "there is a rebuttable presumption that the basic child support obligation at the up-

permost level of the guidelines is the *minimum* presumptive amount of support." *In re Marriage of LeBlanc,* 800 P.2d 1384, 1388 (Colo.App.1990) (emphasis in original). Further, that court has held that it is an abuse of discretion for a trial judge to mechanically extrapolate from the guidelines without making a determination regarding the needs of the child. *In re Marriage of Van Inwegen,* 757 P.2d 1118, 1121 (Colo.App.1988).

authorize virtually unlimited discretion as soon as the combined adjusted actual income of the parties exceeds $10,000 per month.

As the Court's opinion points out, the legislature adopted an Income Shares Model when it enacted Senate Bill 49 in 1989. The Bill Analysis prepared for the Senate Judicial Proceedings Committee explains the basic concepts of this model in the following language:

> The Income Shares model is based on the premise that the child should receive the same proportion of parental income he or she would receive if the parents lived together. Under this model, a basic child support obligation is computed based on the combined income of the parents (replicating total income in an intact household). This basic obligation is then prorated in proportion to each parent's adjusted gross income. Prorated shares of child care costs and extraordinary medical expenses are added to each parent's basic obligation.

The economic assumptions underlying this model are based on recent studies estimating expenditures on children as a proportion of household consumption.

The chancellor followed one of these policies when he allocated the share of each parent in accordance with their share of the total income. He apparently ignored, however, the "recent studies estimating expenditures on children as a proportion of household consumption" which underlay the legislature's approved model, and instead reverted to an earlier practice of attempting to determine the needs of a child based upon the custodial parent's estimated allocation to the child of a portion of fixed expenses of the family. As the Court of Special Appeals cogently observed in *Tannehill v. Tannehill,* 88 Md.App. 4, 11, 591 A.2d 888 (1991), one of the principal purposes for adopting the guidelines was "to improve the consistency and equity of child support awards." *See also Richardson v. Richardson,* 12 Va.App. 18, 401 S.E.2d 894, 895 (1991) (child support guidelines were intended to "decrease the disparity in the amount of awards, which, without the guidelines, range from unreasonably low to unrealistically high").

I believe the Income Shares Model adopted by the legislature provides informed guidance for the fixing of child support obligations even when the combined adjusted actual income exceeds $10,000 per month, while still granting the discretion referred to in § 12–204(d) of the Family Law Article, Maryland Code (1991 Repl.Vol.). The schedule of basic child support obligations, based upon data that the legislature found acceptable, shows that above the poverty level the percentage of parental income dedicated to child-rearing expenses decreases as the parental income increases. I do not agree with the father that the curve which can be plotted from the schedule must be projected to establish child support obligations beyond the limits of the schedule; that argument is contrary to the express intention of the legislature to grant a measure of discretion to the court when incomes exceed the highest income listed on the schedule. But that does not mean that the entire concept of the schedule, or its underlying data, should be jettisoned as soon as the upper limit of the schedule is passed. The legislative objective may be carried forward by using the schedule to establish presumptive maximum and minimum amounts for basic child support.

Specifically, I suggest that the amount calculated in accordance with the schedule for child support when the combined income equals $10,000 per month should serve as the presumptive floor for awards based upon combined income in excess of that amount. It makes no sense to hold the parents who would be required to provide $1,040 per month for the support of a child when their combined monthly income is $10,000 would be permitted to pay less if their income were $10,050 per month. Similarly, I believe the presumptive maximum base payment for one child should be 10.4 percent of the combined income of the parents, which is the percentage that the maximum scheduled payment bears to the maximum combined income ($1,040 to $100,000).

As I have noted above, the studies upon which the schedule is based demonstrate that the percentage of combined income of families living together that is dedicated to support of a child decreases as the income increases. Thus, it would hardly be inequitable to the child to establish as a maximum the percentage fixed by the schedule for a lesser amount of combined income. It should be kept in mind, however, that it is the *percentage* of income that remains as a constant presumptive ceiling—the amount of dollars to be paid for the support of the child obviously increases as the combined income increases.

I certainly would not fault a chancellor for utilizing a projection of the schedule for combined incomes above $10,000 a month as a presumptive child support payment where other factors did not suggest a different amount, but I agree that such a projection is not required. The legislature expressly reserved a considerable range of discretion to the chancellor when the combined monthly income of the parties exceeds $10,000, and thus there is no authority for requiring a mathematical projection. It was, however, the intent of the legislature that this discretion be exercised in a manner consistent with the principles approved by the passage of subtitle 2 of Chapter 12 of the Family Law Article (Child Support Guidelines). Accordingly, the presumptive maximum and minimum support payments should be dictated by those policies.

Applying these principles to this case, the presumptive minimum base payment would be $1,040 (the payment established by the schedule for $10,000), and the presumptive maximum would be $1,517 (10.4 percent of combined income of $14,583). Adding $400 of child care expenses to the presumptive maximum figure produces a total of $1,917, and multiplying that amount by 83 percent to arrive at the contribution to be made by the father produces a total presumptive maximum payment of $1,591. The monthly payment ordered in this case was $1,550. Although calculated by a method which I believe is at variance with the approach intended by the legislature, the payment ordered here falls within the range of discretion which I believe the legislature intended to grant to trial judges, and I would therefore affirm the decision in this case.

NOTE

Guideline formulae vary in several respects, including how high a weekly or monthly income amount they specifically include. Whether and how guidelines should be applied in cases involving high-income, noncustodial parents have generated court contests in some states with statutes that are silent or unclear on the subject. In Battersby v. Battersby, 218 Conn. 467, 590 A.2d 427 (1991), the Supreme Court of Connecticut noted that

> the [trial] court found that the plaintiff's weekly disposable income alone was in excess of the highest income listed on the state Guidelines for Support Standards (Guidelines) chart. It further concluded that the Guidelines do not apply when the combined weekly disposable income of the parties exceeds $750. The court considered the financial status of the parties, their living arrangements, the tax consequences of the original unallocated order, and the tax benefit of awarding the personal exemptions for the two children to the defendant. An order was entered requiring that the plaintiff pay $260 per week support for both children and allocating the tax exemptions to the defendant.

On appeal, the defendant urged that

> . . . the trial court improperly held that: (1) when the combined weekly disposable income of the parties exceeds $750, the Guidelines are not applicable; and (2) since the parties' combined disposable income exceeded $750, that fact alone is sufficient to find that the application of the Guidelines would be inequitable or inappropriate.

In response to the defendant's assertion that the trial court's refusal to apply the Guidelines contradicted the language of the child support statute, the Supreme Court responded that

> The statute does not . . . require the trial courts to apply the Guidelines to all determinations of child support, but creates only a rebuttable presumption as to the amount of child support. It requires only that the trial court consider the Guidelines. Moreover, the Guidelines do not contain provisions for disposable incomes in excess of $750. . . .

> There are no provisions for extrapolating to higher income levels the percentages or award amounts set forth in the Guidelines chart. If the legislature or commission had intended to provide for such extrapolation of the chart, it could have said so. . . .

> General Statutes § 46b–215b(b) provides that in any proceeding for the establishment or modification of a child support award, the Guidelines "shall be considered in addition to and not in lieu of" the criteria established in General Statutes § 46b–84(b) and other statutes not applicable to this proceeding. In addition, the Guidelines themselves list several factors that may be relevant to the determination of support amount, including the "needs of a second or prior family" and "other reasonable considerations."

In reaching its decision, the trial court considered the parties' financial affidavits and the fact that the plaintiff pays $200 per week, pursuant to the order of another court, for the support of one child from a subsequent marriage. It further considered the tax ramifications of modifying the original order of unallocated child support and alimony to an order of simple child support, and of awarding the personal exemptions for the two children to the defendant. The court also explained how the Guidelines work and why they do not apply to these parties.

The defendant's claim that the trial court contradicted the plain language of General Statutes § 46b–215b is without merit. The record shows that the court considered the Guidelines, found the chart inapplicable for arriving at a presumptive support amount, and considered the statutory criteria and other Guideline factors in arriving at its decision.

The defendant urged the trial court to extrapolate from the chart by applying the percentage listed at the $750 level (44 percent) to the plaintiff's income. The court found that applying the Guidelines chart to incomes in excess of $750 would be inequitable because the statistical basis for the chart loses its validity as the disposable income of the family increases; that is, the proportion of household income spent on children declines as household income increases. R. Williams, "Guidelines for Setting Levels of Child Support Orders," 21 Fam.L.Q., No. 3, 281, 288 (1987). The final report prepared by the 1985 commission on child support which recommended the statewide adoption of the Guidelines itself noted: "It is generally accepted that the guidelines are of minimal value in framing support obligations at both the high and low ends of the income scale." Obviously, while a family earning $750 a week may spend 44 percent of its income supporting two children, a family earning $2000 per week ordinarily spends a lower percentage. Since the purpose of a child support order is to provide for the care and well-being of minor children, and not to equalize the available income of divorced parents, the trial court had the authority to reject the defendant's suggested extrapolation of the Guidelines' percentage as inappropriate and inequitable in the circumstances before it.

Nash v. Mulle

Supreme Court of Tennessee, 1993.
846 S.W.2d 803.

■ Daughtrey, Justice.

The essential facts in this case are not in dispute. What is contested is the extent of the child support obligation of Charles Mulle, who fathered Melissa Alice Matlock as the result of an extramarital affair with the appellant, Helen Nash, in 1981 but has since had nothing to do with mother or child. After an order was entered establishing his paternity in 1984, the Juvenile Court also ordered him to pay $200.00 each month in child support, in addition to other specified expenses. In 1990, Helen Nash filed this action seeking an increase in the amount of his payments because of Charles Mulle's dramatically increased income.[1] The Juvenile Court then ordered Mulle to pay $3,092.62 per month, with $1,780.17 reserved for a trust fund established for Melissa's college education. The Court of Appeals reversed, limiting the award to $1,312.00 per month, or exactly 21 percent of $6,250.00, the top monthly income to which the child support guidelines explicitly apply. The Court of Appeals also disallowed the trust, finding that it improperly extended the parental duty of support beyond the age of majority. Because the facts are not disputed, we review de novo the questions of law presented on appeal.

Child support in Tennessee is statutorily governed by T.C.A. § 36–5–101. Section 36–5–101(e)(1) provides that "[i]n making its determination concerning the amount of support of any minor child ... of the parties, the court shall apply as a rebuttable presumption the child support guidelines as provided in this subsection." The General Assembly adopted the child support guidelines promulgated by the Tennessee Department of Human Services in order to maintain compliance with the Family Support Act of 1988, codified in various sections of 42 U.S.C.[2] While they add a measure of consistency to child support awards statewide, the guidelines provide more than simple percentages to be applied against the net incomes of non-custodial parents. They also embody "the rules promulgated by the Department of Human Services in compliance with [the] requirements [of the Family Support Act of 1988]."[3] Hence, the purposes, premises, guidelines for compliance, and criteria for deviation from the guidelines carry what amounts to a legislative mandate.

The first issue presented concerns the proper measure of child support to be awarded in this case in view of the fact that Charles Mulle's monthly income exceeds $6,250.00. The guidelines apply in all cases awarding financial support to a custodial parent for the maintenance of a child, whether or not the child is a welfare recipient, and whether or not the child's parents are married. The guidelines are based, however, on several goals; they make many assumptions; and they permit deviation in circumstances that do not always comport with the assumptions. In studying the

---

1. Mr. Mulle's income has risen substantially since the original award, thus justifying this review under T.C.A. § 36–5–101(a), which permits a change in child support only "upon a showing of a substantial and material change of circumstances." Whereas his income when the first award was made was approximately $30,000.00 annually, his gross annual income has risen considerably. In 1988 his gross income was approximately $192,000.00; in 1989, he earned approximately $292,000.00; and in 1990, his income was approximately $260,000.00. These figures contrast with Ms. Nash's 1989 gross annual income of approximately $42,000.00. In its calculation under the guidelines, the Juvenile Court increased Mulle's payments to reflect a more appropriate contribution in light of his present earnings.

2. Under 42 U.S.C. §§ 651, 652, and 654, a "state plan" is essential in order to assure the state's receipt of federal money for child support enforcement. 42 U.S.C. § 667(a) requires that "[e]ach state, as a condition for having its State plan approved ..., must establish guidelines for child support award amounts within the state."

3. Tenn.Comp.R. and Regs. ch. 1240–2–4–.01(6) (1989).

goals, premises, and criteria for deviation, we are convinced that the guidelines permit a monthly award greater than $1,312.00 without a specific showing of need by the custodial parent.

One major goal expressed in the guidelines is "[t]o ensure that when parents live separately, the economic impact on the child(ren) is minimized and to the extent that either parent enjoys a higher standard of living, the child(ren) share(s) in that higher standard." Tenn.Comp.R. and Regs. ch. 1240–2–4–.02(2)(e). This goal becomes significant when, as here, one parent has vastly greater financial resources than the other. It reminds us that Tennessee does not define a child's needs literally, but rather requires an ward to reflect both parents' financial circumstances. This goal is consistent with our long-established common law rule, which requires that a parent must provide support "in a manner commensurate with his means and station in life." Evans v. Evans, 125 Tenn. 112, 119, 140 S.W. 745, 747 (1911).

The guidelines are currently structured to require payment by the non-custodial parent of a certain percentage of his or her net income, depending upon the number of children covered by the support order (21 percent for one child, 32 percent for two children, etc.). The statute promulgating the use of the guidelines creates a "rebuttable presumption" that the scheduled percentages will produce the appropriate amounts to be awarded as monthly child support.[4] However, they are subject to deviation upward or downward when the assumptions on which they are based do not pertain to a particular situation. For example, one assumption on which the percentages are based is that the "children are living primarily with one parent but stay overnight with the other parent as often as every other weekend . . ., two weeks in the summer and two weeks during holidays. . . ."[5] The criteria for deviation provide that when this level of visitation does not occur, child support should be adjusted upward to provide for the additional support required of the custodial parent. Additionally, "[e]xtraordinary educational expenses and extraordinary medical expenses not covered by insurance" are given as reasons for deviation. The guidelines thus recognize that "unique case circumstances will require a court determination on a case-by-case basis."

Among the "unique cases" specifically anticipated in the guidelines are those cases in which the income of the parent paying support exceeds $6,250.00 per month. In the criteria for deviation the guidelines provide that among the "cases where guidelines are neither appropriate nor equitable" are those in which "the net income of the obligor exceeds $6,250 per month." In the present case, the Juvenile Court calculated Charles Mulle's net monthly income to be $14,726.98, a figure well above the $6,250.00 figure justifying deviation from the guidelines. Yet the total award of $3,092 ordered by the trial judge is exactly 21 percent of Mulle's monthly income.

4. T.C.A. § 36–5–101(a)(2); Tenn. Comp.R. & Regs. ch. 1240–2–4–.02(8).

5. Tenn.Comp.R. & Regs. ch. 1240–2–4–.02(7).

Obviously, to treat the monthly income figure of $6,250.00 as a cap and automatically to limit the award to 21 percent of that amount for a child whose non-custodial parent makes over $6,250.00 may be "neither appropriate nor equitable." Such an automatic limit fails to take into consideration the extremely high standard of living of a parent such as Charles Mulle, and thus fails to reflect one of the primary goals of the guidelines, i.e., to allow the child of a well-to-do parent to share in that very high standard of living. On the other hand, automatic application of the 21 percent multiplier to every dollar in excess of $6,250.00 would be equally unfair.

We conclude that the courts below found themselves at such polar extremes in this case due to a misreading of the criteria for deviation in the guidelines. The Juvenile Court placed the burden "on Mr. Mulle to convince the Court of the inequity or inappropriateness of the guidelines in this case," i.e., to prove that the court should award less than 21 percent of his income in excess of $6,250.00. That court ultimately found that Mulle had shown no "extraordinary burden" on his budget or other reason justifying deviation downward from the presumptive award of 21 percent, and awarded that amount. The Court of Appeals, on the other hand, held that "to obtain support larger than 21% of $6,250.00 for one child, the [custodial parent] has the burden of showing such need." Thus, to receive more than $1,312.00 per month for the child, Helen Nash would have to demonstrate exactly why the additional money was required. Rather than adopting either of these diametrically opposed approaches, we conclude that the trial court should retain the discretion to determine—as the guidelines provide, "on a case-by-case basis"—the appropriate amount of child support to be paid when an obligor's net income exceeds $6,250.00 per month, balancing both the child's need and the parents' means.

The guidelines' very latitude reflects this need for an exercise of discretion. Twenty-one percent of an enormous monthly income may provide far more money than most reasonable, wealthy parents would allot for the support of one child. However, it would also be unfair to require a custodial parent to prove a specific need before the court will increase an award beyond $1,312.00. At such high income levels, parents are unlikely to be able to "itemize" the cost of living. Moreover, most parents living within their means would not be able to present lists of expenditures made in the mere anticipation of more child support. Until the guidelines more specifically address support awards for the children of high-income parents, we are content to rely on the judgment of the trial courts within the bounds provided them by those guidelines. In this case, although the child support award may be appropriate, we think it expedient to remand this case to the Juvenile Court, thus providing the trial judge an opportunity to reconsider his opinion in light of the fact that he is not limited to the $1,312.00 cap imposed by the Court of Appeals, nor is he bound to award 21 percent of Charles Mulle's full net income, but may exercise his discretion as the facts warrant.

II.

As he did before the Court of Appeals, Charles Mulle contends that the establishment of an educational trust fund for his daughter unlawfully requires him to support her past her minority. Citing Garey v. Garey, 482 S.W.2d 133 (Tenn.1972), and Whitt v. Whitt, 490 S.W.2d 159, 160 (Tenn. 1973), he argues that the trust fund is incompatible with Tennessee case law. In Garey, this Court held that "[b]y lowering the age of majority from 21 to 18 years of age the Legislature has completely emancipated the minor from the control of the parents and relieved the parents of their attendant legal duty to support the child." 482 S.W.2d at 135. Because the trust fund is intended for Melissa's college education, her father insists that it unlawfully requires post-minority support.

We conclude, to the contrary, that the establishment of the trust fund in this case does not conflict with the holding in Garey. Although child support payments may not extend beyond the child's minority (except in extraordinary circumstances involving physical or mental disability), the benefits from such payments can. Hence, it is consistent with established rules of Tennessee law to hold, as we do here, that funds ordered to be accumulated during a child's minority that are in excess of the amount needed to supply basic support may be used to the child's advantage past the age of minority.

In reaching this conclusion, we must recognize the obvious fact that responsible parents earning high incomes set aside money for their children's future benefit and often create trusts for that purpose. They save for unforeseen emergencies; they accumulate savings for trips and other luxuries; and they may, and usually do, save for their children's college educations. Melissa's mother has expressed her intention to send her daughter to college. As all parents realize, however, the goal of sending a child to college often requires the wise management of money through savings. For a child of Melissa's age, assumed to begin college in the fall of 2000, it has been estimated that a parent must invest $457.00 per month for a public college education, or $964.00 per month for a private education, in order to save the $61,571.00 or $129,893.00, respectively, that will be required to fund a college education beginning that year.[11] Lacking the resources to write a check for the full amount of college tuition, room, board, and other expenses when that time arrives, Helen Nash must accumulate these savings over the course of the child's minority, or be forced to borrow the money later on. Such savings in this case would inevitably deplete Melissa's child support award. While in many cases parents undergo serious financial sacrifices to make college possible for their children, in this case, as the Juvenile Court found, Charles Mulle's income can afford Melissa a high standard of living that also includes savings for college.

We believe that an approach that refuses to recognize the laudable goal of post-secondary education and instead provides only for the child's

---

11. See The Tennessean, Nov. 14, 1992, at 1E, col. 4.

immediate needs, would not be a responsible approach. If the most concerned, caring parents do not operate in such a haphazard way, surely the courts cannot be expected to award child support in such a fashion. Thus, we conclude that establishing a program of savings for a college education is a proper element of child support when, as in this case, the resources of the non-custodial parent can provide the necessary funds without hardship to that parent.

Moreover, the use of a trust fund for just such a purpose is explicitly approved by the guidelines. In the section on criteria for deviation, the guidelines provide: There are ... cases where guidelines are neither appropriate nor equitable when a court so finds. Guidelines are inappropriate in cases including but not limited to, the following: (a) In cases where the net income of the obligor ... exceeds $6,250 per month. *These cases may require such things as the establishment of educational or other trust funds* for the benefit of the child(ren) or other provisions as may be determined by the court. Tenn.Comp.R. & Regs., ch. 1240–2–4–.04(2)(a) (emphasis added). Thus, the guidelines specifically recommend a trust fund in cases in which a large cash award may be inappropriate. Moreover, the guidelines do not limit expenditures from such trusts to the child's minority. We defer to the policy judgment of the legislature in adopting the guidelines and uphold the use of the trust in this case.

In addition to adhering to the guidelines and providing a mechanism for this laudable use of savings, a trust fund for college education achieves several other goals. First, in a case such as this one involving a large difference in the parents' incomes, the trust allows for equitable contributions from each parent while avoiding an immediate cash windfall to one of them. When a large award given to a custodial parent with a much lower income would result in a windfall to the custodial parent, a trust fund helps to ensure that money earmarked for the child actually inures to the child's benefit. Thus, the trust fund is properly used to minimize unintended benefits to the custodial parent.

We also note the need for a trust as protection for the child of an uncaring non-custodial parent. When the Supreme Court of Washington upheld an order requiring a parent to fund the college education of his three sons, it noted "the long standing special powers the courts have had (in equity, regardless of legislation) over the children of broken homes to assure that their disadvantages are minimized." Childers v. Childers, 89 Wash.2d 592, 575 P.2d 201, 207 (1978). Later, quoting Esteb v. Esteb, 138 Wash. 174, 184, 244 P. 264, 267 (1926), the Childers court continued, "Parents, when deprived of the custody of their children very often refuse to do for such children what natural instinct would ordinarily prompt them to do." 575 P.2d at 208. When a non-custodial parent has shown normal parental concern for a child, a trust fund may be unnecessary to ensure that his or her feelings are reflected in spending. However, when a non-custodial parent shows a lack of care, the court may step in and require the parent to support his or her child. The establishment of a trust is simply one discretionary mechanism used in the endeavor.

Thus, Charles Mulle's argument that the absence of a relationship with Melissa obviates the need to fund her college education is simply backwards. Child support is designed to prevent a non-custodial parent from shirking responsibility for the child he or she willingly conceived. It is precisely when natural feelings of care and concern are absent, and no parent-child relationship has been developed, that the court must award child support in a manner that best mirrors what an appropriate contribution from an interested parent would be. In fact, at least one court has gone beyond the acknowledgment of this lack of parental interest, and has spoken in terms of compensating the child for the parent's lack of concern. In Cohen v. Cohen, 193 Misc. 106, 82 N.Y.S.2d 513, 514 (1948), the court stated that the non-custodial parent "should be obliged to make up for his neglect, and to contribute towards his son's education as much as lies within his power." While we do not adhere to this compensatory view of child support, we do believe that an appropriate child support award should reflect an amount that would normally be spent by a concerned parent of similar resources.

We thus find no merit to Charles Mulle's complaint that the order deprives him of the freedom to decide his daughter's educational fate, arguing that a requirement is being imposed upon him that does not exist for married parents. He contends in his brief that "some parents plan for the future education of their children and some do not"; he argues that "[s]urely a divorce decree or a paternity order should not give children rights that children who are living with their parents who are married do not have." This argument overlooks the obvious fact that divorced and unmarried parents face a substantial loss of parental autonomy whenever a court must step in to exercise responsibility for their children in the absence of parental cooperation. Married parents may choose to rear their children in an extravagant or miserly fashion; they may send their children to expensive private schools and universities; or they may require their children to make their ways in the world at age 18. Nevertheless, when children become the subject of litigation, courts must judge the children's needs. Long-standing Tennessee law requires the courts to evaluate children's needs not in terms of life's essentials, but in terms of the parents' "means and station in life." See Atchley v. Atchley, 29 Tenn.App. 124, 127, 194 S.W.2d 252, 253 (1945) (citing Evans v. Evans, supra, 140 S.W. at 747). The guidelines' requirement that child support allow a child to share in the higher standard of living of a high-income parent continues this objective. Thus, Mulle's complaint about the alleged unfairness of the court's judgment concerning the benefits his standard of living should afford Melissa is misplaced.

Moreover, as the court stated in Atchley, "[r]eason, as well as the public policy of this state, favorable as it is to higher learning, permits no other conclusion. The high esteem in which college training is held in this state is unmistakably indicated by the numerous colleges found in the various parts of this state." 29 Tenn.App. at 129, 194 S.W.2d at 254 (citing Jackman v. Short, 165 Or. 626, 109 P.2d 860 (1941)). When the Illinois court in Maitzen v. Maitzen, 24 Ill.App.2d 32, 163 N.E.2d 840, 845 (1959), required a parent to provide a college education to a child over the age of majority in the absence of legislative approval, it stated in a similar vein: The public policy of this state, that a college education be given children whenever possible, is evidenced by the many institutions of higher education maintained by the state.... A divorced parent should not ... expect his children to rely on the bounty of others when he has ample means to provide for them. Id., 163 N.E.2d at 845 (citing state and federal college aid statutes).... The Washington Supreme Court likewise reasoned in Childers, saying, "[The fact that] it is the public policy of the state that a college education should be had, if possible, by all its citizens, is made manifest by the fact that the state of Washington maintains so many institutions of higher learning at public expense." Id. 575 P.2d at 206. Given the public policy favoring higher education in Tennessee, likewise evidenced by our many colleges and universities, it would be highly improper in this case to cast the burden of Melissa's higher education entirely on her mother, or on the "bounty of the state," when her father can provide for her education without unduly burdening himself.

In ruling the trust in this case illegal because it "has no relation to the support of the child during minority," the Court of Appeals relied for authority on prior Tennessee case law discussed earlier in this section, as well as cases from other jurisdictions, primarily Illinois and Hawaii. But, the Tennessee precedents predate the enactment of the Child Support Guidelines, which specifically authorize the use of trusts in cases involving non-custodial parents with high income, without limiting expenditures to the beneficiary's minority. Moreover the courts and legislatures of many other states have approved the funding of a college education by non-custodial parents who can afford such an expense. Indeed, several courts have done so without explicit statutory permission. In Pennsylvania, for example, the rule that a parent owes no duty of support for a child's college education is subject to an important exception. A parent may be ordered to provide such support if that parent has the "earning capacity or income to enable him to do so without undue hardship to himself." See Commonwealth v. Thomas, 243 Pa.Super. 599, 364 A.2d 410, 411 (1976); see also Brake v. Brake, 271 Pa.Super. 314, 413 A.2d 422 (1979). Therefore, in appropriate cases, the Pennsylvania courts require college support, even though the age of majority in that jurisdiction is 18.[12] An Alabama court, similarly, has required the establishment of a trust during a child's minority for educational expenses incurred after the age of majority. See Armstrong v. Armstrong, 391 So.2d 124, 126 (Ala.Civ.App.1980). The Iowa Supreme Court decreed in Hart v. Hart, 239 Iowa 142, 30 N.W.2d 748 (1948), that a non-custodial parent should provide his sons with four-year college educations despite the fact that college funding would likely require support beyond the 21–year–old age of majority in existence at that time.[13] New Hampshire courts also have the discretion to award college support

---

12. 23 Pa.Cons.Stat.Ann. § 4321.

13. Iowa Code § 599.1 (1981) now makes the age of majority 18. In 1972 the age was reduced to 19 from 21, and a year later the age was reduced again to 18 (see historical notes).

past the age of majority. See Gnirk v. Gnirk, 134 N. 199, 589 A.2d 1008, 1011–12 (1991). These courts have used their equitable powers to require wealthy non-custodial parents to fund their children's college educations past the age of majority.

In yet other states, the authority of the courts to require non-custodial parents to fund a college education for their children is provided by statute. In Washington, after the child support statute was amended to include support for "dependents," the Washington Supreme Court declared that a college education could be included in the duty of support in cases where it "works the parent no significant hardship and . . . the child shows aptitude." Childers v. Childers, supra, 575 P.2d at 207. Oregon, similarly, allows courts to award support to children until the age of 21, three years past the age of majority, if they attend school. See Or.Rev.Stat. § 107.108 (1991); In the Matter of the Marriage of Wiebe, 113 Or.App. 535, 537, 833 P.2d 333, 334 (1992). Indiana allows child support for college expenses if the parent has the financial ability and the child has the aptitude. Ind.Code § 31–1–11.5–12(b) (1991); see also Martin v. Martin, 495 N.E.2d 523 (Ind.1986).

Other legislatures have taken the lead from court decisions allowing college support and now statutorily provide for such support. For example, Illinois has codified prior case law that had established a parent's duty to provide for his or her child's education whether the child was of minority or majority age. Ill.Ann.Stat. ch. 40, para. 513 (Smith–Hurd (1980)) (codifying Maitzen v. Maitzen, 24 Ill.App.2d 32, 163 N.E.2d 840 (1959)). In addition, a New York statute permits an award for post-secondary educational expenses when the court determines that the award is appropriate in light of "the circumstances of the case and of the respective parties and the best interests of the child and as justice requires." N.Y.Jud.Law § 413(1)(c)(7) (McKinney 1992). New York's statute replaces years of case law holding that a college education could be a "special circumstance" meriting support past minority. See Gamble v. Gamble, 71 A.D.2d 649, 418 N.Y.S.2d 800 (1979); Brundage v. Brundage, 100 A.D.2d 887, 889, 474 N.Y.S.2d 546, 549 (1984); Shapiro v. Shapiro, 116 Misc.2d 40, 45, 455 N.Y.S.2d 157, 160–61 (1982). Thus, whether based on statute or rooted in the courts' equitable powers in family matters, the efforts of these states to provide for the college educations of children with wealthy parents persuade us that reason and public policy permit the use of a trust fund in this case.

In light of the guidelines' explicit provision for the use of trusts in cases involving high-income parents, the goals promoted by the use of a trust in this instance, and the reasoned support of other state courts and legislatures, we find the use of an educational trust in this case to be proper. As noted in Section I, however, there remains the question of the level at which the trust should be funded in this case. We therefore reverse the judgment of the Court of Appeals, and remand the case to the Juvenile Court for calculation of an award in accordance with this opinion. . . .

NOTES

Contribution to College Expenses. Gimlett v. Gimlett, 95 Wn.2d 699, 629 P.2d 450 (1981), the Supreme Court of Washington was faced with interpreting terms of a decree requiring support "until said children are emancipated". The question was whether the term "emancipate" means attaining majority or ceasing to be dependent. While recognizing that support can be granted after majority, as explained in *Childers,* in view of the facts and an examination of the original decree it was obvious that the judge equated emancipation with reaching the majority age of 18 years. In a later decision in the same jurisdiction it was held that the phrase "so long as the children remain dependent" did not automatically end the support obligation at their majority. *See* In re Marriage of Anderson, 49 Wash.App. 867, 746 P.2d 1220 (1987).

Before widespread legislative action lowered the age of majority to 18, many states had developed rules requiring contribution to college education in accordance with a child's capacity and a parent's financial ability to pay. In some jurisdictions, distinctions were made according to whether an order to contribute had been entered before or after the child had reached majority. With the lowering of the majority age, some courts held that their power to require such contribution ended at the age when most college students entered their first year. *See, e.g.,* Riegler v. Riegler, 259 Ark. 203, 532 S.W.2d 734 (1976); Eaton v. Eaton, 215 Va. 824, 213 S.E.2d 789 (1975); Sillman v. Sillman, 168 Conn. 144, 358 A.2d 150 (1975). Others disagreed. *See, e.g.,* French v. French, 117 N.H. 696, 378 A.2d 1127 (1977). Some state legislatures, such as Washington's, adopted legislation specifically dealing with the issue.

The most recent litigation has centered on constitutional challenges regarding whether states can require greater support contribution for children of divorced marriages. In LeClair v. LeClair, 137 N.H. 213, 624 A.2d 1350 (1993), the Supreme Court of New Hampshire held that a statute authorizing such a contribution was constitutional even though another statute provides for termination of child support when a child finishes high school. However, in Curtis v. Kline, 542 Pa. 249, 666 A.2d 265 (1995), the Supreme Court of Pennsylvania held that a statute requiring only separated or divorced parents to provide post-secondary education to their adult children constituted unconstitutional discrimination. State courts have rejected *Curtis* and held that the state has a rational purpose in requiring parents of divorce children to pay for college education that satisfies equal protection. Children of divorced parents suffer economic disadvantages and requiring parents to contribute to their children's education fosters the state goal of having an educated population. *See* In re McGinley, 172 Or.App. 717, 19 P.3d 954 (2001). Furthermore, the Supreme Court of Mississippi has held that a parent may be held responsible for the child's college education, to include car insurance and sorority fees, even though the child has substantial financial assets of her own. *See* Saliba v. Saliba, 753 So.2d 1095 (Miss.2000); Lindsay Cohen, *Daddy Will You Buy Me a College Education? Children of Divorce and the Constitutional Impli-*

cations of Noncustodial Parents Providing for Higher Education, 66 Mo. L. REV. 187 (2001); Judith G. McMullen, *Father (or Mother) Knows Best: An Argument Against Including Post–Majority Educational Expenses in Court–Ordered Child Support,* 34 IND. L. REV. 343 (2001). For resources in all fifty states, *see* www.childsupport.ws/; or www.divorcenet.com. Child support calculation reports may be found at www.divorcesource.com and at www.adrr.com/law1/csp11.htm.

The trust device. In *In re* Paternity of Tukker M.O., 199 Wis.2d 186, 544 N.W.2d 417 (1996), the Supreme Court of Wisconsin held that the state's child support standards did not preclude the family court's establishment in a paternity proceeding of both a trust fund to pay for a child's postminority higher education expenses and a discretionary fund from which the mother could withdraw funds without court approval when monthly child support needs were not met. The father was a professional athlete with a high current income.

In re Barrett

Supreme Court of New Hampshire, 2004.
150 N.H. 520, 841 A.2d 74.

■ DALIANIS, J.

The respondent, John T. Coyne, appeals an order recommended by a Marital Master (*Harriet J. Fishman*, Esq.) and approved by the Portsmouth Family Division (*DeVries*, J.). We vacate and remand.

The record supports the following facts. Coyne and the petitioner, Susan C. Barrett, were divorced on August 22, 1996, in the Commonwealth of Pennsylvania. The parties agreed to share joint legal custody of their two daughters, Kathryn and Jacqueline, with Barrett having primary physical custody. Additionally, Coyne was ordered to pay child support.

Barrett and the children moved to New Hampshire in 1998. At approximately the same time, Coyne ceased communication with them, although he continued to pay child support. Kathryn attended Winnacunnet High School, a public secondary school in Hampton, during her freshman year. Kathryn had been diagnosed in 1997 with attention deficit disorder and she suffered emotional problems due to her estranged relationship with Coyne. As a result of both conditions, she failed her freshman year. Although Barrett met with the Winnacunnet administration, Kathryn was neither coded for special education nor provided with other assistance.

In order to help her daughter, Barrett decided to enroll her in private school. Kathryn took summer courses and qualified for acceptance as a sophomore at Tilton School (Tilton), a private secondary school. Despite the high cost of private school, Barrett believed that unless Kathryn attended private school she would continue to fail. When requested by Tilton to provide financial information, Coyne submitted the necessary forms without objection. Because of Coyne's and Barrett's financial status, Tilton did not give Kathryn significant financial aid.

Kathryn's grades improved upon her enrollment at Tilton and she passed both her sophomore and junior years. In 2002 Barrett suffered financial difficulties and asked Coyne to pay for Kathryn's tuition to enable her to attend Tilton in her senior year. Coyne refused Barrett's request.

Barrett filed a motion in the Portsmouth Family Division seeking an order that Coyne contribute financially towards Kathryn's senior year at Tilton. The trial court initially found, on October 2, 2002, that Coyne "[did] not have the ability to pay" any amount towards Kathryn's senior year at Tilton.

Barrett filed a motion for reconsideration, arguing that Coyne's ability to pay was greater than that presented to the court because Coyne had failed to include his current wife's income in his financial statements. The trial court reconsidered and ordered Coyne to pay $8,000 of Kathryn's school tuition.

On appeal, Coyne argues that the trial court erred in applying an "ability to pay" standard when ordering him to pay for Kathryn's private school tuition in addition to child support. We will uphold the trial court's decision unless it is unsupported by the evidence or tainted by an error of law. *In the Matter of Peirce and Peirce,* 146 N.H. 611, 613, 777 A.2d 874 (2001).

While we have considered the issue of college education expenses, *see In the Matter of Breault & Breault,* 149 N.H. 359, 821 A.2d 1118 (2003), the award of private secondary education expenses for a minor child is an issue of first impression for this court. Two statutes are relevant to our analysis: (1) RSA 458:17, I (1992), which provides that "the court shall make such . . . decree in relation to the support, education, and custody of the children as shall be most conducive to their benefit and may order a reasonable provision for their support and education"; and (2) RSA chapter 458–C (Supp. 2002), the child support guidelines, adopted by the legislature "to establish a uniform system to be used in the determination of the amount of child support," RSA 458–C:1.

In cases of statutory interpretation, we are the final arbiter of the legislature's intent as expressed in the words of the statute considered as a whole. *In the Matter of Coderre & Coderre,* 148 N.H. 401, 403, 807 A.2d 1245 (2002). We interpret legislative intent from the statute as written, and, therefore, we will not consider what the legislature might have said or add words that the legislature did not include. *Id.* Furthermore, we interpret statutes in the context of the overall statutory scheme and not in isolation. *Id.*

There exists an inconsistency between RSA 458:17, I, and RSA chapter 458–C. RSA 458:17, I, on its face appears to authorize an award of education expenses in addition to an award for child support. RSA chapter 458–C, adopted after RSA 458:17, I, however, purports to allow for deviations from the child support guidelines only when "the application of the guidelines would be unjust or inappropriate," RSA 458–C:4, II, IV, because of "special circumstances," RSA 458–C:5, which include "ongoing extraordinary . . . education expenses," RSA 458–C:5, I(a).

We consider all statutes concerning the same subject matter in interpreting any one of them and, where reasonably possible, we construe statutes as consistent with each other. *Coderre,* 148 N.H. at 404, 807 A.2d 1245. When interpreting two statutes that deal with a similar subject matter, we construe them so that they do not contradict each other, and so that they lead to reasonable results and effectuate the legislative purpose of each statute. *Id.*

The purpose of RSA chapter 458–C is not only to ensure uniformity in determining the amount of child support, but also to ensure that both the custodial and non-custodial parents share in the support responsibility for their children, according to the relative percentage of each parent's income. *See* RSA 458–C:1; *see also* RSA 458–C:2, II, IX, XI; RSA 458–C:3, I, II, III.

Through a complex scheme of definitions and formulae, the legislature provided guidelines from which the trial court first determines a parent's total child support obligation. *See* RSA 458–C:2, II, XI; RSA 458–C:3. The legislature has also authorized the trial court to deviate from those guidelines when "the application of the guidelines would be unjust or inappropriate," RSA 458–C:4, II, IV, because of the existence of "special circumstances," RSA 458–C:5. Such "special circumstances" include, as noted above, "ongoing extraordinary . . . education expenses." RSA 458–C:5, I(a).

Under normal circumstances a trial court need not consider private secondary education expenses when determining a non-custodial parent's child support obligation because all children are entitled to a public education. Instead, it is only when the trial court finds that "special circumstances" exist that it may require an obligor parent to contribute to private or specialized education. RSA 458–C:5, I(a). So, while RSA 458:17, I, read separately from the rest of the child support scheme, on its face would appear to authorize an award of private secondary education expenses in addition to the amount awarded under the child support guidelines, such a deviation, absent "special circumstances," would be inconsistent with the child support guidelines. *See* RSA 458–C:5. Therefore, a trial court may deviate from the child support guidelines to account for private secondary education expenses only after a finding that "the application of the guidelines would be unjust or inappropriate," RSA 458–C:4, II, IV, because of "special circumstances," RSA 458–C:5.

While this is an issue of first impression in New Hampshire, other jurisdictions have addressed the parameters of "special circumstances" for the purpose of ordering a non-custodial parent to contribute towards the private education of a minor child. These jurisdictions focus upon two conditions: (1) a demonstrated "special need" of the child; and (2) the non-custodial parent's "ability to pay." *See Solomond v. Ball,* 22 Va.App. 385, 470 S.E.2d 157, 160 (1996); *In re Marriage of Stern,* 57 Wash.App. 707, 789 P.2d 807, 813 (1990); *In re Marriage of Aylesworth,* 106 Cal.App.3d 869, 165 Cal.Rptr. 389, 394 (1980). This approach is consistent with our own statute. *See* RSA 458–C:5.

Therefore, when making a finding that "special circumstances" exist that warrant a deviation from the child support guidelines so as to require a non-custodial parent to contribute toward private secondary education expenses, the trial court must find that both the child has a demonstrated "special need" and the non-custodial parent has "an ability to pay." Furthermore, when determining whether a demonstrated "special need" exists, the trial court may consider such factors as: (1) the child's attendance at private school prior to the separation and divorce; (2) the availability of satisfactory public education, including special education; (3) the child's academic performance; (4) the child's family and/or religious tradition; and (5) the child's particular emotional and/or physical needs. *See Ley v. Forman,* 144 Md.App. 658, 800 A.2d 1, 14 (Sp.Ct.App.2002); *Lee v. Maier,* 728 A.2d 154, 156 (Me.1999); *Solomond,* 470 S.E.2d at 160; *Wilson v. Wilson,* 559 So.2d 698, 700 (Fla.Ct.App.1990); *Stern,* 789 P.2d at 814; *Aylesworth,* 165 Cal.Rptr. at 394.

In this case the trial court required Coyne to contribute to the cost of Kathryn's private education without a finding of "special circumstances." We hold that this was error and remand for consideration of whether Kathryn's private education expenses constitute "special circumstances."

Additionally, Coyne argues that the trial court may not consider his current wife's income when determining whether to order him to contribute towards Kathryn's tuition. Coyne points to RSA 458–C:2, IV(b), which provides that when determining the gross income of a parent, that parent's spouse's income "shall not be considered as gross income to the parent unless the parent resigns from or refuses employment or is voluntarily unemployed or underemployed," and contends that, because neither condition is present in this case, such income may not, therefore, be considered. The circumstances in this case, however, deal, not with determining Coyne's gross income, but rather with determining whether to allow for a deviation from the child support guidelines. RSA 458–C:5, I(c) expressly allows the trial court to consider "[t]he economic consequences of the presence of stepparents." Therefore, upon remand the trial court may consider Coyne's current wife's income for the purpose of determining whether "special circumstances" exist so as to justify a deviation from the child support guidelines. *See* RSA 458–C:5, I(c).

Finally, we turn to Coyne's arguments that the trial court is precluded from awarding Barrett private secondary education expenses because she: (1) failed to pursue certain State and federal remedies; and (2) failed to inform Coyne of her decision to send Kathryn to private school, thus eliminating his ability to pursue those remedies.

Concerning the former argument, we hold that "the availability of a public education program and extensive federal and state guidelines regarding special education does not preclude a parent's decision to place a child in a private school." *Lee,* 728 A.2d at 156. Rather, in evaluating the placement of a child in private school, the court should determine whether "special circumstances" warrant such placement and may consider the "availability of satisfactory public education, including special education" in its analysis of "special needs."

As to the latter argument, Coyne points to RSA 186–C:16–b, I and II, under which there exist statutory periods within which to pursue certain "special education" remedies. Coyne contends that because Barrett failed to inform him of her decision to place Kathryn in private school, she eliminated his ability to pursue those remedies on Kathryn's behalf, since by the time he knew of such placement the statutory periods had expired. We begin by noting that Coyne and Barrett share joint legal custody of Kathryn. "Legal custody refers to the responsibility for making major decisions affecting the child's welfare," 59 Am. Jur. 2d *Parent and Child* § 26 (2002), and legal custodians are entitled to make the major decisions regarding the health, education and religious upbringing of the child, *Chandler v. Bishop,* 142 N.H. 404, 412, 702 A.2d 813 (1997). Thus, either Barrett or Coyne is entitled to bring a petition for "special education" on behalf of Kathryn, if they are unable to make a joint decision.

The trial court, in ruling against Coyne, found that Coyne "had knowledge of his daughter's attendance at [Tilton]" and did nothing to pursue "special education" on her behalf, thus defeating his argument that his opportunity to pursue such education was eliminated. We have not been provided with a record of the first trial court hearing on October 2, 2002. Absent such a record, we assume, for the purposes of appeal, that the evidence supported the trial court's findings, and we limit our review to legal errors apparent on the record available to us. *See Dombrowski v. Dombrowski,* 131 N.H. 654, 663, 559 A.2d 828 (1989).

Though the trial court found that Coyne had knowledge of Kathryn's attendance at Tilton, it did not specify whether that knowledge arose within the relevant statutory time period. It is clear from the limited record available to us that Coyne knew of Kathryn's attendance at Tilton because he filled out the forms to determine her financial aid. Though it is not clear from the record exactly when he filled out those forms, we infer from the trial court's ruling denying him relief that his knowledge must have arisen within the relevant statutory time period. Coyne does not argue that the lack of a record has prejudiced him. The trial court did not commit any legal error and Coyne has presented us with no basis to overturn its ruling.

Coyne also argues that his rights to due process and equal protection under the law were violated by the trial court's order. Because Coyne's constitutional arguments were not adequately briefed and argued, we decline to address them. *State v. Schultz,* 141 N.H. 101, 104, 677 A.2d 675 (1996).

Vacated and remanded.

■ Broderick, C.J., and Nadeau and Duggan, JJ., concurred; Brock, C.J., retired, specially assigned under RSA 490:3, concurred.

CALIFORNIA FAMILY CODE (West 2004)

§ 3901. Duration of duty of support

(a) The duty of support imposed by Section 3900 continues as to an unmarried child who has attained the age of 18 years, is a full-time high school student, and who is not self-supporting, until the time the child completes the 12th grade or attains the age of 19 years, whichever occurs first.

(b) Nothing in this section limits a parent's ability to agree to provide additional support or the court's power to inquire whether an agreement to provide additional support has been made.

VERMONT STATUTES ANN. (1989)

Title 15, § 296 Liability of stepparents

A stepparent has a duty to support a stepchild if they reside in the same household and if the financial resources of the natural or adoptive parents are insufficient to provide the child with a reasonable subsistence consistent with decency and health. The duty of a stepparent to support a stepchild under this section shall be coextensive with and enforceable according to the same terms as the duty of a natural or adoptive parent to support a natural or adoptive child including any such duty of support as exists under the common law of this state, for so long as the marital bond creating the step relationship shall continue.

NOTE

In Ainsworth v. Ainsworth, 154 Vt. 103, 574 A.2d 772 (1990), the parties were divorced and the defendant father was ordered to pay support for the couple's two children. Defendant paid the support as ordered, but later remarried and established a home with his new wife and her son from a previous marriage. There was no preexisting order for defendant to support his stepchild and the issue before the court was whether the discretionary provision in the support guidelines allowed consideration of this obligation. In permitting consideration of such a factor they explained that

It would be unfair ... to consider amounts paid under existing support obligations only when they are the subject of court orders. By allowing consideration of payments made to discharge support obligations in instances where they have been scrutinized by a court and can be fit within mathematical formulas and allowing courts to deviate from support amounts calculated under the guidelines when such amounts are "inequitable," the Legislature must have intended that the courts use their discretion to consider the expenses connected with second families. The use of discretion in this area prevents the guideline system from being wholly arbitrary.

In reaching the conclusion that the court could consider the expenses of supporting other families under § 659, we also rely on the fact that the courts in Colorado, the state with a guideline system closest to that adopted in Vermont,[3] have reached the same conclusion. The Colorado

---

3. Colorado and Vermont use an income-share approach to setting guidelines. See Williams, Guidelines for Setting Levels of Child Support Orders, 21 Fam. L.Q. at 291.

courts have held that support obligations to other dependents may be evaluated in determining the extent to which a deviation from the guidelines is necessary to avoid an "inequitable" support order. See People in Interest of C.D., 767 P.2d at 811; In re Marriage of Rosser, 767 P.2d 807 (Colo.Ct.App.1988). In Rosser, the court reversed a trial court order that failed to take into account the fact that the noncustodial parent was living in New York City and was supporting another child. 767 P.2d at 809 ("the trial court abused its discretion in not deviating from the unjust result achieved by application of guideline calculations"). In C.D., the court analyzed the difference between support obligations liquidated and reduced to orders and those not so liquidated. It found that the Legislature required automatic consideration of liquidated support orders because they have been found to be "necessary and reasonable in amount in proper judicial proceedings." 767 P.2d at 811. Support for dependents without an order does not have a judicial evaluation and, therefore, the noncustodial parent must prove amounts paid are "reasonable and necessary" under the circumstances. See also In re Paternity of B.W.S., 131 Wis.2d 301, 319–20, 388 N.W.2d 615, 623 (1986) (fundamentally unreasonable to determine father's support obligation under percentage-of-income standards used in Wisconsin where there are "children in several households").

. . . . The trial court may, under § 659, find that calculating a support order based on the guidelines would be inequitable because of a parent's expenses in supporting other dependents.

Margaret M. Mahoney, in her book STEPFAMILIES AND THE LAW (1994), argues that the underlying issue affecting the stepparent-child relationship is whether they comprise a family relationship in the eyes of the law. The answer is unclear because each state controls the outcome of the status, so it depends on where you live; (2) issues are resolved on an *ad hoc* basis so there is little continuity of thinking; and (3) the traditional family model remains the basis and everything else seems to be the exception. The future, however, will certainly see an increase in the number of stepchildren and stepparents and this eventually will have an impact on the law.

M.H.B. v. H.T.B.

Supreme Court of New Jersey, 1985.
100 N.J. 567, 498 A.2d 775.

■ PER CURIAM.

The members of the Court being equally divided, the judgment of the Appellate Division is affirmed.

As noted earlier, Colorado has adopted an exclusion from income for the amount of preexisting child support obligations actually paid. Colorado also allows a deviation from the guidelines where their application would be inequitable. See Colo.Rev.Stat.Ann. § 14–10–115(3)(a).

■ HANDLER, J., concurring.

We have recently recognized that upon a divorce, one spouse may be obligated under principles of equitable estoppel to provide financial support for his or her stepchildren who are the children of the other spouse. Miller v. Miller, 97 N.J. 154, 167, 478 A.2d 351 (1984). In this appeal, we consider the circumstances that can give rise to an equitable estoppel forbidding a divorced stepparent from denying the validity of a previous voluntary commitment to provide financial support for a stepchild. The child in this case was born while the defendant was married to the child's mother. However, the defendant knew shortly after the child's birth that he probably was not her natural father. Nevertheless, throughout the marriage and for five years following the divorce, the defendant consistently conducted himself as the child's father, successfully gained the child's love and affection, and established himself as the little girl's parental provider of emotional and material support. Under such circumstances, I believe that the stepfather is obligated to provide continuing financial support for his stepchild.

The parties in this case (referred to by their initials or first names in order to protect the child who is the object of the controversy) were married in 1966. The couple settled in New Jersey where, during their first five years together, they conceived two sons, G.B. and M.B. The marriage turned sour during 1975, however, and sometime thereafter the plaintiff-wife, Marilyn, had a brief extra-marital affair. In 1977, while still married to the defendant-husband, Henry, Marilyn gave birth to a daughter, K.B.

Three months later, Henry first learned that he might not be K.B.'s biological father. He discovered a letter, or a diary entry, implicating Marilyn's former paramour as K.B.'s natural father. Henry then confronted Marilyn with this evidence of her infidelity, and moved out of the family residence. Following this separation, the marriage continued for almost three years. After living for six months in the same town as the rest of his family, however, Henry moved twice, first to California and then to Wisconsin, where he continues to live. During this period of separation, Henry maintained close bonds with all of the children, K.B. as well as the two sons, through phone calls, letters, gifts, and visits.

Marilyn also moved several times with the children. Between March and September 1978, she cohabitated with her erstwhile paramour, K.B.'s purported natural father, whom she briefly considered marrying. In December 1978, however, Marilyn brought herself and the children to Henry's home in Wisconsin, and for six months the parties attempted to reconcile their differences. Henry then professed to Marilyn that he would always love K.B., and that he did not want the child's illegitimacy to interfere with the couple's future together.

The reconciliation attempt failed, however, and, in June 1979, the couple signed a separation agreement covering financial support obligations, child custody, and visitation. Marilyn assumed custody of all three children, then ages 2, 7, and 10, and Henry undertook to pay $600 per month as family support, based on his annual income of over $34,000 at a time when Marilyn had no income. Marilyn thereafter moved back to New Jersey with all three children.

It is undisputed that K.B.'s purported father then lived and still lives nearby to the child and her mother. Marilyn testified, however, that she last saw this man in December 1979, six months after returning to New Jersey, and has not seen him since. Further, although after the separation Marilyn dated several men, none, including the alleged natural father, ever replaced Henry as a father-figure to K.B.

In March 1980, the couple obtained a divorce in Wisconsin under terms established by an extensive written settlement agreement. The parties, Henry as well as Marilyn, stipulated that all three children were born of the marriage. They further agreed that Marilyn would have custody of the children during the school year, and that Henry would get custody during the three summer months. Although at this point Henry earned about $51,000 each year while Marilyn still had no income, Henry promised only to continue paying $200 per month per child in Marilyn's custody. These payments would have totalled about $5,400 annually if three children had lived with their mother for nine months each year; however, by the parties' agreement, M.B. lived with his father for most of the post-divorce period, and therefore Henry's annual support obligation came to about $3,600. No alimony was awarded, and the couple's remaining, limited assets were divided in half.

All three minor children remained objects of Henry's affection, attention, and solicitude throughout the post-divorce period. In particular, Henry expressed interest in and concern for K.B. As found by the trial judge,

> K.B. bears Henry's surname, is registered on all of her records as bearing his surname, knows no other father, and is ignorant of the facts surrounding her paternity. Henry made innumerable representations to K.B. and to the world that he was her father.... The testimony related many tender moments between father and daughter. He sent her roses on her birthdays and comforted her in his bed during thunder and lightening storms.

Thus, Henry treated K.B. exactly as he treated his own son G.B., who was also in Marilyn's custody. Both K.B. and G.B. received Christmas gifts in 1979, 1980, and 1981. Further, Henry willingly provided child support payments on behalf of both children through the end of 1981. Based on all of the evidence, the trial judge concluded that Henry had become K.B.'s "psychological, if not biological parent."

Then, in March of 1981, Henry remarried. The following summer, both K.B. and G.B. visited and remained with Henry. By September 1981, however, Marilyn and Henry's second wife did not get along. The relationship between Marilyn and Henry deteriorated and Henry began withholding child support payments.

In January 1982 Henry petitioned a Wisconsin court to grant him custody of all three children, including K.B. The Wisconsin judge transferred the case to the New Jersey courts based on the children's best interests and the absence of local jurisdictional prerequisites. Marilyn filed a separate complaint, in March 1982, in New Jersey, seeking to retain custody of G.B. and K.B., and to obtain an increase in child support. Consistent with the petition he had filed in Wisconsin, Henry filed a counterclaim requesting custody of these children, K.B. as well as G.B. Later, by a pre-trial motion, Henry amended his counterclaim, claiming, in the alternative, that he should be under no duty to provide child support for K.B., and seeking to litigate the issue of the child's paternity. This was the first time that Henry had ever attempted to repudiate his paternal relationship with K.B. Without conceding Henry's right to contest paternity, Marilyn consented to allow the completion of Human Leucocyte Analysis blood test in December 1982. The results of the test excluded Henry as K.B.'s biological father.

A plenary hearing on the custody and support applications took place over several days in April and May of 1983. In addition to the foregoing facts, including Henry's knowledge in 1977 that he might not be K.B.'s natural father, the trial judge found that

> [i]t is clear Henry intended to be K.B.'s father and that she relied on that fact. . . . Even Henry's [second] wife . . . described Henry's relationship with K.B. as that of "a loving father-daughter relationship." . . . K.B. relied upon Henry's representations and has treated H.B. as her father, giving to him and receiving back from him all of the love and affection that the parent-child relationship should naturally evoke.
>
> Henry is certainly K.B.'s psychological, if not biological parent. . . . Henry is the only father K.B. knows or has ever known. . . . To permit Henry now to repudiate his intent to support K.B. . . . would cause irreparable harm to the child.

Based on these findings, the trial judge concluded that the doctrine of equitable estoppel was applicable to preclude Henry from denying the duty to provide child support on behalf of K.B. This aspect of his decision was affirmed by a divided court in the Appellate Division, and presents the sole issue on the appeal that Henry filed with this Court as of right under *R.* 2:2–1(a).

The framework for analysis of the issue on this appeal is provided by Miller v. Miller, 97 N.J. 154, 478 A.2d 351 (1984). In that case, the Court recognized that the doctrine of equitable estoppel could properly be applied in the context of a matrimonial controversy in which the interests of individual children were at stake. Because we were dealing with responsibilities that may flow from familial relationships that are inherently complicated and subtle, we acknowledged that the application of equitable principles called for great sensitivity, caution, and flexibility.

The *Miller* case involved two girls whose mother remarried after divorcing their father. During the mother's second marriage the defendant, her second husband, assumed sole responsibility for the girls' financial support, as well as other parental privileges and obligations. He also discouraged his wife and stepchildren from maintaining any personal or financial relationship with the children's natural father. The second marriage ended in divorce after seven years, at which time the mother sought to receive continuing child support from the girls' stepfather.

The Court ruled in *Miller* that, before a duty of child support could be imposed based on equitable considerations, it must first be shown that, by a course of conduct, the stepparent affirmatively encouraged the child to rely and depend on the stepparent for parental nurture and financial support. We specifically recognized that such conduct could interfere with the children's relationship to their natural father. Under the facts, we held that the stepfather would be equitably estopped to deny his duty to continue to provide child support on behalf of his stepchildren, if it could be shown that the children would suffer financial harm if the stepparent were permitted to repudiate the parental obligations he had assumed. We further held that the natural father could continue to be legally liable for the support of these children.

Applying the principles set forth in *Miller,* the evidence in this case compels the imposition of equitable estoppel to prevent Henry from denying the duty to provide financial support for K.B. Henry's actions throughout the marriage and following the divorce constituted a continuous course of conduct toward the child that was tantamount to a knowing and affirmative representation that he would support her as would a natural father. By both deed and word, Henry repeatedly and consistently recognized and confirmed the parent-child relationship between himself and K.B. He acted in every way like a father toward his own child. He also stipulated to the child's paternity. At the time of his divorce he promised to pay child support, which obligation was incorporated into the judgment of divorce.

The volitional nature of Henry's conduct is underscored by Henry's persistent attempts to gain custody of K.B., efforts that he continued on appeal from the trial court's award of custody to Marilyn. He thus sought child custody even after blood tests conclusively demonstrated that, biologically, he was not K.B.'s father. Consequently, there can be no suggestion that Henry's prior actions were merely accidental or inadvertent. His actions attest to the previously well-developed father-daughter bond, and convey all possible indicia of an affirmative and purposeful representation of continuing support, which constitutes a primary element of equitable estoppel.

There was clearly reasonable reliance upon Henry's purposeful conduct. The obvious expectations engendered by Henry's conduct were that K.B. fully accepted and reasonably believed Henry to be her father. Significantly, the court found that Henry became K.B.'s psychological father, a finding that imports much more than mere affection. See generally Goldstein, Freud & Solnit, Beyond the Best Interests of the Child 9–28 (1973). The strength and durability of a psychological parent-child relationship is perhaps the most relevant consideration in defining a child's best interests. Further, it is not disputed that K.B. never knew any person other than Henry to be her natural father. As found by the trial judge, Henry's absorption of the child's time and affection as her father effectively stultified the development of any other filial relationship between K.B. and anyone else.

In these circumstances, Henry's conduct assuredly engendered material and emotional consequences for K.B.—consequences that would be demonstrably adverse to K.B. if Henry were now permitted to repudiate all his prior actions. This becomes understandable upon a consideration of the nature of filial bonding. This bonding is indispensable in fostering the optimum psychological and emotional development of the child because it is the vehicle of parental love. This love of the parent for the child is a cohesive that binds parent and child and, further, gives unique strength and durability to the natural loyalty that the parent holds for the child. The parent-child bond thus serves to anchor the material and financial, as well as emotional, support that are vital to the well-being of a child. In this frame of reference, the critical factor is K.B.'s total filial dependence on Henry. Were Henry permitted to disavow the parent-child relationship that he created and fostered and to repudiate the parental responsibility that flowed from that relationship, K.B. would suffer demonstrable harm fully commensurate with her dependent condition.

The detrimental character of reliance in such situations has led courts to impose an estoppel against a man whose wife gives birth to another man's child if the husband then knowingly "represents himself to both the child and the community as the natural father." Miller, supra, 97 N.J. at 165, 478 A.2d 351 (citing Clevenger v. Clevenger, 189 Cal.App.2d 658, 11 Cal.Rptr. 707 (Dist.Ct.App.1961); Hall v. Rosen, 50 Ohio St.2d 135, 363 N.E.2d 725 (1977)); . . .

. . .

Defendant cites two reasons why he should not be responsible for his stepchild's financial support. He urges that the New Jersey Parentage Act, requires that if a man is found not to be a child's biological father, then he cannot be held liable to support that child, at least if the biological father may be identified. Defendant also contends that *Miller* stands for the proposition that Marilyn had a duty to bring the purported natural father into court and that, because she did not, we should remand to consider whether that person should be liable for K.B.'s support. Neither argument is persuasive.

With respect to the argument based on the New Jersey Parentage Act, N.J.S.A. 9:17–45a provides that "a man alleged . . . to be the father [of a child] . . . or any person with an interest recognized as justiciable by the court may bring . . . an action . . . for the purpose of determining the existence or nonexistence of the parent and child relationship." N.J.S.A. 9:17–45d further provides that "[r]egardless of its terms, an agreement, other than an agreement approved by the court in accordance with [N.J.S.A. 9:17–48c] between an alleged or presumed father and the mother of the child, shall not bar an action under this section." Henry alleges that these provisions shield him, as a stepparent, from child support obligations.

The statute, however, draws a distinction between paternity and the duty of support. The statute also recognizes the need for flexibility in determining child support. Thus, under N.J.S.A. 9:17–53c, after a court determines paternity and clarifies birth records, "[t]he judgment or order may contain any other provision directed against the *appropriate* party to the proceeding, concerning the duty of support, the custody . . . of the child, visitation privileges . . . , or any other matter *in the best interests of the child*." (Emphasis added.) This provision assures that in custody and support cases the children's best interests trump any determination of parentage. Clearly the Legislature did not intend to preclude the equitable imposition of a duty of child support upon a stepparent when the evidence assessed in accordance with principles of equity demand that result.

With respect to the other contention, in *Miller* there was undisputed evidence of a pre-existing and continuing relationship between the natural father and the daughters prior to the mother's remarriage to the defendant stepfather. There was also considerable testimony regarding the continuing viability of that relationship. In this case, by contrast there is no competent evidence as to K.B.'s natural parentage. Moreover, the uncontroverted testimony revealed no contact whatsoever between K.B. and her alleged natural father, nor any inkling on K.B.'s part that Henry was not her actual father. In addition there was evidence in *Miller* that the natural father had acknowledged in the past his financial ability and willingness to support his daughters. There is no comparable evidence in this case.

We recognized in *Miller* that a natural parent ordinarily is the primary source of financial support of a child, and that such a legal obligation is not abrogated by imposing a current obligation of child support upon a stepparent under principles of equitable estoppel. In that case, the Court felt it would be in the best interests of the child to consider whether the natural father, if available, should be made to honor his legal obligation to support his children. In this case, the circumstances are markedly different because no person, other than Henry, has ever emerged in K.B.'s life as her father.

A determination to affix a present obligation upon a stepfather does not in any way mean that we exonerate or condone a biological father who abdicates his responsibility to support his child. I fully acknowledge the statutory and common law requirement that the primary responsibility of child raising and support is that of the natural parent. Consequently, any decision to impose liability for child support on a stepparent must recognize the exceptional nature of such relief, as we have done in this case.

Notwithstanding the existence of exceptional circumstances and an equitable basis to impose a child support obligation on a child's stepparent, that relief remains mutable; it is subject to changing circumstances as these may affect the child's best interests. Indeed, in appropriate cases a stepparent, or any other person entitled to represent the interest of the child, may demonstrate the existence of changed circumstances justifying the assumption of liability for child support by the biological parent. That assumption of child support will be required if changed circumstances show that it would be in the best interest of the child, fair to the stepparent, and legally just as to the biological father. The record in this case, however, does not present these issues, and hence we cannot deal with them further.

For the reasons expressed, I would affirm the judgment below. Chief Justice Wilentz and Justice O'Hern join in this opinion.

■ POLLOCK, J., concurring in part and dissenting in part.

. . . Today's concurring opinion . . . would impose on a stepparent a duty of support not on the basis of estoppel but of a perceived emotional bonding between stepparent and child. From that premise, the opinion then proceeds to force the facts of the present case within its expanded interpretation of *Miller.*

I believe that the expansion of the *Miller* opinion is unwise and unnecessary. I further believe that the better practice would be to remand the matter to the Chancery Division for reconsideration in light of *Miller.* Pending that determination, I would continue to require Henry to support K.B.

. . .

Notwithstanding the contentions of the concurring opinion to the contrary, the record is devoid of any proof that Henry directly interfered with the natural father's relationship with K.B. In this regard, the facts of the present case differ from those in *Miller,* where the stepparent actively interfered with the natural parent's attempt to support his children. For example, the stepfather in *Miller* tore up the natural father's support checks, which eventually induced the natural father to discontinue his support payments. Here, the natural father has never claimed K.B. as his child and has been content to allow Henry to support her. The tragic fact is that neither Henry nor the natural father has spent much time with K.B.

Although the concurrence purports to rely on Miller v. Miller, supra, it actually stands the *Miller* opinion on its head. *Miller* recognized "that in appropriate cases, the doctrine of equitable estoppel may be invoked to impose on a stepparent the duty to support a stepchild after a divorce from the child's natural parent." We admonished, however, that the doctrine was to be invoked "cautiously."

Accordingly, we held that a stepparent could be equitably estopped from denying an obligation to support a stepchild on proof of three conditions. First, the stepparent must have made a representation to either the children or the natural parent that he or she would provide support. Second, that representation must have been relied on by either the children or the natural parent. We declined to rely on these two conditions alone to establish estoppel because such a rule would penalize a "stepparent who tried to create a warm family atmosphere with his or her stepchildren." Consistent with that concern, we imposed a third condition, one that required a showing that "the children will suffer future financial detriment as a result of the stepparent's representation or conduct that caused the children to be cut off from their natural parent's financial support." Such financial detriment could be shown if the custodial parent cannot locate or does not know the whereabouts of the natural parent, or cannot obtain legal jurisdiction over the natural parent, and the natural parent's unavailability is attributable to the actions of the stepparent. Thus, a stepparent is responsible for the unavailability of a natural parent only when he or she takes "positive action interfering with the natural parent's support obligation." Id. at 170, 478 A.2d 351. Accordingly, in *Miller,* we remanded the matter to the trial court to determine whether the stepfather had detrimentally affected his stepchildren's ability to obtain future support by interfering with the children's relationship with the natural father.

. . .

I continue to be counselled by *Miller's* warning not to impose a child-support obligation on a stepfather merely because he developed a close relationship with the stepchildren. Without further proof, I would not alter *Miller's* requirement that when the natural parent can be located and is financially able, he or she remains principally responsible to pay permanent child support.

The concurring opinion in the present case reflects the understandable desire to spare K.B. the painful knowledge that Henry is not her biological father. As painful as that discovery may be, however, it is inevitable that one day K.B. will learn the facts. For example, Marilyn has already revealed to G.B. and M.B., K.B.'s stepbrothers, the identity of K.B.'s natural father. In addition, Marilyn advises that she intends to inform K.B. at a later date that Henry is not her natural father. As well-intentioned as the concurrence may be, it cannot spare K.B. whatever anguish she will feel when she learns the identity of her natural father.

This case stands in stark contrast to *Miller,* where the evidence was that the stepparent actively resisted the natural father's attempt to maintain relations with his children. Here, the whereabouts of the natural father are known; he is in the next town. Most importantly, Henry has not done anything to interfere directly with the natural father's relationship with K.B. On the present record, the absence of financial support from the natural father is as attributable to his insouciance as it is to Henry's conduct.

In seeking an appropriate judicial response, I am guided, as are the concurring justices, by the best interests of the child. Like my colleagues who join in the concurring opinion, I believe that Henry is obliged to provide support for K.B., but I would require Henry to meet that obligation only until such time as a support order may be entered against the natural father. Hence, I would remand the matter to the Chancery Division for reconsideration in light of *Miller.* Of course, support obligations are always subject to modification because of changed circumstances, such as the ability of the natural father to satisfy the child's support needs. Because of Henry's previous agreement, included in his divorce decree, to support K.B., I would place the burden upon him to show that it is in the best interest of K.B. to obtain support from the natural father. If for any reason such an order cannot be entered against the natural father, I would continue to require Henry to support K.B.

NOTE

In Knill v. Knill, 306 Md. 527, 510 A.2d 546 (1986), the Maryland Court of Appeals held that a husband was not equitably estopped in a divorce action from denying any support duty to a child born to his wife during the marriage but not his natural child. The husband had undergone a vasectomy a year and a half before the child's birth, and the parties already had two children at that time. It was agreed that the husband was not the father, but he continued to live with his wife for twelve years afterward and treated the third child as a member of the family. The child first learned that the mother's husband was not his father when the mother revealed it to him after a family argument some two years before the parents separated. In allowing the defense of estoppel to be raised, the court found that although the elements of representation and reliance were present, the evidence did not show any financial detriment incurred as a result of the husband's course of conduct. They explained that "if any detriment was incurred by [the child] it was emotional and attributable to his mother", who had "ripped the 'cloak of legitimacy' off the boy following a family dispute. . . ." They pointed out that because there is no longer a statute of limitations in paternity cases in Maryland, the mother could still bring a statutory paternity suit against the natural father to establish his support duty.

In NPA v. WBA, 8 Va.App. 246, 380 S.E.2d 178 (1989), a husband who was not the biological father of his wife's child had reared and supported the child for five years after birth under the erroneous belief that he was the child's father. In a divorce proceeding, the Court of Appeals of Virginia held that the husband could not be required to support (1) because Virginia does not recognize "common law adoption"; (2) because the theory of *in loco parentis* extends legally cognizable rights "only so long as the relationship which gave rise to the rights continues to exist"; (3) there was no finding of an implied agreement to support a child who he had not fathered; and (4) Virginia courts have never applied equitable estoppel in the context of child support, and on the facts before the court the requirements for an estoppel were not met.

For another set of issues involving stepparents and stepchildren, *see* Margaret M. Mahoney, *Stepfamilies in the Law of Intestate Succession and Wills*, 22 U.C. DAVIS L.REV. 917 (1989).

CHILD SUPPORT RECOVERY ACT OF 1992
18 U.S.C. § 228 (2000)

§ 228.   Failure to pay legal child support obligations

(a) Offense.—Any person who—

(1) willfully fails to pay a support obligation with respect to a child who resides in another State, if such obligation has remained unpaid for a period longer than 1 year, or is greater than $5,000;

(2) travels in interstate or foreign commerce with the intent to evade a support obligation, if such obligation has remained unpaid for a period longer than 1 year, or is greater than $5,000; or

(3) willfully fails to pay a support obligation with respect to a child who resides in another State, if such obligation has remained unpaid for a period longer than 2 years, or is greater than $10,000; shall be punished as provided in subsection (c).

(b) Presumption.—The existence of a support obligation that was in effect for the time period charged in the indictment or information creates a rebuttable presumption that the obligor has the ability to pay the support obligation for that time period.

(c) Punishment.—The punishment for an offense under this section is—

(1) in the case of a first offense under subsection (a)(1), a fine under this title, imprisonment for not more than 6 months, or both; and

(2) in the case of an offense under paragraph (2) or (3) of subsection (a), or a second or subsequent offense under subsection (a)(1), a fine under this title, imprisonment for not more than 2 years, or both.

(d) Mandatory restitution.—Upon a conviction under this section, the court shall order restitution under section 3663A in an amount equal to the total unpaid support obligation as it exists at the time of sentencing.

(e) Venue.—With respect to an offense under this section, an action may be inquired of and prosecuted in a district court of the United States for—

(1) the district in which the child who is the subject of the support obligation involved resided during a period during which a person described in subsection (a) (referred to in this subsection as an "obliger") failed to meet that support obligation;

(2) the district in which the obligor resided during a period described in paragraph (1); or

(3) any other district with jurisdiction otherwise provided for by law.

(f) Definitions.—As used in this section—

(1) the term "Indian tribe" has the meaning given that term in section 102 of the Federally Recognized Indian Tribe List Act of 1994 (25 U.S.C. 479a);

(2) the term "State" includes any State of the United States, the District of Columbia, and any commonwealth, territory, or possession of the United States; and

(3) the term "support obligation" means any amount determined under a court order or an order of an administrative process pursuant to

the law of a State or of an Indian tribe to be due from a person for the support and maintenance of a child or of a child and the parent with whom the child is living.

NOTE

Federal involvement and impact in the area of child support enforcement has increased significantly during the past two decades. This should not be surprising, in view of the enormous economic interest of the federal government in support of child and family support programs whether or not they are administered by the states. The basic pattern of providing what might be described realistically as family law regulations that might affect only persons who are participants in public assistance or other state financed social schemes goes back a considerable stretch in time.

The Child Support and Establishment of Paternity amendments of 1974[1] and 1975[2] to Title IV of the Social Security Act added sharper teeth to the existing state law framework for support enforcement. The stated purposes of the new legislation were "enforcing the support obligations owed by absent parents to their children, locating absent parents, establishing paternity, and obtaining child support...."[3] A separate organizational unit, established by the HEW Secretary, was mandated with setting standards for state programs which will qualify for federal assistance, with operating a Parent Locator Service, and with undertaking such general housekeeping roles as evaluating, auditing and providing technical assistance for various state programs.[4]

A key feature of the new law was a waiver of sovereign immunity by the United States with regard to child support or alimony payments due from federal employees, including service persons, thereby making it possible to subject federal salaries to garnishment proceedings.[5] Another provision, unusual in light of the longstanding reluctance of the federal courts to hear domestic relations cases, provides for establishment of a separate organizational unit reporting to the Secretary of HEW

"... to receive applications from States for permission to utilize the courts of the United States to enforce court orders for support against absent parents and, upon a finding that (A) another State has not undertaken to enforce the court order of the originating State against the absent parent within a reasonable time, and (B) that utilization of the Federal courts is the only reasonable method of enforcing such order, approve such applications; ..."[6]

Under another provision a mechanism could be established for referring certain delinquent, court ordered support payments to the Secretary of

1. Act of Jan. 4, 1975, Public Law 93–647, 88 Stat. 2351. The Act, along with the later amendments, are codified at 42 U.S.C.A. §§ 651–660.

2. Act of Aug. 9, 1975, Public Law 94–88.

3. 42 U.S.C.A. § 651.

4. 42 U.S.C.A. § 653.

5. Id. at § 659.

6. Id. at § 652(a)(8).

the Treasury for collection when they have been assigned to a State with an approved plan and diligent efforts to collect have been made.[7]

The Parent Locator Service provided in the legislative scheme can utilize records and files of HEW and other federal agencies when requested under appropriate circumstances and procedures by the Secretary of HEW.

Even though the new amendments operate within the sphere of state-federal cooperation, analogous to the general approach in public assistance, they nevertheless constitute a substantial federal step into the family law field. In this regard the Act's provisions on what a state plan for child and spousal support must include is of special impact.[8] The goal of paring the cost of welfare expenditures has obviously provided the basis for such a role.

The Child Support Amendments of 1984[9] constituted a further step toward dealing with child support on a national basis and to effectively require states to enact more stringent enforcement legislation. Key among the latter is the establishment of nonbinding support guidelines to be made available to judges.

The Family Support Act of 1988[10] introduced further changes and is specially significant because of its impact outside the realm of persons on public assistance. It makes adherence to established support guidelines more nearly the rule than the exception (there is a rebuttable presumption that requires a specific finding about why applications of the guidelines would be "unjust or inappropriate in a particular case"). "Performance standards" for state paternity establishment programs are introduced, and wage withholding is to begin sooner after default. Automatic tracking and monitoring systems are made mandatory, and beginning in 1992 states must meet federal standards for establishing paternity for children born out of wedlock. The Act calls for appointment of a special Commission on Interstate Child Support.

Whether the latest of these statutory measures will be the opening gambit toward even greater federal involvement in family law regulation beyond the fiscally based support area remains to be seen.[11] For now, the Child Support Recovery Act continues to be the focus of litigation. The Supreme Court allowed to stand a holding that the Act does not unconstitutionally burden a defendant's right to travel decided in the Ninth Circuit. Sutton v. U.S., 533 U.S. 952, 121 S.Ct. 2597, 150 L.Ed.2d 755 (2001); the Second Circuit has ruled that a custodial parent cannot bring a private enforcement action under CSRA to obtain court-ordered support payments

7. Id. at § 652(b). See also 26 U.S.C.A. § 6305.

8. 42 U.S.C.A. § 654.

9. Pub.L. 98–378, 98 Stat. 1305. For a discussion of these amendments and their potential impact on one state's law, see Gallen, Congress Demands Stricter Child–Support Enforcement: Florida Requires Major Reforms to Comply, 10 Nova L.J. 1371 (1986).

10. Pub.L. 100–485.

11. For a thorough historical background of the workings of the original federal program and the law it complemented, see Harry Krause, Child Support in America (1981).

from a non-custodial parent who fled the state and ignored the support order. Salahuddin v. Alaji, 232 F.3d 305 (2d Cir.2000). Four federal circuits have upheld the authority of Congress under the Commerce Clause to enact the CSRA, only the Sixth Circuit has held the Act unconstitutional. United States v. Faasse, 227 F.3d 660 (6th Cir.2000). *See also* FULL FAITH AND CREDIT FOR STATE SUPPORT ORDERS, 28 U.S.C.A. § 1738B (West 2005).

Kansas v. United States

Tenth Circuit Court of Appeals, 2000.
214 F.3d 1196.

■ SEYMOUR, CHIEF JUDGE.

Kansas brought this action for declaratory and injunctive relief in response to changes in child support enforcement policy brought about by Title III of the Personal Responsibility and Work Opportunity Reconciliation Act (PRWORA). Pub.L. No. 104–193, 110 Stat. 2105 (1996). The district court granted the United States' motion to dismiss for failure to state a claim, and Kansas appeals. We review this decision de novo. . . .

The PRWORA, also known as "welfare reform," made sweeping changes in social policy relating to low-income people. It replaced the Aid to Families with Dependent Children (AFDC) program with the Temporary Assistance to Needy Families (TANF) program. The new program consists of federal block grants that are distributed to states, which then use the money to provide cash assistance and other supportive services to low-income families within their borders. Although this funding structure gives the states greater flexibility in designing their own public assistance programs, they are required to work toward program goals, satisfy a maintenance-of-effort requirement for the expenditure of state funds, and abide by federal regulations.

Title III of the PRWORA amended the Child Support Enforcement Program (IV–D)[12], which provides federal money to assist states in collecting child support from absent parents. *See* 42 U.S.C. §§ 651–669. State IV–D programs must currently provide child support services to all cases in which the custodial parent either receives temporary assistance under TANF or Medicaid, or requests IV–D assistance.

The PRWORA imposes greater federal oversight and control over the states' participation in the IV–D program in an effort to increase efficiency in child support enforcement, particularly in interstate cases, through information sharing, mass case processing, and uniformity. Among other things, the states must establish a Case Registry which contains all child support orders within the state, *see id.* § 653a, and a Directory of New Hires, *see id.* § 654a. These databases are regularly matched against one another and against a Federal Case Registry and National Directory of New

---

12. The Child Support Enforcement Program is commonly called IV–D because of its location in Subchapter IV, Part D of the Social Security Act.

Hires, which function as part of the existing Federal Parent Locator Service. *See id.* § 653.

The PRWORA also requires states to adopt the Uniform Interstate Family Support Act. *See id.* § 666(f). This act, which has been passed by the legislatures of all fifty states, allows state agencies to send income-withholding orders across state lines directly to employers. In addition, the PRWORA requires states to pass laws facilitating genetic testing and paternity establishment, *see id.* § 666(a)(5), and authorizing state child support agencies to take expedited enforcement action against non-paying noncustodial parents, *see id.* § 666(c). When a parent fails to pay child support, the PRWORA requires states to revoke passports, suspend professional and other licenses, place liens on property, and notify consumer credit reporting agencies, *see id.* §§ 652(k), 666(a)(1)–(4), (6)–(7), (16).

Significantly, states are not required to participate in the IV–D program. A state that elects to receive the federal block grant under the TANF program, however, must operate a child support enforcement program that meets IV–D's requirements. If a state's child support enforcement program fails to conform to the requirements of IV–D, the state risks the denial of both its IV–D child support enforcement funding and its TANF funding. The parties do not dispute that in fiscal year 1996, Kansas received $29.3 million in IV–D money from the federal government, and $101.9 million in TANF funding. These federal funds provide 66% of Kansas' IV–D program operating costs, and 80% of the expenditures relating to its computerized data systems. *See id.* § 655(a)(2)(C), (3)(B).

Kansas argues that the amended IV–D program requirements are too onerous and expensive, necessitate too much manpower, and encroach upon its ability to determine its own laws. Because of the amount of money at stake, Kansas contends it is being coerced into implementing the program requirements in violation of two provisions of the United States Constitution, specifically the Spending Clause of Article 1, § 8 and the Tenth Amendment. These claims are essentially mirror images of each other: if the authority to act has been delegated by the Constitution to Congress, then it may act pursuant to Article I; if not, the power has been reserved to the states by the Tenth Amendment. *See New York v. United States,* 505 U.S. 144, 156, 112 S.Ct. 2408, 120 L.Ed.2d 120 (1992). Because the legislation at issue was enacted pursuant to Congress' spending power, we will address the issue as arising under the Spending Clause.

A. *Spending Clause Challenges Generally*

Congress' spending power enables it "to further broad policy objectives by conditioning receipt of federal moneys upon compliance by the recipient with federal statutory and administrative directives." *Fullilove v. Klutznick,* 448 U.S. 448, 474, 100 S.Ct. 2758, 65 L.Ed.2d 902 (1980). The most instructive case on the Spending Clause issue is *South Dakota v. Dole,* 483 U.S. 203, 107 S.Ct. 2793, 97 L.Ed.2d 171 (1987), in which the Supreme Court upheld a legislative provision directing the Secretary of Transportation to withhold federal highway money from states refusing to raise their legal drinking age to 21.

The Court in *Dole* recognized four general restrictions on Congress' exercise of power under the Spending Clause. First, Congress' object must be in pursuit of "the general welfare." *Id.* at 207, 107 S.Ct. 2793. In considering whether an expenditure falls into this category, courts should defer substantially to the judgment of Congress. *See, e.g., Helvering v. Davis,* 301 U.S. 619, 640–41, 57 S.Ct. 904, 81 L.Ed. 1307 (1937). Second, if Congress desires to place conditions on the state's receipt of federal funds, it must do so unambiguously so that states know the consequences of their decision to participate. *See Dole,* 483 U.S. at 207, 107 S.Ct. 2793. Third, the conditions must be related to the federal interest in the particular program. *See id.* The required degree of this relationship is one of reasonableness or minimum rationality. *See New York,* 505 U.S. at 167, 112 S.Ct. 2408 (conditions must "bear some relationship to the purpose of the federal spending"); *id.* at 172, 112 S.Ct. 2408 (conditions imposed are "reasonably related to the purpose of the expenditure"). Fourth, there can be no independent constitutional bar to the conditions. *See Dole,* 483 U.S. at 208, 107 S.Ct. 2793. The Tenth Amendment itself does not act as a constitutional bar; rather, the fourth restriction stands for the more general proposition that Congress may not induce the states to engage in activities that would themselves be unconstitutional. *See id.* at 210, 107 S.Ct. 2793.

Kansas does not seriously argue that the IV–D conditions in the PRWORA violate the four restrictions outlined in *Dole.* The first two restrictions are easily dispensed with. As the district court noted in its opinion below, the "general welfare" test is substantially deferential to Congress, and can clearly be met here.[4] And although contending that some of the requirements associated with the computerized database are vague, Kansas fails to assert that the alleged ambiguity resulted in its inability to exercise its choice to accept the funds knowingly and "cognizant of the

---

4. In its brief to this court, Kansas tries to downplay the seriousness of the problem of unpaid child support, perhaps in an attempt to argue that the general welfare requirement is not met. Kansas makes numerous references to "the perceived need to crack down on the elusive and rumored population of 'deadbeat dads' " "believed to be running from state to state," and the "rare" "so-called dead-beat dads allegedly fleeing from State to State," *Plaintiff's Br.* at 8, 10, 19, 29. These characterizations do nothing to advance Kansas' argument. Congress made clear that non-payment of child support, particularly in interstate cases, is a widespread problem which has significant deleterious effects on children, particularly those in low-income families. The changes in IV–D's requirements were made in response to the widespread belief that the system of pursuing child support across state lines was "far too sluggish to be effective" and "universally regarded as broken." H.R. Rep. No. 104–651, at 1405, *reprinted in* 1996 U.S.C.C.A.N. 2183, 2464. For example, Congress found that in 1992 only 54% of single-parent families with children had a child support order established and, of that 54%, only about one-half received the full amount due. 42 U.S.C. § 601 note. Only 18% of the cases enforced through the public child support enforcement system resulted in a collection. *Id.* Interstate cases represent almost 30% of all child support orders, yet yield only 10% of collections. *See* H.R. Rep. No. 104–651, at 1405, *reprinted in* 1996 U.S.C.C.A.N. 2183, 2464. While lawyers may legitimately debate the application of the laws which address the non-payment of child support, no one is served by denying the existence of the problem.

consequences of ... participation," as required by *Dole. Id.* at 207, 107 S.Ct. 2793 (citing *Pennhurst State Sch. & Hosp. v. Halderman,* 451 U.S. 1, 17, 101 S.Ct. 1531, 67 L.Ed.2d 694 (1981)). The PRWORA unambiguously attaches its many conditions to the TANF and IV–D funds, and Kansas does not claim it accepted the money without knowledge of those conditions.

Regarding the third *Dole* requirement, under which the conditions must be related to the federal interest in the program, Kansas asserts that the IV–D conditions are not sufficiently related to the larger TANF program. This contention is based on Justice O'Connor's dissent in *Dole,* in which she argued for a closer correlation between the funding condition and the federal interest, stating that the drinking age condition was "far too over and under-inclusive" in addressing the problem of drunk driving. *Id.* at 214–15, 218, 107 S.Ct. 2793 (O'Connor, J., dissenting). The majority in *Dole,* however, endorsed a much less demanding test and determined that the drinking age condition was reasonably related to the highway program because of the connection between the drinking age and highway fatalities.

The TANF program, which provides financial support for low-income families, is clearly related to the IV–D program and its requirements, which assist low-income families in collecting child support from absent parents. *See* H.R.Rep. No. 104–651, at 1410 (1996), *reprinted in,* 1996 U.S.C.C.A.N. 2183, 2469 (noting IV–D complements the TANF program because establishing paternity and collecting child support may enable families to reduce dependence on the welfare system). Indeed, child support enforcement was conceived of as a related component of the AFDC system. *See* S.Rep. No. 93–1356 (1974), *reprinted in,* 1974 U.S.C.C.A.N. 8133, 8145–48 (discussing the interrelationship between the welfare system and non-support of children by absent parents). It is no coincidence that the AFDC/TANF and the child support programs are both set forth in the same subchapter of the Social Security Act, which bears the heading "Grants to States for Aid and Services to Needy Families with Children and for Child–Welfare Services."[5]

Finally, Kansas makes a few cursory arguments to the effect that the United States is requiring it to violate the privacy and procedural due process rights of its citizens. These claims center around the requirements that the state keep a directory of new hires, and that it take automatic enforcement action against those parents found to be in arrears on child support. Neither of these arguments is developed in the brief, and neither appears to have merit. In fact, Congress has expressly required participating states to adopt safeguards to protect against the unauthorized use or disclosure of confidential information handled by a state child support enforcement agency. *See* 42 U.S.C. § 654(26). Moreover, the states are free to adopt other measures to protect the information they receive.

---

5. As stated previously, child support enforcement falls under Subchapter IV, Part D of the statute. The TANF program is contained in Subchapter IV, Part A.

In general, Kansas bears a very heavy burden in seeking to have the PRWORA declared unconstitutional. There are no recent relevant instances in which the Supreme Court has invalidated a funding condition. ... On the other hand, there have been many cases in which the Supreme Court has upheld conditions placed on the receipt of federal funds. . . .

Federal courts of appeal have been similarly reluctant to invalidate funding conditions. For example, in *Schweiker,* 655 F.2d 401, the D.C. Circuit upheld Congress' conditioning of Medicaid funds on state implementation of a provision in the Supplemental Security Income program. *See also California v. United States,* 104 F.3d 1086 (9th Cir.1997) (upholding conditioning receipt of Medicaid funds on agreement to provide emergency medical services to illegal aliens); *Padavan v. United States,* 82 F.3d 23, 28–29 (2d Cir.1996) (same); *Planned Parenthood v. Dandoy,* 810 F.2d 984 (10th Cir.1987) (upholding Medicaid funding condition which required changes in state law regarding the provision of family planning advice to minors) (per curiam); *New Hampshire v. Marshall,* 616 F.2d 240 (1st Cir.1980) (upholding requirements in the Federal Unemployment Tax Act).

Virginia v. Riley, 106 F.3d 559 (4th Cir.1997) (en banc) (per curiam) (superseded by statute), represents the rare case in which a federal court invalidated a funding condition. In *Riley,* the Fourth Circuit found that conditions in the Individuals with Disabilities Education Act were not sufficiently clear and unambiguous to satisfy *Dole's* second requirement. Specifically, the court objected to conditions requiring every state to provide a free, appropriate education to learning disabled students, which the United States Department of Education later interpreted to apply even where school authorities had expelled a student for behavioral problems unrelated to the learning disability. Because we have determined that the conditions at issue in the present case do not violate *Dole's* ambiguity restriction, however, *Riley* is inapposite.

B.   Coercion Theory

In addition to the four categorical restrictions, the Court in *Dole* articulated a fifth, indistinct limit on the spending power: "[I]n some circumstances the financial inducement offered by Congress might be so coercive as to pass the point at which 'pressure turns into compulsion.'" *Dole,* 483 U.S. at 211, 107 S.Ct. 2793 (quoting *Steward Mach. Co. v. Davis,* 301 U.S. 548, 590, 57 S.Ct. 883, 81 L.Ed. 1279 (1937)). It is this coercion theory upon which Kansas primarily relies. The crux of Kansas' argument is that the size of its IV–D and TANF grants, totalling over $130 million, leaves it no choice but to accept the PRWORA's many requirements. In this connection, Kansas correctly argues that the Court in *Dole* specifically pointed out that the federal government there was only threatening to withhold 5% of South Dakota's federal highway funds:

When we consider ... that all South Dakota would lose if she adheres to her chosen course as to a suitable minimum drinking age is 5% of the funds otherwise obtainable under specified highway grant programs, the argument as to coercion is shown to be more rhetoric than fact.

Id.

This passage does not get Kansas far. It is merely an instance in which the Court acknowledged circumstances *not* sufficient to constitute coercion. In fact, the cursory statements in *Steward Machine* and *Dole* mark the extent of the Supreme Court's discussion of a coercion theory.[7] The Court has never employed the theory to invalidate a funding condition, and federal courts have been similarly reluctant to use it. "The coercion theory has been much discussed but infrequently applied in federal case law, and never in favor of the challenging party." *Nevada v. Skinner,* 884 F.2d 445, 448 (9th Cir.1989). Most of the treatment given the theory in the federal courts has been negative.

The boundary between incentive and coercion has never been made clear, and courts have found no coercion in situations where similarly large amounts of federal money were at stake. For example, numerous courts have upheld conditions on Medicaid grants even where the removal of Medicaid funding would devastate the state's medical system. In *Schweiker,* 655 F.2d 401, Oklahoma argued that the threat of losing all Medicaid funding was so drastic that it had no choice but to comply in order to prevent the collapse of its medical system. The D.C. Circuit stated: "[t]he courts are not suited to evaluating whether the states are faced here with an offer they cannot refuse or merely with a hard choice.... We therefore follow the lead of other courts that have explicitly declined to enter this thicket when similar funding conditions have been at issue." *Id.* at 414. *See also California,* 104 F.3d 1086 (conditioning receipt of Medicaid funds); *Padavan,* 82 F.3d at 28–29 (same); *Planned Parenthood v. Dandoy,* 810 F.2d 984 (upholding Medicaid funding condition). *But see Virginia v. Riley,* 106 F.3d at 561 (noting in dicta that a "substantial constitutional question under the Tenth Amendment would be presented," if the provision were not already being struck down on ambiguity grounds, because it "resembles impermissible coercion").

In any event, the coercion theory is unclear, suspect, and has little precedent to support its application. Indeed, in *Steward Machine,* the first case to articulate the coercion theory, the Court minimized its force, observing, "to hold that motive or temptation is equivalent to coercion is to plunge the law in endless difficulties. The outcome of such a doctrine is the acceptance of a philosophical determinism by which choice becomes impossible." 301 U.S. at 589–90, 57 S.Ct. 883. For all these reasons, we hold that the conditioning of TANF funds on Kansas' compliance with the requirements contained in IV–D does not present a situation of impermissible coercion.[8]

. . .

---

7. The Court also acknowledged the coercion theory in passing in *College Sav. Bank v. Florida Prepaid Postsecondary Educ. Expense Bd.,* 527 U.S. 666, 119 S.Ct. 2219, 2231, 144 L.Ed.2d 605 (1999). The Court merely quoted the language from *Dole* and *Steward Machine* but did not have an occasion to apply it.

8. Moreover, IV–D contains a "safety valve" provision which allows states to be

Kansas has invited us to forge new ground in Spending Clause jurisprudence by invalidating the child support enforcement conditions Congress attached to its social welfare funding program. In doing so, it asks that we expand the concept of "coercion" as it applies to relations between the state and federal governments, and find a large federal grant accompanied by a set of conditional requirements to be coercive because of the powerful incentive it creates for the states to accept it. We decline the invitation. In this context, a difficult choice remains a choice, and a tempting offer is still but an offer. If Kansas finds the IV–D requirements so disagreeable, it is ultimately free to reject both the conditions and the funding, no matter how hard that choice may be. *See* Kathleen M. Sullivan, *Unconstitutional Conditions,* 102 HARV. L.REV. 1413, 1428 (May 1989) (discussing the resilience of the argument that "offers of conditioned benefits expand rather than contract the options of the beneficiary class, and so present beneficiaries with a free choice"). Put more simply, Kansas' options have been increased, not constrained, by the offer of more federal dollars.

The requirements contained in IV–D represent a reasoned attempt by Congress to ensure that its grant money is used to further the state and federal interest in assisting needy families, in part through improved child support enforcement. This is a valid exercise of Congress' spending power, and the requirements do not render the PRWORA unconstitutional.

We AFFIRM the judgment of the district court.

NOTE

The Personal Responsibility and Work Opportunity Reconciliation Act became law on August 22, 1996. The Act ended the federal government's Aid to Families with Dependent Children (AFDC) program of providing income to poor children and their parent or parents, and replaced it with capped block grants to the states and income paid to support low-income families is now called Temporary Assistance to Needy Families, or TANF. The states may also receive block grants for child care and social services, high performance grants for success in reducing illegitimacy and placing welfare recipients in paid employment. States are given far greater flexibility in expenditure of the grant money, but the federal legislation has provided some significant requirements: (1) each state must adopt the Uniform Interstate Family Support Act; (2) each state must adopt expedited collection procedures including suspension of licenses and seizure of assets; (3) imposition of a five year limit on benefits, although as many as twenty percent of families may be allowed exceptions in hardship cases; (4) allows states access to federal and private information related to such items as military locator service, state and local tax records, public utilities, banks

exempted from requirements that will not increase the effectiveness and efficiency of their CSE programs. *See* 42 U.S.C. § 666(d). In light of this, Kansas' prediction that it will be forced to labor under a cumbersome and byzantine set of regulations appears to be overstated.

and credit agencies, motor vehicle departments and cable television companies. *See generally* Louis Kaplow and Steven Shavell, *Fairness Versus Welfare*, 114 Harv. L. Rev. 961–1388 (2001); Cary LaCheen, *Using Title II of the Americans With Disabilities Act on Behalf of Clients in TANF Programs*, 8 Geo. J. on Poverty L. & Pol'y 1 (2001); Parvin R. Huda, *Singled Out: A Critique of the Representation of Single Motherhood in Welfare Discourse*, 7 Wm. & Mary J. Women and L. 341 (2001); Thomas Massaro, Catholic Social Teaching and United States Welfare Reform (1998).

F. The Scope of Antenuptial Contracting

Agreements between persons planning to marry long were used primarily by wealthy (and often older) persons to assure that their separate estates would be passed along family or other lines of their choice. Objection to some of the economic and legal incidents of marriage established by statute or judicial decree has lead to far greater use of such premarital contracts. Other factors that contributed to the increase include (1) female and male role changes regarding property management and career choices, (2) popular awareness that marriages may not last for life, and therefore it may be advisable to plan for dissolution before the tensions of marital discord make negotiating more difficult, (3) desire of the parties to retain their identity in a world where concern with pressures for conformity has greatly increased, and (4) clearer delineation of the permissible legal scope of such contracts, as well as expansion of that scope.

Antenuptial contracts typically are viewed by lawyers as dealing largely with matters of property and support. Agreements drafted by the individual parties sometimes include many additional stipulations ranging from their proposed relationships with third persons (including other family members), to their various personal habits. Because not all such provisions are legally enforceable, problems of interpretation and even overall validity of such agreements may be faced when a marriage breaks down.

Many of the past cases focused on whether antenuptial agreements that seemed unfair or that were the product of overreaching conduct should be invalidated. Some of these decisions now appear to be obsolete because of their presumptions concerning relative disabilities and disadvantages based on sex. A newer group of cases centers on the permissible scope of the parties' rearrangement of the traditional legal incidents of marriage as well as their relative economic obligations after dissolution. Many of the subjects touched on as possible items for inclusion in antenuptial agreements might just as easily be includible in contracts in lieu of marriage. The California Supreme Court's decision in Marvin v. Marvin, makes it important to consider the potential legal impact of the latter alternative for couples who wish to forego the traditional marriage approach. Finally, statutes such as the Uniform Premarital Agreements Act have given parties great latitude to order their marital rights and duties by contract in advance of marrying. Because of the variation in approaches, it is important to understand the differing frameworks that continue to coexist.

Matter of Estate of Benker

Supreme Court of Michigan, 1982.
416 Mich. 681, 331 N.W.2d 193.

■ WILLIAMS, JUSTICE.

. . .

On December 15, 1976, Charles Benker died intestate leaving as his sole heirs at law his widow, Elizabeth Benker, and Ruth Counts, a daughter from a previous marriage, who was appointed administratrix of his estate. Three days prior to the marriage, Mrs. Benker, defendant in this case, and the decedent entered into an antenuptial agreement, the subject of this litigation.

The decedent and his widow each had been married once before, and each had one child from the previous marriage. The couple was married in 1963 after knowing each other for over 20 years through employment at Ex–Cell–O Corporation. Decedent was in charge of maintenance prior to retiring in 1959, and defendant worked in maintenance and later in the inspection department. Decedent was 71 years old when the marriage took place, and defendant was 60 years old.

Decedent left a very substantial estate when he died, $640,500, of which $221,500 was in a trust account at First Federal Savings and Loan Association for the benefit of his daughter. Despite the worth of his estate, decedent had a modest lifestyle. He did not display his wealth at all and was somewhat secretive about it. He lived in a most modest neighborhood in Highland Park, his house was valued at $3,000, and he drove a car worth approximately $500. His daughter testified that she did not realize the extent of her father's estate.

She first became involved in assessing her father's wealth when she was appointed guardian on April 14, 1976, when decedent was adjudicated legally incompetent by the Wayne County Probate Court. At that time, she estimated his estate at $9,500.

The surviving widow has also been adjudicated legally incompetent and therefore was unavailable to testify at the trial. On September 28, 1976, her son was appointed guardian with assets of the guardianship estate being estimated at $110,000. The guardianship continues in effect.

The antenuptial agreement at issue here was signed by Elizabeth Stewart and Charles Benker on May 29, 1963. The agreement contains no reference to the assets of either party, generally or specifically, nor does it make any statement at all regarding disclosure of assets by the parties to the agreement. The agreement provides for a complete waiver of rights by the widow to take by the laws of descent and distribution, provided by the following language of the contract:

"(8) The party of the second part likewise waives all right of inheritance, under the laws of descent and distribution of property of any jurisdiction in or to any estate or property of the party of the first part dying intestate, and does also waive all rights as a widow, in the event of death of the party of the first part, to elect to take against or contrary to any last will and testament or codicil executed by the party of the first part and admitted to probate."

But the agreement failed to state whether there was an understanding on her part that the husband's rights in her estate were far less substantial than the wife's rights in his estate and that therefore she was waiving far more than he was.

The attorney who prepared the agreement, Mr. William Dye, testified in a deposition on September 12, 1977. He could not recall specifically the steps taken for this particular agreement, but testified as to his "normal procedure" in such a situation which would include a discussion of assets. Mr. Dye later testified as follows in response to a question asking how he insured that there was full disclosure of assets by each party:

"Well, I didn't press the full disclosure matter, for the simple reason that once you outline to your clients the purpose of a prenuptial agreement, then they disclose their assets to you. You don't press them for undisclosed assets, or at least I didn't."

Mr. Dye also stated that the main objective of an antenuptial agreement, in general, was to retain the status quo of each party, and that he was not concerned with what Mrs. Benker would receive upon Mr. Benker's death. He represented both parties in executing this agreement and felt that he had an obligation to make sure that this was "an arm's length transaction" between the two of them. He was acquainted with Mr. Benker through his father's association with Ex–Cell–O Corporation as general counsel. Mr. Dye could not recall much of the events leading up to the execution of the subject agreement.

The antenuptial agreement became the subject of controversy when plaintiff, as administratrix of her father's estate, petitioned the probate court to determine the validity of the antenuptial agreement and to instruct as to the assignment of the residue of the estate. After hearing testimony on the issue, the probate court allowed the parties to submit briefs as to which party had the burden of proof and whether there was a presumption of nondisclosure on the part of the deceased husband in light of the facts presented. On January 9, 1978, the probate court, without deciding which party had the burden of proof in attacking the validity of antenuptial agreements for failure of disclosure, held that there was a presumption of nondisclosure and that the evidence presented was not sufficient to rebut the presumption. Therefore, the agreement was held to be invalid. This decision was appealed to the circuit court which summarily affirmed. The Court of Appeals reversed and remanded, holding that the trial court erred by not allocating the burden of proof to defendant widow, the party seeking to invalidate the antenuptial contract. . . .

It is now generally recognized that antenuptial agreements which relate to the parties' rights upon the death of one of the parties are favored by public policy. M.C.L. § 557.28; M.S.A. § 26.165(8) recognizes such contracts and provides that:

> "A contract relating to property made between persons in contemplation of marriage shall remain in full force after marriage takes place."

Such agreements, while recognized as valid instruments, are of a special nature because of the fact that they originate between parties contemplating marriage.[3] This relationship is one of extreme mutual confidence and, thus, presents a unique situation unlike the ordinary commercial contract situation where the parties deal at arm's length.

In order for an antenuptial agreement to be valid, it must be fair, equitable, and reasonable in view of the surrounding facts and circumstances. It must be entered into voluntarily by both parties, with each understanding his or her rights and the extent of the waiver of such rights. Hockenberry v. Donovan, 170 Mich. 370, 380, 136 N.W. 389 (1912). Antenuptial agreements give rise to a special duty of disclosure not required in ordinary contract relationships so that the parties will be fully informed before entering into such agreements. The Legislature has recognized the validity of agreements that provide for the waiver of rights by a surviving spouse in the decedent's estate, but specifically requires fair disclosure:

> "The rights of the surviving spouse to an estate or to dower under sections 1 to 29 of chapter 66 of the Revised Statutes of 1846, as amended, homestead allowance, election, exempt property, and family allowance or any of them, may be waived, wholly or partially, before or after marriage, by a written contract, agreement, or waiver signed by the party waiving *after fair disclosure*." M.C.L. § 700.291; M.S.A. § 27.5291. (Emphasis added.)

The duty of disclosure is recognized by numerous jurisdictions and is succinctly described in Anno: Setting Aside Antenuptial Agreement Based on Non–Disclosure, 27 A.L.R.2d 883, 886, as follows:

> "Where, as is usually the case, the parties to an antenuptial property settlement occupy a confidential relationship toward one another, and the agreement substantially affects the property interests which one or the other would otherwise acquire by the marriage, each is under an affirmative duty to disclose to the other the nature of his property interests so that the effect of the agreement can be understandingly assessed, and in the absence of such a full and frank disclosure, the courts will refuse to give effect to such an agreement attacked by the spouse to whom disclosure should have been made."

---

3. Marriage alone is sufficient consideration for the antenuptial agreement, and it need not be recited in the agreement. Rich-ard v. Detroit Trust Co., 269 Mich. 411, 413–414, 257 N.W. 725 (1934).

It is clear that there is a duty to disclose one's assets to the other party entering into an antenuptial agreement. The Court of Appeals here properly interpreted the law of this state as placing the burden of proof on the party seeking to invalidate the agreement on the basis of fraud. . . .

Even if the burden of proof is on the party seeking to invalidate the antenuptial agreement on the basis of non-disclosure, there will be instances where there is sufficient evidence to raise a rebuttable presumption of non-disclosure. Many jurisdictions apply such a presumption when the antenuptial agreement provides a disproportionately small allowance for the wife.

. . .

We do not here adopt a presumption of non-disclosure based merely on a disproportionately small allowance for the wife, but hold that the presumption is properly invoked when the facts are, in general, as follows. One, the antenuptial agreement provides for a complete waiver of all rights of inheritance and rights of election by the widow and does not make any provision for her upon her husband's death. Two, the husband's estate is very ample in comparison to the wife's. Three, the decedent was shown to be rather secretive about his financial affairs, lived very modestly, and gave no outward appearance of his wealth. Four, the agreement makes no reference whatsoever, in general or specific terms, to whether the parties had been fully informed of the property interests held by each other. Five, the widow was not represented by independent counsel. Six, the attorney who drafted the subject agreement testified in a deposition as to his normal procedure in such a matter and stated that he normally would discuss the assets of the parties, but that he did not press the full disclosure matter. Seven, the scrivener testified that he was not concerned with what the widow would get. These factors support the trial judge's decision to invoke the presumption of non-disclosure. A discussion of each of these factors is helpful.

1) and 2) The antenuptial agreement provides for a complete waiver by the widow of her rights in her husband's estate and her right of election. There was no provision whatsoever to compensate her for the waiver of her rights given by law in the husband's estate. The lack of any provision whatsoever, especially considering the size of the decedent's estate and the extent of the widow's rights in the property absent the antenuptial agreement, along with the other facts in this case, gives rise to a presumption of non-disclosure. See Juhasz v. Juhasz, 134 Ohio St. 257, 263–265, 16 N.E.2d 328 (1938).

It should also be considered that the parties' estates were not of equal value. Mr. Benker's estate turned out to be worth $640,500, while Mrs. Benker's estate was estimated at $110,000. Thus, the parties were not in equal positions when executing the antenuptial agreement. Clearly, Mrs. Benker waived rights in her spouse's estate which turned out to be of a much greater value than the rights waived by the decedent. An antenuptial agreement that so substantially alters a person's rights must be entered into with full knowledge and understanding. If the contract is so entered into, the lack of provision for the party waiving rights will not invalidate the agreement. But when there are allegations of non-disclosure along with no provision at all for the widow, the agreement and surrounding circumstances must be carefully scrutinized. See Rosenberg v. Lipnick, 377 Mass. 666, 389 N.E.2d 385 (1979).

3) The decedent in this case was shown to be rather secretive about his financial affairs, lived very modestly and gave no outward appearance of his wealth. These facts, along with the others discussed, support the application of the presumption of non-disclosure. The property status of the decedent was not such that Mrs. Benker should have been aware of his wealth at the time of executing the agreement. See 27 A.L.R.2d 898–901 and cases cited therein. It was not as if he had a general reputation for wealth and therefore that she should have been fully aware of the value of his assets regardless of disclosure on his part. See *Hockenberry*, 170 Mich. 370, 378, 136 N.W. 389. It was quite the contrary. He lived in a $3,000 home in a lower-middle-class neighborhood in Highland Park, drove a car valued at $500, and had a modest lifestyle. His daughter testified that they had always lived modestly and that she was not aware of the trust left in her name nor of the total value of her father's estate. When the guardianship papers were filed in 1976 for Mr. Benker, his assets were valued at $9,500; yet he left an estate valued at $640,500 upon his death. We agree with the probate court that it was not sufficient that the decedent and defendant were both employed by Ex–Cell–O Corporation to support an argument that she should have been aware of his wealth. The argument that Mrs. Benker was or should have been aware of the decedent's wealth from other sources making the duty to disclose a mere ritual is not supported by the evidence.

4) The antenuptial agreement made no reference whatsoever, in general or specific terms, to whether the parties had been fully informed for the property interests held by each other. Such a statement is usually included in an antenuptial agreement to avoid a challenge at a later date. See *Snyder Estate*, 375 Pa. 185, 100 A.2d 67 (1953). Some contracts specifically itemize the property of the parties so that there is no manner in which to challenge the agreement on the basis of non-disclosure. Neither approach was taken here. The antenuptial agreement makes absolutely no mention of disclosure of assets by the parties. That is not to say that the inclusion or absence of such a statement or inventory is necessarily conclusive, but it is a factor to be weighed. See 27 A.L.R.2d 895–898 and cases cited therein.

5) The widow was not represented by independent counsel. Mr. Dye represented both parties in drafting and executing the antenuptial agreement. Representation of both parties by one attorney is allowed by the Code of Professional Responsibility

"if it is obvious that he can adequately represent the interest of each and if each consents to the representation after full disclosure of the possible effect of such representation on the exercise of his independent professional judgment on behalf of each." DR 5–105(C).[7]

There is no indication whether such disclosure was made, or whether the wife was fully informed as to the extent of the rights she was waiving, which were far greater than those waived by her husband. The fact that she did not have independent counsel before signing an antenuptial agreement that totally eliminated any right in her husband's estate, along with the other factors in this case, supports the application of the presumption of non-disclosure. See Allison v. Stevens, 269 Ala. 288, 112 So.2d 451 (1959).

6) The attorney who drafted the subject agreement testified in a deposition as to his normal procedure in such a matter and stated that he usually would discuss the assets of the parties, but that he did not press the full disclosure matter.[9] Mr. Dye did not recall the specifics of the circum-

---

7. DR 5–105(C) applies to situations covered by DR 5–105, subds. (A) and (B), which provide:

"(A) A lawyer shall decline proffered employment if the exercise of his independent professional judgment in behalf of a client will be or is likely to be adversely affected by the acceptance of the proffered employment, or if it would be likely to involve him in representing different interests, except to the extent permitted under DR 5–105(C).

"(B) A lawyer shall not continue multiple employment if the exercise of his independent professional judgment in behalf of a client will be or is likely to be adversely affected by his representation of another client, or if it would be likely to involve him in representing different interests, except to the extent permitted under DR 5–105(C)."

9. A few excerpts from Mr. Dye's testimony regarding disclosure of assets are provided below:

"*A.* Well, with the reservation that I would have handled all antenuptial agreements in the same fashion, I would normally bring the people in, discuss their assets with them, discuss the purpose of an antenuptial agreement with them, prepare the document based upon that, then bring them in again, have them review the document, that is both parties, and then if all things being equal, that they were then satisfied with that agreement, and again being a prenuptial agreement, then I would conduct

the ceremony, so to speak, of executing the agreement before a notary.

"*Q.* Do you recall, Mr. Dye, specifically the steps you took with respect to this particular antenuptial agreement?

"*A.* Not really.

"*Q.* This would be what you just outlined previously would be your normal—

"*A.* Yes, the basic purpose, as both you gentlemen know as attorneys, of a prenuptial agreement is to protect the—more or less to retain the status quo, so to speak." Appellee's Appendix, pp. 4b–5b.

. . .

"*Q.* Do you recall, Mr. Dye, whether or not in this particular case you discussed the assets of the parties with both parties?

"*A.* Well, again I can only say in response to that, that the purpose of a prenuptial agreement, it follows from that purpose that you would. I always discuss their assets, because that's the only reason for it. If people go into a second marriage, so to speak, with very little or no assets, there would be no reason for this. So obviously, I did discuss their assets." Appellee's Appendix, p. 6b . . .

"*Q.* What steps if any did you employ in your typical practice, and in particular to this instance, if you can recall, to insure that there was a full disclosure by each to the other as far as assets?

stances surrounding the execution of the antenuptial agreement and, therefore, he testified as to his normal procedure in handling such a transaction. He stated that he normally would discuss the assets and review the document with the parties. He later stated, however, that he did not press for undisclosed assets. This statement, coupled with the fact that Mrs. Benker did not have independent counsel and with the fact that Mr. Dye felt this was an arm's length transaction between the two of them, raises some doubt as to whether there was an adequate disclosure of assets. Mr. Dye was the only person involved in the transaction who was available to testify as to the events surrounding the execution of the antenuptial contract because Mrs. Benker has been declared legally incompetent and Mr. Benker is deceased. The evidence regarding disclosure is weak, especially considering that Mr. Dye could not recall the specifics but could only testify as to his normal procedure.

7) The attorney who was the only one involved in the drafting of the antenuptial agreement testified that his interest was to see that the parties retained the status quo and that he was not concerned with what the widow would get. This attitude along with the scrivener's lack of interest in the disclosure of possible undisclosed assets and the fact that the wife-to-be was not represented by independent counsel combine to create a climate where full and fair disclosure might not have been obtained, thereby warranting a rebuttable presumption of non-disclosure.

The presumption of non-disclosure was properly invoked in this case on the basis of all the facts discussed earlier. We must now address the nature of this presumption and its effect. The presumption of non-disclosure is a rebuttable one. Once the presumption is proper, it is incumbent upon the opposite party to introduce evidence to rebut the presumption. . . . We agree with the trial court that the rebuttal evidence presented was not sufficient to overcome the presumption.

The evidence presented in this case consisted of the testimony of Mrs. Counts, the daughter of the deceased, the deposition testimony of Mr. Dye, the attorney who drafted the agreement, and the testimony of Mr. Stewart, the son of Mrs. Benker. The evidence presented did not contain facts sufficient to rebut the presumption of non-disclosure applicable in this case. Mrs. Counts testified that she was not aware of any of her father's financial matters and only became aware of the safe in his home (where most of his assets were kept) when she was informed about it when Mr. Benker went on a trip to Germany. Mr. Stewart testified that he was aware of the antenuptial agreement, but had never seen it. He was also not aware of his mother's financial affairs. The testimony of the daughter and son shed little light on whether there was or was not a disclosure of assets when the antenuptial agreement was executed.

"A. Well, I didn't press the full disclosure matter, for the simple reason that once you outline to your clients the purpose of a prenuptial agreement, then they disclose their assets to you. You don't press them for undisclosed assets, or at least I didn't." Appellee's Appendix, p. 9b.

The only other testimony was that given by Mr. Dye, the attorney who drafted the agreement. His testimony did not establish what the circumstances surrounding this particular transaction were, and even as to his normal procedure the testimony was ambiguous. He did testify that he would normally discuss the parties' assets and go over the agreement with them point by point. But as to the possibility of undisclosed assets, he testified that he did not press the matter. Thus, the evidence presented is not enough to rebut the presumption of non-disclosure. We therefore hold that the antenuptial agreement entered into between the decedent and the defendant is invalid on the basis of the fact that there was not sufficient evidence to rebut the presumption of non-disclosure.

. . .

The judgment of the Court of Appeals is reversed.

NOTE

The Statute of Frauds must be considered if an attempt is made to enforce an oral agreement. An imaginative circumvention of this obstacle is found in T . . . v. T . . ., 216 Va. 867, 224 S.E.2d 148 (1976). The plaintiff wife, before her marriage to defendant, was pregnant by another man. With full knowledge of this, defendant promised plaintiff that if she would forego her plans to move to another state and place the child for adoption, he "would care for the child after it was born 'as if it were his own' ''. Plaintiff changed her plans and married defendant. Several years later the parties divorced and plaintiff sought support for the child in accordance with the oral antenuptial agreement. VA.CODE ANN. § 11-2 (2004), the Statute of Frauds, provides:

No action shall be brought in any of the following cases: . . .

> (5) Upon any agreement made upon consideration of marriage;

. . .

> Unless the promise, contract, agreement, representation, assurance, or ratification, or some memorandum or note thereof, be in writing and signed by the party to be charged thereby. . . .

The Supreme Court of Virginia reversed the trial court's holding that the unwritten promise was unenforceable. They explained (somewhat surprisingly) that:

The object of the statute of frauds is to prevent frauds and perjuries, and not to perpetrate them, so that the statute is not enforced when to do so would cause a fraud and a wrong to be perpetrated.

The court also found that there had been part performance sufficient to take the case out of the statute. Although marriage alone is not enough for this, the plaintiff's change of plans as to her job and the relinquishment of her child for adoption were deemed sufficient.

Osborne v. Osborne

Supreme Judicial Court of Massachusetts, Norfolk, 1981.
384 Mass. 591, 428 N.E.2d 810.

■ Hennessey, Chief Justice.

. . .

The relevant facts as found by the master are summarized. The parties, Barbara E. Mallinckrodt (Barbara) and David P. Osborne, Jr. (David), met and became engaged while they were both attending medical school. They were married on August 19, 1967. Barbara is an heiress to a large family fortune amounting to nearly $17,000,000, most of which is held in trust. Barbara's income from these funds was approximately $540,000 in 1976. At the time of their engagement, David had no assets of significant value. A few hours before their wedding they executed an antenuptial agreement containing, among others, the following pertinent provisions: "Barbara now has sufficient property to provide adequate means for her own support and David, by reason of his becoming a member of the medical profession, contemplates that he will have adequate earning power for his own support"; "Barbara and David intend this agreement to be in full discharge of all . . . statutory marital property rights under the statutes or law of any state in which they are now or may hereafter be domiciled"; "neither, upon or subsequent to said marriage, shall acquire any interest, right or claim in or to the property, real and personal, of whatever kind or wherever situated, which the other now owns, possesses or is entitled to, or which the other may own, possess or become entitled to hereafter"; that if their "marriage is legally terminated in accordance with the laws of any jurisdiction in which they or either of them may be domiciled, then . . . neither shall be entitled to any alimony, support money, costs, attorneys fees, or to any other money by virtue thereof. This provision may be cited by either party by any court of competent jurisdiction, as a waiver and release of any money payment as aforesaid, by one to the other." Attached to the agreement was a schedule accurately showing Barbara's wealth and expectation of inheritance. David read the agreement before he signed it.

Two children were born of the marriage. During the marriage the parties maintained a high standard of living which was financed completely by the income from Barbara's trust accounts. Barbara maintained joint checking accounts upon which either party could draw funds. These accounts were funded with monies from her separate trust accounts. During the marriage the parties acquired furniture, and fixtures worth approximately $15,000, jewelry valued at approximately $225,000, art valued at approximately $428,545, a wine collection worth $60,000, and three parcels of real estate valued at $100,000, $60,000, and $40,000. The husband claims an ownership interest in all these items of property. Both parties are now practicing physicians and earn respectable salaries. . . .

Validity of the Antenuptial Agreement.

... This court has not previously passed on the validity of an antenuptial agreement that attempts to regulate the rights of the parties in the event of their subsequent divorce. The majority of Massachusetts cases dealing with the validity of antenuptial contracts concern the rights of the parties to modify those property rights that would otherwise arise during the marriage or upon the death of one of the parties. See, e.g., Rosenberg v. Lipnick, 377 Mass. 666, 389 N.E.2d 385 (1979) (abandoning the rule of Wellington v. Rugg, 243 Mass. 30, 136 N.E. 831 [1922], that common law fraud must be proved in order to invalidate an antenuptial contract); French v. McAnarney, 290 Mass. 544, 195 N.E. 714 (1935). These contracts have generally been upheld where there has been no fraudulent conduct on the part of either party, or, more recently, where the parties have acted honestly and fairly and have fully disclosed their assets one to the other. Antenuptial contracts are recognized by statute and at common law.

In many jurisdictions it has been held that an antenuptial contract made in contemplation of divorce is void as against public policy. The reasons most frequently given for invalidating such contracts are (1) they are not compatible with and denigrate the status of marriage, (2) they tend to facilitate divorce by providing inducements to end the marriage, and (3) a contract waiving or minimizing alimony may turn a spouse into a ward of the State....

In Fox v. Davis, 113 Mass. 255, 257–258 (1873), this court stated: "The great weight of authority sustains the validity of such contracts, where the separation has taken place, or is to take place immediately. But where the agreement is made in contemplation of future separation, the current of authority is against its validity." Had the issue come before this court several decades ago, the law as stated in *Fox* might well have been held to be controlling. In French v. McAnarney, 290 Mass. 544 (1935), it was held that an antenuptial contract wherein the wife agreed not to make any claim for support against the husband was void as against public policy. The facts of the case are distinguishable in that there the parties were not divorced; yet the rationale is applicable. The court in *French* concluded that certain rights and duties incident to the marital relation, including the duty of the husband to support his wife, could not be avoided by an antenuptial contract. Under the case law of the time, this same reasoning would have applied to the rights of the parties upon divorce, since the obligation of the husband to pay alimony was also based on the husband's legal duty to support his wife.

Perhaps the closest this court has come to addressing the issue is in Kovler v. Vagenheim, 333 Mass. 252, 130 N.E.2d 557 (1955). *Kovler* involved a premarital contract between the husband and the brothers of the wife, whereby the brothers, in consideration of the husband's marrying their sister, promised to indemnify the husband for any support and maintenance that he might be obliged to pay for his wife and child. After obtaining a divorce, the husband sought to enforce the contract. The court upheld the contract, concluding that since it was not in derogation of, but rather in aid of marriage, there was no violation of public policy in its enforcement. The court in *Kovler* did, however, state that "a contract tending to divest a husband of any obligation incidental to his marriage is invalid" (citing French v. McAnarney, supra), thus suggesting that if the husband's obligations had somehow been contractually divested, for example through a waiver of rights by the wife, then a different result would have been reached.

In 1970 the Florida Supreme Court took the lead in departing from this approach.[6] In Posner v. Posner, 233 So.2d 381 (Fla.1970), the court held that antenuptial agreements settling alimony and property rights upon divorce are not void ab initio as contrary to public policy. The court disagreed with the traditional assumption that such agreements tended to facilitate divorce, suggesting that such contracts are no more likely to encourage divorce than antenuptial contracts in contemplation of death. With respect to public policy, the court stated: "We know of no community or society in which the public policy that condemned a husband and wife to a lifetime of misery as an alternative to the opprobrium of divorce still exists. And a tendency to recognize this change in public policy and to give effect to the antenuptial agreements of the parties relating to divorce is clearly discernible." Id. at 384. A number of jurisdictions have followed the approach of the *Posner* case. . . .

We conclude that we shall follow the reasoning of the *Posner* case and its progeny and uphold the contract. While the matter is not free from dispute, it is apparent that the significant changes in public policy during the last decade in the area of domestic relations warrant a tolerant approach to the use of antenuptial contracts as vehicles for settling the property rights of the parties in the event of divorce. In recent years the Legislature has abolished the doctrine of recrimination and recognized irretrievable breakdown as a ground for divorce. G.L. c. 208, § 1, as appearing in St.1975, c. 698, § 1. The Legislature itself has thus removed significant obstacles to unhappy couples wishing to obtain a divorce. There is no reason not to allow persons about to enter into a marriage the freedom to settle their rights in the event their marriage should prove unsuccessful, and thus remove a potential obstacle to their divorce. We therefore hold that an antenuptial contract settling the alimony or property rights of the parties upon divorce is not per se against public policy and may be specifically enforced. We express no opinion on the validity of antenuptial contracts that purport to limit the duty of each spouse to support the other during the marriage.

Legal Limitations upon Antenuptial Agreements.

We note that the freedom of the parties to limit or waive their legal rights in the event of a divorce is not appropriately left unrestricted. We therefore set forth some guidelines to be used in determining the extent to which such agreements should be enforced, observing at the same time that

---

6. One pre–1970 case, Hudson v. Hudson, 350 P.2d 596 (Okl.1960), upheld an antenuptial contract in which each spouse waived alimony rights upon divorce; however, the decision met with virtual nonacceptance by other courts. See Gamble, The Antenuptial Contract, 26 U.Miami L.Rev. 692, 715 (1972).

none of these comments are relevant or applicable to the decision in the case before us. At the outset, the validity of such agreements should be judged by the same "fair disclosure" rules set forth by this court in Rosenberg v. Lipnick, 377 Mass. 666, 389 N.E.2d 385 (1979). Consistent with our holding in *Rosenberg*, those rules should be applied prospectively from the date of our decision in that case. In addition, antenuptial agreements that settle the alimony and property rights of the parties in the event of a divorce should be binding on the courts to the same extent as postnuptial separation agreements. The public policies that underlie the laws regulating separation agreements are equally applicable whether the agreement is entered into before the marriage or after the marriage and in expectation of separation or divorce. Accordingly, the agreement must be fair and reasonable at the time of entry of the judgment nisi, and it may be modified by the courts in certain situations, for example, where it is determined that one spouse is or will become a public charge, or where a provision affecting the right of custody of a minor child is not in the best interests of the child. See generally Knox v. Remick, 371 Mass. 433, 358 N.E.2d 432 (1976).[7] See also Restatement (Second) of Contracts § 191 (1981). In any case where the issue is whether payment shall be ordered in excess of that provided in the agreement, the agreement can be raised as a potential bar in the same proceeding. Knox v. Remick, supra at 436, 358 N.E.2d 432. Finally, we recognize that certain contracts may so unreasonably encourage divorce as to be unenforceable on grounds of public policy. See Restatement (Second) of Contracts § 190 (1981).

After-acquired Property.

David argues that even if the antenuptial agreement is not contrary to public policy, it is ineffective as to property acquired after the parties were married. His argument is based on the language of G.L. c. 209, § 25: "At any time before marriage, the parties may make a written contract providing that, after the marriage is solemnized, the whole or any designated part of the real or personal property or any right of action, of which either party may be seized or possessed at the time of the marriage, shall remain or become the property of the husband or wife, according to the terms of the contract." David contends that the words "at the time of the marriage" prohibit the application of the terms of the antenuptial contract to after-acquired property. However, this statute, enacted in 1845 (St.1845, c. 208, § 1), was designed to abrogate the old common law doctrine that precluded a man and a woman from entering into an enforceable contract with each other to be performed during their subsequent marriage. It does not affect the rights of the parties to determine their property rights upon termination of the marriage. . . .General Laws c. 209, § 25, therefore, does not preclude the parties from determining in advance of the marriage their rights with respect to property acquired during the marriage. We see no

---

7. See also Unander v. Unander, 265 Or. 102, 107, 506 P.2d 719 (1973), holding that the antenuptial agreement will be en- forceable unless the spouse is deprived of support she cannot otherwise secure.

reason to impose such a restriction ourselves, and we therefore decline to do so.

Duress.

David alleges that the antenuptial contract is invalid because it was entered into under duress.[8] David saw the contract for the first time a few hours before the wedding ceremony when it was presented to him by Barbara's attorney for signing. However, the master whose report was adopted by the Probate Court found that on several occasions before the marriage Barbara had told David that she intended to have her money pass to her legitimate descendants and their descendants. The master also found that at some point after their engagement and before the wedding they had discussed the antenuptial agreement. The master concluded that the husband had entered into the agreement "of his own free will ... without any fraud, coercion, undue influence or duress." On review of the record, we conclude that there was ample evidence to support the master's findings and that they are therefore not clearly erroneous.

. . .

NOTE

In Rosenberg v. Lipnick, 377 Mass. 666, 389 N.E.2d 385 (1979), referred to in *Osborne* as the standard for determining validity of antenuptial agreements in general, the court stated:

> ... [I]n future cases involving agreements drawn after the publication date of this opinion, we shall feel free to hold that the parties by definition occupy a confidential relationship and that the burden of disclosure rests upon both of them.

> In judging the validity of such an antenuptial agreement, other relevant factors which we may consider are whether (1) it contains a fair and reasonable provision as measured at the time of its execution for the party contesting the agreement; (2) the contesting party was fully informed of the other party's worth prior to the agreement's execution, or had, or should have had, independent knowledge of the other party's worth; and (3) a waiver by the contesting party is set forth. It is clear that the reasonableness of any monetary provision in an antenuptial contract cannot ultimately be judged in isolation. Rather, reference may appropriately be made to such factors as the parties' respective worth, the parties' respective ages, the parties' respective intelligence, literacy, and business acumen, and prior family ties or commitments.

. . .

8. There is no claim of fraud here, since David was fully aware of the extent and nature of Barbara's assets. A full schedule of Barbara's property was attached to the antenuptial contract and was read by David before he signed it.

The right to make antenuptial agreements settling property rights in advance of marriage is a valuable personal right which courts should not regulate destructively. Neither should the exercise of that right be looked upon with disfavor. Thus, we recognize that antenuptial agreements must be so construed as to give full effect to the parties' intentions, but we are concerned that such agreements be executed fairly and understandingly and be free from fraud, imposition, deception, or over-reaching.

389 N.E.2d at 388–89.

Stregack v. Moldofsky

Supreme Court of Florida, 1985.
474 So.2d 206.

■ McDONALD, JUSTICE.

We have for review Moldofsky v. Stregack, 449 So.2d 918 (Fla. 3d DCA 1984), which directly and expressly conflicts with Coleman v. Estate of Coleman, 439 So.2d 1016 (Fla. 1st DCA 1983).... The issue here is whether a surviving spouse may challenge an antenuptial agreement based upon fraudulent nondisclosure of assets by a decedent spouse, in light of section 732.702, Florida Statutes (1983), which requires no disclosure for a valid antenuptial agreement in probate. We quash *Moldofsky* because nondisclosure in any form cannot invalidate an antenuptial agreement in probate proceedings of a deceased spouse.

When Manuel Moldofsky died, his will contained no provision for his wife, Sally Moldofsky, beyond a reference to an antenuptial agreement between them. Mrs. Moldofsky filed a notice of elective share after the circuit court probate division admitted the will to probate. Susan Stregack, Mr. Moldofsky's daughter and personal representative of his estate, moved to strike the notice of elective share based upon an antenuptial agreement executed by the parties, in which Mr. and Mrs. Moldofsky waived all rights in each other's estate. Mrs. Moldofsky then filed an action in the circuit court general jurisdiction division seeking cancellation of the antenuptial agreement for fraud. The probate court struck Moldofsky's motion for elective share. Following this order, the trial court dismissed on mootness and res judicata grounds the pending action to cancel the antenuptial agreement.

The district court reversed both orders on appeal. While acknowledging that section 732.702 eliminated the disclosure requirement for an antenuptial agreement to be valid in probate, the district court held that a surviving spouse could challenge an antenuptial agreement for fraudulent nondisclosure by the deceased spouse. The district court declined to follow the contrary holding in *Coleman*.

In Del Vecchio v. Del Vecchio, 143 So.2d 17 (Fla.1962), this Court held that a valid antenuptial agreement must either contain fair and reasonable provisions for the spouse waiving his or her rights or else the spouse obtaining the waiver of rights must make a full and fair disclosure of assets to the other spouse. Id. at 20. The legislature changed this rule by enacting subsection 732.702(2), which provides: "Each spouse shall make a fair disclosure to the other of his or her estate if the agreement, contract, or waiver is executed after marriage. *No disclosure shall be required for an agreement, contract, or waiver executed before marriage.*" (Emphasis added). We held this statute constitutional against access to courts, due process, and equal protection challenges. Estate of Roberts, 388 So.2d 216 (Fla.1980).

Relying on subsection 732.702(2), the *Coleman* court affirmed the denial of a surviving spouse's motion to amend pleadings and attack an otherwise valid antenuptial agreement for nondisclosure by the decedent spouse before execution of the antenuptial agreement. *Coleman* held that nondisclosure, however pled, could not constitute a basis for invalidating an antenuptial agreement in probate proceedings because the statute required no disclosure in such cases. 439 So.2d at 1018–19. In the present case, on the other hand, the district court interpreted subsection 732.702(2) to eliminate the disclosure duty before marriage, but not the duty that any disclosure be made truthfully. According to the third district, fraudulent nondisclosure would provide a basis to challenge the antenuptial agreement because the surviving spouse's signature was "otherwise improperly obtained" under *Roberts*. 388 So.2d at 217. We disagree.

Nondisclosure, whether fraudulent or not, is precisely what the legislature intended to eliminate from consideration on the validity of antenuptial agreements. Many older Florida residents want to marry again but also want to keep their assets separate. Often this is the desire of both parties contemplating marriage. Section 732.702 allows complete control over assets accumulated over a lifetime without fear that a partial disclosure before marriage may trigger an unwanted disposition of those assets. We cannot accept the district court decision which rewards the totally silent spouse and punishes the spouse who attempts some disclosure.

We also reject the argument that fraudulent nondisclosure may render the surviving spouse's signature improperly obtained. The quoted language from *Roberts* would apply where the surviving spouse had been misled about what he or she was signing, i.e., a marriage license application instead of an antenuptial agreement. Such fraud could provide grounds to set aside an antenuptial agreement.

. . .

■ Ehrlich, Justice, dissenting.

I cannot disagree with the majority when it says that "nondisclosure in any form cannot invalidate an antenuptial agreement in probate proceedings of a deceased spouse," and with its further holding that fraudulent nondisclosure does not render the surviving spouse's signature improperly obtained. However, that is not what this case is all about.

The case was decided at the pleadings stage of two proceedings. The widow initially filed a timely notice of elective share pursuant to section

732.212, Florida Statutes. The personal representative moved to strike this election, attaching to the motion an antenuptial agreement wherein the parties had purportedly waived all rights in one another's estate. The widow attacked the validity of the agreement, claiming that decedent had affirmatively misled her as to his actual assets in obtaining her assent. The probate court granted the motion to strike. On another front, the widow had filed an action for declaratory judgment in the general jurisdiction division of the circuit court seeking to cancel the antenuptial agreement on the ground of fraud. She alleged that decedent had grossly misrepresented his net worth "stating to plaintiff that he had no assets, when, in truth and in fact, his assets at the time had a net value of approximately two hundred and fifty thousand ($250,000) dollars" and that at the time he made these representations he knew they were false and that plaintiff would be relying on them to her detriment in entering into the antenuptial agreement and that if she had known the truth as to decedent's net worth she would not have entered into the agreement. After the probate division's ruling on the motion to strike, the general jurisdiction division dismissed the action for cancellation with prejudice on the grounds of res judicata and mootness.

The agreement provides in part that decedent "is the owner of real and personal property in his own right" and that "the agreement is entered into by the parties hereto with full knowledge on the part of each of the extent and probable value of all of the property or estate of the other."

Section 732.702, Florida Statutes[1] relieved each party from making a disclosure of his or her assets, and so long as neither made any disclosure, the agreement could not be set aside, but if either party, in my opinion, made any disclosure of his or her assets, then it was incumbent upon that party to make a truthful disclosure and one that was not misleading. The widow alleged fraud on decedent's part and the statute does not protect him from that. Whether she could have proved fraud or not is another matter.

Thus, as I see it, we are not dealing with a case of nondisclosure or fraudulent nondisclosure, but one wherein one of the parties claims that there was a disclosure in fact and that fraud was practiced. She should have had an opportunity to prove her allegations of fraud.

I dissent and would approve the opinion of the district court of appeal.

Avitzur v. Avitzur

Court of Appeals of New York, 1983.
58 N.Y.2d 108, 459 N.Y.S.2d 572, 446 N.E.2d 136.

■ WACHTLER, JUDGE.

This appeal presents for our consideration the question of the proper role of the civil courts in deciding a matter touching upon religious

---

1. In pertinent part the statute provides: no disclosure shall be required for an agreement, contract, or waiver executed before a marriage.

concerns. At issue is the enforceability of the terms of a document, known as a Ketubah, which was entered into as part of the religious marriage ceremony in this case. The Appellate Division, 86 A.D.2d 133, 449 N.Y.S.2d 83, held this to be a religious covenant beyond the jurisdiction of the civil courts. However, we find nothing in law or public policy to prevent judicial recognition and enforcement of the secular terms of such an agreement. There should be a reversal.

Plaintiff and defendant were married on May 22, 1966 in a ceremony conducted in accordance with Jewish tradition. Prior to the marriage ceremony, the parties signed both a Hebrew/Aramaic and an English version of the "Ketubah". According to the English translation, the Ketubah evidences both the bridegroom's intention to cherish and provide for his wife as required by religious law and tradition and the bride's willingness to carry out her obligations to her husband in faithfulness and affection according to Jewish law and tradition. By signing the Ketubah, the parties declared their "desire to . . . live in accordance with the Jewish law of marriage throughout [their] lifetime" and further agreed as follows: "[W]e, the bride and bridegroom . . . hereby agree to recognize the Beth Din of the Rabbinical Assembly and the Jewish Theological Seminary of America or its duly appointed representatives, as having authority to counsel us in the light of Jewish tradition which requires husband and wife to give each other complete love and devotion, and to summon either party at the request of the other, in order to enable the party so requesting to live in accordance with the standards of the Jewish law of marriage throughout his or her lifetime. We authorize the Beth Din to impose such terms of compensation as it may see fit for failure to respond to its summons or to carry out its decision."

Defendant husband was granted a civil divorce upon the ground of cruel and inhuman treatment on May 16, 1978. Notwithstanding this civil divorce, plaintiff wife is not considered divorced and may not remarry pursuant to Jewish law, until such time as a Jewish divorce decree, known as a "Get", is granted. In order that a Get may be obtained plaintiff and defendant must appear before a "Beth Din", a rabbinical tribunal having authority to advise and pass upon matters of traditional Jewish law. Plaintiff sought to summon defendant before the Beth Din pursuant to the provision of the Ketubah recognizing that body as having authority to counsel the couple in the matters concerning their marriage.

Defendant has refused to appear before the Beth Din, thus preventing plaintiff from obtaining a religious divorce. Plaintiff brought this action, alleging that the Ketubah constitutes a marital contract, which defendant has breached by refusing to appear before the Beth Din, and she seeks relief both in the form of a declaration to that effect and an order compelling defendant's specific performance of the Ketubah's requirement that he appear before the Beth Din. Defendant moved to dismiss the complaint upon the grounds that the court lacked subject matter jurisdiction and the complaint failed to state a cause of action, arguing that resolution of the dispute and any grant of relief to plaintiff would involve the civil court in impermissible consideration of a purely religious matter. Plaintiff, in addition to opposing the motion, cross-moved for summary judgment.

Special Term denied defendant's motion to dismiss, noting that plaintiff sought only to compel defendant to submit to the jurisdiction of the Beth Din, an act which plaintiff had alleged defendant bound himself to do. That being the only object of the lawsuit, Special Term was apparently of the view that the relief sought could be granted without impermissible judicial entanglement in any doctrinal issue. The court also denied plaintiff's motion for summary judgment, concluding that issues concerning the translation, meaning and effect of the Ketubah raised factual questions requiring a plenary trial.

The Appellate Division modified, granting defendant's motion to dismiss. Inasmuch as the Ketubah was entered into as part of a religious ceremony and was executed, by its own terms, in accordance with Jewish law, the court concluded that the document constitutes a liturgical agreement. The Appellate Division held such agreements to be unenforceable where the State, having granted a civil divorce to the parties, has no further interest in their marital status.

Accepting plaintiff's allegations as true, as we must in the context of this motion to dismiss, it appears that plaintiff and defendant, in signing the Ketubah, entered into a contract which formed the basis for their marriage. Plaintiff has alleged that, pursuant to the terms of this marital contract, defendant promised that he would, at plaintiff's request, appear before the Beth Din for the purpose of allowing that tribunal to advise and counsel the parties in matters concerning their marriage, including the granting of a Get. It should be noted that plaintiff is not attempting to compel defendant to obtain a Get or to enforce a religious practice arising solely out of principles of religious law. She merely seeks to enforce an agreement made by defendant to appear before and accept the decision of a designated tribunal.

Viewed in this manner, the provisions of the Ketubah relied upon by plaintiff constitute nothing more than an agreement to refer the matter of a religious divorce to a nonjudicial forum. Thus, the contractual obligation plaintiff seeks to enforce is closely analogous to an antenuptial agreement to arbitrate a dispute in accordance with the law and tradition chosen by the parties. There can be little doubt that a duly executed antenuptial agreement, by which the parties agree in advance of the marriage to the resolution of disputes that may arise after its termination, is valid and enforceable, similarly, an agreement to refer a matter concerning marriage to arbitration suffers no inherent invalidity (Hirsch v. Hirsch, 37 N.Y.2d 312, 372 N.Y.S.2d 71, 333 N.E.2d 371; see Bowmer v. Bowmer, 50 N.Y.2d 288, 293, 428 N.Y.S.2d 902, 406 N.E.2d 760). This agreement—the Ketubah—should ordinarily be entitled to no less dignity than any other civil contract to submit a dispute to a nonjudicial forum, so long as its enforcement violates neither the law nor the public policy of this State.

Defendant argues, in this connection, that enforcement of the terms of the Ketubah by a civil court would violate the constitutional prohibition against excessive entanglement between church and State, because the court must necessarily intrude upon matters of religious doctrine and practice. It is urged that the obligations imposed by the Ketubah arise solely from Jewish religious law and can be interpreted only with reference to religious dogma. Granting the religious character of the Ketubah, it does not necessarily follow that any recognition of its obligations is foreclosed to the courts.

It is clear that judicial involvement in matters touching upon religious concerns has been constitutionally limited in analogous situations, and courts should not resolve such controversies in a manner requiring consideration of religious doctrine. In its most recent pronouncement on this issue, however, the Supreme Court, in holding that a State may adopt any approach to resolving religious disputes which does not entail consideration of doctrinal matters, specifically approved the use of the "neutral principles of law" approach as consistent with constitutional limitations (Jones v. Wolf, supra, 443 U.S. at p. 602, 99 S.Ct. at 3024). This approach contemplates the application of objective, well-established principles of secular law to the dispute thus permitting judicial involvement to the extent that it can be accomplished in purely secular terms.

The present case can be decided solely upon the application of neutral principles of contract law, without reference to any religious principle. Consequently, defendant's objections to enforcement of his promise to appear before the Beth Din, based as they are upon the religious origin of the agreement, pose no constitutional barrier to the relief sought by plaintiff. The fact that the agreement was entered into as part of a religious ceremony does not render it unenforceable. Solemnization of the marital relationship often takes place in accordance with the religious beliefs of the participants, and this State has long recognized this religious aspect by permitting duly authorized pastors, rectors, priests, rabbis and other religious officials to perform the ceremony. Similarly, that the obligations undertaken by the parties to the Ketubah are grounded in religious belief and practice does not preclude enforcement of its secular terms. Nor does the fact that all of the Ketubah's provisions may not be judicially recognized prevent the court from enforcing that portion of the agreement by which the parties promised to refer their disputes to a nonjudicial forum. The courts may properly enforce so much of this agreement as is not in contravention of law or public policy.

In short, the relief sought by plaintiff in this action is simply to compel defendant to perform a secular obligation to which he contractually bound himself. In this regard, no doctrinal issue need be passed upon, no implementation of a religious duty is contemplated, and no interference with religious authority will result. Certainly nothing the Beth Din can do would in any way affect the civil divorce. To the extent that an enforceable promise can be found by the application of neutral principles of contract law, plaintiff will have demonstrated entitlement to the relief sought.

Consideration of other substantive issues bearing upon plaintiff's entitlement to a religious divorce, however, is appropriately left to the forum the parties chose for resolving the matter.

Accordingly, the order of the Appellate Division should be reversed, with costs, and defendant's motion to dismiss the complaint denied.

■ Jones, Judge (dissenting).

We are of the opinion that to grant the relief plaintiff seeks in this action, even to the limited extent contemplated by the majority, would necessarily violate the constitutional prohibition against entanglement of our secular courts in matters of religious and ecclesiastical content. Accordingly, we would affirm the order of the Appellate Division.

We start on common ground. Judicial intervention in disputes with respect to religious and ecclesiastical obligation is constitutionally proscribed, save with respect to a narrow class of issues, as to which, under "neutral principles of law", the secular component of the religious and ecclesiastical rights and obligations may be resolved without impermissible trespass on or even reference to religious dogma and doctrine. We depart from the conclusion of the majority that in this case the courts may discern one or more discretely secular obligations which may be fractured out of the "Ketubah", indisputably in its essence a document prepared and executed under Jewish law and tradition.

. . .

The majority's reference to the fact that marriage relationships solemnized within a religious context are recognized by the civil law is not determinative of the question here presented where what is sought to be enforced is an aspect of the relationship peculiar to the religion within which the ceremony creating it took place. No authority is cited in which a civil court has enforced a concomitant undertaking required by the ecclesiastical authority under which the marriage ceremony was solemnized. That no such civil enforcement of the obligation to appear before the Beth Din was contemplated either by the drafter of the Ketubah or by the parties as its signatories is evident from the inclusion of explicit authorization to the Beth Din "to impose such terms of compensation as it may see fit for failure to respond to its summons or to carry out its decision". Nothing in the record suggests that it was the intention of the parties when they signed this religious document that the civil courts of the State of New York were to have jurisdiction to determine the substantive rights created thereby or to invoke civil procedures and remedies for the enforcement of such rights. Indeed, any conclusion on the part of our courts that this express provision was not intended by the parties as the exclusive remedy available to them for any breach of their obligations under the Ketubah would itself necessarily entail examination of Jewish law and tradition.

Finally, the evident objective of the present action—as recognized by the majority and irrefutably demonstrated by the complaint—even if procedural jurisdiction were to be assumed, is to obtain a religious divorce, a matter well beyond the authority of any civil court. (Again supplying her own interpretation of the Ketubah, the wife alleges: "That pursuant to the terms of the Ketubah, the plaintiff and defendant agreed that in the event of any civil divorce decree that the husband grant and the wife accept a Jewish divorce decree in accordance with the authority vested in the Beth Din of the Rabbinical Assembly".) As was noted at the Appellate Division, the interest of the civil authorities of the State of New York in the status of the marriage between these parties was concluded when the final judgment of divorce was entered in 1978.

NOTE

In Victor v. Victor, 177 Ariz. 231, 866 P.2d 899 (App.1994), an Arizona Court of Appeals held that a Ketubah which set forth the husband's financial obligations to his wife under Jewish law was not an enforceable antenuptial agreement under which the husband could be ordered to obtain religious divorce document or "get." However, in Scholl v. Scholl, 621 A.2d 808 (Fam.Del.1992), a Delaware Family Court determined that an order to enforce a stipulation of settlement between the parties in which the husband agreed to cooperate in obtaining an Orthodox get (he had obtained a get from a Conservative body but his wife was Orthodox) would not be an excessive entanglement with religion. For another example of judicial enforcement of a Ketubah, *see* In re Marriage of Goldman, 196 Ill.App.3d 785, 143 Ill.Dec. 944, 554 N.E.2d 1016 (1990). In Aziz v. Aziz, 127 Misc.2d 1013, 488 N.Y.S.2d 123 (1985), the court held that secular terms of the mahr, an agreement entered into by the parties as part of a religious ceremony under Islamic law, were enforceable as a contractual obligation. For a discussion of *Avitzur*, see Comment, *Avitzur v. Avitzur: Jewish Divorce and the First Amendment,* 36 RUTGERS L.REV. 887 (1984). *See generally* David Novak, *Jewish Marriage and Civil Law: A Two Way Street?* 68 GEO. WASH. L. REV. 1059 (2000); Jesse Choper, *A Century of Religious Freedom,* 88 CAL. L. REV. 1709 (2000).

NEW YORK DOMESTIC RELATIONS LAW (McKinney 1999)

§ 253.   Removal of barriers to remarriage

1.   This section applies only to a marriage solemnized in this state or in any other jurisdiction by a person specified in subdivision one of section eleven of this chapter.

2.   Any party to a marriage defined in subdivision one of this section who commences a proceeding to annul the marriage or for a divorce must allege, in his or her verified complaint: (i) that, to the best of his or her knowledge, that he or she has taken or that he or she will take, prior to the entry of final judgment, all steps solely within his or her power to remove any barrier to the defendant's remarriage following the annulment or divorce; or (ii) that the defendant has waived in writing the requirements of this subdivision.

3. No final judgment of annulment or divorce shall thereafter be entered unless the plaintiff shall have filed and served a sworn statement: (i) that, to the best of his or her knowledge, he or she has, prior to the entry of such final judgment, taken all steps solely within his or her power to remove all barriers to the defendant's remarriage following the annulment or divorce; or (ii) that the defendant has waived in writing the requirements of this subdivision.

4. In any action for divorce based on subdivisions five and six of section one hundred seventy of this chapter in which the defendant enters a general appearance and does not contest the requested relief, no final judgment of annulment or divorce shall be entered unless both parties shall have filed and served sworn statements: (i) that he or she has, to the best of his or her knowledge, taken all steps solely within his or her power to remove all barriers to the other party's remarriage following the annulment or divorce; or (ii) that the other party has waived in writing the requirements of this subdivision.

5. The writing attesting to any waiver of the requirements of subdivision two, three or four of this section shall be filed with the court prior to the entry of a final judgment of annulment or divorce.

6. As used in the sworn statements prescribed by this section "barrier to remarriage" includes, without limitation, any religious or conscientious restraint or inhibition, of which the party required to make the verified statement is aware, that is imposed on a party to a marriage, under the principles held by the clergyman or minister who has solemnized the marriage, by reason of the other party's commission or withholding of any voluntary act. Nothing in this section shall be construed to require any party to consult with any clergyman or minister to determine whether there exists any such religious or conscientious restraint or inhibition. It shall not be deemed a "barrier to remarriage" within the meaning of this section if the restraint or inhibition cannot be removed by the party's voluntary act. Nor shall it be deemed a "barrier to remarriage" if the party must incur expenses in connection with removal of the restraint or inhibition and the other party refuses to provide reasonable reimbursement for such expenses. "All steps solely within his or her power" shall not be construed to include application to a marriage tribunal or other similar organization or agency of a religious denomination which has authority to annul or dissolve a marriage under the rules of such denomination.

7. No final judgment of annulment or divorce shall be entered, notwithstanding the filing of the plaintiff's sworn statement prescribed by this section, if the clergyman or minister who has solemnized the marriage certifies, in a sworn statement, that he or she has solemnized the marriage and that, to his or her knowledge, the plaintiff has failed to take all steps solely within his or her power to remove all barriers to the defendant's remarriage following the annulment or divorce, provided that the said clergyman or minister is alive and available and competent to testify at the time when final judgment would be entered.

8. Any person who knowingly submits a false sworn statement under this section shall be guilty of making an apparently sworn false statement in the first degree and shall be punished in accordance with section 210.40 of the penal law.

9. Nothing in this section shall be construed to authorize any court to inquire into or determine any ecclesiastical or religious issue. The truth of any statement submitted pursuant to this section shall not be the subject of any judicial inquiry, except as provided in subdivision eight of this section.

UNIFORM PREMARITAL AGREEMENT ACT (1983)

SECTION 1.   DEFINITIONS.

As used in this Act:

(1) "Premarital agreement" means an agreement between prospective spouses made in contemplation of marriage and to be effective upon marriage.

(2) "Property" means an interest, present or future, legal or equitable, vested or contingent, in real or personal property, including income and earnings.

SECTION 2.   FORMALITIES.

A premarital agreement must be in writing and signed by both parties. It is enforceable without consideration.

SECTION 3.   CONTENT.

(a) Parties to a premarital agreement may contract with respect to:

(1) the rights and obligations of each of the parties in any of the property of either or both of them whenever and wherever acquired or located;

(2) the right to buy, sell, use, transfer, exchange, abandon, lease, consume, expend, assign, create a security interest in, mortgage, encumber, dispose of, or otherwise manage and control property;

(3) the disposition of property upon separation, marital dissolution, death, or the occurrence or nonoccurrence of any other event;

(4) the modification or elimination of spousal support;

(5) the making of a will, trust, or other arrangement to carry out the provisions of the agreement;

(6) the ownership rights in and disposition of the death benefit from a life insurance policy;

(7) the choice of law governing the construction of the agreement; and

(8) any other matter, including their personal rights and obligations, not in violation of public policy or a statute imposing a criminal penalty.

(b) The right of a child to support may not be adversely affected by a premarital agreement.

SECTION 4.   EFFECT OF MARRIAGE.

A premarital agreement becomes effective upon marriage.

SECTION 5.   AMENDMENT, REVOCATION.

After marriage, a premarital agreement may be amended or revoked only by a written agreement signed by the parties. The amended agreement or the revocation is enforceable without consideration.

SECTION 6.   ENFORCEMENT.

(a) A premarital agreement is not enforceable if the party against whom enforcement is sought proves that:

(1) that party did not execute the agreement voluntarily; or

(2) the agreement was unconscionable when it was executed and, before execution of the agreement, that party:

(i) was not provided a fair and reasonable disclosure of the property or financial obligations of the other party;

(ii) did not voluntarily and expressly waive, in writing, any right to disclosure of the property or financial obligations of the other party beyond the disclosure provided; and

(iii) did not have, or reasonably could not have had, an adequate knowledge of the property or financial obligations of the other party.

(b) If a provision of a premarital agreement modifies or eliminates spousal support and that modification or elimination causes one party to the agreement to be eligible for support under a program of public assistance at the time of separation or marital dissolution, a court, notwithstanding the terms of the agreement, may require the other party to provide support to the extent necessary to avoid that eligibility.

(c) An issue of unconscionability of a premarital agreement shall be decided by the court as a matter of law.

SECTION 7.   ENFORCEMENT: VOID MARRIAGE.

If a marriage is determined to be void, an agreement that would otherwise have been a premarital agreement is enforceable only to the extent necessary to avoid an inequitable result.

SECTION 8.   LIMITATION OF ACTIONS.

Any statute of limitations applicable to an action asserting a claim for relief under a premarital agreement is tolled during the marriage of the parties to the agreement. However, equitable defenses limiting the time for enforcement, including laches and estoppel, are available to either party.

[Sections 9–13, which deal with application and construction, short title, severability, time of taking effect, and repeal of other statutes have been omitted.]

NOTE

Some states adopting the preceding Act have added amendments that could prove more than cosmetic. Virginia's act, for example, does not include UPAA §§ 3(b) and 6(b), and VA. CODE § 20–150.4 (the equivalent of UPAA § 3(a)(4)) refers simply to "Spousal support". Two years after first adopting the UPAA, Virginia also added § 20–155, which provides that:

> Married persons may enter into agreements with each other for the purpose of settling the rights and obligations of either or both of them. To the extent, with the same effect, and subject to the same conditions, as provided in §§ 20–147 through 20–154 [the Virginia version of the UPAA] for agreements between prospective spouses, except that such marital agreements shall become effective immediately upon their execution.

California's version of the UPAA omits § 3(a)(4) (the modification or elimination of spousal support), thus it appears that spousal support may not be modified or eliminated. Nonetheless, the California Supreme Court, citing agreement with 41 other jurisdictions, allows waiver of spousal support even though it was thought in the past that such a waiver would encourage divorce. Pendleton v. Fireman, 24 Cal.4th 39, 99 Cal.Rptr.2d 278, 5 P.3d 839 (2000).

In addition to the Uniform Premarital Agreement Act drafted by the National Conference of Commissioners on Uniform State Laws, the American Law Institute Principles provide their own provisions expressly applicable to premarital agreements. The Institute provisions specifically state that they could be applicable to domestic partnerships and civil unions. When comparing the Commissioners' and the Institute's acts, both require that for a premarital agreement to be valid, it must (1) be in writing and signed by both of the parties; (2) that the agreement may affect the property of the parties in the context of marital dissolution or death, even allowing the parties to eliminate support obligations; (3) result from voluntary motives; (4) be based on full and fair disclosure with reasonable opportunity to adequately acquire knowledge of the property or financial obligations of the other party; and (5) if the subsequent marriage is declared void, the agreement is enforceable only to the extent necessary to avoid an inequitable result. Additionally, the Commissioners' Act creates a rebuttable presumption that the agreement is valid. The Institute takes the position that the agreement is presumptively valid only if the agreement was entered into (1) at least 30 days prior to the actual marriage, partnership or union; (2) both parties were advised to obtain independent counsel and had opportunity to do so, and (3) if there was no independent counsel obtained, the agreement is written in such a way that persons of ordinary intelligence with no legal training could understand any adverse consequences that would occur because of the agreement. PRINCIPLES OF THE LAW OF FAMILY DISSOLUTION: ANALYSIS AND RECOMMENDATIONS §§ 7.04, 7.05, 7.04(c) (2002). Attorneys representing couples or persons executing the agreements must be careful to provide full and adequate disclosure, the opportunity to consult with legal counsel, the possibility of future acquisitions, the timing of the agreement in reference to the wedding or similar ceremony, and the possibility of a presumption arising from the agreement. Failure to be attentive to these issues may arise in disciplinary action against the attorney. *See, e.g.,* Antone v. Mirviss, 694 N.W.2d 564 (Minn. Ct. App. 2005)(attorney successfully sued for malpractice sixteen years after drafting a faulty premarital agreement), *rev'd* 720 N.W.2d 331 (Minn. 2006).

G. Postnuptial Support Contracts and Separation Agreements

Reform of the grounds for divorce has made the attorney's role in marriage dissolution more that of a negotiator than a litigator. Today an attorney needs to consider carefully the implications of tax, estate and property law in order to represent a client properly in negotiating a divorce settlement. The process can call for the negotiating skills of a labor lawyer as well as an estate planner's careful attention to details and consideration of future eventualities.

Not long ago separation and settlement agreements were regarded with suspicion, if not hostility, by the courts. This reflected the then strong public policy against fomenting or even encouraging divorce. With the introduction of nonfault divorce grounds—particularly those involving separation of the parties for a specified period before the grounds mature—separation agreements gained increasing popularity and legislatures began to enact statutes facilitating their use. Persons contemplating divorce may, on separating, execute an agreement that will order their economic relationship during the period before divorce as well as afterward. Problems remain in some jurisdictions about whether (or how) such agreements can be modified after divorce and the means available for enforcing their terms through judicial action. However, there is increasing movement toward a system of private ordering in which such agreements retain their contractual integrity even after they have been incorporated into judicial decrees. This has the effect of permitting modification only in accordance with the terms of the contract or by subsequent agreement between the parties. At the same time, there has been movement toward providing for increased enforcement through such judicial remedies as contempt.

Inconsistent use of terminology, by courts and legislatures as well as lawyers, has caused much confusion. The terms "incorporate", "merge", "ratify", and "affirm" probably have produced the most difficulty. In some jurisdictions they have become words of art, to be used with considerable care according to the result desired. In others, some of the terms may be interchangeable. The key distinction to be made is whether parts of a settlement agreement included in a divorce decree, either by reference or by specifically incorporating the language of the agreement into the court's order, retain their contractual identity or are subsumed into the decree and so changed in character that the executory portions are subject to statutory rules such as those regarding future modification or termination of alimony.

It is generally an alternative for the parties to make no mention of the terms of their settlement agreement to the court at the time of divorce and simply to rely on enforcing it as an ordinary contract. A variation of this, practiced regularly in some jurisdictions in the past, is to have the court pass on the fairness of such an agreement without jeopardizing its contractual nature. This procedure developed out of concern for insuring against future invalidation of an agreement for unconscionability or any other reason. Prior validation was particularly important in jurisdictions that only permitted alimony awards to be made at the time of the divorce; if a settlement agreement in such a state were set aside after divorce there would be no avenue for seeking a judicial award of support subsequently.

For a discussion of some of the problems of separation agreements and private ordering versus public policy, and negotiation in the context of separation and divorce, *see* Richard A. Corwin, *Ethical Considerations: the Attorney–Client Relationship*, 75 TUL. L. REV. 1327 (2001); Martha M. Ertman, *Marriage as a Trade: Bridging the Private/Public Distinction*, 36 Harv. C.R.-C.L. L. REV. 79 (2001); Brian H. Bix, *State of the Union: The States' Interest in the Marital Status of Their Citizens*, 55 U. MIAMI L. REV. 1 (2000); John Witte, Jr., *The Goods and Goals of Marriage,* 76 NOTRE DAME L. REV. 1019 (2001); Elizabeth S. Scott, *Social Norms and the Legal Regulation of Marriage*, 86 VA. L. REV. 1901 (2000); 7 WEST'S LEGAL FORMS, 339–740 (2d ed. 1995).

Johnston v. Johnston

Court of Appeals of Maryland, 1983.
297 Md. 48, 465 A.2d 436.

■ COUCH, JUDGE.

Although the parties have raised four issues in this case, the issue, as we see it, is whether a separation agreement approved and incorporated but not merged in a divorce decree may be collaterally attacked. For reasons to be discussed herein, we hold that it may not be where, as here, its validity is conclusively established by the decree which operates as *res judicata*.

The parties hereto were married in June of 1948 and lived together 23 years prior to separating in June of 1971. During the marriage, four children were born all of whom have now reached their majority. Subsequent to their separation, each party retained counsel and negotiated an agreement the purpose of which was "to effect a final and permanent settlement of their respective property rights." The agreement was executed by the parties in February of 1973 and provided, *inter alia*, for the support and maintenance of Mrs. Johnston and the four children, the transfer of certain property interests, the execution of testamentary designations, and the creation of various trusts. The agreement was made in contemplation of divorce proceedings and provided:

> "This agreement shall be offered in evidence in any such suit, and if acceptable to the court, shall be incorporated by reference in the decree that may be granted therein. *Notwithstanding such incorporation, this agreement shall not be merged in the decree, but shall survive the same and shall be binding and conclusive on the parties for all time.*" (Emphasis supplied).

The agreement also provided:

> "No modification or waiver of any of the terms of this agreement shall be valid unless in writing and executed with the same formality as this agreement."

Mr. Johnston filed a "Bill of Complaint for Divorce A *Vinculo Matrimonii* "in the Circuit Court for Baltimore City, specifically requesting "[t]hat the Agreement of the parties dated February 16, 1973 be incorporated by reference in any decree that may be granted herein." A "Decree of Divorce" was entered June 27, 1973, stating in relevant part:

> "It is further ADJUDGED, ORDERED AND DECREED that the Plaintiff provide for maintenance, and support of Defendant and of the infant children of the parties, all as provided in the Agreement between the parties dated February 16, 1973 and filed in this cause of action, *said Agreement being hereby approved and made a part hereof as if fully set forth herein....*" (Emphasis added).

In May, 1981, Mr. Johnston filed a "Petition to Set Aside and Void Agreement" on the basis that "consultations [with professionals] ha[d] disclosed that [he] suffered from a mental disease and/or mental defect during the negotiations and subsequent execution of the aforesaid Agreement which severely impaired [his] mental competency at that time." The petition further asserted that Mr. Johnston's mental incompetency justified the voiding of the separation agreement. Mrs. Johnston in turn filed a "Motion to Strike and Motion Raising Preliminary Objection" contending that the four children were necessary parties as they were affected by the agreement, the allegations in the petition were insufficient to advise her of the nature of Mr. Johnston's mental disease or defect, that Mr. Johnston had failed to state whether he is presently mentally competent, and that she and other members of the family have relied upon and continue to rely upon the terms of the agreement. She also asserted that the relief requested should be denied because of laches and public policy. In addition, Mrs. Johnston argued that Mr. Johnston was actually seeking to have the enrolled decree set aside but had failed to allege "fraud, mistake or irregularity" as required by Maryland Rule 625.[1]

---

1. Md. Rule 625a states:

"For a period of thirty days after the entry of a judgment, or thereafter pursuant to motion filed within such period, the court shall have revisory power and control over such judgment. After the expiration of such period the court shall have revisory power and control over such judgment, only in case of fraud, mistake or irregularity."

Following a hearing on the matter, the chancellor granted Mrs. Johnston's motion to strike stating in pertinent part:

> "I do not feel that you can bifurcate the Agreement and the divorce decree. I think that they have merged and that they are one and the same.
>
> It is obvious that if, in fact, any attack is made on the Agreement, that attack is also made on the divorce decree. The divorce decree here is the court document, which is the binding document on the parties. The document that has set up the custody, visitation, the property rights, support, alimony and so on. This decree was enrolled within 30 days. There has been no attack on this decree until ten years later. Strike that. There has been no attack on this decree until eight years later. Mr. Johnston now comes in and says the divorce decree in reality should be set aside.
>
> Now, I think that is a play on words. I don't think there is any question that regardless of what counsel labels the petition, whether it is a petition to set aside the Agreement or to set aside what it is, it is clear in the Court's mind that the petition is seeking to either modify or set aside an enrolled judgment.
>
> There is no question about the law, that the parties have a right to enter into a contract as to their matrimonial disputes and put those contractual obligations in a decree for divorce.
>
> There is no question that the rule is clear as to Rule 625, that I cannot set aside this decree unless the parties can show any fraud, mistake or irregularity under the law.
>
> There is no question here, and I don't think it is necessary at this time to rule on the question of laches.
>
> .   .   .
>
> [A]nd I think that based on the pleadings as I have seen them here, and based on the law as I understand Rule 625, and based on laches, I would at this time grant the motion to strike."

The chancellor further held that the children were necessary parties as "they have individual rights in [the] various trusts." Mrs. Johnston's request for counsel fees was denied. The Court of Special Appeals affirmed the chancellor's ruling, stating in relevant part:

> "Mr. Johnston asserts that the chancellor erred, and that the case should be permitted to go to trial on Johnston's petition because the responsive pleadings are insufficient to constitute a demurrer. What appellant, Johnston, would have us do is substitute form for substance and, thereby, subject an enrolled decree to an assault it should not have to endure. We decline to subvert the enrolled decree and submit it to the indignity of an attack such as Mr. Johnston would make. If there ever was a time when the niceties of pleadings should be ignored in the

interest of a just result, this is that time." Hamilos v. Hamilos, 52 Md.App. 488, 493, 450 A.2d 1316, 1320 (1982).[2]

We believe that the threshold issue, which neither the chancellor nor the intermediate appellate court discussed, is whether the separation agreement merged in the decree so as to be superseded by the decree.[3] The decree expressly approved and incorporated the agreement. However, the agreement explicitly provided that it was not to merge in the decree but was to survive the decree. As observed by the Supreme Court of Arizona in McNelis v. Bruce, 90 Ariz. 261, 367 P.2d 625, 631 (1961) (en banc):

"It is the rule that the mere approval of a property settlement in the divorce decree does not operate to make it a part of and enforceable as a decree. If the language of the agreement shows an intent to make it part of the divorce decree and the agreement is actually incorporated in the decree, the provisions of the agreement may be enforced as an order of the court. As soon as a property settlement agreement is incorporated into the decree the agreement is superceded by the decree and the obligations imposed are not those imposed by contract but are those imposed by the decree since the contract is merged in the decree." (Citations omitted).

The language of the agreement in *McNelis* was similar to that in the instant case, providing: " 'This agreement shall be offered in evidence in such action and if acceptable to the court shall be incorporated by reference in any decree that may be granted herein. Notwithstanding such incorporation, this agreement shall not be merged in the decree but shall survive the same and shall be binding and conclusive upon the parties for all time.' " Id. 367 P.2d at 631–32.

In determining whether the agreement merged in the decree so as to be modifiable by the court, the court looked to the intent of the parties, stating in pertinent part:

"The foregoing clause manifests the intention of the parties to the agreement. It was not disapproved by the court but rather adopted as part of the agreement; it therefore must be taken as speaking the intention of not only the parties but of the court that the agreement was not to be merged in the judgment." Id. 367 P.2d at 632.

The Supreme Court of California has also had occasion to discuss the issue of merger:

"Merger is the substitution of rights and duties under the judgment or the decree for those under the agreement or cause of action

---

2. Upon motion by the parties, the Court of Special Appeals consolidated the *Johnston* and *Hamilos* cases. We were not requested to do so and have treated them separately although the issues are similar. See Hamilos v. Hamilos, 297 Md. 99, 465 A.2d 445 (1983), and argued the same date.

3. "Merger" is defined as the "[s]ubstitution of rights and duties under judgment or decree for those under property settlement agreement." Black's Law Dictionary 892 (5th ed. 1979); Flynn v. Flynn, 42 Cal.2d 55, 265 P.2d 865, 866 (1954) (en banc); Roesbery v. Roesbery, 88 Idaho 514, 401 P.2d 805, 807 (1965).

sued upon. The question as to what extent, if any, a merger has occurred, when a separation agreement has been presented to the court in a divorce action, arises in various situations. Thus, it may be necessary to determine whether or not contempt will lie to enforce the agreement, whether or not other judgment remedies, such as execution or a suit on the judgment, are available, whether or not an action may still be maintained on the agreement itself, and whether or not there is an order of the court that may be modified. . . .

In any of these situations it is first necessary to determine whether the parties and the court intended a merger. If the agreement is expressly set out in the decree, and the court orders that it be performed, it is clear that a merger is intended. On the other hand, the parties may intend only to have the validity of the agreement established, and not to have it become a part of the decree enforceable as such. Whether or not a merger is intended, the agreement may be incorporated into the decree either expressly or by reference. If a merger is not intended, the purpose of incorporation will be only to identify the agreement so as to render its validity res judicata in any subsequent action based upon it. If a merger is intended, the purpose of incorporation is, of course, to make the agreement an operative part of the decree." Flynn v. Flynn, 42 Cal.2d 55, 265 P.2d 865, 866 (1954) (en banc) (numerous citations omitted).

The agreement in *Flynn* provided that it could be approved by the court and incorporated in the decree. However, there was no provision, as in the instant case, that it would not merge. The decree ratified, approved, and incorporated the agreement. The court concluded that the parties and the court had clearly intended the agreement to merge in the decree and, accordingly, the court had jurisdiction to modify the provision for monthly payments.

In our view, where, as in the instant case, the agreement provides that it shall be *incorporated but not merged* in the decree, it is patent that the parties did not intend merger and the agreement survives as a separate and independent contractual arrangement between the parties. On the other hand, where, as in *Flynn* supra, the agreement does not include a non-merger clause and it is incorporated in the decree, the agreement is superseded by the decree. See also Wallace v. Wallace, 1 Hawaii Ct.App. 315, 619 P.2d 511, 513 (1980); Bowman v. Bennett, 250 N.W.2d 47, 50 (Iowa 1977). The agreement, once incorporated and merged in the decree, is enforceable through contempt proceedings and may be modified by the court. See, e.g., Early v. Early, 6 Ariz.App. 110, 430 P.2d 456, 460–61 (1967); *Flynn*, supra. It has also been stated that where the court incorporates the agreement as a whole, including the non-merger clause, the court approves the clause against merger so that the contract survives.

It is undisputed that pursuant to Maryland Rule S77 b[5] a separation agreement may be incorporated in the divorce decree. Moreover, there are

5. Md.Rule S77 b provides:

"A deed, agreement or settlement between husband and wife as described in Art. 16, Sec. 28 of the Annotated Code of Maryland may be received in evidence and made a part of the record in an action for divorce, annulment or alimony and may be incorporated, insofar as the court may deem proper, into the decree."

numerous cases previously decided by this Court that firmly establish that once incorporated, the contractual provisions become part of the decree, modifiable by the court where appropriate and enforceable through contempt proceedings.... It is significant to note that the issue of merger has simply never arisen as none of the incorporated agreements contained a non-merger clause. On the other hand, it appears to be well established that separation agreements not incorporated in divorce decrees remain separate enforceable instruments. For example, we have observed that:

> "A support or property agreement is not invalid nor unenforceable merely because it is not embodied in the divorce decree, if not in conflict with such decree. If the divorce decree does not provide for alimony, it does not terminate liability of the husband to make the payments provided for by a separation agreement. A support or property agreement is not affected by the subsequent decree of divorce, if such settlement is neither incorporated in the decree, disapproved by the decree, nor superseded by provisions of the decree." Shacter v. Shacter, 251 Md. 304, 307–08, 247 A.2d 268, 270 (1968) (quoting 1 Nelson on Divorce, Ch. 13, § 13.54 (2d ed. 1945)).

In *Shacter*, the separation agreement was not incorporated as there were no grounds for divorce. However, its validity was clearly recognized as the court entered judgment for the wife against the husband in the amount due under the agreement. See also Coffman v. Hayes, 259 Md. 708, 270 A.2d 808 (1970), where the wife was allowed to recover arrearages for child support and medical payments as provided in the separation agreement. Although the agreement had been incorporated in the divorce decree, the arrearages occurred after the separation agreement but prior to the decree.

In our view, the cases from other jurisdictions as well as the various treatises concerning the doctrine of merger, as discussed hereinabove at length, are very persuasive. On the basis of such authority, we hold that where the parties intend a separation agreement to be incorporated but not merged in the divorce decree, the agreement remains a separate, enforceable contract and is not superseded by the decree. In the case *sub judice*, the agreement expressly provided that it was to be incorporated but not merged in the decree. The decree approved the agreement as a whole and made it a part of the decree as if it were *fully* set forth, thus approving the non-merger clause. Accordingly, the agreement remained an independent contract which in some instances could be attacked separately from the decree and thus the trial judge erred in granting the motion to strike on the basis that the requirements of Md.Rule 625 had not been met.

It has been stated that:

> "Where there is a valid bilateral divorce—the divorce court having had jurisdiction of the parties and the subject matter—and the court

approves the separation agreement, which is then incorporated in the decree, the court will be deemed to have passed on its legality, and subsequent collateral attack on it will not be countenanced. The validity of the agreement is then *res judicata*; and if the decree approving it is that of a sister state, full faith and credit bars collateral attack on the agreement elsewhere. To put it concretely, the husband cannot in such a case evade his obligations under the agreement by claiming that it is illegal because it was in consideration of divorce, or that it is voidable because it was procured through fraud. Nor can the wife upset the agreement on the ground of misrepresentation or coercion.

On the other hand, where the agreement is not approved by or incorporated in an out-of-state decree, the parties are not estopped, as a matter of law, from later challenging its validity elsewhere. And this despite the fact that it may have been brought to the court's attention and may have been referred to in the findings." 2 A. Lindey, Separation Agreements and Ante–Nuptial Contracts §§ 31–50 to 51 (1962) (footnotes omitted).

In addition, at least two of our sister jurisdictions have held that where the separation agreement is incorporated in the divorce decree but no merger is intended, the purposes of incorporation are to identify the agreement and to render its validity *res judicata*. See *McNelis*, supra, 367 P.2d at 632; *Flynn*, supra, 265 P.2d at 866.

Although the parties in the instant case have not precisely raised the issue of *res judicata*, we believe that in the interests of judicial economy it is appropriate for us to address it as it is dispositive of the matter before us. . . .

In the instant case, the separation agreement was executed "[w]hereas the Husband desire[d] to make provision for the Wife's and children's support and maintenance, and the parties desire[d] to effect a final and permanent settlement of their respective property rights." Both parties were represented by competent counsel at the time of the execution of the agreement as well as during the divorce proceeding. The agreement, consisting of 17 pages and numerous exhibits, was submitted to the court for its approval. By its own terms, it was to be incorporated in the decree only if it were acceptable to the court. Mr. Johnston testified at the divorce hearing and was questioned by the chancellor regarding the separation agreement:

"Q Now, you and your wife have entered into a separation agreement. Is that correct?

A That is correct.

Q And that agreement is dated February 16th, 1973, and you have requested the court to incorporate that agreement into any decree that may be granted in this case. Do you understand what that means?

A Yes, Your Honor.

Q That the agreement will become a part of this decree, and you will be required to comply with the terms and conditions of the agreement. Do you understand that?

A Yes, Your Honor. . . .

Q All right, Mr. Johnston, I show you this agreement and ask whether the agreement is signed by you and your wife?

A Yes, Your Honor.''

The divorce decree expressly approved the agreement, which was filed as an exhibit, and ordered, at the request of the parties, that it be sealed due to the confidential nature of various matters and facts contained therein.

In our view the property rights of the parties were determined in the divorce proceeding. Moreover, the approval and incorporation of the agreement conclusively established the validity of the agreement and precludes a collateral attack by either party. . . .

. .   .

For the reasons stated herein, we conclude that where, as in the instant case, the property settlement agreement is presented to the court for approval and is approved by the court and incorporated in the divorce decree, the validity of the agreement is conclusively established and the doctrine of *res judicata* operates so as to preclude a collateral attack on the agreement.

In accordance with the above, we hold that Mrs. Johnston's motion to strike was properly granted by the chancellor although for reasons different from those assigned by the Court of Special Appeals.

NOTE

In Mendelson v. Mendelson, 75 Md.App. 486, 541 A.2d 1331 (1988), the Court of Special Appeals of Maryland, relying on Johnston v. Johnston, held that:

> an agreement for spousal support that is not merged into the divorce decree remains entirely contractual and passes beyond the court's power to modify it for any reason—other than the one provided for in the contract—once the decree is enrolled.

UNIFORM MARRIAGE AND DIVORCE ACT (1973)

§ 306. [Separation Agreement]

(a) To promote amicable settlement of disputes between parties to a marriage attendant upon their separation or the dissolution of their marriage, the parties may enter into a written separation agreement containing provisions for disposition of any property owned by either of them, maintenance of either of them, and support, custody, and visitation of their children.

(b) In a proceeding for dissolution of marriage or for legal separation, the terms of the separation agreement, except those providing for the support, custody, and visitation of children, are binding upon the court unless it finds, after considering the economic circumstances of the parties and any other relevant evidence produced by the parties, on their own motion or on request of the court, that the separation agreement is unconscionable.

(c) If the court finds the separation agreement unconscionable, it may request the parties to submit a revised separation agreement or may make orders for the disposition of property, maintenance, and support.

(d) If the court finds that the separation agreement is not unconscionable as to disposition of property or maintenance, and not unsatisfactory as to support:

(1) unless the separation agreement provides to the contrary, its terms shall be set forth in the decree of dissolution or legal separation and the parties shall be ordered to perform them, or

(2) if the separation agreement provides that its terms shall not be set forth in the decree, the decree shall identify the separation agreement and state that the court has found the terms not unconscionable.

(e) Terms of the agreement set forth in the decree are enforceable by all remedies available for enforcement of a judgment, including contempt, and are enforceable as contract terms.

(f) Except for terms concerning the support, custody, or visitation of children, the decree may expressly preclude or limit modification of terms set forth in the decree if the separation agreement so provides. Otherwise, terms of a separation agreement set forth in the decree are automatically modified by modification of the decree.

NOTE

Federal Tax Liability for Alimony: To qualify as alimony, a payment must be: (1) made under a valid divorce or separation instrument incident to a divorce decree; (2) made in cash; (3) between two former spouses who do not occupy the same household when the payments are made; (4) there is no requirement that the payments are to continue after the death of the payee spouse; (5) the former spouses do not file joint returns with each other; and (6) payments made as child support do not constitute alimony. If all of the conditions are met, the payor may deduct the amount paid and the payee must include the alimony as income. *See* Internal Revenue Code §§ 62(a)(10); 71 and 215. No gain or loss is recognized to the payor on a transfer of property between spouses of former spouses incident to a divorce, nor is the value of the property transferred included in the gross income of the payee. *Id.* at §§ 1041(1), 1041(b)(1)–1041(c). A transfer between spouses is incident to a divorce and complies with these rules if it occurs within one year after the marriage ceases or is related to the cessation of the marriage. Additional material will be provided, *infra*.

Glickman v. Collins

Supreme Court of California, 1975.
13 Cal.3d 852, 120 Cal.Rptr. 76, 533 P.2d 204.

■ WRIGHT, CHIEF JUSTICE.

Defendant Hilda Collins appeals from a judgment in favor of plaintiff Claire Glickman in the sum of $8,852.80 plus attorney's fees and costs found by the court to be due under an agreement wherein defendant guaranteed the obligation of plaintiff's former husband Gerald Glickman to make alimony and child support payments to plaintiff. Defendant contends that the agreement is void as against public policy because it was intended to induce plaintiff to divorce Mr. Glickman. [The guaranty was executed after plaintiff and Mr. Glickman had separated. Plaintiff had instructed her attorney to advise defendant that plaintiff would not sign a new property settlement agreement with Mr. Glickman or proceed to secure a divorce unless defendant executed the guaranty. After defendant executed the guaranty and the property agreement was signed by plaintiff and Mr. Glickman, plaintiff obtained a divorce in Nevada. Mr. Glickman and defendant then married. Later, defendant obtained a divorce from Mr. Glickman. At about the time that defendant's divorce action was instituted, Mr. Glickman ceased sending plaintiff the payments required under the separation agreement. Plaintiff obtained a judgment against him for arrearages that has not been satisfied.]

Defendant first contends that the guaranty agreement is unenforceable as being contrary to public policy because its effect was to promote the dissolution of the Glickmans' marriage. "Public policy seeks to foster and protect marriage, to encourage parties to live together, and to prevent separation." (Hill v. Hill (1943) 23 Cal.2d 82, 93, 142 P.2d 417, 422.) Thus we have voided, as promotive of divorce and hence contrary to public policy, a contingent fee agreement between the plaintiff in a divorce action and her attorney. (Newman v. Freitas (1900) 129 Cal. 283, 289–293, 61 P. 907.) We have likewise voided an agreement between a husband and wife which provided for payment of a specified sum to the wife in release of all property rights in the event of a future divorce if the husband should subsequently give her grounds for such a divorce. (Pereira v. Pereira (1909) 156 Cal. 1, 4–5, 103 P. 488.)

Notwithstanding the foregoing we have applied a different rule where the marriage relationship had irreparably broken down before the parties entered into a property settlement agreement. We have upheld such an agreement even though the husband would not have signed it absent the wife's promise to obtain a divorce, and the wife would not have obtained the divorce absent the husband's execution of the agreement. (Hill v. Hill, supra, 23 Cal.2d 82, 142 P.2d 417.) We held that "public policy does not discourage divorce where the relations between husband and wife are such that the legitimate objects of matrimony have been utterly destroyed. In the absence of fraud, collusion or imposition upon the court, public policy does not prevent parties who have separated from entering into a contract disposing of their property rights which shall become effective only in the event one of the parties obtains a divorce, even though such a contract may be a factor in persuading a party who has a good cause for divorce to proceed to establish it.''

A similar result has been reached not only in cases involving agreements between the two spouses but also in cases of contracts between one of the spouses and a third party. In one such instance the plaintiff wife told her aunt, the defendant, that she had decided to divorce her husband. The defendant, concerned about the adverse social effect of the ensuing publicity, promised the plaintiff that if she would obtain the divorce in Nevada rather than locally she would thereafter support the plaintiff and her children. After obtaining a Nevada divorce, the plaintiff returned to California, lived with her aunt and continued to be supported by her until a quarrel arose several years later. We held the agreement was not contrary to public policy, noting that the plaintiff had had a good cause of action for divorce and had determined to procure such a legal separation prior to the time the defendant had proposed to support the plaintiff and her children upon the condition that she would secure the divorce in Nevada. (Howard v. Adams (1940) 16 Cal.2d 253, 105 P.2d 971).

In a case similar to that now before the court, the defendant had promised the plaintiff, a married woman, that if she would divorce her husband and marry defendant, he would support her and her children and divide his property with her. We again held that public policy did not invalidate their agreement, noting that the objects of the marriage had theretofore been destroyed, that the marriage was beyond saving at the time the defendant made his offer to the plaintiff, that there was little likelihood of reconciliation and that whatever possibility of reconciliation existed was not barred by the offer. (Spellens v. Spellens (1957) 49 Cal.2d 210, 225, 317 P.2d 613.)[2]

In determining whether public policy forbids the enforcement of an agreement "promotive" of the dissolution of a particular marriage, we must look not solely to the terms of the agreement but also to the viability of the marriage in question at the time the contract was entered into. If the marriage had so deteriorated that legitimate grounds for divorce existed and if there was little hope of reconciliation, the dissolution of such a

---

2. *Spellens* refers to the divorce obtained in the circumstances of that case as being "merely incidental to the agreement." The distinction between contracts deemed "promotive of divorce" and those to which divorce is merely "incidental" is of little practical value other than as a means of expressing the legal conclusion that the marriage had so deteriorated prior to the agreement that public policy against the encouragement of divorce is not applicable. "[T]his terminology is not always accurate or descriptive. The validity of such contracts must be determined in light of the factual background of each case and considerations of public policy appropriate thereto." (Hill v. Hill, supra, 23 Cal.2d 82, 93, 142 P.2d 417, 422.)

marriage is not contrary to public policy. Divorce is often, in fact, the preferred solution.[3]

There is no question that, as the trial court found on substantial evidence, the Glickman marriage was beyond redemption in September and October 1967 when the property settlement and the guaranty agreement were executed. The Glickmans had been separated for over a year and one of the parties was living in Los Angeles, the other in Portland, Oregon. For several months Mr. Glickman had been living with another woman, defendant, whom he had informed plaintiff he desired to marry. Unquestionably, plaintiff had ample grounds for divorce under the law then existing in California. The guaranty agreement was of no consequence in the promotion of a legal separation, both spouses having previously decided upon a divorce and plaintiff having already established residence in Nevada for the purpose of initiating such a proceeding. Moreover, plaintiff testified that even if defendant had refused to sign the guaranty and if plaintiff had consequently abandoned the divorce action, she did not plan to effect a reconciliation with Mr. Glickman. Instead she would have remained apart from him and brought an action for separate maintenance or for divorce in a state other than Nevada. Reconciliation was never considered as a serious possibility. Under these circumstances no policy of the State of California would have been served by maintaining this marriage, and the guaranty agreement that facilitated its dissolution was therefore not invalid as against public policy.

[The judgment was modified to eliminate $252.80 of payments for items covered by the separation agreement but not by defendant's guaranty. The decree was affirmed as to the rest of the amount.]

NOTE

In Capazzoli v. Holzwasser, 397 Mass. 158, 490 N.E.2d 420 (1986), a wife had contracted to abandon her marriage in exchange for a promise of support from another man. She later sought to enforce the promise. In refusing to enforce such a provision the court explained:

> We declare, as an expression of public policy, that a contract containing as an essential provision the requirement that one of the contracting parties will abandon that party's marriage to a third person, is unenforceable in this Commonwealth on a contract, quantum meruit, or any other theory.

---

3. Although the Family Law Act (Civ. Code, § 4000 et seq.) had not been enacted in 1967 and is not therefore directly relevant to this case, the results expressed herein are consistent with the policy of that legislation. As set forth in the Assembly Committee Report of 1969 Divorce Reform Legislation such policy is to permit dissolution whenever the marriage has irreparably broken down, looking at the marriage as a whole and making the possibility of reconciliation the important issue. (4 Assem.J. (1969 Reg.Sess.) 8054, 8058).

Boulter v. Boulter

Supreme Court of Nevada, 1997.
113 Nev. 74, 930 P.2d 112.

■ PER CURIAM:

After a thirty-seven year marriage, appellant Ronald Boulter filed a complaint for divorce against his wife, respondent Noleen Boulter, on April 18, 1990. Subsequently, Ronald and Noleen executed a property settlement agreement. The district court entered a decree of divorce which, by its terms, ratified, merged and incorporated the property settlement agreement. Eight months later, Noleen filed a motion for an order compelling enforcement of the divorce decree. Specifically, she asked for enforcement of paragraph 4(E) of the property settlement agreement.[1]

When Ronald turned 65, he refused to apply for social security benefits, and refused to directly deposit the equivalent of one-half of his benefits (as if he were receiving them), into Noleen's bank account. Noleen contends that paragraph 4(E) required Ronald, upon reaching age 65, to pay her a sum equal to one-half of his monthly social security entitlement earned prior to the end of 1990. Pursuant to the agreement, Noleen sought attorney's fees and costs for filing the motion.[2]

Ronald opposed the motion, arguing that federal law prohibits the division of social security benefits in a marital dissolution proceeding. Alternatively, he argued that Noleen's motion should be denied because the language of the property settlement agreement neither required Ronald to apply for benefits at a certain age nor required him to pay Noleen one-half of his benefits at a certain age, and only required the equalization and payment of benefits actually received by the parties.

The district court granted Noleen's motion because the property settlement agreement equalizing social security benefits was not in violation of federal social security statutes. Moreover, the district court held that since Ronald's former attorney prepared the agreement, any ambiguity should be resolved against Ronald. Finally, the district court determined that Noleen

---

1. Paragraph 4E states: Each party is eligible to receive Social Security Benefits at normal retirement age. The parties have agreed to equalize Social Security Benefits as they are received during their joint lifetimes. Husband agrees to pay to wife one-half of each monthly Social Security check he receives. Wife agrees likewise to split equally with husband each Social Security check she receives. The parties will arrange with Social Security to have the Social Security checks deposited directly into their respective bank accounts, and shall arrange with their banks for an automatic transfer of the other party's share as set forth herein. It is the parties' intention that Social Security benefits be di-

vided, if possible, only to the extent that they were earned prior to the end of 1990. Accordingly, if the parties can obtain from Social Security within one hundred and eighty days of the date hereof, sufficient information to ascertain the benefits derived solely from earning prior to December 31, 1990, the parties specifically agree to amend this portion of this Agreement to include such specific monthly amounts.

2. The agreement provides for an award of attorney's fees to the prevailing party in any action by which the court's assistance is sought to enforce the agreement.

was entitled to an award of attorney's fees and costs under the agreement as prevailing party. This appeal ensued.

DISCUSSION

In pertinent part, the federal Social Security Act provides that: The right of any person to any future payment under this subchapter shall not be transferable or assignable, at law or in equity, and none of the moneys paid or payable or rights existing under this subchapter shall be subject to execution, levy, attachment, garnishment, or other legal process, or to the operation of any bankruptcy or insolvency law. 42 U.S.C. § 407(a) (1983).

Ronald contends that his right to future social security payments is being subjected to legal process in violation of § 407(a) because the district court incorporated the property settlement agreement into the divorce decree and because this court is now employed to enforce that decree. We agree.

Any state action is preempted by a conflicting federal law, such as the Social Security Act, under the Supremacy Clause of the United States Constitution, Article VI, Clause 2. Kirk v. Kirk, 577 A.2d 976, 979 (R.I. 1990).

> The [Social Security Act], consistent with its remedial purpose, provides for the various contingencies of life including the dissolution of marriage. Since the statute itself provides for an equitable distribution of its benefits to ... divorced spouses, ... we will not disturb the statutory scheme by suggesting *any* award of *any* part of the actual social security retirement benefits to which respondent may be entitled upon his reaching retirement age.

In re Marriage of Hawkins, 160 Ill.App.3d 71, 111 Ill.Dec. 897, 901, 513 N.E.2d 143, 147 (1987) (citations omitted) (emphasis added); see also Olson v. Olson, 445 N.W.2d 1, 11 (N.D.1989) (social security is immune to adjustment by state courts in dividing marital property); Umber v. Umber, 591 P.2d 299, 301–02 (Ok.1979) (Congress intended to provide distribution of social security benefits between spouses at time of divorce, thus placing the subject beyond state control); Matter of Marriage of Swan, 301 Or. 167, 720 P.2d 747, 751–52 (1986) (Congress intended to preempt state property division law as applied to social security benefits of a spouse upon divorce); Richard v. Richard, 659 S.W.2d 746, 749 (Tex.App.1983) (Congress exempted social security benefits from state law regarding property division since divorced spouse is provided social security benefits).

The United States Supreme Court has construed § 407(a) to impose "a broad bar against the use of any legal process to reach all social security benefits." Philpott v. Essex County Welfare Bd., 409 U.S. 413, 417, 93 S.Ct. 590, 592, 34 L.Ed.2d 608 (1973). In enacting such anti-assignment statutes, "Congress has afforded recipients [protection] from creditors, taxgatherers, and all those who would 'anticipate' the receipt of benefits...." Hisquierdo v. Hisquierdo, 439 U.S. 572, 575–76, 99 S.Ct. 802, 805, 59 L.Ed.2d 1 (1979), superseded in part by 45 U.S.C. § 231m (1986).[3]

---

3. In Hisquierdo, the United States Supreme Court considered whether benefits provided under the Federal Railroad Retirement Act of 1974 could be divided upon di-

In the instant case, the district court merged the property settlement agreement that equalized social security benefits into the divorce decree. We hold that under Philpott, the district court's decree constitutes state action that has been preempted by the federal Social Security Act. Philpott, 409 U.S. at 417, 93 S.Ct. at 592–93. Because the court was without power to take any action regarding the parties' social security benefits, paragraph 4E was not properly incorporated into the divorce decree. Accordingly, this court may not sustain the district court order enforcing paragraph 4(E) of the decree. We must therefore determine whether the lower court may nevertheless order enforcement of a private agreement dividing future payments of social security.

In U.S. v. Eggen, 984 F.2d 848 (7th Cir.1993), the court held that once social security benefits "are paid over to the recipient, . . . he can use them to satisfy his preexisting obligations." Id. at 850 (citing Ponath v. Hedrick, 22 Wis.2d 382, 126 N.W.2d 28, 31 (1964)). In Ponath the court stated that, Federal cases construing 42 U.S.C.A. § 407, hold that the provision seeks to prevent transfer of benefits prior to receipt. . . . The section [407] is intended to preclude a person entitled to benefits . . . from transferring his right before, but not after the Administrator has recognized it. The provisions of section 407 apply to the assignment of future receipts, not to received benefits. . . .

Noleen contends that the division of social security benefits was a voluntary agreement between two private individuals to divide the benefits once they were received, and not an agreement dividing future social security benefits.

Although social security recipients may use the proceeds of their social security, after their receipt, to satisfy preexisting obligations, they may not contract to transfer their unpaid social security benefits. Thus, in contracting to give Noleen one-half of his benefits before he was eligible to receive them, Ronald ineffectually "transferred his right" to the benefits. Because Ronald and Noleen attempted to transfer their rights to future benefits in violation of 42 U.S.C. § 407(a), the agreement was invalid and neither this court nor the district court may order its enforcement.

Moreover, the fact that the property settlement agreement was entered into voluntarily by the parties is without relevance. As another court correctly ruled, "Congress' clear and stringent interpretation of the prohibition on transfer or assignment of benefits in section 207(b) . . . compels us to strictly interpret that clause to prohibit voluntary as well as involuntary transfers or assignments." Ellender v. Schweiker, 575 F.Supp. 590,

vorce. The anti-assignment statute in that case, 45 U.S.C. § 231m(a), is virtually identical to the Social Security Act's anti-assignment clause, 42 U.S.C. § 407(a). That statute provides: [N]otwithstanding any other law of the United States, or of any State, territory, or the District of Columbia, no annuity or supplemental annuity shall be assignable or be subject to any tax or to garnishment, attachment, or to other legal process under any circumstances whatsoever, nor shall the payment thereof be anticipated. 45 U.S.C. § 231m(a).

599 (S.D.N.Y.1983), appeal dismissed, 781 F.2d 314 (2d Cir.1986). If voluntary assignments and transfers of future benefits were allowed, the "security" aspect of the social security program would frequently be jeopardized. Moreover, as discussed above, the agreement in this case is prohibited by federal statute.

Even if the benefits were received by Ronald and directly deposited in his account, the court is not empowered to compel Ronald to pay those benefits to Noleen. "It is clear from the U.S. Supreme Court's opinion in Philpott v. Essex County Welfare Board, ... that if a bank account contains social security funds, the funds are exempt from legal process." Hatfield v. Cristopher, 841 S.W.2d 761, 767 (Mo.App.Ct.1992).

Noleen cites Owens v. Owens, 591 S.W.2d 57 (Mo.App.Ct.1980), in support of her position that the court can compel Ronald to transfer one-half of his social security benefits to Noleen once they are paid to Ronald. Owens held that "once social security funds have been paid to the recipient, the funds are his personal property and no longer exempt from execution on the sole ground that the government was the source of those payments." Id. at 58. The Owens case was followed in Fraser v. Deppe, 770 S.W.2d 479 (Mo.App.Ct.1989).

However, in Collins, Webster and Rouse v. Coleman, 776 S.W.2d 930 (Mo.App.Ct.1989), without overruling either Owens or Fraser, the same court held that social security benefits deposited in a bank account were exempt from process by a creditor under Philpott. The court held that Philpott was controlling and "was apparently not considered in Owens, nor cited in Fraser ... which follows Owens." Thus, Noleen's reliance on Owens is unavailing. In any event, we agree with Hatfield's interpretation of Philpott, concluding that if a bank account contains social security funds, the funds are exempt from legal process. Hatfield, 841 S.W.2d at 767.

In view of our ruling that the contested paragraph of the property settlement agreement was neither enforceable nor properly incorporated into the divorce decree, we need not consider Ronald's contention that the district court improperly interpreted the agreement.

Finally, Ronald notes that paragraph 8(D) of the agreement provides for an award of reasonable attorney's fees and costs to the prevailing party in an action that challenges or seeks to enforce the property settlement agreement. The district court awarded attorney's fees and costs to Noleen as the prevailing party. However, as a result of our reversal of the order entered by the district court, that award will have to be vacated.

CONCLUSION

Under 42 U.S.C. § 407(a), the district court was without jurisdiction to enforce an award of Ronald's social security benefits to Noleen pursuant to paragraph 4(E) of the property settlement agreement. Although the agreement was the product of the voluntary negotiations of the parties, the enforcement of the contested paragraph is nevertheless prohibited by the federal statute.

For the reasons expressed above, we reverse the order entered below, including the district court's ruling with regard to the property settlement agreement, vacate the award of attorney's fees and costs to Noleen, and remand this matter to the district court with instructions to reconsider the property distribution to the parties, and the issue of attorney's fees and costs.

NOTE

The decision illustrates the fact that state courts may not treat federal benefits as divisible marital property. Previously we have seen restrictions on state power to divide property in association with ERISA-protected pensions (Boggs v. Boggs), and with military retirement pay elected to be taken as disability in association with Uniformed Services Former Spouses' Protection Act (Mansell v. Mansell). The Maine Supreme Judicial Court, while not dividing Social Security benefits themselves, did anticipate the economic worth of the benefits that were earned during the marriage and allowed this to be a factor in dividing the couple's other existing marital property. Depot v. Depot, 893 A.2d 995 (Me. 2006).

H. TAX ISSUES AND INCIDENTS

The Deficit Reduction Act of 1984 made some highly significant changes in Internal Revenue Code provisions dealing with the tax implications of divorce. Prior tax law will, of course, continue to have significance for many years to come. This factor and the complexity of some of the new provisions make it important for domestic relations practitioners to have a basic grounding in tax law or to be willing to associate a tax specialist in many instances.

As anticipated, the rule of United States v. Davis, 370 U.S. 65, 82 S.Ct. 1190, 8 L.Ed.2d 335 (1962) that gain or loss was recognized upon transfer of property between spouses for release of marital claims, was repealed except in the case of a nonresident alien transferor. Internal Revenue Code § 1041 now provides that no gain or loss will be recognized on property transferred between spouses or former spouses if the transfer is incident to divorce. A transfer between spouses (or former spouses) will be treated like a gift in that the transferee's basis in the property will be the adjusted basis of the transferor.

Less expected was the 1984 Act's overruling of Commissioner v. Lester, 366 U.S. 299, 81 S.Ct. 1343, 6 L.Ed.2d 306 (1961), which held that undifferentiated alimony and child support might qualify in its entirety for the treatment now afforded only alimony or maintenance. Even more surprising was the inclusion of new provisions designed to prevent "front-end loading" of alimony payments. The special set of recapture rules designed for that goal may have special impact on what had been a trend toward rehabilitative alimony, though a further revision in 1986 may lessen this. Other changes include liberalizing the "innocent spouse" rule, more flexible child dependency provisions, and new rules for alimony trusts.

The new alimony rules were intended to assimilate qualifying (i.e., taxable) payments to payments that were thought to resemble support or maintenance payments under local substantive law. Thus, for example, qualifying payments must terminate on the death of the payee (who no longer needs support). However, recent developments in the substantive law of support and its relationship to determination of marital property rights raise important questions about the relevance of any concept of support to the tax incidents. For example, it can be questioned whether the conditions imposed on taxable alimony accurately reflect state law concepts of support or maintenance? Or whether these conditions appropriate in defining the tax consequences of post-divorce payments?

One way of thinking about such questions is to consider all economic resources of a married couple as resources available to fund the needs of a divided household after divorce, just as they were available to the household before divorce. These resources include traditional types of "property"—stocks and bonds, personal effects, automobiles, the personal residence—as well as newer but equally important intangible assets, such as interests in retirement plans. Also included are the earning capacity of both spouses, a resource which has been discussed in some recent literature as analytically equivalent to more traditional kinds of capital—that is to say, as human capital. The rules tend to treat this form of "capital" differently, with payments out of future income governed by maintenance or alimony concepts, but the effect of these rules is to give the economically disadvantaged spouse a share in the future earning capacity of the other spouse when there is insufficient traditional "property" in the marital "community" to meet his or her needs (or rights). This perspective extends the partnership analysis to include rights to future, as yet unearned, income.

The amendments repealing the *Lester* rule governing the taxability of child support payments were adopted because of the view held by some that support obligations are personal matters which should not be deductible. In particular, child support is not deductible under other circumstances (e.g., when paid by an unmarried parent to support his illegitimate child), and so should not be deductible in divorce. One can take issue with this view. Both parents are obligated to support their child; they can decide as between themselves how that burden should be allocated. Presumably, they can also decide who should control the spending of support money, and if so, which one should bear the tax cost. The *Lester* rule, by permitting the discretionary allocation of the tax burden on support payments between two parents, recognized the flexibility given to parents (or to the courts if the parents were unwilling or unable to reach voluntary agreement) to make these allocations. When family support payments are spent within the household of receipt (the custodial parent's household), the tax cost of earning those payments might appropriately be determined by the tax status of that household, rather than the household of the payor. From this perspective, the issue is not the deductibility *vel non* of child support, but rather which parent should bear the tax and whether the law should permit them to allocate it between themselves.

The Tax Reform Act of 1986 revised the front-end loading rules of § 71(f). Under the earlier version of the statute a six year period was required and the recapture determination applied to alimony or separate maintenance payments in excess of $10,000 during any calendar year. These provisions were criticized because of their possible effect on providing for rehabilitative alimony.

Finally, on January 18, 2000, the Internal Revenue Service issued Revenue Procedure 2000–15, providing guidelines for divorced and separated spouses to seek "equitable relief" when one spouse did not know of tax problems occasioned by the other spouse. The Ruling also allows for equitable relief if payment would cause undue hardship and provides a list of seven factors which the Internal Revenue Service will consider. *See* IRS Procedure, 26 CFR 601.105: Examination of Returns and Claims for Determination of Correct Tax Liability (2000). *But see* Hegg v. Internal Revenue Service, 28 P.3d 1004 (Idaho 2001), holding that community assets may be reached to satisfy a debt incurred through a spouse's fraud even if his or her spouse is completely innocent.

A course in family law does not provide time for detailed coverage of taxation but at least these basic rules and issues need to be understood if only to alert practitioners about the need to seek advice from a tax expert, in some instances. Selected, important provisions from the Internal Revenue Code follow.

INTERNAL REVENUE CODE (2000)

§ 71. Alimony and Separate Maintenance Payments

(a) General Rule.—Gross income includes amounts received as alimony or separate maintenance payments.

(b) Alimony or Separate Maintenance Payments Defined.—For purposes of this section—

(1) In General.—The term "alimony or separate maintenance payment" means any payment in cash if—

(A) such payment is received by (or on behalf of) a spouse under a divorce or separation instrument,

(B) the divorce or separation instrument does not designate such payment as a payment which is not includible in gross income under this section and not allowable as a deduction under section 215,

(C) in the case of an individual legally separated from his spouse under a decree of divorce or of separate maintenance, the payee spouse and the payor spouse are not members of the same household at the time such payment is made, and

(D) there is no liability to make any such payment for any period after the death of the payee spouse and there is no liability to make any payment as a substitute for such payments after the death of the payee spouse.

(2) Divorce or Separation Instrument.—The term "divorce or separation instrument" means—

(A) a decree of divorce or separate maintenance or a written instrument incident to such a decree,

(B) a written separation agreement, or

(C) a decree (not described in subparagraph (A)) requiring a spouse to make payments for the support or maintenance of the other spouse.

(c) Payments to Support Children.—

(1) In General.—Subsection (a) shall not apply to that part of any payment which the terms of the divorce or separation instrument fix (in terms of an amount of money or a part of the payment) as a sum which is payable for the support of children of the payor spouse.

(2) Treatment of Certain Reductions Related to Contingencies Involving Child.—For purposes of paragraph (1), if any amount specified in the instrument will be reduced—

(A) on the happening of a contingency specified in the instrument relating to a child (such as attaining a specified age, marrying, dying, leaving school, or a similar contingency), or

(B) at a time which can clearly be associated with a contingency of a kind specified in subparagraph (A), an amount equal to the amount of such reduction will be treated as an amount fixed as payable for the support of children of the payor spouse.

(3) Special Rule Where Payment Is Less Than Amount Specified in Instrument.—For of this subsection, if any payment is less than the amount specified in the instrument, then so much of such payment as does not exceed the sum payable for support shall be considered a payment for such support.

(d) Spouse.—For purposes of this section, the term "spouse" includes a former spouse.

(e) Exception for Joint Returns.—This section and section 215 shall not apply if the spouses make a joint return with each other.

[Subsection (f) provides the formula to be used in recomputation in cases of excess front-loading of alimony payments.]

(A) Where Payment Ceases by Reason of Death or Remarriage.—Paragraph (1) shall not apply if—

(i) either spouse dies before the close of the 3rd post-separation year, or the payee spouse remarries before the close of the 3rd post-separation year, and

(ii) the alimony or separate maintenance payments cease by reason of such death or remarriage.

(B) Support Payments.—For purposes of this subsection, the term "alimony or separate maintenance payment" shall not include any payment received under a decree described in subsection (b)(2)(C).

(C) Fluctuating Payments not Within Control of Payor Spouse.— For purposes of this subsection, the term "alimony or separate maintenance payment" shall not include any payment to the extent it is made pursuant to a continuing liability (over a period of not less than 3 years) to pay a fixed portion or portions of the income from a business or property or from compensation for employment or self-employment.

(6) Post–Separation Years.—For purposes of this subsection, the term "1st years" means the 1st calendar year in which the payor spouse paid to the payee spouse alimony or separate maintenance payments to which this section applies. The 2nd and 3rd post-separation years shall be the 1st and 2nd succeeding calendar years, respectively.

§ 215. Alimony, etc., payments

(a) General Rule.—In the case of an individual, there shall be allowed as a deduction an amount equal to the alimony or separate maintenance payments paid during such individual's taxable year.

(b) Alimony or Separate Maintenance Payments Defined.—For purposes of this section, the term "alimony or separate maintenance payment" means any alimony or separate maintenance payment (as defined in section 71(b)) which is includible in the gross income of the recipient under section 71.

(c) Requirement of Identification Number.—The Secretary may prescribe regulations under which—

(1) any individual receiving alimony or separate maintenance payments is required to furnish such individual's taxpayer identification number to the individual making such payments, and

(2) the individual making such payments is required to include such taxpayer identification number on such individual's return for the taxable year in which such payments are made.

(d) Coordination With Section 682.—No deduction shall be allowed under this section with respect to any payment if, by reason of section 682 (relating to income of alimony trusts), the amount thereof is not includible in such individual's gross income.

§ 682. Income of an estate or trust in case of divorce, etc.

(a) Inclusion in Gross Income of Wife.—There shall be included in the gross income of a wife who is divorced or legally separated under a decree of divorce or of separate maintenance (or who is separated from her husband under a written separation agreement) the amount of the income of any trust which such wife is entitled to receive and which, except for this section, would be includible in the gross income of her husband, and such amount shall not, despite any other provision of this subtitle, be includible in the gross income of such husband. This subsection shall not apply to that part of any such income of the trust which the terms of the decree, written separation agreement, or trust instrument fix, in terms of an amount of money or a portion of such income, as a sum which is payable for the support of minor children of such husband. In case such income is less than the amount specified in the decree, agreement, or instrument, for the purpose of applying the preceding sentence, such income, to the extent of such sum payable for such support, shall be considered a payment for such support.

(b) Wife Considered a Beneficiary.—For purposes of computing the taxable income of the estate or trust and the taxable income of a wife to whom subsection (a) applies, such wife shall be considered as the beneficiary specified in this part.

§ 1041. Transfers of property between spouses or incident to divorce

(a) General Rule.—No gain or loss shall be recognized on a transfer of property from an individual to (or in trust for the benefit of)—

(1) a spouse, or

(2) a former spouse, but only if the transfer is incident to the divorce.

(b) Transfer Treated as Gift; Transferee Has Transferor's Basis.—In the case of any transfer of property described in subsection (a)—

(1) for purposes of this subtitle, the property shall be treated as acquired by the transferee by gift, and

(2) the basis of the transferee in the property shall be the adjusted basis of the transferor.

(c) Incident to Divorce.—For purposes of subsection (a)(2), a transfer of property is incident to the divorce if such transfer—

(1) occurs within 1 year after the date on which the marriage ceases, or

(2) is related to the cessation of the marriage.

(d) Special Rule Where Spouse Is Nonresident Alien.—Subsection (a) shall not apply if the spouse (or former spouse) of the individual making the transfer is a nonresident alien.

(e) Transfers in Trust Where Liability Exceeds Basis.—Subsection (a) shall not apply to the transfer of property in trust to the extent that—

(1) the sum of the amount of the liabilities assumed, plus the amount of the liabilities to which the property is subject, exceeds

(2) the total of the adjusted basis of the property transferred.

Proper adjustment shall be made under subsection (b) in the basis of the transferee in such property to take into account gain recognized by reason of the preceding sentence.

I. DISCHARGE IN BANKRUPTCY

In the BANKRUPTCY ACT, § 523 of 11 U.S.C.A.(West 2006), provides:

(a) A discharge under section 727, 1141, 1228(a), 1228(b), or 1328(b) of this title does not discharge an individual debtor from any debt–

(1) for a tax or a customs duty–

(A) of the kind and for the periods specified in section 507(a)(3) or 507(a)(8) of this title, whether or not a claim for such tax was filed or allowed;

(B) with respect to which a return, or equivalent report or notice, if required–

(i) was not filed or given; or

was filed or given after the date on which such return, report, or notice was last due, under applicable law or under any extension, and after two years before the date of the filing of the petition; or

(C) with respect to which the debtor made a fraudulent return or willfully attempted in any manner to evade or defeat such tax;

(2) for money, property, services, or an extension, renewal, or refinancing of credit, to the extent obtained by–

false pretenses, a false representation, or actual fraud, other than a statement respecting the debtor's or an insider's financial condition;

(B) use of a statement in writing–

(i) that is materially false;

(ii) respecting the debtor's or an insider's financial condition;

(iii) on which the creditor to whom the debtor is liable for such money, property, services, or credit reasonably relied; and

(iv) that the debtor caused to be made or published with intent to deceive; or

(C)(i) for purposes of subparagraph (A)—

(I) consumer debts owed to a single creditor and aggregating more than $500 for luxury goods or services incurred by an individual debtor on or within 90 days before the order for relief under this title are presumed to be nondischargeable; and

(II) cash advances aggregating more than $750 that are extensions of consumer credit under an open end credit plan obtained by an individual debtor on or within 70 days before the order for relief under this title, are presumed to be nondischargeable; and

(ii) for purposes of this subparagraph–

(I) the terms "consumer", "credit", and "open end credit plan" have the same meanings as in section 103 of the Truth in Lending Act; and

(II) the term "luxury goods or services" does not include goods or services reasonably necessary for the support or maintenance of the debtor or a dependent of the debtor.

(3) neither listed nor scheduled under section 521(1) of this title, with the name, if known to the debtor, of the creditor to whom such debt is owed, in time to permit–

(A) if such debt is not of a kind specified in paragraph (2), (4), or (6) of this subsection, timely filing of a proof of claim, unless such creditor had notice or actual knowledge of the case in time for such timely filing; or

(B) if such debt is of a kind specified in paragraph (2), (4), or (6) of this subsection, timely filing of a proof of claim and timely request for a determination of dischargeability of such debt under one of such paragraphs, unless such creditor had notice or actual knowledge of the case in time for such timely filing and request;

(4) for fraud or defalcation while acting in a fiduciary capacity, embezzlement, or larceny;

(5) for a domestic support obligation;

(6) for willful and malicious injury by the debtor to another entity or to the property of another entity;

(7) to the extent such debt is for a fine, penalty, or forfeiture payable to and for the benefit of a governmental unit, and is not compensation for actual pecuniary loss, other than a tax penalty–

(A) relating to a tax of a kind not specified in paragraph (1) of this subsection; or

(B) imposed with respect to a transaction or event that occurred before three years before the date of the filing of the petition;

(8) unless excepting such debt from discharge under this paragraph would impose an undue hardship on the debtor and the debtor's dependents, for–

(A)(i) an educational benefit overpayment or loan made, insured, or guaranteed by a governmental unit, or made under any program funded in whole or in part by a governmental unit or nonprofit institution; or

(ii) an obligation to repay funds received as an educational benefit, scholarship, or stipend; or

(B) any other educational loan that is a qualified education loan, as defined in section 221(d)(1) of the Internal Revenue Code of 1986, incurred by a debtor who is an individual;

(9) for death or personal injury caused by the debtor's operation of a motor vehicle, vessel, or aircraft if such operation was unlawful because the debtor was intoxicated from using alcohol, a drug, or another substance;

(10) that was or could have been listed or scheduled by the debtor in a prior case concerning the debtor under this title or under the Bankruptcy Act in which the debtor waived discharge, or was denied a discharge under section 727(a)(2), (3), (4), (5), (6), or (7) of this title, or under section 14c(1), (2), (3), (4), (6), or (7) of such Act;

(11) provided in any final judgment, unreviewable order, or consent order or decree entered in any court of the United States or of any State, issued by a Federal depository institutions regulatory agency, or contained in any settlement agreement entered into by the debtor, arising from any act of fraud or defalcation while acting in a fiduciary capacity committed with respect to any depository institution or insured credit union;

(12) for malicious or reckless failure to fulfill any commitment by the debtor to a Federal depository institutions regulatory agency to maintain the capital of an insured depository institution, except that this paragraph shall not extend any such commitment which would otherwise be terminated due to any act of such agency; or

(13) for any payment of an order of restitution issued under title 18, United States Code;

(14) incurred to pay a tax to the United States that would be nondischargeable pursuant to paragraph (1);

(14A) incurred to pay a tax to a governmental unit, other than the United States, that would be nondischargeable under paragraph (1);

(14B) incurred to pay fines or penalties imposed under Federal election law;

(15) to a spouse, former spouse, or child of the debtor and not of the kind described in paragraph (5) that is incurred by the debtor in the course of a divorce or separation or in connection with a separation agreement, divorce decree or other order of a court of record, or a determination made in accordance with State or territorial law by a governmental unit;

(16) for a fee or assessment that becomes due and payable after the order for relief to a membership association with respect to the debtor's interest in a unit that has condominium ownership, in a share of a cooperative corporation, or a lot in a homeowners association, for as long as the debtor or the trustee has a legal, equitable, or possessory ownership interest in such unit, such corporation, or such lot, but nothing in this paragraph shall except from discharge the debt of a debtor for a membership association fee or assessment for a period arising before entry of the order for relief in a pending or subsequent bankruptcy case;

(17) for a fee imposed on a prisoner by any court for the filing of a case, motion, complaint, or appeal, or for other costs and expenses assessed with respect to such filing, regardless of an assertion of poverty by the debtor under subsection (b) or (f)(2) of section 1915 of title 28 (or a similar non-Federal law), or the debtor's status as a prisoner, as defined in section 1915(h) of title 28 (or a similar non-Federal law);

(18) owed to a pension, profit-sharing, stock bonus, or other plan established under section 401, 403, 408, 408A, 414, 457, or 501(c) of the Internal Revenue Code of 1986, under—

(A) a loan permitted under section 408(b)(1) of the Employee Retirement Income Security Act of 1974, or subject to section 72(p) of the Internal Revenue Code of 1986; or

(B) a loan from a thrift savings plan permitted under subchapter III of chapter 84 of title 5, that satisfies the requirements of section 8433(g) of such title;

but nothing in this paragraph may be construed to provide that any loan made under a governmental plan under section 414(d), or a contract or account under section 403(b), of the Internal Revenue Code of 1986 constitutes a claim or a debt under this title; or

(19) that—

(A) is for—

(i) the violation of any of the Federal securities laws (as that term is defined in section 3(a)(47) of the Securities Exchange Act of 1934), any of the State securities laws, or any regulation or order issued under such Federal or State securities laws; or

(ii) common law fraud, deceit, or manipulation in connection with the purchase or sale of any security; and

(B) results, before, on, or after the date on which the petition was filed, from—

(i) any judgment, order, consent order, or decree entered in any Federal or State judicial or administrative proceeding;

(ii) any settlement agreement entered into by the debtor; or

(iii) any court or administrative order for any damages, fine, penalty, citation, restitutionary payment, disgorgement payment, attorney fee, cost, or other payment owed by the debtor.

For purposes of this subsection, the term "return" means a return that satisfies the requirements of applicable nonbankruptcy law (including applicable filing requirements). Such term includes a return prepared pursuant to section 6020(a) of the Internal Revenue Code of 1986, or similar State or local law, or a written stipulation to a judgment or a final order entered by a nonbankruptcy tribunal, but does not include a return made pursuant to section 6020(b) of the Internal Revenue Code of 1986, or a similar State or local law.

NOTE

The non-dischargeability of spousal support in a bankruptcy proceeding was the issue raised in *In re* Duffy, 331 B.R. 137 (S.D.N.Y. 2005). In this case the husband and wife had been married for ten years and had two children. The husband was a successful physician when the wife left him for another man and filed for divorce. Upon divorce, the court ordered the husband to pay the wife $2,000 in monthly spousal support for a term of ten years. The court's order specifically stated that the support received by the former wife was non-dischargeable in bankruptcy and was due irrespective of the wife's remarriage of cohabitation. For several years, the husband paid the monthly support but then lost his medical license because of allegations of professional misconduct. He suffered severe depression and was unable to find new employment n spite of good faith efforts, resulting in the deletion of his savings and assets. The husband's father paid part of the amount due the wife, keeping him from debtors' prison, but when the remainder was due the husband knew he could not pay and filed under Chapter 7 of the Bankruptcy Code for discharge of his debt to his wife. The court, referencing the Bankruptcy Code, distinguished between alimony and maintenance payments (Section 523(a)(5)) and equitable division of marital property (Section 523(a)(15)). The former is not dischargeable in bankruptcy, but the latter may be. Furthermore, the determination of what constitutes alimony, maintenance, or support will be determined under bankruptcy laws, not state laws. In looking to the "substance, and not just to the form" of the payments, the court ruled that the payments were termed spousal support to make them deductible by the husband. But the substance of the arrangement was that the payments were in fact a division of the medical practice of the physician-husband, an equitable asset. The court then ruled that the debt may be discharged in bankruptcy and that the good faith of the husband and his lack of financial resources justify discharge of the remaining debt to the former wife.

J. Special Problems of Enforcement

Hicks on Behalf of Feiock v. Feiock

Supreme Court of the United States, 1988.
485 U.S. 624, 108 S.Ct. 1423, 99 L.Ed.2d 721.

■ Justice White delivered the opinion of the Court.

. . .

On January 19, 1976, a California state court entered an order requiring respondent, Phillip Feiock, to begin making monthly payments to his ex-wife for the support of their three children. Over the next six years, respondent only sporadically complied with the order, and by December 1982 he had discontinued paying child support altogether. His ex-wife sought to enforce the support orders. On June 22, 1984, a hearing was held in California state court on her petition for ongoing support payments and for payment of the arrearage due her. The court examined respondent's financial situation and ordered him to begin paying $150 per month commencing on July 1, 1984. The court reserved jurisdiction over the matter for the purpose of determining the arrearages and reviewing respondent's financial condition.

Respondent apparently made two monthly payments but paid nothing for the next nine months. He was then served with an order to show cause why he should not be held in contempt on nine counts of failure to make the monthly payments ordered by the court. At a hearing on August 9, 1985, petitioner made out a *prima facie* case of contempt against respondent by establishing the existence of a valid court order, respondent's knowledge of the order, and respondent's failure to comply with the order. Respondent defended by arguing that he was unable to pay support during the months in question. This argument was partially successful, but respondent was adjudged to be in contempt on five of the nine counts. He was sentenced to five days in jail on each count, to be served consecutively, for a total of 25 days. This sentence was suspended, however, and respondent was placed on probation for three years. As one of the conditions of his probation, he was ordered once again to make support payments of $150 per month. As another condition of his probation, he was ordered, starting the following month, to begin repaying $50 per month on his accumulated arrearage, which was determined to total $1650.

At the hearing, respondent had objected to the application of Cal.Civ. Proc.Code Ann. § 1209.5 (1982) against him, claiming that it was unconstitutional under the Due Process Clause of the Federal Constitution because it shifts to the defendant the burden of proving inability to comply with the order, which is an element of the crime of contempt.[1] This objection was rejected, and he renewed it on appeal. The intermediate state appellate court agreed with respondent and annulled the contempt order, ruling that the state statute purports to impose "a mandatory presumption compelling a conclusion of guilt without independent proof of an ability to pay," and is therefore unconstitutional because "the mandatory nature of the presumption lessens the prosecution's burden of proof." 180 Cal.App.3d 649, 654, 225 Cal.Rptr. 748, 751 (1986).[2] In light of its holding that the statute as previously interpreted was unconstitutional, the court went on to adopt a different interpretation of that statute to govern future proceedings: "For future guidance, however, we determine the statute in question should be construed as authorizing a permissive inference, but not a mandatory presumption." The court explicitly considered this reinterpretation of the statute to be an exercise of its "obligation to interpret the statute to

1. California Civ.Proc.Code Ann. § 1209.5 (1982) states that "[w]hen a court of competent jurisdiction makes an order compelling a parent to furnish support ... for his child, proof that ... the parent was present in court at the time the order was pronounced and proof of noncompliance therewith shall be prima facie evidence of a contempt of court."

2. Although the court mentioned one state case among the cases it cited in support of this proposition, the court clearly rested on federal constitutional grounds as articulated in this Court's decisions, as did the other state case it cited.

preserve its constitutionality whenever possible." The California Supreme Court denied review, but we granted certiorari.

Three issues must be decided to resolve this case. First is whether the ability to comply with a court order constitutes an element of the offense of contempt or, instead, inability to comply is an affirmative defense to that charge. Second is whether § 1209.5 requires the alleged contemnor to shoulder the burden of persuasion or merely the burden of production in attempting to establish his inability to comply with the order. Third is whether this contempt proceeding was a criminal proceeding or a civil proceeding, i.e., whether the relief imposed upon respondent was criminal or civil in nature.

Petitioner argues that the state appellate court erred in its determinations on the first two points of state law. . . . Although petitioner marshals a number of sources in support of the contention that the state appellate court misapplied state law on these two points, the California Supreme Court denied review of this case and we are not free in this situation to overturn the state court's conclusions of state law.

The third issue, however, is a different matter: the argument is not merely that the state court misapplied state law, but that the characterization of this proceeding and the relief given as civil or criminal in nature, for purposes of determining the proper applicability of federal constitutional protections, raises a question of federal law rather than state law. This proposition is correct as stated. The fact that this proceeding and the resultant relief were judged to be criminal in nature as a matter of state law is thus not determinative of this issue, and the state appellate court erred insofar as it sustained respondent's challenge to the statute under the Due Process Clause simply because it concluded that this contempt proceeding is "quasi-criminal" as a matter of California law.

The question of how a court determines whether to classify the relief imposed in a given proceeding as civil or criminal in nature, for the purposes of applying the Due Process Clause and other provisions of the Constitution, is one of long standing, and its principles have been settled at least in their broad outlines for many decades. When a State's proceedings are involved, state law provides strong guidance about whether or not the State is exercising its authority "in a nonpunitive, noncriminal manner," and one who challenges the State's classification of the relief imposed as "civil" or "criminal" may be required to show "the clearest proof" that it is not correct as a matter of federal law. Nonetheless, if such a challenge is substantiated, then the labels affixed either to the proceeding or to the relief imposed under state law are not controlling and will not be allowed to defeat the applicable protections of federal constitutional law. This is particularly so in the codified laws of contempt, where the "civil" and "criminal" labels of the law have become increasingly blurred.[4]

---

4. California is a good example of this modern development, for although it defines civil and criminal contempts in separate stat- utes, compare Cal.Civ.Proc.Code Ann. § 1209 (Supp.1988) with Cal.Penal Code Ann. § 166 (1970), it has merged the two kinds of pro-

Instead, the critical features are the substance of the proceeding and the character of the relief that the proceeding will afford. "If it is for civil contempt the punishment is remedial, and for the benefit of the complainant. But if it is for criminal contempt the sentence is punitive, to vindicate the authority of the court." Gompers v. Bucks Stove & Range Co., 221 U.S. 418, 441, 31 S.Ct. 492, 498, 55 L.Ed. 797 (1911). The character of the relief imposed is thus ascertainable by applying a few straightforward rules. If the relief provided is a sentence of imprisonment, it is remedial if "the defendant stands committed unless and until he performs the affirmative act required by the court's order," and is punitive if "the sentence is limited to imprisonment for a definite period." Id., at 442, 31 S.Ct. at 498. If the relief provided is a fine, it is remedial when it is paid to the complainant, and punitive when it is paid to the court, though a fine that would be payable to the court is also remedial when the defendant can avoid paying the fine simply by performing the affirmative act required by the court's order. These distinctions lead up to the fundamental proposition that criminal penalties may not be imposed on someone who has not been afforded the protections that the Constitution requires of such criminal proceedings, including the requirement that the offense be proved beyond a reasonable doubt.[5]

. . .

The distinction between relief that is civil in nature and relief that is criminal in nature has been repeated and followed in many cases. An unconditional penalty is criminal in nature because it is "solely and exclusively punitive in character." Penfield Co. v. SEC, 330 U.S. 585, 593, 67 S.Ct. 918, 922, 91 L.Ed. 1117 (1947). A conditional penalty, by contrast, is civil because it is specifically designed to compel the doing of some act. "One who is fined, unless by a day certain he [does the act ordered], has it in his power to avoid any penalty. And those who are imprisoned until they obey the order, 'carry the keys of their prison in their own pockets.'" Id., at 590, 67 S.Ct. at 921, quoting In re Nevitt, 117 F. 448, 461 (C.A.8 1902)....

Shillitani v. United States, 384 U.S. 364, 86 S.Ct. 1531, 16 L.Ed.2d 622 (1966), adheres to these same principles. There two men were adjudged guilty of contempt for refusing to obey a court order to testify under a grant of immunity. Both were sentenced to two years of imprisonment, with the proviso that if either answered the questions before his sentence ended, he would be released. The penalties were upheld because of their "conditional nature," even though the underlying proceeding lacked certain constitutional protections that are essential in criminal proceedings.

ceedings under the same procedural rules. See Cal.Civ.Proc.Code Ann. §§ 1209–1222 (1982 and Supp.1988).

5. We have recognized that certain specific constitutional protections, such as the right to trial by jury, are not applicable to those criminal contempts that can be classi-fied as petty offenses, as is true of other petty crimes as well. Bloom v. Illinois, 391 U.S. 194, 208–210, 88 S.Ct. 1477, 1485–1486, 20 L.Ed.2d 522 (1968). This is not true, however, of the proposition that guilt must be proved beyond a reasonable doubt. Id., at 205, 88 S.Ct. at 1484.

Any sentence "must be viewed as remedial," and hence civil in nature, "if the court conditions release upon the contemnor's willingness to [comply with the order]." By the same token, in a civil proceeding the court "may also impose a determinate sentence *which includes a purge clause.*" (emphasis added). "On the contrary, a criminal contempt proceeding would be characterized by the imposition of an unconditional sentence for punishment or deterrence."

In repeatedly stating and following the rules set out above, the Court has eschewed any alternative formulation that would make the classification of the relief imposed in a State's proceedings turn simply on what their underlying purposes are perceived to be. Although the purposes that lie behind particular kinds of relief are germane to understanding their character, this Court has never undertaken to psychoanalyze the subjective intent of a State's laws and its courts, not only because that effort would be unseemly and improper, but also because it would be misguided. In contempt cases, both civil and criminal relief have aspects that can be seen as either remedial or punitive or both: when a court imposes fines and punishments on a contemnor, it is not only vindicating its legal authority to enter the initial court order, but it also is seeking to give effect to the law's purpose of modifying the contemnor's behavior to conform to the terms required in the order. As was noted in *Gompers:*

"It is true that either form of [punishment] has also an incidental effect. For if the case is civil and the punishment is purely remedial, there is also a vindication of the court's authority. On the other hand, if the proceeding is for criminal contempt and the [punishment] is solely punitive, to vindicate the authority of the law, the complainant may also derive some incidental benefit from the fact that such punishment tends to prevent a repetition of the disobedience. But such indirect consequences will not change [punishment] which is merely coercive and remedial, into that which is solely punitive in character, or *vice versa.*" 221 U.S., at 443, 31 S.Ct. at 498.

For these reasons, this Court has judged that conclusions about the purposes for which relief is imposed are properly drawn from an examination of the character of the relief itself.

There is yet another reason why the overlapping purposes of civil and criminal contempt proceedings have prevented this Court from hinging the classification on this point. If the definition of these proceedings and their resultant relief as civil or criminal is made to depend on the federal courts' views about their underlying purposes, which indeed often are not clearly articulated in any event, then the States will be unable to ascertain with any degree of assurance how their proceedings will be understood as a matter of federal law. The consequences of any such shift in direction would be both serious and unfortunate. Of primary practical importance to the decision in this case is that the States should be given intelligible guidance about how, as a matter of federal constitutional law, they may lawfully employ presumptions and other procedures in their contempt proceedings. It is of great importance to the States that they be able to understand clearly and in advance the tools that are available to them in ensuring swift and certain compliance with valid court orders—not only orders commanding payment of child support, as in this case, but orders that command compliance in the more general area of domestic relations law, and in all other areas of the law as well.

The States have long been able to plan their own procedures around the traditional distinction between civil and criminal remedies. The abandonment of this clear dividing line in favor of a general assessment of the manifold and complex purposes that lie behind a court's action would create novel problems where now there are rarely any—novel problems that could infect many different areas of the law. And certainly the fact that a contemnor has his sentence suspended and is placed on probation cannot be decisive in defining the civil or criminal nature of the relief, for many convicted criminals are treated in exactly this manner for the purpose (among others) of influencing their behavior. What is true of the respondent in this case is also true of any such convicted criminal: as long as he meets the conditions of his informal probation, he will never enter the jail. Nonetheless, if the sentence is a determinate one, then the punishment is criminal in nature, and it may not be imposed unless federal constitutional protections are applied in the contempt proceeding.[8]

The proper classification of the relief imposed in respondent's contempt proceeding is dispositive of this case. As interpreted by the state court here, § 1209.5 requires respondent to carry the burden of persuasion on an element of the offense, by showing his inability to comply with the court's order to make the required payments. If applied in a criminal proceeding, such a statute would violate the Due Process Clause because it would undercut the State's burden to prove guilt beyond a reasonable doubt. If applied in a civil proceeding, however, this particular statute would be constitutionally valid, and respondent conceded as much at the argument.[9]

The state court found the contempt proceeding to be "quasi-criminal" in nature without discussing the point. There were strong indications that the proceeding was intended to be criminal in nature, such as the notice sent to respondent, which clearly labeled the proceeding as "criminal in nature," and the participation of the District Attorney in the case. Though

---

8. This does not even suggest, of course, that the State is unable to suspend the sentence imposed on either a criminal contemnor or a civil contemnor in favor of a term of informal probation. That action may be appropriate and even most desirable in a great many cases, especially when the order that has been disobeyed was one to pay a sum of money. This also accords with the repeated emphasis in our decisions that in wielding its contempt powers, a court "must exercise 'the least possible power adequate to the end proposed.'" Shillitani v. United

States, 384 U.S. 364, 371, 86 S.Ct. 1531, 1536, 16 L.Ed.2d 622 (1966), quoting Anderson v. Dunn, 6 Wheat. 204, 231 (1821).

9. Our precedents are clear, however, that punishment may not be imposed in a civil contempt proceeding when it is clearly established that the alleged contemnor is unable to comply with the terms of the order. United States v. Rylander, 460 U.S. 752, 757, 103 S.Ct. 1548, 1552, 75 L.Ed.2d 521 (1983); *Shillitani*, supra, at 371, *Oriel*, 278 U.S., at 366, 49 S.Ct. at 175.

significant, these facts are not dispositive of the issue before us, for if the trial court had imposed only civil coercive remedies, as surely it was authorized to do, then it would be improper to invalidate that result merely because the Due Process Clause, as applied in *criminal* proceedings, was not satisfied. It also bears emphasis that the purposes underlying this proceeding were wholly ambiguous. Respondent was charged with violating nine discrete prior court orders, and the proceeding may have been intended primarily to vindicate the court's authority in the face of his defiance. On the other hand, as often is true when court orders are violated, these charges were part of an ongoing battle to force respondent to conform his conduct to the terms of those orders, and of future orders as well.

Applying the traditional rules for classifying the relief imposed in a given proceeding requires the further resolution of one factual question about the nature of the relief in this case. Respondent was charged with nine separate counts of contempt, and was convicted on five of those counts, all of which arose from his failure to comply with orders to make payments in past months. He was sentenced to five days in jail on each of the five counts, for a total of 25 days, but his jail sentence was suspended and he was placed on probation for three years. If this were all, then the relief afforded would be criminal in nature.[11] But this is not all. One of the conditions of respondent's probation was that he begin making payments on his accumulated arrearage, and that he continue making these payments at the rate of $50 per month. At that rate, all of the arrearage would be paid before respondent completed his probation period. Not only did the order therefore contemplate that respondent would be required to purge himself of his past violations, but it expressly states that "[i]f any two payments are missed, whether consecutive or not, the entire balance shall become due and payable." What is unclear is whether the ultimate satisfaction of these accumulated prior payments would have purged the determinate sentence imposed on respondent. Since this aspect of the proceeding will vary as a factual matter from one case to another, depending on the precise disposition entered by the trial court, and since the trial court did not specify this aspect of its disposition in this case, it is not surprising that neither party was able to offer a satisfactory explanation of this point at

---

11. That a determinate sentence is suspended and the contemnor put on probation does not make the remedy civil in nature, for a suspended sentence, without more, remains a determinate sentence, and a fixed term of probation is itself a punishment that is criminal in nature. A suspended sentence with a term of probation is not equivalent to a conditional sentence that would allow the contemnor to avoid or purge these sanctions. A determinate term of probation puts the contemnor under numerous disabilities that he cannot escape by complying with the dictates of the prior orders, such as: any conditions of probation that the court judges to be reasonable and necessary may be imposed; the term of probation may be revoked and the original sentence (including incarceration) may be reimposed at any time for a variety of reasons without all the safeguards that are ordinarily afforded in criminal proceedings; and the contemnor's probationary status could affect other proceedings against him that may arise in the future (for example, this fact might influence the sentencing determination made in a criminal prosecution for some wholly independent offense).

argument. If the relief imposed here is in fact a determinate sentence with a purge clause, then it is civil in nature.

The state court did not pass on this issue because of its erroneous view that it was enough simply to aver that this proceeding is considered "quasi-criminal" as a matter of state law. And, as noted earlier, the court's view on this point, coupled with its view of the Federal Constitution, also led it to reinterpret the state statute, thus softening the impact of the presumption, in order to save its constitutionality. Yet the Due Process Clause does not necessarily prohibit the State from employing this presumption as it was construed by the state court, *if* respondent would purge his contempt judgment by paying off his arrearage. In these circumstances, the proper course for this Court is to vacate the judgment below and remand for further consideration of § 1209.5 free from the compulsion of an erroneous view of federal law. If on remand it is found that respondent would purge his sentence by paying his arrearage, then this proceeding is civil in nature and there was no need for the state court to reinterpret its statute to avoid conflict with the Due Process Clause.[13]

We therefore vacate the judgment below and remand for further proceedings consistent with this opinion.

■ Justice O'Connor, with whom The Chief Justice and Justice Scalia join, dissenting.

This case concerns a contempt proceeding against a parent who repeatedly failed to comply with a valid court order to make child support payments. In my view, the proceeding is civil as a matter of federal law. Therefore, the Due Process Clause of the Fourteenth Amendment does not prevent the trial court from applying a legislative presumption that the parent remained capable of complying with the order until the time of the contempt proceeding.

. . .

The California Court of Appeal has erected a substantial obstacle to the enforcement of child support orders. As petitioner vividly describes it, the judgment turns the child's support order into "a worthless piece of scrap." The judgment hampers the enforcement of support orders at a time when strengthened enforcement is needed. "The failure of enforcement efforts in this area has become a national scandal. In 1983, only half of custodial parents received the full amount of child support ordered; approximately 26% received some lesser amount, and 24% received nothing at

---

13. Even if this relief is judged on remand to be criminal in nature because it does not allow the contemnor to purge the judgment by satisfying the terms of the prior orders, this result does not impose any real handicap on the States in enforcing the terms of their orders, for it will be clear to the States that the presumption established by § 1209.5 can be imposed, consistent with the Due Process Clause, in any proceeding where the relief afforded is civil in nature as defined by this Court's precedents. In addition, the state courts remain free to decide for themselves the state law issues we have taken as having been resolved in this case by the court below, and to judge the lawfulness of statutes that impose similar presumptions under the provisions of their own state constitutions.

all." Brief for Women's Legal Defense Fund et al. as *Amici Curiae* 26 (footnote omitted). The facts of this case illustrate how easily a reluctant parent can evade a child support obligation. Congress recognized the serious problem of enforcement of child support orders when it enacted the Child Support Enforcement Amendments of 1984. The California legislature responded to the problem by enacting the presumption described in § 1209.5. Now, says petitioner, the California Court of Appeal has sabotaged the California legislature's effort.

Contempt proceedings often will be useless if the parent seeking enforcement of valid support orders must prove that the obligor can comply with the court order. The custodial parent will typically lack access to the financial and employment records needed to sustain the burden imposed by the decision below, especially where the noncustodial parent is self-employed, as is the case here. Serious consequences follow from the California Court of Appeal's decision to invalidate California's statutory presumption that a parent continues to be able to pay the child support previously determined to be within his or her means.

. . .

The linchpin of the Court of Appeal's opinion is its determination that the contempt proceeding against respondent was criminal in nature. . . .

The characterization of a state proceeding as civil or criminal for the purpose of applying the Due Process Clause of the Fourteenth Amendment is itself a question of federal law. The substance of particular contempt proceedings determines whether they are civil or criminal, regardless of the label attached by the court conducting the proceedings. Civil contempt proceedings are primarily coercive; criminal contempt proceedings are punitive. As the Court explained in *Gompers:* "The distinction between refusing to do an act commanded,—remedied by imprisonment until the party performs the required act; and doing an act forbidden,—punished by imprisonment for a definite term; is sound in principle, and generally, if not universally, affords a test by which to determine the character of the punishment." Failure to pay alimony is an example of the type of act cognizable in an action for civil contempt.

Whether a particular contempt proceeding is civil or criminal can be inferred from objective features of the proceeding and the sanction imposed. The most important indication is whether the judgment inures to the benefit of another party to the proceeding. A fine payable to the complaining party and proportioned to the complainant's loss is compensatory and civil. Because the compensatory purpose limits the amount of the fine, the contemnor is not exposed to a risk of punitive sanctions that would make criminal safeguards necessary. By contrast, a fixed fine payable to the court is punitive and criminal in character.

An analogous distinction can be drawn between types of sentences of incarceration. Commitment to jail or prison for a fixed term usually operates as a punitive sanction because it confers no advantage on the other party. But if a contemnor is incarcerated until he or she complies with a court order, the sanction is civil. Although the imprisonment does not compensate the adverse party directly, it is designed to obtain compliance with a court order made in that party's favor. . . .

Several peculiar features of California's contempt law make it difficult to determine whether the proceeding in this case was civil or criminal. All contempt proceedings in California courts are governed by the same procedural rules. Because state law provides that defendants in civil contempt proceedings are entitled to most of the protections guaranteed to ordinary criminal defendants, the California courts have held that civil contempt proceedings are quasi-criminal under state law. Therefore, indications that the California Superior Court conducted respondent's hearing as a criminal proceeding do not conclusively demonstrate for purposes of federal due process analysis that respondent was tried for criminal contempt.

Certain formal aspects of the proceeding below raise the possibility that it involved criminal contempt. The orders to show cause stated that "[a] contempt proceeding is criminal in nature" and that a violation would subject the respondent to "possible penalties." The orders advised respondent of his right to an attorney. During the hearing, the trial judge told respondent that he had a constitutional right not to testify. Finally, the judge imposed a determinate sentence of five days in jail for each count of contempt, to be served consecutively. See Cal.Civ.Proc. Code Ann. § 1218 (West 1982) (contempt may be punished by a fine not exceeding $500, or imprisonment not exceeding five days, or both); cf. Cal.Civ.Proc.Code Ann. § 1219 (West 1982) (contempt may be punished by imprisonment until an act is performed, if the contempt is the omission to perform the act).

Nevertheless, the substance of the proceeding below and the conditions on which the sentence was suspended reveal that the proceeding was civil in nature. Mrs. Feiock initiated the underlying action in order to obtain enforcement of the child support order for the benefit of the Feiock children. The California District Attorney conducted the case under a provision of the URESA that authorizes him to act on Mrs. Feiock's behalf. As the very caption of the case in this Court indicates, the District Attorney is acting on behalf of Mrs. Feiock, not as the representative of the State of California in a criminal prosecution. Both of the provisions of California's enactment of the URESA that authorize contempt proceedings appear in a chapter of the Code of Civil Procedure entitled "Civil Enforcement." It appears that most States enforce child and spousal support orders through civil proceedings like this one, in which the burden of persuasion is shifted to the defendant to show inability to comply. J. Atkinson, Modern Child Custody Practice 556 (1986); H. Krause, Child Support in America 65 (1981); Annot., 53 A.L.R.2d 591, 607–616 (1957 and Supp.1987).

These indications that the proceeding was civil are confirmed by the character of the sanction imposed on respondent. The California Superior Court sentenced respondent to a fixed term of 25 days in jail. Without more, this sanction would be punitive and appropriate for a criminal contempt. But the court suspended the determinate sentence and placed respondent on three years' informal probation on the conditions that he comply with the support order in the future and begin to pay on the arrearage that he had accumulated in the past. These special conditions aim exclusively at enforcing compliance with the existing child support order.

Our precedents indicate that such a conditional sentence is coercive rather than punitive. Thus in *Gompers,* we observed that civil contempt may be punished by an order that "the defendant stand committed *unless* and until he performs the affirmative act required by the court's order." 221 U.S., at 442, 31 S.Ct. at 498 (emphasis added). In *Shillitani,* we decided that civil contempt could be punished by a prison sentence fixed at two years if it included a proviso that the contemnor would be released as soon as he complied with the court order. 384 U.S., at 365, 86 S.Ct. at 1533. In this case, if respondent performs his obligations under the original court order, he can avoid going to jail at all. Like the sentence in *Shillitani,* respondent's prison sentence is coercive rather than punitive because it effectively "conditions release upon the contemnor's willingness to [comply]." Id., at 370, 86 S.Ct. at 1535.

It is true that the order imposing the sentence does not expressly provide that, *if* respondent is someday incarcerated and *if* he subsequently complies, he will be released immediately. The parties disagree about what will happen if this contingency arises, and there is no need to address today the question of whether the failure to grant immediate release would render the sanction criminal. In the case before us respondent carries something even better than the "keys to the prison" in his own pocket: as long as he meets the conditions of his informal probation, he will never enter the jail.

It is critical that the only conditions placed on respondent's probation, apart from the requirement that he conduct himself generally in accordance with the law, are that he cure his past failures to comply with the support order and that he continue to comply in the future.* The sanction imposed on respondent is unlike ordinary criminal probation because it is collateral to a civil proceeding initiated by a private party, and respondent's sentence is suspended on the condition that he comply with a court order entered for the benefit of that party. This distinguishes respondent's sentence from suspended criminal sentences imposed outside the contempt context.

This Court traditionally has inquired into the substance of contempt proceedings to determine whether they are civil or criminal, paying particu-

---

* Unlike the Court, I find no ambiguity in the court's sentencing order that hints that respondent can purge his jail sentence by paying off the arrearage alone. The sentencing order suspends execution of the jail sentence and places respondent on probation on the conditions that he *both* make future support payments at $150 per month *and* pay $50 per month on the arrearage. If respon-dent pays off the arrearage before the end of his probation period, but then fails to make a current support payment, the suspension will be revoked and he will go to jail. See People v. Chagolla, 151 Cal.App.3d 1045, 199 Cal. Rptr. 181 (1984) (explaining that if a court suspends a sentence on conditions, and any condition is violated, the court *must* reinstate the original sentence).

lar attention to whether the sanction imposed will benefit another party to the proceeding. In this case, the California Superior Court suspended respondent's sentence on the condition that he bring himself into compliance with a court order providing support for his children, represented in the proceeding by petitioner. I conclude that the proceeding in this case should be characterized as one for civil contempt, and I would reverse the judgment below.

NOTE

After the case was remanded, the California Court of Appeal held that the proceedings against the father were criminal in nature but that the statute did not create a mandatory presumption of ability to pay but rather made ability to pay an affirmative defense in a contempt proceeding. In re Feiock, 215 Cal.App.3d 141, 263 Cal.Rptr. 437 (1989). The court said:

> Court decisions have long upheld the constitutionality of legislation making issues such as inability to pay matters of defense. As noted in Martin v. Ohio [480 U.S. 228, 235], "[T]he common law rule was that affirmative defenses, . . ., were matters for the defendant to prove. 'This was the rule when the Fifth Amendment was adopted, and it was the American rule when the Fourteenth Amendment was ratified.'" Thus, there is no constitutional impediment to making inability to pay an affirmative defense, at least if there is some rational basis for doing so.

> Common sense dictates that the contemnor raise inability to pay. The contemnor is the person in the best position to know whether inability to pay is even a consideration in the proceeding and also has the best access to evidence on the issue, particularly in cases of self-employment. Considerations of policy and convenience have led courts to sanction placement of the burden of establishing a defense on defendants under similar circumstances.

> Making inability to pay a matter of defense does not place too harsh a burden on the contemnor. Since inability to pay goes to the heart of the contempt, the contemnor's task is merely to raise the issue of his ability to pay. The petitioner's burden then remains to prove the contempt beyond a reasonable doubt, including ability to pay. (People v. Figueroa (1986) 41 Cal.3d 714, 721, 224 Cal.Rptr. 719, 715 P.2d 680; . . .) It also eliminates the district attorney's concern that proof of the contempt would be unreasonably difficult if ability to pay were an element, yet minimizes the prospect that a truly indigent contemnor will end up in what is tantamount to debtor's prison.

Federal legislation requires that one state enforce the support orders of another state so long as the support order is consistent with due process of law. The legislation was enacted in 1994, two years after the introduction of the Uniform Interstate Family Support Act, but prior to the federal requirement that every state adopt the UIFSA. Collection for child support has increased due to federal efforts and to concomitant efforts to strengthen interstate collection. For an example of state enforcement using the

FFCCSOA, see Auclair v. Bolderson, 6 A.D.3d 892, 775 N.Y.S.2d 121 (2004)(a state must have continuing jurisdiction under the legislation or, if there is no continuing jurisdiction, have personal jurisdiction over the parties). For current statistics on child support enforcement, see U.S. Department of Health and Human Services, Office of Child Support Enforcement at www.acf.hhs.gov/programs/cse/pubs/2003/reports/prelim_ datareport/Table 9. For current commentary on the status of child support, see Stacey Brustin, *The Intersection Between Welfare Reform and Child Support Enforcement*, 52 CATH. U. L. REV. 621 (2003); Jane C. Murphy, *Legal Images of Fatherhood: Welfare Reform, Child Support Enforcement, and Fatherless Children,* 81 NOTRE DAME L. REV. 325–386 (2005).

UNIFORM INTERSTATE FAMILY SUPPORT ACT (UIFSA) (1996, Amended 2001)

9 U.L.A. Pt. IB 159 *et seq.* (2005)

The uniform legislation was first promulgated by the National Conference of Commissioners on Uniform State Laws in 1992, but was revised in 1996. When Congress enacted sweeping changes to federal welfare legislation in 1996 through the Personal Responsibility and Work Opportunity Reconciliation Act of 1996 (PRWORA), part of this legislation required states to adopt the UIFSA. Of particular importance is the Act's provisions expanding personal jurisdiction over a nonresident obligor, the establishment of one order of support throughout any enforcement process, the curtailment of an enforcing state's ability to modify the support order, and provisions making it easier for states to garnish an obligor's wages. The Act also allows for interstate production of obligors charged with the crime of failure to provide support. See UIFSA Home Page, http://www.uifsa.com. For an example of the Act's wording, see Case v. Case, 103 P.3d 171 (Utah Ct. App. 2004).

Internationally, the UIFSA allows for enforcement of a foreign country's laws and procedures if they are substantially similar to the standards established by the Act. For commentary on the Act and for spousal and child support in general, see Dana Johnson, *Child Support Obligations That Result From Male Sexual Victimization: An Examination of the* Requirement of Support, 25 N. ILL. U. L. REV. 515–538 (2005); James W. Paulsen, *Acquiring Separate Property on Credit: A Review and Proposed Revision of Texas Marital Property Doctrine*, 37 ST. MARY'S L. J. 675–752 (2006); Laura A. Rosenbury, *Two Ways to End a Marriage: Divorce or Death*, 2004 UTAH L. REV. 1227–1290; Cynthia Lee Starnes, *Mothers As Suckers: Pity, Partnership, and Divorce Discourse*, 90 IOWA L. REV. 1513–1552 (2005).

K. WELLINGTON V. WELLINGTON: NEGOTIATING A SETTLEMENT AGREEMENT

Several months ago, Dr. Erik Wellington told his wife Glenda that he wanted a divorce. He explained to her that (1) he wanted to spend the rest of his life with someone who can converse knowledgeably about medicine and who appreciates the special stresses faced by a practicing physician; (2) he was disenchanted with Glenda's "arty" friends; and (3) he no longer loved her. He did not tell Glenda that he wishes to marry Dr. Katherine Ernst, a urologist he met some five months ago. Glenda had never met Dr. Ernst and had no idea that a serious relationship existed between Erik and Katherine or any other woman.

Glenda urged Erik to join her in counseling before making a final decision. Erik refused, saying that he thought the next step should be to have a lawyer "finalize things" for them. He assured Glenda that she and their two minor children, who he assumed would stay with her, would be supported appropriately. Several days later Erik announced that he was going to pack his belongings and move to an apartment in a few days. He gave Glenda a copy of the "Draft Separation Agreement" that follows, explaining that she should make an appointment with "their" lawyer who had prepared it so that it could be explained to her before she signed it. Glenda advised Erik that she would retain her own attorney. Somewhat surprised by that response, Erik moved out of the house immediately.

Glenda has presented the draft to you for evaluation, revision, or whatever action you deem appropriate. She also has told you that presently she has no thoughts about remarriage, and that she would like to return to graduate school to complete a Ph.D. in Art History. She wishes to become a museum curator, which she believes would be personally gratifying and would enable her to achieve financial independence. A major logistical obstacle to implementing this is the fact that the nearest university offering such a program is 200 miles away. Glenda has made it clear that she does not want to return to her old job under any circumstances, although she has been told that it would be available to her.

In reviewing the draft and advising Glenda about her possible alternatives, the following information may be helpful.

Background Facts

The Wellingtons were married in 1990. Erik, then a fourth year medical student, was 25. Glenda, then 23, had graduated from college a year earlier with an art history degree and a superb academic record. When Glenda and Erik met, she was a receptionist-secretary at the medical center where Erik was a student. She had planned to return to graduate school the following year, but instead the couple married six months later. Glenda remained in the same basic job, receiving salary increases and increased responsibilities, until Erik obtained his medical degree and completed a three year internal medicine residency in 1994. During that time all of Glenda's income was applied toward the couple's basic living costs. During the final year of medical school, her income and his student loans were their sole support. When Erik began receiving a salary during his residency training they started repaying some of his student loans from Glenda's salary and his residency income.

On finishing his residency, Erik joined an established private group practice with a guaranteed income of $90,000 the first year, a commitment for additional participation in the profits of the group after the first year, and the opportunity to become a partner after three years of satisfactory practice with the group. Glenda was several months pregnant with their first child when Erik began practice and she then resigned from her job. Since that time she has been a homemaker, mother and wife, and she has managed the couple's personal records and financial affairs. Their first child, a daughter they named Erika, was born in 1996. Their second child, a son Glen, was born in 1997.

Erik was a highly successful practitioner from the outset. He became a partner in the medical group in less than three years and by now Erik's educational loans have been repaid. In 1995 he and Glenda purchased a home in joint tenancy for $200,000, with a 30 year, $160,000 mortgage carrying a variable interest rate. The monthly mortgage payment (currently consisting almost entirely of interest) is now $1,000 and less than $7,000 has been paid toward principal. The annual property tax is $4,000, based on the $380,000 current fair market value assessment of the property. Their utility bills (heat, water, electricity) during the past year have averaged approximately $650 monthly.

This month's basic household bills have been paid and there is $1,000 in a household account in Glenda's name that she uses for current family needs. A savings account in her name alone has a balance of $7,500, the amount of a legacy she received from her grandmother's estate a year ago which has been kept in a separate account ever since.

Erik owns 300 shares of a local bank stock that he inherited from his mother ten years ago. The stock has an income tax basis of $30,000 and a current market value of $60,000. It is pledged as collateral for a bank loan of $50,000 that was taken out initially by Erik to buy into the group medical partnership; the loan has been renewed regularly and interest payments are current but there has been no reduction of the principal. Erik's 5 year old BMW has been fully depreciated as a business asset. The estimated value of Erik's interest in the group medical partnership is approximately $85,000. Erik also has a vested retirement plan that is administered through the partnership. The current value of his interest in the plan is $200,000.

The adjusted gross income on page 1 of the Wellingtons' joint federal income tax form for the most recent taxable year was $250,000. Almost all of this was Erik's income from the medical partnership, after payments made into his retirement plan. Basic liabilities are the home mortgage (a joint obligation) and the previously mentioned bank loan (evidenced by Erik's individual promissory note). In addition to Glenda's household account, Erik and Glenda have a joint checking account with a present balance of $3,000 and a money market mutual fund with a balance of approximately $5,000. Glenda has no insurance on her life; Erik has a $200,000 group term insurance policy on his life, purchased through a medical society of which he is a member. The policy has no cash surrender value and the designated beneficiary is the insured's "legal wife". Erik also has a whole life policy in the face amount of $100,000 with a present cash surrender value of $6,000; Erika and Glen are currently designated as beneficiaries of that policy.

The following is the text of the document that Erik gave Glenda:

DRAFT SEPARATION AGREEMENT

Erik and Glenda Wellington, referred to respectively as Husband and Wife, execute this agreement voluntarily with full understanding of their respective rights and knowledge of their individual assets and liabilities.

Husband and Wife were married on February 3, 1990. There are two children of the marriage: Erika, born October 4, 1996, and Glen, born December 21, 1997. They are hereinafter referred to as the Children.

Because of irreconcilable differences between them, Husband and Wife separated on _____. They intend to remain separate and apart from each other, and they wish to settle their respective property rights and to provide for the maintenance of the Wife and the custody and support of the Children, whose welfare is of primary concern to both Husband and Wife.

In consideration of the premises and the following mutual covenants and undertakings, it is agreed by Husband and Wife that:

1.   Henceforth each of them shall be free from interference by the other as fully as though they were not married to each other. Each one may engage in any employment, profession or business he or she may choose, and shall be free to contract without the consent of the other.

2.   There has been a mutually satisfactory division of all personal property owned by them.

3.   Neither Husband nor Wife will incur further debts, liabilities or obligations in the name of or upon the credit of the other. Husband will pay all household bills incurred through _____.

4.   Wife shall have primary custody of the Children, subject to the specific provisions of this agreement, but all decisions with regard to choice of schools and determination of what medical care is appropriate will be made jointly by Husband and Wife.

5.   If Wife predeceases Husband or becomes unable to care adequately for the Children because of mental or physical incapacity or any other reason, then husband shall have primary custody of the Children during the remainder of their minority.

6.   So long as Wife has custody of either or both of the Children, Husband can exercise the right to visit them by giving Wife reasonable advance notice. Husband also can have both children or either of them reside with him during each summer vacation period for a reasonable time that can include a period of as many as 30 consecutive days.

7.   Each of the Children, upon reaching age 14, can elect to live with and be in the primary custody of Husband rather than Wife. If a change of

custody is effected under this provision, then Wife shall have visitation rights equal to those accorded Husband under clause 6.

8. Husband agrees that Wife will have exclusive use and possession of their house at _____ for so long as she makes it the principal residence for herself and at least one of the minor Children. The house will continue to be owned by Husband and Wife as tenants in common, and Husband agrees that as long as Wife has exclusive possession under this agreement he will (a) make the monthly payments toward principal and interest required by the amortization schedule of the existing mortgage on the property; (b) pay all real estate taxes lawfully assessed against the property; and (c) maintain adequate insurance coverage for the structure. Wife agrees that during her use and possession of the property she will pay for all utilities (including water, electricity, gas and telephone). She also will pay all maintenance costs.

9. Husband agrees to pay Wife $_____ monthly for the next 10 years for her support and maintenance. Payments shall be made no later than the first day of each calendar month directly to Wife or to a bank account designated by her.

10. Husband agrees to pay $_____ monthly for each Child until the Child reaches the age of majority, dies or marries, whichever comes sooner. Payments shall be made no later than the first day of each calendar month directly to Wife or to a bank account designated by her.

11. Husband agrees to transfer to Wife his interest in the Volvo station wagon registered in his name. Wife relinquishes to Husband any interest she has in the BMW sedan registered in the name of Husband.

12. Husband agrees to make a reasonable contribution to the tuition costs of college for each Child at institutions approved by both Husband and Wife for so long as the child is making satisfactory progress and for a maximum period of four years.

13. Husband agrees that during the minority of each of the Children he will continue for their benefit the Blue Cross, Blue Shield and major medical insurance policies currently in effect or provide equivalent insurance coverage in its place.

14. Husband agrees to pay the reasonable fees of an attorney for preparing this agreement.

15. Except as otherwise expressly provided herein, Husband and Wife release each other from all liabilities or obligations to each other, including any right to dower, curtesy, or inheritance, or to renounce or take against the will or testament of the other.

16. Wife agrees that for federal and state tax purposes, Husband shall be entitled to claim all deductions and exemptions attributable to support of the children.

17. Husband and Wife agree that all disputes concerning interpretation of this agreement shall be submitted to arbitration before an arbitrator selected by them. If Husband and Wife cannot agree upon selection of an

arbitrator, each party will select one arbitrator and the two arbitrators so selected shall select a third and sit as a panel to make decisions by a majority vote. All decisions made by an arbitrator selected by the parties, or by a panel selected in accordance with this paragraph, will be binding on Husband and Wife, who will share equally in the costs of the arbitration.

18.   This agreement is made and shall be performed and construed in accordance with the laws of the State of _____.

———

Glenda has asked you to advise her and to identify and evaluate the problems and pitfalls of the preceding draft. As noted already, she has some fairly clear ideas about her preferred approach to establishing financial and professional independence after divorce. Aware that under the law of the jurisdiction she may delay but not block a divorce, Glenda has decided to concentrate on protecting her financial well being and her children.

Glenda wants custody of Erika and Glen. However she is annoyed and concerned by what she perceives as Erik's willingness to have her do all the work in raising them, while holding on to what she regards as too many "strings" that could hamper her parental effectiveness. She realizes that except for repaying student loans she and Erik have been spending the bulk of their increasing income ever since they married and that there is little in the way of liquid assets to be divided. Glenda says that both she and Erik regard their jointly owned house as a splendid long term investment because of its historic and architectural significance, its location in an older area now undergoing increased popularity in the real estate market, and the substantial amount of money and individual effort (the latter mostly Glenda's) that has been expended in restoring and maintaining it. The restoration already has played a significant role in enhancing the property's value. Neither Erik nor Glenda anticipates receiving any significant inheritance. Glenda has a thorough knowledge of the business aspects of Erik's medical partnership and she expects his income to increase when several older partners retire soon. She believes that Erik expects her to ask for somewhat high monthly payments and that he probably would agree to make them if the contract otherwise remains intact.

Explain to Glenda:

(1) What you view as problems with the draft and your assessment of its appropriateness;

(2) Alternative approaches that would better fulfill her goals for life after divorce and also work to the benefit of both spouses.

Would it make any difference in advising Glenda if she were aware of Erik's relationship with Katherine and knew that he wishes to marry her as soon as he can, and that he anticipates having children in his second family?

CHAPTER VI

PARENT AND CHILD: LEGAL AND BIOLOGICAL RELATIONSHIPS

A. LEGITIMATE AND ILLEGITIMATE STATUS

Zepeda v. Zepeda

Appellate Court of Illinois, 1963.
41 Ill.App.2d 240, 190 N.E.2d 849, cert. denied 379 U.S. 945, 85 S.Ct. 444, 13 L.Ed.2d 545 (1964).

■ DEMPSEY, PRESIDING JUSTICE.

The plaintiff is the infant son of the defendant. He seeks damages from his father because he is an illegitimate child. He appeals from an order dismissing his suit and striking his complaint for its failure to state a cause of action. . . .

The factual averments of the complaint, which were admitted by the motion to strike, are: the defendant is the plaintiff's father; the defendant induced the plaintiff's mother to have sexual relations by promising to marry her; this promise was not kept and could not be kept because, unbeknown to the mother, the defendant was already married. The complaint charges that the promise was fraudulent, that the acts of the defendant were willful and that the defendant injured the plaintiff in his person, property and reputation by causing him to be born an adulterine bastard. The plaintiff seeks damages for the deprivation of his right to be a legitimate child, to have a normal home, to have a legal father, to inherit from his father, to inherit from his paternal ancestors and for being stigmatized as a bastard.

[Defendant did not contest the appeal, but at the suggestion of plaintiff's counsel, Professor Max Rheinstein, a distinguished family law scholar, was asked to participate as amicus curiae. He pointed out that:]

"Such a claim is novel. There is no statutory or judicial recognition of such a claim in Illinois or elsewhere in the United States. There is no adverse decision either. In fact, no such claim seems ever to have been raised in any court in Illinois, of any other Common Law jurisdiction, or in any Civil Law country either."

The plaintiff raises constitutional questions and presents two theories of recovery, one in tort and the other in contract. [The court concluded that it lacked jurisdiction to consider the constitutional arguments because the case had been appealed directly to the Illinois Supreme Court which then transferred it to the Court of Appeal, indicating no constitutional issues are involved or are to be considered material. The court did not consider the contract theory of third party beneficiary because the complaint sounded in tort.]

The first of the many interesting questions prompted by the unique averments of the complaint is this: was the act of the defendant a legal wrong, a tortious act? From the admitted facts we can draw the conclusion that the defendant's act was willful and, perhaps, criminal. It was willful in that the defendant was completely indifferent to the foreseeable consequences of his act. He pursued a course of conduct which showed a conscious disregard for the rights of others. He knew he could not marry the woman and he knew that if a child were born as a result of his act he could not legitimatize that child. The act may have been criminal in that the defendant, a married man, and the mother, an unmarried woman, were living together in the mother's apartment. If this cohabitation as husband and wife was openly done, it was a criminal offense: adultery on the part of the defendant, fornication on the part of the mother. The criminal aspect of the act accentuates its gravity. It was not only a moral wrong but was, under the aggravated circumstances of this case, tortious in its nature.

We need not be concerned whether a tort was committed upon the mother by the defendant's false promise of marriage which induced her to have intercourse with him. Our problem is whether a tort was committed upon the child. Thus, the second question to confront us is, can a tort be inflicted upon a being simultaneously with its conception?

[The opinion traces the evolution of tort theory to permit recovery for prenatal injuries.]

But what if the wrongful conduct takes place before conception? Can the defendant be held accountable if his act was completed before the plaintiff was conceived? Yes, for it is possible to incur, as Justice Holmes phrased it in the Dietrich case, "a conditional prospective liability in tort to one not yet in being." [Dietrich v. Inhabitants of Northampton, 138 Mass. 14 (1884).] It makes no difference how much time elapses between a wrongful act and a resulting injury if there is a causal relation between them. . . . Suppose a manufacturer prepared and sold a drug for human consumption which had not been adequately tested; that, while it was beneficial for the purpose intended, it proved to be harmful if taken by women in the very early stage of pregnancy in that it arrested the development of infants' bodies, causing them to be born with abnormal arms or legs. Would not a child so born have a right of action in tort? In the second case the child was injured soon after conception. So let us go still further and take a third suppositive case, where the wrongful act also takes place before conception but the injury attaches at the moment of conception. Physicists and geneticists declare that thermonuclear radiation can so affect the reproductive cells of future parents that their offspring may be born with physical and mental defects. If a child is born malformed or an imbecile because of the genetic effect on his father and mother of a negligently or intentionally caused atomic explosion, will he be denied recovery because he was not in being at the time of the explosion?

. . .

Returning to the present case, we have seen that it is not too important whether the plaintiff's life began during or subsequent to the act of procreation. There is no certainty as to the exact moment conception takes place. It occurs when the male semen contacts and fertilizes the female ovum and this may happen at the time of coition or within a few hours thereafter. If the plaintiff was conceived before the completion of the act he became a living, human organism concurrently with the wrongful act. If his conception took place after the act, he was a potential being with essential reality at the time of the act. . . . The defendant's wrongful act simultaneously procreated the being whom it injured.

In neither event was the plaintiff a "person" as that word has been historically understood in the law of torts. We do not think this is too material for we are not concerned with some abstract ontological proposition as to the instant a human entity becomes a person. The plaintiff is a person now and he was a potential person with full capacity for independent existence at the time of the original wrong. . . . When he became a person the nature of the wrong became fixed. From a moral wrong and a criminal act against the public, it became a legal wrong and a tortious act against the individual.

This brings us to the next question to be considered, the character of the plaintiff's injury. Injuries other than physical or to property are compensable in law and the plaintiff in the case at bar endeavors to come within the coverage of two of them: mental suffering and defamation. This court, in the first case in Illinois involving the right of privacy, considered the interrelationship between right of privacy and mental suffering and concluded that actions were permissible for intentionally caused mental suffering. Eick v. Perk Dog Food Co., 347 Ill.App. 293, 106 N.E.2d 742 (1952). . . . The present complaint, however, does not charge mental distress. The nearest approach to this is the allegation that "His father has wilfully injured and wronged him . . . in stigmatizing him as an adulterine bastard." To some persons the shame of being an adulterine bastard might cause as genuine and severe emotional distress as that resulting from other serious provocation. However, in the absence of proper and adequate averments, we must hold that the complaint states no cause of action for this tort. If it did outline such an action, it would be an interesting speculation whether a charge of mental distress and emotional suffering could be made and sustained in behalf of an infant.

Likewise the complaint does not state a cause of action for defamation. . . .

The plaintiff further complains of being deprived of the normal home that might have been his and of equality with the legitimate child he might have been. A legitimate child has the natural right to be wanted, loved and cared for. He also has an interest in preserving his family life and he may protect this interest against outside disturbance. However, a legitimate child cannot maintain an action against his own parents for lack of affection, for failure to provide a pleasant home, for disrupting the family life or for being responsible for a divorce which has broken up the home. An illegitimate child cannot be given rights superior to those of a legitimate child, and the plaintiff has no cause of action on this account.

But it would be pure fiction to say that the plaintiff suffers no injury. The lot of a child born out of wedlock, who is not adopted or legitimatized, is a hard one. The community itself has come to understand this hardship. After centuries of stagnation, an evolution has been taking place and illegitimate children are now being treated with more consideration. The contrast between the common law and present day statutes is striking.

Under the common law an illegitimate child was called "filius nullius" son of no one, or "filius populi" son of the people. His position in the community was one of ignominy and he had no rights in law. Since he was the child of no one he was without a name; his parents had no right to his custody and no subsequent act of theirs could make him legitimate, only a special act of Parliament could do so. He could not compel his parents to support him, he could not inherit and he could have no heirs except his widow and the issue of his own body.

In most American jurisdictions, illegitimate children were also treated harshly, but in recent years a more compassionate sense of social justice has brought about the enactment of beneficent legislation which has alleviated some of the oppression long visited upon these unfortunates. The whole climate has changed nationally, with variations in degree from state to state. . . . More euphonious terms are also being used in the statutes. "Bastard" is giving way to "illegitimate child," to "a child born out of wedlock," and to "a natural child"; "Bastardy Acts" have yielded to "Family Acts" and "Paternity Acts."

This liberalization is reflected in the statutes of Illinois: an illegitimate child has the right to his father's surname; either or both of his parents may be compelled to support and educate him until he becomes 18 years of age; his parents have custodial rights; he may be legitimatized by the marriage of his parents; if a birth certificate has been issued a new one is issued in the same form as for a legitimate child and the old certificate is impounded; if he is born following an attempted marriage, where some form of a lawful marriage ceremony has been performed, he is considered legitimate; if he is born of an adulterous relation he may be legitimatized if his parents intermarry and his father acknowledges him to be his child; in order to facilitate his legitimation, the certificate of negative finding as to venereal disease in his parents, a prerequisite to marriage, is waived; he is not considered as illegitimate if, after his conception or birth, the marriage of his parents is declared void; the consent of his father is not necessary for his adoption; the word "illegitimate" and the phrase "born out of wedlock" cannot be used in his adoption petition or decree; he may inherit from his mother and his maternal ancestors; if his mother has died he may inherit from those from whom she might have inherited; his issue may take what he would have taken if he were living; not only his wife and descendants inherit from him, but his mother and her descendants can also.

. . .

All these measures spring from the conscience of man disturbed by the severity of the common law and the patent injustices long suffered by innocent children, damned by the sins of their parents. By these benign statutes an illegitimate child's material inequality has been lessened, his legitimation made easier and his succession rights improved. Praiseworthy as they are, they do not, and no law can, make these children whole. Children born illegitimate have suffered an injury. If legitimation does not take place, the injury is continuous. If legitimation cannot take place, the injury is irreparable.

The injury is not as tangible as a physical defect but it is as real. This is acknowledged by the State itself. The statutory provisions that a child's illegitimacy must be suppressed, in certain public records, is an admission of the hardship that can be caused by its disclosure. How often during his life does an illegitimate try to conceal his parentage and how often does he wince in shame when it is revealed? Public opinion may bring about more laws ameliorating further his legal status, but laws cannot temper the cruelty of those who hurl the epithet "bastard" nor ease the bitterness in him who hears it, knowing it to be true. This, however is but one phase, one manifestation of the basic injury, which is in being born and remaining an illegitimate. An illegitimate's very birth places him under a disability.

It is of this that the plaintiff complains. His adulterine birth has placed him under a permanent disability. He protests not only the act which caused him to be born but birth itself. Love of life being what it is, one may conjecture whether, if he were older, he would feel the same way. As he grows from infancy to maturity the natural instinct to preserve life may cause him to cherish his existence as much as, through his next friend, he now deplores it. Be that as it may, the quintessence of his complaint is that he was born and that he is. Herein lies the intrinsic difficulty of this case, a difficulty which gives rise to this question: are there overriding legal, social, judicial or other considerations which should preclude recognition of a cause of action?

. . . [O]n the one hand, we believe that the elements of a willful tort are presented by the allegations of the complaint and, on the other hand, we approach with restraint the creation, by judicial sanction, of the new action required by the complaint.

Recognition of the plaintiff's claim means creation of a new tort: a cause of action for wrongful life. The legal implications of such a tort are vast, the social impact could be staggering. If the new litigation were confined just to illegitimates it would be formidable. In 1960 there were 224,330 illegitimate births in the United States, 14,262 in Illinois and 10,182 in Chicago. Not only are there more such births year after year (in Illinois and in Chicago the number in 1960 was twice that of 1950) but the ratio between illegitimate and legitimate births is increasing. . . .

That the doors of litigation would be opened wider might make us proceed cautiously in approving a new action, but it would not deter us. The plaintiff's claim cannot be rejected because there may be others of equal merit. It is not the suits of illegitimates which give us concern, great in numbers as these may be. What does disturb us is the nature of the new action and the related suits which would be encouraged. Encouragement would extend to all others born into the world under conditions they might regard as adverse. One might seek damages for being born of a certain color, another because of race; one for being born with a hereditary disease, another for inheriting unfortunate family characteristics; one for being born into a large and destitute family, another because a parent has an unsavory reputation.

The present case could be just a forerunner of those which may confront the courts in the future. Without stimulating them, we may have suits for wrongful life just as we now have for wrongful death. Cases are appearing in the domestic relations field concerning children born as a result of artificial insemination.... How long will it be before a child so produced sues in tort those responsible for its being?

... If there are public sperm banks in future years and if there are sperm injections like present day blood transfusions, with donors and donees unknown to each other, will there not be a basis for an action for wrongful life?

. . .

If we are to have a legal action for such a radical concept as wrongful life, it should come after thorough study of the consequences. This would be so even if the new action were to be restricted to illegitimates or even adulterine illegitimates. A study, of the depth and scope warranted by the gravity of this action, can best be made by the General Assembly which, as we have seen, has been steadily whittling away at the legal handicaps shackling bastards and has given them rights almost equivalent to those born legitimate. Changing economic, social or political conditions, or scientific advancements, produce new problems which are constantly thrust upon the courts. These problems often require the remolding of the law, the extension of old remedies or the creation of new and instant remedies— but no recent development is presented by this case which demands an immediate remedy to keep abreast of progress. Although the legal questions unfolded are new, the problem is not; the social conditions producing the problem have existed since the advent of man.

We have decided to affirm the dismissal of the complaint. We do this, despite our designation of the wrong committed herein as a tort, because of our belief that lawmaking, while inherent in the judicial process should not be indulged in where the result could be as sweeping as here....

NOTE

"Bastard," the term long used by courts and legislatures to denote illegitimate status, can carry opprobrious social connotations. Reflecting this, gentler terminology has been widely substituted in the legal lexicon.

After reviewing the cases that follow, speculate on whether the facts in *Zepeda* would state a viable cause of action today? Was the court's concern about "line drawing" realistic in light of subsequent judicial treatment of illegitimacy?

GEORGIA CODE ANN. (2004 & Supp. 2006)

§ 19–7–20. What children are legitimate; disproving legitimacy; legitimation by marriage of parents and recognition of child.

(a) All children born in wedlock or within the usual period of gestation thereafter are legitimate.

(b) The legitimacy of a child born as described in subsection (a) of this Code section may be disputed. Where possibility of access exists, the strong presumption is in favor of legitimacy and the proof must be clear to establish the contrary. If pregnancy existed at the time of the marriage and a divorce is sought and obtained on that ground, the child, although born in wedlock, will not be legitimate.

(c) The marriage of the mother and reputed father of a child born out of wedlock and the recognition by the father of the child as his shall render the child legitimate; in such case the child shall immediately take the surname of his father.

§ 19–7–21. When children conceived by artificial insemination legitimate.

All children born within wedlock or within the usual period of gestation thereafter who have been conceived by means of artificial insemination are irrebuttably presumed legitimate if both spouses have consented in writing to the use and administration of artificial insemination.

§ 19–7–22. Petition to legitimatize child

(a) A father of a child born out of wedlock may render his relationship with the child legitimate by petitioning the superior court of the county of the residence of the child's mother or other party having legal custody or guardianship of the child; provided, however, that if the mother or other party having legal custody or guardianship of the child resides outside the state or cannot, after due diligence, be found within the state, the petition may be filed in the county of the father's residence or the county of the child's residence. If a petition for the adoption of the child is pending, the father shall file the petition for legitimation in the county in which the adoption petition is filed.

(b) The petition shall set forth the name, age, and sex of the child, the name of the mother, and, if the father desires the name of the child to be changed, the new name. If the mother is alive, she shall be named as a party and shall be served and provided an opportunity to be heard as in other civil actions under Chapter 11 of Title 9, the "Georgia Civil Practice Act."

(c) Upon the presentation and filing of the petition, the court may pass an order declaring the father's relationship with the child to be legitimate, and that the father and child shall be capable of inheriting from each other in the same manner as if born in lawful wedlock and specifying the name by which the child shall be known.

(d) A legitimation petition may be filed, pursuant to paragraph (2) of subsection (e) of Code Section 15–11–28, in the juvenile court of the county in which a deprivation proceeding regarding the child is pending.

(e) Except as provided by subsection (f) of this Code section, the court shall upon notice to the mother further establish such duty as the father may have to support the child, considering the facts and circumstances of the mother's obligation of support and the needs of the child as provided under Code Section 19–6–15.

(f) After a petition for legitimation is granted, if a demand for a jury trial as to support has been properly filed by either parent, then the case shall be transferred from juvenile court to superior court for such jury trial.

(f.1) The petition for legitimation may also include claims for visitation or custody. If such claims are raised in the legitimation action, the court may order, in addition to legitimation, visitation or custody based on the best interests of the child standard. In a case involving allegations of family violence, the provisions of paragraph (2) of subsection (a) of Code Section 19–9–1 shall also apply.

(g)(1) In any petition to establish paternity pursuant to paragraph (4) of subsection (a) of Code Section 19–7–43, the alleged father's response may assert a third-party action for the legitimation of the child born out of wedlock. Upon the determination of paternity or if a voluntary acknowledgment of paternity has been made and has not been rescinded pursuant to Code Section 19–7–46.1, the court or trier of fact as a matter of law and pursuant to the provisions of Code Section 19–7–51 may enter an order or decree legitimating a child born out of wedlock, provided that such is in the best interest of the child. Whenever a petition to establish the paternity of a child is brought by the Department of Human Resources, issues of name change, visitation, and custody shall not be determined by the court until such time as a separate petition is filed by one of the parents or by the legal guardian of the child, in accordance with Code Section 19–11–8; if the petition is brought by a party other than the Department of Human Resources or if the alleged father seeks legitimation, the court may determine issues of name change, visitation, and custody in accordance with subsections (b) and (f.1) of this Code section. Custody of the child shall remain in the mother unless or until a court order is entered addressing the issue of custody.

(2) In any voluntary acknowledgment of paternity which has been made and has not been rescinded pursuant to Code Section 19–7–46.1, when both the mother and father freely agree and consent, the child may be legitimated by the inclusion of a statement indicating a voluntary acknowledgment of legitimation.

§ 19-7-23. "Child born out of wedlock" defined.

The term "child born out of wedlock" means:

(1) A child whose parents are not married when that child is born or who do not subsequently intermarry;

(2) A child who is the issue of adulterous intercourse of the wife during wedlock; or

(3) A child who is not legitimate within the meaning of Code Section 19-7-20.

§ 19-7-24. Parents' obligation to child born out of wedlock

It is the joint and several duty of each parent of a child born out of wedlock to provide for the maintenance, protection, and education of the child until the child reaches the age of 18 or becomes emancipated, except to the extent that the duty of one parent is otherwise or further defined by court order.

§ 19-7-25. In whom parental power over a child born out of wedlock lies.

Only the mother of a child born out of wedlock is entitled to his custody, unless the father legitimates him as provided in Code Section 19-7-22. Otherwise, the mother may exercise all parental power over the child.

§ 19-7-26. Mother of child born out of wedlock not to be discriminated against in action to recover for its injury or death.

In an action brought by the mother of a child born out of wedlock in her own right or in her capacity as guardian, executor, or administrator for damages for the child's injury or death, the mother shall not be discriminated against because of her child's having been born out of wedlock.

CALIFORNIA FAMILY CODE (West 2004)

§ 7601. Parent and child relationship; defined

"Parent and child relationship" as used in this part means the legal relationship existing between a child and the child's natural or adoptive parents incident to which the law confers or imposes rights, privileges, duties, and obligations. The term includes the mother and child relationship and the father and child relationship.

§ 7602. Application regardless of marital status of parents

The parent and child relationship extends equally to every child and to every parent, regardless of the marital status of the parents.

NOTE

The California provisions above were based on sections 1 and 2 of the Uniform Parentage Act (1973), one of the most significant acts proposed by the National Conference of Commissioners on Uniform State Laws. Even though it was adopted in less than half of the states, its perspective on the equality of all children and its presumptions of paternity influenced many other jurisdictions. Eventually states began to grapple with such issues as the rights of putative fathers, standing to establish paternity, and advances in testing to establish paternity. This produced demands for revision and in 2000 a new Uniform Paternity Act was promulgated. Only with amendments added in 2002 was the new act approved by the Commissioners. Contributions of the final Act include recognition of scientific developments in determining paternity, voluntary acknowledgment of paternity, registry of paternity, and enforcement of gestational agreements.

VIRGINIA CODE ANN. (2004)

§ 20–31.1. If a person, having had a child, shall afterwards intermarry with the mother or father, such child if recognized by both of them, as their own child, jointly or separately, before or after marriage, shall be deemed legitimate.

The issue of marriages prohibited by law, deemed null or void or dissolved by a court shall nevertheless be legitimate.

Levy v. Louisiana

Supreme Court of the United States, 1968.
391 U.S. 68, 88 S.Ct. 1509, 20 L.Ed.2d 436.

■ Mr. Justice Douglas delivered the opinion of the Court.

Appellant sued on behalf of five illegitimate children to recover, under a Louisiana statute[1] (La.Civ.Code Ann. Art. 2315 (Supp.1967)) for two kinds of damages as a result of the wrongful death of their mother: (1) the damages to them for the loss of their mother; and (2) those based on the survival of a cause of action which the mother had at the time of her death

---

1. "Every act whatever of man that causes damage to another obliges him by whose fault it happened to repair it.

"The right to recover damages to property caused by an offense or quasi offense is a property right which, on the death of the obligee, is inherited by his legal, instituted, or irregular heirs, subject to the community rights of the surviving spouse.

"The right to recover all other damages caused by an offense or quasi offense, if the injured person dies, shall survive for a period of one year from the death of the deceased in favor of: (1) the surviving spouse and child or children of the deceased, or either such spouse or such child or children; (2) the surviving father and mother of the deceased, or either of them, if he left no spouse or child

surviving; and (3) the surviving brothers and sisters of the deceased, or any of them, if he left no spouse, child, or parent surviving. The survivors in whose favor this right of action survives may also recover the damages which they sustained through the wrongful death of the deceased. A right to recover damages under the provisions of this paragraph is a property right which, on the death of the survivor in whose favor the right of action survived, is inherited by his legal, instituted, or irregular heirs, whether suit has been instituted thereon by the survivor or not.

"As used in this article, the words 'child,' 'brother,' 'sister,' 'father,' and 'mother' include a child, brother, sister, father, and mother, by adoption, respectively."

for pain and suffering. Appellees are the doctor who treated her and the insurance company.

We assume in the present state of the pleadings that the mother, Louise Levy, gave birth to these five illegitimate children and that they lived with her; that she treated them as a parent would treat any other child; that she worked as a domestic servant to support them, taking them to church every Sunday and enrolling them, at her own expense, in a parochial school. [The trial court's dismissal was affirmed by the Louisiana Court of Appeal which held that "child" in Article 2315 meant "legitimate child." Denial of an action to illegitimate children was "based on morals and general welfare because it discourages bringing children into the world out of wedlock." 192 So.2d 193, 195. The Supreme Court of Louisiana denied certiorari.]

. . .

We start from the premise that illegitimate children are not "nonpersons." They are humans, live, and have their being.[3] They are clearly "persons" within the meaning of the Equal Protection Clause of the Fourteenth Amendment.

While a State has broad power when it comes to making classifications, it may not draw a line which constitutes an invidious discrimination against a particular class. Though the test has been variously stated, the end result is whether the line drawn is a rational one.

In applying the Equal Protection Clause to social and economic legislation, we give great latitude to the legislature in making classifications. Even so, would a corporation, which is a "person," for certain purposes, within the meaning of the Equal Protection Clause be required to forgo recovery for wrongs done its interests because its incorporators were all bastards? However that might be, we have been extremely sensitive when it comes to basic civil rights and have not hesitated to strike down an invidious classification even though it had history and tradition on its side. The rights asserted here involve the intimate, familial relationship between a child and his own mother. When the child's claim of damage for loss of his mother is in issue, why, in terms of "equal protection," should the tortfeasors go free merely because the child is illegitimate? Why should the illegitimate child be denied rights merely because of his birth out of wedlock? He certainly is subject to all the responsibilities of a citizen, including the payment of taxes and conscription under the Selective Service Act. How under our constitutional regime can he be denied correlative rights which other citizens enjoy?

Legitimacy or illegitimacy of birth has no relation to the nature of the wrong allegedly inflicted on the mother. These children, though illegitimate, were dependent on her; she cared for them and nurtured them; they

---

3. See Note, The Rights of Illegitimates Under Federal Statutes, 76 Harv.L.Rev. 337 (1962).

were indeed hers in the biological and in the spiritual sense; in her death they suffered wrong in the sense that any dependent would.[5]

We conclude that it is invidious to discriminate against them when no action, conduct, or demeanor of theirs[6] is possibly relevant to the harm that was done the mother.[7]

NOTE

Decided along with *Levy* was Glona v. American Guarantee & Liability Ins. Co., 391 U.S. 73, 88 S.Ct. 1515, 20 L.Ed.2d 441 (1968), in which the court held that Louisiana's wrongful death statute was unconstitutional in barring recovery for damages to the parent of an illegitimate child while allowing such recovery to the parent of a legitimate child. The opinion by Justice Douglas explained:

> ... [W]e see no possible rational basis for assuming that if the natural mother is allowed recovery for the wrongful death of her illegitimate child, the cause of illegitimacy will be served. It would, indeed, be farfetched to assume that women have illegitimate children so that they can be compensated for damages for their death. A law which creates open season on illegitimates in the area of automobile accidents gives a windfall to tortfeasors. But it hardly has a causal connection with the "sin", which is, we are told, the historic reason for the creation of the disability. To say that the test of equal protection should be the "legal" rather than the biological relationship is to avoid the issue. For the Equal Protection Clause necessarily limits the authority of a State to draw such "legal" lines as it chooses.

In a dissent to both *Levy* and *Glona,* Justice Harlan was joined by Justices Black and Stewart. After opening with the statement that the two decisions "can only be classed as constitutional curiosities", the opinion later stated:

> The Court today, for some reason which I am at a loss to understand, rules that the State must base its arbitrary definition of the plaintiff class on biological rather than legal relationships. Exactly how this makes the Louisiana scheme even marginally more "rational" is not clear, for neither a biological nor legal acknowledgment is indicative of the love or economic dependence that may exist between two persons. It is, frankly, preposterous to suggest that the State has

---

5. Under Louisiana law both parents are under a duty to support their illegitimate children. La.Civ.Code Ann. Arts. 239, 240 (1952).

6. We can say with Shakespeare: "Why bastard, wherefore base? When my dimensions are as well compact, My mind as generous, and my shape as true, As honest madam's issue? Why brand they us With base? with baseness? bastardy? base, base?" King Lear, Act I, Scene 2.

7. Under Louisiana's Workmen's Compensation Act (La.Rev.Stat.Ann. §§ 23:1231, 23:1252, 23:1253 (1964)) an illegitimate child, who is a dependent member of the deceased parent's family, may recover compensation for his death. See Thompson v. Vestal Lumber & Mfg. Co., 208 La. 83, 22 So.2d 842 (1945). Employers are entitled to recover from a wrongdoer workmen's compensation payments they make to the deceased's dependent illegitimate children.

made illegitimates into "nonpersons", or that, by analogy with what Louisiana has done here it might deny illegitimates constitutional rights or the benefits of doing business in corporate form. The rights at issue here stem from the existence of a family relationship, and the State has decided only that it will not recognize the family relationship unless the formalities of marriage, or of the acknowledgment of children by the parent in question, have been complied with.

There is obvious justification for this decision. If it be conceded, as I assume it is, that the State has power to provide that people who choose to live together should go through the formalities of marriage and, in default, that people who bear children should acknowledge them, it is logical to enforce these requirements by declaring that the general class of rights that are dependent upon family relationships shall be accorded only when the formalities as well as the biology of those relationships are present.

Three years after deciding *Levy* and *Glona,* the Supreme Court upheld another Louisiana statute disqualifying an illegitimate child from sharing in intestate distribution of the estate of her father. Labine v. Vincent, 401 U.S. 532, 91 S.Ct. 1017, 28 L.Ed.2d 288 (1971). The Court's opinion, written by Justice Black, did not find illegitimacy a "suspect classification", which meant that the state had only to establish a rational basis for the statute. Although some suggested that *Labine* had effectively contained any expansion of the *Levy* doctrine, it was reinvigorated the following year by the Court's decision in Weber v. Aetna Casualty and Surety Co., 406 U.S. 164, 92 S.Ct. 1400, 31 L.Ed.2d 768 (1972), which held that excluding illegitimate children from claiming under workers' compensation on behalf of a deceased father denied the claimants both equal protection and due process.

Mathews v. Lucas, 427 U.S. 495, 96 S.Ct. 2755, 49 L.Ed.2d 651 (1976), involved a challenge of a Social Security Act provision requiring special proof of dependency by illegitimate children claiming benefits based on their father's death. Again determining that illegitimacy was not entitled to strict scrutiny, the Court held that differential treatment was rationally related to problems of proof.

Gomez v. Perez

Supreme Court of the United States, 1973.
409 U.S. 535, 93 S.Ct. 872, 35 L.Ed.2d 56.

■ Per Curiam.

The issue presented by this appeal is whether the laws of Texas may constitutionally grant legitimate children a judicially enforceable right to support from their natural fathers and at the same time deny that right to illegitimate children.

In 1969, appellant filed a petition in Texas District Court seeking support from appellee on behalf of her minor child. After a hearing, the state trial judge found that appellee is "the biological father" of the child, and that the child "needs the support and maintenance of her father," but concluded that because the child was illegitimate "there is no legal obligation to support the child and the Plaintiff take nothing." The Court of Civil Appeals affirmed this ruling over the objection that this illegitimate child was being denied equal protection of law. 466 S.W.2d 41. The Texas Supreme Court refused application for a Writ of Error. . . .

In Texas, both at common law and under the statutes of the State, the natural father has a continuing and primary duty to support his legitimate children. That duty extends even beyond dissolution of the marriage, and is enforceable on the child's behalf in civil proceedings and, further, is the subject of criminal sanctions. The duty to support exists despite the fact that the father may not have custody of the child. The Court of Civil Appeals has held in this case that nowhere in this elaborate statutory scheme does the State recognize any enforceable duty on the part of the biological father to support his illegitimate children and that, absent a statutory duty to support, the controlling law is the Texas common-law rule that illegitimate children, unlike legitimate children, have no legal right to support from their fathers. It is also true that fathers may set up illegitimacy as a defense to prosecutions for criminal nonsupport of their children.

In this context, appellant's claim on behalf of her daughter that the child has been denied equal protection of the law is unmistakably presented. Indeed, at argument here, the attorney for the State of Texas, appearing as *amicus curiae,* conceded that but for the fact that this child is illegitimate she would be entitled to support from appellee under the laws of Texas.

We have held that under the Equal Protection Clause of the Fourteenth Amendment a State may not create a right of action in favor of children for the wrongful death of a parent and exclude illegitimate children from the benefit of such a right. Levy v. Louisiana, 391 U.S. 68 (1968). Similarly, we have held that illegitimate children may not be excluded from sharing equally with other children in the recovery of workmen's compensation benefits for the death of their parent. Weber v. Aetna Casualty & Surety Co., 406 U.S. 164 (1972). Under these decisions, a State may not invidiously discriminate against illegitimate children by denying them substantial benefits accorded children generally. We therefore hold that once a State posits a judicially enforceable right on behalf of children to needed support from their natural fathers there is no constitutionally sufficient justification for denying such an essential right to a child simply because its natural father has not married its mother. For a State to do so is "illogical and unjust." Weber v. Aetna Casualty & Surety Co., supra, at 175. We recognize the lurking problems with respect to proof of paternity. Those problems are not to be lightly brushed aside, but neither can they be made into an impenetrable barrier that works to shield otherwise invidious discrimination.

The judgment is reversed and the case remanded for further proceedings not inconsistent with this opinion.

■ [The dissenting opinion of JUSTICE STEWART, in which JUSTICE REHNQUIST joined, is omitted.]

Stanley v. Illinois

Supreme Court of the United States, 1972.
405 U.S. 645, 92 S.Ct. 1208, 31 L.Ed.2d 551.

■ MR. JUSTICE WHITE delivered the opinion of the Court.

Joan Stanley lived with Peter Stanley intermittently for 18 years during which time they had three children. When Joan Stanley died, Peter Stanley lost not only her but also his children. Under Illinois law the children of unwed fathers become wards of the State upon the death of the mother. Accordingly, upon Joan Stanley's death, in a dependency proceeding instituted by the State of Illinois, Stanley's children were declared wards of the State and placed with court appointed guardians. Stanley appealed, claiming that he had never been shown to be an unfit parent and that since married fathers and unwed mothers could not be deprived of their children without such a showing, he had been deprived of the equal protection of the laws guaranteed him by the Fourteenth Amendment. The Illinois Supreme Court accepted the fact that Stanley's own unfitness had not been established but rejected the equal protection claim, holding that Stanley could properly be separated from his children upon proof of the single fact that he and the dead mother had not been married. Stanley's actual fitness as a father was irrelevant. In re Stanley, 45 Ill.2d 132, 256 N.E.2d 814 (1970).

Stanley presses his equal protection claim here. The State continues to respond that unwed fathers are presumed unfit to raise their children and that it is unnecessary to hold individualized hearings to determine whether particular fathers are in fact unfit parents before they are separated from their children.

At the outset we reject any suggestion that we need not consider the propriety of the dependency proceeding that separated the Stanleys because Stanley might be able to regain custody of his children as a guardian or through adoption proceedings. The suggestion is that if Stanley has been treated differently from other parents, the difference is immaterial and not legally cognizable for the purposes of the Fourteenth Amendment. This Court has not, however, embraced the general proposition that a wrong may be done if it can be undone. . . .

It is clear, moreover, that Stanley does not have the means at hand promptly to erase the adverse consequences of the proceeding in the course of which his children were declared wards of the State. It is first urged that Stanley could act to adopt his children. . . . Insofar as we are informed, Illinois law affords him no priority in adoption proceedings. It would be his burden to establish not only that he would be a suitable parent but also that he would be the most suitable of all who might want custody of the children. Neither can we ignore that in the proceedings from which this action developed, the "probation officer," the assistant state's attorney, and the judge charged with the case, made it apparent that Stanley, unmarried and impecunious as he is, could not now expect to profit from adoption proceedings.

Before us, the State focuses on Stanley's failure to petition for "custody and control"—the second route by which, it is urged, he might regain authority for his children. Passing the obvious issue whether it would be futile or burdensome for an unmarried father—without funds and already once presumed unfit—to petition for custody, this suggestion overlooks the fact that legal custody is not parenthood or adoption. A person appointed guardian in an action for custody and control is subject to removal at any time without such cause as must be shown in a neglect proceeding against a parent. Ill.Rev.Stat., c. 37, § 705–8. He may not take the children out of the jurisdiction without the court's approval. He may be required to report to the court as to his disposition of the children's affairs. Ill.Rev.Stat., c. 37, § 705–8. Obviously then, even if Stanley were a mere step away from "custody and control," to give an unwed father only "custody and control" would still be to leave him seriously prejudiced by reason of his status.

We must therefore examine the question which Illinois would have us avoid: Is a presumption which distinguishes and burdens all unwed fathers constitutionally repugnant? We conclude that as a matter of due process of law, Stanley was entitled to a hearing on his fitness as a parent before his children were taken from him and that by denying him a hearing and extending it to all other parents whose custody of their children is challenged the State denied Stanley the equal protection of the law guaranteed by the Fourteenth Amendment.

Illinois has two principal methods of removing non-delinquent children from the homes of their parents. In a dependency proceeding it may demonstrate that the children are wards of the State because they have no surviving parent or guardian. In a neglect proceeding it may show that children should be wards of the State because the present parent(s) or guardian does not provide suitable care.

The State's right—indeed duty—to protect minor children through a judicial determination of their interests in a neglect proceeding is not challenged here. Rather we are faced with a dependency statute which empowers state officials to circumvent neglect proceedings on the theory that an unwed father is not a "parent" whose existing relationship with his children must be considered. "Parents," says the State, "means the father and mother of a legitimate child, or the survivor of them, or the natural mother of an illegitimate child, and includes any adoptive parent," Ill.Rev. Stat., c. 37, § 701–14, but the term does not include unwed fathers....

The private interest here, that of a man in the children he has sired and raised, undeniably warrants deference and, absent a powerful countervailing interest, protection. It is plain that the interest of a parent in the companionship, care, custody, and management of his or her children "come[s] to this Court with a momentum for respect lacking when appeal is made to liberties which derive merely from shifting economic arrangements." Kovacs v. Cooper, 336 U.S. 77, 95 (1949) (concurring opinion).

The Court has frequently emphasized the importance of the family. The rights to conceive and to raise one's children have been deemed "essential," Meyer v. Nebraska, 262 U.S. 390, 399 (1923), "basic civil rights of man," Skinner v. Oklahoma, 316 U.S. 535, 541 (1942), and "[r]ights far more precious ... than property rights," May v. Anderson, 345 U.S. 528, 533 (1953). "It is cardinal with us that the custody, care and nurture of the child reside first in the parents, whose primary function and freedom include preparation for obligations the state can neither supply nor hinder." Prince v. Massachusetts, 321 U.S. 158, 166 (1944). The integrity of the family unit has found protection in the Due Process Clause of the Fourteenth Amendment, Meyer v. Nebraska, supra, at 399, the Equal Protection Clause of the Fourteenth Amendment, Skinner v. Oklahoma, supra, at 541, and the Ninth Amendment, Griswold v. Connecticut, 381 U.S. 479, 496 (1965) (Goldberg, J., concurring).

Nor has the law refused to recognize those family relationships unlegitimized by a marriage ceremony. The Court has declared unconstitutional a state statute denying natural, but illegitimate, children a wrongful death action for the death of their mother, emphasizing that such children cannot be denied the right of other children because familial bonds in such cases were often as warm, enduring, and important as those arising within a more formally organized family unit. Levy v. Louisiana, 391 U.S. 68, 71–72 (1968).

These authorities make it clear that, at the least, Stanley's interest in retaining custody of his children is recognizable and substantial.

For its part, the State has made its interest quite plain: Illinois has declared that the aim of the Juvenile Court Act is to protect "the moral, emotional, mental and physical welfare of the minor and the best interests of the community" and to "strengthen the minor's family ties whenever possible, removing him from the custody of his parents only when his welfare or safety or the protection of the public cannot be adequately safeguarded without removal...." Ill.Rev.Stat., c. 37, §§ 701–702. These are legitimate interests well within the power of the State to implement. We do not question the assertion that neglectful parents may be separated from their children.

But we are here not asked to evaluate the legitimacy of the state ends, but rather to determine whether the means used to achieve these ends are constitutionally defensible. What is the state interest in separating children from fathers without a hearing designed to determine whether the father is unfit in a particular disputed case? We observe that the State registers no gain towards its declared goals when it separates children from the custody of fit parents. Indeed, if Stanley is a fit father, the State spites its own articulated goals when it needlessly separates him from his family.

In Bell v. Burson, 402 U.S. 535 (1971), we found a scheme repugnant to the Due Process Clause because it deprived a driver of his license without reference to the very factor (there fault in driving, here fitness as a parent) which the State itself deemed fundamental to its statutory scheme. Illinois would avoid the self-contradiction which rendered the Georgia license suspension system invalid by arguing that Stanley and all other unmarried fathers can reasonably be presumed to be unqualified to raise their children.

It may be, as the State insists, that most unmarried fathers are unsuitable and neglectful parents.[6] It may also be that Stanley is such a parent and that his children should be placed in other hands. But all unmarried fathers are not in this category; some are wholly suited to have custody of their children.[7] This much the State readily concedes, and nothing in this record indicates that Stanley is or has been a neglectful father who has not cared for his children. Given the opportunity to make his case, Stanley may have been seen to be deserving of custody of his offspring. Had this been so, the State's statutory policy would have been furthered by leaving custody in him.

... [I]t may be argued that unmarried fathers are so seldom fit that Illinois need not undergo the administrative inconvenience of inquiry in any case, including Stanley's. The establishment of prompt efficacious procedures to achieve legitimate state ends is a proper state interest worthy of cognizance in constitutional adjudication. But the Constitution recognizes higher values than speed and efficiency. Indeed, one might fairly say of the Bill of Rights in general, and the Due Process Clause in particular, that they were designed to protect the fragile values of a vulnerable citizenry from the overbearing concern for efficiency and efficacy which may characterize praiseworthy government officials no less, and perhaps more, than mediocre ones.

Procedure by presumption is always cheaper and easier than individualized determination. But when, as here, the procedure forecloses the determinative issues of competence and care, when it explicitly disdains present realities in deference to past formalities, it needlessly risks running

---

6. The State speaks of "the general disinterest of putative fathers in their illegitimate children" and opines "In most instances the natural father is a stranger to his children."

7. See in re Mark T., 8 Mich.App. 122, 154 N.W.2d 27 (1967). There a panel of the Michigan Court of Appeals in unanimously affirming a circuit court's determination that the father of an illegitimate son was best suited to raise the boy, said:

"The appellants' presentation in this case proceeds on the assumption that placing Mark for adoption is inherently preferable to rearing by his father, that uprooting him from the family which he knew from birth until he was a year and a half old, secretly institutionalizing him

and later transferring him to strangers is so incontrovertibly better that no court has the power even to consider the matter. Hardly anyone would even suggest such a proposition if we were talking about a child born in wedlock.

"We are not aware of any sociological data justifying the assumption that an illegitimate child reared by his natural father is less likely to receive a proper upbringing than one reared by his natural father who was at one time married to his mother, or that the stigma of illegitimacy is so pervasive it requires adoption by strangers and permanent termination of a subsisting relationship with the child's father." Id., at 39.

roughshod over the important interests of both parent and child. It there-fore cannot stand.[9]

Bell v. Burson held that the State could not, while purporting to be concerned with fault in suspending a driver's license, deprive a citizen of his license without a hearing which would assess fault. Absent fault, the State's declared interest was so attenuated that administrative convenience was insufficient to excuse a hearing where evidence of fault could be considered. That drivers involved in accidents, as a statistical matter, might be very likely to have been wholly or partially at fault did not foreclose hearing and proof in specific cases before licenses were suspended.

We think the Due Process Clause mandates a similar result here. The State's interest in caring for Stanley's children is *de minimis* if Stanley is shown to be a fit father. It insists on presuming rather than proving Stanley's unfitness solely because it is more convenient to presume than to prove. Under the Due Process Clause that advantage is insufficient to justify refusing a father a hearing when the issue at stake is the dismem-berment of his family.

The State of Illinois assumes custody of the children of married parents, divorced parents, and unmarried mothers only after a hearing and proof of neglect. The children of unmarried fathers, however, are declared dependent children without a hearing on parental fitness and without proof of neglect. Stanley's claim in the state courts and here is that failure to afford him a hearing on his parental qualifications while extending it to other parents denied him equal protection of the laws. We have concluded that all Illinois parents are constitutionally entitled to a hearing on their fitness before their children are removed from their custody. It follows that denying such a hearing to Stanley and those like him while granting it to other Illinois parents is inescapably contrary to the Equal Protection Clause.

The judgment of the Supreme Court of Illinois is reversed and the case is remanded to that court for proceedings not inconsistent with this opinion.

■ MR. CHIEF JUSTICE BURGER, with whom MR. JUSTICE BLACKMUN, concurs, dissenting. . . .

No due process issue was raised in the state courts; and no due process issue was decided by any state court. . . .

---

9. We note in passing that the incre-mental cost of offering unwed fathers an op-portunity for individualized hearings on fit-ness appears to be minimal. If unwed fathers, in the main, do not care about the disposition of their children, they will not appear to demand hearings. If they do care, under the scheme here held invalid, Illinois would ad-mittedly at some later time have to afford them a properly focused hearing in a custody or adoption proceeding.

Extending opportunity for hearing to un-wed fathers who desire and claim competence to care for their children creates no constitu-tional or procedural obstacle to foreclosing those unwed fathers who are not so inclined. The Illinois law governing procedure in juve-nile cases, Ill.Rev.Stat., c. 37, § 704-1 et seq., provides for personal service, notice by certi-fied mail or for notice by publication when personal or certified mail service cannot be had or when notice is directed to unknown respondents under the style of "all whom it may concern." Unwed fathers who do not promptly respond cannot complain if their children are declared wards of the State. Those who do respond retain the burden of proving their fatherhood.

All of those persons in Illinois who may have followed the progress of this case will, I expect, experience no little surprise at the Court's opinion handed down today. Stanley will undoubtedly be surprised to find that he has prevailed on an issue never advanced by him. . . .

In regard to the only issue which I consider properly before the Court, I agree with the State's argument that the Equal Protection Clause is not violated when Illinois gives full recognition only to those father-child relationships that arise in the context of family units bound together by legal obligations arising from marriage or from adoption proceedings. Quite apart from the religious or quasi-religious connotations which marriage has—and has historically enjoyed—for a large proportion of this Nation's citizens, it is in law an essentially contractual relationship, the parties to which have legally enforceable rights and duties, with respect both to each other and to any children born to them. Stanley and the mother of these children never entered such a relationship. The record is silent as to whether they ever privately exchanged such promises as would have bound them in marriage under the common law. . . . In any event, Illinois has not recognized common law marriages since 1905. . . . Stanley did not seek the burdens when he could have freely assumed them.

Where there is a valid contract of marriage, the law of Illinois presumes that the husband is the father of any child born to the wife during the marriage; as the father, he has legally enforceable rights and duties with respect to that child. When a child is born to an unmarried woman, Illinois recognizes the readily identifiable mother, but makes no presumption as to the identity of the biological father. It does, however, provide two ways, one voluntary and one involuntary, in which that father may be identified. First, he may marry the mother and acknowledge the child as his own; this has the legal effect of legitimating the child and gaining for the father full recognition as a parent. Ill.Rev.Stat., c. 3, § 12–8. Second, a man may be found to be the biological father of the child pursuant to a paternity suit initiated by the mother; in this case, the child remains illegitimate, but the adjudicated father is made liable for the support of the child until the latter attains age 18 or is legally adopted by another. . . .

Stanley argued before the Supreme Court of Illinois that the definition of "parents," set out in Ill.Rev.Stat., c. 37, § 701–14, as including "the father and mother of a legitimate child, or the survivor of them, or the natural mother of an illegitimate child, [or] ... any adoptive parent,"[3]

---

3. The Court seems at times to ignore this statutory definition of "parents," even though it is precisely that definition itself whose constitutionality has been brought into issue by Stanley. In preparation for finding a purported similarity between this case and Bell v. Burson, 402 U.S. 535 (1971), the Court quotes the legislatively declared aims of the Juvenile Court Act to "strengthen the minor's family ties whenever possible, removing him from the custody of his *parent* only when his welfare or the safety or the protection of the public cannot be adequately safeguarded without removal." (Emphasis added.) The Court then goes on to find a "self-contradiction" between that stated aim and

violates the Equal Protection Clause in that it treats unwed mothers and unwed fathers differently. Stanley then enlarged upon his equal protection argument when he brought the case here; he argued before this Court that Illinois is not permitted by the Equal Protection Clause to distinguish between unwed fathers and any of the other biological parents included in the statutory definition of legal "parents."

The Illinois Supreme Court correctly held that the State may constitutionally distinguish between unwed fathers and unwed mothers. Here, Illinois' different treatment of the two is part of that State's statutory scheme for protecting the welfare of illegitimate children. In almost all cases, the unwed mother is readily identifiable, generally from hospital records and alternatively by physicians or others attending the child's birth. Unwed fathers, as a class are not traditionally quite so easy to identify and locate. Many of them either deny all responsibility or exhibit no interest in the child or its welfare; and, of course, many unwed fathers are simply not aware of their parenthood.

Furthermore, I believe that a State is fully justified in concluding, on the basis of common human experience, that the biological role of the mother in carrying and nursing an infant creates stronger bonds between her and the child than the bonds resulting from the male's often casual encounter. This view is reinforced by the observable fact that most unwed mothers exhibit a concern for their offspring either permanently or at least until they are safely placed for adoption, while unwed fathers rarely burden either the mother or the child with their attentions or loyalties. Centuries of human experience buttress this view of the realities of human conditions and suggest that unwed mothers of illegitimate children are generally more dependable protectors of their children than are unwed fathers. While these, like most generalizations, are not without exceptions, they nevertheless provide a sufficient basis to sustain a statutory classification whose objective is not to penalize unwed parents but to further the welfare of illegitimate children in fulfillment of the State's obligations as *parens patriae*.

Stanley depicts himself as a somewhat unusual unwed father, namely, as one who has always acknowledged and never doubted his fatherhood of these children. He alleges that he loved, cared for, and supported these children from the time of their birth until the death of their mother. He contends that he consequently must be treated the same as a married father of legitimate children. Even assuming the truth of Stanley's allegations, I am unable to construe the Equal Protection Clause as requiring Illinois to tailor its statutory definition of "parents" so meticulously as to include such unusual unwed fathers, while at the same time excluding those unwed, and generally unidentified, biological fathers who in no way share Stanley's professed desires.

the Act's non-recognition of unwed fathers. There is, of course, no such contradiction. The word "parent" in the statement of legis- lative purpose obviously has the meaning given to it by the definitional provision of the Act.

Indeed, the nature of Stanley's own desires is less than absolutely clear from the record in this case. Shortly after the death of the mother, Stanley turned these two children over to the care of a Mr. and Mrs. Ness; he took no action to gain his own recognition as a father, through adoption, or as a legal custodian, through a guardianship proceeding. Eventually it came to the attention of the State that there was no living adult who had any legally enforceable obligation for the care and support of the children; it was only then that the dependency proceeding here under review took place and that Stanley made himself known to the juvenile court in connection with these two children.[5] Even then, however, Stanley did not ask to be charged with the legal responsibility for the children. He asked only that such legal responsibility be given to no one else. He seemed, in particular, to be concerned with the loss of the welfare payments he would suffer as a result of the designation of others as guardians of the children.

Not only, then, do I see no ground for holding that Illinois' statutory definition of "parents" on its face violates the Equal Protection Clause; I see no ground for holding that any constitutional right of Stanley has been denied in the application of that statutory definition in the case at bar....

NOTE

Is *Stanley* more a case on sex discrimination than parental rights? Whatever the issue that was being pressed by the parties or that the court felt they were addressing, the impact of footnote 9 of the opinion on adoption law and practice was considerable. This led to a series of later cases dealing with constitutional challenges to state provisions seeking to clarify the rights of unwed fathers and their children in the adoption context, discussed in Chapter 9.

Like Griswold v. Connecticut, *Stanley* has become one of those decisions that is cited for many meanings that often seem difficult to extrapolate from the opinion of the court.

B.   ESTABLISHING LEGAL PARENTAGE

For centuries, biological (genetic) and legal parentage were equated. However during much of the period, establishing biological parentage was done largely through the presumption that a child born to a married woman cohabiting with her husband was the child of both husband and wife. Scientific tests that were developed in the middle of the 20th century could be used to establish that the husband was not the genetic father in

---

5. As the majority notes, Joan Stanley gave birth to three children during the 18 years Peter Stanley was living "intermittently" with her. At oral argument, we were told by Stanley's counsel that the oldest of these three children had previously been declared a ward of the court pursuant to a neglect proceeding which was "proven against" Stanley at a time, apparently, when the juvenile court officials were under the erroneous impression that Peter and Joan Stanley had been married.

certain, limited instances, but they were largely ineffective at affirmatively proving paternity. Also, courts often were reluctant to use them, ostensibly basing their concern on whether they were scientifically accepted even though the concern actually might be declaring a child illegitimate. Even though tests have become more sophisticated in establishing paternity, some reluctance to use them still remains. The key questions now are whether we really want to know who the genetic father is, particularly when the child is living in an intact family where both husband and wife regard the child as theirs regardless of the lack of a genetic tie to the husband. Such cases thus may call for recognition of legal paternity independent of biological paternity. In a time when assisted conception using the semen of someone other than the husband of the inseminated wife is widely used, and when surrogacy or gestational parentage is being undertaken on a larger scale (even though unresolved legal issues remain worrisome), the issues become even more complex. Older rules prohibiting testimony of a parent that would illegitimate a child have eroded substantially. Disputes now often center on whether a putative or alleged father has standing to bring an action seeking to establish his paternity of a married woman's child, or whether he can seek to prove this through blood testing.

In sum, the old rules were designed largely to protect children and deal with the fact that biological paternity could not be readily established through scientific methods. Now that we have the scientific methods, the question becomes whether we should utilize them in some or all cases where the issue of paternity arises.

Practical and legal issues continue to face lawyers regarding the use of scientific testing. For a discussion *see* Christopher Blakesley, *Scientific Testing and Proof of Paternity: Some Controversy and Key Issues for Family Law Counsel*, 57 LA. L. REV. 379 (1997). For two provocative assessments of differing ways in which issues of genetic kinship or paternity have been and might be approached, *see* Janet Dolgin, *Just a Gene: Judicial Assumptions About Parenthood*, 40 U.C.L.A. L. REV. 637 (1993), and Barbara Bennett Woodhouse, *Hatching the Egg: A Child–Centered Perspective on Parents' Rights*, 14 CARDOZO L. REV. 1747 (1993). *See also* WALTER WADLINGTON and RAYMOND C. O'BRIEN, FAMILY LAW IN PERSPECTIVE (2d ed.2007).

NEW YORK FAMILY COURT ACT (McKinney 1999)

§ 532.   Blood genetic marker tests; costs of tests; admissibility of test results

(a) The court shall advise the parties of their right to one or more genetic marker tests or DNA tests and, on the court's own motion or the motion of any party, shall order the mother, her child and the alleged father to submit to one or more genetic marker or DNA tests of a type generally acknowledged as reliable by an accreditation body designated by the secretary of the federal department of health and human services and performed by a laboratory approved by such an accreditation body and by the commissioner of health or by a duly qualified physician to aid in the determination of whether the alleged father is or is not the father of the child. No such test shall be ordered, however, upon a written finding by the court that it is not in the best interests of the child on the basis of res judicata, equitable estoppel, or the presumption of legitimacy of a child born to a married woman. The record or report of the results of any such genetic marker or DNA test ordered pursuant to this section or pursuant to section one hundred eleven-k of the social services law shall be received in evidence by the court pursuant to subdivision (e) of rule forty-five hundred eighteen of the civil practice law and rules where no timely objection in writing has been made thereto and that if such timely objections are not made, they shall be deemed waived and shall not be heard by the court. If the record or report of the results of any such genetic marker or DNA test or tests indicate at least a ninety-five percent probability of paternity, the admission of such record or report shall create a rebuttable presumption of paternity, and shall establish, if unrebutted, the paternity of and liability for the support of a child pursuant to this article and article four of this act.

(b) Whenever the court directs a genetic marker or DNA test pursuant to this section, a report made as provided in subdivision (a) of this section may be received in evidence pursuant to rule forty-five hundred eighteen of the civil practice law and rules if offered by any party.

(c) The cost of any test ordered pursuant to subdivision (a) of this section shall be, in the first instance, paid by the moving party. If the moving party is financially unable to pay such cost, the court may direct any qualified public health officer to conduct such test, if practicable; otherwise, the court may direct payment from the funds of the appropriate local social services district. In its order of disposition, however, the court may direct that the cost of any such test be apportioned between the parties according to their respective abilities to pay or be assessed against the party who does not prevail on the issue of paternity, unless such party is financially unable to pay.

Witso v. Overby

Supreme Court of Minnesota, 2001.
627 N.W.2d 63.

■ STRINGER, JUSTICE.

Respondent Benjamin Witso (Witso) seeks custody and visitation rights with his putative child M.R.O. and petitioned under the Minnesota Parentage Act (MPA)[6] for a court order to compel the child's mother, appellant Mary Overby (Overby), and M.R.O. to undergo blood or genetic testing to determine whether he is a presumed biological father of M.R.O. The district court granted Witso's petition but, on Overby's motion, certified as important and doubtful the following question as recast by the court of appeals:

---

6. The MPA is codified in Minn.Stat.
§§ 257.51–.74 (2000).

Must a paternity action be dismissed for lack of standing when the petitioning putative father shows the requisite sexual contact but has not had genetic testing, which might establish the genetic basis for standing that arises from a positive genetic test?

The court of appeals answered the question in the negative and affirmed the district court. We now affirm the court of appeals.

Overby gave birth to M.R.O. on April 27, 1998. At the time of M.R.O.'s birth Overby was married to James Overby, and therefore, by statute, James Overby is M.R.O.'s presumed biological father. Minn.Stat. § 257.55, subd. 1(a) (2000). Witso alleges however, that he and Overby became involved in a two-year extra-marital affair that included frequent sexual contact during the period in which M.R.O. was conceived and that he is M.R.O.'s biological father. He supports his claim with an affidavit asserting that he and Overby had an intimate relationship over the time period alleged and that Overby admitted that he was M.R.O.'s biological father. Overby's responsive affidavit denies the two-year affair but admits that she and Witso had one sexual encounter that could have resulted in the conception of M.R.O. Overby denies that she told Witso that M.R.O. was his child and contends that she and her husband were trying to have a second child and had frequent sexual contact during the period in which M.R.O. was conceived. Overby maintains that James Overby is M.R.O.'s biological father.

The issue in the certified question is one of statutory interpretation and is therefore a question of law that this court reviews de novo. *In re Welfare of G.L.H.*, 614 N.W.2d 718, 720 (Minn.2000).

The right to bring a proceeding to establish paternity is totally a creature of the MPA. In the MPA the legislature adopted, with some modifications, the Uniform Parentage Act, a comprehensive set of laws designed to provide "substantive legal equality for all children regardless of the marital status of their parents * * * [including] the *sine qua non* of equal rights—the identification of the person against whom these rights may be asserted."[7] The MPA establishes that the father and child relationship may exist regardless of the marital status of the parents. Minn.Stat. §§ 257.52, 257.53 (2000).

The MPA provides the exclusive bases for standing to bring an action to determine paternity. *Morey v. Peppin*, 375 N.W.2d 19, 22 (Minn.1985). Whether and when a person may bring a paternity action depends on which presumptions of paternity, if any, apply. *See* Minn.Stat. § 257.57 (2000). Nine presumptions of paternity are set forth in section 257.55, generally divided between those based on marriage, Minn.Stat. § 257.55, subd. 1(a)–(c) (2000), and those based on circumstances other than marriage, Minn. Stat. § 257.55, subd. 1(d)–(I) (2000). Standing to bring a paternity action with respect to these presumptions is also based on statute.[8]

---

7. The MPA is codified in Minn.Stat. §§ 257.51–.74 (2000).

8. Standing to bring a paternity action is provided in Minn.Stat. § 257.57, subds. 1–

The issue here is whether Witso, a putative father who is not a presumed father under section 257.55, can bring an action to require Overby, the mother, and M.R.O., the putative child, to submit to blood or genetic testing to establish whether he is a presumed father under section 257.55, subd. 1(f) when M.R.O. already has a presumed father. Section 257.55, subd. 1(f) provides that if "blood or genetic testing establishes the likelihood that he is the father of the child, calculated with a prior probability of no more than 0.5 (50 percent), is 99 percent or greater" then Witso is presumed to be the biological father. Witso thus seeks to establish a presumption of paternity in himself, and if successful, to proceed in district court to seek custody and visitation rights with M.R.O. as provided in Minn.Stat. § 257.541, subd. 2(b) (2000). Whether he is ultimately granted any such rights is not before us.

The court of appeals held that Witso is a party to this paternity action under Minn.Stat. § 257.57, subd. 2(1) (2000),[9] and as a party has the right to compel Overby and M.R.O. to submit to blood or genetic testing under Minn.Stat. § 257.62 (2000)[10] by alleging by affidavit sufficient bases for the requisite sexual contact. *Witso v. Overby,* 609 N.W.2d at 621–23. The court expressed concern that its ruling might open the door to casual assertions of paternity but concluded that the affidavit requirement in section 257.62, subdivision 1(a) provided the district court with adequate discretion to determine whether a factual basis exists to reasonably conclude that there was sexual contact sufficient for conception to occur.

The court of appeals states that Minn.Stat. § 257.57, subd. 1(b) limits the time one can use blood or genetic tests to challenge a marriage-based presumption to no more than three years after the child is born. *Witso v. Overby,* 609 N.W.2d 618, 622–23 (Minn.App.2000). The court is correct in so far as a child, biological mother or presumed father under Minn.Stat. § 257.55, subd. 1(a), (b), or (c) may not use blood or genetic tests to declare the nonexistence of the presumed father's paternity after three years have passed since the child's birth. But that section would not prevent a putative father from bringing an action to declare his competing presumption of paternity.

3 (2000). Subdivision 1 provides standing with respect to presumptions based on marriage, subdivision 2 provides standing with respect to presumptions based on evidence other than marriage and subdivision 3 provides standing when there is no presumption.

9. Minnesota Statutes § 257.57, subd. 2 (2000) provides:

The child, the mother, or * * * a man alleged or alleging himself to be the father, * * * may bring an action: at any time for the purpose of declaring the existence of the father and child relationship presumed under section 257.55, subdivision 1, paragraph (d), (e), (f), (g), or (h), or the nonexistence of the father and

child relationship presumed under clause (d) of that subdivision * * *.

10. Minnesota Statutes § 257.62, subd. 1(a) provides:

The court or public authority may, and upon request of a party shall, require the child, mother, or alleged father to submit to blood or genetic tests. A mother or alleged father requesting the tests shall file with the court an affidavit either alleging or denying paternity and setting forth facts that establish the reasonable possibility that there was, or was not, the requisite sexual contact between the parties.

The Overbys argue that Witso does not have standing because the phrase "declaring the existence of the father and child relationship presumed" in section 257.57, subdivision 2 requires that Witso have evidence of blood or genetic tests establishing that he is a presumed biological father before he is permitted to commence a paternity action. In effect, the Overbys argue that Witso is foreclosed from bringing an action to conduct blood or genetic tests to determine whether he is a presumed father because he does not possess test results that show he is a presumed father. We disagree, as we do not believe that the legislative scheme posits such a chicken-or-egg dilemma. If a putative father were required to be a presumed father under Minn.Stat. § 257.55, subd. 1(f), the mother could foreclose the putative father from obtaining the test results to prove paternity. Further, the terms "alleged" or "alleging" in section 257.57, subd. 2 providing for who may bring an action would have no meaning independent from the term "presumed," clearly ignoring the important statutory distinction between the terms "alleged" or "alleging" and "presumed."

The structure and terminology of section 257.57 also evidence a clear legislative purpose to give putative fathers, in contrast to those already presumed to be fathers under Minn.Stat. § 257.55, subd. 1 (2000), a cause of action to establish a presumption of paternity. On the one hand subdivision 1 protects marriage-based presumptions by strictly limiting those who may directly challenge the existence of a presumption of paternity based on marriage to the child, the *biological* mother and a man *presumed* to be the child's father by virtue of Minn.Stat. § 257.55, subd. 1(a), (b) or (c). Minn.Stat. § 257.57, subd. 1.[11] On the other hand subdivision 2 of section 257.57 expands the category of those eligible to bring an action to declare the existence or nonexistence of the father and child relationship based on evidence outside of a marriage to mothers who are not necessarily biological mothers, a personal representative of the child, public authorities charged with support of the child, a personal representative or parent of the mother or an alleged father if the mother or alleged father has died or is a minor and men *alleged or alleging* themselves to be the father. Minn.Stat. § 257.57, subd. 2. Importantly subdivision 2 is not limited to the class of men who can bring an action under Minn.Stat. § 257.57, subd. 1. Putative fathers alleged and alleging themselves to be fathers, but not necessarily presumed fathers—e.g., Witso—are specifically authorized to bring an action under Minn.Stat. § 257.57, subd. 2 to establish their paternity.[12]

11. Minnesota Statutes § 257.57, subd. 1 provides: A child, the child's biological mother, or a man presumed to be the child's father under section 257.55, subdivision 1, paragraph (a), (b), or (c) may bring an action:

    (a) At any time for the purpose of declaring the existence of the father and child relationship presumed under section

257.55, subdivision 1, paragraph (a), (b), or (c); * * *.

12. The dissent contends that the use of the word "the" in "the father and son relationship" in section 257.57, subd. 2(1) instead of the word "a" indicates that the statute refers to a specific preexisting presumed relationship. The use of "the" rather than "a" establishes nothing of the kind, as

That an alleging father need not also be a presumed father is further evident from section 257.60, relating to who may and who must be made a party to a paternity action.[13] The section distinguishes those presumed to be fathers from those alleging themselves to be fathers when it provides that a "man presumed to be a father under section 257.55, or a man who alleges himself to be the father" may bring an action to "declare" the existence of the father-child relationship. Minn.Stat. § 257.60(3) (2000). If a putative father brings a paternity action and the mother denies the existence of the father and child relationship, the section requires the court to make the child a party to the action. Judicial opinions from other jurisdictions have held that putative fathers of children born to women married to other men have protectable interests in establishing their paternity. In Colorado, even before it legislatively adopted a presumption of paternity based on blood or genetic testing similar to Minnesota law, the supreme court held that a putative father was denied his right to equal protection when he was prevented from proving his paternity through blood or genetic tests under the state's parentage act. *R. McG. v. J.W.,* 200 Colo. 345, 615 P.2d 666, 672 (1980). After the presumption was adopted, the Colorado Court of Appeals, citing *R. McG. v. J.W.,* construed its parentage act to give a putative father standing to compel a mother and child to submit to blood or genetic testing. *See In re S.R.H.,* 981 P.2d 199, 202 (Colo.Ct.App.1998), *rev'd on other grounds sub nom., N.A.H. v. S.L.S.,* 9 P.3d 354, 366 (Colo.2000). Five members of the U.S. Supreme Court agreed that a biological father might have "a constitutionally protected interest in his relationship with a child whose mother is married to, and cohabiting with, another man at the time of the child's conception and birth." *Michael H. v. Gerald D.,* 491 U.S. 110, 133, 136, 157, 109 S.Ct. 2333, 105 L.Ed.2d 91 (1989) (Stevens, J., concurring in the judgment; Brennan, J., with Marshall and Blackmun, JJ., dissenting; White, J., with

the use of the term "a" would suggest multiple fathers.

The dissent also seeks to support its position by suggesting that "declare" in "declare the existence of the father and child relationship presumed under section 257.55" in section 257.57, subd. 2(1) must imply the preexistence of a presumption of fatherhood because subdivision 3 uses the word "determine" rather than "declare" in "determine the existence of the father and child relationship with respect to a child who has no presumed father under section 257.55 * * *." Minn.Stat. § 257.57, subd. 3 (2000). The difference in meaning between "declare" and "determine" in this context is de minimis—certainly insufficient to support the dissent's position. First, the definitions of the terms overlap making a distinction based on the dictionary or thesaurus tenuous at best. "Declare" can mean to "make

evident or give evidence of"; "determine" can mean "to fix conclusively or authoritatively." Webster's Third New International Dictionary 586, 616. (1961). Second, even assuming that the terms differ in meaning, they are not necessarily mutually exclusive. A determination may be made as part of a declaration of legal rights and status. Finally, unlike the terms "alleged/alleging" and "presumed", the terms "declare" and "determine" are not used in contradistinction to each other in the Parentage Act.

13. Minnesota Statutes § 257.60 (2000) provides: "The child shall be made a party whenever: * * * (3) an action to declare the existence of the father and child relationship is brought by a man presumed to be the father under section 257.55, or a man who alleges to be the father, and the mother of the child denies the existence of the father and child relationship."

Brennan, J., dissenting). Justice Stevens concurred in the judgment denying the putative father an opportunity to establish his paternity only after concluding that under the California statute at issue the putative father "was given a fair opportunity to show that he is [the child's] natural father, that he developed a relationship with her, and that her interests would be served by granting him visitation rights." *Id.* at 135–36, 109 S.Ct. 2333.

We conclude that a party alleging he is a child's father has standing to bring a paternity action under section 257.57, subdivision 2 to compel blood or genetic testing as provided in section 257.62, subdivision 1 even though he does not at the time the action is commenced possess blood or genetic tests that establish he is the child's presumed father under section 257.55, subdivision 1(f). Witso thus has standing to bring this paternity action.

Our conclusion does not open the door to unfettered challenges to the sanctity of marriages, family unity and parent-child relationships. By vesting in the courts the safeguard of a judicial determination that a putative father has asserted by affidavit sufficient grounds to determine that sexual contact occurred between him and the child's mother that could reasonably have resulted in the child's conception as provided in Minn.Stat. § 257.62, subd. 1 (2000)[14] additional protection is provided against frivolous claims of paternity and a balance is achieved between the interests in the preservation and protection of familial relationships and the interests of the putative father to establish his paternity. In any event, here Overby has admitted that she had sexual contact with Witso that could have resulted in the conception of M.R.O.—thus there is no question that Witso's affidavit alleges sufficient facts establishing requisite sexual contact.

Finally, we note again that even if blood or genetic tests show that Witso is M.R.O.'s presumed biological father under section 257.55, subd. 1(f), James Overby is also a presumed biological father based on his marriage to Overby at the time of M.R.O.'s birth. Section 257.55, subdivision 2 requires the court to weigh the conflicting presumptions, and "the presumption which on the facts is founded on the weightier considerations of policy and logic controls." Minn.Stat. § 257.55, subd. 2 (2000). Thus, even though Witso may establish a presumption of biological fatherhood, whether he should be granted custodial or visitation rights with respect to M.R.O. is for an independent determination later to be made by the district court. We affirm the court of appeals and answer the certified question in the negative.

The dissent's concern that the court's holding may be abused by a rapist or any man armed with an affidavit is overstated. The trial court clearly has discretion to determine whether the affidavit meets the statuto-

---

14. Section 257.62 as originally enacted required the court to order a mother or child to submit to blood or genetic testing upon the request of a party to the action. Minn.Stat. § 257.62, subd. 1 (1980). In 1997 the legislature amended section 257.62, subd. 1 by adding: "A mother or alleged father requesting the tests shall file with the court an affidavit either alleging or denying paternity and setting forth facts that establish the reasonable possibility that there was, or was not, the requisite sexual contact between the parties." Act of May 29, 1997, ch. 203, art. 6, § 21, 1997 Minn. Laws 1587, 1766.

ry requirement in section 257.62, subd. 1. In any event however, it is not for this court to interpret a statute to mean something different than what the legislature clearly intended in order to avoid a potential abuse in a hypothetical circumstance not before the court. As noted above, the statutory framework establishes the putative father's right to obtain blood and genetic testing subject to statutory preconditions, and those preconditions are met in the matter before the court.

Affirmed.

■ LANCASTER, JUSTICE (dissenting)

Because the majority has fundamentally misconstrued the Minnesota Parentage Act and reached a result not contemplated by the statute, I respectfully dissent. As I read Minn.Stat. § 257.57, subd. 1(a) (2000), Benjamin Witso has no standing to bring a cause of action to challenge James Overby's marital presumption of paternity. Furthermore, absent a presumption in Witso's favor, he cannot bring suit to declare his own paternity under Minn.Stat. § 257.57, subd. 2(1) (2000).

. . .

Although Witso allegedly seeks only to declare the existence of his paternity under Minn.Stat. § 257.57, subd. 2, as opposed to challenging Overby's presumption of paternity under section 257.57, subdivision 1, it is necessary to consider both subdivisions to clarify the error in the majority's reading of the statute. Section 257.57, subdivision 1, reads in relevant part:

> A child, the child's biological mother, or a man presumed to be the child's father under section 257.55, subdivision 1, paragraph (a), (b), or (c) may bring an action:

> . . .

> (b) For the purpose of declaring the nonexistence of the father and child relationship presumed under section 257.55, subdivision 1, paragraph (a), (b), or (c) [only within certain time limitations].

As described by the majority, Minn.Stat. § 257.55, subd. 1(a)–(c), discusses the presumptions of paternity based on marriage. Thus, section 257.57, subdivision 1, allows only "a man presumed to be the father" under a marital presumption to bring suit to declare the nonexistence of his own or another man's marital presumption of paternity. Because Witso has no marital presumption in his favor, he has no standing under subdivision 1 to challenge James Overby's marital presumption.

There is a very clear policy reason for this limitation on the ability to challenge a marital presumption; once a family unit has been established, it is very often in the best interests of the child to leave it undisturbed. *See Michael H. v. Gerald D.*, 491 U.S. 110, 124, 109 S.Ct. 2333, 105 L.Ed.2d 91 (1989) ("[T]he institution of the family is deeply rooted in this Nation's history and tradition."); *see also In re Marriage of Ross*, 245 Kan. 591, 783 P.2d 331, 335 (1989) (recognizing, in a UPA state, "the ancient presumption of the legitimacy of a child born in wedlock is one of the strongest presumptions known to the law''); *B.H. v. K.D.*, 506 N.W.2d 368, 376 (N.D.1993) ("[P]arenting and the family unit are important considerations worthy of constitutional protection."). Even if, as the majority implies, an unmarried man like Witso could have a due process interest in a father-child relationship where there is already a presumed father in place, that interest would not arise when he has nothing more than a biological relationship. *See generally Michael H.*, 491 U.S. at 133, 136, 157–58, 109 S.Ct. 2333 (Stevens, J., concurring in judgment; Brennan, J., with Marshall and Blackmun, JJ., dissenting; White, J., dissenting) (agreeing that a biological father might have a constitutionally-protected interest in his relationship with a child whose mother was married to another man at the time the child was born). Rather, "an unwed father's biological link to his child does not, in and of itself, guarantee him a constitutional stake in his relationship with that child, [but] such a link combined with a substantial parent-child relationship will do so." 491 U.S. at 142–43, 109 S.Ct. 2333 (Brennan, J., with Marshall and Blackmun, JJ., dissenting). Here, the record contains no evidence demonstrating the existence of a "substantial parent-child" relationship. In any event, Witso never raised a due process or equal protection argument and therefore conjecture like that engaged in by the majority today is fruitless.

Minnesota Statutes § 257.57, subd. 2, also does not give Witso standing to bring suit to declare the existence of his own father and child relationship with M.R.O. Subdivision 2 states:

> The child, the mother, or * * * a man alleged or alleging himself to be the father * * * may bring an action:

> (1) at any time for the purpose of declaring the existence of the father and child relationship presumed under section 257.55, subdivision 1, paragraph (d), (e), (f), (g), or (h) * * *.

Witso and the majority would have us believe that section 257.57, subdivision 2(1), gives Witso, a man "alleging himself to be the father," standing to obtain blood tests and establish a section 257.55, subdivision 1(f), genetic testing presumption of paternity in himself. But this interpretation ignores the explicit language of section 257.57, subdivision 2, which allows any putative father to bring an action to declare the existence of "*the* father and child relationship presumed under section 257.55." Minn. Stat. § 257.57, subd. 2(1) (emphasis added). The use of "*the* father and child relationship" instead of "*a* father and child relationship" indicates that the statute is referring to a specific preexisting presumed relationship. Section 257.57, subdivision 2, thereby requires that Witso's genetic testing presumption must have existed before he could have standing to declare the existence of a father and child relationship based on that presumption. Because Witso does not have that preexisting presumption, he has no standing to bring the instant suit.[1]

---

1. This is not to say that a putative father would never have standing to declare the existence of his, or another's, paternity. Section 257.57, subdivision 2, gives any putative father standing to declare the existence or nonexistence of his own paternity if there

The majority's characterization of this plain reading interpretation as creating a "chicken-or-egg dilemma" not only glosses over the statutory significance of each section, but also usurps the legislature's rightful role in setting public policy. The majority is wrong, I believe, in failing to acknowledge that important public policies are advanced by Minnesota's legislative adaptation of the UPA. The North Dakota Supreme Court recognized those policies when interpreting North Dakota's parentage statute, which is also based on the UPA and recognizes a paternity presumption based on genetic testing. *B.H. v. K.D.*, 506 N.W.2d at 373–75. Like the present case, *B.H. v. K.D.* involved a man who had no presumptions in his favor but alleged to be the father of a child who already had a presumed father based on a marital presumption. *Id.* at 370. The alleging father moved the district court to order blood tests in order to aid him in proving his paternity. *Id.* Interpreting statutory provisions strikingly similar to those now before this court, the North Dakota Supreme Court held:

> There must be genetic tests already in existence which satisfy the statistical qualifications of the statute. Without the requisite test results, an individual like [the alleging father] cannot bring such an intrusive action, disrupting an established family, hoping that tests ordered by the court will subsequently vest him with standing to proceed. Too much irreparable damage will have occurred to the family in the meantime; the potential for abuse is too great.

Id. at 375.

The error of the majority's decision is further shown by Minn.Stat. § 257.57, subd. 3 (2000). Subdivision three permits an action to determine the existence of a father and child relationship when the child has no presumed father. Under subdivision 3, a putative father would not attempt to "*declar*[e]" the existence of the father and child relationship presumed under section 257.55" as in subdivisions one or two, but would bring "[a]n action to *determine* the existence of the father and child relationship with respect to a child who has no presumed father under section 257.55." Minn.Stat. § 257.57, subd. 3 (emphasis added). While making much of the difference between "presumed" and "alleged" in the MPA, the majority ignores the differences between "determine" and "declare" as used within section 257.57. A party bringing an action to "declare" the existence of a father and child relationship presumed in section 275.55 seeks to "make known clearly or officially" the preexisting factual presumption. *Roget's*

are preexisting facts—such as a signed recognition of parentage or evidence that the putative father received the child into his home and held the child out as his biological child—indicating the putative father was a presumed father. A putative father without a presumption in his favor could also bring suit if he were seeking to declare the nonexistence of *another man's* presumption of paternity based on that man's blood tests or recognition of parentage. Other portions of the MPA also confirm that a putative father will have standing to bring a paternity suit in certain circumstances. Minn.Stat. § 257.60 (2000) ("The child shall be made a party whenever * * * (3) an action to declare the existence of the father and child relationship is brought by a man presumed to be the father under section 257.55, or a man who alleges to be the father * * *."). The facts of this case do not present one of those circumstances.

21st Century Thesaurus *201 (2d ed.1999). In contrast, an action to "determine" the existence of a father and child relationship suggests a process of discovering whether such a relationship, and thus a presumption, exists.*[2] See id. at 222 (listing "discover" as synonym to "determine," but not listing "declare"). In any event, Witso can bring neither action because in the first instance (under section 257.57, subd. 2(1)) he has no preexisting presumption in his favor, and in the second instance (under section 257.57, subd. 3) a presumed father already exists.*

. . .

. . . [T]he majority denies that its holding creates the potential for abuse by "open[ing] the door to unfettered challenges to the sanctity of marriage" and asserts that baseless and intrusive paternity challenges will not follow from its holding because section 257.62, subdivision 1, requires a putative father who is requesting genetic tests to file an affidavit alleging facts regarding sexual contact with the mother at the relevant time. Contrary to the majority's assertions, section 257.62 does not provide an adequate safeguard against the very real potential for abuse of today's holding. Any man with an affidavit claiming that he had sexual contact with the mother during the period of conception may, after today's opinion, intrude upon an established family unit. Minn.Stat. § 257.62, subd. 1(a) ("A mother or alleged father requesting the tests shall file with the court an affidavit either alleging or denying paternity and setting forth facts that establish the reasonable possibility that there was, or was not, the requisite sexual contact between the parties."). Although the majority emphasizes that in this case Mary Overby admitted the sexual contact, it is irrelevant under section 257.62 whether the mother admits or denies the contact.

Finally, even if the mother admits the sexual contact, the majority's reading, taken to its logical conclusion, would give any man who raped the mother standing to obtain blood tests and therefore assert his paternity of the resulting child.[5] See Minn.Stat. § 257.62, subd. 1(a). If the legislature had meant for this statute to create such an intrusive and extreme result, surely it would have stated so explicitly. See In re J.A.V., 547 N.W.2d at 377 (stating that, if the legislature had intended to radically change the parent-child relationship, "it surely would have done so in language of greater clarity than we find here."). See generally Michael H., 491 U.S. at 124 n. 4, 109 S.Ct. 2333 (recognizing the grave problems with giving a rapist a liberty interest in establishing a father and child relationship with a child potentially begotten by rape). Because I cannot see that the legislature intended the result at which the majority arrives, I must dissent.

2. This distinction is highlighted in other states' parentage acts. In Colorado, for instance, "[a]ny interested party * * * may bring an action at any time for the purpose of *determining* the existence or nonexistence of the father and child relationship" under the nonmarital presumptions. Colo.Rev.Stat. § 19–4–107, subd. 2 (2000) (emphasis added). However, only the mother, child, or presumed father may bring an action to "*declar[e]* the existence" or nonexistence of a father-child relationship under the marital presumptions. *Id.,* subd. 1(a)–(b) (2000).

5. This point was conceded at oral argument.

■ [Chief Justice Blatz and Justice Russell A. Anderson joined in the dissent by Justice Lancaster.]

NOTES

Judicial discretion. Note that N.Y. Fam. Ct. Act § 532 (McKinney 1999) provides that

No such test shall be ordered, however, upon a written finding by the court that it is not in the best interests of the child on the basis of res judicata, equitable estoppel, or the presumption of legitimacy of a child born to a married woman.

This "escape hatch" seemingly could permit establishment of legal paternity in one man, even though it is deemed highly probable that another is the biological father.

UNIFORM PARENTAGE ACT (2002)

SECTION 701. SCOPE OF ARTICLE. This [article] does not apply to the birth of a child conceived by means of sexual intercourse [, or as the result of a gestational agreement as provided in [Article] 8].

SECTION 702. PARENTAL STATUS OF DONOR. A donor is not a parent of a child conceived by means of assisted reproduction.

SECTION 703. PATERNITY OF CHILD OF ASSISTED REPRODUCTION. A man who provides sperm for, or consents to, assisted reproduction by a woman as provided in Section 704 with the intent to be the parent of her child, is a parent of the resulting child.

SECTION 704. CONSENT TO ASSISTED REPRODUCTION.

(a) Consent by a woman, and a man who intends to be a parent of a child born to the woman by assisted reproduction must be in a record signed by the woman and the man. This requirement does not apply to a donor.

(b) Failure a man to sign a consent required by subsection (a), before or after birth of the child, does not preclude a finding of paternity if the woman and the man, during the first two years of the child's life resided together in the same household with the child and openly held out the child as their own.

SECTION 705. LIMITATION ON HUSBAND'S DISPUTE OF PATERNITY.

(a) Except as otherwise provided in subsection (b), the husband of a wife who gives birth to a child by means of assisted reproduction may not challenge his paternity of the child unless:

(1) within two years after learning of the birth of the child he commences a proceeding to adjudicate his paternity; and

(2) the court finds that he did not consent to the assisted reproduction, before or after birth of the child.

(b) A proceeding to adjudicate paternity may be maintained at any time if the court determines that:

(1) the husband did not provide sperm for, or before or after the birth of the child consent to, assisted reproduction by his wife;

(2) the husband and the mother of the child have not cohabited since the probable time of assisted reproduction; and

(3) the husband never openly held out the child as his own.

(c) The limitation provided in this section applies to a marriage declared invalid after assisted reproduction.

SECTION 706. EFFECT OF DISSOLUTION OF MARRIAGE OR WITHDRAWAL OF CONSENT.

(a) If a marriage is dissolved before placement of eggs, sperm, or embryos, the former spouse is not a parent of the resulting child unless the former spouse consented in a record that if assisted reproduction were to occur after a divorce, the former spouse would be a parent of the child.

(b) The consent of a woman or a man to assisted reproduction may be withdrawn by that individual in a record at any time before placement of eggs, sperm, or embryos. An individual who withdraws consent under this section is not a parent of the resulting child.

SECTION 707. PARENTAL STATUS OF DECEASED INDIVIDUAL.

If an individual who consented in a record to be a parent by assisted reproduction dies before placement of eggs, sperm, or embryos, the deceased individual is not a parent of the resulting child unless the deceased spouse consented in a record that if assisted reproduction were to occur after death, the deceased individual would be a parent of the child.

Cleo A. E. v. Rickie Gene E.

Supreme Court of Appeals of West Virginia, 1993.
190 W.Va. 543, 438 S.E.2d 886.

■ WORKMAN, CHIEF JUSTICE:

The Child Advocate Office ("CAO") brought this appeal to challenge the voluntary bastardization of a minor child. Having examined the record in this matter in conjunction with the issue presented, this Court concludes that the best interests of the child standard precludes the parties from entering into a stipulation which has as its effect the bastardization of a child born to the parties during their marriage.

Cleo and Rickie E. were married on May 24, 1981, in Mason County, West Virginia. Cleo and Rickie E. had two children—Sheila E. on January 19, 1981, and Amber Dawn E. ("Amber Dawn") on July 9, 1983. Cleo and Rickie E. last cohabited in July 1985 and Cleo E. filed for a divorce on July 10, 1986. Through the final order of divorce, which was entered by the Mason County Circuit Court on August 11, 1986, Cleo E. was awarded custody of both children. No child support was awarded, however, based on the fact that Cleo E. had not made a request for support during the divorce proceedings.

On July 2, 1987, Cleo and Rickie E. entered into a written agreement whereby Rickie E. agreed to pay Cleo E. $250 per month for child support. The record bears no indication that this agreement was ever ratified by the circuit court, but the parties do not dispute the document's existence. In late 1991, the CAO located Rickie E. in Marion County, Florida, through its efforts to collect child support. The CAO filed a petition in the Circuit Court of Cabell County, West Virginia, on February 13, 1992, pursuant to the Uniform Reciprocal Enforcement of Support Act ("URESA"), West Virginia Code §§ 48A–7–1 to–41 (1992 & Supp.1993) to collect support payments.

On May 21, 1992, a hearing was held before the Circuit Court for the Fifth Judicial Circuit in Marion County, Florida, on the URESA petition. Rickie E. appeared and challenged the petition's claim that he was the father of Amber Dawn.[1] He requested that HLA blood testing be performed to determine whether he was in fact the natural father of Amber Dawn. The Florida court ordered Rickie E. to pay $31.24 per week to the court as temporary support. Following the submission of briefs on the issue of whether Rickie E. could properly challenge the paternity of a child conceived during marriage in the Florida court, a second hearing was held on September 15, 1992, in Florida. At this hearing the court ruled that Rickie E. was the father of Amber Dawn and entered an order requiring Rickie E. to pay $62.40 per week to the court beginning September 7, 1992, for support arrearages which totaled $18,074 as of December 31, 1991. The Florida court reserved jurisdiction to modify both support and arrears retroactively upon its receipt of a modified final order of divorce from a West Virginia court.[2]

An amended final order of divorce was entered in West Virginia by the Mason County Circuit Court on October 26, 1992. The order referenced and attached a stipulation which set forth, inter alia, that Rickie E. was not the natural father of Amber Dawn.[3] It is unclear whether the circuit court held an actual hearing on this matter, but its order provides no reasoning for its decision to approve an amendment to the final order of divorce which had as its primary objective the bastardization of one of the children born to the

---

1. Rickie E. claims that he learned through hearsay in late 1991 or early 1992 that a cousin of his was the true father of Amber Dawn.

2. The order of the Circuit Court of Marion County, Florida, dated September 15, 1992, does not state any reason for its finding that Rickie E. is the father of Amber Dawn. However, because the Florida court reserved jurisdiction to modify its order regarding both support and arrears retroactively upon its receipt of a modified final order from a West Virginia court, the implication is that

the court thought that only the West Virginia courts would have jurisdiction to make such a finding. See W.Va.Code § 48A–7–26 (URESA permits court to adjudicate paternity issue "if both of the parties are present at the hearing or the proof required in the case indicates that the presence of either or both of the parties is not necessary").

3. The stipulation was signed by Rickie E. on October 2, 1992, in Florida and by Cleo E. on October 26, 1992, in West Virginia.

parties during their marriage. The CAO brings this appeal seeking to have the amended final order of divorce set aside.

The CAO premises its position on the "nearly universal concept that a child born in wedlock is presumptively legitimate." As this Court explained in Michael K.T. v. Tina L.T., 182 W.Va. 399, 387 S.E.2d 866 (1989): "Historically, society has frowned upon the bastardization of children. Thus, many states like West Virginia view a child as being presumptively legitimate if the child was born or conceived during a marriage." Id. at 402, 387 S.E.2d at 869. Recognizing that this presumption of legitimacy is rebuttable, we ruled in Michael K.T. that blood test evidence offered to disprove paternity should only be admitted after an in camera hearing has been held and various factors considered to determine "whether the equities surrounding the particular facts and circumstances of the case warrant admission of blood test results." See id. at 404, 387 S.E.2d at 871 and Syl. Pt. 2, in part. This Court further instructed in syllabus point four of Michael K.T. that "[a] guardian ad litem should be appointed to represent the interests of the minor child whenever an action is initiated to disprove a child's paternity." Id. at 400, 387 S.E.2d at 867.

The CAO argues that the guidelines established in Michael K.T. regarding the admissibility of blood test evidence should be extended to cases such as this which involve a stipulated disavowal of paternity. In Michael K.T., we instructed courts to consider these factors: (1) the length of time following when the putative father first was placed on notice that he might be the biological father before he acted to contest paternity; (2) the length of time during which the individual desiring to challenge paternity assumed the role of father to the child; (3) the facts surrounding the putative father's discovery of nonpaternity; (4) the nature of the father/child relationship; (5) the age of the child; (6) the harm which may result to the child if paternity were successfully disproved; (7) the extent to which the passage of time reduced the chances of establishing paternity and a child support obligation in favor of the child; and (8) all other factors which may affect the equities involved in the potential disruption of the parent/child relationship or the chances of undeniable harm to the child. Id. at 405, 387 S.E.2d at 872.

We determine initially that the parties to a domestic proceeding cannot by stipulation agree to bastardize children born during their marriage. Our conclusion is not founded on the traditional arguments against bastardization: the social stigma imposed on the child and the financial burden imposed on the state. As we discussed in Michael K.T., "[t]hese two historical bases for opposing bastardization have been significantly vitiated given the modernization of society and legislation drafted to address the problems of bastardization." 182 W.Va. at 402–03, 387 S.E.2d at 869. Rather, we are once again guided by the cardinal principle that "the best interests of the child is the polar star by which decisions must be made which affect children." Id. at 405, 387 S.E.2d at 872. Furthermore, a child has a right to an establishment of paternity and a child support obligation, and a right to independent representation on matters affecting his or her substantial rights and interests.

Because it appears that consideration of Amber Dawn's best interests were totally ignored in the proceedings below, we conclude that a court cannot properly adjudicate the issue of paternity based on a stipulation between the parties. Given the serious and long-lasting effects of bastardization, resolution of the paternity issue should be accomplished with the active participation of the court, rather than involvement that is limited to reviewing a previously-executed document. This is necessary to guarantee that the issue of paternity is not used as a bargaining tool, perhaps to secure a favorable monetary award or some other preferred attainment. But, more importantly, it is required to secure proper consideration of the facts of the case in light of the best interests of the child and with due regard to the rights of the child. Accordingly, the guidelines which this Court identified in Michael K.T., regarding the admission of blood test evidence on the issue of paternity, should similarly be utilized when making a ruling which has as its effect the bastardization of a minor child. See 182 W.Va. at 405, 387 S.E.2d at 872.

This case demonstrates vividly the need for a court-appointed attorney to represent the interests of a child whose paternity is at issue. Not only were the interests of Amber Dawn unrepresented during the drafting of the stipulation, but the court's approval of the document was also apparently made without any consideration for its impact upon her. Further, a hearing should have been held for the presentation of evidence on the factors enumerated in Michael K.T. such as: the length of time following when Rickie E. allegedly learned that he was not the natural father of Amber Dawn and when he took action to disprove paternity; the period of time during which Rickie E. assumed the role of father to Amber Dawn and the nature of their relationship; the harm which might result through disestablishment of paternity; and the extent to which the passage of time reduced the possibility that paternity can be established and child support obtained. See id.

Although historically courts have addressed issues affecting children primarily in the context of competing adults' rights, the present trend in courts throughout the country is to give greater recognition to the rights of children, including their right to independent representation in proceedings affecting substantial rights. Consequently, we extend our previous ruling in Michael K.T. regarding the appointment of a guardian ad litem.[4] A guardian ad litem should be appointed to represent the interests of a minor child whenever the issue of disproving paternity is involved in a proceeding,

---

4. In response to the Michael K.T. decision the Legislature amended West Virginia Code § 48–2–11 (Supp.1993) to include subsection (b) which reads as follows: If, in an action for divorce or annulment, either party shall allege that a person, other than the husband, is the father of a child born during the marriage of the parties, the court shall appoint a competent attorney to act as guardian ad litem on behalf of the child. The attorney shall be appointed without motion and prior to an entry of any order requiring blood testing. W.Va.Code § 48–2–11(b).

regardless of whether the proceeding was initiated for the sole purpose of disproving paternity.[5] Furthermore, if paternity of a child is abrogated, the guardian ad litem should seek to establish legal paternity and child support.[6]

The CAO suggests that a finding of fraud against Cleo E. is necessary to overcome the res judicata doctrine established by this Court in State ex. rel. West Virginia Dep't of Health and Human Resources v. Cline, 185 W.Va. 318, 406 S.E.2d 749 (1991). We ruled in Cline in syllabus point two that "[a]n adjudication of paternity, which is expressed in a divorce order, is res judicata as to the husband and wife in any subsequent proceeding." 185 W.Va. at 319, 406 S.E.2d at 750 (quoting Syl. Pt. 1, in part, Nancy Darlene M. v. James Lee M., Jr., 184 W.Va. 447, 400 S.E.2d 882 (1990)). The Cline decision also referenced this Court's statement in Michael K.T. that "absent evidence of fraudulent conduct which prevented the putative father from questioning paternity, this Court will not sanction the disputation of paternity through blood test evidence if there has been more than a relatively brief passage of time." 185 W.Va. at 321, 406 S.E.2d at 752 (quoting Michael K.T., 182 W.Va. at 405, 387 S.E.2d at 872). Certainly, evidence of fraud on the part of Cleo E. of withholding information from Rickie E. concerning the identity of Amber Dawn's biological father would be relevant on remand if the circuit court is required to rule on blood testing, or ultimately, when it makes its ruling regarding the paternity of Amber Dawn.

Based on the foregoing, the decision of the Circuit Court of Mason County is hereby reversed and remanded for additional proceedings consistent with this opinion.

NOTES

Spousal testimony and the presumption of legitimacy. In its strictest form, the presumption of legitimacy would virtually preclude testimony by the mother or her husband that would cause the child to be deemed illegitimate. Many jurisdictions have modified this rule substantially. *See, e.g.*, Cassady v. Martin, 220 Va. 1093, 266 S.E.2d 104 (1980).

---

5. This Court's decision in Michael K.T. arguably permits the appointment of a guardian ad litem presently in such cases given the directive contained therein that "a guardian ad litem should be appointed to represent the interests of the minor child whenever the issue of disproving paternity is raised outside of a proceeding contemplated by W.Va.Code § 48A–6–1." 182 W.Va. at 406, 387 S.E.2d at 873. Because, however, the issue of Amber Dawn's paternity was resolved through a stipulation rather than any specific court proceeding, we resolve any potential confusion by creating a separate syllabus point addressing this issue; in actuality, our ruling regard-

ing the required appointment of a guardian ad litem is more of a clarification than an extension.

6. In Michael K.T., we pointed out that the fees of a guardian ad litem in a divorce or related domestic relations action should be paid by the party most able to bear that cost. 182 W.Va. at 406, 387 S.E.2d at 873. In the event paternity is disproved, the court should appoint the guardian for the child, and the guardian should act expeditiously to establish actual paternity and to obtain entry of a child support award.

Special statutory tests or criteria. Statutes establishing special benefit or insurance schemes, such as workers' compensation, may provide their own definitions or standards of proof regarding parentage and dependency. *See, e.g.,* VA. CODE § 65.2–515 (Michie 1995); Allstate Messenger Service v. James, 220 Va. 910, 266 S.E.2d 86 (1980).

The child as a party. Section 603 of the Uniform Parentage Act (2002) requires that the mother of the child and a man whose paternity of the child is to be adjudicated be joined as parties to a paternity action. Section 612 provides that a minor child is a permissible but not a necessary party, rejecting the view that a child necessarily has independent standing in a parentage proceeding. However, if the child is not a party this may be of importance with regard to later support actions in some jurisdictions. As a general rule the parent-child relationship does not automatically establish privity and thus a child is not necessarily bound by a judgment against the parent. *See* Note, *Privity, Preclusion, and the Parent–Child Relationship,* 1977 B.Y.U.L.REV. 612 (1972).

Little v. Streater

Supreme Court of the United States, 1981.
452 U.S. 1, 101 S.Ct. 2202, 68 L.Ed.2d 627.

■ CHIEF JUSTICE BURGER delivered the opinion of the Court.

This appeal presents the question whether a Connecticut statute which provides that in paternity actions the cost of blood grouping tests is to be borne by the party requesting them, violates the Due Process and Equal Protection Clauses of the Fourteenth Amendment when applied to deny such tests to indigent defendants.

On May 21, 1975, appellee Gloria Streater, while unmarried, gave birth to a female child, Kenyatta Chantel Streater. As a requirement stemming from her child's receipt of public assistance, appellee identified appellant Walter Little as the child's father to the Connecticut Department of Social Services. See Conn.Gen.Stat. § 46b–169 (1981). The Department then provided an attorney for appellee to bring a paternity suit against appellant in the Court of Common Pleas at New Haven to establish his liability for the child's support.

At the time the paternity action was commenced, appellant was incarcerated in the Connecticut Correctional Institution at Enfield. Through his counsel, who was provided by a legal aid organization, appellant moved the trial court to order blood grouping tests on appellee and her child pursuant to Conn.Gen.Stat. § 52–184 (1977), which ... includes the provision that "[t]he costs of making such tests shall be chargeable against the party making the motion." Appellant asserted that he was indigent and asked that the State be ordered to pay for the tests. The trial court granted the motion insofar as it sought blood grouping tests but denied the request that they be furnished at the State's expense.

For "financial reasons," no blood grouping tests were performed even though they had been authorized. The paternity action was tried to the court on September 28, 1978. Both appellee and appellant, who was still a state prisoner, testified at trial. After listening to the testimony, the court found that appellant was the child's father. Following a subsequent hearing on damages, the court entered judgment against appellant in the amount of $6,974.48, which included the "lying-in" expenses of appellee and the child, "accrued maintenance" through October 31, 1978, and the "costs of suit plus reasonable attorney's fees." In addition, appellant was ordered to pay child support at the rate of $2 per month—$1 toward the arrearage amount of $6,974.48 and $1 toward a current monthly award of $163.58—directly to Connecticut's Department of Finance and Control.[5]

... Appellant argues that his [Fourteenth Amendment] right to due process was abridged by the refusal, under Conn.Gen.Stat. § 46b–168 (1981), to grant his request based on indigency for state-subsidized blood grouping tests.

. . .

The application of blood tests to the issue of paternity results from certain properties of the human blood groups and types: (a) the blood group and type of any individual can be determined at birth or shortly thereafter; (b) the blood group and type of every individual remain constant throughout life; and (c) the blood groups and types are inherited in accordance with Mendel's laws. [S. Schatkin, Disputed Paternity Proceedings (1975)], § 5.03. If the blood groups and types of the mother and child are known, the possible and impossible blood groups and types of the true father can be determined under the rules of inheritance. For example, a group AB child cannot have a group O parent, but can have a group A, B, or AB parent. Similarly, a child cannot be type M unless one or both parents are type M, and the factor cannot appear in the blood of a child unless present in the blood of one or both parents. Id., §§ 5.03 and 6.02. Since millions of men belong to the possible groups and types, a blood grouping test cannot conclusively establish paternity. However, it can demonstrate nonpaternity, such as where the alleged father belongs to group O and the child is group AB. It is a negative rather than an affirmative test with the potential to scientifically exclude the paternity of a falsely accused putative father.

The ability of blood grouping tests to exonerate innocent putative fathers was confirmed by a 1976 report developed jointly by the American Bar Association and the American Medical Association. Miale, Jennings, Rettberg, Sell, & Krause, Joint AMA–ABA Guidelines: Present Status of Serologic Testing in Problems of Disputed Parentage, 10 Family L.Q. 247 (Fall 1976). The joint report recommended the use of seven blood test

---

5. The minimal sum of $2 was ordered presumably because appellant was indigent and incarcerated. However, his payments to the State are subject to future increase pursuant to Conn.Gen.Stat. § 46b–171 (1981), which provides that "[a]ny order for the payment of [child] support ... may at any time thereafter be set aside or altered by any court issuing such order."

"systems"—ABO, Rh, MNSs, Kell, Duffy, Kidd, and HLA—when investigating questions of paternity. These systems were found to be "reasonable" in cost and to provide a 91% cumulative probability of negating paternity for erroneously accused Negro men and 93% for white men.

The effectiveness of the seven systems attests the probative value of blood test evidence in paternity cases. The importance of that scientific evidence is heightened because "[t]here are seldom accurate or reliable eyewitnesses since the sexual activities usually take place in intimate and private surroundings, and the self-serving testimony of a party is of questionable reliability." Larson, Blood Test Exclusion Procedures in Paternity Litigation: The Uniform Acts and Beyond, 13 J.Fam.L. 713 (1973–1974). . . .

Appellant emphasizes that, unlike a common dispute between private parties, the State's involvement in this paternity proceeding was considerable and manifest, giving rise to a constitutional duty. Because appellee's child was a recipient of public assistance, Connecticut law compelled her, upon penalty of fine and imprisonment for contempt, "to disclose the name of the putative father under oath and to institute an action to establish the paternity of said child." Conn.Gen.Stat. § 46b–169 (1981). See Maher v. Doe, 432 U.S. 526, 97 S.Ct. 2474, 53 L.Ed.2d 534 (1977); Roe v. Norton, 422 U.S. 391, 95 S.Ct. 2221, 45 L.Ed.2d 268 (1975). The State's Attorney General automatically became a party to the action, and any settlement agreement required his approval or that of the Commissioner of Human Resources or Commissioner of Income Maintenance. The State referred this mandatory paternity suit to appellee's lawyer "for prosecution" and paid his fee as well as all costs of the litigation. In addition, the State will be the recipient of the monthly support payments to be made by appellant pursuant to the trial court's judgment. "State action" has undeniably pervaded this case. Accordingly, appellant need not, and does not, contend that Connecticut has a constitutional obligation to fund blood tests for an indigent's defense in ordinary civil litigation between private parties.

The nature of paternity proceedings in Connecticut also bears heavily on appellant's due process claim. Although the State characterizes such proceedings as "civil," see Robertson v. Apuzzo, 170 Conn. 367, 372–373, 365 A.2d 824, 827–828 cert. denied 429 U.S. 852 (1976), they have "quasi-criminal" overtones. Connecticut Gen.Stat. § 46b–171 (1981) provides that if a putative father "is found *guilty*, the court shall order him to stand charged with the support and maintenance of such child" (emphasis added); and his subsequent failure to comply with the court's support order is punishable by imprisonment under Conn.Gen.Stat. §§ 46b–171, 46b–215, and 53–304 (1981).

Moreover, the defendant in a Connecticut paternity action faces an unusual evidentiary obstacle. Connecticut's original "bastardy" statute was enacted in 1672, and from 1702 until 1902 it stated in pertinent part: "And if such woman shall continue constant in her accusation, being put to the discovery in the time of her travail, and also examined on the trial of the cause, it shall be prima facie evidence that such accused person is the father of such child." Mosher v. Bennett, 108 Conn. 671, 672, 144 A. 297 (1929). . . .

. . . In its modern form, Conn.Gen.Stat. § 46b–160 (1981) simply states that "if such mother or expectant mother continues constant in her accusation, it shall be evidence that the respondent is the father of such child." Nevertheless, in Mosher v. Bennett, supra, at 674, 144 A., at 298, the Connecticut Supreme Court held:

> "The mother still has the right to rely upon the prima facie case made out by constancy in her accusation. She is no longer required under oath to make discovery at the time of her travail. *The prima facie case so made out places upon the reputed father the burden of showing his innocence of the charge, and under our practice he must do this by other evidence than his own."* (Emphasis added.)

Under Connecticut law, therefore, the defendant in a paternity suit is placed at a distinct disadvantage in that his testimony alone is insufficient to overcome the plaintiff's prima facie case. Among the most probative additional evidence the defendant might offer are the results of blood grouping tests, but if he is indigent, the State essentially denies him that reliable scientific proof by requiring that he bear its cost. In substance, the State has created an adverse presumption regarding the defendant's testimony by elevating the weight to be accorded the mother's imputation of him. If the plaintiff has been "constant" in her accusation of paternity, the defendant carries the burden of proof and faces severe penalties if he does not meet that burden and fails to comply with the judgment entered against him. Yet not only is the State inextricably involved in paternity litigation such as this and responsible for an imbalance between the parties, it in effect forecloses what is potentially a conclusive means for an indigent defendant to surmount that disparity and exonerate himself. Such a practice is irreconcilable with the command of the Due Process Clause.

Our holding in Mathews v. Eldridge, 424 U.S., at 335, 96 S.Ct., at 903, set forth three elements to be evaluated in determining what process is constitutionally due: the private interests at stake; the risk that the procedures used will lead to erroneous results and the probable value of the suggested procedural safeguard; and the governmental interests affected. Analysis of those considerations weighs in appellant's favor.

The private interests implicated here are substantial. Apart from the putative father's pecuniary interest in avoiding a substantial support obligation and liberty interest threatened by the possible sanctions for noncompliance, at issue is the creation of a parent-child relationship. . . . Through the judicial process, the State properly endeavors to identify the father of a child born out of wedlock and to make him responsible for the child's maintenance. Obviously, both the child and the defendant in a paternity action have a compelling interest in the accuracy of such a determination.

Given the usual absence of witnesses, the self-interest coloring the testimony of the litigants, and the State's onerous evidentiary rule and refusal to pay for blood grouping tests, the risk is not inconsiderable that an indigent defendant in a Connecticut paternity proceeding will be erroneously adjudged the father of the child in question. See generally H. Krause, Illegitimacy: Law and Social Policy 106–108 (1971). Further, because of its recognized capacity to definitively exclude a high percentage of falsely accused putative fathers, the availability of scientific blood test evidence clearly would be a valuable procedural safeguard in such cases. Connecticut has acknowledged as much in § 46b–168 of its statutes by providing for the ordering of blood tests and the admissibility of negative findings. Unlike other evidence that may be susceptible to varying interpretation or disparagement, blood test results, if obtained under proper conditions by qualified experts, are difficult to refute. Thus, access to blood grouping tests for indigent defendants such as appellant would help to insure the correctness of paternity decisions in Connecticut.

The State admittedly has a legitimate interest in the welfare of a child born out of wedlock who is receiving public assistance, as well as in securing support for the child from those legally responsible. In addition, it shares the interest of the child and the defendant in an accurate and just determination of paternity. Nevertheless, the State also has financial concerns; it wishes to have the paternity actions in which it is involved proceed as economically as possible and, hence, seeks to avoid the expense of blood grouping tests.[10] Pursuant to 42 U.S.C. § 655(a)(1) (1976 ed. and Supp. III), however, the states are entitled to reimbursement of 75% of the funds they expend on operation of their approved child support plans, and regulations promulgated under authority of 42 U.S.C. § 1302 make clear that such federal financial participation is available for the development of evidence regarding paternity, "including the use of . . . blood tests." 45 CFR § 304.20(b)(2)(i)(B) (1980). Moreover, following the example of other states, the expense of blood grouping tests for an indigent defendant in a Connecticut paternity suit could be advanced by the State and then taxed as costs to the parties. We must conclude that the State's monetary interest "is hardly significant enough to overcome private interests as important as those here." Lassiter v. Department of Social Services, 452 U.S., at 28, 101 S.Ct., at 2160.

Assessment of the Mathews v. Eldridge factors indicates that appellant did not receive the process he was constitutionally due. Without aid in obtaining blood test evidence in a paternity case, an indigent defendant, who faces the State as an adversary when the child is a recipient of public assistance and who must overcome the evidentiary burden Connecticut imposes, lacks "a meaningful opportunity to be heard." Boddie v. Connecticut, 401 U.S., at 377, 91 S.Ct., at 785. Therefore, "the requirement of

---

10. Laboratories surveyed in a 1977 study sponsored by the Department of Health, Education and Welfare (now in part the Department of Health and Human Services) charged an average of approximately $245 for a battery of test systems that led to a minimum exclusion rate of 80%. HEW Office of Child Support Enforcement, Blood Testing to Establish Paternity 35–37 (1977 Condensed Report). According to appellant, blood grouping tests were available at the Hartford Hospital for $250 at the time this paternity action was pending trial, but the cost has since been increased to $460.

'fundamental fairness'" expressed by the Due Process Clause was not satisfied here.

"[A] statute . . . may be held constitutionally invalid as applied when it operates to deprive an individual of a protected right although its general validity as a measure enacted in the legitimate exercise of state power is beyond question." Boddie v. Connecticut, 401 U.S., at 379, 91 S.Ct., at 786. Thus, "a cost requirement, valid on its face, may offend due process because it operates to foreclose a particular party's opportunity to be heard." Id., at 380, 91 S.Ct., at 787. We hold that, in these specific circumstances, the application of Conn.Gen.Stat. § 46b–168 (1981) to deny appellant blood grouping tests because of his lack of financial resources violated the due process guarantee of the Fourteenth Amendment. Accordingly, the judgment of the Appellate Session of the Connecticut Superior Court is reversed, and the case is remanded for further proceedings not inconsistent with this opinion.

G.P. v. State

Florida District Court of Appeals, 2003.
842 So.2d 1059.

■ STONE, J.

We reverse a declaratory judgment in which the trial court found that sections 63.087–088(5), Florida Statutes, relating to private adoptions under the Florida Adoption Act, were not unconstitutional. The Attorney General of Florida has intentionally failed to file a contesting brief and neither the attorney general nor the Palm Beach County State Attorney appeared at the hearing below.

Appellants are four women who have each executed a formal consent for adoption of their children and have authorized an intermediary to file a petition to terminate their parental rights. Because, in each case, the identity of the fathers is unknown, constructive notice is required under the challenged statutory provisions.

Appellants moved for declaratory relief, challenging sections 63.087 and 63.088(5) as violative of their right to privacy guaranteed under the Fourteenth Amendment of the United States Constitution and Article I, § 23 of the Florida Constitution. Although the trial court agreed that the provisions violated Appellants' right to privacy, the court found that Appellants had failed to prove that the state did not have a compelling interest to invade their privacy or that the interest could be achieved through less intrusive means. The court did find that the statutes were unconstitutional as to the women whose pregnancy was a result of sexual battery.

Under the challenged statutes, Appellants would be forced to publish information relating to their sexual relations that may have led to the child's conception. Section 63.087(6)(f) provides, in relevant part:

(f) The petition must include:

1. The minor's name, gender, date of birth, and place of birth. The petition must contain all names by which the minor is or has been known, excluding the minor's prospective adoptive name but including the minor's legal name at the time of the filing of the petition, to allow interested parties to the action, including parents, persons having legal custody of the minor, persons with custodial or visitation rights to the minor, and persons entitled to notice pursuant to the Uniform Child Custody Jurisdiction Act or the Indian Child Welfare Act, to identify their own interest in the action.

2. If the petition is filed before the day the minor is 6 months old and if the identity or location of the father is unknown, each city in which the mother resided or traveled, in which conception may have occurred, during the 12 months before the minor's birth, including the county and state in which that city is located.

3. Unless a consent to adoption or affidavit of nonpaternity executed by each person whose consent is required under s. 63.062 is attached to the petition, the name and the city of residence, including the county and state in which that city is located, of:

a. The minor's mother;

b. Any man who the mother reasonably believes may be the minor's father. . . .

§ 63.087(6)(f)1–3, Fla. Stat. (2002).

Notice and service requirements are governed by section 63.088, Florida Statutes. Appellants challenge only subsection (5) of section 63.088, which states:

(5) LOCATION UNKNOWN OR IDENTITY UNKNOWN. This subsection only applies if, as to any person whose consent is required under s. 63.062 and who has not executed an affidavit of nonpaternity, the location or identity of the person is unknown and the inquiry under subsection (3) fails to identify the person or the diligent search under subsection (4) fails to locate the person. The unlocated or unidentified person must be served notice under subsection (2) by constructive service in the manner provided in chapter 49 in each county identified in the petition, as provided in s. 63.087(6). The notice, in addition to all information required in the petition under s. 63.087(6) and chapter 49, must contain a physical description, including, but not limited to, age, race, hair and eye color, and approximate height and weight of the minor's mother and of any person the mother reasonably believes may be the father; the minor's date of birth, and any date and city, including the county and state in which the city is located, in which conception may have occurred. If any of the facts that must be included in the notice under this subsection are unknown and cannot be reasonably ascertained, the notice must so state.

§ 63.088(5), Fla. Stat.

Article I, section 23 of the Florida Constitution, recognizes a right to privacy in this state and provides: "[e]very natural person has the right to be let alone and free from governmental intrusion into the person's private life as otherwise provided herein." This right to privacy encompasses at least two different categories of interest. The first is "the individual interest in avoiding disclosure of personal matters[.]" *Rasmussen v. S. Fla. Blood Serv., Inc.*, 500 So.2d 533, 536 (Fla.1987)(quoting *Whalen v. Roe*, 429 U.S. 589, 599–600, 97 S.Ct. 869, 51 L.Ed.2d 64 (1977)). The second is "the interest in independence in making certain kinds of important decisions." *Id.* In deciding whether this constitutional right is impacted, the courts consider both the individual's subjective expectation and the values of privacy that our society seeks to foster. *Jackson v. State*, 833 So.2d 243 (Fla. 4th DCA 2002).

The concern as to sections 63.087 and 63.088(5) is that the offending provisions substantially interfere with both a woman's independence in choosing adoption as an alternative and with the right not to disclose the intimate personal information that is required when the father is unknown. We deem the invasion of both of these interests so patent in this instance as to not require our analysis of cases interpreting this constitutional provision. *See generally, Von Eiff v. Azicri*, 720 So.2d 510 (Fla.1998); *In re T.W.*, 551 So.2d 1186 (Fla.1989).

Having thus determined that the statutes violate a fundamental right to privacy, the burden of proof shifted to the state to justify the intrusion on the mothers' privacy. *See Von Eiff*, 720 So.2d at 514. The standard is one of strict scrutiny. The state has the burden of demonstrating that the challenged statutes serve a compelling state interest and that they accomplish the intended result, i.e., notice to fathers, through the use of the least intrusive means. *Id.; Fla. Bd. of Bar Examiners Re: Applicant*, 443 So.2d 71, 74 (Fla.1983)("The compelling state interest or strict scrutiny standard imposes a heavy burden of justification upon the state to show an important societal need and the use of the least intrusive means to achieve that goal.").

The legislature's intent in enacting the stringent notice provisions was to finalize private adoptions by ensuring that all possible avenues of affording parents their due process have been exhausted and to protect the child by ensuring that any future challenge to the adoption based on lack of notice would be unsuccessful.

The state has failed to demonstrate, however, how any compelling interest of either the putative father or the state outweighs the privacy rights of the mother and child in not being identified in such a personal, intimate, and intrusive manner.

We do not address the alternative proposals that have been raised by the appellants which are designed to ensure that notice is sufficient to protect the due process rights of the unknown fathers, such as by registration with a state or national database, or simply by a more narrowly tailored statute.

It is sufficient, here, given the state's effective waiver of interest, to simply recognize that the state failed to demonstrate a sufficiently compelling interest for such an invasion of privacy and that the interests sought to be achieved could not have been accomplished by less intrusive means. Strict scrutiny imposes a heavy burden on the state. *Fla. Bd. of Bar Examiners,* 443 So.2d at 74. Thus, the trial court erred in placing the burden on Appellants to prove the state did not have a compelling interest and that the means used were not the least intrusive.

We conclude that the state failed to meet its burden of proof in demonstrating the validity of the challenged provisions. The state has, in effect, conceded that the statutes cannot survive a strict scrutiny challenge. Accordingly, the order on appeal is reversed. We remand for further proceedings as governed by the remainder of the statute.

■ WARNER and HAZOURI, JJ., concur.

NOTE

In Lavertue v. Niman, 196 Conn. 403, 493 A.2d 213 (1985), the Supreme Court of Connecticut held that indigent defendants in state-supported paternity actions have a constitutional right, under both U.S. and Connecticut constitutions, to have court-appointed counsel at state expense. The court declined to adopt a "case-by-case" approach to appointment of counsel not only because of the special evidentiary problems of the Connecticut statute but also because of the difficulties of assessing the complexities of a given paternity trial in advance.

Lalli v. Lalli

Supreme Court of the United States, 1978.
439 U.S. 259, 99 S.Ct. 518, 58 L.Ed.2d 503.

■ MR. JUSTICE POWELL announced the judgment of the Court in an opinion, in which THE CHIEF JUSTICE and MR. JUSTICE STEWART join.

This case presents a challenge to the constitutionality of § 4–1.2 of New York's Estates, Powers, and Trusts Law, which requires illegitimate children who would inherit from their fathers by intestate succession to provide a particular form of proof of paternity. Legitimate children are not subject to the same requirement.

Appellant Robert Lalli claims to be the illegitimate son of Mario Lalli who died intestate on January 7, 1973, in the State of New York. Appellant's mother, who died in 1968, never was married to Mario. After Mario's widow, Rosamond Lalli, was appointed administratrix of her husband's estate, appellant petitioned the Surrogate's Court for Westchester County for a compulsory accounting, claiming that he and his sister Maureen Lalli were entitled to inherit from Mario as his children. Rosamond Lalli opposed the petition. She argued that even if Robert and Maureen were Mario's children, they were not lawful distributees of the estate because they had failed to comply with § 4–1.2, which provides in part:

> "An illegitimate child is the legitimate child of his father so that he and his issue inherit from his father if a court of competent jurisdiction has, during the lifetime of the father, made an order of filiation declaring paternity in a proceeding instituted during the pregnancy of the mother or within two years from the birth of the child."

Appellant conceded that he had not obtained an order of filiation during his putative father's lifetime. He contended, however, that § 4–1.2, by imposing this requirement, discriminated against him on the basis of his illegitimate birth in violation of the Equal Protection Clause of the Fourteenth Amendment. Appellant tendered certain evidence of his relationship with Mario Lalli, including a notarized document in which Lalli, in consenting to appellant's marriage, referred to him as "my son," and several affidavits by persons who stated that Lalli had acknowledged openly and often that Robert and Maureen were his children.

. . .

We begin our analysis with *Trimble* [v. Gordon, 430 U.S. 762, 97 S.Ct. 1459, 52 L.Ed.2d 31 (1977)]. At issue in that case was the constitutionality of an Illinois statute providing that a child born out of wedlock could inherit from his intestate father only if the father had "acknowledged" the child and the child had been legitimated by the intermarriage of the parents. The appellant in *Trimble* was a child born out of wedlock whose father had neither acknowledged her nor married her mother. He had, however, been found to be her father in a judicial decree ordering him to contribute to her support. When the father died intestate, the child was excluded as a distributee because the statutory requirements for inheritance had not been met.

We concluded that the Illinois statute discriminated against illegitimate children in a manner prohibited by the Equal Protection Clause. Although ... classifications based on illegitimacy are not subject to "strict scrutiny," they nevertheless are invalid under the Fourteenth Amendment if they are not substantially related to permissible state interests. Upon examination, we found that the Illinois law failed that test.

Two state interests were proposed which the statute was said to foster: the encouragement of legitimate family relationships and the maintenance of an accurate and efficient method of disposing of an intestate decedent's property. Granting that the State was appropriately concerned with the integrity of the family unit, we viewed the statute as bearing "only the most attenuated relationship to the asserted goal." We again rejected the argument that "persons will shun illicit relationships because the offspring may not one day reap the benefits" that would accrue to them were they legitimate. Weber v. Aetna Casualty & Surety Co., 406 U.S. 164, 173, 92 S.Ct. 1400, 1405, 31 L.Ed.2d 768 (1972). The statute therefore was not defensible as an incentive to enter legitimate family relationships.

Illinois' interest in safeguarding the orderly disposition of property at death was more relevant to the statutory classification. We recognized that devising "an appropriate legal framework" in the furtherance of that interest "is a matter particularly within the competence of the individual States." *Trimble,* supra, 430 U.S. at 771, 97 S.Ct. at 1465. An important aspect of that framework is a response to the often difficult problem of proving the paternity of illegitimate children and the related danger of spurious claims against intestate estates. These difficulties, we said, "might justify a more demanding standard for illegitimate children claiming under their fathers' estates than that required either for illegitimate children claiming under their mothers' estates or for legitimate children generally."

The Illinois statute, however, was constitutionally flawed because, by insisting upon not only an acknowledgment by the father, but also the marriage of the parents, it excluded "at least some significant categories of illegitimate children of intestate men [whose] inheritance rights can be recognized without jeopardizing the orderly settlement of estates or the dependability of titles to property passing under intestacy laws." We concluded that the Equal Protection Clause required that a statute placing exceptional burdens on illegitimate children in the furtherance of proper State objectives must be more "carefully tuned to alternative considerations," than was true of the broad disqualification in the Illinois law.

The New York statute, enacted in 1965, was intended to soften the rigors of previous law which permitted illegitimate children to inherit only from their mothers. By lifting the absolute bar to paternal inheritance, § 4–1.2 tended to achieve its desired effect. As in *Trimble,* however, the question before us is whether the remaining statutory obstacles to inheritance by illegitimate children can be squared with the Equal Protection Clause.

At the outset we observe that § 4–1.2 is different in important respects from the statutory provision overturned in *Trimble.* The Illinois statute required, in addition to the father's acknowledgment of paternity, the legitimation of the child through the intermarriage of the parents as an absolute precondition to inheritance. This combination of requirements eliminated "the possibility of a middle ground between the extremes of complete exclusion and case-by-case determination of paternity." *Trimble,* supra, 430 U.S. at 770–771, 97 S.Ct. at 1465. As illustrated by the facts in *Trimble,* even a judicial declaration of paternity was insufficient to permit inheritance.

Under § 4–1.2, by contrast, the marital status of the parents is irrelevant. The single requirement at issue here is an evidentiary one—that the paternity of the father be declared in a judicial proceeding sometime before his death.[5] The child need not have been legitimated in order to

---

5. Section 4–1.2 requires not only that the order of filiation be made during the lifetime of the father, but that the proceeding in which it is sought be commenced "during the pregnancy of the mother or within two years from the birth of the child." The New York Court of Appeals declined to rule on the constitutionality of the two-year limitation in

inherit from his father. Had the appellant in *Trimble* been governed by § 4–1.2, she would have been a distributee of her father's estate.

A related difference between the two provisions pertains to the state interests said to be served by them. The Illinois law was defended, in part, as a means of encouraging legitimate family relationships. No such justification has been offered in support of § 4–1.2.

. . .

Our inquiry, therefore, is focused narrowly. We are asked to decide whether the discrete procedural demands that § 4–1.2 places on illegitimate children bear an evident and substantial relation to the particular state interests this statute is designed to serve.

The primary state goal underlying the challenged aspects of § 4–1.2 is to provide for the just and orderly disposition of property at death.[6] We long have recognized that this is an area with which the States have an interest of considerable magnitude.

This interest is directly implicated in paternal inheritance by illegitimate children because of the peculiar problems of proof that are involved. Establishing maternity is seldom difficult.... Proof of paternity, by contrast, frequently is difficult when the father is not part of a formal family unit....

Thus, a number of problems arise that counsel against treating illegitimate children identically to all other heirs of an intestate father. These were the subject of a comprehensive study by the Temporary State Commission on the Modernization, Revision and Simplification of the Law of Estates. This group, known as the Bennett Commission, consisted of individuals experienced in the practical problems of estate administration. The Commission issued its report and recommendations to the Legislature in 1965. The statute now codified as § 4–1.2 was included.

Although the overarching purpose of the proposed statute was "to alleviate the plight of the illegitimate child," Commission Report 37, the Bennett Commission considered it necessary to impose the strictures of § 4–1.2 in order to mitigate serious difficulties in the administration of the estates of both testate and intestate decedents. The Commission's perception of some of these difficulties was described by Surrogate Sobel, a

both of its opinions in this case because appellant concededly had never commenced a paternity proceeding at all. Thus, if the rule that paternity be judicially declared during his father's lifetime were upheld, appellant would lose for failure to comply with that requirement alone. If, on the other hand, appellant prevailed in his argument that his inheritance could not be conditioned on the existence of an order of filiation, the two-year limitation would become irrelevant since the paternity proceeding itself would be unnecessary. As the New York Court of Appeals has not passed upon the constitutionality of the two-year limitation, that question is not before us. Our decision today therefore sustains § 4–1.2 under the Equal Protection Clause only with respect to its requirement that a judicial order of filiation be issued during the lifetime of the father of an illegitimate child.

6. The presence in this case of the State's interest in the orderly disposition of a decedent's property at death distinguishes it from others in which that justification for an illegitimacy-based classification was absent.

member of "the busiest [surrogate's] court in the State measured by the number of intestate estates which traffic daily through this court," and a participant in some of the Commission's deliberations:

"An illegitimate, if made an unconditional distributee in intestacy, must be served with process in the estate of his parent or if he is a distributee in the estate of the kindred of a parent.... And, in probating the will of his parent (though not named a beneficiary) or in probating the will of any person who makes a class disposition to 'issue' of such parent, the illegitimate must be served with process.... How does one cite and serve an illegitimate of whose existence neither family nor personal representative may be aware? And of greatest concern, how achieve finality of decree in *any* estate when there always exists the possibility however remote of a secret illegitimate lurking in the buried past of a parent or an ancestor of a class of beneficiaries? Finality in decree is essential in the Surrogate's Courts since title to real property passes under such decree. Our procedural statutes and the Due Process Clause mandate notice and opportunity to be heard to all necessary parties. Given the right to intestate succession, *all* illegitimates must be served with process. This would be no real problem with respect to those few estates where there are 'known' illegitimates. But it presents an almost insuperable burden as regards 'unknown' illegitimates. The point made in the [Bennett] commission discussions was that instead of affecting only a few estates, procedural problems would be created for many—some members suggested a majority—of estates."

Even where an individual claiming to be the illegitimate child of a deceased man makes himself known, the difficulties facing an estate are likely to persist. Because of the particular problems of proof, spurious claims may be difficult to expose. The Bennett Commission therefore sought to protect "innocent adults and those rightfully interested in their estates from fraudulent claims of heirship and harassing litigation instituted by those seeking to establish themselves as illegitimate heirs."

As the State's interests are substantial, we now consider the means adopted by New York to further these interests. In order to avoid the problems described above, the Commission recommended a requirement designed to ensure the accurate resolution of claims of paternity and to minimize the potential for disruption of estate administration. Accuracy is enhanced by placing paternity disputes in a judicial forum during the lifetime of the father. As the New York Court of Appeals observed in its first opinion in this case, the "availability [of the putative father] should be a substantial factor contributing to the reliability of the fact-finding process." In re Lalli, 38 N.Y.2d, at 82, 378 N.Y.S.2d, at 355, 340 N.E.2d, at 724. In addition, requiring that the order be issued during the father's lifetime permits a man to defend his reputation against "unjust accusations in paternity claims," which was a secondary purpose of § 4–1.2.

The administration of an estate will be facilitated, and the possibility of delay and uncertainty minimized, where the entitlement of an illegitimate child to notice and participation is a matter of judicial record before the administration commences. Fraudulent assertions of paternity will be much less likely to succeed, or even to arise, where the proof is put before a court of law at a time when the putative father is available to respond, rather than first brought to light when the distribution of the assets of an estate is in the offing.[8]

Appellant contends that § 4–1.2, like the statute at issue in *Trimble*, excludes "significant categories of illegitimate children" who could be allowed to inherit "without jeopardizing the orderly settlement" of their intestate fathers' estates. *Trimble,* supra, 430 U.S. at 771, 97 S.Ct. at 1465. He urges that those in his position—"known" illegitimate children who, despite the absence of an order of filiation obtained during their fathers' lifetimes, can present convincing proof of paternity—cannot rationally be denied inheritance as they pose none of the risks § 4–1.2 was intended to minimize.[9]

We do not question that there will be some illegitimate children who would be able to establish their relationship to their deceased fathers without serious disruption of the administration of estates and that, as applied to such individuals, § 4–1.2 appears to operate unfairly. But few statutory classifications are entirely free from the criticism that they sometimes produce inequitable results. Our inquiry under the Equal Protection Clause does not focus on the abstract "fairness" of a state law, but on whether the statute's relation to the state interests it is intended to promote is so tenuous that it lacks the rationality contemplated by the Fourteenth Amendment.

The Illinois statute in *Trimble* was constitutionally unacceptable because it effected a total statutory disinheritance of children born out of wedlock who were not legitimated by the subsequent marriage of their parents. The reach of the statute was far in excess of its justifiable purposes. Section 4–1.2 does not share this defect. Inheritance is barred only where there has been a failure to secure evidence of paternity during

---

8. In affirming the judgment below, we do not, of course, restrict a State's freedom to require proof of paternity by means other than a judicial decree. Thus a State may prescribe any *formal* method of proof, whether it be similar to that provided by § 4–1.2 or some other regularized procedure that would assure the authenticity of the acknowledgment. As we noted in *Trimble,* such a procedure would be sufficient to satisfy the State's interests.

9. Appellant claims that in addition to discriminating between illegitimate and legitimate children, § 4–1.2, in conjunction with N.Y.Dom.Rel.Law § 24 (McKinney 1977), impermissibly discriminates between classes of illegitimate children. Section 24 provides that a child conceived out of wedlock is nevertheless legitimate if, before or after his birth, his parents marry, even if the marriage is void, illegal or judicially annulled. Appellant argues that by classifying as "legitimate" children born out of wedlock whose parents later marry, New York has, with respect to these children, substituted marriage for § 4–1.2's requirement of proof of paternity. Thus, these "illegitimate" children escape the rigors of the rule unlike their unfortunate counterparts whose parents never marry.

Under § 24, one claiming to be the legitimate child of a deceased man would have to prove not only his paternity but also his maternity and the fact of the marriage of his parents. These additional evidentiary requirements make it reasonable to accept less exacting proof of paternity and to treat such children as legitimate for inheritance purposes.

the father's lifetime in the manner prescribed by the State. This is not a requirement that inevitably disqualifies an unnecessarily large number of children born out of wedlock.

. . .

Even if, as Mr. Justice Brennan believes, § 4–1.2 could have been written somewhat more equitably, it is not the function of a court "to hypothesize independently on the desirability or feasibility of any possible alternative[s]" to the statutory scheme formulated by New York. Mathews v. Lucas, 427 U.S., at 515, 96 S.Ct. at 2767. "These matters of practical judgment and empirical calculation are for [the State]. . . . In the end, the precise accuracy of [the State's] calculations is not a matter of specialized judicial competence; and we have no basis to question their detail beyond the evident consistency and substantiality." Id., at 515–516, 96 S.Ct. at 2767.[11]

We conclude that the requirement imposed by § 4–1.2 on illegitimate children who would inherit from their fathers is substantially related to the

---

11. The dissent of Mr. Justice Brennan would reduce the opinion in Trimble v. Gordon, 430 U.S. 762, 97 S.Ct. 1459, 52 L.Ed.2d 31 (1977), to a simplistic holding that the Constitution *requires* a State, in a case of this kind, to recognize as sufficient any "formal acknowledgment of paternity." This reading of *Trimble* is based on a single phrase lifted from a footnote. Id., at 772 n. 14, 97 S.Ct. at 1466. It ignores both the broad rationale of the Court's opinion and the context in which the note and the phrase relied upon appear. The principle that the footnote elaborates is that the States are free to recognize the problems arising from different forms of proof and to select those forms "carefully tailored to eliminate imprecise and unduly burdensome methods of establishing paternity." Ibid. The New York Legislature, with the benefit of the Bennett Commission's study, exercised this judgment when it considered and rejected the possibility of accepting evidence of paternity less formal than a judicial order.

The "formal acknowledgment" contemplated by *Trimble* is such as would minimize post-death litigation, i.e., a regularly prescribed, legally recognized method of acknowledging paternity. It is thus plain that footnote 14 in *Trimble* does not sustain the dissenting opinion. Indeed, the document relied upon by the dissent is not an acknowledgment of paternity at all. It is a simple "Certificate of Consent" that apparently was required at the time by New York for the marriage of a minor. It consists of one sentence:

> "This is to certify that I, who have hereto subscribed my name, do hereby consent that Robert Lalli who is my son and who is under the age of 21 years, shall be united in marriage to Janice Bivens by a minister of the gospel or other person authorized by law to solemnize marriages."

Mario Lalli's signature to this document was acknowledged by a notary public, but the certificate contains no oath or affirmation as to the truth of its contents. The notary did no more than confirm the identity of Lalli. Because the certificate was executed for the purpose of giving consent to marry, not of proving biological paternity, the meaning of the words "my son" is ambiguous. One can readily imagine that had Robert Lalli's half-brother, who was not Mario's son but who took the surname Lalli and lived as a member of his household, sought permission to marry, Mario might also have referred to him as "my son" on a consent certificate.

The important state interests of safeguarding the accurate and orderly disposition of property at death, emphasized in *Trimble* and reiterated in our opinion today, could be frustrated easily if there were a constitutional rule that any notarized but unsworn statement identifying an individual as a "child" must be accepted as adequate proof of paternity regardless of the context in which the statement was made.

important state interests the statute is intended to promote. We therefore find no violation of the equal Protection Clause.

. . .

For the reasons stated in his dissent in Trimble v. Gordon, 430 U.S. 762, 777, 97 S.Ct. 1459, 1468, 52 L.Ed.2d 31 (1977), Mr. Justice Rehnquist concurs in the judgment of affirmance.

■ Mr. Justice Stewart, concurring.

It seems to me that Mr. Justice Powell's opinion convincingly demonstrates the significant differences between the New York law at issue here and the Illinois law at issue in Trimble v. Gordon, 430 U.S. 762, 97 S.Ct. 1459, 52 L.Ed.2d 31. Therefore, I cannot agree with the view expressed in the concurring opinion that Trimble v. Gordon is now "a derelict," or with the implication that in deciding the two cases the way it has this Court has failed to give authoritative guidance to the courts and legislatures of the several States.

■ Mr. Justice Blackmun, concurring in the judgment.

I agree with the result the Court has reached and concur in its judgment. I also agree with much that has been said in the plurality opinion. My point of departure, of course, is at the plurality's valiant struggle to distinguish, rather than overrule, Trimble v. Gordon, 430 U.S. 762, 97 S.Ct. 1459, 52 L.Ed.2d 31 (1977), . . . Four Members of the Court, like the Supreme Court of Illinois, found the case "constitutionally indistinguishable from Labine v. Vincent, 401 U.S. 532, 91 S.Ct. 1017, 28 L.Ed.2d 288 (1971)," and were in dissent.

It seems to me that the Court today gratifyingly reverts to the principle set forth in Labine v. Vincent. . . .

I would overrule *Trimble,* but the Court refrains from doing so on the theory that the result in *Trimble* is justified because of the peculiarities of the Illinois Probate Act there under consideration. This, of course, is an explanation, but, for me, it is an unconvincing one. I therefore must regard *Trimble* as a derelict, explainable only because of the overtones of its appealing facts and offering little precedent for constitutional analysis of State intestate succession laws. If *Trimble* is not a derelict, the corresponding statutes of other States will be of questionable validity until this Court passes them, one by one, as being on the *Trimble* side of the line, or the *Vincent–Lalli* side.

■ Mr. Justice Brennan, with whom Mr. Justice White, Mr. Justice Marshall, and Mr. Justice Stevens join, dissenting.

. . .

The present case illustrates the injustice of the departure from *Trimble* worked by today's decision sustaining the New York rule. All interested parties concede that Robert Lalli is the son of Mario Lalli. Mario Lalli supported Robert during his son's youth. Mario Lalli formally acknowledged Robert Lalli as his son. Yet, for want of a judicial order of filiation entered during Mario's lifetime, Robert Lalli is denied his intestate share of his father's estate.

There is no reason to suppose that the injustice of the present case is aberrant. Indeed it is difficult to imagine an instance in which an illegitimate child acknowledged and voluntarily supported by his father, would ever inherit intestate under the New York scheme. Social welfare agencies, busy as they are with errant fathers, are unlikely to bring paternity proceedings against fathers who support their children. Similarly, children who are acknowledged and supported by their father are unlikely to bring paternity proceedings against him. First, they are unlikely to see the need for such adversary proceedings. Second, even if aware of the rule requiring judicial filiation orders, they are likely to fear provoking disharmony by suing their father. For the same reasons, mothers of such illegitimates are unlikely to bring proceedings against the father. Finally, fathers who do not even bother to make out wills (and thus die intestate) are unlikely to take the time to bring formal filiation proceedings. Thus, as a practical matter, by requiring judicial filiation orders entered during the lifetime of the father, the New York statute makes it virtually impossible for acknowledged and freely supported illegitimate children to inherit intestate.

Two interests are said to justify this discrimination against illegitimates. First, it is argued, reliance upon mere formal public acknowledgements of paternity would open the door to fraudulent claims of paternity. I cannot accept this argument. I adhere to the view that when "a father has formally acknowledged his child . . . there is no possible difficulty of proof, and no opportunity for fraud or error. This purported interest [in avoiding fraud] . . . can offer no justification for distinguishing between a formally acknowledged illegitimate child and a legitimate one." Labine v. Vincent, 401 U.S. 532, 552, 91 S.Ct. 1017, 1028, 28 L.Ed.2d 288 (1971) (Brennan, J., dissenting).

But even if my confidence in the accuracy of formal public acknowledgements of paternity were unfounded, New York has available less drastic means of screening out fraudulent claims of paternity. In addition to requiring formal acknowledgements of paternity, New York might require illegitimates to prove paternity by an elevated standard of proof, e.g., clear and convincing evidence, or even beyond a reasonable doubt. Certainly here, where there is no factual dispute as to the relationship between Robert and Mario Lalli, there is no justification for denying Robert Lalli his intestate share.

. . .

I see no reason to retreat from our decision in Trimble v. Gordon. The New York statute on review here, like the Illinois statute in *Trimble,* excludes "forms of proof which do not compromise the State['s] interests." Trimble v. Gordon, 430 U.S. 762, 772 n. 14, 97 S.Ct. 1459, 1466, 52 L.Ed.2d 31. The statute thus discriminates against illegitimates through means not substantially related to the legitimate interests that the statute purports to promote. I would invalidate the statute.

NOTES

Reed v. Campbell. In Reed v. Campbell, 476 U.S. 852, 106 S.Ct. 2234, 90 L.Ed.2d 858 (1986), the Supreme Court of the United States held that Trimble v. Gordon applied to a case involving a similarly limiting Texas statute. In the opinion of the Court, Justice Stevens explained:

> The state interest in the orderly disposition of decedents' estates may justify the imposition of special requirements upon an illegitimate child who asserts a right to inherit from her father, and, of course, it justifies the enforcement of generally applicable limitations on the time and the manner in which claims may be asserted. After an estate has been finally distributed, the interest in finality may provide an additional, valid justification for barring the belated assertion of claims, even though they may be meritorious and even though mistakes of law or fact may have occurred during the probate process. We find no such justification for the State's rejection of appellant's claim in this case.

One parent's approach to equal treatment. Thorpe v. Thorpe, 260 Ga. 799, 400 S.E.2d 620 (1991), involved a situation in which a child born out of wedlock contested the will of her father. In an earlier judicial proceeding the plaintiff's mother alleged that the child's father had promised, among other things, to treat the plaintiff "equally with his other children". A trial court found this promise valid and ordered the father, who had three legitimate children, to create a will awarding the child "the same amount of property ... that he awards to each of his children." The father responded by making a will that left all his property to his wife. After the father's subsequent death, the Supreme Court of Georgia upheld the will because all of the children were treated equally under it.

Rivera v. Minnich

Supreme Court of the United States, 1987.
483 U.S. 574, 107 S.Ct. 3001, 97 L.Ed.2d 473.

■ Justice Stevens delivered the opinion of the Court.

The Pennsylvania statute governing proceedings brought against a defendant to establish his paternity of a child born out of wedlock specifies that the "burden of proof shall be by a preponderance of the evidence." This appeal presents the question whether a determination of paternity by that evidentiary standard complies with the Due Process Clause of the Fourteenth Amendment. We agree with the Supreme Court of Pennsylvania's conclusion that applying the preponderance standard to this determination is constitutionally permissible.

On May 28, 1983, appellee Jean Marie Minnich, an unmarried woman, gave birth to Cory Michael Minnich. Three weeks later, appellee filed a complaint for child support in the Common Pleas Court of Lancaster County, Pennsylvania, against appellant Gregory Rivera, alleging that he was the father of her son. In advance of trial appellant requested the court to rule that the statutory burden of proof of paternity violated the Due

Process Clause of the Fourteenth Amendment and to instruct the jury that paternity must be established by clear and convincing evidence. The trial judge denied the motion. Applying the preponderance standard, the jury unanimously found that appellant is the father of the child. On appellant's post-trial motions, the trial judge reconsidered his ruling on the burden of proof issue and granted appellant's motion for a new trial. Appellee appealed directly to the Pennsylvania Supreme Court, which held that the statute is constitutional and reinstated the jury's verdict.

The State Supreme Court noted that the standard was entitled to the presumption that legislative enactments are valid, and is the same as that approved by a majority of the jurisdictions that regard paternity suits as civil proceedings. Then, after reviewing the respective interests of the putative father, the mother, and the child, as well as "the interest of the Commonwealth in seeing that fathers support their children who are born out of wedlock so that those children do not become public charges," the court concluded that the preponderance standard is one that "does not unduly risk the erroneous deprivation of any of them." The Chief Justice of that court dissented. Relying on our holding in Santosky v. Kramer, 455 U.S. 745 (1982), that the Constitution requires clear and convincing evidence before the State may terminate the parental relationship, he reasoned that the same degree of proof should be required to create the relationship.

.   .   .

The preponderance of the evidence standard that the Pennsylvania Legislature has prescribed for paternity cases is the standard that is applied most frequently in litigation between private parties in every State. More specifically, it is the same standard that is applied in paternity litigation in the majority of American jurisdictions that regard such proceedings as civil in nature. . . .

Appellant's principal argument is that the standard of proof required by our holding in *Santosky* to terminate the parent-child relationship is also constitutionally required to create it. This view of *Santosky* rests on the tacit assumption of an equivalence between the State's imposition of the legal obligations accompanying a biological relationship between parent and child and the State's termination of a fully existing parent-child relationship. We are unable to accept this assumption. The collective judgment of the many state legislatures which adhere to a preponderance standard for paternity proceedings rests on legitimate and significant distinctions between termination and paternity proceedings.

First, there is an important difference between the ultimate results of a judgment in the two proceedings. Resolving the question whether there is a causal connection between an alleged physical act of a putative father and the subsequent birth of the plaintiff's child sufficient to impose financial liability on the father will not trammel any pre-existing rights; the putative father has no legitimate right and certainly no liberty interest in avoiding financial obligations to his natural child that are validly imposed by state law. In the typical contested paternity proceeding, the defendant's nonadmission of paternity represents a disavowal of any interest in providing the training, nurture, and loving protection that are at the heart of the parental relationship protected by the Constitution. Rather, the primary interest of the defendant is in avoiding the serious economic consequences that flow from a court order that establishes paternity and its correlative obligation to provide support for the child. In contrast, in a termination proceeding the State is seeking to destroy permanently all legal recognition of the parental relationship. In *Santosky,* we described the parent's desire for, and right to, the companionship, care, and custody of his or her children as "an interest far more precious than any property right." 455 U.S., at 758–759. The State's determination that the relationship between a parent and his or her child ought to be stripped of legal recognition abrogates many aspects of this precious interest. The difference between the two types of proceedings is thus a difference that is directly related to the degree of proof that is appropriately required. For, as we have said in explanation of the need for clear and convincing evidence in certain proceedings, "rights once confirmed should not be lightly revoked."

Second, there is an important distinction between the parties' relationship to each other in the two proceedings. As is true of the other types of proceedings in which the Court has concluded that the Constitution demands a higher standard of proof than a mere preponderance of the evidence, the contestants in a termination proceeding are the State and an individual. Because the State has superior resources, and because an adverse ruling in a criminal, civil commitment, or termination proceeding has especially severe consequences for the individuals affected, it is appropriate for society to impose upon itself a disproportionate share of the risk of error in such proceedings. Unlike those proceedings, in a paternity suit the principal adversaries are the mother and the putative father, each of whom has an extremely important, but nevertheless relatively equal, interest in the outcome. Each would suffer in a similar way the consequences of an adverse ruling; thus, it is appropriate that each share roughly equally the risk of an inaccurate factual determination. Nor does the child's interest in the proceeding favor placing a disproportionate share of the risk of error on either party. Surely, from the child's point of view, a lower standard of proof increases the possibility of an erroneous determination that the defendant is his or her father, while a higher standard of proof increases the risk of a mistaken finding that the defendant is not his or her true father and thus may not be required to assume responsibility for his or her support. The equipoise of the private interests that are at stake in a paternity proceeding supports the conclusion that the standard of proof normally applied in private litigation is also appropriate for these cases.[8]

8. Unlike the State Supreme Court, we place no reliance on the State's interest in avoiding financial responsibility for children born out of wedlock. If it were relevant, the State's financial interest in the outcome of the case would weigh in favor of imposing a disproportionate share of the risk of error upon it by requiring a higher standard of proof. In our view, however, the State's legitimate interest is in the fair and impartial

Finally, there is an important difference in the finality of judgment in favor of the defendant in a termination proceeding and in a paternity proceeding. As we pointed out in *Santosky,* "natural parents have no 'double jeopardy' defense" against the State's repeated efforts to terminate parental rights. 455 U.S., at 764. If the State initially fails to win termination, as New York did in that case, it always can try once again as family circumstances change or as it gathers more or better evidence. "[E]ven when the parents have attained the level of fitness required by the State, they have no similar means by which they can forestall future termination efforts." Id., at 764. The imposition of a higher standard of proof protects the parents, and to some degree the child, from renewed efforts to sever their familial ties. In contrast, a paternity suit terminates with the entry of a final judgment that bars repeated litigation of the same issue under normal principles of civil litigation. There is no "striking asymmetry in [the parties'] litigation options." Ibid.

The judgment of the Supreme Court of Pennsylvania is therefore affirmed.

■ JUSTICE O'CONNOR, concurring in the judgment.

I believe that the judgment of the Pennsylvania Supreme Court should be affirmed for the reasons set forth by Justice Rehnquist in dissent in Santosky v. Kramer, 455 U.S. 745, 770–791 (1982). "Both theory and the precedents of this Court teach us solicitude for state interests, particularly in the field of family and family-property arrangements." United States v. Yazell, 382 U.S. 341, 352 (1966). Particularly in light of that special solicitude, I cannot find that the flexible concept of due process, Santosky v. Kramer, supra, at 774–776 (REHNQUIST, J., dissenting), bars Pennsylvania from providing that the litigants to a civil paternity suit are to bear the risk of factual error in roughly equal fashion. I do not find it necessary to this conclusion to rely upon the fact that the majority of American jurisdictions apply the same rule as Pennsylvania does. Nor do I agree that the differences between termination and paternity proceedings are substantial enough to justify the different conclusion reached in *Santosky.* Accordingly, I concur in the Court's judgment but not its opinion.

■ JUSTICE BRENNAN, dissenting.

I cannot agree with the Court that a determination of paternity is no more significant than the resolution of " 'a monetary dispute between private parties.' " What is at stake for a defendant in such a proceeding is not merely the prospect of a discrete payment in satisfaction of a limited obligation. Rather, it is the imposition of a life-long relationship with significant financial, legal, and moral dimensions.

Financially, a paternity determination results in ongoing, open-ended support responsibility. A parent is responsible for supporting a child at least until the child is 18, and perhaps longer. The father cannot be certain

adjudication of all civil disputes, including paternity proceedings. This interest is served by the State's independent judiciary, which presumably resolves these disputes unaffected by the State's interest in minimizing its welfare expenditures.

of the amount of support that will be necessary, for this will depend on the needs of the particular child over the years. If his child receives any form of public assistance, all the father's real and personal property are deemed available to the State for reimbursement. The financial commitment imposed upon a losing defendant in a paternity suit is thus far more onerous and unpredictable than the liability borne by the loser in a typical civil suit.

The obligation created by a determination of paternity is enforced by significant legal sanctions. Failure to comply with a support obligation may result in the attachment of income, and a 10% penalty may be imposed for any amount in arrears for more than 30 days if the failure to pay is deemed willful. In addition, a father's state and federal income tax refunds may be confiscated to pay alleged arrearages. Furthermore, failure to satisfy the support obligation may result in incarceration. A delinquent father may be declared in contempt of court and imprisoned for up to six months, and may also be found guilty of a misdemeanor punishable by imprisonment for up to two years. A paternity determination therefore establishes a legal duty whose assumption exposes the father to the potential loss of both property and liberty.

"Apart from the putative father's pecuniary interest in avoiding a substantial support obligation and liberty interest threatened by the possible sanctions for noncompliance, at issue is the creation of a parent-child relationship." Little v. Streater, 452 U.S. 1, 13 (1981). The judgment that a defendant is the father of a particular child is the pronouncement of more than mere financial responsibility. It is also a declaration that a defendant assumes a cultural role with distinct moral expectations. Most of us see parenthood as a lifelong status whose responsibilities flow from a wellspring far more profound than legal decree. Some men may find no emotional resonance in fatherhood. Many, however, will come to see themselves far differently, and will necessarily expand the boundaries of their moral sensibility to encompass the child that has been found to be their own. The establishment of a parental relationship may at the outset have fewer emotional consequences than the termination of one. It has, however, the potential to set in motion a process of engagement that is powerful and cumulative, and whose duration spans a lifetime. In this respect, a paternity determination is far more akin to the proceeding involved in Santosky v. Kramer, 455 U.S. 745 (1982), than to a suit for breach of contract.

Finally, the losing defendant in a paternity suit is subject to characterization by others as a father who sought to shirk responsibility for his actions.... He is seen as a parent apparently impervious to the moral demands of that role, who must instead be coerced by law to fulfill his obligation. Regardless of whether a satisfying parent-child relationship ultimately develops, the father will be seen as a person whose initial participation in it was involuntary. By contrast, the losing party in a civil suit is rarely the target of such social opprobrium.[2]

---

2. Of course, a child also has an interest in not being stigmatized as illegitimate. As we have stressed, however, an illegitimate child cannot be held responsible for his or her

A paternity proceeding thus implicates significant property and liberty interests of the defendant. These can be protected without significantly burdening the interests of the mother, the child, or the State. Modern blood-grouping tests, such as the human leukocyte antigen (HLA) test used in this case, provide an extremely reliable means of determining paternity in most cases. The probability of paternity in this case, for instance, was calculated at 94.6%, a level of certainty achieved quite frequently through the use of such tests.

It is likely that the requirement that paternity be proved by clear and convincing evidence would make a practical difference only in cases in which blood test results were not introduced as evidence. . . .

Clark v. Jeter

Supreme Court of the United States, 1988.
486 U.S. 456, 108 S.Ct. 1910, 100 L.Ed.2d 465.

■ JUSTICE O'CONNOR delivered the opinion of the Court.

Under Pennsylvania law, an illegitimate child must prove paternity before seeking support from his or her father, and a suit to establish paternity ordinarily must be brought within six years of an illegitimate child's birth. By contrast, a legitimate child may seek support from his or her parents at any time. We granted certiorari to consider the constitutionality of this legislative scheme.

I

On September 22, 1983, petitioner Cherlyn Clark filed a support complaint in the Allegheny County Court of Common Pleas on behalf of her minor daughter, Tiffany, who was born out of wedlock on June 11, 1973. Clark named respondent Gene Jeter as Tiffany's father. The court ordered blood tests, which showed a 99.3% probability that Jeter is Tiffany's father.

Jeter moved to dismiss the complaint on the ground that it was barred by the 6–year statute of limitations for paternity actions. In her response, Clark contended that this statute is unconstitutional under the Equal Protection and Due Process Clauses of the Fourteenth Amendment. In the alternative, she argued that the statute was tolled by fraudulent and misleading actions of the welfare department, or by threats and assaults by Jeter.

The trial court upheld the statute of limitations on the authority of *Astemborski v. Susmarski,* 499 Pa. 99, 451 A.2d 1012 (1982), vacated, 462 U.S. 1127, 103 S.Ct. 3105, 77 L.Ed.2d 1360 (1983), reinstated on remand, 502 Pa. 409, 466 A.2d 1018 (1983). The Pennsylvania Supreme Court there

status. See Trimble v. Gordon, 430 U.S. 762 (1977). By contrast, the stigma that attaches to the father of such a child reflects a judgment regarding moral culpability. In addi-

tion, as I discuss in text this page, I believe that the child's interest in legitimation would not be significantly burdened by the employment of a "clear and convincing" standard.

had considered and rejected constitutional challenges similar to Clark's. The trial court also rejected Clark's argument that the statute should be tolled, specifically finding that any fear that Clark may have had of Jeter had subsided more than six years before she filed her support complaint. Therefore, the trial court entered judgment for Jeter.

Clark appealed to the Superior Court of Pennsylvania, again raising her constitutional challenges to the 6–year statute of limitations. Before the court decided her case, the Pennsylvania Legislature enacted an 18–year statute of limitations for actions to establish paternity. Act of Oct. 30, 1985, No. 66, § 1, subch. C, 1985 Pa.Laws 270, codified at 23 Pa.Cons.Stat. § 4343(b) (1985). Pennsylvania thereby brought its law into compliance with a provision of the federal Child Support Enforcement Amendments of 1984 that requires all States participating in the federal child support program to have procedures to establish the paternity of any child who is less than 18 years old. 98 Stat. 1307, 42 U.S.C. § 666(a)(5) (1982 ed., Supp. IV). The Superior Court concluded, however, that Pennsylvania's new 18–year statute of limitations did not apply retroactively, and that it would not revive Clark's cause of action in any event. It affirmed the trial court's conclusions that the 6–year statute of limitations was constitutional, and that Clark's tolling argument was without merit. Thereafter, the Superior Court denied Clark's motion for reargument. The Pennsylvania Supreme Court denied her petition for allowance of appeal. We granted Clark's petition for certiorari.

Clark's first argument to this Court is that Pennsylvania's 6–year statute of limitations is invalid because it conflicts with the federal Child Support Enforcement Amendments of 1984, which she says require States to adopt retroactive 18–year statutes of limitations in paternity cases. See 42 U.S.C. § 666(a)(5) (1982 ed., Supp. IV). Because this argument raises an issue of statutory interpretation, we ordinarily would address it before reaching the constitutional claims. Having reviewed the record, however, we find that Clark did not adequately present a federal pre-emption argument to the lower courts. It is our practice, when reviewing decisions by state courts, not to decide federal claims that were not "pressed or passed upon" below. *Bankers Life & Casualty Co. v. Crenshaw*, 486 U.S. 71, 79–80, 108 S.Ct. 1645, FN8. Currently, a minority of states have passed legislation addressing in vitro fertilization. *See, e.g., Cal.Penal Code* § 367g (West 1999) (permitting use of preembryos only pursuant to written consent form); *Fla. Stat.* ch. 742.17 (1997) (establishing joint decision-making authority regarding disposition of preembryos); *La.Rev.Stat. Ann.* §§ 121–33 (West 1991) (establishing fertilized human ovum as biological human being that cannot be intentionally destroyed); *Okla. Stat. Ann.* tit. 10, § 556 (West 2001) (requiring written consent for embryo transfer); *Tex. Family Code Ann.* § 151.103 (West 1996) (establishing parental rights over child resulting from preembryo).

The Pennsylvania Legislature passed the 18–year statute of limitations on October 30, 1985. At that time, Clark already had filed her brief on appeal to the Superior Court. Clark immediately suggested a remand to determine the retroactivity of the new Pennsylvania statute. But the

Superior Court instead itself decided that the 6–year statute of limitations would continue to apply to cases like Clark's. The court reasoned that, under Pennsylvania law, a statute is retroactive only if the legislature clearly and manifestly so intends, and it found insufficient evidence of such an intent. The decision did not address the relevance of the federal Child Support Enforcement Amendments to the continuing validity of the 6–year statute of limitations. 358 Pa.Super., at 553–555, 518 A.2d 278.

In her application for reargument in the Superior Court and in her petition for appeal to the Pennsylvania Supreme Court, Clark argued that the Superior Court had overlooked Pennsylvania cases which had applied similar statutes of limitations retroactively, as well as indications that the federal Child Support Enforcement Amendments required States to adopt retroactive 18–year statutes of limitations or their equivalent. See 42 U.S.C. § 666(a)(5) (1982 ed., Supp. III); 50 Fed.Reg. 19608, 19631 (1985). But Clark did not expressly assert that the 6–year statute of limitations was pre-empted by the new federal law. We interpret Clark's argument to be that the Pennsylvania Legislature intended to comply with the new conditions on the federal spending program, which arguably showed that it clearly and manifestly intended its new statute to be retroactive. This question of how to interpret the Pennsylvania statute ultimately is a matter of state law. We find that Clark's argument below was not adequate to raise a federal pre-emption claim. Accordingly, we do not address it here and proceed to her equal protection claim.

In considering whether state legislation violates the Equal Protection Clause of the Fourteenth Amendment, U.S. Const., Amdt. 14, § 1, we apply different levels of scrutiny to different types of classifications. At a minimum, a statutory classification must be rationally related to a legitimate governmental purpose. Classifications based on race or national origin, *e.g., Loving v. Virginia,* 388 U.S. 1, 11, 87 S.Ct. 1817, 1823, 18 L.Ed.2d 1010 (1967), and classifications affecting fundamental rights, *e.g., Harper v. Virginia Bd. of Elections,* 383 U.S. 663, 672, 86 S.Ct. 1079, 1084–85, 16 L.Ed.2d 169 (1966), are given the most exacting scrutiny. Between these extremes of rational basis review and strict scrutiny lies a level of intermediate scrutiny, which generally has been applied to discriminatory classifications based on sex or illegitimacy. See, *e.g., Mississippi University for Women v. Hogan,* 458 U.S. 718, 723–724, and n. 9, 102 S.Ct. 3331, 3336, and n. 9, 73 L.Ed.2d 1090 (1982); *Mills v. Habluetzel,* 456 U.S. 91, 99, 102 S.Ct. 1549, 1554–55, 71 L.Ed.2d 770 (1982); *Craig v. Boren,* 429 U.S. 190, 197, 97 S.Ct. 451, 456–57, 50 L.Ed.2d 397 (1976); *Mathews v. Lucas,* 427 U.S. 495, 505–506, 96 S.Ct. 2755, 2762–2763, 49 L.Ed.2d 651 (1976).

To withstand intermediate scrutiny, a statutory classification must be substantially related to an important governmental objective. Consequently we have invalidated classifications that burden illegitimate children for the sake of punishing the illicit relations of their parents, because "visiting this condemnation on the head of an infant is illogical and unjust." *Weber v. Aetna Casualty & Surety Co.,* 406 U.S. 164, 175, 92 S.Ct. 1400, 1406, 31 L.Ed.2d 768 (1972). Yet, in the seminal case concerning the child's right to support, this Court acknowledged that it might be appropriate to treat illegitimate children differently in the support context because of "lurking problems with respect to proof of paternity." *Gomez v. Perez,* 409 U.S. 535, 538, 93 S.Ct. 872, 875, 35 L.Ed.2d 56 (1973).

This Court has developed a particular framework for evaluating equal protection challenges to statutes of limitations that apply to suits to establish paternity, and thereby limit the ability of illegitimate children to obtain support.

> "First, the period for obtaining support ... must be sufficiently long in duration to present a reasonable opportunity for those with an interest in such children to assert claims on their behalf. Second, any time limitation placed on that opportunity must be substantially related to the State's interest in avoiding the litigation of stale or fraudulent claims." *Mills v. Habluetzel,* 456 U.S., at 99–100, 102 S.Ct., at 1554.

In *Mills,* we held that Texas' 1–year statute of limitations failed both steps of the analysis. We explained that paternity suits typically will be brought by the child's mother, who might not act swiftly amidst the emotional and financial complications of the child's first year. And, it is unlikely that the lapse of a mere 12 months will result in the loss of evidence or appreciably increase the likelihood of fraudulent claims. *Id.,* at 100–101, 102 S.Ct., at 1555–56. A concurring opinion in *Mills* explained why statutes of limitations longer than one year also may be unconstitutional. *Id.,* at 102–106, 102 S.Ct., at 1556–58 (O'CONNOR, J., joined by Burger, C.J., and BRENNAN and BLACKMUN, JJ., and joined as to Part I by Powell, J., concurring). First, the State has a countervailing interest in ensuring that genuine claims for child support are satisfied. Second, the fact that Texas tolled most other causes of action during a child's minority suggested that proof problems do not become overwhelming during this period. Finally, the practical obstacles to filing a claim for support are likely to continue after the first year of the child's life.

In *Pickett v. Brown,* 462 U.S. 1, 103 S.Ct. 2199, 76 L.Ed.2d 372 (1983), the Court unanimously struck down Tennessee's 2–year statute of limitations for paternity and child support actions brought on behalf of certain illegitimate children. Adhering to the analysis developed in *Mills,* the Court first considered whether two years afforded a reasonable opportunity to bring such suits. The Tennessee statute was relatively more generous than the Texas statute considered in *Mills* because it did not limit actions against a father who had acknowledged his paternity in writing or by furnishing support; nor did it apply if the child was likely to become a public charge. Nevertheless, the Court concluded that the 2–year period was too short in light of the persisting financial and emotional problems that are likely to afflict the child's mother. Proceeding to the second step of the analysis, the Court decided that the 2–year statute of limitations was not substantially related to Tennessee's asserted interest in preventing stale and fraudulent claims. The period during which suit could be brought was only a year longer than the period considered in *Mills,* and this incremental difference would not create substantially greater proof and fraud problems. Furthermore, Tennessee tolled most other actions during a child's minority, and even permitted a support action to be brought on behalf of a child up to 18 years of age if the child was or was likely to become a public charge. Finally, scientific advances in blood testing had alleviated some problems of proof in paternity actions. For these reasons, the Tennessee statute failed to survive heightened scrutiny under the Equal Protection Clause.

In light of this authority, we conclude that Pennsylvania's 6–year statute of limitations violates the Equal Protection Clause. Even six years does not necessarily provide a reasonable opportunity to assert a claim on behalf of an illegitimate child. "The unwillingness of the mother to file a paternity action on behalf of her child, which could stem from her relationship with the natural father or . . . from the emotional strain of having an illegitimate child, or even from the desire to avoid community and family disapproval, may continue years after the child is born. The problem may be exacerbated if, as often happens, the mother herself is a minor." *Mills, supra,* at 105, n. 4, 102 S.Ct., at 1558, n. 4. (O'CONNOR, J., concurring). Not all of these difficulties are likely to abate in six years. A mother might realize only belatedly "a loss of income attributable to the need to care for the child," *Pickett, supra,* 462 U.S. at 12, 103 S.Ct., at 2206. Furthermore, financial difficulties are likely to increase as the child matures and incurs expenses for clothing, school, and medical care. See, *e.g., Moore v. McNamara,* 40 Conn.Supp. 6, 11, 12, 478 A.2d 634, 637 (1984) (invalidating a 3–year statute of limitations). Thus it is questionable whether a State acts reasonably when it requires most paternity and support actions to be brought within six years of an illegitimate child's birth.

We do not rest our decision on this ground, however, for it is not entirely evident that six years would necessarily be an unreasonable limitations period for child support actions involving illegitimate children. We are, however, confident that the 6–year statute of limitations is not substantially related to Pennsylvania's interest in avoiding the litigation of stale or fraudulent claims. In a number of circumstances, Pennsylvania permits the issue of paternity to be litigated more than six years after the birth of an illegitimate child. The statute itself permits a suit to be brought more than six years after the child's birth if it is brought within two years of a support payment made by the father. And in other types of suits, Pennsylvania places no limits on when the issue of paternity may be litigated. For example, the intestacy statute, 20 Pa. Cons. Stat. § 2107(3) (1982), permits a child born out of wedlock to establish paternity as long as "there is clear and convincing evidence that the man was the father of the child." Likewise, no statute of limitations applies to a father's action to establish paternity. *In re Mengel,* 287 Pa.Super. 186, 429 A.2d 1162 (1981). Recently, the Pennsylvania Legislature enacted a statute that tolls most other civil actions during a child's minority. 42 Pa. Cons. Stat. § 5533(b) (Supp.1987). In *Pickett* and *Mills,* similar tolling statutes cast doubt on the State's purported interest in avoiding the litigation of stale or fraudulent claims. 462 U.S., at 15–16, 103 S.Ct., at 2207–08; 456 U.S., at 104–105, 102 S.Ct., at 1557–58 (O'CONNOR, J., concurring); *id.,* at 106, 102 S.Ct., at 1558 (Powell, J., concurring in judgment). Pennsylvania's tolling statute has the same implications here.

A more recent indication that Pennsylvania does not consider proof problems insurmountable is the enactment by the Pennsylvania Legislature in 1985 of an 18–year statute of limitations for paternity and support actions. 23 Pa. Cons. Stat. § 4343(b) (1985). To be sure the legislature did not act spontaneously, but rather under the threat of losing some federal funds. Nevertheless, the new statute is a tacit concession that proof problems are not overwhelming. The legislative history of the federal Child Support Enforcement Amendments explains why Congress thought such statutes of limitations are reasonable. Congress adverted to the problem of stale and fraudulent claims, but recognized that increasingly sophisticated tests for genetic markers permit the exclusion of over 99% of those who might be accused of paternity, regardless of the age of the child. H.R.Rep. No. 98–527, p. 38 (1983). This scientific evidence is available throughout the child's minority, and it is an additional reason to doubt that Pennsylvania had a substantial reason for limiting the time within which paternity and support actions could be brought.

We conclude that the Pennsylvania statute does not withstand heightened scrutiny under the Equal Protection Clause. We therefore find it unnecessary to reach Clark's due process claim. The judgment of the Superior Court is reversed, and the case is remanded for further proceedings not inconsistent with this opinion.

NOTE

In Opinion of the Justices, the New Hampshire Supreme Court determined that earlier statutes of limitation on paternity actions that were tolled short of 18 years after a child's birth were violative of the U.S. Constitution. They also opined that it would violate the New Hampshire Constitution to impair a putative father's right to assert res judicata as a defense to a subsequent action when an earlier one was dismissed based on untimeliness because of a previous, shorter statute of limitations. 588 A.2d 454 (N.H. 1989). As to the latter issue, in B.M.L. v. Cooper, 919 S.W.2d 855 (Tex.App.1996), the Court of Appeals of Texas held that a paternity suit was not precluded by determination of nonpaternity in a prior child support suit brought by the state, absent establishment by the father that the parties to the prior suit so fully represented the child's interests as to establish identity of interests.

C. Special Issues of the New and Old Technologies

1. Steps to Avoid Child Bearing

a. CONTRACEPTION

Griswold v. Connecticut

Supreme Court of the United States, 1965.
381 U.S. 479, 85 S.Ct. 1678, 14 L.Ed.2d 510.

For the opinion in this case, *see* p. 74 *supra*.

Eisenstadt v. Baird

Supreme Court of the United States, 1972.
405 U.S. 438, 92 S.Ct. 1029, 31 L.Ed.2d 349.

For the opinion in this case, *see* p. 78 *supra*.

NOTE

Starting with the 1873 Comstock Law, 17 Stat. 598, there were major legal problems in importing contraceptive devices, or in mailing or introducing into interstate commerce material dealing with contraception. In 1944 it required favorable action by a United States Court of Appeals before a Consumers Union Report could be delivered through the mail (and then only to married couples). *See* Consumers Union of United States v. Walker, 145 F.2d 33 (D.C.Cir.1944). Times have changed. One of the last barriers was removed in 1977 when the Supreme Court of the United States struck down a New York law that made it a criminal offense to sell or distribute contraceptives of any kind to minors under age 16, allowing only licensed pharmacists to distribute contraceptives, and prohibiting anyone (including license pharmacists) to advertise or display contraceptives. *See* Carey v. Population Services International, 431 U.S. 678, 97 S.Ct. 2010, 52 L.Ed.2d 675 (1977). For further discussion, *see* Walter Wadlington and Raymond C. O'Brien, Family Law in Perspective (2d ed.2007).

b.   STERILIZATION

Buck v. Bell

Supreme Court of the United States, 1927.
274 U.S. 200, 47 S.Ct. 584, 71 L.Ed. 1000.

■ Mr. Justice Holmes delivered the opinion of the Court.

This is a writ of error to review a judgment of the Supreme Court of Appeals of the State of Virginia, affirming a judgment of the Circuit Court of Amherst County, by which the defendant in error, the superintendent of the State Colony for Epileptics and Feeble Minded, was ordered to perform the operation of salpingectomy upon Carrie Buck, the plaintiff in error, for the purpose of making her sterile. 143 Va. 310, 130 S. E. 516. The case comes here upon the contention that the statute authorizing the judgment is void under the Fourteenth Amendment as denying to the plaintiff in error due process of law and the equal protection of the laws.

Carrie Buck is a feeble-minded white woman who was committed to the State Colony above mentioned in due form. She is the daughter of a feeble-minded mother in the same institution, and the mother of an illegitimate feeble-minded child. She was eighteen years old at the time of the trial of her case in the Circuit Court in the latter part of 1924. An Act of Virginia approved March 20, 1924 (Laws 1924, c. 394) recites that the health of the patient and the welfare of society may be promoted in certain cases by the sterilization of mental defectives, under careful safeguard, etc.; that the sterilization may be effected in males by vasectomy and in females by salpingectomy, without serious pain or substantial danger to life; that the Commonwealth is supporting in various institutions many defective persons who if now discharged would become a menace but if incapable of procreating might be discharged with safety and become self-supporting with benefit to themselves and to society; and that experience has shown that heredity plays an important part in the transmission of insanity, imbecility, etc. The statute then enacts that whenever the superintendent of certain institutions including the abovenamed State Colony shall be of opinion that it is for the best interest of the patients and of society that an inmate under his care should be sexually sterilized, he may have the operation performed upon any patient afflicted with hereditary forms of insanity, imbecility, etc., on complying with the very careful provisions by which the act protects the patients from possible abuse.

The superintendent first presents a petition to the special board of directors of his hospital or colony, stating the facts and the grounds for his opinion, verified by affidavit. Notice of the petition and of the time and place of the hearing in the institution is to be served upon the inmate, and also upon his guardian, and if there is no guardian the superintendent is to apply to the Circuit Court of the County to appoint one. If the inmate is a minor notice also is to be given to his parents, if any, with a copy of the petition. The board is to see to it that the inmate may attend the hearings if desired by him or his guardian. The evidence is all to be reduced to writing, and after the board has made its order for or against the operation, the superintendent, or the inmate, or his guardian, may appeal to the Circuit Court of the County. The Circuit Court may consider the record of the board and the evidence before it and such other admissible evidence as may be offered, and may affirm, revise, or reverse the order of the board and enter such order as it deems just. Finally any party may apply to the Supreme Court of Appeals, which, if it grants the appeal, is to hear the case upon the record of the trial in the Circuit Court and may enter such order as it thinks the Circuit Court should have entered. There can be no doubt that so far as procedure is concerned the rights of the patient are most carefully considered, and as every step in this case was taken in scrupulous compliance with the statute and after months of observation, there is no doubt that in that respect the plaintiff in error has had due process at law.

The attack is not upon the procedure but upon the substantive law. It seems to be contended that in no circumstances could such an order be justified. It certainly is contended that the order cannot be justified upon the existing grounds. The judgment finds the facts that have been recited and that Carrie Buck "is the probable potential parent of socially inadequate offspring, likewise afflicted, that she may be sexually sterilized without detriment to her general health and that her welfare and that of society will be promoted by her sterilization," and thereupon makes the order. In view of the general declarations of the Legislature and the specific findings of the Court obviously we cannot say as matter of law that the grounds do not exist, and if they exist they justify the result. We have seen more than once that the public welfare may call upon the best citizens for their lives. It would be strange if it could not call upon those who already sap the strength of the State for these lesser sacrifices, often not felt to be such by those concerned, in order to prevent our being swamped with incompetence. It is better for all the world, if instead of waiting to execute degenerate offspring for crime, or to let them starve for their imbecility, society can prevent those who are manifestly unfit from continuing their kind. The principle that sustains compulsory vaccination is broad enough to cover cutting the Fallopian tubes. Jacobson v. Massachusetts, 197 U. S. 11, 25 S. Ct. 358, 49 L. Ed. 643, 3 Ann. Cas. 765. Three generations of imbeciles are enough.

But, it is said, however it might be if this reasoning were applied generally, it fails when it is confined to the small number who are in the institutions named and is not applied to the multitudes outside. It is the usual last resort of constitutional arguments to point out shortcomings of this sort. But the answer is that the law does all that is needed when it does all that it can, indicates a policy, applies it to all within the lines, and seeks to bring within the lines all similarly situated so far and so fast as its means allow. Of course so far as the operations enable those who otherwise must be kept confined to be returned to the world, and thus open the asylum to others, the equality aimed at will be more nearly reached.

Judgment affirmed.

■ Mr. Justice Butler dissents.

NOTES

A legislature apologizes. The eugenics movement, popular in the first half of the 20th century, led to many legal abuses. The first eugenics-based sterilization law was enacted in Indiana in 1907, with Connecticut following shortly afterward. The Virginia law at issue in Buck v. Bell was enacted in 1924. That was the same year in which the state's Racial Integrity Law, at issue in Loving v. Virginia, discussed in Chapter 1, was adopted. Ironically, we now know that Justice Holmes's pithy comment that "Three generations of imbeciles are enough" reflected not only a lack of scientific knowledge but also involved a person who was not an imbecile. See Paul Lombardo, *Three Generations, No Imbeciles: New Light on Buck v. Bell*, 30 N.Y.U. L. Rev. 30 (1985); Paul Lombardo, *Medicine, Eugenics, and the Supreme Court: From Coercive Sterilization to Reproductive Freedom*, 13 J. Contemp. Health Law & Pol'y 1 (1996); Michael Ollove, *The Lessons of Lynchburg*, The Baltimore Sun, May 6, 2001 at 7F.

In 2001, the Virginia General Assembly passed a Resolution expressing that body's "profound regret over the Commonwealth's role in the eugenics movement in this country and the incalculable human damage done in the name of eugenics.... Va. House Jt. Res. 607 (2001). The Resolution noted that some 8,000 involuntary sterilizations had taken place in Virginia since Buck v. Bell and stated that

... in practice, the eugenics laws were used to target virtually any human shortcoming or malady, including alcoholism, syphilis, and criminal behavior...."

Another Supreme Court test. In 1942 the Supreme Court of the United States visited the area of compulsory sterilization in a different context in Skinner v. Oklahoma ex rel. Williamson, 316 U.S. 535, 62 S.Ct. 1110, 86 L.Ed. 1655 (1942). The court overturned an Oklahoma criminal law that permitted the state to order sterilization of "habitual criminals" who had committed "felonies involving moral turpitude". They bypassed reconsideration of Buck v. Bell as well as arguments about cruel and inhuman punishment, deciding the case on the basis of the Equal Protection Clause. This stemmed from a provision in the law that exempted some serious offenses (such as embezzlement, usually regarded as a white collar crime) while retaining others such as chicken theft. Despite the limited scope of the decision, the opinion of the Court by Justice Douglas stated that

> We are dealing here with legislation which involves one of the basic civil rights of man. Marriage and procreation are fundamental to the very existence and survival of the race. The power to sterilize, if exercised, may have subtle, far-reaching and devastating effects.

This language has been widely quoted.

Regulating voluntary sterilization. Limitations, or at least time delays, also have been placed on voluntary sterilization in some states. Current VA. CODE ANN. § 54.1–2974 (2004) provides that

> It shall be lawful for any physician licensed by the Board of Medicine to perform a vasectomy, salpingectomy, or other surgical sexual sterilization procedure on any person eighteen years of age or older, who has the capacity to give informed consent, when so requested in writing by such person. Prior to or at the time of such request, a full, reasonable, and comprehensible medical explanation as to the meaning and consequences of such an operation and as to alternative methods of contraception shall be given by the physician to the person requesting the operation. No such operation shall be performed prior to thirty days from the date of the written request therefor upon a person who has not previously become the natural or adoptive parent of a child.

Sterilization of minors is discussed in Chapter 7.

c. ABORTION

Roe v. Wade

Supreme Court of the United States, 1973.
410 U.S. 113, 93 S.Ct. 705, 35 L.Ed.2d 147.

For the opinion in this case, *see* p. 85, supra.

NOTE

In a series of decisions following *Roe* the Supreme Court has focused on what restrictions can and cannot be imposed by states. For example, a requirement of parental consent for adolescents was set aside in Planned Parenthood v. Danforth, 428 U.S. 52, 96 S.Ct. 2831, 49 L.Ed.2d 788 (1976), but a law requiring parental notification was upheld at least in its application to other than mature minors. H.L. v. Matheson, 450 U.S. 398, 101 S.Ct. 1164, 67 L.Ed.2d 388 (1981). The right to unobstructed access to abortion clinics has been upheld. Madsen v. Women's Health Center, 512 U.S. 753, 114 S.Ct. 2516, 129 L.Ed.2d 593 (1994). Further litigation almost inevitably will continue and many of the issues have been very divisive and politically charged as in the *Carhart* decision.

2. Assisted Conception

"Assisted conception" is one of several terms now used in referring to a broad range of techniques including artificial insemination, fertilization *in vitro,* and surrogate embryo transfer. Although it may not yet be the standard, it received a boost in that direction when it was selected by the National Conference of Commissioners on Uniform State Laws in the title for its 1989 Uniform Status of Children of Assisted Conception Act. Regardless of its availability as an "umbrella" term, acronyms such as AID, AIH, IVF, and SET will remain in use, though new labels are being offered for some of them as well.

a. ARTIFICIAL INSEMINATION

Walter Wadlington, *Artificial Conception: The Challenge for Family Law*, 69 Va.L.Rev. 465, 468–473 (1983).

. . .

Artificial insemination (AI) today is a widely accepted, nonexperimental medical procedure. In what is probably its best known form, heterologous artificial insemination (appropriately dubbed AID, the acronym for Artificial Insemination, Donor), a woman is impregnated with semen from a man not her husband in a simple procedure that can be accomplished with a syringe.[12] Through modern cryogenic capabilities, semen can be frozen and stored for future use in sperm banks. Some banks operate as commercial enterprises, though, unlike their counterparts in the financial field, they are virtually free from state licensing and other regulation.[14]

---

12. *See* W. Finegold, Artificial Insemination (2d ed. 1976); W. Finegold, Artificial Insemination With Husband Sperm (1980).

14. . . . Recently the Ad Hoc Committee on Artificial Insemination of The American Fertility Society published a proposal for model legislation that would impose certain requirements on sperm banks, including obtaining a family medical history, performing a physical examination, and screening potential donors for sexually transmitted disease. *See* The American Fertility Society, Report of the Ad Hoc Committee on Artificial Insemination 16 (1980). For an account of the rapid growth of the sperm bank business and the advertising campaign that business has un-

A second method that poses fewer legal problems is homologous artificial insemination (AIH). A married woman is impregnated with the semen of her husband when normal copulation fails because of various medical problems. A child conceived through AIH is the biological offspring of both the woman and her husband.

In a third variation of the practice, "confused" or "combined" artificial insemination (CAI), a married woman is inseminated with a mixture of her husband's and a donor's sperm. This procedure has no medical superiority over the usual AID process, and it is much less popular today than it was a decade or two ago.

AID presents the problem of determining who bears paternity obligation—the sperm donor or the female's husband—and the concomitant difficulty of identifying the sperm donor. In fact, these concerns spurred the development of the CAI procedure. One basis for CAI contemplates a possible psychological benefit to a sterile husband who might rationalize that he, rather than the sperm donor, had fathered the child conceived by his wife. This structured opportunity for fantasy disturbed some who feared that persons in need of such support would be poor AID candidates. A more telling reason for CAI was the hope that it might obviate an undesired legal result in paternity suits following artificial insemination. A court which otherwise might hold that the donor was the father could use CAI to support a finding that the husband was the biological father.[18] The

---

dertaken see Pendleton, Advertising Age, May 14, 1979, at 30. Not long ago considerable publicity centered on the establishment of a specialized sperm bank that would only accept deposits from Nobel laureates or other persons of exceptional intelligence. This institution originally was named the Herman J. Muller Repository for Germinal Choice after the distinguished geneticist who won a Nobel Prize in 1946 and who advocated sperm banks for exceptional people. The announcement of the bank, established more than a decade after Muller's death, met with considerable criticism when it was learned that one of the few Nobel Prize winners who had admitted making a deposit was Stanford professor William B. Shockley, a controversial figure because of his papers on race and genetics. Professor Muller's widow also objected to the use of her late husband's name in connection with the project. For accounts of the establishment of the sperm bank and responses to it, see *A Bank for Nobel Sperm*, 207 Sci. 1326 (1980); N.Y. Times, Mar. 1, 1980, at 6, col. 2. One commentator recalled how George Bernard Shaw declined a beautiful woman's proposal that she should bear a child by him, asking what would happen if the child were to have her mind and his

looks. O'Toole, *Hers*, N.Y. Times, June 4, 1981, at C2, col. 1. A winner of the Nobel Prize in Medicine described creation of the sperm bank as having "the undertones of a spoof," adding that "only someone who does not know the Nobel Prize winners would want to reproduce them in thousands of specimens." Jacob, *Fish Got to Swim, Man Got to Fly*, N.Y. Times, Mar. 25, 1980, at A19, col. 1. Commenting on speculation about whether such genetic selection would in fact give some children an edge, a mathematics professor pointed out that at least four children of Nobel laureates have won Nobel Prizes, indicating that the child of a Nobel winner is several thousand times more likely to win such an award than a child selected randomly. N.Y. Times, Mar. 20, 1980, at A26, col. 4. According to newspaper accounts, one of the first returns on a deposit in that institution was a child conceived through artificial insemination by a woman who previously had lost custody of her children for abusing them, her abuse ostensibly motivated by a desire to drive them to intellectual success. See Wash. Post, July 14, 1982, at A6, col. 1.

18. See W. Finegold, Artificial Insemination 66, 75 (1964).

concern that a court might designate the donor the biological father precipitated certain AI practices. For example, it is a widespread practice to use semen from different donors when multiple inseminations are performed during one AID cycle to make actual donor identification difficult.[19]

Although the medical literature has discussed AID for many years, there still is surprisingly little data on the incidence of its use and the customary medical standards for its practice. The most informative review of these facets of AID is a study published in 1979.[21] Its authors sent questionnaires to 711 physicians considered likely to be performing AID. Of 471 respondents, 379 acknowledged performing AID. The primary reason doctors gave for performing AID was husband infertility, but forty percent of the respondents also had used it for other reasons such as avoiding possible transmission of genetic disease. Nearly ten percent also said they had used AID to help women without male partners have children.

Only 65.7% of the respondents answered a question asking for the maximum number of pregnancies achieved from any one donor's sperm. Among those who did reply, a maximum of six pregnancies per donor was typical, though one respondent attributed fifty pregnancies to a donor. The small percentage of answers may be attributed to uncertainty (an AID practitioner may use semen from several different donors sequentially during a donee's treatment cycle thus preventing an accurate conclusion as to the "successful" donor) as well as a desire to ensure donor anonymity.

The study also addressed donor selection. It has long been known that the term "donor" is a euphemism and that, in fact, "donors" receive standard payments for "donations" in various localities. The most frequent practice among respondents was to use donors selected by themselves or their medical associates, typically medical students and hospital residents, or, less often, other university and graduate students. A large number of physicians acknowledged attempts to match certain traits or characteristics between a donor and the donee's husband either routinely or on request.

---

19. In this study, 31.8% of the respondents said that during a single cycle they used different donors. Id. at 587. An acknowledged purpose of this serial use of donors was to foster uncertainty as to the genetic father's identity. Id. at 589.

Another ploy sometimes used to avoid designation of the sperm donor, rather than the AID mother's infertile husband, as father of her child calls for the baby's delivery by a physician unaware of the method of conception. The doctor presumably would routinely list the husband as father on birth registration documents if not otherwise instructed. Id.

One distinguished practitioner indicated his willingness to "carry out the white lie of according paternity to the legal father, even if he was not the biological father, on the birth certificate," adding that he was happy to deliver his own AID patients. Guttmacher, *Artificial Insemination*, 97 Annals N.Y. Acad. of Sci. 623, 628 (1962). Many physicians may take a similar stance even though the laws of their states fixing legal parentage on the basis of biological kinship may make their characterization of the wife's husband as father more "wishful" than "legal." Oregon's AID statute, the most comprehensive to date, requires an AID mother and her husband to give notice of the child's birth to the physician who performed the AID procedure. Or. Rev.Stat. § 677.365(4) (1981).

21. Curie–Cohen, Luttrell & Shapiro, *Current Practice of Artificial Insemination by Donor in the United States*, 300 New Eng. J. Med. 585, 587 (1979) (hereinafter cited as Current Practice).

The study concluded that there was little effective genetic screening of donors in the sample. Family histories usually were superficial, and biochemical testing was rarely done. Inadequately trained physicians performed most screening. Although 94.7% of respondents said they would reject a carrier of Tay–Sachs disease, less than one percent tested for the carrier state. Less than twenty-nine percent of the respondents conducted biochemical tests on donors aside from blood typing, and the major purpose of such testing was to detect communicable diseases. Some responses even indicated that lack of knowledge about genetics may have resulted in unnecessary exclusion of some donors.

Based on survey answers and a projection of the total number of physicians performing artificial insemination, the authors concluded that between 6,000 and 10,000 AID children are born annually. Previous estimates had ranged as high as 20,000 births annually, though some probably were little more than guesses. The study confirmed that the degree of recordkeeping, particularly with regard to donors and children conceived by AID, is minimal, making it impossible to produce "hard" birth numbers. This lack of recordkeeping in a milieu of increasing concern about the need for documentation both to protect physicians and to protect their patients' health reflects a near obsession with confidentiality, particularly with regard to donor identity. Among responding physicians, 82.6% opposed legislation requiring that records be kept of AID donors or children.

. . .

NOTES

The OTA Survey. A 1987 Survey conducted by the Office of Technology Assessment of the U.S. Congress shed further light on artificial insemination practice. It concluded that during 1986 approximately 172,000 women in the U.S. underwent artificial insemination; that more than 30,000 babies were conceived using semen from anonymous sperm donors; and that half the physicians regularly engaged in artificial insemination practice maintain records of genetic parentage but virtually none would release that information to the child. Under the OTA study on criteria for rejection of recipients, which used as a base physicians who had accepted 4 or more patients for artificial insemination during the past year, 32% of respondents had rejected patients who were unmarried without partners. Twenty-nine percent indicated they would be likely to reject on that basis but 37% indicated they would not be likely to reject. Sixty-three percent said they would be likely to reject patients who were psychologically immature, 48% would be likely to reject homosexuals, 82% would be likely to reject persons where there was evidence of child abuse, 79% where there was evidence of drug or alcohol abuse, 79% where there was evidence of serious genetic disorders, and 88% where there was a positive HIV testing.

With regard to diagnostic testing of donors, the OTA study confirmed that recognition of the transmissibility of AIDS virus through semen has affected the diagnostic testing of donors. In a study using a similar physician base, 44% of those responding indicated that they had started testing donors for HIV in all cases. Testing for other diseases or conditions was not so prevalent. Only 28% tested for syphilis, 27% for gonorrhea, and 26% for hepatitis serum in all cases. None took a herpes culture in all cases. One per cent tested for inheritable disease in all cases and 6% tested in some cases. See U.S. CONGRESS, OFFICE OF TECHNOLOGY ASSESSMENT, ARTIFICIAL INSEMINATION PRACTICE IN THE UNITED STATES: SUMMARY OF A 1987 SURVEY (USGPO, August 1988).

The Impact of AIDS. As the OTA study reflects, recognition that the AIDS virus can be transmitted through semen, and therefore through AID, had significant effect. And it is likely to have even greater long term implications. (The closeness of the two acronyms also has led some to argue further that the AID label for donor artificial insemination should be replaced to avoid confusion.) The first effect has been seen in increased testing and selectivity in sperm donors. Because an initial ELISA test at the time of the donation may not be conclusive as to whether the donor is HIV positive, the recommended protocol is to freeze the semen and have a second test (usually a "Western blot") taken after six months or more. (This was recommended by the Center for Disease Control in February 1988.) Concern about control of such an elaborate practice has led some hospitals to maintain their own sperm banks. New York, through its State Health Department, was the first state to require so-called "anonymous" sperm bank donors to undergo at least two tests for AIDS before their semen can be used. The regulation also requires special licensing of sperm banks. It does not apply to donations of sperm between husband and wife. See *New York, in Move to Bar AIDS, Puts New Limits on Sperm Banks*, N.Y. TIMES, Oct. 4, 1989, col. 1, p. B–1.

While secrecy and anonymity once were the order of the day, fostered by sparse or non-existent records about donors, the new concerns about AIDS already have caused major change. Additional desires for information about genetic make-up, already an issue in adoption, hold the promise for greater record keeping and corresponding less anonymity. This in turn should force a closer look at status issues and standing to raise them. *See generally* Walter Wadlington, *Baby M: Catalyst for Family Law Reform?*, 5 J.CONTEMP.HEALTH LAW AND POLICY 1 (1989). As in the case of surrogate parenting, one may ask whether different treatment should be accorded to the status problems of children sired through AID and those conceived through normal sexual intercourse. The potential for emotional attachments may, of course, be smaller in the AID situation. Movie viewers who saw "The Big Chill" or "Hannah and Her Sisters" will recall the varying reactions of a potential sperm donor approached by a friend and in another instance of a man who was asked to father a child for an unmarried female friend through sexual intercourse with her.

In re M.J.

Supreme Court of Illinois, 2003.
203 Ill.2d 526, 272 Ill.Dec. 329, 787 N.E.2d 144.

■ JUSTICE KILBRIDE delivered the opinion of the court.

Appellant, Alexis Mitchell, brought this action against appellee, Raymond Banary, her former paramour, seeking to establish paternity and to impose support obligations for twin boys conceived through artificial insemination by an anonymous donor. The circuit court of Cook County dismissed Alexis' suit. The appellate court affirmed. 325 Ill.App.3d 826, 259 Ill.Dec. 641, 759 N.E.2d 121. We allowed Alexis' petition for leave to appeal.... We now affirm in part, reverse in part, and hold that the Illinois Parentage Act does not bar common law claims for child support.

    . . .

    Alexis is a single woman who was 40 years old at the time of the filing of her complaint, and Raymond is a male who was 57 years old at the time of the filing of the complaint. Alexis and Raymond first met in 1986 and began an intimate relationship lasting 10 years. When they met, Raymond introduced himself to Alexis as "Jim Richardson" and told her that he was divorced.

    During their 10–year relationship, the parties discussed marriage. Alexis and Raymond are of different races and, according to Alexis, Raymond told her that he would have to wait until retirement to marry because his community would not accept a mixed-race marriage. Raymond promised Alexis that upon his retirement, they would move to another community and be married.

    The parties also discussed Alexis' desire to have children with Raymond. Despite their attempts to conceive, Alexis did not become pregnant, and it became apparent that Raymond could not father children. In 1991, Raymond suggested to Alexis that she become artificially inseminated by an anonymous donor as a means to have their child. Artificial insemination by a donor is also known as heterologous artificial insemination. Alexis claims that Raymond promised her that he would provide financial support for any child born by means of artificial insemination. However, Raymond's written consent to the procedure was never obtained. Alexis contends that Raymond orally consented to the procedure and that but for Raymond's promise to support the children, Alexis would not have completed the procedure.

    According to Alexis, with Raymond's continuing consent and active encouragement, she attempted to become pregnant through artificial insemination. Raymond provided financial assistance for the insemination procedure; accompanied Alexis to the doctor's office for examinations; injected Alexis with medication designed to enhance her fertility; and participated in selecting the donor so that the offspring would appear to be a product of their relationship.

    On the fifth attempt, Alexis became pregnant and gave birth to twin boys in 1993. Raymond participated in selecting names for the children. After the births, Raymond acknowledged the children as his own. He also provided support for them in the form of monthly payments of cash and the purchase of food, clothing, furniture, toys, and play equipment. In her complaint, Alexis further describes many family vacations with Raymond to

10 different states and Mexico, and alleges that Raymond also paid for the children's medical, travel, and entertainment expenses.

In 1996, Alexis discovered that Raymond was not named Jim Richardson and that he was married. Upon discovering Raymond's true name and marital status, Alexis ended their relationship. Since 1996, Raymond has provided no financial support for the children.

Alexis filed a three-count complaint against Raymond seeking to establish paternity and impose a support obligation for the benefit of the twin boys. In the first two counts, Alexis sought to impose child support obligations by invoking common law theories of breach of an oral agreement and promissory estoppel. In the remaining count of her complaint, Alexis sought a declaration of paternity and establishment of child support pursuant to the Illinois Parentage Act (750 ILCS 40/1 *et seq.* (West 1998)).

Raymond filed a motion to dismiss, arguing that Alexis' common law claims, contained in counts I and II, were unenforceable under the provisions of the Frauds Act (740 ILCS 80/0.01 *et seq.* (West 1998)) and contravened Illinois public policy. Raymond also argued that all three counts should be dismissed pursuant to section 2–615 of the Code (735 ILCS 5/2–615 (West 1998)) because Alexis failed to set forth a legally recognized basis for the imposition of a father-child relationship or for child support under the Illinois Parentage Act (750 ILCS 40/1 *et seq.* (West 1998)).

The circuit court granted Raymond's motion and dismissed Alexis' complaint. The circuit court interpreted the Illinois Parentage Act as requiring that a husband consent in writing before he is treated in law as the natural father of a child conceived to his wife by means of artificial insemination. The circuit court commented that it would not be rational that unmarried couples would have fewer safeguards in such a matter. The circuit court therefore held that Alexis' common law theories were not actionable because the Illinois Parentage Act expressly requires written consent. The circuit court did not refer to the Frauds Act in its dismissal of the complaint.

Alexis appealed the circuit court's decision, and the appellate court majority determined that Alexis' common law theories for child support fail because the Illinois Parentage Act governs artificial insemination and requires that the "husband's consent must be in writing." The appellate court held that written consent is required before an unmarried man becomes legally obligated to support a child born as a result of artificial insemination. Based on its decision, the appellate court did not reach the issue concerning the Frauds Act.

.   .   .

In construing a statute, this court must give effect to the intent of the legislature. *Antunes v. Sookhakitch*, 146 Ill.2d 477, 484, 167 Ill.Dec. 981, 588 N.E.2d 1111 (1992). To ascertain legislative intent, we must examine the language of the entire statute and consider each part or section in connection with every other part or section. *Castaneda v. Illinois Human*

Rights Comm'n, 132 Ill.2d 304, 318, 138 Ill.Dec. 270, 547 N.E.2d 437 (1989). Where the language is clear and unambiguous, we must apply the statute without resort to further aids of statutory construction. *Davis v. Toshiba Machine Co., America,* 186 Ill.2d 181, 184–85, 237 Ill.Dec. 769, 710 N.E.2d 399 (1999). With these principles in mind, we now turn to the interpretation of the Illinois Parentage Act.

In 1984, the General Assembly enacted the Illinois Parentage Act (750 ILCS 40/1 *et seq.* (West 1998)) "to define the legal relationships of a child born to a wife and husband requesting and consenting to * * * artificial insemination." Pub. Act 83–1026, eff. January 5, 1984. Section 3 of the Illinois Parentage Act provides:

> "(a) If, under the supervision of a licensed physician and with the consent of her husband, a wife is inseminated artificially with semen donated by a man not her husband, the husband shall be treated in law as if he were the natural father of a child thereby conceived. The husband's consent must be in writing executed and acknowledged by both the husband and wife. The physician who is to perform the technique shall certify their signatures and the date of the insemination, and file the husband's consent in the medical record where it shall be kept confidential and held by the patient's physician. However, the physician's failure to do so shall not affect the legal relationship between father and child. All papers and records pertaining to the insemination, whether part of the permanent medical record held by the physician or not, are subject to inspection only upon an order of the court for good cause shown.
>
> (b) The donor of the semen provided to a licensed physician for use in artificial insemination of a woman other than the donor's wife shall be treated in law as if he were not the natural father of a child thereby conceived." 750 ILCS 40/3(a) (West 1998).

Any child born as a result of artificial insemination is considered the legitimate child of the husband and wife consenting to the use of the technique. 750 ILCS 40/2 (West 1998). Our interpretation of the express language of this provision of the statute indicates that the primary purpose of the Illinois Parentage Act is to provide a legal mechanism for a husband and wife to obtain donor sperm for use in artificial insemination and to ensure that a child is considered the legitimate child of the husband and wife requesting and consenting to the artificial technique.

Section 3(b) of the Illinois Parentage Act also provides a statutory vehicle for women to obtain semen for artificial insemination without fear that the donor may claim paternity. 750 ILCS 40/3(b) (West 1998). Additionally, section 3(b) protects sperm donors from claims of paternity and liability for child support.

The parties dispute whether, under section 3(a) of the Illinois Parentage Act, the failure to provide written consent will preclude the establishment of a parent-child relationship and the imposition of a support obligation. This court has not conclusively interpreted the written-consent provision of the Act. We have, however, commented that the provision in the Act that "the husband's consent to the [artificial insemination] procedure 'must be in writing' *could be* considered a mandatory requirement for establishing a parent-child relationship pursuant to the statute." (Emphasis added.) *In re Marriage of Adams,* 133 Ill.2d 437, 444, 141 Ill.Dec. 448, 551 N.E.2d 635 (1990), citing *Andrews v. Foxworthy,* 71 Ill.2d 13, 21, 15 Ill.Dec. 648, 373 N.E.2d 1332 (1978) (the word "must" is generally construed in a mandatory sense.)

Whether a statutory provision is deemed mandatory or merely directory depends upon the intent of its drafters. *People v. Youngbey,* 82 Ill.2d 556, 562, 45 Ill.Dec. 938, 413 N.E.2d 416 (1980). An important aid in the determination of whether a provision is mandatory or directory is the form of the verb used in the statute. *Youngbey,* 82 Ill.2d at 562, 45 Ill.Dec. 938, 413 N.E.2d 416. If the provision merely directs a manner of conduct, it is directory. *Andrews,* 71 Ill.2d at 21, 15 Ill.Dec. 648, 373 N.E.2d 1332. If the conduct is, however, prescribed in order to safeguard one's rights, the statute is mandatory. *Andrews,* 71 Ill.2d at 21, 15 Ill.Dec. 648, 373 N.E.2d 1332.

The first sentence of section 3(a) provides for the establishment of a parent-child relationship by consent. The second sentence of section 3(a) unequivocally requires that the consent for establishment of a parent-child relationship be in writing. This provision is clearly designed to safeguard rights concerning parentage. In light of the purpose of the written-consent requirement, we must conclude that the written-consent provision of section 3(a) of the Illinois Parentage Act is mandatory. Thus, section 3(a) of the Illinois Parentage Act mandates that written consent be obtained before parental responsibility may be established. Consequently, the failure to provide or obtain written consent will preclude a claim for paternity and child support under the Illinois Parentage Act. Accordingly, the appellate court did not err in affirming the circuit court's dismissal of count III of Alexis' complaint.

We note that the language of the Illinois Parentage Act was largely adopted from section 5 of the Uniform Parentage Act (UPA) (Unif. Parentage Act § 5, 9B U.L.A. 377 (1973)), as approved by the National Conference of Commissioners on Uniform State Laws. The commentary to section 5 of the UPA states:

> "This Act does not deal with the many complex and serious legal problems raised by the practice of artificial insemination. It was though [*sic*] useful, however, to single out and cover in this Act at least one fact situation that occurs frequently. Further consideration of other legal aspects of artificial insemination has been urged on the National Conference of Commissioners on Uniform State Laws and is recommended to state legislators." Unif. Parentage Act § 5, 9B U.L.A. 408, Comment (1973).

At the time the Illinois Parentage Act was enacted, the legislature intended to clarify the legal relationships among the parties involved in the artificial insemination procedure. See L. Smith, *The AID Child and In re*

Marriage of Adams: Ambiguities in the Illinois Parentage Act, 21 Loy. U. Chi. L.J. 1173, 1192–93 (1990). However, as recognized by the commentary to section 5 of the UPA, the artificial insemination legislation "does not deal with the many complex and serious legal problems raised by the practice of artificial insemination." Unif. Parentage Act § 5, 9B U.L.A. 408, Comment (1973). Accordingly, the UPA comment urges that state legislators consider other legal aspects of artificial insemination.

In its current form, the Illinois Parentage Act fails to address the full spectrum of legal problems facing children born as a result of artificial insemination and other modern methods of assisted reproduction. The rapid evolution of assisted reproduction technology will continue to produce legal problems similar to those presented in this case. We urge the Illinois legislature to enact laws that are responsive to these problems in order to safeguard the interests of children born as a result of assisted reproductive technology.

The need for reform to the Illinois Parentage Act is clear where, as here, we are compelled to apply the statute, in its current form, to a complex legal situation that the legislature did not anticipate when it passed the Illinois Parentage Act nearly 20 years ago.

Based on our determination that written consent is a prerequisite for invoking the protections of the Illinois Parentage Act, we need not and do not make any determination with regard to whether the Illinois Parentage Act applies to unmarried persons. Section 3(a) of the Illinois Parentage Act is simply not satisfied in this case because written consent was lacking.

Our determination that Alexis may not maintain an action under the Illinois Parentage Act does not end our inquiry. We must now determine whether the Illinois Parentage Act precludes common law claims for child support. Two Illinois appellate court cases have addressed this issue. These cases are *In re Marriage of Adams,* 174 Ill.App.3d 595, 124 Ill.Dec. 184, 528 N.E.2d 1075 (1988), *rev'd on other grounds,* 133 Ill.2d 437, 141 Ill.Dec. 448, 551 N.E.2d 635 (1990), and *In re Marriage of Witbeck–Wildhagen,* 281 Ill.App.3d 502, 217 Ill.Dec. 329, 667 N.E.2d 122 (1996). Each case reached a different result based on its unique facts.

In *Adams,* the appellate court held that the Illinois Parentage Act does not bar the imposition of a support obligation under an estoppel or waiver theory and that the failure to execute a written consent did not bar further inquiry into the circumstances surrounding the decision to use artificial insemination. *Adams,* 174 Ill.App.3d at 610–11, 124 Ill.Dec. 184, 528 N.E.2d 1075. The appellate court affirmed the trial court's finding that there was "actual consent" by the husband to the insemination procedure, who twice attempted to have his vasectomy reversed, had knowledge of and paid for tests and medical bills, accepted joint responsibility for the child, and listed the child as a dependent on his federal income tax return. *Adams,* 174 Ill.App.3d at 613–15, 124 Ill.Dec. 184, 528 N.E.2d 1075. This court reversed and remanded the cause, on other grounds, holding that Florida law governed because the parties had resided in that state when the procedure was performed. *Adams,* 133 Ill.2d at 448, 141 Ill.Dec. 448, 551

N.E.2d 635. We did not, however, reach the issue of whether a cause of action for child support could be maintained under common law theories.

In *Witbeck–Wildhagen,* 281 Ill.App.3d 502, 217 Ill.Dec. 329, 667 N.E.2d 122, the husband made it clear that he did not consent to the procedure, and the wife acknowledged that he did not consent. Nonetheless, the wife petitioned to have the husband declared the legal father of her child and she sought child support. The appellate court upheld the trial court's finding that the husband did not consent to the insemination procedure since there was no evidence of the husband's consent, written or otherwise. *Witbeck–Wildhagen,* 281 Ill.App.3d at 506–07, 217 Ill.Dec. 329, 667 N.E.2d 122. The appellate court specifically stated that it was not deciding whether the failure to obtain written consent would be an absolute bar to the establishment of the father-child relationship where the conduct of the father otherwise demonstrated his consent. *Witbeck–Wildhagen,* 281 Ill. App.3d at 506–07, 217 Ill.Dec. 329, 667 N.E.2d 122. The appellate court recognized that this was not a case where the husband was "attempting to evade responsibility for his own actions in helping to conceive or encouraging the conception of a child." *Witbeck–Wildhagen,* 281 Ill.App.3d at 507, 217 Ill.Dec. 329, 667 N.E.2d 122.

Although the appellate court reached opposite conclusions in *Adams* and *Witbeck–Wildhagen,* a finding of the existence or nonexistence of consent was based on an examination of the specific facts in each case.

In interpreting the Illinois Parentage Act, this court has specifically noted that "[i]t may be the case that a support obligation will be found even in the absence of a parent-child relationship." *In re Marriage of Adams,* 133 Ill.2d 437, 445, 141 Ill.Dec. 448, 551 N.E.2d 635 (1990). In *Adams,* this court recognized its duty, in an action where the interests of a minor are at stake, to ensure that the rights of the child are adequately protected. *Adams,* 133 Ill.2d at 445, 141 Ill.Dec. 448, 551 N.E.2d 635, citing *Muscarello v. Peterson,* 20 Ill.2d 548, 170 N.E.2d 564 (1960). We also suggested that estoppel might be available to prove consent. *Adams,* 133 Ill.2d at 448, 141 Ill.Dec. 448, 551 N.E.2d 635.

Illinois has articulated its public policy recognizing the right of every child to the physical, mental, emotional, and monetary support of his or her parents. See 750 ILCS 45/1.1 (West 1998). Public policy considerations also seek to prevent children born as a result of assisted reproductive technology procedures from becoming public charges. See *Department of Public Aid ex rel. Cox v. Miller,* 146 Ill.2d 399, 411–12, 166 Ill.Dec. 922, 586 N.E.2d 1251 (1992) (concluding that the legislature intends to provide parental support for all minor children and commenting that "[l]egislative common sense dictates that if parents do not support their children, an already strained State welfare system must do so"). Illinois has a strong interest in protecting and promoting the welfare of its children. See *In re Marriage of Lappe,* 176 Ill.2d 414, 431, 223 Ill.Dec. 647, 680 N.E.2d 380 (1997). We believe that, consistently with this important public policy, cases involving assisted reproduction must be decided based on the particular circumstances presented.

In considering the reach of the Illinois Parentage Act, we note that the statute contains only three sections: (1) the title section; (2) a section declaring that children conceived as a result of artificial insemination are deemed the same as the naturally conceived legitimate child of the husband and wife; and (3) a section concerning consent procedures of the "husband," and protections for and against the sperm donor. In interpreting a statute, courts should not add requirements or impose limitations that are inconsistent with the plain meaning of the enactment. *Nottage v. Jeka,* 172 Ill.2d 386, 392, 217 Ill.Dec. 298, 667 N.E.2d 91 (1996). Our examination of these three sections of the Illinois Parentage Act finds nothing to prohibit common law actions to establish parental responsibility, and the state's public policy considerations support a finding in favor of allowing common law actions. Moreover, this court has a duty to ensure that the rights of children are adequately protected. *Adams,* 133 Ill.2d at 445, 141 Ill.Dec. 448, 551 N.E.2d 635.

We believe that if the legislature had intended to bar common law actions for child support, it would have clearly stated its intent, and we will not imply a legislative intent where none is expressed. See *Nottage,* 172 Ill.2d at 395, 217 Ill.Dec. 298, 667 N.E.2d 91. We therefore determine that the best interests of children and society are served by recognizing that parental responsibility may be imposed based on conduct evincing actual consent to the artificial insemination procedure.

The courts of other states have reached similar results and have assigned parental responsibility based on conduct evincing consent to the artificial insemination. See *Gursky v. Gursky,* 39 Misc.2d 1083, 242 N.Y.S.2d 406 (1963) (husband held liable for support of a child conceived by artificial insemination under either the basis of implied consent to support or the application of the doctrine of estoppel); *K.S. v. G.S.,* 182 N.J.Super. 102, 440 A.2d 64 (1981) (oral consent of husband was effective at the time pregnancy occurs unless established by clear and convincing evidence that consent has been revoked or rescinded); *In re Marriage of L.M.S.,* 105 Wis.2d 118, 122–23, 312 N.W.2d 853, 855 (App.1981) (sterile man who suggested to his wife that she become pregnant by another man and promised that he would acknowledge the child as his own has a legal obligation "to support the child for whose existence he is responsible"); *In re Baby Doe,* 291 S.C. 389, 353 S.E.2d 877 (1987) (husband's consent to artificial insemination may be express, or implied from conduct).

Here, Raymond's *alleged* conduct evinces a powerful case of actual consent. The allegations demonstrate a deliberate course of conduct with the precise goal of causing the birth of these children. In comparison, statutes and case law do not equivocate in imposing child support obligations for other children born out of wedlock. Moreover, a state may not discriminate against a child based on the marital status of the parties at the time of the child's birth. See *Miller,* 146 Ill.2d at 405, 166 Ill.Dec. 922, 586 N.E.2d 1251; *Gomez v. Perez,* 409 U.S. 535, 538, 93 S.Ct. 872, 875, 35 L.Ed.2d 56, 60 (1973); *Mills v. Habluetzel,* 456 U.S. 91, 92, 102 S.Ct. 1549, 1551, 71 L.Ed.2d 770, 773 (1982). Thus, if an unmarried man who biologically causes conception through sexual relations without the premeditated intent of birth is legally obligated to support a child, then the equivalent resulting birth of a child caused by the deliberate conduct of artificial insemination should receive the same treatment in the eyes of the law. Regardless of the method of conception, a child is born in need of support. Under the alleged facts of this case, to hold otherwise would deprive the children of financial support merely because of deception and a technical oversight. Simply put, we cannot accept Raymond's argument that these children and their mother must be left to fend for themselves.

Claims of parentage and support of children produced as a result of assisted reproductive technologies are unique and must be decided based on the particular facts in each case. We hold that the Illinois Parentage Act does not preclude Alexis' claims based on common law theories of oral contract or promissory estoppel. Accordingly, the circuit court erred in dismissing counts I and II of Alexis' complaint on this basis, and the appellate court erred in affirming that order. We make no determination on the merits of Alexis' claims, or Raymond's affirmative defenses, including the Frauds Act, since these claims and defenses must be developed in the circuit court.

Our holding is limited to the unique circumstances of this case. We do not address issues raised by the *amicus,* because these issues were not previously raised by the parties to this appeal. See *Burger v. Lutheran General Hospital,* 198 Ill.2d 21, 62, 259 Ill.Dec. 753, 759 N.E.2d 533 (2001).

For the foregoing reasons, we affirm that part of the appellate court judgment affirming the circuit court's dismissal of count III of Alexis' complaint, we reverse that part of the judgment of the appellate court affirming the dismissal of Alexis' claim for child support under counts I and II, and we remand the cause to the circuit court of Cook County for further proceedings not inconsistent with this opinion.

Judgments affirmed in part and reversed in part; cause remanded.

NOTE

In C.M. v. C.C., 152 N.J.Super. 160, 377 A.2d 821 (Juv. & Dom.1977), cited in the preceding opinion, a New Jersey Juvenile and Domestic Relations Court faced one of the problems left unresolved by the artificial insemination statutes. C.C. had a child conceived through artificial insemination practiced by C.C. herself with a syringe containing the semen of C.M. (A doctor at a sperm bank had refused to allow C.C. to use its facilities.) After birth of the child the court held that C.M., the natural father, was entitled to visitation rights with the child, saying:

> It is in a child's best interests to have two parents whenever possible. The court takes no position as to the propriety of the use of artificial insemination between unmarried persons, but must be concerned with the best interests of the child in granting custody or visitation, and for such consideration will not make any distinction

between a child conceived naturally or artificially.... In this situation a man wants to take upon himself the responsibility of being a father to a child he is responsible for helping to conceive. The evidence does not support C.C.'s argument that he is unfit. The evidence demonstrates that C.M. attempted to establish a relationship with the child but was thwarted in his attempts by C.C. Contrary to C.C.'s argument, C.M. has shown a genuine interest in the child; he is ... financially capable of contributing to his support. C.M.'s consent and active participation in the procedure leading to conception should place upon him the responsibilities of fatherhood. The court will not deny him the privileges of fatherhood. His motion for the right of visitation is granted.

Inasmuch as the court has found C.M. to be the natural father, the court must consider support and maintenance of the child and payment of any expenses incurred in his birth. Proper application shall be made by the parties to effect the above.

In a sequel, C.M. v. C.C., 170 N.J.Super. 586, 407 A.2d 849 (Juv. & Dom.1979), the natural father sought and obtained the court's assistance in requiring the mother to cooperate in executing documents necessary to change the birth certificate to reflect the father's identity without altering the child's surname.

Hecht v. Kane

Court of Appeal, Second District, 1993.
16 Cal.App.4th 836, 20 Cal.Rptr.2d 275.

■ LILLIE, PRESIDING JUSTICE.

Petitioner, the girlfriend of decedent William E. Kane, seeks a peremptory writ of mandate/prohibition to vacate a January 4, 1993 order directing the personal representative of decedent's estate to destroy all of the decedent's sperm in the custody and control of California Cryobank, Inc. The real parties in interest are the administrator of the decedent's estate, (Robert L. Greene) and the decedent's adult son (William E. Kane, Jr.) and adult daughter (Katharine E. Kane). We issued an order to show cause and order staying execution of the January 4, 1993 order.

This proceeding presents several matters of first impression involving the disposition of cryogenically-preserved sperm of a deceased. We conclude that the trial court's order constituted an abuse of discretion in the procedural posture of this case which compels us to set aside such order.

FACTUAL AND PROCEDURAL BACKGROUND

At the age of 48, William E. Kane took his own life on October 30, 1991, in a Las Vegas hotel. For about five years prior to his death, he had been living with petitioner, 38–year–old Deborah Hecht. Kane was survived by two college-aged children of his former wife whom he had divorced in 1976.

In October 1991, decedent deposited 15 vials of his sperm in an account at California Cryobank, Inc., a Los Angeles sperm bank (hereinafter sperm bank). On September 24, 1991, he signed a "Specimen Storage Agreement" with sperm bank which provided in pertinent part that "In the event of the death of the client [William E. Kane], the client instructs the Cryobank to: ... [¶] Continue to store [the specimens] upon request of the executor of the estate [or] [r]elease the specimens to the executor of the estate." A provision captioned "Authorization to Release Specimens" states, "I, William Everett Kane, ... authorize the [sperm bank] to release my semen specimens (vials) to Deborah Ellen Hecht. I am also authorizing specimens to be released to recipient's physician Dr. Kathryn Moyer."[22]

. . .

On September 27, 1991, decedent executed a will which was filed with the Los Angeles County Superior Court and admitted to probate. The will named Hecht as executor of the estate, and provides, "I bequeath all right, title, and interest that I may have in any specimens of my sperm stored with any sperm bank or similar facility for storage to Deborah Ellen Hecht." A portion of the will entitled "Statement of Wishes" provided, "It being my intention that samples of my sperm will be stored at a sperm bank for the use of Deborah Ellen Hecht, should she so desire, it is my wish that, should [Hecht] become impregnated with my sperm, before or after my death, she disregard the wishes expressed in Paragraph 3 above [pertaining to disposition of decedent's "diplomas and framed mementoes,"] to the extent that she wishes to preserve any or all of my mementoes and diplomas and the like for our future child or children."

. . .

On December 3, 1991, in open court, counsel for the special administrator orally placed on the record a "tentative agreement" to resolve "all matters relating to the estate between the children and Miss Hecht and to provide a 'global' resolution" pertaining to two will contests filed by the children and "one or two petitions under Probate Code [section] 9860 seeking the termination of title in the estate to various assets." Pursuant to the agreement, Hecht had in her possession and was to keep as her sole and separate property the sum of $80,000, an automobile, and some items of household furniture; the children were entitled to keep some personal effects and furnishings located at decedent's rented property in Malibu and his Monterey County house, and were entitled to proceeds of an insurance policy. "The balance of all assets over which the decedent had dominion or control or ownership, whether in the possession of Miss Hecht, the children

---

22. On our record, it is unclear whether the "Authorization to Release Specimens" applies to the release of specimens only during Kane's lifetime or includes release of specimens after his death. It is also unclear whether the contract's reference to "executor" means Hecht. In light of the fact that decedent's will names Hecht as executor, decedent may have intended "executor" to refer to Hecht. However, for reasons not clear in our record, Hecht is not the present executor of the estate.

or any third party shall be subject to administration in the decedent's estate."

After payment of all specific bequests and debts and obligations, the parties agreed that "Sums in excess of $190,000 net available for distribution will be distributed 20 percent to Deborah Hecht, 40 percent to Katharine E. Kane and 40 percent to William Everett Kane, Jr." Further, "the parties will request that said last will and testament be admitted to probate subject to the terms of the formalized version of this stipulation." The foregoing stipulation was not to be binding until each of the parties and counsel discussed it and obtained approval; the reporter was also instructed to put signature lines at the bottom of the transcript for each party and his or her counsel. According to the copy of the transcript and signature page in our record, the stipulation was signed by William Kane, Jr., and Katharine Kane and her attorney. In court on December 6, 1991, Hecht stated that she agreed with the terms of the stipulation and her counsel indicated that Hecht had signed a copy of the reporter's transcript.

According to real parties, six months after the first settlement agreement of December 1991 (hereinafter First Settlement Agreement), Hecht's counsel attempted to claim the sperm from the sperm bank by letter; the sperm bank refused to release it to Hecht, who contacted the media and asserted claims to the sperm in that forum. Hecht alleges in the instant petition that real parties breached the First Settlement Agreement which is unenforceable and refiled their will contests in direct violation of the agreement. She also alleges that the First Settlement Agreement did not mention the decedent's sperm, which was not an "asset" of the estate and does not fall under the catch-all provision of the agreement because decedent gifted it to her before his death. Real parties William Kane, Jr., and Katharine Kane contended, and still contend, that the First Settlement Agreement is valid and binding.

In October 1992, the administrator of decedent's estate filed under Probate Code sections 9837 and 9860 "Petition for Order Authorizing Compromise and Settlement of Action by Estate and Authorizing and Directing Transfer of Property from Estate," which alleged that real parties and Hecht had entered into a settlement agreement and release (herein Second Settlement Agreement); pursuant to the Second Settlement Agreement, the estate will assign to Hecht any interest the estate may have in decedent's sperm, and Hecht will agree to "defend, indemnify, and hold harmless the Estate of William Kane [and real parties, their heirs, successors, and assigns] from and against all claims, demands, and causes of action by or on behalf of any William Kane Unborn Child. . . ." The Second Settlement Agreement also provided in part that "This Agreement is subject to the condition subsequent of approval by the probate court on the application of Greene [administrator] for approval of this Agreement. . . ."

Hecht alleges that she, as well as William Kane, Jr., and Katharine Kane, signed the Second Settlement Agreement prior to October 10, 1992; on that date, at the hearing on the petition, an estate creditor named Barbara Kelly objected to the settlement, and the court set the matter for trial. According to Hecht, decedent's children attempted to withdraw from the Second Settlement Agreement but the court refused to permit such withdrawal, ruling that the interested parties were entitled to trial on the confirmation of the Second Settlement Agreement. According to the children, they effectively withdrew from the agreement because it had never become binding on the parties because not signed by Greene and approved by the court.

On November 5, 1992, Greene, as administrator, filed a "Petition for Alternative Relief (Instructions to Destroy Decedent's Frozen Sperm or Order for Preliminary Distribution of Said Sperm and Order of Determination of Whether Children Conceived from Said Sperm Shall Be Entitled to Distribution and Instructions Concerning Administration of Estate Pending Conception and Birth of Said Children)." Greene sought relief under Probate Code section 9611 (instruction from or confirmation by court), section 11620 (petition for preliminary distribution) and section 11700 (petition for determination of persons entitled to distribution), stating in his petition that "decedent's children have requested that Petitioner Petition this Court for Instructions to order the sperm destroyed, on public policy grounds, or in the alternative, for an Order for preliminary distribution of either 100% or 80% of the sperm to them upon alternative theories of entitlement. These theories include a claim based on the children's being the next of kin to the decedent and his sperm and claims based upon the terms of the Settlement Agreement."

Greene requested the court to select one of four alternative dispositions: (1) order destruction of the sperm; (2) order distribution of the sperm to decedent's children; (3) order distribution of 80 percent of the sperm to decedent's children and 20 percent to Hecht, and determine whether any children subsequently conceived by use of the sperm shall be entitled to distribution of estate assets; and (4) order distribution of the sperm to Hecht, but reserve one or two vials for future DNA/paternity testing, and determine to what extent any children subsequently conceived shall be entitled to estate assets.

Real parties Katharine Kane and William Kane, Jr., filed a statement of interested parties in which they argued that ordering destruction of decedent's sperm would "help guard the family unit in two different ways": First, such an order would prevent the birth of children who will never know their father and "never even have the slightest hope of being raised in a traditional family." Second, such an order would "prevent the disruption of existing families by after-born children," and would "prevent additional emotional, psychological and financial stress on those family members already in existence." They characterized the desire to father children after one's death as "egotistic and irresponsible," and stated that they "have lost their father to a tragic death which Hecht could easily have prevented; they do not wish to suffer any more at her hands. Further, they do not wish to be troubled for the rest of their lives with worries about the fate of their half-sibling(s)."

Hecht filed a Brief in response to the administrator's petition. She argued that neither the estate nor the children currently hold any property interest in, or right to distribution of, the sperm; it was gifted to her at the time of its deposit into the sperm bank and is either an inter vivos gift or a gift causa mortis. Hecht also maintained that even if the semen is an asset of the estate, the estate should be directed to distribute it to her because (1) the parties entered into a settlement agreement providing she is entitled to sole possession and control of the semen; (2) the will specifically directs that she is to be the sole beneficiary of the sperm; (3) destruction of the semen against her wishes would violate her rights to privacy and procreation under the federal and California Constitutions; and (4) she faces irreparable harm if the semen is not quickly distributed to her because her "advanced maternal age" will adversely affect her ability to conceive using the semen.

At the December 9, 1992, hearing on the petition, the court ordered that the sperm be destroyed.[3] On January 4, 1993, the court entered an order authorizing and directing the administrator "to destroy all of the decedent's sperm in the custody and control of California Cryobank, Inc., and in connection therewith, to instruct California Cryobank, Inc., to destroy all of the decedent's sperm in its custody and control." On March 5, 1993, Hecht filed in this court a petition for peremptory writ of mandate/prohibition to vacate the January 4, 1993 order, and requested an immediate stay. Although the trial court's order stayed execution for 60 days, on March 8, 1993, we issued an order staying execution of the January 4, 1993 order. On March 25, 1993, we issued order to show cause; oral argument has been had thereon.

PROBATE PRINCIPLES

. . .

As we hereinafter explain, the decedent's interest in his frozen sperm vials, even if not governed by the general law of personal property, occupies "an interim category that entitles them to special respect because of their potential for human life" (See Davis v. Davis (Tenn.1992) 842 S.W.2d 588, 597), and at the time of his death, decedent had an interest, in the nature of ownership, to the extent that he had decision making authority as to the sperm within the scope of policy set by law. (Ibid.) Thus, decedent had an interest in his sperm which falls within the broad definition of property in Probate Code section 62, as "anything that may be the subject of ownership and includes both real and personal property and any interest therein."

---

3. When Hecht's counsel asked for the legal basis of the ruling, the court stated, "It really does not matter, does it? If I am right, I am right and if I am wrong, I am wrong. As you know, I am persuaded by the arguments in the moving papers. This is something that is going to have to be decided by the appellate courts. Let's get a decision." Before ruling, the court also stated, "Obviously we are all agreed that we are forging new frontiers because science has run ahead of common law. And we have got to have some sort of appellate decision telling us what rights are in these uncharted territories."

II NATURE OF RIGHTS IN SEMEN

"The present legal position toward property rights in the human body is unsettled and reflects no consistent philosophy or approach. Until recently, the common law either refused to recognize a property right in human bodies or recognized only a quasi-property right.... [The court in Moore v. Regents of University of California, supra, 51 Cal.3d 120, 271 Cal.Rptr. 146, 793 P.2d 479] did not resolve the debate over the existence or extent of a property interest in one's body. Nor does the existing statutory scheme quiet the debate. The statutes that address individuals' control over their bodies delineate the extent of that control in specific situations, but do not establish a general principle." (Note, Personalizing Personalty: Toward a Property Right in Human Bodies (1990) 69 Tex. L.Rev. 209, 220, fns. omitted.)

As also recognized by the court in Moore, "the laws governing such things as human tissues, transplantable organs, blood, fetuses, pituitary glands, corneal tissue, and dead bodies deal with human biological materials as objects sui generis, regulating their disposition to achieve policy goals rather than abandoning them to the general law of personal property. It is these specialized statutes, not the law of conversion, to which courts ordinarily should and do look for guidance on the disposition of human biological materials." (51 Cal.3d at p. 137, 271 Cal.Rptr. 146, 793 P.2d 479, fn. omitted.)

Although real parties argue that Health and Safety Code section 7054.4 supports the proposition that decedent did not "own" his stored sperm, the court in Moore expressly stated that "It may be that some limited right to control the use of excised cells does survive the operation of this statute. There is, for example, no need to read the statute to permit 'scientific use' contrary to the patient's expressed wish." (51 Cal.3d at p. 141, 271 Cal.Rptr. 146, 793 P.2d 479.) The court also explained: "Clearly the Legislature did not specifically intend this statute to resolve the question of whether a patient is entitled to compensation for the nonconsensual use of excised cells. A primary object of the statute is to ensure the safe handling of potentially hazardous biological waste material. Yet one cannot escape the conclusion that the statute's practical effect is to limit, drastically, a patient's control over excised cells." (Id. at p. 140, 271 Cal.Rptr. 146, 793 P.2d 479, fn. omitted.)

Consistent with Moore, we conclude that the Legislature did not intend Health and Safety Code section 7054.4 to resolve the issue of the "property" rights retained by the donor of sperm, let alone the issue of insemination with the sperm of a deceased donor. These are issues separate and apart from the issue of the paternity of a child conceived through artificial insemination, which latter issue has been addressed in state statutes modeled after the Uniform Parentage Act, as well as by the courts.

One commentator recently noted that although some sperm banks operate as commercial enterprises, they are virtually free from state licensing and other regulation. (Wadlington, Artificial Conception: The Challenge for Family Law (1983) 69 Va.L.Rev. 465, 468.) The various state statutes modeled after the Uniform Parentage Act (see, e.g., Civ.Code, § 7000 et seq.) address the issue of the legal relationship between the sperm donor and the child born by artificial insemination. However, "[n]one of the statutes on artificial insemination indicate who owns the sperm donation, but sperm banks generally require those donors who are to be anonymous to sign a written waiver of any rights to the deposit and any paternity claims to children born from it. In return, the sperm bank guarantees the donor's anonymity. Thus, according to the contract between the parties, the donor no longer 'owns' the sperm. [P] Men who use sperm banks to store their sperm for their own future use, however, do own their donation(s) of sperm and are required to pay for its maintenance and its later withdrawal. Upon notice of the death of the donor, however, many storage agreements authorize the sperm bank to dispose of the deposit. Requests from the widow of the donor to be inseminated with the sperm, as a matter of practice, are denied absent express instructions in the donor's will or a court order." (Shapiro & Sonnenblick, The Widow and the Sperm: The Law of Post–Mortem Insemination (1986) 1 J. Law & Health 229, 243–244, fns. omitted [discussing the language in the storage agreement used by Idant Laboratory in New York, which permits Idant, upon the death of the donor, to discard the sperm or use it in scientific research, "except that no Specimen will be used, without the Client's written consent, for the purpose of causing pregnancy by means of artificial insemination." (Id., at p. 243, fn. 115)].)

The American Fertility Society, in its Ethical Statement on in vitro fertilization, has written that "It is understood that the gametes and concepti are the property of the donors. The donors therefore have the right to decide at their sole discretion the disposition of these items, provided such disposition is within medical and ethical guidelines...." (York v. Jones (E.D.Va.1989) 717 F.Supp. 421, 426, fn. 5, citing Ethics Com. of the Am. Fertility Society, Ethical Considerations of the New Reproductive Technologies (1986) 46 Fertility and Sterility 89s.)

Although Davis v. Davis, supra, 842 S.W.2d 588, involved the disposition of frozen preembryos (four-to-eight-celled entities)[5] of a married couple

---

5. According to the scientific testimony in Davis, the process of fertilization of the egg with the sperm results in a one-cell zygote which contains a new hereditary constitution (genome) contributed to by both parents through the union of sperm and egg; the stage subsequent to the zygote is cleavage, during which the single cell undergoes successive equal divisions with little or no intervening growth; the resulting cells, (blastomeres) become smaller, while the size of the total aggregate of cells remains the same; after three such divisions, the aggregate contains eight cells in relatively loose association; each blastomere, if separated from the others, has the potential to develop into a complete adult; " '[s]tated another way, at the 8–cell stage, the developmental singleness of one person has not been established.' " (842 S.W.2d at p. 593.) "Today, under federal law and all state statutory law except Louisiana, embryos [created by in vitro fertilization] do not possess rights or have legal status. In Louisiana, embryos have been given rights and limits have been imposed on how embryos may be treated." (Poole, Allocation of Decision–Making Rights to Frozen Embryos (1990) 4 Amer.J. of Fam.Law 67, 84–85.) The Louisiana statute defines "human embryo" as "an in vitro fertilized human ovum" and prohibits its destruction unless it fails to develop further over a 36 hour period,

who had attempted to bear a child through in vitro fertilization but divorced before they could do so, the court's discussion of the legal status of preembryos is informative. For various reasons, not pertinent to our discussion, the Supreme Court of Tennessee concluded that the preembryos could not be considered "persons" under Tennessee law. The court also refused to characterize the interest of the Davises in the preembryos as a property interest under general property law; rather they "occupy an interim category that entitles them to special respect because of their potential for human life. It follows that any interest that Mary Sue Davis and Junior Davis have in the preembryos in this case is not a true property interest. However, they do have an interest in the nature of ownership, to the extent that they have decision-making authority concerning disposition of the preembryos, within the scope of policy set by law." (842 S.W.2d at p. 597.)

The court in Davis found persuasive a report of the Ethics Committee of The American Fertility Society, which identified three major ethical positions that have been articulated in the debate over preembryo status. At one extreme is the view that the preembryo is a human subject after fertilization, which requires that it be accorded the rights of a person; the opposite extreme is the view that the preembryo has a status no different from any other human tissue; a third view, " 'one that is most widely held—takes an intermediate position between the other two. It holds that the preembryo deserves respect greater than that accorded to human tissue but not the respect accorded to actual persons. The preembryo is due greater respect than other human tissue because of its potential to become a person and because of its symbolic meaning for many people. Yet, it should not be treated as a person, because it has not yet developed the features of personhood, is not yet established as developmentally individual, and may never realize its biologic potential.' " (Davis v. Davis, supra, 842 S.W.2d at p. 596.)

The Davis court also notes that The American Fertility Society suggests that " 'Within the limits set by institutional policies, decision-making authority regarding preembryos should reside with the persons who have provided the gametes.... As a matter of law, it is reasonable to assume that the gamete providers have primary decision-making authority regarding preembryos in the absence of specific legislation on the subject. A person's liberty to procreate or to avoid procreation is directly involved in most decisions involving preembryos.' " (842 S.W.2d at p. 597.)

Sperm which is stored by its provider with the intent that it be used for artificial insemination is thus unlike other human tissue because it is "gametic material" (Davis v. Davis, supra, 842 S.W.2d 588, 597) that can be used for reproduction. Although it has not yet been joined with an egg to form a preembryo, as in Davis, the value of sperm lies in its potential to

except when the embryo is in a state of cryopreservation. (Id., at pp. 78–79.) In Poole's opinion, the Louisiana statute may be unconstitutional under federal law because "it infringes on individual's right of procreative choice at a stage where the state has no compelling interest in the embryo." (Id. at p. 85.)

create a child after fertilization, growth, and birth. We conclude that at the time of his death, decedent had an interest, in the nature of ownership, to the extent that he had decision making authority as to the use of his sperm for reproduction. Such interest is sufficient to constitute "property" within the meaning of Probate Code section 62. Accordingly, the probate court had jurisdiction with respect to the vials of sperm.

In concluding that the sperm is properly part of decedent's estate, we do not address the issue of the validity or enforceability of any contract or will purporting to express decedent's intent with respect to the stored sperm. In view of the nature of sperm as reproductive material which is a unique type of "property," we also decline petitioner's invitation to apply to this case the general law relating to gifts of personal property or the statutory provisions for gifts in view of impending death. (See Prob.Code, § 5700 et seq.)

We now address the propriety of the trial court's order that the sperm be destroyed. In order to do so, we examine several theories proffered by the parties to explain or uphold the trial court's order.

In this case, the trial court could not have properly ordered the sperm destroyed by applying the provisions of the will; Hecht is not only the residual beneficiary specified but the will evidences the decedent's intent that Hecht, should she so desire, is to receive his sperm stored in the sperm bank to bear his child posthumously. Moreover, there is no indication that the trial court itself purported to apply the terms of the will or was adjudicating the issue of the validity of the will. There is also no indication in our record that the trial court's order was based upon a theory the will was invalid or subject to revocation. . . .

Real parties attempt to justify the order as premised upon the theory that even if decedent had sufficient right of possession or ownership of the sperm so as to bring it within the jurisdiction of the probate court, his assumed intended use or disposition of the sperm—artificial insemination of Hecht—is invalid on two purported public policy grounds: (1) public policy forbids the artificial insemination of an unmarried woman, and (2) public policy forbids artificial insemination of Hecht with the stored sperm of a deceased man.

Before addressing the merits of the public policy arguments, we must emphasize that we are not adjudicating the validity or invalidity of the will or any contract or settlement agreement at issue in this case; we also do not purport to adjudicate any claims of decedent's competence or Hecht's undue influence. For the purpose of addressing this rationale for the trial court's order, we assume, arguendo, a particular intention on the part of the decedent. Thus, the issues of decedent's actual intention and the right of any party to actual distribution or possession of the sperm are not before us and must await the resolution of other issues in this case. For these same reasons, we must deny that part of Hecht's petition which seeks a writ directing the Superior Court to distribute the sperm to her. Such a writ is premature because many issues remain unadjudicated.

We thus proceed to address the argument that public policy forbids the artificial insemination of Hecht because she is an unmarried woman.

III ARTIFICIAL INSEMINATION AND UNMARRIED WOMEN

Although artificial insemination in itself is not new, having been performed on animals for centuries, the first recorded successful human artificial insemination was performed in England in 1770. (Shapiro & Sonnenblick, The Widow and the Sperm: The Law of Post–Mortem Insemination, supra, 1 J. Law & Health 229, 234; hereinafter Shapiro & Sonnenblick.) Although the practice was slow to be accepted in the United States until the mid–20th century, artificial insemination has now gained widespread acceptance as "medical technology has made it increasingly available and inexpensive to the estimated fifteen percent of all married couples who are infertile." (Ibid., fns. omitted.) Artificial insemination was made available to the astronauts in 1961 so they could still father healthy children using stored sperm even if space travel were to harm their reproductive systems. (Ibid.)

By 1986, it was estimated that as many as 20,000 women each year were artificially inseminated in the United States; by one estimate, 1,500 of these women were unmarried. (Jhordan C. v. Mary K. (1986) 179 Cal. App.3d 386, 389, fn. 1, 224 Cal.Rptr. 530.)

In Jhordan C. v. Mary K., supra, 179 Cal.App.3d 386, 224 Cal.Rptr. 530, the court interpreted Civil Code section 7005, subdivision (b), part of the Uniform Parentage Act (UPA),[6] as affording "unmarried as well as married women a statutory vehicle for obtaining semen for artificial insemination without fear that the donor may claim paternity, and has likewise provided men with a statutory vehicle for donating semen to married and unmarried women alike without fear of liability for child support." (179 Cal.App.3d at p. 392, 224 Cal.Rptr. 530.)

In Jhordan C., an unmarried woman artificially inseminated herself at home with the semen of a known donor and gave birth to a child, which she wanted to raise jointly with a close woman friend; the donor obtained a paternity judgment from which the mother appealed. In affirming the judgment, the court held that "where impregnation takes place by artificial insemination, and the parties have failed to take advantage of this statuto-

---

6. Civil Code section 7005 provides: "(a) If, under the supervision of a licensed physician and with the consent of her husband, a wife is inseminated artificially with semen donated by a man not her husband, the husband is treated in law as if he were the natural father of a child thereby conceived. The husband's consent must be in writing and signed by him and his wife. The physician shall certify their signatures and the date of the insemination, and retain the husband's consent as part of the medical record, where it shall be kept confidential and in a sealed file. However, the physician's failure to do so does not affect the father and child relationship. All papers and records pertaining to the insemination, whether part of the permanent record of a court or of a file held by the supervising physician or elsewhere, are subject to inspection only upon an order of the court for good cause shown. [¶] (b) The donor of semen provided to a licensed physician for use in artificial insemination of a woman other than the donor's wife is treated in law as if he were not the natural father of a child thereby conceived."

ry basis for preclusion of paternity [by providing semen to a licensed physician], the donor of semen can be determined to be the father of the child in a paternity action." (179 Cal.App.3d 386, 389, 224 Cal.Rptr. 530.)

The court in Jhordan C. was careful to stress "that our opinion in this case is not intended to express any judicial preference toward traditional notions of family structure or toward providing a father where a single woman has chosen to bear a child. Public policy in these areas is best determined by the legislative branch of government, not the judicial. *Our Legislature has already spoken and has afforded to unmarried women a statutory right to bear children by artificial insemination (as well as a right of men to donate semen) without fear of a paternity claim, through provision of the semen to a licensed physician.* We simply hold that because Mary omitted to invoke Civil Code section 7005, subdivision (b), by obtaining Jhordan's semen through a licensed physician, and because the parties by all other conduct preserved Jhordan's status as a member of Devin's [the child's] family, the trial court properly declared Jhordan to be Devin's legal father." (179 Cal.App.3d at pp. 397–398, 224 Cal.Rptr. 530; emphasis added.)

The court in Jhordan C. based its conclusion that the Legislature had "already spoken" on the issue of an unmarried woman's right to artificial insemination, because "Section 7005 is derived almost verbatim from the UPA as originally drafted, with one crucial exception. The original UPA restricts application of the nonpaternity provision of subdivision (b) to a *'married* woman other than the donor's wife.' (9A West's U.Laws Ann., op. cit. supra, § 5 subd. (b), p. 593; . . . .) The word 'married' is excluded from subdivision (b) of section 7005, so that in California, subdivision (b) applies to all women, married or not." (179 Cal.App.3d at p. 392, 224 Cal.Rptr. 530; original emphasis.) We agree with the reasoning in Jhordan C.; had the Legislature intended to express a public policy against procreative rights of unmarried women or against artificial insemination of unmarried women, it would not have excluded the word "married" from section 7005, subdivision (b). Colorado, Washington, Wisconsin and Wyoming have also eliminated the word "married" from subsection (b) in their adoption of the UPA. (Shapiro & Sonnenblick, supra, 1 J. Law & Health 229, 240, fn. 93.)

In light of the foregoing, we reject real parties' argument that we are operating in a legal vacuum and are "free to establish policies with respect to the access of an unmarried woman to a non-coital reproductive technique (artificial insemination)."

Citing Civil Code section 4600, subdivision (a), dealing with the custody of children whose parents are separated or divorced, real parties contend that the latter "demonstrates the state's recognition that a child is better off with two living parents, whether living apart or living together, rather than with just one parent." Section 4600, subdivision (a) declares the Legislature's policy "to assure minor children of frequent and continuing contact with both parents after the parents have separated or dissolved their marriage, and to encourage parents to share the rights and responsibilities of child rearing. . . ." The foregoing statute is neither pertinent to, nor implicated in, the instant case where we are concerned with the procreative rights of an unmarried woman. Real parties fail to cite any pertinent authority which indicates that the state has a policy of preventing the formation of single-parent families. We also point out that, at this time, the issue is speculative, as it assumes that Hecht will bear a child into a single-parent family.

We also note that in a case dealing with the right of an unwed father to withhold his consent to his child's adoption by third parties, the California Supreme Court had an opportunity to comment that the state did not have a sufficiently strong interest in providing two-parent families to discriminate against unwed fathers in its application of Civil Code section 7004, subdivision (a): "We cannot conclude in the abstract that adoption is itself a sufficient objective to allow the state to take whatever measures it deems appropriate. Nor can we merely assume, either as a policy or factual matter, that adoption is necessarily in a child's best interest. This assumption is especially untenable in light of the rapidly changing concept of family. As recently as only a few years ago, it might have been reasonable to assume that an adopted child would be placed into a two-parent home and thereby have a more stable environment than a child raised by a single father. The validity of that assumption is now highly suspect in light of modern adoption practice. Recent statistics show that a significant percentage of children placed for independent adoption—7.7 percent—are adopted by a single parent. [Citation.] The figure is even higher—21.9 percent—for children placed with agencies for adoption. [Citation.] We note that New York's high court also recently rejected the argument that the state has a sufficiently strong interest in providing two-parent families to discriminate against unwed fathers. [Citation.] [¶] If the possible benefit of adoption were by itself sufficient to justify terminating a parent's rights, the state could terminate an unwed mother's parental rights based on nothing more than a showing that her child's best interest would be served by adoption. Of course, that is not the law; nor do the parties advocate such a system. We simply do not in our society take children away from their mothers— married or otherwise—because a 'better' adoptive parent can be found.... Respondents seem to suggest that a child is inherently better served by adoptive parents than by a single, biological father but that the child is also inherently better served by a single, biological mother than by adoptive parents. The logic of this view is not apparent, and there is no evidence in the record to support such a counterintuitive view." (Adoption of Kelsey S. (1992) 1 Cal.4th 816, 845–846, 4 Cal.Rptr.2d 615, 823 P.2d 1216.)

Given the foregoing we also find without merit the argument of real parties that "The state's interest in protecting the institutions of family and marriage dictates petitioner should be denied access to the sperm." Clearly the institution of marriage is not implicated in this case, especially where there was no existing marriage relationship involving decedent at the time of his death and obviously there can be none after his death. (See Jhordan C. v. Mary K., supra, 179 Cal.App.3d 386, 395, 224 Cal.Rptr. 530.) It is also premature for us to address the issue of family integrity and, in any case, there is no factual basis in this record to support any contention that the artificial insemination of Hecht would have an impact on any other family, including any family involving decedent's surviving adult children.

We thus conclude that real parties fail to establish with any pertinent authority that the public policy of California prohibits the artificial insemination of Hecht because of her status as an unmarried women.

IV   POST–MORTEM ARTIFICIAL INSEMINATION

We are aware of only one other court which has addressed the issue of the right of a woman to the sperm of a decedent. In 1984, in Parpalaix v. CECOS, the French Tribunaux de grande instance ordered CECOS, a government run sperm bank in a Paris suburb, to return stored sperm of a decedent to a doctor chosen by his surviving wife. In light of the discussion in the preceding section pertaining to unmarried women, we find the Parpalaix case instructive and pertinent to the issue before us although it dealt with a married couple. We glean the following facts and decision in the Parpalaix case from a discussion of it in Shapiro and Sonnenblick, supra, 1 Journal of Law and Health at pages 229–233.[7]

In 1981, Alain Parpalaix, suffering from testicular cancer, made one deposit of sperm at CECOS but left no instructions as to the future use of the sperm. At the time of the deposit, he was living with Corinne, whom he later married on December 23, 1983; as his condition was rapidly deteriorating, Alain died on December 25, 1983 at the age of 26. Corinne requested Alain's sperm deposit from CECOS, which denied the request as other centers had denied the requests of other widows. Corinne, joined by her in-laws, pursued the matter in court, where they contended that as Alain's natural heirs (spouse and parents), they had become the owners of the sperm and CECOS had broken the contract, which was in the nature of a bailment; they also argued they had a moral right to the sperm.

CECOS contended that (1) its only legal obligation was to the donor, not the wife; (2) sperm is an indivisible part of the body, much like a limb or organ and is therefore not inheritable absent express instructions; and (3) the act of depositing sperm was strictly for therapeutic purposes, to aid Alain psychologically, and giving birth was not a therapeutic matter.

"Before discussing the parties' contentions, the [court] acknowledged and briefly described the difficulties that French laws governing inheritance rights and illegitimacy would impose on a child born 'post-mortem.' By strict interpretation of the Civil Code (based on the Napoleonic Code from the early 19th Century), any child born more than 300 days after the putative father's death is deemed illegitimate. Even if the reach of the article were to be miraculously interpreted or legislatively altered to establish paternity, the child would be barred from inheriting through his

---

7. Shapiro and Sonnenblick obtained their information concerning the Parpalaix case from the Gazette du Palais, September 15, 1984, at pages 11 to 14. It is not clear whether the latter is an official or unofficial report of the trial court's opinion. At any event, Shapiro and Sonnenblick's characterization of the French court's opinion is consistent with reports of it in the English-language press. We have not been able to obtain a copy of the Gazette du Palais.

father pursuant to another article of the code which states that to inherit, the child must exist at the time of death and then expressly disqualifies '[o]ne who is not yet conceived.' ''[8] (Shapiro & Sonnenblick, supra, 1 J. Law & Health at pp. 231–232; fns. omitted.)

According to Shapiro & Sonnenblick, the French court offered no solutions to the obstacles created by the foregoing laws, but implied that, given the various new methods of procreation, the laws were outdated. The French court also expressly declined to apply ordinary contract principles raised by both parties, finding "it is impossible to characterize human sperm as movable, inheritable property within the contemplation of the French legislative scheme." (Shapiro & Sonnenblick, supra, 1 J. Law & Health at p. 232.) The court also disagreed with the position of CECOS that the sperm is an indivisible part of the body, characterizing sperm instead as " 'the seed of life . . . tied to the fundamental liberty of a human being to conceive or not to conceive.' This fundamental right must be jealously protected, and is not to be subjected to the rules of contracts. Rather the fate of the sperm must be decided by the person from whom it is drawn. Therefore, the sole issue becomes that of intent." (Ibid.; fns. omitted.) Property rights and status became irrelevant to that decision. (Id., at p. 233.) The court framed the issues it had to decide as only whether Alain Parpalaix intended his widow to be artificially inseminated with his sperm and whether that intent was "unequivocable." The court found that the testimony of the widow and Alain's parents established his "deep desire" to make his wife "the mother of a common child." (Ibid.) CECOS did not appeal the decision of the court and Corinne was artificially inseminated in November 1984; due to the small quantity and poor quality, she did not become pregnant. (Ibid.)

"Although the Parpalaix decision has been generally acclaimed as eminently humane, it has been criticized by doctors and lawyers alike. The court's order is a victory for the widow and even for the father who can sire a child from the grave, but it may be detrimental to the child. Though the court permitted Corinne Parpalaix to continue expressing her love for Alain by bearing his child, nowhere in the Parpalaix decision did it address and

---

8. In California, Probate Code section 6407 provides that "Relatives of the decedent conceived before the decedent's death, but born thereafter inherit as if they had been born in the lifetime of the decedent." "For purposes of intestate succession, section 6408 provides the rules for determining parent-child relationships and inheritance rights. Under subdivision (c)(1), a natural parent-child relationship or paternity is established when there is a presumption of the parent-child relationship under Civil Code section 7004 and that presumption has not been rebutted. Subdivision (c)(2), with its 'may' language, merely allows other provisions of the Uniform Parentage Act to be used to estab-lish a natural parent-child relationship provided that a court decree declaring paternity was entered while the father was alive or there is clear and convincing evidence that the father, while alive, had openly and notoriously held out the child as his own. . . . Therefore, here, where there is no unrebutted presumption of paternity and there is neither a court decree declaring paternity entered during Sanders's lifetime nor clear and convincing evidence that he had openly and notoriously held out Laurel as his child, section 6408 does not contemplate any means of establishing paternity." (Estate of Sanders (1992) 2 Cal.App.4th 462, 471, 3 Cal.Rptr.2d 536, original emphasis, fn. omitted.)

consider the best interests of the child. Commentators have suggested that the child could suffer psychologically from being conceived by a dead man. How such psychological effects would differ from those experienced by a child born to an unmarried woman by AID [artificial insemination by donor] or a child who, at a very young age, loses his father, remains to be explained." (Shapiro & Sonnenblick, supra, 1 J. Law & Health at pp. 246–247; fns. omitted.)

Echoing some of the concerns expressed by Shapiro and Sonnenblick, real parties argue that "this court should adopt a state policy against posthumous conception," because it is "in truth, the creation of orphaned children by artificial means with state authorization," a result which they characterize as "tragic." However, real parties do not cite any authority establishing the propriety of this court, or any court, to make the value judgment as to whether it is better for such a potential child not to be born, assuming that both gamete providers wish to conceive the child. In other words, assuming that both Hecht and decedent desired to conceive a child using decedent's sperm, real parties fail to establish a state interest sufficient to justify interference with that decision. As in Tennessee, we are aware of no statutes in California which contain a "statement of public policy which reveals an interest that could justify infringing on gamete-providers' decisional authority. . . ." (Davis v. Davis, supra, 842 S.W.2d 588, 602.)

We also disagree with real parties' claim that any order other than destruction of the sperm is tantamount to "state authorization" of posthumous conception of children, i.e., the creation of a public policy in favor of such conception. In such a case, the state is simply acknowledging that "no other person or entity has an interest sufficient to permit interference with the gamete-providers' decision ... because no one else bears the consequences of these decisions in the way that the gamete-providers do." (Davis v. Davis, supra, 842 S.W.2d at p. 602.)

Citing Davis, real parties also urge this court to uphold the trial court's order on the ground that Hecht "can easily procreate by a variety of other means," and she "cannot bear a child using [decedent's] sperm without encroaching upon the family integrity of [decedent's] existing children." As pointed out above, our record is inadequate to address the issue of real parties' "family integrity."

As to the issue of whether Hecht has other means to bear a child, the issue is a factual one which our record fails to address. Moreover, it must be pointed out that the court in Davis was called upon to resolve a dispute involving the disposition of preembryos where the gamete-providers disagreed as to their disposition and where there was no written agreement of the parties or state statute governing such disposition. Under those circumstances, the court held as follows: "[W]e hold that disputes involving the disposition of preembryos produced by in vitro fertilization should be resolved, first, by looking to the preferences of the progenitors. If their wishes cannot be ascertained, or if there is dispute, then their prior agreement concerning disposition should be carried out. If no prior agreement exists, then the relative interests of the parties in using or not using the preembryos must be weighed. Ordinarily, the party wishing to avoid procreation should prevail, assuming that the other party has a reasonable possibility of achieving parenthood by means other than use of the preembryos in question. If no other reasonable alternatives exist, then the argument in favor of using the preembryos to achieve pregnancy should be considered. However, if the party seeking control of the preembryos intends merely to donate them to another couple, the objecting party obviously has the greater interest and should prevail." (Davis v. Davis, supra, 842 S.W.2d 588, 604.)

Given the procedural posture of this case, and the fact that, for purposes of addressing real parties' arguments, we are assuming that decedent intended to allow Hecht to use his sperm for posthumous artificial insemination, it is premature for us to apply the Davis test. At this point, the only issue which we address is whether artificial insemination with the sperm of a decedent violates public policy. There is nothing in Davis which indicates that such artificial insemination violates public policy.[9]

Real parties also intimate that the birth of a child by Hecht using decedent's sperm will create psychological burdens on them, decedent's surviving adult children, as well as financial burdens on society and on the estate.

In light of the UPA and Probate Code sections 6407 and 6408, (ante, fn. 8), it is unlikely that the estate would be subject to claims with respect to any such children. If the Second Settlement Agreement is enforceable against Hecht, the estate may also be protected from any claims with respect to such children.

The interest of heirs and courts in the finality of probate rulings was recognized by the committee which drafted the Uniform Status of Children of Assisted Conception Act.... Section 4 of that Act provides in pertinent part that [Except as otherwise provided in Sections 5 through 9:] ... "(b) An individual who dies before implantation of an embryo, or before a child is conceived other than through sexual intercourse, using the individual's egg or sperm, is not a parent of the resulting child." The exceptions, dealing with surrogacy agreements, are not pertinent here.

The Committee Comment states that "Subsection 4(b) is designed to provide finality for the determination of parenthood of those whose genetic material is utilized in the procreation process after their death. The death of the person whose genetic material is either used in conceiving an embryo

---

9. It is only if the trier of fact determines that decedent's intent cannot be ascertained, or is contrary to Hecht's intent to bear decedent's child, that the Davis balancing test would be pertinent. As we have already explained, the pleadings in this case call into question the decedent's capacity, the validity of the will, the validity of the sperm bank contract, and the enforceability of the first and second settlement agreements. These issues are also inextricably bound up with the issue of decedent's intent to posthumously father a child with Hecht. Accordingly, the actual disposition of decedent's sperm is an issue which must await resolution of many other issues.

or in implanting an already existing embryo into a womb would end the potential parenthood of the deceased. . . .

Real parties also fail to establish that the estate would be subject to a claim in the event a child born to Hecht using decedent's sperm is supported by public assistance. . . ."

Decedent's adult children also fail to provide any legal or factual basis to support their contention that the birth of a child through the artificial insemination of Hecht with decedent's sperm implicates their "fundamental right to protection of their family integrity," and thus their psychological well-being.

At this point, it is also entirely speculative as to whether any child born to Hecht using decedent's sperm will be a burden on society. Real parties also offer no authority for their suggestion that if the sperm is to be distributed to Hecht, the probate court should first treat the matter as a surrogacy arrangement or adoption and appoint a guardian ad litem for the unborn child(ren) and conduct a fitness hearing as to Hecht's fitness to bear a child. We know of no authority which would authorize the probate court to proceed in the foregoing manner, much less provide it authority to address the issue of Hecht's fitness to bear a child.

As recently stated by our Supreme Court in a case involving a surrogacy contract: "It is not the role of the judiciary to inhibit the use of reproductive technology when the Legislature has not seen fit to do so; any such effort would raise serious questions in light of the fundamental nature of the rights of procreation and privacy." (Johnson v. Calvert (1993) 5 Cal.4th 84, 101, 19 Cal.Rptr.2d 494, 851 P.2d 776.)

For the foregoing reasons we conclude that the trial court abused its discretion in ordering decedent's sperm destroyed.

. . .

Let a peremptory writ of mandate issue directing the superior court to (1) vacate its January 4, 1993 order, (2) enter a new order denying the "petition for alternative relief [instructions to destroy decedent's frozen sperm or order for preliminary distribution of said sperm and order of determination of whether children conceived from said sperm shall be entitled to distribution and instructions concerning administration of estate pending conception and birth of said children]," and (3) conduct further proceedings consistent with the views expressed herein. Upon compliance with this writ, our order staying execution of the January 4, 1993 order is discharged.

NOTE

The dispute continued in the courts after the preceding decision. In Kane v. Superior Court, 37 Cal.App.4th 1577, 44 Cal.Rptr.2d 578 (1995), the dispute over decedent's frozen sperm again came before the court. The trial court ordered the administrator of the estate to distribute sperm to prevent imminent injury or loss; the Court of Appeal, Johnson, J., held that the appeal did not stay enforcement of the order directing distribution of sperm to prevent injury or loss.

GEORGIA CODE ANN. (2004)

§ 19-7-21. When children conceived by artificial insemination legitimate.

All children born within wedlock or within the usual period of gestation thereafter who have been conceived by means of artificial insemination are irrebuttably presumed legitimate if both spouses have consented in writing to the use and administration of artificial insemination.

§ 43-34-42. Persons authorized to perform artificial insemination; civil liability of physician or surgeon who obtains written authorization from husband and wife to perform artificial insemination.

(a) Physicians and surgeons licensed to practice medicine in accordance with and under this article shall be the only persons authorized to administer or perform artificial insemination upon any female human being. Any other person or persons who shall attempt to administer or perform or who shall actually administer or perform artificial insemination upon any female human being shall be guilty of a felony and, upon conviction thereof, shall be punished by imprisonment in the penitentiary for not less than one year nor more than five years.

(b) Any physician or surgeon who obtains written authorization signed by both the husband and the wife authorizing him to perform or administer artificial insemination shall be relieved of civil liability to the husband and wife or to any child conceived by artificial insemination for the result or results of said artificial insemination, provided that the written authorization provided for in this Code section shall not relieve any physician or surgeon from any civil liability arising from his own negligent administration or performance of artificial insemination.

OREGON REVISED STATUTES (2005)

§ 109.239 **Rights and obligations of children resulting from artificial insemination; rights and obligations of donor of semen.** If the donor of semen used in artificial insemination is not the mother's husband:

(1) Such donor shall have no right, obligation or interest with respect to a child born as a result of the artificial insemination; and

(2) A child born as a result of the artificial insemination shall have no right, obligation or interest with respect to such donor.

§ 109.243 **Relationship of child resulting from artificial insemination to mother's husband.** The relationship, rights and obligation between a child born as a result of artificial insemination and the mother's husband shall be the same to all legal intents and purposes as if the child had been naturally and legitimately conceived by the mother and the mother's husband if the husband consented to the performance of artificial insemination.

§ 109.247   Application of law to children resulting from artificial insemination. Except as may be otherwise provided by a judicial decree entered in any action filed before October 4, 1977, the provisions of ORS 109.239 to 109.247, 677.355 to 677.365 and 677.990(3) apply to all persons conceived as a result of artificial insemination.

§ 677.355   "Artificial insemination" defined. As used in ORS 109.239 to 109.247, 677.355 to 677.365 and 677.990(3), "artificial insemination" means introduction of semen into a woman's vagina, cervical canal or uterus through the use of instruments or other artificial means.

§ 677.360   Who may select donors and perform procedure. Only physicians licensed under this chapter and persons under their supervision may select artificial insemination donors and perform artificial insemination.

§ 677.365   Consent required; filing with State Registrar of Vital Statistics; notice to physician. (1) Artificial insemination shall not be performed upon a woman without her prior written request and consent and, if she is married, the prior written request and consent of her husband.

(2) Whenever a child is born who may have been conceived by the use of semen of a donor who is not the woman's husband, a copy of the request and consent required under subsection (1) of this section shall be filed by the physician who performs the artificial insemination with the State Registrar of Vital Statistics. The state registrar shall prescribe the form of reporting.

(3) The information filed under subsection (2) of this section shall be sealed by the state registrar and may be opened only upon an order of a court of competent jurisdiction.

(4) If the physician who performs the artificial insemination does not deliver the child conceived as a result of the use of semen of a donor who is not the woman's husband, it is the duty of the woman and the husband who consented pursuant to subsection (1) of this section to give that physician notice of the child's birth. The physician who performs the artificial insemination shall be relieved of all liability for noncompliance with subsection (2) of this section if the noncompliance results from lack of notice to the physician about the birth.

§ 677.370   Who may be donor. No semen shall be donated for use in artificial insemination by any person who:

(1) Has any disease or defect known by him to be transmissible by genes; or

(2) Knows or has reason to know he has a venereal disease.

NOTE

Rights of a sperm donor. In McIntyre v. Crouch, 98 Or.App. 462, 780 P.2d 239 (1989) the Court of Appeals of Oregon upheld the provision that in the absence of agreement, a sperm donor has no parental rights as to the child that respondent, an unmarried woman, conceived by artificial insemination with petitioner's semen. However the court explained that

> It is not disputed that, if petitioner and respondent had mutually agreed that he should have the rights and responsibilities of fatherhood and, in reliance thereon, he gave her his semen by sexual intercourse, the legislature could not declare that he has no claim to be the father.

Not all states have followed the practice of specifically severing rights of a sperm donor in their legislation on artificial insemination, even though potential claims might exist under the rationale of Stanley v. Illinois, and subsequent decisions interpreting it. In the face of a statute containing no such specific language, the Court of Appeals of Virginia held in Welborn v. Doe, 10 Va.App. 631, 394 S.E.2d 732 (1990), that the husband of a mother who conceived a child through AID with her husband's consent could bring an adoption action. The court explained that while the Virginia law established a presumption that the husband was the natural father, it did not specifically terminate all possible parental rights of a donor. During 1991 the Virginia General Assembly modified Va. Code Ann. § 32.1–25.7.D (West 2001) to provide that:

> For the purpose of birth registration in the case of a child resulting from assisted conception, . . . the birth certificate of such child shall contain full information concerning the mother's husband as the father of the child and the gestational mother as the mother of the child. Donors of sperm or ova shall not have any parental rights or duties for any such child.

Fixing "parentage" for custody of children of same sex relationships.

Many of the decisions involving artificial insemination involve lesbians and the evolving arena of same sex relationships. In seeking to determine parentage and attendant benefits and responsibilities, courts often borrow from existing cases involving opposite-sex parties. For example, in King v. S.B. (*In re* the Parentage of A.B.), 818 N.E.2d 126 (Ind. Ct. App. 2004), two women in a nine-year domestic relationship agreed that one would conceive a child through artificial insemination and after birth, both of the women would raise the child as parents. In holding that both women were parents, the court stressed that both women acted in good faith in deciding to co-parent and the biological parent cannot unilaterally abrogate the resulting parenting roles.

Clifford K. and Tina B. v. Paul S., 217 W.Va. 625, 619 S.E.2d 138 (W. Va. 2005), involved a contest for primary custody of the minor child, Z.B.S. who Tina B. had raised from infancy with her now-deceased partner, Christina S. The child was conceived by Christina S. about a year after she and Tina B. commenced their relationship. Sperm from Clifford K. was utilized to help Christina S. conceive Z.B.S. After Christina's death, her father, Paul S., sought custody of Z.B.S. In her petition for custody, Tina B. was joined as a party by Clifford K. (However, the Supreme Court explains in its opinion that "Clifford K. not only acquiesces in an award of custody to Tina B; he has not actively sought custody of his son and has chosen not to participate in the instant appeal.") Initially the Family Court held that Tina B. had standing to seek custody as a psychological parent due to the relation with the child prior to the death of Christina S. An award of primary custody was granted to Tina B. with visitation rights to Paul S. and his wife (Christina's mother) and Clifford K. On appeal, the circuit court found that Tina B. lacked standing and therefore remanded the case to the Family Court for a determination of permanent custody of Z.B.S. to either Paul S. or Clifford K. However the West Virginia Supreme Court upheld a finding that although Tina B. could not participate in the custodial determinations as the "legal parent" of Z.B.S., she could participate as an intervenor under W.Va.Code 48–9–103 (2004) which provides that

> (3) Persons who were parties to a prior order establishing custody and visitation, or who, under a parenting plan, were allocated custodial responsibility or decision-making responsibility.

> (b) In exceptional cases the court may, in its discretion, grant permission to intervene to other persons or public agencies whose participation in the proceedings under this article it determines is likely to serve the child's best interests. The court may place limitations on participation by the intervening party as the court determines to be appropriate. Such persons or public agencies do not have standing to initiate an action under this article.

Emphasizing that the child's best interests was the key factor, and after reviewing prior instance of psychological parenthood before the courts, primary custody was awarded to Tina B.

3.   IN VITRO FERTILIZATION

Walter Wadlington, *Artificial Conception: The Challenge for Family Law*

69 VA.L.REV. 465, 473–474 (1983).

AID offers a possible answer for child-seeking couples when the male partner is infertile. In vitro fertilization (IVF) and embryo transfer can enable women previously unable to conceive to bear children. It can be a special boon to women with blocked or damaged Fallopian tubes. And IVF has even greater potential. It could enable the merged egg and sperm of one couple to be carried to term in the womb of a second female. Thus a husband's sperm could fertilize ova of a third party donor to produce an embryo, or conceptus, implantable in the body of a wife incapable of ovulation. Alternatively, the conceptus from the egg and sperm of wife and husband (or third party donor) could be implanted in a borrowed womb because of a wife's medical problems or simply for personal convenience.

To achieve conception through IVF, a physician removes ova from a female through laparoscopy, a procedure involving insertion of a tube through which follicles containing mature ova can be located visually and withdrawn. The physician then places the ova in a laboratory medium with male sperm for fertilization. Several cell divisions later the physician places the embryo in the uterus of the female egg donor (or possibly that of another female whose hormonal cycle is at approximately the same stage). In the desired course of events, implantation, development, and birth of a child will ensue.[37] IVF followed by embryo transfer still is considered widely to be an experimental procedure, although more than 120 babies have been born through the process. Though popular concern about the possibility of an abnormal number of congenital defects in IVF children may remain, there are reassuring statements from within the scientific community that the risks are little or no greater than those associated with pregnancies commencing in normal fashion. This would make the risks less than those accepted by couples who elect to have a child when aware of a recessive genetic defect.[39]

Several years ago the Department of Health, Education and Welfare made federal research support for human IVF contingent upon a finding by its Ethics Advisory Board that such research is ethically acceptable. In a May 1979 report, the board concluded that such research is acceptable upon satisfaction of certain conditions. Of special relevance is the report's recommendation favoring development of a model law to clarify the legal status of children born through IVF and embryo transfer.

Like AID, IVF poses problems of establishing paternity when the sperm came from a donor other than the husband. In addition, it poses a parallel problem of establishing maternity when the egg came from someone other than the wife. IVF also raises potential new concerns about the rights and obligations of a female whose uterus may be borrowed for maturation and delivery.

NOTE

Currently ova cannot be frozen and then thawed with assurance that there has been no DNA damage. Such a procedure is considered experiment, generally. However embryos can be frozen, and such a practice allows potential use of multiple eggs removed the same time. It also has produced an ongoing series of legal disputes. In April 1984 a baby was born

---

37. For more detailed explanation of the process, see Edwards, Steptoe & Purdy, *Establishing Full–Term Human Pregnancies Using Cleaving Embryos Grown In Vitro,* 87 Brit. J. Obstetrics & Gynaecology 737 (1980); Mettler, Seki, Baukloh & Semm, Human Ovum *Recovery Via Operative Laparoscopy* *and In Vitro Fertilization,* 38 Fertility & Sterility 30 (1982).

39. For further discussion see Biggers, *In Vitro Fertilization and Embryo Transfer in Human Beings,* 304 New Eng.J.Med. 336, 341 (1981).

in Australia through use of an embryo that had been frozen and stored before transfer. The use of cryostorage can serve to minimize the possible need for multiple laparoscopies and also can permit the "banking" of embryos. Many perplexing issues might be envisioned as a result of such technology. For example, if a couple "bank" an embryo (using their sperm and ova) for future use, who should control its use if they subsequently divorce? After a wealthy California couple died in 1983 it was found that two embryos produced from their sperm and ova in 1981, when the wife had undergone an unsuccessful IVF procedure, remained frozen in Australia. Because of freezing techniques at the time, physicians subsequently considered it unlikely the embryos could survive thawing and implantation. *See* WASHINGTON POST, June 18, 1984, at A2, col. 2. How would you advise the parties' executors under such circumstances? Suppose only the mother had died, leaving a will making her husband heir if they had no children?

J.B. v. M.B. and C.C.

Supreme Court of New Jersey, 2001.
170 N.J. 9, 783 A.2d 707.

■ The opinion of the Court was delivered by PORITZ, C.J.

In this case, a divorced couple disagree about the disposition of seven preembryos[1] that remain in storage after the couple, during their marriage, undertook in vitro fertilization procedures. We must first decide whether the husband and wife have entered into an enforceable contract that is now determinative on the disposition issue. If not, we must consider how such conflicts should be resolved by our courts.

Although the reproductive technology to accomplish in vitro fertilization has existed since the 1970s, there is little caselaw to guide us in our inquiry.

J.B. and M.B. were married in February 1992. After J.B. suffered a miscarriage early in the marriage, the couple encountered difficulty conceiving a child and sought medical advice from the Jefferson Center for Women's Specialties. Although M.B. did not have infertility problems, J.B. learned that she had a condition that prevented her from becoming pregnant. On that diagnosis, the couple decided to attempt in vitro fertilization at the Cooper Center for In Vitro Fertilization, P.C. (the Cooper Center).

The in vitro fertilization procedure requires a woman to undergo a series of hormonal injections to stimulate the production of mature oocytes[2] (egg cells or ova). The medication causes the ovaries to release multiple egg

---

1. A preembryo is a fertilized ovum (egg cell) up to approximately fourteen days old (the point when it implants in the uterus). *The American Heritage Stedman's Medical Dictionary* 667 (1995). Throughout this opinion, we use the term "preembryo," rather than "embryo," because preembryo is technically descriptive of the cells' stage of development when they are cryopreserved (frozen).

2. Oocytes are cells from which an egg or ovum develops. *Id.* at 578.

cells during a menstrual cycle rather than the single egg normally produced. The egg cells are retrieved from the woman's body and examined by a physician who evaluates their quality for fertilization. Egg cells ready for insemination are then combined with a sperm sample and allowed to incubate for approximately twelve to eighteen hours. Successful fertilization results in a zygote[3] that develops into a four-to eight-cell preembryo. At that stage, the preembryos are either returned to the woman's uterus for implantation or cryopreserved at a temperature of–196 C and stored for possible future use.

A limited number of preembryos are implanted at one time to reduce the risk of a multiple pregnancy. Cryopreservation of unused preembryos reduces, and may eliminate, the need for further ovarian stimulation and egg retrieval, thereby reducing the medical risks and costs associated with both the hormone regimen and the surgical removal of egg cells from the woman's body. Cryopreservation also permits introduction of the preembryos into the uterus at the optimal time in the natural cycle for pregnancy. Egg cells must be fertilized before undergoing cryopreservation because unfertilized cells are difficult to preserve and, once preserved, are difficult to fertilize.

The Cooper Center's consent form describes the procedure:

> IVF [or in vitro fertilization] will be accomplished in a routine fashion: that is, ovulation induction followed by egg recovery, insemination, fertilization, embryo development and embryo transfer of up to three or four embryos in the stimulated cycle. With the couple's consent, any "extra" embryos beyond three or four will be cryopreserved according to our freezing protocol and stored at–196 C. Extra embryos, upon thawing, must meet certain criteria for viability before being considered eligible for transfer. These criteria require that a certain minimum number of cells composing the embryo survive the freeze-thaw process. These extra embryos will be transferred into the woman's uterus in one or more future menstrual cycles for the purpose of establishing a normal pregnancy. The physicians and embryologists on the IVF team will be responsible for determining the appropriate biological conditions and the timing for transfers of cryopreserved embryos.

The consent form also contains language discussing the control and disposition of the preembryos:

> The control and disposition of the embryos belongs to the Patient and her Partner. You will be asked to execute the attached legal statement regarding control and disposition of cryopreserved embryos. The IVF team will not be obligated to proceed with the transfer of any cryopreserved embryos if experience indicates the risks outweigh the benefits.

Before undertaking in vitro fertilization in March 1995, the Cooper Center gave J.B. and M.B. the consent form with an attached agreement for their signatures. The agreement states, in relevant part:

---

3. A zygote is a fertilized ovum before it undergoes cell division. *Id.* at 906.

I, J.B. (patient), and M.B. (partner), agree that all control, direction, and ownership of our tissues will be relinquished to the IVF Program under the following circumstances:

1. A dissolution of our marriage by court order, unless the court specifies who takes control and direction of the tissues. . . .

The in vitro fertilization procedure was carried out in May 1995 and resulted in eleven preembryos. Four were transferred to J.B. and seven were cryopreserved. J.B. became pregnant, either as a result of the procedure or through natural means, and gave birth to the couple's daughter on March 19, 1996. In September 1996, however, the couple separated, and J.B. informed M.B. that she wished to have the remaining preembryos discarded. M.B. did not agree.

J.B. filed a complaint for divorce on November 25, 1996, in which she sought an order from the court "with regard to the eight[4] frozen embryos." In a counterclaim filed on November 24, 1997, M.B. demanded judgment compelling his wife "to allow the (8) eight frozen embryos currently in storage to be implanted or donated to other infertile couples." J.B. filed a motion for summary judgment on the preembryo issue in April 1998 alleging, in a certification filed with the motion, that she had intended to use the preembryos solely within her marriage to M.B. She stated:

Defendant and I made the decision to attempt conception through in vitro fertilization treatment. Those decisions were made during a time when defendant and I were married and intended to remain married. Defendant and I planned to raise a family together as a married couple. I endured the in vitro process and agreed to preserve the preembryos for our use in the context of an intact family.

J.B. also certified that "[t]here were never any discussions between the Defendant and I regarding the disposition of the frozen embryos should our marriage be dissolved."

M.B., in a cross-motion filed in July 1998, described his understanding very differently. He certified that he and J.B. had agreed prior to undergoing the in vitro fertilization procedure that any unused preembryos would not be destroyed, but would be used by his wife or donated to infertile couples. His certification stated:

Before we began the I.V.F. treatments, we had many long and serious discussions regarding the process and the moral and ethical repercussions. For me, as a Catholic, the I.V.F. procedure itself posed a dilemma. We discussed this issue extensively and had agreed that no matter what happened the eggs would be either utilized by us or by other infertile couples. In fact, the option to donate [the preembryos] to infertile couples was the Plaintiff's idea. She came up with this idea because she knew of other individuals in her work place who were having trouble conceiving. M.B.'s mother, father, and sister also certi-

---

4. As noted above, seven had actually been cryopreserved.

fied that on several occasions during family gatherings J.B. had stated her intention to either use or donate the preembryos.

The couple's final judgment of divorce, entered in September 1998, resolved all issues except disposition of the preembryos. Shortly thereafter, the trial court granted J.B.'s motion for summary judgment on that issue. The court found that the reason for the parties' decision to attempt in vitro fertilization—to create a family as a married couple—no longer existed. J.B. and M.B. had become parents and were now divorced. Moreover, M.B. was not infertile and could achieve parenthood in the future through natural means. The court did not accept M.B.'s argument that the parties undertook the in vitro fertilization procedure to "create life," and found no need for further fact finding on the existence of an agreement between them, noting that there was no written contract memorializing the parties' intentions. Because the husband was "fully able to father a child," and because he sought control of the preembryos "merely to donate them to another couple," the court concluded that the wife had "the greater interest and should prevail."

The Appellate Division affirmed. *J.B. v. M.B.*, 331 *N.J.Super.* 223, 751 A.2d 613 (2000). The court noted the inconsistency between the trial court's finding that "the parties engaged in IVF to create their child within the context of their marriage" and M.B.'s claim that the couple had entered into an agreement to donate or use, and not to destroy, the preembryos. *Id.* at 228, 751 A.2d 613. Before the Appellate Division, the husband argued that his constitutional right to procreate had been violated by the ruling of the trial court and sought a remand to establish the parties' understanding regarding the disposition of the preembryos. *Ibid.*

The Appellate Division understood this case to "involv[e] an attempt to enforce an alleged agreement to use embryos to create a child." *Id.* at 231, 751 A.2d 613. It initially examined that "attempt" in the context of two fundamental rights, "the right to procreate and the right not to procreate," citing *Skinner v. Oklahoma,* 316 *U.S.* 535, 541, 62 *S.Ct.* 1110, 1113, 86 *L. Ed.* 1655, 1660 (1942), and *Roe v. Wade,* 410 *U.S.* 113, 152–53, 93 *S.Ct.* 705, 726, 35 *L. Ed.*2d 147, 176–77 (1973), among other cases. *J.B., supra,* 331 *N.J.Super.* at 231–32, 751 A.2d 613. The court found that, on the facts presented, the conflict between those rights was "more apparent than real." *Id.* at 232, 751 A.2d 613. It observed that destruction of the preembryos would not seriously impair M.B.'s constitutional right to procreate since "he retains the capacity to father children." *Ibid.* In contrast, allowing donation or use of the preembryos would impair J.B.'s right not to procreate "[e]ven if [she was] relieved of the financial and custodial responsibility for her child" because she would then have been forced to allow strangers to raise that child. *Ibid.* In those circumstances, and assuming "that the Fourteenth Amendment applies," the court found no impairment of the husband's constitutional rights. *Ibid.*

Nonetheless, the court chose not to decide this case on constitutional grounds.... In affirming the judgment of the trial court in favor of J.B., the panel considered the parties' views and the trial court's opinion, and determined that destruction of the preembryos was required.

M.B. contends that the judgment of the court below violated his constitutional rights to procreation and the care and companionship of his children. He also contends that his constitutional rights outweigh J.B.'s right not to procreate because her right to bodily integrity is not implicated, as it would be in a case involving abortion. He asserts that religious convictions regarding preservation of the preembryos, and the State's interest in protecting potential life, take precedence over his former wife's more limited interests. Finally, M.B. argues that the Appellate Division should have enforced the clear agreement between the parties to give the preembryos a chance at life. He believes that his procedural due process rights have been violated because he was not given an opportunity to introduce evidence demonstrating the existence of that agreement, and because summary judgment is inappropriate in a case involving novel issues of fact and law.

J.B. argues that the Appellate Division properly held that any alleged agreement between the parties to use or donate the preembryos would be unenforceable as a matter of public policy. She contends that New Jersey has "long recognized that individuals should not be bound by agreements requiring them to enter into family relationships or [that] seek to regulate personal intimate decisions relating to parenthood and family life." J.B. also argues that in the absence of an express agreement establishing the disposition of the preembryos, a court should not imply that an agreement exists. It is J.B.'s position that requiring use or donation of the preembryos would violate her constitutional right not to procreate. Discarding the preembryos, on the other hand, would not significantly affect M.B.'s right to procreate because he is fertile and capable of fathering another child.

. . .

M.B. contends that he and J.B. entered into an agreement to use or donate the preembryos, and J.B. disputes the existence of any such agreement. As an initial matter, then, we must decide whether this case involves a contract for the disposition of the cryopreserved preembryos resulting from in vitro fertilization. We begin, therefore, with the consent form provided to J.B. and M.B. by the Cooper Center.... That form states, among other things:

> The control and disposition of the embryos belongs to the Patient and her Partner. You will be asked to execute the attached legal statement regarding control and disposition of cryopreserved embryos.

The attachment, executed by J.B. and M.B., provides further detail in respect of the parties' "control and disposition": I, J.B. (patient), and M.B. (partner) agree that all control, direction, and ownership of our tissues will be relinquished to the IVF Program under the following circumstances:

> 1. A dissolution of our marriage by court order, unless the court specifies who takes control and direction of the tissues, or

2. In the event of death of both of the above named individuals, or unless provisions are made in a Will, or

3. When the patient is no longer capable of sustaining a normal pregnancy, however, the couple has the right to keep embryos maintained for up to two years before making a decision [regarding a] "host womb" or

4. At any time by our/my election which shall be in writing, or

5. When a patient fails to pay periodic embryo maintenance payment.

The consent form, and more important, the attachment, do not manifest a clear intent by J.B. and M.B. regarding disposition of the preembryos in the event of "[a] dissolution of [their] marriage." Although the attachment indicates that the preembryos "will be relinquished" to the clinic if the parties divorce, it carves out an exception that permits the parties to obtain a court order directing disposition of the preembryos. That reading is consistent with other provisions of the attachment allowing for disposition by a last will and testament "[i]n the event of death," or "by our/my election ... in writing." Clearly, the thrust of the document signed by J.B. and M.B. is that the Cooper Center obtains control over the preembryos unless the parties choose otherwise in a writing, or unless a court specifically directs otherwise in an order of divorce.

The conditional language employed in the attachment stands in sharp contrast to the language in the informed consents provided by the hospital in *Kass v. Kass,* 91 *N.Y.*2d 554, 673 *N.Y.S.*2d 350, 696 *N.E.*2d 174 (N.Y.1998). In *Kass,* the New York Court of Appeals enforced a couple's memorialized decision to donate their preembryos for scientific research when they could not agree on disposition. The court found that the parties had signed an unambiguous contract to relinquish control of their preembryos to the hospital for research purposes in the event of a dispute. In that case, the parties executed several forms before undergoing in vitro fertilization. Informed Consent No. 2 stated:

> In the event of divorce, we understand that legal ownership of any stored pre-zygotes[5] must be determined in a property settlement and will be released as directed by order of a court of competent jurisdiction.

Addendum No. 2–1 further elaborated:

> In the event that we ... are unable to make a decision regarding the disposition of our stored, frozen pre-zygotes, we now indicate our desire for the disposition of our pre-zygotes and direct the IVF Program to (choose one):

> Our frozen pre-zygotes may be examined by the IVF Program for biological studies and be disposed of by the IVF Program for approved research investigation as determined by the IVF Program.

---

5. The term "pre-zygote" is used in the forms and in the opinion of the New York court where this opinion uses the term "preembryo."

Moreover, before the parties divorced, they drafted and signed an "'uncontested divorce' agreement" indicating that their preembryos "should be disposed of [in] the manner outlined in our consent form and [neither party] will lay claim to custody of these pre-zygotes." *Id.* at 177.[6]

The *Kass* court found that the parties had agreed to donate their preembryos for IVF research if they could not together decide on another disposition. The court interpreted the provision of the consent form dealing directly with divorce to indicate only that the parties' agreement would be embodied in a document of divorce, noting that the couple had, indeed, endorsed an "'uncontested divorce' instrument" ratifying the consent forms they had signed earlier. That holding is based on language entirely different from the language in the form in this case. Here, the parties have agreed that on the dissolution of their marriage the Cooper Center obtains control of the preembryos unless the court specifically makes another determination. Under that provision, the parties have sought another determination from the court.

M.B. asserts, however, that he and J.B. jointly intended another disposition. Because there are no other writings that express the parties' intentions, M.B. asks the Court either to remand for an evidentiary hearing on that issue or to consider his certified statement. In his statement, he claims that before undergoing in vitro fertilization the couple engaged in extensive discussions in which they agreed to use the preembryos themselves or donate them to others. In opposition, J.B. has certified that the parties never discussed the disposition of unused preembryos and that there was no agreement on that issue.

We find no need for a remand to determine the parties' intentions at the time of the in vitro fertilization process. Assuming that it would be possible to enter into a valid agreement at that time irrevocably deciding the disposition of preembryos in circumstances such as we have here, a formal, unambiguous memorialization of the parties' intentions would be required to confirm their joint determination. The parties do not contest the lack of such a writing. We hold, therefore, that J.B. and M.B. never entered into a separate binding contract. . . .

In essence, J.B. and M.B. have agreed only that on their divorce the decision in respect of control, and therefore disposition, of their cryopreserved preembryos will be directed by the court. In this area, however, there are few guideposts for decision-making. Advances in medical technology have far outstripped the development of legal principles to resolve the inevitable disputes arising out of the new reproductive opportunities now available. For infertile couples, those opportunities may present the only way to have a biological family. Yet, at the point when a husband and wife decide to begin the in vitro fertilization process, they are unlikely to anticipate divorce or to be concerned about the disposition of preembryos on divorce. As they are both contributors of the genetic material comprising

---

6. Although the agreement was never finalized, it was accepted by the New York court as "reaffirm[ing] the [parties'] earlier understanding. . . ." *Id.* at 181.

the preembryos, the decision should be theirs to make. *See generally Davis v. Davis,* 842 *S.W.*2d 588, 597 (Tenn.1992) (stating that donors should retain decision-making authority with respect to their preembryos), *reh'g granted in part,* 1992 WL 341632, at *1 (Nov. 23, 1992), *and cert. denied, Stowe v. Davis,* 507 *U.S.* 911, 113 *S.Ct.* 1259, 122 *L. Ed.*2d 657 (1993); Carl H. Coleman, *Procreative Liberty and Contemporaneous Choice: An Inalienable Rights Approach to Frozen Embryo Disputes,* 84 *Minn. L.Rev.* 55, 83 (1999) ("Because the embryos are the products of the couple's shared procreative activity, any decision to use them should be the result of the couple's mutual choice."); *cf.* Paul Walter, *His, Hers, or Theirs—Custody, Control, and Contracts: Allocating Decisional Authority Over Frozen Embryos,* 29 *Seton Hall L.Rev.* 937, 959–62 (1999) (discussing approaches to disposition of preembryos, including grant of "sole authority to the biological provider(s)").

But what if, as here, the parties disagree. Without guidance from the Legislature, we must consider a means by which courts can engage in a principled review of the issues presented in such cases in order to achieve a just result. Because the claims before us derive, in part, from concepts found in the Federal Constitution and the Constitution of this State, we begin with those concepts.

Both parties and the ACLU *Amici* invoke the right to privacy in support of their respective positions. More specifically, they claim procreational autonomy as a fundamental attribute of the privacy rights guaranteed by both the Federal and New Jersey Constitutions. Their arguments are based on various opinions of the United States Supreme Court that discuss the right to be free from governmental interference with procreational decisions. See *Eisenstadt v. Baird,* 405 *U.S.* 438, 453, 92 *S.Ct.* 1029, 1038, 31 *L. Ed.*2d 349, 362 (1972); *Griswold v. Connecticut,* 381 *U.S.* 479, 485–86, 85 *S.Ct.* 1678, 1682, 14 *L. Ed.*2d 510, 515–16 (1965); *Skinner v. Oklahoma,* 316 *U.S.* 535, 541, 62 *S.Ct.* 1110, 1113, 86 *L. Ed.* 1655, 1660 (1942).

. . .

This Court also has recognized the fundamental nature of procreational rights. In *In re Baby M,* we considered a custody dispute between a father and a surrogate mother. 109 *N.J.* 396, 537 *A.*2d 1227 (1988). Although the case involved the enforceability of a surrogacy contract, the father asserted that his right to procreate supported his claim for custody of Baby M. We held that the right to procreate was not implicated by the custody battle, which dealt with parental rights after birth. We observed, however, that "the rights of personal intimacy, of marriage, of sex, of family, of procreation . . . are fundamental rights protected by both the federal and state Constitutions." *Id.* at 447, 537 *A.*2d 1227; *see also In re Grady,* 85 *N.J.* 235, 247–48, 426 *A.*2d 467 (1981) (recognizing that decisions in *Griswold* and *Eisenstadt* ended "any doubt about a personal right to prevent conception," and holding that "an individual's constitutional right of privacy includes the right to undergo sterilization voluntarily"); *cf. Schroeder v. Perkel,* 87 *N.J.* 53, 66, 432 *A.*2d 834 (1981) (allowing recovery against defendants whose negligent diagnosis deprived mother of right to choose not to conceive child with genetic defect).

Those decisions provide a framework within which disputes over the disposition of preembryos can be resolved. In *Davis, supra,* for example, a divorced couple could not agree on the disposition of their unused, cryopreserved preembryos. 842 *S.W.*2d at 589. The Tennessee Supreme Court balanced the right to procreate of the party seeking to donate the preembryos (the wife), against the right not to procreate of the party seeking destruction of the preembryos (the husband). *Id.* at 603. The court concluded that the husband's right would be significantly affected by unwanted parenthood "with all of its possible financial and psychological consequences." *Ibid.* In his case, that burden was the greater because, as a child, he had been separated from his parents after they divorced and his mother suffered a nervous breakdown. *Id.* at 603–04. Because of his personal experiences, the husband was "vehemently opposed to fathering a child that would not live with both parents." *Id.* at 604.

Against that interest, the court weighed the wife's "burden of knowing that the lengthy IVF procedures she underwent were futile, and that the preembryos to which she contributed genetic material would never become children." *Ibid.* Although that burden was not insignificant, the court found that it did not outweigh the father's interest in avoiding procreation. *Ibid.* The court held that the scales "[o]rdinarily" would tip in favor of the right not to procreate if the opposing party could become a parent through other reasonable means. *Ibid.*

We agree with the Tennessee Supreme Court that "[o]rdinarily, the party wishing to avoid procreation should prevail." *Ibid.* Here, the Appellate Division succinctly described the "apparent" conflict between J.B. and M.B.:

> In the present case, the wife's right not to become a parent seemingly conflicts with the husband's right to procreate. The conflict, however, is more apparent than real. Recognition and enforcement of the wife's right would not seriously impair the husband's right to procreate. Though his right to procreate using the wife's egg would be terminated, he retains the capacity to father children.

[*J.B., supra,* 331 *N.J.Super.* at 232, 751 A.2d 613.]

In other words, M.B.'s right to procreate is not lost if he is denied an opportunity to use or donate the preembryos. M.B. is already a father and is able to become a father to additional children, whether through natural procreation or further in vitro fertilization. In contrast, J.B.'s right not to procreate may be lost through attempted use or through donation of the preembryos. Implantation, if successful, would result in the birth of her biological child and could have life-long emotional and psychological repercussions.[7] See Patricia A. Martin & Martin L. Lagod, *The Human Preem-*

---

7. The legal consequences for J.B. also are unclear. *See N.J.A.C.* 8:2–1.4(a) (stating "the woman giving birth shall be recorded as a parent"). We note without comment that a

bryo, the Progenitors, and the State: Toward a Dynamic Theory of Status, Rights, and Research Policy, 5 *High Tech. L.J.* 257, 290 (1990) (stating that "[g]enetic ties may form a powerful bond . . . even if the progenitor is freed from the legal obligations of parenthood"). Her fundamental right not to procreate is irrevocably extinguished if a surrogate mother bears J.B.'s child. We will not force J.B. to become a biological parent against her will.

The court below "conclude[d] that a contract to procreate is contrary to New Jersey public policy and is unenforceable." 331 *N.J.Super.* at 234, 751 *A.*2d 613. That determination follows the reasoning of the Massachusetts Supreme Judicial Court in *A.Z. v. B.Z.*, wherein an agreement to compel biological parenthood was deemed unenforceable as a matter of public policy. 431 *Mass.* 150, 725 *N.E.*2d 1051, 1057–58 (2000). The Massachusetts court likened enforcement of a contract permitting implantation of preembryos to other contracts to enter into familial relationships that were unenforceable under the laws of Massachusetts, *i.e.*, contracts to marry or to give up a child for adoption prior to the fourth day after birth. *Id.* at 1058. In a similar vein, the court previously had refused to enforce a surrogacy contract without a reasonable waiting period during which the surrogate mother could revoke her consent, and a contract to abandon or to prevent marriage. *Id.* at 1059. Likewise, the court declined to enforce a contract that required an individual to become a parent. *Id.* at 1058.

As the Appellate Division opinion in this case points out, the laws of New Jersey also evince a policy against enforcing private contracts to enter into or terminate familial relationships. 331 *N.J.Super.* at 234–35, 751 *A.*2d 613. New Jersey has, by statute, abolished the cause of action for breach of contract to marry. *N.J.S.A.* 2A:23–1. Private placement adoptions are disfavored, *Sees v. Baber,* 74 *N.J.* 201, 217, 377 *A.*2d 628 (1977), and may be approved over the objection of a parent only if that parent has failed or is unable to perform "the regular and expected parental functions of care and support of the child." *N.J.S.A.* 9:3–46; *see N.J.S.A.* 9:3–48 (stating statutory requirements for private placement adoption).

That public policy also led this Court to conclude in *Baby M, supra,* that a surrogacy contract was unenforceable. 109 *N.J.* at 433–34, 537 *A.*2d 1227. We held that public policy prohibited a binding agreement to require a surrogate, there the biological mother, to surrender her parental rights. *Id.* at 411, 537 *A.*2d 1227. The contract in *Baby M* provided for a $10,000 payment to the surrogate for her to be artificially inseminated, carry the

recent case before the Chancery Division in Bergen County concluded that seventy-two hours must pass before a non-biological surrogate mother may surrender her parental rights and the biological mother's name may be placed on the birth certificate. *A.H.W. v. G.H.B.,* 339 *N.J.Super.* 495, 505, 772 *A.*2d 948 (2000). In Arizona, an appellate court determined that a statute allowing a biological father but not a biological mother to prove paternity violated the Equal Protection Clause. *Soos v. Superior Court,* 182 *Ariz.* 470, 897 *P.*2d 1356, 1361 (1995). In California, the legal mother is the person who "intended to bring about the birth of a child that she intended to raise as her own." *Johnson v. Calvert,* 5 *Cal.*4th 84, 19 *Cal.Rptr.*2d 494, 851 *P.*2d 776, 782 (Cal.1993), *cert. denied,* 510 *U.S.* 874, 114 *S.Ct.* 206, 126 *L. Ed.*2d 163, *and cert. dismissed, Baby Boy J. v. Johnson,* 510 *U.S.* 938, 114 *S.Ct.* 374, 126 *L. Ed.*2d 324 (1993).

child to term, and then, after the child's birth, relinquish parental rights to the father and his wife. *Id.* at 411–12, 537 A.2d 1227. The surrogate mother initially surrendered the child to the father, but subsequently reconsidered her decision and fled with Baby M. In an action by the father to enforce the surrogacy contract, we held that the contract conflicted with "(1) laws prohibiting the use of money in connection with adoptions; (2) laws requiring proof of parental unfitness or abandonment before termination of parental rights is ordered or an adoption is granted; and (3) laws that make surrender of custody and consent to adoption revocable in private placement adoptions." *Id.* at 423, 537 A.2d 1227. Our decision was consistent with the policy expressed earlier in *Sees, supra,* that consent to terminate parental rights was revocable in all but statutorily approved circumstances. 74 *N.J.* at 212, 377 *A.2d* 628.

Enforcement of a contract that would allow the implantation of preembryos at some future date in a case where one party has reconsidered his or her earlier acquiescence raises similar issues. If implantation is successful, that party will have been forced to become a biological parent against his or her will. We note disagreement on the issue both among legal commentators and in the limited caselaw on the subject. *Kass, supra,* held that "[a]greements between progenitors, or gamete donors, regarding disposition of their prezygotes should generally be presumed valid and binding, and enforced in a dispute between them. . . ." 673 *N.Y.S.2d* 350, 696 *N.E.2d* at 180. The New York court emphasized that such agreements would "avoid costly litigation," "minimize misunderstandings and maximize procreative liberty by reserving to the progenitors the authority to make what is in the first instance a quintessentially personal private decision."; see also New York State Task Force on Life and the Law, *Executive Summary of Assisted Reproductive Technologies: Analysis and Recommendations for Public Policy* (last modified Aug. 1999) <www.health. state.ny.us/nysdoh/taskfce/execsum.htm> (stating that "[i]ndividuals or couples who have excess embryos no longer desired for assisted reproduction have a strong interest in controlling the fate of those embryos"); John A. Robertson, *Prior Agreements For Disposition of Frozen Embryos,* 51 *Ohio St. L.J.* 407, 409–18 (1990) (arguing that enforcement of advance directives maximizes reproductive freedom, minimizes disputes, and provides certainty to couples and in vitro fertilization programs); Peter E. Malo, *Deciding Custody of Frozen Embryos: Many Eggs Are Frozen But Who Is Chosen?,* 3 *DePaul J. Health Care L.* 307, 332 (2000) (favoring mandatory preembryo disposition agreements). Yet, as discussed above, the Massachusetts Supreme Judicial Court as well as our Appellate Division have declared that when agreements compel procreation over the subsequent objection of one of the parties, those agreements are violative of public policy. *A.Z., supra,* 725 *N.E.2d* at 1057–58; *J.B., supra,* 331 *N.J.Super.* at 234, 751 A.2d 613; *cf.* Coleman, *supra,* 84 *Minn. L.Rev.* at 83–84 (suggesting that party objecting to implantation should prevail against infertile party seeking use of preembryos).

We recognize that persuasive reasons exist for enforcing preembryo disposition agreements. *See Kass, supra,* 673 *N.Y.S.2d* 350, 696 *N.E.2d* at

179 (noting "need for clear, consistent principles to guide parties in protecting their interests and resolving their disputes"); *Davis, supra,* 842 *S.W.2d* at 597 (discussing benefit of guidance to parties undertaking in vitro fertilization procedures). We also recognize that in vitro fertilization is in widespread use, and that there is a need for agreements between the participants and the clinics that perform the procedure. We believe that the better rule, and the one we adopt, is to enforce agreements entered into at the time in vitro fertilization is begun, subject to the right of either party to change his or her mind about disposition up to the point of use or destruction of any stored preembryos.

The public policy concerns that underlie limitations on contracts involving family relationships are protected by permitting either party to object at a later date to provisions specifying a disposition of preembryos that that party no longer accepts. Moreover, despite the conditional nature of the disposition provisions, in the large majority of cases the agreements will control, permitting fertility clinics and other like facilities to rely on their terms. Only when a party affirmatively notifies a clinic in writing of a change in intention should the disposition issue be reopened. Principles of fairness dictate that agreements provided by a clinic should be written in plain language, and that a qualified clinic representative should review the terms with the parties prior to execution. Agreements should not be signed in blank . . . or in a manner suggesting that the parties have not given due consideration to the disposition question. Those and other reasonable safeguards should serve to limit later disputes.

Finally, if there is disagreement as to disposition because one party has reconsidered his or her earlier decision, the interests of both parties must be evaluated. Because ordinarily the party choosing not to become a biological parent will prevail, we do not anticipate increased litigation as a result of our decision. In this case, after having considered that M.B. is a father and is capable of fathering additional children, we have affirmed J.B.'s right to prevent implantation of the preembryos. We express no opinion in respect of a case in which a party who has become infertile seeks use of stored preembryos against the wishes of his or her partner, noting only that the possibility of adoption also may be a consideration, among others, in the court's assessment.

Under the judgment of the Appellate Division, the seven remaining preembryos are to be destroyed. It was represented to us at oral argument, however, that J.B. does not object to their continued storage if M.B. wishes to pay any fees associated with that storage. M.B. must inform the trial court forthwith whether he will do so; otherwise, the preembryos are to be destroyed.

The judgment of the Appellate Division is affirmed as modified.

■ Verniero, J., concurring.

I join in the disposition of this case and in all but one aspect of the Court's opinion. I do not agree with the Court's suggestion, in *dicta,* that the right to procreate may depend on adoption as a consideration.

I also write to express my view that the same principles that compel the outcome in this case would permit an infertile party to assert his or her right to use a preembryo against the objections of the other party, if such use were the only means of procreation. In that instance, the balance arguably would weigh in favor of the infertile party absent countervailing factors of greater weight. I do not decide that profound question today, and the Court should not decide it or suggest a result, because it is absent from this case.

■ ZAZZALI, J., concurring.

I join in the Court's opinion, except as noted by Justice Verniero's concurring opinion, which I also join. I write separately to note that these difficult disputes all too often prompt dire predictions. And yet, most assuredly, developing technologies will give rise to many more such controversies in the future. The resolution of those controversies depends on the amount of caution, compassion, and common sense we summon up as we balance the competing interests. The significance of those interests underscores the need for continued careful and deliberate decisionmaking, infused with equity, in this developing jurisprudence.

NOTE

In Davis v. Davis, 842 S.W.2d 588 (Tenn.1992), discussed in several of the preceding cases, the Supreme Court of Tennessee noted that the parties at the time of their donations were not even asked to sign any consent forms, evidently because the clinic was in the process of moving and they did not wish to delay the procedure while the forms were being located. In their conclusion, the court summarized:

> . . . [W]e hold that disputes involving the disposition of preembryos produced by in vitro fertilization should be resolved, first, by looking to the preferences of the progenitors. If their wishes cannot be ascertained, or if there is dispute, then their prior agreement concerning disposition should be carried out. If no prior agreement exists, then the relative interests of the parties in using or not using the preembryos must be weighed. Ordinarily, the party wishing to avoid procreation should prevail, assuming that the other party has a reasonable possibility of achieving parenthood by means other than use of the preembryos in question. If no other reasonable alternatives exist, then the argument in favor of using the preembryos to achieve pregnancy should be considered. However, if the party seeking control of the preembryos intends merely to donate them to another couple, the objecting party obviously has the greater interest and should prevail.

> But the rule does not contemplate the creation of an automatic veto, and in affirming the judgment of the Court of Appeals, we would not wish to be interpreted as so holding.

York v. Jones, 717 F.Supp. 421 (E.D.Va.1989), involved a dispute over disposition of a frozen pre-zygote of by a childless couple who had unsuccessfully attempted to have a child through IVF at the fertility institute of defendants. During the process they signed an agreement providing three alternatives for the disposition of any frozen pre-zygotes should plaintiffs determine that they did not wish to initiate a pregnancy through them. The alternatives were donation to another infertile couple, donation for research, or thawing. Plaintiffs later sought to have their frozen pre-zygote transferred to a fertility center in another state, but defendants refused to grant approval for this unscheduled alternative.

A U.S. District Court rejected defendants' motion to dismiss for failure to state a claim upon which relief can be granted, noting that "the requisite elements of a bailment are present" and determining that a state human research statute was inapplicable to bar plaintiffs from asserting a property interest. The court added that the "three fates" included in the written agreement were not described therein as exclusive.

What procedures would you advise a fertility clinic to establish for dealing with the various scenarios that might be anticipated and other scenarios that are unexpected?

Scientific advances continue; for example, today there can be nonsurgical human ovum transfer. At some point it probably will be feasible to freeze ova in a process that will not endanger DNA. When this occurs, will the legal issues be basically the same as those pertaining to artificial insemination?

In a Report on Donor Gametes in IVF, the Committee to Consider the Social, Ethical and Legal Issues Arising from In Vitro Fertilization, appointed by the government of Victoria, Australia (1983), reached several conclusions that might be controversial in this country. They recommended prohibiting payments to donors of either male or female gametes beyond reimbursement for costs such as medical expenses. This was based on the view that "it would be inhuman to traffic in human tissue." Id. at 18. They also recommended that donors should be selected on the basis not only of medical but also social and psychological considerations, and that each donor should receive comprehensive information about the implications of gamete donation, "including the use to be made of the donated material, and the consequences of its successful use in an IVF programme." Id. at 21. While the committee expressed reservations about the use of "known donors" (persons who are known to, and perhaps selected by the couple who intend to be parents through use of donated gametes), it nevertheless recommended that use of known donors should be permitted where both partners request that it be done. Id. at 23. The committee concluded that children born in Victoria through use of donor gametes would be illegitimate, and it recommended legislation that would make children conceived through use of donor sperm or ova legitimate (in much the same fashion as the statutes presently in existence in the U.S. operate at least with regard to AID).

In August 1984 the Victoria Committee issued a Report on The Disposition of Embryos Produced by In Vitro Fertilization. Recommendations included allowing embryos to be frozen; providing for authorization of some hospitals to conduct cryopreservation programs, though banning them from banking large numbers of frozen embryos that may be disposed of as the hospital sees fit; and limiting research to the excess embryos produced by patients in an IVF program. Also recommended were that an embryo should be frozen only with permission of the couple whose gametes were used in its formation, that such a couple should not be allowed to "sell or casually dispose of the embryo", and that they should be required to indicate in their consent document what disposition is to be made of the embryo "in the event of accident, death or dissolution." If no such instructions were given, it is recommended that the frozen embryo "be removed from storage" on the occurrence of any such event.

4.   CONTRACTS TO BEAR A CHILD

Surrogate Parenting Associates, Inc. v. Commonwealth ex rel. Armstrong

Supreme Court of Kentucky, 1986.
704 S.W.2d 209.

■ LEIBSON, JUSTICE.

In March 1981, the Attorney General, acting pursuant to KRS 271A.470, instituted proceedings against Surrogate Parenting Associates, Inc. (SPA), a Kentucky corporation, seeking to revoke SPA's corporate charter on grounds of abuse and misuse of its corporate powers detrimental to the interest and welfare of the state and its citizens. The suit alleges that SPA's surrogate parenting procedure is in violation of the following Kentucky statutes:

A) KRS 199.590(2), which prohibits sale, purchase or procurement for sale or purchase of "any child for the purpose of adoption";[1]

B) KRS 199.601(2), which prohibits filing a petition for voluntary termination of parental rights "prior to five (5) days after the birth of a child"; and

C) KRS 199.500(5), which specifies that a "consent for adoption" shall not "be held valid if such consent for adoption is given prior to the fifth day after the birth of the child."

The case was decided on the basis of a "Stipulation of Facts" setting out SPA's manner of doing business. Franklin Circuit Court held that SPA's activities were not illegal and not an abuse of corporate powers, and dismissed the complaint. The Court of Appeals reversed. Having accepted discretionary review, we reverse the Court of Appeals and affirm the judgment of Franklin Circuit Court.

---

1. This statute was changed to this present form in 1984. Since the question to be answered turns on whether the services being offered by the corporation are illegal, the issue must be decided on the current state of the law.

SPA operates a medical clinic which assists infertile couples in obtaining a child biologically-related to the husband (the biological father) through artificial insemination of a "surrogate mother." The contract for conception and delivery is between the biological father and the surrogate mother. The arrangement contemplates that after delivery of the child the parental rights of the surrogate mother will be terminated, leaving the biological father with custody. The husband of the surrogate mother, if there is one, also agrees to give up any claim to the child. The paternity of the biological father is confirmed by new methods of genetic testing with almost complete scientific certainty.

The wife of the biological father, if there is one, is not party to these contractual arrangements. Of course, after entry of a judgment terminating the parental rights of the surrogate mother, the wife of the biological father can avail herself of the legal procedure available for adoption by a stepparent. KRS 199.470(4)(a).

Before being artificially inseminated, the prospective surrogate mother agrees with the prospective father that she will voluntarily terminate all parental rights subsequent to the birth, thereby extinguishing any rights she might have to participate in any subsequent adoptive proceeding by the biological father's wife.

The surrogate mother receives a fee from the biological father, part of which is paid before delivery of the child and the remainder of which is paid after entry of a judgment terminating the parental rights of the surrogate mother. In addition, the father assumes responsibility for medical, hospital, travel, laboratory and other necessary expenses of the pregnancy.

Each party must be represented by independent counsel, and the father's counsel is to prepare all agreements and documents in connection with the surrogate parenting process. The biological father pays the attorneys' fees.

SPA and its president, Richard M. Levin, M.D., are paid a fee by the biological father for selection and artificial insemination of the surrogate mother, for obstetrical care and testing during pregnancy, and for actual delivery.

. . .

The question for us to decide is one of statutory interpretation: Has the legislature spoken? The fundamental question is whether SPA's involvement in the surrogate parenting procedure should be construed as participation in the buying and selling of babies as prohibited by KRS 199.590(2). We conclude that it does not, that there are fundamental differences between the surrogate parenting procedure in which SPA participates and the buying and selling of children as prohibited by KRS 199.590(2) which place this surrogate parenting procedure beyond the purview of present legislation.

There is no doubt but that KRS 199.590 is intended to keep baby brokers from overwhelming an expectant mother or the parents of a child with financial inducements to part with the child. But the central fact in the surrogate parenting procedure is that the agreement to bear the child is entered into *before* conception. The essential considerations for the surrogate mother when she agrees to the surrogate parenting procedure are *not* avoiding the consequences of an unwanted pregnancy or fear of the financial burden of child rearing. On the contrary, the essential consideration is to assist a person or couple who desperately want a child but are unable to conceive one in the customary manner to achieve a biologically related offspring. The problem is caused by the wife's infertility. The problem is solved by artificial insemination. The process is not biologically different from the reverse situation where the husband is infertile and the wife conceives by artificial insemination.

No one suggests that where the husband is infertile and conception is induced by artificial insemination of the wife that the participants involved, the biological father, the physicians who care for the mother and deliver the child, or the attorneys who arranged the procedure, have violated the statutes now in place. Although this is tampering with nature in the same manner as the surrogate parenting procedure here involved, we recognize "[t]he decision whether or not to beget or bear a child is at the very heart ... of constitutionally protected choices." Carey v. Population Services, Int'l, 431 U.S. 678, 97 S.Ct. 2010, 52 L.Ed.2d 675 (1977).

When KRS 199.590 was amended in 1984 the following language was added:

> "Nothing in this section shall be construed to prohibit in vitro fertilization. For purposes of this section 'in vitro fertilization' means the process whereby an egg is removed from a woman, then fertilized in a receptacle by the sperm of the husband of the woman in whose womb the fertilized egg will thereafter be implanted."[3]

The Attorney General contends that by including this "in vitro" fertilization procedure in the statute while leaving out the surrogate parenting procedure presently under consideration, the legislature was legislating against surrogate parenting. We do not divine any such hidden meanings. All we can derive from this language is that the legislature has expressed itself about one procedure for medically assisted conception while remaining silent on others. To this extent the legislature puts its stamp of approval on tampering with nature in the interest of assisting a childless couple to conceive. The "in vitro" fertilization procedure sanctioned by the statute and the surrogate parenting procedure as described in the Stipulation of Facts are similar in that both enable a childless couple to have a baby biologically related to one of them when they could not do so otherwise. The fact that the statute now expressly sanctions one way of doing this does not rule out other ways by implication. In an area so

---

3. Presumably, in this procedure a husband and wife bear a child utilizing an egg taken from another woman, fertilized by the husband, and then implanted in the womb of the wife. Donor "in vitro fertilization" differs from SPA's procedure only in who carries the fertilized egg. Donor "in vitro fertilization" and "surrogate parenting" are virtually indistinguishable from the standpoint of biological engineering.

fundamental as medically assisting a childless couple to have a child, such a prohibition should not be implied.

As stated in the circuit court opinion:

"Because of the existence of a legal relationship between the father and the child, any dealing between the father and the surrogate mother in regard to the child cannot properly be characterized as an adoption."

As between the biological father, who is both contractually acknowledged and scientifically confirmed, and the biological mother, *if* there is no subsequent termination of the mother's parental rights, the only legal question between the parties would relate to which biological parent should have *custody.* KRS 403.270 prepares for a resolution of this dilemma by stating:

"The court shall determine custody in accordance with the best interest of the child and equal consideration shall be given to each parent."

SPA has freely acknowledged that the initial contractual arrangements regarding the mother's surrender of custody and termination of parental rights are voidable. The surrogate mother's consent given before five days following birth of the baby is no more legally binding than the decision of an unwed mother during her pregnancy that she will put her baby up for adoption. The five days' consent feature in the termination of parental rights statute (KRS 199.601(2)) and in the consent to adoption statute (KRS 199.500(5)) take precedence over the parties' contractual commitments, meaning that the surrogate mother is free to change her mind. The policy of the voluntary termination statute and the consent to adoption statute is to preserve to the mother her right of choice regardless of decisions made before the birth of the child. This policy is not violated by the existence of the contractual arrangements previously made. The policy of these statutes is carried out because the law gives the mother the opportunity to reconsider her decision to fulfill the role as surrogate mother and refuse to perform the voluntary termination procedure. Should she elect to do so, the situation would be no different than had she never entered into the procedure. She would be in the same position vis-a-vis the child and the biological father as any other mother with a child born out of wedlock. The parental rights and obligations between the biological father and mother, and the obligations they owe to the child, would then be the rights and obligations imposed by pertinent statutes rather than the obligations imposed by the contract now vitiated.

Kentucky has taken the position that custody contracts are voidable, not illegal and void. In Edleson v. Edleson, 179 Ky. 300, 200 S.W. 625 (1918), we held that, while the court is not compelled to enforce such a contract because the statutory rights are preemptive, such a contract is not *per se* illegal. The surrogate mother who changes her mind before going through with her contractual obligation stands in the same legal position as a woman who conceives without benefit of contractual obligations. She has forfeited her rights to whatever fees the contract provided, but both the mother, child and biological father now have the statutory rights and obligations as exist in the absence of contract.

The advances of biomedical science have carried us forward, willingly or otherwise into a new era of genetics.

If there are social and ethical problems in the solutions science offers, these are problems of public policy that belong in the legislative domain, not in the judicial, under our constitutional doctrine of separation of powers. Ky. Const. Sections 27 and 28. It is only when a proposed solution violates individual constitutional rights that the courts have place in the controversy.

But that is not the question here because the threshold question is whether the legislation on the books declares the procedure impermissible. Short of such legislation it is not for the courts to cut off solutions offered by science.

In Bedinger v. Graybill's Executor & Trustee, Ky., 302 S.W.2d 594 (1957), we considered and rejected a request that the court, under the guise of legislative "interpretation," hold that an adoption by a husband of his wife, making her his heir at law, violated Kentucky "public policy" not-withstanding statutory language which addressed the subject and failed to forbid the arrangement challenged. We stated:

> "The courts are bound by statutory law as written and cannot write into it an exception that the legislature did not make." 302 S.W.2d at 599.

We have consistently held that our Kentucky Constitution empowers the legislative branch, but not the judicial branch, of government to articulate public policy regarding health and welfare. The questions of whether and how new medical services of the type offered by SPA offend public policy and should be prohibited by legislation are addressed to the legislature, not the courts.

The courts should not shrink from the benefits to be derived from science in solving these problems simply because they may lead to legal complications. The legal complications are not insolvable. Indeed, we have no reason to believe that the surrogate parenting procedure in which SPA participates will not, in most instances, proceed routinely to the conclusion desired by all of the parties at the outset—a woman who can bear children assisting a childless couple to fulfill their desire for a biological-related child.

We agree with the trial court that if there is a judgment to be made outlawing such a procedure, it is a matter for the legislature. The surrogate parenting procedure as outlined in the Stipulation of Facts is not foreclosed by legislation now on the books. The judgment of the Court of Appeals is reversed. The judgment of the trial court is affirmed.

■ VANCE, JUSTICE, dissenting.

Respectfully, I dissent.

When the activities of Surrogate Parenting Associates are placed in their best light by the majority, the fact remains that its primary purpose is to locate women who will readily, for a price, allow themselves to be used as human incubators and who are willing to sell, for a price, all of their parental rights in a child thus born.

The parties stipulate that a surrogate mother is paid a fee, part of which is paid to the mother before delivery of the child, and the rest to be paid after she carries the child to term and upon entry of a judgment terminating her parental rights. In other words, a portion of the fee is paid in advance for the use of her body as an incubator, but a portion of the payment is withheld and is not paid until her living child is delivered unto the purchaser, along with the equivalent of a bill of sale, or quit-claim deed, to wit—the judgment terminating her parental rights. How can it be denied that this last portion of the payment is in fact a payment for the baby, because if the baby is not delivered and parental rights not surrendered, the last part of the fee need not be paid.

Whether or not the transaction is for the purpose of adoption or otherwise is immaterial. It violates K.R.S. 199.590 in either event.

K.R.S. 199.590(2) provides:

"No person, agency, institution or intermediary may sell or purchase *or procure for sale or purchase* and child for the purpose of adoption or *any other purpose, including termination of parental rights . . . .*" (Emphasis added.)

It is stipulated that Surrogate Parenting Associates is an intermediary which offers to assist infertile couples in obtaining a child biologically related to the father through the process of artificial insemination of a surrogate mother. I view the subsequent delivery of the child together with an agreed judgment terminating the parental rights of the natural mother in exchange for a monetary consideration to be no less than the sale of a child. It cannot be gainsaid that Surrogate Parenting Associates is an intermediary in this process, and thus it violates the statute. The revocation of its Charter is therefore appropriate.

I would affirm the Court of Appeals.

■ WINTERSHEIMER, JUSTICE, dissenting.

I respectfully dissent from the majority opinion because the legislative intent to prohibit the buying and selling of children is abundantly clear in regard to KRS 199.590(2). I fully agree with the dissent written by Justice Vance.

In my view, the people of the Commonwealth of Kentucky have not abdicated their sovereignty to a self-appointed group of scientists-kings. The tolerance of the many can easily lead to the tyranny of a few. The attractiveness of assistance to childless couples should not be a cosmetic facade for unnecessary tampering with human procreation.

Animals are reproduced; human beings are procreated.

The procedure endorsed by the majority is nothing more than a commercial transaction in which a surrogate mother receives money in exchange for terminating her natural and biological rights in the child. This permits the infant to be adopted by the infertile wife and apparent biological father.

The apparent biological father is obviously not adopting his own child but actually purchasing the right to have the child adopted by his own infertile wife. Regardless of the good intentions that may give rise to such a practice, the commercialization of this type of personal problem is exactly what KRS 199.590(2) is intended to prevent.

The Kentucky legislature has not been silent on the public policy question of surrogate parenting. When the General Assembly was given the opportunity to authorize surrogate parenting in Kentucky, that body refused to adopt language which would legalize such a procedure. During the 1984 General Assembly, House Bill 421 was adopted so as to permit certain forms of genetic engineering. A similar Senate amendment to the original statute would have provided for surrogate parenting. The legislature rejected surrogate parenting. It is totally proper to interpret this recent legislative activity and history as a clear indication that surrogate parenting violates the current statute and its policy against the unauthorized purchase and sale of children for adoption by this type of processing. Frequently we have heard complaints of an absence of legislative history. In this situation, we have the opportunity to review the legislative record and the majority chooses to ignore it.

It is curious to note that the majority states that "There is no doubt but that KRS 199.590 is intended to keep baby brokers from overwhelming an expectant mother or the parents of a child with financial inducements to part with that child." However, the majority apparently loses its judicial insight into the proper interpretation of the activities of the General Assembly when it comes to surrogate parenting.

Surrogate parenting obviously contemplates adoption by the infertile wife of the apparent biological father. The infertile wife is prominently included in all definitions of surrogate parenting which we have examined.

The corporate charter of this entity acknowledges her in its statement of purpose which is to assist infertile *couples* in obtaining a biologically related child. Once the obvious certainty of the infertile wife's presence is recognized, it cannot be logically denied that the certainty of adoption must logically follow. The termination of parental rights by the surrogate mother is a necessary predicate to a subsequent adoption by the infertile wife. The apparent biological father and/or husband is only an intermediary who acquires and assists the transfer of the parental rights of the two females involved.

The contracts employed in this case go to great length to avoid mentioning adoption or including any specific reference to the infertile wife. As noted by the Court of Appeals, this does not prevent a reviewing court from recognizing the true nature of the commercial transaction involved. The purpose of the language of the contract is merely to avoid KRS 199.590(2). It is an obvious subterfuge.

Adoption made possible through paid termination of a surrogate's parental rights, is an essential part of the surrogating procedure. Accordingly it is in direct contradiction to the policy and the expressed language of KRS 199.590(2), which prohibits the purchase and sale of children.

I am not at all unmindful of the precious gift of life demonstrated by the birth of a child to infertile couples. Certainly this is a most attractive prospect. However, it still remains that the end does not justify the means.

The fact that a woman's infertility can be cured is a matter that evokes serious questions of medical and public policy. The prospect of host-mothers with wombs for hire is immediately possible. There are already sperm banks and egg banks could be next. It is entirely possible, as we have seen in this case, that reproduction can be arranged by contract and financial payment. In my view the consequences which could arise from the opening of the human uterus to commercial medical technology does not contribute to the emancipation of women. In my opinion, the safeguarding of marriage and the family is essential to the continuation of human society as we know it. The possibility of exploitation of women as surrogate mothers is totally undesirable.

There is no question that our age is one of expanding biomedical technology. In every era people believe they are at a "turning point" on the threshold of new development. There are some moments in history when such an impression is justified. The law must be stable, yet it cannot stand still. Our legal system is workable only because it has been continually restructured to meet society's changing needs. The *Brave New World* of Aldous Huxley seems to be upon us. The intrusion of government into the private lives of individuals forecast in George Orwell's *1984,* seems to be here.

I certainly agree that the legal system should not avoid the necessary legal problems that arise from the advances of sciences.

I agree with the majority that decisions relating to the outlawing of surrogate parenting are better left with the legislature. In my view the legislature has already indicated their displeasure with the type of commercial transaction involved in this case.

Our consideration of public policy in this regard should include the possible exploitation of financially-needy women. Although there may be some altruistic women who will volunteer as surrogate mothers, the greater prospect is that monetary payment will have to be made to surrogates. The offer of financial payment will undoubtedly persuade financially needy women to sell their reproductive faculties for the benefit of those who can pay. The price at which a woman will sell her reproductive capacity may depend on her financial status.

Another public policy factor relating to surrogate mothering is the long-standing interest in society for the preservation of the traditional family. The family unit has been under severe attack from almost every element of our modern commercial society, yet it continues as the bedrock of the world as we know it. Any practice which threatens the stability of the family unit is a direct threat to society's stability. The question is whether the introduction of a third contracting party, the surrogate mother, substantially deviates from and threatens the traditional family concept. I believe that the legislature has already expressed their opinion that surrogate mothering tends to violate public policy.

Certainly important practical results from the growing ability to scientifically control biological reproduction demands legislative attention.

The decision to become pregnant parallels the fundamental right of reproductive privacy. The adopting couple's claimed right of reproductive privacy does not appear to be sufficiently similar. The emphasis in reproductive privacy is on the right of the individual to control his or her reproductive faculties. To give a second party the right to control another person's reproductive capacity would appear to be contradictory. Although a surrogate mother's decision to become pregnant is a fundamental right, another party would not have the right to contract for the control of her pregnancy. . . .

Matter of Baby M

Supreme Court of New Jersey, 1988.
109 N.J. 396, 537 A.2d 1227.

■ WILENTZ, C.J.

In this matter the Court is asked to determine the validity of a contract that purports to provide a new way of bringing children into a family. For a fee of $10,000, a woman agrees to be artificially inseminated with the semen of another woman's husband; she is to conceive a child, carry it to term, and after its birth surrender it to the natural father and his wife. The intent of the contract is that the child's natural mother will thereafter be forever separated from her child. The wife is to adopt the child, and she and the natural father are to be regarded as its parents for all purposes. The contract providing for this is called a "surrogacy contract," the natural mother inappropriately called the "surrogate mother."

We invalidate the surrogacy contract because it conflicts with the law and public policy of this State. While we recognize the depth of the yearning of infertile couples to have their own children, we find the payment of money to a "surrogate" mother illegal, perhaps criminal, and potentially degrading to women. Although in this case we grant custody to the natural father, the evidence having clearly proved such custody to be in the best interests of the infant, we void both the termination of the surrogate mother's parental rights and the adoption of the child by the wife/stepparent. We thus restore the "surrogate" as the mother of the child. We remand the issue of the natural mother's visitation rights to the trial court, since that issue was not reached below and the record before us is not sufficient to permit us to decide it *de novo*.

We find no offense to our present laws where a woman voluntarily and without payment agrees to act as a "surrogate" mother, provided that she is not subject to a binding agreement to surrender her child. Moreover, our holding today does not preclude the Legislature from altering the current statutory scheme, within constitutional limits, so as to permit surrogacy contracts. Under current law, however, the surrogacy agreement before us is illegal and invalid.

I. FACTS

In February 1985, William Stern and Mary Beth Whitehead entered into a surrogacy contract. It recited that Stern's wife, Elizabeth, was infertile, that they wanted a child, and that Mrs. Whitehead was willing to provide that child as the mother with Mr. Stern as the father.

The contract provided that through artificial insemination using Mr. Stern's sperm, Mrs. Whitehead would become pregnant, carry the child to term, bear it, deliver it to the Sterns, and thereafter do whatever was necessary to terminate her maternal rights so that Mrs. Stern could thereafter adopt the child. Mrs. Whitehead's husband, Richard,[1] was also a party to the contract; Mrs. Stern was not. Mr. Whitehead promised to do all acts necessary to rebut the presumption of paternity under the Parentage Act. N.J.S.A. 9:17–43a(1),–44a. Although Mrs. Stern was not a party to the surrogacy agreement, the contract gave her sole custody of the child in the event of Mr. Stern's death. Mrs. Stern's status as a nonparty to the surrogate parenting agreement presumably was to avoid the application of the baby-selling statute to this arrangement.

Mr. Stern, on his part, agreed to attempt the artificial insemination and to pay Mrs. Whitehead $10,000 after the child's birth, on its delivery to him. In a separate contract, Mr. Stern agreed to pay $7,500 to the Infertility Center of New York ("ICNY"). The Center's advertising campaigns solicit surrogate mothers and encourage infertile couples to consider surrogacy. ICNY arranged for the surrogacy contract by bringing the parties together, explaining the process to them, furnishing the contractual form,[2] and providing legal counsel.

The history of the parties' involvement in this arrangement suggests their good faith. William and Elizabeth Stern were married in July 1974, having met at the University of Michigan, where both were Ph.D. candidates. Due to financial considerations and Mrs. Stern's pursuit of a medical degree and residency, they decided to defer starting a family until 1981.

---

1. Subsequent to the trial court proceedings, Mr. and Mrs. Whitehead were divorced, and soon thereafter Mrs. Whitehead remarried. Nevertheless, in the course of this opinion we will make reference almost exclusively to the facts as they existed at the time of trial, the facts on which the decision we now review was reached. We note moreover that Mr. Whitehead remains a party to this dispute. For these reasons, we continue to refer to appellants as Mr. and Mrs. Whitehead.

2. The Stern–Whitehead contract (the "surrogacy contract") and the Stern–ICNY contract are reproduced below as Appendix A and B respectively. Other ancillary agreements and their attachments are omitted.

Before then, however, Mrs. Stern learned that she might have multiple sclerosis and that the disease in some cases renders pregnancy a serious health risk. Her anxiety appears to have exceeded the actual risk, which current medical authorities assess as minimal. Nonetheless that anxiety was evidently quite real, Mrs. Stern fearing that pregnancy might precipitate blindness, paraplegia, or other forms of debilitation. Based on the perceived risk the Sterns decided to forego having their own children. The decision had a special significance for Mr. Stern. Most of his family had been destroyed in the Holocaust. As the family's only survivor, he very much wanted to continue his bloodline.

Initially the Sterns considered adoption, but were discouraged by the substantial delay apparently involved and by the potential problem they saw arising from their age and their differing religious backgrounds. They were most eager for some other means to start a family.

The paths of Mrs. Whitehead and the Sterns to surrogacy were similar. Both responded to advertising by ICNY. The Sterns' response, following their inquiries into adoption, was the result of their longstanding decision to have a child. Mrs. Whitehead's response apparently resulted from her sympathy with family members and others who could have no children (she stated that she wanted to give another couple the "gift of life"); she also wanted the $10,000 to help her family.

Both parties, undoubtedly because of their own self-interest, were less sensitive to the implications of the transaction than they might otherwise have been. Mrs. Whitehead, for instance, appears not to have been concerned about whether the Sterns would make good parents for her child; the Sterns, on their part, while conscious of the obvious possibility that surrendering the child might cause grief to Mrs. Whitehead, overcame their qualms because of their desire for a child. At any rate, both the Sterns and Mrs. Whitehead were committed to the arrangement; both thought it right and constructive.

Mrs. Whitehead had reached her decision concerning surrogacy before the Sterns, and had actually been involved as a potential surrogate mother with another couple. After numerous unsuccessful artificial inseminations, that effort was abandoned. Thereafter, the Sterns learned of the Infertility Center, the possibilities of surrogacy, and of Mary Beth Whitehead. The two couples met to discuss the surrogacy arrangement and decided to go forward. On February 6, 1985, Mr. Stern and Mr. and Mrs. Whitehead executed the surrogate parenting agreement. After several artificial inseminations over a period of months, Mrs. Whitehead became pregnant. The pregnancy was uneventful and on March 27, 1986, Baby M was born.

Not wishing anyone at the hospital to be aware of the surrogacy arrangement, Mr. and Mrs. Whitehead appeared to all as the proud parents of a healthy female child. Her birth certificate indicated her name to be Sara Elizabeth Whitehead and her father to be Richard Whitehead. In accordance with Mrs. Whitehead's request, the Sterns visited the hospital unobtrusively to see the newborn child.

Mrs. Whitehead realized, almost from the moment of birth, that she could not part with this child. She had felt a bond with it even during pregnancy. Some indication of the attachment was conveyed to the Sterns at the hospital when they told Mrs. Whitehead what they were going to name the baby. She apparently broke into tears and indicated that she did not know if she could give up the child. She talked about how the baby looked like her other daughter, and made it clear that she was experiencing great difficulty with the decision.

Nonetheless, Mrs. Whitehead was, for the moment, true to her word. Despite powerful inclinations to the contrary, she turned her child over to the Sterns on March 30 at the Whiteheads' home.

The Sterns were thrilled with their new child. They had planned extensively for its arrival, far beyond the practical furnishing of a room for her. It was a time of joyful celebration—not just for them but for their friends as well. The Sterns looked forward to raising their daughter, whom they named Melissa. While aware by then that Mrs. Whitehead was undergoing an emotional crisis, they were as yet not cognizant of the depth of that crisis and its implications for their newly-enlarged family.

Later in the evening of March 30, Mrs. Whitehead became deeply disturbed, disconsolate, stricken with unbearable sadness. She had to have her child. She could not eat, sleep, or concentrate on anything other than her need for her baby. The next day she went to the Sterns' home and told them how much she was suffering.

The depth of Mrs. Whitehead's despair surprised and frightened the Sterns. She told them that she could not live without her baby, that she must have her, even if only for one week, that thereafter she would surrender her child. The Sterns, concerned that Mrs. Whitehead might indeed commit suicide, not wanting under any circumstances to risk that, and in any event believing that Mrs. Whitehead would keep her word, turned the child over to her. . . .

The struggle over Baby M began when it became apparent that Mrs. Whitehead could not return the child to Mr. Stern. Due to Mrs. Whitehead's refusal to relinquish the baby, Mr. Stern filed a complaint seeking enforcement of the surrogacy contract. He alleged, accurately, that Mrs. Whitehead had not only refused to comply with the surrogacy contract but had threatened to flee from New Jersey with the child in order to avoid even the possibility of his obtaining custody. The court papers asserted that if Mrs. Whitehead were to be given notice of the application for an order requiring her to relinquish custody, she would, prior to the hearing, leave the state with the baby. And that is precisely what she did. After the order was entered, *ex parte,* the process server, aided by the police, in the presence of the Sterns, entered Mrs. Whitehead's home to execute the order. Mr. Whitehead fled with the child, who had been handed to him through a window while those who came to enforce the order were thrown off balance by a dispute over the child's current name.

The Whiteheads immediately fled to Florida with Baby M. They stayed initially with Mrs. Whitehead's parents, where one of Mrs. Whitehead's children had been living. For the next three months, the Whiteheads and Melissa lived at roughly twenty different hotels, motels, and homes in order to avoid apprehension. From time to time Mrs. Whitehead would call Mr. Stern to discuss the matter; the conversations, recorded by Mr. Stern on advice of counsel, show an escalating dispute about rights, morality, and power, accompanied by threats of Mrs. Whitehead to kill herself, to kill the child, and falsely to accuse Mr. Stern of sexually molesting Mrs. Whitehead's other daughter.

Eventually the Sterns discovered where the Whiteheads were staying, commenced supplementary proceedings in Florida, and obtained an order requiring the Whiteheads to turn over the child. Police in Florida enforced the order, forcibly removing the child from her grandparents' home. She was soon thereafter brought to New Jersey and turned over to the Sterns. The prior order of the court, issued *ex parte,* awarding custody of the child to the Sterns *pendente lite,* was reaffirmed by the trial court after consideration of the certified representations of the parties (both represented by counsel) concerning the unusual sequence of events that had unfolded. Pending final judgment, Mrs. Whitehead was awarded limited visitation with Baby M.

The Sterns' complaint, in addition to seeking possession and ultimately custody of the child, sought enforcement of the surrogacy contract. Pursuant to the contract, it asked that the child be permanently placed in their custody, that Mrs. Whitehead's parental rights be terminated, and that Mrs. Stern be allowed to adopt the child, *i.e.,* that, for all purposes, Melissa become the Sterns' child.

The trial took thirty-two days over a period of more than two months.... Soon after the conclusion of the trial, the trial court announced its opinion from the bench. 217 N.J.Super. 313, 525 A.2d 1128 (1987). It held that the surrogacy contract was valid; ordered that Mrs. Whitehead's parental rights be terminated and that sole custody of the child be granted to Mr. Stern; and, after hearing brief testimony from Mrs. Stern, immediately entered an order allowing the adoption of Melissa by Mrs. Stern, all in accordance with the surrogacy contract. Pending the outcome of the appeal, we granted a continuation of visitation to Mrs. Whitehead, although slightly more limited than the visitation allowed during the trial.

Although clearly expressing its view that the surrogacy contract was valid, the trial court devoted the major portion of its opinion to the question of the baby's best interests. The inconsistency is apparent. The surrogacy contract calls for the surrender of the child to the Sterns, permanent and sole custody in the Sterns, and termination of Mrs. Whitehead's parental rights, all without qualification, all regardless of any evaluation of the best interests of the child. As a matter of fact the contract recites (even before the child was conceived) that it is in the best interests of the child to be placed with Mr. Stern. In effect, the trial court awarded custody to Mr. Stern, the natural father, based on the same kind of evidence and analysis as might be expected had no surrogacy contract existed. Its rationalization, however, was that while the surrogacy contract was valid, specific performance would not be granted unless that remedy was in the best interests of the child. The factual issues confronted and decided by the trial court were the same as if Mr. Stern and Mrs. Whitehead had had the child out of wedlock, intended or unintended, and then disagreed about custody. . . .

On the question of best interests—and we agree, but for different reasons, that custody was the critical issue—the court's analysis of the testimony was perceptive, demonstrating both its understanding of the case and its considerable experience in these matters. We agree substantially with both its analysis and conclusions on the matter of custody.

The court's review and analysis of the surrogacy contract, however, is not at all in accord with ours. The trial court concluded that the various statutes governing this matter, including those concerning adoption, termination of parental rights, and payment of money in connection with adoptions, do not apply to surrogacy contracts. It reasoned that because the Legislature did not have surrogacy contracts in mind when it passed those laws, those laws were therefore irrelevant.

. . .

Mrs. Whitehead contends that the surrogacy contract, for a variety of reasons, is invalid. She contends that it conflicts with public policy since it guarantees that the child will not have the nurturing of both natural parents—presumably New Jersey's goal for families. She further argues that it deprives the mother of her constitutional right to the companionship of her child, and that it conflicts with statutes concerning termination of parental rights and adoption. With the contract thus void, Mrs. Whitehead claims primary custody (with visitation rights in Mr. Stern) both on a best interests basis (stressing the "tender years" doctrine) as well as on the policy basis of discouraging surrogacy contracts. She maintains that even if custody would ordinarily go to Mr. Stern, here it should be awarded to Mrs. Whitehead to deter future surrogacy arrangements.

In a brief filed after oral argument, counsel for Mrs. Whitehead suggests that the standard for determining best interests where the infant resulted from a surrogacy contract is that the child should be placed with the mother absent a showing of unfitness. All parties agree that no expert testified that Mary Beth Whitehead was unfit as a mother; the trial court expressly found that she was *not* "unfit," that, on the contrary, "she is a good mother for and to her older children," 217 N.J.Super. at 397, 525 A.2d 1128; and no one now claims anything to the contrary.

. . .

The Sterns claim that the surrogacy contract is valid and should be enforced, largely for the reasons given by the trial court. They claim a constitutional right of privacy, which includes the right of procreation, and the right of consenting adults to deal with matters of reproduction as they see fit. . . .

Of considerable interest in this clash of views is the position of the child's guardian *ad litem,* wisely appointed by the court at the outset of the litigation. As the child's representative, her role in the litigation, as she viewed it, was solely to protect the child's best interests. She therefore took no position on the validity of the surrogacy contract, and instead devoted her energies to obtaining expert testimony uninfluenced by any interest other than the child's. We agree with the guardian's perception of her role in this litigation. She appropriately refrained from taking any position that might have appeared to compromise her role as the child's advocate. She first took the position, based on her experts' testimony, that the Sterns should have primary custody, and that while Mrs. Whitehead's parental rights should not be terminated, no visitation should be allowed for five years. As a result of subsequent developments, mentioned infra, her view has changed. She now recommends that no visitation be allowed at least until Baby M reaches maturity.

. . . The trial court, consistent in this respect with its view that the surrogacy contract was valid, did not deal at all with the question of visitation. Having concluded that the best interests of the child called for custody in the Sterns, the trial court enforced the operative provisions of the surrogacy contract, terminated Mrs. Whitehead's parental rights, and granted an adoption to Mrs. Stern. . . .

II.   INVALIDITY AND UNENFORCEABILITY OF SURROGACY CONTRACT

We have concluded that this surrogacy contract is invalid. Our conclusion has two bases: direct conflict with existing statutes and conflict with the public policies of this State, as expressed in its statutory and decisional law.

One of the surrogacy contract's basic purposes, to achieve the adoption of a child through private placement, though permitted in New Jersey "is very much disfavored." Sees v. Baber, 74 N.J. 201, 217, 377 A.2d 628 (1977). Its use of money for this purpose—and we have no doubt whatsoever that the money is being paid to obtain an adoption and not, as the Sterns argue, for the personal services of Mary Beth Whitehead—is illegal and perhaps criminal. N.J.S.A. 9:3–54. In addition to the inducement of money, there is the coercion of contract: the natural mother's irrevocable agreement, prior to birth, even prior to conception, to surrender the child to the adoptive couple. Such an agreement is totally unenforceable in private placement adoption. Even where the adoption is through an approved agency, the formal agreement to surrender occurs only *after* birth and then, by regulation, only after the birth mother has been counseled. Integral to these invalid provisions of the surrogacy contract is the related agreement, equally invalid, on the part of the natural mother to cooperate with, and not to contest, proceedings to terminate her parental rights, as well as her contractual concession, in aid of the adoption, that the child's best interests would be served by awarding custody to the natural father and his wife—all of this before she has even conceived, and, in some cases, before she has the slightest idea of what the natural father and adoptive mother are like.

The foregoing provisions not only directly conflict with New Jersey statutes, but also offend long-established State policies. These critical terms, which are at the heart of the contract, are invalid and unenforceable; the conclusion therefore follows, without more, that the entire contract is unenforceable.

A. Conflict with Statutory Provisions

The surrogacy contract conflicts with: (1) laws prohibiting the use of money in connection with adoptions; (2) laws requiring proof of parental unfitness or abandonment before termination of parental rights is ordered or an adoption is granted; and (3) laws that make surrender of custody and consent to adoption revocable in private placement adoptions.

(1) Our law prohibits paying or accepting money in connection with any placement of a child for adoption. N.J.S.A. 9:3–54a. Violation is a high misdemeanor. N.J.S.A. 9:3–54c. Excepted are fees of an approved agency (which must be a nonprofit entity, N.J.S.A. 9:3–38a) and certain expenses in connection with childbirth. N.J.S.A. 9:3–54b.

Considerable care was taken in this case to structure the surrogacy arrangement so as not to violate this prohibition. The arrangement was structured as follows: the adopting parent, Mrs. Stern, was not a party to the surrogacy contract; the money paid to Mrs. Whitehead was stated to be for her services—not for the adoption; the sole purpose of the contract was stated as being that "of giving a child to William Stern, its natural and biological father"; the money was purported to be "compensation for services and expenses and in no way . . . a fee for termination of parental rights or a payment in exchange for consent to surrender a child for adoption"; the fee to the Infertility Center ($7,500) was stated to be for legal representation, advice, administrative work, and other "services." Nevertheless, it seems clear that the money was paid and accepted in connection with an adoption.

The Infertility Center's major role was first as a "finder" of the surrogate mother whose child was to be adopted, and second as the arranger of all proceedings that led to the adoption. Its role as adoption finder is demonstrated by the provision requiring Mr. Stern to pay another $7,500 if he uses Mary Beth Whitehead again as a surrogate, and by ICNY's agreement to "coordinate arrangements for the adoption of the child by the wife." The surrogacy agreement requires Mrs. Whitehead to surrender Baby M for the purposes of adoption. The agreement notes that Mr. *and Mrs.* Stern wanted to have a child, and provides that the child be "placed" with Mrs. Stern in the event Mr. Stern dies before the child is born. The payment of the $10,000 occurs only on surrender of custody of the child and "completion of the duties and obligations" of Mrs. Whitehead, including termination of her parental rights to facilitate adoption by Mrs. Stern.

As for the contention that the Sterns are paying only for services and not for an adoption, we need note only that they would pay nothing in the event the child died before the fourth month of pregnancy, and only $1,000 if the child were stillborn, even though the "services" had been fully rendered. Additionally, one of Mrs. Whitehead's estimated costs, to be assumed by Mr. Stern, was an "Adoption Fee," presumably for Mrs. Whitehead's incidental costs in connection with the adoption.

Mr. Stern knew he was paying for the adoption of a child; Mrs. Whitehead knew she was accepting money so that a child might be adopted; the Infertility Center knew that it was being paid for assisting in the adoption of a child. The actions of all three worked to frustrate the goals of the statute. It strains credulity to claim that these arrangements, touted by those in the surrogacy business as an attractive alternative to the usual route leading to an adoption, really amount to something other than a private placement adoption for money.

. . .

(2) The termination of Mrs. Whitehead's parental rights, called for by the surrogacy contract and actually ordered by the court, fails to comply with the stringent requirements of New Jersey law. Our law, recognizing the finality of any termination of parental rights, provides for such termination only where there has been a voluntary surrender of a child to an approved agency or to the Division of Youth and Family Services ("DYFS"), accompanied by a formal document acknowledging termination of parental rights, or where there has been a showing of parental abandonment or unfitness.

. . .

As the trial court recognized, without a valid termination there can be no adoption. This requirement applies to all adoptions, whether they be private placements, or agency adoptions.

Our statutes, and the cases interpreting them, leave no doubt that where there has been no written surrender to an approved agency or to DYFS, termination of parental rights will not be granted in this state absent a very strong showing of abandonment or neglect. . . . It is clear that a "best interests" determination is never sufficient to terminate parental rights; the statutory criteria must be proved.

. . .

Since the termination was invalid, it follows, as noted above, that adoption of Melissa by Mrs. Stern could not properly be granted.

. . .

The provision in the surrogacy contract whereby the mother irrevocably agrees to surrender custody of her child and to terminate her parental rights conflicts with the settled interpretation of New Jersey statutory law. There is only one irrevocable consent, and that is the one explicitly provided for by statute: a consent to surrender of custody and a placement with an approved agency or with DYFS. The provision in the surrogacy contract, agreed to before conception, requiring the natural mother to surrender custody of the child without any right of revocation is one more indication of the essential nature of this transaction: the creation of a contractual system of termination and adoption designed to circumvent our statutes.

B. Public Policy Considerations

The surrogacy contract's invalidity, resulting from its direct conflict with the above statutory provisions, is further underlined when its goals and means are measured against New Jersey's public policy. The contract's basic premise, that the natural parents can decide in advance of birth which one is to have custody of the child, bears no relationship to the settled law that the child's best interests shall determine custody....

The surrogacy contract guarantees permanent separation of the child from one of its natural parents. Our policy, however, has long been that to the extent possible, children should remain with and be brought up by both of their natural parents.... This is not simply some theoretical ideal that in practice has no meaning. The impact of failure to follow that policy is nowhere better shown than in the results of this surrogacy contract. A child, instead of starting off its life with as much peace and security as possible, finds itself immediately in a tug-of-war between contending mother and father.

The surrogacy contract violates the policy of this State that the rights of natural parents are equal concerning their child, the father's right no greater than the mother's....

The policies expressed in our comprehensive laws governing consent to the surrender of a child stand in stark contrast to the surrogacy contract and what it implies. Here there is no counseling, independent or otherwise, of the natural mother, no evaluation, no warning.

The only legal advice Mary Beth Whitehead received regarding the surrogacy contract was provided in connection with the contract that she previously entered into with another couple. Mrs. Whitehead's lawyer was referred to her by the Infertility Center, with which he had an agreement to act as counsel for surrogate candidates. His services consisted of spending one hour going through the contract with the Whiteheads, section by section, and answering their questions. Mrs. Whitehead received no further legal advice prior to signing the contract with the Sterns.

Mrs. Whitehead was examined and psychologically evaluated, but if it was for her benefit, the record does not disclose that fact. The Sterns regarded the evaluation as important, particularly in connection with the question of whether she would change her mind. Yet they never asked to see it, and were content with the assumption that the Infertility Center had made an evaluation and had concluded that there was no danger that the surrogate mother would change her mind. From Mrs. Whitehead's point of view, all that she learned from the evaluation was that "she had passed." It is apparent that the profit motive got the better of the Infertility Center.

Although the evaluation was made, it was not put to any use, and understandably so, for the psychologist warned that Mrs. Whitehead demonstrated certain traits that might make surrender of the child difficult and that there should be further inquiry into this issue in connection with her surrogacy. To inquire further, however, might have jeopardized the Infertility Center's fee. The record indicates that neither Mrs. Whitehead nor the Sterns were ever told of this fact, a fact that might have ended their surrogacy arrangement.

Under the contract, the natural mother is irrevocably committed before she knows the strength of her bond with her child. She never makes a totally voluntary, informed decision, for quite clearly any decision prior to the baby's birth is, in the most important sense, uninformed, and any decision after that, compelled by a pre-existing contractual commitment, the threat of a lawsuit, and the inducement of a $10,000 payment, is less than totally voluntary. Her interests are of little concern to those who controlled this transaction.

Although the interest of the natural father and adoptive mother is certainly the predominant interest, realistically the *only* interest served, even they are left with less than what public policy requires. They know little about the natural mother, her genetic makeup, and her psychological and medical history. Moreover, not even a superficial attempt is made to determine their awareness of their responsibilities as parents.

Worst of all, however, is the contract's total disregard of the best interests of the child. There is not the slightest suggestion that any inquiry will be made at any time to determine the fitness of the Sterns as custodial parents, of Mrs. Stern as an adoptive parent, their superiority to Mrs. Whitehead, or the effect on the child of not living with her natural mother.

This is the sale of a child, or, at the very least, the sale of a mother's right to her child, the only mitigating factor being that one of the purchasers is the father. Almost every evil that prompted the prohibition of the payment of money in connection with adoptions exists here.

The differences between an adoption and a surrogacy contract should be noted, since it is asserted that the use of money in connection with surrogacy does not pose the risks found where money buys an adoption. Katz, "Surrogate Motherhood and the Baby–Selling Laws," 20 Colum.J.L. & Soc.Probs. 1 (1986).

First, and perhaps most important, all parties concede that it is unlikely that surrogacy will survive without money. Despite the alleged selfless motivation of surrogate mothers, if there is no payment, there will be no surrogates, or very few. That conclusion contrasts with adoption; for obvious reasons, there remains a steady supply, albeit insufficient, despite the prohibitions against payment. The adoption itself, relieving the natural mother of the financial burden of supporting an infant, is the equivalent of payment.

Second, the use of money in adoptions does not *produce* the problem— conception occurs, and usually the birth itself, before illicit funds are offered. With surrogacy, the "problem," if one views it as such, consisting of the purchase of a woman's procreative capacity, at the risk of her life, is caused by and originates with the offer of money.

Third, with the law prohibiting the use of money in connection with adoptions, the built-in financial pressure of the unwanted pregnancy and the consequent support obligation do not lead the mother to the highest paying, ill-suited, adoptive parents. She is just as well off surrendering the child to an approved agency. In surrogacy, the highest bidders will presumably become the adoptive parents regardless of suitability, so long as payment of money is permitted.

Fourth, the mother's consent to surrender her child in adoption is revocable, even after surrender of the child, unless it be to an approved agency, where by regulation there are protections against an ill-advised surrender. In surrogacy, consent occurs so early that no amount of advice would satisfy the potential mother's need, yet the consent is irrevocable.

The main difference, that the plight of the unwanted pregnancy is unintended while the situation of the surrogate mother is voluntary and intended, is really not significant. Initially, it produces stronger reactions of sympathy for the mother whose pregnancy was unwanted than for the surrogate mother, who "went into this with her eyes wide open." On reflection, however, it appears that the essential evil is the same, taking advantage of a woman's circumstances (the unwanted pregnancy or the need for money) in order to take away her child, the difference being one of degree.

In the scheme contemplated by the surrogacy contract in this case, a middleman, propelled by profit, promotes the sale. Whatever idealism may have motivated any of the participants, the profit motive predominates, permeates, and ultimately governs the transaction. The demand for children is great and the supply small. The availability of contraception, abortion, and the greater willingness of single mothers to bring up their children has led to a shortage of babies offered for adoption. The situation is ripe for the entry of the middleman who will bring some equilibrium into the market by increasing the supply through the use of money.

Intimated, but disputed, is the assertion that surrogacy will be used for the benefit of the rich at the expense of the poor. See, e.g., Radin, "Market Inalienability," 100 Harv.L.Rev. 1849, 1930 (1987). In response it is noted that the Sterns are not rich and the Whiteheads not poor. Nevertheless, it is clear to us that it is unlikely that surrogate mothers will be as proportionately numerous among those women in the top twenty percent income bracket as among those in the bottom twenty percent. Put differently, we doubt that infertile couples in the low-income bracket will find upper income surrogates.

In any event, even in this case one should not pretend that disparate wealth does not play a part simply because the contrast is not the dramatic "rich versus poor." At the time of trial, the Whiteheads' net assets were probably negative—Mrs. Whitehead's own sister was foreclosing on a second mortgage. Their income derived from Mr. Whitehead's labors. Mrs. Whitehead is a homemaker, having previously held part-time jobs. The Sterns are both professionals, she a medical doctor, he a biochemist. Their combined income when both were working was about $89,500 a year and their assets sufficient to pay for the surrogacy contract arrangements.

The point is made that Mrs. Whitehead *agreed* to the surrogacy arrangement, supposedly fully understanding the consequences. Putting aside the issue of how compelling her need for money may have been, and how significant her understanding of the consequences, we suggest that her consent is irrelevant. There are, in a civilized society, some things that money cannot buy.

. . .

The long-term effects of surrogacy contracts are not known, but feared—the impact on the child who learns her life was bought, that she is the offspring of someone who gave birth to her only to obtain money; the impact on the natural mother as the full weight of her isolation is felt along with the full reality of the sale of her body and her child; the impact on the natural father and adoptive mother once they realize the consequences of their conduct. Literature in related areas suggests these are substantial considerations, although, given the newness of surrogacy, there is little information.

The surrogacy contract creates, it is based upon, principles that are directly contrary to the objectives of our laws. It guarantees the separation of a child from its mother; it looks to adoption regardless of suitability; it totally ignores the child; it takes the child from the mother regardless of her wishes and her maternal fitness; and it does all of this, it accomplishes all of its goals, through the use of money.

Beyond that is the potential degradation of some women that may result from this arrangement. In many cases, of course, surrogacy may bring satisfaction, not only to the infertile couple, but to the surrogate mother herself. The fact, however, that many women may not perceive surrogacy negatively but rather see it as an opportunity does not diminish its potential for devastation to other women.

In sum, the harmful consequences of this surrogacy arrangement appear to us all too palpable. In New Jersey the surrogate mother's agreement to sell her child is void. Its irrevocability infects the entire contract, as does the money that purports to buy it.

III. TERMINATION

. . .

Nothing in this record justifies a finding that would allow a court to terminate Mary Beth Whitehead's parental rights under the statutory standard. It is not simply that obviously there was no "intentional abandonment or very substantial neglect of parental duties without a reasonable expectation of reversal of that conduct in the future," N.J.S.A. 9:3–48c(1), quite the contrary, but furthermore that the trial court never found Mrs. Whitehead an unfit mother and indeed affirmatively stated that Mary Beth Whitehead had been a good mother to her other children. 217 N.J.Super. at 397, 525 A.2d 1128.

Although the best interests of the child is dispositive of the custody issue in a dispute between natural parents, it does not govern the question of termination. It has long been decided that the mere fact that a child would be better off with one set of parents than with another is an insufficient basis for terminating the natural parent's rights. Furthermore, it is equally well settled that surrender of a child and a consent to adoption through private placement do not alone warrant termination. It must be noted, despite some language to the contrary, that the interests of the child are not the only interests involved when termination issues are raised. The parent's rights, both constitutional and statutory, have their own independent vitality.

. . .

IV. CONSTITUTIONAL ISSUES

Both parties argue that the Constitutions—state and federal—mandate approval of their basic claims. The source of their constitutional arguments is essentially the same: the right of privacy, the right to procreate, the right to the companionship of one's child, those rights flowing either directly from the fourteenth amendment or by its incorporation of the Bill of Rights, or from the ninth amendment, or through the penumbra surrounding all of the Bill of Rights. They are the rights of personal intimacy, of marriage, of sex, of family, of procreation. Whatever their source, it is clear that they are fundamental rights protected by both the federal and state Constitutions. The right asserted by the Sterns is the right of procreation; that asserted by Mary Beth Whitehead is the right to the companionship of her child. . . .

. . . The right to procreate very simply is the right to have natural children, whether through sexual intercourse or artificial insemination. It is no more than that. Mr. Stern has not been deprived of that right. Through artificial insemination of Mrs. Whitehead, Baby M is his child. The custody, care, companionship, and nurturing that follow birth are not parts of the right to procreation; they are rights that may also be constitutionally protected, but that involve many considerations other than the right of procreation. To assert that Mr. Stern's right of procreation gives him the right to the custody of Baby M would be to assert that Mrs. Whitehead's right of procreation does *not* give her the right to the custody of Baby M; it would be to assert that the constitutional right of procreation includes within it a constitutionally protected contractual right to destroy someone else's right of procreation.

We conclude that the right of procreation is best understood and protected if confined to its essentials, and that when dealing with rights concerning the resulting child, different interests come into play. There is nothing in our culture or society that even begins to suggest a fundamental right on the part of the father to the custody of the child as part of his right to procreate when opposed by the claim of the mother to the same child. We therefore disagree with the trial court: there is no constitutional basis whatsoever requiring that Mr. Stern's claim to the custody of Baby M be sustained. Our conclusion may thus be understood as illustrating that a person's rights of privacy and self-determination are qualified by the effect on innocent third persons of the exercise of those rights.

Mr. Stern also contends that he has been denied equal protection of the laws by the State's statute granting full parental rights to a husband in relation to the child produced, with his consent, by the union of his wife with a sperm donor. N.J.S.A. 9:17–44. The claim really is that of Mrs. Stern. It is that she is in precisely the same position as the husband in the statute: she is presumably infertile, as is the husband in the statute; her spouse by agreement with a third party procreates with the understanding that the child will be the couple's child. The alleged unequal protection is that the understanding is honored in the statute when the husband is the infertile party, but no similar understanding is honored when it is the wife who is infertile.

It is quite obvious that the situations are not parallel. A sperm donor simply cannot be equated with a surrogate mother. The State has more than a sufficient basis to distinguish the two situations—even if the only difference is between the time it takes to provide sperm for artificial insemination and the time invested in a nine-month pregnancy—so as to justify automatically divesting the sperm donor of his parental rights without automatically divesting a surrogate mother. Some basis for an equal protection argument might exist if Mary Beth Whitehead had contributed her egg to be implanted, fertilized or otherwise, in Mrs. Stern, resulting in the latter's pregnancy. That is not the case here, however.

... By virtue of our decision Mrs. Whitehead's constitutional complaint—that her parental rights have been unconstitutionally terminated—is moot.

. . .

V. CUSTODY

... Under the Parentage Act the claims of the natural father and the natural mother are entitled to equal weight, i.e., one is not preferred over the other solely because it is the father or the mother. N.J.S.A. 9:17–40. The applicable rule given these circumstances is clear: the child's best interests determine custody.

. . .

The circumstances of this custody dispute are unusual and they have provoked some unusual contentions. The Whiteheads claim that even if the child's best interests would be served by our awarding custody to the Sterns, we should not do so, since that will encourage surrogacy contracts—contracts claimed by the Whiteheads, and we agree, to be violative of important legislatively-stated public policies. Their position is that in order that surrogacy contracts be deterred, custody should remain in the surrogate mother unless she is unfit, regardless of the best interests of the child. We disagree. Our declaration that this surrogacy contract is unenforceable and illegal is sufficient to deter similar agreements. We need not sacrifice the child's interests in order to make that point sharper....

. . .

... Our reading of the record persuades us that the trial court's decision awarding custody to the Sterns (technically to Mr. Stern) should be affirmed since "its findings ... could reasonably have been reached on sufficient credible evidence present in the record."

Our custody conclusion is based on strongly persuasive testimony contrasting both the family life of the Whiteheads and the Sterns and the personalities and characters of the individuals. The stability of the Whitehead family life was doubtful at the time of trial. Their finances were in serious trouble (foreclosure by Mrs. Whitehead's sister on a second mortgage was in process). Mr. Whitehead's employment, though relatively steady, was always at risk because of his alcoholism, a condition that he seems not to have been able to confront effectively. Mrs. Whitehead had not worked for quite some time, her last two employments having been part-time. One of the Whiteheads' positive attributes was their ability to bring up two children, and apparently well, even in so vulnerable a household. Yet substantial question was raised even about that aspect of their home life. The expert testimony contained criticism of Mrs. Whitehead's handling of her son's educational difficulties. Certain of the experts noted that Mrs. Whitehead perceived herself as omnipotent and omniscient concerning her children. She knew what they were thinking, what they wanted, and she spoke for them. As to Melissa, Mrs. Whitehead expressed the view that she alone knew what that child's cries and sounds meant. Her inconsistent stories about various things engendered grave doubts about her ability to explain honestly and sensitively to Baby M—and at the right time—the nature of her origin. Although faith in professional counseling is not a *sine qua non* of parenting, several experts believed that Mrs. Whitehead's contempt for professional help, especially professional psychological help, coincided with her feelings of omnipotence in a way that could be devastating to a child who most likely will need such help. In short, while love and affection there would be, Baby M's life with the Whiteheads promised to be too closely controlled by Mrs. Whitehead. The prospects for a wholesome independent psychological growth and development would be at serious risk.

The Sterns have no other children, but all indications are that their household and their personalities promise a much more likely foundation for Melissa to grow and thrive. There *is* a track record of sorts—during the one-and-a-half years of custody Baby M has done very well, and the relationship between both Mr. and Mrs. Stern and the baby has become very strong. The household is stable, and likely to remain so. Their finances are more than adequate, their circle of friends supportive, and their marriage happy. Most important, they are loving, giving, nurturing, and open-minded people. They have demonstrated the wish and ability to nurture and protect Melissa, yet at the same time to encourage her independence. Their lack of experience is more than made up for by a willingness to learn and to listen, a willingness that is enhanced by their professional training, especially Mrs. Stern's experience as a pediatrician. They are honest; they can recognize error, deal with it, and learn from it. They will try to determine rationally the best way to cope with problems in their relationship with Melissa. When the time comes to tell her about her origins, they will probably have found a means of doing so that accords with the best interests of Baby M. All in all, Melissa's future appears solid, happy, and promising with them.

Based on all of this we have concluded, independent of the trial court's identical conclusion, that Melissa's best interests call for custody in the Sterns....

. . .

Some comment is required on the initial *ex parte* order awarding custody *pendente lite* to the Sterns (and the continuation of that order after a plenary hearing). The issue, although irrelevant to our disposition of this case, may recur; and when it does, it can be of crucial importance. When father and mother are separated and disagree, at birth, on custody, only in an extreme, truly rare, case should the child be taken from its mother *pendente lite,* i.e., only in the most unusual case should the child be taken from its mother before the dispute is finally determined by the court on its merits. The probable bond between mother and child, and the child's need, not just the mother's, to strengthen that bond, along with the likelihood, in most cases, of a significantly lesser, if any, bond with the father—all counsel against temporary custody in the father. A substantial showing that the mother's continued custody would threaten the child's health or welfare would seem to be required.

In this case, the trial court, believing that the surrogacy contract might be valid, and faced with the probable flight from the jurisdiction by Mrs. Whitehead and the baby if *any* notice were served, ordered, *ex parte,* an immediate transfer of possession of the child, i.e., it ordered that custody be transferred immediately to Mr. Stern, rather than order Mrs. Whitehead not to leave the State. We have ruled, however, that the surrogacy contract is unenforceable and illegal. It provides no basis for either an *ex parte,* a plenary, an interlocutory, or a final order requiring a mother to surrender custody to a father. Any application by the natural father in a surrogacy dispute for custody pending the outcome of the litigation will henceforth require proof of unfitness, of danger to the child, or the like, of so high a quality and persuasiveness as to make it unlikely that such application will succeed. Absent the required showing, all that a court should do is list the matter for argument on notice to the mother. Even her threats to flee should not suffice to warrant any other relief unless her unfitness is clearly shown. At most, it should result in an order enjoining such flight. The erroneous transfer of custody, as we view it, represents a greater risk to the child than removal to a foreign jurisdiction, unless parental unfitness is clearly proved. Furthermore, we deem it likely that, advised of the law and knowing that her custody cannot seriously be challenged at this stage of the litigation, surrogate mothers will obey any court order to remain in the jurisdiction.

VI. VISITATION

The trial court's decision to terminate Mrs. Whitehead's parental rights precluded it from making any determination on visitation. Our reversal of the trial court's order, however, requires delineation of Mrs. Whitehead's rights to visitation. It is apparent to us that this factually sensitive issue, which was never addressed below, should not be determined *de novo* by this Court. We therefore remand the visitation issue to the trial court for an abbreviated hearing and determination as set forth below.[19]

.   .   .

We join those who want this litigation to end for the benefit of this child. To spare this two-year-old another sixty to ninety days of litigation, however, at the risk of wrongly deciding this matter, which has life-long consequences for the child and the parties, would be unwise.

We also note the following for the trial court's consideration: First, this is not a divorce case where visitation is almost invariably granted to the non-custodial spouse. To some extent the facts here resemble cases where the non-custodial spouse has had practically no relationship with the child, see Wilke v. Culp, supra, 196 N.J.Super. 487, 483 A.2d 420; but it only "resembles" those cases. In the instant case, Mrs. Whitehead spent the first four months of this child's life as her mother and has regularly visited the child since then. Second, she is not only the natural mother, but also the legal mother, and is not to be penalized one iota because of the surrogacy contract. Mrs. Whitehead, as the mother (indeed, as a mother who nurtured her child for its first four months—unquestionably a relevant consideration), is entitled to have her own interest in visitation considered. Visitation cannot be determined without considering the parents' interests along with those of the child.

In all of this, the trial court should recall the touchstones of visitation: that it is desirable for the child to have contact with both parents; that besides the child's interests, the parents' interests also must be considered; but that when all is said and done, the best interests of the child are paramount.

---

19. As we have done in similar situations, we order that this matter be referred on remand to a different trial judge by the vicinage assignment judge. The original trial judge's potential "commitment to its findings," New Jersey Div. of Youth & Family Servs. v. A.W., supra, 103 N.J. at 617, 512 A.2d 438, and the extent to which a judge "has already engaged in weighing the evidence," In re Guardianship of R, 155 N.J.Super. 186, 195, 382 A.2d 654 (App.Div.1977), persuade us to make that change. On remand the trial court will consider developments subsequent to the original trial court's opinion, including Mrs. Whitehead's divorce, pregnancy, and remarriage.

We have decided that Mrs. Whitehead is entitled to visitation at some point, and that question is not open to the trial court on this remand. The trial court will determine what kind of visitation shall be granted to her, with or without conditions, and when and under what circumstances it should commence....

. . .

We would expect that after the visitation issue is determined the trial court, in connection with any other applications in the future, will attempt to assure that this case is treated like any other so that this child may be spared any further damaging publicity.

While probably unlikely, we do not deem it unthinkable that, the major issues having been resolved, the parties' undoubted love for this child might result in a good faith attempt to work out the visitation themselves, in the best interests of their child.

CONCLUSION

This case affords some insight into a new reproductive arrangement: the artificial insemination of a surrogate mother. The unfortunate events that have unfolded illustrate that its unregulated use can bring suffering to all involved. Potential victims include the surrogate mother and her family, the natural father and his wife, and most importantly, the child. Although surrogacy has apparently provided positive results for some infertile couples, it can also, as this case demonstrates, cause suffering to participants, here essentially innocent and well-intended.

We have found that our present laws do not permit the surrogacy contract used in this case. Nowhere, however, do we find any legal prohibition against surrogacy when the surrogate mother volunteers, without any payment, to act as a surrogate and is given the right to change her mind and to assert her parental rights. Moreover, the Legislature remains free to deal with this most sensitive issue as it sees fit, subject only to constitutional constraints.

If the Legislature decides to address surrogacy, consideration of this case will highlight many of its potential harms. We do not underestimate the difficulties of legislating on this subject. In addition to the inevitable confrontation with the ethical and moral issues involved, there is the question of the wisdom and effectiveness of regulating a matter so private, yet of such public interest. Legislative consideration of surrogacy may also provide the opportunity to begin to focus on the overall implications of the new reproductive biotechnology—*in vitro* fertilization, preservation of sperm and eggs, embryo implantation and the like. The problem is how to enjoy the benefits of the technology—especially for infertile couples—while minimizing the risk of abuse. The problem can be addressed only when society decides what its values and objectives are in this troubling, yet promising, area.

The judgment is affirmed in part, reversed in part, and remanded for further proceedings consistent with this opinion.

NOTES

Appendixes to the opinion reproduce the agreements between the various parties. Contained in the basic "SURROGATE PARENTING AGREEMENT" are the following provisions:

[4.] (C) William Stern, Natural Father, shall pay the expenses incurred by Mary Beth Whitehead, Surrogate, pursuant to her pregnancy, more specifically defined as follows:

(1) All medical, hospitalization, and pharmaceutical, laboratory and therapy expenses incurred as a result of Mary Beth Whitehead's pregnancy, not covered or allowed by her present health and major medical insurance, including all extraordinary medical expenses and all reasonable expenses for treatment of any emotional or mental conditions or problems related to said pregnancy, but in no case shall any such expenses be paid or reimbursed after a period of six (6) months have elapsed since the date of the termination of the pregnancy, and this Agreement specifically excludes any expenses for lost wages or other non-itemized incidentals (see Exhibit "B") related to said pregnancy.

(2) William Stern, Natural Father, shall not be responsible for any latent medical expenses occurring six (6) weeks subsequent to the birth of the child, unless the medical problem or abnormality incident thereto was known and treated by a physician prior to the expiration of said six (6) week period and in written notice of the same sent to ICNY, as representative of William Stern by certified mail, return receipt requested, advising of this treatment.

(3) William Stern, Natural Father, shall be responsible for the total costs of all paternity testing. Such paternity testing may, at the option of William Stern, Natural Father, be required prior to release of the surrogate fee from escrow. In the event William Stern, Natural Father, is conclusively determined not to be the biological father of the child as a result of an HLA test, this Agreement will be deemed breached and Mary Beth Whitehead, Surrogate, shall not be entitled to any fee. William Stern, Natural Father, shall be entitled to reimbursement of all medical and related expenses from Mary Beth Whitehead, Surrogate, and Richard Whitehead, her husband.

(4) Mary Beth Whitehead's reasonable travel expenses incurred at the request of William Stern, pursuant to this Agreement.

5. Mary Beth Whitehead, Surrogate, and Richard Whitehead, her husband, understand and agree to assume all risks, including the risk of death, which are incidental to conception, pregnancy, childbirth, including but not limited to, postpartum complications. A copy of said possible risks and/or complications is attached hereto and made a part hereof (see Exhibit "C").

6.   Mary Beth Whitehead, Surrogate, and Richard Whitehead, her husband, hereby agree to undergo psychiatric evaluation by Joan Einwohner, a psychiatrist as designated by William Stern or an agent thereof. William Stern shall pay for the cost of said psychiatric evaluation. Mary Beth Whitehead and Richard Whitehead shall sign, prior to their evaluations, a medical release permitting dissemination of the report prepared as a result of said psychiatric evaluations to ICNY or William Stern and his wife.

7.   Mary Beth Whitehead, Surrogate, and Richard Whitehead, her husband, hereby agree that it is the exclusive and sole right of William Stern, Natural Father, to name said child.

8.   "Child" as referred to in this Agreement shall include all children born simultaneously pursuant to the inseminations contemplated herein.

9.   In the event of the death of William Stern, prior or subsequent to the birth of said child, it is hereby understood and agreed by Mary Beth Whitehead, Surrogate, and Richard Whitehead, her husband, that the child will be placed in the custody of William Stern's wife.

10.   In the event that the child is miscarried prior to the fifth (5th) month of pregnancy, no compensation, as enumerated in paragraph 4(A), shall be paid to Mary Beth Whitehead, Surrogate. However, the expenses enumerated in paragraph 4(C) shall be paid or reimbursed to Mary Beth Whitehead, Surrogate. In the event the child is miscarried, dies or is stillborn subsequent to the fourth (4th) month of pregnancy and said child does not survive, the Surrogate shall receive $1,000.00 in lieu of the compensation enumerated in paragraph 4(A). In the event of a miscarriage or stillbirth as described above, this Agreement shall terminate and neither Mary Beth Whitehead, Surrogate, nor William Stern, Natural Father, shall be under any further obligation under this Agreement.

11.   Mary Beth Whitehead, Surrogate, and William Stern, Natural Father, shall have undergone complete physical and genetic evaluation, under the direction and supervision of a licensed physician, to determine whether the physical health and well-being of each is satisfactory. Said physical examination shall include testing for venereal diseases, specifically including but not limited to, syphilis, herpes and gonorrhea. Said venereal disease testing shall be done prior to, but not limited to, each series of inseminations.

12.   In the event that pregnancy has not occurred within a reasonable time, in the opinion of William Stern, Natural Father, this Agreement shall terminate by written notice to Mary Beth Whitehead, Surrogate, at the residence provided to the ICNY by the Surrogate, from ICNY, as representative of William Stern, Natural Father.

13.   Mary Beth Whitehead, Surrogate, agrees that she will not abort the child once conceived except, if in the professional medical opinion of the inseminating physician, such action is necessary for the

physical health of Mary Beth Whitehead or the child has been determined by said physician to be physiologically abnormal. Mary Beth Whitehead further agrees, upon the request of said physician to undergo amniocentesis (see Exhibit "D") or similar tests to detect genetic and congenital defects. In the event said test reveals that the fetus is genetically or congenitally abnormal, Mary Beth Whitehead, Surrogate, agrees to abort the fetus upon demand of William Stern, Natural Father, in which event, the fee paid to the Surrogate will be in accordance to Paragraph 10. If Mary Beth Whitehead refuses to abort the fetus upon demand of William Stern, his obligations as stated in this Agreement shall cease forthwith, except as to obligations of paternity imposed by statute.

14.   Despite the provisions of Paragraph 13, William Stern, Natural Father, recognizes that some genetic and congenital abnormalities may not be detected by amniocentesis or other tests, and therefore, if proven to be the biological father of the child, assumes the legal responsibility for any child who may possess genetic or congenital abnormalities. (See Exhibits "E" and "F").

15.   Mary Beth Whitehead, Surrogate, further agrees to adhere to all medical instructions given to her by the inseminating physician as well as her independent obstetrician. Mary Beth Whitehead also agrees not to smoke cigarettes, drink alcoholic beverages, use illegal drugs, or take non-prescription medications or prescribed medications without written consent from her physician. Mary Beth Whitehead agrees to follow a prenatal medical examination schedule to consist of no fewer visits than: one visit per month during the first seven (7) months of pregnancy, two visits (each to occur at two-week intervals) during the eighth and ninth months of pregnancy.

Visitation. A visitation plan determined by the New Jersey Superior Court, Bergen County, that Ms. Whitehead Gould is entitled to one eight hour visitation period weekly, with an increase in September 1988 to two days every other week. There is also a provision for visits overnight after a year and for two weeks during summer 1989. *See* 14 Fam.Law Rep. 1276, Apr. 12, 1988.

Some typical procedures. Although the number of children born through the practice is still small, surrogate parenting has caught the attention of the mass media and is thus a subject of wide discussion. Some of its supporters profess considerable ambition and optimism about its future. One entrepreneur interviewed about her surrogate matchmaking service expressed the hope that her company would become "the Coca–Cola of the surrogate parenting industry." Wash. Post, Jan. 25, 1983, at C5, col. 1. While the term "surrogate mother" can refer to a number of different situations, including that in which gestation takes place in a womb other than that of the egg donor, it is widely used today in the United States to describe the woman who conceives a child by heterologous artificial insemination, carries it to term, and then relinquishes it to the sperm donor in accord with a contract executed before the child's conception. Ordinarily the surrogate mother in such a scenario receives a fee or honorarium from the sperm donor, who also pays for all the expenses of the procedure. There can be many variations of such a contract, but they center on a promise that the biological mother will relinquish the child to the biological father immediately after birth, renouncing all rights to the child and consenting to adoption if this is deemed necessary. Other typical provisions include agreements for genetic screening and psychiatric evaluation, cooperation with medical directions during pregnancy, submission to amniocentesis if this is deemed appropriate medically, and abstention from teratogens such as alcohol during pregnancy.

Some intermediaries in the surrogate parenting field prefer to use married women who have borne at least one healthy child. This requires additional contractual provisions to ensure that the surrogate mother's husband will relinquish any legal rights he may have to the child and will submit to testing to confirm that he is not the biological father.

Generally a married sperm donor's wife will not be a contracting party. Indeed it is asserted by some that her nonparticipation is important in order that she can state later in an adoption proceeding that she did not pay for the biological mother's relinquishment of the child for adoption.

Conception the old fashioned way. *In re* Marriage of L.M.S. v. S.L.S., 105 Wis.2d 118, 312 N.W.2d 853 (App.1981), mentioned R.S. v. R.S., dealt with allegations that a husband had agreed to his wife's conceiving a child through sexual intercourse, rather than artificial insemination, with another man. A similar assertion was made in *In re* Adoption of McFadyen, 108 Ill.App.3d 329, 64 Ill.Dec. 43, 438 N.E.2d 1362 (1982), which involved the issue of whether a husband's consent to adoption of his wife's child was necessary. The husband sought to establish that the child was conceived through "surrogate insemination", described in one pleading as "artificial insemination by means of a surrogate donor's penis." The court determined that it need not address the particular issue because the existence of such an agreement between the husband and wife had not been established. Should there be a difference in the result reached in surrogate parent agreements according to whether the child was conceived through artificial insemination or normal intercourse? Does our ability to fix paternity make a difference in the rules that should be applied in the cases?

A surrogate intermediary's duty of care. The Michigan legislature has enacted criminal sanctions for surrogate parentage brokerage. A tort action brought against such an intermediary before such legislation was initially dismissed on summary judgment at the trial level but the United States Court of Appeal reversed the decision and remanded the case for trial. Stiver v. Parker, 975 F.2d 261 (6th Cir.1992). The child born to the surrogate mother was diagnosed with cytomegalic inclusion disease (CID) at birth, was microcephalic and suffers from hearing loss, mental retardation, and severe neuromuscular disorders. It was determined that the father of the child was the surrogate mother's husband. The surrogate mother, who obviously had contracted the disease at the time of conception or early in pregnancy, brought suit against the surrogacy broker, another attorney and certain physicians for damages. The Court of Appeals held that the defendants owed a duty of protection to mother, and that there were jury questions as to negligence and causation.

Johnson v. Calvert

Supreme Court of California, In Bank, 1993.
5 Cal.4th 84, 19 Cal.Rptr.2d 494, 851 P.2d 776.

■ Panelli, Justice.

In this case we address several of the legal questions raised by recent advances in reproductive technology. When, pursuant to a surrogacy agreement, a zygote formed of the gametes of a husband and wife is implanted in the uterus of another woman, who carries the resulting fetus to term and gives birth to a child not genetically related to her, who is the child's "natural mother" under California law? Does a determination that the wife is the child's natural mother work a deprivation of the gestating woman's constitutional rights? And is such an agreement barred by any public policy of this state?

. . .

Mark and Crispina Calvert are a married couple who desired to have a child. Crispina was forced to undergo a hysterectomy in 1984. Her ovaries remained capable of producing eggs, however, and the couple eventually considered surrogacy. In 1989 Anna Johnson heard about Crispina's plight from a coworker and offered to serve as a surrogate for the Calverts.

On January 15, 1990, Mark, Crispina, and Anna signed a contract providing that an embryo created by the sperm of Mark and the egg of Crispina would be implanted in Anna and the child born would be taken into Mark and Crispina's home "as their child." Anna agreed she would relinquish "all parental rights" to the child in favor of Mark and Crispina. In return, Mark and Crispina would pay Anna $10,000 in a series of installments, the last to be paid six weeks after the child's birth. Mark and Crispina were also to pay for a $200,000 life insurance policy on Anna's life.[4]

The zygote was implanted on January 19, 1990. Less than a month later, an ultrasound test confirmed Anna was pregnant.

Unfortunately, relations deteriorated between the two sides. Mark learned that Anna had not disclosed she had suffered several stillbirths and miscarriages. Anna felt Mark and Crispina did not do enough to obtain the required insurance policy. She also felt abandoned during an onset of premature labor in June.

In July 1990, Anna sent Mark and Crispina a letter demanding the balance of the payments due her or else she would refuse to give up the child. The following month, Mark and Crispina responded with a lawsuit,

---

4. At the time of the agreement, Anna already had a daughter, Erica, born in 1987.

seeking a declaration they were the legal parents of the unborn child. Anna filed her own action to be declared the mother of the child, and the two cases were eventually consolidated. The parties agreed to an independent guardian ad litem for the purposes of the suit.

The child was born on September 19, 1990, and blood samples were obtained from both Anna and the child for analysis. The blood test results excluded Anna as the genetic mother. The parties agreed to a court order providing that the child would remain with Mark and Crispina on a temporary basis with visits by Anna.

At trial in October 1990, the parties stipulated that Mark and Crispina were the child's genetic parents. After hearing evidence and arguments, the trial court ruled that Mark and Crispina were the child's "genetic, biological and natural" father and mother, that Anna had no "parental" rights to the child, and that the surrogacy contract was legal and enforceable against Anna's claims. The court also terminated the order allowing visitation. Anna appealed from the trial court's judgment. The Court of Appeal for the Fourth District, Division Three, affirmed. We granted review.

Determining Maternity Under the Uniform Parentage Act

The Uniform Parentage Act (the Act) was part of a package of legislation introduced in 1975 as Senate Bill No. 347. The legislation's purpose was to eliminate the legal distinction between legitimate and illegitimate children. The Act followed in the wake of certain United States Supreme Court decisions mandating equal treatment of legitimate and illegitimate children. . . .

The pertinent portion of Senate Bill No. 347, which passed with negligible opposition, became Part 7 of Division 4 of the California Civil Code, sections 7000–7021.[5]

. . .

Passage of the Act clearly was not motivated by the need to resolve surrogacy disputes, which were virtually unknown in 1975. Yet it facially applies to any parentage determination, including the rare case in which a child's maternity is in issue. We are invited to disregard the Act and decide this case according to other criteria, including constitutional precepts and our sense of the demands of public policy. We feel constrained, however, to decline the invitation. Not uncommonly, courts must construe statutes in factual settings not contemplated by the enacting legislature. . . . We therefore proceed to analyze the parties' contentions within the Act's framework.

These contentions are readily summarized. Anna, of course, predicates her claim of maternity on the fact that she gave birth to the child. The Calverts contend that Crispina's genetic relationship to the child establishes that she is his mother. Counsel for the minor joins in that contention

---

5. Effective January 1, 1994, Civil Code sections 7000–7021 have been repealed and replaced with equivalent provisions in the Family Code. (Stats.1992, ch. 162, § 4; see Fam.Code, §§ 7600–7650 [eff. Jan. 1, 1994].)

and argues, in addition, that several of the presumptions created by the Act dictate the same result. As will appear, we conclude that presentation of blood test evidence is one means of establishing maternity, as is proof of having given birth, but that the presumptions cited by minor's counsel do not apply to this case.

We turn to those few provisions of the Act directly addressing the determination of maternity. "Any interested party," presumably including a genetic mother, "*may* bring an action to determine the existence ... of a mother and child relationship." (Civ.Code, § 7015.) Civil Code section 7003 provides, in relevant part, that between a child and the natural mother a parent and child relationship "may be established by proof of her having given birth to the child, or under [the Act]." (Civ.Code, § 7003, subd. (1), emphasis added.) Apart from Civil Code section 7003, the Act sets forth no specific means by which a natural mother can establish a parent and child relationship. However, it declares that, insofar as practicable, provisions applicable to the father and child relationship apply in an action to determine the existence or nonexistence of a mother and child relationship. (Civ.Code, § 7015.) Thus, it is appropriate to examine those provisions as well.

A man can establish a father and child relationship by the means set forth in Civil Code section 7004. Paternity is presumed under that section if the man meets the conditions set forth in section 621 of the Evidence Code. The latter statute applies, by its terms, when determining the questioned paternity of a child born to a married woman, and contemplates reliance on evidence derived from blood testing. (Evid.Code, § 621, subds. (a), (b);[6] see Evid.Code, §§ 890–897 [Uniform Act on Blood Tests to Determine Paternity].) Alternatively, Civil Code section 7004 creates a presumption of paternity based on the man's conduct toward the child (e.g., receiving the child into his home and openly holding the child out as his natural child) or his marriage or attempted marriage to the child's natural mother under specified conditions.

In our view, the presumptions contained in Civil Code section 7004 do not apply here. They describe situations in which substantial evidence points to a particular man as the natural father of the child. In this case, there is no question as to who is claiming the mother and child relationship, and the factual basis of each woman's claim is obvious. Thus, there is no need to resort to an evidentiary presumption to ascertain the identity of

---

6. Evidence Code section 621 provides in relevant part as follows: "(a) Except as provided in subdivision (b), the issue of a wife cohabiting with her husband, who is not impotent or sterile, is conclusively presumed to be a child of the marriage. [P] (b) Notwithstanding subdivision (a), if the court finds that the conclusions of all the experts, as disclosed by the evidence based upon blood tests performed pursuant to Chapter 2 (commencing with Section 890) of Division 7, are that the husband is not the father of the child, the question of paternity of the husband shall be resolved accordingly." Effective January 1, 1994, Evidence Code sections 621 and 890 through 897 have been repealed and replaced with equivalent provisions of the Family Code. (Stats.1992, ch. 162, §§ 8, 9; see Fam.Code, §§ 7500–7501, 7550–7557 [eff. Jan. 1, 1994].)

the natural mother. Instead, we must make the purely legal determination as between the two claimants.

Significantly for this case, Evidence Code section 892 provides that blood testing may be ordered in an action when paternity is a relevant fact. When maternity is disputed, genetic evidence derived from blood testing is likewise admissible. The Evidence Code further provides that if the court finds the conclusions of all the experts, as disclosed by the evidence based on the blood tests, are that the alleged father is not the father of the child, the question of paternity is resolved accordingly. (Evid.Code, § 895.) By parity of reasoning, blood testing may also be dispositive of the question of maternity. Further, there is a rebuttable presumption of paternity (hence, maternity as well) on the finding of a certain number of genetic markers. (Evid.Code, § 895.5.)

Disregarding the presumptions of paternity that have no application to this case, then, we are left with the undisputed evidence that Anna, not Crispina, gave birth to the child and that Crispina, not Anna, is genetically related to him. Both women thus have adduced evidence of a mother and child relationship as contemplated by the Act. Yet for any child California law recognizes only one natural mother, despite advances in reproductive technology rendering a different outcome biologically possible.[8]

We see no clear legislative preference in Civil Code section 7003 as between blood testing evidence and proof of having given birth.[9] "May" indicates that proof of having given birth is a permitted method of establishing a mother and child relationship, although perhaps not the exclusive one. The disjunctive "or" indicates that blood test evidence, as prescribed in the Act, constitutes an alternative to proof of having given birth. It may be that the language of the Uniform Parentage Act merely reflects "the ancient dictum mater est quam [gestation] demonstrat (by gestation the mother is demonstrated). This phrase, by its use of the word 'demonstrated,' has always reflected an ambiguity in the meaning of the presumption. It is arguable that, while gestation may demonstrate maternal status, it is

8. We decline to accept the contention of amicus curiae the American Civil Liberties Union (ACLU) that we should find the child has two mothers. Even though rising divorce rates have made multiple parent arrangements common in our society, we see no compelling reason to recognize such a situation here. The Calverts are the genetic and intending parents of their son and have provided him, by all accounts, with a stable, intact, and nurturing home. To recognize parental rights in a third party with whom the Calvert family has had little contact since shortly after the child's birth would diminish Crispina's role as mother.

9. The Court of Appeal interpreted Civil Code section 7003, subdivision (1), to mean that only a "natural" mother can establish a mother and child relationship by proof of having given birth, and that a woman must first demonstrate, through blood test evidence, that she is the "natural" mother of the child before her evidence of having given birth can establish that she is the child's natural mother. We disagree with the Court of Appeal's reading of the statute. In our view, the term "natural" as used in subdivision (1) of Civil Code section 7003 simply refers to a mother who is not an adoptive mother. Section 7003 does not purport to answer the question before us, i.e., who is to be deemed the natural mother when the biological functions essential to bringing a child into the world have been allocated between two women.

not the sine qua non of motherhood. Rather, it is possible that the common law viewed genetic consanguinity as the basis for maternal rights. Under this latter interpretation, gestation simply would be irrefutable evidence of the more fundamental genetic relationship." (Hill, What Does It Mean to Be a "Parent"? The Claims of Biology As the Basis for Parental Rights (1991) 66 N.Y.U.L.Rev. 353, 370, fns. omitted.) This ambiguity, highlighted by the problems arising from the use of artificial reproductive techniques, is nowhere explicitly resolved in the Act.

Because two women each have presented acceptable proof of maternity, we do not believe this case can be decided without enquiring into the parties' intentions as manifested in the surrogacy agreement. Mark and Crispina are a couple who desired to have a child of their own genetic stock but are physically unable to do so without the help of reproductive technology. They affirmatively intended the birth of the child, and took the steps necessary to effect in vitro fertilization. But for their acted-on intention, the child would not exist. Anna agreed to facilitate the procreation of Mark's and Crispina's child. The parties' aim was to bring Mark's and Crispina's child into the world, not for Mark and Crispina to donate a zygote to Anna. Crispina from the outset intended to be the child's mother. Although the gestative function Anna performed was necessary to bring about the child's birth, it is safe to say that Anna would not have been given the opportunity to gestate or deliver the child had she, prior to implantation of the zygote, manifested her own intent to be the child's mother. No reason appears why Anna's later change of heart should vitiate the determination that Crispina is the child's natural mother.

We conclude that although the Act recognizes both genetic consanguinity and giving birth as means of establishing a mother and child relationship, when the two means do not coincide in one woman, she who intended to procreate the child—that is, she who intended to bring about the birth of a child that she intended to raise as her own—is the natural mother under California law.[10]

. . .

---

10. Thus, under our analysis, in a true "egg donation" situation, where a woman gestates and gives birth to a child formed from the egg of another woman with the intent to raise the child as her own, the birth mother is the natural mother under California law. The dissent would decide parentage based on the best interests of the child. Such an approach raises the repugnant specter of governmental interference in matters implicating our most fundamental notions of privacy, and confuses concepts of parentage and custody. Logically, the determination of parentage must precede, and should not be dictated by, eventual custody decisions. The implicit assumption of the dissent is that a recognition of the genetic intending mother as the natural mother may sometimes harm the child. This assumption overlooks California's dependency laws, which are designed to protect all children irrespective of the manner of birth or conception. Moreover, the best interest standard poorly serves the child in the present situation: it fosters instability during litigation and, if applied to recognize the gestator as natural mother, results in a split of custody between the natural father and the gestator, an outcome not likely to benefit the child. Further, it may be argued that, by voluntarily contracting away any rights to the child, the gestator has, in effect, conceded the best interest of the child is not with her.

In deciding the issue of maternity under the Act we have felt free to take into account the parties' intentions, as expressed in the surrogacy contract, because in our view the agreement is not, on its face, inconsistent with public policy.

Preliminarily, Mark and Crispina urge us to interpret the Legislature's 1992 passage of a bill that would have regulated surrogacy as an expression of this state's public policy despite the fact that Governor Wilson's veto prevented the bill from becoming law. Senate Bill No. 937 contained a finding that surrogate contracts are not against sound public and social policy. Had Senate Bill No. 937 become law, there would be no room for argument to the contrary. The veto, however, raises a question whether the legislative declaration truly expresses California's public policy.

In the Governor's veto message we find not unequivocal agreement with the Legislature's public policy assessment, but rather reservations about the practice of surrogate parenting. "Surrogacy is a relatively recent phenomenon. The full moral and psychological dimensions of this practice are not yet clear. In fact, they are just beginning to emerge. Only two published court opinions in California have treated this nettlesome subject.... Comprehensive regulation of this difficult moral issue is premature.... To the extent surrogacy continues to be practical, it can be governed by the legal framework already established in the family law area." (Governor's veto message to Sen. on Sen. Bill No. 937 (Sept. 26, 1992) Sen. Daily File (1991–1992 Reg.Sess.) p. 68.) Given this less than ringing endorsement of surrogate parenting, we conclude that the passage of Senate Bill No. 937, in and of itself, does not establish that surrogacy contracts are consistent with public policy. (Of course, neither do we draw the opposite conclusion from the fact of the Governor's veto.)

Anna urges that surrogacy contracts violate several social policies. Relying on her contention that she is the child's legal, natural mother, she cites the public policy embodied in Penal Code section 273, prohibiting the payment for consent to adoption of a child. She argues further that the policies underlying the adoption laws of this state are violated by the surrogacy contract because it in effect constitutes a prebirth waiver of her parental rights.

We disagree. Gestational surrogacy differs in crucial respects from adoption and so is not subject to the adoption statutes. The parties voluntarily agreed to participate in in vitro fertilization and related medical procedures before the child was conceived; at the time when Anna entered into the contract, therefore, she was not vulnerable to financial inducements to part with her own expected offspring. As discussed above, Anna was not the genetic mother of the child. The payments to Anna under the contract were meant to compensate her for her services in gestating the fetus and undergoing labor, rather than for giving up "parental" rights to the child. Payments were due both during the pregnancy and after the child's birth. We are, accordingly, unpersuaded that the contract used in this case violates the public policies embodied in Penal Code section 273 and the adoption statutes. For the same reasons, we conclude these contracts do not implicate the policies underlying the statutes governing termination of parental rights.

It has been suggested that gestational surrogacy may run afoul of prohibitions on involuntary servitude. We see no potential for that evil in the contract at issue here, and extrinsic evidence of coercion or duress is utterly lacking. We note that although at one point the contract purports to give Mark and Crispina the sole right to determine whether to abort the pregnancy, at another point it acknowledges: "All parties understand that a pregnant woman has the absolute right to abort or not abort any fetus she is carrying. Any promise to the contrary is unenforceable." We therefore need not determine the validity of a surrogacy contract purporting to deprive the gestator of her freedom to terminate the pregnancy.

Finally, Anna and some commentators have expressed concern that surrogacy contracts tend to exploit or dehumanize women, especially women of lower economic status. Anna's objections center around the psychological harm she asserts may result from the gestator's relinquishing the child to whom she has given birth. Some have also cautioned that the practice of surrogacy may encourage society to view children as commodities, subject to trade at their parents' will.

We are all too aware that the proper forum for resolution of this issue is the Legislature, where empirical data, largely lacking from this record, can be studied and rules of general applicability developed. However, in light of our responsibility to decide this case, we have considered as best we can its possible consequences.

We are unpersuaded that gestational surrogacy arrangements are so likely to cause the untoward results Anna cites as to demand their invalidation on public policy grounds. Although common sense suggests that women of lesser means serve as surrogate mothers more often than do wealthy women, there has been no proof that surrogacy contracts exploit poor women to any greater degree than economic necessity in general exploits them by inducing them to accept lower-paid or otherwise undesirable employment. We are likewise unpersuaded by the claim that surrogacy will foster the attitude that children are mere commodities; no evidence is offered to support it. The limited data available seem to reflect an absence of significant adverse effects of surrogacy on all participants.

The argument that a woman cannot knowingly and intelligently agree to gestate and deliver a baby for intending parents carries overtones of the reasoning that for centuries prevented women from attaining equal economic rights and professional status under the law. To resurrect this view is both to foreclose a personal and economic choice on the part of the surrogate mother, and to deny intending parents what may be their only means of procreating a child of their own genetic stock. Certainly in the present case it cannot seriously be argued that Anna, a licensed vocational nurse who had done well in school and who had previously borne a child, lacked the intellectual wherewithal or life experience necessary to make an informed decision to enter into the surrogacy contract.

Constitutionality of the Determination That Anna Johnson Is Not the Natural Mother

. . .

First, we note the constitutional rights that are not implicated here.

There is no issue of procedural due process: although Anna broadly contends that the procedures prescribed for adoptions should be followed in the situation of a gestational surrogate's relinquishment to the genetic parents of the child she has carried and delivered, she cites no specific deficiency in the notice or hearing this matter received.

Furthermore, neither Anna nor amicus curiae ACLU articulates a claim under the equal protection clause, and we are unable to discern in these facts the necessary predicate to its operation. This is because a woman who voluntarily agrees to gestate and deliver to a married couple a child who is their genetic offspring is situated differently from the wife who provides the ovum for fertilization, intending to mother the resulting child.

Anna relies mainly on theories of substantive due process, privacy, and procreative freedom, citing a number of decisions recognizing the fundamental liberty interest of natural parents in the custody and care of their children. Most of the cases Anna cites deal with the rights of unwed fathers in the face of attempts to terminate their parental relationship to their children. These cases do not support recognition of parental rights for a gestational surrogate. Although Anna quotes language stressing the primacy of a developed parent-child relationship in assessing unwed fathers' rights, certain language in the cases reinforces the importance of genetic parents' rights. (Lehr v. Robertson, 463 U.S. at p. 262, 103 S.Ct. at p. 2993 ["The significance of the biological connection is that it offers the natural father an opportunity that no other male possesses to develop a relationship with his offspring. If he grasps that opportunity and accepts some measure of responsibility for the child's future, he may enjoy the blessings of the parent-child relationship and make uniquely valuable contributions to the child's development."]; see also Adoption of Kelsey S. (1992) 1 Cal.4th 816, 838, 4 Cal.Rptr.2d 615, 823 P.21216 ["The biological connection between father and child is unique and worthy of constitutional protection if the father grasps the opportunity to develop that biological connection into a full and enduring relationship."].)

Anna's argument depends on a prior determination that she is indeed the child's mother. Since Crispina is the child's mother under California law because she, not Anna, provided the ovum for the in vitro fertilization procedure, intending to raise the child as her own, it follows that any constitutional interests Anna possesses in this situation are something less than those of a mother. As counsel for the minor points out, the issue in this case is not whether Anna's asserted rights as a natural mother were unconstitutionally violated, but rather whether the determination that she is not the legal natural mother at all is constitutional.[11]

---

11. The trial court analogized Anna's relationship with the child to that of a foster mother, whose liberty interest, if any, in her relationship with the foster child is surely

Anna relies principally on the decision of the United States Supreme Court in Michael H. v. Gerald D. (1989) 491 U.S. 110, 109 S.Ct. 2333, 105 L.Ed.2d 91, to support her claim to a constitutionally protected liberty interest in the companionship of the child, based on her status as "birth mother." In that case, a plurality of the court held that a state may constitutionally deny a man parental rights with respect to a child he fathered during a liaison with the wife of another man, since it is the marital family that traditionally has been accorded a protected liberty interest, as reflected in the historic presumption of legitimacy of a child born into such a family. (491 U.S. at pp. 124–125, 109 S.Ct. at pp. 2342–2343 (plur. opn. by Scalia, J.).) The reasoning of the plurality in Michael H. does not assist Anna. Society has not traditionally protected the right of a woman who gestates and delivers a baby pursuant to an agreement with a couple who supply the zygote from which the baby develops and who intend to raise the child as their own; such arrangements are of too recent an origin to claim the protection of tradition. To the extent that tradition has a bearing on the present case, we believe it supports the claim of the couple who exercise their right to procreate in order to form a family of their own, albeit through novel medical procedures.

Moreover, if we were to conclude that Anna enjoys some sort of liberty interest in the companionship of the child, then the liberty interests of Mark and Crispina, the child's natural parents, in their procreative choices and their relationship with the child would perforce be infringed. Any parental rights Anna might successfully assert could come only at Crispina's expense. As we have seen, Anna has no parental rights to the child under California law, and she fails to persuade us that sufficiently strong policy reasons exist to accord her a protected liberty interest in the companionship of the child when such an interest would necessarily detract from or impair the parental bond enjoyed by Mark and Crispina.

Amicus curiae ACLU urges that Anna's right of privacy, embodied in the California Constitution (Cal. Const., art. I, § 1), requires recognition and protection of her status as "birth mother." We cannot agree. Certainly it is true that our state Constitution has been construed to provide California citizens with privacy protections encompassing procreative decisionmaking—broader, indeed, than those recognized by the federal Constitution.... However, amicus curiae fails to articulate persuasively how Anna's claim falls within even the broad parameters of the state right of privacy. Amicus curiae appears to assume that the choice to gestate and deliver a baby to its genetic parents pursuant to a surrogacy agreement is the equivalent, in constitutional weight, of the decision whether to bear a child of one's own. We disagree. A woman who enters into a gestational surrogacy arrangement is not exercising her own right to make procreative choices; she is agreeing to provide a necessary and profoundly important

---

more attenuated than that of the natural parents with the child. (See Smith v. Organization of Foster Families, supra, 431 U.S. at pp. 845–847, 97 S.Ct. at pp. 2110–2111 [declining to define the constitutional contours of the foster relationship].)

service without (by definition) any expectation that she will raise the resulting child as her own.

Drawing an analogy to artificial insemination, Anna argues that Mark and Crispina were mere genetic donors who are entitled to no constitutional protection. That characterization of the facts is, however, inaccurate. Mark and Crispina never intended to "donate" genetic material to anyone. Rather, they intended to procreate a child genetically related to them by the only available means. Civil Code section 7005, governing artificial insemination, has no application here.

Finally, Anna argues that the Act's failure to address novel reproductive techniques such as in vitro fertilization indicates legislative disapproval of such practices. Given that the Act was drafted long before such techniques were developed, we cannot agree. Moreover, we may not arrogate to ourselves the power to disapprove them. It is not the role of the judiciary to inhibit the use of reproductive technology when the Legislature has not seen fit to do so; any such effort would raise serious questions in light of the fundamental nature of the rights of procreation and privacy. Rather, our task has been to resolve the dispute before us, interpreting the Act's use of the term "natural mother" (Civ.Code, § 7003, subd. (1)) when the biological functions essential to bringing a child into the world have been allocated between two women.

[The separate, concurring opinion of ARABIAN, JUSTICE, is omitted.]

■ KENNARD, JUSTICE, dissenting.

When a woman who wants to have a child provides her fertilized ovum to another woman who carries it through pregnancy and gives birth to a child, who is the child's legal mother? Unlike the majority, I do not agree that the determinative consideration should be the intent to have the child that originated with the woman who contributed the ovum. In my view, the woman who provided the fertilized ovum and the woman who gave birth to the child both have substantial claims to legal motherhood. Pregnancy entails a unique commitment, both psychological and emotional, to an unborn child. No less substantial, however, is the contribution of the woman from whose egg the child developed and without whose desire the child would not exist.

For each child, California law accords the legal rights and responsibilities of parenthood to only one "natural mother." When, as here, the female reproductive role is divided between two women, California law requires courts to make a decision as to which woman is the child's natural mother, but provides no standards by which to make that decision. The majority's resort to "intent" to break the "tie" between the genetic and gestational mothers is unsupported by statute, and in the absence of appropriate protections in the law to guard against abuse of surrogacy arrangements, it is ill-advised. To determine who is the legal mother of a child born of a gestational surrogacy arrangement, I would apply the standard most protective of child welfare—the best interests of the child.

[Omitted sections of the opinion trace the factual background of the case, analyze the policy considerations, and discuss provisions of legislative models such as the Uniform Status of Children of Assisted Conception Act.]

VII. ANALYSIS OF THE MAJORITY'S "INTENT" TEST

Faced with the failure of current statutory law to adequately address the issue of who is a child's natural mother when two women qualify under the UPA, the majority breaks the "tie" by resort to a criterion not found in the UPA—the "intent" of the genetic mother to be the child's mother.

... [I]n making the intent of the genetic mother who wants to have a child the dispositive factor, the majority renders a certain result preordained and inflexible in every such case: as between an intending genetic mother and a gestational mother, the genetic mother will, under the majority's analysis, always prevail. The majority recognizes no meaningful contribution by a woman who agrees to carry a fetus to term for the genetic mother beyond that of mere employment to perform a specified biological function.

The majority's approach entirely devalues the substantial claims of motherhood by a gestational mother such as Anna. True, a woman who enters into a surrogacy arrangement intending to raise the child has by her intent manifested an assumption of parental responsibility in addition to her biological contribution of providing the genetic material. (See Adoption of Kelsey S., supra, 1 Cal.4th at pp. 838, 849, 4 Cal.Rptr.2d 615, 823 P.2d 1216.) But the gestational mother's biological contribution of carrying a child for nine months and giving birth is likewise an assumption of parental responsibility. (See Dolgin, Just a Gene: Judicial Assumptions About Parenthood (1993) 40 UCLA L.Rev. 637, 659.) A pregnant woman's commitment to the unborn child she carries is not just physical; it is psychological and emotional as well. The United States Supreme Court made a closely related point in Lehr v. Robertson (1983) 463 U.S. 248, 103 S.Ct. 2985, 77 L.Ed.2d 614, explaining that a father's assertion of parental rights depended on his having assumed responsibility for the child after its birth, whereas a mother's "parental relationship is clear" because she "carries and bears the child." (Id. at p. 260, fn. 16, 103 S.Ct. at p. 2992, fn. 16, quoting Caban v. Mohammed (1979) 441 U.S. 380, 397, 99 S.Ct. 1760, 1770, 60 L.Ed.2d 297 (dis. opn. of Stewart, J.).)[3] This court too has

---

3. In my view, the United States Supreme Court's decision in Lehr v. Robertson, 463 U.S. 248, 103 S.Ct. 2985, does not, despite the language I have just quoted, compel a conclusion that either the gestational mother or the genetic mother in a gestational surrogacy arrangement has, at the birth of the child, a fully vested and matured constitutional right to be a parent. Rather, I read the quoted language as indicating that the high court considers that a woman who conceives by traditional means and carries a fetus to term is a parent, and that a critical indicator of parenting status for a woman is gestation. Gestation is neither necessary nor sufficient to establish motherhood; it is, however, a factor the significance of which cannot be ignored, as the majority in effect does. This reading of Lehr v. Robertson seems consistent with the plurality opinion in Michael H. v. Gerald D., 491 U.S. 110, 123, 109 S.Ct. 2333, 2342, 105 L.Ed.2d 91, holding that a claim to fatherhood premised on biology plus "an established parental relationship" did

acknowledged that a pregnant woman and her unborn child comprise a "unique physical unit" and that the welfare of each is "intertwined and inseparable." (Burgess v. Superior Court (1992) 2 Cal.4th 1064, 1080, 9 Cal.Rptr.2d 615, 831 P.2d 1197.) Indeed, a fetus would never develop into a living child absent its nurturing by the pregnant woman. A pregnant woman intending to bring a child into the world is more than a mere container or breeding animal; she is a conscious agent of creation no less than the genetic mother, and her humanity is implicated on a deep level. Her role should not be devalued.

To summarize, the woman who carried the fetus to term and brought a child into the world has, like the genetic mother, a substantial claim to be the natural mother of the child. The gestational mother has made an indispensable and unique biological contribution, and has also gone beyond biology in an intangible respect that, though difficult to label, cannot be denied. Accordingly, I cannot agree with the majority's devaluation of the role of the gestational mother.

VIII. THE BEST INTERESTS OF THE CHILD

As I have discussed, in California the existing statutory law applicable to this case is the UPA, which was never designed to govern the new reproductive technology of gestational surrogacy. Under the UPA, both the genetic mother and the gestational mother have equal rights to be the child's natural mother. But the UPA allows one natural mother for each child, and thus this court is required to make a choice. To break this "tie" between the genetic mother and the gestational mother, the majority uses the legal concept of intent. In so doing, the majority has articulated a rationale for using the concept of intent that is grounded in principles of tort, intellectual property and commercial contract law.

But, as I have pointed out, we are not deciding a case involving the commission of a tort, the ownership of intellectual property, or the delivery of goods under a commercial contract; we are deciding the fate of a child. In the absence of legislation that is designed to address the unique problems of gestational surrogacy, this court should look not to tort, property or contract law, but to family law, as the governing paradigm and source of a rule of decision.

The allocation of parental rights and responsibilities necessarily impacts the welfare of a minor child. And in issues of child welfare, the standard that courts frequently apply is the best interests of the child. Indeed it is highly significant that the UPA itself looks to a child's best interests in deciding another question of parental rights. This "best interests" standard serves to assure that in the judicial resolution of disputes affecting a child's well-being, protection of the minor child is the foremost consideration. Consequently, I would apply "the best interests of the child" standard to determine who can best assume the social and legal responsibil-

not necessarily warrant constitutional protection. The court's precedents are, however, not entirely clear as to what will establish motherhood in a gestational surrogacy case, undoubtedly because the court has never dealt with such a case.

ities of motherhood for a child born of a gestational surrogacy arrangement.

The determination of a child's best interests does not depend on the parties' relative economic circumstances, which in a gestational surrogacy situation will usually favor the genetic mother and her spouse. (See Matter of Baby M., supra, 537 A.2d at p. 1249.) As this court has recognized, however, superior wealth does not necessarily equate with good parenting. (See Burchard v. Garay (1986) 42 Cal.3d 531, 540, 229 Cal.Rptr. 800, 724 P.2d 486.)

Factors that are pertinent to good parenting, and thus that are in a child's best interests, include the ability to nurture the child physically and psychologically (Cahill, The Ethics of Surrogate Motherhood: Biology, Freedom, and Moral Obligation, in Surrogate Motherhood, supra, at p. 160), and to provide ethical and intellectual guidance (see In re Marriage of Carney (1979) 24 Cal.3d 725, 739, 157 Cal.Rptr. 383, 598 P.2d 36). Also crucial to a child's best interests is the "well recognized right" of every child "to stability and continuity." (Burchard v. Garay, supra, 42 Cal.3d at p. 546, 229 Cal.Rptr. 800, 724 P.2d 486 (conc. opn. of Mosk, J.).) The intent of the genetic mother to procreate a child is certainly relevant to the question of the child's best interests; alone, however, it should not be dispositive.

Here, the child born of the gestational surrogacy arrangement between Anna Johnson and Mark and Crispina Calvert has lived continuously with Mark and Crispina since his birth in September 1990. The trial court awarded parental rights to Mark and Crispina, concluding that as a matter of law they were the child's "genetic, biological and natural" parents.[5] In reaching that conclusion, the trial court did not treat Anna's statutory claim to be the child's legal mother as equal to Crispina's, nor did the trial court consider the child's best interests in deciding between those two equal statutory claims. Accordingly, I would remand the matter to the trial court to undertake that evaluation.

CONCLUSION

Recent advances in medical technology have made it possible for the human female reproductive role to be divided between two women, the genetic mother and the gestational mother. Such gestational surrogacy arrangements call for sensitivity to each of the adult participants. But the paramount concern must be the well-being of the child that gestational surrogacy has made possible.

The model legislation proposed by the National Conference of Commissioners on Uniform Laws would protect such children's well-being by precisely defining their parentage. Such precision is not possible using a "best interests of the child" standard, which requires a case-by-case evaluation after the birth of the child. But that evaluation would afford many protections similar to those set out in USCACA, such as judicial oversight,

---

5. It is uncontested that Mark is the natural father of this child.

legal counsel, and an opportunity for the court to determine who best can provide for the child.

I recognize that, for couples such as Mark and Crispina, gestational surrogacy offers the only hope of raising a child who is genetically related to both. But the desire for a genetically related child does not diminish the substantial concerns expressed by a broad spectrum of commentators that surrogacy left unregulated poses a fundamental threat to the well-being of women and children. This threat could largely be allayed by legislation permitting gestational surrogacy, but under court supervision and with the type of procedural requirements proposed in the USCACA that serve to protect all of those affected by a gestational surrogacy arrangement, particularly the child. In my view, the Legislature should turn its attention to the complex issues posed by gestational surrogacy.

In this opinion, I do not purport to offer a perfect solution to the difficult questions posed by gestational surrogacy; perhaps there can be no perfect solution. But in the absence of legislation specifically designed to address the complex issues of gestational surrogacy and to protect against potential abuses, I cannot join the majority's uncritical validation of gestational surrogacy.

I would reverse the judgment of the Court of Appeal, and remand the case to the trial court for a determination of disputed parentage on the basis of the best interests of the child.

Buzzanca v. Buzzanca

Court of Appeal, Fourth District, Division 3, California, 1998.
61 Cal.App.4th 1410, 72 Cal.Rptr.2d 280.

■ SILLS, PRESIDING JUSTICE.

Jaycee was born because Luanne and John Buzzanca agreed to have an embryo genetically unrelated to either of them implanted in a woman—a surrogate—who would carry and give birth to the child for them. After the fertilization, implantation and pregnancy, Luanne and John split up, and the question of who are Jaycee's lawful parents came before the trial court.

Luanne claimed that she and her erstwhile husband were the lawful parents, but John disclaimed any responsibility, financial or otherwise. The woman who gave birth also appeared in the case to make it clear that she made no claim to the child.

The trial court then reached an extraordinary conclusion: Jaycee had *no* lawful parents. First, the woman who gave birth to Jaycee was not the mother; the court had—astonishingly—already accepted a stipulation that neither she nor her husband were the "biological" parents. Second, Luanne was not the mother. According to the trial court, she could not be the mother because she had neither contributed the egg nor given birth. And John could not be the father, because, not having contributed the sperm, he had no biological relationship with the child.

We disagree. Let us get right to the point: Jaycee never would have been born had not Luanne and John both agreed to have a fertilized egg implanted in a surrogate.

The trial judge erred because he assumed that legal motherhood, under the relevant California statutes, could *only* be established in one of two ways, either by giving birth or by contributing an egg. He failed to consider the substantial and well-settled body of law holding that there are times when *fatherhood* can be established by conduct apart from giving birth or being genetically related to a child. The typical example is when an infertile husband consents to allowing his wife to be artificially inseminated. As our Supreme Court noted in such a situation over 30 years ago, the husband is the "lawful father" because he *consented* to the procreation of the child. (See *People v. Sorensen* (1968) 68 Cal.2d 280, 284–286, 66 Cal.Rptr. 7, 437 P.2d 495.)

The same rule which makes a husband the lawful father of a child born because of his consent to artificial insemination should be applied here—by the same parity of reasoning that guided our Supreme Court in the first surrogacy case, *Johnson v. Calvert* (1993) 5 Cal.4th 84, 19 Cal.Rptr.2d 494, 851 P.2d 776—to both husband and wife. Just as a husband is deemed to be the lawful father of a child unrelated to him when his wife gives birth after artificial insemination, so should a husband *and* wife be deemed the lawful parents of a child after a surrogate bears a biologically unrelated child on their behalf. In each instance, a child is procreated because a medical procedure was initiated and consented to by intended parents. The only difference is that in this case—unlike artificial insemination—there is no reason to distinguish between husband and wife. We therefore must reverse the trial court's judgment and direct that a new judgment be entered, declaring that both Luanne and John are the lawful parents of Jaycee.[1]

John filed his petition for dissolution of marriage on March 30, 1995, alleging there were no children of the marriage. Luanne filed her response on April 20, alleging that the parties were expecting a child by way of surrogate contract. Jaycee was born six days later. In September 1996 Luanne filed a separate petition to establish herself as Jaycee's mother. Her action was consolidated into the dissolution case. In February 1997, the court accepted a stipulation that the woman who agreed to carry the child, and her husband, were not the "biological parents" of the child.[2] At a

---

1. ... When we refer to artificial insemination in this opinion we are only referring to the heterologous variety.

2. John's attorney was present at the hearing when the court accepted the stipulation that the surrogate was not the "biological" parent of Jaycee. He made no objection. Yet in the respondent's brief on appeal and in oral argument, he has argued that the surrogate is the lawful mother of Jaycee by virtue of the biological connection of having given birth.

One reaction to this inconsistency might be to hold, simply, that John is barred from arguing the point that the surrogate is the lawful mother because he did not object to the surrogate being let off the hook when he had the chance at the trial level. We reject that course of analysis because in this case of first impression it would be an intellectual cheat. Particularly in matters regarding children and parental responsibilities, courts must be wary of allowing lawyers from trying to cleverly (or inadvertently) maneuver a case into a posture where the court's decision does not reflect the underlying legal reality.

hearing held in March, based entirely on oral argument and offers of proof, the trial court determined that Luanne was not the lawful mother of the child and therefore John could not be the lawful father or owe any support.

The trial judge said: "So I think what evidence there is, is stipulated to. And I don't think there would be any more. One, there's no genetic tie between Luanne and the child. Two, she is not the gestational mother. Three, she has not adopted the child. That, folks, to me, respectfully, is clear and convincing evidence that she's not the legal mother."

After another hearing on May 7, regarding attorney fees, a judgment on reserved issues in the dissolution was filed, terminating John's obligation to pay child support, declaring that Luanne was not the legal mother of Jaycee, and declining "to apply any estoppel proposition to the issue of John's responsibility for child support." Luanne then filed a petition for a writ of supersedeas to stay the judgment; she also filed an appeal from it. This court then granted a stay which had the effect of keeping the support order alive for Jaycee. We also consolidated the writ proceeding with the appeal.

In his respondent's brief in this appeal, John tries to intimate—though he stops short of actually saying it—that Jaycee was not born as a result of a surrogacy agreement with his ex-wife. He points to the fact that the actual written surrogacy agreement was signed on August 25, 1994, but the implantation took place a little less than two weeks before, on August 13, 1994. The brief states: "At the time that the implantation took place, no surrogacy contract had been executed by the parties to this action."

Concerned with the implication made in John's respondent's brief, members of this court questioned John's attorney at oral argument about it. It turned out that the intimation in John's brief was a red herring, based merely on the fact that John did not sign a *written* contract until after implantation. Jaycee was nonetheless born as a result of a surrogacy agreement on the part of both Luanne *and* John; it was just that the agreement was an *oral* one prior to implantation. The written surrogacy agreement, John's attorney acknowledged in open court, was the written memorialization of that oral contract.

Members of this panel also pressed John's attorney to state whatever factually based defenses John might have offered if the case had actually been tried. John's attorney had not specifically stated such defenses at the hearing in March 1996; he had only vaguely indicated that "the facts as testified to would be somewhat different than" those which the trial court had "assumed."

Again, there was less than was intimated. John's signature on the written surrogacy agreement was not forged, or anything of the sort. His one trump card, finessed out only after repeated questioning and the importuning of one of our panel to articulate his "best facts," was this: John would offer testimony to the effect that Luanne told him that she would assume all responsibility for the care of any child born. Luanne alone would assume "the burdens of childrearing."

Therefore, even though there was no actual trial in front of the trial court on the matter, this appellate court will assume arguendo that if there had been a trial the judge would have believed John's evidence on the point and concluded that Luanne had indeed promised not to hold John responsible for the child contemplated by their oral surrogacy agreement.

DISCUSSION

The Statute Governing Artificial Insemination Which Makes a Husband the Lawful Father of a Child Unrelated to Him Applies to Both Intended Parents In This Case

Perhaps recognizing the inherent lack of appeal for any result which makes Jaycee a legal orphan, John now contends that the surrogate is Jaycee's legal mother; and further, by virtue of that fact, the surrogate's husband is the legal father. His reasoning goes like this: Under the Uniform Parentage Act (the Act), and particularly as set forth in section 7610 of California's Family Code, there are only two ways by which a woman can establish legal motherhood, i.e., giving birth or contributing genetically. Because the genetic contributors are not known to the court, the only candidate left is the surrogate who must therefore be deemed the lawful mother. And, as John's counsel commented at oral argument, if the surrogate and her husband cannot support Jaycee, the burden should fall on the taxpayers.

The law doesn't say what John says it says. It doesn't say: "The legal relationship between mother and child shall be established only by either proof of her giving birth or by genetics." The statute says "may," not "shall," and "under this part," *not* "by genetics." Here is the complete text of section 7610: "The parent and child relationship may be established as follows: [§] (a) Between a child and the natural mother, it may be established by proof of her having given birth to the child, or under this part. [§] (b) Between a child and the natural father, it may be established under this part. [§] (c) Between a child and an adoptive parent, it may be established by proof of adoption."

The statute thus contains no direct reference to genetics (i.e., blood tests) at all. The *Johnson* decision teaches us that genetics is simply *subsumed* in the words "under this part." In that case, the court held that genetic consanguinity was equally "acceptable" as "proof of maternity" as evidence of giving birth. (*Johnson v. Calvert, supra,* 5 Cal.4th at p. 93, 19 Cal.Rptr.2d 494, 851 P.2d 776.)

It is important to realize, however, that in construing the words "under this part" to include genetic testing, the high court in *Johnson* relied on several statutes in the Evidence Code (former Evid.Code, §§ 892, 895, and 895.5) all of which, by their terms, only applied to *paternity.* (See *Johnson v. Calvert, supra,* 5 Cal.4th at pp. 90–92, 19 Cal.Rptr.2d 494, 851 P.2d 776.) It was only by a "parity of reasoning" that our high court concluded those statutes which, on their face applied only to men, were also "dispositive of the question of maternity." (5 Cal.4th at p. 92, 19 Cal. Rptr.2d 494, 851 P.2d 776.)

The point bears reiterating: It was only by a parity of reasoning from statutes which, on their face, referred only to *paternity* that the court in *Johnson v. Calvert* reached the result it did on the question of *maternity*. Had the *Johnson* court reasoned as John now urges us to reason—by narrowly confining the means under the Uniform Parentage Act by which a woman could establish that she was the lawful mother of a child to texts which on their face applied only to motherhood (as distinct from father-hood)—the court would have reached the opposite result.[5]

In addition to blood tests there are several other ways the Act allows paternity to be established. Those ways are not necessarily related at all to any biological tie. Thus, under the Act, paternity may be established by:

—marrying, remaining married to, or attempting to marry the child's mother when she gives birth (see § 7611, subds. (a) & (b));

—marrying the child's mother after the child's birth and either con-senting to being named as the father on the birth certificate (§ 7611, subd. (c)(1)) or making a written promise to support the child (see § 7611, subd. (c)(2)).

A man may also be deemed a father under the Act in the case of artificial insemination of his wife, as provided by section 7613 of the Family Code.[6] To track the words of the statute: "If, under the supervision of a

---

5. In *In re Marriage of Moschetta* (1994) 25 Cal.App.4th 1218, 1224–1226, 30 Cal.Rptr.2d 893, the court refused to apply certain *presumptions* regarding paternity found in the Act to overcome the claim of a woman who was both the genetic and birth mother. Relying on *In re Zacharia D.* (1993) 6 Cal.4th 435, 24 Cal.Rptr.2d 751, 862 P.2d 751, we observed that there may be times when the Act cannot be applied in a gender interchangeable manner. (See *Moschetta, su-pra,* 25 Cal.App.4th at p. 1225, fn. 8, 30 Cal.Rptr.2d 893.)

It made sense in *Moschetta* not to apply the paternity statutes cited by the father to the biologically unrelated intended mother because those statutes merely embody pre-sumptions. The statutes were: (1) the pre-sumption that a child of a wife cohabiting with her husband at the time of birth is conclusively presumed to be a child of the marriage unless the husband is impotent or sterile (see Fam.Code, § 7540), and (2) the presumption that a man is the natural father if he receives the child into his home and openly holds out the child as his own (Fam.

Code, § 7611, subd. (d)). We rejected applica-tion of these presumptions because, even as-suming they could be applied to a woman, they were only presumptions and, just like a paternity case, could be overcome by blood tests showing an actual genetic relationship. (*Moschetta, supra,* 25 Cal.App.4th at pp. 1225–1226, 30 Cal.Rptr.2d 893.) Most funda-mentally, as we pointed out on page 1226, 30 Cal.Rptr.2d 893 of the opinion, the presump-tions were inapposite because they arose out of the "old law of illegitimacy" and were designed as evidentiary devices to make a determination of a child's biological father.

Moschetta thus cannot be read for the proposition that statutes which are part of the Act and refer to an individual of one sex can never be applied to an individual of an-other. For one reason, *Moschetta* never said that. For another, such a broad proposition would contradict the rationale used by a higher court in *Johnson*.

6. California Family Code section 7613 is California's enactment of the artificial in-semination provision of section 5 of the Uni-form Parentage Act.

licensed physician and surgeon and with the consent of her husband, a wife is inseminated artificially with semen donated by a man not her husband, the husband is treated in law as if he were the natural father of a child thereby conceived."[7]

As noted in *Johnson,* "courts must construe statutes in factual settings not contemplated by the enacting legislature." (*Johnson v. Calvert, supra,* 5 Cal.4th at p. 89, 19 Cal.Rptr.2d 494, 851 P.2d 776.) So it is, of course, true that application of the artificial insemination statute to a gestational surrogacy case where the genetic donors are unknown to the court may not have been contemplated by the legislature. Even so, the two kinds of artificial reproduction are *exactly* analogous in this crucial respect: Both contemplate the procreation of a child by the consent to a medical procedure of someone who intends to raise the child but who otherwise does not have any biological tie.

If a husband who consents to artificial insemination under section 7613 is "treated in law" as the father of the child by virtue of his consent, there is no reason the result should be any different in the case of a married couple who consent to in vitro fertilization by unknown donors and subsequent implantation into a woman who is, as a surrogate, willing to carry the embryo to term for them. The statute is, after all, the clearest expression of past legislative intent when the legislature did contemplate a situation where a person who caused a child to come into being had no biological relationship to the child.

Indeed, the establishment of fatherhood and the consequent duty to support when a husband consents to the artificial insemination of his wife is one of the well-established rules in family law. The leading case in the country (so described by a New York family court in *Adoption of Anonymous* (1973) 74 Misc.2d 99, 345 N.Y.S.2d 430, 433) is *People v. Sorensen, supra,* 68 Cal.2d 280, 66 Cal.Rptr. 7, 437 P.2d 495, in which our Supreme Court held that a man could even be *criminally* liable for failing to pay for

---

7. The entire statute reads as follows: "If, under the supervision of a licensed physician and surgeon and with the consent of her husband, a wife is inseminated artificially with semen donated by a man not her husband, the husband is treated in law as if he were the natural father of a child thereby conceived. The husband's consent must be in writing and signed by him and his wife. The physician and surgeon shall certify their signatures and the date of the insemination, and retain the husband's consent as part of the medical record, where it shall be kept confidential and in a sealed file. However, the physician and surgeon's failure to do so does not affect the father and child relationship. All papers and records pertaining to the insemination, whether part of the permanent record of a court or of a file held by the supervising physician and surgeon or elsewhere, are subject to inspection only upon an order of the court for good cause shown. [§] (b) The donor of semen provided to a licensed physician and surgeon for use in artificial insemination of a woman other than the donor's wife is treated in law as if he were not the natural father of a child thereby conceived."

California's Family Code section 7613 varies from the promulgated version in that it omits the word "married" in subdivision (b) in front of the word "woman," a textual indication that the California Legislature contemplated use of artificial insemination by single women.

the support of a child born to his wife during the marriage as a result of artificial insemination using sperm from an anonymous donor.

In *Sorensen,* the high court emphasized the role of the husband in *causing* the birth, even though he had no biological connection to the child: "[A] reasonable man who ... actively participates and consents to his wife's artificial insemination in the hope that a child will be produced whom they will treat as their own, *knows that such behavior carries with it the legal responsibilities of fatherhood and criminal responsibility for non-support.*"(*Id.* at p. 285, 66 Cal.Rptr. 7, 437 P.2d 495, emphasis added.) The court went on to say that the husband was "directly responsible" for the "existence" of the child and repeated the point that "without defendant's active participation and consent the child would not have been procreated." (*Ibid.*)

Sorensen expresses a rule universally in tune with other jurisdictions. "Almost exclusively, courts which have addressed this issue have assigned parental responsibility to the husband based on conduct evidencing his consent to the artificial insemination." *In re Baby Doe* (1987) 291 S.C. 389, 353 S.E.2d 877, 878; accord, *Gursky v. Gursky* (1963) 39 Misc.2d 1083, 242 N.Y.S.2d 406, 411–412 [even though child was not technically "legitimate" under New York law at the time, husband's conduct in consenting to the artificial insemination properly invoked application of the doctrine of equitable estoppel requiring him to support the child]; *Anonymous v. Anonymous* (1964) 41 Misc.2d 886, 246 N.Y.S.2d 835, 836–837 [following *Gursky*]; *K.S. v. G.S.* (1981) 182 N.J.Super. 102, 440 A.2d 64, 68 [because husband did not offer clear and convincing evidence that he had *withdrawn* his consent to artificial insemination procedure, he was bound by initial consent given earlier and accordingly held to be lawful father of the child]; ... One New York family court even went so far as to hold the lesbian partner of a woman who was artificially inseminated responsible for the support of two children where the partner had dressed as a man and the couple had obtained a marriage license and a wedding ceremony had been performed prior to the inseminations. (*Karin T. v. Michael T.* (1985) 127 Misc.2d 14, 484 N.Y.S.2d 780.) Echoing the themes of causation and estoppel which underlie the cases, the court noted that the lesbian partner had "by her course of conduct in this case ... brought into the world two innocent children" and should not "be allowed to benefit" from her acts to the detriment of the children and public generally. (484 N.Y.S.2d at p. 784.)

Indeed, in the one case we are aware of where the court did not hold that the husband had a support obligation, the reason was *not* the absence of a biological relationship as such, but because of actual lack of consent to the insemination procedure. (See *In re Marriage of Witbeck–Wildhagen* (1996) 281 Ill.App.3d 502, 217 Ill.Dec. 329, 331–332, 667 N.E.2d 122, 125–126 [it would be "unjust" to impose support obligation on husband who never consented to the artificial insemination].)

It must also be noted that in applying the artificial insemination statute to a case where a party has caused a child to be brought into the world, the statutory policy is really echoing a more fundamental idea—a sort of *grundnorm* to borrow Hans Kelsen's famous jurisprudential word— already established in the case law. That idea is often summed up in the legal term "estoppel." Estoppel is an ungainly word from the Middle French (from the word meaning "bung" or "stopper") expressing the law's distaste for inconsistent actions and positions—like consenting to an act which brings a child into existence and then turning around and disclaiming any responsibility.

While the *Johnson v. Calvert* court was able to predicate its decision on the Uniform Parentage Act rather than making up the result out of whole cloth, it is also true that California courts, prior to the enactment of the Act, had based certain decisions establishing paternity merely on the common law doctrine of estoppel. . . . [This was] the basis for establishing paternity and its concomitant responsibility as far back as the 1961 decision of *Clevenger v. Clevenger* (1961) 189 Cal.App.2d 658, 662, 11 Cal.Rptr. 707 (husband who took illegitimate child into his home and held child out as his own "estopped" to assert illegitimacy and "avoid liability for its support").

There is no need in the present case to predicate our decision on common law estoppel alone, though the doctrine certainly applies. The estoppel concept, after all, is *already* inherent in the artificial insemination statute.

. . .

John argues that the artificial insemination statute should not be applied because, after all, his wife did not give birth. But for purposes of the statute with its core idea of estoppel, the fact that Luanne did not give birth is irrelevant. The statute contemplates the establishment of lawful fatherhood in a situation where an intended father has no biological relationship to a child who is procreated as a result of the father's (as well as the mother's) *consent* to a medical procedure.

Luanne is the Lawful Mother of Jaycee, Not the Surrogate, and Not the Unknown Donor of the Egg

In the present case Luanne is situated like a husband in an artificial insemination case whose consent triggers a medical procedure which results in a pregnancy and eventual birth of a child. Her motherhood may therefore be established "under this part," by virtue of that consent. In light of our conclusion, John's argument that the surrogate should be declared the lawful mother disintegrates. The case is now postured like the *Johnson v. Calvert* case, where motherhood could have been "established" in either of two women under the Act, and the tie broken by noting the intent to parent as expressed in the surrogacy contract. (See *Johnson v. Calvert, supra,* 5 Cal.4th at p. 93, 19 Cal.Rptr.2d 494, 851 P.2d 776.) The only difference is that this case is not even close as between Luanne and the surrogate. Not only was Luanne the clearly intended mother, no bona fide attempt has been made to establish the surrogate as the lawful mother.[12]

We should also add that neither could the woman whose egg was used in the fertilization or implantation make any claim to motherhood, even if she were to come forward at this late date. Again, as between two women who would both be able to establish motherhood under the Act, the *Johnson* decision would mandate that the tie be broken in favor of the intended parent, in this case, Luanne.

Our decision in *In re Marriage of Moschetta, supra,* 25 Cal.App.4th 1218, 30 Cal.Rptr.2d 893, relied on by John, is inapposite and distinguishable. In *Moschetta*, this court held that a contract giving rise to a "traditional" surrogacy arrangement where a surrogate was simply inseminated with the husband's sperm could not be *enforced* against the surrogate by the intended father. (*Id.* at p. 1231, 30 Cal.Rptr.2d 893.) In order for the surrogate not to be the lawful mother she would have to give the child up for adoption. (See *id.* at pp. 1231, 1233, 30 Cal.Rptr.2d 893.)

In *Moschetta*, the surrogate was the mother both by birth and genes; the woman contemplated as the intended mother in the surrogacy contract gave up any claim to the child. (*Id.* at pp. 1223–1225, 30 Cal.Rptr.2d 893.) In fact, at the appellate level, she went so far as to file a brief in favor of the birth mother's claim.

Moschetta is inapposite because this court never had occasion to consider or discuss whether the original intended mother's participation in the surrogacy arrangement, which brought about the child's birth, might have formed the basis for holding her responsible as a parent. She had given up her claim; the issue was not before the court. Unlike the *Johnson* case there was no tie to break between two women both of whom could be held to be mothers under the Act. (See *ibid.* ["There is no 'tie' to break."].) When courts do not consider propositions, their subsequent decisions are not precedent for them.

Moschetta is distinguishable because it involved the claim of a woman who both gave birth to the child, "contributed" the egg, and who wanted the child enough to go to court to seek custody. (See *Moschetta, supra,* 25 Cal.App.4th at p. 1223, 30 Cal.Rptr.2d 893.) The only alternative was a woman who did not give birth, did not contribute genes, and who gave up her claim. (*Id.* at pp. 1224–1225, 30 Cal.Rptr.2d 893.) Only if the surrogacy contract were *specifically enforced* in *Moschetta* could this court have ruled in favor of the father's claim to *exclusive* parenthood.

There is a difference between a court's *enforcing* a surrogacy agreement and making a legal determination based on the intent *expressed in* a surrogacy agreement. (See *id.* at pp. 1230, 1235, fn. 23, 30 Cal.Rptr.2d 893.) By the same token, there is also an important distinction between enforcing a surrogacy contract and making a legal determination based on the

---

12. As noted in footnote 2 above, John's attorney did nothing to object when the trial court accepted a stipulation taking the surrogate and her husband out of this case. Accordingly, nothing in this opinion is intended to address the question of who might be responsible for a child when *only* the surrogate mother is available.

fact that the contract itself *sets in motion* a medical procedure which results in the birth of a child.

In the case before us, we are not concerned, as John would have us believe, with a question of the enforceability of the oral and written surrogacy contracts into which he entered with Luanne. This case is not about "transferring" parenthood pursuant to those agreements. We are, rather, concerned with the consequences of those agreements as *acts* which *caused the birth* of a child.

The legal paradigm adopted by the trial court, and now urged upon us by John, is one where all forms of artificial reproduction in which intended parents have no biological relationship with the child result in legal parentlessness. It means that, absent adoption, such children will be dependents of the state. One might describe this paradigm as the "adoption default" model: The idea is that by not specifically addressing some permutation of artificial reproduction, the Legislature has, in effect, set the default switch on adoption. The underlying theory seems to be that when intended parents resort to artificial reproduction without biological tie the Legislature wanted them to be *screened* first through the adoption system. (Thus John, in his brief, argues that a surrogacy contract must be "subject to state oversight.")

The "adoption default" model is, however, inconsistent with both statutory law and the Supreme Court's *Johnson* decision. As to the statutory law, the Legislature has already made it perfectly clear that public policy (and, we might add, common sense) favors, whenever possible, the establishment of legal parenthood with the concomitant responsibility. Family Code section 7570, subdivision (a) states that "There is a compelling state interest in establishing paternity for all children." The statute then goes on to elaborate why establishing paternity is a good thing: It means someone besides the taxpayers will be responsible for the child: "Establishing paternity is the first step toward a child support award, which, in turn, provides children with equal rights and access to benefits...." (*Ibid.*) In light of this strong public policy, the statutes which follow section 7570, subdivision (a) seek to provide a "simple system allowing for the establishment of voluntary paternity." (See Fam.Code, § 7570, subd. (b).)

Section 7570 necessarily expresses a legislative policy applicable to maternity as well. It would be lunatic for the Legislature to declare that establishing paternity is a compelling state interest yet conclude that establishing maternity is not. The obvious reason the Legislature did not include an explicit parallel statement on "maternity" is that the issue almost never arises except for extraordinary cases involving artificial reproduction.

Very plainly, the Legislature has declared its preference for assigning *individual* responsibility for the care and maintenance of children; not leaving the task to the taxpayers. That is why it has gone to considerable lengths to insure that parents will live up to their support obligations. (Cf. *Moss v. Superior Court* (1998) 17 Cal.4th 396, 424, 71 Cal.Rptr.2d 215, 950

P.2d 59 [noting legislative priority put on child support obligations].) The adoption default theory flies in the face of that legislative value judgment.

As this court noted in *Jaycee B. v. Superior Court* (1996) 42 Cal. App.4th 718, 731, 49 Cal.Rptr.2d 694, the *Johnson* court had occasion, albeit in dicta, to address "pretty much the exact situation before us." The language bears quoting again: "In what we must hope will be the extremely rare situation in which neither the gestator nor the woman who provided the ovum for fertilization is willing to assume custody of the child after birth, a rule recognizing the intending parents as the child's legal, natural parents should best promote certainty and stability." (*Johnson v. Calvert, supra,* 5 Cal.4th at pp. 94–95, 19 Cal.Rptr.2d 494, 851 P.2d 776.) This language quite literally describes precisely the case before us now: Neither the woman whose ovum was used nor the woman who gave birth have come forward to assume custody of the child after birth.

John now argues that the Supreme Court's statement should be applied only in situations, such as that in the *Johnson* case, where the intended parents have a genetic tie to the child. The context of the *Johnson* language, however, reveals a broader purpose, namely, to emphasize the intelligence and utility of a rule that looks to intentions.

... The *Johnson* court had just enunciated its conclusion that in cases of "genetic consanguinity" and "giving birth" the intended mother is to be held the lawful mother.[13] The court then found "support" for its conclusions in the writings of several legal commentators (*id.* at p. 93, 19 Cal.Rptr.2d 494, 851 P.2d 776), the first of whom, Professor Hill, had made the point that the intended parents are the " 'first cause, or prime movers, of the procreative relationship.' " (*Id.* at p. 94, 19 Cal.Rptr.2d 494, 851 P.2d 776, quoting Hill, *What Does It Mean to Be a "Parent"? The Claims of Biology as the Basis for Parental Rights* (1991) 66 N.Y.U.L.Rev. 353, 415.) The court then quoted two more law review articles, both of which emphasized the same theme as Professor Hill.[14] This laid the foundation for the court's next point, which was that people who " 'choose' " to bring a child into being are likely to have the child's best interest at heart, which the court immediately juxtaposed against the surrogate's position which would result in a woman becoming the legal mother *against* her expecta-

---

13. This rule, incidentally, has the salutary effect of working both ways. Thus if an intended mother who could carry a baby to term but had no suitable eggs was implanted with an embryo in which the egg was from a donor who did not intend to parent the child, the law would still reflect the intentions of the parties rather than some arbitrary or imposed preference.

14. The *Johnson* court quoted Professor Schulz to the effect that " 'intentions that are voluntarily chosen, deliberate, express and bargained-for ought presumptively to determine legal parenthood' " (*Johnson v.*

Calvert, supra, 5 Cal.4th at p. 94, 19 Cal. Rptr.2d 494, 851 P.2d 776, quoting Schultz, *Reproductive Technology and Intent–Based Parenthood: An Opportunity for Gender Neutrality* (1990) Wis.L.Rev. 297, 323) and a Yale Law Journal Note that the " '[m]ental concept of the child *is a controlling factor of its creation*' " (*Johnson v. Calvert, supra,* 5 Cal.4th at p. 94, 19 Cal.Rptr.2d 494, 851 P.2d 776, quoting Note, *Redefining Mother: A Legal Matrix for New Reproductive Technologies* (1986) 96 Yale L.J. 187, 196 (our emphasis).)

tions. Then came the sentence which we have already quoted addressing the "extremely rare situation" where—as is precisely the case before us now—neither the woman who has given birth nor the woman who provided the ovum were "willing to assume custody of the child after birth"—and therefore recognizing intentions as the best rule to promote certainty and stability for the child. (*Id.* at pp. 94–95, 19 Cal.Rptr.2d 494, 851 P.2d 776.)

In context, then, the high court's considered dicta is directly applicable to the case at hand. The context was not limited to just *Johnson*-style contests between women who gave birth and women who contributed ova, but to any situation where a child would not have been born " 'but for the efforts of the intended parents.' " (*Id.* at p. 94, 19 Cal.Rptr.2d 494, 851 P.2d 776, quoting Hill, *op. cit., supra*, 66 N.Y.U.L.Rev. at p. 415.)

Finally, in addition to its contravention of statutorily enunciated public policy and the pronouncement of our high court in *Johnson,* the adoption default model ignores the role of our dependency statutes in protecting children. Parents are not screened for the procreation of their *own* children; they are screened for the adoption of *other* people's children. It is the role of the dependency laws to protect children from neglect and abuse from their own parents. The adoption default model is essentially an exercise in circular reasoning, because it assumes the idea that it seeks to prove; namely, that a child who is born as the result of artificial reproduction is somebody else's child from the beginning.

In the case before us, there is absolutely no dispute that Luanne caused Jaycee's conception and birth by initiating the surrogacy arrangement whereby an embryo was implanted into a woman who agreed to carry the baby to term on Luanne's behalf. In applying the artificial insemination statute to a gestational surrogacy case where the genetic donors are unknown, there is, as we have indicated above, no reason to distinguish *between* husbands and wives. Both are equally situated from the point of view of consenting to an act which brings a child into being. Accordingly, Luanne should have been declared the lawful mother of Jaycee.

John is the Lawful Father of Jaycee Even If Luanne Did Promise to Assume All Responsibility for Jaycee's Care

The same reasons which impel us to conclude that Luanne is Jaycee's lawful mother also require that John be declared Jaycee's lawful father. Even if the written surrogacy contract had not yet been signed at the time of conception and implantation, those occurrences were nonetheless the direct result of actions taken pursuant to an oral agreement which envisioned that the fertilization, implantation and ensuing pregnancy would go forward. Thus, it is still accurate to say, as we did the first time this case came before us, that for all practical purposes John caused Jaycee's conception every bit as much as if things had been done the old-fashioned way. (*Jaycee B., supra,* 42 Cal.App.4th at p. 730, 49 Cal.Rptr.2d 694.)

When pressed at oral argument to make an offer of proof as to the "best facts" which John might be able to show if this case were tried, John's attorney raised the point that Luanne had (allegedly, we must add) promised to assume all responsibility for the child and would not hold him responsible for the child's upbringing. However, even if this case were returned for a trial on this point (we assume that Luanne would dispute the allegation) it could make no difference as to John's lawful paternity. It is well established that parents cannot, by agreement, limit or abrogate a child's right to support.[17]

> . . .

The rule against enforcing agreements obviating a parent's child support responsibilities is also illustrated by *Stephen K. v. Roni L.* (1980) 105 Cal.App.3d 640, 164 Cal.Rptr. 618, a case which is virtually on point about Luanne's alleged promise. In *Stephen K.*, a woman was alleged to have falsely told a man that she was taking birth control pills. In "reliance" upon that statement the man had sexual intercourse with her. (*Id.* at p. 642, 164 Cal.Rptr. 618.) The woman became pregnant and brought a paternity action. While the man did not attempt to use the woman's false statement as grounds to avoid paternity, he did seek to achieve the same result by cross-complaining against the woman for damages based on her fraud.

The trial court dismissed the cross-complaint on demurrer and the appellate court affirmed. The cross-complaint was "nothing more than asking the court to supervise the promises made between two consenting adults as to the circumstances of their private sexual conduct." (*Id.* at pp. 644–645, 164 Cal.Rptr. 618.)

There is no meaningful difference between the rule articulated in *Stephen K.* and the situation here—indeed, the result applies a fortiori to the present case: If the man who engaged in an act which merely opened the possibility of the procreation of a child was held responsible for the consequences in *Stephen K.*, how much more so should a man be held responsible for giving his express consent to a medical procedure that was *intended* to result in the procreation of a child. Thus, it makes no difference that John's wife Luanne did not become pregnant. John still engaged in

---

17. The legal consequences of John's allegation that Luanne would assume sole responsibility were briefed. Minor's appointed counsel specifically anticipated the point on page 11, footnote 11 of the minor's opening brief. Rather than attempt to show that Luanne's alleged promise *would* make a difference, John's respondent's brief merely alludes to a vague need to consider "[a]ll of the aspects of contract formation . . . including, but not limited to, the issues of mistake of law or fact, fraud, coercion and duress" and claims that John had been precluded from presenting evidence on these issues by the "preemptive ruling of the trial court." Three times now—when this case was here before (*Jaycee B. v. Superior Court, supra,* 42 Cal. App.4th 718, 49 Cal.Rptr.2d 694), at the trial, and in his respondent's brief—John has had the opportunity to present offers of proof of facts to the court which would change the result which would otherwise flow from his oral and written consent to the surrogacy. Having chosen not to respond to a point made by minor's counsel in her opening brief, John cannot now be heard to complain that he didn't have the opportunity to brief it. Then again, to be fair, John's attorney may himself have recognized that Luanne's alleged promise was of no consequence and it would be almost frivolous to press the issue at the appellate level. Every family law attorney knows that courts will not enforce promises by one parent to hold the other parent harmless from any claims of child support.

"procreative conduct." In plainer language, a deliberate procreator is as responsible as a casual inseminator.

CONCLUSION

Even though neither Luanne nor John are biologically related to Jaycee, they are still her lawful parents given their initiating role as the intended parents in her conception and birth. And, while the absence of a biological connection is what makes this case extraordinary, this court is hardly without statutory basis and legal precedent in so deciding. Indeed, in both the most famous child custody case of all time,[19] and in our Supreme Court's *Johnson v. Calvert* decision, the court looked to *intent to parent* as the ultimate basis of its decision.[20] Fortunately, as the *Johnson* court also noted, intent to parent " 'correlate[s] significantly' " with a child's best interests. (*Johnson v. Calvert, supra,* 5 Cal.4th at p. 94, 19 Cal.Rptr.2d 494, 851 P.2d 776, quoting Schultz, *op. cit. supra,* Wis.L.Rev., at p. 397.) That is far more than can be said for a model of the law that renders a child a legal orphan.[21]

Again we must call on the Legislature to sort out the parental rights and responsibilities of those involved in artificial reproduction. No matter what one thinks of artificial insemination, traditional and gestational surrogacy (in all its permutations), and—as now appears in the not-too-distant future, cloning and even gene splicing—courts are still going to be faced with the problem of determining lawful parentage. A child cannot be ignored. Even if all means of artificial reproduction were outlawed with draconian criminal penalties visited on the doctors and parties involved, courts will still be called upon to decide who the lawful parents really are and who—other than the taxpayers—is obligated to provide maintenance and support for the child. These cases will not go away.

Courts can continue to make decisions on an ad hoc basis without necessarily imposing some grand scheme, looking to the imperfectly de-signed Uniform Parentage Act and a growing body of case law for guidance in the light of applicable family law principles. Or the Legislature can act to impose a broader order which, even though it might not be perfect on a

---

19. See I Kings 3: 25–26 (dispute over identity of live child by two single women, each of whom had recently delivered a child but one child had died, resolved by novel evidentiary device designed to ferret out intent to parent).

20. While in each case intent to parent was used as a tie-breaker as between two claimants who either had or claimed a biological connection, it is still undeniable that, when push came to shove, the court employed a legal idea that was *unrelated* to any necessary biological connection.

21. It is significant that even if the *Johnson* majority had adopted the position of Justice Kennard advocating best interest as

the more flexible and better rule (see *id.* at p. 118, 19 Cal.Rptr.2d 494, 851 P.2d 776 (dis. opn. of Kennard, J.)) there is no way the trial court's decision could stand. Luanne has cared for Jaycee since infancy; she is the only parent Jaycee has ever known. It would be unthinkable, given the facts of this case and her role as caregiver for Jaycee, for Luanne not to be declared the lawful mother under a best interest test.

As for the father, John would not be the first man whose responsibility was based on having played a role in causing a child's procreation, regardless of whether he really wanted to assume it.

case-by-case basis, would bring some predictability to those who seek to make use of artificial reproductive techniques. As jurists, we recognize the traditional role of the common (i.e., judge-formulated) law in applying old legal principles to new technology. (See, e.g., *Hurtado v. State of California* (1884) 110 U.S. 516, 530, 4 S.Ct. 111, 118, 28 L.Ed. 232 ["This flexibility and capacity for growth and adaptation is the peculiar boast and excellence of the common law."]; *Rodriguez v. Bethlehem Steel Corp.* (1974) 12 Cal.3d 382, 394, 115 Cal.Rptr. 765, 525 P.2d 669 ["in the common law system the primary instruments of evolution are the courts, adjudicating on a regular basis the rich variety of individual cases brought before them"].) However, we still believe it is the Legislature, with its ability to formulate general rules based on input from all its constituencies, which is the more desirable forum for lawmaking.

That said, we must now conclude the business at hand.

(1) The portion of the judgment which declares that Luanne Buzzanca is not the lawful mother of Jaycee is reversed. The matter is remanded with directions to enter a new judgment declaring her the lawful mother. The trial court shall make all appropriate orders to ensure that Luanne Buzzanca shall have legal custody of Jaycee, including entering an order that Jaycee's birth certificate shall be amended to reflect Luanne Buzzanca as the mother.

(2) The judgment is reversed to the extent that it provides that John Buzzanca is not the lawful father of Jaycee. The matter is remanded with directions to enter a new judgment declaring him the lawful father. Consonant with this determination, today's ruling is without prejudice to John in future proceedings as regards child custody and visitation as his relationship with Jaycee may develop.[22] The judgment shall also reflect that the birth certificate shall be amended to reflect John Buzzanca as the lawful father.

(3) To the degree that the judgment makes no provision for child support it is reversed. The matter is remanded to make an appropriate permanent child support order. Until that time, the temporary child support order shall remain in effect. (See *Jaycee B. v. Superior Court, supra,* 42 Cal.App.4th at p. 730, 49 Cal.Rptr.2d 694.)

Luanne and Jaycee will recover their costs on appeal.

---

22. Luanne has had actual physical custody of Jaycee from the beginning. Obviously, it would be frivolous of John to seek custody of Jaycee right now in light of that fact. However, as the lawful father he certainly must be held to have the right, consistent with Jaycee's best interest, to visitation. Our decision today leaves Luanne and John in the same position as any other divorced couple with a child who has been exclusively cared for by the mother since infancy.

And while it may be true that John's consent to the fertilization, implantation and pregnancy was done as an accommodation to allow Luanne to surmount a formality, who knows what relationship he may develop with Jaycee in the future? Human relationships are not static; things done merely to help one individual overcome a perceived legal obstacle sometimes become much more meaningful. (See, e.g., Nicholson, Shadowlands (1990) (play based on true story of prominent British author who married American citizen in Britain in perfunctory civil ceremony to allow her to remain in country; a deeper relationship then developed).)

NEW YORK DOMESTIC RELATIONS LAW (McKinney 1999)

§ 122. Public policy

Surrogate parenting contracts are hereby declared contrary to the public policy of this state, and are void and unenforceable.

§ 123. Prohibitions and penalties

1. No person or other entity shall knowingly request, accept, receive, pay or give any fee, compensation or other remuneration, directly or indirectly, in connection with any surrogate parenting contract, or induce, arrange or otherwise assist in arranging a surrogate parenting contract for a fee, compensation or other remuneration, except for:

(a) payments in connection with the adoption of a child permitted by subdivision six of section three hundred seventy-four of the social services law and disclosed pursuant to subdivision eight of section one hundred fifteen of this chapter; or

(b) payments for reasonable and actual medical fees and hospital expenses for artificial insemination or in vitro fertilization services incurred by the mother in connection with the birth of the child.

2. (a) A birth mother or her husband, a genetic father and his wife, and, if the genetic mother is not the birth mother, the genetic mother and her husband who violate this section shall be subject to a civil penalty not to exceed five hundred dollars.

(b) Any other person or entity who or which induces, arranges or otherwise assists in the formation of a surrogate parenting contract for a fee, compensation or other remuneration or otherwise violates this section shall be subject to a civil penalty not to exceed ten thousand dollars and forfeiture to the state of any such fee, compensation or remuneration in accordance with the provisions of subdivision (a) of section seven thousand two hundred one of the civil practice law and rules, for the first such offense. Any person or entity who or which induces, arranges or otherwise assists in the formation of a surrogate parenting contract for a fee, compensation or other remuneration or otherwise violates this section, after having been once subject to a civil penalty for violating this section, shall be guilty of a felony.

§ 124. Proceedings regarding parental rights, status or obligations

In any action or proceeding involving a dispute between the birth mother and (i) the genetic father, (ii) the genetic mother, (iii) both the genetic father and genetic mother, or (iv) the parent or parents of the genetic father or genetic mother, regarding parental rights, status or obligations with respect to a child born pursuant to a surrogate parenting contract:

1. the court shall not consider the birth mother's participation in a surrogate parenting contract as adverse to her parental rights, status, or obligations; and

2. the court, having regard to the circumstances of the case and of the respective parties including the parties' relative ability to pay such fees and expenses, in its discretion and in the interests of justice, may award to either party reasonable and actual counsel fees and legal expenses incurred in connection with such action or proceeding. Such award may be made in the order or judgment by which the particular action or proceeding is finally determined, or by one or more orders from time to time before the final order or judgment, or by both such order or orders and the final order or judgment; provided, however, that in any dispute involving a birth mother who has executed a valid surrender or consent to the adoption, nothing in this section shall empower a court to make any award that it would not otherwise be empowered to direct.

NOTE

About a dozen states have adopted specific statutory provisions dealing with surrogacy. The bulk of them bar or invalidate commercial agreements. Virginia, the second state (and one of the very few) to adopt a version of the Uniform Status of Children of Assisted Conception Act (but with much more elaborate language and procedural provisions), allows surrogacy agreements under limited circumstances but provides criminal sanctions that can be invoked against surrogacy brokers as well as damages of treble the amount of compensation that they would have received under a contract. *See* Va. Code Ann. § 20–156 (West 2001).

CHAPTER VII

RAISING CHILDREN: COMPETING INTERESTS OF PARENT, CHILD AND STATE

INTRODUCTION

As with custody and termination decisions involving children, parents, third parties, and the state, the judicial system increasingly is being asked to mediate between parents, protect the physical and educational interests of children, and protect the historical rights of the parent in the raising of children. Many of the issues of custody and termination appear within this material. For instance: When may the state remove a child from the custody of a parent? What constitutional rights do children have separate and apart from a parent? What can a parent expect from the state in support of the traditional parental role of guardian?

The cases and materials demonstrate that there is increasing state involvement in rearing children. Issues presented within this chapter are affected by many often competing interests, but all have an impact on the parties and sociology involved. To begin, consider a few of the statistics and recommendations set forth in the report of the NATIONAL COMMISSION ON CHILDREN, UNITED STATES, BEYOND RHETORIC: A NEW AMERICAN AGENDA FOR CHILDREN AND FAMILIES: FINAL REPORT OF THE NATIONAL COMMISSION ON CHILDREN 24 (1991).

> Today, children are the poorest Americans. One in five lives in a family with an income below the federal poverty level. One in four infants and toddlers under the age of three is poor. Nearly 13 million children live in poverty, more than 2 million more than a decade ago. Many of these children are desperately poor; nearly 5 million live in families with incomes less than half the federal poverty level.
>
> . . .
>
> Today, one in four children in the United States is raised by just one parent, usually a divorced or unmarried mother. Many grow up without the consistent presence of a father in their lives. *Id*. at 4. Nearly 75 percent of all American children growing up in single-parent families experience poverty for some period during their first 10 years, compared to 20 percent of children in two-parent families. Among children living only with their mothers, sustained poverty for seven or

more years is common; among children living with both parents, it is rare. *Id.* at 83.

The family has primary responsibility for teaching values and creating the ethical context that is fundamental to our society and our democracy. Children learn to love others by being loved. They learn to respect and value the rights of others by being respected and valued themselves. They learn to trust when they have unwavering support from parents and the other adults closest to them. The capacity for understanding and valuing the feelings of others is present in every child, and it flowers when children are encouraged to empathize with others.... From the time they are very young, children learn responsibility and commitment, freedom and dissent in small, manageable steps. Experiences within the family provide them with the moral and ethical framework for their lives as adults. *Id.* at 360–1.

The [National Commission on Children] strongly urges all programs and services for youth to make special efforts to involve parents and to respect their values, taking care not to undermine parents' important role and influence in adolescent decision making. Parents are the first people youngsters should turn to for the support and guidance they need to avoid high-risk behaviors and for help in exploring life options. Whenever possible, programs should build upon and encourage strong parent-child relationships. *Id.* at 237.

A. THE INTEREST IN ASSURING AN EDUCATION

Wisconsin v. Yoder

Supreme Court of the United States, 1972.
406 U.S. 205, 92 S.Ct. 1526, 32 L.Ed.2d 15.

■ MR. CHIEF JUSTICE BURGER delivered the opinion of the Court.

[We granted certiorari to review a] Wisconsin Supreme Court holding that respondents' convictions for violating the State's compulsory school-attendance law were invalid under the Free Exercise Clause of the First Amendment to the United States Constitution made applicable to the States by the Fourteenth Amendment.... [W]e affirm the judgment of the Supreme Court of Wisconsin.

[Respondents were Wisconsin residents and members of either the Old Order Amish religion or the Conservative Amish Mennonite Church. Their children, ages 14 and 15 were not enrolled in any public or private school, although Wisconsin's compulsory school-attendance law requires parents to cause their children to attend school until they reach age 16. Respondents were convicted of violating the law and fined $5 each.]

... The trial testimony showed that respondents believed, in accordance with the tenets of Old Order Amish communities generally, that their children's attendance at high school, public or private, was contrary to the Amish religion and way of life. They believed that by sending their children to high school, they would not only expose themselves to the danger of the censure of the church community, but, as found by the county court, also endanger their own salvation and that of their children. The State stipulated that respondents' religious beliefs were sincere.

In support of their position, respondents presented as expert witnesses scholars on religion and education whose testimony is uncontradicted. They expressed their opinions on the relationship of the Amish belief concerning school attendance to the more general tenets of their religion, and described the impact that compulsory high school attendance could have on the continued survival of Amish communities as they exist in the United States today....

Formal high school education beyond the eighth grade is contrary to Amish beliefs, not only because it places Amish children in an environment hostile to Amish beliefs with increasing emphasis on competition in class work and sports and with pressure to conform to the styles, manners, and ways of the peer group, but also because it takes them away from their community, physically and emotionally, during the crucial and formative adolescent period of life. During this period, the children must acquire Amish attitudes favoring manual work and self-reliance and the specific skills needed to perform the adult role of an Amish farmer or housewife. They must learn to enjoy physical labor. Once a child has learned basic reading, writing, and elementary mathematics, these traits, skills, and attitudes admittedly fall within the category of those best learned through example and "doing" rather than in a classroom. And, at this time in life, the Amish child must also grow in his faith and his relationship to the Amish community if he is to be prepared to accept the heavy obligations imposed by adult baptism. In short, high school attendance with teachers who are not of the Amish faith—and may even be hostile to it—interposes a serious barrier to the integration of the Amish child into the Amish religious community. Dr. John Hostetler, one of the experts on Amish society, testified that the modern high school is not equipped, in curriculum or social environment, to impart the values promoted by Amish society.

The Amish do not object to elementary education through the first eight grades as a general proposition because they agree that their children must have basic skills in the "three R's" in order to read the Bible, to be good farmers and citizens, and to be able to deal with non-Amish people when necessary in the course of daily affairs. They view such a basic education as acceptable because it does not significantly expose their children to worldly values or interfere with their development in the Amish community during the crucial adolescent period. While Amish accept compulsory elementary education generally, wherever possible they have established their own elementary schools in many respects like the small local schools of the past. In the Amish belief higher learning tends to develop values they reject as influences that alienate man from God.

On the basis of such considerations, Dr. Hostetler testified that compulsory high school attendance could not only result in great psychological harm to Amish children, because of the conflicts it would produce, but would also, in his opinion, ultimately result in the destruction of the Old Order Amish church community as it exists in the United States today....

... [A] State's interest in universal education, however highly we rank it, is not totally free from a balancing process when it impinges on fundamental rights and interests, such as those specifically protected by the Free Exercise Clause of the First Amendment, and the traditional interest of parents with respect to the religious upbringing of their children so long as they, in the words of Pierce [v. Society of Sisters], "prepare [them] for additional obligations." 268 U.S., at 535, 45 S.Ct., at 573.

It follows that in order for Wisconsin to compel school attendance beyond the eighth grade against a claim that such attendance interferes with the practice of a legitimate religious belief, it must appear either that the State does not deny the free exercise of religious belief by its requirement, or that there is a state interest of sufficient magnitude to override the interest claiming protection under the Free Exercise Clause. Long before there was general acknowledgment of the need for universal formal education, the Religion Clauses had specifically and firmly fixed the right to free exercise of religious beliefs, and buttressing this fundamental right was an equally firm, even if less explicit, prohibition against the establishment of any religion by government. The values underlying these two provisions relating to religion have been zealously protected, sometimes even at the expense of other interests of admittedly high social importance. The invalidation of financial aid to parochial schools by government grants for a salary subsidy for teachers is but one example of the extent to which courts have gone in this regard, notwithstanding that such aid programs were legislatively determined to be in the public interest and the service of sound educational policy by States and by Congress. Lemon v. Kurtzman, 403 U.S. 602, 91 S.Ct. 2105, 29 L.Ed.2d 745 (1971).

The essence of all that has been said and written on the subject is that only those interests of the highest order and those not otherwise served can overbalance legitimate claims to the free exercise of religion. We can accept it as settled, therefore, that, however strong the State's interest in universal compulsory education, it is by no means absolute to the exclusion or subordination of all other interests.

We come then to the quality of the claims of the respondents concerning the alleged encroachment of Wisconsin's compulsory school-attendance statute on their rights and the rights of their children to the free exercise of the religious beliefs they and their forbears have adhered to for almost three centuries. In evaluating those claims we must be careful to determine whether the Amish religious faith and their mode of life are, as they claim, inseparable and interdependent....

... [T]he record in this case abundantly supports the claim that the traditional way of life of the Amish is not merely a matter of personal preference, but one of deep religious conviction, shared by an organized group, and intimately related to daily living....

... [T]he unchallenged testimony of acknowledged experts in education and religious history, almost 300 years of consistent practice, and strong evidence of a sustained faith pervading and regulating respondents' entire mode of life support the claim that enforcement of the State's requirement of compulsory formal education after the eighth grade would gravely endanger if not destroy the free exercise of respondents' religious beliefs.

. . .

We turn ... to the State's broader contention that its interest in its system of compulsory education is so compelling that even the established religious practices of the Amish must give away.

. . .

The State advances two primary arguments in support of its system of compulsory education. It notes, as Thomas Jefferson pointed out early in our history, that some degree of education is necessary to prepare citizens to participate effectively and intelligently in our open political system if we are to preserve freedom and independence. Further, education prepares individuals to be self-reliant and self-sufficient participants in society. We accept these propositions.

However, the evidence adduced by the Amish in this case is persuasively to the effect that an additional one or two years of formal high school for Amish children in place of their long-established program of informal vocational education would do little to serve those interests. Respondents' experts testified at trial, without challenge, that the value of all education must be assessed in terms of its capacity to prepare the child for life. It is one thing to say that compulsory education for a year or two beyond the eighth grade may be necessary when its goal is the preparation of the child for life in modern society as the majority live, but it is quite another if the goal of education be viewed as the preparation of the child for life in the separated agrarian community that is the keystone of the Amish faith. See *Meyer v. Nebraska*, 262 U.S., at 400, 43 S.Ct., at 627, 67 L.Ed. 1042.

The State attacks respondents' position as one fostering "ignorance" from which the child must be protected by the State. No one can question the State's duty to protect children from ignorance but this argument does not square with the facts disclosed in the record. Whatever their idiosyncrasies as seen by the majority, this record strongly shows that the Amish community has been a highly successful social unit without our society, even if apart from the conventional "mainstream." Its members are productive and very law-abiding members of society; they reject public welfare in any of its usual modern forms. The Congress itself recognized their self-sufficiency by authorizing exemption of such groups as the Amish from the obligation to pay social security taxes.[11]

---

11. Title 26 U.S.C. § 1402(h) authorizes the Secretary of Health, Education, and Welfare to exempt members of "a recognized religious sect" existing at all times since December 31, 1950, from the obligation to pay social security taxes if they are, by reason of

It is neither fair nor correct to suggest that the Amish are opposed to education beyond the eighth grade level. What this record shows is that they are opposed to conventional formal education of the type provided by a certified high school because it comes at the child's crucial adolescent period of religious development. Dr. Donald Erickson, for example, testified that their system of learning-by-doing was an "ideal system" of education in terms of preparing Amish children for life as adults in the Amish community....

We must not forget that in the Middle Ages important values of the civilization of the Western World were preserved by members of religious orders who isolated themselves from all worldly influences against great obstacles. There can be no assumption that today's majority is "right" and the Amish and others like them are "wrong." A way of life that is odd or even erratic but interferes with no rights or interests of others is not to be condemned because it is different.

The State, however, supports its interest in providing an additional one or two years of compulsory high school education to Amish children because of the possibility that some such children will choose to leave the Amish community, and that if this occurs they will be ill-equipped for life. The State argues that if Amish children leave their church they should not be in the position of making their way in the world without the education available in the one or two additional years the State requires. However, on this record, that argument is highly speculative. There is no specific evidence of the loss of Amish adherents by attrition, nor is there any showing that upon leaving the Amish community Amish children, with their practical agricultural training and habits of industry and self-reliance, would become burdens on society because of educational shortcomings. Indeed, this argument of the State appears to rest primarily on the State's mistaken assumption, already noted, that the Amish do not provide any education for their children beyond the eighth grade, but allow them to grow in "ignorance." To the contrary, not only do the Amish accept the necessity for formal schooling through the eighth grade level, but continue to provide what has been characterized by the undisputed testimony of expert educators as an "ideal" vocational education for their children in the adolescent years.

There is nothing in this record to suggest that the Amish qualities of reliability, self-reliance, and dedication to work would fail to find ready markets in today's society. Absence some contrary evidence supporting the State's position, we are unwilling to assume that persons possessing such valuable vocational skills and habits are doomed to become burdens on

the tenets of their sect, opposed to receipt of such benefits and agree to waive them, provided the Secretary finds that the sect makes reasonable provision for its dependent members. The history of the exemption shows it was enacted with the situation of the Old Order Amish specifically in view. H.R.Rep. No. 213, 89th Cong., 1st Sess., 101–102 (1965).

The record in this case establishes without contradiction that the Green County Amish had never been known to commit crimes, that none had been known to receive public assistance, and that none were unemployed.

society should they determine to leave the Amish faith, nor is there any basis in the record to warrant a finding that an additional one or two years of formal school education beyond the eighth grade would serve to eliminate any such problem that might exist.

.   .   .

The requirement for compulsory education beyond the eighth grade is a relatively recent development in our history. Less than 60 years ago, the educational requirements of almost all of the States were satisfied by completion of the elementary grades, at least where the child was regularly and lawfully employed. The independence and successful social functioning of the Amish community for a period approaching almost three centuries and more than 200 years in this country are strong evidence that there is at best a speculative gain, in terms of meeting the duties of citizenship, from an additional one or two years of compulsory formal education. Against this background it would require a more particularized showing from the State on this point to justify the severe interference with religious freedom such additional compulsory attendance would entail.

We should also note that compulsory education and child labor laws find their historical origin in common humanitarian instincts, and that the age limits of both laws have been coordinated to achieve their related objectives. In the context of this case, such considerations, if anything, support rather than detract from respondents' position. The origins of the requirement for school attendance to age 16, an age falling after the completion of elementary school but before completion of high school, are not entirely clear. But to some extent such laws reflected the movement to prohibit most child labor under age 16 that culminated in the provisions of the Federal Fair Labor Standards Act of 1938. It is true, then, that the 16–year child labor age limit may to some degree derive from a contemporary impression that children should be in school until that age. But at the same time, it cannot be denied that, conversely, the 16–year education limit reflects, in substantial measure, the concern that children under that age not be employed under conditions hazardous to their health, or in work that should be performed by adults.

The requirement of compulsory schooling to age 16 must therefore be viewed as aimed not merely at providing educational opportunities for children, but as an alternative to the equally undesirable consequence of unhealthful child labor displacing adult workers, or, on the other hand, forced idleness. The two kinds of statutes—compulsory school attendance and child labor laws—tend to keep children of certain ages off the labor market and in school; this regimen in turn provides opportunity to prepare for a livelihood of a higher order than that which children could pursue without education and protects their health in adolescence.

In these terms, Wisconsin's interest in compelling the school attendance of Amish children to age 16 emerges as somewhat less substantial than requiring such attendance for children generally. For, while agricultural employment is not totally outside the legitimate concerns of the child labor laws, employment of children under parental guidance and on the family farm from age 14 to age 16 is an ancient tradition that lies at the periphery of the objectives of such laws. There is no intimation that the Amish employment of their children on family farms is in any way deleterious to their health or that Amish parents exploit children at tender years. Any such inference would be contrary to the record before us. Moreover, employment of Amish children on the family farm does not present the undesirable economic aspects of eliminating jobs that might otherwise be held by adults.

Finally, the State, on authority of Prince v. Massachusetts, argues that a decision exempting Amish children from the State's requirement fails to recognize the substantive right of the Amish child to a secondary education, and fails to give due regard to the power of the State as *parens patriae* to extend the benefit of secondary education to children regardless of the wishes of their parents. Taken at its broadest sweep, the Court's language in *Prince,* might be read to give support to the State's position. However, the Court was not confronted in *Prince* with a situation comparable to that of the Amish as revealed in this record; this is shown by the Court's severe characterization of the evils that it thought the legislature could legitimately associate with child labor, even when performed in the company of an adult. 321 U.S., at 169–170, 64 S.Ct., at 443–444. The Court later took great care to confine *Prince* to a narrow scope in Sherbert v. Verner, when it stated:

> "On the other hand, the Court has rejected challenges under the Free Exercise Clause to governmental regulation of certain overt acts prompted by religious beliefs or principles, for 'even when the action is in accord with one's religious convictions, [it] is not totally free from legislative restrictions.' Braunfeld v. Brown, 366 U.S. 599, 603, 81 S.Ct. 1144, 1146, 6 L.Ed.2d 563. The conduct or actions so regulated have invariably posed some substantial threat to public safety, peace or order. See, e.g., Reynolds v. United States, 98 U.S. 145, 25 L.Ed. 244; Jacobson v. Massachusetts, 197 U.S. 11, 25 S.Ct. 358, 49 L.Ed. 643; Prince v. Massachusetts, 321 U.S. 158, 64 S.Ct. 438, 88 L.Ed. 645...."
> 374 U.S., at 402–403, 83 S.Ct., at 1793.

This case, of course, is not one in which any harm to the physical or mental health of the child or to the public safety, peace, order, or welfare has been demonstrated or may be properly inferred. The record is to the contrary, and any reliance on that theory would find no support in the evidence.

Contrary to the suggestion of the dissenting opinion of Mr. Justice Douglas, our holding today in no degree depends on the assertion of the religious interest of the child as contrasted with that of the parents. It is the parents who are subject to prosecution here for failing to cause their children to attend school, and it is their right of free exercise, not that of their children, that must determine Wisconsin's power to impose criminal penalties on the parent. The dissent argues that a child who expresses a desire to attend public high school in conflict with the wishes of his parents should not be prevented from doing so. There is no reason for the Court to consider that point since it is not an issue in the case. The children are not parties to this litigation. The State has at no point tried this case on the theory that respondents were preventing their children from attending school against their expressed desires, and indeed the record is to the contrary. The State's position from the outset has been that it is empowered to apply its compulsory-attendance law to Amish parents in the same manner as to other parents—that is, without regard to the wishes of the child. That is the claim we reject today.

Our holding in no way determines the proper resolution of possible competing interests of parents, children, and the State in an appropriate state court proceeding in which the power of the State is asserted on the theory that Amish parents are preventing their minor children from attending high school despite their expressed desires to the contrary. Recognition of the claim of the State in such a proceeding would, of course, call into question traditional concepts of parental control over the religious upbringing and education of their minor children recognized in this Court's past decisions. It is clear that such an intrusion by a State into family decisions in the area of religious training would give rise to grave questions of religious freedom comparable to those raised here and those presented in Pierce v. Society of Sisters, 268 U.S. 510, 45 S.Ct. 571, 69 L.Ed. 1070 (1925). On this record we neither reach nor decide those issues.

The State's argument proceeds without reliance on any actual conflict between the wishes of parents and children. It appears to rest on the potential that exemption of Amish parents from the requirements of the compulsory-education law might allow some parents to act contrary to the best interests of their children by foreclosing their opportunity to make an intelligent choice between the Amish way of life and that of the outside world. The same argument could, of course, be made with respect to all church schools short of college. There is nothing in the record or in the ordinary course of human experience to suggest that non-Amish parents generally consult with children of ages 14–16 if they are placed in a church school of the parents' faith.

Indeed it seems clear that if the State is empowered, as *parens patriae,* to "save" a child from himself or his Amish parents by requiring an additional two years of compulsory formal high school education, the State will in large measure influence, if not determine, the religious future of the child. Even more markedly than in *Prince,* therefore, this case involves the fundamental interest of parents, as contrasted with that of the State, to guide the religious future and education of their children. The history and culture of Western civilization reflect a strong tradition of parental concern for the nurture and upbringing of their children. This primary role of the parents in the upbringing of their children is now established beyond debate as an enduring American tradition. If not the first, perhaps the most significant statements of the Court in this area are found in Pierce v. Society of Sisters, in which the Court observed:

"Under the doctrine of Meyer v. Nebraska, 262 U.S. 390, 43 S.Ct. 625, 67 L.Ed. 1042, we think it entirely plain that the Act of 1922 unreasonably interferes with the liberty of parents and guardians to direct the upbringing and education of children under their control. As often heretofore pointed out, rights guaranteed by the Constitution may not be abridged by legislation which has no reasonable relation to some purpose within the competency of the State. The fundamental theory of liberty upon which all governments in this Union repose excludes any general power of the State to standardize its children by forcing them to accept instruction from public teachers only. The child is not the mere creature of the State; those who nurture him and direct his destiny have the right, coupled with the high duty, to recognize and prepare him for additional obligations." 268 U.S., at 534–535, 45 S.Ct., at 573.

The duty to prepare the child for "additional obligations," referred to by the Court, must be read to include the inculcation of moral standards, religious beliefs, and elements of good citizenship. *Pierce,* of course, recognized that where nothing more than the general interest of the parent in the nurture and education of his children is involved, it is beyond dispute that the State acts "reasonably" and constitutionally in requiring education to age 16 in some public or private school meeting the standards prescribed by the State.

However read, the Court's holding in *Pierce* stands as a charter of the rights of parents to direct the religious upbringing of their children. And, when the interests of parenthood are combined with a free exercise claim of the nature revealed by this record, more than merely a "reasonable relation to some purpose within the competency of the State" is required to sustain the validity of the State's requirement under the First Amendment. To be sure, the power of the parent, even when linked to a free exercise claim, may be subject to limitation under *Prince* if it appears that parental decisions will jeopardize the health or safety of the child, or have a potential for significant social burdens. But in this case, the Amish have introduced persuasive evidence undermining the arguments the State has advanced to support its claims in terms of the welfare of the child and society as a whole. The record strongly indicates that accommodating the religious objections of the Amish by forgoing one, or at most two, additional years of compulsory education will not impair the physical or mental health of the child, or result in an inability to be self-supporting or to discharge the duties and responsibilities of citizenship, or in any other way materially detract from the welfare of society.

In the face of our consistent emphasis on the central values underlying the Religion Clauses in our constitutional scheme of government, we cannot accept a *parens patriae* claim of such all-encompassing scope and with such sweeping potential for broad and unforeseeable application as that urged by the State.

For the reasons stated we hold, with the Supreme Court of Wisconsin, that the First and Fourteenth Amendments prevent the State from compelling respondents to cause their children to attend formal high school to age 16. Our disposition of this case, however, in no way alters our recognition of the obvious fact that courts are not school boards or legislatures, and are ill-equipped to determine the "necessity" of discrete aspects of a State's program of compulsory education. This should suggest that courts must move with great circumspection in performing the sensitive and delicate task of weighing a State's legitimate social concern when faced with religious claims for exemption from generally applicable educational requirements. It cannot be overemphasized that we are not dealing with a way of life and mode of education by a group claiming to have recently discovered some "progressive" or more enlightened process for rearing children for modern life.

Aided by a history of three centuries as an identifiable religious sect and a long history as a successful and self-sufficient segment of American society, the Amish in this case have convincingly demonstrated the sincerity of their religious beliefs, the interrelationship of belief with their mode of life, the vital role that belief and daily conduct play in the continued survival of Old Order Amish communities and their religious organization, and the hazards presented by the State's enforcement of a statute generally valid as to others. Beyond this, they have carried the even more difficult burden of demonstrating the adequacy of their alternative mode of continuing informal vocational education in terms of precisely those overall interests that the State advances in support of its program of compulsory high school education. In light of this convincing showing, one that probably few other religious groups or sects could make, and weighing the minimal difference between what the State would require and what the Amish already accept, it was incumbent on the State to show with more particularity how its admittedly strong interest in compulsory education would be adversely affected by granting an exemption to the Amish.

Nothing we hold is intended to undermine the general applicability of the State's compulsory school-attendance statutes or to limit the power of the State to promulgate reasonable standards that, while not impairing the free exercise of religion, provide for continuing agricultural vocational education under parental and church guidance by the Old Order Amish or others similarly situated. The States have had a long history of amicable and effective relationships with church-sponsored schools, and there is no basis for assuming that, in this related context, reasonable standards cannot be established concerning the content of the continuing vocational education of Amish children under parental guidance, provided always that state regulations are not inconsistent with what we have said in this opinion.

Affirmed.

■ Mr. Justice Powell and Mr. Justice Rehnquist took no part in the consideration or decision of this case.

■ Mr. Justice Stewart with whom Mr. Justice Brennan joins, concurring.

This case involves the constitutionality of imposing criminal punishment upon Amish parents for their religiously based refusal to compel their children to attend public high schools. Wisconsin has sought to brand these parents as criminals for following *their* religious beliefs, and the Court today rightly holds that Wisconsin cannot constitutionally do so.

This case in no way involves any questions regarding the right of the children of Amish parents to attend public high schools, or any other institutions of learning, if they wish to do so. As the Court points out, there is no suggestion whatever in the record that the religious beliefs of the children here concerned differ in any way from those of their parents. Only one of the children testified. The last two questions and answers on her cross-examination accurately sum up her testimony:

"Q. So I take it then, Frieda, the only reason you are not going to school, and did not go to school since last September, is because of *your* religion?

"A. Yes.

"Q. That is the only reason?

"A. Yes." (Emphasis supplied.)

It is clear to me, therefore, that this record simply does not present the interesting and important issue discussed in Part II of the dissenting opinion of Mr. Justice Douglas. With this observation, I join the opinion and the judgment of the Court.

■ Mr. Justice White, with whom Mr. Justice Brennan and Mr. Justice Stewart join, concurring.

... In the present case, the State is not concerned with the maintenance of an educational system as an end in itself, it is rather attempting to nurture and develop the human potential of its children, whether Amish or non–Amish: to expand their knowledge, broaden their sensibilities, kindle their imagination, foster a spirit of free inquiry, and increase their human understanding and tolerance. It is possible that most Amish children will wish to continue living the rural life of their parents, in which case their training at home will adequately equip them for their future role. Others, however, may wish to become nuclear physicists, ballet dancers, computer programmers, or historians, and for these occupations, formal training will be necessary.... [A]lthough the question is close, I am unable to say that the State has demonstrated that Amish children who leave school in the eighth grade will be intellectually stultified or unable to acquire new academic skills later....

... I join the Court because the sincerity of the Amish religious policy here is uncontested, because the potentially adverse impact of the state requirement is great, and because the State's valid interest in education has already been largely satisfied by the eight years the children have already spent in school.

■ Mr. Justice Douglas, dissenting in part.

. . . The Court's analysis assumes that the only interests at stake in the case are those of the Amish parents on the one hand, and those of the State on the other. The difficulty with this approach is that, despite the Court's claim, the parents are seeking to vindicate not only their own free exercise claims, but also those of their high-school-age children.

It is argued that the right of the Amish children to religious freedom is not presented by the facts of the case, as the issue before the Court involves only the Amish parents' religious freedom to defy a state criminal statute imposing upon them an affirmative duty to cause their children to attend high school.

First, respondents' motion to dismiss in the trial court expressly asserts, not only the religious liberty of the adults, but also that of the children, as a defense to the prosecutions. It is, of course, beyond question that the parents have standing as defendants in a criminal prosecution to assert the religious interests of their children as a defense.[1] Although the lower courts and a majority of this Court assume an identity of interest between parent and child, it is clear that they have treated the religious interest of the child as a factor in the analysis.

Second, it is essential to reach the question to decide the case, not only because the question was squarely raised in the motion to dismiss, but also because no analysis of religious-liberty claims can take place in a vacuum. If the parents in this case are allowed a religious exemption, the inevitable effect is to impose the parents' notions of religious duty upon their children. Where the child is mature enough to express potentially conflicting desires, it would be an invasion of the child's rights to permit such an imposition without canvassing his views. As in Prince v. Massachusetts, 321 U.S. 158, 64 S.Ct. 438, 88 L.Ed. 645, it is an imposition resulting from this very litigation. As the child has no other effective forum, it is in this litigation that his rights should be considered. And, if an Amish child desires to attend high school, and is mature enough to have that desire respected, the State may well be able to override the parents' religiously motivated objections. Religion is an individual experience. It is not necessary, nor even appropriate, for every Amish child to express his views on the subject in a prosecution of a single adult. Crucial, however, are the views of the child whose parent is the subject of the suit. Frieda Yoder has in fact testified that her own religious views are opposed to high-school

---

1. Thus, in Prince v. Massachusetts, 321 U.S. 158, 64 S.Ct. 438, 88 L.Ed. 645, a Jehovah's Witness was convicted for having violated a state child labor law by allowing her nine-year-old niece and ward to circulate religious literature on the public streets. There, as here, the narrow question was the religious liberty of the adult. There, as here, the Court analyzed the problem from the point of view of the State's conflicting interest in the welfare of the child. But, as Mr. Justice Brennan, speaking for the Court, has so recently pointed out, "The Court [in *Prince*] implicitly held that the custodian had standing to assert alleged freedom of religion . . . rights of the child that were threatened in the very litigation before the Court and that the child had no effective way of asserting herself." Eisenstadt v. Baird, 405 U.S. 438, 446 n. 6, 92 S.Ct. 1029, 1034, 31 L.Ed.2d 349. Here, as in *Prince,* the children have no effective alternate means to vindicate their rights. The question, therefore, is squarely before us.

education. I therefore join the judgment of the Court as to respondent Jonas Yoder. But Frieda Yoder's views may not be those of Vernon Yutzy or Barbara Miller. I must dissent, therefore, as to respondents Adin Yutzy and Wallace Miller as their motion to dismiss also raised the question of their children's religious liberty.

. . .

These children are "persons" within the meaning of the Bill of Rights. We have so held over and over again. . . .

. . .

On this important and vital matter of education, I think the children should be entitled to be heard. While the parents, absent dissent, normally speak for the entire family, the education of the child is a matter on which the child will often have decided views. He may want to be a pianist or an astronaut or an oceanographer. To do so he will have to break from the Amish tradition.

It is the future of the student, not the future of the parents, that is imperiled by today's decision. If a parent keeps his child out of school beyond the grade school, then the child will be forever barred from entry into the new and amazing world of diversity that we have today. The child may decide that that is the preferred course, or he may rebel. It is the student's judgment, not his parents', that is essential if we are to give full meaning to what we have said about the Bill of Rights and of the right of students to be masters of their own destiny.[3] If he is harnessed to the Amish way of life by those in authority over him and if his education is truncated, his entire life may be stunted and deformed. The child, therefore, should be given an opportunity to be heard before the State gives the exemption which we honor today.

The views of the two children in question were not canvassed by the Wisconsin courts. The matter should be explicitly reserved so that new

---

3. The court below brushed aside the students' interests with the offhand comment that "[w]hen a child reaches the age of judgment, he can choose for himself his religion." 49 Wis.2d 430, 440, 182 N.W.2d 539, 543. But there is nothing in this record to indicate that the moral and intellectual judgment demanded of the student by the question in this case is beyond his capacity. Children far younger than the 14- and 15-year-olds involved here are regularly permitted to testify in custody and other proceedings. Indeed, the failure to call the affected child in a custody hearing is often reversible error. See, e.g., Callicott v. Callicott, 364 S.W.2d 455 (Tex. Civ.App.) (reversible error for trial judge to refuse to hear testimony of eight-year-old in custody battle). Moreover, there is substan- tial agreement among child psychologists and sociologists that the moral and intellectual maturity of the 14-year-old approaches that of the adult. See, e.g., J. Piaget, The Moral Judgment of the Child (1948); D. Elkind, Children and Adolescents 75–80 (1970); Kohl- berg, Moral Education in the Schools: A De- velopment View, in R. Muuss, Adolescent Be- havior and Society 193, 199–200 (1971); W. Kay, Moral Development 172–183 (1968); A. Gesell & F. Ilg, Youth: The Years From Ten to Sixteen 175–182 (1956). The maturity of Amish youth, who identify with and assume adult roles from early childhood, see M. Goodman, The Culture of Childhood 92–94 (1970), is certainly not less than that of chil- dren in the general population.

hearings can be held on remand of the case.[4]

. . .

NOTE

What should be the outcome if, as was suggested by Justice Douglas in *Yoder*, there were significant differences of opinion between the children and the parents regarding educational opportunities? In allowing the Amish parents to withdraw the children from school, did the Court also allow the parents to pre-empt a world-view for their children? What effect does *Yoder* have upon the desire of some parents to educate their children at home and not within any established school? If the state sought to force the parent's home-school arrangement to comply with state regulations, would the parent have a Free Exercise argument? *See* Jon S. Lerner, *Protecting Home Schooling Through the Casey Undue Burden Standard*, 62 U. Chi. L. Rev. 363 (1995).

In Jackson v. Benson, 218 Wis.2d 835, 578 N.W.2d 602 (1998), *cert. denied*, 525 U.S. 997, 119 S.Ct. 466, 142 L.Ed.2d 419 (1998), the Wisconsin Supreme Court upheld the Milwaukee's Parental Choice Program. But in Simmons–Harris v. Goff, 86 Ohio St.3d 1, 711 N.E.2d 203 (1999), the public scholarship program of the Cleveland City school district was found to be unconstitutional under the state constitution. And the Sixth Circuit Court of Appeals had held that school voucher programs violate the Establishment Clause of the United States Constitution. The Supreme Court of the United States, in a 5–4 decision, has ruled that Cleveland's school voucher program is constitutional because it vests private individuals with genuine and independent choices. Zelman v. Simmons–Harris, 536 U.S. 639, 122 S.Ct. 2460,, 153 L.Ed.2d 604 (2002). Because of the extensive public policy debate over school vouchers and the continuing litigation in courts over its constitutionality, the issue is likely to be resolved only in the Supreme Court. For commentary, *see* Angela Slate Rawls, Comment, *Eliminating Options Through Choice: Another Look at Private School Vouchers*, 50 Emory L.Rev. 363 (2001); Robert K. Vischer, *Racial Segregation in American Churches and Its Implications for School Vouchers*, 53 Fla. L. Rev. 193 (2001); Frank R. Kemerer, *Reconsidering the Constitutionality of Vouchers*, 30 J. L. & Educ. 435 (2001); Catharine V. Ewing, Comment, *Constitutional Law: Vouchers, Sectarian Schools, and Constitutional Certainty: Choices for the United States Supreme Court and the States*, 53 Okla. L. Rev. 437 (2000); James E. Ryan, *The Supreme Court and Public Schools*, 86 Va. L. Rev. 1335 (2000); Emily Buss, *The Adolescent's Stake in the Allocation of Educational Control Between Parent and State*, 67 U. Chi. L. Rev. 1233 (2000); www.childrenfirstamerica.org/legislation.html. For a general com-

---

4. Canvassing the views of all school-age Amish children in the State of Wisconsin would not present insurmountable difficulties. A 1968 survey indicated that there were at that time only 256 such children in the entire State. Comment, 1971 Wis.L.Rev. 832, 852 n. 132.

mentary on child autonomy, *see* Yochai Benkler, *Siren Songs and Amish Children: Autonomy, Information, and Law*, 76 N.Y.U. L. REV. 23 (2001).

Smith v. Ricci

Supreme Court of New Jersey, 1982.
89 N.J. 514, 446 A.2d 501.

■ CLIFFORD, J.

Appellants challenge a regulation of the State Board of Education (Board) that requires each local school district to develop and implement a family life education program in the public elementary and secondary curricula. N.J.A.C. 6:29–7.1. Appellants contend that such a program impinges upon the free exercise of their religion and constitutes an establishment of religion in violation of the United States Constitution. U.S.Const. amend. I. . . .

The Board adopted the regulation on August 6, 1980. Appellants then sought review in the Appellate Division, R. 2:2–3(a)(2). Before argument was heard in the Appellate Division we certified the matter directly.

In January 1979 the Board appointed a committee, called the Family Life Committee, to make recommendations concerning the teaching of family life and human sexuality in the public schools. Prior to that time the Board's policy toward sex education was embodied in a resolution that had been adopted in 1967. That policy recommended but did not require that local school boards develop programs for sex education. A survey by the Department of Education, conducted at the Family Life Committee's request, determined that under the "recommended-but-not-required" policy, only 40 per cent of the state's public school pupils were receiving sex education. See Report of the Family Life Committee of the New Jersey State Board of Education, August 1979 (hereinafter Report).

In the Report, the Family Life Committee pointed out several sociological factors and statistics that it believed reinforced the need for sex education. Although the source of these statistics is not given, there is nothing to indicate that they are unreliable nor do appellants dispute them. The Report sets forth the following: in the United States one in five births is to a teenager between 15 and 19; in 1977 one million babies were born to girls between the ages of 10 and 18; in New Jersey in 1977, twelve thousand babies were born to girls between 15 and 19; 60% of these girls were unmarried; of the teenagers who do become pregnant when in school, about 80% drop out and do not return to complete their education; research studies continue to show that babies born to adolescent mothers are more apt to be premature and underweight; babies of low birth weight often suffer from a lag in development through their early years which affects their ability to learn in school; the incidence of venereal disease in both males and females continues to rise.

The Committee also cited the results of a 1978 Gallup poll indicating that 77 per cent of the public and 95 per cent of the students favored sex education in the schools. However, the Committee pointed out that no research studies had been found that showed a correlation between teaching about human sexuality and a reduction in teenage pregnancy or venereal disease.

The Committee then made the following recommendations: that the study of family life education as part of the sequential comprehensive kindergarten through twelfth grade curriculum be required; that the State Board's regulation provide for an excusal policy from sections of the curriculum dealing directly with sex education on parental grounds of conscience; that the districts provide appropriate services to assist pregnant teenagers and teenage parents; that the Department of Education be directed to prepare for consideration of the board, administrative code regulations to implement the above recommendations. [Report, supra, at 8–10.]

Thereafter, the Commissioner of Education submitted a proposed regulation to the Board, which considered it at its February 6, 1980 meeting. At this meeting members of the public offered comments, both for and against the proposed regulations. The Board then approved the publication of the proposed regulation. The regulation, along with an invitation for comment, was published in the March 1980 New Jersey Register, 12 N.J.R. 105 (1980).

At its April 8, 1980 meeting the Board again heard extensive public comment on the proposed regulation. Although a variety of objections were raised, the common theme of those opposed to the family life education program was the fear that it would destroy the prerogative of parents to educate their children on matters involving sexual morality, and would inculcate in pupils concepts and attitudes, especially as related to sexuality, that conflict with their parents' views. Those in favor of the program stressed the need for young people to receive information about family life and sexuality, and saw the program as supplementing rather than replacing parental and religious efforts in this area. At the conclusion of this meeting the Board adopted the regulation by a vote of nine to one.

Less than a month later the New Jersey Senate passed a resolution directing the Board to reconsider the Family Life Education regulation. See Senate Resolution No. 24 (May 1, 1980). In response, the Board reviewed the regulations and made some changes at its meeting on June 11, 1980. The revised regulation was published in the July New Jersey Register, 12 N.J.R. 388 (1980), and was adopted at the August 6, 1980 meeting.

The regulation required each local district to institute, by September 1981, a policy that would begin the development of a family life education program. The local programs were to be developed through consultation with and participation of teachers, administrators, parents, pupils in grades nine through twelve, physicians, members of the clergy, and other community members. N.J.A.C. 6:29–7.1(b). Each year the district must give parents an outline of the curriculum and a list of instructional material, and must permit parents to review all the materials prior to their use in the classroom. The regulation also listed the teaching staff members authorized to teach in the program and provided for in-service preparation for those teachers. It also permitted districts to use "resource people," such as physicians, clergymen, attorneys, and psychologists, to assist with the program's development, and required the Department of Education to give technical assistance to local districts in developing their programs.

The regulation devotes one paragraph to defining "family life education programs." It says: (a) As used in this subchapter, "family life education program" means instruction to develop an understanding of the physical, mental, emotional, social, economic, and psychological aspects of interpersonal relationships; the physiological, psychological and cultural foundations of human development, sexuality, and reproduction, at various stages of growth; the opportunity for pupils to acquire knowledge which will support the development of responsible personal behavior, strengthen their own family life now, and aid in establishing strong family life for themselves in the future thereby contributing to the enrichment of the community. [N.J.A.C. 6:29.7.1(a)]

As part of its technical assistance to local districts, the Department of Education has provided the districts with curriculum guidelines that clarify the above definition. These guidelines indicate that although the emphasis of the program is on teaching about human sexuality, that is not its only focus. Other areas of study include such topics as "Family Structure," "Growing Up Emotionally," and "Dating." Although a wide range of physical, psychological, and social phenomena are suggested as appropriate areas of study, the final decision as to what specific topics are appropriate for each district is left to that district. However, local districts must provide a program that satisfies the definition of family life education as given in the regulation.

Finally, the regulation includes an "excusal clause," which states: (i) The local board of education shall establish procedures whereby any pupil, whose parent or guardian presents to the school principal a signed statement that any part of the instruction in family life education is in conflict with his/her conscience, or sincerely held moral or religious beliefs, shall be excused from that portion of the course where such instruction is being given and no penalties as to credit or graduation shall result therefrom. [N.J.S.A. 18A:35–4.6 et seq.] [N.J.A.C. 6:29.7.1(i)][1]

Under the excusal policy a pupil will receive instruction in all aspects of the family life education program unless a parent or guardian objects. In such a case, the pupil will be excused, but only from those parts of the program that the parent finds morally, conscientiously, or religiously objectionable.

Appellants' principal objection to the regulation is that it violates both the Free Exercise and Establishment clauses of the First Amendment.

---

1. Even if this paragraph were not included in the regulation, such an excusal policy would be required by statute, N.J.S.A. 18A:35–4.7, the wording of which is nearly identical to that used in the regulation.

Free Exercise Clause

Appellants assert that by teaching about human reproduction, sexuality, and the development of personal and social values, the schools will "inhibit the moral concepts held by those students who have received them through their Judeo–Christian and other home teaching." As a result, children will be exposed to attitudes, goals, and values that are contrary to their own and to those of their parents, and will thereby be inhibited in the practice of their religion. We do not question that this argument is sincerely made. Whether or not it is well reasoned we need not now decide, for we believe that the simple fact that parents can remove their children from any objectionable part of the program is dispositive. If the program violates a person's beliefs, that person is not required to participate. Where there is no compulsion to participate in this program, there can be no infringement upon appellants' rights freely to exercise their religion. See Medeiros v. Kiyosaki, 52 Haw. 436, 478 P.2d 3124 (1970); Citizens for Parental Rights v. San Mateo County Bd. of Ed., 51 Cal.App.3d 1, 124 Cal.Rptr. 68 (Ct.App.1975), appeal dismissed, 425 U.S. 908, 96 S.Ct. 1502, 47 L.Ed.2d 759 (1976); Hopkins v. Hamden Board of Education, 29 Conn. Sup. 397, 289 A.2d 914 (Ct.Com.Pls.1970), appeal dismissed, 305 A.2d 536 (Conn.1973).

Even though the program permits excusal, appellants argue that it nonetheless inhibits the free exercise of their religion. They assert that requiring pupils affirmatively to assert their objection to the program in front of teachers and peers exerts an intolerable pressure on those pupils such that they may be compelled to abandon their beliefs and to choose not to exercise their option to be excused. Relying on School District of Abington Township v. Schempp, 374 U.S. 203, 83 S.Ct. 1560, 10 L.Ed.2d 844 (1963), they argue that such pressure is constitutionally unacceptable.

We do not doubt that the exercise of the right to be excluded may be difficult for some. The constitution does not guarantee, however, that the exercise of religion will be without difficulty. The Supreme Court repeatedly has upheld neutral laws of general applicability even though such laws have somehow burdened the exercise of some religions....

Appellants' reliance upon Schempp is misplaced. What the Court said in Schempp was that an excusal policy would not save the challenged program (Bible reading in school) from a claim of unconstitutionality under the Establishment Clause. 374 U.S. at 224–25, 83 S.Ct. at 1572–1573, 10 L.Ed.2d at 859. That holding lends no support to appellants' contentions that a family life education program that allows for conscientious excusal will coerce or cajole pupils into abandoning the exercise of their religion.

Courts in at least two states have addressed the validity of sex education curricula in light of free exercise considerations. In both instances the courts held that where there was adequate provision for excusal on the grounds of conscientiously-held belief, sex education or family life education programs did not offend the Free Exercise Clause. The Supreme Court of Hawaii specifically rejected a Schempp-based coercion argument in Medeiros v. Kiyosaki, supra, 52 Haw. at 442, 478 P.2d at 318, holding that where excusal was permitted, no government compulsion inhibiting religion existed. The California Court of Appeals has also rejected appellant's argument that coercion exists despite an excusal policy. Citizens for Parental Rights v. San Mateo County Bd. of Ed., supra, 51 Cal.App.3d at 17–18, 124 Cal.Rptr. at 81–82.

Indeed, both the Hawaii and California courts pointed out that accepting the argument that public schools may not offer curricula that offend the religious or moral views of a particular group would be tantamount to enshrining that group's views as state policy, thereby violating the Establishment Clause. In Epperson v. Arkansas, 393 U.S. 97, 89 S.Ct. 266, 21 L.Ed.2d 228 (1968) the Supreme Court said, "There is and can be no doubt that the First Amendment does not permit the State to require that teaching and learning must be tailored to the principles or prohibitions of any religious sect or dogma." Id. at 106, 89 S.Ct. at 271, 21 L.Ed.2d at 235. The Court in Epperson held that the prohibition of teaching one point of view (evolution) because it was contrary to the religious views of some constituted an impermissible establishment of religion. Appellants' argument is essentially the same as the one rejected in Epperson.

Thus, appellants' argument based on the Free Exercise Clause is flawed in two ways. First, the regulation, because of the excusal clause, does not inhibit the free exercise of religion. Second, to permit the appellants to control what others may study because the subject may be offensive to appellants' religious or moral scruples would violate the Establishment Clause.

Establishment Clause

Appellants contend that the regulation violates the Establishment Clause in that the family life education program will establish secularism (or "Secular Humanism") as a religion and inhibit all traditional religions to the point of establishing secularism as a religion. Appellants' argument focuses on a single part of the Lemon tripartite test (Lemon v. Kurtzman, 403 U.S. 602, 91 S.Ct. 2105, 29 L.Ed.2d 745 (1971)) that the Supreme Court has articulated for identifying the boundaries between church and state. In order to withstand constitutional scrutiny the challenged regulation must have a secular purpose, its primary effect must neither advance nor inhibit religion, and it must not create excessive government entanglement with religion.

Appellants do not contend that the regulation is nonsecular; their argument assumes its secularity. Nor do they present a valid argument that the regulation fosters excessive governmental entanglement with religion.[2] The gravamen of their Establishment Clause argument is that the regulation, because it is secular, will in its primary effect inhibit religion.

---

2. Appellants only "excessive entanglement" argument—that because the regulation permits consultation with members of the clergy in developing the program it fosters excessive entanglement—is clearly without merit. Indeed, although we need not decide the issue here, it appears that if members of the community in general are

This argument is unpersuasive. There is absolutely nothing in the regulation or in the curriculum guidelines that gives even the slightest indication that the program favors a "secular" view of its subject matter over a "religious" one. The program is, as it must be, neither antagonistic toward religion nor supportive of non-religion. The mention of religion in the classroom is not forbidden. Indeed, it might be entirely appropriate in the context of discussing sexuality for a teacher to mention that different religions have different views as to the morality of certain aspects of sexual behavior and to encourage the students to seek guidance from their parents and clergymen. As one writer has stated, As long as the state does not unfairly represent any moral views that might undercut the teaching of a child's religion, sex is as unobjectionable a classroom subject as lyric passages from the Bible. Further, such a course need not be "dehumanizing," or constitute a "religion of secularism". Competing moral interpretations of sex may still be discussed, provided that one particular interpretation is not stressed to the exclusion of others. [Comment, Sex Education: The Constitutional Limits of State Compulsion, 48 S.Cal.L.Rev. 548, 563 (1970) (footnotes omitted).]

The regulation is barren of any requirement that a point of view, be it secular or religious, must be stressed to the exclusion of others. We therefore hold that this program does not contravene any of the three requirements of the Lemon test and does not constitute an establishment of religion.

Appellants argue that the Board's action in adopting N.J.A.C. 6:29–7.1 violates the Due Process Clause of the Fourteenth Amendment because the Board did not show a reasonable relationship between the goals of the family life education program and the means adopted.

The Board, on the other hand, maintains that the Family Life Committee Report, as well as the testimony of knowledgeable people such as the Commissioner of the Department of Health and the Commissioner of Human Services, supports the view that not only is there a relationship between the program and the reduction of teenage pregnancy, venereal disease, and other social problems, but also the program is necessary if these problems are to be ameliorated.

It is well established that a presumption of reasonableness attaches to the actions of an administrative agency and that the burden of proving unreasonableness falls upon those who challenge the validity of the action. Appellants have offered no evidence to meet that burden but instead merely assert that there are no data that prove that the program will have any effect on the societal ills that it attacks. This bare assertion does not satisfy appellants' burden of proving that the regulation is unreasonable.

In addition, the record reveals a sufficient factual basis for the Board's conclusion that the family life education program is a reasonable, desirable,

being consulted, members of the clergy could not be excluded without violating their right of free exercise of religion....

and necessary method of dealing with readily identifiable educational and social problems. If the Board were required to prove the efficacy of each curricular program before implementing it, the Board's ability to operate would be severely and unnecessarily encumbered. No such proof is required.

. . .

The action of the State Board of Education is:

Affirmed.

NOTE

The incidence of home schooling is increasing in America. What are the limits suggested by the previous case concerning parents or the state?

In 1999, Florida became the first state to enact a plan for high school education that targets adolescents in an effort to teach them about marriage and relationship skills. *See* 1998 Fla. Sess. Law Serv. 403 (West) (codified in scattered sections of FLA. STAT. ANN. (West Supp. 1999)).The effort is an attempt to reduce the number of divorces. The issue concerns the ability of the state to intervene in the parent-child relationship in issues which often involve religion and other parental prerogatives concerning the education of their children. For further commentary, *see* Jane Rutherford, *Religion, Rationality, and Special Treatment*, 9 WM. & MARY BILL RTS. J. 303 (2001); Richard W. Garnett, *Taking Pierce Seriously: The Family, Religious Education, and Harm to Children*, 76 NOTRE DAME L. REV. 109 (2000); Michael W. McConnell, *The Problem of Singling Out Religion*, 50 DEPAUL L. REV. 1 (2000); Jesse H. Choper, *A Century of Religious Freedom*, 88 CAL. L. REV. 1709 (2000); Frederick Mark Gedicks, *Towards a Defensible Free Exercise Doctrine*, 68 GEO. WASH. L. REV. 925 (2000).

Board of Ed., Plainfield v. Cooperman

Supreme Court of New Jersey, 1987.
105 N.J. 587, 523 A.2d 655.

■ HANDLER, J.

Acquired Immune Deficiency (AIDS) is a disease that disables the body from fighting infection. The cause of the disease is infection by the Human T-Lymphotropic Virus, Type III (HLTV–III, also known as Human Immunodeficiency Virus (HIV)). Three categories of outcomes result from infection by HTLV–III. The first, AIDS, is the most severe form of the infection; and most victims of the disease die within two years. The second possible form of infection is AIDS–Related Complex (ARC), a milder degree of immunodeficiency. The third and most common form of infection is asymptomatic, resulting in no abnormal infections.

On August 30, 1985, the State Commissioners of Health and Education jointly announced the adoption of policy guidelines for the admission to schools of children with AIDS, ARC, or HTLV–III antibody. These guidelines were promulgated by a representative of the Commissioner of Education (Commissioner) to county school superintendents on September 3, 1985.

According to the Commissioner, these policy guidelines were based upon epidemiological studies indicating "that AIDS is not transmitted through casual contact as would be present in the school environment." Pursuant to these guidelines, children with AIDS/ARC or HTLV–III antibody were required to be admitted to regular school attendance, unless the following exceptional conditions were evident:

a. The student is not toilet-trained or is incontinent, or otherwise is unable to control drooling.

b. The student is unusually physically aggressive with a documented history of biting or harming others.

The guidelines also established a Medical Advisory Panel (MAP or Panel), comprised of independent medical experts appointed by the Board of Health, to review local school board decisions to exclude a child. In reaching its decision, the Panel was empowered to consider written statements of reasons as well as other "written documentation submitted by the local district and/or such personal testimony as may be necessary." The Panel was required to render a written recommendation to the Commissioner of Education "as to whether the district has met its burden of proof to deny admission of the child."

The present case results from the efforts of two local school boards to exclude students with AIDS or ARC from the classroom. On September 3, 1985, the Plainfield Board of Education excluded from its pre-school program a female child named "I.C." The child was diagnosed as having AIDS and was living in foster care under the guardianship of the Division of Youth and Family Services (DYFS).

The Plainfield Board initially sought the opinion of James M. Oleskie, M.D., the Director of the Division of Allergy, Immunology, and Infectious Diseases at the University of Medicine and Dentistry of New Jersey, who served as I.C.'s treating physician. On receiving Dr. Oleskie's recommendation that I.C. be admitted to the classroom, the School Board sought a second opinion, this time of Lawrence F. Frenkel, M.D., a professor of Clinical Pediatrics and Director of the Division of Immunology, Allergy and Infectious Diseases at Rutgers Medical School. Dr. Frenkel's report concluded, "it is my strong opinion that the students should not be kept out of schools and do not seem to pose a risk to other children in their environment." Notwithstanding these reports, the school board continued to exclude I.C. from its pre-school program.

The Plainfield Board next assembled a "Child Study Team" comprised of a psychologist, a learning disability consultant, a speech therapist, a school worker, and a physician, to ascertain whether I.C. should be eligible for special education. Pending completion of the Study Team's report, I.C. was excluded from regular kindergarten education and received two hours of home instruction per day. DYFS filed a petition with the Commissioner of Education for declaratory judgment to determine the validity of the Commissioner's action.

The exclusion was reviewed by the Medical Advisory Panel, which had been constituted under the Commissioner's guidelines. The Panel considered letters and evaluations submitted by I.C.'s and the school's doctor, as well as written psychological evaluations from two other doctors. In addition, the school's physician personally appeared before the Panel. Dr. Oleskie, I.C.'s treating physician, recommended the admission of I.C., concluding that the student did not pose a risk of transmission to others in the school environment. Dr. John E. Hampton, the school's medical inspector, recommended that I.C. be excluded as a result of her reduced immunity to infection. The Plainfield Board had no contact with the Panel throughout its deliberation process.

On October 2, 1985, the Panel concluded that the data that it considered "describe no tendencies toward behavior which could possibly be related to spread of infection." The Panel then issued a decision directing that the Plainfield Board "immediately admit I.C. to regular classroom attendance in the same manner and on the same basis as [it] would admit any other child eligible for school attendance." Although I.C. was neurologically impaired and thus being evaluated for possible classification as educationally handicapped, the Commissioner ordered the board not to use this as an excuse "for not placing I.C. in a regular classroom environment."

The Plainfield Board responded by requesting an additional 30 days to determine the appropriate placement of the child. Notwithstanding this request, on October 10 the Division of Youth and Family Services brought an action in Superior Court, Chancery Division, to enforce compliance with the Commissioner's order. On October 15, 1985, prior to the return date of the order to show cause issued by the Chancery Division, the Commissioner responded to the Plainfield Board's "30 day" request. The Commissioner's letter stated that even if I.C. is to be classified for a special education program, she should be placed in regular kindergarten class pending transfer to a special class within the school. I.C., the Commissioner ordered, was to be admitted to school no later than October 21.

On October 17, the Plainfield Board appealed the Commissioner's September 3 guidelines and October 3 order. The Appellate Division, with the consent of both parties, transferred the appeal to the State Board of Education. On October 31, 1985, the Chancery Division ordered I.C. admitted to school immediately but stayed its order until November 8. The State Board affirmed the Commissioner's order on November 8. In addition the State Board determined that in accordance with N.J.A.C. 6:2–1.14, "oral argument [was not] necessary in order for it to arrive at a fair determination of the case." Due process, the Board concluded, "does not require a trial type hearing as to nonfactual issues; trial procedure is not required on issues of law, policy or discretion. Thus, once the medical determination was made that I.C.'s conditions did not warrant excluding her from school," the Commissioner was within his authority to direct I.C.'s admittance. The Plainfield Board appealed the State Board's decision to the Appellate Division.

The appeal was joined with the case of "Jane Doe," a five-year-old child diagnosed as having ARC who was refused admission to kindergarten by the Washington Borough Board of Education. The Medical Advisory Panel, after considering behavioral and pathological data and the oral testimony of one physician, concluded that Jane Doe should be admitted to school. When the school board refused the Commissioner's order to admit Jane Doe, a Chancery Division action ensued and the Appellate Division granted leave to appeal under Rule 2:2–3(b).

The Appellate Division issued its opinion in these appeals on March 15, 1986. Board of Educ. of City of Plainfield v. Cooperman, 209 N.J.Super. 174. The court held that the Commissioner's "Policy Guidelines" were of such widespread, continuing and prospective effect as to amount to administrative rules, which should have been promulgated under formal rulemaking procedures. Because the proceedings regarding I.C. and Jane Doe were conducted pursuant to invalid guidelines, the order requiring the immediate admittance of the two students was reversed and remanded to the Commissioner for hearings.

In addition, the Appellate Division concluded that the proceedings held pursuant to the Commissioner's guidelines violated "fundamental due process." Neither the local school boards nor the excluded children were provided the opportunity to be heard or to present or cross-examine witnesses regarding their written reports.

The Appellate Division next addressed the issue of whether the students should be admitted to the classroom pending "a sufficient showing of a potential risk of exposure to contagious disease." The Appellate Division concluded that the hearings should precede the admission of the children to the classroom. . . .

As to the two children for whom this action was originally brought, this case is moot. I.C. was admitted to a class for neurologically impaired children after a stipulation of dismissal was concluded between the Plainfield Board of Education and the DYFS. Jane Doe has since moved from Washington Borough. Thus, hearings regarding the admission to school of these two children are no longer necessary.

On August 4, 1986, the State Board of Education proposed new regulations under the formal rulemaking procedures mandated by the Appellate Division. After receipt and consideration of public comment, the State Board of Education adopted (with minor modifications) the proposed rules. . . . The two regulations are codified at N.J.A.C. 6:29–4.4, 8:61–1.1.

The appellant boards of education argue that the power to exclude students from public schools due to health reasons resides in the schools and the local school boards. . . .

The Commissioner argues that while these statutes do place power in local school officials, that power is limited by two sets of constraints. First, the power must be exercised reasonably. Like other government actors, the school board cannot act in an arbitrary fashion, especially when a child's right to an education is at stake. Reasonableness in the present context clearly involves appropriate deference to medical expertise. In the case of Jane Doe and I.C., all the medical experts and medical authorities agreed that the presence of the AIDS virus in the children did not by itself pose any danger to other children or to the child the board wished to exclude.

The second set of constraints on local school officials is the preemptive regulations of the State Commissioner and State Board of Education adopted pursuant to the school laws. Local boards of education must act in conformity to the regulating guidelines promulgated by the Commissioner and the State Board of Education as part of their duties to execute the Education Clause of the New Jersey Constitution....

The authority granted the Commissioner to promulgate regulations and to resolve disputes has always been interpreted broadly.... Though the authorizing statute does not speak specifically of the power to promulgate regulations on the issue of excluding children from the classroom due to health reasons, that specific power can be inferred from the broad powers that are granted to the Department. The regulations in question fit within this context: they are thoughtful efforts intended to protect both school children's health and school children's right to a public education.[2]

The regulations promulgated by the State Board of Education establish the following procedures for any exclusion from school of Human Immuno-deficiency Virus (HIV) infected children. The board can exclude the pupil only under very limited circumstances. First, exclusion is allowed if the district medical officer, the pupil's parent(s) or guardian(s), and the pupil's physician all agree that the pupil fits the criteria listed in N.J.A.C. 8:61–1.1.[3] A HIV-infected pupil cannot be excluded from attending school before the district medical officer concludes that the pupil does fit the regulatory criteria. Once the district medical officer so concludes, the board is authorized to exclude the child from school.

If the district medical officer disagrees with the pupil's physician as to whether the pupil manifests the relevant conditions, the case then goes before the Medical Advisory Panel established by the Department of

---

2. In School Board of Nassau County v. Arline, 480 U.S. 1123, 107 S.Ct. 1123, 94 L.Ed.2d 307 (1987), the United States Supreme Court held that a person afflicted with a contagious disease may be a "handicapped individual" for the purposes of Section 504. *Arline* involved tuberculosis, not AIDS, but the Court's reasoning and holding applied broadly to all contagious diseases and not merely to the specific facts before the Court. This may suggest that the Federal Rehabilitation Act may be relevant to cases involving the exclusion of children with AIDS from public education involving particular programs. Section 504 of the Rehabilitation Act of 1973, 29 U.S.C. § 794, provides that no otherwise qualified handicapped individual shall, solely by reason of her handicap, be excluded from participating in any program receiving federal financial assistance.

3. The criteria are as follows:

1. The pupil is not toilet-trained or is incontinent, or is unable to control drooling.

2. The pupil is unusually physically aggressive with a documented history of biting or harming others. [N.J.A.C. 8:61–1.1(b).]

Health. The district board of education passes on to the Panel all medical information that was before the board, medical information submitted to the board by the pupil's parent(s) or guardian(s), and a recent evaluation of the child's behavior—as that behavior is relevant to N.J.A.C. 8:61–1.1.

The board has the burden of proof. Each party can submit additional written information; and "[t]he Panel shall call for any oral and/or written information it deems necessary for it to reach a determination."

The Panel shall render a written conclusion with supporting reasons and analysis included. The parties may file with the Commissioner of Education written exceptions on issues of fact and of law. The Commissioner, after reviewing the Panel's opinion and the filed exceptions, can do one of three things: 1) direct the pupil's immediate enrollment, 2) confirm the board's decision to exclude the pupil, or 3) "[d]etermine that the matter is a contested case and direct that it be transmitted to the Office of Administrative Law for further determinations."

It is contended that the procedures established fail to protect the parties' constitutional rights to due process.[5] The United States Supreme Court has described the Due Process Clause as guaranteeing "that deprivation of life, liberty or property by adjudication be preceded by notice and opportunity for hearing appropriate to the nature of the case," Mullane v. Central Hanover Trust Co., 339 U.S. 306, 313, 70 S.Ct. 652, 656, 94 L.Ed. 865, 873 (1950), "the timing and content of the hearing [depending] on appropriate accommodation of the competing interests involved," Goss v. Lopez, 419 U.S. 565, 579, 95 S.Ct. 729, 738, 42 L.Ed.2d 725, 737 (1975).

In Mathews v. Eldridge, 424 U.S. 319, 96 S.Ct. 893, 47 L.Ed.2d 12 (1976), the Supreme Court offered three factors to be considered in evaluating whether a particular procedure is sufficient to satisfy the requirements of due process:

> first, the private interest that will be affected by the official action; second, the risk of an erroneous deprivation of such interest through the procedures used, and the probable value, if any, of additional or substitute procedural safeguards; and finally, the Government's interest, including the function involved and the fiscal and administrative burdens that the additional or substitute procedural requirement would entail. [Id. at 335, 96 S.Ct. at 903, 47 L.Ed.2d at 33.]

The interests at stake include the pupil's interests in receiving an education and having that education be in a classroom setting, the concurring government interest that children receive an education and having that education be in a classroom setting, and the government's interest in protecting its citizens from dangerous diseases. See N.J. Const. of 1947, art. VIII, § 4, para. 1 (constitutional right to an education); Goss v. Lopez, 419

5. This applies to the individual parties involved in the dispute, not to the school boards. The school boards are State agencies, public entities whose power is delegated to them by the state legislature. See N.J.S.A. 18A:10–1 to 18A:12–20. Because school boards are themselves agents of the State, it would be a misstatement in this context to ascribe to school boards due process rights against improper state action.

U.S. 565, 95 S.Ct. 729, 42 L.Ed.2d 725 (1975) (due process protections against suspension from school); Jacobson v. Massachusetts, 197 U.S. 11, 25 S.Ct. 358, 49 L.Ed. 643 (1905) (compulsory vaccination) (societal interests in health sometimes overcomes individual rights). Both the interest in education and the interest in public health underscore the importance of having accurate proceedings, and speedy hearings to the extent that such is compatible with accuracy. The government also has an interest in relatively informal hearings to reduce the fiscal and administrative burdens of the procedures.

In evaluating how well the procedures in question serve the interests mentioned, we use as a guidepost Professor Davis' list of four elements necessary to a fair trial:

> (1) adequate notice, (2) a chance to know the opposing evidence and argument and to present evidence and argument in response, (3) a chance to confront and to cross-examine adverse witnesses, and (4) an impartial deciding officer. [2 K. Davis, Administrative Law Treatise § 10:6, at 327 (2nd ed.1979).]

No problem of notice exists because the procedure commences only after it is determined that the board's medical inspector disagrees with the pupil's physician on whether the child fits the relevant criteria. The regulations contain procedures through which the pupil's parent(s) or guardian(s) are informed of the opposing evidence and argument, and through which that party can present evidence and argument in response. There is little doubt that the Panel is an impartial deciding body.

The regulations do not contain an explicit authorization or prohibition of cross-examination or the right to produce witnesses. However, those overseeing the hearings have discretion in the conduct of hearings.

The Appellate Division determined that both the school children and the school boards have the right to present witnesses and to engage in cross-examination. We note and emphasize that the discretion delegated under the rules to the Medical Panel expressly includes the power to allow any party to call witnesses and to allow cross-examination. In cases where the child's admissibility is being disputed, the contested issues will almost always be fact-sensitive. Because of the importance of the rights at stake as well as the dire consequences that could result from an erroneous decision, the right to call witnesses with the attendant right of cross-examination must be provided automatically upon the request of the parties.

In sum, the discretionary authority delegated to the Medical Panel under the regulations promulgated by the Commissioner expressly and impliedly imports the obligation to summon witnesses with the attendant right of cross-examination on its own initiative or upon the application of any party before it. As construed, the regulations prescribing this discretionary authority are clearly sufficient to protect the constitutional and statutory interests implicated by the proceedings that will be conducted under these regulations.

In view of the fact that, pursuant to the Appellate Division's judgment, the Commissioners of the Department of Education and the Department of Health have promulgated formal regulations, the judgment is modified, and as modified is affirmed, and further, the regulations, as interpreted herein, are upheld.

NOTES

The Department of Health and Human Services, through the Centers for Disease Control and Prevention (CDC), provides surveillance reports on the HIV/AIDS epidemic in the United States and dependent areas. The following statistics were reported in CDC, *HIV/AIDS Surveillance Report, 2005*, Vol. 17 (2006). The report is available at http://cdc.gov/hiv/topics. surveillance/resources/reports/.

(1) From 2001 through 2005, thirty-three states accounted for approximately 63% of the epidemic. At the end of 2005, an estimated 476,095 persons in those states were living with HIV/AIDS. *Id.* at 5. Three states, California, Florida and New York reported 43% of the commutative AIDS cases through 2005. *Id.* at 9. In all fifty states and the District of Columbia, the estimated rate of AIDS cases was 14.9 per 100,000 population. *Id.* at 6.

(2) In all fifty states, the largest number of HIV/AIDS cases occurred among persons aged 40–44 years and accounted for 20% of all cases in 2005. During the period 2001–2005, the estimated number of cases decreased 51% among children less than 13 years of age. *Id.*

(3) In all fifty states and the District of Columbia in 2005, the rates of AIDS cases were 59 per 100,000 in the black population; 19.8 per 100,000 in the Hispanic population; 8 per 100,000 in the American Indian/Alaska Native population; 6.3 per 100,000 in the white population; and 4 per 100,000 in the Asian/Pacific Islander population. *Id.*

(4) Males accounted for 73% of all AIDS cases diagnosed in 2005. *Id.* at 7.

(5) In 2005, there were 430 cases of HIV infection in children and 93 cases of AIDS in children. *Id.* at 9.

For statistics concerning the global HIV/AIDS epidemic, see http:// www.unaids.org/en/HIV_data/2006GlobalReport/default.asp (providing link to United Nations *Report on the Global Epidemic*). In addition, for general information see http://www.cdc.gov/hiv/stts/cumilati.htm. Many of the issues involving discrimination and HIV/AIDS are addressed through the Federal Americans With Disabilities Act and the Rehabilitation Act, but some states have enacted legislation addressing the special needs of children, partially in response to the HIV/AIDS epidemic. *See, e.g.,* Walter Wadlington and Raymond C. O'Brien, Family Law Statutes, International Conventions and Uniform Laws, 200–330 (3d ed. 2007) (providing the Safe Haven Statute, the Standby Guardianship statute, and the Virginia long term foster care statute). For an analysis of how HIV/AIDS may affect the broad spectrum of family relationships, *see* Raymond C. O'Brien, *AIDS: Perspectives on the American Family*, 34 VILL. L. REV. 209 (1989).

B. CHILDREN BEYOND PARENTAL CONTROL

L.A.M. v. State

Supreme Court of Alaska, 1976.
547 P.2d 827.

■ ERWIN, JUSTICE.

L.A.M. seeks review of the superior court's order dated July 26, 1973, declaring her a delinquent child for violation of AS 09.50.010,[2] i.e., willful failure to comply with certain court orders made after a prior adjudication that she was a child in need of supervision.[3]

In order to understand L.A.M.'s arguments and place her situation in context, it will be necessary to set out her history at some length.

L.A.M. was born in Canada in 1958 and was adopted by the M.'s shortly thereafter. The M.'s soon were divorced and Mrs. M. moved with L.A.M. to Alaska. In 1971 Mrs. M. married Mr. C. and retired from work, intending to spend more time with L.A.M. Difficulties arose almost immediately with L.A.M. neglecting to return home after staying with friends.

L.A.M. began a consistent pattern of running away in the Spring and Summer of 1972. During this period two petitions were filed seeking to have her declared a child in need of supervision, but in both cases the petitions were dismissed on stipulation and the matter handled informally.[4]

---

2. AS 09.50.010 provides in relevant part:

Acts or omissions constituting contempt. The following acts or omissions in respect to a court of justice or court proceedings are contempts of the authority of the court:

. . .

(5) disobedience of a lawful judgment, order, or process of the court....

3. AS 47.10.290 provides in relevant part:

In this chapter, unless the context otherwise requires,

. . .

(7) "child in need of supervision" is a minor whom the court determines is within the provisions of (AS 47.10.010(a)(2), (3), (4), and (6)). [Matter in parentheses supplied.]

AS 47.10.010(a)(2), (3) and (6) respectively provide:

[B]y reason of being wayward or habitually disobedient is uncontrolled by his parent, guardian or custodian;

[I]s habitually truant from school or home, or habitually so conducts himself as to injure or endanger the morals or health of himself or others;

. . .

[A]ssociates with vagrant, vicious or immoral people, or engages in an occupation or is in a situation dangerous to life or limb or injurious to the health, morals, or welfare of himself or others....

4. Children's Rule 4(d) provides:

Informal Disposition. If the intake officer, after investigation, believes that in the best interest of the child the matter should be handled on an informal basis,

On November 2, 1972, a new petition was filed. At the hearing L.A.M. admitted the allegations of the petition and was declared a child in need of supervision. She was ordered detained at the McLaughlin Youth Center pending adjudication.

On December 12, 1972, the disposition hearing was continued and L.A.M. was released to her parents. One week later the court was informed that she had run away. A pick-up order was issued and the minor was brought back to court on December 27, 1972, at which time she was detained pending disposition. The disposition hearing was finally held on January 11, 1973. Upon listening to testimony, the Master for the Family Court filed his recommendation that the minor be "released to her parents." A superior court judge adopted the finding and executed a release.

On March 19, 1973, L.A.M. was brought back to court by an intake officer who informed the court that she had "been a runaway almost constantly since the time the court released her." The intake officer then filed a petition with the court alleging that the minor was a "child in need of supervision" by virtue of having been truant from school in violation of AS 47.10.010(a)(3) and AS 14.30.010 (truancy).[5] At the hearing the court was informed that Mrs. C. had obtained a child psychiatrist who had met with the child and her mother, and together they had worked out some program of counseling. The parties agreed that L.A.M. would be placed in a foster home during a period of counseling and the judge accepted a stipulation to that effect. Having previously explained to L.A.M. that if she violated a court order she could be held in contempt of court and incarcerated, the judge informed the child that she was not to leave the foster home without contacting her psychiatrist, her social worker, or her mother. She agreed. The minor was released from McLaughlin on March 31, 1973, and placed in a foster home. She ran away on April 2, without notification, and was not apprehended until May 4.

[A CINS petition was filed by an intake officer.] The court denied the motion [to dismiss] but permitted the State to file an amended petition alleging as a separate count an act of delinquency predicated upon "criminal contempt."

A petition alleging delinquency was filed on May 23, 1973, at which time a hearing was held. In responding to the petition L.A.M. denied the allegations and requested a trial. Pending trial, she was placed at the Alaska Children's Services receiving home. A written order was entered on

---

he may thereafter refrain from filing a petition and shall thereafter on behalf of the court, counsel with the child and parents, guardian or custodian, and with their consent and cooperation establish such informal supervision or disposition of the child matter as the circumstances may require.

5. AS 14.30.010 provides in relevant part:

When attendance compulsory. (a) Every child between seven and 16 years of age shall attend school at the public school in the district in which the child resides during each school term. Every parent, guardian or other person having the responsibility for or control of a child between seven and 16 years of age shall insure that the child is not absent from attendance.

June 8, 1973, specifically setting out the conditions under which L.A.M. would reside at the receiving home pending her adjudication hearing. Specifically, it provided that "[T]he child is not to remain away from the Anchorage Children's Christian Home overnight without the permission of the appropriate adult authorities of the home."

[After this order was entered L.A.M. ran away four times.]

. . .

On March 18, 1974, Ms. Lankford [of the Division of Corrections Probation Department] filed a further petition seeking revocation of probation. In it she alleged that on February 20, 1974, the minor ran away from the receiving home and remained away until March 16, 1974, when she was apprehended by the police. At the hearing on the petition, held on March 22, 1974, the court found the minor had violated the conditions of her probation and had run away from the receiving home. The court considered the minor's objections presented by her attorney and, after considering the evidence and the argument of the parties, directed that the minor be institutionalized.

L.A.M. seeks to have her adjudication of delinquency set aside on two grounds. She contends that both as a matter of statutory interpretation and constitutional law, a child in need of supervision may not be prosecuted for criminal contempt; or, in the alternative, if such a prosecution is allowable, such prosecution cannot result in incarceration. Upon discussing the nature of contempt in this case, each of these grounds be dealt with in order.

. . .

[T]he contempt order issued by the court would obviously be classified as "criminal." Were L.A.M. an adult, her failure to abide by court orders would be characterized as a "crime" under AS 09.50.010(5). Hence, L.A.M. could properly be declared a delinquent under AS 47.10.010(a)(1) after a proceeding in the Children's Court.

L.A.M. grounds her constitutional argument in Breese v. Smith,[9] where this court ruled that the right to liberty set out in Art. I, Sec. 1, of the Alaska State Constitution[10] guarantees every Alaskan regardless of age "... total personal immunity from governmental control: the right to be let alone ...," which L.A.M. contends the supreme court qualified only to the extent that it "... must yield when [it] intrudes upon the freedom of others...." Therefore, she continues, a citizen's right to liberty as enunciated in *Breese,* supra, (bolstered by the more recently enacted "right to

---

9.   501 P.2d 159, 168–170 (Alaska 1972).

10.   Art. I of the declaration of rights of the Alaska Constitution, § 1, provides:

Inherent Rights. This constitution is dedicated to the principles that all persons have a natural right to life, liberty, the pursuit of happiness, and the enjoyment of the rewards of their own industry; that all persons are equal and entitled to equal rights, opportunities, and protection under the law; and that all persons have corresponding obligations to the people and to the State.

privacy")[11] cannot be infringed by preventing her from doing anything that does not injure a specific definable victim. Consequently, L.A.M. concludes since her conduct, i.e. running away from home and foster home placement, did not injure anyone (except perhaps herself, which she contends has not been proved), it necessarily follows that it cannot constitutionally be interfered with by the State because there is no compelling state interest to justify such an interference.

L.A.M. assumes that the only interest to be protected by legislation in this area is that of the children. This is simply not the case. The parents' interest as well as the State's must be considered.

Proceedings against children alleged to be in need of supervision are in substance and effect custody disputes where the contestants are parent and child, and the parent appeals to the court to vindicate and enforce his custody rights in the child against that child.[13] Viewed in this light, the statutes creating the status "child in need of supervision" provide a judicial remedy and discourage resort to self-help and the attendant risk of violence.[14]

Thus, before L.A.M. can sustain her case that the child in need of supervision procedure, including the invocation of the court's contempt power to enforce orders made pursuant to it, is an unconstitutional invasion of her liberty and privacy, she must first establish that her mother

---

11. Alaska Constitution, Art. I, § 22, provides:

Right of Privacy. The right of the people to privacy is recognized and shall not be infringed. The legislature shall implement this section.

13. While there is much discussion of parental rights in reported cases, few cases attempt to define those rights making discussion difficult. A careful review of the literature, including case law, treatise and law review, indicates that the following have been listed as "parental rights" protected to varying degrees by the Constitution:

(1) Physical possession of the child which, in the case of a custodial parent includes the day-to-day care and companionship of the child. In the case of a non-custodial parent, possession is tantamount to the right to visitation.

(2) The right to discipline the child, which includes the right to inculcate in the child the parent's moral and ethical standards.

(3) The right to control and manage a minor child's earnings.

(4) The right to control and manage a minor child's property.

(5) The right to be supported by an adult child.

(6) The right to have the child bear the parent's name.

(7) The right to prevent an adoption of the child without the parents' consent.

Of these so called residual parental rights, those that remain after custody is placed in another include the right to consent to an adoption and to withhold consent to prevent an adoption, the right to visitation and the right to have the child bear the parents' name. See the discussion in Burt, Forcing Protection on Children and Their Parents, 69 Michigan 1259 (1971); Dobson, The Juvenile Court and Parental Rights, 4 Family Law Quarterly 393 (1970). . . .

14. By withdrawing court assistance (and police assistance) from embattled parents, the state is not inducing compromise but may encourage violence, since parents have the right under Alaska law to physically control their children. See AS 11.15.110(1) as interpreted in State v. England, 220 Or. 395, 349 P.2d 668 (1960), and compare the civil liability of parents for disciplining their children which is discussed in Hebel v. Hebel, 435 P.2d 8, 14–15 (Alaska 1967).

has no legally enforceable right to her custody and the State thus has no right to enforce such an order. We note at the outset, however, that there is more to the parent-child relationship than simple custody. It is love and trust and a responsibility toward each other which cannot be defined legally. It is impossible to discuss severing this relationship without considering the heartache and anguish of the parents who must ultimately live with themselves and the decision after the child reaches adulthood. Further, the consideration of such an issue must accept the limitations of the State to be a parent; good intentions are not adequate substitutes for the day-to-day relationship which we have come to accept as necessary to the growth of children into responsible adults. True, like all legal rights, a parent's right to the custody of his child is not absolute and may be lost through divorce, by conduct depriving the child of the necessities of life, by abandonment, by the child's emancipation or, subject to constitutional limitations, where the welfare of the child requires a limitation or termination of parental rights.

L.A.M. was given an opportunity to show any of the foregoing as a defense to a finding that she was a "child in need of supervision" or, subsequent thereto, to a finding that she had committed criminal contempt of court and was therefore delinquent by violating orders regarding her placement; but she failed to do so.

Runaway children of L.A.M.'s age are generally incapable of providing for or protecting themselves. As a result, police spend a substantial amount of time protecting these youths from those who would prey upon them, as well as protecting the community from those who are ultimately driven to criminal activity to provide themselves with the necessities of life.

Various other social agencies also expend considerable efforts attempting to protect and shelter runaways in an effort to provide both an alternative to criminal activities and counseling in lieu of that they received from their parents. Without question these children's matters are of broad public interest and concern. They go to all aspects of the physical and mental well being of such children.

The family, school, social agency and police resources allocated to aid the runaway are enormous. In this case, the child had continuing aid and support of (1) her mother and step-father, (2) a private psychiatrist hired by her mother, (3) counseling with social workers in Division of Family and Children's Services, (4) probation officers in Division of Corrections, (5) school counselors, (6) psychologists and psychiatrists from Langdon Clinic, (7) Alaska Youth Advocates, (8) group home counselors, (9) her court-appointed attorney, and (10) the court. To assert that the State has no interest in this child is to deny that the function of government is to protect its citizens. All of this presupposes the heartache and anguish of the parents, who in the first instance have been unable to deal with this problem but who must also live with the solution.

This court has previously found that there is sufficient State interest to justify restrictive measures on much less substantial grounds. Further, this court has noted that distinct government interests with reference to children may justify legislation that could not properly be applied to adults.

The State has a legitimate interest in protecting children from venereal disease, from exposure to the use of dangerous and illicit drugs, from attempted rape, and from physical injury, all of which occurred in this case. Doubtless the State will never be entirely successful in its efforts. It does, however, have the right and obligation to *try* to protect its young people from such conditions. The test set out by this court in Ravin v. State,[24] is whether the means chosen by the State are closely and substantially related to an appropriate government interest. Clearly they are here.

While it may be argued that the necessary "supervision" contemplated by the statute is simply the furnishing of food, clothing, shelter and schooling in lieu of that which would otherwise have been provided by a parent, this argument begs the question, for the purpose of the supervision or treatment contemplated by the creation of the child in need of supervision and its predecessor non-criminal delinquency was reintegration of the child into her family and resumption of parental custody including parental control (cf. AS 47.10.280). Thus, the State's efforts regarding the child are not directed solely at providing an alternate living situation (as they are in a true case of dependency) but at putting the child back in her own home. The reestablishment of her mother's custody and supervision over her and any foster placement is merely a means to that end, not an end in itself. Thus, by rejecting these efforts L.A.M. defeats, or at least slows, this reintegration process and thereby prejudices her mother's right to her custody and control, subjecting herself to the more severe sanction contemplated by AS 09.50.020.

We note that L.A.M.'s primary argument in this case is that as a child in need of supervision whose conduct from the inception of the case to the present has not changed, she may not be placed in a closed setting, i.e. one where the doors may be locked. However, the cases upon which L.A.M. relies proceed to a different point, namely that the child should not be placed in a state training school. In Colorado, California, Illinois and New York, children in need of supervision can at the first instance be placed in juvenile halls or youth centers, i.e. places with locked doors, but cannot be placed at the state training school, i.e. maximum security institutions. The McLaughlin Youth Center in Anchorage is more the equivalent of a juvenile hall than it is a state training school. It should be noted that Alaska has contracts with Colorado and California to place Alaska delinquents who are too sophisticated for McLaughlin in the state institutions in those states. Thus L.A.M. is not to be placed at either the California or Colorado training schools; she is threatened with placement at the McLaughlin Youth Center.

Substantial evidence was introduced during the many hearings of this case regarding the population at the McLaughlin Youth Center. Based upon that evidence, it is clear that the kind of children who are extremely

---

24. 537 P.2d 494 (Alaska 1975).

aggressive, and extremely hardened in delinquency, are not treated at McLaughlin Youth Center but are sent outside for placement at schools in Colorado and California under contract with the State of Alaska. While the population at McLaughlin is made up at the present time exclusively of "delinquents," the evidence introduced at trial convinces us that while delinquency in some form is a prerequisite to gaining admission to McLaughlin, it is not the real reason that the child is at McLaughlin. The overwhelming majority of delinquents with strong family ties are treated in the community. Those delinquents who end up at McLaughlin are by and large there for the same reason that L.A.M. may be there, namely an unwillingness to remain at home or a home substitute and heed parental or a custodian's regulations. Based upon the evidence, it appears that L.A.M. and other chronic runaways would not be distinguishable in sophistication, exposure to criminal activity, etc., from the average child in the population at McLaughlin and that therefore the reasoning of the cases cited by L.A.M. should not apply to Alaska.

Whether we characterize L.A.M. as a delinquent child, a child in need of supervision, a dependent child, or merely a child whose custody is disputed in a domestic relations proceeding, the court has authority, upon extending all procedural safeguards, to make orders affecting her custody. It is argued, however, that this is a situation where the court has no power to enforce its order, and thus the court must release L.A.M. This view is contrary to the inherent power of the court to enforce its orders or decrees. While the court may have limitations on its power to act, there are only due process limitations on its authority to compel enforcement of its orders. Hence, we reject the argument that the superior court lacked the authority to enforce specific orders against L.A.M. in this case.

The lower court determined that L.A.M. would not abide by any orders it entered regarding her supervision under AS 47.10.080(j). This behavior constitutes willful criminal contempt of the court's authority; were she an adult, her actions would be characterized as a "crime" under Alaska statutes. She was, therefore, properly declared a delinquent and subject to those sanctions available for the correction of a delinquent minor's behavior. Certainly, conciliation should precede coercion; and if coercion is necessary, mild sanctions should first be tried before more severe sanctions are imposed. However, where mild sanctions fail, the court's orders must be enforced and severe sanctions should be imposed if necessary. In the instant case, all available sanctions, save institutionalization, were tried and found unsuccessful. Thus, the lower court determined that it had no choice but to order L.A.M. institutionalized.

. . .

■ BOOCHEVER, JUSTICE, with whom RABINOWITZ, CHIEF JUSTICE, joins, concurring.

I concur in the court's opinion based on the last three paragraphs thereof. I would not reach the other issues discussed in the opinion. Protection of parental rights to care, custody and supervision do not seem to me to be an appropriate rationale for placing a child in an institution. In my opinion, the court's efforts were devoted primarily to furthering the welfare of the child, a subject in which the state does have an interest. There was ample testimony to indicate that L.A.M.'s conduct was harmful to her.[2]

On the basis of the record, I do not believe that we can conclude that police spend countless hours protecting the community from anti-social conduct of runaway children. Recent studies indicate that status offenders (such as runaways) are not a source of general harm to others as contrasted with children who have committed offenses which, if perpetrated by adults, would be crimes.[3] I concur in the opinion since I believe that the state has an interest in the welfare of children justifying the entry of appropriate orders. In cases involving status offenders, only after all else fails, should placement in a closed setting be justified. But under the facts of this case, the trial judge had no alternative.

Matter of Andrew R.

Family Court, Richmond County, New York, 1982.
115 Misc.2d 937, 454 N.Y.S.2d 820.

■ Daniel D. Leddy, Jr., Judge:

In dismissing the instant Person in Need of Supervision (PINS) proceeding this court holds that thirteen-year old Andrew R. was legally justified in resisting his parents' efforts to return him to foster care against his will. Reaching this decision, the court concludes that his placement at Hawthorne Cedar Knolls (Hawthorne) for over seven months under a so-called voluntary placement without any review by a neutral fact-finder violated his fundamental liberty interest as protected by the due process clause of the Fourteenth Amendment to the United States Constitution.

Andrew is an intelligent, appealing boy who desperately wishes to remain at home on Staten Island. His parents are equally determined to return him to Hawthorne, a residential treatment center, to which he had been sent by them under a so-called voluntary placement instrument. Social Services Law Sec. 384–a. The parent-child conflict culminated in the instant PINS proceeding.

Thus, on August 16, 1982, Andrew's father filed a petition with this court alleging that his son was a Person in Need of Supervision (PINS) in that

"... he is beyond the lawful control of his parents. Respondent on this date, threatened petitioner with a knife and damaged household prop-

---

2. While a runaway, L.A.M. was truant from school; was allegedly the victim of a rape as reported in a call to the police; contracted gonorrhea; suffered an injured jaw and broken teeth from a fall, which injuries had not received medical attention.

3. Clarke, Stevens H., "Some Implications for North Carolina of Recent Research in Juvenile Delinquency," Journal of Research in Crime and Delinquency, January 1975.

erty. Respondent had been voluntarily placed with Hawthorne Cedar Knolls from January, 1982 up until about a week ago, at which time he ran away and returned home."

The petition was subsequently amended to add an additional allegation that

"Respondent truanted from school for over two years and truanted while in placement."

A fact-finding hearing was held during which the only witnesses were Andrew and his father. During the hearing, the assistant corporation counsel, representing the petitioner-father, attempted to elicit testimony about additional alleged misbehavior on the part of Andrew other than that specifically set forth in the petition. In offering this testimony, the petitioner argued that it was sufficiently pleaded under the umbrella allegation that Andrew "is beyond the lawful control of his parents". The court sustained the law guardian's objection as a matter of both statutory law and constitutional due process.

Section 732(a) of the Family Court Act provides that a PINS proceeding is initiated by the filing of a petition, alleging that

"the respondent is an habitual truant or is incorrigible, ungovernable, or habitually disobedient and beyond the lawful control of his parents ... and *specifying the acts on which the allegations are based and the time and place they allegedly occurred;*" (emphasis supplied).

This statutory provision evidences clear legislative intent to accord a PINS respondent adequate notice of the charges. It is consistent with longstanding judicial recognition that a PINS proceeding is quasi-criminal in nature, involving the potential for significant governmental interference in the liberty of the child. FCA Secs. 754; 756. Therefore, the due process rights accorded to a respondent in a juvenile delinquency proceeding apply with equal force to a PINS respondent.... Matter of Reynaldo R., 73 Misc.2d 390, 341 N.Y.S.2d 998; Matter of George C., 91 Misc.2d 875, 398 N.Y.S.2d 936.

For these reasons, a general allegation that a respondent is beyond the lawful control of his parents may not be utilized as a predicate to subject the child's life to parental attack.

As was stated in Matter of Reynaldo R., (supra)

"... no petition alleging a person to be in need of supervision can stand unless the acts complained of are set forth in specific terms with dates and frequency, the nature of the behavior and conduct charged.... Otherwise, there is a violation of child's constitutional rights to notice of charges against him *in time to prepare for trial, not at the time of trial.* None of these rights can be taken away from children merely because their conduct is noncriminal or the subject of a PINS petition. (Matter of Gault, 387 U.S. 1 [87 S.Ct. 1428, 18 L.Ed.2d 527])" 73 Misc.2d at 394, 341 N.Y.S.2d 998.

In January of 1982, while under the so-called "voluntary placement" Andrew was sent to Hawthorne, a residential treatment center in Hawthorne, New York. At the hearing, the petitioner-father testified that his son agreed to the placement at Hawthorne. Andrew disputed this, maintaining that he never wanted to leave home and that, in effect, he was tricked into going by a promise from his father that his stay would be no longer than a month. The court believes Andrew and concludes that he was induced to go to Hawthorne by a representation that was at least misleading, if not purposely false.

In August of this year, the respondent ran away from Hawthorne and returned home, refusing to return. When pressed by his father to go back to the facility, Andrew reacted with threats against him. On one occasion, he threatened to kill his father. In response thereto, his father handed him a knife and told him to go ahead and do it. Andrew thereupon proceeded to thrust the knife into a household item.

While in school at Hawthorne, the respondent cut a number of classes, although he attended his academic subjects for the most part.

Hawthorne is anxious to have Andrew return since it believes that he can be helped by their program. In fact, it was at the urging of Hawthorne personnel that the petitioner initiated this proceeding. It has been apparent at the outset that the petitioner is utilizing the PINS procedure to compel his son's return to Hawthorne.

Stripped of all euphemism, the term "voluntary placement" is dangerously misleading. A review of Sec. 384–a of the Social Services Law reveals that the child is not a party to the instrument effecting the foster care placement. Nor is there a requirement that the wishes of the child be considered or even solicited.

It is readily evident, therefore, that there is no reason to assume that any "voluntary placement" is truly voluntary on the part of the child.

This is significant since, in this case, there can be no doubt that Andrew's placement at Hawthorne against his will involves a substantial deprivation of liberty. . . .

The deprivation of liberty extends beyond the mere fact of confinement in a residential treatment center. A child so placed loses the daily consortium of family and friends, schoolmates, and participation in community affairs and activities.

In his concurring and dissenting opinion in Parham v. J.R., 442 U.S. 584, 626, 99 S.Ct. 2493, 61 L.Ed.2d 101, Mr. Justice Brennan referred to commitment to a mental institution as involving a "massive curtailment of liberty" since it restricts not only physical liberty but also contacts with "friends, family and community".

Andrew's liberty interest has been further impaired by the fact that he has been sent to a facility that contains both juvenile delinquents and PINS, children who are entitled to treatment measured by their need for rehabilitation. Thus, where there is a commingling of voluntarily placed children, PINS, and juvenile delinquents, it may well be that the "basic care" to which a foster child is entitled is in jeopardy.

It is more than ironic that Andrew arrived at Hawthorne by a process that accorded him absolutely no legal rights while others, with whom he came into daily contact, enjoyed all of the procedural and substantive protection that apply to PINS and juvenile delinquency cases.[3] At least in this case, the problem created by this disparity in treatment reaches constitutional dimensions.

New York has virtually ignored the feelings of children who are placed in foster care against their will. Section 358–a of the Social Services Law provides for judicial approval of a voluntary placement instrument in any instance where the child is likely to remain in foster care for in excess of thirty consecutive days. The statute requires that the review proceeding be filed "as soon as practicable, but in no event later than thirty days following removal of the child from the home." SSL Sec. 358–a(1). This should be contrasted with a PINS proceeding where a child is entitled to a probable cause hearing within three days of any remand to a foster care facility, FCA Sec. 739(b). What is critically important, however, is that while SSL Sec. 358–a mandates the filing of a petition within thirty days of the removal from home, there is no statutory time limitation within which the court proceeding must take place. And in Andrew's case, a review of the records of the Family Court Foster Care review term in Manhattan reveals that no petition has yet been filed to review the voluntary placement instrument which is now over seven months old.

It is apparent that the protection accorded to a child under Sec. 358–a is anywhere from minimal to non-existent. This is consistent with a finding that the statute is, in reality, a "funding device to trigger the flow of Federal dollars" and that the issue at a hearing thereunder is "the voluntariness of a parent's transfer of custody, not whether a placement by the state is in the child's best interests". Sinhogar v. Parry, 53 N.Y.2d 424, 446, 442 N.Y.S.2d 438, 425 N.E.2d 826. (Fuchsberg, J., dissenting.)

To reach a decision in this case, the court need not consider whether New York's statutory scheme for effecting voluntary placements violates the child's right to due process of law. The holding herein must be limited to the facts of this case. Thus, the issue is whether Andrew R., an intelligent youngster, "mature enough to have (his contrary) desire respected" (Wisconsin v. Yoder, 406 U.S. 205, 242, 92 S.Ct. 1526, 1546, 32 L.Ed.2d 15) suffered a constitutionally infirmed deprivation of liberty by being kept in foster care at Hawthorne against his will for over seven months without any hearing or other review by a neutral factfinder. The issue is thus framed since it is fundamental that a child may not be adjudicated a PINS for refusing to comply with a directive that violates his constitutional rights

---

3. These include, *inter alia,* the right to counsel, to adequate notice of the charges, to confront and cross-examine witnesses, to the exercise of the privilege against self-incrimination, and to have the stated charges proven beyond a reasonable doubt.

or is otherwise unlawful. Matter of Mary P., 111 Misc.2d 532, 444 N.Y.S.2d 545.

.   .   .

In Parham v. J.R. (supra), the United States Supreme Court held that a child has a substantial liberty interest in not being confined unnecessarily for medical treatment. Accordingly,

"... the risk of error inherent in the parental decision to have a child institutionalized for mental health care is sufficiently great that some kind of inquiry should be made by a 'neutral factfinder' to determine whether the statutory requirements for admission are satisfied.... That inquiry must carefully probe the child's background using all available sources, including, but not limited to, parents, schools, and other social agencies. Of course, the review must also include an interview with the child. It is necessary that the decisionmaker have the authority to refuse to admit any child who does not satisfy the medical standards for admission." 442 U.S. 584, 606, 607, 99 S.Ct. 2493, 2506, 2507, 61 L.Ed.2d 101.

As has already been established, Andrew has a liberty interest that suffers substantial infringement by his placement at Hawthorne against his will. For the purposes of this decision, however, it is not necessary to decide whether due process required a formal hearing either before Andrew was placed in foster care or even immediately thereafter.

Given the posture of the case, the court need only decide whether his running away from Hawthorne in August and his refusal to return constitutes PINS behavior. The court concludes that it does not and finds that the failure to afford Andrew any review of his foster care placement by a neutral factfinder for over seven months violated his constitutional right to due process of law.

It must follow, therefore, that the boy may not be penalized in any manner whatsoever for running away and staying away from Hawthorne. For the same reasons, his failure to cooperate with the school program at Hawthorne may not subject him to the stigma of a PINS finding.

The court is aware that Andrew made threats against his father as a result of his placement at Hawthorne and in response to his father's desire to implement that placement. And it must be emphasized that this court in no way condones this behavior on Andrew's part. Nevertheless, those threats (and they remained just that) must be evaluated against all the facts in this case. An intelligent, sensitive youngster is placed against his will in a facility that houses juvenile delinquents and PINS and is denied review of that parental decision for over seven months. He lacks the resources to challenge the placement through legal means and resorts to threats to enunciate his liberty interest. On the facts of this case, those threats are more attributable to the failure of the state to provide the boy with an opportunity to be heard rather than PINS intent on his part.

Furthermore, in handing Andrew a knife at a time when the boy threatened to kill him, the petitioner demonstrated remarkably poor judgment. The inappropriate nature of this behavior on the part of the petitioner is exceeded only by his temerity in charging the boy with threatening him with a knife.

"A parent in a PINS petition has no divine right to be right. Their actions and conduct must be more carefully screened than those of the accused child." Matter of Reynaldo R. (supra), 73 Misc.2d at page 394, 341 N.Y.S.2d 998.

While at Hawthorne, Andrew's attendance at school was less than exemplary. He cut several classes a week even though there is no evidence to controvert his assertion that he was present for his academic subjects. Nevertheless, Andrew's failure to attend school while at Hawthorne must be viewed in the same light as his refusal to stay at that facility. His truancy was simply another manifestation of his deep-seated desire not to be at Hawthorne, a desire that was never evaluated in a manner consistent with constitutional due process.

Accordingly, the court cannot find that Andrew had the requisite intent to truant from school or to disobey the mandates of Article 65 of the Education Law.

The court also finds that the petitioner has failed to establish beyond a reasonable doubt that Andrew was sufficiently truant from school prior to placement in order to sustain a finding that he is "incorrigible, ungovernable or habitually disobedient and beyond the lawful control" of his parents. FCA Sec. 712(b). In that regard, it should be noted that the petitioner chose not to allege specifically a violation of Article 65 of the Education Law, preferring instead, to make the allegation of truancy following the assertion that Andrew "is beyond the lawful control of his parents".

Section 3233 of the Education Law makes absence from school for even one day a violation and provides a stated penalty. However, even if measured by the dictates of Article 65 of the Education Law, Andrew's sporadic absences prior to placement cannot support a PINS finding. To interpret Article 65 as justifying state interference in the parent-child relationship as a result of a few absences from school would render the statute unconstitutional as an arbitrary and unreasonable interference in the affairs of both parent and child.

In order to sustain a PINS finding on the basis of truancy, there must be a substantial and intentional failure to attend school. Such has not been established here.

For all of the foregoing reasons, the petition is dismissed. Furthermore, incidental to the order of dismissal and at the request of the law guardian, a final order of protection is issued to the child directing the petitioner to cease and desist in his efforts to have Andrew return to Hawthorne under the instant voluntary placement instrument. Since his continued placement there offends his constitutionally protected liberty interests, any attempt by the parents to force his return against his will is conduct that is "offensive" to the child within the meaning of Sec. 759(c) of the Family Court Act. The petitioner is warned that any violation of the order of protection may result in a six-month jail term.

. . .

This is a sad commentary on the degree of our society's commitment to treating children with the respect they deserve as citizens. This case demonstrates in graphic terms the need to avoid granting to agencies unfettered discretion over the liberties of children, something that is certain to occur if, as some would have it, PINS cases are removed from the jurisdiction of the Family Court.

C. NEGLECT (ENDANGERMENT) AND DEPENDENCY

CALIFORNIA WELFARE AND INSTITUTIONS CODE (West Supp. 2007)

§ 300. Children subject to jurisdiction; legislative intent and declarations; guardian defined

Any child who comes within any of the following descriptions is within the jurisdiction of the juvenile court which may adjudge that person to be a dependent child of the court:

(a) The child has suffered, or there is a substantial risk that the child will suffer, serious physical harm inflicted nonaccidentally upon the child by the child's parent or guardian. For the purposes of this subdivision, a court may find there is a substantial risk of serious future injury based on the manner in which a less serious injury was inflicted, a history of repeated inflictions of injuries on the child or the child's siblings, or a combination of these and other actions by the parent or guardian which indicate the child is at risk of serious physical harm. For purposes of this subdivision, "serious physical harm" does not include reasonable and age-appropriate spanking to the buttocks where there is no evidence of serious physical injury.

(b) The child has suffered, or there is a substantial risk that the child will suffer, serious physical harm or illness, as a result of the failure or inability of his or her parent or guardian to adequately supervise or protect the child, or the willful or negligent failure of the child's parent or guardian to adequately supervise or protect the child from the conduct of the custodian with whom the child has been left, or by the willful or negligent failure of the parent or guardian to provide the child with adequate food, clothing, shelter, or medical treatment, or by the inability of the parent or guardian to provide regular care for the child due to the parent's or guardian's mental illness, developmental disability, or substance abuse. No child shall be found to be a person described by this subdivision solely due to the lack of an emergency shelter for the family. Whenever it is alleged that a child comes within the jurisdiction of the court on the basis of the parent's or guardian's willful failure to provide adequate medical treatment or specific decision to provide spiritual treatment through prayer, the court shall give deference to the parent's or guardian's medical treatment, nontreatment, or spiritual treatment through prayer alone in accordance with the tenets and practices of a recognized church or religious denomination, by an accredited practitioner thereof, and shall not assume jurisdiction unless necessary to protect the child from suffering serious physical harm or illness. In making its determination, the court shall consider (1) the nature of the treatment proposed by the parent or guardian, (2) the risks to the child posed by the course of treatment or nontreatment proposed by the parent or guardian, (3) the risk, if any, of the course of treatment being proposed by the petitioning agency, and (4) the likely success of the courses of treatment or nontreatment proposed by the parent or guardian and agency. The child shall continue to be a dependent child pursuant to this subdivision only so long as is necessary to protect the child from risk of suffering serious physical harm or illness.

(c) The child is suffering serious emotional damage, or is at substantial risk of suffering serious emotional damage, evidenced by severe anxiety, depression, withdrawal, or untoward aggressive behavior toward self or others, as a result of the conduct of the parent or guardian or who has no parent or guardian capable of providing appropriate care. No child shall be found to be a person described by this subdivision if the willful failure of the parent or guardian to provide adequate mental health treatment is based on a sincerely held religious belief and if a less intrusive judicial intervention is available.

(d) The child has been sexually abused, or there is a substantial risk that the child will be sexually abused, as defined in Section 11165.1 of the Penal Code, by his or her parent or guardian or a member of his or her household, or the parent or guardian has failed to adequately protect the child from sexual abuse when the parent or guardian knew or reasonably should have known that the child was in danger of sexual abuse.

(e) The child is under the age of five years and has suffered severe physical abuse by a parent, or by any person known by the parent, if the parent knew or reasonably should have known that the person was physically abusing the child. For the purposes of this subdivision, "severe physical abuse" means any of the following: any single act of abuse which causes physical trauma of sufficient severity that, if left untreated, would cause permanent physical disfigurement, permanent physical disability, or death; any single act of sexual abuse which causes significant bleeding, deep bruising, or significant external or internal swelling; or more than one act of physical abuse, each of which causes bleeding, deep bruising, significant external or internal swelling, bone fracture, or unconsciousness; or the willful, prolonged failure to provide adequate food. A child may not be removed from the physical custody of his or her parent or guardian on the basis of a finding of severe physical abuse unless the social worker has made an allegation of severe physical abuse pursuant to Section 332.

(f) The child's parent or guardian caused the death of another child through abuse or neglect.

(g) The child has been left without any provision for support; physical custody of the child has been voluntarily surrendered pursuant to Section 1255.7 of the Health and Safety Code and the child has not been reclaimed within the 14–day period specified in subdivision (e) of that section; the child's parent has been incarcerated or institutionalized and cannot arrange for the care of the child; or a relative or other adult custodian with whom the child resides or has been left is unwilling or unable to provide care or support for the child, the whereabouts of the parent are unknown, and reasonable efforts to locate the parent have been unsuccessful.

(h) The child has been freed for adoption by one or both parents for 12 months by either relinquishment or termination of parental rights or an adoption petition has not been granted.

(i) The child has been subjected to an act or acts of cruelty by the parent or guardian or a member of his or her household, or the parent or guardian has failed to adequately protect the child from an act or acts of cruelty when the parent or guardian knew or reasonably should have known that the child was in danger of being subjected to an act or acts of cruelty.

(j) The child's sibling has been abused or neglected, as defined in subdivision (a), (b), (d), (e), or (i), and there is a substantial risk that the child will be abused or neglected, as defined in those subdivisions. The court shall consider the circumstances surrounding the abuse or neglect of the sibling, the age and gender of each child, the nature of the abuse or neglect of the sibling, the mental condition of the parent or guardian, and any other factors the court considers probative in determining whether there is a substantial risk to the child.

It is the intent of the Legislature that nothing in this section disrupt the family unnecessarily or intrude inappropriately into family life, prohibit the use of reasonable methods of parental discipline, or prescribe a particular method of parenting. Further, nothing in this section is intended to limit the offering of voluntary services to those families in need of assistance but who do not come within the descriptions of this section. To the extent that savings accrue to the state from child welfare services funding obtained as a result of the enactment of the act that enacted this section, those savings shall be used to promote services which support family maintenance and family reunification plans, such as client transportation, out-of-home respite care, parenting training, and the provision of temporary or emergency in-home caretakers and persons teaching and demonstrating homemaking skills. The Legislature further declares that a physical disability, such as blindness or deafness, is no bar to the raising of happy and well-adjusted children and that a court's determination pursuant to this section shall center upon whether a parent's disability prevents him or her from exercising care and control. The Legislature further declares that a child whose parent has been adjudged a dependent child of the court pursuant to this section shall not be considered to be at risk of abuse or neglect solely because of the age, dependent status, or foster care status of the parent.

As used in this section, "guardian" means the legal guardian of the child.

In re M.L.

Supreme Court of Pennsylvania, 2000.
562 Pa. 646, 757 A.2d 849.

■ CASTILLE, JUSTICE.

Allowance of appeal was granted in this matter limited to the issue of whether a court may properly adjudge a child to be dependent where the non-custodial parent is ready, willing and able to provide the child with proper parental care and control. The Superior Court affirmed the trial court's finding of dependency in the instant case even though the child's father was available and willing to provide adequate care for the child. We hold that a child, whose non-custodial parent is ready, willing and able to provide adequate care to the child, cannot be found dependent and, therefore, reverse.

Appellant is the natural mother of the child, born February 6, 1995, and R.G. is the child's natural father. The child's parents never married but shared custody of the child from the time of her birth. A January 1997 custody dispute ended with appellant having primary physical custody and the father having partial custody every other weekend. In May of 1996, appellant contacted Cambria County Children and Youth Service (CYS) to complain that the father did not care for the child properly during her weekends with him in that he lacked supplies for the child and did not feed her appropriately.

Then, in August of 1996, appellant began alleging that the father was sexually abusing the child. Between August 1996 and January 1997, appellant subjected the child to six separate physical examinations for possible sexual abuse at either the hospital emergency room or the child's pediatrician's office. Each examining physician reported that the child had diaper rash or normal redness for a child of her age wearing diapers; no signs of sexual abuse were found in any of the examinations. Despite the lack of evidence, appellant continued to allege that the father was sexually abusing the child, leading CYS to file a petition for dependency. Following two evidentiary hearings on February 24 and March 19, 1997, the trial court found, on March 25, 1997, that the child was a dependent child and awarded custody to her father.[4]

---

4. The trial court's decision was based upon a finding that appellant suffers from factitious disorder by proxy, that she had repeatedly subjected the child to physical examinations which revealed nothing more than diaper rash, and that appellant's mental illness had the strong potential to escalate to the point where appellant would actually harm the child physically in order to provide substantiation of her abuse allegations against the child's father. Factitious disorder by proxy means, in this case, that appellant

The sole issue for our determination is whether the trial court erred in finding that the child was a dependent child when her father was ready, willing and able to provide adequate care to her. Two earlier panels of the Superior Court reached conflicting decisions as to whether a child can be found dependent and then placed in the custody of the non-custodial parent.

. . .

A dependent child is defined in pertinent part at 42 Pa.C.S. § 6302 as:

A child who:

(1) is without proper parental care or control, subsistence, education as required by law, or other care or control necessary for his physical, mental or emotional health, or morals; (2) has been placed for care or adoption in violation of law;

(3) has been abandoned by his parents, guardian, or other custodian;

(4) is without parent, guardian, or legal custodian;

* * *

A court is empowered by 42 Pa.C.S. § 6341(a) and (c) to make a finding that a child is dependent if the child meets the statutory definition by clear and convincing evidence. If the court finds that the child is dependent, then the court may make an appropriate disposition of the child to protect the child's physical, mental and moral welfare, including allowing the child to remain with the parents subject to supervision, transferring temporary legal custody to a relative or a private or public agency, or transferring custody to the juvenile court of another state. 42 Pa.C.S. § 6351(a).

The definition of a dependent child contained in section 6302 clearly states that a child must lack a parent, guardian or other legal custodian who can provide appropriate care to the child. A child whose non-custodial parent is ready, willing and able to provide such care does not meet this definition. In *Justin S.*, 375 Pa.Super. at 104, 543 A.2d at 1200, the Superior Court stated:

[I]t is the duty of the trial court to determine whether the non-custodial parent is capable and willing to render proper parental control prior to adjudicating a child dependent. If the court determines that the custodial parent is unable to provide proper parental care and control "at this moment" and that the non-custodial parent is "immediately available" to provide such care, the child is not dependent under the provisions of the Juvenile Act. Consequently, the court must grant custody of the allegedly dependent child to the non-custodial parent. Once custody is granted to the non-custodial parent, "the care, protection, and wholesome mental and physical development of the

transferred to the child her own psychological difficulties such that she claimed that the child was experiencing symptoms of abuse that the child did not actually experience.

child" can occur in a family environment as the purpose of the Juvenile Act directs. 42 Pa.C.S. § 6301(b).

We are in accord with the Superior Court's decision in *Justin S.* The plain language of the statutory definition of a dependent child compels the conclusion that a child is not dependent if the child has a parent who is willing and able to provide proper care to the child. When a court adjudges a child dependent, that court then possesses the authority to place the child in the custody of a relative or a public or private agency. Where a non-custodial parent is available and willing to provide care to the child, such power in the hands of the court is an unwarranted intrusion into the family. Only where a child is truly lacking a parent, guardian or legal custodian who can provide adequate care should we allow our courts to exercise such authority. Accordingly, we hold that where a non-custodial parent is ready, willing and able to provide adequate care to a child, a court may not adjudge that child dependent.

Therefore, she does not meet the statutory definition of a dependent child, and the trial court erred in adjudging her dependent. Therefore, the decision of the Superior Court affirming the trial court's finding that the child is a dependent child is reversed.

[The concurring opinion of Justice NEWMAN and the dissenting opinion of Justice CAPPY have not been reproduced. In the latter the Justice stated agreement with the majority's ultimate result that the child should remain with her non-custodial parent but states his belief that the majority "fundamentally misapprehended the nature of dependency proceedings" and its reversal of the decision of the Superior Court violated both the language and intent of the Juvenile Act, 42 Pa.C.S. § 6301 *et seq.*]

In re Juvenile Appeal (83–CD)

Supreme Court of Connecticut, 1983.
189 Conn. 276, 455 A.2d 1313.

■ SPEZIALE, CHIEF JUSTICE.

This is an appeal by the defendant, mother of five children, from the order of the Superior Court for juvenile matters granting temporary custody of her children to the plaintiff commissioner of the department of children and youth services.

The defendant and her six children lived in a small apartment in New Haven. They had been receiving services from the department of children and youth services (hereinafter DCYS) as a protective service family[1] since 1976, and were supported by the Aid to Families with Dependent Children program. Michelle Spicknall, a DCYS caseworker, was assigned to the defendant's case in January 1979. In the next nine months she visited the

---

1. A protective services family is one which has come to the attention of DCYS as having a potential for abuse, neglect, abandonment, or sexual exploitation. DCYS then investigates the family and, where appropriate, provides "support systems to bolster family functioning." DCYS: Programs and Priorities, FY 1979.

defendant's home twenty-seven times. She considered the family situation "marginal," but noted that the children were "not abused [or] neglected." It was Spicknall's opinion that the children were very happy and active, and that they had a "very warm" relationship with their mother.

During the night of September 4–5, 1979, the defendant's youngest child, nine month old Christopher, died. The child was brought by ambulance to Yale–New Haven Medical Center where resuscitation was unsuccessfully attempted by his pediatrician, Dr. Robert Murphy. No cause of death could be determined at that time, but the pediatrician noticed some unexplained superficial marks on Christopher's body.

Because of Christopher's unexplained death, the plaintiff commissioner of children and youth services seized custody of the defendant's five remaining children on September 5, 1979, under authority of the "96–hour hold" provision of General Statutes § 17–38a(e),[3] which permits summary seizure if the commissioner has probable cause to believe that a child is "suffering from serious physical illness or serious physical injury or is in immediate physical danger from his surroundings, and that immediate removal from such surroundings *is necessary to insure the child's safety*...." (Emphasis added.)

On September 7, 1979, in the Juvenile Court for New Haven, DCYS filed petitions of neglect under General Statutes § 46b–129(a) for each of the defendant's children. Accompanying each petition was an affidavit for orders of temporary custody asking that the court issue temporary ex parte orders to keep the five children in DCYS custody under authority of § 46b–129(b)(2).[5] The petitions alleged, in addition to Christopher's unexplained

---

3. General Statutes § 17–38a(e) provides: "Agencies or institutions receiving reports of child abuse as provided in this section shall, within twenty-four hours, transfer such information to the commissioner of children and youth services or his agent, who shall cause the report to be investigated immediately. If the investigation produces evidence that the child has been abused in the manner described in subsection (b), he shall take such measures as he deems necessary to protect the child, and any other children similarly situated, including but not limited to the removal of the child or children from his home with the consent of his or their parents or guardian or by order of the superior court. If the commissioner of children and youth services or his designee, after such investigation, has probable cause to believe that the child is suffering from serious physical illness or serious physical injury or is in immediate physical danger from his surroundings, and that immediate removal from such surroundings is necessary to insure the child's safety, the commissioner, or his designee, may au-

thorize any employee of his department or any law enforcement officer to remove the child from such surroundings without the consent of the child's parent or guardian. Such removal and temporary custody shall not exceed ninety-six hours during which time either a petition shall be filed with the superior court or the child shall be returned to his parent or guardian. If the commissioner determines that there are grounds to believe the child may be properly cared for in his own home, the parents or guardian, as the case may be, shall be aided to give such proper care under the supervision of the commissioner. Such supervised custody may be terminated when the commissioner finds a safe environment has been provided the child; but if the commissioner, after a reasonable time, finds this condition cannot be achieved in the child's own home under such supervision, he may petition the superior court for commitment of the child."

5. General Statutes § 46b–129(b) provides: "If it appears from the allegations of the petition and other verified affirmations of

death, that the defendant's apartment was dirty, that numerous roaches could be found there, that beer cans were to be found in the apartment, that the defendant had been observed drinking beer, that on one occasion the defendant may have been drunk, that a neighbor reported that the children once had been left alone all night,[6] and that the two older children had occasionally come to school without having eaten breakfast. On the basis of these allegations, on September 7, 1979, the court granted, ex parte, temporary custody to the commissioner pending a noticed hearing on temporary custody set for September 14, 1979, within ten days of the ex parte order as required by § 46b–129(b)(2). The court also set October 1, 1979, for a hearing on the neglect petitions.[7]

At the September 14 temporary custody hearing, DCYS presented testimony of Spicknall confirming and elaborating on the conditions of the defendant's home and on the defendant's beer drinking. Christopher's pediatrician testified concerning Christopher's treatment and physical appearance when the child was brought to the hospital on September 5. The doctor also testified that, although the pathologist's report on the autopsy was not complete,[8] the external marks on Christopher's body were not a cause of death, that no internal injuries were found, and that the child had had a viral lung infection. He also explained, on cross-examination, the term "sudden infant death syndrome" and its pathology. At the conclusion of the state's case, the court found "probable cause" and ordered temporary custody of the children to remain with the plaintiff commissioner of children and youth services.

The defendant appealed to this court claiming that General Statutes § 46b–129(b) violates the due process clause of the fourteenth amendment

---

fact accompanying the petition, or subsequent thereto, that there is reasonable cause to find that the child's or youth's condition or the circumstances surrounding his care require that his custody be immediately assumed to safeguard his welfare, the court shall either (1) issue an order to the parents or other person having responsibility for the care of the child or youth to show cause at such time as the court may designate why the court shall not vest in some suitable agency or person the child's or youth's temporary care and custody pending a hearing on the petition, or (2) vest in some suitable agency or person the child's or youth's temporary care and custody pending a hearing upon the petition which shall be held within ten days from the issuance of such order on the need for such temporary care and custody. The service of such orders may be made by any officer authorized by law to serve process, or by any probation officer appointed in accordance with section 46b–123, investigator from the department of administrative services, state police officer or indifferent per-

son. The expense for any temporary care and custody shall be paid by the town in which such child or youth is at the time residing, and such town shall be reimbursed therefor by the town found liable for his support, except that where a state agency has filed a petition pursuant to the provisions of subsection (a) of this section, the agency shall pay such expense."

6. The report was allegedly made by an upstairs neighbor of the defendant. At the hearing, the neighbor denied having made such a report at any time.

7. The hearing on the neglect petitions was continued when additional evidence on the temporary custody petitions was heard on October 1, 1979. It was never rescheduled.

8. The final autopsy report was not complete at the time of the hearing. Preliminary findings were available, however, and the cause of death could not be determined. No evidence available at the hearing connected the death with any sort of neglect or abuse.

both because it is an impermissible infringement on her right to family integrity, and because the statute is unconstitutionally vague. The defendant also claims error in the trial court's determination that "probable cause" is the standard of proof in a temporary custody proceeding. We conclude that § 46b–129(b) is constitutional; however, we do find that the trial court erred when it decided that "probable cause" is the standard of proof in a temporary custody proceeding.

As hereinafter set forth, we hold: (1) that § 46b–129(b) is constitutional because it must be read together with § 17–38a which contains adequate criteria for determining whether temporary custody of children may be taken from the parent by court order; and (2) that the standard of proof applicable to temporary custody proceedings pursuant to § 46b–129(b) is a fair preponderance of the evidence.

. . .

Where fundamental rights are concerned we have a two-part test: "[1] regulations limiting these rights may be justified only by a 'compelling state interest,' and . . . [2] legislative enactments must be narrowly drawn to express only the legitimate state interests at stake." Roe v. Wade, 410 U.S. 113, 155, 93 S.Ct. 705, 727, 35 L.Ed.2d 147 (1973). The state has a substantial interest in protecting minor children; intervention in family matters by the state is justified, however, only when such intervention is actually "in the best interests of the child," a standard long used in this state.

Studies indicate that the best interests of the child are usually served by keeping the child in the home with his or her parents. "Virtually all experts, from many different professional disciplines, agree that children need and benefit from continuous, stable home environments." Institute of Judicial Administration—American Bar Association, Juvenile Justice Standards Project, Standards Relating to Abuse and Neglect, p. 45 (Tentative draft, 1977) (IJA–ABA, STDS). The love and attention not only of parents, but also of siblings, which is available in the home environment, cannot be provided by the state. Unfortunately, an order of temporary custody often results in the children of one family being separated and scattered to different foster homes with little opportunity to see each other. Even where the parent-child relationship is "marginal," it is usually in the best interests of the child to remain at home and still benefit from a family environment.[11]

---

11. Uninterrupted home life "comports . . . with each child's biological and psychological need for unthreatened and unbroken continuity of care by his parents. No other animal is for so long a time after birth in so helpless a state that its survival depends upon continuous nurture by an adult. Although breaking or weakening the ties to the responsible and responsive adults may have different consequences for children of different ages, there is little doubt that such breaches in the familial bond will be detrimental to a child's well-being." (Footnotes omitted.) Goldstein, "Medical Care for the Child at Risk: On State Supervision of Parental Autonomy," 865 Yale L.J. 645, 649 (1977). Separation from his or her parents for any significant time has damaging effects on a child, even when the parents are minimally supportive of the child's needs. See Goldstein,

The defendants' challenge to the temporary custody statute, § 46b–129(b), must be addressed in light of the foregoing considerations. The defendant contends that only when the child is "at risk of harm" does the state's interest become a compelling one, justifying even temporary removal of the child from the home. We agree.

In custody proceedings, any criteria used to determine when intervention is permissible must take into account the competing interests involved. The parent has only one interest, that of family integrity; and the state has only one compelling interest, that of protecting minor children.... The child, however, has two distinct and often contradictory interests. The first is a basic interest in safety; the second is the important interest, discussed above, in having a stable *family* environment. Connecticut's child welfare statutes recognize both the conflicting interests and the constitutional limitations involved in any intervention situation. Thus, under the criteria of General Statutes § 17–38a(e), summary assumption of temporary custody is authorized only when there is probable cause to believe that "the child is suffering from serious physical illness or serious physical injury or is in *immediate* physical danger from his surroundings, *and* that *immediate* removal from such surroundings is *necessary* to insure the child's safety...." (Emphasis added.)

The language of § 17–38a(e) clearly limits the scope of intervention to cases where the state interest is compelling ... Intervention is permitted only where "serious physical illness or serious physical injury" is found or where "immediate physical danger" is present. It is at this point that the child's interest no longer coincides with that of the parent, thereby diminishing the magnitude of the parent's right to family integrity; In re Angelia P., 28 Cal.3d 908, 916–17, 171 Cal.Rptr. 637, 623 P.2d 198 (1981); and therefore the state's intervention as parens patriae to protect the child becomes so necessary that it can be considered paramount. Alsager v. District Court, 406 F.Supp. 10, 22–23 (S.D.Iowa 1975). A determination that the state interest is compelling does not alone affirm the constitutionality of the statute. More is needed. The second part of the due process analysis of Roe v. Wade, supra, requires that statutes affecting fundamental rights be "narrowly drawn to express only the legitimate state interests at stake." General Statutes § 17–38a(e) meets this part of the test by requiring, in addition to the compelling need to protect the child, that the assumption of temporary custody by the commissioner be immediately "necessary to insure the child's safety." This phrase requires that various

Freud and Solnit, Before the Best Interests of the Child, pp. 6–12 (1979); Wald, "State Intervention on Behalf of 'Neglected' Children: Standards for Removal of Children from Their Homes, Monitoring the Status of Children in Foster Care, and Termination of Parental Rights," 28 Stan.L.Rev. 623 (1976); Goldstein, Freud and Solnit, Beyond the Best Interests of the Child, p. 20 (1973). "Even when placed in good environments, which is often not the case, they suffer anxiety and depression from being separated from their parents, they are forced to deal with new caretakers, playmates, school teachers, etc. As a result they often suffer emotional damage and their development is delayed." Wald, "Thinking About Public Policy Toward Abuse and Neglect of Children," 78 Mich. L.Rev. 645, 662 (1980).

steps short of removal from the home be used when possible in preference to disturbing the integrity of the family. The statute itself mentions supervised in-home custody, but a wide range of other programs short of removal are a part of existing DCYS procedure. See DCYS: Programs and Priorities, FY 1979.

The challenged statute, § 46b–129(b), does not contain the "serious physical illness or serious physical injury" or "immediate physical danger" language of § 17–38a(e). We note, however, that § 46b–129(b) does limit the temporary custody order to those situations in which "the child or youth's condition or the circumstances surrounding his care require that his custody be immediately assumed to safeguard his welfare." It is axiomatic that statutes on a particular subject be "considered as a whole, with a view toward reconciling their separate parts in order to render a reasonable overall interpretation.... We must avoid a consequence which fails to attain a rational and sensible result which bears most directly on the object which the legislature sought to obtain." This is no less true when the legislature has chosen to place related laws in different parts of the General Statutes. Therefore, the language limiting coercive intervention in chapter 301 ("Child Welfare"), § 17–38a, must be read as applying equally to such intervention in chapter 815t ("[Family Law] Juvenile Matters"), § 46b–129. Because we hold that General Statutes § 46b–129(b) may be applied only on the basis of the criteria enunciated in § 17–38a, we reject the defendant's claim that § 46b–129(b) is unconstitutional.[12]

---

12. The American Bar Association Juvenile Justice Standards Project, after a thorough study of the competing individual, societal, and legal interests involved when state intervention into family affairs is contemplated, developed model Standards Relating to Abuse and Neglect (Tentative Draft, 1977). The basic policy assumptions underlying the study mirror our own law, i.e, "[s]tate intervention should promote family autonomy and family life.... [B]ut where a child's needs ... conflict with his/her parents' interests, the child's needs should have priority." ABA Standard 1.5. When interpreting the "at risk" criteria set forth in General Statutes § 17–38a(e), the following guidelines may be considered insofar as they help to define more clearly our own statutes pertaining to temporary custody orders:

"Courts should ... assume jurisdiction in order to condition continued parental custody upon the parents' accepting supervision or to remove a child from his/her home only when a child is endangered in a manner specified in subsection A.–F.:

"A. a child has suffered, or there is a substantial risk that a child will immi-

nently suffer, a physical harm, inflicted nonaccidentally upon him/her by his/her parents, which causes, or creates a substantial risk of causing disfigurement, impairment of bodily functioning, or other serious physical injury;

"B. a child has suffered, or there is a substantial risk that the child will imminently suffer, physical harm causing disfigurement, impairment of bodily functioning, or other serious physical injury as a result of conditions created by his/her parents or by the failure of the parents to adequately supervise or protect him/her;

"C. a child is suffering serious emotional damage, evidenced by severe anxiety, depression, or withdrawal, or untoward aggressive behavior toward self or others, and the child's parents are not willing to provide treatment for him/her;

"D. a child has been sexually abused by his/her parent or a member of his/her household ...;

"E. a child is in need of medical treatment to cure, alleviate, or prevent him/her from suffering serious physical harm

In the instant case, no substantial showing was made at the temporary custody hearing that the defendant's five children were suffering from either serious physical illness or serious physical injury, or that they would be in immediate physical danger if they were returned to the defendant's home. The DCYS caseworker admitted at trial, as did the state's counsel at argument before this court, that without the unexplained death of Christopher there was no reason for DCYS to have custody of the other children. The medical evidence at the hearing indicated no connection between Christopher's death and either the defendant or the conditions in her home. While the final autopsy report was not available at the hearing, the pediatrician testified that the marks on Christopher's body were *not* related to the child's death. There was, therefore, no evidence before the court to indicate whether his death was from natural causes or was the result of abuse. Yet with nothing before it but subjective suspicion, the court granted the commissioner custody of the defendant's other children. It was error for the court to grant to the commissioner temporary custody when no immediate risk of danger to the children was shown.

It appears from this record that DCYS has not heeded the suggestion of this court that the agency bears a responsibility of continuing review of cases it is litigating. In In re Juvenile Appeal (Anonymous), 177 Conn. 648, 662, 420 A.2d 875 (1979), we stated that when the cause for the commitment of children to DCYS custody ends, the state bears the burden of showing the necessity to continue the commitment. Although that holding concerned a parent's petition for revocation of a commitment, implicit in our holding was that the state had a duty to seek the best interests of the child even after adversary proceedings with the parent had begun. In this case, at some time shortly after the orders of temporary custody were granted, the state received the final autopsy report which effectively exonerated the defendant from any wrongdoing in Christopher's death. The reason for the custody order then no longer existed. It was then incumbent on DCYS to reunite the family. "In this situation, the state cannot constitutionally 'sit back and wait' for the parent to institute judicial proceedings. It 'cannot ... [adopt] for itself an attitude of if you don't like it, sue.'" Duchesne v. Sugarman, 566 F.2d 817, 828 (2d Cir.1977).[13]

which may result in death, disfigurement, or substantial impairment of bodily functions, and his/her parents are unwilling to provide or consent to the medical treatment;

"F. a child is committing delinquent acts as a result of parental encouragement, guidance, or approval." ABA Standard 2.1.

13. We recognize that there are three parties to litigation in the Superior Court for juvenile matters—DCYS, the parent, and the child (through a guardian ad litem appointed pursuant to Practice Book § 484) and that any of these parties could have moved to terminate this litigation in a number of ways.

We are saying only that DCYS, acting as parens patriae, had a duty to do so.

This court notes, however, that the defendant mother took no steps either to revoke custody under General Statutes § 46b–129(f) or to pursue a judicial resolution of the neglect petitions. We are even more concerned that the attorney for the children took no steps to protect their interests in family integrity by insisting on a resolution of the neglect petitions, and failed to represent their interests before this court. This court, therefore, is appreciative of the fact that the interests of the children have been ably represented by the Connecticut Civil Liberties Union as amicus curiae on this appeal.

Petitions for neglect and for temporary custody orders, like the petitions to terminate parental rights in Duchesne v. Sugarman, supra, or in In re Juvenile Appeal (Anonymous), supra, "are particularly vulnerable to the risk that judges or social workers will be tempted, consciously or unconsciously, to compare unfavorably the material advantages of the child's natural parents with those of prospective adoptive parents [or foster parents]." In re Juvenile Appeal (Anonymous), supra, 177 Conn. 672, 420 A.2d 875.

This case clearly shows that these dangers do exist; it is shocking that the defendant's children have been in "temporary" custody for more than three years. This is a tragic and deplorable situation, and DCYS must bear full responsibility for this unwarranted and inexcusable delay. Too often the courts of this state are faced with a situation where, as here, litigation has continued for years while the children, whose interests are supposed to be paramount, suffer in the insecurity of "temporary" placements. The well-known deleterious effects of prolonged temporary placement on the child, which we have discussed above, makes continuing review by DCYS of all temporary custody and commitment cases imperative. Where appropriate, the agency can and must take unilateral action either to reunite families or to terminate parental rights as expeditiously as possible to free neglected children for placement and adoption in stable family settings.

The failure of DCYS properly to administer § 46b–129 does not, however, affect its constitutionality. The statute is constitutional because when it is read together with § 17–38a, as it must be, it is justified by a compelling state interest and is narrowly drawn to express only that legitimate state interest.

. . .

NOTES

When may the state refuse to propose a treatment plan that would result in the reunification of a child with a parent? The Court of Appeals of South Carolina, in Dorchester County Dep't of Soc. Serv. v. Miller, 324 S.C. 445, 477 S.E.2d 476 (App.1996), held that the state is not required to submit a plan for reunification of parent and child when the abuse is so chronic that there is no realistic possibility that the children can be reunited with a parent and to do so would pose a threat of harm to the children and thus be contrary to their best interest. In a California decision, Baby Boy L., 24 Cal.App.4th 596, 29 Cal.Rptr.2d 654 (1994), the baby boy was born with a toxic condition indicating cocaine addiction, which could only have come from the mother, then fourteen years of age, using cocaine during pregnancy. Upon birth the child was placed in protective custody and had been in two placements by the time of a six month review of the case. The boy remained in a single foster home and by his first birthday had bonded with his foster parents who wished to adopt him. The father of the child was incarcerated and the mother was told that if she wished a contested hearing on the issue of instituting reunification, she would need to file a petition for implementation of a permanent plan. Shortly thereafter, she was arrested and jailed for sale of a controlled substance. No petition for reunification was filed. Nonetheless, when the mother was released from jail, the court ordered her to participate in drug and alcohol counseling and to submit to drug testing. The mother's attorney did not submit proof of clean drug tests to the court at a subsequent hearing on the future of Baby Boy and it was proven that the mother had only visited the child once in nearly two years. Because of these facts, the court terminated parental rights without offering reunification services in accordance with California Welfare and Institutions Code §§ 361.5 and 366.21. And in a sharp criticism of the judicial delay which resulted in Baby Boy about to turn five years of age, the court stated the County attorneys should avoid requests for extension of time except in the most compelling circumstances.

How important is the role of the social worker assigned to the case? Both compensation and case loads have been criticized in recent years as limiting recruitment and adequate attention to many cases. The National Commission on Children, United States, Beyond Rhetoric: A New American Agenda for Children and Families: Final Report of the National Commission on Children 334 (1991), reported that social workers were averaging between 50 and 70 cases at any given time, with some caseworkers reporting that they were carrying more than 200 cases simultaneously.

D. RESPONDING TO CHILD ABUSE

Johnson v. State

Supreme Court of Florida, 1992.
602 So.2d 1288.

■ HARDING, JUSTICE.

We have for review Johnson v. State, 578 So.2d 419, 420 (Fla. 5th DCA 1991), in which the Fifth District Court of Appeal certified the following question as one of great public importance: WHETHER THE INGESTION OF A CONTROLLED SUBSTANCE BY A MOTHER WHO KNOWS THE SUBSTANCE WILL PASS TO HER CHILD AFTER BIRTH IS A VIOLATION OF FLORIDA LAW?

. . .

The issue before the court is whether section 893.13(1)(c)(1), Florida Statutes (1989), permits the criminal prosecution of a mother, who ingested a controlled substance prior to giving birth, for delivery of a controlled substance to the infant during the thirty to ninety seconds following the infant's birth, but before the umbilical cord is severed.

Johnson presents four arguments attacking the applicability of section 893.13(1)(c)(1) to her conviction: 1) the district court's interpretation of the statute violates the legislature's intent; 2) the plain language of the statute prevents her conviction; 3) the conviction violates her constitutional rights of due process and privacy; and 4) the State presented insufficient evidence to show that she intentionally delivered cocaine to a minor.... The State contends that the district court correctly found that the statute's plain language prohibits the delivery of the controlled substance to a minor, and that the conviction does not violate Johnson's constitutional rights.

We adopt Judge Sharp's analysis concerning the insufficiency of the evidence to support Johnson's conviction and her analysis concerning the legislature's intent in section 893.13(1)(c)(1). However, we note that Judge Sharp's analysis did not clearly state the rules of statutory construction in the criminal context. Although Judge Sharp correctly applied the rule of strict construction, she failed to apply the other paramount rule of criminal statutory construction, the rule of lenity. § 775.021(1), Fla. Stat. (1989).

The rules of statutory construction require courts to strictly construe criminal statutes, and that "when the language is susceptible to differing constructions, [the statute] shall be construed most favorably to the accused." § 775.021(1). In strictly construing criminal statutes, we have held that only those terms which are " 'clearly and intelligently described in [a penal statute's] very words, as well as manifestly intended by the Legislature' " are to be considered as included in the statute. State v. Wershow, 343 So.2d 605, 608 (Fla.1977), quoting Ex parte Amos, 93 Fla. 5, 112 So. 289 (1927). We find that the legislative history does not show a manifest intent to use the word "delivery" in the context of criminally prosecuting mothers for delivery of a controlled substance to a minor by way of the umbilical cord. This lack of legislative intent coupled with uncertainty that the term "delivery" applies to the facts of the instant case, compels this Court to construe the statute in favor of Johnson. The text of Judge Sharp's dissent is as follows:

Johnson appeals from two convictions for delivering a controlled substance to her two minor children in violation of section 893.13(1)(c)1., Florida Statutes (1989).[1] The state's theory of the case was that Johnson "delivered" cocaine or a derivative of the drug to her two children via blood flowing through the children's umbilical cords in the sixty-to-ninety second period after they were expelled from her birth canal but before their cords were severed. The application of this statute to this concept of "delivery"

---

1. Section 893.13(1)(c)1., Florida Statutes (1989) provides as follows: 893.13 Prohibited acts; penalties.—

* * *

(c) Except as authorized by this chapter, it is unlawful for any person 18 years of age or older to deliver any controlled substance to a person under the age of 18 years, or to use or hire a person under the age of 18 years as an agent or employee in the sale or delivery of such a substance, or to use such person to assist in avoiding detection or apprehension for a violation of this chapter. Any person who violates this provision with respect to: 1. A controlled substance ... is guilty of a felony of the first degree....

presents a case of first impression in this state. Because I conclude that section 893.13(1)(c)1. was not intended to apply to these facts, I would vacate the convictions and remand for the entry of a judgment of acquittal.

The record in this case establishes the following facts. On October 3, 1987, Johnson delivered a son. The birth was normal with no complications. There was no evidence of fetal distress either within the womb or during the delivery. About one and one-half minutes elapsed from the time the son's head emerged from his mother's birth canal to the time he was placed on her stomach and the cord was clamped.

The obstetrician who delivered Johnson's son testified he presumed that the umbilical cord was functioning normally and that it was delivering blood to the baby after he emerged from the birth canal and before the cord was clamped. Johnson admitted to the baby's pediatrician that she used cocaine the night before she delivered. A basic toxicology test performed on Johnson and her son was positive for benzoylecgonine, a metabolite or "breakdown" product of cocaine.

In December 1988, Johnson, while pregnant with a daughter, suffered a crack overdose. Johnson told paramedics that she had taken $200 of crack cocaine earlier that evening and that she was concerned about the effects of the drug on her unborn child. Johnson was then taken to the hospital for observation.

Johnson was hospitalized again on January 23, 1989, when she was in labor. Johnson told Dr. Tompkins, an obstetrician, that she had used rock cocaine that morning while she was in labor. With the exception of finding meconium stain fluid in the amniotic sack,[2] there were no other complications with the birth of Johnson's baby daughter. Approximately sixty-to-ninety seconds elapsed from the time the child's head emerged from her mother's birth canal until her umbilical cord was clamped.

The following day, the Department of Health and Rehabilitative Services investigated an abuse report of a cocaine baby concerning Johnson's daughter. Johnson told the investigator that she had smoked pot and crack cocaine three to four times every-other-day throughout the duration of her pregnancy with her daughter. Johnson's mother acknowledged that Johnson had been using cocaine for at least three years during the time her daughter and son were born.

At Johnson's trial, Dr. Tompkins testified that a mother's blood passes nutrients, oxygen and chemicals to an unborn child by a diffusion exchange at the capillary level from the womb to the placenta. The umbilical cord then circulates the baby's blood (including the exchange from its mother) between the placenta and the child. Metabolized cocaine derivatives in the mother's blood thus diffuse from the womb to the placenta, and then reach the baby through its umbilical cord. Although the blood flow is somewhat restricted during the birthing process, a measurable amount of blood is

---

2. This condition may indicate that the baby is normal or that its neurological func-   tion has been compromised.

transferred from the placenta to the baby through the umbilical cord during delivery and after birth.

Dr. Shashi Gore, a pathologist and toxicologist, testified that cocaine has a half life of about one hour. This means that half of the amount of the drug remains in a person's blood stream for about one hour. The remainder gradually decreases over a period of forty-eight to seventy-two hours. The liver metabolizes the cocaine into benzoylecgonine which travels through the kidneys and into the urine until it is voided.

When Dr. Gore was asked whether a woman who had smoked cocaine at 10:00 p.m. and again between 6:00 and 7:00 a.m. the following morning and delivered a child at 1:00 p.m. that afternoon would still have cocaine or benzoylecgonine present in her blood stream at the time of delivery, the response was yes. When asked whether a woman who had smoked cocaine sometime the night before delivering a child at 8:00 in the morning would still have cocaine or benzoylecgonine in her system at the time of the child's birth, the response again was yes.

Dr. Stephen Kandall, a neonatologist, testified for the defense that it was impossible to tell whether the cocaine derivatives which appeared in these children's urine shortly after birth were the result of the exchange from the mother to her children before or after they were born because most of it took place from womb to the placenta before the birth process was complete.

He also testified that blood flow to the infant from the placenta through the umbilical cord to the child is restricted during contractions. Cocaine also constricts the passage of blood dramatically but benzoylecgonine does not. Dr. Kandall admitted that it is theoretically possible that cocaine or other substances can pass between a mother and her baby during the thirty-to-sixty second period after the child is born and before the umbilical cord is cut, but that the amount would be tiny.

I submit there was no medical testimony adequate to support the trial court's finding that a "delivery" occurred here during the birthing process, even if the criminal statute is applicable. The expert witnesses all testified about blood flow from the umbilical cord to child. But that blood flow is the child's and the placenta through which it flows, is not part of the mother's body. No witness testified in this case that any cocaine derivatives passed from the mother's womb to the placenta during the sixty-to-ninety seconds after the child was expelled from the birth canal. That is when any "delivery" would have to have taken place under this statute, from one "person" to another "person."

Further, there was no evidence that Johnson timed her dosage of cocaine so as to be able to transmit some small amount after her child's birth. Predicting the day or hour of a child's birth is difficult to impossible even for experts. Had Johnson given birth one or two days later, the cocaine would have been completely eliminated, and no "crime" would have occurred. But since she went into labor which progressed to birth after taking cocaine when she did, the only way Johnson could have prevented the "delivery" would have been to have severed the cord before the child was born which, of course, would probably have killed both herself and her child. This illustrates the absurdity of applying the delivery-of-a-drug statute to this scenario.

However, in my view, the primary question in this case is whether section 893.13(1)(c)1. was intended by the Legislature to apply to the birthing process. Before Johnson can be prosecuted under this statute, it must be clear that the Legislature intended for it to apply to the delivery of cocaine derivatives to a newborn during a sixty-to-ninety second interval, before severance of the umbilical cord. I can find no case where "delivery" of a drug was based on an involuntary act such as diffusion and blood flow.[3] Criminal statutes must be strictly—not loosely—construed.

Further, in construing a statute, we must consider its history, the evil to be corrected, the intention of the Legislature, the subject to be regulated and the objects to be attained. Legislative intent is the polestar by which the courts must be guided. Legislative intent may be express or it may be gathered from the purpose of the act, the administrative construction of it, other legislative acts bearing upon the subject, and all the circumstances surrounding and attendant upon it. My review of other pertinent legislative enactments, specifically chapter 415, leads me to conclude in this case that the Legislature expressly chose to treat the problem of drug dependent mothers and newborns as a public health problem and that it considered but rejected imposing criminal sanctions, via section 893.13(1)(c)1.

In 1982, sections 415.501–514 were enacted to deal with the problem of child abuse and neglect. The Legislature determined that because of the impact that abuse or neglect has on a victimized child, siblings, family structure, and inevitably on all citizens of the state, the prevention of child abuse and neglect is a priority of this state. § 415.501, Fla. Stat. (1989). To further this end, the Legislature required that a comprehensive approach for the prevention of abuse and neglect of children be developed for the state. Id. The statute defined an "abused or neglected child" as a child

---

3. As examples of delivery of a controlled substance, see State v. Medlin, 273 So.2d 394 (Fla.1973) (defendant's conviction for delivering a barbiturate affirmed where a defendant gave sixteen-year-old girl a capsule, advising her that it would make her go up and gave her another pill to be taken when she came down); Gelsey v. State, 565 So.2d 876 (Fla. 5th DCA 1990) (defendant's conviction for delivery of a controlled substance affirmed where he met with officers and exchanged crack and cash for powdered cocaine); Roberts v. State, 557 So.2d 685 (Fla. 5th DCA 1990) (defendant's conviction for delivery of cocaine affirmed where he sold one rock of cocaine to undercover officer); Willingham v. State, 541 So.2d 1240 (Fla. 2d DCA), rev. denied, 548 So.2d 663 (Fla.1989) (delivery of cocaine convictions affirmed where defendant offered two pieces of rock cocaine to officer, officer bought one and defendant retained the other); Newman v. State, 522 So.2d 71 (Fla. 4th DCA 1988) (defendant's conviction for trafficking in cocaine by constructive delivery affirmed where cocaine was sampled and cocaine and money not yet exchanged); King v. State, 336 So.2d 1200 (Fla. 2d DCA 1976), cert. denied, 345 So.2d 424 (Fla.), cert. dismissed, King v. Florida, 434 U.S. 802, 98 S.Ct. 30, 54 L.Ed.2d 60 (1977) (defendant guilty of delivery of narcotics by writing prescriptions in bad faith); State v. Vinson, 298 So.2d 505 (Fla. 2d DCA 1974) (physician who issued prescription for drug in bad faith guilty of delivery).

whose physical or mental health or welfare was harmed, or threatened with harm, by the acts of omissions of the parent or other person responsible for the child's welfare. As originally defined, "harm" included physical or mental injury, sexual abuse, exploitation, abandonment, and neglect. § 415.503(7), Fla. Stat. (1983)

In 1987, a bill was proposed to broaden the definition of "harm" to include physical dependency of a newborn infant upon certain controlled drugs. However, there was a concern among legislators that this language might authorize criminal prosecutions of mothers who give birth to drug-dependent children. Comment, A Response to "Cocaine Babies"—Amendment of Florida's Child Abuse and Neglect Laws to Encompass Infants Born Drug Dependent, 15 Fla.S.U.L.Rev. 865, 877 (1987).[4] The bill was then amended to provide that no parent of a drug-dependent newborn shall be subject to criminal investigation solely on the basis of the infant's drug dependency. In the words of the sponsor of the House bill:

> This clearly states that the individual would not be subject to any investigation solely upon the basis of the infant's drug dependency.
>
> The prime purpose of this bill is to keep the families intact. It's not for the purpose of investigation.
>
>   . . .
>
> Again, there is a well-founded anxiety that we are looking to arrest Moms. We're not looking to do that. What we are looking to do is we're looking to intervene on behalf of many different state policies. . . .

The bill was passed by the Legislature and the changes were codified in section 415.503(9)(a)2.

From this legislative history, it is clear that the Legislature considered and rejected a specific statutory provision authorizing criminal penalties against mothers for delivering drug-affected children who received transfer of an illegal drug derivative metabolized by the mother's body, in utero. In light of this express legislative statement, I conclude that the Legislature never intended for the general drug delivery statute to authorize prosecutions of those mothers who take illegal drugs close enough in time to childbirth that a doctor could testify that a tiny amount passed from mother to child in the few seconds before the umbilical cord was cut. Criminal prosecution of mothers like Johnson will undermine Florida's express policy of "keeping families intact" and could destroy the family by incarcerating the child's mother when alternative measures could protect the child and stabilize the family. Comment, A Response to "Cocaine Babies", 15 Fla.S.U.L.Rev. at 881.

In similar cases in which charges have been brought against mothers after delivery of drug-affected newborns, those charges have been dismissed. See People v. Hardy, 188 Mich.App. 305, 469 N.W.2d 50 (1991);

---

4. The staff analysis of this bill noted that the legislation, as written, provided a likelihood that a parent could be criminally prosecuted under chapter 893 for delivering a drug dependent child.

People v. Bremer, No. 90–32227–FH (Mich.Cir.Ct. January 31, 1991); State v. Gray, 1990 WL 125695, No. L–89–239 (Ohio Ct.App. August 31, 1990), jurisdictional motion allowed, 57 Ohio St.3d 711, 568 N.E.2d 695 (1991). In People v. Bremer, the defendant was charged with delivery of cocaine to her newborn daughter after urine samples from the defendant and child following birth tested positive for benzoylecgonine. The circuit court concluded that the Michigan Legislature never intended to include the action of the defendant under the delivery statute: To interpret this section to cover ingestion of cocaine by a pregnant woman would be a radical incursion upon existing law. A person may not be punished for a crime unless her acts fall clearly within the language of the statute. The specific language of this act does not allow the strained construction advanced by the prosecution. Neither judges nor prosecutors can make criminal laws. This is the purview of the Legislature. If the Legislature wanted to punish the uterine transfer of cocaine from a mother to her fetus, it would be up to the Legislature to consider the attending public policy and constitutional arguments and then pass its legislation. The Legislature has not done so and the court has no power to make such a law.

The Michigan court also rejected the prosecutor's argument that charging women with delivery of controlled substances to their newborns provides a strong deterrent against unlawful use of drugs by pregnant women and prompts them to drug treatment. The court noted that prosecution of these women would likely have the opposite effect. A woman may abort her child or avoid prenatal care or treatment out of fear of prosecution. Thus the court concluded that the state's interest was better served by making treatment programs available to pregnant addicts rather than driving them away from treatment by criminal sanctions.

In State v. Gray, the defendant was indicted for child endangering based on her use of cocaine during the last trimester of pregnancy. The trial court concluded that the child endangering statute did not apply to this situation and dismissed the charge against her. On appeal, the state of Ohio argued that the trial court had failed to consider the time the fetus is a child and still attached to the mother and the duty of care created at that point. The appellate court concluded that the Ohio General Assembly did not intend to criminalize the passage of harmful substances from a mother to a child in the brief moments from birth to the severance of the umbilical cord. "To construe the statute in this manner would mean that every expectant woman who ingested a substance with the potential of harm to her child, e.g., alcohol or nicotine, would be criminally liable under [the child endangering statute]. We do not believe such result was intended by the General Assembly."

There can be no doubt that drug abuse is one of the most serious problems confronting our society today. National Treasury Employees Union v. Von Raab, 489 U.S. 656, 109 S.Ct. 1384, 1395, 103 L.Ed.2d 685 (1989). Of particular concern is the alarming rise in the number of babies born with cocaine in their systems as a result of cocaine use by pregnant women. Some experts estimate that as many as eleven percent of pregnant women have used an illegal drug during pregnancy, and of those women, seventy-five percent have used cocaine. Report of the American Medical Association Board of Trustees, Legal Interventions During Pregnancy, 264 JAMA 2663 (Nov. 28, 1990). Others estimate that 375,000 newborns per year are born to women who are users of illicit drugs. American Public Health Association 1990 Policy Statement.

It is well-established that the effects of cocaine use by a pregnant woman on her fetus and later on her newborn can be severe. On average, cocaine-exposed babies have lower birth weights, shorter body lengths at birth, and smaller head circumferences than normal infants. 264 JAMA at 2666. Cocaine use may also result in sudden infant death syndrome, neural-behavioral deficiencies as well as other medical problems and long-term developmental abnormalities. American Public Health Association 1990 Policy Statement. The basic problem of damaging the fetus by drug use during pregnancy should not be addressed piecemeal, however, by prosecuting users who deliver their babies close in time to use of drugs and ignoring those who simply use drugs during their pregnancy.

Florida could possibly have elected to make *in utero* transfers criminal. But it chose to deal with this problem in other ways. One way is to allow evidence of drug use by women as a ground for removal of the child to the custody of protective services, as was done in this case. Some states have responded to this crisis by charging women with child abuse and neglect. See In re Baby X, 97 Mich.App. 111, 293 N.W.2d 736 (1980) (newborn suffering from narcotics withdrawal symptoms due to prenatal maternal drug addiction is neglected and within jurisdiction of the probate court); In re Smith, 128 Misc.2d 976, 492 N.Y.S.2d 331 (N.Y.Fam.Ct.1985) (person under Family Court Act includes unborn child who is neglected as the result of mother's conduct); In re Ruiz, 27 Ohio Misc.2d 31, 27 O.B.R. 350, 500 N.E.2d 935 (Com.Pl.1986) (mother's use of heroin close to baby's birth created substantial risk to the health of the child and constituted child abuse).

However, prosecuting women for using drugs and "delivering" them to their newborns appears to be the least effective response to this crisis.[5]

5. As the AMA Board of Trustees Report notes, possession of illicit drugs already results in criminal penalties and pregnant women who use illegal substances obviously are not deterred by existing sanctions. Thus the goal of deterrence is not served. To punish a person for substance abuse ignores the impaired capacity of these individuals to make rational decisions concerning their drug use. "In all but a few cases, taking a harmful substance such as cocaine is not meant to harm the fetus but to satisfy an acute psychological and physical need for that particular substance. If a pregnant woman suffers from a substance dependency, it is the physical impossibility of avoiding an impact on fetal health that causes severe damage to the fetus, not an intentional or malicious wish to cause harm." 264 JAMA at 2667–2668. Punishment is simply not an effective way of curing a dependency or preventing future substance abuse. Id. at 2667. See also National Treasury Employees Union, 109 S.Ct. at 1396 ("Addicts may be unable to abstain even for a limited period of time, or may be unaware of the 'fade-away affect' of certain drugs."). Stated another way: However the initial use of a drug might be characterized, its continued use by addicts is rarely, if any, truly voluntarily. Drug addiction tends to obliterate rational, autonomous decision

Rather than face the possibility of prosecution, pregnant women who are substance abusers may simply avoid prenatal or medical care for fear of being detected. Yet the newborns of these women are, as a group, the most fragile and sick, and most in need of hospital neonatal care. A decision to deliver these babies "at home" will have tragic and serious consequences. As the Board of Trustees Reports notes:

> [C]riminal penalties may exacerbate the harm done to fetal health by deterring pregnant substance abusers from obtaining help or care from either the health or public welfare professions, the very people who are best able to prevent future abuse. The California Medical Association has noted:
>
> > While unhealthy behavior cannot be condoned, to bring criminal charges against a pregnant woman for activities which may be harmful to her fetus is inappropriate. Such prosecution is counterproductive to the public interest as it may discourage a woman from seeking prenatal care or dissuade her from providing accurate information to health care providers out of fear of self-incrimination. This failure to seek proper care or to withhold vital information concerning her health could increase the risks to herself and her baby.
>
> Florida's Secretary of Health and Rehabilitative Services has also observed that potential prosecution under existing child abuse or drug use statutes already "makes many potential reporters reluctant to identify women as substance abusers." (footnotes omitted)

264 JAMA at 2669. See also Commonwealth v. Pellegrini, No. 87970 (Mass. Superior Court Oct. 15, 1990) (by imposing criminal sanctions, women may turn away from seeking prenatal care for fear of being discovered, undermining the interests of the state in protecting potential human life). Prosecution of pregnant women for engaging in activities harmful to their fetuses or newborns may also unwittingly increase the incidence of abortion.[6]

Such considerations have led the American Medical Association Board of Trustees to oppose criminal sanctions for harmful behavior by a pregnant woman toward her fetus and to advocate that pregnant substance abusers be provided with rehabilitative treatment appropriate to their specific psychological and physiological needs. 264 JAMA at 2670. Likewise, the American Public Health Association has adopted the view that the use

---

making about drug use. Drugs become a necessity for dependent users, even when they would much prefer to escape their addiction. In virtually all instances, a user specifically does not want to harm her fetus, yet she cannot resist the drive to use the drug. Thus it is not plausible to attribute to drug-using women a motive of causing harm to the fetus. Mariner, Glantz and Annas, Pregnancy, Drugs and the Perils of Prosecution, 9 Crimi-

nal Justice Ethics 30, 36 (Winter/Spring 1990).

6. See 264 JAMA at 2667; Rush, Prenatal Care Taking: Limits of State Intervention With and Without Roe, 39 Univ.Fla.L.Rev. 55, 68 n. 38 (1986). A woman could simply "opt out" of the scope of any criminal regulations by terminating the pregnancy through abortion. 39 Univ.Fla.L.Rev. at 68 n. 38.

of illegal drugs by pregnant women is a public health problem. It also recommends that no punitive measures be taken against pregnant women who are users of illicit drugs when no other illegal acts, including drug-related offenses, have been committed. See 1990 Policy Statement.

In summary, I would hold that section 893.13(1)(c)1. does not encompass "delivery" of an illegal drug derivative from womb to placenta to umbilical cord to newborn after a child's birth. If that is the intent of the Legislature, then this statute should be redrafted to clearly address the basic problem of passing illegal substances from mother to child in utero, not just in the birthing process.

. . . At oral argument the State acknowledged that no other jurisdiction has upheld a conviction of a mother for delivery of a controlled substance to an infant through either the umbilical cord or an *in utero* transmission; nor has the State submitted any subsequent authority to reflect that this fact has changed. The Court declines the State's invitation to walk down a path that the law, public policy, reason and common sense forbid it to tread. Therefore, we quash the decision below, answer the certified question in the negative, and remand with directions that Johnson's two convictions be reversed.

NOTES

In **Whitner v. State**, 328 S.C. 1, 492 S.E.2d 777 (1997), *cert. denied* 523 U.S. 1145, 118 S.Ct. 1857, 140 L.Ed.2d 1104 (1998), a woman in South Carolina was sentenced to eight years in prison for criminal child neglect when she took crack cocaine during her pregnancy and the child was subsequently stillborn. Subsequently the South Carolina Supreme Court held unconstitutional a public hospital's practice of identifying and testing pregnant women suspected of using controlled substances. If presence of narcotics was discovered the hospital referred the women to law enforcement officials for eventual prosecution. The court held that such testing violated the Fourth Amendment prohibition of warrantless searches and were not conducted with consent of the women. More recently, the state's supreme court permitted a mother to be charged with "homicide by child abuse" when the mother's baby was stillborn. The mother's use of cocaine during pregnancy was deemed to be the cause of the baby's death. South Carolina v. McKnight, 352 S.C. 635, 576 S.E.2d 168 (2003). For additional information on controlled substances and protection of children, *see* www.calib.com/nccanch/pubs/usermanuals/subabuse/biblio.cfm. Drug testing with or without knowledge and possibility of third-party notification is of particular concern as the HIV/AIDS pandemic continues. *See generally* Michael Flannery and Raymond C. O'Brien, *Mandatory HIV Testing for Boxers*, 31 U.C. DAVIS L. REV. 409 (1998); Raymond C. O'Brien, *The Legal Dilemma of Partner Notification During the HIV Epidemic: A Commentary*, 4 J. CLINICAL. ETH. 245 (1993).

The Supreme Court of Connecticut, in *In re* Valerie D., 223 Conn. 492, 613 A.2d 748 (1992), held that its state statute allowing termination of parental rights if a child has been denied care necessary for its well being by acts of parental commission or omission did not authorize termination of parental rights of a mother based on her prenatal conduct of injecting cocaine several hours before onset of labor. Further, where the assertion of custody over the child immediately after birth led directly to the condition supporting termination of parental rights (no ongoing parent-child relationship), the state could not terminate mother's parental rights on that basis.

Fetal protection. Increasing controversy is developing over how to cope with what some label "fetal abuse". The term describes maternal conduct during pregnancy that would endanger a child's health or development. Most prominent is substance abuse leading to fetal alcohol syndrome or impairment from cocaine. In State ex rel. Angela M.W. v. Kruzicki, 209 Wis.2d 112, 561 N.W.2d 729 (1997), the Supreme Court of Wisconsin held that the definition of "child" in the children's code as a "person who is less than 18 years of age," does not include a viable fetus for purposes of protection and services afforded to children in need. A Circuit Judge had held to the contrary and ordered that the mother be held in protective custody within a hospital so as to isolate her and her baby from cocaine and other drugs which were found within the mother's blood during tests at pregnancy. *See, also* Reinesto v. Superior Court, 182 Ariz. 190, 894 P.2d 733 (App.1995) (court refused to criminally prosecute mother for child abuse when she gave birth to a heroin-addicted child); and Pima County Juvenile Severance Action No. S–120171, 183 Ariz. 546, 905 P.2d 555 (App.1995) (fetal abuse cannot be the basis of termination of parental rights).

A few states have modified their child protection laws to provide greater latitude in dealing with substance abuse affecting children immediately after birth. Provisions such as these may be used to intervene after birth for the protection of such children. However, some persons would like to take measures to protect the fetus before birth at least in cases of extreme or well defined danger. This obviously raises serious legal and ethical questions about the extent to which the state can intervene to regulate maternal life styles and habits. In a widely publicized case in the District of Columbia during 1988, a pregnant woman was convicted of forging some $700 of checks and sentenced to jail during the remainder of her pregnancy. The checks were against an account of her employer, who previously had paid for a private rehabilitation program to help the employee deal with cocaine addiction. The judge explained that even though the offense normally might not have resulted in a jail term, the purpose was to protect the fetus against the mother's cocaine use. *See* WASH. POST, July 23, 1988, page 1, col. 1. The mother remained in jail until she went to the hospital and gave birth to a normal child. Intervention before birth is increasingly disallowed. In an opinion which explores other state practices, the Oklahoma Supreme Court held that a fetus is not a child for purposes of child abuse and neglect law. The court reasoned that even though the child may be the subject of homicide and its biological parents may recover for wrongful death, medical science cannot furnish evidence as to whether a fetus might be mentally, physically, or intellectually deprived within the meaning of the Children's Code. Only if the legislature changes the language of the code would there be applicability to a viable or nonviable fetus. Starks v. State (In re Unborn Child), 18 P.3d 342 (Okla.2001).

Authority to take affirmative action before birth has been asserted by some courts in requiring a cesarean section over a mother's objection— cases that also are controversial. *See, e.g.,* Jefferson v. Griffin Spalding County Hospital Authority, 247 Ga. 86, 274 S.E.2d 457 (1981). However, in Matter of A.C., 573 A.2d 1235 (D.C.1990), the D. C. Court of Appeals held that when a pregnant patient with a viable fetus is near death, the decision whether to undergo a cesarean is for the patient to make unless she is incompetent or unable to give informed consent. In the latter instance, according to the court, her decision must be ascertained through substituted judgment. The court explained their view of such a process:

> ... [T]o determine the subjective desires of the patient, the court must consider the totality of the evidence, focusing particularly on written or oral directions concerning treatment to family, friends, and health-care professionals. The court should also take into account the patient's past decisions regarding medical treatment, and attempt to ascertain from what is known about the patient's value system, goals, and desires what the patient would decide if competent.
>
> After considering the patient's prior statements, if any, the previous medical decisions of the patient, and the values held by the patient, the court may still be unsure what course the patient would choose. In such circumstances the court may supplement its knowledge about the patient by determining what most persons would likely do in a similar situation. When the patient is pregnant, however, she may not be concerned exclusively with her own welfare. Thus it is proper for the court, in a case such as this, to weigh (along with all the other factors) the mother's prognosis, the viability of the fetus, the probable result of treatment or non-treatment for both mother and fetus, and the mother's likely interest in avoiding impairment for her child together with her own instincts for survival.
>
> Additionally, the court should consider the context in which prior declarations, treatment decisions, and expressions of personal values were made, including whether statements were made casually or after contemplation, or in accordance with deeply held beliefs. Finally, in making a substituted judgment, the court should become as informed about the patient's condition, prognosis, and treatment options as one would expect any patient to become before making a treatment decision. Obviously, the weight accorded to all of these factors will vary from case to case.

For more detailed review of some of the various issues, *see* Christ J. Richer, Note. *Fetal Abuse Law: Punitive Approach and the Honorable Status of Motherhood, 50* SYRACUSE L. REV. *1127 (2000);* Kay Levine and Virginia Mellea, *Strategizing the Street: How Law Matters in the Lives of Women in the Street–Level Drug Economy* (Reviewing PATRICIA EWICK AND

SUSAN S. SILBEY, THE COMMON PLACE OF LAW: STORIES FROM EVERYDAY LIFE.), 26 LAW & SOC. INQUIRY 169 (2001); Michael T. Flannery, *Court–Ordered Prenatal Intervention: A Final Means to the End of Gestational Substance Abuse*, 30 J. FAM. L. 519 (1991); Robin–Vergeer, *The Problem of the Drug–Exposed Newborn: A Return to Principled Intervention*, 42 STAN.L.REV. 745 (1990); and Note, *Maternal Rights and Fetal Wrongs: The Case Against the Criminalization of "Fetal Abuse"*, 101 HARV.L.REV. 994 (1988).

INDIANA CODE ANN. (LexisNexis 2003)

31–34–1–9   Disabled child deprived of necessary nutrition or medical or surgical intervention

Sec. 9. A child in need of services under section 1, 2, 3, 4, 5, 6, 7, or 8 of this chapter includes a child with a disability who:

(1) is deprived of nutrition that is necessary to sustain life; or

(2) is deprived of medical or surgical intervention that is necessary to remedy or ameliorate a life threatening medical condition;

if the nutrition or medical or surgical intervention is generally provided to similarly situated children with or without disabilities.

Sanders v. State

Supreme Court of Georgia, 1983.
251 Ga. 70, 303 S.E.2d 13.

■ BELL, JUSTICE.

Lillian Sanders appeals her conviction and life sentence for the murder of her infant daughter, Cassandra Denise Sanders. There was evidence at trial showing that Cassandra was born September 11, 1981. She was twelve weeks premature and had a low birth weight, a hernia, and anemia. She was hospitalized for treatment of these ailments and was discharged November 6. On November 17 she was treated at a pediatric clinic for fussiness stemming from a suspected allergy, and on November 30 for a cold and a fungus infection. The clinic's record of the November 30 examination had a notation that Cassandra had gained weight, but did not indicate that bruises or other injuries had been found.

At about three p.m. on December 3, 1981 appellant used a neighbor's phone to call the police. She told the police dispatcher her baby was sick, and asked for an ambulance. The dispatcher later said appellant was not sobbing, and her voice seemed normal; appellant's neighbor testified she seemed worried. After making the call Sanders returned to her own home, from which the neighbor then heard crying and hollering. When the county emergency medical service arrived at appellant's residence a few minutes later, the technicians found her holding Cassandra in her arms. One technician asked what the trouble was and she replied the baby had been crying and had just stopped. She also repeatedly told them, "Please don't let my baby die." The technicians gave Cassandra a quick examination and found multiple bruises on her face, neck, chest and abdomen. A patch of skin was missing from her neck, and one side of her head was mushy due to blood and fluid under the skin. The child was gasping for breath, had a high pulse and low respiration, and appeared unconscious. The technicians then took Cassandra and her mother to the emergency room of Archbold Hospital, arriving about 3:20 p.m. At the emergency room Dr. Randolph Malone examined the infant, who had stopped breathing and was being given artificial respiration. At that point she was unconscious and appeared dead. Because she had suffered a severe head injury and had unusual bruise marks around the neck he had the police notified, and he questioned Lillian about what had happened. She told him she didn't know, even though she had been with the baby right until she left to call the ambulance.

Forest Roberts, a child protective services worker with the Thomas County Department of Family and Children Services, was summoned to the hospital and was told that Sanders was suspected of child abuse. She questioned appellant, who first told her that she didn't know what had happened to the baby, that there had been nothing wrong with her earlier, and that she had gone in to check on her and found her like that. She said she might have "popped" her to make her stop crying, but insisted she hadn't hurt her. However, Sanders admitted after more questioning that she hadn't felt well that morning and had been depressed. She had been alone with Cassandra and her older child, Chrishenbo Lashan, that afternoon. The baby had begun to cry so she changed her and gave her some milk. When Roberts asked how the child had gotten its neck bruises appellant maintained she didn't know, but then a few minutes later she said some milk had dried and caked around Cassandra's neck, and that she had scrubbed her neck to remove the milk, and might have bruised and scratched her in the process. Roberts left the room, then returned and told her the child was seriously ill, that it didn't appear she'd gotten that way by herself, and appellant needed to tell her what happened. Lillian said she may have dropped the baby but didn't remember, then she said the baby cried all the time and she must have dropped it. Sanders appeared upset and nervous during this interrogation, but was not hysterically crying or otherwise showing a lot of emotion. While Roberts was questioning Sanders the police arrived. They were present during some of the questioning, and at some point read Sanders *Miranda* warnings. In the course of their interrogation she told them that the child had fallen out of her hands when she reached for something on a table or chest of drawers in the bedroom. She was asked if the child had struck anything except the floor, and she said she hadn't. Her demeanor during this inquiry was confused but otherwise normal, except that a few minutes later she cried.[1]

The baby was pronounced dead at 5:30 that afternoon. Appellant was taken to the police station where shortly after seven that evening she was

---

1. The trial court conducted a *Jackson-Denny* hearing and found by a preponderance of the evidence that Sander's statements given to or in the presence of the police were freely and voluntarily given.

again questioned after being given *Miranda* warnings, and again she said she'd dropped the baby, that it hadn't hit anything except the floor, and she didn't know how she had been that badly injured. During this interrogation Sanders expressed concern about what would happen to her and asked if she told the truth she would still have to go to court or jail. The police told her they couldn't promise anything, whereupon she volunteered she'd been upset, was pregnant, and didn't want another baby. Sanders consented to a search of her house, during which she pointed out the spot where she claimed the baby had fallen and again denied the baby had hit anything except the floor. Sanders was allowed to go home for the night, but was questioned again at the police station shortly after six p.m. the next day. After being advised a third time about *Miranda* rights, she told the police she'd gone downtown the previous day, leaving Cassandra in her sister's care. When she returned the child had no scratches, bruises, or other apparent injuries. After she related this story, the police then told her she was being charged with murder, and she asked them about securing bond. When queried about Cassandra's head injury, she said she may have mashed her head while picking her up.

Dr. Larry Howard, forensic pathologist and Director of the State Crime Laboratory, performed the autopsy. He testified that the primary cause of death was a severe crushing type head injury which consisted of a circular skull fracture on the right side of the head. There was severe damage to the brain, including much bleeding into the brain tissue and laceration of the brain by the edges of the skull fracture. There were numerous bruises on the face, chest, and abdomen. The neck had considerable bruising and abrasions which were possible fingernail marks, indicating pressure may have been applied to the neck with a hand. Similar possible fingernail abrasions were found on the chest and the back of the right hand. The upper right arm was broken, probably by someone placing tension on it until it snapped. The liver had been split, which was an injury consistent with a blow to the front of the chest. This injury was at least four and possibly twelve hours older than many of the others, which appeared fresh. Some of the bruises were lined up as if caused by a blunt instrument with several projections, which would have been consistent with the child having been struck by the knuckles of a hand. In his opinion these injuries were not consistent with the child having been dropped on a floor, and he described them as evidencing a typical battered child syndrome. Moreover, he testified they would have been impossible for another young child to inflict.

The defense rested without introducing evidence, and the jury returned a verdict of guilty. Sanders was sentenced to life imprisonment and appealed without having moved for a new trial.

1) Although appellant has not raised the general grounds we have nevertheless reviewed the evidence in a light most favorable to the jury's verdict. We conclude that a rational trier of fact could reasonably have found Sanders guilty of murder beyond a reasonable doubt.

2) In her first enumeration of error appellant complains that the trial court should not have admitted into evidence the state's thirteenth exhibit, which was an autopsy photograph of the victim with her scalp reflected to show the fractured skull, lacerated brain, and blood from hemorrhaging, on the ground that it was an intentional distortion of the original evidence and was gruesome and inflammatory. Although the photograph is gruesome, we find its admission was necessary to show the cause of death, which had become apparent only because of the autopsy. Brown v. State, 250 Ga. 862(5), 302 S.E.2d 347 (1983).

3) In her second enumeration Sanders claims the state impermissibly placed her character in issue. The record shows that three employees of the Department of Family and Children Services ("the Department") testified for the prosecution. Their combined testimony established certain aspects of appellant's personal history and the fact that appellant had sought the Department's help on several occasions. Specifically, they testified that during the period 1976–81 Sanders had moved several times and had asked the Department for help in locating housing; that she had sought food stamps; that both her children had been problem pregnancies; that appellant's mother had contacted the Department and complained about the quality of care Chrishenbo was receiving and about appellant's attitude toward the child; that Lillian was counseled about child care and a stable living environment; and that appellant's mother's own family had been supervised by the Department for several years. Following this testimony about appellant's background, Dr. Wallace Kennedy, a clinical psychologist, took the stand to testify about the "battering parent syndrome."[2] After his qualifications as an expert in the field of clinical and family psychology and child abuse were established, Dr. Kennedy constructed a profile of the typical abusive parent.[3] He testified that the characteristics of an adult who abuses a child in a life threatening fashion almost always are, first, that the parent herself is the product of a violent, abusive environment and usually commits violent acts with growing frequency; second, that the parent is under some kind of chronic environmental stress, caused by, for example, money or housing problems, and is frequently a single parent; third, that the parent has a history of poor social judgment, in that she tends to be impulsive or explosive under stress; fourth, that the child she abuses is the product of an unplanned, difficult, and unpleasant pregnancy and is prematurely born; fifth, that the abused child is a chronically difficult child, either sickly or frequently crying. The following exchange between the prosecutor and Dr. Kennedy then took place: Q. "Is there a difference between a child that's suffering from a lethal abuse where as (sic) just random spanking abuse, Doctor?" A. "Yes." Q. "What's the difference, please sir?" A. "The main difference in the history is that a parent who is likely to kill a child is a person who has engaged in some kind of life

---

2. This term is not Dr. Kennedy's, but clearly represents his concept. See Loebach v. State, 310 N.W.2d 58 (Minn.1981).

3. Although Dr. Kennedy indicated he had researched this area and was familiar with the relevant literature, he cited no specific source for his profile and he attempted no showing of its scientific validity.

threatening behavior in the past. That is, pulling knives on people, threatening people with sticks or engaging in lethal behavior. That is, I personally have not had a circumstance in all the twenty-three (23) years which (sic) you have a person who has killed a child that has not had a previous history of violence unless it was a psychotic mother where the killing of the child—" MR. ANDREWS: "—Your Honor, if I may at this time I'd like to object and move for a mistrial."

This motion was denied and the state, without further objection from defense counsel, proceeded to retrace much of the same ground, eliciting substantially similar testimony about the second through fifth criteria. Sanders appeals from the denial of her motion for mistrial.

We have held that under appropriate circumstances a woman who kills her husband or boyfriend and raises the defense of self-defense may, as evidence of whether she acted in fear of her life, have an expert witness describe the "battered woman syndrome", apply that model to the facts, and conclude that the woman falls within the profile. Smith v. State, 247 Ga. 612, 277 S.E.2d 678 (1981).[4] We also observed in *Smith* that it is accepted practice for the state to offer expert opinion testimony that a child is a victim of "battered child syndrome" and that its injuries are not accidental. Id. at 617, 277 S.E.2d 678.[5] In addition, we cited the case of State v. Baker, 120 N.H. 773, 424 A.2d 171 (N.H.1980). In *Baker* the defendant husband claimed his attempt to kill his wife was the result of insanity, but the state contended it was but a single episode in a recurring pattern of domestic violence. Baker called two psychiatrists who testified that in their opinion he was insane at the time of the crime, and the New Hampshire Supreme Court held that the state then could properly call an expert on domestic violence to testify regarding the battered wife syndrome and to give his opinion that mental illness is not an important cause of wife beating. It was also proper, the court ruled, for the state's expert to state his opinion that, based on prior testimony by Baker's wife and daughter that he had physically abused them, Baker's marriage probably fell within the contours of the battered woman syndrome. We have not previously been faced with a case wherein the state has seized the initiative and attempted to use a profile in its case-in-chief as an affirmative weapon

---

4. The other primary issue in *Smith* concerned the admissibility of expert opinion testimony on issues of ultimate fact. Not considered were whether the particular clinical psychologist whom Smith sought to use was qualified to give an opinion in that area (her qualifications were not contested by the state), and whether the state of the art of the study of battered women and the application of diagnostic profiles to particular defendants has reached a scientific stage of verifiable certainty, Harper v. State, 249 Ga. 519(1), 292 S.E.2d 389 (1982).

5. As support for this principle we cited State v. Wilkerson, 295 N.C. 559, 247 S.E.2d

905 (N.C.1978). However, the Wilkerson court took pains to indicate the limits of the use of the battered child syndrome. Although an expert may diagnose a particular child as a "battered child," explain the use of that term, and give his opinion regarding the usual cause of the syndrome, i.e., that it is usually intentionally inflicted by some physical custodian of the child, the expert may not testify that the injuries were in fact caused by any particular person or class of persons engaged in any particular activity or class of activities, nor may he give his opinion as to the defendant's guilt or innocence. *Wilkerson*, id. 247 S.E.2d at 911.

against the defendant; however, this question has been confronted by another appellate court, Loebach v. State, 310 N.W.2d 58 (Minn.1981). In that case Loebach appealed his conviction for murdering his infant son. At trial the state had called an expert on child abuse, Dr. Robert ten Bensel, to testify that, based on the child's injuries, in his opinion the child had suffered from nonaccidental physical abuse over a period of time and accordingly was a victim of battered child syndrome. Ten Bensel also testified over objection that battering parents tend to have similar personality traits and personal histories; he described those characteristics but did not suggest Loebach possessed any of them. However, evidence about Loebach's past was introduced through other witnesses. On appeal the Minnesota Supreme Court found that the testimony about Loebach's personal history and personality was nothing more than character evidence, introduced for the purpose of showing Loebach fit within ten Bensel's battering parent profile, and it held that since Loebach had not placed his character in issue, admission of the testimony was error. The court then announced a prospective rule that the prosecution would not be permitted to introduce evidence of the battering parent syndrome or establish a defendant's character as a battering parent unless the defendant first raised that issue. However, the court went on to rule that there was overwhelming evidence of Loebach's guilt without the battering parent testimony, which was only a small percentage of the evidence, and held the error was not prejudicial.

Turning to the instant case, we find that the disputed portion of Dr. Kennedy's testimony clearly implicated Sanders's character. It matters little that, as the state points out, Kennedy never expressly drew the conclusion that appellant fit his profile of battering parents; his construction of the profile, coupled with the previous testimony that appellant possessed many characteristics which Kennedy's profile identified as being shared by the typical battering parent, could lead a reasonable juror to no other inference than that the state was implying that this parent had a history of violent behavior, and, more important, that this parent fit within the syndrome, and had in fact murdered her baby. We hold that unless a defendant has placed her character in issue or has raised some defense which the battering parent syndrome is relevant to rebut, the state may not introduce evidence of the syndrome, nor may the state introduce character evidence showing a defendant's personality traits and personal history as its foundation for demonstrating the defendant has the characteristics of a typical battering parent. Accordingly, the trial court in the instant case erred in admitting the portion of Dr. Kennedy's testimony which was challenged.

However, we find that it is highly probable that the error did not contribute to the verdict, since the evidence of guilt was otherwise overwhelming. Moreover, we find the error was harmless for the additional reason that testimony covering substantially the same area, including the testimony about appellant's personal history and most of Dr. Kennedy's testimony, was introduced without challenge.

. . .

Judgment affirmed.

NOTES

The Battered Child Syndrome. A now classic article by Dr. Henry Kempe and his associates in 1962 established a label for classification of child abuse as a medical condition. *See* Kempe, Silverman, Steele, Droegemuller & Silver, *The Battered Child Syndrome*, 181 J.A.M.A. 17 (1962). The phrase came to "characterize a clinical condition in young children who have received serious physical abuse, generally from a parent or foster parent". In 1963, another article appeared in a distinguished medical journal suggesting that the "battered child syndrome" terminology, with its connotation of violence, was not sufficiently broad. Another term was suggested: "maltreatment syndrome". See Fontana, Donovan & Wong, *The "Maltreatment Syndrome", in Children*, 269 NEW ENG. J. MED. 1389 (1963). For a review of historical and contemporary approaches in medical as well as legal contexts, see MARY E. HELFER, RUTH S. KEMPE, AND RICHARD D. KRUGMAN, THE BATTERED CHILD (5th ed. 1997).

New York state has, by statute, established a res ipsa loquitur approach to certain types of child abuse, denominating certain types of injuries as prima facie evidence of abuse or neglect. *See* N.Y. FAM. CT. ACT § 1046(a)(ii) (McKinney 2001):

> [P]roof of injuries sustained by a child or of the condition of a child of such a nature as would ordinarily not be sustained or exist except by reason of the acts or omissions of the parent or other person responsible for the care of such child shall be prima facie evidence of child abuse or neglect, as the case may be, of the parent or other person legally responsible.

Whiplash shaken baby syndrome (WSIS), a common form of child abuse, has been held to be such an injury, justifying custodial limitations on a parent. See Dietz v. Damas, 932 F.Supp. 431 (E.D.N.Y.1996).

The neglectful or abusing parent may suffer from a condition that makes the prospect of future abuse or neglect of another child highly probable and there is no reasonable basis for improvement. For instance, pedophilia. But what of other emotional disabilities? What of being a product of abusive parents? Is prospective abuse or "derivative" abuse sufficient for termination of parental rights? *See* Smith v. Department of Health and Rehab. Serv., 665 So.2d 1153 (Fla.Dist.Ct.App.1996).

The Lawyer's Role. Child advocacy is a fairly recent phenomenon and is necessitated because the child's interest is often diametrically opposed to the competing interests of parents, third parties and sometimes, social services. The Child Abuse Prevention and Treatment Act provided federal financial assistance to state protective services if the state provided a court appointed guardian ad-litem for each child, but there is no requirement that each child have an attorney. Recent cases and articles suggest such a requirement. For further discussion *see* David R. Katner, *Coming to*

Praise, Not to Bury, the New ABA Standards of Practice for Lawyers Who Represent Children in Abuse and Neglect Cases, 14 GEO. J. LEGAL ETHICS, 103 (2000); Guardianship of S.A.W. v. Torres, 856 P.2d 286 (Okla.1993) (child has a right to independent representation in an action for termination of parental rights when the parents have such a right under statute); Leonard P. Edwards and Inger J. Sagatun, *Who Speaks for the Child?*, 2 U. CHI. L. SCH. ROUNDTABLE 67 (1995); Marvin R. Ventrell, *Rights and Duties: An Overview of the Attorney–Child Client Relationship*, 26 LOY. U. CHI. L.J. 259 (1995); Robin A. Rosencrantz, *Rejecting "Hear No Evil, Speak No Evil": Expanding the Attorney's Role in Child Abuse Reporting*, 8 GEO. J. LEGAL ETHICS 327 (1995).

People v. Jennings

Supreme Court of Colorado, 1982.
641 P.2d 276.

■ DUBOFSKY, JUSTICE.

On July 18, 1979 the defendant, John Jennings, was convicted in Garfield County District Court of child abuse resulting in serious bodily injury under section 18–6–401(1)(c), C.R.S.1973 (1978 Repl. Vol. 8).[1] Subsequently, the trial court granted the defendant's motion to dismiss based on the vagueness of the criminal child abuse statute. The People appealed the trial court's ruling, and we reverse.

The child abuse charge arises from an incident which occurred on August 16, 1978. On that day, the defendant left work at about noon because he felt ill, went home, and dismissed the babysitter who was caring for his stepson, Jason, aged three, and his four-month-old daughter, Christina. The defendant testified that from the time he arrived home, Christina was "fussy." He attempted to calm her, then lay down and tried to take a nap, but the baby continued to cry. The defendant got up, checked Christina's diaper and tried to give her a bottle. She continued crying. The defendant testified that he was going to pick her up, but instead he struck her on the head with his open hand. The following colloquy regarding the slap took place at trial:

"Q. Okay. Now, how many times did you hit Christina?

"A. One time.

"Q. Why did you do that?

"A. I don't know.

---

1. At the time of the defendant's conviction child abuse resulting in serious bodily injury to the child was a class 3 felony, while all other instances of child abuse were classified as class 2 misdemeanors. Subsequent to the defendant's conviction section 18–6–401(7), C.R.S.1973 (1978 Repl. Vol. 8) was amended to classify the offense of child abuse depending on the state of mind of the defendant and the extent of injury to the victim. For example, subsection 18–6–401(7)(a)(i), C.R.S.1973 (1981 Supp.) provides: "When a person acts knowingly, . . . and the child abuse results in death to the child, it is a class 2 felony."

"Q. Were you trying to punish her?

"A. No, I wasn't trying to punish her.

"Q. Do you think a four-month-old child knows the meaning of discipline?

"A. No.

"Q. Had you intended to slap her?

"A. No. . . .

"Q. Did you mean to hurt her?

"A. No.

"Q. Did it ever occur to you, John, that by hitting a child that young in the face that it might cause serious bodily injury?

"A. I never really gave it that much thought because I never wanted to hit my children anywhere. . . ."

Apparently as a result of the slap, Christina stopped breathing for a time, causing brain damage which resulted in blindness and arrested mental development. After the defendant's trial, on November 3, 1979, Christina died. The defendant stipulated before trial that Christina suffered serious bodily injury as a result of his single slap to her head. The only question for the jury was whether the slap resulting in brain damage constituted felony child abuse, defined under section 18–6–401(1)(c) as "knowingly, intentionally, or negligently, and without justifiable excuse," causing or permitting a child to be "abandoned, tortured, cruelly confined or cruelly punished." In response to the defendant's request for a bill of particulars, the prosecution alleged that the child had been "cruelly punished."

The jury found the defendant guilty of felony child abuse. The defendant filed a new trial motion and renewed his pre-trial motion to dismiss, which the court had taken under advisement. At a hearing on November 6, 1979, the court found the language "cruelly punished" unconstitutionally vague because of the subjective nature of the words "cruel" and "punish."

. . .

The vagueness challenge to the child abuse statute centers on the statutory phrase "cruelly punished."[4] The defendant argues that the words "cruel" and "punish," while they may have generally understood meanings in day-to-day usage, are, in the context of the child abuse statute, unclear and susceptible of subjective interpretation. The defendant contends that the absence of a statutory definition of these words forces jurors to import their subjective impressions as to what punishment is cruel. The defendant

---

4. In People v. Hoehl, 193 Colo. 557, 568 P.2d 484 (1977) we upheld the child abuse statute against a vagueness challenge based on the language of section 18–6–401(1)(a) which provides that a person commits child abuse if he causes or permits a child to be "placed in a situation that may endanger the child's life or health. . . ." We construed the word "may" to mean a reasonable probability that the child's life or health will be endangered from the situation in which the child is placed.

cites State v. Meinert, 225 Kan. 816, 594 P.2d 232 (1979), in which the Kansas Supreme Court, interpreting that state's criminal child abuse statute, stated:

> "Some persons do not believe in any form of corporal punishment and to them any such treatment would be unjustified. On the other hand, others may believe any correction, however severe, which produces temporary pain only, and no lasting injury or disfigurement, is justified. The statute can conceivably cover anything from a minor spanking or slapping to severe beating depending upon the personal beliefs of the individual."

594 P.2d at 234–35.

At the outset, we note that the defendant's argument is a broad one, amounting to a contention that in light of the wide divergence in personal views as to what constitutes cruel punishment of a child, a statute which does not define in detail each act proscribed cannot delineate an enforceable standard. We disagree; the prohibition in the child abuse statute against cruel punishment is sufficiently precise to satisfy due process requirements.

This Court has on numerous occasions enunciated the standard a statute challenged on vagueness grounds must satisfy to accord due process. As a preliminary matter, a statute claimed to be impermissibly vague must be closely scrutinized. If a challenged statute is capable of alternate constructions, one of which is constitutional, the constitutional interpretation must be adopted.

A penal statute is unconstitutionally vague if it "forbids or requires the doing of an act in terms so vague that men of common intelligence must necessarily guess as to its meaning and differ as to its application...." Connally v. General Construction Co., 269 U.S. 385, 46 S.Ct. 126, 70 L.Ed. 322 (1926); ... Criminal statutes should be framed with sufficient clarity so as to inform the persons subject to them of the standards of conduct imposed and to give fair warning of which acts are forbidden. The vagueness doctrine also seeks to minimize arbitrary and discriminatory enforcement of laws by providing police and prosecutors with clearly defined standards. Such standards serve as well to inform a court and jury whether a crime has been committed and proved.

The vagueness standard, while frequently enunciated, is nevertheless difficult to apply. Here, the defendant's contention is that the distinction between mere "punishment" and "cruel punishment" is impermissibly vague. The distinction between the two centers on the meaning of the word "cruel." Webster's Third New International Dictionary (1961) defines "cruel" as "disposed to inflict pain, especially in a wanton, insensate, or vindictive manner," and "cruelly" as "so as to cause pain or hurt."

That a distinction can be made between permissible punishment and "cruel" punishment is supported by the traditional common law rule concerning parental discipline of children. At common law the parent of a minor child or one standing *in loco parentis* was privileged in using a reasonable amount of force upon a child for purposes of safeguarding or promoting the child's welfare. Bowers v. State, 283 Md. 115, 389 A.2d 341 (Ct.App.1978); Boyd v. State, 88 Ala. 169, 7 So. 268–69 (1890); W. LaFave & A. Scott, Handbook on Criminal Law § 52, at 389–90 (1972); Restatement of Torts (Second) § 147(1); Paulsen, The Legal Framework for Child Protection, 66 Colum.L.Rev. 679 (1966). While at common law the precise test of what constituted permissible force varied from jurisdiction to jurisdiction, as a general proposition, so long as the chastisement was moderate and reasonable in light of the child's age and condition, the misconduct being punished, the kind of punishment inflicted, the degree of harm done to the child and other relevant circumstances, the parent or custodian would incur neither civil nor criminal liability, even though identical behavior against a stranger would be grounds for an action in tort or prosecution for assault and battery or a similar offense.

This common law privilege has been codified in Colorado in section 18–1–703(1)(a), C.R.S.1973 (1978 Repl.Vol. 8), which provides:

> "The use of physical force upon another person which would otherwise constitute an offense is justifiable and not criminal under any of the following circumstances:
>
> . . .
>
> A parent, guardian or other person entrusted with the care and supervision of a minor or an incompetent person, ... may use reasonable and appropriate physical force upon the minor or incompetent person when and to the extent it is reasonably necessary and appropriate to maintain discipline or promote the welfare of the minor or incompetent person."

The parental privilege to inflict moderate, reasonable and appropriate corporal punishment has never shielded from liability parental acts which cannot be justified as salutary discipline. Before the adoption of statutes specifically proscribing child abuse, "cruel and outrageous" treatment of a child defeated the parental privilege and subjected the parent to the penal sanctions normally applicable to the acts committed. Paulsen, supra, 66 Colum.L.Rev. at 686–87.

This discussion of the common law background to the present child abuse statute illustrates that rather than existing in a vacuum, the parental privilege set out in section 18–1–703(1)(a) and the definition of criminal child abuse in section 18–6–401 codify common law principles concerning the limits of permissible parental chastisement. As the Maryland Court of Appeals said in Bowers v. State, supra:

> "Since the contours of the common law privilege have been subject for centuries to definition and refinement through careful and constant judicial decisionmaking, terms like 'cruel' or 'inhumane' and 'malicious' have acquired a relatively widely accepted connotation in the law."

389 A.2d at 348.

In addition to the criminal sanctions in section 18–6–401, the General Assembly has enacted other statutes to prevent cruelty to children. They evidence the legislature's parallel intent to protect children from unwarranted abuse while permitting parents to discipline those in their charge within the limits of the traditional privilege. For example, Article 10 of the Children's Code, which concerns the reporting of child abuse to the proper authorities, defines abuse in section 19–10–103(1)(a) as "an act or omission ... which seriously threatens the health or welfare of a child" including:

> "(i) Any case in which a child exhibits evidence of skin bruising, bleeding, malnutrition, failure to thrive, burns, fracture of any bone, subdural hematoma, soft tissue swelling, or death...."

Paragraph (b) of the same subsection provides:

> "Nothing in this subsection (1) shall refer to acts which could be construed to be a reasonable exercise of parental discipline."

Child abuse may also trigger the commencement of proceedings to terminate the parent-child relationship under Article 11 of the Children's Code, sections 19–11–101 through–110. In an action for termination of a parent-child relationship, criteria which support the determination that a parent is unfit include:

> "(b) Conduct towards the child of a physically or sexually abusive nature; ...
>
> (d) A single incident of life-threatening or gravely disabling injury or disfigurement of the child."

Section 19–11–105(2)(b) and (d).

Implicit in our decisions upholding as constitutionally sound the definition of child abuse in the termination of parental rights statute is the proposition that a meaningful distinction can be made between permissible discipline and abusive treatment. See People in the Interest of C.S., Colo., 613 P.2d 1304 (1980); People in the Interest of V.A.E.Y.H.D., 199 Colo. 148, 605 P.2d 916 (1980); People in the Interest of D.A.K., 198 Colo. 11, 596 P.2d 747 (1979). In the context of a termination proceeding where the definition of child abuse is at issue we have recognized that "fundamental fairness does not require a statute to enunciate in all-encompassing examples, or exactly described acts, precisely how poorly a parent can treat a child before risking loss of parental rights." While termination of parental rights actions are civil cases and distinguishable from this criminal prosecution, we scrutinize the child abuse standard at issue in these cases with special care, reasoning that "although no criminal sanction is involved, a serious and substantial parental interest is at stake, which in many, if not most, cases is as important to the parents as their freedom."

Given the statutory and common law context in which the "cruelly punished" language of section 18–6–401 is set, we are satisfied that this language is intelligible and capable of nonarbitrary enforcement. Although the criminal child abuse standard is enunciated in general terms, this is not a fatal flaw. Scientific exactitude in statutory language is not required as long as the statute meets the minimal requirements of due process.... The relationship between parents or guardians and children is a delicate and complex one, and standards designed to regulate this relationship must necessarily provide some flexibility while at the same time effectuating the state policy of protecting children from abuse.

The defendant also argues that the mental state requirements in the statute are too broad to have meaning and that even if the mental states can be defined with sufficient clarity, the defendant did not have the mens rea required by the term "punished." At both the time of the defendant's act and when his trial was conducted, section 18–6–401 provided that child abuse is committed when a person "knowingly, intentionally, or negligently, and without justifiable excuse, causes or permits a child to be: ... (a) cruelly punished."[5] The defendant specifically argues that negligently causing cruel punishment is impossible to understand and therefore unconstitutionally vague. However, in People v. Taggart, Colo., 621 P.2d 1375 (1981), we ruled that the inclusion of "negligently" as a state of mind in section 18–6–401 does not render the child abuse statute unconstitutionally vague:

> "[A] person may negligently cause or permit a child to be placed in a situation so debilitating to the child's physical well-being that a reasonable juror, looking at the effect of the offender's conduct on the child, would consider it torture or cruel punishment. The term 'negligently' is not irreconcilably at odds with 'tortured' and 'cruelly punished', and the statutory definition of child abuse is sufficiently particular as to furnish adequate notice to potential wrongdoers of the proscribed conduct and to protect against discriminatory enforcement [citations omitted]."

621 P.2d at 1375. See People v. Noble, Colo., 635 P.2d 203, 210 (1981).

In addition, we note that the child abuse statute proscribes acts of mistreatment which include inaction as well as action. The inclusion of a range of states of mind can deal, for example, with a parent who "negligently ... permits" a child to be abused in some way. See State v. Zobel, 81 S.D. 260, 134 N.W.2d 101 cert. denied 382 U.S. 833, 86 S.Ct. 74, 15 L.Ed.2d 76 (1965) (father who had never actively mistreated two infant daughters convicted of child abuse for leaving them with his insane wife, who he knew beat them and deprived them of food, and who eventually killed them).

> The defendant's argument that "punished" implies a mens rea which he did not possess is also without merit. As we made clear in People v. Taggart, supra:

" 'Tortured' and 'cruelly punished' do not refer to the *mens rea* of the crime of child abuse. Rather, these words refer to the *actus reus* as measured by the consequences wrought on the child."

5. Section 18–6–401(1) has since been amended to add "recklessly" to the mental states applicable to commission of child abuse.

621 P.2d at 1383. The defendant's testimony that he did not mean to punish Christina does not preclude a jury from finding that he caused her to be "cruelly punished."

Reversed and remanded for a new trial.

NOTES

The Maine Supreme Judicial Court made a distinction between criminal and civil litigation involving parents and corporal punishment of their children. In a criminal proceeding the parent is entitled to a parental control justification and the state must disprove this by a standard beyond a reasonable doubt. But in a civil proceeding involving removal of the child from the home, the justification defense does not apply and the state need only show that the child would or may be subject to more serious harm if returned to the parent. *See* In re Dorothy V., 774 A.2d 1118 (Me.2001).

Baltimore City Dept. Social Services v. Bouknight

Supreme Court of the United States, 1990.
493 U.S. 549, 110 S.Ct. 900, 107 L.Ed.2d 992.

■ JUSTICE O'CONNOR delivered the opinion of the Court.

In this action, we must decide whether a mother, the custodian of a child pursuant to a court order, may invoke the Fifth Amendment privilege against self-incrimination to resist an order of the Juvenile Court to produce the child. We hold that she may not.

Petitioner Maurice M. is an abused child. When he was three months old, he was hospitalized with a fractured left femur, and examination revealed several partially healed bone fractures and other indications of severe physical abuse. In the hospital, respondent Bouknight, Maurice's mother, was observed shaking Maurice, dropping him in his crib despite his spica cast, and otherwise handling him in a manner inconsistent with his recovery and continued health. Hospital personnel notified Baltimore City Department of Social Services (BCDSS) of suspected child abuse. In February 1987, BCDSS secured a court order removing Maurice from Bouknight's control and placing him in shelter care. Several months later, the shelter care order was inexplicably modified to return Maurice to Bouknight's custody temporarily. Following a hearing held shortly thereafter, the Juvenile Court declared Maurice to be a "child in need of assistance," thus asserting jurisdiction over Maurice and placing him under BCDSS's continuing oversight. BCDSS agreed that Bouknight could continue as custodian of the child, but only pursuant to extensive conditions set forth in a court-approved protective supervision order. The order required Bouknight to "cooperate with BCDSS," "continue in therapy," participate in parental aid and training programs, and "refrain from physically punishing [Maurice]." The order's terms were "all subject to the further Order of the Court." Bouknight's attorney signed the order, and Bouknight in a separate form set forth her agreement to each term.

Eight months later, fearing for Maurice's safety, BCDSS returned to Juvenile Court. BCDSS caseworkers related that Bouknight would not cooperate with them and had in nearly every respect violated the terms of the protective order. BCDSS stated that Maurice's father had recently died in a shooting incident and that Bouknight, in light of the results of a psychological examination and her history of drug use, could not provide adequate care for the child. On April 20, 1988, the Court granted BCDSS's petition to remove Maurice from Bouknight's control for placement in foster care. BCDSS officials also petitioned for judicial relief from Bouknight's failure to produce Maurice or reveal where he could be found. The petition recounted that on two recent visits by BCDSS officials to Bouknight's home, she had refused to reveal the location of the child or had indicated that the child was with an aunt whom she would not identify. The petition further asserted that inquiries of Bouknight's known relatives had revealed that none of them had recently seen Maurice and that BCDSS had prompted the police to issue a missing persons report and referred the case for investigation by the police homicide division. Also on April 20, the Juvenile Court, upon a hearing on the petition, cited Bouknight for violating the protective custody order and for failing to appear at the hearing. Bouknight had indicated to her attorney that she would appear with the child, but also expressed fear that if she appeared the State would "snatch the child." The court issued an order to show cause why Bouknight should not be held in civil contempt for failure to produce the child. Expressing concern that Maurice was endangered or perhaps dead, the court issued a bench warrant for Bouknight's appearance.

Maurice was not produced at subsequent hearings. At a hearing one week later, Bouknight claimed that Maurice was with a relative in Dallas. Investigation revealed that the relative had not seen Maurice. The next day, following another hearing at which Bouknight again declined to produce Maurice, the Juvenile Court found Bouknight in contempt for failure to produce the child as ordered. There was and has been no indication that she was unable to comply with the order. The court directed that Bouknight be imprisoned until she "purge[d] herself of contempt by either producing [Maurice] before the court or revealing to the court his exact whereabouts." The Juvenile Court rejected Bouknight's subsequent claim that the contempt order violated the Fifth Amendment's guarantee against self-incrimination. The court stated that the production of Maurice would purge the contempt and that "[t]he contempt is issued not because she refuse[d] to testify in any proceeding . . . [but] because she has failed to abide by the Order of this Court, mainly [for] the production of Maurice M." While that decision was being appealed, Bouknight was convicted of theft and sentenced to 18 months' imprisonment in separate proceedings. The Court of Appeals of Maryland vacated the Juvenile Court's judgment upholding the contempt order. In re Maurice M., 314 Md. 391, 550 A.2d 1135 (1988). The Court of Appeals found that the contempt order unconstitutionally compelled Bouknight to admit through the act of production "a measure of continuing control and dominion over Maurice's person" in circumstances in which "Bouknight has a reasonable apprehension that she will be prosecuted." Chief Justice Rehnquist granted BCDSS's application for a stay of the judgment and mandate of the Maryland Court of Appeals, pending disposition of the petition for a writ of certiorari. We granted certiorari, and we now reverse.

The Fifth Amendment provides that "No person . . . shall be compelled in any criminal case to be a witness against himself." The Fifth Amendment's protection "applies only when the accused is compelled to make a *testimonial* communication that is incriminating." Fisher v. United States, 425 U.S. 391, 408 (1976); . . . The courts below concluded that Bouknight could comply with the order through the unadorned act of producing the child, and we thus address that aspect of the order. When the government demands that an item be produced, "the only thing compelled is the act of producing the [item]." The Fifth Amendment's protection may nonetheless be implicated because the act of complying with the government's demand testifies to the existence, possession, or authenticity of the things produced. But a person may not claim the Amendment's protections based upon the incrimination that may result from the contents or nature of the thing demanded. Bouknight therefore cannot claim the privilege based upon anything that examination of Maurice might reveal, nor can she assert the privilege upon the theory that compliance would assert that the child produced is in fact Maurice (a fact the State could readily establish, rendering any testimony regarding existence or authenticity insufficiently incriminating.) Rather, Bouknight claims the benefit of the privilege because the act of production would amount to testimony regarding her control over and possession of Maurice. Although the State could readily introduce evidence of Bouknight's continuing control over the child—e.g., the custody order, testimony of relatives, and Bouknight's own statements to Maryland officials before invoking the privilege—her implicit communication of control over Maurice at the moment of production might aid the State in prosecuting Bouknight.

The possibility that a production order will compel testimonial assertions that may prove incriminating does not, in all contexts, justify invoking the privilege to resist production. Even assuming that this limited testimonial assertion is sufficiently incriminating and "sufficiently testimonial for purposes of the privilege," Bouknight may not invoke the privilege to resist the production order because she has assumed custodial duties related to production and because production is required as part of a noncriminal regulatory regime.

The Court has on several occasions recognized that the Fifth Amendment privilege may not be invoked to resist compliance with a regulatory regime constructed to effect the State's public purposes unrelated to the enforcement of its criminal laws. . . .

. . .

These principles readily apply to this case. Once Maurice was adjudicated a child in need of assistance, his care and safety became the particular object of the State's regulatory interests. See 314 Md., at 404,

550 A.2d, at 1141; Md.Cts. & Jud. Proc. Code §§ 3–801(e), 3–804(a) (Supp.1989); see also App. 105 ("This court has jurisdiction to require at all times to know the whereabouts of the minor child. We asserted jurisdiction over that child in the spring of 1987 . . . "). Maryland first placed Maurice in shelter care, authorized placement in foster care, and then entrusted responsibility for Maurice's care to Bouknight. By accepting care of Maurice subject to the custodial order's conditions (including requirements that she cooperate with BCDSS, follow a prescribed training regime, and be subject to further court orders), Bouknight submitted to the routine operation of the regulatory system and agreed to hold Maurice in a manner consonant with the State's regulatory interests and subject to inspection by BCDSS. In assuming the obligations attending custody, Bouknight "has accepted the incident obligation to permit inspection." Wilson, 221 U.S. at 382, 31 S.Ct., at 545. The State imposes and enforces that obligation as part of a broadly directed, noncriminal regulatory regime governing children cared for pursuant to custodial orders. See Md.Cts. & Jud.Proc.Code Ann. § 3–802(a) (1984) (setting forth child protective purposes of subtitle, including "provid[ing] for the care, protection, and wholesome mental and physical development of children coming within the provisions of this subtitle"); see also Md.Cts. & Jud.Proc.Code Ann. §§ 3–820(b), (c) (Supp. 1989); In re Jessica M., 312 Md. 93, 538 A.2d 305 (1988).

Persons who care for children pursuant to a custody order, and who may be subject to a request for access to the child, are hardly a "selective group inherently suspect of criminal activities." Marchetti, 390 U.S. at 57 (quoting Albertson v. Subversive Activities Control Board, 382 U.S., at 79). The Juvenile Court may place a child within its jurisdiction with social service officials or "under supervision in his own home or in the custody or under the guardianship of a relative or other fit person, upon terms the court deems appropriate." Md.Cts. & Jud.Proc.Code Ann. § 3–820(c)(1)(i) (Supp.1989). Children may be placed, for example, in foster care, in homes of relatives, or in the care of state officials. Even when the court allows a parent to retain control of a child within the court's jurisdiction, that parent is not one singled out for criminal conduct, but rather has been deemed to be, without the State's assistance, simply "unable or unwilling to give proper care and attention to the child and his problems." Md.Cts. & Jud.Proc.Code Ann. § 3–801(e) (Supp.1989); see In re Jertrude O., 56 Md.App. 83, 466 A.2d 885 (1983), cert. denied, 298 Md. 309, 469 A.2d 863 (1984). The provision that authorized the Juvenile Court's efforts to gain production of Maurice reflects this broad applicability. See Md.Cts. & Jud.Proc.Code Ann. § 3–814(c) (1984) ("If a parent, guardian, or custodian fails to bring the child before the court when requested, the court may issue a writ of attachment directing that the child be taken into custody and brought before the court. The court may proceed against the parent, guardian, or custodian for contempt"). This provision "fairly may be said to be directed at . . . parents, guardians, and custodians who accept placement of juveniles in custody." 314 Md., at 418, 550 A.2d, at 1148 (McAuliffe, J., dissenting).

Similarly, BCDSS's efforts to gain access to children, as well as judicial efforts to the same effect, do not "focu[s] almost exclusively on conduct which was criminal." Many orders will arise in circumstances entirely devoid of criminal conduct. Even when criminal conduct may exist, the court may properly request production and return of the child, and enforce that request through exercise of the contempt power, for reasons related entirely to the child's well-being and through measures unrelated to criminal law enforcement or investigation. See Maryland Cts. & Jud.Proc. Code Ann. § 3–814(c) (1984). This case provides an illustration: concern for the child's safety underlay the efforts to gain access to and then compel production of Maurice. Finally, production in the vast majority of cases will embody no incriminating testimony, even if in particular cases the act of production may incriminate the custodian through an assertion of possession, the existence, or the identity of the child. These orders to produce children cannot be characterized as efforts to gain some testimonial component of the act of production. The government demands production of the very public charge entrusted to a custodian, and makes the demand for compelling reasons unrelated to criminal law enforcement and as part of a broadly applied regulatory regime. In these circumstances, Bouknight cannot invoke the privilege to resist the order to produce Maurice.

We are not called upon to define the precise limitations that may exist upon the State's ability to use the testimonial aspects of Bouknight's act of production in subsequent criminal proceedings. But we note that imposition of such limitations is not foreclosed. The same custodial role that limited the ability to resist the production order may give rise to corresponding limitations upon the direct and indirect use of that testimony. The State's regulatory requirement in the usual case may neither compel incriminating testimony nor aid a criminal prosecution, but the Fifth Amendment protections are not thereby necessarily unavailable to the person who complies with the regulatory requirement after invoking the privilege and subsequently faces prosecution.

. . .

The judgment of the Court of Appeals of Maryland is reversed and the cases remanded to that court for further proceedings not inconsistent with this opinion.

■ JUSTICE MARSHALL, with whom JUSTICE BRENNAN joins, dissenting.

. . . The State's goal of protecting children from abusive environments through its juvenile welfare system cannot be separated from criminal provisions that serve the same goal. When the conduct at which a civil statute aims—here, child abuse and neglect—is frequently the same conduct subject to criminal sanction, it strikes me as deeply problematic to dismiss the Fifth Amendment concerns by characterizing the civil scheme as "unrelated to criminal law enforcement investigation". A civil scheme that inevitably intersects with criminal sanctions may not be used to coerce, on pain of contempt, a potential criminal defendant to furnish evidence crucial to the success of her own prosecution.

I would apply a different analysis, one that is more faithful to the concerns underlying the Fifth Amendment. This approach would target the respondent's particular claim of privilege, the precise nature of the testimony sought, and the likelihood of self-incrimination caused by this respondent's compliance. "To sustain the privilege, it need only be evident from the implications of the question, in the setting in which it is asked, that a responsive answer to the question or an explanation of why it cannot be answered might be dangerous because injurious disclosure could result." Hoffman v. United States, 341 U.S. 479, 486–487, 71 S.Ct. 814, 818–819, 95 L.Ed.2d 1118 (1951). This analysis unambiguously indicates that Bouknight's Fifth Amendment privilege must be respected to protect her from the serious risk of self-incrimination.

An individualized inquiry is preferable to the Court's analysis because it allows the privilege to turn on the concrete facts of a particular case, rather than on abstract characterizations concerning the nature of a regulatory scheme. Moreover, this particularized analysis would not undermine any appropriate goals of civil regulatory schemes that may intersect with criminal prohibitions. Instead, the ability of a State to provide immunity from criminal prosecution permits it to gather information necessary for civil regulation, while also preserving the integrity of the privilege against self-incrimination. The fact that the State throws a wide net in seeking information does not mean that it can demand from the few persons whose Fifth Amendment rights are implicated that they participate in their own criminal prosecutions. Rather, when the State demands testimony for its citizens, it should do so with an explicit grant of immunity.

.   .   .

Although I am disturbed by the Court's willingness to apply inapposite precedent to deny Bouknight her constitutional right against self-incrimination, especially in light of the serious allegations of homicide that accompany this civil proceeding, I take some comfort in the Court's recognition that the State may be prohibited from using any testimony given by Bouknight in subsequent criminal proceedings (leaving open the question of the "State's ability to use the testimonial aspects of Bouknight's act of production" in such criminal proceedings).[2] Because I am not content to deny Bouknight the constitutional protection required by the

---

2. I note, with both exasperation and skepticism about the bona fide nature of the State's intentions, that the State may be able to grant Bouknight use immunity under a recently enacted immunity statute, even though it has thus far failed to do so. See 1989 Md. Laws, Ch. 288 (amending § 9–123). Although the statute applies only to testimony "in a criminal prosecution or a proceeding before a grand jury of the State," Md.Cts. & Jud.Proc.Code Ann. § 9–123(b)(1) (Supp. 1989), the State represented to this Court that "[a]s a matter of law, [granting limited use immunity for the testimonial aspects of Bouknight's compliance with the production order] would now be possible". If such a grant of immunity has been possible since July 1989 and the State has refused to invoke it so that it can litigate Bouknight's claim of privilege, I have difficulty believing that the State is sincere in its protestations of concern for Maurice's well-being.

Fifth Amendment *now* in the hope that she will not be convicted *later* on the basis of her own testimony, I dissent.

NOTES

Jacqueline L. Bouknight, a 29–year–old woman, was released from prison on November 1, 1995, after 7 ½ years behind bars for contempt. The judge said that continued imprisonment was no longer an effective tool to learn the location of her son, Maurice. The son remained missing.

CHILD ABUSE REPORTING STATUTES

The proliferation of state statutes mandating the reporting of abuse or neglect attest to their popularity; the statutes have also progressively expanded the scope of who must report. For instance, some statutes require anyone who suspects child abuse to report, while other statutes specify a particular class of persons. Still other statutes include a permissive reporting provision, stating that any person not included under the mandatory provision may report suspected abuse. Some persons are exempted from reporting because of state confidential communication privileges normally granted to attorney-client, doctor-patient, priest-penitent. Nonetheless, with the increase of abuse, some states have abrogated the privilege. For example, GA. CODE ANN. § 19–7–5(g) (Supp. 2006) provides:

> Suspected child abuse which is required to be reported by any person pursuant to this Code section shall be reported notwithstanding that the reasonable cause to believe such abuse has occurred or is occurring is based in whole or in part upon any communication to that person which is otherwise made privileged or confidential by law.

States give reporters immunity from civil or criminal liability for reporting suspected child abuse as long as they act in good faith. Others, who are mandated to report and do not do so, can be found criminally liable and also, civilly liable for failure to report under negligence or a malpractice cause of action. For instance: ALA. CODE § 26–14–13 (Michie 1992) provides that failure to report is a misdemeanor, publishable by no more than six months in jail or by a fine of not more than $500.00. ARK. CODE ANN. § 12–12–504(b) (LEXIS 1999) provides that "Any person, official, or institution required ... to make notification of suspected child maltreatment who wilfully fails to do so shall be civilly liable for damages proximately caused by that failure." In a leading case, Landeros v. Flood, 17 Cal.3d 399, 131 Cal.Rptr. 69, 551 P.2d 389 (1976), the California Supreme Court upheld the potential liability of a physician with a duty to report suspected abuse, for negligently failing to diagnose a case of battered child syndrome and subsequently failing to report it.

Computers, expanded reporting requirements, and the anonymous nature of most reports, must be balanced against individual privacy, the limits of search and seizure and traditional notions of confidentiality. For instance, if the state has abrogated all confidential communication privileges and requires all persons who suspect abuse of a child to report this suspicion to the authorities, must a member of the clergy report a conversation confined to a confessional? *See* Raymond C. O'Brien & Michael T. Flannery, *The Pending Gauntlet to Free Exercise: Mandating That Clergy Report Child Abuse*, 25 LOY. L.A. L. REV. 1 (1991); and Raymond C. O'Brien, *Clergy, Sex and the American Way*, 31 PEPPERDINE L. REV. 363, 430–435 (2004). Is it justifiable to provide for a data bank in each hospital emergency room to obtain computerized information about past reports of actual or possible child abuse of a specific child, or about the number of times a particular child has been brought to the attention of a physician or had suffered physical injury requiring emergency room attention at other facilities?

Finally, reporting requirements have embraced dependent adults and the elderly, who often are subjected to abuse. *See, e.g.,* CALIF. WELF. AND INST. CODE § 15630 (West 2001).

WHO IS AN ABUSED CHILD?

The definition of an abused child varies from state to state and should be distinguished from neglect and abandonment. Also, is abuse physical, emotion, sexual? What are the limits on parental discipline? When may a parent assert the free exercise of religion as a defense against an accusation of abuse or neglect? VA. CODE § 63.2–100 (as amended 2007) contains the following definition:

§ 63.2–100. Definitions

As used in this title, unless the context requires a different meaning

"Abused or neglected child" means any child less than 18 years of age:

1. Whose parents or other person responsible for his care creates or inflicts, threatens to create or inflict, or allows to be created or inflicted upon such child a physical or mental injury by other than accidental means, or creates a substantial risk of death, disfigurement, or impairment of bodily or mental functions, including but not limited to, a child who is with his parent or other person responsible for his care either (i) during the manufacture or attempted manufacture of a Schedule I or II controlled substance, or (ii) during the unlawful sale of such substance by that child's parents or other person responsible for his care, where such manufacture, or attempted manufacture or unlawful sale would constitute a felony violation of § 18.2–248;

2. Whose parents or other person responsible for his care neglects or refuses to provide care necessary for his health. However, no child who in good faith is under treatment solely by spiritual means through prayer in accordance with the tenets and practices of a recognized church or religious denomination shall for that reason alone be considered to be an abused or neglected child. Further, a decision by parents who have legal authority for the child or, in the absence of parents with legal authority for the child, any person with legal authority for the child, who refuses a particular medical treatment for a child with a life-threatening condition shall not be deemed a refusal

to provide necessary care if (i) such decision is made jointly by the parents or other person with legal authority and the child; (ii) the child has reaced 14.

3. Whose parents or other person responsible for his care abandons such child;

4. Whose parents or other person responsible for his care commits or allows to be committed any act of sexual exploitation or any sexual act upon a child in violation of the law;

5. Who is without parental care or guardianship caused by the unreasonable absence or the mental or physical incapacity of the child's parent, guardian, legal custodian or other person standing in loco parentis; or

6. Whose parents or other person responsible for his care creates a substantial risk of physical or mental injury by knowingly leaving the child alone in the same dwelling, including an apartment as defined in § 55–79.2, with a person to whom the child is not related by blood or marriage and who the parent or other person responsible for his care knows has been convicted of an offense against a minor for which registration is required as a violent sexual offender pursuant to § 9.1–902.

If a civil proceeding under this title is based solely on the parent having left the child at a hospital or rescue squad, it shall be an affirmative defense that such parent safely delivered the child to a hospital that provides 24–hour emergency services or to an attended rescue squad that employs emergency medical technicians, within 14 days of the child's birth. For purposes of terminating parental rights pursuant to § 16.1–283 and placement for adoption, the court may find such a child is a neglected child upon the ground of abandonment.

Procedures to remove children under abuse statutes are civil in nature and only require preponderance of the evidence, Many states have established res ipsa loquitur approaches to certain types of child abuse. For instance, N.Y. FAM. CT. ACT § 1046(a)(ii) (West Supp. 2001) states that:

[P]roof of injuries sustained by a child or of the condition of a child of such a nature as would ordinarily not be sustained or exist except by reason of the acts or omissions of the parent or other person responsible for the care of such child shall be prima facie evidence of child abuse or neglect, as the case may be, of the parent or other person legally responsible.

In the case of Dietz v. Damas, 932 F.Supp. 431 (E.D.N.Y.1996), the abuse to the child occurred when he, then six-months old, was blinded by being shaken violently (Shaken Infant Syndrome), and the failure of the mother to offer any reasonable explanation for the physical injuries satisfied preponderance of the evidence standard resulting in temporary removal of the child and placement with the maternal grandparents until a hearing could be held. How would you establish the time criteria by which a court may evaluate temporary removal against procedural due process under the United States Constitution?

In re Michael C.

Supreme Court of Rhode Island, 1989.
557 A.2d 1219.

■ KELLEHER, JUSTICE.

The parents of Michael C. are before this court on their respective appeals from a judgment of the Family Court in which the trial justice found that the couple's thirteen-year-old son had been sexually abused by his father[1] and neglected by both parents.

At the Family Court hearing, counsel for the Department of Children and Their Families (DCF), acting pursuant to G.L.1956 (1985 Reenactment) § 9–17–14, called both parents as adverse witnesses. The mother testified that at the time of the events in question she had been married to Michael's father for seven years. The mother would leave for work early in the morning. The father, who had been injured in a work-related incident and was receiving Workers' Compensation benefits, remained at home. Consequently, he had the responsibility of awakening Michael and ensuring his readiness for school.

The mother testified that on two occasions in the spring of 1987 Michael told her that her husband was "after his body." When she relayed this information to her husband, he denied any such intent. Michael was told by his mother to stay away from his father and not to bother him.

In his appearance as an adverse witness, the father denied ever having engaged in any sexual activity with Michael. When his wife first told him of Michael's accusations, the father asserted, he thought she was joking.

Prior to Michael's testifying, an attorney for DCF and Michael's guardian ad litem explained to the trial justice that Michael had "expressed a great deal of anxiety about testifying in open court." He was described as being "most reticent and embarrassed to testify in open court."

It should be noted at this point that the trial justice decided that Michael's testimony was to be given in camera before him, with a stenographer recording the proceedings. After Michael had been questioned by the trial justice, his testimony was read back to the attorneys for the parents. The attorneys were then permitted to formulate written questions for cross-examination, which would also be posed by the trial justice in camera. The father's attorney submitted some fifty inquiries. The mother's attorney submitted an almost equal number.

Michael told the trial justice of various episodes involving the father's stripping him of his pants and pajamas and stroking his genitalia and, apparently on other occasions, committing what might be described as first-

---

1. Michael was adopted by John C. in May 1984.

degree sexual assault. When Michael informed the mother of what was occurring, she did not believe him.

On cross-examination Michael denied that he complained about his father because he was afraid of being punished for a report card that did not measure up to parental expectations. He also denied that he was attempting to retaliate against the father after he had been punished for beating up a boy in school. The punishment included confinement to his room for a six-week period with the knob on the television set turned to the off position.

The parents, for their part, denied any wrongdoing by either party and described Michael's testimonial efforts as an attempt to gain revenge for his father's "failure to give him a motorcycle" or because of the parental discipline that had been imposed. The trial justice found Michael's testimony to be forthright, clear, and convincing. He rejected the parents' defense of fabrication, and he specifically ruled that the father's testimony was not worthy of belief.

The trial justice found that the father had sexually abused Michael and that the mother was "confused and bewildered . . . and perhaps torn between the love for the child and loyalty to her husband." Consequently the trial justice committed Michael to the custody of DCF after finding that he was an abused and neglected child. He also restrained the father from having any contact with Michael.

In their appeals both the mother and the father claim that the trial justice erred in allowing the in-camera testimony of Michael. They also claim that their due-process rights were violated by the trial justice's technique and their right to confrontation unduly restricted.

The father also argues that the trial justice erred in not permitting him to call Michael as an adverse witness.

The mother claims that DCF violated Rule 13(b) of the Rules of Juvenile Proceedings because its petition did not explicitly state the facts on which DCF relied to show that Michael had been abused and neglected. She also faults the trial justice for considering the argument presented by the guardian ad litem who was not present on the first day of the hearing. The DCF sees little merit in these contentions, and neither does this court.

The sole critical issue in this familial dispute concerns the trial justice's refusal to have Michael testify in open court. All the litigants recognize that this court, in In re James A., 505 A.2d 1386 (R.I.1986), approved an approach taken by another Family Court justice who authorized a procedure somewhat similar to that used in the case at bar. Initially the trial justice submitted questions to the child with the attorneys for both parties present. After the child became upset, the trial justice cleared the chambers and continued questioning the child with only the stenographer present. Later the questions and answers were read back, and the attorneys were permitted to formulate follow-up questions. There the father argued before us that this procedure, because it did not permit confrontation, failed to accord him his constitutional right of confrontation.

After noting that there is no constitutional right to confrontation in noncriminal proceedings, this court stated that the issue was whether due process necessitated the father's being permitted to cross-examine. There this court emphasized that such a determination "must be made in light of the particular facts and circumstances of the particular case."

This court found no abuse of discretion in the trial justice's decision to protect the child from a potentially "severe psychological trauma" by reason of testifying in court.

Here virtually the same procedure was followed. The only significant difference is that Michael was thirteen years of age at the time of the hearing whereas the child in *In re James A.* was five years old. Naturally Michael's mother and father argue that there was no need to protect the sensitivities of a thirteen-year-old boy.

While the trial justice in *In re James A.* expressed concern for the tender years of the child, we are of the belief that a similar trauma may await an adolescent boy when testifying about sexual acts performed upon him by an adult male. However, it was argued that the emotional impact upon an adolescent boy of thirteen, after testifying about sexual acts performed upon him by an adult male, may be substantially less severe than the impact experienced by a younger child testifying about sexual abuse. This concept is highly debatable.

We believe that this issue is best resolved at the trial level where the trial justice is in a position to see and hear the witnesses. Thus such a decision is one that lies within the discretion of the trial justice after consideration of the best interests of the child as weighed against the interests of the parents and the state. The adoption of a special procedure in order to protect a child, if the trial justice deems it appropriate, is a discretionary matter. The record before us discloses no abuse of that discretion.

Proof of the correctness of the trial justice's decision can be found during the cross-examination of the father, when he was asked if he had threatened to punch Michael after Michael had told his mother what was going on at home. After replying in the negative, the father continued, "I threatened to strangle the little bugger if he took a swing at his mother or any other member of the family again. . . . I told him if he ever did it again, I would kill him and put him through the wall because I was furious." We believe that these shocking remarks provide a sufficient evidentiary basis for the trial justice's conclusion that Michael's testimony would be given in camera.

While this controversy was on appeal, counsel were asked to comment on whether the holding in Coy v. Iowa, 487 U.S. 1012, 108 S.Ct. 2798, 101 L.Ed.2d 857 (1988), is applicable to this litigation. Counsel for the parents argued that it is. However, *Coy* has no relevancy to the issues that were pending before the trial justice. *Coy* was a criminal appeal involving the defendant's constitutional right to confront his accusers, two thirteen-year-old girls. Here we are concerned with a civil proceeding in which the petition speaks in terms of the parents' neglect and abuse and seeks a change in the care, custody, and control of Michael from his parents to DCF. In such proceedings the parents have no right to face-to-face confrontation with Michael.

Accordingly the mother's and the father's appeals are denied and dismissed.

NOTE

The preceding case involved child testimony within a civil context of due process in conjunction with an action similar to that defined in CAL. FAM. CODE § 7507 (West 2004):

> The abuse of parental authority is the subject of judicial cognizance in a civil action brought by the child, or by the child's relative within the third degree, or by the supervisors of the county where the child resides; and when the abuse is established, the child may be freed from the dominion of the parent, and the duty of support and education enforced.

Clearly, the role of the attorneys representing the children and the adults is a crucial one in determining both facts and resolution. *See* Bruce A. Boyer, *Ethical Issues in the Representation of Parents in Child Welfare Cases*, 64 FORDHAM L. REV. 1621 (1996) (argues that zealous parent advocacy can accomplish much for the parents and the children); Marvin R. Ventrell, *Rights & Duties: An Overview of the Attorney–Child Client Relationship*, 26 LOY. U. CHI. L.J. 259 (1995) (argues that children historically have not been given equal advocacy with parents and attorneys have an obligation to promote children's interests); Robin A. Rosencrantz, *Rejecting "Hear No Evil Speak No Evil": Expanding the Attorney's Role in Child Abuse Reporting*, 8 GEO. J. LEGAL ETHICS 327 (1995) (recommends an expanded role for attorneys in child abuse reporting). For further discussion of the child as witness in sexual abuse cases, *see* Bennett L. Gershman, *Child Witnesses and Procedural Fairness*, 24 AM. J. TRIAL ADVOC. 585 (2001); Randi Mandelbaum, *Revisiting the Question of Whether Young Children in Child Protection Proceedings Should be Represented by Lawyers*, 32 LOY. U. CHI. L. J. 1 (2000); Mary Ann Mason, *A Judicial Dilemma: Expert Witness Testimony in Child Sex Abuse Cases*, 19 J. PSYCHIATRY & L. 185 (1991); John E.B. Myers, et al., *Expert Testimony in Child Sexual Abuse Litigation*, 68 NEB. L. REV. 1 (1989); John E.B. Myers, *The Child Witness: Techniques for Direct Examination, Cross–Examination, and Impeachment*, 18 PAC. L.J. 801 (1987).

The criminal prosecution of child sexual abuse and the concomitant constitutional guarantee of the Sixth Amendment ("In all criminal prosecutions, the accused shall enjoy the right ... to be confronted with the witnesses against him.") were the subject of Maryland v. Craig, 497 U.S. 836, 110 S.Ct. 3157, 111 L.Ed.2d 666 (1990). In this case, a six-year-old child had attended a kindergarten and prekindergarten operated by a woman. The woman was charged with child abuse, first and second degree sexual offenses, perverted sexual practices, assault and battery. During the trial the State sought to receive the testimony of the child through a one-way closed circuit television in the presence of the prosecutor and the defense counsel. Nonetheless, the judge, the defendant and the jury remained in the courtroom outside the physical presence of the child.

In her majority opinion, Justice Sandra Day O'Connor weighed the state's interest in protecting children from abuse with the Sixth Amendment's guarantee of the right to confront one's accuser. The Court held that a state's interest in the well-being of child abuse victims may be sufficiently important, in some cases, to outweigh a defendant's right to face his or her accusers in court. Justice O'Connor continued, that the general rules of law that grant protections such as those offered by the Sixth Amendment, "however beneficent in their operation and valuable to the accused, must occasionally give way to considerations of public policy and the necessity of the case." The constitutionally protected interest in confrontation may in fact "disserve" the Confrontation Clause's truth-seeking goal by causing significant emotional distress in the child and inhibiting the child's testimony.

Before the child may be sequestered and the accused denied confrontation with his or her witness accuser, the child must be very susceptible to the trauma of testifying and the state must employ special procedures. In his dissent, Justice Scalia, argued the procedure is not permitted by the plain wording of the Constitution, and impliedly, because children are more prone to fantasy, face-to-face confrontation is better to arrive at truth. For further discussion, *see* Hon. Barbara Gilleran–Johnson and Timothy R. Evans, *The Criminal Courtroom: Is It Childproof?*, 26 Loy. U. Chi. L.J. 681 (1995); Robert P. Mosteller, *Remaking Confrontation Clause and Hearsay Doctrine Under the Challenge of Child Sexual Abuse Prosecutions*, 1993 U. Ill. L. Rev. 691.

After Maryland v. Craig, the United States Congress enacted the Child Victims' and Witnesses' Rights Act, 18 U.S.C.A. § 3509, allowing for a child's testimony to be given beyond the sight of the defendant if any of the following occur: (1) The child is unable to testify because of fear; (2) The child is likely to suffer emotional trauma from testifying; (3) The child suffers from a mental or other infirmity; (4) Conduct of the defendant or defense counsel causes the child to be unable to testify. The federal statute has been found constitutional. *See* United States v. Garcia, 7 F.3d 885 (9th Cir.1993) and United States v. Carrier, 9 F.3d 867 (10th Cir.1993).

For an important discussion of the problem of evaluating the broader danger to other siblings of a victimized child, see Robin Fretwell Wilson, *The Cradle of Abuse: Evaluating the Danger Posed by a Sexually Predatory Parent to the Victim's Siblings*, 51 Emory L. J. 241 (2002).

DeShaney v. Winnebago County DSS

Supreme Court of the United States, 1989.
489 U.S. 189, 109 S.Ct. 998, 103 L.Ed.2d 249.

■ Chief Justice Rehnquist delivered the opinion of the Court.

.   .   .

The facts of this case are undeniably tragic. Petitioner Joshua DeShaney was born in 1979. In 1980, a Wyoming court granted his parents a divorce and awarded custody of Joshua to his father, Randy DeShaney. The father shortly thereafter moved to Neenah, a city located in Winnebago County, Wisconsin, taking the infant Joshua with him. There he entered into a second marriage, which also ended in divorce.

The Winnebago County authorities first learned that Joshua DeShaney might be a victim of child abuse in January 1982, when his father's second wife complained to the police, at the time of their divorce, that he had previously "hit the boy causing marks and [was] a prime case for child abuse." The Winnebago County Department of Social Services (DSS) interviewed the father, but he denied the accusations, and DSS did not pursue them further. In January 1983, Joshua was admitted to a local hospital with multiple bruises and abrasions. The examining physician suspected child abuse and notified DSS, which immediately obtained an order from a Wisconsin juvenile court placing Joshua in the temporary custody of the hospital. Three days later, the county convened an ad hoc "Child Protection Team"—consisting of a pediatrician, a psychologist, a police detective, the county's lawyer, several DSS caseworkers, and various hospital personnel—to consider Joshua's situation. At this meeting, the Team decided that there was insufficient evidence of child abuse to retain Joshua in the custody of the court. The Team did, however, decide to recommend several measures to protect Joshua, including enrolling him in a preschool program, providing his father with certain counselling services, and encouraging his father's girlfriend to move out of the home. Randy DeShaney entered into a voluntary agreement with DSS in which he promised to cooperate with them in accomplishing these goals.

Based on the recommendation of the Child Protection Team, the juvenile court dismissed the child protection case and returned Joshua to the custody of his father. A month later, emergency room personnel called the DSS caseworker handling Joshua's case to report that he had once again been treated for suspicious injuries. The caseworker concluded that there was no basis for action. For the next six months, the caseworker made monthly visits to the DeShaney home, during which she observed a number of suspicious injuries on Joshua's head; she also noticed that he had not been enrolled in school and that the girlfriend had not moved out. The caseworker dutifully recorded these incidents in her files, along with her continuing suspicions that someone in the DeShaney household was physically abusing Joshua, but she did nothing more. In November 1983, the emergency room notified DSS that Joshua had been treated once again for injuries that they believed to be caused by child abuse. On the caseworker's next two visits to the DeShaney home, she was told that Joshua was too ill to see her. Still DSS took no action.

In March 1984, Randy DeShaney beat 4-year-old Joshua so severely that he fell into a life-threatening coma. Emergency brain surgery revealed a series of hemorrhages caused by traumatic injuries to the head inflicted over a long period of time. Joshua did not die, but he suffered brain damage so severe that he is expected to spend the rest of his life confined to an institution for the profoundly retarded. Randy DeShaney was subsequently tried and convicted of child abuse.

Joshua and his mother brought this action under 42 U.S.C. § 1983 in the United States District Court for the Eastern District of Wisconsin against respondents Winnebago County, its Department of Social Services, and various individual employees of the Department. The complaint alleged that respondents had deprived Joshua of his liberty without due process of law, in violation of his rights under the Fourteenth Amendment, by failing to intervene to protect him against a risk of violence at his father's hands of which they knew or should have known. The District Court granted summary judgment for respondents.

The Court of Appeals for the Seventh Circuit affirmed, 812 F.2d 298 (1987), holding that petitioners had not made out an actionable § 1983 claim for two alternative reasons. First, the court held that the Due Process Clause of the Fourteenth Amendment does not require a state or local governmental entity to protect its citizens from "private violence, or other mishaps not attributable to the conduct of its employees." Id., at 301. In so holding, the court specifically rejected the position endorsed by a divided panel of the Third Circuit in Estate of Bailey by Oare v. County of York, 768 F.2d 503, 510–511 (C.A.3 1985), and by dicta in Jensen v. Conrad, 747 F.2d 185, 190–194 (C.A.4 1984), cert. denied, 470 U.S. 1052, 105 S.Ct. 1754, 84 L.Ed.2d 818 (1985), that once the State learns that a particular child is in danger of abuse from third parties and actually undertakes to protect him from that danger, a "special relationship" arises between it and the child which imposes an affirmative constitutional duty to provide adequate protection. Second, the court held, in reliance on our decision in Martinez v. California, 444 U.S. 277, 285, 100 S.Ct. 553, 559, 62 L.Ed.2d 481 (1980), that the causal connection between respondents' conduct and Joshua's injuries was too attenuated to establish a deprivation of constitutional rights actionable under § 1983. The court therefore found it unnecessary to reach the question whether respondents' conduct evinced the "state of mind" necessary to make out a due process claim after Daniels v. Williams, 474 U.S. 327, 106 S.Ct. 662, 88 L.Ed.2d 662 (1986), and Davidson v. Cannon, 474 U.S. 344, 106 S.Ct. 668, 88 L.Ed.2d 677 (1986).

Because of the inconsistent approaches taken by the lower courts in determining when, if ever, the failure of a state or local governmental entity or its agents to provide an individual with adequate protective services constitutes a violation of the individual's due process rights, and the importance of the issue to the administration of state and local governments, we granted certiorari. We now affirm.

The Due Process Clause of the Fourteenth Amendment provides that "[no State shall ... deprive any person of life, liberty, or property, without due process of law." Petitioners contend that the State deprived Joshua of his liberty interest in "freedom] from ... unjustified intrusions on personal security," by failing to provide him with adequate protection against his father's violence. The claim is one invoking the substantive rather than procedural component of the Due Process Clause; petitioners do not claim that the State denied Joshua protection without according him appropriate procedural safeguards, but that it was categorically obligated to protect him in these circumstances.

But nothing in the language of the Due Process Clause itself requires the State to protect the life, liberty, and property of its citizens against invasion by private actors. The Clause is phrased as a limitation on the State's power to act, not as a guarantee of certain minimal levels of safety and security. It forbids the State itself to deprive individuals of life, liberty, or property without "due process of law," but its language cannot fairly be extended to impose an affirmative obligation on the State to ensure that those interests do not come to harm through other means. Nor does history support such an expansive reading of the constitutional text. Like its counterpart in the Fifth Amendment, the Due Process Clause of the Fourteenth Amendment was intended to prevent government "from abusing [its] power, or employing it as an instrument of oppression," Davidson v. Cannon, supra, at 348, 106 S.Ct., at 670; . . . Its purpose was to protect the people from the State, not to ensure that the State protected them from each other. The Framers were content to leave the extent of governmental obligation in the latter area to the democratic political processes.

Consistent with these principles, our cases have recognized that the Due Process Clauses generally confer no affirmative right to governmental aid, even where such aid may be necessary to secure life, liberty, or property interests of which the government itself may not deprive the individual. . . .

Petitioners contend, however, that even if the Due Process Clause imposes no affirmative obligation on the State to provide the general public with adequate protective services, such a duty may arise out of certain "special relationships" created or assumed by the State with respect to particular individuals. Petitioners argue that such a "special relationship" existed here because the State knew that Joshua faced a special danger of abuse at his father's hands, and specifically proclaimed, by word and by deed, its intention to protect him against that danger. Having actually undertaken to protect Joshua from this danger—which petitioners concede the State played no part in creating—the State acquired an affirmative "duty," enforceable through the Due Process Clause, to do so in a reasonably competent fashion. Its failure to discharge that duty, so the argument goes, was an abuse of governmental power that so "shocks the conscience," Rochin v. California, 342 U.S. 165, 172, 72 S.Ct. 205, 209, 96 L.Ed. 183 (1952), as to constitute a substantive due process violation.

We reject this argument. It is true that in certain limited circumstances the Constitution imposes upon the State affirmative duties of care and protection with respect to particular individuals. In Estelle v. Gamble, 429 U.S. 97, 97 S.Ct. 285, 50 L.Ed.2d 251 (1976), we recognized that the Eighth Amendment's prohibition against cruel and unusual punishment, made applicable to the States through the Fourteenth Amendment's Due Process Clause, Robinson v. California, 370 U.S. 660, 82 S.Ct. 1417, 8

L.Ed.2d 758 (1962), requires the State to provide adequate medical care to incarcerated prisoners. 429 U.S., at 103–104, 97 S.Ct., at 290–291.[5] We reasoned that because the prisoner is unable " 'by reason of the deprivation of his liberty [to] care for himself,' 'it is only' 'just' " that the State be required to care for him. Ibid., quoting Spicer v. Williamson, 191 N.C. 487, 490, 132 SE 291, 293 (1926).

In Youngberg v. Romeo, 457 U.S. 307, 102 S.Ct. 2452, 73 L.Ed.2d 28 (1982), we extended this analysis beyond the Eighth Amendment setting, holding that the substantive component of the Fourteenth Amendment's Due Process Clause requires the State to provide involuntarily committed mental patients with such services as are necessary to ensure their "reasonable safety" from themselves and others. As we explained, "[i]f it is cruel and unusual punishment to hold convicted criminals in unsafe conditions, it must be unconstitutional [under the Due Process Clause] to confine the involuntarily committed—who may not be punished at all—in unsafe conditions."

But these cases afford petitioners no help. Taken together, they stand only for the proposition that when the State takes a person into its custody and holds him there against his will, the Constitution imposes upon it a corresponding duty to assume some responsibility for his safety and general well-being.... The rationale for this principle is simple enough: when the State by the affirmative exercise of its power so restrains an individual's liberty that it renders him unable to care for himself, and at the same time fails to provide for his basic human needs—e.g., food, clothing, shelter, medical care, and reasonable safety—it transgresses the substantive limits on state action set by the Eighth Amendment and the Due Process Clause. The affirmative duty to protect arises not from the State's knowledge of the individual's predicament or from its expressions of intent to help him, but from the limitation which it has imposed on his freedom to act on his own behalf.... In the substantive due process analysis, it is the State's affirmative act of restraining the individual's freedom to act on his own behalf—through incarceration, institutionalization, or other similar restraint of personal liberty—which is the "deprivation of liberty" triggering the protections of the Due Process Clause, not its failure to act to protect his liberty interests against harms inflicted by other means.

The ... analysis simply has no applicability in the present case. Petitioners concede that the harms Joshua suffered did not occur while he was in the State's custody, but while he was in the custody of his natural father, who was in no sense a state actor. While the State may have been aware of the dangers that Joshua faced in the free world, it played no part

---

5. To make out an Eighth Amendment claim based on the failure to provide adequate medical care, a prisoner must show that the state defendants exhibited "deliberate indifference" to his "serious" medical needs; the mere negligent or inadvertent failure to provide adequate care is not enough.

Estelle v. Gamble, 429 U.S., at 105–106, 97 S.Ct., at 291–292. In Whitley v. Albers, 475 U.S. 312, 106 S.Ct. 1078, 89 L.Ed.2d 251 (1986), we suggested that a similar state of mind is required to make out a substantive due process claim in the prison setting. Id., at 326–327, 106 S.Ct., at 1088.

in their creation, nor did it do anything to render him any more vulnerable to them. That the State once took temporary custody of Joshua does not alter the analysis, for when it returned him to his father's custody, it placed him in no worse position than that in which he would have been had it not acted at all; the State does not become the permanent guarantor of an individual's safety by having once offered him shelter. Under these circumstances, the State had no constitutional duty to protect Joshua.

It may well be that, by voluntarily undertaking to protect Joshua against a danger it concededly played no part in creating, the State acquired a duty under state tort law to provide him with adequate protection against that danger.... But the claim here is based on the Due Process Clause of the Fourteenth Amendment, which, as we have said many times, does not transform every tort committed by a state actor into a constitutional violation. A State may, through its courts and legislatures, impose such affirmative duties of care and protection upon its agents as it wishes. But not "all common-law duties owed by government actors were ... constitutionalized by the Fourteenth Amendment." Daniels v. Williams, supra, 474 U.S. at 335, 106 S.Ct., at 678. Because, as explained above, the State had no constitutional duty to protect Joshua against his father's violence, its failure to do so—though calamitous in hindsight—simply does not constitute a violation of the Due Process Clause.[10]

Judges and lawyers, like other humans, are moved by natural sympathy in a case like this to find a way for Joshua and his mother to receive adequate compensation for the grievous harm inflicted upon them. But before yielding to that impulse, it is well to remember once again that the harm was inflicted not by the State of Wisconsin, but by Joshua's father. The most that can be said of the state functionaries in this case is that they stood by and did nothing when suspicious circumstances dictated a more active role for them. In defense of them it must also be said that had they moved too soon to take custody of the son away from the father, they would likely have been met with charges of improperly intruding into the parent-child relationship, charges based on the same Due Process Clause that forms the basis for the present charge of failure to provide adequate protection.

The people of Wisconsin may well prefer a system of liability which would place upon the State and its officials the responsibility for failure to act in situations such as the present one. They may create such a system, if they do not have it already, by changing the tort law of the State in

---

10.   Because we conclude that the Due Process Clause did not require the State to protect Joshua from his father, we need not address respondents' alternative argument that the individual state actors lacked the requisite "state of mind" to make out a due process violation. See Daniels v. Williams, 474 U.S., at 334, n. 3, 106 S.Ct., at 677, n. 3. Similarly, we have no occasion to consider whether the individual respondents might be entitled to a qualified immunity defense, see Anderson v. Creighton, 483 U.S. 635, 107 S.Ct. 3034, 97 L.Ed.2d 523 (1987), or whether the allegations in the complaint are sufficient to support a § 1983 claim against the county and its Department of Social Services under Monell v. New York City Dept. of Social Services, 436 U.S. 658, 98 S.Ct. 2018, 56 L.Ed.2d 611 (1978), and its progeny.

accordance with the regular law-making process. But they should not have it thrust upon them by this Court's expansion of the Due Process Clause of the Fourteenth Amendment.

■ JUSTICE BRENNAN, with whom JUSTICE MARSHALL and JUSTICE BLACKMUN join, dissenting.

"The most that can be said of the state functionaries in this case," the Court today concludes, "is that they stood by and did nothing when suspicious circumstances dictated a more active role for them." Because I believe that this description of respondents' conduct tells only part of the story and that, accordingly, the Constitution itself "dictated a more active role" for respondents in the circumstances presented here, I cannot agree that respondents had no constitutional duty to help Joshua DeShaney.

It may well be, as the Court decides, that the Due Process Clause as construed by our prior case creates no general right to basic governmental services. That, however, is not the question presented here; indeed, that question was not raised in the complaint, urged on appeal, presented in the petition for certiorari, or addressed in the briefs on the merits. No one, in short, has asked the Court to proclaim that, as a general matter, the Constitution safeguards positive as well as negative liberties.

This is more than a quibble over dicta; it is a point about perspective, having substantive ramifications. In a constitutional setting that distinguishes sharply between action and inaction, one's characterization of the misconduct alleged under § 1983 may effectively decide the case. Thus, by leading off with a discussion (and rejection) of the idea that the Constitution imposes on the States an affirmative duty to take basic care of their citizens, the Court foreshadows—perhaps even preordains—its conclusion that no duty existed even on the specific facts before us. This initial discussion establishes the baseline from which the Court assesses the DeShaneys' claim that, when a State has—"by word and by deed,"—announced an intention to protect a certain class of citizens and has before it facts that would trigger that protection under the applicable state law, the Constitution imposes upon the State an affirmative duty of protection.

The Court's baseline is the absence of positive rights in the Constitution and a concomitant suspicion of any claim that seems to depend on such rights. From this perspective, the DeShaneys' claim is first and foremost about inaction (the failure, here, of respondents to take steps to protect Joshua), and only tangentially about action (the establishment of a state program specifically designed to help children like Joshua). And from this perspective, holding these Wisconsin officials liable—where the only difference between this case and one involving a general claim to protective services is Wisconsin's establishment and operation of a program to protect children—would seem to punish an effort that we should seek to promote.

I would begin from the opposite direction. I would focus first on the action that Wisconsin *has* taken with respect to Joshua and children like him, rather than on the actions that the State failed to take. Such a method is not new to this Court. Both Estelle v. Gamble, 429 U.S. 97, 97 S.Ct. 285,

50 L.Ed.2d 251 (1976), and Youngberg v. Romeo, 457 U.S. 307, 102 S.Ct. 2452, 73 L.Ed.2d 28 (1982), began by emphasizing that the States had confined J.W. Gamble to prison and Nicholas Romeo to a psychiatric hospital. This initial action rendered these people helpless to help themselves or to seek help from persons unconnected to the government. See Estelle, supra, 429 U.S. at 104, 97 S.Ct., at 291 ("'[I]t is but just that the public be required to care for the prisoner, who cannot by reason of the deprivation of his liberty, care for himself'"); Youngberg, supra, 457 U.S. at 317, 102 S.Ct., at 2458 ("When a person is institutionalized—and wholly dependent on the State—it is conceded by petitioners that a duty to provide certain services and care does exist"). Cases from the lower courts also recognize that a State's actions can be decisive in assessing the constitutional significance of subsequent inaction. For these purposes, moreover, actual physical restraint is not the only State action that has been considered relevant. See, e.g., White v. Rochford, 592 F.2d 381 (C.A.7 1979) (police officers violated due process when, after arresting the guardian of three young children, they abandoned the children on a busy stretch of highway at night).

. . .

Wisconsin has established a child-welfare system specifically designed to help children like Joshua. Wisconsin law places upon the local departments of social services such as respondent (DSS or Department) a duty to investigate reported instances of child abuse. See Wis.Stat.Ann. § 48.981(3) (1987 and Supp.1988–1989). While other governmental bodies and private persons are largely responsible for the reporting of possible cases of child abuse, see § 48.981(2), Wisconsin law channels all such reports to the local departments of social services for evaluation and, if necessary, further action. § 48.981(3). Even when it is the sheriff's office or police department that receives a report of suspected child abuse, that report is referred to local social services departments for action, see § 48.981(3)(a); the only exception to this occurs when the reporter fears for the child's immediate safety. § 48.981(3)(b). In this way, Wisconsin law invites—indeed, directs—citizens and other governmental entities to depend on local departments of social services such as respondent to protect children from abuse.

The specific facts before us bear out this view of Wisconsin's system of protecting children. Each time someone voiced a suspicion that Joshua was being abused, that information was relayed to the Department for investigation and possible action. When Randy DeShaney's second wife told the police that he had " 'hit the boy causing marks and [was] a prime case for child abuse,' " the police referred her complaint to DSS. When, on three separate occasions, emergency room personnel noticed suspicious injuries on Joshua's body, they went to DSS with this information. When neighbors informed the police that they had seen or heard Joshua's father or his father's lover beating or otherwise abusing Joshua, the police brought these reports to the attention of DSS. And when respondent Kemmeter, through these reports and through her own observations in the course of nearly 20 visits to the DeShaney home, compiled growing evidence that Joshua was being abused, that information stayed within the Department—chronicled by the social worker in detail that seems almost eerie in light of her failure to act upon it. (As to the extent of the social worker's involvement in and knowledge of Joshua's predicament, her reaction to the news of Joshua's last and most devastating injuries is illuminating: "I just knew the phone would ring some day and Joshua would be dead." 812 F.2d 298, 300 (C.A.7 1987).)

Even more telling than these examples is the Department's control over the decision whether to take steps to protect a particular child from suspected abuse. While many different people contributed information and advice to this decision, it was up to the people at DSS to make the ultimate decision (subject to the approval of the local government's Corporation Counsel) whether to disturb the family's current arrangements. When Joshua first appeared at a local hospital with injuries signaling physical abuse, for example, it was DSS that made the decision to take him into temporary custody for the purpose of studying his situation—and it was DSS, acting in conjunction with the Corporation Counsel, that returned him to his father. Unfortunately for Joshua DeShaney, the buck effectively stopped with the Department.

In these circumstances, a private citizen, or even a person working in a government agency other than DSS, would doubtless feel that her job was done as soon as she had reported her suspicions of child abuse to DSS. Through its child-welfare program, in other words, the State of Wisconsin has relieved ordinary citizens and governmental bodies other than the Department of any sense of obligation to do anything more than report their suspicions of child abuse to DSS. If DSS ignores or dismisses these suspicions, no one will step in to fill the gap. Wisconsin's child-protection program thus effectively confined Joshua DeShaney within the walls of Randy DeShaney's violent home until such time as DSS took action to remove him. Conceivably, then, children like Joshua are made worse off by the existence of this program when the persons and entities charged with carrying it out fail to do their jobs.

It simply belies reality, therefore, to contend that the State "stood by and did nothing" with respect to Joshua. Through its child-protection program, the State actively intervened in Joshua's life and, by virtue of this intervention, acquired ever more certain knowledge that Joshua was in grave danger. These circumstances, in my view, plant this case solidly within the tradition of cases like *Youngberg* and *Estelle*.

It will be meager comfort to Joshua and his mother to know that, if the State had "selectively den[ied] its protective services" to them because they were "disfavored minorities," ante, at 1004, n. 3, their § 1983 suit might have stood on sturdier ground. Because of the posture of this case, we do not know why respondents did not take steps to protect Joshua; the Court, however, tells us that their reason is irrelevant so long as their inaction was not the product of invidious discrimination. Presumably, then, if respondents decided not to help Joshua because his name began with a "j," or because he was born in the spring, or because they did not care enough about him even to formulate an intent to discriminate against him based on an arbitrary reason, respondents would not be liable to the DeShaneys because they were not the ones who dealt the blows that destroyed Joshua's life.

I do not suggest that such irrationality was at work in this case; I emphasize only that we do not know whether or not it was. I would allow Joshua and his mother the opportunity to show that respondents' failure to help him arose, not out of the sound exercise of professional judgment that we recognized in *Youngberg* as sufficient to preclude liability, see 457 U.S., at 322–323, 102 S.Ct., at 2461–2462, but from the kind of arbitrariness that we have in the past condemned. . . .

Youngberg's deference to a decisionmaker's professional judgment ensures that once a caseworker has decided, on the basis of her professional training and experience, that one course of protection is preferable for a given child, or even that no special protection is required, she will not be found liable for the harm that follows. (In this way, *Youngberg's* vision of substantive due process serves a purpose similar to that served by adherence to procedural norms, namely, requiring that a State actor stop and think before she acts in a way that may lead to a loss of liberty.) Moreover, that the Due Process Clause is not violated by merely negligent conduct, means that a social worker who simply makes a mistake of judgment under what are admittedly complex and difficult conditions will not find herself liable in damages under § 1983.

As the Court today reminds us, "the Due Process Clause of the Fourteenth Amendment was intended to prevent government 'from abusing [its] power, or employing it as an instrument of oppression.'" My disagreement with the Court arises from its failure to see that inaction can be every bit as abusive of power as action, that oppression can result when a State undertakes a vital duty and then ignores it. Today's opinion construes the Due Process Clause to permit a State to displace private sources of protection and then, at the critical moment, to shrug its shoulders and turn away from the harm that it has promised to try to prevent. Because I cannot agree that our Constitution is indifferent to such indifference, I respectfully dissent.

■ JUSTICE BLACKMUN, dissenting.

Today, the Court purports to be the dispassionate oracle of the law, unmoved by "natural sympathy." But, in this pretense, the Court itself retreats into a sterile formalism which prevents it from recognizing either the facts of the case before it or the legal norms that should apply to those facts. As Justice Brennan demonstrates, the facts here involve not mere passivity, but active state intervention in the life of Joshua DeShaney— intervention that triggered a fundamental duty to aid the boy once the State learned of the severe danger to which he was exposed.

The Court fails to recognize this duty because it attempts to draw a sharp and rigid line between action and inaction. But such formalistic reasoning has no place in the interpretation of the broad and stirring clauses of the Fourteenth Amendment. Indeed, I submit that these clauses were designed, at least in part, to undo the formalistic legal reasoning that infected antebellum jurisprudence, which the late Professor Robert Cover analyzed so effectively in his significant work entitled *Justice Accused* (1975).

Like the antebellum judges who denied relief to fugitive slaves, the Court today claims that its decision, however harsh, is compelled by existing legal doctrine. On the contrary, the question presented by this case is an open one, and our Fourteenth Amendment precedents may be read more broadly or narrowly depending upon how one chooses to read them. Faced with the choice, I would adopt a "sympathetic" reading, one which comports with dictates of fundamental justice and recognizes that compassion need not be exiled from the province of judging. . . .

Poor Joshua! Victim of repeated attacks by an irresponsible, bullying, cowardly, and intemperate father, and abandoned by respondents who placed him in a dangerous predicament and who knew or learned what was going on, and yet did essentially nothing except, as the Court revealingly observes, ante, at 1001, "dutifully recorded these incidents in [their] files." It is a sad commentary upon American life, and constitutional principles— so full of late of patriotic fervor and proud proclamations about "liberty and justice for all," that this child, Joshua DeShaney, now is assigned to live out the remainder of his life profoundly retarded. Joshua and his mother, as petitioners here, deserve—but now are denied by this Court— the opportunity to have the facts of their case considered in the light of the constitutional protection that 42 U.S.C. § 1983 is meant to provide.

NOTES

Compare Justice Blackmun's dissent in 1989 in *DeShaney* (Poor Joshua!) with his majority opinion in 1982 in Santosky v. Kramer, to be discussed in Chapter 9: "The fundamental liberty interest of natural parents in the care, custody, and management of their child does not evaporate simply because they have not been model parents or have lost temporary custody of their child to the state." The issue of parental rights versus children's rights is at issue in both cases. In *Santosky*, the court terminated parental rights after the three children remained in foster care for four years. What is the standard by which you should balance the due process rights of the child against the due process rights of the parents?

The majority in *DeShaney* held that the Constitution imposes on the state affirmative duties of care and protection whenever the state takes a person into its custody and holds him or her there against his or her will. Custody creates substantive and procedural due process claims enforceable under § 1983. Liability in other circumstances depends on the state's assumption of affirmative duties. When does the state assume duties? In one case, the District of Columbia government was aware that the mother of a minor might be unable to feed and care for her three minor children. Thus, when her two and one-half year old daughter was severely burned when she was submerged in scalding water by a friend of her mother with whom she was staying, the minor sued the District of Columbia for failure to investigate and protect her from abuse and neglect. The minor argued that a provision of the federal Child Abuse Prevention and Treatment Act required reports of child abuse and neglect and this was sufficient to support a claim under 42 U.S.C. § 1983; a duty to investigate was a custodial arrangement. The U.S. Court of Appeals for the District of Columbia denied relief saying the Act was vague—generalized—in what constitutes a prompt investigation, and this lack of specificity deprives the minor of an enforceable right. The court held that "by codifying procedures for investigating child abuse and neglect reports. D.C. has not assumed a constitutional obligation to protect children from such abuse and neglect." Doe v. District of Columbia, 93 F.3d 861 (D.C.Cir.1996).

In LaShawn A. v. Kelly, 990 F.2d 1319 (D.C.Cir.1993), the court held that the Prevention of Child Abuse and Neglect Act of the District of Columbia did in fact provide a scheme for the protection and care of foster children. Indeed, the court held that children not yet in custodial care, but reported to have been abused or neglected, have a private cause of action claim against the District of Columbia under the Act. See Turner v. District of Columbia, 532 A.2d 662 (D.C.1987), and followed by District of Columbia v. Harris, 770 A.2d 82 (D.C.2001). Problems persist in the District of Columbia, often resulting in the death of children under the custodial care of the city's Child and Family Services. The Washington Post published a series of articles describing the agency's shortfalls and the effects upon children. For the first of the articles, see Sari Horwitz, Scott Higham, Sarah Cohen, *"Protected" Children Died as Government Did Little,* WASH POST, Sept. 9, 2001, at A1. Children in foster care may thus have enforceable rights against the state when the state's conduct is either a substantial departure from a professional standard, *see, e.g.,* Tyler v. Gray, 1996 WL 355335 (E.D.Pa.1996), or reckless indifference, *see, e.g.,* Lintz v. Skipski, 25 F.3d 304 (6th Cir.1994). Often foster parents are not considered "state actors" thus there is no extending liability to the state for any failure of the foster parents. *See, e.g.,* Rayburn v. Hogue, 241 F.3d 1341 (11th Cir.2001). Sometimes the state defines the foster parents as state employees and because of this status, the foster parents enjoy sovereign immunity from suit. *See, e.g.,* Williams v. Reed, 164 Fed.Appx. 908 (11th Cir.2006).In another case, a county that licensed foster homes was not liable when a foster parent licenses by the county sexually abused a child placed in the home. Waubanascum v. Shawano County, 416 F.3rd 658 (7th Cir. 2005). Likewise, attorneys involved in administrative enforcement of child neglect suits are entitled to absolute immunity because they perform functions analogous to a criminal prosecutor. Since both functions demand decision free from intimidation and harassment, attorneys should have absolute immunity. See Gray v. Poole, 243 F.3d 572 (D.C.Cir.2001).

Cities and states grapple with increasing child abuse and neglect, providing services, and nonetheless seeking to limit liability which drains dwindling city and state coffers. In Marisol A. v. Giuliani, 929 F.Supp. 662 (S.D.N.Y.1996), eleven children, all having endured a wide range of abuses, "reflect the dire situation facing children in the system." The court held that the children have a right to be free from unreasonable and unnecessary intrusion into their emotional well being and to family integrity which is associated with this well being. The court then found that New York's Child Protective Services laws are more than mere procedural guidelines and, in fact, give plaintiffs an entitlement to protective services of which they may not be deprived without due process of law. This entitlement and further court-sanctioned claims under the Adoption Assistance and Child Welfare Act, the Child Abuse Prevention and Treatment Act, the Americans With Disabilities Act, and the Rehabilitation Act, signal continuing contest between state agencies and private citizens seeking more or suffering from too little, government care. Seeking to reform its child welfare system, New York City has appointed a new commissioner of children's services and published a new plan of action for the administration of children's services: Protecting the Children of New York: A Plan of Action for the Administration for Children's Services (1996).

E.   Medical Decision Making For and By Children

Hermanson v. State

Supreme Court of Florida, 1992.
604 So.2d 775.

■ Overton, Justice.

. . .

In this tragic case, Amy Hermanson, the daughter of William and Christine Hermanson, died from untreated juvenile diabetes. The Hermansons, members of the First Church of Christ, Scientist, were charged and convicted of child abuse resulting in third-degree murder for failing to provide Amy with conventional medical treatment. The Hermansons received four-year suspended prison sentences on their murder convictions and were ordered to serve fifteen years' probation. The district court, finding that the spiritual treatment accommodation provision of section 415.503(7)(f), Florida Statutes (1985), did not prevent their prosecution and conviction, affirmed the trial court's sentence and certified the above question. In summary, we find that sections 827.04(1) and 415.503(7)(f), when considered together, are ambiguous and result in a denial of due process because the statutes in question fail to give parents notice of the point at which their reliance on spiritual treatment loses statutory approval and becomes culpably negligent. We further find that a person of ordinary intelligence cannot be expected to understand the extent to which reliance on spiritual healing is permitted and the point at which this reliance constitutes a criminal offense under the subject statutes. The statutes have created a trap that the legislature should address. Accordingly, we quash the decision of the district court.

Statutory History

The statutory provisions are critical to the legal and constitutional issues presented in this case. Florida's child abuse statute, section 827.04(1)–(2), Florida Statutes (1985), provides:

(1) Whoever, willfully or by culpable negligence, deprives a child of, or allows a child to be deprived of, necessary food, clothing, shelter, or medical treatment, or who, knowingly or by culpable negligence, permits physical or mental injury to the child, and in so doing causes great bodily harm, permanent disability, or permanent disfigurement to such child, shall be guilty of a felony of the third degree....

(2) Whoever, willfully or by culpable negligence, deprives a child of, or allows a child to be deprived of, necessary food, clothing, shelter, or medical treatment, or who, knowingly or by culpable negligence, permits physical or mental injury to the child, shall be guilty of a misdemeanor of the first degree....

The third-degree murder provision of section 782.04(4), Florida Statutes (1985), provides that the killing of a human being while engaged in the commission of child abuse constitutes murder in the third degree and is a felony of the second degree. Section 415.503 provides, in part, as follows:

(1) "Abused or neglected child" means a child whose physical or mental health or welfare is harmed, or threatened with harm, by the acts or omissions of the parent or other person responsible for the child's welfare....

(7) "Harm" to a child's health or welfare can occur when the parent or other person responsible for the child's welfare: ...

(f) Fails to supply the child with adequate food, clothing, shelter, *or health care,* although financially able to do so or although offered financial or other means to do so; *however, a parent or other person responsible for the child's welfare legitimately practicing his religious beliefs, who by reason thereof does not provide specified medical treatment for a child, may not be considered abusive or neglectful for that reason alone,* but such an exception does not:

1. Eliminate the requirement that such a case be reported to the department;

2. Prevent the department from investigating such a case; or

3. Preclude a court from ordering, when the health of the child requires it, the provision of medical services by a physician, as defined herein, or treatment by a duly accredited practitioner who relies solely on spiritual means for healing in accordance with the tenets and practices of a well-recognized church or religious organization.

(Emphasis added)[1]

---

1. [The court lists statutes in 27 other states that provide some form of religious exemption.]

The religious accommodation provision in section 415.503(7)(f) was initially passed by the legislature in 1975 as section 827.07(2), Florida Statutes (1975), the same chapter that contained the child abuse provision under which the Hermansons were prosecuted. The senate staff analysis of the religious accommodation provision stated that these provisions were "a defense for parents who decline medical treatment for legitimate religious reasons." Staff of Fla. S. Comm. Crim. Just., SB 1186 (1975) Staff Analysis 1 (final May 26, 1975) (available at Fla. Dep't of State, Div. of Archives, Tallahassee, Fla.). In 1983, the Division of Statutory Revision moved the above religious accommodation provision from chapter 827 to chapter 415.

Facts

The facts of this case, as stipulated to by the parties in the trial court, are as follows:

1. The Defendant, William F. Hermanson, is 39 years of age. Mr. Hermanson is married to the Defendant, Christine Hermanson, who is 36 years of age. Since June of 1973, Mr. and Mrs. Hermanson have resided in Sarasota, Florida. At all times material to this case, they resided at.... Mr. Hermanson is a bank vice president, and Mrs. Hermanson is the director of the Sarasota Fine Arts Academy. Mr. and Mrs. Hermanson have graduate degrees from Grand Valley State College and the University of Michigan, respectively. Neither Mr. nor Mrs. Hermanson has ever been arrested for, or convicted of, a crime.

2. Mr. and Mrs. Hermanson were married on May 30, 1970. There have been two children born of this marriage: Eric Thomas Hermanson, date of birth 8/26/77 and Amy Kathleen Hermanson (deceased) date of birth 7/16/79. There are no facts indicating that Mr. or Mrs. Hermanson ever deprived their children of necessary food, clothing or shelter as those terms are used in section 827.04, Florida Statutes.

3. According to the autopsy report of the Medical Examiner, James C. Wilson, M.D., on September 30, 1986, at approximately 1:55 p.m., Amy Hermanson died. Dr. Wilson found the cause of death to be diabetic ketoacidosis due to juvenile onset diabetes mellitus. Additional autopsy findings of dehydration and weight loss were consistent with the disease process. Dr. Wilson believes that the disease could have been diagnosed by a physician prior to death and, within the bounds of medical probability, Amy's death could have been prevented even up to several hours before her death with proper medical treatment.

4. At the time of Amy's death, the Hermanson family, including William, Christine, Eric and Amy, were regular attenders of the First Church of Christ, Scientist in Sarasota. William Hermanson has been a member of the Christian Science Church since childhood, and Christine Hermanson has been a member of the Church of Christ, Scientist since 1969. The Church of Christ, Scientist is a well-recognized church or religious organization, as that term is used in Section 415.503, Florida Statutes.

5. Christian Scientists believe in healing by spiritual means in accordance with the tenets and practices of the Christian Science Church. William and Christine Hermanson, at all times material to the facts in this case, followed the religious teachings of their church and relied upon Christian Science healing in the care and treatment of Amy Hermanson.

6. On or about September 22, 1986, the Hermansons became aware that something was particularly wrong with Amy Hermanson which they believed to be of an emotional nature. They contacted Thomas Keller, a duly-accredited practitioner of the First Church of Christ, Scientist for consultation and treatment in accordance with the religious tenets and beliefs of the Christian Science Religion. Thomas Keller treated Amy from September 22, 1986 until September 30, 1986.

7. On or about September 25, 1986, the Hermansons traveled to Indianapolis, Indiana to attend an annual Christian Science conference on healing and left their children in the care of one Marie Beth Ackerman, age 24, a Christian Scientist employed by the Christian Science Committee on Publications and who was residing with the Hermanson family in Sarasota County, Florida and assisting Mrs. Hermanson as an administrator at the Sarasota Fine Arts Academy. The Hermansons returned to their home in Sarasota County, Florida at approximately 2 a.m. on September 29, 1986.

8. After their arrival, the Hermansons noticed a worsening of Amy's condition. They decided to seek the assistance of a local Christian Science practitioner and at approximately 9 a.m. on September 29, 1986, the Hermansons contacted one Frederick Hillier, a duly-accredited Christian Science practitioner of the First Church of Christ, Scientist whom they secured as a practitioner for Amy. Thereafter, until Amy's death, Hillier provided treatment for Amy relying solely on spiritual means for healing in accordance with the tenets and practices of the First Church of Christ, Scientist.

9. On Monday, September 29, 1986, William Hermanson had a discussion with Jack Morton, the father of Christine Hermanson, wherein Mr. Morton expressed his concern for the health of Amy and suggested the possibility that Amy had diabetes.

10. At approximately 9:30 a.m. on September 30, 1986, Hillier went to the Hermanson home to continue treatment and, due to the fact the Hermansons had been up all night with Amy, suggested that a Christian Science nurse be called to help care for Amy.

11. At approximately 10 a.m. on Tuesday, September 30, 1986, one Molly Jane Sellers was called to the Hermanson residence to assist in the care of Amy Hermanson. Molly Jane Sellers is recognized as a Christian Science nurse by the First Church of Christ, Scientist and has been so recognized for twenty years. In preparation for such accreditation by the Church, Sellers completed a three and one-half year training course. Her area of care primarily relates to the physical

needs of the patients and would be closely related to the duties performed by a licensed practical nurse.

12.   On September 30, 1986 at approximately 11 a.m., William Hermanson was contacted by a counselor from the Department of Health and Rehabilitative Services (Willy Torres) who informed him that they had received a complaint alleging child abuse of his daughter, Amy Hermanson and that a hearing pursuant to said allegation had been set before the Juvenile Court for 1:30 p.m. Torres further informed Mr. Hermanson that the purpose of the hearing was to determine if medical treatment would be court ordered or if treatment as prescribed by the Christian Science practitioner would be ordered at that time.

13.   At approximately 12:30 p.m., Mr. Hermanson left his home and traveled to the Sarasota County Courthouse for the hearing pursuant to the notification from Willy Torres. While at the hearing, at approximately 1:27 p.m., Mr. Hermanson received a telephone call from an individual at the Hermanson home who reported that Amy had "taken a turn for the worse and an ambulance had been called." Such information was related to the Court and an order was entered which required that Amy Hermanson be examined by a licensed medical doctor. When paramedics arrived they found that Amy had died.

14.   Prior to her death, Amy Hermanson continued under the care and treatment of Frederick Hillier with the assistance of Molly Jane Sellers until approximately 1:27 p.m. September 30, 1986 at which time Amy had died.

15.   On or about October 7, 1986, the Department of Health and Rehabilitative Services notified Mr. and Mrs. William Hermanson that it had completed its investigation and had classified the report as unfounded.

Hermanson, 570 So.2d at 324–27.

The district court summarized the facts presented at trial as follows:

In the month or so before her death Amy was having a marked and dramatic weight loss, that she was almost skeletal in her thinness and this was a big change in her appearance. There were great dark circles under her eyes that had never been there before. Her behavior was very different from the usual; she was lethargic and complaining whereas previously she had been bubbly, vivacious, and outgoing. She was seen lying down on the floor to sleep during the day when accompanying her mother to visit music students and lying down on the floor after school at her mother's fine arts academy. She often complained of not feeling well, that her stomach hurt and that she wasn't sleeping well. She was too tired during the day to participate in gym class at school. There was a bluish tint to her skin. Her breath smelled funny, one observer called it a "fruity" odor. The pathologist who performed the autopsy testified to Amy's skeletal appearance, that her vertebrae and shoulder blades were prominent and her abdomen distended as if she were undernourished. Her eyes were quite sunken, due to the dehydration, although her parents had told the pathologist that on the day before her death she was drinking a lot of fluids but urinating frequently too. They also told him that they had noticed changes in Amy starting about a month previously. Amy had complained of constipation during the last week of her life but at no time seemed feverish although there was intermittent vomiting.

The pathologist opined that the illness was chronic, not acute. According to her parents' talk with the pathologist, Amy seemed incoherent on the evening before her death although the next morning she seemed better. The pathologist also testified that vomiting and dehydration are compatible with flu-like symptoms but these, added to a four-week-long history of weight loss with the more severe conditions reported, would not be indicative of flu. Finally, the jury was shown photographs of Amy taken shortly after she died before her body was removed from the home by the paramedics as well as some taken before the autopsy was performed.

Id. at 336–37.

The evidence and the stipulated facts established that the Hermansons treated Amy in accordance with their Christian Science beliefs. On the day of Amy's death, a Christian Science nurse had been summoned to the home to care for her. The nurse testified that Amy was unresponsive and that, when she began vomiting and her condition worsened, she recommended that an ambulance should be called. The Christian Science practitioner who was present advised the nurse that the church headquarters in Boston should be contacted before an ambulance was called. After placing a call to Boston, an ambulance was summoned.

In its argument to the jury, the State asserted that the Hermansons' reliance on Christian Science healing practices under these circumstances constituted culpable negligence. The basis of its argument was that the Hermansons were not legitimately practicing their religious beliefs. Drawing on the evidence that the Christian Science nurse had called an ambulance when Amy began vomiting, the State suggested that the Christian Science Church recognizes conventional medical care and, therefore, the Hermansons had not been legitimately practicing their religious beliefs when they failed to seek medical care before Amy's death. No specific evidence was introduced by either side on the question of when, if at all, the Christian Science faith allows its members to call for medical attention. The Hermansons, on the other hand, argued to the jury that they should not be convicted of a criminal offense because they were "legitimately" practicing their faith in accordance with the accommodation provision of section 415.503(7)(f).

The jury, after one and one-half hours of deliberation, sought the answer to three questions: "(1) As a Christian Scientist do they have a choice to go to a medical doctor if they want to? (2) Or if not, can they call a doctor at a certain point? (3) Do they need permission first?" In response, the court advised the jurors that they must look to the evidence presented during the trial to find the answers. Counsel for both parties had previously agreed to this response by the trial court. The jury found the Hermansons guilty of felony child abuse and third-degree murder, and they were sentenced to four-year suspended prison sentences, with fifteen years' probation, on condition that they provide regular medical examinations and treatment for their surviving children.

On appeal, the district court affirmed, finding that the statutory accommodation section in 415.503(7)(f) applied only to matters contained in chapter 415 and that that provision did not provide any protection from criminal penalties for actual child abuse or neglect in chapters 782 and 827, Florida Statutes (1985). The district court rejected the Hermansons' claim that the evidence did not establish that they had acted willfully or with culpable negligence under the circumstances of this case. The district court agreed with the trial court that, when they returned from Indiana thirty-six hours before Amy's death and had seen that her condition had worsened, the Hermansons were placed on notice "that their attempts at spiritual treatment were unavailing and [that] it was time to call in medical help." The district court concluded that those facts justified the issue's being submitted to the jury and the verdict finding the Hermansons guilty of culpable negligence. The district court also rejected the Hermansons' claim of a due process violation for lack of notice of when their conduct became criminal. In rejecting this contention, the district court relied on the decision of the California Supreme Court in Walker v. Superior Court, 47 Cal.3d 112, 253 Cal.Rptr. 1, 21, 763 P.2d 852, 872 (1988), cert. denied, 491 U.S. 905 (1989), in which that court stated:

> "[T]he law is full of instances where a man's fate depends on his estimating rightly, that is, as the jury subsequently estimates it, some matter of degree ... 'An act causing death may be murder, manslaughter, or misadventure according to the degree of danger attending it' by common experience in the circumstances known to the actor." (Nash v. United States (1913) 229 U.S. 373, 377; see also Coates v. City of Cincinnati, (1971) 402 U.S. 611, 614.) The "matter of degree" that persons relying on prayer treatment must estimate rightly is the point at which their course of conduct becomes criminally negligent. In terms of notice, due process requires no more.

Hermanson, 570 So.2d at 332.

In this appeal, the Hermansons challenge the district court decision on the following four issues: (1) that the Florida Statutes under which they were convicted did not give them fair warning of the consequences of practicing their religious belief and their conviction was, therefore, a denial of due process; (2) that the Hermansons were entitled to a judgment of acquittal because the evidence presented at trial failed to establish culpable negligence beyond a reasonable doubt; (3) that permitting a jury to decide the reasonableness of the Hermansons in following their religious beliefs was a violation of the First Amendment freedom of religion; and (4) that the trial court erred in not granting a mistrial when the prosecutor stated in closing argument that Christian Science recognizes conventional medical treatment, which was not supported by any evidence in the record. We choose to discuss only the first issue because we find that it is dispositive.

Due Process

In asserting that they were denied due process, the Hermansons claim that the statutes failed to give them sufficient notice of when their treatment of their child in accordance with their religious beliefs became criminal. They argue that their position is supported by (1) the fact that it took the district court of appeal nine pages to explain how it arrived at its conclusion that the exemption for spiritual treatment was only part of the civil child abuse statute, not the criminal child abuse statute and (2) the trial court's construing the statute differently, holding that they were protected by the provision of section 415.503(7)(f) to the extent of making it a jury issue.

The United States Supreme Court, in United States v. Cardiff, 344 U.S. 174 (1952), stated that confusion in lower courts is evidence of vagueness which violates due process. Furthermore, in Linville v. State, 359 So.2d 450, 453–54 (Fla.1978), we held that due process is lacking where "a man of common intelligence cannot be expected to discern what activity the statute is seeking to proscribe." In State v. McKown, 461 N.W.2d 720 (Minn.Ct.App.1990), aff'd, 475 N.W.2d 63 (Minn.1991), cert. denied, ___ U.S.___, 112 S.Ct. 882, 116 L.Ed.2d 786 (1992), a child's parents utilized a Christian Science practitioner and a Christian Science nurse, but did not seek conventional medical treatment. The McKowns were indicted for second-degree manslaughter when their child died of untreated diabetes. The issue in that case was whether the child abuse statute, which contained an exception for spiritual treatment similar to the Florida statute, was to be construed in conjunction with a manslaughter statute that was based on culpable negligence resulting in death. In finding a violation of due process, the Minnesota court concluded that there was a "lack of clarity in the relationship between the two statutes." Id. at 723.

> [T]he state would have us conclude that the choice of spiritual treatment, which has been put on legal footing equal to that of orthodox medical care by the child neglect statute, can result in a manslaughter indictment, simply because of its outcome. That is unacceptably arbitrary, and a violation of due process.

Id. at 724. The court further stated:

> Evidence before the trial court suggests that, due to the sensitive nature of this issue, many Christian Scientists, including the McKowns, were specifically aware of the statutory provisions relating to use of spiritual means and prayer. They may have indeed "mapped out" their behavior based upon the statute. While the cases in this area are more likely to involve reliance by the defendant on administrative pronouncements, there is nothing inherent in the concept which would make it inapplicable to an argument of reliance on a specific statutory enactment. The state in this instance has attempted to take away with

the one hand—by way of criminal prosecution—that which it apparently granted with the other hand, and upon which defendants relied. This it cannot do, and meet constitutional requirements.

Id. at 724–25.

The State, in this instance, relies primarily on the decision of the Supreme Court of California in Walker. In Walker, a child died from untreated meningitis as a result of her mother's reliance on spiritual means in treating the child's illness. The mother, charged with manslaughter and felony child endangerment, argued that a religious accommodation provision found in a California misdemeanor child neglect statute, similar to chapter 415, barred her prosecution under the California manslaughter statute. The mother argued that "the statutory scheme violate[d] her right to fair notice by allowing punishment under sections 192(b) and 273(a)(1) for the same conduct that is assertedly accommodated under section 270." In rejecting this claim, the California Supreme Court explained that the statutes were clearly distinguishable and, in light of their differing objectives, the statutes could not be said to constitute inexplicably contradictory commands with respect to their respective requirements

In addressing the lack of notice claim, the State relies on the previously quoted statements in the Walker decision, particularly the conclusion that "persons relying on prayer treatment must estimate rightly" to avoid criminal prosecution because "due process requires no more." Walker, 253 Cal.Rptr. at 20–21, 763 P.2d at 871–72. Pennsylvania and Indiana have taken a similar view and rejected similar due process arguments. See Commonwealth v. Barnhart, 345 Pa.Super. 10, 497 A.2d 616 (1985), cert. denied, 488 U.S. 817 (1988); Hall v. State, 493 N.E.2d 433 (Ind.1986). The State asserts that we should also reject the Minnesota court's reasoning in McKown in part because the spiritual treatment exception in that case was contained in a criminal child abuse statute, while the provision in the Florida statute is contained in the child dependency statute.

The United States Supreme Court has stated that one of the purposes of due process is "to insure that no individual is convicted unless 'a fair warning [has first been] given to the world in language that the common world will understand, of what the law intends to do if a certain line is passed.'" Mourning v. Family Publications Serv., Inc., 411 U.S. 356 (1973) (quoting McBoyle v. United States, 283 U.S. 25, 27 (1931)). In Linville, this Court explained that a person of common intelligence must be able to determine what type of activity the statute is seeking to proscribe.

We disagree with the view of the Supreme Court of California in Walker that, in considering the application of this type of religious accommodation statute, persons relying on the statute and its allowance for prayer as treatment are granted only the opportunity to guess rightly with regard to their utilization of spiritual treatment. In commenting on this type of situation, one author has stated: "By authorizing conduct in one statute, but declaring that same conduct criminal under another statute, the State trapped the Hermansons, who had no fair warning that the State would consider their conduct criminal." Christine A. Clark, Religious

Accommodation and Criminal Liability, 17 Fla.St.U.L.Rev. 559, 585 (1990) (footnotes omitted). We agree.

To say that the statutes in question establish a line of demarcation at which a person of common intelligence would know his or her conduct is or is not criminal ignores the fact that, not only did the judges of both the circuit court and the district court of appeal have difficulty understanding the interrelationship of the statutes in question, but, as indicated by their questions, the jurors also had problems understanding what was required.

In this instance, we conclude that the legislature has failed to clearly indicate the point at which a parent's reliance on his or her religious beliefs in the treatment of his or her children becomes criminal conduct. If the legislature desires to provide for religious accommodation while protecting the children of the state, the legislature must clearly indicate when a parent's conduct becomes criminal. As stated by another commentator: "Whatever choices are made . . . both the policy and the letter of the law should be clear and clearly stated, so that those who believe in healing by prayer rather than medical treatment are aware of the potential liabilities they may incur." Catherine W. Laughran, Comment, Religious Beliefs and the Criminal Justice System: Some Problems of the Faith Healer, 8 Loy.L.A.L.Rev. 396, 431 (1975).

Accordingly, for the reasons expressed, we quash the decision of the district court of appeal and remand this case with directions that the trial court's adjudication of guilt and sentence be vacated and the petitioners discharged.

NOTES

Walker v. Superior Court. The *Walker* case, 47 Cal.3d 112, 253 Cal.Rptr. 1, 763 P.2d 852 (1988), *cert. denied* 491 U.S. 905, 109 S.Ct. 3186, 105 L.Ed.2d 695 (1989), discussed but not followed by the Florida Supreme Court in *Hermanson*, carefully detailed the legislative provisions of California law that contained a religious exception in some statutes but not in those for involuntary manslaughter and felony child endangerment. After explaining that imposing felony liability for failure to seek medical care for a seriously ill child is justified by a compelling state interest, the court added that even so, to survive a First Amendment challenge the policy also must represent "the least restrictive alternative available to the state." They pointed out that:

> Defendant and the Church argue that civil dependency proceedings advance the governmental interest in a far less intrusive manner. This is not evident. First, we have already observed the profoundly intrusive nature of such proceedings; it is not clear that parents would prefer to lose custody of their children pursuant to a disruptive and invasive judicial inquiry than to face privately the prospect of criminal liability. Second, child dependency proceedings advance the governmental interest only when the state learns of a child's illness in time to take protective measures, which quite likely will be the exception rather

than the rule.... Finally, the imposition of criminal liability is reserved for the actual loss or endangerment of a child's life and thus is narrowly tailored to those instances when governmental intrusion is absolutely compelled.

We conclude that an adequately effective and less restrictive alternative is not available to further the state's compelling interest in assuring the provision of medical care to gravely ill children whose parents refuse such treatment on religious grounds. Accordingly, the First Amendment and its California equivalent do not bar defendant's criminal prosecution.

Accordingly, the court held that prosecution of the defendant for involuntary manslaughter and felony child endangerment did not violate statutory law or either the California or federal Constitution. In a separate concurring opinion, Justice Mosk notes that the majority chose not to reach the Attorney General's contention that extending the religious exemption of § 270 to the felony prosecution "would import into the proceeding a defense that offends the establishment clauses of the state and federal Constitutions." 47 Cal.3d 112, 253 Cal.Rptr. 1, 763 P.2d 852, at 873. Noting that the issue had been "timely raised and thoroughly briefed, and its importance is manifest", he expresses the view that "the statutory exemption as it now reads plainly violates the establishment clauses." Justice Broussard, in a separate dissenting and concurring opinion, states that he would direct the Court of Appeal to grant the writ of prohibition insofar as it seeks dismissal of the § 723a charge and deny it as to dismissal of the manslaughter charge.

If a state chooses to have no religious exemptions in any of its neglect, dependency or felony child endangerment statutes, would this make a difference with regard to a defense of vagueness?

The state as monitor. In Matter of Appeal in Cochise County, 133 Ariz. 157, 650 P.2d 459 (1982), the Supreme Court of Arizona was called on to determine whether there was sufficient evidence to justify "state interference with the fundamental right of a parent to the custody and control of his or her child, particularly to 'monitor' the health of the child when there is known medical danger and when providing medical care is contrary to the parent's religious beliefs." After the death of one of her children through septicemia and peritonitis secondary to a strangulated inguinal hernia, the mother explained to Department of Economic Security (D.E.S.) case workers that "she had faith that miracles would safeguard her children" and that she would not seek medical help if any of her other seven children became ill. A juvenile court judge declined to find the children "dependent" in light of their otherwise seemingly satisfactory home life, but that decision was reversed by the Court of Appeals. The latter based its finding of present abuse on the threatened passive conduct of the mother in possibly failing to provide medical care in the future. The Supreme Court, reversing the intermediate appellate court, noted that the cases cited in justification of their decision were distinguishable because they upheld state intervention in cases in which there was present rather than future need of medical attention. However, the Supreme Court emphasized that the state continued to maintain broad supervisory powers and that the D.E.S. could "keep a close eye" on the children's progress. Also, it might be prompted to investigate further based on something less than would be required in a more typical situation.

Newmark v. Williams

Supreme Court of Delaware, 1991.
588 A.2d 1108.

■ MOORE, JUSTICE.

Colin Newmark,[1] a three year old child, faced death from a deadly aggressive and advanced form of pediatric cancer known as Burkitt's Lymphoma. We were presented with a clash of interests between medical science, Colin's tragic plight, the unquestioned sincerity of his parents' religious beliefs as Christian Scientists, and the legal right of the State to protect dependent children from perceived neglect when medical treatment is withheld on religious grounds. The Delaware Division of Child Protective Services ("DCPS") petitioned the Family Court for temporary custody of Colin to authorize the Alfred I. duPont Institute ("duPont Institute"), a nationally recognized children's hospital, to treat Colin's condition with chemotherapy. His parents, Morris and Kara Newmark, are well educated and economically prosperous. As members of the First Church of Christ, Scientist ("Christian Science") they rejected medical treatment proposed for Colin, preferring instead a course of spiritual aid and prayer.[2] The parents rely upon provisions of Delaware law, which exempt those who treat their children's illnesses "solely by spiritual means" from the abuse and neglect statutes. Thus, they opposed the State's petition. See 10 Del.C. § 901(11) & 16 Del.C. § 907 (emphasis added). The Newmarks also claimed that removing Colin from their custody would violate their First Amendment right, guaranteed under the United States Constitution, to freely exercise their religion.

The Family Court rejected both of these arguments and awarded custody of Colin to DCPS. The trial court, however, issued a stay permitting the Newmarks to file an immediate appeal to this Court.

---

1. We have used pseudonyms to protect the privacy of Colin and his family.

2. Mary Baker Eddy, the founder of the Christian Science Church, professed a deep belief in spirituality. She preached that sickness was a manifestation of a diseased mind. See Eddy, Sermon Subject Christian Science Healing 7–8 (Pamphlet 1886). Eddy therefore claimed that "[m]edicine will not arrive at the Science of treating disease until disease is treated mentally and man is healed morally and physically." Id. at 17. Accordingly, Christian Scientists do not treat most sicknesses with medical care. Rather, they rely on prac-

titioners who administer spiritual aid. See Schneider, Christian Science and the Law: Room for Compromise? 1 Colum.J.L. & Soc. Probs. 81, 81 (1965). Eddy also believed that childhood illnesses were more manifestations of their parents' own spiritual infirmities. She reasoned that "[t]he law of mortal mind and [parents'] own fears govern [their] own child more than the child's mind governs itself and they produce the very results which might have been prevented through the opposite." M. EDDY, SCIENCE AND HEALTH WITH KEY TO THE SCRIPTURES 154 (1934).

We heard this appeal on an emergency basis. After argument on September 14, 1990, we issued an order reversing the Family Court and returned custody of Colin to his parents. At that time we noted that this more detailed opinion would follow in due course.

We have concluded that Colin was not an abused or neglected child under Delaware law. Parents enjoy a well established legal right to make important decisions for their children. Although this right is not absolute, the State has the burden of proving by clear and convincing evidence that intervening in the parent-child relationship is necessary to ensure the safety or health of the child, or to protect the public at large. DCPS did not meet this heavy burden. This is especially true where the purpose of the custody petition was to administer, over the objections of Colin's parents, an extremely risky, toxic and dangerously life threatening medical treatment offering less than a 40% chance for "success".

I.

Colin was the youngest of the three Newmark children. In late August, 1990, the Newmarks noticed that he had lost most of his appetite and was experiencing frequent vomiting. The symptoms at first appeared occasionally but soon worsened. The Newmarks reluctantly took Colin to the duPont Institute for examination. The parties stipulated that this violated the Newmarks' Christian Science beliefs in the effectiveness of spiritual healing. The parties further stipulated that the Newmarks acted out of concern for their potential criminal liability, citing a Massachusetts case which held parents liable for manslaughter for foregoing medical treatment and treating their minor child only in accordance with Christian Science tenets.

Dr. Charles L. Minor, a duPont Institute staff pediatric surgeon, examined Colin and ordered X-rays of his stomach. Dr. Minor found the X-rays inconclusive and suggested that Colin remain at the hospital for further testing. The Newmarks refused and took Colin home. Colin remained at home for approximately one week while receiving treatments under the care of a Christian Science practitioner. Colin's symptoms nonetheless quickly reappeared and the Newmarks returned him to the hospital.

Dr. Minor ordered a second set of X-rays and this time discovered an obstruction in Colin's intestines. The doctor suggested immediate surgery and, again, the Newmarks consented. The Newmarks considered the procedure "mechanical" and therefore believed that it did not violate their religious beliefs.

During the operation, Dr. Minor discovered a large mass 10 to 15 centimeters wide connecting Colin's large and small bowels. He also noticed that some of Colin's lymph nodes were unusually large. Dr. Minor removed the mass and submitted tissue samples for a pathological report. There were no complications from the surgery and Colin was recovering "well."

The pathology report confirmed that Colin was suffering from a non-Hodgkins Lymphoma. Five pathologists from Children's Hospital, Philadelphia, Pennsylvania, confirmed the diagnosis. Dr. Minor, after receiving the pathology report, contacted Dr. Rita Meek, a board certified pediatric hematologist-oncologist and an attending physician at the duPont Institute.

Dr. Meek ordered two blood tests which indicated the presence of elevated levels of uric acid and LHD in Colin's system. The presence of these chemicals indicated that the disease had spread. Dr. Meek then conducted an external examination and detected a firm mass growing above Colin's right testicle. She diagnosed Colin's condition as Burkitt's Lymphoma, an aggressive pediatric cancer.[3] The doctor recommended that the hospital treat Colin with a heavy regimen of chemotherapy.

Dr. Meek opined that the chemotherapy offered a 40% chance of "curing" Colin's illness. She concluded that he would die within six to eight months without treatment. The Newmarks, learning of Colin's condition only after the surgery, advised Dr. Meek that they would place him under the care of a Christian Science practitioner and reject all medical treatment for their son. Accordingly, they refused to authorize the chemotherapy. There was no doubt that the Newmarks sincerely believed, as part of their religious beliefs, that the tenets of their faith provided an effective treatment.

II.

We start with an overview of the relevant Delaware statutory provisions. Delaware law defines a neglected child as: [A] child whose physical, mental or emotional health and well-being is threatened or impaired because of inadequate care and protection by the child's custodian, who has the ability and financial means to provide for the care but does not or will not provide adequate care; or a child who has been abused or neglected as defined by § 902 of Title 16. 10 Del.C. § 901(11). Section 902 further defines abuse and neglect as: [P]hysical injury by other than accidental means, injury resulting in a mental or emotional condition which is a result of abuse or neglect, negligent treatment, sexual abuse, maltreatment, mistreatment, nontreatment, exploitation or abandonment, of a child under the age of 18. Sections of the Delaware Code, however, contain spiritual treatment exemptions which directly affect Christian Scientists. Specifically, the exemptions state: No child who in good faith is under treatment solely by spiritual means through prayer in accordance with the tenets and practices of a recognized church or religious denomination by a duly accredited practitioner thereof shall for that reason alone be considered a neglected child for purposes of this chapter. 10 Del.C. § 901(11) & 16 Del.C. § 907. These exceptions reflect the intention of the Delaware General Assembly to provide a "safe harbor" for parents, like the Newmarks, to pursue their own religious beliefs. This is evident from the limited legislative history available on the subject.

---

3. Dr. Meek testified that Burkitt's Lymphoma cancer cells double more rapidly than any other form of pediatric cancer which inevitably results in a fast growing tumor.

As originally enacted in 1972, one of the spiritual healing exemptions appeared in the child abuse reporting section of the Code, under the general heading of "Immunity from liability." The statute included both the spiritual treatment exemption and an immunity provision applicable to reporting child abuse. See 58 Del. Laws 154 (1972). The General Assembly later amended this section of the Code in 1976 and placed the spiritual treatment exemption under a separate heading entitled "Child Under Treatment By Spiritual Means Not Neglected." See 60 Del. Laws 494 (1976); 16 Del.C. s 907. The amendment reflects the legislature's apparent intent to clarify the meaning of the exemption and to magnify its importance. The accuracy of this conclusion is less in doubt after considering the legislative history of the other identical exemption.

The General Assembly also amended the meaning of a "neglected child" in the section of the Code dealing with the Family Court. See 10 Del.C. § 901(11). The statute originally defined a neglected child as one "whose custodian refuses to provide him with adequate care." 58 Del. Laws 114 (1971). In 1978, the legislature changed the definition of a "neglected child" to include the spiritual treatment exemption found in 16 Del.C. § 907. See 61 Del. Laws 334 (1978). The amendment clearly reflects the General Assembly's intent to provide protection for parents who treat their children through statutorily defined spiritual means. Accordingly, our ruling from the bench noted that the spiritual treatment exemptions reflect, in part, "[t]he policy of this State with respect to the quality of life" a desperately ill child might have in the caring and loving atmosphere of his or her family, versus the sterile hospital environment demanded by physicians seeking to prescribe excruciating, and life threatening, treatments of doubtful efficacy.

With the considerable reflection that time has now permitted us in examining these issues, we recognize the possibility that the spiritual treatment exemptions[4] may violate the ban against the establishment of an official State religion guaranteed under both the Federal and Delaware Constitutions. Clearly, in both reality and practical effect, the language providing an exemption only to those individuals practicing "in accordance" with the "practices of a recognized church or religious denomination by a duly accredited practitioner thereof" is intended for the principal benefit of Christian Scientists.[7] Our concern is that it possibly forces us to

---

4. We express no view, and indeed, this case does not concern the good faith healing defense contained in the Delaware Criminal Code. See 11 Del.C. § 1104.

7. The terminology used in the spiritual treatment exemption indicates that the statute was enacted as a result of a Christian Science lobbying effort. See In Child Deaths, a Test for Christian Science, N.Y. Times, Aug. 6, 1990, at 1, col. 2 (exemptions to neglect statutes passed at behest of Christian Science Church in forty state legislatures).

Specifically, the requirement that a person must be a "duly accredited practitioner" mirrors the Christian Science belief that only "practitioners" receiving approval from the Christian Science Mother Church can conduct spiritual healing. See Schneider, Christian Science and the Law: Room for Compromise?, 1 Colum.J.L. & Soc.Probs. 81, 81 (1965); see also Walker v. Super. Ct. Sacramento Co., 47 Cal.3d 112, 147–48, 763 P.2d 852, 875, 253 Cal.Rptr. 1, 24 (1988) (Mosk, J., concurring), cert. denied, 491 U.S. 905, 109

impermissibly determine the validity of an individual's own religious beliefs.[8]

Neither party challenged the constitutionality of the spiritual treatment exemptions in either the Family Court or on appeal. Thus, except to recognize that the issue is far more complicated than was originally presented to us, we must leave such questions for another day.

III.

Addressing the facts of this case, we turn to the novel legal question whether, under any circumstances, Colin was a neglected child when his parents refused to accede to medical demands that he receive a radical form of chemotherapy having only a forty percent chance of success. Other jurisdictions differ in their approaches to this important and intensely personal issue. Some courts resolved the question on an ad hoc basis, without a formal test, concluding that a child was neglected if the parents refused to administer chemotherapy in a life threatening situation. See In re Willmann, 24 Ohio App.3d 191, 199, 493 N.E.2d 1380, 1389 (1986); In re Hamilton, 657 S.W.2d 425, 429 (Tenn.Ct.App.1983). The California Court of Appeals in In re Ted B., 189 Cal.App.3d 996, 235 Cal.Rptr. 22 (1987), employed the best interests test to determine if a child was neglected when his parents refused to permit treatment of his cancer with "mild" chemotherapy following more intense treatment. Id. at 1006, 235 Cal.Rptr. at 27. Ted B. weighed the gravity, or potential gravity of the child's illness, the

S.Ct. 3186, 105 L.Ed.2d 695 (1989) (Christian Scientists sponsored spiritual treatment exception to abuse and neglect law in California and therefore it is "more than a fortuity that the word 'practitioner'" appears in California spiritual healing statute). The influence of the Church of Christ Scientist on the Delaware exemptions is also apparent when those statutes are compared with the federal spiritual healing exemption, which the Department of Health, Education and Welfare ("HEW") adopted in response to the Child Abuse Prevention and Treatment Act of 1974. See 45 C.F.R. s§ 1340.1 (1990). The federal regulation provides that "[n]othing in this part should be construed as requiring or prohibiting a finding of negligent treatment or maltreatment when a parent practicing his or her religious beliefs does not, for that reason alone, provide medical treatment for a child...." 45 C.F.R. s 1340.2(d)(2)(ii) (1990). (Emphasis added). The states were required to enact statutes similar to the HEW regulations to qualify for federal funds. See Comment, Faith Healing and Religious Treatment Exemptions To Child Endangerment Laws: Should Parental Religious Practices Excuse The Failure To Provide Necessary Medical Care To Children?, 13 U.Dayton L.Rev. 79,

96 (1987) (written by LeClair). Tellingly, the statute the General Assembly enacted to adopt the Child Abuse Prevention and Treatment Act of 1974 in Delaware merely incorporated the prior version of the Delaware exemption including the language "duly accredited practitioner" and "recognized religion." See 16 Del.C. s 907; 60 Del.Laws 494 (1976) (synopsis). It is perhaps more than coincidental that the legislature merely carried over the exemption without amending it to conform with the new federal regulations. Certainly, any statute passed as the result of the efforts of one religious group to benefit that one particular group to the exclusion of others bears a strong presumption against its validity as a direct violation of the Establishment Clause.

8. At least one state has ruled that a statutory exemption to a criminal abuse and neglect statute, containing identical language as the Delaware statutes, violated both the Establishment Clause and the Equal Protection Clause of the Fourteenth Amendment. See State v. Miskimens, 22 Ohio Misc.2d 43, 43–46, 490 N.E.2d 931, 933–936 (Ohio Ct. Com.Pl.1984)....

treating physician's medical evaluation of the course of care, the riskiness of the treatment and the child's "expressed preferences" to ultimately judge whether his parents' decision to withhold chemotherapy served his "best interests." Finally, the Supreme Judicial Court of Massachusetts, in Custody Of A Minor, 375 Mass. 733, 379 N.E.2d 1053 (1978), utilized a tripartite balancing test which weighed the interests of the parents, their child and the State to determine whether a child was neglected when his parents refused to treat his leukemia with non-invasive chemotherapy.

In the present case, the Family Court did not undertake any formal interest analysis in deciding that Colin was a neglected child under Delaware law. Instead, the trial court used the same ad hoc approach as the Ohio and Tennessee courts respectively employed in Willmann and Hamilton. Specifically, the Family Court rejected the Newmarks' proposal to treat Colin by spiritual means under the care of a Christian Science practitioner. The trial judge considered spiritual treatment an inadequate alternative to chemotherapy. The court therefore concluded that "[w]ithout any other factually supported alternative" the Newmarks' decision to refuse chemotherapy "constitute[d] inadequate parental care for their son who is in a life threatening situation and constitute[d] neglect as defined in the Delaware statute."

This Court reviews the trial court's application of legal precepts involving issues of law de novo. While we do not recognize the primacy of any one of the tests employed in other jurisdictions, we find that the trial court erred in not explicitly considering the competing interests at stake. The Family Court failed to consider the special importance and primacy of the familial relationship, including the autonomy of parental decision making authority over minor children. The trial court also did not consider the gravity of Colin's illness in conjunction with the invasiveness of the proposed chemotherapy and the considerable likelihood of failure. These factors, when applied to the facts of this case, strongly militate against governmental intrusion.

A.

Any balancing test must begin with the parental interest. The primacy of the familial unit is a bedrock principle of law. See Stanley v. Illinois, 405 U.S. 645, 651 (1972) (citing cases); . . . ("State and society in general have a fundamental interest in preserving and protecting the family unit."); . . . We have repeatedly emphasized that the parental right is sacred which can be invaded for only the most compelling reasons. Indeed, the Delaware General Assembly has stated that the preservation of the family is "fundamental to the maintenance of a stable, democratic society. . . ." 10 Del.C. § 902(a); see 16 Del.C. § 901 (abuse, neglect reporting statute designed to ensure strength of "parental care.")

Courts have also recognized that the essential element of preserving the integrity of the family is maintaining the autonomy of the parent-child relationship. In Prince v. Commonwealth of Massachusetts, 321 U.S. 158, 166 reh'g denied, 321 U.S. 804 (1944), the United States Supreme Court announced: It is cardinal with us that the custody, care and nurture of the child reside first in the parents, whose primary function and freedom include preparation for obligations the state can neither supply nor hinder. Parental autonomy to care for children free from government interference therefore satisfies a child's need for continuity and thus ensures his or her psychological and physical well-being.

Parental authority to make fundamental decisions for minor children is also a recognized common law principle. A doctor commits the tort of battery if he or she performs an operation under normal circumstances without the informed consent of the patient. Tort law also assumes that a child does not have the capacity to consent to an operation in most situations. Thus, the common law recognizes that the only party capable of authorizing medical treatment for a minor in "normal" circumstances is usually his parent or guardian.

Courts, therefore, give great deference to parental decisions involving minor children. In many circumstances the State simply is not an adequate surrogate for the judgment of a loving, nurturing parent. See Baskin, supra, at 1386. As one commentator aptly recognized, the "law does not have the capacity to supervise the delicately complex interpersonal bonds between parent and child."

B.

We also recognize that parental autonomy over minor children is not an absolute right. Clearly, the State can intervene in the parent-child relationship where the health and safety of the child and the public at large are in jeopardy. Accordingly, the State, under the doctrine of parens patriae, has a special duty to protect its youngest and most helpless citizens.

The parens patriae doctrine is a derivation of the common law giving the State the right to act on behalf of minor children in certain property and marital disputes. See In Re Hudson, 13 Wash.2d 673, 126 P.2d 765, 777 (1942). More recently, courts have accepted the doctrine of parens patriae to justify State intervention in cases of parental religious objections to medical treatment of minor children's life threatening conditions. The Supreme Court of the United States succinctly described the parens patriae concept in Prince, 321 U.S. at 170, 64 S.Ct. at 444. The Court found that parental autonomy, under the guise of the parents' religious freedom, was not unlimited. Rather, the Court held: Parents may be free to become martyrs themselves. But it does not follow they are free, in identical circumstances, to make martyrs of their children before they have reached the age of full and legal discretion when they can make that choice for themselves.

The basic principle underlying the parens patriae doctrine is the State's interest in preserving human life. See Cruzan v. Director, Missouri Dept. of Health, 497 U.S. 261, 110 S.Ct. 2841, 2853, 111 L.Ed.2d 224 (1990) (State may "assert an unqualified interest in the preservation of human life...."); Custody Of A Minor, 375 Mass at 755, 379 N.E.2d at 1066. Yet this interest and the parens patriae doctrine are not unlimited. In its recent Cruzan opinion, the Supreme Court of the United States announced that the state's interest in preserving life must "be weighed against the constitutionally protected interests of the individual." 497 U.S. 261, 110 S.Ct. 2841, 2853 (1990).

The individual interests at stake here include both the Newmarks' right to decide what is best for Colin and Colin's own right to life. We have already considered the Newmarks' stake in this case and its relationship to the parens patriae doctrine. The resolution of the issues here, however, is incomplete without a discussion of Colin's interests.

C.

All children indisputably have the right to enjoy a full and healthy life. Colin, a three year old boy, unfortunately lacked the ability to reach a detached, informed decision regarding his own medical care.[9] This Court must therefore substitute its own objective judgment to determine what is in Colin's "best interests."

There are two basic inquiries when a dispute involves chemotherapy treatment over parents' religious objections. The court must first consider the effectiveness of the treatment and determine the child's chances of survival with and without medical care. The court must then consider the nature of the treatments and their effect on the child.

The "best interests" analysis is hardly unique or novel. Federal and State courts have unhesitatingly authorized medical treatment over a parent's religious objection when the treatment is relatively innocuous in comparison to the dangers of withholding medical care.... [C]ourts are reluctant to authorize medical care over parental objection when the child is not suffering a life threatening or potential life threatening illness. See In re Green, 448 Pa. 338, 348–49, 292 A.2d 387, 392 (1972) (court refused to authorize corrective spine surgery on minor); In re Seiferth, 309 N.Y. 80, 85–86, 127 N.E.2d 820, 823 (1955) (no authorization to correct cleft palate and harelip on fourteen year old minor); but cf. In re Sampson, 65 Misc.2d 658, 675–76, 317 N.Y.S.2d 641, 657–58 (N.Y.Fam.Ct.1970), aff'd, 29 N.Y.2d 900, 328 N.Y.S.2d 686, 278 N.E.2d 918 (1972) (authorizing corrective surgery on minor where parents' only objection was blood transfusion).

---

9. Other jurisdictions have respected and upheld a minor's decision regarding his own medical care only when the child presented clear and convincing evidence that he was mature enough to exercise an adult's judgment and understood the consequences of his decision. See, e.g., In re E.G., 133 Ill.2d 98, 103, 139 Ill.Dec. 810, 815–16, 549 N.E.2d 322, 327–28 (1989); cf. In re Application of L.I. Jewish Med. Ctr., 147 Misc.2d at 730, 557 N.Y.S.2d at 243. Although we decline to comment on the applicability of the "mature minor doctrine" under Delaware law, it is doubtful that even the most precocious three year old could meet the standard. Yet, while not dispositive, there was evidence that Colin overheard some hospital discussion about treating him with chemotherapy. His reaction was one of fright that the proposed treatment would "kill" him. Thus, even at his young age, Colin was able to perceive the very real dangers of the treatment. Given the admittedly poor odds of its success, Colin's fear of chemotherapy was not unjustified.

The linchpin in all cases discussing the "best interests of a child", when a parent refuses to authorize medical care, is an evaluation of the risk of the procedure compared to its potential success. This analysis is consistent with the principle that State intervention in the parent-child relationship is only justifiable under compelling conditions. The State's interest in forcing a minor to undergo medical care diminishes as the risks of treatment increase and its benefits decrease.

The New Jersey Supreme Court implicitly recognized this principle in the seminal Quinlan case decided over a decade ago. See In re Quinlan, 70 N.J. 10, 355 A.2d 647, cert. denied, 429 U.S. 922 (1976). In deciding that a legal custodian could authorize the termination of artificial life support in certain circumstances, Quinlan noted that: [T]he State's interest contra weakens and the individual's right to privacy grows as the degree of bodily invasion increases and the prognosis dims. Ultimately there comes a point at which the individual's rights overcome the State interest. It is for that reason that we believe Karen's choice, if she were competent to make it, would be vindicated by the law. Her prognosis is extremely poor,—she will never resume cognitive life. And the bodily invasion is very great,—she requires 24 hour intensive nursing care, antibiotics, the assistance of a respirator, a catheter and feeding tube. Similarly, most courts which have authorized medical treatment on a minor over parental objection have also noted that a different situation exists when the treatment is inherently dangerous and invasive. See, e.g., In re Cabrera, 381 Pa.Super. at 111, 552 A.2d at 1119; Muhlenberg Hospital, 128 N.J.Super. at 503, 320 A.2d at 521 ("if the disputed procedure involved a significant danger to the infant, the parents' wishes would be respected."); Perricone, 37 N.J. at 479–80, 181 A.2d at 760 (strong argument for parents if "there were substantial evidence that the treatment itself posed a significant danger to the infant's life"); Labrenz, 411 Ill. at 624–25, 104 N.E.2d at 773 (same); In re Hudson, 126 P.2d at 777 (court not permitted to authorize treatment "which would probably result in merciful release by death from [minor's] physical . . . handicap.").

Applying the foregoing considerations to the "best interests standard" here, the State's petition must be denied. The egregious facts of this case indicate that Colin's proposed medical treatment was highly invasive, painful, involved terrible temporary and potentially permanent side effects, posed an unacceptably low chance of success, and a high risk that the treatment itself would cause his death. The State's authority to intervene in this case, therefore, cannot outweigh the Newmarks' parental prerogative and Colin's inherent right to enjoy at least a modicum of human dignity in the short time that was left to him.

IV.

Dr. Meek originally diagnosed Colin's condition as Burkitt's Lymphoma. She testified that the cancer was "a very bad tumor" in an advanced disseminated state and not localized to only one section of the body. She accordingly recommended that the hospital begin an "extremely intensive" chemotherapy program scheduled to extend for at least six months.

The first step necessary to prepare Colin for chemotherapy involved an intravenous hydration treatment. This process, alone, posed a significant risk that Colin's kidneys would fail. Indeed, these intravenous treatments had already begun and were threatening Colin's life while the parties were arguing the case to us on September 14, 1990. Thus, if Colin's kidneys failed he also would have to undergo dialysis treatments. There also was a possibility that renal failure could occur during the chemotherapy treatments themselves. In addition, Dr. Meek recommended further pretreatment diagnostic tests including a spinal tap and a CAT scan.

Dr. Meek prescribed "maximum" doses of at least six different types of cancer-fighting drugs during Colin's chemotherapy. This proposed "maximum" treatment represented the most aggressive form of cancer therapy short of a bone marrow transplant. The side effects would include hair loss, reduced immunological function creating a high risk of infection in the patient, and certain neurological problems. The drugs also are toxic to bone marrow.

The record demonstrates that this form of chemotherapy also would adversely affect other parts of Colin's body. Dr. Meek stated that the doctors would have to administer the treatments through injections in the veins and spinal fluid. The chemotherapy would reduce Colin's white blood count, and it would be extremely likely that he would suffer numerous infections. Colin would require multiple blood transfusions with a resultant additional risk of infection.

The treating physicians also would have to install a catheter in Colin's chest to facilitate a constant barrage of tests and treatments. Colin also would receive food through the catheter because the chemotherapy would depress his appetite. The operation to set the catheter in place would take approximately one hour. The doctors proposed to perform biopsies on both Colin's bone marrow and the lump in his groin during the procedure.

The physicians planned to administer the chemotherapy in cycles, each of which would bring Colin near death. Then they would wait until Colin's body recovered sufficiently before introducing more drugs. Dr. Meek opined that there was no guarantee that drugs alone would "cure" Colin's illness. The doctor noted that it would then be necessary to radiate Colin's testicles if drugs alone were unsuccessful. Presumably, this would have rendered him sterile.

Dr. Meek also wanted the State to place Colin in a foster home after the initial phases of hospital treatment. Children require intensive home monitoring during chemotherapy. For example, Dr. Meek testified that a usually low grade fever for a healthy child could indicate the presence of a potentially deadly infection in a child cancer patient. She believed that the Newmarks, although well educated and financially responsible, were incapable of providing this intensive care because of their firm religious objections to medical treatment.[10]

Dr. Meek ultimately admitted that there was a real possibility that the chemotherapy could kill Colin. In fact, assuming the treatment did not itself prove fatal, she offered Colin at "best" a 40% chance[11] that he would "survive."[12] Dr. Meek additionally could not accurately predict whether, if Colin completed the therapy, he would subsequently suffer additional tumors.

A.

No American court, even in the most egregious case, has ever authorized the State to remove a child from the loving, nurturing care of his parents and subject him, over parental objection, to an invasive regimen of treatment which offered, as Dr. Meek defined the term, only a forty percent chance of "survival." For example, the California Court of Appeals ruled in Eric B., that the State could conduct various procedures as part of an "observation phase" of chemotherapy over the objection of his parents. 189 Cal.App.3d at 1008–1009, 235 Cal.Rptr. at 29. The treatment included bone scans, CT scans, spinal taps and biopsies. The court specifically found that "[t]he risks entailed by the monitoring are minimal." The court also noted that the child would enjoy a 60% chance of survival with the treatments.

The Tennessee Court of Appeals awarded custody of a minor suffering from Ewing's Sarcoma to the State after her parents refused to treat the cancer with medical care. See In re Hamilton, 657 S.W.2d at 429. The child in that case enjoyed an at least 80% chance of temporary remission and a 25%–50% opportunity for long-term "cure". The court specifically noted that various hospitals had successfully treated Ewing's Sarcoma in "a significant number of patients." There was no testimony in Hamilton, however, concerning the magnitude of the proposed chemotherapy.

The Supreme Judicial Court of Massachusetts took custody away from parents who refused to administer "mild" cancer fighting drugs after the child had already undergone more "vigorous" treatment. See Custody of a Minor, 375 Mass. at 755–56, 379 N.E.2d at 1058, 1067. The trial judge, in that case, specifically found that aside from some minor side effects, including stomach cramps and constipation, the chemotherapy "bore no chance of leaving the child physically incapacitated in any way." The trial

---

10. A doctor in a recent related case in Connecticut involving state intervention over a mother's decision to treat her minor child with traditional Chinese remedies rather than "conventional surgery" remarked that " '[i]f you do something where you need the cooperation of the entire family for the child to get better, when it's against the family's wishes your probability of success is vastly reduced.' " N.Y. Times, Dec. 13, 1990, at B5, col. 1.

11. Dr. Meek based her estimate on "historical" data compiled from children who have suffered from Burkitt's Lymphoma.

12. Dr. Meek testified that there was no available medical data to conclude that Colin could survive to adulthood. Rather, she stated that the term "survival", as applied to victims of leukemia or lymphoma, refers only to the probability that the patient will live two years after chemotherapy without a recurrence of cancer.

court also ruled that the chemotherapy gave the child not only a chance to enjoy a long life "but also a 'substantial' chance for cure."

The Ohio Court of Appeals awarded custody of a minor suffering from Osteogenic Sarcoma to the state when his parents consented to chemotherapy, but later refused to authorize an operation to partially remove his shoulder and entire left arm. In re Willmann, 24 Ohio App.3d at 193, 199, 493 N.E.2d at 1383, 1390. Although amputation is ultimately the most invasive type of surgery, there was at least a 60% chance in Willmann that the child would survive with the operation. The court also significantly noted that the child remained at home while receiving the lower court's mandated chemotherapy treatments.

Finally, the New York Supreme Court most recently ruled that the State could intervene and order chemotherapy treatments over a parent's religious objections when the medical care presented a 75% chance of short-term remission but only a 25–30% chance for "cure." See In re Application of L.I. Jewish Med. Ctr., 147 Misc.2d at 725, 557 N.Y.S.2d at 241. The seventeen year old minor in that case suffered from an advanced case of Rhabdomyosarcoma, a type of pediatric cancer affecting potential muscle tissue. This case, however, is not dispositive given the fact that the parents were not wholly opposed to chemotherapy.

The minor and his parents in L.I. Jewish Med. Ctr., were both members of the Jehovah's Witnesses religion and only objected to blood transfusions which were an incidental part of the prescribed medical treatment. There was no evidence that either party objected to the chemotherapy, which included radiation treatments. The treatments were also probably "radical" in nature given the fact that the disease had spread throughout the child's body. This New York decision is therefore in perfect accord with other well-established precedent. Courts have consistently authorized state intervention when parents object to only minimally intrusive treatment which poses little or no risk to a child's health. See supra Part III.C.

B.

The aggressive form of chemotherapy that Dr. Meek prescribed for Colin was more likely to fail than succeed. The proposed treatment was also highly invasive and could have independently caused Colin's death. Dr. Meek also wanted to take Colin away from his parents and family during the treatment phase and place the boy in a foster home. This certainly would have caused Colin severe emotional difficulties given his medical condition, tender age, and the unquestioned close bond between Colin and his family.

In sum, Colin's best interests were served by permitting the Newmarks to retain custody of their child. Parents must have the right at some point to reject medical treatment for their child. Under all of the circumstances here, this clearly is such a case. The State's important and legitimate role in safeguarding the interests of minor children diminishes in the face of this egregious record.

Parents undertake an awesome responsibility in raising and caring for their children. No doubt a parent's decision to withhold medical care is both deeply personal and soul wrenching. It need not be made worse by the invasions which both the State and medical profession sought on this record. Colin's ultimate fate therefore rested with his parents and their faith.[13]

The judgment of the Family Court is, REVERSED.

TREATMENT FOR CHILDREN IN LIFE THREATENING CIRCUM-STANCES

The Blood Transfusion Cases. Usually the cases involve disputes between parent and state about whether medical treatment should be given to a child. The "life threatening" exception developed largely through cases involving parental opposition to blood transfusions. Despite the religious basis for such objections, courts asserted their authority and willingness to intervene to protect the life of a child. *See, e.g.*, People ex rel. Wallace v. Labrenz, 104 N.E.2d 769 (Ill.1952); State v. Perricone, 181 A.2d 751 (N.J.1962). In Raleigh Fitkin–Paul Morgan Memorial Hospital v. Anderson, 201 A.2d 537 (N.J.1964), the New Jersey Supreme Court held that blood transfusions might be administered to a pregnant mother against her wishes for the purpose of saving the life of the unborn child. The Nebraska Supreme Court upheld a state law that required a blood test for newborns, holding that such a law does not violate a parent's right of free exercise when the parent opposes the test on religious grounds. The court held that the blood test was rationally related to the state's interest in preventing the spread of disease and is a neutral requirement of general applicability. Douglas County v. Anaya, 694 N.W. 2d 601 (Neb. 2005).

The Choice of Therapy Cases. One of the more widely publicized cases involving the clash between the state and a child's parents over choice of medical care involved Chad Green, a minor afflicted with acute lymphocytic leukemia. In Custody of a Minor, 379 N.E.2d 1053 (Mass. 1978), the Supreme Judicial Court of Massachusetts, after a fairly elaborate explanation of the interests of the child, parent and state which must be balanced in making such a decision, determined that an order removing legal (but not physical) custody of the child from the parents was warranted under the circumstances. Key to the decision were findings that leukemia is fatal in children if untreated and that the risk of chemotherapy (the only medical treatment considered to offer a hope for cure) were minimal in comparison with the consequences of not treating the disease. The parents had been unwilling to continue chemotherapy for their child. The case again came before the court in Custody of a Minor, 393 N.E.2d 836 (Mass.1979) in an appeal from denial of the parent's petition that an alternative treatment, "metabolic therapy" (consisting of administration of laetrile, vitamins A and C, enzyme enemas, and folic acid), be substituted for chemotherapy. Finding that such a regimen was contrary to the best interests of the child, the court continued the restrictions on the parents,

---

13. Tragically, Colin died shortly after we announced our oral decision.

who by this time had left the jurisdiction. The child later died. When the parents returned to Massachusetts afterward, a judge held them in contempt but did not impose a fine or sentence on them on the theory that they already had suffered enough.

A different tack was taken by the Court of Appeals of New York in Matter of Hofbauer, 393 N.E.2d 1009 (N.Y.1979). A County Commissioner of Social Services sought to have a child with Hodgkins disease adjudged to be neglected because his parents failed to follow the advice of one attending physician, which would have led to conventional methods of treatment (including radiation and possibly chemotherapy) and instead elected to follow the advice of another physician to treat the child with a form of nutritional therapy and laetrile. The Court of Appeals (and the two courts below) did not find the child neglected. It noted that the child was receiving treatment by a physician licensed to practice in New York, and explained that a court cannot "assume the role of a surrogate parent and establish as the objective criteria with which to evaluate a parent's decision its own judgment as to the exact method or degree of medical treatment which should be provided, for such standard is fraught with subjectivity. Rather, in our view, the court's inquiry should be whether the parents, once having sought accredited medical assistance, and having been made aware of the seriousness of their child's affliction and the possibility of cure if a certain mode of treatment is undertaken, have provided for their child a treatment which is recommended by their physician and which has not been totally rejected by all responsible medical authority."

Parham v. J.R.

Supreme Court of the United States, 1979.
442 U.S. 584, 99 S.Ct. 2493, 61 L.Ed.2d 101.

■ MR. CHIEF JUSTICE BURGER delivered the opinion of the Court.

The question presented in this appeal is what process is constitutionally due a minor child whose parents or guardian seek state administered institutional mental health care for the child and specifically whether an adversary proceeding is required prior to or after the commitment.

(a) Appellee, J.R., a child being treated in a Georgia state mental hospital, was a plaintiff in this class-action suit based on 42 U.S.C. § 1983, in the District Court for the Middle District of Georgia. Appellants are the State's Commissioner of the Department of Human Resources, the Director of the Mental Health Division of the Department of Human Resources and the Chief Medical Officer at the hospital where appellee was being treated. Appellee sought a declaratory judgment that Georgia's voluntary commitment procedures for children under the age of 18, Ga.Code, §§ 88–503.1, 88–503.2,[3] violated the Due Process Clause of the Fourteenth Amendment and requested an injunction against its future enforcement.

3. Section 88–503.1 provides:

"The superintendent of any facility may receive for observation and diagno-

sis ... any individual under 18 years of age for whom such application is made by his parent or guardian.... If found to

... [A three-judge District Court] held that Georgia's statutory scheme was unconstitutional because it failed to protect adequately the appellees' due process rights. J.L. v. Parham, 412 F.Supp. 112, 139 (M.D.Ga.1976).

To remedy this violation the court enjoined future commitments based on the procedures in the Georgia statute. It also commanded Georgia to appropriate and expend whatever amount was "reasonably necessary" to provide nonhospital facilities deemed by the appellant state officials to be the most appropriate for the treatment of those members of plaintiffs' class, who could be treated in a less drastic, nonhospital environment.

Appellants challenged all aspects of the District Court's judgment....

(b) J.L., a plaintiff before the District Court who is now deceased, was admitted in 1970 at the age of six years to Central State Regional Hospital in Milledgeville, Ga. Prior to his admission, J.L. had received outpatient treatment at the hospital for over two months. J.L.'s mother then requested the hospital to admit him indefinitely.

The admitting physician interviewed J.L. and his parents. He learned that J.L.'s natural parents had divorced and his mother had remarried. He also learned that J.L. had been expelled from school because he was uncontrollable. He accepted the parents' representation that the boy had been extremely aggressive and diagnosed the child as having a "hyperkinetic reaction to childhood."

J.L.'s mother and stepfather agreed to participate in family therapy during the time their son was hospitalized. Under this program J.L. was permitted to go home for short stays. Apparently his behavior during these visits was erratic. After several months the parents requested discontinuance of the program.

In 1972, the child was returned to his mother and stepfather on a furlough basis, i.e., he would live at home but go to school at the hospital. The parents found they were unable to control J.L. to their satisfaction which created family stress. Within two months they requested his readmission to Central State. J.L.'s parents relinquished their parental rights to the county in 1974.

Although several hospital employees recommended that J.L. should be placed in a special foster home with "a warm, supported, truly involved couple," the Department of Family and Children Services was unable to place him in such a setting. On October 24, 1975, J.L. filed this suit

show evidence of mental illness and to be suitable for treatment, such person may be given care and treatment at such facility and such person may be detained by such facility for such period and under such conditions as may be authorized by law."

Section 88–503.2 provides:
"The superintendent of the facility shall discharge any voluntary patient who has recovered from his mental illness or who has sufficiently improved that the superintendent determines that hospitalization of the patient is no longer desirable."

requesting an order of the court placing him in a less drastic environment suitable to his needs.

(c) Appellee, J.R., was declared a neglected child by the county and removed from his natural parents when he was three months old. He was placed in seven different foster homes in succession prior to his admission to Central State Hospital at the age of seven.

Immediately preceding his hospitalization, J.R. received out-patient treatment at a county mental health center for several months. He then began attending school where he was so disruptive and incorrigible that he could not conform to normal behavior patterns. Because of his abnormal behavior J.R.'s seventh set of foster parents requested his removal from their home. The Department of Family and Children Services then sought his admission at Central State. The agency provided the hospital with a complete sociomedical history at the time of his admission. In addition, three separate interviews were conducted with J.R. by the admission team of the hospital.

It was determined that he was borderline retarded, and suffered an "unsocialized, aggressive reaction to childhood." It was recommended unanimously that he would "benefit from the structured environment" of the hospital and would "enjoy living and playing with boys of the same age."

J.R.'s progress was re-examined periodically. In addition, unsuccessful efforts were made by the Department of Family and Children Services during his stay at the hospital to place J.R. in various foster homes. On October 24, 1975, J.R. filed this suit requesting an order of the court placing him in a less drastic environment suitable to his needs.

(d) GA.CODE ANN. § 19–7–5(g) (Supp.2006) provides for the voluntary admission to a state regional hospital of children such as J.L. and J.R. Under that provision admission begins with an application for hospitalization signed by a "parent or guardian." Upon application the superintendent of each hospital is given the power to admit temporarily any child for "observation and diagnosis." If, after observation, the superintendent finds "evidence of mental illness" and that the child is "suitable for treatment" in the hospital, then the child may be admitted "for such period and under such conditions as may be authorized by law."

Georgia's mental health statute also provides for the discharge of voluntary patients. Any child who has been hospitalized for more than five days may be discharged at the request of a parent or guardian. § 88–503.3(a). Even without a request for discharge, however, the superintendent of each regional hospital has an affirmative duty to release any child "who has recovered from his mental illness or who has sufficiently improved that the superintendent determines that hospitalization of the patient is no longer desirable." § 88–503.2.

Georgia's Mental Health Director has not published any statewide regulations defining what specific procedures each superintendent must employ when admitting a child under 18. Instead, each regional hospital's superintendent is responsible for the procedures in his or her facility. [Noting that "substantial variation" exists between them, the Court reviews and details procedures of the different hospitals.]

. . .

Although most of the focus of the District Court was on the State's mental hospitals, it is relevant to note that Georgia presently funds over 50 community mental health clinics and 13 specialized foster care homes. The State has built seven new regional hospitals within the past 15 years and it has added a new children's unit to its oldest hospital. The State budget in fiscal year 1976 was almost $150 million for mental health care. Georgia ranks 22d among the States in per capita expenditures for mental health and 15th in total expenditures.

The District Court nonetheless rejected the State's entire system of providing mental health care on both procedural and substantive grounds. The District Court found that 46 children could be "optimally cared for in another, less restrictive, non-hospital setting if it were available." These "optimal" settings included group homes, therapeutic camps and home care services. The Governor of Georgia and the Chairmen of the two Appropriations Committees of its legislature, testifying in the District Court, expressed confidence in the Georgia program and informed the court that the State could not justify enlarging its budget during fiscal year 1977 to provide the specialized treatment settings urged by appellees in addition to those then available.

In holding unconstitutional Georgia's statutory procedure for voluntary commitment of juveniles the District Court first determined that commitment to any of the eight regional hospitals constitutes a severe deprivation of a child's liberty. The court defined this liberty interest both in terms of a freedom from bodily restraint and freedom from the "emotional and psychic harm" caused by the institutionalization. Having determined that a liberty interest is implicated by a child's admission to a mental hospital, the court considered what process is required to protect that interest. It held that the process due "includes at least the right after notice to be heard before an impartial tribunal." 412 F.Supp., at 137.

In requiring the prescribed hearing, the court rejected Georgia's argument that no adversary-type hearing was required since the State was merely assisting parents who could not afford private care by making available treatment similar to that offered in private hospitals and by private physicians. The court acknowledged that most parents who seek to have their children admitted to a state mental hospital do so in good faith. It, however, relied on one of appellees' witnesses who expressed an opinion that "some still look upon mental hospitals as a 'dumping ground.' " Id., at 138.[8] No specific evidence of such "dumping," however, can be found in the record.

---

8. In light of the District Court's holding that a judicial or quasi-judicial body should review voluntary commitment decisions, it is at least interesting to note that

The District Court also rejected the argument that review by the superintendents of the hospitals and their staffs was sufficient to protect the child's liberty interest. The court held that the inexactness of psychiatry, coupled with the possibility that the sources of information used to make the commitment decision may not always be reliable, made the superintendent's decision too arbitrary to satisfy due process.

In an earlier day, the problems inherent in coping with children afflicted with mental or emotional abnormalities were dealt with largely within the family. Sometimes parents were aided by teachers or a family doctor. While some parents no doubt were able to deal with their disturbed children without specialized assistance, others, especially those of limited means and education, were not. Increasingly, they turned for assistance to local, public sources or private charities. Until recently, most of the states did little more than provide custodial institutions for the confinement of persons who were considered dangerous.

As medical knowledge about the mentally ill and public concern for their condition expanded, the states, aided substantially by federal grants, have sought to ameliorate the human tragedies of seriously disturbed children. Ironically, as most states have expanded their efforts to assist the mentally ill, their actions have been subjected to increasing litigation and heightened constitutional scrutiny. Courts have been required to resolve the thorny constitutional attacks on state programs and procedures with limited precedential guidance. In this case appellees have challenged Georgia's procedural and substantive balance of the individual, family and social interests at stake in the voluntary commitment of a child to one of its regional mental hospitals.

The parties agree that our prior holdings have set out a general approach for testing challenged state procedures under a due process claim. Assuming the existence of a protectible property or liberty interest, the Court has required a balancing of a number of factors:

> "First, the private interest that will be affected by the official action; second, the risk of an erroneous deprivation of such interest through the procedures used, and the probable value, if any, of additional or substitute procedural safeguards; and finally, the Government's interest, including the function involved and the fiscal and administrative burdens that the additional or substitute procedural requirement would entail." Mathews v. Eldridge, 424 U.S. 319, 335, 96 S.Ct. 893, 903, 47 L.Ed.2d 18 (1976); Smith v. Offer, 431 U.S. 816, 847–848, 97 S.Ct. 2094, 2111–2112, 53 L.Ed.2d 14 (1977).

In applying these criteria, we must consider first the child's interest in not being committed. Normally, however, since this interest is inextricably

the witness who made the statement quoted in the text was not referring to parents as the people who "dump" children into hospitals. This witness opined that some juvenile court judges and child welfare agencies misused the hospitals. See also Rolfe & MacClintock, The Due Process Rights of Minors "Voluntarily Admitted" to Mental Institutions, 4 J. Psych. & L. 333, 351 (1976), (hereinafter Rolfe & MacClintock).

linked with the parents' interest in and obligation for the welfare and health of the child, the private interest at stake is a combination of the child's and parents' concerns. Next we must examine the State's interest in the procedures it has adopted for commitment and treatment of children. Finally, we must consider how well Georgia's procedures protect against arbitrariness in the decision to commit a child to a state mental hospital.

(a) It is not disputed that a child, in common with adults has a substantial liberty interest in not being confined unnecessarily for medical treatment and that the State's involvement in the commitment decision constitutes state action under the Fourteenth Amendment. See Addington v. Texas, 441 U.S. 418, at 425–426, 99 S.Ct. 1804, at 1809, 60 L.Ed.2d 323 (1979); In re Gault, 387 U.S. 1, 27, 87 S.Ct. 1428, 1443, 18 L.Ed.2d 527 (1967). We also recognize that commitment sometimes produces adverse social consequences for the child because of the reaction of some to the discovery that the child has received psychiatric care.

This reaction, however, need not be equated with the community response resulting from being labeled by the state as delinquent, criminal, or mentally ill and possibly dangerous. The state through its voluntary commitment procedures does not "label" the child; it provides a diagnosis and treatment that medical specialists conclude the child requires. In terms of public reaction, the child who exhibits abnormal behavior may be seriously injured by an erroneous decision not to commit. Appellees overlook a significant source of the public reaction to the mentally ill, for what is truly "stigmatizing" is the symptomatology of a mental or emotional illness. The pattern of untreated, abnormal behavior—even if nondangerous—arouses at least as much negative reaction as treatment that becomes public knowledge. A person needing, but not receiving, appropriate medical care may well face even greater social ostracism resulting from the observable symptoms of an untreated disorder.

However, we need not decide what effect these factors might have in a different case. For purposes of this decision, we assume that a child has a protectible interest not only in being free of unnecessary bodily restraints but also in not being labeled erroneously by some because of an improper decision by the state hospital superintendent.

(b) We next deal with the interests of the parents who have decided, on the basis of their observations and independent professional recommendations, that their child needs institutional care. Appellees argue that the constitutional rights of the child are of such magnitude and the likelihood of parental abuse is so great that the parents' traditional interests in and responsibility for the upbringing of their child must be subordinated at least to the extent of providing a formal adversary hearing prior to a voluntary commitment.

Our jurisprudence historically has reflected Western Civilization concepts of the family as a unit with broad parental authority over minor children. Our cases have consistently followed that course; our constitutional system long ago rejected any notion that a child is "the mere creature of the State" and, on the contrary, asserted that parents generally "have the right, coupled with the high duty, to recognize and prepare [their children] for additional obligations." Pierce v. Society of Sisters, 268 U.S. 510, 535, 45 S.Ct. 571, 573, 69 L.Ed. 1070 (1924). See also Wisconsin v. Yoder, 406 U.S. 205, 213, 92 S.Ct. 1526, 1532, 32 L.Ed.2d 15 (1972); Prince v. Massachusetts, 321 U.S. 158, 166, 64 S.Ct. 438, 442, 88 L.Ed. 645 (1944); Meyer v. Nebraska, 262 U.S. 390, 400, 43 S.Ct. 625, 627, 67 L.Ed. 1042 (1923). Surely, this includes a "high duty" to recognize symptoms of illness and to seek and follow medical advice. The law's concept of the family rests on a presumption that parents possess what a child lacks in maturity, experience, and capacity for judgment required for making life's difficult decisions. More important, historically it has recognized that natural bonds of affection lead parents to act in the best interests of their children. 1 W. Blackstone, Commentaries *447; 2 Kent, Commentaries on American Law *190.

As with so many other legal presumptions, experience and reality may rebut what the law accepts as a starting point; the incidence of child neglect and abuse cases attests to this. That some parents "may at times be acting against the interests of their child" as was stated in Bartley v. Kremens, 402 F.Supp. 1039, 1047–1048 (E.D.Pa.1975), vacated, 431 U.S. 119, 97 S.Ct. 1709, 52 L.Ed.2d 184 (1977), creates a basis for caution, but is hardly a reason to discard wholesale those pages of human experience that teach that parents generally do act in the child's best interests. The statist notion that governmental power should supersede parental authority in *all* cases because *some* parents abuse and neglect children is repugnant to American tradition.

Nonetheless, we have recognized that a state is not without constitutional control over parental discretion in dealing with children when their physical or mental health is jeopardized. See Wisconsin v. Yoder, supra, 406 U.S., at 230, 92 S.Ct., at 1540; Prince v. Massachusetts, supra, 321 U.S., at 166, 64 S.Ct., at 442. Moreover, the Court recently declared unconstitutional a state statute that granted parents an absolute veto over a minor child's decision to have an abortion. Planned Parenthood of Missouri v. Danforth, 428 U.S. 52, 96 S.Ct. 2831, 49 L.Ed.2d 788 (1976). Appellees urge that these precedents limiting the traditional rights of parents, if viewed in the context of the liberty interest of the child and the likelihood of parental abuse, require us to hold that the parents' decision to have a child admitted to a mental hospital must be subjected to an exacting constitutional scrutiny, including a formal, adversary, preadmission hearing.

Appellees' argument, however, sweeps too broadly. Simply because the decision of a parent is not agreeable to a child or because it involves risks does not automatically transfer the power to make that decision from the parents to some agency or officer of the state. The same characterizations can be made for a tonsillectomy, appendectomy or other medical procedure. Most children, even in adolescence, simply are not able to make sound judgments concerning many decisions, including their need for medical care or treatment. Parents can and must make those judgments. Here there is no finding by the District Court of even a single instance of bad faith by any parent of any member of appellees' class. We cannot assume that the result in Meyer v. Nebraska, supra, and Pierce v. Society of Sisters, supra, would have been different if the children there had announced a preference to learn only English or a preference to go to a public, rather than a church, school. The fact that a child may balk at hospitalization or complain about a parental refusal to provide cosmetic surgery does not diminish the parents' authority to decide what is best for the child. Neither state officials nor federal courts are equipped to review such parental decisions.

Appellees place particular reliance on *Planned Parenthood,* arguing that its holding indicates how little deference to parents is appropriate when the child is exercising a constitutional right. The basic situation in that case, however, was very different; *Planned Parenthood* involved an absolute parental veto over the child's ability to obtain an abortion. Parents in Georgia in no sense have an absolute right to commit their children to state mental hospitals; the statute requires the superintendent of each regional hospital to exercise independent judgment as to the child's need for confinement.

In defining the respective rights and prerogatives of the child and parent in the voluntary commitment setting, we conclude that our precedents permit the parents to retain a substantial, if not the dominant, role in the decision, absent a finding of neglect or abuse, and that the traditional presumption that the parents act in the best interests of their child should apply. We also conclude, however, that the child's rights and the nature of the commitment decision are such that parents cannot always have absolute and unreviewable discretion to decide whether to have a child institutionalized. They, of course, retain plenary authority to seek such care for their children, subject to a physician's independent examination and medical judgment.

(c) The State obviously has a significant interest in confining the use of its costly mental health facilities to cases of genuine need. The Georgia program seeks first to determine whether the patient seeking admission has an illness that calls for in-patient treatment. To accomplish this purpose, the State has charged the superintendents of each regional hospital with the responsibility for determining, before authorizing an admission, whether a prospective patient is mentally ill and whether the patient will likely benefit from hospital care. In addition, the State has imposed a continuing duty on hospital superintendents to release any patient who has recovered to the point where hospitalization is no longer needed.

The State in performing its voluntarily assumed mission also has a significant interest in not imposing unnecessary procedural obstacles that may discourage the mentally ill or their families from seeking needed psychiatric assistance. The *parens patriae* interest in helping parents care for the mental health of their children cannot be fulfilled if the parents are unwilling to take advantage of the opportunities because the admission process is too onerous, too embarrassing or too contentious. It is surely not idle to speculate as to how many parents who believe they are acting in good faith would forego state-provided hospital care if such care is contingent on participation in an adversary proceeding designed to probe their motives and other private family matters in seeking the voluntary admission.

The State also has a genuine interest in allocating priority to the diagnosis and treatment of patients as soon as they are admitted to a hospital rather than to time-consuming procedural minutes before the admission. One factor that must be considered is the utilization of the time of psychiatrists, psychologists and other behavioral specialists in preparing for and participating in hearings rather than performing the task for which their special training has fitted them. Behavioral experts in courtrooms and hearings are of little help to patients.

The *amicus* brief of the American Psychiatric Association points out at page 20 that the average staff psychiatrist in a hospital presently is able to devote only 47% of his time to direct patient care. One consequence of increasing the procedures the state must provide prior to a child's voluntary admission will be that mental health professionals will be diverted even more from the treatment of patients in order to travel to and participate in—and wait for—what could be hundreds—or even thousands—of hearings each year. . . .

(d) We now turn to consideration of what process protects adequately the child's constitutional rights by reducing risks of error without unduly trenching on traditional parental authority and with out undercutting "efforts to further the legitimate interests of both the state and the patient that are served by" voluntary commitments. Addington v. Texas, 441 U.S., at 419–420, 99 S.Ct., at 1806. We conclude that the risk of error inherent in the parental decision to have a child institutionalized for mental health care is sufficiently great that some kind of inquiry should be made by a "neutral factfinder" to determine whether the statutory requirements for admission are satisfied. That inquiry must carefully probe the child's background using all available sources, including, but not limited to, parents, schools and other social agencies. Of course, the review must also include an interview with the child. It is necessary that the decisionmaker have the authority to refuse to admit any child who does not satisfy the medical standards for admission. Finally, it is necessary that the child's continuing need for commitment be reviewed periodically by a similarly independent procedure.

We are satisfied that such procedures will protect the child from an erroneous admission decision in a way that neither unduly burdens the state nor inhibits parental decisions to seek state help.

Due process has never been thought to require that the neutral and detached trier of fact be law-trained or a judicial or administrative officer. Surely, this is the case as to medical decisions for "neither judges nor administrative hearing officers are better qualified than psychiatrists to render psychiatric judgments." In re Roger S., 19 Cal.3d 921, 941, 141 Cal.Rptr. 298, 569 P.2d 1286, 1299 (1977) (Clark, J., dissenting). Thus, a staff physician will suffice, so long as he or she is free to evaluate independently the child's mental and emotional condition and need for treatment.

It is not necessary that the deciding physician conduct a formal or quasi-formal hearing. A state is free to require such a hearing, but due process is not violated by use of informal traditional medical investigative techniques. Since well-established medical procedures already exist, we do not undertake to outline with specificity precisely what this investigation must involve. The mode and procedure of medical diagnostic procedures is not the business of judges. What is best for a child is an individual medical decision that must be left to the judgment of physicians in each case. We do no more than emphasize that the decision should represent an independent judgment of what the child requires and that all sources of information that are traditionally relied on by physicians and behavioral specialists should be consulted.

What process is constitutionally due cannot be divorced from the nature of the ultimate decision that is being made. Not every determination by state officers can be made most effectively by use of "the procedural tools of judicial or administrative decisionmaking." Board of Curators of U. of Missouri v. Horowitz, 435 U.S. 78, 90, 98 S.Ct. 948, 955, 55 L.Ed.2d 124 (1978).

Here the questions are essentially medical in character: whether the child is mentally or emotionally ill and whether he can benefit from the treatment that is provided by the state. While facts are plainly necessary for a proper resolution of those questions, they are only a first step in the process. In an opinion for a unanimous Court, we recently stated in Addington v. Texas, supra, 441 U.S., at 429–430, 99 S.Ct., at 1811, "whether [a person] is mentally ill ... turns on the *meaning* of the facts which must be interpreted by expert psychiatrists and psychologists."

Although we acknowledge the fallibility of medical and psychiatric diagnosis, we do not accept the notion that the shortcomings of specialists can always be avoided by shifting the decision from a trained specialist using the traditional tools of medical science to an untrained judge or administrative hearing officer after a judicial-type hearing. Even after a hearing, the nonspecialist decision-maker must make a medical-psychiatric decision. Common human experience and scholarly opinions suggest that the supposed protections of an adversary proceeding to determine the appropriateness of medical decisions for the commitment and, treatment of mental and emotional illness may well be more illusory than real.

Another problem with requiring a formalized, factfinding hearing lies in the danger it poses for significant intrusion into the parent-child relationship. Pitting the parents and child as adversaries often will be at odds with the presumption that parents act in the best interests of their child. It is one thing to require a neutral physician to make a careful review of the parents' decision in order to make sure it is proper from a medical standpoint; it is a wholly different matter to employ an adversary contest to ascertain whether the parents' motivation is consistent with the child's interests.

Moreover, it is appropriate to inquire into how such a hearing would contribute to the long range successful treatment of the patient. Surely, there is a risk that it would exacerbate whatever tensions already existed between the child and the parents. Since the parents can and usually do play a significant role in the treatment while the child is hospitalized and even more so after release, there is a serious risk that an adversary confrontation will adversely affect the ability of the parents to assist the child while in the hospital. Moreover, it will make his subsequent return home more difficult. These unfortunate results are especially critical with an emotionally disturbed child; they seem likely to occur in the context of an adversary hearing in which the parents testify. A confrontation over such intimate family relationships would distress the normal adult parents and the impact on a disturbed child almost certainly would be significantly greater.[18]

It has been suggested that a hearing conducted by someone other than the admitting physician is necessary in order to detect instances where parents are "guilty of railroading their children into asylums" or are using "voluntary commitment procedures in order to sanction behavior of which they disapprove." Ellis, Volunteering Children: Parental Commitment of Minors to Mental Institutions, 62 Calif.L.Rev. 840, 850–851 (1974). Curiously it seems to be taken for granted that parents who seek to "dump" their children on the state will inevitably be able to conceal their motives and thus deceive the admitting psychiatrists and the other mental health professionals who make and review the admission decision. It is elementary that one early diagnostic inquiry into the cause of an emotional disturbance of a child is an examination into the environment of the child. It is unlikely if not inconceivable that a decision to abandon an emotionally normal, healthy child and thrust him into an institution will be a discrete act leaving no trail of circumstances. Evidence of such conflicts will emerge either in the interviews or from secondary sources. It is unrealistic to believe that trained psychiatrists, skilled in eliciting responses, sorting medically relevant facts and sensitive to motivational nuances will often be deceived about the family situation surrounding a child's emotional disturbance.[19] Surely a lay, or even law-trained factfinder, would be no more skilled in this process than the professional.

---

18. While not altogether clear, the District Court opinion apparently contemplated a hearing preceded by a written notice of the proposed commitment. At the hearing the child presumably would be given an opportunity to be heard and present evidence, and the right to cross-examine witnesses, including, of course, the parents. The court also required an impartial trier of fact who would render a written decision reciting the reasons for accepting or rejecting the parental application.

Since the parents in this situation are seeking the child's admission to the state institution, the procedure contemplated by the District Court presumably would call for some other person to be designated as a guardian *ad litem* to act for the child. The guardian, in turn, if not a lawyer, would be empowered to retain counsel to act as an advocate of the child's interest.

Of course, a state may elect to provide such adversary hearings in situations where it perceives that parents and a child may be at odds, but nothing in the Constitution compels such procedures.

19. In evaluating the problem of detecting "dumping" by parents, it is important to keep in mind that each of the regional hospitals has a continuing relationship with the

By expressing some confidence in the medical decisionmaking process, we are by no means suggesting it is error free. On occasion parents may initially mislead an admitting physician or a physician may erroneously diagnose the child as needing institutional care either because of negligence or an overabundance of caution. That there may be risks of error in the process affords no rational predicate for holding unconstitutional an entire statutory and administrative scheme that is generally followed in more than 30 states. "[P]rocedural due process rules are shaped by the risk of error inherent in the truthfinding process as applied to the generality of cases, not the rare exceptions." Mathews v. Eldridge, 424 U.S. 319, 344, 96 S.Ct. 893, 907, 47 L.Ed.2d 18 (1976). In general, we are satisfied that an independent medical decisionmaking process, which includes the thorough psychiatric investigation described earlier followed by additional periodic review of a child's condition, will protect children who should not be admitted; we do not believe the risks of error in that process would be significantly reduced by a more formal, judicial-type hearing. The issue remains whether the Georgia practices, as described in the record before us, comport with these minimum due process requirements.

(e) Georgia's statute envisions a careful diagnostic medical inquiry to be conducted by the admitting physician at each regional hospital. The *amicus* brief of the Solicitor General explains, at pp. 7–8:

> "[I]n every instance the decision whether or not to accept the child for treatment is made by a physician employed by the State....
>
> "That decision is based on interviews and recommendations by hospital or community health center staff. The staff interviews the child and the parent or guardian who brings the child to the facility ... [and] attempts are made to communicate with other possible sources of information about the child...."

Focusing primarily on what it saw as the absence of any formal mechanism for review of the physician's initial decision, the District Court unaccountably saw the medical decision as an exercise of "unbridled discretion." 412 F.Supp., at 136. But extravagant characterizations are no substitute for careful analysis and we must examine the Georgia process in its setting to determine if, indeed, any one person exercises such discretion.

In the typical case the parents of a child initially conclude from the child's behavior that there is some emotional problem—in short, that "something is wrong." They may respond to the problem in various ways, but generally the first contact with the State occurs when they bring the child to be examined by a psychologist or psychiatrist at a community mental health clinic.

Department of Family and Children Services. The staffs at those hospitals refer cases to the Department when they suspect a child is being mistreated and thus are sensitive to this problem. In fact, J.L.'s situation is in point. The family conflicts and problems were well documented in the hospital records. Equally well documented, however, were the child's severe emotional disturbances and his need for treatment.

Most often, the examination is followed by outpatient treatment at the community clinic. In addition, the child's parents are encouraged, and sometimes required, to participate in a family therapy program to obtain a better insight into the problem. In most instances, this is all the care a child requires. However, if, after a period of outpatient care, the child's abnormal emotional condition persists, he may be referred by the local clinic staff to an affiliated regional mental hospital.

At the regional hospital an admissions team composed of a psychiatrist and at least one other mental health professional examines and interviews the child—privately in most instances. This team then examines the medical records provided by the clinic staff and interviews the parents. Based on this information, and any additional background that can be obtained, the admissions team makes a diagnosis and determines whether the child will likely benefit from institutionalized care. If the team finds either condition not met, admission is refused.

If the team admits a child as suited for hospitalization, the child's condition and continuing need for hospital care are reviewed periodically by at least one independent, medical review group. For the most part, the reviews are as frequent as weekly, but none are less often than once every two months. Moreover, as we noted earlier the superintendent of each hospital is charged with an affirmative statutory duty to discharge any child who is no longer mentally ill or in need of therapy.[21]

As with most medical procedures, Georgia's are not totally free from risk of error in the sense that they give total or absolute assurance that every child admitted to a hospital has a mental illness optimally suitable for institutionalized treatment. But it bears repeating that "procedural due process rules are shaped by the risk of error inherent in the truth-finding process as applied to the generality of cases, not the rare exceptions." Mathews v. Eldridge, supra, 424 U.S., at 344, 96 S.Ct., at 907.

Georgia's procedures are not "arbitrary" in the sense that a single physician or other professional has the "unbridled discretion" the District Court saw to commit a child to a regional hospital. To so find on this record would require us to assume that the physicians, psychologists and mental health professionals who participate in the admission decision and who review each others' conclusions as to the continuing validity of the initial decision are either oblivious or indifferent to the child's welfare—or that they are incompetent. We note, however, the District Court found to the contrary; it was "impressed by the conscientious, dedicated state employed psychiatrists who, with the help of equally conscientious dedicated state employed psychologists and social workers, faithfully care for the plaintiff children. . . ." 412 F.Supp., at 138.

---

21. While the record does demonstrate that the procedures may vary from case to case, it also reflects that no child in Georgia was admitted for indefinite hospitalization without being interviewed personally and without the admitting physician checking with secondary sources, such as school or work records.

This finding of the District Court also effectively rebuts the suggestion made in some of the briefs *amici* that hospital administrators may not actually be "neutral and detached" because of institutional pressure to admit a child who has no need for hospital care. That such a practice may take place in some institutions in some places affords no basis for a finding as to Georgia's program; the evidence in the record provides no support whatever for that charge against the staffs at any of the State's eight regional hospitals. Such cases, if they are found, can be dealt with individually;[22] they do not lend themselves to class-action remedies.

We are satisfied that the voluminous record as a whole supports the conclusion that the admissions' staffs of the hospitals have acted in a neutral and detached fashion in making medical judgments in the best interests of the children....

Although our review of the record in this case satisfies us that Georgia's general administrative and statutory scheme for the voluntary commitment of children is not *per se* unconstitutional, we cannot decide on this record, whether every child in appellees' class received an adequate, independent diagnosis of his emotional condition and need for confinement under the standards announced earlier in this opinion. On remand, the District Court is free to and should consider any individual claims that initial admissions did not meet the standards we have described in this opinion.

In addition, we note that appellees' original complaint alleged that the State had failed to provide adequate periodic review of their need for institutional care and claimed that this was an additional due process violation. Since the District Court held that the appellees' original confinement was unconstitutional, it had no reason to consider this separate claim. Similarly, we have no basis for determining whether the review procedures of the various hospitals are adequate to provide the process called for or what process might be required if a child contests his confinement by requesting a release. These matters require factual findings not present in the District Court's opinion. We have held that the periodic reviews described in the record reduce the risk of error in the initial admission and thus they are necessary. Whether they are sufficient to justify continuing a voluntary commitment is an issue for the District Court on remand. The District Court is free to require additional evidence on this issue.

... Some members of appellees' class, including J.R., were wards of the State of Georgia at the time of their admission. Obviously their situation differs from those members of the class who have natural parents. While the determination of what process is due varies somewhat when the state, rather than a natural parent, makes the request for commitment, we conclude that the differences in the two situations do not justify requiring

---

22. One important means of obtaining individual relief for these children is the availability of habeas corpus. As the appellants' brief explains, "Ga.Code § 88–502.11 provides that at any time and without notice a person detained in a facility, or a relative or friend of such person, may petition for a writ of habeas corpus to question the cause and legality of the detention of the person." Brief for Appellants 36–37.

different procedures at the time of the child's initial admission to the hospital.

For a ward of the State, there may well be no adult who knows him thoroughly and who cares for him deeply. Unlike with natural parents where there is a presumed natural affection to guide their action, Blackstone *447; Kent *190, the presumption that the state will protect a child's general welfare stems from a specific state statute. Ga.Code Ann. § 24A–101. Contrary to the suggestion of the dissent, however, we cannot assume that when the State of Georgia has custody of a child it acts so differently from a natural parent in seeking medical assistance for the child. As Mr. Justice Stewart's concurring opinion points out, post, at p. 2514, no one has questioned the validity of the statutory presumption that the State acts in the child's best interest. Nor could such a challenge be mounted on the record before us. There is no evidence that the State, acting as guardian, attempted to admit any child for reasons unrelated to the child's need for treatment. Indeed, neither the District Court nor the appellees has suggested that wards of the State should receive any constitutional treatment different from children with natural parents.

Once we accept that the State's application of a child for admission to a hospital is made in good faith, then the question is whether the medical decisionmaking approach of the admitting physician is adequate to satisfy due process. We have already recognized that an independent medical judgment made from the perspective of the best interests of the child after a careful investigation is an acceptable means of justifying a voluntary commitment. We do not believe that the soundness of this decisionmaking is any the less reasonable in this setting.

Indeed, if anything, the decision with regard to wards of the State may well be even more reasonable in light of the extensive written records that are compiled about each child while in the State's custody. In J.R.'s case, the admitting physician had a complete social and medical history of the child before even beginning the diagnosis. After carefully interviewing him and reviewing his extensive files, three physicians independently concluded that institutional care was in his best interests.

Since the state agency having custody and control of the child *in loco parentis* has a duty to consider the best interests of the child with respect to a decision on commitment to a mental hospital, the State may constitutionally allow that custodial agency to speak for the child, subject, of course, to the restrictions governing natural parents. On this record, we cannot declare unconstitutional Georgia's admission procedures for wards of the State.

(b) It is possible that the procedures required in reviewing a ward's need for continuing care should be different from those used to review a child with natural parents. As we have suggested earlier, the issue of what process is due to justify continuing a voluntary commitment must be considered by the District Court on remand. In making that inquiry the District Court might well consider whether wards of the State should be treated with respect to continuing therapy differently from children with natural parents.

The absence of an adult who cares deeply for a child has little effect on the reliability of the initial admission decision, but it may have some effect on how long a child will remain in the hospital. We noted in Addington v. Texas, supra, 441 U.S., at 428, 99 S.Ct., at 1811, "the concern of family and friends generally will provide continuous opportunities for an erroneous commitment to be corrected." For a child without natural parents, we must acknowledge the risk of being "lost in the shuffle." Moreover, there is at least some indication that J.R.'s commitment was prolonged because the Department of Family and Children Services had difficulty finding a foster home for him. Whether wards of the State generally have received less protection than children with natural parents, and, if so, what should be done about it, however, are matters that must be decided in the first instance by the District Court on remand, if the Court concludes the issue is still alive.

It is important that we remember the purpose of Georgia's comprehensive mental health program. It seeks substantively and at great cost to provide care for those who cannot afford to obtain private treatment and procedurally to screen carefully all applicants to assure that institutional care is suited to the particular patient. The State resists the complex of procedures ordered by the District Court because in its view they are unnecessary to protect the child's rights, they divert public resources from the central objective of administering health care, they risk aggravating the tensions inherent in the family situation and they erect barriers that may discourage parents from seeking medical aid for a disturbed child.

On this record we are satisfied that Georgia's medical factfinding processes are reasonable and consistent with constitutional guarantees. Accordingly, it was error to hold unconstitutional the State's procedures for admitting a child for treatment to a state mental hospital. . . .

Reversed and remanded.

■ [The concurring opinion of Mr. Justice Stewart is omitted.]

■ [In a separate opinion Mr. Justice Brennan, joined by Mr. Justice Marshall and Mr. Justice Stevens concurred in part and dissented in part.

While finding the present Georgia admission procedures "reasonably consistent" with the constitutional principles they outlined, they regard the postadmission procedures as "simply not enough to qualify as hearings—let alone reasonably prompt hearings. The procedures lack all the traditional due process safeguards." As to juvenile wards of the State, the Justices find that "the special considerations that justify postponement of formal commitment proceedings whenever parents seek to hospitalize their children are absent when the children are wards of the State and are being committed upon recommendations of their social workers." In the absence of "exigent circumstances" they would require preadmission commitment hearings for such juveniles.]

NOTES

In *In re* Roger S., 19 Cal.3d 921, 141 Cal.Rptr. 298, 569 P.2d 1286 (1977), the Supreme Court of California held that minors who have reached age 14 and object to being institutionalized for mental illness or psychiatric problems are entitled to an administrative hearing to determine whether commitment is appropriate for them. The practical effect of that decision is discussed in Carol K. Dillon, Margaret R. Roisman, Joel S. Sanders & Betsy B. Adler, *In re Roger S.: The Impact of a Child's Due Process Victory on the California Mental Health System*, 70 Calif.L.Rev. 373 (1982).

The tendency of some judges to make assumptions about societal facts, with or without competence or sensitivity to do so, is particularly of concern in the field of family law. For a sensitive appraisal of this problem in the context of the *Parham* case, *see* Gail S. Perry and Gary B. Melton, *Precedential Value of Judicial Notice of Social Facts: Parham as an Example*, 22 J.Fam.Law 633 (1984).

Stump v. Sparkman

Supreme Court of the United States, 1978.
435 U.S. 349, 98 S.Ct. 1099, 55 L.Ed.2d 331.

■ Mr. Justice White delivered the opinion of the Court.

. . .

The relevant facts underlying respondent's suit are not in dispute. On July 9, 1971, Ora Spitler McFarlin, the mother of respondent Linda Kay Spitler Sparkman, presented to Judge Harold D. Stump of the Circuit Court of DeKalb County, Ind., a document captioned "Petition To Have Tubal Ligation Performed On Minor and Indemnity Agreement." The document had been drafted by her attorney, a petitioner here. In this petition Mrs. McFarlin stated under oath that her daughter was 15 years of age and was "somewhat retarded," although she attended public school and had been promoted each year with her class. The petition further stated that Linda had been associating with "older youth or young men" and had stayed out overnight with them on several occasions. As a result of this behavior and Linda's mental capabilities, it was stated that it would be in the daughter's best interest if she underwent a tubal ligation in order "to prevent unfortunate circumstances...." In the same document Mrs. McFarlin also undertook to indemnify and hold harmless Dr. John Hines, who was to perform the operation, and the DeKalb Memorial Hospital, where the operation was to take place, against all causes of action that might arise as a result of the performance of the tubal ligation.

The petition was approved by Judge Stump on the same day. He affixed his signature as "Judge, DeKalb Circuit Court," to the statement that he did "hereby approve the above Petition by affidavit form on behalf of Ora Spitler McFarlin, to have Tubal Ligation performed upon her minor daughter, Linda Spitler, subject to said Ora Spitler McFarlin covenanting and agreeing to indemnify and keep indemnified Dr. John Hines and the

DeKalb Memorial Hospital from any matters or causes of action arising therefrom."

On July 15, 1971, Linda Spitler entered the DeKalb Memorial Hospital, having been told that she was to have her appendix removed. The following day a tubal ligation was performed upon her. She was released several days later, unaware of the true nature of her surgery.

Approximately two years after the operation, Linda Spitler was married to respondent Leo Sparkman. Her inability to become pregnant led her to discover that she had been sterilized during the 1971 operation. As a result of this revelation, the Sparkmans filed suit in the United States District Court for the Northern District of Indiana against Mrs. McFarlin, her attorney, Judge Stump, the doctors who had performed and assisted in the tubal ligation, and the DeKalb Memorial Hospital. Respondents sought damages for the alleged violation of Linda Sparkman's constitutional rights; also asserted were pendent state claims for assault and battery, medical malpractice, and loss of potential fatherhood.

Ruling upon the defendants' various motions to dismiss the complaint, the District Court concluded that each of the constitutional claims asserted by respondents required a showing of state action and that the only state action alleged in the complaint was the approval by Judge Stump, acting as Circuit Court Judge, of the petition presented to him by Mrs. McFarlin. The Sparkmans sought to hold the private defendants liable on a theory that they had conspired with Judge Stump to bring about the allegedly unconstitutional acts. The District Court, however, held that no federal action would lie against any of the defendants because Judge Stump, the only state agent, was absolutely immune from suit under the doctrine of judicial immunity. . . .

. . .

The governing principle of law is well established and is not questioned by the parties. As early as 1872, the Court recognized that it was "a general principle of the highest importance to the proper administration of justice that a judicial officer, in exercising the authority vested in him, [should] be free to act upon his own convictions, without apprehension of personal consequences to himself." Bradley v. Fisher [13 Wall. 335, 347 (1872)]. For that reason the Court held that "judges of courts of superior or general jurisdiction are not liable to civil actions for their judicial acts, even when such acts are in excess of their jurisdiction, and are alleged to have been done maliciously or corruptly." Later we held that this doctrine of judicial immunity was applicable in suits under § 1 of the Civil Rights Act of 1871, 42 U.S.C. § 1983, for the legislative record gave no indication that Congress intended to abolish this long-established principle. Pierson v. Ray, 386 U.S. 547, 87 S.Ct. 1213, 18 L.Ed.2d 288 (1967).

The Court of Appeals correctly recognized that the necessary inquiry in determining whether a defendant judge is immune from suit is whether at the time he took the challenged action he had jurisdiction over the subject matter before him. Because "some of the most difficult and embarrassing questions which a judicial officer is called upon to consider and determine relate to his jurisdiction ...," *Bradley,* supra, at 352, the scope of the judge's jurisdiction must be construed broadly where the issue is the immunity of the judge. A judge will not be deprived of immunity because the action he took was in error, was done maliciously, or was in excess of his authority; rather, he will be subject to liability only when he has acted in the "clear absence of all jurisdiction."[7] 13 Wall., at 351.

We cannot agree that there was a "clear absence of all jurisdiction" in the DeKalb County Circuit Court to consider the petition presented by Mrs. McFarlin. As an Indiana Circuit Court Judge, Judge Stump had "original exclusive jurisdiction in all cases at law and in equity whatsoever ...," jurisdiction over the settlement of estates and over guardianships, appellate jurisdiction as conferred by law, and jurisdiction over "all other causes, matters and proceedings where exclusive jurisdiction thereof is not conferred by law upon some other court, board or officer." Ind.Code § 33–4–4–3 (1975). This is indeed a broad jurisdictional grant; yet the Court of Appeals concluded that Judge Stump did not have jurisdiction over the petition authorizing Linda Sparkman's sterilization.

In so doing, the Court of Appeals noted that the Indiana statutes provided for the sterilization of institutionalized persons under certain circumstances, see Ind.Code §§ 16–13–13–1 through 16–13–13–4 (1973), but otherwise contained no express authority for judicial approval of tubal ligations. It is true that the statutory grant of general jurisdiction to the Indiana circuit courts does not itemize types of cases those courts may hear and hence does not expressly mention sterilization petitions presented by the parents of a minor. But in our view, it is more significant that there was no Indiana statute and no case law in 1971 prohibiting a circuit court, a court of general jurisdiction, from considering a petition of the type presented to Judge Stump. The statutory authority for the sterilization of institutionalized persons in the custody of the State does not warrant the inference that a court of general jurisdiction has no power to act on a petition for sterilization of a minor in the custody of her parents, particularly where the parents have authority under the Indiana statutes to "consent to and contract for medical or hospital care or treatment of [the minor] including surgery." Ind.Code § 16–8–4–2 (1973). The District Court concluded that Judge Stump had jurisdiction under § 33–4–4–3 to entertain and act upon Mrs. McFarlin's petition. We agree with the District Court, it appearing that neither by statute nor by case law has the broad jurisdiction granted to the circuit courts of Indiana been circumscribed to foreclose consideration of a petition for authorization of a minor's sterilization.

7. In *Bradley,* the Court illustrated the distinction between lack of jurisdiction and excess of jurisdiction with the following examples: if a probate judge, with jurisdiction over only wills and estates, should try a criminal case, he would be acting in the clear absence of jurisdiction and would not be immune from liability for his action; on the other hand, if a judge of a criminal court should convict a defendant of a nonexistent crime, he would merely be acting in excess of his jurisdiction and would be immune. Id., at 352.

The Court of Appeals also concluded that support for Judge Stump's actions could not be found in the common law of Indiana, relying in particular on the Indiana Court of Appeals' intervening decision in A.L. v. G.R.H., 163 Ind.App. 636, 325 N.E.2d 501 (1975). In that case the Indiana court held that a parent does not have a common-law right to have a minor child sterilized, even though the parent might "sincerely believe the child's adulthood would benefit therefrom." Id., at 638, 325 N.E.2d, at 502. The opinion, however, speaks only of the rights of the parents to consent to the sterilization of their child and does not question the *jurisdiction* of a circuit judge who is presented with such a petition from a parent. Although under that case a circuit judge would err as a matter of law if he were to approve a parent's petition seeking the sterilization of a child, the opinion in A.L. v. G.R.H. does not indicate that a circuit judge is without jurisdiction to entertain the petition. Indeed, the clear implication of the opinion is that, when presented with such a petition, the circuit judge should deny it on its merits rather than dismiss it for lack of jurisdiction.

Perhaps realizing the broad scope of Judge Stump's jurisdiction, the Court of Appeals stated that, even if the action taken by him was not foreclosed under the Indiana statutory scheme, it would still be "an illegitimate exercise of his common law power because of his failure to comply with elementary principles of procedural due process." This misconceives the doctrine of judicial immunity. A judge is absolutely immune from liability for his judicial acts even if his exercise of authority is flawed by the commission of grave procedural errors....

... Because the court over which Judge Stump presides is one of general jurisdiction, neither the procedural errors he may have committed nor the lack of a specific statute authorizing his approval of the petition in question rendered him liable in damages for the consequences of his actions.

The respondents argue that even if Judge Stump had jurisdiction to consider the petition presented to him by Mrs. McFarlin, he is still not entitled to judicial immunity because his approval of the petition did not constitute a "judicial" act. It is only for acts performed in his "judicial" capacity that a judge is absolutely immune, they say. We do not disagree with this statement of the law, but we cannot characterize the approval of the petition as a nonjudicial act.

... [Respondents] argue that Judge Stump's approval of the petition was not a judicial act because the petition was not given a docket number, was not placed on file with the clerk's office, and was approved in an *ex parte* proceeding without notice to the minor, without a hearing, and without the appointment of a guardian *ad litem*.

. . .

The relevant cases demonstrate that the factors determining whether an act by a judge is a "judicial" one relate to the nature of the act itself, i.e., whether it is a function normally performed by a judge, and to the expectations of the parties, i.e., whether they dealt with the judge in his judicial capacity. Here, both factors indicate that Judge Stump's approval of the sterilization petition was a judicial act. State judges with general jurisdiction not infrequently are called upon in their official capacity to approve petitions relating to the affairs of minors, as for example, a petition to settle a minor's claim. Furthermore, as even respondents have admitted, at the time he approved the petition presented to him by Mrs. McFarlin, Judge Stump was "acting as a county circuit court judge." See supra, at 1106. We may infer from the record that it was only because Judge Stump served in that position that Mrs. McFarlin, on the advice of counsel, submitted the petition to him for his approval. Because Judge Stump performed the type of act normally performed only by judges and because he did so in his capacity as a Circuit Court Judge, we find no merit to respondents' argument that the informality with which he proceeded rendered his action nonjudicial and deprived him of his absolute immunity.

. . .

The Indiana law vested in Judge Stump the power to entertain and act upon the petition for sterilization. He is, therefore, under the controlling cases, immune from damages liability even if his approval of the petition was in error. Accordingly, the judgment of the Court of Appeals is reversed, and the case is remanded for further proceedings consistent with this opinion.

■ Mr. Justice Brennan took no part in the consideration or decision of this case.

■ [The dissenting opinion of Mr. Justice Stewart, with whom Mr. Justice Marshall and Mr. Justice Powell join, is omitted.]

VIRGINIA CODE ANN. (2004)

§ 54.1–2975. Sterilization operations for certain children incapable of informed consent.

It shall be lawful for any physician licensed by the Board of Medicine to perform a vasectomy, salpingectomy, or other surgical sexual sterilization procedure on a person fourteen years of age or older and less than eighteen years of age when:

1. A petition has been filed in the circuit court of the county or city wherein the child resides by the parent or parents having custody of the child or by the child's guardian, spouse, or next friend requesting that the operation be performed;

2. The court has made the child a party defendant, served the child, the child's guardian, if any, the child's spouse, if any, and the child's parent who has custody of the child with notice of the proceedings and appointed for the child an attorney-at-law to represent and protect the child's interests;

3. The court has determined that a full, reasonable, and comprehensible medical explanation as to the meaning, consequences, and risks of the

sterilization operation to be performed and as to alternative methods of contraception has been given by the physician to the child upon whom the operation is to be performed, to the child's guardian, if any, to the child's spouse, if any, and, if there is no spouse, to the parent who has custody of the child;

4.   The court has determined by clear and convincing evidence that the child's mental abilities are so impaired that the child is incapable of making his or her own decision about sterilization and is unlikely to develop mentally to a sufficient degree to make an informed judgment about sterilization in the foreseeable future;

5.   The court, to the greatest extent possible, has elicited and taken into account the views of the child concerning the sterilization, giving the views of the child such weight in its decision as the court deems appropriate;

6.   The court has complied with the requirements of § 54.1–2977; and

7.   The court has entered an order authorizing a qualified physician to perform the operation not earlier than thirty days after the date of the entry of the order, and thirty days have elapsed. The court order shall state the date on and after which the sterilization operation may be performed.

§ 54.1–2969.

. . .

D.   A minor shall be deemed an adult for the purpose of consenting to:

1.   Medical or health services needed to determine the presence of or to treat venereal disease or any infectious or contagious disease which the State Board of Health requires to be reported;

2.   Medical or health services required in case of birth control, pregnancy or family planning except for the purposes of sexual sterilization;

3.   Medical or health services needed in the case of outpatient care, treatment or rehabilitation for substance abuse . . . ;

4.   Medical or health services needed in the case of outpatient care, treatment or rehabilitation for mental illness or emotional disturbance.

E.   Except for the purposes of sexual sterilization, any minor who is or has been married shall be deemed an adult for the purpose of giving consent to surgical and medical treatment.

NOTE

Many states have adopted statutes permitting minors to give valid consent to treatment for specific illnesses or conditions. Some such laws provided no specific age floor, others a much lower floor than that for general emancipation. Although it might be assumed that such laws were enacted as part of a movement toward greater autonomy for minors, they were largely rooted in expediency. Parental consent often is not needed for crisis counseling, birth control, or treatment for substance abuse or contagious disease—situations in which there is concern that minors might not want to seek assistance or consent from their parents. If they cannot consent to treatment by themselves, they might not obtain medical care, which would be detrimental to themselves and society generally. The statutes thus illustrate legislative recognition of a major, disturbing change that has occurred in the counseling and consultative relationship between too many parents and their children.

Another variation of this approach is codification of a mature minor doctrine, sometimes greatly expanding the exception created judicially. An Arkansas statute, for example, permits consent to treatment by "Any unemancipated minor of sufficient intelligence to understand and appreciate the consequences of the proposed surgical or medical procedures, for himself. . . ." ARK. CODE 20–9–602(7) (LEXIS 2000).

THE JUVENILE JUSTICE STANDARDS RELATING TO RIGHTS OF MINORS (1980) start with the premise that medical services should not be provided without prior parental consent, but then add a series of exceptions (mental or emotional disorder, venereal disease chemical dependency, emergency treatment). The Standards also provide some criteria for when a physician should override a minor's decision regarding confidentiality extending to parents. Section 4.3(C) of the Standards tries to assure that although the minor may be financially responsible that will not remove an insurer from liability even when the parent has not consented. Section 403(D) adds that

> A public or private health insurer should not inform a parent or policy holder that a minor has filed a claim or received a benefit under a health insurance policy or plan of which the minor is a beneficiary, unless the physician has previously notified the parent of the treatment for which the claim is submitted.

Persons accustomed to dealing with the billing practices of health insurers in general will recognize the ambitiousness if not the futility of such a proposal.

For further discussion of the issues and approaches, *see* Walter Wadlington, *Medical Decision Making For and By Children: Tensions Between Parent, State and Child*, 1994 ILL.L.REV. 301; and Walter Wadlington, *Minors and Health Care: The Age of Consent*, 11 OSGOODE HALL L.J. 115 (1973).

In re Green

Supreme Court of Pennsylvania, 1972.
448 Pa. 338, 292 A.2d 387.

■ JONES, C.J. [Ricky Green, age fifteen, was the subject of a neglect petition seeking the appointment of a guardian who would consent to corrective surgery. The petition was dismissed but that decision was reversed by the Superior Court.]

. . . Ricky suffers from paralytic scoliosis (94% curvature of the spine).

Due to this curvature of the spine, Ricky is presently a "sitter," unable to stand or ambulate due to the collapse of his spine; if nothing is done, Ricky could become a bed patient. Doctors have recommended a "spinal fusion" to relieve Ricky's bent position, which would involve moving bone from Ricky's pelvis to his spine. Although an orthopedic specialist testified, "there is no question that there is danger in this type of operation," the mother did consent conditionally to the surgery. The condition is that, since the mother is a Jehovah's Witness who believes that the Bible proscribes any blood transfusions which would be necessary for this surgery, she would not consent to any blood transfusions. Initially, we must recognize that, while the operation would be beneficial, there is no evidence that Ricky's life is in danger or that the operation must be performed immediately. Accordingly, we are faced with the situation of a parent who will not consent to a dangerous operation on her minor son requiring blood transfusions solely because of her religious beliefs....

Almost a century ago, the United States Supreme Court enunciated the twofold concept of the Free Exercise clause: "Laws are made for the government of actions, and while they cannot interfere with mere religious belief and opinions, they may with practices." Reynolds v. United States, 98 U.S. 145, 166 (1878). Thus, it was stated in Prince v. Massachusetts, 321 U.S. 158, 166–167, 64 S.Ct. 438, 442, 88 L.Ed. 645 (1944):

> "But the family itself is not beyond regulation in the public interest, as against a claim of religious liberty. Reynolds v. United States, 98 U.S. 145, 25 L.Ed. 244; Davis v. Beason, 133 U.S. 333, 10 S.Ct. 299. And neither rights of religion nor rights of parenthood are beyond limitation. Acting to guard the general interest in youth's well being the state as *parens patriae* may restrict the parent's control by requiring school attendance [footnote omitted], regulating or prohibiting the child's labor [footnote omitted] and in many other ways [footnote omitted]. Its authority is not nullified merely because the parent grounds his claim to control the child's course of conduct on religion or conscience. Thus, he cannot claim freedom from compulsory vaccination for the child more than for himself on religious grounds [footnote omitted]. The right to practice religion freely does not include liberty to expose the community or the child to communicable disease or the latter to ill health or death. People v. Pierson, 176 N.Y. 201, 68 N.E. 243 [footnote omitted]. The catalogue need not be lengthened. It is sufficient to show what indeed appellant hardly disputes, that the state has a wide range of power for limiting parental freedom and authority in things affecting the child's welfare; and that this includes, to some extent, matters of conscience and religious conviction."

On the other hand, the United States Supreme Court recently stated, "to agree that religiously grounded conduct must often be subject to the broad police power of the State is not to deny that there are areas of conduct protected by the Free Exercise Clause of the First Amendment and thus beyond the power of the State to control, even under regulations of general applicability." Wisconsin v. Yoder, 406 U.S. 205, 92 S.Ct. 1526 (1972). "The conduct or actions so regulated have invariably posed some substantial threat to public safety, peace or order." Sherbert v. Verner, 374 U.S. 398, 403, 83 S.Ct. 1790, 1793 (1963). Without appearing callous, Ricky's unfortunate condition, unlike polygamy, vaccination, child labor and the like, does not pose a substantial threat to society; in this fashion, [the earlier cases] are readily distinguishable....

Turning to the situation where an adult refuses to consent to blood transfusions necessary to save the life of his infant son or daughter, other jurisdictions have uniformly held that the state can order such blood transfusions over the parents' religious objections.

In our view, the penultimate question presented by this appeal is whether the state may interfere with a parent's control over his or her child in order to enhance the child's physical well-being when the child's life is in no immediate danger and when the state's intrusion conflicts with the parent's religious beliefs. Stated differently, does the State have an interest of sufficient magnitude to warrant the abridgment of a parent's right to freely practice his or her religion when those beliefs preclude medical treatment of a son or daughter whose life is not in immediate danger? We are not confronted with a life or death situation as in the cases cited earlier in this opinion. Nor is there any question in the case at bar of a parent's omission or neglect for non-religious reasons....

[The Court discusses In re Sampson, 29 N.Y.2d 900, 328 N.Y.S.2d 686, 278 N.E.2d 918 (1972). The court states that the New York Court of Appeals opinion made the observation that "religious objections to blood transfusions do not 'present a bar at least where the transfusion is necessary to the success of the required surgery.'" It then adds:]

... [W]e disagree with [this] observation in a non-fatal situation and express no view of the propriety of that statement in a life or death situation. If we were to describe this surgery as "required," like the Court of Appeals, our decision would conflict with the mother's religious beliefs. Aside from religious considerations, one can also question the use of that adjective on medical grounds since an orthopedic specialist testified that the operation itself was dangerous. Indeed, one can question who, other than the Creator, has the right to term certain surgery as "required." This fatal/nonfatal distinction also steers the courts of this Commonwealth away from a medical and philosophical morass: if spinal surgery can be ordered, what about a hernia or gall bladder operation or a hysterectomy? The problems created by *Sampson* are endless. We are of the opinion that as between a parent and the state, the state does not have an interest of sufficient magnitude outweighing a parent's religious beliefs when the child's life is *not immediately imperiled* by his physical condition.

Unlike *Yoder* and *Sampson*, our inquiry does not end at this point since we believe the wishes of this sixteen-year-old boy should be ascertained; the ultimate question, in our view, is whether a parent's religious beliefs are paramount to the possibly adverse decision of the child. In *Yoder*, Mr. Justice Douglas, dissenting in part, wanted to remand the matter in order to determine whether the Amish children wished to continue their education in spite of their parents' beliefs: "if an Amish child desires to attend high school, and is mature enough to have that desire respected, the State may well be able to override the parents' religiously motivated objections," 406 U.S. at 242, 92 S.Ct. at 1546. The majority opinion as well as the concurring opinion of Mr. Justice Stewart did not think it wise to reach this point for two principal reasons: (1) it was the parents, not the children, who were criminally prosecuted for their religious beliefs; and (2) the record did not indicate a parent-child conflict as the testimony of the lone child witness coincided with her parents' religious beliefs. While the record before us gives no indication of Ricky's thinking, it is the child rather than the parent in this appeal who is directly involved which thereby distinguishes *Yoder's* decision not to discuss the beliefs of the parents vis-a-vis the children. In *Sampson,* the Family Court judge decided not to "evade the responsibility for a decision now by the simple expedient of foisting upon this boy the responsibility for making a decision at some later day...." 65 Misc.2d 658, 317 N.Y.S.2d at 655. While we are cognizant of the realistic problems of this approach enunciated by Judge (now Chief Judge) Fuld in his *Seaforth** dissent, we believe that Ricky should be heard.

It would be most anomalous to ignore Ricky in this situation when we consider the preference of an intelligent child of sufficient maturity in determining custody.... Moreover, we have held that a child of the same age can waive constitutional rights and receive a life sentence.... Indeed, minors can now bring a personal injury action in Pennsylvania against their parents. We need not extend this litany of the rights of children any further to support the proposition that Ricky should be heard. The record before us does not even note whether Ricky is a Jehovah's Witness or plans to become one. We shall, therefore, reserve any decision regarding a possible parent-child conflict and remand the matter for an evidentiary hearing similar to the one conducted in *Seaforth* in order to determine Ricky's wishes.

* [In In re Seiferth, 309 N.Y. 80, 127 N.E.2d 820 (1955), the father of a fourteen year old boy with a cleft palate and harelip refused to permit corrective surgery, instead preferring to "let the natural forces of the universe work on the body". The court refused to declare the child neglected and appoint someone to consent to the surgery, saying that there was no serious threat to his health or life and, in effect, that the boy would be able to make his own decision after a few more years. Fuld, J., dissenting, stated:

"Every child has a right, so far as is possible, to lead a normal life and, if his parents, through viciousness or ignorance, act in such a way as to endanger that right, the courts should, as the legis-

lature has provided, act in his behalf. Such is the case before us.

. . .

"The welfare and interests of a child are at stake. A court should not place upon his shoulders one of the most momentous and far-reaching decisions of his life. The court should make the decision, as the statute contemplates, and leave to the good sense and sound judgment of the public authorities the job of preparing the boy for the operation and of getting him as adjusted to it as possible. We should not put off the decision on the chance that the child may change his mind and submit at some future time to the operation."—EDS.]

The order of the Superior Court is reversed and the matter remanded to the Court of Common Pleas of Philadelphia, Family Division, Juvenile Branch, for proceedings consistent with the views expressed in this opinion. . . .

■ EAGAN, JUSTICE (dissenting). With all due deference to the majority of this Court, I am compelled to dissent. I would affirm the order of the Superior Court.

The Court's analysis presumes there are two primary interests at stake, that of the state to protect its citizens, and that of the mother to follow her religious convictions. The difficulty, and what I believe to be the fatal flaw in this reasoning, is that too little consideration and attention is given to the interests of the health and well-being of this young boy. Although the mother's religious beliefs must be given the fullest protection and respect, I do not believe the mother's religious convictions should be our primary consideration. As Mr. Justice Rutledge aptly stated:

> "Parents may be free to become martyrs themselves. But it does not follow they are free, in identical circumstances, to make martyrs of their children before they have reached the age of full and legal discretion when they can make that choice for themselves."

Prince v. Commonwealth, 321 U.S. 158, 170, 64 S.Ct. 438, 444 (1944). . . . The court below determined that the mother's exercise of control here would undoubtedly expose the child to progressively worsening ill health, but it still refused to assert the State's power by finding the child neglected. . . .

The statute only speaks in terms of "health" not life or death. If there is a substantial threat to health, then I believe the courts can and should intervene to protect Ricky. By the decision of this Court today, this boy may never enjoy any semblance of a normal life which the vast majority of our society has come to enjoy and cherish.

Lastly, I must take issue with the manner in which the majority finally disposes of the case. I do not believe that sending the case back to allow Ricky to be heard is an adequate solution. We are herein dealing with a young boy who has been crippled most of his life, consequently, he has been under the direct control and guidance of his parents for that time. To now presume that he could make an independent decision as to what is best for his welfare and health is not reasonable. See In Matter of Seiferth, 309 N.Y. 80, 85, 127 N.E. 820, 823 (1955) (dissenting opinion, Fuld, J.). Moreover, the mandate of the Court presents this youth with a most painful choice between the wishes of his parents and their religious convictions on the one hand, and his chance for a normal, healthy life on the other hand. We should not confront him with this dilemma.

NOTES

On Remand. The lower court held an evidentiary hearing to determine Ricky's wishes respecting the proposed surgery. He indicated that he did not wish to submit to surgery. His decision was not based solely on religious grounds. He also stated that he had been in the hospital a long time already and that no one said "it is going to come out right." *In re Green*, 452 Pa. 373, 307 A.2d 279 (1973).

In re **Sampson.** In the *Sampson* case, with which the majority decision in *Green* expressed disagreement, Kevin Sampson, fifteen-years-old at the time his case came before a New York family court, had suffered since childhood from neurofibromatosis. A large, bag-like growth enveloped one side of his face. It caused one ear, cheek, and eyelid to droop and one side of his face to be roughly twice as large as the other. Because of his deformity, he had not attended school for several years. A lengthy and dangerous operation, followed by prolonged treatment, might alleviate his condition cosmetically but would not effect a cure. The surgery required transfusions of whole blood, but because of her beliefs as a Jehovah's Witness, Kevin's mother would allow only the use of plasma. In a proceeding instituted by the County Health Commissioner, the Family Court declared Kevin a "neglected" child and ordered his mother to permit such surgery as the Commissioner deemed necessary. The Appellate Division upheld the order, carefully pointing out that Kevin was "neglected" only in a technical sense, for his mother was not shown to have failed her son except in this one decision. The Court of Appeals affirmed per curiam. Not one judge dissented as the case passed through the state's entire judicial process.

The *Sampson* facts did not present a general pattern of abuse or culpable neglect but only a single, controversial parental decision, albeit a major one. Both the Family Court and the Appellate Division explicitly recognized that inaction did not mean probable death and that the operation would remove only some of the unsightly growth. Plastic surgery and several years of continuing treatment would be necessary. One surgeon described the initial operation as "a risky surgical procedure" of six to eight hours duration and occasioning great loss of blood. And far from demanding immediate action, according to the witness, the operation would be less hazardous if postponed until the boy reached maturity. Then the potential blood loss would be less in relation to his body's total supply. In short, it might be said that it was not the mother's refusal to consent but the operation itself that was life-threatening.

The trial court justified overriding the objections lodged both by the child's mother and his law guardian by a humane desire to salvage some semblance of a normal life for Kevin Sampson:

> I am persuaded that if this court is to meet its responsibilities to this boy it can neither shift the responsibility onto his shoulders nor can it permit his mother's religious beliefs to stand in the way of obtaining through corrective surgery whatever chance he may have for a normal, happy existence, which ... is difficult of attainment under the most propitious circumstances, but will unquestionably be impossible if the disfigurement is not corrected.

In re Sampson, 65 Misc.2d 658, 317 N.Y.S.2d 641, 657 (1970), affirmed per curiam 29 N.Y.2d 900, 328 N.Y.S.2d 686, 278 N.E.2d 918 (1972)

Hart v. Brown

Superior Court of Connecticut, Fairfield County, 1972.
29 Conn.Sup. 368, 289 A.2d 386.

■ Testo, Judge. This matter is before this court by way of an action for a declaratory judgment. General Statutes § 52–29; Practice Book § 307.

The plaintiffs are Peter Hart and Eleanor Hart, the parents and natural guardians of Katheleen A. Hart and Margaret H. Hart, minors, identical twins, age seven years and ten months. The minor twins appear herein by court-appointed guardians ad litem: Attorney Thomas Dolan for the minor, Margaret, and Mrs. Sylvia Chandler for the minor Katheleen. The defendants are practicing physicians licensed in this state and the Yale–New Haven Hospital, Inc., a duly organized Connecticut corporation located in the city and county of New Haven.

The plaintiff minor Katheleen A. Hart is presently a patient in the Yale–New Haven Hospital awaiting a kidney transplant. It is reasonably probable that if such procedure does not occur soon she will die. The defendant physicians have in the past performed successful kidney transplantation operations, and they are of the opinion that a successful transplantation operation can be performed on the plaintiff minors, Katheleen A. Hart as donee and Margaret H. Hart as donor.

The plaintiffs Peter Hart and Eleanor Hart, each of whom had originally offered a kidney, have requested as parents and natural guardians of the identical twins the transplantation operation of the kidney, but the defendant physicians are unwilling to perform this operation and the defendant hospital refuses the use of its facilities unless this court declares that the parents and/or guardians ad litem of the minors have the right to give their consent to the operation upon the minor twins.

The equity powers of a court must be cautiously and sparingly exercised and only in rare instances should they be exercised. The need must be urgent, the probabilities of success should be most favorable, and the duty must be clear. If it were otherwise, a court of equity, in a case such as this might assume omnipotent powers; to do so is not the function of the court and must be avoided.

The inherent power of a court of equity to grant the relief sought herein has been decided previously in our American courts. In earlier decisions, the English courts took a broader view of this power, with respect to incompetents. Ex parte Whitbread, 2 Mer. 99, 35 Eng.Rep. 878 (Ch.1816). That case held that a court of equity has the power to make provisions for a needy brother from the estate of an incompetent. This inherent rule was followed in this country in New York; Re Willoughby, 11 Paige 257 (N.Y.Ch.1844); where the court stated that a chancellor has the power to deal with the estate of an incompetent in the same manner as the incompetent if he had his faculties. This rule has been extended to cover not only property matters but also the personal affairs of an incompetent. 27 Am.Jur.2d 592, Equity, § 69. "[A] court of equity has full and complete jurisdiction over the persons of those who labor under any legal disability.... The court's action ... is not limited by any narrow bounds, but it is empowered to stretch forth its arm in whatever direction its aid ... may be needed. While this indeed is a special exercise of equity jurisdiction, it is beyond question that by virtue thereof the court may pass upon purely personal rights." Ibid. The right to act for an incompetent has been recognized as the "doctrine of substituted judgment" and is broad enough to cover all matters touching on the well-being of legally incapacitated persons. The doctrine has been recognized in American courts since 1844.

This court is not being asked to act where a person is legally incompetent. The matter, however, does involve two minors who do not have the legal capacity to consent. This situation was dealt with in three earlier unreported cases decided in our sister state of Massachusetts. The commonwealth of Massachusetts ruled that a court of equity does have the power to permit the natural parents of minor twins to give their consent to a procedure such as is being contemplated by this court. Those cases involved minors of the ages of nineteen, fourteen and fourteen. In a similar case, Strunk v. Strunk, 445 S.W.2d 145 (Ky.1969), a court of equity was confronted with whether or not it had the power to permit the natural parent of a twenty-seven-year-old mental incompetent with a mentality of a six-year-old to give her consent to a kidney transplantation operation. The Kentucky case dealt with a transplant from the mental incompetent to his twenty-eight-year-old brother. The court held that a court of equity does have such power, applying also the "doctrine of substituted judgment."

Therefore, this court is of the opinion that it has the power to act in this matter.

The facts of the case as testified to by competent medical witnesses are as follows: Katheleen Hart is a minor of the age of seven years and ten months and is suffering from a hemolytic uremic syndrome. This is a disorder of the kidneys with clots within the small blood vessels. This disease has no known etiology and is prevalent primarily in young children. The diagnosis was confirmed on November 29, 1971, after a kidney biopsy was performed. Hemodialysis treatments were commenced on December 8, 1971, along with other treatment to correct this disorder. On February 1, 1972, her kidney was biopsied for the second time because of the onset of a malignant type of blood pressure elevation, and this biopsy disclosed a new and more disastrous lesion—malignant hypertension—which could prove fatal. On February 17, 1972, a bilateral nephrectomy was performed with removal of both kidneys to control the situation. As of that date, Katheleen became a patient with fixed uremia with no potential kidney function and required dialysis treatments twice weekly. The prospect of survival is, because of her age, at best questionable. It was medically advised that she not continue this dialysis therapy but rather that a kidney transplantation take place.

The types of kidney transplantations discussed in this matter were a parental homograft—transfer of tissue from one human being to another—and an isograft, that is, a one-egg twin graft from one to another. The parental homograft always presents a serious problem of rejection by the donee. Because the human body rejects any foreign organs, the donee must be placed upon a program of immunosuppressive drugs to combat such rejection. An isograft transplantation, on the other hand, is not presented with the problem of rejection. A one-egg twin carries the same genetic material, and, because of this, rejection is not a factor in the success rate of the graft.

The chance of Katheleen's surviving dialysis therapy for a period of five years was estimated at fifty-fifty, with the possibility of many other complications setting in. The ultimate purpose of dialysis treatment in a child this age is to keep the patient alive until a kidney transplant is found. Because of the many complications involved in a transplantation procedure other than with the minor identical twin as donor, it has been medically advised that an isograft transplantation be recommended.

Since 1966, it is reported in the Ninth Report of the Human Renal Transplant Registry, twelve twin grafts have been performed. All twelve have been successful, as reported by the Registry, at one-and two-year follow-ups. In the identical-twin donations since 1966, grafts are functioning at 100 percent. Before 1966, because of technical matters, the survival rate was about 90 percent. Of all isografts followed since 1966, all are successful. In this type of a graft there is substantially a 100 percent chance that the twins will live out a normal life span—emotionally and physically.

If a parent donates the kidney, the statistics show less success. The average percent of success in that type of transplant has been 70 percent at one year and 65 percent or so over a two-year period. The falloff thereafter runs another 5 to 10 or more percent per year. The long-range survival of a parent transplant runs around 50 to 55 percent over a period of five years and appears to fall off to about 37 percent over a period of seven years.

The side effects of the immunosuppressive drugs in a parental homograft are numerous and include the possibility of bone marrow toxicity, liver damage, and a syndrome called Cushing syndrome—a roundish face, a "buffalo hump" on the back of the neck, and growth retardation. Some less common side effects are a demineralization of the bone mass which will result in the collapsing of bones of the spine; aseptic necrosis of the femoral head of the hip, making a person unable to walk; peptic ulcer disease with bleeding; hairiness; sexual immaturity; and cataracts of the eyes. It has also been reported that two suicides have occurred because of the psychological effect upon young girls resulting from immunosuppressive drugs. An overall percentage of around 70 to 77 percent would be expected to survive two years from a parental graft. It is also possible that 40 to 50 percent of the patients might still be surviving at near ten years with a parental graft.

Of 3000 recorded kidney operations of live donors, there is reported only one death of a donor, and even this death may have been from causes unrelated to the procedure. The short-range risk to a donor is negligible.

The operating surgeon testified that the surgical risk is no more than the risk of the anesthesia. The operative procedure would last about two and one-half hours. There would be some minor post-operative pain but no more than in any other surgical procedure. The donor would be hospitalized for about eight days and would be able to resume normal activities in thirty days. Assuming an uneventful recovery, the donor would thereafter be restricted only from violent contact sports. She would be able to engage in all of the normal life activities of an active young girl. Medical testimony indicated that the risk to the donor is such that life insurance actuaries do not rate such individuals higher than those with two kidneys. The only real risk would be trauma to the one remaining kidney, but testimony indicated that such trauma is extremely rare in civilian life.

The tests to be performed on the donor are an intravenous pyelogram and an aortagram. The former would permit the examiner to visualize the structure and anatomy of the kidneys, while the latter would outline the blood vessels that supply the blood to the kidneys. Both tests involve a single needle puncture—one into a vein and one into an artery. There might be a skin graft test performed if necessary to confirm the fact that donor and donee are identical twins. The operation would not be performed if the medical team was not fully satisfied that the donor and the donee are identical twins.

A psychiatrist who examined the donor gave testimony that the donor has a strong identification with her twin sister. He also testified that if the expected successful results are achieved they would be of immense benefit to the donor in that the donor would be better off in a family that was happy than in a family that was distressed and in that it would be a very great loss to the donor if the donee were to die from her illness.

The donor has been informed of the operation and insofar as she may be capable of understanding she desires to donate her kidney so that her sister may return to her. A clergyman was also a witness and his testimony was that the decision by the parents of the donor and donee was morally and ethically sound. The court-appointed guardian ad litem for the donor gave testimony that he conferred with the parents, the physicians, the donor, and other men in the religious profession, and he has consented to the performance of the operation.

The medical testimony given at this hearing clearly indicates that scientifically this type of procedure is a "perfect" transplant.

The court has weighed the testimony of the clergyman who stated that the natural parents are making a morally sound decision. Also, the testimony of the court-appointed guardians ad litem was that they are giving their consent to the procedure. The psychiatric testimony is of limited value only because of the ages of the minors. The testimony of the natural parents was reviewed by this court, and it is apparent that they came to their decision only after many hours of agonizing consideration.

One of the legal problems in this matter presents a balancing of the rights of the natural parents and the rights of minor children—more directly the rights of the donor child. Because of the unusual circumstances of this case and the fact of great medical progress in this field, it would appear that the natural parents would be able to substitute their consent for that of the minor children after a close, independent and objective investigation of their motivation and reasoning. This has been accomplished in this matter by the participation of a clergyman, the defendant physicians, an attorney guardian ad litem for the donor, the guardian ad litem for the donee, and, indeed, this court itself.

A further question before this court is whether it should abandon the donee to a brief medically complicated life and eventual death or permit the natural parents to take some action based on reason and medical probability in order to keep both children alive. The court will choose the latter course, being of the opinion that the kidney transplant procedure contemplated herein—an isograft—has progressed at this time to the point of being a medically proven fact of life. Testimony was offered that this type of procedure is not clinical experimentation but rather medically accepted therapy.

There is authority in our American jurisdiction that nontherapeutic operations can be legally permitted on a minor as long as the parents or other guardians consent to the procedure. Bonner v. Moran, 75 U.S.App. D.C. 156, 126 F.2d 121 (1941). That case involved skin grafting from a fifteen-year-old boy to his cousin, who was severely burned. The year of the case was 1941, when such skin homografting—transferring tissue from one human being to another—was relatively novel. "[H]ere we have a case of a surgical operation not for the benefit of the person operated on but for another, and also so involved in its technique as to require a mature mind to understand precisely what the donor was offering to give." Id., 123. The court held that the consent of the parent was necessary.

In Strunk v. Strunk, 445 S.W.2d 145 (Ky.1969), the adult donor was a legal incompetent. The court in the commonwealth of Kentucky authorized the parent to give her consent. The incompetent had the mental capacity of a six-year-old. The court further held that the saving of the life of the incompetent's brother would be of benefit to the donor. In the instant case, it has been stated that the donor would enjoy a better future life if her ailing twin sister were kept alive. The difference between the cases is subtle. The donor here is almost eight years old. In the *Strunk* case, the donor was an adult with the mentality of a six-year-old. The risks to the donee in the *Strunk* case were more than what are presented here, the procedure there being a related homograft as compared to an isograft in this case, as discussed earlier in this opinion. The accomplished results in that matter and in this matter are identical.

Thus, also, in the Massachusetts cases discussed above, where the doctrine of "grave emotional impact" to the donors was first used, the courts of that state permitted the procedures.

This court is confronted with a combination of the *Strunk* case and the Massachusetts cases in that the procedures in the latter involved minor identical twins and in the former a legally incompetent adult with the mental capacity of an infant. In the case at bar we have an identical twin donor almost eight years old. Justice was accomplished in all of the aforementioned cases. Justice will be accomplished in this case.

This court can and will make a determination of this matter, using the doctrines of law as stated in the *Strunk* case, in the *Bonner* case, and in the Massachusetts cases.

The court understands that the operation on the donee is a necessity for her continued life; that there are negligible risks involved to both donor and donee; that to subject the donee to a parental homograft may be cruel and inhuman because of the possible side effects of the immunosuppressive drugs; that the prognosis for good health and long life to both children is excellent; that there is no known opposition to having the operations performed; that it will be most beneficial to the donee; and that it will be of some benefit to the donor. To prohibit the natural parents and the guardians ad litem of the minor children the right to give their consent under these circumstances, where there is supervision by this court and other persons in examining their judgment, would be most unjust, inequitable and injudicious. Therefore, natural parents of a minor should have the right to give their consent to an isograft kidney transplantation procedure when their motivation and reasoning are favorably reviewed by a community representation which includes a court of equity.

It is the judgment of this court that Eleanor Hart and Peter Hart have the right, under the particular facts and circumstances of this matter, to give their consent to the operations on both minor children and to give their consent to the defendant physicians to conduct the further medical tests that the defendants deem necessary prior to the performing of the operations, provided the defendant physicians medically establish the children to be identical twins and a report of their findings is filed with this court.

Judgment accordingly.

NOTE

In Strunk v. Strunk, 445 S.W.2d 145 (Ky.1969), the court authorized the transplant of a kidney from a retarded adult to his brother who was facing end stage renal disease and needed a transplant. The court justified the decision as a benefit to the donor by explaining that the donor's well being "would be jeopardized more severely by the loss of his brother than by removal of a kidney." In Curran v. Bosze, 141 Ill.2d 473, 153 Ill.Dec. 213, 566 N.E.2d 1319 (1990), the Supreme Court of Illinois confronted a situation in which an eight year old with undifferentiated leukemia needed a bone transplant. The father of the child and his stepbrother were not HLA identical. Several years earlier Mr. Bosze had fathered identical twins from an affair with Ms. Curran. The father filed suit seeking to have the twins submit for bone marrow harvesting over the objection of their mother. The court held that the substituted judgment doctrine was not applicable and that the best interests of the twins was not served by having them tested for compatibility when they would not benefit medically and there was some risk of harm to them in the procedure.

With advances in immunosuppression drugs and surgical and medical techniques, and programs to encourage organ donation, organ transplantation has increased substantially. No longer is the sibling relationship so critical, and thus the primary problem faced in *Hart* and *Strunk* is much less important in most cases. A new issue that has risen concerns the decision of parents to bear another child in order to assist their existing child through tissue transplantation. For discussion of the ethical issues involved, *see* Mark P. Aulisio, Thomas May, and Geoffrey D. Block, *Procreation for Donation: The Moral and Political Permissibility of "Having a Child to Save a Child"*, 110 CAMBRIDGE QUARTERLY OF HEALTHCARE ETHICS 408 (2001).

CALIFORNIA FAMILY CODE (West 2004)

§ 6910. Medical treatment of minor; adult entrusted with consensual power

The parent, guardian, or caregiver of a minor who is a relative of the minor and who may authorize medical care and dental care under Section 6550, may authorize in writing an adult into whose care a minor has been entrusted to consent to medical care or dental care, or both, for the minor.

NOTE

See, also, the discussion of Standby Guardianship *infra* at p. 1332 in Chapter 9.

In re Doe

Supreme Court of Georgia, 1992.
262 Ga. 389, 418 S.E.2d 3.

■ CLARKE, JUSTICE.

In this appeal from a final order in a declaratory judgment action, we face several difficult issues relating to medical decision-making for a terminally ill child. Jane Doe, a 13–year–old child, had experienced medical problems since birth. In May, 1991, she was admitted to Scottish Rite Hospital following a mild choking episode. Initially her attending physicians expected she would recover. Over the next weeks, however, her condition degenerated and she became limp and unresponsive. The doctors described her condition as "stuporous" or varying between stupor and coma states, and noted her brain stem was shrinking or degenerating. She also suffered from various systemic illnesses. The doctors agreed that she suffered from a degenerative neurological disease, but none could make a certain diagnosis.

In late May her doctors placed Jane on a respirator. By mid-July she had suffered recurrent infections and mental decline. At that time the doctors decided it was necessary to insert tracheostomy and gastronomy (feeding and breathing) tubes surgically. They discussed the possibility of a "Do Not Resuscitate" (DNR) order with her parents in case Jane suffered cardiac arrest during the procedure. Jane's mother, Susan Doe, agreed to a DNR order; her father, John Doe, did not. In August, Jane Doe's condition continued to decline. The doctors began to discuss whether deescalation of life support[1] and a DNR order might be appropriate. In early September, Susan Doe supported deescalation of life support and a DNR order. John Doe did not. At Susan Doe's request, Jane's medical situation was presented to Scottish Rite's Bioethics Committee. The Committee considered and evaluated Jane's condition and recommended the hospital back Jane's mother's desire to enter a DNR order and deescalate medical treatment.

At the time of the hearing, she favored a DNR order, but not deescalation of treatment. After an evidentiary hearing, the trial judge entered an order enjoining the hospital from deescalating treatment or from enforcing a DNR order unless both parents agreed to such a course of treatment. The state filed this appeal.[2]

1. We find no merit to the state's contention that the hospital had no standing to bring this declaratory judgment action. We must construe the declaratory judgment statute liberally. The statute is available in situations presenting an " 'actual controversy' ... where interested parties are asserting adverse claims upon a state of facts wherein a legal judgment is sought that would control or direct future action." Darnell v. Tate, 206 Ga. 576, 580, 58 S.E.2d 160 (1950).

Here, the hospital was charged with a duty of care to an incompetent patient whose parents disagreed as to the appropriate course of medical treatment. Neither precedent nor statute provided a clear answer to the hospital's dilemma. Meanwhile, Jane Doe's condition continued to deteriorate and the likelihood that she would experience cardiac arrest increased daily. Without guidance as to which parent's instructions to follow, the hospital could not determine its legal obligation to its patient. On these facts, we conclude that the hospital adequately demonstrated a need for a legal judgment that would control its future action. A declaratory judgment action was appropriate.[3]

---

1. Deescalation is the discontinuation of medical measures, such as a ventilator. A DNR order means that extreme lifesaving procedures like countershock, chest compression and administration of medication to support heart rate and blood pressure will not be instituted in the event of cardiac or respiratory failure.

2. Although Jane Doe died several weeks after the final order was entered in the declaratory judgment action below, this appeal is not moot because it is among those

cases which are "capable of repetition yet evading review." In re L.H.R., 253 Ga. 439, 321 S.E.2d 716 (1984) (quoting Gerstein v. Pugh 420 U.S. 103, 95 S.Ct. 854, 43 L.Ed.2d 54 (1975)).

3. Contrary to the state's suggestion, this action does not fall within the exclusive jurisdiction of Juvenile Court. See OCGA § 15–11–5. The action did not seek to terminate the legal parent-child relationship or to wrest custody or control from Jane Doe's

2. The state next contends the trial court erred in considering the hospital's petition because Jane Doe did not meet the criteria for withdrawal of life support established in In re: L.H.R., 253 Ga. 439, 321 S.E.2d 716 (1984). In In re: L.H.R. we held that, in the absence of any conflicting state interest, a patient has a right to refuse medical treatment which right is not lost because of the youth or incompetence of the patient. We went on to say: We conclude that the right to refuse treatment may be exercised by the parents or legal guardian of the infant after diagnosis that the infant is terminally ill with no hope of recovery and that the infant exists in a chronic vegetative state with no reasonable possibility of attaining cognitive function. The above diagnosis must be made by the attending physician. Two physicians with no interest in the outcome of the case must concur in the diagnosis and prognosis. Although prior judicial approval is not required, the courts remain available in the event of disagreement between the parties, any case of suspected abuse, or other appropriate instances. In this case the state emphasizes Jane Doe's doctors could not diagnose with certainty the disease causing her neurological degeneration. The state also points out Jane Doe was not in a chronic vegetative state and death was not imminent.[4] Therefore, the state asserts, the hospital could not raise the issue of deescalation of medical treatment and the trial court should have dismissed the case.

(a) First, we reject the state's argument that the trial court should have dismissed this case because Jane Doe did not meet the criteria expressed in In re L.H.R. In In re L.H.R. we addressed a specific set of circumstances and decided that the parents and physicians caring for the infant could decide whether to proceed with deescalation of medical treatment without seeking judicial approval. The opinion set up guidelines to protect the rights of incompetent patients without involving the court in the medical decision-making process for every incompetent patient. The opinion did not preclude considering the propriety of deescalation under other circumstances. During the years since we considered In re L.H.R., the legislature has enacted or amended several statutes governing the legal propriety of proxy health care decisions. See, OCGA § 31–32–1, et seq. (Living Wills); OCGA § 31–36–1, et seq. (Durable Power of Attorney for Health Care); and OCGA § 31–39–1, et seq. (Cardiopulmonary Resuscitation). Also, other courts have recognized that incompetent patients have the right to refuse life sustaining treatment even though they are not in a chronic vegetative state.[5] Thus, while medical technology and society's

parents. Further, Jane Doe was not a "deprived child," because both parents actively sought the best available care and treatment for her.

4. Imminence of death is not a criterion for deescalation of medical treatment under In re L.H.R. or under the current provisions of the Living Will statute. See OCGA § 31–32–1 (1992). See also State v. McAfee, 259 Ga. 579, 385 S.E.2d 651 (1989). This court

and the Georgia legislature have recognized, as have numerous other courts, scholars, and ethicists, that medical technology can extend the dying process almost indefinitely, so that technical death might not occur for many years if artificial support systems are continued.

5. See, e.g., Superintendent of Belchertown State Sch. v. Saikewicz, 373 Mass. 728, 370 N.E.2d 417 (1977) (chemotherapy treat-

understanding of death and dying continue to evolve and change, we cannot mandate a single, static formula for deciding when deescalation of medical treatment may be appropriate. Rather, we endorse the view that medical decision-making for incompetent patients is most often best left to the patient's family (or other designated proxy) and the medical community, ... and the courts remain available to decide controversial cases.

(b) We further reject the state's argument that Jane Doe's parents could not legally have decided to deescalate her medical treatment. The medical staff attending to Jane Doe agreed that she was in the final stages of some degenerative neurological disease, and that she vacillated between coma and stupor, responding only to deep pain stimulus. She required artificial means to support all her bodily functions. The doctors agreed she lacked the ability for any cognitive function or interactive activity, and did not have any reasonable hope for her recovery. They also agreed there was no known medical treatment that could improve her condition or halt the neurological deterioration. It was apparent that the life support system was prolonging her death, rather than her life. There was no state interest in maintaining life support systems. Thus, we conclude that those legally responsible for Jane Doe could have refused treatment on her behalf without seeking prior judicial approval.

(c) A corollary to the above statement is that Jane Doe's parents also could have consented to treatment on her behalf. See OCGA § 31–9–2 (Persons authorized to consent to medical or surgical treatment). At the time of the hearing, both parents opposed deescalation of treatment. No party in this case argues that the parents' mutual decision to continue life support measures should have been overridden under the facts of this case.[6]

ment could be withheld from a profoundly retarded and disoriented man suffering from leukemia, where the chemotherapy would not cure his disease but merely prolong his suffering); In re Spring, 380 Mass. 629, 405 N.E.2d 115 (1980) (life-prolonging but noncurative hemodialysis treatment could be withheld from conscious but profoundly senile patient suffering from kidney disease); In re Hier, 18 Mass.App. 200, 464 N.E.2d 959 (1984) (surgery necessary for insertion of a stomach feeding tube could be withheld from incompetent person suffering from delusions and severe mental illness); In re Conroy, 98 N.J. 321, 486 A.2d 1209 (1985) (right to terminate life-sustaining treatment could be exercised on behalf of an incompetent person with serious and permanent mental and physical impairments and a life expectancy less than 1 year); Foody v. Manchester Mem. Hosp., 40 Conn.Sup. 127, 482 A.2d 713 (1984) (life-sustaining treatment could be withheld from semicomatose patient described as "awake but unaware").

6. The law recognizes that parents "possess what a child lacks in maturity, experience and capacity for judgment required for making life's difficult decisions. More importantly, ... natural bonds of affection lead parents to act in the best interests of their children." In re L.H.R., 253 Ga. 439, 321 S.E.2d 716 (1984) (quoting Parham v. J.R., 442 U.S. 584, 602, 99 S.Ct. 2493, 2504, 61 L.Ed.2d 101 (1979)). Therefore, the law presumes that the parents are the appropriate parties to make their children's medical decisions. For this reason in In re L.H.R., supra, we held that, under certain circumstances, the parents of an incompetent child may exercise the child's right to refuse medical treatment without prior judicial approval. We have never held, however, that parents have an absolute right to make medical decisions for their children. See, e.g., Jefferson v. Griffin Spalding County Hospital Authority, 247 Ga. 86, 274 S.E.2d 457 (1981); In the Interest of C.R., 160 Ga.App. 873, 288 S.E.2d 589 (1982). The United States Supreme Court

This appeal does not present and we do not reach any issue regarding "medical abuse." Therefore, the trial court correctly enjoined the hospital from deescalating treatment over both parents' objection.[7]

3. The state next asserts the trial court erred in holding that a DNR order requires the concurrence of both parents of the child. The statute requires the agreement of both parents, if both parents are present and actively participating in the medical decision-making process for the child. OCGA § 31–39–1 allows "any parent"[8] to consent to a DNR order for a minor child. OCGA § 31–39–6 allows "any parent" to revoke consent to an order not to resuscitate. The result is as follows: One parent may consent. If there is no second parent, if the other parent is not present, or if the other parent simply prefers not to participate in the decision, the consent of one parent to a DNR order is legally sufficient under the statute. However, if there is a second custodial parent who disagrees with the decision to forego cardiopulmonary resuscitation, the second parent may revoke consent under the terms of OCGA § 31–39–6(b). We reject the argument that only the parent who has given consent may effectively revoke consent. Where two parents have legal custody of a child, each parent shares equal decision-making responsibility for that child. If consent to a DNR order is revoked under the provision of OCGA § 31–39–6(b), the hospital must follow the statutory presumption that every patient is presumed to consent to resuscitation.[9] See OCGA § 31–39–3(a). Thus, because the father revoked consent, the trial court correctly determined the hospital could not enter a DNR order.

■ HUNT, JUSTICE, concurring.

I write in response to the state's motion for reconsideration.

The state urges that we further delineate the limits of a hospital's standing in cases like this one. In particular, the state asks us to hold, as did the trial court, that a hospital would not have standing to advocate an alternative course of treatment where the parents or legal guardians agree about the course of treatment for their child. We make no such holding, and our opinion should not be read to confer standing for a hospital under circumstances other than those presented here; that is, where the parents disagree about the course of such medical treatment. This is not to imply that, when a case presents the issue, we would interpret a hospital's standing either more broadly or more narrowly than we have done here. Compare Jefferson v. Griffin Spalding County Hospital Authority, 247 Ga. 86, 274 S.E.2d 457 (1981).

similarly does not recognize an absolute right of a parent to make medical decisions for a child. See Parham v. J.R., supra.

7. This appeal does not present any issue regarding what should have been done if Jane Doe's parents had disagreed at trial or thereafter about the propriety of deescalating treatment.

8. Note that the statute defines "parent" as a parent who has custody of a minor. OCGA § 31–39–2(10).

9. The statutory presumption governs only consent to emergency cardio-pulmonary resuscitation. No statutory or other presumption governs the issue of consent to other, non-emergency medical procedures.

Montalvo v. Borkavec

Court of Appeals of Wisconsin, 2002.
256 Wis.2d 472, 647 N.W.2d 413, appeal denied, 257 Wis.2d 118, 653 N.W.2d 890, cert. denied, 124 S.Ct. 1485 (2003).

■ Before WEDEMEYER, P.J., FINE and SCHUDSON, JJ.

■ WEDEMEYER, P.J.

Nancy Montalvo, Brian Vila and Emanuel L. Vila (by his guardian ad litem, Timothy J. Aiken) appeal from judgments entered after the trial court dismissed their complaint against Dr. Brent W. Arnold, Dr. Jonathan H. Berkoff, St. Mary's Hospital of Milwaukee, the Wisconsin Patients Compensation Fund and Physicians Insurance Co. of Wisconsin. The complaint alleged that the defendants were negligent for failing to sufficiently inform Montalvo and Vila of the risk of disability to Emanuel following his premature birth by cesarean section.

Montalvo, Vila, and Emanuel raise ten arguments[1] We address only those arguments necessary to the resolution of this case. Because under our current rules of pleading and procedure, substantive law, and public policy the plaintiffs' claims cannot be pursued, we affirm.

I. BACKGROUND

On November 21, 1996, Montalvo entered St. Mary's Hospital in Milwaukee, Wisconsin, with pre-term labor symptoms. An ultrasound revealed that the baby was 23 and 3/7 weeks old, and weighed 679 grams. Attempts to interrupt her labor and delay the birth were unsuccessful. Prior to delivery of the child, the parents executed an informed consent agreement for a cesarean procedure.

Dr. Terre Borkovec performed the cesarean section. At birth, Emanuel was "handed off" to Dr. Arnold, a neonatologist, who successfully performed life-saving resuscitation measures.

On November 19, 1999, Montalvo filed a complaint against Borkovec and Arnold alleging that both physicians violated the informed consent statute, Wis. Stat. § 448.30, in performing the cesarean section. The complaint also alleged that Arnold, Berkoff, and St. Mary's Hospital were negligent for violating the same informed consent statute when they performed "life-saving measures" for Emanuel. The complaint alleged that

---

1. They argue: (1) Montalvo had a right to informed consent prior to the cesarean procedure; (2) the decision to use potentially harmful therapy is subject to informed consent; (3) Wisconsin abortion law does not apply to this situation; (4) with the exception of the drug/alcohol abuse provisions of ch. 48, expectant mothers have the absolute right to control the manner of delivery; (5) the concept of "viability" cannot mean preservation of life at any cost; (6) the lifelong ramifications of perinatal treatment decisions mandate that such decisions be made by the parents only after being fully informed of all the risks and alternatives; (7) federal funding statutes do not control Wisconsin informed consent law; (8) the Americans with Disabilities Act does not control this case; (9) there is no constitutional basis for federal or state government interference in the medical decision-making process; and (10) compelling parents to agree to surgeries or therapies whose benefit versus risk analysis is unclear puts an unfair burden on parents.

because the physicians failed to advise the parents of "the risks or potential consequences of a child born at 23 or 24 weeks gestation and/or with a birth weight of less than 750 grams," consent was not informed and a variety of damages resulted.

Berkoff, Arnold, and St. Mary's Hospital moved to dismiss the claims contending that the complaint failed to state a claim upon which relief could be granted pursuant to Wis. Stat. § 802.06(2)(a)6. During a hearing on the motions, and prior to rendering a decision, the trial court ascertained that the plaintiffs were not alleging harm to Emanuel as the result of "extraordinary care measures" but were claiming that the decision to use "extraordinary care measures" should have been relegated to them as parents rather than left to the physicians. Lastly, the plaintiffs were not alleging that Emanuel was disabled by any actions taken by the physicians or St. Mary's Hospital.

The trial court dismissed the complaint ruling first that the only claim pled for a violation of the informed consent statute in performing the cesarean section was against Arnold.[2] Because, however, he was only a bystander to the delivery, he was not required under the statute to provide informed consent because he did not perform the procedure. Second, the trial court ruled that Wisconsin law does not leave the resuscitation decision upon the birth of a child solely to the parents because of the community's interest in protecting children, and the physicians' commitment to preserving life. Montalvo now appeals.

II. ANALYSIS

Standard of Review

A motion to dismiss a complaint for failure to state a claim upon which relief may be granted tests the legal sufficiency of the pleading. *Evans v. Cameron,* 121 Wis.2d 421, 426, 360 N.W.2d 25 (1985). As a question of law, we review the trial court's decision independently, keeping in mind the value we accord the trial court's analysis. We must affirm a judgment dismissing a complaint for failure to state a claim if, upon review of the complaint, as liberally construed, it is quite clear that under no conditions can the plaintiff recover based upon the facts alleged and inferences reasonably drawn. *Bartley v. Thompson,* 198 Wis.2d 323, 332, 542 N.W.2d 227 (Ct.App.1995). With these rubrics of review in mind, we now examine the issues dispositive of this appeal.

A. *Rules of Pleading and Procedure.*

The original defendants in this case were Drs. Borkovec, Arnold, Berkoff and St. Mary's Hospital. Borkovec, who performed the cesarean section, was voluntarily dismissed from the case. That left Arnold as the only target allegedly negligent for failure to obtain a properly informed

---

2. For reasons undisclosed in the rec- ord, Dr. Terre Borkovec was voluntarily dis- missed from the action.

consent for the performance of the cesarean section. Yet, it was undisputed that Arnold, although present when the cesarean section occurred, did not participate in the procedure. The trial court construed Wis. Stat. § 448.30 to provide that only the treating physician, here Borkovec, owed the responsibility of informed consent to the parents. Borkovec, however, was no longer a party to the action. The statute does not impose the duty of informed consent on non-treating physicians. Because Arnold neither participated nor assisted, he was not a treating physician with respect to the cesarean procedure, and did not have a duty to comply with the informed consent statute.

Thus, the trial court concluded that with respect to the cesarean procedure, no claim had been properly pleaded upon which relief could be granted. We know of no authority to the contrary. In this respect, the trial court did not err. On appeal, Montalvo has not contested this ruling. Consequently, the only claims remaining to be addressed by the trial court were the failure to properly obtain informed consent relating to resuscitation efforts by Arnold, Berkoff, and St. Mary's Hospital.

B. Substantive Law and Statutory Law.

On the remaining informed consent issue relating to the resuscitation efforts, the essential question is whether the complaint states a legally cognizable claim against the remaining defendants. The trial court ruled it did not.

Our informed consent law requires a physician to disclose information necessary for a reasonable person to make an intelligent decision with respect to the choices of treatment or diagnosis. *Kuklinski v. Rodriguez,* 203 Wis.2d 324, 329, 552 N.W.2d 869 (Ct.App.1996). It is a right found in both the common law of this state and in statutory provisions. Wisconsin Stat. § 448.30 codified the duty-to-disclose law recognized by *Scaria v. St. Paul Fire & Marine Ins. Co.,* 68 Wis.2d 1, 13, 227 N.W.2d 647 (1975), and reads:

Information on alternate modes of treatment. Any physician who treats a patient shall inform the patient about the availability of all alternate, viable medical modes of treatment and about the benefits and risks of these treatments. The physician's duty to inform the patient under this section does not require disclosure of:

(1) Information beyond what a reasonably well-qualified physician in a similar medical classification would know.

(2) Detailed technical information that in all probability a patient would not understand.

(3) Risks apparent or known to the patient.

(4) Extremely remote possibilities that might falsely or detrimentally alarm the patient.

(5) Information in emergencies where failure to provide treatment would be more harmful to the patient than treatment.

(6) Information in cases where the patient is incapable of consenting.

The statute is basically divided into two parts: what information a treating physician is obligated to convey to a patient and what information he/she need not convey. The plain language of the statute places an obligation on a physician to provide information only about available and viable options of treatment.

In addressing the obligatory first part of the statute, our supreme court has declared: "[W]hat a physician must disclose is contingent upon what, under the circumstances of a given case, a reasonable person in the patient's position would need to know in order to make an intelligent and informed decision." *Johnson v. Kokemoor,* 199 Wis.2d 615, 639, 545 N.W.2d 495 (1996). Restricting the application of the obligation, we declared in *Mathias v. St. Catherine's Hospital, Inc.,* 212 Wis.2d 540, 569 N.W.2d 330 (Ct.App.1997): "The law in Wisconsin on informed consent is well settled. . . . the duty to advise a patient of the risks of treatment lies with the doctor. . . . The court was explicit in pointing out that the duty to obtain informed consent lay with the doctor, not the hospital." *Id.* at 548, 569 N.W.2d 330 (citations omitted)[3]. Thus, St. Mary's Hospital was not a proper defendant. We continue the analysis then only as the second claim applies to Arnold and Berkoff . . .

Doubtless, the doctrine of informed consent comes into play only when there is a need to make a choice of available, viable alternatives. In other words, there must be a choice that can be made. The process of decision-making necessarily implies assessing and selecting an available alternative. In the context of treatment required after the cesarean procedure was performed on Emanuel, there are two reasons why no available, viable alternative existed to give rise to the obligation to engage in the informed consent process. First, requiring the informed consent process here presumes that a right to decide not to resuscitate the newly born child or to withhold life-sustaining medical care actually existed. This premise is faulty. In *Edna M.F. v. Eisenberg,* 210 Wis.2d 557, 568, 563 N.W.2d 485 (1997), our supreme court set forth the preconditions required for permitting the withholding or withdrawal of life-sustaining medical treatment. There, the appointed guardian of her incompetent sister, Edna, sought permission to direct the withholding of medical care from Edna even though she was not in a persistent vegetative state. *Id.* at 559–60, 563 N.W.2d 485. She claimed that Edna would not want to live in her condition, completely dependent on others for her care and existence, non-responsive and immobile. *Id.* at 560–61, 563 N.W.2d 485. The court, in refusing to extend the right to refuse life-sustaining medical treatment beyond individuals in a persistent vegetative state, relied on the analysis of the United States Supreme Court in *Cruzan v. Director, Missouri Department of Health,* 497 U.S. 261, 110 S.Ct. 2841, 111 L.Ed.2d 224 (1990): "[W]e think a State may properly decline to make judgments about the 'quality' of life

---

3. The dismissal of St. Mary's Hospital at the complaint stage has not been addressed by the plaintiffs. We therefore deem the issue abandoned. *See Reiman Assocs. v. R/A Adver. Inc.,* 102 Wis.2d 305, 306 n. 1, 306 N.W.2d 292 (Ct.App.1981)

that a particular individual may enjoy, and simply assert an unqualified interest in the preservation of human life to be weighed against the constitutionally protected interests of the individual." *Edna M.F.*, 210 Wis.2d at 563, 563 N.W.2d 485 (quoting *Cruzan*, 497 U.S. at 282, 110 S.Ct. 2841, 111 L.Ed.2d 224).

The *Edna* court, in examining the sensitive issues before it and the need to balance the interests of the individual versus those of the state, was quick to appreciate the consequences of ultimate decisions made by third-party surrogates for those who cannot speak for themselves. It thus concluded that either withholding or withdrawing life-sustaining medical treatment is not in the best interests of any patient who is not in a persistent vegetative state. *Edna M.F.*, 210 Wis.2d at 566–68, 563 N.W.2d 485. Thus, in Wisconsin, in the absence of a persistent vegetative state, the right of a parent to withhold life-sustaining treatment from a child does not exist. It is not disputed here that there was no evidence that Emanuel was in "a persistent vegetative state." Accordingly, the alternative of withholding life-sustaining treatment did not exist.

The second reason why a viable alternative did not exist to trigger informed consent is the existence of the United States Child Abuse Protection and Treatment Act (CAPTA) of 1984, Pub.L. No. 98–457, 98 Stat. 1749 (codified at 42 U.S.C. § 5101 et seq.). Because Wisconsin has fulfilled the necessary obligations to receive federal funds under CAPTA, CAPTA and its regulations are fully applicable in this state. *Jeanine B. v. Thompson*, 967 F.Supp. 1104, 1111–12, 1118 (E.D.Wis.1997).

CAPTA was enacted to establish eligibility for states to obtain federal funding for the prevention of child abuse and to develop and implement a successful and comprehensive child and family protection strategy. Under CAPTA, states must have in place procedures for responding to child neglect. 42 U.S.C. § 5106(b)(4)(C). The Act includes a provision preventing "the withholding of medically indicated treatment from a disabled infant with a life-threatening condition." 45 C.F.R. § 1340.15(b)(1). In the regulations enacted under the statute, "withholding of medically indicated treatment" is defined as "the failure to respond to the infant's life-threatening conditions by providing treatment ... which, in the treating physician's ... reasonable medical judgment, will be most likely to be effective in ... correcting all such conditions...." 45 C.F.R. § 1340.15(b)(2). The regulations further include the "authority to initiate legal proceedings ... to prevent the withholding of medically indicated treatment from disabled infants with life-threatening conditions." 45 C.F.R. § 1340.15(c)(2)(iii). The implied choice of withholding treatment, proposed by the plaintiffs, is exactly what CAPTA prohibits.

It is noteworthy that in the complaint, plaintiffs did not allege that Emanuel was born with a known disability or that they would have chosen to withhold life-sustaining treatment. Instead, they allege that they were not given the statistics about the possible risks that he could develop a disability if he lived, and they should have been given the opportunity to withhold life-saving measures immediately after Emanuel's birth. Under the common law of Wisconsin and federal statutory law, however, Emanuel's parents did not have the right to withhold or withdraw immediate postnatal care from him. Thus, no viable alternative health treatment existed to trigger the informed consent process.[4]

We now examine the applicability of the second part of the informed consent statute; i.e., the six exception sections, providing conditions under which the treating physician is not obligated to inform the patient. Germane to our analysis is subsection (5) which renders unnecessary the disclosure of "information in emergencies where failure to provide treatment would be more harmful to the patient than treatment."

The complaint alleges that "attempts . . . to interrupt the preterm labor . . . [were] unsuccessful" resulting in Emanuel's premature birth by cesarean section, and that "upon Emanuel Vila's delivery, he was immediately handed off to defendant Brent Arnold, M.D. who initiated heroic and extraordinary life saving measures" on him. The allegations suggest that an emergency arose requiring an immediate response, which occurred. Montalvo does not suggest that all emergency actions should have ceased while Arnold explained possible options. Such an argument would be frivolous. Given the allegations of the complaint, it cannot be gainsaid that failure to provide treatment would have been more harmful than treatment.

Although Montalvo concedes that as parents they have "no right to terminate the child's life," they assert that if "there is a balance between giving therapies that help, but which may also seriously harm, the parents should be the final arbiters of that choice." In the exigent circumstances confronting the treating physician here, no "balance" existed as proposed by the parents. Failure to treat was tantamount to a death sentence. Under the pleaded circumstances, informed consent was not required.

C. *Public Policy.*

24 The trial court, in rendering its oral decision reasoned:

That as far as I can read from reading the materials in the complaint that presumes that the parents had a legally enforceable right to reject or withhold treatment. From what is alleged in the complaint there was no gap, space in time for which they could sit down and discuss statistics or any other manners of dealing with the situation. It was a life or death situation. When a child is not breathing there is no time—

---

4. In *Iafelice v. Zarafu,* 221 N.J.Super. 278, 534 A.2d 417 (1987), the New Jersey Appellate Division examined the exact same issue presented by this appeal and exclaimed:

The mistaken premise of this appeal is that allowing the child to die untreated was a legally viable alternative . . . we find no support for the belief that a newborn child may be put to death through [allowing a natural delivery with no resuscitation efforts upon birth] on the mere expectation that she will, in some unquantified way, be a defective person. As the Supreme Court wrote in *Berman v. Allan,* 80 N.J. 421, 430, 404 A.2d 8 (1979), "It is life itself, that is jealously safeguarded, not life in a perfect state."

Id. at 418.

there is no time. Any—any amount of loss of oxygen could be devastating to the child certainly....

... What the doctors did was save this child's life, and I understand the legal position of the parents is that was a decision they should make, but I don't believe that's one that we as a community in our public policy that's been adopted by our state and our court can place wholly in the hands of the parents.

Protection of children is something that the community has an interest, in and a parent does not have the right to withhold necessary emergency treatment, and I agree entirely that had the doctors acted in any other way they would face not only civil—civil cases against them but possibly criminal cases. We simply can't say that the possibility that this child could be disabled or even the probability if it is that strong is sufficient to withhold li[f]e-saving measures and decide this child does not deserve to live.

Without a doubt, a major underpinning of the court's decision was public policy.

In Wisconsin, the interest in preserving life is of paramount significance. In re *L.W.*, 167 Wis.2d 53, 90, 482 N.W.2d 60 (1992). As a result, there is a presumption that continued life is in the best interests of a patient. *Id.* at 86, 482 N.W.2d 60. In the absence of proof of a persistent vegetative state, our courts have never decided it is in the best interests of a patient to withhold or withdraw life-sustaining medical care. When appropriate circumstances are present, Wisconsin courts have not hesitated to dismiss complaints on public policy grounds, particularly where allowing recovery would place an unreasonable burden on physicians or where allowing recovery would provoke an exercise that has no sensible or just terminal point. *Rieck v. Medical Protective Co.*, 64 Wis.2d 514, 518–19, 219 N.W.2d 242 (1974).

The physicians involved in the resuscitation measures could be faced with a "damned if you do, damned if you don't" dilemma as demonstrated by the result of *Burks v. St. Joseph's Hospital*, 227 Wis.2d 811, 596 N.W.2d 391 (1999). In *Burks*, the physicians made a decision not to resuscitate based upon a judgment that a premature baby was not viable. *Id.* at 813, 596 N.W.2d 391. The baby died. *Id.* The parents brought a claim under the Emergency Medical Treatment and Active Labor Act (EMTALA) against the physician who determined that the infant was not viable and who did not resuscitate the child. *Id.* at 814, 596 N.W.2d 391. The claim was allowed because a hospital is required to provide emergency room patients with a medical screening examination including care to stabilize them. *Id.* at 817–18, 596 N.W.2d 391. If treating physicians can be sued for failing to resuscitate a baby they feel is not viable, and for resuscitating a viable baby such as Emanuel, they are placed in a continuing "damned" status. The public policy of Wisconsin does not tolerate such a "lose-lose" enigma.

If the parents' claim is allowed to proceed, courts will be required to decide which potential imperfections or disabilities are, as characterized in appellant's brief, "worse than death." They will have to determine which disability entitles a child to live and which disability allows a third-party surrogate to withhold or withdraw life-sustaining treatment with the intent to allow a disabled person to die. This determination could vary greatly based on the parents' beliefs. One set of parents may view a particular disability as "worse than death," while another set of parents would not. Such a process, not unreasonably, has kaleidoscopic, unending implications. The trial court did not err in reaching its conclusion based upon public policy reasons.

Judgments affirmed.

NOTE

In *In re* E.G., 133 Ill.2d 98, 139 Ill.Dec. 810, 549 N.E.2d 322 (1989), the Supreme Court of Illinois held that a 17 year old minor with leukemia could reject blood transfusions that both she and her mother opposed on religious grounds, even though the choice could be fatal. Although she had not reached the age of legal majority, it was determined that she was mature enough to make health care choices of her own, with the court noting that minors could make decisions in many other contexts ranging from freedom of expression to abortion. The court explained that:

> The State's parens patriae authority fades ... as the minor gets older and disappears upon her reaching adulthood.

Modern Natural Death Acts, which provide a means through which a person can make an advance election about what treatment will be rendered during a terminal illness, generally do not permit minors to execute a declaration. The Virginia Health Care Decisions Act, which applies to "competent adults", provides in VA. CODE ANN. § 54.1–2992 (2004) that:

> The provisions of this article are cumulative with existing law regarding an individual's right to consent or refuse to consent to medical treatment and shall not impair any existing rights or responsibilities which a health care provider, a patient, including a minor or incapacitated patient, or a patient's family may have in regard to the providing, withholding or withdrawal of life-prolonging medical procedures under the common law or statutes of the Commonwealth; however, this section shall not be construed to authorize violations of § 54.1–2990.

In response to publicity concerning a young man's wish to avoid a particular repeat treatment in connection with a major illness, "Abraham's law" was enacted by the Virginia General Assembly in 2007 as an amendment to Va. Code Ann. § 63.2–100, the State's child abuse law. Subsection 2 of the atatute, (the amended part) is reproduced below. The italicized portion includes the new language.

> "Abused or neglected child means any child less than 18 years of age:
>
> . . . .
>
> 2. Whose parents or other person responsible for his care neglects or refuse to provide care necessary for his health. However, no

child who in good faith is under treatment solely by spiritual means through prayer in accordance with the tenets and practices of a recognized church or religious denomination shall for that reason alone be considered to be an abused or neglected child. *Further, a decision by parents who have legal authority for the child or, in the absence of parents with legal authority for the child, any person with legal authority for the child, who refuses a particular medical treatment for a child with a life-threatening condition shall not be deemed a refusal to provide necessary care if (i) such decision is made jointly by the parents or other person with legal authority and the child; (ii) the child has reached 14 years of age and is sufficiently mature to have an informed opinion on the subject of his medical treatment; (iii) the parents or other peron with legal authority and the child have considered alternative treatment options; and (iv) the parents or other person with legal authority, and the child believe in good faith that such decision is in the child's best interest. Nothing in this subdivision shall be construed to limit the provisions of § 16.1–278.4.*

F.   A Tort Action Between Parent and Child?

Newman v. Cole

Supreme Court of Alabama.
872 S.2d 138 (Ala. 2003).

■ Per Curiam.

In this wrongful-death action, Anna Belle Newman, the personal representative of the estate of the decedent, Clinton Patterson Cole ("Clinton"), sued Clinton's father, John Cole, and his stepmother, Tara Cole (sometimes referred to hereinafter collectively as "the Coles"), for allegedly causing Clinton's death. Newman's complaint asserted claims of negligence, wantonness, and willful and intentional conduct.

The Coles moved to dismiss the complaint based on the doctrine of parental immunity. That doctrine was judicially created in the case of *Hewellette v. George,* 68 Miss. 703, 9 So. 885 (Miss.1891), abrogated by *Glaskox v. Glaskox,* 614 So.2d 906 (Miss.1992), and was adopted by the this Court in *Owens v. Auto Mutual Indemnity Co.,* 235 Ala. 9, 177 So. 133 (Ala.1937). The present form of the doctrine in this State was most recently discussed by the Court of Civil Appeals:

> "Under Alabama law, '[t]he parental immunity doctrine prohibits all civil suits brought by unemancipated minor children against their parents for the torts of their parents.' *Mitchell v. Davis,* 598 So.2d 801, 803 (Ala.1992). Only one exception to this rule has emerged-when a child alleges sexual abuse by a parent, the parental immunity doctrine

will not bar an action against the parent, although proof of the alleged conduct must be tested under a 'clear and convincing' standard. *Hurst v. Capitell,* 539 So.2d 264, 266 (Ala.1989)."

Hinson v. Holt, 776 So.2d 804, 811 (Ala.Civ.App.1998).

On July 3, 2002, the trial court granted the Coles' motion to dismiss the complaint. Newman appealed, arguing that this Court should abolish the doctrine, or, in the alternative, craft an exception to the doctrine that encompasses the facts alleged in this case.

I. Facts

Clinton was 16 years old at the time of his death, which occurred during an altercation with his father over Clinton's failure to perform household chores; Newman asserts that the altercation ended with the father's striking Clinton repeatedly in the chest and then holding him on the ground in a "choke hold" while Tara Cole sprayed him in the face with water from a garden hose. The father held Clinton on the ground for approximately 20 minutes; he let go of Clinton when a police officer arrived. Clinton was unconscious, and he was taken to a local hospital; he died the next day.

II. The Legal Issue

Although the facts in this case are tragic and compelling, the legal issue is clear-cut: Whether this Court should abolish the doctrine of parental immunity, or to what extent, if any, it should modify the application of the doctrine in light of the circumstances of this case. We hold that a further exception to the doctrine should be recognized where it is shown by clear and convincing evidence that a parent's willful and intentional injury caused the death of his or her child.

Newman asserts that Alabama is the last state not to have entirely abrogated or significantly modified the doctrine. Newman's argument, supported by the briefs of amici curiae National Crime Victims Bar Association and Alabama Trial Lawyers Association, asserts that to apply the parental-immunity doctrine in the circumstances of this case is fundamentally unjust and contrary to long-settled principles of tort law. Newman and the amici support their argument by noting the large number of other states that have abrogated, or significantly modified, the doctrine.[1] Newman argues that this Court should abrogate the doctrine entirely, or, alternatively, either craft an exception to the doctrine in the case of a parent who intentionally or willfully and wantonly injures his or her child, or craft an exception for a wrongful-death action in which a parent is accused of causing a child's death. Newman and the amici assert, without significant rebuttal from the Coles, that Alabama's application of the

---

1. Six states—Hawaii, Nevada, North Dakota, South Dakota, Utah, and Vermont, and the District of Columbia—have declined to adopt the doctrine ..... Eleven states ... adopted the doctrine at some point but subsequently abolished it.... The remaining 33 states all retain the doctrine in some form, usually with one or more significant exceptions.

doctrine is the strictest imposition of parental immunity against minors in the United States.

. . .

The Coles, on the other hand, argue that the Legislature is the entity that should make any changes to the settled doctrine of parental immunity, and that abrogation of the doctrine would adversely impact families and give rise to unwarranted lawsuits by unemancipated minors against their parents.

Thus, the parties' arguments offer the Court three options: (1) we might simply decline to interfere with the doctrine, (2) we might abrogate the doctrine entirely, or (3) we might craft an exception to the doctrine, as we did in *Hurst v. Capitell,* 539 So.2d 264 (Ala.1989), to fit the circumstances of this case.

We discussed the history of the doctrine in this State, and the rationale for crafting an exception, in *Hurst:*

> "The parental immunity doctrine had its genesis in the United States in *Hewellette v. George,* 68 Miss. 703, 9 So. 885 (1891), abrogated by *Glaskox v. Glaskox,* 614 So.2d 906 (Miss.1992), in which a minor daughter was precluded from suing her deceased mother's estate for damages resulting from mental suffering and injury to her character incurred during her confinement in an asylum for 11 days caused by her mother. The court gave this reason for its holding:

> " 'The peace of society, and of the families composing society, and a sound public policy, designed to subserve the repose of families and the best interests of society, forbid to the minor child a right to appear in court in the assertion of a claim to civil redress for personal injuries suffered at the hands of the parent. The state, through its criminal laws, will give the minor child protection from parental violence and wrongdoing, and this is all the child can be heard to demand.'

"68 Miss. at 711, 9 So. at 887.

> "The parental immunity doctrine was not based upon English common law, statutes, or previous cases; rather, it was judicially created by the Mississippi Supreme Court. In fact, even the *Hewellette* opinion recognized the limitation on the application of parental immunity to those cases involving unemancipated children:

> " 'If ... the relation of parent and child had been finally dissolved, insofar as that relationship imposed the duty upon the parent to protect and care for and control, and the child to aid and comfort and obey, *then it may be the child could successfully maintain an action against the parent for personal injuries.* But so long as the parent is under obligation to care for, guide, and control, and the child is under reciprocal obligation to aid and comfort and obey, no such action as this can be maintained.'

"*Id.,* 68 Miss. at 711, 9 So. at 887. (Emphasis added [in *Hurst*].)

"The first Alabama case addressing the issue of parental immunity, *Owens v. Auto Mut. Indemnity Co.*, 235 Ala. 9, 177 So. 133 (1937), quoted from a New Hampshire case that states a similar reason for the rule:

" 'It is declared in *Lloyd Dunlap v. Dunlap*, 84 N.H. 352, 150 A. 905, 71 A.L.R. 1055 [1930] that the' disability of a child to sue the parent for an injury negligently inflicted by the latter upon the former while a minor *is not absolute, but is imposed for the protection of family control and harmony, and exists only where the suit, or the prospect of a suit, might disturb the family relations.*"

"235 Ala. at 10, 177 So. at 134. (Emphasis added [in *Hurst*].)

"We reaffirmed the doctrine in *Hill v. Giordano*, 447 So.2d 164 (Ala.1984) (Jones, J., dissenting), based on the authority of *Owens*, supra, and held that 'any modification or abolition of the parental immunity doctrine should be left to the prerogative of the legislature.' 447 So.2d at 164. However, we also stated three months later in *Lloyd v. Service Corporation of Alabama, Inc.*, 453 So.2d 735 (Ala.1984):

" 'While the preferred method for modification of a rule of law is by legislative action, it is clearly within the power of the judiciary, and, at times, appropriate for the judiciary, to change an established rule of law. . . .

" '. . . [W]here a judicial creation has become outmoded or unjust in application, it is more often appropriate for the judicial body to act to modify the law.'

"(Emphasis added [in *Hurst*].)

"*Because the doctrine was judicially created, it is not exclusively a legislative issue and it may be judicially qualified.* Since our decision in *Hill* to defer to the Legislature on this issue, the Legislature has declined to act in regard to the doctrine, while the incidents of sexual abuse involving children have continued to occur. To leave children who are victims of such wrongful, intentional, heinous acts without a right to redress those wrongs in a civil action is unconscionable, especially where the harm to the family fabric has already occurred through that abuse. Because we see no reason to adhere to the doctrine of parental immunity when the purpose for that immunity is no longer served, as in Melissa's case, we are today creating an exception to the doctrine, limited to sexual abuse cases only.

"In creating this exception for sexual abuse cases, we believe it is unnecessary to spell out a separate body of procedural and substantive rules to govern such cases. Traditional rules of tort law relating to intentional infliction of personal injury are generally sufficient for the governance of such claims and the defenses asserted thereto.

"In the interest of preserving the unqualified right of parents to reasonably discipline their children, we do deem it appropriate, however, to require that the proof of alleged sexually abusive conduct be tested under a 'clear and convincing' standard, as opposed to a mere 'substantial evidence' standard. Because we are restricting this exception to the general rule to cases involving 'sexual abuse,' and requiring a 'clear and convincing' standard of proof, we do not perceive of our recognition of this narrow exception as posing an undue risk of limiting the parents' legitimate role in the disciplining of their children.''

539 So.2d at 265–66 (last emphasis added).

At this time, some 14 years after *Hurst* was decided, the Legislature has made no other modification to the doctrine. During that same time, we considered the doctrine once more in *Mitchell v. Davis,* 598 So.2d 801 (Ala.1992), holding that the doctrine of parental immunity applied to foster parents and recognizing the exception crafted in *Hurst.* As stated in *Hurst,* the doctrine was judicially created, and it is therefore subject to judicial modification. But this Court still attaches great importance to the underlying reason for the doctrine-to avoid unduly limiting the legitimate interest of parents in rearing and disciplining their children. In *Broadwell v. Holmes,* 871 S.W.2d 471 (Tenn.1994), the Supreme Court of Tennessee articulated well the importance of this interest:

"The parental right to govern the rearing of a child has been afforded protection under both the federal and state constitutions. This Court has stated, 'Tennessee's historically strong protection of parental rights and the reasoning of federal constitutional cases convince us that parental rights constitute a fundamental liberty interest under Article I, Section 8 of the Tennessee Constitution.' *Hawk v. Hawk,* 855 S.W.2d 573, 579 (Tenn.[1993]); see also *Davis v. Davis,* 842 S.W.2d 588, 601 (Tenn.1992)[,] *cert. denied,* 507 U.S. 911, 113 S.Ct. 1259, 122 L.Ed.2d 657 (1993); *Bellotti v. Baird,* 443 U.S. 622, 638, 99 S.Ct. 3035, 3045, 61 L.Ed.2d 797 (1979) (recognition of parents' right to be free of undue, adverse interference by state); *Quilloin v. Walcott,* 434 U.S. 246, 255, 98 S.Ct. 549, 554, 54 L.Ed.2d 511 (1978) (recognition that parent-child relationship is constitutionally protected); *Wisconsin v. Yoder,* 406 U.S. 205, 232, 92 S.Ct. 1526, 1541, 32 L.Ed.2d 15 (1972) (recognition of parents' primary role in child rearing as a 'fundamental interest' and 'an enduring American tradition'); *Prince v. Massachusetts,* 321 U.S. 158, 166, 64 S.Ct. 438, 442, 88 L.Ed. 645 (1944) (recognition that the custody, care and nurture of the child 'reside first in the parents, whose primary function and freedom include preparation for obligations the state can neither supply nor hinder'). The integrity of the family unit has found protection against arbitrary state interference in the Due Process Clause of the Fourteenth Amendment, *Cleveland Board of Education v. LaFleur,* 414 U.S. 632, 639–40, 94 S.Ct. 791, 796–97, 39 L.Ed.2d 52 (1974); *Roe v. Wade,* 410 U.S. 113, 152–53, 93 S.Ct. 705, 726–27, 35 L.Ed.2d 147 (1973); *Meyer v. Nebraska,* 262 U.S. 390, 399, 43 S.Ct. 625, 626, 67 L.Ed. 1042 (1923); the equal protection clause of the Fourteenth Amendment, *Skinner v. Oklahoma,* 316 U.S. 535, 541, 62 S.Ct. 1110, 1113, 86 L.Ed. 1655

(1942); and the Ninth Amendment. [*Griswold*] *v. Connecticut*, 381 U.S. 479, 496, 85 S.Ct. 1678, 1688, 14 L.Ed.2d 510 (1965) (Goldberg, J., concurring).

"Courts have expressed a concern that without the imposition of parent-child immunity, juries would feel free to express their disapproval of what they consider to be unusual or inappropriate child rearing practices by awarding damages to children whose parents' conduct was only unconventional. See, e.g., *Pedigo v. Rowley*, 101 Idaho 201, 205, 610 P.2d 560, 564 (1980); *Holodook v. Spencer*, [36 N.Y.2d 35,] 364 N.Y.S.2d [859] at 869–71, 324 N.E.2d [338] at 345–46 (N.Y.1974). Courts also properly have found that parents whose '[p]hysical, mental or financial weakness [causes them] to provide what many a reasonable man would consider substandard maintenance, guidance, education and recreation for their children, and in many instances to provide a family home which is not reasonably safe as a place of abode,' should not be liable to the child for these 'unintended injuries.' *Chaffin v. Chaffin*, 239 Or. 374, 397 P.2d 771, 774 (1964) (*en banc*), *overruled by Heino v. Harper*, 306 Or. 347, 759 P.2d 253 (1988) (abolishing interspousal immunity); *accord Cannon v. Cannon*, 287 N.Y. 425, 40 N.E.2d 236, 237–38 (1942), *overruled by Gelbman v. Gelbman*, 23 N.Y.2d 434, 297 N.Y.S.2d 529, 245 N.E.2d 192, 193 (1969) (abolishing bar to intrafamily lawsuits), *but see Holodook v. Spencer*, 364 N.Y.S.2d at 865, 324 N.E.2d at 342 (negligent failure to supervise child not recognized as a tort). Such imposition of liability could effectively curtail the exercise of constitutionally guaranteed parental discretion in matters of child rearing. Consequently, it reasonably can be argued that parental immunity that relates to the right and duty to rear children implements a constitutional right. *See Hawk v. Hawk*, 855 S.W.2d at 579 (recognizing a fundamental constitutional right of parents to care for their children without unwarranted state intervention)."

871 S.W.2d at 475–76.

This Court has been equally loathe to interfere with the parent-child relationship:

" '... So strong is the presumption, that "the care which is prompted by the parental instinct, and responded to by filial affection, is most valuable of all"; and so great is the reluctance of the court to separate a child of tender years from those who according to the ordinary laws of human nature, must feel the greatest affection for it, and take the deepest interest in its welfare-that the parental authority will not be interfered with, except in case of gross misconduct or where, from some other cause, the parent wants either the capacity or the means for the proper nurture and training of the child.' "

Ex parte Sullivan, 407 So.2d 559, 563 (Ala.1981) (quoting *Striplin v. Ware*, 36 Ala. 87, 89–90 (1860)). See also *R.J.D. v. Vaughan Clinic, P.C.*, 572 So.2d 1225, 1228 (Ala.1990).

Given the weight we assign to the sanctity of the parent-child relationship, we decline to follow the example of many of our sister states and wholly abrogate the doctrine of parental immunity. Further, we decline to consider any exception to the doctrine that would permit a claim by an injured child against a parent where the injury was not willful and intentional. In *Hurst* we held that the exception to the parental-immunity doctrine giving the injured child a right to redress was in response to "wrongful, intentional, heinous acts," 539 So.2d at 266, committed by the parent. Most recently, in *Mitchell,* supra, we held that the parental-immunity doctrine also protected foster parents as to any claim by a foster child based upon the foster parents' alleged negligence. As the court stated in *Broadwell:*

> "[T]he rights, responsibilities, and privileges of parents in relation to their children are so unique that the ordinary standards of care which regulate conduct between others are not applicable to conduct incident to the particular relationship of parent and child. That relationship includes responsibilities not owed by parents to any persons other than their children; these responsibilities are inseparable from the privileges that parents have in rearing their children which are not recognized in any other relationship."

871 S.W.2d at 475.

In view of this unique and special relationship, we note first that this opinion leaves the doctrine unchanged with respect to the protection afforded a parent from any claim by his or her child based upon unintentional conduct. Further, we consider only the specific circumstances of the case before us and apply our holding only to the situation where it can be shown by clear and convincing evidence that a parent's willful and intentional infliction of injury resulted in the death of his or her child.

As we noted in *Hurst,* supra, this Court declined to modify the doctrine in *Hill,* supra, a wrongful-death case in which the father's alleged negligence in piloting a plane resulted in the deaths of his two minor sons. However, the holding in *Hurst* makes clear that the rationale that supported *Hill,* i.e., deference to the Legislature, is no longer a dispositive basis for not modifying the judicially created doctrine. Accordingly, we cannot overlook the fact that the wrongful death of a child profoundly impacts the parent-child relationship. Plainly, the death of a child removes the parental interests the doctrine was intended to protect with respect to that child. Certainly, the parent's responsibilities to the child and the child's dependence upon the parent are terminated by the child's death. See, e.g., *Floyd v. Abercrombie,* 816 So.2d 1051 (Ala.Civ.App.2001) ; *Anderson v. Loper,* 689 So.2d 118 (Ala.Civ.App.1996)(discussing a parent's duties toward his or her unemancipated child). As Justice Jones, dissenting from the majority's opinion in *Hill,* aptly stated:

> "The purpose of the wrongful death statute [Ala.Code 1975, § 6–5–410] is to prevent homicide by wrongful act, omission, or negligence 'without respect to personal condition or disability of the person so protected.' *Breed v. Atlanta, B. & C.R.R.,* 241 Ala. 640, 642, 4 So.2d

315, 316 (1941). The parental immunity doctrine has its basis in domestic harmony. Isn't the commission of the tort, in and of itself, disruptive to domestic harmony?"

447 So.2d at 168.

In assessing the balance between the unique nature and critical importance of the parent-child relationship and the right of any victim for redress for a willful or intentional injury, we find the analysis of the Supreme Court of West Virginia instructive. In *Courtney v. Courtney,* 186 W.Va. 597, 413 S.E.2d 418 (1991), that court considered claims by a mother and her son against her ex-husband and the son's father for a number of intentional assaults. The court stated:

> "Courts have recognized that not every physical touching of a child will result in liability. Parents are able to discipline their children by administering reasonable physical punishment. However, when such punishment becomes excessive and results in substantial traumatic injury to the child, liability arises. Several courts have quoted this language from the California Supreme Court in *Emery v. Emery,* 45 Cal.2d 421, 429–30, 289 P.2d 218, 224 (1955):

> " 'Since the law imposes on the parent a duty to rear and discipline his child and confers the right to prescribe a course of reasonable conduct for its development, the parent has a wide discretion in the performance of his parental functions, but that discretion does not include the right wilfully to inflict personal injuries beyond the limits of reasonable parental discipline. No sound public policy would be subserved by extending it beyond those limits. While it may seem repugnant to allow a minor to sue his parent, we think it more repugnant to leave a minor child without redress for the damage he has suffered by reason of his parent's wilful or malicious misconduct. A child, like every other individual, has a right to freedom from such injury.'

> "See *Attwood v. Attwood's Estate,* 276 Ark. 230, 633 S.W.2d 366 (1982); *Rodebaugh v. Grand Trunk W.R.R. Co.,* 4 Mich.App. 559, 145 N.W.2d 401 (1966).

> "Thus, the general rule is that parental immunity is abrogated where the parent causes injury or death to his or her child from intentional or wilful conduct, but liability does not arise from reasonable corporal punishment for disciplinary purposes."

186 W.Va. at 607, 413 S.E.2d at 428.

Similarly, we recognize an exception to the doctrine of parental immunity in this State for a civil wrongful-death action by the personal representative of a decedent child against the child's parent where the parent willfully and intentionally inflicted the injury that caused the child's death. As in *Hurst,* supra, "in the interest of preserving the unqualified right of parents to reasonably discipline their children," 539 So.2d at 266, we require that the proof of the alleged willful and intentional nature of the injury that caused the child's death be tested under the clear-and-convincing-evidence standard rather than the substantial-evidence standard.

Accordingly, the judgment of the trial court is affirmed with respect to Newman's wrongful-death claims based on negligence and wantonness; the judgment is reversed with respect to Newman's wrongful-death claim based upon willful and intentional conduct, to the extent that claim implicates a willful and intentional injury, and the cause is remanded for further proceedings consistent with this opinion.

AFFIRMED IN PART; REVERSED IN PART; AND REMANDED.

■ Johnstone and Woodall, JJ., concur; Houston and Harwood, JJ., concur in the result;

■ Lyons, J., concurs in the result in part and dissents in part; Moore, C.J., and See, Brown, and Stuart, JJ., dissent.

■ Harwood, Justice (concurring in the result).

I concur in the result. I would prefer that the exception recognized today to the parental-immunity doctrine require only that the parental conduct in question, whether negligent, wanton, or willful and intentional, result in the death of the minor. The doctrine does not preclude an emancipated or adult child from suing a parent in tort, in recognition of the cessation of parent-child reciprocal rights and duties upon a child's emancipation or reaching adulthood. What more final cessation of those rights and duties could there be than that occasioned by death? Accordingly, I would go further than the per curiam opinion and hold that any wrongful-death action predicated on the death of a minor could be brought against his or her parent or parents pursuant to Ala.Code 1975, § 6–5–391.

■ Houston, J., concurs.

■ Lyons, Justice (concurring in the result in part and dissenting in part).

I concur in the result in that portion of the per curiam opinion reversing the trial court's judgment so as to permit the action to proceed as to Newman's wrongful-death claim based on willful and intentional conduct. For the reasons set forth below, I dissent from that portion of the per curiam opinion affirming the trial court's judgment dismissing the claims based on negligence and wantonness.

The genesis of the parental-immunity doctrine is an opinion of the Supreme Court of Mississippi in *Hewellette v. George,* 68 Miss. 703, 9 So. 885 (1891), *abrogated on other grounds, Glaskox ex rel. Denton v. Glaskox,* 614 So.2d 906 (Miss.1992). The per curiam opinion quotes that portion of *Hewellette* in which the court observed that if the relationship of parent and child has been finally dissolved, "then it may be the child could successfully maintain an action against the parent for personal injuries." 68 Miss. at 711, 9 So. at 887. Continuing, the Mississippi court noted, "But so long as the parent is under obligation to care for, guide, and control, and the child is under reciprocal obligation to aid and comfort and obey, no such action as this can be maintained." 68 Miss. at 711, 9 So. at 887.

The per curiam opinion states that "the death of the child removes the parental interests the doctrine was intended to protect." 872 So.2d at 145. One might assume that the death of a parent would have the same effect.

However, the Mississippi court must have contemplated dissolution of the relationship of parent and child by some mechanism other than death when it made the foregoing observation about when an action by a child could be maintained against the parent. This is so because in the case before the Supreme Court of Mississippi, a minor daughter was attempting to sue the estate of her *deceased* mother; the court, notwithstanding the absence of an ongoing parent-child relationship, refused to permit the action to proceed. Therefore, the denial of immunity in *Hewellette* could not have been based upon a public policy against such actions only in instances where there existed the possibility of a viable parent-and-child relationship at the time of the pendency of the action. I conclude that the public policy the Mississippi court was protecting related to the need to shield the parent from liability as to decisions made while the parent was under a duty to protect, care for, and control the child, and the child was under a concomitant duty to aid, comfort, and obey the parent. In this setting, the Mississippi court's standard should be read as follows:

> "But so long as the parent is under obligation to care for, guide, and control, and the child is under reciprocal obligation to aid and comfort and obey [*at the time of the conduct made the basis of the action*], no such action as this can be maintained."

This Court, in *Hurst v. Capitell,* 539 So.2d 264 (Ala.1989), embraced an exception to the parental-immunity doctrine in instances where a child can prove by clear and convincing evidence sexual abuse by the parent. The Court noted that "the harm to the family fabric has already occurred through that abuse." 539 So.2d at 266. Could we not just as easily say that harm to the family fabric would occur through a brutal assault not involving sexual abuse? I am not persuaded that "harm to the family fabric" or the termination of the parent-child relationship by death are meaningful bases upon which to chip away at the parental-immunity doctrine.

I prefer to view the rationale for creating the parental-immunity doctrine as a means of protecting the parent in the discharge of his or her duties from second-guessing in subsequent litigation, where hindsight is always crystal clear. Under this view, an after-the-fact analysis of whether there has been "harm to the family fabric" or whether either the parent or the child or both are dead does not offer meaningful justification for reconsidering the wisdom of applying the parental-immunity doctrine to a given situation.

I would prefer to address the prospect for exceptions by formulating a standard sufficient to protect the child when a parent causes injury under circumstances where no reasonable person could expect immunity from the consequences of his or her action, such as where the conduct had been made a felony by the Legislature or is a misdemeanor with respect to conduct directed toward children below an age limit that is irrelevant to the duties imposed by the parent-child relationship. See, e.g., § 13A–6–67, Ala.Code 1975, defining the Class A misdemeanor of second-degree sexual abuse as occurring when a person 19 years old or older subjects another person who is less than 16 years old, but no more than 12 years old, to sexual contact.

Under the above-stated standard, a parent acting in good faith could discipline a child, yet remain secure in the knowledge that only the most egregious acts committed in the course of parenting would expose him or her to the prospect of civil liability in an action brought on behalf of a child. We would thereby recognize the wisdom in permitting a parent to discipline a child without concern over subsequently being required to answer in court for what the child deems excessive corporal punishment. Likewise, negligence not amounting to criminal negligence (§ 13A–2–2(4), Ala.Code 1975) or other breach of duty not amounting to recklessness (§ 13A–2–2(3)) would not become the basis for a civil action, even where the parent-child relationship has been terminated by the child's death. On the other hand, conduct constituting the felonies of manslaughter (§ 13A–6–3, Ala.Code 1975) or criminally negligent homicide (§ 13A–6–4) would not be subject to the defense of parental immunity in a civil action against the parent.

The allegations of the complaint in this action, if proven, would constitute the criminal offense of murder (§ 13A–6–2, Ala.Code 1975). As previously noted, I therefore concur in the result as to the per curiam opinion's reversal of the trial court's judgment dismissing Newman's wrongful-death claim based on willful and intentional conduct. I dissent from that portion of the per curiam opinion affirming the trial court's judgment dismissing the claims alleging negligence and wantonness, because the facts in this case relating to the Coles' negligence or wantonness could be determined to be sufficient to fall under the heading of the felony offenses of either manslaughter or criminally negligent homicide. Under these circumstances, no reasonable person could expect immunity from the consequences of his or her action, and the doctrine of parental immunity should not bar the action.

I agree with the per curiam opinion's insistence upon a standard of proof by clear and convincing evidence in instances where the defense of parental immunity is rejected. I would require the trial court to apply this standard of proof to the elements of the analogous crime in the Alabama Code.

■ The dissenting opinions of Chief Justice Moore and Justices See, Stuart and Brown are omitted.

G. Emancipation: "Divorce" Between Parent and Child?

There can be two sides to a possible "divorce" between parent and child. First, may a parent voluntarily "divorce" a child? When a non-marital son was born to a couple in Wisconsin the father was ordered to pay 17% of his gross income as child support. After nearly four years of non-payment, the support arrearage totaled $16,279. Plea negotiations led to an agreement in which Gerald agreed to terminate his parental rights and pay a lump sum of $20,506 in exchange for the district attorney dropping nonsupport charges. The mother opposed the petition to terminate the father's parental rights to the child and the court said that the best interest of the child was the paramount consideration. In arriving at the best interest for the child, the Wisconsin Court of Appeals concluded that abandonment and failure to pay child support are not sufficient to make voluntary termination of parental rights in the best interest of the child. To allow for termination, other factors would have to be present, such as the father having a negative impact on the child or the possibility of a stepparent adoption. Neither factor was present and thus the father could not walk away from the child through termination. Gerald O. v. Cindy R., 203 Wis.2d 148, 551 N.W.2d 855 (Wis.App.1996).

The second side of emancipation raises the issue of whether a child should be able to ''divorce'' a parent. Professor Bruce Hafen has suggested that the result in a 1975 Washington decision, *In re* Welfare of Snyder, 85 Wash.2d 182, 532 P.2d 278 (1975), implies that even when a family problem does not reach the level of the juvenile court, a dissatisfied child should be permitted to leave the family at his or her own request when discontent is serious enough to indicate that the court may intervene and additional stress may be alleviated. He implies that there is thus an argument that the child should be able to divorce the parent on the ground of ''incompatibility.'' He thus suggests that resolving the effects of a collision between modern notions of individualism and the family may be ''one of the critical problems of our time.'' *See* Bruce Hafen, *Children's Liberation and the New Egalitarianism: Some Reservations About Abandoning Youth to Their ''Rights'',* 1976 B.Y.U. L. REV. 605, 608–9. Since the date of the article, children have made no progress in divorcing their parents. *See generally* Linda S. Beres & Thomas D. Griffith, *Demonizing Youth,* 34 LOY. L. REV. 747 (2001); Calvin Massey, *Juvenile Curfews and Fundamental Rights Methodology,* 27 HAST. CONST. L. Q. 775 (2000); Elizabeth S. Scott, *The Legal Construction of Adolescence,* 29 HOFSTRA L. REV. 547 (2000). David B. Wexler, *Just Some Juvenile Thinking About Delinquent Behavior: A Therapeutic Jurisprudence Approach to Relapse Prevention Planning and Youth Advisory Juries,* 69 UMKC L. REV. 93 (2000); Franklin E. Zimring, *The Common Thread: Diversion in Juvenile Justice,* 88 CAL. L. REV. 2477 (2000); Rhonda Gay Hartman, *Adolescent Autonomy: Clarifying an Ageless Conundrum,* 51 HAST. L. J. 1265 (2000); *Websites on Juvenile Issues,* 5 UC DAVIS J. JUV. L. & POL'Y 17 (2000).

Strictly speaking, emancipation generally has not been considered tantamount to divorce. It has the practical effect of making the child an adult, with corresponding rights and duties. The common law of emancipation was often unclear because it depended on a factual determination. Often it was accomplished in part, at least, by some act or omission of the parent. Indeed, it has been described by one commentator as ''a legal doctrine designed primarily for parents.'' *See* H. Jeffrey Gottesfeld, *The Uncertain Status of the Emancipated Minor: Why We Need a Uniform Statutory Emancipation of Minors Act (USEMA),* 15 U.S.F. L.REV. 473 (1981).Whether emancipation has taken place was a question of fact to be decided by the courts, which have few guidelines to use in this determination. *See, e.g.,* Lawson v. Brown, 349 F.Supp. 203 (W.D.Va.1972); Brumfield v. Brumfield, 194 Va. 577, 74 S.E.2d 170 (1953). *See also,* Francis C. Cady, *Emancipation of Minors,* 12 CONN. L. REV. 62 (1979); Sanford N. Katz, et al., *Emancipating Our Children—Coming of Legal Age in America,* 7 FAM. L.Q. 211 (1973). It required establishment of that a child had attained independent status financially, with some minimum statutory age or educational status, and usually required at least acquiescence by the parents.

Increasingly states have enacted statutes establishing standards and formal procedures for emancipation and clearly delineating its legal effects. Some early examples of such statutes dealt only with minors active in sports or entertainment professions. Today's statutes are much broader in scope, as illustrated by the following California statute.

CALIFORNIA FAMILY CODE (West 2004 & Supp. 2007)

§ 7001.   Purpose of Part

It is the purpose of this part to provide a clear statement defining emancipation and its consequences and to permit an emancipated minor to obtain a court declaration of the minor's status. This part is not intended to affect the status of minors who may become emancipated under decisional case law that was in effect before the enactment of Chapter 1059 of the Statutes of 1978.

§ 7002.   Emancipated minor; description

A person under the age of 18 years is an emancipated minor of any of the following conditions is satisfied:

(a) The person has entered into a valid marriage, whether or not the marriage has been dissolved.

(b) The person is on active duty with the armed forces of the United States.

(c) The person has received a declaration of emancipation pursuant to Section 7122.

§ 7120.   Petitions for declaration of emancipation; contents

(a) A minor may petition the superior court of the county in which the minor resides or is temporarily domiciled for a declaration of emancipation.

(b) The petition shall set forth with specificity all of the following facts:

(1) The minor is at least 14 years of age.

(2) The minor willingly lives separate and apart from the minor's parents or guardian with the consent or acquiescence of the minor's parents or guardian.

(3) The minor is managing his or her own financial affairs. As evidence of this, the minor shall complete and attach a declaration of income and expenses as provided in Judicial Council form FL–150.

(4) The source of the minor's income is not derived from any activity declared to be a crime by the laws of this state or the laws of the United States.

§ 7122.   Findings of court; issuance of declaration of emancipation

(a) The court shall sustain the petition if it finds that the minor is a person described by Section 7120 and that emancipation would not be contrary to the minor's best interest.

(b) If the petition is sustained, the court shall forthwith issue a declaration of emancipation, which shall be filed by the clerk of the court.

(c) A declaration is conclusive evidence that the minor is emancipated.

NOTE

A 1979 Connecticut statute did permit a minor age sixteen to petition for emancipation in circumstances that were comparable to divorce for irretrievable breakdown. It stayed in effect only a short time. The law as originally adopted is shown below, with amendments and additions to the text made by the legislature in 1980. Additions are shown by capital letters and deletions are indicated by ~~strikeouts~~. The former section of the code provided:.

§ 46b–150b.

If the court, after hearing, finds that: (1) The minor has entered into a valid marriage, whether or not that marriage has been terminated by dissolution; or (2) the minor is on active duty with any of the armed forces of the United States of America; or (3) the minor willingly lives separate and apart from his parents or guardian, with or without the consent of the parents or guardian, and that the minor is managing his own financial affairs, regardless of the source of any lawful income; or (4) [~~other facts exist which demonstrate that the parent child relationship has irretrievably broken down~~] FOR GOOD CAUSE SHOWN, IT IS IN THE BEST INTEREST OF EITHER OR BOTH PARTIES, the court [~~shall~~] MAY enter an order declaring that the minor is emancipated.

It was replaced by amended CONN. GEN. STAT ANN. § 46b–150d (West 2004 & Supp. 2006):

§ 46b–150d. Effect of emancipation

An order that a minor is emancipated shall have the following effects:

(1) The minor may consent to medical, dental or psychiatric care, without parental consent, knowledge or liability;

(2) the minor may enter into a binding contract;

(3) the minor may sue and be sued in such minor's own name;

(4) the minor shall be entitled to such minor's own earnings and shall be free of control by such minor's parents or guardian;

(5) the minor may establish such minor's own residence;

(6) the minor may buy and sell real and personal property;

(7) the minor may not thereafter be the subject of a petition under section 46b–129 as an abused, dependent, neglected or uncared for child or youth;

(8) the minor may enroll in any school or college, without parental consent;

(9) the minor shall be deemed to be over eighteen years of age for purposes of securing an operator's license under section 14–36 and a marriage license under subsection (b) of section 46b–30 or a civil union license under section 46b–38jj without parental consent;

(10) the minor shall be deemed to be over eighteen years of age for purposes of registering a motor vehicle under section 14–12;

(11) the parents of the minor shall no longer be the guardians of the minor under section 45a–606;

(12) the parents of a minor shall be relieved of any obligations respecting such minor's school attendance under section 10–184;

(13) the parents shall be relieved of all obligation to support the minor;

(14) the minor shall be emancipated for the purposes of parental liability for such minor's acts under section 52–572;

(15) the minor may execute releases in such minor's own name under section 14–118; and

(16) the minor may enlist in the armed forces of the United States without parental consent.

§ 46b–150e. Emancipation under common law

Nothing in sections 46b–150 to 46b–150e, inclusive, shall affect the status of minors who are or may become emancipated under the common law of this state.

CHAPTER VIII

Vying for Custody

Custody determinations are the most difficult decisions for courts, for attorneys, for parents, and most of all for children. Any decision illustrates the axiom of Oliver Wendell Holmes, Jr., writing in The Common Law, that "The life of the law has not been logic; it has been experience." Experience dictates that custody decisions, involving a minor unable to enter into the contractual arrangements available to parents and remaining within the *parens patriae* authority of the state, are the most modifiable and least settled decisions within family law litigation.

Custody decisions involve three constructs, each with appropriate presumptions. First, most of the cases involve a parent versus parent construct. Second, in a parent versus third party construct, such as a psychological parent, courts have been all too willing to apply a presumption in favor of the natural parent. And third, in increasing numbers of cases involving abuse and neglect, there is a parent versus state construct, in which the child is removed from the parent's custody by the state, but the courts are again usually willing to apply a presumption in favor of the parent. Often the constructs overlap; for example, increasing recognition of psychological parentage in some jurisdictions may largely merge the first two constructs as to the applicable rules or guidelines. And often the child is shifted from one construct to another in the course of changing tensions and problems.

Difficult questions arise throughout the materials: Is an adversary style judicial proceeding truly in the best interest of the child? What is the influence of individual values or beliefs in judicial determinations? Would non-judicial mediation be a better process for determination? What is the appropriate role of an attorney for a parent or child? Is it wise to make distinctions between legal and physical custody, or to create presumptions or preferences for newer approaches such as joint custody? Would federal control be preferable to the historic state approach? Do statutes unduly deprive courts of flexibility and can they be updated as needed within a reasonable time frame?

A. Parent Versus Parent

1. Sole Custody With Visitation Rights

CALIFORNIA FAMILY CODE (West 2004)

§ 3011. Best interest of child: Considerations

In making a determination of the best interest of the child in a proceeding described in Section 3021, the court shall, among any other factors it finds relevant, consider all of the following:

(a) The health, safety, and welfare of the child.

(b) Any history of abuse by one parent or any other person seeking custody against any of the following:

(1) Any child to whom he or she is related by blood or affinity or with whom he or she has had a caretaking relationship, no matter how temporary.

(2) The other parent.

(3) A parent, current spouse, or cohabitant, of the parent or person seeking custody, or a person with whom the parent or person seeking custody has a dating or engagement relationship.

As a prerequisite to the consideration of allegations of abuse, the court may require substantial independent corroboration, including, but not limited to, written reports by law enforcement agencies, child protective services or other social welfare agencies, courts, medical facilities, or other public agencies or private nonprofit organizations providing services to victims of sexual assault or domestic violence. As used in this subdivision, "abuse against a child" means "child abuse" as defined in Section 11165.6 of the Penal Code and abuse against any of the other persons described in paragraph (2) or (3) means "abuse" as defined in Section 6203 of this code.

(c) The nature and amount of contact with both parents, except as provided in Section 3046.

(d) The habitual or continual illegal use of controlled substances or habitual or continual abuse of alcohol by either parent. Before considering these allegations, the court may first require independent corroboration, including, but not limited to, written reports from law enforcement agencies, courts, probation departments, social welfare agencies, medical facilities, rehabilitation facilities, or other public agencies or nonprofit organizations providing drug and alcohol abuse services. As used in this subdivision, "controlled substances" has the same meaning as defined in the California Uniform Controlled Substances Act, Division 10 (commencing with Section 11000) of the Health and Safety Code.

(e)(1) Where allegations about a parent pursuant to subdivision (b) or (d) have been brought to the attention of the court in the current proceeding, and the court makes an order for sole or joint custody to that parent, the court shall state its reasons in writing or on the record. In these circumstances, the court shall ensure that any order regarding custody or visitation is specific as to time, day, place, and manner of transfer of the child as set forth in subdivision (b) of Section 6323.

(2) The provisions of this subdivision shall not apply if the parties stipulate in writing or on the record regarding custody or visitation.

§ 3020.   Legislative findings and declarations; health, safety, and welfare of children; continuing contact with parents

(a) The Legislature finds and declares that it is the public policy of this state to assure that the health, safety, and welfare of children shall be the court's primary concern in determining the best interest of children when making any orders regarding the physical or legal custody or visitation of children. The Legislature further finds and declares that the perpetration of child abuse or domestic violence in a household where a child resides is detrimental to the child.

(b) The Legislature finds and declares that it is the public policy of this state to assure that children have frequent and continuing contact with both parents after the parents have separated or dissolved their marriage, or ended their relationship, and to encourage parents to share the rights and responsibilities of child rearing in order to effect this policy, except where the contact would not be in the best interest of the child, as provided in Section 3011.

(c) Where the policies set forth in subdivisions (a) and (b) of this section are in conflict, any court's order regarding physical or legal custody or visitation shall be made in a manner that ensures the health, safety, and welfare of the child and the safety of all family members.

NOTE

The *ALI Principles* recommend that a child's best interest is served by facilitating all of the following: (1) parental planning and agreement about the child's custodial arrangements and upbringing; (2) continuity of existing parent-child attachments; (3) meaningful contact between child and each parent; (4) a caretaking relationship by adults who love the child, know how to provide for the child's needs, and place a high priority on doing so; (5) security from exposure to conflict and violence; (6) expeditious, predictable decisionmaking and avoidance of prolonged uncertainty respecting arrangements for the child's care and control. PRINCIPLES OF THE LAW OF FAMILY DISSOLUTION: ANALYSIS AND RECOMMENDATIONS 23 (2000). States are willing to consider the child's preference in making a custody decision. West Virginia, for example, has as one of its objectives the accommodation of the firm and reasonable preference of a child who is sufficiently matured to give an intelligent opinion. W. VA. CODE ANN. § 48–9–206(a)(2) (West 2004). But the child's preference is not determinative, only one factor to be considered among many. *See, e.g., In re* Marriage of Kimbrell, 34 Kan. App.2d 413, 119 P.3d 684 (2005).

Johnson v. Johnson

Supreme Court of Alaska, 1977.
564 P.2d 71, cert. denied 434 U.S. 1048, 98 S.Ct. 896, 54 L.Ed.2d 800 (1978).

■ BURKE, JUSTICE.

In this case, appellant Rudy Johnson challenges the superior court's reliance on the tender years presumption in awarding custody of his young children to their mother, Linda Johnson.

Rudy and Linda Johnson were married in 1966. Their daughter, April, was born in 1968 and their son, Darrin, in 1970. Several years after their marriage, Rudy and Linda became involved with the Jehovah's Witnesses, and both were baptized into the congregation. However, in 1974, Rudy Johnson became disenchanted with the religion and was excommunicated or "disfellowshipped" from the congregation for willfully smoking cigarettes. Although Rudy attempted to persuade Linda to abandon the religious principles which he had rejected, Linda remained with the church, and a severe strain was placed upon the marriage. Rudy filed for divorce on April 8, 1975, and the children were temporarily placed in his custody, pending trial.

Judge Carlson presided over the five day trial in this divorce action, the only issue at trial being the custody of the two Johnson children. At the time of trial April was seven and Darrin five. The heart of Rudy Johnson's case was that if he were denied custody of the children, he would have virtually no input into their lives because of his disfellowshipped status. Testimony was adduced at trial that since a disfellowshipped member of the Jehovah's Witnesses is believed to be under, or in danger of coming under, satanic control, members of the congregation will not associate with him.

Rudy Johnson also introduced evidence that his children's development would be better served by an award of their custody to him. Dr. LaVere Edwin Clawson, a psychologist, and his wife Darleen Morel, a family counselor, concluded that the children should be awarded to their father since he appeared more willing to offer them "increased exposure to the usual experiences of children their age." Rudy testified to the same effect, stating that Linda had not taught the children such simple tasks as counting money, washing themselves, and helping to clean around the house. He also emphasized the fact that Linda would not allow the children to celebrate holidays, birthdays or allow them to join such organizations as the Brownies. She also does not believe in college for the children. In short, Rudy's case centered around the fact that Linda's plan to raise the children in strict accordance with the church's rules and decrees would not serve the children's best interest.

Aside from rebutting Rudy's testimony and that of Dr. Clawson and Ms. Morel, Linda's evidence focused on Rudy's instability, as evidenced by threats of suicide and an unsuccessful suicide attempt, and his capacity for violence when frustrated. Linda offered proof that Rudy was unreasonable about Linda's visitation during the period in which he had temporary custody and introduced into evidence the deposition of Marilyn Kerr, a court-appointed social worker, who recommended that Linda have custody of April and Darrin.

The trial court, in extensive findings of fact, concluded that both parents were fit to have custody of the children and based its award of physical custody of the children to Linda on the tender years presumption. After citing AS 09.55.205[1] for the proposition that his award of custody should be guided by the best interests of the children, the trial judge stated:.

The statute has been interpreted in several cases and the following principles have emerged:

. . .

2. a mother of young children will generally be given preference for custody if the other factors are evenly balanced. Harding v. Harding, 477 [377] P.2d 378 (Alaska 1962); Sheridan v. Sheridan, 466 P.2d 821, 824 (Alaska 1970).

The trial court further reasoned:

The reasons for my conclusion that the best interests of the children are served by awarding their primary physical custody to Mrs. Johnson are the ages of April and Darrin and the fact that until their interim custody was awarded to Mr. Johnson in April, 1975, Mrs. Johnson had attended to nearly all of the physical needs of the children.

Judge Carlson awarded legal custody of the children to both parents so that Rudy could consent to medical care for them.

Appellant Rudy Johnson appeals the trial court's decision on two grounds. First, he contends that the trial court erred in applying the tender years presumption to the facts since that presumption is inconsistent with the statute's requirement that the best interests of the child be considered. He also argues that the tender years doctrine constitutes a denial of equal protection. Rudy's second argument is that the trial court abused its discretion in failing to award the children to him.

Appellee Linda Johnson cross appeals, contending that the trial court erred in failing to award her costs and attorney's fees.

---

1. AS 09.55.205 provides in part:

[I]n awarding custody the court is to be guided by the following considerations:

(1) by what appears to be for the best interests of the child and if the child is of a sufficient age and intelligence to form a preference, the court may consider that preference in determining the question;

(2) as between parents adversely claiming the custody neither parent is entitled to it as of right.

Trial courts have wide discretion in determining custody issues, but that discretion is not unlimited. This court must determine on review "whether that discretion has been abused, perhaps by assigning too great a weight to some factors while ignoring others. . . ." Horton v. Horton, 519 P.2d 1131, 1132 (Alaska 1974). Furthermore, if we find that the trial court has used an impermissible criterion in its determination, we will remand the case for a decision in which proper factors are considered. In the instant case, we must determine whether the trial court assigned too great a weight to the age of the Johnson children and whether the tender years doctrine is now an impermissible criterion for the trial courts in Alaska to use.

Appellant challenges the trial court's reliance on the doctrine of tender years on two grounds. He first argues that the doctrine is no longer the law in Alaska and is inconsistent with AS 09.55.205, which provides that the courts should consider the best interests of the child in determining custody matters. The trial court viewed the tender years doctrine as a judicial interpretation of AS 09.55.205. However, Sheridan v. Sheridan, 466 P.2d 821 (Alaska 1970), and other cases decided since the enactment of AS 09.55.205 in 1968 reflect a growing trend away from use of the tender years doctrine or any other mechanical formula in determining custody issues.

In *Sheridan,* we noted our disapproval of the "mechanistic application" of custody rules and reversed the trial court's award of the children to their mother on the ground that:

> It appears that the basis for resolution of the custody issue was the tender years' doctrine to the exclusion of any other legal criteria or relevant factual considerations. Seemingly ignored in the decisional process was the paramount criterion of the welfare and best interests of the children which should be determinative. (footnote omitted) 466 P.2d at 825.

Clearly we did not, in *Sheridan,* equate the tender years doctrine with the best interests of the child as the trial court appeared to do. . . .

Although the age of the children in a custody dispute is one factor which may be considered by the trial court in its determination of the best interests of the child, it is only one factor, to be weighed with many others. In Turner v. Pannick, 540 P.2d 1051 (Alaska 1975), we suggested factors which a trial court might wish to consider in its deliberations.

> [U]nder the "best interests' test, the court is free to consider a number of factors including the moral fitness of the two parties; the home environment offered by the parties; the emotional ties to the parties by the child; the emotional ties to the child by the parties; the age, sex or health of the child; the desirability of continuing an existing child-third party relationship; and the preference of the child." 540 P.2d at 1054.

Certainly the trial court's use of the tender years presumption is inconsistent with the delicate weighing and balancing process suggested in *Pannick* as a method of determining the child's best interests.

Courts in other jurisdictions have also held the tender years doctrine to be inconsistent with a "best interests" statute. In State ex rel. Watts v. Watts, 77 Misc.2d 178, 350 N.Y.S.2d 285 (1973), the court reversed a custody decision which was based on the tender years presumption. New York's domestic relations statute is similar to Alaska's in that it affords no prima facie right to custody to either party, the controlling consideration being the best interest of the child. The *Watts* court reasoned that the statute was designed to eliminate such sex-based presumptions in favor of the best interests of the child.

The *Watts* court . . . concluded that the tender years doctrine should be discarded since it is based on "outdated social stereotypes."

> Studies of maternal deprivation have shown that the essential experience for the child is that of mothering—the warmth, consistency and continuity of the relationship rather than the sex of the individual who is performing the mothering function. (citations omitted) 350 N.Y.S.2d at 290.

As the court in In Re Marriage of Bowen, 219 N.W.2d 683 (Iowa 1974), remarked in abandoning the tender years doctrine:

> The real issue is not the sex of the parent but which parent will do better in raising the children. Resolution of that issue depends upon what the evidence actually reveals in each case, not upon what someone predicts it will show in many cases.
>
> . . .
>
> We do not think either parent should have a greater burden than the other in attempting to obtain custody in a dissolution proceeding. It is neither necessary or useful to infer in advance that the best interests of young children will be better served if their custody is awarded to their mothers instead of their fathers. 219 N.W.2d at 688.

We conclude that the doctrine of tender years is not an appropriate criterion for determination of the best interests of the child under AS 09.55.205. Due to our disposition of this issue, we need not reach appellant's contention that use of the tender years doctrine violated his right to equal protection of the laws.

Appellant next argues that in light of all the evidence presented at trial, the trial court abused its discretion in not awarding the children to him. Appellant cites three main areas in support of this contention. First, he argues that he will be allowed little, if any, access to his children by virtue of his disfellowshipped status. Second, he argues that Linda will restrict his children's educational and cultural environment. He states that he plans to send the children to college, while Linda does not. Third, he cites the psychologists' reports in support of the contention that he will provide the expansive atmosphere necessary for the children's emotional development, while Linda would restrict them in their development. All of these factors center around Linda's plans to raise the children as Jehovah's Witnesses, and this court cannot deem the trial court's decision to award the children to Linda an abuse of discretion simply because of these plans. In Carle v. Carle, 503 P.2d 1050, 1055 (Alaska 1972), we found that the trial court erred in deciding the issue of custody on the premise that the child's best interest would be served by assimilation into the dominant culture and stated:

> It is not the function of our courts to homogenize Alaskan society. Recently, we had occasion to observe that "The United States of America, and Alaska in particular, reflect a pluralistic society, grounded upon such basic values as the preservation of maximum individual choice, protection of minority sentiments, and appreciation for divergent lifestyles." citing Breese v. Smith, 501 P.2d 159, 169 (Alaska 1972).

Certainly, we cannot use Linda's continued membership in the Jehovah's Witnesses as a basis for directing the trial court to award the children to Rudy. To do so would be violative of her right to freedom of religion under the First Amendment to the United States Constitution and of the principles articulated by this court in *Carle*. Furthermore, liberal and specific visitation rights with the children, such as those directed by the trial court, would give Rudy the access which he desires.

. . .

In view of the fact that the trial court based its award of physical custody of the children to Linda on the tender years presumption, it is necessary to remand the case to the trial court for further consideration of the custody issue in accordance with the criteria set forth in this opinion.

. . .

NOTE

The Supreme Court of Colorado took a different tack in *In re* Marriage of Short, 698 P.2d 1310 (Colo.1985) with regard to a motion *in limine* by a mother in a custody dispute who sought to exclude "all evidence concerning the beliefs or the practices or any other facet of the Jehovah's Witness religion or any participants thereof". In expanding the limited test for admissibility of such evidence applied by an intermediate appellate court, they explained:

> Courts are precluded by the free exercise of religion clause from weighing the comparative merits of the religious tenets of the various faiths or basing its custody decisions solely on religious considerations. However, the religious beliefs and practices of the parent may be a relevant factor, along with other circumstances, which bears upon the child's best interests and general welfare. Among the diverse religious faiths are philosophies and practices which might reasonably imperil the physical or mental health of a child. While courts must remain sensitive to first amendment concerns, a court in a custody proceeding must not blind itself to evidence of religious beliefs or practices of a

party seeking custody which may impair or endanger the child's welfare.

The free exercise of religion is a factor within child custody awards. See e.g. Jerry Bergman, Dealing With Jehovah's Witness Custody Cases, 29 Creighton L. Rev. 1483 (1996); Carl E. Schneider, Religion and Child Custody, 25 U. Mich. J.L. Reform 879 (1992). Are there limits on the parent's right to free exercise and how does this affect the child's rights under the constitution? The Colorado Court of Appeals in In re Marriage of Michelle Oswald, 847 P.2d 251 (Colo.App. 1993), held that the trial court improperly interfered with custodial mother's right to determine her children's religious training by awarding visitation rights to the grandmother to take the children to church on Sunday mornings.

May the courts enforce through contempt power agreements between the parents that incorporate religious practices? Religious schools? What is the difference between enforcement of religion conditions in child custody and enforcement of religion conditions in divorce? See discussion of judicial enforcement of a Jewish religious agreement (the Ketubah) in regard to one spouse obtaining a Jewish divorce (the Get) in Chapter 5. And what should be the role of the judge in sensitive custody determinations involving unique religious beliefs? For instance, in Muhammad v. Muhammad, 622 So.2d 1239 (Miss.1993), the Supreme Court of Mississippi affirmed the determination of the chancellor awarding custody to mother over the objections of the Black Muslim father that the chancellor had injected into the proceedings personal opinions including his disagreement with the Nation of Islam's teaching that white people are devils.

In re Marriage of Carney

Supreme Court of California, 1979.
157 Cal.Rptr. 383, 24 Cal.3d 725, 598 P.2d 36.

■ MOSK, JUSTICE.

Appellant father (William) appeals from that portion of an interlocutory decree of dissolution which transfers custody of the two minor children of the marriage from himself to respondent mother (Ellen).

In this case of first impression we are called upon to resolve an apparent conflict between two strong public policies: the requirement that a custody award serve the best interests of the child, and the moral and legal obligation of society to respect the civil rights of its physically handicapped members, including their right not to be deprived of their children because of their disability. As will appear, we hold that upon a realistic appraisal of the present-day capabilities of the physically handicapped, these policies can both be accommodated. The trial court herein failed to make such an appraisal, and instead premised its ruling on outdated stereotypes of both the parental role and the ability of the handicapped to fill that role. Such stereotypes have no place in our law.

Accordingly, the order changing custody on this ground must be set aside as an abuse of discretion.

William and Ellen were married in New York in December 1968. Both were teenagers. Two sons were soon born of the union, the first in November 1969 and the second in January 1971. The parties separated shortly afterwards, and by written agreement executed in November 1972 Ellen relinquished custody of the boys to William. For reasons of employment he eventually moved to the West Coast. In September 1973 he began living with a young woman named Lori Rivera, and she acted as stepmother to the boys. In the following year William had a daughter by Lori, and she proceeded to raise all three children as their own.

In August 1976, while serving in the military reserve, William was injured in a jeep accident. The accident left him a quadriplegic, i.e., with paralyzed legs and impaired use of his arms and hands. He spent the next year recuperating in a veterans' hospital; his children visited him several times each week, and he came home nearly every weekend.[1] He also bought a van, and it was being fitted with a wheelchair lift and hand controls to permit him to drive.

In May 1977 William filed the present action for dissolution of his marriage. Ellen moved for an order awarding her immediate custody of both boys. It was undisputed that from the date of separation (Nov. 1972) until a few days before the hearing (Aug. 1977) Ellen did not once visit her young sons or make any contribution to their support. Throughout this period of almost five years her sole contact with the boys consisted of some telephone calls and a few letters and packages. Nevertheless the court ordered that the boys be taken from the custody of their father, and that Ellen be allowed to remove them forthwith to New York State.[2] Pursuant to stipulation of the parties, an interlocutory judgment of dissolution was entered at the same time. William appeals from that portion of the decree transferring custody of the children to Ellen.

William contends the trial court abused its discretion in making the award of custody.[3] Several principles are here applicable. First, since it was

---

1. He was scheduled to be discharged shortly after the trial proceedings herein.

2. The court also imposed substantial financial obligations on William. He was ordered to pay all future costs of transporting his sons back to California to visit him, plus $400 a month for child support, $1,000 for Ellen's attorney's fees, $800 for her travel and hotel expenses, and $750 for her court costs.

3. He also contends the ruling violated his right to equal protection and due process of law. (Adoption of Richardson (1967) 251 Cal.App.2d 222, 239–240, 59 Cal.Rptr. 323, see generally Achtenberg, Law and the Physically Disabled: An Update with Constitution-

al Implications (1976) 8 Sw.U.L.Rev. 847; Burgdorf & Burgdorf, A History of Unequal Treatment: The Qualifications of Handicapped Persons as a "Suspect Class" Under the Equal Protection Clause (1975) 15 Santa Clara Law. 855; Comment, The Equal Protection and Due Process Clauses: Two Means of Implementing "Integrationism" for Handicapped Applicants for Public Employment (1978) 27 DePaul L.Rev. 1169; Note, Abroad in the Land: Legal Strategies to Effectuate the Rights of the Physically Disabled (1973) 61 Geo.L.J. 1501.) In the view we take of the case we need not reach the constitutional issues at this time. William further complains that the trial court erred in declining several offers of evidence of alleged misconduct of

amended in 1972 the code no longer requires or permits the trial courts to favor the mother in determining proper custody of a child "of tender years." (E. g., White v. White (1952) 109 Cal.App.2d 522, 523, 240 P.2d 1015.) Civil Code section 4600 now declares that custody should be awarded "To either parent according to the best interests of the child." (Id., subd. (a).) Regardless of the age of the minor, therefore, fathers now have equal custody rights with mothers; the sole concern, as it should be, is "the best interests of the child." (See Taber v. Taber (1930) 209 Cal. 755, 756–757, 290 P. 36, 37.)

Next, those "best interests" are at issue here in a special way: this is not the usual case in which the parents have just separated and the choice of custody is being made for the first time. In such instances the trial court rightly has a broad discretion. (Gudelj v. Gudelj (1953) 41 Cal.2d 202, 208–209, 259 P.2d 656.) Here, although this is the first actual court order on the issue, we deal in effect with a complete change in custody: after the children had lived with William for almost five years virtually all their lives up to that point Ellen sought to remove them abruptly from the only home they could remember to a wholly new environment some 3,000 miles away.

It is settled that to justify ordering a change in custody there must generally be a persuasive showing of changed circumstances affecting the child. (Goto v. Goto (1959) 52 Cal.2d 118, 122–123, 338 P.2d 450.) And that change must be substantial: a child will not be removed from the prior custody of one parent and given to the other "unless the material facts and circumstances occurring subsequently are of a kind to render it essential or expedient for the welfare of the child that there be a change." (Washburn v. Washburn (1942) 49 Cal.App.2d 581, 588, 122 P.2d 96, 100.1) The reasons for the rule are clear: "It is well established that the courts are reluctant to order a change of custody and will not do so except for imperative reasons; that it is desirable that there be an end of litigation and undesirable to change the child's established mode of living." (Connolly v. Connolly (1963) 214 Cal.App.2d 433, 436, 29 Cal.Rptr. 616, 618, and cases cited.)[4]

Moreover, although a request for a change of custody is also addressed in the first instance to the sound discretion of the trial judge, he must

Ellen occurring at various times prior to the hearing. We have reviewed the relevant portions of the record and conclude that certain of the offers were properly refused because the evidence in question was too remote (Prouty v. Prouty (1940) 16 Cal.2d 190, 194), while others should probably have been accepted but failure to do so could not have resulted in prejudice (People v. Watson (1956) 46 Cal.2d 818, 836, 299 P.2d 243).

4. Ellen relies on Loudermilk v. Loudermilk (1962) 208 Cal.App.2d 705, 707–708, 25 Cal.Rptr. 434, which held that the foregoing rule is "not applicable" when custody was originally awarded pursuant to an agreement between the parties rather than a judicial decree. But the opinion gave scant authority for this asserted exception, and it has since been cited only once in dictum. It is also wrong in principle: regardless of how custody was originally decided upon, after the child has lived in one parent's home for a significant period it surely remains "undesirable" to uproot him from his "established mode of living," and a substantial change in his circumstances should ordinarily be required to justify that result. To the extent it declares a contrary rule, Loudermilk is disapproved.

exercise that discretion in light of the important policy considerations just mentioned. For this reason appellate courts have been less reluctant to find an abuse of discretion when custody is changed than when it is originally awarded, and reversals of such orders have not been uncommon. (E. g., In re Marriage of Kern (1978) 87 Cal.App.3d 402, 410–411, 150 Cal.Rptr. 860; In re Marriage of Russo (1971) 21 Cal.App.3d 72, 98 Cal.Rptr. 501; Denham v. Martina (1963) 214 Cal.App.2d 312, 29 Cal.Rptr. 377; Ashwell v. Ashwell (1955) 135 Cal.App.2d 211, 286 P.2d 983; Sorrels v. Sorrels (1951) 105 Cal.App.2d 465, 234 P.2d 103; Bemis v. Bemis (1948) 89 Cal.App.2d 80, 200 P.2d 84; Juri v. Juri (1945) 69 Cal.App.2d 773, 160 P.2d 73; Washburn v. Washburn (1942) supra, 49 Cal.App.2d 581, 122 P.2d 96.)

Finally, the burden of showing a sufficient change in circumstances is on the party seeking the change of custody. (Prouty v. Prouty (1940) supra, 16 Cal.2d 190, 193, 105 P.2d 295; In re Marriage of Kern (1978) supra, 87 Cal.App.3d 402, 410–411, 150 Cal.Rptr. 860; In re Marriage of Mehlmauer (1976) 60 Cal.App.3d 104, 108–109, 131 Cal.Rptr. 325.) In attempting to carry that burden Ellen relied on several items of testimony given at the hearing; even when these circumstances are viewed in their totality, however, they are insufficient for the purpose.

First, Ellen showed that although she had been unemployed when William was given custody in 1972, at the time of trial she had a job as a medical records clerk in a New York hospital. But her gross income from that job was barely $500 per month, and she admitted she would not be able to support the boys without substantial financial assistance from William. (See fn. 2, Ante.) By contrast, at the time of the hearing William's monthly income from a combination of veteran's disability compensation payments and social security benefits had risen to more than $1,750 per month, all tax-free.

Ellen next pointed to the fact that William's relationship with Lori might be in the process of terminating.[5] From this evidence Ellen argued that if Lori were to leave, William would have to hire a baby-sitter to take care of the children. On cross-examination, however, Ellen admitted that if custody were transferred to her she would likewise be compelled because of her job to place the children "in a child care center under a baby-sitter nine hours a day," and she intended to do so. During that period, of course, the children would not be under her supervision; by contrast, William explained that because he is not employed he is able to remain at home "to see to their upbringing during the day as well as the night."

Additional claims lacked support in the record. Thus Ellen impliedly criticized William's living arrangements for the boys, and testified that if she were given custody she intended to move out of her one-bedroom apartment into an apartment with "at least" two bedrooms. Yet it was

---

5. Lori candidly testified she had been "thinking about" leaving. She added, however, that "Bill and I have had some problems, just like anyone else in our situation would have, and we are going to get counseling, and hopefully that will settle the matters." And she declared that she loved both of the boys and wanted to continue being their "substitute mother."

undisputed that the boys were presently residing in a private house containing in effect four bedrooms, with a large living room and a spacious enclosed back yard; despite additional residents, there was no showing that the accommodations were inadequate for the family's needs. Ellen further stated that in her opinion the older boy should be seen by a dentist; there was no expert testimony to this effect, however, and no evidence that the child was not receiving normal dental care. She also remarked that the younger boy seemed to have a problem with wetting his bed but had not been taken to a doctor about it; again there was no evidence that medical intervention in this matter was either necessary or desirable. We obviously cannot take judicial notice of the cause of, or currently recommended cure for, childhood enuresis.[6]

In short, if the trial court had based its change of custody order on the foregoing circumstances alone, it would in effect have revived the "mother's preference" rule abrogated by the Legislature in 1972. The record discloses, however, that the court gave great weight to another factor William's physical handicap and its presumed adverse effect on his capacity to be a good father to the boys. Whether that factor will support the reliance placed upon it is a difficult question to which we now turn.

Ellen first raised the issue in her declaration accompanying her request for a change of custody, asserting that because of William's handicap "it is almost impossible for (him) to actually care for the minor children," and "since (he) is confined to a hospital bed, he is never with the minor children and thus can no longer effectively care for the minor children or see to their physical and emotional needs." When asked at the hearing why she believed she should be given custody, she replied inter alia, "Bill's physical condition." Thereafter she testified that according to her observations William is not capable of feeding himself or helping the boys prepare meals or get dressed; and she summed up by agreeing that he is not able to do "anything" for himself.

The trial judge echoed this line of reasoning throughout the proceedings. Virtually the only questions he asked of any witness revolved around William's handicap and its physical consequences, real or imagined. Thus although William testified at length about his present family life and his future plans, the judge inquired only where he sat when he got out of his wheelchair, whether he had lost the use of his arms, and what his medical prognosis was. Again, when Lori took the stand and testified to William's

---

6. In the only testimony on the point Ellen reported that William's cousin, who had been living with the family explained to her the reason the boy wet the bed is "because he wears himself out so much playing that he just doesn't get up at night." Ellen advanced other grounds for a change of custody that are even more insubstantial. Thus she claimed she wanted to enroll the boys in "some kind of church" a choice of words scarcely indicative of a deep religious commit- ment on her part. And she complained that because William had moved several times in the past five years the boys had not had a chance to "get established" in a school or neighborhood a strange objection coming from one who proposed to move them 3,000 miles. In any event, the record indicated that most of William's moves were job-related and took place prior to the date of his injury, and hence were irrelevant to the family's present situation.

good relationship with his boys and their various activities together, the judge interrupted to ask her in detail whether it was true that she had to bathe, dress, undress, cook for and feed William. Indeed, he seemed interested in little else.

The final witness was Dr. Jack Share, a licensed clinical psychologist specializing in child development, who had visited William's home and studied his family.[7] Dr. Share testified that William had an IQ of 127, was a man of superior intelligence, excellent judgment and ability to plan, and had adapted well to his handicap. He observed good interaction between William and his boys, and described the latter as self-disciplined, sociable, and outgoing. On the basis of his tests and observations, Dr. Share gave as his professional opinion that neither of the children appeared threatened by William's physical condition; the condition did not in any way hinder William's ability to be a father to them, and would not be a detriment to them if they remained in his home; the present family situation in his home was a healthy environment for the children; and even if Lori were to leave, William could still fulfill his functions as father with appropriate domestic help.

Ellen made no effort on cross-examination to dispute any of the foregoing observations or conclusions, and offered no expert testimony to the contrary. The judge then took up the questioning, however, and focused on what appears to have been one of his main concerns in the case i. e., that because of the handicap William would not be able to participate with his sons in sports and other physical activities. Thus the court asked Dr. Share, "It's very unfortunate that he's in this condition, but when these boys get another two, three years older, would it be better, in your opinion, if they had a parent that was able to actively go places with them, take them places, play Little League baseball, go fishing? Wouldn't that be advantageous to two young boys?" Dr. Share replied that "the commitment, the long-range planning, the dedication" of William to his sons were more important, and stated that from his observations William was "the more consistent, stable part of this family regardless of his physical condition at this point." The judge nevertheless persisted in stressing that William "is limited in what he can do for the boys," and demanded an answer to his question as to "the other activities that two growing boys should have with a natural parent." Dr. Share acknowledged William's obvious physical limitations, but once more asserted that "on the side dealing with what I have called the stability of the youngsters, which I put personally higher value on, I would say the father is very strong in this area." Finally, when asked on redirect examination what effect William's ability to drive will have, Dr. Share explained, "this opens up more vistas, greater alternatives when he's more mobile such as having his own van to take them places...."

7. Dr. Share is also a credentialed schoolteacher and a licensed marriage counselor.

We need not speculate on the reasons for the judge's ensuing decision to order the change of custody, as he candidly stated them for the record. First he distinguished a case cited by William, emphasizing "There was no father there or mother that was unable to care for the children because of physical disabilities...." Next he found William and Ellen to be "both good, loving parents," although he strongly chided the latter for failing to visit her sons for five years, saying "She should have crawled on her hands and knees out here if she had to get the children...." The judge then returned to the theme of William's physical inability to personally take care of the children: speculating on Lori's departure, the judge stressed that in such event "a housekeeper or a nursery" would have to be hired overlooking the admitted fact that Ellen would be compelled to do exactly the same herself for nine hours a day. And he further assumed "There would have to be pick up and probably delivery of the children even though (William) drives his van" a non sequitur revealing his misunderstanding of the purpose and capabilities of that vehicle.

More importantly, the judge conceded that Dr. Share "saw a nice, loving relationship, and that's absolutely true. There's a great relationship between (William) and the boys...." Yet despite this relationship the judge concluded "I think it would be detrimental to the boys to grow up until age 18 in the custody of their father. It wouldn't be a normal relationship between father and boys." And what he meant by "normal" was quickly revealed: "It's unfortunate (William) has to have help bathing and dressing and undressing. He can't do anything for the boys himself except maybe talk to them and teach them, be a tutor, which is good, but it's not enough. I feel that it's in the best interests of the two boys to be with the mother even though she hasn't had them for five years." (Italics added.)

Such a record approaches perilously close to the showing in Adoption of Richardson (1967) supra, 251 Cal.App.2d 222, 59 Cal.Rptr. 323. There the trial court denied a petition to adopt an infant boy because of the physical handicap of the proposed adoptive parents, who were deaf-mutes. As here, professional opinions were introduced and remained uncontradicted stating that the petitioners had adjusted well to their handicap and had a good relationship with the child, and that their disability would have no adverse effects on his physical or emotional development. Nevertheless, in language strangely similar to that of the judge herein, the trial court reasoned: "Is this a normally happy home? There is no question about it, it is a happy home, but is it a normal home? I don't think the Court could make a finding that it is a normal home when these poor unfortunate people, they are handicapped, and what can they do in the way of bringing this child up to be the type of citizen we all want him to be." (Id. at p. 228, 59 Cal.Rptr. at p. 327.) The Court of Appeal there concluded from this and other evidence that the trial judge was prejudiced by a belief that no deaf-mute could ever be a good parent to a "normal" child. While recognizing the rule that the granting or denial of a petition for adoption rests in the discretion of the judge, the appellate court held that such discretion had been abused and accordingly reversed the judgment. (Id. at p. 237, 59 Cal.Rptr. 323.)

While it is clear the judge herein did not have the totally closed mind exhibited in Richardson, it is equally plain that his judgment was affected by serious misconceptions as to the importance of the involvement of parents in the purely physical aspects of their children's lives. We do not mean, of course, that the health or physical condition of the parents may not be taken into account in determining whose custody would best serve the child's interests. In relation to the issues at stake, however, this factor is ordinarily of minor importance; and whenever it is raised whether in awarding custody originally or changing it later it is essential that the court weigh the matter with an informed and open mind.

In particular, if a person has a physical handicap it is impermissible for the court simply to rely on that condition as prima facie evidence of the person's unfitness as a parent or of probable detriment to the child; rather, in all cases the court must view the handicapped person as an individual and the family as a whole. To achieve this, the court should inquire into the persons's actual and potential physical capabilities, learn how he or she has adapted to the disability and manages its problems, consider how the other members of the household have adjusted thereto, and take into account the special contributions the person may make to the family despite or even because of the handicap. Weighing these and all other relevant factors together, the court should then carefully determine whether the parent's condition will in fact have a substantial and lasting adverse effect on the best interests of the child.[8]

The record shows the contrary occurred in the case at bar. To begin with, the court's belief that there could be no "normal relationship between father and boys" unless William engaged in vigorous sporting activities with his sons is a further example of the conventional sex-stereotypical thinking that we condemned in another context in Sail'er Inn v. Kirby (1971) 5 Cal.3d 1, 95 Cal.Rptr. 329, 485 P.2d 529. For some, the court's emphasis on the importance of a father's "playing baseball" or "going fishing" with his sons may evoke nostalgic memories of a Norman Rockwell cover on the old Saturday Evening Post. But it has at least been understood that a boy need not prove his masculinity on the playing fields of Eton, nor must a man compete with his son in athletics in order to be a good father: their relationship is no less "normal" if it is built on shared experiences in such fields of interest as science, music, arts and crafts, history or travel, or in pursuing such classic hobbies as stamp or coin collecting. In short, an afternoon that a father and son spend together at a museum or the zoo is surely no less enriching than an equivalent amount of time spent catching either balls or fish.[9]

---

8. A recent statute makes the point in a closely related context: a child may be made a ward of the court because of lack of parental care and control, but "No parent shall be found to be incapable of exercising proper and effective parental care or control solely because of a physical disability. . . ." (Welf. & Inst. Code, s 300, subd. (a); see, e. g., In re W.

O. (1979) 88 Cal.App.3d 906, 910, 152 Cal. Rptr. 130 (mother's epilepsy no ground for removing children from her custody).)

9. The sex stereotype, of course, cuts both ways. If the trial court's approach herein were to prevail, in the next case a divorced mother who became physically handicapped

Even more damaging is the fact that the court's preconception herein, wholly apart from its outdated presumption of proper gender roles, also stereotypes William as a person deemed forever unable to be a good parent simply because he is physically handicapped. Like most stereotypes, this is both false and demeaning. On one level it is false because it assumes that William will never make any significant recovery from his disability. There was no evidence whatever to this effect. On the contrary, it did appear that the hearing was being held only one year after the accident, that William had not yet begun the process of rehabilitation in a home environment, and that he was still a young man in his twenties. In these circumstances the court could not presume that modern medicine, helped by time, patience, and determination, would be powerless to restore at least some of William's former capabilities for active life.

Even if William's prognosis were poor, however, the stereotype indulged in by the court is false for an additional reason: it mistakenly assumes that the parent's handicap inevitably handicaps the child. But children are more adaptable than the court gives them credit for; if one path to their enjoyment of physical activities is closed, they will soon find another. Indeed, having a handicapped parent often stimulates the growth of a child's imagination, independence, and self-reliance. Today's urban youngster, moreover, has many more opportunities for formal and informal instruction than his isolated rural predecessor. It is true that William may not be able to play tennis or swim, ride a bicycle or do gymnastics; but it does not follow that his children cannot learn and enjoy such skills, with the guidance not only of family and friends but also the professional instructors available through schools, church groups, playgrounds, camps, the Red Cross, the YMCA, the Boy Scouts, and numerous service organizations. As Dr. Share pointed out in his testimony, ample community resources now supplement the home in these circumstances.

In addition, it is erroneous to presume that a parent in a wheelchair cannot share to a meaningful decree in the physical activities of his child, should both desire it. On the one hand, modern technology has made the handicapped increasingly mobile, as demonstrated by William's purchase of a van and his plans to drive it by means of hand controls. In the past decade the widespread availability of such vans, together with sophisticated and reliable wheelchair lifts and driving control systems, have brought about a quiet revolution in the mobility of the severely handicapped. No longer are they confined to home or institution, unable to travel except by special vehicle or with the assistance of others; today such persons use the streets and highways in ever-growing numbers for both business and pleasure. Again as Dr. Share explained, the capacity to drive such a vehicle "opens more vistas, greater alternatives" for the handicapped person.

At the same time the physically handicapped have made the public more aware of the many unnecessary obstacles to their participation in

could be deprived of her young daughters because she is unable to participate with them in embroidery, Haute cuisine, or the fine arts of washing and ironing. To state the proposition is to refute it.

community life. Among the evidence of the public's change in attitude is a growing body of legislation intended to reduce or eliminate the physical impediments to that participation, i. e., the "architectural barriers" against access by the handicapped to buildings, facilities, and transportation systems used by the public at large....

While there is obviously much room for continued progress in removing these barriers, the handicapped person today need not remain a shut-in. Although William cannot actually play on his children's baseball team, he may nevertheless be able to take them to the game, participate as a fan, a coach, or even an umpire and treat them to ice cream on the way home. Nor is this companionship limited to athletic events: such a parent is no less capable of accompanying his children to theaters or libraries, shops or restaurants, schools or churches, afternoon picnics or long vacation trips. Thus it is not true that, as the court herein assumed, William will be unable "to actively go places with (his children), take them places, ..."

On a deeper level, finally, the stereotype is false because it fails to reach the heart of the parent-child relationship. Contemporary psychology confirms what wise families have perhaps always known that the essence of parenting is not to be found in the harried rounds of daily carpooling endemic to modern suburban life, or even in the doggedly dutiful acts of "togetherness" committed every weekend by well-meaning fathers and mothers across America. Rather, its essence lies in the ethical, emotional, and intellectual guidance the parent gives to the child throughout his formative years, and often beyond. The source of this guidance is the adult's own experience of life; its motive power is parental love and concern for the child's well-being; and its teachings deal with such fundamental matters as the child's feelings about himself, his relationships with others, his system of values, his standards of conduct, and his goals and priorities in life. Even if it were true, as the court herein asserted, that William cannot do "anything" for his sons except "talk to them and teach them, be a tutor," that would not only be "enough" contrary to the court's conclusion it would be the most valuable service a parent can render. Yet his capacity to do so is entirely unrelated to his physical prowess: however limited his bodily strength may be, a handicapped parent is a whole person to the child who needs his affection, sympathy, and wisdom to deal with the problems of growing up. Indeed, in such matters his handicap may well be an asset: few can pass through the crucible of a severe physical disability without learning enduring lessons in patience and tolerance.

No expert testimony was necessary to establish these facts. As the Court of Appeal correctly observed in a somewhat different context, "It requires no detailed discussion to demonstrate that the support and, even more, the control of the child is primarily a mental function to which soundness of mind is a crucial prerequisite. It is also well known that physical handicaps generally have no adverse effect upon mental functions.... It is also a matter of common knowledge that many persons with physical handicaps have demonstrated their ability to adequately support and control their children and to give them the benefits of stability and security through love and attention." (In re Eugene W. (1972) 29 Cal. App.3d 623, 629–630, 105 Cal.Rptr. 736, 741, 742.)

We agree, and conclude that a physical handicap that affects a parent's ability to participate with his children in purely physical activities is not a changed circumstance of sufficient relevance and materiality to render it either "essential or expedient" for their welfare that they be taken from his custody. This conclusion would be obvious if the handicap were heart dysfunction, emphysema, arthritis, hernia, or slipped disc; it should be no less obvious when it is the natural consequence of an impaired nervous system. Accordingly, pursuant to the authorities cited above the order changing the custody of the minor children herein from William to Ellen must be set aside as an abuse of discretion.

Both the state and federal governments now pursue the commendable goal of total integration of handicapped persons into the mainstream of society: the Legislature declares that "It is the policy of this state to encourage and enable disabled persons to participate fully in the social and economic life of the state...." (Gov. Code, § 19230, subd. (a).) Thus far these efforts have focused primarily on such critical areas as employment, housing, education, transportation, and public access.... No less important to this policy is the integration of the handicapped into the responsibilities and satisfactions of family life, cornerstone of our social system. Yet as more and more physically disabled persons marry and bear or adopt children or, as in the case at bar, previously nonhandicapped parents become disabled through accident or illness custody disputes similar to that now before us may well recur. In discharging their admittedly difficult duty in such proceedings, the trial courts must avoid impairing or defeating the foregoing public policy. With the assistance of the considerations discussed herein, we are confident of their ability to do so.

Lastly, we recognize that during the pendency of this appeal, additional circumstances bearing on the best interests of the children herein may have developed. Any such circumstances may, of course, be considered by the trial court on remand. (See In re Marriage of Russo (1971) supra, 21 Cal.App.3d 72, 93–94, 98 Cal.Rptr. 501.)

The portion of the interlocutory decree of dissolution transferring custody of appellant's minor children to respondent is reversed.

NOTE

Human Immunodeficiency Virus (HIV), the virus which precipitates opportunistic infections then classified as AIDS, may increasingly become a factor in of custody litigation. The Court of Appeals of Kentucky was asked in Newton v. Riley, 899 S.W.2d 509 (Ky.App.1995) whether the cohabitation of a custodial parent with an HIV-infected stepparent is, taken alone, sufficient grounds for modifying custody in favor of the non-custodial parent. Relying on federal and state case law upholding the right of HIV-infected children to attend school and the fact that medical testimony that

HIV is not transmitted through sharing of household functions, the court refused any modification of the custody.

HIV and AIDS are often associated with a homosexual lifestyle. While the Supreme Court's decision of Lawrence v. Texas, 539 U.S. 558, 123 S.Ct. 2472, 156 L.Ed.2d 508 (2003), holding that the liberty interest under the Due Process Clause of the Fourteenth Amendment protects adults engaging in private conduct, has no direct applicability to child custody decisions, it may have lessened the stigma associated with homosexuality. The *Lawrence* decision overruled Bowers v. Hardwick, 478 U.S. 186, 106 S.Ct. 2841, 92 L.Ed.2d 140 (1986), a decision that allowed for states to continue to prosecute sodomy. As a result, all of the sodomy statutes are unconstitutional as applied to consenting adults and by implication, homosexual conduct between consenting adults is to be considered in the same fashion as heterosexual conduct. *See generally* Martha Chamallas, *Deepening the Legal Understanding of Bias: On Devaluation and Biased Prototypes*, 74 S. CAL. L. REV. 747 (2001). Likewise, the Wyoming Supreme Court rejected a trial judge's custody award of the boys to the father and the girls to the mother. In ordering a new hearing, the court stated that gender is an appropriate consideration, but that it cannot be the sole consideration. The court called upon the attorneys to articulate and place all factors in the record so that an appeals court may properly consider if any one factor was impermissibly relied upon in making a determination. *See* Pace v. Pace, 22 P.3d 861 (Wyo.2001).

Palmore v. Sidoti

Supreme Court of the United States, 1984.
466 U.S. 429, 104 S.Ct. 1879, 80 L.Ed.2d 421.

■ CHIEF JUSTICE BURGER delivered the opinion of the Court.

We granted certiorari to review a judgment of a state court divesting a natural mother of the custody of her infant child because of her remarriage to a person of a different race.

When petitioner Linda Sidoti Palmore and respondent Anthony J. Sidoti, both Caucasians, were divorced in May 1980 in Florida, the mother was awarded custody of their three-year-old daughter.

In September 1981 the father sought custody of the child by filing a petition to modify the prior judgment because of changed conditions. The change was that the child's mother was then cohabiting with a Negro, Clarence Palmore, Jr., whom she married two months later. Additionally, the father made several allegations of instances in which the mother had not properly cared for the child.

After hearing testimony from both parties and considering a court counselor's investigative report, the court noted that the father had made allegations about the child's care, but the court made no findings with respect to these allegations. On the contrary, the court made a finding that "there is no issue as to either party's devotion to the child, adequacy of housing facilities, or respect[a]bility of the new spouse of either parent."

The court then addressed the recommendations of the court counselor, who had made an earlier report "in [another] case coming out of this circuit also involving the social consequences of an interracial marriage. Niles v. Niles, 299 So.2d 162." From this vague reference to that earlier case, the court turned to the present case and noted the counselor's recommendation for a change in custody because "[t]he wife [petitioner] has chosen for herself and for her child, a life-style unacceptable to her father *and to society....* The child ... is, or at school age will be, subject to environmental pressures not of choice."

The court then concluded that the best interests of the child would be served by awarding custody to the father. The court's rationale is contained in the following:

> "The father's evident resentment of the mother's choice of a black partner is not sufficient to wrest custody from the mother. It is of some significance, however, that the mother did see fit to bring a man into her home and carry on a sexual relationship with him without being married to him. Such action tended to place gratification of her own desires ahead of her concern for the child's future welfare. *This Court feels that despite the strides that have been made in bettering relations between the races in this country, it is inevitable that Melanie will, if allowed to remain in her present situation and attains school age and thus more vulnerable to peer pressures, suffer from the social stigmatization that is sure to come.*" App. to Pet. for Cert. 26–27 (emphasis added).

The Second District Court of Appeal affirmed without opinion, thus denying the Florida Supreme Court jurisdiction to review the case. We granted certiorari, and we reverse.

The judgment of a state court determining or reviewing a child custody decision is not ordinarily a likely candidate for review by this Court. However, the court's opinion, after stating that the "father's evident resentment of the mother's choice of a black partner is not sufficient" to deprive her of custody, then turns to what it regarded as the damaging impact on the child from remaining in a racially-mixed household. This raises important federal concerns arising from the Constitution's commitment to eradicating discrimination based on race.

The Florida court did not focus directly on the parental qualifications of the natural mother or her present husband, or indeed on the father's qualifications to have custody of the child. The court found that "there is no issue as to either party's devotion to the child, adequacy of housing facilities, or respect[a]bility of the new spouse of either parent." This, taken with the absence of any negative finding as to the quality of the care provided by the mother, constitutes a rejection of any claim of petitioner's unfitness to continue the custody of her child.

The court correctly stated that the child's welfare was the controlling factor. But that court was entirely candid and made no effort to place its holding on any ground other than race. Taking the court's findings and rationale at face value, it is clear that the outcome would have been different had petitioner married a Caucasian male of similar respectability.

A core purpose of the Fourteenth Amendment was to do away with all governmentally-imposed discrimination based on race. Classifying persons according to their race is more likely to reflect racial prejudice than legitimate public concerns; the race, not the person, dictates the category. Such classifications are subject to the most exacting scrutiny; to pass constitutional muster, they must be justified by a compelling governmental interest and must be "necessary . . . to the accomplishment" of its legitimate purpose, McLaughlin v. Florida, 379 U.S. 184, 196, 85 S.Ct. 283, 290, 13 L.Ed.2d 222 (1964). See Loving v. Virginia, 388 U.S. 1, 11, 87 S.Ct. 1817, 1823, 18 L.Ed.2d 1010 (1967).

The State, of course, has a duty of the highest order to protect the interests of minor children, particularly those of tender years. In common with most states, Florida law mandates that custody determinations be made in the best interests of the children involved. Fla. Stat. § 61.13(2)(b)(1) (1983). The goal of granting custody based on the best interests of the child is indisputably a substantial governmental interest for purposes of the Equal Protection Clause.

It would ignore reality to suggest that racial and ethnic prejudices do not exist or that all manifestations of those prejudices have been eliminated. There is a risk that a child living with a step-parent of a different race may be subject to a variety of pressures and stresses not present if the child were living with parents of the same racial or ethnic origin.

The question, however, is whether the reality of private biases and the possible injury they might inflict are permissible considerations for removal of an infant child from the custody of its natural mother. We have little difficulty concluding that they are not.[2] The Constitution cannot control such prejudices but neither can it tolerate them. Private biases may be outside the reach of the law, but the law cannot, directly or indirectly, give them effect. "Public officials sworn to uphold the Constitution may not avoid a constitutional duty by bowing to the hypothetical effects of private racial prejudice that they assume to be both widely and deeply held." Palmer v. Thompson, 403 U.S. 217, 260–261, 91 S.Ct. 1940, 1962, 29 L.Ed.2d 438 (1971) (White, J., dissenting).

. . .

Whatever problems racially-mixed households may pose for children in 1984 can no more support a denial of constitutional rights than could the stresses that residential integration was thought to entail in 1971. The

---

2. In light of our holding based on the Equal Protection Clause, we need not reach or resolve petitioner's claim based on the Fourteenth Amendment's Due Process Clause.

effects of racial prejudice, however real, cannot justify a racial classification removing an infant child from the custody of its natural mother found to be an appropriate person to have such custody.

NOTE

Consideration of race in making a custody determination continues to be the subject of commentary. *See generally* Katherine T. Bartlett, *Comparing Race and Sex Discrimination in Custody Cases*, 28 HOFSTRA L. REV. 877 (2000). Courts allow race to be but one factor in making a custody award. *See, e.g.*, Ebirim v. Ebirim, 9 Neb.App. 740, 620 N.W.2d 117 (2000), where the court held the biracial identity of the child is not the overriding factor in making a custody determination. Should race matter in adoptions? The federal INDIAN CHILD WELFARE ACT OF 1978, 25 U.S.C. § 1901 *et seq.* (West 1983 & Supp. 2000) provides Native American heritage must be considered in placement of Native American children. *See, e.g.*, McKenzie Cty. Social Service Bd. v. C.G., 633 N.W.2d 157 (N.D.2001). But the federal INTERETH-NIC ADOPTION ACT, 42 U.S.C.A. § 1996b (West 1994 & Supp. 1999), which specifically exempts Native Americans, prohibits delay or denial of placement of children based on race, color or national origin; and a state statute, CAL. FAM. CODE § 7950, does the same. These issues will be further explored in Chapter 9.

2. JOINT LEGAL AND/OR PHYSICAL CUSTODY

CALIFORNIA FAMILY CODE (West 2004)

§ 3003. Joint legal custody

"Joint legal custody" means that both parents shall share the right and the responsibility to make the decisions relating to the health, education, and welfare of a child.

§ 3004. Joint physical custody

"Joint physical custody" means that each of the parents shall have significant periods of physical custody. Joint physical custody shall be shared by the parents in such a way as to assure a child of frequent and continuing contact with both parents, subject to Sections 3001 and 3020.

§ 3006. Sole legal custody

"Sole legal custody" means that one parent shall have the right and the responsibility to make the decisions relating to the health, education, and welfare of a child.

§ 3007. Sole physical custody

"Sole physical custody" means that a child shall reside with and be under the supervision of one parent, subject to the power of the court to order visitation.

§ 3040. Order of preference

(a) Custody should be granted in the following order of preference according to the best interest of the child as provided in Sections 3011 and 3020:

(1) To both parents jointly pursuant to Chapter 4 (commencing with Section 3080) or to either parent. In making an order granting custody to either parent, the court shall consider, among other factors, which parent is more likely to allow the child frequent and continuing contact with the noncustodial parent, consistent with Section 3011 and 3020, and shall not prefer a parent as custodian because of that parent's sex. The court, in its discretion, may require the parents to submit to the court a plan for the implementation of the custody order.

(2) If to neither parent, to the person or persons in whose home the child has been living in a wholesome and stable environment.

(3) To any other person or persons deemed by the court to be suitable and able to provide adequate and proper care and guidance for the child.

(b) This section establishes neither a preference nor a presumption for or against joint legal custody, joint physical custody, or sole custody, but allows the court and the family the widest discretion to choose a parenting plan that is in the best interest of the child.

§ 3080. Presumption of joint custody

There is a presumption, affecting the burden of proof, that joint custody is in the best interest of the minor child, subject to Section 3011, where the parents have agreed to joint custody or so agree in open court at a hearing for the purpose of determining the custody of the minor child.

In re Marriage of Weidner

Supreme Court of Iowa, 1983.
338 N.W.2d 351.

■ WOLLE, JUSTICE.

Appellant Marvin Weidner (Marvin) appeals from several provisions of a dissolution decree under which appellee Betsy Weidner (Betsy) was granted sole custody of the parties' two children. The principal issue is whether the court should have provided for joint custody as requested by Marvin. Marvin also contends that if joint custody was not appropriate then he, rather than Betsy, should have received custody of the children. We first address the issue of child custody, then the economic and other issues raised by the parties.

Marvin and Betsy Weidner were married on August 29, 1970, and two children were born of the marriage, Elizabeth (Libby) born on December 18, 1971 and Seth born on December 27, 1974. After Marvin and Betsy graduated from Iowa Wesleyan College in 1972, Marvin received his degree in theology from Garrett Theological Seminary in Evanston, Illinois. Marvin then served Methodist churches in Humboldt, Iowa until 1975 and Burlington, Iowa until 1977, when the parties moved to Des Moines. Marvin is now Director of the Iowa Refugee Service Center. Betsy obtained a teaching certificate in college, but she did not work outside the home on a full time basis until the parties moved to Des Moines. She has had several part time jobs and now is employed full time as an office receptionist in a Des Moines department store.

As early as 1975, disagreements between Marvin and Betsy caused them to live apart for one week. More serious difficulties later arose. Marvin moved out of the family home between June and November of 1980, and after living together for nine more months the parties separated permanently in August of 1981. During the sixteen months between the final separation and the entry of the court's decree Betsy was the primary physical custodian of the children, but Marvin was with them almost half the time. In general Betsy was the person who took care of the children's day-to-day activities, such as getting them ready for school, packing lunches, doing laundry and taking care of them while they were ill. Marvin was with the children every weekend and one other day each week; he also maintained daily contact with the children both by personal visits to the home and through phone calls. Even though both parties spent equivalent amounts of time with the children, by the time of their final separation the parties neither trusted each other nor enjoyed being in each other's company. The friction which this lack of trust and frequent contact created was exacerbated by Marvin's friendship with a woman friend with whom he often spent considerable time while he had physical custody of the children.

Considering these and other circumstances hereafter discussed we must decide if the trial court properly placed Libby and Seth in the custody of Betsy subject to specified periods of visitation for Marvin rather than providing in the decree for joint custody or sole custody in Marvin.

I. *Principles Governing Joint Custody—Background.* The primary issue in this case is whether the trial court should have provided for joint custody rather than awarding custody to Betsy. Until recently, the principles governing joint custody awards were those set forth in In Re Marriage of Burham, 283 N.W.2d 269 (Iowa 1979)....

Effective July 1, 1982, section 598.21(6) was changed to make joint custody awards subject to the more explicit statutory guidelines which are now codified in section 598.41....

Iowa Code section 598.41 (1983) provides in pertinent part as follows:

Custody of children.

1. The court, insofar as is reasonable and in the best interest of the child, shall order the custody award, including liberal visitation rights where appropriate, which will assure a minor child frequent and continuing contact with both parents after the parents have separated or dissolved the marriage, and which will encourage parents to share the rights and responsibilities of raising the child. Unless otherwise ordered by the court in the custody decree, both parents shall have

legal access to information concerning the child, including but not limited to medical, educational and law enforcement records.

2. On the application of either parent, the court shall consider granting joint custody in cases where the parents do not agree to joint custody. If the court does not grant joint custody under this subsection, the court shall state in its decision the reasons for denying joint custody. Before ruling upon the joint custody petition in these cases, the court may require the parties to participate in custody mediation counseling to determine whether joint custody is in the best interest of the child. The court may require the child's participation in the mediation counseling insofar as the court determines the child's participation is advisable.

The costs of custody mediation counseling shall be paid in full or in part by the parties and taxed as court costs.

3. In considering what custody arrangement under either subsection 1 or 2 is in the best interests of the minor child, the court shall consider the following factors:

a. Whether each parent would be a suitable custodian for the child.

b. Whether the psychological and emotional needs and development of the child will suffer due to lack of active contact with and attention from both parties.

c. Whether the parents can communicate with each other regarding the child's needs.

d. Whether both parents have actively cared for the child before and since the separation.

e. Whether each parent can support the other parent's relationship with the child.

f. Whether the custody arrangement is in accord with the child's wishes or whether the child has strong opposition, taking into consideration the child's age and maturity.

g. Whether one or both the parents agree or are opposed to joint custody.

h. The geographic proximity of the parents.

4. Joint legal custody does not require joint physical care. When the court determines such action would be in the child's best interest, physical care may be given to one joint custodial parent and not to the other. However, physical care given to one parent does not affect the other parent's rights and responsibilities as a legal custodian of the child.

It may be instructive to note that this statutory language which encourages courts to consider and grant joint custody was enacted within a few months after publication of In re Marriage of Castle, 312 N.W.2d 147 (Iowa App.1981). There the Iowa Court of Appeals in a three to two decision denied a request for joint custody primarily on the ground that our *Burham* decision seemed to allow one party to veto joint custody by expressing disapproval of such arrangements. The specially concurring judges in *Castle* suggested that the law should presume joint custody to be in the best interests of children. In enacting section 598.41 the legislature did not use the word presumption and we find no such presumption in Iowa law. Clearly, however, our statutes now express a preference for joint custody over other custodial arrangements and do not allow one-party vetoes. One parent's opposition to joint custody is only one of the several factors which the court must consider when the other parent has requested joint custody.

These new principles governing joint custody, and the specific listed factors which are to be considered when a parent requests joint custody, are the bench marks by which our courts are to determine whether joint custody is in the best interest of children of dissolved marriages. Applying them we now must determine whether under the evidence here joint custody should have been granted as being in the best interests of the Weidner children Libby and Seth.

II.   *Is Joint Custody Appropriate in This Case?*

. . .

The trial court's findings of fact demonstrate that before awarding Betsy sole custody of the children, the court carefully considered Marvin's request for joint custody. The court said:

> While this case was awaiting trial, the parties attempted to have the children with each parent approximately one-half of the time. Originally the children, even during the school year, were with the petitioner from Tuesday morning until Wednesday morning of each week and from Friday morning until Sunday night of each week. When the children returned to the custody of the respondent, they were tired, somewhat crabby and did not want the fun they had been having (while with petitioner) to stop. It was difficult for the respondent and for the children, for the children to get back into the routine of going to school.

> On a number of occasions an argument arose over who was going to have the children at a particular time. On one of these occasions when the respondent had the children with her in her car, the petitioner came upon them while he was in his car. The respondent drove into a driveway at a fire station and petitioner did, too. The police were called and arrived upon the scene. No court order was in effect at the time as to who was to have the children, and the officer would not intercede except to keep the peace. Following this incident a court order was entered giving respondent temporary custody and the petitioner visitation for the times he previously had the children with him, except that the weekend visitation ended on Sunday morning.

> The court after a consideration of all the evidence finds that joint custody should not be granted in this case. While the parties are both

fit and suitable to act as a custodial parent, they have not demonstrat-ed that they are able to communicate and give priority to the welfare of the children by reaching shared decisions that are in the best interests of the children.

The trial court also highlighted certain other matters in its findings of fact, providing us further insight into why it decided against joint custody. The findings of fact emphasize the complication in the lives of Marvin and the children caused by the presence of his woman friend. According to the trial court's findings, Marvin and she "had had an open, ongoing, intimate relationship for about a year." The trial court indicated this relationship had been a serious concern of the court-appointed family therapist who had based his recommendation of joint custody in part upon recommending minimal involvement of other adults in the relationship between the parents and their children. The trial court found that Marvin used poor judgment in discussing frightening ideas, such as a nuclear holocaust, with the children shortly before returning them to Betsy. It expressed concern about the petitioner's discussions with the children concerning his relation-ship with his woman friend and other matters pertaining to the dissolution case which caused them anxiety.

There is solid support in the record for each and all of the trial court's findings of fact and expressions of concern about the feasibility of joint custody for these particular parents. The court not only commented on the parties' general inability to communicate and reach shared child-raising decisions, but also focused upon specific unpleasant scenes from the failing marriage when the parties' dislike and mistrust of each other was made painfully clear to the children. Such incidents seem truly to have wreaked havoc in the lives of the parents and, more importantly, the day-to-day lives of their children. We need not further encumber these printed pages with the details of each unpleasant event which followed the final separation of Marvin and Betsy. Suffice it to say that neither party seems now to respect the other. Neither parent has been able to function well except when completely separated from the other. For example, Marvin's repeated efforts to speak with and visit the children on occasions when they have been in the physical care of Betsy have been stressful for Betsy and the children. Marvin's tape recording of some of his phone conversations with Betsy is symptomatic of the extent to which the parents dislike each other. This attempt by Marvin to obtain evidence for trial led Betsy to communi-cate with him exclusively through written notes.

We are here primarily concerned not with the effect upon Marvin and Betsy of this regular pattern of highly unpleasant episodes, but rather with the adverse effect upon Libby and Seth, their children. This is reflected not only in the parties' testimony but also in the written report and testimony of the court-appointed therapist who performed testing, interviewed the family members on several occasions, and then provided recommendations to the court. Marvin relied heavily on the therapist's recommendation of joint custody, but we find much in the report which seems inconsistent with that recommendation. His first recommendation was

> That joint custody be reconsidered for the children's sake, if both Betsy and Marvin are willing to work toward its success . . . and if Marvin and Betsy each follow recommendations listed below for extensive therapy. Without compliance joint custody does not appear a promising alternative.

The recommendation included 10 to 12 months of post-decree therapeutic work. He indicated this was needed for several reasons; these reasons themselves reflect how serious had been the strife created by the parents and thrust upon the children. He reported that neither child had truly accepted or understood the parent's bitterness and sense of failure. It appears the post-separation period of living first with one parent and then the other was confusing to both children. The older child Libby (then "an intelligent, sensitive young girl of 10") was reported by the therapist as "trapped in a loyalty conflict", feeling herself to be a comforter for both parents and responsible for the hurt that might result from either parent's loss of custody. The family therapist was also "concerned about Seth's adjustment" during the period of parental separation. He reported that the children both "have already endured a sense of rootlessness in their development, with the family moves and continued uncertainty of their parents' marriage." He opined also that the children "need frequent time alone with each parent, without the regular involvement of other adults being present with the parent—even other relatives." On cross examination he explained that the "grieving process" needed for repairing and understanding emotional scars of the bad marriage was still in process for the parents and had not even started for these two young children—"they're denying how much disruption is going on." He attributed this in part to the entry of Marvin's woman friend into this situation. In this regard he stated:

> But again, in light of the whole thing of restructuring their primary contacts and their emotional bonds with each individual parent, it's going to be imperative that they have as much time as they want, not as much time as the individual parent wants, to have alone with that natural parent, be that their father or their mother.

It is reasonable to conclude from his testimony that a joint custody arrangement probably would not work unless the parties both would change their recent pattern of behavior, believe in the positive effects of such an arrangement, and respond satisfactorily to about a year of active post-marital counseling and therapy. We agree with the trial court in concluding that those pre-conditions to successful joint custody arrangements are unlikely to be satisfactorily met, based on the parties' demonstrated antagonism toward each other since the marriage failed.

We would be remiss if we did not mention and correct certain misconceptions counsel and trial courts may have concerning joint custody. None of the eight factors which judges must weigh in the balance are conditions precedent to a joint custody determination. The trial court should consider and express itself in writing on those factors among the eight listed which are pertinent in disputed cases, but there is no magic number of the factors which, when satisfied, will mandate a decision for or against joint custody. The quality of the total family custodial setting rather than a given quantity of the listed factors should be determinative on the issue of joint custody. Here, no factor alone has dissuaded us from putting in place a joint custody arrangement. We have concluded, however, that on the record in this case Marvin and Betsy would be unable adequately to communicate with each other regarding their children's needs, neither parent would be adequately supportive of the other parent's relationship with the children, and Betsy is opposed to joint custody for reasons reasonably attributable in substantial part to the actions and attitude of Marvin.

Furthermore, no parent and no attorney representing a party should be concerned that a request for joint custody is a sign of weakness, a suggestion to the court that if joint custody is not decreed the party opposing joint custody may have an edge in obtaining sole custody. Conversely, and as was noted in our recent *Bolin* decision, a court may properly consider that a parent's unreasonable or obdurate resistance to joint custody is a factor which can weigh in favor of awarding sole custody to the other parent. In re Marriage of Bolin, 336 N.W.2d [441], at 446 [Iowa 1983].

In the last analysis, the custodial determination must reflect and accomplish whatever is in the best interest of the affected children. Joint custody is preferred because, properly tailored to the parties' circumstances, joint custodial arrangements will often go a long way toward encouraging both parents to share the rights, responsibilities, and frequently joyful and meaningful experiences of raising their children.

We reluctantly but firmly conclude, as did the trial court, that the circumstances here are not conducive to a workable joint custody arrangement which would be in the best interests of the parties' children Libby and Seth.

. . .

We therefore affirm the trial court's decree . . .

WISCONSIN STATUTES ANN. (West 2001)

767.24. Custody and physical placement

. . .

(2) Custody to party; joint or sole. (a) Subject to pars. (am), (b) and (c), based on the best interest of the child and after considering the factors under sub. (5), the court may give joint legal custody or sole legal custody of a minor child.

(a) The court shall presume that joint legal custody is in the best interest of the child.

(b) The court may give sole legal custody only if it finds that doing so is in the child's best interest and that either of the following applies:

1.   Both parties agree to sole legal custody with the same party.

2.   The parties do not agree to sole legal custody with the same party, but at least one party requests sole legal custody and the court specifically finds any of the following:

a.   One party is not capable of performing parental duties and responsibilities or does not wish to have an active role in raising the child.

b.   One or more conditions exist at that time that would substantially interfere with the exercise of joint legal custody.

c.   The parties will not be able to cooperate in the future decision making required under an award of joint legal custody. In making this finding the court shall consider, along with any other pertinent items, any reasons offered by a party objecting to joint legal custody. Evidence that either party engaged in abuse, as defined in § 813.122(1)(a), of the child, as defined in § 48.02(2), or evidence of interspousal battery, as described under s. 940.19 or 940.20(1m), or domestic abuse, as defined in § 813.12(1)(a), creates a rebuttable presumption that the parties will not be able to cooperate in the future decision making required.

(c) The court may not give sole legal custody to a parent who refuses to cooperate with the other parent if the court finds that the refusal to cooperate is unreasonable . . .

. . .

NOTE

Joint custody arrangements often retain close supervision of the trial court in the raising of children. Is this desirable? For instance, in Birnbaum v. Birnbaum, 211 Cal.App.3d 1508, 260 Cal.Rptr. 210 (1989), the Court of Appeals of California was asked to review a trial court order whereby joint legal and physical custody of three daughters, then aged three, five and seven, was structured in the following manner. One child was given a "primary residence" with her mother, another with her father, and the third to alternate yearly. During the school year all three were to live with the mother during the week and spend weekends and Wednesday afternoons with the father.

The mother unilaterally removed the two older children "from the environment where they had started their lives and the school careers without the opportunity for [the father] to have any input." The court was then asked to intervene in petitions by each parent for sole custody. The appellate court affirmed the continuation of the joint custody arrangement decided upon by the trial court, but made the following comments concerning joint custody:

> In actions to dissolve marriages, it has become quite common to include requests for joint custody of children. It is doubtful that any two words mean as many different things to as many different people as the words "joint custody." The statutory definition, having to cover the wide variety of arrangements parents make when they have joint custody, is necessarily broad and does not provide much guidance.

There seems to be a popular misconception that joint physical custody means the children spend exactly one-half their time with each parent. Such an arrangement, of course, leaves the child with no time of his or her own to spend with friends. It also elevates parental rights over children's rights and virtually treats the child as the parents' possession. It fails to take into account that the maximum personal growth and development of a child occurs from both a loving and supportive relationship within the family and the development of personal relationships outside the family. Parents' demands for equal amounts of the child's time constitute a disservice to the child, usually creating stress and preventing the child from fully achieving his or her potential. In some cases the nature of the relationship between the parents may necessitate this kind of inflexibility. Usually it is temporary, and when the former spouses have adjusted to their new and limited relationship as parents of the same children, mathematical exactitude of time is no longer necessary. That has not occurred here.

Equal division of a child's time between the parents is not the hallmark of joint custody ... Although time is important to the parents, the determining factor as to whether joint physical custody is in the best interest of the child is the nature of the parenting relationship between the parents.

Joint custody arrangements are affected by either of the parties subsequently seeking a modification into sole physical custody. *See, e.g., In re* Pasquale, 146 N.H. 652, 777 A.2d 877 (2001), where the New Hampshire Supreme Court held that in a petition to modify a joint custody arrangement, the court should apply the best interest of the child test, rather than require a significant change of circumstances. Recognizing that the standard for modification is usually whether the child would suffer harm if left in the present custody arrangement, but when both parents admit the joint custody arrangement is not working, then the court should rule as if it were making an initial custody award. Giving deference to the decisions of the parents through arbitration is argued by: E. Gary Spitko, *Reclaiming the "Creatures of the State": Contracting for Child Custody Decisionmaking in the Best Interests of the Family*, 57 WASH. & LEE L. REV. 1139 (2000). *But see* Kelm v. Kelm, 92 Ohio St.3d 223, 749 N.E.2d 299 (2001), rejecting parental provision allowing for arbitration in custody and visitation disputes.

B. PARENT VERSUS THIRD PARTY

Painter v. Bannister

Supreme Court of Iowa, 1966.
258 Iowa 1390, 140 N.W.2d 152, *cert. denied* 385 U.S. 949.

■ STUART, JUSTICE. We are here setting the course for Mark Wendell Painter's future. Our decision on the custody of this 7 year old boy will have a marked influence on his whole life. The fact that we are called upon many times a year to determine custody matters does not make the exercising of this awesome responsibility any less difficult. Legal training and experience are of little practical help in solving the complex problems of human relations. However, these problems do arise and under our system of government, the burden of rendering a final decision rests upon us. It is frustrating to know we can only resolve, not solve, these unfortunate situations.

The custody dispute before us in this habeas corpus action is between the father, Harold Painter, and the maternal grandparents, Dwight and Margaret Bannister. Mark's mother and younger sister were killed in an automobile accident on December 6, 1962 near Pullman, Washington. The father, after other arrangements for Mark's care had proved unsatisfactory, asked the Bannisters to take care of Mark. They went to California and brought Mark to their farm home near Ames in July, 1963. Mr. Painter remarried in November, 1964 and about that time indicated he wanted to take Mark back. The Bannisters refused to let him leave and this action was filed in June, 1965. Since July, 1965 he has continued to remain in the Bannister home under an order of this court staying execution of the judgment of the trial court awarding custody to the father until the matter could be determined on appeal. For reasons hereinafter stated, we conclude Mark's better interests will be served if he remains with the Bannisters.

Mark's parents came from highly contrasting backgrounds. His mother was born, raised and educated in rural Iowa. Her parents are college graduates. Her father is agricultural information editor for the Iowa State University Extension Service. The Bannister home is in the Gilbert Community and is well kept, roomy and comfortable. The Bannisters are highly respected members of the community. Mr. Bannister has served on the school board and regularly teaches a Sunday school class at the Gilbert Congregational Church. Mark's mother graduated from Grinnell College. She then went to work for a newspaper in Anchorage, Alaska, where she met Harold Painter.

Mark's father was born in California. When he was 2 ½ years old, his parents were divorced and he was placed in a foster home. Although he has kept in contact with his natural parents, he considers his foster parents, the McNelly's as his family. He flunked out of a high school and a trade school because of a lack of interest in academic subjects, rather than any lack of ability. He joined the navy at 17. He did not like it. After receiving an honorable discharge, he took examinations and obtained his high school diploma. He lived with the McNelly's and went to college for 2 ½ years under the G.I. bill. He quit college to take a job on a small newspaper in Ephrata, Washington in November 1955. In May 1956, he went to work for the newspaper in Anchorage which employed Jeanne Bannister.

Harold and Jeanne were married in April, 1957. Although there is a conflict in the evidence on the point, we are convinced the marriage, overall, was a happy one with many ups and downs as could be expected in the uniting of two such opposites.

We are not confronted with a situation where one of the contesting parties is not a fit or proper person. There is no criticism of either the Bannisters or their home. There is no suggestion in the record that Mr. Painter is morally unfit. It is obvious the Bannisters did not approve of their daughter's marriage to Harold Painter and do not want their grandchild raised under his guidance. The philosophies of life are entirely different. As stated by the psychiatrist who examined Mr. Painter at the request of Bannisters' attorneys: "It is evident that there exists a large difference in ways of life and value systems between the Bannisters and Mr. Painter, but in this case, there is no evidence that psychiatric instability is involved. Rather, these divergent life patterns seem to represent alternative normal adaptations."

It is not our prerogative to determine custody upon our choice of one of two ways of life within normal and proper limits and we will not do so. However, the philosophies are important as they relate to Mark and his particular needs.

The Bannister home provides Mark with a stable, dependable, conventional, middleclass, middlewest background and an opportunity for a college education and profession, if he desires it. It provides a solid foundation and secure atmosphere. In the Painter home, Mark would have more freedom of conduct and thought with an opportunity to develop his individual talents. It would be more exciting and challenging in many respects, but romantic, impractical and unstable. . . .

Our conclusion as to the type of home Mr. Painter would offer is based upon his Bohemian approach to finances and life in general. We feel there is much evidence which supports this conclusion. His main ambition is to be a free lance writer and photographer. He has had some articles and picture stories published, but the income from these efforts has been negligible. At the time of the accident, Jeanne was willingly working to support the family so Harold could devote more time to his writing and photography. In the 10 years since he left college, he has changed jobs seven times. He was asked to leave two of them; two he quit because he didn't like the work; two because he wanted to devote more time to writing and the rest for better pay. He was contemplating a move to Berkeley at the time of trial. His attitude toward his career is typified by his own comments concerning a job offer:

"About the Portland news job, I hope you understand when I say it took guts not to take it; I had to get behind myself and push. It was very, very tempting to accept a good salary and settle down to a steady, easy routine. As I approached Portland, with the intention of taking the job, I began to ask what, in the long run, would be the good of this job: 1, it was not *really* what I wanted; 2, Portland is just another big farm town, with none of the stimulation it takes to get my mind sparking. Anyway, I decided Mark and myself would be better off if I went ahead with what I've started and the hell with the rest, sink, swim or starve."

There is general agreement that Mr. Painter needs help with his finances. Both Jeanne and Marilyn, his present wife, handled most of them.

Purchases and sales of books, boats, photographic equipment and houses indicate poor financial judgment and an easy come easy go attitude. He dissipated his wife's estate of about $4300, most of which was a gift from her parents and which she had hoped would be used for the children's education.

The psychiatrist classifies him as "a romantic and somewhat of a dreamer". An apt example are the plans he related for himself and Mark in February 1963: "My thought now is to settle Mark and myself in Sausalito, near San Francisco; this is a retreat for wealthy artists, writers, and such aspiring artists and writers as can fork up the rent money. My plan is to do expensive portraits ($150 and up), sell prints ($15 and up) to the tourists who flock in from all over the world...."

The house in which Mr. Painter and his present wife live, compared with the well kept Bannister home, exemplifies the contrasting ways of life. In his words "it is a very old and beat up and lovely home ...". They live in the rear part. The interior is inexpensively but tastefully decorated. The large yard on a hill in the business district of Walnut Creek, California, is of uncut weeds and wild oats. The house "is not painted on the outside because I do not want it painted. I am very fond of the wood on the outside of the house."

The present Mrs. Painter has her master's degree in cinema design and apparently likes and has had considerable contact with children. She is anxious to have Mark in her home. Everything indicates she would provide a leveling influence on Mr. Painter and could ably care for Mark.

Mr. Painter is either an agnostic or atheist and has no concern for formal religious training. He has read a lot of Zen Buddhism and "has been very much influenced by it". Mrs. Painter is Roman Catholic. They plan to send Mark to a Congregational Church near the Catholic Church, on an irregular schedule.

He is a political liberal and got into difficulty in a job at the University of Washington for his support of the activities of the American Civil Liberties Union in the university news bulletin.

There were "two funerals" for his wife. One in the basement of his home in which he alone was present. He conducted the service and wrote her a long letter. The second at a church in Pullman was for the gratification of her friends. He attended in a sport shirt and sweater.

These matters are not related as a criticism of Mr. Painter's conduct, way of life or sense of values. An individual is free to choose his own values, within bounds, which are not exceeded here. They do serve however to support our conclusion as to the kind of life Mark would be exposed to in the Painter household. We believe it would be unstable, unconventional, arty, Bohemian, and probably intellectually stimulating.

Were the question simply which household would be the most suitable in which to raise a child, we would have unhesitatingly chosen the Bannister home. We believe security and stability in the home are more important than intellectual stimulation in the proper development of a child. There are, however, several factors which have made us pause.

First, there is the presumption of parental preference, which though weakened in the past several years, exists by statute.... We have a great deal of sympathy for a father, who in the difficult period of adjustment following his wife's death, turns to the maternal grandparents for their help and then finds them unwilling to return the child. There is no merit in the Bannister claim that Mr. Painter permanently relinquished custody. It was intended to be a temporary arrangement. A father should be encouraged to look for help with the children, from those who love them without the risk of thereby losing the custody of the children permanently. This fact must receive consideration in cases of this kind. However, as always, the primary consideration is the best interest of the child and if the return of custody to the father is likely to have a seriously disrupting and disturbing effect upon the child's development, this fact must prevail....

Second, Jeanne's will named her husband guardian of her children and if he failed to qualify or ceased to act, named her mother. The parent's wishes are entitled to consideration....

Third, the Bannisters are 60 years old. By the time Mark graduates from high school they will be over 70 years old. Care of young children is a strain on grandparents and Mrs. Bannister's letters indicate as much.

We have considered all of these factors and have concluded that Mark's best interest demands that his custody remain with the Bannisters. Mark was five when he came to their home. The evidence clearly shows he was not well adjusted at that time. He did not distinguish fact from fiction and was inclined to tell "tall tales" emphasizing the big "I". He was very aggressive toward smaller children, cruel to animals, not liked by his classmates and did not seem to know what was acceptable conduct. As stated by one witness: "Mark knew where his freedom was and he didn't know where his boundaries were." In two years he made a great deal of improvement. He now appears to be well disciplined, happy, relatively secure and popular with his classmates, although still subject to more than normal anxiety.

We place a great deal of reliance on the testimony of Dr. Glenn R. Hawks, a child psychologist. The trial court, in effect, disregarded Dr. Hawks' opinions stating: "The court has given full consideration to the good doctor's testimony, but cannot accept it at full face value because of exaggerated statements and the witness' attitude on the stand." We, of course, do not have the advantage of viewing the witness' conduct on the stand, but we have carefully reviewed his testimony and find nothing in the written record to justify such a summary dismissal of the opinions of this eminent child psychologist.

Dr. Hawks is head of the Department of Child Development at Iowa State University. However, there is nothing in the record which suggests that his relationship with the Bannisters is such that his professional opinion would be influenced thereby. Child development is his specialty and he has written many articles and a textbook on the subject. He is recognized nationally, having served on the staff of the 1960 White House Conference on Children and Youth and as consultant on a Ford Foundation program concerning youth in India. . . .

Between June 15th and the time of trial, he spent approximately 25 hours acquiring information about Mark and the Bannisters, including appropriate testing of and "depth interviews" with Mark. Dr. Hawks' testimony covers 70 pages of the record and it is difficult to pinpoint any bit of testimony which precisely summarizes his opinion. He places great emphasis on the "father figure" and discounts the importance of the "biological father". "The father figure is a figure that the child sees as an authority figure, as a helper, he is a nutrient figure, and one who typifies maleness and stands as maleness as far as the child is concerned."

His investigation revealed: ". . . the strength of the father figure before Mark came to the Bannisters is very unclear. Mark is confused about the father figure prior to his contact with Mr. Bannister." Now, "Mark used Mr. Bannister as his father figure. This is very evident. It shows up in the depth interview, and it shows up in the description of Mark's life given by Mark. He has a very warm feeling for Mr. Bannister."

Dr. Hawks concluded that it was not for Mark's best interest to be removed from the Bannister home. He is criticized for reaching this conclusion without investigating the Painter home or finding out more about Mr. Painter's character. He answered:

"I was most concerned about the welfare of the child, not the welfare of Mr. Painter, not about the welfare of the Bannisters. In as much as Mark has already made an adjustment and sees the Bannisters as his parental figures in his psychological make-up, to me this is the most critical factor. Disruption at this point, I think, would be detrimental to the child even tho Mr. Painter might well be a paragon of virtue. I think this would be a kind of thing which would not be in the best interest of the child. I think knowing something about where the child is at the present time is vital. I think something about where he might go, in my way of thinking is essentially untenable to me, and relatively unimportant. It isn't even helpful. The thing I was most concerned about was Mark's view of his own reality in which he presently lives. If this is destroyed I think it will have rather bad effects on Mark. I think then if one were to make a determination whether it would be the parents' household, or the McNelly household, or X-household, then I think the further study would be appropriate."

Dr. Hawks stated: "I am appalled at the tremendous task Mr. Painter would have if Mark were to return to him because he has got to build the relationship from scratch. There is essentially nothing on which to build at the present time. Mark is aware Mr. Painter is his father, but he is not very clear about what this means. In his own mind the father figure is Mr. Bannister. I think it would take a very strong person with everything in his favor in order to build a relationship as Mr. Painter would have to build at this point with Mark."

It was Dr. Hawks' opinion "the chances are very high (Mark) will go wrong if he is returned to his father". This is based on adoption studies which "establish that the majority of adoptions in children who are changed, from ages six to eight, will go bad, if they have had a prior history of instability, some history of prior movement. When I refer to instability I am referring to where there has been no attempt to establish a strong relationship." Although this is not an adoption, the analogy seems appropriate, for Mark who had a history of instability would be removed from the only home in which he has a clearly established "father figure" and placed with his natural father about whom his feelings are unclear.

We know more of Mr. Painter's way of life than Dr. Hawks. We have concluded that it does not offer as great a stability or security as the Bannister home. Throughout his testimony he emphasized Mark's need at this critical time is stability. He has it in the Bannister home.

Other items of Dr. Hawks' testimony which have a bearing on our decision follow. He did not consider the Bannisters' age anyway disqualifying. He was of the opinion that Mark could adjust to a change more easily later on, if one became necessary, when he would have better control over his environment.

He believes the presence of other children in the home would have a detrimental effect upon Mark's adjustment whether this occurred in the Bannister home or the Painter home.

The trial court does not say which of Dr. Hawks' statements he felt were exaggerated. We were most surprised at the inconsequential position to which he relegated the "biological father". He concedes "child psychologists are less concerned about natural parents than probably other professional groups are." We are not inclined to so lightly value the role of the natural father, but find much reason for his evaluation of this particular case.

Mark has established a father-son relationship with Mr. Bannister, which he apparently had never had with his natural father. He is happy, well adjusted and progressing nicely in his development. We do not believe it is for Mark's best interest to take him out of this stable atmosphere in the face of warnings of dire consequences from an eminent child psychologist and send him to an uncertain future in his father's home. Regardless of our appreciation of the father's love for his child and his desire to have him with him, we do not believe we have the moral right to gamble with this child's future. He should be encouraged in every way possible to know his father. We are sure there are many ways in which Mr. Painter can enrich Mark's life.

For the reasons stated, we reverse the trial court and remand the case for judgment in accordance herewith.

NOTE

Mark was reunited with his father after a couple of visits to his father's home in California. Mark ultimately expressed a desire to stay with his father; the grandparents did not oppose the change of custody. Mr. Painter was given temporary custody by a California court on Aug. 8, 1968 and published a book on the subject, MARK, I LOVE YOU, in 1969. The State of California subsequently adopted the following statute:

CALIFORNIA FAMILY CODE (West 2004)

§ 3041. Custody award to nonparent; findings of court; hearing

(a) Before making an order granting custody to a person or persons other than a parent, over the objection of a parent, the court shall make a finding that granting custody to a parent would be detrimental to the child and that granting custody to the nonparent is required to serve the best interest of the child. Allegations that parental custody would be detrimental to the child, other than a statement of that ultimate fact, shall not appear in the pleadings. The court may, in its discretion, exclude the public from the hearing on this issue.

(b) Subject to subdivision (d), a finding that parental custody would be detrimental to the child shall be supported by clear and convincing evidence.

(c) As used in this section, "detriment to the child" includes the harm of removal from a stable placement of a child with a person who has assumed, on a day-to-day basis, the role of his or her parent, fulfilling both the child's physical needs and the child's psychological needs for care and affection, and who has assumed that role for a substantial period of time. A finding of detriment does not require any finding of unfitness of the parents.

(d) Notwithstanding subdivision (b), if the court finds by a preponderance of the evidence that the person to whom custody may be given is a person described in subdivision (c), this finding shall constitute a finding that the custody is in the best interest of the child and that parental custody would be detrimental to the child absent a showing by a preponderance of the evidence to the contrary.

(e) Notwithstanding subdivisions (a) to (d), inclusive, if the child is an Indian child, when an allegation is made that parental custody would be detrimental to the child, before making an order granting custody to a person or persons other than a parent, over the objection of a parent, the court shall apply the evidentiary standards described in subdivisions (d), (e), and (f) of Section 1912 of the Indian Child Welfare Act (25 U.S.C. Sec. 1901 et seq.) and Sections 224.6 and 361.7 of the Welfare and Institutions Code and the placement preferences and standards set out in Section 361.31 of the Welfare and Institutions Code and Section 1922 of the Indian Child Welfare Act (25 U.S.C. Sec. 1901 et seq.).

NOTE

Grandparents, as appear in the preceding decision, have become prolific litigators in seeking custody and visitation rights with their grandchildren. The Supreme Court of the United States dealt a setback to any third party, including grandparents, in a suit against a natural parent in Troxel v. Granville, 530 U.S. 57, 120 S.Ct. 2054, 147 L.Ed.2d 49 (2000), which may be found under the visitation materials *infra*. The Court reaffirmed the due process presumptive right of a parent to the custody and visitation decisions affecting his or her child. But there are instances when a parent may be denied custody of his or her child. *See, e.g.*, Adams v. Tessener, 354 N.C. 57, 550 S.E.2d 499 (N.C. 2001), when the father did nothing to assist the mother of the child during her pregnancy nor six months after birth, the court may properly rebut his constitutionally protected interest and award the child's custody to the grandparents under a best interest test. But it seems clear that before the best interest of the child may be the focus, there must first be a determination that the child will suffer physical or emotional harm if the child is returned to the parent. *See, e.g.*, Clark v. Wade, 273 Ga. 587, 544 S.E.2d 99 (2001).

Bennett v. Jeffreys

Court of Appeals of New York, 1976.
40 N.Y.2d 543, 387 N.Y.S.2d 821, 356 N.E.2d 277.

■ BREITEL, CHIEF JUDGE.

Petitioner is the natural mother of Gina Marie Bennett, now an eight-year-old girl. The mother in this proceeding seeks custody of her daughter from respondent, to whom the child had been entrusted since just after birth. Family Court ruled that, although the mother had not surrendered or abandoned the child and was not unfit, the child should remain with the present custodian, a former schoolmate of the child's grandmother. The Appellate Division reversed, one Justice dissenting, and awarded custody to the mother. Respondent custodian appeals.[1]

The issue is whether the natural mother, who has not surrendered, abandoned, or persistently neglected her child, may, nevertheless, be deprived of the custody of her child because of a prolonged separation from the child for most of its life.

There should be a reversal and a new hearing before the Family Court. The State may not deprive a parent of the custody of a child absent surrender, abandonment, persisting neglect, unfitness or other like extraordinary circumstances. If any such extraordinary circumstances are present, the disposition of custody is influenced or controlled by what is in the best interest of the child. In the instant case extraordinary circumstances, namely, the prolonged separation of mother and child for most of the child's life, require inquiry into the best interest of the child. . . .

Some eight years ago, the mother, then 15 years old, unwed, and living with her parents, gave birth to the child. Under pressure from her mother,

---

1. The child is currently with her mother and will remain there pending final determination of this litigation, a stay of the Appellate Division order having been denied by that court.

she reluctantly acquiesced in the transfer of the newborn infant to an older woman, Mrs. Jeffreys, a former classmate of the child's grandmother. The quality and quantity of the mother's later contacts with the child were disputed. The Family Court found, however, that there was no statutory surrender or abandonment. Pointedly, the Family Court found that the mother was not unfit. The Appellate Division agreed with this finding.

There was evidence that Mrs. Jeffreys intended to adopt the child at an early date. She testified, however, that she could not afford to do so and admitted that she never took formal steps to adopt.

The natural mother is now 23 and will soon graduate from college. She still lives with her family, in a private home with quarters available for herself and the child. The attitude of the mother's parents, however, is changed and they are now anxious that their daughter keep her child.

Mrs. Jeffreys, on the other hand, is now separated from her husband, is employed as a domestic and, on occasion, has kept the child in a motel. It is significant that Mrs. Jeffreys once said that she was willing to surrender the child to the parent upon demand when the child reached the age of 12 or 13 years.

At the outset, it is emphasized that not involved is an attempted revocation of a voluntary surrender to an agency or private individual for adoption (see Social Services Law, § 383, subd. 5; People ex rel. Scarpetta v. Spence–Chapin Adoption Serv., 28 N.Y.2d 185, 321 N.Y.S.2d 65, 269 N.E.2d 787, cert. den. 404 U.S. 805), . . . Nor is abandonment involved. Nor does the proceeding involve an attempted permanent termination of custody (Family Ct. Act, § 614, subd. 1; § 631) . . . Nor is there involved the temporary placement into foster care by an authorized agency which is obliged to conduct an investigation and to determine the qualification of foster parents before placement of a child in need of such care (see Social Services Law, § 383, subds. 1–3; Matter of Jewish Child Care Assn. of N.Y. [Sanders], 5 N.Y.2d 222, 224–225, 183 N.Y.S.2d 65, 66, 156 N.E.2d 700, 701; . . .

Instead, this proceeding was brought by an unwed mother to obtain custody of her daughter from a custodian to whom the child had been voluntarily, although not formally, entrusted by the mother's parents when the mother was only 15 years old. Thus, as an unsupervised private placement, no statute is directly applicable, and the analysis must proceed from common-law principles.

Absent extraordinary circumstances, narrowly categorized, it is not within the power of a court, or, by delegation of the Legislature or court, a social agency, to make significant decisions concerning the custody of children, merely because it could make a better decision or disposition. The State is *parens patriae* and always has been, but it has not displaced the parent in right or responsibility. Indeed, the courts and the law would, under existing constitutional principles, be powerless to supplant parents except for grievous cause or necessity. Examples of cause or necessity permitting displacement of or intrusion on parental control would be fault or omission by the parent seriously affecting the welfare of a child, the preservation of the child's freedom from serious physical harm, illness or death, or the child's right to an education, and the like. . . .

The parent has a "right" to rear its child, and the child has a "right" to be reared by its parent. However, there are exceptions created by extraordinary circumstances, illustratively, surrender, abandonment, persisting neglect, unfitness, and unfortunate or involuntary disruption of custody over an extended period of time. It is these exceptions which have engendered confusion, sometimes in thought but most often only in language.

The day is long past in this State, if it had ever been, when the right of a parent to the custody of his or her child, where the extraordinary circumstances are present, would be enforced inexorably, contrary to the best interest of the child, on the theory solely of an absolute legal right. Instead, in the extraordinary circumstance, when there is a conflict, the best interest of the child has always been regarded as superior to the right of parental custody. Indeed, analysis of the cases reveals a shifting of emphasis rather than a remaking of substance. This shifting reflects more the modern principle that a child is a person, and not a subperson over whom the parent has an absolute possessory interest. A child has rights too, some of which are of a constitutional magnitude.

Earlier cases emphasized the right of the parent, superior to all others, to the care and custody of the child. This right could be dissolved only by abandonment, surrender, or unfitness. Of course, even in these earlier cases, it was recognized that parental custody is lost or denied not as a moral sanction for parental failure, but because "the child's welfare compels awarding its custody to the nonparent".

Although always recognizing the parent's custodial rights, the concern in the later cases, given the extraordinary circumstances, was consciously with the best interest of the child. . . . [I]n People ex rel. Scarpetta v. Spence–Chapin Adoption Serv., 28 N.Y.2d 185, 321 N.Y.S.2d 65, 269 N.E.2d 787, . . . the court held "that the record before us supports the finding by the courts below that the surrender was improvident and that the child's best interests—moral and temporal—will be best served by its return to the natural mother", p. 194, 321 N.Y.S.2d p. 72, 269 N.E.2d p. 792.

Finally in Matter of Spence–Chapin Adoption Serv. v. Polk, 29 N.Y.2d 196, 204, 324 N.Y.S.2d 937, 944, 274 N.E.2d 431, 436, the court rejected any notion of absolute parental rights. The court restated the abiding principle that the child's rights and interests are "paramount" and are not subordinated to the right of parental custody, as important as that right is, p. 204, 324 N.Y.S.2d p. 944, 274 N.E.2d p. 436. Indeed, and this is key, the rights of the parent and the child are ordinarily compatible, for "the generally accepted view [is] that a child's best interest is that it be raised by its parent unless the parent is disqualified by gross misconduct" p. 204, 324 N.Y.S.2d p. 944, 274 N.E.2d 436.

Recently enacted statute law, applicable to related areas of child custody such as adoption and permanent neglect proceedings, has explicitly required the courts to base custody decisions solely upon the best interest of the child (Social Services Law, § 383, subd. 5; Domestic Relations Law, § 115–b, subd. 3, par. [d], cl. [v]; Family Ct. Act, § 614, subd. 1, par. [e]; § 631) ... Under these statutes, there is no presumption that the best interest of the child will be promoted by any particular custodial disposition. Only to this limited extent is there a departure from the pre-existing decisional rule, which never gave more than rebuttable presumptive status, however strongly, to the parent's "right."

. . .

But neither decisional rule nor statute can displace a fit parent because someone else could do a "better job" of raising the child in the view of the court (or the Legislature), so long as the parent or parents have not forfeited their "rights" by surrender, abandonment, unfitness, persisting neglect or other extraordinary circumstance. These "rights" are not so much "rights", but responsibilities which reflect the view, noted earlier, that, except when disqualified or displaced by extraordinary circumstances, parents are generally best qualified to care for their own children and therefore entitled to do so.

Indeed, as said earlier, the courts and the law would, under existing constitutional principles, be powerless to supplant parents except for grievous cause or necessity ...

But where there is warrant to consider displacement of the parent, a determination that extraordinary circumstances exist is only the beginning, not the end, of judicial inquiry. Extraordinary circumstances alone do not justify depriving a natural parent of the custody of a child. Instead, once extraordinary circumstances are found, the court must then make the disposition that is in the best interest of the child.

Although the extraordinary circumstances trigger the "best interests of the child" test, this must not mean that parental rights or responsibilities may be relegated to a parity with all the other surrounding circumstances in the analysis of what is best for the child. So for one example only, while it is true that disruption of custody over an extended period of time is the touchstone in many custody cases, where it is voluntary the test is met more easily but where it is involuntary the test is met only with great difficulty, for evident reasons of humanity and policy.

The child's "best interest" is not controlled by whether the natural parent or the nonparent would make a "better" parent, or by whether the parent or the nonparent would afford the child a "better" background or superior creature comforts. Nor is the child's best interest controlled alone by comparing the depth of love and affection between the child and those who vie for its custody. Instead, in ascertaining the child's best interest, the court is guided by principles which reflect "considered social judgments in this society respecting the family and parenthood" (Matter of Spence–Chapin Adoption Serv. v. Polk, 29 N.Y.2d 196, 204, 324 N.Y.S.2d 937, 944,

274 N.E.2d 431, 436). These principles do not, however, dictate that the child's custody be routinely awarded to the natural parent.

. . .

To recapitulate: intervention by the State in the right and responsibility of a natural parent to custody of her or his child is warranted if there is first a judicial finding of surrender, abandonment, unfitness, persistent neglect, unfortunate or involuntary extended disruption of custody, or other equivalent but rare extraordinary circumstance which would drastically affect the welfare of the child. It is only on such a premise that the courts may then proceed to inquire into the best interest of the child and to order a custodial disposition on that ground.

In custody matters parties and courts may be very dependent on the auxiliary services of psychiatrists, psychologists, and trained social workers. This is good. But it may be an evil when the dependence is too obsequious or routine or the experts too casual. Particularly important is this caution where one or both parties may not have the means to retain their own experts and where publicly compensated experts or experts compensated by only one side have uncurbed leave to express opinions which may be subjective or are not narrowly controlled by the underlying facts.

The court's determination may be influenced by whether the child is in the present custody of the parent or the nonparent. Changes in conditions which affect the relative desirability of custodians, even when the contest is between two natural parents, are not to be accorded significance unless the advantages of changing custody outweigh the essential principle of continued and stable custody of children. . . .

Moreover, the child may be so long in the custody of the nonparent that, even though there has been no abandonment or persisting neglect by the parent, the psychological trauma of removal is grave enough to threaten destruction of the child. Of course, such a situation would offer no opportunity for the court, under the guise of determining the best interest of the child, to weigh the material advantages offered by the adverse parties. . . .

Before applying these principles to this case, a factor should be mentioned which, although not here present, often complicates custody dispositions. The resolution of cases must not provide incentives for those likely to take the law into their own hands. Thus, those who obtain custody of children unlawfully, particularly by kidnapping, violence, or flight from the jurisdiction of the courts, must be deterred. Society may not reward, except at its peril, the lawless because the passage of time has made correction inexpedient. Yet, even then, circumstances may require that, in the best interest of the child, the unlawful acts be blinked.

In this case, there were extraordinary circumstances present, namely, the protracted separation of mother from child, combined with the mother's lack of an established household of her own, her unwed state, and the attachment of the child to the custodian. Thus, application of the principles discussed required an examination by the court into the best interest of the child.

In reaching its conclusion that the child should remain with the nonparent custodian, the Family Court relied primarily upon the seven-year period of custody by the nonparent and evidently on the related testimony of a psychologist. The court did not, however, adequately examine into the nonparent custodian's qualifications and background. Also, the court apparently failed to consider the fact that, absent a finding of abandonment or neglect by the mother, or her consent, the nonparent cannot adopt the child. Family Court's disposition, if sustained, would therefore have left the child in legal limbo, her status indefinite until the attainment of her majority. For a single example, a question could arise as to whose consent, the parent's or the nonparent custodian's, would be necessary for the child to marry while underage (see Domestic Relations Law, § 15, subd. 2 [consent of "parent" or "guardian" required]). A similar question could arise with respect to many situations affecting employment and entry into occupations, an adoption, and any other matters requiring the consent of a parent or legal guardian.

On the other hand, the Appellate Division, in awarding custody to the mother, too automatically applied the primary principle that a parent is entitled to the custody of the child. This was not enough if there were extraordinary circumstances, as indeed there were. Other than to agree with Family Court that she was not "unfit", the court did not pursue a further analysis. Most important, no psychological or other background examination of the mother had ever been obtained. There was, therefore, no consideration of whether the mother is an adequate parent, in capacity, motivation, and efficacious planning. Nevertheless, the Appellate Division determination may well be right.

Thus, a new hearing is required because the Family Court did not examine enough into the qualifications and background of the long-time custodian, and the Appellate Division did not require further examination into the qualifications and background of the mother. Each court was excessive in applying abstract principles, a failing, however important those principles are.

At the cost of some repetition, perhaps unnecessary, it should be said, given the extraordinary circumstances present in this case, in determining the best interest of the child, the age of the child, and the fact and length of custody by the nonparent custodian are significant. Standing alone, these factors may not be sufficient to outweigh the mother's "right" to custody. However, taken together with the testimony of the psychologist that return to her mother would be "very traumatic for the child", the relatively lengthy period of nonparent custody casts the matter in sufficient doubt with respect to the best interest of the child to require a new hearing. At this hearing, the mother's adequacy may be explored and positively established, and if so, in connection with the parent's past visiting it might well weight the balance in her favor. Then too, the circumstances and environment of the custodian, the stability of her household, her inability to adopt, her age, and any other circumstances bearing upon the fitness or adequacy of a child's custodian over the whole period of childhood, are all relevant.

In all of this troublesome and troubled area there is a fundamental principle. Neither law, nor policy, nor the tenets of our society would allow a child to be separated by officials of the State from its parent unless the circumstances are compelling. Neither the lawyers nor Judges in the judicial system nor the experts in psychology or social welfare may displace the primary responsibility of child-raising that naturally and legally falls to those who conceive and bear children. Again, this is not so much because it is their "right", but because it is their responsibility. The nature of human relationships suggests over-all the natural workings of the child-rearing process as the most desirable alternative. But absolute generalizations do not fulfill themselves and multifold exceptions give rise to cases where the natural workings of the process fail, not so much because a legal right has been lost, but because the best interest of the child dictates a finding of failure.

Accordingly, the order of the Appellate Division should be reversed, without costs, and the proceeding remitted to Family Court for a new hearing.

■ FUCHSBERG, JUDGE (concurring).

I welcome the express recognition the court today gives to the concept that, under evolving child custody law in New York, circumstances other than the statutory and traditional ones of abandonment, surrender, permanent neglect and unfitness may form the basis for termination of a biological parent-child relationship, and I agree with the result it reaches. However, in concurring, the strength of my conviction that even greater movement in this area of the law is long overdue requires me to indicate the nature of some of my reservations.

Security, continuity and "long-term stability" in an on-going custodial relationship, whether maintained with a natural parent or a third party, are vital to the successful personality development of a child, and authorities (cited therein). Indeed, that is one of the soundest justifications for the priority which our society accords natural parents when the continuance of their status as parents is under legal attack.

The same considerations, however, it seems to me, dictate that, where a natural parent has affirmatively brought about or acquiesced in the creation of a secure, stable and continuing parent-child relationship with a third party who has become the psychological parent,[1] there comes a point where the "rebuttable presumption" which, absent such a change, is employed to favor the natural parent, disappears, as evidentiary presumptions usually do in the face of facts. Accordingly, when that point is reached, the determination of whether the original parental relationship

---

1. (Goldstein, Freud and Solnit, Beyond the Best Interests of the Child [1973]; Erikson, Growth and Crisis of the "Healthy Personality" in Personality, in Nature, Society and Culture [1955], 185–225; Bowley, Child Care and Growth of Love [1953]; Freud, Some Remarks on Infant Observation, 8 Psychoanalytic Study of the Child.)

has terminated should proceed without such bolstering of the natural parent's position vis-à-vis that of the child, the custodial parent or any other proper parties in interest. Generally speaking, when displaced by a state of facts contraindicating their further utility in a fact-finding setting, presumptions can only get in the way of substance, and, as a practical matter, when that happens, the less they are relied upon the better. I would, therefore, that we had spelled out an evidentiary balance consistent with these principles for application in custody litigation, always bearing in mind that each custody case, dealing as it does with emotion-laden and highly sensitive human relationships, is unique.[2]

Further, I do not agree that inquiry into the best interests of a child must await a determination that, because of surrender, abandonment, neglect or "extraordinary" circumstances, a natural parent's "rights" to a child are at an end. Willy-nilly, concern for the best interests of the child must play a central and unavoidable role in the resolution of such questions.

Moreover, even under prior law, when only a finding of abandonment, surrender or neglect could defeat the presumption in favor of natural parents, the best interests of the child were involved from the very outset. Unfitness, for instance, cannot be determined abstractly or in isolation, but only relative to the psychological needs of a particular child, given its age, its mental health, its physical well-being and the like. And the very same conduct which constitutes clear neglect towards one child might not be so at all with regard to another child whose level of independence and emotional requirements are different. It follows that evidence offered to show that the State must intervene in a natural parent-child relationship is, by its very nature, evidence as to the best interests of the child. In short, termination or intervention, on the one hand, and best interests, on the other, are not discrete matters. Pragmatically, they are closely interrelated. Proof of one overlaps the other and I do not believe they should be considered separately.

I would add too that I am not completely convinced that there was not a sufficient basis for the decision of the Trial Judge, despite the unfortunate limitation on resources available to the Family Court and, often, the parties who appear before it (see Gordon, Terminal Placements of Children and Permanent Termination of Parental Rights: The New York Permanent

2. Commentators point out that presumptions and the burden to rebut them should be allocated "on the basis of pragmatic considerations of fairness, convenience, and policy" (James, Burdens of Proof, 47 Va.L.Rev. 51, 60). Thus, where the burden of proof is allocated on policy grounds, it is most often done in order to "handicap" a party whose cause is disfavored (at p. 61). That was the historical basis for casting the entire burden of rebutting the presumption in favor of natural parents on third parties in custody proceedings, the resulting substantive effect varying with the extent to which the "handicap", combined with other evidentiary strictures, rendered the nonparent's case difficult to maintain. In those jurisdictions where that policy was fully developed, it produced essentially the same results as were obtained under the old theory that children were the chattels of their parents (see Note, Alternatives to "Parental Right" in Child Custody Disputes Involving Third Parties, 73 Yale L.J. 151, 154, n. 18, and accompanying text).

Neglect Statute, 46 St. John's L. Rev. 215, 256, n. 204, and citations therein). Among other things, the trial court here fully heard out both Mrs. Jeffreys and Ms. Bennett, conducted an *in camera* interview with the child following which he concluded that she was a "happy, well-adjusted young girl" who "was most adamant about the fact that she wished to continue residing with Mrs. Jeffreys", and, in aid of his determination, sought and had the benefit of a formal psychological study. Nevertheless, since painstaking fact finding is so far superior to presumptions and assumptions, and, therefore, should be encouraged, I join in the decision to remit this case for further information-gathering, noting, in doing so, that it is clear that it should not be controlling that Ms. Bennett, the natural mother, because she is now pursuing collegiate studies may at some time in the future be more likely to afford greater creature comforts for the child than is Mrs. Jeffreys, whose modest position on the vocational social scale did not prevent her from undertaking to act as surrogate mother and thus to form psychological bonds between the child and herself. And, needless to say, any profession by Mrs. Jeffreys that she would have been willing to return the child to her biological mother when she was older *if* it were in the best interests of the child for her to do so would be an evidence of altruistic maternal concern that would win the approval of every sound practitioner of child psychiatry from King Solomon on.

Bennett v. Marrow

New York Supreme Court, Appellate Division, Second Department, 1977.
59 A.D.2d 492, 399 N.Y.S.2d 697.

■ O'CONNOR, JUSTICE.

There is here presented one of the most difficult and disturbing problems known to the law—the custody of a child. The problem is, of course, compounded when, as here, the conflict rages between the natural mother and a foster mother. The Family Court awarded custody of the child to the foster mother and, after carefully studying this meticulously compiled record, we conclude that the order should be affirmed.

[The court reviews the custody determination principles from the opinion in Bennett v. Jeffreys, which remitted this case to Family Court for a hearing.]

The new hearing extended over a four-week period and contains the testimony of some 26 witnesses; that record and the order entered thereon are now before us for review.

We are here concerned with an unsupervised, private placement and, hence, any analysis of the decision of the Family Court must be predicated not upon statute, but upon common law principles.

Fortunately, the hearing was held before the same Judge who had presided at the first hearing some two years before. Predicated upon his observations and findings at the 1975 hearing, the court was in a rather unique position to completely re-examine and re-evaluate the testimony of those witnesses who had testified at both hearings. In the light of his intimate knowledge of the background and history of the case, he was able to conduct a more in-depth examination of the psychiatrists, psychologists, social workers, teachers and other witnesses called by the parties. Most importantly, the court was enabled to clearly and closely observe for a second time the conduct and deportment of the principals, namely the petitioner-appellant (the natural parent), the respondent (the foster parent) and Gina Marie (the infant involved). His comments therefore concerning the changes he found in the personality and demeanor of Gina Marie become all the more significant and persuasive in view of the fact that the child, in the intervening 15 months, had been living in the home of the petitioner, her natural mother.

The trial court, after noting that during the first hearing Gina Marie appeared to be a well-adjusted, happy child, went on to say that "the fact is that notwithstanding a period of some 15 months spent in the home of her mother, Gina Marie has not settled into the household. She does not feel comfortable there, she is not happy there. She continues unswerving in her request to be restored to the custody of Mrs. Marrow."

These surface observations, while bearing some significance, are certainly not controlling; but the court's conclusions concerning the natural mother are perhaps more revealing. The court said: "To the extent that the petitioner has responded to Gina Marie's needs to be housed, to be clothed, to be fed, she could be considered to have performed adequately as a parent. But she has not begun to respond to Gina Marie's emotional needs." At another point the court observed: "I am constrained to consider that Miss Bennett's motivation in seeking custody of Gina Marie stems from a feeling that she is her child and should reside with her. That she has feeling for Gina Marie I am certainly prepared to believe, but in view of the testimony presented during the course of these proceedings, I have serious reservations that she is capable of giving Gina Marie the emotional support so vital to her well-being."

The court then concluded: "This Court was asked to determine whether the mother is an adequate parent. As stated previously, she has provided materially for Gina Marie. That is to say, she has made available to Gina Marie what Welfare has provided in the first instance. But that is virtually all she has given Gina Marie. She had not given significantly of herself. I find that an emotional void exists between mother and daughter that shows no signs of being bridged despite the time they have resided together. This child continues to mourn the loss of her 'mother.' "

Addressing itself then to the relationship between the respondent and Gina Marie, the court gave credence to the testimony of a witness called by the Law Guardian, Dr. Sally Provence, a child psychiatrist from Yale University. Finding her to be "certainly the most impressive expert witness who appeared in this proceeding", the hearing court accepted Dr. Provence's testimony that a psychological parent-child relationship had developed between respondent and the child and the court noted that such bond "appears as strong today as when this case was first heard."

It was Dr. Provence's further testimony, in substance, that to remove the child from such a relationship would endanger the development of the child in many ways and could affect her academic success and her motivation to learn.

This testimony is all the more significant in view of the record, which discloses that in January, 1977 an intelligence test was administered to Gina Marie resulting in a score of 84, in the low-normal range, whereas in April, 1975 she had scored 113. Despite efforts to explain away this rather disturbing pattern, it seems to be, at least to some extent, buttressed by the obvious and drastic decline in the physical, mental and emotional make-up of Gina Marie.

Reflection upon the totality of the testimony and careful consideration of all of the factors involved leads but to one conclusion, the order of the Family Court should be affirmed.

We note in closing that that order properly and fully protects petitioner's rights of visitation but, under the extraordinary circumstances here presented, the best interests of the child require that custody of Gina Marie be awarded to respondent.

NOTE

The New York Court of Appeals has demonstrated considerable doubt over its holding in Bennett v. Jeffreys, especially when permanent parental rights may be affected, as in allegations of abandonment and termination. *See, e.g.*, Dickson v. Lascaris, 53 N.Y.2d 204, 440 N.Y.S.2d 884, 423 N.E.2d 361 (1981); Matter of Sanjivini K., 47 N.Y.2d 374, 418 N.Y.S.2d 339, 391 N.E.2d 1316 (1979); Corey L. v. Martin L., 45 N.Y.2d 383, 408 N.Y.S.2d 439, 380 N.E.2d 266 (1978). *But see* C.C.R.S. v. T.A.M., 892 P.2d 246 (Colo.1995), where the court allowed foster parents to retain custody of child over the objection of the mother because it found that the foster parents had become psychological parents and the child would suffer harm were that bond severed. Perhaps the issue is how the court defines the impact of permanent custody. Is this really termination of parental rights? In a decision by the Supreme Court of Nebraska, *In re* Interest of Amber G., 250 Neb. 973, 554 N.W.2d 142 (1996) the court decided that "permanent guardianship does not result in a de facto termination of parental rights. A termination of parental rights is a final and complete severance of the child from the parent and removes the entire bundle of parental rights." The court then went on to say, that legal custody is not parenthood or adoption, that a person appointed guardian is subject to removal at any time, the parent retains visitation rights and may petition for restoration of custody at any time.

Does it make a difference that Mrs. Jeffreys was seeking to retain custody of Gina Marie Bennett, and not termination of the mother's parental rights which would allow for adoption of the girl? Should custody and termination proceedings be treated differently by the courts? What are the legal standards to be applied? What are the factors which are important?

CALIFORNIA FAMILY CODE (West Supp. 2004)

§ 3042. Preference of child; examination of child witnesses; alternatives

(a) If a child is of sufficient age and capacity to reason so as to form an intelligent preference as to custody, the court shall consider and give due weight to the wishes of the child in making an order granting or modifying the custody.

(b) In addition to the requirements of subdivision (b) of Section 765 of the Evidence Code, the court shall control the examination of the child witness so as to protect the best interests of the child. The court may preclude the calling of the child as a witness where the best interests of the child so dictates and may provide alternative means of obtaining information regarding the child's preferences.

Guardianship of Phillip B.

Court of Appeals, First District, Division 1, 1983.
139 Cal.App.3d 407, 188 Cal.Rptr. 781.

■ RACANELLI, PRESIDING JUSTICE.

Few human experiences evoke the poignancy of a filial relationship and the pathos attendant upon its disruption in society's effort to afford every child a meaningful chance to live life to its fullest promise. This appeal, posing a sensitive confrontation between the fundamental right of parental custody and the well being of a retarded child, reflects the deeply ingrained concern that the needs of the child remain paramount in the judicial monitoring of custody. In reaching our decision to affirm, we neither suggest nor imply that appellants' subjectively motivated custodial objectives affront conventional norms of parental fitness; rather, we determine only that on the unusual factual record before us, the challenged order of guardianship must be upheld in order to avert potential harm to the minor ward likely to result from appellants' continuing custody and to subserve his best interests.

. . .

On February 23, 1981, respondents Herbert and Patsy H. filed a petition for appointment as guardians of the person and estate of Phillip B., then 14 years of age. Phillip's parents, appellants Warren and Patricia B., appeared in opposition to the petition.

On August 7, 1981, following a 12–day trial, the trial court filed a lengthy memorandum of decision ordering—inter alia—1) the issuance of letters of guardianship to respondents with authority to permit a heart catheterization to be performed on Phillip, and 2) the immediate delivery (by appellants) of Phillip to the Sheriff and Juvenile Authority of Santa

Clara County. That same day appellants filed a notice of appeal from both orders followed by a petition to this court for a writ of supersedeas which we summarily denied.

On August 20, 1981, the California Supreme Court granted appellants' petition for hearing, stayed the trial court's order authorizing heart catheterization and retransferred the cause to this court with directions to issue an order to show cause why a writ of supersedeas should not issue.

Meanwhile, on September 24, the trial court filed formal findings of fact and conclusions of law and entered a "final order" confirming issuance of letters of guardianship and authorizing a heart catheterization. A second notice of appeal specifying both orders was thereafter filed by appellants.

On October 19, 1981, we again denied supersedeas in an unpublished opinion.

On November 18, 1981, the California Supreme Court granted a second petition for hearing, issued its writ of supersedeas limited to the trial court's orders of August 7 and September 24 "insofar as they give authority for a heart catheterization upon Phillip B.," and retransferred the cause to this court for determination of the merits of the appeal upon the completed record and full briefing. Thereafter, the matter was duly argued and submitted for decision.

Appellants raise several claims of reversible error relating to the sufficiency of evidence to support the findings, the admissibility of certain evidence and procedural due process. For the reasons which we explain, we find no error as claimed and affirm the order or judgment appealed.

. . .

Phillip B. was born on October 16, 1966, with Down's Syndrome, a chromosomal anomaly—usually the presence of an extra chromosome attached to the number 21 pair—resulting in varying degrees of mental retardation and a number of abnormal physical characteristics. Down's Syndrome reportedly occurs in approximately 1/10 of 1 percent of live births.

Appellants, deeply distraught over Phillip's disability, decided upon institutionalization, a course of action recommended by a state social worker and approved by appellants' pediatrician. A few days later, Phillip was transferred from the hospital to a licensed board and care facility for disabled youngsters. Although the facility was clean, it offered no structured educational or developmental programs and required that all the children (up to 8 years of age) sleep in cribs. Appellants initially visited Phillip frequently; but soon their visits became less frequent and they became more detached from him.

When Phillip was three years old a pediatrician informed appellants that Phillip had a congenital heart defect, a condition afflicting half of Down's Syndrome children. Open heart surgery was suggested when Phillip attained age six. However appellants took no action to investigate or remedy the suspected medical problem.

After the board and care facility had been sold during the summer of 1971, appellants discovered that the condition of the facility had seriously deteriorated under the new management; it had become dirty and cluttered with soiled clothing, and smelled strongly of urine. Phillip was very thin and listless and was being fed watery oatmeal from a bottle. At appellants' request, a state social worker arranged for Phillip's transfer in January, 1972, to We Care, a licensed residential facility for developmentally disabled children located in San Jose, where he remained up to the time of trial.

At that time, the facility—which cared for about 20 children more severely handicapped than Phillip—operated under very limited conditions: it had no programs of education or therapy; the children were not enrolled in outside programs; the facility lacked an outdoor play area; the building was in poor repair; and the kitchen had only a two-burner hot plate used to cook pureed food.

In April 1972, We Care employed Jeanne Haight (later to become program director and assistant administrator of the facility) to organize a volunteer program. Mrs. Haight quickly noticed Phillip's debilitated condition. She found him unusually small and thin for his age (five); he was not toilet trained and wore diapers, still slept in a crib, walked like a toddler, and crawled down stairs only inches high. His speech was limited and mostly unintelligible; his teeth were in poor condition.

Mrs. Haight, who undertook a recruitment program for volunteers, soon recruited respondent Patsy H., who had helped to found a school for children with learning disabilities where Mrs. Haight had once been vice-principal. Mrs. H. began working at We Care on a daily basis. Her husband, respondent Herbert H., and their children, soon joined in the volunteer activities.

Mrs. H., initially assigned to work with Phillip and another child, assisted Phillip in experimenting with basic sensory experiences, improving body coordination, and in overcoming his fear of steps. Mr. H. and one of the H. children helped fence the yard area, put in a lawn, a sandbox, and install some climbing equipment.

Mrs. Haight promptly initiated efforts to enroll Phillip in a preschool program for the fall of 1972, which required parental consent.[4] She contacted Mr. B. who agreed to permit Phillip to participate provided learning aptitude could be demonstrated. Mrs. H. used vocabulary cards to teach Phillip 25 to 50 new words and to comprehend word association. Although Mr. B. failed to appear at the appointed time in order to observe what Phillip had learned, he eventually gave his parental consent enabling Phillip to attend Hope Preschool in October, 1972.

---

4. Apparently, Phillip had received no formal preschool education for the retarded even though such training programs were available in the community. Expert testimony established that early introduction to preschool training is of vital importance in preparing a retarded child for entry level public education.

Respondents continued working with Phillip coordinating their efforts with his classroom lessons. Among other things, they concentrated on development of feeding skills and toilet training and Mr. H. and the two eldest children gradually became more involved in the volunteer program.

Phillip subsequently attended a school for the trainable mentally retarded (TMR) where the children are taught basic survival words. They are capable of learning to feed and dress themselves appropriately, doing basic community activities such as shopping, and engaging in recreational activities. There is no attempt to teach them academics, and they are expected to live in sheltered settings as adults. In contrast, children capable of attending classes for the educable mentally retarded (EMR) are taught reading, writing, and simple computation, with the objective of developing independent living skills as adults.

A pattern of physical and emotional detachment from their son was developed by appellants over the next several years. In contrast, during the same period, respondents established a close and caring relationship with Phillip. Beginning in December, 1972, Phillip became a frequent visitor at respondents' home; with appellants' consent, Phillip was permitted to spend weekends with respondents, a practice which continued regularly and often included weekday evenings. At the same time respondents maintained frequent contact with Phillip at We Care as regular volunteer visitors. Meanwhile, appellants visited Phillip at the facility only a few times a year; however, no overnight home visits occurred until after the underlying litigation ensued.

Respondents played an active role in Phillip's behavioral development and educational training. They consistently supplemented basic skills training given Phillip at We Care.[5]

Phillip was openly accepted as a member of the H. family whom he came to love and trust. He eventually had his own bedroom; he was included in sharing household chores. Mr. H. set up a workbench for Phillip and helped him make simple wooden toys; they attended special Boy Scout meetings together. And Philip regularly participated in family outings. Phillip referred to the H. residence as "my house." When Phillip began to refer to the H. as "Mom" and "Dad," they initially discouraged the familiar reference, eventually succeeding in persuading Phillip to use the discriminate references "Mama Pat" and "Dada Bert" and "Mama B." and "Daddy B."[6]. Both Mrs. Haight and Phillip's teacher observed significant improvements in Phillip's development and behavior. Phillip had developed, in Mrs. Haight's opinion, "true love and strong [emotional] feelings" for respondents.

---

5. In addition to their efforts to improve Phillip's communication and reading skills through basic sign language and word association exercises, respondents toilet-trained Phillip and taught him to use eating utensils and to sleep in a regular bed (the latter frequently monitored during the night).

6. At respondents' suggestion, Mrs. Haight requested a photograph of appellants to show Phillip who his parents were; but appellants failed to provide one.

Meanwhile, appellants continued to remain physically and emotionally detached from Phillip. The natural parents intellectualized their decision to treat Phillip differently from their other children. Appellants testified that Phillip, whom they felt would always require institutionalization, should not be permitted to form close emotional attachments which—upon inevitable disruption—would traumatize the youngster.

In matters of Phillip's health care needs, appellants manifested a reluctant—if not neglectful—concern. When Dr. Gathman, a pediatric cardiologist, diagnosed a ventricular septal defect[7] in Phillip's heart in early 1973 and recommended catheterization (a medically accepted pre-surgery procedure to measure pressure and to examine the interior of the heart), appellants refused their consent.

In the spring of 1977, Dr. Gathman again recommended heart catheterization in connection with the anticipated use of general anesthesia during Phillip's major dental surgery. Appellants consented to the preoperative procedure which revealed that the heart defect was surgically correctable with a maximum risk factor of 5 percent. At a conference attended by appellants and Mrs. Haight in June, 1977, Dr. Gathman recommended corrective surgery in order to avoid a progressively deteriorating condition resulting in a "bed-to-chair existence" and the probability of death before the age of 30.[8] Although Dr. Gathman—as requested by Mrs. B.—supplied the name of a parent of Down's Syndrome children with similar heart disease, no contact was ever made. Later that summer, appellants decided—without obtaining an independent medical consultation—against surgery. Appellants' stated reason was that Dr. Gathman had "painted" an inaccurate picture of the situation. They felt that surgery would be merely life-prolonging rather than life-saving, presenting the possibility that they would be unable to care for Phillip during his later years.[9] A few months later, in early 1978, appellants' decision was challenged in a juvenile dependency proceeding initiated by the district attorney on the ground that the withholding of surgery constituted neglect within the meaning of Welfare and Institutions Code section 300 subdivision (b); the juvenile court's dismissal of the action on the basis of inconclusive evidence was ultimately sustained on appeal (In re Phillip B. (1979) 92 Cal.App.3d 796, 156 Cal.Rptr. 48, cert. den. sub nom. Bothman v. Warren B. (1980) 445 U.S. 949, 100 S.Ct.1597, 63 L.Ed.2d 784).

In September, 1978, upon hearing from a staff member of We Care that Phillip had been regularly spending weekends at respondents' home,

---

7. The disease, found in a large number of Down's Syndrome children, consists of an opening or "hole" between the heart chambers resulting in elevated blood pressure and impairment of vascular functions. The disease can become a progressive, and ultimately fatal, disorder.

8. Dr. Gathman's explicit description of the likely ravages of the disease created anger and distrust on the part of appellants and motivated them to seek other opinions and to independently assess the need for surgery.

9. Oddly, Mr. B. expressed no reluctance in the hypothetical case of surgery for his other two sons if they had the "same problem," justifying the distinction on the basis of Phillip's retardation.

Mr. B. promptly forbade Phillip's removal from the facility (except for medical purposes and school attendance) and requested that respondents be denied personal visits with Phillip at We Care. Although respondents continued to visit Phillip daily at the facility, the abrupt cessation of home visits produced regressive changes in Phillip's behavior: he began acting out violently when respondents prepared to leave, begging to be taken "home"; he resorted to profanity; he became sullen and withdrawn when respondents were gone; bed-wetting regularly occurred, a recognized symptom of emotional disturbance in children. He began to blame himself for the apparent rejection by respondents; he began playing with matches and on one occasion he set his clothes afire; on another, he rode his tricycle to respondents' residence a few blocks away proclaiming on arrival that he was "home." He continuously pleaded to return home with respondents. Many of the behavioral changes continued to the time of trial.

Appellants unsuccessfully pressed to remove Phillip from We Care notwithstanding the excellent care he was receiving. However, in January, 1981, the regional center monitoring public assistance for residential care and training of the handicapped, consented to Phillip's removal to a suitable alternate facility. Despite an extended search, none could be found which met Phillip's individualized needs. Meanwhile, Phillip continued living at We Care, periodically visiting at appellants' home. But throughout, the strong emotional attachment between Phillip and respondents remained intact.

Evidence established that Phillip, with a recently tested I.Q. score of 57,[11] is a highly functioning Down's Syndrome child capable of learning sufficient basic and employable skills to live independently or semi-independently in a non-institutional setting.

Courts generally may appoint a guardian over the person or estate of a minor "if it appears necessary or convenient." (Prob.Code, § 1514, subd. (a).) But the right of parents to retain custody of a child is fundamental and may be disturbed " '... only in extreme cases of persons acting in a fashion incompatible with parenthood.' " (In re Angelia P. (1981) 28 Cal.3d 908, 916, 171 Cal.Rptr. 637, 623 P.2d 198, quoting In re Carmaleta B. (1978) 21 Cal.3d 482, 489, 146 Cal.Rptr. 623, 579 P.2d 514.) Accordingly, the Legislature has imposed the stringent requirement that before a court may make an order awarding custody of a child to a nonparent without consent of the parents, "it shall make a finding that an award of custody to a parent would be detrimental to the child and the award to a nonparent is required to serve the best interests of the child." (Civ.Code, § 4600, subd. (c); see In re B.G. (1974) 11 Cal.3d 679, 695–699, 114 Cal.Rptr. 444, 523 P.2d 244.)[12] That requirement is equally applicable to guardianship pro-

---

11. A retarded child within an I.Q. range of 55–70 is generally considered as mildly retarded and classified as educable under California school standards.

12. Civil Code section 4600 was enacted in response to the celebrated case of Painter v. Bannister (1966) 258 Iowa 1390, 140 N.W.2d 152, cert. den. 385 U.S. 949, 87 S.Ct. 322, 17 L.Ed.2d 227 in which the state court awarded custody of a young boy to his grandparents because it disapproved of the father's "Bohemian" lifestyle in California (see In re

ceedings under Probate Code section 1514, subdivision (b). The legislative shift in emphasis from parental unfitness to detriment to the child did not, however, signal a retreat from the judicial practice granting custodial preference to nonparents "only in unusual or extreme cases." (In re B.G., supra, 11 Cal.3d 679, 698, 114 Cal.Rptr. 444, 523 P.2d 244, see Guardianship of Marino (1973) 30 Cal.App.3d 952, 958, 106 Cal.Rptr. 655.)

The trial court expressly found that an award of custody to appellants would be harmful to Phillip in light of the psychological or "de facto" parental relationship established between him and respondents. Such relationships have long been recognized in the fields of law and psychology. As Justice Tobriner has cogently observed, "The fact of biological parenthood may incline an adult to feel a strong concern for the welfare of his child, but it is not an essential condition; a person who assumes the role of parent, raising the child in his own home, may in time acquire an interest in the 'companionship, care, custody and management' of that child. The interest of the 'de facto parent' is a substantial one, recognized by the decision of this court in Guardianship of Shannon (1933) 218 Cal. 490 [23 P.2d 1020] and by courts of other jurisdictions and deserving of legal protection." (In re B.G., supra, 11 Cal.3d 679, 692–693, 114 Cal.Rptr. 444, 523 P.2d 244 [fns. omitted], citing the seminal study of Goldstein, Freud & Solnit, Beyond the Best Interests of the Child (1973) pp. 17–20, hereafter Goldstein.) Persons who assume such responsibility have been characterized by some interested professional observers as "psychological parents": "Whether any adult becomes the psychological parent of a child is based . . . on day-to-day interaction, companionship, and shared experiences. The role can be fulfilled either by a biological parent or by an adoptive parent or by any other caring adult—but never by an absent, inactive adult, whatever his biological or legal relationship to the child may be." (Goldstein, supra, p. 19.)

Appellants vigorously challenge the evidence and finding that respondents have become Phillip's de facto or psychological parents since he did not reside with them full-time, as underscored in previous California decisions which have recognized de facto parenthood. They argue that the subjective concept of psychological parenthood, relying on such nebulous factors as "love and affection" is susceptible to abuse and requires the countervailing element of objectivity provided by a showing of the child's long-term residency in the home of the claimed psychological parent.

We disagree. Adoption of the proposed standard would require this court to endorse a novel doctrine of child psychology unsupported either by a demonstrated general acceptance in the field of psychology or by the record before us. Although psychological parenthood is said to result from "day-to-day attention to [the child's] needs for physical care, nourishment, comfort, affection, and stimulation" (Goldstein, supra, p. 17), appellants fail to point to any authority or body of professional opinion that equates daily attention with full-time residency. To the contrary, the record con-

B.G., supra, 11 Cal.3d at pp. 697–698, 114 Cal.Rptr. 444, 523 P.2d 244, citing Report of   Assembly Judiciary Committee, 4 Assem.J. (1969 Reg.Sess. pp. 8060–8061)).

tains uncontradicted expert testimony that while psychological parenthood usually will require residency on a "24–hour basis," it is not an absolute requirement; further, that the frequency and quality of Phillip's weekend visits with respondents, together with the regular weekday visits at We Care, provided an adequate foundation to establish the crucial parent-child relationship.

Nor are we persuaded by appellants' suggested policy considerations concerning the arguably subjective inquiry involved in determining psychological parenthood. Trial fact-finders commonly grapple with elusive subjective legal concepts without aid of "countervailing" objective criteria.... Moreover, the suggested standard is itself vulnerable to a claim of undue subjectivity in its vague requirement of residency for a "considerable period of time."[15]

Appellants also challenge the sufficiency of the evidence to support the finding that their retention of custody would have been detrimental to Phillip. In making the critical finding, the trial court correctly applied the "clear and convincing" standard of proof necessary to protect the fundamental rights of parents in all cases involving a nonparent's bid for custody....

The record contains abundant evidence that appellants' retention of custody would cause Phillip profound emotional harm. Notwithstanding Phillip's strong emotional ties with respondents, appellants abruptly foreclosed home visits and set out to end all contact between them. When Phillip's home visits terminated in 1978, he displayed many signs of severe emotional trauma: he appeared depressed and withdrawn and became visibly distressed at being unable to return to "my house," a request he steadily voiced up until trial. He became enuretic, which a psychologist, Dr. Edward Becking, testified indicates emotional stress in children.... Dr. Becking testified to other signs of emotional disturbance which were present nearly three years after the termination of home visits.

Our law recognizes that children generally will sustain serious emotional harm when deprived of the emotional benefits flowing from a true parent-child relationship.

There was uncontroverted expert testimony that Phillip would sustain further emotional trauma in the event of total separation from respondents: that testimony indicated that, as with all children, Phillip needs love and affection, and he would be profoundly hurt if he were deprived of the

---

15. Appellants also fear that, absent a full-time residency requirement, anyone who visits an institutionalized child can lay claim to psychological parenthood. As earlier discussed, development of a parent-child relationship requires long-term nurturing and fulfillment of the child's total needs which can rarely occur without full-time residency. But it was manifested here only as a direct result of respondents' unique relationship with Phillip as We Care volunteers, their previously uninterrupted weekend close contacts and appellants' physical and emotional detachment from the child. All of such important factors contributed to respondents' ability to devote the enormous amount of time and loving care essential to fill the tangible and emotional needs in Phillip's life.

existing psychological parental relationship with respondents in favor of maintaining unity with his biological parents.

Phillip's conduct unmistakably demonstrated that he derived none of the emotional benefits attending a close parental relationship largely as a result of appellants' individualized decision to abandon that traditional supporting role. Dr. Becking testified that no "bonding or attachment" has occurred between Phillip and his biological parents, a result palpably consistent with appellants' view that Phillip had none of the emotional needs uniquely filled by natural parents. We conclude that such substantial evidence adequately supports the finding that parental custody would have resulted in harmful deprivation of these human needs contrary to Phillip's best interests.

Finally, there was also evidence that Phillip would experience educational and developmental injury if parental custody remains unchanged. At Phillip's functioning level of disability, he can normally be expected to live at least semi-independently as an adult in a supervised residential setting and be suitably trained to work in a sheltered workshop or even a competitive environment (e.g., performing assembly duties or custodial tasks in a fast-food restaurant). Active involvement of a parent figure during the formative stages of education and habilitation is of immeasurable aid in reaching his full potential. Unfortunately, appellants' deliberate abdication of that central role would effectively deny Phillip any meaningful opportunity to develop whatever skills he may be capable of achieving. Indeed, Dr. Becking testified that further separation from respondents would not only impair Phillip's ability to form new relationships but would "for a long while" seriously impair Phillip's development of necessary prevocational and independent-living skills for his future life.

Nor can we overlook evidence of potential physical harm to Phillip due to appellants' passive neglect in response to Phillip's medical condition. Although it appears probable that the congenital heart defect is no longer correctible by surgery,[18] the trial court could have reasonably concluded that appellants' past conduct reflected a dangerously passive approach to Phillip's future medical needs.[19]

It is a clearly stated legislative policy that persons with developmental disabilities shall enjoy—inter alia—the right to treatment and rehabilitation services, the right to publicly supported education, the right to social interaction, and the right to prompt medical care and treatment. (Welf. &

---

18. A pediatric cardiologist estimated that the surgery now might have a one-third chance of harming him, a one-third chance of helping him and a one-third chance of causing no appreciable change in his condition. Dr. Gathman testified that it is "highly probable" that Phillip's condition is no longer correctible by surgery, but that a heart catheterization is required to be certain.

19. Notably, the failure to obtain competent medical advice concerning the heart disease and the admitted willingness to forego medical treatment solely by reason of Phillip's retarded condition. The gravity of such dangerous inaction was dramatically illustrated by Mr. B.'s reaction to Phillip's recent undiagnosed episodes of apparent semi-consciousness—discounting their existence without even the benefit of a medical consultation.

Inst. Code, § 4502.) Moreover, the legislative purpose underlying Civil Code section 4600 is to protect the needs of children generally " '... to be raised with love, emotional security and physical safety.' " (In re D.L.C., supra, 54 Cal.App.3d 840, 851, 126 Cal.Rptr. 863.) When a trial court is called upon to determine the custody of a developmentally disabled or handicapped child, as here, it must be guided by such overriding policies rather than by the personal beliefs or attitudes of the contesting parties, since it is the child's interest which remains paramount.... Clearly, the trial court faithfully complied with such legislative mandate in exercising its sound discretion based upon the evidence presented. We find no abuse as contended by appellants.

We strongly emphasize, as the trial court correctly concluded, that the fact of detriment *cannot* be proved solely by evidence that the biological parent has elected to institutionalize a handicapped child, or that nonparents are able and willing to offer the child the advantages of their home in lieu of institutional placement. Sound reasons may exist justifying institutionalization of a handicapped child. But the totality of the evidence under review permits of no rational conclusion other than that the detriment caused Phillip, and its possible recurrence, was due not to appellants' choice to institutionalize but their calculated decision to remain emotionally and physically detached—abdicating the conventional role of competent decisionmaker in times of demonstrated need—thus effectively depriving him of *any* of the substantial benefits of a true parental relationship. *It is the emotional abandonment of Phillip, not his institutionalization,* which inevitably has created the unusual circumstances which led to the award of limited custody to respondents. We do not question the sincerity of appellants' belief that their approach to Phillip's welfare was in their combined best interests. But the record is replete with substantial and credible evidence supporting the trial court's determination, tested by the standard of clear and convincing proof, that appellants' retention of custody has caused and will continue to cause serious detriment to Phillip and that his best interests will be served through the guardianship award of custody to respondents. In light of such compelling circumstances, no legal basis is shown to disturb that carefully considered determination.

. . .

NOTE

Beyond the Best Interests of the Child. A celebrated book by Joseph Goldstein, Anna Freud, and Albert Solnit, Beyond the Best Interests of the Child, was an important influence on the court's decision in Guardianship of Phillip B. (The concepts explained in it also were important in the decision in Bennett v. Marrow.) The focal part of the book is a statutory model, Selected Provisions for the Child Placement Code of Hampstead–Haven (hereinafter the Act), The rest of the book is an extended commentary to this statute. The authors, strongly influenced by their psychoanalytic backgrounds, place great importance on the value of continuity and stability in child placements. Para. 10.2 of the Act defines a wanted child as "one who receives affection and nourishment on a continuing basis from at least one adult and who feels that he or she is and continues to be valued by those who take care of him or her." A psychological parent is "one who, on a continuing, day-to-day basis, through interaction, companionship, interplay, and mutuality, fulfills the child's psychological needs for a parent, as well as the child's physical needs." Under Para. 10.3 a psychological parent can be "a biological, adoptive, foster, or common-law parent, or any other person"; after initial assignment of the child to the biological child at birth, there is no presumption in favor of any of them.

The Act specifically recognizes a "common-law parent-child relationship", defined as "a psychological parent-wanted child relationship" which developed outside of adoption, assignment by custody in separation or divorce proceedings, or the initial assignment at birth of child to his or her biological parents. Although some commentators and jurists cite the text as supportive of traditional "best interests of the child" approach, such a simplistic appraisal belies the fact that the Act sets up a new set of presumptions, heavily emphasizing the maintenance of continuity and stability and minimizing disruption of relationships between psychological parent and child. Key to this is the desire for the least detrimental child placement, defined as "that placement and procedure which maximizes, in accord with the child's sense of time, the child's opportunity for being wanted and for maintaining on a continuous, unconditional, and permanent basis a relationship with at least one person who is or will become the child's psychological parent." Para. 10.6.

Any entity, (person, state, or institution) wishing to disrupt a continuing relationship between psychological parent and child is designated an intervenor. Para. 30.2. There is a presumption in favor of the current placement, and to change this the intervenor must establish that the child is unwanted, and that the placement is not the least detrimental alternative. Para. 30.3. The child is made a party to such proceedings and will be represented by independent counsel. Courts are mandated to conduct trials and appeals as rapidly as possible. Para. 30.5 makes all placements "unconditional and final"; accordingly, a court will not retain continuing jurisdiction over a parent-child relationship and will not establish or enforce conditions such as visitation.

Perhaps taking their cue from Joseph Goldstein, Anna Freud, and Albert Solnit, some recent decisions have allowed for two non-marital cohabitants to contract with one another in reference to raising a child. Once done, courts have demonstrated a willingness to declare that the non-biological parent is a "de facto parent" or a "parent by estoppel." *See, e.g., In re* Shockley, 123 S.W.3d 642 (Tex. App. 2003)(biological parent equitably estopped from denying parenthood of other contractual "parent" when biological parent facilitates notions of parenthood through contract and conduct); Smith v. Smith, 893 A.2d 934 (Del. 2006)(biological parent may consent to de facto parental status of non-biological partner, thereby establishing parenthood). Most cases exhibit a "pattern of immaturity" or a course of conduct on the part of the biological parent, that allows for the child to develop a bond with the non-biological party that then rebuts the parental presumption allowing for a best interest test to prevail. *See, e.g.,* Karen P. v. Christopher J.B., 163 Md.App. 250, 878 A.2d 646 (2005), *cert. denied sub nom*; Pope v. Brush, 390 Md. 501, 889 A.2d 419 (2006).

Robert H. Mnookin, in *The Guardianship of Phillip B.: Jay Spears' Achievement*, 40 Stan. L. Rev. 841 (1988), provides a follow up on Phillip Becker–Heath, who turned twenty-one years old in late 1987. Phillip eventually was adopted by the Heaths and underwent successful open heart surgery. He enrolled in school, obtained a part-time job, and became a Joe Montana fan. Professor Mnookin's account of the poignant case is especially sensitive and it carries a sorrowful message. While the outcome for Phillip B. was far more favorable than most observers expected, the article appears as one of a series of memorial tributes to Jay Spears, the young lawyer whose enormous efforts and commitment were key to the case and who died in December 1986.

C. Parent Versus State

1. Foster Placement

NEW JERSEY STATUTES ANN. (West Supp. 2006)

30:4C–26.1. "Resource family home" defined

As used in this act "resource family home" means and includes private residences wherein any child in the care, custody or guardianship of the Department of Children and Families may be placed by the department, or with its approval, for care, and shall include any private residence maintained by persons with whom any such child is placed by the Division of Youth and Family Services for the purpose of adoption until the adoption is finalized.

Smith v. Organization of Foster Families for Equality & Reform

Supreme Court of the United States, 1977.
431 U.S. 816, 97 S.Ct. 2094, 53 L.Ed.2d 14.

■ Mr. Justice Brennan delivered the opinion of the Court.

Appellees, individual foster parents[1] and an organization of foster parents, brought this civil rights class action pursuant to 42 U.S.C.A.

[1] Appellee Madeleine Smith is the foster parent with whom Eric and Danielle Gandy have been placed since 1970. The Gandy children, who are now 12 and 9 years old respectively, were voluntarily placed in foster care by their natural mother in 1968, and have had no contact with her at least since being placed with Mrs. Smith. The foster care

§ 1983 in the United States District Court for the Southern District of New York, on their own behalf and on behalf of children for whom they have provided homes for a year or more. They sought declaratory and injunctive relief against New York State and New York City officials, alleging that the procedures governing the removal of foster children from foster homes provided in New York Social Services Law §§ 383(2) and 400, and in Title 18, New York Codes Rules and Regulations § 450.14 violated the Due Process and Equal Protection Clauses of the Fourteenth Amendment. The District Court appointed independent counsel for the foster children to forestall any possibility of conflict between their interests and the interests asserted by the foster parents. A group of natural mothers of children in foster care[5] were granted leave to intervene on behalf of themselves and others similarly situated.

A divided three-judge District Court concluded that "the preremoval procedures presently employed by the State are constitutionally defective," holding that "before a foster child can be peremptorily transferred from the foster home in which he has been living, be it to another foster home or to the natural parents who initially placed him in foster care, he is entitled to a hearing at which all concerned parties may present any relevant information to the administrative decisionmaker charged with determining the future placement of the child," 418 F.Supp. 277, 282 (1976).... We reverse.

. . .

agency has sought to remove the children from Mrs. Smith's care because her arthritis, in the agency's judgment makes it difficult for her to continue to provide adequate care....

Appellees Ralph and Christiane Goldberg were the foster parents of Rafael Serrano, now 14. His parents placed him in foster care voluntarily in 1969 after an abuse complaint was filed against them. It is alleged that the agency supervising the placement had informally indicated to Mr. and Mrs. Goldberg that it intended to transfer Rafael to the home of his aunt in contemplation of permanent placement. This effort has apparently failed.... The Goldbergs are now separated, Mrs. Goldberg having moved out of the house, taking her own child but leaving Rafael. The child is now in a residential treatment center, where Mr. Goldberg continues to visit him....

Appellees Walter and Dorothy Lhotan were foster parents of the four Wallace sisters, who were voluntarily placed in foster care by their mother in 1970. The two older girls were placed with the Lhotans in that

year, their two younger sisters in 1972. In June 1974, the Lhotans were informed that the agency had decided to return the two younger girls to their mother and transfer the two older girls to another foster home. The agency apparently felt that the Lhotans were too emotionally involved with the girls and were damaging the agency's efforts to prepare them to return them to their mother. The state courts have ordered that all the Wallace children be returned to their mother.... We are told that the children have been returned and are adjusting successfully....

5. Intervenor Naomi Rodriguez, who is blind, placed her newborn son Edwin in foster care in 1973 because of marital difficulties. When Mrs. Rodriguez separated from her husband three months later, she sought return of her child. Her efforts over the next nine months to obtain return of the child were resisted by the agency, apparently because it felt her handicap prevented her from providing adequate care. Eventually she sought return of her child in the state courts, and finally prevailed, three years after she first sought return of the child....

The expressed central policy of the New York system is that "it is generally desirable for the child to remain with or be returned to the natural parent because the child's need for a normal family life will usually best be met in the natural home and ... parents are entitled to bring up their own children unless the best interests of the child would be thereby endangered," Soc.Serv.L. § 384–b(1)(a)(ii). But the State has opted for foster care as one response to those situations where the natural parents are unable to provide the "positive, nurturing family relationships" and "normal family life in a permanent home" that "offer the best opportunity for children to develop and thrive." Id., § 384–b(1)(b), (1)(a)(i).

Foster care has been defined as "[a] child welfare service which provides substitute family care for a planned period for a child when his own family cannot care for him for a temporary or extended period and when adoption is neither desirable nor possible." Child Welfare League of America, Standards for Foster Family Care, 5 (1959). Thus, the distinctive features of foster care are first, "that it is care in a *family*, it is noninstitutional substitute care," and second, "that it is for a *planned* period—either temporary or extended. This is unlike adoptive placement, which implies a *permanent* substitution of one home for another." Kadushin, Child Welfare Services, 355 (1967).

Under the New York scheme children may be placed in foster care either by voluntary placement or by court order. Most foster care placements are voluntary.[9] They occur when physical or mental illness, economic problems, or other family crises make it impossible for natural parents, particularly single parents, to provide a stable home life for their children for some limited period.[10] Resort to such placements is almost compelled when it is not possible in such circumstance to place the child with a relative or friend, or to pay for the services of a homemaker or boarding school.

Voluntary placement requires the signing of a written agreement by the natural parent or guardian, transferring the care and custody of the child to an authorized child welfare agency.[11] Soc.Serv.L. § 384–a(1). Al-

---

9. The record indicates that as many as 80% of the children in foster care in New York City are voluntarily placed.... Other studies from New York and elsewhere variously estimate the percentage of voluntary placements between 50% and 90....

10. Experienced commentators have suggested that typical parents in this situation might be "[a] divorced parent in a financial bind, an unwed mother still too immature to rear a child, or a welfare mother confronted with hospitalization and therefore temporarily incapable of caring for her child." Weiss and Chase, The Case for Repeal of Section 383 of the New York Social Services Law, 4 Colum.Human Rts.L.Rev. 325,

326 (1972).... Other studies suggest, however, that neglect, abuse, abandonment and exploitation of children, which presumably account for most of the children who enter foster care by court order, ... are also involved in many cases of voluntary placement.

11. "Authorized agency" is defined in Soc.Serv.L. § 371(10) and "includes any local public welfare children's bureau, such as defendants New York City Bureau of Child Welfare and Nassau County Children's Bureau, and any voluntary child-care agency under the supervision of the New York State Board of Social Welfare, such as the defendant Catholic Guardian Society of New York." 418 F.Supp., at 278 n. 5....

though by statute the terms of such agreements are open to negotiation, Soc.Serv.L. § 384–a(2)(a), it is contended that agencies require execution of standardized forms. The agreement may provide for return of the child to the natural parent at a specified date or upon occurrence of a particular event, and if it does not, the child must be returned by the agency, in the absence of a court order, within 20 days of notice from the parent. Soc.Serv.L. § 384–a(2)(a).

The agency may maintain the child in an institutional setting, Soc. Serv.L. §§ 374–b, 374–c, 374–d, but more commonly acts under its authority to "place out and board out" children in foster homes. Soc.Serv.L. § 374(1).[13] Foster parents, who are licensed by the State or an authorized foster care agency, Soc.Serv.L. §§ 376, 377, provide care under a contractual arrangement with the agency, and are compensated for their services. The typical contract expressly reserves the right of the agency to remove the child on request. Conversely, the foster parent may cancel the agreement at will.[15]

The New York system divides parental functions among agency, foster parents and natural parents, and the definitions of the respective roles are often complex and often unclear.[16] The law transfers "care and custody" to the agency, Soc.Serv.L. § 384–a; see also Soc.Serv.L. § 383(2), but day-to-day supervision of the child and his activities, and most of the functions ordinarily associated with legal custody, are the responsibility of the foster parent. Nevertheless, agency supervision of the performance of the foster parents takes forms indicating that the foster parent does not have the full authority of a legal custodian.[18] Moreover, the natural parent's placement of the child with the agency does not surrender legal guardianship;[19] the

---

13. The record indicates that at the end of 1973, of 48,812 children in foster care under the supervision of the New York State Board of Social Welfare and the New York State Department of Social Services, 35,287 (about 72%) were placed in foster family homes, and the rest in institutions or other facilities.

15. ... Evidence in the record indicates that as many as one-third of all transfers within the foster-care system are at the request of the foster parents....

16. The resulting confusion not only produces anomalous legal relationships but also affects the child's emotional status. The foster child's loyalties, emotional involvements, and responsibilities are often divided among three adult authority figures—the natural parent, the foster parent, and the social worker representing the foster-care agency.

18. ... Agencies frequently prohibit corporal punishment; require that children over a certain age be given an allowance;

forbid change in the child's sleeping arrangements or vacations out-of-State without agency approval; require the foster parent to discuss the child's behavioral problems with the agency. Furthermore, since the cost of supporting the child is borne by the agency, the responsibility, as well as the authority, of the foster parent is shared with the agency.

19. Voluntary placement in foster care is entirely distinct from the "surrender" of both "the guardianship of the person and the custody" of a child under Soc.Serv.L. § 384, which frees the child for adoption. Soc.Serv.L. § 384(2). "Adoption is the legal proceeding whereby a person takes another person into the legal relation of child and thereby acquires the rights and incurs the responsibilities of parent in respect of such other person." Dom.Rel.L. § 110. A child may also be freed for adoption by abandonment or consent. Dom.Rel.L. § 111; Soc. Serv.L. § 384–b.

parent retains authority to act with respect to the child in certain circumstances.[20] The natural parent has not only the right but the obligation to visit the foster child and plan for his future; failure of a parent with capacity to fulfill the obligation for more than a year can result in a court order terminating the parent's rights on the ground of neglect.

Children may also enter foster care by court order. The Family Court may order that a child be placed in the custody of an authorized child-care agency after a full adversary judicial hearing under Art. 10 of the New York Family Court Act, if it is found that the child has been abused or neglected by his natural parents. F.C.A. §§ 1052, 1055. In addition, a minor adjudicated a juvenile delinquent, or "person in need of supervision" may be placed by the court with an agency. F.C.A. §§ 753, 754, 756. The consequences of foster care placement by court order do not differ substantially from those for children voluntarily placed, except that the parent is not entitled to return of the child on demand pursuant to Soc.Serv.L. § 384–a(2)(a); termination of foster care must then be consented to by the court. Soc.Serv.L. § 383(1).[22]

The provisions of the scheme specifically at issue in this case come into play when the agency having legal custodianship determines to remove the foster child from the foster home, either because it has determined that it would be in the child's best interests to transfer him to some other foster home, or to return the child to his natural parents in accordance with the statute or placement agreement. Most children are removed in order to be transferred to another foster home.[23] The procedures by which foster parents may challenge a removal made for that purpose differ somewhat from those where the removal is made to return the child to his natural parent.

Soc.Serv.L. § 383(2), supra, n. 3, provides that the "authorized agency placing out or boarding [a foster] child ... may in its discretion remove such child from the home where placed or boarded." Administrative regulations implement this provision. The agency is required, except in emergencies, to notify the foster parents in writing 10 days in advance of any removal. The notice advises the foster parents that if they object to the child's removal they may request a "conference" with the social services department. The department schedules requested conferences within 10 days of the receipt of the request. The foster parent may appear with

---

20. "[A]lthough the agency usually obtains legal custody in foster family care, the child still legally 'belongs' to the parent and the parent retains guardianship. This means that, for some crucial aspects of the child's life, the agency has no authority to act. Only the parent can consent to surgery for the child, or consent to his marriage, or permit his enlistment in the armed forces, or represent him at law." Kadushin, ... [Child Welfare Services, at 355 (1967)].

22. The Family Court is also empowered permanently to sever the ties of parent and child if the parent fails to maintain contact with the child while in foster care. Soc. Serv.L. § 384–b(4)–7....

23. The record shows that in 1973–1974 approximately 80% of the children removed from foster homes in New York State after living in the foster home for one year or more were transferred to another foster placement. 13% were returned to the biological parents, and 7% were adopted....

counsel at the conference, where he will "be advised of the reasons [for the removal of the child], and be afforded an opportunity to submit reasons why the child should not be removed." The official must render a decision in writing within five days after the close of the conference, and send notice of his decision to the foster parents and the agency. The proposed removal is stayed pending the outcome of the conference.

If the child is removed after the conference, the foster parent may appeal to the department of social services for a "fair hearing," that is, a full adversary administrative hearing, under Soc.Serv.L. § 400, the determination of which is subject to judicial review under N.Y.C.P.L.R. Art. 78; however, the removal is not automatically stayed pending the hearing and judicial review.

This statutory and regulatory scheme applies statewide. In addition, regulations promulgated by the New York City Human Resources Administration, Department of Social Services—Special Services for Children (SSC) provide even greater procedural safeguards there. Under SSC Procedure No. 5 (April 5, 1974), in place of or in addition to the conference provided by the state regulations, the foster parents may request a full trial-type hearing *before* the child is removed from their home. This procedure applies, however, only if the child is being transferred to another foster home, and not if the child is being returned to his natural parents.

One further preremoval procedural safeguard is available. Under Soc. Serv.L. § 392, the Family Court has jurisdiction to review, on petition of the foster parent or the agency, the status of any child who has been in foster care for 18 months or longer.[30]

Foster care of children is a sensitive and emotion-laden subject.... New York would have us view the scheme as described in its brief:

> "Today New York premises its foster care system on the accepted principle that the placement of a child into foster care is solely a temporary, transitional action intended to lead to the future reunion of the child with his natural parent or parents, or if such reunion is not possible, to legal adoption and the establishment of a new permanent home for the child."

Some of the parties and *amici* argue that this is a misleadingly idealized picture....

From the standpoint of natural parents, such as the appellant intervenors here, foster care has been condemned as a class-based intrusion into the family life of the poor. See, e.g., Jenkins, Child Welfare as a Class System, in Children and Decent People, 3 (Schorr ed. 1974). It is certainly true that the poor resort to foster care more often than other citizens. For example, over 50% of all children in foster care in New York City are from

---

30. The agency is required to initiate such a review when a child has remained in foster care for 18 months, Soc.Serv.L. § 392(2)(a), and if the child remains in foster care, the court "shall rehear the matter whenever it deems necessary or desirable, or upon petition by any party entitled to notice in proceedings under this section, but at least every twenty-four months." Soc.Serv.L. § 392(10).

female-headed families receiving Aid to Families with Dependent Children. Minority families are also more likely to turn to foster care; 52.3% of the children in foster care in New York City are black and 25.5% are Puerto Rican. This disproportionate resort to foster care by the poor and victims of discrimination doubtless reflects in part the greater likelihood of disruption of poverty stricken families. Commentators have also noted, however, that middle-and upper-income families who need temporary care services for their children have the resources to purchase private care. The poor have little choice but to submit to state-supervised child care when family crises strike.

The extent to which supposedly "voluntary" placements are in fact voluntary has been questioned on other grounds as well. For example, it has been said that many "voluntary" placements are in fact coerced by threat of neglect proceedings and are not in fact voluntary in the sense of the product of an informed consent. Studies also suggest that social workers of middle-class backgrounds, perhaps unconsciously, incline to favor continued placement in foster care with a generally higher-status family rather than return the child to his natural family, thus reflecting a bias that treats the natural parents' poverty and lifestyle as prejudicial to the best interests of the child. This accounts,[35] it has been said, for the hostility of agencies to the efforts of natural parents to obtain the return of their children.

Appellee foster parents as well as natural parents question the accuracy of the idealized picture portrayed by New York. They note that children often stay in "temporary" foster care for much longer than contemplated by the theory of the system. The District Court found as a fact that the median time spent in foster care in New York was over four years. Indeed, many children apparently remain in this "limbo" indefinitely. Mnookin [Child–Custody Adjudication: Judicial Functions in the Face of Indeterminacy, 39 Law and Contemp. Probs.] 226, 273 [Summer 1975]. The District Court also found that the longer a child remains in foster care, the more likely it is that he will never leave: "the probability of a foster child being returned to his biological parents declined markedly after the first year in foster care." 418 F.Supp., at 279 n. 6. It is not surprising then that many children, particularly those that enter foster care at a very early age and have little or no contact with their natural parents during extended stays in foster care, often develop deep emotional ties with their foster parents.[40]

---

35. Other factors alleged to bias agencies in favor of retention in foster care are the lack of sufficient staff to provide social work services needed by the natural parents to resolve their problems and prepare for return of the child; policies of many agencies to discourage involvement of the natural parent in the care of the child while in foster care; and systems of foster-care funding that encourage agencies to keep the child in foster care....

[A discussion of these problems is found in Wald, *State Intervention on Behalf of "Neglected" Children*, 28 Stan.L.Rev. 623, 677 (1977).—Ed.]

40. The development of such ties points up an intrinsic ambiguity of foster care that is central to this case. The warmer and more home-like environment of foster care is intended to be its main advantage over institutional child care, yet because in theory foster care is intended to be only temporary, foster

Yet such ties do not seem to be regarded as obstacles to transfer of the child from one foster placement to another. The record in this case indicates that nearly 60% of the children in foster care in New York City have experienced more than one placement, and about 28% have experienced three or more. The intended stability of the foster home management is further damaged by the rapid turnover among social work professionals who supervise the foster care arrangements on behalf of the State. Moreover, even when it is clear that a foster child will not be returned to his natural parents, it is rare that he achieves a stable home life through final termination of parental ties and adoption into a new permanent family. Fanshel, Status Changes of Children in Foster Care, 55 Child Welfare 143, 145, 157 (1976); . . .

. . . [W]e present this summary in the view that some understanding of those criticisms is necessary for a full appreciation of the complex and controversial system with which this lawsuit is concerned.[41] But the issue presented by the case is a narrow one. . . . Our task is only to determine whether the District Court correctly held that the present procedures preceding the removal from a foster home of children resident there a year or more are constitutionally inadequate. To that task we now turn.

Our first inquiry is whether appellees have asserted interests within the Fourteenth Amendment's protection of "liberty" and "property." Board of Regents v. Roth, 408 U.S. 564, 571 (1972).

parents are urged not to become too attached to the children in their care. . . . Indeed, the New York courts have upheld removal from a foster home for the very reason that the foster parents had become too emotionally involved with the child. In re Jewish Child Care Assn. (Sanders), 5 N.Y.2d 222, 183 N.Y.S.2d 65, 156 N.E.2d 700 (1959). . . .

On the other hand, too warm a relation between foster parent and foster child is not the only possible problem in foster care. Qualified foster parents are hard to find, . . . and very little training is provided to equip them to handle too often complicated demands of their role, . . . it is thus sometimes possible that foster homes may provide inadequate care. Indeed, situations in which foster children were mistreated or abused have been reported. . . . And the social work services that are supposed to be delivered to both the natural and foster families are often limited, due to the heavy caseloads of the agencies. . . . Given these problems, and given that the very fact of removal from even an inadequate natural family is often traumatic for the child, . . . it is not surprising that one commentator has found "rather persuasive, if still incomplete, evidence that throughout the United States, children in foster care are experiencing high rates of psychiatric disturbance." Eisenberg, The Sins of the Fathers: Urban Decay and Social Pathology, 32 Amer.J. of Orthopsychiatry 5, 14 (1962).

41. It must be noted, however, that both appellee foster parents and intervening natural parents present incomplete pictures of the foster-care system. Although seeking relief applicable to all removal situations, foster parents focus on intrafoster-care transfers, portraying a foster-care system in which children neglected by their parents and condemned to a permanent limbo of foster care are arbitrarily shuttled about by social workers whenever they become attached to a foster home. The natural parents, who focus on foster children being returned to their parent, portray a system under which poor and minority parents, deprived of their children under hard necessity and bureaucratic pressures, are obstructed in their efforts to maintain relationships with their children and ultimately to regain custody, by hostile agencies and meddling foster parents. . . . [T]here are elements of truth in both pictures. But neither represents the whole truth about the system.

The appellees have not renewed in this Court their contention, rejected by the District Court, 418 F.Supp., at 280–281, that the realities of the foster-care system in New York gave them a justified expectation amounting to a "property" interest that their status as foster parents would be continued. . . .

The appellees' basic contention is that when a child has lived in a foster home for a year or more, a psychological tie is created between the child and the foster parents which constitutes the foster family the true "psychological family" of the child. See J. Goldstein, A. Freud and A. Solnit, Beyond the Best Interests of the Child (1973). That family, they argue, has a "liberty interest" in its survival as a family protected by the Fourteenth Amendment. Upon this premise they conclude that the foster child cannot be removed without a prior hearing satisfying due process. Appointed counsel for the children, appellants in No. 76–5200, however, disagrees, and has consistently argued that the foster parents have no such liberty interest independent of the interests of the foster children, and that the best interest of the children would not be served by procedural protections beyond those already provided by New York law. The intervening natural parents of children in foster care, appellants in 76–5193, also oppose the foster parents, arguing that recognition of the procedural right claimed would undercut both the substantive family law of New York, which favors the return of children to their natural parents as expeditiously as possible . . . and their constitutionally protected right of family privacy, by forcing them to submit to a hearing and defend their rights to their children before the children could be returned to them.

. . .

We . . . turn to appellees' assertion that they have a constitutionally protected liberty interest—in the words of the District Court, a "right to familial privacy," 418 F.Supp., at 279—in the integrity of their family unit.[45] This assertion clearly presents difficulties.

It is of course true that "freedom of personal choice in matters of . . . family life is one of the liberties protected by the Due Process Clause of the Fourteenth Amendment." Cleveland Board of Education v. LaFleur, 414 U.S. 632, 639–640 (1974). There does exist a "private realm of family life which the state cannot enter," Prince v. Massachusetts, 321 U.S. 158, 166 (1944), that has been afforded both substantive and procedural protection. But is the relation of foster parent to foster child sufficiently akin to the concept of "family" recognized in our precedents to merit similar protection? Although considerable difficulty has attended the task of defining "family" for purposes of the Due Process Clause, see Moore v. City of East Cleveland, supra, n. 42, 431 U.S. 494, 97 S.Ct., at 1934 (plurality opinion of Powell, J.); id., at 97 S.Ct., at 1952 (Stewart, J., dissenting); id., at 97 S.Ct., at 1957 (White, J., dissenting), we are not without guides to some of the

---

45. There can be, of course, no doubt of appellees' standing to assert this interest, which, to whatever extent it exists, belongs to the foster parents as much as to the foster children.

elements that define the concept of "family" and contribute to its place in our society.

First, the usual understanding of "family" implies biological relationships, and most decisions treating the relation between parent and child have stressed this element. Stanley v. Illinois, 405 U.S. 645, 651, 92 S.Ct. 1208, 1212, 31 L.Ed.2d 551 (1972), for example, spoke of "[t]he rights to conceive and raise one's children" as essential rights. . . .

A biological relationship is not present in the case of the usual foster family. But biological relationships are not exclusive determination of the existence of a family. The basic foundation of the family in our society, the marriage relationship, is of course not a matter of blood relation. . . .

Thus the importance of the familial relationship, to the individuals involved and to the society, stems from the emotional attachments that derive from the intimacy of daily association, and from the role it plays in "promot[ing] a way of life" through the instruction of children, as well as from the fact of blood relationship. No one would seriously dispute that a deeply loving and interdependent relationship between an adult and a child in his or her care may exist even in the absence of blood relationship.[51] At least where a child has been placed in foster care as an infant, has never known his natural parents, and has remained continuously for several years in the care of the same foster parents, it is natural that the foster family should hold the same place in the emotional life of the foster child, and fulfill the same socializing functions, as a natural family.[52] For this reason, we cannot dismiss the foster family as a mere collection of unrelated individuals.

But there are also important distinctions between the foster family and the natural family. First, unlike the earlier cases recognizing a right to family privacy, the State here seeks to interfere not with a relationship having its origins entirely apart from the power of the State, but rather with a foster family which has its source in state law and contractual arrangements. The individual's freedom to marry and reproduce is "older than the Bill of Rights," Griswold v. Connecticut, 381 U.S., at 486. Accordingly, unlike the property interests that are also protected by the Fourteenth Amendment, the liberty interest in family privacy has its source, and its contours are ordinarily to be sought, not in state law,[53] but

51. Adopting, for example, is recognized as the legal equivalent of biological parenthood. See, e.g., N.Y.Dom.Rel.L. § 110 n. 19.

52. The briefs dispute at some length the validity of the "psychological parent" theory propounded in Goldstein, Freud and Solnit, Beyond the Best Interests of the Child (1973). The book, on which appellee foster parents relied to some extent in the District Court, is indeed controversial. See, e.g., Strauss and Strauss, Book Review, 74 Colum.L.Rev. 996 (1974) . . . But this case turns not on the disputed validity of any particular psychological theory, but on the legal consequences of the undisputed fact that the emotional ties between foster parent and foster child are in many cases quite close, and undoubtedly in some as close as those existing in biological families.

53. The legal status of families has never been regarded as controlling: "Nor has the [Constitution] refused to recognize those family relationships unlegitimized by a marriage ceremony." Stanley v. Illinois, supra, 405 U.S., at 651, 92 S.Ct. at 1213.

in intrinsic human rights, as they have been understood in "this Nation's history and tradition." Here, however, whatever emotional ties may develop between foster parent and foster child have their origins in an arrangement in which the State has been a partner from the outset.... In this case, the limited recognition accorded to the foster family by the New York statutes and the contracts executed by the foster parents argue against any but the most limited constitutional "liberty" in the foster family.

A second consideration related to this is that ordinarily procedural protection may be afforded to a liberty interest of one person without derogating from the substantive liberty of another. Here, however, such a tension is virtually unavoidable. Under New York law, the natural parent of a foster child in voluntary placement has an absolute right to the return of his child in the absence of a court order obtainable only upon compliance with rigorous substantive and procedural standards, which reflect the constitutional protection accorded the natural family. Moreover, the natural parent initially gave up his child to the State only on the express understanding that the child would be returned in those circumstances. These rights are difficult to reconcile with the liberty interest in the foster family relationship claimed by appellees. It is one thing to say that individuals may acquire a liberty interest against arbitrary governmental interference in the family-like associations into which they have freely entered, even in the absence of biological connection or state-law recognition of the relationship. It is quite another to say that one may acquire such an interest in the face of another's constitutionally recognized liberty interest that derives from blood relationship, state law sanction, and basic human right—an interest the foster parent has recognized by contract from the outset. Whatever liberty interest might otherwise exist in the foster family as an institution, that interest must be substantially attenuated where the proposed removal from the foster family is to return the child to his natural parents.

. . . [A]ppellees' claim to a constitutionally protected liberty interest raises complex and novel questions. It is unnecessary for us to resolve those questions definitively in this case, however, for like the District Court, we conclude that "narrower grounds exist to support" our reversal. We are persuaded that, even on the assumption that appellees have a protected "liberty interest," the District Court erred in holding that the preremoval procedures presently employed by the State are constitutionally defective.

Where procedural due process must be afforded because a "liberty" or "property" interest is within the Fourteenth Amendment's protection, there must be determined "what process is due" in the particular context....

It is true that "[b]efore a person is deprived of a protected interest, he must be afforded opportunity for some kind of hearing, 'except for extraordinary situations where some valid governmental interest is at stake that justifies postponing the hearing until after the event.' " Board of Regents v.

Roth, 408 U.S., at 570 n. 7 . . . But the hearing required is only one "appropriate to the nature of the case." Mullane v. Central Hanover Bank & Trust Co., 339 U.S. 306, 313 (1950). . . . Only last Term, the Court held that "identification of the specific dictates of due process generally requires consideration of three distinct factors: first, the private interest that will be affected by the official action; second, the risk of an erroneous deprivation of such interest through the procedures used, and the probable value, if any, of additional or substitute procedural safeguards; and finally, the Government's interest, including the function involved and the fiscal and administrative burdens that the additional or substitute procedural requirement would entail." Mathews v. Eldridge, 424 U.S. 319, 335 (1976). Consideration of the procedures employed by the City and State of New York in light of these three factors requires the conclusion that those procedures satisfy constitutional standards.

. . .

Reversed.

■ MR. JUSTICE STEWART, with whom THE CHIEF JUSTICE and MR. JUSTICE REHNQUIST join, concurring in the judgment. . . .

Clearly, New York has deprived nobody of his life in these cases. It seems to me just as clear that the State has deprived nobody of his liberty or property. Their argument seems to be that New York, by providing foster children with the opportunity to live in a foster home and to form a close relationship with foster parents, has created "liberty" or "property" that it may not withdraw without complying with the procedural safeguards that the Due Process Clause confers. . . . New York confers no right on foster families to remain intact, defeasible only upon proof of specific acts or circumstances. . . .

. . . New York law provides no basis for a justifiable expectation on the part of foster families that their relationship will continue indefinitely. The District Court in this litigation recognized as much, noting that the typical foster care contract gives the agency the right to recall the child "upon request," and commenting that the discretionary authority vested in the agency "is on its face incompatible with plaintiffs' claim of legal entitlement." 418 F.Supp., at 281. To be sure, the New York system has not operated perfectly. As the state legislature found, foster care has in many cases been unnecessarily protracted, no doubt sometimes resulting in the expectation on the part of some foster families that their relationship will continue indefinitely. But as already noted, the New York Court of Appeals has unequivocally rejected the notion that under New York law prolonged third-party custody of children creates some sort of "squatters' rights." [Citing In re Bennett v. Jeffreys, 40 N.Y.2d 543, 387 N.Y.S.2d 821, 356 N.E.2d 277, 285.]

This is not to say that under the law of New York foster children are the pawns of the State, who may be whisked from family to family at the whim of state officials. . . . [T]he protection that foster children have is simply the requirement of state law that decisions about their placement be determined in the light of their best interests. This requirement is not "liberty or property" protected by the Due Process Clause, and it confers no right or expectancy of any kind in the continuity of the relationship between foster parents and children. . . .

What remains of the appellees' argument is the theory that the relation of the foster parent to the foster child may generate emotional attachments similar to those found in natural families. The Court surmises that foster families who share these attachments might enjoy the same constitutional interest in "family privacy" as natural families. . . .

But under New York's foster care laws, any case where the foster parents had assumed the emotional role of the child's natural parents would represent not a triumph of the system, to be constitutionally safe-guarded from state intrusion, but a failure. The goal of foster care, at least in New York, is not to provide a permanent substitute for the natural or adoptive home, but to prepare the child for his return to his real parents or placement in a permanent adoptive home by giving him temporary shelter in a family setting. . . . Perhaps it is to be expected that children who spend unduly long stays in what should have been temporary foster care will develop strong emotional ties with their foster parents. But this does not mean, and I cannot believe, that such breakdowns of the New York system must be protected or forever frozen in their existence by the Due Process Clause of the Fourteenth Amendment.

One of the liberties protected by the Due Process Clause, the Court has held, is the freedom to "establish a home and bring up children." Meyer v. Nebraska, supra, at 399. If a State were to attempt to force the breakup of a natural family, over the objections of the parents and their children, without some showing of unfitness and for the sole reason that to do so was thought to be in the children's best interest, I should have little doubt that the State would have intruded impermissibly on "the private realm of family life which the state cannot enter." Prince v. Massachusetts, 321 U.S. 158, 166. But this constitutional concept is simply not in point when we deal with foster families as New York law has defined them. The family life upon which the State "intrudes" is simply a temporary status which the State itself has created. It is a "family life" defined and controlled by the law of New York, for which New York pays, and the goals of which New York is entitled to and does set for itself.

NOTE

In a sensitive review and appraisal of Smith v. Offer, Professors David Chambers and Michael Wald point out that seven years after the restraining order had been entered, the courts approved an adoption petition by Mrs. Smith to adopt the children. *See* David Chambers and Michael Wald, *Smith v. Offer*, in ROBERT MNOOKIN, IN THE INTEREST OF CHILDREN 68, 114 (1985). Recent federal decisions support the holding in *Smith*. *See, e.g.,* Rodriguez v. McLoughlin, 214 F.3d 328 (2d Cir.2000), *cert. denied,* 532 U.S. 1051, 121 S.Ct. 2192, 149 L.Ed.2d 1023 (2001), where the court held that foster parents have no liberty interest, under New York law, in their relationship with foster children, and that removal of the foster children from the foster parent's home without prompt hearing and notice does not violate the due process clause of the Fourteenth Amendment.

In Matter of Michael B., 80 N.Y.2d 299, 590 N.Y.S.2d 60, 604 N.E.2d 122 (1992), the New York Court of Appeals faced the situation in which a child's biological father was pitted against state designated foster parents. The dispute centered on the meaning of the term "best interest of the child" in the context of a foster placement. The child, born in 1985 with a positive toxicology for cocaine, had been voluntarily relinquished by the natural mother. No father was listed on the birth certificate. At three months the child, described as then "in need of extraordinary care", was placed by an agency with foster parents who initially were assured that this was a "preadoptive" placement. Legal proceedings to terminate the rights of both natural parents were begun in 1987, after the father had been identified. The mother did not appear and a finding of permanent neglect was made as to her. The father appeared and agreed to a finding of permanent neglect and to placing Michael and his siblings with two godmothers. This agreement was later vacated because the children had not been so placed. The father then entered an 18–month drug rehabilitation program. In 1988 the agency and the Law Guardian agreed to suspend the permanent neglect judgment for 12 months on condition that the father remain drug-free, obtain suitable housing, and submit a plan for the children's care during the day. As this period neared an end, the Law Guardian for Michael entered a report that the child might suffer "severe psychological damage" if removed from his foster home, requesting the Family Court to conduct a "best interests" hearing pursuant to the Court's earlier holding in Bennett v. Jeffreys, supra at 666. Family Court then questioned whether it had authority to rehear the issue on the basis of the child's best interests.

The Court of Appeals distinguished the case from Bennett v. Jeffreys initially because the latter concerned an "unsupervised private placement". The court determined that because a foster parent (even a long term one) was involved, that standard of "best interests" under the applicable statute on voluntary placements was controlling. In such a case, the fitness of the natural parent was deemed to be a primary factor. The court noted that "there are three possible dispositions after foster care review with respect to a child not freed for adoption: continued foster care; release to a parent, guardian, relative or other suitable person; and institution of parental termination proceedings." Based on what were described as "new circumstances", the case was remitted to Family Court for an expedited hearing on the fitness of the parent.

CALIFORNIA FAMILY CODE (West 2004)

§ 7950.   Relatives; race, color or national origin

(a) With full consideration for the proximity of the natural parents to the placement so as to facilitate visitation and family reunification, when a placement in foster care is being made, the following considerations shall be used:

(1) Placement shall, if possible, be made in the home of a relative, unless the placement would not be in the best interest of the child. Diligent efforts shall be made by an agency or entity to which this subdivision applies, to locate an appropriate relative. Before any child may be placed in long-term foster care, the court shall find that the agency or entity to which this subdivision applies has made diligent efforts to locate an appropriate relative and that each relative whose name has been submitted to the agency or entity as a possible caretaker, either by himself or herself or by other persons, has been evaluated as an appropriate placement resource.

(2) No agency or entity that receives any state assistance and is involved in foster care placements may do either of the following:

(A) Deny to any person the opportunity to become a foster parent on the basis of the race, color, or national origin of the person or the child involved.

(B) Delay or deny the placement of a child into foster care on the basis of the race, color, or national origin of the foster parent or the child involved.

(b) Subdivision (a) shall not be construed to affect the application of the Indian Child Welfare Act (25 U.S.C. Sec. 1901 and following).

(c) Nothing in this section precludes a search for an appropriate relative being conducted simultaneously with a search for a foster family . . .

§ 7952.   **Statement to court by minor**

A minor 10 years of age or older being considered for placement in a foster home has the right to make a brief statement to the court making a decision on placement. The court may disregard any preferences expressed by the minor. The minor's right to make a statement is not limited to the initial placement, but continues for any proceedings concerning continued placement or a decision to return to parental custody.

2.   PERMANENT OR LONG TERM FOSTER PLACEMENT

MAINE REVISED STATUTES ANN., TITLE 22 (2004)

§ 4064.   **Long-term foster care**

1.   Defined. "Long-term foster care" means a foster family placement for a child in the custody of the department in which the department retains custody of the child while delegating to the foster parents the duty and authority to make certain decisions. The placement is intended to continue until the child becomes 18 years old, unless altered or terminated in the best interests of the child.

2. Authority for placement. The department may place in long-term foster care a child in its custody, if:

A. The child has been in foster care for 6 months or parental rights have been terminated;

B. The department has decided that it is not likely that the child can be returned to his parents and has so notified the parents;

C. In the judgment of the department, it is not likely that the child can be placed in an adoptive home;

D. The prospective foster parents have met standards established by the department for a placement; and

E. A written agreement between the foster parents and the department has been completed which specifies the duty and authority delegated by the department to the foster parents and the rights retained by the department and the parents, and includes an individual plan for the care of the child. A foster child at least 14 years old may participate in the development of the agreement. The department shall, after consultation with the foster parents, review and, if necessary, revise the plan at least once every 6 months.

3. Duty and authority delegated by the department. The foster parents may make the following decisions:

A. Consent to emergency medical treatment;

B. Consent to the application for a driver's license; and

C. Permit travel by the child outside of the State.

4. Rights of department. Except as delegated in this section or by agreement, the department shall retain custody of the child and all custody rights as provided by court order, statute or rule.

5. Rules. The department may adopt rules for long-term foster care placements in accordance with the Maine Administrative Procedure Act, Title 5, section 8001, et seq. These rules may include, among other things, standards for settings appropriate for long-term foster care, methods of supervising of those settings, procedures for selecting children and foster parents, methods for establishing and reviewing individual plans, additional rights or powers that may be delegated and requirements or conditions for exercising the delegated authority.

D. THE VISITATION DILEMMA

Schutz v. Schutz

Supreme Court of Florida, 1991.
581 So.2d 1290.

■ KOGAN, JUSTICE.

... A final judgment dissolving the six-year marriage of petitioner, Laurel Schutz (mother) and respondent, Richard R. Schutz (father) was entered by the trial court on November 13, 1978. Although custody of the parties' minor children was originally granted to the father, the final judgment was later modified in 1979. Under the modified judgment, the mother was awarded sole custody of the children, and the father was both granted visitation rights and ordered to pay child support.

As noted by the trial court, the ongoing "acrimony and animosity between the adult parties" is clear from the record. The trial court found that in February 1981 the mother moved with the children from Miami to Georgia without notifying the father. After moving, the mother advised the father of their new address and phone number. Although the father and children corresponded after the move, he found an empty house on the three occasions when he traveled to Georgia to visit the children. The father was not notified that after only seven months in Georgia the mother and children had returned to Miami. Four years later in 1985, upon discovering the children's whereabouts, the father visited the children only to find that they "hated, despised, and feared" him due to his failure to support or visit them. After this visit, numerous motions concerning visitation, custody and support were filed by the parties.

After a final hearing on the motions, the trial court found that "the cause of the blind, brainwashed, bigoted belligerence of the children toward the father grew from the soil nurtured, watered and tilled by the mother." The court further found that "the mother breached every duty she owed as the custodial parent to the noncustodial parent of instilling love, respect and feeling in the children for their father." The trial court's findings are supported by substantial competent evidence.

Based on these findings, the trial court ordered the mother "to do everything in her power to create in the minds of [the children] a loving, caring feeling toward the father ... [and] to convince the children that it is the mother's desire that they see their father and love their father." The court further ordered that breach of the obligation imposed "either in words, actions, demeanor, implication or otherwise" would result in the "severest penalties ..., including contempt, imprisonment, loss of residential custody or any combination thereof."

Although the district court construed the above quoted portions of the order to require the mother to "instruct the children to love and respect their father," 522 So.2d at 875, it concluded that she was not " 'protected' by the first amendment from a requirement that she fulfil her legal obligation to undo the harm she had already caused." Id.

We begin our analysis by noting our agreement with the district courts of appeal that have found a custodial parent has an affirmative obligation to encourage and nurture the relationship between the child and the noncustodial parent. This duty is owed to both the noncustodial parent and the child. This obligation may be met by encouraging the child to interact with the noncustodial parent, taking good faith measures to ensure that the child visit and otherwise have frequent and continuing contact with the noncustodial parent and refraining from doing anything likely to undermine the relationship naturally fostered by such interaction.

Consistent with this obligation, we read the challenged portion of the order at issue to require nothing more of the mother than a good faith effort to take those measures necessary to restore and promote the frequent and continuing positive interaction (e.g., visitation, phone calls, letters) between the children and their father and to refrain from doing or saying anything likely to defeat that end. There is no requirement that petitioner express opinions that she does not hold, a practice disallowed by the first amendment....

Under this construction of the order, any burden on the mother's first amendment rights is merely "incidental."[2] Therefore, the order may be sustained against a first amendment challenge if "it furthers an important or substantial governmental interest . . . and if the incidental restriction on alleged First Amendment freedoms is no greater than is essential to the furtherance of that interest." United States v. O'Brien, 391 U.S. 367, 377, 88 S.Ct. 1673, 1679, 20 L.Ed.2d 672 (1968). Accordingly, we must balance the mother's right of free expression against the state's parens patriae interest in assuring the well-being of the parties' minor children. However, as with all matters involving custody of minor children, the interests of the father and of the children, which here happen to parallel those of the state, must also factor into the equation.

In this case, the court, acting on behalf of the state as parens patriae, sought to resolve the dispute between the parties in accordance with the best interests of their children by attempting to restore a meaningful relationship between the children and their father by assuring them unhampered, frequent and continuing contact with him.... In resolving the matter, the court also properly considered the father's constitutionally protected "inherent right" to a meaningful relationship with his children,[3] a personal interest which in this case is consistent with the state's interest in promoting meaningful family relationships.

There is no question that the state's interest in restoring a meaningful relationship between the parties' children and their father, thereby promoting the best interests of the children, is at the very least substantial. Likewise, any restriction placed on the mother's freedom of expression is essential to the furtherance of the state's interests because affirmative measures taken by the mother to encourage meaningful interaction between the children and their father would be for naught if she were allowed to contradict those measures by word or deed.

2. The burden is "incidental" because the state interests which are furthered by the order are "unrelated to the suppression of free expression." United States v. O'Brien, 391 U.S. 367, 377, 88 S.Ct. 1673, 1679, 20 L.Ed.2d 672 (1968).

3. Frazier v. Frazier, 109 Fla. 164, 172, 147 So. 464, 467 (1933) (noncustodial father is "entitled to have and enjoy [child's] society for a reasonably sufficient length of time each year to enable him to inculcate in her mind a spirit of love, affection and respect for her father," if such is not contrary to best interest of child)....

Moreover, as evinced by this record, the mother as custodial parent has the ability to undermine the association to which both the father and the parties' children are entitled.... Therefore, not only is the incidental burden placed on her right of free expression essential to the furtherance of the state's interests as expressed in chapter 61, but also it is necessary to protect the rights of the children and their father to the meaningful relationship that the order seeks to restore.

Accordingly, construing the order as we do, we find no abuse of discretion by the trial court, nor impermissible burden on the petitioner's first amendment rights. Although we do not approve the district court's construction of that portion of the order under review, nor the analysis employed below, the result reached is approved....

NOTE

Courts have not been shy in ordering innovative approaches to allow communications between parents and children. *See, e.g.*, Burke v. Burke, 2001 WL 921770 (Tenn.App.2001), where the court ordered the mother to install a point-to-point video telecommunications device on her home computer so that a couple's two children may communicate with their father when in her physical custody. The father was ordered to pay for the device and the installation. And courts have protected a person's right to make threatening speech against the other parent as long as there is no history of domestic violence and the other parent was at no time in fear of immediate or soon-to-be-inflicted harm. Lawrence v. Delkamp, 620 N.W.2d 151 (N.D. 2000).

MICHIGAN COMPILED LAWS ANN. (West 2005)

552.642. Makeup parenting time policy for wrongful denial of parenting time

Sec. 42. (1) Each circuit shall establish a makeup parenting time policy under which a parent who has been wrongfully denied parenting time is able to make up the parenting time at a later date. The policy does not apply until it is approved by the chief circuit judge. A makeup parenting time policy established under this section shall provide all of the following:

(a) That makeup parenting time shall be at least the same type and duration of parenting time as the parenting time that was denied, including, but not limited to, weekend parenting time for weekend parenting time, holiday parenting time for holiday parenting time, weekday parenting time for weekday parenting time, and summer parenting time for summer parenting time.

(b) That makeup parenting time shall be taken within 1 year after the wrongfully denied parenting time was to have occurred.

(c) That the wrongfully denied parent shall choose the time of the makeup parenting time.

(d) That the wrongfully denied parent shall notify both the office of the friend of the court and the other parent in writing not less than 1 week before making use of makeup weekend or weekday parenting time or not less than 28 days before making use of makeup holiday or summer parenting time.

(2) If wrongfully denied parenting time is alleged and the friend of the court determines that action should be taken, the office of the friend of the court shall send each party a notice containing the following statement in boldfaced type of not less than 12 points:

"FAILURE TO RESPOND IN WRITING TO THE OFFICE OF THE FRIEND OF THE COURT WITHIN 21 DAYS AFTER THIS NOTICE WAS SENT SHALL BE CONSIDERED AS AN AGREEMENT THAT PARENTING TIME WAS WRONGFULLY DENIED AND THAT THE MAKEUP PARENTING TIME POLICY ESTABLISHED BY THE COURT WILL BE APPLIED.".

(3) If a party to the parenting time order does not respond in writing to the office of the friend of the court, within 21 days after the office sends the notice required under subsection (2), to contest the application of the makeup parenting time policy, the office of the friend of the court shall notify each party that the makeup parenting time policy applies. If a party makes a timely response to contest the application of the makeup parenting time policy, the office of the friend of the court shall utilize a procedure authorized under section 41 other than the application of the makeup parenting time policy.

Matter of Cabalquinto

Supreme Court of Washington, 1983.
100 Wn.2d 325, 669 P.2d 886.

■ Dolliver, Justice.

Ernest Cabalquinto and his former wife Cheryll Grover are involved in a dispute over Ernest's rights of visitation with their 8–year–old son Michael. Ernest Cabalquinto appeals from a King County Superior Court decision denying his request for an order allowing visitation with Michael in California.

Ernest and Cheryll Cabalquinto were married on March 3, 1973. The couple resided in Colorado Springs, Colorado, where Cheryll gave birth to their son Michael on January 7, 1974. On July 30, 1976, the Cabalquintos were divorced in Colorado Springs.

In the divorce decree, the District Court for El Paso County, Colorado granted custody of Michael to Cheryll. The Colorado court awarded Ernest the following visitation rights:

2. That the Respondent, Ernest Cabalquinto, be allowed reasonable rights of visitation, which rights are to be liberally construed considering the distance involved between the parties, so that the

Respondent be allowed liberal rights particularly during the summer months, and that the parties hereto alternate the major holidays so that each shall have the opportunity to have the minor child with him or her for those major holidays in different years.

Shortly before the Colorado court entered the custody decree, Cheryll moved to King County, Washington with Michael. She has now remarried and lives in Renton with her husband Ronald Grover. Soon thereafter, Ernest moved to San Francisco, California. He now resides in Concord, California, a suburb of San Francisco.

For approximately 4 years after the divorce, Ernest visited his son Michael in King County, where Ernest's parents also reside. During that time Ernest visited his son on an average of one or two times a year. The length of the stay ranged from a few days to over a week for each of these instances. Ernest was given the opportunity to see Michael in the Seattle area whenever he so desired.

In 1980, however, Ernest decided he would like Michael to visit in California instead. When Cheryll refused to allow Michael to go to California, Ernest filed a motion in King County Superior Court for an order clarifying his visitation rights under the Colorado divorce decree. Ernest asked the court to establish a visitation schedule whereby the court would allow Michael to visit him in California for substantial periods in the summer months and on several holidays throughout the year. Cheryll objected, arguing that a modification of the decree, as opposed to an interpretation, would be necessary to enable Ernest to take the child outside the King County court's jurisdiction. The King County court avoided the procedural problem by treating Ernest's petition as one to clarify the Colorado decree and, in the alternative, as a petition to modify the divorce decree.

After a hearing on August 14, 1980, the trial court denied Ernest's request for the California visitation. The court found the existing pattern of visitation in King County at the home of Ernest's parents to be "fair, reasonable and in the best interest of the child." The existing visitation rights were found to have "resulted in a close relationship between the father and the son and [was] one which has been accomplished without undue expense or inconvenience." Clerk's Papers, at 6. Ernest's visitation with Michael in the Seattle area at the home of his parents was held to be a reasonable fulfillment of the Colorado decree of dissolution and was in the best interests of the child. The court further held it was not in the best interests of the child for the father to be permitted to remove the child from Washington for visitation at the home of the father in California.

In matters dealing with the welfare of children, trial courts are given broad discretion. A trial court's disposition of a case involving rights of custody and visitation will not be disturbed on appeal unless the court manifestly abused its discretion. Therefore, the issue presented by this case is whether the trial court manifestly abused its discretion by refusing to change the existing pattern of visitation.

Ordinarily, with the facts as presented heretofore, we would find no manifest abuse of discretion and would affirm the trial court. The trial court found the existing arrangement of visitation presented Ernest with reasonable rights of visitation, a finding with which we are inclined to agree. There is, however, one additional fact. Ernest is homosexual. At the time of the marriage Ernest advised Cheryll he was bisexual. The record indicates his homosexual behavior was a factor in breaking up the marriage. Ernest is presently living with his avowed homosexual lover in Concord, California.

In his oral opinion, the trial judge expressed a strong antipathy to homosexual living arrangements. He expressed the view that "a child should be led in the way of heterosexual preference, not be tolerant of this thing [homosexuality]" and that "it can[not] do the boy any good to live in such an environment. It might do some harm."

Ernest points out the undisputed testimony of his witnesses was that the visitation would not be harmful. There is no evidence in the record to the contrary. Furthermore, the trial court made no findings a visitation could endanger the physical, mental, or emotional health of the child. See RCW 26.09.240. There is nothing in the record to indicate the visitation proposals of Ernest were unreasonable. This does not mean, however, that the only reasonable rights of visitation are those claimed by Ernest.

In reviewing the entire record before us, we cannot tell what standards of law the trial court followed in reaching its decision on visitation rights. While the findings and conclusions of law suggest the homosexuality of the father was not the determining factor the unfortunate and unnecessary references by the trial court to homosexuality generally indicate the contrary.

It is the function of the trial court to weigh the facts and make its ruling. It is the function of this court to state the appropriate legal standards against which the facts must be weighed. We now make specific the rule of law which was subsumed in the decision in Schuster v. Schuster, [90 Wash.2d 626, 585 P.2d 130 (1978)]: homosexuality in and of itself is not a bar to custody or to reasonable rights of visitation. This rule is consistent with the decisions of other state courts. See, e.g., D.H. v. J.H., Ind.App., 418 N.E.2d 286 (1981); Di Stefano v. Di Stefano, 60 A.D.2d 976, 401 N.Y.S.2d 636 (1978); Nadler v. Superior Court, 255 Cal.App.2d 523, 63 Cal.Rptr. 352 (1967); Bezio v. Patenaude, 381 Mass. 563, 410 N.E.2d 1207 (1980). See also Rivera, Our Straight–Laced Judges: The Legal Position of Homosexual Persons in the United States, 30 Hastings L.J. 799, 883 (1979); Campbell, Child Custody, When One Parent Is a Homosexual, 17 Judges' J., No. 2, at 38 (1978). It is also consistent with our view that custody and visitation privileges are not to be used to penalize or reward parents for their conduct.

It seems apparent from the record the trial court did not grasp the significance of Schuster v. Schuster, supra. Visitation rights must be determined with reference to the needs of the child rather than the sexual preferences of the parent. The best interests of the child remain paramount. RCW 26.09.240. Since we are unable to determine the basis for the trial court's ruling, we are unable to determine whether the ruling was an abuse of discretion.

The case is remanded to the King County Superior Court for further consideration and a determination, consistent with this opinion, of the visitation rights of Ernest Cabalquinto.

■ STAFFORD, JUSTICE (concurring in part and dissenting in part).

I do not attempt to pass judgment on the subject of homosexuality per se or on the overtones of societal opinion concerning morality or immorality. These issues are not before this court. Rather, the question is whether the trial court, in the context of the facts herein, abused its discretion by giving primary consideration to homosexuality in its ultimate disposition of the case.

In its desire to avoid actually coming to grips with specific application of the correct law, the majority has resorted to a rather transparent discussion of "abuse of discretion." By concluding that the record provides an insufficient basis from which to evaluate the trial court's exercise of discretion, the majority has given judicial condonation to the personal feelings of the trial judge.

Even a broad grant of discretion does not excuse a trial court's failure to consider *relevant* issues within the established statutory framework. In making the father's homosexuality its primary consideration, the trial court lost sight of the duties owed both to the child and to his father. While I agree with the majority that a parent's sexual preference, standing alone, cannot be used to restrict visitation rights, I cannot agree with the majority's disposition of the visitation issue. I therefore must dissent.

The majority correctly notes the broad discretion granted to trial courts in domestic relations cases. Indeed we have consistently deferred to trial courts in such cases except where there has been a manifest abuse of discretion. Where there is such abuse, however, this court has a duty to reverse the trial court.

Under the domestic relations law of this State, the best interests of the child must be the paramount concern of the court. As important as this consideration is, however, it must nevertheless be balanced against a parent's fundamental right to be a parent. This right is of constitutional magnitude and cannot be restricted without a rational reason for doing so. *See* Stanley v. Illinois, 405 U.S. 645, 92 S.Ct. 1208, 31 L.Ed.2d 551 (1972). Further, our State Legislature recognized the necessity of balancing the rights of the parent with the best interests of the child by providing:

> The court may modify an order granting or denying visitation rights whenever modification would serve the best interests of the child *but the court shall not restrict a parent's visitation rights unless it finds that the visitation would endanger the child's physical, mental, or emotional health.*

(Italics mine.) RCW 26.09.240.

This statute requires that a court make a finding of specific harm to the child before restricting a parent's visitation rights. The majority suggests that as long as Mr. Cabalquinto had the alternative of visiting his son in Seattle, his visitation rights were not unreasonable. I cannot agree. In totally prohibiting Michael from visiting his father in California, the trial court clearly restricted Mr. Cabalquinto's visitation rights. Moreover, this restriction was imposed without the requisite concurrent finding of harm to the child.

If the course of action chosen by a particular court is based on unreasonable or erroneous grounds, the court has abused its discretion. We cannot avoid overturning a decision such as this in which the trial judge clearly allowed his personal feelings to dictate the result. A decision which is based on untenable or erroneous grounds rather than upon objectivity and impartiality must, by definition, be the product of manifest abuse of discretion. Under the circumstances of this case, I would find that not only was the basis for the trial court's decision inherently unreasonable, but its chosen course of action clearly was unsupported by the evidence or the law.

An examination of the record below leaves no doubt the trial judge allowed his declared views on homosexuality to color his evaluation of the evidence. In finding of fact 6, the trial court states in part:

> Therefore, because the father is living in a homosexual relationship in California and because he has reasonable rights of visitation here, the court finds it is not necessary to direct that the child be removed from the jurisdiction and be placed in the father's home in California in order to fulfill the visitation.

The majority correctly holds that homosexuality is not in and of itself a bar to either custody or reasonable visitation rights. The majority nevertheless holds that because it is unable to determine the basis for the trial court's ruling, it is thus unable to determine whether the ruling is an abuse of discretion. I might agree if the trial court had not clearly declared that Mr. Cabalquinto's avowed homosexuality was a deciding factor. Unlike the majority, I do not choose to sweep this difficult problem under the rug. I am willing to accept the trial court's findings of fact and oral opinion at face value and therefore have no problem finding an abuse of discretion.

In its oral opinion, the trial court repeatedly commented on the immorality of homosexuality while at the same time acknowledging that "everything about" Mr. Cabalquinto had made a favorable impression. The trial court stated:

> The father frankly states he wants his boy to choose the kind of life he wants to live. Well, in my view a child should be led in the way of heterosexual preference, not be tolerant of this thing. God Almighty made the two sexes not only to enjoy, but to perpetuate the human race. And after all, that is the most valuable aspect of sexual behavior, perpetuating the human race.
>
> I certainly can't find that the boy's best interest would be served by being subjected to this tolerant attitude, in view of the fact that I do

think also that the rights of the father have to be considered, and he can in all reason come to know this boy, enjoy his company, free from this environment which could be harmful to him.

The court's comments on homosexuality must be juxtaposed against the trial court's findings which clearly favor the proposed visitation. As noted above, the trial court failed to make any finding indicating that a visit to Mr. Cabalquinto's home in California would in any way be harmful to the child. To the contrary, the uncontroverted evidence clearly shows Mr. Cabalquinto is a loving father with a stable home environment. A psychologist specializing in gender identification testified that a child's sexual preference is developed early in life and that a child of Michael's age would not be influenced by his father's homosexuality provided the father did not flaunt his sexuality. The trial court accepted this testimony as well as that of the social worker who after investigating both Mr. Cabalquinto and his partner, recommended that Michael be allowed to visit in California. Mr. Cabalquinto emphasized his belief that a display of affection should be left behind closed doors and promised not to be indiscreet in his conduct. Finally, the trial court disagreed with the former Mrs. Cabalquinto and found that Michael was old enough to spend 2 weeks with his father 1,000 miles away from his home in Seattle.

Despite the overwhelming evidence supporting the proposed visitation, however, the trial court, nevertheless found that a visit to the father's home was not in the child's best interests. This conclusion is unsupportable absent the trial court's finding of some specific harm to the child. The trial court found only that the child might be harmed by exposure to a homosexual environment, which standing alone does not comply with the law concerning homosexual parents. The trial court's decision restricts the liberal visitation rights granted in the original Colorado decree with virtually no evidence in the record to support the restriction. The State may not restrict a parent's reasonable visitation rights merely because that parent's lifestyle is not within the societal mainstream. Bezio v. Patenaude, 381 Mass. 563, 410 N.E.2d 1207 (1980).

Under the circumstances of this case, I cannot agree with the majority that the record provides an insufficient basis from which to determine an abuse of discretion. The trial court misconstrued the law and improperly relied on that misconception in denying the requested visitation. In the absence of evidence or findings suggesting any particular harm to the child, I would hold that the trial court abused its discretion. Further, nothing would be gained by the wholly undirected remand employed by the majority. This is particularly true if the case is to be remanded to the trial judge who clearly relied on his own personal views to arrive at incorrect reasons for the ultimate ruling. I would specifically direct that the cause be reversed and remanded for a new trial consistent with the law of this State as expressed herein.

NOTE

Homosexual orientation continues to be a factor in visitation and custody determinations. Courts may adopt the rationale of the Missouri

Court of Appeals in S.E.G. v. R.A.G., 735 S.W.2d 164 (Mo.App.1987) in restricting a lesbian mother's visitation rights so as to prevent "extreme exposure of the situation to the minor children." The court wrote: "We are not forbidding Wife from being a homosexual, from having a lesbian relationship, or from attending gay activist or overt homosexual outings. We are restricting her from exposing these elements of her 'alternative life style' to her minor children." Or courts may adopt the rationale of the Family Court in Kings County, New York, in In the Matter of the Guardianship of Astonn H., 167 Misc.2d 840, 635 N.Y.S.2d 418 (N.Y.Fam. Ct.1995), in holding: "Only if a sexual lifestyle, homosexual or heterosexual, was shown to be detrimental to the child's well being would it be considered." In Sherman v. Sherman, 1994 WL 649148 (Tenn.Ct.App.1994) the Court of Appeals of Tennessee refused to restrict the visitation rights of a father to see his two adolescent daughters simply because he lived with his homosexual and HIV-infected brother. So too, In North v. North, 102 Md.App. 1, 648 A.2d 1025 (Md.App.1994), the Court of Special Appeals of Maryland, over strong dissents, held that a father's overnight visitation rights could not be denied because of fear the husband would display or discuss his homosexual lifestyle with his children.

For custody, the Virginia Supreme Court in Bottoms v. Bottoms, 249 Va. 410, 457 S.E.2d 102 (1995), reinstated the trial court's finding that living daily under conditions stemming from the active lesbianism practiced in the home by the mother living with her female lover, may impose a burden upon the child by reason of the "social condemnation" attached to such an arrangement that will inevitable afflict the child's relationship with its "peers and the community at large." The court then rejected the traditional parental presumption of custody and awarded custody of the girl to her grandmother. Subsequently, in a contest involving visitation, the Virginia Court of Appeals held that a parent's homosexuality does not per se render him or her an unfit parent. The appeals court held that the trial judge had misconstrued the case law by requiring that the visitation disposition consider only the mother's homosexuality. *See* Bottoms v. Bottoms, 1997 WL 421218 (1997).

Sexual orientation continues to appear as a factor in decisions affecting visitation, often with facts similar to *Cabalquinto. See, e.g., In re* Dorworth, 33 P.3d 1260 (Colo.App.2001), where the Colorado Court of Appeals held the trial judge in error for imposing limitations on a divorced, bisexual father's parenting time with his nine-year-old daughter without first determining if the daughter would be at risk without the limitations. The father should be able to incorporate the child into his home and social activities unless any of these would impair the child's physical or emotional development. A plethora of articles have arisen discussing the rights of gay and lesbian persons in such issues as custody and visitation pursuits. *See, e.g.,* Ruthann Robson, *Our Children: Kids of Queer Parents and Kids Who Are Queer: Looking at Sexual Minority Rights From a Different Perspective*, 64 ALB. L. REV. 915 (2001); Marc S. Spindelman, *Reorienting Bowers v. Hardwick,* 79 N.C. L. REV. 359 (2001); Tod Brower, *Of Courts and Closets: A Doctrinal and Empirical Analysis of Lesbian and Gay Identity in the*

Courts, 38 San Diego L. Rev. 565 (2001); William N. Eskridge, Jr., *No Promo Homo: the Sedimentation of Antigay Doctrine and the Channeling Effect of Judicial Review,* 75 N.Y.U. L. Rev. 1327 (2000); David Orentlicher, *Beyond Cloning: Expanding Reproductive Options for Same–Sex Couples,* 66 Brook. L. Rev. 651 (2000–2001); Mark Strasser, *Equal Protection at the Crossroads: On Baker, Common Benefits, and Facial Neutrality,* 42 Ariz. L. Rev. 935 (2000); Susan J. Becker, *Child Sexual Abuse Allegations Against a Lesbian or Gay Parent in a Custody or Visitation Dispute: Battling the Overt and Insidious Bias of Experts and Judges,* 74 Denv. U. L. Rev. 75 (1996).

Alison D. v. Virginia M.

Court of Appeals of New York, 1991.
77 N.Y.2d 651, 569 N.Y.S.2d 586, 572 N.E.2d 27.

■ Per Curiam.

. . .

Petitioner Alison D. and respondent Virginia M. established a relationship in September 1977 and began living together in March 1978.* In March 1980, they decided to have a child and agreed that respondent would be artificially inseminated. Together, they planned for the conception and birth of the child and agreed to share jointly all rights and responsibilities of child-rearing. In July 1981, respondent gave birth to a baby boy, A.D.M., who was given petitioner's last name as his middle name and respondent's last name became his last name. Petitioner shared in all birthing expenses and, after A.D.M.'s birth, continued to provide for his support. During A.D.M.'s first two years, petitioner and respondent jointly cared for and made decisions regarding the child.

In November 1983, when the child was 2 years and 4 months old, petitioner and respondent terminated their relationship and petitioner moved out of the home they jointly owned. Petitioner and respondent agreed to a visitation schedule whereby petitioner continued to see the child a few times a week. Petitioner also agreed to continue to pay one half of the mortgage and major household expenses. By this time, the child had referred to both respondent and petitioner as "mommy". Petitioner's visitation with the child continued until 1986, at which time respondent bought out petitioner's interest in the house and then began to restrict petitioner's visitation with the child. In 1987 petitioner moved to Ireland to pursue career opportunities, but continued her attempts to communicate with the child. Thereafter, respondent terminated all contact between petitioner and the child, returning all of petitioner's gifts and letters. No dispute exists that respondent is a fit parent. Petitioner commenced this

---

* Given the procedural posture of the case, the facts are those alleged by petitioner in her habeas corpus petition.

proceeding seeking visitation rights pursuant to Domestic Relations Law § 70.

Supreme Court dismissed the proceeding concluding that petitioner is not a parent under Domestic Relations Law § 70 and, given the concession that respondent is a fit parent, petitioner is not entitled to seek visitation pursuant to section 70. The Appellate Division affirmed . . .

Pursuant to Domestic Relations Law § 70 "either parent may apply to the supreme court for a writ of habeas corpus to have such minor child brought before such court; and [the court] may award the natural guardianship, charge and custody of such child to either parent * * * as the case may require". Although the Court is mindful of petitioner's understandable concern for and interest in the child and of her expectation and desire that her contact with the child would continue, she has no right under Domestic Relations Law § 70 to seek visitation and, thereby, limit or diminish the right of the concededly fit biological parent to choose with whom her child associates. She is not a "parent" within the meaning of section 70.

Petitioner concedes that she is not the child's "parent"; that is, she is not the biological mother of the child nor is she a legal parent by virtue of an adoption. Rather she claims to have acted as a "de facto" parent or that she should be viewed as a parent "by estoppel". Therefore, she claims she has standing to seek visitation rights. These claims, however, are insufficient under section 70. Traditionally, in this State it is the child's mother and father who, assuming fitness, have the right to the care and custody of their child, even in situations where the nonparent has exercised some control over the child with the parents' consent (see, Matter of Ronald FF. v. Cindy GG., 70 N.Y.2d 141, 144, 517 N.Y.S.2d 932, 511 N.E.2d 75, citing People ex rel. Kropp v. Shepsky, 305 N.Y. 465, 468–469, 113 N.E.2d 801). "It has long been recognized that, as between a parent and a third person, parental custody of a child may not be displaced absent grievous cause or necessity" (Matter of Ronald FF. v. Cindy GG., supra, 70 N.Y.2d at 144, 517 N.Y.S.2d 932, 511 N.E.2d 75; see also, Matter of Bennett v. Jeffreys, 40 N.Y.2d 543, 549, 387 N.Y.S.2d 821, 356 N.E.2d 277). To allow the courts to award visitation—a limited form of custody—to a third person would necessarily impair the parents' right to custody and control (id.). Petitioner concedes that respondent is a fit parent. Therefore she has no right to petition the court to displace the choice made by this fit parent in deciding what is in the child's best interests.

Section 70 gives parents the right to bring proceedings to ensure their proper exercise of their care, custody and control Where the Legislature deemed it appropriate, it gave other categories of persons standing to seek visitation and it gave the courts the power to determine whether an award of visitation would be in the child's best interests (see, e.g., Domestic Relations Law § 71 [special proceeding or habeas corpus to obtain visitation rights for siblings]; § 72 [special proceeding or habeas corpus to obtain visitation rights for grandparents]; . . .). We decline petitioner's invitation to read the term parent in section 70 to include categories of nonparents who have developed a relationship with a child or who have had prior relationships with a child's parents and who wish to continue visitation with the child. While one may dispute in an individual case whether it would be beneficial to a child to have continued contact with a nonparent, the Legislature did not in section 70 give such nonparent the opportunity to compel a fit parent to allow them to do so (see, Matter of Ronald FF. v. Cindy GG., 70 N.Y.2d 141, 517 N.Y.S.2d 932, 511 N.E.2d 75, supra; compare, Oregon Rev.Stat.Ann. § 109.119[1] [giving "(a)ny person including but not limited to a foster parent, stepparent, grandparent * * * who has established emotional ties creating a child-parent relationship with a child" the right to seek visitation or other right of custody]).

Accordingly, the order of the Appellate Division should be affirmed, with costs.

■ KAYE, JUDGE (dissenting).

The Court's decision, fixing biology[1] as the key to visitation rights, has impact far beyond this particular controversy, one that may affect a wide spectrum of relationships—including those of longtime heterosexual stepparents, "common-law" and nonheterosexual partners such as involved here, and even participants in scientific reproduction procedures. Estimates that more than 15.5 million children do not live with two biological parents, and that as many as 8 to 10 million children are born into families with a gay or lesbian parent, suggest just how widespread the impact may be (see, Polikoff, This Child Does Have Two Mothers: Redefining Parenthood to Meet the Needs of Children in Lesbian–Mother and other Nontraditional Families, 78 Geo.L.J. 459, 461, n. 2 [1990]; Bartlett, Rethinking Parenthood as an Exclusive Status: The Need for Legal Alternatives When the Premise of the Nuclear Family has Failed, 70 Va.L.Rev. 879, 880–881 [1984]; see generally, Developments in the Law—Sexual Orientation and the Law, 102 Harv.L.Rev. 1508, 1629 [1989]).

But the impact of today's decision falls hardest on the children of those relationships, limiting their opportunity to maintain bonds that may be crucial to their development. The majority's retreat from the courts' proper role—its tightening of rules that should in visitation petitions, above all, retain the capacity to take the children's interests into account—compels this dissent.

In focusing the difference, it is perhaps helpful to begin with what is not at issue. This is not a custody case, but solely a visitation petition. The issue on this appeal is not whether petitioner should actually have visitation rights. Nor is the issue the relationship between Alison D. and Virginia M. Rather, the sole issue is the relationship between Alison D. and A.D.M., in particular whether Alison D.'s petition for visitation should even be considered on its merits. I would conclude that the trial court had jurisdiction to hear the merits of this petition.

The relevant facts are amply described in the Court's opinion. Most significantly, Virginia M. agrees that, after long cohabitation with Alison D.

---

1. While the opinion speaks of biological and legal parenthood, this Court has not yet passed on the legality of adoption by a second mother.

and before A.D.M.'s conception, it was "explicitly planned that the child would be theirs to raise together." It is also uncontested that the two shared "financial and emotional preparations" for the birth, and that for several years Alison D. actually filled the role of coparent to A.D.M., both tangibly and intangibly. In all, a parent-child relationship—encouraged or at least condoned by Virginia M.—apparently existed between A.D.M. and Alison D. during the first six years of the child's life.

While acknowledging that relationship, the Court nonetheless proclaims powerlessness to consider the child's interest at all, because the word "parent" in the statute imposes an absolute barrier to Alison D.'s petition for visitation. That same conclusion would follow, as the Appellate Division dissenter noted, were the coparenting relationship one of 10 or more years, and irrespective of how close or deep the emotional ties might be between petitioner and child, or how devastating isolation might be to the child. I cannot agree that such a result is mandated by section 70, or any other law.

Domestic Relations Law § 70 provides a mechanism for "either parent" to bring a habeas corpus proceeding to determine a child's custody. Other State Legislatures, in comparable statutes, have defined "parent" specifically . . . Significantly, the Domestic Relations Law contains no such limitation. Indeed, it does not define the term "parent" at all. That remains for the courts to do, as often happens when statutory terms are undefined.

The majority insists, however, that, the word "parent" in this case can only be read to mean biological parent; the response "one fit parent" now forecloses all inquiry into the child's best interest, even in visitation proceedings. We have not previously taken such a hard line in these matters, but in the absence of express legislative direction have attempted to read otherwise undefined words of the statute so as to effectuate the legislative purposes. The Legislature has made plain an objective in section 70 to promote "the best interest of the child" and the child's "welfare and happiness." (Domestic Relations Law § 70.) Those words should not be ignored by us in defining standing for visitation purposes—they have not been in prior case law.

Domestic Relations Law § 70 was amended in 1964 to broaden the category of persons entitled to seek habeas corpus relief. Previously, only a husband or wife living within the State, and legally separated from the spouse, had standing to bring such a proceeding. The courts, however, refused to apply the statute so literally. In amending the statute to make domicile of the child the touchstone, and eliminate the separation requirement, the Legislature acted to bring section 70 into conformity with what the courts were already doing. . . .

This amendment to bring the statute into line with the practice reflects Supreme Court's equitable powers that complement the special habeas statute. In Finlay v. Finlay, 240 N.Y. 429, 433, 148 N.E. 624, this Court established that where the section 70 writ is denied to the petitioner seeking custody "there would remain his remedy by petition to the chancellor or to the court that has succeeded to the chancellor's prerogative [and] [n]othing in the habeas corpus act affects that jurisdiction." In such an action, the Chancellor "may act at the intervention or on the motion of a kinsman * * * but equally he may act at the instance of any one else." (240 N.Y., at 434, 148 N.E. 624.) Jurisdiction rests on the parens patriae power—concern for the welfare of the child. . . .

As the Court wrote in Matter of Bennett v. Jeffreys, 40 N.Y.2d 543, 546, 387 N.Y.S.2d 821, 356 N.E.2d 277—even in recognizing the superior right of a biological parent to the custody of her child—"when there is a conflict, the best interest of the child has always been regarded as superior to the right of parental custody. Indeed, analysis of the cases reveals a shifting of emphasis rather than a remaking of substance. This shifting reflects more the modern principle that a child is a person, and not a subperson over whom the parent has an absolute possessory interest."

Apart from imposing upon itself an unnecessarily restrictive definition of "parent," and apart from turning its back on a tradition of reading of section 70 so as to promote the welfare of the children, in accord with the parens patriae power, the Court also overlooks the significant distinction between visitation and custody proceedings.

While both are of special concern to the State, custody and visitation are significantly different.[2] Custody disputes implicate a parent's right to rear a child—with the child's corresponding right to be raised by a parent (see, Matter of Bennett v. Jeffreys, 40 N.Y.2d, at 546, 387 N.Y.S.2d 821, 356 N.E.2d 277, (supra)). Infringement of that right must be based on the fitness—more precisely the lack of fitness—of the custodial parent.

Visitation rights also implicate a right of the custodial parent, but it is the right to choose with whom the child associates (see, Matter of Ronald FF. v. Cindy GG., 70 N.Y.2d, at 144, 517 N.Y.S.2d 932, 511 N.E.2d 75, supra). Any burden on the exercise of that right must be based on the child's overriding need to maintain a particular relationship (see, Weiss v. Weiss, 52 N.Y.2d, at 174–175, 436 N.Y.S.2d 862, 418 N.E.2d 377, supra). Logically, the fitness concern present in custody disputes is irrelevant in visitation petitions, where continuing contact with the child rather than severing of a parental tie is in issue. For that reason, we refused to extend the Bennett "extraordinary circumstances" doctrine—which relates to the fitness of the custodial parent—to visitation petitions (Matter of Ronald FF. v. Cindy GG., 70 N.Y.2d 141, 517 N.Y.S.2d 932, 511 N.E.2d 75, supra).

The Court now takes the law a step beyond Ronald FF. by establishing the Bennett "extraordinary circumstances" test as the only way to reach the child's best interest in a section 70 proceeding. In that Ronald FF. determined that extraordinary circumstances are irrelevant in the visitation context, our holding today thus firmly closes the door on all consider-

---

2. The majority's opinion rests on a fundamental inconsistency. It cannot be that visitation is the same as custody—"a limited form of custody" (majority opn. at 656, at 588 of 569 N.Y.S.2d, at 29 of 572 N.E.2d)—and yet at the same time different from custody in that the "extraordinary circumstances" doctrine is inapplicable.

ation of the child's best interest in visitation proceedings such as the one before us, unless petitioner is a biological parent.

Of course there must be some limitation on who can petition for visitation. Domestic Relations Law § 70 specifies that the person must be the child's "parent," and the law additionally recognizes certain rights of biological and legal parents. Arguments that every dedicated caretaker could sue for visitation if the term "parent" were broadened, or that such action would necessarily effect sweeping change throughout the law, over-look and misportray the Court's role in defining otherwise undefined statutory terms to effect particular statutory purposes, and to do so narrowly, for those purposes only.

Countless examples of that process may be found in our case law, the Court looking to modern-day realities in giving definition to statutory concepts. Only recently, we defined the term "family" in the eviction provisions of the rent stabilization laws so as to advance the legislative objective, making abundantly clear that the definition was limited to the statute in issue and did not effect a wholesale change in the law (see, Braschi v. Stahl Assocs. Co., 74 N.Y.2d 201, 211–213, 544 N.Y.S.2d 784, 543 N.E.2d 49).

In discharging this responsibility, recent decisions from other jurisdictions, for the most part concerning visitation rights of stepparents, are instructive (see, e.g., Gribble v. Gribble, 583 P.2d 64 [Utah]; Spells v. Spells, 250 Pa.Super. 168, 378 A.2d 879). For example in Spells, 250 Pa.Super. at 172–173, 378 A.2d, at 881–882, the court fashioned a test for "parental status" or "in loco parentis" requiring that the petitioner demonstrate actual assumption of the parental role and discharge of parental responsibilities. It should be required that the relationship with the child came into being with the consent of the biological or legal parent, and that the petitioner at least have had joint custody of the child for a significant period of time (see, Rethinking Parenthood as an Exclusive Status, op. cit., 70 Va.L.Rev. at 945–946). Other factors likely should be added to constitute a test that protects all relevant interests—much as we did in Braschi. . . .

It is not my intention to spell out a definition but only to point out that it is surely within our competence to do so. It is indeed regrettable that we decline to exercise that authority in this visitation matter, given the explicit statutory objectives, the courts' power, and the fact that all consideration of the child's interest is, for the future, otherwise absolutely foreclosed.

I would remand the case to Supreme Court for an exercise of its discretion in determining whether Alison D. stands in loco parentis to A.D.M. and, if so, whether it is in the child's best interest to allow her the visitation rights she claims.

NOTE

Changes in cohabitation patterns have prompted an evolution in parental status. Two persons may now become parents through a contract to have an embryo genetically related to neither of them implanted in a third person. *In re* Marriage of Buzzanca, 61 Cal.App.4th 1410, 72 Cal.Rptr.2d 280 (1998); *In re* C.K.G., 173 S.W.3d 714 (Tenn. 2005)(holding that genetics is not the only factor establishing parenthood). The California Supreme Court has ruled that a woman who orally agreed to raise children born to her lesbian partner through artificial insemination from an anonymous sperm donor was nonetheless a parent to the resulting children. The crucial factor in establishing parenthood was the agreement between the two women and the resulting conduct that ratified the agreement. Elisa B. v. Superior Court, 37 Cal.4th 108, 33 Cal.Rptr.3d 46, 117 P.3d 660 (2005). Many of these cases evolve in the context of same sex relationships and the agreement between the two partners is written or oral. *See, e.g.,* King v. S.B., 837 N.E.2d 965 (Ind. 2005)(allowing woman to proceed with parental rights determination for child born when she and her lesbian partner consented to artificial insemination by anonymous donor); Jones v. Jones, 884 A.2d 915 (Pa. Super. Ct. 2005)(biological mother lost custody to child's de facto parent, the mother's former lesbian partner). For additional commentary, see generally David Orentlicher, *Beyond Cloning: Expanding Reproductive Options for Same–Sex Couples,* 66 Brook. L. Rev. 651 (2002–2001); Ryiah Lilith, *Comment, The G.I.F.T. of Two Biological and Legal Mothers,* 9 Am. U. J. Gender Soc. Pol'y & L. 207 (2001); John Charles Kunich, *Mother Frankenstein, Doctor Nature and the Environmental Law of Genetic Engineering,* 74 Cal. L. Rev. 807 (2001).

Troxel v. Granville

Supreme Court of the United States, 2000.
530 U.S. 57, 120 S.Ct. 2054, 147 L.Ed.2d 49.

■ Justice O'Connor announced the judgment of the Court and delivered an opinion, in which The Chief Justice, Justice Ginsburg, and Justice Breyer join.

Section 26.10.160(3) of the Revised Code of Washington permits "[a]ny person" to petition a superior court for visitation rights "at any time," and authorizes that court to grant such visitation rights whenever "visitation may serve the best interest of the child." Petitioners Jenifer and Gary Troxel petitioned a Washington Superior Court for the right to visit their grandchildren, Isabelle and Natalie Troxel. Respondent Tommie Granville, the mother of Isabelle and Natalie, opposed the petition. The case ultimately reached the Washington Supreme Court, which held that § 26.10.160(3) unconstitutionally interferes with the fundamental right of parents to rear their children.

Tommie Granville and Brad Troxel shared a relationship that ended in June 1991. The two never married, but they had two daughters, Isabelle and Natalie. Jenifer and Gary Troxel are Brad's parents, and thus the paternal grandparents of Isabelle and Natalie. After Tommie and Brad separated in 1991, Brad lived with his parents and regularly brought his daughters to his parents' home for weekend visitation. Brad committed suicide in May 1993. Although the Troxels at first continued to see Isabelle and Natalie on a regular basis after their son's death, Tommie Granville informed the Troxels in October 1993 that she wished to limit their visitation with her daughters to one short visit per month.

In December 1993, the Troxels commenced the present action by filing, in the Washington Superior Court for Skagit County, a petition to obtain visitation rights with Isabelle and Natalie. The Troxels filed their petition under two Washington statutes, Wash. Rev.Code §§ 26.09.240 and 26.10.160(3) (1994). Only the latter statute is at issue in this case. Section 26.10.160(3) provides: "Any person may petition the court for visitation rights at any time including, but not limited to, custody proceedings. The court may order visitation rights for any person when visitation may serve the best interest of the child whether or not there has been any change of circumstances." At trial, the Troxels requested two weekends of overnight visitation per month and two weeks of visitation each summer. Granville did not oppose visitation altogether, but instead asked the court to order one day of visitation per month with no overnight stay. In 1995, the Superior Court issued an oral ruling and entered a visitation decree ordering visitation one weekend per month, one week during the summer, and four hours on both of the petitioning grandparents' birthdays.

Granville appealed, during which time she married Kelly Wynn. Before addressing the merits of Granville's appeal, the Washington Court of Appeals remanded the case to the Superior Court for entry of written findings of fact and conclusions of law. On remand, the Superior Court found that visitation was in Isabelle and Natalie's best interests:

The Petitioners [the Troxels] are part of a large, central, loving family, all located in this area, and the Petitioners can provide opportunities for the children in the areas of cousins and music.

"... The court took into consideration all factors regarding the best interest of the children and considered all the testimony before it. The children would be benefitted from spending quality time with the Petitioners, provided that that time is balanced with time with the childrens' [sic] nuclear family. The court finds that the childrens' [sic] best interests are served by spending time with their mother and stepfather's other six children." App. 70a.

Approximately nine months after the Superior Court entered its order on remand, Granville's husband formally adopted Isabelle and Natalie.

The Washington Court of Appeals reversed the lower court's visitation order and dismissed the Troxels' petition for visitation, holding that non-parents lack standing to seek visitation under § 26.10.160(3) unless a custody action is pending. In the Court of Appeals' view, that limitation on nonparental visitation actions was "consistent with the constitutional restrictions on state interference with parents' fundamental liberty interest in the care, custody, and management of their children." 87 Wash.App., at 135, 940 P.2d, at 700 (internal quotation marks omitted). Having resolved the case on the statutory ground, however, the Court of Appeals did not expressly pass on Granville's constitutional challenge to the visitation statute.

The Washington Supreme Court granted the Troxels' petition for review and, after consolidating their case with two other visitation cases, affirmed. The court disagreed with the Court of Appeals' decision on the statutory issue and found that the plain language of § 26.10.160(3) gave the Troxels standing to seek visitation, irrespective of whether a custody action was pending. The Washington Supreme Court nevertheless agreed with the Court of Appeals' ultimate conclusion that the Troxels could not obtain visitation of Isabelle and Natalie pursuant to § 26.10.160(3). The court rested its decision on the Federal Constitution, holding that § 26.10.160(3) unconstitutionally infringes on the fundamental right of parents to rear their children. In the court's view, there were at least two problems with the nonparental visitation statute. First, according to the Washington Supreme Court, the Constitution permits a State to interfere with the right of parents to rear their children only to prevent harm or potential harm to a child. Section 26.10.160(3) fails that standard because it requires no threshold showing of harm. Id., at 15–20, 969 P.2d, at 28–30. Second, by allowing " 'any person' to petition for forced visitation of a child at 'any time' with the only requirement being that the visitation serve the best interest of the child," the Washington visitation statute sweeps too broadly. "It is not within the province of the state to make significant decisions concerning the custody of children merely because it could make a 'better' decision." Ibid., 969 P.2d, at 31. The Washington Supreme Court held that "[p]arents have a right to limit visitation of their children with third persons," and that between parents and judges, "the parents should be the ones to choose whether to expose their children to certain people or ideas." Four justices dissented from the Washington Supreme Court's holding on the constitutionality of the statute.

We granted certiorari, 527 U.S. 1069, 120 S.Ct. 11, 144 L.Ed.2d 842 (1999), and now affirm the judgment.

The demographic changes of the past century make it difficult to speak of an average American family. The composition of families varies greatly from household to household. While many children may have two married parents and grandparents who visit regularly, many other children are raised in single-parent households. In 1996, children living with only one parent accounted for 28 percent of all children under age 18 in the United States. U.S. Dept. of Commerce, Bureau of Census, Current Population Reports, 1997 Population Profile of the United States 27 (1998). Understandably, in these single-parent households, persons outside the nuclear family are called upon with increasing frequency to assist in the everyday tasks of child rearing. In many cases, grandparents play an important role. For example, in 1998, approximately 4 million children—or 5.6 percent of all children under age 18—lived in the household of their grandparents. U.S. Dept. of Commerce, Bureau of Census, Current Population Reports, Marital Status and Living Arrangements: March 1998 (Update), p. *i* (1998).

The nationwide enactment of nonparental visitation statutes is assuredly due, in some part, to the States' recognition of these changing realities of the American family. Because grandparents and other relatives undertake duties of a parental nature in many households, States have sought to ensure the welfare of the children therein by protecting the relationships those children form with such third parties. The States' nonparental visitation statutes are further supported by a recognition, which varies from State to State, that children should have the opportunity to benefit from relationships with statutorily specified persons—for example, their grandparents. The extension of statutory rights in this area to persons other than a child's parents, however, comes with an obvious cost. For example, the State's recognition of an independent third-party interest in a child can place a substantial burden on the traditional parent-child relationship. Contrary to Justice STEVENS' accusation, our description of state nonparental visitation statutes in these terms, of course, is not meant to suggest that "children are so much chattel." *Post,* at 2072 (dissenting opinion). Rather, our terminology is intended to highlight the fact that these statutes can present questions of constitutional import. In this case, we are presented with just such a question. Specifically, we are asked to decide whether § 26.10.160(3), as applied to Tommie Granville and her family, violates the Federal Constitution.

The Fourteenth Amendment provides that no State shall "deprive any person of life, liberty, or property, without due process of law." We have long recognized that the Amendment's Due Process Clause, like its Fifth Amendment counterpart, "guarantees more than fair process." The Clause also includes a substantive component that "provides heightened protection against government interference with certain fundamental rights and liberty interests." . . .

The liberty interest at issue in this case—the interest of parents in the care, custody, and control of their children—is perhaps the oldest of the fundamental liberty interests recognized by this Court. More than 75 years ago, in Meyer v. Nebraska, 262 U.S. 390, 399, 401, 43 S.Ct. 625, 67 L.Ed. 1042 (1923), we held that the "liberty" protected by the Due Process Clause includes the right of parents to "establish a home and bring up children" and "to control the education of their own." Two years later, in Pierce v. Society of Sisters, 268 U.S. 510, 534–535, 45 S.Ct. 571, 69 L.Ed. 1070 (1925), we again held that the "liberty of parents and guardians" includes the right "to direct the upbringing and education of children under their control." We explained in Pierce that "[t]he child is not the mere creature of the State; those who nurture him and direct his destiny have the right, coupled with the high duty, to recognize and prepare him for additional obligations." Id., at 535, 45 S.Ct. 571. We returned to the subject in Prince v. Massachusetts, 321 U.S. 158, 64 S.Ct. 438, 88 L.Ed. 645 (1944), and again confirmed that there is a constitutional dimension to the right of parents to direct the upbringing of their children. "It is cardinal with us that the custody, care and nurture of the child reside first in the parents, whose primary function and freedom include preparation for obligations the state can neither supply nor hinder." Id., at 166, 64 S.Ct. 438.

In subsequent cases also, we have recognized the fundamental right of parents to make decisions concerning the care, custody, and control of their children. See, *e.g.,* Stanley v. Illinois, 405 U.S. 645, 651, 92 S.Ct. 1208, 31 L.Ed.2d 551 (1972) ("It is plain that the interest of a parent in the companionship, care, custody, and management of his or her children 'come[s] to this Court with a momentum for respect lacking when appeal is made to liberties which derive merely from shifting economic arrangements' " (citation omitted)); Wisconsin v. Yoder, 406 U.S. 205, 232, 92 S.Ct. 1526, 32 L.Ed.2d 15 (1972) ("The history and culture of Western civilization reflect a strong tradition of parental concern for the nurture and upbringing of their children. This primary role of the parents in the upbringing of their children is now established beyond debate as an enduring American tradition"); Quilloin v. Walcott, 434 U.S. 246, 255, 98 S.Ct. 549, 54 L.Ed.2d 511 (1978) ("We have recognized on numerous occasions that the relationship between parent and child is constitutionally protected"); Parham v. J. R., 442 U.S. 584, 602, 99 S.Ct. 2493, 61 L.Ed.2d 101 (1979) ("Our jurisprudence historically has reflected Western civilization concepts of the family as a unit with broad parental authority over minor children. Our cases have consistently followed that course"); Santosky v. Kramer, 455 U.S. 745, 753, 102 S.Ct. 1388, 71 L.Ed.2d 599 (1982) (discussing "[t]he fundamental liberty interest of natural parents in the care, custody, and management of their child"); Glucksberg, supra, at 720, 117 S.Ct. 2258 ("In a long line of cases, we have held that, in addition to the specific freedoms protected by the Bill of Rights, the 'liberty' specially protected by the Due Process Clause includes the righ[t] . . . to direct the education and upbringing of one's children" (citing Meyer and Pierce)). In light of this extensive precedent, it cannot now be doubted that the Due Process Clause of the Fourteenth Amendment protects the fundamental right of parents to make decisions concerning the care, custody, and control of their children.

Section 26.10.160(3), as applied to Granville and her family in this case, unconstitutionally infringes on that fundamental parental right. The Washington nonparental visitation statute is breathtakingly broad. According to the statute's text, "*[a]ny person* may petition the court for visitation rights *at any time,*" and the court may grant such visitation rights whenever "visitation may serve *the best interest of the child.*" § 26.10.160(3) (emphases added). That language effectively permits any third party seeking visitation to subject any decision by a parent concerning visitation of the parent's children to state-court review. Once the visitation petition has been filed in court and the matter is placed before a judge, a parent's decision that visitation would not be in the child's best interest is accorded no deference. Section 26.10.160(3) contains no requirement that a court accord the parent's decision any presumption of validity or any weight whatsoever. Instead, the Washington statute places the best-interest determination solely in the hands of the judge. Should the judge disagree with the parent's estimation of the child's best interests, the judge's view necessarily prevails. Thus, in practical effect, in the State of Washington a court can disregard and overturn *any* decision by a fit custodial parent concerning visitation whenever a third party affected by the decision files a visitation petition, based solely on the judge's determination of the child's best interests. The Washington Supreme Court had the opportunity to give § 26.10.160(3)a narrower reading, but it declined to do so. See, *e.g.,* 137 Wash.2d, at 5, 969 P.2d, at 23 ("[The statute] allow[s] any person, at any time, to petition for visitation without regard to relationship to the child, without regard to changed circumstances, and without regard to harm"); id., at 20, 969 P.2d, at 30 ("[The statute] allow[s] 'any person' to petition for forced visitation of a child at 'any time' with the only requirement being that the visitation serve the best interest of the child").

Turning to the facts of this case, the record reveals that the Superior Court's order was based on precisely the type of mere disagreement we have just described and nothing more. The Superior Court's order was not founded on any special factors that might justify the State's interference with Granville's fundamental right to make decisions concerning the rearing of her two daughters. To be sure, this case involves a visitation petition filed by grandparents soon after the death of their son—the father of Isabelle and Natalie—but the combination of several factors here compels our conclusion that § 26.10.160(3), as applied, exceeded the bounds of the Due Process Clause.

First, the Troxels did not allege, and no court has found, that Granville was an unfit parent. That aspect of the case is important, for there is a presumption that fit parents act in the best interests of their children. As this Court explained in Parham:

> "[O]ur constitutional system long ago rejected any notion that a child is the mere creature of the State and, on the contrary, asserted that parents generally have the right, coupled with the high duty, to recognize and prepare [their children] for additional obligations.... The law's concept of the family rests on a presumption that parents possess what a child lacks in maturity, experience, and capacity for judgment required for making life's difficult decisions. More important, historically it has recognized that natural bonds of affection lead parents to act in the best interests of their children." 442 U.S., at 602, 99 S.Ct. 2493 (alteration in original) (internal quotation marks and citations omitted).

Accordingly, so long as a parent adequately cares for his or her children (*i.e.,* is fit), there will normally be no reason for the State to inject itself into the private realm of the family to further question the ability of that parent to make the best decisions concerning the rearing of that parent's children.

The problem here is not that the Washington Superior Court intervened, but that when it did so, it gave no special weight at all to Granville's determination of her daughters' best interests. More importantly, it appears that the Superior Court applied exactly the opposite presumption. In reciting its oral ruling after the conclusion of closing arguments, the Superior Court judge explained:

> "The burden is to show that it is in the best interest of the children to have some visitation and some quality time with their grandparents. I think in most situations a commonsensical approach [is that] it is normally in the best interest of the children to spend quality time with the grandparent, unless the grandparent, *[sic]* there are some issues or problems involved wherein the grandparents, their lifestyles are going to impact adversely upon the children. That certainly isn't the case here from what I can tell." Verbatim Report of Proceedings in *In re Troxel,* No. 93–3–00650–7 (Wash.Super.Ct., Dec. 14, 19, 1994), p. 213 (hereinafter Verbatim Report).

The judge's comments suggest that he presumed the grandparents' request should be granted unless the children would be "impact[ed] adversely." In effect, the judge placed on Granville, the fit custodial parent, the burden of *disproving* that visitation would be in the best interest of her daughters. The judge reiterated moments later: "I think [visitation with the Troxels] would be in the best interest of the children and I haven't been shown it is not in [the] best interest of the children." Id., at 214, 113 S.Ct. 1439.

The decisional framework employed by the Superior Court directly contravened the traditional presumption that a fit parent will act in the best interest of his or her child. In that respect, the court's presumption failed to provide any protection for Granville's fundamental constitutional right to make decisions concerning the rearing of her own daughters. Cf., *e.g.,* Cal. Fam.Code Ann. § 3104(e) (West 1994) (rebuttable presumption that grandparent visitation is not in child's best interest if parents agree that visitation rights should not be granted); Me.Rev.Stat. Ann., Tit. 19A, § 1803(3) (1998) (court may award grandparent visitation if in best interest of child and "would not significantly interfere with any parent-child relationship or with the parent's rightful authority over the child"); Minn.Stat. § 257.022(2)(a)(2) (1998) (court may award grandparent visitation if in best interest of child and "such visitation would not interfere with the parent-child relationship"); Neb.Rev.Stat. § 43–1802(2) (1998) (court must find "by clear and convincing evidence" that grandparent visitation "will not adversely interfere with the parent-child relationship"); R.I. Gen. Laws § 15–5–24.3(a)(2)(v) (Supp.1999) (grandparent must rebut, by clear and convincing evidence, presumption that parent's decision to refuse grandparent visitation was reasonable); Utah Code Ann. § 30–5–2(2)(e) (1998) (same); Hoff v. Berg, 595 N.W.2d 285, 291–292 (N.D.1999) (holding North Dakota grandparent visitation statute unconstitutional because State has no "compelling interest in presuming visitation rights of grandparents to an unmarried minor are in the child's best interests and forcing parents to accede to court-ordered grandparental visitation unless the parents are first able to prove such visitation is not in the best interests of their minor child"). In an ideal world, parents might always seek to cultivate the bonds between grandparents and their grandchildren. Needless to say, however, our world is far from perfect, and in it the decision whether such an intergenerational relationship would be beneficial in any specific case is for the parent to make in the first instance. And, if a fit parent's decision of the kind at issue here becomes subject to judicial review, the court must accord at least some special weight to the parent's own determination.

Finally, we note that there is no allegation that Granville ever sought to cut off visitation entirely. Rather, the present dispute originated when Granville informed the Troxels that she would prefer to restrict their visitation with Isabelle and Natalie to one short visit per month and special holidays. See 87 Wash.App., at 133, 940 P.2d, at 699; Verbatim Report 12. In the Superior Court proceedings Granville did not oppose visitation but instead asked that the duration of any visitation order be shorter than that requested by the Troxels. While the Troxels requested two weekends per month and two full weeks in the summer, Granville asked the Superior Court to order only one day of visitation per month (with no overnight stay) and participation in the Granville family's holiday celebrations. See 87 Wash.App., at 133, 940 P.2d, at 699; Verbatim Report 9 ("Right off the bat we'd like to say that our position is that grandparent visitation is in the best interest of the children. It is a matter of how much and how it is going to be structured") (opening statement by Granville's attorney). The Superior Court gave no weight to Granville's having assented to visitation even before the filing of any visitation petition or subsequent court intervention. The court instead rejected Granville's proposal and settled on a middle ground, ordering one weekend of visitation per month, one week in the summer, and time on both of the petitioning grandparents' birthdays. See 87 Wash.App., at 133–134, 940 P.2d, at 699; Verbatim Report 216–221. Significantly, many other States expressly provide by statute that courts may not award visitation unless a parent has denied (or unreasonably denied) visitation to the concerned third party. See, *e.g.,* Miss.Code Ann. § 93–16–3(2)(a) (1994) (court must find that "the parent or custodian of the child unreasonably denied the grandparent visitation rights with the child"); Ore.Rev.Stat. § 109.121(1)(a)(B) (1997) (court may award visitation if the "custodian of the child has denied the grandparent reasonable opportunity to visit the child"); R.I. Gen. Laws § 15–5–24.3(a)(2)(iii)–(iv) (Supp.1999) (court must find that parents prevented grandparent from visiting grandchild and that "there is no other way the petitioner is able to visit his or her grandchild without court intervention").

Considered together with the Superior Court's reasons for awarding visitation to the Troxels, the combination of these factors demonstrates that the visitation order in this case was an unconstitutional infringement on Granville's fundamental right to make decisions concerning the care, custody, and control of her two daughters. The Washington Superior Court failed to accord the determination of Granville, a fit custodial parent, any material weight. In fact, the Superior Court made only two formal findings in support of its visitation order. First, the Troxels "are part of a large, central, loving family, all located in this area, and the [Troxels] can provide opportunities for the children in the areas of cousins and music." App. 70a. Second, "[t]he children would be benefitted from spending quality time with the [Troxels], provided that that time is balanced with time with the childrens' [sic] nuclear family." *Ibid*. These slender findings, in combination with the court's announced presumption in favor of grandparent visitation and its failure to accord significant weight to Granville's already having offered meaningful visitation to the Troxels, show that this case involves nothing more than a simple disagreement between the Washington Superior Court and Granville concerning her children's best interests. The Superior Court's announced reason for ordering one week of visitation in the summer demonstrates our conclusion well: "I look back on some personal experiences.... We always spen[t] as kids a week with one set of grandparents and another set of grandparents, [and] it happened to work out in our family that [it] turned out to be an enjoyable experience. Maybe that can, in this family, if that is how it works out." Verbatim Report 220–221. As we have explained, the Due Process Clause does not permit a State to infringe on the fundamental right of parents to make childrearing decisions simply because a state judge believes a "better" decision could be made. Neither the Washington nonparental visitation statute generally—which places no limits on either the persons who may petition for visitation or the circumstances in which such a petition may be granted—nor the Superior Court in this specific case required anything more. Accordingly, we hold that § 26.10.160(3), as applied in this case, is unconstitutional.

Because we rest our decision on the sweeping breadth of § 26.10.160(3) and the application of that broad, unlimited power in this case, we do not consider the primary constitutional question passed on by the Washington Supreme Court—whether the Due Process Clause requires all nonparental visitation statutes to include a showing of harm or potential harm to the child as a condition precedent to granting visitation. We do not, and need not, define today the precise scope of the parental due process right in the visitation context.... Because much state-court adjudication in this context occurs on a case-by-case basis, we would be hesitant to hold that specific nonparental visitation statutes violate the Due Process Clause as a *per se* matter.

．　．　．

Accordingly, the judgment of the Washington Supreme Court is affirmed.

．　．　．

■ Justice Stevens, dissenting.

The Court today wisely declines to endorse either the holding or the reasoning of the Supreme Court of Washington. In my opinion, the Court would have been even wiser to deny certiorari. Given the problematic character of the trial court's decision and the uniqueness of the Washington statute, there was no pressing need to review a State Supreme Court decision that merely requires the state legislature to draft a better statute.

Having decided to address the merits, however, the Court should begin by recognizing that the State Supreme Court rendered a federal constitutional judgment holding a state law invalid on its face. In light of that judgment, I believe that we should confront the federal questions presented directly. For the Washington statute is not made facially invalid either because it may be invoked by too many hypothetical plaintiffs, or because it leaves open the possibility that someone may be permitted to sustain a relationship with a child without having to prove that serious harm to the child would otherwise result.

.   .   .

The task of reviewing a trial court's application of a state statute to the particular facts of a case is one that should be performed in the first instance by the state appellate courts. In this case, because of their views of the Federal Constitution, the Washington state appeals courts have yet to decide whether the trial court's findings were adequate under the statute.... Any as-applied critique of the trial court's judgment that this Court might offer could only be based upon a guess about the state courts' application of that State's statute, and an independent assessment of the facts in this case—both judgments that we are ill-suited and ill-advised to make.

.   .   .

As I read the State Supreme Court's opinion, In re Smith, 137 Wash.2d 1, 19–20, 969 P.2d 21, 30–31 (1998), its interpretation of the Federal Constitution made it unnecessary to adopt a definitive construction of the statutory text, or, critically, to decide whether the statute had been correctly applied in this case. In particular, the state court gave no content to the phrase, "best interest of the child," Wash. Rev.Code § 26.10.160(3) (Supp.1996)—content that might well be gleaned from that State's own statutes or decisional law employing the same phrase in different contexts, and from the myriad other state statutes and court decisions at least nominally applying the same standard.

.   .   .

We are thus presented with the unconstrued terms of a state statute and a State Supreme Court opinion that, in my view, significantly misstates the effect of the Federal Constitution upon any construction of that statute. Given that posture, I believe the Court should identify and correct the two flaws in the reasoning of the state court's majority opinion, and remand for further review of the trial court's disposition of this specific case.

In my view, the State Supreme Court erred in its federal constitutional analysis because neither the provision granting "any person" the right to petition the court for visitation, 137 Wash.2d, at 20, 969 P.2d, at 30, nor the absence of a provision requiring a "threshold . . . finding of harm to the child," ibid., provides a sufficient basis for holding that the statute is invalid in all its applications. I believe that a facial challenge should fail whenever a statute has "a 'plainly legitimate sweep,'" Washington v. Glucksberg, 521 U.S. 702, 739–740 and n. 7, 117 S.Ct. 2258 (1997) (STEVENS, J., concurring in judgment).... Under the Washington statute, there are plainly any number of cases—indeed, one suspects, the most common to arise—in which the "person" among "any" seeking visitation is a once-custodial caregiver, an intimate relation, or even a genetic parent. Even the Court would seem to agree that in many circumstances, it would be constitutionally permissible for a court to award some visitation of a child to a parent or previous caregiver in cases of parental separation or divorce, cases of disputed custody, cases involving temporary foster care or guardianship, and so forth. As the statute plainly sweeps in a great deal of the permissible, the State Supreme Court majority incorrectly concluded that a statute authorizing "any person" to file a petition seeking visitation privileges would invariably run afoul of the Fourteenth Amendment.

The second key aspect of the Washington Supreme Court's holding— that the Federal Constitution requires a showing of actual or potential "harm" to the child before a court may order visitation continued over a parent's objections—finds no support in this Court's case law. While, as the Court recognizes, the Federal Constitution certainly protects the parent-child relationship from arbitrary impairment by the State, see *infra,* at 2071–2072 we have never held that the parent's liberty interest in this relationship is so inflexible as to establish a rigid constitutional shield, protecting every arbitrary parental decision from any challenge absent a threshold finding of harm.... The presumption that parental decisions generally serve the best interests of their children is sound, and clearly in the normal case the parent's interest is paramount. But even a fit parent is capable of treating a child like a mere possession.

. . .

Cases like this do not present a bipolar struggle between the parents and the State over who has final authority to determine what is in a child's best interests. There is at a minimum a third individual, whose interests are implicated in every case to which the statute applies—the child.

. . .

Despite this Court's repeated recognition of . . . significant parental liberty interests, these interests have never been seen to be without limits. In Lehr v. Robertson, 463 U.S. 248, 103 S.Ct. 2985, 77 L.Ed.2d 614 (1983), for example, this Court held that a putative biological father who had never established an actual relationship with his child did not have a constitutional right to notice of his child's adoption by the man who had married the child's mother. As this Court had recognized in an earlier case, a parent's liberty interests " 'do not spring full-blown from the biological connection between parent and child. They require relationships more enduring.' " Id., at 260, 103 S.Ct. 2985 (quoting Caban v. Mohammed, 441 U.S. 380, 397, 99 S.Ct. 1760, 60 L.Ed.2d 297 (1979)).

Conversely, in Michael H. v. Gerald D., 491 U.S. 110, 109 S.Ct. 2333, 105 L.Ed.2d 91 (1989), this Court concluded that despite both biological parenthood and an established relationship with a young child, a father's due process liberty interest in maintaining some connection with that child was not sufficiently powerful to overcome a state statutory presumption that the husband of the child's mother was the child's parent. As a result of the presumption, the biological father could be denied even visitation with the child because, as a matter of state law, he was not a "parent." A plurality of this Court there recognized that the parental liberty interest was a function, not simply of "isolated factors" such as biology and intimate connection, but of the broader and apparently independent interest in family. See, *e.g.*, id., at 123, 109 S.Ct. 2333; see also Lehr, 463 U.S., at 261, 103 S.Ct. 2985; Smith v. Organization of Foster Families For Equality & Reform, 431 U.S. 816, 842–847, 97 S.Ct. 2094, 53 L.Ed.2d 14 (1977); Moore v. East Cleveland, 431 U.S. 494, 498–504, 97 S.Ct. 1932, 52 L.Ed.2d 531 (1977).

. . .

While this Court has not yet had occasion to elucidate the nature of a child's liberty interests in preserving established familial or family-like bonds, 491 U.S., at 130, 109 S.Ct. 2333 (reserving the question), it seems to me extremely likely that, to the extent parents and families have fundamental liberty interests in preserving such intimate relationships, so, too, do children have these interests, and so, too, must their interests be balanced in the equation. At a minimum, our prior cases recognizing that children are, generally speaking, constitutionally protected actors require that this Court reject any suggestion that when it comes to parental rights, children are so much chattel ... The constitutional protection against arbitrary state interference with parental rights should not be extended to prevent the States from protecting children against the arbitrary exercise of parental authority that is not in fact motivated by an interest in the welfare of the child.

. . .

This is not, of course, to suggest that a child's liberty interest in maintaining contact with a particular individual is to be treated invariably as on a par with that child's parents' contrary interests. Because our substantive due process case law includes a strong presumption that a parent will act in the best interest of her child, it would be necessary, were the state appellate courts actually to confront a challenge to the statute as applied, to consider whether the trial court's assessment of the "best interest of the child" incorporated that presumption.

. . .

But presumptions notwithstanding, we should recognize that there may be circumstances in which a child has a stronger interest at stake than mere protection from serious harm caused by the termination of visitation by a "person" other than a parent. The almost infinite variety of family relationships that pervade our ever-changing society strongly counsel against the creation by this Court of a constitutional rule that treats a biological parent's liberty interest in the care and supervision of her child as an isolated right that may be exercised arbitrarily. It is indisputably the business of the States, rather than a federal court employing a national standard, to assess in the first instance the relative importance of the conflicting interests that give rise to disputes such as this. Far from guaranteeing that parents' interests will be trammeled in the sweep of cases arising under the statute, the Washington law merely gives an individual—with whom a child may have an established relationship—the procedural right to ask the State to act as arbiter, through the entirely well-known best-interests standard, between the parent's protected interests and the child's. It seems clear to me that the Due Process Clause of the Fourteenth Amendment leaves room for States to consider the impact on a child of possibly arbitrary parental decisions that neither serve nor are motivated by the best interests of the child.

Accordingly, I respectfully dissent.

■ [The concurring opinions of JUSTICES SOUTER and THOMAS, and the dissenting opinions of JUSTICES KENNEDY and SCALIA are omitted.]

CALIFORNIA FAMILY CODE (West 2004)

§ 3101. Stepparent's visitation rights

(a) Notwithstanding any other provision of law, the court may grant reasonable visitation to a stepparent, if visitation by the stepparent is determined to be in the best interest of the minor child.

(b) If a protective order, as defined in Section 6218, has been directed to a stepparent to whom visitation may be granted pursuant to this section, the court shall consider whether the best interest of the child requires that any visitation by the stepparent be denied.

(c) Visitation rights may not be ordered under this section that would conflict with a right of custody or visitation of a birth parent who is not a party to the proceeding.

(d) As used in this section:

(1) "Birth parent" means "birth parent" as defined in Section 8512.

(2) "Stepparent" means a person who is a party to the marriage that is the subject of the proceeding, with respect to a minor child of the other party to the marriage.

§ 3102. Deceased parent; visitation rights of close relatives; adoption of child

(a) If either parent of an unemancipated minor child is deceased, the children, siblings, parents, and grandparents of the deceased parent may be granted reasonable visitation with the child during the child's minority upon a finding that the visitation would be in the best interest of the minor child.

(b) In granting visitation pursuant to this section to a person other than a grandparent of the child, the court shall consider the amount of personal contact between the person and the child before the application for the visitation order.

(c) This section does not apply if the child has been adopted by a person other than a stepparent or grandparent of the child. Any visitation rights granted pursuant to this section before the adoption of the child automatically terminate if the child is adopted by a person other than a stepparent or grandparent of the child.

§ 3104. Grandparent's rights; petition by grandparent

(a) On petition to the court by a grandparent of a minor child, the court may grant reasonable visitation rights to the grandparent if the court does both of the following:

(1) Finds that there is a preexisting relationship between the grandparent and the grandchild that has engendered a bond such that visitation is in the best interest of the child.

(2) Balances the interest of the child in having visitation with the grandparent against the right of the parents to exercise their parental authority.

(b) A petition for visitation under this section may not be filed while the natural or adoptive parents are married, unless one or more of the following circumstances exist:

(1) The parents are currently living separately and apart on a permanent or indefinite basis.

(2) One of the parents has been absent for more than one month without the other spouse knowing the whereabouts of the absent spouse.

(3) One of the parents joins in the petition with the grandparents.

(4) The child is not residing with either parent.

At any time that a change of circumstances occurs such that none of these circumstances exist, the parent or parents may move the court to terminate grandparental visitation and the court shall grant the termination.

(c) The petitioner shall give notice of the petition to each of the parents of the child, any stepparent, and any person who has physical custody of the child, by personal service pursuant to Section 415.10 of the Code of Civil Procedure.

(d) If a protective order as defined in Section 6218 has been directed to the grandparent during the pendency of the proceeding, the court shall consider whether the best interest of the child requires that any visitation by that grandparent should be denied.

(e) There is a rebuttable presumption that the visitation of a grandparent is not in the best interest of a minor child if the natural or adoptive parents agree that the grandparent should not be granted visitation rights.

(f) There is a rebuttable presumption affecting the burden of proof that the visitation of a grandparent is not in the best interest of a minor child if the parent who has been awarded sole legal and physical custody of the child in another proceeding or with whom the child resides if there is currently no operative custody order objects to visitation by the grandparent.

(g) Visitation rights may not be ordered under this section if that would conflict with a right of custody or visitation of a birth parent who is not a party to the proceeding.

(h) Visitation ordered pursuant to this section shall not create a basis for or against a change of residence of the child, but shall be one of the factors for the court to consider in ordering a change of residence.

(i) When a court orders grandparental visitation pursuant to this section, the court in its discretion may, based upon the relevant circumstances of the case:

(1) Allocate the percentage of grandparental visitation between the parents for purposes of the calculation of child support pursuant to the statewide uniform guideline (Article 2 (commencing with Section 4050) of Chapter 2 of Part 2 of Division 9).

(2) Notwithstanding Sections 3930 and 3951, order a parent or grandparent to pay to the other, an amount for the support of the child or grandchild. For purposes of this paragraph, "support" means costs related to visitation such as any of the following:

(A) Transportation.

(B) Provision of basic expenses for the child or grandchild, such as medical expenses, day care costs, and other necessities.

(j) As used in this section, "birth parent" means "birth parent" as defined in Section 8512.

NOTE

Third party visitation statutes, to include the one in *Troxel* and the three in the California Family Code listed *supra*, are common in the state codes; especially in the case of grandparents, they are very often the subject of litigation. Following *Troxel*, states such as Missouri have interpreted the Supreme Court's decision. That is, that parents have a fundamental constitutional right to rear their children, including who shall educate and socialize them. McRaven v. Thomsen, 55 S.W.3d 419 (Mo.App.2001). But an Illinois court sustained its own state grandparent visitation statute, saying that the issue only arises in the context of when judicial intervention is sought. Whenever this happens, for whatever reason, the court must look to the best interest of the child and this may include the possibility of grandparent visitation as long as there are specific relevant factors to be considered. The Illinois statute has a list of factors that the court must consider in determining the best interest of the child and this distinguishes the statute from the Washington state statute in *Troxel*. In re Mehring, 324 Ill.App.3d 262, 258 Ill.Dec. 28, 755 N.E.2d 109 (2001). *See also* State ex rel. Brandon L. v. Moats, 209 W.Va. 752, 551 S.E.2d 674 (2001), upholding statute in part because it provides a list of 12 specific factors in making a determination of what is in the child's best interest. And in Zeman v. Stanford, 789 So.2d 798 (Miss.2001), the state Supreme Court upheld the Mississippi statute in part because of identifiable factors.

Other states have decided to reconsider visitation decision made prior to *Troxel*. For example, an Indiana court interprets *Troxel* as requiring a presumption that a fit parent acts in the best interest of his or her child or children and the grandparent must rebut that presumption before visitation may be ordered against the wishes of the parent. Crafton v. Gibson, 752 N.E.2d 78 (Ind.Ct.App.2001). A Kansas Supreme Court decision provides the parent with a presumption that he or she acts in the best interest of the child and found its statute unconstitutional because it did not afford the parent that presumption prior to ordering visitation by a third party. State Dept. of Social and Rehab. Services v. Paillet, 270 Kan. 646, 16 P.3d 962 (2001). What is the difference between the Illinois and the Indiana/Kansas approach? Which of the two approaches best conforms to *Troxel*? Does it matter if the statute allows visitation for "any person" or is restricted to grandparents? *See, e.g.*, Punsly v. Ho, 87 Cal.App.4th 1099, 105 Cal.Rptr.2d 139 (2001), holding that state statute allowing visitation rights to a deceased parent's blood relatives if such visitation is found in the child's best interest is unconstitutional because it unduly infringes the parent's fundamental rights. Furthermore, any order of visitation over the objection of the parent must survive strict scrutiny that the parent was not acting in the best interest of the child.

For a review, *see* David D. Meyer, *Lochner Redeemed: Family Privacy After Troxel and Carhart*, 48 UCLA L. REV. 1125 (2001); Maegen E. Peek, Note. *Grandparent Visitation Statutes: Do Legislatures Know the Way to Cary the Sleigh Through the Wide and Drifting Law?*, 53 FLA. L. REV. 321 (2001); Eric B. Martin, Comment. *Grandma Got Run Over by the Supreme Court: Suggestions for Constitutional Nonparental Visitation Statute After (Troxel v. Granville, 530 U.S. 57, 120 S.Ct. 2054, 147 L.Ed.2d 49 (2000))*, 76 WASH. L. REV. 571 (2001); Sara Elizabeth Culley, *Legislative Reform. Troxel v. Granville and Its Effect on the Future of Grandparent Visitation Statutes*, 27 J. LEGIS. 237 (2001).

CALIFORNIA FAMILY CODE (West 2004)

§ 3170. Setting matters for mediation; guidelines for handling domestic violence cases

(a) If it appears on the face of a petition, application, or other pleading to obtain or modify a temporary or permanent custody or visitation order that custody, visitation, or both are contested, the court shall set the contested issues for mediation.

(b) Domestic violence cases shall be handled by Family Court Services in accordance with a separate written protocol approved by the Judicial Council. The Judicial Council shall adopt guidelines for services, other than services provided under this chapter, that counties may offer to parents who have been unable to resolve their disputes. These services may include, but are not limited to, parent education programs, booklets, videotapes, or referrals to additional community resources.

§ 3171.   Stepparent or grandparent visitation; setting matter for mediation; waiver of parental right to object or require a hearing

(a) If a stepparent or grandparent has petitioned, or otherwise applied, for a visitation order pursuant to Chapter 5 (commencing with Section 3100), the court shall set the matter for mediation.

(b) A natural or adoptive parent who is not a party to the proceeding is not required to participate in the mediation proceeding, but failure to participate is a waiver of that parent's right to object to a settlement reached by the other parties during mediation or to require a hearing on the matter.

E.   CONTENDING WITH THE ADVERSARY PROCESS

1.   APPOINTMENT OF COUNSEL TO REPRESENT CHILD

CALIFORNIA FAMILY CODE (West 2004)

§ 3150.   Appointment of private counsel

(a) If the court determines that it would be in the best interest of the minor child, the court may appoint private counsel to represent the interests of the child in a custody or visitation proceeding.

(b) Upon entering an appearance on behalf of a child pursuant to this chapter, counsel shall continue to represent that child unless relieved by the court upon the substitution of other counsel by the court or for cause.

§ 3151.5.   Judicial determinations of custody or visitation; consideration of statements by child's counsel

If a child is represented by court appointed counsel, at every hearing in which the court makes a judicial determination regarding custody or visitation the court shall consider any statement of issues and contentions of the child's counsel. Any party may subpoena as a witness any person listed in the statement of issues and contentions as having provided information to the attorney, but the attorney shall not be called as a witness.

§ 3151.   Duties and rights of private counsel

(a) The child's counsel appointed under this chapter is charged with the representation of the child's best interests. The role of the child's counsel is to gather facts that bear on the best interests of the child, and present those facts to the court, including the child's wishes when counsel deems it appropriate for consideration by the court pursuant to Section 3042. The counsel's duties, unless under the circumstances it is inappropriate to exercise the duty, include interviewing the child, reviewing the court files and all accessible relevant records available to both parties, and making any further investigations as the counsel considers necessary to ascertain facts relevant to the custody or visitation hearings.

(b) At the court's request, counsel shall prepare a written statement of issues and contentions setting forth the facts that bear on the best interests of the child. The statement shall set forth a summary of information received by counsel, a list of the sources of information, the results of the counsel's investigation, and such other matters as the court may direct. The statement of issues and contentions shall not contain any communication subject to Section 954 of the Evidence Code. The statement of issues and contentions shall be filed with the court and submitted to the parties or their attorneys of record at least 10 days before the hearing, unless the court orders otherwise. At the court's request, counsel may orally state the wishes of the child if that information is not a privileged communication subject to Section 954 of the Evidence Code, for consideration by the court pursuant to Section 3042. Counsel shall not be called as a witness in the proceeding. Counsel may introduce and examine counsel's own witnesses, present arguments to the court concerning the child's welfare, and participate further in the proceeding to the degree necessary to represent the child adequately. In consultation with representatives of the Family Law Section of the State Bar and the Senate and Assembly Judiciary Committees, the Judicial Council may specify standards for the preparation of the statement of issues and contentions and may promulgate a model statement of issues and contentions, which shall include simple instructions regarding how to subpoena a witness, and a blank subpoena form.

(c) The child's counsel shall have the following rights:

(1) Reasonable access to the child.

(2) Standing to seek affirmative relief on behalf of the child.

(3) Notice of any proceeding, and all phases of that proceeding, including a request for examination affecting the child.

(4) The right to take any action that is available to a party to the proceeding, including, but not limited to, the following: filing pleadings, making evidentiary objections, and presenting evidence and being heard in the proceeding, which may include, but shall not be limited to, presenting motions and orders to show cause, and participating in settlement conferences, trials, seeking writs, appeals, and arbitrations.

(5) Access to the child's medical, dental, mental health, and other health care records, school and educational records, and the right to interview school personnel, caretakers, health care providers, mental health professionals, and others who have assessed the child or provided care to the child. The release of this information to counsel shall not constitute a waiver of the confidentiality of the reports, files, and any disclosed communications. Counsel may interview mediators; however, the provisions of Sections 3177 and 3182 shall apply.

(6) The right to reasonable advance notice of and the right to refuse any physical or psychological examination or evaluation, for purposes of the proceeding, which has not been ordered by the court.

(7) The right to assert or waive any privilege on behalf of the child.

(8) The right to seek independent psychological or physical examination or evaluation of the child for purposes of the pending proceeding, upon approval by the court.

§ 3153. Compensation and expenses of private counsel

(a) If the court appoints counsel under this chapter to represent the child, counsel shall receive a reasonable sum for compensation and expenses, the amount of which shall be determined by the court. Except as provided in subdivision (b), this amount shall be paid by the parties in the proportions the court deems just.

(b) Upon its own motion or that of a party, the court shall determine whether both parties together are financially unable to pay all or a portion of the cost of counsel appointed pursuant to this chapter, and the portion of the cost of that counsel which the court finds the parties are unable to pay shall be paid by the county. The Judicial Council shall adopt guidelines to assist in determining financial eligibility for county payment of counsel appointed by the court pursuant to this chapter.

NOTE

How often should children who are the subjects of custody disputes be represented by independent counsel? In some special instances, such as situations involving child abuse, such representation is not uncommon. However, broadening the scope of such appointments is being advocated by many today. One argument in favor of this is that without such representation children may be the pawns in negotiations involving other matters, such as property.

Appointment of a guardian *ad litem* is within the authority of courts in many jurisdictions today when there are specific conflicts of interest between parent and child, but there is often uncertainty about the exact role of such a guardian, particularly with regard to matters going beyond the specific item in conflict. *See, e.g.,* Knock v. Knock, 224 Conn. 776, 621 A.2d 267 (1993). Some see it as little more than demanding strict proof of facts involving the child. Although it is quite common, though not always necessary, that a guardian ad litem is an attorney, many persons in the role do not consider themselves as occupying a traditional attorney-client role in the sense that the their role is to follow the preferences or directions of their client (in this case, the child), whose prime concern might be assuring that the parents do not obtain a divorce. If the role is a very limited one, however, it can appropriately be asked whether merely having one more person offer a personal assessment materially improves a custody hearing, or even whether this usurps the role of the judge. There is the further concern about "running up the meter" by adding what can be significant expenses that usually are assessed against the parties if they can afford to pay them.

2. COUNSELING

FLORIDA STATUTES ANN. (West 2007)

§ 61.21. Parenting course authorized; fees; required attendance authorized; contempt

(1) Legislative findings; purpose.—It is the finding of the Legislature that:

(a) A large number of children experience the separation or divorce of their parents each year. Parental conflict related to divorce is a societal concern because children suffer potential short-term and long-term detrimental economic, emotional, and educational effects during this difficult period of family transition. This is particularly true when parents engage in lengthy legal conflict.

(b) Parents are more likely to consider the best interests of their children when determining parental arrangements if courts provide families with information regarding the process by which courts make decisions on issues affecting their children and suggestions as to how parents may ease the coming adjustments in family structure for their children.

(c) It has been found to be beneficial to parents who are separating or divorcing to have available an educational program that will provide general information regarding:

1. The issues and legal procedures for resolving custody and child support disputes.

2. The emotional experiences and problems of divorcing adults.

3. The family problems and the emotional concerns and needs of the children.

4. The availability of community services and resources.

(d) Parents who are separating or divorcing are more likely to receive maximum benefit from a program if they attend such program at the earliest stages of their dispute, before extensive litigation occurs and adversarial positions are assumed or intensified.

(2) The Department of Children and Family Services shall approve a parenting course which shall be a course of a minimum of 4 hours designed to educate, train, and assist divorcing parents in regard to the consequences of divorce on parents and children.

(a) The parenting course referred to in this section shall be named the Parent Education and Family Stabilization Course and may include, but need not be limited to, the following topics as they relate to court actions between parents involving custody, care, visitation, and support of a child or children:

1.   Legal aspects of deciding child-related issues between parents.

2.   Emotional aspects of separation and divorce on adults.

3.   Emotional aspects of separation and divorce on children.

4.   Family relationships and family dynamics.

5.   Financial responsibilities to a child or children.

6.   Issues regarding spousal or child abuse and neglect.

7.   Skill-based relationship education that may be generalized to parenting, workplace, school, neighborhood, and civic relationships.

(b) Information regarding spousal and child abuse and neglect shall be included in every parent education and family stabilization course. A list of local agencies that provide assistance with such issues shall also be provided.

(c) The parent education and family stabilization course shall be educational in nature and shall not be designed to provide individual mental health therapy for parents or children, or individual legal advice to parents or children.

(d) Course providers shall not solicit participants from the sessions they conduct to become private clients or patients.

(e) Course providers shall not give individual legal advice or mental health therapy.

(3) Each course provider offering a parenting course pursuant to this section must be approved by the Department of Children and Family Services.

(a) The Department of Children and Family Services shall provide each judicial circuit with a list of approved course providers and sites at which the parent education and family stabilization course may be completed. Each judicial circuit must make information regarding all course providers approved for their circuit available to all parents.

(b) The Department of Children and Family Services shall include on the list of approved course providers and sites for each circuit at least one site in that circuit where the parent education and family stabilization course may be completed on a sliding fee scale, if available.

(c) The Department of Children and Family Services shall include on the list of approved course providers, without limitation as to the area of the state for which the course is approved, a minimum of one statewide approved course to be provided through the Internet and one statewide approved course to be provided through correspondence. The purpose of the Internet and correspondence courses is to ensure that the parent education and stabilization course is available in the home county of each state resident and to those out-of-state persons subject to this section.

(d) The Department of Children and Family Services may remove a provider who violates this section, or its implementing rules, from the list of approved court providers.

(e) The Department of Children and Family Services shall adopt rules to administer subsection (2) and this subsection.

(4) All parties to a dissolution of marriage proceeding with minor children or a paternity action that involves issues of parental responsibility shall be required to complete the Parent Education and Family Stabilization Course prior to the entry by the court of a final judgment. The court may excuse a party from attending the parenting course, or from completing the course within the required time, for good cause.

(5) All parties required to complete a parenting course under this section shall begin the course as expeditiously as possible. For dissolution of marriage actions, unless excused by the court pursuant to subsection (4), the petitioner must complete the course within 45 days after the filing of the petition, and all other parties must complete the course within 45 days after service of the petition. For paternity actions, unless excused by the court pursuant to subsection (4), the petitioner must complete the course within 45 days after filing the petition, and any other party must complete the course within 45 days after an acknowledgment of paternity by that party, an adjudication of paternity of that party, or an order granting visitation to or support from that party. Each party to a dissolution or paternity action shall file proof of compliance with this subsection with the court prior to the entry of the final judgment.

(6) All parties to a modification of a final judgment involving shared parental responsibilities, custody, or visitation may be required to complete a court-approved parenting course prior to the entry of an order modifying the final judgment.

(7) A reasonable fee may be charged to each parent attending the course.

(8) Information obtained or statements made by the parties at any educational session required under this statute shall not be considered in the adjudication of a pending or subsequent action, nor shall any report resulting from such educational session become part of the record of the case unless the parties have stipulated in writing to the contrary.

(9) The court may hold any parent who fails to attend a required parenting course in contempt, or that parent may be denied shared parental responsibility or visitation or otherwise sanctioned as the court deems appropriate.

(10) Nothing in this section shall be construed to require the parties to a dissolution of marriage to attend a court-approved parenting course together.

(11) The court may, without motion of either party, prohibit the parenting course

F.   PROBLEMS OF ENFORCEMENT

1.   THE COURT AS TIE-BREAKER

Griffin v. Griffin

Supreme Court of Colorado, En Banc, 1985.
699 P.2d 407.

■ DUBOFSKY, JUSTICE.

We granted certiorari to review In re Marriage of Griffin, 666 P.2d 1105 (Colo.App.1982), in which the Court of Appeals held that, where a dissolution decree provides for joint parental selection of their child's school, the parents may request the district court to select the school when the parents cannot agree. We reverse.

The marriage of Mary Q. Griffin (the mother) and Clarence A. Griffin (the father) was dissolved on September 14, 1979. The decree of dissolution incorporated a separation agreement between the mother and the father that contained the following provisions concerning the custody and upbringing of their son, Hardy:

3. *Custody and Visitation*

A. *Joint Decisions and Deadlocks:*

The wife shall have custody of Hardy Micajah Griffin. The husband shall have certain full legal rights set forth in this Agreement. The District Court of Boulder County, Colorado, shall have continuing jurisdiction over the welfare of the child and to enforce the rights of either party to joint decision making, visitation and custody so long as either party is domiciled in Colorado. . . .

. . .

C. *Education*

Both parents shall fully and equally participate in the education of their child. Schools shall be selected jointly. To promote a close family environment, both parents shall participate in Parent–Teacher Conferences and other school-related parental obligations such as trips, carpools and fundraising. These are the legal and binding rights of both parties.

On August 26, 1980 the father filed a motion in the Boulder County District Court entitled "Motion to Enforce Decree and Separation Agreement by Requiring that Child Be Placed in a Public or Private School by Joint Decision of Parties." The father alleged that the mother planned to enroll their son in the Vidya School in Boulder over the father's objections, denying the father his right under the separation agreement to participate in the selection of their son's school. The father further alleged that the

Vidya School was sponsored by the Boulder Tibetan Buddhist Community, and that enrollment of the son in such a school would hamper his development by placing him outside "the broad stream of the American cultural community...."

At a hearing before the district court on September 19, 1980, the mother testified that the father had failed to investigate or visit the school although the mother had arranged for him to do so. Both the father and the Vidya School director confirmed that the father had broken an appointment to visit the Vidya School, and had failed to make any further arrangements to investigate the school. At the conclusion of the hearing, the court denied the father's motion, finding that the father had had an opportunity to exercise his right under the agreement to participate in the selection of his son's school, but had failed to avail himself of the opportunity.

On May 8, 1981, the father again filed in the Boulder County District Court a motion to enforce the separation agreement and dissolution decree, alleging that Hardy had been enrolled in the Vidya School for the 1980–81 school year, and that the mother had refused to discuss Hardy's schooling or allow the father "to participate in the selection of the school." A different district court judge heard the motion on September 4, 1981. At the hearing, the father requested that the court require the parties to meet in order to select a school, and that the court choose a school for the parties if they were unable to agree.[3] The court denied the motion, determining that the separation agreement made no provision for the resolution of disagreement concerning the selection of schools. In the absence of such provision, the court ruled, section 14–10–130, 6 C.R.S. (1973) provides that decisions concerning the child's education are to be made by the custodial parent. Therefore, the court concluded, the father's motion was "meaningless" because the statute does not permit the court either to substitute its own judgment for that of the custodial parent or to force the custodial parent to compromise on any educational decisions.

The Court of Appeals reversed the district court order, holding that "the intention of the parties was to create equal decision-making authority" over the selection of schools, that the agreement supersedes the statute granting authority over the child's upbringing to the custodial parent, and that consequently "the court must determine the issue of choice of schools" in case of parental deadlock. 666 P.2d at 1106–07. We disagree. In our view the "joint selection of schools" provision is unenforceable and the custodial parent therefore retains the ultimate authority to select the child's school.

Section 14–10–130(1) allocates the authority to make child rearing decisions following an award of custody:

3. At the hearing, the father attempted to testify concerning his evaluation of the Vidya School and his discussions with the mother concerning their child's education. The district court ruled that the testimony was unnecessary because the father's motion presented a purely legal question.

Except as otherwise agreed by the parties in writing at the time of the custody decree, the custodian may determine the child's upbringing, including his education, health care, and religious training, unless the court, after hearing and upon motion by the noncustodial parent, finds that, in the absence of a specific limitation of the custodian's authority, the child's physical health would be endangered or his emotional development significantly impaired. (Emphasis added.)

The father here contends that the parties have agreed to joint authority over their son's education, thereby limiting the mother's power under this statute to control educational decisions.[4]

The agreement at issue required that the parents consult concerning their child's education and jointly select his school. The agreement neither selected a school nor provided a means of resolving deadlocks over school selection. In essence, the parties merely "agreed to agree," to negotiate and reach agreement at some future time concerning their child's education. Ordinarily, such agreements are unenforceable because the court has no power to force the parties to reach agreement and cannot grant a remedy. In Jenks v. Jenks, 385 S.W.2d 370 (Mo.App.1964), the Missouri Court of Appeals applied this general rule to an agreement similar to the one before us. There, the parties agreed to consult concerning the education of their children and to agree in writing upon the schools that their children would attend.[5] The court held that the agreement was unenforceable because courts cannot force parties to reach agreement; given this powerlessness, it would be futile to order the parties to meet and negotiate. Id. at 376.

We agree with the court in *Jenks* that the general rule rendering "agreements to agree" unenforceable is particularly applicable to agreements of the type before us. Determinations affecting the custody and welfare of children must always be made in accordance with the best interests of the child. § 14–10–124, 6 C.R.S. (1973 & 1984 Supp.); In re Marriage of Short, 698 P.2d 1310, 1312 (Colo.1985); Kelley v. Kelley, 161 Colo. 486, 490, 423 P.2d 315, 317 (1967). The validity of agreements concerning custody and upbringing of children must be judged against this standard. In re Marriage of Lawson, 44 Colo.App. 105, 107, 608 P.2d 378, 380 (1980) (trial court must determine that custody agreement is in best interests of child before it may be incorporated into dissolution decree). Both the legislature and courts of Colorado have recognized that child custody arrangements that promote discord between the parents are not in the best interests of the child. . . .

Enforcing an agreement, such as this one, that requires the parents to meet and agree after they already have demonstrated their inability to agree exposes the child to further discord and surrounds the child with an atmosphere of hostility and insecurity. See Cleveland v. Cleveland, 165

4. The father does not contend here that the child's physical health would be endangered or his emotional development significantly impaired by the mother's choice of school.

5. The parties also had agreed to arbitration in case of deadlock, but stipulated before the Court of Appeals that the arbitration provision was unenforceable in equity.

Conn. 95, 328 A.2d 691, 695 (1973) (agreement providing for choice of school by noncustodial parent deleted from separation agreement because it would lead to further parental conflict); cf. Rhoades v. Rhoades, 188 Colo. 423, 428, 535 P.2d 1122, 1125 (1975) (statute awarding child rearing decisions to custodial parent has rational basis because it will avoid the "constant buffeting of a child between two parents who disagree on the issues of the child's upbringing, including his education, health care and religious training...."). Therefore, any attempt to enforce the agreement by requiring the parents to negotiate and reach a future agreement would be not only futile, but adverse to the interests of the child as well.[6]

Moreover, the court is not in a position to enforce this agreement by substituting its choice of schools for that of the parents. The court, a stranger to both child and parents, is ill-equipped to understand and act upon the needs of the child. As the court stated in *Jenks:*

> Courts are not so constituted as to be able to regulate the details of a child's upbringing. It exhausts the imagination to speculate on the difficulties to which they would subject themselves were they to enter the home or the school or the playground and undertake to exercise on all occasions the authority which one party or the other would be bound to ascribe to them. Considerations of the most practical kind, therefore, dictate that in these cases the duty of attending to the details of the child's rearing be delegated to a custodian....

385 S.W.2d at 377. See also Kilgrow v. Kilgrow, 268 Ala. 475, 107 So.2d 885 (1959) (court has no power to determine details of upbringing where parents are not separated); Bennett v. Bennett, 73 So.2d 274 (Fla.1954) (court has no power to choose school for child of divorced parents). Resort to the courts, like forced negotiations between parents, is likely to foster and magnify parental discord to the detriment of the child.

In addition, where the selection of a school is intertwined with religious considerations, court control over educational decisions may be constitutionally impermissible. The father here objects to the school chosen by the mother because it is associated with the Buddhist religion and therefore allegedly will remove his child from the mainstream of American life. However, the father has not demonstrated any relation between the purportedly Buddhist curriculum of the Vidya School and the mental or physical health of his child;[7] the court could respond to the father's claim

---

6. Empirical studies have suggested that parental post-divorce conflict adversely affects the adjustment and development of the child. See Wexler, Rethinking the Modification of Child Custody Decrees, 94 Yale L.J. 757, 789–92 (1985) (hereinafter "Wexler").

7. Although the father in both of his motions and in his testimony at the September 19 hearing asserted that his son was suffering psychologically as a result of practices at the Vidya School, he was unable to specify any particular school or religious practices that might result in such harm. Rather, the father objected to the Vidya School because he feared that his child would be exposed to "Buddhist teaching" and because he read an article describing the Vidya School "as a place where non-aggression occurs...." Placing the issue before a court without evidence of specifically harmful practices is tantamount to asking the court to decide whether Buddhism is an acceptable religion for this child.

only by determining the abstract propriety of sending the child to a Buddhist school. That determination would be repugnant to the free exercise of religion clauses of both the United States and Colorado Constitutions. U.S. Const.Amend. 1; Colo. Const. Art. II, Sec. 4. In In re Marriage of Short, 698 P.2d 1310, we held that "a court may not properly inquire into or make judgments regarding the abstract wisdom of a particular religious value or belief. Evidence of religious beliefs or practices is admissible only as it reasonably relates to potential mental or physical harm to the welfare of the child." At 1313. See also Siegel v. Siegel, 122 Misc.2d 932, 472 N.Y.S.2d 272 (1984) (separation agreement requiring court to choose religious training for child is unenforceable; decision remains with custodial parent).

In sum, we hold that the agreement of the parents to jointly select a school for their child is unenforceable. Because no enforceable agreement concerning the child's education exists, the power to control the child's education remains with the mother as custodial parent under section 14–10–130(1). The Court of Appeals erred in reversing the district court's denial of the father's motion to enforce the agreement.

2. Tort Remedies for Interference With Custody Rights

In Wasserman v. Wasserman, 671 F.2d 832 (4th Cir.1982), a court permitted a former wife to bring an action for child enticement and intentional infliction of emotional harm against her former husband and others who she alleged had removed the children from her custody, prevented them from contacting her, and concealed their location from her. The argument that the case was a "dispute involving child custody" and thus within the domestic relations exception to federal diversity jurisdiction, was rejected on the ground that the complaint alleged "generally cognizable common law torts." For an earlier decision in another federal circuit upholding a jury award to a mother of $65,000 in compensatory damages and $65,000 in punitive damages based on intentional infliction of mental anguish through child concealment, *see* Fenslage v. Dawkins, 629 F.2d 1107 (5th Cir.1980). The court in *Fenslage* quoted with approval Restatement (Second) of Torts § 700, which states:

> One who, with knowledge that the parent does not consent, abducts or otherwise compels or induces a minor child to leave a parent legally entitled to its custody or not to return to the parent after it has been left to him, is subject to liability to the parent.

Administrators of the federal Witness Protection Program also have been sued both for money damages and injunctive relief based on supplying new identities for informants and their families that results in practical severance of the relationship with a natural parent. In Franz v. United States, 707 F.2d 582 (D.C.Cir.1983), it was held that a natural father stated a cause of action for abrogation of his rights and those of his children after the mother and her husband, an informant, were given new identities along with the three children of plaintiff by a previous marriage to the mother. The appeals court, in overruling the district court's dismissal of the complaint for failure to state a claim upon which relief can be granted, found that there had not been adequate showing of equally effective alternative solutions that would have been less restrictive of the rights of the natural father and the children.

3.   LIMITATIONS ON HABEAS CORPUS IN FEDERAL COURTS

In Lehman v. Lycoming County Children's Services Agency, 458 U.S. 502, 102 S.Ct. 3231, 73 L.Ed.2d 928 (1982), the Supreme Court of the United States held that the federal habeas corpus statute, 29 U.S.C.A. § 2254, does not confer jurisdiction on federal courts to consider collateral challenges to state court judgments terminating parental rights. Earlier, in Doe v. Doe, 660 F.2d 101 (4th Cir.1981), it was held that federal habeas corpus was not available in a federal court in a suit between private parties with the object of ascertaining custody of a child or the right to rear a child. In *Doe*, the court noted that there was an ongoing state proceeding that would resolve the same issues. For a thorough assessment of the limitations on federal jurisdiction today, *see* Martin Guggenheim, *State Intervention in the Family: Making a Federal Case Out of It*, 45 OHIO ST.L.J. 399 (1984). For an example of habeas corpus limitation in the context of an extradition proceeding, *see* California v. Superior Court, San Bernardino County (Smolin), 482 U.S. 400, 107 S.Ct. 2433, 96 L.Ed.2d 332 (1987).

4.   ACROSS STATE LINES

Holder v. Polanski

Supreme Court of New Jersey, 1988.
111 N.J. 344, 544 A.2d 852.

■ POLLOCK, J.

Plaintiff, Virginia Holder (formerly Polanski), and defendant, Benjamin H. Polanski, formerly husband and wife, separated on April 1, 1985, and were divorced by a judgment dated September 19, 1986. Holder had a son by a prior marriage, and two children were born of her marriage to Polanski: Katie in 1980 and Melissa in 1982. The trial court denied Holder permission to move to Connecticut with the children. In an unreported opinion, the Appellate Division affirmed. We granted certification, 108 N.J. 656, 532 A.2d 236 (1987), and now reverse and remand to the Chancery Division, Matrimonial Part. We conclude that Holder justified her move to Connecticut but because Polanski has had residential custody of the children for nearly two years, a further hearing is necessary to determine the custodial arrangement that will be in the best interests of the children.

The record is sparse, but contains sufficient facts for the determination of this appeal. In the interim between their separation and divorce, Holder, who had physical custody of the children, stated that she wanted to move to

Connecticut. Holder's reasons for the move included a desire to live near her sister and brother-in-law, who could provide her with emotional and financial support. Furthermore, her brother-in-law had offered her employment, and she planned to attend the University of Bridgeport. Finally, she said she wanted to put behind her the trauma of her divorce and the recent death of her parents. Polanski opposed the move for various reasons, primarily because of the distance between Flemington, New Jersey, where they lived, and New Canaan, Connecticut. He contended that the housing, educational, and employment opportunities available to Holder in Connecticut were also available in New Jersey, and that there was no comparative advantage to her or their children in moving to Connecticut.

At the divorce trial, which was held on July 3, 1986, the court reserved decision on Holder's request to relocate with the children and directed her to provide more specific information on housing, education, and employment, which she provided on August 1, 1986. On September 2, 1986, the divorce judgment not yet having been entered, Holder renewed her request. In the interim, she had signed a one-year lease on a house in Connecticut, enrolled her son in high school, paid one-half year's tuition at a nursery school for Melissa, and signed a contract for the balance.

On September 19, 1986, the trial court denied Holder's motion. After acknowledging the sincerity of both parties, the court stated:

> There is no question in my mind that the move to Connecticut is in fact something which is beneficial to Virginia Holder * * * [a]nd I'm sure that in somewhat of a traditional sense she is willing to do her best and would in fact do her best to avoid inconveniencing Mr. Polanski, to avoid in any way alienating the children from him, that in fact she would or will in any event, no matter what happens here today, I think foster a relationship between the children and Mr. Polanski.

Although the benefits to her appeared to be substantial, the court found that Holder had not shown that the same benefits were not available in New Jersey. Nor had she established that it was in the best interests of the children to be away from Polanski. Consequently, the court entered an order denying Holder "permission to move to the State of Connecticut with the two children of the marriage; and she shall not remove the children from New Jersey without permission of defendant." In the divorce judgment, also entered on September 19, 1986, the court awarded physical custody of the children to Holder, and granted Polanski visitation rights on alternate weekends, certain holidays, and during the summer vacation. Because of her prior commitments, Holder nonetheless moved to Connecticut and filed a motion to grant Polanski physical custody, as a result of which the court awarded him "residential custody" of the children and granted Holder visitation rights comparable to those previously granted to Polanski under the divorce judgment.

In every divorce, the family unit is broken, and the relationship between the parties irrevocably changed. When children are involved, one parent receives physical or residential custody and the other parent receives visitation rights. Alternatively, the parents may enter into an arrangement for joint custody. Formerly, custody of children of tender years was generally awarded to the mother. With increasing frequency, however, mothers and fathers now share the responsibility for the care and custody of their children and the support of the family. Consequently, courts have begun to make more frequent awards of custody to fathers and, in appropriate cases, to make joint custody awards. Nonetheless, in many instances, the mother still receives custody of the children, and the father is awarded visitation rights. Implicit in that arrangement is the right of the father to move elsewhere for virtually any reason. D'Onofrio v. D'Onofrio, 144 N.J.Super. 200, 207, 365 A.2d 27 (Ch.Div.), aff'd o.b., 144 N.J.Super. 352, 365 A.2d 716 (App.Div.1976). As men and women approach parity, the question arises when a custodial mother wants to move from one state to another, why not? Until today, our response has included the requirement that the custodial parent establish, among other things, a real advantage to that parent from the move. Cooper v. Cooper, 99 N.J. 42, 56, 491 A.2d 606 (1984). We now modify that requirement and hold that a custodial parent may move with the children of the marriage to another state as long as the move does not interfere with the best interests of the children or the visitation rights of the non-custodial parent.

Our analysis begins with N.J.S.A. 9:2–2, which provides:

> [when] such children are natives of this State, or have resided five years within its limits, they shall not be removed out of its jurisdiction without their own consent, if of suitable age to signify the same, nor while under that age without the consent of both parents, unless the court, upon cause shown, shall otherwise order.

The heart of the statute is the requirement of establishing "cause" to justify removal of the children from this to another state. The purpose of that requirement, manifested also in the abiding concern of courts for children, "is to preserve the rights of the noncustodial parent and the child to maintain and develop their familial relationship." Cooper v. Cooper, supra, 99 N.J. at 50, 491 A.2d 606; see also D'Onofrio v. D'Onofrio, supra, 144 N.J.Super. at 204–05, 365 A.2d 27 (purpose of anti-removal statute is preservation of the mutual rights of the children and noncustodial parent to maintain and develop their relationship). Our problem is to balance those rights with the right of the custodial parent to seek a better life for himself or herself in this or another state.

As previously noted, the calculus for solving this problem includes the custodial parent's interest in freedom of movement as qualified by his or her custodial obligation, the State's interest in protecting the best interests of the child, and the competing interests of the noncustodial parent. Under *Cooper,* "the custodial parent initially must show that there is a real advantage to that parent in the move and that the move is not inimical to the best interests of the children." Once the custodial parent has made this threshold showing, courts must then consider three factors: the prospective advantages of the move, including its capacity for maintaining or improving the general quality of life of both the custodial parent and the children; the integrity of the custodial parent's motives in seeking to move, as well as the noncustodial parent's motives in seeking to restrain the move; and whether a realistic and reasonable visitation schedule can be reached if the move is allowed.

In this case, the lower courts concluded with respect to the threshold showing that the move to Connecticut would not be inimical to the best interests of the children, but that Holder had failed to show a real advantage for the move. Both courts noted that she had failed to establish that the cost of living was lower in Connecticut or that superior housing, educational or job opportunities, or child care were available in that state. Although Holder could derive personal satisfaction and receive emotional support from her sister and brother-in-law, these benefits were not considered sufficient to satisfy the "real advantage" test of *Cooper*. But see Vertrees v. Vertrees, 24 Mass.App.Ct. 918, 919, 508 N.E.2d 868, 869 (1987) (Massachusetts' "real advantage" requirement satisfied by a showing of emotional and social advantages to be gained from moving closer to family members); Signorelli v. Albano, 21 Mass.App.Ct. 939, 940, 486 N.E.2d 750, 751 (1985) ("real advantage" requirement satisfied when custodial mother's new husband, with whom she had just had a baby, moved to New Jersey to start a higher paying job).

In reaching that result, the Appellate Division decision is in line with other decisions of that court supporting the requirement that more than a personal advantage to the custodial parent is required for permission to remove children to another state. See Helentjaris v. Sudano, 194 N.J.Super. 220, 224–25, 476 A.2d 828 (App.Div.) (in addition to moving closer to family members, proposed area provided job with better hours and working conditions and lower cost of living), certif. den., 99 N.J. 200, 491 A.2d 699 (1984); Middlekauff v. Middlekauff, 161 N.J.Super. 84, 94–95, 390 A.2d 1202 (App.Div.1978) (relocation permitted because custodial mother could not otherwise attend higher education classes in Manhattan and continue to spend time with the children); D'Onofrio v. D'Onofrio, supra, 144 N.J.Super. at 208–11, 365 A.2d 27 (relocation allowed because, in addition to benefit to custodial mother in being closer to her family, standard of living and physical environment of mother and children will be considerably improved).

We believe, however, that the focus of the "cause" requirement should not be on the benefits that will accrue to the custodial parent but on the best interests of the children and on the preservation of their relationship with the noncustodial parent. From that perspective, the "cause" requirement of N.J.S.A. 9:2–2 implicates the best interests of the child as manifested through visitation with the noncustodial parent. Short of an adverse effect on the noncustodial parent's visitation rights or other aspects of a child's best interests, the custodial parent should enjoy the same freedom of movement as the noncustodial parent. This construction of N.J.S.A. 9:9–2, while recognizing the values that underlie her constitutional argument, avoids the necessity of addressing Holder's challenge to the statute as violative of her constitutional right to travel and to equal protection of the laws. See Frontiero v. Richardson, 411 U.S. 677, 93 S.Ct. 1764, 36 L.Ed.2d 583 (1973) (unconstitutional discrimination to require servicewomen to demonstrate that their husbands are dependent on them for support without requiring servicemen to make same showing regarding their wives).

To this extent, we modify the "cause" test that we announced in *Cooper* by holding that any sincere, good-faith reason will suffice, and that a custodial parent need not establish a "real advantage" from the move. If the court should find that the purpose of the move is to thwart the noncustodial parent's visitation rights, that obviously will not satisfy the test. Here, however, Holder's motivation was to live closer to her relatives and to make a fresh start in life. This clearly was a sufficient explanation to justify her move to Connecticut.

The modification precipitates a further adjustment of the *Cooper* formula. Once the court finds that the custodial parent wants to move for a good-faith reason, it should then consider whether the move will be inimical to the best interests of the children or adversely affect the visitation rights of the noncustodial parent. Not every change in a visitation schedule will prejudice those rights, particularly if the noncustodial parent has not exercised them before the custodial parent seeks to move from the state. If the move will not substantially change the visitation rights, then the court should determine whether the move would be inimical to the best interests of the children.

If, however, the move will require substantial changes in the visitation schedule, proofs concerning the prospective advantages of the move, the integrity of the motives of the party, and the development of a reasonable visitation schedule remain important. The emphasis, however, should not be on whether the children or the custodial parent will benefit from the move, but on whether the children will suffer from it. Motives are relevant, but if the custodial parent is acting in good faith and not to frustrate the noncustodial parent's visitation rights, that should suffice. Maintenance of a reasonable visitation schedule by the noncustodial parent remains a critical concern, but in our mobile society, it may be possible to honor that schedule and still recognize the right of a custodial parent to move. In resolving the tension between a custodial parent's right to move and a noncustodial parent's visitation rights, the beacon remains the best interests of the children.

On the record before us, it appears that Polanski's visitation rights would not have been substantially affected by Holder's move to Connecticut. Indeed, Holder persuasively argues that she could have moved to several places in New Jersey without contravening the statute and with a more adverse impact on Polanski's visitation rights. See Helentjaris v. Sudano, supra, 194 N.J.Super. at 230, 476 A.2d 828 (noting that mother's move to Ohio imposed no greater visitation burden than would have resulted from a move to southern New Jersey). Furthermore, the move apparently would have left the children as well situated as they are in New Jersey with respect to medical treatment or educational opportunities.

Consequently, we conclude that Holder should have been permitted in 1986 to move to Connecticut with her children. We recognize, however, that in this as in many custody cases, we are confronted with a living record. Accordingly, a remand is necessary to reconsider the best interests of the children. In remanding, we acknowledge that Polanski has had "residential custody" of the children for the past two years. Although Holder should have been permitted to move to Connecticut in 1986, the issue on remand will not be, as it was then, whether she should move to that state, but what custodial arrangement is in the best interests of the children at the present time.

The judgment of the Appellate Division is reversed. . . .

NOTE

Litigation involving a custodial parent's efforts to physically remove the child from one jurisdiction so as to bring about a permanent move typically are referred to as relocations. On April 23, 2001, the Supreme Court of New Jersey attempted to better define the standard by which relocation could be assessed. *See* Baures v. Lewis, 167 N.J. 91, 770 A.2d 214 (2001). In its opinion the court stated there was a growing trend among the states to ease restrictions on the custodial parent's ability to relocate with the child. Furthermore, in New Jersey there is a two-pronged test: first, a good faith reason to make the move, and second, that the child will not suffer from the move. The court then listed twelve factors that the court should consider in evaluating the custodial parent's petition. Primarily, these factors center on the child and his or her best interest. After the custodial parent has established a prima facie case for the relocation, the noncustodial parent then has the burden of proving that the move is being sought in bad faith or that it will be harmful to the child. Decisions in other states range from a presumption in favor of relocation to presumptions against the relocation. Some states apply a best interest test. The following cases are representative.

In Burgess v. Burgess, 13 Cal.4th 25, 51 Cal.Rptr.2d 444, 913 P.2d 473 (1996), the Supreme Court of California considered whether a mother with physical custody of the two children, aged three and four, for over a year, needed to establish a "necessity" to move forty miles away for employment reasons. The father of the children would still be able to maintain his visitation schedule with the children. The court of appeals held that a trial court may not award sole physical custody of the children to a parent unless he or she remains in the same locality or establishes that relocation is necessary. The Supreme Court reversed, holding that relocation is similar to any other modification of custody or visitation. The custody parent has the presumptive right to make decisions, including the right to relocate. That is, the parent whose visitation rights may be affected, must demonstrate that a significant change in circumstances would not be in the child's best interest. Until this is shown, the relocation is in the best interest of the child.

A unanimous New York Court of Appeals, in Tropea v. Tropea, 87 N.Y.2d 727, 642 N.Y.S.2d 575, 665 N.E.2d 145 (1996) rejected a three-step formula for evaluating relocation requests and replaced it with a non-exclusive list of factors with which to evaluated each relocation request, but with the best interest of the child the ultimate yardstick. The decision will make it easier for custodial parents to relocate, more difficult to accommodate visitation, and evidences a shift towards starting over again, versus holding the dissolved family unit together.

Other jurisdictions are prepared to exert considerable control over the choice of a custodial parent to move to another jurisdiction after divorce if this will significantly affect or curtail visitation rights of the noncustodial parent. (Joint custody cases may be specially difficult.) In Carpenter v. Carpenter, 220 Va. 299, 257 S.E.2d 845 (1979), a custodial mother wished to move from Virginia to New York City. She explained that her employment opportunities as a chemist would be better and that the children would have greater cultural and educational advantages there. The father prayed that custody be granted to him because such a move would be contrary to the best interests of the children. The Supreme Court of Virginia upheld the chancellor's refusal to allow the mother to remove the children, pointing to the chancellor's findings as to the good relationship between the children and their father and the fact that they were well adjusted in school. The chancellor had noted that the father would be required to reduce his visits if the children were to move (and also had found that the cultural and educational advantages in New York City were not significantly greater than the "cultural, educational and recreational advantages in Tidewater, Virginia"). Subsequently, in Gray v. Gray, 228 Va. 696, 324 S.E.2d 677 (1985), the same court explained that the *Carpenter* holding merely meant that before a court permits a custodial parent to remove children from the Commonwealth, it must determine that removal is in the child's best interest.

In denying the custodial parent the ability to relocate, courts rely on the burden the custodial parent must meet in establishing a qualitative advantage to the children and the custodial parent, the good faith motive of the custodial parent in seeking the move, the good faith motive of the non-custodial parent in opposing the move, and the whether a realistic visitation schedule can me maintained. This burden is still the test in many states today. *See, e.g.,* Momb v. Ragone, 132 Wash.App. 70, 130 P.3d 406 (2006)(upholding state statute requiring consideration of eleven factors prior to allowing relocation). Rejecting this approach, some courts, as *Holder* indicates, simply focus on the best interest of the child and how separation from the non-custodial parent will affect this. *See, e.g.,* Bodne v. Bodne, 277 Ga. 445, 588 S.E.2d 728 (2003); Lenz v. Lenz, 79 S.W.3d 10 (Tex. 2002). Other states require the non-custodial parent to rebut the presumption that the custodial parent may relocate with the child. *See, e.g., In re* Marriage of Brown & Yana, 37 Cal.4th 947, 38 Cal.Rptr.3d 610, 127 P.3d 28 (2006); Fenwick v. Fenwick, 114 S.W.3d 767 (Ky. 2003).

In Mize v. Mize, 621 So.2d 417 (Fla.1993), the Supreme Court of Florida adopted an approach articulated by Judge Schwartz in an earlier District Court of Appeals decision, Hill v. Hill, 548 So.2d 705 (Fla.3d DCA 1989), review denied 560 So.2d 233 (Fla.1990). The opinion in *Mize* explains:

As Judge Schwartz stated: [S]o long as the parent who has been granted the primary custody of the child desires to move for a well-intentioned reason and founded belief that the relocation is best for that parent's—and, it follows, the child's—well-being, rather than from a vindictive desire to interfere with the visitation rights of the other parent, the change in residence should ordinarily be approved. However, Judge Schwartz recognized that circumstances may exist that would justify a departure from the general rule. For example, when older children are involved, the trauma of leaving friends, other family members, and school may outweigh the trauma in separating from the primary residential parent. Thus, in making the ultimate decision, trial courts must consider and weigh factors discussed by Judge Nesbitt, such as: 1. Whether the move would be likely to improve the general quality of life for both the primary residential spouse and the children. 2. Whether the motive for seeking the move is for the express purpose of defeating visitation. 3. Whether the custodial parent, once out of the jurisdiction, will be likely to comply with any substitute visitation arrangements. 4. Whether the substitute visitation will be adequate to foster a continuing meaningful relationship between the child or children and the noncustodial parent. 5. Whether the cost of transportation is financially affordable by one or both of the parents. 6. Whether the move is in the best interests of the child. (This sixth requirement we believe is a generalized summary of the previous five.)

■ SHAW, J., concurring only in the result, concluded:

The majority's liberal standard favoring removal will work no inequity in those cases where the noncustodial parent has failed to exercise decisionmaking and visitation rights or has done so in a negative manner. However, where the noncustodial parent has exercised extensive parenting and visitation rights, perhaps at great personal sacrifice, and has worked hard to create a loving bond with the child, the majority opinion will invite clear injustice—as well as immeasurable heartbreak—for that parent and child, in case after case within our state. To my mind, when a parent is granted the great benefits of primary physical residence he or she may reasonably be expected to shoulder the responsibilities as well, and this may at times include reasonable geographical limitations during the child's minority.

Half a century ago in Fields v. Fields, 143 Fla. 886, 890, 197 So. 530, 531 (1940), this Court embraced the then-popular "tender years" doctrine, ruling: "Other things being equal ... the mother of infants of tender years [is] best fitted to bestow the motherly affection, care, companionship, and early training suited to their needs." Today's majority opinion is a throwback to those days—in fact, today's opinion actually expands the "tender years" doctrine to hold that the convenience of the custodial parent is tantamount to the best interests of the child. This mindset ignores virtually the entire weight of social and psychological data in the intervening half century, summarized above, which indicates that the interests of the child are best served by shared parenting and "frequent and continuing contact with both parents"—a fact long recognized by our Legislature.

At what point might it be argued effectively that restrictions on geographical relocation, particularly when a custodial parent remarries, amount to an unconstitutional infringement on the right to travel?

In re Amberley D.

Supreme Judicial Court of Maine, 2001.
775 A.2d 1158.

■ ALEXANDER, J.

Joann R., mother of Amberley D., appeals the judgment of the Waldo County Probate Court appointing Diana and Richard B. coguardians of Amberley pursuant to 18–A M.R.S.A. § 5–204 (1998 & Supp.2000). On appeal, Joann contends that: (1) the court erred by appointing temporary guardians without notice to her; (2) the court lacked jurisdiction and venue over the guardianship petition; (3) no clear and convincing evidence supported the petition; and (4) the guardianship statute is unconstitutional as applied. We affirm the judgment.

Amberley D. was born on January 19, 1985, and grew up with her mother, Joann R., her stepfather, Charles R., and her two siblings, moving many times and living in Maine, Vermont and several other states.[1] Joann and Charles separated several times, during which Joann and the children utilized various temporary living arrangements, including friends' homes, motels, and a shelter.

In the spring of 1999, Joann and Charles separated and filed for divorce in Vermont. Joann and the children then moved to New Hampshire, staying in motels and with friends. Amberley, who was in the eighth grade, stopped going to school. By this time, she had been enrolled in approximately twenty-seven different schools. Amberley testified that Joann was abusing drugs and alcohol, providing them to her, staying out all night drinking, and engaging in sexual activity in front of her. Amberley also testified that she had been sexually molested several times, and that she reported this to Joann, who had done nothing.

In late 1999, Amberley ran away on two occasions. She was found at her boyfriend's home and then at Charles' home, and returned to Joann. In January 2000, Amberley ran away again to Charles' home in Vermont. Charles drove her to a friend's place in Massachusetts. From there,

---

1. Amberley's biological father, Mark M., never developed a relationship with her and did not participate in the proceedings.

Amberley took a bus to Augusta to meet Charles' parents, Diana and Richard B., who reside in Stockton Springs. Joann notified law enforcement agencies that Amberley was missing, then departed for a California vacation. Upon her return, she was informed by the Waldo County Sheriff's Office that Amberley was with Diana and Richard B.

Shortly after Amberley's arrival, Diana and Richard B. filed a petition requesting appointment as temporary coguardians of a minor pursuant to 18–A M.R.S.A. § 5–207(c) (Supp.2000).[2] After a hearing, the court granted a temporary, six-month guardianship, finding that Amberley was in an intolerable living situation at her mother's, inadequately cared for, and subject to abuse by others. Joann was served with notice of the appointment and, representing herself, filed a motion to dismiss the temporary guardianship. Subsequently, through counsel, she filed another motion to dismiss the guardianship and an answer to the petition. After a hearing, the court denied the motion.

A hearing on full guardianship was held, which Joann had notice of and participated in. The court found by clear and convincing evidence a history of abuse, neglect, and mistreatment, and a living situation that was at least temporarily intolerable for Amberley, and that the guardians would provide a living situation in her best interest. *See* 18–A M.R.S.A. § 5–204(c). The court then entered an order appointing Diana and Richard B. full coguardians of Amberley pursuant to 18–A M.R.S.A. § 5–204.[3]

The record does not indicate that there was any other prior or pending order from any other court in any state addressing custody or parental rights for Amberley during this time.

Joann brought this appeal from the Probate Court's order.

The Probate Court, in appointing Diana and Richard B. temporary guardians of Amberley, waived notice of hearing to Amberley's parents pursuant to 18–A M.R.S.A. § 5–207, which states that "[u]pon a showing of good cause, the court may waive service of the notice of hearing on any person, other than the minor, if the minor is at least 14 years of age."

---

2. Section 5–207(c) states that "[i]f necessary, the court may appoint a temporary guardian, with the status of an ordinary guardian of a minor, but the authority of a temporary guardian may not last longer than 6 months."

3. Section 5–204 states in relevant part:

The court may appoint a guardian or coguardians for an unmarried minor if:

(a) All parental rights of custody have been terminated or suspended by circumstance or prior court order;

(b) Each living parent whose parental rights and responsibilities have not been terminated or the person who is the legal custodian of the unmarried minor consents to the guardianship and the court finds that the consent creates a condition that is in the best interest of the child; or

(c) The person or persons whose consent is required under subsection (b) do not consent, but the court finds by clear and convincing evidence that the person or persons have failed to respond to proper notice or a living situation has been created that is at least temporarily intolerable for the child even though the living situation does not rise to the level of jeopardy required for the final termination of parental rights, and that the proposed guardian will provide a living situation that is in the best interest of the child.

Joann contends that the Uniform Child Custody Jurisdiction, and Enforcement Act (UCCJEA), 19–A M.R.S.A. §§ 1731–1783 (Supp.2000), which defers to state notice provisions for child custody determinations, is preempted by the Parental Kidnapping Prevention Act (PKPA), 28 U.S.C. § 1738A (1994 & Supp.2000), and that she was entitled to notice of the emergency guardianship hearing under the PKPA.

The UCCJEA provides that notice to persons outside the state "may be given in a manner prescribed by the law of this State for service of process or by the law of the state in which the service is made." 19–A M.R.S.A. § 1738(1). In the event of a conflict, the PKPA preempts the UCCJEA. However, the PKPA addresses jurisdictional issues only when existing orders have been entered by courts of other states concerning the custody or visitation of a child. *See Thompson v. Thompson*, 484 U.S. 174, 177, 108 S.Ct. 513, 98 L.Ed.2d 512 (1988) ("[a]s the legislative scheme suggests, and as Congress explicitly specified, one of the chief purposes of the PKPA is to avoid jurisdictional competition and conflict between State courts") (citation omitted). The PKPA is not applicable in this case because no competing custody order regarding Amberley was pending or entered in another state[4].

Joann also contends that 18–A M.R.S.A. § 5–207, as applied, violates due process by depriving her of fundamental parental rights. In assessing what process is due, we apply the *Mathews* factors:

> First, the private interest that will be affected by the official action; second, the risk of an erroneous deprivation of such interest through the procedures used, and the probable value, if any, of additional or substitute procedural safeguards; and finally, the Government's interest, including the function involved and the fiscal and administrative burdens that the additional or substitute procedural requirement would entail.

In re Heather C., 2000 ME 99, § 22, 751 A.2d 448, 454 (citing *Mathews v. Eldridge*, 424 U.S. 319, 335, 96 S.Ct. 893, 47 L.Ed.2d 18 (1976)). *See also Rideout v. Riendeau*, 2000 ME 198, § 14, 761 A.2d 291, 297–98 ("[i]f we can reasonably interpret a statute as satisfying those constitutional requirements, we must read it in such a way, notwithstanding other possible unconstitutional interpretations of the same statute").

Joann has a fundamental parental right, and the government has a significant interest in protecting children. *See Heather C.*, 2000 ME 99, §§ 23–28, 751 A.2d at 454–56. The risk of a due process violation occurs when an emergency guardian may be appointed without notice to parents, temporarily depriving them of parental rights, before a hearing takes place. However, section 5–207(c) limits the emergency guardianship to six months. Further, upon notice that a guardian has been appointed, a parent can petition for removal of the guardian pursuant to 18–A M.R.S.A. § 5–

---

4. However, the PKPA is relevant to initial custody determinations by providing guidelines to prevent jurisdictional disputes. *See Wambold v. Wambold*, 651 A.2d 330, 332 (Me.1994).

212 (1998),[5] entitling them to a hearing. At the hearing, the guardian has the burden of demonstrating that continuation of the guardianship is in the child's best interest. 18–A M.R.S.A. § 5–212(d). Joann received notice of the six-month guardianship appointment, filed a motion to dismiss, and a prompt hearing was held on her motion, at which her attorneys were present. She also received notice of and participated in the hearing on full guardianship. Thus, the guardianship statute, providing for waiver of notice in limited circumstances, but with subsequent opportunity to be heard, did not violate Joann's due process rights.

Joann contends that New Hampshire has jurisdiction over the guardianship petition pursuant to the PKPA and the UCCJEA. As set forth above, the PKPA is not directly at issue where no competing court order is involved. However, the jurisdictional requirements of the PKPA, which are similar but not identical to the UCCJEA, must be met, or the decree risks being denied full faith and credit by courts of other states. *See Wambold v. Wambold,* 651 A.2d 330, 333 (Me.1994).

Both the PKPA and the UCCJEA provide that a state has jurisdiction over a child custody proceeding if the state is the "home state" of the child on the date the proceeding is commenced, or was the home state within six months before the date the proceeding is commenced[6]. *See* 28 U.S.C. § 1738A(c); 19–A M.R.S.A. § 1745. The PKPA and the UCCJEA define the home state as the state in which the child lived with a parent, or a person acting as a parent, for at least six consecutive months immediately before the commencement of a child custody proceeding, and include periods of temporary absence as part of the period. 28 U.S.C. § 1738A(b)(4); 19–A M.R.S.A. § 1732(7).

Immediately prior to the filing of the temporary guardianship petition, Amberley lived in New Hampshire, but for less than six months. Nevertheless, Joann contends that New Hampshire is Amberley's home state because she lived there for almost six months, last attended school there, and had contacts with individuals providing services in the state, such as her physician and the New Hampshire Department of Health and Human Services' workers concerning her truancy. However, this evidence is inadequate because the six-month requirement was not met, due to Joann and Amberley's transitory living situation. New Hampshire cannot be considered Amberley's home state.

---

5. Section 5–212 reads in relevant part:

(a) Any person interested in the welfare of a ward, or the ward, if 14 or more years of age, may petition for removal of a guardian on the ground that removal would be in the best interest of the ward. A guardian may petition for permission to resign. A petition for removal or for permission to resign may, but need not, include a request for appointment of a successor guardian.

(b) After notice and hearing on a petition for removal or for permission to resign, the court may terminate the guardianship and make any further order that may be appropriate

6. The UCCJEA's child custody jurisdiction provisions generally track the PKPA's, although they differ slightly in some respects. *See Wambold,* 651 A.2d at 332–33; 19–A M.R.S.A. § 1745 comment (2000); 19–A M.R.S.A. § 1748 comment (2000).

When the child has no home state, the PKPA and the UCCJEA require the court to examine whether a sufficiently significant connection and substantial evidence exists to exercise jurisdiction. Pursuant to the PKPA, in the absence of a home state, a state can exercise jurisdiction when it is in the child's best interest because "the child and his parents, or the child and at least one contestant, have a significant connection with such State other than mere physical presence," and "substantial evidence" is available in the state concerning the child's care. 28 U.S.C. § 1738A(c)(2)(B). The corresponding UCCJEA provision, which does not include the "best interest" language, states that jurisdiction is proper when "the child and at least one parent or a person acting as a parent" has a significant connection with the state. 19–A M.R.S.A. § 1745(1)(B)(1).

Diana and Richard B. are residents of Maine. They have had physical custody and care of Amberley since her arrival in this state, and they are the parents of her stepfather. The record indicates that Amberley has visited them on a regular basis in the past, and that she lived and attended school in Maine for periods during 1991–97. Consequently, the significant connection and substantial evidence requirements were satisfied under the UCCJEA and the PKPA, and the Probate Court has jurisdiction over the guardianship petition. *See Gabriel W.*, 666 A.2d at 509–10.

Regarding Joann's claim that venue did not exist, under 18–A M.R.S.A. § 5–205 (1998), venue for guardianship proceedings for minors is "in the place where the minor resides or is present." Amberley's presence within Maine was determinative in establishing venue. *See Guardianship of Zachary Z.*, 677 A.2d 550, 552–53 (Me.1996).

Pursuant to 18–A M.R.S.A. § 5–204(c), absent the consent of a parent or legal custodian to the guardianship appointment, the Probate Court must find by clear and convincing evidence that "a living situation has been created that is at least temporarily intolerable for the child even though the living situation does not rise to the level of jeopardy required for the final termination of parental rights, and that the proposed guardian will provide a living situation that is in the best interest of the child." Neither the child protective statute, 22 M.R.S.A. §§ 4001–4091 (1992 & Supp.2000), nor the protection from abuse statute, 19–A M.R.S.A. §§ 4001–4014 (1998 & Supp.2000), prohibits the Probate Court from appointing emergency guardians for minors, absent parental consent, when the requisite findings are made.

On a direct appeal from the Probate Court, we review the court's findings for clear error. *See Conservatorship of Justin R.*, 662 A.2d 232, 234 (Me.1995) (citing *Estate of Paine*, 609 A.2d 1150, 1152 (Me.1992)). In its guardianship order, the court found that the testimony established a history of abuse, neglect and mistreatment of Amberley by her mother. Among the evidence cited by the court was the unstable living arrangement involving multiple moves, and Amberley's fear for her own safety. The court further cited the testimony that Joann used alcohol and marijuana and provided them to Amberley, and that she engaged in sexual activity in Amberley's presence. In addition, the court cited Joann's apparent disregard for Amberley's well-being in taking a vacation when she was missing. The court determined that Diana and Richard B., with whom Amberley had spent considerable time during her life, offer her a stable, loving home and have met her physical, educational, emotional, and social needs.

The evidence is sufficient to support the court's findings that a living situation was created that was at least temporarily intolerable for Amberley and that Diana and Richard B. provide a living situation in her best interests. Joann claims that the testimony presented at the hearing was self-interested and conflicting. However, it is the factfinder's responsibility to assess the credibility of witnesses and the weight and significance of the evidence. *Guardianship of Boyle*, 674 A.2d 912, 913 (Me.1996) (citation omitted). Absent clear error, we defer to that assessment. *Id.*

Amberley's age and her participation in the proceedings further supports the court's best interest determination. Amberley was fifteen at the time the petition was filed and granted, and the record indicates she nominated Diana and Richard B. to be her guardians pursuant to 18–A M.R.S.A. § 5–206 (1998).[7] Minors who are older are permitted, under certain circumstances, to exercise a greater degree of choice. *See, e.g.,* 15 M.R.S.A. § 3506–A (Supp.2000) (allowing sixteen-year-olds to seek emancipation). The court did not err in appointing guardians based on this evidence.

Apart from her notice claim, Joann challenges the constitutionality of the guardianship statute by contending her parental rights have effectively been terminated, but that unlike a child protective termination proceeding, no home study was made, and no agency or individual will work with Joann towards reunification. However, guardianship determinations are not final. Under 18–A M.R.S.A. § 5–212(a), any person who is interested in the welfare of the ward, or the ward if over fourteen years old, may petition for removal of the guardian. When the guardian does not consent to removal, the guardian has the burden of showing, by a preponderance of the evidence, that continuation of the guardianship is in the best interest of the ward pursuant to 18–A M.R.S.A. § 5–212(d).[8] Because the parent retains the right to regain custody, the same degree of procedural safeguards as in termination proceedings is not constitutionally required. *See, e.g., In re Sabrina M.,* 460 A.2d 1009, 1015–16 (Me.1983) ("the nature of the interests concerned in a child protection proceeding significantly differs from that in a proceeding to terminate parental rights").

Finally, we do not address the question of visitation. The record does not indicate that Joann has made an effort to obtain contact with Amberley, or that Diana and Richard B. attempted to restrict visitation between them. As a result, this issue is not reached.

The entry is: Judgment affirmed.

---

7. Section 5–206 states in relevant part that "[t]he court shall appoint a person nominated by the minor, if the minor is 14 years of age or older, unless the court finds the appointment contrary to the best interests of the minor."

8. Because Joann has not yet petitioned for removal of the guardian, we do not reach her claims that the process for such a petition would violate her due process rights.

NOTE

The UCCJEA replaced the earlier UCCJA, the latter being in partial conflict with the federal Parental Kidnapping Prevention Act of 1980 (PKPA), 28 U.S.C. § 1738A. Specifically, the federal legislation (PKPA) demands that if there is a "home state," defined as a state in which the child has lived with a parent or person acting as a parent for six months immediately preceding the time of the petition, then this "home state" has precedence for jurisdictional purposes. If the child is less than six months old, then the state in which the child has lived since birth is the "home state." Because the UCCJA did not share such a preference for "home state" jurisdiction it was replaced by the UCCJEA. *See* Shute v. Shute, 158 Vt. 242, 607 A.2d 890 (1992). In addition, the UCCJEA provides that the first state making a custody determination retains jurisdiction until the child, the child's parents or any other person acting as a parent no longer resides in the initial state. The goal of the newly enacted UCCJEA is identical to that of the former UCCJA, that is, to limit the ability of sister-states to modify custody decrees. The federal Parental Kidnapping Prevention Act (PKPA) shares this goal. *See generally* Kelly Gaines Stoner, *The Uniform Child Custody Jurisdiction & Enforcement Act (UCCJEA)—A Metamorphosis of the Uniform Child Custody Jurisdiction Act (UCCJA)*, 75 N. Dakota. L. Rev. 301 (1999). Consider then the following decision made famous by extensive media coverage.

Thompson v. Thompson

Supreme Court of the United States, 1988.
484 U.S. 174, 108 S.Ct. 513, 98 L.Ed.2d 512.

■ Justice Marshall delivered the opinion of the Court.

We granted certiorari in this case to determine whether the Parental Kidnaping Prevention Act of 1980, 28 U.S.C. § 1738A, furnishes an implied cause of action in federal court to determine which of two conflicting state custody decisions is valid.

The Parental Kidnaping Prevention Act (PKPA or Act) imposes a duty on the States to enforce a child custody determination entered by a court of a sister State if the determination is consistent with the provisions of the Act. In order for a state court's custody decree to be consistent with the provisions of the Act, the State must have jurisdiction under its own local law and one of five conditions set out in § 1738A(c)(2) must be met. Briefly put, these conditions authorize the state court to enter a custody decree if the child's home is or recently has been in the State, if the child has no home State and it would be in the child's best interest for the State to assume jurisdiction, or if the child is present in the State and has been abandoned or abused. Once a State exercises jurisdiction consistently with the provisions of the Act, no other State may exercise concurrent jurisdiction over the custody dispute, § 1738A(g), even if it would have been empowered to take jurisdiction in the first instance,[1] and all States must accord full faith and credit to the first State's ensuing custody decree.

As the legislative scheme suggests, and as Congress explicitly specified, one of the chief purposes of the PKPA is to "avoid jurisdictional competition and conflict between State courts." This case arises out of a jurisdictional stalemate that came to pass notwithstanding the strictures of the Act. In July 1978, respondent Susan Clay (then Susan Thompson) filed a petition in Los Angeles Superior Court asking the court to dissolve her marriage to petitioner David Thompson and seeking custody of the couple's infant son, Matthew. The court initially awarded the parents joint custody of Matthew, but that arrangement became infeasible when respondent decided to move from California to Louisiana to take a job. The court then entered an order providing that respondent would have sole custody of Matthew once she left for Louisiana. This state of affairs was to remain in effect until the court investigator submitted a report on custody, after which the court intended to make a more studied custody determination.

Respondent and Matthew moved to Louisiana in December of 1980. Three months later, respondent filed a petition in Louisiana state court for enforcement of the California custody decree, judgment of custody, and modification of petitioner's visitation privileges. By order dated April 7, 1981, the Louisiana court granted the petition and awarded sole custody of Matthew to respondent. Two months later, however, the California court, having received and reviewed its investigator's report, entered an order awarding sole custody of Matthew to petitioner. Thus arose the current impasse.

In August 1983, petitioner brought this action in the District Court for the Central District of California. Petitioner requested an order declaring the Louisiana decree invalid and the California decree valid, and enjoining the enforcement of the Louisiana decree. Petitioner did not attempt to enforce the California decree in a Louisiana state court before he filed suit in federal court. The District Court granted respondent's motion to dismiss the complaint for lack of subject matter and personal jurisdiction. The Court of Appeals for the Ninth Circuit affirmed.... 798 F.2d 1547 (C.A.9 1986). Canvassing the background, language, and legislative history of the PKPA, the Court of Appeals held that the Act does not create a private right of action in federal court to determine the validity of two conflicting custody decrees.

In determining whether to infer a private cause of action from a federal statute, our focal point is Congress' intent in enacting the statute....

We examine initially the context of the PKPA with an eye toward determining Congress' perception of the law that it was shaping or reshaping. At the time Congress passed the PKPA, custody orders held a peculiar

---

1. The sole exception to this constraint occurs where the first State either has lost jurisdiction or has declined to exercise continuing jurisdiction. See § 1738A(f).

status under the full faith and credit doctrine, which requires each State to give effect to the judicial proceedings of other States, see U.S. Const., Art. IV, § 1; 28 U.S.C. § 1738. The anomaly traces to the fact that custody orders characteristically are subject to modification as required by the best interests of the child. As a consequence, some courts doubted whether custody orders were sufficiently "final" to trigger full faith and credit requirements, see e.g., Hooks v. Hooks, 771 F.2d 935, 948 (C.A.6 1985); McDougald v. Jenson, 596 F.Supp. 680, 684–685 (N.D.Fla.1984), aff'd 786 F.2d 1465 (C.A.11), cert. denied, 479 U.S. 860, 107 S.Ct. 207, 93 L.Ed.2d 137 (1986), and this Court had declined expressly to settle the question. See Ford v. Ford, 371 U.S. 187, 192, 83 S.Ct. 273, 276, 9 L.Ed.2d 240 (1962). Even if custody orders were subject to full faith and credit requirements, the Full Faith and Credit Clause obliges States only to accord the same force to judgments as would be accorded by the courts of the State in which the judgment was entered. Because courts entering custody orders generally retain the power to modify them, courts in other States were no less entitled to change the terms of custody according to their own views of the child's best interest. See New York ex rel. Halvey v. Halvey, 330 U.S. 610, 614–615, 67 S.Ct. 903, 906, 91 L.Ed. 1133 (1947). For these reasons, a parent who lost a custody battle in one State had an incentive to kidnap the child and move to another State to relitigate the issue. This circumstance contributed to widespread jurisdictional deadlocks like this one, and more importantly, to a national epidemic of parental kidnaping. At the time the PKPA was enacted, sponsors of the Act estimated that between 25,000 and 100,000 children were kidnapped by parents who had been unable to obtain custody in a legal forum.

A number of States joined in an effort to avoid these jurisdictional conflicts by adopting the Uniform Child Custody Jurisdiction Act. The UCCJA prescribed uniform standards for deciding which State could make a custody determination and obligated enacting States to enforce the determination made by the State with proper jurisdiction. The project foundered, however, because a number of States refused to enact the UCCJA while others enacted it with modifications. In the absence of uniform national standards for allocating and enforcing custody determinations, noncustodial parents still had reason to snatch their children and petition the courts of any of a number of haven States for sole custody.

The context of the PKPA therefore suggests that the principal problem Congress was seeking to remedy was the inapplicability of full faith and credit requirements to custody determinations. Statements made when the Act was introduced in Congress forcefully confirm that suggestion. The sponsors and supporters of the Act continually indicated that the purpose of the PKPA was to provide for nationwide enforcement of custody orders made in accordance with the terms of the UCCJA....

The significance of Congress' full faith and credit approach to the problem of child snatching is that the Full Faith and Credit Clause, in either its constitutional or statutory incarnations, does not give rise to an implied federal cause of action. Rather, the clause "only prescribes a rule by which courts, Federal and state, are to be guided when a question arises in the progress of a pending suit as to the faith and credit to be given by the court to the public acts, records, and judicial proceedings of a State other than that in which the court is sitting." Because Congress' chief aim in enacting the PKPA was to extend the requirements of the Full Faith and Credit Clause to custody determinations, the Act is most naturally construed to furnish a rule of decision for courts to use in adjudicating custody disputes and not to create an entirely new cause of action. It thus is not compatible with the purpose and context of the legislative scheme to infer a private cause of action.

The language and placement of the statute reinforce this conclusion. The PKPA is an addendum to the full faith and credit statute, 28 U.S.C. § 1738. This fact alone is strong proof that the Act is intended to have the same operative effect as the full faith and credit statute. Similarly instructive is the heading to the PKPA: "Full faith and credit given to child custody determinations." As for the language of the Act, it is addressed entirely to States and state courts. Unlike statutes that explicitly confer a right on a specified class of persons, the PKPA is a mandate directed to state courts to respect the custody decrees of sister States. We agree with the Court of Appeals that "[i]t seems highly unlikely Congress would follow the pattern of the Full Faith and Credit Clause and section 1738 by structuring section 1738A as a command to state courts to give full faith and credit to the child custody decrees of other states, and yet, without comment, depart from the enforcement practice followed under the Clause and section 1738." 798 F.2d, at 1556.

Finally, the legislative history of the PKPA provides unusually clear indication that Congress did not intend the federal courts to play the enforcement role that petitioner urges. Two passages are particularly revealing. The first of these is a colloquy between Congressmen Conyers and Fish. Congressman Fish had been the sponsor of a competing legislative proposal—ultimately rejected by Congress—that would have extended the District Courts' diversity jurisdiction to encompass actions for enforcement of state custody orders. In the following exchange, Congressman Conyers questioned Congressman Fish about the differences between his proposal and "the Bennett proposal," which was a precursor to the PKPA.

> "Mr. Conyers: Could I just interject, the difference between the Bennett proposal and yours: You would have, enforcing the full faith and credit provision, the parties removed to a Federal court. Under the Bennett provision, his bill would impose the full faith and credit enforcement on the State court.

> "It seems to me that that is a very important difference. The Federal jurisdiction, could it not, Mr. Fish, result in the Federal court litigating between two State court decrees; whereas, in an alternate method previously suggested, we would be imposing the responsibility of the enforcement upon the State court, and thereby reducing, it seems to me, the amount of litigation.

"Do you see any possible merit in leaving the enforcement at the State level, rather than introducing the Federal judiciary?

"Mr. Fish: Well, I really think that it is easier on the parent that has custody of the child to go to the nearest Federal district court....

"Mr. Conyers: Of course you know that the Federal courts have no experience in these kinds of matters, and they would be moving into this other area. I am just thinking of the fact that they have [many areas of federal concern and] on the average of a 21–month docket, you would now be imposing custody matters which it seems might be handled in the courts that normally handle that...." Parental Kidnaping: Hearing on H.R. 1290 Before the Subcommittee on Crime of the House Committee on the Judiciary, 96th Cong., 2d Sess., 14 (1980).

Section 23 of the UCCJA provides:

The general policies of this Act extend to the international area. The provisions of this Act relating to the recognition and enforcement of custody decrees of other states apply to custody decrees and decrees involving legal institutions similar in nature to custody, rendered by appropriate authorities of other nations if reasonable notice and opportunity to be heard were given to all affected persons.

This section was generally included in the laws of the states which have adopted the Act, though at least one jurisdiction (Ohio) omitted it. Several state appeals courts used their versions of the UCCJA provision in reconciling disputes across national borders. See, e.g., Middleton v. Middleton, 314 S.E.2d 362 (Va., 1984); Miller v. Superior Court of Los Angeles County, 587 P.2d 723 (Cal.1978).

This exchange suggests that Congress considered and rejected an approach to the problem that would have resulted in a "[f]ederal court litigating between two State court decrees." Ibid.

The second noteworthy entry in the legislative history is a letter from then Assistant Attorney General Patricia Wald to the Chairman of the House Judiciary Committee, which was referred to extensively during the debate on the PKPA. The letter outlined a variety of solutions to the child-snatching problem. It specifically compared proposals that would "grant jurisdiction to the federal courts to enforce state custody decrees" with an approach, such as was proposed in the PKPA, that would "impose on states a federal duty, under enumerated standards derived generally from the UCCJA, to give full faith and credit to the custody decrees of other states." The letter endorsed the full faith and credit approach that eventually was codified in the PKPA. More importantly, it "strongly oppose[d] ... the creation of a federal forum for resolving custody disputes." Id., at 108. Like Congressman Conyers, the Justice Department reasoned that federal enforcement of state custody decrees would increase the workload of the federal courts and entangle the federal judiciary in domestic relations disputes with which they have little experience and which traditionally have been the province of the States. That the views of the Justice Department and Congressman Conyers prevailed, and that Congress explicitly opted for a full faith and credit approach over reliance on enforcement by the federal courts, provide strong evidence against inferring a federal cause of action.

Petitioner discounts these portions of the legislative history. He argues that the cause of action that he asks us to infer arises only in cases of an actual conflict between two State custody decrees, and thus is substantially narrower than the cause of action proposed by Congressman Fish and rejected by Congress. The Fish bill would have extended federal-diversity jurisdiction to permit federal courts to enforce custody orders in the first instance, before a second State had created a conflict by refusing to do so. This cause of action admittedly is farther reaching that that which we reject today. But the considerations that prompted Congress to reject the Fish bill also militate against the more circumscribed role for the federal courts that petitioner proposes. Instructing the federal courts to play Solomon where two State courts have issued conflicting custody orders would entangle them in traditional state-law questions that they have little expertise to resolve.[4] This is a cost that Congress made clear it did not want the PKPA to carry.[5]

In sum, the context, language, and history of the PKPA together make out a conclusive case against inferring a cause of action in federal court to determine which of two conflicting state custody decrees is valid. Against this impressive evidence, petitioner relies primarily on the argument that failure to infer a cause of action would render the PKPA nugatory. We note, as a preliminary response, that ultimate review remains available in this Court for truly intractable jurisdictional deadlocks. In addition, the unspoken presumption in petitioner's argument is that the States are

---

4. Petitioner argues that determining which of two conflicting custody decrees should be given effect under the PKPA would not require the federal courts to resolve the merits of custody disputes and thus would not offend the long-standing tradition of reserving domestic-relations matters to the States. Petitioner contends that the cause of action he champions would require federal courts only to analyze which of two States is given exclusive jurisdiction under a federal statute, a task for which the federal courts are well-qualified. We cannot agree with petitioner that making a jurisdictional determination under the PKPA would not involve the federal courts in substantive domestic-relations determinations. Under the Act, jurisdiction can turn on the child's "best interest" or on proof that the child has been abandoned or abused. See §§ 1738A(c)(2)(B), (C), and (D). In fact, it would seem that the jurisdictional disputes that are sufficiently complicated as to have provoked conflicting state-court holdings are the most likely to require resolution of these traditional domes-

tic-relations inquiries. See Rogers v. Platt, 259 U.S.App.D.C. 154, 162, 814 F.2d 683, 691 (1987). Cf. Cort v. Ash, 422 U.S. 66, 84, 95 S.Ct. 2080, 2090–2091, 45 L.Ed.2d 26 (1975) (possibility that implied federal cause of action *may* in certain instances turn on state-law issues counsels against inferring such an action).

5. Moreover, petitioner's argument serves to underscore the extraordinary nature of the cause of action he urges us to infer. Petitioner essentially asks that federal district courts exercise appellate review of state-court judgments. This is an unusual cause of action for Congress to grant, either expressly or by implication. Petitioner's proposal is all the more remarkable in the present case, in which he seeks to have a California District Court enjoin enforcement of a Louisiana state-court judgment before the intermediate and supreme courts of Louisiana even have had an opportunity to review that judgment.

either unable or unwilling to enforce the provisions of the Act. This is a presumption we are not prepared, and more importantly, Congress was not prepared, to indulge. State courts faithfully administer the Full Faith and Credit Clause every day; now that Congress has extended full faith and credit requirements to child custody orders, we can think of no reason why the courts' administration of federal law in custody disputes will be any less vigilant. Should state courts prove as obstinate as petitioner predicts, Congress may choose to revisit the issue. But any more radical approach to the problem will have to await further legislative action; we "will not engraft a remedy on a statute, no matter how salutary, that Congress did not intend to provide." The judgment of the Court of Appeals is affirmed.

NOTES

Prosecution for child stealing. In People v. Howard, 36 Cal.3d 852, 206 Cal.Rptr. 124, 686 P.2d 644 (1984), the Supreme Court of California reversed the conviction of a father for stealing his children. The father and mother had obtained an interlocutory judgment of dissolution of their marriage, the mother being awarded child custody and the father visitation rights. Subsequently the parties resumed living together for almost two years during which neither sought to enforce the provisions of the interlocutory decree which had dealt with matters such as community property division and payment of child support by the husband to the wife. The husband left the state at the end of that period, later returning to take the children to Colorado with him after telling their babysitter that he wanted to take them out "for an hour or two." Afterward he refused to allow contact between the children and their mother, who then filed the criminal charges against him. In reversing his conviction, the court held that the parties' reconciliation before a final judgment of dissolution served to cancel the interlocutory decree and thus one essential element, an existing child custody order, was missing from the state's case.

Chief Justice Bird wrote both the majority opinion and a separate concurrence. In the latter she urged that "an erroneous good faith belief in the invalidity of a child custody order" constitutes a defense to a prosecution for child stealing. (The accused also had asserted that the trial court erred in not instructing the jury on the effect of good faith mistake of law.) Justice Mosk, in dissent, responded with his opinion that adding "a subjective belief that the custody decree is valid" as an element of the offense

> would make child-stealing prosecutions extremely difficult, regardless of how egregious the offense, and it would encourage self-help rather than resort to legal process. Thereafter, rare indeed would be the defendant in a child-stealing case who did not assert his subjective belief that a prior custody award was invalid and hence the abduction of the child was permissible.

The crime of custodial interference. In State v. Carver, 113 Wash.2d 591, 781 P.2d 1308 (1989), the Supreme Court of Washington upheld the validity of the State's custodial interference statute, finding that it was not unconstitutionally vague and that it did not define the offense in such a way as to encourage arbitrary or discriminatory enforcement. The key portions of the statute, WASH.REV.CODE ANN. § 9A.40.060, provide that:

(1) A relative of a child under the age of eighteen or of an incompetent person is guilty of custodial interference in the first degree if, with the intent to deny access to the child or incompetent person by a parent, guardian, institution, agency, or other person having a lawful right to physical custody of such person, the relative takes, entices, retains, detains, or conceals the child or incompetent person from a parent, guardian, institution, agency, or other person having a lawful right to physical custody of such person and:

(a) Intends to hold the child or incompetent person permanently or for a protracted period; or

(b) Exposes the child or incompetent person to a substantial risk of illness or physical injury; or

(c) Causes the child or incompetent person to be removed from the state of usual residence; or

(d) Retains, detains, or conceals the child or incompetent person in another state after expiration of any authorized visitation period with intent to intimidate or harass a parent, guardian, institution, agency, or other person having lawful right to physical custody or to prevent a parent, guardian, institution, agency, or other person with lawful right to physical custody from regaining custody.

INTERNATIONAL CHILD ABDUCTION

Delvoye v. Lee

United States Court of Appeals, Third Circuit, 2003.
329 F.3d 330.

■ SCHWARZER, SENIOR DISTRICT JUDGE.

This is an appeal from an order of the district court denying Wim Delvoye's petition to return Baby S to Belgium under the *Hague Convention on the Civil Aspects of International Child Abduction,* Oct. 25, 1980; T.I.A.S. No. 11670, 19 I.L.M. 1501 (the "Convention"). The district court found and concluded that petitioner had failed to meet his burden of proving that Baby S was an habitual resident of Belgium and thus was wrongfully removed from that country. We affirm.

FACTUAL AND PROCEDURAL BACKGROUND

Petitioner and respondent met in New York early in 2000. Petitioner resided in Belgium but made several trips to visit respondent. On his visits to New York, a romantic relationship developed between them. In August 2000, respondent moved into petitioner's New York apartment. While continuing to live in Belgium, petitioner spent about a quarter of his time in New York. In September 2000, respondent learned that she was pregnant with petitioner's child. Respondent began prenatal care in New York, but because petitioner refused to pay the cost of delivery of the baby in the United States and Belgium offered free medical services, respondent agreed to have the baby in Belgium. In November 2000, she traveled to Belgium on a three-month tourist visa, bringing along only one or two suitcases. She left the rest of her belongings, including her non-maternity clothes, in the New York apartment. While in Belgium respondent lived out of her suitcases. When her visa expired she did not extend it. The baby was born on May 14, 2001. By then the relationship between the parties had deteriorated. After initially resisting, petitioner signed the consent form that enabled respondent to get an American passport for Baby S and agreed to respondent's return to the United States with Baby S in July 2001. Over the next two months, petitioner made several trips to the United States and the parties made several attempts to reconcile. When those efforts failed, petitioner filed this petition. Following an evidentiary hearing, the district court denied the petition. This appeal followed. Because the order is a final disposition of the petition, we have jurisdiction under 28 U.S.C. § 1291.

DISCUSSION

Article 3 of the Convention provides in relevant part:

> The removal ... of a child is to be considered wrongful where—a) it is in breach of rights of custody attributed to a person ... either jointly or alone, under the law of the State in which the child was *habitually resident* immediately before the removal....

(Emphasis added.)

The determination of a person's habitual residence is a mixed question of fact and law. We review the district court's findings of historical and narrative facts for clear error, but exercise plenary review over the court's application of legal precepts to the facts. *Feder v. Evans–Feder,* 63 F.3d 217, 222 n. 9 (3d Cir.1995); *see also Mozes v. Mozes,* 239 F.3d 1067, 1073 (9th Cir.2001).

The issue before us is whether Baby S was "habitually resident" in Belgium at the time of his removal to the United States. In *Feder,* we defined the relevant concept:

> [A] child's habitual residence is the place where he ... has been physically present for an amount of time sufficient for acclimatization and which has a "degree of settled purpose" from the child's perspective.... [A] determination of whether any particular place satisfies this standard must focus on the child and consists of an analysis of the child's circumstances in that place and the parents' present, shared intentions regarding their child's presence there.

63 F.3d at 224.

The district court held that petitioner had failed to meet his burden of proving that Baby S was an habitual resident of Belgium. It reasoned that a two-month-old infant, who is still nursing, has not been present long enough to have an acclimatization apart from his parents.

This case then presents the unique question of whether and when a very young infant acquires an habitual residence. It differs from the run of decisions under the Convention where the child is assumed to have an habitual residence initially and the controversy is over a change of that residence. No decisions have squarely addressed the issue before us. The leading treatise on the Convention provides some general guidance:

> There is general agreement on a theoretical level that because of the factual basis of the concept there is no place for habitual residence of dependence. However, in practice it is often not possible to make a distinction between the habitual residence of a child and that of its custodian. Where a child is very young it would, under ordinary circumstances, be very difficult for him ... to have the capability or intention to acquire a separate habitual residence.

Paul Beaumont & Peter McEleavy, *The Hague Convention on International Child Abduction* 91 (1999). An English court has said: "The habitual residence of the child is where it last had a settled home which was in essence where the matrimonial home was." *Dickson v. Dickson,* 1990 SCLR 692. And an Australian court has stated: "A young child cannot acquire habitual residence in isolation from those who care for him. While 'A' lived with both parents, he shared their common habitual residence or lack of it." *Re F* (1991) 1 F.L.R. 548, 551.[2]

Where a matrimonial home exists, i.e., where both parents share a settled intent to reside, determining the habitual residence of an infant presents no particular problem, it simply calls for application of the analysis under the Convention with which courts have become familiar. Where the parents' relationship has broken down, however, as in this case, the character of the problem changes. Of course, the mere fact that conflict has developed between the parents does not *ipso facto* disestablish a child's habitual residence, once it has come into existence. But where the conflict is contemporaneous with the birth of the child, no habitual residence may ever come into existence.

That is not to say that the infant's habitual residence automatically becomes that of his mother. In *Nunez–Escudero v. Tice–Menley,* 58 F.3d 374 (8th Cir.1995), Nunez–Escudero and Tice–Menley married in Mexico in August 1992. A child was born there in July 1993. In September, Tice–Menley left Mexico with her two-month-old infant and returned to the United States. Nunez–Escudero filed a petition under the Convention

---

2. These cases assume that the parents had joint custody. This is true under Belgian law regardless of whether the parents are married. *See* H. Bocken and W. DeBondt, *Introduction to Belgian Law* 150 (cohabiting parents) (2001). But the situation is different where only one parent has custody rights. Thus, "where a child of [two years of age] [was] in the sole lawful custody of the mother, his situation with regard to habitual residence will necessarily be the same as hers." *In re J (C v. S)* [1990] 2 AC 562, 579.

alleging that his son had been wrongfully removed. The district court denied the petition on the ground that return of the child would subject him to a grave risk of harm. The court of appeals reversed and remanded. The mother contended that the court should affirm, notwithstanding the erroneous grave risk of harm determination, on the ground that the infant was not an habitual resident of Mexico. The court rejected the argument and remanded for a determination of the child's habitual residence, stating.

> To say that the child's habitual residence derived from his mother would be inconsistent with the Convention, for it would reward an abducting parent and create an impermissible presumption that the child's habitual residence is where the mother happens to be.

58 F.3d at 379.

The instant case differs from *Nunez–Escudero.* Because the petitioner and respondent had married in Mexico and lived there together for nearly a year before the child was born, a basis existed for finding the child's habitual residence to be in Mexico. Here, in contrast, the district court found that respondent, at petitioner's urging, had traveled to Belgium to avoid the cost of the birth of the child and intended to live there only temporarily. She retained her ties to New York, not having taken her non-maternity clothes, holding only a three-month visa and living out of the two suitcases she brought with her. Thus, there is lacking the requisite "degree of common purpose" to habitually reside in Belgium. As explained in *Re Bates,*

> There must be a degree of settled purpose.... All that is necessary is that the purpose of living where one does has a sufficient degree of continuity to be properly described as settled.

No. CA 122–89, High Court of Justice, Family Div'l Ct. Royal Courts of Justice, United Kingdom (1989), quoted in *Feder,* 63 F.3d at 223.

Because petitioner and respondent lacked the "shared intentions regarding their child's presence [in Belgium]," *Feder,* 63 F.3d at 224, Baby S did not become an habitual resident there. Even if petitioner intended that he become an habitual resident, respondent evidenced no such intention. Addressing the status of a newborn child, one Scottish commentator said:

> [A] newborn child born in the country where his ... parents have their habitual residence could normally be regarded as habitually resident in that country. Where a child is born while his ... mother is temporarily present in a country other than that of her habitual residence it does seem, however, that the child will normally have no habitual residence until living in a country on a footing of some stability.

Dr. E.M. Clive, "The Concept of Habitual Residence," *The Juridical Review part 3,* 138, 146 (1997).

Based on the district court's factual findings, which have not been challenged, we conclude that petitioner failed to prove that Baby S was habitually resident in Belgium.

We affirm the district court's order.

Friedrich v. Friedrich

United States Court of Appeals, Sixth Circuit, 1996.
78 F.3d 1060.

■ Boggs, Circuit Judge.

For the second time, we address the application of the Hague Convention on the Civil Aspects of International Child Abduction ("the Convention") and its implementing legislation, the International Child Abduction Remedies Act ("the Act"), 42 U.S.C. §§ 11601–11610, to the life of Thomas Friedrich, now age six. We affirm the district court's order that Thomas was wrongfully removed from Germany and should be returned.

Thomas was born in Bad Aibling, Germany, to Jeana Friedrich, an American servicewoman stationed there, and her husband, Emanuel Friedrich, a German citizen. When Thomas was two years old, his parents separated after an argument on July 27, 1991. Less than a week later, in the early morning of August 2, 1991, Mrs. Friedrich took Thomas from Germany to her family home in Ironton, Ohio, without informing Mr. Friedrich. Mr. Friedrich sought return of the child in German Family Court, obtaining an order awarding him custody on August 22. He then filed this action for the return of his son in the United States District Court for the Southern District of Ohio on September 23.

We first heard this case three years ago. Friedrich v. Friedrich, 983 F.2d 1396 (6th Cir.1993) ("Friedrich I"). At that time, we reversed the district court's denial of Mr. Friedrich's claim for the return of his son to Germany pursuant to the Convention. We outlined the relevant law on what was then an issue of first impression in the federal appellate courts, and remanded with instructions that the district court determine whether, as a matter of German law, Mr. Friedrich was exercising custody rights to Thomas at the time of removal. We also asked the district court to decide if Mrs. Friedrich could prove any of the four affirmative defenses provided by the Convention and the Act. Thomas, meanwhile, remained with his mother and his mother's parents in Ohio.

On remand, the district court allowed additional discovery and held a new hearing. The court eventually determined that, at the time of Thomas's removal on August 1, 1991, Mr. Friedrich was exercising custody rights to Thomas under German law, or would have been exercising such rights but for the removal. The court then held that Mrs. Friedrich had not established any of the affirmative defenses available to her under the Convention. The court ordered Mrs. Friedrich to return Thomas to Germany "forthwith," but later stayed the order, upon the posting of a bond by Mrs. Friedrich, pending the resolution of this appeal.[1]

---

1. The stay of the judge's order pending appeal, hotly contested below, is not now challenged by Mr. Friedrich. It may have been improvident. Staying the return of a child in an action under the Convention should hardly be a matter of course. The aim of the Convention is to secure prompt return of the child to the correct jurisdiction, and any unnecessary delay renders the subsequent return more difficult for the child, and subsequent adjudication more difficult for the foreign court.

Mrs. Friedrich's appeal raises two issues that are central to the young jurisprudence of the Hague Convention. First, what does it mean to "exercise" custody rights? Second, when can a court refuse to return a child who has been wrongfully removed from a country because return of the abducted child would result in a "grave" risk of harm?

In answering both these questions, we keep in mind two general principles inherent in the Convention and the Act, expressed in Friedrich I, and subsequently embraced by unanimous federal authority. First, a court in the abducted-to nation has jurisdiction to decide the merits of an abduction claim, but not the merits of the underlying custody dispute. Hague Convention, Article 19; 42 U.S.C. § 11601(b)(4); Friedrich I, 983 F.2d at 1400; Rydder v. Rydder, 49 F.3d 369, 372 (8th Cir.1995); Feder v. Evans–Feder, 63 F.3d 217, 221 (3d Cir.1995); Journe v. Journe, 911 F.Supp. 43 (D.P.R.1995). Second, the Hague Convention is generally intended to restore the pre-abduction status quo and to deter parents from crossing borders in search of a more sympathetic court. Pub. Notice 957, 51 Fed.Reg. 10494, 10505 (1986); Friedrich I, 983 F.2d at 1400; Rydder, 49 F.3d at 372; Feder, 63 F.3d at 221; Wanninger v. Wanninger, 850 F.Supp. 78, 80 (D.Mass.1994).

The removal of a child from the country of its habitual residence is "wrongful" under the Hague Convention if a person in that country is, or would otherwise be, exercising custody rights to the child under that country's law at the moment of removal. Hague Convention, Article 3. The plaintiff in an action for return of the child has the burden of proving the exercise of custody rights by a preponderance of the evidence. 42 U.S.C. § 11603(e)(1)(A). We review the district court's findings of fact for clear error and review its conclusions about American, foreign, and international law de novo. See Fed.R.Civ.P. 44.1 (a district court's determination of foreign law should be reviewed as a ruling on a question of law); ...

The district court held that a preponderance of the evidence in the record established that Mr. Friedrich was exercising custody rights over Thomas at the time of Thomas's removal. Mrs. Friedrich alleges that the district court improperly applied German law. Reviewing de novo, we find no error in the court's legal analysis. Custody rights "may arise in particular by operation of law or by reason of a judicial or administrative decision, or by reason of an agreement having legal effect under the law of the State." Hague Convention, Article 3. German law gives both parents equal de jure custody of the child, German Civil Code 1626(1), and, with a few exceptions, this de jure custody continues until a competent court says otherwise. See Currier v. Currier, 845 F.Supp. 916, 920 (D.N.H.1994) ("under German law both parents retain joint rights of custody until a decree has been entered limiting one parent's rights"); Wanninger, 850 F.Supp. at 78 (D.Mass.1994).

Mrs. Friedrich argues that Mr. Friedrich "terminated" his custody rights under German law because, during the argument on the evening of July 27, 1991, he placed Thomas's belongings and hers in the hallway outside of their apartment. The district court properly rejected the claim that these actions could end parental rights as a matter of German law. We agree. After examining the record, we are uncertain as to exactly what happened on the evening of July 27, but we do know that the events of that night were not a judicial abrogation of custody rights. Nor are we persuaded by Mrs. Friedrich's attempts to read the German Civil Code provisions stipulated to by the parties in such a way as to create the ability of one parent to terminate his or her custody rights extrajudicially.[2]

Mrs. Friedrich also argues that, even if Mr. Friedrich had custody rights under German law, he was not exercising those custody rights as contemplated by the Hague Convention. She argues that, since custody rights include the care for the person and property of the child, Mr. Friedrich was not exercising custody rights because he was not paying for or taking care of the child during the brief period of separation in Germany.

The Hague Convention does not define "exercise." As judges in a common law country, we can easily imagine doing so ourselves. One might look to the law of the foreign country to determine if custody rights existed de jure, and then develop a test under the general principles of the Hague Convention to determine what activities—financial support, visitation—constitute sufficient exercise of de jure rights. The question in our immediate case would then be: "was Mr. Friedrich's single visit with Thomas and plans for future visits with Thomas sufficient exercise of custodial rights for us to justify calling the removal of Thomas wrongful?" One might even approach a distinction between the exercise of "custody" rights and the exercise of "access" or "visitation" rights.[3] If Mr. Friedrich, who has de jure custody, was not exercising sufficient de facto custody, Thomas's removal would not be wrongful.

We think it unwise to attempt any such project. Enforcement of the Convention should not to be made dependent on the creation of a common law definition of "exercise." The only acceptable solution, in the absence of a ruling from a court in the country of habitual residence, is to liberally find "exercise" whenever a parent with de jure custody rights keeps, or seeks to keep, any sort of regular contact with his or her child.

2. Mrs. Friedrich cites German Civil Code s 1629, which says that a parent who exercises parental care alone can also represent the child in legal matters alone. Obviously, the ability of one parent to "represent" the child does not imply that the other parent has no custody rights. Mrs. Friedrich also cites German Civil Code s 1631, which says that the Family Court, if petitioned, can assist the parents in providing parental care. We have no idea how this provision, which is essentially no more than a grant of jurisdiction to appoint and direct a family services officer, can support Mrs. Friedrich's claim that "a German parent can certainly relin- quish custody or parental rights absent a judicial determination." Defendants–Appellants' Brief at 15.

3. Article 21 of the Hague Convention instructs signatory countries to protect the "rights of access" of non-custodial parents to their children. Courts have yet to address the question whether Article 21 implies that a custodial parent can remove a child from its country of habitual residence without the permission of a parent whose rights that country's courts have expressly limited to "visitation." See infra n. 4.

We see three reasons for this broad definition of "exercise." First, American courts are not well suited to determine the consequences of parental behavior under the law of a foreign country. It is fairly easy for the courts of one country to determine whether a person has custody rights under the law of another country. It is also quite possible for a court to determine if an order by a foreign court awards someone "custody" rights, as opposed to rights of "access."[4] Far more difficult is the task of deciding, prior to a ruling by a court in the abducted-from country, if a parent's custody rights should be ignored because he or she was not acting sufficiently like a custodial parent. A foreign court, if at all possible, should refrain from making such policy-oriented decisions concerning the application of German law to a child whose habitual residence is, or was, Germany.

Second, an American decision about the adequacy of one parent's exercise of custody rights is dangerously close to forbidden territory: the merits of the custody dispute. The German court in this case is perfectly capable of taking into account Mr. Friedrich's behavior during the August 1991 separation, and the German court presumably will tailor its custody order accordingly. A decision by an American court to deny return to Germany because Mr. Friedrich did not show sufficient attention or concern for Thomas's welfare would preclude the German court from addressing these issues—and the German court may well resolve them differently.

Third, the confusing dynamics of quarrels and informal separations make it difficult to assess adequately the acts and motivations of a parent. An occasional visit may be all that is available to someone left, by the vagaries of marital discord, temporarily without the child. Often the child may be avoided, not out of a desire to relinquish custody, but out of anger, pride, embarrassment, or fear, vis a vis the other parent.[5] Reading too much into a parent's behavior during these difficult times could be inaccurate and unfair. Although there may be situations when a long period of unexplainable neglect of the child could constitute non-exercise of otherwise valid custody rights under the Convention, as a general rule, any attempt to maintain a somewhat regular relationship with the child should constitute "exercise." This rule leaves the full resolution of custody issues, as the Convention and common sense indicate, to the courts of the country of habitual residence.

We are well aware that our approach requires a parent, in the event of a separation or custody dispute, to seek permission from the other parent

---

4. For a particularly difficult situation, ably resolved, see David S. v. Zamira, 151 Misc.2d 630, 574 N.Y.S.2d 429 (Fam.Ct. 1991), aff'd In re Schneir, 17 F.L.R. 1237 (N.Y.App.Div.2d Dep't). The court here held that an order giving the non-custodial parent visitation rights and restricting the custodial parent from leaving the country constitutes an order granting "custodial" rights to both parents under the Hague Convention.

5. When Mrs. Friedrich took Thomas and her belongings from the family apartment on the morning of July 28, she was accompanied by some friends from work: soldiers of the United States Army. Mr. Friedrich testified that he was "intimidated" by the presence of the soldiers, and discouraged from making a stronger objection to the removal of his child.

or from the courts before taking a child out of the country of its habitual residence. Any other approach allows a parent to pick a "home court" for the custody dispute ex parte, defeating a primary purpose of the Convention. We believe that, where the reason for removal is legitimate, it will not usually be difficult to obtain approval from either the other parent or a foreign court. Furthermore, as the case for removal of the child in the custody of one parent becomes more compelling, approval (at least the approval of a foreign court) should become easier to secure.

Mrs. Friedrich argues that our approach cannot adequately cope with emergency situations that require the child and parent to leave the country. In her case, for example, Mrs. Friedrich claims that removal of Thomas to Ohio was necessary because she could no longer afford to have the child stay at the army base, and Mr. Friedrich refused to provide shelter. Examining the record, we seriously doubt that Mr. Friedrich would have refused to lodge Thomas at his expense in Germany. In any event, even if an emergency forces a parent to take a child to a foreign country, any such emergency cannot excuse the parent from returning the child to the jurisdiction once return of the child becomes safe. Nor can an emergency justify a parent's refusal to submit the child to the authority of the foreign court for resolution of custody matters, including the question of the appropriate temporary residence of the child. See Viragh v. Foldes, 415 Mass. 96, 612 N.E.2d 241 (1993) (child removed to America by one parent without notification to other parent may remain in America in light of decision by Hungarian court in parallel proceeding that best interests of the child require exercise of sole custody by parent in America).

We therefore hold that, if a person has valid custody rights to a child under the law of the country of the child's habitual residence, that person cannot fail to "exercise" those custody rights under the Hague Convention short of acts that constitute clear and unequivocal abandonment of the child.[6] Once it determines that the parent exercised custody rights in any manner, the court should stop—completely avoiding the question whether the parent exercised the custody rights well or badly. These matters go to the merits of the custody dispute and are, therefore, beyond the subject matter jurisdiction of the federal courts. 42 U.S.C. § 11601(b)(4).

In this case, German law gave Mr. Friedrich custody rights to Thomas. The facts before us clearly indicate that he attempted to exercise these rights during the separation from his wife. Mr. and Mrs. Friedrich argued during the evening of July 27, 1991, and separated on the morning of July 28. Mrs. Friedrich left with her belongings and Thomas. She stayed on the army base with the child for four days. Mr. Friedrich telephoned Mrs. Friedrich on July 29 to arrange a visit with Thomas, and spent the

---

6. The situation would be different if the country of habitual residence had a legal rule regarding the exercise of custody rights clearly tied to the Hague concept of international removal. If, for example, Germany had a law stating that, for the purposes of the Convention, mere visitation without financial support during a period of informal separation does not constitute the "exercise" of custody rights, we would, of course, be bound to apply that law in this case.

afternoon of that day with his son. Mr. and Mrs. Friedrich met on August 1 to talk about Thomas and their separation. The parties dispute the upshot of this conversation. Mrs. Friedrich says that Mr. Friedrich expressed a general willingness that Thomas move to America with his mother. Mr. Friedrich denies this. It is clear, however, that the parties did agree to immediate visitations of Thomas by Mr. Friedrich, scheduling the first such visit for August 3. Shortly after midnight on August 2, Mrs. Friedrich took her son and, without informing her husband,[7] left for America by airplane.

Because Mr. Friedrich had custody rights to Thomas as a matter of German law, and did not clearly abandon those rights prior to August 1, the removal of Thomas without his consent was wrongful under the Convention, regardless of any other considerations about Mr. Friedrich's behavior during the family's separation in Germany.

Once a plaintiff establishes that removal was wrongful, the child must be returned unless the defendant can establish one of four defenses. Two of these defenses can be established by a preponderance of the evidence, 42 U.S.C. § 11603(e)(2)(B): the proceeding was commenced more than one year after the removal of the child and the child has become settled in his or her new environment, Hague Convention, Article 12; or, the person seeking return of the child consented to or subsequently acquiesced in the removal or retention, Hague Convention, Article 13a. The other two defenses must be shown by clear and convincing evidence, 42 U.S.C. § 11603(e)(2)(A): there is a grave risk that the return of the child would expose it to physical or psychological harm, Hague Convention, Article 13b; or, the return of the child "would not be permitted by the fundamental principles of the requested State relating to the protection of human rights and fundamental freedoms," Hague Convention, Article 20.[8]

All four of these exceptions are "narrow," 42 U.S.C. § 11601(a)(4). They are not a basis for avoiding return of a child merely because an American court believes it can better or more quickly resolve a dispute. See Rydder, 49 F.3d at 372 (citing Friedrich I, 983 F.2d at 1400). In fact, a federal court retains, and should use when appropriate, the discretion to return a child, despite the existence of a defense, if return would further the aims of the Convention. Feder, 63 F.3d at 226 (citing Pub. Notice 957, 51 Fed.Reg. 10494, 10509 (1986)).

Mrs. Friedrich alleges that she proved by clear and convincing evidence in the proceedings below that the return of Thomas to Germany would cause him grave psychological harm. Mrs. Friedrich testified that Thomas has grown attached to family and friends in Ohio. She also hired an expert psychologist who testified that returning Thomas to Germany would be

---

7. Q. You didn't call your husband, Mrs. Friedrich, because you didn't want him to know you were leaving; isn't that the reason? A. Yes it is. Transcript of October 16, 1991, Proceedings at 36.

8. The situation changes somewhat when the child is older. The Hague Convention allows a court in the abducted-to country to "refuse to order the return of the child if it finds that the child objects to being returned and has attained an age and degree of maturity at which it is appropriate to take account of its views." Hague Convention, Article 13.

traumatic and difficult for the child, who was currently happy and healthy in America with his mother. [Thomas] definitely would experience the loss of his mother ... if he were to be removed to Germany. Than that would be a considerable loss. And there then would be the probabilities of anger both towards his mother, who it might appear that she has abandoned him [sic], and towards the father for creating that abandonment. [These feelings] could be plenty enough springboard for other developmental or emotional restrictions which could include nightmares, antisocial behavior, a whole host of anxious-type behavior. Blaske Deposition at 28–29.

If we are to take the international obligations of American courts with any degree of seriousness, the exception to the Hague Convention for grave harm to the child requires far more than the evidence that Mrs. Friedrich provides. Mrs. Friedrich alleges nothing more than adjustment problems that would attend the relocation of most children. There is no allegation that Mr. Friedrich has ever abused Thomas. The district court found that the home that Mr. Friedrich has prepared for Thomas in Germany appears adequate to the needs of any young child. The father does not work long hours, and the child's German grandmother is ready to care for the child when the father cannot. There is nothing in the record to indicate that life in Germany would result in any permanent harm or unhappiness.

Furthermore, even if the home of Mr. Friedrich were a grim place to raise a child in comparison to the pretty, peaceful streets of Ironton, Ohio, that fact would be irrelevant to a federal court's obligation under the Convention. We are not to debate the relevant virtues of Batman and Max und Moritz, Wheaties and Milchreis. The exception for grave harm to the child is not license for a court in the abducted-to country to speculate on where the child would be happiest. That decision is a custody matter, and reserved to the court in the country of habitual residence.

Mrs. Friedrich advocates a wide interpretation of the grave risk of harm exception that would reward her for violating the Convention. A removing parent must not be allowed to abduct a child and then—when brought to court—complain that the child has grown used to the surroundings to which they were abducted.[9] Under the logic of the Convention, it is the abduction that causes the pangs of subsequent return. The disruption of the usual sense of attachment that arises during most long stays in a single place with a single parent should not be a "grave" risk of harm for the purposes of the Convention.

In thinking about these problems, we acknowledge that courts in the abducted-from country are as ready and able as we are to protect children. If return to a country, or to the custody of a parent in that country, is dangerous, we can expect that country's courts to respond accordingly. Cf. Nunez–Escudero v. Tice–Menley, 58 F.3d 374, 377 (8th Cir.1995) (if parent in Mexico is abusive, infant returned to Mexico for custody determination

---

9. We forgo the temptation to compare this behavior to the standard definition of "chutzpah." See A. Kozinski & E. Volokh, Lawsuit, Shmawsuit, 103 Yale L.J. 463, 467 (1993).

can be institutionalized during pendency of custody proceedings). And if Germany really is a poor place for young Thomas to grow up, as Mrs. Friedrich contends, we can expect the German courts to recognize that and award her custody in America. When we trust the court system in the abducted-from country, the vast majority of claims of harm—those that do not rise to the level of gravity required by the Convention—evaporate.

The international precedent available supports our restrictive reading of the grave harm exception. In Thomson v. Thomson, 119 D.L.R.4th 253 (Can.1994), the Supreme Court of Canada held that the exception applies only to harm "that also amounts to an intolerable situation." Id. at 286. The Court of Appeal of the United Kingdom has held that the harm required is "something greater than would normally be expected on taking a child away from one parent and passing him to another." In re A., 1 F.L.R. 365, 372 (Eng.C.A.1988). And other circuit courts in America have followed this reasoning in cases decided since Friedrich I. See Nunez–Escudero, 58 F.3d at 377 (citing Thomson, 119 D.L.R.4th at 286, and In re A., 1 F.L.R. at 372); Rydder, 49 F.3d at 373 (affirming district court order for return of child over abducting parent's objection that return would cause grave harm). Finally, we are instructed by the following observation by the United States Department of State concerning the grave risk of harm exception. This provision was not intended to be used by defendants as a vehicle to litigate (or relitigate) the child's best interests. Only evidence directly establishing the existence of a grave risk that would expose the child to physical or emotional harm or otherwise place the child in an intolerable situation is material to the court's determination. The person opposing the child's return must show that the risk to the child is grave, not merely serious. A review of deliberations on the Convention reveals that "intolerable situation" was not intended to encompass return to a home where money is in short supply, or where educational or other opportunities are more limited than in the requested State. An example of an "intolerable situation" is one in which a custodial parent sexually abuses the child. If the other parent removes or retains the child to safeguard it against further victimization, and the abusive parent then petitions for the child's return under the Convention, the court may deny the petition. Such action would protect the child from being returned to an "intolerable situation" and subjected to a grave risk of psychological harm. Public Notice 957, 51 FR 10494, 10510 (March 26, 1986) (emphasis added).

For all of these reasons, we hold that the district court did not err by holding that "[t]he record in the instant case does not demonstrate by clear and convincing evidence that Thomas will be exposed to a grave risk of harm." Although it is not necessary to resolve the present appeal, we believe that a grave risk of harm for the purposes of the Convention can exist in only two situations. First, there is a grave risk of harm when return of the child puts the child in imminent danger prior to the resolution of the custody dispute—e.g., returning the child to a zone of war, famine, or disease. Second, there is a grave risk of harm in cases of serious abuse or neglect, or extraordinary emotional dependence, when the court in the country of habitual residence, for whatever reason, may be incapable or unwilling to give the child adequate protection. Psychological evidence of the sort Mrs. Friedrich introduced in the proceeding below is only relevant if it helps prove the existence of one of these two situations.[10]

Mrs. Friedrich also claims that the district court erred in ordering Thomas's return because Mrs. Friedrich proved by a preponderance of the evidence that Mr. Friedrich (i) consented to, and (ii) subsequently acquiesced in, the removal of Thomas to America.[11]

Mrs. Friedrich bases her claim of consent to removal on statements that she claims Mr. Friedrich made to her during their separation. Mr. Friedrich flatly denies that he made these statements. The district court was faced with a choice as to whom it found more believable in a factual dispute. There is nothing in the record to suggest that the court's decision to believe Mr. Friedrich, and hold that he "did not exhibit an intention or a willingness to terminate his parental rights," was clearly erroneous. In fact, Mr. Friedrich's testimony is strongly supported by the circumstances of the removal of Thomas—most notably the fact that Mrs. Friedrich did not inform Mr. Friedrich that she was departing. Supra n. 7. The deliberately secretive nature of her actions is extremely strong evidence that Mr. Friedrich would not have consented to the removal of Thomas. For these reasons, we hold that the district court did not abuse its discretion in finding that Mrs. Friedrich took Thomas to America without Mr. Friedrich's consent.

Mrs. Friedrich bases her claim of subsequent acquiescence on a statement made by Mr. Friedrich to one of her commanding officers, Captain Michael Farley, at a cocktail party on the military base after Mrs. Friedrich had left with Thomas. Captain Farley, who cannot date the conversation exactly, testified that: During the conversation, Mr. Friedrich indicated that he was not seeking custody of the child, because he didn't have the means to take care of the child. Farley Deposition at 13. Mr. Friedrich denies that he made this statement. The district court made no specific finding regarding this fact.

We believe that the statement to Captain Farley, even if it was made, is insufficient evidence of subsequent acquiescence. Subsequent acquiescence requires more than an isolated statement to a third-party. Each of the words and actions of a parent during the separation are not to be scrutinized for a possible waiver of custody rights. See Wanninger, 850 F.Supp. at 81–82 (refusing to construe father's personal letters to wife and priest as sufficient evidence of acquiescence where father consistently attempted to keep in contact with child). Although we must decide the

---

10. The only other circuit addressing the issue had its own doubts about whether a psychological report concerning the difficulty that a child would face when separated from the abducting parent is ever relevant to a Hague Convention action. Nunez–Escudero, 58 F.3d at 378 (such reports are not per se irrelevant, but they are rarely dispositive).

11. Article 13a provides a defense to an action for return if the petitioner "consented to or subsequently acquiesced in the removal or retention" of the child. The Convention does not define consent or acquiescence in any more definite manner, and there is no statement to guide us in the text or legislative history of the Act.

matter without guidance from previous appellate court decisions, we believe that acquiescence under the Convention requires either: an act or statement with the requisite formality, such as testimony in a judicial proceeding;[12] a convincing written renunciation of rights;[13] or a consistent attitude of acquiescence over a significant period of time.

By August 22, 1991, twenty-one days after the abduction, Mr. Friedrich had secured a German court order awarding him custody of Thomas. He has resolutely sought custody of his son since that time. It is by these acts, not his casual statements to third parties, that we will determine whether or not he acquiesced to the retention of his son in America. Since Mrs. Friedrich has not introduced evidence of a formal renunciation or a consistent attitude of acquiescence over a significant period of time, the judgment of the district court on this matter was not erroneous.

The district court's order that Thomas be immediately returned to Germany is AFFIRMED, and the district court's stay of that order pending appeal is VACATED. Because Thomas's return to Germany is already long-overdue, we order, pursuant to Fed.R.App.P. 41(a), that our mandate issue forthwith.

INTERNATIONAL CHILD ABDUCTION REMEDIES ACT OF 1988

42 U.S.C.A. § 11601 et seq. (West 2005)

§ 11601. Findings and declarations

(a) Findings

The Congress makes the following findings:

(1) The international abduction or wrongful retention of children is harmful to their well-being.

(2) Persons should not be permitted to obtain custody of children by virtue of their wrongful removal or retention.

(3) International abductions and receptions of children are increasing, and only concerted cooperation pursuant to an international agreement can effectively combat this problem.

(4) The Convention on the Civil Aspects of International Child Abduction, done at The Hague on October 25, 1980, establishes legal rights and

---

12. In Journe v. Journe, 911 F.Supp. 43 (D.P.R.1995), a French father instituted custody proceedings in France after the mother took the children to Puerto Rico. The mother returned to France, presumably without the children, to participate in the proceedings. The father voluntarily dismissed the French custody proceedings, but continued to pursue Hague Convention remedies The district court held that the father had waived his rights to have a French court determine cus-tody issues by virtue of the voluntary dismissal of his French case. Id. at 48. The court reached that decision because of "its equitable powers," not because the dismissal constituted "acquiescence" for the purposes of the Convention.

13. A hastily-drafted and soon-rued written agreement was found insufficient indication of consent in Currier v. Currier, 845 F.Supp. 916 (D.N.H.1994).

procedures for the prompt return of children who have been wrongfully removed or retained, as well as for securing the exercise of visitation rights. Children who are wrongfully removed or retained within the meaning of the Convention are to be promptly returned unless one of the narrow exceptions set forth in the Convention applies. The Convention provides a sound treaty framework to help resolve the problem of international abduction and retention of children and will deter such wrongful removals and receptions.

(b) Declarations

The Congress makes the following declarations:

(1) It is the purpose of this chapter to establish procedures for the implementation of the Convention in the United States.

(2) The provisions of this chapter are in addition to and not in lieu of the provisions of the Convention.

(3) In enacting this chapter the Congress recognizes—

(A) the international character of the Convention; and

(B) the need for uniform international interpretation of the Convention.

(4) The Convention and this chapter empower courts in the United States to determine only rights under the Convention and not the merits of any underlying child custody claims.

§ 11602. Definitions

For the purposes of this chapter—

(1) the term "applicant" means any person who, pursuant to the Convention, files an application with the United States Central Authority or a Central Authority of any other party to the Convention for the return of a child alleged to have been wrongfully removed or retained or for arrangements for organizing or securing the effective exercise of rights of access pursuant to the Convention;

(2) the term "Convention" means the Convention on the Civil Aspects of International Child Abduction, done at The Hague on October 25, 1980;

(3) the term "Parent Locator Service" means the service established by the Secretary of Health and Human Services under section 653 of this title;

(4) the term "petitioner" means any person who, in accordance with this chapter, files a petition in court seeking relief under the Convention;

(5) the term "person" includes any individual, institution, or other legal entity or body;

(6) the term "respondent" means any person against whose interests a petition is filed in court, in accordance with this chapter, which seeks relief under the Convention;

(7) the term "rights of access" means visitation rights;

(8) the term "State" means any of the several States, the District of Columbia, and any commonwealth, territory, or possession of the United States; and

(9) the term "United States Central Authority" means the agency of the Federal Government designated by the President under section 11606(a) of this title.

§ 11603. Judicial remedies

(a) Jurisdiction of the courts

The courts of the States and the United States district courts shall have concurrent original jurisdiction of actions arising under the Convention.

(b) Petitions

Any person seeking to initiate judicial proceedings under the Convention for the return of a child or for arrangements for organizing or securing the effective exercise of rights of access to a child may do so by commencing a civil action by filing a petition for the relief sought in any court which has jurisdiction of such action and which is authorized to exercise its jurisdiction in the place where the child is located at the time the petition is filed.

(c) Notice

Notice of an action brought under subsection (b) of this section shall be given in accordance with the applicable law governing notice in interstate child custody proceedings.

(d) Determination of case

The court in which an action is brought under subsection (b) of this section shall decide the case in accordance with the Convention.

(e) Burdens of proof

(1) A petitioner in an action brought under subsection (b) of this section shall establish by a preponderance of the evidence—

(A) in the case of an action for the return of a child, that the child has been wrongfully removed or retained within the meaning of the Convention; and

(B) in the case of an action for arrangements for organizing or securing the effective exercise of rights of access, that the petitioner has such rights.

(2) In the case of an action for the return of a child, a respondent who opposes the return of the child has the burden of establishing—

(A) by clear and convincing evidence that one of the exceptions set forth in article 13b or 20 of the Convention applies; and

(B) by a preponderance of the evidence that any other exception set forth in article 12 or 13 of the Convention applies.

(f) Application of the Convention

For purposes of any action brought under this chapter—

(1) the term "authorities", as used in article 15 of the Convention to refer to the authorities of the state of the habitual residence of a child, includes courts and appropriate government agencies;

(2) the terms "wrongful removal or retention" and "wrongfully removed or retained", as used in the Convention, include a removal or retention of a child before the entry of a custody order regarding that child; and

(3) the term "commencement of proceedings", as used in article 12 of the Convention, means, with respect to the return of a child located in the United States, the filing of a petition in accordance with subsection (b) of this section.

(g) Full faith and credit

Full faith and credit shall be accorded by the courts of the States and the courts of the United States to the judgment of any other such court ordering or denying the return of a child, pursuant to the Convention, in an action brought under this chapter.

(h) Remedies under the Convention not exclusive

The remedies established by the Convention and this chapter shall be in addition to remedies available under other laws or international agreements.

§ 11604. Provisional remedies

(a) Authority of courts

In furtherance of the objectives of article 7(b) and other provisions of the Convention, and subject to the provisions of subsection (b) of this section, any court exercising jurisdiction of an action brought under section 11603(b) of this title may take or cause to be taken measures under Federal or State law, as appropriate, to protect the well-being of the child involved or to prevent the child's further removal or concealment before the final disposition of the petition.

(b) Limitation on authority

No court exercising jurisdiction of an action brought under section 11603(b) of this title may, under subsection (a) of this section, order a child removed from a person having physical control of the child unless the applicable requirements of State law are satisfied.These cases assume that the parents had joint custody.

§ 11605. Admissibility of documents

With respect to any application to the United States Central Authority, or any petition to a court under section 11603 of this title, which seeks relief under the Convention, or any other documents or information included with such application or petition or provided after such submission which relates to the application or petition, as the case may be, no authentication of such application, petition, document, or information shall be required in order for the application, petition, document, or information to be admissible in court.

§ 11606.   United States Central Authority

(a) Designation

The President shall designate a Federal agency to serve as the Central Authority for the United States under the Convention.

(b) Functions

The functions of the United States Central Authority are those ascribed to the Central Authority by the Convention and this chapter.

(c) Regulatory authority

The United States Central Authority is authorized to issue such regulations as may be necessary to carry out its functions under the Convention and this chapter.

(d) Obtaining information from Parent Locator

The United States Central Authority may, to the extent authorized by the Social Security Act [42 U.S.C.A. § 301 et seq.], obtain information from the Parent Locator Service.

(e) Grant Authority

The United States Central Authority is authorized to make grants to, or enter into contracts or agreements with, any individual, corporation, other Federal, State, or local agency, or private entity or organization in the United States for purposes of accomplishing its responsibilities under the Convention and this chapter.

(f) Limited liability of private entities acting under the direction of the United States central authority

(1) Limitation on liability

Except as provided in paragraphs (2) and (3), a private entity or organization that receives a grant from or enters into a contract or agreement with the United States Central Authority under subsection (e) of this section for purposes of assisting the United States Central Authority in carrying out its responsibilities and functions under the Convention and this chapter, including any director, officer, employee, or agent of such entity or organization, shall not be liable in any civil action sounding in tort for damages directly related to the performance of such responsibilities and functions as defined by the regulations issued under subsection (c) of this section that are in effect on October 1, 2004

(2) Exception for intentional, reckless, or other misconduct

The limitation on liability under paragraph (1) shall not apply in any action in which the plaintiff proves that the private entity, organization, officer, employee, or agent described in paragraph (1), as the case may be, engaged in intentional misconduct or acted, or failed to act, with actual malice, with reckless disregard to a substantial risk of causing injury without legal justification, or for a purpose unrelated to the performance of responsibilities or functions under this chapter.

(3) Exception for ordinary business activities

The limitation on liability under paragraph (1) shall not apply to any alleged act or omission related to an ordinary business activity, such as an activity involving general administration or operations, the use of motor vehicles, or personnel management.

§ 11607. Costs and fees

(a) Administrative costs

No department, agency, or instrumentality of the Federal Government or of any State or local government may impose on an applicant any fee in relation to the administrative processing of applications submitted under the Convention.

(b) Costs incurred in civil actions

(1) Petitioners may be required to bear the costs of legal counsel or advisors, court costs incurred in connection with their petitions, and travel costs for the return of the child involved and any accompanying persons, except as provided in paragraphs (2) and (3).

(2) Subject to paragraph (3), legal fees or court costs incurred in connection with an action brought under section 11603 of this title shall be borne by the petitioner unless they are covered by payments from Federal, State, or local legal assistance or other programs.

(3) Any court ordering the return of a child pursuant to an action brought under section 11603 of this title shall order the respondent to pay necessary expenses incurred by or on behalf of the petitioner, including court costs, legal fees, foster home or other care during the course of proceedings in the action, and transportation costs related to the return of the child, unless the respondent establishes that such order would be clearly inappropriate.

§ 11608. Collection, maintenance, and dissemination of information

(a) In general

In performing its functions under the Convention, the United States Central Authority may, under such conditions as the Central Authority prescribes by regulation, but subject to subsection (c) of this section, receive from or transmit to any department, agency, or instrumentality of the Federal Government or of any State or foreign government, and receive from or transmit to any applicant, petitioner, or respondent, information necessary to locate a child or for the purpose of otherwise implementing the Convention with respect to a child, except that the United States Central Authority—

(1) may receive such information from a Federal or State department, agency, or instrumentality only pursuant to applicable Federal and State statutes; and

(2) may transmit any information received under this subsection notwithstanding any provision of law other than this chapter.

(b) Requests for information

Requests for information under this section shall be submitted in such manner and form as the United States Central Authority may prescribe by regulation and shall be accompanied or supported by such documents as the United States Central Authority may require.

(c) Responsibility of government entities

Whenever any department, agency, or instrumentality of the United States or of any State receives a request from the United States Central Authority for information authorized to be provided to such Central Authority under subsection (a) of this section, the head of such department, agency, or instrumentality shall promptly cause a search to be made of the files and records maintained by such department, agency, or instrumentality in order to determine whether the information requested is contained in any such files or records. If such search discloses the information requested, the head of such department, agency, or instrumentality shall immediately transmit such information to the United States Central Authority, except that any such information the disclosure of which—

(1) would adversely affect the national security interests of the United States or the law enforcement interests of the United States or of any State; or

(2) would be prohibited by section 9 of Title 13;

shall not be transmitted to the Central Authority. The head of such department, agency, or instrumentality shall, immediately upon completion of the requested search, notify the Central Authority of the results of the search, and whether an exception set forth in paragraph (1) or (2) applies. In the event that the United States Central Authority receives information and the appropriate Federal or State department, agency, or instrumentality thereafter notifies the Central Authority that an exception set forth in paragraph (1) or (2) applies to that information, the Central Authority may not disclose that information under subsection (a) of this section.

(d) Information available from Parent Locator Service

To the extent that information which the United States Central Authority is authorized to obtain under the provisions of subsection (c) of this section can be obtained through the Parent Locator Service, the United States Central Authority shall first seek to obtain such information from the Parent Locator Service, before requesting such information directly under the provisions of subsection (c) of this section.

(e) Record keeping

The United States Central Authority shall maintain appropriate records concerning its activities and the disposition of cases brought to its attention.

[EDITORS' NOTE: Sections 11609 and 11610 are omitted. The first provides for designation of persons (some of whom may be private citizens) to monitor operation of the Convention and to provide advice on its implementation. The latter section authorizes annual appropriations.]

NOTES

(1) The Hague Convention on the Civil Aspects of International Child Abduction was adopted by the Hague Conference on Private International Law in1980 and was ratified by the United States in 1988. *See* Westbrook, *Law and Treaty Responses to International Child Abduction*, 20 VA.J.INT. LAW 669 (1980). It was implemented in the United States in 1988 through adoption of the International Child Abduction Remedies Act, 42 U.S.C.A. §§ 11601et seq. The text of the convention can be found in WALTER WADLINGTON AND RAYMOND C. O'BRIEN, FAMILY LAW STATUTES, INTERNATIONAL CONVENTIONS AND UNIFORM LAWS. (3d ed. 2007).

There are a number of practical problems regarding the Hague Convention. It calls for the designation of a Central Authority in each country; in the United States this is the Department of State. Not all states have adequately implemented it. The cost and availability of counsel also can serve as impediments. *See* 3d B. Whitman, *Recent Development. The Second Circuit Limits "Custody Rights" Under the Hague Convention on the Civil Aspects of International Child Abduction.* 9 TUL. J. INT'L & COMP. L. 605 (2001); Peter Pfund, *The Hague Convention on International Child Abduction, the International Child Abduction Remedies Act, and the Need for Availability of Counsel for All Petitioners,* 24 FAM.L.Q. 35 (1990). For more details about the convention, *see* the *Legal Analysis of the Hague Convention on the Civil Aspects of International Child Abduction,* 51 FED. REG. 10,503, 10,505 (1993).

(2) Section 23 of the UCCJA provides:

> The general policies of this Act extend to the international area. The provisions of this Act relating to the recognition and enforcement of custody decrees of other states apply to custody decrees and decrees involving legal institutions similar in nature to custody, rendered by appropriate authorities of other nations if reasonable notice and opportunity to be heard were given to all affected persons.

This section was generally included in the laws of the states which have adopted the Act, though at least one jurisdiction (Ohio) omitted it. Several state appeals courts used their versions of the UCCJA provision in reconciling disputes across national borders. *See, e.g.,* Middleton v. Middleton, 227 Va. 82, 314 S.E.2d 362 (1984); Miller v. Superior Court of Los Angeles County, 22 Cal.3d 923, 151 Cal.Rptr. 6, 587 P.2d 723 (1978).

Sections 301 and 302 of the UCCJEA (reprinted earlier in this Chapter) provide that a state may enforce an order for return of a child made under the Hague Convention on the Civil Aspects of International Child Abduction.

INTERNATIONAL PARENTAL KIDNAPPING CRIME ACT OF 1993

18 U.S.C.A. § 1204 (West 2006)

§ 1204. International parental kidnapping

(a) Whoever removes a child from the United States or retains a child (who has been in the United States) outside the United States with intent to obstruct the lawful exercise of parental rights shall be fined under this title or imprisoned not more than 3 years, or both.

(b) As used in this section—

(1) the term "child" means a person who has not attained the age of 16 years; and

(2) the term "parental rights", with respect to a child, means the right to physical custody of the child—

(A) whether joint or sole (and includes visiting rights); and

(B) whether arising by operation of law, court order, or legally binding agreement of the parties.

(c) It shall be an affirmative defense under this section that—

(1) the defendant acted within the provisions of a valid court order granting the defendant legal custody or visitation rights and that order was obtained pursuant to the Uniform Child Custody Jurisdiction Act and was in effect at the time of the offense;

(2) the defendant was fleeing an incidence or pattern of domestic violence;

(3) the defendant had physical custody of the child pursuant to a court order granting legal custody or visitation rights and failed to return the child as a result of circumstances beyond the defendant's control, and the defendant notified or made reasonable attempts to notify the other parent or lawful custodian of the child of such circumstances within 24 hours after the visitation period had expired and returned the child as soon as possible.

(d) This section does not detract from The Hague Convention on the Civil Aspects of International Parental Child Abduction, done at The Hague on October 25, 1980.

NOTE

The principal mechanism by which abducted children may be returned to the United States is the Hague Convention on the Civil Aspects of

International Law. If a child is taken to a non-signatory country, however, the treaty may not be implemented. To fill this vacuum in the Hague Convention's coverage, Congress enacted the preceding statute.

For a discussion of possible ways for dealing with abduction to escape from domestic violence, *see* Merle H. Weiner, *International Child Abduction and The Escape from Domestic Violence*, 69 FORDHAM L.REV. 593 (2000).

CHAPTER IX

Parental Rights Termination and Adoption

A. Severing Parental Rights Involuntarily

Involuntary termination of parental rights typically occurs within the context of abuse, neglect abandonment or parental incapacity. Because of the peremptory nature of a termination decree, unlike a custody decision, issues of due process loom importantly *See* Raymond C. O'Brien, *An Analysis of Realistic Due Process Rights of Children Versus Parents,* 26 Conn. L. Rev.1209 (1994). Issues of timing often are difficult because undue delay may impair the prospects of placing a child in a stable home, though it would be preferable in many cases that families remain intact. In 1991, the final report of the National Commission on Children, *Beyond Rhetoric,* acknowledged that termination of parental rights may not always be in the best interest of a child, but nevertheless stated that:

> Children need strong, stable, one-to-one relationships with their parents. When parents are unable or unwilling to provide consistent care and nurturing, children should have an opportunity to develop stable, trusting relationships with other caring adults. Accordingly, the Commission encourages states to review their judicial policies regarding termination of parental rights and take steps to accelerate the adoption process in cases where babies have been abandoned at birth and where repeated attempts to reunite older children and their parents have been unsuccessful. Some commissioners recommend terminating parental rights for abandoned infants after 90 days, in order to ensure that these very young children are able to be placed in loving homes and to begin the process of bonding with their adoptive parents as early as possible. While the 90 day period may be used as a guideline, all commissioners believe that social workers and judges must review cases on an individual basis to account for special circumstances that may warrant longer or shorter stays in foster care.

The preceding statement reflects the often close relationship between termination proceedings and adoption. The age of a child at the time of major family disintegration can be a major factor in affecting timing for termination of parental rights with an eye to adoption. The older child may have some specific preferences that should be considered. However, many of the cases that reach the courts seem to boil down to a question of whether the rights and interests of children will be accorded at least equal weight with those of parents.

1. CONSTITUTIONAL DIMENSIONS

Santosky v. Kramer

Supreme Court of the United States, 1982.
455 U.S. 745, 102 S.Ct. 1388, 71 L.Ed.2d 599.

■ JUSTICE BLACKMUN delivered the opinion of the Court.

Under New York law, the State may terminate, over parental objection, the rights of parents in their natural child upon a finding that the child is "permanently neglected." N.Y. Soc. Serv. Law §§ 384–b.4.(d), 384–b.7.(a). The New York Family Court Act § 622 requires that only a "fair preponderance of the evidence" support that finding. Thus, in New York, the factual certainty required to extinguish the parent-child relationship is no greater than that necessary to award money damages in an ordinary civil action.

Today we hold that the Due Process Clause of the Fourteenth Amendment demands more than this. Before a State may sever completely and irrevocably the rights of parents in their natural child, due process requires that the State support its allegations by at least clear and convincing evidence.

New York authorizes its officials to remove a child temporarily from his or her home if the child appears "neglected," within the meaning of Art. 10 of the Family Court Act. Once removed, a child under the age of 18 customarily is placed "in the care of an authorized agency," usually a state institution or a foster home. At that point, "the state's first obligation is to help the family with services to ... reunite it...." But if convinced that "positive, nurturing parent-child relationships no longer exist," the State may initiate "permanent neglect" proceedings to free the child for adoption.

The State bifurcates its permanent neglect proceeding into "factfinding" and "dispositional" hearings. Fam.Ct.Act §§ 622, 623. At the factfinding stage, the State must prove that the child has been "permanently neglected," as defined by Fam.Ct.Act §§ 614.1.(a)–(d) and Soc.Serv.Law § 384–b.7.(a). The Family Court judge then determines at a subsequent dispositional hearing what placement would serve the child's best interests.

At the factfinding hearing, the State must establish, among other things, that for more than a year after the child entered state custody, the agency "made diligent efforts to encourage and strengthen the parental relationship." Fam.Ct.Act §§ 614.1.(c), 611. The State must further prove that during that same period, the child's natural parents failed "substantially and continuously or repeatedly to maintain contact with or plan for the future of the child although physically and financially able to do so." § 614.1.(d). Should the State support its allegations by "a fair preponderance of the evidence," § 622, the child may be declared permanently neglected. § 611. That declaration empowers the Family Court judge to terminate permanently the natural parents' rights in the child. §§ 631(c),

634. Termination denies the natural parents physical custody, as well as the rights ever to visit, communicate with, or regain custody of the child.

New York's permanent neglect statute provides natural parents with certain procedural protections.[2] But New York permits its officials to establish "permanent neglect" with less proof than most States require. Thirty-three States, the District of Columbia, and the Virgin Islands currently specify a higher standard of proof, in parental rights termination proceedings, than a "fair preponderance of the evidence." . . . The question here is whether New York's "fair preponderance of the evidence" standard is constitutionally sufficient.

Petitioners John Santosky II and Annie Santosky are the natural parents of Tina and John III. In November 1973, after incidents reflecting parental neglect, respondent Kramer, Commissioner of the Ulster County Department of Social Services, initiated a neglect proceeding under Fam.Ct. Act § 1022 and removed Tina from her natural home. About 10 months later, he removed John III and placed him with foster parents. On the day John was taken, Annie Santosky gave birth to a third child, Jed. When Jed was only three days old, respondent transferred him to a foster home on the ground that immediate removal was necessary to avoid imminent danger to his life or health.

In October 1978, respondent petitioned the Ulster County Family Court to terminate petitioners' parental rights in the three children. Petitioners challenged the constitutionality of the "fair preponderance of the evidence" standard specified in Fam.Ct.Act § 622. The Family Court judge rejected this constitutional challenge, and weighed the evidence under the statutory standard. While acknowledging that the Santoskys had maintained contact with their children, the judge found those visits "at best superficial and devoid of any real emotional content." After deciding that the agency had made " 'diligent efforts' to encourage and strengthen the parental relationship," he concluded that the Santoskys were incapable, even with public assistance, of planning for the future of their children. The judge later held a dispositional hearing and ruled that the best interests of the three children required permanent termination of the Santoskys' custody.[5]

Petitioners appealed, again contesting the constitutionality of § 622's standard of proof. The New York Supreme Court, Appellate Division, affirmed, holding application of the preponderance of the evidence standard "proper and constitutional." In re John AA, 75 App.Div.2d 910, 427 N.Y.S.2d 319, 320 (1980). That standard, the court reasoned, "recognizes

---

2. Most notably, natural parents have a statutory right to the assistance of counsel and of court-appointed counsel if they are indigent. Fam.Ct.Act § 262(a)(iii).

5. Since respondent took custody of Tina, John III, and Jed, the Santoskys have had two other children, James and Jeremy.

The State has taken no action to remove these younger children. At oral argument, counsel for respondent replied affirmatively when asked whether he was asserting that petitioners were "unfit to handle the three older ones but not unfit to handle the two younger ones."

and seeks to balance rights possessed by the child ... with those of the natural parents...." Ibid.

The New York Court of Appeals then dismissed petitioners' appeal to that court "upon the ground that no substantial constitutional question is directly involved." ...

Last term, in Lassiter v. Department of Social Services, 452 U.S. 18, 101 S.Ct. 2153, 68 L.Ed.2d 640 (1981), this Court, by a 5–4 vote, held that the Fourteenth Amendment's Due Process Clause does not require the appointment of counsel for indigent parents in every parental status termination proceeding. The case casts light, however, on the two central questions here—whether process is constitutionally due a natural parent at a State's parental rights termination proceeding, and, if so, what process is due.

In *Lassiter,* it was "not disputed that state intervention to terminate the relationship between [a parent] and [the] child must be accomplished by procedures meeting the requisites of the Due Process Clause." The absence of dispute reflected this Court's historical recognition that freedom of personal choice in matters of family life is a fundamental liberty interest protected by the Fourteenth Amendment.

The fundamental liberty interest of natural parents in the care, custody, and management of their child does not evaporate simply because they have not been model parents or have lost temporary custody of their child to the State. Even when blood relationships are strained, parents retain a vital interest in preventing the irretrievable destruction of their family life. If anything, persons faced with forced dissolution of their parental rights have a more critical need for procedural protections than do those resisting state intervention into ongoing family affairs. When the State moves to destroy weakened familial bonds, it must provide the parents with fundamentally fair procedures.

In *Lassiter,* the Court and three dissenters agreed that the nature of the process due in parental rights termination proceedings turns on a balancing of the "three distinct factors" specified in Mathews v. Eldridge, 424 U.S. 319, 335, 96 S.Ct. 893, 903, 47 L.Ed.2d 18 (1976): the private interests affected by the proceeding; the risk of error created by the State's chosen procedure; and the countervailing governmental interest supporting use of the challenged procedure.

. . .

In *Lassiter,* to be sure, the Court held that fundamental fairness may be maintained in parental rights termination proceedings even when some procedures are mandated only on a case-by-case basis, rather than through rules of general application. 452 U.S., at 31–32, 101 S.Ct., at 2161–2162 (natural parent's right to court-appointed counsel should be determined by the trial court, subject to appellate review). But this Court never has approved case-by-case determination of the proper *standard of proof* for a given proceeding. Standards of proof, like other "procedural due process rules[,] are shaped by the risk of error inherent in the truth-finding process as applied to the *generality of cases,* not the rare exceptions." Mathews v. Eldridge, 424 U.S., at 344, 96 S.Ct., at 907 (emphasis added). Since the litigants and the factfinder must know at the outset of a given proceeding how the risk of error will be allocated, the standard of proof necessarily must be calibrated in advance. Retrospective case-by-case review cannot preserve fundamental fairness when a class of proceedings is governed by a constitutionally defective evidentiary standard.

In parental rights termination proceedings, the private interest affected is commanding; the risk of error from using a preponderance standard is substantial; and the countervailing governmental interest favoring that standard is comparatively slight. Evaluation of the three *Eldridge* factors compels the conclusion that use of a "fair preponderance of the evidence" standard in such proceedings is inconsistent with due process.

"The extent to which procedural due process must be afforded the recipient is influenced by the extent to which he may be 'condemned to suffer grievous loss.'" Whether the loss threatened by a particular type of proceeding is sufficiently grave to warrant more than average certainty on the part of the factfinder turns on both the nature of the private interest threatened and the permanency of the threatened loss.

Lassiter declared it "plain beyond the need for multiple citation" that a natural parent's "desire for and right to 'the companionship, care, custody, and management of his or her children'" is an interest far more precious than any property right. 452 U.S, at 27, 101 S.Ct., at 2160, quoting Stanley v. Illinois, 405 U.S., at 651, 92 S.Ct., at 1212. When the State initiates a parental rights termination proceeding, it seeks not merely to infringe that fundamental liberty interest, but to end it. "If the State prevails, it will have worked a unique kind of deprivation.... A parent's interest in the accuracy and justice of the decision to terminate his or her parental status is, therefore, a commanding one." 452 U.S., at 27, 101 S.Ct., at 2160.

In government-initiated proceedings to determine juvenile delinquency, this Court has identified losses of individual liberty sufficiently serious to warrant imposition of an elevated burden of proof. Yet juvenile delinquency adjudications, civil commitment, deportation, and denaturalization, at least to a degree, are all *reversible* official actions. Once affirmed on appeal, a New York decision terminating parental rights is *final* and irrevocable. Few forms of state action are both so severe and so irreversible.

Thus, the first *Eldridge* factor—the private interest affected—weighs heavily against use of the preponderance standard at a State-initiated permanent neglect proceeding. We do not deny that the child and his foster parents are also deeply interested in the outcome of that contest. But at the factfinding stage of the New York proceeding, the focus emphatically is not on them.

The factfinding does not purport—and is not intended—to balance the child's interest in a normal family home against the parents' interest in raising the child. Nor does it purport to determine whether the natural parents or the foster parents would provide the better home. Rather, the factfinding hearing pits the State directly against the parents. The State alleges that the natural parents are at fault. The questions disputed and decided are what the State did—"made diligent efforts," § 614.1.(c)—and what the natural parents did not do—"maintain contact with or plan for the future of the child." § 614.1.(d). The State marshals an array of public resources to prove its case and disprove the parents' case. Victory by the State not only makes termination of parental rights possible; it entails a judicial determination that the parents are unfit to raise their own children.[10]

At the factfinding, the State cannot presume that a child and his parents are adversaries. After the State has established parental unfitness at that initial proceeding, the court may assume at the *dispositional* stage that the interests of the child and the natural parents do diverge. But until the State proves parental unfitness, the child and his parents share a vital interest in preventing erroneous termination of their natural relationship.[11] Thus, at the factfinding, the interests of the child and his natural parents coincide to favor use of error-reducing procedures.

However substantial the foster parents' interests may be, they are not implicated directly in the factfinding stage of a State-initiated permanent neglect proceeding against the natural parents. If authorized, the foster parents may pit their interests directly against those of the natural parents by initiating their own permanent neglect proceeding. Fam.Ct.Act §§ 615, 1055(d); Soc.Serv.Law § 392.7.(c). Alternatively, the foster parents can make their case for custody at the dispositional stage of a State-initiated proceeding, where the judge already has decided the issue of permanent neglect and is focusing on the placement that would serve the child's best interests. Fam.Ct.Act §§ 623, 631. For the foster parents, the State's failure to prove permanent neglect may prolong the delay and uncertainty until their foster child is freed for adoption. But for the natural parents, a finding of permanent neglect can cut off forever their rights in their child.

---

10. The Family Court judge in the present case expressly refused to terminate petitioners' parental rights on a "non-statutory, no-fault basis." Nor is it clear that the State constitutionally could terminate a parent's rights *without* showing parental unfitness. See Quilloin v. Walcott, 434 U.S. 246, 255, 98 S.Ct. 549, 554, 54 L.Ed.2d 511 (1978) ("We have little doubt that the Due Process Clause would be offended '[i]f a State were to attempt to force the breakup of a natural family, over the objections of the parents and their children, without some showing of unfitness and for the sole reason that to do so was thought to be in the children's best interest,' " quoting Smith v. Organization of Foster Families, 431 U.S. 816, 862–863, 97 S.Ct. 2094, 2119, 53 L.Ed.2d 14 (1977) (Stewart, J., concurring in the judgment)).

11. For a child, the consequences of termination of his natural parents' rights may well be far-reaching. In Colorado, for example, it has been noted: "The child loses the right of support and maintenance, for which he may thereafter be dependent upon society; the right to inherit; and all other rights inherent in the legal parent-child relationship not just for [a limited] period ..., but forever." In re K.S., 33 Colo.App. 72, 76, 515 P.2d 130, 133 (1973). Some losses cannot be measured. In this case, for example, Jed Santosky was removed from his natural parents' custody when he was only three days old; the judge's finding of permanent neglect effectively foreclosed the possibility that Jed would ever know his natural parents.

Given this disparity of consequence, we have no difficulty finding that the balance of private interests strongly favors heightened procedural protections.

Under Mathews v. Eldridge, we next must consider both the risk of erroneous deprivation of private interests resulting from use of a "fair preponderance" standard and the likelihood that a higher evidentiary standard would reduce that risk. . . .

In New York, the factfinding stage of a State-initiated permanent neglect proceeding bears many of the indicia of a criminal trial. The Commissioner of Social Services charges the parents with permanent neglect. They are served by summons. The factfinding hearing is conducted pursuant to formal rules of evidence. The State, the parents, and the child are all represented by counsel. The State seeks to establish a series of historical facts about the intensity of its agency's efforts to reunite the family, the infrequency and insubstantiality of the parents' contacts with their child, and the parents' inability or unwillingness to formulate a plan for the child's future. The attorneys submit documentary evidence, and call witnesses who are subject to cross-examination. Based on all the evidence, the judge then determines whether the State has proved the statutory elements of permanent neglect by a fair preponderance of the evidence.

At such a proceeding, numerous factors combine to magnify the risk of erroneous factfinding. Permanent neglect proceedings employ imprecise substantive standards that leave determinations unusually open to the subjective values of the judge. In appraising the nature and quality of a complex series of encounters among the agency, the parents, and the child, the court possesses unusual discretion to underweigh probative facts that might favor the parent.[12] Because parents subject to termination proceedings are often poor, uneducated, or members of minority groups, such proceedings are often vulnerable to judgments based on cultural or class bias.

The State's ability to assemble its case almost inevitably dwarfs the parents' ability to mount a defense. No predetermined limits restrict the sums an agency may spend in prosecuting a given termination proceeding. The State's attorney usually will be expert on the issues contested and the procedures employed at the factfinding hearing, and enjoys full access to all public records concerning the family. The State may call on experts in family relations, psychology, and medicine to bolster its case. Furthermore, the primary witnesses at the hearing will be the agency's own professional

---

12. For example, a New York court appraising an agency's "diligent efforts" to provide the parents with social services can excuse efforts *not* made on the grounds that they would have been "detrimental to the moral and temporal welfare of the child." Fam.Ct.Act § 614.1.(c). In determining whether the parent "substantially and continuously or repeatedly" failed to "maintain contact with . . . the child." § 614.1.(d), the judge can discount actual visits or communications on the grounds that they were insubstantial or "overtly demonstrat[ed] a lack of affection and concerned parenthood." Soc. Serv.Law § 384–b.7.(b). When determining whether the parent planned for the child's future, the judge can reject as unrealistic plans based on overly optimistic estimates of physical or financial ability. § 384.b.7.(c). . . .

caseworkers whom the State has empowered both to investigate the family situation and to testify against the parents. Indeed, because the child is already in agency custody, the State even has the power to shape the historical events that form the basis for termination.[13]

The disparity between the adversaries' litigation resources is matched by a striking asymmetry in their litigation options. Unlike criminal defendants, natural parents have no "double jeopardy" defense against repeated state termination efforts. If the State initially fails to win termination, as New York did here, it always can try once again to cut off the parents' rights after gathering more or better evidence. Yet even when the parents have attained the level of fitness required by the State, they have no similar means by which they can forestall future termination efforts.

Coupled with a "preponderance of the evidence" standard, these factors create a significant prospect of erroneous termination. A standard of proof that by its very terms demands consideration of the quantity, rather than the quality, of the evidence may misdirect the factfinder in the marginal case. Given the weight of the private interests at stake, the social cost of even occasional error is sizable.

. . .

The Appellate Division approved New York's preponderance standard on the ground that it properly "balanced rights possessed by the child . . . with those of the natural parents. . . ." 75 App.Div.2d, at 910, 427 N.Y.S.2d, at 320. By so saying, the court suggested that a preponderance standard properly allocates the risk of error *between* the parents and the child. That view is fundamentally mistaken.

The court's theory assumes that termination of the natural parents' rights invariably will benefit the child.[15] Yet we have noted above that the

13. In this case, for example, the parents claim that the State sought court orders denying them the right to visit their children, which would have prevented them from maintaining the contact required by Fam.Ct. Act § 614.1.(d). The parents further claim that the State cited their rejection of social services they found offensive or superfluous as proof of the agency's "diligent efforts" and their own "failure to plan" for the children's future.

We need not accept these statements as true to recognize that the State's unusual ability to structure the evidence increases the risk of an erroneous factfinding. Of course, the disparity between the litigants' resources will be vastly greater in States where there is no statutory right to court-appointed counsel. . . .

15. This is a hazardous assumption at best. Even when a child's natural home is

imperfect, permanent removal from that home will not necessarily improve his welfare. See, e.g., Wald, State Intervention on Behalf of "Neglected" Children: A Search for Realistic Standards, 27 Stan.L.Rev. 985, 993 (1975) ("In fact, under current practice, coercive intervention frequently results in placing a child in a more detrimental situation than he would be in without intervention.").

Nor does termination of parental rights necessarily ensure adoption. See Brief for Community Action for Legal Services, Inc., et al., as *Amicus Curiae* 22–23 (in 1979; only 12% of the adoptable children in foster care in New York City were actually adopted, although some had been waiting for years, citing Redirecting Foster Care, A Report to the Mayor of the City of New York 69, 43 (1980)). Even when a child eventually finds an adoptive family, he may spend years moving between state institutions and "temporary"

parents and the child share an interest in avoiding erroneous termination. Even accepting the court's assumption, we cannot agree with its conclusion that a preponderance standard fairly distributes the risk of error between parent and child. Use of that standard reflects the judgment that society is nearly neutral between erroneous termination of parental rights and erroneous failure to terminate those rights. Cf. In re Winship, 397 U.S., at 371, 90 S.Ct., at 1076 (Harland, J., concurring). For the child, the likely consequence of an erroneous failure to terminate is preservation of an uneasy status quo.[16] For the natural parents, however, the consequence of an erroneous termination is the unnecessary destruction of their natural family. A standard that allocates the risk of error nearly equally between those two outcomes does not reflect properly their relative severity.

Two state interests are at stake in parental rights termination proceedings—a *parens patriae* interest in preserving and promoting the welfare of the child and a fiscal and administrative interest in reducing the cost and burden of such proceedings. A standard of proof more strict than preponderance of the evidence is consistent with both interests.

"Since the State has an urgent interest in the welfare of the child, it shares the parent's interest in an accurate and just decision" at the *factfinding* proceeding. As *parens patriae,* the State's goal is to provide the child with a permanent home. Yet while there is still reason to believe that positive, nurturing parent-child relationships exist, the *parens patriae* interest favors preservation, not severance, of natural familial bonds.[17] § 384–b.1.(a)(ii). "[T]he State registers no gain towards its declared goals when it separates children from the custody of fit parents." Stanley v. Illinois, 405 U.S., at 652, 92 S.Ct., at 1213.

The State's interest in finding the child an alternative permanent home arises only "when it is *clear* that the natural parent cannot or will not provide a normal family home for the child." Soc.Serv.Law § 384–b.1.(a)(iv) (emphasis added). At the factfinding, that goal is served by procedures that promote an accurate determination of whether the natural parents can and will provide a normal home.

foster placements after his ties to his natural parents have been severed. See Smith v. Organization of Foster Families, 431 U.S., at 833–838, 97 S.Ct., at 2103–06 (describing the "limbo" of the New York foster care system).

16. When the termination proceeding occurs, the child is not living at his natural home. A child cannot be adjudicated "permanently neglected" until, "for a period of more than a year," he has been in "the care of an authorized agency." Soc.Serv.Law § 384–b.7.(a); Fam.Ct.Act § 614.1.(d). See also dissenting opinion, at 20–21.

Under New York law, a judge has ample discretion to ensure that, once removed from his natural parents on grounds of neglect, a child will not return to a hostile environment. In this case, when the State's initial termination effort failed for lack of proof, see n. 4, supra, the court simply issued orders under Fam.Ct.Act § 1055(b) extending the period of the child's foster home placement. See App. 19–20. See also Fam.Ct.Act § 632(b) (when State's permanent neglect petition is dismissed for insufficient evidence, judge retains jurisdiction to reconsider underlying orders of placement); § 633 (judge may suspend judgment at dispositional hearing for an additional year).

17. Any *parens patriae* interest in terminating the natural parents' rights arises only at the dispositional phase, *after* the parents have been found unfit.

Unlike a constitutional requirement of hearings, or court-appointed counsel, a stricter standard of proof would reduce factual error without imposing substantial fiscal burdens upon the State. . . .

Nor would an elevated standard of proof create any real administrative burdens for the State's factfinders. New York Family Court judges already are familiar with a higher evidentiary standard in other parental rights termination proceedings not involving permanent neglect. . . . New York also demands at least clear and convincing evidence in proceedings of far less moment than parental rights termination proceedings.

. . .

We . . . express no view on the merits of petitioners' claims. At a hearing conducted under a constitutionally proper standard, they may or may not prevail. Without deciding the outcome under any of the standards we have approved, we vacate the judgment of the Appellate Division and remand the case for further proceedings not inconsistent with this opinion.

■ JUSTICE REHNQUIST, with whom THE CHIEF JUSTICE, JUSTICE WHITE, and JUSTICE O'CONNOR join, dissenting.

. . . New York has created an exhaustive program to assist parents in regaining the custody of their children and to protect parents from the unfair deprivation of their parental rights. And yet the majority's myopic scrutiny of the standard of proof blinds it to the very considerations and procedures which make the New York scheme "fundamentally fair."

[The opinion reviews the procedures of the New York statute both with regard to temporary removal of children from the home and termination of parental rights.]

The three children to which this case relates were removed from petitioners' custody in 1973 and 1974, before petitioners' other two children were born. The removals were made pursuant to the procedures detailed above and in response to what can only be described as shockingly abusive treatment.[10] At the temporary removal hearing held before the Family Court on September 30, 1974, petitioners were represented by counsel, and allowed the Ulster County Department of Social Services ("Department") to take custody of the three children.

---

10. Tina Apel, the oldest of petitioners' five children, was removed from their custody by court order in November 1973 when she was two years old. Removal proceedings were commenced in response to complaints by neighbors and reports from a local hospital that Tina had suffered injuries in petitioners' home including a fractured left femur, treated with a homemade splint; bruises on the upper arms, forehead, flank, and spine; and abrasions of the upper leg. The following summer John Santosky III, petitioners' sec-

ond oldest child, was also removed from petitioners' custody. John, who was less than one year old at the time, was admitted to the hospital suffering malnutrition, bruises on the eye and forehead, cuts on the foot, blisters on the hand, and multiple pin pricks on the back. Jed Santosky, the third oldest of petitioners' children, was removed from his parents' custody when only three days old as a result of the abusive treatment of the two older children.

Temporary removal of the children was continued at an evidentiary hearing held before the Family Court in December 1975, after which the court issued a written opinion concluding that petitioners were unable to resume their parental responsibilities due to personality disorders. Unsatisfied with the progress petitioners were making, the court also directed the Department to reduce to writing the plan which it had designed to solve the problems at petitioners' home and reunite the family.

A plan for providing petitioners with extensive counseling and training services was submitted to the court and approved in February 1976. Under the plan, petitioners received training by a mother's aide, a nutritional aide, and a public health nurse, and counseling at a family planning clinic. In addition, the plan provided psychiatric treatment and vocational training for the father, and counseling at a family service center for the mother. Between early 1976 and the final termination decision in April 1979, the State spent more than $15,000 in these efforts to rehabilitate petitioners as parents.

Petitioners' response to the State's effort was marginal at best. They wholly disregarded some of the available services and participated only sporadically in the others. As a result, and out of growing concern over the length of the childrens' stay in foster care, the Department petitioned in September 1976 for permanent termination of petitioners' parental rights so that the children could be adopted by other families. Although the Family Court recognized that petitioners' reaction to the State's efforts was generally "non-responsive, even resentful," the fact that they were "at least superficially cooperative" led it to conclude that there was yet hope of further improvement and an eventual reuniting of the family. Accordingly, the petition for permanent termination was dismissed.

Whatever progress petitioners were making prior to the 1976 termination hearing, they made little or no progress thereafter. In October 1978, the Department again filed a termination petition alleging that petitioners had completely failed to plan for the childrens' future despite the considerable efforts rendered in their behalf. This time, the Family Court agreed. The court found that petitioners had "failed in any meaningful way to take advantage of the many social and rehabilitative services that have not only been made available to them but have been diligently urged upon them." In addition, the court found that the "infrequent" visits "between the parents and their children were at best superficial and devoid of any real emotional content." The court thus found "nothing in the situation which holds out any hope that [petitioners] may ever become financially self sufficient or emotionally mature enough to be independent of the services of social agencies. More than a reasonable amount of time has passed and still, in the words of the case workers, there has been no discernible forward movement. At some point in time, it must be said 'enough is enough.' "

In accordance with the statutory requirements set forth above, the court found that petitioners' failure to plan for the future of their children, who were then seven, five, and four years old and had been out of petitioners' custody for at least four years, rose to the level of permanent neglect. At a subsequent dispositional hearing, the court terminated petitioners' parental rights, thereby freeing the three children for adoption.

As this account demonstrates, the State's extraordinary four-year effort to reunite petitioners' family was not just unsuccessful, it was altogether rebuffed by parents unwilling to improve their circumstances sufficiently to permit a return of their children. At every step of this protracted process petitioners were accorded those procedures and protections which traditionally have been required by due process of law. Moreover, from the beginning to the end of this sad story all judicial determinations were made by one family court judge. After four and one-half years of involvement with petitioners, more than seven complete hearings, and additional periodic supervision of the State's rehabilitative efforts, the judge no doubt was intimately familiar with this case and the prospects for petitioners' rehabilitation.

It is inconceivable to me that these procedures were "fundamentally unfair" to petitioners. Only by its obsessive focus on the standard of proof and its almost complete disregard of the facts of this case does the majority find otherwise.[11] ... [S]uch a focus does not comport with the flexible

---

11. The majority finds, without any reference to the facts of this case, that "numerous factors [in New York termination proceedings] combine to magnify the risk of erroneous factfinding." Among the factors identified by the majority are the "unusual discretion" of the family court judge "to underweigh probative facts that might favor the parent"; the often uneducated, minority status of the parents and their consequent "vulnerab[ility] to judgments based on cultural or class bias"; the "State's ability to assemble its case," which "dwarfs the parents' ability to mount a defense" by including an unlimited budget, expert attorneys, and "full access to all public records concerning the family"; and the fact that "natural parents have no 'double jeopardy' defense against repeated state" efforts, "with more or better evidence," to terminate parental rights "even when the parents have attained the level of fitness required by the State." In short, the majority characterizes the State as a wealthy and powerful bully bent on taking children away from defenseless parents. Such characterization finds no support in the record.

The intent of New York has been stated with eminent clarity: "the [S]tate's *first obligation* is to *help* the family with services to *prevent* its break-up or to *reunite* it if the child has already left home." SSL § 384–b(1)(a)(iii) (emphasis added). There is simply no basis in fact for believing, as the majority does, that the State does not mean what it says; indeed, the facts of this case demonstrate that New York has gone the extra mile in seeking to effectuate its declared purpose. More importantly, there should be no room in the jurisprudence of this Court for decisions based on unsupported inaccurate assumptions.

A brief examination of the "factors" relied upon by the majority demonstrates its error. The "unusual" discretion of the family court judge to consider the "affectio[n] and concer[n]" displayed by parents during visits with their children, is nothing more than discretion to consider reality; there is not one shred of evidence in this case suggesting that the determination of the family court was "based on cultural or class bias"; if parents lack the "ability to mount a defense," the State provides them with the full services of an attorney, FCA § 262, and they, like the State, have "full access to all *public* records concerning the family" (emphasis added); and the absence of "double jeopardy" protection simply recognizes the fact that family problems are often ongoing and may in the future warrant action that currently is unnecessary. In this case the family court dismissed the first termination petition because it desired to give petitioners "the benefit of the doubt," and a second opportunity to raise themselves to "an acceptable minimal level of competency as parents." It was their complete failure to do so that prompted the second, successful termination petition.

standard of fundamental fairness embodied in the Due Process Clause of the Fourteenth Amendment.

In addition to the basic fairness of the process afforded petitioners, the standard of proof chosen by New York clearly reflects a constitutionally permissible balance of the interests at stake in this case. The standard of proof "represents an attempt to instruct the factfinder concerning the degree of confidence our society thinks he should have in the correctness of factual conclusions for a particular type of adjudication." In re Winship, 397 U.S. 358, 370, 90 S.Ct. 1068, 1076, 25 L.Ed.2d 368 (1970) (Harlan, J. concurring); Addington v. Texas, 441 U.S. 418, 423, 99 S.Ct. 1804, 1807, 60 L.Ed.2d 323 (1979). In this respect, the standard of proof is a crucial component of legal process, the primary function of which is "to minimize the risk of erroneous decisions."[12]

In determining the propriety of a particular standard of proof in a given case, however, it is not enough simply to say that we are trying to minimize the risk of error. Because errors in factfinding affect more than one interest, we try to minimize error as to those interests which we consider to be most important. As Justice Harlan explained in his well-known concurrence to In re Winship:

> "In a lawsuit between two parties, a factual error can make a difference in one of two ways. First, it can result in a judgment in favor of the plaintiff when the true facts warrant a judgment for the defendant. The analogue in a criminal case would be the conviction of an innocent man. On the other hand, an erroneous factual determination can result in a judgment for the defendant when the true facts justify a judgment in plaintiff's favor. The criminal analogue would be the acquittal of a guilty man.

12. It is worth noting that the significance of the standard of proof in New York parental termination proceedings differs from the significance of the standard in other forms of litigation. In the usual adjudicatory setting, the factfinder has had little or no prior exposure to the facts of the case. His only knowledge of those facts comes from the evidence adduced at trial, and he renders his findings solely upon the basis of that evidence. Thus, normally, the standard of proof is a crucial factor in the final outcome of the case, for it is the scale upon which the factfinder weighs his knowledge and makes his decision.

Although the standard serves the same function in New York parental termination proceedings, additional assurances of accuracy are present in its application. As was adduced at oral argument, the practice in New York is to assign one judge to supervise a case from the initial temporary removal of the child to the final termination of parental rights. Therefore, as discussed above, the factfinder is intimately familiar with the case before the termination proceedings ever begin. Indeed, as in this case, he often will have been closely involved in protracted efforts to rehabilitate the parents. Even if a change in judges occurs, the Family Court retains jurisdiction of the case and the newly assigned judge may take judicial notice of all prior proceedings. Given this familiarity with the case, and the necessarily lengthy efforts which must precede a termination action in New York, decisions in termination cases are made by judges steeped in the background of the case and peculiarly able to judge the accuracy of evidence placed before them. This does not mean that the standard of proof in these cases can escape due process scrutiny, only that additional assurances of accuracy attend the application of the standard in New York termination proceedings.

The standard of proof influences the relative frequency of these two types of erroneous outcomes. If, for example, the standard of proof for a criminal trial were a preponderance of the evidence rather than proof beyond a reasonable doubt, there would be a smaller risk of factual errors that result in freeing guilty persons, but a far greater risk of factual errors that result in convicting the innocent. Because the standard of proof affects the comparative frequency of these two types of erroneous outcomes, the choice of the standard to be applied in a particular kind of litigation should, in a rational world, reflect an assessment of the comparative social disutility of each." 397 U.S., at 370–372, 90 S.Ct., at 1076.

When the standard of proof is understood as reflecting such an assessment, an examination of the interests at stake in a particular case becomes essential to determining the propriety of the specified standard of proof. Because proof by a preponderance of the evidence requires that "[t]he litigants ... share the risk of error in a roughly equal fashion," Addington v. Texas, supra, 441 U.S., at 423, 99 S.Ct. at 1808, it rationally should be applied only when the interests at stake are of roughly equal societal importance. The interests at stake in this case demonstrate that New York has selected a constitutionally permissible standard of proof.

On one side is the interest of parents in a continuation of the family unit and the raising of their own children. The importance of this interest cannot easily be overstated. Few consequences of judicial action are so grave as the severance of natural family ties. Even the convict committed to prison and thereby deprived of his physical liberty often retains the love and support of family members. "This Court's decisions have by now made plain beyond the need for multiple citation that a parent's desire for and right to 'the companionship, care, custody and management of his or her children' is an important interest that 'undeniably warrants deference and, absent a powerful countervailing interest, protection.' Stanley v. Illinois, 405 U.S. 645, 651 [92 S.Ct. 1208, 1212, 31 L.Ed.2d 551]." Lassiter v. Department of Social Services, 452 U.S. 18, 27, 101 S.Ct. 2153, 2161, 68 L.Ed.2d 640 (1981). In creating the scheme at issue in this case, the New York legislature was expressly aware of this right of parents "to bring up their own children." SSL § 384–b(1)(a)(ii).

On the other side of the termination proceeding are the often countervailing interests of the child.[13] A stable, loving homelife is essential to a

---

13. The majority dismisses the child's interest in the accuracy of determinations made at the factfinding hearing because "[t]he factfinding does not purport ... to balance the child's interest in a normal family life against the parents' interest in raising the child," but instead "pits the State directly against the parents." Only "[a]fter the State has established parental unfitness," the majority reasons, may the court "assume ...

that the interests of the child and the natural parents do diverge."

This reasoning misses the mark. The child has an interest in the outcome of the factfinding hearing independent of that of the parent. To be sure, "the child and his parents share a vital interest in preventing *erroneous* termination of their natural relationship." (emphasis added). But the child's interest in a continuation of the family unit exists only

child's physical, emotional, and spiritual well-being. It requires no citation of authority to assert that children who are abused in their youth generally face extraordinary problems developing into responsible, productive citizens. The same can be said of children who, though not physically or emotionally abused, are passed from one foster home to another with no constancy of love, trust, or discipline. If the Family Court makes an incorrect factual determination resulting in a failure to terminate a parent-child relationship which rightfully should be ended, the child involved must return either to an abusive home or to the often unstable world of foster care. The reality of these risks is magnified by the fact that the only families faced with termination actions are those which have voluntarily surrendered custody of their child to the State, or, as in this case, those from which the child has been removed by judicial action because of threatened irreparable injury through abuse or neglect. Permanent neglect findings also occur only in families where the child has been in foster care for at least one year.

In addition to the child's interest in a normal homelife, "the State has an urgent interest in the welfare of the child." Lassiter v. Department of Social Services, supra, at 27, 101 S.Ct., at 2160.[16] Few could doubt that the most valuable resource of a self-governing society is its population of children who will one day become adults and themselves assume the responsibility of self-governance. "A democratic society rests, for its continuance, upon the healthy, well-rounded growth of young people into full maturity as citizens, with all that implies." Prince v. Massachusetts, 321 U.S. 158, 168, 64 S.Ct. 438, 443, 88 L.Ed. 645 (1944). Thus, "the whole community" has an interest "that children be both safeguarded from

to the extent that such a continuation would not be harmful to him. An error *in the factfinding hearing* that results in a failure to terminate a parent-child relationship which rightfully should be terminated may well detrimentally affect the child

The preponderance of the evidence standard, which allocates the risk of error more or less evenly, is employed when the social disutility of error *in either direction* is roughly equal—that is, when an incorrect finding of fault would produce consequences as undesirable as the consequences that would be produced by an incorrect finding of *no* fault. Only when the disutility of error in one direction discernibly outweighs the disutility of error in the other direction do we choose, by means of the standard of proof, to reduce the likelihood of the more onerous outcome. See In re Winship, 397 U.S. 358, 370–372, 90 S.Ct. 1068, 1075–1077, 25 L.Ed.2d 368 (1970) (Harlan, J., concurring).

New York's adoption of the preponderance of the evidence standard reflects its conclusion that the undesirable consequence

of an erroneous finding of parental unfitness—the unwarranted termination of the family relationship—is roughly equal to the undesirable consequence of an erroneous finding of parental fitness—the risk of permanent injury to the child either by return of the child to an abusive home or by the child's continued lack of a permanent home. Such a conclusion is well within the province of state legislatures. It cannot be said that the New York procedures are unconstitutional simply because a majority of the members of this Court disagree with the New York legislature's weighing of the interests of the parents and the child in an error-free factfinding hearing.

16. The majority's conclusion that a state interest in the child's well-being arises only after a determination of parental unfitness suffers from the same error as its assertion that the child has no interest, separate from that of its parents, in the accuracy of the factfinding hearing.

abuses and given opportunities for growth into free and independent well-developed ... citizens." Id., at 165.

When, in the context of a permanent neglect termination proceeding, the interests of the child and the State in a stable, nurturing homelife are balanced against the interests of the parents in the rearing of their child, it cannot be said that either set of interests is so clearly paramount as to require that the risk of error be allocated to one side or the other. Accordingly, a State constitutionally may conclude that the risk of error should be borne in roughly equal fashion by use of the preponderance of the evidence standard of proof. . . .

For the reasons heretofore stated, I believe that the Court today errs in concluding that the New York standard of proof in parental-rights termination proceedings violates due process of law. The decision disregards New York's earnest efforts to *aid* parents in regaining the custody of their children and a host of procedural protections placed around parental rights and interests. The Court finds a constitutional violation only by a tunnel-vision application of due process principles that altogether loses sight of the unmistakable fairness of the New York procedure.

Even more worrisome, today's decision cavalierly rejects the considered judgment of the New York legislature in an area traditionally entrusted to state care. The Court thereby begins, I fear, a trend of federal intervention in state family law matters which surely will stifle creative responses to vexing problems. Accordingly, I dissent.

NOTES

In M. L. B. v. S. L. J., 519 U.S. 102, 117 S.Ct. 555, 136 L.Ed.2d 473 (1996), the Supreme Court of the United States held that a Mississippi statute conditioning appeal from a trial court's termination of a mother's parental rights on advance payment of record preparation fees (estimated at $2,352.36 in the particular case) violated both equal protection and due process guarantees of the Fourteenth Amendment. The appellant mother's application to appeal in forma pauperis had been denied by the Mississippi Supreme Court because the state allowed in forma pauperis proceedings only at the trial level in civil cases. In a 6–3 decision, the court noted that although the trial judge's order stated that the decision to terminate parental rights was based on clear and convincing evidence, the order contained no description of the evidence for this conclusion. The decision of the Supreme Court pointed out two lines of cases that were of importance to their decision. One was based on two family law cases: Boddie v. Connecticut, 401 U.S. 371, 91 S.Ct. 780, 28 L.Ed.2d 113 (1971) (holding that a state could not deny access to judicial proceedings for divorce because of inability to pay court costs); and Lassiter v. Department of Social Services, 452 U.S. 18, 101 S.Ct. 2153, 68 L.Ed.2d 640 (1981) (discussed in the *Santosky* opinion). The other stems from Griffin v. Illinois, 351 U.S. 12, 76 S.Ct. 585, 100 L.Ed. 891 (1956) and Mayer v. Chicago, 404 U.S. 189, 92 S.Ct. 410, 30 L.Ed.2d 372 (1971). The court noted their past recognition that termination of parental rights cases were "apart from mine run civil actions, even from other domestic relations matters such as divorce, paternity, and child custody."

In Lassiter v. Department of Social Services, 452 U.S. 18, 101 S.Ct. 2153, 68 L.Ed.2d 640 (1981), discussed in *Santosky*, the petitioner-mother's infant son had been declared a neglected child and placed in custody of a state agency in 1975. The mother was convicted of second-degree murder a year afterward and began serving a 25–40 year prison term. A termination proceeding was commenced in 1978 and petitioner was brought from prison to the hearing. Finding that she had been given ample time to obtain counsel and that her failure to do so was without just cause, the court declined to postpone the proceeding. Counsel was not appointed for petitioner because she did not aver that she was indigent. During the hearing, petitioner and her mother responded to questions by the court, and petitioner cross-examined a social worker. Determining that she had "willfully failed to maintain concern or responsibility for the welfare of the minor," the court terminated petitioner's parental rights, On appeal the issue was whether failure to appoint counsel for petitioner was a denial of due process.

Explaining how to determine whether counsel need be appointed in a particular case, the opinion of the Court stated:

The case of Mathews v. Eldridge, 424 U.S. 319, 335, 96 S.Ct. 893, 47 L.Ed.2d 18, propounds three elements to be evaluated in deciding what due process requires, viz., the private interests at stake, the government's interest, and the risk that the procedures used will lead to erroneous decisions. We must balance these elements against each other, and then set their net weight in the scales against the presumption that there is a right to appointed counsel only where the indigent, if he is unsuccessful, may lose his personal freedom.

This Court's decisions have by now made plain beyond the need for multiple citation that a parent's desire for and right to "the companionship, care, custody and management of his or her children" is an important interest that "undeniably warrants deference and, absent a powerful countervailing interest, protection." Stanley v. Illinois, 405 U.S. 645, 651. Here the State has sought not simply to infringe upon that interest but to end it. If the State prevails, it will have worked a unique kind of deprivation. Cf. May v. Anderson, 345 U.S. 528, 533; Armstrong v. Manzo, 380 U.S. A parent's interest in the accuracy and justice of the decision to terminate his or her parental status is, therefore a commanding one.[3]

Since the State has an urgent interest in the welfare of the child, it shares the parent's interest in an accurate and just decision. For this

---

3. Some parents will have an additional interest to protect. Petitions to terminate parental rights are not uncommonly based on alleged criminal activity. Parents so accused may need legal counsel to guide them in understanding the problems such petitions may create.

reason, the State may share the indigent parent's interest in the availability of appointed counsel. If, as our adversary system presupposes, accurate and just results are most likely to be obtained through the equal contest of opposed interests, the State's interest in the child's welfare may perhaps best be served by a hearing in which both the parent and the State acting for the child are represented by counsel, without whom the contest of interests may become unwholesomely unequal. North Carolina itself acknowledges as much by providing that where a parent files a written answer to a termination petition, the State must supply a lawyer to represent the child. N.C.G.S. § 7A–289.29.

The State's interests, however, clearly diverge from the parent's insofar as the State wishes the termination decision to be made as economically as possible and thus wants to avoid both the expense of appointed counsel and the cost of the lengthened proceedings his presence may cause. But though the State's pecuniary interest is legitimate, it is hardly significant enough to overcome private interests as important as those here, particularly in light of the concession in the respondent's brief that the "potential costs of appointed counsel in termination proceedings ... is [*sic*] admittedly *de minimis* compared to the costs in all criminal actions."

Finally, consideration must be given to the risk that a parent will be erroneously deprived of his or her child because the parent is not represented by counsel.

. . .

The respondent argues that the subject of a termination hearing—the parent's relationship with her child—far from being abstruse, technical, or unfamiliar, is one as to which the parent must be uniquely well informed and to which the parent must have given prolonged thought. The respondent also contends that a termination hearing is not likely to produce difficult points of evidentiary law, or even of substantive law, since the evidentiary problems peculiar to criminal trials are not present and since the standards for termination are not complicated. In fact, the respondent reports, the North Carolina Departments of Social Services are themselves sometimes represented at termination hearings by social workers instead of by lawyers.

Yet the ultimate issues with which a termination hearing deals are not always simple, however commonplace they may be. Expert medical and psychiatric testimony, which few parents are equipped to understand and fewer still to confute, is sometimes presented. The parents are likely to be people with little education, who have had uncommon difficulty in dealing with life, and who are, at the hearing, thrust into a distressing and disorienting situation. That these factors may combine to overwhelm an uncounselled parent is evident from the findings some courts have made. Thus, courts have generally held that the State must appoint counsel for indigent parents at termination proceedings. The respondent is able to point to no presently authoritative case, except for the North Carolina judgment now before us, holding that an indigent parent has no due process right to appointed counsel in termination proceedings.

The dispositive question . . . is whether the three *Eldridge* factors, when weighed against the presumption that there is no right to appointed counsel in the absence of at least a potential deprivation of physical liberty, suffice to rebut that presumption and thus to lead to the conclusion that the Due Process Clause requires the appointment of counsel when a State seeks to terminate an indigent's parental status. To summarize the above discussion of the *Eldridge* factors: the parent's interest is an extremely important one (and may be supplemented by the dangers of criminal liability inherent in some termination proceedings); the State shares with the parent an interest in a correct decision, has a relatively weak pecuniary interest, and, in some but not all cases, has a possibly stronger interest in informal procedures; and the complexity of the proceeding and the incapacity of the uncounselled parent could be, but would not always be, great enough to make the risk of an erroneous deprivation of the parent's rights insupportably high.

If, in a given case, the parent's interests were at their strongest, the State's interests were at their weakest, and the risks of error were at their peak, it could not be said that the *Eldridge* factors did not overcome the presumption against the right to appointed counsel, and that due process did not therefore require the appointment of counsel. But since the *Eldridge* factors will not always be so distributed, and since "due process is not so rigid as to require that the significant interests in informality, flexibility and economy must always be sacrificed," Gagnon v. Scarpelli, supra, 411 U.S., at 788, 93 S.Ct., at 1762, neither can we say that the Constitution requires the appointment of counsel in every parental termination proceeding. We therefore adopt the standard found appropriate in Gagnon v. Scarpelli, and leave the decision whether due process calls for the appointment of counsel for indigent parents in termination proceedings to be answered in the first instance by the trial court, subject, of course, to appellate review.

. . .

In its Fourteenth Amendment, our Constitution imposes on the States the standards necessary to ensure that judicial proceedings are fundamentally fair. A wise public policy, however, may require that higher standards be adopted than those minimally tolerable under the Constitution. Informed opinion has clearly come to hold that an indigent parent is entitled to the assistance of appointed counsel not only in parental termination proceedings, but in dependency and neglect proceedings as well. Most significantly, 33 States and the District of Columbia provide statutorily for the appointment of counsel in termination cases. The Court's opinion today in no way implies that the standards increasingly urged by informed public opinion and now widely followed by the States are other than enlightened and wise.

For further discussion of *Lassiter* and some subsequent review issues and standards, *see* Bruce A. Boyer, *Justice, Access to the Courts, and the Right to Free Counsel for Indigent Parents: The Continuing Scourge of Lassiter v. Department of Social Services of Durham*, 36 Loy. U. Chi. L.J. 363 (2005); William Wesley Patton, *The Right to Appointed Counsel in Child Protection and Parental Severance Cases*, 27 Loy. U. Chi. L.Rev. 195 (1996).

Provisions for appointing counsel for children in parental rights termination cases are made by several states. What role should such counsel play? The March 1996 Fordham Law Review is devoted in its entirety to Ethical Issues in the Legal Representation of Children.

Standard of Proof in an Action by a Parent. *Santosky* involved a state's action to terminate parental rights. In In re T.R., 502 Pa. 165, 465 A.2d 642 (1983), the Pennsylvania Supreme Court held that although proceedings undertaken by an individual (in the particular case, a parent) may not involve as great a disparity in litigating resources, "the same 'particularly important' parental interests are at stake." Also "the private interest affected is commanding; the risk of error from using a preponderance standard is substantial; and the countervailing governmental interest favoring that standard is comparatively slight." Thus the "clear and convincing" standard was held to apply in all proceedings to terminate parental rights involuntarily.

Constitutional attacks based on vagueness. Parental rights termination laws have been the subject of constitutional challenge based on the "void for vagueness" doctrine in a number of states. *See, e.g.*, Alsager v. District Court of Polk Cty., 406 F.Supp. 10 (S.D.Iowa 1975). Usually these have involved statutes that supplied limited criteria such as "unfitness". For examples of judicial opinions rejecting such attacks see Matter of Doe, 100 N.M. 92, 666 P.2d 771 (N.M.1983), and In re Brooks, 228 Kan. 541, 618 P.2d 814 (1980). Newer statutes generally are more specific about what action or inaction can be used to establish unfitness for the purpose of terminating parental rights.

Would it be possible (and constitutionally permissible) to clearly define a minimum level of parental capacity or involvement below which rights of a parent could be terminated in order to enable a child's early placement in a home where he or she is clearly wanted? Would such a standard need to be tied to overt, dangerous conduct or flagrant inaction by a parent? How much is the movement toward recognition of greater rights in nonbiological parents likely to cause us to focus on questions such as these?

2. Safe Haven Laws

In recent years many states have enacted what are known as "safe haven" statutes. There is considerable variation among them but their basic approach is to provide that a parent who anonymously leaves a newborn child or young infant at a certain designated location (hospitals, emergency medical service facilities, or a fire station are among locations that have been specified) may avoid giving personal information and prosecution for abandonment except when child abuse is evident. This "legally condoned abandonment" is designed to deal with the significant number of cases in which newborns have been abandoned anonymously, and sometimes found only after their death. A presumption of abandonment arises but the statutes differ regarding the legal procedures that must be taken to assure that parental rights can terminated under constitutional standards. Once the rights of the parent have been terminated, an adoption or other placement can take place.

Some statutes are worded in such a fashion as to appear that they apply to a surrender by either a father or a mother, but it has been suggested that they serve largely to permit anonymous surrender by unmarried, genetic mothers who under many statutes need not identify the genetic fathers (or perhaps even themselves). This has raised serious constitutional questions about whether they contravene the spirit, if not the letter, of modern decisions and statutes ostensibly protecting the parental rights of unwed fathers. For further commentary on the statutes, see Annette R. Appell, *Safe Havens to Abandon Babies: Part I: The Law*, 5 (4) ADOPTION Q. 59 (2002); Appell, *supra, Part II: The Fit*, 6 (1) ADOPTION Q. 61 (2002); Appell, *supra, Part III: The Effects*, 6 (2) ADOPTION Q. 67 (2002); Jeffrey A. Parness, *Deserting Mothers, Abandoned Babies, Lost Fathers: Dangers in Safe* Havens, 24 QLR 335–349 (2006); Carol Sanger, *Infant Safe Haven Laws: Legislating in the Culture of Life*, 106 COLUM. L. REV. 753–829 (2006); Christina A. Zawisza, *Taking Hold of the Elephant in Child Dependency and Neglect Cases*, 17 ST. THOMAS L. REV. 531–559 (2005). *See, also,* Stanley v. Illinois, at p. 680, *supra*.

FLORIDA STATUTES ANN. §§ 383.50–51 (West 2002 & Supp. 2006)

§ 383.50.   Treatment of abandoned newborn infant.

(1) As used in this section, the term "newborn infant" means a child that a licensed physician reasonably believes to be approximately 3 days old or younger at the time the child is left at a hospital, emergency medical services station, or fire station.

(2) There is a presumption that the parent who leaves the newborn infant in accordance with this section intended to leave the newborn infant and consented to termination of parental rights.

(3) Each emergency medical services station or fire station staffed with full-time firefighters, emergency medical technicians, or paramedics shall accept any newborn infant left with a firefighter, emergency medical technician, or paramedic. The firefighter, emergency medical technician, or paramedic shall consider these actions as implied consent to and shall:

(a) Provide emergency medical services to the newborn infant to the extent he or she is trained to provide those services, and

(b) Arrange for the immediate transportation of the newborn infant to the nearest hospital having emergency services.

A licensee as defined in § 401.23, a fire department, or an employee or agent of a licensee or fire department may treat and transport a newborn infant pursuant to this section. If a newborn infant is placed in the physical custody of an employee or agent of a licensee or fire department, such placement shall be considered implied consent for treatment and transport. A licensee, a fire department, or an employee or agent of a licensee or fire department is immune from criminal or civil liability for acting in good faith pursuant to this section. Nothing in this subsection limits liability for negligence.

(4) Each hospital of this state subject to § 395.1041 shall, and any other hospital may, admit and provide all necessary emergency services and care, as defined in § 395.002(10), to any newborn infant left with the hospital in accordance with this section. The hospital or any of its licensed health care professionals shall consider these actions as implied consent for treatment, and a hospital accepting physical custody of a newborn infant has implied consent to perform all necessary emergency services and care. The hospital or any of its licensed health care professionals is immune from criminal or civil liability for acting in good faith in accordance with this section. Nothing in this subsection limits liability for negligence.

(5) Except where there is actual or suspected child abuse or neglect, any parent who leaves a newborn infant with a firefighter, emergency medical technician, or paramedic at a fire station or emergency medical services station, or brings a newborn infant to an emergency room of a hospital and expresses an intent to leave the newborn infant and not return, has the absolute right to remain anonymous and to leave at any time and may not be pursued or followed unless the parent seeks to reclaim the newborn infant.

(6) A parent of a newborn infant left at a hospital, emergency medical services station, or fire station under this section may claim his or her newborn infant up until the court enters a judgment terminating his or her parental rights. A claim to the newborn infant must be made to the entity having physical or legal custody of the newborn infant or to the circuit court before whom proceedings involving the newborn infant are pending.

(7) Upon admitting a newborn infant under this section, the hospital shall immediately contact a local licensed child-placing agency or alternatively contact the statewide central abuse hotline for the name of a licensed child-placing agency for purposes of transferring physical custody of the newborn infant. The hospital shall notify the licensed child-placing agency that a newborn infant has been left with the hospital and approximately when the licensed child-placing agency can take physical custody of the child. In cases where there is actual or suspected child abuse or neglect, the hospital or any of its licensed health care professionals shall report the actual or suspected child abuse or neglect in accordance with §§ 39.201 and 395.1023 in lieu of contacting a licensed child-placing agency.

(8) Any newborn infant admitted to a hospital in accordance with this section is presumed eligible for coverage under Medicaid, subject to federal rules.

(9) A newborn infant left at a hospital, emergency medical services station, or fire station in accordance with this section shall not be deemed abandoned and subject to reporting and investigation requirements under § 39.201 unless there is actual or suspected child abuse or until the department takes physical custody of the child.

(10) A criminal investigation shall not be initiated solely because a newborn infant is left at a hospital under this section unless there is actual or suspected child abuse or neglect.

§ 383.51. Confidentiality; identification of parent leaving newborn infant at hospital, emergency medical services station, or fire station.

The identity of a parent who leaves a newborn infant at a hospital, emergency medical services station, or fire station in accordance with § 383.50 is confidential and exempt from the provisions of § 119.07(1) and § 24(a), Art. I of the State Constitution. The identity of a parent leaving a child shall be disclosed to a person claiming to be a parent of the newborn infant. This section is subject to the Open Government Sunset Review Act of 1995 in accordance with § 119.15, and shall stand repealed on October 2, 2007, unless reviewed and saved from repeal through reenactment by the Legislature.

3. JUSTIFYING PEREMPTORY INTERVENTION

23 PENNSYLVANIA STATUTES ANN. (West 2004)

§ 2511. Grounds for involuntary termination

(a) General rule.—The rights of a parent in regard to a child may be terminated after a petition filed on any of the following grounds:

(1) The parent by conduct continuing for a period of at least six months immediately preceding the filing of the petition either has evidenced a settled purpose of relinquishing parental claim to a child or has refused or failed to perform parental duties.

(2) The repeated and continued incapacity, abuse, neglect or refusal of the parent has caused the child to be without essential parental care, control or subsistence necessary for his physical or mental well-being and the conditions and causes of the incapacity, abuse, neglect or refusal cannot or will not be remedied by the parent.

(3) The parent is the presumptive but not the natural father of the child.

(4) The child is in the custody of an agency, having been found under such circumstances that the identity or whereabouts of the parent is unknown and cannot be ascertained by diligent search and the parent does not claim the child within three months after the child is found.

(5) The child has been removed from the care of the parent by the court or under a voluntary agreement with an agency for a period of at least six months, the conditions which led to the removal or placement of the child continue to exist, the parent cannot or will not remedy those conditions within a reasonable period of time, the services or assistance reasonably available to the parent are not likely to remedy the conditions which led to the removal or placement of the child within a reasonable period of time and termination of the parental rights would best serve the needs and welfare of the child.

(6) In the case of a newborn child, the parent knows or has reason to know of the child's birth, does not reside with the child, has not married the child's other parent, has failed for a period of four months immediately preceding the filing of the petition to make reasonable efforts to maintain substantial and continuing contact with the child and has failed during the same four-month period to provide substantial financial support for the child.

(7) The parent is the father of a child conceived as a result of a rape or incest.

(8) The child has been removed from the care of the parent by the court or under a voluntary agreement with an agency, 12 months or more have elapsed from the date of removal or placement, the conditions which led to the removal or placement of the child continue to exist and termination of parental rights would best serve the needs and welfare of the child.

(b) Other considerations.—The court in terminating the rights of a parent shall give primary consideration to the developmental, physical and emotional needs and welfare of the child. The rights of a parent shall not be terminated solely on the basis of environmental factors such as inadequate housing, furnishings, income, clothing and medical care if found to be beyond the control of the parent. With respect to any petition filed pursuant to subsection (a)(1), (6) or (8), the court shall not consider any efforts by the parent to remedy the conditions described therein which are first initiated subsequent to the giving of notice of the filing of the petition.

(c) Right to file personal and medical history information.—At the time the decree of termination is transmitted to the parent whose rights have been terminated, the court shall advise the parent, in writing, of his or her continuing right to place and update personal and medical history information, whether or not the medical condition is in existence or discoverable at the time of adoption, on file with the court and with the Department of Public Welfare pursuant to section 2905(d) (relating to impounding of proceedings and access to records).

In re K.A.W.

Supreme Court of Missouri, En Banc, 2004.
133 S.W.3d 1.

■ Richard B. Teitelman, Judge.

K.A.W. and K.A.W. (twins) are minor children born to T.W. ("Mother"). Mother's parental rights were terminated on December 11, 2002, pursuant to section 211.447, and she appeals. Mother argues that the trial court's findings with respect to sections 211.447.4(2), (3) and (6) and 211.447.6 were insufficient. She also contends that the trial court erred because it failed to make required findings.

This case was transferred to this Court prior to disposition by the court of appeals because of this Court's desire to resolve this case forthwith in accordance with the admonition of section 453.011.1 that cases involving termination of parental rights and adoption be given priority.

The judgment is reversed, and the cause is remanded. If further proceedings include the termination of Mother's parental rights, the trial court is directed to consider and make findings on each of the statutorily required subdivisions or factors for all grounds for termination of parental rights on which the trial court bases its decision.

When Mother was pregnant with the twins she was already raising three other young children on her own while trying to hold a job. Overwhelmed, she struggled with the question of whether it was best to place her twins up for adoption. Eventually, Mother decided that she should place them up for adoption because, as she later testified, she wanted them "to have a better life."

The twin girls were born in June 2000, approximately three months premature. They required a two-month hospital stay. Although Mother had decided to place her twins for adoption, she did not abandon them. Rather, she visited the twins in the hospital daily and continued caring for them, holding, feeding and talking to them. Mother expressed breastmilk for their best care rather than allowing them to be fed formula. She took a special class to learn more about how to care for her premature twins. When the twins were released from the hospital, Mother woke hourly to feed and administer medicine to them, while still maintaining her obligations to her other children and her job.

While caring for her children, Mother carefully tried to investigate prospective families that might be suitable for the twins. She obtained the help of adoption professionals and attorneys. She expressed interest in an "open adoption" so that she could maintain contact with the twins and continue to support them. Mother was told she would need to look beyond Missouri, which does not allow "open adoption."[4]

An adoption facilitator presented a prospective family from California. Mother visited the couple for 10 days to be sure they were fit. Later, Mother became convinced that the California couple was not as good a placement as she originally believed (among other things, they were becom-

---

4. Subsequent media reports that Mother sold her twins on the internet were investigated by the state and revealed to be completely false. There was some evidence that Mother accepted small gifts, including earrings, but no gift was worth more than $100 and nothing in the record supports the media suggestions that Mother was attempting to sell the twins.

ing reluctant to maintain contact), so when she was in California for a visit, she retained the twins in her custody and began to seek another placement. Mother was advised that a British couple was still interested in adopting her babies. Mother had previously investigated the couple and believed them to be excellent candidates. The husband was an attorney, and the couple supported doing an open adoption. The British couple came to California, and the twins, Mother and the couple traveled a circuitous route from California to Arkansas by car. Mother was counseled by a British social worker and three attorneys that she should complete the adoption there because open adoption was not permitted in Missouri. Mother was advised to claim that she was an Arkansas resident. She refused, but she did provide an Arkansas address that belonged to a relative. An Arkansas judge approved the adoption.

Eventually, British officials determined that the British couple was unfit. The twins were taken into the custody of a British children's services agency. The Arkansas court entered an order setting aside the adoption decree for lack of jurisdiction because none of the parties were Arkansas residents. The twins were returned to Missouri, where they were placed in the custody of the Missouri division of family services (DFS).

When Mother learned that the second adoption effort had failed, she decided that adoption was not the appropriate option, and she resolved to rear the babies herself and rally the support of her family so that she could do it well.[5]

The record indicates that, once DFS gained jurisdiction of the twins, Mother's equivocation ceased other than a few week period shortly after DFS took jurisdiction, when she considered allowing the foster parents to adopt the children but ultimately rejected that alternative and strove to gain back custody of the twins instead. After DFS gained jurisdiction of the twins, there is no evidence that any of Mother's conduct would indicate a likelihood of future problems. Instead, all of the evidence indicates that Mother remedied every potential problem noted by DFS. She complied fully with DFS's entire parenting plan, which had as its ostensible goal reunification:

- The plan required Mother to take parenting classes. Mother took parenting classes, and her instructor testified that Mother was the most involved and participatory member of the class.

- The plan required Mother to visit the twins regularly. Mother visited the twins as often as the court would allow and fought for the right to visit more frequently.

- The plan required Mother to provide financial support for the twins. Mother did so and frequently paid in advance.

---

5. Mother twice failed in her efforts to find a suitable placement for her twins, yet this is not uncommon. The difficulty in finding safe permanent homes for children is illustrated by data that children in the custody of Missouri DFS are moved from placement to placement an average of over three times per child. Citizens for Missouri's Children, Children's Trust Fund, *KIDS COUNT in Missouri 2002 Data Book,* 36 (2003).

- Mother was required to undergo a psychological examination, and she did so willingly. On her own initiative, she also obtained counseling.

- She submitted to drug screenings (which she passed) although there was no allegation of drug use.

A DFS worker later testified that Mother complied with everything that had been asked of her including every element of the plan. Nevertheless, the juvenile officer filed a petition to terminate Mother's parental rights. The petition alleged that termination was warranted according to sections 211.447.4(2), (3) and (6) and that termination was in the twins' best interests.

The trial court conducted a hearing and issued "Findings, Conclusions and Judgment Terminating Parental Rights." The trial court's findings incorporated its earlier "Findings and Judgment of Disposition" and "Permanency Planning Order." The trial court terminated Mother's parental rights under subdivisions (2), (3) and (6) of section 211.447.4, ruling:

15. .... "Mother" has abused and neglected "The Twins". Section 211.447.4(2), RSMo.

(a) "Mother" has committed severe and recurrent acts of emotional abuse toward "The Twins." Section 211.447.4(2)(c), RSMo. These acts include the multiple, unstable, inappropriate, temporary placements including, but not limited to, placements in California, Arkansas, and Great Britain within a span of a few months during the first months of "The Twins" lives....

16. .... [T]he conditions which caused this Court to assume jurisdiction over "The Twins" or conditions of a potentially harmful nature continue to exist and will not be remedied at an early date to permit return of "The Twins" in the near future to the custody of "Mother", and under all the circumstances, continuation of any relationship between the "Mother" and "The Twins" greatly diminishes the prospects of "The Twins" for early integration into a stable and permanent home. Section 211.447.4(3), RSMo. These conditions include, but are not limited to, the multiple placements of "The Twins" during the first months of their lives and the resulting instability; "Mother's" continued stress and being overwhelmed with the reality of The Twins; the continued indecisiveness of "Mother" in dealing with "The Twins"; and the lack of family support for "Mother" in caring for the needs of "The Twins." Additionally, further movement of "The Twins" from the stability of their environment since April 18, 2001, would be harmful to "The Twins" in light of the Reactive Detachment [sic] Disorder in Partial Remission, a major mental disorder, suffered by "The Twins" as a result of the multiple placements and resulting instability....

17. .... "Mother" is unfit to be a party to the parent-child relationship with "The Twins" because of her consistent pattern of emotional abuse and, additionally, because of specific conditions direct-

ly relating to her relationship with "The Twins", all of which are of a duration and nature rendering "Mother" unable for the reasonably foreseeable future to care appropriately for the ongoing physical, mental and emotional needs of "The Twins". Section 211.447.4(6), RSMo. These considerations include, but are not limited to, "Mother's" continued indecisiveness in dealing with the lives of "The Twins" and their welfare; and the lack of family support for "Mother" in caring for health and welfare of "The Twins". . . .

. . .

19. . . . . [T]here are no emotional ties between "The Twins" and "Mother". This is a direct result of the actions of "Mother" in her multiple placements of "The Twins" and resulting instability and emotional harm suffered by "The Twins". Section 211.447.6(1), RSMo.

20. . . . . "The Twins" are not bonded with "Mother". This is a direct result of the deliberate acts of "Mother", who knew or should have known said acts would subject "The Twins" to a substantial and real risk of physical and mental harm. Section 211.447.6(7), RSMo.

. . .

22. The multiple placements and instability of "Mother" have caused emotional harm to "The Twins", and these actions by "Mother" continue to affect "The Twins" to this day, and "Mother" is unwilling or unable to provide "The Twins" with the stability necessary for their overall welfare.

23. Termination of the parental rights of "Mother" is necessary to serve the best interests of "The Twins", in light of all the evidence, and . . . the evidence supporting termination of the parental rights of "Mother" is clear, cogent and convincing. Section 211.447.5, RSMo.

. . .

25. This Court has considered all subsections of Section 211.447.4 and Section 211.447.6, RSMo, and except as expressly provided herein, finds the subsections irrelevant because there was inadequate evidence of their applicability presented during the evidentiary hearing.

. . .

27. The parental rights of "Mother" . . . with "The Twins" . . . shall be, and hereby are, terminated.

Mother appeals, arguing that the trial court's findings with respect to sections 211.447.4(2), (3) and (6) and 211.447.6 were insufficient. She also contends that the trial court erred because it failed to make required findings.

"Courts typically terminate parental rights under a 'parental fault' standard, in which the court focuses on the behavior of the parent or parents, a 'best interests of the child' standard, in which the court focuses on the effect of termination of parental rights on the child, or a combination of both." 2 Am Jur 2d *Adoption* sec. 134 (2003). Missouri, through section 211.447, terminates parental rights under a combination of both standards. Additionally, section 211.443 provides that Missouri uses a rule of construction for section 211.447, that it:

[S]hall be construed so as to promote the best interests and welfare of the child as determined by the juvenile court in consideration of the following:

(1) The recognition and protection of the constitutional rights of all parties in the proceedings;

(2) The recognition and protection of the birth family relationship when possible and appropriate; and

(3) The entitlement of every child to a permanent and stable home.

. . .

An essential part of any determination whether to terminate parental rights is whether, considered at the time of the termination and looking to the future, the child would be harmed by a continued relationship with the parent. A prospective analysis is required to determine whether grounds exist and what is in the best interests of the child for the reasonably foreseeable future. Obviously, it is difficult to predict the future. Section 211.447 provides for detailed consideration of the parent's past conduct as well as the parent's conduct following the trial court's assumption of jurisdiction as good evidence of future behavior. *In the Interest of M.E.W.,* 729 S.W.2d 194, 196 (Mo. banc 1987) (court needs to consider existing conditions, which may have arisen or were discovered after it assumed jurisdiction); *In the Interest of C.L.W.,* 115 S.W.3d 354, 356 (Mo.App.2003) (court must look at totality of parent's conduct both prior to and after filing of termination petition); *In the Interest of S.H.,* 915 S.W.2d 399, 404–5 (Mo.App.1996) (past patterns provide vital clues to present and future conduct). However, it is insufficient merely to point to past acts, note that they resulted in abuse or neglect and then terminate parental rights. *In the Interest of C.L.W.,* 115 S.W.3d at 356. Past behavior can support grounds for termination, but only if it is convincingly linked to predicted future behavior. There must be some explicit consideration of whether the past acts provide an indication of the likelihood of future harm. *In the Interest of L.G.,* 764 S.W.2d 89, 95 (Mo. banc 1989) (state met its burden by proving likely harm to child would occur in future). "A judge may properly be guided by evidence demonstrating reason to believe that a parent will correct a condition or weakness that currently disables the parent from serving his or her child's best interests." 2 Am Jur 2d *Adoption* sec. 135 (2003).

Courts have required that abuse or neglect sufficient to support termination under section 211.447.4(2) be based on conduct at the time of termination, not just at the time jurisdiction was initially taken. *In the Interest of B.C.K. and K.S.P.,* 103 S.W.3d at 328; *In the Interest of T.A.S.,*

32 S.W.3d 804, 812 (Mo.App.2000) (*T.A.S. I*). Similarly, courts have required that a failure to rectify sufficient to support termination under section 211.447.4(3) be based on a determination that conditions of a potentially harmful nature continued to exist as of the termination, rather than a mere finding that conditions that led to the assumption of jurisdiction still persisted. *In the Interest of T.A.S.*, 62 S.W.3d 650, 656–7 (Mo.App. 2001) (*T.A.S. II*). Section 211.447.4(6) explicitly requires analysis of the "reasonably foreseeable future." *In the Interest of C.W. and S.J.W.*, 64 S.W.3d 321, 325 (Mo.App.2001). Findings supporting earlier determinations are not irrelevant, but they must be updated to address the extent to which they describe the time of the termination and the potential for future harm. *T.A.S. I* at 812; *T.A.S. II* at 656–7. To that end, a trial court cannot support a termination by merely incorporating earlier findings supporting its assumption of jurisdiction or some other earlier disposition.

. . .

Another essential part of any determination whether to terminate parental rights is whether the cited conduct of the parent has had or will have a detrimental impact upon the child. *In the Interest of P.C., B.M., and C.M.*, 62 S.W.3d 600, 604 (Mo.App.2001) (the trial court must hear some evidence describing what impact the questioned conduct has had on the children). Poor conduct or character flaws are not relevant unless they could actually result in future harm to the child. For example, sections 211.447.4(2)(a) and 211.447.4(3)(c) provide that the parent's mental condition is a factor supporting termination only if it "renders the parent unable to knowingly provide the child the necessary care, custody and control."

Another essential part of any determination whether to terminate parental rights is whether the cited acts or conditions of the parent, and their accompanying impact upon the child, are severe enough to constitute abuse or neglect. *In the Interest of P.C., B.M., and C.M.*, 62 S.W.3d at 604 (parent's acts may have been inappropriate but were not severe enough to support termination). Some parental conduct will harm a child without constituting abuse or neglect. *In the Interest of B.C.K. and K.S.P.*, 103 S.W.3d at 328. It is essential that the trial court determine whether the parent's acts are of sufficient severity.

For some types of parenting problems, the required level of severity the court must find is specified by the statute. For example, sections 211.447.4(2)(b) and 211.447.4(3)(d) provide that chemical dependency is of sufficient severity to support termination if it "prevents the parent from consistently providing the necessary care, custody and control over the child and which cannot be treated so as to enable the parent to consistently provide such care, custody and control." For another example, not every criminal act committed by the parent is severe enough to be abuse or neglect. Section 211.447.4(4) provides that it will be a grounds for termination of parental rights if the "parent has been found guilty or pled guilty to a felony violation of chapter 566, RSMo [sexual offenses], when the child or any child in the family was a victim, or a violation of section 568.020, RSMo [incest], when the child or any child in the family was a victim."

Section 211.447.6(6) provides for consideration of the "conviction of the parent of a felony offense that the court finds is of such a nature that the child will be deprived of a stable home for a period of years...." These sections provide guidance as to how severe a parent's criminal conduct must be to constitute abuse.[7]

Isolated abusive acts or conditions may not support termination when considered individually, but if they form a consistent pattern, are recurrent or are repeated, they can, when considered in combination, rise to the level of abuse and support termination. Sec. 211.447.4(2)(c), (2)(d), (3), (6).

. . .

The trial court found that Mother's acts included "multiple, unstable, inappropriate, temporary placements including, but not limited to, placements in California, Arkansas, and Great Britain within a span of a few months during the first months of 'The Twins' lives."

There is no dispute that Mother twice attempted to place her twins for adoption. However, the record does not contain evidence that the first placement in California was unstable or inappropriate. The "placements in ... Arkansas and Great Britain" refer to the single attempted adoption of the twins in Arkansas by the couple from Great Britain and, thus, constitute but one placement.

The two attempts at placement of the twins for adoption may have been mistakes, and may even have harmed the twins, but no reported Missouri case has ever held that placing a child up for adoption more than once rises to the level of abuse, and there is no reason to consider it abuse in this case. Mother's two attempts at placing her twins for adoption are not an indication of potential future harm to the twins, especially without evidence that she would try to again place the twins for adoption if she regains custody of them. There is no evidence in the record that Mother intends to do anything other than regain permanent custody of her twins.

The trial court erred in concluding that these placements support findings that Mother committed "severe and recurrent acts of emotional abuse" and that Mother created "conditions of a potentially harmful nature [that] continue to exist and will not be remedied at an early date." There is no evidence that the placements were abusive or that they indicate a likelihood of future harm. Therefore, they do not constitute evidence that "instantly tilts the scales in favor of termination." *T.A.S. II* at 655.

. . .

Mother's mental state cannot constitute abuse unless it rises to the level described by sections 211.447.4(2)(a) and (3)(c): "[a] mental condition

---

7. Although it was not explicitly relied upon by the trial court in the termination of parental rights, Mother pleaded guilty to welfare fraud because she provided false information and failed to provide required information to the state. Considering the severity of the crimes described in subdivisions 211.447.4(4) and 211.447.6(6), welfare fraud of this nature is not abuse, and the trial court correctly declined to include it as supporting termination.

which is shown by competent evidence either to be permanent or such that there is no reasonable likelihood that the condition can be reversed and which renders the parent unable to knowingly provide the child the necessary care, custody and control."[8] *In the Interest of C.L.W.*, 115 S.W.3d at 360-1 (Prewitt, J., dissenting); Mark Hardin and Robert Lancour, *Early Termination of Parental Rights: Developing Appropriate Statutory Grounds*, 14 (1996) (more required than just presence of mental or emotional disability—incapacity must be so severe that parent is incapable of providing minimally acceptable care).

It is hard to imagine a single working mother of five children living in poverty without enormous stress. Feeling overwhelmed in this context is not an indication of emotional instability, nor is it child abuse; rather, it is normal. DFS hired an expert to evaluate Mother's mental ability to care for her children. The expert found that Mother's "difficulties in parenting are not substantially different from those of many other single parents caring for large families . . ., she appears to be an adequate parent, and there is no evidence that her parental rights should be terminated."

Sections 211.447.4(2)(a) and 211.447.4(3)(c) provide that a mental or emotional condition must be analyzed in three prongs to make an adequate finding: (1) documentation—whether the condition is supported by competent evidence; (2) duration—whether the condition is permanent or such that there is no reasonable likelihood that it can be reversed; and (3) severity of effect—whether the condition is so severe as to render the parent unable to knowingly provide the child necessary care, custody and control.

Considering each of these three prongs, the problems cited by the trial court (stress, feeling overwhelmed and indecisiveness) do not support termination of parental rights. The expert evidence as to Mother's mental state did not constitute competent evidence that these problems were abnormal. These problems were situational and not necessarily permanent; therefore, the importance of the parenting or reunification plan and the services provided by DFS to Mother. There is evidence that Mother complied with the plan and that the services helped. The trial court's use of the word "continued" is without any support in the record. Even if there was reason to believe that these problems "continued," there is no evidence in the record that such a combination of problems ever caused abuse or would cause future harm. The only evidence on this question was provided

---

8. "Before the court can use mental incapacity as the basis for terminating a parent's rights, it must find that the mental defect or disability renders the parent unable to provide for the needs and well-being of his or her children. . . . It is sufficient to show that the parent's emotional problems are so severe as to prevent the maintenance of any meaningful relationship with his or her children. In such cases, it is often necessary to provide expert testimony that the parent's emotional instability is not likely to improve in the future. . . . In order to prevail in a termination proceeding based on mental incapacity, the petition should present sufficient evidence of the adverse effects which the parent's incapacity has on the well-being of the child. Absent such a showing, most courts will be reluctant to order termination on this ground alone." 32 Am Jur Proof of Facts 3d *Parental Rights* sec. 5 (2003).

by the DFS expert who concluded that these reactions were expectable and not a potential cause of future harm.

Therefore, these findings do not support the termination of Mother's parental rights.

The trial court found that the twins suffered from "Reactive Detachment Disorder in Partial Remission, a major mental disorder, suffered by 'The Twins' as a result of the multiple placements and resulting instability." This opinion was rendered by only one of the several physicians who evaluated the twins—Dr. Luby. Dr. Luby actually diagnosed the twins with Reactive *Attachment* Disorder in Partial Remission. The trial court also omitted a modifier used by Dr. Luby: "moderate" (Dr. Luby testified that the condition can be severe, moderate or mild). Dr. Luby asked to be allowed to see the twins interact with Mother, but the request was denied—significantly undermining the reliability of the diagnosis. The two experts who evaluated the twins in the presence of Mother did not agree with Dr. Luby's diagnosis.

Furthermore, Dr. Luby acknowledged that she did not document any of the standard diagnostic criteria for Reactive Attachment Disorder. Even DFS showed little confidence in Dr. Luby's assessment. DFS did not arrange for treatment and did not inform the foster parents of the diagnosis. Moreover, despite the diagnosis, even Dr. Luby acknowledged that she could see no harm in placing the twins back with Mother.

The two psychologists who evaluated the twins *and witnessed their interaction with Mother* strongly disagreed with Dr. Luby's diagnosis. Dr. Dean Rosen, a clinical psychologist, found that the twins were comfortable with Mother, paying little or no attention to others when their mother was in the room. He observed no signs of Reactive Attachment Disorder. Dr. Rosen found a "good indication there was a bond with [their] mother" and that Mother demonstrated appropriate parenting skills. Dr. Rosen testified that there would be no harm in returning the twins to their mother.

Dr. Daniel Cuneo, a clinical psychologist, was also allowed to observe the twins with their mother. He concluded that the twins showed no signs of Reactive Attachment Disorder. He found that the twins played with and appropriately modeled their mother's behavior, that the children were comfortable and that Mother set limits for the twins while showing affection toward them. Dr. Cuneo observed that the twins showed affection for their mother. He also found no reason to expect the twins to be harmed by being returned to their mother.

A primary focus of a proceeding to terminate parental rights is the relationship between the parent and the child. The findings of experts who have had the opportunity to observe and evaluate that relationship should be given great weight.

The trial court's finding that the twins suffer from "Reactive Detachment [sic] Disorder in Partial Remission, a major mental disorder" that would be worsened by their being placed in Mother's custody, is not supported by clear, cogent and convincing evidence. The evidence only supports a conclusion that the twins may have been emotionally harmed by having been placed multiple times, but that such harm has been ameliorated and that the continuation of Mother's parental rights does not pose a threat of future harm. Therefore, this finding does not support a termination of Mother's parental rights.

Section 211.447.4(2) provides for termination of parental rights if:

The child has been abused or neglected. In determining whether to terminate parental rights pursuant to this subdivision, the court shall consider and make findings on the following conditions or acts of the parent:

(a) A mental condition which is shown by competent evidence either to be permanent or such that there is no reasonable likelihood that the condition can be reversed and which renders the parent unable to knowingly provide the child the necessary care, custody and control;

(b) Chemical dependency which prevents the parent from consistently providing the necessary care, custody and control of the child and which cannot be treated so as to enable the parent to consistently provide such care, custody and control;

(c) A severe act or recurrent acts of physical, emotional or sexual abuse toward the child or any child in the family by the parent, including an act of incest, or by another under circumstances that indicate that the parent knew or should have known that such acts were being committed toward the child or any child in the family; or

(d) Repeated or continuous failure by the parent, although physically or financially able, to provide the child with adequate food, clothing, shelter, or education as defined by law, or other care and control necessary for the child's physical, mental, or emotional health and development;

The trial court concluded that it had considered all applicable subdivisions or factors and omitted those it determined to be irrelevant or supported by inadequate evidence of applicability. Section 211.447 does not provide the trial court with such discretion. *In the Interest of L.G.,* 764 S.W.2d 89, 94 (Mo. banc 1989). "The court is required to make specific findings on *each* of these four factors [or subdivisions]. If a factor is not relevant to the case, the court should state why the given factor is not relevant." *T.A.S. I* at 810 (emphasis in original); *In the Interest of B.C.K. and K.S.P.,* 103 S.W.3d at 327 (trial court must consider and make findings on four factors). "Strict and literal compliance with the statutory requirements is necessary in termination of parental rights cases." *T.A.S. I.* "Statutory mandates to make findings may not be overlooked on appeal." *In re A.P.,* 988 S.W.2d 59, 62 (Mo.App.1999). Section 211.447.4(2) provides that the trial court "shall consider and make findings" on all four factors, (a) through (d). Yet, the trial court only considered factor (c).

As to factor (c), the trial court's finding that Mother "has committed severe and recurrent acts of emotional abuse toward 'The Twins' " by placing the twins with two families within a span of a few months is not sufficient, as discussed above.

As to factors (a), (b) and (d), the evidence indicates that, rather than being irrelevant or unsupported, many of the omitted findings would have supported Mother's claims. There is no question that Mother has neither a mental condition nor chemical dependency that would preclude her from having custody of her children. Therefore, factors (a) and (b) favor Mother. Factor (d) also strongly favors Mother, in that she has continuously (even when the children were in DFS custody and foster care) provided the twins with monetary and emotional support.

Therefore, the trial court's findings as to section 211.447.4(2) are either absent or insufficient, and the trial court's reliance upon section 211.447.4(2) as grounds for termination is error.

. . .

Section 211.447.4(6) provides for termination of parental rights if:

The parent is unfit to be a party to the parent and child relationship because of a consistent pattern of committing a specific abuse, including but not limited to, abuses as defined in section 455.010, RSMo, child abuse or drug abuse before the child or of specific conditions directly relating to the parent and child relationship either of which are determined by the court to be of a duration or nature that renders the parent unable, for the reasonably foreseeable future, to care appropriately for the ongoing physical, mental or emotional needs of the child. It is presumed that a parent is unfit to be a party to the parent-child relationship upon a showing that within a three-year period immediately prior to the termination adjudication, the parent's parental rights to one or more other children were involuntarily terminated pursuant to subsection 2 or 3 of this section or subdivisions (1), (2), (3) or (4) of subsection 4 of this section or similar laws of other states.

The trial court found that Mother had abused the twins in such a way as to satisfy both prongs of section 211.447.4(6)—finding both a "consistent pattern of committing a specific abuse" and "specific conditions directly relating to the parent and child relationship." Both prongs must be (and were) accompanied by a finding that they will "be of a duration or nature that renders the parent unable, for the reasonably foreseeable future, to care appropriately for the ongoing physical, mental or emotional needs of the child." *In the Interest of C.W. and S.J.W.*, 64 S.W.3d at 325.

Subdivision (6) describes findings that the parent continues to have parenting problems that endanger the child coupled with an inability to remedy those problems within the reasonably foreseeable future. *See* Roya R. Hough, *Juvenile Law: A Year in Review*, 63 Mo. L.Rev. 459, 465–66 (1998) (focus in broad language of subdivision (6) is on "kid time"— whether "from the child's perspective, the amount of time necessary for the parent to overcome the barriers to reunification is unreasonable, as measured by the child's need for permanency at the earliest possible date").

Past abuse alone cannot be a basis for terminating parental rights under subdivision (6). Instead, the abuse must be of such a duration and nature that the trial court determines that the parent will not remedy the problem and so it renders the parent unfit for the reasonably foreseeable future. *In the Interest of P.C., B.M., and C.M.,* 62 S.W.3d at 606.

In support of termination under this subdivision, the trial court cited:

> ... "Mother's" continued stress and being overwhelmed with the reality of "The Twins"; "Mother's" continued indecisiveness in dealing with the lives of "The Twins" and their welfare; and the lack of family support for "Mother" in caring for health and welfare of "The Twins".

As discussed above, these findings are insufficient to support termination, even in combination. They are particularly inappropriate for section 211.447.4(6). They do not describe a parent that continues to have parenting problems that endanger a child coupled with an inability to remedy those problems within the reasonably foreseeable future. They are specific past acts or conditions and the record indicates that all of them ended by the time of the termination proceedings. Regardless of the past, section 211.447.4(6) "requires the trial court to determine that the parent is *currently* unfit ... to be a party to the parent and child relationship." *T.A.S. I* at 815 (emphasis added). Such a determination must be supported by findings as to acts or conditions that persist at the time of termination. *Id.*

Therefore, the trial court's findings as to section 211.447.4(6) are insufficient, and the trial court's reliance upon section 211.447.4(6) as grounds for termination is error.

Mother's parental rights were terminated because of little more than her efforts to find an adoptive family for her twins. There is not substantial evidence in the record that Mother did so for personal gain, and the evidence is that she consistently sought to protect her twins by finding a good adoptive family that would allow her to retain contact with the twins. This cannot, without more, provide grounds for termination of parental rights.

Countless psychological and child development studies have shown that children—especially infants and young children under the age of five—who are needlessly separated from their familiar parent suffer resulting deficits in their emotional and intellectual development. Joseph Goldstein, Albert J. Solnit, Sonja Goldstein and Anna Freud, *The Best Interests of the Child: The Least Detrimental Alternative,* 20 (1996). The complex and vital parent-child interactions necessary for healthy child development "thrive in the protective enclave of family life under guardianship by parents who are autonomous." *Id.* at 90. "When family integrity is broken or weakened by state intrusion, [the child's] needs are thwarted.... The effect on the child's developmental progress is likely to be detrimental." *Id.* Accordingly, courts should follow an approach of cautious restraint in intruding on the family relationship—an approach that recognizes that parents are generally entitled to raise their children as they think best, free from state interference, and that favors the minimum amount of state intervention necessary consistent with the best interests of the child. Parental rights should be terminated only when it is clearly necessary to ensure safe and permanent homes for children. Donald N. Duquette and Mark Hardin, *Adoption 2002: The President's Initiative on Adoption and Foster Care, Guidelines for Public Policy and State Legislative Governing Permanence for Children*, VI–1 (1999). "A parent's interest in retaining custody of his children is both legally cognizable and substantial, and may not be overridden in the absence of persuasive evidence that the children's well-being requires that custody be placed elsewhere." 59 Am Jur 2d *Parent and Child* sec. 36 (2003).

Many of the findings necessary to support a termination of Mother's parental rights as to the twins are absent from the trial court's ruling. The findings actually provided by the trial court are insufficient to support termination.

The judgment is reversed and the cause is remanded. If further proceedings include the termination of Mother's parental rights, the trial court is directed to consider and make findings on each of the statutorily required subdivisions or factors for all grounds for termination of parental rights on which the trial court bases its decision.[9]

■ WHITE, C.J., WOLFF and STITH, JJ., concur. PRICE, J., dissents in separate opinion filed.

■ BENTON and LIMBAUGH, JJ., concur in opinion of PRICE, J.

■ WILLIAM RAY PRICE, JR., JUDGE, dissenting.

. . .

In termination of parental rights cases, appellate courts should defer to the trial court's ability to judge the credibility of witnesses and should sustain the judgment unless there is no substantial evidence to support it, it is contrary to the evidence, or it erroneously declares or applies the law. *In the Interest of M.E.W.*, 729 S.W.2d 194, 195–96 (Mo. banc 1987). Appellate courts also should review conflicting evidence in the light most favorable to the judgment of the trial court. *Id.* at 196. "Clear, cogent and convincing" evidence is required to support the trial court's finding that a ground for termination of parental rights exists, and appellate courts must take that into account when reviewing whether "substantial evidence" supports the trial court's judgment. *See* sec. 211.447.5.

Appellate courts should recognize that the trial court occupies a "superior position" from which to "judge the credibility of witnesses and their character, sincerity, and other intangibles that might not be completely shown in the cold record." *Young v. Young*, 59 S.W.3d 23, 29 (Mo.App.

---

9. As the judgment is reversed and the cause is remanded, Mother's other claims of error need not be reviewed. Because the case is remanded for further proceedings on all three grounds for termination, the issue of whether the termination was in the twins' best interests is not reached.

2001). In considering witness testimony, "[a] trial court is free to believe or disbelieve all, part, or none" of a witness's testimony. *Id.*

The trial court found that Mother engaged in a "consistent pattern of emotional abuse" of the twins. *See* sec. 211.447.4(6). Mother's pattern of behavior toward the twins supports this finding, particularly her failure to consider their well-being when making decisions about their care and in her repeated placement and subsequent withdrawal of the twins for adoption.[4]

The trial court also found that Mother's pattern of abuse was "of a duration or nature that renders [her] unable, for the reasonably foreseeable future, to care appropriately for the ongoing physical, mental, or emotional needs" of the twins. Sec. 211.447.4(6). The following evidence in the record is substantial and clearly, cogently, and convincingly supports these findings. *See M.E.W.*, 729 S.W.2d at 195–96; sec. 211.447.5.

The record reveals that when Mother was pregnant, her doctor prescribed a medication for her to prevent premature labor. Mother quit taking the medicine of her own accord, and she later told a psychologist that she stopped taking the medicine because "she was tired of being pregnant." The twins were born at 28 weeks, or approximately three months prematurely, and they weighed slightly more than two pounds each. Mother had similarly stopped taking this medication in a previous pregnancy because "she didn't like to be on medication," and that child was also premature.

The twins' pediatrician testified that, after their release from the hospital, Mother missed their first appointment and three weeks elapsed between their release and first visit to him. He described the twins at that time as having "numerous medical problems" and said this initial visit for the twins after their departure from the hospital was "very important."[5] As a result of missed appointments, the doctor sent a letter to DFS stating that "[n]ot showing up for routine medical visits for the twins is not acceptable care."

Mother testified she first considered adoption because the twins' father told her no man would want her with three children, much less five of them. A disturbing statement in its own right, it prefaced Mother's chain of

---

4. Since the twins returned to the United States on April 18, 2001, they have been in the custody of their foster parents. The foster parents have an adopted son who is approximately nine months older than the twins. The son was placed with the foster parents prior to the twins' arrival and has remained in the parents' custody since that initial placement. The foster parents' adoption of the twins was approved at the circuit court level, but Mother moved to stay that adoption pending the resolution of this appeal.

Mother's court-ordered visits and child support obligations to the twins concluded on June 23, 2002, by order of the trial court. The twins turned two years old three days after that last visit. They are nearly four years old now.

5. The pediatrician testified that Mother had repeatedly missed visits with him for her other children. With her oldest son, J.G., who has a heart problem, Mother missed at least six appointments, and she missed at least four appointments with the twins' sister, N.W.

decisions predicated on her own desires that demonstrated her "unfit to be a party to the parent and child relationship." Sec. 211.447.4(6).

Mother first attempted to place the twins with R.A. and V.A., a married couple residing in California. She admitted placing the twins with them "because they were well off financially." Mother acknowledged that she was aware of V.A.'s criminal record before placing the twins with them. After leaving the twins in the custody of R.A. and V.A., Mother surreptitiously removed the twins from their home a month and a half later because she heard a rumor "they were strapped for money or they were filing for bankruptcy" and because when Mother called them, V.A. "acted nonchalant."[6] She told R.A. and V.A. she was taking them out for a visit, when in fact she took them to a hotel where A.K. and J.K., a married couple residing in the United Kingdom, met her two days later.

After driving from California to Arkansas with A.K. and J.K., Mother transferred custody of the twins to them. A child abuse investigator from DFS testified that Mother said she had placed her children with A.K. and J.K. because they were going to allow her to come to the United Kingdom every year on the twins' birthday, which would be a good experience for her, and that she thought they would pay her airfare for those annual visits.

Mother's first objection to A.K. and J.K. having custody of the twins occurred approximately on January 16, 2001, as a response to media reports that she had sold the twins over the Internet.[7] British authorities rendered the placement with A.K. and J.K. short-term by taking custody of the twins on January 18, 2001, approximately two and a half weeks after their arrival in the United Kingdom, based on allegations of A.K.'s and J.K.'s unfitness.[8]

Both placements of the twins, with R.A. and V.A. and with A.K. and J.K., were illegal under Missouri law. The transfer of custody from Mother to both couples violated section 453.110, the purpose of which is "to prohibit the indiscriminate transfer of children" and to prevent parents

---

6. Mother testified that she called or talked to V.A. "practically every day" when the twins were in R.A. and V.A.'s custody, which was from approximately October 19 through November 29, 2001. Mother stated V.A. made her feel like she "was being a pest" and V.A. "act[ed] nonchalant, like why was [Mother] calling her" one day when Mother called. Mother cited this conversation and reports of their financial problems as the only reasons she withdrew the children from R.A. and V.A.'s custody.

7. As Mother put it, "January 16th is when my life was on the news." She expressed no concern as to any effect this media exposure may have had on the twins.

8. During the summer of 2001, Mother resumed her attempts to place the twins for adoption. She requested a meeting with the twins' foster parents in July to speak with them about adopting the twins. By the end of August, however, she had changed her mind again and withdrawn her offer to consent to adoption.

Even though she had previously declined to attempt to place the twins with her family and her mother had indicated earlier she did not want the twins, in April 2002 Mother testified that she would be amenable to letting her mother adopt the twins because then she could stay with them at her mother's.

from passing them on "like chattel to a new owner." *In re Baby Girl* 64, 850 S.W.2d 64, 68 (Mo. banc 1993).

Mother also admitted that she gave a false address to the Arkansas court to effect the twins' placement with A.K. and J.K. Mother told a psychologist that she knew she was required to be an Arkansas resident to ensure the twins' adoption there, so she used an aunt's Arkansas address instead of her own. Relying on her falsified information, the probate court of Pulaski County, Arkansas, entered an adoption decree for the twins on December 22, 2000. After learning that none of the parties was an Arkansas resident at the time the adoption decree was entered, the Arkansas court entered an order on March 6, 2001, to set aside that decree for lack of jurisdiction.

. . .

The majority cites, in its conclusion, studies showing that children needlessly separated from their parents suffer resulting deficits in their emotional and intellectual development. This point is undisputed. Even Mother, despite her initial testimony that she had never considered the emotional impact on the twins of her consistent pattern of placing and removing them and that she was the victim in this case, admitted subsequently that the twins were harmed by the multiple placements.

The majority also relies on authority that a child's developmental progress can be hampered by state intrusion. The majority ignores, however, that since the twins were released from the hospital in August 2000, they have been in Mother's sole care, custody, and control for 52 days. The absence of the twins from her custody was not her choice after DFS removed them upon their return from the United Kingdom, but the failed placements were direct consequences of her decisions and actions accomplished without mention of concern for the twins' well-being. The majority ignores that Mother voluntarily succumbed the custody of the twins to others—both times purportedly permanently—and that the state intervened only after the second placement was deemed unfit by foreign authorities acting on behalf of the twins' welfare. Any compromise in her family's integrity was accomplished directly as a result of Mother's decisions made without consideration of the twins' well-being.

The reality of this case is that the twins were born on June 26, 2000, and have been in the custody of foster parents since April 18, 2001, where they also have an adopted sibling. The testimony revealed that the twins need a stable environment and special attention to their emotional and physical needs, and Mother has never exhibited any ability to provide that for them.

When the trial court has received conflicting evidence, as in the instant case, the role of this Court is to "review the facts in the light most favorable to the trial court's judgment." *M.E.W.*, 729 S.W.2d at 196. In its review, the Court should "give due regard to the trial court's opportunity to judge the credibility of witnesses and sustain the decree unless there is no substantial evidence to support it, it is contrary to the evidence or it erroneously declares or applies the law." *Id.* at 195–96. "As long as the record contains credible evidence upon which the trial court could have formulated its beliefs," an appellate court should not "substitute its judgment for that of the trial court." *Patton v. Patton,* 973 S.W.2d 139, 145 (Mo.App.1998).

The standard of review precludes this Court from searching the record for facts that could have supported a contrary judgment from the trial court. Unfortunately, that is exactly what the majority has chosen to do. Perhaps more unfortunately, the majority has chosen to sacrifice the best interests and welfare of two innocent children in favor of a parent who has demonstrated, time and again, her inability to make appropriate decisions concerning their care. In doing so, the majority deviates from the dictate of section 211.443, which requires courts to interpret the termination of parental rights statutes "so as to promote the best interests and welfare of the child."

Substantial clear, cogent, and convincing evidence supports the trial court's finding that termination of Mother's parental rights was justified pursuant to section 211.447.4(6) and that termination was in the twins' best interests. I would affirm the judgment.

Matter of Gregory B.

Court of Appeals of New York, 1989.
74 N.Y.2d 77, 544 N.Y.S.2d 535, 542 N.E.2d 1052.

■ ALEXANDER, JUDGE.

The common issue presented on these appeals is whether the evidence adduced in each case supported a finding that the incarcerated parent "permanently neglected" his child within the meaning of Social Services Law § 384–b(7)(a), thus justifying the termination of his parental rights and the concomitant freeing of his child for adoption. For the reasons that follow, we conclude that the termination of parental rights was, in each case, proper and supported by clear and convincing evidence.

Matter of Gregory B.

Evidence was presented at the fact-finding hearing that respondent father has been incarcerated since August 1980 and is currently serving a prison sentence of 10 to 20 years at Green Haven Correctional Facility upon his felony conviction. His children, Gregory and Kareem, were born on December 28, 1979 and November 20, 1980 respectively. Should respondent serve the maximum term imposed, his children will be well into their majorities by the time of his release.[1] Gregory, now 9 years old, and Kareem, now 8 years old, entered foster care on October 24, 1981 pursuant to voluntary placement agreements executed by their mother placing them under the supervision of petitioner St. Dominic's Home, an authorized child care agency. Petitioner placed Gregory and Kareem, along with their

---

1. Respondent will not become eligible for parole until June 1990.

older half-brother Quaron,[2] in the same foster family with whom all three boys have resided since November 1981. Although it appears that Gregory and Kareem suffer from various physical and psychological maladies, with Kareem having required periodic hospitalization for an asthmatic condition, both children continue to thrive in their original foster home and their foster parents apparently wish to adopt them.

In July 1986, petitioner filed petitions in Family Court under Social Services Law § 384–b(7) seeking to terminate the rights of both biological parents on the ground of permanent neglect and to free the children for adoption. At the fact-finding hearing petitioner presented evidence of having actively encouraged and nurtured the parent-child relationship by arranging numerous visits between respondent and his children at prison and by attempting to secure the assistance of relatives offered by respondent as possible custodians for Gregory and Kareem. Respondent's initial plan was to have the children live with his mother until his release from prison. In a foster care review proceeding held in 1985, however, it was determined that discharge of the children to their paternal grandmother was not a viable option because she was neither physically nor emotionally up to the task of raising two young children with Gregory's and Kareem's special needs. No appeal was taken from this ruling. When advised of the court's decision, respondent's only alternative plan was to have his children remain in foster care until his eventual return to society.

Based on this evidence, Family Court concluded that the children had been permanently neglected by both parents "despite the agency's efforts to nurture all available familial resources" and specifically noted that "[t]he term of imprisoned parents must be a factor in evaluating the viability of their plan for the future of their children." After holding a dispositional hearing at which it concluded that the best interests of both children would be served by the termination of parental rights, the court terminated the parental rights of both biological parents and transferred guardianship and custody of the children to petitioner and the Commissioner of Social Services for the purpose of adoption. On respondent's appeal from Family Court's order, the Appellate Division affirmed, without opinion.[3] 143 A.D.2d 548, 538 N.Y.S.2d 889.

Matter of Willie John B.

Matter of Delores B.

Evidence was presented at the joint fact-finding hearing that respondent father has been incarcerated since April 1979 and is currently serving two concurrent sentences of 25 years to life for murder at the Green Haven Correctional Facility. His children, Willie and Delores, were born on August 10, 1975 and August 16, 1979 respectively. Willie, who is now 13 years old, has been in the care of petitioner Cardinal McCloskey Children's and

---

2. Respondent is not the father of Quaron who already has been adopted by the foster family.

3. The mother has not appealed from Family Court's order terminating her parental rights.

Family Services since July 1, 1977 and his foster parents wish to adopt him; Delores, now 9 years old, has been in the care of petitioner since July 31, 1980 and her foster parents wish to adopt her also. The minorities of both children will be over if and when respondent is finally released from prison.

In June 1984, petitioner instituted two separate proceedings in Family Court to terminate the parental rights of respondent and to free the children for adoption.[4] It was established at the fact-finding hearing that petitioner was diligent in its efforts to foster the parent-child relationship by bringing the children to prison to meet with their father and by contacting relatives who might be able to care for the children. Petitioner's efforts to assist respondent secure a permanent home for the children, however, proved futile because the relatives contacted—respondent's two sisters and his mother—were either unwilling, unable, or ill-suited to the task of raising Willie and Delores. The only other plan respondent offered, like that of the respondent in *Matter of Gregory B.,* was to keep his children in foster care until such time as he might be released from prison.

Notwithstanding respondent's failure to provide either Willie or Delores with a realistic alternative to foster care, Family Court dismissed the petition relating to Delores, concluding that respondent did all he could in light of his status of incarceration to maintain contact with and plan for the future of his daughter. The court reasoned that the 1983 statutory reforms pertaining to incarcerated parents—precluding a court from terminating parental rights solely on the basis of incarceration—compelled the conclusion that "adoption can be prevented by a prisoner who expresses real interest in his child and maintains contact insofar as possible although he has never been and can never be a real parent no matter how great his desires" (*Matter of Delores B.,* 130 Misc.2d 484, 485, 496 N.Y.S.2d 930). With respect to Willie, however, the court made a finding of permanent neglect, concluding that even prior to his incarceration respondent had failed to plan for Willie's future. After a dispositional hearing, the court terminated respondent's parental rights in respect to Willie and transferred guardianship and custody of Willie to petitioner and the Commissioner of Social Services for the purpose of adoption.[5]

A majority of the Appellate Division reversed the order of Family Court dismissing the petition relating to Delores, concluding that court had erred in determining that the 1983 statutory reforms precluded a finding of permanent neglect by the incarcerated father. The Appellate Division therefore granted the petition and ordered that the matter be remitted to Family Court for a dispositional hearing. On remand, Family Court ad-

4. The mother was not a party to the proceedings. It appears that she executed a surrender for Willie's adoption in May 1981 and subsequently had her parental rights relating to Delores terminated by order of Family Court in September 1983.

5. Family Court also ordered a specific psychological evaluation of Willie to determine whether visits between Willie and respondent would be helpful to Willie and, further, directed that there be visitation between Willie and Delores until such time as Willie is adopted.

judged Delores to be a permanently neglected child, terminated respondent's parental rights in respect to her, and authorized petitioner and the Commissioner of Social Services to consent to her adoption. In respect to Willie, the Appellate Division majority affirmed Family Court's order, concluding that the record evidence supported that court's finding of permanent neglect.

Justice Ellerin, concurring in part and dissenting in part, agreed with the majority that the evidence supported a finding of permanent neglect as to both children but questioned whether, in light of the potential emotional harm that might result from a permanent severing of ties between the children and their biological father, "the termination of parental rights here should be coupled with provision for the continuation of some contacts between these children and their biological father" (141 A.D.2d 100, 117, 533 N.Y.S.2d 706). Noting that the record in the case was not sufficiently developed to permit the court to decide what type of continuing contacts, if any, might be appropriate, Justice Ellerin suggested that there should be a hearing held in conjunction with any future adoption proceedings "to determine whether the child's best interests will be served by providing for some continued contacts with the biological father and, if so, the nature and extent of such contacts" (141 A.D.2d at 118, 533 N.Y.S.2d 706, supra).

Justice Carro dissented separately, concluding that respondent's incarceration imposed "an external impossibility on his ability to provide a home for his children" and therefore precluded a finding of permanent neglect. Justice Carro reasoned that respondent did not seek to abdicate his parental obligations but merely sought to fulfill them "through a combination of meaningful contacts with his children and long-term foster care" and that such long-term foster care was a viable option under the statutory scheme in the circumstances presented. Justice Carro argued further that if termination of parental rights is indicated, then hearings should be held to determine whether the best interests of the children would be served by "open" adoptions permitting continuing contacts between the children and their biological father.

. . . .

Before an order may be entered terminating parental rights upon the ground of permanent neglect, "the statute requires proof before Family Court that [the parent] failed to maintain contact with or plan for the future of [his or her] child for a period of one year after the child came into the custody of an authorized agency notwithstanding the agency's diligent efforts to encourage and strengthen the parental relationship" (Matter of Star Leslie W., 63 N.Y.2d 136, 140, 481 N.Y.S.2d 26, 470 N.E.2d 824; Social Services Law § 384–b[7]). The threshold determination to be made in any neglect proceeding, of course, is whether the child care agency exercised diligent efforts to strengthen and nurture the parent-child relationship. "Those efforts must include counseling, making suitable arrangements for visitation, providing assistance to the parents to resolve or ameliorate the problems preventing discharge of the child to their care and advising the parent at appropriate intervals of the child's progress and development"

(Matter of Star Leslie W., 63 N.Y.2d at 142, 481 N.Y.S.2d 26, 470 N.E.2d 824, supra).

Here, the record amply supports the determinations of the lower courts that the respective petitioners fulfilled their statutory obligation to nurture the parent-child relationship; in each case, the agency arranged for visitation between respondent and his child, communicated with respondent and kept him apprised of his child's progress, and assisted respondent in formulating a plan for his child's future. The requirement of due diligence by the agency having been satisfied, therefore, the focus of our analysis turns to an examination of the individual efforts of each respondent to maintain contact with and plan for the future of his children.

As we noted in Matter of Star Leslie W., 63 N.Y.2d at 142–143, 481 N.Y.S.2d 26, 470 N.E.2d 824, supra, "[t]he requirement is several: the parent must maintain contact with the child and also realistically plan for [his or her] future. A default in performing either may support a finding of permanent neglect" (see, Matter of Orlando F., 40 N.Y.2d 103, 110, 386 N.Y.S.2d 64, 351 N.E.2d 711). Although both respondents in the instant appeals clearly satisfied the contact requirement of the statute by periodically meeting with their children at their places of incarceration and by communicating with the social workers assigned to their respective cases, the lower courts determined that they had each failed to adequately plan for the future of their children. "[T]he planning requirement contemplates that the parent shall take such steps as are necessary to provide a home that is adequate and stable, under the financial circumstances existing, within a reasonable period of time. Good faith alone is not enough; the plan must be realistic and feasible" (Matter of Star Leslie W., 63 N.Y.2d at 143, 481 N.Y.S.2d 26, 470 N.E.2d 824, supra). Whether or not the planning requirement will be deemed satisfied will, of course, vary depending on the facts and circumstances which, we have noted, "must be scrutinized and weighed carefully in rendering decisions in such delicate human affairs" (Matter of Orlando F., 40 N.Y.2d at 111–112, 386 N.Y.S.2d 64, 351 N.E.2d 711, supra).

In each of the instant cases, respondent's initial plan was to place his children with a relative pending his release from prison. In *Matter of Gregory B.*, respondent sought to place his children with his mother; in *Matter of Willie John B.* and *Matter of Delores B.*, respondent first sought to place his children with his sister and then attempted to contact another sister before turning to his mother as a possible custodian for the children. When these plans proved unworkable, the only other plan offered by each respondent was to keep his children in foster care while maintaining contact with them during the period of incarceration. Such plan, however, was rejected by the Appellate Division in each case as being neither viable nor realistic.

On these appeals, respondents argue that the 1983 statutory reforms precluding the termination of parental rights based solely on the fact of incarceration do not permit a court to make a finding of permanent neglect where an incarcerated father has maintained contact with his children but simply does not have the family resources to provide a realistic alternative to foster care during the period of his incarceration. Thus, respondents contend, the lower courts erred in terminating their parental rights merely because they could not produce a relative who was willing and able to care for their children while they remained in prison. We disagree.

Until the Legislature amended the Social Services Law in 1983, an incarcerated parent was presumed unable to maintain contact with or plan for the future of his child and thus a finding of permanent neglect while the parent was incarcerated was precluded. Yet, although the incarcerated parent was excused from the contact and planning requirements of the statute, the consent of such parent was not required before his or her child could be released for adoption. To correct this anomaly in the statutory scheme and to prevent the automatic termination of parental rights of incarcerated persons, the Legislature changed the law by removing the status of incarceration as a basis for the termination of parental rights and by recognizing the continuing parental obligations of incarcerated parents to their children. The amended law requires the incarcerated parent to cooperate with the authorized child care agency in planning for the child and in arranging visits and further requires the agency to exercise diligent efforts to arrange visitation between the child and the incarcerated parent within the correctional facility (*see,* Social Services Law § 384–b[7][e][ii]; [f][5], *see also,* Correction Law § 619).

In its findings accompanying the statutory reforms, the Legislature declared: "A parent who has been incarcerated *should also fulfill, while actually incarcerated, the obligations of a parent as described in the provisions of section three hundred eighty-four-b of the social services law relating to the termination of parental rights upon the ground of permanent neglect.* However, such ground of permanent neglect should recognize the special circumstances and need for assistance of an incarcerated parent to substantially and continuously or repeatedly maintain contact with, or plan for the future of his or her child. An incarcerated parent who has failed to fulfill these obligations may have his or her parental rights terminated upon such ground" (Legislative findings, L.1983, ch. 911, § 1 [emphasis supplied]). It is plain from these findings that the enacted reforms were in no way intended to excuse incarcerated parents from the requirement that they plan for their child's future. To the contrary, the statutory amendments explicitly recognize the planning responsibilities of incarcerated parents and state that the failure to meet those responsibilities may result, as with any other parent, in the termination of parental rights.

It is true that the Legislature acknowledged the "special circumstances" of an incarcerated parent and intended that those circumstances be considered in evaluating such parent's efforts to meet the statutory contact and planning requirements. Certainly, in light of the drastic consequences of failing to plan, courts should not set unrealistically high standards in evaluating a parent's planning efforts and this directive undoubtedly applies with special force in cases where the parent is incarcerated and thus severely hampered in the ability to act on behalf of his or her child.

This does not mean, however, that the Legislature intended to approve a plan of indefinite foster care for the child of an incarcerated parent who is serving a lengthy prison term and who cannot provide the child with an alternative living arrangement. Although the statutory scheme favors keeping a child with the natural parent where practicable and stresses the importance of exercising diligent efforts to foster and maintain the cohesiveness of the family unit, "permanence in a child's life also has been given a priority, because the Legislature has determined that a normal family life in a *permanent* home offers the best opportunity for a child to develop and thrive" (Matter of Joyce T., 65 N.Y.2d 39, 47, 489 N.Y.S.2d 705, 478 N.E.2d 1306; Social Services Law § 384–b[1][a]). Thus, we have acknowledged that a primary purpose of the statute is to provide "a fair and timely basis to free a child for adoption" and that "[w]hen it is clear that natural parents cannot offer a normal home for a child, and 'continued foster care' is not an appropriate plan, the statute directs that a permanent home be sought" (Matter of Joyce T., 65 N.Y.2d at 47, 489 N.Y.S.2d 705, 478 N.E.2d 1306, supra; Social Services Law § 384–b[1][a][I], [iv]).

As we explained in Matter of Joyce T., 65 N.Y.2d at 47–48, 489 N.Y.S.2d 705, 478 N.E.2d 1306, supra [emphasis supplied]: "[T]he Legislature in section 384–b clearly *did not contemplate foster care as a permanent condition, or even a desired goal for the long, indefinite duration,* because prolonged foster care is not in a child's best interests. The Legislature found that *unnecessarily protracted stays in foster care deprive children of positive, nurturing family relationships,* and therefore—by section 384–b— it provided timely procedures for termination of parental rights, thus furthering the best interests, needs and rights of the child by freeing the child for adoption. *In connection with parental termination, in this State, foster care is viewed as a temporary way station to adoption or return to the natural parents, not the purposeful objective for a permanent way of life.*" In light of the plainly expressed understanding of the Legislature regarding the specific, limited role of foster care and the special importance of permanency in the life of a child, we conclude that an incarcerated parent may not satisfy the planning requirement of the statute where the only plan offered is long-term foster care lasting potentially for the child's entire minority. Put simply, relegating a child to foster care until he or she is no longer a child is not a viable plan because it is patently inconsistent with the purpose of foster care and, more importantly, it deprives the child of that quality of "permanency" found by the Legislature to be so essential to proper growth and development.

Finally, we are not unmindful of the psychological harm that may possibly result from severing the bonds between a child and his or her biological parent, particularly where the child is older and has strong emotional attachments to the birth family. Such concerns have been increasingly well documented in recent years, prompting some to advocate "open" adoptions in which the court supplements an order of adoption with a provision directing that the adopted child have continuing contacts and visitation with members of his or her biological family....

New Jersey Division of Youth and Family Services v. B.G.S.

Superior Court of New Jersey, Appellate Division, 1996.
291 N.J.Super. 582, 677 A.2d 1170.

■ Petrella, P.J.A.D.

B.G.S. challenges an order of the Chancery Division, Family Part, which terminated her parental rights as natural mother to her son, M.A.S. The order, prompted by an application made by the Division of Youth and Family Services (DYFS), conditioned the termination upon visitation between B.G.S. and M.A.S. until the initiation of adoption proceedings, at which time B.G.S. was to be given notification to permit her to pursue post-adoption visitation.[1] Although B.G.S. concedes her inability to care for M.A.S. and seeks neither removal of her son from his legal guardian nor interference with his custody, she asserts that the statutory criteria for termination were not satisfied by clear and convincing evidence. DYFS cross-appeals nunc pro tunc to strike from the orders any mandated post-termination visitation or notification provisions.[2]

Our review of the record in light of the arguments presented satisfies us that there is overwhelming evidence supporting the propriety of the termination order. The conditions imposed in that order relating to post-termination visitation and notification of adoption are, however, in contravention of applicable law and are thus stricken.

B.G.S. was forty-two years old in 1994 when the DYFS complaint for termination of her parental rights proceeded to trial. She had abused drugs and alcohol since she was thirteen; her longest period of sobriety had been one year. Her first hospitalization for mental illness occurred at seventeen. She now suffers from bipolar disorder and polysubstance dependence. M.A.S.'s father, A.R., has apparently shared a history of substance abuse as well.

DYFS first became aware of M.A.S. when his paternal grandfather reported on December 19, 1988, that B.G.S. had left M.A.S., her one-month-old infant son,[3] alone in her Irvington apartment and had travelled to the grandfather's South Orange home without either a coat or shoes. As there was no family member able to care for M.A.S., B.G.S. voluntarily placed him into foster care and sought hospitalization for herself. B.G.S.

---

1. At oral argument, we were informed that B.G.S. paid a "final visit" to her son in June 1995. She has not sought to exercise her right to visitation during the pendency of this appeal.

2. Although originally acquiescing, DYFS has objected to the visitation and notification provisions being included in the Family Part's termination order. During the pendency of this appeal, DYFS moved for summary disposition to strike those provi-

sions from the order. That motion was only considered recently and was denied in the face of the imminent consideration of this calendared appeal.... After oral argument DYFS moved for leave to file the cross-appeal nunc pro tunc. We have granted that motion as well as its motions for stay of the visitation and notification provisions of the order.

3. M.A.S. was born on November 15, 1988.

regained custody of M.A.S. on October 17, 1989, when he was eleven months old.

On April 17, 1990, B.G.S. contacted DYFS to report that A.R. had physically abused her and her son. In addition, B.G.S. stated that M.A.S. may have been sexually abused, either by his baby-sitter or A.R. During a DYFS investigation, the baby-sitter reported that B.G.S. had been abusing drugs and that M.A.S. had been poorly clothed, dirty, and smelly. B.G.S. was later apprehended by Summit police while she was driving eastbound in the westbound lanes of Route 24 with M.A.S. in the back seat. She had apparently suffered an acute incidence of substance abuse. When A.R. declined to care for M.A.S., DYFS again took custody of the child on July 29, 1990.

B.G.S. was initially permitted supervised overnight visitations with M.A.S. in his paternal grandmother's home. At first, he had difficulty during and in concluding these visits, throwing tantrums and pulling out his own hair. On one occasion, he had returned with bruises that appeared not to have been accidental but were nonetheless possibly attributable to his grandmother's attempts to restrain him during those tantrums. These home visits eventually ceased after M.A.S.'s grandmother declined further supervision following A.R.'s attempt to break into her home while intoxicated. In any event, DYFS had already discovered that B.G.S. had circumvented supervision by taking M.A.S. to her apartment, where he was allowed unauthorized contact with A.R.

M.A.S. was psychologically evaluated in foster care for tantrums, self-abusive behavior, and unprovoked aggression towards other children, the results of which indicated that he was developmentally delayed. His aggression towards other children in his first foster home caused M.A.S. to be moved to another foster home and then to an interim foster home on August 23, 1991. The record indicates that M.A.S. was placed in his current foster home on August 27, 1991, where he has since remained.

By the spring of 1991, M.A.S. had begun to flourish in foster care and to approximate normal levels for his age despite his developmental delay. In accordance with his observations of April 12, 1991, psychologist David Sard had recommended that M.A.S. could be returned to B.G.S. if she continued to progress in her treatment. In a progress report covering the period from May through August 1991, a therapist had cautiously reported progress, but had emphasized that reunification should occur only when mother and child were likely to remain together.

While M.A.S. was in foster care, B.G.S. regularly visited with him, demonstrating interest and concern for him as well as showing some improvement in her parenting skills. B.G.S. periodically participated in therapy but soon relapsed into bouts of mental illness and substance abuse. She also separated from A.R. but later resumed cohabitation with him. The record indicates that domestic violence was commonplace in their relationship. A.R. infrequently visited with M.A.S., occasionally while under the influence of an intoxicating substance. A.R. was generally uncooperative with DYFS.

Although scheduled to return to B.G.S. on December 15, 1991, M.A.S. remained in foster care because B.G.S. had relapsed into substance abuse and mental illness following her reconciliation with A.R. Indeed, M.A.S.'s therapist reported in February 1992 that he was progressing, but that B.G.S. was experiencing difficulty. DYFS then shifted its objective from reconciliation to adoption.

DYFS's expert psychologist, Frank Dyer, concluded that M.A.S. had bonded to his foster mother, that it was in his best interest not to be moved again, and that visitation with B.G.S. should therefore cease. The psychologist characterized an attempt to relocate M.A.S. as likely to be a "devastating psychological blow" of potentially permanent impact. In a June 1993 report, Dyer reiterated that it would be catastrophic to remove M.A.S. from his foster family. Dyer opined at trial that removal of M.A.S. from his foster home would likely cause "extreme psychological harm" that would be a "disaster" likely to affect his self-esteem, basic trust, and capacity to have relationships with new caretakers. The expert considered M.A.S.'s foster parents to be his "only hope for developing into a psychologically well-functioning adult."

Dyer also opined that any short-term problem posed by ending visitation with B.G.S. would not constitute a significant loss to M.A.S. According to the psychologist, it would be harmful to M.A.S. if he remained in foster care indefinitely because it promised no stability and was likely to create anxiety and uncertainty. In fact, M.A.S. had told Dyer that he wished to remain with his foster family. Although he said he would feel sad if he no longer visited with B.G.S., M.A.S. responded "maybe not" when asked whether he would like to live with B.G.S.

B.G.S.'s expert psychologist, Donald Skinner, agreed that M.A.S. had bonded to his foster family and that separation was likely to cause M.A.S. serious, long-term psychological harm. He added that separating M.A.S. from B.G.S. would similarly represent a loss, albeit not to the degree that separation from the foster family would jeopardize his mental health.

In a March 1993 psychiatric evaluation of B.G.S., Dr. Stephen Simring, a psychiatrist, concluded that B.G.S. was unable to function as a parent, but not solely because of her mental health. He determined that she was mentally capable to surrender her parental rights. An April 1994 psychiatric evaluation prepared by Dr. Ellen Platt indicated that B.G.S. was then psychiatrically stable, but involved in a highly dysfunctional relationship with A.R., with whom she still cohabitated. Platt confirmed that B.G.S. could not parent M.A.S. and that her maximal relationship with him could only be supervised visitation.

According to Platt, B.G.S. was afflicted with a bipolar disorder, manic depression, the nature of which is the unpredictability of its cycles. A person with the disorder may suddenly become psychologically unstable for no apparent reason, even if faithfully taking medication. The inherent instability of the disease is exacerbated by drug abuse. Because B.G.S. lacked a support system, Platt concluded that B.G.S. was not capable of caring for M.A.S. on a sustained basis. Moreover, she testified that B.G.S. had impaired judgment and limited ability to cope with stress.

By May 1994, A.R. was HIV-positive and had continued to abuse drugs and alcohol. B.G.S. nevertheless justified her continued cohabitation with A.R. on the ground that she could not abandon him because he was sick and his family had rejected him. B.G.S. claimed that she would discontinue her relationship with A.R. if necessary to continue seeing M.A.S. B.G.S. admitted, however, that DYFS had always made it clear to her that she could not regain custody of M.A.S. so long as she cohabitated with A.R. Furthermore, B.G.S. conceded that she could not parent M.A.S. and offered no plan for M.A.S. other than indefinite foster care until such time as she overcame her mental illness and drug abuse. As of the time of trial, B.G.S. had purportedly abstained from illicit drugs and alcohol for five and one-half months. Even so, M.A.S.'s foster parents wish to adopt him and object strenuously to any post-termination visitation or notice to B.G.S. of the adoption proceeding.

B.G.S.'s contention that DYFS has failed to prove the statutory criteria by clear and convincing evidence is without merit. R. 2:11–3(e)(1)(A) and (E). The Family Part Judge's finding that B.G.S. was not able to care for M.A.S. and that he had so bonded to his foster parents that removal would cause him irreparable harm are fully supported in the record. Indeed, the judge emphasized that clear and compelling evidence had persuasively established the need to terminate B.G.S.'s parental rights despite the fact that he also authorized post-termination visitation.

Notwithstanding their profound nature, parental rights are not inviolate when a child's physical or mental health is jeopardized. New Jersey Division of Youth & Family Services v. A.W., 103 N.J. 591, 599, 512 A.2d 438 (1986). N.J.S.A. 30:4C–15.1 codifies the four-prong test set forth in A.W. and provides that DYFS shall initiate an action to terminate parental rights in the child's best interest if a. [t]he child's health and development have been or will continue to be endangered by the parental relationship; b. [t]he parent is unwilling or unable to eliminate the harm facing the child or is unable or unwilling to provide a safe and stable home for the child and the delay of permanent placement will add to the harm. Such harm may include evidence that separating the child from his foster parents would cause serious and enduring emotional or psychological harm to the child; c. [t]he division has made diligent efforts to provide services to help the parent correct the circumstances which led to the child's placement outside the home and the court has considered alternatives to termination of parental rights; and d. [t]ermination of parental rights will not do more harm than good. Each of these statutory elements must be established by clear and convincing evidence. In re Guardianship of J.C., 129 N.J. 1, 10, 608 A.2d 1312 (1992). These standards are "fully consistent with constitutional doctrine." Id. at 9, 608 A.2d 1312.

The judge found that B.G.S.'s ability to adequately care for M.A.S. has endangered his health and development. We reject B.G.S.'s contention that the first prong of the statute could not have been satisfied because M.A.S.'s mental and emotional well-being improved in foster care despite her visits. Overwhelming evidence clearly and convincingly established that M.A.S. was initially harmed by B.G.S.'s inability adequately to care for him and to protect him from A.R. and that M.A.S. is subject to continued psychological damage because of his need for a permanent home and identity. Evidence of serious emotional injury or developmental delay satisfies this prong. In re Guardianship of K.L.F., 129 N.J. 32, 44, 608 A.2d 1327 (1992).

Moreover, harms attributable to a biological parent include the prolonged inattention to a child's needs, which encourages the development of a stronger, "bonding relationship" to foster parents, "the severing of which would cause profound harm...." In re Guardianship of J.C., supra, 129 N.J. at 18, 608 A.2d 1312. The experts agreed that M.A.S. had bonded with his foster family and would suffer serious, long-term psychological harm if removed from the foster home.

The record clearly evinces B.G.S.'s inability or unwillingness to resolve the problems with respect to her mental health and substance abuse, thus satisfying the second prong of the A.W. test. M.A.S.'s long participation in foster care distinguishes this case from In re A., 277 N.J.Super. 454, 471–472, 649 A.2d 1310 (App.Div.1994), where there was disagreement with the permanency of the harm to the child resulting from separation from the foster parents.

Unlike the situation in In re A., B.G.S. conceded her inability to parent or care for M.A.S. Her drug and alcohol addiction was complicated by chronic mental illness as well as by her continued cohabitation with A.R. in direct contravention of DYFS's clear admonition that M.A.S. could not be returned to her under such circumstances. We are convinced, therefore, that it would not be in the best interest of M.A.S. to prolong the resolution of his status by indefinitely extending his current foster care placement.[4] N.J.S.A. 30:4C–53.4 and 30:4C–60(d) effectuate the legislative policy that children be placed in "stable and permanent homes" instead of indefinite long-term foster care. See N.J.S.A. 30:4C–53.1d. The record amply demonstrates that M.A.S. needs stability and relief from the anxiety associated with his lack of permanency. The Family Part Judge appropriately concluded that further delay would harm M.A.S.

As to the third prong, there is little dispute that DYFS was diligent in its efforts to assist B.G.S. When DYFS's efforts to remedy the underlying family problems indicated that there was no prospect of rehabilitation and no available family member to provide care for M.A.S., the lack of any alternative to foster care became readily apparent. The child's need for stability and attachment had become paramount. See DYFS v. A.W., supra, 103 N.J. at 609–610, 512 A.2d 438.

The fourth prong of the A.W. test addresses the effect of termination. A court should hesitate to terminate parental rights in the absence of a

---

4. We note that M.A.S. had been in foster care for most of his five and one-half years by the time of the trial.

permanent plan that will satisfy the child's needs. See id. at 610–611, 512 A.2d 438. The Family Part Judge appropriately concluded that termination here would not do more harm than good as DYFS had a permanent plan in the form of adoption.

B.G.S. nonetheless contends that this prong could not have been satisfied in light of expert testimony that M.A.S. would be saddened if visitation with B.G.S. ceased, even though he wished to remain with his foster parents and was better off doing so. In determining whether the child's bonding with the foster parent in itself justifies termination of parental rights, "[t]he standard is not that the end result cause no pain or trauma but that the child be kept from its parents only to avoid serious and lasting harm." In re Guardianship of K.L.F., supra, 129 N.J. at 45, 608 A.2d 1327. Thus, the child's separation from the foster parents must be shown to threaten "serious and enduring emotional or psychological harm." In re Guardianship of J.C., supra, 129 N.J. at 19, 608 A.2d 1312. Such was the case here. In any event, the present termination action was not predicated upon bonding, but rather reflected M.A.S.'s need for permanency and B.G.S.'s inability to care for him in the foreseeable future. The record supports the conclusion that greater harm is likely to befall M.A.S. by perpetuating any relationship with his natural mother. DYFS satisfied the four-prong test in A.W., and the Family Part Judge accomplished the goal of securing a permanent resolution of M.A.S.'s status through his decision. DYFS v. A.W., supra, 103 N.J. at 610, 512 A.2d 438.

We turn next to DYFS's objection to the termination order inasmuch as it authorized B.G.S. to continue visitation with M.A.S. pending adoption proceedings, of which she was to be notified presumably to allow her the opportunity to seek continued visitation rights or to object to the adoption. In imposing the visitation and notice conditions on termination, the Family Part Judge acknowledged that his authority to order post-termination visitation between the child and the biological parent was by no means clear under present law. His stated intention was to provide visitation in M.A.S.'s best interest "until some Appellate Court . . . tells me I . . . can't do that."

At the outset, we distinguish between visitation acquiesced in by foster or adoptive parents and visitation ordered by a court notwithstanding termination of parental rights. Although some of our cases have discussed potential continued visitation by natural parents after termination of parental rights or adoption,[5] we hold that the definition of best interest

---

[5.] Our Supreme Court has declined to reach the question of when post-termination visitation may be appropriate. See In re Adoption of a Child by D.M.H., 135 N.J. 473, 494, 641 A.2d 235, cert. denied sub nom., Hollingshead v. Hoxworth, 513 U.S. 967, 115 S.Ct. 433, 130 L.Ed.2d 345 (1994); In re Guardianship of J.C., supra, 129 N.J. at 26, 608 A.2d 1312. N.J.S.A. 9:3–37 does advocate liberal construction of the adoption act to promote the child's best interest. Relying upon Kattermann v. DiPiazza, 151 N.J.Super. 209, 376 A.2d 955 (App.Div.1977), and In re Adoption of Children by F., 170 N.J.Super. 419, 406 A.2d 986 (Ch.Div.1979), one commentator has suggested that New Jersey law thus permits post-termination visitation to promote the child's best interest. See Annota-

does not include post-termination visitation where an objection is raised. Our Supreme Court explained in In re Adoption of a Child by D.M.H., 135 N.J. 473, 491, 641 A.2d 235, cert. denied sub nom., Hollingshead v. Hoxworth, 513 U.S. 967, 115 S.Ct. 433, 130 L.Ed.2d 345 (1994), that New Jersey courts, like those of most jurisdictions, do not recognize the parental right of visitation following a final order of adoption by non-relative, adoptive parents.

In New Jersey Division of Youth & Family Services v. D.C., 118 N.J. 388, 395, 571 A.2d 1295 (1990), termination under N.J.S.A. 30:4C–11 to – 24 was held to have ended a child's visitation with its biological parents. "Termination of parental rights permanently cuts off the relationship between children and their biological parents." In re Guardianship of J.C., supra, 129 N.J. at 10, 608 A.2d 1312. The potential harm in cutting off access to a biological parent is an inherent feature of termination, necessary to achieve the greater good of securing for the child a permanent home. Id. at 26, 608 A.2d 1312.

We have acknowledged the absolute nature of the language in N.J.S.A. 30:4C–20 to–22 as to the post-termination guardianship authority of DYFS. See In re Guardianship of R.O.M.C., 243 N.J.Super. 631, 633–634, 581 A.2d 113 (App.Div.1990). The natural parent in R.O.M.C. had intended the "open adoption"[6] of her children by foster parents. Even though intervening events could have disturbed that plan, we upheld the absolute authority of DYFS to allow visitation there on an informal basis. We nonetheless reversed and remanded a portion of the termination order, however, on the ground that the judge could not order continued visitation, especially given the unconditional authority of DYFS over the child following termination. 243 N.J.Super. at 634, 581 A.2d 113; see New Jersey Division of Youth &

tion, Postadoption Visitation by Natural Parent, 78 A.L.R. 4th 218, 239–242 (1990). In Kattermann v. DiPiazza, supra, 151 N.J.Super. at 213, 376 A.2d 955, we considered a situation in which the adoptive grandparents of a fifteen-year-old child had consented to extensive informal visitation, including long periods of child care while they worked, between the biological mother and child until shortly before the court action. We did not order visitation there, however, but rather remanded for a plenary hearing to determine whether visitation was in the child's best interest, noting under the "highly unusual" facts presented that the policy of protecting adoptive parents from disruption within the context of intra-family adoptions was "outside the zone of primary concern of the Legislature in enacting N.J.S.A. 9:3–17 et seq." Id. at 212–214, 376 A.2d 955. The intra-family context presented by Kattermann thus distinguishes that case from the instant appeal. Nor does In re Adoption of Children by F.,

supra, 170 N.J.Super. 419, 406 A.2d 986 support post-termination visitation here. The applicable statute there was the former version of N.J.S.A. 9:3–50a, amended by P.L. 1993, c. 345, which had provided that adoption would not alter the relationship between the child and the biological parent consenting to the adoption by a step-parent. 170 N.J.Super. at 422, 406 A.2d 986.

6. An "open adoption" is one in which the final judgment incorporates the parties' pre-adoption written agreement "that the child will have continuing contact with one or more members of his or her biological family after the adoption is completed." Amadio and Deutsch, Open Adoption: Allowing Adopted Children To "Stay In Touch" With Blood Relatives, 22 J.Fam.L., 59, 60 (1983–1984). Insofar as the record and our research discloses, theories of the advocates of non-consensual open adoptions have not been shown to be workable.

Family Services v. Torres, 185 N.J.Super. 234, 242, 447 A.2d 1372 (J. & D.R. Ct.1980), aff'd. o.b., 185 N.J.Super. 182, 447 A.2d 1343 (App.Div. 1982).

The New York Court of Appeals has similarly concluded that post-adoptive visitation between a child and the biological family, regardless of the desirability of such "open adoptions," could not be incorporated into a termination order where a New York statute spoke unequivocally of termination of all parental duties and responsibilities. See In re Gregory B., 74 N.Y.2d 77, 544 N.Y.S.2d 535, 542, 542 N.E.2d 1052, 1059, reargument denied sub nom., In re Willie John B., 74 N.Y.2d 880, 547 N.Y.S.2d 841, 547 N.E.2d 96 (1989). The same result would appear inevitable under New Jersey's recently amended private adoption statute, N.J.S.A. 9:3–50a, which likewise provides for the complete termination of parental rights upon the entry of an adoption judgment.[7] See In re Adoption of Child by D.M.H., supra, 135 N.J. at 491, 641 A.2d 235 (articulating New Jersey's policy of protecting adoptive parents from interference in relationship with child by natural parents whose parental rights had been voluntarily surrendered or judicially severed); see also N.J.S.A. 9:3–45(b)(2) (expressly precluding notice of adoption proceeding to parent whose rights have been previously terminated).

We view the legislative policy of protecting adoptive families from disruption as strongest in cases where DYFS must take legal action to terminate parental rights. As DYFS argued in In re Guardianship of R.O.M.C., supra, 243 N.J.Super. at 633, 581 A.2d 113, the adoption prospects of all of its wards would be diminished if prospective adoptive parents learned that orders terminating the biological parents' rights could be conditional. The biological mother in R.O.M.C. opposed termination but favored the adoption. Although the parties in that case had agreed to continue visitation voluntarily, DYFS and the adoptive parents had opposed the mandatory order because they feared that it would have required continued visitation even if the biological mother's mental illness worsened to such a degree as to make continued visitation inimical to the child's best interest. Ibid. In this case, where B.G.S. has actively sought to retain parental rights, the foster (prospective adoptive) parents have essentially invoked this State's policy of protecting adoptive families from disruption by adamantly opposing post-adoption visitation here for comparable reasons.

7. D.M.H. also analyzed the legislative history of recent amendments to the private adoption statute and noted the Senate Judiciary Committee's express omission of provisions relating to "open adoptions," described by the committee as a "significant policy issue which should be addressed in separate legislation." In re Adoption of Child by D.M.H., supra, 135 N.J. at 494, 641 A.2d 235 (quoting Senate Judiciary Committee, State-ment to Senate Bill No. 685 (1993)). In the absence of express provisions for "open adoption" in the private-adoption statute, D.M.H. thus concluded that post-termination visitation may not be judicially mandated without regard to the validity of a visitation provision in a voluntary and consensual pre-adoption agreement between the biological and adoptive parents. Ibid.

Where termination is based solely upon the child's bonding with its foster parents, we have suggested alternatives that have included either a gradual transition back to the custody of the biological family or continued foster care with regular visitation of the biological parents, but not termination with continued visitation by the biological parents. See New Jersey Division of Youth & Family Services v. T.C., 251 N.J.Super. 419, 440–441, 598 A.2d 899 (App.Div.1991). We find unpersuasive the reasoning of cases in other jurisdictions, which have addressed the voluntary surrendering of parental rights subject to visitation in a manner supporting notification of adoption proceedings and perhaps post-adoption visitation when found to be in the child's best interest. See, e.g., In re S.A.H., 537 N.W.2d 1, 6–7 (S.D.1995); Petition of Dep't of Social Services to Dispense with Consent to Adoption, 392 Mass. 696, 702, 467 N.E.2d 861, 866 (Mass.1984); In re Adoption of Francisco A., 116 N.M. 708, 714, 866 P.2d 1175, 1181 (App. 1993).

Nor does any theory advocating such visitation and notification provisions demonstrate the propriety of compulsory post-adoption visitation here.[8] Permitting voluntary agreements for visitation where biological parents voluntarily surrender their right is not the same as authorizing courts to mandate post-adoption visitation in involuntary termination cases.[9] See, e.g., Michaud v. Wawruck, 209 Conn. 407, 414, 551 A.2d 738, 741 (Conn.1988) (enforcing as not violative of public policy pre-adoption agreement between biological and adoptive parents providing for post-adoption visitation if in child's best interest); Weinschel v. Strople, 56 Md.App. 252, 261, 466 A.2d 1301, 1305 (1983) (biological mother's consent to step-mother's adoption of child may be conditioned upon post-adoption visitation).

In In re Adoption of Ridenour, 61 Ohio St.3d 319, 326–328, 574 N.E.2d 1055, 1062–1063 (Ohio 1991), the Ohio Supreme Court concluded that the finality of adoption and the establishment of the adoptive family is ulti-

---

8. See, e.g., Appell, Blending Families through Adoption: Implications for Collaborative Adoption Law and Practice, 75 B.U. L.Rev. 997, 1040 (1995) (observing that "[c]ourts have ordered postadoption visitation when the parties have agreed that such visitation should occur and when the courts have found such visitation is in the best interest of the child.") (footnote omitted and emphasis supplied); Amadio and Deutsch, supra (22 J. Fam. L. at 83–86) (discussing feasibility of open adoptions "where the child, the birth parents and the foster family desired the foster parents to adopt the child and where all parties to the adoption desired the biological parent or parents to maintain some contact with the child and adoptive family") (footnotes omitted and emphasis supplied). Under the circumstances of this case, we find no advantage for M.A.S. in compelling his

visitation with his mother, who has been diagnosed with bipolar disorder and polysubstance dependence, based solely upon the application of a social theory that has not been tested in the crucible of the sobering reality now facing this child.

9. Furthermore, cases that grant grandparents visitation rights are also distinguishable because such rights are often created by statute. See, e.g., N.J.S.A. 9:2–7.1; Bopp v. Lino, 110 Nev. 1246, 1251 n. 2, 885 P.2d 559, 562 n. 2 (Nev.1994); Oregon ex rel. Costello v. Cottrell, 318 Or. 338, 345, 867 P.2d 498, 502 (Or.1994); In re Robinson, 517 So.2d 477, 479 (La.Ct.App.1987); Scranton v. Hutter, 40 A.D.2d 296, 339 N.Y.S.2d 708, 711 (1973). The same is true with respect to siblings. See, e.g., In re Adoption of Anthony, 113 Misc.2d 26, 448 N.Y.S.2d 377, 380 n. 14 (N.Y.Fam.Ct.1982).

mately in the child's best interest and that the biological family's desire to maintain some relationship must succumb to the paramount need to cement the new family relationship. Likewise, our termination statute is expressly predicated upon termination being in the child's best interest. N.J.S.A. 30:40C–15.1; In re Guardianship of J.C., supra, 129 N.J. at 8, 608 A.2d 1312.

Even if post-termination visitation may be in the best interest of some child, the record here did not support the Family Part Judge's findings with respect to B.G.S.'s right to visitation with her son. No witness in this case contended that continued visitation was in M.A.S.'s best interest. To the contrary, Dyer characterized M.A.S.'s loss of his relationship to B.G.S. as a short-term problem, not a significant loss. Skinner also described it as a loss, but not one that would jeopardize M.A.S.'s mental health.

The order of termination of parental rights of B.G.S. is affirmed. The visitation and notification provisions of the judge's termination order are reversed.

NOTE

For further discussion of open adoption, *see* p. 1351 *infra*.

CALIFORNIA FAMILY CODE (West 2004)

§ 7826. Parent declared developmentally disabled or mentally ill; right to action

A proceeding under this part may be brought where both of the following requirements are satisfied:

(a) The child is one whose parent or parents have been declared by a court of competent jurisdiction, wherever situated, to be developmentally disabled or mentally ill.

(b) In the state or country in which the parent or parents reside or are hospitalized, the Director of Mental Health or the Director of Developmental Services, or their equivalent, if any, and the superintendent of the hospital, if any, of which the parent or parents are inmates or patients, certify that the parent or parents so declared to be developmentally disabled or mentally ill will not be capable of supporting or controlling the child in a proper manner.

§ 7827. Mentally disabled parent; right to action

(a) "Mentally disabled" as used in this section means that a parent or parents suffer a mental incapacity or disorder which renders the parent or parents unable to care for and control the child adequately.

(b) A proceeding under this part may be brought where the child is one whose parent or parents are mentally disabled and are likely to remain so in the foreseeable future.

(c) Except as provided in subdivision (d), the evidence of any two experts, each of whom shall be either a physician and surgeon, certified either by the American Board of Psychiatry and Neurology or under Section 6750 of the Welfare and Institutions Code, or a licensed psychologist who has a doctoral degree in psychology and at least five years of postgraduate experience in the diagnosis and treatment of emotional and mental disorders, is required to support a finding under this section.

(d) If the parent or parents reside in another state or in a foreign country, the evidence required by this section may be supplied by the affidavits of two experts, each of whom shall be either of the following:

(1) A physician and surgeon who is a resident of that state or foreign country, and who has been certified by a medical organization or society of that state or foreign country to practice psychiatric or neurological medicine.

(2) A licensed psychologist who has a doctoral degree in psychology and at least five years of postgraduate experience in the diagnosis and treatment of emotional and mental disorders and who is licensed in the state or authorized to practice in that country.

(e) If the rights of a parent are sought to be terminated pursuant to this section, and the parent has no attorney, the court shall appoint an attorney for the parent pursuant to Article 4 (commencing with Section 7860) of Chapter 3, whether or not a request for the appointment is made by the parent.

NOTE

In Adoption of Gregory, 434 Mass. 117, 747 N.E.2d 120 (2001), the Supreme Judicial Court of Massachusetts held that noncompliance of a state agency with the federal Americans with Disabilities Act could not be used as a defense in a proceeding to terminate parental rights. The father who attempted to raise the defense had a history of mental health problems and substance abuse and suffers from cognitive and attention deficit disorders. The child has medical and developmental problems that require substantial assistance in daily activities. The court determined that the parents were unfit to care for their son (the mother's rights also were terminated). The Massachusetts court noted that other state courts had determined that termination proceedings are not "services, program, or activities" with the ADA. The court added that provisions in both the ADA and state law requiring accommodation of parents' special needs in providing assistance to improve parenting skills before termination had in fact been met.

In Richmond Department of Social Services v. L. P., 35 Va.App. 573, 546 S.E.2d 749 (2001), a trial judge held that although the evidence clearly supported termination of a mother's residual parental rights in all other respects, her mental deficiency, which prevented her from properly caring for her child, constituted "good cause" under Va. Code § 16.1–283(C)(2) for her inability to timely remedy the condition that led to the placement of her son in foster care. The Virginia Court of Appeals reversed the trial court's judgment, concluding that

> a parent's mental deficiency that is of such severity that there is no reasonable expectation that such a parent will be able within a reasonable period of time befitting the child's best interests to undertake responsibility for the care needed by the child in accordance with the child's age and stage of development does not constitute "good cause" under Code § 16.1–283(C)(2).

In re Jeffrey E.

Supreme Judicial Court of Maine, 1989.
557 A.2d 954.

■ CLIFFORD, JUSTICE.

Linda and James E., the parents of Jeffrey E., appeal from an order of the District Court terminating their parental rights ... On appeal they contend the District Court's termination order is not supported by clear and convincing evidence. We affirm the District Court.

At the hearing on a petition filed by the Department of Human Services (Department) for the termination of the parental rights of Linda and James E., the District Court would have been warranted in finding the following facts.

Jeffrey E. was born on February 1, 1984 to Linda and James E. He has three brothers who currently reside with Linda and James. Linda is the primary caretaker of the children, while James is an unusually passive parent who contributes virtually nothing toward the care of the children and does not assist in performing any household duties.

Jeffrey suffered from pneumonia and was hospitalized several times in 1984 and 1985. In the spring of 1985, Jeffrey was hospitalized and spent time in a Boston hospital with pneumonia and a collapsed lung. When he returned home, he was put on a regimented treatment program that was essential for a healthy recovery. Linda and James, however, were unable to follow through with providing the medications and therapies ordered by Jeffrey's physician, even with the help of a nurse from Androscoggin Home Health Associates. Consequently, Jeffrey became ill and had to be hospitalized again.

In July of 1985, Jeffrey was temporarily removed from his parents' home and placed in foster care, see 22 M.R.S.A. § 4034 (Supp.1988), and in 1986, after a hearing on the Department's Petition for a Final Protection Order, the District Court found Jeffrey to be in circumstances of jeopardy to his health and welfare should he be returned to the custody of his parents and awarded custody to the Department.

When he arrived at the foster home, Jeffrey was seventeen months old; he spoke only two words; he was unable to understand simple sentences;

and he was not using a cup or spoon. After a great deal of work and attention, Jeffrey's medical condition improved and he advanced developmentally. Within a few days in the foster home, he was able to close his mouth enough to drink out of a cup. He was walking within six weeks and had increased his vocabulary from two to thirty words within three months of his arrival at the foster home. His medical condition improved with his foster mother's strict attention to the complicated medical instructions.

The Department pursued three reunification plans, in the form of written service agreements, in accordance with 22 M.R.S.A. § 4041 (Supp. 1988). The reunification plans addressed three areas of concern: the family's health, the discipline and structure in the home, and the formulation of ways to stimulate the learning and development of Jeffrey. Because Linda and James did not comply with the terms of the agreement and the Department's service providers did not see any improvement in Linda's or James' parenting abilities, the Department discontinued reunification efforts in October of 1987 and petitioned the court for termination of the parental rights of Jeffrey's parents. See 22 M.R.S.A. § 4052 (Supp.1988). After a hearing in June 1988, the District Court ordered that the parental rights of Linda and James be terminated. This appeal followed.

Pursuant to the requirements for the termination of parental rights set out in 22 M.R.S.A. § 4055,[1] the court found by clear and convincing evidence that the parents were unwilling or unable to protect Jeffrey from jeopardy and that those circumstances were unlikely to change within a time which is reasonably calculated to meet the needs of Jeffrey (22 M.R.S.A. § 4055(1)(B)(2)(b)(i)), and that they were unwilling or unable to take responsibility for Jeffrey within a time which is reasonably calculated to meet his needs (22 M.R.S.A. § 4055(1)(B)(2)(b)(ii)). In addition, the court found that Linda and James had failed to make a good-faith effort to rehabilitate and reunify with Jeffrey pursuant to 22 M.R.S.A. § 4041 (22 M.R.S.A. § 4055(1)(B)(2)(b)(iv)). The court also made the requisite finding that termination of the parental rights of Linda and James was in the best interest of Jeffrey. 22 M.R.S.A. § 4055(1)(B)(2)(a).

In reviewing the District Court's findings, we examine the entire record to determine whether the court rationally could have found clear and convincing evidence in support of its factual conclusions. When clear

---

1. Pursuant to 22 M.R.S.A. § 4055 (Supp.1988), parental rights may be terminated if the court finds by clear and convincing evidence that:

(a) Termination is in the best interest of the child; and

(b) Either:

(i) The parent is unwilling or unable to protect the child from jeopardy and these circumstances are unlikely to change within a time which is reasonably calculated to meet the child's needs;

(ii) The parent has been unwilling or unable to take responsibility for the child within a time which is reasonably calculated to meet the child's needs;

(iii) The child has been abandoned; or

(iv) The parent has failed to make a good faith effort to rehabilitate and reunify with the child pursuant to section 4041.

and convincing evidence is required, we review whether the factfinder could reasonably have been persuaded that the required factual findings were proved to be highly probable.

A finding of jeopardy may be based on the parents' inability to meet a child's special needs. In re Dean A., 491 A.2d 572, 574–75 (Me.1985). These needs may be developmental, and they may include health care. 22 M.R.S.A. § 4002(6)(B).[2] Linda and James contend that it was improper for the court to consider their inability to provide medical attention to Jeffrey because Jeffrey was in good health at the time of the termination proceeding. We disagree.

In order for a court to take into account the special medical needs of a child, a present medical emergency need not exist, nor does such a medical emergency have to be imminent or even certain to recur. The evidence in this case disclosed that, because of past medical history, Jeffrey was susceptible to medical problems that parents with average skills easily would be able to treat at home, but that Linda and James clearly would be unable to cope with. According to a nurse who worked closely with the family for three years, Linda and James have not improved at all in their ability to provide medical care for themselves or their children. Indeed, Linda testified that she does not force her children to take medications, and does not even have a thermometer in her home. Moreover, in the years between Jeffrey's placement in foster care and the current termination proceeding, Linda did not properly seek medical care for herself when she had pneumonia, or for her youngest son to alleviate his numerous upper respiratory ailments.

In addition to Jeffrey's special medical needs, there was evidence as to his special developmental needs. A psychologist testified that Jeffrey is much more dependent on stimulation from his environment than the average child in order to develop intellectually. Without constant intensive encouragement Jeffrey would regress and fall behind his peers. According to the testimony of the service providers who worked with the family, the home of Linda and James E. would not provide such a nurturing atmosphere. The testimony established that Linda and James did not appropriately discipline their children, did not provide intellectual stimulation in their home and provided their children with a home environment that the court justifiably found to be chaotic. For example, Linda testified that "the arguing and fighting gets sickening when it happens every day." Service providers further testified that in response to kicking, screaming and hitting among the boys in the household, Linda would scream and swear at the children.

2. 22 M.R.S.A. § 4002(6)(B) (1988) provides:

"Jeopardy to health or welfare" or "jeopardy" means serious abuse or neglect as evidenced by: . . .

B. Deprivation of adequate food, clothing, shelter, supervision or care, including health care when that deprivation causes a threat of serious harm.

Given the special medical and developmental needs of Jeffrey, we conclude that the District Court could reasonably have been persuaded that it was highly probable that Linda and James were unable to protect Jeffrey from jeopardy and unable to take responsibility for him within a time which is reasonably calculated to meet the child's needs. Dean A., 491 A.2d at 574–75. Having found that the District Court was justified in finding that Linda and James E. were unable to protect their child from jeopardy and take responsibility within a time reasonably calculated to meet the child's needs, we need not and do not address the court's determination that the parents failed to make a good-faith effort to rehabilitate and reunify with the child, an alternative ground for terminating the parental rights of Linda and James. See In re Randy Scott B., 511 A.2d 450, 455 (Me.1986) (under 22 M.R.S.A. § 4055(1)(B)(2)(b), court's findings of inability to protect from jeopardy and to take responsibility for the child are each independently adequate to justify termination).

We further conclude that there was substantial evidence on the record, including evidence of the inability of Linda and James to protect Jeffrey from jeopardy or to take responsibility for him, to reasonably persuade the court that it was highly probable that termination of the parental rights was in the best interest of Jeffrey.

NOTE

The Adoption and Safe Families Act

Federal incursions into state public policy concerning families, children, and parental rights reached a significant plateau with the passage by Congress of the Adoption and Safe Families Act of 1997, Pub. L. No. 105–89, 111 Stat. 2115 (codified as amended in scattered sections of 2, 42 U.S.C.). The Act was passed during a period of change in government policy. Congress had previously passed the Personal Responsibility and Work Opportunity Reconciliation Act of 1996 (PRWORA), Pub. L. No. 104–193, 110 Stat. 2105, and both Congressional acts transformed government's attitude. Previously, before PRWORA, the emphasis of federal public policy was the reunification of the family and providing services to parents to eventually integrate a dependent child back into the home. Support and services were provided to accommodate these goals. But with the term limits, TANF block grants, and federal supervision, the unlimited support of families heretofore associated with Aid to Families With Dependent Children ceased.

The Adoption and Safe Families Act was a further reversal. Instead of seemingly endless time for parents to comply with state efforts at reunification—and concomitant time spent by children in foster care—the new federal legislation imposed time limits to curtail parental incertitude. Thus, under the new statute:

> [I]n the case of a child who has been in foster care under the responsibility of the State for 15 of the most recent 22 months, or, if a court of competent jurisdiction has determined a child to be an

abandoned infant . . . or has made a determination that the parent has committed murder of another child of the parent, committed voluntary manslaughter of another child of the parent, aided or abetted, attempted, conspired, or solicited to commit such a murder or such a voluntary manslaughter, or committed a felony assault that has resulted in serious bodily injury to the child or to another child of the parent, the State shall file a petition to terminate the parental rights of the child's parents . . . and, concurrently, to identify, recruit, process, and approve a qualified family for adoption . . .

§ 475(5) of the SOCIAL SECURITY ACT (42 U.S.C. 675(s)).

The Act has been the subject of intense debate. *See, e.g.,* Sally Day, *Mothers in Prison: How The Adoption and Safe Families Act of 1997 Threatens Parental Rights,* 20 WIS. WOMEN'S L. J. 217–242 (2005); Kimberly Carpenter Emery, *Family Ties Dismissed: The Unintended Consequences of ASFA,* 12 VA. J. SOC. POL'Y & L. 400–408 (2005).

B.   ADOPTION

1.   A VENERABLE INSTITUTION WITH A MODERN GLOSS

Adoption is a method for establishing a parent-child relationship legally between persons not already so related.[1] Blood ties between adopter and adoptee are unnecessary. In some early societies adoption was used to perpetuate family religious rites or serve a function similar to that of the modern will. It reached a high degree of formal development in Roman law and on more than one occasion was used to determine imperial succession.[2] However, Roman adoption law existed largely to gratify the wishes of adopters, a characteristic that was passed along to modern civil law in those countries that used the earlier Roman legal system as a base.

In France adoption as a formal institution had almost disappeared by the time of the Revolution. Its revival and subsequent incorporation into the 1804 Civil Code included the limitation that the adopter must be at least fifty years of age and without legitimate child or other descendant at the time of the adoption; no adoption could take place until the adoptee had reached majority.[3] Not until well into the 20th century, with the introduction of a process known as adoptive legitimation, did French law provide a method for adopting an infant and fully integrating the child into a normal family situation at an early age.

---

1. In some jurisdictions a natural father also can formally adopt his biological child born out of wedlock for purposes of legitimation. See, e.g., Bridges v. Nicely, 304 Md. 1, 497 A.2d 142 (1985).

2. Justinian, for example, was adopted by his uncle, Justin I.

3. Civil Code arts. 343, 346 (Fr.1804). See, also, Walter Wadlington, *Minimum Age Difference as a Requisite for Adoption,* 1966 DUKE L.J. 392, 396–7.

The common law did not recognize adoption, and it was not introduced by statute in England until 1926.[4] Thus the law in the United States on the subject grew independently of English influence except to the extent that our courts were hampered at first by the tenet requiring strict construction of statutory provisions that were in derogation of the common law. Although adoption in the civil law sense was the first to exist in this country because of Spanish influence in Louisiana and Texas,[5] this is relatively unimportant to present considerations because those provisions were considerably different in purpose and effect from the later American version and they disappeared early here.

The American version of adoption must be considered as drawing to some extent on the civil law model, but application of the process has been far different in this country. It is through development of a system of adoption with the principal object of promoting child welfare that our law has made its great contribution. This in turn has led to many procedural and consequential differences from any earlier models. As one commentator has put it, adoption in the United States is "a process of selecting fit parents for children, not finding children for parents."[6]

The oldest of adoption statutes in the modern American mold is the 1851 Massachusetts law[7] which served as a model for a number of other states. The 1865 Civil Code of New York, commonly known as the Field Code, included an extensive section on adoption. Though not adopted by the New York legislature, the Field Code greatly influenced the private law in a number of our western states and its adoption provisions were enacted in many of these without substantial change.

More recent influences on state adoption legislation have included the Uniform Adoption Act of 1953 and the suggested language for "An Act for the Adoption of Children", published by the Children's Bureau of the Department of Health, Education and Welfare. A Revised Uniform Adoption Act was approved by the National Conference of Commissioners on Uniform State Laws in 1969. A new and far more elaborate Uniform Adoption Act was promulgated by the National Conference of Commissioners on Uniform Laws in 1994.[8] Despite the proliferation of model language, however, in many states the legislative development of adoption statutes has been a patchwork process. Early in this century the most prominent variations between state laws concerned such matters as the need for judicial intervention and approval (as opposed to adoption by deed or

---

4. Adoption of Children Act, 1926, 16 & 17 Geo. 5, c. 29. For discussion of the background of adoption in England, see Presser, *The Historical Background of the American Law of Adoption*, 11 J.FAM.LAW 443 (1971).

5. See, e.g., Vidal v. Commagère, 13 La.Ann. 516 (1858); Fuselier v. Masse, 4 La. 423 (1832); Teal v. Sevier, 26 Tex. 516 (1863).

6. Katz, *Community Decision—Makers and the Promotion of Values in the Adoption of Children*, 4 J.FAM.LAW 7, 8 (1964).

7. Mass. Gen. Laws 18367–1853, ch. 324, at 752 (1874).

8. 9 U.L.A. 1 (Supp. 1999). The Act also is reproduced in WALTER WADLINGTON and RAYMOND C. O'BRIEN, FAMILY LAW STATUTES, INTERNATIONAL CONVENTIONS AND UNIFORM LAWS 1 (3rd ed. 2007).

contract), the need for investigation of the adoptive home for fitness, and the civil effects produced by an adoption decree. Today judicial intervention and investigation of the adoptive home are standard practices, and most states try to equate the relationship of adopter-adoptee with that of parent and legitimate child by blood kinship in all legal respects. Perhaps the most innovative development of the past decade or two, however, has come in the area of subsidized adoption.

It is common to categorize the adoption process from both legal and record-keeping standpoints either by the method through which a child is placed with prospective adoptive parents or by the prior existence of close ties through consanguinity or affinity. "Independent" or "private" placements are those made by parents either directly to prospective adopters or through a non-licensed intermediary such as a physician, lawyer, relative, or friend. Agency placements are those made by a licensed private adoptive agency or an official state bureau designated to serve such a function. In the agency placement the child usually is formally "surrendered" or "relinquished" by the parents to the agency, which then acts in place of the parents in seeking to effect a desirable adoptive placement. Agencies also may receive children through judicial disposition in cases where parental rights have been terminated.

What does the future hold for the adoption process? Changing attitudes concerning legitimacy, widespread dissemination of information about birth control, the availability of legal abortion and a declining birth rate already have had considerable impact on adoption and on the network of licensed agencies through which the bulk of nonrelative placements traditionally have been made. The extent of this change may have been cushioned by the fact that many children, typically those with physical handicaps and some members of minority racial groups, had long remained largely outside the adoption process. There has been substantial effort to include such persons in recent years, and the success of these initiatives is reflected in the continued high number of adoptions even after the number of available neonates has declined sharply.

Ironically we must note that orphanages, once the popular beneficiaries of major philanthropists who wanted to help young people but could not afford to endow a college or university, reached a point some years ago when some had large assets but few orphans in their care. Diversion of their assets was sought in some instances through application of the *cy pres* doctrine. *See* In re Milne's Succession, 230 La. 729, 89 So.2d 281 (1956). This reflected in part a change in attitudes toward how unwanted or parentless children could best be cared for, as well as changing views toward accepting outsiders into family groups.

For a perceptive advancement of a rationale for appropriately and effectively expanding adoption today, see Barbara Bennett Woodhouse. *Waiting for Loving: The Child's Fundamental Right to Adoption,* 34 CAPITAL U. L. REV.297 (2005).

2.   BALANCING THE RIGHT OF THE PARTIES

Adoption of Tammy

Supreme Judicial Court of Massachusetts, Middlesex, 1993.
416 Mass. 205, 619 N.E.2d 315.

■ GREANEY, JUSTICE.

In this case, two unmarried women, Susan and Helen, filed a joint petition in the Probate and Family Court Department under G.L. c. 210, § 1 (1992 ed.) to adopt as their child Tammy, a minor, who is Susan's biological daughter. Following an evidentiary hearing, a judge of the Probate and Family Court entered a memorandum of decision containing findings of fact and conclusions of law. Based on her finding that Helen and Susan "are each functioning, separately and together, as the custodial and psychological parents of [Tammy]," and that "it is the best interest of said [Tammy] that she be adopted by both," the judge entered a decree allowing the adoption. Simultaneously, the judge reserved and reported to the Appeals Court the evidence and all questions of law, in an effort to "secure [the] decree from any attack in the future on jurisdictional grounds." ... We conclude that the adoption was properly allowed under G.L. c. 210.[1]

We summarize the relevant facts as found by the judge. Helen and Susan have lived together in a committed relationship, which they consider to be permanent, for more than ten years. In June, 1983, they jointly purchased a house in Cambridge. Both women are physicians specializing in surgery. At the time the petition was filed, Helen maintained a private practice in general surgery at Mount Auburn Hospital and Susan, a nationally recognized expert in the field of breast cancer, was director of the Faulkner Breast Center and a surgical oncologist at the Dana Farber Cancer Institute. Both women also held positions on the faculty of Harvard Medical School.

For several years prior to the birth of Tammy, Helen and Susan planned to have a child, biologically related to both of them, whom they would jointly parent. Helen first attempted to conceive a child through artificial insemination by Susan's brother. When those efforts failed, Susan successfully conceived a child through artificial insemination by Helen's biological cousin, Francis. The women attended childbirth classes together and Helen was present when Susan gave birth to Tammy on April 30, 1988. Although Tammy's birth certificate reflects Francis as her biological father, she was given a hyphenated surname using Susan and Helen's last names.

---

1. The judge also decreed, as an alternative to the adoption ordered under G.L. c. 210, "[I]t would be in the best interest of the child to permit [Helen] to adopt [Tammy] and [Susan] to retain postadoptive parental rights of custody and visitation pursuant to its equitable powers, under G.L. c. 215." Be- cause we conclude that the adoption was properly allowed under G.L. c. 210, we need not consider the alternative equitable ground relied on by the judge in permitting Helen to adopt Tammy and Susan to maintain post- adoptive rights.

Since her birth, Tammy has lived with, and been raised and supported by, Helen and Susan. Tammy views both women as her parents, calling Helen "mama" and Susan "mommy." Tammy has strong emotional and psychological bonds with both Helen and Susan. Together, Helen and Susan have provided Tammy with a comfortable home, and have created a warm and stable environment which is supportive of Tammy's growth and over-all well being. Both women jointly and equally participate in parenting Tammy, and both have a strong financial commitment to her. During the work week, Helen usually has lunch at home with Tammy, and on weekends both women spend time together with Tammy at special events or running errands. When Helen and Susan are working, Tammy is cared for by a nanny. The three vacation together at least ten days every three to four months, frequently spending time with Helen's and Susan's respective extended families in California and Mexico. Francis does not participate in parenting Tammy and does not support her. His intention was to assist Helen and Susan in having a child, and he does not intend to be involved with Tammy, except as a distant relative. Francis signed an adoption surrender and supports the joint adoption by both women.

Helen and Susan, recognizing that the laws of the Commonwealth do not permit them to enter into a legally cognizable marriage, believe that the best interests of Tammy require legal recognition of her identical emotional relationship to both women. Susan expressed her understanding that it may not be in her own long-term interest to permit Helen to adopt Tammy because, in the event that Helen and Susan separate, Helen would have equal rights to primary custody. Susan indicated, however, that she has no reservation about allowing Helen to adopt. Apart from the emotional security and current practical ramifications which legal recognition of the reality of her parental relationships will provide Tammy, Susan indicated that the adoption is important for Tammy in terms of potential inheritance from Helen. Helen and her living issue are the beneficiaries of three irrevocable family trusts. Unless Tammy is adopted, Helen's share of the trusts may pass to others. Although Susan and Helen have established a substantial trust fund for Tammy, it is comparatively small in relation to Tammy's potential inheritance under Helen's family trusts.

Over a dozen witnesses, including mental health professionals, teachers, colleagues, neighbors, blood relatives and a priest and nun, testified to the fact that Helen and Susan participate equally in raising Tammy, that Tammy relates to both women as her parents, and that the three form a healthy, happy, and stable family unit. Educators familiar with Tammy testified that she is an extremely well-adjusted, bright, creative, cheerful child who interacts well with other children and adults. A priest and nun from the parties' church testified that Helen and Susan are active parishioners, that they routinely take Tammy to church and church-related activities, and that they attend to the spiritual and moral development of Tammy in an exemplary fashion. Teachers from Tammy's school testified that Helen and Susan both actively participate as volunteers in the school community and communicate frequently with school officials. Neighbors testified that they would have no hesitation in leaving their own children in the care of Helen or Susan. Susan's father, brother, and maternal aunt, and Helen's cousin testified in favor of the joint adoption. Members of both women's extended families attested to the fact that they consider Helen and Susan to be equal parents of Tammy. Both families unreservedly endorsed the adoption petition.

The Department of Social Services (department) conducted a home study in connection with the adoption petition which recommended the adoption, concluding that "the petitioners and their home are suitable for the proper rearing of this child." Tammy's pediatrician reported to the department that Tammy receives regular pediatric care and that she "could not have more excellent parents than Helen and Susan." A court-appointed guardian ad litem, Dr. Steven Nickman, assistant clinical professor of psychiatry at Harvard Medical School, conducted a clinical assessment of Tammy and her family with a view toward determining whether or not it would be in Tammy's best interests to be adopted by Helen and Susan. Dr. Nickman considered the ramifications of the fact that Tammy will be brought up in a "non-standard" family. As part of his report, he reviewed and referenced literature on child psychiatry and child psychology which supports the conclusion that children raised by lesbian parents develop normally. In sum, he stated that "the fact that this parent-child constellation came into being as a result of thoughtful planning and a strong desire on the part of these women to be parents to a child and to give that child the love, the wisdom and the knowledge that they possess ... [needs to be taken into account].... The maturity of these women, their status in the community, and their seriousness of purpose stands in contrast to the caretaking environments of a vast number of children who are born to heterosexual parents but who are variously abused, neglected and otherwise deprived of security and happiness." Dr. Nickman concluded that "there is every reason for [Helen] to become a legal parent to Tammy just as [Susan] is," and he recommended that the court so order. An attorney appointed to represent Tammy's interests also strongly recommended that the joint petition be granted.

Despite the overwhelming support for the joint adoption and the judge's conclusion that joint adoption is clearly in Tammy's best interests, the question remains whether there is anything in the law of the Commonwealth that would prevent this adoption. The law of adoption is purely statutory, is to be strictly followed in all its essential particulars. To the extent that any ambiguity or vagueness exists in the statute, judicial construction should enhance, rather than defeat, its purpose. The primary purpose of the adoption statute, particularly with regard to children under the age of fourteen, is undoubtedly the advancement of the best interests of the subject child.... With these considerations in mind, we examine the statute to determine whether adoption in the circumstances of this case is permitted.

1.   The initial question is whether the Probate Court judge had jurisdiction under G.L. c. 210 to enter a judgment on a joint petition for

adoption brought by two unmarried cohabitants in the petitioners' circumstances. We answer this question in the affirmative.

There is nothing on the face of the statute which precludes the joint adoption of a child by two unmarried cohabitants such as the petitioners. Chapter 210, § 1, provides that "[a] person of full age may petition the probate court in the county where he resides for leave to adopt as his child another person younger than himself, unless such other person is his or her wife or husband, or brother, sister, uncle or aunt, of the whole or half blood."[2] Other than requiring that a spouse join in the petition, if the petitioner is married and the spouse is competent to join therein, the statute does not expressly prohibit or require joinder by any person.[3] Although the singular "a person" is used, it is a legislatively mandated rule of statutory construction that "[w]ords importing the singular number may extend and be applied to several persons" unless the resulting construction is "inconsistent with the manifest intent of the law-making body or repugnant to the context of the same statute." G.L. c. 4, § 6 (1992 ed.). In the context of adoption, where the legislative intent to promote the best interests of the child is evidenced throughout the governing statute, and the adoption of a child by two unmarried individuals accomplishes that goal, construing the term "person" as "persons" clearly enhances, rather than defeats, the purpose of the statute. Furthermore, it is apparent from the first sentence of G.L. c. 210, § 1, that the Legislature considered and defined those combinations of persons which would lead to adoptions in violation of public policy. Clearly absent is any prohibition of adoption by two unmarried individuals like the petitioners.

2. There is no question that Helen and Susan each individually satisfy the identity requirements of G.L. c. 210, § 1. Although the adoption statute, as it first appeared (St. 1851, c. 324) precluded a person from adopting his or her own child by birth, the statute was amended to permit adoption by the child's natural parents. Curran, Petition of, 314 Mass. 91, 49 N.E.2d 432 (1943) (natural mother of child born out of wedlock proper party to adoption petition). None of the prohibitions to adoption set forth in § 1 is applicable. Furthermore, there is nothing in the statute that prohibits adoption based on gender or sexual orientation. Contrast Fla.Stat. § 63.042(3) (1991) (prohibiting homosexuals from adopting); N.H.Rev.Stat.Ann. § 170–B:4 (1990) (same). 381 Mass. 563, 579, 410 N.E.2d 1207 (1980).

3. The provision concerning joinder of spouses is a requirement that has been present in the statute since its enactment in 1851.... Adoption by a married person has the effect of changing the legal duties of both spouses because the "infant who is adopted becomes the child not of one but of both." Lee v. Wood, 279 Mass. 293, 295, 181 N.E. 229 (1932). Both spouses must freely consent to join in the adoption petition. If a person falsely claims to be the legal spouse of another, the Probate Court may vacate the adoption decree. The required joinder of spouses, which is jurisdictional in nature, does not by its terms apply to joint petitions by unmarried persons who seek to adopt. See Adoption of B.L.V.B., 628 A.2d 1271 (Vt.1993) (requirement of joinder of spouses in Vermont adoption statute does not bar adoption by same sex partner of children's natural mother); Matter of A.J.J., 108 Misc.2d 657, 659–660, 438 N.Y.S.2d 444 (N.Y.Sur.Ct.1981) (natural parents decided not to marry; natural father permitted, with mother's consent, to adopt as if he were married to mother); Matter of the Adoption of a Child by A.R., 152 N.J.Super. 541, 545, 378 A.2d 87 (1977) (natural father permitted to adopt his illegitimate child without marrying mother or terminating mother's legal relationship to child).

While the Legislature may not have envisioned adoption by same sex partners, there is no indication that it attempted to define all possible categories of persons leading to adoptions in the best interests of children.[4] Rather than limit the potential categories of persons entitled to adopt (other than those described in the first sentence of § 1), the Legislature used general language to define who may adopt and who may be adopted. The Probate Court has thus been granted jurisdiction to consider a variety of adoption petitions. See Adoption of Thomas, 408 Mass. 446, 449–451, 559 N.E.2d 1230 (1990). The limitations on adoption that do exist derive from the written consent requirements contained in § 2,[5] from specific conditions set forth in § 2A, which must be satisfied prior to the adoption of a child under the age of fourteen,[6] and from several statutory and judicial directives[7] which essentially restrict adoptions to those which have been

---

4. Children in earlier times who lacked two married and living parents, just as many children today, were often adopted into "non-standard" families. See e.g., Curran, petitioner, supra (child born out of wedlock adopted by unmarried natural mother); Delano v. Bruerton, 148 Mass. 619, 20 N.E. 308 (1889) (grandfather adopted grandson, child of his deceased son). By permitting adoption by unmarried persons, the Legislature clearly sanctioned adoption into "non-standard" families. Moreover, the Legislature could easily have contemplated circumstances leading to adoption by more than one unmarried party, albeit in circumstances different from this case. For example, orphaned children are frequently taken in and raised by relatives, who may be unmarried siblings, aunts or uncles, or cousins of their parents. See, e.g., Merrill v. Berlin, 316 Mass. 87, 89, 54 N.E.2d 674 (1944) (court found that it was in the best interests of two orphaned boys to be raised by their deceased mother's aunt and two female cousins, despite the "wholly feminine" nature of the household).

5. General Laws c. 210, § 2 (1992 ed.), provides in relevant part: "A decree of adoption shall not be made, except as provided in this chapter, without the written consent of the child to be adopted, if above the age of twelve; of the child's spouse, if any; of the lawful parents, who may be previous adoptive parents, or surviving parent; or of the mother only if the child was born out of wedlock and not previously adopted. A person whose consent is hereby required shall not be prevented from being the adoptive parent." Susan's request to adopt her own child and her consent to Helen's adoption of Tammy satisfies the statute. Although not required by the statute, Francis, the biological father, has

provided his written consent to the joint adoption. The written consent of the child's natural parents is not required if the court has terminated the natural parents' legal rights to the child because there has been a showing by clear and convincing evidence that the natural parents are unfit. G.L. c. 210, § 3 (1992 ed.).

6. A decree of adoption may not be entered unless one of five preconditions set forth in G.L. c. 210, § 2A, is satisfied. These preconditions include a showing that "the petitioner is a blood relative of the child sought to be adopted" or that "[t]he petition for adoption has been approved in writing by the department of social services or by an agency authorized by said department." Because both Susan and Helen are blood relatives of Tammy, and the department has approved the adoption, two of the preconditions have been satisfied in this case.

7. The judge is directed to consider "all factors relevant to the physical, mental and moral health of the child" and a decree of adoption may be entered only after the judge has determined that the adopting parties are "of sufficient ability to bring up the child and provide suitable support and education for it, and that the child should be adopted." G.L. c. 210, §§ 5B, 6. Additionally, we have stated, with regard to establishing the status of legal parent, that the judge "must look at the relationship [between the parent and the child] as a whole, and consider emotional bonds, economic support, custody of the child, the extent of personal association, the commitment of the [parent] to attending to the child's needs, the consistency of the [parent's] expressed interest ... and any other

found by a judge to be in the best interests of the subject child. See Merrill v. Berlin, supra, 316 Mass. at 89, 54 N.E.2d 674 (in dismissing elderly grandparents' petition to adopt following death of children's parents, and retaining custody with three female testamentary guardians, the court stated "[t]he only question [to be considered] is whether the best interests of the children would be served by their adoption").

In this case all requirements in §§ 2 and 2A are met, and there is no question that the judge's findings demonstrate that the directives set forth in §§ 5B and 6, and in case law, have been satisfied. Adoption will not result in any tangible change in Tammy's daily life; it will, however, serve to provide her with a significant legal relationship which may be important in her future. At the most practical level, adoption will entitle Tammy to inherit from Helen's family trusts and from Helen and her family under the law of intestate succession, to receive support from Helen, who will be legally obligated to provide such support, to be eligible for coverage under Helen's health insurance policies, and to be eligible for social security benefits in the event of Helen's disability or death.

Of equal, if not greater significance, adoption will enable Tammy to preserve her unique filial ties to Helen in the event that Helen and Susan separate, or Susan predeceases Helen.[8] As the case law and commentary on the subject illustrate, when the functional parents of children born in circumstances similar to Tammy separate or one dies, the children often remain in legal limbo for years while their future is disputed in the courts. Polikoff, This Child Does Have Two Mothers: Redefining Parenthood to Meet the Needs of Children in Lesbian–Mother and Other Nontraditional Families, 78 Geo.L.J. 459, 508–522 (1990); Comment, Second Parent Adoption for Lesbian–Parented Families: Legal Recognition of the Other Mother, 19 U.C.Davis L.Rev. 729, 741–745 (1986). In some cases, children have been denied the affection of a functional parent who has been with them since birth, even when it is apparent that this outcome is contrary to the children's best interests.[9] Adoption serves to establish legal rights and

factors which bear on the nature of the alleged parent-child relationship." C.C. v. A.B., 406 Mass. 679, 690, 550 N.E.2d 365 (1990).

8. Although Susan has designated Helen guardian of Tammy in her will, Helen's custody of Tammy could conceivably be contested in the event of Susan's death, particularly by Francis, members of his family or members of Susan's family. Absent adoption, Helen would not have a dispositive legal right to retain custody of Tammy, because she would be a "legal stranger" to the child.

9. Cases from other jurisdictions demonstrate the difficulties resulting from the lack of an established legal relationship between a child and its second functional parent. See, e.g., In re the Interest of Z.J.H., 162 Wis.2d 1002, 1033, 471 N.W.2d 202 (1991)

(Bablitch, J., dissenting) (former lesbian partner of child's adoptive mother, who had planned on adoption, cultivated "parent-like" relationship with child since his birth, and had been child's primary caretaker, denied both visitation and custody after partners' separation due to lack of legal relationship with child; court refused to consider issue of child's best interests); Nancy S. v. Michele G., 228 Cal.App.3d 831, 840 & n. 8, 279 Cal.Rptr. 212 (1991) (two children conceived by artificial insemination during lesbian couple's relationship deemed legal children of natural mother only, who was granted sole physical and legal custody following the couple's separation; appellate court recognized that adoption would avoid this "unfortunate situation" noting that "we see nothing in

responsibilities so that, in the event that problems arise in the future, issues of custody and visitation may be promptly resolved by reference to the best interests of the child within the recognized framework of the law. See G.L. c. 209C, § 10. See also Adoption of B.L.V.B., 628 A.2d 1271 (Vt.1993). There is no jurisdictional bar in the statute to the judge's consideration of this joint petition. The conclusion that the adoption is in the best interests of Tammy is also well warranted.

2. The judge also posed the question whether, pursuant to G.L. c. 210, § 6 (1992 ed.), Susan's legal relationship to Tammy must be terminated if Tammy is adopted. Section 6 provides that, on entry of an adoption decree, "all rights, duties and other legal consequences of the natural relation of child and parent shall . . . except as regards marriage, incest or cohabitation, terminate between the child so adopted and his natural parents and kindred." Although G.L. c. 210, § 2, clearly permits a child's natural parent to be an adoptive parent, § 6 does not contain any express exceptions to its termination provision. The Legislature obviously did not intend that a natural parent's legal relationship to its child be terminated when the natural parent is a party to the adoption petition.

Section 6 clearly is directed to the more usual circumstances of adoption, where the child is adopted by persons who are not the child's natural parents (either because the natural parents have elected to relinquish the child for adoption or their parental rights have been involuntarily terminated). The purpose of the termination provision is to protect the security of the child's newly-created family unit by eliminating involvement with the child's natural parents. Although it is not uncommon for a natural parent to join in the adoption petition of a spouse who is not the child's natural parent, the statute has never been construed to require the termination of the natural parent's legal relationship to the child in these circumstances. Nor has § 6 been construed to apply when the natural mother petitions alone to adopt her child born out of wedlock. See Curran, petitioner, 314 Mass. 91, 49 N.E.2d 432 (1943). Reading the adoption statute as a whole, we conclude that the termination provision contained in § 6 was intended to apply only when the natural parents (or parent) are not parties to the adoption petition.[10]

[our statutory] provisions [similar to those in Massachusetts] that would preclude a child from being jointly adopted by someone of the same sex as the natural parent"); In re Pearlman, 15 Fam.L.Rep. (BNA) 1355 (Fla.Cir.Ct. 1989) (unreported) (custody of child conceived by artificial insemination during lesbian couple's relationship awarded to "de facto" parent after four years of litigation with child's maternal grandparents following death of natural mother; child, who had been separated from her functional parent and suffered anxiety as a result, told the court "for

Christmas I don't really want a present. All I want is to live with Neenie ['de facto' parent]").

10. In interpreting a provision similar to G.L. c. 210, § 6, the Vermont Supreme Court, citing support from trial courts in other jurisdictions, likewise concluded that the natural or prior adoptive parent's legal relationship to the child does not terminate when the child is adopted by the same sex partner of the child's legal parent. See Adoption of B.L.V.B., 628 A.2d 1271 (Vt. 1993) . . . .

3. We conclude that the Probate Court has jurisdiction to enter a decree on a joint adoption petition brought by the two petitioners when the judge has found that joint adoption is in the subject child's best interests. We further conclude that, when a natural parent is a party to a joint adoption petition, that parent's legal relationship to the child does not terminate on entry of the adoption decree.

4. So much of the decree as allows the adoption of Tammy by both petitioners is affirmed. So much of the decree as provides in the alternative for the adoption of Tammy by Helen and the retention of rights of custody and visitation by Susan is vacated.

■ NOLAN, JUSTICE (dissenting).

I write separately in dissent only because I do not agree with the sentiments expressed by my brother Lynch in the first few sentences of his dissent. His dissent is otherwise a faultless analysis of our existing jurisprudence to which I subscribe.

■ LYNCH, JUSTICE (dissenting, with whom O'CONNOR, JUSTICE, joins).

At the outset I wish to make clear that my views are not motivated by any disapproval of the two petitioners here or their life-style. The judge has found that the petitioners have provided the child with a healthy, happy, stable family unit. The evidence supports the judge's findings. Nor is my disagreement with the court related to the sexual orientation of the petitioners. I am firmly of the view that a litigant's expression of human sexuality ought not determine the outcome of litigation as long as it involves consenting adults and is not harmful to others. However, the court's decision, which is inconsistent with the statutory language, cannot be justified by a desire to achieve what is in the child's best interests. Indeed, those interests can be accommodated without doing violence to the statute by accepting the alternative to joint adoption suggested by the Probate Court judge; that is, permitting Helen to adopt Tammy while allowing Susan to retain all her parental rights and obligations. This is essentially what the court accomplishes in part 2 of its opinion. By this simple expedient, all of the court's concerns about protecting filial ties and avoiding legal limits are put to rest without invading the prerogatives of the Legislature and giving legal status to a relationship by judicial fiat that our elected representatives and the general public have, as yet, failed to endorse.

The court concludes that the Probate and Family Court has jurisdiction to grant a joint petition for adoption by two unmarried cohabitants because they meet the statutory requirements of G.L. c. 210, § 1, and it is in the child's best interests to be adopted by both. General Laws c. 210, § 1, enumerates who may petition for adoption. In accordance with the statute, a petitioner of full age may petition to adopt. If a person is married and has a competent spouse, the spouse is required to join in the petition to adopt. If a husband and wife fail jointly to petition for adoption, a decree or judgment granting the adoption is void. A minor may petition for adoption of his or her natural child or may join in the petition of his or her spouse when the child is the natural child of one of the parties. G.L. c. 210, § 1. The court has also interpreted the statute as permitting a biological parent of full age to petition for the adoption of his or her own child. Curran, petitioner, 314 Mass. 91, 95, 49 N.E.2d 432 (1943). There is, however, nothing in the statute indicating a legislative intent to allow two or more unmarried persons jointly to petition for adoption.[2]

Massachusetts became the first common law jurisdiction to authorize judicially approved adoption with parental consent by statute. General jurisdiction over adoptions is granted to the Probate and Family Court, G.L. c. 215, § 3, and can be exercised only as provided by the Legislature with the paramount concern, purpose, and focus of adoption proceedings being the welfare of the child. Since adoption is a creature of the Legislature, and in derogation of the common law, the statute must be strictly construed. The plain meaning of a statute cannot be expanded or altered where the Legislature establishes specific criteria or classifications to be satisfied. Unless one of the enumerated potential petitioners brings an adoption petition, the court lacks the jurisdiction to entertain the petition. In the present case, the petitioners are two unmarried persons seeking to adopt a child. The statute only permits joint petitions for adoption by married persons. See Adoption of Meaux, 417 So.2d 522, 523 (La.Ct.App. 1982) (unmarried natural parents may not jointly adopt own illegitimate child); Matter of Adams, 189 Mich.App. 540, 544, 473 N.W.2d 712 (1991) (inconsistent with purpose and scope of adoption statute to allow joint adoption of two unmarried petitioners); In re Jason C., 129 N.H. 762, 765, 533 A.2d 32 (1987) (two unmarried persons may not jointly adopt child). Contra Adoption of B.L.V.B., 628 A.2d 1271 (Vt.1993) (92–321) (permitting joint petition to adopt by two unmarried persons).

The court opines that the use of the singular form "a person" in the first sentence of the statute should not be construed as prohibiting joint petitions by unmarried persons because such an interpretation would not be in the best interests of the child. I have already demonstrated that, whether the petition be singular or joint, has nothing to do with the best interests of the child. The court's reasoning in part 2 of its opinion amounts to a tacit agreement with this position. Furthermore, on examining § 1 as a whole, I find no inconsistent use of the singular form from the first sentence that "[a] person ... may ... adopt ... another person younger than himself," to the final sentence pertaining to nonresidents who wish to adopt. Throughout the section, the singular is preserved. The only time a second petitioner is contemplated is where the initial petitioner has a living, competent spouse. There is nothing in the statute to suggest that joint petitions other than by spouses are permitted.

---

2. There is nothing based on sexual orientation in the statute which would prohibit a homosexual from singly adopting a child. Additionally, a parent may not be deprived of custody of his or her children simply because he or she is a homosexual. Bezio v. Patenaude, 381 Mass. 563, 579, 410 N.E.2d 1207 (1980). Contra Fla.Stat.Ann. § 63.042 (1985) (prohibiting homosexuals from adopting); N.H.Rev.Stat.Ann. § 170–B:4 (1990) (same).

A biological mother may petition alone for the adoption of her child. Curran, petitioner, supra. Helen also meets the statutory requirements and may petition alone for the adoption of Tammy with Susan's consent. G.L. c. 210, § 2. Despite the admirable parenting and thriving environment being provided by these two unmarried cohabitants for this child, the statute does not permit their joint petition for adoption of Tammy.

NOTES

In In the Interest of Angel Lace M., 184 Wis.2d 492, 516 N.W.2d 678 (1994), the Supreme Court of Wisconsin reached a different result, holding that their statute would not allow a mother's female cohabitant to adopt the child of the mother even though the trial court had held that such an adoption would be in the child's best interests. The court also concluded that the adoption statute containing the limitation did not violate either the minor's due process or equal protection rights or the cohabitant's equal protection rights. However, the Court of Appeals of New York, in In the Matter of Jacob, 86 N.Y.2d 651, 636 N.Y.S.2d 716, 660 N.E.2d 397 (1995),held that an unmarried heterosexual couple could be permitted to adopt under New York law. The New York court also held that the unmarried partner of a child's biological mother, whether heterosexual or homosexual, who is raising the child together with the biological parent, can become the child's second parent by means of adoption. They further noted that a single homosexual could adopt a child.

Effect of Divorce. In *In re* Jason C., 129 N.H. 762, 533 A.2d 32 (1987), the Supreme Court of New Hampshire refused to allow a divorced husband of an adoption petitioner to be treated as a copetitioner. The couple had been foster parents to the child for some two years before their divorce, and the former husband explained that his action was undertaken "in order to recognize the importance of each of them as a psychological parent to the child." *Id.* at 33. The former wife did not formally oppose the petition though it was indicated that she did not wish to have him obtain standing to request physical custody in the future. The Division of Children and Youth Service opposed the former husband's petition, which was denied by the trial court. In affirming that decision the appellate court reviewed the categories of adults who are eligible to adopt in New Hampshire and explained

> Applicants who will fall within most, if not all, of these categories share a common characteristic: their domestic circumstances do not threaten to disrupt the living arrangements they will provide for the child to be adopted. Married applicants who apply jointly demonstrate a sense of common purpose. The unmarried applicant who applies alone presents a household with no apparent risk of splitting up. The married applicant who is separated from a spouse by desertion or legal decree may be in the same practical position as someone who is legally single.

We may infer, then, that it was the legislature's intent to confine adoption to applicants who will probably provide a unified and stable household for the child. This objective is not likely to be served by authorizing two unmarried applicants to adopt jointly, as this case illustrates. The applicants do not share living quarters, and if the court were to entertain and grant their joint petition, its next task would presumably be to decide whom the child would live with. That is, it would have to make a custody determination quite separate from the decree of adoption itself. RSA chapter 170–B does not, however, appear to contemplate such a process. The statute evidently assumes that the adopted child will have one "home," and this assumption apparently explains why the chapter makes no provision for an award of custody except in those instances in which the adoption petition is dismissed. . . .

Sexual Orientation. Fla. Stat. Ann. § 63.042(3), preventing adoption by practicing homosexuals, has been upheld as constitutional by the United States Court of Appeals for the Eleventh Circuit. Lofton v. Secretary of Department of Children and Family Services, 358 F.3d 804, *cert. denied* 543 U.S. 1081, 125 S.Ct. 869, 160 L.Ed.2d 825 (2005). Holding that there is no fundamental right to adopt, the court holds that the state may rationally choose to place children in adoptive homes with a mother and a father. And this family model may provide a legitimate basis for the legislature's exclusion of practicing homosexual persons. In 2002, the American Academy of Pediatrics endorsed adoptions by same sex partners. *See* http:/www.aap.org/policy/020008.html. Another issue is the recognition of out-of-state adoptions when the out-of-state adoption would not be allowed in the state asked to give recognition. One federal court has ruled that Oklahoma had to recognize out-of-state adoptions (one in California and one in New Jersey) by same sex couples. The court held that an amendment to the Oklahoma adoption code barring recognition of foreign adoption decrees violated full faith and credit, equal protection, and due process of law. Finstuen v. Edmondson, No. CIV–04–1152–C, 2006 WL 1445354 (W.D. Okla. May 19, 2006).

CALIFORNIA FAMILY CODE (West 2004 & 2006)

§ 9000. Petition for adoption; caption; contents; guardianship petition; order of adoption

(a) A stepparent desiring to adopt a child of the stepparent's spouse may for that purpose file a petition in the county in which the petitioner resides.

(b) A domestic partner, as defined in Section 297, desiring to adopt a child of his or her domestic partner may for that purpose file a petition in the county in which the petitioner resides.

(c) The caption of the adoption petition shall contain the names of the petitioners, but not the child's name. The petition shall state the child's sex and date of birth and the name the child had before adoption.

(d) If the child is the subject of a guardianship petition, the adoption petition shall so state and shall include the caption and docket number or have attached a copy of the letters of the guardianship or temporary guardianship. The petitioners shall notify the court of any petition for guardianship or temporary guardianship filed after the adoption petition. The guardianship proceeding shall be consolidated with the adoption proceeding.

(e) The order of adoption shall contain the child's adopted name, but not the name the child had before adoption.

(f) If the petitioner has entered into a postadoption contact agreement with the birth parent as set forth in Section 8616.5, the agreement, signed by the participating parties, shall be attached to and filed with the petition for adoption.

(g) For the purposes of this chapter, stepparent adoption includes adoption by a domestic partner, as defined in Section 297.

INTERETHNIC ADOPTION
42 U.S.C.A. § 1996b (West 2003)

(1) Prohibited conduct

A person or government that is involved in adoption or foster care placements may not—

(A) deny to any individual the opportunity to become an adoptive or a foster parent, on the basis of the race, color, or national origin of the individual, or of the child, involved; or

(B) delay or deny the placement of a child for adoption or into foster care, on the basis of the race, color, or national origin of the adoptive or foster parent, or the child, involved.

(2) Enforcement

Noncompliance with paragraph (1) is deemed a violation of title VI of the Civil Rights Act of 1964 [42 U.S.C.A. § 2000d et seq.].

(3) No effect on the Indian Child Welfare Act of 1978

This section shall not be construed to affect the application of the Indian Child Welfare Act of 1978 [25 U.S.C.A. § 1901 et seq.].

NOTE

Note that § B(3) specifically excludes application of the Indian Child Welfare Act. Without giving formal weight to ethnicity, a court nevertheless may give a preference to a relative placement in some states. *See, e.g.,* In Matter of Welfare of D.L., 486 N.W.2d 375 (Minn.1992).

Stanley v. Illinois
Supreme Court of the United States, 1972.
405 U.S. 645, 92 S.Ct. 1208, 31 L.Ed.2d 551.

(The opinion is reproduced at p. 680, *supra.*)

NOTE

It can be argued that *Stanley* was a case that turned largely on sex discrimination. However, its impact has been much broader and today it is cited widely for propositions ranging from the rights of fathers of illegitimate children to guarantees that parents should be free from intervention in raising their children absent disqualifying conduct or capacity.

From a practical standpoint, the decision has had its greatest impact on adoption. At the time when it was decided, many states provided that an unacknowledged illegitimate child could be legally relinquished for adoption by the mother acting alone. Courts and attorney general staff members soon construed *Stanley* to conflict with such statutes. Legislative responses have varied considerably. Issues regarding their constitutionality are still being resolved in the courts.

Stanley may well have been a case in which the court wrote its opinion without sufficient understanding of its potential impact (particularly through footnote 9) for adoption law and practice. Had you been commissioned to file a brief *amicus curiae* for an organization concerned with the rights of children, what approach would you have urged the court to follow?

Lehr v. Robertson

Supreme Court of the United States, 1983.
463 U.S. 248, 103 S.Ct. 2985, 77 L.Ed.2d 614.

■ STEVENS, JUSTICE.

The question presented is whether New York has sufficiently protected an unmarried father's inchoate relationship with a child whom he has never supported and rarely seen in the two years since her birth. The appellant, Jonathan Lehr, claims that the Due Process and Equal Protection Clauses of the Fourteenth Amendment, as interpreted in Stanley v. Illinois, 405 U.S. 645, 92 S.Ct. 1208, 31 L.Ed.2d 551 (1972), and Caban v. Mohammed, 441 U.S. 380, 99 S.Ct. 1760, 60 L.Ed.2d 297 (1979), give him an absolute right to notice and an opportunity to be heard before the child may be adopted. We disagree.

Jessica M. was born out of wedlock on November 9, 1976. Her mother, Lorraine Robertson, married Richard Robertson eight months after Jessica's birth.[1] On December 21, 1978, when Jessica was over two years old, the Robertsons filed an adoption petition in the Family Court of Ulster County, New York. The court heard their testimony and received a favorable report from the Ulster County Department of Social Services. On March 7, 1979, the court entered an order of adoption. In this proceeding, appellant contends that the adoption order is invalid because he, Jessica's putative father, was not given advance notice of the adoption proceeding.[3]

---

1. Although both Lorraine and Richard Robertson are appellees in this proceeding, for ease of discussion the term "appellee" will hereafter be used to identify Lorraine Robertson.

3. Appellee has never conceded that appellant is Jessica's biological father, but for purposes of analysis in this opinion it will be assumed that he is.

The State of New York maintains a "putative father registry." A man who files with that registry demonstrates his intent to claim paternity of a child born out of wedlock and is therefore entitled to receive notice of any proceeding to adopt that child. Before entering Jessica's adoption order, the Ulster County Family Court had the putative father registry examined. Although appellant claims to be Jessica's natural father, he had not entered his name in the registry.

In addition to the persons whose names are listed on the putative father registry, New York law requires that notice of an adoption proceeding be given to several other classes of possible fathers of children born out of wedlock—those who have been adjudicated to be the father, those who have been identified as the father on the child's birth certificate, those who live openly with the child and the child's mother and who hold themselves out to be the father, those who have been identified as the father by the mother in a sworn written statement, and those who were married to the child's mother before the child was six months old. Appellant admittedly was not a member of any of those classes. He had lived with appellee prior to Jessica's birth and visited her in the hospital when Jessica was born, but his name does not appear on Jessica's birth certificate. He did not live with appellee or Jessica after Jessica's birth, he has never provided them with any financial support, and he has never offered to marry appellee. Nevertheless, he contends that the following special circumstances gave him a constitutional right to notice and a hearing before Jessica was adopted.

On January 30, 1979, one month after the adoption proceeding was commenced in Ulster County, appellant filed a "visitation and paternity petition" in the Westchester County Family Court. In that petition, he asked for a determination of paternity, an order of support, and reasonable visitation privileges with Jessica. Notice of that proceeding was served on appellee on February 22, 1979. Four days later appellee's attorney informed the Ulster County Court that appellant had commenced a paternity proceeding in Westchester County; the Ulster County judge then entered an order staying appellant's paternity proceeding until he could rule on a motion to change the venue of that proceeding to Ulster County. On March 3, 1979, appellant received notice of the change of venue motion and, for the first time, learned that an adoption proceeding was pending in Ulster County. On March 7, 1979, appellant's attorney telephoned the Ulster County judge to inform him that he planned to seek a stay of the adoption proceeding pending the determination of the paternity petition. In that telephone conversation, the judge advised the lawyer that he had already signed the adoption order earlier that day. According to appellant's attorney, the judge stated that he was aware of the pending paternity petition but did not believe he was required to give notice to appellant prior to the entry of the order of adoption.

Thereafter, the Family Court in Westchester County granted appellee's motion to dismiss the paternity petition, holding that the putative father's right to seek paternity "... must be deemed severed so long as an order of adoption exists." Appellant did not appeal from that dismissal.[6] On June 22, 1979, appellant filed a petition to vacate the order of adoption on the ground that it was obtained by fraud and in violation of his constitutional rights.

.   .   .

Appellant has now invoked our appellate jurisdiction. He offers two alternative grounds for holding the New York statutory scheme unconstitutional. First, he contends that a putative father's actual or potential relationship with a child born out of wedlock is an interest in liberty which may not be destroyed without due process of law; he argues therefore that he had a constitutional right to prior notice and an opportunity to be heard before he was deprived of that interest. Second, he contends that the gender-based classification in the statute, which both denied him the right to consent to Jessica's adoption and accorded him fewer procedural rights than her mother, violated the Equal Protection Clause.

The Due Process Claim.

.   .   .

The intangible fibers that connect parent and child have infinite variety. They are woven throughout the fabric of our society, providing it with strength, beauty, and flexibility. It is self-evident that they are sufficiently vital to merit constitutional protection in appropriate cases. In deciding whether this is such a case, however, we must consider the broad framework that has traditionally been used to resolve the legal problems arising from the parent-child relationship.

In the vast majority of cases, state law determines the final outcome. Rules governing the inheritance of property, adoption, and child custody are generally specified in statutory enactments that vary from State to State. Moreover, equally varied state laws governing marriage and divorce affect a multitude of parent-child relationships. The institution of marriage has played a critical role both in defining the legal entitlements of family members and in developing the decentralized structure of our democratic society.[12] In recognition of that role, and as part of their general overarching concern for serving the best interests of children, state laws almost universally express an appropriate preference for the formal family.

In some cases, however, this Court has held that the Federal Constitution supersedes state law and provides even greater protection for certain formal family relationships. In those cases, as in the state cases, the Court has emphasized the paramount interest in the welfare of children and has noted that the rights of the parents are a counterpart of the responsibilities

---

6. Without trying to intervene in the adoption proceeding, appellant had attempted to file an appeal from the adoption order. That appeal was dismissed.

12. See Hafen, Marriage, Kinship and Sexual Privacy, 81 Mich.L.Rev. 463, 479–481 (1983) (hereinafter Hafen).

they have assumed.... There are also a few cases in which this Court has considered the extent to which the Constitution affords protection to the relationship between natural parents and children born out of wedlock. In some we have been concerned with the rights of the children. In this case, however, it is a parent who claims that the state has improperly deprived him of a protected interest in liberty. This Court has examined the extent to which a natural father's biological relationship with his illegitimate child receives protection under the Due Process Clause in precisely three cases: Stanley v. Illinois, 405 U.S. 645, 92 S.Ct. 1208, 31 L.Ed.2d 551 (1972), Quilloin v. Walcott, 434 U.S. 246, 98 S.Ct. 549, 54 L.Ed.2d 511 (1978), and Caban v. Mohammed, 441 U.S. 380, 99 S.Ct. 1760, 60 L.Ed.2d 297 (1979).

Stanley involved the constitutionality of an Illinois statute that conclusively presumed every father of a child born out of wedlock to be un unfit person to have custody of his children. The father in that case had lived with his children all their lives and had lived with their mother for eighteen years. There was nothing in the record to indicate that Stanley had been a neglectful father who had not cared for his children. 405 U.S., at 655, 92 S.Ct., at 1214. Under the statute, however, the nature of the actual relationship between parent and child was completely irrelevant. Once the mother died, the children were automatically made wards of the state. Relying in part on a Michigan case[14] recognizing that the preservation of "a subsisting relationship with the child's father" may better serve the child's best interest than "uprooting him from the family which he knew from birth," the Court held that the Due Process Clause was violated by the automatic destruction of the custodial relationship without giving the father any opportunity to present evidence regarding his fitness as a parent.

Quilloin involved the constitutionality of a Georgia statute that authorized the adoption of a child born out of wedlock over the objection of the natural father. The father in that case had never legitimated the child. It was only after the mother had remarried and her new husband had filed an adoption petition that the natural father sought visitation rights and filed a petition for legitimation. The trial court found adoption by the new husband to be in the child's best interests, and we unanimously held that action to be consistent with the Due Process Clause.

Caban involved the conflicting claims of two natural parents who had maintained joint custody of their children from the time of their birth until they were respectively two and four years old. The father challenged the validity of an order authorizing the mother's new husband to adopt the children; he relied on both the Equal Protection Clause and the Due Process Clause. Because this Court upheld his equal protection claim, the majority did not address his due process challenge. The comments on the latter claim by the four dissenting Justices are nevertheless instructive, because they identify the clear distinction between a mere biological relationship and an actual relationship of parental responsibility.

14. In re Mark T., 8 Mich.App. 122, 154 N.W.2d 27 (1967).

Justice Stewart correctly observed:

"Even if it be assumed that each married parent after divorce has some substantive due process right to maintain his or her parental relationship, cf. Smith v. Organization of Foster Families, 431 U.S. 816, 862–863 [97 S.Ct. 2094, 2119, 53 L.Ed.2d 14] (opinion concurring in judgment), it by no means follows that each unwed parent has any such right. *Parental rights do not spring full-blown from the biological connection between parent and child. They require relationships more enduring.*" 441 U.S., at 397, 99 S.Ct., at 1770 (emphasis added).[16] In a similar vein, the other three dissenters in *Caban* were prepared to "assume that, *if and when one develops,* the relationship between a father and his natural child is entitled to protection against arbitrary state action as a matter of due process." Caban v. Mohammed, 441 U.S. 380, 414, 99 S.Ct. 1760, 1779, 60 L.Ed.2d 297 (emphasis added).

The difference between the developed parent-child relationship that was implicated in *Stanley* and *Caban,* and the potential relationship involved in *Quilloin* and this case, is both clear and significant. Where an unwed father demonstrates a full commitment to the responsibilities of parenthood by "com[ing] forward to participate in the rearing of his child," *Caban,* 441 U.S., at 392, 99 S.Ct., at 1768, his interest in personal contact with his child acquires substantial protection under the due process clause. At that point it may be said that he "act[s] as a father toward his children." But the mere existence of a biological link does not merit equivalent constitutional protection. The actions of judges neither create nor sever genetic bonds. "[T]he importance of the familial relationship, to the individuals involved and to the society, stems from the emotional attachments that derive from the intimacy of daily association, and from the role it plays in 'promot[ing] a way of life' through the instruction of children as well as from the fact of blood relationship." Smith v. Organization of Foster Families for Equality and Reform, 431 U.S. 816, 844, 97 S.Ct. 2094, 2109–2110, 53 L.Ed.2d 14 (1977) (quoting Wisconsin v. Yoder, 406 U.S. 205, 231–233, 92 S.Ct. 1526, 1541–1542, 32 L.Ed.2d 15 (1972)).

---

16. In the balance of that paragraph Justice Stewart noted that the relation between a father and his natural child may acquire constitutional protection if the father enters into a traditional marriage with the mother or if "the actual relationship between father and child" is sufficient.

"The mother carries and bears the child, and in this sense her parental relationship is clear. The validity of the father's parental claims must be gauged by other measures. By tradition, the primary measure has been the legitimate familial relationship he creates with the child by marriage with the mother. By definition, the question before us can arise only when no such marriage has taken place. In some circumstances the actual relationship between father and child may suffice to create in the unwed father parental interests comparable to those of the married father. Cf. Stanley v. Illinois, supra. But here we are concerned with the rights the unwed father may have when his wishes and those of the mother are in conflict, and the child's best interests are served by a resolution in favor of the mother. It seems to me that the absence of a legal tie with the mother may in such circumstances appropriately place a limit on whatever substantive constitutional claims might otherwise exist by virtue of the father's actual relationship with the children."

Ibid.

The significance of the biological connection is that it offers the natural father an opportunity that no other male possesses to develop a relationship with his offspring. If he grasps that opportunity and accepts some measure of responsibility for the child's future, he may enjoy the blessings of the parent-child relationship and make uniquely valuable contributions to the child's development.[18] If he fails to do so, the Federal Constitution will not automatically compel a state to listen to his opinion of where the child's best interests lie.

In this case, we are not assessing the constitutional adequacy of New York's procedures for terminating a developed relationship. Appellant has never had any significant custodial, personal, or financial relationship with Jessica, and he did not seek to establish a legal tie until after she was two years old.[19] We are concerned only with whether New York has adequately protected his opportunity to form such a relationship.

The most effective protection of the putative father's opportunity to develop a relationship with his child is provided by the laws that authorize formal marriage and govern its consequences. But the availability of that protection is, of course, dependent on the will of both parents of the child. Thus, New York has adopted a special statutory scheme to protect the unmarried father's interest in assuming a responsible role in the future of his child.

After this Court's decision in *Stanley*, the New York Legislature appointed a special commission to recommend legislation that would accommodate both the interests of biological fathers in their children and the children's interest in prompt and certain adoption procedures. The commission recommended, and the legislature enacted, a statutory adoption scheme that automatically provides notice to seven categories of putative fathers who are likely to have assumed some responsibility for the care of their natural children.[20] If this scheme were likely to omit many responsi-

---

18. Of course, we need not take sides in the ongoing debate among family psychologists over the relative weight to be accorded biological ties and psychological ties, in order to recognize that a natural father who has played a substantial role in rearing his child has a greater claim to constitutional protection than a mere biological parent. New York's statutory scheme reflects these differences, guaranteeing notice to any putative father who is living openly with the child, and providing putative fathers who have never developed a relationship with the child the opportunity to receive notice simply by mailing a postcard to the putative father registry.

19. This case happens to involve an adoption by the husband of the natural mother, but we do not believe the natural father has any greater right to object to such an adoption than to an adoption by two total strangers. If anything, the balance of equities

tips the opposite way in a case such as this. In denying the putative father relief in *Quilloin*, we made an observation equally applicable here:

"Nor is this a case in which the proposed adoption would place the child with a new set of parents with whom the child had never before lived. Rather, the result of the adoption in this case is to give full recognition to a family unit already in existence, a result desired by all concerned, except appellant. Whatever might be required in other situations, we cannot say that the State was required in this situation to find anything more than that the adoption, and denial of legitimation, were in the 'best interests of the child.' " 434 U.S., at 255, 98 S.Ct., at 555.

20. In a report explaining the purpose of the 1976 Amendments to § 111–a of the New York Domestic Relations Law, the temble fathers, and if qualification for notice were beyond the control of an interested putative father, it might be thought procedurally inadequate. Yet, as all of the New York courts that reviewed this matter observed, the right to receive notice was completely within appellant's control. By mailing a postcard to the putative father registry, he could have guaranteed that he would receive notice of any proceedings to adopt Jessica. The possibility that he may have failed to do so because of his ignorance of the law cannot be a sufficient reason for criticizing the law itself. The New York legislature concluded that a more open-ended notice requirement would merely complicate the adoption process, threaten the privacy interests of unwed mothers, create the risk of unnecessary controversy, and impair the desired finality of adoption decrees. Regardless of whether we would have done likewise if we were legislators instead of judges, we surely cannot characterize the state's conclusion as arbitrary.[22]

Appellant argues, however, that even if the putative father's opportunity to establish a relationship with an illegitimate child is adequately protected by the New York statutory scheme in the normal case, he was nevertheless entitled to special notice because the court and the mother knew that he had filed an affiliation proceeding in another court. This argument amounts to nothing more than an indirect attack on the notice provisions of the New York statute. The legitimate state interests in facilitating the adoption of young children and having the adoption proceeding completed expeditiously that underlie the entire statutory scheme also justify a trial judge's determination to require all interested parties to adhere precisely to the procedural requirements of the statute. The Constitution does not require either a trial judge or a litigant to give special

porary state commission on child welfare that was responsible for drafting the legislation stated, in part:

> "The measure will dispel uncertainties by providing clear constitutional statutory guidelines for notice to fathers of out-of-wedlock children. It will establish a desired finality in adoption proceedings and will provide an expeditious method for child placement agencies of identifying those fathers who are entitled to notice through the creation of a registry of such fathers within the State Department of Social Services. Conversely, the bill will afford to concerned fathers of out-of-wedlock children a simple means of expressing their interest and protecting their rights to be notified and have an opportunity to be heard. It will also obviate an existing disparity of Appellate Division decisions by permitting such fathers to be petitioners in paternity proceedings.
>
> "The measure is intended to codify the minimum protections for the putative fa-

ther which *Stanley* would require. In so doing it reflects policy decisions to (a) codify constitutional requirements; (b) clearly establish, as early as possible in a child's life, the rights, interests and obligations of all parties; (c) facilitate prompt planning for the future of the child and permanence of his status; and (d) through the foregoing, promote the best interest of children."

22. Nor can we deem unconstitutionally arbitrary the state courts' conclusion that appellant's absence did not distort its analysis of Jessica's best interests. The adoption does not affect Jessica's relationship with her mother. It gives legal permanence to her relationship with her adoptive father, a relationship they had maintained for 21 months at the time the adoption order was entered. Appellant did not proffer any evidence to suggest that legal confirmation of the established relationship would be unwise; he did not even know the adoptive father.

notice to nonparties who are presumptively capable of asserting and protecting their own rights. Since the New York statutes adequately protected appellant's inchoate interest in establishing a relationship with Jessica, we find no merit in the claim that his constitutional rights were offended because the family court strictly complied with the notice provisions of the statute.

The Equal Protection Claim.

. . .

The legislation at issue in this case, sections 111 and 111a of the New York Domestic Relations Law, is intended to establish procedures for adoptions. Those procedures are designed to promote the best interests of the child, protect the rights of interested third parties, and ensure promptness and finality. To serve those ends, the legislation guarantees to certain people the right to veto an adoption and the right to prior notice of any adoption proceeding. The mother of an illegitimate child is always within that favored class, but only certain putative fathers are included. Appellant contends that the gender-based distinction is invidious.

As we noted above, the existence or non-existence of a substantial relationship between parent and child is a relevant criterion in evaluating both the rights of the parent and the best interests of the child. In Quilloin v. Walcott, supra, we noted that the putative father, like appellant, "ha[d] never shouldered any significant responsibility with respect to the daily supervision, education, protection, or care of the child. Appellant does not complain of his exemption from these responsibilities...." 434 U.S., at 256, 98 S.Ct., at 555. We therefore found that a Georgia statute that always required a mother's consent to the adoption of a child born out of wedlock, but required the father's consent only if he had legitimated the child, did not violate the Equal Protection Clause. Because, like the father in *Quilloin,* appellant has never established a substantial relationship with his daughter, the New York statutes at issue in this case did not operate to deny appellant equal protection.

We have held that these statutes may not constitutionally be applied in that class of cases where the mother and father are in fact similarly situated with regard to their relationship with the child. In Caban v. Mohammed, the Court held that it violated the Equal Protection Clause to grant the mother a veto over the adoption of a four-year-old girl and a six-year-old boy, but not to grant a veto to their father, who had admitted paternity and had participated in the rearing of the children. The Court made it clear, however, that if the father had not "come forward to participate in the rearing of his child, nothing in the Equal Protection Clause [would] preclude[ ] the State from withholding from him the privilege of vetoing the adoption of that child." 441 U.S., at 392, 99 S.Ct., at 1768.

Jessica's parents are not like the parents involved in *Caban.* Whereas appellee had a continuous custodial responsibility for Jessica, appellant never established any custodial, personal, or financial relationship with her. If one parent has an established custodial relationship with the child and the other parent has either abandoned or never established a relationship, the Equal Protection Clause does not prevent a state from according the two parents different legal rights.

The judgment of the New York Court of Appeals is

Affirmed.

■ JUSTICE WHITE, with whom JUSTICE MARSHALL and JUSTICE BLACKMUN join, dissenting.

. . .

It is axiomatic that "[t]he fundamental requirement of due process is the opportunity to be heard 'at a meaningful time and in a meaningful manner.'" Mathews v. Eldridge, 424 U.S. 319, 333, 96 S.Ct. 893, 902, 47 L.Ed.2d 18 (1976), quoting Armstrong v. Manzo, 380 U.S. 545, 552, 85 S.Ct. 1187, 1191, 14 L.Ed.2d 62 (1965). As Jessica's biological father, Lehr either had an interest protected by the Constitution or he did not.[1] If the entry of the adoption order in this case deprived Lehr of a constitutionally protected interest, he is entitled to notice and an opportunity to be heard before the order can be accorded finality.

According to Lehr, he and Jessica's mother met in 1971 and began living together in 1974. The couple cohabited for approximately 2 years, until Jessica's birth in 1976. Throughout the pregnancy and after the birth, Lorraine acknowledged to friends and relatives that Lehr was Jessica's father; Lorraine told Lehr that she had reported to the New York State Department of Social Services that he was the father.[2] Lehr visited Lorraine and Jessica in the hospital every day during Lorraine's confinement. According to Lehr, from the time Lorraine was discharged from the hospital, until August, 1978, she concealed her whereabouts from him. During this time Lehr never ceased his efforts to locate Lorraine and Jessica and achieved sporadic success until August, 1977, after which time he was unable to locate them at all. On those occasions when he did determine Lorraine's location, he visited with her and her children to the extent she was willing to permit it. When Lehr, with the aid of a detective agency, located Lorraine and Jessica in August, 1978, Lorraine was already married to Mr. Robertson. Lehr asserts that at this time he offered to provide financial assistance and to set up a trust fund for Jessica, but that Lorraine refused. Lorraine threatened Lehr with arrest unless he stayed away and refused to permit him to see Jessica. Thereafter Lehr retained

1. The majority correctly assumes that Lehr is in fact Jessica's father. Indeed, Lehr has admitted paternity and sought to establish a legal relationship with the child. It is also noteworthy that the mother has never denied that Lehr is the father.

2. Under 18 NYCRR § 369.2(b), recipients of public assistance in the Aid to Families with Dependent Children program are required as a condition of eligibility to provide the name and address of the child's father. Lorraine apparently received public assistance after Jessica's birth; it is unclear whether she received public assistance after that regulation went into effect in 1977.

counsel who wrote to Lorraine in early December, 1978, requesting that she permit Lehr to visit Jessica and threatening legal action on Lehr's behalf. On December 21, 1978, perhaps as a response to Lehr's threatened legal action, appellees commenced the adoption action at issue here.

. . .

Lehr's version of the "facts" paints a far different picture than that portrayed by the majority. The majority's recitation, that "[a]ppellant has never had any significant custodial, personal, or financial relationship with Jessica, and he did not seek to establish a legal tie until after she was two years old," obviously does not tell the whole story. Appellant has never been afforded an opportunity to present his case. The legitimation proceeding he instituted was first stayed, and then dismissed, on appellees' motions. Nor could appellant establish his interest during the adoption proceedings, for it is the failure to provide Lehr notice and an opportunity to be heard there that is at issue here. We cannot fairly make a judgment based on the quality or substance of a relationship without a complete and developed factual record. This case requires us to assume that Lehr's allegations are true—that but for the actions of the child's mother there would have been the kind of significant relationship that the majority concedes is entitled to the full panoply of procedural due process protections.[3]

I reject the peculiar notion that the only significance of the biological connection between father and child is that "it offers the natural father an opportunity that no other male possesses to develop a relationship with his offspring." A "mere biological relationship" is not as unimportant in determining the nature of liberty interests as the majority suggests.

"[T]he usual understanding of 'family' implies biological relationships, and most decisions treating the relation between parent and child have stressed this element." Smith v. Organization of Foster Families, supra, 431 U.S., at 843, 97 S.Ct., at 2109. The "biological connection" is itself a relationship that creates a protected interest. Thus the "nature" of the interest is the parent-child relationship; how well-developed that relationship has become goes to its "weight," not its "nature."[4] Whether Lehr's interest is entitled to constitutional protection does not entail a searching

---

3. In response to our decision in Caban v. Mohammed, 441 U.S. 380, 99 S.Ct. 1760, 60 L.Ed.2d 297 (1979), the statute governing the persons whose consent is necessary to an adoption has been amended to include certain unwed fathers. The State has recognized that an unwed father's failure to maintain an actual relationship or to communicate with a child will not deprive him of his right to consent if he was "prevented from doing so by the person or authorized agency having lawful custody of the child." N.Y.Dom.Rel. Law § 111(1)(d) (as amended by Chap. 575, L.1980). Thus, even the State recognizes that before a lesser standard can be applied con-

sistent with due process requirements, there must be a determination that there was no significant relationship and that the father was not prevented from forming such a relationship.

4. The majority's citation of *Quilloin* and *Caban* as examples that the Constitution does not require the same procedural protections for the interests of all unwed fathers is disingenuous. Neither case involved notice and opportunity to be heard. In both, the unwed fathers were notified and participated as parties in the adoption proceedings.

inquiry into the quality of the relationship but a simple determination of the *fact* that the relationship exists—a fact that even the majority agrees must be assumed to be established.

Beyond that, however, because there is no established factual basis on which to proceed, it is quite untenable to conclude that a putative father's interest in his child is lacking in substance, that the father in effect has abandoned the child, or ultimately that the father's interest is not entitled to the same minimum procedural protections as the interests of other putative fathers. Any analysis of the adequacy of the notice in this case must be conducted on the assumption that the interest involved here is as strong as that of *any* putative father. That is not to say that due process requires actual notice to every putative father or that adoptive parents or the State must conduct an exhaustive search of records or an intensive investigation before a final adoption order may be entered. The procedures adopted by the State, however, must at least represent a reasonable effort to determine the identity of the putative father and to give him adequate notice.

In this case, of course, there was no question about either the identity or the location of the putative father. The mother knew exactly who he was and both she and the court entering the order of adoption knew precisely where he was and how to give him actual notice that his parental rights were about to be terminated by an adoption order.[5] Lehr was entitled to due process, and the right to be heard is one of the fundamentals of that right, which "has little reality or worth unless one is informed that the matter is pending and can choose for himself whether to appear or default, acquiesce or contest." Schroeder v. City of New York, 371 U.S. 208, 212, 83 S.Ct. 279, 282, 9 L.Ed.2d 255 (1962), quoting Mullane v. Central Hanover Trust Co., 339 U.S. 306, 314, 70 S.Ct. 652, 657, 94 L.Ed. 865 (1950).

The State concedes this much but insists that Lehr has had all the process that is due to him. It relies on § 111–a, which designates seven categories of unwed fathers to whom notice of adoption proceedings must be given, including any unwed father who has filed with the State a notice of his intent to claim paternity. The State submits that it need not give notice to anyone who has not filed his name, as he is permitted to do, and who is not otherwise within the designated categories, even if his identity and interest are known or are reasonably ascertainable by the State.

I am unpersuaded by the State's position. In the first place, § 111–a defines six categories of unwed fathers to whom notice must be given even

---

5. Absent special circumstances, there is no bar to requiring the mother of an illegitimate child to divulge the name of the father when the proceedings at issue involve the permanent termination of the father's rights. Likewise, there is no reason not to require such identification when it is the spouse of the custodial parent who seeks to adopt the child. Indeed, the State now requires the mother to provide the identity of the father if she applies for financial benefits under the Aid to Families with Dependent Children Program. The state's obligation to provide notice to persons before their interests are permanently terminated cannot be a lesser concern than its obligation to assure that state funds are not expended when there exists a person upon whom the financial responsibility should fall.

though they have not placed their names on file pursuant to the section. Those six categories, however, do not include fathers such as Lehr who have initiated filiation proceedings, even though their identity and interest are as clearly and easily ascertainable as those fathers in the six categories. Initiating such proceedings necessarily involves a formal acknowledgment of paternity, and requiring the State to take note of such a case in connection with pending adoption proceedings would be a trifling burden, no more than the State undertakes when there is a final adjudication in a paternity action. Indeed, there would appear to be more reason to give notice to those such as Lehr who acknowledge paternity than to those who have been adjudged to be a father in a contested paternity action.

The State asserts that any problem in this respect is overcome by the seventh category of putative fathers to whom notice must be given, namely those fathers who have identified themselves in the putative father register maintained by the State. Since Lehr did not take advantage of this device to make his interest known, the State contends, he was not entitled to notice and a hearing even though his identity, location and interest were known to the adoption court prior to entry of the adoption order. I have difficulty with this position. First, it represents a grudging and crabbed approach to due process. The State is quite willing to give notice and a hearing to putative fathers who have made themselves known by resorting to the putative fathers' register. It makes little sense to me to deny notice and hearing to a father who has not placed his name in the register but who has unmistakably identified himself by filing suit to establish his paternity and has notified the adoption court of his action and his interest. I thus need not question the statutory scheme on its face. Even assuming that Lehr would have been foreclosed if his failure to utilize the register had somehow disadvantaged the State, he effectively made himself known by other means, and it is the sheerest formalism to deny him a hearing because he informed the State in the wrong manner.

No state interest is substantially served by denying Lehr adequate notice and a hearing. The State no doubt has an interest in expediting adoption proceedings to prevent a child from remaining unduly long in the custody of the State or foster parents. But this is not an adoption involving a child in the custody of an authorized state agency....

The State's undoubted interest in the finality of adoption orders likewise is not well served by a procedure that will deny notice and a hearing to a father whose identity and location are known. As this case well illustrates, denying notice and a hearing to such a father may result in years of additional litigation and threaten the reopening of adoption proceedings and the vacation of the adoption....

Because in my view the failure to provide Lehr with notice and an opportunity to be heard violated rights guaranteed him by the Due Process Clause, I need not address the question whether § 111–a violates the Equal Protection Clause by discriminating between categories of unwed fathers or by discriminating on the basis of gender.

Respectfully, I dissent.

NOTE

In Matter of Jessica XX, 54 N.Y.2d 417, 446 N.Y.S.2d 20, 430 N.E.2d 896 (1981), the Court of Appeals of New York had refused to vacate the final order of adoption and reopen the adoption proceeding. In the opinion of the court, Jones, J., explained that the statute "was intended to codify the minimum protections which *Stanley* would require and to achieve finality as early as possible."

Robert O. v. Russell K.

Court of Appeals of New York, 1992.
80 N.Y.2d 254, 590 N.Y.S.2d 37, 604 N.E.2d 99.

■ SIMONS, JUDGE.

Petitioner, an unwed father, seeks to vacate a final order approving the adoption of his son. . . .

The courts below found the following facts.

In December 1987, petitioner Robert O. and Carol A. became engaged and petitioner moved into Carol's home. Disagreements arose, however, and in February 1988, petitioner moved out and terminated all contact with Carol. At that time Carol was pregnant but she did not tell petitioner, apparently because she believed he would feel she was trying to coerce him into marriage. Over the next few weeks, Carol approached her friends, respondents Russell K. and his wife Joanne K., and obtained their agreement to adopt her child. On October 1, 1988, Carol gave birth to a boy, who was delivered to respondents upon her discharge from the hospital. Carol later executed a judicial consent and, in May 1989, the adoption was finalized.

Carol was never asked by the adoption court to identify the father. She did sign a statement indicating, accurately, that there was no one entitled to notice of the adoption under Domestic Relations Law § 111–a or whose consent was required under Domestic Relations Law § 111.

Between the time Carol and petitioner separated in March 1988 and January 1990, petitioner made no attempt to contact Carol although she continued to live in the same house and, as the courts below found, did nothing to conceal her whereabouts or her pregnancy. In January 1990, petitioner and Carol reconciled and subsequently married. In March 1990—nearly 18 months after the birth and 10 months after the completed adoption—Carol informed petitioner that the child had been born. In a belated effort to meet the statutory requirements for notice and consent, petitioner reimbursed Carol for her medical expenses, filed with the Putative Father Registry, and commenced this proceeding to vacate the adoption (see, Domestic Relations Law §§ 111, 111–a).

Family Court rejected petitioner's claim that there had been either fraud or concealment of a material fact in the adoption. In addition, it concluded that petitioner had no constitutional right to notice of the adoption proceedings or to veto or consent to the adoption. The Appellate Division unanimously affirmed. . . .

[Based on the trial court's factual findings, the court rejected petitioner's claim of fraud through deception or concealment of Carol and respondents.]

Petitioner concedes that the applicable statutes do not require notice to one in his position or require his consent to the adoption. Domestic Relations Law § 111–a(2) provides the father of a child born outside wedlock can qualify for notice of an adoption proceeding in any one of several ways: by having been adjudicated to be the father, by filing a timely notice of intent to claim paternity, by living openly with the mother and child and holding himself out as the father, by having been named the father in a sworn statement by the mother, by having married the mother subsequent to the birth, or by filing with the Putative Father Registry. As petitioner notes, these actions generally presume that the father knows he has a child before the adoption is finalized and he had no such knowledge.

Domestic Relations Law § 111(1)(e), the consent statute relevant here because the child was younger than six months at the time he was placed for adoption, did not require the petitioner's consent because he had not held himself out as the father or met the other statutory requirements.[3]

Petitioner contends that because these New York laws fail to require notice and consent from a father in his position, they deny biological fathers a constitutional liberty interest. He maintains that before an adoption is finalized, the courts must be required to resolve the factual issue of who the biological father is and determine whether he has had sufficient opportunity to establish a relationship with the child, in part by requiring the mother to testify as to paternity.

The nature of the constitutional interest possessed by unwed fathers has been addressed previously by both the Supreme Court and this Court.

The Supreme Court, beginning with Stanley v. Illinois, 405 U.S. 645, 92 S.Ct. 1208, 31 L.Ed.2d 551, has recognized that some unwed fathers, by their conduct in relation to their children, enjoy parental rights protected by the Federal Constitution (see, Quilloin v. Walcott, 434 U.S. 246, 98 S.Ct. 549, 54 L.Ed.2d 511; Caban v. Mohammed, 441 U.S. 380, 99 S.Ct. 1760, 60 L.Ed.2d 297; Lehr v. Robertson, 463 U.S. 248, 103 S.Ct. 2985, 77 L.Ed.2d 614). The guiding principle has been that the biological connection between father and child is not sufficient, in and of itself, to create a protected

---

3. We struck down that section as unconstitutional in Matter of Raquel Marie X., 76 N.Y.2d 387, 406–407, 559 N.Y.S.2d 855, 559 N.E.2d 418, after this adoption became final, because the provision of section 111(1)(e) that premised the father's right to consent on his living with the mother was not sufficiently related to the State's legitimate interest in the quality of the relationship between the father and the child and it allowed the mother to block a willing father's attempt to assert his parental rights. By referring to that decision throughout the opinion, we do not mean to imply that Raquel Marie has any retrospective application to this case or to adoptions finalized before it was announced. It does not. Its reasoning, however, provides a useful starting point for analysis in the case before us.

interest for the father. Only if the unwed father "grasps the opportunity" to form a relationship with his child will the inchoate right created by biology blossom into a protected liberty interest under the Constitution. The Lehr Court stated it thus: "When an unwed father demonstrates a full commitment to the responsibilities of parenthood * * * his interest in personal contact with his child acquires substantial protection under the Due Process Clause * * * But the mere existence of a biological link does not merit equivalent constitutional protection" (Lehr v. Robertson, supra, at 261, 103 S.Ct. at 2993).

We subsequently followed this reasoning to hold that the unwed father of a newborn infant has a right to veto an adoption if he manifests a willingness to assume full custody of the child (Matter of Raquel Marie X., 76 N.Y.2d 387, 559 N.Y.S.2d 855, 559 N.E.2d 418). In making that determination of willingness, courts are to consider such factors as whether the father paid the medical bills related to the pregnancy, whether he held himself out as the father, and, "[p]erhaps most significantly", whether his manifestations of willingness took place promptly (id., at 408, 559 N.Y.S.2d 855, 559 N.E.2d 418). Like the notice statute, the standards set forth in Raquel Marie presuppose that the father knows he is a father.

Manifestly, the unwed father of an infant placed for adoption immediately at birth faces a unique dilemma should he desire to establish his parental rights. Any opportunity he has to shoulder the responsibility of parenthood may disappear before he has a chance to grasp it, no matter how willing he is to do so. Accordingly, we have acknowledged that in some instances the Constitution protects an unwed father's opportunity to develop a relationship with his infant son or daughter. This constitutional right to the opportunity to develop a qualifying relationship does not extend to all unwed fathers or arise from the mere fact of biology. The right exists only for the unwed father who manifests his willingness to assume full custody of the child and does so promptly.

Petitioner asks us to extend Raquel Marie's protection to him—i.e., to find that the Constitution also protects the custodial opportunity of the "unknowing" unwed father who does nothing to manifest his parental willingness before placement because he is unaware of the child's existence. His claim necessarily supposes the existence of some liberty interest that he has and that the State has improperly denied. Absent such interest, our inquiry is finished and we need inquire no further into the constitutional adequacy of New York's adoption procedures.

Petitioner finds evidence that this liberty interest exists from a statement in Lehr and our holding in Matter of Baby Girl S., 141 Misc.2d 905, 535 N.Y.S.2d 676 (the companion case to Raquel Marie). In Lehr, a New York unwed father who had not been actively involved in his child's life commenced a paternity action in one county, unaware that the mother and her husband had initiated adoption proceedings in another. The adoption court, though aware of the paternity action, proceeded to finalize the adoption. The Supreme Court rejected the unwed father's argument that he was entitled to notice, noting that he could have guaranteed his right to notice by registering with the Putative Father Registry (Lehr v. Robertson, supra, at 264, 103 S.Ct. at 2995). The Court stated in passing, and petitioner seizes this as central to his argument, "if qualification for notice were beyond the control of an interested putative father, [New York's statutory scheme] might be thought procedurally inadequate" (id., at 264, 103 S.Ct. at 2994).[4]

In Raquel Marie, we followed that theme, finding that the father in a companion case, Matter of Baby Girl S. (see, 141 Misc.2d 905, 535 N.Y.S.2d 676), had gained a protected liberty interest, even though he failed to meet the statutory requirements of Domestic Relations Law § 111(1)(e), because he had done "everything possible to manifest and establish his parental responsibility". His failure to meet the statutory requirements promptly was due not to his own failings but to the concerted actions of the mother and the adopting parents to frustrate his efforts. Under those circumstances, we held that "a father who has promptly taken every available avenue to demonstrate that he is willing and able to enter into the fullest possible relationship with his under-six-month-old child should have an equally fully protected interest in preventing termination of the relationship by strangers, even if he has not as yet actually been able to form that relationship".

Petitioner analogizes his situation to that of the father in Baby Girl S. In his rendering of the events, as soon as he became aware of the child's existence, he manifested his willingness to assume full parental responsibility by taking those steps available to get legal custody of the child. Petitioner correctly reads Lehr and Raquel Marie to stand for the proposition that an unwed father who has promptly done all that he could to protect his parental interest is entitled to constitutional protection. His argument falters, however, in its conclusion that he has met that standard.

We made clear in our decision in Raquel Marie that the timing of the father's actions is the "most significant" element in determining whether an unwed father has created a liberty interest. States have a legitimate concern for prompt and certain adoption procedures and their determination of the rights of unwed fathers need not be blind to the "vital importance" of creating adoption procedures possessed of "promptness and finality," promoting the best interests of the child, and protecting the rights of interested third parties like adoptive parents (Lehr v. Robertson, supra, n. 25). Recognizing those competing interests—all of which are jeopardized when an unwed father is allowed to belatedly assert his rights—we stressed in Raquel Marie that the period in which the biological father must manifest his parental interest is limited in duration: if the father's actions are untimely, the State can deny a right of consent. In Raquel Marie we limited the period in which the father must act to the six

---

4. Lehr dealt solely with the procedural issue of notice under Domestic Relations Law § 111–a and not with consent under section 111. Consequently, it is not clear that even had the father there succeeded in his argument he would have received anything more than the right to be heard on the best interests of the child at the adoption proceeding (see, Domestic Relations Law § 111–a[3]).

continuing months immediately preceding the child's placement for adoption.

To conclude that petitioner acted promptly once he became aware of the child is to fundamentally misconstrue whose timetable is relevant. Promptness is measured in terms of the baby's life not by the onset of the father's awareness. The demand for prompt action by the father at the child's birth is neither arbitrary nor punitive, but instead a logical and necessary outgrowth of the State's legitimate interest in the child's need for early permanence and stability. The competing interests at stake in an adoption—and the complications presented by petitioner's position—are clearly illustrated here: nearly a year and a half after the baby went to live with the adoptive parents, and more than 10 months after they were told by the court that the baby was legally theirs, petitioner sought to rearrange those lives by initiating his present legal action.

During the first months of his son's life, petitioner's only connection to the infant was biological. That he now asserts that he was willing to be a custodial parent, had he only known, adds nothing to his argument, even if we accept the dubious proposition that a willingness so abstract and amorphous has some legal significance. Something more than an assertion of custody is required. There must be manifestation through action on the part of the unwed father. Absent that, the biological link of the father is insufficient to create a constitutionally protected interest, and petitioner's due process claim fails.

Petitioner's argument confuses the meaning of the constitutionally protected "opportunity" we recognized in Raquel Marie. The opportunity at issue there, and the one we found constitutionally protected, was the opportunity "to develop a qualifying relationship with the infant" (Matter of Raquel Marie X., supra, at 401, 559 N.Y.S.2d 855, 559 N.E.2d 418). That opportunity arose and became protected only after the father had manifested his willingness to be a custodial parent. The opportunity petitioner seeks to protect is different and quite separate. It is the opportunity to manifest his willingness. No one, however, let alone any State actor, prevented petitioner from finding out about Carol's pregnancy. His inaction, however regrettable and with whatever unfortunate consequences, was solely attributable to him. Nothing in Raquel Marie or the Supreme Court decisions on which it rests suggests that the protections of constitutional due process must or should be extended to him under these circumstances.

The concurrence analyzes the case somewhat differently. It takes what the Court has referred to as an "opportunity" and relabels it an "interest." While conceding that it is an interest arising exclusively from the father's biological connection to the child, the concurrence believes that in some instances this "interest" would nonetheless warrant constitutional protection under its due process analysis. It concludes that the biological father must lose in this case because of the "sensitive balancing" of interests entailed in a due process inquiry. However, a due process analysis properly begins by defining the nature of the liberty interest claimed. Here there is only the biological connection. Whether that gives rise to an "opportunity" or a "parental interest," the cases make clear that when the State decides to finalize the adoption the father has no right that requires balancing. While the outcome is the same in this case, the implication of the concurrence's analysis is that under other circumstances, where the balance is different, the State may be compelled under due process principles to extend protection to the biological father. That result would run counter to the established principle that biology alone is not enough to warrant constitutional protection. But what is more troubling, despite the concurrence's assurances to the contrary, is that a holding that this "right" requires due process recognition would logically and inevitably lead to inhibiting a State's interest in prompt and efficient efforts to finalize adoption proceedings and limiting a mother's right to privacy.... Indeed, even if it were constitutionally permissible to compel disclosure, the State has not chosen to do so and the Constitution does not compel it.

Finally, the Court's decision is not, as the concurrence maintains, contrary to the holding in Raquel Marie. The Court does not hold today that the biological father's ability to assert an interest was "completely extinguished once the State acted by proceeding with the adoption". Had petitioner promptly manifested his willingness to take on parental responsibilities, he, like the unwed father in Baby Girl S., would have enjoyed the protection of the Constitution even though the State had begun adoption proceedings. The concurrence similarly errs when it attempts to read Raquel Marie as holding that " 'where a child is placed for adoption before any real relationship can exist,' an unwed father has some continuing interest". It overlooks the fact that the interest spoken of in the relevant portion of Raquel Marie supra, at 401–402, 559 N.Y.S.2d 855, 559 N.E.2d 418 is nothing more than the "biological parental interest"—i.e., the opportunity, of limited duration, to manifest a willingness to be a parent. As Raquel Marie made clear, and we reaffirm today, that opportunity becomes protected only if grasped.

. . .

... [T]he order of the Appellate Division should be affirmed....

■ Titone, Judge (concurring).

I agree that due process does not require the unraveling of a 10–month-old adoption at the behest of a biological father whose identity was unknown and unknowable at the time the adoption became final, but I cannot agree that in all circumstances "biology alone is not enough to warrant constitutional protection". Additionally, I cannot agree with the majority's reliance on the purported fault of this biological father in "fail[ing] to take any steps to discover the pregnancy or the birth of the child" until after the child was adopted. In my view, the adoption should be left undisturbed despite petitioner's competing interest in the child not because petitioner is blameworthy, but rather because the strong public policies favoring the finality of adoptions outweigh the interest of a biological father who, through no fault of his own, has been deprived of the opportunity to "manifest and establish his parental responsibility" toward the child.

. . .

I would submit, most respectfully, that a rule which places the onus on the man to investigate whether a woman with whom he is no longer intimate has become pregnant is simply out of step with modern mores and the realities of contemporary heterosexual liaisons. In this age of readily accessible birth control devices, men have greatly diminished reason, in most circumstances, to suspect that a woman with whom they have been intimate has become pregnant. Accordingly, there is little to prompt them to pursue their former lovers to satisfy themselves on that point. Moreover, a rule that requires men to foist continued contact on women with whom they are no longer involved overlooks women's interest in preserving their own privacy after the relationship has been terminated.

Contrary to the majority's suggestion my conclusion that the law should not hold petitioner accountable for failing to discover his former fiancee's pregnancy does not lead me to the further conclusion that "the protections of constitutional due process must or should be extended to him under these circumstances". Although petitioner is innocent of any untoward neglect and, in fact, had a constitutionally cognizable interest in a parental relationship with his biological child, that interest does not outweigh the State's countervailing interest in ensuring the finality of adoptions and, thus, it was not entitled to constitutional protection.

The central importance of finality in the adoption process has been recognized by both the Legislature and the courts. While the State must make every effort to protect the rights of biological parents in adoption proceedings (see, e.g., Lehr v. Robertson, 463 U.S. 248, 103 S.Ct. 2985, 77 L.Ed.2d 614; Caban v. Mohammed, 441 U.S. 380, 99 S.Ct. 1760, 60 L.Ed.2d 297), there also must come a point where the matter is deemed irrevocably closed, so that the parties can go forward with their lives, secure in the certainty that their legal and familial status can no longer be disturbed.

The importance of finality in the lives of the children involved in the adoption process is so obvious as to require little elaboration. One of the most crucial elements of a healthy childhood is the availability of a stable home in which each family member has a secure and definite place. In addition to the stake of the adopted child, the adoptive family is unquestionably adversely affected by any lingering uncertainty about the permanence of the adoption. . . .

If petitioner's position were to be embraced by the Court, the critical goal of finality could never be achieved for the substantial number of children whose biological fathers have not been apprised of their existence. Such children—as well as their adoptive families—would be forever relegated to a state of legal limbo in which their familial relationship would remain subject to the possibility that their biological fathers might suddenly learn of their birth and appear to reclaim them. Clearly, such a result is one that cannot be tolerated in a legal system that concerns itself with humane values.

While due-process principles may give unmarried fathers the right to an opportunity to develop relationships with their biological children, there is nothing in the State or Federal Constitutions that compels States to protect that right at all costs. To the contrary, the due-process inquiry necessarily entails a sensitive balancing of the biological parents' interests against "[t]he legitimate state interests in facilitating the adoption of young children and having the adoption proceeding completed expeditiously" (Lehr v. Robertson, supra, at 265, 103 S.Ct. at 2995).

In situations such as this one, the interests of the biological father are relatively slight, since he has not developed a relationship with the child. On the other hand, his interests cannot simply be disregarded or deemed extinguished, since, unlike the biological fathers in Lehr ... and Quilloin ..., petitioner had no realistic opportunity to manifest his parental commitment and, accordingly, cannot be treated as though he knowingly relinquished that opportunity.

Nonetheless, petitioner's interest is not entitled to constitutional protection, since it simply cannot be accommodated without sacrificing the paramount State interest in finality. When the slender interest petitioner has is compared to this very weighty competing interest of the State, we are duty bound to opt for a legal rule that promotes the former, even though that rule may well omit many potentially responsible fathers in petitioner's position (see, Lehr v. Robertson, supra, 103 S.Ct. at 2995).*

. . .

The third societal interest that the majority identifies—efficiency—stands on an entirely different footing. While perhaps desirable, efficiency is simply not, by itself, the kind of goal that warrants the solicitude we might give to the privacy rights of unwed mothers or the finality of adoptions....

NOTE

Would you have considered *Lehr* a good case in which to test the constitutionality of New York's putative father registry statute? What, if anything, does the *Lehr* decision seem to indicate regarding the probable

---

* The difference between the majority's position and my own is not simply a matter of how the biological father's "interest" is characterized or labelled. Rather, we differ on the more fundamental question of whether the father's interests arising from his biological connection, however they are characterized, were completely extinguished once the State acted by proceeding with the adoption.... Like the majority, I would answer that question in the negative here, where adoption proceedings had already begun and, in fact, been finalized before petitioner learned of the child's existence and came forward. However, unlike the majority, I would not go so far as to assert the sweeping conclusion that biology alone can never be enough to warrant some constitutional protection, regardless of the context or the consequences. There is simply nothing in the relevant case law that requires such an extreme position.

interpretation and application of other schemes designed to respond to problems created for adoption by the *Stanley* opinion? For further discussion *see* Elizabeth Buchanan, *The Constitutional Rights of Unwed Fathers Before and After Lehr v. Robertson*, 45 OHIO ST.L.J. 313 (1984).

D.A. v. D.R.L.

Supreme Court of Alaska, 1986.
727 P.2d 768.

■ RABINOWITZ, CHIEF JUSTICE.

D.A. brings this appeal from the superior court's denial of his petition to adopt L.R.A. In his petition D.A. alleged that L.R.A.'s natural father failed significantly without justifiable cause to meaningfully communicate with her for a period of over one year, thereby obviating the necessity of obtaining the natural father's consent to the adoption.[1] The child's natural father, D.R.L., failed to appear at the first scheduled hearing on the adoption petition. At that time, Judge Gonzales ruled that notice to the natural father of the filing of the adoption petition and of the time and place of hearing was inadequate to meet the provisions of AS 25.23.100. The adoption hearing was continued until the natural father could be served with adequate notice. Subsequently, a second hearing was held before Judge Cutler.

D.R.L. and L.A. were married in December 1980 and L.R.A. was born in June 1981. The couple separated in September 1982, and were divorced on December 20, 1982. D.R.L. visited his daughter twice in the three-month period between the separation and the divorce. In the months following the divorce, D.R.L. visited his daughter about once a month until his former wife married D.A. in October 1983. From October 1983 until July 1984, except for February through April when the new family vacationed in Arizona, D.R.L. telephoned L.A. approximately once a month to inquire about L.R.A. or to arrange visits to see her—none of which he carried out. From July through November 1984, D.R.L. did not contact L.A. In November 1984, D.A. filed the subject petition to adopt L.R.A.

D.A. testified that during his marriage to L.A., D.R.L. had sent no Christmas or birthday cards to L.R.A. On cross-examination L.A. revealed that D.R.L. had requested and been refused several visits with L.R.A. L.A. testified that the reason for these refusals was that she was uncomfortable being alone with her former husband and that D.A. (her present husband) was not at home when D.R.L. requested the visits.

At the conclusion of the cross-examination of D.A. the superior court asked the natural father's counsel if he wished to have D.R.L. testify.

---

1. AS 25.23.050(a)(2)(A) provides that:

Consent to adoption is not required of . . .

(2) a parent of a child in the custody of another, if the parent for a period of at least one year has failed significantly without justifiable cause . . . (A) to communicate meaningfully with the child. . . .

D.R.L.'s counsel declined to present any evidence, instead moving for a directed verdict. This motion was based on two grounds. First, for three months of the one year and two weeks that had elapsed between D.R.L.'s last visit with L.R.A. and the filing of the petition for adoption, the new family had been in Arizona. Second, the petitioners failed to show by clear and convincing evidence that there was no justifiable cause for the natural father's failure to meaningfully communicate with L.R.A.

The superior court granted the motion and dismissed the petition for adoption. It held that petitioners had not shown that the natural father's failure to communicate was without justifiable cause, for several reasons. First, the court considered the fact that D.A. and L.A. took the child to Arizona for three months of the year, and found that this absence made it less reasonable for the natural father to exercise his visitation rights. Second, it considered the fact that L.R.A. was only between two and three years old during the year in question, an age which made meaningful communication through phone calls or letters difficult. Third, it considered the fact that during 1983, the natural father had seen L.R.A. almost every month. Finally, the court considered the youth of the divorced natural parents, and its effect on the difficult situation of the natural father visiting L.R.A. in the presence of his ex-wife and her new husband.

. . .

Appellants contend that the superior court erred in denying their petition for adoption. We conclude that the superior court's decision should be affirmed.

As indicated above, Alaska's forfeiture of consent statute provides in part that consent to adoption is not required of a noncustodial parent if that parent for a period of at least one year has failed significantly without justifiable cause to communicate meaningfully with the child.[3] In past decisions this court has strictly construed these statutory consent provisions, in order to protect the rights of the natural parent. S.M.K. v. R.G.G., 702 P.2d 620, 623 (Alaska 1985); R.N.T. v. J.R.G., 666 P.2d 1036, 1040 (Alaska 1983); D.L.J. v. W.D.R., 635 P.2d 834, 837 (Alaska 1981); Matter of Adoption of K.M.M., 611 P.2d 84, 87–88 (Alaska 1980). We also have read the term "meaningful communication" broadly. See K.M.M., 611 P.2d at 88. Contra In re: J.J.J., 718 P.2d 948 (Alaska 1986). Thus, in circumstances where the child is too young to read or communicate over the telephone, we have relaxed the requirement of meaningful communication under the "without justifiable cause" language of AS 25.23.050(a)(2)(A). S.M.K., 702 P.2d at 624.[4]

Considering that petitioners had the burden of proving by clear and convincing evidence that the natural father failed to communicate meaningfully without justifiable cause for a period of one year, we hold that the superior court's findings of fact, which were basic to its conclusion that the

---

3. For the test of AS 25.23.050(a)(2)(A) see note 1, supra.

4. See also, R.N.T., 666 P.2d at 1039; D.L.J., 635 P.2d at 840.

petition should be denied, are not clearly erroneous.[5] In other words, we conclude that there is an adequate evidentiary basis for the superior court's findings relating to the issue of the natural father's justification for failing to communicate with his child. In this regard, we hold that the following controlling findings of fact were not clearly erroneous: the superior court's finding that the natural father's failure to communicate was justified since the child was too young to talk on the telephone or understand gifts or letters from her father; the natural mother's postponement of certain requested visitations and the natural father's emotional difficulty in visiting with the new family justified his failure to communicate with the child;[7] and the new family's absence from Alaska for three months during the critical year period made it less reasonable for the natural father to exercise his visitation rights.[8]

The superior court's dismissal of the petition for adoption is AFFIRMED.

. . .

■ MOORE, JUSTICE, dissenting.

I would reverse and remand this case for two reasons. First, the trial court ordered dismissal of the adoption petition without regard for the procedural requirements of Rule 41(b), Alaska R.Civ.P. The plurality opinion does not address this procedural error. Second, the trial court did not apply the correct decisional law regarding what constitutes justifiable cause for noncommunication. The plurality glosses over this error by ignoring our decision in In re J.J.J., 718 P.2d 948 (Alaska 1986). The plurality's suggestion that D.L.'s failure to communicate was justified by the emotional difficulty of visiting his child in the home of his ex-wife and her new husband is diametrically opposed to our holding in *J.J.J.*, Id. at 953. Furthermore, I cannot agree with the plurality's inference that a child's absence from the state automatically tolls the one-year statutory period.

---

5. See S.M.K., 702 P.2d 620; R.N.T., 666 P.2d 1036; D.L.J., 635 P.2d 884. In S.M.K., 702 P.2d at 624 n. 11, we said in part:

This court has developed the following heightened burden of proof for the consent exceptions:

[T]he adoptive parent has the burden of proving by clear and convincing evidence that the natural parent failed significantly to communicate with ... the child. Because only the natural parent could explain why he or she failed to communicate with or to provide support for the child, fairness requires that he or she then bear the burden of coming forward with evidence of justifiable cause for such omissions before justification be-

comes an issue.... Thereafter, the burden of proving by clear and convincing evidence that the natural parent's omissions were not justified rests with the adoptive parent. On review, we will subject the findings to the clearly erroneous test generally used for review of questions of fact.

7. See K.M.M., 611 P.2d at 88 (finding emotional trauma of natural father who saw ex-wife living with former best friend to be justifiable cause for failure to visit children).

8. A failure to communicate must be willful and take place during a period when the parent is able to communicate with the child. S.M.K., 702 P.2d at 624; R.N.T., 666 P.2d at 1039.

After L.A. and her husband had testified, the trial court asked the natural father's counsel if he wished to have D.L. testify. D.L.'s counsel did not, as the plurality states, "decline to present any evidence." Rather, counsel did not answer the court's question but instead moved for a "directed verdict." Since this was a non-jury proceeding and the petitioner had completed his case in chief, counsel's motion should have been termed one for involuntary dismissal under Civil Rule 41(b).[1]

The trial court erred in granting the motion and dismissing the petition for adoption. Our decisions under Civil Rule 41(b) hold that the motion should be denied if the petitioner has made out a prima facie case based on unimpeached evidence.

. . .

In an adoption case based on AS 25.23.050(a)(2)(A), the petitioner only need show that the natural parent failed significantly to meaningfully communicate with his or her child for a period of over one year to avoid an involuntary dismissal. The natural parent then must come forward with evidence of a justifiable cause for such omissions. Thereafter, the adoptive parent must prove by clear and convincing evidence that the natural parent's omissions were not justified. Even if the evidence establishes that the failure to communicate was not justified and the natural parent's consent to adoption is therefore unnecessary, the court still may decline to order an adoption if it would not be in the child's best interests.[3] The trial court, however, did not reach this issue because it found that justifiable cause existed for D.L.'s failure to communicate.

Here, viewing the uncontested evidence in the light most favorable to the petitioners, a prima facie case clearly was made out that D.L. had failed significantly to meaningfully communicate with L.R.A. for a period in excess of one year.

. . .

Because the trial court's role in deciding the Rule 41(b) motion was limited to determining whether petitioners had presented evidence sufficient to establish a prima facie case of noncommunication, the court erred in granting a dismissal. The case should be remanded for the purpose of completing the trial or, if necessary, for a new trial.

---

1. Alaska R.Civ.P. 41(b) provides in part:

> After the plaintiff, in an action tried by the court without a jury, has completed the presentation of his evidence, the defendant, without waiving his right to offer evidence in the event the motion is not granted, may move for a dismissal on the ground that upon the facts and the law the plaintiff has shown no right to relief. The court as trier of the facts may then determine them and render judgment against the plaintiff or may decline to render any judgment until the close of all the evidence.

3. AS 25.23.120(c) provides: If at the conclusion of the hearing the court determines that the required consents have been obtained or excused *and that the adoption is in the best interest of the person to be adopted,* it may issue a final decree of adoption. (Emphasis added.)

Notwithstanding the procedural error, a remand is necessary in any event because the trial court did not apply the correct decisional law. The court held that petitioners had not shown that D.L.'s failure to communicate was without justifiable cause, citing several reasons. The reasons included: the child's absence from the state for three months of the year, which made it less reasonable for the natural father to exercise his visitation rights; the child's young age, which made meaningful communication through phone calls or letters difficult; and the emotionally difficult situation of D.L. visiting his child in the home of his ex-wife and her new husband.

The plurality affirms these findings as not clearly erroneous and holds that petitioners did not prove that the natural father failed to meaningfully communicate without justifiable cause for a period of one year. In so holding, the plurality flatly contradicts controlling decisional law. In *J.J.J.* we specifically stated that

> in order for a noncustodial parent to block a stepparent adoption, he or she must have maintained *meaningful* contact with a child, . . . unless prevented from doing so by circumstances beyond the noncustodial parent's control. Circumstances resulting from the noncustodial parent's own conduct cannot excuse such a parent's significant failure to provide support or maintain meaningful communication. Moreover, *failure to support or to maintain contact with a child should not be excused by the emotional antagonism or awkwardness that may exist between former spouses.*

J.J.J., 718 P.2d at 953 (emphasis added in last sentence).

We recognize the emotional trauma that may be involved when a noncustodial parent visits a child in the home of a former spouse who has remarried. However, there are ways to avoid this situation, such as visitation in a neutral setting. A child's need for parental contact is simply too important to justify a parent's failure to meaningfully communicate for this reason. Under our case law, the trial court clearly erred in considering this factor as justification for D.L.'s noncommunication.

I also am troubled by the plurality's treatment of the issue of the child's absence from the state. To the extent that the plurality infers that such an absence could automatically toll the one-year statutory period, I strongly disagree. If the statute is tolled automatically when a custodial parent takes a child from the state, a stepparent in many instances could never adopt a stepchild even though the noncustodial natural parent remaining in Alaska had essentially forgotten about the child.

A court could, however, properly consider a child's absence from the state when determining whether there was justification for a parent's noncommunication. If the custodial parent concealed the child's location or otherwise affirmatively hindered visitation, or the noncustodial parent lacked the financial ability to travel to visit his or her child, these factors could properly be considered when deciding the justification issue.

Here, the record is silent as to whether D.L. knew his daughter's address in Arizona, whether he had inquired, or whether the information had been withheld. Therefore, the proper disposition of this case would be to remand with instructions for the court to consider such factors when deciding whether D.L.'s failure to communicate was justified.

■ COMPTON, JUSTICE, dissenting.

I concur with the remarks made by Justice Moore. However, I believe one matter warrants further discussion.

Most of the plurality opinion can be explained by its refusal to accept the holding in In the Matter of J.J.J., 718 P.2d 948 (Alaska 1986). Less explicable and very troubling is its apparent acknowledgment that L.R.A.'s brief absence from the state constitutes justifiable cause for D.R.L.'s failure to communicate meaningfully with her.

L.R.A. was between two years eight months and two years ten months of age when she was visiting in Arizona. While we would all agree that it is a very rare child who can read at that age, it is equally obvious that such a child can talk on the telephone, for instance. Of course, if D.R.L. does not call L.R.A., her capability in that regard is of no consequence. There is no suggestion that D.R.L. did not know where his daughter was during her absence from the state. It appears uncontested that there was no communication between them during this period. There is no evidence that D.R.L. even tried to communicate with her during this period. Further, the opinion merely notes that the family's absence from Alaska made it "less reasonable for the natural father to exercise his visitation right." Yet nothing in our statutes or decisional law equates exercise of visitation rights with meaningful communication.

Stripped of its trappings, the critical factor that leads to the result here is the mere absence of L.R.A. from the state. This is new law. No authority is cited to support it. No reasoning is advanced to justify it.

This court should not adopt a rule that mere absence from the state tolls in some manner the one year period, and thus excuses a non-custodial parent's failure to communicate meaningfully with his or her child. If by leaving the state for whatever benign reason the period is tolled, a stepparent may never be able to adopt a stepchild, even though for all intents and purposes the non-custodial parent has forgotten about the child. Stepparents who move from the state are in jeopardy of losing the opportunity to adopt a stepchild for years. Those who leave only for a vacation will be in a quandary whether a trial court will toll the time they are "outside." And if the non-custodial parent must move elsewhere, that will make it "less reasonable for the natural father to exercise his visitation rights." Presumably tolling will result.

Since the absence from the state in this case was only temporary, and no malignant motive is remotely suggested, it should be sufficient to say that the absence does not toll any part of the one year period. D.R.L. did nothing to communicate with L.R.A. during her absence. He should not be able to argue an advantage because of it.

NOTES

Overruling a natural parent's objection. In Matter of the Adoption of R.S., 928 P.2d 1194 (Alaska 1996), the Supreme Court of Alaska upheld the adoption by maternal grandparents of a child whose father had been convicted of murdering the child's mother. (The two were unmarried but were living together at the time of her death and raising the child.) Relying on Alaska St. 25.23.180(c)(2), which provides for termination of parental rights "on the grounds that a parent who does not have custody is unreasonably withholding consent to adoption, contrary to the best interests of the child," the trial court found that under the circumstances the evidence was clear and convincing that the father does not have custody of the child and will be incarcerated until he is an adult; that the evidence was clear and convincing that it is in the child's best interest to be adopted by the grandparents and that the father's withholding of consent to the adoption was unreasonable in those circumstances.

In Dyer v. Howell, 212 Va. 453, 184 S.E.2d 789 (1971), adoption by a maternal aunt and uncle was permitted over objection of the natural father under this provision. The natural father killed his wife (the child's mother) but was acquitted of murder by reason of insanity. He subsequently was released from a mental institution, remarried, appeared to be making good progress in readjustment, and sought a return of custody of the child. The custodial aunt and uncle then sought to adopt. The Court granted their petition without the father's consent because the child then "desperately" needed the security and stability they felt she could get in the adoptive home.

The importance of notice. The requirement of notice remains a safeguard in cases of legally implied waiver of consent on the ground of abandonment or unfitness on the part of the noncustodial parent when there has been no formal termination of parental rights in a separate proceeding. Some state courts first denied any constitutional necessity for notice but in 1965, in Armstrong v. Manzo, 380 U.S. 545, 85 S.Ct. 1187, 14 L.Ed.2d 62 (1965), the Supreme Court of the United States set aside an adoption of a child by his stepfather because the divorced, natural father had not been given adequate notice of the adoption proceeding. The Texas statute involved was not of the type specifically dispensing with the consent requirement after loss of custody in divorce or because divorce was granted on a particular ground; it provided that a court could consent on behalf of a parent who had abandoned his child or failed to contribute substantially to his support for a specified period. A juvenile court, finding that there had been no substantial contribution by the natural father for some two years, permitted the adoption without the latter's consent and without giving him notice of the proceeding even though his whereabouts were known. The decision was affirmed by a Texas court, 371 S.W.2d 407 (Tex.Ct.Civ.App. 1963), but reversed by the United States Supreme Court, which also stated that a subsequent hearing at which the natural father appeared after being given notice did not serve to cure the initial defect of lack of notice because of the burden then placed on him of overcoming the factual finding of the first judge.

Negotiating for continued parental rights. Some divorcing parents worry enough about future adoption by a stepparent that they seek to include specific bans against this in separation agreements, whether or not such provisions ultimately would be enforceable. In Weinschel v. Strople, 56 Md.App. 252, 466 A.2d 1301 (1983), however, the issue before the Court of Special Appeals of Maryland was the validity and enforceability of a contractual provision in such an agreement consenting to a future stepparent adoption but allowing the noncustodial natural parent to retain her visitation rights. A "Marital Settlement Agreement" executed between the parties noted that the husband/father, who was awarded custody of the two children of the marriage, had indicated an intention to marry a specific person. The wife/mother agreed to consent to an adoption of the children by that person, but the contract provided that in that event her "rights to visit as set forth in this Agreement shall not be impaired or diminished...." After the divorce, the husband remarried as indicated and the former wife consented to the adoption by the husband's new spouse, reserving in the written consent document the rights set forth in the settlement agreement. The adoption was granted by the chancellor, without a hearing. For some reason not fully explained, the court two years later issued *sua sponte* to all three parties an order to show cause why the adoption should not be set aside. After a hearing the court set aside the adoption decree on the basis that there should have been a hearing beforehand because the adoption was conditioned on visitation.

On appeal, the trial judge's decree setting aside the order was vacated. The court explained that although visitation between a natural parent and an adoptive child is "unusual", that "does not make it illegal, against public policy, or contrary to the best interest of the child." Perceiving nothing in the legislative purpose or the substantive provisions of the adoption statute precluding such an agreement, the court held that it could be specifically enforced, noting that an agreement of this sort

> will not ordinarily impede adoptions, but might even foster them in those cases where the natural parent and adoptive parent are known to each other and the natural parent is reluctant to yield all contact with his or her child.

Mississippi Band of Choctaw Indians v. Holyfield

Supreme Court of the United States, 1989.
490 U.S. 30, 109 S.Ct. 1597, 104 L.Ed.2d 29.

■ Justice Brennan delivered the opinion of the Court.

This appeal requires us to construe the provisions of the Indian Child Welfare Act that establish exclusive tribal jurisdiction over child custody proceedings involving Indian children domiciled on the tribe's reservation.

The Indian Child Welfare Act of 1978 (ICWA), 92 Stat. 3069, 25 U.S.C. §§ 1901–1963, was the product of rising concern in the mid–1970's over the consequences to Indian children, Indian families, and Indian tribes of abusive child welfare practices that resulted in the separation of large numbers of Indian children from their families and tribes through adoption or foster care placement, usually in non-Indian homes. Senate oversight hearings in 1974 yielded numerous examples, statistical data, and expert testimony documenting what one witness called "the wholesale removal of Indian children from their homes, ... the most tragic aspect of Indian life today." Indian Child Welfare Program, Hearings before the Subcommittee on Indian Affairs of the Senate Committee on Interior and Insular Affairs, 93d Cong., 2d Sess., 3 (hereinafter 1974 Hearings) (statement of William Byler). Studies undertaken by the Association on American Indian Affairs in 1969 and 1974, and presented in the Senate hearings, showed that 25 to 35 percent of all Indian children had been separated from their families and placed in adoptive families, foster care, or institutions. Adoptive placements counted significantly in this total: in the State of Minnesota, for example, one in eight Indian children under the age of 18 was in an adoptive home, and during the year 1971–1972 nearly one in every four infants under one year of age was placed for adoption. The adoption rate of Indian children was eight times that of non-Indian children. Approximately 90% of the Indian placements were in non-Indian homes. A number of witnesses also testified to the serious adjustment problems encountered by such children during adolescence,[1] as well as the impact of the adoptions on Indian parents and the tribes themselves.

Further hearings, covering much the same ground, were held during 1977 and 1978 on the bill that became the ICWA. While much of the testimony again focused on the harm to Indian parents and their children who were involuntarily separated by decisions of local welfare authorities, there was also considerable emphasis on the impact on the tribes them-

---

1. For example, Dr. Joseph Westermeyer, a University of Minnesota social psychiatrist, testified about his research with Indian adolescents who experienced difficulty coping in white society, despite the fact that they had been raised in a purely white environment:

"[T]hey were raised with a white cultural and social identity. They are raised in a white home. They attended, predominantly white schools, and in almost all cases, attended a church that was predominantly white, and really came to understand very little about Indian culture, Indian behavior, and had virtually no viable Indian identity. They can recall such things as seeing cowboys and Indians on TV and feeling that Indians were a historical figure but were not a viable contemporary social group.

"Then during adolescence, they found that society was not to grant them the white identity that they had. They began to find this out in a number of ways. For example, a universal experience was that when they began to date white children, the parents of the white youngsters were against this, and there were pressures among white children from the parents not to date these Indian children....

"The other experience was derogatory name calling in relation to their racial identity....

. . .

"[T]hey were finding that society was putting on them an identity which they didn't possess and taking from them an identity that they did possess." 1974 Hearings, at 46.

selves of the massive removal of their children. For example, Mr. Calvin Isaac, Tribal Chief of the Mississippi Band of Choctaw Indians and representative of the National Tribal Chairmen's Association, testified as follows:

> "Culturally, the chances of Indian survival are significantly reduced if our children, the only real means for the transmission of the tribal heritage, are to be raised in non-Indian homes and denied exposure to the ways of their People. Furthermore, these practices seriously undercut the tribes' ability to continue as self-governing communities. Probably in no area is it more important that tribal sovereignty be respected than in an area as socially and culturally determinative as family relationships."

Chief Isaac also summarized succinctly what numerous witnesses saw as the principal reason for the high rates of removal of Indian children:

> "One of the most serious failings of the present system is that Indian children are removed from the custody of their natural parents by nontribal government authorities who have no basis for intelligently evaluating the cultural and social premises underlying Indian home life and childrearing. Many of the individuals who decide the fate of our children are at best ignorant of our cultural values, and at worst contemptful of the Indian way and convinced that removal, usually to a non-Indian household or institution, can only benefit an Indian child."[4]

The congressional findings that were incorporated into the ICWA reflect these sentiments. The Congress found:

> "(3) that there is no resource that is more vital to the continued existence and integrity of Indian tribes than their children ...;

> "(4) that an alarmingly high percentage of Indian families are broken up by the removal, often unwarranted, of their children from them by nontribal public and private agencies and that an alarmingly high percentage of such children are placed in non-Indian foster and adoptive homes and institutions; and

---

4. One of the particular points of concern was the failure of non-Indian child welfare workers to understand the role of the extended family in Indian society. The House Report on the ICWA noted: "An Indian child may have scores of, perhaps more than a hundred, relatives who are counted as close, responsible members of the family. Many social workers, untutored in the ways of Indian family life or assuming them to be socially irresponsible, consider leaving the child with persons outside the nuclear family as neglect and thus as grounds for terminating parental rights." At the conclusion of the 1974 Senate hearings, Senator Abourezk noted the role that such extended families played in the care of children: "We've had testimony here that in Indian communities throughout the Nation there is no such thing as an abandoned child because when a child does have a need for parents for one reason or another, a relative or a friend will take that child in. It's the extended family concept." 1974 Hearings 473. See also Wisconsin Potowatomies of Hannahville Indian Community v. Houston, 393 F.Supp. 719 (W.D.Mich.1973) (discussing custom of extended family and tribe assuming responsibility for care of orphaned children).

"(5) that the States, exercising their recognized jurisdiction over Indian child custody proceedings through administrative and judicial bodies, have often failed to recognize the essential tribal relations of Indian people and the cultural and social standards prevailing in Indian communities and families." 25 U.S.C. § 1901.

At the heart of the ICWA are its provisions concerning jurisdiction over Indian child custody proceedings. Section 1911 lays out a dual jurisdictional scheme. Section 1911(a) establishes exclusive jurisdiction in the tribal courts for proceedings concerning an Indian child "who resides or is domiciled within the reservation of such tribe," as well as for wards of tribal courts regardless of domicile. Section 1911(b), on the other hand, creates concurrent but presumptively tribal jurisdiction in the case of children not domiciled on the reservation: on petition of either parent or the tribe, state-court proceedings for foster care placement or termination of parental rights are to be transferred to the tribal court, except in cases of "good cause," objection by either parent, or declination of jurisdiction by the tribal court.

Various other provisions of ICWA Title I set procedural and substantive standards for those child custody proceedings that do take place in state court. The procedural safeguards include requirements concerning notice and appointment of counsel; parental and tribal rights of intervention and petition for invalidation of illegal proceedings; procedures governing voluntary consent to termination of parental rights; and a full faith and credit obligation in respect to tribal court decisions. See §§ 1901–1914. The most important substantive requirement imposed on state courts is that of § 1915(a), which, absent "good cause" to the contrary, mandates that adoptive placements be made preferentially with (1) members of the child's extended family, (2) other members of the same tribe, or (3) other Indian families.

The ICWA thus, in the words of the House Report accompanying it, "seeks to protect the rights of the Indian child as an Indian and the rights of the Indian community and tribe in retaining its children in its society." It does so by establishing "a Federal policy that, where possible, an Indian child should remain in the Indian community," ibid., and by making sure that Indian child welfare determinations are not based on "a white, middle-class standard which, in many cases, forecloses placement with [an] Indian family."

This case involves the status of twin babies, known for our purposes as B.B. and G.B., who were born out of wedlock on December 29, 1985. Their mother, J.B., and father, W.J., were both enrolled members of appellant Mississippi Band of Choctaw Indians (Tribe), and were residents and domiciliaries of the Choctaw Reservation in Neshoba County, Mississippi. J.B. gave birth to the twins in Gulfport, Harrison County, Mississippi, some 200 miles from the reservation. On January 10, 1986, J.B. executed a consent-to-adoption form before the Chancery Court of Harrison County.[7]

---

7. Section 1913(a) of the ICWA requires that any voluntary consent to termination of parental rights be executed in writing and recorded before a judge of a "court of compe-

W.J. signed a similar form.[8] On January 16, appellees Orrey and Vivian Holyfield filed a petition for adoption in the same court, and the chancellor issued a Final Decree of Adoption on January 28. Id., at 13–14.[10] Despite the court's apparent awareness of the ICWA, the adoption decree contained no reference to it, nor to the infants' Indian background.

Two months later the Tribe moved in the Chancery Court to vacate the adoption decree on the ground that under the ICWA exclusive jurisdiction was vested in the tribal court.[12] On July 14, 1986, the court overruled the motion, holding that the Tribe "never obtained exclusive jurisdiction over the children involved herein...." The court's one-page opinion relied on two facts in reaching that conclusion. The court noted first that the twins' mother "went to some efforts to see that they were born outside the confines of the Choctaw Indian Reservation" and that the parents had promptly arranged for the adoption by the Holyfields. Second, the court stated: "At no time from the birth of these children to the present date have either of them resided on or physically been on the Choctaw Indian Reservation."

The Supreme Court of Mississippi affirmed. 511 So.2d 918 (1987). It rejected the Tribe's arguments that the state court lacked jurisdiction and that it, in any event, had not applied the standards laid out in the ICWA. The court recognized that the jurisdictional question turned on whether the twins were domiciled on the Choctaw Reservation. It answered that question as follows:

> "At no point in time can it be said the twins resided on or were domiciled within the territory set aside for the reservation. Appellant's argument that living within the womb of their mother qualifies the

tent jurisdiction," who must certify that the terms and consequences of the consent were fully explained and understood. Section 1913(a) also provides that any consent given prior to birth or within 10 days thereafter is invalid. In this case the mother's consent was given 12 days after the birth.

8. W.J.'s consent to adoption was signed before a notary public in Neshoba County on January 11, 1986. Record 11–12. Only on June 3, 1986, however—well after the decree of adoption had been entered and after the Tribe had filed suit to vacate that decree—did the chancellor of the Chancery Court certify that W.J. had appeared before him in Harrison County to execute the consent to adoption. Id., at 12–A.

10. Mississippi adoption law provides for a 6–month waiting period between interlocutory and final decrees of adoption, but grants the chancellor discretionary authority to waive that requirement and immediately enter a final decree of adoption. See Miss. Code Ann. § 93–17–13 (1972). The chancellor did so here, Record 14, with the result that the final decree of adoption was entered less than one month after the babies' birth.

12. The ICWA specifically confers standing on the Indian child's tribe to participate in child custody adjudications. Section 1914 authorizes the tribe (as well as the child and its parents) to petition a court to invalidate any foster care placement or termination of parental rights under state law "upon a showing that such action violated any provision of sections 1911, 1912, and 1913" of the ICWA. See also § 1911(c) (Indian child's tribe may intervene at any point in state-court proceedings for foster care placement or termination of parental rights). "Termination of parental rights" is defined in § 1903(1)(ii) as "any action resulting in the termination of the parent-child relationship."

children's residency on the reservation may be lauded for its creativity; however, apparently it is unsupported by any law within this state, and will not be addressed at this time due to the far-reaching legal ramifications that would occur were we to follow such a complicated tangential course."

The court distinguished Mississippi cases that appeared to establish the principle that "the domicile of minor children follows that of the parents". It noted that "the Indian twins ... were voluntarily surrendered and legally abandoned by the natural parents to the adoptive parents, and it is undisputed that the parents went to some efforts to prevent the children from being placed on the reservation as the mother arranged for their birth and adoption in Gulfport Memorial Hospital, Harrison County, Mississippi." Therefore, the court said, the twins' domicile was in Harrison County and the state court properly exercised jurisdiction over the adoption proceedings. Indeed, the court appears to have concluded that, for this reason, none of the provisions of the ICWA was applicable.... In any case, it rejected the Tribe's contention that the requirements of the ICWA applicable in state courts had not been followed....

... We now reverse.

Tribal jurisdiction over Indian child custody proceedings is not a novelty of the ICWA. Indeed, some of the ICWA's jurisdictional provisions have a strong basis in pre–ICWA case law in the federal and state courts.... In enacting the ICWA Congress confirmed that, in child custody proceedings involving Indian children domiciled on the reservation, tribal jurisdiction was exclusive as to the States.

The state-court proceeding at issue here was a "child custody proceeding." That term is defined to include any " 'adoptive placement' which shall mean the permanent placement of an Indian child for adoption, including any action resulting in a final decree of adoption." 25 U.S.C. § 1903(1)(iv). Moreover, the twins were "Indian children." See 25 U.S.C. § 1903(4). The sole issue in this case is, as the Supreme Court of Mississippi recognized, whether the twins were "domiciled" on the reservation.[16]

The meaning of "domicile" in the ICWA is, of course, a matter of Congress' intent. The ICWA itself does not define it. The initial question we must confront is whether there is any reason to believe that Congress intended the ICWA definition of "domicile" to be a matter of state law....

---

16. "Reservation" is defined quite broadly for purposes of the ICWA. See 25 U.S.C. § 1903(10). There is no dispute that the Choctaw Reservation falls within that definition.

Section 1911(a) does not apply "where such jurisdiction is otherwise vested in the State by existing Federal law." This proviso would appear to refer to Pub.L. 280, 67 Stat. 588, as amended, which allows States under certain conditions to assume civil and criminal jurisdiction on the reservations. ICWA § 1918 permits a tribe in that situation to reassume jurisdiction over child custody proceedings upon petition to the Secretary of the Interior. The State of Mississippi has never asserted jurisdiction over the Choctaw Reservation under Public Law 280. See F. Cohen, Handbook of Federal Indian Law 362–363, and nn. 122–125 (1982);....

First, and most fundamentally, the purpose of the ICWA gives no reason to believe that Congress intended to rely on state law for the definition of a critical term; quite the contrary. It is clear from the very text of the ICWA, not to mention its legislative history and the hearings that led to its enactment, that Congress was concerned with the rights of Indian families and Indian communities vis-à-vis state authorities. More specifically, its purpose was, in part, to make clear that in certain situations the state courts did *not* have jurisdiction over child custody proceedings. Indeed, the congressional findings that are a part of the statute demonstrate that Congress perceived the States and their courts as partly responsible for the problem it intended to correct.... Under these circumstances it is most improbable that Congress would have intended to leave the scope of the statute's key jurisdictional provision subject to definition by state courts as a matter of state law.

Second, Congress could hardly have intended the lack of nationwide uniformity that would result from state-law definitions of domicile. An example will illustrate. In a case quite similar to this one, the New Mexico state courts found exclusive jurisdiction in the tribal court pursuant to § 1911(a), because the illegitimate child took the reservation domicile of its mother at birth—notwithstanding that the child was placed in the custody of adoptive parents two days after its off-reservation birth and the mother executed a consent to adoption ten days later. In re Adoption of Baby Child, 102 N.M. 735, 737–738, 700 P.2d 198, 200–201 (App.1985). Had that mother traveled to Mississippi to give birth, rather than to Albuquerque, a different result would have obtained if state-law definitions of domicile applied. The same, presumably, would be true if the child had been transported to Mississippi for adoption after her off-reservation birth in New Mexico. While the child's custody proceeding would have been subject to exclusive tribal jurisdiction in her home State, her mother, prospective adoptive parents, or an adoption intermediary could have obtained an adoption decree in state court merely by transporting her across state lines. Even if we could conceive of a federal statute under which the rules of domicile (and thus of jurisdiction) applied differently to different Indian children, a statute under which different rules apply from time to time to the same child, simply as a result of her transport from one State to another, cannot be what Congress had in mind.[21]

We therefore think it beyond dispute that Congress intended a uniform federal law of domicile for the ICWA.

It remains to give content to the term "domicile" in the circumstances of the present case. The holding of the Supreme Court of Mississippi that the twin babies were not domiciled on the Choctaw Reservation appears to have rested on two findings of fact by the trial court: (1) that they had never been physically present there, and (2) that they were "voluntarily surrendered" by their parents. The question before us, therefore, is wheth-

---

21. For this reason, the general rule that domicile is determined according to the law of the forum, see Restatement (Second) of Conflict of Laws § 13 (1971) (hereinafter Restatement), can have no application here.

er under the ICWA definition of "domicile" such facts suffice to render the twins nondomiciliaries of the reservation.

. . .

That we are dealing with a uniform federal rather than a state definition does not, of course, prevent us from drawing on general state-law principles to determine "the ordinary meaning of the words used." Well-settled state law can inform our understanding of what Congress had in mind when it employed a term it did not define. Accordingly, we find it helpful to borrow established common-law principles of domicile to the extent that they are not inconsistent with the objectives of the congressional scheme.

"Domicile" is, of course, a concept widely used in both federal and state courts for jurisdiction and conflict-of-laws purposes, and its meaning is generally uncontroverted. "Domicile" is not necessarily synonymous with "residence," and one can reside in one place but be domiciled in another. For adults, domicile is established by physical presence in a place in connection with a certain state of mind concerning one's intent to remain there. Texas v. Florida, 306 U.S. 398, 424 (1939). One acquires a "domicile or origin" at birth, and that domicile continues until a new one (a "domicile of choice") is acquired. Since most minors are legally incapable of forming the requisite intent to establish a domicile, their domicile is determined by that of their parents. In the case of an illegitimate child, that has traditionally meant the domicile of its mother. Under these principles, it is entirely logical that "[o]n occasion, a child's domicil of origin will be in a place where the child has never been." Restatement § 14, Comment *b*.

It is undisputed in this case that the domicile of the mother (as well as the father) has been, at all relevant times, on the Choctaw Reservation. Thus, it is clear that at their birth the twin babies were also domiciled on the reservation, even though they themselves had never been there. The statement of the Supreme Court of Mississippi that "[a]t no point in time can it be said the twins . . . were domiciled within the territory set aside for the reservation," 511 So.2d, at 921, may be a correct statement of that State's law of domicile, but it is inconsistent with generally accepted doctrine in this country and cannot be what Congress had in mind when it used the term in the ICWA.

Nor can the result be any different simply because the twins were "voluntarily surrendered" by their mother. Tribal jurisdiction under § 1911(a) was not meant to be defeated by the actions of individual members of the tribe, for Congress was concerned not solely about the interests of Indian children and families, but also about the impact on the tribes themselves of the large numbers of Indian children adopted by non-Indians. . . .

In addition, it is clear that Congress' concern over the placement of Indian children in non-Indian homes was based in part on evidence of the detrimental impact on the children themselves of such placements outside their culture. Congress determined to subject such placements to the ICWA's jurisdictional and other provisions, even in cases where the parents consented to an adoption, because of concerns going beyond the wishes of individual parents. As the 1977 Final Report of the congressionally established American Indian Policy Review Commission stated, in summarizing these two concerns, "[r]emoval of Indian children from their cultural setting seriously impacts a long-term tribal survival and has damaging social and psychological impact on many individual Indian children."[25]

These congressional objectives make clear that a rule of domicile that would permit individual Indian parents to defeat the ICWA's jurisdictional scheme is inconsistent with what Congress intended. See In re Adoption of Child of Indian Heritage, 111 N.J. 155, 168–171, 543 A.2d 925, 931–933 (1988). The appellees in this case argue strenuously that the twins' mother went to great lengths to give birth off the reservation so that her children could be adopted by the Holyfields. But that was precisely part of Congress' concern. Permitting individual members of the tribe to avoid tribal exclusive jurisdiction by the simple expedient of giving birth off the reservation would, to a large extent, nullify the purpose the ICWA was intended to accomplish.[27] The Supreme Court of Utah expressed this well in its scholarly and sensitive opinion in what has become a leading case on the ICWA:

> "To the extent that [state] abandonment law operates to permit [the child's] mother to change [the child's] domicile as part of a scheme to facilitate his adoption by non-Indians while she remains a domiciliary of the reservation, it conflicts with and undermines the operative scheme established by subsections [1911(a)] and [1913(a)] to deal with children of domiciliaries of the reservation and weakens considerably the tribe's ability to assert its interest in its children. The protection of this tribal interest is at the core of the ICWA, which recognizes that the tribe has an interest in the child which is distinct from but on a parity with the interest of the parents. This relationship between Indian tribes and Indian children domiciled on the reservation finds no parallel in other ethnic cultures found in the United States. It is a

---

25. While the statute itself makes clear that Congress intended the ICWA to reach voluntary as well as involuntary removal of Indian children, the same conclusion can also be drawn from the ICWA's legislative history. For example, the House Report contains the following expression of Congress' concern with both aspects of the problem:

> "One of the effects of our national paternalism has been to so alienate some Indian [parents] from their society that they abandon their children at hospitals or to welfare departments rather than entrust them to the care of relatives in the extended family. Another expression of it is the involuntary, arbitrary, and unwarranted separation of families."

27. It appears, in fact, that all Choctaw women give birth off the reservation because of the lack of appropriate obstetric facilities there. In most cases, of course, the mother and child return to the reservation after the birth, and this would presumably be sufficient to make the child a reservation domiciliary even under the Mississippi court's theory. Application of the Mississippi domicile rule would, however, permit state authorities to avoid the tribal court's exclusive § 1911(a) jurisdiction by removing a newborn from an allegedly unfit mother while in the hospital, and seeking to terminate her parental rights in state court.

relationship that many non-Indians find difficult to understand and that non-Indian courts are slow to recognize. It is precisely in recognition of this relationship, however, that the ICWA designates the tribal court as the exclusive forum for the determination of custody and adoption matters for reservation-domiciled Indian children, and the preferred forum for nondomiciliary Indian children. [State] abandonment law cannot be used to frustrate the federal legislative judgment expressed in the ICWA that the interests of the tribe in custodial decisions made with respect to Indian children are as entitled to respect as the interests of the parents." In re Adoption of Halloway, 732 P.2d 962, 969–970 (1986).

We agree with the Supreme Court of Utah that the law of domicile Congress used in the ICWA cannot be one that permits individual reservation-domiciled tribal members to defeat the tribe's exclusive jurisdiction by the simple expedient of giving birth and placing the child for adoption off the reservation. Since, for purposes of the ICWA, the twin babies in this case were domiciled on the reservation when adoption proceedings were begun, the Choctaw tribal court possessed exclusive jurisdiction pursuant to 25 U.S.C. § 1911(a). The Chancery Court of Harrison County was, accordingly, without jurisdiction to enter a decree of adoption; under ICWA § 1914 its decree of January 28, 1986, must be vacated.

We are not unaware that over three years have passed since the twin babies were born and placed in the Holyfield home, and that a court deciding their fate today is not writing on a blank slate in the same way it would have in January 1986. Three years' development of family ties cannot be undone, and a separation at this point would doubtless cause considerable pain.

Whatever feelings we might have as to where the twins should live, however, it is not for us to decide that question. We have been asked to decide the legal question of *who* should make the custody determination concerning these children—not what the outcome of that determination should be. The law places that decision in the hands of the Choctaw tribal court. Had the mandate of the ICWA been followed in 1986, of course, much potential anguish might have been avoided, and in any case the law cannot be applied so as automatically to "reward those who obtain custody, whether lawfully or otherwise, and maintain it during any ensuing (and protracted) litigation." It is not ours to say whether the trauma that might result from removing these children from their adoptive family should outweigh the interest of the Tribe—and perhaps the children themselves— in having them raised as part of the Choctaw community.[28] Rather, "we must defer to the experience, wisdom, and compassion of the [Choctaw] tribal courts to fashion an appropriate remedy."

---

28. We were assured at oral argument that the Choctaw court has the authority under the tribal code to permit adoption by the present adoptive family, should it see fit to do so.

The judgment of the Supreme Court of Mississippi is reversed and the case remanded for further proceedings not inconsistent with this opinion.

■ Justice Stevens, with whom The Chief Justice and Justice Kennedy join, dissenting.

The parents of these twin babies unquestionably expressed their intention to have the state court exercise jurisdiction over them. J.B. gave birth to the twins at a hospital 200 miles from the Reservation, even though a closer hospital was available. Both parents gave their written advance consent to the adoption and, when the adoption was later challenged by the Tribe, they reaffirmed their desire that the Holyfields adopt the two children. As the Mississippi Supreme Court found, "the parents went to some efforts to prevent the children from being placed on the reservation as the mother arranged for their birth and adoption in Gulfport Memorial Hospital, Harrison County, Mississippi." 511 So.2d 918, 927 (1987). Indeed, both parents appear before us today, urging that Vivian Holyfield be allowed to retain custody of B.B. and G.B.

Because J.B.'s domicile is on the reservation and the children are eligible for membership in the Tribe, the Court today closes the state courthouse door to her. I agree with the Court that Congress intended a uniform federal law of domicile for the Indian Child Welfare Act of 1978 (ICWA), and that domicile should be defined with reference to the objectives of the congressional scheme.... I cannot agree, however, with the cramped definition the Court gives that term. To preclude parents domiciled on a reservation from deliberately invoking the adoption procedures of state court, the Court gives "domicile" a meaning that Congress could not have intended and distorts the delicate balance between individual rights and group rights recognized by the ICWA.

The ICWA was passed in 1978 in response to congressional findings that "an alarmingly high percentage of Indian families are broken up by the *removal,* often unwarranted, of their children from them by nontribal public and private agencies" and that "the States, exercising their recognized jurisdiction over Indian child custody proceedings through administrative and judicial bodies, have often failed to recognize the essential tribal relations of Indian people and the cultural and social standards prevailing in Indian communities and families." 25 U.S.C. § 1901(4), (5). (Emphasis added.) The Act is thus primarily addressed to the unjustified removal of Indian children from their families through the application of standards that inadequately recognized the distinct Indian culture.

The most important provisions of the ICWA are those setting forth minimum standards for the placement of Indian children by state courts and providing procedural safeguards to insure that parental rights are protected. The Act provides that any party seeking to effect a foster care placement of, or involuntary termination of parental rights to, an Indian child must establish by stringent standards of proof that efforts have been made to prevent the breakup of the Indian family and that the continued custody of the child by the parent is likely to result in serious emotional or physical damage to the child. §§ 1912(d), (e), (f). Each party to the proceeding has a right to examine all reports and documents filed with the court and an indigent parent or custodian has the right to appointment of counsel. §§ 1912(b), (c). In the case of a voluntary termination, the ICWA provides that consent is valid only if given after the terms and consequences of the consent have been fully explained, may be withdrawn at any time up to the final entry of a decree of termination or adoption, and even then may be collaterally attacked on the grounds that it was obtained through fraud or duress. § 1913. Finally, because the Act protects not only the rights of the parents, but also the interests of the tribe and the Indian children, the Act sets forth criteria for adoptive, foster care, and preadoptive placements that favor the Indian child's extended family or tribe, and that can be altered by resolution of the tribe. § 1915.

The Act gives Indian tribes certain rights, not to restrict the rights of parents of Indian children, but to complement and help effect them. The Indian tribe may petition to transfer an action in state court to the tribal court, but the Indian parent may veto the transfer. § 1911(b). The Act provides for a tribal right of notice and intervention in involuntary proceedings but not in voluntary ones. §§ 1911(c), 1912(a). Finally, the tribe may petition the court to set aside a parental termination action upon a showing that the provisions of the ICWA that are designed to protect parents and Indian children have been violated. § 1914.[5]

While the Act's substantive and procedural provisions effect a major change in state child custody proceedings, its jurisdictional provision is designed primarily to preserve tribal sovereignty over the domestic relations of tribe members and to confirm a developing line of cases which held that the tribe's exclusive jurisdiction could not be defeated by the temporary presence of an Indian child off the reservation.

. . .

Although parents of Indian children are shielded from the exercise of state jurisdiction when they are temporarily off the reservation, the Act also reflects a recognition that allowing the tribe to defeat the parents' deliberate choice of jurisdiction would be conducive neither to the best interests of the child nor to the stability and security of Indian tribes and families. Section 1911(b), providing for the exercise of concurrent jurisdiction by state and tribal courts when the Indian child is not domiciled on the reservation, gives the Indian parents a veto to prevent the transfer of a state court action to tribal court.[8] "By allowing the Indian parents to 'choose' the forum that will decide whether to sever the parent-child relationship, Congress promotes the security of Indian families by allowing

---

5. Significantly, the tribe can not set aside a termination of parental rights on the grounds that the adoptive placement provisions of § 1915, favoring placement with the tribe, have not been followed.

8. The explanation of this subsection in the House Committee Report reads as follows:

"Subsection (b) directs a State court, having jurisdiction over an Indian child custody proceeding to transfer such proceeding, absent good cause to the contrary, to the appropriate tribal court upon the petition of the parents or the Indian tribe. Either parent is given the right to veto such transfer. The subsection is intended to permit a State court to apply a modified doctrine of forum

the Indian parents to defend in the court system that most reflects the parents' familial standards." Jones, 21 Ariz.L.Rev., at 1141. As Mr. Calvin Isaac, Tribal Chief of the Mississippi Band of Choctaw Indians stated in testimony to the House Subcommittee on Indian Affairs and Public Lands with respect to a different provision:

> "The ultimate responsibility for child welfare rests with the parents and we would not support legislation which interfered with that basic relationship."

If J.B. and W.J. had established a domicile off the Reservation, the state courts would have been required to give effect to their choice of jurisdiction; there should not be a different result when the parents have not changed their own domicile, but have expressed an unequivocal intent to establish a domicile for their children off the Reservation. The law of abandonment, as enunciated by the Mississippi Supreme Court in this case, does not defeat, but serves the purposes of the Act. An abandonment occurs when a parent deserts a child and places the child with another with an intent to relinquish all parental rights and obligations. Restatement (Second) of Conflict of Laws § 22, Comment e (1971) (hereinafter Restatement); In re Adoption of Halloway, 732 P.2d 962, 966 (Utah 1986). If a child is abandoned by his mother, he takes on the domicile of his father; if the child is abandoned by his father, he takes on the domicile of his mother. If the child is abandoned by both parents, he takes on the domicile of a person other than the parents who stands in loco parentis to him. To be effective, the intent to abandon or the actual physical abandonment must be shown by clear and convincing evidence.

When an Indian child is temporarily off the reservation, but has not been abandoned to a person off the reservation, the tribe has an interest in exclusive jurisdiction. The ICWA expresses the intent that exclusive tribal jurisdiction is not so frail that it should be defeated as soon as the Indian child steps off the reservation. Similarly, when the child is abandoned by one parent to a person off the reservation, the tribe and the other parent domiciled on the reservation may still have an interest in the exercise of exclusive jurisdiction. That interest is protected by the rule that a child abandoned by one parent takes on the domicile of the other. But when an Indian child is deliberately abandoned by both parents to a person off the reservation, no purpose of the ICWA is served by closing the state court-house door to them. The interests of the parents, the Indian child, and the

non conveniens, in appropriate cases, to insure that the rights of the child as an Indian, the Indian parents or custodian, and the tribe are fully protected." Id., at 21.

In commenting on the provision, the Department of Justice suggested that the section should be clarified to make it perfectly clear that a state court need not surrender jurisdiction of a child custody proceeding if the Indian parent objected. The Department of Justice letter stated:

"Section 101(b) should be amended to prohibit clearly the transfer of a child placement proceeding to a tribal court when any parent or child over the age of 12 objects to the transfer." Id., at 32.

Although the specific suggestion made by the Department of Justice was not in fact implemented, it is noteworthy that there is nothing in the legislative history to suggest that the recommended change was in any way inconsistent with any of the purposes of the statute.

tribe in preventing the unwarranted removal of Indian children from their families and from the reservation are protected by the Act's substantive and procedural provisions. In addition, if both parents have intentionally invoked the jurisdiction of the state court in an action involving a non-Indian, no interest in tribal self-governance is implicated.

The interpretation of domicile adopted by the Court requires the custodian of an Indian child who is off the reservation to haul the child to a potentially distant tribal court unfamiliar with the child's present living conditions and best interests. Moreover, it renders any custody decision made by a state court forever suspect, susceptible to challenge at any time as void for having been entered in the absence of jurisdiction.[12] Finally, it forces parents of Indian children who desire to invoke state court jurisdiction to establish a domicile off the reservation. Only if the custodial parent has the wealth and ability to establish a domicile off the reservation will the parent be able use the processes of state court. I fail to see how such a requirement serves the paramount congressional purpose of "promot[ing] the stability and security of Indian tribes and families." 25 U.S.C. § 1902.

The Court concludes its opinion with the observation that whatever anguish is suffered by the Indian children, their natural parents, and their adoptive parents because of its decision today is a result of their failure to initially follow the provisions of the ICWA. By holding that parents who are domiciled on the reservation cannot voluntarily avail themselves of the adoption procedures of state court and that all such proceedings will be void for lack of jurisdiction, however, the Court establishes a rule of law that is virtually certain to ensure that similar anguish will be suffered by other families in the future. Because that result is not mandated by the language of the ICWA and is contrary to its purposes, I respectfully dissent.

Adoption of F.H.

Supreme Court of Alaska, 1993.
851 P.2d 1361.

■ COMPTON, JUSTICE.

The Native Village of Noatak (Noatak) and the State of Alaska, Division of Family and Youth Services (DFYS), opposed the adoption of

---

12. The facts of In re Adoption of Halloway, 732 P.2d 962 (Utah 1986), which the Court cites approvingly, vividly illustrate the problem. In that case, the mother, a member of an Indian Tribe in New Mexico, voluntarily abandoned an Indian child to the custody of the child's maternal aunt off the Reservation with the knowledge that the child would be placed for adoption in Utah. The mother learned of the adoption two weeks after the child left the Reservation and did not object and, two months later, she executed a consent to adoption. Nevertheless, some two years after the petition for adoption was filed, the Indian Tribe intervened in the proceeding and set aside the adoption. The Tribe argued successfully that regardless of whether the Indian parent consented to it, the adoption was void because she resided on the Reservation and thus the tribal court had exclusive jurisdiction. Although the decision in *Halloway,* and the Court's approving reference to it, may be colored somewhat by the fact that the mother in that case withdrew her consent (a fact which would entitle her to relief even if there were only concurrent jurisdiction, see 25 U.S.C. § 1913(c)), the rule set forth by the majority contains no such limitation. As the Tribe acknowledged at oral argument, any adoption of an Indian child effected through a state court will be susceptible of challenge by the Indian tribe no matter how old the child and how long it has lived with its adoptive parents.

F.H., an Indian child, by the Hartleys, a non-Indian couple. Superior Court Judge Elaine M. Andrews determined that F.H.'s case presented good cause to deviate from the Indian Child Welfare Act (ICWA) adoptive placement preferences. Noatak and DFYS appeal this determination.

F.H. was born on February 24, 1990. Her mother, E.P.D., had a blood alcohol level of about .275 at the time of birth. F.H.'s biological father is unknown. F.H. is an Indian child as defined by ICWA. 25 U.S.C. § 1903. She and her mother are members of the Native Village of Noatak.

DFYS took custody of F.H. shortly after her birth, based on her mother's homelessness and high blood alcohol level at the time of birth. DFYS filed a Child in Need of Aid (CINA) petition (3AN–90–159) and notified Noatak. DFYS filed a petition to terminate parental rights in August 1990.[1]

F.H. has experienced a number of medical problems, symptomatic of Fetal Alcohol Syndrome (FAS) or Fetal Alcohol Effects (FAE). The Alaska Area Native Health Service has determined that F.H. does not have FAS, but is at high risk for FAE, which is not as severe. Her prenatal exposure to alcohol has placed her at risk for developmental delay and learning and behavioral problems.

F.H. lived in four different foster homes before she was adopted by the Hartleys in March 1992. The Hartleys were her third foster placement. F.H. lived with them from June 1990 until June 1991, when Carol Hartley was transferred to Washington State. F.H. now lives with the Hartleys in Kennewick, Washington.

While F.H. was in foster homes, E.P.D. expressed an interest in relinquishing her custody to at least five different people, including her cousin, Mary Penn, and the Hartleys. As E.P.D.'s cousin, Mary Penn is a first place adoptive placement preference under ICWA. 25 U.S.C. § 1915(a). Based upon a favorable home study, DFYS concluded that F.H. should be placed with Mary Penn, though F.H. never lived with her. Trial on the petition to terminate parental rights was set for September 18, 1991.

On September 16, E.P.D. executed three documents before Probate Master Lucinda McBurney relinquishing her parental rights to the Hartleys. Her relinquishment was conditioned upon the Hartleys' adoption of F.H., F.H.'s retention of inheritance rights from E.P.D., and E.P.D.'s and her family's retention of contact and visitation rights with F.H. The next day, the Hartleys filed a Petition for Adoption. Since signing the papers, E.P.D. has consistently supported an adoption by the Hartleys.

E.P.D. has not been to Noatak for several years and plans never to return. She abuses alcohol. Her father died of alcoholism. Her mother was

---

1. The CINA proceeding was briefly consolidated with the adoption proceeding. That consolidation was vacated and the adop-tion trial was held first. The CINA petition was dismissed when the Hartleys' petition for adoption was granted.

murdered by her brother. None of her siblings were raised in Noatak. F.H. has never been to Noatak. E.P.D. believes she could visit F.H. more easily in Kennewick, Washington, than in Noatak.

An early interventionist, who worked with F.H. in the Hartleys' home twice a month for almost one year, believes F.H. made a lot of progress during that period and that F.H.'s bond with Nancy Hartley is the best F.H. will ever have. Both guardians ad litem assigned to F.H. testified that they believe F.H.'s best interest is to be placed with the Hartleys. The DFYS social worker assigned to F.H.'s case until June 1991 believed that F.H. should have stayed with the Hartleys.

After several hearings at which Noatak,[2] E.P.D., the Hartleys, DFYS, and F.H. were represented, Probate Master John E. Duggan recommended that the superior court find good cause to deviate from ICWA preferences. The primary basis for his recommendation was the "strong and consistent preference of the biological mother for this open adoption by the petitioners and against placement of her daughter in the village of Noatak." Secondary considerations included 1) the bond between Nancy Hartley and F.H., 2) the uncertainty of F.H.'s future if the adoption were not allowed, and 3) the "open adoption" petition allowing E.P.D. access to F.H. and possibly giving F.H. exposure to her Native American heritage.

Judge Andrews accepted Master Duggan's recommendation. Judge Andrews stressed the importance of the mother's preference, which was based in part on the adoption of F.H. being "open." E.P.D. retained contact and visitation rights, while F.H. retained her inheritance rights from E.P.D. In contrast, "[t]here is no written evidence suggesting that the proposed Penn adoption would be 'open.'"

In support of its Motion for Reconsideration, Noatak submitted the affidavit of Mary Penn and an excerpt from a study of Northwest Alaskan Family traditions to show that E.P.D. and others in F.H.'s blood family would have access to F.H. if she lived with Mary Penn. Judge Andrews denied the motion.

Superior Court Judge Brian C. Shortell conducted a hearing on the remaining issues. He granted the Decree of Adoption on March 5, 1992. This appeal followed.

A. Standard of Review

The question on appeal is whether the superior court erred in concluding that good cause existed to deviate from the adoptive placement prefer-

---

2. The Hartleys assert that Noatak's opposition to their adoption is barred by the doctrine of laches. Noatak was sent notices of F.H.'s CINA case in March and August 1990. In October 1991 Noatak received notice of the Hartleys' adoption petition and only then moved to intervene in both the adoption and the CINA cases. Alaska Adoption Rule 12(a) states that "[i]n any adoption or relinquish- ment proceeding involving an Indian child, the Indian child's tribe and an Indian custo- dian, if any, may intervene as a matter of right at any stage in the proceeding." (Em- phasis added). In light of this rule, it is doubtful laches may be raised as a defense to intervention "at any stage in the proceed- ing." In view of our decision on the merits, we need not address laches.

ences mandated under ICWA (25 U.S.C. §§ 1901–1963). Under state law, the Hartleys have the burden of proof by a preponderance of the evidence that there is good cause for allowing a non-preferred placement. Alaska Adoption Rule 11(f). A good cause determination is within the superior court's discretion. See In re Adoption of M., 66 Wash.App. 475, 832 P.2d 518, 522–23 (1992); In re Appeal in Coconino County Juvenile Action No. J–10175, 153 Ariz. 346, 349–50, 736 P.2d 829, 832–33 (App.1987). We will reverse an adoptive placement preference determination only if convinced that the record as a whole reveals an abuse of discretion or if controlling factual findings are clearly erroneous. Farrell v. Farrell, 819 P.2d 896, 898 (Alaska 1991). Abuse of discretion is established if the superior court considered improper factors or improperly weighted certain factors in making its determination. See id. Whether there is good cause to deviate in a particular case depends on many factors including, but not necessarily limited to, the best interests of the child, the wishes of the biological parents, the suitability of persons preferred for placement and the child's ties to the tribe. In re Adoption of M., 832 P.2d at 522.

B.   Good Cause Determination

ICWA was enacted to discourage the separation of Indian children from their families and tribes through adoption or foster care placement to non-Indian homes. 25 U.S.C. § 1901; Mississippi Band of Choctaw Indians v. Holyfield, 490 U.S. 30, 36, 109 S.Ct. 1597, 1601, 104 L.Ed.2d 29 (1989). Congress found that no resource "is more vital to the continued existence and integrity of Indian tribes than their children." 25 U.S.C. § 1901(3); Holyfield, 490 U.S. at 38, 109 S.Ct. at 1603. In order "to protect the best interests of Indian children and to promote the stability and security of Indian tribes and families," Congress established minimum federal standards for the placement of Indian children in foster or adoptive homes. 25 U.S.C. § 1902.

ICWA provides preferences in placing Indian children for adoption. In any adoptive placement of an Indian child under State law, a preference shall be given, in the absence of good cause to the contrary, to a placement with (1) a member of the child's extended family; (2) other members of the Indian child's tribe; or (3) other Indian families. 25 U.S.C. § 1915(a). ICWA does not define "good cause."[3]

Master Duggan found good cause to deviate from ICWA's preferences. The factual bases upon which Master Duggan made his determination were E.P.D.'s preference for the Hartleys, the bond between Nancy Hartley and F.H., the uncertainty of F.H.'s future if the adoption were not allowed, and the "openness" of the Hartleys' adoption.

1.   Maternal Preference.

At a hearing in which the terms and consequences were fully explained to her, E.P.D. signed three documents relinquishing her parental rights on

---

3. Noatak's argument that the three ICWA preferential placements must be rejected before consideration of an alternative ignores the "good cause" exception.

condition that the Hartleys adopt F.H. Four months later, at a hearing in front of Master Duggan, E.P.D. testified that she wanted F.H. to be adopted by the Hartleys.

Noatak argues that under Holyfield, parental preference cannot defeat the interests of the tribe. In Holyfield, the United States Supreme Court held that parents can not defeat tribal jurisdiction by giving birth off a reservation. Id. at 53, 109 S.Ct. at 1610. Since jurisdiction is not an issue in this case, Holyfield is not apposite.

ICWA states, with regard to the order of the preferences, "[w]here appropriate, the preference of the Indian child or parent shall be considered." 25 U.S.C. § 1915(c). The Bureau of Indian Affairs publication "Guidelines for State Courts; Indian Child Custody Proceedings" (Guidelines) provides that good cause not to follow the order of preference may be based on parental preference. 44 Fed.Reg. 67584, § F.3 (1979). Although the Guidelines do not have binding effect, this court has looked to them for guidance. In re L.A.M., 727 P.2d 1057, 1060 n. 6 (Alaska 1986). ICWA and the Guidelines indicate that courts may consider parental preference when determining whether there is good cause to deviate from ICWA preferences. E.P.D.'s preference for the Hartleys was an appropriate factor for the superior court to consider in its finding of good cause.

Noatak argues that even if a mother's preference constitutes good cause to deviate from ICWA placement preferences, E.P.D.'s relinquishment should be given little weight since it was neither reasonable nor knowledgeable. E.P.D. had offered to relinquish F.H. to several different people, including Mary Penn. At least once she adamantly opposed placement with the Hartleys. She admitted that when she signed the relinquishment to the Hartleys she was so mixed up she would have signed anything. Noatak argues that E.P.D.'s decision was based in part on her belief that F.H. had serious health problems.

However, Master McBurney certified that E.P.D. understood and voluntarily signed the documents. Since signing them, E.P.D. has consistently supported an adoption by the Hartleys. E.P.D. gave several reasons she would not want to return to Noatak or have her daughter raised there. The finding that E.P.D. preferred that the Hartleys adopt F.H. was not clearly erroneous.

2. Bond between Nancy Hartley and F.H.

Both guardians ad litem testified to a strong bond between Nancy Hartley and F.H. An early interventionist stated that F.H.'s bond with Nancy Hartley is the best she will ever have. Bonding between Nancy Hartley and F.H. was a proper factor for the superior court to consider. The finding of bonding was not clearly erroneous.

3. F.H.'s Need for Permanent Placement.

Master Duggan recognized that F.H.'s situation would be uncertain if the Hartleys' adoption petition were dismissed and E.P.D. withdrew her conditional relinquishment. E.P.D.'s relinquishment was conditional on the

Hartleys' adoption of F.H. If the Hartleys' adoption petition were dismissed, F.H. would have continued to be in DFYS' temporary custody. DFYS' petition to terminate permanently E.P.D.'s parental rights had not been granted. No other petition to adopt F.H. had been filed. Although DFYS expressed an intent to place F.H. with Mary Penn immediately, further legal proceedings would have been necessary for a permanent adoption by Mary Penn. The superior court properly considered F.H.'s situation if the adoption petition were dismissed. It was not clearly erroneous for the superior court to find that F.H.'s uncertain situation would have continued if the Hartleys were not allowed to adopt F.H.

4.   Openness of Hartley Adoption.

Master Duggan and Judge Andrews found that an adoption by the Hartleys would be open, since E.P.D. and her family would have access to F.H. Noatak argues that an adoption by Mary Penn would ensure access to F.H. by E.P.D. and other relatives. E.P.D. testified that she could visit F.H. more easily in Kennewick, Washington than in Noatak. The finding that an adoption by the Hartleys would be open was not clearly erroneous and was a proper factor for the superior court to consider.

Given the possibility of a placement with a relative in Noatak, this case presented a close question to the superior court. However, the factual findings which supported deviation from ICWA preferences are not clearly erroneous. Further, they address factors which are proper to consider in determining whether good cause exists to deviate from the preferences. The record as a whole reveals no abuse of discretion. Therefore, the order approving Master Duggan's finding of good cause is AFFIRMED and the decision to grant the Hartleys' Petition for Adoption is AFFIRMED.

NOTE

In *In re* Adoption of T.N.F., 781 P.2d 973 (Alaska 1989), *cert. denied* 494 U.S. 1030, 110 S.Ct. 1480, 108 L.Ed.2d 616 (1990), the Supreme Court of Alaska held that the Indian Child Welfare Act was applicable to an action by a non-Indian wife of an Indian husband who sought as a stepparent to adopt her husband's child who had been born to her own sister (also a non-Indian) under a surrogate parentage agreement in which petitioner's husband was the sperm donor. Although such an interpretation might have served to disrupt an Indian family, the court noted that

> in enacting the ICWA, Congress did not simply seek to protect the interests of individual Indian parents. Rather, Congress sought to also protect the interests of Indian tribes and communities, and the interests of the Indian children themselves.

The court, however, did determine that the ICWA incorporates state statutes of limitation for actions to set aside consents that are invalid under the ICWA except when the challenges are based on fraud or duress. No allegations of the latter having been raised, the court held that an action by the natural mother to vacate the adoption by her sister that had been granted by an Alaska state court was barred by the Alaska one year statute of limitations for actions to set aside adoption decrees.

In Matter of Adoption of Riffle, 277 Mont. 388, 922 P.2d 510 (Mont. 1996), The Supreme Court of Montana rejected the application of the "best interests of the child" test in determining whether the good cause exception in ICWA applied.

In Matter of Adoption of a Child of Indian Heritage, 111 N.J. 155, 543 A.2d 925 (1988), the Supreme Court of New Jersey held that the fact that an unwed mother had voluntarily relinquished her child for a private adoptive placement without having lived with an Indian family or in an Indian environment did not preclude application of the Indian Child Welfare Act (ICWA). Because the mother was only 9/32 Rosebud Sioux, the child was ineligible for tribal membership unless the father's lineage would establish that the child had a quarter or more of Rosebud Sioux blood.

A putative father, who was 17/32 Rosebud Sioux and an enrolled member of the tribe, sought to establish his paternity and vacate the private placement adoption that had taken place with the mother's consent. At the time of the hearing, the tribe had refused to enroll the child for membership. However the putative father's ancestry seemingly would have made the child eligible for membership if his paternity were established. The ICWA, in 25 U.S.C.A. § 1903(9), refers to

> any biological parent or parents of an Indian child or any Indian person who has lawfully adopted an Indian child, including adoptions under tribal law or custom. It does not include the unwed father where paternity has not been acknowledged or established.

The ICWA provides no standard for establishing paternity. The court therefore applied the New Jersey Parentage Act, which was patterned after the Uniform Parentage Act (1973). The court held that the putative father, who had been living with the mother within a month of the child's birth and knew of the adoptive placement but took no steps to protect his paternal rights for twenty-one months, had not satisfied the requirements of the Parentage Act before a final adoption was effected and had not made "timely acknowledgment of paternity within the contemplation of the ICWA". The trial court's refusal to vacate the adoption therefore was upheld.

In *In re* Marinna J., 90 Cal.App.4th 731, 109 Cal.Rptr.2d 267 (2001), the California Court of Appeal held that the requirement of notice to the tribe of a child whose parental rights were being terminated was mandatory under 25 U.S.C.A. § 1912. The issue did not arise until an appeal from a termination of parental rights, but the court nevertheless held that the statutory did not provide for a waiver by the parents. A purpose of giving notice is to protect tribal interests.

For further discussion of the Indian Child Welfare Act and adoption, *see* David H. Getches, *Conquering the Cultural Frontier: The New Subjectivism of the Supreme Court in Indian Law*, 84 CALIF. L. REV. 1573 (1996); Philip P. Frickey, *Congressional intent, Practical reasoning, and the Dy-*

namic Nature of Federal Indian Law, 78 CALIF. L. REV. 1137 (1990); Barbara Ann Atwood, *Fighting Over Indian Children: The Uses and Abuses of Jurisdictional Ambiguity*, 36 UCLA L. REV. 1051 (1989).

3.   SPECIAL ISSUES OF THE PLACEMENT PROCESS

a.   A PLACING AGENCY'S SPECIAL ROLE AND DUTIES

CALIFORNIA FAMILY CODE (West 2004 & Supp. 2006)

§ 8700.   Relinquishment of child to department or a licensed adoption agency; minor parents; rescission; termination of parental rights

(a) Either birth parent may relinquish a child to the department or a licensed adoption agency for adoption by a written statement signed before two subscribing witnesses and acknowledged before an authorized official of the department or agency. The relinquishment, when reciting that the person making it is entitled to the sole custody of the child and acknowledged before the officer, is prima facie evidence of the right of the person making it to the sole custody of the child and the person's sole right to relinquish.

(b) A relinquishing parent who is a minor has the right to relinquish his or her child for adoption to the department or a licensed adoption agency, and the relinquishment is not subject to revocation by reason of the minority.

(c) If a relinquishing parent resides outside this state and the child is being cared for and is or will be placed for adoption by the department or a licensed adoption agency, the relinquishing parent may relinquish the child to the department or agency by a written statement signed by the relinquishing parent before a notary on a form prescribed by the department, and previously signed by an authorized official of the department or agency, that signifies the willingness of the department or agency to accept the relinquishment.

(d) If a relinquishing parent and child reside outside this state and the child will be cared for and will be placed for adoption by the department or a licensed adoption agency, the relinquishing parent may relinquish the child to the department or agency by a written statement signed by the relinquishing parent, after that parent has satisfied the following requirements:

(1) Prior to signing the relinquishment, the relinquishing parent shall have received, from a representative of an agency licensed or otherwise approved to provide adoption services under the laws of the relinquishing parent's state of residence, the same counseling and advisement services as if the relinquishing parent resided in this state.

(2) The relinquishment shall be signed before a representative of an agency licensed or otherwise approved to provide adoption services under the laws of the relinquishing parent's state of residence whenever possible

or before a licensed social worker on a form prescribed by the department, and previously signed by an authorized official of the department or agency, that signifies the willingness of the department or agency to accept the relinquishment.

(e)(1) The relinquishment authorized by this section has no effect until a certified copy is sent to, and filed with, the department. The licensed adoption agency shall send that copy by certified mail, return receipt requested, or by overnight courier or messenger, with proof of delivery, to the department no earlier than the end of the business day following the signing thereof. The relinquishment shall be final 10 business days after receipt of the filing by the department, unless any of the following apply:

(A) The department sends written acknowledgment of receipt of the relinquishment prior to the expiration of that 10–day period, at which time the relinquishment shall be final.

(B) A longer period of time is necessary due to a pending court action or some other cause beyond control of the department.

(2) After the relinquishment is final, it may be rescinded only by the mutual consent of the department or licensed adoption agency to which the child was relinquished and the birth parent or parents relinquishing the child.

(f) The relinquishing parent may name in the relinquishment the person or persons with whom he or she intends that placement of the child for adoption be made by the department or licensed adoption agency.

(g) Notwithstanding subdivision (e), if the relinquishment names the person or persons with whom placement by the department or licensed adoption agency is intended and the child is not placed in the home of the named person or persons or the child is removed from the home prior to the granting of the adoption, the department or agency shall mail a notice by certified mail, return receipt requested, to the birth parent signing the relinquishment within 72 hours of the decision not to place the child for adoption or the decision to remove the child from the home.

(h) The relinquishing parent has 30 days from the date on which the notice described in subdivision (g) was mailed to rescind the relinquishment.

(1) If the relinquishing parent requests rescission during the 30–day period, the department or licensed adoption agency shall rescind the relinquishment.

(2) If the relinquishing parent does not request rescission during the 30–day period, the department or licensed adoption agency shall select adoptive parents for the child.

(3) If the relinquishing parent and the department or licensed adoption agency wish to identify a different person or persons during the 30–day period with whom the child is intended to be placed, the initial relinquishment shall be rescinded and a new relinquishment identifying the person or persons completed.

(i) If the parent has relinquished a child, who has been found to come within Section 300 of the Welfare and Institutions Code or is the subject of a petition for jurisdiction of the juvenile court under Section 300 of the Welfare and Institutions Code, to the department or a licensed adoption agency for the purpose of adoption, the department or agency accepting the relinquishment shall provide written notice of the relinquishment within five court days to all of the following:

(1) The juvenile court having jurisdiction of the child.

(2) The child's attorney, if any.

(3) The relinquishing parent's attorney, if any.

(j) The filing of the relinquishment with the department terminates all parental rights and responsibilities with regard to the child, except as provided in subdivisions (g) and (h).

(k) The department shall adopt regulations to administer the provisions of this section.

§ 8702. Statement presented to birth parents at time of relinquishment; content; form

(a) The department shall adopt a statement to be presented to the birth parents at the time a relinquishment is signed and to prospective adoptive parents at the time of the home study. The statement shall, in a clear and concise manner and in words calculated to ensure the confidence of the birth parents in the integrity of the adoption process, communicate to the birth parents of a child who is the subject of an adoption petition all of the following facts:

(1) It is in the child's best interest that the birth parent keep the department or licensed adoption agency to whom the child was relinquished for adoption informed of any health problems that the parent develops that could affect the child.

(2) It is extremely important that the birth parent keep an address current with the department or licensed adoption agency to whom the child was relinquished for adoption in order to permit a response to inquiries concerning medical or social history.

(3) Section 9203 of the Family Code authorizes a person who has been adopted and who attains the age of 21 years to request the department or the licensed adoption agency to disclose the name and address of the adoptee's birth parents. Consequently, it is of the utmost importance that the birth parent indicate whether to allow this disclosure by checking the appropriate box provided on the form.

(4) The birth parent may change the decision whether to permit disclosure of the birth parent's name and address, at any time, by sending a notarized letter to that effect, by certified mail, return receipt requested, to the department or to the licensed adoption agency that joined in the adoption petition.

(5) The relinquishment will be filed in the office of the clerk of the court in which the adoption takes place. The file is not open to inspection by any persons other than the parties to the adoption proceeding, their attorneys, and the department, except upon order of a judge of the superior court.

(b) The department shall adopt a form to be signed by the birth parents at the time the relinquishment is signed, which shall provide as follows:

"Section 9203 of the Family Code authorizes a person who has been adopted and who attains the age of 21 years to make a request to the State Department of Social Services, or the licensed adoption agency that joined in the adoption petition, for the name and address of the adoptee's birth parents. Indicate by checking one of the boxes below whether or not you wish your name and address to be disclosed:

[ ] YES

[ ] NO

[ ] UNCERTAIN AT THIS TIME; WILL NOTIFY AGENCY AT LATER DATE."

§ 8706. Medical report; background of child and biological parents; contents; blood sample

(a) An agency may not place a child for adoption unless a written report on the child's medical background and, if available, the medical background of the child's biological parents so far as ascertainable, has been submitted to the prospective adoptive parents and they have acknowledged in writing the receipt of the report.

(b) The report on the child's background shall contain all known diagnostic information, including current medical reports on the child, psychological evaluations, and scholastic information, as well as all known information regarding the child's developmental history and family life.

(c)(1) The biological parents may provide a blood sample at a clinic or hospital approved by the State Department of Health Services. The biological parents' failure to provide a blood sample shall not affect the adoption of the child.

(2) The blood sample shall be stored at a laboratory under contract with the State Department of Health Services for a period of 30 years following the adoption of the child.

(3) The purpose of the stored sample of blood is to provide a blood sample from which DNA testing can be done at a later date after entry of the order of adoption at the request of the adoptive parents or the adopted child. The cost of drawing and storing the blood samples shall be paid for by a separate fee in addition to the fee required under Section 8716. The amount of this additional fee shall be based on the cost of drawing and storing the blood samples but at no time shall the additional fee be more than one hundred dollars ($100).

(d)(1) The blood sample shall be stored and released in such a manner as to not identify any party to the adoption.

(2) Any results of the DNA testing shall be stored and released in such a manner as to not identify any party to the adoption.

NOTE

The California statute is more elaborate than many, but it reflects the trend of specifying in detail what must be done in the process of relinquishment to and placement by an agency. In Tyler v. Children's Home Society of California, 29 Cal.App.4th 511, 35 Cal.Rptr.2d 291 (1994), *cert. denied* 515 U.S. 1160, 115 S.Ct. 2614, 132 L.Ed.2d 857 (1995), birth parents who had relinquished their child to a licensed private agency for adoption sought to void their relinquishments due to failure of the agency and one of its employees to comply with Department of Social Services (DSS) regulations. In addition to accusations of coercion and intimidation, the plaintiffs asserted that the agency failed to give plaintiffs full counseling, copies of the signed and filed forms, and to obtain a full medical history from the father. The agency employee admitted noncompliance in that she did not discuss the option of placement with extended family members or educational or employment resources, and did not give plaintiffs copies of the executed documents or obtain the father's medical history before the relinquishments were signed. Concluding that the plaintiffs failed to show prejudice from any of the regulatory violations, the California Court of Appeal, Third District, affirmed the judgment below refusing to void the relinquishment agreement.

At one time it was not uncommon that a relinquishing parent could legally withdraw consent as a matter of right before an interlocutory decree of adoption had been rendered. Legislative provisions generally were added to limit or bar revocation of consent upon relinquishment to an agency or at least after the child had been placed by an agency. Sometimes the easier revocation rule remained for private placement cases. Today the widely accepted approach is not only to require that revocation must take place prior to adoption, but also to limit revocation very substantially even before adoption has taken place. The latest Uniform Adoption Act (1994) provides separate, detailed requirements for revocation of consent from a private individual or guardian, (section 2–408) and revocation of a relinquishment to an agency (Section 2–409). Many states provide that a consent to relinquish is not valid unless executed a certain number of days after birth of the child. *See, e.g.,* KY.REV.STAT. § 199.500(5) (West Supp. 2001) (consent not valid if given before 72 hours after birth). This can provide a safeguard to problems of relinquishment during a period of postpartum stress.

One situation in which a placing agency might wish to remove a child before adoption has taken place is when the potential adopters are a couple whose marriage is troubled. For a decision upholding an agency's authority to remove a child in such an instance if adequate procedures to insure fairness are followed, *see* Marten v. Thies, 99 Cal.App.3d 161, 160 Cal.Rptr. 57 (1979), *cert. denied* 449 U.S. 831, 101 S.Ct. 99, 66 L.Ed.2d 36 (1980).

M.H. and J.L.H. v. Caritas Family Services

Supreme Court of Minnesota, 1992.
488 N.W.2d 282.

■ Wahl, Justice.

We are asked to decide whether public policy precludes an action against an adoption agency for alleged negligent misrepresentations made during the placement of a child in adoption proceedings. . . .

Plaintiffs M.H. and J.L.H., who married in 1977, sought to adopt a child after learning J.L.H. was unlikely to conceive a child. Plaintiffs first contacted Caritas Family Services, a Catholic social service agency active in placing children for adoption, in early 1980. In May of that year, they filled out an application for adoption during an interview in their home by a Caritas social worker.

On November 23, 1981, Caritas conducted a second home visit. The purpose of the second visit was, according to Caritas' adoption summary, "to explore with [the H.s] their feelings regarding a child with incest in the background." According to the summary, the H.s "appeared open to any child except one with a very serious mental deficiency."

Two days later, in a telephone conversation, Sister Cathan Culhane, a Caritas social worker, told J.L.H. that Caritas had a child the H.s might wish to adopt. According to J.L.H., Sister Culhane told her there was a "possibility of incest in the family." J.L.H. said she told sister Culhane, "Well, it's a baby. We're happy. As long as it's in the family, it didn't affect him." Sister Culhane described the baby as having a plugged tear duct and an undescended testicle, but otherwise in good health.

Two days after this telephone call, the H.s met with Sister Culhane in Caritas' office in St. Cloud. Sister Culhane again raised the question of incest and, according to M.H. and J.L.H., asked "Did it matter if there was incest in the family's background?" M.H. said he replied, "No problem, didn't matter to me in the background." According to M.H., Sister Culhane said there was a slight chance that the child might have abnormalities related to incest in his "background." The H.s asked no further questions and there was no more discussion of incest.

At this meeting, Caritas gave the H.s a document with information about the child, including his name, birth date, birth weight and length, cultural heritage, and a description of the genetic parents. The health of the genetic parents was described as follows: HEALTH Both parents of normal intelligence and in good health as are their parents, brothers and sisters. Older members of their families—(Grandparents' generation) have had coronary trouble, Muscular Dystrophy and also nervous breakdown. One cousin of the natural mother is retarded and an uncle had an ulcer.

Both parents planned for the adoption of their child because they are young, still in school, and unable to assume the role of parents at this time.

The H.s took the baby, C.H., home with them that day. He was 45 days old. The H.s soon noticed that C.H. was jumpy, nervous, cried a lot, and did not sleep very much. The H.s consulted their physician who wanted information as to whether C.H.'s genetic mother had taken drugs during pregnancy. Mrs. H. contacted Sister Culhane who said that the genetic mother was not on drugs during pregnancy.

Sometime between November 1981 and when the adoption became final in September 1982, Caritas sent the H.s a document saying the birth mother was 17 years old instead of 13 as they had been previously told. The document also mentioned the "possibility of incest" but said nothing more specific on the subject. The H.s inquired about the discrepancy in the genetic mother's age and were assured by Sister Culhane that the original information given them about the genetic mother's age (that she was 13) was correct and a new document was sent to replace the mistaken one. Neither the H.s or Sister Culhane discussed incest at this time.

Throughout his childhood, C.H. has had serious behavioral and emotional problems. He has been diagnosed as having attention deficit hyperactivity disorder. He has exhibited hyperactivity, violent behavior when upset (i.e. kicking, biting, pulling hair), and has set fires indoors. On one occasion, he struck, punched, bit, and scratched J.L.H. while she took him to an appointment with his psychiatrist. He has difficulty with small motor skills and has had social problems in school. He is not mentally retarded, however, and his adoptive parents characterize him as smart.

The H.s consulted psychologists to help C.H. regarding his behavior. In 1987, one of the psychologists asked for more information regarding C.H.'s genetic background. In response to this request, Caritas produced and gave to the H.s a 2–page document entitled "Background History of [C.H.]" in December 1987. This document revealed to the H.s, for the first time, that C.H.'s genetic parents were a 17–year old boy and his 13–year old sister. Caritas admits that it knew of this relationship from the time it first considered placing C.H. with the H.s.

Caritas subsequently also disclosed that the genetic father was considered "borderline hyperactive" which caused problems for him in school; that he had tested in the low average range of intelligence; and that he had been seen at the local mental health center at age of 11 for six weeks, but was discharged from treatment because he was not cooperating with his therapist. The H.s were also told that a physician, possibly a neurologist, had prescribed medication for the genetic father's hyperactivity. Caritas has denied knowing this information about the genetic father's mental health history until its inquiry in 1987.

After learning these facts regarding H.'s genetic parents, the H.s filed an action against Caritas in October 1989. Count I of their complaint alleged that Caritas failed to disclose the relationship of C.H.'s genetic parents and all relevant history known to Caritas concerning the birth parents with the intent to induce the H.s to adopt the child. Count II alleged that Caritas negligently failed to disclose that information as well as other relevant information it had about the child's genetic parents. The complaint also alleged that because of the misrepresentations, whether intentional or negligent, the plaintiffs had suffered mental pain and anguish and had incurred considerable expense.

During discovery Caritas refused to reveal information relating to what it knew about C.H.'s genetic parents prior to adoption, its attempts to place him with other families, and its sources of information about the genetic parents without a court order permitting it to do so, citing the state adoption statute (Minn.Stat. ch. 259), the Minnesota Government Data Practices Act (Minn.Stat. ch. 13), and unspecified federal regulations. Caritas agreed to stipulate to a court order to permit it to disclose its discussions held between the agency's employees and the adoptive parents, but not its written records. No such order was ever requested, however, or granted by the court.

On October 8, 1990, Caritas moved for summary judgment on both counts of the complaint, the intentional misrepresentation claim on the grounds of insufficient evidence and the negligent misrepresentation claim on grounds of public policy. Caritas also moved for summary judgment on a count of intentional infliction of emotional distress that it anticipated the respondents would try to add to their complaint. Plaintiffs then did move to amend their complaint to add allegations of intentional and negligent infliction of emotional distress and a prayer for punitive damages. They also moved to compel discovery of Caritas' pre-adoption records.

The district court granted Caritas' motions for summary judgment, except as to negligent misrepresentation. The court certified the question we have before us....

Plaintiffs in the case before us allege that the adoption agency disclosed information about the child's genetic parents but negligently failed to communicate that information fully and accurately and that such negligence caused them damages. Whether public policy precludes an action against an adoption agency for alleged negligent misrepresentation during the placement of a child in adoption proceedings is a question of law and a question of first impression in Minnesota. A review at the outset of cases from jurisdictions that have considered the issue is instructive, however. See generally Mary E. Schwartz, *Note, Fraud in the Nursery: Is the Wrongful Adoption Remedy Enough?*, 26 VAL.U.L.REV. 807 (1992). On the one hand, the cases seem to agree that adoption agencies may be held liable for damages caused by intentional, affirmative misrepresentations of facts regarding the child to the adopting parents. See, e.g., Michael J. v. County of Los Angeles, 201 Cal.App.3d 859, 247 Cal.Rptr. 504, 512–13 (1988) (public policy does not condone concealment or intentional misrepresentation that misleads adopting parents); Burr v. Board of County Comm'rs of Stark County, 23 Ohio St.3d 69, 491 N.E.2d 1101, 1109 (Ohio 1986) (same). On the other hand, there is agreement that an adoption agency cannot be expected to be "a guarantor of the infant's future good health" and negligence suits tending to have that effect have been rejected. Richard P. v. Vista Del Mar Child Care Serv., 106 Cal.App.3d 860, 165 Cal.Rptr. 370, 374 (1980); see also Foster v. Bass, 575 So.2d 967, 980 (Miss.1990). The question we are asked to decide falls between these two extremes: whether public policy bars actions holding adoption agencies liable for damages for negligent misrepresentation of facts concerning the child's genetic parents and medical history.

We have recognized the tort of negligent misrepresentation, Bonhiver v. Graff, 311 Minn. 111, 121–23, 248 N.W.2d 291, 298–99 (1976), but conduct actionable against one class of defendant is not automatically actionable against another class of defendants. Tort liability in the first instance always depends on whether the party accused of the tort owes a duty to the accusing party. If such a duty is owed, then one who undertakes to act must, under common law principles, act with reasonable care. No duty is owed, however, unless the plaintiff's interests are entitled to legal protection against the defendant's conduct. Whether the plaintiff's interests are entitled to legal protection against the defendant's conduct is a matter of public policy. Which brings us to the certified question stated somewhat more precisely: Does public policy favor legal protection of the interests of adoptive parents against the negligent conduct of adoption agencies?

Caritas and amici adoption agencies emphatically answer that question in the negative. They ask this court to hold as a matter of law that public policy precludes recognition of a legal duty of care with regard to negligent representations of fact by adoption agencies to adoptive parents. They argue that recognition of such a duty would place an unreasonable burden on adoption agencies by requiring them to independently verify family histories given them by the genetic parent. Adoptions would be discouraged, they say, if agencies were required to disclose information that might render certain children more difficult to place or would unnecessarily stigmatize them once adopted. They further argue it is unreasonable to impose liability on agencies for negligently failing to discover certain aspects of a child's genetic history when the number of genetic-related conditions and the cost of tests to discover them are increasing at a rapid rate. Finally, Caritas and amici argue that requiring adoption agencies to defend negligent misrepresentation suits would conflict with confidentiality policies required by state and federal law to protect the identity of genetic parents.

We appreciate that these are legitimate policy concerns. We recognize the unique nature and mission of adoption agencies as they seek to meet both the need of adoptive parents to experience the joys and challenges of parenthood and the need of every child to have a stable, loving family. We also recognize, however, the compelling need of adoptive parents for full disclosure of medical background information that may be known to the agency on both the child they may adopt and the child's genetic parents, not only to secure timely and appropriate medical care for the child, but also to make vital personal, health and family decisions.

While under other circumstances the policy concerns of the adoption agencies may preclude a cause of action, on the facts of this case, the policy concerns are not implicated. Plaintiffs do not allege that Caritas insufficiently investigated C.H.'s background: Caritas knew from the start of these adoption proceedings that C.H.'s genetic parents were brother and sister. Neither do plaintiffs assert that Caritas had a duty to test C.H. for genetic abnormalities. There is no suggestion nor do plaintiffs allege that Caritas had an affirmative common law duty to disclose facts surrounding C.H.'s parentage beyond those required by statute or administrative rule.[5] Furthermore, confidentiality policies are necessary to protect the identity of the genetic parents, not to inhibit communication of vital health and medical information. Plaintiffs assert only that once Caritas undertook to disclose the information that incest existed in C.H.'s background, it assumed a duty to use due care that its disclosure be complete and adequate to ensure that the adoptive parents were not misled as to the true nature of their son's genetic parentage. This is the common law duty plaintiffs allege Caritas breached.

We long ago recognized that even if one has no duty to disclose a particular fact, if one chooses to speak he must say enough to prevent the words from misleading the other party. We have also held that a duty to disclose facts may exist "when disclosure would be necessary to clarify information already disclosed, which would otherwise be misleading," particularly when a confidential or fiduciary relationship exists between the parties. L & H Airco, 446 N.W.2d at 380. We are not persuaded that adoption agencies should be immune from this common law rule.[6] Recognition of this duty imposes no extraordinary or onerous burden on adoption agencies. It merely requires them to use due care to ensure that when they undertake to disclose information about a child's genetic parents and medical history, they disclose that information fully and adequately so as not to mislead prospective adoptive parents. Caritas had a legal duty to not mislead plaintiffs by only partially disclosing the truth.

The district court, in denying Caritas' motion for summary judgment on negligent misrepresentation on policy grounds, and the court of appeals in affirming that denial, relied on Meracle v. Children's Serv. Soc. of Wis., 149 Wis.2d 19, 437 N.W.2d 532 (1989). In Meracle, the Wisconsin Supreme Court recognized a cause of action where an adoption agency negligently told adoptive parents that, though the child's paternal grandmother had Huntington's Disease, the child's genetic father had tested negative for that disease, thus negating the child's chances of developing the disease. In fact no such test existed and the father could not have been tested. Id. 437 N.W.2d at 533. The court recognized that public policy requires that adoption agencies should not be exposed to unlimited liability or be made

---

5. See, e.g., Minn.R. 9560.0060 (1991) (adoption agencies required to provide adoptive parents with written health history of the child that is understandable and meaningful to the adoptive family).

6. If there are policy considerations that should override the agency's common law liability for misrepresentation, the legislature is the appropriate body to extend such immunity.

guarantors of the health of children they place in adoptive homes. Id. at 537. It held, however, that public policy did not bar a negligent misrepresentation action when the agency assumed a duty of informing adoptive parents about the child's health history but did so negligently. "To avoid liability, agencies simply must refrain from making affirmative misrepresentations about a child's health." Id. See also Roe v. Catholic Charities, 588 N.E.2d 354, 365 (Ill.App.1992).

We, like the court of appeals, find Meracle persuasive. Like the Meracle court, we reject the argument that potential liability will inhibit adoptions. "Indeed, [our decision] will give potential parents more confidence in the adoption process and in the accuracy of the information they receive. Such confidence would be eroded if we were to immunize agencies from liability for false statements made during the adoption process." Meracle, 437 N.W.2d at 537. This is particularly true because adoption agencies are the adoptive parents' only source of information about the child's medical and genetic background.

We hold that public policy does not preclude a negligent misrepresentation action against an adoption agency where the agency, having undertaken to disclose information about the child's genetic parents and medical background to the adoptive parents, negligently withholds information in such a way that the adoptive parents were misled as to the truth. We affirm the court of appeals and answer the certified question in the negative.

The district court granted Caritas summary judgment on plaintiffs' intentional misrepresentation claim because it found that Caritas had made no affirmative misrepresentation to plaintiffs. Plaintiffs argue that Caritas made two discrete misrepresentations, one regarding the incest in C.H.'s background and the other by affirmatively stating that C.H.'s genetic father was in "good health." Plaintiffs argue that either representation was specific enough to support their claim of intentional misrepresentation. The court of appeals agreed and reinstated the claim for both representations.

An intentional misrepresentation claim requires plaintiffs to allege that defendant (1) made a representation (2) that was false (3) having to do with a past or present fact (4) that is material (5) and susceptible of knowledge (6) that the representor knows to be false or is asserted without knowing whether the fact is true or false (7) with the intent to induce the other person to act (8) and the person in fact is induced to act (9) in reliance on the representation (10) that the plaintiff suffered damages (11) attributable to the misrepresentation. A misrepresentation may be made either (1) by an affirmative statement that is itself false or (2) by concealing or not disclosing certain facts that render the facts that are disclosed misleading.

The statements Caritas made regarding incest were of the latter type. Their falsity arose, if at all, from Caritas' failure to disclose additional facts, not from the statements themselves which were true on their face. Plaintiffs, however, have not alleged any facts or produced any evidence implying that Caritas intended to mislead plaintiffs by deliberately withholding the full facts regarding incest in C.H.'s background. Indeed, the evidence suggests the opposite: if Caritas intended to mislead plaintiffs, it is unlikely it would have raised the question of incest with them at all. In the absence of evidence that the statements regarding incest were calculated to mislead plaintiffs, they were insufficient as a matter of law to establish a case of intentional misrepresentation.[7]

Neither will Caritas' statement regarding the genetic father's "good health" support an intentional misrepresentation claim because plaintiffs have not shown it was either false on its face or deliberately misleading. Caritas' statement in 1981 that the genetic father was in good health is not made false by the fact that the genetic father had been hyperactive and had undergone psychiatric treatment several years before. Plaintiffs must, therefore, produce evidence that Caritas intentionally misled them by withholding the information. Even if Caritas knew of the genetic father's mental health history in 1981,[8] plaintiffs have not produced any facts to suggest that Caritas' failure to disclose that fact was intended to mislead them.

We reverse the court of appeals and hold that the district court properly granted defendant Caritas summary judgment on the intentional misrepresentation claim.

Plaintiffs moved the trial court to amend their complaint to add claims for intentional infliction of emotional distress, negligent infliction of emotional distress, and punitive damages. The trial court denied the motion, holding that the dismissal of the intentional misrepresentation claim left the record bare of allegations of outrageous and willful misconduct required for either claim of infliction of emotional distress and the punitive damages claim. The court of appeals, having reinstated the intentional misrepresentation claim, reversed.

Infliction of emotional distress, whether intentional or negligent, generally requires plaintiffs to suffer a physical injury as evidence of their severe emotional distress. Because plaintiffs have alleged no physical injury resulting from their alleged emotional distress, their motion to amend was properly denied unless they alleged a "direct invasion" of their rights by "willful, wanton, or malicious conduct." State Farm Mut. Auto. Ins. Co. v. Village of Isle, 265 Minn. 360, 367–68, 122 N.W.2d 36, 41 (1963). There is no evidence of such a direct invasion of plaintiffs' rights, or of willful, wanton, or malicious conduct on the part of Caritas. Plaintiffs have provided no evidence that Caritas deliberately misled them, much less wantonly did so.... [T]he district court did not abuse its discretion in

---

7. Plaintiffs contend that Caritas' refusal to grant them access to its pre-adoption records should estop it from receiving summary judgment on this claim. The records might contain direct evidence of Caritas' intent to mislead plaintiffs by deliberately referring to the incest in an oblique manner calculated to obscure the actual truth. Plaintiffs did not file a motion to compel discovery of these records until more than a year and three months after the suit was filed and over three months after Caritas filed its motion for summary judgment, however. Having delayed so long, they cannot now complain that they lack the facts to support their complaint.

8. Caritas asserts it did not learn of those problems until 1987.

denying plaintiffs leave to amend their complaint to add claims of intentional and negligent infliction of emotional distress.

Similarly, plaintiffs have not alleged sufficient facts to support a finding that there is "clear and convincing evidence that the acts of the defendant show a deliberate disregard for the rights or safety of others" required to recover punitive damages The court of appeals is therefore reversed and the district court's denial of leave to add a claim for punitive damages is affirmed.

. . .

Case remanded for trial.

NOTE

An action for "Wrongful Adoption"? In Burr v. Board of County Com'rs of Stark Cty., 23 Ohio St.3d 69, 491 N.E.2d 1101 (1986), adoptive parents brought an action described as "Wrongful Adoption", alleging that they were fraudulently misled to their detriment by material misrepresentations of an adoption agency about the condition and background of the infant placed with them. They asserted, for example, that they were told that the child was "a nice, big, healthy baby boy" surrendered to the agency by an eighteen-year-old mother who was leaving the state for better employment. In fact, the mother was a thirty-one year old mental patient. After suffering from a series of physical and mental problems, the child was diagnosed as suffering from Huntington's disease when he reached high school age. The Supreme Court of Ohio stated that to recover, the parents must prove each element of the tort of fraud, described in the Syllabus by the Court as:

(a) a representation or, where there is a duty to disclose, concealment of a fact,

(b) which is material to the transaction at hand,

(c) made falsely, with knowledge of its falsity, or with such utter disregard and recklessness as to whether it is true or false that knowledge may be inferred,

(d) with the intent of misleading another into relying upon it,

(e) justifiable reliance upon the representation or concealment, and

(f) a resulting injury proximately caused by the reliance.

The court further held that while the cause of action must be commenced within four years of its accrual, it does not begin to accrue until actual discovery of the fraud and the wrongdoer.

In Mallette v. Children's Friend and Service, 661 A.2d 67 (R.I.1995), the Rhode Island Supreme Court held that the tort of negligent misrepresentation could be extended to the context of adoption through placement agencies. *See also,* Mohr v. Commonwealth, 421 Mass. 147, 653 N.E.2d 1104 (1995).

In Dahlin v. Evangelical Family Agency, 2001 WL 840347 (N.D.Ill. 2001), an adopted child was not allowed to continue an action against an adoption agency that placed her, for failing to give information about her biological family to her or to her adoptive parents after she reached age 18. The adoptee alleged that she had experienced severe behavioral problems and depression during her childhood and that failure to disclose the information impeded her medical treatment and thereby exacerbated her medical problems. The court pointed out while cases had established that the agency owes a duty to adoptive parents, a similar duty to an adoptee had not been established under Illinois law.

b. ENCOURAGING OR LIMITING THIRD PARTY PARTICIPATION IN THE PLACEMENT PROCESS

Licensure. Some states have enacted legislation to discourage or bar adoption through private (nonagency) placements. A typical approach is to limit or bar the involvement of third persons who are paid for acting as intermediaries unless they obtain a license to place children. *See, e.g.,* DEL. CODE ANN. tit. 13, § 904; D.C. CODE ANN. §§ 32–1002,–1009; MASS.GEN.LAWS ANN. ch. 210, § 11A; N.J.STAT.ANN. §§ 9:3–39.1.

A "Market" for Babies? It has been suggested that some of the current demand for children to adopt could be satisfied through allowing the transfer of unwanted children for compensation. One postulate is that it would induce some women with unwanted pregnancies to forgo abortion, bear the children and then receive payment for relinquishing them for adoption. Market factors might even induce the mother to avoid possibly dangerous acts or conduct during gestation that might injure the child. The idea was discussed in an article by Elizabeth M. Landes and Richard A. Posner, *The Economics of the Baby Shortage*, 7 J. LEGAL STUD. 323, 343 (1978). The proposal was revisited in a symposium published in 67 B.U.L.REV. 1 (1987). Professor Jane Maslow Cohen, in *Posnerism, Pluralism, Pessimism*, 67 B.U.L.REV. 105 (1987), places the family law issues of such a proposal in important perspective. Though the debate still has not centered on issues of surrogate parent agreements, it seems inevitable that it will.

Implementation of any such proposals would run afoul of existing laws in a number of states. Oklahoma has created a separate crime of "trafficking in children", OKLA.STAT.ANN. tit. 21, §§ 866–867 (West 2001 Supp.), and some other jurisdictions maintain criminal statutes against child selling. *See, e.g.,* UTAH CODE ANN. § 76–7–203 (LEXIS 1999).

The term "grey market" is sometimes applied to independent placements made through usually well meaning persons ranging from physicians and lawyers to family or friends of the parties. The term has unfortunate connotations and should be distinguished from what has been dubbed the "black market" in which children were literally bought and sold for adoption by unscrupulous parties who operated rather widely just a decade or so ago. Hearings before a subcommittee of the Senate Judiciary Committee in 1955 revealed harrowing accounts of the latter experiences.

4.   SUBSIDIZED ADOPTION

MODEL STATE SUBSIDIZED ADOPTION ACT (1976)

Section 1. [Purpose]. The purpose of this Act is to supplement the [State] adoption statutes by making possible through public financial subsidy the most appropriate adoption of each child certified by the [Department of Social Services] as requiring a subsidy to assure adoption.

Section 2. [Definition of "child."] As used in this Act, except as otherwise required by the context, "child" means a minor as defined by [State] statute, who is (a) a dependent of a public or voluntary licensed child-placing agency, (b) legally free for adoption, and (c) in special circumstances either (1) because he has established significant emotional ties with prospective adoptive parents[1] while in their care as a foster child, or (2) because he is not likely to be adopted by reason of one or more conditions, such as:

1. Physical or mental disability,

2. Emotional disturbance,

3. Recognized high risk of physical or mental disease,

4. Age,

5. Sibling relationship,

6. Racial or ethnic factors, or

7. Any combination of these conditions.

Section 3. [Administration and Funding.] The [Department of Social Services] shall establish and administer an ongoing program of subsidized adoption. Subsidies and services for children under this program shall be provided out of funds appropriated to the [Department of Social Services] for the maintenance of children in foster care or made available to it from other sources.

Section 4. [Eligibility.] Whenever significant emotional ties have been established between a child and his foster parents, and the foster parents seek to adopt the child, the child shall be certified as eligible for a subsidy conditioned upon his adoption under applicable [State] adoption procedures by the foster parents.

In all other cases, after reasonable efforts have been made and no appropriate adoptive family without the use of subsidy has been found for a child, the [Department of Social Services] shall certify the child as eligible for a subsidy in the event of adoption.

---

1. As used in this Act and Comments, "parents" represents either one or two parents.

If the child is the dependent of a voluntary licensed child-placing agency, that agency shall present to the [Department of Social Services] (1) evidence of significant emotional ties between the child and his foster parents or (2) evidence of inability to place the child for adoption due to any of the conditions specified in Section 2 of this Act. In the latter case, the agency shall present evidence that reasonable efforts have been made to place the child without subsidy, such as recruitment of potential parents, use of adoption resource exchanges, and referral to appropriate specialized adoption agencies.

Section 5. [Subsidy Agreement.] When parents are found and approved for adoption of a child certified as eligible for subsidy, and before the final decree of adoption is issued, there must be a written agreement between the family entering into the subsidized adoption and the [Department of Social Services.] Adoption subsidies in individual cases may commence with the adoption placement or at the appropriate time after the adoption decree, and will vary with the needs of the child as well as the availability of other resources to meet the child's needs. The subsidy may be for special services only, or for money payments, and either for a limited period, or for a long term, or for any combination of the foregoing. The amount of the time-limited or long-term subsidy may in no case exceed that which would be allowable from time to time for such child under foster family care, or, in the case of a special service, the reasonable fee for the service rendered.

When subsidies are for more than one year, the adoptive parents shall present an annual sworn certification that the adopted child remains under their care and that the condition(s) that caused the child to be certified continue(s) to exist. The subsidy agreement shall be continued in accordance with its terms but only as long as the adopted child is the legal dependent of the adoptive parents and the child's condition continues, except that, in the absence of other appropriate resources provided by law and in accordance with [State] regulations, it may be continued after the adopted child reaches majority. Termination or modification of the subsidy agreement may be requested by the adoptive parents at any time.

A child who is a resident of this [State] when eligibility for subsidy is certified shall remain eligible and receive subsidy, if necessary for adoption, regardless of the domicile or residence of the adopting parents at the time of application for adoption, placement, legal decree of adoption or thereafter.

All records regarding subsidized adoption shall be confidential and may be disclosed only in accordance with the [relevant provisions of the State adoption act.]

[Sections 6–9 deal with appeals under state administrative procedures, promulgation of regulations, the title of the Act and its effective date.]

NOTE

Although a subsidized adoption provision was adopted as early as 1968, there was initial reluctance by most states to introduce the approach. This prompted one early commentator to remark that "In a society in which two of the most cherished values are children and money, it is surprising that a proposal holding promise of saving both has met with much resistance." *See* Kenneth W. Watson, *Subsidized Adoption: A Crucial Investment*, 51 CHILD WELFARE 220, 224 (1972).

The preceding model law was disseminated by the Office of Child Development of what is now the Department of Health and Human Services. A model set of regulations accompanied the statutory proposal, along with a comparison of the Model Act with then existing laws. The regulations explained that:

> Subsidized adoption is an ongoing program ... intended to make adoption possible for children who otherwise may not be adopted. It is designed as a supplement to the [State] adoption statutes and as an effective addition to regular recruitment efforts. It is meant to provide the benefits of family security, love and nurture for children in special circumstances, presently under the care of public or licensed voluntary agencies.

Subsidized adoption was given a strong boost by a provision in Public Law 96–272 (1980) requiring state plans for adoption assistance under 42 U.S.C.A. § 602(a)(20). In 1981 the Department also published a MODEL ACT FOR ADOPTION OF CHILDREN WITH SPECIAL NEEDS. *See* 46 FED.REG. 50,022 (1981). The elaborate and comprehensive proposal, which includes special sections on terminating parental rights of children with special needs, complemented the Model Subsidized Adoption Act.

For an overview of the adoption assistance program and a perceptive analysis of problems that have arisen under it, including coordination of medical care payments for children of interstate placements, see Alice Bussiere, *Federal Adoption Assistance for Children with Special Needs*, 1985 CLEARINGHOUSE REV. 587.

5. CIVIL EFFECTS

a. STATUTORY FRAMEWORK

NEW YORK DOMESTIC RELATIONS LAW (McKinney Supp. 2007)

§ 117. Effect of adoption

1.(a) After the making of an order of adoption the birth parents of the adoptive child shall be relieved of all parental duties toward and of all responsibilities for and shall have no rights over such adoptive child or to his property by descent or succession, except as hereinafter stated.

(b) The rights of an adoptive child to inheritance and succession from and through his birth parents shall terminate upon the making of the order of adoption except as hereinafter provided.

(c) The adoptive parents or parent and the adoptive child shall sustain toward each other the legal relation of parent and child and shall have all the rights and be subject to all the duties of that relation including the rights of inheritance from and through each other and the birth and adopted kindred of the adoptive parents or parent.

(d) When a birth or adoptive parent, having lawful custody of a child, marries or remarries and consents that the stepparent may adopt such child, such consent shall not relieve the parent so consenting of any parental duty toward such child nor shall such consent or the order of adoption affect the rights of such consenting spouse and such adoptive child to inherit from and through each other and the birth and adopted kindred of such consenting spouse.

(e) Notwithstanding the provisions of paragraphs (a), (b) and (d) of this subdivision, as to estates of persons dying after the thirty-first day of August, nineteen hundred eighty-seven, if:

(1) the decedent is the adoptive child's birth grandparent or is a descendant of such grandparent, and

(2) an adoptive parent

(i) is married to the child's birth parent,

(ii) is the child's birth grandparent, or

(iii) is descended from such grandparent,

the rights of an adoptive child to inheritance and succession from and through either birthparent shall not terminate upon the making of the order of adoption.

However, an adoptive child who is related to the decedent both by birth relationship and by adoption shall be entitled to inherit only under the birth relationship unless the decedent is also the adoptive parent, in which case the adoptive child shall then be entitled to inherit pursuant to the adoptive relationship only.

(f) The right of inheritance of an adoptive child extends to the distributees of such child and such distributees shall be the same as if he were the birth child of the adoptive parent.

(g) Adoptive children and birth children shall have all the rights of fraternal relationship including the right of inheritance from each other. Such right of inheritance extends to the distributees of such adoptive children and birth children and such distributees shall be the same as if each such child were the birth child of the adoptive parents.

(h) The consent of the parent of a child to the adoption of such child by his or her spouse shall operate to vest in the adopting spouse only the rights as distributee of a birth parent and shall leave otherwise unaffected the rights as distributee of the consenting spouse.

(i) This subdivision shall apply only to the intestate descent and distribution of real and personal property.

2.(a) Except as hereinafter stated, after the making of an order of adoption, adopted children and their issue thereafter are strangers to any birth relatives for the purpose of the interpretation or construction of a disposition in any instrument, whether executed before or after the order of adoption, which does not express a contrary intention or does not expressly include the individual by name or by some classification not based on a parent-child or family relationship.

(b) As to the wills of persons executed after the thirty-first day of August, nineteen hundred eighty-six, or to lifetime instruments executed after such date whether executed before or after the order of adoption, a designation of a class of persons described in section 2–1.3 of the estates, powers and trusts law shall, unless the will or instrument expresses a contrary intention, be deemed to include an adoptive child who was a member of such class in his or her birth relationship prior to adoption, and the issue of such child, only if:

(1) an adoptive parent (i) is married to the child's birth parent, (ii) is the child's birth grandparent, or (iii) is a descendant of such grandparent, and

(2) the testator or creator is the child's birth grandparent or a descendant of such grandparent.

(c) A person who, by reason of this subdivision, would be a member of the designated class, or a member of two or more designated classes pursuant to a single instrument, both by birth relationship and by adoption shall be entitled to benefit only under the birth relationship, unless the testator or creator is the adoptive parent, in which case the person shall then be entitled to benefit only under the adoptive relationship.

(d) The provisions of this subdivision shall not impair or defeat any rights which have vested on or before the thirty-first day of August, nineteen hundred eighty-six, or which have vested prior to the adoption regardless of when the adoption occurred.

3.   The provisions of law affected by the provisions of this section in force prior to March first, nineteen hundred sixty-four shall apply to the estates or wills of persons dying prior thereto and to lifetime instruments theretofore executed which on said date were not subject to grantor's power to revoke or amend.

NOTE

State adoption laws generally include a basic statement to the effect that adopted children are to be fully integrated into their new adoptive families. New York Domestic Relations Law § 114, dealing with what will be contained in an adoption order, states that the order approving an adoption will direct "that the adoptive child shall thenceforth be regarded and treated in all respects as the child of the adoptive parents or parent."

Because adoption was regarded as abrogating the common law, a rule of strict construction often resulted in judicial decisions of a limiting nature, particularly in the area of inheritance rights. This would in due time be followed by a specific statutory amendment to overcome the limitation. In some jurisdictions, such as New York, this has produced increasingly detailed provisions.

b. MARRIAGE BANS BASED ON ADOPTIVE KINSHIP

As noted in Chapter 3, some states now specifically preclude intermarriage between siblings related only through adoption. Given the approach of encouraging early adoptive placement through agencies that can accord anonymity to insulate the adoptive and natural parents from knowing anything about each other, is it important to provide specific exceptions to incest laws in order to avoid sibling or parent-child intermarriage? When close adoptive relationship is made a bar to intermarriage, should distinction be made between whether the parties were adopted as infants or after reaching adolescence?

c. INHERITANCE

Despite enactment of general statutes that would appear to equate the rights of adoptive and natural children, problems of succession or inheritance by adopted children were caused by narrow construction of such widely used legal terms as "issue". For example, in Crumpton v. Mitchell, 303 N.C. 657, 281 S.E.2d 1 (1981), the North Carolina Supreme Court held that the word "issue" in a deed did not include persons adopted out of the family unless a contrary intent appeared plainly from its terms. And in Morgan v. Mayes, 170 W.Va. 687, 296 S.E.2d 34 (1982), the Supreme Court of Appeals of West Virginia held that when inheritance rights are broadened by a statute of descent and distribution, the law in effect at the death of one from whom an adopted child would take controls rather than the law in effect at the time when the adoption took place. Some statutes, such as Massachusetts Gen.Laws Ann., ch. 210, § 8 (inheritance from grandparents), and Conn.Gen.Stat. § 45–64a deal specifically with concerns of this sort. In MacCallum v. Seymour, 165 Vt. 452, 686 A.2d 935 (1996), the Supreme Court of Vermont held that a Vermont statute denying an adopted person the right to inherit from collateral kin violated the common benefits provision of the Vermont Constitution. A person adopted as a child had brought the action to enforce the right to inherit from a brother of the adopting father.

6. VISITATION AFTER ADOPTION

a. OPEN ADOPTION

Michaud v. Wawruck

Supreme Court of Connecticut, 1988.
209 Conn. 407, 551 A.2d 738.

■ PETERS, CHIEF JUSTICE.

The sole issue in this case is whether a written visitation agreement between a genetic mother and adoptive parents violates the public policy of this state. The plaintiff, Jacqueline Michaud, filed a complaint seeking specific enforcement of an "Open Adoption and Visitation Agreement" between herself and the defendants, James Wawruck and Cynthia Wawruck. The defendants filed a motion to strike the complaint, which was granted by the trial court, Barall, J., and was the basis for the subsequent rendering of a judgment in favor of the defendants by the trial court, Kaplan, J. The plaintiff's appeal to the Appellate Court has been transferred to this court pursuant to Practice Book § 4023. We find error and remand the case for further proceedings.

Since this appeal is from a judgment following the granting of a motion to strike, we must take the facts to be those alleged in the plaintiff's complaint and construe the complaint in the manner most favorable to sustaining its legal sufficiency. Accordingly, we assume the following factual circumstances concerning the "Open Adoption and Visitation Agreement" negotiated by the parties. The Ellington Probate Court, on August 31, 1981, terminated the plaintiff's parental rights with respect to her child born on February 5, 1979. The same Probate Court terminated the father's parental rights on January 6, 1982. At some time thereafter, in 1982, the plaintiff filed a Superior Court action against the commissioner of children and youth services to set aside the Probate Court's decree terminating her parental rights, on the ground that her consent to that proceeding had been fraudulently procured by the child's father. The child's foster parents, who were then seeking to adopt the child, were permitted to intervene as defendants in the Superior Court action. The plaintiff agreed to withdraw her lawsuit, and to allow the adoption to go forward, in exchange for the defendant's agreement to permit regular visitation between the plaintiff and the child during the child's minor years.[1]

---

1. The "Open Adoption and Visitation Agreement" provides in relevant part:

"1. *Adoption.* The parties shall all cooperate fully with the state DCYS in the orderly completion of an adoption of the child by the adopting parents.

2. *Termination of Rights.* The natural mother will withdraw her legal challenge . . . as soon as the adopting parents have approval of their adoption application by DCYS.

3. *Visitation.* The adopting parents will cooperate fully with the natural-mother in the natural mother's visits with the child both now and after the adoption takes place until the child's 18th birthday. The parties agree to be guided in carrying out this provision by the present laws of Connecticut regarding reasonable visitation, which are partly em-

bodied in Connecticut General Statutes Section 46b–56, as they pertain to visitation rights of non-custodial parents in dissolutions of marriage. The tender age of the child and her high sensitivity to her, up to the present, state of uncertainty shall be taken into account by the parties.

Each of the parties shall at all times in good faith endeavor to maintain in the child respect and affection for the other parties.

The rights of visitation shall not be exercised by the natural mother at any time or in such a manner as to interfere with the education and normal social and school activities of the child.

Visitation shall be twice a month for three (3) hours each visit at the Wawrucks' home."

The agreement between the parties was placed on record in the Superior Court on September 16, 1983. Acquiescence in the agreement was noted, in open court, by counsel for the plaintiff, for the defendants, for the commissioner, and for the minor child. The agreement was not, however, made part of the subsequent decree of the Probate Court permitting the defendants to adopt the child, although the parties to that proceeding, having all appeared in the Superior Court action, were fully aware of its terms. After the adoption had been finalized, the defendants terminated all visitation between the plaintiff and the child.

The trial court, after reviewing these facts, granted the defendants' motion to strike the plaintiff's complaint because, in its view, enforcement of the "Open Adoption and Visitation Agreement" would violate Connecticut's adoption statutes. According to the trial court, adoption, as a creature of statute, must comply strictly with statutory requirements, and the existing statutes governing adoption preclude private "side agreements" that would serve to perpetuate a relationship, after adoption, between a genetic parent and an adopted child. The court noted that termination of parental rights, under General Statutes § 45–61b(g), operates as a "complete severance by court order of the legal relationship ... between the child and his parent...." Furthermore, under General Statutes § 45–64a,[3]

---

3. General Statutes § 45–64a provides in relevant part: "EFFECTS OF FINAL DECREE OF ADOPTION. SURVIVING RIGHTS. A final decree of adoption, whether issued by a court of this state or a court of any other jurisdiction, shall have the following effect in this state:

"(1) All rights, duties and other legal consequences of the genetic relation of child and parent shall thereafter exist between the adopted person and the adopting parent and his relatives. Such adopted person shall be treated as if he were the genetic child of the adopting parent, for all purposes including the applicability of statutes which do not expressly exclude an adopted person in their operation or effect;

"(2) The adopting parent and the adopted person shall have rights of inheritance from and through each other and the genetic and adopted relatives of the adopting parent. The right of inheritance of an adopted person extends to the heirs of such adopted person, and such heirs shall be the same as if such adopted person were the genetic child of the adopting parent;

"(3) The adopted person and the genetic children and other adopted children of the adopting parent shall be treated, unless otherwise provided by statute, as siblings, having rights of inheritance from and through each other. Such rights of inheritance extend to the heirs of such adopted person and of the genetic children and other adopted children, and such heirs shall be the same as if each such adopted person were the genetic child of the adopting parent;

"(4) The adopted person shall, except as hereinafter provided, be treated as if he were the genetic child of the adopting parent for purposes of the applicability of all documents and instruments, whether executed before or after the adoption decree is issued, which do not expressly exclude an adopted person in their operation or effect. The words 'child,' 'children,' 'issue,' 'descendant,' 'descendants,' 'heir,' 'heirs,' 'lawful heirs,' 'grandchild' and 'grandchildren,' when used in any will or trust instrument shall include legally adopted persons unless such document clearly indicates a contrary intention. Nothing in this section shall be construed to alter or modify the provisions of section 45–162 regarding children born through A.I.D.;

"(5) The legal relationship between the adopted person and his genetic parent or parents and the relatives of such

adoption creates new legal relationships in which the adopting parents are completely substituted for the genetic parents of an adopted person. Finally, the trial court observed that General Statutes § 45–63 requires agreements about adoption to be in writing and filed in the Probate Court. Relying on these statutory provisions, and a number of out-of-state cases, the court concluded that the contract between the parties could not confer upon the plaintiff a specifically enforceable right to visitation after completion of the adoption process.

Although the plaintiff's appeal purports to raise three issues about the enforceability of her "Open Adoption and Visitation Agreement," there is really only one question that we must resolve: did the trial court err in concluding that this agreement violated the public policy reflected in our adoption statutes?[5] We disagree with the trial court's ruling.

The validity of an "open adoption" agreement is a matter of first impression for this court. Before we address the merits of this question, we should note that the title "open adoption," which has apparently become the standard characterization of such agreements,[6] conveys a misleading impression of what such agreements intend to accomplish. The plaintiff does not seek to "open," to set aside or to diminish in any way the adoptive process that has substituted the defendants as the legal parents of the child. The plaintiff's rights are not premised on an ongoing genetic relationship that somehow survives a termination of parental rights and an adoption. Instead, the plaintiff is asking us to decide whether, as an adult who has had an ongoing personal relationship with the child, she may contract with the adopting parents, prior to adoption, for the continued right to visit with the child, so long as that visitation continues to be in the

---

genetic parent or parents is terminated for all purposes, including the applicability of statutes which do not expressly include such an adopted person in their operation and effect. The genetic parent or parents of the adopted person is relieved of all parental rights and responsibilities;

"(6) The genetic parent or parents and their relatives shall have no rights of inheritance from or through the adopted person, nor shall the adopted person have any rights of inheritance from or through his genetic parent or parents and their relatives, except as provided in this section;

"(7) The legal relationship between the adopted person and his genetic parent or parents and the relatives of such genetic parent or parents is terminated for purposes of the construction of the documents and instruments, whether executed before or after the adoption decree is issued, which do not expressly include the individual by name or by some designation not based on a parent and child or blood relationship, except as provided in this section."

5. The plaintiff's three issues ask us to rule separately about whether the "Open Adoption and Visitation Agreement," which is "supported by mutual consideration," is: (1) void and unenforceable as against public policy; (2) specifically enforceable as a contract right after the completion of the adoption process; or (3) violative of the public policy expressed in the Connecticut statutes governing adoption. The defendants' motion to strike was not premised on any deficiency in consideration, as the transcript of the hearing before the trial court, Barall, J., makes clear.

6. See C. Amadio & S. Deutsch, "Open Adoption: Allowing Children to 'Stay in Touch' with Blood Relatives," 22 J.Fam.L. 59 (1983–84).

best interest of the child.[7]

Our statutes recognize that visitation encompasses considerations that differ from those that govern custody, guardianship or parental status. The plaintiff reminds us that, in the adoption statutes themselves, while an application for adoption must disclose pending proceedings "affecting the custody of the child to be adopted ... [f]or the purposes of [such disclosure], visitation rights granted by any court shall not be considered as affecting the custody of the child." General Statutes § 45–63(a)(2). The defendants maintain that this statutory distinction merely reflects the fact that Probate Court adoption proceedings necessarily must take outstanding custody orders into account, while visitation rights are not so implicated. This explanation for the distinction contained in § 45–63 may well be accurate but it does not eradicate the existence of the distinction and thus supports the plaintiff's position that the adoption statutes do not expressly make a visitation agreement void as against public policy.

Even more significantly, our visitation statute, General Statutes § 46b–59, permits the Superior Court, upon a proper application, to "grant the right of visitation with respect to any minor child ... to any person.... In making, modifying or terminating such an order, the court shall be guided by the best interest of the child.... Visitation rights granted in accordance with this section shall not be deemed to have created parental rights in the person ... to whom such visitation rights are granted. The grant of visitation rights shall not prevent any court of competent jurisdiction from thereafter acting upon the custody of such child, the parental rights with respect to such child or the adoption of such child and any such court may include in its decree an order terminating such visitation rights." In Temple v. Meyer, 208 Conn. 404, 410, 544 A.2d 629 (1988), we recently noted that this statute "leaves great latitude for the exercise of judicial discretion because it does not focus on the legal relationship of the parties involved.... The only criterion under § 46b–59 is the best interest of the child." All this plaintiff seeks is a court order consistent with the statutory constraints imposed on visitation by § 46b–59.

In light of these statutes, we are unpersuaded that the agreement between the parties in this case violates the public policy of Connecticut. It would be elevating form over substance to allow the plaintiff to obtain

---

7. The plaintiff's complaint did not clearly articulate that her claim for specific enforcement of the "Open Adoption and Visitation Agreement" was conditioned upon her ability to persuade a trier of fact that her visitation with the child would be in the child's best interest. At the trial court hearing on the motion to strike, however, the plaintiff expressly and consistently limited her claim to relief in this fashion. Obliged as we are, in ruling upon a motion to strike, to construe a complaint in the manner most favorable to sustaining its legal sufficiency; Blancato v. Feldspar Corporation, 203 Conn. 34, 36, 522 A.2d 1235 (1987); Norwich v. Silverberg, 200 Conn. 367, 370, 511 A.2d 336 (1986); we conclude that the complaint should be construed to incorporate a "best interest of the child" standard. We note that, although the trial court raised a question about the sufficiency of the complaint in this regard at the hearing, the defendants did not premise their motion to strike on this ground. Furthermore, the proposition that any and all visitation rights are impliedly premised on a factual finding "guided by the best interest of the child" finds statutory support in General Statutes § 46b–59.

visitation rights by filing an appropriate "application" in the Superior Court, but to deny her the opportunity to seek such rights under a contractual umbrella.

Case law in other jurisdictions does not persuade us that we should strike down the visitation agreement in this case. To a significant extent, the cases turn on legislative determinations that vary from state to state. We note nonetheless that People ex rel. Sibley v. Sheppard, 54 N.Y.2d 320, 429 N.E.2d 1049, 445 N.Y.S.2d 420 (1981), concluded, as do we, that the statutory creation of an adoptive family does not automatically require complete severance of the child from all further contact with former relatives. Similarly, Weinschel v. Strople, 56 Md.App. 252, 261, 466 A.2d 1301 (1983), concluded, as do we, that as long as the best interest of the child is the determinative criterion, public policy does not forbid an agreement about visitation rights between a genetic parent and adoptive parents. In re Custody of Atherton, 107 Ill.App.3d 1006, 63 Ill.Dec. 582, 438 N.E.2d 513 (1982), on which the trial court relied, is distinguishable because that decision focused on the impropriety of parental bargaining about post-adoption custody when, according to the court, the purpose of the parties' contract was to bypass judicial determinations of custody. That is not this case.

Traditional models of the nuclear family have come, in recent years, to be replaced by various configurations of parents, step-parents, adoptive parents and grandparents. We are not prepared to assume that the welfare of children is best served by a narrow definition of those whom we permit to continue to manifest their deep concern for a child's growth and development. The record of the 1982 Superior Court proceedings to set aside the termination of the plaintiff's parental rights demonstrates that, in the present case, the "Open Adoption and Visitation Agreement" was openly and lovingly negotiated, in good faith, in order to promote the best interest of the child. The attorney for the child reported that the child thought the agreement between her mother and her soon-to-be adoptive parents would be "the best world that she could imagine." This agreement did not violate public policy, either ab initio or upon the subsequent entry of a decree of adoption.

We therefore remand this case to the trial court for a hearing on the merits of the plaintiff's claim that visitation would now be in the best interest of the child. Our observations about the genesis of the "Open Adoption and Visitation Agreement" are intended to express no opinion about how that claim should be resolved in light of the circumstances presently confronting the child.

· · ·

New Jersey Division of Youth and Family Services v. B.G.S.

Superior Court of New Jersey, Appellate Division, 1996.
291 N.J.Super. 582, 677 A.2d 1170.

(The opinion in this case can be found at p. 1249, *supra*.)

NEW MEXICO STATUTES ANN. § 32A–5–35 (West 2006)

§ 32A–5–35. Open adoptions.

A. The parents of the adoptee and the petitioner may agree to contact between the parents and the petitioner or contact between the adoptee and one or more of the parents or contact between the adoptee and relatives of the parents. An agreement shall, absent a finding to the contrary, be presumed to be in the best interests of the child and shall be included in the decree of adoption. The contact may include exchange of identifying or nonidentifying information or visitation between the parents or the parents' relatives and the petitioner or visitation between the parents or the parents' relatives and the adoptee. An agreement entered into pursuant to this section shall be considered an open adoption.

B. The court may appoint a guardian ad litem for the adoptee. The court shall adopt a presumption in favor of appointing a guardian ad litem for the adoptee when visitation between the biological family and the adoptee is included in an agreement; however, this requirement may be waived by the court for good cause shown. When an adoptive placement is made voluntarily through an agency or pursuant to Section 32A–5–13 NMSA 1978, the court may, in its discretion, appoint a guardian ad litem. If the child is fourteen years of age or older, the court may appoint an attorney for the child. In all adoptions other than those in which the child is placed by the department, the court may assess the parties for the cost of services rendered by the guardian ad litem or the child's attorney. The duties of the guardian ad litem or child's attorney end upon the filing of the decree, unless otherwise ordered by the court.

C. In determining whether the agreement is in the adoptee's best interests, the court shall consider the adoptee's wishes, but the wishes of the adoptee shall not control the court's findings as to the best interests of the adoptee.

D. Every agreement entered into pursuant to provisions of this section shall contain a clause stating that the parties agree to the continuing jurisdiction of the court and to the agreement and understand and intend that any disagreement or litigation regarding the terms of the agreement shall not affect the validity of the relinquishment of parental rights, the adoption or the custody of the adoptee.

E. The court shall retain jurisdiction after the decree of adoption is entered, if the decree contains an agreement for contact, for the purpose of hearing motions brought to enforce or modify an agreement entered into pursuant to the provisions of this section. The court shall not grant a request to modify the agreement unless the moving party establishes that there has been a change of circumstances and the agreement is no longer in the adoptee's best interests.

NOTE

The changing legal landscape. There is movement today toward legally permitting open adoption, at least in instances in which the adoptive parent agrees to such an arrangement. Such a possibility was not anticipated in most adoption laws until recently, as the previous case explains illustrates. The preceding statute illustrates some legal recognition of this approach.

How would you assess the problems and promise of open adoption? In framing your response, consider the pros and cons of utilizing some form of this approach in each of the following situations:

a.   The defective neonate whose parent(s) cannot adequately cope with the child's special needs;

b.   The biological (but not legal) parent of a child conceived through assisted conception;

c.   The child of a parent who is disabled or lacks competence to be an adequate parent;

d.   The child who otherwise would be likely to remain in long term foster care, for whatever reason (including the possibility of parental refusal to relinquish for adoption);

e.   Stepparent adoption, where the noncustodial parent wishes to retain contacts;

f.   Allowing post-adoptive contact between the child and a former foster parent with whom a good relationship had been established.

Standby guardianship. This approach is designed to permit designation of a standby guardian by parental agreement or possible judicial action who would be available to assume authority for a minor upon the incapacity or death of a parent. It is generally thought of as a way to deal with the parent who anticipates a significant decline in physical or medical condition.

Though not actually open adoption, it is considered by some as a partial variation on it.

MARYLAND CODE ANN., EST. & TRUSTS §§ 13–901 et seq. (LexisNexis 2001)

§ 13–901.   Definitions.

(a) In this subtitle the following words have the meanings indicated.

(b)(1) "Attending physician" means a physician who has primary responsibility for the treatment and care of a parent described under this subtitle.

(2) If more than one physician shares the responsibility for the treatment and care of a parent or if another physician is acting on the attending physician's behalf, any physician described in this paragraph may act as the attending physician under this subtitle.

(3) If no physician has responsibility for the treatment and care of a parent, any physician who is familiar with the parent's medical condition may act as the attending physician under this subtitle.

(c)(1) "Debilitation" means a person's chronic and substantial inability, as a result of a physically incapacitating illness, disease, or injury, to care for the person's dependent minor child.

(2) "Debilitated" means the state of having a debilitation.

(d)(1) "Incapacity" means a person's chronic and substantial inability, as a result of mental impairment, to understand the nature and consequences of decisions concerning the care of the person's dependent minor child, and a consequent inability to care for the child.

(2) "Incapacitated" means the state of having an incapacity.

(e) "Standby guardian" means a person:

(1) Appointed by a court under § 13–903 of this subtitle as standby guardian of the person or property of a minor, whose authority becomes effective on the incapacity or death of the minor's parent, or on the consent of the parent; or

(2) Designated under § 13–904 of this subtitle as standby guardian of the person or property of a minor, whose authority becomes effective on the incapacity of the minor's parent, or on the debilitation and consent of the parent.

§ 13–902. Application.

Except as otherwise provided in this subtitle, the provisions of this title concerning a guardian of the person or property of a minor shall apply to standby guardians.

§ 13–903. Petition for appointment of standby guardian.

(a)(1) Subject to the provisions of paragraphs (2) and (3) of this subsection, a petition for the judicial appointment of a standby guardian of the person or property of a minor under this section may be filed only by a parent of the minor, and if filed, shall be joined by each person having parental rights over the minor.

(2) If a person who has parental rights cannot be located after reasonable efforts have been made to locate the person, the parent may file a petition for the judicial appointment of a standby guardian.

(3) If the petitioner submits documentation, satisfactory to the court, of the reasonable efforts to locate the person who has parental rights, the court may issue a decree under this section.

(b) A petition for the judicial appointment of a standby guardian shall state:

(1) The duties of the standby guardian;

(2) Whether the authority of the standby guardian is to become effective on the petitioner's incapacity, on the petitioner's death, or on whichever occurs first; and

(3) That there is a significant risk that the petitioner will become incapacitated or die, as applicable, within 2 years of the filing of the petition, and the basis for this statement.

(c) If the petitioner is medically unable to appear, the petitioner's appearance in court may not be required, except on a motion and for good cause shown.

(d)(1) If the court finds that there is a significant risk that the petitioner will become incapacitated or die within 2 years of the filing of the petition and that the interests of the minor will be promoted by the appointment of a standby guardian of the person or property of the minor, the court shall issue a decree accordingly.

(2) A decree under this subsection shall:

(i) Specify whether the authority of the standby guardian is effective on the receipt of a determination of the petitioner's incapacity, on the receipt of the certificate of the petitioner's death, or on whichever occurs first; and

(ii) Provide that the authority of the standby guardian may become effective earlier on written consent of the petitioner in accordance with subsection (e)(3) of this section.

(3) If at any time before the beginning of the authority of the standby guardian the court finds that the requirements of paragraph (1) of this subsection are no longer satisfied, the court may rescind the decree.

(e)(1)(i) If a decree under subsection (d) of this section provides that the authority of the standby guardian is effective on receipt of a determination of the petitioner's incapacity, the standby guardian's authority shall begin on the standby guardian's receipt of a copy of a determination of incapacity made under § 13–906 of this subtitle.

(ii) A standby guardian shall file a copy of the determination of incapacity with the court that issued the decree within 90 days of the date of receipt of the determination.

(iii) If a standby guardian fails to comply with subparagraph (ii) of this paragraph, the court may rescind the standby guardian's authority.

(2)(i) If a decree under subsection (d) of this section provides that the authority of the standby guardian is effective on receipt of a certificate of the petitioner's death, the standby guardian's authority shall begin on the standby guardian's receipt of a certificate of death.

(ii) The standby guardian shall file a copy of the certificate of death with the court that issued the decree within 90 days of the date of the petitioner's death.

(iii) If the standby guardian fails to comply with subparagraph (ii) of this paragraph, the court may rescind the standby guardian's authority.

(3)(i) Notwithstanding paragraphs (1) and (2) of this subsection, a standby guardian's authority shall begin on the standby guardian's receipt of the petitioner's written consent to the beginning of the standby guardian's authority signed by:

1. The petitioner in the presence of two witnesses at least 18 years of age, neither of whom may be the standby guardian; and

2. The standby guardian.

(ii) 1. If the petitioner is physically unable to sign a written consent to the beginning of the standby guardian's authority, another person may sign the consent on the petitioner's behalf and at the petitioner's direction.

2. A consent under this subparagraph to the beginning of the standby guardian's authority shall be signed in the presence of the petitioner and two witnesses at least 18 years of age, neither of whom may be the standby guardian.

3. A standby guardian also shall sign a written consent to the beginning of the standby guardian's authority under this subparagraph.

(iii) The standby guardian shall file the written consent with the court that issued the decree within 90 days of the date of receipt of the written consent.

(iv) If the standby guardian fails to comply with subparagraph (iii) of this paragraph, the court may rescind the standby guardian's authority.

(f) The petitioner may revoke a standby guardianship created under this section by:

(1) Executing a written revocation;

(2) Filing the revocation with the court that issued the decree; and

(3) Promptly notifying the standby guardian of the revocation.

(g) A person who is judicially appointed as a standby guardian under this section may at any time before the beginning of the person's authority renounce the appointment by:

(1) Executing a written renunciation;

(2) Filing the renunciation with the court that issued the decree; and

(3) Promptly notifying in writing the petitioner of the revocation.

§ 13–904. Designation of standby guardian.

(a)(1) A parent may designate a standby guardian by means of a written designation:

(i) Signed in the presence of two witnesses, at least 18 years old, neither of whom is the standby guardian; and

(ii) Signed by the standby guardian.

(2)(i) If a parent is physically unable to sign a written designation, another person may sign the designation on the parent's behalf and at the parent's direction.

(ii)1. A designation under this paragraph shall be signed in the presence of the parent and two witnesses at least 18 years of age, neither of whom may be the standby guardian.

2. The standby guardian also shall sign a designation under this paragraph.

(b)(1) A designation of a standby guardian shall identify the parent, the minor, and the person designated to be the standby guardian, state the duties of the standby guardian, and indicate that the parent intends for the standby guardian to become the minor's guardian in the event the parent either:

(i) Becomes incapacitated; or

(ii) Becomes debilitated and consents to the beginning of the standby guardian's authority.

(2) A parent may designate an alternate standby guardian in the same writing and by the same manner as the designation of a standby guardian.

. . .

[The omitted portion of this article provides examples of language that may be used in making a designation of standby guardianship.]

. . .

(c) The authority of the standby guardian under a designation shall begin on:

(1) The standby guardian's receipt of a copy of a determination of incapacity under § 13–906 of this subtitle; or

(2) The standby guardian's receipt of:

(i) A copy of a determination of debilitation under § 13–906 of this subtitle;

(ii) A copy of the parent's written consent to the beginning of the standby guardianship, signed by the parent in the presence of two witnesses at least 18 years of age, neither of whom is the standby guardian, and signed by the standby guardian; and

(iii) A copy of the birth certificate for each child for whom the standby guardian is designated.

(d)(1) If a parent is physically unable to sign a written consent to the beginning of the standby guardianship, another person may sign the written consent to the beginning of the standby guardianship on the parent's behalf and at the parent's direction.

(2) A consent under this subsection to the beginning of the stand-by guardianship shall be signed in the presence of the parent and two witnesses at least 18 years of age, neither of whom may be the standby guardian.

(3) The standby guardian also shall sign a consent to the beginning of the standby guardianship under this subsection.

(e)(1) A standby guardian shall file a petition for judicial appointment within 180 days of the date of the beginning of the standby guardianship under this section.

(2) If the standby guardian fails to file the petition within the time specified in this subsection, the standby guardian's authority shall terminate 180 days from the date of the beginning of the standby guardianship.

(3) The standby guardian's authority shall begin again on the filing of the petition.

(f)(1) A standby guardian shall file a petition for appointment as guardian after receipt of:

(i) A copy of a determination of incapacity made under § 13–906 of this subtitle; or

(ii) Copies of:

1. A determination of debilitation made under § 13–906 of this subtitle; and

2. The parent's written consent to the beginning of the standby guardianship under this section.

(2) Subject to the provisions of paragraphs (3) and (4) of this subsection, the petition shall be accompanied by:

(i) The written designation of the standby guardian signed, or consented to, by each person having parental rights over the child;

(ii) A copy of:

1. The determination of incapacity of the parent; or

2. The determination of debilitation and the parental consent to the beginning of the standby guardianship; and

(iii) If the petition is filed by a person designated as alternate standby guardian, a statement that the person designated as standby guardian is unwilling or unable to act as standby guardian, and the basis for the statement

(3) If a person who has parental rights cannot be located after reasonable efforts have been made to locate the person, the standby guardian may file a petition under this section without the consent of the person to the designation of the standby guardian.

(4) If the standby guardian submits documentation, satisfactory to the court, of the reasonable efforts to locate the person who has

parental rights, the court may appoint a standby guardian under this section.

(g) The court shall appoint a person to be a standby guardian under this section if the court finds that:

(1) The person was duly designated as standby guardian;

(2) A determination of incapacity, or a determination of debilitation and parental consent to the beginning of the standby guardianship, has been made under this section;

(3) The interests of the minor will be promoted by the appointment of a standby guardian of the person or property of the minor; and

(4) If the petition is by a person designated as alternate standby guardian, the person designated as standby guardian is unwilling or unable to act as standby guardian.

(h) A parent may revoke a standby guardianship created under this section:

(1) Before the filing of a petition, by notifying the standby guardian verbally or in writing or by any other act that is evidence of a specific intent to revoke the standby guardianship; and

(2) If a petition has been filed by:

(i) Executing a written revocation;

(ii) Filing the revocation with the court in which the petition was filed; and

(iii) Promptly notifying the standby guardian of the revocation.

(i) A person who is judicially appointed as a standby guardian under this section may at any time before the beginning of the person's authority renounce the appointment by:

(1) Executing a written renunciation;

(2) Filing the renunciation with the court that issued the decree; and

(3) Promptly notifying in writing the parent of the revocation.

§ 13–905. Alternative methods of guardian appointment; appending of designation.

A standby guardian may also file a petition for appointment as guardian in any other manner permitted by this title, on notice to the parent, and may append a designation of a standby guardian to the petition for consideration by the court in the determination of the petition.

§ 13–906. Determination of incapacity or debilitation.

(a)(1) A determination of incapacity or debilitation under this subtitle shall:

(i) Be made by the attending physician to a reasonable degree of medical certainty;

(ii) Be in writing; and

(iii) Contain the attending physician's opinion regarding the cause and nature of the parent's incapacity or debilitation, and the extent and probable duration of the incapacity or debilitation.

(2) If a standby guardian's identity is known to an attending physician, the attending physician shall provide a copy of a determination of incapacity or debilitation to the standby guardian.

(b) If requested by a standby guardian, an attending physician shall make a determination regarding the parent's incapacity or debilitation for purposes of this subtitle.

(c) If the parent is able to comprehend the information, a standby guardian shall inform the parent of:

(1) The beginning of the standby guardian's authority as a result of a determination of incapacity; and

(2) The parent's right to revoke the authority promptly after receipt of the determination of incapacity.

§ 13–907. Authority of standby guardian.

(a) The beginning of a standby guardian's authority in accordance with a determination of incapacity, determination of debilitation, or consent may not, itself, divest a parent of any parental or guardianship rights.

(b) The authority of a standby guardian with respect to the minor is limited to the express authority granted to the standby guardian by a court under this subtitle.

§ 13–908. Bond of standby guardian.

The furnishing of a bond by a standby guardian shall be governed by the provisions of § 13–208 of this title.

7. EQUITABLE ADOPTION

John Jeffries, Equitable Adoption: They Took Him Into Their Home and Called Him Fred*

58 VA.L.REV. 727, 727–31 (1972).†

Though not legally adopted, a foster child may in some cases participate in the estate of an intestate foster parent. Courts reach this result under a number of different labels: equitable or virtual adoption, or adoption by estoppel. Generally, "equitable adoption" describes the provi-

---

* Kuchenig v. California Co., 410 F.2d 222, 224 (5th Cir.1969).

† Copyright 1972, Virginia Law Review. Reprinted with permission.

sion of some judicial remedy for an unperformed contract for legal adoption. Although this doctrine arises in a variety of factual contexts, it most commonly involves a child's effort to share in the intestate estate of someone who has agreed to adopt him but has not done so. Typically the foster parents contract for legal adoption with the child, his natural parents, or someone *in loco parentis*. The child lives with his foster parents, takes their name, loves and obeys them as would a natural child. Upon the death of the foster parents, the child asks a court to treat him as if he were a legally adopted child for purposes of intestate succession.

Whatever remedy is provided, the result is startling: A child's share of the estate goes to one who, in the eyes of the law, stands as a stranger to the deceased. Eight states refuse to allow any such recovery on an unperformed adoption contract. These courts note that adoption is everywhere a creature of statute and insist on strict construction of statutes in derogation of common law. In these jurisdictions the statutory scheme provides the exclusive method of adoption, and no private agreement will suffice to bring the child within the statutes of descent and distribution.

One may ask why any court would consider a claim of equitable adoption in the face of an unambiguous statutory scheme. The answer lies in the extraordinarily persuasive factual situations which may arise. For example, in Wooley v. Shell Petroleum Corporation[8] Mr. and Mrs. Fowler agreed with a widower to adopt his twin infant daughters. Three years later the father and the foster parents apprenticed the girls to the Fowlers, apparently thinking that this proceeding constituted a legal adoption. The Fowlers took the children into their home and raised them as their own. In return, the girls helped and cared for the Fowlers during the apparent poverty of their declining years:

> Evidence could not show more loyal or faithful performance of duty than these girls rendered to the Fowlers. Hardships and privations which they endured in their faithfulness to Mr. and Mrs. Fowler evoke sympathy and consideration, as well as admiration, from all acquainted with the facts.[9]

Courts of some twenty-five other jurisdictions have similarly demonstrated their willingness to go beyond the statutory scheme to meet the demands of conscience.

. . .

Theory of Recovery

At the outset one must distinguish a contract to adopt from a contract to make a will. The latter agreement necessarily involves the disposition of property and may come within the Statute of Frauds, but if written or removed from the Statute by part performance, such a contract will be enforced quite apart from any purported adoption. An agreement to adopt stands on a different footing. Although frequently discussed in relation to

---

8. 39 N.M. 256, 45 P.2d 927 (1935).   **9.** Id. at 261, 45 P.2d at 930.

an adoption agreement, the Statute of Frauds does not invalidate such a contract. It can be performed within one year and within the lifetime of the promisor, and it need not involve the disposition of property since the promisor remains free to disinherit a child by will. Of course, a single case may involve both a contract to make a will and a contract to adopt, and courts sometimes fail to distinguish between them; but the essence of equitable adoption is the provision of a judicial remedy for an unperformed adoption agreement.

Courts that endorse the doctrine of equitable adoption recognize no right in law; they merely agree to provide an equitable and discretionary remedy in a proper case: "Equity, abhorring injustice, and having its origin in the inadequacy of legal remedies, and possessing powers all its own, has developed the remedy ... the granting or denial of which rests in sound discretion."[15] Some courts rest their decisions solely and squarely on the principles of equity. More commonly, courts employ one of several more sophisticated techniques to reach the desired result.

Specific Performance

The most popular theory of recovery is specific performance of the contract to adopt. Courts grant this remedy only against the estate of a deceased promisor; a child cannot enforce an adoption agreement during the lifetime of his adoptive parent:

> The [adoption] statute involves action by the court, looking always to the best interest of the child. Such action could not have been compelled in a suit for specific performance.... [A]doption is not a contract alone between the parties. It requires judicial determination of the advisability of permitting such action, and if a court decrees otherwise, it is not within the power of one person to adopt another. The relationship of parent and child is of the most intimate, personal nature. Equity will not ordinarily enforce a contract to create such relationship.[17]

As against the defaulting promisor's estate, courts characteristically require an adoption agreement and valid consideration for the promise of adoption. This conceptual framework leads to discussions of the authority of the contracting parties and the sufficiency of consideration. Generally, custody of the child, filial companionship and obedience, or change in the child's domestic status will support the promise of the adoptive parent. Transfer of custody to the prospective spouse of the child's natural parent may suffice, but some courts hold that neither the marriage nor the benefits of association consequently enjoyed by the stepparent constitute consideration. Misconduct of the child, including abandonment of the adoptive family, may amount to a failure of consideration, but only where the conduct is flagrant.

---

15. Wooley v. Shell Petroleum Corp., 39 N.M., 256, 264, 45 P.2d 927, 932 (1935).

17. Besche v. Murphy, 190 Md. 539, 544, 59 A.2d 499, 501–02 (1948).

Despite its currency, the theory of specific performance of the adoption agreement fits the facts of these cases only passing well. For one thing, courts will grant relief only against the estate of a deceased promisor. Furthermore, a proven contract to adopt will fail to determine custody in a contest between the natural and foster parents. Most importantly, courts that follow this theory do not order specific performance. A deceased promisor cannot adopt the child, and no court has held that the equitably adopted child attains the status of legal adoption. In allowing participation in the estate of a foster parent, the courts do not specifically enforce the contract but merely provide an equitable remedy, limited in application and result.

NOTE

Some states have gradually adopted the doctrine of equitable adoption in the context of intestate succession, allowing for the child equitably adopted to take "from" but not "through" the equitably adopting parent under the state's intestate laws. *See, e.g.*, Lankford v. Wright, 347 N.C. 115, 489 S.E.2d 604 (1997)(acknowledging that twenty-seven other states have recognized and adopted equitable adoption). In *In re* Estate of Ford, 32 Cal.4th 160, 8 Cal.Rptr.3d 541, 82 P.3d 747 (2004), the Supreme Court of California ruled that the doctrine may only apply if the parties' conduct and statements clearly and convincingly demonstrate an intent to adopt. A close relationship between an adopter and an adoptee is not sufficient to invoke the doctrine of equitable adoption. There must be statements and acts indicating an intent to adopt, or the "parent" consistently holding the child out as the child of the parent.

8. THE QUEST FOR BIOLOGICAL IDENTITY

State statutes that seal adoption records, usually allowing them to be unsealed on a showing of good cause), remain widespread. They have generated largely unsuccessful constitutional attacks from adopted persons or adopters. In one widely cited decision, *In re* Roger B., 84 Ill.2d 323, 49 Ill. Dec. 731, 418 N.E.2d 751, appeal dismissed 454 U.S. 806, 102 S.Ct. 80, 70 L.Ed.2d (1981) the Supreme Court of Illinois addressed a plaintiff adoptee's arguments that such a statute

> is invalid in that it (1) infringes upon a fundamental right, (2) creates a suspect classification, in violation of the equal protection clause of the United States Constitution, and (3) violates plaintiff's right to receive information.

In rejecting these arguments, the court determined that

> Although information regarding one's background, heritage, and heredity is important to one's identity, it does not fall within any heretofore delineated zone of privacy implicitly protected within the Bill of Rights. We believe the adoptee does not have any fundamental right to examine his adoption records.

Since they found no fundamental right, the court viewed the validity of the statute in terms of whether it was arbitrary and did not bear a rational relationship to a legitimate state objective. The court noted that the statutory scheme represented a considered legislative determination that confidentiality under the circumstances to promote integrity of the adoption process. They explained that

> The natural parents, having determined that it is in the best interests of themselves and the child, have placed the child for adoption. This process is done not only with the expectation of anonymity, but also with the statutory assurance that his or her identity as the child's parent will be shielded from public disclosure.

The opinion further noted that confidentiality is needed to protect the right of the adopting parents. In an earlier case that also upheld the validity of a "sealed adoption records" case, a federal court rejected the further argument that the statutes violated a fundamental right to "personhood". *See* Alma Society, Inc. v. Mellon, 601 F.2d 1225 (2d Cir. 1979).

With the statutes regarded as constitutional, there remains the question of what constitutes "good cause" for opening them. The definition is not always clear, and probably only a few cases calling for construction of it have reached the appellate level and produced a published opinion. However, it seems clear that the requirements remain strict in most jurisdictions. The basic reasons mentioned previously are given as the explanation for not relaxing the restrictions. Reasons such as curiosity, or the thought that there may be an inheritance out there somewhere, are insufficient. The most persuasive are some arguments regarding medical needs. This has been lessened somewhat by increased availability of the natural parent's genetic or other medical history from adoptive placing agencies. Such information, if in fact needed, often can be supplied without revealing the identity of the natural parents in many instances. The Iowa Supreme Court, in *In re* Adoption of S.J.D., 641 N.W.2d 794 (2002), found that the adoptee who wishes to obtain information from the sealed record must show a "compelling need" for the information, adding that what constitutes such a need "depends on the circumstances of each case". But the court concluded that

> Under our statute, we think that good cause to invade the privacy of biological parents by revealing their identities without their consent should include no less than a showing of a medical need to save the life of or prevent great harm to an adult adopted person requesting the identifying information. This showing should be made upon competent medical evidence.

It remains to be seen whether there will be significant legislative relaxation of the "sealed records" laws, although some states are considering or have adopted schemes such as voluntary registries that might result in some reunions of biological parent and child, analogous to the Kentucky statute which follows regarding siblings. Increasing acceptance of some form of open adoption, as seen in the New Mexico statute at p. 1351, could allow more examples of situations in which the biological parents' identities are not fully confidential from the birth of the adopter.

KENTUCKY REVISED STATUTES ANN. (LexisNexis Supp. 2005)

In situations where a preadoptive brother or sister relationship existed, and one (1) or more of these siblings was then adopted, the following procedures shall be followed on an inquiry by one (1) or more of the siblings to the Cabinet for Health and Family Services seeking information about his brother or sister:

(1) In all cases, an adopted person eighteen (18) years of age or older or a pre-adoptive sibling eighteen (18) years of age or older of an adopted person may file information concerning himself, his present location, and his known antecedents with the Cabinet for Health and Family Services, stating his interest in being reunited with his pre-adoptive siblings and authorizing the cabinet to release such information to his pre-adoptive siblings who may make similar inquiry.

(2) In any case in which a person eighteen (18) years of age or older requests information about or expresses a desire in being reunited with a pre-adoptive sibling, the cabinet shall first determine whether such sibling has made similar inquiry pursuant to subsection (1) of this section. If the sibling has previously authorized release of information about himself, the cabinet shall release the information to the sibling making inquiry.

NOTE

Placement of siblings. Some states have a policy of trying to avoid separation of siblings in foster and adoptive placements. West Virginia Code Ann. § 49–2–14(e) (LexisNexis 2004) provides that

(e) When a child is in a foster care arrangement and is residing separately from a sibling or siblings who are in another foster home or who have been adopted by another family and the parents with whom the placed or adopted sibling or siblings reside have made application to the department to establish an intent to adopt or to enter into a foster care arrangement regarding a child so that said child may be united or reunited with a sibling or siblings, the state department shall upon a determination of the fitness of the persons and household seeking to enter into a foster care arrangement or seek an adoption which would unite or reunite siblings, and if termination and new placement are in the best interests of the children, terminate the foster care arrangement and place the child in the household with the sibling or siblings: Provided, That if the department is of the opinion based upon available evidence that residing in the same home would have a harmful physical, mental or psychological effect on one or more of the sibling children or if the child has a physical or mental disability which the existing foster home can better accommodate, or if the department can document that the reunification of the siblings would not be in the best interest of one or all of the children, the state department may petition the circuit court for an order allowing the separation of the siblings to continue: Provided, however, That if the child is twelve years of age or older, the state department shall provide the child the option of remaining in the existing foster care arrangement if remaining is in the best interests of the child. In any proceeding brought by the department to maintain separation of siblings, such separation may be ordered only if the court determines that clear and convincing evidence supports the department's determination. In any proceeding brought by the department seeking to maintain separation of siblings, notice shall be afforded, in addition to any other persons required by any provision of this code to receive notice, to the persons seeking to adopt a sibling or siblings of a previously placed or adopted child and said persons may be parties to any such action.

9. ADOPTION OF ADULTS

Adoption of Swanson

Supreme Court of Delaware, 1993.
623 A.2d 1095.

■ MOORE, JUSTICE.

Richard Sorrels appeals the denial of his petition in the Family Court to adopt James A. Swanson,[1] a consenting adult.[2] We confront an issue of first impression: Is a pre-existing parent-child relationship required under our adult adoption statutes, 13 Del.C. §§ 951–56, in order for one adult to adopt another?

. . .

When Richard Sorrels sought to adopt James Swanson, his companion of 17 years, they were, respectively, 66 and 51 years of age. The adoption had two purposes—to formalize the close emotional relationship that had existed between them for many years and to facilitate their estate planning. Apparently, they sought to prevent collateral claims on their respective estates from remote family members, and to obtain the reduced inheritance tax rate which natural and adopted children enjoy under Delaware law. Admittedly, there was no pre-existing parent-child relationship between them, and on that basis the Family Court denied the petition.

Adult adoptions in Delaware are governed by our Domestic Relations Law, 13 Del.C. §§ 951 through 956. Section 953 provides that "[i]f the petition complies with the requirements of §§ 951 and 952 of this title, and if the person or persons to be adopted appear in court and consent to the

---

1. Pseudonyms have been used for both parties to this adoption proceeding.

2. Although not required by Delaware law, Mr. Swanson's natural father also consented to the adoption.

adoption, the Family Court may render a decree ordering the issuance of a certificate of adoption to the petitioner.'"[3] Although the statute mentions no other requirements beyond those listed in Sections 951–952, the Family Court sua sponte concluded that approval of an adult adoption was contingent upon a pre-existing family relationship.

Indisputably, the legislature, by providing for adoption of minors, intended to allow for the creation and formalization of parent-child relationships between nonrelated adults and children. It is reasonable to infer that the legislature, by providing for adult adoptions, sought to extend this principle to those situations where no adoption occurred before the age of majority or where the parent-child relationship developed during adulthood. It is reasonable to infer that the legislature, by providing for adult adoptions, intended to allow for the formalization of the parent-child relationship where there is an existing parent-child relationship between nonrelated individuals.... It is simply illogical that the legislature enacted the adult adoption statute to make familial inheritance rights available to all. Furthermore, it is unlikely that the legislature intended to extend adoption to all other kinds of relationships, including friendships and sexual relationships. Petitioner's interpretation of the statute would lead to these results.

Thus, the Family Court implied a new requirement into the adult adoption process. As a result, we are faced with a simple question of statutory construction—did the Family Court err as a matter of law in formulating or applying legal principles when it interpreted Section 953 to require a preexisting parent-child relationship?

We begin with the basic rule of statutory construction that requires a court to ascertain and give effect to the intent of the legislature. If the statute as a whole is unambiguous and there is no reasonable doubt as to the meaning of the words used, the court's role is limited to an application of the literal meaning of those words. However, where, as here, the Court is faced with a novel question of statutory construction, it must seek to ascertain and give effect to the intention of the General Assembly as expressed by the statute itself.

There is no reference in Section 953 to any condition of a pre-existing parent-child relationship. Instead, the statute only compels a person seeking an adult adoption to sign and file a petition containing certain basic personal data. If, after having done so, the adoptee appears in court and consents to the adoption, the Family Court may grant the petition for adoption. 13 Del.C. § 953.[4]

---

3. 13 Del.C. § 951 provides that: Any person, or any husband and wife jointly, desiring to adopt any person or persons upwards of 18 years of age, shall file a petition in the Family Court of the county in which the petitioner or the person to be adopted resides. 13 Del.C. § 952 describes the contents of the petition: The petition shall state the name, sex and date of birth of the person or persons whose adoption is sought and that the petitioner or petitioners desire to adopt such person or persons. The petition shall be signed by the petitioner or petitioners.

4. Although the use of the verb "shall" in legislation generally connotes a mandatory requirement, while the verb "may" is

When statutory language is clear, unambiguous, and consistent with other provisions of the same legislation, the court must give effect to its intent. Moreover, 13 Del.C. § 953, the relevant adult adoption statute, has existed in equivalent form since 1915, without any material change by the General Assembly. That is indicative of legislative satisfaction with the provisions of the statute.

Regardless of one's views as to the wisdom of the statute, our role as judges is limited to applying the statute objectively and not revising it. A court may not engraft upon a statute language which has been clearly excluded therefrom. Thus, where, as here, provisions are expressly included in one part of a statute, but omitted from another, it is reasonable to conclude that the legislature was aware of the omission and intended it. As a result, the omission from the adult adoption procedure for investigation and supervision of prospective placements, found in the requirements for adopting minors, persuades us that it was not the result of an accident. If anything, it is the best evidence of a legislative policy against imposing unnecessary conditions upon the adult adoption process.

Many jurisdictions limit inquiry into the motives or purposes of an adult adoption. However, most recognize that adult adoptions for the purpose of creating inheritance rights are valid. In one of the earliest cases, the Supreme Judicial Court of Massachusetts upheld an adoption of three adults, aged 43, 39 and 25 respectively, by a 70 year old person who intended the adoption to operate in lieu of a will. Collamore v. Learned, Mass.Supr., 171 Mass. 99, 50 N.E. 518 (1898). The court ruled that motive, although proper in that case, had no effect on the validity of the adoption.

A similar result obtained in Sheffield v. Franklin, 151 Ala. 492, 44 So. 373 (1907). The court concluded that the law placed no limit on the age of the person to be adopted even if it altered inheritance rights. Likewise, in Ex parte Libertini, 244 Md. 542, 224 A.2d 443 (1966), the Maryland Court of Appeals permitted the adoption of an unmarried thirty-five year old woman by an unmarried fifty-six year old woman, initiated for reasons of inheritance and maternal feelings. The court rejected outright the lower court's conclusion that granting the adoption would pervert the entire adoptive process. The court noted that an adoption for the purpose of inheritance does not change the social or domestic relationship of the parties. Rather, its purpose and effect bestows on the adoptee the right of a natural heir to inherit property. This motive was not improper, the court concluded, and therefore had no bearing on a determination of the adoption's propriety.

Cases upholding adoptions for the purpose of improving the adoptee's inheritance rights continue to grow. In Berston v. Minnesota Dept. of Public Welfare, 206 N.W.2d 28 (Minn.1973), the trial court denied the adoption of an adult woman by her natural son on the public policy ground that the purpose of the adoption—to make the petitioner's mother his heir

---

deemed permissive, we have cautioned that use of this test is contextual, and thus, mere use of the term "may" does not control legislative intent where, as here, the full setting of the statute suggests a different construction. Miller v. Spicer, Del.Supr., 602 A.2d 65, 67 (1991).

in order to bring her into the terms of a trust established by the petitioner's father after he divorced the mother—would thwart the intent of the settlor of the trust. The Minnesota Supreme Court ruled that the broad language of the adult adoption statute unequivocally foreclosed any limiting construction.[6] Thus, considerations of public policy were matters for reappraisal by legislative amendment. See also Harper v. Martin, Ky.App., 552 S.W.2d 690 (1977) (approving of the adoption of a forty-seven year old male by a terminally ill petitioner for the express purpose of making him the heir at law of a third person); Matter of Fortney's Estate, 5 Kan.App.2d 14, 611 P.2d 599, 604–05 (1980) (upholding an adult adoption originally effectuated for purposes of inheritance); but see Matter of Griswold's Estate, 140 N.J.Super. 35, 354 A.2d 717 (1976) (ruling that an adoption to make an adoptee a beneficiary of a trust was an abuse of the adoption process). If anything, Griswold's Estate is contrary to well established Delaware law. See Haskell v. Wilmington Trust Co., Del.Supr., 304 A.2d 53, 54–5 (1973); Riggs Nat. Bank v. Zimmer, Del.Ch., 304 A.2d 69, 74, aff'd sub nom. Jackson v. Riggs Nat. Bank, Del.Supr., 314 A.2d 178, 182 (1973).

The general disinclination to examine the motives of the petitioner has been extended beyond the area of inheritance rights. In 333 East 53rd Street Associates v. Mann, 1st Dept., 121 A.D.2d 289, 503 N.Y.S.2d 752 (1986), a petitioner adopted an adult woman in order to ensure that she would succeed to the tenancy of a rent controlled apartment. The building's owner sought a declaratory judgment that the adoptee had no rights in the apartment. The appellate court found nothing inherently wrong with an adoption intended to confer an economic benefit on the adopted person.

On the other hand, the New York Court of Appeals ruled that a fifty-seven year old man could not adopt a fifty year old male with whom he shared a homosexual relationship. Matter of Adoption of Robert Paul P., 63 N.Y.2d 233, 481 N.Y.S.2d 652, 471 N.E.2d 424 (1984). The court reasoned that adoption is not a quasi-matrimonial device to provide unmarried partners with a legal imprimatur for their sexual relationship.[7] Id. 481 N.Y.S.2d at 653, 471 N.E.2d at 425. The court also determined that New York's adult adoption process requires the adoption to be in the best interests of the adoptee, and thus, the financial and emotional condition of the petitioner must still be investigated. Delaware's adult adoption process clearly abandons the requirement for such an investigation. It suggests no

---

6. Minn.St. 259.21 to 259.32 governed adoption in Minnesota at that time. There were only two references to adult adoptions in these sections. Section 259.22 stated in part that any person who resided in the state for one year or more may petition to adopt a child or an adult. Section 259.24, which dealt with consent, provided that in the adoption of an adult, written consent only shall be required. As in Delaware, the other sections of the statute dealing with notice, investigation and a hearing on the petition, referred only to the adoption of a minor.

7. There remains, however, an active debate, Bowers v. Hardwick, 478 U.S. 186, 106 S.Ct. 2841, 92 L.Ed.2d 140 (1986), notwithstanding, whether such relationships enjoy constitutionally protected status under the Equal Protection Clause. See Symposium, Life After Hardwick, 27 Harv.C.R.–C.L.L.Rev. 531 (1992); Tracey Rich, Note, Sexual Orientation in the Wake of Bowers v. Hardwick, 22 Ga.L.Rev. 773 (1988).

corresponding need to determine that an adult adoption be in the best interests of the adoptee. We also note the compelling dissent in Matter of Adoption of Robert Paul P., 481 N.Y.S.2d at 656, 471 N.E.2d at 428 (Meyer, J., dissenting), taking the majority to task for imposing limitations on the process that are not found in New York's adult adoption statute.

There are, of course, common sense limitations on any adult adoption. That is why our statute appears to confer reasonable discretion upon the Family Court's approval of an adult adoption. Solely by way of example, no court should countenance an adoption to effect a fraudulent, illegal or patently frivolous purpose. See, e.g., In re Jones, 122 R.I. 716, 411 A.2d 910 (1980), where an older married man sought to adopt his 20 year old paramour to the economic detriment of his wife and family. Delaware law is not necessarily inconsistent with the results in Adoption of Robert Paul P. and In re Jones, supra. Adult adoptions intended to foster a sexual relationship would be against public policy as violative of the incest statute. See 11 Del.C. § 766(b), which defines the crime of incest to include sexual intercourse between a parent and child "without regard to ... relationships by adoption."

A statute cannot be construed to produce an absurd, meaningless or patently inane result. However, where, as here, the petition contemplates an adoption that is not only within the scope of the statute, but which is also widely recognized as a proper exercise of the authority granted by the statute, we can divine no reason why this petition should be denied.

Since the primary object of statutory construction is to reach a result in conformity with legislative policy, once that policy is determined we need only test the construction by the rules of reasonableness and conformity with that policy. In this case, our construction of the statute—permitting the adoption of one adult by another for economic reasons—is consistent with a policy promoting limited judicial inquiry into the purposes or motives behind such a relationship.

. . . It is beyond the province of courts to question the policy or wisdom of an otherwise valid law. Instead, each judge must take and apply the law as they find it, leaving any changes to the duly elected representatives of the people. . . . Accordingly, the order of the Family Court dismissing the petition is REVERSED. The Family Court is directed to issue an appropriate decree of adoption.

CALIFORNIA FAMILY CODE (West 2004)

§ 9303.   Restrictions on adoption of more than one unrelated adult

(a) A person may not adopt more than one unrelated adult under this part within one year of the person's adoption of an unrelated adult, unless the proposed adoptee is the biological sibling of a person previously adopted pursuant to this part or unless the proposed adoptee is disabled or physically handicapped.

(b) A person may not adopt an unrelated adult under this part within one year of an adoption of another person under this part by the prospective adoptive parent's spouse, unless the proposed adoptee is a biological sibling of a person previously adopted pursuant to this part.

NOTE

Adoption laws in a majority of the states either specifically authorize adult adoptions or are worded so broadly that they would seem to permit adoptions regardless of the adoptee's age. Use of the word "child", for example, can be interpreted to refer to relationship rather than age. For further discussion, *see* Walter Wadlington, *Adoption of Adults: A Family Law Anomaly*, 54 CORNELL L.REV. 566, 570 (1969). Some states limit adult adoptions to cases in which there has been some "in loco parentis" type of relationship before the adoptee reached majority.

Civil effects of adoptions of adults and minor adoptions generally are not distinguished by statute, but limitations may be added through judicial gloss. In Minary v. Citizens Fidelity Bank & Trust Co., 419 S.W.2d 340 (Ky.1967), the Supreme Court of Kentucky refused to hold that the widow of a surviving life beneficiary of a trust, adopted by the life beneficiary long after the death of the testatrix, was an heir entitled to the remainder interest under a will which provided that on the death of the last surviving beneficiary the remainder should be distributed to "my then surviving heirs" according to descent and distribution laws of the state. The court said:

> The time has come to face again this problem which has persistently perplexed the court when an adult is adopted for the sole purpose of making him or her an heir and claimant to the estate of an ancestor under the terms of a testamentary instrument known and in existence at the time of the adoption. Even though the statute permits such adoption and even though it expressly provides that it shall be "with the same legal effect as the adoption of a child," we, nevertheless, are constrained to view this practice to be an act of subterfuge which in effect thwarts the intent of the ancestor whose property is being distributed and cheats the rightful heirs. We are faced with a situation wherein we must choose between carrying out the intent of deceased testators or giving a strict and rigid construction to a statute which thwarts that intent.

419 S.W.2d at 343.

At one time some adults in same sex relationships used adoption for estate or other purposes. Whether this will occur more frequently with the adoption of more state limitations on the effects of same sex relationships remains to be seen.

A requirement that an adopter must be older than the adoptee, often by a number of years representing the normal minimum age difference between a biological mother or father and child, dates at least from Roman law. Once found in a number of our states, it has largely disappeared in the United States. *See* Walter Wadlington, *Minimum Age Difference as a Requisite for Adoption*, 1966 DUKE L.J. 392.

INDEX

1371

†